ROBERT NORTH S.J.

ELENCHUS OF BIBLICA

1989

EDITRICE PONTIFICIO ISTITUTO BIBLICO
ROMA 1992

ROBERT NORTH S.J.

ELENCHUS OF BIBLICA
1989

EDITRICE PONTIFICIO ISTITUTO BIBLICO
ROMA 1992

© 1992 – E.P.I.B. – Roma

ISBN 88-7653-598-5

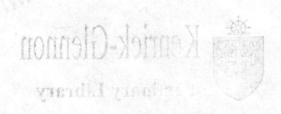

Editrice Pontificio Istituto Biblico
Piazza della Pilotta, 35 - 00187 Roma

Nota Bene – in citing titles from this Elenchus

Adhibemus:
Intra titulum **;**
ante subtitulum
[non sicut originale]

1. We strive to give the original form of titles as accurately and identically as possible. But every bibliography has certain 'conventions' or adaptations in the interest of its own internal clarity and consistency; thus for example a title is never given in ALL CAPITALS even when it is so in the original. Our major warning is this: we use the **semicolon** [**;**] to set off the **subtitle**, where the original uses a colon, dot, or separate line. Also, like many bibliography and library catalogues, we do **not** capitalize every word in English-language titles.

Semper
'[" "]'
non **,** *'* *vel* «».

For **quotation-marks**, we are following always British usage:

Normally ' ';

Quotes-within-quotes " "

even where the original may have „ " or «».

Pretium numero
rotundo: $20 pro
$19.95, etiam
contra *fontem*
ibidem citatum.

2. The **price** is rounded off, in the interest of brevity, clarity, and coping with inflation. Thus $12.95 will appear as $13 even where the cited source has $12.95. Less often: £20 for 19.90; DM 50 for 49,80.

Annus voluminis
late interpretandus;
sub 1989
etiam 1989-90, vel
1989 tarde
editum, vel
(numerus voluminis
sine anno) pro
fonte libri 1989.

3. In principle each volume contains only books and articles published **within that year** or earlier; thus this volume 5 contains the writings dated 1989. However, to be as up-to-date as possible, we include: *a*) periodicals officially dated 1989 even though published late; *b*) periodical-volumes including **partly** 1989, but also the part published in 1990 (= 1989s); *c*) **Source** for 1989 books, usually by volume-number (without year-number) of a later periodical [thus TDig 36,182; but BL 91,35 since it has no volume-numbers]; so also for **dissertations**.

Datur tendentia
movendi titulos
non biblicos ab
initio versus
finem libri;
sic compilationes
in voluminibus
post primam
mentionem.

4. We have progressively been moving **away from the front** those materials which are less directly biblical. Thus a book given in A-section for its first appearance (so that its number can be used for → renvoi), if repeated in later volumes (with book-reviews), will be in the section where it fits best. — 'Summary reports of meetings' (not needed for renvoi) are now shunted from A2.2 to Y7.2. 'Revelation', formerly B3.2, is now H1.7. Hermeneutic materials not strictly biblical have been moved from B2 to J9 (linguistic analysis).

Index systematicus
(et synopticus)
monstrat
innovationes;
e.g. nunc
4.4-6 de influxu
biblico in
litteraturam.

5. The Table of Contents (systematic index, p. 4-5) prints in **boldface** those categories which have been relocated, or new categories which have just been introduced: thus the former B4.5, 'The Bible as Literature', has now been subdivided into B4.4 'The Bible itself as literature'; B4.5, 'Biblical influence on secular literature in general'; B4.6, 'Bible-influence on individual authors'.

AA	Ann Arbor
Amst	Amsterdam
B	Berlin
Ba/BA	Basel/Buenos Aires
Barc	Barcelona
Bo/Bru	Bologna/Brussel
CasM	Casale Monferrato
CinB	Cinisello Balsamo
C	Cambridge, England
CM	Cambridge, Mass.
Ch	Chicago
Da: Wiss	Darmstadt, WissBuchg
DG	Downers Grove IL
Dü	Düsseldorf
E	Edinburgh
ENJ	EnglewoodCliffs NJ
F	Firenze
FrB/FrS	Freiburg-Br/Schw
Fra	Frankfurt/M
GCNY	Garden City NY
Gö	Göttingen
GR	Grand Rapids MI
Gü	Gütersloh
Ha	Hamburg
Heid	Heidelberg
Hmw	Harmondsworth
J	Jerusalem
K	København
L	London
LA	Los Angeles
Lp	Leipzig
Lv(N)	Leuven (L-Neuve)
M/Mi	Madrid/Milano
Mkn/Mp	Maryknoll/Minneapolis
Mü	München
N	Napoli
ND	NotreDame IN
Neuk	Neukirchen/Verlag
NHv	New Haven
Nv	Nashville
NY	New York
Ox	Oxford
P/Pd	Paris/Paderborn
Ph	Philadelphia
R/Rg	Roma/Regensburg
S/Sdr	Salamanca/Santander
SF	San Francisco
Sto	Stockholm
Stu	Stuttgart
T/TA	Torino/Tel Aviv
Tü	Tübingen
U/W	Uppsala/Wien
WL	Winona Lake IN
Wmr	Warminster
Wsb	Wiesbaden
Wsh	Washington
Wsz	Warszawa
Wu/Wü	Wuppertal/Würzburg
Z	Zürich

Index systematicus – Contents

Pag.

We have gradually begun indicating more exactly our sources. Thus ZIT (which is precious though giving only table of contents, thus no book-reviews, for publications which we cannot get) is now indicated by year and page; so also **BL**, and now **OIAc**. But **ZAW**, **NTAbs**, and **TDig** are indicated by volume and page.

The sign < meaning 'coming from' is used normally to indicate only a periodical-article taken from sources such as those indicated above. For **books**, it is more normal for us to cite from a secondary listing; and then the sign < is not used: only the source, in brackets [ZAW 103,220].

Book-reviews as such are usually taken only from up to the year specified for this volume of the Elenchus (1989). But in order to be able to indicate our source for **books** dated within this year, we put after them in brackets and without R a source published only later, in 1990 or 1991. Most such indications come from purely bibliographical publications, in which the critical comment or contents-summary is very brief, like those mentioned above. But in some few cases the indicated later source is a genuine and lengthy book-review, which will not then be repeated in a later Elenchus. Also in some few cases the briefly-indicated later source in brackets is retained, even if it is followed by a normal book-review of the proper year but discovered by us only later.

The numbering of the items in this Elenchus may seem capricious. It does not go straight forward for every item from 1 to k997, so that the user would know at once the total number of items in the volume. The numbers from 6480 to 6999 (this year) are not used at all. This is because we now *begin* editing and sending to the printer the materials on biblical theology and other subjects rather on the fringe of exegesis proper. Thus we can keep on inserting until the last moment the articles actually dealing with the biblical books and verses, as was explained on p. 3 of Elenchus 4 (1988). We cannot know until that last minute how many of the numbers before 7000 will be needed for NT titles.

The prefix-letters for the higher numbers are not used with consistent regularity, because only from experience we discovered that *t* and *f* are mistaken for (number) 1; *h* for *b*; *c* and *p* for circa and page.

Moreover, many of the item-numbers are used for more than one item. Those subdivided into *a*, *b*, *c* ... are generally those which have been excerpted from one single book or periodical-issue, and all pertain more or less directly to the same category of the Elenchus. Again, many of the numbers have an asterisk *. This is because we discovered these items too late to put them in their regular numbering order, or to re-number the whole section or volume. Conversely, some numbers are skipped entirely, usually because we noticed only at a later stage that the same item is given in a different category where it fits (maybe) better. Thus though the actual numbers from 1 to k997 amount only to some 16,000 (or some 800 less for the numbers skipped), still the total number of items is much larger, possibly 18 to 20 thousand apart from book-reviews.

Nuper magis exacte indicamus fontem nostrae informationis [vol. (secus ann.) + p.; praefixo < pro articulis, non libris]: sine R si fons est post 1989 (si est vera recensio, non repetetur in Elencho sequenti). Non supprimitur tale indicium etsi addatur (decursu redactionis) vera recensio.

Numeratio rerum citatarum est irregularis sed cum motivis. Numeri 6480-6999 (hoc anno) omittuntur quia redactio nunc incipit a categoriis posterioribus minus exegeticis. Sic inseri possunt plura et recentiora stricte exegetica.

*Litterae praefixae pro numeris post 9999 variantur inquantum possunt creare confusionem (c vel p pro circa/ pagina; f, t pro numero 1). Unus numerus aliquoties adhibetur pro pluribus rebus: sive cum asterisco * (generatim pro rebus inventis post numerationem) sive pro pluribus articulis ex uno fonte ad eandem categoriam appartenentibus. Alias numerus prorsus omittitur, si decursu redactionis invenitur idem titulus alibi.*

Hinc nostri numeri ab 1 ad k997 repraesentant circa 18 milia titulorum praeter recensiones.

Acronyms: Periodica - Series (small). *8 fig.* = ISSN; *10 fig.* = ISBN; *6/7* = DissA.

❹: *arabice,* in Arabic.

AAR [Aids]: American Academy of Religion (➤ JAAR, not PAAR) [Aids for the Study of Religion; Chico CA].

AAS: Acta Apostolicae Sedis; Vaticano. 0001-5199.

AASOR: Annual of the American Schools of Oriental Research; CM.

Abh: Abhandlungen Gö Lp Mü etc.; ➤ DOG / DPV.

AbhChr.JüDial: Abhandlungen zum christlich-jüdischen Dialog; Mü, Kaiser.

AbrNahr: Abr-Nahrain; Lv, Peeters.

AcAANorv: Acta ad archaeologiam et artium historiam spectantia, Inst. Norvegiae; Roma.

AcArchLov: Acta archaeologica Lovaniensia; Lv.

AcBg: Académie royale de Belgique; Bru.

Acme; Mi, Fac. Lett. Filos. 0001-494X.

AcNum: Acta Numismatica; Barc. 0211-8386 [15 (1985)].

AcSém: Actes sémiotiques; Paris [5 (1983)].

Act: Actes/Acta (Congrès, Colloque).

ActAntH: Acta Antiqua Academiae Scientiarum Hungaricae; Budapest.

Acta PIB: Acta Pontificii Instituti Biblici: Roma.

ActArchH/K: Acta Archaeologica, Hungarica, Budapest. 0001-5210 / København. 0065-101X.

ActClasSAfr: Acta Classica; Cape Town.

ActIran: Acta Iranica; Téhéran/Leiden.

ActOrH/K: Acta Orientalia: Budapest, Academia Scientiarum Hungarica; 0044-5975 / K (Societates Orientales Danica, Norveigica). 0001-6438.

ActPraeh: Acta Praehistorica et Archaeologica; B.

ActSum: Acta Sumerologica; Hiroshima, Univ. Linguistics. 0387-8082.

ActuBbg: Actualidad Bibliográfica; Barc. 0211-4143.

ADAJ: Annual of the Department of Antiquities, Jordan; 'Amman.

ADPF: Association pour la diffusion de la pensée française; Paris ➤ RCiv.

Aeg: Aegyptus; Milano. 0001-9046.

ÄgAbh: Ägyptologische Abhandlungen; Wb.

ÄgAT: Ägypten und Altes Testament; Wiesbaden. 0720-9061.

AegHelv: Aegyptiaca Helvetica: Basel Univ. Äg. Sem. (Univ. Genève).

AevA: Aevum Antiquum; Mi, Univ. Cattolica/ViPe. [1 (1988)]. 88-348-1701-5.

Aevum; Milano [anche Univ. Catt.].

AfER: African Ecclesial Review; Eldoret, Kenya.

AfJB: African Journal of Biblical Studies; Ibadan. [1,1 (1986)].

AfO: Archiv für Orientforschung; Graz. 3-85028-141-8.

AfTJ: Africa Theological Journal; Arusha, Tanzania. 0856-0048.

AGJU: Arbeiten zur Geschichte des Antiken Judentums und des Urchristentums; Leiden.

AIBL: Académie des Inscriptions et Belles-Lettres; P ➤ CRAI. – **AIEMA** ➤ BMosA.

AION [-Clas]: Annali (dell')Istituto Universitario Orientale [Classico] ➤ ArchStorAnt di Napoli.

AIPHOS: Annuaire de l'Institut de Philologie et d'Histoire Orientales et Slaves; Bru. 2-8004-0881-2.

AJA: American Journal of Archaeology; Princeton NJ. 0002-9114.

AJS: Association for Jewish Studies Review; CM 0364-0094 [6 (1981); Newsletter (10, 1985) 0278-4033].

Akkadica; Bruxelles/Brussel.

al.: et alii, and other(s).

ALGHJ: Arbeiten zur Literatur und Geschichte des hellenistischen Judentums; Leiden.

Al-Kibt, The Copts, die Kopten; Ha.

ALLC: Association for Literary and Linguistic Computing Bulletin; Stockport, Cheshire.

Altertum (Das); oB. 0002-6646.

AltOrF: Altorientalische Forschungen; B. 0232-8461.

AltsprU: Der altsprachliche Unterricht.

AmBapQ: American Baptist Quarterly; Valley Forge PA. 0015-8992.

AmBenR: American Benedictine Review; Richardton ND. 0002-7650.

Ambrosius, bollettino liturgico; Milano. 0392-5757.

America; NY. 0002-7049.

AmHR: American Historical Review; NY.

AmJAncH: American Journal of Ancient History; CM.

AmJPg: American Journal of Philology; Baltimore. 0002-9475.

AmJTPh: American Journal of Theology and Philosophy; W. Lafayette IN.

AmMessianJ: The American Messianic Jew; Ph [68 (1983)].

AmNumM: American Numismatic Society Museum Notes; NY.

AmPhTr: Transactions of the American Philosophical Society; Ph.

AmstCah: Amsterdamse cahiers voor exegese en bijbelse theologie; Kampen.

AmstMed ➔ Mededelingen.

AmStPapyr: American Studies in Papyrology; NHv.

AnAASyr: Annales Archéologiques Arabes Syriennes; Damas.

Anadolu; Ankara, Univ.

Anagénnēsis (none ☺), papyrology; Athēnai [2 (1982)].

Anatolica; Istanbul. 0066-1554.

AnatSt: Anatolian Studies; London.

AnAug: Analecta Augustiniana; R.

ANaut: Archaeonautica; Paris. 0154-1854 [4 (1984)].

AnBib: Analecta Biblica. Investigationes scientificae in res biblicas; R. 0066-135X.

AnBoll: Analecta Bollandiana; Bruxelles. 0003-2468.

AnBritAth: Annual of the British School at Athens; London.

AnCalas: Analecta Calasanctiana (religioso–cultural–histórica); Salamanca. 0569-9789.

AnCÉtRel: Annales du Centre d'Études des Religions; Bru.

AncHB: Ancient History Bulletin; Calgary/Chicago. 0835-3638.

AnChile: Anales de la Facultad de Teología; Santiago, Univ. Católica.

AnchorB: Anchor Bible; Garden City NY.

AncHRes: Ancient History ['Ancient Society' till 1987]; Resources for Teachers; Sydney. 0310-5814.

AnCist: Analecta Cisterciensia; Roma. 0003-2476.

AnClas: Annales Universitatis, sectio classica; Budapest.

AnClémOchr: Annuaire de l'Académie de théologie 'St. Clément d'Ochrida' [27 (1977s) paru 1982].

AnCracov: Analecta Cracoviensia (Polish Theol. Soc.); Kraków. 0209-0864.

AncSoc: Ancient Society. Katholieke Universiteit; Leuven. 0066-1619.

AnCTS: Annual Publication of the College Theological Society; Chico CA [not = ➔ ProcC(ath)TS].

AncW: The Ancient World; Chicago. 0160-9645.

AndrUnS: Andrews University Seminary Studies; Berrien Springs, Mich. 0003-2980.

AnÉCS: Annales Économies Sociétés Civilisations; P, 0395-2649.

AnEgBbg: Annual Egyptological Bibliography; Leiden.

AnÉPH: Annuaire ➔ ÉPHÉ.

AnÉth: Annales d'Éthiopie; Addis-Ababa.

AnFac: Let: Annali della facoltà di lettere, Univ. (Bari/Cagliari/Perugia).

— **Ling/T:** Annal(es) Facultat(is); linguarum, theologiae.

AnFg: Anuario de Filología; Barc.

Ang: Angelicum; Roma. 0003-3081.

AnglTR: Anglican Theological Review; Evanston IL. 0003-3286.

AnGreg: Analecta (Pont. Univ.) Gregoriana; Roma. 0066-1376.

AnHArt: Annales d'histoire de l'art et d'archéologie: Bru.

AnHConc: Annuarium Historiae Conciliorum; Paderborn.

ANilM: Archéologie du Nil Moyen; Lille. 0299-8130 [1 (1986)].

AnItNum: Annali (dell')Istituto Italiano di Numismatica; Roma.

AnJapB: Annual of the Japanese Biblical Institute; Tokyo ❶ ➔ Sei-Ron.

AnLetN: Annali della Facoltà di lettere e filosofia dell'Univ.; Napoli.

AnLovBOr: Analecta Lovaniensia Biblica et Orientalia; Lv.

AnnTh: Annales Theologici; Roma [1,1 (1987) 88-384-4000-6].

AnOchr: Annuaire de Théologie d'Ochrida; Sofya.

AnOr: Analecta Orientalia: Roma.

AnOrdBas: Analecta Ordinis S. Basilii Magni; Roma.

AnPg: L'Année Philologique; Paris.

AnPisa: Annali della Scuola Normale Superiore; Pisa.

AnPraem: Analecta Praemonstratensia; Averbode.

AnRIM: Annual Review of the Royal Inscriptions of Mesopotamia Project; Toronto. 0822-2525.

AnRSocSR: Annual Review of the Social Sciences of Religion; The Hague. 0066-2062.

ANRW: Aufstieg und Niedergang der römischen Welt → 878.

AnSacTar: Analecta Sacra Tarraconensia; Barcelona.

AnSemClas: Annali del Seminario di Studi del Mondo Classico, sezione Archeologia e Storia Antica; Napoli, Ist. Univ. Orientale [5 (1983)].

AnStoEseg: Annali di Storia dell'Esegesi; Bologna. 88-10-20255-4.

AntAb: Antike und Abendland; Berlin. 0003-5696.

AntAfr: Antiquités africaines; Paris. 0066-4871.

AntClas: L'Antiquité Classique; Bru.

AntClCr: Antichità classica e cristiana; Brescia.

Anthropos; 1. Fribourg/Suisse. 0003-5572. / [2. Rivista sulla famiglia; Roma 1 (1985)].

Anthropotes; R, Città Nuova [3 (1987)].

AntiqJ: Antiquaries Journal; London. 0003-5815.

Antiquity; Gloucester. 0003-5982.

Ant/ka: Ⓖ Anthropologiká: Thessaloniki.

AntKu: Antike Kunst; Basel. 0003-5688.

Anton: Antonianum; Roma. 0003-6064.

AntRArch: Antiqua, Rivista d'Archeologia e d'Architettura; Roma.

AnTVal: Anales de la Cátedra de Teología en la Universidad de Valencia [1 (1984)].

AntWelt: Antike Welt; Feldmeilen.

Anvil, Anglican Ev. theol.; Bramcote, Nottingham. 0003-6226.

AnzAltW: Anzeiger für die Altertumswissenschaft; Innsbruck. 0003-6293.

AnzW: Anzeiger der österreichischen Akademie (phil./hist.); Wien. 0378-8652.

AOAT: Alter Orient und Altes Testament: Kevelaer/Neukirchen.

AOtt: Univ. München, Arbeiten zu Text und Sprache im AT; St. Ottilien.

Apollonia: Afro-Hellenic studies, under patronage of Alexandria Patriarchate; Johannesburg, Rand Afrikaans Univ. [1 (1982)].

Aram: Oxford [1 (1989)].

ArBegG: Archiv für Begriffsgeschichte (Mainz, Akad.); Bonn.

ArbGTL: Arbeiten zur Geschichte und Theologie des Luthertums, Neue Folge; B.

ArbKiG: Arbeiten zur Kirchengeschichte; B.

ArbNTJud: Arbeiten zum NT und zum Judentum: Frankfurt/M. 0170-8856.

ArbNtTextf: Arbeiten zur Neutestamentlichen Textforschung; B/NY.

ArbT: Arbeiten zur Theologie (Calwer); Stu.

ARCE → J [News] AmEg.

Archaeología; Wrocław. 0066-605X.

Archaeology; Boston. 0003-8113.

Archaeometry; L. 0003-813X.

Archaiognōsía Ⓖ; Athenai [2 (1981)].

ArchAnz: Archäologischer Anzeiger; Berlin. 0003-8105.

ArchAth: Ⓖ Archaiología; Athēna [sic; 1 (1981); 2-5 (1982)].

ArchBbg: Archäologische Bibliographie zu JbDAI; Berlin.

ArchClasR: Archeologia Classica; R.

Archeo, attualità del passato; Milano [1-10 (1985)].

Archéo-Log: archéologie informatique; Liège, Univ. groupe Diapré. [1 (1986)].

Archéologia; (ex-Paris) Dijon, Faton. 0570-6270 → Dossiers.

ArchEph: Ⓖ Archaiologikē Ephēmeris; Athēnai.

ArchInf: Archäologische Informationen; Bonn. 3-7749-2202-0.

Architectura; München. 0044-863X.

ArchMIran: Archäologische Mitteilungen aus Iran, N.F.; Berlin.

ArchNews: Archaeological News; Tallahassee FL. 0194-3413. [13 (1984)].

ArchRCamb: Archaeological Reviews from Cambridge (Eng.). 0261-4332.

ArchRep: Archaeological Reports; Wmr, British Sch. Athens. 0570-6084.

ArchStorAnt: [= a third AION] Archeologia e Storia Antica; Napoli, Univ. Ist. Or./Cl. 0393-070X.

Arctos, Acta Philologica Fennica; Helsinki. 0570-734X.

Areopagus: Hong Kong [1 (1987) incorporates vol. 11 of Aarhus Dialog].

ArEspArq: Archivo Español de Arqueología; Madrid. 0066-6742.

ARET/S: Archivi Reali di Ebla, Testi/Studi; R.

Arethusa... wellspring of Western man; Buffalo NY. 0004-0975.

ArFrancHist: Archivum Franciscanum Historicum; Grottaferrata.

ArGlottIt: Archivio Glottologico Italiano; Firenze. 0004-0207.

ArHPont: Archivum Historiae Pontificiae; Roma.

ArKulturg: Archiv für Kulturgeschichte; Köln. 0003-9233.

ArLtgW: Archiv für Liturgiewissenschaft; Regensburg. 0066-6386.

ArOr: Archiv Orientální; Praha. 0044-8699.

ArPapF: Archiv für Papyrusforschung; Leipzig. 0066-6459.

ArRefG: Archiv für Reformationsgeschichte; Gütersloh.

ArchRep: Archaeological Reports; Wmr, British School at Athens. 0570-6084.

ArSSocRel: Archives de Sciences Sociales des Religions; Paris.

ARTANES: Aids and Research Tools in Ancient Near Eastern Studies; Malibu.

ArTGran: Archivo Teológico Granadino; Granada. 0210-1629.

ArztC: Arzt und Christ; Salzburg.

ASAE: Annales du Service des Antiquités de l'Égypte; Le Caire.

AsbTJ: Asbury Theological Journal; Wilmore, KY.

AshlandTJ: Theological J. (Ohio).

AsiaJT: Asia Journal of Theology; Tokyo.

AsMis: Assyriological Miscellanies; K, Univ. [1 (1980)].

ASOR: American Schools of Oriental Research; CM (**diss.**: Dissertation Series).

Asprenas... Scienze Teologiche; Napoli.

ASTI: Annual of the [Jerusalem] Swedish Theological Institute; Leiden.

At[AcBol/Tor/Tosc]: Atti [dell'Accademia... di Bologna / di Torino / Toscana].

ATANT: Abhandlungen zur Theologie des Alten & Neuen Testaments; Zürich.

ATD: Das Alte Testament Deutsch. Neues Göttinger Bibelwerk; Gö.

AteDial: Ateismo e Dialogo; Vaticano.

AtenRom: Atene e Roma; Firenze. 0004-6493.

Athenaeum: Letteratura e Storia dell'antichità; Pavia.

`Atiqot, English edition; J, Dept. Ant.

AtKap: Ateneum Kapłańskie; Włocławek. 0208-9041.

ATLA: American Theological Library Association; Menuchen, NJ.

AtSGlot: Atti Sodalizio Glottologico; Mi.

Atualização, Revista de Divulgação Teológica; Belo Horizonte, MG.

AuCAfr: Au cœur de l'Afrique; Burundi [22 (1982)].

AugL: Augustinus-Lexikon ➤ 879.

AugLv: Augustiniana; Leuven.

AugM: Augustinus; Madrid.

AugR: Augustinianum; Roma.

AugSt: Augustinian Studies; Villanova PA.

AulaO: Aula Orientalis; Barc [1 (1983)].

AusgF: Ausgrabungen und Funde; B.

AustinSB: Austin (TX) Sem. Bulletin.

AustralasCR: Australasian Catholic Record; Sydney. 0727-3215.

AustralBR: Australian Biblical Review; Melbourne.

AVA: ➤ Bei AVgA.

BA: Biblical Archaeologist; CM. 0006-0895.

Babel, international organ of translation; Budapest, Akad.

BaBernSt: Basler und Berner Studien zur historischen und systematischen Theologie; Bern.

Babesch: Bulletin Antieke Beschaving; Haag. 0165-9367.

BaghMit: Baghdader Mitteilungen DAI; Berlin.

BAH: Bibliothèque Archéologique et Historique (IFA-Beyrouth).

BAngIsr: Bulletin of the Anglo-Israel Archaeological Soc.; L. 0266-2442.

BangTF: Bangalore Theological Forum. [18 (1986)].

BaptQ: Baptist [Historical Soc.] Quarterly; Oxford. 0005-576X.

BArchAfr: Bulletin archéologique des travaux historiques et scientifiques (A. Antiquités nationales) B. Afrique du Nord: P.

BArchAlg: Bulletin d'Archéologie Algérienne; Alger.

BarIlAn: Bar-Ilan Annual; Ramat-Gan. 0067-4109.

BAR (-Int): British Archaeology Reports; Oxford.

BAR-W: Biblical Archaeology Review; Washington. 0098-9444.

BArte: Bollettino d'Arte; Roma.

BAsEspOr: Boletín de la Asociación Española de Orientalistas; Madrid.

BASOR: Bulletin of the American Schools of Oriental Research; CM. 0003-097X.

BASP: Bulletin, American Society of Papyrologists; NY. 0003-1186.

BAusPrax: Biblische Auslegung für die Praxis; Stuttgart.

Bazmaveb (Pazmavep; Armenian); Venezia.

BBArchäom: Berliner Beiträge zur Archäometrie; Berlin. 0344-5098. [6 (1985)].

BBB: ➤ BiBasB & BoBB.

BbbOr: Bibbia e Oriente; Bornato BS.

BBelgRom: Bulletin de l'Institut Historique Belge de Rome; R. 0073-8530. [59 (1989)].

BBudé: Bulletin de l'Association G. Budé; Paris.

BBVO: Berliner Beiträge zum Vorderen Orient: B, Reimer.

BCanadB: Bulletin of the Canadian Society of Biblical Studies; Ottawa.

BCanMed: Bulletin of the Canadian Mediterranean Institute [= BCIM].

BCentPrei: Bollettino del Centro Camuno di Studi Preistorici; Brescia. 0057-2168.

BCentProt: Bulletin du Centre Protestant d'Études; Genève.

BCH: Bulletin de Correspondance Hellénique; Paris. 0007-4217.

BChinAc: Bulletin of the China Academy; Taipei.

BCILL: Bibliothèque des Cahiers de l'Institut de Linguistique; Lv, Peeters/P, Cerf.

BCNH-T: Bibliothèque Copte de Nag Hammadi -Textes; Québec.

BEcuT: Bulletin of ecumenical theology; Enugu, Nigeria [2,1 (1989)].

Bedi Kartlisa, (44) ➤ RÉtGC (1).

BeerSheva: ❿ Annual: Bible/ANE; J.

BÉF: Bibliothèque des Écoles françaises d'Athènes et de Rome; R. ➤ MÉF.

BEgS: Bulletin of the Egyptological Seminar; NY.

BeitATJ: Beiträge zur Erforschung des Alten Testaments und des Antiken Judentums; Bern. 0722-0790.

BeitAVgArch: Beiträge zur allgemeinen und vergleichenden Archäologie; Mü, Beck.

BeitBExT: Beiträge zur biblischen Exegese und Theologie [ipsi: BET]; Frankfurt/M.

BeitEvT: Beiträge zur evangelischen Theologie; München.

BeitGbEx: Beiträge zur Geschichte der biblischen Exegese; Tübingen.

BeitHistT: Beiträge zur Historischen Theologie; Tübingen.

BeitNam: Beiträge zur Namenforschung N. F.; Heid. 0005-8114.

BeitÖkT: Beiträge zur ökumenischen Theologie; München, Schöningh. 0067-5172.

BeitRelT: Beiträge zur Religionstheologie; Mödling.

BeitSudan: Beiträge zur Sudanforschung; Wien, Univ.

Belleten (Türk Tarih Kurumu); Ankara.

Benedictina; Roma.

Berytus (Amer. Univ. Beirut); København.

BethM: ❿ Beth Mikra; Jerusalem. 0005-979X.

BÉtOr: Bulletin d'Études Orientales; Damas, IFAO.

BFaCLyon: Bulletin des Facultés Catholiques; Lyon. 0180-5282.

Bib ➤ Biblica; Roma. 0006-0887.

BibAfr: La Bible en Afrique [francophone]; Lomé, Togo.

BiBasB: Biblische Basis Bücher; Kevelaer/ Stuttgart.

BiBei: Biblische Beiträge, Schweizerisches Kath. Bibelwerk; Fribourg.

BibFe: Biblia y Fe; Bibel Heute; Stu, KBW, M. 0210-5209.

BibIll: Biblical Illustrator; Nv.

BibKonf: Biblische Konfrontationen; Stu, Kohlhammer.

Bible Bhashyam: Kottayam. 0970-2288.

BiblEscB/EstB: Biblioteca Escuela Bíblica; M / de Estudios Bíblicos, Salamanca.

BiblETL: Bibliotheca, ETL; Leuven.

BiblHumRef: Bibliotheca Humanistica et Reformatorica; Nieuwkoop, de Graaf.

BiblHumRen: Bibliothèque d'Humanisme et Renaissance; Genève/ Paris.

Biblica: commentarii Pontificii Instituti Biblici; Roma. 0006-0887.

Biblica-Lisboa (Capuchinos: given also as Revista Bíblica).

BiblMesop: Bibliotheca Mesopotamica; Malibu CA.

Biblos 1. Coimbra; 2. Wien.

BiblScRel: Biblioteca di Scienze religiose; Roma, Salesiana.

BibNot: Biblische Notizen; Bamberg. 0178-2967.

BibOrPont: Biblica et Orientalia, Pontificio Istituto Biblico; Roma.

BibTB: Biblical Theology Bulletin; St. Bonaventure NY. 0146-1079.

BibTPaid: Biblioteca Teologica; Brescia, Paideia.

BibTSt: Biblisch-Theologische Studien; Neukirchen-Vluyn. 0930-4800.

BibUnt: Biblische Untersuchungen; Regensburg.

BICLyon: Bulletin de l'Institut Catholique de Lyon [cf. ➤ RICathP].

BIFAO: Bulletin de l'Institut Français d'Archéologie Orientale; Le Caire. 0255-0962.

Bijd: Bijdragen, Filosofie en Theologie; Nijmegen.

BijH: Bijbels Handboek; Kampen = World of the Bible; GR ➤ 880.

BiKi: Bibel und Kirche; Stuttgart.

BInfWsz: Bulletin d'Information de l'Académie de Théologie Catholique; Warszawa. 0137-7000.

BInstArch: Bulletin of the Institute of Archaeology; London. 0076-0722.

BIP[Br]: Books in Print, U.S., annual; NY, Bowker [British, L, Whitaker].

BiRes: Biblical Research; Chicago. 0067-6535.

Biserica ... Ortodoxă Română; Bucureşti.

BIstFGrec: Bollettino dell'Istituto di Filologia Greca, Univ. di Padova; Roma.

Bits and bytes review; Whitefish MT.

BiWelt: Die Bibel in der Welt; Stu.

BJG: Bulletin of Judaeo-Greek Studies; Cambridge Univ. [1 (1987)].

BJRyL: Bulletin of the John Rylands Library; Manchester. 0301-102X.

BKAT: Biblischer Kommentar AT; Neuk.

BL: Book List, The Society for Old Testament Study. 0309-0892.

BLCéramEg: Bulletin de liaison ... céramique égyptienne; Le Caire, IFAO. 0255-0903 [10 (1985)].

BLitEc [Chr]: Bulletin de Littérature Ecclésiastique [Chronique]. Toulouse. 0007-4322 [0495-9396].

BLtg: Bibel und Liturgie; Wien-Klosterneuburg.

BMB: Bulletin du Musée de Beyrouth.

BMes: Bulletin, the Society for Mesopotamian Studies; Toronto [2-4 (1982)].

BMonde ➤ CahTrB.

BMosA [ipsi AIEMA]: Bulletin d'information de l'Association internationale pour l'étude de la mosaïque antique; Paris. 0761-8808.

BO: Bibliotheca Orientalis; Leiden. 0006-1913.

BoBB: Bonner Biblische Beiträge; Königstein.

BogSmot: Bogoslovska Smotra; Zagreb. 0352-3101.

BogTrud: Ⓖ Bogoslovskiye Trudi; Moskva.

BogVest: Bogoslovni Vestnik; Ljubljana [46 (1986)].

BonnJb: Bonner Jahrbücher.

Boreas [1. Uppsala, series]; 2. Münsterische Beiträge zur Archäologie. 0344-810X.

BOriento: Biblia kaj Oriento (Esperanto) [1 (1986)].

BPast: Biblical pastoral bulletin; Nairobi, BICAM. [6 (1987)].

BR: Bible Review; Wsh. 8755-6316 [1 (1985)].

BREF: Bibliographie religieuse en français; Dourgne ➤ 1,1042*.

BRefB: Bulletin of the Institute for Reformation Biblical Studies: Fort Wayne [1 (1989)].

BRevuo ➤ BOriento.

BritJREd: British Journal of Religious Education; London [5 (1983)].

BrownJudSt/StRel: Brown Judaic Studies / Studies in Religion; Atlanta.

BS: Bibliotheca Sacra; Dallas, TX. 0006-1921.

BSAA: Boletín del Seminario de Estudios de Arte y Arqueología; Valladolid.

BSAC: Bulletin de la Société d'Archéologie Copte; Le Caire.

BSeptCog: Bulletin of the International Organization for Septuagint and Cognate Studies; ND.

BSignR: Bulletin Signalétique, religions; Paris. 0180-9296.

BSLP: Bulletin de la Société de Linguistique; Paris.

BSNAm: Biblical Scholarship in North America; Atlanta, SBL.

BSNEJap ➤ Oriento.

BSO: Bulletin of the School of Oriental and African Studies; London. 0041-977X.

BSoc[Fr]Ég: Bulletin de la Société [Française] d'Égyptologie; Genève [Paris].

BSoGgIt: Bollettino della Società Geografica Italiana; R. 0037-8755.

BSpade: Bible and Spade; Ballston NY.

BStLat: Bollettino di Studi Latini; N.

BStor: Biblioteca di storia e storiografia dei tempi biblici; Brescia.

BSumAg: Bulletin on Sumerian Agriculture; Cambridge. 0267-0658.

BTAfr: Bulletin de Théologie Africaine; Kinshasa.

BTAM: Bulletin de Théologie Ancienne et Médiévale; Louvain. ➤ RTAM.

BThemT: Bibliothek Themen der Theologie; Stuttgart.

BToday: The Bible Today; Collegeville MN. 0006-0836.

BTrans: The Bible Translator [Technical/ Practical, each 2 annually]; Stuttgart. 0260-0943.

BtSt: Biblisch-theologische Studien (ex-Biblische Studien); Neukirchen.

BTT: Bible de tous les temps; P.

BTZ: Berliner Theologische Zeitschrift; Berlin. 0724-6137.

BUBS: Bulletin of the United Bible Societies; Stu.

BudCSt: Buddhist-Christian Studies; Honolulu, Univ. 0882-0945 [4 (1984)].

Burgense; Burgos.

BurHist: Buried History; Melbourne.

BVieChr: Bible et Vie Chrétienne NS; Paris.

BViewp: Biblical Viewpoint; Greenville SC, B. Jones Univ. 0006-0925.

BW: Beiträge zur Wissenschaft vom Alten und Neuen Testament; Stuttgart.

BySlav: Byzantinoslavica; Praha. 0007-7712.

ByZ: Byzantinische Zeitschrift; München. 0007-7704.

Ⓖ Byzantina; Thessaloniki.

Byzantion; Bruxelles.

ByzFor: Byzantinische Forschungen; Amsterdam. 90-256-0619-9.

BZ: Biblische Zeitschrift; Paderborn. 0006-2014.

BZA[N]W: Beihefte zur ➤ ZAW[ZNW].

CAD: [Chicago] Assyrian Dictionary; Glückstadt. ➤ 890.

CADIR: Centre pour l'Analyse du Discours Religieux; Lyon ➤ SémBib.

CAH: Cambridge Ancient History rev; Cambridge Univ. ➤ 785.

CahArchéol: Cahiers Archéologiques; Paris. 2-7084-0131-9.

CahCMéd: Cahiers de Civilisation Médiévale; Poitiers.

CahDAFI: Cahiers de la Délégation Archéologique Française en Iran; Paris. 0765-104X.

CahÉv: Cahiers Évangile; Paris. 0222-8741.

CahHist: Cahiers d'Histoire; Lyon.

CahIntSymb: Cahiers Internationaux de Symbolique; Mons, Belgique.

CahLV: Cahiers voor Levensverdieping; Averbode.

CahRechScRel: Cahiers de Recherche en Sciences de la Religion; Québec.

CahRenan: Cahiers du Cercle Ernest Renan; Paris.

CahSpIgn: Cahiers de spiritualité ignatienne; Québec.

CahSPR: Cahiers de l'École des Sciences Philosophiques et Religieuses, Fac. Univ. St-Louis; Bru [3s (1988)].

CahTrB: Cahiers de traduction biblique; Pierrefitte France. 0755-1371.

CahTun: Les Cahiers (de la Faculté des Lettres) de Tunisie; Tunis.

CalvaryB: Calvary Baptist Theological Journal; Lansdale PA. 8756-0429 [1 (1985)].

CalvinT: Calvin Theological Journal; Grand Rapids MI. 0008-1795.

CalwTMon: Calwer Theologische Monographien (A: Biblisch); Stuttgart.

CamCW: Cambridge Commentary on Writings of the Jewish and Christian World 200 BC to AD 200: C. 0-521-28554-2.

CanadB: Canadian Society of Biblical Studies Bulletin; Toronto [49 (1989)].

CanadCR: Canadian Catholic Review; Saskatoon.

Carmel: Tilburg.

Carmelus: Roma. 0008-6673.

CARNES: Computer-aided research in Near Eastern Studies; Malibu CA. 0742-2334.

Carthaginensia; Murcia, Inst. Teol. 0213-4381 [1 (1985)].

CathCris: Catholicism in crisis; ND.

CathHR: Catholic Historical Review; Wsh. 0008-8080.

Catholica (Moehler-Institut, Paderborn); Münster.

Catholicisme: Paris ➤ 882.

Catholic Studies, Tokyo ➤ Katorikku.

CathTR: Catholic Theological Review; Clayton, Australia (NTAbs 30,150: Hong Kong) [6 (1984)].

CathTSocAmPr: ➤ PrCTSAm [AnCTS].

CATSS: Computer assisted tools for Septuagint studies: Atlanta ➤ SBL.

CBQ: Catholic Biblical Quarterly; Washington, DC. 0008-7912.

CC: La Civiltà Cattolica; R. 0009-8167.

CCGraec/Lat/Med: Corpus Christianorum, series graeca / latina / continuatio mediaev.; Turnhout.

CdÉ: Chronique d'Égypte; Bruxelles.

CEB: Commentaire évangelique de la Bible; Vaux/Seine ➤ Édifac.

CédCarthB: Centre d'Études et de Documentation de la Conservation de Carthage, Bulletin; Tunis.

Center Journal; Notre Dame.

CERDAC: (Atti) Centro di Ricerca e Documentazione Classica; Milano.

CETÉDOC: Centre de Traitement Électronique des Documents; Lv.

CGL: Coptic Gnostic Library ➤ NHS.

CGMG: Christlicher Glaube in moderner Gesellschaft; FrB.

ChCu: Church and Culture; Vatican [1 (1984)].

CHermProt: Centre d'Herméneutique Protestante.

ChH: Church History; Berne, Ind.

CHH: Center for Hermeneutical Studies in Hellenistic and Modern Culture; Berkeley CA.

Chiea [ChAfC]: Nairobi, Catholic Higher Institute of Eastern Africa.

CHIran: Cambridge History of Iran; C ➤ 883.

Chiron: Geschichte, Epigraphie; München.

CHistEI: ⊕ Cathedra, History of Eretz-Israel; Jerusalem.

CHist-J: Jerusalem Cathedra.

CHJud: Cambridge History of Judaism; C ➤ 884.

Chm: Churchman 1. (Anglican); London: 0009-661X / 2. (Humanistic); St. Petersburg FL: 0009-6628.

ChrCent: Christian Century; Chicago.

Christus; 1. Paris; 2. México.

Chr.JRel: Christian Jewish Relations; L.

ChrNIsr: Christian News from Israel; J.

ChrOost: Het Christelijk Oosten; Nijmegen.

ChrSchR: Christian Scholar's Review; Houston TX.

ChrT: Christianity Today; Carol Stream IL. 0009-5761.

ChSt: Chicago Studies; Mundelein IL.

Church: NY, Nat. Pastoral Life.

ChWoman: The Church Woman [Protestant, Roman Catholic, Orthodox, other Christian]; NY. 0009-6598.

CistSt: Cistercian Studies; ed. Getsemani KY; pub. Chimay, Belgium.

Citeaux; Achel, Belgium. 0009-7497.

Cithara: Essays in the Judaeo-Christian Tradition; St. Bonaventure (NY) Univ.

CiTom: Ciencia Tomista; Salamanca.

CiuD: Ciudad de Dios; M. 0009-7756.

CivClCr: Civiltà classica e cristiana; Genova. 0392-8632.

CiVit: Città di Vita; Firenze. [0]009-7632.

Claret: Claretianum; Roma.

ClasA: [formerly California Studies in] Classical Antiquity; Berkeley.

ClasB: Classical Bulletin; Ch. 0009-8137.

ClasJ: Classical Journal; Greenville SC. 0009-8353.

ClasMed: Classica et Mediaevalia; København. 0106-5815.

ClasModL: Classical and Modern Literature; Terre Haute IN.

ClasOutl: The Classical Outlook; Ch [ed. Miami Univ. OH]. 0009-8361.

ClasPg: Classical Philology; Chicago. 0009-8361.

ClasQ: Classical Quarterly NS; Oxford. 0009-8388.

ClasR: Classical Review NS; Oxford. 0009-840X.

ClasWo: Classical World; Pittsburgh. 0009-8148.

CLehre: Die Christenlehre; Berlin.

CleR: Clergy Rev. [➤ PrPeo 1 (1987)].

ClubH: Club des Hébraïsants; Boran.

CMatArch: Contributi e materiali di archeologia orientale; Roma, Univ. [1 (1986)].

CNRS: Conseil National de Recherche Scientifique; Paris.

CogF: Cogitatio Fidei; Paris.

ColcCist: Collectanea Cisterciensia; Forges, Belgique.

ColcFranc: Collectanea Franciscana; Roma. 0010-0749.

ColcT: Collectanea Theologica; Warszawa. 0137-6985.

ColcTFu: Collectanea theol. Universitatis Fujen = Shenhsileh Lunchi; Taipei.

CollatVL: Collationes, Vlaams... Theologie en Pastoraal; Gent.

Colloquium; Auckland, Sydney.

ColStFen: Collezione di Studi Fenici; Roma, Univ.

ComLtg: Communautés et Liturgies; Ottignies (Belgique).

Commentary; NY. 0010-2601.

CommBras: Communio Brasiliensis: Rio de Janeiro.

CommND: Communio USA; Notre Dame. 0094-2065.

CommRevue: Communio [various languages, not related to ComSev]: revue catholique internationale; Paris.

CommStrum: Communio, strumento internazionale per un lavoro teologico; Milano.

Communio deutsch ➤ IkaZ.

ComOT: Commentaar op het Oude Testament. Kampen.

CompHum: Computers and the Humanities; Osprey FL. 0010-4817.

CompINT: Compendium rerum Iudaicarum ad NT; Assen.

Compostellanum; Santiago de Compostela.

ComRatisbNT: Comentario de Ratisbona; Barc.

ComRelM: Commentarium pro Religiosis et Missionariis; Roma.

ComSev: Communio; Sevilla. 0010-3705.

ComSpirAT/NT: Commenti spirituali dell'Antico / Nuovo Testamento; Roma.

ComTeolNT: Commentario Teologico del NT; Brescia.

ComViat: Communio Viatorum; Praha. 0010-7133.

ConBib: Coniectanea Biblica OT/NT; Malmö.

Conc: Concilium, variis linguis; P,E, etc. [deutsch = ➤ IZT].

ConcordJ: Concordia Journal; St. Louis. 0145-7233.

ConcordTQ: Concordia Theological Quarterly; Fort Wayne.

ConoscRel: Conoscenza religiosa; Firenze.

Consensus: Canadian Lutheran; Winnipeg.

ConsJud: Conservative Judaism; NY. 0010-6542.

Contacts/Orthodoxe, de théologie et spiritualité; P. 0045-8325.

ContrIstStorAnt: Contributi dell'Istituto di Storia Antica; Milano, Univ. Sacro Cuore.

Coptologia [also for Egyptology]: Thunder Bay ONT, Lakehead Univ.

CouStR: Council for the Study of Religion Bulletin; Macon GA, Mercer Univ.

CovQ: Covenant Quarterly; Chicago.

CRAI: Comptes rendus de l'Académie des Inscriptions et Belles-Lettres; Paris.

Creation; Oakland CA.

Cretan Studies; Amst. [1 (1988) 90-256-0949-X; 52-X].

CRIPEL ➤ SocUÉg.

CriswT: Criswell Theological Review; Dallas [1 (1986)].

Criterio; Buenos Aires. 0011-1473.

CrkvaSv: Crkva u Svijetu; Split.

CrNSt: Cristianesimo nella Storia; Bologna. 0393-3598.

CroatC: Croatica Christiana; Zagreb.

CrossC: Cross Currents; West Nyack NJ. 0011-1953.

Crux: Vancouver. 0011-2186.

CSacSN: Corpus Sacrae Scripturae Neerlandicae Medii Aevi; Leiden.

CSCO: Corpus Scriptorum Christianorum Orientalium; Lv. 0070-0401.

CuadJer: Cuadernos Bíblicos, Institución S. Jerónimo; Valencia.

CuadFgClás: Cuadernos de Filología Clásica; M, Univ.

CuadTeol: Cuadernos de Teología; Buenos Aires [6,3 (1983)].

CuadTrad: Cuadernos de Traducción y Interpretación; Barc.

CuBíb: Cultura Bíblica; M: AFEBE. 0211-2493.

CuesT: Cuestiones Teológicas; Medellín [14 (1987)].

CuH: Culture and History; K.

CurrTMiss: Currents in Theology and Mission; St. Louis. 0098-2113.

CyrMeth: Cyrillomethodianum; Thessaloniki.

D: director (in Indice etiam *auctor*) Dissertationis.

DAFI: Délégation Archéologique Française en Iran (Mém); Paris.

DAI: Deutsches Archäologisches Institut (Baghdad etc.) ➤ Mi(tt).

DanTTs: Dansk Teologisk Tidsskrift; København.

DanVMed/Skr: Det Kongelige Danske Videnskabornes Selskap, Historisk-Filosofiske Meddelelser / Skriften; K.

DBS [= SDB], Dictionnaire de la Bible, Supplément; P ➤ 809.

Dedalo: São Paulo.

DeltChr: Deltion tes christianikēs archaiologikēs hetaireias: Athēna [4,12 (for 1984: 1986)].

DeltVM: ☉ Deltío vivlikôn meletôn (= Bulletin des Études Bibliques); Athēnai.

DHGE: Dictionnaire d'Histoire et de Géographie Ecclésiastiques; P ➤ 885.

Diachronica, international journal for historical linguistics; Hildesheim [1 (1984)].

Diakonia; Mainz/Wien [13 (1982)] 0341-9592; Stu [8 (1982)].

DialArch: Dialoghi di Archeologia; Mi.

DiálEcum: Diálogo Ecuménico; Salamanca. 0210-2870.

Dialog; Minneapolis. 0012-2033.

DialTP: Diálogo teológico; El Paso TX.

DictSpir: Dictionnaire de Spiritualité; P. ➤ 886.

Didascalia; Rosario ARG.

Didaskalia; Lisboa.

DielB: Dielheimer Blätter zum Alten Testament [ipsi DBAT]; Heid.

Dionysius: Halifax, Dalhousie University. 0705-1085.

Direction; Fresno CA.

DiscEg: Discussions in Egyptology; Oxford. 0268-3083 [1 (1985)].

Disciple, the (Disciples of Christ); St. Louis. 0092-8372.

Diss [= ᴰ, etiam Director]: Dissertation.

DissA: Dissertation Abstracts International; AA/L. -A [= US]: 0419-4209 [C = Europe. 0307-6075].

DissHRel: Dissertationes ad historiam religionum (supp. Numen); Leiden.

Divinitas, Pont. Acad. Theol. Rom. (Lateranensis); Vaticano. 0012-4222.

DivThom: Divus Thomas; Piacenza. 0012-4257.

DJD: Discoveries in the Judaean Desert; Oxford.

DLZ: Deutsche Literaturzeitung; Berlin. 0012-043X.

DMA: Dictionary of the Middle Ages; NY ➤ 887.

DocCath: Documentation Catholique; Paris.

DoctCom: Doctor Communis; Vaticano.

DoctLife: Doctrine and Life; Dublin.

DOG: Deutsche Orient-Gesellschaft: B.

Dor ➤ JBQ.

DosB: Les dossiers de la Bible; P.

DossHA: Histoire et archéologie, les dossiers; Dijon.

DowR: Downside Review; Bath. 0012-5806.

DPA: Dizionario patristico e di antichità cristiane; Casale Monferrato ➤ 888.

DrevVost: ❸ Drevnij Vostok; Moskva.

DrewG: The Drew [Theological School] Gateway; Madison NJ.

DumbO: Dumbarton Oaks Papers; CM. 0070-7546.

DutchMgA: Dutch Monographs in Ancient History and Archaeology; Amst.

E: editor, Herausgeber, *a cura di*.

EAfJE: East African Journal of Evangelical Theology; Machakos, Kenya.

EAsJT: East Asia Journal of Theology [combining NE & SE AJT]; Tokyo. 0217-3859.

EAPast: East Asian Pastoral Review; Manila. 0040-0564.

ÉcAnn: Écoutez et Annoncez, mensuel; Lomé, Togo [6 (1984)].

ÉchMClas: Échos du Monde Classique/ Classical Views; Calgary. 0012-9356.

ÉchSM: Les Échos de Saint-Maurice; Valais, Abbaye.

EcOr: Ecclesia Orans, periodica de scientiis liturgicis; R, Anselmiano [1,1 (1984)].

ÉcoutBib: Écouter la Bible; Paris.

EcuR: Ecumenical Review; Geneva. 0013-0790.

EDIFAC: Éditions de la Faculté libre de Théologie Évangélique; Vaux/Seine.

EfMex: Efemerides Mexicana; Tlalpan.

Egb: Ergänzungsband.

ÉglRur après 488 (1987) ➤ Sève.

ÉglT: Église et Théologie; Ottawa.

EgVO: Egitto e Vicino Oriente; Pisa.

ÉHRel: Études d'histoire des religions.

Einzb: Einzelband.

EkK [Vor]: Evangelischer-katholischer Kommentar zum NT; Z/Köln; Neukirchen-Vluyn ['Vorarbeiten'].

EkkT: ❺ Ekklēsía kaì Theología; L.

Elenchos, ... pensiero antico; Napoli.

Elliniká; ❺ Thessaloniki.

Emerita: (lingüística clásica); M.

Emmanuel: St. Meinrads IN/NY. 0013-6719.

Enc. Biblica ➤ EnṣMiqr.

EncHebr: ❺ Encyclopaedia Hebraica; J/TA.

Enchoria, Demotistik/Koptologie; Wiesbaden. 3-447-02807-6.

EncIran: Encyclopaedia Iranica; London [I,1 (1982)] ➤ 975.

EncIslam: Encyclopédie de l'Islam. Nouvelle édition; Leiden/P ➤ 890.

EncKat: Encyklopedia Katolicka; Lublin ➤ 891.

Encounter (theol.); Indianapolis.

EncRel: (1) ᴱ*Eliade* M., The encyclopedia of religion; NY ➤ 892; (2) Enciclopedia delle Religioni; Firenze.

EncTF: Enciclopedia di Teologia Fondamentale; Genova ➤ 3, 858.

EnṣMiqr: ❸ Enṣiqlopediya miqrā'ît, Encyclopaedia Biblica; Jerusalem.

Entschluss: Wien. 0017-4602.

EnzMär: Enzyklopädie des Märchens; B ➤ 3, 860.

EOL: Ex Oriente Lux ➤ 1.Jb/2. Phoenix.

Eos, ... philologia; Wsz. 0012-7825.

EpAnat: Epigraphica anatolica; Bonn.

ÉPHÉ[H/R]: École Pratique des Hautes-Études, Annuaire [Hist.-Pg. / Sc. Rel.]; Paris.

EpHetVyzSpoud: ❺ Ephēmeris tēs Hetaireías tōn Vyzantinōn Spoudōn; Athēnai.

EphLtg: Ephemerides Liturgicae; R.

EphMar: Ephemerides Mariologicae; Madrid.

ÉPR: Études préliminaires aux religions orientales dans l'Empire romain; Leiden.

Eranos[/Jb]: Acta Philologica Suecana; Uppsala / Jahrbuch; Frankfurt/M (< Z).

ErbAuf: Erbe und Auftrag; Beuron.

Eretz-Israel (partly ❸), 'annual'; Jerusalem. 0071-108X.

ErfTSt/Schr: Erfurter Theologische Studien/ Schriften.

ErtFor: Ertrag der Forschung; Da, Wiss. 0174-0695.

EscrVedat: Escritos del Vedat [del Torrente]; Valencia. 0210-3133.

EsprVie: Esprit et Vie: 1. [< Ami du Clergé]; Langres; 2. (series) Chambray.

EstAgust: Estudio Agustiniano; Valladolid.

EstBíb: Estudios Bíblicos; Madrid. 0014-1437.

EstDeusto: Estudios Universidad Deusto: Madrid.

EstE: Estudios Eclesiásticos; Madrid. 0210-1610.

EstFranc: Estudios Franciscanos; Barcelona.

EstJos: Estudios Josefinos; Valladolid.

EstLul: Estudios Lulianos; Mallorca.

EstMar: Estudios Marianos; Madrid.

EstMonInstJer: Estudios y Monografias, Institución S. Jerónimo (bíblica); Valencia.

EstTrin: Estudios Trinitarios; Salamanca.

EstudosB: Estudos Bíblicos; Petrópolis [no longer part of **REB**].

ÉtBN: Études Bibliques, Nouvelle Série; Paris. 0760-3541.

ÉtClas: Les études classiques; Namur. 0014-200X.

Eternity; Philadelphia [34 (1983)].

ÉtFranc: Études Franciscaines; Blois.

ÉtIndE: Études Indo-Européennes; Lyon.

ETL: Ephemerides Theologicae Lovanienses; Leuven. 0013-9513.

ÉtPapyr: Études [Société Égyptienne] de Papyrologie; Le Caire.

ÉtPgHist: Études de Philologie et d'Histoire; Genève, Droz.

ÉTRel: Études Théologiques et Religieuses; Montpellier. 0014-2239.

ÉtTrav: Études et Travaux; Varsovie.

Études; Paris. 0014-1941.

Euhemer (❷ hist. rel.); Warszawa. 0014-2298

EuntDoc: Euntes Docete; Roma.

EurHS: Europäische Hochschulschriften / Publ. Universitaires Européennes; Bern.

Evangel; Edinburgh. 0265-4547.

EvErz: Der evangelische Erzieher; Frankfurt/M. 0014-3413.

EvJ: Evangelical Journal; Myerstown PA [3 (1985)].

EvKL: Evangelisches Kirchenlexikon; ➤ 894.

EvKom: Evangelische Kommentare; Stuttgart. 0300-4236.

EvQ[RT]: Evangelical Quarterly [Review of Theology]; Exeter.

EvT: Evangelische Theologie, NS; München. 0014-3502.

EWest: East and West | 1. L / 2. R.

EWSp: Encyclopedia of World Spirituality; NY/L.

ExAud: Ex auditu, ongoing symposium annual: Princeton (sb. Pickwick) 0883-0053 ➤ 4,567.

ExcSIsr: Excavations and Surveys in Israel ➤ Ḥadašot; Jerusalem. [Winona Lake: Eisenbrauns $10]. 0334-1607.

Expedition (archaeol., anthrop.); Philadelphia. 0014-4738.

Explor [sic]; Evanston. 0362-0876.

ExpTim: The Expository Times; Edinburgh. 0014-5246.

F&R: Faith and Reason; Front Royal VA. 0098-5449.

FascBíb: Fascículos bíblicos; Madrid.

Faventia: classica; Barc. 0210-7570.

fg./fil.: filologico, filosofico.

FgNt: Filologia neotestamentaria; Córdoba, Univ. [1 (1988)].

FidH: Fides et Historia; Longview TX [20 (1988)].

FilRTSt: Filosofia della Religione, Testi e Studi; Brescia.

FilT: Filosofia e teologia; Napoli.

Fønix [6 (1982)].

FoiTemps: La Foi et le Temps. NS; Tournai.

FoiVie: Foi et Vie; Paris. 0015-5357.

FolOr: Folia Orientalia, Polska Akademia Nauk; Kraków. 0015-5675.

Fondamenti; Brescia, Paideia [4 (1986)].

ForBib: Forschung zur Bibel; Wü/Stu.

ForBMusB: Forschungen und Berichte, Staatliche Museen zu Berlin.

ForGLehrProt: Forschungen zur Geschichte und Lehre des Protestantismus; Mü.

ForJüdChrDial: Forschungen zum jüdisch-christlichen Dialog; Neuk.

ForKiDG: Forschungen zur Kirchen- und Dogmengeschichte; Gö.

Fornvännen (Svensk Antikvarisk Forskning); Lund. 0015-7813.

ForSystÖ: Forschungen zur Systematischen & Ökumenischen Theologie; Gö.

ForTLing: Forum Theologiae Linguisticae; Bonn.

Forum [= Foundations & Facets]; Bonner MT. 0883-4970.

ForumKT: Forum Katholische Theologie; Münster. 0178-1626 [1 (1985)].

FOTLit: Forms of OT Literature; GR, Eerdmans.

FraJudBei: Frankfurter Judaistische Beiträge: Fra.

FranBog: Franciscanum, ciencias del espíritu; Bogotá. 0120-1468.

FrancSt: Franciscan Studies; St. Bonaventure, NY. 0080-5459.

FranzSt: Franziskanische Studien; Pd.

FraTSt: Frankfurter Theologische Studien; Fra, S. Georgen.

FreibRu: Freiburger Rundbrief. ... christlich-jüdische Begegnung; FrB.

FreibTSt: Freiburger Theologische Studien; Freiburg/Br.

FreibZ: Freiburger Zeitschrift für Philosophie und Theologie; Fribourg/ Suisse.

FRL: Forschungen zur Religion und Literatur des Alten und NTs; Gö.

FutUo: Il futuro dell'uomo; Firenze, Assoc. Teilhard. 0390-217X [12 (1985)].

❻ *Graece*; title in Greek.

GCS: Die Griechischen Christlichen Schriftsteller der ersten Jahrhunderte; oBerlin.

GDE / UTET: Grande dizionario enciclopedico; Torino, Unione Tipografica.

GdT: Giornale di Teologia; Brescia.

GeistL: Geist und Leben; Wü.

Genava (archéologie, hist. art); Genève. 0072-0585.

GenLing: General Linguistics; University Park PA.

Georgica: Jena/Tbilissi. 0232-4490.

GerefTTs: Gereformeerd Theologisch Tijdschrift; Kampen. 0016-8610.

Gerión, revista de Historia Antigua; Madrid, Univ. 0213-0181.

GGA: Göttingische Gelehrte Anzeigen; Göttingen. 0017-1549.

GidsBW: Gidsen bij de Bijbelwetenschap; Kampen, Kok.

GItFg: Giornale italiano di filologia; Napoli. 0017-0461.

GLA/NT: Grande Lessico dell'A/NT (< TWA/NT); Brescia ➔ 895.

GLÉCS: (Comptes rendus) Groupe Linguistique d'Études Chamito-Sémitiques; Paris.

GLern: Glaube und Lernen; Zeitschrift für theologische Urteilsbildung; Göttingen, VR [2 (1987)].

GLeven: Geest en leven [continuing OnsGLev] 65 (1988); Eindhoven.

Glotta: griech.-lat.; Göttingen. 0017-1298.

Gnomon; klass. Altertum; München. 0017-1417.

GöMiszÄg: Göttinger Miszellen ... zur ägyptologischen Diskussion; Göttingen. 0344-385X.

GöOrFor: Göttinger Orientforschungen; Würzburg.

GöTArb: Göttinger Theologische Arbeiten; Göttingen.

GraceTJ: Grace Theological Journal; Winona Lake IN. 0198-666X.

GraecChrPrim: Graecitas Christianorum Primaeva; Nijmegen, van den Vegt.

Grail, ecumenical quarterly; Waterloo ONT, St. Jerome's College [1,1 (1985)].

GrArab: Graeco-Arabica; Athenai.

GreeceR: Greece and Rome; Oxford.

Greg[LA]: Gregorianum; R, Pontificia Universitas Gregoriana [Liber Annualis].

GrenzfTP: Grenzfragen zwischen Theologie und Philosophie; Köln.

GRIC: Groupe de recherches islamo-chrétien; P.

GrOrTR: Greek Orthodox Theological Review; Brookline MA. 0017-3894.

GrPT: Growing Points in Theology.

GrRByz: Greek, Roman and Byzantine Studies; CM. 0017-3916.

GrSinal: Grande Sinal, revista de espiritualidade; Petrópolis.

Gymn: Gymnasium; Heid. 0342-5231.

❶ *(Neo-)hebraice*; (modern) Hebrew.

HaBeiA: Hamburger Beiträge zur Archäologie. 0341-3152.

Ḥadašôt arkeologiyôt **❶** [News]; J, Education ministry museum dept. ➔ ExcSIsr.

HalleB: Hallesche Beiträge zur Orientwissenschaft; Halle. 0233-2205.

Hamdard Islamicus [research]; Pakistan. 0250-7196.

Handes Amsorya [armen.]; Wien.

HarvSemMon/Ser: Harvard Semitic Monographs / (Museum) Series; CM.

HarvStClasPg: Harvard Studies in Classical Philology; CM.

HarvTR: The Harvard Theological Review; CM. 0017-8160.

HbAltW: Handbuch der Altertumswissenschaft; München.

HbAT/NT: Handbuch zum Alten/Neuen Testament; Tübingen.
HbDG: Handbuch der Dogmengeschichte; Freiburg/B.; ➤ 1,896.
HbDTG: Handbuch der Dogmen- und Theologiegeschichte; Göttingen ➤ 4, 799.
HbFT: Handbuch der Fundamentaltheologie; FrB ➤ 896.
HbOr: Handbuch der Orientalistik; Leiden.
HbRelG: Handbuch der Religionsgeschichte; Göttingen.
HbRwG: Handbuch Religionswissenschaftlicher Grundbegriffe; Stuttgart ➤ 897.
HDienst: Heiliger Dienst; Salzburg. 0017-9620.
HebAnR: Hebrew Annual Review; Columbus, Ohio State Univ.
HebBWJud: Hebräische Beiträge zur Wissenschaft des Judentums deutsch angezeigt: Heidelberg. [1/1s (1985)].
HebSt: Hebrew Studies; Madison WI. 0146-4094.
Hekima; Nairobi, Jesuit School of Theology [1,1 (1988)].
Helikon (Tradizione e Cultura Classica, Univ. Messina); Roma.
Hellenika; Bochum. 0018-0084; ➤ *Elliniká*.
Helmántica (humanidades clásicas, Univ.); Salamanca.
Henceforth, journal for Advent Christian thought; Lenox MA [14 (1985s)].
Henoch (ebraismo): Torino (Univ.).
Hephaistos, Theorie / Praxis Arch.; Ha.
HerdKor: Herder-Korrespondenz; Freiburg/Br. 0018-0645.
HerdTKom, NT: Herders Theologischer Kommentar zum NT; FrB.
Heresis, revue d'hérésiologie médiévale; Villegly/Carcassonne, Centre Nat. Ét. Cathares. 0758-3737 [4s (1985)].
Hermathena; Dublin. 0018-0750.
Hermeneus, antieke cultuur; Amersfoort.
Hermeneutica; Urbino, Univ.
Hermes, Klassische Philologie; Wiesbaden. 0018-0777.
HermUnT: Hermeneutische Untersuchungen zur Theologie; Tü. 0440-7180.
HervTS: Hervormde Teologiese Studies; Pretoria.

Hesperia (American School of Classical Studies at Athens); Princeton. 0018-098X.
Hethitica. Travaux édités; Lv.
HeythJ: Heythrop Journal; London. 0018-1196.
HistJ: Historical Journal; Cambridge.
HistJb: Historisches Jahrbuch; Mü.
Historia; 1. Baden-Baden: 0018-2311; 2. Santiago, Univ. Católica Chile.
HistRel: History of Religions; Chicago. 0018-2710.
HLand[S]: Das Heilige Land (Deutscher Verein) Köln [(Schw. Verein); Luzern].
Hokhma; Lausanne. 0379-7465.
HolyL: Holy Land: J, OFM. 0333-4851 [5 (1985)]. ➤ **TerraS.**
Homoousios (consustancial); Buenos Aires, Ortodoxía antioquena [1 (1986)].
HomPastR: Homiletic and Pastoral Review; New York. 0018-4268.
HomRel: Homo religiosus (histoire des religions); Louvain-la-Neuve.
HorBibT: Horizons in Biblical Theology (Old & NT); Pittsburgh. 0195-9085.
Horeb: Histoire Orientation Recherche Exégèse Bible; Sèvres.
Horizons (College Theology Society); Villanova PA. 0360-9669.
Hsientai Hsüehyüan (= Universitas); Taipei.
HSprF: Historische Sprachforschung ab 101 (1988) = **ZvglSpr.** 0044-3646.
HUC|A: Hebrew Union College [+ Jewish Institute of Religion] Annual; Cincinnati.
Humanitas; 1. Brescia; 2. Tucuman.
HumT: Humanística e Teologia; Porto [6 (1985)].
HWomenRel: History of women religious, news and notes; St. Paul MN. [1,3 (1988)].
Hydra, Middle Bronze Age studies; Uppsala, Univ. [1 (1985)].
Hypom: Hypomnemata; Göttingen, VR.
HZ: Historische Zeitschrift; München. 0018-2613.
IAJS: ➤ **RAMBI.**

IBMiss: International (formerly Occasional) Bulletin of Missionary Research; Minneapolis (Lutheran).

ICC: International Critical Commentary; Edinburgh.

ICI: Informations Catholiques Internationales; Paris.

IClasSt: Illinois Classical Studies; Urbana. 0363-1923 [11 (1985)].

IFA: Institut Français d'Archéologie (Orientale, Le Caire / Beyrouth).

IglV: Iglesia Viva; Valencia/Madrid.

IkaZ: Internationale Kath. Zeitschrift, Communio; Rodenkirchen. 0341-8693.

IkiZ: Internationale kirchliche Zeitschrift; Bern. 0020-9252.

ILN: Illustrated London News; London. 0019-2422.

Immanuel (ecumenical); J. 0302-8127.

Index Jewish Studies → RAMBI.

IndIranJ: Indo-Iranian Journal; (Canberra-) Leiden. 0019-7246.

IndJT: Indian Journal of Theology; Serampore.

IndMissR: Indian Missiological Review; Shillong. [7 (1985)].

IndogF: Indogermanische Forschungen; Berlin. 0019-7262.

IndTSt: Indian Theological Studies; Bangalore, St. Peter's.

InnsBeiKultW/SpraW/TS: Innsbrucker Beiträge zur Kulturwissenschaft / Sprachwissenschaft / Theologische Studien.

Inst. Jerón. → EstMon.

IntBbg[R/Z]: Internationale Bibliographie | der Rezensionen wissenschaftlicher Literatur [10 (1980)] / der Zeitschriftenliteratur aus allen Gebieten des Wissens [16 (1980)]; Osnabrück.

IntCathRCom → CommND.

Interp: Interpretation; Richmond VA. 0020-9643.

IntJNaut: International Journal of Nautical Archaeology L/NY. 0305-7445.

IntJPhR: International Journal for the Philosophy of Religion; The Hague.

IntJSport: International Journal of the history of sport; L. [5 (1988)].

IntRMiss: International Review of Mission; London. 0020-8582.

Iran; London, British Institute Persian Studies. 0578-6967.

IrAnt: Iranica Antiqua; Leiden.

Iraq; L, British School of Archaeology. 0021-0889.

IrBSt: Irish Biblical Studies; Belfast. 0268-6112.

Irén: Irénikon; Chevetogne. 0021-0978.

IrTQ: Irish Theological Quarterly; Maynooth. 0021-1400.

ISBEnc: International Standard Bible Encyclopedia³; GR, Eerdmans → 898.

Islam, Der: Berlin. 0021-1818.

Islamochristiana; Roma, Pontificio Istituto di Studi Arabi. 0392-7288.

IsrEJ: Israel Exploration Journal; Jerusalem. 0021-2059.

IsrJBot/Zool: Israel Journal of Botany 0021-213X / Zoology 0021-2210: Jerusalem.

IsrLawR: Israel Law Review; Jerusalem. 0021-2237.

IsrMusJ: Israel Museum Journal; Jerusalem.

IsrNumJ[SocB]: Israel Numismatic Journal, J [Society Bulletin: TA].

IsrOrSt: Israel Oriental Studies; Tel Aviv.

Istina; Paris. 0021-2423.

IVRA (Jura); Napoli.

IZBG: Internationale Zeitschriftenschau für Bibelwissenschaft und Grenzgebiete; Pd. 0074-9745.

IZT: Internationale Zeitschrift für Theologie [= Concilium deutsch].

JAAR: Journal of the American Academy of Religion; Atlanta. 0002-7189.

J[News]AmEg: Journal [Newsletter] of the American Research Center in Egypt; Winona Lake IN.

JAmScAff: Journal of the American Scientific Affiliation (evang.); Ipswich MA. 0003-0988.

JANES: Journal of the Ancient Near Eastern Society; NY, Jewish Theol. Sem. 0010-2016.

JanLing[Pract]: Janua Linguarum [Series Practica]; The Hague / Paris.

JAOS: Journal of the American Oriental Society; NHv. 0003-0279.

JapJRelSt: Japanese Journal of Religious Studies; Nagoya.

JapRel: Japanese Religions; Tokyo.

JArchSc: Journal of Archaeological Science; London/New York.

JAs: Journal Asiatique; P. 0021-762X.

JAsAf: Journal of Asian and African Studies (York Univ., Toronto); Leiden.

Javeriana → TXav.

Jb: Jahrbuch [Heid, Mainz...]; Jaarbericht.

JbAC: Jahrbuch für Antike und Christentum; Münster i. W.

JbBerlMus: Jahrbücher der Berliner Museen; wBerlin.

JbBTh: Jahrbuch für biblische Theologie; Neukirchen.

JbEOL: Jaarbericht van het Vooraziatisch-Egyptisch Genootschap Ex Oriente Lux; Leiden.

JbEvHL: Jahrbuch des Deutschen Evangelischen Instituts für Altertumswissenschaft des Heiligen Landes; Firth [1 (1989)].

JBL: Journal of Biblical Literature; Atlanta. 0021-9231.

JBlackT: Journal of Black Theology; Atteridgeville SAf. [1 (1987)].

JbLtgH: Jahrbuch für Liturgik und Hymnologie; Kassel. [3-7982-0182-X: 4 (1984)].

JbNumG: Jahrbuch für Numismatik und Geldgeschichte; Regensburg.

JbÖsByz: Jahrbuch der Österreichischen Byzantinistik; W. 0378-8660.

JBQ: Jewish Biblical Quarterly = Dor le Dor since 18,1 (1989s); J. 0792-3910.

JbRP: Jahrbuch der Religionspädagogik; Neukirchen [2 (1985)].

JChrEd: Journal of Christian Education; Sydney. 0021-9657 [82s (1985)].

JCS: Journal of Cuneiform Studies; CM. 0022-0256.

JDharma: Journal of Dharma; Bangalore.

JdU: Judentum und Umwelt; Frankfurt/M.

JEA: Journal of Egyptian Archaeology; London. 0307-5133.

JEcuSt: Journal of Ecumenical Studies; Ph, Temple Univ. 0022-0558.

Jeevadhara; Alleppey, Kerala.

JEH: Journal of Ecclesiastical History; Cambridge. 0022-0469.

JEmpT: Journal of empirical theology; Kampen. [1 (1988)].

JerusSt: Jerusalem studies in Jewish thought; Jerusalem [2 (1982)].

JESHO: Journal of Economic and Social History of the Orient; Leiden.

JEvTS: Journal of the Evangelical Theological Society; Wheaton IL.

JewishH: Jewish History; Leiden. 0334-701X [4 (1989)].

JFemR: Journal of Feminist Studies in Religion; Chico CA. 8755-4178.

JField: Journal of Field Archaeology; Boston, Univ. 0093-4690.

JGlass: Journal of Glass Studies; Corning, NY. 0075-4250.

JHistId: Journal of the History of Ideas; Ph, Temple Univ. 0022-5037.

JHMR: Judaica, Hermeneutics, Mysticism, and Religion; Albany, SUNY.

JhÖsA: Jahreshefte des Österreichischen Archäologischen Institutes; Wien. 0078-3579.

JHS: Journal of Hellenic Studies; London. 0075-4269.

JIndEur: Journal of Indo-European Studies; Hattiesburg, Miss.

JIntdenom: Journal of the Interdenominational Theological Center; Atlanta GA.

JIntdis: Journal of the Society for Interdisciplinary History; CM, MIT.

JJC: Jésus et Jésus-Christ; Paris.

JJS: Journal of Jewish Studies; Oxford. 0022-2097.

JJurPap: Journal of Juristic Papyrology; Warszawa [revived 19 (1983)].

JLawA: Jewish Law Annual (Oxford).

JLawRel: Journal of Law and Religion; St. Paul. [3 (1985)].

JMeditArch: Journal of Mediterranean Archeol.; Sheffield. 0952-7648.

JMedRenSt: Journal of Medieval and Renaissance Studies; Durham NC.

JMoscPatr: [Engl.] Journal of the Moscow Patriarchate; Moscow.

JNES: Journal of Near Eastern Studies; Chicago, Univ. 0022-2968.

JNWS: Journal of Northwest Semitic Languages; Leiden.

Journal für Geschichte; Braunschweig.

JPrehRel: Journal of Prehistoric Religion; Göteborg. 0283-8486 [1 (1987)].

JPseud: Journal for the Study of the Pseudepigrapha; Sheffield. 0951-8207 [1 (1987)].

JPsy&C: Journal of Psychology and Christianity; Farmington Hills MI. 0733-4273.

JPsy&Jud: Journal of Psychology and Judaism; New York.

JPsy&T: Journal of Psychology and Theology; La Mirada / Rosemead CA.

JQR: Jewish Quarterly Review (Ph, Dropsie Univ.); Winona Lake IN. 0021-6682.

JRArch: Journal of Roman Archaeology; AA [1 (1988)].

JRAS: Journal of the Royal Asiatic Society; London.

JRefJud: Journal of Reform Judaism; NY. 0149-712X.

JRel: Journal of Religion; Chicago. 0022-4189.

JRelAf: Journal of Religion in Africa; Leiden. 0022-4200.

JRelEth: Journal of Religion and Ethics; ND (ᴱRutgers). 0384-9694.

JRelHealth: The Journal of Religion and Health; New York.

JRelHist: Journal of Religious History; Sydney, Univ. 0022-4227.

JRelPsyR: Journal of Religion and Psychical Research; Bloomfield CT.

JRelSt: Journal of Religious Studies; Cleveland.

JRelTht: Journal of Religious Thought; Washington DC.

JRit: Journal of ritual studies; Pittsburgh/Waterloo ON.

JRPot: Journal of Roman Pottery Studies: Ox. [2 (1989)].

JRS: Journal of Roman Studies; London. 0075-4358.

JSArm: Journal of the Society for Armenian Studies; LA [1 (1984)].

JSav: Journal des Savants: Paris.

JScStR: Journal for the Scientific Study of Religion; NHv. 0021-8294.

JSem: Journal for Semitics / Tydskrif vir Semitistiek; Pretoria, Unisa.

JSHZ: Jüdische Schriften aus hellenistischer und römischer Zeit; Gütersloh.

JSS: Journal of Semitic Studies; Manchester. 0022-4480.

JSStEg: Journal of the Society for the Study of Egyptian Antiquities [ipsi SSEA]; Toronto. 0383-9753.

JStJud: Journal for the Study of Judaism in the Persian, Hellenistic, & Roman Periods; Leiden. 0047-2212.

JStJTht: Jerusalem Studies in Jewish Thought.

JStNT/OT: Journal for the Study of the NT/OT; Sheffield, Univ. 0142-064X / 0309-0892. ⇒ JPseud.

JStRel: Journal for the study of religion [formerly Religion in Southern Africa]; Pietermaritzburg, Natal [1,1 (1988)].

JTS: Journal of Theological Studies, N.S.: Oxford/London. 0022-5185.

JTSAfr: Journal of Theology for Southern Africa; Rondebosch.

Judaica; Zürich.

Judaism; NY. 0022-5762.

JudTSt: Judaistische Texte und Studien; Hildesheim.

JWarb: Journal of the Warburg and Courtauld Institutes; London.

JwHist: Jewish History; Haifa.

JWomen&R: Journal of Women and Religion; Berkeley [4,2 (1985)].

JyskR: Religionsvidenskabeligt Tidsskrift; Århus, Jysk [Jutland] Selskap.

Kadmos; Berlin. 0022-7498.

Kairos (Religionswiss.); Salzburg.

Karawane (Die); Ludwigsburg.

Karthago (archéologie africaine); P.

KAT: Kommentar zum AT: Gütersloh.

KatBlät: Katechetische Blätter; Mü.

KatKenk: Katorikku Kenkyu < Shingaku; Tokyo, Sophia. 0387-3005.

KBW: Katholisches Bibelwerk; Stu [bzw. Österreich, Schweiz].

KeK: Kritisch-exegetischer Kommentar über das NT; Göttingen.

KerDo: Kerygma und Dogma; Göttingen. 0023-0707.

KerkT: Kerk en Theologie; Wageningen. 0165-2346.

Kernos, religion grecque; Liège [1 (1988)].

Kerygma (on Indian missions); Ottawa. 0023-0693.

KGaku: ❶ Kirisutokyo Gaku (Christian Studies) NS; Tokyo St. Paul's Univ. 0387-6810 [29 (1987)].

KingsTR: King's College Theological Review; London.

KirSef: ❻ Kiryat Sefer, Bibliographical Quarterly; J, Nat.-Univ. Libr. 0023-1851. ➤ Rambi.

KIsr: Kirche und Israel, theologische Zeitschrift; Neukirchen. 0179-7239. [1 (1986)].

KkKS: Konfessionskundliche und Kontroverstheologische Studien; Pd. Bonifacius.

KkMat: Konfessionskundliches Institut, Materialdienst; Bensheim [39 (1988)].

KleinÄgTexte: Kleine ägyptische Texte; Wb.

Kler: ❻ Klēronomia (patristica); Thessaloniki.

Klio: oBerlin. 0075-6334.

KLK: Katholisches Leben und Kirchenreform im Zeitalter der Glaubensspaltung; Münster.

KölnJbVFG: Kölner Jahrbuch für Vor-und Frühgeschichte; Berlin, Mann. 0075-6512.

KomBeiANT: Kommentare und Beiträge zum Alten und N.T.; Düsseldorf, Patmos.

KosmosŒ: Kosmos en Œkumene: Amsterdam.

Kratylos (Sprachwissenschaft); Wsb.

KřestR [TPřil]: Křest'anská revue [Theologická Příloha]; Praha.

KTB/KUB: Keilschrifttexte/urkunden aus Boghazköi; wB,Mann/oB,Akademie.

Ktema; Strasbourg, CEDEX.

KuGAW: Kulturgeschichte der Antiken Welt; Mainz.

KvinnerA: Kvinner i [women in] arkeologi i Norge; Bergen, Historisk Museum [1 (1985)].

KZg: Kirchliche Zeitgeschichte; Gö [1 (1988)].

LA: Liber Annuus; Jerusalem, SBF.

Labeo, diritto romano; N. 0023-6462.

Landas: Journal of Loyola School of Theology; Manila. [1,1 (1987)].

Language; Baltimore.

LAPO: Littératures Anciennes du Proche-Orient; Paris, Cerf. 0459-5831.

Lateranum; R, Pont. Univ. Lateranense.

Latomus (Ét. latines); Bru. 0023-8856.

Laur: Laurentianum; R. 0023-902X.

LavalTP: Laval Théologique et Philosophique; Québec.

LDiv: Lectio Divina; Paris, Cerf.

LebSeels: Lebendige Seelsorge; Wü/FrB.

LebZeug: Lebendiges Zeugnis; Paderborn. 0023-9941.

Lěšonénu (Hebrew Language); J.

LetPastB: Lettura pastorale della Bibbia; Bologna, Dehoniane.

Levant (archeology); London.

LexÄg: Lexikon der Ägyptologie; Wb ➤ 899.

LexMA: Lexikon des Mittelalters; Mü/Z ➤ 901.

LexTQ: Lexington [KY] Theological Quarterly. 0024-1628.

LGB: Lexikon des Gesamten Buchwesens²; Stu ➤ 950.

LIAO: Lettre d'Information Archéologie Orientale; Valbonne, CNRS. 0750-6279.

LIGHT: Laughter in God, History, and Theology; Fort Worth.

LIMC: Lexicon iconographicum mythologiae classicae; Z. ➤ 852.

LimnOc: Limnology & Oceanography; AA.

LinceiR/Scavi/BClas: Accademia Nazionale dei Lincei. Rendiconti / Notizie degli Scavi / Bollettino Classico. 0391-8270: Roma.

LingBib: Linguistica Biblica; Bonn. 0342-0884.

Lire la Bible; P, Cerf. 0588-2257.

Listening: Romeoville IL.

LitLComp: Literary and Linguistic Computing; Ox. 0268-1145. [4 (1989)].

LitRelFrühjud: Literatur und Religion des Frühjudentums; Wü/Gü.

LitTOx: Literature and theology; Oxford. [1,1 (1987)].

LivLight: The Living Light (US Cath. Conf.); Huntington. 0024-5275.

LivWord: Living Word; Alwaye, Kerala.

LOB: Leggere oggi la Bibbia; Brescia, Queriniana.

LogosPh: Logos, philosophic issues in Christian perspective; Santa Clara, Univ. [5 (1984)].

Logotherapie, Zeitschrift der Deutschen Gesellschaft für ~; Bremen [1 (1986); ColcT 58,1 (1988) 153-8].

LOrA: Langues orientales anciennes, philologie et linguistique; Lv. 0987-7738. [1 (1988)].

LStClas: London studies in classical philology [8, Corolla Londiniensis 1]; Amst.

LtgJb: Liturgisches Jahrbuch; Münster/Wf.

Lucentum; prehistoria, arqueología e historia antigua; Alicante, Univ.

LumenK: Lumen; København.

LumenVr: Lumen; Vitoria.

LumièreV: Lumière et Vie; Lyon. 0024-7359.

Luther (Gesellschaft) [Jb]; Hamburg. 0340-6210 [Gö 3-525-87419-7].

LuthMonh: Lutherische Monatshefte; Hamburg. 0024-7618.

LuthTJ: Lutheran Theological Journal; North Adelaide, S. Australia.

LuthTKi: Lutherische Theologie und Kirche; Oberursel. 0170-3846.

LVitae: Lumen Vitae; Bru. 0024-7324.

LvSt: Louvain Studies.

Ⓜ magyar: *hungarice*, en hongrois.

ᴹ: *mentio, de eo*; author commented upon.

Maarav; Winona Lake IN. 0149-5712.

MadMitt [B/F]: DAI Madrider Mitteilungen (Mainz: 3-8053-0831-0) [Beiträge/Forschungen].

MAGA: Mitteilungen zur Alten Geschichte und Archäologie; oB [13 (1985)].

Maia (letterature classiche); Messina. 0025-0538.

MaisD: La Maison-Dieu; P. 0025-0937.

MANE: Monographs on the Ancient Near East; 1. Leiden; 2. Malibu.

Manresa (espiritualidad ignaciana); Azpeitia-Guipúzcoa.

Manuscripta; St. Louis.

Mara: tijdschrift voor feminisme en theologie; [1: TsTNijm 27 (1987) 396].

MarbTSt: Marburger Theologische Studien; Marburg.

MARI: Mari, Annales de Recherches Interdisciplinaires; Paris [2 (1983)].

Marianum; Roma.

MariolSt: Mariologische Studien; Essen.

MarŠipri; Boston, Baghdad ASOR [1 (1988)].

MarSt: Marian Studies; Washington.

Masca: Museum Applied Science Center for Archaeology Journal; Ph, Univ. [3 (1984s)].

Massorot; J, Univ.

MasSt: (SBL) Masoretic Studies; Chico CA.

MatDClas: Materiali e discussioni per l'analisi dei testi classici; Pisa. 0392-6338.

MatKonfInst: Materialdienst des konfessionskundlichen Instituts; Bensheim.

MatPomWykBib: Materiały pomocznicze do wykładów z biblistyki; Lublin.

Mayéutica (Agustinos Recoletos); Marcilla (Navarra).

MDOG: Mitteilungen der Deutschen Orientgesellschaft; B. 0342-118X.

Meander: Wsz Akad. 0025-6285.

Med: Mededelingen [Amst, ...]; Meddelander.

MeditArch: Mediterranean Archaeology; Sydney. 1030-8482.

MedHum: Mediaevalia et Humanistica (Denton, N. Texas Univ.); Totowa NJ.

MeditHistR: Mediterranean historical review Tel Aviv Univ.; L. 0951-8967.

MeditLg: Mediterranean Language Review: Wiesbaden [1 (1983)].

MÉF [= **MélÉcFrR**]: Mélanges de l'École Française de Rome/Ath; Ant. 0223-5102.

MélSR: Mélanges de Science Religieuse; Lille.

Mém: Mémoires ➤ AIBL ... AcSc, T...

MenQR: Mennonite Quarterly Review; Goshen, Ind.

Mensaje; Chile.

Meroit: Meroitic Newsletter / Bulletin d'informations méroitiques: Paris, CNRS [24 (1985)].

MESA: Middle East Studies Association (Bulletin); Tucson, Univ. AZ.

MesopK: Mesopotamia: Copenhagen Studies in Assyriology; København.

MesopT: Mesopotamia (Archeologia, Epigrafia, Storia... Torino); (pub. F).

Mesorot [Language-tradition researches]; Jerusalem [1983s: Lešonenu 50 (1985s) 252-260].

MESt: Middle Eastern Studies; L.

MetB: Metropolitan Museum Bulletin; New York. 0026-1521.

MethT: Method and theory in the study of religion; Toronto [1,1 (1989)].

Mêtis, Revue d'anthropologie du monde grec ancien; Philologie — histoire — archéologie; P. [1 (1986)].

Mg: Monograph (-ie, -fia); → CBQ, SBL, SNTS.

MGraz: Mitteilungen der archäologischen Gesellschaft; Graz [1 (1987)].

MHT: Materialien zu einem hethitischen Thesaurus; Heidelberg.

MiDAI-A/K/M/R: Mitteilungen des Deutschen Archäologischen Instituts: Athen / Kairo 3-8053-0885-X. / Madrid / Rom 0342-1287.

MidAmJT: Mid-America Journal of Theology: Orange City, Iowa [4 (1988)].

Mid-Stream, Disciples of Christ; Indianapolis. – Midstream (Jewish); NY. 0026-332X.

Mikael; Paraná, Arg. (Seminario).

MilltSt: Milltown Studies (philosophy, theology); Dublin. 0332-1428.

Minerva: filología clásica; Valladolid [1 (1987)].

Minos (Filología Egea); Salamanca. 0544-3733.

MiscCom: Miscelánea Comillas, estudios históricos; M. 0210-9522.

MiscFranc: Miscellanea Francescana; Roma (OFM Conv.).

Mishkan, a theological forum on Jewish evangelism; Jerusalem, United Christian Council [1 (1984)].

Missiology; Scottdale PA.

MissHisp: Missionalia hispanica; Madrid, CSIC Inst. E. Flores [40,117 (1983)].

Mitt: Mitteilungen [Gö Septuaginta; Berliner Museen...]; → MiDAI.

Mnemosyne, Bibliotheca Classica Batava [+ Supplements]; Leiden.

ModChm: Modern Churchman; Leominster, Herf.

ModJud: Modern Judaism; Baltimore.

ModT: Modern Theology, quarterly review; Oxford, Blackwell [1,1 (1984)].

Mon → Mg.

MonastSt: Monastic Studies; Montreal [14 (1983)].

MondeB: Le Monde de la Bible: 1. P. 0154-9049. – 2. Genève.

Monde Copte, Le: 0399-905X.

MonStB: Monographien und Studienbücher; Wu/Giessen.

Month (Christian Thought and World Affairs); London. 0027-0172.

Moralia; Madrid [6 (1984)].

MsME: Manuscripts of the Middle East; Leiden. 0920-0401. [1 (1986)].

MüÄgSt: Münchener Ägyptologische Studien; München/Berlin.

MüBei[T]PapR: Münchener Beiträge zur [Theologie] Papyruskunde und antiken Rechtsgeschichte; Mü.

MünstHand: Münsterische Beiträge zur Antiken Handelsgeschichte; St. Katharinen. 0722-4532.

MüStSprW: Münchener Studien zur Sprachwissenschaft; Mü. → AOtt.

MüTZ: Münchener Theologische Zeitschrift; St. Ottilien. 0580-1400.

Mundus (German Research, in English); Stuttgart. 0027-3392.

Mus: Le Muséon; LvN. 0771-6494.

MusHelv: Museum Helveticum; Basel.

MusTusc: Museum Tusculanum; København. 0107-8062.

MuzTA: ⊕ Muzeon Ha-Areş NS; TA.

NABU: Nouvelles assyriologiques brèves et utilitaires; 0989-5671 [4 (1989)].

NachGö: Nachrichten der Akademie der Wissenschaften; Göttingen.

Naos: notes and materials for the linguistic study of the sacred; Pittsburgh Univ. [3,1 (1987)].

NarAzAfr: ⊕ *Narody:* Peoples of Asia and Africa; Moskva.

NatGeog: National Geographic; Washington. 0027-9358.

NatGrac: Naturaleza y Gracia; Salamanca (OFM Cap.).

NBL: Neues Bibel-Lexikon 1988 → 902.

NBlackfr: New Blackfriars; London. 0028-4289.

NCent: The New Century Bible Commentary (reedited); Edinburgh / GR.

NChrIsr: Nouvelles Chrétiennes d'Israël: Jérusalem.

NduitseGT: Nederduits-Gereformeerde Teologiese Tydskrif; Kaapstad. 0028-2006.

NedTTs: Nederlands Theologisch Tijdschrift; Wageningen. 0028-212X.

Neotestamentica; Pretoria; NTWerk.

NEphS: Neue Ephemeris für semitische Epigraphik; Wiesbaden.

Nestor, Classical Antiquity, Indiana Univ.; Bloomington. 0028-2812.

NESTR: Near East School of Theology Review; Beirut.

News: Newsletter: Anat[olian Studies; NHv]; Targ[umic and Cognate Studies; Toronto]; ASOR [CM]; Ug[aritic Studies; Calgary]; → JAmEg.

NewTR: New theology review: Ch, Catholic Theological Union [publ. Wilmington, Glazier [1,1 (1988)]. 0896-4297.

NHC: Nag Hammadi Codices, Egypt UAR Facsimile edition; Leiden.

NHL/S: Nag Hammadi Library in English / Studies; Leiden.

NHLW: Neues Handbuch der Literaturwissenschaft: Wb, Athenaion.

Nicolaus (teol. ecumenico-patristica); Bari.

NICOT: New International Commentary OT; Grand Rapids, Eerdmans.

NigJT: The Nigerian Journal of Theology; Owerri [1,4 (1988)].

NIGT: New International Greek Testament Commentary; Exeter/GR, Paternoster/Eerdmans.

NJBC: New Jerome Biblical Commentary → 384.

NOrb: NT & Orbis Antiquus; FrS/Gö.

NorJ: Nordisk Judaistik.

NorTTs: Norsk Teologisk Tidsskrift; Oslo. 0029-2176.

NotSocTLv: Notes de la Société Théologique de Louvain; Lv-N.

NOxR: New Oxford Review; Berkeley.

NRT: Nouvelle Revue Théologique; Tournai. 0029-4845.

NS [NF]: Nova series, nouvelle série.

NSys: Neue Zeitschrift für systematische Theologie und Religionsphilosophie; Berlin. 0028-3517.

NT: Novum Testamentum; Leiden. 0048-1009.

NTAbh: Neutestamentliche Abhandlungen. [N.F.]; Münster.

NTAbs: New Testament Abstracts; CM. 0028-6877.

NTDt: Das Neue Testament deutsch; Gö.

NTS: New Testament Studies; L (SNTS).

NubChr: Nubia Christiana; Warszawa, Akad. Teol. Kat. [1 (1983)].

NumC: Numismatic Chronicle; London. 0078-2696.

Numisma; Madrid. 0029-0015.

NumZ: Numismatische Zeitschrift; Wien. 0250-7838.

Numen (International Association for the History of Religions); Leiden.

NuovaUm: Nuova Umanità; Roma.

Nuovo Areopago (Il), trimestrale di cultura; Bologna, CSEO [1,1.2 (1982)].

NVFr/Z: Nova et Vetera; 1. Fribourg S. / 2. Zamora [10 (1985)].

NYarm: Newsletter of the Institute of Archaeology and Anthropology, Yarmuk Univ.; Irbid [1 (1987)].

NZMissW: Neue Zeitschrift für Missionswissenschaft; Beckenried, Schweiz. 0028-3495.

NZSysT → NSys.

ObnŽiv: Obnovljeni Život (Erneuertes religiöses Leben); Zagreb.

OBO: Orbis Biblicus et Orientalis: FrS/Gö.

OEIL: Office d'édition et d'impression du livre; Paris.

ÖkRu: Ökumenische Rundschau; Stuttgart. 0029-8654.

ÖkTbKom, NT: Ökumenischer Taschenbuchkommentar; Gütersloh / Würzburg.

ÖsterrBibSt: Österreichische Biblische Studien; Klosterneuburg.

Offa, ... Frühgeschichte; Neumünster. 0078-3714.

Ohio → JRelSt: Cleveland.

OIC/P/Ac: Oriental Institute Communications / Publications / Acquisitions; Ch.

OikBud: Oikumene; historia antiqua classica et orientalis; Budapest.

Olivo (El), diálogo jud.-cr.: Madrid.

OLZ: Orientalistische Literaturzeitung; ab 1987 Berlin. 0030-5383.

OMRO: Oudheidkundige Mededelingen, Rijksmuseum van Oudheden; Leiden.

OneInC: One in Christ (Catholic Ecumenical); Turvey, Bedfordshire.

OnsGErf: Ons Geestelijk Erf; Antwerpen.

OnsGLev: Ons Geestelijk Leven; ab 65 (1988) ➤ **GLeven.**

OpAth/Rom: Opuscula Atheniensia 91-85086-80-0 / Romana 91-7042-099-8; Swedish Inst.

OPTAT: Occasional Papers in Translation and Textlinguistics: Dallas [1,1 (1987)].

Opus, rivista internazionale per la storia economica e sociale dell'antichità (Siena); R.

Or: ➤ Orientalia; Roma.

OraLab: Ora et Labora; Roriz, Portugal.

OrAnt[Coll]: Oriens Antiquus [Collectio]; Roma.

OrBibLov: Orientalia et Biblica Lovaniensia; Lv.

OrChr: Oriens Christianus; Wiesbaden. 3-447-02532-8.

OrChrPer[An]: Orientalia Christiana Periodica [Analecta]; R, Pontificium Inst. Orientalium Stud. 0030-5375.

OrGand: Orientalia Gandensia; Gent.

Orientalia (Ancient Near East); Rome, Pontifical Biblical Institute. 0030-5367.

Orientierung; Zürich. 0030-5502.

Orient-Japan: Orient, Near Eastern Studies Foreign Language Annual; Tokyo. 0743-3851; cf. ➍ Oriento. 0030-5219.

Origins; Washington Catholic Conference. 0093-609X.

OrJog: Orientasi, Annual ... Philosophy and Theology; Jogjakarta.

OrLovPer[An]: Orientalia Lovaniensia Periodica [Analecta]; Lv.

OrMod: Oriente Moderno; Napoli. 0030-5472.

OrOcc: Oriente-Occidente. Buenos Aires, Univ. Salvador.

OrPast: Orientamenti Pastorali; Roma.

Orpheus; Catania.

OrSuec: Orientalia Suecana; Uppsala.

OrtBuc: Ortodoxia; Bucureşti.

OrthF: Orthodoxes Forum; München, Univ. [1,1 (1987)].

OrTrad: Oral Tradition; Columbia MO, Univ. [1 (1986)].

OrVars: Orientalia Varsoviensia; Wsz. 0860-5785. [1 (1987)].

OstkSt: Ostkirchliche Studien; Würzburg. 0030-6487.

OTAbs: Old Testament Abstracts; Washington. 0364-8591.

OTEssays: Old Testament essays; Pretoria. 1010-9919. [1,1 (1988)].

OTS: Oudtestamentische Studiën; Leiden. 0169-9555.

OTWerkSuidA: Die Ou Testamentiese Werkgemeenskap Suid-Afrika; Pretoria.

OudKMed: Oudheidkundige Mededelingen uit het Rijksmuseum van Oudheden; Leiden.

OvBTh: Overtures to Biblical Theology; Philadelphia.

Overview; Ch St. Thomas More Asn.

OxJArch: Oxford Journal of Archaeology; Ox. 0262-5253.

➋: *polonice,* in Polish.

p./pa./pl.: page(s)/paperback/plate(s).

PAAR: Proceedings of the American Academy for Jewish Research; Ph.

Pacifica: Australian theological studies; Melbourne Brunswick East [1,1 (1988)].

PacTR: Pacific theological review: SanAnselmo, SF Theol.Sem. 21, 1 (1987).

Palaeohistoria; Haarlem.

PalCl: Palestra del Clero; Rovigo.

PaléOr: Paléorient; Paris.

PalSb: ➌ Palestinski Sbornik; Leningrad.

PapBritSR: Papers of the British School at Rome; London.

PAPS: Proceedings of the American Philosophical Society; Ph.

PapTAbh: Papyrologische Texte und Abhandlungen; Bonn, Habelt.

PapyrolColon: Papyrologica Coloniensia; Opladen. 0078-9410.

Parabola (Myth and the Quest for Meaning); New York.

Paradigms; Louisville KY [1 (1985)].

ParOr: Parole de l'Orient; Kaslik [12 (1984s)].

ParPass: Parola del Passato; Napoli. 0031-2355.

ParSpV: Parola, Spirito e Vita, quaderni di lettura biblica; Bo, Dehoniane.

ParVi: Parole di Vita; T-Leumann.

PasT: Pastoraltheologie; Göttingen.

PastScPast: Pastoral / Sciences pastorales; psych.sociol.théol.; Ottawa, St. Paul Univ. [5 (1986)].

PatByzR: Patristic and Byzantine Review; Kingston NY [1 (1982)].

Patr&M: Patristica et Mediaevalia; Buenos Aires [I. 1975; ... II. 1981 - VII. 1986: RHE 83,491].

PatrStudT: Patristische Studien und Texte; B. 0553-4003.

PBSB: Petite bibliothèque des sciences bibliques; Paris, Desclée.

PenséeC: La Pensée Catholique; P.

PEQ: Palestine Exploration Quarterly; London. 0031-0328.

PerAz: Peredneaziatskij Sbornik; Moskva.

Persica: Leiden.

PerspRelSt: Perspectives in Religious Studies (Baptist); Danville VA.

PerspT: Perspectiva Teológica; Belo Horizonte [before 1981 São Leopoldo].

Pg/Ph: philolog-/philosoph-.

PgOrTb: Philologia Orientalis (Georgian Ac. Sc.); Tbilisi.

Phase; Barcelona.

PhilipSa: Philippiniana Sacra; Manila.

Philologus; oB. 0031-7985.

Phoenix; Toronto. 0031-8299.

PhoenixEOL; Leiden (not = JbEOL). 0031-8329.

Phronema: St. Andrew's Greek Orthodox Theological College, Australia [annual; 1 (1986) TAth 58 (1987) 645s].

Phronesis; Assen. 0031-8868.

PiTMon: Theological Monograph Series; Pittsburgh.

PJungG: Projekte und Modelle zum Dialog mit der jungen Generation; Stu.

Pneuma, Pentecostal Studies; Pasadena [7 (1985)].

PoinT: Le Point Théologique; P.

Polin: Polish-Jewish Studies; Oxford [1 (1986)].

PontAcc, R/Mem: Atti della Pontificia Accademia Romana di Archeologia, Rendiconti/Memorie; Vaticano.

PrPeo [< *CleR*]: Priests and People; L.

PracArch: Prace Archeologiczne; Kraków, Univ. 0083-4300.

PraehZ: Praehistorische Zeitschrift; Berlin. 0079-4848.

PrakT: Praktische theologie ... pastorale wetenschappen; Zwolle.

PraktArch: ☺ Praktika, Archeology Society Athens.

PrAmPhilSoc: ➤ PAPS.

PrCambPg: Proceedings of the Cambridge Philological Society; England. 0068-6735.

PrCTSAm: Proceedings Catholic Theological Society of America; Villanova.

PredikOT/NT: De Prediking van het OT / van het NT; Nijkerk.

Presbyteri (Spiritualità pastorale); Trento.

Presbyterion; St. Louis.

PresPast: Presenza Pastorale; Roma.

PrêtreP: Prêtre et Pasteur; Montréal. 0385-8307.

Priest (The); Washington.

PrincSemB: Princeton Seminary Bulletin; Princeton NJ.

PrIrB: Proceedings of the Irish Biblical Association; Dublin, 'published annually'.

Prism; St. Paul, United Church of Christ [1 (1986)].

PrIsrAc: Proceedings of the Israel Academy of Sciences & Humanities; Jerusalem.

ProbHistChr: Problèmes de l'Histoire du Christianisme; Bruxelles, Univ.

ProcClas: Proceedings of the Classical Association; London [35 (1988)].

ProcCom: Proclamation Commentaries; Ph.

ProcGLM: Proceedings of the Eastern Great Lakes and Midwest Bible Societies; Buffalo.

Prooftexts; Baltimore.

PrOrChr: Proche-Orient Chrétien; Jérusalem. 0032-9622.

Prot: Protestantesimo; R. 0033-1767.

Proyección (Teología y mundo actual); Granada.

ProySal: Proyecto Centro Salesiano de Estudios; Buenos Aires [1 (1989)].

PrPrehS: Proceedings of the Prehistoric Society; Cambridge (Univ. Museum).

PrSemArab: Proceedings of the Seminar for Arabian Studies; London.

Prudentia (Hellenistic, Roman); Auckland.

PrzOr[Tom/Pow]: Przegląd Orientalistyczny, Wsz: [Tomisticzny 1 (1984) Wsz / Powszechny, Kraków].

PT: Philosophy/Theology: Milwaukee, Marquette Univ. [1 (1986)].

PubTNEsp: Publicaciones de la Facultad Teológica del Norte de España; Burgos.

PUF: Presses Universitaires de France; P.

Qadm: Qadmoniot ❸ Quarterly of Dept. of Antiquities; Jerusalem.

Qardom, ❸ mensuel pour la connaissance du pays; Jerusalem, Ariel.

QDisp: Quaestiones Disputatae; FrB.

Qedem: Monographs of the Institute of Archaeology: Jerusalem, Hebr. Univ.

QEtnR: Quaderni di etnologia religiosa; Milano.

QLtg: Questions Liturgiques; Lv.

QRMin: Quarterly Review [for] Ministry; Nv. 0270-9287.

QuadCatan / Chieti: Quaderni, Catania / Chieti [3 (1982)]; Univ.

QuadSemant: Quaderni di Semantica; Bologna.

QuadSemit: Quaderni di Semitistica; Firenze.

QuadUrb: Quaderni Urbinati di Cultura Classica; Urbino. 0033-4987.

Quaerendo (Low Countries: Manuscripts and Printed Books); Amst.

QuatreF: Les quatre fleuves: Paris.

QüestVidaCr: Qüestions de Vida Cristiana; Montserrat.

❸: *russice,* in Russian.

ᴿ: *recensio,* book-review(er).

RAC: Reallexikon für Antike und Christentum; Stuttgart ➤ 904.

Radiocarbon; NHv, Yale. 0033-8222.

RAfrT: Revue Africaine de Théologie; Kinshasa/Limete.

RAg: Revista Agustiniana [de Espiritualidad hacia 18 (1977)] Calahorra.

RAMBI: Rešimat Ma'amarim bemadda'ê ha-Yahedût, Index of articles on Jewish Studies; J. 0073-5817.

RaMIsr: Rassegna mensile di Israel; Roma.

RArchéol: Revue Archéologique; Paris. 0035-0737.

RArchéom: Revue d'Archéométrie; Rennes.

RArtLv: Revue des Archéologues et Historiens d'Art; Lv. 0080-2530.

RasEtiop: Rassegna di Studi Etiopici; R/N.

RAss: Revue d'Assyriologie et d'Archéologie Orientale; P. 2-13-039142-7.

RasT: Rassegna di Teologia; Roma [ᴱNapoli]. 0034-9644.

Raydan:

RazF: Razón y Fe; Madrid.

RB: Revue Biblique; J/P. 0035-0907.

RBén: Revue Bénédictine; Maredsous. 0035-0893.

RBgNum: Revue Belge de Numismatique et Sigillographie; Bruxelles.

RBgPg: Revue Belge de Philologie et d'Histoire; Bruxelles.

RBBras: Revista Bíblica Brasileira; Fortaleza [1 (1984)].

RBíbArg: Revista Bíblica; Buenos Aires. 0034-7078.

RBkRel: The Review of Books and Religion; Durham NC, Duke Univ. [10 c. 1984].

RCatalT: Revista Catalana de Teología; Barcelona, St. Pacià.

RCiv: Éditions Recherche sur les [Grandes] Civilisations [Mém(oires) 0291-1655]. Paris ➤ ADPF.

RClerIt: Rivista del Clero Italiano; Mi.

RCuClaMed: Rivista di Cultura Classica e Medioevale; Roma.

RÉAnc: Revue des Études Anciennes; Bordeaux. 0035-2004.

RÉArmén: Revue des Études Arméniennes. 0080-2549.

RÉAug: Revue des Études Augustiniennes; Paris. 0035-2012.

REB: Revista Eclesiástica Brasileira; Petrópolis.

RÉByz: Revue des Études Byzantines; Paris.

RECAM: Regional Epigraphic Catalogues of Asia Minor [AnSt].

RechAug: Recherches Augustiniennes; Paris. 0035-2021.

RechSR: Recherches de Science Religieuse; Paris. 0034-1258.

RecTrPO: Recueil de travaux et communications de l'association des études du Proche-Orient ancien / Collected papers of the Society for Near Eastern Studies; Montréal [2 (1984)].

RefEgy: Református Egyház; Budapest. 0324-475X.

ReferSR: Reference Services Review; Dearborn MI, Univ.

RefF: Reformiertes Forum; Zürich.

RefGStT: Reformationsgeschichtliche Studien und Texten: Münster.
RefJ: The Reformed Journal; Grand Rapids. 0486-252X.
Reformatio; Zürich.
RefR: Reformed Review; New Brunswick NJ / Holland MI.
RefTR: Reformed Theological Review; Hawthorn, Australia. 0034-3072.
RefW: The Reformed World; Geneva.
RÉG: Revue des Études Grecques; Paris. 0035-2039.
RÉgp: Revue d'Égyptologie; Paris. 2-252-02201-9.
RÉJ: Revue des Études Juives; Paris. 0035-2055.
RÉLat: Revue des Études Latines; P.
RelCult: Religión y Cultura; M.
RelEdn: Religious Education (biblical; Jewish-sponsored); NHv.
RelHum: Religious Humanism; Yellow Springs OH.
Religion [... and Religions]; Lancaster. 0048-721X.
RelIntL: Religion and Intellectual Life; New Rochelle NY, College. 0741-0549 [2 (1985)].
RelPBei: Religionspädagogische Beiträge; Kaarst. [17 (1986)].
RelSoc: Religion and Society; B/Haag.
RelSt: Religious Studies; Cambridge. 0034-4125.
RelStR: Religious Studies Review; Waterloo, Ont. 0319-485X.
RelStT: Religious Studies and Theology; Edmonton. 0829-2922.
RelTAbs: Religious and Theological Abstracts; Myerstown, Pa.
RelTrad: Religious Traditions; Brisbane. 0156-1650.
RencAssInt: Rencontre Assyriologique Internationale, Compte-Rendu.
RencChrJ: Rencontre Chrétiens et Juifs; Paris. 0233-5579.
Renovatio: 1. Zeitschrift für das interdisziplinäre Gespräch; Köln [38 (1982)]: 2. (teologia); Genova.
RepCyp: Report of the Department of Antiquities of Cyprus; Nicosia.
RépertAA: Répertoire d'art et d'archéologie; Paris. 0080-0953.

REPPAL: Revue d'Études Phéniciennes-Puniques et des Antiquités Libyques; Tunis [1 (1985)].
REspir: Revista de Espiritualidad; San Sebastián.
ResPLit: Res Publica Litterarum; Kansas.
RestQ: Restoration Quarterly; Abilene TX.
Résurrection, bimestriel catholique d'actualité et de formation [9-12 (1987)].
RET: Revista Española de Teología; Madrid.
RÉtGC: Revue des Études Géorgiennes et Caucasiennes; Paris. 0373-1537. [1 (1985) = Bedi Kartlisa 44].
RevCuBíb: Revista de Cultura Bíblica; São Paulo.
RevSR: Revue des Sciences Religieuses; Strasbourg. 0035-2217.
RExp: Review and Expositor; Louisville. 0034-6373.
RFgIC: Rivista di Filologia e di Istruzione Classica; Torino. 0035-6220.
RgStTh: Regensburger Studien zur Theologie; Fra/Bern, Lang.
RgVV: Religionsgeschichtliche Versuche und Vorarbeiten; B/NY, de Gruyter.
RHDroit: Revue historique de Droit français et étranger; Paris.
RHE: Revue d'Histoire Ecclésiastique; Louvain. 0035-2381.
RheinMus: Rheinisches Museum für Philologie; Frankfurt. 0035-449X.
Rhetorik [Jb]; Stu / Bad Cannstatt.
RHist: Revue Historique; Paris.
RHPR: Revue d'Histoire et de Philosophie Religieuses; Strasbourg. 0035-2403.
RHR: Revue de l'Histoire des Religions; Paris. 0035-1423.
RHS ➤ RUntHö; **RU** ➤ ZRUnt.
RHText: Revue d'Histoire des Textes; Paris. 0373-6075.
Ribla: Revista de interpretación bíblica latinoamericana; San José CR. 1 (1988) [Actu Bbg 26,198].
RIC: Répertoire bibliographique des institutions chrétiennes; Strasbourg, CERDIC.
RICathP: Revue de l'Institut Catholique de Paris. 0294-4308 [cf. ➤ BICLyon].

RicStoB: Ricerche storico bibliche; Bo. 0394-980X [1 (1989)].

RicStorSocRel: Ricerche di Storia Sociale e Religiosa; Roma.

RIDA: Revue Internationale des Droits de l'Antiquité; Bruxelles.

RIMA: Royal Inscriptions of Assyria; Toronto.

RINASA: Rivista dell'Istituto Nazionale di Archeologia e Storia dell'Arte; Roma.

RitFg: Rivista italiana di Filologia Classica.

RItNum: Rivista Italiana di Numismatica e scienze affini; Milano.

RivArCr: Rivista di Archeologia Cristiana; Città del Vaticano. 0035-6042.

RivArV: Rivista di Archeologia, Univ. Venezia; Roma.

RivAscM: [non Nuova] Rivista di Ascetica e Mistica; Roma.

RivB: Rivista Biblica Italiana; (da 1985) Bo, Dehoniane. 0393-4853.

RivLtg: Rivista di Liturgia; T-Leumann.

RivPastLtg: Rivista di Pastorale Liturgica; Brescia. 0035-6395.

RivScR: Rivista di Scienze Religiose; Molfetta.

RivStoLR: Rivista di Storia e Letteratura Religiosa; F. 0035-6573.

RivStorA: Rivista Storica dell'Antichità; Bologna.

RivVSp: Rivista di Vita Spirituale; Roma. 0035-6638.

RLA: Reallexikon der Assyriologie & vorderasiatischen Archäologie; B ➤ 905.

RLatAmT: Revista Latinoamericana de Teología; El Salvador.

RNouv: La Revue Nouvelle; Bruxelles. 0035-3809.

RNum: Revue Numismatique; Paris.

RoczOr: Rocznik Orientalistyczny; Warszawa. 0080-3545.

RoczTK: Roczniki Teologiczno-Kanoniczne; Lublin. 0035-7723.

RömQ: Römische Quartalschrift für Christliche Altertumskunde...; Freiburg/Br. 0035-7812.

RomOrth: Romanian Orthodox Church News, French Version [sic]; Bucureşti.

RPg: Revue de Philologie, de Littérature et d'Histoire anciennes; Paris, Klincksieck. 0035-1652.

RQum: Revue de Qumrân; P. 0035-1725.

RRéf: Revue Réformée; Saint-Germain-en-Laye.

RRel: Review for Religious; St. Louis. 0034-639X.

RRelRes: Review of Religious Research; New York. 0034-673X.

RRns: The Review of Religions; Wsh. 0743-5622.

RSO: Rivista degli Studi Orientali; Roma. 0392-4869.

RSocietà; Roma [1,1 (1986)].

RSPT: Revue des Sciences Philosophiques et Théologiques; [Le Saulchoir] Paris. 0035-2209.

RStFen: Rivista di Studi Fenici: R.

RStPomp: Rivista di Studi Pompeiani: Roma. [1 (1987)].

RSzem: Református Szemle; Budapest.

RTAM: Recherches de Théologie Ancienne et Médiévale; Louvain. 0034-1266. ➤ BTAM.

RTBat: Revista Teológica (Sem. Batista); Rio de Janeiro.

RThom: Revue Thomiste; Toulouse/Bru. 0035-4295.

RTLim: Revista Teológica; Lima.

RTLv: Revue théologique de Louvain. 0080-2654.

RTPhil: Revue de Théologie et de Philosophie; CH-1066 Épalinges. 0035-1784.

RuBi: Ruch Biblijny i Liturgiczny; Kraków. 0209-0872.

RUntHö: Religionsunterricht an höheren Schulen; Düsseldorf.

RVidEsp: Revista vida espiritual [replacing Vida espiritual with 85 (1986)]; Bogotá.

RZaïrTP: Revue Zaïroise de Théologie Protestante; [2 (1988)].

SAA[B]: State Archives of Assyria [Bulletin]; Helsinki [1/1 (1987)].

SacEr: Sacris Eruditi; Steenbrugge. Saeculum; FrB/Mü. 0080-5319.

SAfJud: South African Judaica; Johannesburg, Witwatersrand Univ. [1 (1984)].

Sales: Salesianum; Roma. 0036-3502.

Salm: Salmanticensis; Salamanca. 0036-3537.

SalT: Sal Terrae; Santander. 0211-4569.

Sandalion (Sassari); R, Herder.

SAOC: Studies in Ancient Oriental Civilization: Ch, Univ. 0081-7554.

Sap: Sapienza; Napoli. 0036-4711.

SapCro: La Sapienza della Croce; R.

sb.: subscription; price for members.

SBF/Anal/Pub [min]: Studii Biblici Franciscani: 0081-8933 / Analecta / Publicationes series maior 0081-8971 [minor]; Jerusalem. → LA.

SBL [AramSt / CR / Mg / Diss / GRR / MasSt / NAm / SemP / TexTr]: Society of Biblical Literature: Aramaic Studies / Critical Review of Books in Religion / Monograph Series / Dissertation Series / Graeco-Roman Religion / Masoretic Studies / Biblical Scholarship in North America / Seminar Papers 0145-2711 / Texts and Translations. → **JBL; CATSS.**

SborBrno: Sborník praci filozoficke fakulty; Brno, Univ.

SBS [KBW]: Stuttgarter Bibelstudien; Stuttgart, Katholisches Bibelwerk.

ScandJOT: Scandinavian Journal of the Old Testament; Aarhus.

ScChrB: Science and Christian Belief; Exeter [1 (1989)].

ScEsp: Science et Esprit; Montréal. 0316-5345.

SCHN: Studia ad Corpus Hellenisticum NT; Leiden.

Schönberger Hefte; Fra.

Scholars Choice; Richmond VA.

SChr: Sources Chrétiennes; P. 0750-1978.

SciTHV: Science, technology and human values; NY [8 (1983)].

ScotBEv: The Scottish Bulletin of Evangelical Theology; E. 0265-4539.

ScotJT: Scottish Journal of Theology; Edinburgh. 0036-9306.

ScotR: Scottish Journal of Religious Studies; Stirling.

ScrCiv: Scrittura [scrivere] e Civiltà; T.

ScrClasIsr: Scripta Classica Israelica; J.

ScriptB: Scripture Bulletin; London. 0036-9780.

Scriptorium; Bruxelles.

ScripTPamp: Scripta theologica; Pamplona, Univ. Navarra. 0036-9764.

Scriptura; Stellenbosch.

ScriptVict: Scriptorium Victoriense; Vitoria, España.

ScrMedit: Scripta Mediterranea; Toronto, Univ. [3 (1982)].

ScuolC: La Scuola Cattolica; Venegono Inferiore, Varese. 0036-9810.

SDB [= DBS]: Supplément au Dictionnaire de la Bible; Paris → 906.

SDH: Studia et documenta historiae et iuris; Roma, Pont. Univ. Later.

SDJ: Studies on the Texts of the Desert of Judah; Leiden.

Search: Dublin [5 (1982)].

SecC: The Second Century; Malibu CA. 0276-7899.

Sefarad; Madrid. 0037-0894.

SEG: Supplementum epigraphicum graecum; Withoorn.

Segmenten; Amsterdam, Vrije Univ.

SeiRon: Seisho-gaku ronshū; Tokyo, Japanese Biblical Institute.

SelT: Selecciones de Teología; Barc.

SémBib: Sémiotique et Bible; Lyon → CADIR. 0154-6902.

Semeia (Biblical Criticism) [Supplements]; Chico CA, SBL. 0095-571X.

Seminarios ... sobre los ministerios en la Iglesia; Salamanca, Inst. Vocacional 'M. Ávila' [29 (1983)].

Seminarium; Roma.

Seminary Review; Cincinnati.

Semiotica; Amsterdam.

Semitica; Paris. 2-7200-1040-5.

Semitics; Pretoria. '84: 0-86981-312-9.

Sens; juifs et chrétiens; Paris.

SeptCogSt: → B[ulletin].

Servitium, quaderni di spiritualità; Bergamo, priorato S. Egidio; publ. Casale Monferrato. 88-211-9031-5.

SEST: South-Eastern [Baptist Sem.] Studies; Wake Forest NC.

Sevārtham; Ranchi (St. Albert's College).

Sève = Église aujourd'hui [non plus 'en monde rural' (→ ÉglRur) à partir du Nᵒ 488, mai 1987]; P. 0223-5854.

SGErm: ⊕ Soobščeniya gosudarstvennovo Ermitaža, Reports of the State Hermitage Museum; Leningrad. 0432-1501.

ShinKen: ❽ *Shinyaku Kenkyū,* Studia Textus Novi Testamenti; Osaka.

ShnatM: ❺ Shnaton la-Mikra (Annual, Biblical and ANE Studies); Tel Aviv. ➤ **SMišpat.**

SicArch: Sicilia archaeologica; Trapani.

SicGym: Siculorum Gymnasium; Catania.

Sidra, a journal for the study of Rabbinic literature; Ramat-Gan [1 (1985)].

SIMA: Studies in Mediterranean Archaeology; Göteborg.

SixtC: The Sixteenth Century Journal; St. Louis (Kirksville). 0361-0160.

SkK: Stuttgarter (KBW) kleiner Kommentar.

SkrifK: Skrif en Kerk; Pretoria, Univ.

SMEA: Studi Micenei ed Egeo-Anatolici (Incunabula Graeca); Roma, Consiglio Naz.

SMišpat: Šnaton ha-Mišpaṭ ha-Ivri, Annual of the Institute for Research in Jewish Law [9s (1983)].

SMSR: Studi e Materiali di Storia delle religioni: Roma. [1977-82 'Studi Storico Religiosi'].

SNTS (Mg.): Studiorum Novi Testamenti Societas (Monograph Series); C.

SNTU-A/B: Studien zum NT und seiner Umwelt; Linz [Periodica / Series].

SocAnRel: Sociological analysis, a journal in the sociology of religion; Chicago [49 (1989)].

SocUÉg: Sociétés Urbaines en Égypte et au Soudan [= CRIPEL jusqu'à 1985]; Lille.

SocWB: The Social World of Biblical Antiquity; Sheffield.

Soundings; Nashville, Vanderbilt Univ. [65 (1983)].

SovArch: ❻ Sovyetskaja Archeologija; Moskva. 0038-5034.

Speculum (Medieval Studies); CM. 0038-7134.

SPg: Studia Philologica.

SpirC, SpirNC: La Spiritualità cristiana / non-cristiana; R ➤ 907.

Spiritus; Paris. 0038-7665.

SpirLife: Spiritual Life; Washington. 0038-7630.

Sprache; Wien. 0038-8467.

SR: Studies in Religion / Sciences Religieuses; Waterloo, Ont. 0008-4298.

ST: (Vaticano) Studi e Testi.

ST: Studia Theologica [Oslo till 43 (1989)] K. 0039-338X.

StAChron: Studies in Ancient Chronology; London. 0952-4975 [1 (1987)].

Stadion, Geschichte des Sports; Sankt Augustin. 0178-4029.

StAltägK: Studien zur altägyptischen Kultur; Hamburg. 0340-2215.

StAns: Studia Anselmiana; Roma.

StANT: Studien zum Alten und Neuen Testament; München.

StAntCr: Studi di Antichità Cristiana; Città del Vaticano.

Star: St. Thomas Academy for Research; Bangalore.

StArchWsz: Studia archeologiczne; Warszawa, Univ.

Staurós, Bollettino trimestrale sulla teologia della Croce: Pescara [7 (1981)].

StBEC: Studies in the Bible and Early Christianity; Lewiston NY.

StSp: Storia della Spiritualità ➤ 908.

StSpG: Storia della Spiritualità, ᴱ*Grossi* V. ➤ 909.

StBib: Dehon/Paid/Leiden: Studi Biblici; Bo, Dehoniane / Brescia, Paideia / Studia Biblica; Leiden [1 (1983)].

StBoğT: Studien zu den Boğazköy-Texten; Wiesbaden.

STBuc: Studii Teologice; Bucureşti.

StCatt: Studi cattolici; Milano. 0039-2901.

StCEth: Studies in Christian Ethics; E [1 (1989)].

StChHist: Studies in Church History; Oxford [21 (1984)].

StChrAnt: Studies in Christian Antiquity; Wsh.

StChrJud: Studies in Christianity and Judaism; Waterloo ON.

StClasBuc: Studii Clasice; Bucureşti.

StClasOr: Studi Classici e Orientali; P.

StCompRel: Studies in Comparative Religion; Bedfont, Middlesex.

StDelitzsch: Studia Delitzschiana (Institutum Judaicum Delitzschianum, Münster); Stuttgart. 0585-5071.

StEbl: Studi Eblaiti; Roma, Univ.

StEcum: Studi Ecumenici; Verona. 0393-3687 [2 (1984)].

StEgPun: Studi di Egittologia e di Antichità Puniche, Univ. Bologna: Pisa.

StEpL: Studi Epigrafici e Linguistici sul Vicino Oriente antico; Verona.

STEv: Studi di Teologia dell'Istituto Biblico Evangelico [Roma fino a 1 (1989)]; Padova.

StFormSp: Studies in Formative Spirituality; Pittsburgh, Duquesne.

StGnes: Studia Gnesnensia; Gniezno.

StHCT: Studies in the History of Christian Thought; Leiden.

StHJewishP: Studies in the History of the Jewish People; Haifa.

StHPhRel: Studies in the History and Philosophy of Religion; CM.

StHRel [= Numen Suppl.] Studies in the History of Religions; Leiden.

StIsVArh: Studii şi cercetări de Istorie Veche şi arheologie; Bucureşti. 0039-4009.

StIran: Studia Iranica; Leiden.

StIsVArh: Studii şi cercetări de Istorie Veche şi arheologie; Bucureşti. 0039-4009.

StItFgC: Studi Italiani di Filologia Classica; Firenze.

StiZt: Stimmen der Zeit; FrB. 0039-1492.

StJudLA: Studies in Judaism in Late Antiquity; Leiden.

StLeg: Studium Legionense; León.

StLtg: Studia Liturgica; Nieuwendam.

StLuke: St. Luke's Journal of Theology; Sewanee TN.

StMiss: Studia Missionalia, Annual; Rome, Gregorian Univ.

StMor: Studia Moralia; R, Alphonsianum.

StNT: Studien zum Neuen Testament; Gütersloh; **STNT** → Shin-Ken.

StNW: Studies of the NT and its World; E.

StOr: Studia Orientalia; Helsinki, Societas Orientalis Fennica. 0039-3282.

StOrRel: Studies in Oriental Religions; Wiesbaden.

StOvet: Studium Ovetense; Oviedo ('La Asunción').

StPatav: Studia Patavina; Padova. 0039-3304.

StPatrist: Studia Patristica; oBerlin.

StPhilonAn: Studia Philonica Annual, revival of Studia Philonica 1-6 (1972-80) + (7) 1984, S. Sandmel memorial; Atlanta [1 (1989) 1-55540-399-9].

StPostB: Studia Post-Biblica; Leiden.

StPrace: Studia i Prace = Études et Travaux, Centre d'Archéologie Méditerranéenne; Warszawa [12 (1983)].

Streven: 1. cultureel maatschappelijk maandblad; Antwerpen [50 (1982s)] 0039-2324; 2. S.J., Amst [35 (1982)].

StRicOrCr: Studi e Ricerche dell'Oriente Cristiano; Roma [5 (1982)].

StRom: Studi Romani; Roma.

Stromata (< Ciencia y Fe); San Miguel, Argentina. 0049-2353.

StRz: Studia Religioznawcze (Filozofii i Socjologii); Wsz, Univ.

StSemLgLing: Studies in Semitic Language and Linguistics; Leiden.

StTGg: Studien zur Theologie und Geistesgeschichte des 19. Jdts.; Gö, VR.

StTNeunz: Studien zur Theologie und Geistesgeschichte des Neunzehnten Jahrhunderts; Gö.

StudiaBT: Studia Biblica et Theologica; Pasadena CA. 0094-2022.

Studies; Dublin. 0039-3495.

StudiesBT: Studies in Biblical Theology; L.

Studium; 1. Madrid; 2. R. 0039-4130.

StVTPseud: Studia in Veteris Testamenti Pseudepigrapha; Leiden.

STWsz: Studia theologica Varsaviensia; Warszawa.

SubsB: Subsidia Biblica; R, Pontifical Biblical Institute.

SudanTB: Sudan Texts Bulletin; Ulster, Univ. 0143-6554. [7 (1985)].

Sumer (Archaeology-History in the Arab World); Baghdad, Dir. Ant.

SUNT: Studien zur Umwelt des NTs; Göttingen.

SUNY: State University of New York; Albany etc.

Supp.: Supplement → NT, JStOT, SDB, SEG.

Supplément, Le: autrefois 'de VSp'; P.

SvEx: Svensk Exegetisk Årsbok; U.

SVlad: St. Vladimir's Theological Quarterly; Tuckahoe NY. 0036-3227.

SvTKv: Svensk Teologisk Kvartalskrift; Lund.

SWJT: Southwestern Journal of Theology; Fort Worth. 0038-4828.

Symbolae (graec-lat.); Oslo. 0039-7679.

Symbolon: 1. Ba/Stu; 2. Köln.

Synaxe, annuale dell'Istituto per la Documentazione e la Ricerca S. Paolo; Catania [1 (1983)].

Syria (Art Oriental, Archéologie); Paris, IFA Beyrouth.

SyrMesSt: Syro-Mesopotamian Studies (Monograph Journals); Malibu CA.

Szb: Sitzungsberichte [Univ.], phil.-hist. Klasse (Bayr./Mü. 0342-5991).

Szolgalat ⓜ ['Dienst']; Eisenstadt, Österreich.

ⓣ: *lingua turca,* Turkish; – ᵀtranslator.

Tablet; London. 0039-8837.

TAik: Teologinen Aikakauskirja / Teologisk Tidskrift; Helsinki.

TaiwJT: Taiwan [Presbyterian Sem.] Journal of Theology; Taipei.

TAJ: Tel Aviv [Univ.] Journal of the Institute of Archaeology. 0334-4355.

TAn: Theology Annual; Hongkong.

ṬanṭurYb: Ecumenical Institute for Theological Research Yearbook; J, Ṭanṭur.

TArb: Theologische Arbeiten; Stu/oB.

Tarbiẓ ⓞ (Jewish Studies); Jerusalem, Hebr. Univ. 0334-3650.

TArg: Teología; Buenos Aires.

TAth: ⓖ Theología; Athēnai, Synodos.

TAVO: Tübinger Atlas zum Vorderen Orient [Beih(efte)]: Wiesbaden.

TBei: Theologische Beiträge; Wuppertal.

TBer: Theologische Berichte: Z/Köln.

TBR: Theological Book Review; Guildford, Survey.

TBraga: Theologica; Braga.

TBud: Teologia; Budapest, Ac. Cath.

TBüch: Theologische Bücherei. (Neudrucke und Berichte 20. Jdt.); München.

TCN: Theological College of Northern Nigeria Research Bulletin; Bukuru.

TContext: Theology in Context, English ed. [5,1 (1988) ➤ **TKontext** 9,1]. 0176-1439.

TDeusto: Teología-Deusto; Bilbao/M [16 (1982)].

TDienst: Theologie und Dienst; Wuppertal.

TDig: Theology Digest; St. Louis. 0040-5728.

TDNT: Theological Dictionary of the NT [< TWNT]; Grand Rapids ➤ 811.

TDocStA: Testi e documenti per lo studio dell'Antichità; Milano, Cisalpino.

TDOT: Theological Dictionary of the Old Testament [< TWAT] GR ➤ 910.

TEdn: Theological Education; Vandalia OH [20 (1983s)].

TEdr: Theological Educator; New Orleans.

TEFS: Theological Education [Materials for Africa, Asia, Caribbean] Fund, Study Guide; London.

Telema (réflexion et créativité chrétiennes en Afrique); Kinshasa-Gombe.

Teocomunicação; [12 (1982)].

Teresianum [ex-EphCarm]; Roma.

TerraS / TerreS: Terra Santa: 0040-3784. / La Terre Sainte; J (Custodia OFM). ➤ **HolyL.**

TEspir: Teología Espiritual; Valencia.

TEuph: Transeuphratène [Syrie perse]; P [1 (1989) 2-85021-036-6].

TEV: Today's English Version (Good News for Modern Man); L, Collins.

TEvca: Theologia Evangelica; Pretoria, Univ. S. Africa.

TExH: Theologische Existenz heute; München.

Text; The Hague. 0165-4888.

TextEstCisn: Textos y Estudios 'Cardenal Cisneros'; Madrid, C.S.I.C.

TextPatLtg: Textus patristici et liturgici; Regensburg, Pustet.

Textus, Annual of the Hebrew Univ. Bible Project; J. 0082-3767.

TFor: Theologische Forschung; Hamburg.

TGegw: Theologie der Gegenwart in Auswahl; Münster, Regensberg-V.

TGL: Theologie und Glaube; Paderborn.

THandkNT: Theologischer Handkommentar zum NT; oB.

THAT: Theologisches Handwörterbuch zum AT; München. ➤ 1,908.

Themelios; L. 0307-8388.

ThemTT: Themen und Thesen der Theologie; Dü.

Theokratia, Jahrbuch des Institutum Delitzschianum; Leiden/Köln.

Ho Theológos [sic], quadrimestrale Fac. Teol. Sicilia 'S. Giovanni Ev.'; Palermo [NS 1 (1983)].

30D: Thirty days in the Church and in the world [< Trenta giorni]; SF, Ignatius. [1,1 (1988)].

THist: Théologie Historique; P. 0563-4253.

This World; NY [3 (1982)].

Thomist, The; Wsh. 0040-6325.

Thought; Bronx NY, Fordham Univ.

TierraN: Tierra Nueva.

Tikkun; Oakland CA. [1,1 (1986)].

TimLitS: Times Literary Supplement; London.

TltSett: Teologia; Brescia (Fac. teol. Italia settentrionale).

Tiusi: Teología, Instituto Universitario Seminario Interdiocesano; Caracas [3-4 (1989)].

TJb: Theologisches Jahrbuch; Leipzig.

TKontext: Theologie im Kontext; Aachen. 0724-1682. ➤ **TContext.**

TLond: Theology; London. 0040-571X.

TLZ: Theologische Literaturzeitung; Berlin. 0040-5671.

TolkNT: Tolkning [commentarius] av Nya Testamentet; Stockholm.

TorJT: Toronto Journal of Theology [1 (1985)].

TPast: Theologie en pastoraat; Zwolle.

TPhil: Theologie und Philosophie; Freiburg/Br. 0040-5655.

TPQ: Theologisch-praktische Quartalschrift; Linz, Ös. 0040-5663.

TPract: Theologia Practica; München/Hamburg. 0720-9525.

TR: Theologische Revue; Münster. 0040-568X.

Traces; annuel des religions; Turnhout. [1 (1986); 2 (1987)].

TradErn: Tradition und Erneuerung (religiös-liberales Judentum); Bern.

Traditio; Bronx NY, Fordham Univ.

Tradition, a journal of orthodox Jewish thought; New York.

TRE: Theologische Realenzyklopädie; Berlin ➤ 911.

TRef: Theologia Reformata; Woerden.

TRevNE: ➤ NESTR.

TRicScR: Testi e ricerche di scienze religiose; Brescia.

TrierTZ: Trierer Theologische Zeitschrift; Trier. 0041-2945.

TrinJ: Trinity Journal; Deerfield IL. 0360-3032.

TrinSemR: Trinity Seminary Review; Columbus [11 (1989)].

TrinT: Trinity theological journal, Singapore [1 (1989)].

TrinUn [St/Mon] Rel: Trinity University Studies [Monographs] in Religion, San Antonio TX.

Tripod; Hong Kong, Holy Spirit Study Centre [2 (1981)].

TRu: Theologische Rundschau; Tübingen. 0040-5698.

TS: Theological Studies; Baltimore. 0040-5639.

TsGesch: Tijdschrift voor Geschiedenis; Groningen.

TsLtg: Tijdschrift voor Liturgie; Lv.

TStAJud: Texte und Studien zum Antiken Judentum; Tübingen. 0721-8753.

TsTKi: Tidsskrift for Teologi og Kirke; Oslo. 0040-7194.

TsTNijm: Tijdschrift voor Theologie; Nijmegen (redactie). 0168-9959.

TSzem: Theologiai Szemle; Budapest. 0133-7599.

TTod: Theology Today; Princeton.

TU: Texte und Untersuchungen, Geschichte der altchristlichen Literatur; oBerlin.

Tü [ÄgBei] ThS: Tübinger [Ägyptologische Beiträge; Bonn, Habelt] Theologische Studien; Mainz, Grünewald.

[Tü]TQ: [Tübinger] Theologische Quartalschrift; Mü. 0342-1430.

TürkArk: Türk Arkeoloji dergisi; Ankara [23 (1989)].

TUmAT: Texte aus der Umwelt des ATs; Gütersloh ➤ 912.

TVers: Theologische Versuche; oB. 0437-3014.

TViat: Theologia Viatorum, Jb.; B; to 15 (1979s); ➤ **BTZ.**

TVida: Teología y Vida; Santiago, Chile. 0049-3449.

TWAT: Theologisches Wörterbuch zum Alten Testament; Stu ➤ 913.

TWiss: Theologische Wissenschaft, Sammelwerk für Studium und Beruf; Stu.

TWNT: Theologisches Wörterbuch zum NT; Stuttgart (➤ GLNT; TDNT).

TXav: Theologica Xaveriana; Bogotá.

TxK: Texte und Kontexte (Exegese); Stu.

Tyche, Beiträge zur alten Geschichte, Papyrologie und Epigraphik; Wien.

Tychique (Chemin Neuf); Lyon.

TyndB: Tyndale Bulletin; Cambridge.

TZBas: Theologische Zeitschrift; Basel.

UF: Ugarit-Forschungen; Kevelaer/ Neukirchen. 0342-2356.

Universitas; 1. Stuttgart. 0041-9079; 2. Bogotá. 0041-9060.

UnivT: Universale Teologica; Brescia.

UnSa: Una Sancta: 1. Augsburg-Meitingen; 2. Brooklyn.

UnSemQ: Union Seminary Quarterly Review; New York.

UPA: University Press of America; Wsh/ Lanham MD.

Update [new religious movements]; Aarhus [7 (1983)].

URM: Ultimate Reality and Meaning; Toronto [12 (1989)].

VAeg: Varia Aegyptiaca; San Antonio. 0887-4026 [1 (1985)].

VBGed: Verklaring van een Bijbelgedeelte; Kampen.

VChrét: Vie Chrétienne; P. 0767-3221.

VComRel: La vie des communautés religieuses; Montréal.

VDI: ❻ Vestnik Drevnej Istorii; Moskva. 0321-0391.

Veleia, (pre-) historia, arqueología filología clásicas; Vitoria-Gasteiz, Univ. País Vasco [1 (1984)].

Verbum; 1. SVD; R; 2. Nancy [5 (1983)].

Veritas; Porto Alegre, Univ. Católica.

VerkF: Verkündigung und Forschung; München.

VerVid: Verdad y Vida; Madrid.

VestB: Vestigia Biblica; Hamburg.

VetChr: Vetera Christianorum; Bari.

Vidyajyoti (Theological Reflection); Ranchi (Delhi, Inst. Rel.St.).

VieCons: La Vie Consacrée; P/Bru.

VigChr: Vigiliae Christianae; Leiden. 0042-6032.

ViMon: Vita Monastica; Camaldoli, Arezzo.

ViPe: Vita e Pensiero: Mi, Univ. S. Cuore.

VisLang: Visible Language; Cleveland.

VisRel: Visible Religion, annual for religious iconography; Leiden [3 (1984) 90-04-07496-1].

VitaCons: Vita Consacrata; Milano.

VizVrem: ❻ Vizantijskij Vremennik; Moskva. 0136-7358.

VO: Vicino Oriente; Roma.

Vocation; Paris.

VoxEvca: Vox Evangelica; London. 0263-6786.

VoxEvi: Vox Evangelii; Buenos Aires [NS 1 (1984)].

VoxRef: Vox Reformata; Geelong, Australia.

VoxTh: Vox Theologica; Assen.

VSp: La Vie Spirituelle; Paris. 0042-4935; **S(up).** 0083-5859.

VT: Vetus Testamentum; Leiden.

WDienst: Wort und Dienst; Bielefeld. 0342-3085.

WegFor: Wege der Forschung; Da, Wiss.

WeltOr: Welt des Orients; Göttingen. 0043-2547.

WesleyTJ: Wesleyan Theological Journal; Marion IN. 0092-4245.

WestTJ: Westminster Theological Journal; Philadelphia. 0043-4388.

WEvent: Word + Event, World Catholic Federation for the Biblical Apostolate; Stuttgart; printed in Hong Kong, also in Spanish ed.

WienerSt: Wiener Studien; Wien.

Wiss: Wissenschaftliche Buchhandlung; Da.

WissPrax: Wissenschaft und Praxis in Kirche und Gesellschaft; Göttingen.

WissWeish: Wissenschaft und Weisheit; Mü-Gladbach. 0043-678X.

WM: Wissenschaftliche Monographien zum Alten und Neuen Testament; Neukirchen.

WoAnt: Wort und Antwort; Mainz.

Word and Spirit; Still River MA.

WorldArch: World Archaeology; Henley.

World Spirituality ➤ EWSp.

Worship; St. John's Abbey, Collegeville, Minn. 0043-9414.

WrocST: Wrocławskie Studia Teologiczne / Colloquium Salutis; Wrocław. 0239-7714.

WUNT: Wissenschaftliche Untersuchungen zum NT: Tübingen.

WVDOG: Wissenschaftliche Veröffentlichungen der Deutschen Orient-Gesellschaft; Berlin.

WWorld: Word and World; St. Paul.

WZ: Wissenschaftliche Zeitschrift [... Univ.].

WZKM: Wiener Zeitschrift für die Kunde des Morgenlandes; Wien. 0084-0076.

Xilotl, revista nicaraguense de teología [5 (1989)].

YaleClas: Yale Classical Studies; NHv.

Yuval: Studies of the Jewish Music Research Centre [incl. Psalms]; Jerusalem.

ZäSpr: Zeitschrift für Ägyptische Sprache und Altertumskunde; Berlin. 0044-216X.

ZAHeb: Zeitschrift für Althebraistik; Stuttgart. 0932-4461 [1,1 (1988)].

ZAss: Zeitschrift für Assyriologie & Vorderasiatische Archäologie; Berlin. 0048-5299.

ZAW: Zeitschrift für die Alttestamentliche Wissenschaft; Berlin. 0044-2526.

ZDialT: Zeitschrift für dialektische Theologie; Kampen [1 (1985)].

ZDMG: Zeitschrift der Deutschen Morgenländischen Gesellschaft; Wiesbaden.

ZDPV: Zeitschrift des Deutschen Palästina-Vereins; Stu. 0012-1169.

ZeichZt: Die Zeichen der Zeit, Evangelische Monatschrift; oBerlin.

Zeitwende (Die neue Furche); Gü.

ZeKUL: Zeszyty Naukowe Katolickiego Uniwersytetu Lubelskiego; Lublin. 0044-4405.

Zephyrus; Salamanca. 0514-7336.

ZEthnol: Zeitschrift für Ethnologie; Braunschweig. 0044-2666.

ZEvEthik: Zeitschrift für Evangelische Ethik; Gütersloh. 0044-2674.

ZfArch: Zeitschrift für Archäologie: oBerlin. 0044-233X.

ZGPred: Zeitschrift für Gottesdienst und Predigt; Gü. [1 (1983)].

Zion: ❶; Jerusalem. 0044-4758.

ZIT: Zeitschriften Inhaltsdienst Theologie; Tübingen. 0340-8361.

ZKG: Zeitschrift für Kirchengeschichte; Stuttgart. 0044-2985.

ZkT: Zeitschrift für katholische Theologie; Innsbruck. 0044-2895.

ZMissRW: Zeitschrift für Missionswissenschaft und Religionswissenschaft; Münster. 0044-3123.

ZNW: Zeitschrift für die Neutestamentliche Wissenschaft und die Kunde des Alten Christentums; Berlin. 0044-2615.

ZPapEp: Zeitschrift für Papyrologie und Epigraphik; Bonn. 0084-5388.

ZPraxRU: Zeitschrift für die Praxis des Religionsunterrichts; Stu.

ZRGg: Zeitschrift für Religions- und Geistesgeschichte; Köln. 0044-3441.

ZSavR: Zeitschrift der Savigny-Stiftung (Romanistische) Rechtsgeschichte: Weimar. 0323-4096.

ZSprW: Zeitschrift für Sprachwissenschaft; [3 (1984)].

ZTK: Zeitschrift für Theologie und Kirche; Tübingen. 0513-9147.

ZvgSpr: Zeitschrift für vergleichende Sprachforschung; ➜ HSpF ab 1988.

Zwingliana; Zürich [17 (1986-8) 3-290-11532-1].

Zygon; Winter Park FL. 0044-5614.

I. Bibliographica

A1 *Opera collecta* .1 **Festschriften,** memorials.

1 Collected essays [now separately signed]: CBQ 51 (1989) 170-185. 388-397. 578-587. 765-781; – EErnst Juliette, AnPg 58 (1989 pour 1987); – ETL 65,2s (1989) 7*-14*, opera collecta (15*s, bibliographiae a parte). – *Fretheim* Terence E. [OT], *Epp* Eldon J., Collected essays: JBL 108 (1989) 173-180. 361-374. 555-561. – Collected essays: JQR 80 (1989s) 438-446. – *Langlamet* F., Recueils et mélanges: RB 96 (1989) 120-5. 289-294. 423-432. 595s.

2 **Zeller** Otto & Wolfram, Internationale Jahresbibliographie der Festschriften 7 (for 1986). Osnabrück 1988, Dietrich. 695 [+] 948 [+] 449 p. [AnPg 59, p. 969, with data also on 1 (1980/2)-6 (1985/8)].

3 ABRAMSKY Chimen: Jewish history; essays in honour of ~, ᴱ**Rapaport-Albert** Ada, *Zipperstein* Steven J. L 1988, Halban. xi-700 p. £30. – ᴿJJS 40 (1989) 272-4 (H.-D. *Löwe*).

4 ADRIANI Achille [† 1982]: Alessandria e il mondo ellenistico-romano: Univ. Palermo, Studi e Materiali 4-6. R 1983s, Bretschneider. XIX-IX-XII + 877 p. (3 vol.); CXLVI pl.; 5 plans; bibliog. 1, XV-XIX (*Epifanio* E.). – ᴿLatomus 48 (1989) 490-2 (J. *Debergh*).

5 AKURGAL Ekrem: Armağan = Anadolu 21 (1978-80) [1987] 236 p. + bibliog. 30 art., 10 infra.

6 ALBINI Umberto: Heptachordos lyra, ᴱ**Sisti** Franco, *Maltese* Enrico V. Genova 1988, Univ. Sez. ellenica. 95 p. [AnPg 59 p. 969].

7 ALFARO Juan: Fides quae per caritatem operatur, 75° cumpleaños, ᴱ**Lera** José M. [Bilbao 1989, Mensajero (TS 51,187)] = Estudios Eclesiásticos 64, 248s (1989). 269 p. [+ p. 273-554, fasc. 250s]; portr.; biobibliog. 9-14; 15-36, *Miguel* José M. de, La teología de J. A.; 37-52, *Rovira Belloso* Josep P., La obra reciente de J. A. [NRT 112,614, R. *Escol*; RET 50,473-5, F. *de Carlos Otto*; ScripTPamp 22,625-7, L. F. *Mateo-Seco*].

8 ALLONI N. mem.: ❺ Ešel Be'er-Scheva, essays in Jewish studies 3 (1986) [JStJud 20,275].

9 ALMAGRO BOSCH Martin: Homenaje a ~, Kalathos 5s (Teruel 1985s). 395 p. [AnPg 59 p. 969].

10 AMPE Albert: Ons Geestelijk Erf 63, 2-4 (1989) p. 119-416 (bibliog. 121-154, phot., *Hendrickx* Frans) + 64,1-3 (1990) 1-308.

11 ANDERSSON Thorsten: Studia onomastica, Festskrift till ~. Sto 1989, Almqvist & W. 454 p. 52 art. – ᴿBeiNam 24 (1989) 420s (H. *Beck*).

12 AUGUSTO TAVARES António, Estudos de alta antiguidade. Lisboa 1983, Presença. 254 p. – ᴿRB 95 (1988) 438s (F. J. *Gonçalves*).

13 AUTENRIETH Johanne: Litterae Medii Aevi, 65. Gb., ᴱ**Borgolte** Michael, *Spilling* Herrad: Sigmaringen 1988, Thorbecke. xiv-394 p.; 29 pl. – ᴿRBén 99 (1989) 377s (P. *Verbrake*).

14 AVI-YONAH Michael mem., ᴱ**Barag** D., Eretz Israel 19, 1987 ➤ 3,13: ᴿJStJud 20 (1989) 222-6 (M. *Mach*: tit. pp. & detailed analyses).

15 BACHI Roberto, Studies in the population of Israel in honor of ~, ᴱ**Schmelz** Uriel O., *Gad* Nathan. J 1986, Hebrew Univ. – ᴿRÉJ 146 (1987) 198s (M. L. *Lévy*).

16 BALTL Hermann: Recht und Geschichte, 70. Gb., ᴱ**Valentinitsch** H. Graz 1988, Leykam. 664 p. – ᴿSchweizerische Zts für Geschichte 38 (1988) 451s (H. *Herold*); Mitteilungen Inst. Österr. Geschichtsforschung 97 (1989) 133-5 (W. *Goldinger*) [RHE 84,227*].

17 BARTELINK Gerard J. M.: Fructus centesimus, mélanges... 65ᵉ anniv., ᴱ**Bastiaensen** A. A. R., *al.*: Instrumenta Patristica 19. Steenbrugge / Dordrecht 1989, Abdij S. Pieter / Kluwer. xxxiii-427 p.; portr.; bibliog. p. vii-ix. 28 art.; 6 infra [AnBoll 108,192-7, P. *Devos*; JTS 41,692, W. *Frend*; NRT 112,439, N. *Plumat*]. – ᴿTR 85 (1989) 426s (tit. pp.); TsTNijm 29 (1989) 413 (P. van de *Paverd*); VigChr 43 (1989) 414s (tit. pp.).

18 BARTH Karl: *a)* Theology beyond Christendom; essays on the centenary of the birth of Karl Barth, ᴱ**Thompson** J.: PrincTMg 6. Allison Park PA 1986, Pickwick. IX-350 p. [ETL 65,14*]. – *b)* Centenary essays. NY 1989, Cambridge-UP. 171 p. $37.50. 0-521-34184-1 [TDig 37,68]. –

c) Reckoning with Barth... centenary, EBiggar Nigel. L 1988, Mowbray. xi-214 p. £25.

19 BAUM Gregory: Faith that transforms, 60th b. (1983), ELeddy Mary Jo, *Hinsdale* Mary Ann. Mahwah NJ 1987, Paulist. vi-196 p.; 42-p. bibliog. – RSR 18 (1989) 99 (J. R. *Williams*: unfair choice of contributors); TsTNijm 29 (1989) 81 (A. van *Harskamp*, also on Baum's 1987 collected essays).

21 BEASLEY-MURRAY George R.: Eschatology and the New Testament, essays in honor of ~, EGloer W. Hulitt. Peabody MA 1988, Hendrickson. xix-154 p.; phot.; bibliog. p. xiii-xvii. 0-943575-01-X. 8 art.; infra.

22 BECK Heinrich: Actualitas omnium actuum, 60 Gb., ESchadel Erwin: Schriften zur Triadik und Ontodynamik 3. Fra 1989, Lang. 712 p. [TPhil 64,632]. – RForumKT 5 (1989) 302-4 (H. *Müller*).

23 BECKER Alfons, Deus qui mutat tempora; Menschen und Institutionen im Wandel des Mittelalters, EHehl E.-D., *al.* Sigmaringen 1987, Thorbecke. ix-386 p.; 9 fig.; map. – RMitteilungen des Instituts für Österreichische Geschichtsforschung 97 (1989) 135-7 (H. *Weigl*) [< RHE 84,227*].

24 BEER Ellen Judith: Nobile claret opus, 60. Gb. Z 1986, Schwegler. 180 p.; ill. – RRHÈ 84 (1989) 293s (Thérèse *Poilvache-Lambert*: surtout sur les manuscrits enluminés).

25 BEINART Haim: Exile and diaspora, 70th. b., EMirsky A., *al.* J 1988, Ben-Zvi. 606 p. [JQR 81,228, tit. Ⓗ sans pp.]. – RSefarad 49 (1989) 420-3 (M. *Orfali*).

26 BENDER Ernest [editor 1964-88]: JAOS 109,4 (1989), ERiccardi Theodore, *Insler* Stanley. AA 1989. p. x (biobibliog.; portr.) 509-658. 20 art., all on Southeast Asia.

27 BEN-GURION and the Bible — the people and its land, ECogan Mordechai. Beer-Sheva 1989, Ben Gurion University of the Negev. – Not clear whether intended as a Festschrift, nor whether the name is that of the person or of the university.

28 BERGHE Louis Vanden: Archaeologia iranica et orientalis, EMeyer L. De, *Haerinck* E. Gent 1989, Peeters. xlv-573 p. (bibliog. xiii-xiv); p. 575-1054. 90-6831-185-9. 35 + 27 art.; 37 infra.

28* BEYERHAUS Peter: Wie gewinnt die Mission ihre Gewissheit? Martyria, 60. Gb., EMoritzen Niels-Peter Wu/Z 1989, Brockhaus. 12 art., 5 infra [TR 85 (1989) 425, but 344, 'Bayerhaus'] 256-270 Bibliog. DM 29,80.

29 BIEŻUŃSKA-MALOWIST Iza: Świat antyczny; stosunki spółeczne, ideologia i polityka, religia. Wsz 1988, PWN. 328 p.; ill. [AnPg 59, p. 970].
FBITTEL Kurt, Colloquium 1987/8 → 777.

30 BLANC Haim (1926-1984) mem.: Studia linguistica et orientalia, EWexler Paul, *al.*: TA Mediterranean Language and Culture 6. Wsb 1989, Harrassowitz. viii-314 p.; portr.; biobibliog. 1-10 (Somekh Sasson). 27 art.; 13 infra.

31 BOOMS Hans: Aus der Arbeit der Archive; Beiträge zum Archivwesen, zur Quellenkunde und zur Geschichte, EKahtenberg F.-P.; Schriften des Bundesarchivs 36. Boppard 1989, Boidt. xxii-988 p.; ill. DM 96 [RHE 85,63*].

32 BOUCHET Jean-René † 15.XII.1987: VSp 142,5 (1988) p. 617-782.

33 BOUGEROL Jacques-Guy, OFM: Bonaventuriana, miscellanea in onore di, ~ EChavero Bianco F. de A.: Bibl. Antonianum 27s. R 1988, Pont. Athenaeum Antonianum. vii-786 p. (2 vol.); biobibliog. 11-16. Lit. 40.000. – RRSPT 73 (1989) 100s (L. *Bataillon*, tit. pp.).

BREKELMANS C. H. W., 'cordialement dédié à ~' ➤ 614, ᴱVermeylen J., The book of Isaiah 1987/9.

34 BRIDEL Claude: Pratique et théologie, ᴱAmsler S., al.: Pratiques 1. Genève 1989, Labor & F. 224 p. Fs 32. 2-8309-0141-X [ETRel 64,674; JTS 41,346; RTLv 21,387, P. Weber; RÉAug 36,212, P. Fédou].

35 BRINK C. O.: Studies in Latin literature and its tradition, 80th b., ᴱDiggle J., al.: Proc. Sup. 15. C 1989, Pg. Soc. v-145 p. 0-906014-14-X. 10 art. 1 infra [ClasR 40,447, N. Horsfall; REAug 36,211, M. Fédou]. – ᴿArctos 23 (1989) 253s (O. Merisalo).

36 BROWN R. Allen: Studies in medieval history, 65th. b. (shortly before his death), ᴱHarper-Bill Christopher, al. Woodbridge 1989, Boydell. xvi-360 p.; ill.; bibliog. (Brown Vivien). £39.50 [RHE 85,241, D. Bradley; Speculum 65,793s, tit. pp.].

36* BRUNHÖLZL Franz, Tradition und Wertung, 65. Gb., ᴱBernt G., al. Sigmaringen 1989, Thorbecke. xi-332 p.; 6 pl. DM 120 [TLZ 115,667, tit. pp.].

37 BUCHNER Edmund, 65 Gb. = Chiron 18. Mü 1988, Beck. viii-507 p. [AnPg 59, p. 978].

38 BURGHARDT Walter J.: Preaching in the patristic age; studies in honor of ~, ᴱHunter David G. NY 1989, Paulist. vi-217 p. $15. 0-8091-3079-3 [CalvinT 25,280, C. Zylstra; TS 51,560, E. C. Muller]. 10 art., infra.

38* CHADWICK Henry: The making of orthodoxy, ᴱWilliams R., C 1989, Univ. xxv-340 p.; portr. £35 [NRT 112,927, A. Harvengt]. 16 art., 7 infra.

39 CLÈRE Jacques Jean, 1906-1989, mém.: Revue d'Égyptologie 40 (1989). IX (biobibliog.) – 222 p.; phot. 2-252-02201-9.

40 COLPE Carsten: JbAC 32 (1989), portr.

41 CORETH Emerich: Sinngestalten; Metaphysik in der Vielfalt menschlichen Fragens, ᴱMuck Otto. Innsbruck 1989, Tyrolia. 408 p.; Bibliog. p. 389-408. DM 58 [TPQ 138,392, U. G. Leinsle; TR 85,337].

42 COSTANZA Salvatore: Polyanthema, studi di letteratura cristiana antica offerti a ~, ᴱCalderone Salvatore (De Salvio Lietta), al.: Univ. Messina, Studi tardoantichi 7. Messina 1989, Sicania. xxvii-434 p.; portr.; biobibliog. i-xiii (S. Leanza), xv-xix. 29 art.; 8 infra.

43 COTTLE Basil: Medieval literature and antiquities, ᴱStokes M., Burton T. L. C 1987, Brewer. xxii-201 p. [RHE 85,63*].

44 CRAEYBECKX E., SCHOLLIERS E., Arbeit in veelvoud; en huldeboek. Bru 1988, Vrije Univ. 335 p. – ᴿBijdragen tot de Geschiedenis 71 (1988) 192s (B. Blondé) [RHE 84,227*].

44* CRISWELL W. A.: Essays in honor of ~, ᴱMathews K. A., Dockery David S. = CriswTR 1,2 (Dallas 1987) 229-399; ill.; biobibliog. p. 237-255-267, Patterson Paige; Cooper James E. 8 art.; infra.

45 DEISSLER Alfons: Der Weg zum Menschen; zur philosophischen und theologischen Anthropologie, 75. Gb., ᴱMosis Rudolf, Ruppert Lothar. FrB 1989, Herder. x-344 p.; Bibliog. 341-4. DM 58. 3-451-21441-5. 20 art., infra [TLZ 115,94, tit. pp.]. – ᴿNRT 111 (1989) 925 (V. Roisel).

46 DELANEY Tom mem.: Studies in medieval archaeology and history, ᴱMacNiocaill G., Wallace P. F. Galway 1989, Univ. xvi-622 p.; ill. £49.50 [RHE 85,63*].

47 DELCOURT Albert: Mélanges: Histoire et archéologie athoises 8. Ath 1989, Le Cercle. 216 p.; 27 fig. [RHE 85,63*].

47* DEMBOWSKI Hermann, 'Das unsere Augen aufgetan werden ...', 60. Gb., ᴱGutheil Jörn-Erik, Zoske Sabine. Fra 1989, Lang. 237 p. 3-631-40582-0. 13 art. [ZIT 89,830], 3 infra.

48 DIMIER Anselme: Mélanges à la mémoire [I,1s, c. 1984; II,1s, c. 1985] I [? de nouveau], 1, L'homme, l'œuvre; 2. Travaux inédits et rééditions, ᴱChauvin Benoit. Arbois 1987, Chauvin. 506 p.; p. 515-861; ill. – ᴿRBén [95,364; 96,193] 99 (1989) 208s (J. *Lefèvre*).

49 DRERUP Heinrich: Bathron, Beiträge zur Architektur und verwandten Kunsten, 80. Gb., ᴱBüsing Hermann, *Hiller* Friedrich: Saarbrücker Studien zur Archäologie und Alten Geschichte 3. Saarbrücker-V. 1988. 433 p.; ill.; Bibliog. p. 9-12. 3-925036-21-0. 38 art.; 5 infra.

50 DUBUISSON Pierrette: Agronymes; mélanges de toponymie et de dialectologie. Dijon 1987, Assoc. Bourguignonne de Dialectologie et d'Onomastique. vi-152 p. – ᴿSalesianum 51 (1989) 392 (R. *Bracchi*).

51 EBOROWICZ Wacław: Miscellanea patristica in honorem (Venceslai) ~ = Vox Patrum 15 (1988) 551-1160; portr.; biobibliog. 557-563-574 (A. *Eckmann* / Cz. *Mazur*). 88-228-0141-6. 32 art.; 4 infra.

52 Otto-EISSFELDT-Ehrung 100. Gb. 1.X.1987, ᴱ*Wallis* G.: Wiss. Beit. 1988/36. Halle 1988. 119 p. S. 19-44, *Zobel* H.-J., als Theologe; 67-98, *Hillmann* H., für die orientalische Religionsgeschichte; 99-104, *Reinelt* H., für die katholische Bibelwissenschaft; 105-113, *Beyse* K.-M., Geschichte Alt-Israels [< ZAW 101, 456].

52* ELTON Geoffrey: Politics and society in reformation Europe; essays for Sir ~, 65th b., ᴱ**Kouri** E. I., *Scott* T. NY 1987, St. Martin's. xix-568 p. $45. 25 art. – ᴿChH 58 (1989) 106-8 (L. H. *Zuck*); EngHR 104 (1989) 688s (E. *Cameron*).

53 ERVIN Howard, Essays on apostolic themes, ᴱ**Elbert** Paul, 1985 ↠ 2,28: ᴿEvQ 60 (1988) 71-74 (R. P. *Menzies*: detailed).

54 ETTINGER Shmuel: ☉ Essays in honor of ~, ᴱ**Almog** Shmuel, *al.*, I. Israel and the nations; II. Transition and change in modern Jewish history. J 1987, Shazar Center. 375-cxlvi p.; 568-cxxvii p. – ᴿRÉJ 147 (1988) 435-8 (Esther *Benbassa*: tit. pp.; many on antisemitism; none notably biblical).

55 ÉVRARD Étienne, a) Le nombre et le texte; hommage à ~: Revue informatique 24 (1988). xiv-161 p. – b) *Eis pollà ètē*, ad multos annos: Cahiers de l'analytique des données 13. P 1988, Dumont. 152 p. [AnPg 59, both p. 971].

56 FASOLA Umberto Maria: Quaeritur invenitur colitur, Miscellanea: Studi di Antichità cristiana 40. Vaticano 1989, Pont. Ist. Arch. Cr. 827 p.; ill. Lit. 200.000 [RHE 85,63*].

57 FERGUSON Charles A.: The Fergusonian impact, 65th b., ᴱ**Fishman** J. A., *al.*, I. From phonology to society; II. Sociolinguistics and the sociology of language: Contrib. Soc. Lang. 42. B 1986, Mouton de Gruyter. xii-598 p.; xii-545 p. – ᴿBSOAS 51 (1988) 123s (J. *Wansbrough*).

58 FINEGAN Jack: Chronos, kairos, Christos; Nativity and chronological studies, 80th b., ᴱ**Vardaman** Jerry, *Yamauchi* Edwin M., WL 1989, Eisenbrauns. xxiii-240 p.; portr.; biobibliog. ix-xii (*Van Elderen* B.), xv-xxiii. $25. 0-931464-50-1. 13 art., infra.

59 FINET André: Reflets des deux fleuves, ᴱ**Lebeau** Marc, *Talon* Philippe: Akkadica supp. 6. Lv 1989, Peeters. viii-193 p.; ill.; p. 191-3 bibliog. (*Scouflaire* M.). 90-6831-181-6 [OIAc S89]. 31 art., 10 infra.

60 FITZMYER Joseph A.: [I. = CBQ 48,3 (1986) ↠ 2,32; II:] To touch the text; biblical and related studies in honor of ~, ᴱ**Horgan** Maurya P., *Kobelski* Paul J. NY 1989, Crossroad. xiv-418 p., bibliog. 390-412 (490 items). $40. 0-8245-0807-1. 25 art., infra [NRT 112,896, titres sans pp.].

61 FLETCHER Domingo: (III) Archivo de Prehistoria Levantina 19 (1989). Valencia 1989, Diputación.

62 FRANZ Heinrich G.: Orient und Okzident im Spiegel der Kunst, 70. Gb., ᴱBrucher Günter, *al.* Graz 1986, Akad. XI-498 p.; p. 501-670, pl. (+ portr.); Bibliog. p. 477-498. 3-201-01296-3. 32 art.; 2 infra.

63 FREHNER Paul: Im Gespräch mit der Bibel; Beiträge aus der Erwachsenenbildung, 75. Gb., ᴱWeymann V. Z 1987, Theol.-V. 80 p. Fs 12. 3-290-10013-8 [NTAbs 33,237: *Schweizer* E. on 1 Pt 2,1-10, priesthood of all believers].

64 GARCIA BELLIDO M.: Homenaje V: Gerión Anejos 1. M 1988, Univ. Complutense. 410 p. [AnPg 59, p. 971].

65 GARZYA Antonio: Taláriskos, studia graeca, 60° compleanno. N 1987, d'Auria. 481 p. [AnPg 59, p. 971].

65* GEISSER Hans Friedrich: Theologische Kaprizen, 60. Gb., ᴱBaumgartner Markus. Z 1988, Univ. Theol. Fak. Inst. Hermeneutik. 572 p.; ill. 37 Art. [ZIT 89,832], 7 infra.

66 GILKEY Langdon: The whirlwind in culture; frontiers in theology, ᴱMusser Donald W., *Price* Joseph L. Bloomington IN 1988, Meyer-Stone. ix-273 p. $40; pa. $20. 0-940989-43-3; 39-5 [TDig 36,393].

67 GINER María C.: Stephanion, homenaje a ~, ᴱCodoñer Carmen, *al.*: Acta Salmanticensia. Salamanca 1988, Univ. 254 p. [AnPg 59, p. 971].

67* GINNEKEN Grietje van: En zij lachte en het lichtte; scepsis als grondslag voor het zien van vrouwen [Abschied Amst.], ᵀDoorsen H. van, *al.* Voorburg 1989, Prot. Bib./Lectuur. 97 p. ƒ27,50. 90-6495-192-6. – ᴿTsTNijm 29 (1989) 418 (Annelies de *Bont*).

68 GNILKA Joachim: Vom Urchristentum zu Jesus, ᴱFrankemölle Hubert, *Kertelge* Karl. FrB 1989, Herder. 536 p. 3-451-21410-5. 29 art., infra [TLZ 115,33, tit. pp.; NRT 112,902 titres]. – ᴿTsTNijm 29 (1989) 406 (S. van *Tilborg*).

69 GOEDERT Joseph: Mélanges, ᴱTrausch G., *Vekene* E. van der. Luxembourg 1983, Bibl. Nat. 396 p. 18 art.; p. 228-239 (3 pl.) *Schroeder* J., Älteste Echternacher Bibelfragmente. – ᴿRHE 84 (1989) 810 (R. *Aubert*).

69* GOMÀ I CIVIT Isidre: In medio Ecclesiae, miscel·lània en homenatge al prof. dr. ~, ᴱRius Camps Joseph, *Sanchez Bosch* Jordi, *Pié i Ninot* Salvador = RCatalT 14 (1989) 578 p. 48 art.; 45 infra (16 en castellano).

70 GORDON Colin D. mem.: Syneisphora McGill 1. Papers in Greek archaeology and history, ᴱFossey John M. Amst 1987, Gieben. 155 p.; 25 fig.; 17 pl.; biobibliog. p. 11-13 (Paola *Valeri-Tomaszuk*). 90-5063-009-X. 9 art.; 6 infra.

71 GRANT John W.: Canadian Protestant and Catholic missions 1820s-1960s; historical essays in honour of ~, ᴱMoir J.S., *McIntire* C.T.: Toronto Studies in Religion 3. NY 1988, Lang. xix-266 p. Fs 53 [TR 85,527].

72 GROSS David A.: Anniversary volume, an anthology of history, education, literature and research [13 art. (mostly on modern Hebrew) + some of his writings and several tributes], 70th b., ᴱKodesh Shlomo. J 1983, Hamatmid. 142 p. + ☉359; 23 pl.

73 GÜNTHER Rigobert, 60. Gb. = Klio 71/2 (1989) 321-538. 25 art., 2 infra.

74 GUIRAL Pierre: Hommes, idées, journaux, ᴱGili Jean-Antoine, *Schor* Ralph: 'France XIXᵉ-XXᵉ s.' 29. P 1988, Sorbonne. 400 p.; ill. F 210 [RHE 85,226, J.-P. *Hendrickx*].

75 GURDON Edmund: The threshold of Paradise, a memoir, ᴱHogg J.: Analecta Carthusiana. Salzburg 1988, Inst. Anglistik. xii-144 p. – ᴿRHE 84 (1989) 789 (J. De *Grauwe*).

GUTIÉRREZ Gustavo: multiple anniversary meeting 1988/9 → 671.

76 HANDY Robert T.: Altered landscapes; Christianity in America 1935-1985, ᴱLotz David W. *al.* GR 1989, Eerdmans. 387 p. $28; pa $18. 21 art. [ZIT 90,148]; *Fogarty* G./*Gaustad* E. on Catholic/Protestant biblical scholarship. – ᴿTTod 46 (1989s) 344s (E. B. *Holifield*).

77 HARRISON Roland K.: Israel's apostasy and restoration, ᴱGileadi Avraham. GR 1988, Baker. xi-325 p. $25. 0-8010-3830-8. 26 art. [TDig 36,375; CBQ 52,772; 24 art., OT; tit. pp.; some analyses, L. F. *Asma*].

78 HEERMA VAN VOSS M. S. H. G.: Funerary symbols and religion [... retirement], ᴱKamstra J. H., *al.* Kampen 1988, Kok. xi-182 p.; portr.; bibliog. p. 1-11. 90-242-4430-2. 15 art.; 11 infra.

79 Heidelberger Seminar für Alte Geschichte, Gedenk- und Jubiläumsvortrage, Vom frühen Griechentum bis zur römischen Kaiserzeit, ᴱAlföldy Géza. Stu 1989, Steiner. 108 p.; ill. 3-515-05190-2. 6 art., 1 infra.

80 HELCK Wolfgang: Miscellanea aegyptologica, 75. Gb., ᴱAltenmüller Hartwig, *Germer* Renate. Ha 1989, Univ. Archäol. Inst. vii-195 p.; ix pl. 13 art.; 8 infra.

81 HELD Moshe: ❿ Linguistic studies in memory of ~, ᴱCogan Mordechai: Beer-Sheva 3. J 1988, Magnes [for Ben-Gurion Univ.]. 178 p. + 14 Eng. 0334-2255 [OIAc Ja90; BL 91,16, J. A. *Emerton*].

82 HEMMERLE Klaus, Der dreieine Gott und die eine Menschheit, 60. Gb. FrB 1989, Herder. 215 p.; ill. DM 38 [TR 85,161; TPQ 138,180].

83 HIGHFIELD J. R. I.: God and man in medieval Spain, ᴱLomax D. W., *Mackenzie* D. Wmr 1989, Aris & P. xxiv-168 p.; portr. [RHE 85,64*; JEH 41,701s, R. B. *Tate*].

84 HILL David: NT Essays in honour of ~, ᴱTuckett Christopher: JStNT 37 (1989) [not 1988 as cover]. 135 p. 1-85075-245-1. 8 art.; infra.

85 HINZ Christoph: '... und Frieden auf Erden'; Beiträge zur Friedensantwortung von Kirche und Israel, 60. Gb., ᴱLux R. B 1988, Inst. Kirche und Judentum. – ᴿTLZ 114 (1989) 875s (tit. pp.).

86 HOECK Abt Johannes: Primum Regnum Dei 1986 [his Konzilsrede 19.X.1965, ᴱGahbauer R. for Hoeck's 85th birthday, with other contributions]. Mü 1986, 212 p. – ᴿOrChrPer 55 (1989) 232-5 (W. de *Vries*).

87 HOLM-NIELSEN Svend, 70th b.: Skriv synet tydeligt på tavler [Hab 2,2]; om problemerne ved en ny bibeloversettelse. K 1989, Gad. 168 p. 87-12-01895-3. 16 art. in Danish on Bible-translation in Danish [BL 90,18].

88 HOMMEL Hildebrecht: Charisteria, 85. Gb., ᴱKiefner Gottfried: Spudasmata 40. Hildesheim 1988, Olms. viii-309 p.; 10 pl. [AnPg 59, p. 972].

89 HOURS Francis: hommage à ~, ᴱCauvin Jacques, *al.* Lyon 1989, Maison de l'Orient. 47 p. [OIAc N89].

90 HÜBENER Wolfgang: Fs. für ~, ᴱLüdtke Hartwig, *al.* Neumünster 1989, Wachholtz. 348 p.; 216 fig. bibliog. 11-15 (H. *Heine*, A. *Hübener*). 3-529-01357-9. – ᴿArchAustriaca 73 (1989) 223s (E. *Lauermann*).

91 HÜBNER Kurt: Zur Kritik der wissenschaftlichen Rationalität; 65. Gb., ᴱLenk Hans. FrB 1986, Alber. 579 p. [AnPg 59, p. 972].

92 HÜNERMANN Peter: Christologie und Metaphysikkritik, 60. Gb., ᴱHattrup Dieter, *Hoping* Helmut. Münster 1989, Aschendorff. vi-162 p.; Bibliog. p. 141-157 (*Eckholt* Margit). DM 48. 5 art., 1 infra [TPhil 65,308, J. *Splett*].

93 HUMBACH Helmut; Studia grammatica iranica, ᴱSchmitt Rüdiger, *Skjærvø* Prods O.: MüStSprW Beih 13. Mü 1986, Kitzinger. xxxii-524. –

ᴿJAOS 109 (1989) 443s (R. N. *Frye*: interesting details without 'Auseinandersetzung' or tit. pp.).

94 HUSSEY Joan: Kathegetria, 80th b. Camberley 1988, Porphyrogenitus. 576 p. [RelStR 16,348]. – ᴿMuséon 102 (1989) 388s (J. *Mossay*: 'Kathigitria').

95 IERSEL Bas van: Intertextuality in biblical writings, ᴱ**Draisma** Sipke. Kampen 1989, Kok. 207 p.; portr.; bibliog. p. 205-7. ƒ40. 90-242-5050-1. 15 art., infra. – ᴿStreven 57 (1989) 1047s (P. *Beentjes*).

96 IGLESIAS Juan: Estudios en homenaje al Prof. ~. M 1988, Semin. U. Alvarez. xxiv-1688 p. (3 vol.) [AnPg 59, p. 972].

97 IRIARTE DE ASPURZ [ITURRI] Lázaro: Homenaje, ᴱ*Elizondo* Jacinto = Estudios Franciscanos 89,391s (1988) 492 p., portr.; bibliog. 9-44 (Casimiro *Pérez Aguirre*). – ᴿColcFran 59 (1989) 450s (C. *Cargnoni*).

98 IRMSCHER Johannes: Antikerezeption, Antikeverhältnis, Antikebegegnung in Vergangenheit und Gegenwart, ᴱ**Dummer** Jürgen, *Kunze* Max: Winckelmann-Ges. 6 (1983). Stendal 1988. 620 p. (3 vol.) [AnPg 59, p. 972].

99 JAGER Okke: Tegendraads; opstellen aangeboden aan ~† ᴱ**Buck** Pieterjan de. Baarn 1988, Ten Have. 247 p.; Bibliog. p. 226-233. ƒ30 [TR 85,521].

100 JAKOBOVITS Immanuel: Tradition and transition; essays presented to Chief Rabbi Sir ~, ᴱ**Sacks** Jonathan. L 1986, Jews College. [OTAbs 11,214].

101 JANÁCEK Karel: Zprávy Jednóty klasických filologii 28s (1986s). Praha 1989. 157 p. [AnPg 59, p. 972].

102 JANSSENS Louis: Personalist morals, essays in honor of ~, ᴱ**Selling** Joseph A.: BiblETL 83. Lv 1988, Univ./Peeters. viii-344 p. portr.; bibliog. p. 329-334. Fb 1200. 90-6186-286-8 / 90-6831-136-0. 18 art.; 4 infra. – ᴿETL 65 (1989) 145-9 (J. *Étienne* mentionne l'Écriture à propos de BURGGRAEVE R.); TsTNijm 29 (1989) 424 (H. M. *Kuitert*).

103 JOHNSON S. Lewis: Continuity and discontinuity; perspectives on the relationship between the Old and New Testaments, ᴱ**Feinberg** John S. Westchester IL 1988, Crossway. 410 p. 13 art. [JBL 108,184].

104 KAISER Matthäus: Recht als Heilsdienst, 65. Gb., ᴱ**Schulz** Winfried. Pd 1989, Bonifatius. 299 p., Bibliog. *Heinrichsmeier* Clemens. DM 38 [TR 86,85; TPQ 138,395, J. *Hirnsperger*].

105 KAISER Otto: Prophet und Prophetenbuch, 65. Gb., ᴱ**Fritz** Volkmar, *al.*: BZAW 185. B 1989, de Gruyter. viii-284 p. 3-11-011339-2 [TR 86,161, tit. pp.], 19 art., infra.

106 KANTOR Helene J.: Essays in Ancient Civilization, ᴱ**Leonard** Albert, *Williams* Bruce B.: SAOC 47. Ch 1989, Univ. Oriental Institute. xxxix-387 p.; 52 fig.; 72 pl.; bibliog. xxxi-xxxix. 0-918986-57-5. 25 art.; 22 infra.

107 KAPPEN Sebastian: Religion, ideology and counter-culture, ᴱ**Mathew** Philip, *Muricken* Ajit. Bangalore 1987, Horizon. 228 p. rs 75. – ᴿVidyajyoti 52 (1988) 354s (J. F. *Raj*).

108 KAUFMANN Hans Bernard: Glaube im Dialog; 30 Jahre religionspädagogische Reform, 60. Gb., ᴱ**Gossmann** Klaus; Vorw. *Nipkow* K. E. Gü 1987, Mohn. 308 p. – ᴿTZBas 45 (1989) 385s (W. *Neidhart*).

109 KOENIGSBERGER H. G.: Politics and culture in early modern Europe, ᴱ**Mack** Phyllis, *Jacob* Margaret C. C 1987, Univ. 219 p. $49.50. – ᴿEngHR 104 (1989) 689s (E. *Cameron*); RelStR 15 (1989) 270 (R. M. *Golden*).

110 KOHLER Werner (1920-1984): Gedenkschrift, Mitten im Tod — von Leben umfangen, ᴱHesse Jochanan: Studien zur interkulturellen Geschichte des Christentums 48. Fra 1988, Lang. 276 p. – ᴿTContext 6,2 (1989) 108 (G. *Evers*).

111 KOLB Herbert: 65. Gb., ᴱMatzel Klaus, *al.* Fra 1989, Lang. xiv-804 p. 43 art. – ᴿBeiNam 24 (1989) 392-6 (G. *Lohse*).

113 KRAAY Colin M. 1918-1982, MORKHOLM Otto 1930-1983: Numismatic studies in memory of ~, ᴱLe Rider Georges, *al.*: Numismatica Lovaniensia 10. LvN 1989, Univ. xxiii-321 p.; LXXII pl.; biog. IXs (Margaret *Thompson*); bibliog. Kraay XI-XIV; portr. (G. K. *Jenkins*) Morkholm XV-XIX, portr. (J. S. *Jensen*). 30 art.; 3 infra.
KRIARAS (M.) E., 80th b. ➔ 687.

114 LATOURELLE René: Gesù rivelatore, teologia fondamentale; 70° genetliaco, ᴱFisichella Rino. CasM 1988, Piemme. 267 p. Lit. 35.000. 88-384-1315-7. – ᴿActuBbg 26 (1989) 207 (J. *Boada*); Lateranum 55 (1989) 476-8 (N. *Ciola*); Gregorianum 70 (1989) 402s (*Fisichella*).

115 LECHNER Odilo: Welte des Herzens, Welte des Lebens; Beiträge zum Christsein in moderner Gesellschaft, Mü Abtei S. Bonifaz. Rg 1989, Pustet. 674 p.; 591 p. DM 68 [TR 85,337].

116 LEEUWEN C. van: Door het oog van de profeten; exegetische studies ~, ᴱBecking B., *al.*: Utrechtse Theol. 8. Utrecht/Franeker 1989, Univ./ Wever. 171 p. portr.; bibliog. 169-171. ƒ29,20. 90-72235-08-8 [BL 90,9: topics; ZAW 102,298s, tit. pp.]. 13 art., infra.

117 LENZENWEGER Josef: Ecclesia peregrinans (Titel nur zufällig = *Kötting* B. Aufsätze 1988). 1986 ➔ 2,60. – ᴿTLZ 114 (1989) 175s (G. *Haendler*).

118 LÉVÊQUE P. Melanges 1. Religion: ᴱMactoux M., *Geny* E.: Univ. Besançon ann. litt. 367, hist. anc. 79. P 1988, BLettres. lxiii-330 p.; ill. 2-251-60367-0 [JRS 79,274]. – ᴿLatomus 48 (1989) 950 (J. *Debergh*).

119 LIENHARDT Godfrey: Vernacular Christianity; essays in the social anthropology of religion, ᴱJames Wendy, *Johnson* Douglas H. NY 1988, Barber. xiv-196 p.; 17 phot. $44. 0-936508-23-X. 14 art. [TDig 37,93]. – ᴿJScStR 29 (1989) 136 (K. *Perry*).

120 LOHSE Eduard, Wissenschaft und Kirche, 65. Gb., ᴱAland K., *Meurer* S.: Texte und Arbeiten zur Bibel 4. Bielefeld 1989, Luther. 404 p.; portr. [TR 86,162, tit. pp.]. 23 art.; 22 infra. – ᴿTLZ 114 (1989) 874s (G. *Heintze*).

121 London Institute of Archaeology Golden Jubilee volume, ᴱClayton Peter A. = Bulletin 24 (1987) 240 p.; ill. £20. 0076-0722. – ᴿAntiqJ 68 (1988) 329-332 (G. *Clark*).

122 LOON Maurits N. van, To the Euphrates and beyond, ᴱHaex Odette M. C., *al.* Rotterdam 1989, Baikema. 304 p.; bibliog. p. 301-4. 90-6191-866-9 [OIAc S89; DLZ 111,508, B. *Brentjes*]. 20 art., 10 infra.

123 Lux Mundi centenary [1889 book by 11 Oxford dons, ᴱGore Charles], *a)* Keeping the faith, ᴱWainwright Geoffrey. Ph 1988, Fortress/Pickwick (L, SPCK). xxv-399 p. $35. 0-8006-0876-3 [TDig 36,376; RelStR 16,241, P. C. *Hodgson*; EvT 50,83-87, G. *Sauter*; TS 51,347, H. J. *Ryan*]. – ᴿExpTim 100 (1988s) 477 (B. M. G. *Reardon*); – *b)* ᴱMorgan Robert, The religion of the Incarnation. Bristol 1989, Classical. xx-217 p. £20; pa. £8 [TLond 93,227; JTS 41,310-5, H. *Willmer*: both excellent].

124 [MACHEN J. Gresham, founder] Pressing toward the mark; essays commemorating fifty years of the Orthodox Presbyterian Church, ᴱDennison Charles G., *Gamble* Richard C. Ph 1986, Committee. 489 p. $20. –

ᴿCalvinT 24 (1989) 140-2 (J. A. *DeJong*: mostly on Machen; includes R. *Gaffin* on Sabbath-idea in Heb; G. *Knight* limiting Church offices to two).
ᶠMACKINNON Donald: Christ, ethics and tragedy 1989 ➤ 701.

125 MCNICOLL Anthony W.: = Mediterranean Archaeology 1 (Sydney 1988).

126 MACUCH Rudolf, *Ḥokmôt bānᵉtâ beytâ*; studia semitica necnon iranica, 70 Gb., ᴱ**Macuch** Maria, *al.* Wsb 1989, Harrassowitz. xliv-418 p.; portr.; Biobibliog. ix-xxiii (*Powels* Sylvia, *Pohl* Heinz); xxv-xxxii. 3-447-02936-6. 31 art.; 18 infra [BL 91,19, tit. pp.].

MAGNINO Domenico ~ 155, QUARTIROLI.

127 MALLOCH A. E.: Literature and ethics, ᴱ**Wild** Gary, *Williams* David. Montreal 1988, McGill-Queen's Univ. xvi-152 p. 9 art. – ᴿSR 18 (1989) 388 (C. *Ridd*).

128 MARC'HADOUR Germain: Miscellanea Moreana, ᴱ**Murphy** Clare M., *al.*: MedRenTSt 61. Binghamton 1989, SUNY. xxxiii-569 p.; 18 fig. [RHE 85,131*].

129 MARÓTI Egon, ⓂStudia in honorem Aegonis Maróti sexagenarii. Szeged 1987, Acta Univ. Antiqua supp 6. 129 p.; bibliog. p. 5-14 (*M. Korchmáros* Valéria). 16 art.; 2 infra. 0567-7246.

130 MARTYN J. Louis: Apocalyptic and the New Testament, ᴱ**Marcus** Joel, *Soards* Marion L.: JStNT supp 24. Sheffield 1989, Academic. 351 p. £25. 1-85075-175-7. 16 art.; 14 infra [JBL 109,748, tit. pp.]. – ᴿExpTim 101 (1989s) 122s (D. S. *Russell*).

131 MARXSEN Willi: Jesu Rede von Gott und ihre Nachgeschichte im frühen Christentum; Beiträge zur Verkündigung Jesu und zum Kerygma der Kirche, 70. Gb., ᴱ**Koch** Dietrich-A., *al.* Gü 1989, Mohn. 679 p.; Bibliog. 459-472. DM 96. 29 art. [TR 86,74, tit. pp.; infra].

132 MAYER Cornelius P., O.S.A.: Signum pietatis, ᴱ**Zumkeller** A. Wü 1989, Augustinus. lxiv-670 p. DM 248 [MüTZ 40,378; TR 85,252, tit. pp.; auch TLZ 115,574]. 38 art.; 3 infra. – ᴿTüTQ 169 (1989) 314-6 (H. J. *Vogt*).

133 MEAD Sidney E., The lively experiment continued, ᴱ**Brauer** Jerald C. Macon GA 1987, Mercer Univ. xix-250 p. $19. 10 art., one by M. *Marty*. – ᴿJRel 69 (1989) 557s (P. *Williams*); RelStR 15 (1989) 87 (P. N. *Moore*).

134 MERHART Gero von: Gedenkschrift zum 100. Gb., ᴱ**Frey** Otto-Herman, *al.*: Marburger Studien zur Vor- und Frühgeschichte 7. Marburg 1986, Hitzeroth. 235 p.; portr. + 16 pl.; Biog. 1-16 (*Kossack* Georg) 3-925944-06-0. 12 art.; 2 infra. – ᴿAcPraeh 21 (1989) 140s (B. *Hänsel*).

135 METCZAK Sebastian, The wisdom of faith; essays in honor of Dr. ~, ᴱ**Thompson** Henry O. Lanham MD 1989, UPA. 191 p. [JAAR 57,890].

136 MEYER Harding: Einheit der Kirche; neue Entwicklungen und Perspektiven, 60. Gb., ᴱ**Gassmann** Günther, *Nørgaard-Hojen* Peter. Fra 1988. Lambeck. 180 p.; Bibliog. 166-177. DM 48 [TR 85,83 tit. pp.]. 12 art.; ➤ 7967*. – ᴿIrénikon 62 (1989) 132-5 (E. *Lanne*); ÖkRu 38 (1989) 111s (E. *Geldbach*).

MORKHOLM Otto mem. 1988 ➤ 113.

MORTON W. H., 'dedicated to …': Studies in the Mesha inscription and Moab 1989 ➤ 392.

137 MROWIEC Karol: ❷ Musicae sacrae ars et scientia, 70. b., ᴱ**Dąbek** Stanisław, *Pawlak* Ireneusz = RoczTK 34,7 (1987). 458 p.; portr. zł. 950; biobibliog. 5-17; 36 art.; 2 infra.

138 MÜLLER Wolfgang: ArchPapF 33 (1987). – ᴿCdÉ 64 (1989) 362s (A. *Martin*).

139 MULDER Martin J. [retirement; and Oudtestamentisch Werkgezelschap 50th year], New Avenues in the Study of the OT, EWoude A. S. van der [English of the Dutch lectures Oct. 1989]: OTS 25. Leiden 1989, Brill. ix-166 p. ƒ110. 90-04-09125-4 [BL 90,28, topics; TR 86,73, tit. pp.]. 16 art., infra.

140 MUNARI Francis: Kontinuität und Wandel, Lateinische Poesie von Naevius bis Baudelaire. 65. Gb. EStache Ulrich J., al. Hildesheim 1986, Weidmann. xv-714 p. DM 128. 3-615-00012-9.

141 NOCENT Adrien: Traditio et progressio; studi liturgici, EFarnedi Giustino: StudAnselm 95 / AnalLtg 12. R 1988, Abbazia S. Paolo. 692 p.; [bio-] bibliog. p. 12-23. [25-34, Scicolone Ildebrando]. Lit. 60.000. 30 art.; 3 infra [TR 85,175, tit. pp.]. – ᴿRSPT 73 (1989) 112s (P.-M. Gy: tit. pp.).

142 OEHLER Klaus: Gedankenzeichen 60 Gb., EClaussen Regina, Daube-Schachat Roland. Tü 1988, Stauffenburg. xiv-364 p. [AnPg 59, p. 974].

143 OGDEN Schubert M.: Witness and existence; essays in honor of ~, EDevenish Philip E., Goodwin George L. Ch 1989, Univ. 252 p. bibliog. p. 229s. $20 [JAAR 57,692; ZIT 90,372 tit. pp.]. 10 art., 4 infra.

144 OLSEN Olaf: Festskrift til ~, 60-år. K 1988, Oldskriftselskab. xxviii-334 p.; ill. Dk 250. 87-87-48309-2. 29 art. [AntiqJ 68,381].

145 OLSSON Karl A.: Amicus Dei, essays on faith and friendship, 75th b., EAnderson Philip J. = Covenant Quarterly 46,2s (Ch 1988). xv-293 p.; 215-293 bibliog. $14 [TR 85,425].

146 OPELT Ilona: Roma renascens; Beiträge zur Spätantike und Rezeptionsgeschichte, EWissemann Michael. Fra 1988, Lang. 450 p. [AnPg 59,973].

147 OTTOSSON Magnus: SvEx 54 (1989), frontispiece with Hebrew dedication (60th b.).

148 OTZEN Benedikt: 60. Gb. = Dansk Teologisk Tidskrift 52,4 (1989) [ZAW 102,274].

149 PALAZZINI Pietro, card.; Studi in onore, ELeoni F.: BiblStRel 5. Pisa 1987, Giardini. 239 p. [ETL 65,12*].

150 PEKÁRY Thomas: Migratio et commutatio; Studien zur Alten Geschichte und deren Nachleben, 60. Gb., EDrexhage Hans-Joachim, Sünskes Julia. St. Katharinen 1989, Mercatura. xix-377 p.; 12 fig.; Bibliog. p. XIV-XIX. 3-92261-71-8. 28 art., 10 infra.

151 PETERS George W.: Bilanz und Plan; Mission an der Schwelle zum dritten Jahrtausend, 80. Gb., EKasdorf Hans, Müller Klaus W. Bad Liebenzell 1988, Liebenzeller Mission. 504 p.; ill.; Bibliog. p. 43-50. DM 34,80 [TR 85,433].

152 PIEL Joseph M.: Homenagem, 85° aniv., EKremer Dieter. Inst. Portug.-Galega. Tü 1988, Niemeyer. xiv-798 p. [AnPg 59, p. 973].

153 POLOMÉ Edgar C.: Languages and cultures, EJazayery Mohammad Ali, Winter Werner: Trends in Linguistics StMg 36. B 1988, Mouton de Gruyter. xvi-791 p.; portr.; biobibliog. p. 1-20. 3-11-010204-8. 64 art., 6 infra.

ᶠPOŁOTSKY H. J. [I-II 1985-6/6-7 → 4,711.712] III 1988 → 9475*.

154 PUGLIESE CARRATELLI Giovanni: Eōthen; Studi di storia e di filologia anatolica ~, EImparati Fiorella. Firenze 1988, ELITE. 310 p.; portr. 29 art.; 10 infra.

155 QUARTIROLI Anna M., MAGNINO Domenico, Storia e filologia classica ... Como 1987, New Press. xii-356 p. [AnPg 59, p. 973].

156 QUASTEN Johannes: 'to the memory of' (co-founder): Traditio 44 (1988). 571 p.

157 RATZINGER Joseph, Kard.: Weisheit Gottes – Weisheit der Welt, ᴱBaier W. al. 1987 ⇥ 3,135: ᴿDivThom 91 (1988) 156-169 (L. J. Elders).

158 READ Allen W.: Festschrift, ᴱSeits Laurence C.: Publ. 2. Dekalb IL 1988, North Central Name Soc. XXIV-151 p. 11 art. – ᴿBeiNam 24 (1989) 476-9 (K. Schneider).

159 RÉMY Paul mem.: Studia occitanica 2, The narrative philology, ᴱKeller H.-E., al. Kalamazoo 1986, Medieval Institute. 441 p.; maps. – ᴿSpeculum 64 (1989) 725-7 (W. D. Paden).

159* RIBUOLI Riccardo: Commemoratio, studi di filologia in ricordo di ∼, ᴱPrete Sesto. Sassoferrato 1986, Ist. Studi Piceni. 133 p. [SicGym 43,345, F. Corsaro].

160 RICHARD Marcel: Texte und Textkritik, eine Aufsatzsammlung ⇥ 3,489, ᴱDümmer Jürgen, al.: TU 133 (also 124, 1987 and 133, 1981). B 1987, Akademie. 638 p. DM 150. – ᴿJTS 40 (1989) 229s (H. Chadwick).

160* ROBINSON James M., The Jesus of Q = Forum 5,2 (1989) 192 p.; tributes 4-6.

161 RODILLA ZANÓN Antonio: Santidad y cultura, homenaje a ∼. Valencia 1986.

Römisches Institut der Görres-Gesellschaft und RömQ 100-Jahr ⇥ 732, symposia.

162 RONCONI Alessandro: Munus amicitiae [I. 1986 ⇥ 3,140]; II. QuadFgLat 4/2. F 1988, Le Monnier. 147 p. [AnPg 57, p. 760; 59, p. 974].

163 RONIG Franz J.: Ars et ecclesia, 60. Gb., ᴱStork Hans-Walter, al.: Bistumsarchiv Trier 26. Trier 1989, Paulinus. 467 p.; Bibliog. p. 401-7. DM 98 [TR 86,73].

164 RUBINACCI Roberto: Studi arabo-islamici, 70° compleanno (1985), ᴱSarnelli Cerqua Clelia. N 1988, Ist. Univ. Orientale. I. 428 p.; II. p. 429-807; bibliog. p. ix-xiii. 52 art.; 2 infra. – ᴿBAsEspOr 24 (1988) 497s (M. Arribas); Islamochristiana 15 (1989) 320 (tit. pp.).

165 RYAN Dermot, abp., mem.: Back to the sources; biblical and Near Eastern studies in honour of ∼, ᴱCathcart Kevin J., Healey John F. Dublin 1989, Glendale. 191 p. £19.50. 0-907606-61-X [BL 90,12: some titles]. 8 art.; 7 infra.

166 SACHS Abraham: A scientific humanist, studies in memory of ∼ [1915-1983], ᴱLeichty Erle, al.: Kramer Fund, Occas. Publ. 9. Ph 1988, Univ. Museum. xvii-378 p.; portr.; bibliog. p. 375s (Pingree David). 0-934718-90-3 [BO 47,371-5, M. Stol]. 27 art.; 19 infra.

167 SANFILIPPO Cesare: Studi in onore [6, 1985] 7: Univ. Catania, Fac. Giurisprudenza 96. Mi 1987, Giuffrè. 812 p. 88-14-01057-9. 27 art.

168 St. Augustin [Bonn] Missionspriesterseminar, 75.-J.: Theologie im Dienste der Weltkirche, ᴱPrawdzik Werner: Wort und Werk 38. Nettetal 1988, Steyler. 321 p. DM 40. [TR 85 (1989) 256s, tit. pp.]. – ᴿVerbumSVD 30 (1989) 97-102 (J. Kuhl); ZkT 111 (1989) 377s (J. Wicki, 12 Art.).

169 SCHARBERT Josef: Die Väter Israels; Beiträge zur Theologie der Patriarchenüberlieferungen im AT, 70. Gb., ᴱGörg Manfred (Müller Augustin R.). Stu 1989, KBW. 461 p.; Bibliog. 431-461 (W. Berg). 3-460-32841-X [TR 86,81, tit. pp]. 24 art., infra.

170 SCHENKEVELD D. M.: Ophelos, zes studies voor ∼, ᴱSlings S. R., Slutter I. Amst 1988, V. U. 100 p. [AnPg 59, p. 974].

171 SCHMALE Franz-Josef: Ecclesia et Regnum; Beiträge zur Geschichte von Kirche, Recht und Staat im Mittelalter, 65. Gb., ᴱBerg D., Goetz H.-W. Bochum 1989, Winkler. xxii-365 p.; ill. DM 85 [RHE 84,230*; TR 85,525 (with different title!) tit. pp.].

172 SCHMIDT Martin A.: Fs 70. Gb. = Theologische Zeitschrift 45,2s (Basel 1989) 101-273; portr.; Bibliog. p. 267-273 [ZIT 89,694]. 13 Art. mittelalterlichen Denkens.

173 SCHNACKENBURG Rudolf, 75. Gb.: Neues Testament und Ethik, EMerklein Helmut. FrB 1989, Herder. 597 p.; portr.; Bibliog. 589-597. 3-451-21008-8. 29 art., infra. – RBogSmot 59 (1989) 491-6 (M. Zovkić) & 496s (M. Valković).

174 SCHNEEMELCHER Wilhelm: Oecumenica et patristica, 75. Gb., EPapandreou Damaskinos, al. Stu 1989, Kohlhammer. 405 p.; portr.; Bibliog. 397-405. 3-17-010792-5 [EcuR 42,355, H. W. Tajra; TR 86,164, tit. pp.]. 22 art.; 14 infra.

175 SCHODER Raymond V. † 1987: Daidalikon, studies in memory of ~, S.J., ESutton Robert F. Wauconda IL 1989, Bolchazy-Carducci. xii-424 p.; portr.; ill.; bibliog. p. 1-7; appreciation 9-11 (Wild Robert A.). 0-86516-200-X; pa. 1-8. 31 art., 8 infra (some of the papers are from a symposium in his presence Apr. 11-12, 1986).

SCHOLLIERS E., Huldeboek 1988 → 44.

176 SCHWARTZ Ben memorial: A linguistic happening [not apparently a meeting]; studies in Anatolian, Italic and other Indo-European languages, EArbeitman Yoel L.: Cah. Inst. Linguistique Lv 42. LvN 1988, Peeters. 598 p. [AnPg 59, p. 974].

177 SCHWARZ Reinhard: Von Wittenberg nach Memphis; 60. Gb., EHomolka Walter, Ziegelmeier Otto. Gö 1989, Vandenhoeck & R. 271 p.; Bibliog. 256-9 (Zschoch Helmut). 3-525-58150-3. 14 art.; 10 infra.

178 SERBAT F. Guy: Etudes de linguistique générale et de linguistique latine, EGrimal Pierre. P 1987, Soc. Inform. Gramm. 431 p. [AnPg 58, p. 815].

178* SEUMOIS André: Chiesa locale e inculturazione nella missione: Studia Urbaniana 30. Bo 1987, Ed. Missionaria. 390 p. – RLateranum 55 (1989) 511 (O. Pasquato: autori-temi).

179 SEVERUS Emmanuel von: Itinera Domini [I, 1984; II:] 80. Gb. Gesammelte Aufsätze [von Anderen!]: Beit. G. Mönchtums 5. Münster 1988, Aschendorff. 370 p. – RTüTQ 169 (1989) 248s (R. Reinhardt).

180 SHARWOOD-SMITH John: Greek religion and society, EEasterling P. E., Muir J. V., 1985 → 1,425 ... 3,b120 (notF): RHeythJ 30 (1989) 100 (J. Ferguson: a deserved symposium in honour of Sharwood-Smith).

181 SHINNIE Peter L.: Nubian studies in Canada, 75th b.: JSSEg [= SSEA] 17,1s (1987). 66 p.; XI pl. 6 art.; infra.

182 SIEVERS Angelika, Pilgrimage in world religions; 75th b., EBhardwaj S. M., Rinschede G.: Geographia religionum 4. B 1988, Reimer. 200 p.; 2 foldouts. DM 38. 7 art. – RRelStR 15 (1989) 339 (G. Yocum).

183 SJÖBERG Ake W.: DUMU-E₂-DUB-BA-E, 65th b., EBehrens Hermann, al.: Kramer Fund Occas. Publ. 11. Ph 1989, Univ. Museum. xxiii-599 p.; portr.; ill.; bibliog. p. 593-5 (Heimerdinger Jane). 0-934718-98-9. 57 art.; 39 infra.

SKUTSCH Otto, 'vir bonus discendi peritus' 1988 → 806.

184 SLADEK Paulus: Begegnung und Entfremdung im Spannungsfeld von Volk und Glaube, Fs. für P. ~ O.S.A. Mü 1988, Institutum Bohemicum Ackermann-Gemeinde. P. 65-78, Scharbert J., Volk, Heimat und Vertreibung in der Bibel [< ZAW 101 (1989) 453].

185 SMITH Ralph L.: SWJT 32,3 (1989s); 7-16 bibliog. (H. B. Hunt); phot. p. 5.

186 STEINBAUER Karl: Gott mehr gehorchen, 80. Gb., EMildenberger F., Seitz M., Mü 1986, Claudius. 141 p. – RScotJT 42 (1989) 557-9 (A. Heron,

also or really only on Steinbauer's 4 vol. Einander das Zeugnis gönnen 1983-7).

187 STIENNON Jacques: Clio et son regard; mélanges d'histoire, d'histoire de l'art et d'archéologie (25 ans enseignement), ELejeune R., *Deckers* J. Liège 1982, Mardaga. 692 p. [AnPg 57, p. 760].

188 STOGIANNOS Vasilios: Diakonia, aphierōma stē mnēmē. Thessaloniki 1988, Univ.

189 STROHM Johannes, 80. Gb.: WienerSt 101 (1988). 353 p.

190 TAILLARDAT Jean; *Hēdiston logódeipnon*, Logopédies; mélanges de philosophie et de linguistique grecques: SELAF 276. P 1988. Peeters. xiv-262 p. [AnPg 59, 974]. 2-87723-003-1. 22 art.; 2 infra.

191 TAYLOR H. M.: The Anglo Saxon Churches; papers on history, architecture, and archaeology, EButler A. S. *Morris* R. K.; Research Report 60. L 1986, Humanities (for Council for British Archaeology). xi-226 p. $45. – RChH 57 (1988) 81 (M. *Gatch*).

192 THILL Andrée: De Virgile a Jacob Balde, hommage à Mᵐᵉ ~, EFreyburger Gérard: Mulhouse Fac. Lettres, Bull. 15. P 1987, BLettres. 300 p. [Latomus 49,254-6, R. *Chevallier*]. – RRÉLat 66 (1988) 400-2 (J. *Chomarat*).

193 THOM Alexander: Records in stone; papers in memory of ~, ERuggles Clive. C 1988, Univ. xviii-518 p.; 139 fig. £50. 0-521-33381-4. – RAntiquity 63 (1989) 183s (Julian *Thomas*: astroarchaeology i.e. archaeoastronomy).

194 THOMPSON Edward A.: Nottingham Medieval Studies 32 special (1988). 227 p. [AnPg 59, p. 974].

195 TOYNBEE Jocelyn M. C.: Image and mystery in the Roman world; three papers given in memory of ~, Zanker P., *al.* Gloucester 1988, Sutton. viii-80 p.; 25 pl. 0-9514135-0-3 [JRS 79,279].

196 TRENDALL A. D.: 80th b., = Mediterranean Archaeology 2 [Sydney; due to appear July 1989 (AJA 93, after p. 494)]. 205 p.

197 TRILLING Wolfgang: Christus bezeugen, 65. Gb., EKertelge Karl, *al.*: Erfurter Theol. Studien 19. Lp 1989, St. Benno. 317 p.; Bibliog. 299-317. 3-7462-0440-2. 24 art., infra.

197* TRIZNA Jazeps: RArtLv 20 (1987). vii-350 p.; phot.

198 TROLLER Alois: Formalismus und Phänomenologie im Rechtsdenken der Gegenwart, 80. Gb., EKrawietz Werner, *Ott* Walter. B 1987, Dunckler & H. xii-574 p. – RTPhil 64 (1989) 152-4 (N. *Brieskorn*, etwas über F. TÖNNIES und M. WEBER).

199 TUILIER André: Mélanges de la Bibliothèque de la Sorbonne 8; préf. *Ahrweiler* Hélène. P 1988, Aux Amateurs des livres. 317 p.; ill. [AnPg 59, p. 974].

200 ULLENDORFF Edward, 70th b. = JSS 34,2 (1989) 147-512; biobibliog. 253-289 (S. *Hopkins*).

201 VANNESTE Alfred, mgr.: Théologie et cultures, EDimandja Eluy'a Kondo, *Mbonyinkebe Sebahire*. LvN 1988, NORAF [ETL 65, p. 10*]. 442 p. – RTContext 6,2 (1989) 107 (B. *Abeng*: for the founder of Africa's first theological faculty, Kinshasa 1957).

202 VERNANT Jean-Pierre, Poíkilia: Recherches d'histoire et de sciences sociales 26, 1987 ► 4, 146*; 2-7132-0891-2; F 350; 24 art.: RÉchMClas 33 (1989) 99-104 (N. *Robertson*).

203 VERVLIET H. D. L.: Liber amicorum ~, Het oude en het nieuwe boek; de oude en de nieuwe bibliotheek, EBorm J. Van, *Simons* L. Kapellen, Belgium 1988, Pelckmans. 664 p.; 30 fig. [RHE 84,271*].

203* VILNAY Zev: ❹ Selection of [? his own] articles on Yᵉdi̇̄at ha-Areṣ, ᴱSchiller Ely. J 1987, Ariel. 182 p. [KirSef 62 (1988s) p. 185].
WAGNER Heinz, Leben im Diakonat 1987 → 764.
204 WALLE Baudouin van de [21.X.1909-26.XII.1988], mém.: Chronique d'Égypte 64, 127s (1989). 374 p.; portr.; p. 5-15 biog. (A. Mekhitarian), 16-23 bibliog. (M. Maline).
205 WALSER Gerold: Labor omnibus unus, zum 70. Gb., ᴱHerzig Heinz E., Frei-Stolba Regula: Historia Einz. 60. Stu 1989 [→ 4, 147*, 1988], Steiner, xvi-287 p.; bibliog. p. xii-xvi. 3-515-04393-4 [ClasAnt 59,65, J. Wankenne; ClasR 40,409, M. Roxan; RÉLat 68,239, D. Briquel]. 21 art., 4 infra. – ᴿMünstHand 8,2 (1989) 96-106 (J. Engels).
206 WEBSTER T. B. L.: Studies in honour of ~ [I 1986 → 3,167]; II, ᴱBetts J. H., al. Bristol 1988, Classical. xii-159 p.; 132 pl. – ᴿClasR 39 (1989) 424s (J. Boardman).
207 WEIGAND Rudolf: Ius et historia, 60. Gb., ᴱHöhl Norbert: Forschungen zur Kirchenrechtswissenschaft 6. Wü 1989, Echter. 476 p.; ill. [RHE 85, 95-98, G. Fransen]. 13 art., 1 infra.
208 WEILER Cyrus: Gevuroth haromah, Jewish Studies, rabbi ~, 80th b., ᴱFalk Zev. J 1987, Mesharim. 24 art. ❹ + Eng. [Dor 18,120].
208* WEIMA Jan: Religieuze Ervaring, een veelvormig perspectief op de zin an bestaan [Afscheid ...], ᴱBouritius G., al.: TFT-studies 9. Tilburg 1988, Univ. ix-120 p. f25. 90-361-9971-9. – ᴿTsTNijm 29 (1989) 88 (D. Hutsebaut).
209 WERNER Robert: Fs. 65. Gb., ᴱDahlheim Werner, al.: Xenia 22. Konstanz 1989, Univ. 321 p.; 6 pl. DM 120. 3-87940-356-2 [ClasR 40,526, B. Levick; JRS 79,280]. 16 art., 6 infra.
210 WESSEL Klaus: (70 Gb., teils; teils:) In memoriam, ᴱRestle Marcell. Mü 1988, Maris. 384 p.; p. 385-453 phot.; bibliog. p. 7-19 (Daisy Wessel) 3-925801-02-2. 30 art., 6 infra.
211 WESTERINK Leendert G., Gonimos; Neoplatonic and Byzantine studies, 75th b., ᴱDuffy John, Peradotto John. Buffalo 1988, Arethusa. xiv-370 p.; 1 phot. $25. – ᴿRÉByz 47 (1989) 295 (Marie-Hélène Congourdeau: Byzantine titles only).
212 WESTERMANN Claus: Schöpfung und Befreiung, 80. Gb., ᴱAlbertz R., al. Stu 1989, Calwer. 284 p. DM 48. 3-7668-3034-1. 19 art.; 17 infra [BL 90,7; TR 86,73, tit. pp.].
213 WILLIAMS R. D.: ᴱHunley Herbert H., = Proceedings of the Virgil Society 19 (London Univ. College 1988). 77 p. [AnPg 59, p. 975].
214 WINTER Johanna Maria von, Convivium. Hilversum 1988, Verloren. 223 p.; Bibliog. 201-216. f30 [TR 85,73].
215 WIRTH G., Zu Alexander dem Grossen, Fs. ~, 60. Gb. (1986), ᴱWill W. (Heinrichs J.). Amst 1988, Hakkert. [2 or more vol.: BTAM 14 p. 573] / II. p. 657-1322; 10 pl. 90-256-0933-3. 5 art. infra.
216 WOHLFEIL Rainer: Reformation und Revolution: Beiträge zum politischen Wandel und den sozialen Kräften am Beginn der Neuzeit, ᴱPostel Rainer, Kopitzsch Franklin. Stu 1989, Steiner-Wsb. 329 p.; bibliog. p. 23-32 [TR 85,167: tit. pp.].
217 WOLFSGRUBER K., Kunst und Kirche in Tirol, ᴱNössing Josef, Stampfer Helmut. Bozen 1987, Athesia. 460 p.; 168 fig. + 18 color. Bibliog. p. 449-56 (H. Griessmair). Sch 360. – ᴿZkT 111 (1989) 120s (H. B. Mayer, tit. pp.: 28 Art.; p. 413-430, Gschnitzer H., Das AT auf Zillertaler Möbeln).
218 YADIN Yigael: [21.III.1917-28.VI.1984 → 568] Memorial volume, ᴱBen-Tor A., al., = Eretz Israel 20. J 1989, Exploration Soc./Hebr. Univ./

HUC, 371 p. ❺ + 208* Eng.; ill.; i-xvi ❺ phot., bibliog.; x-xxiv Eng. appreciations. 46 art. ❺ (Eng. summaries) + 19 Eng., 5 franç.; infra.
219 ZAWADZKI Tadeusz: Historia testis; mélanges d'épigraphie, d'histoire ancienne et de philologie, ᴱPiérart M., *Curty* O. FrS 1989, Univ. xiv-276 p.; 6 pl. [RHE 85,63*; RÉLat 68,272, J. P. *Callu*].
220 ZENGER Erich; Vom Sinai zum Horeb; Stationen alttestamentlicher Glaubensgeschichte, ᴱHossfeld Frank-Lothar. Wü 1989, Echter. 197 p.; ill. 3-429-01248-1. 6 art.; infra.
221 ZIEGLER Josef Georg, Sein und Handeln in Christus; Perspektiven einer Gnadenmoral, 70 Gb., ᴱKleber Karl-Heinz, *Piegsa* Joachim: Moralth. St. Syst. 15. St. Ottilien 1988, EOS. 231 p. DM 46 [TLZ 115,140, G. *Keil*]. – ᴿTR 85 (1989) 317-320 (H. *Doblosch*: stress on Polish theologians: 108 have 'referiert' in Mainz since 1971, while 38 from Mainz lectured in Poland).
222 ZURAYK Constantine K.: Arab civilization, challenges and responses; studies in honor of ~, ᴱAtiyeh George N., *Oweiss* Ibrahim. Albany 1988, SUNY. xii-365 p. [JAOS 109,341].

A1.2 **Miscellanea** *unius* auctoris.

223 **Abrams** M. H., Doing things with texts; essays in criticism and critical theory. ᴱ*Fischer* Michel. NY 1989, Norton. xiii-429 p. 0-393-02713-9. 17 art.
224 **Alberigo** Giuseppe, Nostalgie di unità; saggi di storia dell'ecumenismo: Dabar 8. Genova 1989, Marietti. 175 p. Lit. 22.000. 88-211-6800-X [Greg 70,827].
225 **Alt** Albrecht, Essays on Old Testament history and religion [Kleine Schriften I-III, 1953/59/64], ᵀ*Wilson* R. A. [1966 ⟶ 48,1248; reprinted]: Biblical Seminar 7. Sheffield 1989, JStOT. x-274 p. $18; £11 [CBQ 52,194]. 1-85075-204-4. 5 art., infra.
226 **Altmann** Alexander, Von der mittelalterlichen zur modernen Aufklärung; Studien zur jüdischen Geistesgeschichte: TStMedEMJud 2. Tü 1987, Mohr. vii-336 p. DM 128. 10 art. – ᴿJudaica 44 (1988) 109s (S. *Schreiner*); RÉJ 146 (1987) 393-7 (M.-R. *Hayoun*: 2 inédits; plusieurs déjà réimprimés).
227 **Applebaum** Shimon, Judaea in Hellenistic and Roman times; historical and archaeological essays: StJudLA 40. Leiden 1989, Brill. x-175 p. 90-04-08821-0. 13 art.; 6 infra.
228 **Ayalon** David, Outsiders in the lands of Islam; Mamluks, Mongols and eunuchs. L 1988, Variorum. xii-316 p. – ᴿIslam 66 (1989) 150s (B. *Spuler*).
229 **Barbé** Dominique, A theology of conflict and other writings on nonviolence. Mkn 1989, Orbis. xviii-181 p. $12 pa. [CBQ 52,379].
230 **Barbieri** Guido, Scritti minori [1933-1981]: Univ. Roma; Vetera III. R 1988, Quasar. xvii-481 p.; bibliog. p. xv-xvii (*Leone* E., *Licordari* A.) [AnPg 59, p. 975].
231 **Beckwith** John, Studies in Byzantine and medieval Western art. L 1989, Pindar. 362 p.; 4 pl.
232 **Bennett** Anne M., ᴱ*Hunt* Mary E., From woman-pain to woman-vision, writings in feminist theology [lectures, poems ...]. Ph 1988, Fortress. $11 [CurrTM 16,385 adv.].
233 **BENZING** Johannes: Kritische Beiträge zur Altaistik und Turkologie, Fs. für ~, ᴱ**Johanson** Lars, *Schönig* Claus: Turkologie 3. Wsb 1988,

Harrassowitz.   xxvi-210 p.; portr.   DM 98.   3-447-02766-5.   52 art.   by Benzing. – ᴿBO 46 (1989) 502s (H. E. *Boeschoten*).

234 **Birley** Eric,   The Roman army papers 1929-1986 [45 art., also on frontiers and Hadrian's wall]: Mavors 4.   Amsterdam 1988, Gieben.   x-457 p. 90-5063-007-3. – ᴿClasR 39 (1989) 324s (L. *Keppie*); JRS 79 (1989) 225-7 (J. *Wilkes*, also on ALFÖLDY G., 1986/7).

235 **Blázquez** R.,   La Iglesia del Concilio Vaticano II: Verdad e Imagen 107. Salamanca 1988, Sígueme.   510 p. – ᴿRET 49 (1989) 458-460 (E. *Bueno de la Fuente*).

236 **Böhlig** Alexander,   Gnosis und Synkretismus; gesammelte Aufsätze zur spätantiken Religionsgeschichte: WUNT 47s.   Tü 1989, Mohr.   xxii-370 p.; p. 373-765.   3-16-145299-2; 454-5.   8 art.; 10 infra.

237 **Boff** Leonardo,   Una prospettiva di liberazione; la teologia, la Chiesa, i poveri.   T 1987, Einaudi.   xix-220 p.   Lit. 14.000.   13 art. – ᴿCC 140 (1989,3) 195-7 (F. A. *Pastor*: sentenze difficilmente accettabili).

238 **Bommer** Josef,   Gemeinde auf dem Weg Jesu; Anregungen und Predigten zu einer neuen Theologie der Gemeinde.   Mü 1988, Pfeiffer.   151 p. – ᴿAtKap 113 (1989) 154-7 (M. *Marczewski* ☉).

239 **Bosworth** A. B.,   From Arrian to Alexander; studies in historical interpretation.   Ox 1988, Clarendon.   x-225 p.

240 **Brinkman** Bruno R.,   To the lengths of God; truth and the ecumenical age.   L 1988, Sheed & W.   xv-334 p.   £25. – ᴿHeythJ 30 (1989) 63s (P. *Avis*).

241 **Brunt** P. A.,   The fall of the Roman Republic, and related essays [4 reprints, several inedita].   Ox 1988, Clarendon.   xi-545 p.   0-19-814849-6. – ᴿJRS 79 (1989) 151-6 (J. *North*: a Roman counter-revolution); RÉLat 67 (1989) 336 (J.-L. *Ferrary*: un livre majeur, qui fera date).

242 **Buri** Fritz,   Verantwortung übernehmen, ein Lesebuch [80. Gb.], ᴱ**Hauff** Günther.   Bern/Tü 1987.   Haupt/Katzmann.   160 p.   Fs 16,50. – ᴿTZBas 45 (1989) 380s (W. A. *Sommer*).

243 **Casaldáliga** Pedro, bispo,   Na procura do Reino [150 art., 60 anos de idade].   São Paulo 1988, FTD.   280 p. – ᴿREB 49 (1989) 233-5 (E. F. *Alves*).

244 **Casalis** Georges,   Un semeur est sorti pour semer [reprints]; préf. *Klein* J. L.: Parole présente.   P 1988, Cerf.   220 p. – ᴿRSPT 73 (1989) 158s (M. *Barth*).

245 **Casson** Lionel,   Ancient trade and society ➤ 65,d184 [selection of his essays].   Detroit 1984, Wayne State Univ.   284 p.; 12 maps. $25. – ᴿInt-JNaut 17 (1988) 275s (D. *Blackman*).

246 **Coppola** C.,   Esegesi e grammatica; raccolta di scritti e testimonianza, ᴱ*Gallo* Italo.   Salerno 1988, Laveglia.   173 p. [AnPg 59, p. 976].

247 **Cothenet** Édouard,   Exégèse et liturgie; préf. *Gy* Pierre-M.: LDiv 133, 1988 ➤ 4,9233: ᴿEsprVie 99 (1989) 235-8 (L. *Walter*); Études 371 (1989) 136s (P. *Gibert*); RThom 89 (1989) 151s (G.-H. *Masson*).

248 **Cox** Harvey,   Many mansions; a Christian's encounter with other faiths [4 reprints, 5 inedita].   Boston 1988, Beacon.   216 p. $19. – ᴿTTod 46 (1989s) 203s (P. *Knitter*).

249 **Curti** Carmelo,   Eusebiana I. Commentarii in Psalmos [15 reprints 1968-88].   Catania 1989², Univ. – ᴿAthenaeum 77 (1989) 176 (F. *Gasti*); Gregorianum 70 (1989) 176 (G. *Pelland*); Koinonia 13 (1989) 395 (F. *Conti Bizzarro*).

250 **Dack** Edmond van 't,   Ptolemaica selecta; études [1948-1985] sur l'armée et l'administration lagides: StHellen 29.   Lv 1988, Orientaliste.   xxvii-409 p. [AnPg 59,976].

251 **Daumer** Georg F., Pan und Madonna, ausgewählte Schriften, ᴱ*Kluncker* Karlhans: Abh. Ph. Ps. Pedag. 210. Bonn 1988, Bouvier. 176 p. [AnPg 59, p. 976].

252 **Davies** R. W., Service in the Roman Army, ᴱ*Breeze* D., *Maxfield* V. A. E 1989, Univ. xii-336 p.; 86 fig. £35. 0-85224-495-9; pa. 648-X [JRS 79,271]. 10 reprints. – ᴿAntiqJ 69 (1989) 167 (B. *Dobson*).

253 **Derrett** J. D. M., The sea-change of the Old Testament in the New: Studies in the NT 5. Leiden 1989, Brill. xii-245 p. 90-04-09110-6 [NRT 112,590, X. *Jacques*]. 19 art., 3 infra.

254 **Drexler** Hans, Politische Grundbegriffe der Römer. Da 1988, Wiss. viii-226 p. [AnPg 59, p. 976].

255 **Eco** Umberto, *a*) Über Gott und die Welt, Essays und Glossen, ᵀ*Kroeber* B.² Mü 1988, Deutscher Tb-V. 305 p. DM 12,80. – *b*) Apokalyptiker und Integrierte; zur kritischen Kritik der Massenkultur, ᵀ*Looser* M.: Wiss.-Tb. 1480. Fra 1987, Fischer. 312 p. – ᴿTLZ 114 (1989) 255-9 (W. *Engermann*).

256 **Edelstein** Ludwig, Selected papers, ᴱ*Tarán* Leonardo: GkLatPh 15. NY 1987, Garland. Original paginations.

257 **Esposito** Mario [8 art. 1907-1937], ᴱ*Lapidge* Michael, Latin learning in mediaeval Ireland, I. L 1988, Variorum. x-326 p. £34 [RHE 85,232, D. *Bradley*].

258 **Finley** Moses I., Sur l'histoire ancienne; la matière, la forme et la méthode [6 art.], ᵀ*Carlier* Jeannie. P 1987, Découverte. 215 p. – ᴿRPLH 62 (1988) 319-326 (É. *Will*).

259 **Fishbane** Michael, The garments of Torah; essays in biblical hermeneutics [since 1975]: StudBibLit. Bloomington 1989, Indiana Univ. xi-155 p. 0-253-32217-0. 9 art., infra.

259* **Flusser** David, Ontdekkingen in het NT; Woorden van Jezus en hun overlevering [1974-87: 1987 ➤ 4,191], ᵀ. Baarn 1988, Ten Have. 568 p. *f* 25. – ᴿStreven 56 (1988s) 663 (P. *Beentjes*).

260 **Fontaine** Jacques, Tradition et actualité chez Iꜱɪᴅᴏʀᴇ de Séville [13 art. 1945...]. L 1988, Variorum. xiv-336 p. £34. – ᴿRHE 84 (1989) 616s (G. *Corcoran*).

261 **Frend** W. H. C., Archeology and history in the study of early Christianity: Collected Studies 282. L 1988, Variorum. 318 p.; 47 fig. – ᴿOrChrPer 55 (1989) 482s (V. *Poggi*).

262 **Frieling** R., Old Testament studies [... R. Sᴛᴇɪɴᴇʀ philosophy; world, tabernacle, vestments all produced in seven phases]. E 1987, Floris. 159 p. £11. 0-86315-057-8. – ᴿBL (1989) 105 (F. F. *Bruce*).

263 **Fuchs** Josef, Für eine menschliche Moral; Grundfragen der theologischen Ethik, I. Normative Grundlegung: Studien zur theologischen Ethik 25. FrS/FrB 1988, Univ./Herder. 335 p. – ᴿFreibZ 36 (1989) 225-7 (C. *Kissling*); TPQ 137 (1989) 408s (J. *Janda*).

264 **Garbini** Giovanni, Il Semitico nordoccidentale [articoli e recensioni, non = (²) Semitico di nord-ovest 1960]: StSemitici NS 5. R 1988, Univ. VIII-172 p. – ᴿZAW 101 (1989) 459 (J. A. *Soggin*).

265 **Gese** Hartmut, *a*) Zur biblischen Theologie; alttestamentliche Vorträge³ [¹1977, ²1983]. Tü 1989, Mohr. 239 p. 2-16-145526-6. – *b*) Sulla teologia biblica [²1983], ᵀ*Odasso* Giovanni: BiblCuRel 54. Brescia 1989, Paideia. 285 p. 88-394-0420-1.

266 **Görg** Manfred, Beiträge zur Zeitgeschichte der Anfänge Israels; Dokumente — Materialien — Notizen [< BibNot]: ÄgAT 2. Wsb 1989, Harrassowitz. [viii-]225 p.; 40 pl. 3-447-02185-3 [ZAW 102,301, tit. pp.].

267 **Gonnet** Giovanni, Il grano e le zizzanie; tra eresia e riforma (secoli XII-XVII). Soveria Mannelli 1989, Rubbettino. 1586 p. (3 vol.). – ᴿComViat 32 (1989) 261-6 (A. *Molnár*).

268 **González Montes** Adolfo, Reforma luterana y tradición católica [reprints]: Bibl. Salm. 100. Salamanca 1987, Univ. Pont. 257 p. – ᴿScripTPamp 718 (J. M. *Odero*).

268* GOODENOUGH [Erwin R.] on the history of religion and on Judaism → 3, e417 [a choice of his own articles], ᴱ*Frerichs* E., *Neusner* J.: BrownJudSt 121. Atlanta 1986, Scholars. xxi-146 p. $30.

269 **Greenstein** Edward L., Essays on biblical method and translation: BrownJudSt 92. Atlanta 1989, Scholars. xvi-147 p. $45. 1-55540-122-8 [OIAc N89].

270 **Griffith** John G., Festinus senex, or An old man in a hurry, unpublished essays on problems in Greek and Latin literature and archaeology + 3 reprints. Ox 1988, Oxbow. 134 p.; 1 pl. [AnPg 59, p. 977].

271 **Guelluy** Robert, Mais il y a Jésus-Christ [10 reprints + 7 inédits]. P 1989, Duculot. 197 p. – ᴿETL 65 (1989) 468 (J. *Étienne*).

272 **Gutmann** Joseph, Sacred images; studies in Jewish art from antiquity to the Middle Ages. Northampton 1989, Variorum. x-276 p.; portr.; ill. 0-86078-251-4. 18 art. in the original pagination.

273 **Gyula** Nagy, bp. Ⓜ *Az Egyház kincse*, The treasure of the church [(his) sermons and studies, 70th b.]. Budapest 1985, Evangelical. – ᴿTSzem 32 (1989) 58s (J. *Szigeti*).

274 **Hall** Robert A.ᴶ, Linguistics and pseudo-linguistics [12 art. 1965-85]; AmstLing 4/55. Amst 1987, Benjamins. 147 p. – ᴿSalesianum 51 (1989) 903 (R. *Della Casa*).

275 **Harder** Günther †1978, Kirche und Israel; Arbeiten zum christlich-jüdischen Verhältnis, ᴱ*Osten-Sacken* Peter von der: Studien zu jüdischem Volk und christlicher Gemeinde 7. B 1986, Inst. Kirche und Judentum. 281 p. DM 17,80. – ᴿTR 85 (1989) 408s (C. *Thoma*).

276 **Hastings** Adrian, African Catholicism; essays in discovery [12 art., some reprinted]. L/Ph 1989, SCM/Trinity. xiv-208 p. $15. 0-334-00019-X [TDig 37,58]. – ᴿTsTNijm 29 (1989) 432 (J. *Heijke*).

277 **Hauerwas** Stanley M., Christian existence today; essays on Church, world and living in between. Durham [ɴᴄ] 1988, Labyrinth. 266 p. $15. – ᴿTTod 46 (1989s) 425-7 (J. W. *McClendon*).

278 **Heinemann** Gustav W., Es gibt schwierige Vaterländer ... Aufsätze und Reden 1919-1969, ᴱ*Lindemann* H.: Tb 24. Mü 1988 [reprint], Kaiser. 391 p. DM 24. – ᴿTLZ 114 (1989) 99s (E. *Winkler*).

279 **Henninger** Joseph, Arabica varia; Aufsätze zur Kulturgeschichte Arabiens und seiner Randgebiete [i. 1981, OBO 40 → 62,229; ii:]: OBO 90. FrS/Gö 1989, Univ/VR. 498 p. Fs 120. 3-7278-0638-9 / 3-525-53720-4. 11 art. (3 infra) + 8 reviews 1938-75 [BL 90,121, W. *Johnstone*].

280 **Hofius** Otfried, Paulusstudien: WUNT 51. Tü 1989, Mohr. viii-321 p. 3-16-145532-0; pa. 04-5. 12 art., some infra.

281 **Hollenbach** David, Justice, peace, and human rights; American Catholic social ethics in a pluralistic world [14 reprints 1977-88]. NY 1988, Crossroad. xi-260 p. $17. – ᴿTS 50 (1989) 815-7 (J. B. *Benestad*).

283 **Isaac** Glynn, The archaeology of human origins; papers, ᴱ*Isaac* Barbara. C 1989, Univ. xxv-447 p.; portr.; ill. 0-521-36573-2. 18 art.; 2 infra → b974.

284 **Jaki** Stanley L., The absolute beneath the relative and other essays. Lanham ᴹᴰ 1989, UPA/Intercollegiate. 233 p. $27; pa. $12.75. 0-8191-7182-4; 3-2. – ᴿDowR 107 (1989) 152s (P. *Hodgson*).

285 **Jenkins** David E. (bishop of Durham, lectures since 1983), God, politics and the future. L 1988, SCM. xvii-139 p. £5 pa. – ᴿTLond 92 (1989) 220-2 (R. E. *Pahl*: clear message, p. 31: 'Put your faith in God and *think*'; What can be controversial about that?).

286 **Jossua** Jean-Pierre, La foi de jour en jour [100 art. d'une page < Réforme 1985s]. P 1988, Beauchesne. 168 p. F 90. – ᴿEsprVie 99 (1989) 574 (L. *Barbey*: p. 51 objects to the expression 'meet God' but p. 9 and 77 say 'God is human'...).

287 **Jüngel** Eberhard, Theological essays, selected & ᵀᴱ*Webster* J. B. E 1989, Clark. xii-235 p. $30. 0-567-09502-9 [TDig 37,67].

288 **Käsemann** Ernst, Saggi esegetici [< 1960/4 ; 9 art]: Dabar 3. CasM 1985, Marietti. XXI-174 p. – ᴿLaurentianum 30 (1989) 226s (L. *Martignani*).

289 **Katz** Jacob, Jewish emancipation and self-emancipation. Ph 1986, Jewish Publ. ix-179 p. $15. – ᴿJRel 68 (1988) 148s (M. A. *Meyer*).

290 **KATZOFF** Louis *zal.*, Memorial volume (editor of Dor 1972-87; selection of his writings). $20 [JBQ 18,164 adv.].

291 **KELLER** C. A., Communication avec l'ultime [florilège de ses écrits pour son éméritat; p. 17-40 sur l'AT]: Religions en perspective 1. Genève 1987, Labor et Fides. 281 p.; portr. – ᴿNRT 111 (1989) 292s (J. *Masson*).

292 **Klauck** Hans-Josef, Gemeinde — Amt — Sakrament; neutestamentliche Perspektiven. Wü 1989, Echter. 452 p. DM 68, pa. 48. 3-429-01181-7; pa. -2-5. 22 art.; 7 infra. – ᴿClaretianum 29 (1989) 422-4 (B. *Proietti*); GeistL 62 (1989) 311-3 (Johanna *Schreiner*).

293 **Kötting** Bernhard, Ecclesia peregrinans; das Gottesvolk unterwegs, Gesammelte Aufsätze I-II: Münsterische BeitT 54. Münster 1988, Aschendorff. viii-548 p.; portr.; iii-339 p. DM 120 [TR 86,207-211, W. D. *Hauschild*]. – ᴿTLZ 114 (1989) 176-8 (G. *Haendler*: title suggestively but only by chance echoes ᶠ*Lenzenweger* 1986).

294 **Köves-Zulauf** Thomas, Kleine Schriften, ᴱ*Heinrichs* Achim. Heid 1988, Winter. viii-415 p. [AnPg 59, p. 977].

295 **Kreeft** Peter, Fundamentals of the faith, essays in Christian apologetics [46 < National Catholic Register]. SF 1988, Ignatius. 300 p. $10. 0-89870-202-X [TDig 36,377].

296 **Latham** John D., From Muslim Spain to Barbary; Studies in the history and culture of the Muslim West [nineteen, 1960-84]. L 1986, Variorum. 348 p. – ᴿDer Islam 65 (1988) 153s (O. *Hegyi*).

297 **Levi della Vida** Giorgio, Pitagora, Bardesane e altri studi siriaci, ᴱ*Contini* Riccardo: Univ. Roma, StOr 8. R 1989, Bardi. xxi-194 p. 7 art., 1 infra → a494.

298 **Levinas** Emmanuel, Aan gene zijde van het vers; talmoedische studies en essays. Hilversum 1989, Gooi. 250 p. ƒ 49,50. – ᴿStreven 57 (1989s) 953s (P. *Beentjes*).

299 **LODS** Marc [† 13.XII.1988], Protestantisme et tradition de l'Église [16 art. 1958-, pour ses 80 ans], ᴱ*Pérès* J.-N., *Dubois* J.-D.: Patrimoines Christianisme. P 1988, Cerf. 368 p. F 270. 2-204-03039-2. – ᴿÉTRel 64 (1989) 444s (J.-M. *Prieur*); RTLv 20 (1989) 385 (A. de *Halleux*).

300 **Lohfink** Gerhard, Studien zum Neuen Testament: Aufsatzb. 5. Stu 1989, KBW. 408 p. 3-460-06051-4. 19 art., 5 infra.

301 **Lohfink** Norbert, Unsere neuen Fragen und das Alte Testament; wiederentdeckte Lebensweisung [Aufsätze 1965-83]: Tb 1594. FrB 1989, Herder. 157 p. DM 13. 3-451-08594-1 [BL 90,107, J. W. *Rogerson*; TPQ

138,184s, B. *Baldauf*]. – ᴿBiKi 44 (1989) 89 (M. *Helsper*); OTAbs 12 (1989) 230s (R. E. *Murphy*); TLZ 114 (1989) 728s (K.-H. *Bernhardt*).

302 **Lohfink** Norbert, Il sapore della speranza nella Bibbia e nella teologia [Konferenzen Wü 1982 < Ordensnachrichten ecc.], ᵀ*Russo* Giovanni. CasM 1989, Piemme. 111 p. Lit. 15.000. 88-384-1414-9.

303 **Lonergan** Bernard, Collection [16 early compositions as published in 1967 plus notes]: Collected works 4 [of 22 projected, ᴱ*Crowe* F. E., *Doran* R. M.]. Toronto 1988, Univ. xiii-350 p. – ᴿSR 18 (1989) 373s (Cathleen M. *Going*).

304 **Lortz** Joseph, Erneuerung und Einheit; Aufsätze zur Theologie- und Kirchengeschichte, 100. Gb. [† 1975], ᴱ*Manns* Peter: Inst. Europ. Gesch. 126. Stu 1987, Steiner. ix-895 p. [TLZ 115,11, S. *Bräuer*]. – ᴿTPhil 64 (1989) 272s (H. J. *Sieben*).

305 **Lubac** Henri de, Theological fragments [Théologies d'occasion 1984 65,209; 1,203], ᵀ*Balinski* Rebecca H. SF 1989, Ignatius. 441 p. $20. 0-89870-236-4 [TDig 37,71].

306 **Lubsczyk** Hans, Die Einheit der Schrift; gesammelte Aufsätze, ᴱ*Hentschel* Georg, *Richter* Heribert. Lp 1989, St. Benno. 259 p.; Bibliog. 245-7. 3-7462-0369-4. 13 art.; 8 infra.

307 **Lyonnet** Stanislas, Études sur l'Épître aux Romains [en partie ᵀ*Morel* J.]: AnBib 120. R 1989, Pont. Ist. Biblico. ix-387 p. Lit. 48.000. 88-7653-120-3. 22 art.; → 5911.

307* **Mass** F., Er is meer God dan we denken [essays over spiritualiteit < diss. ᴰ*Schillebeeckx*]: CahLV 53. Averbode/Kampen 1989, Altiora/ Kok. 191 p. ƒ27,90. 90-317-0792-9 / 90-242-0989-7. – ᴿTsTNijm 29 (1989) 420 (J. A. P. *Peters*).

308 **McCormick** Richard A., The critical calling; reflections on moral dilemmas since Vatican II [22 essays, partly already published]. Wsh 1989, Georgetown Univ. xii-414 p. $30; pa. $17. 0-87840-463-5; 4-3 [TDig 37,72]. – ᴿAmerica 161 (1989) 216s (W. C. *Spohn*).

309 **Maddalena** Antonio †, Letture dai Vangeli [scritti postumi inediti]: Culture Antiche 1. Alessandria 1989, Orso. XII-81 p. Lit. 20.000. – ᴿSileno 15 (R 1989) 337-341 (V. *Messana*).

310 **Manns** Peter: Vater im Glauben; [11 1965-86] Studien zur Theologie M. *Luthers*, Festgabe zum 65. Gb., ᴱ*Decot* Rolf: Mainz Inst. Eur. Gesch. 131. Stu 1988, Steiner. ix-534 p. DM 72. 3-515-05055-8. – ᴿGregorianum 70 (1989) 800s (J. E. *Vercruysse*); RHE 84 (1989) 783 (J.-F. *Gilmont*).

311 **Mansfeld** Jaap, Studies in later Greek philosophy and Gnosticism: CS 292. L 1989, Variorum. Original pagination; portr.

312 **Maron** Gottfried, Zum Gespräch mit Rom; Beiträge aus evangelischer Sicht [60 Gb.]: Bensheimer Hefte 69. Gö 1988, Vandenhoeck & R. 314 p. DM 25. – ᴿTLZ 114 (1989) 852s (H. *Kirchner*).

314 **Martin** Roland, Architecture et urbanisme, préf. *Pouilloux* J., *Vallet* G.: Coll. Éc. Fr. Rome 99. P 1987, de Boccard. x-364 p.; 18 pl. [AnPg 58, p. 818].

314* **Martini** Carlo M., Unterwegs zur Stadt Gottes; ein neues soziales Engagement der Christen. Salzburg 1986, O. Müller. 88 p. Sch 198. – ᴿTPQ 137 (1989) 212 (F. *Reisinger*).

315 **Mazal** Otto, Bibliothekswesen und Forschung [27 (seiner) Art., 50. Gb.], ᴱ*Németh* István (Bibliog. 309-314): Studien zur Bibliotheksgeschichte 4. Graz 1982, Akad. XXII-316 p. – ᴿResPLit 9 (1986) 271-3 (M. *Palma*).

316 **Meland** Bernard E., Essays in constructive theology, a process perspective [20 art. 1938-80]. Ch 1988, Exploration. 329 p. $27; pa. $15. – RTTod 46 (1989s) 249s (M. *Welker*).

317 **Mendelssohn** Moses, Schriften zum Judentum (Psaumes, Ct, Jg 5 ...) 4, E*Weinberg* Werner, *al.*: Gesammelte Schriften 10,1s. Stu 1985, Frommann. 652 p. – RRÉJ 146 (1987) 417-9 (M.-R. *Hayoun*).

318 **Mette** Hans J., Kleine Schriften, E*Mette* Adelheid, *Seidensticker* Bernd: Alt.-Wiss. 184. Fra 1988, Athenäum. XXV-367 p.; ill. [AnPg 59, p. 977]. – RClasR 39 (1989) 373s (W. C. *Arnott*).

319 **Meyer** Ben F., Critical realism and the New Testament; Princeton Theol. Mg 17. Allison Park PA 1989, Pickwick. xv-225 p. $20. 0-915138-97-2 [NTAbs 33,380: four essays dated 1981-7 + 3 inedita, JBL 108,569].

320 **Meyer** Rudolf, Zur Geschichte und Theologie des Judentums in hellenistisch-römischer Zeit; ausgewählte Abhandlungen, E*Bernhardt* Waltraut. Neuk 1989, Neuk.-V. 226 p. 3-7887-1314-4. 8 art.; 4 infra.

321 **Miccoli** G., Fra mito della cristianità e secolarizzazione; studi [nove, dal 1965-85] sul rapporto chiesa-società nell'età contemporanea: Dabar 4. CasM 1985, Marietti. 510 p. – RCrNSt 9 (1988) 458-461 (M. *Guasco*).

322 **Mildenberger** F., Zeitgemässes zur Unzeit; Texte zum Frieden, zum Verstehen des Evangeliums und zur Erfahrung Gottes: Theologie im Gespräch 1. Essen 1987, Blaue Eule. 178 p. DM 27 pa. 3-89206-138-6 [NTAbs 33,122]. 18 art.

323 **Momigliano** Arnaldo, Saggi di storia della religione romana; studi e lezioni 1983-1986, E*Di Donato* Riccardo. Brescia 1988, Morcelliana. 205 p. Lit. 25.000. – RCC 140 (1989,3) 540s (A. *Ferrua*).

324 **Morris** Meaghan, The pirate's fiancée; feminism, reading, postmodernism. L 1988, Verso. x-287 p. $50; pa. $17. 0-86091-212-4; 926-9 [RelStR 16, 137, Kathryn A. *Rabuzzi*: dazzling for the few who are up to it].

325 **Morris** Thomas V., Anselmian explorations [13 reprints]. ND 1987, Univ. 253 p. £26. – RScotJT 42 (1989) 600-3 (J. *McIntyre*).

325* **MÜLLER** Gerhard, Causa reformationis; [seine] Beiträge zur Reformationsgeschichte und zur Theologie M. LUTHERS [60. Gb.], E*Maron* G., *Seebass* G. Gü 1989, Mohn. 588 p. DM 68 [TLZ 115,879, J. *Rogge*].

326 **Mueller** Reimar, Polis und Res publica; Studien zum antiken Gesellschafts- und Geschichtsdenken. Weimar 1987, Böhlau. 384 p. [AnPg 59, p. 978].

326* *Mulack* Christa, Im Anfang war die Weisheit; feministische Kritik des männlichen Gottesbildes. Stu 1988, Kreuz. 119 p. DM 16,80. 3-7831-0946-9. – RTsTNijm 29 (1989) 420 (C. *Halkes*).

327 **Nazir-Ali** Michael, Frontiers in Muslim-Christian encounter [17 art., mostly reprints]. Ox 1987, Regnum. 191 p. £6.50. 1-870345-05-3. – RÉTRel 64 (1989) 105s (J.-P. *Gabus*: the author is a Pakistani Christian, assistant to the Archbishop of Canterbury); Vidyajyoti 52 (1988) 307s (C. W. *Troll*).

328 **Neusner** Jacob, Ancient Judaism and modern category-formation; 'Judaism', 'midrash', 'messianism' and canon in the past quarter-century [4 reprints, reworked and with two new prefaces]. Lanham MD 1986, UPA. xiv-124 p. $9.75 pa. [JBL 108, 372 titles, pp., sources].

329 **Neusner** Jacob, Method and meaning in Judaism / in ancient Judaism [lectures 1989 etc.] first/fourth series: BrownJudSt 179/168. Atlanta 1989, Scholars. xi-159 p.; xiii-287 p. -/$50. 1-55540-323-9 [NTAbs 33,419]. 9 art.

330 **Neusner** J., Paradigms in passage; patterns of change in the contemporary study of Judaism [13 art.]: Studies in Judaism. Lanham MD 1988, UPA. xvii-200 p. $19. 0-8191-6899-8 [NTAbs 33,132].

331 **Neusner** Jacob, The religious study of Judaism, I. Description, analysis, and interpretation; II. The centrality of context. Lanham MD 1986, UPA. xvi-172 p., $11.75; xiv-216 p.; $12.75 pa. [JBL 108, 372: titles, pp.].

332 **Neusner** Jacob, The social study of Judaism, essays and reflections [8 + 7 articles, largely on economics], 1s: BrownJudSt 160.162. Atlanta 1988, Scholars. xv-252 p.; xvi-162 p. $45 each. 1-55540-306-9 [NTAbs 33,419, gives same ISBN number for both].

332* **Noordmans** O., De kerk en het leven: Versamelde werken 6, E*Hasselaar* J. M., *al.* Kampen 1986, Kok. 659 p. *f*87,50. 90-242-2609-0. – RBijdragen 50 (1989) 458s (J. *Wissink*).

333 **North** J.D., Stars, minds and fate; essays in ancient and medieval cosmology. L 1989, Hambledon. xi-429 p.; ill. [RHE 85,128*].

334 **Oroz Reta** José, San AGUSTÍN, cultura clásica y cristianismo [reprints]; Bibl. Salm. 110. Salamanca 1988, Univ. Pont. 359 p. – RScripTPamp 21 (1989) 706s (C. *Basevi*).

335 **Paglia** Vincenzo, Città secolare e Vangelo [< giornale Il Popolo]. R 1988, Cinque Lune. 241 p. Lit. 24.000. – RCC 140 (1989,2) 509s (G. *Salvini*).

336 **Panikkar** Raimundo, Il dialogo intrareligioso. Assisi 1989, Cittadella. 207 p. – RAngelicum 66 (1989) 647s (A. *Lobato*).

337 **Penco** Gregorio, Spiritualità monastica; aspetti e momenti [1960-86]: Scritti Monastici 9. Praglia 1988, Abbazia. 536 p. [AnPg 59, p. 978].

Pieris Aloysius, Love meets wisdom; a Christian experience of Buddhism 1988 → b272.

339 **Pötscher** Walter, Hellas und Rom; Beiträge und kritische Auseinandersetzung mit der inszwischen erschienenen Literatur: Collectanea 21. Hildesheim 1988, Olms. xxii-670 p. – RAnzAltW 42 (1989) 145s (J. T. *Hooker*).

340 **Poorthuis** Marcel, Hamer op de rots; artikelen over teksten en hun uitleg in jodendom en christendom. Voorburg 1989, Lectuurvorziening. 152 p. *f*32,50. – RStreven 57 (1989s) 1047s (P. *Beentjes*).

341 **Rade** Martin, Ausgewählte Schriften 3. Recht und Glaube; Einl. *Schwöbel* C. Gü 1988, Mohn. 211 p. DM 64. – RTLZ 114 (1989) 43s (M. *Greschat*).

342 **Ratzinger** Joseph, Servitori della vostra gioia [8 omelie]. Mi 1989, Àncora. 137 p. Lit. 20.000. – RCC 140 (1989,4) 512s (G. *Caprile*).

343 **Riezu** Jorge, Religión y sociedad. Salamanca 1989, San Esteban. 227 p. – RCarthaginensia 5 (1989) 339 (F. *Martínez Fresneda*).

344 **Robert** Louis, Documents d'Asie Mineure [< BCH 1977-85]: BÉF 239 bis. P 1987, de Boccard. viii-568 p.; 202 fig. [AnPg 59, p. 979].

345 **Santiago-Otero** H., Fe y cultura en la edad media [20 art.]: Mediaevalia et humanistica 4. M 1988, Cons. Sup. 302 p. – RRSPT 73 (1989) 156s (L.-J. *Bataillon*).

346 **Scannone** Juan Carlos, Teología de la liberación y doctrina social de la Iglesia. M 1987, Cristiandad. 285 p. RRLatAmT 6,16 (1989) 134s (J.A.C.).

347 **Schilling** Robert, Dans le sillage de Rome; religion, poésie, humanisme: Études & comm. 101. P 1988, Klincksieck. 286 p. [AnPg 59, p. 979].

348 **Schmidt** Ernst G., Erworbenes Erbe; Studien zur antiken Literatur und ihrer Nachwirkung; Universal-Bibl. 1259. Lp 1988, Reclam. 471 p. [AnPg 59, p. 979].

349 **Schottroff** Luise & Willy, Die Macht der Auferstehung, sozialgeschichtliche Bibelauslegung [allerart; nichts über Auferstehung]: Tb 30.
Mü 1988, Kaiser. 132 p. DM 12,80. – ᴿTsTNijm 29 (1989) 404 (L.
Grollenberg); ZAW 101 (1989) 327 (H.-C. *Schmitt* gives most of the titles,
without pp.).

350 **Schunck** K.-D., Altes Testament und Heiliges Land; Gesammelte Studien
zum AT und zur biblischen Landeskunde I: BErfAJ 17. Fra 1989, Lang.
276 p. Fs 60. 3-8204-1187-9 [BL 90,25]. 24 art., plures infra.

351 Sᴄʜᴜᴏɴ Frithjof, Avoir un centre [7 reprints, 7 inédits, pour ses 80 ans]:
Métalangage. P 1988, Maisonneuve & L. 160 p. F 150. 2-7068-0968-X.
– ᴿÉTRel 64 (1989) 103s (Jacky *Argaud*).

352 **Schwarz** H., Die biblische Urgeschichte; Gottes Traum von Mensch und
Welt [11 Homilien]: Tb 1608. FrB 1989, Herder. 158 p. DM 12,90. –
ᴿNRT 111 (1989) 938 (J.-L. *Ska*: il ne s'agit pas d'une exégèse de Gn 1-12).

353 **Seckler** Max, Die schiefen Wände des Lehrhauses; Katholizität als
Herausforderung [11 Art. 1965-87]. FrB 1988, Herder. 267 p. DM 30.
ᴿActuBbg 26 (1989) 223s (J. *Boada*); ZkT 111 (1989) 102s (W. *Kern*).

354 **Seckler** Max, Teologia scienza chiesa; saggi di teologia fondamentale,
ᴱ*Coffele* Gianfranco. Brescia 1988, Morcelliana. 290 p. Lit. 28.000.
88-372-1343-3 [Greg 70,411].

355 **Segal** R. A., Religion and the social sciences, essays on the confrontation
[thirteen, 1978-1987]: BrownStRel 3. Atlanta 1989, Scholars. 184 p. $44;
sb. $29. 1-55540-295-X [BL 90, 114, J. W. *Rogerson*].

356 Sᴇɪᴛᴢ Manfred [60. Gb.] Lebenswort; Erlanger Universitätspredigten,
ᴱ*Bub* W., *al.* Erlangen 1988, Junge / Ev.-Luth. Mission. 191 p. DM 20
[TLZ 114, 876].

357 **Shahîd** Irfan, Byzantium and the Semitic Orient before the rise of Islam:
Collected Studies 270. L 1988, Variorum. xiv-318 p.; 4 fig. £32. – ᴿIkiZ
49 (1989) 206 (B. *Spuler*); Muséon 102 (1989) 211s (J. *Mossay*).

358 **Smend** Rudolf, Deutsche Alttestamentler in drei Jahrhunderten [mostly
revised reprints]. Gö 1989, Vandenhoeck & R. 336 p. DM 78. 3-525-
53484-8 [BL 90,25; NTAbs 33,422].

359 **Sobrino** Jon, Spirituality of liberation; toward political holiness [1985
➤ 4,266], ᵀ*Barr* Robert. Maryknoll NY 1988, Orbis. 189 p. $12. –
ᴿCalvinT 24 (1989) 194-7 (J. W. *Cooper*); NewTR 2,3 (1989) 118s (J. M.
Lozano).

360 **Soden** Wolfram von, Aus Sprache, Geschichte und Religion Babyloniens;
Gesammelte Aufsätze, ᴱ*Cagni* Luigi, *Müller* Hans-Peter: Studi Asiatici
min. 32. N 1989, Ist. Univ. Orientale. x-368 p.; ill. [TZBas 45,80, E.
Kellenberger; ZAW 102,460: tit. pp.]. 23 art.; 5 infra.

361 **Speyer** Wolfgang, Frühes Christentum im antiken Strahlungsfeld,
ausgewählte Aufsätze: WUNT 50. Tü 1989, Mohr. x-531 p. DM 150.
3-16-145238-0. 34 art., 5 infra.

362 Sᴛᴏᴇʙᴇ H. J., Geschichte, Schicksal, Schuld und Glaube [18 (seine)
Aufsätze, 1952-80], 80 Gb., ᴱ*Neef* H.-D.: BoBB 72. Fra 1989,
Athenäum. 359 p.; 11-25, Ergänzungen. DM 88. 3-610-09127-4 [ZAW
101,477; JTS 41,569, R. J. *Coggins*], 18 art.; 6 infra.

363 **Surin** Kenneth, The turnings of darkness and light; essays in philosophical and systematic theology. C 1989, Univ. xv-316 p. $49.50 [CBQ
51,786].

364 **Takizawa** Katsumi, Das Heil im Heute, Texte einer japanischen
Theologie, ᴱ*Sundermeier* Theo: Theologie der Ökumene 21. Gö 1987,
Vandenhoeck & R. 220 p. – ᴿTContext 6,2 (1989) 109 (G. *Evers*).

365 **Talmon** Shemaryahu, The world of Qumran from within; collected studies. J/Leiden 1989, Magnes/Brill. 423 p. [OIAc N89]. 90-04-08449-5. 13 art., 6 infra.

366 **Tödt** H. E., Perspektiven theologischer Ethik [13 reprints]. Mü 1988, Kaiser. 285 p. DM 48. 3-459-01745-7. – ᴿTsTNijm 29 (1989) 311 (T. *Veerkamp*).

367 **Trummer** Peter, Aufsätze zum NT: GrazerTSt 12, 1987 ➙ 3,312: ᴿRB 95 (1988) 426 (F. *Langlamet*: tit. pp.).

368 **Tsopanakes** Agapetos G., Ⓖ Symboles stin istoria tis hellenikis glossas [75. Gb., 45 Art., 9 Rez. 1944-1973]. Thessaloniki 1983, Univ. xxxiv-625 p., phot.; 754 p. – ᴿAnzAltW 42 (1989) 27-29 (W. *Lackner*).

369 **Vijlbrief-Charbon** T., *Epistamai* and religio; religion as a source of knowledge and insight and other philologic and folkloristic studies. Dordrecht c. 1988, auct. vi-89 p. ƒ 30. 90-900-2249-X [JRS 79,279].

369* **Vilanova** Evangelista, Esperti i llibertat [20 art.], pról. *Panikkar* Raimon. Montserrat 1988, Sauri-84. 217 p. – ᴿRCatalT 13 (1988) 502s (R. *Pou i Rius*).

370 **Vischer** Eduard, Zur Geschichte der Geschichtsschreibung; eine Nachlese. Bern 1985, Francke. 310 p.; 2 pl. Fs 70. – ᴿDLZ 109 (1988) 250s (H. *Schleier*).

371 **Vögtle** Anton, Die Dynamik des Anfangs; Leben und Fragen der jungen Kirche [erweiterte Vorträge]. FrB 1988, Herder. 206 p. DM 19,80. – ᴿBZ 33 (1989) 153-5 (F. *Mussner*).

372 **Waldenfels** Hans, An der Grenze des Denkbaren [Vorträge & Reprints über] Meditation — Ost und West. Mü 1988, Kösel. 208 p. DM 29,80. – ᴿTR 85 (1989) 421s (G. *Risse*).

372* **West** Cornell, Prophetic fragments. GR/Trenton/Exeter 1988, Eerdmans/AfricaWorld/Paternoster. xi-294 p. £ 13. – ᴿEvQ 61 (1989) 189 (R. J. *Bauckham*: brilliant).

373 **Willebrands** J., Mandatum unitatis; Beiträge zur Ökumene: KkK 16. Pd 1989, Bonifatius. 363 p. DM 48 [RHE 85,107*; TPQ 138,392, C. *Gleixner*].

374 **Wimmel** Walter, Collectanea; Augusteertum und späte Republik. Stu 1987, Steiner. viii-436 p. – ᴿRÉLat 66 (1988) 307 (J.-C. *Richard*).

375 **Wulf** Friedrich, Gott begegnen in der Welt; Erfahrungen des Glaubens. Wü 1988, Echter. 202 p. DM 34. – ᴿTR 85 (1989) 334s (Corona *Bamberg*).

A1.3 *Plurium compilationes* **biblicae.**

376 **Alonso Schökel** Luis present., Creazione e liberazione nei libri dell'Antico Testamento. T-Leumann 1989, Elle Di Ci. 118 p. Lit. 10.000. 88-01-11106-1. 4 art., infra.

377 ᴱ**Anderson** Bernhard W., The books of the Bible; I. The Old Testament, the Hebrew Bible; II. The Apocrypha and the New Testament. NY 1989, Scribner's. xix-435 p.; xii-412 p. $175. 0-684-19098-2; 9-0 [8487-7 both; TDig 37,45: interpretive essays]. 33 + 29 art., infra.

378 ᴱ**Avery-Peck** Alan J., New perspectives on ancient Judaism, 4. The literature of early rabbinic Judaism; issues in Talmudic redaction and criticism. Lanham MD 1989, UPA. 168 p. $18.50 [JAAR 57,681].

379 ᴱ**Bloom** Harold, The Gospels [9 reprints (*Frei* H., *Frye* N., *Schüssler Fiorenza* E.; *Girard* R. ...)]: Modern critical interpretations. NY 1988, Chelsea. vii-187 p. $24.50. 0-87754-911-7 [TDig 36,370].

380 ᴱ**Borgonovo** Gianantonio, I profeti e i libri profetici: Piccola Enc. Biblica. R 1987, Borla. 400 p. Lit. 30.000. – ᴿCC 140 (1989,2) 89s (G. L. *Prato*: quarto volume di una serie programmata da Desclée).

381 ᴱ**Bourg** Dominique, *al.*, Variations johanniques [*Beaude* P.-M., *al.*]: Parole présente. P 1989, Cerf. 266 p. F 120. 2-204-03189-5. 12 art., infra.

382 ᴱ**Bovon** F., *Rouiller* G., Exegesis; problems of method and exercises in reading [Gn 22; Lk 15; 1975 ➤ 56,316... 60,399]: ᵀ*Miller* D. G. Pittsburgh 1978, Pickwick. x-169 p. $15 pa. – ᴿSWJT 32,3 (1989s) 56s (E. E. *Ellis*: nothing on why now).

383 ᴱ**Brekelmans** Chris H. W., Questions disputées d'Ancien Testament²ʳᵉᵛ [ᴱ*Vervenne* M.; ¹1974 ➤ 56,1662] – Continuing questions in Old Testament method and theology: BiblETL 33. Lv 1989, Peeters. 250 p. Fb 1200.

384 ᴱ**Brown** R. E., *Fitzmyer* J. A., *Murphy* R. E., **NJBC:** The New Jerome Biblical Commentary [¹1968 ➤ 50,1419]. ENJ 1990 [actually 1989 ➤ CBQ 51,311; TDig 37,78], Prentice Hall / L 1989 Chapman. xlvii-1484 p.; £60. 0-13-624934-0 / 0-225-66588-3 [BL 90,68s, A. *Auld*] 83 art., infra.

385 ᴱ**Bühler** P., *Habermacher* J.-F., La narration; quand le récit devient communication; postf. *Ricoeur* P.: Lieux Théologiques 12. Genève 1988, Labor et Fides. 310 p. [TR 85,521, some tit. pp.; infra].

386 ᴱ**Burden** J. J., *Prinsloo* W. S., Tweegesprek met God [= Dialogue with God...]: Die Literatuur van die Ou Testament 3. Cape Town 1987, Tafelberg. R 39. – ᴿOTEssays 2,2 (1989) 81ss (Afrikaans; no author).

387 ᴱ**Clements** R. E. [SOTS survey volume] The world of ancient Israel; sociological, anthropological and political perspectives. C 1989, Univ. xi-436 p. £45 ($65). 0-521-34243-0 [BL 90,13]. 18 art., infra.

388 ᴱ**Conn** Harvie M., Inerrancy and hermeneutic; a tradition, a challenge, a debate. GR 1988, Baker. 276 p. 14 art. [JBL 108,566].

389 ᴱ**Crown** A. D., The Samaritans. Tü 1989, Mohr. xxi-865 p. DM 398. 3-16-145237-2 [BL 90,131, J. R. *Bartlett*; RÉJ 149,198 & ZAW 102,160, tit. pp.]. – ᴿArTGran 52 (1989) 348s (A. S. *Muñoz*); TGegw 32 (1989) 312-4 (H. *Giesen*).

390 ᴱ**Davidson** H. E. The Seer in Celtic and other traditions. E 1989, Donald. 0-85976-259-9 [BL 90,152].

391 ᴱ**Day** Peggy L., Gender and difference in ancient Israel. Minneapolis 1989, Fortress. xiii-209 p. 195-202 bibliog. (*Chase* Debra A.). 0-8006-2393-2. 12 art., infra.

392 ᴱ**Dearman** Andrew, Studies in the Mesha inscription and Moab [for MORTON W. H.]: Atlanta 1989, Scholars. xii-324 p. $20; sb./pa. $13. 1-55540-356-4; 7-3 [TDig 37,88]. *Dearman* p. 155-210; *Drinkard* J. F. 132-154; *Graham* M. P. 41-92; *Jackson* K. P. 96-120; *Mattingly* G. L. (religion) 211-238; *Miller* J. M. 1-40.

393 ᴱ**Drewery** Benjamin, *Baulkham* Richard, Scripture, tradition and reason; a study in the criteria of Christian doctrine. 1988, Books Int. 308 p. $33 [JAAR 57,887].

394 ᴱ**Epp** Eldon J., *MacRae* George W.†, The New Testament and its modern interpreters: SBL Bible Mod. Interp. 3. Atlanta/Ph 1989, Scholars/Fortress. xxxii-601 p. 0-89130-881-4; pa. 2-2 / 0-8006-0724-4. 19 art.; infra. – ᴿNewTR 2,4 (1989) 96s (Barbara E. *Reid*).

395 ᴱ**Exum** J. Cheryl, Signs and wonders; biblical texts in literary focus: SBL Semeia Studies 18. Atlanta 1989, Scholars. vii-247 p. 1-555-40249-6; pa. 50-X [TLZ 115,365, tit. pp.]. 6 art. with responses, infra.

396 ᴱ**Filippi** Alfio, [*Bianchi* E., *Sacchi* P., *al.*] *a*) Peccato e male nell'AT / NT / Padri; *b*) 'Ed ebbero vergogna' AT / NT / Padri: ParSpV 19/20 (1989). 256 p./303 p.; Lit. 15.000. → 2175; 2170.

398 ᴱ**Gray** Donald, The Word in season; the use of the Bible in liturgy [... in view of an international ecumenical lectionary]. 1988, Canterbury Press. vii-141 p. £6 pa. – ᴿTLond 92 (1989) 342s (T. *Baker*: risk of a soporific).

399 [*Guimot* J.-N. présent.] Figures de l'Ancien Testament chez les Pères: Biblia Patristica Cah. 2. Strasbourg 1989, Centre d'analyse. 312 p. – ᴿIrénikon 62 (1989) 593s (A. L.).

400 ᴱ**Hacker** Joseph, Shalem, Studies in the history of the Jews in Eretz-Israel [I-IV ...], V. J 1987, Ben-Zvi. x-284 p. – ᴿRÉJ 148 (1989) 164s (G. *Nahon*: 'with English summaries' so presumably in Hebrew).

401 **Horsley** G. H. R., Linguistic essays: New documents illustrating early Christianity 5 ['rather different in conception from its predecessors' p. 1], with cumulative indexes to vol. 1-5 (*Swinn* S. P. p. 153-214; plus addenda and corrigenda 135-52). Sydney 1989, Macquarie Univ. 214 p. $52; pa. A$31. 0-85837-636-9; 44-X.

402 **Kamphaus** Franz [p. 9-16], *al.*, ... und machen einander reich: Beiträge zur Arm/Reich-Problematik reflektiert am Lukas-Evangelium [*Lentzen-Deis* F. → 5096]. Annweiler 1989, Plöger. 118 p. 3-924574-16-2. 4 art. (*Schwarz* Leo 69-93; *Zauzich* Christine 95-118).

403 ᴱ**Kasher** A., ⊕ *Yavan* wᵉ-*Roma*, Greece and Rome in Eretz-Israel, collected essays. J 1989, Yad Ben Zvi. 965-217-059-3 [OIAc S89].

404 ᴱ**Kuhn** Johannes, Manchmal setzt der Himmel Zeichen; die Bibel in meinem Leben [48 answers from important people; D. *Sölle*, H. *Küng*...]. Stu 1989, Quell. 319 p.; photos. 3-7918-1987-9.

405 Lectures anciennes de la Bible: Biblia Patristica Cahier 1, 1987: ᴿBTAM 14 (1989) p. 572, nº 1227 [J. *Winandy*, indicating no relation either to ᶠBᴇɴᴏîᴛ André (→ 3,23) or to ᴱ*Maraval* P. (→ 3,350); tit. pp.].

406 ᴱ**Lindars** Barnabas, Law and religion; essays on the place of the Law in Israel and early Christianity. c. 1988, J. Clarke. £25. 13 art. [TLond 92,349].

408 ᴱ**Lowe** Malcolm, People, land and state of Israel; Jewish and Christian perspectives = Immanuel 22s (1989) 237 p.; bibliog. 215-237 (*Skoog* Lena). 0302-8127. 12 art.; 6 infra.

409 ᴱ**Lukken** Gerard, Semiotiek en christelijke uitingsvormen; de semiotiek van A. J. Gʀᴇɪᴍᴀs en de Parijse school toegepast op bijbel en liturgie [... SEMANET]. Hilversum/Antwerpen 1987, Gooi & S. / Scriptoria. 288 p. ƒ 59.50. – ᴿStreven 55 (1987s) 748-752 (P. *Beentjes*).

410 ᴱ**Meer** W. van der, *Moor* J. C. de, The structural analysis of biblical and Canaanite poetry [15 art.]: JStOT Sup 74, 1988 → 4,3121 [BL 90,85, N. *Wyatt*: '9 authors testing the same theory is perhaps a first outside the physics lab']. – ᴿETL 65 (1989) 431-6 (M. *Vervenne*: 'Kampen circle' not showing sufficient concern for other schools); ExpTim 100 (1988s) 430s (W. G. E. *Watson*).

411 ᴱ**Neusner** Jacob, *al.*, New perspectives on ancient Judaism, I. Religion, literature, and society in ancient Israel; formative Christianity and Judaism; formative Judaism [= ᶠKᴇᴇ Howard C., The social world of formative Christianity and Judaism 1988 → 4,77]; II. Religion, literature, and society in ancient Israel, formative Christianity and Judaism; Ancient Israel and Christianity [also part of ᶠKee]; III. Judaic and Christian interpretation of texts; contents and contexts. Lanham MD 1987 [... s], UPA. xi-172 p.; $13.50 / xi-172 p.; $28.50 / 218 p.; $30.25. 0-8191-651-4-X; 97-2; 63-8 [TDig 37,175: series to continue].

412 **Noort** Ed, *al.*, Sleutelen aan het verbond; biblische en theologische essays. Boxtel/Brugge 1989, KBS/Tabor. 187 p. *f* 22,50. – 90-6173-447-9 / Tabor 90-6597-134-3. 8 art., infra. – ᴿTsTNijm 29 (1989) 421 (T. *Brattinga*).

413 ᴱ**O'Connor** M. P., *Freedman* D. N., Backgrounds for the Bible [= 19 of the articles in The Bible and its traditions 1983 ➤ 64,291 + 5 others] ➤ 3,356: WL 1987, Eisenbrauns. xii-369 p. $17.50. 0-931464-30-7. – ᴿBL (1989) 89 (A. *Gelston*).
ᴱ**Robbins** Gregory A., Genesis 1-3, 1989 ➤ 2171.

416 ᴱ**Sandt** H. van de, *Tongeren* L. van, Naar mijn daden word Ik genoemd; over de betekenis en het gebruik van de Godsnaam [Yʜᴡʜ in translations]. Boxtel/Brugge 1989, KBS/Tabor. 176 p. *f* 21,50. 90-61-73448-7 / 90-6597-144-0. – ᴿStreven 57 (1989s) 272 (P. *Beentjes*); TsTNijm 29 (1989) 405 (A. *Schoors*: authors, topics; no tit. pp.).

417 ᴱ**Schneemelcher** Wilhelm, Neutestamentliche Apokryphen [I.⁵ 1987 ➤ 3, a298*; 4,b1] II.⁵ [some articles revised from ᴱ*Hennecke* E., 1904; introductions all new]. Tü 1989, Mohr. viii-703 p. 3-16-145181-3. 8 art. [Kap. XIII-XXI], infra.

418 ᴱ**Smith** Morton, *Hoffmann* R. J., What the Bible really says about capital punishment, the future, government, marriage and divorce, miracles ... slavery, war, wealth, women. Buffalo 1989, Prometheus. 256 p. 0-87975-468-0. 13 art.; 5 infra; p. 135-155, *Lang* B., Segregation and intolerance (OT esp. Hosea to Josiah 'internal control, punishment, and persecution'; Jesus more tolerant, 'Paul's reestablishment of segregation and intolerance'); p. 8: not true that we cannot understand texts without knowing their backgrounds [< ZAW 102,167]. – ᴿExpTim 101 (1989) 123 (C. S. *Rodd*: attempts the impossible and fails spectacularly).

419 ᴱ**Sola-Solé** J. M., *al.*, Hispania judaica; studies on the history, language, and literature of the Jews in the Hispanic world, III. Language. Barc c. 1988, Puvill. 143 p. – ᴿHenoch 11 (1989) 378s (B. *Chiesa*: 4 art. destinati a confluire in un Atlante linguistico delle comunità giudaiche parlanti judézmo).

420 ᴱ**Stachowiak** L., *Rubinkiewicz* R., ❷ Duch Święty — Duch Boży ... The Holy Spirit; the Spirit of God: Biblical Subsidia 7. Lublin 1985, KUL. 127 p. zł 400. – ᴿJStJud 20 (1989) 89s (Z. J. *Kapera*: Rubinkiewicz and Tʀᴏɴɪᴄᴀ A. utilize pseudepigrapha).

421 ᴱ**Stone** Michael E., *Satran* David, Emerging Judaism; studies on the fourth and third centuries ʙ.ᴄ.ᴇ. Minneapolis 1989, Fortress. xiv-178 p. [RelStR 16,257, W. L. *Humphreys*]. 0-8006-2090-9 [E. *Bickerman* 1949; F. *Cross* 1966, M. *Hengel* 1980; A. *Momigliano* 1975; M. *Smith* 1971; V. *Tcherikover* 1959].

423 ᴱ**Struppe** Ursula, Studien zum Messiasbild im Alten Testament: Stu Biblische Aufsätzbände 6. Stu 1989, KBW. 336 p. DM 39 pa. 3-460-06061-1 [NTAbs 38,266]. 13 art.

424 Studia z biblystyki 4. Wsz 1984, Akad. Teol. Katolickiej. 376 p. – ᴿSTWsz 26,1 (1988) 267-273 (G. *Rafiński*).

425 ᴱ**Swartley** W. M., Essays on war and peace; Bible and early Church: Occas. Papers 9. Elkhart ɪɴ 1986, Institute of Mennonite Studies. 154 p. $6.50. 0-963273-09-7 [NTAbs 33,124: *Fritz* M., OT ḥerem; *Pries* E., scapegoat; *Lind* M., Lᴏʜғɪɴᴋ's Gewalt 1983; *Dyck* P. on Sᴛᴜʜʟᴍᴀᴄʜᴇʀ; *Lugibihl* J.; ... *Friesen* J.].

426 ᴱ**Tyson** J. B., Luke-Acts and the Jewish people. Minneapolis 1988, Augsburg. 160 p. $16. 0-8066-2390-X [ÉTRel 64,674].

427 Wie aktuell ist das AT? Beiträge aus Israel und Berlin 3. B 1985, Inst. Kirche und Judentum. 106 p. – ᴿJEcuSt 26 (1989) 366s (J. A. *Soggin*).
428 Das Zeugnis des Jesaja: Impulse aus dem AT. Stu 1988, KBW. 104 p. – ᴿZAW 101 (1989) 480 (H.-C. *Schmitt*: 6-page items of popularization).

A1.4 *Plurium compilationes* **theologicae.**

429 ᴱAgnes Mario, Dignità e vocazione della donna; per una lettura della 'Mulieris dignitatem' [GIOVANNI PAOLO II, 15.VIII.1988 + 14 commenti]: Oss Rom Quaderno 9. Vaticano 1989. 190 p. 88-209-1613-4.
429* ᴱAltner Günter, Ökologische Theologie; Perspektiven zur Orientierung. Stu 1989, Kreuz. 429 p. DM 36. 3-7831-0959-0 [TsTNijm 29,438]. – ᴿTGL 79 (1989) 625s (W. *Beinert*).
430 **Amos** T. L., *al.*, De ore Domini; preacher and word in the Middle Ages: Studies in medieval culture 27. Kalamazoo 1989, Medieval Inst. xiv-269 p. [RHE 85,113*].
431 ᴱAtkinson Clarissa W., *al.*, Shaping new vision; gender and values in American culture: Harvard Women's Studies in Religion 5. AA 1987, UMI Research. viii-228 p. $35. – ᴿHorizons 16 (1989) 195s (Denise L. *Carmody*).
432 ᴱBan Joseph D., The Christological foundation for contemporary theological education. Macon GA 1988, Mercer Univ. vii-232 p. $30 [JBL 108,377]. 11 art.
433 ᴱBeinert Wolfgang, *Hoeren* Jürgen [SW-Funk], 'Dien leuchtend Angesicht, Maria ...' Das Bild der Mutter Jesu in der Glaubensgeschichte: Tb 1565. FrB 1988, Herder. 125 p. DM 8. – ᴿTR 85 (1989) 403s (F. *Courth*).
434 ᴱBellah Robert N., *Greenspahn* Frederick E., Uncivil religion; interreligious hostility in America. NY 1987, Crossroad. x-235 p. $18. – ᴿHorizons 16 (1989) 165s (J. A. *Coleman*).
435 ᴱBenstock Shari, Feminist issues in literary scholarship. Bloomington 1987, Indiana Univ. viii-242 p. $27.50; pa. $10 [RelStR 16,63, Kathryn A. *Rabuzzi*].
436 ᴱBerger David, History and hate; the dimensions of anti-Semitism [in antiquity: *Feldman* L.; *Cohen* S. ...]. NY 1986, Jewish Publ. ix-138. – ᴿJQR 79 (1988s) 279s (K. R. *Stow*).
439 ᴱabp. Birmingham, The unsealed fountain; essays on the Christian spiritual tradition [Oscott lectures 1983; some OT ...]. Dublin c. 1988, Veritas. 155 p. – ᴿDowR 107 (1989) 149-151 (J. P. H. *Clark*).
440 ᴱBockmühl Klaus, Die Aktualität der Theologie Adolf SCHLATTERS. Giessen 1988, Brunnen. vi-118 p. DM 19,80. – ᴿTLZ 114 (1989) 760s (R. *Marschner*).
441 ᴱBöhme Wolfgang, Evolution und Gottesglaube; ein Lese- und Arbeitsbuch zum Gespräch zwischen Naturwissenschaft und Theologie. Gö 1988, Vandenhoeck & R. 405 p. DM 58. – ᴿTR 85 (1989) 158s (W. *Bröker*).
443 ᴱBraaten Carl E., *Clayton* Philip, The theology of Wolfhart PANNENBERG; twelve American critiques, with an autobiographical essay and response. Minneapolis 1988, Augsburg. 352 p.; bibliog. p. 337-352. $30 [RelStR 16,240, J. *Glasse*].
444 ᴱBrändle R., *Stegemann* E. W., Franz OVERBECKs unerledigte Anfragen an das Christentum [11 essays for 150th anniversary of his birth]. Mü 1988, Kaiser. 237 p. DM 49. 3-459-01755-4 [NTAbs 33,232].

445 ᴱBrockway Allan, al. (Van Buren P., Rendtorff R. ...], The theology of the churches and the Jewish people, statements by WCC and its member churches, with a commentary. Geneva 1988, WCC. x-186 p. Fs 19,50. – ᴿRTLv 20 (1989) 384s (A. de Halleux: satisfying answer except to 'But who do you say that I am?').

446 ᴱBrown Neil, Challenges to ministry: Faith and culture 15. Sydney 1989, Catholic Institute. [vi-] 241 p. 0-908-224-14-1. 14 art.; 2 infra.

447 ᴱBühler Pierre, Humain à l'image de Dieu; la théologie et les sciences humaines face au problème de l'anthropologie: Travaux de 3ᵉ cycle en théologie systématique des Facultés de théologie des Universités romandes 1985-6: Lieux Théologiques 15. Genève 1989, Labor et Fides. 324 p. Fs 32. [TR 86,82, tit. pp.].

448 ᴱCampbell Joseph, Myths, dreams, and religion. Dallas 1988 = 1970, Spring. 255 p. 0-88214-334-4. 11 art., 2 infra (OT-NT).

449 ᴱCamps Arnulf, Oecumenische inleiding in de missiologie; teksten en konteksten van het wereldchristendom. Kampen 1988, Kok. 525 p. ƒ 99. – ᴿTR 85 (1989) 527 (tit. pp.).

450 ᴱCardon P., Dieu, le monde et l'homme; hasard ou projet? 17 réponses [en rapport avec exposition de la 'Mission Intérieure de l'Église Évangélique Luthérienne de France', Paris 1987s]. P 1988, O.E.I.L. 169 p. – ᴿRHPR 69 (1989) 486 (G. Siegwalt: indication du contenu sans pp.).

451 ᴱChernus Ira, Lintenthal Edward T., A shuddering dawn; religious studies and the nuclear age. Albany 1989, SUNY. 227 p. [JAAR 57,682].

452 ᴱCollet Giancarlo, Der Christus der Armen; das Christuszeugnis der lateinamerikanischen Befreiungstheologien. FrB 1988, Herder. 231 p. – ᴿSalesianum 51 (1989) 367s (L. A. Gallo).

453 Communio: strumento internazionale per un lavoro teologico; Milano 1989, Jaca [also Eng. ND; franç. P; deutsch = IkaZ, etc.]. 103. La remissione dei peccati; 104. Per costruire la pace; 105. BALTHASAR; 106. La rivoluzione francese; 107. I miracoli; 108. L'immaginazione religiosa.

454 Concilium (français P 1989, Beauchesne; Eng. etc., numérotés un peu différemment; deutsch = IZT); chaque c. 160 p.; F 65; tous F 230 (étr. 300). – 221. La révolution française et l'Église, ᴱGeffré C., Jossua J.-P. – 222. La musique et l'expérience de Dieu, ᴱCollins Mary. – 223. L'éthique dans les sciences de la nature, ᴱMieth Dietmar, Pohier Jacques. – 224. Catéchisme universel ou inculturation?, ᴱMetz J.-B., Schillebeeckx E. – 225. Sport, société et religion, ᴱColeman John, Baum Gregory. – 226. La maternité; expérience, institution et théologie, ᴱSchüssler Fiorenza Elisabeth, Carr Ann.

455 ᴱCosta Ruy O., One faith, many cultures; inculturation, indigenization, and contextualization. Mkn/CM 1988, Orbis / Boston Theological Institute. xvii-161 p. $11 [TR 85,527].

455* ᴱCurran Charles E., McCormick Richard A., Dissent in the Church: Readings in Moral Theology 6. NY 1988, Paulist. 552 p. $15. – ᴿAmerica 160 (1989) 43s (H. McSorley).

456 ᴱDekker G., Gäbler K. U., Secularisatie in theologisch perspectief: Amst VU Bezinningscentrum 17. Kampen 1988, Kok. 173 p. ƒ 32,50 [TR 85 (1989) 261: tit. pp.].

457 [ᴱDoré J., CERIT] Les chrétiens et leurs doctrines [→ 4,355] Le christianisme et la foi chrétienne 3. P 1987, Desclée. 447 p. – ᴿNRT 111 (1989) 97s (V. Roisel).

458 [E]**Duke** James O., *Streetman* Robert F., BARTH and SCHLEIERMACHER; beyond the impasse? Ph 1988, Fortress. 186 p. 0-8006-0888-7. – [R]RExp 86 (1989) 446s (D. L. *Mueller*).

458* [E]**Eicher** Peter, Der lebendige Gott: Neue Summe Theologie 1. FrB 1988, Herder. 456 p. DM 65. 3-451-20413-4. – [R]TPQ 137 (1989) 415s (R. *Schulte*); TsTNijm 29 (1989) 185s (T. *Schoof*).

459 [E]**Ellwood** Robert S., Eastern spirituality in America; selected writings: Sources of American Spirituality. NY 1987, Paulist. vi-246 p. $17. – [R]RelStR 15 (1989) 373 (J. *Borelli*).

460 [E]**Farnham** Christie, The impact of feminist research in the academy. Bloomington 1987, Indiana Univ. ix-228 p. $27.50; pa. $13. 0-253-32807-1; -20448-4. – [R]AmHR 94 (1989) 700s (Lindoe L. *Clark*); RelStR 15 (1989) 339 (Kathryn A. *Rabuzzi*).

461 [E]**Ferm** Deane W., Liberation theology, North American style: Interreligious Exploration. NY 1988, International Religious Fd. vi-284 p. $10 pa. [Horizons 16,206].

462 [E]**Fernández Rodríguez** Fernando, Estudios sobre la Encíclica 'Laborem exercens': BAC 492. M 1987, Católica. xvi-757 p. 84-220-1295-2. – [R]EstE 64 (1989) 594-6 (G. *Higuera*); NRT 111 (1989) 115s (L. *Volpe*).

463 [E]**Fois** M., *Monachino* V., *Litva* F., [per il 50° anniversario della Facoltà di Storia Eccl. dell'Università Gregoriana] Dalla Chiesa antica alla Chiesa moderna: Miscellanea Historiae Pontificiae 50. R 1983, Pont. Univ. Gregoriana. xxviii-533 p. – [R]RHE 84 (1989) 876-8 (R. *Aubert*).

464 [E]**Gabriel** Karl, Die gesellschaftliche Verantwortung der Kirche; zur Enzyklika Sollicitudo rei socialis: Arbeiterbewegung und Kirche 9. Dü 1988, Patmos. 329 p. DM 29,80 pa. 13 art.; 2 infra [TR 85,349, tit. pp.].

465 [E]**Gordon** Haim, *Grob* Leonard, Education for peace; testimonies from world religions. Mkn 1987, Orbis. 240 p. – [R]TGL 79 (1989) 322-4 (K. J. *Tossou*).

466 [E]**Górka** L., *Hryniewicz* L., ☉ Eucharystia i posłannictwo [mission]. Wsz 1987, Verbinum. 192 p. – [R]AtKap 110 (1988) 151-5 (T. *Lewandowski*).

467 **Gort** J. D., *al.*, Dialogue and syncretism; an interdisciplinary approach: Currents of Encounter. Amst c. 1988, Rodopi. *f*80; pa. 29.50. 17 art. [Kairos 30,29 adv.].

468 [E]**Gunton** Colin E., *Hardy* Daniel W., On being the Church; essays on the Christian community. E 1989, Clark. 263 p. £13. 0-567-09501-0 [TDig 37,176]. – [R]EcuR 41 (1989) 626-9 (A. *Sell*).

469 [E]**Hagen** June, Gender matters; women's studies for the Christian community. GR 1989, Zondervan. $15. ...-23571-5 [JBL 108,554 adv. 'For people who can't not think'].

470 [E]**Hammond** Phillip E., The sacred in a secular age 1985 → 1,354; 2,8684: [R]HeythJ 30 (1989) 84s (R. *Gill*: exciting, useful for sociology of religion course).

471 [E]**Hawley** John S., Saints and virtues. Berkeley 1987, Univ. California. xxiv-256 p. 13 art.; P. *Brown* on Christian late antiquity. – [R]HistRel 29 (1989s) 177-9 (D. A. *Pittman*).

472 [E]**Hough** Joseph C.[J], *Wheeler* Barbara G., Beyond clericalism; the congregation as a focus for theological education [in the spirit of ex-missionary prof. James F. HOPEWELL, † 1984]. Atlanta 1988, Scholars. 151 p. $29; pa. $19. – [R]TTod 46 (1989s) 331.334 (J. R. *Taylor*).

473 [E]**Hudson** Anne, *Wilks* Michael, From Ockham to Wyclif: Studies in Church History, Subsidia 5. NY 1987, Blackwell. xv-486 p. $50. – [R]TS

49 (1988) 743-5 [T. E. *Morrissey*: 'From Ockham's birth (1385) to Wyclif's death (1384)...'??].

474 ᴱ**Hughes** Richard T., The American quest for the primitive Church. Urbana 1988, Univ. Illinois. viii-257 p. $32.50; pa. $13. – ᴿRelStR 15 (1989) 369s (D. G. *Roebuck*).

475 ᴱ**Jones** Ivor H., *Wilson* Kenneth B., Freedom and grace [for 250th anniversary of C. & J. WESLEY conversion]. L 1988, Epworth. vi-201 p. £7 pa. – ᴿTLond 92 (1989) 408s (J. *Kent*; a certain pathos in their all tying John Wesley to BALTHASAR or CUPITT or WHITEHEAD or someone else).

476 ᴱ**Jones** R. Kenneth, Sickness and sectarianism; exploratory studies in medical and religious sectarianism. Aldershot 1985, Gower. ix-158 p. £14.50. – ᴿHeythJ 30 (1989) 85s (R. *Gill*).

477 ᴱ**Kauffman** Christopher J., Makers of the Catholic community; the [bishops-authorized] bicentennial history of the Catholic Church in America: *a*) ᴱ**Kennelly** Karen, American Catholic women; xviii-231 p.; $25. – *b*) **Reher** Margaret M., Catholic intellectual life in America; xxiii-183 p.; $22.50. – *c*) **Liptak** Dolores, Immigrants and their church; xviii-221 p.; $25. – *d*) **Chinnici** Joseph P., Living stones... spiritual life; xxiv-258 p.; $30. – *e*) ᴱ**Fogarty** Gerald P. Patterns of episcopal [i.e. bishops'] leadership; xlvi-306 p.; $30. – *f*) **O'Brien** David, Public Catholicism; xx-281 p.; $30. NY 1989, Macmillan. 0-20-917302-7; 25902-9; 19231-5; 05475-3; 10611-7; 23831-5. All six $160 [TDig 36,173].

478 **Keller** Carl-A., *al.*, Jesus ausserhalb der Kirche; das Jesusverständnis in neuen religiösen Bewegungen: Weltanschauungen im Gespräch 5. FrS/Z 1989, Paulus/Theol.-V. 159 p. DM 22 [TR 85,530].

479 ᴱ**Khoury** A. T., *Hünermann* P., Wozu und wie beten; die Antwort der Weltreligionen: Tb 1644. FrB 1989, Herder. S. 67-99, *Vetter* D., Vom Beten im Judentum [< ZAW 101,479].

480 ᴱ**Kieckhefer** Richard, *Bond* George D., Sainthood; its manifestations in world religions. Berkeley 1988, Univ. California. xii-263 p. $38.50. – ᴿTS 50 (1989) 609s (G. P. *Evans*).

481 ᴱ**King** Karen L., *a*) Images of the feminine in Gnosticism: Studies in Antiquity and Christianity. Ph 1988, Fortress. xxi-455 p. 19 art. + 13 responses (SBL Inst. Ant. Chr., Claremont, Nov. 19-25, 1985). – ᴿExp-Tim 101 (1989s) 216 (C. M. *Tuckett*). – *b*) Women and spirituality; voices of protest and promise: Women in Society. L 1989, Macmillan. xii-273 p. £8. 0- 333-39605-7 / 6-5. – ᴿTsTNijm 29 (1989) 417s (Barbara de *Groot-Kopetzky*).

481* ᴱ**Kirby** John, *Thompson* William M., [Eric] VOEGELIN and the theologian; ten studies in interpretation: Toronto StT 10, 1983 ➜ 65,367: ᴿRelStT 7,1 (1987) 71s (P. J. *Cahill*).

482 ᴱ**Kraemer** Ross S., Maenads, martyrs, matrons, monastics; a source book on women's religions in the Greco-Roman world. Ph 1988, Fortress. xxxii-429 p. $20. 0-8006-0855-0; pa. 2071-2. 36 items translated from EURIPIDES, PHILO, JEROME, Mishna; then 41 by women, largely epitaphs; then 50 on religious office (Montanists etc.) and 12 on the feminine divine (OVID, Odes of Solomon, NagH). – ᴿRelStR 15 (1989) 353 (Ann *Loades*).

483 ᴱ**Lambrecht** J., Hoelang nog en waarom toch? God, mens en lijden: Nikè 18. Lv 1988, Acco. 295 p. [ETL 65,11*].

485 ᴱ**Lee Jung Young**, An emerging theology in world perspective; commentary on Korean Minjung theology. Mystic CT 1988, Twenty-third. vii-211 p. $15. – ᴿTContext 6,2 (1989) 110 (G. *Evers*); TS 50 (1989) 410s

(D. L. *McNamara*: essays by prestigious theologians, R. M. BROWN, H.
COX, Letty RUSSELL, *al.*).
486 ᴱLehmann Karl, *Kasper* Walter, H. U. v. BALTHASAR, Gestalt und Werk.
Köln 1989, Communio. 359 p. DM 48 [TR 86, 32-5, H. *Vorgrimler*: B.s
'bedauerliche Eigentümlichkeiten'].
487 ᴱLienemann W., Die Finanzen der Kirche; Studien zu Struktur,
Geschichte und Legitimation kirchlicher Ökonomie. Mü 1989, Kaiser.
S. 485-524, *Crüsemann* F., Religiöse Abgaben und ihre Kritik im AT
[ZAW 102,147].
488 ᴱLonergan Anne, *Richards* Caroline, Thomas BERRY and the new
cosmology. Mystic CT 1987, Twenty-third. 112 p. $8. – ᴿNewTR 2,1
(1989) 110s (J. P. *Szura*).
489 ᴱLubahn E., *Rodenberg* O., Das Wort vom Kreuz; Geschehen – Denken
– Theologie²: TVG Mg 337. Giessen 1988, Brunnen. v-210 p. DM 26 pa.
3-7655-9337-0 [NTAbs 33,265: *Michel* O. on Phlp 3,2-21 etc.; *Maier* G. on
redemption; *Betz* O. on history of the kerygma ...].
490 ᴱMarx J., Sainteté et martyre dans les religions du livre: ProbHistChr 19.
Bru 1989, Univ. Inst. des religions et de la laicité. 159 p. Fb 700 [RHE
85,110*].
491 ᴱMeier Johannes, Zur Geschichte des Christentums in Lateinamerika:
Kath. Akad. Freiburg. Mü 1988, Schnell & S. 93 p. DM 18 [TLZ
113, 904].
492 ᴱMoll Helmut, The Church and women, a compendium. SF 1988,
Ignatius. 277 p. $15. 0-89870-164-3. 16 art., mostly from German
[TDig 36,350].
493 ᴱMoltmann-Wendel Elisabeth, Weiblichkeit in der Theologie; Verdrängung und Wiederkehr: Siebenstern 494. Gü 1988, Mohn. 188 p.
[ETL 65, 12*].
494 ᴱMüller Hubert, *Pottmeyer* Hermann J., Die Bischofskonferenz; theologischer und juridischer Status [über das 'instrumentum laboris' der
Bischofskongregation]. Dü 1989, Patmos. 304 p. DM 50. – ᴿMüTZ 40
(1989) 375s (F. *Bernard*); NRT 111 (1989) 1038 (L. *Volpe*); TR 85 (1989)
171 (tit. pp.).
495 ᴱMüller H.-P., Was ist Wahrheit? Stu 1989, Kohlhammer. 119 p.
DM 39,80. ⇥ 4,390; 3-17-010532-9 [NTAbs 33,408: his own essay is on
myth and kerygma in biblical theology; there are seven others on the
understanding of truth in various academic disciplines].
496 ᴱMyers Kenneth A., Aspiring to freedom; commentaries on JOHN PAUL
II's Encyclical 'The social concerns of the Church'. GR 1988, Eerdmans.
169 p. – ᴿAnnTh 3,1 (1989) 183-8 (J. M. de *Torre*, Eng.).
498 ᴱNi Chatháin P., *Richter* M., Irland und die Christenheit; Bibelstudien
und Mission: Tü Europa-Zentrum. Stu 1987, Klett-Cotta. xii-523 p. –
ᴿPrzegląd Historyczny 79 (1988) 362-7 (J. *Strzelczyk*) [RHE 84,230*].
499 ᴱNiewiadomski J., Verweigerte Mündigkeit; politisches Kultur und die
Kirche; Theologische Trends 2. Thaur 1989, Österr. Kulturverlag.
254 p. DM 28. 3-85395-131-7 [BL 90,110, R. J. *Coggins*: Ruth FRICK-
PÖDER uses 2 Sam 13,20 and J. M. OESCH Jg-1Sm].
500 ᴱNørgaard-Højen Peder, *al.*, På enhedens vej; Bijdrag til den økumeniske
bevægelses historie i Danmark i det 20. århundrede. Århus 1989, Anis.
393 p. – ᴿSvTKv 65 (1989) 180-2 (H. *Fagerberg*).
501 ᴱPixley Jorge, Hacia una fe evangélica latinoamericana; una perspectiva
bautista. Costa Rica 1988, Dep. Ecuménico. 220 p. $7. – ᴿRExp 86
(1989) 124s (J. *Gros*).

502 ᴱPuech Henri-Charles [capitolo introduttivo di *Pincherle* A., *al.*, < sua Introd. 1978, 3-343], Il cristianesimo: Universale 222. R 1988, Laterza. 407 p.; p. 411-767. Lit. 44.000. 84-420-3205-0.

503 ᴱQuacquarelli Antonio, Complementi interdisciplinari di patrologia. R 1989, Città Nuova. 920 p. Lit. 100.000.

504 ᴱRabil Albertᴶ, Renaissance humanism. Ph 1988, Univ. Pennsylvania. $130. – ᴿJAAR 57 (1989) 829-842 (P. I. *Kaufman*: begins and ends with Paul O. KRISTELLER).

505 ᴱRace Alan, Theology against the nuclear horizon. L 1988, SCM. 181 p. £8.50 pa. – ᴿTLond 92 (1989) 526-8 (P. *Oestreicher*, severe: abstruse and ineffectual).

506 ᴱRanson P., Saint AUGUSTIN [40 art.]: Les Dossiers H. P 1988, Âge d'Homme. 491 p. F 270. – ᴿNRT 111 (1989) 594s (L.-J. *Renard*: full of disagreements based on Augustine's ambiguities).

507 La religion... sans retour ni détour: Esprit (1986, 4s). F 72. 25 art. [ÉTRel 64, 602 sans auteurs, titres, pages].

508 ᴱRussell Letty M., *al.*, Inheriting our mother's gardens; feminist theology in third world perspective. Ph 1988, Westminster. 181 p. $13. – ᴿTTod 46 (1989s) 430-2 (Mary M. *Fulkerson*: feminist recovery of Hispanic, Asian, African roots).

509 [Sassu Marina, *al.*] L'audacia insolente; la cooperazione femminile 1886-1986. Venezia 1986, Marsilio. 352 p. Lit. 35.000. – ᴿStPatav 36 (1989) 230s (S. *Tramontin*).

510 ᴱSchindler David, [*Bohm* David + 6], Beyond mechanism; the universe in recent physics and Catholic thought. Lanham MD 1986, UPA. x-156 p. $24; pa. $11.50. – ᴿZygon 24 (1989) 119s (R. *Ringo*).

512 ᴱSchmid Hans H., Mythos und Rationalität: Veröffentlichungen der Wissenschaftlichen Gesellschaft für Theologie. Gü 1988, Mohn. 396 p. DM 42 [TR 85 (1989) 258, tit. pp.].

513 ᴱSchneider Theodor [*Gössmann* Elisabeth, *al.*] Mann und Frau; Grundproblem theologischer Anthropologie: QDisp 121. FrB 1989, Herder. 222 p. DM 38. – ᴿTR 85 (1989) 529 (tit. pp.).

514 ᴱSchreiter Robert J., *Hilkert* Mary Catherine, The praxis of Christian experience; an introduction to the theology of Edward SCHILLEBEECKX. SF 1989, Harper & R. x-164 p. $19 [RelStR 16,243, Mary L. *Schneider*]. 0-06-067137-5.

515 ᴱSchrotenboer Paul G., Roman Catholicism; a contemporary evangelical perspective. GR 1987, Baker. 99 p. 0-8010-8292-7. – ᴿRExp 86 (1989) 454 (E. G. *Hinson*).

516 Der schwarze Christus; Wege afrikanischer Christologie: Theologie der Dritter Welt 12. FrB 1989, Herder. 205 p. [TContext 7/1, 120, B. *Abeng*].

517 Seybold Michael, Fragen in der Kirche und an die Kirche: Fragen der Theologie und Seelsorge 6. Eichstätt 1988. 203 p. – ᴿForumKT 5 (1989) 227-9 (M. *Hauke*); ScripTPamp 21 (1989) 932-4 (A. *Cattaneo*).

518 ᴱSharma Arvind, Neo-Hindu views of Christianity. L 1988, Brill. vii-218 p. *f*80 [RelStR 16, 179, W. *Cenkner*].

519 ᴱShowalter Elaine, Speaking of gender. NY 1989, Routledge. viii-335 p.; ill. $39.50; pa. $14 [RelStR 16, 138, Kathryn A. *Rabuzzi*].

520 ᴱSpringer Kevin, Power encounters; stories of the work of the Holy Spirit in the world today [Vineyard movement]. SF 1988, Harper & R. 320 p. $11. 0-06-069537-4. – ᴿBS 146 (1989) 460s (K. L. *Sarles*).

521 ᴱStacey John, John WESLEY, contemporary perspectives. L 1988, Epworth. ix-242 p. $9.50 pa. 0-7162-0449-5. 19 contributors. – ᴿExpTim

100 (1988s) 160 (C.S. *Rodd* does not tell us *how* only Methodists pronounce the name correctly); TLond 92 (1989) 409s (J. *Kent*).

522 ᴱ**Swatos** William H., Religious sociology, interfaces and boundaries: Contributions to sociology 64. NY 1987, Greenwood.   xiv-194 p. $38. 12 art. [TR 85,173 tit. pp.].

523 ᴱ**Swinburne** Richard, Miracles [16 classical and modern essays]. NY 1989, Macmillan.   vi-210 p. [RelStR 16, 142, M.P. *Levine*].

524 ᴱ**Toso** Mario, Essere donna; studi sulla lettera apostolica 'Mulieris dignitatem' di GIOVANNI PAOLO II. T-Leumann 1989, Elle Di Ci. 375 p. Lit. 25.000. 98-01-11198-4 [Greg 70,829].

525 ᴱ**Vischer** Lukas, Reformiertes Zeugnis heute; eine Sammlung neuerer Bekenntnistexte aus der reformierten Tradition, ᵀ*Boecker* J., *al.* Neuk 1988, xiv-306 p. DM 48 pa. – ᴿTLZ 114 (1989) 130-3 (E. *Busch*).

526 ᴱ**Vogt** Kari, Religion og menneskesyn. Oslo 1983, Univ.-Forlaget. 139 p. – ᴿTsTKi 59 (1988) 74 (Dagfinn *Rian*).

527 ᴱ**Wood** Ralph C., *Collins* John E., Civil Religion and transcendent experience; studies in theology and history, psychology and mysticism, religion and the social crisis, 3. Macon GA 1988, Mercer Univ.   vii-167 p. [JBL 108,382].

528 ᴱ**Wyschogrod** Edith, *Crownfield* David, *al.*, LACAN [Jacques 1901-81] and theological discourse. Albany 1989, SUNY. $40; pa. $13. 0-7914-0110-3; 1-1 [TDig 37,69].

529 ᴱ**Yew Choo Lak**, Women participation and contribution in Asian Churches: Occas. Paper 5. Singapore 1988, ATESEA. 108 p. [TContext 7/1, 122, G. *Evers*].

A1.5   *Plurium compilationes* philologicae *vel* archaeologicae.

530 ᴱ**[R.-] Alföldi** Maria [p. 1-42], Methoden der antiken Numismatik: WegFo 529. Da 1989, Wiss.   vii-406 p.; 53 pl.

531 ᴱ**Bammesberger** Alfred, Die Laryngaltheorie und die Rekonstruktion des indogermanischen Laut- und Formensystems: IndogB 3. Heid 1988. 585 p. – ᴿHistSprF 102 (1989) 268-297 (F.O. *Lindeman*: quite long critical summaries of all the articles).

532 ᴱ**Brentjes** B., Das Grundeigentum in Mesopotamien: Jb Wirtschaftsgeschichte, Sonderband 1987s. B 1988, Akademie. 186 p. 11 art. – ᴿArOr 57 (1989) 263-7 (B. *Hruška*; with no indication of whether it was a meeting).

533 ᴱ**Cavallo** Guglielmo, *a*) Le strade del testo: Studi e commenti 5. Bari 1987, Adriatica.   159 p. 9 art., 1 infra. – *b*) Le biblioteche nel mondo antico e medievale. R 1988, Laterza. xxxii-206 p. Lit. 25.000 [RHE 84, p. 422*].

534 ᴱ**Christensen** Andrew L., Tracing archaeology's past; the historiography of archaeology. Carbondale 1989, Southern Illinois Univ.   xii-252 p. 0-8093-1523-8 [OIAc N89].

535 ᴱ**Clayton** Peter A., *Price* Martin J. The seven wonders of the ancient world. [→ 4,d631]. L 1988, Routledge. xvi-176 p.; 89 fig. 0-415-00279-6. 7 art., 3 infra.

536 ᴱ**Clemoes** P., *al.*, Anglo-Saxon England 17. C 1988, Univ. ix-335 p.; 8 facsim. → 1817 [RHE 84,336*.376*].

538 ᴱ**Détienne** Marcel, Les savoirs de l'écrire en Grèce ancienne [18 art.]: Cah. Pg. Apparat Critique 14. Lille 1988, Presses Univ. 540 p. – ᴿRÉG 102 (1989) 203s (P. *Cauderlier*).

539 ᴱFerrier R.W., The arts of Persia. NHv 1989, Yale Univ. x-334 p. 0-300-03987-5 [OIAc N89].
540 ᴱFischer-Hansen T., East and West; cultural relations in the ancient world: Danish St. Clas. Arch. 1. K 1988, Mus. Tusc. 167 p.; 18 pl.; maps. Dk 210. 87-7289-061-4 [JRS 79,267].
541 ᴱGessinger Joachim, *Rahden* Wolfert von, Theorien vom Ursprung der Sprache [I...] II. B 1989, de Gruyter. xii-675 p.; viii-593 p. DM 560. 3-11-010189-0 [IndogF 94,377 adv.].
542 ᴱGiardina A., Società romana e impero tardoantico, III. Le merci; gli insediamenti. Roma 1986, Laterza. 941 p. 29 art. – ᴿJRS 78 (1988) 183-193 (C. *Wickham*: massive successor to the 3-volume 1300-page 1981 compilation; this one is 4 volumes and twice as many pages; left unclear whether this review deals with only the third of the 4 new volumes).
543 ᴱGitin Seymour, *Dever* William G., Recent excavations in Israel; studies in Iron Age archaeology: AASOR 49. WL 1989, Eisenbrauns. xii-152 p.; ill. 0-89757-049-9. 9 art., infra.
544 ᴱKluwe Ernst, Kultur und Fortschritt in der Blütezeit der griechischen Polis: Schriften zur Geschichte und Kultur der Antike. B 1985, Akademie. 285 p. – ᴿKlio 71 (1989) 285-290 (A. E. *Raubitschek*).
545 ᴱMeutsch Dietrich, *Viehoff* Reinhold, Comprehension of literary discourse; results and problems of interdisciplinary approaches: Researches in Text Theory 3. B 1989, de Gruyter. [vi-]259 p. 3-11-011111-X. 13 art.; 1 infra.
546 ᴱMommsen Wolfgang J., *Schwentker* Wolfgang, Max WEBER und seine Zeitgenossen: Deutsches Historisches Institut, Veröff. 21. Gö 1988, VR. 799 p. DM 168 [KerDo 35,163 + adv.]. 37 art.
547 ᴱNeukam Peter, Die Antike als Begleiterin; Dialog Schule-Wissenschaft 24. ... c. 1989, Bayerischer Schulbuch-V. ➤ 9791.
548 ᴱRolley Claude, Techniques antiques du bronze; faire un vase – faire un casque – faire une fibule: Centre Techniques gréco-romaines, 12. Dijon 1988, Univ. 92 p., XVIII pl. 2-900119-13-8. 4 art.
549 ᴱSarbatov G. Š., Ⓑ Irano-afrazijske jazykovy kontakty, Irano-Afro-Asiatic language contacts [24 art.]. Moskva 1987, Nauka. 171 p. r 2.10. – ᴿJStJud 20 (1989) 109s (Z.J. *Kapera*: AJCHENVAL'D A.A. on Iranian loanwords in Hebrew and Aramaic p. 4-7; BOGULJUBOV M., Aramaic-Greek epitaph, 30-37).
550 ᴱScheeper M. De, *Nave* F. De, Ex officina plantiniana; studia in memoriam Christophori PLANTINI (ca. 1520-1589): De Oulden Passer 66s (1988s) 1-692; ill.
551 ᴱSchiffer Michael B., Advances in archaeological method and theory [8,1985 ➤ 1,443] 10. San Diego 1987, Academic. 455 p.; 42 fig. 0-12-003110-8 [AJA 93,627].
552 ᴱSchluchter Wolfgang, Max WEBERs Sicht des Islam — Interpretation und Kritik. Fra 1988, Suhrkamp. 365 p. DM 24. – ᴿArOr 57 (1989) 291 (B. *Hruška*, deutsch).
553 ᴱSchneider Laurie, Phrygian art and archaeology: Source notes in the history of art, 7/-14 special. NY 1988, Ars brevis. 71 p. [JAOS 109,723].
554 ᴱSchultz Uwe, Mit dem Zehnten fing es an; eine Kulturgeschichte der Steuer. Mü 1986, Beck. 298 p. [38-, *Baatz* D., Rom; 51-, *Bringmann* K., Judäa]. – ᴿSalesianum 51 (1989) 545 (G. *Gentileschi*).
555 Serta historica antiqua I-II: Univ. Genova, Ist. Stor. Ant. 15s. R 1986-9, Bretschneider. 276 p.; 305 p. Lit. 250.000. 88-7689-016-5.

556 ᴱSiems Andreas K., (Einf. p. 1-15) Sexualität und Erotik in der Antike: WegFor 605. Da 1988, Wiss. vi-456 p. 13 art.
557 ᴱSørensen Jørgen P., Rethinking religion; studies in the Hellenistic process: Opuscula Graecolatina 30. K 1989, Museum Tusculanum. 101 p. 87-7289-079-7 [OIAc Ja90].
558 ᴱThomas Carol G., Paths from ancient Greece. Leiden 1988, Brill. vii-206 p. 90-04-08846-6. 10 art., 3 infra. – ᴿClasR 39 (1989) 376-8 (R. Stoneman).
559 ᴱVan Sertima Ivan, Egypt Revisited²ʳᵉᵛ [= 4 essays < Egypt Revisited 4/2 (1982) plus 300 p.]: Journal of African Civilizations 19. New Brunswick 1989, Transaction. vi-441 p. 0-88738-799-3 [OIAc N89].
560 ᴱWilson B. A., About interpretation; from Plato to Dilthey. NY 1989, Lang. xxii-208 p. $33. – ᴿSWJT 32,3 (1989s) 49s (E. E. Ellis).
561 ᴱZimmermann A., Vuillemin-Diem D., Die Kölner Universität im Mittelalter; geistige Wurzeln und soziale Wirklichkeit: Misc. Mediaevalia 20. B 1989, de Gruyter. ix-537 p. [RHE 85,123*].

A2 Acta congressuum 1. biblica [Notitiae, reports ➤ Y7.2].

562 ᴱAmihai M., al., Narrative research on the Hebrew Bible [11 art. of SBL Narrative Research group]: Semeia 46. Atlanta 1989, Scholars. $15; sb. $10 or 4 for $25 [BL 90, 65, C. S. Rodd: 'Literary approaches to the Bible still lack coherence'].
563 Associazione laica di cultura biblica 'Biblia' ['Dante' 1986/8 ➤ 565]: a) La posizione del debole nella Bibbia; Atti del convegno nazionale, Casale Monferrato, 16-17 maggio 1987; introd. Ghiberti G. p. 9-23. Settimello FI 1988, Biblia. 139 + 21 p. (Bianchi E., Chi sono i poveri oggi? p. 125-139). 7 art.; infra. – b) Abramo, padre di una moltitudine di uomini; Atti del seminario invernale, Rocca di Papa 28-21 gennaio 1988. Settimello 1989, Biblia. 277 p. Lit. 10.000. – c) Il sogno nella Bibbia, Ravenna 7-8 maggio 1988. Settimello 1989. 125 p.; ill. 5 art., infra.
564 ᴱBar-Asher Moshe, Colloque sur les langues juives et les traditions linguistiques des Juifs orientaux, Paris 15-18 oct. 1982: Massorot 2. J 1986, Univ. Language Tradition Project. 180 p. + ❺ 135 p. 13 art. français + 9 ❺.
564* ᴱBar-Asher Moshe, 9th World Congress of Jewish Studies, Jerusalem August 4-12, 1985, Proceedings: B-I, The history of the Jewish people / B-II, Hebrew and Aramaic Languages. J 1986-8, World Union of Jewish Studies. 178 p. + ❺ 171; 57 p. + ❺ 99. 0333-0068.
565 ᴱBarblan G., DANTE e la Bibbia: convegno internazionale 'Biblia', Firenze 26-28.IX.1986: Archivum Romanicum 1/210. F 1988. 371 p. Jacoff P. su Geremia; altri sull'esegesi medievale [ZAW 101,455]. – ᴿAevum 63 (1989) 409 (E. Fumagalli); CC 140 (1989,1) 511s (C. Bortone).
566 ᴱBoice James M., Transforming our world; a call to action [< Second Congress on Bible Inerrancy Sept. 1987]. Portland OR 1988, Multnomah. 157 p. $11. 0-88070-222-2. – ᴿRExp 86 (1989) 282s (D. S. Dockery).
567 ᴱBori Pier Cesare, Pesce Mauro, Studi sulla letteratura esegetica cristiana e giudaica antica, [V, 1987 ➤ 4,472] VI Seminario, Acireale 12-14 ott. 1988: AnStoEseg 6 (1989) 5-300. 15 art., infra.
568 ᴱBrooke George J., Temple Scroll studies [dedicated to Y. YADIN], Manchester Dec. 1987: JPseud Sup 7. Sheffield 1987, Academic. 299 p. $45. 1-85075-200-1 [OIAc S89]. 15 art., infra. – ᴿExpTim 101 (1989s) 215s (J. C. L. Gibson); JJS 40 (1989) 243-5 (G. Vermes).

569 BUBER Martin (1878-1965), Internationales Symposium zum 20. Todestag, ᴱLicharz Werner, *Schmidt* Heinz, I. Dialogik und Dialektik; II. Vom Erkennen zum Tun des Gerechten: Arnoldshainer Texte 57s. Fra 1989, Haag & H. 301 p.; 326 p. DM 48. [TR 85,337].

570 ᴱBusi Giulio, 'Ovadyah Yare da BERTINORO [c. 1500] e la presenza ebraica in Romagna nel Quattrocento; Atti del Convegno di Bertinoro 17-18 maggio 1988: Henoch Quad. 1. T 1989, Zamorani. xvi-111 p.; III pl. Lit. 25.000. 88-7158-001-X. 8 art.; 2 infra.

571 *Campana* B., present., L'Ebraismo [Conferenze S. Carlo, Modena 1986]. Modena 1987, Mucchi. 125 p. 7 art., infra. – ᴿRivB 37 (1989) 227s (M. *Perani*).

572 ᴱCasciaro José M., *al.*, Masculinidad y feminidad en el mundo de la Biblia; estudios exegéticos para una teología bíblica del cuerpo y de la sexualidad de la persona humana. Pamplona 1989, Univ. Navarra. xv-933 p. 84-87146-04-X. 12 art., infra.

572* ᴱCeresa-Gastaldo Aldo, Storia e preistoria dei Vangeli [Seminario Univ. Genova 1986s]. Genova 1989, 'D.AR.FI.CL.ET' (Univ. Fac. Lettere) 'Dipartimento Archeologia, Filologia Classica e loro tradizioni' [0025-0852] 112. 143 p. 7 art.; infra.

573 ᴱCollado B., *Vilar Hueso* V., II Simposio biblico 1985/7 ➤ 3,529: ᴿSefarad 49 (1989) 411-6 (E. *Fernández Tejero*).

574 ᴱCorsani Mary, John WYCLIF e la tradizione degli studi biblici in Inghilterra [convegno dic. 1984, Univ. Genova, Sez. Anglistica]. Genova 1987, Melangolo. 156 p. – ᴿProtestantesimo 44 (1989) 140s (G. *Gonnet*).

575 ᴱDe Lorenzi Lorenzo (introd. p. 5-27), The diakonia of the Spirit (2 Co 4:7-7:4) [Atti dell'XI Colloquio Ecumenico Paolino, Roma 21-26.IX.1987]; Benedictina Mg 10. R 1989, St. Paul's Abbey. 362 p.; 327-362 indici (*Burini* Clara). 7 art. (+ discussioni), infra: conclusions p. 291-304, *Chevallier* Max-Alain.

576 ᴱDelorme Jean, Les paraboles évangéliques, perspectives nouvelles; XIIᵉ Congrès de l'ACFÉB Lyon (1987) [31 août-4 septembre]: LDiv 135. P 1989, Cerf. 452 p.; front. F 230. 2-204-02997-1. 22 art.; infra. – ᴿÉTRel 64 (1989) 631s (E. *Cuvillier*); TsTNijm 29 (1989) 407s (A. van *Schaik*).

577 DORNSEIFF Franz in memoriam; Kolloquium Univ. Lp anlässlich des 20. Todestages, ᴱWerner Jürgen. Amst 1986, Hakkert. 134 p.; portr.; 10 fig. Fs 32. p. 90-99, *Conrad* Joachim, Dornseiffs alttestamentliche Arbeiten; 79-89, *Rudolph* Kurt, D's religionsgeschichtliche Arbeiten. – ᴿDLZ 110 (1989) 799-801 (M. *Maróth*).

577* ᴱDuval Y.-M., Jérôme entre l'Occident et l'Orient; XVIᵉ centenaire du départ de S. Jérôme de Rome et de son installation à Bethléem: Actes du Colloque de Chantilly (Sept. 1986). P 1988, Ét. Aug. 508 p. [RHE 85, p. 97*].

578 Early Jewish Mysticism; Jerusalem 1st conference: Jerusalem Studies in Jewish Thought 5 (1986) 65-120 *Gruenwald* I. (Merkabah and Shiur Komah); 121-138, *Schiffman* L., Hekhalot and Qumran. – 2d Conference, Medieval Europe: Jerusalem Studies in Jewish Thought 6,3s (1987) [1-14 *Pines* S.; < JStJud 20,278].

579 ᴱFuchs Gotthard, *Henrix* Hans H., Zeitgewinn – messianisches Denken nach Franz ROSENZWEIG [zum 100. Gb., Kath. Akad. Aachen]. Fra 1987, Knecht. 190 p. – ᴿJudaica 44 (1988) 61s (F. von *Hammerstein*). ➤ 604.

580 ᴱFuss A. M., Jewish Law Association Oxford conference volume: Papers and Proceedings 3. Atlanta 1987, Scholars. ix-209 p. [ETL 65, p. 11*].

581 ᴱ**Goetschel** Roland, Prière, mystique et Judaïsme (colloque de Strasbourg, 10-12 sept. 1984). P 1987, PUF. 245 p. F 180. – ᴿJJS 40 (1989) 119-121 (D. *Frank*); RÉJ 148 (1989) 413s (J.-P. *Rothschild*).

582 ᴱ**Halperin** Jean, *Lévitte* Georges, Mémoires et histoire; actes du 25ᵉ colloque des intellectuels juifs de langue française. P 1986, Denoël. 190 p. [KirSef 61 (1986s) 597].

584 ᴱ**Jackson** B. S., Touro Conference volume [Dec. 1982]: Jewish Law Association Studies 1. Chico CA 1985, Scholars. viii-156 p. – ᴿRÉJ 146 (1987) 421-5 (J.-P. *Rothschild*).

585 ᴱ**Kapera** Z. J., The first international colloquium on the Dead Sea Scrolls (Mogilany near Cracow; May 31-June 2, 1987): FolOr 25 (1988). 155 p.; 2 phot. zł 1200. 0015-5675. 13 art., infra.

586 ᴱ**Khoury** A. T., *Hünermann* P., Wer ist mein Nächster? Die Antwort der Weltreligionen: Tb 1512. FrB 1988, Herder. S. 83-112, *Vetter* D., Toleranz, Solidarität, Liebe — Stimmen aus dem jüdischen Volk [< ZAW 101,479].

586* *Kiehn* A., al., Bibliodrama [biblische Bilder: Bad Segeberg 1986]. Stu 1987, Kreuz. 158 p. DM 24,80. 3-7831-0848-9. – ᴿTsTNijm 29 (1989) 200 (L. van der *Tuin*).

587 ᴱ**Leibowitz** Joshua O., Proceedings of the Third International Symposium on Medicine in Bible and Talmud: Koroth 9. J 1988, Hebrew Univ. 280 p. 30 art. [JBL 108,569].

587* ᴱ**Liberti** V., La famiglia nella Bibbia [corso L'Aquila 1987]: Studio Biblico Teologico Aquilano 9. R 1989, Dehoniane. 271 p. 88-396-0279-8. 12 art.; infra.

588 ᴱ**Lindars** B., Law and religion; essays on the place of law in Israel and early Christianity [Manchester U. Ehrhardt seminar]. C 1989, Clarke. xvi-209 p. £25. 0-227-67907-3. 13 art. [BL 90,106, B. S. *Jackson*, titles].

589 ᴱ**Lull** David J., Society of Biblical Literature 1989 Seminar Papers, 125th annual meeting 18-21 Nov. 1989, Anaheim CA: Seminar Papers 28. Atlanta 1989, Scholars. ix-655 p. 1-55540-421-9. 38 art.; infra.

590 ᴱ**Merón Arroyo** Ciríaco, *Revuelta Sañudo* Manuel, Fray LUIS DE LEÓN; aproximaciones a su vida y su obra, Coloquio [Santander 1987]: Estudios de literatura y pensamiento hispánicos 6. Santander 1989, Soc. Menendez Pelayo. xxvi-335 p. 84-404-5198-9. 10 art.; p. 203-229, *Fernández Tejero* Emilia, L. L. Hebraista (Ct).

591 *a)* ᴱ**Neuhaus** Richard J., Biblical interpretation in crisis (p. 1-23), the RATZINGER conference [Jan. 1988 NY meeting for his Erasmus lecture]: Encounter 9. GR 1989, Eerdmans. 191 p. $10 pa. 3 other art., infra; p. 102-180, *Stallsworth* Paul T., detailed account of discussion by 21 invited participants. – ᴿHorBT 11,1 (1989) 102 (D. F. *Gowan*). – *b)* ᴱ**Ratzinger** Joseph Kard., Schriftauslegung im Widerstreit [NT 'Erasmus workshop'], ᵀ*Johnson* Susan: QDisp 117. FrB 1989, Herder. 128 p. DM 19,80. 3-451-02117-X. – ᴿTR 85 (1989) 265-272 (F. *Mussner*); TsTNijm 29 (1989) 402s (S. van *Tilborg*).

592 ᴱ**Neusner** Jacob, al. Religious writings and religious systems; systemic analysis of Holy Books in ... I. Islam, Buddhism, Greco-Roman religions, Ancient Israel, & Judaism; II. Christianity [two Brown Univ. seminars 1988]: Brown Studies in Religion 01, 02. Atlanta 1989, Scholars. xxiv-200 p.; xi-201 p. $51 + 48; sb./pa. $45 + 32. 1-55540-296-8; 333-6. 9 + 10 art.; 18 infra.

593 ᴱ**Novak** David, *Samuelson* Norbert, Creation and the end of days; Judaism and scientific cosmology [1984 Meeting, Academy for Jewish

Philosophy]. Lanham MD 1986, UPA. 276 p. $26.75; pa. $14.50. – ᴿZygon 24 (1989) 273-5 (G. L. *Murphy*).

594 La paraula al servei dels homes; XXV jornadas de biblistes catalans (1963-1985). Barc 1989, Claret. [iv-] 176 p. [CBQ 52,378; JStJud 21,133].

595 ᴱ**Parente** F., Aspetti della storiografia ebraica. Atti del IV congresso internazionale dell'Assoc. Italiana per lo Studio del Giudaismo, S. Miniato, 7-10 nov. 1983. R 1987, Carucci. 260 p. 14 art.; infra. – ᴿAthenaeum 67 (1989) 619-622 (A. *Boffi*).

596 ᴱ**Patrick** D., Thinking biblical law [SBL biblical law group]: Semeia 45. $15; sb. $10 [BL 90, 111, B. S. *Jackson*, titles].

597 ᴱ**Penna** Romano, Antipaolinismo; reazioni a Paolo tra il I e il II secolo; Atti del II convegno nazionale di studi neotestamentari (Bressanone, 10-12.IX.1987), Assoc. Biblica Italiana = RicStoB 1,2 (1989). 137 p. 9 art., infra.

598 ᴱ**Pirola** G., *Coppellotti* F., Il 'Gesù storico'; problema della modernità [seminario Torino 1985-7] 1988 ⭢ 4,495*: ᴿNRT 111 (1989) 918 (L. *Renwart*).

599 ᴱ**Prato** Gian Luigi (p. 5-12), Israele alla ricerca di identità tra il III sec. a. C. e il I sec. d. C.; Atti del V convegno di studi veterotestamentari (Bressanone, 7-9.IX.1987), Assoc. Biblica Italiana = RicStoB 1,1 (1989). 269 p. 12 art., infra [ZAW 102,311; no tit. pp.].

600 Proceedings of the Conference on Biblical Interpretation [Ridgecrest NC (1987 ⭢ 4,476); 1988]. Nv 1988, Broadman. 221 p. 0-8054-6005-5 [NTAbs 33,380: authors and subjects, no tit. pp.].

601 ᴱ**Pury** A. de, Le Pentateuque en question; les origines et la composition des cinq premiers livres de la Bible à la lumière des recherches récentes [séminaire 1987 des univ. suisses-fr.]: MondeB. Genève 1989, Labor et Fides. 421 p. 2-8309-0148-7 [BL 90, 90, R. N. *Whybray*: high quality but no index]. 13 art., infra. – ᴿCarthaginensia 5 (1989) 281s (J. F. *Cuenca*).

602 ᴱ**Reventlow** H., *al.*, Historische Kritik und biblischer Kanon in der deutschen Aufklärung [Herzog August Bibliothek Symposium Dez. 1985]: Wolfenbütteler Forschungen 41. Wsb 1988, Harrassowitz. vii-293 p. DM 98. 3-447-02884-X [BL 90,23, J. W. *Rogerson*].

603 ᴱ**Sartori** Luigi (p. 11-40), Popoli messianici; Atti del convegno, Trento 16-17 maggio 1984: IstScRel 11. Bo 1987, Dehoniane. 269 p. Lit. 25.000. 88-10-40361-4. 12 art., 5 infra.

604 ᴱ**Schmied-Kowarzik** Wolfdietrich, Der Philosoph Franz ROSENZWEIG (1886-1929), Internationaler Kongress Kassel 1986; I. Die Herausforderung des jüdischen Lernens; II. Das neue Denken und seine Dimensionen. FrB 1987, Alber. – ᴿTPhil 64 (1989) 435-440 (J. *Splett*). ⭢ 579.

605 Second Asian workshop for the biblical apostolate, Singapore Dec. 11-16, 1988. 224 p. [< TContext 6/2 No. 958; 7/1, p. 30].

606 ᴱ**Sevrin** Jean-Marie, The NT in early Christianity — La réception des Écrits néotestamentaires dans le christianisme primitif [36ᵉ Colloquium Biblicum Lovaniense, 26-28 août 1986]: BiblETL 86. Lv 1989, Univ./Peeters. xvi-410 p. Fb 2500. 90-6186-308-2 / 90-6831-166-2. 15 art., infra. – ᴿETL 65 (1989) 436-9 (C. *Focant*).

607 SOTS bulletin for 1989: 64th winter meeting, L 4-6.I.1989: *Rogerson* J. W., presidential address, *Mah ᵉnoš* (Ps 8,5), the central question of OT theology; *Martin* J. D., Choice and selectivity in Ben Sira's Hymn to the Fathers; *Joyce* -P. M., Ezek 11,16; *Hayward* C., Gn 35,1-15; *Davies* P. R., Does OT study need a dictionary?; *Sawyer* J. F. A., The female

[daughter of Zion] and male [Servant] characters in Is 40-55. – 65th (summer) meeting; Sheffield 18-20.VII.1989: *Rendtorff* R., Covenant in Gn-Ex; *Hayman* A.P., Qohelet & Creation; *Lowy* S., Exodus in early exegesis; *Clines* D., Job; *Provan* I., Lam 3,52-66; *Williams* J., Welsh Bible; *Jeppesen* K., Servant Is. 40-66.

608 ᴱ**Talstra** E., Computer assisted analysis of biblical texts: 'Werkgroep Informatica' 10th anniv. workshop, Amst. Nov. 5-6, 1987: Applicatio 7. Amst 1989, Free Univ. vi-173 p. £36. 6 art. [ZAW 102,442, titles, no pp.].

609 ᴱ**Tambasco** Anthony J., Blessed are the peacemakers; biblical perspectives on peace and its social foundations [< CBA seminar 1982-6]. NY 1989, Paulist. viii-184 p. $9 pa. 0-8091-3027-0 [NTAbs 33,409; TDig 37,150]. – ᴿBibTB 19 (1989) 157 (R.J. *Cassidy*).

610 ᴱ**Thoma** Clemens, *Wyschogrod* Michael, Parable and story in Judaism and Christianity [Lucerne June 2-4, 1986]: StJudChr. NY 1989, Paulist. vi-258 p. $9. 0-8091-3087-4. 10 art., 8 infra.

611 **Toniolo** Ermanno M., present., Come leggere nella Bibbia il mistero di Maria: [Roma 1988, Teresianum] Fine d'anno con Maria 7. R 1989, Centro Cultura Mariana. 207 p. 8 art.; 7 infra.

612 ᴱ**Twersky** Isadore, *Septimus* Bernard, Jewish thought in the seventeenth century [international conference]. CM 1987, Harvard Univ. xxi-521. – ᴿRelStR 15 (1989) 366s (E. *Wolfson*).

613 ᴱ**Van Beek** G.W., The scholarship of W.F. ALBRIGHT; an appraisal [Symposium Rickville MD 1984]: HarvSemSt 33. Atlanta 1989, Scholars. 73 p. $17; sb. $11. 1-55540-314-X [BL 90,28, D.J.*Wiseman*: D. *Freedman* and D. *Hillers* unduly critical; – CBQ 52,774, tit. pp., comments, R. *Althann*].

614 ᴱ**Vermeylen** Jacques, The book of Isaiah / Le livre d'Isaïe; les oracles et leurs relectures; unité et complexité de l'ouvrage [Colloquium Biblicum Lovaniense 37, 1987; *Brekelmans* C.H.W. 65ᵉ anniv.; bibliog.]: BiblETL 81. Lv 1989, Univ./Peeters. x-475 p. Fb 2700. 90-6186-304-X / 90-6831-164-6 [BL 90,94, P.W. *Coxon*, & ZAW 102,144: tit. pp.] 30 art., infra.

615 ᴱ**Wedderburn** A.J.M., Paul and Jesus, collected essays [< meeting; 5 by him, 4 others]: JStNT supp. 37. Sheffield 1989, Academic. 207 p. £20. 1-85075-218-4. Infra → 5784.

616 [ᴱ**Woude** A.S. van der] Crises and perspectives; studies in Ancient Near Eastern polytheism, biblical theology, Palestinian archaeology and intertestamental literature [joint British-Dutch conference, Cambridge 1985]: OTS 24, 1986 → 2,399: ᴿTLZ 114 (1989) 585 (H. *Ringgren*: title inept).

617 ᴱ**Zyl** H.C. van, The resurrection of Jesus in historical perspective; papers read at the annual congress of Die Nuwe-Testamentiese Werkgemeenskap van Suid-Afrika, April 1989 = Neotestamentica 23,2 (1989) 157-361; list of members p. 363-371.

A2.3 Acta congressuum theologica [reports → Y7.4].

618 Actualité de la Réforme: 24 leçons, Univ. Genève 1986: Publ. Fac. Théol. 12. Genève 1987, Labor et Fides. 328 p. – ᴿRHPR 69 (1969) 359s (M. *Lienhard*).

619 ᴱ**Althaus** Heinz, Christentum, Islam und Hinduismus vor den grossen Weltproblemen [Tagung Religionslehrer, Limburg 1987]. Altenberge 1988,

Telos. 145 p. 4 art. – ᴿTPQ 137 (1989) 306s (J. *Janda*); TR 85 (1989) 330 (L. *Hagemann*).

620 ᴱAquino M. P., Aportes para una teología desde la mujer [conferencia Oaxtepec, Méx. 1-6.XII.1986]. M 1988, Biblia y Fe. 158 p. – ᴿBibFe 15 (1989) 169 (M. *Saenz Galache*).

621 ᴱArens Edmund, HABERMAS und die Theologie; Beiträge zur theologischen Rezeption, Diskussion und Kritik der Theorie kommunikativen Handelns. Dü 1989, Patmos. 270 p. DM 39 pa. 22 art. [*Fiorenza* F. S., 115-144; *Lamb* Matthew L. 241-270].

622 AUGUSTINUS: ᴱCaprioli A., *al.*, *a*) Agostino e la conversione 1986/7 ⇥ 4,518*a*; – *b*) L'opera letteraria 1986/7 ⇥ 4,518*b*: ᴿNRT 111 (1989) 470s (L. J. *Renard*).

623 Scanavino G. present., [*Solignac* A., *Corsini* E., *al.*], 'Le confessioni' di AGOSTINO d'Ippona, libri X-XIII: Lectio Augustini, Settimana Agostiniana Pavese [1982-7] 4. Palermo 1987, Augustinus. 114 p. Lit. 15.000. – ᴿTR 85 (1989) 19s (C. *Mayer*).

624 Jornadas Agustinianas, Madrid 22-24 de abril de 1987. Valladolid 1988, Estudio Agustiniano. 400 p. [RHE 85,98*].

625 ᴱBal Mieke, Anti-covenant; counter-reading women's lives in the Hebrew Bible [Harvard women's caucus 1985s]: JStOT Sup 81, BLit 22. Sheffield 1989, Almond. 243 p. £25. 1-85075-207-9 [BL 90,67, G. I. *Emmerson*: a surfeit]. 11 art.; infra.

626 ᴱBekkenkamp J. [Werkgroep, *Dröes* F., *al.*], Proeven van vrouwenstudies, theologie I: IIMO Research Publ. [19,1986 ⇥ 4,525] 25. Leiden/Utrecht 1989, IIMO/Fem. Theol. 262 p. *f* 32,50. 90-6495-193-4. – ᴿStreven 57 (1989s) 754s (P. *Beentjes*); TsTNijm 29 (1989) 417.

627 ᴱBenetollo Ottorino, Il matrimonio e la famiglia; convegno Bologna 23-24 nov. 1988: SacDoc 34,3s (1989) 249-428. 6 art., ⇥ 4990.

628 ᴱBerg J. van den, *Wall* Ernestine G. E. van der, Jewish-Christian relations in the seventeenth century; studies and documents: symposium Leiden 23.I. 1985. Boston 1988, Kluwer. ix-210 p. $77. 90-247-3617-X [TDig 36,375].

629 Bericht über die 27. Internationale Altkatholische Theologenkonferenz in Innsbruck (5.-10. September 1988) = IkiZ 49 (1989), 5 art. + Tagungsbericht, *Lauber* Roland, p. 29-31; Erklärung p. 78.

630 ᴱBirtel Frank T., Religion, science, and public policy [8 Tulane Univ. lectures]. NY 1987, Crossroad. xiii-152 p. $17. – ᴿNewTR 2,1 (1988) 109s (S. *Bevans*); Zygon 24 (1989) 385-8 (Marian *Kaehler*).

631 Boff L., *al.*, Jews, Christians and Liberation Theology; a symposium: Christian Jewish Relations 21,1 (L 1988) [< Judaica 44,189].

632 ᴱBolle Pierre, *Godel* Jean, Spiritualité, théologie et résistance; Yves de MONTCHEUIL, théologien au maquis du Vercors [colloque S.-Hugues-de-Bibiers, Isère 27-29 sept. 1984]. Grenoble 1987, Univ. 381 p.; ill. – ᴿRHE 84 (1989) 498-501 (A. *Dantoing*).

633 ᴱBonamente G., *Nestori* A., I Cristiani e l'Impero nel IV secolo; colloquio sul Cristianesimo nel mondo antico; Atti del convegno (Macerata 17-18 dicembre 1987): Fac. Lett. 47, Atti 9. Macerata 1988, Univ. xx-245 p. Lit. 30.000 [JRS 79,270].

634 ᴱBonner G., *al.*, St. Cuthbert, his cult and his community to AD 1200 [Durham conference 14-18.VII.1987]. Woodbridge 1989, Boydell. xxiii-484 p.; 34 fig.; 60 pl.; maps. £49.50 [Manuscripta 33,3 (1989) 217 (tit. sans pp.) RHE 84, p. 413*]. Two gospel texts ⇥ 1788.

635 ^E**Borgeaud** Philippe [p. 7-20], La mémoire des religions [...son fonctionnement dans les religions; colloque Genève févr. 1986]: Religions en perspective 2. Genève 1988, Labor et Fides. 150 p. 2-8309-0118-5. 8 art., 5 infra. – ^RÉTRel 64 (1989) 101s (Jacky *Argaud*); RÉG 102 (1989) 206s (Yvonne *Vernière*); TR 85 (1989) 345 (tit. pp.).

636 ^E**Botto** Oscar, *Rossi* Pietro, Max WEBER e l'India [Torino 24-25.XI.1983]: SMEO Coll. 1. T 1986, Jollygrafica. 160 p. – ^RJAOS 109 (1989) 318s (L. *Rocher*).

637 ^E**Braaten** Carl E., Our naming of God; problems and prospects of God-talk today [Chicago Lutheran seminars 1986s]. Minneapolis 1989, Fortress. ix-163 p. $13. 0-8006-2301-0 [TDig 37,177].

638 ^E**Bradshaw** Brendan, *Duffy* Eamon, Humanism, reform and the Reformation; the career of Bishop John FISHER [450th commemoration ...]. C 1989, Univ. ix-260 p. £27.50. – ^RJTS 40 (1989) 670-2 (P. N. *Brooks*); Studies 78 (1989) 345 (F. *O'Donoghue*).

639 ^E**Broek** R. van den, *al.*, Knowledge of God in the Graeco-Roman world [symposium Utrecht 26.-30.VI.1986]: ÉPR 112. Leiden 1988, Brill. ix-290 p. 90-04-08688-9. 7 art. infra.

640 ^E**Brown** L. B., Advances in the psychology of religion [1982 meeting, Oxford Wolfson College]. Ox 1985, Pergamon. xii-234 p. $27.50. – ^RJRel 68 (1988) 165s (R. W. *Hood*).

641 ^E**Brown** Stuart E., Meeting in faith; twenty years of Christian-Muslim conversations sponsored by the World Council of Churches. Geneva 1989, WCC. ix-181 p. $11. 2-8254-0949-9 [TDig 37,75].

642 ^E**Bryant** M. Darrol, *Flinn* Frank, Interreligious dialogue, voices from a new frontier [Assembly of world religions, McAfee NJ Nov. 1985]: New Era. NY 1989, Paragon. xx-234 p. $25. 0-89226-067-X [TDig 37,64].

643 ^E**Burgess** Joseph A., *Gros* Jeffrey, Building unity; ecumenical dialogues with Roman Catholic participation in the United States [1965-86]: Ecumenical Documents 4. NY 1988, Paulist. xii-499 p. $15. 0-8091-3040-8 [TDig 36,357].

644 ^E**Cameron** Nigel M. D., Issues in faith and history; papers presented at the second Edinburgh conference on dogmatics, 1987. E 1989, Rutherford. 122 p. £6.90. 0-946068-37-2. 7 art.; 5 infra.

646 CELAN Paul, internationale Symposien: 1985, Psalm und Hawdalah, ^E**Strelka** Joseph P.; — 1986, Datum und Zitat, ^E**Schoham** Chaim, *al.*; — 1987, Argumentum e silentio, ^E**Colin** Amy D.: JbGermanistik A20/21/—. Fra 1987, P. Lang (1985-6); B 1987, de Gruyter. 202 p.; 242 p.; xvi-450 p. – ^RTPhil 64 (1989) 117-121 (J. *Splett*, auch über DERRIDA J., Für Celan).

647 ^E**Chandran** J. Russell, The Cross and the Tanoa; Gospel and culture in the Pacific [Fiji symposium 27-29.VII.1987]. Suva 1988, Lotu Pasifika. 111 p. [TContext 7/1, 127, H. *Janssen*].

648 ^E**Clause** Bonnidell & Robert G., Women in ministry [evangelical symposium; 4 views]. DG 1989, InterVarsity. 250 p. $10. 0-8308-1284-9 [TDig 37, 96].

649 ^E**Cooke** Bernard, The Papacy and the Church in the United States [Worcester MA Holy Cross College conference]. NY 1989, Paulist. 220 p.; ill. $11. 0-8091-3070-X. 9 art. [TDig 37,178].

650 ^E**Coward** Harold G., Modern [Asia] Indian responses to religious pluralism → 3,692 [Calgary meeting]. Albany 1987, SUNY. xii-340 p. 14 art. – ^RSR 18 (1989) 90s (L. T. *Denton*).

651 EDespland Michel, *al.*, Religion et culture; Actes du colloque international du centenaire Paul TILLICH, Université Laval, Québec 1986. Laval 1987, Univ. x-650 p. 47 art. – RSR 18 (1989) 235-7 (R. *Aldwinckle*).

652 Le deuxième concile du Vatican (1959-1965) Actes du Colloque ... avec Univ. Lille/Bologne/Rome 28-30 mai 1986: Collection ÉcFrR 113. R 1989, École Française. xx-867 p. [RHE 85,77*; RSPT 74,151-3, Y. *Congar*]. 2-7283-0188-3. ⇥ k404.

653 EDinzelbacher Peter, *Bauer* Dieter R., Religiöse Frauenbewegung und mystische Frömmigkeit im Mittelalter [Studientagung Weingarten 19.-22.III.1986]: ArKulturGBeih 28. Köln 1988, Böhlau. ix-412 p. [TR 85,84, tit. pp.].

654 d'Onorio J.-B., *al.*, Droits de Dieu et droits de l'homme; Actes du IXᵉ colloque national des juristes catholiques, Paris 11-12 nov. 1988. P 1989, Téqui. 215 p. F 100. – RNRT 111 (1989) 1091 (L. *Volpe*).

655 EEngelhardt Paulus, Glück und glückliches Leben; philosophische und theologische Untersuchungen zur Bestimmung des Lebenszieds [Vorträge der Dominikanerhochschule Walberberg 1977]: Walberberger Studien ph. 7. Mainz 1985, Grünewald. 260 p. DM 42. – RTR 85 (1989) 497s (K. *Müller*).

656 Éthique chrétienne et sociétés africaines: 16ᵉ Sem. Théol. Kinshasa 26 apr.-2 mai 1987. Kinshasa 1987, Fac. Théol. Cath. 272 p. – RStPatav 36 (1989) 246s (G. *Segalla*).

657 EFabella Virginia, *Oduyoye* Mercy Amba, With passion and compassion; third world women doing theology [Oaxtepec Méx. 1-6.XII.1986]. Mkn 1988, Orbis. 192 p. – RRelStR 15 (1989) 245 (Rosemary R. *Ruether*); TContext 6,2 (1989) 114 (G. *Evers*).

658 EFallon Timothy P., *Riley* Philip B., Religion in context; recent studies in Lonergan [Santa Clara symposium 1984]: College Theology Society Resources in Religion 4. Lanham MD 1988, UPA. $26.50; pa. $13.75. 0-8191-7137-9; 8-7 [TDig 37,84].

659 EFarrugia E.G., *Taft* R.F., *Piovesana* G.K., Christianity among the Slavs; the heritage of saints Cyril and Methodius; Acts of the International Congress, XI centenary of the death of Methodius, Rome Oct. 8-11, 1985: OrChrAnt 231. R 1988, Pont. Inst. Studiorum Orientalium. ix-409 p. [RHE 85,111*].

660 EFerretti Giovanni, Temporalità ed escatologia; Atti del Primo Colloquio su Filosofia e Religione (Macerata, 10-12 maggio 1984): Univ. Lett/Fil 30. T 1986, Marietti. 250 p. Lit. 30.000. 88-211-8595-8. – RGregorianum 70 (1989) 789s (R. *Fisichella*).

661 EFilippi Carlo D., [Niels Stensen] Niccolò STENONE 1638-1686, due giornate di studio, F 17-18.XI.1986: FutUomo 14,1s (1987) 182 p.

662 EFreimark Peter, *al.*, LESSING und die Toleranz; Beiträge der vierten internationalen Konferenz der Lessing Society in Hamburg vom 27. bis 29. Juni 1985: Lessing Yearbook Supp. Detroit/Mü 1986, Wayne State Univ. / Text + Kritik. 374 p. DM 58. – RDLZ 109 (1988) 259-262 (W. *Albrecht*).

663 EGarfagnini Gian Carlo, AMBROGIO, traversari nel VI centenario della nascita [convegno Camaldoli-Firenze 15-18.IX.1986]. F 1988, Olschki. viii-532 p. Lit. 90.000. – RCC 140 (1989,4) 506s (G. *Cremascoli*).

664 EGelpi Donald L., Beyond individualism; toward a retrieval of moral discourse in America [J.C. Murray group discussion of R. *Bellah*, who provides an Afterword]. ND 1989, Univ. xi-230 p. $21. 0-268-00680-6 [TDig 37,44].

665 ᴱGerardi Renzo, Pensare e dire Dio oggi [MEIC (Movimento Ecclesiale di Impegno Culturale) settimane estive 1986 e 1987]. R 1989, Studium. 168 p. Lit. 18.000. – ᴿHumBr 44 (1989) 903s (B. *Belletti*).

666 ᴱGibaud H., Les problèmes d'expression dans la traduction biblique: Actes du colloque des 7-8 nov. 1986. Nancy 1988, Univ. Catholique de l'Ouest. – ᴿÉTRel 64 (1989) 429-431 (J.-M. *Babut*: titres sans pages).

667 ᴱGioia M., I giovani nella Bibbia: Studio Biblico Teologico Aquilano. R 1989, Dehoniane. p. 151-171, *Carniti* C.

668 Görg Manfred, *al.*, Christen und Juden in Gespräch [Tagung... Bayern, ev./kath. Akademien]; Bilanz nach 40 Jahren Staat Israel. Rg 1989, Pustet. 108 p. DM 19,80. – ᴿÖkRu 38 (1989) 504s (F.-W. *Marquardt*).

669 ᴱGössmann Elisabeth, *Bauer* Dieter R., Maria — für alle Frauen oder über alle Frauen? [Tagung der Diözese Stu-Rottenburg 27.-28.IX.1986]: frauenforum. FrB 1989, Herder. 216 p. DM 24,80. – ᴿTR 85 (1989) 405-7 (Teresa *Berger*); JEcuSt 26 (1989) 386s (G. C. *Chapman*).

670 Gott und Geschichte, 25. Konferenz Greifswald 8.-12. Juni 1986. Greifswald 1988, Univ. 164 p.; 21-46, *Tengström* S., Die Auffassung von der Geschichte im jahwistischen Werk und im AT [< ZAW 101,154].

671 GUTIÉRREZ Gustavo, The future of liberation theology; essays in honor of ∼, ᴱEllis Maduro O. [meeting at Maryknoll Aug. 1988]. Mkn 1989, Orbis. 336 p. $30 [ETL 66,447-9, V. *Neckebrouck*; JAAR 57,683; NRT 112,615, L. *Volpe*]. 50 art. – ᴿExpTim 101 (1989s) 352s (S. *Mayor*).

672 ᴱHamon Léo, Un siècle et demi d'histoire protestante; Théodore de BÈZE et les protestants sujets du roi [Yonne en Bourgogne]: Entretiens d'Auxerre: P 1989, Sciences de l'homme. 129 p. – ᴿEsprVie 99 (1989) 561 (R. *Epp*).

673 ᴱHart Ray L., Trajectories in the Study of Religion ⇥ 1,583 [AAR 75th, 1984]. Atlanta 1987, Scholars. xi-317 p. $26 [TDig 36,89: Eric VOEGELIN dictated his paper just before his death; 17 others].

674 ᶠHARTSHORNE Charles [90th b. conference, Austin TX 1988]; Hartshorne, process philosophy, and theology, ᴱKane Robert, *Phillips* Stephen H. Albany 1989, SUNY. xiii-198 p. $34.50; pa. $11. 0-7914-0164-2; 5-0 [TDig 37,58].

675 ᴱHilhorst A., De heiligenverering in de eerste eeuwen van het christendom [Genootschap voor Oudchristelijke Studiën (25. Jaar) 14-15.III., Nijmegen]. Nijmegen 1988, Dekker. x-229 p. ƒ29,50. 90-255-0016-1. – ᴿTsTNijm 29 (1989) 69 (F. van de *Paverd*).

676 ᴱHill Henry, Light from the east; a symposium on the [1-5 centuries] Oriental Orthodox and Assyrian [modern; also Armenian, Coptic...] churches [where? when?]. Toronto 1988, Anglican. 164 p. C$10. 0-919891-90-X. – ᴿExpTim 100 (1988s) 393 (G. *Bebawi*); SVlad 33 (1989) 202-5 (C. *Lock*).

677 ᴱHouten Richard Van, Christ's rule; a light for every corner [Zimbabwe Reformed Ecumenical Synod, Zimbabwe 1988]. GR 1988, RES. 252 p. $6.50 pa. – ᴿCalvinT 24 (1989) 373-6 (J. H. *Kromminga*).

678 ᴱHünermann Peter, *Eckholt* Margit, Katholische Soziallehre — Wirtschaft — Demokratie; ein lateinamerikanisch-deutsches Dialogsprogramm [deutsche Arbeitsgruppe; es folgen andere aus Brasilien, Argentinien, Chile, Perú]: Entwicklung und Frieden 51. Mainz/Mü 1989, Grünewald/Kaiser. 346 p. [TR 86, 49-51, N. *Strotmann*].

679 ᴱHutchison William R., Between the times; the travail of the Protestant establishment in America, 1900-1960 [Harvard Colloquium...]. NY 1989, Cambridge UP. xvii-322 p. $39.50. 0-521-36614-0. 13 art. [TDig 37,149].

680 ᴱIngram Paul O., *Streng* Frederick J., Buddhist-Christian dialogue; mutual renewal and transformation [Hawaii conference 1980; 11 papers]. Honolulu 1986, Univ. $10. – ᴿRelStR 15 (1989) 237 (D. K. *Swearer*).

681 Jornadas — Coloquio 'Libertad cristiana y preocupación social': Stromata 45,1s (1989) 1-171.

682 ᴱKalu Ogbu U., African Church historiography; an ecumenical perspective [Nairobi 1986]: Ökumene 4. Bern 1988, Ev. Arbeitsstelle. 223 p. Fs 12,80. – ᴿÖkRu 38 (1989) 114s (G. *Grohs*); TContext 6,2 (1989) 107 (N. *Bitoto Abeng*).

683 ᴱKannengiesser Charles, *Petersen* William L., ORIGEN of Alexandria; his world and his legacy [Colloquy ND 11-13.IV.1986]: Christianity and Judaism in Antiquity 1. ND 1988, Univ. viii-373 p. $25. – ᴿManuscripta 33 (1989) 70s (titles sans pp.).

684 Kartäuserliturgie und Kartäuserschrifttum [2.-5. Sept. 1987,? Pleterje, Yugoslavia]: Analecta carthusiana 16. Salzburg 1988, Institut für Anglistik. 192 p.; 159 p.; 96 p.; 165 p. – ᴿRHE 84 (1989) 187-9. 789-791 (G. *Hendrix*).

685 ᴱKoster Hilda, *Door-Elske* Cazemier, Zin en onzin van de Godin [Univ. Groningen]: Protestantsche Stichting Lectuurvoorziening. Voorburg 1989. 68 p. *f* 14.90. – ᴿStreven 57 (1989) 471 (P. *Beentjes*).

686 ᴱKremers Heinz, *Schoeps* Julius, Das jüdisch-christliche Religionsgespräch [Duisburg, Univ. 1980]; St. Geistesg. 9. Stu 1988, Burg. 234 p. DM 38. – ᴿÖkRu 38 (1989) 502s (J. *Schoneveld*).

687 ᴱKRIARAS (M.) E., Ⓖ Colloque, 3.IV.1987; *Aphierōma... praktika* (Actes). Thessaloniki 1988, Centre de recherches byzantines. 15 art., XIIᵉ-XIXᵉ s. [RHE 84,852].

688 KÜHNER Raphael [Syntax 150th Anniv.] Proceedings of the international colloquium, Amst 1986, ᴱRijksbaron A., *al.* Amst 1988, Gieben. 386 p.

689 ᴱLaubier Patrick de, Visages de l'Église; cours d'ecclésiologie [Genève 1985-7]. FrS 1989, Univ. 386 p. Fs 35. – ᴿEsprVie 99 (1989) 475s (P. *Jay*: souvenir de JOURNET); TR 85 (1989) 435 (tit. pp.).

690 ᴱLegrand Hervé, *Manzanares* Julio, *García y García* Antonio, Naturaleza y futuro de las conferencias episcopales; Actas del Coloquio internacional de Salamanca 3-8 enero 1988. Salamanca 1988, Univ. 505 p. –ᴿETL 65 (1989) 197-9 (A. de *Halleux*); REB 49 (1989) 232s (E. P. *Alves*).

691 ᴱLegrand H., *al.*, Les conférences épiscopales; théologie, statut canonique, avenir; Actes du Colloque international de Salamanque (3-8 janvier 1988): CogF 149. P 1988, Cerf. 530 p. F 175. – ᴿNRT 111 (1989) 1037s (L. *Volpe*).

692 ᴱLegrand Hervé, *al.*, The nature and future of episcopal conferences [Salamanca 3-8.I. 1988 = Jurist 1988)]. Wsh 1988, Catholic Univ. 410 p. $20. – ᴿNewTR 2,2 (1989) 114 (J. M. *Hels*).

693 ᴱLemieux Raymond, *Richard* Reginald, Gnoses d'hier et d'aujourd'hui [Colloque 'ACFAS' 1984, 'Gnosticisme comme le salut par la connaissance]: Cahiers de recherches en sciences de la religion 7. Québec 1986, Univ. Laval. 316 p. 15 art. – ᴿSR 18 (1989) 104s (G. *Martel*).

694 [*Lévêque* J., pneumatologie johannique] Viens Esprit-Saint; rencontre spirituelle et théologique 1987: Centre Notre-Dame de Vie (Vaucluse) Spiritualité 4. Venasque 1988, Carmel. 332 p. F 146. – ᴿRTLv 20 (1989) 389s (A. de *Halleux*).

695 ᴱLevering Miriam, Rethinking Scripture [of various religions], essays from a comparative perspective. Albany 1989, SUNY. ix-276 p. $44.50; pa. $15. 0-88706-613-5; 4-3 [TDig 37,183]. 7 art., 4 infra.

695* ᴱLilienfeld Fairy von, *Ritter* Adolf M., Einheit der Kirche in vor-konstantinischer Zeit [Bern 2.-4.I.1985]: Oikonomia 25. Bamberg 1988, AKU. vii-165 p. DM 20. 7 art., 2 infra.

696 ᴱLivingstone Elizabeth A., Tenth international conference on patristic studies, Oxford 1987: Studia Patristica **19-23.** Lv 1989, Peeters. 5 vol.: **19**, Biblica, apocrypha...; xvi-405 p., 52 art.; 16 infra. – **20.** Critica, classica, orientalia, 408 p.; 57 art.; 8 infra. – **21.** 2 cent. & Athanasius, 455 p.; 50 art.; 10 infra. – **22.** Cappadocians, Chrysostom, Augustine; 386 p.; 52 art.; 3 infra. – **23.** Late Greek/Latin; Nachleben; 313 p.; 42 art.; 5 infra.

697 [*Lobato* A. dir.] GIOVANNI di San Tommaso, O.P. nel IV centenario della sua nascita (1589), Il suo pensiero filosofico, teologico e mistico; Atti del convegno SITA, Roma 25-28.XI.1988 = Angelicum 66,1 (1989) 192 p.

698 ᴱLopez Donald S.ᴶ, *Rockefeller* Steven C., The Christ and the Bodhisattva [Middlebury College Symposium 1984]. Albany 1987, SUNY. 274 p. $44.50; pa. $15. – ᴿNewTR 1,2 (1988) 108s (P. F. *Knitter*).

699 ᴱLucal J., *Laurier* P. de, Travail, cultures, religions [BIT = Institut International d'Études sociales de Genève), 'comme en 1982']. FrS 1988, Univ. 197 p. [NRT 111 (1989) 467s].

700 ᴱLuzzati Michele, *al.*, Ebrei e cristiani nell'Italia medievale e moderna; conversioni, scambi, contrasti; Atti del VI Congresso internazionale dell'A(ssociazione) I(taliana per lo) S(tudio del) G(iudaismo), F, S. Miniato 4-6. nov....: AISG TStudi 6. R 1988, Carucci. 288 p. Lit. 40.000. – ᴿBTAM 14 (1989) 606 (G. *Dahan*).

701 ᶠMacKINNON Donald: Christ, ethics and tragedy; essays in honour of ∼ [conference St. John's, Cambridge, 22-25 July 1986; 75th b.], ᴱSurin Kenneth. C 1989, Univ. xi-206 p. $37.50. 0-521-34137-X [TDig 37,151]. art.; 3 infra ➤ 4637.

702 ᴱMangum John M., The new faith-science debate; probing cosmology, technology and theology [1987 Larnaca consultation]. Minneapolis/ Geneva 1989, Augsburg/WCC. 165 p. $10 pa. – ᴿZygon 24 (1989) 487-9 (P. *Hefner*).

703 **Manna** Salvatore, present., Atti del VII colloquio cattolico-ortodosso [Bari 27-28.V.... (continuando 1985 'Fede, sacramenti e unità della Chiesa')]: Nicolaus 16 (1989) 1-140.

704 ᴱMartin Richard C., Approaches to Islam in religious studies [colloquium...]. Tucson 1985, Univ. Arizona. 243 p. $19. – ᴿDer Islam 66 (1989) 369s (M. A. *Köhler*).

705 ᴱMarty Martin E., *Greenspahn* Frederick E., Pushing the faith; proselytism and civility in a pluralistic world [Denver Judaic Studies Philips Symposium]: Jewish and Christian Traditions 5. NY 1988, Crossroad. xiv-190 p. $20. – ᴿAmerica 160 (1989) 403-5 (Alice L. *Laffey*); TS 50 (1989) 212 (M. H. *Kelleher*).

706 ᴱMarx J., Propagande et contre-propagande religieuses [colloque Religions et Laïcité Bru mai 1987]: ProbHistChr 17. Bru 1987, Univ. 238 p. Fb 760. – ᴿNRT 111 (1989) 596s (B. *Joassart*: histoire de l'oppression du kérygme par la propagande, dit H. SAVON p. 235).

707 ᴱMayer Cornelius, *Chelius* Karl-Heinz, Internationales Symposium über den Stand der Augustinus-Forschung, 12.-16. April 1987, Univ. Giessen; I. Res et signa: Cassiciacum 39/1. Wü 1989, Augustinus. xxv-262 p. DM 128. – ᴿDowR 107 (1989) 297-301 [lengthy and critical summaries, but no reviewer's name, even in Index].

708 ᴱMiglio M., al., Un pontificato ed una città, Sisto IV (1471-1484); Atti del convegno, Roma 3-7 dicembre 1984: Scuola Vaticana di Paleografia, littera antiqua 5. Vaticano 1986, Assoc. Roma nel Rinascimento. xv-826 p.; 65 fig. Lit. 100.000. – ᴿColcFranc 58 (1988) 412-4 (M. D'Alatri) [RHE 84,235*].

709 ᴱMoeller B., Guggisberg H. R., Ketzenverfolgung im 16. und im frühen 17. Jh. [Wolfenbüttel 2.-4. Okt. 1989]. [RHE 85, 157s, J.-F. Gilmont: on attend les Actes, Herzog August Bibliothek].

710 ᴱMoeller Bernd, Theologie in Göttingen; eine Vorlesungsreihe [250.j. Bestehen]: Gö. Univ. Schr. A/1. Gö 1987, Vandenhoeck & R. 412 p.; 44 fig. DM 48. 15 art. – ᴿJTS 40 (1989) 315 (R. Morgan: Nº 1 in biblical studies and church history); TRu 54 (1989) 427-431 (O. Kaiser).

711 ᴱMoingt Joseph, L'acte de croire: colloque Chantilly 28-30 juin 1988 = RechSR 77,1s (1989) 13-111. 165-250 → 7654.

712 Le mouvement confraternel au Moyen Âge, France, Italie, Suisse [Table Ronde Univ. Lausanne 9-11.V.1985]: Coll. ÉcFrR 97. Lausanne/R 1987, Univ./École Française. 420 p. F 350 [TR 85,85].

713 ᴱMoxnes Halvor, 'Feminist reconstruction of early Christian history', Oslo conference Nov. 1988: ST (now subtitled Scandinavian Journal of Theology, Oslo 1989) 1-163.

714 Neo-Fundamentalism and the humanist response [1986 Oslo conference]. Buffalo 1988, Prometheus. 184 p. $23. 11 art. – ᴿJScStR 29 (1989) 135s (J. H. Simpson); TS 50 (1989) 405 (Patrick M. Arnold: except for good essays by G. LARUE, V. BULLOUGH, and G. A. WELLS, fundamentalism is attacked as identical with religion itself by Paul KURTZ and the others).

715 ᴱNeri Emma, Il libro del meeting '89 [Nº 10, Rimini: 'Il paradosso', Albano Laziale] 1989, Meeting per l'amicizia fra i popoli. 460 p.; 42 color. fot. Lit. 18.000. c. 30 art. [più conferenze stampa ecc.], 1 infra.

716 ᴱNeumann Johannes, Fischer Michael W., Toleranz und Repression; zur Lage religiöser Minderheiten in modernen Gesellschaften [Symposium Ziest 1985]. Fra 1987, Campus. 349 p. – ᴿTR 85 (1989) 418s (W. Rüfner).

717 ᴱNicholls William, Modernity and religion [Univ. British Columbia 1981]: SR Sup 19. Waterloo ON 1987, W. Laurier Univ. iv-191 p. – ᴿRelStR 15 (1989) 238 (J. L. Price: '$14.95 Canada, $17.50 U. S.').

718 OCKHAM: International Colloquium on the thought and writings of William of Ockham, Oct. 10-12, 1985, Bonaventure Univ., NY, part 1-3: [= FrancSt 45-47]. St. Bonaventure NY 1984-6 [published 1988], Franciscan Institute. x-352 p.; xxx-264 p.; x-327 p. [TR 85,526].

719 ᴱOzment Steven, Religion and culture in the Renaissance and Reformation [Harvard symposium Nov. 1987]: Sixteenth Century Essays & Studies 11. Kirksville MO 1989, SixtC. 136 p. $30. 0-940474-11-5 [TDig 37,84].

720 ᴱPenzo Giorgio, SCHOPENHAUER e il sacro; atti del seminario, Trento 26-28 aprile 1984: IstScRel Trento 12. Bo 1987, Dehoniane. 195 p. Lit. 18.000.

721 a) ᴱPeretto Elio, Aspetti della presenza di Maria nella Chiesa in cammino verso il duemila; atti del 7. Simposio internazionale mariologico (Roma, 21-23 giugno 1988). R 1989, Marianum. [xvi-] 427 p. Lit. 35.000. 9 art.; 3 infra. – b) Maria nel cammino della Chiesa, Incontro Fac. Teol. Italia Merid. Napoli 26-27.V.1988 = Asprenas 36,2 (1989) 121-281.

722 ᴱPetit Jean-Claude, *Breton* Jean-Claude, Le christianisme d'ici a-t-il un avenir? Questions posées à nos pratiques [Soc. Canad. Théologie, Montréal 1988, Fides. 269 p. − ᴿScEspr 41 (1989) 260-2 (M. *Viau*).

723 ᴱPetri Heinrich, Divergenzen in der Mariologie; zur ökumenischen Diskussion über die Mutter Jesu [Tagung Walldürn Okt. 1986]: Arbeitsgemeinschaft für Mariologie / Mariologische Studien 7. Rg 1989, Pustet. 102 p. DM 28. − ᴿForumKT 5 (1989) 151-3 (M. *Hauke*); ÖkRu 38 (1989) 353 (H. *Vorster*: eher irritierend); TLZ 114 (1989) 854s (W. *Beinert*); TPhil 64 (1989) 621s (W. *Löser*); TPQ 137 (1989) 418s (E. *Röthlin*).

723* ᴱPlaner-Friedrich G., Frieden und Gerechtigkeit; auf dem Weg zu einer ökumenischen Friedensethik [Bad Boll 14-18.XII.1987]. Mü 1989, Kaiser. 231 p. DM 19,80. 3-459-01802-X. − ᴿTsTNijm 29 (1989) 425s (G. *Manenschijn*).

724 Pour une théologie contemporaine du Moyen-Orient; Actes du Iᵉʳ Symposium Interdisciplinaire, Inst. S.-Paul, Harissa 15-18 oct. 1987: Publ. Centre de Théologie pour le Moyen-Orient I. Beyrouth-Jounieh 1988, Saint-Paul. 322 p. $23. − ᴿNRT 111 (1989) 1016 (J. *Masson*).

725 ᴱPrawdzik Werner, [Dritte-Welt-] Wirklichkeit und Theologie; theologische Versuche und pastorale Impulse aus der Weltkirche [Missionstheologische Studienwoche 1987]. Nettetal 1988, Steyler. 164 p. [TR 85,168, tit. pp.].

726 Problemi di storia della Chiesa dal Vaticano I al Vaticano II: Associazione Italiana dei Professori di Storia della Chiesa. R 1988, Dehoniane. 471 p. Lit. 32.000. − P. 107-126, *Garofalo* S., Gli studi biblici in Italia da Leone XIII a Pio XII (1878-1958).

727 ᴱPuthanangady Paul, Sharing worship; communicatio in sacris [Bangalore meeting Jan. 1988]. 812 p. − ᴿTContext 6,2 (1989) 113s (G. *Evers*).

727* ᴱRenz Horst, *Graf* Friedrich W., Umstrittene Moderne; die Zukunft der Neuzeit im Urteil der Epoche Ernst ᴛʀᴏᴇʟᴛꜱᴄʜꜱ [2. T-Kongress]: Troeltsch-Studien [3. 1984 → 1,393] 4. Gü 1987, Mohn. 400 p. DM 75. 0-19-826670-7. − ᴿTsTNijm 29 (1989) 294 (T. *Schoof*).

728 ᴱRies J. (*Limet* H.), Anges et démons; Actes du colloque de Liège et de LvN, 25-26 nov. 1987: Homo religiosus 14. LvN 1989, Centre Hist. Rel. 466 p. Fb 1200. 24 art.; 18 infra. − ᴿRTLv 20 (1989) 363-6 (J. *Étienne*).

729 Ripensare il Concilio [interventi Centro di Teologia e Cultura di Trieste]: Cultura e Teologia 2. CasM 1986, Piemme. 181 p. Lit. 16.000. 88-384-1163-8. − ᴿGregorianum 70 (1989) 352s (R. *Fisichella*).

730 ᴱRobinson-Hammerstein Helga, The transmission of ideas in the Lutheran Reformation [Trinity College symposium 1983]. Dublin 1989, Irish Academic. 192 p., 8 art. − ᴿScripTPamp 21 (1989) 974s (J. *Morales*).

731 ᴱRobson John M., Origin and evolution of the universe; evidence for design? [McGill Univ. symposium 1985]. Montréal 1987, McGill-Queen's Univ. xvi-298 p. − ᴿSR 18 (1989) 240s (B. *Alton*).

732 *a*) Rom und der Norden 14.-16.IX.1987; − *b*) Das Episkopat des hl. Römischen Reiches 1648-1803, 21.-23.IX. 1987; − *c*) Katholische Reform, 26.-29.IX.1988: Symposia im Campo Santo Teutonico: Festschrift zum einhundertjährigen Bestehen der RömQ und des Römischen Instituts der Görres-Gesellschaft = RömQ 83 (1988) 25-210 / 211-396, 32 pl. / 84 (1989) 1-400.

733 ᴱRudavsky Tamar, Divine omniscience and omnipotence in medieval philosophy; Islamic, Jewish, and Christian perspectives → 2,336 [Ohio

State Univ. conference 1982]: Synthese Historical Library 25. Dordrecht 1985, Reidel. ix-299 p. ƒ140. – ᴿJAOS 108 (1988) 494s (B. *Weiss*).
734 Sagesse, éloquence, piété: colloque 11.-12.III.1988, Fac. prot. Strasbourg (450 anniv.; première partie): RHPR 69,1 (1989) 3-49.
735 La Salvezza oggi: Atti del Quinto Congresso Internazionale di Missiologia [5.-8.X.1988]: Studia Urbaniana 34. R 1989, Pont. Univ. Urbaniana. 609 p. Lit. 55.000. 88-401-1034-8. 11 + 26 art.; 9 infra.
736 ᴱSargent Michael G., De cella in seculum; religious and secular life and devotion in late medieval England [800th anniv. of HUGH of Avalon as bishop of Lincoln; Lincoln 20-22 July 1986]: C 1989, Brewer. 244 p.; 24 pl. $86. 0-85991-268-X [TDig 36,365].
737 ᴱSarmiento Augusto, *al.*, La misión del láico en la Iglesia de la Univ. de Navarra, 1987: Teológica 53. Pamplona 1987, Univ. 1094 p. – ᴿRThom 89 (1989) 348s (M. *Rivero*).
738 ᴱSavard Pierre, Actes du Colloque LAMENNAIS: RUnivOt 57,3 (1987, 'avant de rendre l'âme'). 113 p. – ᴿRHE 84 (1989) 567 (G. *Laperrière*).
738* ᴱSchaumberger C., *Schottroff* L., Schuld und Macht; Studien zu einer feministischen Befreiungstheologie [Kassel, Sommer 1987]. Mü 1988, Kaiser. 296 p. DM 49. 4-459-01758-9. – ᴿTsTNijm 29 (1989) 418s (C. *Halkes*).
739 ᴱSchilling Heinz, Die reformierte Konfessionalisierung in Deutschland — das Problem der 'zweiten Reformation' [transit to Calvinism: Göttingen-Reinhausen Okt. 1985]: Verein für Reformationsgeschichte. Gü 1986, Mohn. 480 p. 20 art. – ᴿRHE 84 (1989) 184 (P. *Denis*).
740 Schlegel J.L., *al.*, Le religieux en Occident; pensée des déplacements [session 1987]: Publ. 43. Bru 1988, Fac. univ. S.-Louis. 148 p. Fb 580. – ᴿNRT 111 (1989) 600s (M.J. *Horowitz*); TsTNijm 29 (1989) 416s (G. de *Grunt*).
741 ᴱSchmidt H.H., Mythos und Rationalität: Wiss. Ges. für Theol. [Wien 21.-25.IX.1987]. Gü 1988, Mohn. 396 p. DM 42. 3-579-00177-9. – ᴿTLZ 114 (1989) 795-9 (B. *Hildebrandt*); TsTNijm 29 (1989) 298s (P.A. van *Gennip*: p. 108 localiseert PANNENBERG nuchter in de omstandigheid dat 'heute die mythische Weltauffassung in weit höherem Masse des öffentlichen Interesses würdig zu sein scheint als das Evangelium selber'); ZAW 101 (1989) 163s (tit. pp.).
742 ᴱSchulz H., *Lewek* C., Frau und Mann in Kirche und Gesellschaft, Arbeitsergebnisse des Facharbeitskreises 1972-85, Bund der ev. Kirchen in der DDR. B 1987, Ev.-V. 200 p. DM 12,50. – ᴿZevEth 33 (1989) 75.
742* ᴱSchulz Hans-Joachim, **Speigl** Jakob, Bild und Symbol — glaubenstiftende Impulse: [Symposium kath. Fak. Würzburg, 'Nikaia 787-1987']. Wü 1988, Echter. 207 p. DM 24,80 pa. – ᴿTGL 79 (1989) 204s (W. *Beinert*).
743 Scienze della natura e problematiche religiose; Atti del convegno, Pisa 1987: FutUomo 14,3s (1987) 135 p.
744 ᴱSegl P., Der Hexenhammer; Entstehung und Umfeld des Malleus maleficarum von 1487: Bayreuther Historische Kolloquien 2. Köln 1988, Böhlau. x-255 p. [RHE 84,215*].
745 [Italia Judaica 26.] *a*) *Sermoneta* G., present., (p. 17-35), 'Gli Ebrei in Italia tra rinascimento ed età barocca'; – *b*) ... dalla segregazione alla prima emancipazione, ᴱ*Scandaliato Ciciani* Isotta: Atti del II/III Convegno Internazionale, Genova 10-15 giugno 1984 / TA 15-20 giugno 1986: Ministero per i beni culturali, Saggi 6. 11. R 1986/9. Ist. Poligrafico. 336 p. + ◐ 154: 64 color pl. 88-7125-001-X.

746 ᴱ**Shannon** David T., *Wilmore* Gayraud S.,   Black witness to the apostolic faith: Faith and Order Study Group [< Mid-Stream 24 (Oct. 1985)]. GR 1988, Eerdmans. 104 p. $6. – ᴿJEcuSt 26 (1989) 381s (D. S. *Armentrout*).

747 ᴱ**Sheils** W. J., *Wood* D.,   The churches; Ireland and the Irish; 1987s meetings, Ecclesiastical History Society: Studies in Church History 25. Ox 1989, Blackwell. xiv-418 p. £32.50 [RHE 84,314*].

748 Sogni, visioni e profezie nell'antico cristianesimo: XVII Incontro di Studiosi dell'Antichità Cristiana, R 5-7.V.1988 = (per l'ultima volta) AugR 29 (1989). 610 p.

749 ᴱ**Sookhdeo** Patrick,   New frontiers in mission [Wheaton consultation 1983]. GR/Exeter 1987, Baker/Paternoster.   190 p. £7. – ᴿCalvinT 24 (1989) 166s (C. *Van Gelder*); Themelios 14 (1988s) 112 (P. *Cotterell*).

750 South Pacific Theology, papers from the [first Evangelical] Consultation, Papua-NG 1986,   Ox 1987, Regnum.   109 p. – ᴿTContext 6,2 (1989) 111 (H. *Janssen*).

751 Spiritualità oblativa reparatrice [seminario Frascati 19-31.IX.1988]: Teologia viva, Fede e cultura 4. Bo 1989, Dehoniane.   205 p. Lit. 20.000. 88-10-40909-4.   10 art.; 4 infra.

752 ᴱ**Spykman** Gordon,   Let my people live; faith and struggle in central America [9-member Calvin Center Reformed approach to the crisis].   GR 1988, Eerdmans.   xvi-269 p. $10 pa. – ᴿCalvinT 24 (1989) 362-5 (J. W. *Skillen*).

753 ᴱ**Stivers** Robert L.,   Reformed faith and economics [13 out of many papers at Ghost Ranch ɴᴍ Presbyterian seminars 1985-7]. Lanham ᴍᴅ 1989, UPA. $29.50; pa. $14.75.   0-8191-7380-0; 1-9 [TDig 37,181, no pp.]. – ᴿTTod 46 (1989s) 454. 456 (A. *Geyer*).

754 Summary of the Proceedings of the American Theological Library Association 42. St. Meinrad ɪɴ 1988 [NTAbs 33,301].

755 ᴱ**Swidler** L.,   Toward a universal theology of religion [Temple Univ. symposium, Ph 1984]: Faith Meets Faith.   Mkn 1987, Orbis.   viii-256 p. – ᴿNRT 111 (1989) 598s (J. *Masson*).

756 Tᴇɪʟʜᴀʀᴅ: Atti del colloquio su Scienza conoscenza responsabilità, delle Associazioni francese e italiana Teilhard de Chardin e del Gruppo italiano 'Scienza e fede' (dove?) 23-25 sett. 1988: FutUom 16,2 (1989). 83 p.

757 La teología trinitaria de Jᴜᴀɴ Pᴀʙʟᴏ II [XXII Settimana di Studi Trinitari, 19-21.X.1987]. Salamanca 1988, Segretariado Trinitario.   220 p. – ᴿCC 140 (1989,2) 617s (G. *Caprile*).

758 Teología y comunicación de la fe; Actas de la 1ª Semana de Teología [S. Dámaso], M 26-28. IX.1988 = RET 49,2s (1989) 139-321.

759 ᴱ**Vattioni** Francesco,   Sangue e antropologia nella teologia; atti della VI Settimana, Roma 23-28 novembre 1987: Centro Studi Sanguis Christi 6. R 1989, Pia Unione Prez. Sangue.   I. 630 p.; II. p. 631-1284; III. 1287-1759 + 1761-1813 indice (in parte cumulativo) Sangue I-VI. Lit. 100.000. 63 art.; 27 infra.

760 ᴱ**Verbeke** W.,   The use and abuse of eschatology in the Middle Ages (international conference Lv 14-16.V.1984). Lv 1988, Univ. ix-513 p. – ᴿColcFran 59 (1959) 179-181 (B. de *Armellada*); Salmanticensis 36 (1989) 392s (J. L. *Ruiz de la Peña*).

761 Vivre le célibat sacerdotal; Congrès de l'Assoc. d'Entraide sacerdotal, Chantilly 8-10.III.1988: SuppVSp 166 (1988). 174 p. [Aucun art. ne touche ni suggère l'Écriture].

762 ᴱVorster W. S., Are we killing God's earth? Ecology and theology
[... seminar]. Pretoria 1987, Univ. S. Africa. ix-118 p. 0-86981-525-3. –
ᴿTsTNijm 29 (1989) 89 (T. *Brattinga*).

762* ᴱWacker Marie-Theres, Theologie feministisch; Disziplinen, Schwerpunkte, Richtungen [Rabanus-Maur-Akad. Tagung 1987]. Dü 1988,
Patmos. 204 p. DM 26 pa. – ᴿTGL 79 (1989) 205 (W. *Beinert*).

763 ᴱWagner Harald (*Kruse* Torsten), Ars moriendi; Erwägungen zur Kunst
des Sterbens [kath. Sem. Marburg]: QDisp 118. FrB 1989, Herder.
198 p. 3-451-02118-8 [TLZ 115.145, E. *Winkler*]. 9 art.; 4 infra.

764 [ꟳWAGNER Heinz], Leben im Diakonat der Kirche, Konferenz Halle
14.-18.IX.1987, ᴱ*Freytag* G. Bonn 1987, Kaiserswerther General-
konferenz. 176 p.; ill. 7 art. – ᴿTLZ 114 (1989) 16 (E.-H. *Amberg*).

764* ᴱWalt B. J. van der [→ k170], John Calvin's Institutes; his opus magnum
[proceedings of the 2d SAf. Congress for Calvin research, July 31-Aug. 3,
1984]. Potchefstron 1986, Univ. 528 p. – ᴿEvQ 61 (1989) 283-5 (A. N. S.
Lane).

765 ᴱWilliams Paul L., The Catholic Church's message to United States
citizens of the twenty-first century; proceedings of the tenth convention of
the Fellowship of Catholic Scholars. Pittston ᴘᴀ 1988, Northeast. 256 p.
$11. 0-937374-04-0. 21 art. [TDig 36,359].

766 ᴱWoodberry J. Dudley, Muslims and Christians on the Emmaus road;
crucial issues in witness among Muslims: Lausanne conference in Holland
1987. Monrovia ᴄᴀ 1989, ᴍᴀʀᴄ. xv-392 p. $16. 0-912552-65-4 [TDig
37,77]. – ᴿSWJT 32,3 (1989s) 62s (F. M. *Graham*).

767 ᴱYeow Choo Lak, Doing theology with cultures of Asia [inaugural
workshop, Kyoto 1987]; Occas. Paper 6. Singapore 1988, ᴀᴛᴇꜱᴇᴀ.
148 p. [TContext 7/1, 122, G. *Evers*].

768 ᴱZambelli Paola, 'Astrologi hallucinati'; Stars at the end of the world
in Luther's time [Berlin conference 28-29 May 1984]. B 1986, de Gruyter.
x-294 p. 10 art. – ᴿEngHR 104 (1989) 191s (J. V. *Field*); RTAM 56
(1989) 241s (G. *Hendrix*: tit. sans pp.); Salesianum 51 (1989) 523s (P.
Canaccini); ZKG 100 (1989) 128-132 (Barbara *Bauer*).

769 ᴱZeller Dieter, Menschwerdung Gottes — Vergöttlichung von Menschen
[Seminario Mainz 1986s]: NTOrb 7. FrS/Gö 1989, Univ./Vandenhoeck &
R. 223 p.; 9 fig. DM 82. 3-7278-0604-4 / VR 3-525-53906-1. 7 art.; infra.
– ᴿArTGran 52 (1989) 343s (A. *Segovia*); RivB (1989) 522s (A. *Bonora*);
TR 85 (1989) 528 (some tit. pp.).

770 ᴱZiegler Josef G., *Piegsa* Joachim, 'In Christus', Beiträge zum
ökumenischen Gespräch [Univ. Mainz, Vortragsreihe]: Moralth. Studien
14. St. Ottilien 1987, ᴇᴏꜱ. 168 p. DM 38. – ᴿZkT 111 (1989) 245 (H.
Rotter).

771 ᴱZimmermann A., *Kopp* C., Thomas von AQUIN, Werk und Wirkung im
Licht neuerer Forschungen: Köln, Miscellanea Mediaevalia 19. B 1988,
de Gruyter. xi-507 p. DM 252. – ᴿBTAM 14 (1989) 730-745 (R.
Wielockx); RelStR 15 (1989) 60 (T. B. *Noon*); Scriptorium 43 (1989) 184*s
(also R. *Wielockx*).

A2.5 *Acta* philologica *et* historica [reports → Y7.6].

772 Actes de l'Association (7 nov. 1988-21 juin 1989): RÉG 102,2 (1989)
IX-L.

773 ᴱAllén Sture, Possible worlds in humanities, arts and sciences [IBM
Nordic education center, Nobel symposium 65, Stockholm-Lidingö

Aug. 11-15, 1986]: Research in Text Theory 14. B 1989, de Gruyter. x-453 p.; ill. 3-11-011220-5. 35 art.; 2 infra.

774 ᴱ**Aquilon** P., *Martin* H.-J., Le livre dans l'Europe de la Renaissance; Actes du XXVIIIᵉ colloque internat. d'études humanistes de Tours. P 1988, Promodis. 587 p.; ill. [RHE 84, p. 422*].

775 ᴱ**Arrighetti** Graziano, *al.*, La filologia greca e latina nel secolo XX; Atti del Congresso Internazionale Cons. Naz. Ricerche, 17-21.IX.1984: Biblioteca di Studi Antichi 56. Pisa 1989, Giardini. I. xviii-589 p.; II. p. 591-1180; III. Indice (*Lamedica* Armida) 301 p. 17 + 22 art.; survey of separate modern states, exc. ➤ 9671.

776 ᴱ**Bataillon** L.-J., *al.*, La production du livre universitaire au moyen âge; exemplar et pecia: Actes Grottaferrata mai 1983. P 1988, CNRS. 334 p., 19 pl. – ᴿRSPT 73 (1989) 570-4 (Olga *Weijers*) & 88s (tit. pp.).

777 ᶠBɪᴛᴛᴇʟ Kurt, 80. Gb.: Zivile und militärische Strukturen im Nordwesten der römischen Provinz Raetien, 3. Heidenheimer Archäologie-Colloquium, 9.-10. Okt. 1987; ᴱ**Weimert** Helmut. Heidenheim 1988, Heimat- und Altertumsverein. 173 p. [AnPg 59,970].

778 ᴱ**Blanchard** A., Les débuts du codex, Actes de la journée d'étude P 3-4.VII.1985: Bibliologia 9. Turnhout 1989, Brepols. [197 p.]. – ᴿAegyptus 69 (1989) 282s (S. *Daris*).

779 ᴱ**Campanile** Enrico, *al.*, Bilinguismo e biculturalismo nel mondo antico, Atti del colloquio interdisciplinare Pisa 28-29.IX.1987: Testi linguistici 13. Pisa 1988, Giardini. 100 p. [OIAc S89]. – ᴿBSLP 84,2 (1989) 174s (Françoise *Bader*).

780 ᴱ**Ceard** J., *Margolin* J.-C., Voyager à la Renaissance; Actes du Colloque de Tours, 30 juin-13 juillet 1983. P 1987, Maisonneuve & L. 677 p.; 8 pl. F 298 [RHE 84,303*].

781 ᴱ**Clover** F. M., *Humphreys* R. S., Tradition and innovation in late antiquity [Seminar Madison 25-27.IV.1984 & Ch 18.X.1984]: Studies in Classics. Madison 1989, Univ. Wisconsin. xx-343 p.; 64 fig.; 3 maps; 0-299-12000-7 [AnBoll 108,427s J. *Kluyckens*]. 13 art.; 3 infra.

782 ᴱ**Delcourt** Christiane, Actes du colloque 'Éditer le Texte' [surtout français moyen-âge], Bru Univ 28.I.1989: RBgPg 67,3 (1989) 521-672. 8 art.

782* ᴱ**Descat** Raymond, L'or perse et l'histoire grecque, Table Ronde CNRS Bordeaux, 20-22 mars 1989 = RÉAnc 91,1s (1989) 344 p. F 420. 0035-2004. 20 art.; infra.

783 Deutscher Altphilologenverband, Tagung in Bonn 1988, Vorträge I-II = Gymnasium 96,4s (1989) 8 + 7 art.; 2 infra.

784 ᴱ**Devijver** H., *Lipiński* E., Punic wars; proceedings of the conference held in Antwerp Nov. 22-26, 1988: OrLovAn 33/StPhoen 10. Lv 1989, Peeters. viii-373 p.; ill. 90-6831-219-7. 30 art.; 15 infra.

785 ᴱ**Eck** W., *Wolff* H., Heer und Integrationspolitik; die römischen Militärdiplome als historische Quelle [1984 Kolloquium]: Passauer Hist. For. 2. Köln 1986, Böhlau. [v-]615 p. 3-412-06686-9. – ᴿJRS 79 (1989) 227s (B. *Campbell*).

786 Les écrivains et le sacré [&] La vigne et le vin dans la littérature, I: Actes de l'Association G. Budé, XIIᵉ Congrès, Bordeaux, 17-21 août 1988. P 1989, BLettres. 505 p. 2-251-69012-5. 117 art.; plusieurs infra.

787 ᴱ**Fancy** Margaret, *Cohen* Ivan, Crake lectures 1984 (symposium Sept. 27s). Sackville, New Brunswick 1986. 59 p. 3 art., infra.

788 Fᴏʀʟᴀᴛɪ Tᴀᴍᴀʀᴏ Bruna, Giornata di studio in onore di ∼. Aquileia 1989, Assoc. Naz. 79 p.; ill.

789 ᴱGallo I., Aspetti dello stoicismo e dell'epicureismo in PLUTARCO [2°
congresso 1987]: Quad. Giornale Fg. 9. Ferrara 1988. 142 p. (109-118
Brenk F.). – ᴿREG 102 (1989) 606s (A. *Laks*).

790 ᴱGentili Bruno, *Pretagostini* Roberto, La musica in Grecia [convegno
Urbino 18-20.X.1985]. R 1988, Laterza. xii-317 p. 88-420-3302-2. 19 art.,
2 infra.

790* ᴱGrottanelli Cristiano, *Parise* Nicola F., Sacrificio e società nel mondo
antico [in parte < convegno dell'Univ. di Siena a Pontignano 23-25 sett.
1983]. Bari 1988, Laterza. ix-307 p. 88-420-3267-0. 14 art., infra.

791 ᴱHackens Tony, *Marchetti* Patrick, Histoire économique de l'Antiquité:
réunion Anvers, Univ. Fac. Sint-Ignatius [30.III.1985]. Lv 1987, Sém.
Numismatique M. Hoc. 169 p. 8 art., 6 infra.

792 ᴱHägg Robin, *al.*, Early Greek cult practice; proceedings of the Fifth
International Symposium at the Swedish Institute at Athens, 26-29 June,
1986: Skrifter 4°, 38. Göteborg 1988, Åström. 303 p.; ill. 91-85086-97-5
[Antiquity 63,383].

793 ᴱHankinson R.I., Method, medicine and metaphysics; studies in the
philosophy of ancient science [Montreal McGill Univ. Oct. 2-3, 1986]:
Apeiron 21. Alberta 1988. 194 p. 5 art. – ᴿElenchos 10 (1989) 461-4 (L.
Simeoni).

794 ᴱHermann Joachim, *Müller* Reimar, Die Antike und Europa, Zentrum
und Peripherie in der antiken Welt; Beiträge vom 17. Internationalen
Eirenekongress (Berlin, 11.-15.VIII.1986) = Klio 71/1 (1989) 1-210 [21
art. not included in the 1990 volume of Acta] 6 infra.

795 ᴱJanni Pietro, *Lanzilotta* Eugenio, Geōgraphia, Atti del Secondo Convegno Maceratese su Geografia e Cartografia antica (16-17 apr. 1985).
R 1988, Bretschneider. 222 p. 88-7689-046-7. 9 art.; 3 infra.

796 ᴱLaurens Annie-France, Entre hommes et dieux; le convive, le héros, le
prophète [équipe Univ. Montpellier]: Lire les polythéismes 2 / Annales
Litt. Univ. Besançon 391. P 1989, BLettres. 199 p. 12 art.; 1 infra.

797 Lévêque P., *Mactoux* M.-M., présent., Les grandes figures religieuses
[... héroiques, impériales]; fonctionnement pratique et symbolique dans
l'Antiquité; Besançon 25-26 avril 1984: Centre Hist. Anc. 68/1; Annales
329. P 1986, BLettres. 607 p. – ᴿAJA 93 (1989) 467s (Susan G. *Cole*).

798 ᴱLevi Mario E., *al.*, La città antica come fatto di cultura; Atti del
convegno di Como e Bellagio 16-19.VI.1979 [1900° anniv. morte PLINIO
S.]. Como 1983, Municipio. 410 p.; 40 fig.; 2 foldouts. – ᴿAnzAltW 42
(1989) 78-82 (H. *Grassl*).

799 ᴱNatalini T., Cento anni di cammino; scuola Vaticana di paleografia,
diplomatica e archivistica (1884-1984); Atti delle manifestazioni per il
Centenario della Scuola con documentazione relativa alla sua storia.
Vaticano 1986. 342 p. 28 pl. [RHE 85,262, R. *Aubert*).

800 ᴱPrinz-von *Hohenzollern* J.G., *Liedtke* M., Schreiber-Magister-Lehrer;
zur Geschichte und Funktion eines Berufstandes [Symposion Ichen-
hausen 1.-4.X.1987]. Bad Heilbrunn 1989, Klinkhardt. 362 p. DM 36.
S. 33-50, *Waetzoldt* H., Der Schreiber als Lehrer in Mesopotamien;
51-59, *Wanke* G., Der Lehrer im alten Israel; 60-70, *Fischer-Elfert*
H.W., Der Schreiber als Lehrer in der frühen ägyptischen Hochkultur
[< ZAW 101,475].

801 ᴱRahtz Sebastian, Information technology in the humanities; tools,
techniques and applications. [Univ. Southampton conference 1987].
Chichester 1987, Horwood. [xiv-]184 p. 0-7458-0148-X. 13 art. –
ᴿLitLComp 4 (Ox 1989) 245 (W.J. *Jones*).

802 ᴱRidder-Symoens Mme H. De, *Fletcher* J. M., Academic relations between the Low Countries and the British Isles 1450-1700: first historians of universities conference, Ghent Sept. 30-Oct. 2, 1987: Studia historica gandensia 273. Ghent 1989, Univ. 161 p. Fb 500 [RHE 85, 173, J. *Paquet*].

803 St. Louis [Univ.] Fifteenth/Sixteenth conference on manuscript studies, 14-15 Oct. 1988 / 13-14 Oct. 1989; abstracts of papers: Manuscripta 7,32 (1988) 163-176 / 8,33 (1989) 155-168.

804 Schmidt Wilhelm [1868-1954], un etnologo sempre attuale [Convegno commemorativo Trento 27.IX.1986], ᴱDemarchi Franco: IstScRel 14. Bo 1989, Dehoniane. 251 p. Lit. 28.000. 88-10-40364-8. 12 art.; 5 infra.

805 ᴱSilverman Hugh J., *Ihde* Don, Hermeneutics and deconstruction [Society for Phenomenology and Existential Philosophy 1981-3]. Albany 185, SUNY. xii-309 p. $44.50; pa. $20. – ᴿJRel 68 (1988) 307s (M. C. *Taylor*).

806 Skutsch Otto: Vir bonus discendi peritus, 2-day conference for his 80th b., ᴱHorsfall Nicholas: Bulletin Sup 51. L 1988, Univ. Inst. Clas. ix-188 p.; portr. £30 [ClasR 40,449-452, M. D. *Reeve*]. – ᴿGreeceR 36 (1989) 240 (D. *Fowler*); RÉLat 66 (1988) 402s (H. *Zehnacker*); both have 'discendi', correctly; p. vii attributes the title (without explanation) to Bill Calder and ultimately to Wilamowitz.

807 ᴱValentin Jean-Marie, Jacob Balde [S.J., geb. 1604] und seine Zeit, Akten des Ensisheimer Kolloquiums 15.-16. Oktober 1982 = Jb. Internat. Germanistik A-16. Bern 1986, Lang. 290 p. – ᴿRÉLat 66 (1988) 406s (J. *Chomarat*).

808 ᴱWallace-Hadrill Andrew, Patronage in ancient society: Leicester-Nottingham [1984-6 meetings] Studies in Ancient Society 1. L 1989, Routledge. 255 p. 0-415-00341-5. 11 art.; 4 infra. → g157.

809 ᴱWhittaker C., Pastoral economies in classical antiquity [9th Economic History congress, Bern 1986]. C 1988, Pg. Soc. 218 p. 12 art.; 2 infra. – ᴿAmJPg 110 (1989) 668-675 (R. *Brilliant*: long comment); GreeceR 36 (1989) 112s (T. *Wiedemann*).

A2.7   *Acta* orientalistica.

810 ᴱAbdalla Abdelgadir M., Studies in ancient languages of the Sudan, 2d International Conference 1970: Sudan Studies 3. Khartoum 1974, Univ. x-129 p. [OIAc N89].

811 ᴱAcquaro Enrico, *al.*, Momenti precoloniali [miceneo, fenicio ...] nel Mediterraneo antico; aree d'indagine, evidenze a confronto; Atti del Convegno Internazionale, Roma 14-16 marzo 1985: StFen Collez. 28. R 1988, Cons. Naz. Ricerche. 297 p. 28 art.; 23 infra.

812 Atti del XIII Congresso dell'Union Européenne d'Arabisants et Islamisants [Venezia 1986]: Quaderni di Studi Arabi 5s (for 1987s). Venezia 1988, Dipartimento di Scienze stor/arch/or. 798 p. 62 art. – ᴿJAOS 109 (1989) 718s (Jeanette *Wakin* notes many things but none of biblical interest).

813 ᴱBryer Anthony, *Lowry* Heath, Continuity and change in Late Byzantine and Early Ottoman society; Symposium Dumbarton Oaks, May 1982. Birmingham 1986, Univ. vii-343 p. £12. – ᴿDLZ 110 (1989) 296-300 (K.-P. *Matschke*).

814 ^E**Donadoni** Sergio, *Wenig* Steffen, Studia meroitica 1984; proceedings of the fifth international conference for Meroitic studies: Meroitica 10. B 1989, Akademie. 896 p.; ill. 3-05-000354-5. 45 art., plures infra.

815 ^E**Eber** Irene, Confucianism; the dynamics of tradition [Jerusalem Hebrew Univ. conference 1983]. NY 1986, Macmillan. xxii-234 p. $27.50. – ^RJAOS 108 (1988) 652s (R. L. *Taylor*).

816 ^E**Fahd** T., L'Arabie préislamique et son environnement historique et culturel; Actes du Colloque de Strasbourg, 24-27 juin 1987: Centre Rech. Pr. Orient 10. Leiden 1989, Brill. 584 p. 90-04-09115-7 [OIAc Ja90]. 33 art.; 25 infra.

817 ^E**Goldenberg** Gideon, Ethiopian studies; proceedings of the sixth international conference, Tel-Aviv, 14-17 April 1980. Rotterdam 1986, Balkema. xiv-530 p. *f*135. 27 art. [+ 4 others]. – ^RJAOS 109 (1989) 135s (G. *Hudson*; data on the other meetings); OLZ 84 (1989) 98s (S. *Uhlig*: titles sans pp.); RSO 63 (1989) 320-7 (R. *Contini*).

817* ^E**Haas** Volkert, Hurriter und Hurritisch; Konstanzer Altorientalische Symposien 2.: Xenia 21. Konstanz 1988, Univ. 318 p.; 53 fig.; map. DM 114 [ClasR 40,87, E. *Masson*]. 10 art., 9 infra.

818 ^E**Kramer** Martin, Shi'ism, resistance, and revolution [Univ. TA meeting Dec. 1984]. Boulder/L 1987, Westview/Mansell. x-324 p. – ^RDer Islam 65 (1988) 348s (W. *Ende*).

819 ^E**Potts** D. T., Araby the blest. 1988. [OIAc S89].

820 ^E**Rosenstiehl** Jean-Marc, *a*) Deuxième journée d'Études Coptes [→ 3,777], Strasbourg 25 mai 1984: Cahiers de la Bibliothèque Copte 3. Lv 1986, Peeters. 15 art., 9 infra. – *b*) Troisième Journée d'Études Coptes, Musée du Louvre 23 mai 1986: Cah. Bibliothèque Copte 4. Lv 1989, Peeters. vi-154 p. 90-6831-201-4. 11 art.; 8 infra.

821 ^E**Rippin** Andrew, Approaches to the history of the interpretation of the Qur'an [Calgary Univ. Apr. 1985]. Ox 1988, Clarendon. xi-334 p. $60. 0-19-826546-8. 14 art. [TDig 37,42].

822 ^E**Salles** Jean-François, L'Arabie et ses mers bordières [Séminaire 1985s] 1. Itinéraires et voisinages: Travaux 16. P 1988, Maison de l'Orient. 199 p.; ill. 2-903264-45-7. 10 art., 5 infra. – ^RMesopT 24 (1989) 203-5 (E. *Valtz*).

823 ^E**Schoske** Sylvia, Akten des vierten internationalen Ägyptologen-Kongresses, München 1985 [1. 1988 → 4,770]; 2. Archäologie – Feldforschung – Prähistorie; 3. Linguistik – Philologie – Religion: StAltÄgKBeih. 2s Ha 1989, Buske. viii-359 p.; 24 pl. ix-459 p.; 9 pl. 3-87118-902-2; 3-0. 37 + 43 art., plures infra.

823* ^E**Schuler** E. von, XXIII. Deutscher Orientalistentag, Würzburg 16.-20. Sept. 1985; Ausgewählte Vorträge: ZDMG Sup 7. Stu 1989, Steiner. 717 p. DM 298. 3-515-04961-4.

824 ^E**Théodoridès** Aristide, *al.*, La formazione del diritto nel Vicino Oriente Antico; seminario: Univ. Roma, Diritto Romano 65. R 1988, Ed. Scientifiche [OIAc S89].

825 ^E**Werner** Jürgen, Griechenland – Ägäis – Zypern; Vorträge der wissenschaftlichen Konferenz 'Das moderne Griechenland und das moderne Zypern in der Forschung der sozialistischen Gesellschaft' 1984. Univ. Wiss. Beit. ges. Lp 1987, Univ. 136 p. – ^RDLZ 110 (1989) 253-6 (K. *Szabó*).

826 ^E**Zimmermann** Albert, *al.*, Orientalische Kultur und europäisches Mittelalter [24th Cologne Congress of Medievalists, Sept. 1984, not mentioned in book]: Misc. Mediaevalia 17. x-440 p. DM 212. 3-

11-010531-4. – ᴿBO 46 (1989) 487-493 (M. *Kruk*: some on Crusades and first Latin Qor'an).

A2.9   *Acta* **archaeologica**   [meeting-reports ➤ Y7.8].

827   Actes du XIᵉ Congrès d'Archéologie Chrétienne; Lyon, Vienne, Grenoble, Genève et Aoste (21-28 sept. 1986) ᴱ*Duval* Noël, *al.*: Collection Éc.Fr.R. 123. R 1989, École Française. I. cxxvii-858 p.; II. - p. 2029; III. - p. 2919. 2-7283-0194-8, all [I. - 5-6; II. - 6-4; III. - 7-2]. 24 + 45 + 30 art.; 13 infra.

828   ᴱ**Adam** Anne-Marie, *Rouveret* Agnès,   Guerre et société en Italie aux Vᵉ et IVᵉ siècles avant J.-C.; les indices fournis par l'armement et les techniques de combat: Table Ronde, Équipe de Recherches Étrusco-Italiques, Paris 5 mai 1984. P 1988, École Normale Supérieure. 165 p.; 18 pl. F 140 pa. 3-7288-0135-5 [AJA 93,624].

829   Archaeological Institute of America, 90th meeting, Baltimore 5-9 January 1989, summaries of papers: AJA 93 (1989) 247-283; author index 283s. Some 150 summaries; 9 infra.

830   Archeologia e informatica... Convegno Roma 3-5 marzo 1988 [ᴱ**Liberati** **Silverio** Anna Maria]; DialArchQuad 4. R 1988, Quasar. 192 p. [ArchCalc 1, 311-3, M. *Rendelli*]. 19 art.

830*   Archéologie et médecine, VIIèmes rencontres internationales d'archéologie et d'histoire d'Antibes, 23-25 oct. 1986. Antibes 1987, Musée. 586 p. F 160. 2-904110-08-0. – ᴿAntClas 58 (1989) 396-8 (S. *Byl*: à côté d'un grain excellent, un peu trop d'ivraie).

831   ᴱ**Archi** Alfonso, Eblaite personal names and Semitic name-giving; Symposium Rome July 15-17, 1985: ARES 1. R 1988, Univ. Missione in Siria. XIII-306 p.; ill. 14 art., 10 infra.

831*   ᴱ**Åström** Paul, High, middle or low? Acts of an international colloquium on absolute chronology, Univ. Gothenburg 20-22 Aug. 1987, Part [(I-)II 1987; 88 p., 4 art.] 3: SIMA pocket 80. Göteborg 1989, Åström. 207 p.; ill. 91-86098[65-9]94-2.

832   ᴱ**Aurenche** Olivier, *Cauvin* Jacques,   Néolithisations; proche et moyen orient, Méditerranée orientale, ...: BAR-Int 516.   Ox/Lyon 1989, -/ CNRS-Univ. Lumière.   332 p.   0-86054-657-8 [OIAc N89].

832*   [BALY Dennis mém.] ᴱ**LaBianca** Øystein S., *Hopkins* David C., Early Israelite Agriculture: symposium on HOPKINS, Highlands of Canaan 1985: Inst. Archaeology, Occas.P.1.   Berrien Springs MI 1988, Andrews Univ. xi-55 p. – ᴿLA 39 (1989) 277 (P. *Kaswalder*).

833   ᴱ**Bintliff** John, *al.*, Conceptual issues in environmental archaeology. E 1988, Univ. x-320 p.; 79 fig. £35. 0-85224-545-9. – ᴿAntiquity 63 (1989) 855 (D. F. *Dincuase*: in concluding hints that this is one of 'any number of symposium volumes' but does not hint where or when).

834   ᴱ**Boddington** A., *al.*, Death, decay and reconstruction; approaches to archaeology and forensic science [Leeds Univ. conference 1986]. Manchester 1987, Univ. 250 p.; 71 fig. £27.50. – ᴿAJA 93 (1989) 462 (T. *O'Connor*).

835   **Brentjes** Burchard, *al.*, Das Grundeigentum in Mesopotamien: Jb Wirtschaftsgeschichte Sdb 1987. B 1988, Akademie. 185 p. 3-05000339-1 [OIAc N89].

836   ᴱ**Burnett** A. M., *Crawford* M. H.,   Coinage of the Roman world in the late Republic; colloquium British Museum Sept. 1985: BAR-Int 326. Ox

1987. 186 p.; 12 pl. £15. – ᴿAcNum 17s (Barc 1987s) 355 (L. *Villaronga*: 'Ceawford'); NumC 149 (1989) 245-7 (M. *Amandy*).

837 ᴱ**Campion** Timothy C., Centre and periphery; comparative studies in archaeology [World Archaeological Congress, Southampton 1986]: One World Archaeology 11. L 1989, Unwin Hyman. xxi-240 p.; ill. 0-04-44024-9. 13 art.; 1 infra.

838 ᴱ**Christiansen** Jette, Ancient Greek and related pottery: Congrès int. céramique 3, K Sept. 1987. K 1988, Nationalmuseet. 683 p. 87-7452-91-1 [sic]. 65 art., 4 infra.

840 ᴱ**Deroche** V., *Spieser* J.-M., Recherches sur la céramique byzantine; Actes du colloque Éc. Fr. Athènes / Univ. Strasbourg II (Athènes, 8-10 avril 1987): BCH Sup. 18. P 1989, de Boccard. 330 p.; ill. 2-86958-025-8. 30 art.; 2 infra.

841 ᴱ**Dolce** Rita, 17-48; *Zaccagnini* Carlo, 101-116, Il pane del Re — accumulo e distribuzione dei cereali nell'Oriente Antico [seminario apr. 1985; 49-63, *Frangipane* Marcello; 65-100, *Milano* Lucio; 117-132, *Grottanelli* Cristiano]: Studi di Storia Antica 13. Bo 1989, Coop. Univ. 135 p. Lit. 20.000 [BL 90,120, K. A. *Kitchen*].

842 ᴱ**Englund** Gertie, The religion of the ancient Egyptians; cognitive structures and popular expressions; proceedings of symposia in Uppsala and Bergen 1987s: Boreas 20. Uppsala 1989, Almqvist & W. vii-147 p. 91-554-2433-3 [OIAc Ja90].

843 ᴱ**Fant** J. Clayton, Ancient marble quarrying and trade: AJA colloquium, San Antonio Dec. 1986: BAR-Int 453. xii-165 p.; ill. 0-86054-582-2. 5 art.; 2 infra.

844 ᴱ**Farioli Campanati** R., La Siria araba da Roma a Bisanzio, Colloquio internazionale Ravenna, 22-24 marzo 1988, Univ. Bologna. Ravenna 1989, Lapucci. – ᴿAION 49 (1989) 156s (F. *Vattioni*: in gran parte identico col 'XXXV corso di cultura Ravennate' del Farioli 1988).

845 ᴱ**Hachlili** Rachel, Ancient synagogues in Israel, 3d-7th century C.E.; Proceedings of Symposium, Univ. Haifa May 1987: BAR-Int 499. Ox 1989. iv-105 p.; ill. £12. 0-86054-640-3. 12 art.; infra. – ᴿBAnglIsr 9 (1989s) 59-61 (Claudine *Dauphin*).

ᴱ**Hole** F., Archaeology of Western Iran 1977/87 [4,744] ➤ e268.

846 **Hours** F., Mémoire de l'humanité; du néolithique à la Bible: Colloque Chantilly 4-6 janv. 1986: CahICLyon 17. Lyon 1986, Association des facultés catholiques. 110 p. 2-903583-14-5 [OIAc Ja90].

847 **Kommos** [Crete] Symposium, Toronto Dec. 29, 1984, Proceedings: ᴱ**Shaw** Joseph W. & Maria C.: Scripta Mediterranea 6 (1985). 61 p.; 10 fig.; IV pl. – *Watrous* L.V., p. 7-18; *Betancourt* P., p. 31-44; *LaRose* V., p. 45-58.

848 ᴱ**Lasarov** M., al., Thracia pontica II. Le littoral thrace et son rôle dans le monde ancien [Symposium, Sozopol, Bulgaria, Oct. 1982]. Jambol 1985, Académie Bulgare. 373 p.; 41 pl. 14 maps. – ᴿIntJNaut 18 (1989) 149 (Mensun *Bound*).

ᴱ**Lauvergne** J. J., Populations... ovicaprinae 1986/8 ➤ e990.

849 LAYARD: ᴱ**Fales** F. M., *Hickey* B. J., Austen Henry Layard [1817-1894] tra l'Oriente e Venezia; symposium internazionale Venezia 26-28 ott. 1983: Fenice 8. R 1987, Bretschneider. vii-237 p.; LII pl. 88-7062-632-6. 19 art.; 2 infra ➤ b939.

850 [Lepsius Karl R. 1810-1884] **Freier** Elke, *Reineke* Walter F., ∼, Akten der Tagung anlässlich seines 100. Todestages, 10.-12.VII.1984 in Halle:

Schriften zur Geschichte und Kultur des AO 20. B 1988, Akademie. 324 p. DM 110 [JAOS 109,721].

851 ᴱLesko Barbara S., Women's earliest records: from Ancient Egypt and Western Asia [Brown Univ. Nov. 5-7, 1987]: BrownJudSt 166. Atlanta 1989, Scholars. xl-350 p.; 36 fig. $70; sb. $50; 1-555-40319-0. 13 art. [BL 90,123, G. I. *Emmerson*).

852 ᴱLinders Tullia, *Hellström* Pontus, Architecture and society in Hecatomnid Caria; Proceedings of the Uppsala Symposium 1987: Boreas 17. U 1989, Almqvist & W. 104 p. 91-554-2355-8. 11 art.; infra.

853 ᴱLund Cajsa S., Second conference of the ICTM-study-group on music archaeology, Stockholm 19-23.XI.1984. Sto 1986, Royal Acad. Music. 2 vol. vol. 1, 242 p., 20 art.; 4 infra (vol. 2, 253 p.: 16 art. on bronze 'lur'). 91-85428-48-5.

854 ᴱMaddin Robert [western participants' contributions], The beginning of the use of metals and alloys; papers from the 2d International Conference, Zhengshou, China, 21-26 October 1986. CM 1988, MIT. xiv-393 p.; 300 ill. $55. 0-262-13232-X. $55. – ᴿAntiquity 63 (1989) 835-7 (P. *Craddock*).

855 ᴱMalkin Irad, *Hohlfelder* Robert L., Mediterranean cities; historical perspectives [Haifa 1986 = MeditHistR 3/1]. L 1988, Cass. 200 p.; 21 fig. 13 art. – ᴿAJA 93 (1989) 480s (G. E. *Rickman*).

856 ᴱMastino A., L'Africa romana I-III [Sassari 1983-4-5]. Sassari 1984-5-6, Gallizzi. 226 p.; 286 p.; 457 p. Lit. 40.000 ognuno. – ᴿAION 48 (1988) 155-7 (F. *Vattioni*).

857 ᴱMiroschedji Pierre de, L'urbanisation de la Palestine à l'âge du Bronze Ancien; bilan et perspectives des recherches actuelles; Actes du Colloque d'Emmaüs 20-24 oct. 1986: BAR-Int 527. Ox 85054-670-5 [OIAc Ja90].

858 ᴱMüller Walter, Fragen und Probleme zur bronzezeitlichen ägäischen Glyptik; 3. Symposium Marburg 5.-7.IX.1985: Corpus min./myk. Siegel Beih 3. B 1989, Mann. vii-353 p. 3-7861-1542-7. 23 art.; 6 infra.

859 ᴱNibbi Alessandra, The archaeology, geography and history of the Egyptian Delta in Pharaonic times: proceedings of colloquium, Oxford 29-31 August 1988: DiscEg Sup 1. Ox 1989. 348 p. 22 art.; infra.

860 ᴱNitecki Matthew H. & Doris V., The [paleolithic] evolution of human hunting [9th Field Museum symposium, Chicago 10.V.1986]. NY 1987, Plenum. 464 p. $75. – ᴿAJA 93 (1989) 462-4 (Pamela R. *Willoughby*).

861 ᴱPeltenburg Edgar, Early society in Cyprus [proceedings of the April 1988 Edinburgh conference]: National Museums of Scotland / Leventis Fd. E 1989, Univ. xvi-404 p. 0-85224-633-1 [OIAc N89].

862 ᴱPensabene P., Marmi antichi; problemi d'impiego, di restauro e d'identificazione [incontro 1982, Univ.], Roma Museo dei Gessi: Studi Miscellanei 26. R 1985, Bretschneider. viii-254 p.; ill.; maps. – ᴿJRS 79 (1989) 222s (J. C. *Fant*: useful, though the more technical papers have been surpassed or published elsewhere).

863 ᴱPisano Giovanna, Da Mozia a Marsala, un crocevia della civiltà mediterranea; Convegno nazionale Marsala 4-5 aprile 1987. R c.1989. 186 p. 20 art.; 5 infra.

864 ᴱRaban Avner, Archaeology of coastal changes: Cities on the sea, past and present, International Symposium Haifa Sept. 22-29, 1986: BAR-Int 404. Ox 1988. 0-86054-519-9. 13 art.; 2 infra → d158.

865 ᴱRahtz S. P. Q., Computer and quantitative methods in archaeology [1988 Birmingham meeting]: BAR-Int 446. Ox 1988. 550 p. (2 vol.) [ArchCalc 1, 309-311, Paola *Moscati*].

866 ᴱSlater Elizabeth A., *Tate* James O., Science and archaeology: Proceedings of a conference on the application of scientific techniques to archaeology, Glasgow, Sept. 1987, I-II: BAR-Brit. 196. Ox 1988. xi-303 p., p. 305-650 ill. 0-86054-581-4. 64 art. ➤ 897*.

867 ᴱSoffer Olga, The pleistocene Old World, regional perspectives. NY 1987, Plenum. xxi-380 p.; 72 fig. 23 art. – ᴿAJA 93 (1989) 142 (I. *Davidson*).

868 ᴱSrdoč Dusan, 13th international radiocarbon conference, June 20-25, 1988, Dubrovnik, Yugoslavia = Radiocarbon 31/3 (1989). Pp. xx, 231-1032. 110 art., 2 infra.

869 [*Starcky* Jean, présent.], La Jordanie de l'âge de la pierre à l'époque byzantine: Rencontres École du Louvre. P 1987, La documentation française. 120 p.; ill. 2-11-001786-4. 7 art., infra.

870 ᴱStordeur D., La main et l'outil; manches et emmanchements préhistoriques: Table Ronde CNRS, Lyon 26-29 nov. 1984. P 1988, Maison de l'Orient. 336 p.; 202 fig. 2-903264-44-9. – ᴿAntiquity 63 (1989) 867s (R. *Larick*).

871 ᴱTatton-Brown Veronica, Cyprus and the East Mediterranean in the Iron Age; Proceedings of the Seventh British Museum Classical Colloquium, April 1988. L 1989, British Museum. 196 p. 0-7141-1292-5 [OIAc Ja90].

872 Terminologie und Typologie mittelalterlicher Sachgüter; das Beispiel der Kleidung: Round-Table Gespräch, Krems/Donau 6, Okt. 1986: Inst. Mitt.-a. Realienkunde ph/h 10. W 1988, Österr. Akad. 205 p., 40 fig. [RHE 84,188*].

873 L'Urbs; espace urbain et histoire (Iᵉʳ siècle av. J.-C.-IIIᵉʳ siècle ap. J.-C.) Actes du Colloque internat. [➤ 3,832; *Piétri* C., présent.]: Éc. Française, Rome 8-12 mai 1985: Coll. ÉFR 98. R 1987. vii-833 p. – ᴿAJA 93 (1989) 481s (R. E. A. *Palmer*); Latomus 48 (1989) 697-9 (J. *LeGall*).

874 ᴱVavroušek Petr, *Souček* Vladimir, Šulmu; papers on the Ancient Near East, International Conference of Socialist Countries (Prague, Sept. 30-Oct. 3, 1986). Praha 1988, Charles University. ix-391 p. Kčs 44. 27 art.; 20 infra.

875 ᴱWaldren William H., *Kennard* Rex C., Bell beakers of the western Mediterranean [Oxford conference]: BAR-Int 331. Ox 1987. vi-699 p.; ill. (2 vol.). – ᴿAJA 93 (1989) 147 (R. J. *Rowland*).

876 ᴱZaccagnini Carlo, Production and consumption in the Ancient Near East, a collection of essays [< DialArch 3/3 (1981) 3-160]. Budapest 1989, Univ. Egyptology dept. [viii-]341 p. 96-34624-13-8. 6 art.; infra.

877 ᴱZanardo Aldo, Stato Economia Lavoro nel Vicino Oriente antico, convegno internazionale Firenze, Ist. Gramsci. Mi 1988, Francoangeli. xv-413 p.; ill. Lit. 35.000. 88-204-2313-8. 31 art.; infra.

A3   *Opera consultationis* – **Reference works** .1 *plurium* **separately** *infra.*

878 **ANRW**: Aufstieg und Niedergang der römischen Welt, II. Principat, ᴱHaase W. [10,1; 11,1; 25,5s: 1988 ➤ 4,782] **18,2**, Heidentum – Provinzen. xi + p. 875-1655. – **33,1**, Sprache und Lit. (2 Jh.). xiv-847 p. – **36,3**, Philosophie (Stoizismus). xv + p. 1325-2252. 3-11-010366-6; 75-3; 93-1. – ᴿAntClas 58 (1989) 578s (G. *Raepsaet*, 18/1); AnzAltW 42 (1989) 102-9 (Erna *Diez*; 12,1s) & 177-187 (M. *Baltes*, 36/1s) & 214-8 (G. *Radke*. 18/1); BL (1989) 133s M. A. *Knibb*; 20/2); CdÉ 64 (1989) 348-350 (J. *Bingen*, 10/1); CiuD 202 (1989) 252s. 508 (J. *Gutiérrez*, 20/1s); ÉtClas 57 (1989)

264s (A. *Wankenne*, 25/4); GrazBei 15 (1988) 289-296 (Rosalba *Dimundo*, 32/3); Gymnasium 96 (1989) 561-4 (F. *Börner*, 25/5s; 36); Jewish History 2,2 (Haifa Univ. 1987) 9-28 (D. R. *Schwartz*, 21/2, H. MOEHRING attack on A. SCHALIT) [< JStJud 20,279]; JStNT 35 (1989) 127 (A. T. *Lincoln*, 25/4; but VIVIANO is withdrawn); Latomus 48 (1989) 495, 725 (J. *Debergh*, 25/4; 11/1); RBgPg 67 (1989) 218s (J. *Debergh*, 16/3); RÉJ 147 (1988) 189-195 (M. *Petit*, 21/2); RHR 206 (1989) 221 (P.*Nautin*, 25/4); StPatav 36 (1989) 216-9 (A. *Moda*, 21/1; 25/2s); TR 85 (1989) 522 (25/4-6: tit. pp.); VigChr 43 (1989) 193s & 405-9 (D. T. *Runia*, 25/4; 36/1s).

879 **Aug-L**: Augustinus-Lexikon, ᴱ**Mayer** Cornelius, *al.* 1/3, 1988 ➤ 4,783: ᴿCarthaginensia 5 (1989) 291s (F. *Martinez Fresneda*, 1-3); DowR 107 (1989) 69-71 (D. *Foster*, 1-3); GrazBei 16 (1989) 329s (J.-B. *Bauer*, 1-3); Gregorianum 70 (1989) 808 (F.-A. *Pastor*, 1/3); Klio 71 (1989) 303s (F. *Winkelmann*); RÉAnc 90 (1988) 234-6 (Madeleine *Moreau*); RÉLat 67 (1989) 420s (J.-C. *Fredouille*, 1/3); TPhil 64 (1989) 265s (H. J. *Sieben*, 1/3); TüTQ 169 (1989) 316s (H. J. *Vogt*, 1).

880 **BijH**: [ᴱ**Woude** A. van der], The world of the Bible, OT [I. 1986 ➤ 2,576; 3,847] II, ᵀ*Woodstra* Sierd. GR 1989, Eerdmans. 300 p., $28. 0-8028-2406-4; -0443-8. – ᴿCalvaryB 5,2 (1989) 102 (S. *Horine*, 2: useful despite presuppositions); TRu 54 (1989) 434-6 (L. *Perlitt*, 1).

881 **CAH**: Cambridge Ancient History [now firmly called 2d ed.; ➤ 65,724]: 4. Persia, Greece and the Ancient Mediterranean, c. 529 to 479 B.C., ᴱ**Boardman** J., *al.* 1988 ➤ 4,785: ᴿAntiquity 63 (1989) 522-5 (T. *Spawforth*): GreeceR 36 (1989) 243s (P. J. *Rhodes*); ScrClasIsr 8s (1988) 186-8 (D. *Mandels*, 7/1).

882 Catholicisme, ᴱ**Mathon** G. [XI, 53, 1988➤ 4,786] XII, 54, Psychologie-Ratramne, 259-517. P 1988, Letouzey et A. F 146. 2-7063-0172-4 (t. XII). – ᴿGregorianum 70 (1989) 604s (J. *Galot*, 52); NRT 111 (1989) 785s (L.-J. *Renard*, 52ss, surtout 'Procréation'); RHE 84 (1989) 825s (R. *Aubert*, 52ss).

883 **CHIran**: The Cambridge History of Iran, 2. ᴱ**Gershevitch** Ilya 1985 ➤ 1,885... 4,788: ᴿJAOS 109 (1989) 290-2 (A. *Kuhrt*); ZAss 89 (1989) 157-9 (P. *Calmeyer*).

884 **CHJud** [I. 1984 ➤ 1,886... 4,789]: II. The Hellenistic Age, ᴱ**Davies** W. D., *Finkelstein* Louis. C 1989, Univ. xvii-738 p. 0-521-21929-9 [TDig 37,46]. – ᴿProtestantesimo 44 (1989) 293s (J. A. *Soggin*, 1).

885 **DHGE**: Dictionnaire d'Histoire et de Géographie Ecclésiastiques, ᴱ**Aubert** R., *al.* [XXII, 131 ➤ 4,790] XXIII, 132 – 133s, Hampole-Heerse, col. 257-768; – 135, Heslingen-Hennberg, col. 769-1024. 2-7063-0173-2 (tome XXIII). – ᴿNRT 111 (1989) 786s (N. *Plumat*, 128-132); RHE 84 (1989) 590-3 (H. *Silvestre*, 131-4: numerous additions to the bibliographies).

886 **DictSpir**: Dictionnaire de Spiritualité, ᴱ**Rayez** A., *al.* [XIV, 91, 1988 ➤ 4, 781] 92-94, Savonarola-Spiritualité, col. 385-1152. P 1989, Beauchesne. 2-7010-1168-X. – ᴿDivThom 91 (1988) 279-302 (! G. *Perini*, 86ss); Gregorianum 70 (1989) 589s (M. *Ruiz Jurado*, 89-91); Irénikon 61 (1988) 308s; 62 (1989) 297s (E. *Lanne*, 89-94); NRT 111 (1989) 787s (L.-J. *Renard*, 89-94); NVFr 64 (1989) 77-79 (M. N. 86ss); RET 49 (1989) 107-110 (M. *Gesteira*, 89-91); RHPR 69 (1989) 501s (M. *Chevallier*, 89-91: préfère 'Royaume de Dieu' à 'Royauté de Marie'); Salesianum 51 (1989) 145 (E. *Valentino*, 89-91); VSp 143 (1989) 836-8 (J.-H. *Nicolas*, 89s).

887 **DMA**: Dictionary of the Middle Ages, ᴱ**Strayer** J. R. [XI. 1988 ➤ 4,792] to Textiles (no further volume in 1989).

888 **DPA:** Dizionario patristico e di antichità cristiane, ᴱ**Di Berardino** Angelo, I-III, 1983-8 ➤ 65,731 ... 4,793: ᴿCC 140 (1989,1) 408s (A. *Ferrua*); RHPR 69 (1989) 331s (P. *Maraval*, 3); RivStoLR 25 (1989) 500-3 (F. *Bolgiani*, 1-3).

889 **EncIslam:** Encyclopedia of Islam², ᴱ**Bosworth** C.E., *al.* [VI, 105s, 1988 ➤ 4,794] : (Eng.) VI 107s mar'ashis – māsardjawayh, 513-640; 109s, -masraḥ, –768. Leiden/P 1989, Brill/Maisonneuve. 90-04-09082-7; 084-3; 239-0.

890 **EncIslam: Pearson** H & J.D., ᴱ*Donzel* E. van, Index des Tomes I-V et du Supplément lvi 1-6. Leiden 1989 Brill. vii-295 p.

891 **EncKat:** Encyklopedia Katolicka, ᴱ**Hemperek** Piotr, *al.*, [I-IV. 1973-83 ➤ 60,877 ... 1,736] V. Fabbri-Górzyński. Lublin 1989, KUL. v-1391 p.

892 **EncRel:** Encyclopedia of religion, ᴱ*Eliade* M. 1987 ➤ 2,585 ... 4,795: ᴿJDharma 14 (1989) 217-221 (R. *Panikkar*).

893 [EncRel]: **Harrelson** Walter, Reflections on the value for biblical scholars of the new Encyclopedia of Religion: Council of Societies for the Study of Religion Bulletin 17 (1988) 29.31.

894 **EvKL:** Evangelisches Kirchenlexikon, ᴱ**Fahlbusch** E. [1. 1985 ➤ 1,893 ... 4,798] II. Gö 1987 (bis 480), 1988 (bis 960) 1989, Vandenhoeck & R. xi-1534 col. 3-525-50132-3. – ᴿÉTRel 63 (1988) 627s (J. *Pons*, I); RelStR 15 (1989) 58 (J.P. *Galvin*); TsTNijm 29 (1989) 402 (B.L. de *Groot-Kopetzky*, 4s); ZkT 111 (1989) 229s. 380 (L. *Lies*, 2/4s).

895 **GLAT:** [*Botterweck* G.J. ➤ 913] **Ringgren** Helmer *al.*, Grande Lessico dell'Antico Testamento, ᵀᴱ*Catastini* Alessandro, *Contini* Riccardo, I. Ab-Gala. Brescia 1988, Paideia. xvi-1119 p. 88-394-0416-3. – ᴿIréni-kon 62 (1989) 121 (E. *Lanne*).

896 **HbFT:** Handbuch der Fundamentaltheologie, ᴱ**Kern** Walter, *al.*, 1-4, 1985-8 ➤ 1,898 ... 4,800: ᴿActuBbg 26 (1989) 213s (J. *Boada*); KatKenk 28,55 (1989) 179 [not 197 as cover]-191 (S. *Takayanagi* ❶ 2); NRT 111 (1989) 953s (L. *Renwart*, 4); TR 85 (1989) 42-46 (E. *Lessing*, 4); ZkT 111 (1989) 206-9 (W. *Klausnitzer*, 4).

897 **HbRwG:** Handbuch religionswissenschaftlicher Grundbegriffe, ᴱ**Cancik** Hubert, *al.*, I. [Systematischer Teil; dann] Aberglaube-Antisemitismus. Stu 1988, Kohlhammer. 504 p. DM 145 [TR 85,161]. – ᴿProtestantesimo 44 (1989) 286s (J.A. *Soggin*).

898 **ISBEnc:** International standard Bible encyclopaedia, ᴱ**Bromiley** G.W. [3, 1986 ➤ 2,590; 3,865]; 4 (Q-Z) 1988 ➤ 4,801: ᴿEvQ 60 (1988) 263-5 (R.J. *Bauckham*, 3: BRUCE F. on Paul longest, LASOR W. on Palestine next); HolyL 9 (1989) 94 (S. *Doyle*, unfavorable; but a lengthy article is given on p. 173); RExp 86 (1989) 435s (J.D.W. *Watt*, 4).

899 **LexÄg:** Lexikon der Ägyptologie, ᴱ**Helck** Wolfgang, *Westendorf* Wolfhart. [VI, 49 (Schluss) 1986 ➤ 2,592]: VII, Nachträge, Korrekturen und Indices: Lfg. 1 und 2. Wsb 1989, Harrassowitz. xli-44 (col.)-45-108 (p. Korrekturen) / p. 109-240, Allgemeiner Index. 3-447-02918-8; 73-0.

900 **—— Westendorf** Wolfhart, [bei Göttinger Miszellen, von LexÄg un-abhängig:] Bemerkungen und Korrekturen zum LexÄg. Gö 1989, GöMiszÄg. 140 p. DM 46.

901 **LexMA:** Lexikon des Mittelalters, ᴱ**Mariacher** B. [IV. col. 1568 ➤ 4,803]: IV. Erzkanzler – Hiddensee. Mü 1989 (Lfg 8-10), Artemis. viii-2220 col. 3-7608-8904-2. – ᴿColcFranc 59 (1989) 157-9 (O. *Schmucki*, IV/1-7); RBén 99 (1989) 375s (D. *Misonne*, IV/5-7); RHE 84 (1989) 169s (J. *Pycke*, IV/1-4); TAth 60 (1989) 187-9 (K.G. *Bonis*, IV/5-7); ZkT 111 (1989) 506s (H.B. *Meyer*, IV/1-7).

902 **NBL:** Neues Bibel-Lexikon, ᴱ**Görg** Manfred, *Lang* Bernhard, I. [Lfg. 1, 1988 ➤ 4,804] Lfg. 2, Arwad-Bruderliebe. Z 1989, Benziger. col. 177-336. DM 25. 3-545-23053-8. – ᴿOrientierung 53 (1989) 47s (C. *Locher*, 1); TLZ 114 (1989) 873s (R. *Stahl*, 1).

903 **NDizTB:** Nuovo dizionario di teologia biblica, ᴱ**Rossano** P., *al.*, 1988 ➤ 4,806: ᴿAsprenas 36 (1989) 529-531 (V. *Scippa*); Salesianum 51 (1989) 568s (R. *Sabin*); STEv 1,2 (1989) 209 (P. *Bolognesi*); Teresianum 40 (1989) 275s (V. *Pasquetto*).

904 **RAC:** Reallexikon für Antike und Christentum, ᴱ**Dassmann** Ernst, *al.* [XIV, 102-112] XV, 113 –Hilarius, col. 1-160; 114, –Himyar, –320; 115, –Hippokrates, –480; Stu 1989, Hiersemann. 3-7772-8912-4; 8939-6; 9003-3. – ᴿGnomon 61 (1989) 617-9 (H. D. *Betz*, 13); RHE 84 (1989) 503s (P.-A. *Deproost*, 13s); RHR 206 (1989) 219-221 (P. *Nautin*, 13); TLZ 114 (1989) 337-9 (H. *Seidel*, Sup. 1-3).

905 **RLA:** Reallexikon der Assyriologie und vorderasiatischen Archäologie, ᴱ**Edzard** Dietz O. [VII, 1s, 1987 ➤ 3,871; 4,808] VII, 3s, Lu-huzattija-Maltai, p. 161-320. B 1988, de Gruyter. 3-11-010440-7. – ᴿBO 46 (1989) 346-9 (W. W. *Hallo*, 7/1s); OLZ 84 (1989) 415s (H. *Klengel*, 7/3s).

906 **SDB:** Supplément, Dictionnaire de la Bible, ᴱ**Briend** J., *al.*, XI, 62, 1988 'Salut' ➤ 4,809: ᴿBL (1989) 9 (R. N. *Whybray*, XI, 62).

907 **SpirC, SpirNC:** La spiritualità cristiana (20 vol.), La spiritualità non cristiana (5 vol.), storia e testi, ᴱ**Ancilli** E. R 1986-9. – ᴿRHE 84 (1989) 256s (R. *Aubert* présente toute la série).

908 **StSp:** Storia della Spiritualità ➤ 4,810 ['a cura di L. *Bouyer*, E. *Ancilli*'; ma p. es. vol. 2 NT 'opera originale e nuova, a cura di G. **Barbaglio**', con 9 autori]. Bo 1988, Dehoniane. 378 p. Lit. 30.000. 88-10-30412-8. – ᴿParVi 34 (1989) 156s. 298 (C. *Ghidelli*, 2; 1).

909 **StSpG:** Storia della Spiritualità, ᴱ**Grossi** Vincenzo ➤ 4,810* [1. ᴱ**Fanuli** A., La spiritualità dell'Antico Testamento]. R 1989, Borla.

910 **TDNT:** Theological Dictionary of the NT, ᴱ**Kittel** G., *Bromiley* G., One-vol. abridgment 1985 ➤ 3,873; 4,811. – ᴿAsbTJ 44,1 (1989) 111s (J. A. *Pattengale*).

911 **TRE:** Theologische Realenzyklopädie, ᴱ**Müller** Gerhard, *al.* [XVII. 1988 ➤ 4,813]. XVIII. Katechumenat-Kirchenrecht. B 1989, de Gruyter. 778 p. 3-11-011613-8. – ᴿBL (1989) 20s (R. N. *Whybray*, 17s); BogVest 47 (1987) 190-4 (M. *Smolik*, 11-15); CC 140 (1989,1) 617 (B. *Groth*, 16); CiuD 202 (1989) 255 (J. M. *Ozaeta*, 17); DLZ 110 (1989) 749-752. 1030-2 (G. *Wendelborn*, 16s); ÉTRel 63 (1988) 327. 628s (B. *Reymond*, 15s); ÖkRu 38 (1989) 254s (H. *Krüger*, 17); Protestantesimo 44 (1989) 286 (J. A. *Soggin*, 17); RelStR 15 (1989) 117-9 (J. H. *Elliott*, 1-10); RHPR 69 (1989) 485s (M.-A. *Chevallier*, 16s); SvTKv 65 (1989) 88s (B. *Hägglund*, 17); TLZ 114 (1989) 11-14 (E.-H. *Amberg*, 14s); TPQ 137 (1989) 287s (G. *Bachl*, 16); VerkF 34,1 (1989) 87-95 (G. *Sauter*, 8-17); ZkT 111 (1989) 378s (L. *Lies*, 13.15-17).

912 **TUmAT:** Texte aus der Umwelt des Alten Testament [2/4, 1988 ➤ 4,814] 2/5, ᴱ**Römer** Willem H. P., *Hecker* Karl, Religiöse Texte, Lieder und Gebete 1. Gü 1989, Mohn. p. 641-784. 3-579-00070-5 [OIAc Ja90]. – ᴿBO 46 (1989) 352-7 (S. *Lieberman*, 1/1); TPhil 64 (1989) 252. 578s (N. *Lohfink*, 1/5; I/6, II, 1-4).

913 **TWAT:** Theologisches Wörterbuch zum Alten Textament, ᴱ**Ringgren** Helmer, *al.* [IV/6s, 1988 ➤ 4,815] VI/8-10, *šô'n – qæbær*; VI/11, nur *qôl* und *qûm*, Register. Stu 1989, Kohlhammer. col. 865-1248 (DM 124);

col. 1249-1274 (DM 62,80). 3-17-010230-3; 693-7. – ᴿNRT 111 (1989) 921-3 (J.-L. *Ska*, VI, 3-10; col. 926 en haut, manquent quelques lignes) [N.B. supplied (one line) VI/11 p. 667]; TR 85 (1989) 10 (W. *Kornfeld* †, 4/6s).

A3.2 *Opera consultationis non separatim infra;* **not subindexed.**

914 **Abrams** M. H., A glossary of literary terms⁵ [¹1971]. Fort Worth 1988, Holt-RW. ix-260 p. 0-03-011953-7.

915 ᴱ**Achtemeier** Paul J., Harper's Bible Dictionary 1985 ➤ 1,913 ... 4,816: ᴿCriswT 2 (1987s) 161s (K. A. *Mathews*: leads the field); WestTJ 50 (1988) 167s (L. C. *Sibley*: liberal-critical bias, but contains articles not usually found: art, economics, sociology ...).

916 [ᴱ*Alexander* D. & P.]ᵀ, pref. *Ravasi* G. Enciclopedia illustrata della Bibbia [1978 ➤ 65,752]. R 1983, Paoline. 398 p. Lit. 32.000. – ᴿParVi 34 (1989) 307s (G. *Biguzzi*).

917 ᴱ**Arai** S., *Ishida* T. [revision of Vandenhoeck 1966-9 Biblisch-historisches Handwörterbuch] ❶ Kyuyaku Shinyaku Seisho Dai-jiten. Tokyo 1989, Kyobunkwan. 1454 p.; ill.; 3 maps. Y 46,350. 4-7642-4006-8 C 3516 [BL 90,8].

917* ᴱ**Bäumer** Remigius, *Scheffczyk* Leo, Marienlexikon: Rg Inst. Marianum: I. Aa-Chagall. St. Ottilien 1988, EOS. ➤ 4,819 xxxi-672 p. DM 98. – ᴿForumKT 5 (1989) 149-151 (H.-A. *Klein*); TGL 79 (1989) 206-8 (W. *Beinert*).

918 ᴱ**Beinert** W., Lexikon der katholischen Dogmatik 1987 ➤ 3,884; 4,821: ᴿNRT 111 (1989) 97 (R. *Escol*).

919 **Bellinger** Gerhard J., Knaurs Grosser Religionsführer; 670 Religionen, Kirchen und Kulte, weltanschaulich-religiöse Bewegungen und Gesellschaften sowie religionsphilosophische Schulen. Mü 1986, Knaur. 432 p. – ᴿDer Islam 65 (1988) 189s (B. *Spuler*).

919* *Biedermann* Hans, ²**Riemann** Gerhard, Knaurs Lexikon der Symbole. Mü 1989, Knaur. 591 p. 600 fig. DM 68. – ᴿTGL 79 (1989) 626s (W. *Beinert*).

920 Biographie nationale de Belgique [I. 1866; 'dernier' volume 1987] Nouvelle biographie nationale [un seul volume], fasc. 1. Bru 1988, Académie. 376 p. – ᴿRHE 84 (1989) 523-5 (J.-P. *Hendrickx*: le tout a été repensé *ab ovo*).

921 ᴱ**Boardman** John, *al.*, The Oxford history of the classical world 1986 ➤ 2,603 ... 4,824; Ox 1988 reprint. 882 p.; ill.; 20 colour. pl.; 10 maps. A$ 55. 0-19-872112-9. – ᴿAmHR 94 (1989) 413-5 (M. *Reinhold*: Greek and Roman, 'scintillating distillation'); AncHRes 19 (1989) 184-7 (A. *Harper*).

922 **Bocian** Martin, *al.*, Lexikon der [200] biblischen Personen, mit ihrem Fortleben in Judentum, Christentum, Islam, Dichtung, Musik und Kunst: Tb 460. Stu 1989, Kröner. x-510 p. 3-520-46001-1. – ᴿBeiNam 24 (1989) 369s (R. *Schützeichel*).

923 [**Bogaert** P.-M., *al.*] Dictionnaire encyclopédique de la Bible 1987 ➤ 3,888; 4,805: ᴿAtKap 111 (1988) 349s (B. *Kurzawa*); BibTB 19 (1989) 108s (Justine *Apfeld* singles out ᴿᴏʟʟᴀɴᴅ's Synoptic origins); BZ 33 (1989) 138 (J. *Schreiner*); EstBib 47 (1989) 280 (F. *Pastor-Ramos*); ÉTRel 63 (1989) 447s (D. *Lys*).

ᴱ**Burgess** Stanley M., *al.*, Dictionary of pentecostal and charismatic movements 1988 ➤ 6069.

925 ᴱ**Burkhardt** Helmut, *al.*, Das grosse Bibellexikon [< ᴱ*Bruce* F. F., Illustrated Bible Dictionary 1962/1980] I (1987 ➤ 3,889); II. Haar-Otniel, p. 505-1104. – III. Paddan-Zypern, –1750. Wuppertal/Giessen 1989s, Brockhaus/Brunnen. 3-417-24611-3 (vol. 1-2); 2-1 / 3-7655-5421-9; 2-7 (vol. 2-3).

926 **Calvocoressi** Peter, Who's who in the Bible? 1988 ➤ 4,826; Hmw 1988, Penguin. 0-14-051212-8: ᴿExpTim 100 (1988s) 159 [C. S. *Rodd*: 450 names like Pul and Cozbi].

927 **Cannon** John, The Blackwell dictionary of historians [450; plus sections on difficult terms and on research-areas]. Ox 1988, Blackwell. xiv-480 p. £39.50. – ᴿRHE 84 (1989) 615 (D. *Bradley*).

928 **Cornfeld** G., *Botterweck* G. J. Die Bibel und ihre Welt. Bergisch Gladbach 1988, Lubbe. 1590 p. (3 vol.) 888 fig.

928* ᴱ**Corsten** Severin, *al.*, Lexikon des gesamten Buchwesens² [¹1937], I. A-Buch, xii-639 p. II. Buck-Foster, vii-638 p. Stu 1987/9, Hiersemann. 3-7772-8721-0; 911-6. I, 346-364, Bibel, -druck, -handschriften, -illustration (G. *Franz*, *al.*); II, 145-152, Codex Amiatinus etc. (C. *Eggenberger*, *al.*).

929 ᴱ**Drehsen** Volker von, *Häring* H., *al.*, Wörterbuch des Christentums ➤ 4,831: Gü/Z 1988, Mohn/Benziger. 1439 p. DM 245. 3-579-00059-4 / Z 3-545-22097-3. – ᴿTGL 79 (1989) 322 (W. *Beinert*); TLZ 114 (1989) 413-6 (E.-H. *Amberg*); TsTNijm 29 (1989) 60 (A. *Lascaris*).

930 ᴱ**Dubost** Michel, Théo, nouvelle encyclopédie catholique. P 1989, Droguet-Ardant/Fayard. 1236 p. F 275. – ᴿÉtudes 371 (1989) 136 (R. *Marlé*).

931 ᴱ**Eicher** Peter, Dictionnaire de Théologie ➤ 4,834, ᵀᴱ*Jossua* P. [pour accompagner l'Initiation en 5 vol., et remplacer L'encyclopédie de la foi 1965-7]. P 1988, Cerf. x-838 p. F 650. 2-204-02770-7. – ᴿClaretianum 29 (1989) 412s (B. *Proietti*, deutsch 1985 ➤ 1,935); ÉTRel 64 (1989) 463 (A. *Gounelle*); NRT 111 (1989) 784s (R. *Escol*).

932 **Eicher** Peter, Diccionario de conceptos teológicos I. Amor – Liturgía. Barc c. 1988, Herder. 600 p. – ᴿAnVal 15 (1989) 403s (F. T.).

933 ᴱ**Elwell** Walter A., Baker Encyclopedia of the Bible. GR 1988, Baker. xiv-2210 p. (2 vol.) $80. – ᴿAndrUnS 27 (1989) 140-2 (J. *Paulien*); CalvaryB 5,1 (1989) 104 (G. H. *Lovik*).

934 ᴱ**Ferguson** Sinclair B., *Wright* David F., New dictionary of theology 1988 ➤ 4,838: ᴿSTEv NS 1 (1989) 84 (P. *Guccini*); Themelios 14 (1988s) 27s (A. *McGrath*); Vidyajyoti 52 (1988) 515s (G. *Gispert-Sauch*).

935 **Fritz** Volkmar, Kleines Lexikon der biblischen Archäologie: Bibel Kirche Gemeinde 26. Konstanz 1987, Christl.-VA. 202 p.; 68 fig.; 16 color. pl.; map. DM 24,50. – ᴿZkT 111 (1989) 93s (J. M. *Oesch*).

936 ᴱ**Gehman** H. S., ³*Wright* R. B., The new Westminster dictionary of the Bible. Ph c. 1988, Westminster. xii-1027 p.; 16 maps. – ᴿSalesianum 51 (1989) 589s (G. *Gentileschi*).

937 ᴱ[*Ghisalberti* M. †], **Pavan** Massimiliano, Dizionario biografico degli Italiani, 27 (1982) – 36 (1988), Collenucio... Ponte. – ᴿRHE 84 (1989) 855-861 (R. *Aubert*, analyse détaillée).

938 ᴱ**Härle** W., *Wagner* H., Theologenlexikon, von den Kirchenvätern bis zur Gegenwart: B-Reihe 321, 1987➤ 3,913; 4,841: ᴿTsTNijm 29 (1989) 60s (T. *Schoof*).

939 ᴱ**Harrison** R. K., The new Unger's Bible dictionary [1957 revised]. Ch 1988, Moody. xv-1400 p.; 15 maps. $30. 0-8024-9037-9 [BL 90,15: B. P. *Robinson* disapproves its fundamentalism].

940 **Johnstad** Gunnar, Ord i Bibelen. Oslo 1987, Nor. Bibelselskap. 917 p.
   – ᴿTsTKi 59 (1988) 138 (T. *Stordalen*).
941 ᴱ**Judge** Harry, Oxford illustrated encyclopedia; world history from
   earliest times to 1800. Ox 1988, Univ. 392 p.; 365 ill. £19.50.
   0-19-869135-1 [Antiquity 63,70].
942 ᴱ**Kennedy** George A., The Cambridge history of literary criticism, I.
   Classical criticism. C 1989, Univ. xvii-378 p. 0-521-30006-1.
943 ᴱ**Khoury** Adel T., Lexikon religiöser Grundbegriffe, Judentum/Chri-
   stentum/Islam 1987 ➤ 3,920; 4,846: ᴿDer Islam 65 (1988) 329-331 (B.
   Spuler); MüTZ 40 (1989) 164s (J. *Modesto*).
944 ᴱ**Koch** Klaus, *al.*, Reclams Bibellexikon⁴ʳᵉᵛ. Stu 1987, Reclam. 584 p.;
   138 fig.; 6 maps. DM 59. – ᴿZkT 111 (1989) 95s (J.M. *Oesch*).
945 [*König* Franz] ²ʳᵉᵛ·**Waldenfels** Hans, Lexikon der Religionen 1987
   ➤ 4,847: ᴿZkT 111 (1989) 114s (J. *Thorer*); ZRGg 40 (1989) 371-3 (H.
   Zirker).
946 ᴱ**Komonchak** J. A., *al.*, New dictionary of theology 1987 ➤ 3,923; 4,849:
   ᴿCommonweal 115 (1988) 474 (J. H. *Wright*); ExpTim 99 (1987) 373-375
   (J. *Macquarrie*: no biographies, such as prove useful in *Ferguson*'s
   comparable new volume); IrTQ 55 (1989) 331s (T. *Corbett*); Worship 62
   (1988) 478-480 (Catherine M. *LaCugna*).
947 ᴱ**La Brosse** Olivier de, *al.* Dictionnaire des mots de la foi chrétienne². P
   1989, Cerf. xi-836 col. [NRT 111,745 adv.]. 2-204-04008-8.
948 **Lanczkowski** Günther, Religionen: Kleines Lexikon. Mannheim 1987,
   Meyer. 502 p. – ᴿDer Islam 65 (1988) 378s (B. *Spuler*).
949 *Lesnik* Rafko, Biblični leksikon — njegova uporabnost [*Grabner-Haider*
   A. / *Krašovec* J. Celje 1984]: BogVest 48 (1988) 189-198.
   LGB: Lexikon des gesamten Buchwesens² 1989 ➤ supra 928*.
951 **LIMC:** Lexicon iconographicum mythologiae classicae, ᴱ**Kahil** Lilly: IV,1
   (2 = photos), Eros-Heracles, 1988 ➤ 4,852: ᴿAnzAltW 42 (1989) 239s (H.
   Walter, 3); MusHelv 46 (1989) 176s (K. *Schefold*, 4).
952 ᴱ**Lissner** Anneliese, *Süssmuth* Rita, *Walter* Karin, Frauenlexikon;
   Traditionen, Fakten, Perspektiven² [¹1988 ➤ 4,854]. FrB 1989 [TR
   85,353]. – ᴿForumKT 5 (1989) 285-290 (Jutta *Burggraf*¹).
953 **Maimon** Arye, (*Guggenheim* Yacov), Germania Judaica [I. 1917 ²1963; II.
   1934 ²1968] III. 1350-1519, I. Teilband, Ortschaftsartikel Aach-Lychen.
   Tü 1987, Mohr. xxx-769 p. – ᴿRÉJ 148 (1989) 384-8 (G. *Weill*).
954 **Melton** J. Gordon, The encyclopedia of American religion³. Detroit
   1989, Gale. lxiv-1102 p. $165. 0-8103-2841-0 [TDig 36,158].
955 **Monloubou** Louis, Dictionnaire biblique abrégé: Abrégés (n⁰ 6). P 1989,
   Desclée. 250 p. F 115. – ᴿCiVit 44 (1989) 310 (D. *Camiciotti*); RivB 37
   (1989) 107-9 (A. *Minissale*); RTLv 20 (1989) 369 (J. *Ponthot*: pas
   exactement un résumé de son Dict. B. Universel, Desclée 1984); ScEspr 41
   (1989) 379-381 (J. *Duhaime*).
956 **Morby** John E., Dynasties of the world, a chronological and genealogical
   handbook. Ox 1989, Univ. xv-254 p. 0-19-215872-4 [OIAc N89].
957 ᴱ**Müller** Karl, *Sundermeier* T., Lexikon missionstheologischer Grundbegriffe 1987 ➤ 4,861: ᴿNRT 111 (1989) 774 (J. *Masson*); NZMissW 45
   (1989) 142s (F. *Frei*).
958 ᴱ**Myers** Allen C., The Eerdmans Bible dictionary 1987 ➤ 4,862:
   ᴿSalesianum 51 (1989) 565 (R. *Sabin*); Vidyajyoti 52 (1988) 460 (P. M.
   Meagher).

959 **Nadell** Pamela S., Conservative Judaism in America; a biographical dictionary and sourcebook: Jewish denominations in America. Westport CT 1988, Greenwood. xvi-409 p. $55. 0-313-24205-4 [TDig 36,382].

960 ^E**Poupard** Paul, *a*) Grande dizionario delle religioni 1988 → 4,865*b*: ^RCC 140 (1989,3) 92s (M. *Dhavamony*). – *b*) Diccionario de las religiones 1987 → 4,865*a*: ^RBrotéria 126 (1988) 477s (I. *Ribeiro da Silva*); HumT 10 (1989) 257s (J. *Monteiro*); Proyección 35 (1988) 152s (E. *Barón*).

961 **Proch** U., Breve dizionario dei termini e dei concetti biblico-teologici più usati. T-Leumann 1988, LDC. 134 p. Lit. 8.500 [CC 140/1 cop.]. – ^RClaretianum 29 (1989) 430s (B. *Proietti*).

962 Répertoire international des Médiévistes / International dictionary of medievalists⁶ (to 1980), I. A-K; II. L-Z. P 1987, CNRS. ix-1259 p. DM 298. – ^RDer Islam 65 (1988) 331-3 (B. *Spuler*).

963 ^E**Robbins** Vernon E., Ancient quotes and anecdotes; from crib to crypt: Foundations and Facets Reference. Sonoma 1989, Polebridge. xvii-493 p. $22. 0-944344-03-8. From R. *Funk*'s SBL 'Pronouncement Story' group, including J. *VanderKam*, Pheme *Perkins*, al.

964 ^E**Rocca** G., Dizionario degli Istituti di perfezione 8, S. Saba – Spirituali. R 1988, Paoline. xxxii-2040 col.; ill. – ^RRHE 84 (1989) 861s (R. *Aubert*).

965 ^E**Rodriguez** Ángel Aparicio, *Canals Casas* Jean, Diccionario teológico de la vida consagrada. M 1989, Claretianas. 1957 p. 138 art. – ^RRHE 84 (1989) 813 (T. *Moral*).

966 [*Schmitt* O.] ^E**Wirth** K.-A., Reallexikon zur deutschen Kunstgeschichte, VII, Lfg. 82-84, Felicitas–Fensterladen. Mü 1980s, Beck. col. 1153-1526. – ^RTLZ 114 (1989) 746-750 (Erika *Dinkler-von Schubert*).

967 ^E**Schütz** Christian, Praktisches Lexikon der Spiritualität. FrB 1988, Herder. xv-1504 col. DM 78. – ^RTGL 79 (1989) 211s (K. *Hollmann*); TLZ 114 (1989) 845s (G. *Wolff*); TPQ 137 (1989) 284-6 (S. *Scheuer*).

968 **Spitzing** Günter, Lexikon byzantinisch-christlicher Symbole; die Bilderwelt Griechenlands und Kleinasiens. Mü 1988, Diederichs. 344 p. DM 68. – ^RTGL 79 (1989) 335s (W. *Beinert*).

969 [Tardy, présent.], Dictionnaire des arts, de l'histoire, des lettres et des religions [cover: Dictionnaire des thèmes et décors]: I. Occident classique, thèmes; II. ... décors. P 1987s, Tardy. 539 p. F 350; xii-208 p. + 209-389 = 211 fig.; F 350.

970 **Urech** Edouard, Lexikon christlicher Symbole [Dictionnaire des symboles chrétiens, Neuchâtel 1972]: Bibel-Kirche-Gemeinde 9. Konstanz 1989, Christliche VA. 256 p.; ill. 3-7673-7609-1.

971 ^E**Walker** William O.^J [SBL], Harper's Bible pronunciation guide. SF 1989, Harper & R. xiii-170 p. $16. 0-06-068951-X [BA 53,176, M. A. *Phelps*; TDig 37,161].

972 ^E**Walther** K. K., Lexikon der Buchkunst und Bibliophilie. Mü 1988, Saur. 386 p.; ill. DM 148 [RHE 85,119*].

973 ^E**Wiench** Peter [*Stadler* Wolf], Lexikon der Kunst; Malerei-Architektur-Bildhauerkunst in 12 Bänden; 1. Aac–Barm; 2. Barn–Buc; 3. Bud–Degl; 4. Dego–Gai; 5. Gal–Herr; 6. Hert–Klap; 7. Klas–Mal; 8. Mal–Rel. FrB 1987s, Herder. je 380 p.; DM 178. – ^RZkT 111 (1989) 117-9. 501 (H. B. *Meyer*: who wrote which?).

974 ^E**Wigoder** G. *al.*, Illustrated dictionary and concordance of the Bible 1986 → 2,655*; 3,947: ^RSalesianum 51 (1989) 654s (R. *Sabin*).

975 ᴱYarshater Ehsan, Encyclopaedia Iranica [3/7, 1988 ➤ 4,874] 4/4,
Bolbol-Brick. L 1989, Routledge-KP. p. 337-448. 0-7100-9122-3 [OIAc
N89]. – ᴿArOr 57 (1989) 69-71 (M. *Shaki*, 1, monumental); Der Islam 65
(1988) 166-9 (B. *Spuler*, 1); OLZ 84 (1989) 647-657 (W. *Sundermann*, 1s).

A4 **Bibliographiae** .1 **biblicae.**

975* *Abadie* P., Ancien Testament [bulletin]: TEuph 1 (1989) 165-176.
976 *Abbink* J., A bibliography on the Ethiopian Jews: Studies in Bibliography and Booklore [3 (1957) 9-27, *Leslau* W.] 16 (1986) 37-48 [< OLZ
84,120].
977 *Aletti* Jean-Noël, Bulletin paulinien [28 livres]: RechSR 77 (1989)
113-135.
AnPg ['Testamenta' = NT] ➤ 1096.
978 **Aufrecht** Walter E., A bibliography of Ammonite inscriptions: NewsTarg
Sup. 1 (1983) [< OTAbs 12,258].
978* *Best* Ernest, Recent continental [i.e. all German] NT literature: ExpTim
100 (1988s) 377-382 [*Gnilka* J. Mt; *Lührmann* D., *Schenke* L., Mk.;
Pokorný P. Col; *Schnackenburg* R.].
979 **BL:** ᴱ**Auld** A. Graeme, Society for Old Testament Study Book List, 1989.
167 p. 0-905495-08-X.
980 *Bogaert* P.-M., Bulletin de la Bible latine VI: RBén 98 (1988) [221]-[252].
981 *Briend* Jacques, Bulletin d'exégèse de l'AT: *a*) Pentateuque, livres
historiques [17 ouvrages]; *b*) Livres prophétiques et sapientiaux [17 livres]:
RechSR 76 (1988) 561-577 / 77 (1989) 366-378.
982 **Carson** D. A., New Testament commentary survey [called 3d ed. of
Thiselton A. C., Personal suggestions about a minister's library ²1973,
revised by Carson 1976]. GR 1988, Baker. 79 p. $4. 0-8010-2535-4
[NTAbs 33,233].
983 **Charlesworth** James H., (*Mueller* James R.), The NT Apocrypha and
Pseudepigrapha: ATLA Bibliography 17, 1987 ➤ 3,952; 4,877; also
Folkestone, Bailey. xvi-450 p. $42.50. – ᴿJTS 40 (1989) 219s (S. P.
Brock); NT 31 (1989) 182-5 (J. K. *Elliott*).
983* *Coggins* Richard, [5] German OT studies; *b*) Recent continental
OT literature [also all German, 7 books]. ExpTim 100 (1988s) 390-2 /
413-7.
984 Computerized list of 6000 experts in Jewish studies, available for
purchase. J 1989, World Union of Jewish Studies.
985 *Daniels* Dwight R., *Janowski* Bernd, Literatur zur biblischen Theologie
1985-1988: JbBT 4 (1989) 301-360.
985* *Delcor* Mathias, *Husser* Jean M., Chronique d'Ancien Testament:
BLitEc 90 (1989) 33-53.125-134.
986 *Devillers* Luc, Bulletin d'Écriture Sainte: RThom 89 (1989) 475-491.
987 **Dirksen** P. B., An annotated bibliography of the Peshiṭta of the
Old Testament: Peshiṭta Institute Mg 5. Leiden 1989, Brill. xiv-119 p.
90-04-09017-7.
988 Dissertationes doctorales 1987-8, Lv/LvN: ETL 65 (1989) 220-2 (some 10
each).
988* *Elayi* J., *Sapin* J., Bibliographie, Palestine époque perse: TEuph 1 (1989)
131-145 [177-180, Calendrier, *Lemaire* A., *Elayi* J.].
989 **Gotenburg** Erwin, Bibelwissenschaft [Theologische Bibliographie]: TR 85
(1989) 73-75 [-88]. 161-4 [-176]. 249-251 [-264]. 337-9 [-352]. 425-8 [-440].
521-3 [-534].

990 *Grady* John F., The Bible as a classic: ChSt 27 (1988) 96-108 (despite title, review of BRUEGGEMANN, ACHTEMEIER, COLLINS).
991 **Griffiths** David B., A critical bibliography of writings on Judaism 1/2. Lewiston 1988, Mellen. 804 p. [RelStR 16, 82, M. S. *Jaffee*: superficial].
992 *Guillet* Jacques, Bulletin d'exégèse synoptique [47 livres]: RechSR 77 (1989) 379-416.
993 *Harrington* D. J., Books on the Bible [28, in English]: America 159 (1988) 470-8.
994 Hebrew Annual Review, Index vol. 1-10, 1977-1986: HebAnR 10 (1986) 367-376.
995 *Homan* Martin J., Computer assisted biblical research: ConcordiaJ 14 (1988) 150-7 [< OTAbs 12,6].
996 Interpretation index 1982-6 (vol. 36-40). Richmond 1989. $3 [Int 43,57].
997 **IZBG**: Internationale Zeitschriftenschau für Bibelwissenschaft und Grenzgebiete, ᴱ**Lang** Bernhard, *al.*, 35 (for 1987s, in 1990). 376 p. 3-491-66035-1. – 2374 items, including many more *books* than the 46 which are indexed on p. 359 only for the reviews of them which are here given. – On p. 335, 'Würdigungen' (along with 'Bibliographien') contains a very small sampling of what this Elenchus gives partly as Festschriften and partly as obituaries; but on p. 24 (Nº 162 and 162a) special interest is shown in our obituaries; several are cited from our 1985 and 1986 volumes (remarking 'Simone de Beauvoir, not a biblical scholar': in general we include almost all the obituaries from the 1200 periodicals we excerpt — including famous people on the fringe of biblical scholarship, like popes, bishops, philosophers, Nobel prizewinners).
998 *Kelly* Joseph F., A catalogue of early medieval Hiberno-Latin biblical commentaries, I: Traditio 44 (1988) 537-571 ...
999 *Kiehl* E. H., Building your biblical studies library; a survey of current resources. St. Louis 1988, Concordia. 151 p. $10. 0-570-04489-8 [NTAbs 33,379].
1000 ᴱ**Lange** Nicholas de, *Humphrey* Judith, [53 books, 64 art., since 1982]: Bulletin of Judaeo-Greek Studies 1 (Cambridge Univ. 1987) 21 p. [< RÉJ 147 (1988) 240s: some titles rather remote; the bulletin is to appear twice a year, £4].
1001 **Langevin** Paul-Émile, Bibliographie biblique 1930-1983, III, 1985 ➤ 1,1007 ... 4,896: ᴿTPhil 64 (1989) 262 (N. *Lohfink*).
1002 **Longstaff** Thomas R. W., *Thomas* Page A., The Synoptic Problem, a bibliography, 1716-1988. Macon GA 1989, Mercer Univ. $35. – ᴿParadigms 5 (1989) 163s (S. L. *Cox*).
1003 *a)* Lust J., Scriptura Sacra Veteris Testamenti; – *b)* Neirynck F., *Segbroeck* F. Van, ... Novi Testamenti; Elenchus bibliographicus: ETL 65,2s (1989) 126*-212* / 212*-283*.
1004 *a)* Marshall I. Howard, They set us in new paths [new series, each article to discuss six most influential books of the century]; I. The New Testament, paths without destinations [*Westcott-Hort, Moffatt* J., *Manson* T., *Black* M., *Sanders* E., *Dodd* C.]; – *b)* Carroll Robert P., What gets lost in untranslation [i.e. untranslated books on] The Old Testament [*Procksch* O. 1950; *Duhm* B., *Gunkel*'s Genesis; *Gressmann*'s Messias ..., *Richter* W. 1971]; – *c)* Grayston Kenneth, A century of NT commentaries [*Westcott, Bultmann* on John; *Jackson-Lake* Acts, *Sanday-Headlam, Nygren* Rom. ....); – *d)* Clements R. E., The OT: fresh questions — new gateways [*Wellhausen*'s Prolegomena, *Kirkpatrick*'s Prophets, *Pedersen*'s Israel, *Mowinckel* Psalms, *Eichrodt* Theology]; – *e)* Johnstone William,

Six commentaries on the Bible, 1888-1988 [G.A. *Smith* Is; *Driver* Dt, *Zimmerli* Ezek; *McKane* Prov; *Childs* Ex; *Habel* Job]; – *f*) *Dunn* James D.G., NT, the great untranslated [*Strack-Billerbeck, Wellhausen* Synoptics, *Weiss* 1Cor, *Schlatter* Mt, *Zahn* Rom]; – *g*) *Galloway* A.D., Systematic theology; faith and critical reason, an uneasy partnership [*Gore* Lux Mundi; *Caird* Fundamental Ideas; *Barth* Rom; *Macquarrie, Tillich, Pannenberg*]; – *h*) *Thomas* J. Heywood, Philosophy of religion [*Caird; Webb* C.; *Tennant* F.; *Ramsey* I.; *Wittgenstein; MacKinnon*]: ExpTim 100 (1988s) 9-15 / 44-48 / 84-87 / 124-7 / 164-9 / 203-7 / 244-8 / 284-8.

1005 *Moda* Aldo, Bollettino di Sacra Scrittura [83 libri]: Nicolaus 16 (1989) 241-352.

1006 ᴱ*Muñoz Abad* Carmen, *al.*, Elenco de artículos de revistas: Sefarad 49 (1989) 191-210. 425-444.

1007 *Paul* André, Bulletin du Judaïsme ancien [41 livres]: RechSR 76 (1988) 57-86.

1008 *Piñero* Antonio, Boletín de filología neotestamentaria 3/4: FgNt 2,1 (1989) 125-133; 2,2 (1989) 217-228 [2,1, p.133-6, índice escriturístico cumulativo de 1-3].

1009 ᴱ**Reif** Stefan C., Published material from the Cambridge Genizah collections [(S. *Schechter*), 200,000 items], a bibliography 1896-1980: Genizah Series 6. C 1989, Univ. xiv-608 p. $125. 0-521-33336-9 [TDig 36,358].

1010 Revista Bíblica, Índices acumulativos 1970-1988: RBíbArg 32 (año 50, 1988) 323-443.

1010* *Rodd* C.S., [100th volume bonuses and comments; only four editors in a century, and one (till 1964) was daughter of founder-editor James HASTINGS (till 1922)]: ExpTim 100 (1988s) 1s [403-5 questionnaire-result reassuring, but suggests some changes, especially on sermons; and a reader-reaction column].

1011 *Runia* D.T., *a*) (with *Radice* R., *Satran* D.) A bibliography of Philonic studies 1981-1986; – *b*) Some statistical observations on fifty years of Philonic scholarship; – *c*) An *Index locorum philonicorum* to VÖLKER [Walther, Fortschritt und Vollendung bei Philo: TU 49/1, 1938: the full index, not just a project]: StPhilonAn 1 (1989) 95-123 / 74-81 / 82-93.

1012 Sample list of Israeli university dissertations completed or in progress, in Hebrew or English: BASOR 274 (1989) 86s (S. *Gitin*).

1013 *Scholer* David M., *a*) Bibliographia gnostica supplementum XVIII: NT 31 (1989) 344-378. – *b*) Q bibliography 1989 → 4302.

1014 *Scopello* Madeleine, Bulletin sur la Gnose [... Nag' Ḥammadi]: RechSR 77 (1989) 291-304.

1015 *Sibley* L., Shaking loose biblical fruit [5 general reference books and 7 NT]: Christianity Today 33,3 (1989) 34s [< NTAbs 33,149].

1016 *Stuhlmueller* Carroll, *Senior* Donald, The Old and New Testaments in review: BToday 27 (1989) 54-61. 118-126. 184-192. 247-254. 312-9. 381-8.

1017 *a*) *Suchy* Jerzy, ❷ Polska literatura z zakresu etyki biblijnej za lata 1945-1984; – *b*) *Szier* Barbara, ❷ Polska bibliografia biblijna za rok 1984/5: RoczTK 33,1 (1986) 135-147 / 147-154.

1018 *Thomopoulos* S., ❻ St. Paul, a bibliographic sketch [*schediasma*, 199 titles] (1819-1985): TAth 60 (1989) 457-472 [-5, index].

1019 **Welch** John W., A biblical law bibliography, sorted by subjects and authors. Provo UT, Brigham Young Univ. Clark Law School. c.120 unnumbered pages; c.4000 unnumbered items by category.

1020 **White** Leland J., Jesus the Christ, a bibliography 1988 → 4,918: ᴿCBQ 51 (1989) 385s (P. *Zilonka*).

1021 **Zubatsky** David, Jewish autobiographies and biographies ... in English: Ref. Library Hum. 722. NY 1989, Garland. 370 p. $47 [RelStR 16, 82, R. *Singerman*: inadequate].

A4.2 *Bibliographiae* **theologicae.**

1022 **Andersson-Schmitt** Margarete, *Hedlund* Monika, Mittelalterliche Handschriften der Universitätsbibliothek Uppsala, Katalog über die C-Sammlung 1 (C I-IV 1-50): Acta Bibliothek U 26,1. Sto 1988. viii-162 p. – ᴿTR 85 (1989) 206s (L. *Hödl* gibt nichts über Bibel, viel über Predigtinitien).

1023 *a*) *Bataillon* L. J., Bulletin d'histoire des doctrines médiévales; le treizième siècle; – *b*) *Gy* P.-M., Bulletin de Liturgie: RSPT 73 (1989) 87-104. 585-604 / 104-114.

1024 *Baudry* G.-H., Bulletin teilhardien: MélSR 46 (1989) 29-36.

1024* **Belle** A. van, (*Haverals* M.) Bibliographies: RHE 84 (1989) 1*-185*. 187*-327*. 329*-606*.

1025 *Bertuletti* Angelo, al., I problemi metodologici della teologia sulle Riviste del 1988: TItSett 14 (1989) 318-390 (S. Scr. 333-342).

1026 Bibliographia carmelitana actualis 1987: Carmelus 35 (1988) 291-499; 301-8, S. Scrittura; 309-313, Elia ed Eliseo; 314, Monte Carmelo.

1027 Bibliographical bulletin [in alphabetical order]: TAth 60 (1989) 833-855.

1028 Bijdragen, Register 21-49 (1960-88). Meppel 1989, Krips. 0006-2278.

1029 *Bogaert* P.-M., Bulletin d'anc. litt. chrét. lat. T VI: RBén 99 (1989) [253]-[280].

1030 ᴱ*Boudens* R., al., Elenchus bibliographicus 1989: ETL 65,2s (1989) 601* p., 11283 items; index p. 537*-601* [Les abréviations pour les périodiques se trouvent dans le volume 66 (1980) 454* (-477*)].

1031 *Burghardt* Walter J., A half century of Theological Studies; retrospect and prospect: TS 50,4 (Fiftieth anniversary volume, 'Theology and other disciplines' issue, 1989) 761-785.

1032 Five-Year cumulative index: Calvary Baptist Journal 5,2 (Lansdale PA 1989) 105-114.

1033 *Carrai* G., Indici anni 1946-1988 (dal I al XLIII): Protestantesimo 44,3 (1989) 189-223.

1034 Chronique œcuménique des périodiques: III. Anglicanisme, protestantisme; IV. Œcuménisme, science des religions / I. Bible, théologie: Istina 34 (1989) 83-112 / 248-256: sommaires notablement amples.

1035 Collectanea cisterciensia, Tables générales, tomes 1-50, 1934-1988. Fleurus, Belgique, Abbaye Soleilmont. 135 p.

1036 **d'Agostini** Espedito al., Indice 1967-1989: Servitium 66 (1989) 112 p. (p. 5-16, storia dell'impresa).

1037 **Dawsey** J., A scholar's guide to academic journals in religion [... in view of his/her getting something published]. Metuchen NJ 1988, Scarecrow. xxiii-290 p. $32.50. 0-9108-2135-4 [NTAbs 33,234].

1038 *De Klerk* Peter, CALVIN bibliography 1989: CalvinT 24 (1989) 278-299.

1038* *Dell'Oro* Ferdinando, al., Bollettino Bibliografico: RivLtg 76 (1989) 597-795.

1039 *Dillard* Raymond B., Notes on computing: WestTJ 50 (1988) 243-5. 387-9.

1040 *Dubois* Jean-Daniel, Chronique patristique VI [BCNH-T 15-19...]: ÉTRel 64 (1989) 577-586.

1041 *Durand* G.-M. de, Bulletin de patrologie: RSPT 73 (1989) 453-492.

1042 *Duval* Yves-Marie, Bulletin de patrologie latine [13 éditions, 24 études]: RechSR 77 (1989) 567-601.

1043 Euntes Docete, Indice 1-40 (1948-87): = EuntDoc 42,1s (1989) 363 p.

1044 ᴱEvers Georg, Zeitschriftenschau [120 Zeitschriften aus der Dritten Welt: Titel mit Inhalt kurz deutsch] / Zusammenfassungen ausgewählter Beiträge / (neu) Buchanzeigen / Konferenzberichte: TKontext 10,1 (1989) 15-108 (-112) / 113-123 / 125-136 / 137-157; – 10,2 (1989)...

1045 **TContext**: Theology in context, annotated bibliography... reports of conferences: vol. 6 (Aachen 1989), substantially the equivalent of the German Theologie im Kontext vol. 10, with page-numbers almost identical; we give henceforth below reference to TContext English edition for all articles and reports we have not found elsewhere.

1046 *Évieux* Pierre, Littérature monastique d'Orient [7 livres]: RechSR 77 (1989) 417-430.

1047 *Fares* D. J., *al.*, Fichero de revistas latinoamericanas: Stromata 45 (1989) 481-534 [498-501 S. Escr.].

1048 ᴱFontaine Jacques, *Piétri* Charles, Chronique d'antiquité tardive et du christianisme ancien et médiéval: RÉAnc 90 (1988) 217-260: signed book-reports.

1049 **Gatti** Maria Luisa, Mᴀssɪᴍᴏ il Confessore... bibliog. 1987 ➤ 3,1014: ᴿByzantion 59 (1989) 548-555 (P. van *Deun* supplies 40 titles she overlooked., notably in Rumanian and Greek).

1050 ᴱGaventa Beverly R., Critical review of books in religion [1988 ➤ 4,947*]; 1989?

1051 *Guillemette* Nil, Priestly celibacy — mixed celibate friendships; an annotated bibliography: Landas 2,2 (Manila 1989) 263... [< 89,222].

1052 *Heiser* W. Charles, Theology Digest book survey: TDig 36 (1989) 43-96. 147-195. 247-296. 347-394: the usual amazingly rich collection of titles, with concise description.

1053 *Hendrickx* F., Literatuuroverzicht 1988: OnsGErf 63 (1989) 1-114.

1054 ᴱHenkel W., *Metzler* G., Bibliografia missionaria 52 (1988). R 1989, Pont. Univ. Urbaniana. 408 p. [< RHE 84, p. 335*]. – ᴿNZMissW 44 (1988) 297 (J. *Baumgartner*, vol. 50, 1987 für 1986).

1055 Index international des dissertations doctorales en théologie et en droit canonique présentées en 1988: RTLv 20 (1989) 520-593 (538-547, AT-NT; 522-533, finder par institution).

1056 *Jossua* Jean-Pierre, Bulletin de théologie littéraire: RSPT 73 (1989) 259-280.

1056* ᴱ*Junghans* Helmar, *al.*, Lutherbibliographie 1989: LuJb 56 (1989) 159-203, 1026 items; 204-6, neue Rezensionen; 207-213, index.

1057 **Kominès** Athanasios A., Ⓖ *Patmikē bibliothēkē*... New catalogue of Patmos St. John Monastery manuscripts, I, codices 1-101. Athenai 1988. xxix-277 p. – ᴿRÉByz 47 (1989) 268s (J. *Darrouzès*).

1058 *Kraft* Robert A., Offline; computer assisted research for religious studies 21s: CouStR 18 (1989) 15s / 47-50 / ...

1059 *Ledoyen* H. Aymes, Bulletin d'histoire bénédictine, T. XI/10: indicated on the cover of RBén 99 (1989) as contained within, on pages numbered 409*-448*, between p. 380(-3) and p. [253]; but there is nothing there.

1060 *Lumpe* Adolf, Bibliographie [der Geschichte der Konzilien]: AnHConc 19 (1987) 232-240. 458s.

1061 **McCabe** James P., Critical guide to Catholic reference books³ [¹1971; ²1980]: Research studies in library science 20. Englewood CO 1989, Libraries Unlimited. xiv-323 p. $47. 0-87287-621-7 [TDig 37,72].

1062 *Massein* Pierre, Bulletin d'histoire et de théologie des religions orientales: RechSR 76 (1988) 461-480.

1063 *Mateo-Seco* Lucas-F., *Lama* Enrique de la, Espiritualidad del presbítero secular (boletín bibliográfico): ScripTPamp 21 (1989) 227-287.

1064 *a*) *Mbiye* Lumbala, La théologie africaine, bibliographie sélective (1981-5), VI. Pastorale, évangélisation; – *b*) *Mukuama, al.*, Thèses et mémoires théol. cath. Kinshasa: RAfrT 13 (1989) 277-290 / 137-144. 299-300.

1065 *Meier* Kurt, Literatur zur kirchlichen Zeitgeschichte: TRu 54 (1989) 113-168.

1066 **Nadell** Pamela S., Conservative Judaism in America; a bibliographical dictionary and sourcebook. Westport CT 1988, Greenwood. xvii-408 p. $55. – ᴿTS 50 (1989) 626 (L. E. *Frizzell*).

1067 **Navas** Antonio, Archivo teológico granadino, Indices 26-50, 1963-1987. Granada 1989, Fac, Teol. 205 p.

1068 *Nichols* Aidan, An Yves CONGAR bibliography 1967-1987 [by years, adding 832 items to the 958 of *Jossua* J.-P. 1967]: Angelicum 66 (1989) 422-466.

1069 *Ottlyk* Ernő, Ⓜ Theologiai Szemle is thirty years old [1 (1958)]: TSzem 32 (1989) 50-55.

1070 Pelas revistas: REB 49 (1989) 251-6. 506-512. 763-8. 1011-8.

1071 *Poirier* Paul-Hubert, Ancienne littérature chrétienne et histoire de l'Église: LavalTP 45 (1989) 303-318.

1072 *Rau* Stefan, Ministranten-Literatur [14 (7 + 5?) books about servers at Mass]: TR 85 (1989) 57-63.

1073 Recension des revues: RSPT 73 (1989) 115-150. 315-340. 493-523. 633-639.

1074 Recent dissertations in religion: RelStR 15 (1989) 189-195 [290-295, Dissertations in progress; only a few titles here (and vol. 4)].

1075 Religious Studies Review Index 1-15 (1974-1989). Macon GA 1989, Mercer Univ. 200 p. $35; pa. $20 [RelStR 15,208 adv.].

1076 *Renwart* Léon, Théologie de la vie religieuse; bulletin bibliographique: VieCons 60 (1988) 45-58.

1077 Revista de Revistas: RET 49 (1989) 123-132. 343-354. 465-490.

1078 ᴱ**Ruether** Rosemary R., *Keller* Rosemary S., Women and religion in America [1. 1981; 2. 1983]; 3, 1900-1968; a documentary history. SF 1986, Harper & R. 409 p. $27. – ᴿJAAR 57 (1989) 429s (Dorothy C. *Bass*).

1079 *Sesboüé* Bernard, *a*) Bulletin de théologie patristique grecque; – *b*) Bulletin de théologie dogmatique; Christologie [i. NT, 4 livres; ii. Histoire des doctrines, 9 livres; iii. systématique, 7; iv. sotériologie, 7; philosophie, littérature, 5]: RechSR 76 (1988) 579-613 / 77 (1989) 531-565.

1080 Significant ecumenical journals, table of contents [titles without page-numbers]: EcuR 41 (1989) 145-150. 312-6. 478-482. 641-6 [bibliography (book-titles) 151-3. 317-320. 483-5. 647-650].

1081 *Stover* Mark, Notes on computing; theological reference tools on CD-ROM (Compact Disc — Read Only Memory): WestTJ 51 (1989) 431-4.

1082 *Tallon* Andrew, RAHNER studies 1939-89 [including TDig 21 (1973) 185-192 and 26 (1978) 365-385]: TDig 36 (1989) 321-349 [there is no Volume between 30 (1982) and 31 (1984)]; 37, 17-41: 1089 items.

1083 Tijdschrift voor Liturgie, Register 1910-1985. Hekelgem c. 1986, Abdij Affligem. – ᴿLtgJb 37 (1987) 127s (L. *Brinkhoff*).
1084 *a*) *Vallin* Pierre,   Bulletin d'histoire de l'Église et d'ecclésiologie; – *b*) *Ruello* Francis,   Bulletin d'histoire des idées médiévales: RechSR 76 (1988) 129-158 / 87-114.
1085 *Völker* Alexander, *al.*, Literaturbericht zur Gottesdienst: JbLtgHymn 31 (1987s) 134-197; zur Liturgik, 32 (1989) 198-262 [-289, zur Hymnologie, *Ameln* Konrad & *Marti* Andreas].
1086 *Wainwright* Geoffrey,   Recent continental theology; historical and systematic: ExpTim 100 (1988s) 91-96 (22 books; *Kasper* W., *Sauter* G., *Pannenberg* W.; *Labbe* Y.; *Rohls* J.; *Birmelé* A., *Tillard* J. ...).
1087 ᴱ**Wei-hsun** Charles, *Spiegler* Gerhard E.,   Movements and issues in world religions; a sourcebook and analysis of developments since 1945. Westport CT 1987, Greenwood.   570 p. – ᴿJAAR 57 (1989) 229-232 (H. *Coward*).
1088 Cumulative index, volumes 1-50:   WestTJ 50 (1988) 391-477.

A4.3   *Bibliographiae* philologicae *et* generales.

1088* *Amelotti* Mario,   L'epigrafia giuridica in Italia nell'ultimo decennio: StDocHistJ 53 (1987) 378-385.
1089 **Andrews** Derek, *Greenhalgh* Michael,   Computing for non-scientific applications. Leicester 1987, Univ. 346 p. 0-7185-1252-9. – ᴿLitLComp 4 (Ox 1989) 70 (J. *Hammond*).
1090 ᴱ*Balconi* Carla, *al.*,   Testi recentemente pubblicati [la più parte greci]: Aegyptus 69 (1989) 197-275; bibliografia metodica 303-357, ind. 358-363.
1090* **Beck** F. A. G.,   Bibliography of Greek education and related topics 1986 ➤ 4,991:   ᴿEmerita 57 (1989) 369s (D. *Plácido*).
1091 Bibliographische Beilage (klassische Altertumswissenschaft): Gnomon 61 (1989) Fasz. 1, p. *1-32*; 3. p. *33-72*; 5. p. *73-116*; 7. p. *117-152*.
1092 *Bousquet* Jean,   Bulletin épigraphique: RÉG 101 (1988) 293-491.
1093 **Busa** Roberto,   Fondamenti di informatica linguistica: Trattati e manuali.   Mi 1987, ViPe.   412 p. – ᴿSalesianum 51 (1989) 397s (B. *Amata*).
1094 *Busa* Roberto, *a*) Gli 'instrumenta lexicologica latina' [Lv Centre de Traitement Électronique, ᴰ*Tombeur* P.]:   CC 140 (1989,3) 396-403; – *b*) Storia informatica di parole [i. 'Lessico intellettuale europeo', Univ. Roma; ii. Instrumenta lexicologica latina, Univ. LvN]: Gregorianum 70 (1989) 127-140.
1095 Catalogue général des livres imprimés de la Bibliothèque Nationale: Anonymes XVIᵉ-XVIIᵉ s. [175,000 items], available in progressively updated microfiches [RHE 84,590]. The catalogue of books with known authors up to 1960 was completed 1981.
1096 ᴱ**Ernst** Juliette, *al.*, L'Année philologique, 58 (1987). P 1989, BLettres. xl-911 p. 12971 items.   0184-6949. The biblical items are on p. 301-321 under the heading 'Testamenta' [presumably OT-NT, but all are from NT].
1097 *Friant* Jean,   Informatique et 'intelligence artificielle': EsprVie 99 (1989) 529-543.
1098 *Gauthier* P., *al.*, Bulletin épigraphique: RÉG 102 (1989) 361-509.
1099 *Ijsewijn* J., *al.*, Instrumentum bibliographicum neolatinum: Humanistica Lovaniensia 37 (1988) 278-334; 38 (1989) 323-376.

1100 **Ireland** Norma O.,   Index to fairy tales, I. 1949-1972; II. 1973-1977; III. 1978-1986 with *Sprug* J.W.; ; including folklore, legends, and myths in collections. Metuchen NJ 1985, Scarecrow. 741 p.; 249 p.; 575 p. $39.50; $26; -. 0-8108-1855-8; -2011-0; -2194-X.

1101 *Liviabella Furiani* Patrizia, L'universo femminile del mondo antico: GitFg [38 (1986) 275-282] 41 (1989) 267-274, recensioni.

1101* *a*) **Losfeld** Gérard, Banques de données; cultures et religions antiques; introduction méthodologique: CREDO [Centre de Recherche sur la Documentation dans les Sciences de l'Antiquité]. Villeneuve d'Ascq 1987, Univ. Lille III. 34 p.; annexes. – *b*) Guide d'interrogation 1988, 40 p.; – *c*) Liste des revues dépouillées 1988, 174 + 46 + 42 p. – *d*) Thesaurus thématique 1987, 300 + 762 p. [AntClas 59,431].

1102 **Luey** Beth, Handbook for academic authors. C 1987, Univ. xiii-226 p. 0-521-33682-1 [OIAc N89].

1102* *Modrzejewski* Joseph, Papyrologie documentaire 1982-1984: JJurPap 20 (1988) 169-277.

1103 *Packer* Margaret M., Research in classical studies for University degrees in Great Britain and Ireland: BInstClas 35 (1988) 183-210, in progress; 211-9, completed; 36 (1989) 169-196, in progress; 197-202, completed.

1104 **Pellegrin** Elisabeth, Bibliothèques retrouvées; manuscrits, bibliothèques et bibliophiles du Moyen Âge et de la Renaissance; recueil d'études publiées de 1938 à 1985. P 1988, CNRS. xii-568 p.; 24 pl. – ᴿRBén 99 (1989) 187s (P.-M. *Bogaert*).

1104* Les provinces hellénophones de l'empire romain, de Pompée au milieu du IIIᵉ siècle ap. J.-C.; recueil bibliographique à partir des analyses du BAHR (1962 à 1974): 1986 ➤ 4,1008: ᴿArctos 23 (1989) 283s (M. *Kajava*).

1105 Rassegna bibliographica: Ivra 37 (1986) 244-381; indice 382-396.

1106 **Schepper** M. De, (*Heesakkers* C.L.), Bibliographie de l'humanisme des anciens Pays-Bas [1972], Supplément 1970-1985. Bru 1988, Acad. vi-439 p. – ᴿETL 65 (1989) 171s (F. *Neirynck*: exhaustif, onze titres sur COPPENS; mais pas d'index systématique, et un quatrième titre d'ARTOLA sur LESSIUS omis).

1107 **Sorrentino** Antonio, Saggio di una bibliografia sulla preistoria linguistica dell'Eurasia: AION Quad. Ling. min. 2. N 1988, Univ. Ist. Orientale. 191 p.

1108 *Staritsyn* A.N., Index of literature on the ancient world published in the USSR in 1986: VDI 191 (1989) 165-178.

A4.4   *Bibliographiae* **orientalisticae.**

1109 **Attal** Robert, ❺ A bibliography of the writings of Prof. Nehemya ALLONY [...Arabist], intr. *Morag* Shlomoh: Ešel Be'er-Šebaʻ 3. Beersheba 1984, Ben-Gurion Univ. vi-33 p. – ᴿRÉJ 146 (1987) 172s (J.-P. *Rothschild*).

1110 **Bacharach** Jere L., A Middle East studies handbook. Seattle 1989, University of Washington. xii-160 p. 0-295-96144-9.

1111 Bibliographie 1986 - Nachtrag; 1987: BeiSudan 4 (1989) 187s; 189-229.

1111* ᴱ*Bleibtreu* E. (Archäologie), *al.*, Assyriologie, Register; 1. Realien; 2. Wörter; 3. Textstellen (1986-Feb. 1988): AfO 35 (1988) 261-432.

1112 *Brunsch* Wolfgang, Annotated bibliography for Coptic philology: BSACopte 28 (1986-9) 111-145.

1113 *Deller* Karlheinz, Keilschriftbibliographie: Orientalia, intended for 58,4 (1989, delayed until 60,1, 1991).

1114 *Dohaish* Abdul-Latif A. ibn, Growth and development of Islamic libraries: Der Islam 66 (1989) 289-302.
1115 *Gilliot* Claude, Bulletin d'Islamologie et d'études arabes: RSPT 73 (1989) 423-452.
1116 **Hazai** György, *Kellner-Heinkele* Barbara, Bibliographisches Handbuch der Turkologie; eine Bibliographie der Bibliographien vom 18. Jahrhundert bis 1979, I: Bibliotheca Orientalis Hungarica 30. Wsb/ Budapest 1986, Harrassowitz/Ofenpest. 583 p. – ᴿDer Islam 65 (1988) 173-5 (B. *Spuler*).
1117 **Jones** Charles E., Oriental Institute Research Archives Acquisitions List, Dec. 1989-Jan. 1990 [and four further issues each year, each of some 35 p., about 350 books, plus maps, periodicals, etc.] Ch 1989s. N.B. in this Dec.-Jan. issue, Appendix I contains Chicago University Near Eastern Studies dissertations, not available in DissA.
1118 *Jones* Charles E., Microfilm holdings of the Chicago Univ. Oriental Institute research archives: OIAc S89, 8-page appendix].
1119 **Makar** Ragai N., Egypt: World Bibliog. 86. Ox 1988, Clio. xxxi-307 p. 1-85109-039-8.
1120 *Meinari* I. E., Catalogue des manuscrits arabes découverts récemment au Monastère de Sainte-Catherine au Mont Sinai. Athenai 1985, Organisme National Grec pour la Recherche. 156 + 70 p., 73 pl. + 10 color. – ᴿBSACopte 28 (1986-9) 151s (A. *Khater*).
1121 *Volpe* Michael J., An annotated bibliography of Ethiopian literature in Russian: RasEtiop 32 (1988) 171-193.
1122 **Zonhoven** L. M. J., *al.*, Annual Egyptological bibliography 39 (1985) / Late Reviews 1947-1984. Leiden 1989, Internat. Asn. Egyptologists / Ned. Inst. N.Oosten. x-376 p. / xii-74 p. 90-72147-06-5; 5-7 [OIAc Ja90].

A4.5 *Bibliographiae* **archaeologicae.**

1123 **Barouch** Giovanna, Selected bibliography; publications on archaeological excavations and surveys in Israel 1979-1984: Atiqot Eng. 18 Sup. (1989). 95 p.
1124 *Calmeyer* Peter, Archäologische Bibliographie 1987: ArchMIran 21 (1988) 261-275.
1125 51 Dissertation - Titel: ArchAnz (1989) 101-5 [104, palästin. Weihrauchgefässe mit Reliefszenen aus dem Leben Christi (*Richter* Ilse, Berlin)].
1126 *Gringmuth-Dallmer* E., *al.*, Bibliographie zur Ur- und Frühgeschichte: AusgF 34 (1989) 260-295.
1126* [*Homès-Fredericq* Denyse], La coopération [work in progress], 26ᵉ Rencontre Assyriologique: Akkadica 63 (1989) 27-34; 64s (1989) 20-38.
1127 Numismatic Literature 122 (Sept. 1989). 160 p. by site; plus medals, obituaries etc.
1128 ᴱ*Symonds* R. P., Roman pottery bibliography: JRPot 2 (1989) 106-130 [by sites in Britain; then unclassified Foreign].

> **II. Introductio**

B1   *Introductio* .1 *tota vel VT* – **Whole Bible or OT**

1129 **Augustin** M., *Kegler* J., Bibelkunde des ATs 1987 → 3,1137; 4,1050: ᴿStreven 57 (1989s) 86s (P. *Beentjes*).

1130 **Baldermann** Ingo, Einführung in die Bibel³ [¹Die Bibel, Buch des Lernens 1980] → 61,1569]: Uni 1486, 1988 → 4,1051 ['Uni 1946']: ᴿTLZ 114 (1989) 466s (G. *Kehnscherper*); TR 85 (1989) 99s (O. B. *Knoch*); ZAW 101 (1989) 147 (H.-C. *Schmitt*).

1131 **Barucq** A., *al.*, Écrits de l'Orient ancien et sources bibliques 1986 → 2,602*: ᴿRÉJ 148 (1989) 396s (Mireille *Hadas-Lebel*).

1132 **Barucq** A., *al.*, Scritti dell'Antico Vicino Oriente e fonti bibliche 1988 → 4,1052: ᴿAntonianum 64 (1989) 196s (M. *Nobile*); ParVi 34 (1989) 309-311 (C. *Balzaretti*); RivB 37 (1989) 365-7 (G. L. *Prato*).

1133 ᴱ**Bigger** Stephen, Creating the Old Testament; the emergence of the Hebrew Bible.   Ox 1989, Blackwell.   xx-364 p.   0-631-15909-6; pa. -6249-6. Numerous short chapters, by *Auld* A., *Clines* D., *Whitelam* K., *al.* – ᴿExpTim 101 (1989s) 281 (C. S. *Rodd*).

1134 *Cazelles* Henri,   Israel among the nations [Quelques dettes, in Foi et culture 1981], ᵀ*Moloney* F. J., updated by Cazelles: Pacifica 2 (1989) 47-60.

1135 **Craigie** Peter C.,   The OT, its background, growth, and content 1986 → 2,797... 4,1064:   ᴿAndrUnS 27 (1989) 82s (P. D. *Duerksen*); AsbTJ 44,2 (1989) 101-4 (also P. D. *Duerksen*: balanced); CriswT 2 (1987s) 159-161 (K. A. *Mathews*).

1136 **Drane** John,   Introducing the OT 1987 → 4,1065:   ᴿBibTB 19 (1989) 37s (L. A. *Sinclair*); Paradigms 5 (1989) 156-8 (J. W. *Watts*).

1137 **Flanders** Henry J., *al.*,   People of the covenant; an introduction to the OT³ [¹1963; ²1973].   NY 1988, Oxford UP.   xiii-498 p. $30.   0-19-504438-X [TDig 36,370].

1138 **Fohrer** Georg,   Erzähler und Propheten im AT 1988 → 4,1067:   ᴿBO 46 (1989) 419-422 (P. *Höffken*); ÉTRel 64 (1989) 610 (J. *Rennes*: excellent); TLZ 114 (1989) 21-23 (S. *Herrmann*); ZAW 101 (1989) 151 (H.-C. *Schmitt*).

1139 **Galbiati** Enrico,   História da Salvação [1.] no Antigo Testamento [2. Evangelho; 3. Atos: no prelo]. Petrópolis c. 1989, Vozes. [REB 49/1 adv.].

1140 **Gari** Jaume Llorenç,   Leer y entender el Antiguo Testamento.   Palma de Mallorca 1988.   413 p.   84-7535-125-5 [EstBíb 47,578].

1141 **Gibert** Pierre,   L'Ancien Testament: Parcours.   P 1989, Centurion. 124 p.   F 59 [MondeB 64, 69, F. *Brossier*].

1142 *Goodenough* Erwin R.,   The Bible as product of the ancient world [1960]: → 268*, ᴱ*Frerichs* E., Goodenough['s own essays] 1986, 23-46.

1143 **Gottwald** Norman K.,   The Hebrew Bible; a socio-literary introduction 1985 → 1,1183... 4,1071:   ᴿCriswT 1 (1987) 408s (K. A. *Mathews*); JRel 68 (1988) 447s (B. *Halpern*).

1144 **Gottwald** N. K.,   Introdução sócio-literária à Bíblia Hebraica. São Paulo 1988, Paulinas.   652 p. – ᴿREB 49 (1989) 736s (F. *Orafino*).

1145 *a*) *Harrelson* Walter,   Introduction to the OT; – *b*) *Brown* Raymond E., Introduction to the NT; – *c*) *Anderson* B.,   The Bible as sacred literature: → 377, Books (1989) 1, 11-19 / 2, 117-124 / 1, 1-9.

1146 **Jacob** E.,   L'Antico Testamento, ᵀᴱ*Corsani* B., 1988 → 4,1072; Lit. 18.000:   ᴿProtestantesimo 44 (1988) 123 (J. *Hobbins*: breve ma più completo di RENDTORFF R. ital. 1968).

Josipovici Gabriel,   The book of God [as a literary masterpiece]; a response to the Bible 1988 → 1553.

1148 **Kaiser** Walter C.,   Toward rediscovering the Old Testament.   GR 1987, Zondervan.   219 p. $17. – ᴿBS 146 (1989) 228s (E. H. *Merrill*).

1149 **Keil** C. F., Introduction to the OT, ᵀ*Douglas* G.C.M. (1869). Peabody
MA 1988, Hendrickson. 657 p.; 435 p. $40 (both). – ᴿSWJT 32,2 (1989s)
53s (H. B. *Hunt*).

1150 **Laffey** Alice L., An introduction to the OT; a feminist perspective 1988
→ 4,1075 [not 'Alice B.']: ᴿBibTB 19 (1989) 153s (R. *Gnuse*: she does not
wish to ignore the biblical text completely); CBQ 51 (1989) 720s (Gale A.
Yee); ExpTim 100,2 first choice (1988s) 41s (C. S. *Rodd* 'learned a lot
from this' despite its misuses of Hebrew); Gregorianum 70 (1989) 147-9
(C. *Conroy* approves); Horizons 16 (1989) 374s (Denise D. *Hopkins*:
belongs in every college OT course); TS 50 (1989) 198 (Barbara *Cullom*:
inadequately helps the reader to form her/his own feminist approach).

1151 **LaSor** William S., Das Alte Testament; Entstehung – Geschichte –
Botschaft [OT Survey, Eerdmans 1982 → 63,1050], ᵀᴱ*Egelkraut* Helmuth.
Giessen 1989, Brunnen. xx-799 p.; maps. 3-7655-9344-3.

1152 **Maillot** A., Gros plan sur l'AT 1987 → 4,1079: ᴿProtestantesimo 44
(1989) 57s (G. *Conte*).

1153 **Mannucci** Valerio, La Biblia como palabra de Dios 1985 → 1,1195...
3,1158: ᴿFranBog 30 (1988) 375s (A. *Gil Londoño*).

1154 **Martín Sánchez** B., La Biblia explicada; para mejor entender la Biblia.
S 1987, Hetesa. 552 p. – ᴿProyección 35 (1988) 322 (B. A. O.).

1155 **Möller** Hans, Alttestamentliche Bibelkunde. [B 1986, Ev.-V.]. Gr.
Oesingen 1989, Luth-BH. 326 p. DM 22,80. 3-922534-49-X. – ᴿTLZ 114
(1989) 148s (K.-H. *Bernhardt*: kein wissenschaftlicher Ertrag).

1156 **Moshkowitz** Y. Z., *Hamiel* H., ⊕ Pirkê mābô'... Introduction to the
study of the Bible I. Ramat-Gan 1987, Bar-Ilan Univ. 86 p. 965-
226-088-6 [OIAc Ja90].

1157 ᴱ**Mulder** Martin J., Mikra 1988 → 4,317: ᴿExpTim 100,8 2d-top choice
(1988s) 283s (C. S. *Rodd*: standard).

1158 **Musset** Jacques, Collins Bible handbook [1985-7], ᵀ*Thomas* Sarah,
Stanley-Baker Penny. SF c.1989, Collins Liturgical [Harper & R.].
528 p.; color. ill. $15. 0-00-599134-X [TDig 37,174].

1159 **Ohler** Annemarie, Grundwissen AT, ein Werkbuch 1-3, 1986s
→ 2,810... 4,1084: ᴿTPQ 137 (1989) 413 (A. *Schnider*); ZkT 111 (1989)
98-100 (F. *Mohr*, 1).

1160 **Ohler** Annemarie, Studying the Old Testament; from tradition to canon
[1972], ᵀ*Cairns* David 1985 → 1,1198... 4,1085: ᴿHeythJ 30 (1989) 74s (J.
Blenkinsopp); JRel 68 (1988) 448s (G. *Anderson*: weak).

1161 **Rendtorff** Rolf, The OT 1985 → 1,1200... 4,1088: ᴿHeythJ 30 (1989)
494 (B. R.).

1162 **Rendtorff** Rolf, Introduction à l'Ancien Testament [1983], ᵀ*Smyth*
Françoise, *Winkler* Heinz. P 1989, Cerf. 526 p. F 224. 2-204-02872-X
[ÉTRel 64,609]. – ᴿEsprVie 99 (1989) 670-2 (L. *Monloubou*); PrOrChr 39
(1989) 215s (P. *Ternant*); VSp 143 (1989) 827-9 (J. *Asurmendi*).

1163 **Rogerson** John W., *Davies* Philip R., The Old Testament world
[...archeology, sociology, literature]. C 1989, Univ. 384 p. £19.50.
0-521-34006-3 [BL 90,24]. – ᴿJJS 40 (1989) 240s (P. R. S. *Moorey*).

1164 *Rose* Martin, L'Ancien Testament, livre d'une attente; le concept
d'histoire comme clef d'interprétation dans l'œuvre de Gerhard von RAD:
RTPhil 121 (1989) 407-421.

1165 **Schmidt** W. H., *Thiel* W., *Hanhart* R., Altes Testament: Grundkurs
Theologie 1. Stu 1989, Kohlhammer. 216 p. DM 22. 3-17-010267-5
[NTAbs 33,422]. – ᴿComViat 32 (1989) 201s (J. *Heller*); ZAW 101 (1989)
474 (H.-C. *Schmitt*).

1166 **Schmidt** Werner H., Einführung in das Alte Testament⁴ʳᵉᵛ [¹1979
➤ 60,1309; ³1985 ➤ 1,1204]. B 1989, de Gruyter. x-430 p. DM 22.
3-17-010267-2. – ᴿBO 46 (1989) 687-9 (N. P. *Lemche*,³).

1167 *Schürmann* Heinz, Bibelwissenschaft unter dem Wort Gottes; eine
selbstkritische Besinnung: ➤ 197, ꟳTRILLING W., Christus bezeugen 1989,
11-42.

1168 *a*) *Smith* Wilfred C., The study of religion and the study of the Bible /
Scripture as form and concept; their emergence in the western world; – *b*)
Graham William A., Scripture as spoken word: ➤ 557, Re-thinking
1989 ...

1169 **Soden** Wolfram von, Bibel und Alter Orient: BZAW 162, 1985
➤ 1,247 ... 4,1093: ᴿOLZ 84 (1989) 35-37 (L. *Wächter*).

1170 **Soggin** J. Alberto, Introduction to the Old Testament from its origins to
the closing of the Alexandrian canon³ [1987 ➤ 3,1169], ᵀ*Bowden* John:
OTLibrary. Louisville 1989, Knox/Westminster. xxxii-608 p. $30 [CBQ
52,198].

1171 **Soggin** J. Alberto, Introduzione all'AT⁴ 1987 ➤ 3,1169; 4,1094: ᴿRSO
63 (1989) 171s (G. *Garbini*).

1172 [*Homerski* J.] ²ʳᵉᵛ**Szlaga** J., ❷ Wstęp ogólny ... General introduction to
the Holy Scripture 1986 ➤ 4,1095; zł 500: ᴿJStJud 20 (1989) 115s (Z. J.
Kapera: quite modern, but Temple scroll missing).

1173 **Talmon** Shemaryahu, Gesellschaft und Literatur in der Hebräischen
Bibel: Gesammelte Aufsätze 1 [9, 1958-85] 1988 ➤ 4,271: ᴿÉTRel 64
(1989) 276 (J. *Pons*).

1174 **Taylor** Justin, As it was written; an introduction to the Bible 1987
➤ 3,1171; 4,1098: ᴿEstBíb 47 (1989) 278s (J. P. *Tosaus*).

1175 **Vannini** Marco, M. LUTERO, Prefazioni alla Bibbia; Vorreden ital.:
Ascolta Israele 4. Genova 1987, Marietti. 195 p. [LuJb 56, p. 167].

1176 **Vidal i Cruañas** Albert, Encuentro con la Biblia, pról. *Camprodón*
Jaume: EstBíb 7. M 1989, Paulinas. 412 p.; ill. 84-285-1265-5. –
ᴿActuBbg 26 (1989) 201 (R. de *Sivatte*).

1177 **Walton** John H., Ancient Israelite literature in its cultural context; a
survey of parallels between biblical and Ancient Near Eastern texts:
Library of Biblical Interpretation. GR 1989, Zondervan Regency. 249 p.
0-310-36590-2 [OIAc N89].

1178 **Zeilinger** A., Das AT verstehen I-II, Konstanz 1986-8 ➤ 4,1099:
ᴿZAW 101 (1989) 480 (M. C. *Schmitt*).

B1.2 'Invitations' to Bible or OT.

1179 **Alonso Schökel** Luis, Današni čovjek pred Biblijom: Riječ 15. Zagreb
1986, Kršćanska Sadašnost. 60 p. – ᴿBogSmot 59 (1989) 235s (A. *Rebić*).

1180 **Beauchamp** Paul, Parler d'Écritures saintes 1987 ➤ 3,1177; 4,1105:
ᴿMasses Ouvrières 427 (1989) 110 (X. *Durand*).

1181 **Beauchamp** Paul, Hablar de las Escrituras Santas; perfil del lector actual
de la Biblia [1987 ➤ 3,1177], ᵀ*Arias* J. Barc 1989, Herder. 136 p. –
ᴿNatGrac 36 (1989) 379 (R. *Robles*).

1182 *Beentjes* Panc, Start-bijbel [Een keuze uit het Oude en Nieuwe
Testament; Haarlem/Brussel 1989, Bijbelgenootschap. 379 p.], een nieuw
genre: Streven 57 (1989s) 559-561.

1183 **Charpentier** Étienne, Wegwijs in het Oude/Nieuwe Testament [1980s
➤ 62,1189*a*; 4000*a*],ᵀ. Baarn 1987, Ten Have. 123 p. 128 p. *f* 29,50 each.
– ᴿStreven 55 (1987s) 467s (P. *Beentjes*).

1184 **Chouraqui** André, Il pensiero ebraico [La pensée juive, PUF ³1975], ᵀ*Bigarelli* Alberto: LoB 3.10. Brescia 1989, Queriniana. 113 p. Lit. 15.000. 88-399-1690-3 [Greg 70,828].

1185 **Comblin** José, La forza della Parola [1986], ᵀ*Demarchi* Enzo: La Missione 11. Bo 1989, EMI. xvi-463 p. Lit. 34.000. 88-307-0223-4.

1186 **Daniélou** Jean, I santi pagani dell'Antico Testamento [1956; ital. = 1964 + pref. *Ravasi* G.]. Brescia 1988, Queriniana. 140 p. Lit. 11.000. – ᴿCC 140 (1989,4) 619s (A. *Ferrua*).

1187 **Deshayes** H. [† 1988], Chercher Dieu dans la Bible. P 1989, Letouzey & Â. xii-195 p. F 120. 2-7063-0174-0 [BL 90, 100, R. *Hammer*].

1188 *Dietrich* Walter, Der rote Faden im Alten Testament ['Gerechtigkeit']: EvT 49 (1989) 232-250.

1189 ᴱ**Ferguson** John, [*Goldstein* David, conseiller], Les grands événements de la Bible, ᵀᴱ*Passelecq* G. Turnhout 1987, Brépols. 200 p. F 265. – ᴿEsprVie 99 (1989) 28-*jaune* [E. *Vauthier*]; RThom 89 (1989) 475 (L. *Devillers*: 'gadgets?'). Figures de l'AT chez les Pères 1989 → 399.

1190 **Fitzgerald** Billy, Take and read; a guide to the Bible for lay readers. Dublin 1986, Dominican. vi-178 p. – ᴿAfER 30 (1988) 125s (R. K. P. *Rwehumbiza*).

1190* a) *Guillén Torralba* Juan, La fuerza de la 'Palabra' [... AT; Egipto]; – b) *Esquerda Bifet* Joan, La Paraula contemplada esdevé missió: → 69*, ᶠGOMÀ I., RCatalT 14 (1989) 379-394 castellano, Eng. 394 / 367-378, Eng. 378.

1191 ᴱ**Guinness** A. E., Mysteries of the Bible; the enduring questions of the Scriptures. Pleasantville NY 1988, Reader's Digest. 384 p. 0-89577-293-0 [NTAbs 33,236].

1192 **Hall** Thelma, Too deep for words; rediscovering 'lectio divina' 1988 → 4,1117: ᴿScripB 20 (1989s) 42 (M. *McNamara*).

1193 **Hanegraaf** J., Met de Torah is het begonnen, I. Oecumenische inleiding in het Oude Testament; II. De voortgang van het Woord in Tenach en Septuagint. Nijkerk 1988, Callenbach. 253 p.; ƒ32,50; 354 p., ƒ47,50. 90-266-0162-X. – ᴿStreven 57 (1989s) 273,659 (P. *Beentjes*); TsTNijm 29 (1989) 173 (J. *Holman*).

1194 **Hanson** R. P. C. & A. T., The Bible without illusions. L/Ph 1989, SCM/Trinity. ix-150 p. £7. 0-334-00101-3 [BL 90,15, J. *Barton*: opportunity to reclaim fundamentalists wasted by bad temper]. – ᴿExpTim 101 (1989s) 285s (F. F. *Bruce* approves).

1195 ᴱ**Harpur** James, Great events of Bible times. GCNY 1987, Doubleday. 200 p. $30 [BAR-W 16/1, 12, E. *Yamauchi*].

1195* **Harrington** Wilfrid J., Heroes and heroines of the way [29 biblical characters]: Theology of a pilgrim people. Dublin 1988, Gill & M. 185 p. £8. 0-7171-1617-4. – ᴿExpTim 101 (1989s) 89 (G. *Slater*).

1196 *Harrison* R. K., [Dallas Griffith Lectures Nov. 1988] The [pastor's] critical use of the Old Testament; [2.] Credibility and enthusiasm in preaching the OT; [3.] Learning the lessons of history; [4.] The Gospel in OT preaching: Bibliotheca Sacra 146 (1989) 12-20. 123-131. 243-254. 363-372.

1197 a) *Heflin* Boo, The OT for a twentieth century Christian; a personal testimony; – b) *Johnson* Rick, The OT demand for faith and obedience: → 185, ᶠSMITH R., SWJT 32,3 (1989s) 17-26 / 27-35.

1198 *Helsper* Michael, Zur bildlichen Rekonstruktion des alttestamentlichen Weltbildes: KatBlätt 114 (1989) 356-361 [< ZIT 89,414].

1199 **Hendricks** Lois L., Discovering my biblical dream heritage. San José 1989, Resource. xii-248 p. $10 pa. [CBQ 52,196].

1200 **Hiers** R. H., Reading the Bible book by book; an introductory study guide to the books of the Bible with apocrypha [for first-time readers]. Ph 1988, Fortress. xvii-238 p. $13. 0-8006-2074-7 [NTAbs 33,96].

1201 **Holman** Samuel C., The people of the book; drama, fellowship, and religion. Ch 1987 (pa. = 1983), Univ. xvi-337 p. $13. – ᴿJRel 69 (1989) 138s (M. *Gresser*).

1202 *a) Hruby* K., Judaïsme; les deux branches de la révélation; – *b) Reeber* M., La communication divine en Islam; – *c) Grelot* P., Tradition et Écriture; – *d) Delzant* A., Raison humaine et Révélation; la Bible à l'épreuve de la modernité; – *e) Lathuilière* P., Questions sur le fondamentalisme chrétien; – *f) Sindt* Gérard, Les lecteurs ont la parole; – *g) Varro* R., 'Je choisis tout!' Comment toute la Bible est-elle parole de Dieu?; – *h) Asurmendi* J., 'Ainsi parle le Seigneur'; – *j) Philbert* R., Écriture, parole de Dieu et travail croyant en Église: Masses Ouvrières 427 (1989) 5-10 / 11-20 / 23-36 / 37-48 / 49-55 / 57-66 / 67-73 / 75-83 / 85-93 / 95-107.

1203 **Kopp** Johanna, Das AT – ein Buch für heute; Zugänge zu den Büchern der Geschichte Israels. Pd 1989, Bonifatius. 154 p. DM 18.50. 3-87088-592-0. – ᴿErbAuf 65 (1989) 499s (A. *Schmidt*).

1204 **Lapide** Pinchas, Leggere la Bibbia con un ebreo 1985 → 1,1231; 2,829: ᴿProtestantesimo 44 (1989) 76 (L. *Negro*).

1205 **Lohfink** Gerhard, *a)* Enfin je comprends la Bible; un livre sur la critique des formes [1973 → 55,503]: Essais bibliques 14. Genève 1988, Labor et Fides. 148 p. 2-8309-0109-6. – *b)* ❷ Rozumieć Biblię, wprowadzenie do krytyki form literackich, ᵀWidła Bogusław. Wsz 1987, Pax. 144 p. – ᴿPrzPow 810 (1989) 204-8 (C. *Łukasz*).

1206 **Lys** Daniel, Treize énigmes de l'Ancien Testament [13 paradoxes like 'particularism vs. universalism' on which the reader is supposed to read first an indicated study]: Initiations 1988 → 4,1125: ᴿBL (1989) 85 (B. P. *Robinson*); Carthaginensia 5 (1989) 271 (J. F. *Cuenca*); VSp 143 (1989) 311-3 (J. *Asurmendi*).

1207 ᴱ**Meyer** Ivo, Faszinierende Welt der Bibel; von Menschen und Schicksalen, Schauplätzen und Ereignissen. FrB 1988, Herder. 200 p.; 175 fig. + 84 color.; 35 maps. DM 50. – ᴿTPQ 137 (1989) 75 (Borghild *Baldauf*).

1208 *Molnár* Amadeo, ❶ The Bible, witness, and Europe; historical and cultural aspects, ᵀBóna Zoltán: TSzem 31 (1988) 358-362.

1209 **Oden** R. A., The Bible without theology 1987 → 3,269; 4,1132: ᴿCCurr 38 (1988s) 364-6 (J. C. *Endres*); Horizons 16 (1989) 155s (C. *Mercer*); JRel 68 (1988) 600s (J. J. M. *Roberts*).

1210 *O'Malley* W. J., Scripture from scratch [... Catholics have never really learned to read the biblical message for themselves, without a priest or teacher to explain it]: America 160 (1989) 77-81 [< NTAbs 33,142].

1211 **Orsatti** Mauro, Briciole di Vangelo 1985 → 2,1986: ᴿParVi 33 (1988) 231s (A. *Enbru*).

1212 *Peli* Pinchas H., La Tora aujourd'hui; la Bible nous (p. 3 'vous') parle [< Jerusalem Post], ᵀGugenheim Jean-J. P 1988, D-Brouwer. 258 p. F 98. – ᴿEsprVie 99 (1989) 46s (L. *Monloubou*); Études 371 (1989) 140 (G. *Petitdemange*).

1213 **Ralph** M. N. (ms.) Plain words about biblical images [covenant, Messiah, Kingdom, redemption]; growing in our faith through the

Scriptures. NY 1989, Paulist. vi-241 p. $11. 0-8091-3045-9 [NTAbs 33,380].

1214 *Ravasi* Gianfranco, Per un'estetica biblica: RasT 30 (1989) 5-21.

1215 **Renckens** Han, De Bijbel mee maken; omgangsvormen en proefteksten. Kampen 1988, Kok. 234 p. *f* 39. 90-242-3395-X. – ᴿStreven 56 (1988s) 947 (P. *Beentjes*); TsTNijm 29 (1989) 173 (J. *Holman*).

1216 *Scheffler* E., Searching for meaning in biblical scholarship — reflections with Hermann HESSE: TEv 21,2 (Pretoria 1988) 2-8 [< NTAbs 33,145].

1217 **Simone** R. Thomas, *Sugarman* Richard I., Reclaiming... Greek/biblical worlds 1986 → 4,1138: ᴿCurrTM 16 (1989) 127s (F. M. *Danker*: weak on Bible).

1218 **Steinsaltz** Adin, Biblical images; men and women of the Book [Radio Israel], ᵀ*Hanegbi* Yehuda, *Keshet* Yehudit, 1984 → 1,1498: ᴿCBQ 51 (1989) 541s (Rita J. *Burns*: in the rich tradition of Jewish 'creative exposition').

1219 **Strappazzon** Valentin, 36 questions sur la Bible: C'est-à-dire. P 1989, Centurion. 115 p. F 54 [MondeB 64, 70, F. *Brossier*].

1220 **Stuhlmueller** Carroll, New paths through the Old Testament. NY 1989, Paulist. v-111 p. $6. 0-8091-3094-7.

1221 **VanDevelder** Frank R., The biblical journey of faith; the road of the sojourner. Ph 1988, Fortress. 126 p. $9. – ᴿTTod 46 (1989s) 354 (R. *Boyce*).

B1.3 *Paedagogia biblica* – **Bible-teaching techniques.**

1222 *Alla scoperta della Bibbia* [dal francese 1980] I-II. T-Leumann 1985 LDC. I. AT, 232 p.; II. NT 275 p. Lit. 14.000 ciascuno. 80-01-10082-5; -3-3. – ᴿProtestantesimo 44 (1989) 122s (G. *Anziani*).

1223 *Alves de Lima* Luiz, Biblia y catequesis: Medellín 14,56 (1988) 435-448 [449-486, *al.*; < TContext 6/2, 69].

1224 *Baena* Gustavo, Palabra de Dios y evangelización: TXav 39 (1989) 397-431.

1225 *La Bibbia, prima lettura*; present. *Martini* C. M. R 1984, Piemme. 640 p. Lit. 39.000. – ᴿProtestantesimo 44 (1989) 74s (G. *Scuderi*: antologia, per scuole medie).

1225* *Bible and Children.* L 1988, 'BCC'. 60 p. £2. 0-85169-123-4. – ᴿExpTim 101 (1989s) 94s (J. B. *Bates*: severe, but leaves 'BCC' unexplained).

1226 **Blair** Colin F.N., The United Bible Societies of the Asia Pacific region; a study into the history and possible future development: diss. Fuller, ᴰ*Clinton* R. Pasadena 1989. 287 p. 90-14264. – DissA 50 (1989s) 4002-A [under 'Business Administration'].

1227 *Bloth* Peter C., Kommt die 'pädagogische Gemeinde'? Über Sachtendenz und Konjunkturtrend einer praktisch-theologischen Entwicklung: TRu 54 (1989) 69-108.

1228 **Dodd** Christine, Making Scripture work; a practical guide to using Scripture in the local church. L 1989, Chapman. 167 p. £9. – ᴿPrPeo 3 (1989) 412 (B. *Robinson*: highly recommended).

1228* *a)* *Domman* Fritz, Tradierung des Glaubens zwischen Wissen und Erfahrung; – *b)* *Kirchhofer* Karl, Weitergabe des Glaubens als Prozess; – *c)* *Feifel* Erich, Ist Katechese geschichtsvergessen? Spannung zwischen Tradition und Gegenwart: TBer 18 ('Glaubensvermittlung, theologische und anthropologische Aspekte' 1989) 89-.... / 141-.... / 117-.... [< ZIT 90,174].

1229 **Johannsen** Friedrich, *Reents* Christine, Alttestamentliches Arbeitsbuch für Religionspädagogen: Tb 1041. Stu 1987, Kohlhammer. 224 p. DM 24 pa. – ᴿTR 85 (1989) 493s (J. V. *Sandberger*).

1230 **Karleen** Paul S., The handbook to Bible study with a guide to the Scofield study system. NY 1987, Oxford-UP. 469 p. $25. 0-19-504987-X. – ᴿBS 146 (1989) 106 (R. P. *Lightner*).

1231 *Limelette* Yves et Anita de, La mémorisation de la Parole de Dieu, un chemin de ré-création: LVitae 44 (1989) 303-314.

1234 *Pacomio* Luciano, Epistemologia e didattica teologico-pastorale; approccio biblico: Lateranum 55 (1989) 311-328.

1235 **Pardy** Marion, Teaching children the Bible; new models in Christian education. SF 1988, Harper & R. 170 p. $13. 0-06-254829-8. – ᴿRExp 86 (1989) 141 (T. A. *Lines*).

1236 *Reents* Christine, Kinderbibel: → 911, TRE 18 (1989) 176-182.

1237 **Roxman** James D., Enhancing the adolescent 'biblical self-concept' through Christian education: diss. Biola, ᴰ*McIntosh* G. 1989. 246 p. – DissA 50 (1989s) 3990-A.

1237* *Schwerin* Eckart, Die Bibel in unserer Arbeit mit Kindern: CLehre 42 (1989) 292-8 [< ᴢɪᴛ 89,807].

1238 *Sevin* Marc, *al.*, Lire la Bible ensemble: DossB 29 (1989) 1-14 [-30].

1239 *Stuhlmueller* Carroll, Adult Bible study; norms and goals; NewTR 2,1 (1989) 63-70 [71-83, *al.* Can Bible study really change your life?].

1240 *Wallace* Mark I., Paul Rɪᴄœᴜʀ in the classroom; hermeneutic and the teaching of religion: CouSR 18 (1989) 53.55s.

1241 **Wilhoit** James, *Ryken* Leland, Effective Bible teaching. GR 1988, Baker. 256 p. $12 pa. 0-8010-9685-5 [NTAbs 33,241]. – ᴿBS 146 (1989) 236 (K. O. *Gangel*).

1242 *Yannart* Danielle, Une catéchèse à l'école primaire; de la Bible à la parole de foi des enfants: LVitae 44 (1989) 183-192.

B2.1 Hermeneutica.

1243 **Adams** D. J., Biblical hermeneutics, an introduction[2]: Indian Theological Library 10. Madras 1987, Christian Literature society. xiv-165 p. rs 25 [NTAbs 33,231: the author teaches in Taiwan].

1244 **Aillet** Marc, L'interprétation de l'Écriture Sainte dans la Somme théologique de saint Thomas d'Aqᴜɪɴ; de la 'littera' à la 'res': diss. cath. ᴰ*Pinckaers*: FrS 1988s. – TR 85 (1989) 513.

1245 **Alonso Schökel** Luis, Hermenéutica de la Palabra I-II 1986s → 2,874... 4,1174: ᴿRazF 217 (1988) 442s (J. R. *Busto Saiz*); Religión y Cultura 35 (1989) 138 (A. *Moral*).

1246 **Alonso Schökel** Luis, La palabra inspirada; la Biblia a la luz de la ciencia del lenguaje[3] 1986 → 2,875... 4,1175: ᴿActuBbg 26 (1989) 33 (X. *Alegre S.*).

Artola A., *Sánchez Caro* J., Biblia y palabra de Dios: 1989 → 1447.

1248 **Barr** James, Sémantique du langage biblique[2] [[1]1961, franç. [1]1971] 1988 → 4,1177: ᴿScEspr 41 (1989) 237-9 (S. Elizabeth *Farrell*).

1249 *Barr* James, The literal, the allegorical, and modern biblical scholarship: JStOT 44 (1989) 3-17.

1250 *Brown* Raymond E., [*Schneiders* Sandra M., literary criticism], Hermeneutics: → 384, NJBC (1989) 1146-1165 [1158-60].

1251 *Burton-Christie* Douglas, 'Practice makes perfect'; interpretation of

Scripture in the Apophthegmata Patrum: ➤ 696, StudPatr 10/20 (1987/9) 213-8.

1252 **Caillot** J., L'Évangile de la communication; pour une nouvelle approche du Salut chrétien: CogF 152. P 1989, Cerf. 374 p. F 149 [NRT 112, 913-5, X. *Jacques*].

1253 *Canevet* Mariette, Sens spirituel: ➤ 886, DictSpir 14,92s (1989) 598-617.

1254 ᴱ**Casciaro** José M., *al.*, Biblia y hermenéutica 1985/6 ➤ 2,166*; 4,1183: ᴿCarthaginensia 5 (1989) 304 (R. *Sanz Valdivieso*); CiuD 202 (1989) 507s (J. *Gutiérrez*); RThom 89 (1989) 164 (H. *Ponsot*).

1254* *Casey* Michael, The origins of the hermeneutics of the Churches of Christ, I. The Reformed tradition: RestQ 31 (1989) 75-92 [< ZIT 89,651].

1255 **Cöster** Henry, Skriften i verkligheten; en hermeneutisk studie av förhållandet mellan skrift och historisk verklighet i kristen livsförståelse. Sto 1987, Verbum. 154 p. Sk 165. – ᴿSvTKv 65 (1989) 137-9 (L. O. *Armgard*).

Cotterell P., *Turner* M., Linguistics and biblical interpretation 1989 ➤ 9746.

1256 **Croatto** J. Severino, Biblical hermeneutics 1987 ➤ 3,1252; 4,1187: ᴿAsbTJ 44,1 (1989) 107s (J. B. *Green*).

1257 **Deventer** Louis F. van, Changes in the concept and usage of Scripture as reflected in the discussion on the place of women in Reformed churches: diss. Unisa, ᴰ*König* A. Pretoria 1988. – DissA 50 (1989s) 2949-A.

1258 **Dockery** David S., An examination of hermeneutical development in early Christian thought and its contemporary significance: diss. Univ. Texas, ᴰ*Lackner* B. Arlington TX 1988. 485 p. 89-14110. – DissA 50 (1989s) 975-A.

1259 *Fackre* Gabriel, Evangelical hermeneutics; commonality and diversity: Interpretation 43 (1989) 117-129 [D. *Tracy* 1987 has no evangelical among 300 cited].

1260 **Fishbane** Michael, Biblical interpretation in ancient Israel. Ox 1988 [= 1985 ➤ 1,1308... 4,1193 + addenda p. 545-8], Clarendon. xviii-617 p. £15 pa. 0-19-826699-5 [BL 90,101]. – ᴿJAOS 109 (1989) 679s (I. *Rabinowitz*); JRel 69 (1989) 387-391 (W. *Roth*); VT 39 (1989) 244s (H. *Williamson*).

1261 **Gantke** Wolfgang, Die Bedeutung des hermeneutischen Ansatzes Otto F. BOLLNOWS für die Religionswissenschaft: Diss. Bonn 1987. 565 p. – ᴿTüTQ 169 (1989) 331 (M. *Seckler*).

1262 *Geisler* Norman N., Does purpose determine meaning? A brief response to Professor SILVA: WestTJ [50 (1988) 65-80] 51 (1989) 153-5.

1263 **Graham** William A., Beyond the written word; oral aspects of Scripture in the history of religions 1987 ➤ 4,1200: ᴿRB 96 (1989) 601s (J. J. *Taylor*).

1264 **Grech** Prosper, Ermeneutica e teologia biblica 1986 ➤ 2,166; 4,1201: ᴿEuntDoc 42 (1989) 511s (P. *Miccoli*); ScripTPamp 21 (1989) 343 (J. M. *Casciaro*).

1265 **Groves** Joseph W., Actualization and interpretation in the Old Testament [... Dt 5,1-3; Am 9,11-15; Is 36-39]: SBL diss. 86, 1987 ➤ 3,1263; 4,1202: ᴿBL (1989) 106 (R. *Davidson*); CBQ 51 (1989) 329-331 (J. A. *Sanders*).

1266 *Gruenler* Royce G., New directions in the hermeneutical debate [ᴱ*Carson* D., *Woodbridge* D. 1986]: WestTJ 51 (1989) 133-142.

1267 *Hägglund* Bengt, Om 'Skriftens klarhet' — reformationens bortglömda grundprincip: SvTKv 65 (1989) 162-8.
1268 ᴱKantzer Kenneth S., Applying the Scriptures ... ICBI Summit III, 1987 ➤ 3,548: ᴿSTEv NS 1 (Padova 1989) 85s (P. *Bolognesi*).
1269 **Keegan** Terence J., Interpreting the Bible 1985 ➤ 1,1319 ... 4,1209: ᴿCalvinT 24 (1989) 139s (W. D. *Dennison*).
1270 ᴱKlemm David, Hermeneutical inquiry I-II, 1986 ➤ 3,348 ... 4,1211: ᴿRelStR 15 (1989) 122s (D. R. *Blumenthal*).
1271 *Kossen* P., Interpreting and applying Scripture: VoxRef 50 (1988) 3-38 [< NTAbs 33,6].
1272 **Kugel** James L., *Greer* Rowan A., Early biblical interpretation 1986 ➤ 2,905 ... 4,1213: ᴿAsbTJ 44,1 (1989) 99-101 (L. G. *Stone*); Latomus 48 (1989) 707s (R. *Braun*).
1272* *Langsdorf* Leonore, Current paths toward an objective hermeneutic [*Lundin* R. *al.*, 1985]: CriswTJ 2 (1987s) 145-154.
1273 **Larkin** William J., Culture and biblical hermeneutics 1988 ➤ 4, 1216; $17 pa.: ᴿTrinJ 10 (1989) 223-6 (E. *Rommen*: needs serious revision).
1274 **Laurant** Jean-P., Symbolisme et Écriture; le cardinal Pitra et la 'clef' de MÉLITON de Sardes; préf. *Poulat* E.: Patrimoines 1988 ➤ 4,1217: ᴿRHPR 69 (1989) 341s (D. A. *Bertrand*: not an edition or scholarly inquiry); RTLv 20 (1989) 375s (A. de *Halleux*: symbolisme confinant à l'occultisme des catholiques qui trouvaient la science historique 'allemande et protestante').
1275 *Lindbeck* George, Scripture, consensus and community: ➤ 591*a*, Ratzinger 1988, 74-101.
1276 **Lundin** Roger, [*Thiselton* Anthony C., parables], The responsibility of hermeneutics 1985 ➤ 1,1325 ... 3,1272: ᴿRTLv 20 (1989) 93s (E. *Brito*).
1277 *Mabee* Charles, The violence of American typological revisionism: Forum 5,1 (1989) 3-21.
1277* *McKim* Donald K., A guide to contemporary hermeneutics 1986 ➤ 2,258; 3,1274: ᴿCriswT 2 (1988) 438-440 (C. L. *Bomberg*).
1278 *Mesters* Carlos, O projeto 'Palavra-Vida' ['falta às mais elementares normas hermenêuticas', Nota da Congregação Romana para a Vida Religiosa 3.IV.1989] e a leitura fiel da Biblia de acordo com a Tradição e o Magistério da Igreja: REB 49 (1989) 661-673.
1279 **Molina Palma** M.A., La interpretación de la Escritura en el Espiritu ᴰ1987 ➤ 3,1277; 4,1230: ᴿNRT 111 (1989) 100s (V. *Roisel*); Salmanticensis 36 (1989) 95-97 (J.M. *Sánchez Caro*); ScripTPamp 21 (1989) 342s (F. *Varo*).
1280 **Morgan** Robert, (*Barton* John), Biblical interpretation 1988 ➤ 4,1231; $55; pa. $15; 0-19-213256-3; 7-1: ᴿExpTim 100,6 1st choice (1988s) 201s (C.S. *Rodd*); ModT 6 (1989s) 211-4 (D. B. *Martin*); ScotJT 42 (1989) 587s (C.M. *Tuckett*, also on NEILL-WRIGHT); StPatav 36 (1989) 567-570 (G. *Segalla*); TLond 92 (1989) 298s (F. *Watson*).
1281 ᴱ*Müller* H.-F., Mythos-Kerygma-Wahrheit; zur Hermeneutik einer biblischen Theologie ➤ 495, Was ist Wahrheit? 1989, 53-67.
1282 *Noort* E., Exegese van het Oude Testament, een zwertocht: GerefTTs 89 (1989) 2-22.
1283 **Piret** Pierre, L'Écriture et l'esprit; une étude théologique sur l'exégèse et les philosophies: 'IET' 7, 1987 ➤ 3,1283; 4,1239: ᴿGregorianum 70 (1989) 795s (P. *Gilbert*); NRT 111 (1989) 259s (A. M. *Pelletier*).

1283* *Pou i Rius* Ramon, Llegir la Sagrada Escriptura amb el mateix esperit amb què ha estat escrita: ➤ 69*, ᶠGOMÀ I., RCatalT 14 (1989) 361-6; Eng. 366.

1284 **Prickett** Stephen, Words and the Word; poetics and biblical interpretation 1986 ➤ 2,918 ... 4,1241: ᴿEvQ 61 (1989) 369-371 (A. G. *Newell*); JRel 68 (1988) 340 (Lynn *Poland*).

Ralph M., Plain words about biblical images 1989 ➤ 1213.

1286 **Reiling** J., Het woord van God; over schriftgezag en schriftuitleg. Kampen 1987, Kok. 173 p. *f*26. – ᴿStreven 55 (1987s) 1038 (P. *Beentjes*).

1287 **Resweber** Jean-Paul, Qu'est-ce qu'interpréter? Essai sur les fondements de l'herméneutique. P 1988, Cerf. 179 p. – ᴿQVidCr 145 (1989) 147 (J. *Bosch*); SR 18 (1989) 247 (Anne *Fortin-Melkevik*).

1288 **Rothen** Bernhard, Die Klarheit der Schrift: ev. Diss. ᴰ*Link*. Bern 1988s. – TR 85 (1989) 513.

1289 *Sánchez Caro* José M., Teología sistemática y hermenéutica bíblica: ➤ 758, RET 49,2s (1989) 185-208.

1290 *Scalise* Charles J., The 'sensus literalis'; a hermeneutical key to biblical exegesis [BROWN R. E.; ORIGEN...]: ScotJT 42 (1989) 45-65.

1291 *Schäublin* Christoph, AUGUSTIN, 'De utilitate credendi'; über das Verhältnis des Interpreten zum Text: VigChr 43 (1989) 53-68.

1291* *Schille* Gottfried, Komplementarität als hermeneutisches Modell: TVers 17 (1989) 51-60.

1292 **Schilling** Alfred, 'Verstehst du auch, was du liest?'; vom rechten Umgang mit der Bibel: Tb 1585. FrB 1989, Herder. 157 p. DM 13.

1293 **Schweizer** Harald, Biblische Texte verstehen; Arbeitsbuch zur Hermeneutik und Methodik der Bibelinterpretation [... sémiotique; Osée comme exemple] 1986 ➤ 2,922; 4,1247: ᴿBiKi 44 (1989) 130s (O. *Dangl*); ÉTRel 64 (1989) 114s (T. *Römer*: no praise).

1294 *Stevens* Bernard, Herméneutique philosophique et herméneutique biblique dans l'œuvre de Paul RICŒUR: RTLv 20 (1989) 178-193; Eng. 280.

1295 ᴱ**Tardieu** Michel, Les règles de l'interprétation 1987 ➤ 3,569; 4,1253: ᴿHenoch 11 (1989) 109s (E. *Jucci*); RechSR 77 (1989) 305-8 (C. *Théobald*); StPatav 36 (1989) 573-5 (C. *Corsato*).

1296 **Thoma** C., *Wyschogrod* M., Understanding Scripture; explorations of Jewish and Christian traditions of interpretation 1984/7 ➤ 3,570; 4,1255: ᴿScripB 20 (1989s) 40s (M. *McNamara*).

1297 *Tong Fung-wan*, ☉ Problems in biblical hermeneutics: TaiwanJT 10 (1988) 5-32 [< TContext 7/1, 33].

1298 **Untergassmair** Franz G., *Kappes* Michael, Zum Thema 'Wie wörtlich ist die Bibel zu verstehen?' 1987 ➤ 3,1234: ᴿTPQ 137 (1989) 74s (Roswitha *Unfried*).

1298* *Vines* Jerry, *Allen* David, Hermeneutics, exegesis, and proclamation: ➤ 44*, ᶠCRISWELL W., CriswTJ 1 (1987) 309-334.

1299 a) *Vorster* Willem, Intertextuality and Redaktionsgeschichte; – b) *Voelz* James, Multiple signs and double texts; elements of intertextuality; – c) *Wolde* Ellen Van, Trendy intertextuality?: ➤ 95, ᶠIERSEL B. van 1989, 15-26 / 27-34 / 43-49.

1300 **Whitman** Jon, Allegory; the dynamics of an ancient and medieval technique 1987 ➤ 4,1260: ᴿJAAR 57 (1989) 440-3 (Lynn *Poland*); JRel 69 (1989) 295-7 (M. *Murrin*).

1301 *Wilson* Robert M., Of words and meanings [... is BARR a nominalist?]: ➤ 84, ᶠHILL D., JStNT 37 (1989) 9-15.

1302 **Wood** Patricia C., What language shall we borrow? [linguistic function in Moses, OT prophets, 1542 Geneva liturgy]: diss. Emory, ᴰ*Detweiler* R. Atlanta 1989. 429 p. 89-24721. – DissA 50 (1989s) 2101-A.

1303 *a*) *Young* Frances, Exegetical method and biblical proof — the Bible in doctrinal debate; – *b*) *Hoek* Annewies van den, The concept of *sôma tôn graphôn* in Alexandrian theology: ➤ 696, 10th Patristic, 19 (1989) 291-304 / 250-4.

B2.2 **Structuralismus biblicus** (generalior ➤ J9.4).

1304 **Díaz Castrillón** C., Leer el texto; vivir la palabra; manual de iniciación a la lectura estructural de la Biblia. Estella 1988, VDivino. 246 p. 84-7151-552-0. – ᴿActuBbg 26 (1989) 35s (R. de *Silvatte*); BibFe 15 (1989) 319 (M. *Sáenz Galache*).

1306 **Greenwood** David, Structuralism and the biblical text: Religion and Reason 32, 1985 ➤ 1,1358... 4,1263: ᴿSalesianum 51 (1989) 358 (C. *Bissoli*).

1307 **Milne** Pamela J., Vladimir PROPP and the study of structure in Hebrew biblical literature [...Dan 1-6] 1987 ➤ 3,1309; 4,1264: ᴿBL (1989) 87 (R. P. *Carroll*); ETL 65 (1989) 154 (J. *Lust*: she shows Propp does not fit Dan 1-6); ÉTRel 64 (1989) 610 (D. *Lys*); RB 96 (1988) 603 (G. F. *Davies*); SR 18 (1989) 229s (F. *Landy*); ZAW 101 (1989) 321 (H.-C. *Schmitt*).

1308 *Panier* Louis, Theologische Implikationen einer semiotischen Lektüre biblischer Texte; ᵀ*Hofstetter* Andreas: TüTQ 169 (1989) 223-237.

1309 **Sàvoca** Gaetano, Iniziazione all'analisi biblica strutturalista. Messina 1989, Scienze Umane. 136 p.; Lit. 12.000. 88-85096-09-3. – ᴿRivB 37 (1989) 499 (G. *De Virgilio*: non 'S. Savoca'); StCattMi 33 (1989) 764 (U. *De Martino*); StPatav 36 (1989) 215s (G. *Segalla*).

1310 *Sheppard* G. T., 'Blessed are those who take refuge in him'; biblical criticism and deconstruction: RelIntL 5,2 (1988) 57-66 [< NTAbs 33,10].

B2.4 *Analysis* **narrationis** *biblicae* (generalior ➤ J9.6).

1311 *Ahuis* Ferdinand, Das Märchen im AT: ZTK 86 (1989) 455-476.

1312 **Bar-Efrat** Shimon, Narrative art in the Bible [❶ 1979 ²1984], ᵀwith *Shefer-Vanson* Dorothea: JStOT Sup 70, BLit 17. Sheffield 1989, Almond [Ithaca NY, Cornell Univ.]. 295 p. £26.50. 1-85075-138-2 [TDig 36,350]. – ᴿTLond 92 (1989) 303s (R. *Mason*).

1312* **Boomershine** T. E., Story journey; an invitation to the Gospel as storytelling. Nv 1988, Abingdon. 220 p. $13 pa. 0-687-39662-X [NTAbs 33,382].

1313 ᴱ**Coats** G. W., Saga... Narrative forms OT 1985 ➤ 1,274; 4,1268: ᴿRHPR 69 (1989) 199s (J. G. *Heintz* adds J. SCULLION and other supplements to the bibliography).

1314 *a*) *Culpepper* R. Alan, Commentary on biblical narratives; changing paradigms; – *b*) *Aichele* Georgeᴶ, Literary fantasy and the composition of the Gospels: Forum 5,3 (1989) 87-102 / 42-60.

1315 *Deist* F., Ou-Testamentiese verhale en/as geskiedenis [OT narrative and/as history]: TEv 20,3 (Pretoria 1987) 5-17 [< OTAbs 12,132].

1316 **Eslinger** L., Into the hands of the living God ['narratology' applied to Jos; Jg 1s; 1 Sm 12; 1 Kgs 1-11; 2 Kgs 17]: JStOT 84, BLit 24. Sheffield 1989, Almond. xii-272 p. £20. 1-85075-212-5 [BL 90,73, I. W. *Provan*].

1317 FFREI Hans: Scriptural authority and narrative interpretation, EGreen Garrett, 1987 ➤ 4,52: RJTS 40 (1989) 319-321 (R. *Morgan*).

1318 **Funk** Robert, The poetics of biblical narrative 1988 ➤ 4,1273: RForum 5,3 (1989) 61-68 (H. *Boers*) & 69-78 (J. *Camery-Hoggatt*) & 79-86 (G. A. *Phillips*).

1319 *a*) *Gerhart* Mary, The restoration of biblical narrative; – *b*) *Williams* James G., Between reader and text; a general response: Semeia 46 (1989) 13-29 / 169-179.

1320 *Grottanelli* C., The ancient novel and biblical narrative: QuadUrb 27 (1987) 7-34 [< ZAW 102,284].

Jobling David, The sense of biblical narrative II, 1986 ➤ 2146.

1321 *a*) *Kermode* Frank, New ways with Bible stories; – *b*) *Boadt* Lawrence, Understanding the *mashal* and its value for the Jewish-Christian dialogue in a narrative theology: ➤ 610, Parable & story 1986/9, 121-135 / 159-188.

1322 **Kort** Wesley, Story, text, and Scripture; literary interests in biblical narrative. Univ. Park 1988, Penn. State Univ. xii-159 p. 0-271-00610-2 ➤ 4,1276: RCCurr 39 (1989s) 499s (G. *Aichele*); ExpTim 100,5 2d-top choice (1988s) 162s (C. S. *Rodd*: important though polysyllabic); Horizons 16 (1989) 156s (Irena *Makarushka*); RelSt 25 (1989) 405s (J. L. *Houlden*); TS 50 (1989) 611s (Karen A. *Barta*).

1323 **McCarthy** Carmel, *Riley* William, The OT short story; explorations into narrative spirituality 1986 ➤ 2,8022... 4,1277: RCBQ 51 (1989) 126-8 (J. S. *Coolidge*).

1323* **Marcol** Alojzy, *Kowarz* Jan, Joseph WITTIG — ein Vertreter der 'Narrativen Theologie'; zu einer Habilitationsschrift der Katholischen Akademie Warschau: Archiv für Schlesische Kirchengeschichte 46 (Hildesheim 1988) 161-170 [< ZIT 90,255].

1324 ENeidhart Walter, *Eggenberger* Hans, al., Erzählbuch zur Bibel; Theorie und Beispiele. Dü 1987-9, Kaufmann. I⁵ 1987, 384 p.; II ¹1989, 300 p. 3-491-80020-X; -7-7.

1325 *Nicolet* P., Récits bibliques et théories des jeux [*Brams* S., Biblical games, a strategic analysis of stories in the OT]: ➤ 385, Narration 1988, 21-36.

1326 *a*) *Polak* F. H., Het bijbelverhaal als palimpsest; over de rol van de diachronie in de structurele analyse; – *b*) *Smelik* K. A. D., Vertellingen in de Hebreeuwse Bijbel; de benadering van het bijbelse verhaal door PALACHE, BEEK en diens leerlingen: AmstCah 9 (1988) 22-34 / 8-21.

1327 *Prickett* Stephen, The status of biblical narrative: Pacifica 2 (1989) 26-46.

Ravasi Gianfranco, [Sal 78,3-4] Narrazione ed esegesi, rassegna 1989 ➤ 3133.

1328 *Riva* Franco, L'esegesi narrativa; dimensioni ermeneutiche: RivB 37 (1989) 129-160.

1329 *Saltarini* Brunetto, Le motivazioni religiose della narrativa ebraica: HumBr 44 (1989) 526-547.

1330 **Savran** George W., Telling and retelling; quotation in biblical literature [Gen through 2 Kgs] 1988 ➤ 4,1282 ('in biblical narrative'): RJRel 69 (1989) 397s (Adele *Berlin*); RelStR 15 (1989) 456 (W. L. *Humphreys*).

1331 **Stegner** W., Narrative theology in early Jewish Christianity. Louisville 1989, Westminster/Knox. 141 p. $12 [TS 51,187].

1332 **Sternberg** Meir, The poetics of biblical narrative 1985 ➤ 2,935... 4,1283: RJRel 68 (1988) 426-434 (Lynn *Poland*: 'defending biblical poetics'; he describes the Bible as 'ideological literature').

1332* *Ulonska* Herbert, Biographische Hermeneutik und narrative Theologie: → 47*, ᶠDEMBOWSKI H. 1989, 222-233.
1333 **Virgili** Elizabeth S., Narrative as expression of women's theological voice: diss. Southern California, LA 1988 [RTLv 21, p. 549].
1334 *Vorster* W. S., Oor die Nuwe Testament, vertelkunde en prediking [... narrative]: HervTS 44 (Pretoria 1988) 164-7 [< NTAbs 32,10].
1335 **Wesselius** J. W., Studies in biblical narrative texts: diss. ᴰ*Deurloo* K. Amst 1989. – RTLv 21,542; TsTNijm 30,83.
1336 **Zuidema** Willem, De vergeten taal van het verhaal. Baarn 1989, Ten Have. ƒ22,50. – ᴿStreven 57 (1989s) 753 (P. *Beentjes*).

B2.6 *Critica reactionis lectoris* – **Reader-response criticism.**

1337 *Brown* Schuyler, New directions in biblical interpretation [... reader response]: BToday 27 (1989) 197-202.
1338 *Dockery* D. S., Author? Reader? Text? Toward a hermeneutical synthesis: TEdr 38 (1988) 7-16 [< NTAbs 33,141].
1339 *a) Lategan* Bernard C., Coming to grips with the reader in biblical literature; – *b) Vorster* Willem S., The reader in the text; narrative material; – *c) Wuellner* Wilhelm, Is there an encoded reader fallacy?; – *d) Schenk* Wolfgang, The roles of the readers or the myth of *the* reader: Semeia 48 (1989) 3-17 / 21-39 / 41-54 / 55-80.
1340 **McKnight** E., Postmodern use of the Bible; the emergence of reader-oriented criticism. Nv 1988, Abingdon. 288 p. $16. 0-687-33178-1 [ÉTRel 64,484].
1340* **McKnight** Edgar V., The Bible and the reader 1985 → 1,1658: ᴿCriswT 2 (1988) 437s (D. S. *Dockery*).
1341 **McKnight** Edgar V., Reader perspectives on the New Testament: Semeia 48. Atlanta 1989, Scholars. viii-206 p.
1342 *a) Moore* Stephen D., Doing Gospel criticism as/with a 'reader'; – *b) Kurz* William S., The beloved disciple and implied readers; a socio-narratological approach: BibTB 19 (1989) 85-93 / 100-7.
1343 *Villiers* Pieter G. R. de, New Testament scholarship in South Africa [ᶠMETZGER 1985; reader's social world in interpretation]: Neotestamentica 23 (1989) 119-124.
1344 *Voelz* J. W., The problem of meaning in texts [... reader's role]: Neotestamentica 23 (1989) 33-43.

B3 *Interpretatio ecclesiastica* .1 **Bible and Church.**

1345 *a) Akhtar* Shabbir, The virtues of fundamentalism; – *b) Williams* Cyril G., The status of Scripture; some comparative contours: ScotR 10,1 (Stirling 1989) 41-49 / 22-40 [< ZIT 89,141].
1346 **Ammerman** Nancy T., Bible believers; fundamentalists in the modern world 1987 → 4,1289: ᴿChH 58 (1989) 265s (D. E. *Harrell*); JAAR 57 (1989) 843s (J. L. *Guth*); RelStR 15 (1989) 56 (R. B. *Flowers*).
1347 *a) Antón* Ángel, Magisterio y teología; dos funciones complementarias en la Iglesia; – *b) Stern* J., Le magistère et les théologiens selon J. H. NEWMAN; – *c) Stagliano* A., La teologia che 'serve' la Chiesa; annotazioni sul compito del teologo tra ecclesialità e scientificità; – *d) Grasso* G., Libertà e fedeltà nella ricerca teologica: Seminarium 31 (1989) 351-382 / 383-398 / 399-420 / 421-433; all Eng. 288-291.

1348 **Barlow** Philip L.,   The Bible in Mormonism; diss. Harvard. CM 1988.
303 p. 89-08497. – DissA 50 (1989s) 169-A; RelStR 16,191.
1349 **Barton** John,   People of the Book?The authority of the Bible in
Christianity (Bampton Lectures) 1988 ➤ 4,1294:   ᴿExpTim 100,6 top
choice (1988s) 201-3 (C.S. *Rodd*); TLond 92 (1989) 129s (L. *Houlden*);
TTod 46 (1989) 467 (R. B. *Hays*).
1350 **Bergeron** Richard,   Les fondamentalistes et la Bible; quand la lettre se
fait prison: Rencontres d'aujourd'hui 1. Montréal 1987, Fides.   82 p. –
ᴿSR 18 (1989) 248 (J. *Duhaime*).
1351 **Boone** Kathleen C.,   The Bible tells them so; the discourse of Protestant
fundamentalism [< diss. Buffalo].   Albany 1989, SUNY.   139 p. $34.50;
pap. $11.   0-88706-894-4; 5-2 [TDig 36,148]. – ᴿCalvinT 24 (1989) 383-5
(D. P. *Bergsma*: she uses 'fundamentalist' interchangeably with 'evangelical' for all those for whom the Bible functions as final authority for
doctrine and moral practice); TTod 46 (1989s) 422-5 (J. *Barr*: high praise).
1352 *Boulet* Michel,   Magistère de l'Église et opinion publique: Christus 36
(P 1989) 444-454.
1353 *Brandmüller* Walter,   Die Lehre der Konzilien über die rechte
Schriftinterpretation bis zum I. Vatikanum: AnHConc 19 (1987) 13-61.
1354 **Breck** John,   The power of the word in the worshiping Church 1987
➤ 3,1318; 4,1298:   ᴿSVlad 23 (1989) 105-7 (C. *Lock*).
1355 **Brown** R. E.,   Biblical exegesis and Church doctrine 1985 ➤ 1,159 ...
4,1300:   ᴿKatKenk 26,52 (1987) 171-8 (R. *López Silonis* ❶); RB 96
(1989) 616 (B. T. *Viviano*).
1356 *Brown* Raymond E., *Collins* Thomas A.,   Church pronouncements:
➤ 384, NJBC (1989) 1166-1174.
1357 **Burke** Cormac,   Authority and freedom in the Church 1988 ➤ 4,1302;
also 1988, Four Courts: ᴿPrPeo 3 (1989) 112s (J. *Tolhurst* prefers to E.
Hɪʟʟ's 'tearing down').
1358 **Burke** C.,   Autoridad y libertad en la Iglesia 1988 ➤ 4,1303; pt. 1500:
ᴿProyección 36 (1989) 239 (J. A. *Estrada*); ScripTPamp 21 (1989) 383s
(J. R. *Villar*).
1359 ᴱ**Caplan** Lionel,   Studies in religious fundamentalism: [B]SOAS seminar
[1988 ➤ 4,537], also L 1987, Macmillan. – ᴿRelSt 25 (1989) 250-2 (B. R.
Wilson).
1360 **Chilson** Richard,   Catholic Christianity; a guide to the way, the truth,
and the life. NY 1987, Paulist.   vi-472 p. $7 pa. [TLZ 115,638, R.
Bäumer].
1361 *Coleman* John A.,   Who are the Catholic fundamentslists?:   Commonweal 116 (1989) 42-47.
1362 **Curran** Charles E.,   Faithful dissent 1986 ➤ 2,948 ... 4,1308:   ᴿJRel 68
(1988) 182 (R. B. *Miller*).
1363 **Daniel** Petrino J.,   La lectura de la Sagrada Escritura bajo el regimen de
la organización de los testigos de Jehova; el uso de la Biblia en el 'Salón
del Reino': diss. Pont. Univ. S. Thomae, ᴰ*García Trapiello* J.   R 1989.
351 p.
1364 *Dieten* Jan-Louis van,   Die Rolle der Bibel auf dem Konzil von
Ferrara-Florenz: AnHConc 19 (1987) 392-8.
1365 *a*) *Dobbin* Edmund J.,   Sensus fidelium reconsidered; – *b*) *Gittins*
Anthony J.,   Belief and faith, assent and dissent: NewTR 2,3 (1989)
48-64 / 65-85.
1366 *Duquoc* Christian,   Une coexistence conflictuelle; théologie critique et
magistère en catholicisme: RTPhil 121 (1989) 165-171.

1367 **Ellingsen** Mark, The evangelical movement; growth, impact, controversy, dialog. Minneapolis 1988, Augsburg. 496 p. [TLZ 115, 470-2, Helge *Stadelmann*].

1368 *Evans* Michael, How 'Catholic' is liberal Catholicism? [can be]; PrPeo 3 (1989) 47-54.

1369 **Evans** Rod L., *Berent* Irwin M., Fundamentalism; hazards and heartbreaks. LaSalle IL 1988, Open Court. xxi-175 p. $27; pa. $12 [RelStR 16, 233, D. A. *Foster*].

1370 **Fackre** Gabriel, Authority; Scripture in the Church for the world: The Christian story, a pastoral systematics 2. GR 1987, Eerdmans. 366 p. $15 pa. – ᴿInterpretation 43 (1989) 428.430 (R. K. *Johnston*).

1371 [Freckenhorster Kreis], No podemos callar ante la manera como se ejerce la autoridad en la Iglesia [< Orientierung 53 (1989) 26-29]: ᵀᴱ*Giménez* Josep: SelT 28 (1989) 275-8.

1372 *Fuchs* Josef, Magisterium und Moraltheologie: FreibZ 36 (1989) 395-407.

1372* ᴱ**Geffré** C, *Jossua* J.-P., 1789, The French Revolution and the Church [➤ 454, Concilium (P 221)] E 1989. 144 p. – ᴿExpTim 101 (1989s) 251 (W. S. F. *Pickering*: 'in 1791 Pius VI condemned... the notion of the rights of man'; the Vatican inconsistently now upholds them 'in the world at large but not within the church itself').

1373 *a)* *Gesteira Garza* M., Autoridad y obediencia en la Iglesia; – *b)* *González Montes* A., Tradición, escritura, magisterio y desarrollo doctrinal de la fe: DiálEcum 24, 78 (1989) 141-189 / 75-105 [< ZIT 89,417].

1374 *Gubler* Marie-Louise, Eine biblisch orientierte Pastoral: Diakonia 20,1 (1989) 11-15 [< ZIT 89,194].

1375 **Häring** Bernhard, Meine Erfahrung mit der Kirche; Einl. *Licheri* Gianni [= Fede storia morale, interviste di Gianni *Licheri* (R 1989, Borla)], ᵀ*Häring*. FrB 1989, Herder. 237 p. DM 28. 3-451-21620-5 [TLZ 115, 571-3, H. *Kirchner*].

1376 *Harris* G., The Bible and Church renewal: LexTQ 23,3 (1988) 57-62 [< NTAbs 33,5].

1377 *Hawkes* Gerald, Beyond criticism; Bible study today [... commitment]: JTSAf 65 (1988) 60-72 [< TContext 6/2, 18].

1378 *Hellwig* Monika K., Scholars and bishops: Commonweal 115 (1988) 38s.

1379 *Hill* Edmund, Who does the teaching in the Church? [... no pope or bishop wrote the catechisms we learned from]: NBlackf 70,2 (1989) 67-73 [74-84, *Lash* N.; 85-95, *Williams* R.].

1379* *Houlden* Leslie, The limits of theological freedom: TLond 92 (1989) 268-276. ·

1380 *Janssens* Louis, The non-infallible magisterium and theologians: LvSt 14 (1989) 195 [-259 < ZIT 89,646].

1380* *Jodock* Darrell, The Church's Bible; its contemporary authority. Minneapolis 1989, Fortress. xi-173 p. $12 [TR 86,425].

1381 ᴱ**Johnston** Robert K., The use of the Bible in theology; evangelical options 1985 ➤ 2,960 ... 4,1325: ᴿEvQ 61 (1989) 191s (T. *Lane*); TrinJ 10,1 (1989) 115-9 (J. *Dahl*).

1382 *Joubert* Jacques, Tu transmettras dans la souffrance [... en attente d'une solution définitive... langue-écriture-lecture autant de dangers, d'où le nécessaire recours à ... inspiration, dogme, infaillibilité]; l'Église catholique et la maîtrise de la vérité révélée: RevSR 61 (1987) 208-234; sommaire 253.

1383 *Kasper* Walter, Die Kirche als Ort der Wahrheit: TJb (1989) 215-229.
1384 **Kaufman** Philip S., Why you can disagree... and remain a faithful Catholic. Bloomington IN 1989, Meyer-Stone. xvi-174 p. $10 pa. [JAAR 57,694].
1384* *a*) *Kaufmann* Franz-Xaver, Die Bischofskonferenz im Spannungsfeld von Zentralisierung und Dezentralisierung; – *b*) *Rössler* Andreas, Evangelische Randbemerkungen zum römischen Zentralismus: Diakonia 20 (1989) 400-6 / 392-5 [< ZIT 90,60].
1385 *Langer* Wolfgang, Die lehramtlichen Weisungen zur katholischen Bibelauslegung: BLtg 62 (1989) 2-9.
1385* *Lehmann* Karl, Das Alte Testament in seiner Bedeutung für Leben und Lehre der Kirche heute: TrierTZ 98 (1989) 161-170.
1386 *Lindbeck* G., Scripture, consensus, and community: This World 23 (Rockford IL 1988) 5-24 [< NTAbs 33,7].
1386* *Losada* Joaquín, Teología y Magisterio en la Iglesia; unas relaciones difíciles: SalT 76 (1988) 357-370.
1387 *a*) *McClendon* James W.[J], The concept of authority; a Baptist view: PerspRelSt 16 (1989) 101-8 [< ZIT 90,163]. – *b*) *McCormick* Richard A., A moral magisterium in ecumenical perspective [response, *Bayer* Oswald]: Studies in Christian Ethics 1,1 (Edinburgh 1988) 20-29 [-32; < ZIT 90,125].
1387* **McKim** Donald K., What Christians believe about the Bible 1985 ➤ 1,1237... 3,1346: [R]CriswT 1 (1987) 422s (D. S. *Dockery*).
1388 *Marböck* Johannes, Bibelauslegung in Kirche und Theologie: TPQ 137 (1989) 135-141.
1389 **Marsden** George, Reforming fundamentalism; Fuller Seminary and the New Evangelicalism 1987 ➤ 3,1348; 4,1338: [R]AndrUnS 26 (1988) 304s (G. *Land*); CalvinT 24 (1989) 157-9 (J. A. *DeJong*); EvQ 61 (1989) 187-9 (E. C. *Lucas*); JRel 69 (1989) 415s (D. F. *Durnbaugh*); STEv NS 1 (1989) 97 (P. *Guccini*); WestTJ 50 (1988) 370-4 (W. S. *Barker*).
1390 **Mattai** G., Magistero e teologia; alle radici di un dissenso. Cristianismo 7. Palermo 1989, Augustinus. 109 p. Lit. 16.000 [NRT 112,936, A. *Toubeau*].
1391 [E]**May** William W., Vatican authority and American Catholic dissent 1987 ➤ 3,437; 4,1339: [R]JRel 69 (1989) 259s (R. P. *McBrien*).
1392 *Meurer* Siegfried, Ⓜ The contacts between the Bible Societies and the churches, [T]*Karasszon* István: TSzem 32 (1989) 293-301.
1393 *a*) *Meurer* Siegfried, Die Bibelgesellschaften und die Kirche; – *b*) *Fick* Ulrich, Zwischen Magie und Kritik: ➤ 120, [F]LOHSE E., Wissenschaft 1989, 311-5 / 346-361.
1394 **Meyer** Thomas, Fundamentalismus; Aufstand gegen die Moderne. Ha-Reinbek 1989, Rowohlt. – [R]TGL 79 (1989) 624s (R. M. *Bucher*).
1395 *Moloney* Francis J., Whither Catholic biblical studies? [...'there is nowadays a growing insistence that biblical scholars be stopped from putting the "simple faith" of people at risk']: AustralasCR 66 (1989) 83-93.
1396 **Muesse** Mark W., The significance of contemporary fundamentalism for academic liberal theology: diss. Harvard. CM 1987. – RTLv 21, p. 538.
1397 **Naud** André, [➤ 4,1348] Le Magistère incertain [i.e. 'problèmes contemporains autour du M.... devant la loi naturelle... l'intelligence, conscience]: Héritage et projet 39. Montréal 1987, Fides. 268 p. – [R]NRT 111 (1989) 261s (A. *Toubeau*: dénonce les ambiguités, propose des comportements plus satisfaisants); RTLv 20 (1989) 207-210 (G. *Thils*); ScEspr 40 (1988) 249s (R. *Morency*).

1398 ᴱNiewiadomski József, Eindeutige Antworten? Fundamentalistische Versuchung... 1988 → 4,397: ᴿBogSmot 59 (1989) 500-3 (M. Zovkić); TLZ 114 (1989) 690s (H. Kirchner); ZkT 111 (1989) 84-86 (F. Mohr).

1399 Niewiadomski J., Fundamentalistische Versuchung des Katholizismus: TGegw 32 (1989) 104-115.

1400 Örsy Ladislas, The Church, learning and teaching 1987 → 4,1346: ᴿAngelicum 66 (1989) 345-7 (R. Christian: those familiar with the subject will find nothing new; others will lose their way); Commonweal 115 (1988) 441s (L. S. Cunningham); DocLife 38 (1988) 276s (G. Daly, in relation to RATZINGER J. 1988); Thomist 53 (1989) 519-521 (Susan K. Wood).

1401 Örsy Ladislas, The new profession of faith and oath of fidelity: DocLife 39 (1989) 507-512 [< America 160 (1989) 345-8].

1402 ᴱPapandreou Damaskinos, L'Ancien Testament dans l'Église; Chambésy [10-26.V.1986] 8. 1988. – ᴿÖkRu 38 (1989) 256s (G. Schütz); PrOrChr 38 (1988) 403s (P. Gruber).

1403 Pereira José, Magisterium under fire [Burtchaell James, its fallibilities; Griffiths Bede: Tablet April 8 and May 20 (1989)]: PrPeo 3 (1989) 435-7.

1404 a) Piegsa Joachim, Lehramt — Gehorsam — Gewissen; – b) Ziegenaus Anton, Das Gewissen vor dem Anspruch des Lehramts; – c) Crosby John F., 'Das schöpferische Prinzip aller Religion; das Gewissen bei Kardinal NEWMAN: ForumKT 5 (1989) 162-174 / 175-187 / 188-205.

1405 Pottmeyer Hermann J., Das Lehramt der Bischofskonferenz: → 494, ᴱMüller H., B-konf 1989, (44-87) 116-133.

1406 a) Ratzinger Joseph, Schriftauslegung im Widerstreit; zur Frage nach Grundlagen und Weg der Exegese heute; – b) Lindbeck George, Heilige Schrift, Konsens und Gemeinschaft; – c) Brown Raymond E., Der Beitrag der historischen Bibelkritik zum ökumenischen Austausch zwischen den Kirchen; – d) Lazareth William H., Das 'sola Scriptura' Prinzip M. LUTHERs; Evangeliumstraditionen zur Bestimmung des christlichen Gerechtigkeitsbegriff: → 521b, QDisp 117, 1989, (7-)15-44 / 45-80 / 81-97 / 98-123.

Raurell Frederic, Fe i exegesi; entre el revisionisme i la caricatura 1988 → 1644.

1408 Rémond René, L'intégrisme catholique, portrait intellectuel: Études 370 (1989) 95-105.

1409 Robinson R. B., Roman Catholic exegesis since 'Divino Afflante Spiritu'; hermeneutical implications [diss. Yale 1982]: SBL diss. 111, 1988 → 4,1349: ᴿBL (1989) 115 (B. P. Robinson defends LOHFINK and ALONSO-SCHÖKEL against unwisdom of letting historical criticism in by the back door); CBQ 51 (1989) 570s (D. J. Harrington: reserves); ScotJT 42 (1989) 589s (M. Tower: title inadequate).

1410 Sauter Gerhard, Wozu dogmatische Aussagen? Eine evangelische Stellungnahme: ZkT 111 (1989) 409-419.

1411 Schmied Alois, Vielfältige Autorität in der Vermittlung des Glaubens (1. Primat der .. Heilswahrheit selbst ...): TJb (1989) 83-96.

1411* Schmitz H., 'Professio fidei' und 'iusiurandum fidelitatis', Glaubensbekenntnis und Treueid; Wiederbelebung des Antimodernisteneides?: Archiv für katholisches Kirchenrecht 157 (Mainz 1988) 353-429 [< ZIT 90,137].

1412 Schwager Raymund, Kirchliches Lehramt und Theologie: ZkT 111 (1989) 163-182.

1413 **Silva** Moisés, Has the Church misread the Bible? The history of interpretation in the light of current issues: Foundations of Contemporary Interpretation 1, 1987 ➤ 3,1365; 4,1351: ᴿCalvaryB 5,1 (1989) 108s (G. H. *Lovik*); CBQ 51 (1989) 382s (E. C. *Muller*).

1413* *Storck* Thomas, How we understand the Bible; both fundamentalism and modernism represent naive approaches: HomP 90 (1989) 19-27 [65ss, *Podles* Leon J., Sex in the Bible].

1414 *Theobald* Michael, Die Autonomie der historischen Kritik — Ausdruck des Unglaubens oder theologische Notwendigkeit? Zur Schriftauslegung Romano GUARDINIS: TJb (1989) 13-33.

1415 *Torfs* Rik, Kerk en tegenspraak: Streven 57 (1989s) 99-112.

1416 **Warren** Michael, Faith, culture, and the worshiping community [...catechetics]. NY 1989, Paulist. xvi-214 p. $10 [RelStR 16, 236, Marianne *Sawicki*: a goldmine for Catholics, also others].

1416* **Zehr** Paul M., Biblical criticism in the life of the Church. Scottdale PA 1986, Herald. 109 p. $7 pa. – ᴿCriswT 2 (1988) 447s (D. *Allen*, D. L. *Akin*: interesting mixture of truth and error by a Mennonite).

B3.2 *Homiletica* – **The Bible in preaching.**

1417 *a)* **Adams** Jay E., Essays on biblical preaching. GR 1983, Zondervan. 135 p. $8 pa. – ᴿCriswT 3 (1989) 436s (C. E. *Coulton*). – *b)* **Andrew** John, Nothing cheap and much that is cheerful. GR/Exeter 1988, Eerdmans/Paternoster. 188 p. £11.75. 0-8026-3646-1. – ᴿExpTim 100 (1988s) 317s (J. M. *James*: fits BUTTRICK's 'Today's sermons need plots rather than plans').

1418 **Bailey** Ivor, Prate, prattle or preach 1987 ➤ 4,1360: ᴿAsiaJT 3 (1989) 373s (W. D. *Adams*); Pacifica 2 (1989) 117s (P. *Bishop*).

1419 **Barlé** Helmut, Predigt und Arbeitswelt; Analyse und praktische Anregungen. Stu 1989, Calwer. 133 p. DM 19,80 [TLZ 115, 62, H. *Albrecht*].

1420 **Baumann** J. Daniel, Introduction to contemporary [1972] preaching. GR 1988 reprint, Baker. 302 p. 0-8010-0958-8. – ᴿExpTim 100 (1988s) 318 (J. M. *James*).

1421 **Best** E., From text to sermon; responsible use of the NT in preaching²ʳᵉᵛ [¹1978 USA] 1988 ➤ 4,1362: ᴿRHPR 69 (1989) 221 (M. A. *Chevallier*); TLond 92 (1989) 130 (E. *Franklin*).

1421* *Bindemann* Walther, Vom Predigttext zum Text der Predigt: ZeichZt 43 (1989) 107-114 [< ZIT 89,529].

1422 **BreytenBach** Hermanus S., Beeld en kommunikasie in die prediking [...John's Gospel images]: diss. Unisa, ᴰ*Pieterse* H. Pretoria 1988. – DissA 50 (1989s) 2943-A.

1423 **Burghardt** Walter J., Preaching; the art and the craft 1987 ➤ 3,1374; 4,1364: ᴿCalvinT 24 (1989) 155s (W. M. *Van Dyk*: refreshing); RExp 86 (1989) 463s (R. *Bailey*: high praise).

1424 **Buttrick** David G., Homiletic 1987 ➤ 3,1267; 4,1366: ᴿInterpretation 43 (1989) 82.84.86s (D. *Macleod*); TLZ 114 (1989) 65-67 (H. *Theurich*).

1425 **Buttrick** David G., Preaching Jesus Christ; an exercise in homiletic theology 1988 ➤ 4,1367: ᴿRExp 86 (1989) 286s (C. A. *Loscalzo*).

1425* *Cowen* Gerald, Sermon starters from the Greek New Testament. Nv 1985, Broadman. 179 p. $7 pa. – ᴿCriswT 1 (1987) 402s (J. A. *Millikan*).

1426 ᴱ**Cox** James W., Best sermons [1. 1988 ➤ 4,1371], 2 [winners in Harper's second annual competition; 17 of the 28 are Baptists]. SF 1989,

Harper & R. 422 p. $17. – RSWJT 32,3 (1989s) 73 (G. *Lovejoy*: Elizabeth ACHTEMEIER and W. J. BURGHARDT included).

1427 **Dwyer** Henry F., A critical evaluation of the homiletics of Jay E. ADAMS [... Christ the focus of infallible Scripture]: diss. Unisa, DPieterse H. Pretoria 1988. – DissA 50 (1989s) 2944s-A.

1428 **Fasol** Al, Essentials for biblical preaching; an introduction to basic sermon preparation. GR 1989, Baker. 174 p. 0-8010-3550-3. – RExpTim 101 (1989s) 254 (J. M. *James*); SWJT 32,2 (1989s) 51 (G. L. *Klein*).

1429 **Forbes** James A.,J, The Holy Spirit and preaching [1986 Yale Beecher Lectures on Preaching]. Nv 1989, Abingdon. 108 p. – RSWJT 32,3 (1989s) 71 (G. *Lovejoy*).

1430 **Gräb** Wilhelm, Predigt als Mitteilung des Glaubens; Studien zu einer prinzipiellen Homiletik in praktischer Absicht. Gü 1988, Mohn. 272 p. DM 78 [TLZ 115, 63-65, F. *Mildenberger*].

1431 **Green** Michael P., [➤ 1,508] Illustration for biblical preaching. GR 1989, Baker. 448 p. – RSWJT 32,1 (1989s) 75 (G. *Lovejoy*).

1432 **Greidanus** Sidney, The modern preacher and the ancient text; interpreting and preaching biblical literature. GR/Leicester 1988, Eerdmans/Inter-Varsity. xvi-374 p. $13 pa. 0-8028-0360-1 / IVP 0-85111-573-X [NTAbs 33,236]. – RBS 146 (1989) 472-4 (R. P. *Richard*).

1433 **Larson** Raymond M., Biblical preaching; better communication to stimulate better Christian living: diss. Drew. Madison NJ 1989. 191 p. 89-21831. – DissA 50 (1989s) 1693-A.

1433* **Lawton** George, Reader-preacher. L 1989, Churchman. 286 p. £9. 1-85093-111-9. – RExpTim 101 (1989s) 91s (J. S. *Lampard*: best on historical material).

1434 **Lewis** Ralph L. & (son) Greg, Learning to preach like Jesus. Westchester IL 1989, Crossway. 159 p. $8. 0-89107-536-4. – RSWJT 32,3 (1989s) 68 (A. *Fasol*).

1435 **Long** T. G., Preaching and the literary forms of the Bible. Ph 1989, Fortress. 144 p. $9. 0-8006-2313-4 [NTAbs 33,379].

1436 **McKeown** Eileen A., A theology of preaching based on Karl RAHNER's theology of the word: diss. Fordham, DDych W. NY 1989. 344 p. 89-10759. – DissA 49 (1988s) 3764-A; RelStR 16,187.

1437 EMorenzoni Franco, Thomas de CHOBHAM, Summa de arte praedicandi: CCMed 82. Turnhout 1988, Brepols. lxxxiii-380 p. [JTS 41, 745, G. *Cigman*, D. *Howlett*].

1438 **Papp** Vilmos, ⓜ Warum kann man über das Neue Testament ohne das Alte Testament nicht predigen?: TSzem 32 (1989) 158-161.

1438* TPerelmuter Hayim G., David DARSHAN, ⓞ David's Šîr ha-Ma'alot; and In defense of preachers. Cincinnati 1984, HUC. 183 p. – RJQR 80 (1989s) 192s (H. A. *Sosland*). ➤ 1443.

1439 **Pitt-Watson** Ian, A primer for preachers. GR 1986, Baker. 112 p. $6 pa. – RGraceTJ 10 (1989) 117-9 (A. B. *Luter*: 'primer' is a pun: i. elementary text; ii. as of pump or gun, small charge used to produce much larger one) [are they pronounced the same in Aberdeen?].

1439* **Poensgen** Herbert, Die Not der Predigt des Evangeliums: BLtg 62 (1989) 45-49.

1440 **Reymond** Bernard, Quand le prédicateur se fait exégète: ÉTRel 64 (1989) 593-7.

1441 **Robinson** H. W., Predicare la Bibbia 1984 ➤ 2,999b; Lit. 10.000: RProtestantesimo 44 (1989) 74 (E. *Stretti*).

1442 **Sleeth** Ronald E., God's word and our words; basic homiletics. Atlanta 1986, Knox. 120 p. $8 pa. – ᴿAndrUnS 27 (1989) 157 (R. *Sheppard*).

1443 ᴱ**Sosland** Henry A., ZAHALON Jacob, Or ha-Darshanim, a guide for preachers on composing and delivering sermons; a seventeenth-century Italian preacher's manual: Studies in Jewish History 11. NY 1987, Jewish Publ. xiv-194 + 54* p. $20 [HeythJ 31, 351, A. *Hamilton*]. ➤ 1438*.

1444 **Talbert** John D., Charles H. SPURGEON's Christological homiletics; a critical evaluation of selected sermons from Old Testament texts: diss. SW Baptist Theol. Sem. 1989. 247 p. 90-04365. – DissA 50 (1989s) 2935-A.

1444* **Walker** Alan, Evangelistic preaching. GR 1983 [=] 1988, Zondervan. 110 p. $7. – ᴿCriswT 3 (1988s) 246s (C. R. *Wells*: Australian, good, despite irritants).

1445 *Waznak* Robert P., Preaching the Gospel in an age of technology; NewTR 2,4 (1989) 48-60.

1446 **White** Richard C., Biblical preaching; how to find and remove the barriers. St. Louis 1988, 'CBF.' 141 p. $9. – ᴿSWJT 32,2 (1989s) 83 (G. *Lovejoy*).

1446* **Williamson** Clark M., *Allen* Ronald J., Interpreting difficult texts; anti-Judaism and Christian preaching. L/Ph 1989, SCM/Trinity. viii-133 p. $11 pa. 0-334-02062-X. – ᴿExpTim 101 (1989s) 155 (R. *Lunt*); TLond 92 (1989) 312s (C. J. A. *Hickling*).

B3.3   **Inerrantia, inspiratio** [Revelatio ➤ H1.7].

1447 **Artola** Antonio M., *Sánchez Caro* José M., Biblia y Palabra de Dios: Introducción al Estudio de la Biblia 2. Estella 1989, VDivino. 450 p. 84-7151-608-X.

1448 *Artola* Antonio M., Treinta años de reflexión sobre la inspiración bíblica [Dei Verbum; *Loretz* O., Das Ende der Inspirations-Theologie 1974]: EstBíb 47 (1989) 363-415.

1449 *Bonino* Serge-Thomas, Le rôle de l'image dans la connaissance prophétique [... inspiration scripturaire] d'après saint Thomas d'AQUIN: RThom 89 (1989) 533-568.

Burkhardt Helmut, Die Inspiration heiliger Schriften bei Philo von Alexandrien 1989 ➤ 9934.

1450 *Collins* Raymond F., Inspiration: ➤ 384, NJBC (1989) 1023-1033.

1451 **Diebner** Bernd J., Heilsgeschichte und Schriftprinzip, eine Skizze [*Strange* J., Lemche N. 1989; *Rendtorff* R., *Blum* E.]: DielB Beih 10. Heid 1989. vi-66 p. DM 5 [ZAW 102,442]. Eng. summ. 61; Dansk 62s.

1451* *Dockery* David S., On [*Beale* David O., SBC] Houses on Sand [? (Greenville 1985, Unusual) 232 p.; $5 pa.], holy wars and heresies; a review of the inerrancy controversy in the Southern Baptist Convention: CriswT 2 (1987s) 391-401.

1452 **Dunn** James D., The living Word [... scriptural authority, NT] 1988 ➤ 4,1408: ᴿCurrTM 16 (1989) 467 (E. *Krentz*).

1453 **Farrow** Douglas, The word of truth and disputes about words 1987 ➤ 3,1412: ᴿCBQ 51 (1989) 368s (S. *McKnight*); ExpTim 100 (1988s) 64s (J. *Goldingay* says his response to the 'abstract, abstruse American style' was 'to have my conviction reinforced that actually the very category of inerrancy is an appropriate [sic] one: not that scripture is errant rather than inerrant, but that the debate has a misguided starting-point').

1453* ᴱGarrett Duane A., *Melick* Richard R.ᴶ, Authority and interpretation;
a Baptist perspective [symposium ...] 1987 ➤ 4,303: ᴿCalvaryB 5,2 (1989)
100s (W. *Vanhetloo*); CriswT 3 (1988s) 223-8 (W. *Ward*) & 228-231 (M.
Coppenger: 'about/by/for Southern Baptists').

1454 **Goldingay** John, Theological diversity and the authority of the OT 1987
➤ 3,1415; 4,1412: ᴿCalvinT 24 (1989) 328-331 (G. N. *Knoppers*).

1455 **Goodrick** Edward W., Is my Bible the inspired Word of God?
Portland OR 1988, Multnomah. 114 p. $7. – ᴿBS 146 (1989) 459 (R. P.
Lightner).

1456 *Graham* Ronald W., The inspiration of Scripture: LexTQ 22 (1987)
97-105 [< OTAbs 11,184].

1457 *a) Haykin* Michael, 'The oracles of God'; Andrew FULLER and the
Scriptures; – *b) Burkill* Mark, The principles of Bible interpretation:
Churchman 103,1 (L 1989) 60-... / 40-52 [< ZIT 89,365s].

1458 **Ibáñez Arana** Andrés, *a)* Inspiración, inerrancia e interpretación de la S.
Escritura en el Concilio Vaticano II: ScriptV [➤ 2,1016*: 33 (1986) 5-96.
225-329] 34 (1987) 5-44. – *b)* Inspiración, inerrancia e interpretación ...:
Biblioteca Victoriensis 5. Vitoria 1987, ESETR. 258 p. – ᴿAnnTh 3,1
(1989) 149s (M. A. *Tábet*).

1458* **James** Gordon, Inerrancy and the Southern Baptist Convention.
Dallas 1986, SB-Heritage. 171 p. $13. – ᴿCriswT 2 (1987s) 391-401 (D. S.
Dockery).

1459 *Jelen* Ted G., Biblical literalism and inerrancy; does the difference make
a difference?: SocAnRel 49 (1989) 421-9 [< ZIT 89,353].

1460 *Kantzer* K. S., Why I still believe the Bible is true: Christianity Today
32,14 (1988) 22-25 [< NTAbs 33,6].

1461 *a) Pinnock* Clark H., The Scripture principle 1985 ➤ 1,1461 ... 3,1424:
ᴿCriswT 1 (1987) 440s (D. S. *Dockery*). – *b) Brown* Delwin, Rethinking
authority from the right; a critical review of Clark Pinnock's Scripture
Principle: ChrSchR 19 (1989) 66-72; 73s, response by Pinnock [< ZIT
89,763).
Proceedings of the [1987 Southern Baptist] conference on biblical inerrancy.
1987 ➤ 1453*; 1458*.

1461* **Ruokanen** Miikka, Doctrina divinitus inspirata, M. LUTHER's position
1985 ➤ 2,1023*: ᴿTrierTZ 98 (1989) 238s (A. *Dahm*).

1462 **Saarnivaara** Uuras, Can the Bible be trusted? Old and New Testament
introduction and interpretation 1983 ➤ 65,1260; 1,1463: ᴿLuthTKi 12
(1988) 138-142 (E. *Volk*: reserves).

1463 **Seely** P. H., Inerrant wisdom; science and inerrancy in biblical
perspective. Portland OR 1989, Evangelical Reform. 216 p. $12. 0-
96222950-4 [BL 90,114, F. *Bruce*: abandons his adherence to literal
inerrancy conclave].

1464 *Schneider* Werner, Über die Freiheit und die Autorität der Heiligen
Schrift: EvT 49 (1989) 478-490.

1465 *Silva* Moisés, Old Princeton, Westminster, and inerrancy: WestTJ 50
(1988) 65-80.

1466 *Smith* Graham, 'This is the word of the Lord' [every bit of the Bible?]:
ExpTim 100 (1988s) 137-9.

1467 **Trembath** K. R., Evangelical theories of biblical inspiration; a review
and proposal 1987 ➤ 3,1430; 4,1426: ᴿBL (1989) 118 (C. S. *Rodd*:
evangelical, good; 'inerrancy' an attribute reserved for God alone);
Thomist 53 (1989) 734-9 (L. *Boadt*); TLond 92 (1989) 300-2 (R. P.
Carroll: inspired meaning inspiring, with errors).

1468 *Vanhetloo* Warren, Indications of verbal inspiration: CalvaryB 5,1 (1989) 63-85.

B3.4 **Traditio, canon.**

1469 *Aurelius* Erik, Gamla testamentet i kristendomens bibel: SvTKv 65 (1989) 97-108.

1470 **Beckwith** Roger, The OT canon of the NT church 1985 ➤ 1,1472... 4,1429: ᴿSecC 7 (1989s) 99s (J.J. *Collins*); WestTJ 50 (1988) 172-5 (T. *Longman*).

1471 *Brown* Raymond E., *Collins* Raymond F., Canonicity: ➤ 384, NJBC (1989) 1034-1054.

1472 **Bruce** Frederick F., The canon of Scripture. DG 1988, Inter-Varsity. 349 p. $20. 0-8308-1258-X [NTAbs 33,233]. – ᴿSWJT 32 (1989s) 49 (J.A. *Brooks*).

1473 *Brueggemann* W., Brevard CHILDS' canon criticism; an example of post-critical naiveté: JEvTS 32 (1989) 311-326.

1474 **Bunnenberg** Johannes, Lebendige Treue zum Ursprung; das Traditionsverständnis Yves CONGARS [kath. Diss. Bochum 1988, ᴰ*Pottmeyer* H.: TR 85,514; RTLv 21,567]: Walberberger Studien 14. Mainz 1989, Grünewald. xxxix-392 p. DM 54 [TPhil 64,632].

1475 *Dyck* Elmer, What do we mean by canon?: Crux 25,1 (Vancouver 1989) 17-22 [< OTAbs 12,132].

1476 **Greenwald** Michael R., The New Testament canon and the Mishnah; consolidation of knowledge in the second century C.E.: diss. Boston Univ. 1989, ᴰ*Kee* H. 269 p. 89-15699. – DissA 50 (1989s) 975-A [RelStR 16,189, The 'consolation' of knowledge ...].

1477 *Funke* Alex [interview], Nur die Tradition festhalten, hiesse zum Museum werden: Diakonie 15 (Stu 1989) 70-76 [< ZIT 89,412].

1478 *Gamble* Harry Y., The canon of the NT: ➤ 394, NT/Interpreters 1989, 201-243.

1479 **Hahneman** G.M., The Muratorian Fragment and the development of the canon: diss. Oxford 1989. – RTLv 21,548.

1480 **McDonald** Lee M., The formation of the Christian biblical canon 1988 ➤ 4,1446: ᴿSWJT 32,1 (1989s) 49s (J.A. *Brooks*); TTod 46 (1989s) 248 (R.W. *Wall*).

1481 **Meade** David G., Pseudonymity and canon...: WUNT 39, 1986 ➤ 2,1040... 4,1449: ᴿBL (1989) 137 (C.T.R. *Hayward*); JTS 40 (1989) 588-590 (C.C. *Rowland*); WestTJ 51 (1989) 167-171 (D.G. *McCartney*).

1482 **Metzger** Bruce M., The canon of the NT 1987 ➤ 3,1456; 4,1450: ᴿAsiaJT 3 (1989) 365-7 (H.T. *Ellis*); Biblica 70 (1989) 133-7 (R.J. *Dillon*: first-class); CBQ 51 (1989) 161s (Pheme *Perkins*: classic, but queries 'Neither religious nor artistic works really gain anything by having an official stamp put on them'); EvQ 61 (1989) 274s (I.H. *Marshall*); Interpretation 43 (1989) 410-2 (G.D. *Fee*); JBL 108 (1989) 551s (H.Y. *Gamble*); RB 96 (1989) 146 (B.T. *Viviano*); ScotJT 42 (1989) 420s (D.C. *Parker*).

Meyer Rudolf, Kanontheorie des JOSEFUS 1974/89 ➤ b638.

1483 **Miller** Patricia C., 'Words with an alien voice'; Gnostics, scripture, and canon: JAAR 57 (1989) 459-483.

1484 *Müller* Mogens, Hebraica sive graeca veritas; the Jewish Bible at the time of the New Testament and the Christian Bible: ScandJOT (1989,2) 55-71.

1485 *Oliver* W.G., ORIGEN and the New Testament canon: RestQ 31,1 (Abilene 1989) 13-26 [< NTAbs 33,284].

1486 *Pesce* Mauro, La trasformazione dei documenti religiosi; dagli scritti protocristiani al canone neotestamentario: VetChr 26 (1989) 307-326.

1487 **Pilhofer** Peter, *Presbýteron kreîtton*; der Altersbeweis der jüdischen und christlichen Apologese und seine Vorgeschichte: ev. Diss. ᴰ*Koch* D.-A. 298 p. Münster 1988s. – TR 85 (1989) 517; RTLv 21,548 (> Tü Mohr).

1488 *Readings* Bill, Canon and on; from concept to figure: JAAR 57 (1989) 149-172.

1489 *Rothermund* Dietmar, Der Traditionalismus als Forschungsgegenstand für Historiker und Orientalisten: Saeculum 40 (1989) 142-8.

1490 *a) Rüger* Hans P., Der Umfang des alttestamentlichen Kanons in den verschiedenen kirchlichen Traditionen; – *b) Wilckens* Ulrich, Das historisch ausgelegte Neue Testament als Kanon Heiliger Schrift; – *c) Coggan* Donald, 'Without note or comment' — then & now: ➤ 120, ᶠLOHSE E., Wissenschaft 1989, 336-345 / 13-28 / 305-310.

1491 *Rüger* Hans P., The extent of the Old Testament canon [...Catholic deuterocanonica]: BTrans 40 (1989) 301-8.

1492 **Sanders** James A., From sacred story to sacred text; canon as paradigm 1987 ➤ 3,1466; 4,1457: ᴿRelStR 15 (1989) 97-100-103 (B. W. *Anderson*; W. S. *Towner*).

1493 *a) Starobinski-Safran* Esther, La mémoire, son inscription dans les actes et sa signification spirituelle dans la tradition juive; – *b) Tardieu* Michel, Théorie de la mémoire et fonction prophétique; – *c) Basset* Jean-Claude, L'anamnèse; aux sources de la tradition chrétienne: ➤ 442, Mémoire 1988, 79-90 / 105-113 / 91-104.

1493* *a) Stendebach* Franz J., Der Kanon des Alten Testaments in der katholischen Kirche; – *b) Oikonomos* Elias [*Chadwick* Owen / *Mallau* Hans-H.], Die Bedeutung der deuterokanonischen Schriften in der Orthodoxen [anglikanischen / Baptist-] Kirche; – *c) Fricke* Klaus D., Der Apokryphenteil der Lutherbibel; – *d) Neuser* Wilhelm H., Die Reformierten und die Apokryphen des Alten Testaments: BiWelt 22 (1989) 41-50 / 26-40 [104-116 / 117-120] / 51-82 / 83-103 [< ZIT 90,400].

1494 **Stuhlhofer** Franz, Der Gebrauch der Bibel von Jesus bis Euseb; eine statistische Untersuchung zur Kanonsgeschichte ➤ 4,1461: Wu 1988, Brockhaus. 160 p. DM 28. 3-417-29335-9. – ᴿBL (1989) 116 (J. *Barton*: extremely important presentation of statistics with moderation, elegance, and simplicity); ForumKT 5 (1989) 159 (A. *Ziegenaus*); NRT 111 (1989) 434s (X. *Jacques*); RHE 84 (1989) 779 (R. *Gryson*); TR 85 (1989) 296 (K. S. *Frank*).

1495 *Veltri* Giuseppe, Canone, Scrittura e contesto immanente in alcuni testi del I secolo dopo Cristo (PHILO, Vit. Cont. §25; Lc 24,44; JOS., ContAp 1, cap. 8): Laurentianum 30 (1989) 3-24.

B4 *Interpretatio humanistica* – .1 **The Bible and man.**

1495* *Adamo* David, Suffering in the Old Testament: DeltioVM 18,1 (1989) 30-42 [< ZIT 89,530].

1496 *Bailey* Lloyd, Biblical perspectives on aging; QRMin 9,4 (1989) 48-64.

1497 **Brooks** Holifield E., Health and medicine in the Methodist tradition. NY 1986, Crossroads. xv-198 p. $18. – ᴿJRel 68 (1988) 596 (H. U. *Ashby*).

1498 **Conyer** Christopher C. & Leigh E., Self-defeating life-styles [case studies of unhealthy personalities, some from the Bible, including the disciples at Emmaus]. Nv 1988, Broadman. 140 p. $10. 0-8054-5441-1. – ᴿRExp 86 (1989) 285s (G. W. *Rowatt*).

1499 ᴱ**De Gennaro** G., Lavoro e riposo nella Bibbia 1987 ➤ 3,537: ᴿSalesianum 51 (1989) 350-2 (M. *Cimosa*).

1500 **Dulin** Rachel Z., A crown of glory; a biblical view of aging 1988 ➤ 4,1468: ᴿCBQ 51 (1989) 715s (P. J. *Griffin*, also on J. HARRIS).

1501 ᴱ**Felici** Sergio, Spiritualità del lavoro 1985/6 ➤ 2,432: ᴿCrNSt 10 (1989) 164s (Marcella *Forlin Patrucco*).

1502 Figures de l'Ancien Testament chez les Pères: Biblia Patristica Cah. 2. Strasbourg 1989, Centre d'Analyse et de Documentation Patristique (diffusion Brepols). 316 p. 13 art. – ᴿRHPR 69 (1989) 508 (P. *Maraval*: no names mentioned, but in a rubric where the reviewer is usually the author himself).

1503 *García García* Luis, El trabajo en la sabiduría popular; la laboriosidad en los refranes castellanos, a la luz de enseñanzas bíblicas: StOvet 15 (1987) 7-48.

1503* ᴱ**Gioia** Mario, [*Soggin* J. A., *al.*], I giovani nella Bibbia: StBDeh. R 1988, Dehoniane. 287 p.

1504 **Harris** J. Gordon, Biblical perspectives on aging 1987 ➤ 3,1472: ᴿHorizons 16 (1989) 157s (N. R. *Kollar*).

1505 *Hirth* Volkmar, Die Arbeit als ursprüngliche und bleibende Aufgabe des Menschen; Beobachtungen zum Alten Testament: BZ 33 (1989) 210-221.

1506 *a) Lim Seung-Phil*, ✪ The Word of God and work from the point of view of the OT: – *b) Do Jo-Han*, ✪ The dignity of work according to the Bible: Samok 125 (Seoul 1989) 4-29 / Kyong-Hyang 80,3 (Seoul 1988) 84s [< TContext 7/1, 58.54].

1507 *O'Grady* John F., The biblical doctrine of work: ChSt 28 ('Religion in the marketplace' 1989) 65-78.

1508 *Ravasi* Gianfranco, Per un'estetica biblica [Gn 1,4; Ct; ma Es 20,4, nessuna immagine]: RasT 30 (1989) 36-51.

1508* **Schmidt** William S., A biblical paradigm for selfhood: Journal of Pastoral Care 43 (NY 1989) 337-354 < ZIT 90,199].

1509 *Schwab* C., À pleine vie; jalons bibliques pour naître, vivre et mourir. Aubonne 1989, Moulin. 98 p. [ÉTRel 64,674].

1510 *Sicre* José L., Paro [strike, grève], pobreza y conversion: Proyección 35 (1988) 219-226 [226, obligación de plantearnos un nuevo modelo del trabajo].

1511 *Simundson* D. J., Mental health in the Bible: WWorld 9,2 (St. Paul 1989) 140-6 [< NTAbs 33,361].

1511* *Svoboda* Melannie, Work and leisure; our Judeo-Christian foundations: RRel 48 (1989) 493-7.

B4.2 *Femina, familia;* Woman in the Bible [➤ H8.8s].

1512 *Abe* G. O., The Jewish and Yoruba social institution of marriage; a comparative study; Orita 20,2 (Ibadan 1988) 3-18 [< TContext 7/1, 24].

1513 **Bal** Mieke, Lethal love; feminist literary readings of biblical love stories 1987 ➤ 3,1482: ᴿJRel 69 (1989) 395s (E. L. *Greenstein*).

ᴱ**Bal** Mieke, Anti-covenant; counter-reading women's lives in the Hebrew Bible: JStOT Sup 61, 1989 ➤ 625.

1515 *Barrett* Don, Women and family life in ancient Egypt and Israel: AncHRes 19 (1989) 6-12.

1516 *Baskin* Judith R., Rabbinic reflections on the barren wife: HarvTR 82 (1989) 101-114.

1517 **Becker-Cantarino** Barbara, Der lange Weg zur Mündigkeit: Frau und Literatur (1500-1800). Stu 1987, Metzler. ix-402 p.: I. 37-45 [LuJb 56, p. 175].

1518 **Biale** Rachel, Women and Jewish law 1984 → 1,1507.6630; 2,1067: ᴿJRel 68 (1988) 327-9 (Judith R. *Wegner*, also on BROOTEN T. 1985).

1519 **Brayer** Menachem M., The Jewish woman in rabbinic literature, 1. A psychosocial perspective; 2. A psychohistorical perspective, 1986 → 2, 1068: ᴿRelStR 15 (1989) 174 (Judith R. *Wegner*: 'This volume [which of the two?], possibly the worst on the subject ever to appear...').

1520 **Brenner** Athalya, The Israelite woman 1985 → 1,1510... 4,1483: ᴿCBQ 51 (1989) 112s (Katheryn P. *Darr*).

1521 **Callaway** Mary, Sing, O barren one 1986 → 64,1503... 4,1486: ᴿJQR 79 (1988s) 275-8 (Dvora *Steinmetz*); JRel 68 (1988) 453s (F. J. *Murphy*); RB 96 (1989) 128s (J. *Loza*: thèse de 1978, très en retard).

1522 **Chalier** Catherine, De aartsmoeders; Sara, Rebekka, Rachel en Lea [1985 → 2,1073],ᵀ. Hilversum 1987, Gooi & S. 208 p. ƒ37,50. – ᴿStreven 55 (1987s) 182 (P. *Beentjes*).

ᴱ**Day** Peggy L., Gender and difference in ancient Israel 1989 → 391.

1523 *de Benedetti* P., La donna nell'ebraismo: Sefer 43 (Mi 1989) 1-7 [< Judaica 45,144].

1524 ᴱ*Durand* Jean-Marie, La femme dans le Proche-Orient antique 1986/7 → 3,779: ᴿAfO 35 (1988) 187-190 (J. M. *Sasson*); JNES 48 (1989) 157s (Rivkah *Harris* enumerates the titles, some on Ebla but none on Egypt or Palestine).

1525 *Emmerson* Grace I., Women in ancient Israel: → 378, World 1989, 371-394.

1526 *Fishbane* Michael, Israel and the 'mothers' [< ᴱ*Berger* P., The other side of God 1981, 28-47]: → 259, Garments of Torah 1989, 49-63. 139s.

1527 **Frishman** Judith, *al.*, Sara en Maria; vrouwen in synagoge en kerk: OJEC-5. Kampen 1987, Kok. 104 p. ƒ15,90. – ᴿStreven 55 (1987s) 180 (P. *Beentjes*).

1528 *Frymer-Kensky* Tikva, The ideology of gender in the Bible and the Ancient Near East: → 183, ᶠSJÖBERG Å., Dumu- 1989, 185-191.

1529 *a) Fuchs* Esther, The literary characterization of mothers and sexual politics in the Hebrew Bible; – *b) Bird* Phyllis, The harlot as heroine; narrative art and social presupposition in three OT texts [Gn 38,1-26; Jos 2,1-24; 1 Kgs 3,15-27]; – *c) Furman* Nelly, His story versus her story; male genealogy and female strategy in the Jacob cycle: Semeia 46 (1989) 151-166 / 119-139 / 141-9.

1530 **Gilner** David J., The status of women in ancient Israel: diss. HUC, ᴰ*Brichto* H. Cincinnati 1989, 326 p. 89-16984. – DissA 50 (1989s) 1406-A.

1531 *a) Goeden* Roland, Eine komplizierte Beziehung; die Bibel über 'Mann und Frau' [I AT 1/1] 2; – *b) Ellerbrock* Jochen, Glaube und Persönlichkeit; seine Bibel schafft man sich; Interferenz von Symbolverständnis und Erlebnisstruktur: Religion Heute (Hannover 1989, 3s) [2s, 128-...] 242-5 / 202-225 [< ZIT 90,133].

1532 ᴱ**Greenberg** Simon, The ordination of women as rabbis; studies and responses 1988 → 4,9981; 0-87334-041-4; pa. -2-6: ᴿExpTim 100

(1988s) 357 (Julia *Neuberger*: they try to find answers to questions not asked).

1532* **Krafte-Jacobs** Lori Ellen, Feminism and modern Jewish theological method: diss. Claremont 1989, ᴰ*Cobb* J. 303 p. 90-00184. – DissA 50 (1989s) 3539-A; RelStR 16,187.

1533 *Lachmann* Rainer, Kind [child]: → 911, TRE 18 (1989) 156-176.

1534 *Légasse* Simon, L'enfant dans la Bible: DossB 30 (1989) 3-7 [-30, *al.*].
    ᴱ**Liberti** Vittorio, La famiglia nella Bibbia: Studio Biblico Teologico Aquilano 9, 1989 → 587*.

1536 **Ljung** Inger, Silence or suppression; attitudes towards women in the Old Testament: Ac U Women in Religion 2. Sto 1989, Almqvist & W. 159 p. 91-554-2460-0.

1537 *McHatten* M. Timothy, Prophetic images of women: Emmanuel 94 (1988) 136-141. 162 (216-220. 258-263. 338-341. 352s, covenant) [< OTAbs 12,9].

1538 **Maillot** Alphonse, Ève, ma mère; étude sur la femme dans l'Ancien Testament (et dans quelques civilisations proches). P 1989, Letouzey & Â. 183 p. F 120. 2-7063-0178-3 [BL 90, 108, G. I. *Emmerson*].

1539 **Méroz** Christiane, Waren zij vrije vrouwen? Sarah, Hagar, Rebekka, Rachel en Lea; een essay op de wijze van midrasj. Kampen 1988, Kok. 76 p. *f* 6. 278 p. – ᴿCollatVL 19 (1989) 241s (P. *Kevers*).

1540 **Mollenkott** V. R., Women, men, and the Bible²ʳᵉᵛ [¹1977 → 60, 1968]. NY 1988, Crossroad. x-163 p. $9. 0-8245-0893-9 [NTAbs 33,265].

1541 *Molnár* János, ⑩ Die Frau im AT: Református Szemle 79 (1986) 14-21 [< ZAW 114,236].

1542 **Schirmer** Eva, Eva-Maria; Rollenbilder von Männern für Frauen. Offenbach 1988, Burckhardt. 204 p. DM 22,80. – ᴿTGL 79 (1989) 212s (W. *Beinert*).

1543 ᴱ**Skinner** Marilyn, Rescuing Creusa; new methodological approaches to women in antiquity 1987 → 3,772*: ᴿAntClas 58 (1989) 466s (Marie-Thérèse *Raepsaet-Charlier*).

1544 **Terrien** Samuel, Till the heart sings; a biblical theology of manhood and womanhood 1985 → 1,1545... 3,1517: ᴿSvTKv 65 (1989) 76s (S. *Norin*, svensk except epilogue, 'Women do it better!').

1544* a) *Tolbert* Mary Ann, Protestant feminists and the Bible; on the horns of a dilemma; – b) *Exum* J. Cheryl, Murder they wrote; ideology and the manipulation of female presence in biblical narrative; UnSemQ 43 (1989) 1-18 / 19-40 [< ZIT 90,25].

1545 **Toorn** Karel van der, Van haar wieg tot haar graf; de rol van de godsdienst in het leven van de Israëlitische en de Babylonische vrouw 1987 → 3,1518: ᴿBO 46 (1989) 125s (D. *Snell*: 'in English trendily called the life-span'); CBQ 51 (1989) 543s (W. A. *Vogels*); JBL 108 (1989) 324s (Sara J. *Denning-Bolle*); Streven 55 (1987s) 756 (P. *Beentjes*).

1546 ᴱ**Uglione** Renato, La donna nel mondo antico: Atti Torino 21-23 aprile 1986: Assoc. Ital. di Cultura Classica, 1987 → 4,699: ᴿClasR 39 (1989) 103-5 (Gillian *Clark*).

B4.4   *Exegesis litteraria* – The Bible itself as literature.

1547 ᴱ**Alter** Robert, *Kermode* Frank, The literary guide to the Bible 1987 → 3,324; 4,1520: ᴿAncHRes 19 (1989) 96-98 (M. *Lattke*); Commonweal 115 (1988) 123-5 (Pheme *Perkins*); JAAR 57 (1989) 373-383 (Mieke *Bal*); JAOS 109 (1989) 673-5 (Adele *Berlin*, also on GREENSTEIN E. 1986 and

LONGMAN T. 1987); JRel 69 (1989) 99s (R.L. *Cohn*); Religion and Literature 20,2 (ND 1988) 75-80 (D. *Jasper*: bland, 'the "good book" is in danger of becoming the "nice book"') [< NTAbs 33,3]; WestTJ 51 (1989) 157s (L. *Ryken*).

1548 *Barry* Peter, Exegesis and literary criticism: ScripB 20 (1989s) 28-33.

1549 **Bloom** Harold, Ruin the sacred truths; poetry and belief from the Bible to the present. CM 1989, Harvard. 204 p. $20 [BL 91,9, R. *Carroll*; TS 50,416]. – RCCurr 39 (1989s) 375s. 378 (I. *Stavans*).

1550 **Frye** Northrup, El gran Código; una lectura mitológica y literaria de la Biblia [1982 ➤ 63,1648], TCasals Elisabeth: Esquinas. Barc 1988, Gedisa. 281 p. 84-7432-307-X. – RActuBbg 26 (1989) 37s (X. *Alegre S.*).

1551 **Gabel** J.B., *Wheeler* C.B., The Bible as literature, an introduction 1986 ➤ 2,1106 ... 4,1526: RZAW 101 (1989) 315 (H.-C. *Schmitt*).

1552 **Grabandt** L.G.C., De Bijbel als cultuurhistorisch en literair document; I. OT; II. NT; 1986 ➤ 3,1150: RStreven 55 (1987s) 376 (P. *Beentjes*).

Jasper David, The New Testament and the literary imagination 1987 ➤ 4220.

1553 **Josipovici** Gabriel, The book of God; a response to the Bible [viewed as a single literary masterpiece ...] 1988 ➤ 4,1073: RTS 50 (1989) 786s (L. *Boadt*); TTod 46 (1989s) 323s. 326 (W. *Brueggemann*).

Moore Stephen D., Literary criticism and the Gospels; the theoretical challenge 1989 ➤ 4249.

1555 EPreminger Alex, *Greenstein* Edward L., The Hebrew Bible in literary criticism 1986 ➤ 2,262; 3,1559: RRBgPg 67 (1989) 176-8 (J. *Klener*).

1556 *Seidl* Theodor, Die literaturwissenschaftliche Methode in der alttestamentlichen Exegese; Erträge – Erfahrungen – Projekte; ein Überblick: MüTZ 40 (1989) 27-37.

1557 *Sprinkle* J., Literary approaches to the Old Testament; a survey of recent scholarship: JEvTS 32 (1989) 299-310.

4.5 Influxus biblicus in litteraturam profanam, *generalia.*

1558 **Adey** Lionel, Hymns and the Christian 'myth'. Vancouver 1986, Univ. B.C. xvi-269 p. £20. – REvQ 61 (1989) 371-3 (A.G. *Newell*: tracing a literary and cultural tradition; some imperfections).

1559 **Birney** A.L., The literary lives of Jesus; an international bibliography of poetry, drama, fiction and criticism: Reference Library of the Humanities 735. NY 1989, Garland. xxv-187 p.; 9 pl. $30 [NTAbs 33,242].

1560 **Brzezinski** Monica, Cup of the new covenant; *cleanness* and the *artes praedicandi*: diss. Virginia 1989, 325 p. 90-08169. – DissA 50 (1989s) 3233-A.

1560* **Detweiler** Robert, Breaking the fall; religious readings of contemporary fiction [... 'sacred texts / sacred space']. SF 1989, Harper & R. xvii-198 p. $25 [TS 51, 560, E.J. *Ingebretsen*].

1561 *Dinwiddy* Hugh, Biblical usage and abusage in Kenyan writing: JRelAf 19,1 (1989) 27-47 [< ZIT 89,424].

1562 EHartman G., *Budick* S., Midrash and literature 1986 ➤ 2,249 ... 4,1537: RIrTQ 55 (1989) 329-331 (M. *McNamara*).

1563 *Jean-Nesmy* Claude, *a)* Anglo-Saxons, doublement frères; le roman et l'œuvre littéraire aux États-Unis et dans le Royaume Uni; – *b)* 'Europe, souviens-toi de ton baptême ...' (La littérature et son apport chrétien) [i. Le Portugal; ii. Les nordiques]; – *c)* iii. Europe centrale; [iv. France];

[v. entre-guerres]; EsprVie 99 (1989) 33-42; 273-280; 296-303; 503-510; 673-682.

1564 **Krook** Anne K., The genesis of authority; Scripture, satire, and interpretation in English literature, 1660-1760; diss. Cornell. Ithaca NY 1989. 249 p. 89-15079. – DissA 50 (1989) 691-A.

1565 *Lovsky* F., Quand nos poètes aimaient les Psaumes: FoiVie 88 (1989) 77-81.

1566 **Mosès** Stéphane, Spuren der Schrift, von Goethe bis Celan [... SCHOLEMS KAFKA]. Fra 1987, Athenäum. 151 p. DM 34. – ᴿLuthMon 29 (1989) 373s (Susanne *Heil*); ZRGg 41 (1989) 280s (A. *Silbermann*).

1567 ᴱ**Osborn** Eric, *McIntosh* Lawrence, The Bible and European literature [LuJb 56, p. 180: *Kósa* Irma, The Bible and the formation of the German language, p. 56-64] 1987 → 4,495; 0-958966-8-18; 21 art.: ᴿExpTim 100 (1988s) 308s (M. J. *Townsend*).

1568 **Ray** Rhonda J., The last things; apocalypse and eschatology in British dark romanticism: diss. Emory, ᴰ*Metzger* Lore. Atlanta 1989. 247 p. 89-24701. – DissA 50 (1989s) 2068-A.

1569 **Robinson** Lewis S., Double-edged sword; Christianity and 20th century [Hong Kong - Taiwan] fiction [< diss.]. Hong Kong 1986, Tao Fong Shan Ecumenical Centre. vii-384. – ᴿJRel 68 (1988) 634s (*Wee Wanling*).

1570 **Wood** Ralph C., The comedy of redemption 1988 → 4,1547: ᴿTS 50 (1989) 818-20 (P. C. *Rule*).

1571 ᴱ**Wright** David F., The Bible in Scottish life and literature ... 1988, St. Andrew. 236 p. £7.50. 0-7152-0629-X. – ᴿExpTim 100 (1988s) 310s (F. F. *Bruce*).

1572 **Zemka** Sue, Victorian testaments; the use and abuse of the Bible in early nineteenth century British literature: diss. Stanford 1989. 432 p. 90-11601. – DissA 50 (1989s) 3966-A.

B4.6 *Singuli auctores* – **Bible-influence on individual authors.**

1573 AUSTEN: *Marcus* Joel, Jane Austen's Pride and prejudice; a theological reflection: TTod 46 (1989s) 288-298 [*al.* 256-287 on T. MERTON, C. S. LEWIS, J. STEINBECK, R. DAVIES, U. ECO].

1574 BLAKE: *Ferber* Michael, The social vision of William Blake. Princeton 1985, Univ. xii-254 p. £24.60. – ᴿHeythJ 30 (1989) 109 (Leslie-Ann *Hales*: the Spirit of Christ in us is the Imagination, p. 70).

1575 **Schock** Peter A., The romantic myth of Satan [... in Blake]: diss. Iowa, ᴰ*Grant* J. Iowa City 1989. 636 p. 90-04944. – DissA 50 (1989s) 2914-A.

1576 **Smith** John M., [Blake W.] Los and the science of the Elohim: diss. Univ. W. Ontario 1989, ᴰ*Shroyer* R. – DissA 50 (1989s) 3239-A.

1577 BROWNING: *Nisbet* Patricia, 'How very hard it is to be a Christian' [Robert Browning's mission; Saul; John ...]: ExpTim 100,6 (1988s) 212-5.

1578 BUNYAN: **Batson** Beatrice, John Bunyan's Grace Abounding and The Pilgrim's Progress; an overview of literary studies 1960-1987. NY 1988, Garland. 256 p. $33. 0-8240-6630-8. – ᴿEvQ 61 (1989) 286-8 (N. E. *Arnesen*).

1579 *Graafland* C., De Nederlandse Gereformeerden en Bunyan in de 18ᵉ eeuw: TRef 31 (1988) 328-344 [< GerefTTs 89,128]. → k241.

1579* *Wakefield* Gordon S., Starting with oneself; spiritual confessions, I. John Bunyan, Grace abounding: ExpTim 101 (1989s) 68-72.

1580 CAMUS: **Sutton** Robert C., Authentic responses to evil in Jesus and Albert Camus: diss. Drew. Durham NC 1988. 89-06807. – DissA 50 (1989s) 173-A.

1581 COHEN: *Charbonneau* B., Individu, amour et société; critique de Belle du Seigneur d'Albert Cohen [Gallimard 1968 mais souvent réimprimé]: FoiVie 88 (1989) 87-92.

1582 COLERIDGE: **Crowley** Alan J., Ezekiel's wheels [nothing on Ezekiel; just a term for] reading the performance of assent in NEWMAN and Coleridge: diss. Boston College 1989. 252 p. 89-22272. – DissA 50 (1989s) 2001-A.

1583 **Cutsinger** James S., The form of transformed vision; Coleridge and the knowledge of God. Macon GA 1987, Mercer Univ. 136 p. $25. – RJAAR 57 (1989) 394-6 (C. *Welch*).

1584 **Gowler** Ronald S., Coleridge on the idea and history of Christianity: diss. Iowa 1989, DSpalding J. 222 p. 90-04907. – DissA 50 (1989) 2938-A.

1585 DANTE: *Penna* Romano, Ascendenze apocalittiche della Divina Commedia; Henoch 11 (1989) 41-50; franç. 50 [Inf. 2,28 basato su Visio Pauli, non 2 Cor 12,2s].
EBarblan G., Dante e la Bibbia 1986/8 → 565.

1586 *Placella* Vincenzo, Dante e l'esegesi medievale: Sapienza 42 (1989) 171-193.

1587 DUNNE: *Collinge* William J., John Dunne's journey of the mind, heart, and soul: Horizons 16 (1989) 28-44.

1587* *Davis* Ellen F., Messenger of a metaphorical God; John DONNE's use of Scripture in preaching: AnglTR 71 (1989) 48-62 [< ZIT 89,433].

1588 ELIOT: *Gibert Maceda* María T., Ecos bíblicos en la poesía de T. S. Eliot: RelCult 33 (1987) 609-621.

1588* GIDE: **Parnell** Charles E., André Gide et la Bible: diss. Yale. NHv 1948 (!). 378 p. 90-009793. – DissA 50 (1989s) 3615-A.

1589 HARDY: **Hopkins** Annie H., Biblical plot and character in Thomas Hardy's major novels: diss. Arizona State 1989. 333 p. 89-19610. – DissA 50 (1989s) 1065-A.

1590 HESSE: *Scheffler* Eben, Searching for meaning in biblical scholarship — reflections with Herman Hesse: TEv 21,2 (Pretoria 1988) 2-8 [< OTAbs 12,139].

1591 KAFKA: *Bar-David* Yoram, Kafka et l'appartenance à l'être; écrire l'hébreu avec des mots allemands: RÉJ 147 (1988) 145-166.

1592 **Robertson** Ritchie, Kafka; Judaism, politics, and literature. Ox 1985, Clarendon. xii-330 p. $40. – RJRel 69 (1989) 596s (C. *Koelb*).

1593 LÓPEZ: **Barres-Marlys** Mirta, An edition of the play 'Jael' by Juan José López de Sedano: diss. Pennsylvania, DSebold R. Ph 1989. 279 p. 90-04759. – DissA 50 (1989s) 2918-A.

1594 MANN: **Swensen** Alan J., Gods, angels, and narrators; a metaphysics of narrative in Thomas Mann's 'Joseph und seine Brüder' [seems to demythologize Gn 37-50]: diss. Princeton 1989. 187 p. 89-10886. – DissA 50 (1989s) 695-A.

1595 MILTON: **Boocker** Joseph D., 'Paradise Lost' as Reformation history: diss. Nebraska, DOlson P. A. Lincoln 1988. 208 p. – DissA 50 (1989s) 144-A.

1596 **Lewalski** Barbara K., Paradise Lost and the rhetoric of literary forms. Princeton 1985, Univ. xi-378 p. £38.50. – RHeythJ 30 (1989) 475-7 (D. *Haskin*).

1597 **MacCallum** Hugh, Milton and the Sons of God; the divine image in Milton's epic poetry 1986 ➤ 4,1567: ᴿSR 18 (1989) 230s (D. L. *Jeffrey*).

1598 **Radzinowicz** Mary Ann, Milton's epics and the Book of Psalms. Princeton 1989, Univ. xvii-227 p. 0-691-06759-7.

1598* **Schwartz** Regina M., Remembering and repeating; creation in 'Paradise Lost'. C 1989, Univ. xi-144 p. $30 [RelStR 16, 338, Wendy *Furman*]. – ᴿExpTim 101 (1989s) 59 (M. J. *Townsend*).

1599 **Turk** David F., Joint heirs with Christ; John Milton and the revolutionary sons of God: diss. NYU 1989, ᴰ*Low* A. 428 p. 90-04245. – DissA 50 (1989s) 2949-A.

1600 **Williams** Herbert G., Anabatic movements in Milton's 'Paradise Lost': diss. ᴰ*MacCallum* H. Toronto 1989. – DissA 50 (1989s) 2914-A.

1601 Oz: **Feininger** Bernd, Amos Oz verstehen — Literatur und jüdisches Erbe im heutigen Israel: ArbNTJ 9. Fra 1988, Lang. viii-409 p.; portr. 3-8204-9535-5.

1602 PASCAL: **Edmunds** Bruce T., The Fall of man as temporal and ontological discontinuity in the writings of Blaise Pascal: diss. Stanford 1989. 200 p. 90-11491. – DissA 50 (1989s) 3971-A.

1603 SACHS: **Lermen** Birgit J., Die Hiob-Gestalt in der Lyrik von Nelly Sachs: TGegw 32 (1989) 3-10.

1604 STEINBECK: **Procter-Murphy** Jeffrey M., John Steinbeck's use of biblical imagery in 'The grapes of wrath'; American dreams and realities examined: diss. Claremont 1989. 71 p. 89-25006. – DissA 50 (1989s) 2099-A.

1605 TOLKIEN: *Syme* M. Ruth, Tolkien as Gospel writer: diss. McGill, ᴰ*Hall* D. Montréal 1989. – RTLv 21,571 (microfiche Ottawa, Nat. Library).

B4.7 *Interpretatio* **athea, materialistica, psychiatrica.**

1606 **Beirnaert** Louis († 1985), Aux frontières de l'acte analytique; la Bible, saint IGNACE, FREUD et LACAN. P 1987, Seuil. 254 p. F 99. – ᴿRechSR 76 (1988) 302-4 (F. *Courel*).

1607 ᴱ**Cooper** Howard, Soul searching; studies in Judaism and psychotherapy. L 1988, SCM. xxviii-239 p. £10 pa. – ᴿTLond 92 (1989) 231s (M. B. *Ettlinger*).

1608 **Drewermann** Eugen, Tiefenpsychologie und Exegese 1⁶ 1988 ➤ (65,1386 ...) 4,1584: ᴿRHPR 69 (1989) 200s (J. G. *Heintz*).

1609 **Drewermann** E., 'An ihren Früchten' [*Pesch* R., *Lohfink* G. ➤ 1616], 1988 ➤ 4,1585: ᴿActuBbg 26 (1989) 205 (J. *Boada*: estilo brillante).

1609* *Eckert* Jost, Die tiefenpsychologische Schriftauslegung Eugen DREWERMANNs — ihre Anliegen und Grenzen: TrierTZ 98 (1989) 1-20.

1610 **Frankl** Victor E., Der unbewusste Gott; Psychotherapie und Religion. Mü 1988, Kösel. 156 p. DM 28. 3-466-20302-3. – ᴿActuBbg 26 (1989) 208 (J. *Boada*).

1611 **Gay** Peter, FREUD, a life for our time. NY 1988, Norton. 810 p. [not 1987, 182 p. ➤ 4,1587]. – ᴿJQR 79 (1988s) 251-3 (S. L. *Gilman*: grand definitive biography; echoes A godless Jew 1987).

1612 **Gay** Peter, A godless Jew, FREUD... 1987 ➤ 4,1587: ᴿAmHR 94 (1989) 100s (W. M. *Johnston*).

1613 ᴱ**Görres** Albert, *Kasper* Walter, Tiefenpsychologische Deutungen des Glaubens? Anfragen an E. DREWERMANN: QDisp 113, 1988 ➤ 4,305;

DM 24,80:   RActuBbg 26 (1989) 54s (J. *Boada*); TPhil 64 (1989) 288-290 (R. *Sebott*); TPQ 137 (1989) 405s (J. *Janda*).

1614 **Gresser** Moshe Y., Sigmund FREUD's Jewish identity; a study of his correspondence: diss. D*Browning* D. Chicago 1989. – RelStR 16,186.

1615 **Hall** Brian, The Genesis effect [... moving from image to creative action via the Word]. NY 1986, Paulist. 364 p. $15 pa. – RRRel 48 (1989) 795s (B. *Edens*).

1616 **Lohfink** G., *Pesch* R., Tiefenpsychologie und keine Exegese... DREWERMANN 1987 → 3,1571; 4,1592: RActuBbg 26 (1989) 57s (J. *Boada*).

1617 **Meves** Christa, Salud psíquica y salvación bíblica 1983 → 65,1403; 84-254-1230-7: RActuBbg 26 (1989) 85s (F. *Abel*).

1618 *a*) *Priest* John F., Myth and dream in Hebrew Scripture; – *b*) *Wilder* Amos N., ... in Christian Scripture: → 448, ECampbell J., Myths, dreams and religion 1988 = 1970, 48-65 / 66-90.

1619 **Rebell** Walter, Psychologisches Grundwissen für Theologen; ein Handbuch. Mü 1988, Kaiser. 288 p. DM 49. – RTLZ 114 (1989) 847s (E.-R. *Kiesow*); TR 85 (1989) 326-8 (K. *Thomas*).

1620 **Schmitz** Stefan, In Menschen der Bibel sich wiederfinden; tiefenpsychologische Zugänge; Vorw. *Drewermann* Eugen. Olten 1988, Walter. 227 p. DM 29,80. – RTGL 79 (1989) 212 (K. *Hollmann*).

1620* *a*) *Spiegel* Yorick, Mehr als wilde Exegese; Psychoanalyse und die Interpretation der biblischen Schriften; – *b*) *Altner* Günter, al., Die Bibel, Medium der Selbsterfahrung oder Sprachform des Göttlichen?; – *c*) *Noormann* Harry, Streit um die Bibel; Streit um die 'Wahrheit' des Evangeliums und ihre Vermittlungsfähigkeit; – *d*) *Brömse* Michael, 'Mit der Fackel der Wahrheit den Leuten den Bart versengen'; moderne Klassiker der Bibelwissenschaft: Religion Heute (Hannover 1989, 3s) 180-3 / 144-152 / 184-219 / 220... [174s über DREWERMANN; < ZIT 90,132].

1621 **Stein** Dominique, Lectures psychanalytiques de la Bible 1985 → 2,1131; 4,1599: RLVitae 43 (1988) 353 (A. *Godin*).

1622 *Sudbrack* Josef, Im Gespräch mit Eugen DREWERMANN: GeistL 62 (1989) 325-348.

B5 Methodus exegetica.

1623 **Beattie** D. R. G., First steps in biblical criticism 1988 → 4,1608: RRelStR 15 (1989) 255 (W. L. *Humphreys*).

1624 *Black* C. Clifton II, Keeping up with recent studies XVI. Rhetorical criticism and biblical interpretation [in English]: ExpTim 100 (1988s) 252-8.

1625 *Chernick* Michael, Internal restraints on *gezerah shawah*'s application [exegetical comparison of a term found in unrelated verses]: JQR 80 (1989s) 251-282.

1626* *Crüsemann* Frank, Tendenzen der alttestamentlichen Wissenschaft zwischen 1933 und 1945: WDienst 20 (Bielefeld 1989) 79-104 [< ZIT 89,721].

1626 **Brown** Raymond E., O significado crítico da Biblia, T*Toledo Steidel* Yolanda de. São Paulo 1987, Loyola. 150 p. – RPerspT 20 (1988) 271s (J. *Konings*).

1627 **Eckardt** W., Computergestützte Analyse hebräischer Texte ...: AOtt 29, 1987 → 3,1588: RAION 48 (1988) 71s (J. A. *Soggin*, also on AOtt 21-28).

1628 *Fick* Ulrich, Ⓜ Exegesis between magic and criticism, ᵀ*Karasszon* István: TSzem 32 (1989) 197-202.

1629 *Fitzmyer* Joseph A., Historical criticism; its role in biblical interpretation and Church life: TS 50,2 (Fiftieth anniversary volume, Scripture issue, 1989) 244-259.

1629* **Foley** John M., The theory of oral composition; history and methodology. Bloomington 1988, Indiana Univ. xv-170 p. $35; pa. $10 [ClasR 40, 1, J. B. *Hainsworth*].

1630 *Fowler* Robert M., Postmodern biblical criticism: Forum 5,3 (1989) 3-30 (-35-41, responses, *Moore* Stephen D., *Aichele* George).

1631 ᴱ**Friedman** R. E., The poet and the historian 1983 ↠ 64,264; 2,1142*: ᴿOLZ 84 (1989) 303-5 (H.-J. *Zobel*).

1632 ᴱ**Friedman** Richard E., *Williamson* H. G. M., The future of biblical studies [< 1984 meeting at San Diego U. Cal.] 1987 ↠ 3,541: ᴿJRel 69 (1989) 136s (R. M. *Polzin*).

1633 **Giroud** Jean-Claude, *Panier* Louis, Semiótica [progresos desde 1987]: Cuad. Bib. 59, 1988 ↠ 4,1615; pt. 280; 84-7151-550-4: ᴿActuBbg 26 (1989) 38 (R. de *Sivatte*); EfMex 6 (1988) 457s (E. *Serraima*); RBíbArg 51 (1989) 189s (A. J. *Levoratti*).

1634 *Gnilka* Joachim, Die Wirkungsgeschichte als Zugang zum Verständnis der Bibel: MüTZ 40 (1989) 51-62.

1635 **Guillemette** Pierre, *Brisebois* Mireille, Introduction aux méthodes historico-critiques: Héritage et projet 35, 1987 ↠ 3,1596; 4,1617: ᴿCBQ 51 (1989) 717s (L.-P. *Hoppe*); ÉTRel 64 (1989) 608s (J.-P. *Gardelle*); RThom 89 (1989) 476s (L. *Devillers*).

1636 *a*) *Hanson* A. T., Today and tomorrow in biblical studies, NT; – *b*) *Whybray* R. N., OT; – *c*) *Houlden* J. L., A future for NT studies; – *d*) *Barton* J., Should OT study be more theological?: ExpTim 100 (1988s) 324-8 / 364-8 / 404-8 / 443-8.

1637 *Hardmeier* C., *Talstra* E., Sprachgehalt und Sinngehalt; Wege zu neuen Instrumenten der computergestützten Textwahrnehmung: ZAW 101 (1989) 408-428.

1638 *Hawkes* G., Beyond criticism; Bible study today [*Wink* W. 1973, 1980]: JTSAf 65 (1988) 60-72 [< NTAbs 33,142].

1639 **Hughes** John J., Bits, bytes and biblical studies 1987 ↠ 3,965; 4,1618: ᴿCriswT 3 (1988s) 203-5 (G. L. *Klein*); CurrTM 16 (1989) 291s (E. *Krentz*: reliable); WestTJ 51 (1989) 197s (M. *Silva*).

1640 ᴱ**Knight** D. A., *Tucker* G. M., The Hebrew Bible and its modern interpreters 1985 ↠ 1,293 ... 4,1620: ᴿProtestantesimo 44 (1989) 289-291 (J. A. *Soggin*).

1641 *Lubsczyk* Hans, Die Seele der Theologie, Erfahrungen mit der historisch-kritischen Methode [weder in der Bibliographie S. 245 noch als ineditum]: ↠ 306, Einheit 1989, 9-14.

1642 **Meynet** Roland, L'analyse rhétorique; une nouvelle méthode pour comprendre la Bible; textes fondateurs et exposé systématique; préf. *Beauchamp* Paul: Initiations. P 1989, Cerf. 347 p. F 220. 2-204-04024-X [TR 86,337]. ↠ 5069.

Muñoz León Domingo, Deras... I. targumico y NT 1987 ↠ 4230.

1642* *Nielsen* Kirsten, Hvor er den gammeltestamentlige forskning på veg hen?: DanTTs 52 (1989) 81-91 [< ZIT 89,507].

1643 *Premnath* D. N., Recent developments in biblical studies [interdisciplinarity; latifundialization]: Bangalore Theological Forum 20,3 (1988) 1-7 [< NTAbs 33,143].

1644 *Raurell* F., Fe i exegesi; entre el revisionisme i la caricatura; clima d'unes actituds: EstFranc 89 (1988) 601-620 [< NTAbs 33,143s: H. von BALTHASAR, R. LAURENTIN, and P. TOINET do not seem to understand the real nature of the historical-critical method].

1645 *a*) *Schmeller* Thomas, Soziologisch orientierte Exegese des NTs; – *b*) *Rebell* Walter, Psychologische Bibelauslegung; – *c*) *Fuchs* Ottmar, Kontext und Bedeutung sprachanalytischer Zugänge zur Bibel; – *d*) *Merklein* Helmut, Integrative Bibelauslegung? Methodische und hermeneutische Aspekte: BiKi 44 (1989) 103-110 / 111-7 / 98-103 / 117-123.

1646 **Sluis** Douwe van der, De Bijbel lezen; een inleiding tot de exegesemethoden van de Bijbel; een werkboek. Haag 1988, Boekencentrum. 143 p. *f* 17,90. – ᴿStreven 56 (1988s) 378s (P. *Beentjes*).

1647 **Steck** O. H., Exegese des Alten Testaments; Leitfaden der Methodik, ein Arbeitsbuch für Proseminare, Seminare und Vorlesungen¹²ʳᵉᵛ. Neuk 1989, Neuk.-V. xvii-209 p. DM 28 [ZAW 102, 163, H.-C. *Schmitt*]. 3-7887-1315-5.

1648 **Stenger** Werner, Biblische Methodenlehre 1987 → 3,1617; 4,1645: ᴿBLtg 62 (1989) 55-57 (G. *Steins*, auch über EGGER W.); Salmanticensis 36 (1989) 97-99 (J. M. *Sánchez Caro*).

1649 *Suelzer* Alexa, *Kselman* John S., Modern Old Testament criticism: → 384, NJBC (1989) 1113-1129.

1650 ᴱ**Uffenheimer** B., *Reventlow* H., Creative biblical exegesis; Christian and Jewish hermeneutics through the centuries [TA(/Bochum ev./kath. Fak) 1985]: JStOT Sup 59, 1988 → 4,505: ᴿBL (1989) 119 (R. B. *Salters*: titles, no pp.); ExpTim 100 (1988s) 430 (R. *Morgan*: title misleading; the TA conference was on history of hermeneutics).

1651 *Vallauri* Emiliano, Il metodo storico-critico alla sbarra [*Brown* R. E.; *Ratzinger-Messori*...]: Laurentianum 30 (1989) 174-223.

1652 *Walker* Larry L., Some results and reversals of the higher criticism of the OT: → 44*, ᶠCRISWELL W., CriswTJ 1 (1987) 281-294.

1653 **Weber** Hans-Ruedi, Esperimenti di studio biblico; nuovi metodi e tecniche [1981], ᵀ*Comba* Fernando: PiccBiblTeol 20. T 1989, Claudiana. 240 p. Lit. 24.000. 88-7016-098-X.

1654 *Wimbush* V. L., Historical study as cultural critique; a proposal for the role of biblical scholarship in theological education: TEdn 25,2 (Vandalia OH 1989) 30-43 [< NTAbs 33,289].

1655 ᴱ**Winquist** C. E., Text and textuality: Semeia 40, 1987 → 3,363*b*: ᴿBL (1989) 98s (R. P. *Carroll*: 'nonsense on stilts', 'obscurantist writing' 'the impoverishment which theory can bring'; from p. 1 'Instantiation and ideation mark a text that is not a text at all').

III. Critica Textus, Versiones

D1   **Textual Criticism.**

1656 ᴱ**Barthélemy** D., Critique textuelle de l'AT 2, 1986 → 2,1157... 4,1654: ᴿRB 96 (1989) 395-401 (G. J. *Norton* defends against charge of bias in favour of MT); TütQ 169 (1989) 322-4 (H. J. *Vogt*).

1657 **Beit-Arié** Malachi, al., ⊙ *Asupot* ... Specimens of mediaeval Hebrew scripts, I. Oriental and Yemenite 1987 → 4,1655: ᴿRÉJ 148 (1989) 409s (G. *Nahon*).

ᴱ**Blanchard** A., Les débuts du codex 1985/9 → 778.

1657* **Bologna** Giulia, Illuminated manuscripts; the book before Gutenberg. L 1988, Thames & H. 199 p. £20. – ᴿMonth 250 (1989) 143-6 (P. *Hackett*).

1658 *Brown* Raymond E., *Johnson* D. W., *O'Connell* Kevin G., Texts and versions: ➤ 384, NJBC (1989) 1083-1112.

1659 **Carreras de Nadal** J. R., *al.*, Ramon ROCA-PUIG i la ciència dels papirs. Algerri 1989, Ajuntament / Virgili & P. 226 p.; ill. – ᴿEstFranc 90 (1989) 533s (V. *Serra*).

1660 *Cathcart* Kevin J., The biblical and other early Christian manuscripts of the Chester Beatty library: ➤ 165, Mem. RYAN D., Back to the sources 1989, 129-147 + 148-163, XVI pl.

1661 **Cavallo** Guglielmo, Libri, scritture, scribi a Ercolano 1983 ➤ 1,1675*; 4,1659; ᴿClasR 39 (1989) 358s (P. J. *Parsons*: an event awaited for 200 years).

1662 **Cavallo** Guglielmo, *Maehler* Herwig, Greek bookhands of the early Byzantine period A.D. 300-800: Bulletin supp 47. L 1987, Univ. Inst. Classical Studies. xii-153 p.; pl. – ᴿAevum 63 (1989) 124 (Antonietta *Porro*); CdÉ 64 (1989) 338s (A. *Martin*); ClasR 39 (1989) 127s (N. G. *Wilson*).

1663 **Dukan** Michèle, La réglure des manuscrits hébreux au moyen âge. P 1988, CNRS. 235 p. – ᴿRÉJ 148 (1989) 166-8 (J.-P. *Rothschild*).

1664 **Fackelmann** Michael, Restaurierung von Papyrus und anderen Schriftträgern aus Ägypten: Stud. Amst. Epig. 24 [➤ 1,1678]. Zutphen 1985, Terra. 120 p.; 63 fig. *f* 70. 90-6255-243-9 [BO 46,628]. – ᴿJEA 75 (1989) 295s (A. *Bülow-Jacobsen*: 'I do not know who the other four are' in the whole world capable of this work).

1665 **Fälschungen** im Mittelalter 1986/8 ➤ 4,1662*: ᴿTLZ 114 (1989) 528-531 (G. *Haendler*).

1666 **Fikhman** I. F., ⊕ *Vvedennye*... General and documentary papyrology. Moskva 1987, Nauka. 528 p.; franç. 519-521 [OIAc N89]. – ᴿCdÉ 64 (1989) 340s (G. *Nachtergael*).

1667 **Fuks** L., *Fuks-Mansfeld* R. G., Hebrew typography in the Northern Netherlands 1585-1815; historical evaluation and descriptive bibliography I, 1984, vii-232 p.; II. 1987 ➤ 3,958: ᴿRÉJ 148 (1989) 388-391 (G. *Nahon*).

1668 **Gallo** Italo, Greek and Latin papyrology: Classical Handbooks 1, 1986 ➤ 4,1664: ᴿEmerita 57 (1989) 170s (J. *Ridríguez Somolinos*); RHPL 62 (1988) 380-2 (P. *Cauderlier*).

1669 ᴱ**Glenisson** Jean, Le livre au Moyen Âge 1988 ➤ 4,1666: ᴿRBén 99 (1989) 181s (P.-M. *Bogaert*).

1670 *Godfroy* Marie-France, Rémploi d'un fragment du Pentateuque (XIIIᵉ-XIVᵉ s.), archives de l'Aude [noté comme Lv. 13,25-54 mais possiblement de 13,7 à 14,9, en tout cas illisible]: RÉJ 148 (1989) 361-5.

1671 ᴱ**Gold** Leonard S., A sign and a witness; 2,000 years of Hebrew books and illuminated manuscripts [exhibit]. NY 1989, Public Library/ Oxford-UP. xiii-223 p. (color.) ill. 0-87104-409-9 pa. / Ox 0-19-505619-1: p. 35-47, *Beit-Arié* Malachi, How Hebrew manuscripts are made [47-60 decoration, *Cohen* Evelyn M.; 61-70 as history source, *Schmelzer* M.]; 71-79, *Gutmann* Joseph, Forming the great collections; 80-91, *Glatzer* M., Early Hebrew printing [92-100 *Rosenfeld* Moshe N.; 101-113, *Ruderman* David B., in a Christian world; 125-139, *Avrin* Leila, 20th cent.]; 7-34, *Cross* Frank M., The Dead Sea Scrolls.

1672 ᴱHeide A. van der, *Voolen* E. van. The Amsterdam Mahzor; history, liturgy, illumination: Litterae textuales. Leiden 1989, Brill. 85 p.; 40 pl. 90-04-08971-3.

1673 **Hunger** Herbert, Schreiben und Lesen in Byzanz; die byzantinische Buchkultur: Archäologische Bibliothek. Mü 1989, Beck [DLZ 111,5, H. G. *Thümmel*].

1674 **Hunger** Herbert, *al.*, Die Textüberlieferung der antiken Literatur und der Bibel. Mü 1988 = 1961, Deutscher Tb.-V. 623 p. – ᴿZRGg 41 (1989) 281s (L. *Flaig*).

1675 *Kupiszewski* Henryk, Dal codice-libro al codice-raccolta di precetti giuridici: JJurPap 20 (1988) 83-92.

1676 **Lemaire** J., Introduction à la codicologie: UCL Textes, Études, Congrès 9. LvN 1989, Inst. Ét. Médiévales. xi-265 p.; 49 fig.; XLIII pl. [RHE 85,16*].

1677 ᴱ**Lewis** Naphtali, Papyrology: Yale Clas. St. 28, 1985 ➤ 1,436; £25: ᴿCdÉ 64 (1989) 341-6 (J. *Bingen*).

1678 **Mazal** Otto, Paläographie und Paläotypie; zur Geschichte der Schrift im Zeitalter der Inkunabeln: Bibliothek des Buchwesens 8, 1984 ➤ 2,7884; 4,1672: ᴿResPLit 11 (1988) 330s (S. *Prete*).

1679 *Mazal* O., Handschriften: ➤ 901, LexMA 4 (1988) 1904-8.

1680 **Pächt** Otto, Book illumination in the Middle Ages; an introduction, ᵀ*Davenport* Kay, 1986 ➤ 4,1673: ᴿRelStR 15 (1989) 351 (L. *Nees*).

1681 **Pintaudi** Rosario, *Sijpesteijn* Pieter J., *al.*, Tavolette lignee e cerate da varie collezioni: Papyrol. Florent. 18. F 1989, Gonnelli. 242 p.; 94 pl.

1682 *Robbins* Gregory A., 'Fifty copies of the sacred writings' [EUSEBIUS, Vita Constantini 4,36]; entire Bibles or Gospel books?: ➤ 696, 10th Patristic, 19 (1989) 91-98.

1683 **Roberts** Colin H., *Skeat* T.C., The birth of the codex 1983 ➤ 64,1705 ... 3,1640: ᴿTLond 92 (1989) 56-58 (J. N. *Birdsall*).

1684 ᴿ**Schreiner** Peter, Codices Vaticani graeci 867-932: Bibl. Apost. Vat. codices ms recensiti. R 1988, Bibliotheca Vaticana. xviii-227 p. 88-210-0613-1.

1684* *Simcha* Emanuel, ⊕ Scribal errors: Tarbiz 58 (1988s) 135-145; Eng. v.

1685 *a) Supino Martini* Paola, La scrittura delle Scritture (sec. XI-XII); – *b) Palma* Marco, Modifiche di alcuni aspetti materiali della produzione libraria latina nei secoli XII e XIII: ScrCiv 12 (1988) 101-118 / 119-133.

1685* *Treu* Kurt, Christliche Papyri XIV: ArPapF 35 (1989) 107-116; p. 107, Ps 15s; Röm 6; Eph 4; p. 108, Apocrypha.

1686 *Troncarelli* Fabio, Codicologia e storia della trasmissione dei testi; note e riflessioni: ScrCiv 13 (1989) 547-559.

1687 **Turner** Eric G., Greek manuscripts of the ancient world, ²ʳᵉᵛ**Parsons** P. J.: BInstClas Supp 46, 1987 ➤ 4,1680: ᴿRPg 62 (1988) 316-8 (J. *Irigoin*).

1688 *Waltke* Bruce K., Aims of textual criticism [i. restore the original composition; ii. restore the final text; iii. restore the earliest attested text; iv. restore accepted texts; v. reconstruct final texts]: WestTJ 51 (1989) 93-108.

Wisselink W. F., Assimilation as a criterion for the establishment of the text 1989 ➤ 1750.

1690 *Woude* S. Van der, De Keulse bijbels tussen Bartholomaeus von UNCKEL en Henricus QUENTEL: ➤ 203, ᶠVERVLIET H., Liber amicorum 1988, 45-56; 3 facsim.

1691 **Yakerson** Simeon M., ❽ Yevreyskiye inkunabuly... Hebrew incunabula; description of publications kept in libraries of Moscow and Leningrad. Leningrad 1988, Nauka. 337 p.; 60 pl. – ᴿJQR 80 (1989s) 363-5 (C. *Abramsky*); RÉJ 148 (1989) 441s (Colette *Sirat*: improves on the volume reviewed here in 1986).

1691* *Zamponi* Stefano, Elisione e sovrapposizione nella littera textualis: ScrCiv 12 (1988) 135-176; 8 pl.

D2.1   *Biblia hebraica,* **Hebrew text.**

1692 *Abramowitz* Chaim, *a)* Soferim – Scribes – counters; – *b)* Vavei ha'amudim: Dor 15 (1986s) 248 / 198 [interesting scribal practices, < OTAbs 11,97].

1693 **Busi** G., Edizioni ebraiche del XVI secolo nelle biblioteche dell'Emilia Romagna. Bo 1987, Analisi. 222 p. – ᴿCrNSt 10 (1989) 193s (S. *Giombi*)

1694 **Cassuto** Philippe, Qeré-Ketib et listes massorétiques dans le manuscrit B 19a: JudUmw 26. Fra 1989, Lang. 289 p. – ᴿLA 39 (1989) 347 (A. *Mello*).

1695 *Cassuto* Philippe, La lettre comme forme; les bases d'une édition des divergences de la Bible hébraïque: Henoch 11 (1989) 3-16; ital. 16.

1696 *Ciprotti* Pio, Bibbia ebraica e critica testuale (a proposito di...) [*Barthélemy* D., 'Alliance biblique universelle' I-II 1982-6 (→ 3656)]: StDocHistJ 53 (1987) 313-354.

1697 *Di Segni* R., Nuovi dati sugli incunaboli ebraici di Roma: → 708, Sisto IV 1984/6, 291-304.

1698 **Dotan** Aron, Thesaurus of the Tiberian Masora... Ben Asher school, I. Genesis Leningrad Codex. TA 1977, Univ. polycopié. 218-xxxii-24 p. [cf. → 61,2299]. – ᴿRÉJ 147 (1988) 409-411 (M. *Serfaty*).

1699 *Lorian* A., L'imprimerie hébraïque 1470-1550; ateliers chrétiens et ateliers juifs: → 774, ᴱ*Aquilon* P., Le livre 1988, 219-229.

1700 **McCarter** P. Kyle, Textual criticism ... Hebrew Bible 1986 → 2,1192 ... 4,1686: ᴿAndrUnS 26 (1988) 305s (P. J. *Ray*); CriswT 1 (1987) 409-411 (K. A. *Mathews*).

1701 *May* J. C., The Morgan Library Hebrew Bible; documents, codicology, and art history: Studies in Bibliography and Booklore [14 (1982) N. *Allony*] 16 (1986) 13-36 [< OLZ 84,120: Allony pp. '64-51'].
Ognibeni Bruno, Tradizioni orali ... 17 Ketiv/Qere 1989 → 9185.

1702 *Otter* Joseph, ❽ The masoretic divisions (*sedarim*) in the books of the Prophets and Hagiographa: Tarbiz 58 (1989) 155-189; Eng. i-ii.

1703 *Penkower* Jordan S., ❽ A tenth-century Pentateuchal ms. from Jerusalem (MS C3) corrected by Mishael BEN UZZIEL: Tarbiz 58 (1988s) 49-74; Eng. ii-iii.

1704 *Schmelzer* Hermann I., 'Heilige Kunst' und Buchdruck; vor 400 Jahren erschien die erste gedruckte hebräische Bibel: Orientierung 53 (1989) 81-84.

1705 **Scott** William R., A simplified guide to BHS. SF 1987, Bibal. 88 p. $6. 0-941037-04-5 [ExpTim 100,269].

1705* **Sed-Rajna** Gabrielle, La Bible hébraïque. FrS 1987, Office du Livre. 173 p.; bibliog. 165-8; ill. – ᴿKirSef 62 (1988s) 264s (M. *Beit-Arié* ❽).

1706 **Tov** Emanuel, ❽ The textual criticism of the Bible, an introduction: The Biblical Encyclopedia [EnṣM] Library 4. J 1989, Bialik. xxiv-326 p., 30 pl. 965-342-541-2.

1707 **Valle Rodríguez** Carlos del, Catálogo descriptivo de los manuscritos hebreos de la Biblioteca Nacional. M 1986, Min. Cultura. 225 p. – ᴿRÉJ 146 (1987) 386-9 (J.-P. *Rothschild*).

1709 *VanderKam* J.C., Jubilees and Hebrew texts of Genesis-Exodus [diverges so widely from Septuagint-Vorlage and Samaritan as to invalidate F. CROSS theory of local texts]: Textus 14 (1988) 71-85.

1710 *Vilar Hueso* Vicente, Impresos hebreos en la Biblioteca Universitaria de Valencia [13 Biblias...]: ➤ 3,529, II Simposio Biblico Español 1987, 627-634.

1711 **Würthwein** Ernst, Der Text des Alten Testaments⁵ʳᵉᵛ 1988 ➤ 4,1697: ᴿActuBbg 26 (1989) 203 (R. de *Sivatte*); ScripTPamp 21 (1989) 543 (K. *Limburg*); TLZ 114 (1989) 722-4 (R. *Stahl*).

D2.2 Targum.

1712 **Chester** Andrew, Divine revelation and divine titles in the Pentateuchal Targumim: TStAJ 14, 1986 ➤ 2,1199... 4,1699: ᴿGregorianum 70 (1989) 779-781 (G.L. *Prato*); Judaica 45 (1989) 251s (S. *Schreiner*).

1713 *Chrostowski* Waldemar, ❷ *a*) La nature et la genèse du targumisme; – *b*) Les plus anciennes versions de la Bible en araméen (targums): PrzPow 800 (1988) 82-96; franç. 96 / 811 (1989) 394-411; franç. 411.

1714 ᴱ**Clarke** E.G., *al.*, Targum Pseudo-Jonathan of the Pentateuch 1984 ➤ 65,1487... 3,1660: ᴿJQR 79 (1988s) 227-230 (M.J. *Bernstein*).

1715 **Golomb** David M., A grammar of Targum Neofiti 1985 ➤ 1,1733.8838... 4,1702: ᴿIrTQ 55 (1989) 73s (M. *McNamara*).

1716 **Goshen-Gottstein** Moshe, Fragments of lost targumim I 1983 ➤ 64,1733 ... 3,1663: ᴿJQR 80 (1989s) 376-9 (M.J. *Bernstein*).

1717 **Goshen-Gottstein** M., ❸ Fragments of lost Targumim II (with *Kasher* Rimon): Inst. Jewish Bible Research 3. Ramat Gan 1989, Bar-Ilan Univ. 965-226-098-3 [OIAc S89].

1718 **Grelot** Pierre, Les Targoums 1985 ➤ 1,1735 [español 3,1665]: ᴿRÉJ 146 (1987) 429s (Madeleine *Petit*).

1719 **Grossfeld** Bernard, The Targum Onqelos to Gen / Ex / Lev-Num / Dt 1988 ➤ 4,1703: ᴿVT 39 (1989) 380 (H. *Williamson*).

1720 **Harrington** D.J., *al.*, Targum... Aramaic Bible 10-13, first four to appear, 1987 ➤ 3,1666; 4,1703*: ᴿCBQ 51 (1989) 331s (S.A. *Kaufman*: only Glazier indicated as publisher).

1721 *Hayward* Robert, *a*) The date of Targum Pseudo-Jonathan; some comments: JJS 40 (1989) 7-30; – *b*) Targum Pseudo-Jonathan and anti-Islamic polemic: JSS 34 (1989) 77-93.

1722 *Kaufman* Stephen A., Of beginnings, ends, and computers in targumic studies: ➤ 60, ᶠFITZMYER J., Touch 1989, 52-66.

1723 **Klein** Michael L., Genizah manuscripts of Palestinian Targum to the Pentateuch 1986 ➤ 2,1298... 4,1704: ᴿCBQ 51 (1989) 335-7 (M. *Aberbach*); JQR 80 (1989s) 156-160 (D.M. *Golomb*).

1724 *Klein* Michael L., New fragments of Palestinian Targum from the Cairo Genizah [Ex 36; Gn 15; 37]: Sefarad 49 (1989) 123-133; 4 pl.; español 133.

1725 **Levine** Etan, The Aramaic version of the Bible; contents and context [23 theological themes]: BZAW 174, 1988 ➤ 4,1706: ᴿBLitEc 90 (1989) 131s (M. *Delcor*); EstFran 90 (1989) 516-525 (Madeleine *Taradach*); TLZ 114 (1989) 508-510 (R. *Macuch*); ZAW 101 (1989) 319 (H.-C. *Schmitt*); ExpTim 100 (1988s) 349s (S. *Brock*).

1726 *McCarthy* Carmel, The treatment of biblical anthropomorphisms in Pentateuchal Targums: ➤ 165, Mem. RYAN D., Back to the sources 1989, 45-66.

1727 **Tal** Abraham, Samaritan Targum of the Pentateuch I-III, 1980-3 ➤ 61,2344 / 64,1742 ... 3,1674: ᴿCBQ 51 (1989) 353-5 (M. F. *Collins*).

1728 *Tal* Abraham, Targumic fragments in an Old Samaritan prayerbook (Paris BNat Sam 62): ➤ 126, ᶠMACUCH R., Ḥokmôt 1989, 329-342.

D3.1   *Textus graecus* – Greek NT.

1729 *Aland* Barbara, Die Rezeption des neutestamentlichen Textes in den ersten Jahrhunderten: ➤ 606, Réception 1986/9, 1-38.

1730 **Aland** K. & B., Text of the NT 1987 ➤ 3,1677; 4,1711; ²1989. 0-8028-3662-3 GR / [90-04-08367-7, Brill as before]: ᴿAthenaeum 67 (1989) 344-6 (A. *De Nicola*); HarvTR 82 (1989) 213-229 (E. J. *Epp*); JBL 108 (1989) 139-144 (M. *Holmes*: maybe the most detailed one-volume work of its kind ever written; but their value-judgments obscure as much as enlighten); NRT 111 (1989) 426s (X. *Jacques*); ScotJT 42 (1989) 418-420 (D. C. *Parker*); VigChr 43 (1989) 410s (G. *Quispel*); WestTJ 50 (1988) 195-200 (M. *Silva*).

1731 *Aland* Kurt, Neutestamentliche Textkritik und Exegese: ➤ 120, ᶠLOHSE E., Wissenschaft 1989, 132-148.

1732 *a) Aland* Kurt, Der Text der Kirche?; – *b) Aland* Barbara, Neutestamentliche Handschriften als Interpreten des Textes? P⁷⁵ und seine Vorlagen in Johannes 10: ➤ 131, ᶠMARXSEN W., Jesu Rede 1989, 398-413 / 379-397.

1733 *Aland* Kurt, The text of the Church? [TrinJ 8 (1987) 131-144]: BS 146 (1989) 455s (D. B. *Wallace*).

1734 *[Vaganay* L.] ²**Amphoux** C.-B., Initiation à la critique textuelle du NT 1986 ➤ 2,1224 ... 4,1726: ᴿEstBíb 47 (1989) 275-8 (J. *Trebolle*); RB 96 (1989) 454s (M.-É. *Boismard*); RHPR 69 (1989) 216s (J.-C. *Ingelaere*).

1735 *Cotsonis* John, On some illustrations in the lectionary Athos Dionysiou 587: Byzantion 59 (Bru 1989) 5-19; 16 fig.

1736 **Duplacy** Jean, Études de critique textuelle du NT: BiblETL 88, 1987 ➤ 3,215; 4,1714: ᴿBZ 33 (1989) 144s (G. *Schneider*); EstBíb 47 (1989) 274s (J. *Trebolle*); JTS 40 (1989) 223-5 (J. N. *Birdsall*); RHE 84 (1989) 101-6 (C. B. *Amphoux*, analyses détaillées des 20 art.); ScripTPamp 21 (1989) 944s (A. *García Moreno*); TLZ 114 (1989) 668s (G. D. *Kilpatrick*, Eng.); TR 85 (1989) 103-5 (G. *Mink*).

1737 *Ehrmann* Bart D., A problem of textual circularity; the ALANDs on the classification of New Testament manuscripts: Biblica 70 (1989) 377-388.

1738 **Elliott** J. K., Bibliography of Greek New Testament manuscripts: SNTS Mg 62. C 1989, Univ. 210 p. £30. 0-521-35479-X. – ᴿFgNt 2,1 (1989) 111 (J. *Peláez*).

1739 **Elliott** J. K., A survey of manuscripts used in editions of the Greek NT: NT supp. 57, 1987 ➤ 3,1682; 4,1715: ᴿCBQ 51 (1989) 558s (M. *Silva*); TLZ 114 (1989) 817 (K. *Treu*).

1740 *Epp* Eldon J., *a)* Textual criticism: ➤ 394, NT/Interpreters 1989, 75-126; – *b)* The New Testament papyrus manuscripts in historical perspective: ➤ 60, ᶠFITZMYER J., Touch 1989, 261-288.

1741 **Greenlee** J. Harold, Scribes, scrolls, and Scripture; a student's guide to NT textual criticism 1985 ➤ 1,1681; 2,1169: ᴿCriswT 3 (1988s) 220s (D. L. *Akin*).

1742 *Greeven* Heinrich,   Neues Licht auf den 'Cäsarea-Text' der Evangelien: ZNW 80 (1989) 262 nur.

1743 *Kim Young Kyu*,   Palaeographical dating of P⁴⁶ to the later first century [Biblica 69 (1988) 248-257]: BS (1989) 451 (D.B. *Wallace*: wait and see).

1744 *Leesti* Elizabeth,   A late thirteenth-century Greek Gospel book in Toronto and its relative in Oxford: Byzantion 59 (Bru 1989) 128-136.

1745 **Lilla** Salvator,   Codices Vaticani graeci 2162-2254:   1985 ➤ 3,1688: ᴿRÉByz 45 (1987) 232s (J. *Darrouzès*).

1747 *O'Neill* J.C.,   The rules followed by the editors of the text found in the Codex Vaticanus: NTS 35 (1989) 219-228.

1748 *Petzer* J.H.,   Die betroubaarheid van die Nuwe Testament vanuit 'n tekstkritiese oogpunt: HervTS 44 (Pretoria 1988) 98-138 [< NTAbs 33,11].

1749 *Wallace* Daniel B.,   The Majority Text [*Hodges* Z. 1982 ²1985]; a new collating base?: NTS 35 (1989) 609-618.

1750 **Wisselink** William F.,   Assimilation as a criterion for the establishment of the text; a comparative study on the basis of passages from Matthew, Mark and Luke [diss. Kampen, ᴰ*Bruggen* J. van: RTLv 21,547]. Kampen 1989, Kok.   249 p. *f* 39,50 [TR 86,75]. – ᴿStreven 57 (1989s) 661s (P. *Beentjes*).

D3.2   *Versiones graecae* – **VT, Septuaginta** etc.

1751 *Bajard* J.,   De la Septante au Nouveau Testament; approche quantitative de la Bible grecque: Revue Informatique et Statistique dans les Sciences humaines 24 (1988) 3-29 [< JStJud 20,287].

1752 *Brown* John P.,   The Septuagint as a source of the Greek loan-words in the Targums: Biblica 70 (1989) 194-216; franç. 216.

1753 *a*) **Combs** William W.,   The transmission-history of the Septuagint; – *b*) *Wallace* Daniel B.,   Some second thoughts on the majority text [*Hodges* Z., *Farstad* A., NT 1982]: BS 146 (1989) 255-269 / 270-290.

1754 ᴱ**Cox** Claude E.,   VI Congress Septuagint/Cognate 1986/7 ➤ 3,533; 4,1279: ᴿETL 65 (1989) 420-2 (M. *Vervenne*); JSS 34 (1989) 203-5 (A. *Salvesen*).

1755 **Fernández Marcos** Natalio,   La Septuaginta en la investigación contemporánea 1983/5 ➤ 1,468... 3,1701: ᴿRSO 63 (1989) 172-4 (A. *Catastini*).

1756 **Harl** Marguerite, *Dorival* Gilles, *Munnich* Olivier,   La Bible grecque des Septante; du judaïsme hellénistique au christianisme ancien: Initiations au christianisme ancien 1988 ➤ 4,1732: ᴿFgNt 2 (1989) 105-9 (J. *Trebolle Barrera*); NRT 111 (1989) 747s (X. *Jacques*); RB 96 (1989) 107-111 (G.J. *Norton*); RÉJ 148 (1989) 400s (J. *Schwartz*); VigChr 43 (1989) 203s (J. van *Winden*).

Lowden John,   Illuminated [Byzantine major and minor] prophet books 1988 ➤ 4,3613.

1757 *Müller* Mogens,   Graeca sive hebraica veritas? The defence of the Septuagint in the early Church: ScandJOT (1989,1) 103-124 [< OTAbs 12,137].

1758 **Rehkopf** Friedrich,   Septuaginta-Vokabular [all Greek words of RAHLFs in alphabetical order with German equivalence and some data about occurrence]. Gö 1988, Vandenhoeck & R.   ix-318 p. DM 38.   3-525-50172-2. – ᴿJStJud 20 (1989) 256s (A. *Hilhorst*).

1759 *Simon* Marie, Das Problem der jüdischen Identität in der Literatur des jüdischen Hellenismus [Aristeasbrief]: Kairos 30s (1988s) 41-52.
1760 **Tov** E., A computerized data base for Septuagint studies; the parallel aligned text of the Greek and Hebrew Bible: CATSS 2, 1986 → 4,1742: ᴿJTS 40 (1989) 536-8 (D. R. de *Lacey*).
1761 ᶠWEVERS J. W.: De Septuaginta, ᴱ**Pietersma** A., *Cox* C. 1984 → 65,149: ᴿRivStoLR 25 (1989) 183s (P. G. *Borbone*).

D4   **Versiones orientales.**

1762 ᴱ**Dirksen** P. B., *Mulder* M. J., The Peshitta 1985/8 → 4,480:   ᴿÉTRel 64 (1989) 625s (A. G. *Martin*); VT 39 (1989) 121 (J. A. *Emerton*).
1763 *Borbone* Pier Giorgio, La Pešiṭta; testi, studi, strumenti: Henoch 11 (1989) 339-362.

1764 **Bouvarel-Boud'hors** Anne, Bibl. Nat. fragments coptes I. bibliques [LOrA 1 (1988) 95-116 → 4,1753]: ᴿRB 96 (1989) 459 (M.-É. *Boismard*).
1765 ᴱ**Diebner** Bernd Jörg, *Kasser* Rodolphe, Hamburger Papyrus Bilinguis 1; die alttestamentlichen Texte... der Staats- und Universitätsbibliothek, Ct Lam copt., Eces gr.-copt.: Cah. Orientalisme 18. Genève 1989, Cramer. 531 p.; 53 pl.
1766 **Peters** Melvin K. H., A critical edition of the Coptic (Bohairic) Pentateuch 1.2.5, 1985/6/3 [Dt 1983 → 64,2588... 3,2556]: ᴿJQR 79 (1988s) 243-7 (W.-P. *Funk*).
1767 *Pezin* Michel, Copta Sorbonica [Nm 33s; Ps 1; Am 9; Mi 1; Zach 12s; Is 2; Dan 3]: LOrA 2 (1989) 1-11 + 4 pl.
1768 **Schmitz** Franz-Jürgen, *Mink* Gerd, Liste der koptischen Handschriften des Neuen Testaments [1, 1986 → 1,1242... 4,1756]; 2/1, Die sahidischen Handschriften der Evangelien: ArbNTTextf 13. B 1989, de Gruyter. x-449 p. 3-11-012255-3. – ᴿRB 96 (1989) 459 (M.-É. *Boismard*, 1); Salesianum 51 (1989) 569s (E. *Fontana*, 1).

1769 *Cowley* Roger W., Zakre and Pawli — Ethiopic Bible translators or interpreters: → 200, ᶠULLENDORFF E., JSS 34 (1989) 387-398.
1770 **Kadžaia** Lamara, Die älteste georgische Vier-Evangelien-Handschrift, I. Prolegomena, ᵀ*Greeven* Heinrich, *Job* Michael. Bochum 1989, Brockmeyer. xi-99 p. DM 16,80. 3-88339-725-3.

1771 ᴱ**Shehadeh** Haseeb, The Arabic translation of the Samaritan Pentateuch, I. Genesis-Exodus. J 1989, Israel Academy. vi-447 p. 965-208-089-6.
1772 *Shehadeh* Haseeb, A new unknown version of the Arabic translation of the Samaritan Pentateuch: → 126, ᶠMACUCH R., Ḥokmôt 1989, 303-327.
1773 *Khoury* Raif G., Quelques réflexions sur la première ou les premières Bibles arabes: → 316, L'Arabie 1987/9, 549-561.

D5   **Versiones latinae.**

ᴱ**Ammassari** Antonio, Il salterio latino di Pietro 1987 → 3001.
1774 *Bellavista* Joan, El leccionari de la Missa en el Sacramentari de Barcelona, Ms. Vat. Lat. 3542, de la Biblioteca Apostòlica Vaticana: → 69*, ᶠGOMÀ I., RCatalT 14 (1989) 453-466; Eng. 466.

1775 **Cahn** Walter, Die Bibel in der Romanik (... Illuminationen). Mü 1982, Hirmer. 308 p.; 200 fig. + 60 color. DM 198. – ᴿGeistL 62 (1989) 479s (Vera *Begel*).

1776 **Cavallo** G., *al.*, Codex purpureus rossanensis: Codices Selecti 81. R/Graz 1987, Salerno/Akad. xiv-215 p. DM 185. – ᴿJbAC 32 (1989) 233-240 (Petra *Sevrugian*).

1777 *Chasson* Timothy, New uses for an old text in some early Tuscan Bibles: Manuscripta 8 (1989) 15-28.

Fischer Bonifatius, Die lateinischen Evangelien II. Varianten zu Markus 1989 → 4858.

1778 ᴱ**Fuhrmann** Horst, *Mütherich* Florentine, Das Evangeliar Heinrichs des Löwen und das mittelalterliche Herrscherbild: Bayerische Staatsbibliothek Ausstellungskatalog 35. Mü 1986, Prestel. 84 p. 3-7913-0752-5.

1779 *Haelewyck* Jean-Claude, Le centre de recherches sur la Bible latine à Louvain-la-Neuve: ETL 65 (1989) 484-7.

1780 *Haendler* Gert, Zur Arbeit an altlateinischen Bibelübersetzungen: TLZ 114 (1989) 1-12.

1781 *Mälzer* G., Das Kilians-Evangeliar: Würzburger Diözesangeschichts-blätter 51 (1989) 355-390; 8 fig., 9 facsim. [< RHE 84, p. 336*].

Morano Rodríguez C., Glosas de Vetus Latina 1-2 Samuel 1989 → 2716.

1782 **Nees** Lawrence, The Gundohinus gospels 1987 → 4,1724 ('Laurence', amid Greek NT): $40: ᴿREByz 47 (1989) 319 (C. *Walter*: relation of iconography to Ravenna Vorlage); RHE 84 (1989) 821 (D. *Bradley*: uncial Vulgate, but unusually with 20 brief commentaries inserted in minuscule).

1783 *Palazzo* Éric, L'illustration de l'Évangéliaire au Haut Moyen Âge: MaisD 176 (1989) 67-80.

1784 **Riedinger** Rudolf, Der Codex Vindobonensis 418; seine Vorlage und seine Schreiber: Instrumenta Patristica 17. Steenbrugge 1989, Kluwer Academic. 108 p.; 172 pl.

1785 *Schroeder* J., Älteste Echternacher Bibelfragmente → 69, ᶠGᴏᴇᴅᴇʀᴛ J. 1983, 228-239; 3 pl.

1786 *Stamm* Liselotte E., [fragment complémentaire de la Bible illustrée de Fribourg; RHE 84 (1989) 294]: → 22, ᶠBᴇᴇʀ Ellen J., Nobile claret opus 1986, 113-123.

1787 ᴱ**Stramare** Tarcisio, La Bibbia 'Vulgata' 1985/7 → 3,566; 4,1785: ᴿRivB 37 (1989) 218-222 (G. *Crocetti*).

1788 *a*) *Verey* C.D., The Gospel texts at Lindisfarne at the time of St. Cuthbert; – *b*) *Brown* M.P., The Lindisfarne scriptorium from the late VIIth to the early IXth cent.; – *c*) *Ó Cróinin* D., Is the Augsburg gospel codex a Northumbrian manuscript?: → 634, St. Cuthbert 1989, 143-150 / 151-163 / 189-201.

1789 *Vineis* Edoardo, Le antiche versioni latine dei Vangeli: → 572*, Storia/preistoria Vangeli 1986/8, 61-90.

1790 *Voorwelt* Gebhard, *Leeuwen* Bertulf P. van, L'Évangéliaire de Baltimore; étude critique sur le missel que saint François aurait consulté: ColcFran 59 (1989) 261-321.

D5.5   *Citationes apud Patres* – the Patristic Bible.

1791 Biblia patristica [4, 1987 → 4,1987]; 5. P c. 1989, CNRS. – ᴿBijdragen 50 (1989) 447 (M. *Parmentier*, 4).

1792 **Ehrman** Bart D., Dɪᴅʏᴍᴜs the Blind and the text of the Gospels 1986 → 3,1758: ᴿJBL 108 (1989) 144-6 (M. *Holmes*); RB 96 (1989) 460s (M.-É. *Boismard*).

1793 *García García* Luis, Mayúsculas y minúsculas en los leccionarios y el misal: Burgense 30 (1989) 505-533.

1794 *Herren* Michael W., A copy of ERIUGENA's glossed Greek Gospels: ⇢ 36*, ᶠBRUNHÖLZL F., Tradition 1989, 97-106.

1795 **Jenkins** R. G., The Old Testament quotations of PHILOXENUS of Mabbug: CSCOr 514, subs. 84. Lv 1989, Peeters. xx-206 p. 0070-0844.

1796 *Lehmann* Henning J., Evidence of the Syriac Bible translation in Greek Fathers of the 4th and 5th centuries: ⇢ 696, 10th Patristic, 19 (1989) 366-371.

1797 *Maltese* Enrico V., Osservazioni critiche sul testo delle Epistole di Michele PSELLO: JbÖsByz 38 (1988) 248-255.

1797* *Mensa i Valls* Jaume, Les citacions bíbliques en Català en les obres d'ARNAU de Vilanova: ⇢ 69*, ᶠGOMÀ I., RCatalT 14 (1989) 517-525; Eng. 525.

1798 **Price** William C., The textual relationships of quotations from the four Gospels in IRENAEUS' 'Against Heresies' [closest affinity with Western text-type]: diss. SW Baptist Theol. Sem. 1989. 209 p. 89-22315. – DissA 50 (1989s) 2934-A.

1799 *Rorem* Paul, The biblical allusions and overlooked quotations in the Pseudo-Dionysian corpus: ⇢ 696, StudPatr 10/23 (1987/9) 61-65.

D6   **Versiones modernae**   .1   *romanicae,* **romance.**

1800 **Bagot** Jean-Pierre, *Barrios-Auscher,* La Bible de Jérusalem pour tous, textes présentés; traduction BJér ['revue et simplifiée']. P 1989, Cerf. 432 p.; ill. (J.-O. Heron). F 225. – ᴿEsprVie 99 (1989) 288 (É. *Vauthier).*

1801 ᴱ**Casalis** G., *Roussel* B., [Pierre Robert] OLIVÉTAN, traducteur de la Bible 1985/7 ⇢ 3,527: ᴿBL (1989) 51s (F. F. *Bruce);* BLitEc 90 (1989) 67s (S. *Légasse).*

1802 *Margot* Jean-Claude, Revision of the Français Courant Bible: BTrans 40 (1989) 236-241.

1803 ᴱ**Vesco** J.-L., Le Nouveau Testament, une Parole qui fait vivre [sélections avec des paragraphes assurant la continuité]: Livre de Poche 4280. P 1988, Librairie Générale. 224 p. – ᴿNRT 111 (1989) 615 (A. *Toubeau).*

Mateos J., *Alonso-Schökel* L., Nuevo Testamento 1987 ⇢ 4280.

1804 *Ben Abou* Isaac, À la recherche de la Bible en ladino; une traduction manuscrite du seizième siècle: ⇢ 564, Massorot 2 (1986) 15-24 [**O** 103-118, *Schwarzwald* Ora, Pirqê Abot ladino].

1805 ᴱ**Fernández Lago** Xosé, *al.,* A Biblia, traducción ó galego das linguas orixinais. Santiago de Compostela 1989, Sept. xxiv-1761 p.; 13 maps. 84-7337-036-8.

1806 *Fernández Lago* José, Nova Biblia en Galego, escolma de textos: ⇢ 69*, ᶠGOMÀ I., RCatalT 14 (1989) 395-406, castellano ('Gallego' a parte el título); Eng. 407.

1806* Sigles i abreviatures dels llibres de la Biblia i d'escrits afins jueus i grecs. Barc 1988, Assoc. Bíblica de Catalunya. 24 p. – ᴿRCatalT 13 (1988) 496s (D. *Jové).*

1807 Parola del Signore, la Bibbia; traduzione interconfessionale in lingua corrente (1985), nuova edizione con fotografie a colori e note. T-Leumann/R 1988, Elle Di Ci / A.B.U. 1472 p. Lit. 50.000. – ᴿParVi 34 (1989) 313s (F. *Mosetto).*

1807* La Bibbia, traduzione interconfessionale in lingua corrente. T/R 1985, LDC/ABU. – RBenedictina 35 (1988) 215-8 (L. *De Lorenzi*).

1808 *Barbieri* E., La fortuna della 'Biblia vulgarizata' di Nicolò MALERBI [1471, prima in italiano]: Aevum 63 (1989) 419-500.

1809 TGeymet Enrico, L'Evangeli secondo Matteo, Piemontese. Bo 1984 = 1861 (parte già 1834), CLUEB. lvii-130 p. – RProtestantesimo 44 (1989) 67s (*G. Gonnet*).

D6.2   *Versiones anglicae* – English Bible translations.

1810 [NAB:] EBourke M. M., *al.*, The New American Bible; revised New Testament. GR/Northport NY 1988, Eerdmans / (pa.) Costello. xlvii-774 p. 0-8028-0417-9 / 0-918344-27-1 [NTAbs 33,238].

1811 Cassirer Heinz W., God's new covenant; a NT translation. GR 1989, Eerdmans. xvii-494 p. £12.50 [JTS 41,827]. 0-8028-3673-9.

1812 EDaniell David, [William] TYNDALE's New Testament, translated from the Greek in 1534, with modern spelling. NHv 1989, Yale Univ. xxxiv-429 p.; 1 facsim. $30. 0-300-04419-4 [TDig 36,352].

1813 *Greenspoon* Leonard, Biblical translators in antiquity and in the modern world; a comparative study [MARGOLIS M. and THEODOTION]: HUCA 60 (1989) 91-113.

1814 Lindberg Conrad, The Middle English Bible; the Book of Judges. Oslo 1989, Norwegian Univ. Press. 505 p.

1815 NIV: *Klosterman* N. D., The New International Version: decennial observations: MidAmJT 4,1 (Orange City IA 1988) 7-31 [NTAbs 33,294].

1816 Goddard Burton L., The NIV story; the inside story of the New International Version [-1978]. NY 1989, Vantage. 125 p. $10. 0-533-07929-2 [NTAbs 33,370]. – RExpTim 101 (1989s) 25 (F. F. *Bruce*).

1816* Kohlenberger John R., Words about the Word; a guide to choosing and using your Bible 1987 ➤ 3,1771*: RCriswT 3 (1988s) 202s (R. L. *Alden*).

1817 *Liuzza* R. M., The Yale fragments of the West-Saxon gospels: ➤ 536, Anglo-Saxon 17 (1988) 67-82.

1818 *a) Millet* Robert L., Joseph SMITH's translation of the Bible; impact on Mormon theology: RelStT 7,1 (1987) 43-53. – *b) Barlow* Philip L., Before Mormonism; Joseph Smith's use of the Bible, 1820-1829: JAAR 57 (1989) 739-771.

1818* Murphy G. Ronald, The Saxon savior; the transformation of the Gospel in the ninth-century HELIAND. NY 1989, Oxford-UP. xii-129 p. $25 [TS 51,783, W. P. *Lehmann*].

1819 *O'Grady* John F., Bible translations and commentaries: ChSt 28 (1989) 191-204.

1820 [NEB²] EMcHardy W. D., The revised English Bible with the Apocrypha. Ox/C 1989, Univ. xviii-828 p.; iv-205 p.; iv-236 p. £10. 0-19-101220-3 / 0-521-50724-3. – RCurrTM 16 (1989) 456 (R. W. *Klein*: NEB with DRIVER dethroned); Tablet 243 (1989) 1121s (R. *Fuller*).

1821 EWalker William O.ᴶ, Harper's Bible pronunciation guide. SF 1989, Harper & R. xiii-170 p. 0-06-068951-X.

1822 *Walsh* J. P. M., Contemporary English translations of Scripture: TS 50 (1989) 336-358.

Waltke Bruce K., The New International Version and its textual principles in the Book of Psalms 1989 ➤ 3011.

1823 ᴱWansbrough Henry, The new Jerusalem Bible 1985 (Doubleday $25)
➤ 1,1827 ... 3,1775: ᴿCBQ 51 (1989) 358s (A. A. *Di Lella*: best annotated
Bible in English today).

1824 *Wolfers* David, The Humpty Dumpty principle in biblical translation ['a
word means just what I choose'; criticism of new Jewish translation of Job
14,36; 20,24; 21,21]: JBQ (= Dor) 18 (1989s) 141-7.

D6.3 *Versiones germanicae* – **Deutsche Bibelübersetzungen.**

1825 ᴱHainz Josef, Münchener Neues Testament, Studienübersetzung. Dü
1988, Patmos. xi-506 p. DM 19,80. – ᴿTüTQ 169 (1989) 243s (M. *Reiser*).

1826 *Lannert* Berthold, Die Bibelübersetzung Hermann Menges [MENGE
1841-1889] zwischen Philologie und Theologie: ZTK 86 (1989) 371-388.

1827 **Steurer** Rita Maria, Das AT, Interlinearübersetzung hebräisch-deutsch
und Transkription des hebräischen Grundtextes nach BHS 1986. Stu-
Neuhausen 1989, Hänssler. I. (Gen-Dt) xv-1277 p. 3-7751-1281-2.

1828 ᵀStier Fridolin † (ᴱBeck E., *al.*), Das Neue Testament. Mü/Dü 1989,
Kösel/Patmos. 580 p. DM 19,80 [TLZ 115, 678-682, W. *Scheidacker*].

1829 *Strand* Kenneth A., LUTHER's first edition of the Pentateuch: AndrUnS
27 (1989) 39-48 + 6 pl.

D6.4   **Versiones nordicae** *et variae.*

1830 **Peelen** Gert J., De nieuwe bijbel van een vrij volk; de Statenvertaling
van 1637. Haarlem/Bru 1987, Ned./Belg. Bijbelgenootschap.   95 p.
ƒ12.50. – ᴿStreven 55 (1987s) 82 (P. *Beentjes*).

1831 Det gamle Testamente i ny oversættelse [Danish trial translations being
published since 1977] Ex 16 - Nm 36, Megillot, Job Prov Dan. K 1989,
Dansk. Bibelselskab.   270 + 103 + 187 p. Dk 80; 120; 120. 87-7523-
211-1; 41-3; 37-5 [BL 90,49].

1832 *Kruse-Blinkenberg* Lars, Kompromisets oversættelse: DanTTs 50 (1987)
204-220 [1985 Minor Prophets to replace 1931, scholarly updating without
due literary perceptivity; < OTAbs 11,108].

1833 **Kirby** Ian J., Bible translation in Old Norse [< diss. London 1973].
Genève 1986, Droz. xiii-213 p. – ᴿVigChr 43 (1989) 103s (G. *Quispel*).

1834 *Nikolainen* Aimo T., The new Finnish translation of Holy Scriptures:
BTrans 40 (1989) 434-7.

1835 *Ötvös* László, ⑩ Notes on the Family Bibles [ᵀKároli Gaspar, various
editions]: TSzem 32 (1989) 288-290.

1836 **Frick** David A., Polish sacred philology in the Reformation and the
Counter-Reformation; chapters in the history of the controversies
(1551-1632) [on early Polish Bibles, commended by Bruce *Metzger*]:
Publications in Modern Philology 123. Berkeley 1989, Univ. California.
xi-288 p.

1837 **Strandenaes** Thor, Principles of Chinese Bible translation 1987
➤ 3,1795; 4,1844: ᴿJTS 40 (1989) 220-2 (P. *Ellingworth*).

1838 **Rijks** Piet, A guide to Catholic Bible translations [I. Pacific 1987
➤ 4,1841]; 2. Africa. Stu 1989, World Catholic Federation for Biblical
Apostolate. 583 p.; maps.

D7   *Problemata vertentis* – **Bible translation techniques.**

1839 *Alsop* J. R., Fiesta, a tool for Bible translation [computer program 'Fast
interactive editor of Scripture and text analysis']: Notes on Translation 2,4
(Dallas 1988) 1-17 [NTAbs 33,293].

1840 *André Martín* Melquiades,   En torno a la teoría del traductor en España a principio del siglo XVI: Carthaginensia 5 (1989) 101-113.

1841 a) *Arichea* Daniel C.[J], The Old Testament; some translational issues [Gn 1,2.26; Ps 45,6; 110,1]; – b) *Fehderau* Harold W., Producing [volumes of] Scripture selections: BTrans 40 (1989) 408-415 / 405-8.

1842 *Beentjes* Panc, Auteurs van toen en lezers van nu; de eeuwige tweestrijd van bijbelvertalers: Streven 55 (1987s) 551-9.

1843 a) *Bogaard* L. van den, De functioneel-equivalente vertaaltheorie slecht verdedigt of niet te verdedigen?; – b) *Hemelsoet* B. P. M., De Bijbel en zijn geschiedenis: AmstCah 8 (1987) 136-150 / 45-52 [< GerefTTs 89,61].

1844 *Bria* Ion, The translation of the Bible and the communication of faith today: BTrans 40 (1989) 308-314.

1845 **Buzzetti** Carlo, La Biblia y sus transformaciones [... storia delle traduzioni... 1984], [T]1986 ➤ 2,1160*; 4,1110: [R]ScripTPamp 21 (1989) 344 = 689 (A. *García Moreno*).

1846 **Dedecius** Karl, Vom Übersetzen; Theorie und Praxis: Tb 1258. Fra 1986, Suhrkamp. 204 p. [LuJb 56, p. 179].

1847 [E]**Gibaud** Henri, Les problèmes d'expression dans la traduction biblique 1986/8 ➤ 4,486: [R]RThom 89 (1989) 643-6 (R. *Robert*).

Greenstein E. L., Essays on biblical method and translation 1989 ➤ 269.

1848 *Gueunier* Nicole, Traduction biblique et inégalité des langues: RechSR 77 (1989) 347-364; Eng. 322.

1849 **Howsom** Leslie, The Bible transaction; a publishing history of the British and Foreign Bible Society, 1804-1864: diss. York (Canada) 1989. – DissA 50 (1989s) 2933s-A.

1850 *Huddleston* Mark, Equivalent dynamics; for whom do I translate?: BTrans 39 (1988) 122-5.

1851 **Lehrberger** John, *Bourreau* Laurent, Machine translation; linguistic characteristics of MT systems and general methodology of evaluation: Linguistic Investig. Supp. 15. Amst/Ph 1988, Benjamins. xiii-241 p. – [R]BSLP 84,2 (1989) 112-4 (X. *Mignot*).

1851* *McIvor* J. S., Translators; their method and their problems: IrBSt 11,3 (1989) 106-123 [< ZIT 89,531].

1852 **Margot** Jean-Claude, Traducir sin traicionar; teoría de la traducción aplicada a los textos bíblicos [1979], [T]*Godoy* Rufino: Biblia y lenguaje 8. M 1987, Cristiandad. 459 p. 84-7057-407-4.

1853 **Neusner** Jacob, Translating the classics of Judaism, in theory and in practice: BrownJudSt 176. Atlanta 1989, Scholars. xix-158 p. 1-55540-353-0.

1854 **Newmark** Peter, A textbook of translation. NY 1988, Prentice-Hall. – [R]BTrans 40 (1989) 341s (A. O. *Mojola*).

1855 *Nichols* A. H., Explicitness in translation and the westernization of Scripture: RefTR 47,3 (Melbourne 1988) 78-88.

1856 *Omanson* R. L.,   a) Can you get there from here? Problems in Bible translation: ChrCent 105 (1988) 605-7 [< NTAbs 33,13]; – b) Translations, text and interpretation: EvQ 57 (1985) 195-210.

1857 **Schoder** Raymond V., The art and challenge of translation. Oak Park IL 1987, Bolchazy-Carducci. 107-viii p. – [R]BTrans 40 (1989) 339 (R. G. *Bratcher*: largely identical with his Phlp-Gal tr. 'Paul wrote from the heart').

1858 **Schogt** Henry G., Linguistics, literary analysis, and literary translation. Toronto 1988, Univ. xi-177 p. – [R]BSLP 84,2 (1989) 117s (C. *Hagège*).

1859 *Snell-Hornby* Mary, Translation studies; an integrated approach. Ph 1988, Benjamins [TS 51,497].

1860 **Svejcer** Aleksandr D., Übersetzung und Linguistik [Perevod 1973], ᵀ*Cartellieri* Claus, *Heine* Manfred; ᴱ*Neubert* Albrecht, (*Schrade* Brigitta): Sprache 47. B 1987, Akademie. 331 p. M 18 [DLZ 111, 37-40, W. G. *Scherf*].

1861 *Thomas* Kenneth J., The use of Arabic terminology in biblical translation: BTrans 40 (1989) 101-8.

1862 *Ulrich* Eugene, Double literary editions of biblical narrations and reflections on determining the form to be translated: PerspRelSt 15 (1988) 101-116 [< OTAbs 12,17].

1863 **Waard** J. De, *Nida* E., From one language to another; functional equivalence in Bible translating 1987 → 4,1877: ᴿSalesianum 51 (1989) 353s (C. *Buzzetti*).

1864 *Waard* Jan de, Ⓜ Bible translation and foreign cultures, ᵀ*Karasszon* István: TSzem 32 (1989) 129-131.

1865 **Wendland** Ernst R., The cultural factor in Bible translation; a study of communicating the Word of God in a central African cultural context: UBS Mg 2, 1987 → 3,1825; 4,1878: ᴿJBL 108 (1989) 319s (K. N. *Schoville*); Salesianum 51 (1989) 570-2 (C. *Buzzetti*).

1866 *Wilt* Timothy, Two Zairean Swahili Bibles; dealing with diglossic distances: BTrans 40 (1989) 321-331 [p. 321, the 'diglossictuation'].

1867 *a*) *Yandit* Kirine, [*Renck* Günther] Priorities in translating the Bible; – *b*) *Anis* Pedi, *Waisale* Esikel, The Bible in decision-making; – *c*) *Bosetto* Leslie, ... in land-disputes; – *d*) *Hovey* Kevin, ... in revivals [March 1988 seminar in Papua-NG]: Catalyst 18,4 (1988) 58-60 [61-70] / 16-23 / 24s / 49-53 [< TContext 7/1, 73].

D8   *Concordantiae, lexica specialia* – Specialized dictionaries, synopses.

1868 **Even-Shoshan** Abraham, A new concordance of the Bible; thesaurus of the language of the Bible; Hebrew and Aramaic roots, words, proper names, phrases, and synonyms²ʳᵉᵛ 'easier to use' [¹1983 → 65,1647; 1,1876]. J 1989, Kiryat Sefer.

1869 Grosse Konkordanz zur Lutherbibel²ʳᵉᵛ. Stu 1989, Calwer. xvii-1708 p.

1869* **Jeanne** d'Arc, *al.*, ᵀᴱ*Ghiberti* G., *Pacomio* L., Le concordanze del Nuovo Testamento. Genova 1989, Marietti. xl-728 p. Lit. 120.000 [Asprenas 37, 493-6, V. *Scippa*].

1870 **Manser** Martin H., Chambers Bible quotations. E 1989, Chambers. vii-264 p. 0-550-21010-5.

1871 **Odelain** Olivier, *Séguineau* Raymond, Concordance thématique du Nouveau Testament [115 thèmes, 'aimer-haïr', 'anges-démons' etc.; 300-col. index]. P 1989, Cerf ['format de poche' → 4,1883]. xv-1081 p. F 249. 2-204-02865-7 [NTAbs 33,380]. – ᴿArTGran 52 (1989) 261 (A. *Segovia*).

1872 **Rinaldi** Giancarlo, Biblia gentium; primo contributo per un indice delle citazioni, dei riferimenti e delle allusioni alla Bibbia negli autori pagani, greci e latini, di età imperiale. R 1989, Libreria S. Scr. 752 p. Lit. 80.000. 88-237-8100-0. – ᴿKoinonia 13 (1989) 189s (R. *Maisano*): → g647.

1873 **Schmoller** Alfred, Handkonkordanz zum griechischen Neuen Testament [*Nestle-Aland*²⁶], ᴱ*Köster* B. Stu 1989, Deutsche Bibelges. [x-] 534 p. DM 38. 3-438-06007-8 [TLZ 115, 508, O. *Wittstock*].

1874 **Whitaker** R. W., The Eerdmans analytical concordance to RSV. GR 1988, Eerdmans. xiv-1548 p. $50. 0-8028-2403-X. – ᴿBL (1989) 24

(A. G. *Auld*: adds to YOUNG's AV a Hatch-Redpath style listing of the terms in the original language under each entry; vast indices facilitate judgment on RSV itself).

IV. ➤ K1	V. Exegesis generalis VT vel cum NT

D9 Commentaries on the whole Bible or OT.

1876 ᴱ**Bergant** Dianne, *Karris* Robert J., Collegeville Bible Commentary [OT 25 booklets completed 1986; NT 11 booklets completed 1983; now in one volume]. Collegeville MN 1989, Liturgical. ix-1301 p.; 33 maps. $45. 0-8146-1484-1 [TDig 36,150].

ᴱ**Brown** R. E., *al.*, New Jerome Biblical Commentary 1989 ➤ 384.

1877 ᴱ**Bruce** F. F., The [one-volume] International Bible Commentary [= ²ʳᵉᵛNew Layman's 1979] 1986 ➤ 2,1351 ... 4,1890: ᴿCriswT 2 (1987s) 157s (K. A. *Mathews*).

1878 Christian community Bible². Quezon City / Makari / Manila 1988, Claretian / St. Paul / Divine Word. 1662 p.; 2 maps. $15. 971-501-283-3 [NTAbs 33,375].

1879 **Federici** Tommaso, Per conoscere lui I-III 1987s ➤ 3,216; 4,1892: ᴿCiVit 44 (1989) 96s (D. *Camiciotti*); Teresianum 40 (1989) 600s (M. D. *Sánchez*).

1880 *a) Fee* Gordon D., Reflections on commentary writing; – *b) Perkins* Pheme, Commentaries; windows to the text; – *c) Bruner* F. Dale, The why and how of commentary; – *d) Peterson* Eugene H., Some of my favorites: TTod 46 (1989s) 387-392 / 393-8 / 399-404 / 405-410.

1881 ᴱ**Gaebelein** Frank E., *Polcyn* Richard P., Expositor's Bible Commentary 4. 1 Kings - Job, 1988 ➤ 4,1894: ᴿBS 146 (1989) 466 (T. L. *Constable*: all fine; YAMAUCHI's Ezra 'unusually strong'); CriswT 1 (1987) 413s (G. *Galeotti*, 7); WestTJ 51 (1989) 162s (A. M. *Harman*, 7).

1882 ᴱ**Hoerber** R. G., Concordia self-study Bible [1985 NIV study Bible with indicated Lutheran additions or modifications. St. Louis 1986, Concordia. xxiv-1974 + 156 p.; 59 maps; ill. 0-570-00505-1 [NTAbs 33,93].

1883 ᴱ**Mays** James L., *al.*, Harper's Bible Commentary 1988 ➤ 4,1895: ᴿNewTR 2,3 (1989) 100s (Barbara E. *Reid*); TS 50 (1989) 571-3 (J. P. M. *Walsh*: first-rate); TTod 46 (1989s) 212.214 (F. J. *Matera*).

1884 **Owens** J. J., Analytical key to the Old Testament, 4 [first to appear] Isaiah-Malachi. GR 1989, Baker. xi-941 p. 0-8010-6713-8 [BL 90,149, J. H. *Eaton*].

1885 **Parker** T. H. L., CALVIN's OT commentaries I. 1986 ➤ 2,1357 ... 4,1897: ᴿHeythJ 30 (1989) 202 (Susan H. *Moore*); JBL 108 (1989) 133-5 (R. *Zachman*: his eighth book on Calvin); ScotJT 42 (1989) 125-7 (R. S. *Wallace*).

1886 ᴱ**Sheppard** G. T., The Geneva Bible (the Annotated New Testament, 1602 ed.) [+ *al.*, background essays]: Pilgrim Classic Commentaries 1. NY 1989, Pilgrim. vii-312 p. $30; pa. $15. 0-8298-0789-6; 5-3 [NTAbs 33,378]. – ᴿTTod 46 (1989s) 463 (B. M. *Metzger*).

1887 ᴱ**Smeets** J. R., *al.*, La Bible de MACÉ de la Charité [13ᵉ s.; 1-6 ➤ 3,4160; 4,4391 etc.], 7. Apocalypse, ᴱ**Lops** Ritt: Publications Romanes 10,1-7. Leiden [1964-] 1986, Univ. lxiii-263 p. 90-0406-758-2.

1888 **Solms** Élisabeth de, sr. Bible chrétienne; traduction française sur les textes originaux et choix de commentaires de la Tradition, II Les quatre Évangiles; II* Commentaires, par *Jean-Nesmy* Claude, concordance *Miville-Dechêne* Cécile, [1988, also P/Desclée, 2-7189-0375-9 (Canada 2-88-129078-X) =] 1982 → 64,4135 ... 1,4155: ᴿÉTRel 64 (1989) 285-7 (E. *Cuvillier*: admiration, d'abord, ensuite réserves); NRT 111 (1989) 923s (V. *Roisel*).

1889 **Stanton** Elizabeth C., *al.*, The woman's Bible, I. Comments on Gn [through] Dt; II. Jos-Rev. Salem NH 1988 = 1896, Ayer. 152 p.; 217 p. $25 [RelStR 16, 58, Kathryn A. *Rabuzzi*].

VI. Libri historici VT

E1 **Pentateuchus, Torah** .1 *Textus, commentarii.*

1890 **Bianchi** Enzo, Introduzione al Pentateuco. Magnano VC 1989, Qi-qajon. 37 p.; maps.

1890* *Christensen* Duane L., *Narucki* Marcel, The Mosaic authorship of the Pentateuch: JEvTS 32 (1989) 465-472 [< ZIT 90,228].

1891 ᴱ**Gigineišvili** Bak'ar, *Kikvidze* C'otne, Cignni dzvelisa aġt'k'vmisani nakveti 1: Sesak'misaj, Czamoslvataj: The books of the OT, I. Genesis, Exodus, (in Georgian) from all existing manuscripts: Monuments of Old Georgian Literature 11/1. Tbilisi 1989, Mec'niereb. 640 p.; Russian summary p. 59s.

1892 **Goulet** Richard, La philosophie de Moïse ... préphilonien/Pentateuque 1987 → 3,1849; 4,1902: ᴿAntClas 58 (1989) 388-390 (J. *Wankenne*: scandalisera maints spécialistes); JTS 40 (1989) 590-602 (D. T. *Runia*; really about PHILO); RÉG 102 (1989) 615s (Yvonne *Vernière*); SR 18 (1989) 92s (G. M. de *Durand*).

1893 ᴱ**Radice** Roberto, (*Reale* G.), FILONE di Alessandria, La filosofia mosaica; la creazione del mondo secondo Mosè; le allegorie delle leggi: Classici del Pensiero, 1987 → 4,1906: ᴿNRT 111 (1989) 439-441 (X. *Jacques*); RÉG 102 (1989) 617 (P. *Nautin*); ScripTPamp 21 (1989) 697s (M. *Lluch-Baixauli*); VigChr 43 (1989) 191-3 (D. T. *Runia*: excellent despite impression of untidy bits and pieces).

E1 *Pentateuchus* .2 **Introductio; Fontes JEDP.**

1894 **Friedman** Richard E., Who wrote the Bible? 1987 → 3,1857; 4,1907: ᴿCBQ 51 (1989) 321-3 (L. *Boadt*: narrow viewpoint; chooses questions to which he can give a snap answer; reviewed 'by notable scholars in such bastions of current literary taste as the Los Angeles Times book review section', July 26, 1987 by J. *Sanders*).

1895 *Minette de Tillesse* C., Tradição javista: RBBras 6 (1989) 6-156 [< ZAW 102,284].

1896 *Monloubou* Louis, Du nouveau sur le Pentateuque? [*Rendtorff* R., Introduction*ᵀ* 1989]: EsprVie 99 (1989) 670-2.

1897 *Nicholson* E.W., P as an originally independent source in the Pentateuch [against *Cross* F., *Tengström* S.]: IrBSt 10 (1988) 192-206 [< OTAbs 12, 137].

1898 **Paran** Meir, [d. 1985; ᴱ*Haran* M.], ❺ Forms of the priestly style in the Pentateuch; patterns, language, usages, syntactic structures [diss. 1984]. J 1989, Magnes. 400 p.; Eng. xvi. $23.50. 965-223-692-6 [BL 90,88, J. W. *Rogerson*].

1899 **Paul** Maarten J., Het archimedisch punt van de Pentateuchkritik; een historisch en exegetisch onderzoek naar de verhouding van Deuteronomium en de reformatie van koning Josia (2 Kon. 22-23). Haag 1988, Boekencentrum. 391 p. ƒ55 pa. 90-239-1185-7. – ᴿBS 146 (1989) 108 (E. H. *Merrill*: dates Dt earlier); ETL 65 (1989) 157 (E. *Eynikel*); Streven 56 (1988s) 948s (P. *Beentjes*); TsTNijm 29 (1989) 287 (A. *Schoors*).

1900 **Terino** A., L'origine [mosaica] del Pentateuco 1986 ⇥ 4,1914: ᴿProtestantesimo 44 (1989) 123s (J. A. *Soggin*: non c'è motivo per polemica 'evangelica').

1901 ᴱ**Tigay** Jeffrey H., Empirical models [favor JEPD] 1985 ⇥ 1,315... 4,1915: ᴿTLZ 114 (1989) 590-2 (H.-J. *Zobel*).

1902 — *Baker* David W., 'Reverse archaeology' — disconstruction of texts; a critique of Jeffrey TIGAY: ProcGLM 9 (1989) 34-48.

1903 **Whybray** R. N., The making of the Pentateuch 1987 ⇥ 3,1863; 4,1917: ᴿCBQ 51 (1989) 138s (J. *Blenkinsopp*); RivB 37 (1989) 469-485 (A. *Fanuli*); SWJT 32,1 (1989s) 45s (H. B. *Hunt*); VT 39 (1989) 110-6 (J. A. *Emerton*).

E1.3 *Pentateuchus, themata.*

1904 *Boorer* Suzanne, The importance of a diachronic approach; the case of Genesis-Kings: CBQ 51 (1989) 195-208.

1905 ᵀᴱ**Chavel** Charles B., Encyclopedia of Torah thoughts. NY 1980, Shiloh. xiv-710 p. [cf. ᴱ*Chavel* D., ❺ r. BAHIYA, Be'ur 'al ha-Torah, 400 p. 1977 ⇥ 62,2156].

1906 **Coote** Robert B., *Ord* Daniel R., The Bible's first historian; from Eden to the court of David with the Yahwist [on justice and property]. Ph 1989, Fortress. x-308 p. $25. 0-8006-0878-X [BL 90,71, B. P. *Robinson*]. – ᴿExpTim 101 (1989s) 119 (R. N. *Whybray*: dated under freedom-promoting David, not oppressive Solomon); Paradigms 5 (1989) 160s (K. H. *Wynn*).

1907 *Crüsemann* Frank, Der Pentateuch als Tora; Prolegomena zur Interpretation seiner Endgestalt: EvT 49 (1989) 250-267.

1908 *Domb* Cyril, The Torah concept of leadership: ⇥ 100, ᶠJAKOBOVITZ I., Tradition 1986, 117-130.

1909 *Goodenough* Erwin R., PHILO's exposition of the Law and his De vita Mosis [1933]: ⇥ 268*, ᴱFRERICHS, Goodenough 1986, 63-75.

1910 **Halpern** Baruch, The first historians; the Hebrew Bible and history 1988 ⇥ 4,d139: ᴿBA 52 (1989) 152 (V. *Matthews*); TTod 46 (1989s) 116 (R. D. *Nelson*); TS 50 (1989) 573s (W. T. *Miller*).

1911 **Hughes** Jeremy, The chronology of the Hebrew Bible [schematic in both D and P]: diss. Oxford 1986. 303 p. BRD-85478. – DissA 50 (1989s) 710-A.

1912 **Lohfink** N., Studien zum Pentateuch 1988 ⇥ 4,223: ZAW 101 (1989) 468 (H.-C. *Schmitt*).

1913 *a*) *Pury* Albert de, *Römer* Thomas, Le Pentateuque en question; position du problème et brève histoire de la recherche; – *b*) *Ska* Jean-Louis, Quelques remarques sur Pg et la dernière rédaction du Pentateuque; – *c*) *Vermeylen* Jacques, Les premières étapes littéraires de

la formation du Pentateuque; – *d*) *Crüsemann* Frank, Le Pentateuque, une Tora; prolégomènes à l'interprétation de sa forme finale (ᵀ*Amsler* Samuel): ➤ 601, Pentateuque 1987/9, 9-80 / 95-125 / 149-197 / 339-360.
1914 *Schunck* Klaus-Dietrich, Der alttestamentliche Torabegriff [unveröffentlicht]: ➤ 349, AT 1989, 243-255.
1915 *a*) *Solomon* Anne M., The structure of the Chronicler's history; a key to the organization of the Pentateuch; – *b*) *Coats* George W., The form-critical problem of the Hexateuch: Semeia 46 (1989) 51-64 (3-10) / 65-73.
1916 *Tengström* Sven, Exegetisk metod och dateringsproblem i pentateukforskning: SvEx 54 (1989) 207-225.

E1.4   **Genesis;** *textus, commentarii.*

1917 **Boice** James M., Genesis, an expositional commentary II (12,1-36,43) 1985 ➤ 2,1381; 4,1938: ᴿWestTJ 50 (1988) 175-7 (B. L. *Johnson*).
1918 *Clifford* Richard J., *Murphy* Roland E., Genesis: ➤ 384, NJBC (1989s) 8-43.
1919 **Díez Macho** A., Genesis: Targum Palaestinense 1, 1988 ➤ 4,1700: ᴿCommSev 22 (1989) 87 (M. *de Burgos*).
1920 **Gowan** E., From Eden to Babel [NICOT Gn 1-11]. GR/E 1989, Eerdmans/Handsel. £5. 0-8028-0337-7 / 0-905312-85-6. – ᴿExpTim 100 (1988s) 429 (C. S. *Rodd*).
1921 ᵀᴱ**Harl** Marguerite, La Genèse... Septante 1986: ➤ 2,1384*... 4,1943: ᴿCiuD 202 (1989) 501-3 (J. L. del *Valle*); EstBib 47 (1989) 269-272 (J. *Trebolle*); RechSR 76 (1988) 301s (P. *Lamarche*); RivStoLR 25 (1989) 334-7 (P. *Sacchi*, anche su Lév.); ZkT 111 (1989) 90s (J. M. *Oesch*).
1922 **Hurwitz** Israel M., Jacob ben Isaac ASHKENAZI of Yanow, Ze'enach u-Re'enah, Book of Genesis, ᴱ*Schultz* Joseph P. Ph 1985, Dropsie College. 30 p. + ☻ 418.
1923 **Isabelle de la Source** sr., La Genèse: Lire la Bible avec les Pères 1, 1988 ➤ 4,1944: ᴿBLitEc 90 (1989) 423 (R. *Cabié*); NVFr 63 (1988) 238 (S. *Maza*).
1924 **Kamesar** Adam, Studies in JEROME's 'Quaestiones hebraicae in Genesim'; the work as seen in the context of Greek scholarship: diss. Oxford 1987. 320 p. BRD-85470. – DissA 50 (1989s) 682-A.
1924* *Kasher* Hannah, ☻ The unpublished introduction to KIMḤI's allegorical commentary on Genesis: KirSef 62 (1988s) 873-885.
1925 *Lamirande* Émilien, Le masculin et le féminin dans la tradition alexandrine; le commentaire de DIDYME l'Aveugle sur la 'Genèse': ScEspr 41 (1989) 137-165.
1926 **Neri** U., Genesi... la grande tradizione 1986 ➤ 2,1386... 4,1948: ᴿAnStoEseg 6 (1989) 313-5 (M. *Miegge*); RivStoLR 25 (1989) 370-2 (P. G. *Borbone*).
1927 **Neusner** J., Genesis Rabbah 1985 ➤ 1,1960: ᴿAbr-Nahrain 27 (1989) 184 (T. *Muraoka*).
1928 ᴱ**Paramelle** Joseph, (*Lucchesi* Enzo), PHILON d'Alexandrie, Questions sur la Genèse II 1-7, 1984 ➤ 65,1704... 3,1895: ᴿJAOS 109 (1989) 119s (M. E. *Stone*); StPhilonAn 1 (1989) 134-144 (J. R. *Royse*).
1929 **Petit** F., Catenae Gn Ex II 1986 ➤ 2,1388... 4,1952: ᴿJbÖsByz 39 (1989) 336s (W. *Lackner*).
1930 **Roop** E. F., Genesis. Scottdale 1987, Herald. 350 p. $18. 0-8361-3443-5. – ᴿÉTRel 64 (1989) 110s (J. *Rennes*: ne s'adresse pas aux spécialistes; traduction française souhaitable).

1931 **Ross** Allen P.,   Creation and blessing, a guide to the study and exposition of Genesis 1988 ➤ 4,1952*; $30.   0-8010-7748-6. – ᴿAndrUnS 27 (1989) 155s (H. K. *LaRondelle*).

1932 **Sarna** Nahum M., Genesis: JPS Torah comm.   Ph 1989, Jewish Publ. xxxi-414 p.   0-8276-0326-6 [OIAc N89]. – ᴿSWJT 32,3 (1989s) 50 (F. B. *Huey*); TTod 46 (1989s) 356.358 (P. D. *Miller* both also on *Levine* B. Lv.). **Scharbert** Josef,   Genesis (12-50): NEchter 16, 1986 ➤ 2258.

1933 ᵀᴱ**Strickman** H. N.,   *Silver* A. M.,   Iʙɴ Eᴢʀᴀ's commentary on the Pentateuch; Genesis (Bereshit).   NY 1988, Menorah. 0-9322-3207-8 [BL 90,153].

1934 **Townsend** John T., Midrash Tanhuma (S. *Buber* recension), I. Genesis. Hoboken 1989, ᴋᴛᴀᴠ. xvii-334 p. $39.50.   0-88125-087-2.

1935 **Weitzmann** Kurt, *Kessler* Herbert L.,   The Cotton Genesis 1986 ➤ 2,1395; 4,1955:   ᴿGnomon 61 (1989) 571 (O. *Demus*).

1936 **Wenham** G. J., Genesis 1-15: Word 1987 ➤ 3,1903; 4,1956:   BL (1989) 63 (J. C. L. *Gibson*); EvQ 61 (1989) 86s (R. W. L. *Moberly*); JTS 40 (1989) 151-4 (W. J. *Houston*); RB 96 (1989) 451s (J. *Loza*).

1937 **Westermann** Claus, Genesis, ᵀ*Scullion* J. 1984-7 ➤ 65,1711 ... 4,1957: ᴿCriswT 1 (1987) 404s & 2 (1987s) 162-4 (G. L. *Klein*); JTS 40 (1989) 146-151 (J. A. *Emerton*, lengthy comment on the overall excellent translation).

1938 **Westermann** Claus,   Genesis, a practical commentary 1987, Eerdmans ➤ 3,1906; also E 1988, Clark; £10; 0-567-29160-1:   ᴿBL (1989) 63 (J. *Gibson*) 64 (A. G. *Auld* on the British edition, which does not have the Dutch subtitle, 'a practical commentary'); EvQ 61 (1989) 262s (T. D. *Alexander*).

E1.5   *Genesis, themata.*

1939 *Abela* A., The Genesis genesis: MelT 39 (1988) 155-185 [on Rᴀᴅᴅᴀʏ-Sʜᴏʀᴇ (not exegetes) 1985; Rᴇɴᴅsʙᴜʀɢ G. 1986; OTAbs 12,161 'The Genesis Genesis'].

1940 *Brueggemann* Walter, Genesis: ➤ 377, Books 1 (1989) 21-45.

1941 **Coats** George W.,   Genesis with an introduction to narrative literature: FOTLit 1, 1983 ➤ 64,1953 ... 2,1402:   ᴿBZ 33 (1989) 291-3 (N. *Lohfink*).

1942 **Erffa** Hans M. von,   Ikonologie der Genesis; die christlichen Bildthemen aus dem Alten Testament und ihre Quellen.   Mü 1989, Deutscher Kunstverlag. I. 542 p. 3-422-06034-0.

1943 *a) Fox* Everett,   Can Genesis be read as a book?; – *b) Steinberg* Naomi, The genealogical framework of the family stories in Genesis: Semeia 46 (1989) 31-40 / 41-50.

1944 **Gradwohl** G.,   Uit Joodse bronnen; verklaring bij vijf Genesisteksten. Haag 1988, Boekencentrum. 112 p. ƒ19. – ᴿStreven 57 (1989s) 88 (P. *Beentjes*).

1945 **Jong** Saskia de,   Onvruchtbare moeders; een feministische lezing van Genesis.   Boxtel/Brugge 1989, KBS/Tabor.   109 p. ƒ20. – ᴿStreven 57 (1989s) 755 (P. *Beentjes*).

1946 ᵀᴱ**Maruani** B., *Cohen-Arazi* A., Midrach Rabba I Gn 1987 ➤ 4,1968: ᴿRHR 206 (1989) 171-181 (N. de *Lange*, notes critiques).

1947 **Rendsburg** Gary A.,   The redaction of Genesis 1986 ➤ 2,1412 ... 4,1971: ᴿJAOS 109 (1989) 675-7 (J. A. *Soggin*); RB 96 (1989) 127s (J. *Loza*).

1948 *Rendtorff* Rolf, [Gn 1-11 ‖ Ex 19-34] 'Covenant' as a structuring concept in Genesis and Exodus: JBL 108 (1989) 385-393.

1949 a) *Teske* Roland J., *Homo spiritualis* in St. AUGUSTINE's De Genesi contra Manichaeos; – b) *Vannier* Marie-Anne, Le rôle de l'hexaéméron dans l'interprétation augustinienne de la création: ➤ 696, StudPatr 10/22 (1987/9) 351-5 / 372-381.

1950 **Thompson** Thomas L., The origin tradition of ancient Israel, I. The literary formation of Genesis and Exodus 1-23: JStOT Sup 55, 1987 ➤ 3,1917; 4,1973: ᴿETL 65 (1989) 152-4 (J. *Lust*; refreshing, rewarding; sometimes rash; opposes J. VAN SETERS, supports E. BLUM); ÉTRel 64 (1989) 109s (Françoise *Smyth*); JBL 108 (1989) 327-330 (B.O. *Long*); ScripB 20 (1989s) 43s (J.R. *Duckworth*); RB 96 (1989) 129-131 (J. *Loza*); TLZ 114 (1989) 181s (S. *Herrmann*: 'Mischung aus Missverständnissen... oberflächlichen Argumenten und theologischem Unverständnis').

1950* *Weismann* F.J., Tipología en el 'De Genesi adversus manichaeos' de San AGUSTÍN: RelCult 33 (1987) 247-258.

1951 ᴱ**Youngblood** Ronald, The Genesis debate; persistent questions about Genesis and the Flood. Nv 1986, Nelson. 250 p. $11 pa. – ᴿCriswT 2 (1987s) 158s (P. *Patterson*: yes or no answers from experts).

E1.6 **Creatio, Genesis 1s.**

1952 **Alexandre** Monique, Le commencement du livre Gn I-V ... la Septante: Christianisme antique 3, 1988 ➤ 4,1976: ᴿJJS 40 (1989) 246s (A. *Salvesen*: packed with information but not user-friendly); LA 39 (1989) 339s (F. *Manns*); VigChr 43 (1989) 413s (J. van *Winden*).

1953 ᵀᴱ**Alwan** Khalil, Mar Ya'aqob SERŪGĀGĀ, Quatre homélies métriques sur la création: CSCOr 508s, syri 214s. Lv 1989, Peeters. I. xlvii-108 p.; II. xxvii-135 p. 0070-0452.

1954 **Brito** Emilio, La création selon SCHELLING: Universum / BiblETL 80, 1987 ➤ 4,1980: ᴿRTLv 20 (1989) 72-75 (J. *Étienne*).

1955 *Brooke* George J., Creation in the biblical tradition: Zygon 22 (1987) 227-248 [< OTAbs 12,163].

1956 **Castel** F., 'Dio disse...' I primi undici capitoli della Genesi, ᵀ*Zardi* L., 1987 ➤ 3,1924; Lit. 10,000. 88-215-1218-5: ᴿBL (1989) 70 (J.R. *Porter*).

1957 **Cavedo** Romeo, *Ranon* Angelo, Le origini; i primi tre capitoli della Genesi: Quaderni biblici 5. R 1989, AVE. 87 p.

1958 ᴱ**Dales** R., *Gieben* S., R. GROSSETESTE, Hexaemeron [1232-5] 1982 ➤ 65,1723... 4,1985: ᴿAevum 63 (1989) 383s (P. *Rossi*).

1959 [SUNESEN Andreas, 4th archbishop of Lund, †1128, ᴱ*Gertz* M.C.] **Ebbesen** S., *Mortensen* L.B., Andreae Sunonis filii, Hexaemeron, I. praef. text.; II. Comm. indices: Corpus Philosophorum Danicorum Medii Aevi 11. K 1983/8, Dansk. Sprog./Lit. selskab. 568 p.; 6 pl. Dk 400. – ᴿTPhil 64 (1989) 267s (C.H. *Lohr*: wichtig nicht nur als theologischer Genesiskommentar).

1960 **Eberlein** K., Gott der Schöpfer... exegetisch ᴰ1986 ➤ 2,1423... 4,1987: ᴿÉTRel 63 (1988) 281 (T. *Römer*).

1961 a) *Gibert* P., Le monde comme création de Dieu; – b) *Römer* T., *al.*, La création dans l'AT: ➤ 450, ᴱ*Cardon* P., Dieu 1987/8...

1962 *Gołębiewski* Marian, ❷ Le sens théologique de la création dans l'AT: STWsz 26,1 (1988) 37-52; franç. 52s.

1962* *Gounelle* André, S'intéresser à la création [suivi de '?' en tête des pages mais pas dans le titre]: ÉTRel 64 (1989) 59-69.

1963 *Haag* Ernst, Schöpfungsgeheimnis und Heilsoffenbarung; eine biblische Antwort auf die Herausforderung des christlichen Glaubens durch die Neue Religiosität: RUntHö 32 (1989) 358-366 [< ZIT 90,135].

1963* **Howell** A., Who made you? NY 1989, Praeger. 174 p. $35; pa. $15 [TS 51,187].

1964 *Judisch* Douglas M. L., The length of the days of creation [24 hours; any other hypothesis derives from evolution]: ConcordiaTQ 52 (1988) 265-271 [< OTAbs 12,270].

1965 **Kikawada** I., *Quinn* A., Before Abraham was... Gn 1-11, 1985 ➤ 1,2010 ... 3,1934: RAsbJT 44,2 (1989) 100s (E. E. *Carpenter*).

1965* *a) Lewis* Jack P., The days of creation; an historical survey of interpretation; – *b) Lavallee* Louis, AUGUSTINE on the Creation-days: JEvTS 32 (1989) 433-456 / 457-464 [< ZIT 90,228].

1966 **Marlière** F., Et leurs yeux s'ouvrirent [...la création]. Sainte-Foy QUÉ 1988, Sigier. x-395 p. [NRT 112,143s].

1967 *Moltmann* Jürgen, ⓂTeremtes... Creation, covenant and glory; introduction to a consultation on Karl BARTH's doctrine of creation [Leuenberg 14.VII.1987], T*Szathmáry* S.: TSzem 32 (1989) 140-6.

1968 **O'Shaughnessy** T. J., Creation and the teaching of the Qur'an: BibOrPont 40, 1985 ➤ 1,2018 ... 3,1939: RNRT 111 (1989) 630s (J. *Scheuer*).

1969 *a) Pelikan* Jaroslav, Creation and causality in the history of Western thought; – *b) Clements* R. E., Claus WESTERMANN on Creation in Genesis [+ Clements bibliog.]; – *c) Bellinger* William H., Maker of heaven and earth; the Old Testament and creation theology; – *d) Kirkpatrick* William D., A theology of creation; confession and prolegomena; – *e) Wade* Charles R. [sermon on Romans 1,18-32] Good, but broken: SWJT 32,2 (1989s) 10-16 / 17-24 [25s] / 27-35 / 36-48 / 6-9.

1970 *Pinnock* Clark H., Climbing out of a swamp; the evangelical struggle to understand the creation texts: Interpretation 43 (1989) 143-155.

1971 *Prokurat* Michael, Orthodox perspectives on creation: SVlad 33 (1989) 331-349.

1972 *Prouvost* Géry, Approche herméneutique d'une méthodologie propre à la métaphysique chrétienne... iii. Exégèse de Genèse I,1 - II, 4a et reprise spéculative: RThom 89 (1989) 622 ... 627-9.

E**Radice** Roberto, *al.* (T*Kraus Reggiani* Clara...), FILONE... La creazione 1987 ➤ 1893.

1973 *Rendtorff* Rolf, L'histoire biblique des origines (Gen 1-11) dans le contexte de la rédaction 'sacerdotale' du Pentateuque, T*Amsler* Samuel: ➤ 601, Pentateuque 1987/9, 83-94.

1974 TE**Rosenthal** Franz, El-TABARI, History 1, General introduction and from the Creation to the Flood: Bibl. Persica. Albany 1989, SUNY. xx-413 p. 0-88706-563-5 [OIAc Ja90].

1975 **Savasta** Carmelo, Forme e strutture in Gen. 1-11: Ricerche e Proposte 3, 1988; 160 p. Lit. 15.000; 88-7820-018-2: RBL (1989) 92 (W. G. E. *Watson*: mathematician's chiastic analysis, more suitable for an article); RivB 37 (1989) 246s (A. *Bonora*).

Schubert Mathias, Schöpfungstheologie bei Kohelet, Diss. 1986/9 ➤ 3356.

1976 **Schwarz** H., Die biblische Urgeschichte; Gottes Traum von Mensch und Welt: Tb 1068. FrB 1989, Herder. 158 p. DM 13. 3-451-08608-5. – RZAW 101 (1989) 476 (H. C. *Schmitt*: Predigtreihe; Texte und Inhalt).

1977 *Ska* Jean-Louis,   Creazione e liberazione nel Pentateuco: ➤ 376,
Creazione 1989, (9-) 13-31.

1978 **Tsumura** David T.,   The earth and the waters in Genesis 1 and 2; a
linguistic investigation: JStOT Sup 83. Sheffield 1989. 201 p. £22.50.
1-85075-208-7 [OIAc S89]. – ᴿExpTim 101 (1989s) 211 (J. *Day*: *tiamat* no,
dragon-conflict yes).

1979 *Nodes* Daniel J., [Gen 1,2] Benevolent winds and the Spirit of God in
De laudibus Dei of DRACONTIUS [after 490 A.D.]: VigChr 43 (1989)
282-292.

1980 *Kamienska* Anna, [Gn 1,4...] ✪ 'God saw that it was good'; STWsz
26,1 (1988) 262-6.

Gen. 1,26: imago Dei

1981 **Brown** Richard G.,   The image of God; theological ethics for human
creative genetic engineering: diss. Univ. Pittsburgh 1989. 470 p. 89-21363.
– DissA 50 (1989s) 1701-A.

1981* **Erhueh** H.,   Vatican II; image of God in man. R 1987, Pont. Univ.
Urbaniana. 324 p. [TS 51,187].

1982 **Hall** Douglas J., Imaging God 1986 ➤ 2,1456 ... 4,2015: ᴿRelStT 7,1
(1987) 74s (D. *Skoyles*); TLZ 114 (1989) 59s (D. *Mendt*).

1983 *Hobbel* Arne J.,   The imago Dei in the writings of ORIGEN: ➤ 696, 10th
Patristic, 21 (1989) 301-7.

1984 **Hoekema** Anthony, Created in God's image 1986 ➤ 2,1456; 3,1960:
ᴿCriswT 2 (1987s) 188-190 (D. L. *Akin*).

1984* **Hughes** Philip E., The true image; the origin and destiny of man in
Christ. GR/Leicester 1989, Eerdmans/Inter-Varsity. ix-430 p. £10 [TLZ
115, 914, C. *Frey*]. 0-8028-0314-8 / IVP 0-85110-680-3. – ᴿExpTim 101
(1989s) 218s (T. *Gorringe*).

1985 **Jónsson** Gunnlaugur A.,   The image of God; Genesis 1:26-28 in a
century of OT research [diss. Lund, ᴰ*Mettinger* T.]: ConBib OT 26, 1988
➤ 4,2017; Sk 188: ᴿBL (1989) 80 (R. *Davidson*); CBQ 51 (1989) 737
(M. D. *Guinan*: surprisingly concludes to a current consensus); RB 96
(1989) 608s (J. *Loza*); ZAW 101 (1989) 156s (H.-C. *Schmitt*).

1986 *Klein* Jean-Louis,   L'homme à l'image de Dieu: ÉTRel 64 (1989)
421-8.

1987 **Leavy** Stanley A., In the image of God; a psychoanalyst's view. NHv
1988, Yale Univ. $18. – ᴿCCurr 39 (1989s) 234-6 (K. A. *Loomis*).

1987* *Rava* Eva C., L'uomo immagine e somiglianza di Dio in S. BERNARDO
di Chiaravalle: Lateranum 55 (1989) 345-368.

1988 *Roberts* Carl W., Imagining God; who is created in whose image?:
RRelRes 30 (1989) 325-8 [< zɪᴛ 89,521].

1988* *Ross* Ellen M., Human persons as images of the divine; a reconsideration: UnSemQ 43 (1989) 93-112 [< zɪᴛ 90,25].

1989 *Siotis* Markos A., ✪ 'I am an image of your ineffable glory': TAth 60
(1989) 221-251.

1990 *Stendebach* F. J., *ṣælæm* 'Bild': ➤ 913, TWAT 6,6s (1989) 1046-1055.

1991 *Vogels* Walter, De mens, schepsel en beheerder (Gen 1, 26-28):
CollatVL 19 (1989) 263-291.

1992 **Cohen** Jeremy, 'Be fertile and increase; fill the earth and master it'; the ancient and medieval career of a biblical text. Ithaca NY 1989, Cornell Univ. xv-375 p. $45 [JBL 109,374].

E1.7   *Genesis 1s:*   **Bible and myth [➤ M3.5].**

1993 **Allen** James P., Genesis in Egypt; the philosophy of ancient Egyptian creation accounts. NHv 1988, Yale Univ. x-114 p.; 4 pl. [BO 46,758].

1994 **Anderson** B. W., Creation versus Chaos 1989 = 1987 (= 1967 + 1985 lecture) ➤ 3,1973; 4,2029: ᴿScotJT 42 (1989) 404s (J. *Taylor*: surprisingly little on *ex nihilo*).

1995 **Bilolo** Mubabinge, Le créateur et la création dans la pensée memphite et amarnienne; approche synoptique du 'Document philosophique de Memphis' et du 'Grand Hymne Théologique' d'Echnaton: Académie de la Pensée Africaine 1, La pensée de l'Égypte et de la Nubie ancienne 3. Kinshasa 1988, Publ. Univ. Africaines. 352 p.; ill. [OIAc S89].

1996 **Bottéro** Jean, *Kramer* Samuel N., Lorsque les dieux faisaient l'homme: Mythologie mésopotamienne. P 1989, Gallimard. 755 p. 2-07-071382-2 [OIAc N89].

1997 **Dalley** Stephanie, Myths from Mesopotamia; creation, the flood, Gilgamesh, and others, tr. introd. notes . Ox 1989, Univ. xxi-337 p. £35. 0-19-814397-4 [BL 90, 119, W. G. *Lambert*].

1998 ᴱ**Derousseaux** Louis [*Blanquart* Fabien], La création dans l'Orient Ancien, ACFÉB 1985/7 ➤ 3,521; 4,2032: ᴿBLitEc 90 (1989) 55s (L. *Monloubou*); IndTSt 25 (1988) 101-3 (L. *Legrand*); Protestantesimo 44 (1989) 122 (J. A. *Soggin*); RTPhil 121 (1989) 97s (T. *Römer*); ScEspr 41 (1989) 242s (P.-É. *Langevin*); ZkT 111 (1989) 91s (J. M. *Oesch*).

1999 **Furley** David, [➤ a844] The Greek cosmologists, I. The formation of the atomic theory and its earliest critics 1987 ➤ 4,2035; ᴿClasR 39 (1989) 249s (D. W. *Graham*).

2000 **Gibert** Pierre, Bible, mythes et récits de commencement 1986 ➤ 2,1468*... 4,2036: ᴿCBQ 51 (1989) 323-5 (M. *Kolarcik*: sapiential accounts surprisingly not included).

2001 *Habbi* Joseph, Sangue e creazione dell'uomo nella letteratura mesopotamica: ➤ 759, Sangue VI, 1987/9, 15-24.

2002 *Heller* Jan, Ⓜ The struggle of Old Testament tradition with myth, ᵀ*Fóris* Mrs. Eva: TSzem 32 (1989) 23-25.

2003 *Hood* Robert E., Creation myths in Nigeria; a theological commentary: JRelTht 45,2 (Wsh 1989) 70-... [< ZIT 89,372].

2004 *Hübner* Kurt, Ⓜ Myth, logos and the specifically religious element as the three basic elements of the Christian faith; ᵀ*Fóris* Mrs. Eva: TSzem 32 (1989) 26-32.

2005 **Hutter** Manfred, Altorientalische Vorstellungen von der Unterwelt; Literar- und religionsgeschichtliche Überlegungen zu 'Nergal und Ereškigal': OBO 63, 1985 ➤ 1,2058.a687... 3,1978: ᴿBZ 33 (1989) 129s (V. *Fritz*); OLZ 84 (1989) 163-7 (V. *Afanasieva*, J. *Levin*); ZAss 89 (1989) 124-7 (D. O. *Edzard*).

2006 **Kirkpatrick** Patricia G., The OT and folklore study: JStOT Sup 62, 1988 ➤ 4,2039: ᴿBL (1989) 81 (J. R. *Porter*); ETL 65 (1989) 155s (J. *Lust*); ÉTRel 64 (1989) 429s (D. *Lys*); JTS 40 (1989) 516-8 (B. O. *Long*); OTAbs 12 (1989) 104s (L. *Boadt*); TLZ 114 (1989) 662s (Julia *Männchen*); VT 39 (1989) 256 (J. A. *Emerton*); ZAW 101 (1989) 158 (H.-C. *Schmitt*).

2007 **Kramer** Samuel N., *Maier* John, Myths of Enki, the crafty god. NY 1989, Oxford-UP. viii-272 p. 0-19-505520-0 [OIAc N89].

2008 **Lincoln** Bruce, Myth, cosmos and society 1086 → 2,1477; 4,2043: ᴿJAAR 57 (1989) 654-6 (D. A. *Miller*).

2009 **Miller** James, Measures of wisdom; the cosmic dance in classical and Christian antiquity: Studies in the Relations of Art and Literature 1. Toronto 1986, Univ. xiii-652 p.; 21 fig. [Phoenix-Toronto 44/1, 88-92, J. *Pépin*].

2010 *Moran* William L., Notes on Anzu: AfO 35 (1988) 24-29.

2011 *Müller* Hans-Peter, Eine neue babylonische Menschenschöpfungs-erzählung im Licht keilschriftlicher und biblischer Parallelen — zur Wirklichkeitsauffassung im Mythos: Orientalia 58 (1989) 61-85.

2012 *Otzen* Benedikt, Kult und Mythos im AT aus skandinavischer Sicht [Europ. Theologenkongress W 1987]: KerDo 35 (1989) 23-33; Eng. 33.

2013 *Römer* Thomas, La redécouverte d'un mythe dans l'AT; la création comme combat [Ugarit]: ÉTRel 64 (1989) 561-573; 5 fig.; bibliog. 574s.

2014 *Votto* Silvano, La creazione dell'universo e il destino dell'uomo nel pensiero mesopotamico: → 376, Creazione 1989, 73-114.

2015 *Wambui Gachiri* Ephigenia, Myth on origins and other truths: AfER 39 (1989) 108-120.

E1.8   Genesis 1s: The Bible, the Church, and Science.

2015* a) *Ambrose* M. Devadass, Anthropology of Gen 1-2; – b) *Maroky* P., The Church on the science of evolution: IndTSt 26 (1989) 323-335 / 393-409.

2016 *Andrillat* Henri, L'univers né du vide [... astrophysique]: ÉTRel 64 (1989) 71-82.

2017 **Ballantyne** Edmund C., After DARWIN and the reconciliation of science and religion in nineteenth century North America: diss. ᴰ*Gerrish* B. Chicago 1989. – RelStR 16,190.

2018 **Barbiero** Flavio, La Bibbia senza segreti. Mi 1988, Rusconi. 468 p. Lit. 35.000. – ᴿHumBr 44 (1989) 601s (M. *Orsatti*: romanzo).

2019 **Bartholomew** D. J., God of chance 1984 → 65,1805... 4,3057: ᴿZygon 24 (1989) 109-115 (H. *Rolston*).

2020 **Berry** R. J., God and evolution; creation, evolution and the Bible 1988 → 4,2061: ᴿTLond 92 (1989) 70-72 (P. E. *Hodgson*).

2021 **Blumenberg** Hans, The genesis of the Copernican world [1978], ᵀ*Wallace* Robert M. CM 1987, MIT. xlviii-772 p. $40. – ᴿJRel 69 (1989) 608s (Hope *Cohen*). — pa. 1989; 824 p.; $17.50. 0-268-52144-X.

2022 *Bosshard* Stefan N., Erschafft die Welt sich selbst? 1985 → 1,2081*... 4,2064: ᴿTR 85 (1989) 246-8 (W. *Bröker*).

2023 *Braun* Heinrich, 'Eva' – die Mutter aller Menschen? [Monogenismus] – ein Forschungsbericht: ForumKT 4 (1988) 298s.

2024 *Brooke* John H., Science and the fortunes of natural theology; some historical perspectives: Zygon 24 (1989) 3-22.

2025 **Brown** Frank B., The evolution of DARWIN's religious views 1986 → 3,2011: ᴿJRel 69 (1989) 556s (D. R. *Breed*).

2026 **Brown** Hanbury, The wisdom of science; its relevance to culture and religion. C 1986, Univ. ix-194 p. £20; pa. £7 [HeythJ 31, 221, S. *Talmor*].

2027 **Brungs** Robert A., You see light breaking upon us; doctrinal perspectives on biological advance: ITEST (Institute for Theological

Encounter with Science and Technology). St. Louis 1989, Univ. $13 [TDig 36,357].

2028 **Bulhof** I. N., DARWIN's 'Origin of species'; betoverende wetenschap, een onderzoek naar de relatie tussen literatuur en wetenschap. Baarn 1988, Ambo. 166 p. *f* 39.50. 90-263-0850-7. – RTsTNijm 29 (1989) 86 (T. *Brattinga*).

2029 *Byl* John, Scripture and geologists: WestTJ [49 (1987) 1-34.257-304, *Young* D.] 51 (1989) 143-152; Young's rejoinder, 377-387.

2030 **Campbell** William, Le Coran et la Bible à la lumière de l'histoire et de la science. Marne-la-Vallée 1989, Farel. 328 p. – RIslamochristiana 15 (1989) 264s (J.-M. *Gaudeul*: réponse a M. BUCAILLE, pour lequel le Coran d'un seul auteur est plus 'révélation' que la Bible hétérogène).

2031 *Carroll* William E., Big bang cosmology, quantum tunneling from nothing, and creation: LavalTP 44 (1988) 59-75; franç. 59.

2032 **Catalan** J. F., *Moretti* J. M., Fè/Ciência [La foi devant la science], T. Porto 1989, Perpétuo Socorro. 108 p. – RHumT 10 (1989) 260s (J. *Monteiro*).

2033 *Clark* G. A., Alternative models of Pleistocene biocultural evolution; a response to FOLEY [R., 'cladistic' (not in Oxford Dict.; *kládos* means a branch) view of a single 'Garden of Eden' source in Africa for all human populations]: Antiquity [61 (1987) 380-392] 63 (1989) 153-9; 159-162, rejoinder.

2034 **Clayton** Philip, Explanation from physics to theology; an essay in rationality and religion. NHv 1989, Yale Univ. ix-230 p. $26.50. 0-300-04353-8 [TDig 37,47].

2035 **Coppens** Yves, Préambules; les premiers pas de l'homme. P 1988, Odile Jacob. 248 p. F 110. – RÉtudes 370 (1989) 414s (F. *Russo*).

2035* **Corsi** Pietro, Science and religion; BADEN-POWELL [father of Boy Scout founder] and the Anglican debate, 1800-1860. C 1988, Univ. 346 p. £32.50. 0-521-24245-2. – RExpTim 101 (1989s) 87s (C. A. *Russell*).

2036 *Delumeau* Jean, introd., Le savant et la foi; des scientifiques s'expriment: Présences. P 1989, Flammarion. 310 p. F 95. – REsprVie 99 (1989) 571s (J. *Milet*).

2037 *a*) *Demarchi* Franco, Fede, ideologia e scienza in Wilhelm SCHMIDT; – *b*) *Guariglio* Guglielmo, Valori e limiti del metodo comparativo schmidtiano; – *c*) *Huber* Hugo, Critiche e sviluppi dell'opera scientifica di W. Schmidt: ➤ 804, Schmidt 1986/9, 7-55 / 135-155 / 157-187.

2038 **Denton** Michel, Évolution, une théorie en crise [Eng. 1986 ➤ 4,2073]. P 1988, Londreys. 386 p. F 150. – RÉtudes 370 (1989) 345-350 (F. *Russo*) [> EsprVie 99 (1989) 518s (J. *Daoust*)].

2039 **Drees** W. B., Beyond the Big Bang; quantum cosmologies and God: diss. Vrije Univ. Amst. 1989, DHensen R. vii-236 p. [La Salle IL, Open Court]. – TsTNijm 29 (1989) 282s.

2040 EDurant John, Darwinism and divinity; essays on evolution and religious belief 1985 ➤ 2,426... 4,2077: RIrTQ 55 (1989) 251 (A. P. F. *Sell*); JRel 68 (1988) 180s (P. *Hefner*).

2040* *Emonet* Pierre-Marie, L'évolution, 'le style du Créateur': NVFr 64 (1989) 275-282.

2041 **Facchini** Fiorenzo, Evoluzione, uomo e ambiente; lineamenti di antropologia. T 1988, UTET. xvi-188 p.; ill. Lit. 48.000. – RCC 140 (1989,3) 441s (G. *Blandino*).

2041* **Finocchiaro** Maurice A., The GALILEO affair. Berkeley 1989, Univ. California. 382 p. [TS 51, 177, M. F. *McCarthy*].

2042 **Ford** Norman M., When did I begin? Conception of the human individual in history, philosophy and science. C 1988, Univ. xix-217 p. – ᴿCC 140 (1989,4) 575-585 (A. *Serra*).

2043 *Galleni* Lodovico, I programmi di ricerca scientifica e la teoria dell'evoluzione: FutUom 16,1 (1989) 85-97 [99-107, *Buiatti* M.].

2044 **Geisler** Norman, *Anderson* J. Kerby, Origin sciences [➤ 4,2086 'science']; a proposal for the creation-evolution controversy. GR 1987, Baker. 198 p. $9. – ᴿCriswT 3 (1989) 414-6 (K. *Spencer*).

2045 *Gerhart* Mary, *Russell* Allan M., A generalized conception of text applied to both scientific and religious objects: Zygon 22 (1987) 299-316 [< OTAbs 12,132].

2046 *Giannoni* Paolo, Contro il concordismo [*Hawking* S., Dal big bang 1986; *Davies* P. 1984; *Barrow* J. & *Silk* J. 1985]: FutUomo 16,1 (1989) 59-75.

2047 **Gilkey** Langdon, Creationism on trial 1985 ➤ 2,1505... 4,2087: ᴿJRel 68 (1988) 72-77 (P. *Hefner*).

2048 — *Hefner* Philip, The significance of creationism (GILKEY L. 1985): JRel 68 (Ch 1988) 72-77.

2049 *Gilkey* Langdon, Nature, reality, and the sacred; a meditation in science and religion: Zygon 24 (1989) 283-298.

2050 **Gilson** Étienne, From Aristotle to Darwin and back again [1971], ᵀ*Lyon* J., 1984 ➤ 1,2112; 2,1506: ᴿIrTQ 55 (1989) 81s (J. *McEvoy*).

2051 *Habermas* Gary B., Paradigm shift; a challenge to naturalism: BS 146 (1989) 427-450.

2052 **Hawking** Stephen, Dal Big Bang ai buchi neri, ᵀ*Sosio* Libero. Mi 1988, Rizzoli. 217 p.; ill. Lit. 24.000. – ᴿLetture 44 (1989) 585s (G. *Arledler*: alcuni critici sono troppo mossi dalla compassione).

2053 **Hawking** Stephen W., Eine kurze Geschichte der Zeit; die Suche nach der Urkraft des Universums. Ha 1988, Rowohlt. 238 p. – ᴿTPhil 64 (1989) 140-3 (G. *Brüntrup*).

2054 *a)* *Hefner* Philip, The role of science in PANNENBERG's theological thinking; – *b)* *Tipler* Frank J., The omega point as eschaton; answers to Pannenberg's Questions for Scientists [Zygon 1981]: Zygon 24 (1989) 135-151 / 217-253 [153-185-215, *Wicken* J.; *Eaves* L.; 255-271, Pannenberg rejoinder].

2055 *Heller* Michał, ❷ *a)* L'évolution et la création; – *b)* De l'histoire des relations entre le créationisme et l'évolutionnisme: PrzPow 806 (1988) 66-72; franç. 72 / 808 (1988) 374-384; franç. 384.

2056 **Henderson** Charles P., God and science; the death and rebirth of theism 1986 ➤ 2,1512; 4,2092: ᴿRelStR 15 (1988) 244 (K. *Dodd*).

2057 *a)* **Houghton** John, Does God play dice? Leicester 1988, Inter-Varsity. 160 p. £4. 0-85110-791-5. – ᴿExpTim 100 (1988s) 317 (C. S. *Rodd*: weak on evolution); – *b)* *Stewart* I., Does God play dice? The mathematical chaos. Ox 1989, Blackwell. 317 p. £15; 0-631-16847-8. – ᴿExpTim 101 (1989s) 157s (D. J. *Bartholomew* notes *Houghton* J. same title).

2058 **Hübner** Jürgen, Der Dialog zwischen Theologie und Naturwissenschaften; ein bibliographischer Bericht 1987 ➤ 3,1036; 4,2093: ᴿTLZ 114 (1989) 58s (H.-P. *Gensichen*).

2059 **Hummel** Charles E., The GALILEO connection; resolving conflicts between science and the Bible 1986 ➤ 2,1514... 4,2094: ᴿCriswT 1 (1987) 436-8 (K. *Spencer*).

2060 **Jaki** Stanley L., The savior of science. Wsh 1988, Regnery. 260 p. $11. – ᴿAnnTh 3 (1989) 382-7 (P. *Haffner*); TTod 46 (1989s) 226s (C. B. *Kaiser*: applies Augustinian fall/redemption to science itself).

2061 **Jaki** Stanley L., La strada della scienza e le vie verso Dio [1975s], ᵀ. Mi 1988, Jaca. 482 p. – ᴿAnnTh 3 (1989) 382-7 (P. *Haffner*).

2062 *a*) *Jaki* Stanley L., THOMAS and the universe; – *b*) *Beards* Andrew, Creator and causality, a critique of pre-critical objections: Thomist 53 (1989) 545-572 / 573-586.

2063 *Jans* Henk, Het universum volgens HAWKING [S., Brief history of time 1988]: Streven 57 (1989s) 407-422.

2063* *Jenssen* Hans-H., Der Christ angesichts darwinistischer Entwicklungstheorien / Einige Gedanken zur Vererbungslehre: CLehre 42,9 (1989) 260-9 / 270-4 [< ZIT 89,744].

2064 *Jessberger* Rolf, Creationismus – kritisch betrachtet: Universitas 44 (1989) 342-353.

2065 **Johnson** Michael R., Genesis, geology and catastrophism; a critique of creationist science and biblical literalism. Exeter 1988, Paternoster. 171 p. [RHPR 69,91]. 0-85364-472-1. – ᴿExpTim 100,10 2d-top choice (1988s) 362s (C. S. *Rodd*).

2066 **Kenel** Sally A., Mortal gods; Ernest BECKER and fundamental theology [correlation of scientific and theological analyses]. Lanham MD 1988, UPA. 218 p. $12.75 pa. – ᴿHorizons 16 (1989) 169s (F. *Keck*).

2067 *Krafft* Fritz, KEPLER, Johannes (1571-1630): ➤ 911, TRE 18 (1989) 97-109.

2068 **Kummer** Christian, Evolution als Höherentwicklung des Bewusstseins; über die intentionellen Voraussetzungen der materiellen Selbstorganisation [Diss. 1983]: Symposium 80, 1987 ➤ 4,2104: ᴿTPhil 64 (1989) 144-6 (R. *Koltermann*).

2069 *Leonardi* Giuseppe, Criacionismo; um desaforo à Ciência e à Fé: REB 49 (1989) 144-154.

2069* *Livingstone* David N., The Darwinian diffusion; DARWIN and Darwinism, divinity and design: ChrSchR 19 (1989) 186-... [< ZIT 90,300].

2070 **Livingstone** David N., DARWIN's forgotten defenders; the encounter between evangelical theology and evolutionary thought 1987 ➤ 3,2047; 4,2108; ᴿBS 146 (1989) 103 (F. R. *Howe*); EvQ 61 (1989) 368s (D. W. *Bebbington*); WestTJ 51 (1989) 409-412 (D. G. *Hart*).

2070* **Lonchamp** Jean-Pierre, L'affaire Galilée. P 1988, Cerf-Salidés. 126 p. [RSPT 74, 269].

2071 ᴱLonergan Anne, *Richards* Caroline, Thomas BERRY and the new cosmology (3 items with responses]. Mystic CT c.1988, 23d. 112 p. $8. – ᴿCommonweal 115 (1988) 573s (L. S. *Cunningham*).

2072 *Lopes* António, *a*) Os Jesuitas pioneiros relativamente a Galileu? [*Thuillier* Pierre, La Recherche 195 (Jan. 1988) 88-92]: Brotéria 126 (1988) 499-516 [127 (1988) 375-383, o processo]; – *b*) O processo de Galileu, uma encenação? [*Redondi* P.]: Brotéria 128 (1989) 74-87. 166-180.

2073 *Marcozzi* Vittorio, Controversie evoluzionistiche attuali: CC 140 (1989,1) 31-45.

2074 *a*) *Martelet* Gustav, La teologia della scienza; un compito per domani? ᵀ*Poltronieri* Alberta; – *b*) *Valadier* Paul, La decisione morale, minacciata e necessaria; – *c*) *Ribaut* Jean-Pierre, L'uso rispettoso della natura: ➤ 756, Scienza 1988 = FutUom 16,2 (1989) 31-59 / 61-71 / 73-83.

2075 **Maury** Jean-Pierre, GALILÉE, le messager des étoiles: Découvertes. P 1986, Gallimard. 160 p. – ᴿRThom 89 (1989) 317 (J.-M. *Maldamé*; p. 309-326, 'Science et culture': la modernité, le bluff technologique; philosophies des sciences; nécessité d'une réconciliation des savoirs).

2076 **Mayr** Ernst, Toward a new philosophy of biology; observations of an evolutionist. CM 1988, Harvard/Belknap. 564 p. $35. – ᴿCCurr 39 (1989s) 361-3 (E. *Boyd*).

2077 **Midgley** Mary, Evolution as religion; strange hopes and stranger fears 1985 → 3,2051; $33; pa. $13: ᴿZygon 24 (1989) 275-8 (E. R. *Cruz*).

2077* **Moreland** J. P., Christianity and the nature of science — a philosophical investigation. GR 1989, Baker. 262 p. 0-8010-6249-7. – ᴿExpTim 101 (1989s) 158 (J. *Polkinghorne*).

2078 **Mounier** Frédéric, La création du monde; la Bible et la science face au mystère de nos origines; contradiction ou convergences? le sens caché des récits de la Genèse: Coll. C'est-à-dire 1. P 1989, Centurion. 125 p. F 54. – ᴿEsprVie 99 (1989) 473s (P. *Jay*).

2079 *Nebelsick* H. P., Circles of God; theology and science from the Greeks to Copernicus 1986 → 2,1533; 3,2056: ᴿHeythJ 30 (1989) 241 (J. *Roche*).

2081 **Peacocke** Arthur, God and the new biology 1986 → 2,1540... 4,2119: ᴿModT 6 (1989s) 118s (C. *Knight*).

2082 ᴱ**Pecker** J.-C., L'univers; des faits aux théories. P 1988, Belin. 228 p. 2-9029-1842-9 [ÉTRel 64,484].

2083 *a)* Piveteau J., *al.*, La création et l'évolution de l'homme; – *b)* Gisel P., *al.* [dialogue entre science et foi]: → 450, ᴱ*Cardon* P., Dieu 1987/8,...

2084 **Polkinghorne** John, *a)* One world; the interaction of science and theology 1986 → 2,1544; 4,2123: ᴿHeythJ 30 (1989) 241s (J. *Roche*). – *b)* Scienza e fede 1987 → 4,2124: ᴿFutUom 15,1 (1988) 95-98 (P. *Fortini*).

2085 **Polkinghorne** John, Science and creation; the search for understanding. Boston 1989, Shambhala. 128 p. $9. 0-87773-492-5. – ᴱExpTim 100,2 second-top choice (1988s) 42-44 (C. S. *Rodd*); ModT 6 (1989s) 119s (C. *Knight*); RelSt 25 (C 1989) 537s (K. *Ward*).

2086 **Polkinghorne** John C., Science and Providence; God's interaction with the wotld. L/Boston 1989, SPCK/Shambhala New Science Library. 114 p. $11. 0-281-04398-1 / US 0-87773-490-9. – ᴿExpTim 100,10 first choice (1988s) 361s (C. S. *Rodd*).

2087 **Pollard** William G., Transcendence and Providence; reflections of a physicist and [Anglican] priest. E 1987, Scottish Academic. xi-269 p. $17. – ᴿTS 50 (1989) 395s (F. R. *Haig*).

2088 **Poythress** Vern S., Science and hermeneutics, 6. Foundations of contemporary interpretation [*Kuhn* Thomas, The structure of scientific revelations (explaining hermeneutical shifts)]. GR 1988, Zondervan. 184 p. – ᴿBS 146 (1989) 463s (F. R. *Rowe*); SWJT 32,1 (1989s) 58 (E. E. *Ellis*).

2089 **Puddefoot** John, Logic and affirmation; perspectives in mathematics and theology: Theology and Science 9. E 1987, Scottish Academic (Gower). 212 p. $12.75. 0-7073-0520-9. – ᴿTLond 92 (1989) 435-7 (Chris *Wiltsher*: more serious than FIDDES V.).

2090 **Reale** G., *Antiseri* D., Historia del pensamiento cientifico I-III. Barc 1988, Herder. 617, -822, -1015 p. – ᴿBibFe 15 (1989) 324-6 (A. *Salas*: alabanzas).

2091 **Redondi** Pietro, Galileo heretic [Pope Urban arranged for him to 'cop a plea' and get condemnation for a minor charge (than against transubstantiation) 1983 → 64,2144], ᵀ*Rosenthal* Raymond. Princeton 1987, Univ./Hmw 1988, Penguin. x-356 p. £18. 0-7139-9007-4. – ᴿExpTim 100 (1988s) 280 [C. S. *Rodd* (Paidagogos): erudite-cum-fascinating]; JTS 40 (1989) 356 (G. R. *Evans*); PrzPow 815 (1989) 226-9 (W. *Waslutyński*); RelStR 15 (1989) 172 (D. R. *Janz*); SWJT 32,1 (1989) 73 (J. R. *Bush*: praise).

2092 *Remelts* Glenn A., The Christian Reformed Church and science, 1900-1930; an evangelical alternative to the fundamentalist and modernist responses to science: Fides et Historia 21 (1989) 61-... [< ZIT 89,327].

2093 **Roberts** Jon H., Darwinism and the divine in America; Protestant intellectuals and organic evolution, 1859-1900: 1988 → 4,2133: ᴿJTS 40 (1989) 357s (J. *Barr*); TTod 46 (1989s) 80.82s (C. *Hyers*).

2094 **Rolston** Holmes, Science and religion; a critical survey 1987 → 3,2067; 4,2134: ᴿJRel 68 (1988) 470s (F. *Brown*).

2095 ᴱ**Russell** R. J., *al.*, Physics, philosophy, and theology; a common quest for understanding: Vatican Observatory conference. Vatican 1988. 419 p. $30. 18 art. – ᴿRelSt 25 (1989) 542s (P. *Byrne*).

2096 *Russo* François, L'évolution, une théorie en crise [*Denton* M., 1985, franç. 1988]: Études 370 (1989) 345-350.

2097 *Silva G.* Sergio, ¿Evolución o creación?: TVida 29 (1988) 245-259.

2098 **Spanner** Douglas C., Biblical creation and the theory of evolution 1987 → 3,2073; 4,2142: ᴿEvQ 61 (1989) 183-5 (E. C. *Lucas*).

2098* *Spanner* Douglas, The Bible and Science: Churchman 103 (L 1989) 101-113 [< ZIT 89,573].

2099 **Spirito** Aldo, L'uomo alla ricerca di Dio; riflessioni di un biologo. R 1987, Ed. Internazionali. 137 p. Lit. 25.000. – ᴿCC 140 (1989,1) 406s (A. *Serra*).

2100 **Stanesby** Derek, Science, reason and religion. L 1988, Routledge. 210 p. £9 pa. 0-415-02657-1. – ᴿExpTim 100 (1988s) 439 (J. *Polkinghorne*).

2100* *Stengers* Isabelle, Nouvelle bifurcation; un ou plusieurs procès Galilée? Les affaires Galilée: dans ᴱSerres Michel, Éléments d'histoire des sciences (P 1989, Bordas; 576 p.) 223-250 [< RSPT 74, 252-263, J. *Courcier*].

2101 *Stenhouse* John, Science versus religion in nineteenth century New Zealand; Robert STOUT and Social Darwinism: Pacifica 2 (1989) 61-86.

2101* ᴱ**Stillings** Dennis, The theology of electricity; on the encounter and explanation of theology and science in the 17th and 18th centuries, ᵀ*Taraba* Wolfgang: Princeton Theol. Mg. 19. Allison Park PA 1989, Pickwick. xix-104 p. $12 [TS 51,785, F. R. *Haig*].

2102 **Stuhlhofer** Franz, Charles DARWIN — Weltreise zum Agnostizismus: Telos 2809. Berneck 1988, Schwengeler. 186 p. [TR 86,334-6, H.-J. *Zoche*].

2103 **Stuhlhofer** Franz, Naturforscher und die Frage nach Gott: Telos 522. Berneck 1988, Schwengeler. 134 p. Fs 7,80. – ᴿTPQ 137 (1989) 111s (K. *Rohregger*).

2103* **Taylor** Ian T., In the minds of men; DARWIN and the new world order². Toronto 1987, TFE. 498 p. $30; pa. $20. – ᴿGrace TJ 10 (1989) 105-8 (J. A. *Sproule*).

2104 *a*) *Tshibangu* Tarcisse, Teologia e Scienza; – *b*) *Del Re* Giuseppe, Scienza-Fede o scientismo-religione; La lezione di Teilhard: FutUom 15,1 (1988) 5-18 / 15,2 (1988) 5-22.

2104* **Tupini** Giorgio, Ipotesi sulla creazione; il nostro mondo e la nostra vita. T 1989, SEI. 197 p. Lit. 18.000. – ᴿCC 140 (1989,4) 412s (G. *Mellinato*: quadro sulla storia delle scienze).

2105 *Ullmann* R. A., Evolução e criação: Teocomunicação 81 (1988) 305-324 [< Stromata 45, 491].

2106 *Valera* Edmundo B., BERGSONIAN evolution; a reflection and discussion on the mystery of life: Laurentianum 30 (1989) 390-407.

2107 *Valle* José Luis del, El mundo y su origen; diálogo entre la ciencia y la fe: BibFe 15 (1989) 370-380.
2108 **Van Till** Howard J., *al.*, Science held hostage; what's wrong with creation science *and* evolutionism. DG 1988, Inter-Varsity. 189 p. $8. – ᴿWestTJ 51 (1989) 412-4 (R. C. *Newman*).
2109 *Vicuña* M., Teología bíblica, filosofía y ciencia: Theologika 3,1 (Lima 1988) 40-47 [< NTAbs 33,341].
2110 **Vollmert** Bruno, *al.*, Schöpfung [... Evolution]. Fr 1988, Beruf der Kirche. 112 p. – ᴿForumKT 4 (1988) 314 (M. *Hauke*).
2111 **Wallace** William A., GALILEO and his sources 1984 ➤ 1,2186... 4,2152: ᴿJRel 68 (1988) 110s (B. *Dooley*).
2112 *Wallace* William A., RANDALL *redivivus*; GALILEO and the Paduan Aristotelians: JHistId 49 (1988) 133-149.
2113 **Wells** Jonathan, Charles HODGE's critique of Darwinism; an historical-critical analysis of the 19th century debate: Studies in American Religion 27, 1987 ➤ 4,2153: ᴿWestTJ 51 (1989) 406-9 (K. J. *Howell*).
2114 **Westermann** Claus, Schöpfung — Wie Naturwissenschaft fragt — was die Bibel antwortet: Tb 1630. Stu 1989, Calwer. 40 p. 3-451-08630-1 [BL 91,122: reprint of 1984 enlarged edition of 1973].
2115 **Whitcomb** John C., The early earth²ʳᵉᵛ [¹1972 + 13 reprintings; evaluates UNGER-WALTKE thesis of an original pre-Genesis 1:1 creation]. GR 1986, Baker. 174 p. $9. – ᴿBS 146 (1989) 103 (F. R. *Howe*).
2116 *Wiebe* Donald, Is science really an implicit religion [no; effort to prove it such is futile]: SR 18 (1989) 171-183.
2117 *Zięba* Stanisław, ❾ Galileusz, Galileo GALILEI: ➤ 891, EncKat 5 (1989) 825-7.

E1.9   *Peccatum originale,* **The Sin of Eden,** *Genesis 2-3.*

2118 *Abrego* José M., Reflexiones sobre el pecado en el Antiguo Testamento: Proyección 35 (1988) 91-103.
2119 *a) Ambrose* M. Devadass, The cosmic experience of God according to Genesis; – *b) Luke* K., An Avestan parallel to Genesis 3: IndTSt 26 (1989) 122-133 / 134-151.
2120 *Anderson* Gary, Celibacy or consummation in the garden? Reflections on early Jewish and Christian interpretations of the garden of Eden: HarvTR 82 (1989) 121-148.
2121 *Aranda* Gonzalo, Corporeidad y sexualidad en los relatos de la creación [... *Ausin* Santiago, ... libros proféticos; *Nolli* Gianfranco, ... sapienciales]: ➤ 572, Masculinidad 1989, 19-50 [51-106 / 107-168].
2122 *a)* **Balducci** Corrado, Il diavolo '... esiste e lo si può riconoscere'. CasM 1988, Piemme. 360 p. Lit. 27.500. – *b)* **Franzoni** Giuseppe, Il diavolo, mio fratello, pref. *Balducci.* Soveria Mannelli CZ 1986, Rubettino. 162 p. Lit. 16.000. – ᴿHumBr 44 (1989) 161s (T. *Goffi*).
2123 *Balling* Jacob, [Gn 2s before 1700, especially in AUGUSTINE and LUTHER] Paradisforstællingen som gammelkristen myte: ➤ 148, ᶠOTZEN B., DanTTs 52,4 (1989) 268-286.
2124 *Basetti-Sani* G., Il peccato di Iblīs (Satana) e degli Angeli nel Corano: ➤ 164, ᶠRUBINACCI R., 1985, I, 51-64.
2125 *Béland* Jean-Pierre, La condition de créature dans la dogmatique de 1925 de Paul TILLICH [ᴱ*Schüssler* W. 1986: 'L'existence est le point ou la création et la chute coïncident']: RHPR 69 (1989) 309-324; Eng. 383.

2126 *Blandino* Giovanni, The problem of suffering; the original sin: Teresianum 40 (1989) 149-173.

2127 *a) Bogaert* Pierre-Maurice, Une tradition juive sur la création de l'esprit mauvais au deuxième jour; – *b) Klener* Julien, Démonologie talmudique et ashkénaze; – *c) Leloir* Louis, Anges et démons chez les Pères du Désert; – *d) Ries* Julien, Cultes païens et démons dans l'Apologétique chrétienne de JUSTIN à AUGUSTIN; – *e) Mertens* Michèle, Sur la trace des anges rebelles dans les traditions ésotériques du début de notre ère jusqu'au XVIIe siècle: ➤ 728, Anges 1987/9, 135-146 / 177-201 / 313-335 / 337-352 / 383-398.

2128 **Bur** Jacques, Le péché originel 1988 ➤ 4,2161: RLavalTP 45 (1989) 172s (L. *Létourneau*); ScEspr 41 (1989) 387s (R. *Morency*: 'Buhr').

2129 *Burten* Laurel A., Original sin or original shame?: QRMin 8,4 (1988) 31-41.

2130 **Chauvin** Jacques, Dieu a-t-il vraiment dit? (ou le risque de devenir adulte, selon Genèse 3) 1988 ➤ 4,2162*: RÉTRel 64 (1989) 431 (J. *Rennes*); Protestantesimo 44 (1989) 224 (R. *Subilia*).

2131 **Chiesa** Bruno, Creazione e caduta dell'uomo nell'esegesi giudeo-araba medievale: StBPaid 85. Brescia 1989, Paideia. 209 p. Lit. 15.000. 88-394-0418-X. – RArTGran 52 (1989) 248 (A. S. *Muñoz*).

2132 *Chrysostomos* bp., Demonology in the Orthodox Church; a psychological perspective: GrOrTR 33 (1988) 45-61.

2133 **Deppe** Rupert, Die Erbsünde in der philosophischen Theologie Frederick R. TENNANTs; zur Ortung eines naturwissenschaftlich-evolutiv-psychologischen Ansatzes: kath. Diss. DScheffczyk L. München 1988s. – TR 85 (1989) 517.

2134 **Deurloo** K., De mens als raadsel en geheim; verhalende antropologie in Genesis 2-4. Baarn 1988, Ten Have. 160 p. Fb 498. – RCollatVL 19 (1989) 237 (R. *Hoet*).

2135 **Dohmen** Christoph, Schöpfung und Tod... Gn 2s [Hab. Bonn, DHossfeld]: SBB 17, 1988 ➤ 4,2169: RTR 85 (1989) 191s (H. *Gross*); TüTQ 169 (1989) 240s (W. *Gross*).

2136 **Drewermann** Eugen, Strukturen des Bösen [➤ 4,2170]. Pd 61988, Schöningh. – RCarthaginensia 5 (1989) 293 (J. *García Hernández*).

2137 **Forsyth** Neil, The old enemy, Satan and the combat myth 1987 ➤ 3,2095; 4,2175: RAntClas 58 (1989) 410s (J. *Wankenne*); JBL 108 (1989) 516-8 (Adela Y. *Collins*); JTS 40 (1989) 518-523 (R. P. *Carroll*).

2138 *a) Galot* Jean, Démons et foi chrétienne; – *b) Vauthier* Émile, Deux livres récents [*Tavard* Georges, Satan; *Thomas* Pascal, Le diable oui ou non?]: EsprVie 99 (1989) 209-216 / 217-222.

2139 *García Cordero* Maximiliano, Los espíritus malignos según las creencias judías del tiempo de Jesús: CiTom 116 (1989) 417-456.

2140 *Gibert* Pierre, Péché originel ou problème occidental [... présenté comme fatalisme mythique éloigné de la Bible et du Concile de Trente]: Études 371 (1989) 247-255.

2141 **Goodman** Felicitas D., How about demons? Possession and exorcism in the modern world. Bloomington 1988, Indiana Univ. xvi-142 p. $30; pa. $11. – RJRelRes 31 (1989s) 105s (S. D. *Glazier*).

2142 **Gutting** Ernst, Offensive gegen den Patriarchalismus: für eine menschlichere Welt: Frauenforum 1987 ➤ 3,2096: RTPQ 137 (1989) 313s (Marie-Louise *Gubler*).

2143 *a) Haag* Ernst, Die Ursünde und das Erbe der Gewalt im Licht der biblischen Urgeschichte; – *b) Rémy* Gérard, Erbsündentheologie heute; –

c) *Weier* Reinhold, Die Sündhaftigkeit der Erbsünde: TrierTZ 98 (1989) 21-38 / 171-195 / 196-206.

2144 a) *Hewett* John, Genesis 2:4b-3:31; 4:2-16; 9:20-27; 19: 30-38 (exposition); – b) *McGlone* Lee, Genesis 2:18-24; Ephesians 5:21-6:9: RExp 86 (1989) 237-241 / 243-7.

2145 **Hunter** David G., On the sin of Adam and Eve; a little-known defense of marriage and childbearing by AMBROSIASTER: HarvTR 82 (1989) 283-299.

2146 **Jobling** David, [Gn 2s...] The sense of biblical narrative II 1986 → 2,176; 4,2186: ᴿRelStT 8,3 (1988) 51s (L. *Eslinger*).

2147 **Klein-Braslavy** Sara, ⊕ MAIMONIDES' interpretation of the Adam stories in Genesis; a study in Maimonides' anthropology [sequel to 1978 M. interpretation of the story of creation]. J 1986, Rubin Mass. 342 p. – ᴿRelStR 15 (1989) 274 (N. *Ararat*).

2148 **Kowalski** Aleksander, Perfezione e giustizia di Adamo nel Liber graduum [siriaco; diss. ᴰ*Pelland* G.]: OrChrAn 232. R 1989, Pont. Inst. Orientalium Studiorum. 256 p. [RHE 85,249, A. de *Halleux*].

2149 *Krašovec* Jože, [Gn 1-11] Kazen i rešitev v biblični prazgodovini: BogVest 48 (1988) 209-225; 226, Punishment and salvation in biblical prehistory.

2150 *Laporte* Jean, Models from PHILO in ORIGEN's teaching on original sin: LavalTP 44 (1988) 191-263; franç. 191.

2150* **Levenson** Jon D., Creation and the persistence of evil. SF 1988, Harper & R. 182 p. $19. – ᴿTTod 46 (1989s) 98.100 (M. J. *Haar*).

Maillot Alphonse, Ève, ma mère; la femme dans l'Ancien Testament 1989 → 1538.

2151 **Martelet** Gustave, Libera risposta ad uno scandalo; la colpa originale, la sofferenza e la morte 1987 → 4,2195: ᴿCC 140 (1989,1) 196-9 (G. *Marchesi*: da correggere quelle posizioni dottrinali non pienamente compatibili con l'insegnamento della Chiesa).

2151* [Pablo] *Martín* Juan, La antropología de FILÓN y la de TEÓFILO de Antioquía; sus lecturas de Génesis 2-5: Salmanticensis 36 (1989) 23-70; Eng. 71.

2152 **Melzer** Sara E., Discourses of the Fall [we have fallen away from God and truth into language, which colors everything we say, think, and know]; a study of PASCAL's Pensées 1986 → 2,1587: ᴿRelStR 15 (1989) 57 (B. *Norman*).

2153 *Merrill* Eugene H., Covenant and the Kingdom; Genesis 1-3 as foundation for biblical theology: → 44*, ᶠCRISWELL W. A., CriswT 1 (1987) 295-308.

2154 *Michel* Diethelm, Ihr werdet sein wie Gott; Gedenken zur Sündenfallgeschichte in Genesis 3: → 769, Menschwerdung 1986/9, 61-87.

2155 *Moschetti* Stefano, La teologia del peccato originale; passato, presente, prospettive: CC 140 (1989,1) 245-258.

2156 *Nicolas* Jean-Hervé, Le péché originel et le problème du mal: RThom 89 (1989) 289-308.

2157 **Nothomb** Paul, a) L'homme immortel; nouveau regard sur l'Éden: Bibliothèque de l'Hermétisme. P 1984, A. Michel. – b) L'image de Dieu. Bru 1985, La Longue Vue. – c) La mémoire d'Éden. Bru 1987, La Longue Vue. – ᴿFoiVie 88 (1989) 101-4 (G. *Vahanian*), 104-6, 147s, réponse.

2158 *Odaka* Takeshi, ⊕ The sin of Adam according to ORIGEN: KatKenk 28,56 (1989) 133-161; Eng. xii-xv.

2159 *Olivier* Hannes, Die mensbeeld in die skeppingsverhale van Genesis: JSem 1 (1989) 70-87; Eng. 70.

2160 **Pagels** Elaine, Adam, Eve, and the serpent (Random House) 1988 ► 4,2203; also L 1988, Weidenfeld & N; £15: ᴿChrCent 105 (Ch 1988) 984-6 (R. *Goetz*: her focus on AUGUSTINE is deficient) [< NTAbs 33,228]: NY Review of Books (June 20, 1988) 27-30 (W. H. C. *Frend*, 'The triumph of sin'; scholarly and challenging) & NY Times Book Review (Aug. 21, 1988) 15s (R. *Lane Fox*: 'Sweet are the uses of original sin', clear but not always plausible) [both from NTAbs 33,90]; RSPT 73 (1989) 460-3 (G.-M. de *Durand*: ... Augustine enslaved the Church); Tablet 242 (1989) 200s (H. *Chadwick*); Thomist 53 (1989) 509-512 (J. C. *Cavadini*); TLond 92 (1989) 340s (Rowan *Williams*: important echo of BROWN P. 1989); TS 50 (1989) 201s (R. J. *O'Connell*); VigChr 43 (1989) 100-3 (G. *Quispel*: splendid, original, mature); WestTJ 51 (1989) 183-9 (P. J. *Letthart*: erroneously claims all Western theology built on an aberration).

2161 **Pagels** Elaine, Adam, Ève et le serpent, ᵀ*Miech Chatenay* Michèle. P 1989, Flammarion. 260 p. F 120. – ᴿEsprVie 99 (1989) 140-*jaune* (F. *Daubercies*); Études 371 (1989) 425s (M. *Fédou*).

2162 — *Boswell* J., Trouble in Paradise [*Pagels* E., Adam, Eve, and the Serpent]: New Republic (Wsh. Aug. 8 and 15, 1988) 38-41 [< NTAbs 33,90: she is unclear and oversimplified].

2163 — *Lamberights* M., AUGUSTINE, JULIAN of Aeclanum and E. PAGELS' 'Adam, Eve, and the Serpent': AugLv 39 (1989) 393-435 [< TR 86, 253].

2164 *Parker* D., Original sin; a study in evangelical theory: EvQ 61 (1989) 51-69.

2164* *Perry* Michael, Taking Satan seriously: ExpTim 101 (1989s) 105-112 [266s, reply by *Sweet* J. P. M.].

2165 **Phillips** J. A., [deutsch 1987 ► 4,2204] Eve, the history of an idea. SF 1984, Harper & R. 201 p. $13. – ᴿJRel 68 (1988) 152s (Janet *Summers*).

2166 **Phipps** William E., Genesis and gender; biblical myths of sexuality and their cultural import. NY 1989, Praeger. 144 p. $33 [TS 50,627].

2167 **Piazza** Rosalba, Adamo, Eva e il Serpente. Palermo 1988, Luna. 201 p. Lit. 22.000. – ᴿSandalion 12s (1989s) 278s (Silvana *Fasce*).

2168 *Pottier* Bernard, Interpréter le péché originel sur les traces de G. FESSARD: NRT 111 (1989) 801-823.

2169 [G.-] **Quevedo** Oscar, Antes que os demônios voltem. São Paulo 1989, Loyola. 548 p. – ᴿREB 49 (1989) 490-5 (E. F. *Alves*: os demonófilos têm que rever suas posições).

2170 *a*) *Ravasi* Gianfranco, La vergogna di Adamo ed Eva, Gen 2-3; – *b*) *Bonora* A., Vergogna e pudore in Gen 9,18-27; – *c*) *Festorazzi* F., Le figlie di Lot, Gen 19,30-38; valore della vita o vergogna dell'incesto?; – *d*) *Stefani* P., La vergogna dell'idolatria, Es 32; – *e*) *Cortese* E., La nudità in Lv 18 e 20; – *f*) *Monari* L., '...perché ti vergogni!' Riflessioni su Ezech 16; – *g*) *Virgulin* S., 'Che io non sia svergognato!' La preghiera dei salmisti: ► 396*b*, ParSpV 20 ('Ed ebbero vergogna' 1989) 9-19 [253-270 nei Padri, G. *Sfameni Gasparro*] / 21-32 / 33-39 / 41-52 / 53-62 / 63-73 / 75-86.

2171 ᴱ**Robbins** Gregory A., Genesis 1-3 in the history of exegesis; intrigue in the garden: Studies in Women and Religion 27. Lewiston NY 1988, Mellen. xxviii-282 p. [CBQ 51,592].

2172 **Russell** Jeffrey B., Lucifer 1984 ► 1,2236... 4,2209: ᴿSalesianum 51 (1989) 553s (R. *Della Casa*: esiste in italiano, Laterza 1987).

2173 **Russell** Jeffrey B., Mephistopheles 1986 ➤ 3,2117; 4,2210: ᴿAmHR 94 (1989) 105s (B. *Easlea*); ZKG 100 (1989) 394-6 (G. *Greshake*).

2174 **Russell** Jeffrey B., The prince of darkness 1988 ➤ 4,2211: ᴿNewTR 2,4 (1989) 106 (Z. *Hayes*).

2175 *a) Sacchi* Paolo, Il problema del male nella riflessione ebraica dall'VIII secolo a. C. al I d. C.; – *b) Festorazzi* Franco, La parola non ascoltata (Dt 4,1; 5,1; 6,41; ecc.); – *c) Bonora* Antonio, Il peccato individuale e la sua dimensione sociale nell'AT: ➤ 396*a*, ParSpV 19 ('Liberaci dal male' 1989) 9-28 / 29-41 / 43-56.

2176 *a) Scullion* John J., What of original sin? The convergence of Genesis 1-11 and Romans 5:12; – *b) Liedke* Gerhard, Geschaffen in sieben Tagen; Gen 1 — gehört in der ökologischen Krise: ➤ 212, ᶠWESTERMANN C., Schöpfung 1989, 25-36 / 13-24.

2177 *Segal* B. J., Form and meaning in midrash; Sanhedrin IV:5 [uniqueness of human creation]: JRefJud 35,4 (1988) 41-49 [< NTAbs 33,84].

2178 *Serra* Aristide, La relazione uomo-donna a partire dalle' riletture biblico-giudaiche di Gen 2-3; contributo alla questione del femminile nella Bibbia: ➤ 721*a*, Simposio 7, 1988/9, 7-102.

2179 *Short* Brent, Thomas MERTON on Genesis; a way of seeing: SpirLife 35 (1989) 22-28.

2179* *Soennecken* Silvia, Die Rolle der Frau in AUGUSTINS 'De Genesi ad litteram': ➤ 132, ᶠMAYER C., Signum 1989, 289-300.

2180 *Speranzini* Egidio, La dottrina del Liber de duobus principiis sulla caduta degli angeli e sul problema dell'origine del male: SMSR 55,1 (1989) 45-54.

2181 *Tavard* Georges, Satan: L'horizon du croyant. P/Ottawa 1988, Desclée/Novalis. 156 p. F 65. – ᴿEsprVie 99 (1989) 217-220 (É. *Vauthier*); LavalTP 45 (1989) 463s (M. *Thibault*).

2182 **Testa** Emanuele, La legge del progresso organico ... monogenismo e il peccato originale 1987 ➤ 3,2075: ᴿSalesianum 51 (1989) 587 (B. *Amata*).

2183 *Thomas* Pascal, Le diable oui ou non³ P 1989, Centurion. 245 p. F 89. 2-227-31088-X. – ᴿEsprVie 99 (1989) 220-2 (É. *Vauthier*); NRT 111 (1989) 1045 (B. C.).

2184 **Toorn** Karel van der, Sin and sanction in Israel and Mesopotamia 1985 ➤ 1,2242 ... 4,2217: ᴿBZ 33 (1989) 285-8 (N. *Lohfink*, auch über ADAMIAK R., FORESTI F., MILLER P.: 'göttliche Sanktion für menschliche Sünde'); CBQ 51 (1989) 733s (W. *Harrelson*); Protestantesimo 44 (1989) 128 (J. A. *Soggin*); RÉJ 147 (1988) 225s (M. *Petit*); RHPR 69 (1989) 195s (D. *Bodi*).

2185 *Van Seters* John, The creation of man and the creation of the king: ZAW 101 (1989) 333-342.

2186 **Vermeylen** J., Le mythe d'Adam et Ève; Genèse 2-3 à la lumière de l'exégèse historico-critique: Cah FORel. 1. Charleroi 1988, Centre universitaire. 76 p. [NRT 112, 419s, J.-L. *Ska*].

2187 *Waschke* Ernst-Joachim, Schuld und Schuldbewältigung nach dem prophetischen Zeugnis des Alten Testament: TLZ 115 (1989) 1-10.

2188 **Wolde** E. J. van, A semiotic analysis of Genesis 2-3; a semiotic theory and method of analysis applied to the story of the garden of Eden [diss. Kath. Univ. Nijmegen, ᴰ*Iersel* B. van]. Assen c. 1989, van Gorcum. 247 p. *f* 42,50. 90-232-2433-7. – TsTNijm 29 (1989) 172; RTLv 21,91.

2189 *Zoffoli* Enrico, Il peccato originale secondo San TOMMASO: SacDoc 34 (1989) 492-505.

2190 **Zumkeller** A., Erbsünde 1984 ➤ 1,7295... 4,2224:   ᴿZKG 100 (1989) 117-121 (M. *Schulze*).

2191 *Fabry* H.-J., [Gn 2,21] *ṣēla'* 'Rippe' ['rib'; but 'Brett, board' in Temple-architecture]: ➤ 913, TWAT 6,8s (1989) 1059-1064.
2192 *a*) *Farla* Piet, 'The two shall become one flesh'; Gen. 1.27 and 2.24 in the New Testament marriage texts; – *b*) *Lategan* Bernard, Intertextuality and social transformation; some implications of the family concept in New Testament texts: ➤ 95, ᶠIᴇʀsᴇʟ B. van, 1989, 67-82 / 105-116.
2193 *Chiesa* Bruno, Gen 2,15-3,24 nella più antica esegesi giudeo-araba: ➤ 759, Sangue VI, 1987/9, 987-1095.
2194 *Pizzani* Ubaldo, La dottrina agostiniana dell'origine del linguaggio e l'esegesi di Gen. 2,19-20: ➤ 42, ᶠCᴏsᴛᴀɴᴢᴀ S., Polyanthema 1989, 399-416.
2195 *Lindner* Helga, Spricht Gen 2,24 von der [monogamischen] Ehe?: TBei 19 (1988) 23-32 [yes, against Wᴇsᴛᴇʀᴍᴀɴɴ, von Rᴀᴅ...; < OTAbs 12,46].
2196 *Stoebe* H.-J., *a*) Sündenbewusstsein und Glaubensuniversalismus; Gedanken an Gn Kap 3; – *b*) Gut und Böse in der jahwistischen Quelle des Pentateuchs: ➤ 362, Geschichte 1989, 63-73 / 46-62.
2197 *Hyman* Ronald T., [Gn 3,1-5; Nm 22,28-30] Questions by the serpent and the ass; analysis and parallels with classroom teaching: Dor 16 (1987s) 19-28 [< OTAbs 11,107].
2198 *Bergmann* Jacinto, A figura de Maria em Gênesis 3,15: Teocomunicação 18,82 (1988) 411-423 [< TContext 6/2, 63].
2199 *Ratner* Robert J., 'Garments of skin' (Genesis 3:21): JBQ (= Dor) 18 (1989s) 74-80.

E2.1   **Cain et Abel**; *gigantes, longaevi; Genesis 4s*.

2199* *Cooper* Howard J., Persecution and silence; the myth of Cain and Abel in Jewish-Christian relations: Month 250 (1989) 256-262. 348-354.
2200 **Drijvers** P., *Schilling* P., Hoeder van mijn broeder? Ik? Het verhaal van Kain en Abel. Hilversum 1988, Gooi & S. 158 p. Fb 590. – ᴿCollatVL 19 (1989) 238 (R. *Hoet*).
2201 *Lubsczyk* Hans, *a*) Kain und Abschalom; Sünde und Gnade in der Geschichtsschreibung im davidisch-salomonischen Reich [Rektoratsrede 1973]; – *b*) Mann und Frau in der Theologie des Jahwisten [nicht in der Bibliographie S. 245]: ➤ 306, Einheit 1989, 103-113 / 114-124.
2202 *Poulssen* N., Contouren van de ruimte [space] in Genesis 4,1-26: TsTNijm 29 (1989) 3-17; Eng. 17s.
2203 *Royse* James R., Cain's expulsion from paradise; the text of Pʜɪʟᴏ's Congr 171: JQR 79 (1988s) 219-225.
2204 **Shank** Harold, The sin theology of the Cain and Abel story; an analysis of narrative themes within the context of Genesis 1-11: diss. Marquette, Milwaukee 1988, 261 p. 89-25440. – DissA 50 (1989s) 2527-A.
2205 *Shim Yong-Súb*, ❻ Bible and society; 'I don't know' (Genesis 4:9): Samok 121 (Seoul 1989) 104-111 [122 (1989) 84-89; 124 (1989) 67-76; < TContext 7/1, 56...].
2206 *Soleh* M. Z., ❺ Cain's sin and dwelling in a booth: BethM 32 (1986s) 381s [< OTAbs 11,147].

2206* *a*) *Soggin* J. Alberto, La famiglia, nucleo originario associativo nella Genesi; – *b*) *Fanuli* Antonio, Rapporti tra fratelli nella Genesi: ➤ 587, Famiglia 1987/9, 29-44 / 45-87.

2207 **Szondi** Lipót, ⓦ *Kain*... the violation of law; Moses, the legislator. Budapest 1987 – ᴿTSzem 31 (1988) 249-252 (P. *Hubai*).

2208 **Tijn** Maartje van, De verwarring van goed en kwaad; midrasjin over Kain en Abel, Noach en de torenbouwers van Babel. Haag 1988, B.-centrum. *f* 19,90. – ᴿStreven 56 (1988s) 467 (P. *Beentjes*).

2209 **House** Colin L., The successive, corresponding epochal arrangement of the 'chronogenealogies' of Genesis 5 and 11b in the three textual traditions: LXX-A, SP, and MT: diss. Andrews, ᴰ*Running* Leona G. Berrien Springs MI 1988. 198 p. 89-19891. – DissA 50 (1989s) 1703s-A.

2210 *Alexander* T.D., From Adam to Judah; the significance of the family tree in Genesis: EvQ 61 (1989) 5-19.

2211 *Hess* Richard S., The genealogies of Genesis 1-11 [and 43] and comparative literature [...(HESIOD) Catalogue of Women]: Biblica 70 (1989) 241-254.

2213 *Tabor* James D., [Gn 5,24; Dt 34,5s; 2 Kgs 2,11] 'Returning' to the divinity'; JOSEPHUS's portrayal of the disappearances of Enoch, Elijah and Moses: JBL 108 (1989) 225-238.

2214 **Peters** Ulrike, Wie der biblische Prophet Henoch zum Buddha wurde; die jüdische Henoch-Tradition als frühes Beispiel interkultureller und interreligiöser Vermittlung zwischen Ost und West. Sinzing 1989, Verlag für Theologie. 209 p. – ᴿJBQ (= Dor) 18 (1989s) 181s (S. *Liptzin*).

2215 *Hong* Joseph, Problems in an obscure passage; notes on Genesis 6.1-4: BTrans 40 (1989) 419-436.

  E2.2   *Diluvium,* **The Flood;** Gilgameš (Atraḫasis); **Genesis 6...**

2216 **Bailey** Lloyd R., Noah, the person and the story in history and tradition: Studies in the Personalities of the OT. Columbia 1989, Univ. SC. xi-244 p. $26; pa. $14. – ᴿCBQ 51 (1989) 735-7 (M. D. *Guinan*).

2217 **Cazeaux** Jacques, La trame et la chaîne [I. structures littéraires de PHILON, 1983 ➤ 64,8689], II. Le cycle de Noé dans Philon d'Alexandrie: ALGHJ 20. Leiden 1989, Brill. 298 p. 90-04-09179-3.

2218 ᴱ**Dundes** Alan, The flood myth [reprints] 1988 ➤ 4,2246: ᴿBR 4,6 (1988) 8s (R.S. *Hendel*); BS 146 (1989) 231s (G.H. *Johnston*); JScStR 29 (1989) 126 (J.F. *Baggett*).

2219 *Feldman* L.H., JOSEPHUS' portrait of Noah and its parallels in PHILO, Pseudo-Philo Bibl. Ant. and rabbinic midrashim: PAAR 55 (1988) 37-57 [< NTA 33,359].

2220 ᴱ**Flores D'Arcais** F., Noè, il diluvio... 1987 ➤ 3,557.2157: ᴿBL (1989) 15 (R. *Murray*: some of the lay amateurs are more skilled at attualizzazione than F. ROSSI DE GASPERIS' article).

2221 *Grossmann* Hans-Christoph, Die Möglichkeit der literarischen Abhängigkeit des JOSEPHUS von OVID, dargestellt am Beispiel der Sintfluterzählung: ZRGg 41 (1989) 83-86.

2222 *a*) *Hirsch* Hans, 'The prince and the pauper' [deutsch, zu Gilg. XI,54]; – *b*) *Stol* M., Gilgamesh Epic XI,54: AfO 35 (1988) 109s / 78.

2223 *Kapelrud* Arvid S., [Gn 2s; Gilgameš) Evig liv var ikke gitt ham: SvEx 54 (1989) 101-8.

2224 ᵀᴱ**Kovacs** Maureen G., The epic of Gilgamesh. Stanford 1989, Univ. xxxvi-122 p. 0-8047-1589-0 [OIAc N89].

2225 **Kreis** Rudolf, Dichtung und Umwelt; von Gilgamesch bis zu den 'Physikern'; Das Sprachkunstwerk zwischen Erde, Leib und Geist. Fra 1989, Lang. 304 p. 3-631-41476-5.

2225* *a*) *Lux* R., Noach und das Geheimnis seines Namens; ein Beitrag zur Theologie der Flutgeschichte; – *b*) *Schulz* H., Sintflut und Hoffnung; biblische Motive bei Max FRISCH: ➤ 85, ᶠHINZ C., Frieden 1988, 109-135 / 136-144.

2226 **Papke** Werner, Die Sterne von Babylon; die geheime Botschaft des Gilgamesh — nach 4000 Jahren entschlüsselt. Bergisch Gladbach 1989, Lübbe. 400 p.; 2 loose charts. 3-7857-0498-4 [OIAc Ja90].

2227 *Salvini* Mirjo, Die hurritischen Überlieferungen des Gilgameš-Epos und der Kešši-Erzählung: ➤ 817*, Hurriter 1988, 157-172.

2228 *Stachowiak* Lech, ❷ Gilgamesz: ➤ 891, EncKat 5 (1989) 1078s.

2229 *Dumbrell* William J., [Gn 6,18] Creation, covenant and work: Crux 24,s (Vancouver 1988) 14-24 [< OTAbs 12,165].

2230 *Priest* J., Gen 9:6, a comparative study of bloodshed in Bible and Talmud: JEvTS 31 (1988) 145-152 [< ZAW 102,130].

2231 **Lumeya** Nzash U., [Gn 9,22-27] The curse on Ham's descendants; its missiological impact on Zairian Mbala Mennonite Brethren: diss. Fuller Theol. Sem., ᴰ*Glasser* A. Pasadena 1988, 239 p. 90-05459. – DissA 50 (1989s) 2947-A.

2232 *Arndt* Marian, ❷ Der Noachbund als Beispiel für das Bundes-verständnis in der priesterlichen Tradition (P): RoczTK 33,1 (1986) 5-21; deutsch 21.

2233 *Hamlin* E. John, [Gn 10; Jer 25; Ezek 27] Three metaphors for the inhabited earth: ProcGLM 9 (1989) 49-58.

2234 *Poulssen* Niek, Stad en land in Genesis 10,1-32 en 11,1-9; over de gevoelsruimte van de volkenlijst en het torenbouwerhaal: Bijdragen 50 (1989) 263-277; Eng. 277 [... the emotional space].

2235 *García Santos* Ángel, Gn 11,1-9; crítica literaria y de la redacción: EstBíb 47 (1989) 289-318; Eng. 289.

2236 *Launay* M. B. de, Babel [... interprétation du mythe dans une perspective philosophique]: Revue de Métaphysique et de Morale 94 (1989) 93-105 [< RSPT 73,513].

2236* *Buiatti* Marcello, La modificazione degli esseri viventi ed il mito di Babele: FutUom 15,1 (1988) 25-43.

2237 *Albertz* R., Die Frage des Ursprungs der Sprache im AT ➤ 541, Sprache II (1989) 1-18.

2238 **Uehlinger** Christoph, Die 'eine Rede' und die Weltherrschaft; Studien zur Interpretation der sog. 'Turmbauerzählung' (Gen 11,1-9) mit einer neuen Deutung vor dem Hintergrund altorientalischer Weltherr-schaftsrhetorik: diss. ᴰ*Keel* O. FrS 1989. [> OBO 101]. – RTLv 21,542.

2239 ᴱ**Jeppesen** K., *Cryer* F. H., Tekster og tolkninger — ti [10] studier i Det gamle Testamente 1986 ➤ 2,252 [Gn 11,1-9; Dt 26,5-9 ...]. – ᴿTsTKi 59 (1988) 68s (Helge S. *Kvanvig*).

2240 *Zweifel* Z. S., Los constructores de ciudades; análisis estructural y semiótico de Génesis 11:1-9: Cuadernos de Teología 9 (BA 1988) 111-131 [< Stromata 45,499 'Sweifel'].

2241 *a*) *Ruppert* Lothar, 'Machen wir uns einen Namen ...' (Gen 11,4) — Zur Anthropologie der vorpriesterschriftlichen Urgeschichte; – *b*) *Cazelles*

Henri, Der persönliche Gott Abrahams und der Gott des Volkes Israel, ᵀ*Ohler* A.: ⇢ 45, ᶠDEISSLER A., Weg 1989, 28-45 / 46-61.

2242 *a) Görg* Manfred, [Gen 11,27-32] Abra(ha)m — Wende zur Zukunft; zum Beginn der priesterschriftlichen Abrahamsgeschichte; – *b) Kilian* Rudolf, Nachtrag und Neuorientierung; Anmerkungen zum Jahwisten in den Abrahamserzählungen: ⇢ 169, ᶠSCHARBERT J., Väter 1989, 61-71 / 155-167.

E2.3   **Patriarchae, Abraham;** *Genesis 12s.*

2243 **Abela** Anthony, The themes of the Abraham narrative; thematic coherence within the Abraham literary unit of Genesis 11,27-25,18 [extract of diss. Pont. Ist. Biblico]. Malta 1989, Studia. x-142 p. [AcPIB 9,5 (1988s) 383]. – ᴿOTAbs 12 (1989) 336 (C. T. *Begg*).

2244 **Alt** Albrecht, The God of the Fathers [BW 3/12 (1929)],ᵀ, ⇢ 225, Essays 1989, 1-66 (67-77, the inscriptions).

2245 **Barsotti** Divo, [Abramo, Elia, Giobbe, Tobia] Meditazioni bibliche. Brescia 1987, Queriniana. 245 p. – ᴿTeresianum 40 (1989) 236 (P. *Mantovani*).

2246 **Braselmann** Ruth, Abraham, an dem Gott handelte; Scherenschnitte zu Abrahamgeschichten: Aussaat. Neuk 1988, Neuk.-V. 39 p.; ill. 3-7887-1300-3 / Aussaat 3-7615-4824-9.

2246* *Bray* Gerald, The promises made to Abraham and the destiny of Israel: ScotBEv 7 (1989) 69-87.

2247 **Cerni** Chiara Giovita, La cronologia dei Patriarchi: diss. Pont. Univ. S. Thomae. ᴰ*Zerafa* P. R 1989.

2248 *a) Delaney* Carol, The legacy of Abraham; dubious male dominance and female autonomy; – *b) Marmesh* Ann, Anti-Covenant: ⇢ 625, Anti-Covenant 1989, 27-41 / 43-60.

2249 *a) Fokkelman* J. P., Time and the structure of the Abraham cycle; – *b) Labuschagne* C. J., The life span of the patriarchs: ⇢ 129, ᶠMULDER M., New avenues 1989, 96-109 / 121-7.

2250 **Forsberg** Juhani, Das Abrahamsbild... LUTHERS 1984 ⇢ 1,2288... 4,2269: ᴿTLZ 114 (1989) 831s (M. *Schulze*).

2251 *a) Gross* Heinrich, Zur theologischen Bedeutung von *hālak* (gehen) in den Abrahamgeschichten (Gen 12-25); – *b) Steingrimsson* Sigurdur Ö., Abram in Kana'an; einige literaturwissenschaftliche Beobachtungen zu den Wanderungsberichten in Gen 12-13; – *c) Wahl* Otto, Die Flucht eines Berufenen (Gen 12,10-20); Gedanken zu einer stets aktuellen alten Geschichte; – *d) Müller* Augustin R., Die Mehrungsverheissung und ihre vielfältige Formulierung: ⇢ 169, ᶠSCHARBERT J., Väter 1989, 73-82 / 327-341 / 343-359 / 259-266.

2252 **Guillén Torralba** Juan, Los Patriarcas, historia y leyenda: Bibliografía Básica del Creyente. M 1987, Soc. Atenas. 217 p. 84-7020-238-3. – ᴿActuBbg 26 (1989) 195 (R. de *Sivatte*); RelCu 35 (1989) 483 (M. A. *Martín Juárez*).

2253 *Hernando* Eusebio, Abraham, amigo de Dios: Burgense 30 (1989) 9-29.

2254 *Kieweler* H. V., Abraham und der Preis der Väter bei Ben Sira [44:19-21]: Amt und Gemeinde 37,7s (1986) 70-72 [< JStJud 20,123].

Köckert Matthias, Vätergott und Väterverheissungen ... ALT: FRL 142, 1988 ⇢ 7017.

2254* *McCarter* P. K., The Patriarchal Age: ⇢ b322, ᴱ*Shanks* H., Ancient Israel 1988, 1-29.

2255 *Schmidt* Ludwig, Eine radikale Kritik an der Hypothese von Vätergott und Väterverheissungen [KÖCKERT M. 1988]: TRu 54 (1989) 415-421.

2256 *Luria* B.Z., ☉ *Qadmût*.. early stages of the Hebrews: BethM 34,2 (on Heb. cover) = 121 (1989s, on Eng. cover) 97-123.

2257 **Piper** Vera L., Uprooting traditional interpretation; a consideration of tree worship in the migration of Abraham: diss. SUNY, Buffalo 1989. 158 p. 89-21570. – DissA 50 (1989s) 2043-A.

2258 **Scharbert** Josef, Genesis 12-50: NEchter 16, 1986 ➤ 3,2190: ᴿRB 96 (1989) 452s (J. *Loza*).

2259 **Scheepers** C.L. van W., An evaluation of the science-philosophical model applied by Van Seters to the Abraham traditions: diss. [Afrikaans ➤ 4,2277] Unisa, ᴰ*Deist* F. Pretoria 1988. – DissA 50 (1989s) 2948s-A.

2260 **Siker** Jeffrey S., Disinheriting the Jews; the use of Abraham in early Christian controversy with Judaism from Paul through Justin Martyr: diss. Princeton Theol. Sem. 1989, ᴰ*De Boer* M. 497 p. 89-23111. – DissA 50 (1989s) 2099-A; RelStR 16,190.

2261 *Soggin* J.A., *a)* Abramo fra storia e mito; – *b)* 'Parti dalla tua terra': ➤ 563*b*, Abramo 1988...

2262 *Steinmetz* David C., Abraham and the Reformation, in ᴱ**Masters** G. Mallary, Proceedings of the SE Institute of Medieval and Renaissance Studies 10 (Chapel Hill 1984, Univ. NC) 94-114 [< LuJb 56, p. 181].

2263 **Westermann** Claus, Die Verheissungen an die Väter: FRL 116 [1976 ➤ 57,2192...]: ᴿÉTRel 64 (1989) 432 (T. *Römer*).

2264 *Alexander* T.D., [Gn 12; 20; 26] The wife/sister incidents of Genesis; oral variants?: IrBSt 11 (1989) 2-22 [< OTAbs 12,161].

2265 ᴱ**Becking** Bob, *Smelik* K., Een patriarchale leugen; het verhaal in Genesis 12 verschillend belicht. Baarn 1989, Ten Have. 121 p. Fb 398. – ᴿStreven 57 (1989s) 756 (P. *Beentjes*).

2266 **Niditch** Susan, [Gn 12; 20; 26...] Underdogs and tricksters... folklore 1987 ➤ 3,2189; 4,2288: ᴿBibTB 19 (1989) 39s (A.E. *Zannoni*); Interpretation 43 (1989) 195s (R. *Gnuse*); JAAR 57 (1989) 663-6 (J.L. *Crenshaw*).

2267 *Abela* Anthony, Gen 13; Abraham discovers the land as God's gift: MeliT 38 (1987) 53-80 [< OTAbs 12,166].

E2.4 **Melchisedech, Sodoma;** *Genesis 14.*

2268 *Helderman* Jan, Melchisedeks Wirkung; eine traditionsgeschichtliche Untersuchung eines Motivkomplexes in NHC IX, 1,1 - 27,10 (Melchisedek): ➤ 606, Réception 1986/9, 335-362.

2269 *Lubsczyk* Hans, Melchisedek; Versuch einer Einordnung der Melchisedek-Pericope (Gen 14) in der jahwistischen Erzählungszusammenhang [< ᶠAUFDERBECK Hugo (EThSt 32) Lp 1974, 92-109]: ➤ 306, Einheit 1989, 125-141.

2270 **Mianbé Betoudji** Denis, El... Gn 14, 1986 ➤ 2,1652 ...4,2296: ᴿRTPhil 121 (1989) 98 (T. *Römer*).

E2.5 **The Covenant** (alliance, Bund); *Foedus, Genesis 15...*

Damrosch David, The narrative covenant 1987 ➤ 7266.

2271 *Deurloo* K.A., Abraham, profeet, Gen. 15 en 20: AmstCah 9 (1988) 35-46 [TR 85,425].

2272 **Ha** John, Genesis 15, a theological compendium of Pentateuchal history [diss. Pont. Ist. Biblico, ᴰ*Soggin* J. A., R 1986 ➤ 2,1664]: BZAW 181. B 1989, de Gruyter. xii-241 p. DM 82. 3-11-011206-X / US 0-89925-291-5 [OIAc S89]. – ᴿExpTim 101 (1989s) 211 (G. *Lloyd Jones*).

2273 *a*) *Haag* Ernst, Die Abrahamtradition in Gen 15; – *b*) *Weimar* Peter, Genesis 15; ein redaktionskritischer Versuch; – *c*) *Mosis* Rudolf, 'Glauben' und 'Gerechtigkeit' — zu Gen 15,6; – *d*) *Cazelles* Henri, Abraham au Negeb: ➤ 169, ᶠSCHARBERT J., Väter 1989, 83-106 / 361-411 / 225-257 / 23-32.

2274 **Kreuzer** Siegfried, [Gn 15,13-16; Ex 3; Nm 20,15s; Dt 6,20-25; 26,5-9; Jos 24] Die Frühgeschichte Israels in Bekenntnis und Verkündigung des Alten Testaments: BZAW 178. B 1989, de Gruyter. ix-301 p. DM 120. 3-11-011736-3. – ᴿETL 65 (1989) 423s (J. *Lust*: less radical than T. L. *Thompson*; thinks N. *Lohfink* led a 'Catholic revival' in support of von *Rad*); ExpTim 101 (1989s) 153 (R. *Coggins*); TLZ 114 (1989) 877-9 (E.-J. *Waschke*). ➤ 2597.

2275 **McCarthy** Dennis J., Institution and narrative: AnBib 108, 1985 ➤ 1,204.2309 ... 4,2305: ᴿBZ 33 (1989) 132s (H. *Niehr*).

2276 *a*) *Pury* Albert de, La tradition patriarcale en Genèse 12-35; – *b*) *Seebass* Horst, Que reste-t-il du Yahwiste et de l'Élohiste? À titre d'exemple; réflexions sur Gen 16//21,8-21 et 20,1-18//26,1-33, ᵀ*Pury* Albert de: ➤ 601, Pentateuque 1987/9, 259-270 / 199-232.

2277 **Cairus** Aecio E., Protection and reward; the significance of ancient midrashic expositions on Genesis 15:1-6: diss. Andrews, ᴰ*Doukhan* J. Berrien Springs ᴹɪ 1989. 498 p. 89-22838. – DissA 50 (1989s) 2093-A.

2278 *Légasse* Simon, Songes-rêves, Écriture [*al.*]: ➤ 886, DictSpir 14,92s (1989) 1054-60 [-66].

2279 *a*) *Irsigler* Hubert, Erhörungsmotiv und Ismaelname in Gen 16,11 und 21,17; – *b*) *Krašovec* Jože, Der Ruf nach Gerechtigkeit in Gen 18,16-33; – *c*) *Seidl* Theodor, 'Zwei Gesichter' oder zwei Geschichten? Neuversuch einer Literarkritik zu Gen 20 [par. 12,10-20; 26,1-11 Frau/Schwester]: ➤ 169, ᶠSCHARBERT J., Väter 1989, 107-138 / 169-182 / 305-325.

2280 *Kopciowski* Elia, [Gn 17,7] Stabilirò la mia alleanza come alleanza perenne: StEcum 5 (1987) 193-208; Eng. 208.

2281 *Begrich* Gerhard, Die Freundlichkeit Gottes als Grundform theologischen Redens — ein Nachdenken über Gen 18,1-16a: EvT 49 (1989) 218-231.

2282 **Wright** Rebecca A., [Gn 18s...] Establishing hospitality in the Old Testament; testing the tool of linguistic pragmatics [there is no Hebrew word for 'hospitality', 'guest', or 'host'; exegesis has relied on travel-accounts]: diss. Yale, ᴰ*Wilson* R. NHv 1989. 259 p. 90-12329. – DissA 50 (1989s) 3991-A; RTLv 21,543.

2283 *Bertolini* Marco, I mirabilia di Sodoma (Carmen de Sodoma [Ps.-TERTULLIANO] 121-167): StClasOr 29 (1989) 185-202.

2284 **Rudin-O'Brasky** Talia, ❿ The patriarchs in Hebron and Sodom (Gen 18-19) 1982 ➤ 65,2000; 1,2317: ᴿJQR 79 (1988s) 291-4 (Yair *Zakovitch*).

2285 *Hester* Ralph, The metamorphosis of Sodom; the Ps-CYPRIAN De Sodoma as an Ovidian episode: Traditio 44 (1988) 1-35.

2286 **Mulder** M. J., Sodom en Gomorra, een verhaal van dode steden [< TWAT 5,756-769]: Exegetische Studies 4. Kampen 1988, Kok. 93 p.

*f*17,50. 90-242-3083-7. – ᴿGerefTTs 89 (1989) 185s (A. van der *Wal*); Streven 56 (1988s) 469 (P. *Beentjes*).

2287 *Nicol* George G., [Gen 18s] Building on the silences of texts [*Čapek* Karel, Apocryphal stories (supplementing biblical events), L 1949]: ExpTim 100 (1988s) 368-371.

2288 *Roshwald* Mordecai, [Gn 18,23-32] A dialogue between man and God; shall not the Judge of all the earth do right?: ScotJT 42 (1989) 145-165.

   Niditch Susan, Underdogs and tricksters (Gn 20,1-18; 26,1-17...) 1987 ➤ 2266.

2288* *Alonso Schökel* Luis, *a*) Giocando; esegesi di Gen. 21-1-9; – *b*) L'intercessione di Abramo: ➤ 563*b*, Abramo 1988...

E2.6 The 'Aqedâ; *Isaac, Genesis 22*...

2289 *Breitbart* Sidney, [Gn 22...] Problem of the theodicy: Dor 15 (1986s) 223-233.

2290 *a*) *De Benedetti* P., Il sacrificio di Abramo in alcune grandi letture; – *b*) *Bianchi* U., Il sacrificio del figlio nell'antropologia e nella storia delle religioni; – *c*) *Adinolfi* M., Le donne nel ciclo di Abramo; – *d*) *Gabrieli* F., Abramo e Ismaele nella tradizione islamica; – *e*) *Laras* G., La figura di Abramo nella tradizione ebraica: ➤ 563*b*, Abramo 1988...

2291 *Firestone* Reuven, Abraham's son as the intended sacrifice (*al-dhabīh*, Qur'an 17:99-115); issues in Qur'anic exegesis: JSS 34 (1989) 95-131 [...modern critics generally take Gn 22,1-19 as 'a protest against human sacrifice'].

2292 *a*) *Kreuzer* S., Das Opfer des Vaters — die Gefährdung des Sohnes, Genesis 22; – *b*) *Neubacher* F., Isaaks Opferung in der griechischen Alten Kirche: ➤ 2,99, ᶠSᴀᴜᴇʀ G., Schaut Abraham an, euren Vater! = Amt und Gemeinde 37,1 (1986) 62-70 / 72-76 [< OTAbs 11,150].

2293 *a*) *Landy* Francis, Narrative techniques and symbolic transactions in the Akedah; – *b*) (response) *Fokkelman* Jan P., 'On the mount of the Lord there is no vision': ➤ 395, Signs 1989, 1-40 / 41-57.

2294 **Milgrom** Jo, [Gn 22] The binding of Isaac, the Akedah, a primary symbol in Jewish thought and art (ᴰ1978) 1988 ➤ 4,3329: ᴿExpTim 100 (1988s) 348 (S. *Brock*).

2295 *Nelson* M., The sacrifice of Isaac; a humanistic interpretation: Neuphilologische Mitteilungen (Helsinki) 89 (1988) 286-294 [< RHE 85,100*].

2296 *Veijola* Timo, Abrahams offer (Gen 22) — tid och budskap: SvEx 54 (1989) 236-244.

2296* *Walters* Stanley D., Wood, sand and stars; structure and theology in Gn 22:1-19: TorJT 3 (1987) 301-330.

2297 *Wénin* André, Abraham à la rencontre de ʏʜᴡʜ; une lecture de Gn 22: RTLv 20 (1989) 162-177; Eng. 280.

2298 ᴱ**Zuidema** Willem, Isaak wird geopfert; 'Bindung Isaaks' als Symbol des Leidens Israels, Versuch einer Deutung [...Geschichte der Exegese, MᴀɪᴍᴏɴɪᴅᴇS, Gɪʀᴀʀᴅ]. Neuk 1987. x-250 p. DM 42. – ᴿZkT 111 (1989) 100 (W. *Kern*).

2299 *Maxwell* John F., Gen. 24:12-14; I Sam. 14:6-10; Charismatic renewal and common moral teaching on augury: PrPeo 3 (1989) 265-8, continuing Clergy Review 67 (1982) 1,6-16 on Acts 1,23-26. ➤ 63,6219.

2300 *Jeansonne* Sharon P., [Gn 24...] Images of Rebekah; from modern interpretations to biblical portrayal: BiRes 34 (Ch 1989) 33-52.

E2.7   **Jacob** and Esau; ladder-dream; *Jacob, somnium, Genesis 25 ...*

2301 **Alexandre** Jean,   On l'appellera disait-il Jacob.   Montpellier 1987, Demeret. – ᴿÉTRel 64 (1989) 477s (R. *Chapal*).

2302 **Blum** Erhard, [Gn 25-31] Die Komposition der Vätergeschichte: WM 57, 1984 ➤ 65,1970; 2,1686: ᴿProtestantesimo 44 (1989) 224 (J.A. *Soggin*); TrierTZ 98 (1989) 156 (E. *Haag*); ZkT 111 (1989) 86s (R. *Oberforcher*).

2303 *Lichtenstein* Aaron, [Gn 26,8...] Isaac and laughter: JBQ (= Dor) 18 (1989s) 13-18.

2304 *Safren* Jonathan D., [Gen 26,26-31] Ahuzzath and the pact of Beer-Sheba: ZAW 101 (1989) 184-198.

2305 *Willi-Plein* Ina,   Genesis 27 als Rebekkageschichte; zu einem historiographischen Kunstgriff der biblischen Vätergeschichten: TZBas 45 (1989) 315-334.

2306 *Fabry* Heinz-Josef,   Erst die Erstgeburt, dann der Segen; eine Nachfrage zu Gen 27,1-45. ➤ 220, ᶠZENGER E., Vom Sinai 1989, 51-72.

2307 *Feldman* Louis H.,   Josephus' portrait of Jacob: JQR 79 (1988s) 101-151.

2308 **Hendel** Ronald S.,   The epic of the Pentateuch; Jacob cycle...: HarvSemMg 42, 1987 ➤ 3,2237; 4,2340:   ᴿJBL 108 (1989) 118s (Kathleen A. *Farmer*); TLZ 114 (1989) 263s (E. *Blum*).

2309 *Nagel* Peter, [Gn 28-30] Fragmente eines sahidischen Genesiskodex der Nationalbibliothek zu Paris (BN copte 129ᴵ fol. 8-13): ZägSpr 116 (1989) 71-90.

2310 *Ḥamiel* Ḥ. Y., ◐ The mother of Jacob and Esau (Gen 28,5): BethM 32 (1986s) 332-344 [< OTAbs 11,151].

2311 *Vian* Giovanni M.,   Interpretazioni giudaiche e cristiane antiche del sogno di Giacobbe (Genesi 28,10-22): ➤ 748, Sogni 1988 = AugR 29 (1989) 307-332.

2312 *Pricoco* S.,   La scala di Giacobbe; l'interpretazione ascetica di Gen. 28,12 da FILONE a San BENEDETTO: Regulae Benedicti Studia 14s (1985s) 41-58 [< RHE 84, p. 401*].

2313 **Sherwood** Stephen,   'Had God not been on my side'; an examination of the narrative technique of the story of Jacob and Laban, Genesis 29,1 - 32,2: diss. Pont. Univ. Gregoriana, ᴰConroy C. Roma 1989.   460 p. – RTLv 21,542.

E2.8   **Jacob's wrestling; the Angels;** *lucta, Angelus/mal'ak Gn 31 ...*

2314 *Delery* Mark,   Angels: SpirLife 34 (1988) 163-7; p. 166, 'Angelic messages can also be transmitted through dreams'.

2315 **Fossum** Jarl E.,   The name of God and the angel of the Lord: WUNT 36, 1985 ➤ 1,2344*b*... 4,2355:   ᴿSalesianum 51 (1989) 356s (R. *Farina*).

2316 *Galot* Jean,   Existence personnelle et mission des anges: EsprVie 99 (1989) 257-263.

2317 **Greene** John T.,   The role of the messenger [*ml'k, al.*] and message in the ancient Near East; oral and written communication in the ANE and in the Hebrew Scriptures: BrownJudSt 169; Atlanta 1989, Scholars. xx-346 p. 1-55540-324-7 [BL 90, 121, J. *Sawyer*].

2318 *Kruse* Heinz, **O** God and his messengers: KatKenk 28,56 (1989) 1-34; Eng. i-ii.

2319 *Lacoste* Jean-Yves, Anges et hobbits; le sens des mondes possibles [LEIBNIZ...]: FreibZ 36 (1989) 341-373.

2320 **MacGregor** Geddes, Angels, ministers of grace. NY 1988, Paragon. xxi-230 p. $13. – ᴿTS 50 (1989) 828 (J. R. *Willis*).

1230* **Meier** Samuel A., The messenger in the ancient Semitic world: HarvSemMg 45. Atlanta 1989, Scholars. xvii-269 p.

2321 *a) Ries* Julien, Anges et démons; études récentes et perspectives de notre recherche; – *b) Fontinoy* Charles, Les anges et les démons de l'AT: ➤ 728, Anges 1987/9, 9-17 (399-42) / 117-134.

2322 *a) Schreiner* Josef, Das Gebet Jakobs (Gen 32,10-13); – *b) Bauer* J. B., Jakobs Kampf mit dem Dämon (Gen 32,23-33); – *c) Marböck* Johann, Heilige Orte im Jakobszyklus; einige Beobachtungen und Aspekte: ➤ 169, ᶠSCHARBERT J.: Väter 1989, 287-303 / 17-22 / 211-224.

2323 *Jüngel* Eberhard, [Gn 32] La lutte avec Dieu, ᵀ*Doré* J.: Christus 35 (P 1988) 241-253.

2324 *Masia* Juan, [Gn 32] A orillas del Yaboc; entre la gracia y la des-gracia: SalT 77 (1989) 368-376.

2325 *Lumpe* Adolf, [Gen. 32,23-33] Hinken [limping]: ➤904, RAC 15,115 (1989) 333-342.

2326 *Weimar* Peter, 'O Israel, Erstling im Morgengrauenkampf' (Nelly SACHS); zu Funktion und Theologie der Gotteskampfepisode Gen 32,23-33: MüTZ 40 (1989) 79-113.

2327 *Lipiński* E., Brautpreis [not Gen 34,12; Ex 22,16; 1 Sam 18,25]: ➤ 902, NBL Lfg 2 (1989) 324s.

2328 *Bartel* Aryeh, **O** Studies in the lists of Genesis 36: BethM 32 (1986s) 364-372 [< OTAbs 11,152].

2329 *Westenholz* Joan G., [Gn 38] Tamar, *qedēšâ, qadištu* and sacred prostitution in Mesopotamia: HarvTR 82 (1989) 245-265.

2330 *Mathewson* Steven D., An exegetical study of Genesis 38: BS 146 (1989) 373-392.

E2.9   **Joseph**; Jacob's blessings; *Genesis 37; 39-50.*

2331 **Dietrich** Walter, Die Josephserzählung als Novelle und Geschichts-schreibung; zugleich ein Beitrag zur Pentateuchfrage: BibTSt 14. Neuk 1989, Neuk-V. 78 p. DM 19,80. 3-7887-1306-2 [BL 90, 72, R. N. *Whybray*].

2331* *Greenspahn* F. E., From Egypt to Canaan; a heroic narrative [collective Israel, not specifically Joseph, as a maverick hero who leaves Canaan for Egypt and returns]: ➤ 77, ᶠHARRISON R. 1988, 1-8.

2332 **Humphreys** W. Lee, Joseph and his family; a literary study 1988 ➤ 4,2375; 0-87249-536-1: ᴿCBQ 51 (1989) 519s (J. S. *Ackerman*); Interpretation 43 (1989) 310 (J. *Van Seters* recommends more warmly than HENDEL R.).

2333 *Joines* Karen, Ancient Egypt [chiefly Joseph-era]: BibIll 14 (1987) 41-51 [< OTAbs 11,140].

2334 **Longacre** Robert E., Joseph, a story of divine providence; a text theoretical and textlinguistic analysis of Genesis 37 and 39-48. WL 1989, Eisenbrauns. xiv-322 p. 0-931464-42-0.

2335 *Ruppert* Lothar, Zur neueren Diskussion um die Josefsgeschichte der Genesis: BZ 33 (1989) 92-97.

2336 **Scharbert** Josef, Ich bin Josef, euer Bruder; die Erzählung von Josef und seinen Brüdern, wie sie nicht in der Bibel steht 1988 → 4,2381: ᴿTüTQ 169 (1989) 242 (H. *Schweizer*).
    Croisier F., L'histoire de Joseph... arabe 1989 → 9923.
2337 *Friedman* Mira, More on the Vienna Genesis [37,13-19]: Byzantion 59 (Bru 1989) 64-77.
2338 **Knauf** E. A. [Gn 37,28(.25 → k303 Ismael)], Midian [Hab-Diss. Heidelberg 1986] 1988 → 4,2376: ᴿLA 39 (1989) 276s (P. *Kaswalder*).
2338* *Hollis* Susan T., [Gen 39,7] The woman in ancient examples of the Potiphar's wife motif, K2111: → 391, Gender 1989, 28-42.
2339 *Gessler-Löhr* Beatrix, [Gn 40,1] Bemerkungen zu einigen wb3w njswt ['royal butlers'] der Nach-Amarnazeit: GöMiszÄg 112 (1989) 27-34.
2340 *a) Ringgren* Helmer, Die Versuchung Josefs (Gen 39); – *b) Ruppert* Lothar, Zur Offenbarung des Gottes des Vaters (Gen 46,1-5); traditions- und redaktionsgeschichtliche Überlegungen: → 169, ᶠSCHARBERT J., Väter 1989, 267-270 / 271-286.
2340* *Sarna* N. M., Israel in Egypt: → b322, ᴱ*Shanks* H., Ancient Israel 1988, 31-52.
2341 **Syrén** Roger, [Gn 49; Dt 33] The blessings in the Targums 1986 → 2,1722... 4,2397: ᴿCBQ 51 (1989) 134s (Z. *Garber*); RÉJ 147 (1988) 176-9 (A. *Tal*).
2342 *Nobile* Marco, Le 'benedizioni' a Giuda e a Giuseppe in Gen 49,8-12.22-26 e in Dt 33,7.13-17 nel quadro della redazione Gen-2 Re: Antonianum 64 (1989) 501-517; Eng. 501.
2343 *Rand* Herbert, The Testament of Jacob; an analysis of Gen 49:18: JBQ (= Dor) 18 (1989s) 101-6.

E3.1   **Exodus event and theme;** *textus, commentarii.*

2344 **d'Aviau de Ternay** Henri, **Weiler** Lúcia, Uma reescuta prática da voz do Êxodo; contribuições da teologia narrativa para a teologia da libertação: REB 49 (1989) 60-80.
2345 **Bianchi** Enzo, Esodo, commento esegetico-spirituale. Magnano VC 1987 [data di 'premessa' 1974], Qiqajon. 110 p.
2346 ᵀᴱ**Borret** M., ORIGÈNE, Homélies sur l'Exode: SChr 321, 1985 → 2,1725... 4,2400: ᴿRHR 206 (1989) 88s (J. *Doignon*).
2347 **Cazelles** H., Autour de l'Exode 1987 → 3,201; 4,2402: ᴿCommSev 22 (1989) 263 (M. de *Burgos*); ÉTRel 64 (1989) 278s (D. *Lys*); RHR 206 (1989) 81-3 (A. *Caquot*); RTLv 20 (1989) 218 (P.-M. *Bogaert*); RTPhil 121 (1989) 338 (T. *Römer*).
2348 *Clifford* Richard J., Exodus: → 384, NJBC (1989) 44-60.
2349 **Collins** Nina L., A critical investigation of the provenance and date of the Hellenistic poet Ezekiel [*Exagōgē*], with special reference to the post-biblical traditions of the names of the father-in-law of Moses: diss. Leeds 1989. 454 p. BRD-88400. – DissA 50 (1989s) 3989-A.
    Ezechiel tragicus, Exagoge, ᴱ**Holladay** C. R. 1989 → b678.
2350 **Dunnam** Maxie D., Exodus: Communicator's Comm. Waco 1987, Word. 395 p. $26. 0-8499-0407-2. – ᴿBS 146 (1989) 108 (T. L. *Constable*, 'Dunham': a series of sermons).
2351 **Durham** John J., Exodus: Word Comm. 3, 1987 → 3,2284; 4,2410: ᴿBA 52 (1989) 43 (Rita J. *Burns*); BL (1989) 53 (G. I. *Davies*: in many ways excellent, but misspells his teacher's name, and starts 'The Book of Exodus is the first book of the Bible'); CBQ 51 (1989) 318s (D.

Launderville); CriswT 3 (1989) 380s (E. *Rowell*); RB 96 (1989) 404-6 (J. *Loza*); WestTJ 50 (1988) 177-180 (J. P. *Marcott*).

2352 **Fox** Everett, Now these are the names; a new English rendition of the Book of Exodus 1986 → 2,1729: ᴿCBQ 51 (1989) 119s (J. I. *Hunt*).

2353 **Girón Blanc** Luis-Fernando, Midrás Éxodo Rabbah I: Biblioteca Midrásica P. Valencia 1989, Inst. S. Jerónimo. vi-190 p. 84-86067-32-4 [EstBib 47,578].

2354 *Gottwald* Norman K., El 'Éxodo' como evento y proceso; un estudio de la base bíblica de la teología de la liberación: TXav 39 (1989) 385-396.

2355 **Houtman** C., Exodus vertaald en verklaard I (-7,13) 1986 → 3,2288; 4,2414: ᴿBO 46 (1989) 423-5 (F. C. *Fensham*); Streven 56 (1988s) 947s (P. *Beentjes*); WestTJ 50 (1988) 349 (W. A. *VanGemeren*).

2356 **Houtman** C., Exodus II (7:14-19:25): CommOudT. Kampen 1989, Kok. 413 p. *f* 85. 90-242-0925-0 [BL 90, 56, J. W. *Rogerson*].

2357 ᵀ**LeBoulluec** Alain, Sandevoir Pierre, ᴱ*Dorival* Gilles, *al.*, L'Exode: Bible d'Alexandrie 2. P 1989, Cerf. 397 p. [CBQ 52,195]. 2-204-03066-X. – ᴿIrénikon 62 (1989) 285s (E. *Lanne*).

2357* **Marais** Stephanus, Konteks en resepsie; die Uittogverhaal soos uitgelê door bevrydingsteoloê van die N. G. Sendingskerk (Context and reception; the story of the Exodus as it is interpreted by liberation theologians in the Dutch Reformed Mission Church): diss. ᴰ*Deist* F. Pretoria 1989. 260 p. – RTLv 21,541.

2358 *Nagel* Peter, Textumfang und Textabfolge der sahidischen Version des Buches Exodus: → 138, ᶠMÜLLER C. D. G., Nubica 1988, 181-9.

2359 **Oosthuizen** Marthinus [RTLv 21,541], The God of the Exodus; a study of characterisation in Exodus 1-12: diss. ᴰ*Deist* F. Pretoria 1989. 251 p.

2360 *Ramírez* Z. A., El éxodo israelita: 'Universidad de Antioquía' 214 (Medellín 1988) 31-43 [< Stromata 45, 508].

2361 **Sanderson** Judith E., An Exodus scroll from Qumran... and the Samaritan tradition: HarvSemSt 30, 1986 → 3,1737; 4,2426: ᴿBO 46 (1989) 141-4 (F. *García Martínez*); CBQ 51 (1989) 349s (J. *Duhaime*).

2362 *Sanderson* Judith E., The Old Greek of Exodus in the light of 4QpaleoExodᵐ: Textus 14 (1988) 87-104 [< NTAbs 33,217].

2363 **Sarna** Nahum M., Exploring Exodus 1986 → 2,1738... 4,2428: ᴿCBQ 51 (1989) 730s (J. C. *Endres*).

2364 *Sarna* Nahum M., Exodus: → 377, Books 1 (1989) 47-62. → 2340*.

2365 **Scharbert** Josef, Exodus: NEchter 24. Wü 1989, Echter. 151 p. DM 34; sb. 29. 3-429-01245-7 [BL 90, 61, G. I. *Davies*].

2366 *Schmidt* W. H., Exodus [1-6]: BK AT 2, Lfg. 4, 1988 → 4,2429: ᴿRB 96 (1989) 401-4 (J. *Loza*); ZAW 101 (1989) 147 (H.-C. *Schmitt*).

2366* *Schuller* Eileen, Women of the Exodus in biblical retellings of the Second Temple period: → 391, Gender 1989, 178-194.

2367 ᵀᴱ**Sierra** Sergio L., RASHI de Troyes, Commento all'Esodo: Ascolta Israele 5. Genova 1988, Marietti. xxxii-368 p. Lit. 43.000. 88-211-8456-0 [BL 90,59]. – ᴿAnStoEseg 6 (1989) 316-8 (P. *Stefani*, anche su Rashi Gen 1985); Henoch 11 (1989) 122s (M. *Perani*).

2368 *Sierra* Sergio J., Il commento di RASHI all'Esodo e l'esegesi giudaica medievale: CrNSt 10 (1989) 23-38; Eng. 39.

2369 **Stiebing** William H.ᴶ, Out of the desert? Archaeology and the Exodus/Conquest narratives. Buffalo 1989, Prometheus. 269 p. $22. 0-87975-505-9 [BAR-W 16/1, 8.10, B. *Halpern*: strong indictment of the biblical accounts of the Israelite emergence in Canaan, whether 15th or 12th century; I. FINKELSTEIN also showed that all the towns claimed occupied by the Exodus people were empty before 1100; Stiebing himself relates the Israel takeover to the c. 1200 B.C. unraveling of Mycenean Greece and of the Hittite Empire, and to a microclimatic shift]. – ᴿJScStR 29 (1989) 269s (P. C. *Hammond*: excellent).

2370 *Ullmann* Wolfgang, Exodus und Diabasis; ORIGENES 'Über das Passa' als Beispiel christlicher Auslegung des ATs: BTZ 6 (1989) 234-244.

2371 *Vijver* E., El Éxodo; ¿un modelo para la ética social?; una crítica a la 'Ética comunitaria' de Enrique DUSSEL: Cuadernos de Teología 9 (BA 1988) 177-207 [< Stromata 45,500].

E3.2 **Moyses** – Pharaoh, Goshen – *Exodus 1* ...

Allam S., Trial of Mose [= Mes, Ṣaqqâra scribe] 1989 → 2479*ab*.

2372 **Alonso Schökel** Luis, *Gutiérrez* Guillermo, La misión de Moisés; meditaciones bíblicas: Servidores y Testigos 42. Santander 1989, Sal Terrae. 159 p. [ActaPIB 9,454]. 84-293-0848-2.

2373 *Arichea* Daniel C.ᴶ, The ups und downs of Moses; locating Moses in Exodus 19-33: BTrans 40 (1989) 244-6.

2374 **Aurelius** Erik, Der Fürbitter Israels 1988 → 4,2441: ᴿScandJOT (1989,2) 94-99 (E. *Nielsen*); TLZ 114 (1989) 420-2 (Eva *Osswald*).

2375 **Balout** L., *Roubet* C., La momie de Ramses II 1985 → 4,2442.h275: ᴿArOr 57 (1989) 191s (E. *Strouhal*, Eng.).

2376 *Bietak* Manfred, *a*) Canaanites in the Eastern Nile Delta; – *b*) Comments on the 'Exodus': → 3,834, ᴱ*Rainey* A., Egypt, Israel, Sinai 41-56; 6 fig. / 163-171; map.

2377 *Cazelles* Henri, En busca de Moisés [À la recherche de Moïse ...], ᵀ*Ortiz García* Alfonso. 1981. – FranBog 31 [1989] 329s (H. C.).

2378 **Coats** George W., Moses ...: JStOT Sup 57, 1988 → 4,2448: ᴿBiblica 70 (1989) 539-541 (R. *Martin-Achard*); CBQ 51 (1989) 709-711 (D. M. *Beegle*).

2379 *Cristiani* Marta, Mysticus Moyses; escatologia ed Esodo nel Periphyseon di Giovanni Scoto [ERIUGENA]: CrNSt 10 (1989) 465-481; Eng. 482.

2380 *Garcia López* Félix, El Moisés histórico y el Moisés de la fe [*Miller* J., *Hayes* J., 1986]: Salmanticensis 36 (1989) 5-21; Eng. 21.

2381 *Garthoff* B. W. B., Merenptah's Israel stela; a curious case of Rites de passage?: → 78, ᶠHEERMA VAN VOSS M., Funerary 1988, 23-33.

2382 *Grundlach* Rolf, Der Pharao — eine Hieroglyphe Gottes; zur 'Göttlichkeit' des ägyptischen Königs: → 769, Menschwerdung 1986/9, 13-35.

2383 *Hollerich* Michael J., The comparison of Moses and Constantine in EUSEBIUS of Caesarea's Life of Constantine: → 696, 10th Patristic, 19 (1989) 80-85.

2384 *Sawyer* Vince, The fall of a great leader as illustrated in the life of Moses: CalvaryB 5,1 (1989) 12-27.

2385 *Shea* William H., A further reading for the Hobab inscription from Sinai: AndrUnS [25 (1987) 73] 27 (1989) 193-200; 2 fig.

2386 *Siebert-Hommes* J. C., Twelve women in Exodus 1 and 2; the role of daughters and sons in the stories concerning Moses: AmstCah 9 (1988) 47-58 [TR 85,425].

2387 *Wouters* Werner, Urḫi-Tešub and the Ramses [II]–letters from Boghazköy: JCS 41 (1989) 226-234.

2388 *Holmgren* Frederick C.,   Violence; God's will on the edge, Exodus
2:11-15:   CurrTM 16 (1989) 425-9.

E3.3   Nomen divinum, Tetragrammaton;   *Exodus 3,14 ...*

2389 *Bader* Günter,   Gott nennen; von Götternamen zu göttlichen Namen;
zur Vorgeschichte der Lehre von der göttlichen Eigenschaften: ZTK 86
(1989) 306-354.

2390 **Fischer** Georg,   Jahwe unser Gott; Sprache, Aufbau und Erzähltechnik
in der Berufung des Mose Ex 3-4 [Diss. R 1987s ➤ 4,2470]: OBO 91.
FrS/Gö 1989, Univ./VR. 262 p. Fs 68. 3-7278-0646-X / 3-525-53721-2
[ZAW 102,443, H.-C. *Schmitt*; BL 90,75, R. E. *Clements*].

2391 **Kohata** F.,   Jahwist und Priesterschrift in Ex 3-14: BZAW 166, 1986
➤ 2,1776 ... 4,2472: RRB 96 (1989) 406-411 (J. *Loza*).

2392 **Mettinger** T.,   In search of God; the meaning and message of the
everlasting names 1988 ➤ 4,2477: RRExp 86 (1989) 621s (J. D. W.
Watts).

2393 *Scheifler* José R.,   Revelación y significado del nombre de Yahvé; la
imagen auténtica del Dios de Israel: *a*) SalT 76 (1988) 49-62; – *b*)
Diakonia 12,45 (Managua 1988) 3-17 [< TContext 6/2, 76].

2394 **Stefani** P.,   Il nome e la domanda; dodici volti all'ebraismo. Brescia
1988, Morcelliana. 340 p. Lit. 25.000. – RStPatav 36 (1989) 201s (G.
Segalla).

2395 *Haakma* Garmt J.,   [Ex 3,1-29] Die zahlenmässige Strukturanalyse; eine
kurze Einführung in die Methode und Problematik der Logotechnik oder
zahlenmässige Strukturanalyse [*Schedl* C.]: ComViat 32 (1989) 273-282.

2396 *a*) *Demoustier* Adrien,   Le buisson ardent et la vie quotidienne; – *b*)
Fédou Michel,   L'Exode, figure de la vie chrétienne selon ORIGÈNE:
Christus 36 (P 1989) 146-157 / 281-293.

2397 *Kim Ee Kon*,   Who is Yahweh? based on a contextual reading of
Exodus 3:14: AsiaJT 3 (1989) 108-117.

2398 *Norris* F. W.,   The tetragrammaton in GREGORY Nazianzen (Or. 30.17):
VigChr 43 (1989) 339-344.

2399 *Wehrle* J., *a*) Blutbräutigam [Ex 4,25]; – *b*) [Gn 9,5 ...] Blut: ➤ 902, NBL,
Lfg 2 (1989) 308-310 / 306-8.

2400 *Schneeman* Gisela,   Die Deutung und Bedeutung der Beschneidung nach
Exodus 4,24-26: ComViat 32 (1989) 21-37. 193-200.

2401 **Steingrimsson** Sigurdur Ö.:   Vom Zeichen zur Geschichte... Ex
6,28 - 11,10, 1979 ➤ 60,3105; 61,3378: RRB 96 (1989) 411-3 (J. *Loza*).

2402 *Schmitt* Hans-Christoph,   Tradition der Prophetenbücher in den
Schichten der Plagenerzählung Ex 7,1 - 11,10: ➤ 105, FKAISER O.,
Prophet 1989, 196-216.

E3.4   *Pascha, sanguis, sacrificium:*   **Passover, blood, sacrifice,** *Ex 11 ...*

2403 *Bokser* B. M.,   Changing views of Passover and the meaning of
redemption according to the Palestinian Talmud [mPes 10]: AJS 10,1 (CM
1985) 1-18 [< NTAbs 33,79].

2404 *Klein* M. L.,   Months compete for Passover honor; [six Cairo Genizah]
targumic fragments reveal how Hebrew months vied for Pesach: Moment
14,3 (Wsh 1989) 14-19 [NTAbs 33,362].

2405 *Moster* Julius B.,   Thus they stripped the Egyptians [...stopping the plague by their prayers]: Dor 16 (1987s) 41-44 [< OTAbs 11,153].

2406 *Loza Vera* José,   Éxodo 13,17-14,31; dos perspectivas de lectura: EfMex 6 (1988) 331-366.

2407 **Ska** J. L.,   Le passage de la mer: AnBib 109, ᴰ1986 → 2,1803*... 4,2490: ᴿJAOS 109 (1989) 680s (A. *Cooper*: 'not all has been said', p.178: true, but more than he acknowledges); RB 96 (1989) 297-300 (J. *Loza*); RechSR 76 (1988) 564s (J. *Briend*); RelStR 15 (1989) 69 (D. *Jobling*).

2408 *Görg* M., Baal-Zefon [Ex 14,2.9]: → 902, NBL Lfg. 2 (1989) 225s.

2409 *a) Anderson* Bernhard W.,   The song of Miriam poetically and theologically considered [response, *Brueggemann* W.]; – *b) Hauser* A. J., Two songs of victory; a comparison of Exodus 15 and Judges 5: → 2987, Directions 1987, 285-296 [297-302] / 265-284.

2410 **Brenner** Martin L.,   The song of the sea within its cultic and theological milieu: diss. Angelicum, ᴰ*Zerafa* J.   Dubuque 1989. 214 p.

2411 **Schafran** Philip M.,   The form and function of Exodus 15:1-18; diss. Dallas Theol. Sem. 1988. 240 p. 89-17230. – DissA 50 (1989s) 1342-A.

2412 *Howell* Maribeth,   Exodus 15,1b-18, a poetic analysis: ETL 65 (1989) 5-42.

2413 *Schüngel-Straumann* Helen [Ex 15,20s...] Miryam; comment Miryam fut évincée [1984], ᵀ*Luze* D. de, *Ludwig* Y.: FoiVie 88 (1989) 89-99.

2414 **Burns** Rita J.,   [Ex 15,20s] Has the Lord indeed spoken only through Moses?... Miriam: SBL diss. 84, 1987 → 3,2367; 4,2491: ᴿCBQ 51 (1989) 113-5 (Barbara *Green*); Interpretation 43 (1989) 308 (P. A. *Bird*).

2415 **Turgman** Victor,   De l'autorité de Moïse, Ex 15,22-27: 1987 → 3,2370; 4,2493: ᴿCBQ 51 (1989) 357 (L. J. *Hoppe*); JTS 40 (1989) 523-5 (D. R. *Jones*: hazardous guesses); RB 96 (1989) 612s (J. *Loza*).

2416 *Poniży* Bogdan, ❷ Manna in the biblical traditions: STWsz 26,1 (1988) 96-116; Eng. 116.

2417 **Propp** William H.,   Water in the wilderness; a biblical motif and its mythological background [< diss. Harvard]: HarvSemMg 40. Atlanta 1987, Scholars. xi-144 p. $15. 1-555-40157-0 [TDig 37,83]. – ᴿBZ 33 (1989) 309s (V. *Fritz*).

2417* *Goodnick* Benjamin,   The rise and fall of Israel in the Sinai Desert: JBQ (= Dor) 18 (1989s) 32-36.

2418 *Houtman* C.,   'ʏʜᴡʜ is my banner' — 'A "hand" on the "throne" of ʏʜ', Exodus xvii 15b,16a and their interpretation: → 129, ꟻMULDER M., New avenues 1989, 110-120.

2419 **Maiberger** Paul,   Topographische und historische Untersuchungen zum Sinaiproblem; worauf beruht die Identifizierung des Gebel Musa mit dem Sinai?: OBO 34, 1984 → 65,2128... 4,2507: ᴿJAOS 109 (1989) 117s (T. L. *Thompson*: the 14th century Arabic ineditum gives meaning and value to what is otherwise as WELLHAUSEN said a problem for dilettantes).

2420 **Dozeman** Thomas B.,   God on the mountain; a study of redaction, theology and canon in Exodus 19-24: SBL Mg 37. Atlanta 1989, Scholars. xi-224 p. $27; sb./pa. $18. 1-55540-358-1; 9-X [Bl 90,72, G. I. *Davies*].

2421 *Dozeman* Thomas B.,   Spatial form in Exod 19:1-8 and in the larger Sinai narrative: Semeia 46 (1989) 87-101.

2422 *Sonnet* J.-P.,   Le Sinaï dans l'événement de sa lecture; la dimension pragmatique d'Ex 19-24: NRT 111 (1989) 321-344.

2423 *a) Zenger* Erich, Le thème de la 'sortie d'Égypte' et la naissance du Pentateuque, ^T*Dubois* Éric; – *b) Blum* Erhard, Israël à la montagne de Dieu; remarques sur Ex 19-24; 32-34 et sur le contexte littéraire et historique de sa composition, ^T*Nicolet* Philippe: ➤ 601, Pentateuque 1987/9, 301-321 / 271-295.

2424 *Barbiero* Gianni, *Mamleket koh^anîm* (Es 19,6a); i sacerdoti al potere?: RivB 37 (1989) 427-445; Eng. 445s [universalistic election, against *Moran* W.].

2424* *Wittmann* D., Israels Gotteserfahrung auf dem Wege; Tiefenpsychologische Anmerkungen zu Ex 20,2 und 3: Pastoraltheologie 78 (Gö 1989) 247-256 [< ZIT 89,557].

E3.5 Decalogus, *Ex 20 = Dt 5; Ex 21ss;* Ancient Near East Law.

2425 **Cicchese** M., Le dieci parole 1987 ➤ 4,2512: ^RProtestantesimo 44 (1989) 124s (G. *Conte*).

2426 ^E**Dales** Richard C., *King* Edward B., Robert GROSSETESTE, De decem mandatis [c. 1230 A.D.]: Ox Auctores Britannici Medii Aevi X, 1987 ➤ 3,2889: ^RChH 50 (1989) 507s (G. *Freibergs*); JTS 40 (1989) 288-290 (J. *McEvoy*).

2427 *De Benedetti* Paolo, Lo spirito dei precetti nella tradizione rabbinica: ➤ 571, L'Ebraismo 1986/7, 49-60.

2428 *a) Dohmen* Christoph, Was stand auf den Tafeln vom Sinai und was auf denen vom Horeb? [*nothing* on *either* in the original tradition; the blank stone itself was just a symbol; in a later tradition the Privilegrecht of Ex 34 was for the Sinai-theophany and the Decalog of Dt (9 and) 5 for the Horeb-theophany] Zur Geschichte und Theologie eines Offenbarungsrequisits; – *b) Hossfeld* Frank-L., Zum synoptischen Vergleich der Dekalogfassungen; eine Fortführung des begonnenen Gesprächs: ➤ 220, ^FZENGER E., Vom Sinai zum Horeb 1989, 9-50 / 73-119.

2429 *Feitosa* Neri, Uma redação neotestamentário do Decálogo na renovação da catequese: REB 49 (1989) 136-140.

2430 *Geczö* András, ⓦ Das israelitische Recht und der Dekalog: Református Szemle 80 (1987) 380-9 [< TLZ 115,238].

2431 *Johnstone* William, The 'Ten Commandments'; some recent interpretations: ExpTim 100 (1988s) 453-461 [*Lochman* J., *Crüsemann* F., *Gerstenberger* E. ...].

2432 *Kasher* Rimon, ⓞ *Targum arami l^e'esret ha dibrot* ... Aramaic Targum to the Ten Words according to a new Geniza fragment and its relation to the Piyyuṭ literature of Jewish Kurdistan: HUCA 60 (1989) ⓞ 1-31.

2432* *Lachmann* R., Gebote als Evangelium unterrichten und verkündigen?: Pastoraltheologie 78 (Gö 1989) 535... [< ZIT 90,131].

2433 **Loopik** M. van, [r. Išmael 2 cent. on Ex 20] De tien woorden in de Mekhilta: Sleutelteksten 4. Delft 1987, Meinema. 158 p. *f*27,50. 90-211-6103-6. – ^RTsTNijm 29 (1989) 291 (K. *Waaijman*).

2434 **Loza** José, Las palabras de Yahve; estudio del Decálogo: Biblioteca Mexicana. México DF 1989, Univ. Pontificia. 388 p.

2435 *a) Miller* Patrick D.^J, The place of the Decalogue in the Old Testament and its law; – *b) Fuller* Reginald H., The Decalogue in the New Testament; – *c) Steinmetz* David C., The Reformation and the Ten Commandments: Interpretation 43 (1989) 229-242 / 243-255 / 256-266.

2436 *Rand* Herbert, [Ex 32,15 'from here (the right) and from there (the left)'], The layout of the Decalogue on the tablets and archaeology [engraved in horizontal rows beginning at the center of each tablet as if emanating from God's throne]: Dor 15 (1986s) 177-180 [< OTAbs 11,153].

2437 *Vecchio* Silvana, Il decalogo nella predicazione del XIII secolo: CrNSt 10 (1989) 41-55; Eng. 56.

2438 **Veijola** Timo, Dekalogi; raamatullisen etiikan perusteita: Eks. Seuran Julkaisuja 49. Helsinki 1988, Kirjapaino Raamattutalo. iii-253 p.; 253 summary, Grundlagen biblischer Ethik. 951-9217-04-5.

2439 *Vlachos* Constantinos S., ☉ Israel and the Gentiles; the gkaite and the Decalogue: → 188, Mem. STOGIANNOU V. 1988, 19-34.

2440 *Waschke* Ernst-J., Die 'Zehn Gebote' vom AT her gelesen... Bibelwoche 1989s: Christenlehre 42 (1989) 299-307 [< TLZ 115,343].

2441 *Krašovec* Jože, Ex 20,5-7... Božja dobrota... God's love to thousands, punishment to three or four generations: BogVest 48 (1988) 357-383; Eng. 384.

2442 **Dohmen** C., [Ex 20,4] Das Bilderverbot: BoBB 62, 1985 → 1,1829... 4,2527: ᴿBO 46 (1989) 410-9 (C. *Uehlinger*); CrNSt 10 (1989) 149s (J. A. *Soggin*); VT 39 (1989) 122 (R. P. *Gordon*).

2443 ᴱ**Dohmen** C. [Ex 32, p. 11-23], *Sternberg* T., ... kein Bildnis machen 1987 → 3,395; 4,2528: ᴿETL 65 (1989) 183s (A. de *Halleux*); ZKG 100 (1989) 392-4 (K. *Hoffmann*).

2444 *Dohmen* C., Bild: → 902, NBL, Lfg 2 (1989) 294s (-verbot, 296-8).

2445 *Hossfeld* Frank-L., Du sollst dir kein Bild machen; die Funktion des alttestamentlichen Bilderverbots: TrierTZ 98 (1989) 81-94.

2446 *Mettinger* Tryggve N. D., The study of the Gottesbild — problems and suggestions: SvEx 54 (1989) 135-145.

2447 *Saracino* Francesco, A proposito dell'ermeneutica del 'secondo comandamento' al Niceno II: StEcum 6 (1988) 311-323; Eng. 323.

2448 **Schroer** Silvia, In Israel gab es Bilder...: OBO 74, 1987 → 3,2404; 4,2532: ᴿCBQ 51 (1989) 117-9 (R. *Gnuse*: an encyclopedic work on art and iconography... and, like DOHMEN C., on how religion evolved into monotheism); RB 96 (1989) 297 (J.-M. de *Tarragon*); TüTQ 169 (1989) 70 (W. *Gross*); ZkT 111 (1989) 115s (R. *Oberforcher*).

2449 **Spier** Erich, [Ex 20,8] Der Sabbat: Das Judentum 1. B 1989, Inst. Kirche & Judentum. 220 p. 3-923095-71-6. → 7643*-7651.

2450 *Veijola* Timo, Die Propheten und das Alter des Sabbatgebots: → 105, ᶠKAISER O., Propheten 1989, 246-264.

2451 *Gilbert* Maurice, [Ex 20,12] Il IV comandamento, 'onora tuo padre e tua madre': → 587, Famiglia 1988/9, 89-99.

2452 *Freund* Richard A., [Ex 20,13-15] Murder, adultery and theft? [Ex 20 and Dt 5 in same order; otherwise LXX etc.]: ScandJOT (1989,2) 72-80.

2453 **Gnuse** Robert, [Ex 20,15] Comunidad y propiedad en la tradición bíblica [You shall not steal 1985 → 1,7862... 4,2540], ᵀ*Ruiz-Garrido* Constantino. Estella 1987, VDivino. 303 p. – ᴿFranBog 30 (1988) 97s (A. *Morales D.*).

2454 *Stoebe* Hans J., Das achte Gebot (Exod. 20 v. 16) [< WDienst 3 (1952) 108-126]: → 362, Geschichte 1989, 27-45.

2455 **Osumi** Yuichi, Die Kompositionsgeschichte des Bundesbuches Exodus 20,22b - 23,33: Diss. ᴰ*Crüsemann* F. Kirchliche Hochschule Bethel, 1988s. – TR 85 (1989) 514; RTLv 21,541.

2456 **Otto** Eckart, Rechtsgeschichte der Redaktionen im Kodex Ešnunna und im 'Bundesbuch'; eine redaktionsgeschichtliche und rechtsvergleichende Studie zu altbabylonischen und altisraelitischen Rechtsüberlieferungen: OBO 85. FrS/Gö 1989, Univ./VR. 209 p. Fs 54. 3-7278-0602-8 / VR 3-525-53715-8 [BL 90, 110, B. S. *Jackson*]. – ᴿREB 49 (1989) 737-742 (E. *Bouzon*).

2457 **Otto** E., Wandel der Rechtsbegründungen in der Gesellschaftsgeschichte des antiken Israel; eine Rechtsgeschichte des 'Bundesbuches' Ex XX 22 - XXIII 13: StB 3, 1988 ➤ 4,2543: ᴿTLZ 114 (1989) 802-4 (G. *Sauer*); ZAW 101 (1989) 472s (H.-C. *Schmitt*).

2458 **Schwienhorst-Schönberger** Ludger, Das Bundesbuch; Studien zu seiner Entstehung und Theologie: kath. Diss. ᴰ*Zenger*. Münster 1988s. – TR 85 (1989) 517.

2459 *Schwienhorst-Schönberger* Ludger, 'Hier sind die Rechtsvorschriften, die du ihnen vorlegen sollst'; zur Struktur und Entstehung des Bundesbuches: ➤ 220, ᶠZENGER E., Vom Sinai zum Horeb 1989, 119-143.

2460 **Chirichigno** Gregory C., Debt slavery in the ancient Near East and Israel; an examination of the biblical manumission laws in Exod 21:2-6,7-11; Deut 15:12-18; Lev 25:39-54: diss. Council for [British] Academic Awards. 388 p. BRDX-87660. – DissA 50 (1989s) 337-A.

2461 *Nogah* Rivkah, [Ex 21,4; 1 Sam 15,27; 1 Kgs 11,30; 2 Kgs 8,15; 25,30; Ruth 4,8; 2 Chr 13,20] Ⓗ Biblical verses susceptible to different interpretations: BethM 32 (1986s) 350-4 [< OTAbs 11,111].

2462 *Congdon* Robert N., Exodus 21,22-25 and the abortion debate: BS 146 (1989) 132-147.

2463 *Martin-Achard* Robert, [Ex 21,23 ...; une dizaine de] Récents travaux sur la loi du talion selon l'Ancien Testament [*Crüsemann* F.; *Jüngling* H.-W.; *Otto* E....]: RHPR 69 (1989) 173-188.

2464 *Katzoff* Louis, [Ex 23,10s] Shemittah and the geography of Israel: Dor 15 (1986s) 163-5 [the synagogue—mosaic at Rehov confirms that food grown in pagan cities was exempted from these laws: OTAbs 11,189].

2465 *Alt* Albrecht, The origins of Israelite law [Sächs. Akad. ph/h 86,1 (Lp 1934)], ᵀ ➤ 225, Essays 1989, 79-132.

2466 *Amsler* Samuel, Les documents de la loi et la formation du Pentateuque: ➤ 601, Pentateuque 1987/9, 235-257.

2467 *Barrios* Dominique, L'étranger et la loi dans l'AT: DossB 21 (1988) 6-8 [-26 *al.*, prophètes, Jonas, Jésus ...].

2468 **Dorff** Elliot N., *Rosett* Arthur, A living tree; the roots and growth of Jewish law. Albany 1988, SUNY. xv-502 p. $49.50; pa. $20. – ᴿJRel 69 (1989) 283s (M. *Lockshin*).

2469 **Epsztein** Leon, Social justice 1986 ➤ 2,1860... 4,2559: ᴿInterpretation 43 (1989) 90 (R. D. *Nelson*).

2469* *Hiebert* Paula S., 'Whence shall help come to me?'; the biblical widow [... *'almānâ*; Hammurabi]: ➤ 391, Gender 1989, 125-141.

2470 *Jackson* Bernard S., Ideas of law and legal administration; a semiotic approach: ➤ 378, World of Ancient Israel 1989, 185-202.

2471 *Levitsky* Joseph, The illegitimate child (*mamzer*) in Jewish law: JBQ (= Dor) 18 (1989s) 6-12.

2472 a) *Lohfink* Norbert, Kennt das Alte Testament einen Unterschied von 'Gebot' und 'Gesetz'? Zur bibeltheologischen Einstufung des Dekalogs; – b) *Stemberger* Günter, Der Dekalog im frühen Judentum; – c) *Schmidt* Werner H., Werk Gottes und Tun des Menschen; Ansätze zur

Unterscheidung von 'Gesetz und Evangelium' im AT; – *d*) *Köckert*
Matthias, Leben in Gottes Gegenwart; zum Verständnis des Gesetzes in
der priesterschriftlichen Literatur: JbBT 4 ('Gesetz als Thema biblischer
Theologie' 1989) 63-89 / 91-103 / 11-28 / 29-61.
2473 **Niehr** Herbert, Rechtsprechung in Israel...: SBS 130, 1987 ⇥ 3,2430:
ᴿBL (1989) 112 (A. D. H. *Mayes*); BO 46 (1989) 690-4 (D. R. *Daniels*);
JBL 108 (1989) 686-8 (K. *Whitelam*); TPhil 64 (1989) 257s (R. *Sebott*);
ZAW 101 (1989) 164 (H. C. *Schmitt*).
2474 *a*) *Patrick* Dale, (intr.) Studying biblical law as a humanities; – *b*)
Knierim Rolf, The problem of ancient Israel's prescriptive legal
traditions; – *c*) *Buss* Martin, Logic and Israelite law; – *d*) *Haas* Peter, 'Die
he shall surely die'; the structure of homicide in biblical law; – *e*) *Frymer-
Kensky* Tikva, Law and philosophy; the case of sex in the Bible; – *f*)
Milgrom Jacob, Rationale for cultic law; the case of impurity: Semeia
45 (1989) (1-5) 27-47 / 7-25 / 49-65 / 67-87 / 89-102 / 103-9.
2475 *a*) *Scharbert* J., Autorität; – *b*) *Singer* K. H., Asyl; – *c*) *Lohfink* N.,
Bann: ⇥ 902, NBL Lfg. 2 (1989) 219s / 195s / 237s.
2476 *Schreiner* Josef, 'Deklaratorische Formel' und rechtsgültige Feststellung
im AT: ⇥ 207, ꟳWEIGAND R., Ius et historia 1989, 46-63.
2477 **Van Houten** Christiana D., The legislation of the alien; a study of the
Pentateuchal laws pertaining to the alien: diss. Notre Dame 1989,
ᴰ*Blenkinsopp* J. 304 p. 90-10776. – DissA 50 (1989s) 3630-A; RelStR
16,189 'Christine'.
2478 **Westbrook** Raymond, Studies in biblical and cuneiform law: RB Cah
26, 1988 ⇥ 4,2568: ᴿJBL 108 (1989) 685s (L. *Eslinger*).

2479 *Allam* S., *a*) Some remarks on the trial of Mose [treasury-scribe tomb at
Saqqâra, based on documents from Pi-Ramesses, legitimate though A.
GARDINER's excellent edition interpreted them as a forgery; no dating
here noticeable]: JEA 75 (1989) 103-112; – *b*) Some remarks on the trial of
Mose [*Gaballa* G. 1977; = Mes, *Gardiner* A. 1905=1964]: ⇥ 859, Delta
1988/9, 23-28.
2480 *Boochs* Wolfgang, Das altägyptische Strafverfahren bei Straftaten von
besonderem staatlichen Interesse: Gö MiszÄg 109 (1989) 21-26.
2481 *a*) *Davis* M. Stephen, Polygamy in the ancient world; – *b*) *Cooper* C.
Kenny, Ancient inheritance practice: BibIll 14 (1987) 34-36 / 80-83
[< OTAbs 11,99s].
2482 *Fischer-Elfert* Hans-W., Der ehebrecherische Sohn (P. Deir el-Medineh
27, Stele UC 14.430 und P. Butler verso): GöMiszÄg 112 (1989) 23-26.
2483 *Jankowska* N. B., ❻ Middle-Assyrian act of self-manumission from
debt-slavery; translation of the text: VDI 188 (1989) 82-85; facsimile; 85,
the text only in English.
2484 **Kienast** Burkhart, Das altassyrische Kaufvertragsrecht 1984
⇥ 65,2194... 3,2445: ᴿAfO 35 (1988) 190s (V. *Donbaz*); JNES 48 (1989)
63-65 (G. *Ries*, deutsch: hohe Qualität).
2485 *a*) *Lambert* W. G., The laws of Hammurabi in the First Millennium; –
b) *Kramer* Samuel N., Law and justice; gleanings from Sumerian
literature; – *c*) *Garelli* Paul, L'appel au roi sous l'empire assyrien; – *d*)
Koenig Jean, Traces d'influences babyloniennes dans le judaïsme biblique
et post-biblique: ⇥ 59, ꟳFINET A., Reflets 1989, 95-98 / 77-82 / 45s /
67-75.

2486 **Michalowski** Piotr, *Walker* C. B. F., A new Sumerian 'Law Code': ➤ 103, ᶠSJÖBERG Å., Dumu- 1989, 383-395.
2487 *Petschow* Herbert P. H., Ein Fall von 'Talion' bei falscher Anschuldigung in Ur III: AfO [31 (1984) 9-14] 35 (1988) 105-108.
2488 *Saporetti* Claudio, Qualche considerazione sui §§ 197-198 delle leggi ittite ed i paralleli mesopotamici [morte di adulteri]: ➤ 154, ᶠPUGLIESE CARRATELLI G., 1988, 237-241.
2489 *Théodoridès* Aristide, L'argumentation de Tefnakht dans la stèle de Piânkhy (justice objective et justice subjective): RIDA 36 (1989) 13-54.
2490 **Westbrook** Raymond, Old Babylonian marriage laws: AfO Beih 23, 1988 ➤ 4,2592; Sch 1034 [RB 97, 284, M. *Sigrist*].
2490* *Westbrook* Raymond, Cuneiform law codes and the origins of legislation [upholds against attacks the recent view that they were school-exercises rather than normative legislation]: ZAss 79 (1989) 200-222.
2491 **Wright** David P., The disposal of impurity...: SBL diss. 101 [ᴰ*Milgrom* J. 1984], 1987 ➤ 3,2456; 4,2593: ᴿCBQ 51 (1989) 548s (G. A. *Anderson*); JQR 80 (1989s) 194-8 (S. D. *Sperling*); RB 96 (1989) 609s (J. *Loza*).
2492 **Yaron** Reuven, The laws of Eshnunna²ʳᵉᵛ [¹1969]. J/Leiden 1989, Hebrew Univ./Brill. 355 p. 90-04-08534-3.

E3.6 **Cultus**, *Exodus 24-40*.

2493 *Castelot* John J., *Cody* Aelred, Religious institutions of Israel: ➤ 384, NJBC (1989s) 1253-83.
2494 *Holder* Arthur G., New treasures and old in BEDE's 'De tabernaculo' and 'De templo': RBén 99 (1989) 237-249.
2495 **Nielsen** Kjeld, Incense in ancient Israel [diss. HUC]: VT Sup 38, 1986 ➤ 2,1874... 4,2608: ᴿCBQ 51 (1989) 344-7 (A. *Fitzgerald* prefers DE VAUX viewpoint); OLZ 84 (1989) 45s (H. *Reventlow*).
2496 **Zwickel** Wolfgang, Räucherkult und Räuchergeräte; Studien zum Räucheropfer im Alten Testament und in seiner Umwelt: ev. Diss. ᴰMetzger. Kiel 1988s. – TR 85 (1989) 516.

2497 *Hendel* Ronald S., Sacrifice as a cultural system; the ritual symbolism of Exodus 24,3-8: ZAW 101 (1989) 366-390.
2498 *Steins* Georg, 'Sie sollen mir ein Heiligtum machen'; die Struktur und Entstehung von Ex 24,12-31,18: ➤ 220, ᶠZENGER E., Vom Sinai zum Horeb 1989, 145-167.
Struppe Ursula, [Ex 24-Lev 9] Die Herrlichkeit Jahwes in der Priesterschrift ᴰ1988 ➤ a270.
2499 **Utzschneider** Helmut, Das Heiligtum und das Gesetz; Studien zur Bedeutung der sinaitischen Heiligtumstexte (Ex 25-40; Lev 8-9): OBO 77, 1988 ➤ 4,2604: ᴿAntonianum 64 (1989) 608-610 (M. *Nobile*); BL (1989) 96 (D. G. *Deboys*); TüTQ 169 (1989) 318-320 (W. *Gross*); ZAW 101 (1989) 478 (E. S. *Gerstenberger*).
2500 **Koester** C. R., The dwelling of God; the Tabernacle in the OT, intertestamental Jewish literature, and the NT [diss. Union-NY, ᴰ*Brown* R. E.]: CBQ Mg 22. Wsh 1989, Catholic Biblical Asn. x-328 p. $9; sb. $7.20. 0-915170-21-3. – ᴿLA 39 (1989) 347-9 (G. *Bissoli*).
2501 *Lubsczyk* Hans, Die katechetische Verwertung der Überlieferung von der Bundeslade [< Bibel und Leben 2 (1961) 206-233 (191-208)]: ➤ 306, Einheit 1989, 15-32.

2502 *Guinot* Jean-Noël, [Ex 28,1-39] Sur le vêtement du grand prêtre; le *dêlos* était-il une pierre divinatoire?: VetChr 26 (1989) 23-48.
2503 *Smith* Billy K., The priest: BibIll 14,3 (1988) 51-54 [< OTAbs 12,15].
2504 **Schulz** H., Leviten im vorstaatlichen Israel und im Mittleren Osten ['Orient' ➤ 3,2459] 1987; DM 45: ᴿBL (1989) 41 (G. I. *Davies*).
2505 *a) Sweeney* Marvin A., The wilderness traditions of the Pentateuch; a reassessment of their function and intent in relation to Exodus 32-34; – *b) Dozeman* Thomas B., Horeb-Sinai and the rise of law in the wilderness tradition: ➤ 589, SBL Seminars 1989, 291-9 / 282-290.
2505* *Collins* Alan W. [Ex 32,1-14; Lk 15,1-10], Two images of God: ExpTim 101 (1989s) 112-4.
2506 *Lapostolle* Christine, De Moïse au Veau d'or: CrNSt 10 (1989) 483-507; Eng. 508; ital. ii.
2507 *Letellier* Joël, Le thème du Voile de Moïse chez ORIGÈNE (Exode 34,33-35 et 2 Corinthiens 3,12-18): RevSR 62 (1988) 14-26.
2508 **McCrory** Jefferson H.ᴶ, The composition of Exodus 35-40: diss. Claremont, 1989, ᴰ*Knierim* R. 279 p. 90-00186. – DissA 50 (1989) 2948-A; RelStR 16,189.
2509 *Perani* Mauro, [Es 37s; Lv 3s] Frammenti di manoscritti ebraici nell'archivio di stato di Parma: Henoch 11 (1989) 103-8 [363-5, di Bologna, non biblici].

E3.7 Leviticus.

2510 *Faley* Roland J., Leviticus: ➤ 384, NJBC (1989) 61-79.
2511 *Finkelstein* Louis, The core of the [Lv] Sifra, a temple textbook for priests: JQR 80 (1989s) 15-34.
2512 **Freedman** D. N., *Mathews* K. A., Paleo-Hebraic Leviticus 1985 ➤ 1,2873 ... 4,2612: ᴿCriswT 2 (1987s) 423s (E. S. *Merrill*).
2513 **Harlé** Paul, *Pralon* Didier, Le Lévitique: Bible d'Alexandrie 3, 1988 ➤ 4,2613: ᴿAegyptus 69 (1989) 280s (Anna *Passoni Dell'Acqua*); EsprVie 99 (1989) 46s (L. *Monloubou*); NRT 111 (1989) 746s (X. *Jacques*); JStJud 20 (1989) 90s (A. *Hilhorst*); RHPR 69 (1989) 205s (A. *Marx*: grand intérêt, mais documentation dépassée et trop peu de rapport avec les exégètes).
2514 **Kaddushin** M. [1895-1980], A conceptual commentary on Midrash Leviticus Rabbah; value concepts in Jewish thought: BrownJudSt 126, 1987 ➤ 4,2615 ('Kadushin'): ᴿBL (1989) 136 (S. C. *Reif*).
2515 *Lane* D. L., 'The best words in the best order'; some comments on the 'Syriacing' of Leviticus [Peshiṭta Institute Hull 1982]: VT 39 (1989) 21; 468-479.
2516 **Levine** Baruch A., Leviticus: JPS Torah Comm. Ph 1989, Jewish Publication. xlvi-284 p. 0-8276-0238-2 [OIAc N89].
2517 *Milgrom* Jacob, Leviticus ➤ 377, Books 1 (1989) 63-70.
2518 *Puech* Émile, Notes en marge de 11QPaléo Lévitique; le fragment L, des fragments inédits et une jarre de la grotte 11: RB 96 (1989) 161-184; pl. I-II; inserted p. of 11 corrigenda.
2519 **Wevers** John W., Text history of the Greek Leviticus 1986 ➤ 2,1884*b* ... 4,2620: ᴿCBQ 51 (1989) 545s (B. E. *Shafer*); Salesianum 51 (1989) 364 (M. *Cimosa*); TLZ 114 (1989) 17-19 (Anneli *Aejmelaeus*, Eng.).

2520 **Anderson** Gary A., [Lv 1s] Sacrifices and offerings ... social and political importance 1987 ➤ 3,2476; 4,2622: ᴿBL (1989) 99 (D. G. *Deboys*); CBQ

51 (1989) 704-6 (J. M. *Kennedy*); JBL 108 (1989) 325-7 (D. P. *Wright*); TR 85 (1989) 281s (E. S. *Gerstenberger*).

2521 **Kiuchi** N., The purification offering [Lv 4...16] 1988 ➤ 4,2624: ᴿBL (1989) 82 (J. W. *Rogerson*); ExpTim 100 (1988s) 65 (R. *Mason*); JBL 108 (1989) 504-6 (G. *Anderson*); RB 96 (1989) 610-612 (J. *Loza*); ZAW 101 (1989) 464 (H. C. *Schmitt*).

2522 *Marx* Alfred, [Lv 4,1; 15,31...] Sacrifice pour les péchés ou rite de passage? Quelques réflexions sur la fonction du *ḥaṭṭaʾt*: RB 96 (1989) 27-48; Eng. 27.

2523 *Segal* Peretz, The divine verdict of Leviticus X 3: VT 39 (not 29 as bot; 1989) 91-95.

2524 *Hübner* Ulrich, [Lv 11,7; Dt 14,8] Schweine, Schweineknochen und ein Speiseverbot im alten Israel: VT 39 (1989) 225-236.

2526 *Meier* Sam, House fungus, Mesopotamia and Israel (Lev 14: 33-53): RB 96 (1989) 184-192; franç. 184.

2527 **Dupont** Joanne M., Women and the concept of holiness in the 'holiness code' (Leviticus 16-26); literary, theological and historical context: diss. Marquette, ᴰ*Schmitt* J. Milwaukee 1989. 307 p. 89-25416. – DissA 50 (1989s) 2524s-A.

2528 *Naʾor* B., ✡ [Lev 16] CLEMENT of Alexandria about an unknown practice of the Day-of-Atonement service: Sinai 103,2 (1989) 177s [< JStJud 20,293].

2529 *a)* *Deiana* Giovanni, Il sacrificio del capro nell'AT; – *b)* *Vattioni* Francesco, A proposito di Śeir: ➤ 759, Sangue VI, 1987/9, 641-679 / 681s.

2530 **Mathys** Hans-Peter [Lv 19,18] Liebe deinen Nächsten: OBO 71, 1986: ➤ 2,1895... 4,2636: ᴿRB 96 (1989) 581-4 (J. *Loza*); TLZ 114 (1989) 183s (G. *Sauer*).

2531 *Peleq* Zev, ✡ [Lv 21,6... priests, nezirim] Qiddušim; antique and esthetic: BethM 34,121 (1989s) 138-143.

2532 *Ebach* J., [Lev 25...] Bodenrecht: ➤ 902, NBL Lfg. 2 (1989) 313s.

E3.8 *Numeri;* **Numbers, Balaam.**

2533 **Jagersma** H., Numeri [I. 1983 ➤ 64,2557], deel II: PredikOT, 1988 ➤ 4,2651: ᴿBL (1989) 56 (J. W. *Rogerson*); GerefTTs 89 (1989) 117s (A. van der *Wal*); TsTNijm 29 (1989) 173s (A. *Schoors*).

2534 *L'Heureux* Conrad E., Numbers: ➤ 384, NJBC (1989) 80-93.

2535 **Maarsingh** B., Numbers [1985], ᵀ*Vriend* J. 1987 ➤ 3,2514: ᴿCBQ 51 (1989) 721s (S. *Greenhalgh*); EvQ 61 (1989) 89s (D. G. *Deboys*); WestTJ 50 (1988) 180-2 (A. *Wolters*).

2536 **Maier** Gerhard, Das vierte Buch Mose erklärt; Studienbibel. Wu 1989, Brockhaus. 484 p. DM 49 [TR 86,249].

2537 **Neusner** Jacob, Sifré to Numbers, an American translation I-II: BrownJud 118s, 1986 ➤ 2,1905: ᴿJQR 80 (1989s) 131s (L. M. *Barth*).

2538 ᵀᴱ**Pérez Fernández** Miguel, Midrás Sifre Números: Biblioteca Midrásica 9. Valencia 1989, Soler. 539 p. 84-86067-24-3 [BL 90,154].

2539 *Sakenfeld* Katherine D., Numbers: ➤ 377, Books 1 (1989) 71-87.

2540 *Cartledge* Tony W., [Nm 6,1-21] Were Nazirite vows unconditional?: CBQ 51 (1989) 409-422 [no, against R. de VAUX, Ancient Israel (1961) 2,466; G. von RAD, OT Theology (1962) 1.63 is milder].

2541 **Cartledge** Tony W., [Num 6; Lev 7,16; 22,21 ...] The form and function of vows in the OT: diss. Duke, ^D*Meyers* E. Durham NC 1988. 430 p. 90-02045. – DissA 50 (1989s) 2523s-A; RelStR 16,189.

2542 *Satran* David, [Num.] Fingernails and hair [ungrown; image of Resurrection]; anatomy and exegesis in TERTULLIAN [echoed in JEROME ML 23,383]. JTS 40 (1989) 116-120.

2543 *Barkay* Gabriel, ❿ [Nm 6,29-6] The priestly benediction on the Ketef Hinnom plaques: CHistEI 52 (1989) 37-76 [77-89, *Haran* Menahem, significance]; Eng. 190 [189].

2544 *Korpel* Marjo C. A., [Nm 6,24-26] The poetic structure of the priestly blessing: JStOT 45 (1989) 3-13.

2545 **Jobsen** Aarnoud, [Nm 11-20] Krisis en hoop; een exegetisch-theologisch onderzoek naar de achtergronden en tendensen van de rebelliecyclus in Numeri 11:1-20:13: prot. diss. Bru. 1987. Kampen 1987, Mondiss. 310 p. ƒ 37,50. – ^RGerefTTs 89 (1989) 115-7 (E. *Talstra*); Streven 56 (1988s) 83 (P. *Beentjes*).

2546 *Fuchs* Gotthard, 'Wenn nur der Herr seinen Geist auf sie alle legte' (Num 11,29); der Glaube an den creator spiritus und die Kreativität in der Kirche: BLtg 62 (1989) 235-247.

2547 *Robinson* Bernard P., The jealousy of Miriam; a note on Num 12: ZAW 101 (1989) 428-432.

2548 *Kunin* Robert, [Num 19,9s] The mystery of the red heifer, Dor 15 (1986s) 267-9 [... MAIMONIDES' skill in chemistry].

2549 *Neufeld* Ernest, [Num 19,9-11] The red heifer mystery: JBQ (= Dor) 18 (1989s) 176-180.

2550 *Bar-Ilan* M., ❿ The red heifer in the days of HILLEL: Sinai 100 (1987) 142-165 [< JStJud 20,292; this 'Jubilee volume' 100 is dated 1987; but on p. 293 vol. 103,1 is dated 1988 and 103,2 is 1989].

2551 *Briend* Jacques, [Num 20] La marche des Hébreux au-delà du Jourdain: ➤ 869, Jordanie 1987, 41-46.

2552 *Levine* Baruch A., ❿ [Num 21-25] The triumphs [ṣidqôt] of the Lord: ➤ 218, Mem. YADIN Y., ErIsr 20 (1989) 202-214; Eng. 201*.

2553 *Miller* J. Maxwell, [Num 21,10-20] The Israelite journey through (around) Moab and Moabite toponomy: JBL 108 (1989) 577-595.

2554 *a) Greene* John T., [Num 22-24] Balaam; prophet, diviner, and priest in selected ancient Israelite and Hellenistic Jewish sources; – *b) Berchman* Robert M., Arcana mundi between Balaam and Hecate; prophecy, divination, and magic in Later Platonism: ➤ 589, SBL Seminars 1989, 57-106 / 107-186.

2555 *Gross* W., Bileam: ➤ 902, NBL Lfg 2 (1989) 300s.

2556 *Kellenberger* Edgar, Jahwes unerwarteter Widerstand gegen seinen Beauftragten; Erwägungen zur Episode von Bileams Eselin (Num 22,22-35): TZBas 45 (1989) 69-72.

2557 **Rouillard** Hedwige, La péricope de Balaam (Nb 22-24) 1985 ➤ 1,2627 ... 4,2672: ^RJAOS 109 (1989) 678s (B. A. *Levine*).

2558 *Grimes* Ronald L, [Nm 23,23] Infelicitous performances and ritual criticism [➤ 4,2188c]: Semeia 41 (1988) 103-122.

2559 *Wickler* Wolfgang, Die Irrlehre vom moral-analogen Verhalten der Tiere: Universitas 44 (1989) 644-653; ill.

2560 **Rushing** Ronald L., [Nm 25,12s] Phinehas' covenant of peace: diss. Dallas Theol. Sem. 1988. 260 p. 89-13837. – DissA 50 (1989s) 1341s-A.

2561 *Allan* Nigel, [Nm 26,58 ...] The religious and political significance of the early settlement of the Levites in Judah: IrBSt 10 (1988) 166-177 [< OTAbs 12,155].

2562 *Sakenfeld* Katharine D., [Num 27] *a*) In the wilderness, awaiting the land; the daughters of Zelophehad and feminist interpretation: PrincSemB 9 (1988) 179-196 [cf. her PerspRSt 15,4 (1988) 37.47: < OTAbs 12,171s]; – *b*) Feminist biblical interpretation: TTod 46 (1989s) 154-168.

2563 *Soest* H.J. van, 'Jullie broeders trekken ten strijde en jullie willen hier blijven?' Landtoewijzing voor het aangezicht van JHWH in Numeri 32: AmstCah 9 (1988) 59-76 [TR 85,425].

2564 *Bonato* Antonio, [Nm 35,11-14] Il ruolo universale del sacerdozio di Cristo nell'allegoria delle città-rifugio (Fug. saec. 2,5-13; 3,14-16), una rilettura dell'esegesi FILONIANA da parte di AMBROGIO: StPatav 36 (1989) 57-87; Eng. 87.

E3.9 Liber Deuteronomii.

2565 **Bietenhard** Hans, Der tannaitische Midrasch Sifre Dt: JudChr 8, 1984 ➤ 65,2279 ... 3,2543: ᴿTPhil 64 (1989) 259s (N. *Lohfink*); TRu 54 (1989) 111s (L. *Perlitt*).

2566 *Blenkinsopp* Joseph, Deuteronomy: ➤ 384, NJBC (1989s) 94-109.

2567 **Braulik** Georg, Deuteronomium 1-16: NEchter 16, 1986 ➤ 2,1922 ... 4,2679: ᴿRB 96 (1989) 453s (J. *Loza*).

2568 **Braulik** G., Studien zur Theologie des Dt 1988 ➤ 4,168: ᴿBL (1989) 69 (A.D.H. *Mayes*: a major contribution); TPhil 64 (1989) 579s (H.-W. *Jüngling*).

2569 *Braulik* Georg, Die Entstehung der Rechtfertigungslehre in den Bearbeitungsschichten des Buches Deuteronomium; ein Beitrag zur Klärung der Voraussetzungen paulinischer Theologie: TPhil 64 (1989) 321-333.

2570 **Buchholz** Joachim, Die Ältesten Israels im Dt ᴰ1988 ➤ 4,2681: ᴿBL (1989) 69 (A.D.H. *Mayes*); ÉTRel 64 (1989) 279s (J. *Pons*); TLZ 114 (1989) 345s (W. *Thiel*).

2571 **Bultmann** Christoph, Der Fremde im antiken Juda; eine Untersuchung zum sozialen Typenbegriff im deuteronomischen Gesetz: Diss. ᴰSmend R. Göttingen 1989s. – RTLv 21, p. 539.

2572 **Clements** R.E., Deuteronomy: OT guides. Sheffield 1989, Academic. 104 p. £5. 1-85075-214-1 [BL 90,70].

2573 **Deeley** Mary Katharine, The rhetoric of memory; a study of the persuasive function of the memory commands in Deuteronomy 5-26: diss. Northwestern. Evanston IL 1989. 214 p. 90-02484. – DissA 50 (1989s) 2524-A.

2574 **García López** F., El Deuteronomio; una ley predicada. Estella 1989, VDivino. 63 p. – ᴿRelCu 35 (1989) 680 (M.A. *Martín Juárez*).

2575 ᵀᴱ**Hammer** Reuven, Sifre, a tannaitic commentary on the book of Deuteronomy: Yale Judaica 24, 1986 ➤ 3,2549; 4,2684: ᴿEstFran 90 (1989) 538-541 (E. *Cortès*).

2576 **Hendricks** Herman, Gedenk uw bevrijding; de profetische bijbelboeken van Dt tot Koningen, een werkboek. Lv 1989, Kristenen voor het Socialisme. 199 p. Fb 400. – ᴿStreven 57 (1989s) 1043s (W. *Beuken*).

2577 **Labuschagne** C.J., Deuteronomium Iab: PredikOT, 1987 ➤ 4,2689: ᴿBL (1989) 57s (J.W. *Rogerson*: a strange method, but worthy of serious consideration).

2578 **Labuschagne** C.J., Dt II(-11.32): PredikOT. Nijkerk 1988, Callenbach. 299 p. *f* 78,75. – ᴿStreven 56 (1988s) 469s (P. *Beentjes*).

2579 **McConville** J.G., Law and theology in Dt: JStOT supp 33, 1984 ➤ 65,2294 ... 3,2555: ᴿJQR 80 (1989s) 396-404 (B.M. *Levinson*).

2580 **Mello** Alberto, Deuteronomio; commento esegetico-spirituale. Magnano VC 1989, Qiqajon. 65 p.
2581 *Noort* Ed, Over-lijden en overleven; de verbondsvoorstellingen van de deuteronomistische scholen: ↠ 412, Sleutelen 1989, 7-32.
2582 **Regt** L. J., de, A parametric model... Dt 1-30 ᴰ1988 ↠ 4,2696: ᴿZAW 101 (1989) 324 (H. W. *Hoffmann*).
2583 *Sanders* James A., Deuteronomy: ↠ 377, Books 1 (1989) 89-102.
2584 Shinmeiki (Dt) ◐, Studium Biblicum Franciscanum. Tokyo 1989. Shūō Shuppan-sha. vi-224 p.; map. Y 2800 [BL 90,62].
2585 **Suzuki** Yoshihide, ◑ *Shinmeiki*... Sprachwissenschaftliche Studien zum Deuteronomium. [↠ 4,2699] Tokyo 1987, United Church of Christ Publ. 698 p. Y 7400. – ᴿBZ 33 (1989) 81-98 (K. H. *Walkenhorst*: cognate to the author's 1982 Claremont diss., The 'Numeruswechsel' in Dt; beginning and end too severe on N. *Lohfink*).

2586 **Knapp** Dietrich, Dt 4: GöTheolArb 35, 1987 ↠ 3,2564; 4,2704: ᴿBO 46 (1989) 132s (R. D. *Nelson*); JBL 108 (1989) 119-121 (C. T. *Begg*); RB 96 (1989) 266-286 (G. *Braulik*).
2587 ᴰ**Aschenbach** R., Israel zwischen Verheissung und Gebot; literarkritische Untersuchungen zu Dt 5-11: ev. Diss. Göttingen 1988, ᴰ*Perlitt* L. – TR 85 (1989) 516.
2588 a) *Vazhuthanapally* Ouseph K., [Dt 5] The Decalogue in Deuteronomy; – b) *Kottackal* Joseph, Deuteronomy; the book of the covenant; – c) *de Menezes* Rui, Law and legalism in Deuteronomy: BibleBh 15 (1989) 111-132 / 77-84 / 85-110.
2589 *Fraas* Hans-Jürgen, [p. 270, Gemeinschaft – Geschichte – Persönlichkeit:] Dt 6,20ff als Grundmodell religiöser Sozialisation: ↠ 177, ᶠSᴄʜᴡᴀʀᴢ R., Von Wittenberg 1989, 21-37.
2590 **Langer** G., Von Gott erwählt — Jerusalem; die Rezeption von Dtn 12 im frühen Judentum [Diss. Salzburg 1988, ᴰ*Braulik* G. (↠ 4,2714 '*Fuglister* N.')]: ÖsBSt 8. Klosterneuburg 1988, ÖsKBW. xiv-351 + 22 p. DM 49 [ZAW 102,448, H.-C. *Schmitt*] 3-85396-079-0.
2591 *Lohfink* Norbert, a) Die ḥuqqîm ûmišpāṭîm im Buch Deuteronomium [14-mal] und ihre Neubegrenzung durch Dtn 12,1: Biblica 70 (1989) 1-29; franç. 31; – b) Dtn 12,1 und Gen 15,18; das dem Samen Abrahams geschenkte Land als der Geltungsbereich der deuteronomischen Gesetze: ↠ 169, ᶠSᴄʜᴀʀʙᴇʀᴛ J., Die Väter Israels 1989, 183-210.
2592 *Anderson* Gary, [Dt 16,15] The expression of joy as a halakhic problem in rabbinic sources: JQR 80 (1989s) 221-257.
2593 **Rüterswörden** Udo, Von der politischen Gemeinschaft zur Gemeinde; Studien zu Dt 16,18-18,22: BoBB 65, 1987 ↠ 3,2557; 4,2720: ᴿBL (1989) 91 (A. D. H. *Mayes*); BO 46 (1989) 133s (R. D. *Nelson*).
2594 *Rofé* Alexander, Qumranic paraphrases, the Greek Deuteronomy and the late history of the Biblical nśy [substituted for *melek* in Dt 17,14-20]: Textus 14 (1988) 163-174 [< NTAbs 33,217].
2595 **Vliet** Hendrik van, No single testimony; a study on the adoption of the law of Deut 19:15 par. into the New Testament: diss. Utrecht 1958, Kemink. xv-162 p.
2596 *Locher* Clemens, [Dt 22,13-21] Die Ehre einer Frau in Israel... [ᴰFra St. Georgen 1984]: OBO 70, 1986 ↠ 2,1938... 4,2722: ᴿBO 46 (1989) 425-438 (K. van der *Toorn*); BZ 33 (1989) 133-6 (Helga *Weippert*);

CBQ 51 (1989) 527s (J. F. *Craghan*); WeltOr 20s (1989s) 308-311 (E. *Otto*).
2597 **Kreuzer** Siegfried, [Dt 26 'Aramaic ancestors' the only trace of Israel's premonarchical history] Die Frühgeschichte Israels...: BZAW 178. 1989. ➤ 2274, p. 257.
2598 *Weissblit* Shlomoh, ❻ [Dt 28,47] What was the joy that did not exist?: BethM 34,121 (1989s) 144-8.
2599 *Giordano* M., Per una cultura della vita; 'scegli dunque la vita' (Dt 30,19): RasT 30 (1989) 99-120.
2600 **Basser** Herbert W., [Dt 31,30-32,44] Midrashic interpretations of the Song of Moses: AmerUnivSt 7,2, 1984 ➤ 65,2326... 3,2589: ᴿRÉJ 147 (1988) 450s (Madeleine *Petit*).
2601 **Axelsson** Lars E., [Dt 33,2] The Lord rose up from Seir 1987 ➤ 3,2592; 4,2728: ᴿCBQ 51 (1989) 706s (P. J. *King*); RB 96 (1989) 295s (J.-M. de *Tarragon*); TLZ 114 (1989) 809-811 (E.-J. *Waschke*).
2602 *Rose* Martin, Empoigner le Pentateuque par sa fin? l'investiture de Josué et la mort de Moïse: ➤ 601, Pentateuque 1987/9, 129-147.
2603 *Knowles* Michael P., 'The Rock, his work is perfect'; unusual imagery for God in Deuteronomy XXXII: VT 39 (1989) 307-322.
2604 *Manns* Frédéric, Une altercation doctrinale entre les rabbins et les judéo-chrétiens au début du troisième siècle; Sifre Dt 32,1 (§ 306): VetChr 26 (1989) 49-58.
2605 *Christensen* Duane L., Dtn 33,11 — a curse in the 'blessing of Moses'?: ZAW 101 (1989) 278-282 [*brk* means also 'curse'].

E4.1 *Deuteronomista; Origo Israelis in Canaan;* **Liber Josue.**

2606 *Albertz* Rainer, Die Intentionen und die Träger des deuteronomistischen Geschichtswerkes: ➤ 212, ꟳWESTERMANN C., Schöpfung 1989, 37-53.
2607 **Nelson** Richard D., The double redaction of the Deuteronomistic history [diss. Richmond 1973]: JStOT Sup 18, 1981 ➤ 62,2823; 63,2666...: ᴿRB 96 (1989) 131-3 (F. J. *Gonçalves*).
2608 **O'Brien** M. A., The Deuteronomistic History hypothesis; a reassessment [diss. Melbourne 1987]: OBO 92. FrS/Gö 1989, Univ/VR. xiii-319 p. Fs 86. 3-7278-0647-8 / VR 3-525-537220 [BL 90,87, I. W. *Provan*]. – ᴿExpTim 101 (1989s) 279 (G. H. *Jones*).

2609 **Abu-Qorah** Osamah A., A structural comparison of the Hebrew [OT] conquest and the Arab conquest of Southern Syria [including] Trans-Jordan and Palestine: diss. UCLA 1989, ᴰ*Segert* S., *Morony* M. 369 p. 89-10293. – DissA 50 (1989s) 527s-A.
2610 *Alt* Albrecht, a) The settlement of the Israelites in Palestine [Landnahme 1925/1966]; – b) The formation of the Israelite state in Palestine [Staatenbildung 1930]; – c) The monarchy [VT 1 (1951) 2-22]: ➤ 225, Essays 1989, 133-169 / 171-237 / 239-259.
2611 **Bruce** Larry D., The Israelite Exodus and Conquest in the early Iron Age [Exodus 1180-40; Conquest 1125 B.C.E.]: a synthesis of the archaeological and literary evidence in the light of ethnographic studies: diss. SW Baptist Theol. Sem. 1988. 470 p. 89-08433. – DissA 50 (1989s) 719-A.
2611* *Callaway* J. A. The settlement in Canaan: ➤ b322, ᴱ*Shanks* H., Ancient Israel 1988, 53-84.

2612 **Coote** Robert B., *Whitelam* Keith W., The emergence of early Israel in historical perspective: SocWBA 5, 1987 → 3,2595; 4,2732: ᴿAJA 93 (1989) 289s (C. *Edens*); ETL 65 (1989) 150s (J. *Lust*: risky; shares preoccupations of T. L. THOMPSON); Interpretation 43 (1989) 88 (C. *Mabee*, also on WEBB B. Judges); RB 96 (1989) 142 (J. M. de *Tarragon*); TLZ 114 (1989) 267-9 (W. *Thiel*).

2613 **Finkelstein** Israel, The archaeology of the Israelite settlement 1988 → 4,2733: ᴿBiblica 70 (1989) 290-5 (J. R. *Bartlett*).

2614 **Frick** Frank S., Formation of the state in ancient Israel 1988 → 1,2799*... 4,2735: ᴿJTS 40 (1989) 142s (C. S. *Rodd*); RB 96 (1989) 143s (J. M. de *Tarragon*); TLZ 114 (1989) 510s (H. M. *Niemann*).

2615 **Lemche** Niels P., Early Israel...: VTSup 37, 1985 → 2,1955; 3,2602: ᴿCBQ 51 (1989) 525-7 (A. J. *Hauser*); JBL 108 (1989) 502-4 (R. B. *Coote*: deft critique of GOTTWALD, *al.*); JNES 48 (1989) 136-140 (Diana *Edelman*: a synthesis of this work with AHLSTRÖM and FINKELSTEIN will probably become commonly accepted working model); TLZ 114 (1989) 423-5 (W. *Thiel*); ZDPV 105 (1989) 187-9 (H. N. *Rösel*).

2616 ꟳMENDENHALL George E., The quest for the Kingdom of God, ᴱHuffmon H. B., *al.* 1983 → 64,73: ᴿJNES 48 (1989) 146s (D. *Pardee*, mostly on N. GOTTWALD's 'strange amalgam of religiosity and Marxism' countered by J. FLANAGAN 'squarely within the domain of socio-ethnographic literary analysis').

2617 *Otto* Eckart, Israels Wurzeln in Kanaan; auf dem Weg zu einer neuen Kultur- und Sozialgeschichte des antiken Israels [AHLSTRÖM G. 1986; COOTE R., WHITELAM K., 1987; LEMCHE N. 1988]: TR 85 (1989) 3-10.

2618 *Whitelam* Keith W., Israel's traditions of origin; reclaiming the land: JStOT 44 (1989) 19-42.

2619 *Williamson* H. G. M., The concept of Israel in transition [MENDENHALL, GOTTWALD; LEMCHE; THOMPSON]: → 378, World 1989, 141-161.

2620 **Auld** A. Graeme, Joshua, Judges & Ruth 1984 → 65,2341... 3,2610*: ᴿCriswT 1 (1987) 405-7 (E. R. *Clendenen*).

2621 **Butler** T. C. Joshua: Word Comm 1983 → 64,2640... 2,1959: ᴿAsbTJ 44,1 (1989) 105-7 (O. *Dickens*).

2622 *Chaney* Marvin L., Joshua: → 377, Books 1 (1989) 103-112.

2623 *Coogan* Michael D., Joshua: → 384, NJBC (1989s) 110-131.

2624 **Goslinga** C. J., Joshua, Judges, Ruth 1986 → 3,2615; 4,2747: ᴿVT 39 (1989) 254 (J. A. *Emerton*).

Gray John, Joshua, Judges, Ruth: NCB 1986 → 2604.

2625 **Hamlin** E. John, Inheriting the land; a commentary on the book of Joshua: InternatTheolComm, 1983 → 64,2645... 3,2616: ᴿWestTJ 50 (1988) 182s (T. H. *McAlpine*).

2626 *Hastoupis* Athanasios P., Ⓖ The book of Joshua: TAth 60 (1989) 252-270.

2627 *Malamat* Abraham, Ⓗ Conquest and settlement: → 27, BEN-GURION and the Bible (1989) 19-28; Eng. i.

2628 **Martínez Borobio** E., Targum Jonatan... I. Josué – Jueces: TEstCisn 46, 1989 → 4,2814, 2750 ['1987'] [ZAW 102,155, I. *Kottsieper*].

2629 *Niehaus* J., Joshua and Ancient Near Eastern warfare: JEvTS 31 (1988) 37-50 [< ZAW 102, 130].

2630 **Noort** H., Josua: → 894, EvKL 2 (1989) 849s.

_____

2631 **Eslinger** Lyle, Into the hands of the living God [Jos 1-9; Jg 1s; 1 Sam 12; 1 Kgs 8; 2 Kgs 17]: JStOT Sup 84 / BLit 24. Sheffield 1989, Almond. 284 p. £20; sb. £15. 1-85075-212-5 [JStOT 45,24, adv.]. – RExpTim 101 (1989s) 211s (I. W. *Provan* found it too dismissive of dissent).

2632 *Gacek* Stanisław, Some notes on the book of Joshua [i. historical value of the stories; ii. literary composition of Jos 1,1-9]: FolOr 25 (1988) 227-231.

2633 *Pienaar* D. N., [Jos 1-6] Die stad Jerigo en die boek Josua: JSem 1 (1989) 272-286; Eng. 272.

2634 **Floss** Johannes P., Kunden oder Kundschafter? Literaturwissenschaftliche Untersuchung zu Jos 2 [I. AOtt 16, 1982 → 63, 2687 ... 4, 2757] II. Komposition, Redaktion, Intention: AOtt 26. St. Ottilien 1986, EOS. xiv-187 p. DM 33. – rOLZ 84 (1989) 436-8 (R. *Stahl*); RB 96 (1989) 563-581 (F. *Langlamet*: both).

2635 *Barstad* Hans, The Old Testament personal name *rāḥāb*; an onomastic note: SvEx 54 (1989) 43-49.

2636 *Ottosson* Magnus, Rahab and the spies: → 103, FSJÖBERG Å., Dumu-... 1989, 419-427.

2637 *Rapisarda* Grazia, Raab e Gezabele nell'esegesi patristica: → 567, AnStoEseg 6 (1989) 151-163; Eng. 8.

2638 *Brekelmans* C., Joshua v 10-12, another approach: → 129, FMULDER M., New avenues 1989, 89-95.

2639 *Na'man* Nadav, ❾ [Jos 15 ...] The town-lists of Judah and Benjamin and the kingdom of Judah in the days of Josiah: Zion 59 (1959) 17-71; Eng. i-ii.

2640 *Drews* Robert, [Jos 17,16 + 4 t.] The 'chariots of iron' of Joshua and Judges: JStOT 45 (1989) 15-23.

2641 **Dearman** J. Andrew, [Jos 21,26-27] The Levitical cities of Reuben and Moabite toponymy: BASOR 276 (1989) 55-66; 2 maps.

2642 *Nel* H. W., [Jos 21] Die Levitiese stede; kultiese of staatsadministratiewe setels?: JSem 1 (1989) 257-271; Eng. 257.

2643 *Koopmans* W. T., The poetic prose of Joshua 23: → 410, Structural/ poetry 1988, 119-155.

2644 *Hill* A., The Ebal ceremony as Hebrew land grant?: JEvTS 31 (1988) 399-406 [< ZAW 102, 130].

E4.2 *Liber Judicum:* **Richter, Judges.**

2645 **Abma** H., Profetie en poëzie; verhalen uit het boek Richteren. Kampen 1989, Kok. 138 p. ƒ24,50. 90-242-4518-4 [TsTNijm 29,435].

2646 **Becker** Uwe, Richterbuch und Königtum; redaktionsgeschichtliche Studien zum Richterbuch: ev. Diss. DGunneweg. Bonn 1988s. – TR 85 (1989) 514; RTLv 21, p. 539.

2646* *Block* D. I., The period of the Judges; religious disintegration under tribal rule [Israel its own worst enemy, self-destructive hero who declares holy war against one of its own tribes ...]: → 77, FHARRISON R., Israel's apostasy 1988, 38-57.

2647 *Brettler* Marc, The Book of Judges; literature as politics: JBL 108 (1989) 395-418.
2648 *Hastoupis* Athanasios P., The book of Judges: TAth 60 (1989) 572-592.
2649 *Kempinski* A., ❹ Criticism of FINKELSTEIN I., ❹ Archeology of the Judges period 1986 → 3,2632: ᴿQadmoniot [20 (1984) 59] 22 (1989 for 1985s) 51s (A. *Ofer*).
2650 *King* Philip J., Judges: → 377, Books 1 (1989) 113-121.
2651 **Klein** Lillian R., The triumph of irony in the Book of Judges: JStOT Sup 68 / Bible & Lit 14, 1988 → 4,2763: ᴿBL (1989) 82 (A. G. *Auld*); ExpTim 100 (1988s) 348s (I. *Provan*); RExp 86 (1989) 619s (J. D. W. *Watts*); RHPR 69 (1989) 206s (P. de *Robert*).
2651* **Lindberg** Conrad, The Middle English Bible; the Book of Judges. Oslo 1989, Norwegian Univ. Pr. 82-00-02811-9 [BL 90,153].
2652 **Mayes** A. D. H., Judges: OTGuides 1985 → 1,2735... 3,2633: ᴿHeythJ 30 (1989) 441 (G. C. *Nicol*).
2653 *O'Connor* M., Judges: → 384, NJBC (1989) 132-144.
2654 **Pennant** David F., The significance of rootplay, leading words and thematic links in the Book of Judges: diss. Council for Academic Awards UK. 1988. 524 p. BRDX-86218. – DissA 50 (1989s) 1649-A.
2655 **Soggin** J. Alberto, Le livre des Juges [1970 updated] 1987 → 3,2636; 4,2767: ᴿEstAg 23 (1988) 425 (C. *Mielgo*); RB (1989) 301s (F. *Langlamet*: a dozen corrections of the translation); RechSR 76 (1988) 570s (J. *Briend*); RSO 62 (1988) 173s (G. *Garbini*: anche sul suo Amos).
2656 **Vaux** R. de, ❹ Zoku Isuraeru-Kodai-shi; shishijidai [Histoire ancienne... période des Juges 1973 → 55,6589a], ᵀ*Nashimura* T. Tokyo 1989, Nohon Kirisuto-Kyōdan. 240 p. Y 3400. 4-8184-0014-9 C 9016 [BL 90,42].
2657 **Webb** Barry G., The book of the Judges, an integrated reading [diss. Sheffield]: JStOT Sup 46, 1987 → 3,2638; 4,2769: ᴿCBQ 51 (1989) 359s (L. J. *Hoppe*); ÉTRel 64 (1989) 615s (D. *Lys*, bon avec regrets); EvQ 61 (1989) 87s (R. W. L. *Moberly*); JQR 90 (1989s) 388-390 (L. J. *Greenspoon*); TLZ 114 (1989) 264s (K.-D. *Schunck*).

2658 *Brettler* Marc Z., Jud[icum] 1,1-2,10; from appendix to prologue: ZAW 101 (1989) 433-5.
2658* *Soest* J. van, 'Ga je niet met mij, dan ga ik niet'; de opbouw van Richteren 3 en 4: → 116, ᶠLEEUWEN C. van 1989, 97-108.
2659 *Amit* Yairah, The story of Ehud (Judges 3:12-30); the form and the message [response, *Jobling* David, Right-brained story of left-handed man; an antiphon to Y. Amit]: → 395, Signs 1989, 97-123 [125-131].
2660 *Halpern* Baruch, [Jg 3,12-29] The assassination of Eglon — the first locked-room murder mystery: BR 4,6 (1988) 32-41. 44 [< his First Historians 1988, ch. 3 adapted: OTAbs 12,174].
2661 *Soggin* J. Alberto, 'Ehud und 'Eglon; Bemerkungen zu Richter III 11b-31: VT 39 (nicht 29 wie p. 95 unten; 1989) 95-100.
2662 *Shupak* Nili, [Jg 3,31] New light on Shamgar ben 'Anath [Rameses IV inscription; Dor and other excavations]: Biblica 70 (1989) 517-525.
2663 **Bal** Mieke, [Jg 4] Murder and difference; gender, genre, and scholarship on Sisera's death: Indiana Studies in Biblical Literature, 1988 → 4,2772: ᴿBL (1989) 65 (R. P. *Carroll*); TTod 46 (1989s) 348s (Margaret D. *Zulick*).

2663* *Niditch* Susan, [Jg 4,17-22] Eroticism and death in the tale of Jael: → 391, Gender 1989, 43-57.

2664 *Couturier* Guy, Débora une autorité politico-religieuse aux origines d'Israël: SR 18 (1989) 213-228.

2665 *Gevaryahu* H., Deborah, the wife of Lapidot: JBQ (= Dor) 18 (1989s) 135-140.

2666 *Krašovec* Jože, [in Slovene] Antithetic structure of the Song of Deborah (Judg 5): BogVest 47 (1987) 3-16; Eng. 16s.

2667 **Lepre** Cesare, Il Canto di Debhorah: Studi e Testi 6, 1987 → 3,2695; 4,2775: ᴿRB 96 (1989) 139 (R. J. *Tournay*).

2668 *Stager* Lawrence E., The song of Deborah; why some tribes answered the call and others did not: BAR-W 15,1 (1989) 51-64; (color.) ill.

2669 *Janzen* J. Gerald, The root *pr'* in Judges V2 and Deuteronomy XXXII 42: VT 39 (1989) 393-406.

2670 *Auld* A. Graeme, [Jg 6-8] Gideon; hacking at the heart of the OT: VT 39 (1989) 257-267.

2671 **Lo Pak-Huen** William, Conversion and salvation; a narrative and stylistic analysis of Judges 6-7 [→ 4,2777, not '5-7'; diss. R]. R 1989, Pontifical Biblical Institute. 65 p. excerpt.

2671* *Homerski* Józef, ✪ [Sdz 6] Gedeon: → 891, EncKat 5 (1989) 924s.

2672 *Gerhardsson* Birger, [Jg 9,7-15; 2 Sam 12,1-4; 2 Kgs 14,8-14; Is 5,1-6; Ezek 17,3-10] The narrative meshalim in the Old Testament books and in the Synoptic Gospels: → 60, ᶠFITZMYER J., Touch 1989, 289-304.

2673 *Waard* Jan de, [Jg 9,7-15] Jotham's fable; an exercise in clearing away the unclear: → 120, ᶠLOHSE E., Wissenschaft 1989, 362-370.

2674 *Eshel* Hanan, *Erlich* Ze'ev, [Jg 9,34-41] ✪ Abimelech's first battle with the lords of Shechem: Tarbiz 58 (1988s) 111-6; Eng. v.

2675 **Kaswalder** Pietro A., La disputa diplomatica di Iefte (Gdc 11,12-28) e il problema dell'insediamento di Israele in Transgiordania: diss. ᴰ*Piccirillo* M., SBF. J 1988. xiv-511 p. – LA 39 (1989) 380s.

2675* *Day* Peggy L., [Jg 11,30-39] From the child is born the woman; the story of Jephthah's daughter: → 391, Gender 1989, 58-74.

2676 *Exum* J. Cheryl, [Jg 11,30-39] The tragic vision and biblical narrative; the case of Jephthah [response, *Humphreys* W. Lee]: → 395, Signs 1989, 59-83 [85-96].

2676* a) *Fuchs* Esther, Marginalization, ambiguity, silencing; the story of Jephthah's daughter; – b) *Milne* Pamela J., The patriarchal stamp of Scripture: JFemStRel 5,1 (1989) 35-46 / 17-34 [< ZIT 89,566].

2677 *Hanson* A. T., ORIGEN's treatment of the sacrifice of Jephthah's daughter: → 696, 10th Patristic, 21 (1989) 298-300.

2678 *Parente* James A.ᴶ, The paganization of biblical tragedy; the dramas of Jacob LUMMENAEUS a Marca (1570-1629); Humanistica Lovanensia, Neo-Latin Studies 38 (1989) 209-237 [8 tragedies; Jephte 1608, Amnon 1617, Sampson 1623 ...].

2680 a) *Tapp* Anne Michele, An ideology of expendability; virgin daughter sacrifice in Genesis 19,1-11; Judges 11,30-39 and 19,22-26; – b) *Gerstein* Beth, A ritual processed; a look at Judges 11.40; – c) *Baker* Cynthia, Pseudo-PHILO and the transformation of Jephthah's daughter; – d) *Bal* Mieke, [Jg 11,34] Between altar and wondering rock; toward a feminist philology: → 625, Anti-Covenant 1989, 157-174 / 175-193 / 195-209 / 211-231.

2681 **Bader** Winfried, Simson bei Delila; ein Weg von der EDV-Analyse zur Interpretation durch Ri 13-16: kath. Diss. ᴰ*Schweizer*. Tübingen 1988s. – TR 85 (1989) 518.

2682 **Bal** Mieke, Death and dissymetry [... Delilah; Jephthah's daughter]; the politics of coherence in the Book of Judges. Ch 1988, Univ. 312 p. $50; pa. $17. – ᴿTTod 46 (1989s) 350 (Margaret D. *Zulick*).

2683 **Grosjean** Jean, Samson et Dalila. P 1989, Gallimard. 104 p. F 58. – ᴿEsprVie 99 (1989) 656 (C. *Jean-Nesmy*: 'ton de légen[d]e').

2684 **Kim Jichan**, A stylistic and structural analysis of the Samson story (Judges 13-16): Diss. Calvin Sem. ᴰ*Stek* J. GR 1989, iii-192 p. + bibliog. – CalvinT 24 (1989) 397s.

2684* *Matthews* Victor H., Freedom and entrapment in the Samson narrative; a literary analysis: PerspRelSt 16 (1989) 245-258 [< ᴢɪᴛ 90,164].

2685 *a*) *Merideth* Betsy, Desire and danger; the drama of betrayal in Judges [13-16] and Judith; – *b*) *Rasmussen* Rachel C., Deborah the woman warrior; – *c*) *Hanselman* Stephen W., Narrative theory, ideology, and transformation in Judges 4; – *d*) *Shaw* Jane, Constructions of woman in readings of the story of Deborah: ➤ 625, Anti-Covenant 1989, 63-78 / 79-93 / 95-112 / 113-122.

2686 *Urbrock* W. J., Samson, a play for voices: ➤ 2987, Directions 1987, 232-264.

2687 *Marcus* David, In defense of Micah, Judges 17:2; he was not a thief: Shofar 6 (Purdue 1987) 72-80 [< OTAbs 12,54].

2688 *Schneid-Ofseyer* Miriam, The concubine of Gibeah (Judges 19-21): JBQ (= Dor) 18 (1989s) 111-3.

2689 *Beydon* France, Violence sous silence [*Trible* Phyllis, Jg 19]: FoiVie 88 (1989) 81-87.

E4.3 **Liber Ruth, '*V Rotuli*', The Five Scrolls.**

2690 *Fewell* Danna N., *Gunn* David M., Boaz, pillar of society; measures of worth in the Book of Ruth: JStOT 45 (1989) 45-59 [47 (1990) 120].

2691 *Coxon* Peter W., Was Naomi a scold? A response to Fewell and Gunn: JStOT [40 (1988) 99-108] 45 (1989) 25-37 [39-43 response, 'Is Coxon a scold?'].

2692 *Darr* Katheryn P., Ruth / Esther: ➤ 377, Books 1 (1989) 123-6 / 173-9.

2693 *Gage* Warren A., Ruth upon the threshing floor and the sin of Gibeah; a biblical-theological study: WestTJ 51 (1989) 369-375.

2694 **Gray** John, Joshua, Judges, Ruth: NCent 1986 ➤ 2,1690: ᴿCBQ 51 (1989) 124-6 (Carol *Meyers*, also on ᴊᴏᴜᴏɴ P. Ruth reprint); Grace TJ 10 (1989) 84-86 (R. *Patterson*).

2695 **Hubbard** R. L., The Book of Ruth: NICOT, 1988 ➤ 4,2793*; $27: ᴿExpTim 100 (1988s) 428 (C. S. *Rodd*).

2696 *Laffey* Alice L., Ruth: ➤ 384, NJBC (1989) 553-7.

2697 *Lemaire* André, Une inscription phénicienne découverte récemment [Alanya 1980] et le mariage de Ruth la Moabite: ➤ 218, Mem. ʏᴀᴅɪɴ Y., ErIsr 20 (1989) 124*-129*.

2698 **Sasson** Jack M., Ruth, a new translation with a philological commentary and a formalist-folklorist interpretation²ʳᵉᵛ [¹1979 ➤ 60,3537]: The Biblical Seminar. Sheffield 1989, JStOT. xix-292 p. £14. 1-85075-213-3 [BL 90,61, A. G. *Auld*: foreword regrets having featured Pʀᴏᴘᴘ even modestly].

2699 *Becker* Shlomoh, ❿ [Ruth 1,1] Link between Judges and Ruth: BethM 34,121 (1989s) 149-154.

2700 **Brenner** Athalya, ❶ The love of Ruth, 'who is dearer to you than seven sons'. TA 1988, Meuḥad. 168 p. [RelStR 16, 253, J. M. *Sasson*].

2701 *Min Young-Jin*, Problems in Ruth 2,7: BTrans 40 (1989) 438-441.

2702 *Hubbard* Robert L.ᴶ, [Ruth 3,3] Theological reflections on Naomi's shrewdness: TyndB 40 (1989) 283-292 [the numbering of this fasc. 40,2 is consecutive with vol. 40 (1989), which however is not called 40,1].

E4.4 1-2 Samuel.

2703 *Andersen* Francis I., *Freedman* David N., Another look at 4QSamᵇ: RQum 14 (1989) 7-29.

2704 **Anderson** A. A., 2 Samuel: Word Comm. 11. Dallas 1989, Word. xl-302 p. $25. 0-8499-0210-X [BL 90, 50, I. W. *Provan*]. – ᴿExpTim 101 (1989s) 281s (C. S. *Rodd*); SWJT 32,3 (1989s) 50 (D. G. *Kent*).

2705 *Avalos* Héctor, *Deuro/deute* and the imperatives of *hālak*; new criteria for the 'kaige' recension of Reigns: EstBíb 47 (1989) 165-176; Eng. 165.

2706 **Baldwin** Joyce G., 1 & 2 Samuel: Tyndale OT, 1988 ⟶ 4,2806: ᴿSWJT 32,2 (1989s) 54 (H. B. *Hunt*).

2707 *Birch* Bruce C., I and II Samuel: ⟶ 377, Books 1 (1989) 127-139.

2707* **Briscoe** David O., The implications of Samuel's priestly functions in the setting of the Former Prophets: diss. New Orleans Baptist Theol. Sem., ᴰ*Smith* B. K. 1988. 203 p. 89-11175. – DissA 50 (1989s) 706-A.

2708 *Campbell* Antony F., [*Flanagan* James W.], 1 [2] Samuel: ⟶ 384, NJBC (1989) 145-154 [154-9].

2709 *Campbell* Antony F., Of prophets and kings 1986 ⟶ 2,2012 ... 4,2807: ᴿTLZ 114 (1989) 663-5 (H. J. *Zobel*).

2710 **Chafin** K., 1-2 Samuel. Dallas 1989, Word. 404 p. [TS 51,571].

2711 **Fernández Marcos** N., *Busto Saiz* J. R., El texto antioqueno de la Biblia griega I, 1-2 Samuel: TEstCisn 50. M 1989, ConsSupInv. lxxxix-173 p. 84-00-06971-4 [BL 90, 44, N. de *Lange*].

2712 **Gordon** Robert P., 1 & 2 Samuel, a commentary 1986 ⟶ 2,2016 ... 4,2810: ᴿVT 39 (1989) 253s (J. *Barton*).

2713 **McCarter** P. Kyle, II Samuel: AnchorB 9, 1984 ⟶ 65,2408 ... 2,2019: ᴿJAOS 109 (1989) 681-3 (D. *Marcus*).

2714 **Martínez Borobio** E., I-II Samuel: Targum Jonatán de los Profetas Primeros en tradición babilónica 2/TEstCisn 38, 1987 ⟶ 3,1672.2674; 4,3814; pt. 3500: ᴿBL 89 (1989) 49 (F. *García Martínez*); BO 46 (1989) 145s (M. L. *Klein*); OLZ 84 (1989) 683s (J. *Meier*).

2715 **Miscall** Peter D., 1 Samuel, a literary reading 1986 ⟶ 2,2021; 4,2815: ᴿCriswT 2 (1988) 431s (K. A. *Mathews*).

2716 **Morano Rodríguez** Ciríaca, Glosas marginales de Vetus Latina en las Biblias Vulgatas españolas, 1-2 Samuel: TEstCisn 48. lxxxiii-61 p. M 1989, Cons. Sup. Inv. 84-00-06993-5 [BL 90,45, W. *Watson*: at long last, after failed promises by other scholars, replacement of flawed VER-CELLONE C. 1860-4].

2717 ᴱ**Nautin** Pierre & Marie-Thérèse, ORIGÈNE, Homélies sur Samuel: SChr 328, 1986 ⟶ 3,2676; 4,2816: ᴿRBgPg 67 (1989) 192-5 (J. *Schamp*); RHR 206 (1989) 205s (J. *Doignon*).

2718 **Pisano** Stephen, Additions or omissions in the books of Samuel...: OBO 57, 1984 ⟶ 65,2409 ... 4,2818: ᴿRB 96 (1989) 447s (G. J. *Norton*).

2719 **Polzin** Robert, Samuel and the Deuteronomist; a literary study of the Deuteronomic history, II. 1 Samuel. SF 1989, Harper & R. 328 p. $39. –

ᴿNewTR 2,4 (1989) 95 (L.J. *Hoppe*); TTod 46 (1989s) 458-460 (M.T. *Davis*).

2720 *Polzin* Robert, 1 Samuel; biblical studies and the humanities [MᶜCARTER, 1980; KLEIN, 1983: comm.; 4 others infra]: RelStR 15 (1989) 297-306.

2721 **Schuman** N.A., Messiaans en menselijk; notities bij de boeken Samuël. Kampen 1988, Kok. 130 p. Fb 390. – ᴿCollatVL 19 (1989) 346 (P. *Kevers*).

2722 *Stoebe* Hans-Joachim, Überlegungen zur Exegese historischer Texte — dargestellt an den Samuelisbüchern: TZBas 45 (1989) 290-314.

2723 **Trebolle Barrera** Julio, Centena in libros Samuelis et Regum; variantes textuales y composición literaria en los libros de Samuel y Reyes: TEstCisn 47. M 1989, Cons. Sup. Inv. 235 p. 84-00-06964-1 [BL 90,48].

2724 ᵀᴱVogüé Albert de, GRÉGOIRE le Grand, Commentaire sur le premier livre des Rois I [1 Sam 1-2,28]: SChr 351. P 1989, Cerf. 495 p. – ᴿETL 65 (1989) 451s (A. de *Halleux*); RBén 99 (1989) 338s (L. *Wankenne*).

2725 **Zijl** A.H. van, I Samuel I (1988 → 4,2823) II: PredikOT. Nijkerk 1989, Callenbach. 178 p. *f* 65,50. 90-266-0739-3 (vol. 1), -192-1 [BL 90,155].

2726 **Cook** Joan E., [1 Sam 2,1-10] The song of Hannah; text and contexts: diss. Vanderbilt, ᴰ*Harrelson* W. Nashville 1989. 228 p. 89-19684. – DissA 50 (1989s) 1687-A; RelStR 16,189.

2727 *Banwell* B., A possible meaning of *ephod bad* in 1 Sam 2:18 ['only an ephod']: OTEssays 2,2 (Pretoria 1989) 73s.

2728 *Ben-Reuven* Sara, ⊙ [1 Sam 2.25] Who makes atonement for inter-personal sins?: BethM 32 (1986s) 299s [< OTAbs 11,181].

2729 **Gnuse** Robert K., [1 Sam 3] The dream theophany of Samuel 1984 → 65,2424... 2,2027: ᴿJNES 48 (1989) 145 (D. *Pardee*: original, important).

2730 *Smelik* K.A.D., The Ark narrative reconsidered: → 129, ᶠMULDER M., New avenues 1989, 128-144.

E4.5   *1 Sam 7 ... Initia potestatis regiae,* **Origins of kingship.**

2731 **Berges** Ulrich, Die Verwerfung Sauls; eine thematische Untersuchung [Diss. Pont. Univ. Gregoriana, ᴰ*Conroy* C., R 1988]: ForBi 61. Wü 1989, Echter. xviii-332 p. DM 48. 3-429-01224-4 [TLZ 102,442, H.-C. *Schmitt*].

2732 *Berges* Ulrich, El rechazo de Saul; historia y historiografía en el antiguo Israel, ᵀ*Daum* Jürgen: RTLim 23 (1989) 235-247.

2733 **Brettler** M.Z., God is king; understanding an Israelite metaphor: JStOT 76. Sheffield 1989, Academic. 239 p. £25. 1-85075-224-9 [BL 90,98, R.A. *Mason*].

2734 **Camponovo** Odo, Königtum, Königsherrschaft und Reich Gottes in den frühjüdischen Schriften [ᴰ1983 → 64,2733]: OBO 58, 1984 → 65,2420... 4,2531: ᴿBZ 33 (1989) 127-9 (J. *Maier*); RÉJ 148 (1989) 397-9 (A. *Caquot*).

2735 **Eaton** J.H., Kingship and the Psalms² 1986 (¹1976) → 4,2832*: ᴿVT 39 (1989) 123s (J.A. *Emerton*).

2736 *Finkelstein* Israel, The emergence of the monarchy in Israel; the environmental and socio-economic aspects: JStOT 44 (1989) 43-74.

2737 **Gerbrandt** Gerald E., Kingship according to the Deuteronomistic history SBL diss 87, 1986 ➤ 2,2033 ... 4,2834: ᴿCBQ 51 (1989) 514s (J. C. *Endres*); ÉglT 19 (1988) 95-97 (W. *Vogels*); JQR 80 (1989s) 190s (J. A. *Soggin* gives date as 1960); RB 96 (1989) 133s (F. J. *Gonçalves*); RelStR 15 (1989) 301 (R. *Polzin*); VT 39 (1989) 251s (H. *Williamson*).

2737* *Lemaire* A., The united monarchy: ➤ b322, ᴱ*Shanks* H., Ancient Israel 1988, 85-108.

2738 **Long** V. Philips, The reign and rejection of King Saul; a case for literary and theological coherence: SBL diss 118 [Cambridge, ᴰ*Gordon* R.]. Atlanta 1989, Scholars. xvii-276 p. $23; pa. $11 [TrinJ 10,242]. 1-55540-391-3.

2739 **Polish** David, Give us a king; legal-religious sources of Jewish sovereignty. Hoboken 1989, KTAV. xxi-180 p. $20 [JBL 109,379].

2740 **Rosenberg** Joel, King and kin 1986 ➤ 3,2692; 4,2837: ᴿJAOS 109 (1989) 294s (G. A. *Rendsburg*).

2741 *Seybold* Klaus, Königtum in Israel: ➤ 894, EvKL 2 (1989) 1389-92.

2742 *Stachowiak* Lech, ❷ Saul et David et l'origine de la monarchie israélite: STWsz 26,1 (1988) 15-35; deutsch 35s.

2743 *Whitelam* Keith W., Israelite kingship; the royal ideology and its opponents: ➤ 378, World 1989, 119-140.

2744 **Eslinger** Lyle M., Kingship of God in crisis; a close reading of 1 Samuel 1-12: Bible and Literature 10, 1985 ➤ 1,2808* ... 4,2838: ᴿBL (1989) 72 (R. P. *Carroll*); RelStR 15 (1989) 303s (R. *Polzin*); VT 39 (1989) 126 (R. P. *Gordon*).

2745 **Wénin** André, Samuel et l'instauration de la monarchie (1 S 1-12) [diss Pont. Ist. Biblico 1987] EurHS 23/342, 1988 ➤ 4,2839: ᴿBiblica 70 (1989) 541-4 (L. *Eslinger*); ExpTim 101 (1989s) 139 (R. *Coggins*); NRT 111 (1989) 926-8 (J.-L. *Ska*); RTLv 20 (1989) 356 (P.-M. *Bogaert*: 'post-critique'?).

2746 **Fokkelman** J. P., The crossing fates, 1 Sam 13-31; 2 Sam 1; Narrative art II, 1986 ➤ 2,2042 ... 4,2845: ᴿBO 46 (1989) 431-3 (F. W. *Golka*); JBL 108 (1989) 121s (R. L. *Cohn*: two vulnerabilities); RelStR 15 (1989) 301-3 (R. *Polzin*); JRel 68 (1988) 583s (Adele *Berlin*).

2747 *Stern* Philip D., I Samuel 15; towards an ancient view of the war-ḥerem: UF 21 (1989) 413-420.

2748 *Simotas* Panagiotis S., ❷ [1 Sam 15,33] The death of Agag, king of the Amalikites: TAth 60 (1989) 286-304.

E4.6 *1 Sam 16 ... 2 Sam: Accessio Davidis.* **David's Rise.**

2749 *Catastini* Alessandro, 4QSamᶜ, David e la vendetta del sangue: ➤ 759, Sangue 1987/9, 709-717.

2750 **Dietrich** Walter, David, Saul und die Propheten ...: BW 122, 1987 ➤ 3,2709 ... 4,2853: ᴿCBQ 51 (1989) 713-5 (P. D. *Miscall*); JBL 108 (1989) 123s (J. *Blenkinsopp*).

2751 *Feldman* Louis H., JOSEPHUS' portrait of David: HUCA 60 (1989) 129-174.

2752 **Flanagan** James W., David's social drama; a hologram of Israel's early Iron Age: JStOT supp 73 / SocWB 7, 1988 ➤ 4,2855: ᴿExpTim 101 (1989s) 27s (J. F. *Healey*: hologram, partly as in D. BOHM, aims to illumine the reality by all diverging evidences like archeology and literary citicism without putting them in direct conflict); ZAW 101 (1989) 456s (H.-C. *Schmitt*).

2752* *a*) *Gileadi* Avraham, The Davidic covenant; a theological basis for corporate protection; – *b*) *Lundquist* J. M., Temple, covenant, and law in the Ancient Near East and in the Hebrew Bible; – *c*) *Waltke* B. K., The phenomenon of conditionality within unconditional covenants; – *d*) *Wolf* H. M., The transcendent nature of covenant curse reversals; – *e*) *Dumbrell* W. J., The prospect of unconditionality in the Sinaitic covenant: ⇥ 77, F*HARRISON* R., Israel's apostasy 1988, 157-163 / 293-305 / 128-139 / 319-325 / 141-155.

2753 *a*) *Gunn* David M., In security; the David of biblical narrative; – *b*) (response) *Miscall* Peter D., For David's sake: ⇥ 395, Signs 1989, 133-151 / 153-163.

2754 *Lohfink* Norbert, Welches Orakel gab den Davididen Dauer? Ein Textproblem in 2 Kön 8,19 und das Funktionieren der dynastischen Orakel im deuteronomistischen Geschichtswerk [< (erwartet) F*MORAN* W., HarvSemSt]: ⇥ 423, E*Struppe* Ursula, Studien zum Messiasbild im AT 1989, 127-154.

2755 **Lowery** Richard H., The reforming kings [David, Ahaz, Hezekiah, Josiah]; cult and society in First Temple Judah: diss. Yale, D*Wilson* R. NHv 1989. 334 p. 90-12313. – DissA 50 (1989s) 3986s-A; RTLv 21,541.

2756 **Ollenburger** Ben C., Zion, the city of the great king; a theological symbol of the Jerusalem cult: JStOT sup 41, 1987 ⇥ 3,2718; 4,2861: R*CBQ* 51 (1989) 535s (J. C. *Kesterson*); ScriptB 20 (1989s) 18s (J. E. *Rybolt*).

2757 *Szlaga* Jan, ❷ Filistyni: ⇥ 891, EncKat 5 (1989) 222s.

2758 *Howard* David M.J, The transfer of power from Saul to David in 1 Sam 16:13-14: JEvTS 32 (1989) 473-484 [< ZIT 90,228].

2759 **Barthélemy** D., *al.*, [1 Sam 17] The story of David and Goliath: OBO 73, 1986 ⇥ 2,2060-2062... 4,2863: R*JStJud* 20 (1989) 208-210 (J. *Trebolle*: conclusions not notably advanced beyond starting-points); RB 96 (1989) 448-450 (G. J. *Norton*); Salesianum 51 (1989) 347s (M. *Cimosa*). ⇥ 2783.

2760 *Brueggemann* Walter, [1 Sam 17; Ps 13] Before the giant — surrounded by Mother [= God]: PrincSemB 8,3 (1987) 1-13 [< OTAbs 12,202: commencement address].

2761 *Polzin* Robert, [1 Sam 17] Contributions of biblical studies to Jewish studies [the text as we have it, not imagined pre-texts]: Shofar 7,1 (Purdue 1988) 1-13 [< OTAbs 12,177].

2762 *Rofé* A., ❷ The war between David and Goliath — fairy-tale, theology and eschatology [Persian period early 4th century B.C.E.]: ⇥ 8, Mem. ALLONI N., Ešel BeerŠeba 3 (1986) 55-89.

2763 *Luciani* Ferdinando, *a*) Problemi filologici relativi ad alcuni passi di '1 Sam.' 17,1; '1 Sam.' 17,12b secondo la Volgata; II. Il significato di *iš Jiśrā'ēl* nella proposizione iniziale di '1 Sam.' 17,25: Aevum 63 (1989) 3-16; – *b*) L'ultima frase di 1 Sam 17.24 e la sua posizione nel contesto: RivB 37 (1989) 73-77.

2764 *Luciani* Ferdinando, *a*) La forma e il significato di *wjṭl* [*wajjāṭel*] in 1 Sam 18,11; 20,33; – *b*) La reazione degli Israeliti alla sfida di Golia in 1 Sam 17: RivB 37 (1989) 385-425; Eng. 425s 'Since a long time ...' / 447-460.

2765 *Lawton* Robert B., 1 Samuel 18: David, Merob, and Michal: CBQ 51 (1989) 423-5.

2766 *Stoebe* Hans J., [1 Sam 18,20; 2 Sam 6,16] David und Mikal; Überlegungen zur Jugendgeschichte Davids [< *FEissfeldt* O., BZAW 77 (1958) 224-243]: → 362, Geschichte 1989, 91-110.

2767 *Rebera* Basil A., 'He got up' — or did he? (1 Samuel 20,25): BTrans 40 (1989) 212-8.

2768 **Parmentier** M. F. G., [1 Sam 28] Goddelijke wezens uit de aarde; Griekse kerkvaders over de 'heks' van Endor: Christelijke bronnen 1. Kampen 1989, Kok. 132 p. *f* 24,50. – RStreven 57 (1989s) 471s (P. *Beentjes*).

2769 **Tropper** Josef, Nekromantie; Totenbefragung im Alten Orient und im Alten Testament [kath. Diss. *DWeimar*. Münster 1988s. – TR 85 (1989) 517]: AOAT 228. Neuk/Kevelaer 1989, Neuk-V./Butzon & B. x-398 p. [TR 86,74]. 3-7887-1312-7 Neuk / 3-7666-9639-4 BB.

2770 **Simonetti** Manlio, ORIGENE, EUSTAZIO, GREGORIO de Nisa, La maga di Endor; Biblioteca Patristica 15. F 1989, Nardini. 292 p. 88-404-2015-0.

2771 *Arnold* B., The Amalekite's report of Saul's death; political intrigue or incompatible sources?: JEvTS 32 (1989) 289-298.

2772 *Brueggemann* Walter, Narrative intentionality in 1 Samuel 29: JStOT 43 (1989) 21-35.

2773 *Deboys* D. G., 1 Samuel XXIX 6: VT 39 (1989) 214-9.

2774 *Kleven* Terence, Rhetoric and narrative depiction in 2 Samuel 1:1-16: ProcGLM 9 (1989) 59-73.

2775 *Layton* Scott C., A chain gang in 2 Samuel iii 29? a rejoinder: VT [37 (1987) 370-5, *Holloway* S.] 39 (1989) 81-86.

2776 *Stoebe* H. J., *a*) [2 Sam 5,8] Die Einnahme Jerusalems und der Sinnôr; – *b*) Überlegungen zur Siloahinschrift; – *c*) Die Goliathperikope, 1 Sam XVII,1-XVIII,5; – *d*) Zur Topographie und Überlieferung der Schlacht von Mikmas, 1 Sam 13 und 14; – *e*) David und der Ammoniterkrieg; – *f*) Gedanken zur Heldensage: → 362, Geschichte 1989, 241-267 / 224-240 / 74-90 / 111-122 / 134-144 / 123-133.

2777 **Seow Choon Leong**, [2 Sam 6,14.16] Myth, drama, and the politics of David's dance: HarvSemMg 44. Atlanta 1989, Scholars. xi-272 p. $23; pa. $14. 1-55540-400-6.

2778 **Fokkelman** Jan P. [2 Sam 9-20], Narrative art... Samuel, I: 1981 → 63,2962a... 4,2884: RRelStT 8,1s (1988) 78s (L. *Eslinger*).

2779 **Staats** Carl G., [2 Sam 11] Aspects of negative role modeling in the David/Bathsheba story and its sequel: diss. NYU, *DLevine* B. 1989. 258 p. 89-16090. – DissA 50 (1989s) 978-A.

2780 *a*) *Rosenberg* Joel, The institutional matrix of treachery in 2 Samuel 11; – *b*) *Campbell* Antony F., [1 Sam 18s; 22; 2 Sam 3] The reported story; midway between oral performance and literary art: Semeia 46 (1989) 103-116 / 77-85.

2781 *Pisano* Stephen, La famiglia di Davide; promessa e conflitto: → 587, Famiglia 1989, 101-114.

2782 *Dijk-Hemmes* Fokkelien van, Tamar and the limits of patriarchy; between rape and seduction (2 Samuel 13 and Genesis 38): → 625, Anti-Covenant 1989, 135-156.

2783 *a*) *Moss* Steven A., [2 Sam 21,18-22; 1 Chr 20,4-8] Who killed Goliath?; – *b*) *Wolfers* David, A response to Steven Moss: JBQ 18 (1988s) 37-40 / 114-6.

2784 **Schnabl** Heinrich, Die 'Thronerzählung' Davids: Untersuchungen zur literarkritischen Eigenständigkeit, literarkritischen Abgrenzung und Intention von 2 Sam 21,1-14; 9-20; 1 Kön 1-2 [Diss. Rg.]: Theorie und Forschung 55. Rg 1988, Roderer. XXVII-223 p. [TR 85 (1989) 425].

2785 *Cook* Calvin, [2 Sam 21,1-14] Rizpah's vigil — Stabat mater [... and South Africa]: JTSAf 67 (1989) 77-88 [< TContext 7/1, 22].

2786 *Weisman* Ze'ev, ❻ Legal aspects of David's involvement in the blood-vengeance of the Gibeonites (2 Sam 21: 1-14): Zion 59 (1989) 149-160; Eng. v.

2787 *Rendsburg* Gary A., Additional notes on 'The last words of David' (2 Sam 23,1-17): Biblica [69 (1988) 113-121] 70 (1989) 403-8.

E4.7 *Libri Regum;* **Solomon, Temple: 1 Kings...**

2788 **Auld** A. Graeme, I & II Kings: Daily Study Bible 1986 ⇥ 2,2078; 3,2753: ᴿCBQ 51 (1989) 312s (B. O. *Long*).

2789 **De Vries** Simon J., 1 Kings: Word Comm. 12, 1985 ⇥ 1,2842... 3,2754: ᴿIrTQ 55 (1989) 72s (S. *Goan*, also on T. *Hobbs* 2 Kings, Word 13).

2790 **Hentschel** Georg, 1 Könige: NEchter 10, 1984 ⇥ 65,2463... 3,2756: ᴿRB 96 (1989) 134s (F. J. *Gonçalves*).

2791 *Kohen* Uzzi, ❻ Historical parallels in 1 Kings: BethM 34,121 (1989s) 162-5.

2792 *McConville* J.G., Narrative and meaning in the books of Kings: Biblica 70 (1989) 31-48; franç. 49.

2793 **Mulder** M.J., Koningen vertaald en verklaard, I (1 K 1-7), 1987 ⇥ 4,2904: ᴿGerefTTs 89 (1989) 119s (C. *Houtman*).

2794 **Nelson** Richard D., First and Second Kings: Interpretation Comm. 1987 ⇥ 4,2905: ᴿBL (1989) 59 (G. H. *Jones*).

2795 *Walsh* Jerome T., [*Begg* Christopher T.], 1 [2] Kings: ⇥ 384, NJBC (1989s) 162-175 [175-185 + 160s].

2796 **Würthwein** E., Die Bücher... 1 Kön 17-2 Kön 25 1984 = 1977 ⇥ 1,2875... 3,2760: ᴿRB 96 (1989) 135-7 (F. J. *Gonçalves*).

―――――――――――

2797 *Lasine* Stuart, [1 Kgs 3,17-22] The riddle of Solomon's judgment and the riddle of human nature in the Hebrew Bible: JStOT 45 (1989) 61-86.

2797* *Weippert* Helga & M., Zwei Frauen vor dem Königsgericht; Einzelfragen der Erzählung vom 'Salomonischen Urteil': ⇥ 116, ᶠLEEUWEN C. van 1989, 133-160.

2798 *a) Beuken* W.A.M., No wise king without a wise woman (I Kings iii 16-28); – *b) Deurloo* K.A., The king's wisdom in judgment; narration as example (1 Kings iii); – *c) Dirksen* P.B., Some remarks in connection with the Peshiṭta of Kings; – *d) Hoftijzer* J., Philological notes on 1 Kings xi 14: ⇥ 129, ᶠMULDER M., New avenues 1989, 1-10 / 11-21 / 22-28 / 29-37.

2799 *Naveh* Joseph, ❻ Nameless people? [1 Kgs 4,8-13, patronyms like Ben-Hur without other personal name, also in Is 7 and Ugarit, claimed by A. ALT to indicate inherited position: untenable]: Zion 59 (1989) 1-15; Eng. i.

2800 *Davies* G.I., *'Urwōt* in 1 Kings 5.6 (EVV. 4:26) and the Assyrian horse lists: JSS 34 (1989) 25-38.

2801 **Templum:** a) *Giavini* Giovanni, Il tempio secondo la Bibbia; – b) *Biffi* Inos, Il tempio e i suoi segni: Ambrosius 65 (1989) 461-4 / 509-515.

2802 a) *Kobielus* Stanisław, ❷ Fondements bibliques et symboliques d'une construction sacrale; – b) *Brzegowy* Tadeusz, ❷ La demeure de Dieu sur la terre à la lumière des Psaumes: AtKap 113 (1989) 3-13 / 14-24.

2803 *Hammerschmidt* Ernst, *Uhlig* Siegbert, Ein äthiopischer Text über den Tempel Salomos: ➤ 126, ᶠMACUCH R., Ḥokmôt 1989, 109-139.

2804 **Mulder** M.J., a) Salomo's tempel en JHWH's exclusiviteit. Leiden 1989, Rijksuniv. 21 p. [ÉTRel 64,484]; – b) Solomon's temple and YHWH's exclusivity: ➤ 139, ᶠMULDER & OT Werkgezelschap 1989, 49-62.

2805 *Hirth* Volkmar [1 Kön 6; 22,19; Ezek 10; Ex 25,18-22...] Die Keruben – Vorstellung und Wirklichkeit zur Zeit des Alten Testaments: TVers 17 (1989) 15-22.

2806 a) *Kitchen* Kenneth A., [1 K 6,8-10; not in Chr] Two notes on the subsidiary rooms of Solomons's Temple; – b) *Millard* A., [1 K 6,31.33] The doorways of Solomon's Temple: ➤ 218, Mem. YADIN Y., ErIsr 20 (1989) 107*-112*; 2 fig. / 135*-139*; 2 fig.

2807 *Luria* B.Z., ❸ The walls of the Temple mountain: Sinai 100 (1987) 509-516 [< JStJud 20,293].

2808 a) *Maier* Johann, The architectural history of the Temple in Jerusalem in the light of the Temple Scroll; – b) *Barker* Margaret, The Temple measurements and the solar calendar: ➤ 568, Temple Scroll 1987/9, 23-63; 8 fig. / 63-66.

2809 *Vilar Hueso* Vicente, Los accesos meridionales al templo de Herodes: ➤ 69*, ᶠGOMÀ I., RCatalT 14 (1989) 95-98 castellano; Eng. 98.

2810 ᴱ*Modgley* Graham, John Bunyan [1628-88], Solomon's Temple spiritualized [1687s]; the house of the forest of Lebanon; the water of life: Works 7. Ox 1989, Clarendon. li-236 p. $79. 0-19-812735-9 [TDig 36,357].

2811 *Schottroff* Willy, [1 K 4,6s; 1 Sam 8.13] Der Zugriff des Königs auf die Töchter; zur Fronarbeit von Frauen im alten Israel: EvT 49 (1989) 268-285.

2812 *Flinder* Alexander, [1 Kgs 9,26] Is this Solomon's seaport? [Faraun island 25k SW Eilat]: BAR-W 15,4 (1989) 31-43; color. ill.; plans.

2813 a) *Millard* Alan R., [1 Kgs 9,28; 10,14; 7,49] Does the Bible exaggerate King Solomon's golden wealth?; – b) *Kitchen* Kenneth A., Where did Solomon's gold go?; – Shishak's military campaign in Israel confirmed; BAR-W 15,3 (1989) 20-29.31.34 / 30; 32s; ill.

2814 **Beyer** Rolf, [1 Kön 10,1-13] Die Königin von Saba 1987 ➤ 4,2927; DM 40: ᴿTLZ 114 (1989) 173s (W. *Herrmann*).

2815 ᴱ**Daum** Werner, Die Königin von Saba; Kunst, Legende und Archäologie zwischen Morgenland und Abendland. Stu 1988, Belser. 216 p.; 99 fig.; 2 maps. DM 98. – ᴿDer Islam 66 (1989) 356s (H. *List*); Judaica 45 (1989) 257s (S. *Hurwitz*).

2816 *Kamsler* Harold M., Solomon and Sheba; aggadic roots of the Koran story [Esther, Targum Sheni = Sura 27]: JBQ (= Dor) 18 (1989s) 172-5.

2817 a) *Previn* Dory, Sheba and Solomon; – b) *Fontaine* Carole R., A heifer from thy stable; on goddesses and the status of women in the ancient Near East: UnSemQ 43 (1989) 59-66 / 67-92 [< ZIT 90,25].

2818 *Liptzin* Sol, [1 Kgs 11,8] King Solomon's wives, as envisioned by [1921 Yiddish dramatist] David PINSKI: JBQ (= Dor) 18 (1989s) 19-26.

2818* *Horn* S.H., The divided monarchy: ➤ b322, ᴱ*Shanks* H., Ancient Israel 1988, 85-108.

2819 **Knoppers** Gerald N., [1 Kgs 11-14] 'What share have we in David?' The division of the kingdom in Kings [esp. 3 Reigns 12:24s-z] and Chronicles: diss. Harvard 1988. 542 p. 89-09033. – DissA 50 (1989s) 465-A.
2820 *Steiner* Richard C., [1 Kgs 11,27] New light on the biblical Millo from Hatran inscriptions: BASOR 276 (1989) 15-23; 3 fig.
2821 *Shim Young-Súb,* ◉ [1 Kgs 12,6] Bible and society; 'what answer do you advise me to give this people?': Samok 125 (Seoul 1989) 95-103 [< TContext 7/1, 58].
2822 *Van Winkle* D. W., 1 Kings XIII; true and false prophecy: VT 39 (not 29 as p. 31 top; 1989) 31-43.
2823 *Andersen* Knud T., Noch einmal; die Chronologie der Könige von Israel und Juda: ScandJOT (1989,1) 1-45 [< ZIT 89,176].
2823* *Brincken* Anne-Dorothee von den, Contemporalitas Regnorum; Beobachtungen zum Versuch des SIEGBERT von Gembloux, die Chronik des HIERONYMUS fortzusetzen: → 171, FSCHMALE F., Historiographia 1988, 199-211.
2824 *Hayes* John H., *Hooker* Paul K., A new chronology for the kings... 1988 → 4,2931: RETL 65 (1989) 425s (M. *Vervenne*: attractive, still too tentative).
2825 *Kochavi* Moshe, ◉ [1 Kgs after G 12,24] The identification of Zeredah, home of Jeroboam son of Nebat, king of Israel: → 218, Mem. YADIN Y., ErIsr 20 (1989) 198-201; 5 fig.; Eng. 201*.
2826 *a*) *Gunneweg* Antonius H. J., Die Prophetenlegende 1 Reg 13 — Missdeutung, Umdeutung, Bedeutung; – *b*) *Würthwein* Ernst, Zur Opferprobe Elias I Reg 18,21-39: → 105, FKAISER O., Prophet 1989, 73-81 / 277-284.
2827 *Walsh* Jerome T., The contexts of 1 Kings XIII: VT 39 (1989) 355-370.
2828 *Talmon* Shemaryahu, *Fields* Weston W., The collocation *maštîn beqîr we-'aṣûr we-'āzûb* [1 Kgs 14,10] and its meaning: ZAW 101 (1989) 85-112.
2829 *Müller* A. R., [1 Kön 15,10] Asa: → 902, NBL Lfg. 2 (1989) 179s.
2830 *Ljung* Inger, [1 Kon 16,31...] Om 'Isebel' i Samaria, Tyatira och Frankerriket: SvEx 54 (1989) 127-134.
2831 *Mazar* Benjamin, ◉ The house of Omri: → 218, Mem. YADIN Y., ErIsr 20 (1989) 215-9; Eng. 201*s.

          E4.8   *1 Regum 17-22: Elias,* **Elijah.**

2831* *a*) *Battenfield* J. R., YHWH's refutation of the Baal myth through the actions of Elijah and Elisha; – *b*) *Oswalt* J. N., Golden calves and the 'bull of Jacob'; the impact on Israel of its religious environment; – *c*) *Gilchrist* P. R., Israel's apostasy, catalyst of Assyrian world conquest; – *d*) *Matthews* V. H., Theophanies cultic and cosmic; 'prepare to meet thy God!': → 77, FHARRISON R., Israel's apostasy 1988, 19-37 / 9-18 / 99-113 / 307-317.
2832 *King* Philip J., The eighth, the greatest of centuries: SBL presidential address, Chicago, Nov. 19, 1988: JBL 108 (1989) 3-15.
2833 *Nelson* Richard D., God and the heroic prophet; preaching the stories of Elijah and Elisha: QRMin 9,2 (1989) 93-105.
2834 *Brock* S. P., [1 Kgs 17] A Syriac verse homily on Elijah and the widow of Sarepta [attributed to EPHREM like other 7:7 syllable metre narrative poems]: Muséon 102 (1989) 93-113.
2835 *De Vries* Simon J., The three comparisons in 1 Kings XXII 4b and its parallel [2 Chr 18,3b] and 2 Kings III 7b: VT 39 (1989) 283-306.

2836 *Soards* Marion L., Elijah and the Lord's word; a study of 1 Kings
17:17-24; Studia Biblica et Theologica 13 (Guilford CT 1983) 39-50
[< OTAbs 12 (1989) 179].

2837 *Asurmendi* Jesus, *al.*, Élie au Carmel: MondeB 58 (1989) 5-11 (-40).

2838 *Parker* Simon B., KTU 1.16 III, the myth of the absent God and
1 Kings 18: UF 21 (1989) 283-296.

2839 *Begg* Christopher, 'This thing I cannot do' (1 Kgs 20,9): ScandJOT
(1989,2) 23-27.

2840 *Imhof* Paul, 'Isebel fressen die Hunde...' (1 Kön 21); der Verrat an der
Freiheit: GeistL 62 (1989) 30-37.

2840* *Sandberger* Jörg V., Hermeneutische und didaktische Aspekte der
Naboth-Erzählung 1. Könige 21: ➤ 65*, ᶠGEISSER H. 1988, 466-506.

2841 *Begg* Christopher, [1 K 22] The death of King Ahab according to
JOSEPHUS [A 8,398-420]: Antonianum 64 (1989) 225-245; ital. 225.

2841* *Dorp* J. van, Josafat in Samaria; exegetische aantekeningen bij 1 Kon
22,28: ➤ 116, ᶠLEEUWEN C. van 1989, 41-47.

E4.9   2 Reg 1 ... Elisaeus, Elisha.

2842 **Cogan** M., *Tadmor* H., II Kings: AnchorB 11, 1988 ➤ 4,2952: ᴿCBQ
51 (1989) 711s (C. T. *Begg*: too many typos); JBL 108 (1989) 688-700
(T. R. *Hobbs*); TS 50 (1989) 169-171 (P. M. *Arnold*).

2843 **Reinhold** Gotthard G. G., Die Beziehungen Altisraels zu den
aramäischen Staaten in der israelitisch-jüdischen Königszeit [... zur
Fachbezeichnung 'Biblische Archäologie']: ev. Diss. Fra 1988s, ᴰ*Schottroff*
W. – TR 85 (1989) 515; RTLv 21,543.

2844 *Schäfer-Lichtenberger* Christa, 'Josua' und 'Elischa' — eine biblische
Argumentation zur Begründung der Autorität und Legitimität des
Nachfolgers: ZAW 101 (1989) 198-222.

2845 **Stipp** Hermann-J., Elischa–Propheten–Gottesmänner... 1. Kön 20; 22;
2. Kön 2-7 [Diss. Tü 1985]: AOtt 24, 1987 ➤ 3,2808: ᴿCarthaginensia 5
(1989) 272 (B. *Sanz Valdivieso*); CBQ 51 (1989) 352s (C. T. *Begg*); JBL
108 (1989) 506s (W. *Roth*); TR 85 (1989) 192-4 (H.-C. *Schmitt*).

2846 *Friedman* John B., Bald Jonah and the exegesis of 4 Kings 2.23:
Traditio 44 (1988) 125-144; 20 phot.

2847 *Dijk-Hemmes* F. van, De grote vrouw uit Sunem en de man Gods; een
tweeledige interpretatie van 2 Koningen 4:8-17: Mara 2,2 (1989) 45-53
[< GerefTTs 89,64].

2848 *Trebolle Barrera* Julio, Filiación textual y valor crítico de lecturas de la
Vetus Latina en Samuel y Reyes (2 Re 4,39; 9,33; 12,10; 1 Sam 2,31):
➤ 69*, ᶠGOMÀ I., RCatalT 14 (1989) 65-73 castellano; Eng. 74.

Lohfink Norbert, [2 Kön 8,19] im deuteronomistischen Geschichtswerk 1989
➤ 2754.

2849 *Weimar* P., [2 Kön 8,26] Atalja: ➤ 902, NBL Lfg. 2 (1989) 196s.

2850 **Barré** Lloyd M., The rhetoric of political persuasion... 2 K 9-11, 1988
➤ 4,2959: ᴿArTGran 52 (1989) 243 (A. S. *Muñoz*); BL (1989) 67 (C. S.
Rodd).

2851 **Minokami** Yoshikazu, [2 Kg 9s] Die Revolution des Jehu: GöTArb 38.
Gö 1989, Vandenhoeck & R. 189 p. DM 38. – ᴿZAW 101 (1989) 470s
(H.-C. *Schmitt*).

2852 *Dorp* J. van, De tempelrestauratie van Joas (2 Koningen 12); het gebruik van een motief in het boek Koningen: AmstCah 9 (1988) 77-89
[TR 85,425].

2853 *Wright* Logan S.,   *Mkr* in 2 Kings XII 5-17 and Deuteronomy XVIII 8:
VT 39 (1989) 438-448.

2854 *McFall* Leslie, [2 Kgs 17s] Did THIELE overlook Hezekiah's coregency?:
BS 146 (1989) 393-404.

2855 *Becking* Bob,   Theologie na de Ondergang; enkele opmerkingen bij
2 Koningen 17:   Beiträge zur Förderung christlicher Theologie 49 (1988)
150-174 [< OTAbs 12,60].

2855* *Timm* Stefan, [2 Kön 17] Die Eroberung Samarias aus assyrisch-ba-
bylonischer Sicht: WeltOr 20s (1989s) 62-82.

2856 *Ahlström* Gösta, [2 Kgs 17,4] Kung So och Israels undergång: SvEx 54
(1989) 5-19.

2857 *Christensen* Duane L.,   The identity of 'King So' in Egypt (2 Kings XVII
4): VT 39 (1989) 140-153.

2858 *Brettler* Marc,   Ideology, history and theology in 2 Kings XVII 7-23:
VT 39 (1989) 268-282.

2859 *Thiel* Winfried, [2 Kgs 17,7-23] Verfehlte Geschichte im AT: TBei 17
(1986) 248-266 [< OTAbs 12,140].

2860 **Catastini** A.,   Isaia ed Ezechia; studio di storia della tradizione di II Re
18-20 / Is 36-39: StSemit 6.   R 1989, Univ.   327 p. [ZAW 102, 441, J. A.
Soggin].

2861 *Vera Chamaza* G. W.,   Literarkritische Beobachtung zu 2 Kön 18,1-12:
BZ 33 (1989) 222-231; Bibliog. 232s.

2862 **Vuk** T.,   Wiedererkaufte Freiheit ... 2 Kön 18,13-16, ᴰ1984 ➤ 65,2523;
3,2820: ᴿRB 96 (1989) 137 (F. J. *Gonçalves*).

2863 **Gonçalves** Francolino J., [2 Rois 18,17] L'expédition de Sennacherib 1986
➤ 2,2131 ... 4,2971: ᴿBO 46 (1989) 433-5 (C. van *Leeuwen*); RechSR 76
(1988) 571-3 (J. *Briend*); ZAW 101 (1989) 459s (O. *Kaiser*).

2864 *Dion* Paul E.,   Sennacherib's expedition to Palestine: ÉglT 20 (1989)
5-26.

2865 *Richardson* M. E. J.,   Like the wolf on the fold [Sennacherib expedition
descriptions]: ➤ 200, ᶠULLENDORFF E., JSS 34 (1989) 471-482.

2866 **Camp** Ludger,   Hiskija und Hiskijabild; Analyse und Interpretation
von 2 Kön 18-20: Diss. Münster 1989, ᴰ*Zenger* E. [> Münsteraner
Theologische Abh. 9.   Altenberge 1990, Telos.   339 p. DM 44.   3-
89375- 021-5].

2867 **Provan** Iain W.,   Hezekiah and the books of Kings ... [diss. C 1986]:
BZAW 172, 1988 ➤ 4,2979: ᴿArTGran 52 (1989) 264s (J. L. *Sicre*); CBQ
51 (1989) 725s (R. D. *Nelson*); RHPR 69 (1989) 207 (P. de *Robert*); TR 85
(1989) 282-5 (L. *Camp*); ZkT 111 (1989) 97s (G. *Fischer*).

2868 **Vogt** E.,   Der Aufstand Hiskias ... AnBib 106, 1986 ➤ 2,2136; 4,2981:
ᴿRB 96 (1989) 137-9 (F. J. *Gonçalves*: beau, utile).

2869 *Williams* D. T., [2 Kgs 20] The dial and the boil; some remarks on the
healing of Hezekiah: OTEssays 2/2 (Pretoria 1989) 29-45.

2870 **Tagliacarne** Pierfelice,   'Keiner war wie er'; Untersuchung zur Struktur
von 2 Könige 22-23: Mü Univ AOtt 31.   St. Ottilien 1989, EOS, Erzabtei.
xi-473 p. DM 63.   3-88096-531-5 [BL 90,155].

2871 *Dorp* J. van,   Wat is die steenhoop daar?   Het graf van de man Gods in
2 Koningen 23: AmstCah 8 (1987) 64-79 [< GerefTTs 89,61].

2872 *Erlandsson* Seth, [Is 5,27-29 ...] Kampen om Babels tron — den assyriske
världsfursten som Babels kung: SvEx 54 (1989) 57-69.

2873 *Bruschweiler* Françoise,   Un échange de terrains entre Nabuchodonozor II et un inconnu dans la région de Sippar: RAss 83 (1989) 153-162;
3 phot.

2874 **Eynikel** E.,   De hervorming van Josia en de compositie van de deuteronomistische geschiedenis; diss. Kath. Univ. Leuven, ᴰ*Brekelmans* C., 1989. lxxv-526 p. – TsTNijm 29 (1989) 284s; RTLv 21, p. 540, La réforme de Josias et la composition de l'histoire du deutéronomiste.

2875 **Višaticki** Karlo, [2 K 23] Die Reform des Josija und die religiöse Heterodoxie in Israel: [Diss R 1987 → 4,2992]: Diss. Theol. 21. St. Ottilien 1987, EOS.   ix-329 p. DM 34. – ᴿETL 65 (1989) 157 (E. *Eynikel*: no new insights).

2876 **Delamarter** Stephen,   The death of Josiah; hermeneutics and exegesis in Scripture and tradition: diss. Claremont, ᴰ*Sanders* J. – RelStR 16,189.

2877 *Begg* Christopher, *a)* 'DtrP' in 2 Kings 25; some further thoughts: RB 96 (1989) 49-55; franç. 49; – *b)* JOSEPHUS' Zedekiah: ETL 65 (1989) 96-104.

E5.1   *Chronicorum libri* – **The Chronicler.**

2878 **Becker** Joachim, 1 Chronik: NEchter 18, 1986 → 3,2840; 4,2908: ᴿCBQ 51 (1989) 707s (K. G. *Hoglund*: only Ezra 1-6 may belong to Chr).

2879 **Braun** Roddy L.,   1 Chronicles: Word Comm. 14, 1986 → 2,2144... 4,3000: ᴿCBQ 51 (1989) 111s (R. W. *Klein*); IrTQ 55 (1989) 162s (S. F. *Kealy*, also on WILLIAMSON H., Ezra); RExp 86 (1989) 269 (T. G. *Smothers*); SWJT 32,1 (1989s) 47s (D. G. *Kent*).

2880 **De Vries** Simon J.,   1 and 2 Chronicles: FOTLit 11, GR 1989, Eerdmans. xiv-439 p. $28. 0-8028-0236-2 [BL 90,152]. – ᴿLA 39 (1989) 338s (A. *Niccacci*).

2881 **Dillard** Raymond B.,   2 Chr: Word Comm. 15, 1987 → 3,2485; 4,3002: ᴿGraceTJ 10 (1989) 241-3 (D. *Barker*); SWJT 32,1 (1989s) 48 (D. G. *Kent*).

2882 *Freedman* David N., *Willoughby* Bruce E.,   I and II Chronicles, Ezra, Nehemiah: → 377, Books 1 (1989) 155-171.

2883 *Hernando* Eugenio, El profetismo en los libros de las Crónicas: ScriptV 34 (1987) 45-66.

2884 **Japhet** Sara,   The ideology of the Book of Chronicles and its place in biblical thought [diss. J 1973], ᵀ*Barber* Anna: BeiErfATJ 9. Fra 1989, Lang. viii-553 p. 0-8204-8994-0 [OIAc Ja90].

2885 *Japhet* Sara,   Interchanges of verbal roots in parallel texts in Chronicles: HebSt 28 (1987) 9-50 [OTAbs 11, 163].

2886 **Kegler** Jürgen,   Das Zurücktreten der Exodustradition in der Chronikbücher: → 212, ᶠWESTERMANN C., Schöpfung 1989, 54-66.

2887 *Lorenzin* Tiziano, Osservazioni sull'uso delle preposizioni *lᵉ, bᵉ, min, 'el, 'al* in 1 e 2 Cronache: RivB 37 (1989) 161-6.

2888 **McKenzie** S. L., The Chronicler's use of the deuteronomistic history 1984 → 1,2913 ... 4,3009: ᴿCarthaginensia 5 (1989) 273s (R. *Sanz Valdivieso*).

2889 **Merrill** Eugene H.,   1,2 Chronicles: Bible Study Comm. GR 1988, Zondervan. 173 p. $8 pa. – ᴿBS 146 (1989) 466s (T. L. *Constable*, brief).

2890 *North* Robert, The Chronicler: 1-2 Chronicles [Ezra, Nehemiah]: → 384, NJBC (1989) 362-383 [-398]. [N.B. The author, though not himself convinced by recent (*Japhet* S., *Williamson* H.) abandonment of 'Chronicler' author of Ezra-Nehemiah, proposed to the editors that this subtitle should be withdrawn, and the Ezra-books placed noncommittally in their biblical order before Chronicles. The editors of course had every right not to accept this proposal.]

2891 **Noth** Martin, The Chronicler's history [1943], T*Williamson* H. G. M. 1987 ➤ 3,2847; 4,3011: RJTS 40 (1989) 154s (R. *Mason*).
2892 **Throntveit** Mark A., When kings speak ... SBL diss 93, 1987 ➤ 3,2849; 4,3014: RBiblica 70 (1989) 130-133 (W. E. *Lemke*); CBQ 51 (1989) 355s (L. F. *Asma*).
2893 *Tosato* Angelo, Israele nell'ideologia politica del Cronista: ➤ 597, RicStoB 1,1 (1987/9) 257-269.
2894 *Weinberg* Joel P., Der König im Weltbild des Chronisten: VT 39 (1989) 415-437.

2895 **Kartveit** Magnar, Motive und Schichten der Landtheologie in I Chronik 1-9 [< Israels Land, Diss. Uppsala 1987]: ConBib OT 28. Sto 1989, Almqvist & W. 176 p.; bibliog. p. 168-176. Sk 57. 91-22-01277-X [BL 90,80, G. I. *Davies*].
2896 **Oeming** Manfred, Das wahre Israel; Studien zur Struktur und Intention der 'genealogischen Vorhalle' 1 Chr 1-9: ev. HDiss Bonn, D*Gunneweg* A., 1988s. – TR 85 (1989) 511; RTLv 21,541.
2897 *Szlaga* Jan, ⊕ Genealogie biblijne: ➤ 891, EncKat 5 (1989) 941s.
2898 **Gabriel** Ingeborg G., Die Friedenstheologie der Chronik; eine Untersuchung zu 1 Chronik 10 - 2 Chronik 36: kath. Diss. D*Braulik* G. Wien 1988s. – TR 85 (1989) 512; RTLv 21, p. 540.
2899 *Zalewski* Saul, The purpose of the story of the death of Saul in 1 Chronicles X [... MOSIS R.]: VT 39 (1989) 449-467.
2900 *Sailhamer* John H., 1 Chronicles 21:1 — a study in inner-biblical interpretation: TrinJ 10,1 (1989) 33-48.
2901 **Wright** John W., The origin and function of 1 Chronicles 23-27: diss. D*Blenkinsopp* J. ND 1989. vi-269 p. 89-14870. – OIAc Ja90; RelStR 16,189.
2902 *Perez* Maaravi, ⊕ A vestige of R. Jonah IBN JANAḤ's commentary on the book of Chronicles [I, 28,19-29,11]: Tarbiz 58 (1988s) 283-8; Eng. v.
2903 *Naor* Menaḥem, ⊕ [2 Chr 3,1] King [Ha-] Arauna the Jebusite: BethM 34,121 (1989s) 155-161.
2904 *Herrmann* Siegfried, The so-called 'fortress system of Rehoboam', 2 Chron 11:5-12; theoretical considerations, T*Cryer* F.: ➤ 218, Mem. YADIN Y., ErIsr 20 (1989) 72*-78*.
2904* *Zwickel* Wolfgang, [2 Chr 16,14; 21,19] Über das angebliche Verbrennen von Räucherwerk bei der Bestattung eines Königs: ZAW 101 (1989) 266-277.
2905 **Strübind** Kim, [2 Chr 20] Tradition als Interpretation; die Josaphat-Rezeption in den Chronikbüchern als Beitrag zur Theologie des Chronisten: Diss. D*Welten* P. Berlin 1989s. – RTLv 21,538.
2906 *Knoppers* Gary M., [2 Chr 28,5 ...] A reunited kingdom in Chronicles? [Ahaz, Hezekiah ...]: ProcGLM 9 (1989) 74-88.
2907 *Cranfield* C. E. B., [2 Chr 28,9-15] The prophet Oded: ExpTim 100 (1988s) 383s.
2908 *Abba* Raymond †, [2 Chron 32, undeserved suffering] Unexpected issues: ExpTim 100 (1988s) 144s.

E5.4   *Esdrae libri,* **Ezra-Nehemiah.**

2909 **Blenkinsopp** Joseph, Ezra-Nehemiah: OTLib, 1988 ➤ 4,3032; also L 1989, SCM. 366 p. £15. 0-334-00444-6 [BL 90,51, G. H. *Jones*].

2910 **Bracy** Ron, An examination of the validity of a fourth century B.C. date for Ezra and Nehemiah, and its significance: diss. SW Baptist Theol. Sem. 1988. 233 p. 89-08432. – DissA 50 (1989s) 169-A.

2911 **Clines** D. J., Ezra, Nehemiah, Esther: NCent 1984 ➤ 65,2551 ... 2,2165: ᴿTEuph 1 (1989) 188s (A. *Lemaire*).

2912 *Coggins* Richard J., The origins of the Jewish diaspora: ➤ 378, World 1989, 163-181.

2913 **Eskenazi** Tamara C., In an age of prose 1988 ➤ 4,3036: ᴿTLZ 114 (1989) 511-4 (A. H. J. *Gunneweg*).

2914 *Eskenazi* Tamara C., Ezra-Nehemiah; from text to actuality [response, The force of the text, Clines David J. A.]: ➤ 395, Signs 1989, 165-197 [199-215].

2915 **Hausmann** Jutta, Israels Rest; Studien zum Selbstverständnis der nachexilischen Gemeinde: BW 124, ᴰ1987 ➤ 3,2869; 4,3039: ᴿÉTRel 64 (1989) 277s (T. *Römer*); TLZ 114 (1989) 109s (E.-J. *Waschke*); TPQ 137 (1989) 76s (J. *Scharbert*).

2916 **Hoglund** Kenneth G., Achaemenid imperial administration in Syria-Palestine in the mission of Ezra and Nehemiah: diss. Duke, ᴰ*Meyers* E. Durham NC 1989. – RelStR 16,189.

2917 **Holmgren** Frederick C., Israel alive again; comm. Ezra-Nehemiah 1987 ➤ 3,2870; 4,3040: ᴿRelStT 7,2s (1987) 92s (Kim J. *Parker*); TLZ 114 (1989) 108s (A. H. J. *Gunneweg*); VT 39 (1989) 511 (H. *Williamson*: responsible, bland).

2918 *a*) *Klein* Ralph W., I Esdras; – *b*) *Stone* Michael E., II Esdras: ➤ 377, ᴱ*Anderson* B., Books 2 (1989) 13-19 / 21-34.

2919 **McConville** J. G., Ezra, Nehemiah & Esther 1985 ➤ 1,2932: ᴿCriswT 1 (1987) 407s (E. R. *Clendenen*).

2920 *Mason* Rex, Some Chronistic themes in the 'speeches' in Ezra and Nehemiah: ExpTim 101 (1989s) 72-76.

2920* **Muraoka** T., A Greek-Hebrew/Aramaic index to 1 Esdras: SBL-SeptCog 16. Chico 1984, Scholars. vii-85 p. – ᴿJQR 80 (1989s) 436s (B. G. *Wright*).

2921 **Neusner** Jacob, Self-fulfilling prophecy; exile and return in the history of Judaism [there are many Judaisms but all recapitulate 586-450 B.C.]. Boston 1987, Beacon. 230 p. $25. – ᴿBS 146 (1989) 111 (E. H. *Merrill*).

2922 *North* Robert, Ezra, Nehemiah: ➤ 384, NJBC (1989) 384-398 [➤ 2900].

2922* *Purvis* J. D., Exile and return: ➤ b322, ᴱ*Shanks* H., Ancient Israel 1988, 151-175.

2923 **Smith** Daniel L., The religion of the landless; the social context of the Babylonian Exile. Bloomington IN 1989, Meyer-Stone. xvii-249 p. 0-940989-54-9; pa. -0-6.

ᴱ**Stone** Michael E., **Satran** David, Emerging Judaism; studies on the fourth and third centuries B.C.E. 1989 ➤ 421.

2924 **Vos** Howard F., Ezra, Nehemiah and Esther: Bible Study Comm. GR 1987, Zondervan. 192 p. $9. 0-310-33911-1; pa. -5-1. – ᴿSWJT 32,1 (1989s) 48 (D. G. *Kent*).

2925 **Weiler** Gershon, Jewish theocracy [Ezra put the Jewish people 'on an extended holiday from the normal realities of life': ☉ 1976], ᵀ. L 1988, Brill. xiv-332 p. *f*70. – ᴿJJS 40 (1989) 131s (L. *Kochan*: 'counter-blast to much that passes for religious Zionism'); SWJT 32,2 (1989s) 625s (R. L. *Smith*).

2926 **Williamson** H. G. M.,   Ezra and Nehemiah: OT Study Guides 1987
➤ 3,2881; 4,3046: ᴿCBQ 51 (1989) 546s (J. G. *McConville*); Interpretation 43 (1989) 197s (D. *Hagstrom*, also on COGGINS R., Haggai).

2927 *Sæbø* Magne, [Ezra 1,8; 2,2...] The relation of Sheshbazzar and
Zerubbabel — reconsidered: SvEx 54 (1989) 168-177.
2928 *Sacchi* Paolo, L'esilio e la fine della monarchia davidica [... Zerubabele]:
Henoch 11 (1989) 131-146; franç. 147s.
2929 *Bakon* Shimon, Zerubbabel: JBQ (= Dor) 18 (1989s) 148-156.
2930 *Fassberg* Steven E., [Ezra 4s] The origin of the *Ketib/Qere* in the
Aramaic portions of Ezra and Daniel: VT 39 [top of page wrongly 29]
(1989) 1-12.
2931 *Rubinkiewicz* Ryszard, [Ezra 7s] The book of Noah (1 Enoch 6-11) and
Ezra's reform: ➤ 585, FolOr 25 (1987/8) 151-5.

2932 **Gunneweg** Antonius H. J., Nehemia: KAT 19/2, 1987 ➤ 3,2889 [4,3053,
'1988']: ᴿÉTRel 64 (1989) 622 (J. *Pons*); TLZ 114 (1989) 346s (V. *Hirth*).
2933 *Kilpp* N., Neemias; o perfil de um político: EstudqsT 29 (São
Leopoldo 1989) 175-184 [< Stromata 45,498].
2934 **Tilley** Maureen A., [Neh 8,18...] The use of Scripture in Christian North
Africa; an examination of Donatist hermeneutics [TERTULLIAN to
AUGUSTINE]: diss. Duke, ᴰ*Clark* Elisabeth. 409 p. 90-06748. – DissA 50
(1989s) 3264-A; RelStR 16,190.

2934* *Hamilton* Alastair, The apocryphal apocalypse; 2 Esdras and the
Anabaptist movement: Nederlands Archief voor Kerkgeschiedenis 68,1
(Leiden 1988) 1-16 [< ZIT 89,667].
2935 **Cousin** H., *al.*, Quatrième livre d'Esdras, tr. française, présentation et
index, 1987 ➤ 4,3057: ᴿNRT 111 (1989) 578 (J.-L. *Ska*: la partie la plus
ancienne de 4 Esdras est l'œuvre d'un juif traumatisé par la prise de
Jérusalem en 70 ap. J.-C.).
2936 *Deiana* Giovanni, La crisi d'identità di Israele nel IV Esdra: ➤ 597,
RicStoB 1,1 (1987/9) 193-212.
2937 *Knowles* Michael P., Moses, the Law, and the unity of 4 Ezra: NT 31
(1989) 257-274.
2938 **Stone** Michael E., Features of the eschatology of IV Ezra [diss. ᴰ*Cross*
F., Harvard 1965]: HarvSemSt 35. Atlanta 1989, Scholars. xi-
292 p. + 11 p. index. 1-55540-365-4 [OIAc Ja90].
2939 **Bergren** Theodore A., Fifth Ezra [ch. 1-2 of 4 Ezra or 2 Esdras]; the text,
origin and early history: diss. Pennsylvania, ᴰ*Kraft* R. A. Ph 1988.
512 p. – DissA 50 (1989s) 168-A; RelStR 16,189.
2940 *Bergren* Theodore A., The 'people coming from the East' in 5 Ezra [=
Vulgate 4 Ezra 1-2] 1,38: JBL 108 (1989) 675-683.

E5.5 Libri Tobiae, Judith, Esther.

2941 **Blail** G., Die Apokryphen [i.e. kath. Deuterocanonica], die Schriften
zwischen Altem und Neuem Testament; eine Einführung und Orientierung. Stu 1988, Quell. 93 p. DM 9,80 pa. 3-7918-1900-3 [NTAbs
33,126].

2942 **Gross** Heinrich, Tobit/Judith: NEchter 1987 → 3,2900; 4,3061: ᴿBLtg
62 (1989) 122s (J. *Marböck*).
2943 *Marinoni* Maria Carla, La versione valdese del libro di Tobia 1986
→ 4,3062: ᴿProtestantesimo 44 (1989) 68s (G. *Gonnet*).
2944 *Nowell* Irene, Tobit: → 384, NJBC (1989) 568-571.
2945 *a) Petersen* Norman R., Tobit; – *b) Craven* Toni, Judith: → 377, Books 2
(1989) 35-42 / 43-49.
2946 *Soll* Will, Misfortune and exile in Tobit; the juncture of a fairy tale
source and deuteronomic theology: CBQ 51 (1989) 209-231.
2946* *Virgulin* Stefano, La vita di famiglia nel libro di Tobia: → 587,
Famiglia 1987/9, 159-187.

2947 *Craven* Toni, Judith: → 384, NJBC (1989) 571-6.
2948 *Dubarle* A.-M., Les textes hébreux de Judith [SCHÜRER-VERMES] et les
étapes de la formation du livre: Biblica 70 (1989) 255-266.
2949 *Heltzer* Michael, The Persepolis documents, the Lindos chronicle and
the Book of Judith: ParPass 245 (1989) 81-101.
2950 *a) Roitman* Adolfo D., The function and meaning of Achior in the book
of Judith [5,5-21; 14,5-10]; – *b) Levine* Amy-Jill, Character contruction
and community formation in the book of Judith; – *c) White* Sidnie Ann
[→ 2959*], In the steps of Jael and Deborah; Judith as heroine; – *d)*
Moore Carey A., Why wasn't the book of Judith included in the Hebrew
Bible?: → 589, SBL Seminars 1989, 550-560 / 561-9 / 570-8 / 579-587.

2951 **Busi** G., La istoria de Purim io ve racconto; il libro di Ester secondo un
rabbino emiliano del Cinquecento: Eurasiatica 2. Rimini 1987, Luisè.
107 p. – ᴿRSO 62 (1988) 151s (G. *Garbini*).
2952 **Dorothy** Charles V., The books of Esther; structure, genre, and textual
integrity: diss. Claremont, ᴰ*Sanders* J. 496 p. 90-00175. – DissA 50
(1989s) 2531-A; RelStR 16,189.
2953 *Dumm* Demetrius, Esther: → 384, NJBC (1989) 576-9.
2954 *a) Fox* Nili S., In the spirit of Purim; the hidden hand of God [name of
God nowhere written in Esther]; – *b) Portnoy* Marshall A., Ahasuerus is
the villain: JBQ (= Dor) 18 (1989s) 183-7 / 187-9.
2955 **Grossfeld** Bernard, The first Targum to Esther 1983 → 64,2913...
2,2193: ᴿRB 96 (1989) 111s (T. *Legrand*).
2956 *Huey* F. B.ᴶ, Irony as the key to understanding the book of Esther:
→ 185, ᶠSMITH R., SWJT 32,3 (1989s) 36-39.
2957 *Lacocque* André, Haman dans le livre d'Esther [< HebAnnR 1987,
207-222]: RTPhil 121 (1989) 307-322.
2958 *Perrot* Jean, 'Shoshan ha-birah': → 218, Mem. YADIN Y., ErIsr 20
(1989) 155*-160*; 6 fig.
2959 *Vilar Hueso* Vicente, Notas marginales de San Juan de RIBERA al libro
de Ester: → 161, ᶠRODILLA ZANÓN, Santidad y cultura (Valencia 1986)
73-93.
2959* *White* Sidnie Ann, Esther, a feminine model for Jewish diaspora:
→ 391, Gender 1989, 161-177. → 2950c.

E5.8 *Machabaeorum libri,* 1-2 **Maccabees.**

2960 **Bar-Kochva** Bezalel, Judas Maccabaeus; the Jewish struggle against
the Seleucids [❿ 1980],ᵀ. C 1989, Univ. xvi-672 p.; 4 fig.; 14 pl.; 22

maps. $125. 0-521-32352-5 [NTAbs 33,412]. – ᴿExpTim 101 (1989s) 83 (J. R. *Bartlett*: how and where but not why).

2961 a) *Collins* J. J., Messianism in the Maccabean period; – b) *Goldstein* J. A., How the authors of 1 and 2 Maccabees treated the 'Messianic' promises [they knew Dan 7-12 and perhaps 1 Henoch 85-90 ...]: ↠ 7368, ᴱ*Neusner* J., al., Judaisms and their Messiahs 1987, 97-109 / 69-96 [< JStJud 20,250s].

2962 **Derfler** Steven L., The Hasmonaean revolt; rebellion or revolution?: ANE TSt 5. Lewiston NY 1989, Mellen. vi-115 p. $50 [JBL 109,375].

2963 *Doran* Robert, I and II Maccabees: ↠ 377, Books 2 (1981) 93-114.

2964 **Efron** Joshua, Studies on the Hasmonean period [7 art. ❶ 1980]: StJudLA 39, 1987 ↠ 4,3088: ᴿJStJud 20 (1989) 91-94 (A. S. van der *Woude*: often pure fantasy; dumbfounding that 1 Enoch Similitudes express fundamental Christian beliefs); TLZ 114 (1989) 881-3 (A. H. J. *Gunneweg*).

2965 **Enermalm-Ogawa** Agneta, [1-2 Mcb] Un langage de prière juif en grec [diss. Uppsala 1986]. ConBib NT 17, 1987 ↠ 3,2918; 4,3089: ᴿJStJud 20 (1989) 221s (A. *Hilhorst*); JTS 40 (1989) 171s (H. *Anderson*); RHPR 69 (1989) 215 (D. A. *Bertrand*); Salesianum 51 (1989) 354s (M. *Cimosa*).

2966 **Feldman** L. H., Torah and secular culture; challenge and response in the Hellenistic period: Tradition 23,2 (NY 1988) 26-40 [< NTAbs 33,80].

2967 **Harrington** Daniel J., The Maccabean revolt 1988 ↠ 4,3092: ᴿBibTB 19 (1989) 111s (Betty Jane *Lillie*); JStJud 20 (1989) 229s (F. *García Martínez*); NewTR 2,2 (1989) 95 (L. J. *Hoppe*).

2968 **Jencks** Alden, Maccabees on the Baltic; the biblical apologia of the Teutonic order [I-II Makk rendering]: diss. Washington, ᴰ*Thomas* Carol G. Seattle 1989. 461 p. 90-06965. – DissA 50 (1989s) 3330-A.

2969 **Kampen** John, The Hasideans and the origins of Pharisaism... 1-2 Mcb ᴰ1988 ↠ 4,3093; 1-55540-284-4; pa. -5-2. – ᴿJQR 80 (1989s) 187-9 (D. R. *Schwartz*).

2970 a) *Levine* L. I. A., The age of Hellenism; – b) *Cohen* S. J. D., Roman domination: ↠ b322, ᴱ*Shanks* H., Ancient Israel 1988, 177-204 / 205-235.

2970* *McEleney* Neil J., 1-2 Maccabees: ↠ 384, NJBC (1989) 421-446.

2971 *Maller* A. S., Hanukkah; evolution of a miracle [modern Jewry is more sympathetic to the military-political original than to its spiritualization in intervening Judaism]: Living Light 23,1 (Wsh 1988) 54-58 [< NTAbs 33,362].

2972 **Martola** Nils, Capture and liberation... 1 Mcb 1984 ↠ 1,2971... 3,2923: ᴿBO 46 (1989) 139-141 (J. W. van *Henten*).

2973 *Pesce* Mauro, Movimenti e istituzioni nel giudaismo dai Maccabei a Bar Kokhbah: ↠ 571, L'Ebraismo 1986/7, 9-30.

2974 a) *Prato* Gian Luigi, La persecuzione religiosa nell'ermeneutica maccabaica; l'ellenismo come paganesimo; – b) *Arata Mantovani* Piera, L'identità di Israele alla luce delle fonti epigrafiche tra il III sec. a. C. e il I sec. d. C.: ↠ 597, RicStoB 1,1 (1987/9) 99-122 / 213-227.

2975 **Sandelin** K.-G., Attraction towards pagan cult among Jews during the Hellenistic and Early Imperial era: NordJud 10,1 (Åbo 1989) 27-38 svensk; Eng. summ. [< Judaica 45,268].

2976 *Vivian* A., La Megillat Antiochus; una reinterpretazione dell'epopea maccabaica: ↠ 595, Storiografia 1983/7, 163-195.

2977 *Rubin* Nissan, ❶ [1 Mcb 1,15] On drawing down the prepuce and incision of the foreskin (*peri'ah*) [to avoid being recognized as Jewish in the gymnasium]: Zion 59 (1989) 105-117; Eng. iii.

2978 *Mandell* S., [1 Mcb 8,17s] Was Rome's early diplomatic interaction with the Maccabees legal? [yes; Livy 45,18.1s]: Classical Bulletin 64,3s (ex-St. Louis, now ed. Asbury, pub. Ch. 1988) 87-89 [< NTAbs 33,363].

2978* **Kopidakis** M. Z., ⊖ 3 Mcb. and Aeschylus; Didaktoriki diatribi. Thessaloniki 1982. 148 p.; 145ss franç. [BZ 34,299].
2979 **Klauck** H.-J., 4 Makkabäerbuch: JSHZ 3/6. Gü 1989, Mohn. p. 645-763. DM 88, sb. 78 [ZAW 102, 446, H.-C. *Schmitt*].
2979* *Klauck* Hans-Josef, Hellenistische Rhetorik im Diasporajudentum; das Exordium des vierten Makkabäerbuchs (4 Makk 1.1-12): NTS 35 (1989) 451-465.
2980 *Heininger* Bernhard, Der böse Antiochus; eine Studie zur Erzähltechnik des 4. Makkabäerbuchs: BZ 33 (1989) 43-59.

VII. Libri didactici VT

E6   *Poesis* .1 *metrica*, **Biblical versification.**

2981 **Alonso Schökel** Luis, A manual of Hebrew poetics [1988 ➔ 4,3104], ᵀ*Graffy* Adrian: SubsBPont 11, 1988 ➔ 4,3103: ᴿBiblica 70 (1989) 416-420 & BL (1989) 64 & ScriptB 20 (1989s) 44 (W. G. E. *Watson*); NRT 111 (1989) 920s (J.-L. *Ska*); RB 96 (1989) 286-8 (R. J. *Tournay*); ZAW 101 (1989) 308 (H. W. *Hoffmann*).
2982 **Alonso Schökel** Luis, Manuale di poetica ebraica [1988 ➔ 4,3104], ᵀ. Brescia 1989, Queriniana. 268 p. Lit. 30.000.
2983 *Cloete* W. T. W., The concept of metre in Old Testament studies: JSem 1 (1989) 39-53.
2984 **Fisch** Harold, Poetry with a purpose; biblical poetics and interpretation: Indiana StBLit 11, 1988 ➔ 4,3115: ᴿZAW 101 (1989) 314 (H.-C. *Schmitt*).
2985 *Fitzgerald* Aloysius, Hebrew poetry: ➔ 384, NJBC (1989) 201-8.
2986 **Flender** R., Der biblische Sprechgesang und seine mündliche Überlieferung in Synagoge und griechischer Kirche [< 'Hebräische Psalmodie', Diss. J 1981]. Wilhelmshaven 1988, Noetzel. 206 p.; 8 pl. – ᴿZAW 101 (1989) 457s (H. C. *Schmitt*).
2987 ᴱ**Follis** Elaine R., Directions in biblical Hebrew poetry: JStOT Sup 40, 1987 ➔ 3,540; 4,3116 [13 art., infra]: ᴿCBQ 51 (1989) 579-581 (A. R. *Ceresko*, quite full analyses); VT 39 (1989) 245s (J. A. *Emerton*).
2988 *a*) *Freedman* D. N., Another look at biblical Hebrew poetry [attention to particles used in prose-passages]; – *b*) *Willis* J. T., Alternating (ABA′B′) parallelism in OT psalms and prophetic literature; – *c*) *O'Connor* M., The Pseudosorites, a type of paradox in Hebrew verse: ➔ 2987, Directions 1987, 11-28 / 49-76 / 161-172.
2988* *Green* Yosef, Tiles and bricks in writing poetry [only Dt 32, Jos 12, Est 9 were to be written in double columns]: Dor 15 (1986s) 160-2 [< OTAbs 11,105].
2989 **Grol** Hermanus W. M. van, De versbouw in het klassieke Hebreeuws; fundamentele verkenningen, I. Metriek [diss. Amst 1986, ᴰ*Beuken* W.], 1986 ➔ 4,3118; ᴿCBQ 51 (1989) 135s (W. A. *Vogels*: dense, but invites to

awaiting his view on how meter affects meaning); JSS 34 (1989) 198-201 (T. *Collins*); TR 85 (1989) 194-7 (W. von *Soden*).

2990 **Grossberg** Daniel, Centripetal and centrifugal structures in biblical poetry: SBL mg. 39. Atlanta 1989, Scholars. $20; sb./pa. $13. 1-55540-360-3; 1-1 [TDig 37,56].

2991 *Halle* Morris, Syllable-counting meters and pattern poetry in the Old Testament: → 30, Mem. BLANC H. 1989, 110-120.

2992 *Hunter* J. H., The irony of meaning; intertextuality in Hebrew poetical texts: JSem 1 (1989) 229-243.

2993 *Korpel* M. C. A., *Moor* J. C. de, Fundamentals of Ugaritic and Hebrew poetry: → 410, Structural/poetry 1988, 1-61.

2994 **Loretz** O., *Kottsieper* I., Colometry in Ugaritic and biblical poetry; introduction, illustrations and topical bibliography; Ug-BLit 5, 1987 → 3,2939: ᴿZAW 101 (1989) 469 (H.-C. *Schmitt*).

Meer Willem van der, *Moor* Johannes C. de, The structural analysis of biblical and Canaanite poetry: JStOT supp 74, 1988 → 410.

2995 **Rousseau** François, La poétique fondamentale du texte biblique; le fait littéraire d'un parallélisme élargi et omniprésent: Recherches NS 20. Montréal/P 1989, Bellarmin/Cerf. 280 p. 2-89007-672-5 / P 2-204-02562-3 [EstBíb 47,579].

2996 **Wagner** Ewald, Grundzüge der klassischen arabischen Dichtung, I. Die altarabische Dichtung [500-1000 A.D.]; 2. in islamischer Zeit: Grundzüge 68. Da 1987, Wiss. xii-220 p.; x-213 p. DM 39 + 45. – ᴿMundus 25 (1989) 45-47 & 133-5 (W. W. *Müller*).

2997 **Watson** W. G. E., Classical Hebrew Poetry² 1986 → 3,2945; 4,3126: ᴿBS 146 (1989) 350s (E. H. *Merrill*).

2998 *Watson* Wilfred G. E., *a)* Internal or half-line parallelism in classical Hebrew again: VT 39 (not 29 as p. 44 top; 1989) 44-66; – *b)* Internal or half-line parallelism once more: LA 39 (1989) 27-36.

2999 *Watson* W.G.E., Parallelism with *qtl* in Ugaritic: UF 21 (1989) 435-442.

3000 **Zurro** R. Eduardo, Procedimientos iterativos en la poesía ugarítica y bíblica: BibOrPont 43, 1987 → 3,2947; 4,3128: ᴿJBL 108 (1989) 322-4 (R. H. *McGrath*).

E6.2 **Psalmi, textus.**

3001 **Ammassari** Antonio, Il salterio latino di Pietro 1987 → 3,2949; 4,3129: ᴿNRT 111 (1989) 583s (J.-L. *Ska*).

3002 *Belkin* A., Suicide scenes in Latin Psalters of the thirteenth century as reflection of Jewish midrashic exposition: Man 88 (1988) 75-92 [< REB 49,251].

3003 *a) Böhm* A., Das Psalterium Moguntinum; kann man aufgrund von Satzvarianten verschiedene Auflagen erschliessen?; – *b) Hägele* G., Ein unbekanntes Fragment des Psalterium Benedictinum von 1459 in der Universitätsbibliothek Augsburg: Gutenberg-Jahrbuch 64 (1989) 30-38 / 45s [< RHE 84, p. 423*].

3004 **Diez Macho** A.†, *Navarro Peiro* A., Biblia babilónica; fragmentos de [50] Salmos, Job y Proverbios (MS 508 A del Seminario Teológico Judío de Nueva York): TEstCisn 42, 1987 → 3,2955; 4,3130; pt. 1400. 84-00-06680-4: ᴿBL (1989) 44 (P. *Wernberg-Møller*); JQR 80 (1989s) 419s (J. *Ribera*); ZAW 101 (1989) 310 (I. *Kottsieper*).

3005 **Hiebert** Robert J. V., The 'Syrohexaplaric' Psalter: SeptCog 27. Atlanta 1989, Scholars. xvi-352 p. $30; pa. $20. 1-55540-431-6; pa. -2-4.

3006 *Marrow* J.H., Text and image in two fifteenth-century Dutch Psalters from Delft: ➤ 10, ᶠAMPE A., OnsGErf (1988s) 64, 41-52.

3007 **Mowvley** H., The Psalms, introduced and newly translated for today's readers. L 1989, Collins. Pp. vii-327. £7. 0-00-599172-2 [BL 90,59].

3008 ᴱ**Ochsenbein** Peter, *Scarpatetti* Beat von, Die Folchart-Psalter [ᵀLU-THER 1545] aus der Stiftsbibliothek St-Gallen. FrB 1987, Herder. 240 p.; 149 Farbinitialen + 17 color. pl. DM 490. – ᴿTrierTZ 98 (1989) 158 (E. *Sauser*).

3009 **Reichert** Josua, *al.*, Der Haidholzener Psalter. Mü 1988, Deutscher-Kunstv. 159 p. DM 98. – ᴿErbAuf 65 (1989) 162 (T. *Hogg*).

3010 **Wagenaar** Christofoor, Het Boek der Psalmen naar de Septuagint: Schrift en Liturgie 12, 1988 ➤ 4,3140: ᴿTsTNijm 29 (1989) 287s (K. *Waaijman*: 'volgens de niet-kritische editie van BRATSIOTIS').

3011 *Waltke* B., The NIV and its textual principles in the Book of Psalms: JEvTS 32 (1989) 17-26 [< ZAW 102,279].

3012 **White** Emanuel, A critical edition of the Targum of Psalms; a computer generated text of Books I and II: diss. McGill. Montréal 1988. – DissA 50 (1989s) 172-A; OIAc Ja90.

3013 **Wilson** Gerald H., The editing of the Hebrew Psalter: SBL diss. 76, 1985 ➤ 1,3022... 4,3141: ᴿBijdragen 50 (1989) 210 (F. De *Meyer*).

E6.3 Psalmi, introductio.

3014 **Allen** L.C., Psalms: Word themes. Dallas 1989, Word. 139 p. $10. 0-8499-0789-6 [BL 90,64, R.J. *Coggins*].

3015 *Alonso Schökel* Luis, Interpretación de los Salmos hasta CASIODORO; / desde Casiodoro hasta GUNKEL; síntesis histórica: EstBíb 47 (1989) 5-26.145-164; Eng. 5.145.

3016 **Eriksson** Jan-Erik, The hymns of David interpreted in Syriac; a study of translation technique in the First Book of the Book of Psalms (Ps 1-41) in the Pešiṭta [... *Barr* J.]: diss. Uppsala 1989. – ST 43 (1989) 235s.

3017 **Gerstenberger** Erhard S., Psalms I: FOTLit 14, 1988 ➤ 4,3117: ᴿLA 39 (1989) 336-8 (A. *Niccacci*); VT 39 (1989) 252 (R.P. *Gordon*).

3018 **Longman** Tremper ᴵᴵᴵ, How to read the Psalms 1988 ➤ 4,3144; $8: ᴿBS 146 (1989) 351s (M.F. *Rooker*); ExpTim 100 (1988s) 269s (J. *Eaton*).

3019 **Seybold** Klaus, Die Psalmen, eine Einführung 1986 ➤ 2,2257; 3,2976: ᴿAtKap 113 (1989) 368-370 (J. *Warzecha* ❷).

3020 **Treves** Marco, The dates of the Psalms [all but 45 and 72 from 170-103 B.C.]; history and poetry in ancient Israel 1988 ➤ 4,3149: ᴿJStJud 20 (1989) 119 (A.S. van der *Woude*: totally unfounded); OTAbs 12 (1989) 116 (C.T. *Begg*).

3021 *Warzecha* Julian, ❷ L'analisi strutturale nell'esegesi dei Salmi: STWsz 26,1 (1988) 54-66; ital. 66.

3022 **Zenger** Erich, Mit meinem Gott überspringe ich Mauern; Einführung in das Psalmbuch 1987 ➤ 3,2977; 4,3150: ᴿBiKi 44 (1989) 43 (M. *Helsper*: Auslegung von 24 Pss); TPQ 137 (1989) 198 (J. *Marböck*).

E6.4 Psalmi, commentarii.

3023 **Allen** Leslie C., Psalms 101-150: Word Comm 21, 1983 ➤ 64,2976... 4,3151: ᴿAulaO 7 (1989) 279s (G. del *Olmo Lete*).

Curti Carmelo, Eusebiana I. Commentarii in Psalmos: Saggi e Testi 1, 1987 ➤ 249.

3024 **Gross** Heinrich, *Reinelt* Heinz,   Das Buch der Psalmen: Geistliche Schriftlesung 9,1s. Dü 1989, Patmos. I (Ps. 1-72) 403 p.; II (Ps. 73-150), 452 p. 3-491-77163-3; -4-1.

3025 *a) Jay* P., Jérôme à Bethléem; les Tractatus in Psalmos; – *b) Gourdain* J.-L., Les psaumes dans l'explication de la prière de Jonas (In Ionam 2,2-10): ➤ 579*, Jérôme Occident/Orient 1986/8, 367-380 / 381-9 [RHE 85,37*].

3026 **Kraus** Hans-Joachim, Psalms I. 1-59; II. 60-150 [⁵1978], ᵀ*Oswald* Hilton C. Minneapolis 1988s, Augsburg. II. 587 p., $40. 0-8066-2425-6 [TDig 37,69]. – ᴿCriswT 3 (1989) 378s (G. L. *Klein*, 1).

3027 *Kselman* John S., *Barré* Michael L., Psalms: ➤ 384, NJBC (1989) 523-552.

3028 *Luisier* Guy, Concerto en Dieu Majeur; Marcel MICHELET et les 'Commentaires sur les psaumes' de Saint AUGUSTIN: ÉchSM 19 (1989) 5-14.

3029 *Miller* Patrick D.ᴶ, Psalms: ➤ 377, Books 1 (1989) 203-221.

3030 **Montorsi** G., I Salmi, preghiera di ogni giorno [ordine delle Ore cattoliche] 1987 ➤ 3,3036; 88-7026-669-9: ᴿBL (1989) 111 (R. *Murray*: for each passage, four contexts: author/users, too brief; Jesus; Church; modern individual).

3031 **Ringgren** Helmer, Psaltaren 1-41: Kommentar till Gamla Testamentet, 1987 ➤ 4,3161: ᴿBL (1989) 60 (G. W. *Anderson*); SvTKv 65 (1989) 35 (S. *Norin*).

3032 **Rondeau** Marie-Josèphe, Les commentaires patristiques du Psautier II, 1985 ➤ 1,3047... 4,3164: ᴿTR 85 (1989) 301s (Maria-Barbara von *Stritzky*).

3033 **Sabourin** Léopold, Le livre des Psaumes, traduit et interprété: Recherches NS 18 [➤ 4,3165]: Montréal/P 1988, Bellarmin/Cerf. 631 p. C$24. – ᴿEsprVie 99 (1989) 448 (L. *Monloubou*); NRT 111 (1989) 928 (J.-L. *Ska*: fera certainement progresser la recherche).

3034 ᵀ**Simonetti** Manlio, Sant'AGOSTINO, Commento ai Salmi: Fond. Valla, Scrittori Greci e Latini. Mi 1988, Mondadori. xl-740 p. – ᴿLateranum 55 (1989) 496s (O. *Pasquato*).

3035 *Vian* Giovanni M., Un'antologia esegetica bizantina sui Salmi con inediti di ATANASIO e Giovanni CRISOSTOMO: ➤ 567, AnStoEseg 6 (1989) 125-149; Eng. 8.

3036 **Waaijman** Kees, *Aarnink* Laetitia, Psalm 1-5: Psalmschrift [First of 30 cahiers, awaited 3 per year]. Kampen 1988, Kok. viii-84 p. ƒ22,50. – ᴿStreven 57 (1989s) 87s (P. *Beentjes*); TsTNijm 29 (1989) 174 (B. *Standaert*).

3037 **Westermann** Claus, The living Psalms [Ausgewählte Psalmen 1984 ➤ 65,2657], ᵀ*Porter* J. R. E 1988, Clark. 320 p. £10. 0-567-29156-1. – ᴿExpTim 101 (1989s) 82 (J. *Eaton*: polarizing, assertive); SWJT 32,2 (1989s) 54s (R. L. *Smith*).

3038 **Williams** D., Psalms 73-150: Word comm. Dallas 1989, Word. 543 p. [TS 51,572].

E6.5   **Psalmi, themata.**

3039 **Baldermann** Ingo, Wer hört mein Weinen? Kinder entdecken sich selbst in den Psalmen: Wege des Lernens 4. Neuk 1986, ²1989. – ᴿJbBT 4 (1989) 291-9 (W. *Grünberg*).

3040 **Beer** Stephanus J. de, Die Dawidsverbond in die Psalms [RTLv 21, p. 540 sub *de* Beer]; 'n metodologiese verkenning (The Davidic covenant in the Psalms; a methodological investigation): diss. ᴰ*Burden* J. Pretoria 1989, 272 p.

3041 **Bellinger** W. H.ᴶ, Psalmody and prophecy 1984 ➤ 65,2662... 3,2996*: ᴿBZ 33 (1989) 126s (J. *Becker*).

3042 **Broyles** Craig C., The conflict of faith and experience in the Psalms; a form-critical and theological study: JStOT Sup 52. Sheffield 1989 [Ithaca NY, Cornell Univ.]. 272 p. $42.50. 1-85075-052-1 [TDig 36,356].

3043 **Brzegowy** Tadeusz, 'Miasto Boże' w Psalmach [the city of God in the Psalms]. Kraków 1989, Polskie Towarzystwo Teologiczne. 287 p.; p. 285-7, English summary; p. 273-284, bibliog. 83-05017-50-X.

3044 **Cohen** Mark E., Sumerian hymnology; the Eršemma: HUCA Sup 2, 1981 ➤ 62,3108*; 63,9391: ᴿBZ 33 (1989) 288s (N. *Lohfink*).

3045 *Cortese* Enzo, Pobres y humildes en los Salmos; no confundir las cartas: TArg 24 (1987) 95-106.

3046 **Croft** Steven J. L., The identity of the individual in the Psalms: JStOT Sup 44, 1987 ➤ 3,3003; 4,3173: ᴿCBQ 51 (1989) 314-6 (W. *Brueggemann*); Interpretation 43 (1989) 312.314 (J. L. *Mays*); JBL 108 (1989) 335-7 (L. C. *Allen*); JQR 80 (1989s) 146s (Y. *Gitay*).

3047 *Crüsemann* Frank, Im Netz; zur Frage nach der 'eigentlichen Not' in den Klagen der Einzelnen: ➤ 212, ᶠWESTERMANN C., Schöpfung 1989, 139-148.

3048 *Doignon* Jean, Un témoignage inédit des 'Tractatus super Psalmos' d'HILAIRE de Poitiers contre l'hymnodie païenne: RBén 99 (1989) 35-40.

3049 *Duhaime* Jean, La souffrance dans les Psaumes 3-41; une étude préliminaire: ScEspr 41 (1989) 33-48.

Duin Cornelis van, 'Zal het stof u loven?' Weerlegging van de individualistische uitleg van woorden voor dood en onderwereld in de psalmen 1989 ➤ 3099.

3051 *Gillingham* Sue, The poor in the Psalms: ExpT 100 (1988s) 15-19.

3052 ᶠGROSS Heinrich: Freude... Psalmen, ᴱHaag E., ... 1986 ➤ 2,41; 4,3177: ᴿTPQ 137 (1989) 78s (F. *Hubmann*); TLZ 114 (1989) 178 (K.-H. *Bernhardt*, tit. pp.).

3053 *Grossberg* Daniel, The disparate elements of the inclusio in Psalms: HebAnR 6 (1982) 97-104 [< OTAbs 11,164].

3054 *Hess* Richard S., Hebrew Psalms and Amarna correspondence from Jerusalem; some comparisons and implications: ZAW 101 (1989) 249-265.

3055 *Illman* Karl-Johan, Vän och fiende i bönepsalmerna: SvEx 54 (1989) 90-100.

3056 **Im** Seung-phill, Die 'Unschuldserklärungen' in den Psalmen [diss. Pont. Ist. Biblico, Roma 1987, ᴰ*Simian-Yofre* H. ➤ 3,3008]. Seoul 1989, Logos. viii-539 p. [ActaPIB 9,481].

3057 *Janowski* Bernd, Das Königtum Gottes in den Psalmen [JEREMIAS J. 1987]: ZTK 86 (1989) 389-454.

3058 **Jaschke** Helmut, 'Aus der Tiefe...' Psychotherapie aus den Psalmen. FrB 1989, Herder. 124 p. DM 10. – ᴿGeistL 62 (1989) 309-311 (K. *Murr*).

3059 **Jeremias** Jörg, Das Königtum Gottes in den Psalmen: FRL 141, 1987 ➤ 3,3009; 4,3185: ᴿAntonianum 64 (1989) 199-201 (M. *Nobile*); CrNSt 10 (1989) 615s (A. *Tosato*); ZkT 111 (1989) 89 (R. *Oberforcher*).

3060 *Kirchner* Dankwart, Gruppendynamische Untersuchung zu [WESTERMANN C. 1954] Struktur und Geschichte der Klage im AT: TLZ 114 (1989) 785-796.

3061 **Kraus** Hans-Joachim,   Teologia dei Salmi [1979 ➤ 60,4042], ᵀ: Biblioteca teologica 22. Brescia 1989, Paideia. 362 p.

3062 **Loretz** Oswald,   Ugarit-Texte und Thronbesteigungspsalmen; die Metamorphose des Regenspenders Baal-Jahwe [Ps 24; 29; 93-100; = ²Ps 29 kanaanäisch. 1984 ➤ 3114 infra]: Ug-Bib. Lit. 7. Münster 1988, Ugarit. xiv-550 p.   3-927-120-04-9 [OIAc N89]. – ᴿUF 21 (1989) 471s (W. S. *Prinsloo*).

3063 **Mathias** D.,   Geschichtstheologie der Geschichtssummarien in den Psalmen: H-Diss Lp 1989. ix-290 p. [ZAW 102, 451, H. C. *Schmitt*].

3064 *Monloubou* Louis,   Théologie des Psaumes: EsprVie 99 (1989) 636-9.

3065 **Nasuti** Harry P.,   Tradition history and the psalms of Asaph: diss. Yale; SBL diss. 88, 1988 ➤ 4,3191:   ᴿZAW 101 (1989) 471 (G. *Wanke*).

3066 **Petersen** Claus, [Ps 8...] Mythos im AT... Ps: BZAW 157, 1982 ➤ 63,3146... 1,3066:   ᴿÉTRel 64 (1989) 434s (T. *Römer*).

3067 **Raabe** Paul R.,   Psalm-structures; a study of psalms with refrains: diss. Michigan, ᴰ*Freedman* D. N.   AA 1989. 356 p. 89-20605. – DissA 50 (1989s) 1691-A.

3068 **Rasmussen** Tarald,   Inimici ecclesiae; das ekklesiologische Feindbild in LUTHERs 'Dictata super Psalterium' (1513-1515) im Horizont der theologischen Tradition: Studies in Medieval and Reformation Thought 44. Leiden 1989, Brill. x-242 p.   90-04-08837-7.

3069 *Ruppert* Lothar,   Klage oder Bitte? Zu einer neuen Sicht der individuellen Klagelieder: BZ 33 (1989) 252-5.

3070 *Simonetti* Manlio,   Interpretazione storica e cristologica nei Tractatus super Psalmos di ILARIO: ➤ 42, ᶠCOSTANZA S., Polyanthema 1989, 315-331.

3071 *Speyer* Wolfgang, *a*) Der bisher älteste lateinische Psalmus abecedarius; zur Editio princeps von R. ROCA-PUIG [JbAC 10 (1967) 211-216]; – *b*) Zum Bild des APOLLONIOS von Tyana bei Heiden und Christen [< JbAC 17 (1974) 47-63]; – *c*) Neue Pilatus-Apokryphen [< VigChr 32 (1978) 53-59]; – *d*) Der letzte Mahl Jesu im Lichte des sogenannten Eidopfers [ineditum]: ➤ 361, Frühes Christentum 1989, 64-69 / 176-192 / 228-234 / 477-492.

3072 **Spieckermann** Hermann,   Heilsgegenwart; eine Theologie der Psalmen [Hab.-Diss. Gö]; FRL 148.   Gö 1989, Vandenhoeck & R.   342 p. DM 118; pa. 80.   3-525-53829-4; -30-8 [BL 90, 93, J. H. *Eaton*: not a comprehensive theology of the Psalms, but a skilful tracing of their theological core]. – ᴿNRT 111 (1989) 929s (J.-L. *Ska*: devrait susciter la sympathie).

3073 *Stadelmann* L. I. J.,   As maldições nos Salmos: PerspT 20 (1988) 317-338 [< REB 49,252].

3074 *Velema* —.,   Depressiviteit in het licht van de psalmen: Theologia Reformata 31 (1988) 370-383 [< GerefTTs 89,128].

3075 **Wilson** Jack,   A comparative study of the diction of the oracles and announcements of salvation in Second Isaiah and the diction of the Psalter: diss. Drew, ᴰ*Riemann*. Madison NJ 1989. 282 p. 89-21814. – DissA 50 (1989) 1077-A; RelStR 16,189.

E6.6   *Psalmi: oratio, liturgia;*   **Psalms as prayer.**

3076 **Alonso Schökel** Luis,   Treinta salmos, poesía y oración² [¹1980] 1986 ➤ 2,2298:   ᴿTXav 39 (1989) 369-371 (R. A. *Gallo P.*).

3077 **Anderson** B. W., ❶ Fukaki fuchiyori... [Out of the depths; the Psalms speak for us today [2]1983 ➤ 64,3021; [1]1970], [T]*Nakamura* K. Tokyo 1989, Shinkyō Shuppan-sha. 310 p. Y 2400. 4-400-12378-2 [BL 90,65].

3078 **Brueggemann** Walter, Israel's praise; doxology against idolatry and ideology 1988 ➤ 4,3205: [R]ExpTim 100 (1988s) 66 (J. *Eaton*: merits pastoral attention); NewTR 2,1 (1989) 104 (L. J. *Hoppe*); TS 50 (1989) 611 (A. C. *Mitchell*).

3079 **Brueggemann** Walter, The message of the Psalms 1984 ➤ 65,2687... 2,2260: [R]CriswT 3 (1989) 384s (G. L. *Klein*, also on WESTERMANN C. 1980).

3080 *Cunningham* Lawrence S., Praying the Psalms: TTod 46 (1989s) 39-44.

3081 *Farnés* Pere, L'ús del Saltiri en la litúrgia cristiana: ➤ 69*, [F]GOMÀ I., RCatalT 14 (1989) 433-9; Eng. 440.

3082 **Gerstenberger** E., al., Zu Hilfe, mein Gott; Psalmen und Klagelieder [= [4]Psalmen in der Sprache unserer Zeit]. Neuk/Z 1989, Neuk.-V./Benziger. 256 p. DM 22 [ZAW 102,444].

3083 **Hollmann** Klaus, Verbirg nicht dein Gesicht von mir; mit 20 Psalmen im Gespräch 1986 ➤ 4,3213: [R]TPQ 137 (1989) 79 (Roswitha *Unfried*).

3084 **Larrañaga** I., [17] Salmi per la vita. Padova 1987, Messaggero. 174 p. Lit. 12.000. – [R]HumBr 44 (1989) 155 (M. *Orsatti*).

3085 *McPolin* James M., Psalms as prayers of the poor: ➤ 165, Mem. RYAN D., Back to the sources 1989, 79-103.

3086 **Moriconi** Bruno, Uomini davanti a Dio; spiritualità dei Salmi. Assisi 1989, Cittadella. 188 p. – [R]Teresianum 40 (1989) 625s (V. *Pasquetto*).

3087 *Murillo* A. L., La espiritualidad de los Salmos: Cuestiones Teológicas 42 (Medellín 1988) 49-57 [< Stromata 45,498].

3088 **Neveu** Louis, Au pas des Psaumes; lecture organique à trois voix I. Centre de Linguistique Religieuse Cah. 2, 1988 ➤ 4,3215: [R]NRT 111 (1989) 930 (J.-L. *Ska*).

3089 **Peterson** Eugene H., Answering God; the Psalms as tools for prayer. SF 1989, Harper & R. vii-151 p. $15. 0-06-066502-5 [OTAbs 12,339, R. L. *Murphy*].

3090 *Savarimuthu* A. C., Man and woman before God; the spirituality of the Psalms: IndTSt 26 (1989) 268-283.

3091 **Smith** Mark S., Psalms, the divine journey 1987 ➤ 3,2039; 3,3219: [R]BL (1989) 93 (J. J. *Eaton*); EstBíb 47 (1989) 282s (G. *Flor Serrano*); ScripTPamp 21 (1989) 693s (K. *Limburg*).

3091* **Stanislawski** Michael, Psalms for the Tsar [Alexander II 1864-7, who called his reforms *glasnost*]. NY 1988, Yeshiva/KTAV. 64 p. $23. 0-9620856-0-X [ExpTim 101,63].

3092 **Tournay** Raymond J., Voir et entendre Dieu avec les Psaumes...: CahRB 24, 1988 ➤ 4,3222: [R]Biblica 70 (1989) 269-271 (G. *Ravasi*); EstBíb 47 (1989) 281s (G. *Flor Serrano*); NRT 111 (1989) 582s (J.-L. *Ska*); RB 96 (1989) 95-100 (B. *Renaud*); RHPR 69 (1989) 213s (E. *Jacob*: certainement le meilleur spécialiste des Psaumes en France); RTPhil 121 (1989) 451s (T. *Römer*).

3093 **Vallés** Carlos G., Buscar tu rostro; orar los Salmos: Pozo de Siquem 36. Santander 1989, SalTerrae. 271 p. 84-293-08030-X. – [R]ActuBbg 26 (1989) 243 (R. de *Sivatte*).

3094 *Vogüé* Adalbert de, Psalmodier n'est pas prier: Ecclesia Orans 6 (1989) 7-32.

3095 *Zegarra* Felipe, Salmos; el don de la vida [prayer in Peru]: Páginas 14 (1989) 7-19 [< TContext 7/1, 91].

3096 **Zim** Rivkah, English metrical psalms; poetry as praise and prayer, 1535-1601: 1987 ➤ 3,3044; 4,3324: ᴿRTLv 20 (1989) 369s (J.-F. *Gilmont*); RelStR 15 (1989) 360 (P. *Seaver*: WYATT and 90 others).

E6.7   *Psalmi:* verse-numbers.

3096* *Cruells* Antoni, El just, un arbre sempre verd; el Salm 1: ➤ 69*, ᶠGOMÀ I., RCatalT 14 (1989) 15-28; Eng. 28 (relations to Jeremiah and Amen-Em-Ope).

3097 *Haag* Ernst, Psalm 1. Lebensgestaltung nach dem alttestamentlichen Menschenbild: ➤ 45, ᶠDEISSLER A., Weg 1989, 153-172.

3098 ᴱ**Schreiner** J., Beiträge zur Psalmenforschung, Psalm 2 und 22 [Tagung Salzburg 25.-29.VIII.1987]: ForBi 60, 1988 ➤ 4,3226. – ᴿZAW 101 (1989) 453 (tit. pp.).

3099 **Duin** C. van, [Ps 6; 30; 88; 115; Jes 38,10-20] 'Zal het stof u loven?': Weerlegging van de individualistische uitleg van woorden voor dood en onderwereld in de psalmen: diss. Amst 1989, ᴰ*Deurloo* K. Haag 1989, CIP. xviii-385 p. *f* 60. 90-9002797-1. – TsTNijm 29 (1989) 281; RTLv 21,542 sub Van; ZAW 102,196.

3100 *Albrektson* Bertil, Dibarns mun och havets stigar; randbemärkningar till nyöversättningen av Ps 8: SvEx 54 (1989) 20-32.

3101 *Duarte Castillo* Raúl, La grandeza humana, razón de la gloria divina; Salmo 8: EfMex 7 (1989) 49-65.

3102 *Millet* Marc, Quand Dieu se tait; la prière collective du pauvre; Psaume 9-10: Masses Ouvrières 423 (1989) 57-68.

3103 *Ringgren* Helmer, [Ps 10,8.10.14 ḥlb'ym; Is 14,4 mdhbh; 1QH III,24-26] Two biblical words in the Qumran hymns: ➤ 218, Mem. YADIN Y., ErIsr 20 (1989) 174*s.

3104 *Álvarez Barredo* Miguel, Culto y ética; su conexión en el Salmo 15: Carthaginensia 5 (1989) 3-17.

3105 **Loretz** O., Die Königspsalmen [20s, 72, 101, 144; none in 90s] 1988 ➤ 4,3238: ᴿBL (1989) 85 (J. A. *Emerton*).
    Loretz Oswald, Ugarit-Texte und Thronbesteigungspsalmen [24 ...] 1988 ➤ 3062.

3106 *Gonnelli* Fabrizio, Il salterio esametrico, I. Edizione e traduzione del Ps. 21; II. Commento al Ps. 21: Koinonia 13 (N 1989) 51-59 / 127-151.

3107 **Becker-Ebel** Jochen, Psalm 22; Rettungs- und Loblied eines 'Gottverlassenen': Inaug.-Diss. ᴰ*Ruppert*. Freiburg/B 1988s. 295 p. – TR 85 (1989) 515; RTLv 21, p.539.
    ᴱ**Schreiner** J., Beiträge zu ... Ps 22, 1987/8 ➤ supra 3098.

3108 *Ahroni* Reuben, The unity of Psalm 23: HebAnR 6 (1982) 21-34 [< OTAbs 11,165].

3109 *Uchelen* N.A. van, Psalm xxiii; some regulative linguistic evidence: ➤ 129, ᶠMULDER M., New avenues 1989, 156-162.

3110 *Auffret* Pierre, 'La voix de l'action de grâce'; étude structurelle du Ps 26: NRT 111 (1989) 217-227.

3111 *Bellinger* W.H.ᴶ, Psalm 26 (exposition): RExp 86 (1989) 477-582.

3112 *MacKay* Thomas W., DIDYMUS the Blind on Psalm 28 (LXX); text from unpublished leaves of the Tura commentary: ➤ 696, StudPatr 10/20 (1987/9) 40-49.

3113 **Kloos** Carola, [Ps 29, Ex 15] Yhwh's combat with the sea 1986 ➤ 2,2333 ... 4,3253: ᴿAfO 35 (1988) 229-232 (D. *Pardee*); BASOR 274 (1989) 95s (J. T. *Walsh*).

3114 **Loretz** Oswald, Psalm 29; Kanaanäische El- und Baaltraditionen in jüdischer Sicht 1984 ➤ 65,2315 ... 4,3254 [²1988 ➤ 3062 supra]: ᴿAulaO 7 (1989) 296-8 (G. del *Olmo Lete*); BO 46 (1989) 134s (M. J. *Mulder*).

3115 *Diethart* J. M., *Niederwimmer* K., Ein Psalm [31G, Vind. G 41050] und ein christlicher Hymnus auf Papyrus: JbÖstByz 36 (1986) 1-2 [< ZAW 102,279].

3116 *Auffret* Pierre, 'Allez, fils, entendez-moi!' Étude structurelle du psaume 34 et son rapport au psaume 33: ÉglT 19 (1988) 5-31.

3117 ᴱ**Lifschitz** Daniel, Salmo 34, Benedirò il Signore in ogni tempo: La Tradizione ebraica commenta i Salmi. T-Leumann 1989, Elle Di Ci. 207 p. Lit. 12.000. – ᴿParVi 34 (1989) 312s (F. *Mosetto*).

3117* *Libera* Piotr, Motivo del medico e della medicina nel commento al salmo XXXVII di sant'AMBROGIO: An Cracov 20 (1988) 209-220 [< ZIT 89,433].

3118 *Rahner* Christa-Maria, Leben und Tod – Trauern; Arbeitshilfe zu Psalm 39: CLehre 42 (B 1989) U-161-5 [< ZIT 90,126].

3119 *Auffret* Pierre, 'O bonheurs de l'homme attentif au faible!'; étude structurelle du Psaume 41: Bijdragen 50 (1989) 2-23.

3120 *Auffret* Pierre, La ville de Dieu; étude structurelle du Psaume 46: ScEspr 41 (1989) 323-341.

3121 *Earwood* Greg C., Psalm 46 (exposition): RExp 86 (1989) 79-86.

3122 *Lohfink* Norbert, 'Der den Kriegen einen Sabbat bereitet'; Psalm 46 — ein Beispiel alttestamentlicher Friedenslyrik: BiKi 44 (1989) 148-153.

3123 *Zenger* Erich, Von der Unverzichtbarkeit der historisch-kritischen Exegese; am Beispiel des 46. Psalms: BLtg 62 (1989) 10-20.

3124 *Zenger* Erich, Der Gott Abrahams und die Völker; Beobachtungen zu Psalm 47: ➤ 169, ᶠSCHARBERT J., Väter 1989, 413-430.

3125 *Smith* M. S., God and Zion; form and meaning in Psalm 48: StEpL 6 (1989) 67-77.

3126 **Simms** Rupe, An exegetical and theological study of Psalm 50 [as *ríb*]: diss. Dallas Theol. Sem. 1988. 259 p. 89-13838. – DissA 50 (1989s) 1342-A.

3127 *Schmidt* W. H., [Ps 51 ...] 'Denkt nicht mehr an das Frühere!'; eschatologische Erwartung — Aspekte des ATs: Glauben und Lernen 4 (1989) 17-32 [< ZAW 102,128].

3128 *Ringgren* Helmer, [Ps 54,8] Tacka Herren, ty han är god; ett översättningsproblem: SvEx 54 (1989) 165-7.

3129 *Tournay* R. J., Psaumes 57, 60 et 108; analyse et interprétation: RB 96 (1989) 5-26; Eng. 5.

3129* **Carniti** Cecilia, Il Salmo 68, ᴰ1985 ➤ 1,2146 ... 4,3279: ᴿBenedictina 35 (1988) 220s (L. *De Lorenzi*).

3130 *Renaud* B., De la bénédiction du roi à la bénédiction de Dieu (Ps 72): Biblica 70 (1989) 305-326; Eng. 326.

3131 *Buchanan* George W., [Ps 74] The fall of Jerusalem and the reconsideration of some dates: RQum 14 (1989) 31-48.

3132 *Sollamo* Raija, The simile in Ps 74:5, a wood-cutter entering a forest wielding axes: SvEx 54 (1989) 178-187.

3133 *Ravasi* Gianfranco, 'Ciò che abbiamo udito... lo narreremo' (Sal 78,3-4); narrazione ed esegesi: RivB 37 (1989) 343-350: rassegna sulla 'teologia (ed esegesi) narrativa'.

3134 *Tromp* N. J., Psalm lxxx; form of expression and form of contents: ➤ 129, ᶠMULDER M., New avenues 1989, 145-155.

3135 *Hetényi* Attila, ⓂＩ 'Újíts meg bennünket!' ['tröste uns'; NEB 'restore us']; a short commentary on Ps 80,3: TSzem 32 (1989) 73-75.

3136 *Nebe* G. Wilhelm, Die Masada-Psalmen-Handschrift M 1039-160, nach einem jüngst veröffentlichten Photo mit Text von Psalm 81,2-85,6: RQum 14 (1989) 89-97.

3137 *Boesak* Willa, Exegesis and proclamation; Ps 82, God amidst the gods; JTSAf 64 (Rondebosch 1988) 64-68 [< TContext 6/2, 18].

3138 *Neyrey* Jerome H., I said 'You are gods'; Psalm 82:6 and John 10 [34-36]: JBL 108 (1989) 647-663; ➤ 5555.

3139 *Loretz* O., Ugaritisch *ṭbn* und hebräisch *ṭwb* 'Regen'; Regenrituale beim Neujahrsfest in Kanaan und Israel (Ps 85; 126): UF 21 (1989) 247-258.

3140 **Kim Jungwoo**, Psalm 89; its biblical-theological contribution to the presence of law within the unconditional covenant: diss. Westminster Theol. Sem. 1989, ᴰ*Waltke* B. 453 p. 89-19993. – DissA 50 (1989s) 1704-A.

3141 *Tromp* Nico, Gezegende leeftijd; variaties op het thema van Psalm 90,10: Geest en Leven 65 (1988) 232-4.

3142 *Bonchard* M. N., Una lectura monástica del salmo 90 (91); los sermones de San BERNARDO sobre el salmo Qui habitat: Cuadernos Monásticos 24 (BA 1989) 27-41 [Stromata 45,498].

3143 *Dellazari* Romano, Salmo noventa y cinco; Teocomunicação 18,82 (1988) 425-437 [< TContext 6/2, 63].

3144 **Scoralick** Ruth, Trishagion und Gottesherrschaft; Psalm 99 als Neuinterpretation von Tora und Propheten: SBS 138. Stu 1989, KBW. 124 p. DM 26,80 [TR 86,162].

3145 *Baldermann* Ingo, Ein Psalm zum Atemholen; gekürzte Fassung einer Bibelarbeit über Psalm 103,1-5: EvErz 41,1 (1989) 5-12 [< ZIT 89,413].

3146 *Booij* T., a) Psalm 104,13b, 'The earth is satisfied with the fruit of thy works': Biblica 70 (1989) 409-412; – b) The role of darkness in Psalm CV 28: VT 39 (1989) 209-214.

3147 *Füglister* Notker, Psalm 105 und die Väterverheissung: ➤ 169, ᶠSCHAR-BERT J., Väter 1989, 41-59.

3148 *Bazak* Yaakov, ⒽＩ ➤ 4,3304 [diagrams of the inner geometry of] Psalm 107,15: BethM 32 (1986s) 301-319 [< OTAbs 11,168].

3149 *Meer* W. van der, Psalm 110, a psalm of rehabilitation: ➤ 410, Structural/poetry 1988, 207-234.

3150 *Sherwood* Stephen K., Psalm 112 — a royal wisdom psalm?: CBQ 51 (1989) 50-64.

3151 *Bazak* Yaakov, ⒽＩ Ps 113-8: BethM 34,121 (1989s) 182-191.

3152 *Quecke* Hans, Zur sahidischen Psalmenerzählung [113-117]: ➤ 138, ᶠMÜLLER C. D. G., Nubica 1988, 205-9.

3153 Drei Exegesen zu Psalm 114: Rosch Pina 6 (Mülheim 1989) 3-31 [< Judaica 45,267].

3154 *Botha* P. J., [Ps 119, eight words for Torah] The measurement of meaning — an exercise in field semantics: JSem 1 (1989) 3-22.

3155 ᵀᴱ**Milhau** Marc, [Ps 119H] HILAIRE de Poitiers, Commentaire sur le Psaume 118: SChr 344.347, 1988 ➤ 4,3309: ᴿNRT 111 (1989) 587 (A. *Harvengt*); RB 96 (1989) 627 (M.-J. *Pierre*); RBén 99 (1989) 189.337 (L. *Wankenne*); RechSR 77 (1989) 576-8 (Y.-M. *Duval*); RivStoLR 25 (1989) 557s (L. F. *Pizzolato*).

3156 *Pizzolato* Luigi F., AMBROGIO e PAOLINO di Nola; per una più precisa datazione della Expositio Psalmi CXVIII di Ambrogio: ➤ 42, ᶠCOSTANZA S., Polyanthema 1989, 333-345.

3157 *Tromp* J., The text of Psalm CXX 5-6: VT 39 (1989) 100-3.

3158 *Ceresko* Anthony R., Psalm 121, a prayer of a warrior?: Biblica 70 (1989) 496-510; franç. 510.

3158* *Tromp* N., Psalm 122, eredienst en politiek; lofprijzing en rechtvaardigheid: → 116, FLEEUWEN C. van 1989, 109-127.

3159 *Riemann* Andreas, Psalm 124 — dem Netz entronnen; eine Arbeitshilfe: CLehre 42 (1989) U-177-184 [< ZIT 90,196].

3160 *Prinsloo* W.S., Psalm 126: NduitseGT 28 (1987) 231-242 [< OTAbs 11,168].

3160* *Cimosa* Mario, Due cantici della fecondità familiare (Sal 127 e 128): → 587, Famiglia 1987/9, 137-157.

3161 *Jeremias* Jörg, *a*) 'Aus tiefer Not schrei ich zu dir'; Ps 130 und LUTHERS Psalmlied [p. 270: Psalm 130 im alttestamentlichen Kontext und in Luthers Nachdichtung]: → 177, FSCHWARZ R., Von Wittenberg 1989, 120-136; – *b*) Psalm 130 und Luthers Nachdichtung: TBei 20 (1989) 284-297 [< ZIT 90,22].

3162 **Berlin** A., On the interpretation of Psalm 133: → 2987, Directions 1987, 141-7.

3163 *Zenger* Erich, Vom Segen der Brüderlichkeit; Überlegungen zum Verständnis des 133. Psalms: → 45, FDEISSLER A., Weg 1989, 173-182.

3164 *Auffret* Pierre, Note on the literary structure of Psalm 134 [revision of his Sagesse 1982, p. 511]: JStOT 45 (1989) 87-89.

3165 **Auffret** P., Et comment pourrait-elle chanter? Ps 136 / Thérèse 1985 → 2,2377: RNRT 111 (1989) 272s (J. *Radermakers*); ScEspr 40 (1988) 134s (M. *Girard*).

3166 **Hartberger** Birgit, 'An den Wässern von Babylon...' Psalm 137 / Jeremia 51 [D1985]: BoBB 63, 1986 → 4,3319: RTPQ 137 (1989) 411 (J. *Marböck*).

3167 *Lenowitz* H., The mock-śimḥâ of Psalm 137: → 2987, Directions 1987, 149-159.

3168 *Brunner-Traut* Emma, [Ps 139,16; *Meyrink* G. 1915] Ein Golem in der ägyptischen Literatur: StAltÄgK 16 (1989) 21-26.

3169 *Lindars* Barnabas, The structure of Psalm CXLV: VT 39 (not 29 as top; 1989) 23-30.

3170 *Talmon* S., Extra-canonical psalms from Qumran — Psalm 151 [< Tarbiz 35 (1966) 214-234]: → 365, Qumran 1989, 244-272.

E7.1 **Job, *Textus, commentarii.***

3171 *Aufrecht* Walter E., A bibliography of Job Targumim: NewsTarg sup. 3 (1987) 1-13 [< OTAbs 12,289].

3172 **Bizjak** Jurij, Job. Koper 1989, Ognjišče. 160 p.

3173 **Clines** David J.A., Job [I. ch. 1-20]: Word comm. 17s. Dallas 1989, Word. I. cxv-501 p. 0-8499-0216-9. – RExpTim 101 (1989s) 377s (C.S. *Rodd*: superb).

3174 TDamico Anthony, EYaffe Martin D., Thomas AQUINAS, the literal exposition of Job, a scriptural commentary concerning Providence. [J]AAR classics 7. Atlanta 1989, Scholars. viii-496 p. $60; sb./pa. $40. 1-55540-291-7; 2-5 [TDig 37,90].

3175 **Fleming** David M., [Job 1...] The divine council as type scene in the Hebrew Bible: diss. Southern Baptist Theol. Sem., DWatts J. 1989. 279 p. 90-04715. – DissA 50 (1989s) 2525-A.

3176 **Fohrer** Georg, Das Buch Hiob: KAT 16. Gü 1989, Mohn. 573 p. DM 178. 3-579-64288-2. – RTsTNijm 29 (1989) 405 (N. *Tromp*).
3177 **Gibson** John C. L., Job 1985 → 1,3189: RCBQ 51 (1989) 121s (E. *Hensell*, also on SIMUNDSON D., both 'popular' commentaries).
3178 TGoodman L. E., SAADIEH Ben Joseph al-Fayyūmī, The book of theodicy; translation [from Arabic; first in English] and [philosophic] commentary on the Book of Job: Yale Judaica 25. NHv 1988, Yale Univ. xvii-481 p. [JAOS 109,342].
3179 **Hartley** John E., The book of Job: NICOT, 1988 → 4,3327: RBiblica 70 (1989) 552-5 (J. L. *Sicre*); BL (1989) 54 (J. H. *Eaton*); ExpTim 100 (1988s) 189 (C. S. *Rodd*: immensely interesting); LA 39 (1989) 329-336 (A. *Niccacci*); SWJT 32,2 (1989s) 50s (H. B. *Hunt*); RelStR 15 (1989) 258 (J. L. *Crenshaw*).
3180 TEKreit J., Job, un homme pour notre temps; de saint Thomas d'AQUIN, Exposition littérale sur le livre de Job. 1982 → 63,3235 ... 65,2789: RRSPT 73 (1989) 588 (L.-J. *Bataillon*: useful despite title and some errors of translation).
3181 **McKenna** David L., Job: Communicator's Comm. 1986 → 3,3144 [not 'MacK']; 0-8499-0418-8: RBS 146 (1989) 109s (R. B. *Zuck*).
3182 *MacKenzie* R. A. F., *Murphy* Roland E., Job: ↦ 384, NJBC (1989) 466-488.
3182* [**Sarna** N., *al.* → 61,4267, *Greenberg* M.; 63,3231], The book of Job, a new translation. Ph 1980, Jewish Publ. Soc. xxiii-63 p. – RRSO 63 (1989) 309s (D. *Garrone*).
3183 *Silbermann* Alphons, Soziologische Anmerkungen zum Buch Hiob: ZRGg 41 (1989) 1-11.
3184 ESorlin H., (*Neyrand* L.), Jean CHRYSOSTOME, Commentaire sur Job I (ch. 1-14), II (15-42): SChr 346.348, 1988 → 4,3337: RBiblica 70 (1989) 420s (É. des *Places*, 1); ÉtClas 57 (1989) 270s (F.-X. *Druet*); NRT 111 (1989) 588s (A. *Harvengt*); RÉByz 47 (1989) 274s (A. *Failler*); ScEspr 41 (1989) 383s (G. *Pelland*); TLZ 114 (1989) 824s (G. *Haendler*); VigChr 43 (1989) 306-8 (J. van *Winden*).
3185 *a)* **Wiesel** Elie, *Eisenberg* Josy, Job of God in storm en wind. Hilversum 1989, Gooi. 400 p. *f*37,50. – RStreven 57 (1989) 954 (P. *Beentjes*, also on VOGELS Dutch). – *b)* **Eisenberg** Josy, *Wiesel* Élie, Giobbe o Dio nella tempesta: Religione. T 1989, Soc. Ed. Int. 376 p. 88-05-05063-6.

E7.2 *Job: themata*, **Topics** ... *Versiculi*, **Verse-numbers.**

3186 *Brenner* Athalya, Job the pious? The characterization of Job in the narrative framework of the book: JStOT 43 (1989) 37-52.
3187 *Ceresko* Anthony R., The option for the poor in the book of Job: IndTSt 26 (1989) 105-121.
3188 *Clines* David J. A., Job: ↦ 377, Books 1 (1989) 181-201.
3189 *Dassmann* Ernst, Hiob: ↦ 904, RAC 15,115 (1989) 366-442.
3190 **Dell** K. J., The Book of Job as sceptical literature: diss. Oxford 1988. – RTLv 21, p. 540.
3191 *Elman* Yaakov, The suffering of the righteous in Palestinian and Babylonian sources: JQR 80 (1989s) 315-339.
3192 *Erikson* Gösta, *Jonasson* Kristina, Jobsbokens juridiska grundmönster [juridical pattern of Job]: SvTKv 65 (1989) 64-69.
3193 *Freund* Yosef, Were Job's friends Gentiles?: Dor [17 (1988s) *Corey* L.] 19 (= JBQ 1989) 107-110.

3194 *Gibson* J.C.L., The Book of Job and the cure of souls: ScotJT 42 (1989) 303-317.

3195 **Girard** René, Job, the victim of his people [1985], ^T*Freccero* Yvonne 1987 ➤ 3,3161: ^RCBQ 51 (1989) 515-7 (R. *North*); RelStR 15 (1989) 158 (J.L. *Crenshaw*).

3195* **Girard** R., [Job] De aloude weg der boosdoeners, 1987 ➤ 4,3348; 90-242-2573-3 / 90-289-1281-9: ^RTsTNijm 29 (1989) 206 (A. *Lascaris*).

3196 *a) Bonora* Antonio, Giobbe, capro espiatorio secondo R. GIRARD; – *b) Sequeri* Pierangelo, 'Dare la vita' ed 'essere sacrificato'; il tema della singolarità cristologica nella prospettiva di R. GIRARD: TItSett 14 (1989) 138-142 / 143-153.

3197 **Gutiérrez** Gustavo, On Job; God-talk and the suffering of the innocent 1987 ➤ 3,3165: ^RCurrTM 16 (1989) 50s (J.D. *Rodríguez*) & 129s (C.L. *Nessan*); EglT 19 (1988) 255s (W. *Vogels*); Pacifica 2 (1989) 234-6 (C. *Murray*).

3198 **Gutiérrez** Gustavo, Von Gott sprechen in Unrecht und Leid — Ijob [1986 ➤ 2,2409], ^T*Goldstein* Horst. Mainz/Mü 1988, Grünewald/Kaiser. 154 p. – ^RBiKi 44 (1989) 192s (R. *Baumann*); TGegw 32 (1989) 234s (B. *Häring*).

3199 *Hermisson* Hans-Jürgen, Notizen zu Hiob: ZTK 86 (1989) 125-139.

3200 **Huber** Paul, Hiob – Dulder oder Rebell? Byzantinische Miniaturen zum Buche Hiob in Patmos... 1986 ➤ 2,2411; 4,3356: ^ROrientierung 53 (1989) 11s (Renate *Fechner*); TrierTZ 98 (1989) 231 (E. *Sauser*).

3201 *Long* Thomas G., Ijob; Quere Gedanken im Lande Uz [< TTod 1988s, 5-20]: TGegw 32 (1989) 11-23 [3-10, *Lermen* Birgit ➤ 1601].

3202 **Lübbe** John C., Toward an evaluation of the translation process in 11Qtg Job; a study in methodology: diss. Unisa, ^D*Dreyer* J. Pretoria 1987. – DissA 50 (1989s) 2033-A.

3203 ^E**Moyes** Malcolm R., Richard ROLLE's 'Expositio super novem lectiones mortuorum' [from Job]: Eliz./Ren. St. 92/12. Salzburg 1988, Univ. Inst. Anglistik. vii-104 p.; 298 p. – ^RChH 50 (1989) 508s (R.W. *Pfaff*: does not claim to be a critical edition).

3204 *a) Müller* Hans-Peter, Neue Aspekte der Anfragen Hiobs; – *b) Augustin* Matthias, Sinn des Lebens — Sinn des Leidens; Betrachtungen zur marxistischen Hiob-Interpretation von Milan MACHOVEC als Beitrag zum alttestamentlich-philosophischen Dialog: ➤ 212, ^FWESTERMANN C., Schöpfung 1989, 178-188 / 166-177.

3205 *Oorschot* J. van, Gott als Grenze... Hiob: BZAW 170, 1987 ➤ 3,3175: ^RRivB 37 (1989) 213-8 (G.L. *Prato*).

3206 *Riley* William, The Book of Job and the terrible truth about God: Scripture in Church 18 (Dublin 1988) 322-6 [< OTAbs 12,71].

3207 *O'Connor* Daniel J., *a)* The Keret legend and the prologue-epilogue of Job; – *b)* The hybris of Job: IrTQ 55 (1989) 1-6 / 125-141 [postscript 240-2].

3208 *Pucci* Joseph, Job and Ovid in The Archpoet's Confession [1162]: ClasMedK 40 (1989) 236-250.

3209 *Ravasi* Gianfranco, Giobbe; male fisico e male morale: ParSpV 19 (1989) 83-94.

3210 *Sarrazin* Bernard, Du rire dans la Bible? La théophanie de Job comme parodie: RechSR 76 (1988) 39-55; Eng. 56.

3211 *Schreiner* Susan E., Exegesis and double justice in CALVIN's sermons on Job: ChH 58 (1989) 322-338.

3212 *Seitz* Christopher R., Job; full-structure, movement, and interpretation: Interpretation 43 (1989) 5-17.
3213 **Susman** M., Het boek Job en de lijdensweg van het joodse volk. Kampen 1987, Kok. 127 p. *f* 22,50. 90-242-3162-0. – ᴿTsTNijm 29 (1989) 319 (K. *Waaijman*).
3214 *Tortolone* Gian M., L'enigma di Giobbe; destino dell'uomo e silenzio di Dio: Asprenas 36 (1989) 22-38.
3215 *Townsend* T.P., Soteriology and the Book of Job: Bible Bhashyam 14 (1988) 117-131.
3216 **Unen** C. van, Job, dwarsligger of verbondgenoot? 1987 → 4,3375: ᴿGerefTTs 89 (1989) 118 (C. *Houtman*).
3217 *Vattioni* Francesco, *a*) Il sangue nella fonte di Giobbe; – *b*) Anima e sangue in Epifanio di Salamina: → 759, Sangue 1987/9, 691-708 / 871-887.
3218 **Warner** Martin, Philosophical finesse [Pascal term]; studies in the art of rational persuasion [... in part on Job]. Ox 1989, Clarendon. x-401 p. $64 [TS 51,774s, Z.K. *McKeon*].
3219 **Wilcox** John T., The bitterness of Job; a philosophical reading. AA 1989, Univ. Michigan. xii-243 p. 0-472-10129-3.
3220 **Zahrnt** Heinz, Wie kann Gott das zulassen? Hiob – der Mensch im Leid. Mü 1985, Piper. – ᴿBZ 33 (1989) 297 (E. *Kutsch*).

3221 **Michel** Walter L., Job in the light of Northwest Semitic, I. prologue and first cycle of speeches, Job 1:1-14:22: BibOrPont 42, 1987 → 3,3174; 4,3382: ᴿCBQ 51 (1989) 341-3 (R. *Althann*); JBL 108 (1988) 128-131 (A.R. *Ceresko*: assumes Dahood right until proved wrong); LA 39 (1989) 327-9 (A. *Niccacci*); TLZ 114 (1989) 23s (H.-P. *Müller*).
3222 *Meier* Sam, Job I-II; a reflection of Genesis I-III: VT 39 (1989) 183-193. → 3175.
3223 *Levin* S., [Job 1] Satan; psychologist [< JPsy&J 1980]: JBQ (= Dor) 18 (1989s) 157-164.
3224 **Cotter** David, A study of Job 4-5 in the light of contemporary literary theory: diss. Pont. Univ. Gregoriana, ᴰCox D.; Publ. Nº 3576. R 1989. 394 p. – RTLv 21, p. 540; TR 86,249.
3225 *Miller* James E., [4,12-21] The vision of Eliphaz as foreshadowing in the Book of Job: ProcGLM 9 (1989) 98-112.
3226 *Janzen* J. Gerald, Another look at God's watch over Job (7:12): JBL 108 (1989) 109-114.
3227 *Schwienhorst* Ludger, *Steins* Georg, Zur Entstehung, Gestalt und Bedeutung der Ijob-Erzählung (Ijob 11;42): BZ 33 (1989) 1-24.
3228 *Wolfers* David, 'Greek' logic in the Book of Job (chapter 12): Dor 15 (1986s) 166-172 [< OTAbs 11,169].
3229 *Burns* John B., Support for the emendation *reḥōb meqōmô* in Job XXIV 19-20: VT 39 (1989) 480-5.
3230 *Lugt* P. van der, *a*) The form and function of the refrains in Job 28; some comments relating to the strophic structure of Hebrew poetry; – *b*) Strophes and stanzas in the Book of Job; a historical survey: → 410, Structural/poetry 1988, 265-293 / 235-264.
3230* *Kuhn* Hanni, [Job 30,4] Why are Job's opponents still made to eat broom-root [*Hakham* Amos, Book of Job ⊕ (J 1984, Kook) 226 *roṭem*]:

BTrans 40 (1989) 332-6 (maybe they sold it or used it to warm themselves).
3231 **Mende** sr. M. Theresia, Durch Leiden zur Vollendung; die Elihureden im Buch Ijob (32-37): Diss. ᴰ*Haag* E. Trier 1988s. 507 p. – TR 85 (1989) 518; RTLv 21,541.
3232 *Haggai* Yiśrael, ❻ He gives $z^e mirôt$ at night (Job 35,10): BethM 32 (1986s) 373-380 [< OTAbs 11,169].
3233 *Diewert* David A., Job XXXVI 5 and the root *m's* II: VT 39 (not 29 as bot.; 1989) 71-77.
3234 *Curtis* John B., Some Jewish interpretations of Job 37:6 — midrash or ancient cosmogony?: ProcGLM 9 (1989) 113-123.
3235 *a*) *Scholnick* S. Huberman, Poetry in the courtroom; Job 38-41; – *b*) *Fontaine* C., Folktale structure in the Book of Job; a formalist reading: ➤ 2987, Directions 1987, 185-204 / 205-232.
3236 *Muenchow* Charles, Dust and dirt in Job 42:6: JBL 108 (1989) 597-611.
3237 *Freund* Joseph, ❻ Job 42,7: BethM 34,121 (1989s) 124-130.
3239 *Vattioni* Francesco, Il colofone del libro di Giobbe nel Vat. lat. 5729: Miscellanea Bibliothecae Apostolicae Vaticanae II: ST 331. Vaticano 1988, Biblioteca [329 p. 88-210-0616-6]. p. 267-286.

E7.3 *Canticum canticorum*, **Song of Solomon** – *textus, commentarii*.

3240 *Ceresa-Gastaldo* Aldo, Nuove ricerche sulla storia del testo, le antiche versioni e l'interpretazione del Cantico dei Cantici: ➤ 567, AnStoEseg 6 (1989) 31-38; Eng. 6.
3241 **Deckers-Dys** Mimi, Hooglied: Belichting Bb. Boxtel/Brugge c. 1988, KBS/Tabor. 160 p. ƒ21. – ᴿStreven 57 (1989) 568 (P. *Beentjes*, also on ROZELAAR M.).
ᴱ**Diebner** B., *Kasser* R., Hamburger Papyrus... Cant Lam copt.; Eces gr.-copt. 1989 ➤ 1765.
3242 **Goulder** Michael D., The song of fourteen songs 1986 ➤ 2,3436; 3,3198: ᴿCBQ 51 (1989) 122-4 (J. Cheryl *Exum*).
3242* **Heinevetter** Hans-Josef, 'Komm...' Hoheslied [Diss. 1988 ➤ 4, 3423]: BoBB 69. Fra 1988, Athenäum. 250 p. DM 58. 3-610-09120-7: ᴿExpTim 101 (1989s) 213 (R. *Coggins*, also on STRECKER-SCHMIDT Grundkurs).
3243 ᴱ**Kamin** Sarah, *Saltman* Avrom, Secundum Salomonem; a thirteenth century Latin commentary on the Song of Solomon. Ramat Gan 1989, Bar-Ilan Univ. 101 p. + ❶ 99. 965-226-104-1.
3245 **Knight** George A. F., Revelation of God... The Song of Songs [+ *Golka* F., Jonah]: Int. Theol. Comm. 1988 ➤ 4,3405: ᴿÉTRel 64 (1989) 619s (D. *Lys*).
3246 ᴱ**Moreschini** Claudio, GREGORIO di Nissa, Omelie sul Cantico dei Cantici: Testi Patristici 72. R 1988, Città Nuova. 375 p. Lit. 26.000. 88-311-3072-2. – ᴿCC 140 (1989,3) 202s (A. *Ferrua*); RivStoLR 25 (1989) 559s (F. *Trisoglio*).
3247 **Neri** Umberto, Il Cantico dei Cantici; Targum e antiche interpretazioni ebraiche: Tradizione d'Israele 1, 1987 ➤ 4,3407: ᴿAnnTh 3,1 (1989) 150s (M. A. *Tábet*); BL (1989) 48 (P. S. *Alexander*).
3248 **Neri** Umberto, El Cantar de los Cantares, Targum e interpretaciones hebreas antiguas, ᵀJ. P.: Biblioteca Catecumenal. Bilbao 1988, Desclée de B. 193 p. pt. 1123. 84-330-0747-5. – ᴿActuBbg 26 (1989) 45s (R. de *Sivatte*); LumenVr 38 (1989) 444 (F. *Ortiz de Urtaran*).

3249 *Murphy* Roland E., Canticle of Canticles: ➤ 384, NJBC (1989) 462-5 [447-52, Wisdom lit.].
3250 **Patterson** Paige, Song of Solomon: Everyman's comm. 1986 ➤ 2,2440: ᴿCriswT 2 (1987s) 424s (B. B. *Bayer*).
3251 ᴱ*Raurell* Frederic, [Rupert Maria de MANRESA 1936], Un comentari inèdit del 'Càntic dels Càntics'; l'exegesi catòlica entre 1900-1940: Est Franc 90 (1989) 169-251 (252, printed title-page; 156-158; 253-293, *al.* de Rupert). ➤ k376.
3251* **Tournay** Raymond J., Word of God, song of love 1988 ➤ 4,3411: ᴿExpTim 101 (1989s) 282 (C. S. *Rodd*).
3252 ᴱ**Vregille** B. de, *Neyrand* L., APPONIUS, In Canticum Canticorum expositio: CCLat 19, 1986: ➤ 2,2445: 4,3412: ᴿBijdragen 50 (1989) 96s (M. *Schneiders*); BTAM 14 (1989) p. 586s (P. *Hamblenne*); Gregorianum 70 (1989) 817 (J. *Wicki*); VigChr 43 (1989) 92-95 (K. S. *Frank*).

E7.4   **Canticum**, *themata, versiculi.*

3253 **Brenner** Athalya, The Song of Songs: OT Guides. Sheffield 1989, Academic. 106 p. £5. 1-85075-242-7.
3254 *Brésard* Luc, Un texte d'Origène, l'échelle des Cantiques: PrOrChr 39 (1989) 3-25.
3255 *Brzegowy* Tadeusz, ❷ Vers l'interprétation littérale du Cantique des Cantiques: STWsz 26,1 (1988) 67-94; franç. 94s.
3256 **Casey** Michael, A thirst for God; spiritual desire in BERNARD of Clairvaux's sermons on the Song of Songs: Cistercian Studies 77. Kalamazoo MI 1988, Cistercian. 390 p. – ᴿBTAM 14 (1989) 703s (H. *Brangers*: fort instructive).
3257 *Davidson* Richard M., Theology of sexuality in the Song of Songs; return to Eden: AndrUnS 27 (1989) 1-19.
3258 *Dijk-Hemmes* Fokkelien van, The imagination of power and the power of imagination; an intertextual analysis of two biblical love songs; the Song of Songs and Hosea 2: JStOT 44 (1989) 75-88.
3259 **Elliott** sr. Mary Timothea, The literary unity of the Canticle [diss. Pont. Ist. Biblico 1988 ➤ 4,3419]: EurHS 23/371. Fra 1989, Lang. xiii-383 p. Fs 81 [TR 86,338]. 3-631-42121-4.
3260 **Fox** Michael V., The Song of Songs and ancient Egyptian love songs 1985 ➤ 1,3271 ... 4,3422: ᴿBO 46 (1989) 297-300 (J. J. *Jackson*).
3261 **Mariaselvam** Abraham, The Song of Songs and ancient Tamil love poems [diss. PIB, ᴰ*Gilbert* M. 1987]: AnBib 118, 1988 ➤ 4,3425: ᴿJStOT 45 (1989) 127 (Athalya *Brenner*); NRT 111 (1989) 584 (J. *Masson*); RivB 37 (1989) 519s (A. *Bonora*).
3262 *Murphy* Roland E., Song of Solomon: ➤ 377, Books 1 (1989) 241-6.
3263 *Ohler* Annemarie, Der Mann im Hohelied: ➤ 45, ᶠDEISSLER A., Weg 1989, 183-200.
3264 **Pelletier** Anne-Marie, Lectures du Cantique des Cantiques; de l'énigme du sens aux figures du lecteur. R 1989, Pont. Ist. Biblico. xxi-446 p. Lit. 48.500 [CC 140,4 dopo 520]. 88-7853-121-1.
3265 *Schellekens* J. W. M., De betwisting van RICHARD van St-Victors auteurschap der Expositio in Cantica Canticorum, beschouwd vanuit de handschriften en HADEWIJCH: ➤ 10, ᶠAMPE A. OnsGErf (1988s) 64,107-129.
3266 *Segal* Benjamin J., Four repetitions in the Song of Songs: Dor 16 (1987s) 32-39 [< OTAbs 11,171].

3267 **Triviño** María Victoria, El Cantar de los Cantares vivido en Sor Ángeles Sorazu. Valladolid 1989, Concepcionistas Franciscanas. 104 p. – ᴿEst-Fran 90 (1989) 528 (fr. V. S. de M.).

3268 *Sasson* Victor, [Ct 1,5s] King Solomon and the dark lady in the Song of Songs [Pharaoh's daughter (1 Kgs 3,1; 7,8; 9,24; 11,1s) as already THEODORE of Mopsuestia]: VT 39 (1989) 407-414.
3269 *Dirksen* P. B., Song of Songs III 6-7: VT 39 (1989) 219-225.
3270 *Feuillet* André, Le drame d'amour du Cantique des Cantiques [6,4-8,7] remis en son contexte prophétique II: NVFr 63 (1988) 81-136.
3271 *Alden* R., Song of Songs 8:12a, who said it? [the girl to her brothers]: 31 (1988) 271-8 [< ZAW 102,130].
3272 *Poulssen* Niek, Vluchtwegen in Hooglied 8,14; over de meerzinnigheid van een slotvers: Bijdragen 50 (1989) 72-81; Eng. 82.

E7.5 *Libri sapientiales* – **Wisdom literature.**

3273 *Arens* K. E., El carácter sapiencial de la Biblia: Paginas 14,1 (Lima 1989) 21-29 [< NTAbs 33,344].
3274 **Berger** Klaus, Die Weisheitsschrift [zwei Fragmente, 356 Zeilen, NY und Leningrad] aus der Kairoer Geniza; Erstedition [trotz *Harkavy* RÉJ 1903, *Schechter* JQR 1904], Kommentar und Übersetzung: TArbNZ 1. Tü 1989, Francke. 422 p.; 18 pl. 3-7720-1880-7 [NTS 36,415]. – ᴿTüTQ 169 (1989) 320s (W. *Gross*: wird grosse Beachtung finden).
3275 *Bonora* Antonio, La ricchezza nei libri sapienziali dell'AT: Servitium 3,62 (Bergamo 1989) 155-164.
3276 **Brunner** Helmut, Altägyptische Weisheit 1988 → 4,3439: ᴿTZBas 45 (1989) 375s (T. *Schneider*: biblische Parallelen vom Anhang).
3276* **Büler** Winfried, *Zenobius* Athous, Proverbia [non biblica], I (Prolegomena) - II. Gö 1987/2, Vandenhoeck & R. 434 p. – ᴿSalesianum 51 (1989) 198s (B. *Amata*).
3277 **Cimosa** B. S., Temi di sapienza biblica. R 1989, Dehoniane. 206 p. Lit. 16.000 [RivB 37,529].
3278 **Crenshaw** James L., Old Testament wisdom 1981 → 62,3420 ... 2,2469: ᴿCriswT 2 (1987s) 429-431 (R. L. *Alden*).
3279 *Derchain* Philippe, Éloquence et politique; l'opinion d'Akhtoy [Enseignement pour son fils Mérikaré]: → 39, Mém. CLÈRE J., RÉgp 40 (1989) 37-47.
3280 **Eaton** J., The contemplative face of Old Testament wisdom in the context of world religion. L/Ph 1989, SCM/Trinity. ix-150 p. £7.50. 0-334-01913-3 [BL 90, 100, R. *Davidson*]. – ᴿExpTim 101,9 top choice (1989s) 257s (C. S. *Rodd*).
3280* *Englund* Gertie, The treatment of opposites in temple thinking and wisdom literature: → 842, Bergen 1988/9, 77-88.
3281 *Gladson* Jerry, *Lucas* Ron, Hebrew wisdom and psychotheological dialogue: Zygon 24 (1989) 357-376.
3282 **Goldsworthy** Graeme, Gospel and wisdom; Israel's wisdom literature in the Christian life 1987 → 3,2326; 4,3452: ᴿEvQ 61 (1989) 92s (S. H. *Travis*); STEv NS 1 (1989) 87s (E. *Beriti*).
3283 *Golka* Friedemann W., Die Flecken des Leoparden; biblische und afrikanische Weisheit im Sprichwort: → 212, ᶠWESTERMANN C., Schöpfung 1989, 149-165.

3284 **Grundmann** Walter † 1976, Weisheit im Horizont des Reiches Gottes; Erwägungen zur Christusbotschaft und zum Christusverständnis im Lichte der Weisheit in Israel. Stu 1988, Ev. Kirche Diakonisches Werk. 411 p.; 104 p. notes.

3285 *Kreuzer* Siegfried, Gottesglaube und Welterkenntnis am Beispiel der alttestamentlichen Weisheit: TBei 18 (1987) 43-51 [< OTAbs 12,189].

3286 **Kwasi** Ugira, La problématique de la mort dans les écrits sapientiaux postexiliques; une contribution à la relecture du Yahviste: diss. ᴰ*Chopineau* J. Bru 1988. 363 p. – RTLv 21, p. 540.

3287 **Lichtheim** Miriam, Late Egyptian ... demotic instructions: OBO 52, 1983 ➤ 64,3267 ... 4,3456: ᴿRB 96 (1989) 442 (R. *Beaud*).

3288 *Lubsczyk* Hans, Gotteserkenntnis im Buch der Weisheit; zur Aktualität eines biblischen Buches [< Conoscenza di Dio, NuovaUm 6,32s (1984) 7-26; 17-38]: ➤ 306, Einheit 1989, 155-184.

3289 *Mack* B. L., Wisdom makes a difference; alternatives to 'Messianic' configurations: ➤ 7368, [ᴱ*Neusner* J.] Judaisms and their Messiahs 1987, 15-48 [< JStJud 20,249].

3290 *McNamara* Martin, Some messages of the Wisdom literature: Scripture in Church 19 (Dublin 1989) 217-223.

3291 *Moreno* G. J. [on Diaspora], El Judaismo alejandrino [on Prov., *Senoclain* R.; Wisdom, *Drinberg Woscoboinik* L.; Sirach, *Tapia Adler* R.]: Cuaderno Judaico 13. Santiago 1984, Univ. Centro de Cultura Judaica. iv-72 p. $4 [NTAbs 33,132].

3292 **Morgan** Donn F., Wisdom in the OT traditions 1981 ➤ 63,3334 ... 1,3319: ᴿRelStT 8,1s (1988) 96s (G. C. *Papademetriou*).

3293 ᶠMURPHY Roland E., The listening heart, essays in wisdom and the Psalms, ᴱHoglund K. ... JStOT Sup 58, 1987 ➤ 3,120: ᴿJStJud 20 (1989) 231s (A. S. van der *Woude*: an inspiring collection); SWJT 32,3 (1989s) 55 (B. R. *Ellis*).

Niebuhr Karl-Wilhelm, Gesetz und Paränese; katechismusartige Weisungsreihen in der frühjüdischen Literatur 1987 ➤ a119.

3295 *O'Connor* Kathleen M., The wisdom literature: Message of Biblical Spirituality 5, 1988 ➤ 4,3459: ᴿNewTR 2,3 (1989) 102 (Dianne *Bergant*).

3296 *Pérez* Gabriel, Sabiduría y palabra: StLeg 28 (1987) 9-36.

3297 **Preuss** Horst D., Einführung in die alttestamentliche Weisheitsliteratur: Urban-Tb 383, 1987 ➤ 3,3244: ᴿBO 46 (1989) 135-9 (P. *Höffken*); TPQ 137 (1989) 411s (J. *Marböck*).

3298 **Römheld** K. F. D., Die Weisheitslehre im Alten Orient; Elemente einer Formgeschichte: BibNot Beih 4. Mü 1989. viii-156 p. DM 10 [ZAW 102,457, author same as 'D. Römheld', ᴰ1988 Wege der Weisheit ➤ 3328].

3299 **Sandelin** Karl-Gustav, Wisdom as nourisher 1986 ➤ 2,2488*; 4,3469: ᴿJTS 40 (1989) 530-3 (W. *Horbury*); OrChr 73 (1989) 234 (W. *Gessel*); RHPR 69 (1989) 214s (E. *Jacob*).

3300 *Segalla* Giuseppe, Le figure mediatrici di Israele tra il III e il I sec. a. C.; la storia di Israele tra guida sapienziale e attrazione escatologica: ➤ 597, RicStoB 1,1 (1987/9) 13-65.

3301 *Sellheim* R., *Mathal* [proverb] (in Arabic): ➤ 889, EncIslam 6,111s (Eng. 1989) 815-825.

3302 **Shupak** Nili, Instruction and teaching appellations in Egyptian Wisdom literature (and their biblical counterparts): ➤ 823, Akten IV 3 (1985/9) 193-200.

3303 **Steiert** Franz-Josef, Die Weisheit in Israel und Ägypten: Diss. ᴰ*Deissler* A. Freiburg/B 1988s. – TR 85 (1989) 516; RTLv 21,542.

3304 *Theocharis* A., La notion de la sagesse dans le Livre des Secrets d'Hénoch ou d'Hénoch slave: Klēronomía 18,1 (1986) 95-100 [< ZIT 90,209].

3305 **Thissen** Heinz J., Die Lehre des Anchscheschonqi 1984 → 65,2908 ... 4,3471: ᴿJNES 48 (1989) 51-56 (W. A. *Ward*: translation and glossary; his commentary awaited).

3305* *Tomić* Celestin, Wisdom in the Bible [also NT]: ObnŽiv 44 (1989) 268-278 (Croatian); Eng. 278.

3306 *Virgulin* Stefano, Creazione e liberazione nei libri sapienziali: → 376, Creazione 1989, 55-72.

3307 *Whybray* R. N., The social world of the wisdom writers: → 378, World 1989, 227-250.

E7.6 **Proverbiorum liber**, *themata, versiculi.*

3308 **Camp** Claudia V., Wisdom and the feminine in Proverbs 1985 → 1,3335 ... 4,3476: ᴿJTS 40 (1989) 166-8 (J. G. *Snaith*); OTAbs 12 (1989) 116s (D. C. *Benjamin*).

3309 *Crenshaw* James L., a) Proverbs: → 377, Books 1 (1989) 223-230; – b) Poverty and punishment in the Book of Proverbs: QRMin 9,3 (1989) 30-43.

3310 ᵀᴱ**Géhin** Paul, ÉVAGRE, Scholies aux Proverbes: SChr 340, 1987 → 3,3254; 4,3480: ᴿAntClas 58 (1989) 357-360 (J. *Schamp*); BLitEc 90 (1989) 147s (H. *Crouzel*); EsprVie 99 (1989) 230s (Y.-M. *Duval*); Gregorianum 70 (1989) 176s (G. *Pelland*); MélSR 46 (1989) 47-52 (P.-M. *Humbert*); PrOrChr 39 (1989) 217 (P. *Ternant*); RivStoLR 25 (1989) 157-160 (J. *Mallet*); RHPR 69 (1989) 346s (D. A. *Bertrand*).

3311 a) *Habel* Norman C., Wisdom, wealth, and poverty paradigms in the Book of Proverbs; – b) *Townsend* T. P., The poor in wisdom literature: Bible Bhashyam 14 (1988) 26-49 / 5-25.

3312 **Hubbard** D. A., Proverbs: Communicator's Comm. OT 15A. Dallas 1989, Word. 487 p. [ZAW 102,444, O. *Kaiser*].

3313 **Huwiler** Elizabeth F., [Prov] Control of reality in Israelite wisdom: diss. Duke, ᴰ*Murphy* R. Durham NC 1988. 270 p. 89-19225. – DissA 50 (1989s) 1689-A.

3314 *Koorevaar* H. J., Das Vergeltungsdogma im Buch der Sprüche: Fundamentum 3 (Riehen, Schweiz 1987) 43-50 [< OTAbs 12,73].

3315 **Krispenz-Pichler** Jutta, Spruchkompositionen im Buch Proverbia [Diss. 1987 → 4,3482]: EurHS 23/349. Fra 1989, Lang. 188 p. Fs 43. 3-631-40690-8 [BL 90,81, W. *McKane*).

3316 *McCreesh* Thomas P., Proverbs: → 384, NJBC (1989) 453-461.

3317 *Stadelmann* Andreas, Bemerkungen zur Rolle des Kultus im Proverbienbuch: → 141, ᶠNOCENT A., Traditio 1988, 487-515.

3318 *Tertrais* Max, Proverbes Sukuma: AuCAf 28,4 (Burundi 1988) 334-6 [< TContext 6/2, 20].

3319 *Whybray* R. N., Poverty, wealth, and point of view in Proverbs: ExpTim 100 (1988s) 332-6.

3320 **Woodcock** Eldon, Proverbs. GR 1988, Zondervan. 237 p. $9. – ᴿBS 146 (1989) 352s (R. B. *Zuck*).

3321 *Yee* Gale A., 'I have perfumed my bed with myrrh'; the foreign woman (*išša zârâ*) in Proverbs 1-9: JStOT 43 (1989) 53-68.

3321* *Meinhold* A., Der Gewaltmensch als abschreckendes Beispiel in Prov 1-9: ➤ 85, ᴱHINZ C., Frieden 1988, 82-97.
3322 *Newsom* Carol A., Woman and the discourse of patriarchal wisdom; a study of Proverbs 1-9: ➤ 391, Gender 1989, 142-160.
3323 *Renfroe* F., The effect of redaction on the structure of Prov 1,1-6: ZAW 101 (1989) 290-3.
3324 **Pardee** Dennis, [Prov 2] Ugaritic and Hebrew poetic parallelism...: VT sup 39, 1988 ➤ 4,3490:   ᴿAulaO 7 (1989) 298-300 (W. G. E. *Watson*); UF 21 (1989) 473-5 (O. *Loretz*).
3325 *Toorn* Karel van der, [Prov 7,14.18] Female prostitution in payment of vows in ancient Israel: JBL 108 (1989) 193-205.
3326 *Bonora* Antonio, 'Accogliere la vita' in Pr 11,30: RivB (1989) 313-6.
3327 *Snell* Daniel S., The wheel in Proverbs XX 26 [torture (Hittite, maybe) rather than agriculture as *Alonso-Schökel* L., *Vilchez* L., 1984]: VT 39 (1989) 503-7.
3328 **Römheld** Diethard, Wege der Weisheit; die Lehren Amenemopes und Proverbien 22,17-24,22 [Diss 1988 ➤ 4,3502]: BZAW 184. B 1989, de Gruyter. x-223 p. DM 86. 3-11-011938-7. – ᴿLA 39 (1989) 303-310 (A. *Niccacci*).
3329 **Naré** Laurent, [Prov 25-29] Proverbes salomoniens et... mossi ᴰ1986 ➤ 2,2516... 4,3504:   ᴿCBQ 51 (1989) 343s (J. G. *Williams*: Mossi language is Moor, 'combination of Berber and Arabic', retracted 52,502: it is not related to either); NRT 111 (1989) 773s (J. *Masson*).
3330 **Van Leeuwen** Raymond C., Context and meaning in Proverbs 25-27: SBL diss. 96, 1988 ➤ 4,3905: BL (1989) 96 (W. *McKane*, severe; Prov 27,23-27 allegorizing exegesis bad; devoid of the literary attractiveness it seeks to enhance for the OT); JQR 80 (1989s) 415s (L. G. *Perdue*).
3331 *Durand* Xavier, Un éloge de la femme dans l'AT; le poème de Proverbes 31,10-31: Masses Ouvrières 423 (1989) 76-86.

E7.7   *Ecclesiastes* – **Qohelet,** *themata, versiculi.*

3332 **Anderson** Don, Ecclesiastes, the mid-life crisis 1987 ➤ 4,3511: ᴿBS 146 (1989) 110s (R. B. *Zuck*: for people who have more but enjoy less).
3333 **Crenshaw** James L., Ecclesiastes 1987 ➤ 3,3282; 4,3512: ᴿBL (1989) 52 (A. P. *Hayman*: excellent); BS 146 (1989) 232s (R. B. *Zuck*); Interpretation 43 (1989) 198s (L. G. *Perdue*); ZAW 101 (1989) 148s (O. *Kaiser*).
3334 **Díez Merino** Luis, Targum de Qohelet 1987 ➤ 3,3284; 4,3516: ᴿComm-Sev 22 (1989) 87s (M. de *Burgos*); ETL 65 (1989) 431 (A. *Schoors*); RB 96 (1989) 592-4 (P. *Grelot*).
3335 **Ellul** Jacques, La razón de ser; meditación sobre el Eclesiastés, ᵀ*Arias* Isidro. Barc 1989, Herder. 315 p. 84-254-1645-0. – ᴿActuBbg 26 (1989) 193 (R. de *Sivatte*).
3336 *Fabry* H.-J., *qāhāl* 'Versammlung', *Qohælæt*: ➤ 913, TWAT 6,8s (1989) 1203-1222.
3337 **Fox** Michael V., Qohelet and his contradictions [independent of his 1972 Jerusalem Hebrew Univ. diss.]: JStOT sup. 71. Sheffield 1989, Almond. 384 p. $42.50. 1-85075-148-X [TDig 37,53]. – ᴿExpTim 101 (1989s) 282 (C. S. *Rodd*).
3338 **Fredericks** Daniel C., Qoheleth's language; re-evaluating its nature and date 1988 ➤ 4,3520: ᴿExpTim 100 (1988s) 390 (R. N. *Whybray*); JBL 108 (1989) 698-700 (A. *Schoors*: careful and valuable; mostly a criticism of methodology, but inclines to 700 B.C. date).

3339 **Isaksson** Bo, Studies in the language of Qoheleth ᴰ1987 ⇥ 3,3288; 4,3522: ᴿCBQ 51 (1989) 332s (R. E. *Murphy*); JBL 108 (1989) 510-2 (M. V. *Fox*); RÉJ 147 (1988) 445s (Mireille *Hadas-Lebel*); RSO 63 (1989) 310-2 (F. *Bianchi*).

3340 ᵀᴱ**Japhet** S., *Salters* R. B., Samuel B. MEIR (Rashbam), Commentary on Qohelet 1985 ⇥ 1,3369; 3,3289: ᴿRÉJ 146 (1987) 397-400 (J.-P. *Rothschild*).

3341 *Jarick* John, GREGORY Thaumaturgos' paraphrase of Ecclesiastes: Abr-Nahrain 27 (1989) 37-57.

3342 *Krašovec* Jože, [in Slovene] The problem of God's righteousness in Ecclesiastes: BogVest 47 (1987) 115-125; Eng. 126.

3343 *Kugel* James L., Qohelet and money: CBQ 61 (1989) 32-49.

3344 *Laumann* Maryta, Qoheleth and time: BToday 27 (1989) 305-310.

3345 **Lavoie** Jean-Jacques, Étude exégétique et intertextuelle du Qohélet; rapport entre Qohélet 1-11: diss. ᴰ*Couturier* G. Montréal 1989. 800 p. – RTLv 20, p. 540.

3346 **Loader** J. A., Ecclesiastes 1986 ⇥ 2,2531 ... 4,3524: ᴿWestTJ 50 (1988) 184s (T. *Longman*).

3347 **Maillot** Alphonse, Qohélét ou Ecclésiaste ou La contestation^{2rev} [¹1971], préf. *Caquot* A. P 1987, Bergers & M. xxiii-194 p. F 105. 2-85304-071-2. – ᴿÉTRel 64 (1989) 621 (D. *Lys*).

3348 **Michaud** Robert, Qohélét et l'hellénisme 1987 ⇥ 3,3295; 4,3526: ᴿGregorianum 70 (1989) 782s (G. L. *Prato*); ScEspr 41 (1989) 239-241 (J.-J. *Lavoie*); ScripTPamp 21 (1989) 696 (K. *Limburg*); SR 18 (1989) 94s (aussi J.-J. *Lavoie*).

3349 **Michaud** R., Qohelet y el helenismo, ᵀ*Ortiz García* A. Estella 1988, VDivino. 275 p. – ᴿBibFe 15 (1989) 323 (A. *Salas*); RelCu 35 (1989) 483s (M. A. *Martín Juárez*).

3350 **Michel** Diethelm, [*Lehmann* Reinhard G., Bibliog.], Untersuchungen zur Eigenart des Buches Qohelet: BZAW 183. B 1989, de Gruyter. vii-129 p. DM 118. 3-11-012161-1 [BL 90, 86, R. B. *Salters*].

3351 **Negenman** Johan, Prediker: Belichting BB. Brugge/Boxtel 1988, Tabor/Kath. BS. 110 p. ƒ17,50. – ᴿStreven 56 (1988s) 467 (P. *Beentjes*).

3352 **Niekerk** Martin J. H. van, 'n Ondersoek na die carpe-diem-element in die boek Qohelet: diss. ᴰ*Loader* J. Pretoria [RTLv 542 sub Van, sans date]. 205 p.

3353 **Ogden** Graham, Qoheleth: Readings Comm. 1987 ⇥ 4,3528: ᴿBL (1989) 60 (R. B. *Salters*); ETL 65 (1989) 429s (A. *Schoors*: *hebel* 'mysterious' not 'futile' and other courageous handlings of the Hebrew); RB 96 (1989) 140 (R. J. *Tournay*); ZAW 101 (1989) 165s (O. *Kaiser*).

3354 *Power* John, A surprisingly successful Preacher: Scripture in Church 18 (Dublin) 1988) 470-4 [< OTAbs 12,74].

3355 **Ravasi** Gianfranco, Qohelet 1988 ⇥ 4,3531: ᴿLetture 44 (1989) 273s (E. *Toniutto*); StCattMi 33 (1989) 951 (U. *De Martino*).

3356 **Schubert** Mathias, Schöpfungstheologie bei Kohelet [Diss. Lp 1986, ᴰ*Wagner* S.]: BeiErfAJ 15. Fra 1989, Lang. 212 p. 3-8204-1130-5 [OIAc Ja90].

3357 *Schubert* Mathias, Die Selbstbetrachtungen Kohelets, ein Beitrag zur Gattungsforschung: TVers 17 (1989) 23-34.

3358 *Siméon* Jean-Pierre, Le don du vivre: Qohélet: LumièreV 38, 191 (1989) 17-36.

3359 **Spangenberg** Izak J. J., Poems about death in the book of Ecclesiastes: diss. Unisa, ᴰ*Loader* J. Pretoria 1987. – DissA 50 (1989s) 2117s-A.

3360 **Strothmann** Werner, Das syrische Fragment des Ecclesiastes-Kommentars von THEODOR von Mopsuestia; syrischer Text mit vollständigem Wörterverzeichnis [not identical with → 4,3535-3537 cognates]: GöOrF syr. 28. Wsb 1988, Harrassowitz. xxviii-146 p. DM 36. 3-447-028521-1 [BL 90,47, S. *Brock* with the three others].

3361 *Thurn* Hans, Zum Text des HIERONYMUS-Kommentars zum Kohelet: BZ 33 (1989) 234-244 [etwa 250 wichtige und überraschende Abweichungen von ADRIAEN M., CCL 72,1959].

3362 *Trible* Phyllis, Ecclesiastes: → 377, Books 1 (1989) 231-9.

3363 *Vocht* Constant De, Deux manuscrits perdus de la Catena Trium Patrum in Ecclesiasten (CPG C 100]: Byzantion 59 (Bru 1989) 264-6.

3364 **Whybray** R. N., Ecclesiastes: NCent comm. GR/L 1989, Eerdmans/ Marshall-MS. xxiii-179 p. $14. 0-8028-0406-3 / L 0-551-01853-4. − RExpTim 101 (1989s) 153 (C. S. *Rodd*).

3365 **Whybray** R. N., Ecclesiastes: OT **Guides**. Sheffield 1989, Academic. 88 p. £5. 1-85075-211-7.

3366 *Wiedmann* F., Kohelet: p. 26-42 in: Anstössige Denker; die Wirklichkeit als Natur und Geschichte in der Sicht von Aussenseitern; Wü 1988, Königshausen & N. [ZAW 102,464].

3367 *Wright* Addison G., Ecclesiastes (Qoheleth): → 384, NJBC (1989) 489-495.

3368 *Lohfink* Norbert, *a)* Koh 1,2, 'alles ist Windhauch' — universale oder anthropologische Aussage?: → 45, FDEISSLER A., Weg 1989, 201-216; − *b)* Kohelet und die Banken; zur Übersetzung von Kohelet v 12-16: VT 39 (1989) 488-495.

3369 *Fredericks* Daniel C., Chiasm and parallel structure in Qoheleth 5:6-6:9: JBL 108 (1989) 17-35.

3370 *Garrett* Duane A., Ecclesiastes 7:25-29 and the feminist hermeneutic [...due partly to the expanding job market for women in academia]: CriswT 2 (1987s) 309-321.

3371 *a)* *Hoomissen* Guy van, 'Et je fais l'éloge de la joie' (Qoh 8,15); − *b)* *Tihon* Paul, Dieu nous a faits pour être heureux; − *c)* *Weber* Philippe, Bonheur et plaisirs, valeurs chrétiennes ?: LVitae 43 (1988) 37-46; Eng. 46 / 29-35; Eng. 35 'Are we created to be happy?' / 57-67; Eng. 67.

E7.8 *Liber Sapientiae* – **Wisdom of Solomon.**

3372 **Beentjes** P., Wijsheid van Salomo: Belichting, 1987 → 4,3550: RCollatVL 19 (1989) 229 (P. *Kevers*).

3373 *a)* *Collins* John J., Wisdom of Solomon; − *b)* *Mack* Burton L., Sirach (Ecclesiasticus): → 377, Books 2 (1989) 51-63 / 65-86.

3374 *Duclow* Donald F., Meister ECKHART on the Book of Wisdom; commentary and sermons: Traditio 43 (Fordham 1987) 215-235.

3375 *Gilbert* Maurice, La procréation; ce qu'en sait le Livre de la Sagesse: NRT 111 (1989) 824-841.

3376 *McHenry* Francis, Three daughters of wisdom: Greece [Sap. Sol.], China [Taoism], India [Bhagavadgita]: Living Word 94 (Alwaye 1988) 195-226 [< TContext 6/2, 33].

3377 **Scarpat** Giuseppe, Libro della Sapienza; testo, traduzione, introduzione e commento: Biblica Testi e Studi 1. Paideia 1989, Brescia. I. 478 p. 88-394-0429-5. − RRenovatio 24 (1989) 653s (A. *Ceresa-Gastaldo*).

3378 *Scarpat* G., La morte seconda e la duplice morte dalla Sapienza a S. FRANCESCO: Paideia 42 (1987) 55-62 [< JStJud 20,131 'Sapientia'].

3379 **Schmitt** Armin, Das Buch der Weisheit 1989: 3-429-01212-0 [= 1986 ➤ 2,2547; 4,3554]: ᴿCBQ 51 (1989) 131s (J. M. *Reese*).

3380 *Wright* Addison G., Wisdom: ➤ 384, NJBC (1989) 510-522.

3381 **Kolarcik** Michael, The ambiguity of death in the book of Wisdom 1-6; a study of literary structure and interpretation: diss. Pont. Ist. Biblico, ᴰ*Gilbert* M. R 1989. – AcPIB 9,5 (1988s) 384.423; Biblica 70,443; RTLv 21, p. 540.

3382 *a) Sindt* Gérard, Pour l'amour de la justice (Sagesse 1,16); – *b) Varro* Roger, Quel homme? quels droits? éléments de réflexion biblique [< Courrier de l'Assoc. des Chrétiens pour l'Abolition de la Torture 95 (mai 1989)]: Masses Ouvrières 426 (1989) 65-77 / 79-89.

3383 *Zenger* Erich, 'Du liebst alles, was ist' (Weish 11,24); biblische Perspektiven für einen erneuerten Umgang mit der Schöpfung: BiKi 44 (1989) 138-147.

3384 **Priotto** M., La prima Pasqua in Sap 18,5-25; rilettura e attualizzazione [diss. PIB 1985 ➤ 1,3391]: RivB Sup 15, 1987 ➤ 3,3319: ᴿBL (1989) 142 (R. *Murray*: rich, magisterial); RivB 37 (1989) 502s (F. *Festorazzi*).

3385 *Pié i Ninot* Salvador, Paraula de Déu i saviesa; Sv 18,14-16: ➤ 69*, ᶠGOMÀ I., RCatalT 14 (1989) 29-38; Eng. 39 (most significant chapter on the Word of God in Wisdom).

3386 *Dell'Omo* Mariano, Creazione, storia della salvezza e destino dell'uomo; il significato e l'attualità spirituale del capitolo 19 della Sapienza: RivB 37 (1989) 317-327.

E7.9 *Ecclesiasticus, Siracides;* **Wisdom of Jesus Sirach.**

3387 *Beentjes* Pancratius C., Relations between Ben-Sira and the Book of Isaiah; some methodical observations: ➤ 614, Isaiah Lv 1987/9, 155-9.

3388 *Di Lella* Alexander A., Sirach: ➤ 384, NJBC (1989) 496-509.

3388* **Gastaldi** Casimiro, Sapienza antica e nuova; appunti per una lettura del Siracide: Il seme e il frutto 12. Padova 1989, Messaggero. 115 p.

3389 **Michaud** Robert, Ben-Sira et le Judaïsme 1988 ➤ 4,3562: ᴿEsprVie 99 (1989) 480 (L. *Monloubou*, et non E. *Cothenet* comme indiqué, voir p. 550); EstBíb 47 (1989) 283-5 (G. *Flor Serrano*).

3390 **Minissale** Antonio, Siracide 1988 ➤ 4,3563: ᴿAsprenas 36 (1989) 108s (A. *Rolla*).

3391 *Owens* Robert J., The early Syriac text of Ben Sira in the Demonstration of APHRAHAT: JSS 34 (1989) 39-75.

3392 **Schnabel** Eckhard J., Law and wisdom from Ben Sira to Paul [diss. Aberdeen 1983]: WUNT 2/16, 1985 ➤ 4,3566: ᴿGregorianum 70 (1989) 143-7 (G. L. *Prato*).

3393 **Skehan** P. W. †, *Di Lella* A. A., The Wisdom of Ben Sira ...: AnchorB 39, 1987 ➤ 3,3329; 4,3567: ᴿBiblica 70 (1989) 272-4 (M. *Gilbert*); BL (1989) 62 (J. G. *Snaith*: definitive); CBQ 51 (1989) 350s (R. E. *Hann*); IrTQ 55 (1989) 166-8 (D. *O'Connor*); NRT 111 (1989) 584s (J.-L. *Ska*); TLZ 114 (1989) 111-3 (G. *Sauer*); TsTNijm 29 (1989) 62 (P. *Kevers*).

3394 **Thiele** W., Ecus 11/2, Einl., Schluss: VLat 11, 1988 ➤ 4,3568; Lfg 3, 1,1-3, p. 161-260, 1989: ᴿRHE 84 (1989) 504 (P.-M. *Bogaert*, 1s); TR 85 (1989) 285-7 (C. *Wahl*, 1s).

3395 **Wright** B. G., No small difference; Sirach's relationship to its parent Hebrew text: SeptCog 26. Atlanta 1989, Scholars. xx-354 p.; $20; sb./pa. $13. 1-55540-374-3; 5-1 [BL 90,48].

3395* *Wuckelt* Agnes, 'Hast du Söhne, so halte sie in Zucht... Hast du Töchter, so behüte sie...' (Sir 7,23f); Erziehung aus der Bibel: KatBlätt 114 (Mü 1989) 711-7 [< ZIT 89,746].

3396 *Beentjes* Pancratius C., 'Full wisdom is fear of the Lord'; Ben Sira 19,20 - 20,31; context, composition and concept: EstBíb 47 (1989) 27-45; español 27.

3397 *Wietkamp* Wilhelm, 'Schätze den Arzt — den auch ihn hat Gott erschaffen!' (Sir 38,1): ArztC 35 (1989) 235-8.

3398 *Qimron* Elisha, ❹ New readings [to four marginal notes] in Ben-Sira: Tarbiz 58 (1988s) 117; v: 38,16 bgwytm; 33,9 wtrdwp; 38,10 hsyr; whkr; 34,4 tp'rh.

3399 **Lee** Thomas R., Studies in the form of Sirach 44-50: SBL diss. 75, 1986 ➤ 2,2565... 4,3573: ᴿÉglT 19 (1988) 423s (L. *Laberge*); JSS 34 (1989) 201-3 (J. G. *Snaith*); JQR 80 (1989s) 203-5 (B. G. *Wright*).

3400 *Kieweler* H. V., [Sir 44,19-21] Abraham und der Preis der Väter bei Ben Sira: ➤ 2,99, ꟳSAUER G., Schaut Abraham an, euren Vater! = Amt und Gemeinde 37,7 (1986) 70-72 [OTAbs 11,171].

3401 **Mack** Burton L., [Sir 44,1-50,24] Wisdom and the Hebrew epic 1985 ➤ 1,3403... 4,3574: ᴿÉglT 19 (1988) 425s (L. *Laberge*).

3402 *Beentjes* P. C., Hezekiah and Isaiah; a study on Ben Sira xlviii 15-25: ➤ 129, ꟳMULDER M., New Avenues 1989, 77-88.

VIII. Libri prophetici VT

E8.1 **Prophetismus.**

3403 *Ahlström* G. W., Prophetical echoes of Assyrian growth and decline: ➤ 183, ꟳSJÖBERG A., Dumu- 1989, 1-6.

3404 **Amsler** S., *al.*, Les prophètes 1985 ➤ 2,2575; 3,3341: ᴿBZ 33 (1989) 296s (J. *Scharbert*); RICathP 29 (1989) 103s (J. *Lévêque*).

3405 [**Amsler** S., *al.*] I profeti e i libri profetici [1985]: Picc. Enc. Biblica 4, 1987 ➤ 4,3578: ᴿRivB 37 (1989) 501s (B. *Marconcini*); StPatav 36 (1989) 199-201 (M. *Milani*).

3406 *Árus* Lajos, ❿ Der Dienst der alttestamentlichen Propheten: Református Szemle 79 (1986) 100-111 [< ZAW 114,236].

3407 **Asurmendi** Jesús, El profetismo 1987 ➤ 4,3780: ᴿFranBog 30 (1988) 376s (A. *Morales D.*).

3408 **Barton** John, Oracles... after exile 1986 ➤ 2,2577... 4,3581: ᴿJTS 40 (1989) 159-162 (D. R. *Jones*: 'Prophets' meant 'anything but Torah', and was 'scripture' rather than 'canon'); TTod 46 (1989s) 216.218 (W. *Brueggemann*).

3409 **Beaucamp** Évode, Les prophètes d'Israël, ou le drame d'une alliance: Lire la Bible 75, 1987 ➤ 4,3582: ᴿScEspr 41 (1989) 115s (J.-C. *Filteau*).

3410 **Beaucamp** É., Los profetas de Israel o el drama de una alianza, ᵀOrtiz García A. [1968 = 1958], pról. J. M. *Abrego*. Estella 1988, VDivino. 278 p. 84-7151-588-1. – ᴿActuBbg 26 (1989) 34 (R. de *Sivatte*); BibFe

15 (1989) 170 (M. *Saenz Galache*); EstAgust 24 (1989) 527 (C. *Mielgo*); HumT 10,1 (1989) 118s (J. *Godinho de Lima*).

3411 **Beaucamp** Évode, I profeti d'Israele; o il dramma di un'alleanza: Fame e sete della Parola 3. CinB 1988, Paoline. 308 p. Lit. 18.000. 88-215-1621-0.

3412 *Beentjes* P. C., Oracles against the nations, a central issue in the 'latter prophets': Bijdragen 50 (1989) 203-9.

3413 **Berg** David A., The genre of non-juridical oracles (*ḥrtw*) in ancient Egypt: diss. ^D*Redford* D. Toronto 1989. – DissA 50 (1989s) 1770-A.

3414 **Bohorquez Ramos** Juan F., El temor de Yahweh en los profetas: diss. ^D*Ausín Olmos* S. Pamplona 1989. 343 p. – RTLv 21, p. 539.

^E**Borgonovo** Gianantonio, I profeti e i libri profetici 1987 → 380.

3415 **Bretón** Santiago, Vocación y misión, formulario profético [diss. 1984, ^D*Alonso Schökel* L.]: AnBib 111, 1987 → 3,3350: ^ROTAbs 12 (1989) 340 (C. F. *Mariottini*); VT 39 (1989) 243 (N. de *Lange*: fascinating wider implications); ZAW 101 (1989) 310 (J. A. *Soggin*: vollständig, nützlich).

3416 **Buber** Martin, Der Glaube der Propheten² 1984 → 65,2996; 1,3414: ^ROLZ 84 (1989) 305s (S. *Wagner*).

3417 *Carroll* Robert P., Prophecy and society: → 378, World 1989, 203-226.

3418 *Cimosa* Mario, Creazione e liberazione nei profeti: → 376, Creazione 1989, 33-54.

3419 *Darbanova* E. M., ❻ An ancient Mesopotamian [predictive] dream-book (observations on the structure of a text): VDI 190 (1989) 102-7; Eng. 107-8.

3420 **Dearman** John A., Property rights in the eighth-century prophets; the conflict and its background: SBL diss. 106, 1988 → 4,3595; 1-55540-192-9; pa. -5-3: ^RBL (1989) 103 (R. E. *Clements*); JBL 108 (1989) 693s (D. C. *Hopkins*); JRel 69 (1989) 396s (B. *Halpern*: a credit to Emory's doctorate program); VT 39 (1989) 119 (J. A. *Emerton*).

3421 **Deissler** Alfons, Dann wirst du Gott erkennen; die Grundbotschaft der Propheten 1987 → 3,3359; 4,3595*: ^RTPQ 137 (1989) 80 (Roswitha *Unfried*).

3422 *a) Deist* Ferdinand E., The prophets; are we headed for a paradigm switch?; – *b) Gerstenberger* Erhard S., 'Gemeindebildung' in Prophetenbüchern? Beobachtungen und Überlegungen zum Traditions- und Redaktionsprozess prophetischer Schriften; – *c) Duhm* Bernhard (mitgeteilt von Rudolf *Smend*) De inspiratione prophetarum [Lat. Studentenschrift 1871 'Dt.-Jes utrum propheta sit an poeta']: → 105, ^FKAISER O., Prophet 1989, 1-18 / 44-58 / 217-230.

3422* ^E**Eid** Volker, Prophetie und Widerstand: Theologie zur Zeit 5. Dü 1989, Patmos. p. 90-141, *Kegler* Jürgen, Prophetischer Widerstand [< IZBG 36, p. 91].

3423 *Ellis* Maria D., Observations on Mesopotamian oracles and prophetic texts; literary and historiographic considerations: JCS 41 (1989) 127-186.

3424 *Halpern* Bilhah, ❻ The significance of sacrifices in prophecy and law: BethM 32 (1986s) 358-363 [following Y. *Kaufmann*; < OTAbs 11,185].

3425 **Harbin** Michael A., Blessing and oracle; a study of the use of *brk* in prophetic formulae: diss. Dallas Theol. Sem. 1988. – 332 p. 89-13832. – DissA 50 (1989s) 1358s-A.

3426 *Hidal* Sten, Johannes LINDBLOMs syn på Israels profeter; ett exempel på samverkan mellan olika teologiska miljöer: SvTKv 65 (1989) 16-20.

3427 *Hill* Clifford, Prophecy past and present. L 1989, Highland. 306 p. £7. 0-946616-57-4. – ^RExpTim 101 (1989s) 82s (H. *Mowvley*).

3428 *Horine* Steven, A study of the literary genre of the woe oracle: CalvaryB 5,2 (1989) 74-97.

3429 *Ita* J. M., Biblical prophecy and its challenge to contemporary prophetic movements; a lay viewpoint: AfTJ 18 (Tanzania 1989) 3-16 [< TContext 7/1, 18].

3430 *Jensen* Joseph, Eighth-century prophets and apodictic law: ⇥ 60, ᶠFITZMYER J., Touch 1989, 103-117.

3431 **Keller** C. A., Tu m'as fait prophète; le ministère prophétique dans l'AT. Aubonne 1989, Moulin. 95 p. [ZAW 102, 306, H.-C. *Schmitt*].

3432 **Kraus** H.-J., Profetie vandaag; de actualiteit van de bijbelse profetie in de verkondiging, ᵀPoll E. W. van der. Haag 1988, Boekencentrum. 114 p. f 18,90. 90-239-0820-1. – ᴿGerefTTs 89 (1989) 186s (A. van der *Wal*).

3432* *Kreisel* Howard, ❿ The response of R. Judah b. Benjamin Ibn ROKESH concerning prophecy: KirSef 62 (1988s) 439-444.

3433 *a*) *LaSor* W. S., The Prophets during the monarchy; turning points in Israel's decline; – *b*) *Bullock* C. H., The priestly era in the light of prophetic thought; – *c*) *Hoffmeier* J. K., Egypt as an arm of flesh; a prophetic response; – *d*) *Watts* J. D. W., Babylonian idolatry in the Prophets as a false socio-economic system; – *e*) *Krause* A. E., Historical selectivity; prophetic prerogative or typological imperative?; – *f*) *Youngblood* R., A holistic typology of prophecy and apocalyptic: ⇥ 77, ᶠHARRISON R., Israel's Apostasy 1988, 59-70 / 71-78 / 79-97 / 115-122 / 175-212 / 213-221.

3433* *Malamat* A., Parallels between the new prophecies from Mari [ARM 26] and biblical prophecy: 1. predicting death of an infant; 2. material remuneration for prophetic services: NABU (Nouvelles assyriologiques brèves et utilitaires) 4 (1989) 61-64.

3434 ᴱMays J. L., *Achtemeier* P. J., Interpreting the prophets [< Interpretation 1978-85] 1987 ⇥ 3,352: ᴿBL (1989) 86 (R. P. *Carroll*).

3435 *Michaelsen* Peter, Ecstasy and possession in ancient Israel; a review of some recent contributions [*Petersen* D. 1981; *Parker* S. 1978; *Wilson* R. 1979; *Cryer* F. ...]: ScandJOT (1989,2) 28-54.

3436 **Miller** J. W., Meet the prophets; a beginner's guide to the books of the biblical prophets 1987 ⇥ 3,378; 4,3615: ᴿBL (1989) 87 (R. E. *Clements*); Interpretation 43 (1989) 314.316 (P. V. *Reid*: best in 15 years); RRel 48 (1987) 947s (B. A. *Asen*); ScripTPamp 21 (1989) 694 (S. *Ausín*: esplendido manual).

3437 **Newell** James O., The means of maintaining a right relationship with Yahweh; an investigation of selected passages of the Hebrew prophets of the eighth century B.C.: diss. Baptist Theol. Sem. ᴰSmith B. New Orleans 1988. 196 p. 89-11180. – DissA 50 (1989s) 710-A.

3438 **Overholt** Thomas W., Channels of prophecy; the social dynamics of prophetic activity. Minneapolis 1989, Fortress. xii-193 p. $20 [TR 86,426].

3439 *Porter* J. Roy, The supposed deuteronomic redaction of the prophets; some considerations: ⇥ 212, ᶠWESTERMANN C., Schöpfung 1989, 69-78.

3440 **Rofé** A., The prophetical stories 1988 ⇥ 64,3629: ᴿHenoch 11 (1989) 110-3 (P. *Sacchi*); JStOT 44 (1989) 124 (R. S. *Hess*).

3441 *Rottzoll* Dirk U., Die *kh 'mr* ... – legitimationsformel: VT 39 (1989) 323-340.

3442 **Sawyer** John F.A., Prophecy 1987 → 3,3387; 4,3630: ᴿScotJT 42 (1989) 411s (S.B. *Dawes*).

3442* *a*) *Scharbert* Josef, Der 'Geist' und die Schriftpropheten; – *b*) *Schreiner* Josef, Unter Gottes Treue [... Is]: → 45, ᶠDEISSLER A., Weg 1989, 82-97 / 62-81.

3443 **Schneider** Christoph, Krisis des Glaubens; zur Frage der sogenannten falschen Prophetie im AT: ThArb 46. B 1988, Ev.-VA. 138 p. DM 14,50. – ᴿTLZ 114 (1989) 804 (E. *Osswald*).

3444 **Schultz** Richard L., Prophecy and quotation; a methodological study: diss. ᴰ*Childs* B., Yale. NHv 1989. 465 p. 90-012323. – DissA 50 (1989s) 3932-A; RTLv 21,542.

3445 **Sicre** J.L., 'Con los pobres de la tierra' 1984 → 65,6034... 4,3633: ᴿRechSR 77 (1989) 375s (J. *Briend*); TR 85 (1989) 363s (E.S. *Gerstenberger*).

3446 **Sicre** José L., I profeti d'Israele e il loro messaggio [antologia 1986 → 2,2610], ᵀ*Tosatti* Teodora: Studi e Ricerche Bibliche. R 1989, Borla. 227 p. 88-263-0510-2.

3447 **Sicre** José Luis, *Castillo* José M., *Estrada* Juan A., La Iglesia y los profetas: En torno al Nuevo Testamento 5. Córdoba 1989, Almendro. 143 p. 84-86077-77-X.

3448 *Sicré* José Luis, *a*) La denuncia profética de la idolatría [dioses paganos; más tarde, potencias militares y riqueza]: Proyección 35 (1988) 3-21; – *b*) El Dios de los profetas; contra una imagen 'light' del Dios cristiano: SalT 76 (1988) 419-426.

3449 *Simian-Yofre* Horacio, La famiglia, segno di Dio nella profezia: → 587, Famiglia 1989, 115-135.

3450 **Smith** Gary V., The application of principles from the sociology of knowledge for understanding the setting, tradition, and theology of the Prophets: JEvTS 32 (1989) 145-158 [< ZIT 89,704].

3451 **Soares-Prabhu** George M., The prophet as theologian; biblical prophetism as a paradigm for doing theology today: AsiaJT 2,1 (1988) 3-11.

3452 **Stamey** Gary M., An exposition of prophetic literature as it relates to regeneration: diss. Dallas Theol. Sem. 1988. 277 p. 89-13839. – DissA 50 (1989s) 1343-A.

3453 **Stendebach** Franz J., Rufer wider den Strom; Sachbuch zu den Propheten Israels 1985 → 1,3450: ᴿZkT 111 (1989) 92s (J.M. *Oesch*).

3454 **Tångberg** K.A., Die prophetische Mahnrede...: FRL 143, 1987 → 3,3393; 4,3637: ᴿNRT 111 (1989) 579s (J.L. *Ska*); ZAW 101 (1989) 327s (G. *Wanke*).

3455 **Tomić** Celestin, Veliki proroci. Zagreb 1987, Franj. Konvent. 244 p. – ᴿBogSmot 59 (1989) 230s (A. *Rebić*).

3456 *Vawter* Bruce, Introduction to prophetic literature: → 384, NJBC (1989) 186-200.

3457 **Vernette** Jean, Peut-on prédire l'avenir?: Coll. C'est-à-dire 6. P 1989, Centurion. 126 p. F 54. – ᴿEsprVie 99 (1989) 474s (P. *Jay*: not about prophetism or the Bible; aims to deter dupes of charlatans, but will doubtless just suggest others to seek out).

3458 **Westermann** C., Prophetische Heilsworte: FRL 145, 1987 → 3,3398; 4,3645: ᴿJBL 108 (1989) 330-2 (M.S. *Moore*: adds 'comforting' to 'warning' prophecies of Grundformen 1964); NRT 111 (1989) 580s (J.-L. *Ska*); TsTNijm 29 (1989) 61 (J. *Lust*); ZkT 111 (1989) 87s (R. *Oberforcher*).

3459 **Wolff** Hans Walter, Studien zur Prophetie 1987 ➤ 3,320; 4,3647: ᴿCBQ 51 (1989) 779-781 (D. L. *Petersen*).

E8.2   **Proto-Isaias,** *textus, commentarii.*

3460 **Beuken** W. A. M.,   Jesaja III A-B. Nijkerk 1989, Callenbach.   282 p., 178 p. *f* 79,50; 65,50.   90-266-0204-9; -5-7. – ᴿStreven 57 (1989s) 1044 (P. *Beentjes*).

3461 **Cimosa** Mario,   Isaia, l'evangelista dell'Emmanuele (Is 1-39)²: Picc-BiblTeol 2. R 1988, Dehoniane.   235 p. Lit. 16.000.   88-396-0234-8 [BL 90, 53, C. J. A. *Hickling*]. – ᴿStCattMi 33 (1989) 84 (M. R.).

3461* *a*) *Gitay* Zefira,   Two master portraits of Isaiah [Raphael, Michelangelo]; – *b*) *Gitay* Yehoshua, Isaiah — the impractical prophet: BR 4,6 (1988) 16-19 / 10-15.

3462 **Gryson** Roger,   Esaias [Lfg. 1s ➤ 3,3401; Lfg. 3 (5,8-7,14) 1988 ➤ 4,3654] Lfg. 4 (Is 7,14-10,19): Vetus Latina 12.   FrB 1989, Herder. p. 241-320. – ᴿRCatalT 13 (1988) 244s (M. *Gros i Pujol*, 1); RB 96 (1989) 606s (F. J. *Gonçalves*, 1-3; also on Benedictine Vulgate Duodecim Proph.); RHE 84 (1989) 504 (P.-M. *Bogaert*, 1-3); VigChr 43 (1989) 297s (G. *Bartelink*, 2; also on Sir Heb).

3463 **Gryson** R.,   La tradition manuscrite du commentaire de Jérôme sur Isaïe; état de la question: ➤ 597*, ᴱ*Duval* Y., Jérôme Occident/Orient 1986/8, 403-425.

3464 *Haelewyck* J.-C.,   Le lemme vulgate du commentaire de Jérôme sur Isaïe: ➤ 597*, Jérôme Occident/Orient 1986/8, 391-402 [RHE 85,37*].

3465 **Hayes** J. H., *Irvine* S. A.,   Isaiah 1987 ➤ 4,3656: ᴿVT 39 (1989) 382s (H. *Williamson*).

3466 **Helfmeyer** Franz-Josef,   Isaia; il santo d'Israele tuo redentore [1984] ᵀ*Filippi* Emilio. Assisi 1989, Cittadella.   226 p. Lit. 15.000 [CC 140,3 dopo 448].

3467 **Jacob** Edmond,   Ésaïe 1-12: CommAT 8s, 1987 ➤ 3,3403; 4,3657: ᴿAntonianum 64 (1989) 197s (M. *Nobile*); CBQ 51 (1989) 520s (C. *Stuhlmueller*); ÉglT 20 (1989) 123-5 (L. *Laberge*); Protestantesimo 44 (1989) 292s (P. *Tognina*); SR 18 (1989) 91s (G. *Couturier*); VT 39 (1989) 511 (H. *Williamson*).

3468 **Jay** P.,   L'exégèse de s. JÉRÔME... Isaïe 1985 ➤ 1,3467... 4,3658: ᴿLatomus 48 (1989) 223s (P. *Hamblenne*); RechSR 77 (1989) 588-590 (Y.-M. *Duval*); SecC 7 (1989) 111-3 (P. J. *Gorday*); TR 85 (1989) 300s (K. S. *Frank*).

3469 *Jensen* Joseph, [*Irwin* William H.], Isaiah 1-23 [-39]: 384, NJBC (1989) 229-244 [-248].

3470 *Jeppesen* K.,   Jesajas bog fortolket.   K 1988, D-Bibelselskab.   315 p. Dk 245.   87-7523-238-3 [BL 90, 57, K. *Nielsen*].

3471 **Kaiser** O.,   Isaiah 1-12 [ATD⁵ 1981], ᵀ*Bowden* J. 1983 ➤ 64,3441... 1,3469: ᴿScotJT 42 (1989) 413s (R. *Carroll*).

3472 **Kilian** Rudolf, Jesaja 1-12: NEchter 1986 ➤ 2,2627... 4,3659: ᴿBO 46 (1989) 436-8 (P. *Höffken*); CBQ 51 (1989) 521s (W. E. *Lemke*).

3473 *a*) *Kooij* A. van der,   The Septuagint of Isaiah; translation and interpretation; – *b*) *Haelewyck* J.-C.,   L'édition de la Vetus Latina d'Isaïe; – *c*) *Talstra* Eep,   Grammar and prophetic texts; computer-assisted syntactical research in Isaiah: ➤ 614, Isaiah Lv 1987/9 127-133 / 135-145 / 83-91.

3474 **Mello** Alberto, Isaia, commento esegetico-spirituale. Magnano VC 1988 ['premessa' 1985], Qiqajon. 161 p.

3475 **Ohman** H. M., Een woord gesproken op zijn tijd; hoe lezen wij Jesaja 1-39 (Inaug. 1986). Franeker c. 1988, Van Wijnen. 145 p. f22,75. 90-5194-004-1. – ᴿTsTNijm 29 (1989) 287 (J. *Holman*).

3476 **Oswalt** John N., Is 1-39: NICOT, 1986 → 2,2628... 4,3661: ᴿCriswT 3 (1988s) 207s (G. L. *Klein*); ScriptB 20 (1989s) 17s (R. *Duckworth*).

3477 **Ridderbos** J., Isaiah: Bible Student's comm. 1985 → 1,3473... 4,3664: ᴿWestTJ 50 (1988) 186s (B. L. *Johnson*).

3478 *Syrén* Roger, The Isaiah-Targum and Christian interpretation: ScandJOT (1989,1) 46-65 [< OTAbs 12,193].

3479 **Watts** John D. W., Is 1-33: Word **comm.** 24, 1985 → 2,2632: ᴿCriswT 2 (1987s) 170s (G. *Galeotti*: unacceptable); ScotJT 42 (1989) 414-6 (R. *Carroll*); WestTJ 50 (1988) 188-190 (M. *Futato*).

3480 **Watts** J. D. W., Isaiah 34-66: Word Comm. 25, 1987 → 3,3417; 4,3668: ᴿCBQ 51 (1989) 136-8 (C. *Stuhlmueller*, grateful for 'total canonical approach' and much else); JTS 40 (1989) 155-7 (R. E. *Clements*); TLZ 114 (1989) 804-9 (O. *Kaiser*, 1s).

3481 **Watts** J. D. W., Isaiah: Word-**Themes**. Dallas 1989, Word. xi-120 p. $10. 0-8499-0699-5 [BL 90,95, W. J. *Houston*].

E8.3   [Proto-]**Isaias 1-39**, *themata, versiculi.*

3481 **Bello** Antonio, Sui sentieri di Isaia. Molfetta c. 1989, Meridiana. 240 p. Lit. 18.000. – ᴿStCattMi 33 (1989) 793 (Maria ₍Palmiotti: 'pericoloso sporgersi').

3482 *a) Bovati* Pietro, Le langage juridique du prophète Isaïe; – *b) Davies* G. I., The destiny of the nations in the book of Isaiah; – *c) Begg* C. T., Babylon in the book of Isaiah: → 614, Isaiah Lv 1987/9, 177-196 / 93-120 / 121-5.

3483 *Brekelmans* Christiaan H. W. [to whom the volume is dedicated, with an appreciation and bibliography p. 5-10 by J. *Lust*], Deuteronomistic influence in Isaiah 1-12: → 614, Isaiah Lv 1987/9, 167-176.

3484 *Clements* Ronald E., Isaiah: → 377, Books 1 (1989) 247-279.

3485 *Dietrich* Walter, Jesaja: → 894, EvKL 2 (1988) 813-8.

3486 *Gevaryahu* Hayim M. I., The school of Isaiah; biography and transmission of the book of Isaiah [lecture NYU 1976]: JBQ (= Dor) 18 (1989s) 62-68.

3487 *a) Gitay* Yehoshua, Isaiah – the impractical prophet; – *b) Gitay* Zefira, Two master portraits of Isaiah [Michelangelo, Raphael]: BR 4,6 (1988) 10-15 / 16-19 [< OTAbs 12,193].

3488 **Høgenhaven** Jasper, Gott und Volk bei Jesaja 1988 → 4,3673: ᴿVT 39 (1989) 510 (H. *Williamson*).

3489 *Le Saux* Madeleine, Isaïe dans son temps: DossB 23 (1988) 3-7 [-25, *al.*].

3490 *Ma Wonsuk*, The Spirit (*ruaḥ*) of God in Isaiah 1-39: AsiaJT 3 (1989) 582-596.

3491 **Nielsen** Kristen, There is hope for a tree; the tree as metaphor in Isaiah [1-39]: JStOT Sup 65. Sheffield 1989, Academic. 301 p. £27.50, sb. £20.50. 1-85075-182-X. – ᴿETL 65 (1989) 427s (J. *Lust*: rich content, new methods).

3492 **Schmitt** John J., Isaiah and his interpreters 1986 → 2,2644... 4,3676: ᴿCBQ 51 (1989) 132s (P. J. *Griffin*, unsatisfied); TXav 39 (1989) 498s (R. *Schneck*).

3493 **Seitz** Christopher R.,   Reading and preaching the book of Isaiah. Ph
1988, Fortress. 126 p. 0-8006-2056-9. – ᴿRExp 86 (1989) 115 (J. D. W.
Watts).

3494 **Simian-Yofre** Horacio,   Studi sul Profeta Isaia I-II.   R 1989, Pont. Ist.
Biblico. 166 p. [AcPIB 9/5, 362].

3495 *Talmon* Shemaryahu,   a) Observations on variant readings in the Isaiah
scroll (1QIsaᵃ) [➌ ᶠ*Auerbach* E. 1 (1956) 147-156]; – b) 1QIsaᵃ as a
witness to ancient exegesis of the book of Isaiah [< ASTI 1 (1962) 62-72]:
➤ 365, Qumran 1989, 117-130 / 131-141.

3496 **Troxel** Ronald L.,   Eschatology in the Septuagint of Isaiah: diss.
Wisconsin, ᴰ*Fox* M.   Madison 1989. 309 p. 89-17673. – DissA 50 (1989s)
2941-A.

3497 a) *Vermeylen* Jacques,   L'unité du livre d'Isaïe; – b) *Bogaert* Pierre-
Maurice,   L'organisation des grands recueils prophétiques; – c) *Kaiser*
Otto,   Literarkritik und Tendenzkritik; Überlegungen zur Methode des
Jesajaexegese: ➤ 614, Isaiah Lv 1987/9, 11-53 / 147-153 / 55-71.

3498 **Sweeney** Marvin A.,   Isaiah 1-4 and the post-exilic understanding of the
Isaianic tradition [diss. Claremont 1983, ᴰ*Knierim* R.]: BZAW 171, 1988
➤ 4,3679: ᴿBiblica 70 (1989) 267-9 (H. *Simian-Yofre*); BL (1989) 94
(A. G. *Auld*); BLitEc 90 (1989) 127s (M. *Delcor*); ExpTim 100 (1988s) 65s
(R. *Carroll*); ZkT 111 (1989) 97 (G. *Fischer*).

3499 *Luc* ₐAlex,   Isaiah I as structural introduction: ZAW 101 (1989) 115
only.

3500 *Barbiero* Gianni,   'Venite, discutiamo!' Lettura unitaria di Is 1,2-20:
Salesianum 51 (1989) 811-824.

3501 *Bottino* Adriana,   Il sangue di tori e di agnelli e di capri io non lo
gradisco (Is 1,11): ➤ 750, Sangue VI, 1987/9, 683-690.

3502 *Rogers* Jeffrey S.,   An allusion to coronation in Isaiah 2:6   CBQ 51
(1989) 232-6.

3503 *Baumgarten* Joseph M.,   [Is 5,1-7] 4Q500 and the ancient conception of
the Lord's vineyard: JJS 40 (1989) 1-6.

3504 *Haelewyck* Jean-Claude,   Le cantique de la vigne; histoire du texte vieux
latin d'Is 5,1-7(9a): ETL 65 (1989) 257-279.

3505 *Korpel* M. C. A.,   The literary genre of the Song of the Vineyard (Isa
5,1-7): ➤ 410, Structural/poetry 1988, 119-155.

3506 *Tromp* N. J.,   Un démasquage graduel; lecture immanente d'Is 5,1-7:
➤ 614, Isaiah Lv 1987/9, 197-202.

3507 *Wrembek* Christoph,   Fünf Weinberg-Gleichnisse [Jes 5,1-7; 27,2-6; Mt
21,33-46; Lk 13,6-9; Joh 15,1-8], eine geistliche Schriftbetrachtung:
GeistL 62 (1989) 260-277.

3508 *Hurowitz* Victor (Avigdor),   [Is 6] Isaiah's impure lips and their
purification in light of mouth purification and mouth purity in Akkadian
sources: HUCA 60 (1989) 39-89.

3509 a) *Rendtorff* Rolf,   Jesaja 6 im Rahmen der Komposition des Je-
sajabuches; – b) *Wieringen* Archibald van,   Jesaja 6-12; die Ve-
getationsbildsprache und die prophetische Struktur; – c) *Nobile* Marco,
Jes 6 und Ez 1,1-3,15; Vergleich und Funktion im jeweiligen
redaktionellen Kontext: ➤ 614, Isaiah Lv 1987/9, 73-82 / 203-7 / 209-216.

3510 **Wagner** Renate,   Textexegese als Strukturanalyse; Sprachwissenschaftliche Methode zur Erschliessung althebräischer Texte am Beispiel des

Visionsberichtes Jes 6,1-11; AOtt 32. St. Ottilien 1989, EOS. ix-228 p. DM 45. 3-88096-532-3 [JBL 109,381].

3511 *Bakon* Shimon, [Is 6,1-3] Kedusha – holiness: Dor 16 (1987s) 2-9 [< OTAbs 11,181].

3512 **Evans** Craig A., To see and not perceive; Isaiah 6,9-10 in early Jewish and Christian interpretation: JStOT Supp 64. Sheffield 1989, Academic. 264 p. £23.50 / sb. £17.50. 1-85075-172-2. – ᴿExpTim 101 (1989s) 212 (A. *Hanson*).

3513 *a) Høgenhaven* Jesper, Die symbolischen Namen in Jesaja 7 und 8 im Rahmen der sogenannten 'Denkschrift' des Propheten; – *b) Gitay* Yehoshua, Isaiah and the Syro-Ephraimite war: ⇒ 614, Isaiah Lv 1987/9, 231-5 / 217-230.

3514 *Höffken* Peter, Grundfragen von Jesaja 7,1-17 im Spiegel neuerer Literatur: BZ 33 (1989) 25-42.

3515 **Aubet** Adrian, Die Immanuelperikoop en die Messias vraagstuk (The Immanuel-Pericope and the Messiah problem; a literary-critical and redaction-historical investigation into the memoir of Isaiah): diss. ᴰ*Deist* F. Pretoria 1989. – RTLv 21, p. 539.

3516 **Irvine** Stuart A., King and prophet; Isaiah's relationship with Ahaz during the Syro-Ephraimite war: diss. Emory, ᴰ*Hayes* J. Atlanta 1989. 584 p. 90-06163. – DissA 50 (1989s) 3259-A; RelStR 16, 189; RTLv 21, p. 540.

3517 *Kronholm* Tryggve, Den kommande Hiskia; ett forsök att förstå den messianska interpretationen (Matt 1,18-25) av Immanuelsprofetian (Jes 7,14) i ljuset av några rabbinska texter: SvEx 54 (1989) 109-117.

3518 **Laato** Antti, Who is Immanuel? The rise and the foundering of Isaiah's messianic expectations 1988 ⇒ 4,3687: ᴿBL (1989) 84 (W. J. *Houston*); ETL 65 (1989) 158s (J. *Lust*: logical, not always convincing); ÉTRel 64 (1989) 433s (D. *Lys*: le meilleur depuis VISCHER ÉTRel 1954); TLZ 114 (1989) 665s (C. *Dohmen*).

3519 *Gryson* Roger, Barachie et la prophétesse; exercice de critique textuelle sur Isaïe 8,2-3: RB 96 (1989) 321-337.

3520 *Stachowiak* Lech, ❻ The prince of peace (Is 8,23-9,6): RoczTK 33,1 (1986) 23-35: deutsch 35.

3521 *Jagt* Krijn A. van der, Wonderful counsellor... (Isaiah 9,6) [Dutch 'powerful administrator']: BTrans 40 (1989) 441-5 [rather 'one who plans (and executes) wonders (of salvation)', but this does not sound enough like a title].

3522 *a) Mittmann* Siegfried, 'Wehe ! Assur, Stab meines Zorns' (Jes 10,5-9.13ab-15); – *b) Perlitt* Lothar, Jesaja und die Deuteronomisten: ⇒ 105, ᶠKAISER O., Prophet 1989, 111-132 / 133-149.

3523 *Schroer* Silvia, [Is 10,27-11,9] 'Aus abgehacktem Baumstumpf neues Leben'; Jesajas Vision von Gerechtigkeit, Frieden und Bewahrung der Schöpfung: BiKi 44 (1989) 154-7.

3524 *a) Jenkins* A. K., The development of the Isaiah tradition in Is 13-23; – *b) Clements* R. E., Isaiah 14,22-27; a central passage reconsidered: ⇒ 614, Isaiah Lv 1987/9, 237-251 / 253-262.

3525 **Gosse** Bernard, Isaïe 13,1-14,23...: OBO 78, 1988 ⇒ 4,3691: ᴿAntonianum 64 (1989) 198s (M. *Nobile*); ArTGran 52 (1989) 251s (J. L. *Sicre*); BL (1989) 76 (R. E. *Clements*); JBL 108 (1989) 690-2 (M. A. *Sweeney*).

3526 **Brangenberg** John H.ᴵᴵᴵ, A reexamination of the date, authorship, unity and function of Isaiah 13-23: diss. Golden Gate Baptist Theol. Sem. ᴰ*Eakins* J. K. 1989. 498 p. 89-23157. – DissA 50 (1989s) 2093-A.

3527 *Burns* John B., Does Helel 'go to Hell'? Isaiah 14:12-15: ProcGLM 9 (1989) 89-97.

3528 *Wessels* W. J., Isaiah of Jerusalem and the royal court; Isaiah 22:15-25, a paradigm for restoring just officials: OTEssays 2/2 (Pretoria 1989) 1-13.

3529 **Johnson** Dan G., From chaos to restoration — an integrative reading of Isaiah 24-27 [dated c. 500]: JStOT Sup 61, 1988 ⇒ 4,3696: ᴿBL (1989) 79 (R. P. *Carroll*); ÉTRel 64 (1989) 616 (François *Smyth*); ExpTim 100 (1988s) 270 (R. *Coggins*); RExp 86 (1989) 620s (J. D. W. *Watts*: hidden presumptions).

3530 *Caquot* André, Remarques sur le 'banquet des nations' en Ésaïe 25,6-8 [not invitations to a banquet; not 'God swallows death' but 'death had swallowed']: RHPR 69 (1989) 109-119; Eng. 241.

3531 *Staudigel* Helgalinde, Hermeneutische Überlegungen zu einer triumphalen Glosse in Jesaja 25,6-8: TVers 17 (1989) 9-13.

3532 *Haelewyck* Jean-Claude, Le cantique 'De nocte'; histoire du texte vieux latin d'Is. 26,9b-20(21): RBén 99 (1989) 7-34.

3533 *Graffy* Adrian, 'The Lord however says this'; the prophetic disputation speech [Is 28,14-19; 49,14-25; Ezek 37,11-13]: ScriptB 20 (1989s) 2-8.

3534 *Stewart* Alistair C., [Is 28,15.18] The covenant with death in Isaiah 28: ExpTim 100 (1988s) 375-7.

3535 *Lust* Johan, Isaiah 34 and the *ḥerem*: ⇒ 614, Isaiah Lv 1987/9, 275-286.

3535* *Coetzee* J. H., Is 38,9-20; *Venter* J., Isaiah & Jerusalem: OTEssays 2/3 (1988) 13... / 27...

E8.4 Deutero-Isaias 40-52: commentarii, themata, versiculi.

3536 *Abe* G. O., The messianic theology of Deutero-Isaiah; the challenges of mission to the 20th century African churches: AfTJ 18 (1989) 61-70 [< TContext 7/1, 18].

3537 *André* Gunnel, Deuterojesaja och Jobsboken, en jämförande studie: SvEx 54 (1989) 33-42.

3538 *a*) *Christensen* D. L., A new Israel; the righteous from among all nations; – *b*) *Merrill* E. H., Pilgrimage and procession; motifs of Israel's return; – *c*) *McCready* W. O., 'The day of small things' vs. the Latter Days: historical fulfillment or eschatological hope?; – *d*) *Coleson* J. E., Israel's life cycle from birth to resurrection: ⇒ 77, ᶠHARRISON R., Israel's Apostasy and Restoration 1988, 251-9 / 261-272 / 223-236 / 237-250.

3538* **Fohrer** Georg, Jesaja 40-66; Deuterojesaja / Tritojesaja: Z BK AT 19,3. Z 1986, Theol.-V. 288 p.

3539 **Harner** Philip B., Grace and law Second Isaiah 1988 ⇒ 4,3705: ᴿJBL 108 (1989) 697s (M. C. *Lind*).

3540 *a*) *Hermisson* H. J., Einheit und Komplexität Deuterojesajas; Probleme der Redaktionsgeschichte von Jes 40-55; – *b*) *Goudoever* J. van, The celebration of the Torah in the Second Isaiah: ⇒ 614, Isaiah Lv 1987/9, 287-312 / 313-7.

3541 **Hessler** Eva, Das Heilsdrama; der Weg zur Weltherrschaft Jahwes (Jes 40-55) [< Diss. 1960]: RelWTSt 2. Hildesheim 1988, Olms. 447 p. DM 58. 3-487-09112-7 [ZAW 102, 304, H. C. *Schmitt*].

3542 **Jerger** Günter, Evangelium des ATs; die Grundbotschaft des Propheten Deuterojesaja in ihrer Bedeutung für die Religions-Unterricht [Diss. Fr.]:

SBB 14, 1986 ➤ 2,2681 ... 4,3707:   ᴿBL (1989) 107 (A.*Gelston*: two-thirds is on Freiburg archdiocese Catholic teaching since 1800); RelStR 15 (1989) 69 (C. *Bernas*).

3543 **Knight** George A. F.,   Servant theology; a commentary on the book of Isaiah 40-55: IntTComm 1984 ➤ 65,3125 ... 3,3470:   ᴿRExp 86 (1989) 433 (T. G. *Smothers*).

3544 **Leene** H.,   De vroegere en de nieuwe dingen bij Deuterojesaja [proefschrift ᴰ*Beuken* W.]. Amst 1987, Vrije Univ. xii-331 p. 90-6256-340-6. – ᴿETL 65 (1989) 159s (J. *Lust*: new approach); TsTNijm 29 (1989) 61s (A. *Schoors*).

3545 *Leene* H.,   Deuterojesaja en de val van Babel: AmstCah 8 (1987) 28-39 [40-44, Vervolgreferaat, *Beuken* W.: < GerefTTs 89,61].

3546 *Martin-Achard* R.,   Création et salut; l'exemple du second Ésaïe: ➤ 450, ᴱ*Cardon* P., Dieu 1987/8, ...

3547 **Say Pa** Anna May,   The concept of Israel's role regarding the nations in Isaiah 40-55: diss. Princeton Theol. Sem. 1989, ᴰ*Seow* C.   312 p. 89-23110. – DissA 50 (1989s) 2935s-A; RelStR 16,189.

3548 *Stuhlmueller* Carroll,   Deutero-Isaiah and Trito-Isaiah: ➤ 3984, NJBC (1989) 329-348.

3548* *a) Weippert* Manfred,   Die 'Konfessionen' Deuterojesajas; – *b) Sæbø* Magne,   Vom Individuellen zum Kollektiven; zur Frage einiger innerbiblischer Interpretationen: ➤ 212, ᶠWESTERMANN C., Schöpfung 1989, 104-115 / 116-125.

3549 *Rüterswörden* Udo,   Erwägungen zur Metaphorik des Wassers in Jes 40 ff: ScandJOT (1989,2) 1-22.

3550 *a) Clines* D. J. A.,   The parallelism of greater precision; notes from Isaiah 40 for a theory of Hebrew poetry; – *b) Walsh* J. T.,   A case for the prosecution; Isaiah 41:21-42:17: ➤ 2987, Directions 1987, 77-100 / 101-118.

3551 *Merendino* Rosario P.,   Is 40,1-2, un'analisi del materiale documentario: RivB 37 (1989) 1-64.

3552 **Kern** Brigitte A. A.,   Tröstet ... Jes 40,1, PesR 30 & 29/30: FraJudSt 7, 1986 ➤ 2,2688; 3,3482:   ᴿKairos 30s (1988s) 250s (G. *Stemberger*).

3553 *Fitzgerald* Aloysius,   The technology of Isaiah 40:19-20 + 41:6-7: CBQ 51 (1989) 426-446.

3554 *Fangmeier* Jürgen,   Aufbruch zur Haushalterschaft (Jes 40,26-31): TBei 20 (1989) 281-4 [< ZIT 90,22].

3555 *Hardmeier* Christof,   'Geschwiegen habe ich seit langem ... wie die Gebärende schreie ich jetzt'; zur Komposition und Geschichtstheologie von Jes 42,14-44,23: WDienst 20 (1989) 155-179.

3556 *Helewa* Giovanni,   [Is 43,7] 'Per la mia gloria li ho creati': Teresianum 40 (1989) 435-478.

3557 *Baltzer* Klaus,   Schriftauslegung bei Deuterojesaja? — Jes 43,22-28 als Beispiel: ➤ 169, ᶠSCHARBERT J., Väter 1989, 11-16.

3558 *Sawyer* J. F. A.,   Christian interpretations of Isaiah 45:8 ➤ 614, Isaiah Lv 1987/9, 319-323.

3559 *Texier* Roger,   Le Dieu caché de PASCAL et du Second Isaïe [45,15]: NRT 111 (1989) 3-23.

3560 *Janzen* J. Gerald, An echo of the Shema [Dt 6,4s] in Isaiah 51.1-3: JStOT 43 (1989) 69-82.

E8.5 *Isaiae 53ss, Carmina Servi YHWH:* **Servant-Songs.**

3561 *Beauchamp* Paul, Lecture et relectures du quatrième chant du Serviteur; d'Isaïe à Jean: ⇢ 614, Isaiah Lv 1987/9, 325-355.
3562 **Koenig** J., Oracles et liturgies de l'exil [... Is 40; 53] 1988 ⇢ 4,3713: ᴿJTS 40 (1989) 525-8 (R. N. *Whybray:* the 'Servant' is the 'exilic synagogue' group); Muséon 102 (1989) 195-8 (J.-C. *Haelewyck*); NRT 111 (1989) 931s (J.-L. *Ska*); RB 96 (1989) 614s (R. J. *Tournay*).
3563 **Mettinger** Tryggve N. D., A farewell to the servant songs 1983 ⇢ 64,3525 ... 2,2705: ᴿWeltOr 20s (1989s) 304-7 (B. *Janowski*).
3564 *Ruprecht* Eberhard, Knecht Gottes: ⇢ 894, EvKL 2 (1989) 1315-7.
3565 *Sawyer* John F. A., Daughter of Zion and Servant of the Lord in Isaiah; a comparison: JStOT 44 (1989) 89-107.
3566 **Simian-Yofre** Horacio, I testi del Servitore di Jahwe nel Deuteroisaia. R 1989, Pont. Ist. Biblico. 108 p.; 8 pl. [AcPIB 9/5, 362].

3567 *a)* *Odasso* Giovanni, La missione universale del 'Servo del Signore' (Is 42,1-4); – *b)* *Magnante* Antonio, Missione e consolazione nella Bibbia: EuntDoc 42 (1989) 371-390 / 391-422.
3568 *Syrén* Roger, Targum Isaiah 52:13 - 53:12 and Christian interpretation: JJS 40 (1989) 201-212.
3568* *Cranfield* C. E. B., [Is 53,6] God's costly forgiveness: ExpTim 101 (1989s) 178-180.

3569 *Steck* Odil H., Beobachtungen zur Anlage von Jes 54,1-8: ZAW 101 (1989) 282-5.
3570 *Spykerboer* H. C., Isaiah 55:1-5, the climax of Deutero-Isaiah, an invitation to come to the New Jerusalem: ⇢ 614, Isaiah Lv 1987/9, 357-9.
3571 *Brueggemann* Walter, A poem of summons (Is. 55:1-3) / a narrative of resistance (Dan. 1:1-12): ⇢ 212, ᶠWESTERMANN C., Schöpfung 1989, 126-136.
3572 *Kaiser* Walter C., The unfailing kindnesses promised to David; Isaiah 55.3: JStOT 45 (1989) 91-98.

E8.6 [Trito-] **Isaias 56-66.**

3573 **Polan** Gregory J., In the ways of justice toward salvation ... Is 56-59, ᴰ1986 ⇢ 2,2709: ᴿAngelicum 66 (1989) 326s (J. *Agius*).
3574 **Sekine** S., Die tritojesanische Sammlung (Jes 56-66) redaktionsgeschichtlich untersucht [ev. Diss. München 1984, ᴰ*Jeremias* Jörg]: BZAW 175. B 1989, de Gruyter. xi-303 p. DM 138. 3-11-011633-2 [BL 90, 92, R. N. *Whybray*].
3575 *Kennedy* Charles A., Isaiah 57:5-6; tombs in the rocks: BASOR 275 (1989) 47-52.
3576 *Koenen* Klaus, *a)* Zum Text von Jesaja LVII 12-13A: VT 39 (1989) 236-9; – *b)* Zur Aktualisierung eines Deuterojesajawortes in Jes 58,8: BZ 33 (1989) 255-8.
3577 *Gosse* Bernard, L'alliance d'Isaïe 59,21: ZAW 101 (1989) 116-8.
3578 *a)* *Steck* O. H., Tritojesaja im Jesajabuch; – *b)* *Rofé* Alexander, Isaiah 59:19 and Trito-Isaiah's vision of redemption; – *c)* *Beuken* Wim A. M.,

Servant and herald of good tidings; Isaiah 61 as an interpretation of Isaiah 40-55; – *d*) *Ruiten* J. van, The influence and development of Is 65,17 in 1 En 91,16: ➤ 614, Isaiah Lv 1987/9, 361-406 / 407-410 / 411-442 / 161-6.

3579 **Neufeld** T., God and the saints at war... Is 59: diss. Harvard 1989.

3580 **Langer** Birgit, Gott als 'Licht' in Israel und Mesopotamien; eine Studie zu Jes 60,1-3. 19f: ÖstBSt 7. Klosterneuburg 1989, ÖstKBW. viii-255 p. DM 29,40. 3-85-396-078-2. – ᴿNRT 111 (1989) 932s (J. L. *Ska*).

3581 *Pinto* Henrique, Isaiah 61:1-2a in liberation theology: ChAfChr 5,2 (1989) 11-42 [= Chiea, < TContext 7/1, 19].

3582 *Clifford* Richard J., Narrative and lament in Isaiah 63:7-64:11: ➤ 60, ᶠFITZMYER J., Touch 1989, 93-102.

3583 **Fischer** Irmtraud, Wo ist JHWH, unser Vater? Das Volksklagelied Jes 63,7-64,11 als Ausdruck des Ringens um eine gebrochene Beziehung [kath. Diss. ᴰ*Marböck*; Graz 1988s ➤ 4,3739]: SBB 19. Stu 1989, KBW. vi-326 p. DM 39 [TR 86,249].

3584 *Beuken* Wim, Does Trito-Isaiah reject the Temple? An intertextual inquiry into Isa. 66,1-6: ➤ 95, ᶠIERSEL B. van 1989, 53-66.

E8.7 Jeremias.

3585 **Alba Cecilia** Amparo, Biblia babilónica, Jeremías: TEstCisn 41, 1987 ➤ 3,3510: ᴿJQR 80 (1989s) 417s (E. J. *Revell*); ZAW 101 (1989) 309s (I. *Kottsieper*).

3586 **Brueggemann** Walter, To pluck up, to tear down, Jer 1-25; GR 1988 ➤ 4,3746; also E 1988, Handsel. 222 p. £6.75. 0-9053-1287-2 [ÉTRel 64,481].

3587 **Carroll** Robert F., Jeremiah 1986 ➤ 2,2718... 4,3748: ᴿBASOR 275 (1989) 81-83 (H. T. C. *Sun*); CBQ 51 (1989) 115s (D. E. *Morgan*: balanced; approach open to question); EstAg 23 (1988) 701s (C. *Mielgo*, también su HOLLADAY - I).

3588 **Goldman** Amir P., Origines littéraires de la forme massorétique de Jérémie: diss. cath. ᴰ*Barthélemy* D. Fribourg/S 1988s. 230 p. – TR 85 (1989) 513; RTLv 21, p. 540.

3589 **Guest** John, Jeremiah, Lamentations: Communicator's Comm. Waco 1988, Word. 390 p. $15. 0-8499-0423-4. – ᴿBS 146 (1989) 233 (C. H. *Dyer*); RExp 86 (1989) 619 (J. D. W. *Watts*; fine style but overgeneralizes).

3590 **Herrmann** S., Jeremia (1,1-19): BK AT 12/1, 1986 ➤ 4,3754: ᴿBL (1989) 55 (R. P. *Carroll*: at this rate, 2000 p.).

3591 **Holladay** William L., Jeremiah [I. 1986 ➤ 2,3725... 4,3755]; II (ch. 26-52): Hermeneia comm., ᴱ*Hanson* Paul D. Minneapolis 1989, Fortress. xxxi-543 p. $45. 0-8006-6022-6 [TDig 36,373]. – ᴿCiuD 202 (1989) 500s (J. L. del *Valle*, 1); CriswT 3 (1988s) 205-7 (D. A. *Garrett*, 1); ExpTim 101 (1989s) 275s (C. S. *Rodd*: introduction came too late; both volumes hard to use); ScotJT 42 (1989) 113-6 (R. P. *Carroll*, 1); SWJT 32,1 (1989s) 46 (H. B. *Hunt*, 1); VT 39 (1989) 510s (H. *Williamson*, 1).

3592 **McKane** William, ICC Jeremiah I, 1986 ➤ 2,2728... 4,3761: ᴿAntonianum 64 (1989) 470-3 (M. *Nobile*); EstAg 23 (1988) 426 (C. *Mielgo*).

3593 **Martens** Elmer A., Jeremiah: Believers Comm. 1986 ➤ 2,2729... 4,3746: ᴿWestTJ 51 (1989) 159s (D. A. *Brueggemann*).

3594 *Miller* Merrill P., Is a Targum a systemic document? The case of the Targum of Jeremiah: ➤ 592, Systemic 1 (1989) 143-166.

3594* *Nissinen* Martti, Jeremian kirjan synty [Die Entstehung des Jeremia-buches]: Teologinen Aikakauskirja 94,1 (Helsinki 1989) 15-28 [< IZBG 36, p. 102].

3595 **Soderlund** Sven, The Greek text of Jeremiah 1985 ➤ 2,2741 ... 4,3768: ᴿBZ 33 (1989) 307s (Helga *Weippert*); EstFranc 90 (1989) 302s (F. *Raurell*); ÉTRel 64 (1989) 280 (D. *Bourguet*); HeythJ 30 (1989) 353-5 (J. M. *Dines*).

3596 **Strobel** A., Geremia – Lamentazioni – Baruc; cordoglio per Gerusa-lemme, ᵀ*Pulit* Gianni. Assisi 1989, Cittadella. 181 p. Lit. 12.000 [CC 140,3 dopo 448].

3597 **Stulman** Louis, The other text of Jeremiah 1985 ➤ 2,2743 ... 4,3769: ᴿEstFran 90 (1989) 306s (F. *Raurell*).

3598 *Ball* Jeffrey D., Towards a new understanding of the Jeremiah scroll; the problem and recent scholarship: Studia Biblica et Theologica 13 (1983) 51-75 [< OTAbs 12 (1989) 195s].

3599 *Begg* Christopher, The non-mention of Ezekiel in the book of Jeremiah; an additional consideration: ETL 65 (1989) 94s.

3600 *Berquist* J. L., Prophetic legitimation in Jeremiah: VT 39 (1989) 129-139.

3601 **Bourguet** Daniel, Des métaphores de Jérémie: ÉtBN 9, 1987 ➤ 3,3512; 4,3745: ᴿETL 65 (1989) 428s (J. *Lust*); ÉTRel 64 (1989) 617s (R. *Martin-Achard*); NRT 111 (1989) 678s (J.-L. *Ska*); RB 96 (1989) 100-7 (J. *Loza*).

3602 **Carroll** R. P., Jeremiah: OT **Guides**. Sheffield 1989, Academic. 128 p. £5. 1-85075-146-3 [BL 90,69, G. I. *Emmerson*: subjective; hardly a useful first introduction for students as the series intends]. – ᴿExpTim 101 (1989s) 153 (C. S. *Rodd*); TLond 92 (1989) 309 (R. *Coggins*: his commentary etc. in briefer form, ending 'Jeremiah is an unpleasant book to read').

3603 *Carroll* Robert P., Radical clashes of will and style; recent commentary writing on the Book of Jeremiah: JStOT 45 (1989) 99-114.

3604 *Couturier* Guy P., Jeremiah: ➤ 384. NJBC (1989) 265-297.

3605 **Donnell** David E., An examination of the concept of repentance in the Book of Jeremiah: diss. Baptist Theol. Sem., ᴰ*Cole* D. New Orleans 1988. 248 p. 89-11183. – DissA 50 (1989s) 714-A.

3606 **Friebel** Melvin G., Jeremiah's and Ezekiel's sign-acts; their meaning and function as nonverbal communication and rhetoric: diss. Wisconsin, ᴰ*Fox* M. Madison 1989. 1060 p. 89-15536. – DissA 50 (1989s) 2932-A.

3607 **Graupner** Axel, Auftrag und Geschick; Entstehung, Intention und Her-kunft vordeuteronomistischer Prosa im Jeremiabuch: ev. Diss. ᴰ*Schmidt*. Bonn 1988s. – TR 85 (1989) 514; RTLv 21, p. 540.

3608 *Hamman* A.-G., Jérémie et les Pères de l'Église: MélSR 46 (1989) 181-191; Eng. 192.

3609 *Holt* Else K., The chicken and the egg; or, Was Jeremiah a member of the Deuteronomist Party?: JStOT 44 (1989) 109-122.

3610 *Ibáñez Arana* Andrés, Jeremías, ¿profeta?: ➤ 69*, ᶠGOMÀ I., RCatalT 14 (1989) 53-62 (castellano; Eng. p. 63).

3611 *Kizhakeveettil* Jacob, Jeremiah, a man of prayer, model of an existential encounter between God and man: Living Word 95,1 (Alwaye 1989) 16-34 [< TContext 7/1, 39].

3612 **Klages** Günther, *Heinemeyer* Karl, Prophetie im Unterricht, dargestellt an Jeremia; Modell eines fachspezifischen Kurses 1986 ➤ 2,2726; DM 28: ᴿTLZ 114 (1989) 313s (G. *Kehnscherper*).

3613 *Krašovec* Jože, Kazen in obljuba v Jeremijevi knigi: BogVest 48 (1988) 59-70; 70 Eng. Punishment and promise.

3614 **Liwak** Rüdiger, Der Prophet und die Geschichte ... Jer [Diss. 1984]: BW 121, 1987 ➤ 3,3828; 4,3760: ᴿTLZ 114 (1989) 106s (D. *Vieweger*).

3615 *McKane* Wm., Jeremia, ᵀ*Hoffmann* H., ➤ 894, EvKL 2 (1988) 806-9.

3616 **Odashima** Taro, Heilsworte im Jeremiabuch; Untersuchungen zu ihrer vordeuteronomistischen Bearbeitung [Diss. Bochum, ᴰ*Herrmann* S.]: BW 125. Stu 1989, Kohlhammer. xiii-353 p. DM 79. 3-17-009842-X. – ᴿRHPR 69 (1989) 209 (P. de *Robert*).

3617 **Oosterhoff** B.J., Jeremia en het Woord van God: Apeldoornse Studies 24, 1987 ➤ 4,3765: ᴿGerefTTs 89 (1989) 62s (A.J.O. van der *Wal*).

3618 *Patterson* Richard D., Of bookends, hinges, and hooks; literary clue to the arrangement of Jeremiah's prophecies: WestTJ 51 (1989) 109-131.

3618* *Przybys* Władysław, Theologie der Bekehrung im Buch Jeremia: AnCracov 20 (1988) 265-288 [< ᴢɪᴛ 89,431].

3619 **Ravasi** Gianfranco, Il silenzio di Dio; riflessioni sul libro di Geremia. Mi 1988, Paoline. 196 p. Lit. 10.000. – ᴿStCattMi 33 (1989) 177 (U. *De Martino*).

3620 *Reimer* David J., The 'foe' and the 'north' [ṣapôn] in Jeremiah: ZAW 101 (1989) 223-232.

3621 *Rofé* Alexander, The arrangement of the book of Jeremiah: ZAW 101 (1989) 390-8.

3622 **Seitz** Christopher R., Theology in conflict; reactions to the Exile in the book of Jeremiah: BZAW 176. B 1989, de Gruyter. 329 p. DM 138. 3-11-011223-X. – ᴿExpTim 101 (1989s) 119s (R.P. *Carroll*, brilliant).

3623 *Seitz* Christopher R., The prophet Moses and the canonical shape of Jeremiah: ZAW 101 (1989) 3-27.

3624 *Shoshany* Ronit, Prosodic structures in Jeremiah's poetry: Folia Linguistica Historica 7 (1986) 167-206 [< OTAbs 12,196].

3625 *Stadelmann* Andreas, Geremia; l'alleanza tradita: ParSpV 19 (1989) 57-82.

3626 **Szwarc** Ursula, ❷ Der Sinn des Ausdruckes *haddābār hazzeh* im Buch Jeremia: RoczTK 33,1 (1986) 47-52; deutsch 52.

3627 **Terblanche** Marius D., The function of the traditions in Jeremiah 1-45: diss. ᴰ*Vosloo* W. Pretoria 1989. – DissA 50 (1989s) 1343-A.

3628 **Thondiparambil** Joseph, Prophecy as theatre; an exegetico-theological study of the symbolic acts in the Book of Jeremiah: diss. Pont. Univ. Gregoriana, Nᵒ 3548, ᴰ*Conroy* C. Roma 1989. xix-504 p. – RTLv 21,542.

3628* **Unterman** Jeremiah, From repentance to redemption; Jeremiah's thought in transition: JStOT supp 54, 1988 ➤ 3,3543; 4,3722: ᴿJBL 108 (1989) 332 (A.R.P. *Diamond*).

3629 *Wilson* Robert B., Jeremiah: ➤ 377, Books 1 (1989) 281-301.

3630 *Ruprecht* Eberhard, [Jer 1,1-3] Ist die Berufung Jeremias 'im Jünglingsalter' und seine 'Frühverkündigung' eine theologische Konstruktion der deuteronomistischen Redaktion des Jeremiabuches?: ➤ 212, ᶠWESTERMANN C., Schöpfung 1989, 79-91.

3631 *Ravasi* Gianfranco, [Jer 1,5 ...] 'dal grembo di mia madre mi hai chiamato'; figure e modelli di vocazione nell'AT: Servitium 3,61 (Bergamo 1989) 11-23.

3632 *Thiel* Winfried, 'Vom Norden her wird das Unheil eröffnet'; zu Jeremia 1,11-16: ➤ 105, [F]KAISER O., Prophet 1989, 231-245.

3633 *a) Toorn* Karel van der, Did Jeremiah [1,11s] see Aaron's staff [Nm 17,16-26]?; – *b) Smith* Daniel L., Jeremiah as prophet of nonviolent resistance: JStOT 43 (1989) 83-94 / 95-107.

3634 **Cloete** W. T. W., Versification and syntax in Jeremiah 2-25; syntactical constraints in Hebrew colometry [diss. Stellenbosch 1987]: SBL diss. 117. Atlanta 1989, Scholars. ix-257 p. $17; sb./pa. $11. 1-55540-389-1; 90-5 [BL 90,70, R. P. *Carroll*].

3635 *Schmidt* Andreas [Jer 2,5 LXX; Jos 11,6 LXX] P.Oxy, X 1224, Fragment 2 recto, Col. I: ein neuer Vorschlag: ZNW 80 (1989) 276s.

3636 *Olofsson* Staffan, The translation of Jer 2,18 in the Septuagint; methodological, linguistical and theological aspects: ScandJOT (1988,2) 169-200 [< TR 85,521].

3637 *Gosse* Bernard, L'ouverture de la nouvelle alliance aux nations en Jérémie III 14-18: VT 39 (1989) 385-392.

3638 *Mosis* Rudolf, Umkehr und Vergebung — eine Auslegung von Jer 3,21-4,2: TrierTZ 98 (1989) 39-60.

3639 **Tijn** Maartje van, Een historische inleiding op de Misjna; Vrede en er is gaan vrede! (naar Jer. 6,14; 8,11). Haag 1988, Boekencentrum. 246 p. ƒ30 [TR 85,521].

3640 *Aguilera* Antonio, La fórmula 'Templo de Yahvé, templo de Yahvé, templo de Yahvé' en Jr 7,4: EstBíb 47 (1989) 319-342; Eng. 319.

3641 *Lemche* Niels P., Mysteriet om det forsvundne tempel; oberleveringen om Shilos ødelæggelse i Jer 7,12.14): ➤ 147, [F]OTTOSSON M., SvEx 54 (1989) 118-126.

3642 *Ackerman* Susan, [Jer 7,14; 44,17 ...] 'And the women knead dough'; the worship of the Queen of Heaven in sixth-century Judah: ➤ 391, Gender 1989, 109-124.

3643 **Bartolomeu Barros** José, [Jer 11 ...] Amor e oração nas confissões de Jeremias: diss. [D]*Koch* R. R 1989, Pont. Univ. Lateranensis. xxxiv-266 p.

3644 **Diamond** A. R., [Jer 11 ...] The Confessions of Jeremiah in context [diss. Cambridge 1984]: JStOT Sup 45, 1987 ➤ 3,3521; 4,3783: [R]Biblica 70 (1989) 123-6 (F. D. *Hubmann*); CBQ 51 (1989) 316-8 (L. *Stulman*); JBL 108 (1989) 124-7 (H. E. von *Waldow*); JTS 40 (1989) 157s (R. E. *Clements*); TLZ 114 (1989) 185-7 (W. *Thiel*); VT 39 (1989) 119 (R. P. *Gordon*).

3645 **Mottu** Henry, Les 'Confessions' de Jérémie 1985 ➤ 1,3603 ... 4,3785: [R]CBQ 51 (1989) 128s (Kathleen M. *O'Connor*); ÉglT 19 (1988) 98s (L. *Laberge*).

3646 **O'Connor** Kathleen M., The confessions of Jeremiah ...: SBL diss. 94 (Princeton) 1988 ➤ 4,3784: [R]Biblica 70 (1989) 545-9 (A. R. P. *Diamond*); BL (1989) 89 (A. G. *Auld*); JBL 108 (1989) 694-6 (also A. R. P. *Diamond*); ZAW 101 (1989) 322 (G. *Wanke*).

3647 **Pohlmann** K.-F., Die Ferne Gottes — Studien zum Jeremiabuch; Beiträge zu den 'Konfessionen' im Jeremiabuch und ein Versuch zur Frage nach den Anfängen der Jeremiatradition: BZAW 179. B 1989, de Gruyter. x-232 p. DM 88. 3-11-011828-9. – [E]ExpTim 101 (1989s) 153s (R. C. *Coggins*, also on ODASHIMA T., WALLIS G.); Judaica 45 (1989)

258s (I. *Willi-Plein*); TLZ 114 (1989) 879s (H. *Reventlow*); TR 85 (1989) 455-7 (Helga *Weippert*); ZAW 101 (1989) 322s (H. C. *Schmitt*).

3649 *Luria* B. Z., ☉ [Jer 13,18s] The enemy from the south [*darom*]: BethM 34,121 (1989s) 166-181.

3650 *Taylor* Robert G., The problem with the plaintiff; Jeremiah 15: 10-21: RestQ 31 (1989) 231... [< ZIT 90,168].

3651 *Wessels* W. J., Jeremiah 22,24-30; a proposed ideological reading: ZAW 101 (1989) 232-249.

3652 *Honeycutt* Roy L., Jeremiah 23:9-40 (exposition): RExp 86 (1989) 583-594.

3653 *Walton* John H., Vision narrative wordplay and Jeremiah XXIV: VT 39 (1989) 508s.

3654 *O'Connor* Kathleen M., 'Do not trim a word'; the contributions of chapter 26 to the book of Jeremiah: CBQ 51 (1989) 617-630.

3654* *a) Smelik* K., Jeremia 26 als literaire compositie; – *b) Dijk-Hemmes* Fokkelien van, Betekenissen van Jeremia 31,22*b*: → 116, FLEEUWEN C. van 1989, 79-96 / 31-40.

3655 *a) McKane* William, Jeremiah 27,5-8 — especially 'Nebuchadnezzar, my servant'; – *b) Wanke* Gunther, [Jer 32,6-15] Jeremias Ackerkauf; Heil im Gericht?: → 105, FKAISER O., 1989, 98-110 / 265-276.

3656 *Brandscheidt* Renate, [Jer 28] Der prophetische Konflikt zwischen Jeremia und Hananja: TrierTZ 98 (1989) 61-74.

3657 **Reimer** D. J., [Jer... 28; 34] 'A horror among the nations'; the oracles against Babylon in Jeremiah: diss. Oxford 1989. – RTLv 21,541.

3658 *Becking* Bob, 'I will break his yoke from off your neck'; remarks on Jeremiah xxx 4-11: → 129, FMULDER M., New Avenues 1989, 63-76.

3659 *Gross* Heinrich, Der Mensch als neues Geschöpf (Jer 31; Ez 36; Ps 51): → 45, FDEISSLER A., Weg 1989, 98-109.

3659* *Becking* B., 'Bedrukte Rachel schort dit waren'; Jeremia 31,15-17, Mattheüs 2,18 en Vondels GYSBRECHT: → 116, FLEEUWEN C. van 1989, 9-22.

3660 *Waldman* Nahum M., [Jer 31,29; Ezek 18,1] Parents have eaten sour grapes: JBQ (= Dor) 18 (1989s) 1-5.

3661 **Yu Young Ki**, The new covenant, the promise and its fulfilment; an inquiry into the influence of the new covenant concept of Jer 31.31-34 on later religious thought with particular reference to the Dead Sea Scrolls and the New Testament: diss. Durham UK 1989. 335 p. BRD-86642. – DissA 50 (1989s) 2534-A; RTLv 21,543.

3662 *Kent* Dan G., [Jer 35] The Rechabites; what do we know?: → 185, FSMITH R., SWJT 32,3 (1989s) 40-45.

3663 **Knights** [RTLv 21,543] Christopher H., [Jer 35] The Rechabites in the Bible and in Jewish tradition to the time of Rabbi David KIMHI: diss. Durham 1988.

3663* *Derrett* J. D. M., [... Rechabites] Jewish Brahmins and the tale of Zosimus; a theme common to three religions [< ClasMed 34 (1983) 75-90]: → 253, Sea-Change 1989, 8-23.

3664 **Hardmeier** Christoph, Prophetie im Streit vor dem Untergang Judas; Erzählkommunikative Studien zur Entstehungssituation der Jesaja- und Jeremiaerzählungen in II Reg. 18-20 [cf. Diss. → 4,2974] und Jer 37-40: BZAW 187. B 1989, de Gruyter. 3-11-011735-5 [BL 90,153].

3665 *Weippert* Helga, Schöpfung und Heil in Jer 45: → 212, FWESTERMANN C., Schöpfung 1989, 92-103.

3666 *Amesz* J.G., ...plotseling is Babel gevallen; een onderzoek naar de rol van JHWH en Mardoek in teksten over de val van Babel (Jer 50/51 en Cyrus-Cylinder): AmstCah (1987) 80-86 [< GerefTTS 89,61].

E8.8   **Lamentationes,** *Threni;* **Baruch.**

3667 *Alarcón Sainz* Juan J., Vocablos griegos y latinos en los proemios (*petiḥôt*) de Lamentaciones Rabbah: Sefarad 49 (1989) 3-10.
3668 **Gous** Ignatius G.P., The origin of Lamentations: diss. Unisa, ᴰ*Loader* J. Pretoria 1988. – DissA 50 (1989s) 2945-A.
3669 *Guinan* Michael D., Lamentations; *Fitzgerald* Aloysius, Baruch: ➤ 384, NJBC (1989) 558-562 / 563-7.
3670 *Renkema* J., The literary structure of Lamentations (I-IV): ➤ 410, Structural/poetry 1988, 294-320 / 321-346 / 347-360 / 361-396.
3671 **Michalowski** Piotr, The lamentation over the destruction of Sumer and Ur: MesCiv I. WL 1989, Eisenbrauns. xvi-219 p.; 24 pl. [RelStR 16, 249, J.M. *Sasson*]. 0-931464-43-0.
3672 **Paulus** Beda [➤ 4,3813: non 'P.'] Pascasi RADBERTI expositio in Lamentationes Hieremiae libri quinque: CCMed 85. Turnhout 1988, Brepols. xx-375 p. Fb 4150. – ᴿGregorianum 70 (1989) 815s (J. *Janssens*); RHE 84 (1989) 531 (H. *Silvestre*).
3673 *Westermann* Claus, Lamentations, ᵀ*Anderson* B.: ➤ 377, Books 1 (1989) 303-317.
3674 **Murphy** Frederick J., The structure and meaning of Second Baruch: SBL diss. 78, 1985 ➤ 1,3629... 4,3815: ᴿSecC 7 (1989s) 102-4 (J.G. *Gammie*).
3675 *O'Connor* Kathleen, Baruch, the Letter of Jeremiah, the Prayer of Manasseh: ➤ 377, Books 1 (1989) 87-92.
3676 *Sitarz* E., Baruch: ➤ 902, NBL, Lfg 2 (1989) 246-8.
3677 **Willett** Tom W., Eschatology in the theodicies of 2 Baruch and 4 Ezra [Diss. S. Baptist Sem., ᴰ*Valley* P.]: JPseud supp 4. Sheffield 1989, Academic. 168 p. £22.50 [JTS 41, 570, M. *Barker*]. 1-85075-160-9.

E8.9   **Ezechiel:** *textus, commentarii; themata, versiculi.*

3678 ᴱ**Antoniono** Normando, ORIGENE, Omelie su Ezechiele. R 1987, Città Nuova. 235 p. [RHE 84, p. 350*]. – ᴿBLitEc 90 (1989) 135s (H. *Crouzel*).
3679 **Becker** J., *Fenz* A. Kurt, Ezechiele - Daniele [1971-4, ᵀ*Poletti* Gianni]: Bibbia per tutti. 241 p. Lit. 15.000 [CC 140,3 dopo 448].
3680 ᴱ**Borret** Marcel, ORIGÈNE, Homélies sur Ézéchiel [14, latin de *Jérôme*, éd. Baehrens 1925; grec perdu]: SChr 352. P 1989, Cerf. 526 p. F 292. 2-204-04000-2 [BL 90,51]. – ᴿIrénikon 62 (1989) 432 (E. *Lanne*); PrOrChr 39 (1989) 220s (P. *Ternant*).
3681 **Brownlee** William H., Ezekiel 1-19 [not 1-12 as ➤ 4,3817], ᴱ*Allen* L., Word Comm. 28, 1986 ➤ 2,2777; 3,3587: ᴿAndrUnS 27 (1989) 76-78 (A.M. *Rodríguez*); EvQ 61 (1989) 90-92 (P.E. *Satterthwaite*); ScotJT 42 (1989) 453s (D.C. *Parker*); ScripB 20 (1989s) 43 (A. *Graffy*); WestTJ 50 (1988) 350-2 (W. *VanGemeren*).
3682 **Fuchs** Hans F., Ezechiel I. 1986 ➤ 3,3589; II (Kap. 25-48): NEchter 72, 1988 ➤ 4,3824: ᴿZAW 101 (1989) 152 (H.-C. *Schmitt*, 1s).
3683 *Knibb* Michael A., The Ethiopic text of Ezekiel and the excerpts in Gabra Ḥammamat: ➤ 200, ᶠULLENDORFF E., JSS 34 (1989) 445-454.

3684 **Maarsingh** B., Ezechiël II [16-32]: PredikOT 1988 ➤ 4,3832: ᴿStreven 57 (1989s) 180 (P. *Beentjes*).

3685 **McGregor** Leslie J., The Greek text of Ezekiel; an examination of its homogeneity [diss. Belfast]: SBL SeptCog 18, 1985 ➤ 1,3647... 4,3833: ᴿCBQ 51 (1989) 339-41 (H. V. *Parunak*, also on GOWAN D.).

3686 **Nielsen** K., Ezekiels Bog fortolket; bidrag *Strange* J. K 1988, D-Bibelselskab. 273 p. Dk 245. 87-7523-235-9 [BL 90,59, K. *Jeppesen*].

3687 **Pérez Castro** Federico, El Códice de profetas de El Cairo VI. Ezequiel: TEstCisn 44, 1988 ➤ 3,3603: ᴿBiblica 70 (1989) 549-552 (P.-M. *Bogaert*); BL (1989) 49 (P. *Wernberg-Møller*); ZAW 101 (1989) 148 (I. *Kottsieper*).

3688 **Tidiman** Brian, Le livre d'Ézéchiel: Comm. Év., 1985/7, ➤ 3,3604; 4,3844: ᴿRHPR 69 (1989) 210 (J. de *Waard*).

3689 *Ackroyd* Peter R., Ezekiel: ➤ 377, Books 1 (1989) 319-332.

3690 *Block* Daniel I., The prophet of the Spirit; the use of *rwḥ* in the Book of Ezekiel: JEvTS 32 (1989) 27-50 [< ZIT 89,509].

3691 *Boadt* Lawrence, Ezekiel: ➤ 384, NJBC (1989) 305-328.

3692 **Davis** Ellen F., Swallowing the scroll; textuality and the dynamics of discourse in Ezekiel's prophecy [diss. Yale, ᴰ*Childs* B.]: JStOT supp 78. Sheffield 1989, Almond. 184 p. £22.50. 1-85075-206-0. – ᴿExpTim 101 (1989s) 120 (R. E. *Clements*).

3693 **Hals** Ronald M., Ezekiel: FOTLit 19. GR 1989, Eerdmans. xiii-363 p. $30 [TR 86,162]. 0-8028-0340-7.

3694 **Joyce** Paul, Divine initiative and human response in Ezekiel [diss. Oxford 1983, ᴰ*Barton* J.]: JStOT Sup 51. Sheffield 1989, Academic. 186 p. £25. 1-85075-041-6 [BL 90, 79, R. E. *Clements*].

3695 **Klein** Ralph W., Ezekiel; the prophet and his message: Studies in Personalities of the OT 3. Columbia 1988, Univ. South Carolina. xi-206 p. 0-87249-553-1.

3696 **Krüger** Thomas, Geschichtskonzepte im Ezechielbuch [ev. Diss. München 1986, ᴰ*Baltzer* K.]: BZAW 180. B 1989, de Gruyter. xi-524 p. DM 178. 3-11-011473-9. – ᴿRHPR 69 (1989) 209s (J. G. *Heintz*); ZAW 101 (1989) 466 (H.-C. *Schmitt*).

3697 ᴱ**Lust** Johan, Ezekiel and his book 1985/6 ➤ 2,384... 4,3831: ᴿBZ 33 (1989) 136s (J. *Schreiner*); Laurentianum 30 (1989) 224s (F. *Castellnou*).

3698 **Monari** Luciano, Ezechiele, un sacerdote-profeta: LoB 1.21, 1988 ➤ 4,3834: ᴿParVi 34 (1989) 308s (B. *Marconcini*).

3699 **Smith** Jonathan Z., To take place; toward theory in ritual [... Ezekiel] 1987 ➤ 4,3841: ᴿTLond 92 (1989) 67-69 (J. *Rogerson*).

3700 *Lieb* Michael, [Ezek 1,1-28] Ezekiel's inaugural vision as Jungian archetype: Thought 64 (Fordham 1989) 116-129 [< OTAbs 12,301].

3701 *Davis* Ellen F., [Ezek 3,26] Swallowing hard; reflections on Ezekiel's dumbness [response, *Darr* Kathryn P., 'Write or true?']: ➤ 395, Signs 1989, 217-237 [239-247].

3702 *Dijkstra* Meindert, Legal irrevocability (*lō' yašûb*) in Ezekiel 7.13: JStOT 43 (1989) 109-116.

3703 *Ackerman* Susan, A *marzēaḥ* in Ezekiel 8:7-13?: HarvTR 82 (1989) 267-281.

3704 *Sinclair* Lawrence A., A Qumran biblical fragment; 4QEzek[a] (Ezek.
10,17-11,11): RQum 14 (1989) 99-105, 1 fig.; p. 107s, note, *Puech*
Émile.

3705 *Barthélemy* Dominique, 'Un seul', 'un nouveau ou un autre'? À propos
de l'intervention du Seigneur sur le cœur de l'homme selon Ez 11,19a et des
problèmes de critique textuelle qu'elle soulève: → 45, [F]DEISSLER A., Weg
1989, 329-338.

3706 *Pohlmann* Karl-Friedrich, Zur Frage nach ältesten Texten im
Ezechielbuch — Erwägungen zu Ez 17,19 und 31: → 105, [F]KAISER O.,
Prophet 1989, 150-172.

3707 **Matties** Gordon, Ezekiel 18 and the rhetoric of moral discourse in the
book of Ezekiel: diss. Vanderbilt, [D]*Knight* D. Nv 1989. 441 p. 90-06850.
– DissA 50 (1989s) 3268-A; RelStR 16,189.

3708 *Begg* Christopher, The identity of the princes in Ezekiel 19; some
reflections / The reading in Ezekiel 19,7a; a proposal: ETL 65 (1989)
358-369 / 370-380.

3709 *Allen* L. C., The rejected sceptre in Ezekiel XXI 15b,18a: VT 39 (not 29
as bottom; 1989) 67-71.

3710 *Loretz* O., Der Wohnort Els nach ugaritischen Texten und Ez
28,1-2.6-10: UF 21 (1989) 259-267.

3711 *Goldberg* Ilana, ❺ The poetic structure of the dirge over the king of Tyre
(Ezekiel 28:12-18): Tarbiz 58 (1988s) 277-281; Eng. iv-v.

3711* *Rooy* H. F. van, Esegiël 29:1-16; teen [against] Egipte of teen Israel?:
Scriptura 31 (1989) 1-13 [< IZBG 36, p. 109].

3712 *Gosse* Bernard, Ézéchiel 35,36,1-15 et Ézéchiel 6; la désolation de la
montagne de Séir et la renouveau des montagnes d'Israël: RB 96 (1989)
511-7.

3713 **Swanepoel** Marius G., [Afrikaans] The theology of Ezekiel 33 to 39: diss.
Pretoria, [D]*Prinsloo* W. S. 1988. – DissA 50 (1989s) 176-A.

3714 **Odell** Margaret S., 'Are you he of whom I spoke by my servants the
prophets?'; Ezekiel 38-39 and the problem of history in the Neo-
babylonian context: diss. [D]*Gowan* D. Pittsburgh 1988. 259 p. 89-11284. –
DissA 50 (1989s) 711-A.

3715 *Strange* John, [Ezek 40-48] Architecture and theology [*Ottosson* M. 1980;
→ 147]: SvEx 54 (1989) 199-206; 2 fig.

3716 **Tuell** Steven S., The law of the Temple in Ezekiel 40-48; diss. Union
Theol. Sem., [D]*McBride* S. D. Richmond 1989. 305 p. 90-04120. – DissA
50 (1989s) 2041-A.

3716* *Maarsingh* B., Geen hofkapel [court-chapel] meer, Ezechiel 43,8ab:
→ 116, [F]LEEUWEN C. van 1989, 57-65.

E9.1   Apocalyptica VT.

3717 [E]**Althaus** Heinz, Apokalyptik und Eschatologie; Sinn und Ziel der
Geschichte 1985/7 → 3,579: [R]TPQ 137 (1989) 412 (J. *Marböck*).

3718 *Collins* John J., Old Testament apocalypticism and eschatology
[page-heading: From prophecy to apocalypticism]: → 384, NJBC (1989)
298-304.

3719 *Davies* Philip R., The social world of the apocalyptic writings: → 378,
World 1989, 251-271.

3720 **Delcor** M., Studi sull'apocalittica 1987 → 3,212: [R]VetChr 26 (1989) 185s
(C. *Colafemmina*).

3721 *a) Gritsch* Eric W., Thomas MÜNTZERs Weg in die Apokalyptik; – *b)*
zur Mühlen Karl-Heinz, Heiliger Geist und Heilige Schrift bei T.
Müntzer: Luther 60 (Gö 1989) 53-65 / 131-150.

3722 *Harrington* Wilfrid, Apocalypse: Scripture in Church 19 (Dublin 1989)
212-216 [< OTAbs 12, 202].

3723 [E]**Hellholm** David, Apocalypticism in the Mediterranean world and the
Near East[2] [[1]1983, meeting Uppsala 1979 → 64,274... 4,3865]. Tü 1989,
Mohr. xi-910 p. DM 348. 3-16-145386-7 [TDig 37,63]. – [R]Protes-
tantesimo 44 (1989) 126s (J. A. *Soggin*).

3724 *Kehl* Medart, Aktualisierte Apokalyptik: K. *Rahner*, J. B. *Metz*, E.
Drewermann: TPhil 64 (1989) 1-22.

3725 **Körtner** Ulrich H. J., Weltangst und Weltende... Apokalyptik [D]1988
→ 4,3867: [R]TLZ 114 (1989) 139-141 (G. *Wenz*).

3726 *Körtner* Ulrich H. J., Weltzeit, Weltangst und Weltende; zum Da-
seins- und Zeitverständnis der Apokalyptik: TZBas 45 (1989) 32-52.

3727 **Kvanvig** H. S., Roots of Apocalyptic; the Mesopotamian background of
the Enoch figure and of the Son of Man: WM 61. Neuk 1988, Neuk-V.
xv-656 p. [ZAW 102, 153, H.-C. *Schmitt*].

3728 *Kvanvig* Helge S., The relevance of the biblical visions of the end time;
hermeneutical guidelines to the apocalyptical literature: HorBT 11,1
(1989) 35-58.

3729 **Pagán** Samuel, From crisis to hope; a study of the origins of apocalyptic literature: diss. Jewish Theol. Sem. NY 1989. 193 p. 89-23468. –
DissA 50 (1989s) 2509s-A.

3730 *Rowland* C., Books on Apocalyptic: EpworthR 16,2 (1989) 86-90
[< NTAbs 33,354].

3731 *Sacchi* Paolo, L'apocalittica giudaica: → 571, L'Ebraismo 1986/7, 31-47.

3732 *Sand* Alexander, Jüdische und christliche Apokalyptik: Renovatio 45,1
(Köln 1989) 12-24 [< Judaica 45,205].

3733 *Soušek* Zdeněk, Die Funktion und die Bedeutung der Apokalyptik:
ComViat 32 (1989) 181-192.

3734 *Stadelmann* Andreas, La scarsa presenza dell'apocalittica veterotesta-
mentaria nell'attuale pratica liturgica: Ecclesia Orans 6 (1989) 129-147.

3734* *a) Sturm* Richard E., Defining the word 'apocalyptic'; a problem in
biblical criticism; – *b) Boomershine* Thomas E., Epistemology at the
turn of the ages in Paul, Jesus, and Mark; rhetoric and dialectic in
Apocalyptic and the New Testament: → 130, [F]MARTYN J., 1989, 17-48 /
147-167.

E9.2   **Daniel:** *textus, commentarii; themata, versiculi.*

3735 **Anderson** Robert A., Signs and wonders; a commentary on the book of
Daniel: InternatTheolComm, 1984 → 65,3275... 2,2821: [R]WestTJ 50
(1988) 182-4 (T. H. *McAlpine*).
Becker J., *Fenz* A., Daniele 1989 → 3679.

3736 **Bultema** Harry, Commentary on Daniel, pref. *Bultema* Daniel C. GR
1988, Kregel. 368 p. $13 [TR 86, 162].

3737 **Fenz** Augustinus K., Der Daniel-Memra des SIMEON von Edessa; die
exegetische Bedeutung von BrM 712 Add 12172 Fol 55b-64b; foto-
technische Wiedergabe, Übersetzung und Erklärung seiner alttestamentlichen Grundlage: Studienreihe 1, 1980 → 61,4871: [R]BZ 33 (1989)
125s (J. *Maier*: Memra = 'eine Abhandlung eigentümlicher Art, teils
populären Charakters, aber durchaus belehrend').

3738 *Hartman* Louis F. †, *Di Lella* Alexander A., Daniel: ➤ 384, NJBC (1989) 406-420.
3739 *McCollough* C. Thomas, A Christianity for an age of crisis; THEODORET of Cyrus's Commentary on Daniel: ➤ 592, Systemic 2 (1989) 157-174.
3740 **Naastepad** T. M., Daniel: VBGed. Kampen 1988, Kok. 143 p. *f* 20. – ᴿStreven 56 (1988s) 472 (P. *Beentjes*).
3741 **Russell** D. S., Daniel, an active volcano. E 1989, St. Andrew. 141 p. £5. 0-7152-0632-X [BL 90, 60].
3742 **Stapleton** Russell A., An edition of the book of Daniel and associated apocrypha in Manuscript Sinai Arabic I: diss. Brandeis. Boston 1989. 431 p. 89-10676. – DissA 50 (1989s) 696-A.
3743 *Ulrich* Eugene, Daniel manuscripts from Qumran, II. Preliminary edition of 4QDanᵇ and 4QDanᶜ: BASOR 274 (1989) 3-26; 8 fig.

––––––––––

3744 **Beattie** D. R. G., [Daniel as exemplifying] First steps in biblical criticism. Lanham MD 1988, UPA. 108 p. $14.50. 0-8191-7053-4 [ExpTim 100, 358].
3745 **Bodemann** Reinhard, Naissance d'une exégèse, Daniel ...: BeiGBEx 28, 1986 ➤ 2,2823 ... 4,3876: ᴿBiblica 70 (1989) 421-4 (D. *Satran*); Gregorianum 70 (1989) 174s (A. *Orbe*); HeythJ 30 (1989) 187s (S. G. *Hall*); Protestantesimo 44 (1989) 126 (J. A. *Soggin*); ScripTPamp 21 (1989) 695s (P. *Monod*).
3746 **Davies** P. R., Daniel: OTGuides 1985 ➤ 1,3692 ... 4,3877: ᴿHeythJ 30 (1989) 441s (G. G. *Nicol*); VT 39 (1989) 117 (R. P. *Gordon*).
3747 **Doukhan** Jacques, Daniel, the vision of the end. Berrien Springs MI 1987, Andrews Univ. – ᴿAndrUnS 27 (1989) 84-6 (D. R. *Clark*: some reserves).
3748 **Ferguson** S., Daniel. Waco 1988, Word. 252 p. [TS 50,835].
3749 **Grimm** Werner, Jesus und das Danielbuch, I. Jesu Einspruch gegen das Offenbarungssystem Daniels. NY 1987, Lang. 110 p. $20. – ᴿSWJT 32,1 (1989s) 50 (E. E. *Ellis*).
3750 **Lacocque** André, Daniel in his time [➤ 4,3884 'times']: Studies on Personalities of the OT, 1988: ᴿCBQ 51 (1989) 523s (G. W. *Buchanan*); JRel 69 (1989) 393-5 (R. A. *Pascale*).
3751 **Monod** Philippe, La intervención salvadora de Dios en el Libro de Daniel: diss. ᴰ*Aranda Pérez* G. Pamplona 1989. 447 p. – RTLv 21,541.
3752 **Reid** Stephen B., Enoch and Daniel; a form critical and sociological study of the historical apocalypses: Mg 2. Berkeley 1989, BIBAL. xiii-147 p. $13 pa. [CBQ 52,198]. – ᴿExpTim 101 (1989s) 190 (P. R. *Davies*).
3753 *Stefanovic* Zdravko, Thematic links between the historical and prophetic sections of Daniel: AndrUnS 27 (1989) 121-8.
3754 *Towner* W. Sibley, Daniel and additions: ➤ 377, Books 1 (1989) 333-347.
3755 *Walters* Stanley D., The world will end in 1919 [*Guinness* H. 1835-1910]; Daniel among the Victorians: AsbTJ 44,1 (1989) 29-50.

––––––––––

3756 **Fewell** Danna N., Circle of sovereignty ... Dan 1-6: 1988 ➤ 4,3887: ᴿExpTim 100 (1988s) 471 (J. C. L. *Gibson*).

3757 *Mercer* Mark K., Daniel 1:1 and Jehoiakim's three years of servitude: AndrUnS 27 (1989) 179-192.

3758 **Berriot** F., Exposicions et significacions des songes et Les songes Daniel [sic RHE 85,55*]: Manuscrits français P/B, TravHumRen 234. Genève 1989, Droz. 369 p. F 105.

3759 *a) Semi* A.A., I sogni di Nabucodonosor; – *b) Bonora* A., I sogni e la loro interpretazione nell'AT; – *c) Benedetti* G., I sogni biblici nell'opera di Sigmund FREUD / Il sogno dell'uomo di oggi e il sogno nella Bibbia: ➤ 563c, Sogno 1988...

3760 *Lucas* Ernst C., Daniel's four empires scheme: TyndB 40,2 (1989) 185-202.

3761 *Casey* Maurice, The fourth kingdom in Cosmas INDICOPLEUSTES and the Syrian tradition: RivStoLR 25 (1989) 385-403.

3762 *Aleixandre* Dolores, [Dan 2,31-37] La estatua de Nabucodonosor y otros sueños: SalT 76 (1988) 785-792 [liberación de la mujer].

3763 **Matheny** J.F. & Marjorie, Gold, silver, brass, iron; rethinking the kingdoms of Daniel 2. Enid OK 1988, G. Jay. 173 p. – ᴿBS 146 (1989) 467 (J.A. *Witmer*).

3764 *Leichty* Erle, Feet of clay [not about Daniel 2,33 but about footprints (made for identification?)]: ➤ 183, ᶠSJÖBERG Å., Dumu- 1989, 349-356; 4 fig.

3765 *Margain* Jean, Le livre de Daniel; commentaire philologique du texte araméen 3,1-30: LOrA 2 (1989) 69-78.

3766 *Cook* Edward M., 'In the plain of the wall' (Dan 3:1): JBL 108 (1989) 115s.

3767 *Soesilo* Daud, Belshazzar's scales; towards achieving a balanced translation of Daniel 5: BTrans 40 (1989) 426-432 [< diss. 1988 ➤ 4,3898].

3768 *Walton* J., The decree of Darius the Mede in Daniel 6: JEvTS 31 (1988) 279-286 [< ZAW 102, 130].

3769 **Porter** Paul A., Metaphors and monsters... Dan 7s, 1985 ➤ 1,3715... 3,3663: ᴿTLZ 114 (1989) 472-4 (R.G. *Kratz*).

3770 (Pace) **Jeansonne** Sharon, The Old Greek... Dan 7-12: CBQ 19, 1988 ➤ 4,3900: ᴿETL 65 (1989) 160-3 (J. *Lust*: holds perhaps too strongly that all 'errors' were unintentional); JBL 108 (1989) 700-2 (L. *Greenspoon*: a credit to the series); JTS 40 (1989) 533-5 (H.F.D. *Sparks*); TLZ 114 (1989) 727s (K. *Koch*).

3771 *Caragounis* Chrys C., Greek culture and Jewish piety; the clash and the fourth beast of Daniel 7: ETL 65 (1989) 280-308.

3772 **Bryan** D.J., Cosmos, chaos and the kosher mentality; the roots and rationale of zoomorphic imagery in the animal apocalypse, the Testament of Naphtali and Daniel 7: diss. Oxford 1989. – RTLv 21,539.

3773 *Pierce* Ronald W., Spiritual failure, postponement, and Daniel 9: TrinJ 10 (1989) 211-222.

3774 **Lurie** David H., [Dan 9,3-24] The covenant, the holocaust, and the seventieth week. Coral Gables FL 1988, Messianic Century. xiv-114 p. – ᴿBS 146 (1989) 467-9 (E.H. *Merrill*: intriguing and stimulating, by a Hebrew Christian with science doctorate from Brussels).

3775 ᴱ**Holbrook** Frank B., The Seventy Weeks, Leviticus, and the nature of prophecy: Dan/Rev 3. Wsh 1986, Adventist Biblical. xii-394. $9 pa. – ᴿAndrUnS 27 (1989) 243-5 (R.M. *Davidson*).

3776 **Koch** K., Deuterokanonische Zusätze zum Danielbuch; Entstehung und Textgeschichte [original Aramaic in medieval Chronicle of Jerahmeel, as maintained by Moses *Gaster* in 1894]; 1. Forschungsstand, Programm,

Polyglottensynopse; 2. Exegetische Erläuterungen: AOAT 38, Kevelaer/Neuk 1988 ↦ 3,3645: ᴿBL (1989) 48 (P.W. *Coxon*); TLZ 114 (1989) 589s (H. *Reventlow*).

3777 **Engel** Helmut,   Die Susanna-Erzählung: OBO 61, 1985 ↦ 1,3723 ... 3,3670: ᴿBO 46 (1989) 442-5 (A. *Hilhorst*); TrierTZ 98 (1989) 157 (E. *Haag*).

3778 *Walter* Christopher, [Dan 14,33-38] The iconography of the prophet Habakkuk: RÉByz 47 (1989) 251-260; VIII pl.

E9.3   *Prophetae minores,* **Dodekapropheton ... Hosea, Joel.**

3779 **Azcárraga Servert** María Josefa de,   Minḥat Šay ... Norzi, profetas menores 1987 ↦ 3,3671; 4,3908:   ᴿJBL 108 (1989) 131s (E.J. *Revell*); JQR 80 (1989s) 409s (M.T. *Ortega-Monasterio*); RB 96 (1989) 606 (F.J. *Gonçalves*, with notice of several cognate works).

3780 **Cathcart** Kevin J., *Gordon* Robert P.,   The Targum of the Minor Prophets: Aramaic Bible 14. Wilmington/E 1989, Glazier/Clark. xvi-259 p. 0-89453-489-0 [OIAc Ja90].

3781 **Gelston** A.,   The Peshiṭta of the Twelve Prophets 1987 ↦ 3,3674; 4,3910: ᴿBO 46 (1989) 152-4 (P.B. *Dirksen*); JTS 40 (1989) 162-5 (M.P. *Weitzmann*); ScotJT 42 (1989) 416-8 (A.P. *Hayman*).

3782 [ᴱ**Sainte-Marie** H. de, *al.*] Liber XII prophetarum: Vulgata Benedictina 17, 1987 ↦ 3,3675; 4,3912: ᴿWienerSt 102 (1989) 302s (Michaela *Zelzer*).

3783 ᴱ**Simon** Uriel, ⊕ Abraham Ibn Ezra's two commentaries on the Minor Prophets, I. Hosea-Joel-Amos. Ramat Gan 1989, Bar-Ilan Univ. 332 p. 965-226-103-3.

────────

3784 **Andersen** F.I., *Freedman* D.N., Hosea: AnchorB 24, 1980 (= 1953) ↦ 61,4919 ... 4,3914: ᴿHenoch 11 (1989) 113-9 (P.G. *Borbone*: manca l'essenziale).

3784* *Barker* Kenneth S., Love for the wayward, Hosea ['I once met a man by the name of Hosea Beeri ... he married the town beauty']: ExpTim 101 (1989s) 271-3.

3785 **Beck** Eleonore,   Osea – Amos – Michea; il sogno di Dio, un mondo umano [1972], ᵀ*Pulit* Gianni: Bibbia per tutti. Assisi 1989, Cittadella. 142 p. Lit. 13.000.

3786 **Beeby** H.D.,   Grace abounding; a commentary on the Book of Hosea: IntTheolComm. GR 1989, Eerdmans. x-189 p. 0-905312-95-3.

3786* *a*) *Bird* Phyllis, 'To play the harlot'; an inquiry into an Old Testament metaphor [...'the birth of a metaphor', Hosea]: – *b*) *Leith* Mary Jo W., Verse and reverse; the transformation of the woman, Israel, in Hosea 1-3: ↦ 391, Gender 1989, 75-94 / 95-108.

3787 *Dijk-Hemmes* Fokkelien van,   Herschapen tot een levende tora; het verbond bij Hosea, Jesaja en Jeremia: ↦ 412, Sleutelen 1989, 52-74.

3788 *Fontaine* Carole R., Hosea: ↦ 377, Books 1 (1989) 349-358.

3789 *Hoffman* Yair,   A North Israelite typological myth and a Judaean historical tradition; the Exodus in Hosea and Amos: VT 39 (1989) 169-182.

3790 **Hubbard** David A.,   Hosea; introd. comm.: Tyndale OT. Leicester 1989, Inter-Varsity. 234 p. £6.25. 0-85111-641-8; pa. -843-7 [BL 90, 56, G.I. *Emmerson*: excellent, also Joel-Amos].

Hunter A.V., Hosea 1982 ↦ 3836.

3791 **Israel** Richard D., Prophecies of judgment; a study of the protasis-apodosis text structures in Hosea, Amos and Micah: diss. Claremont 1988, ᴰ*Knierim* R. 429 p. 90-00160. – DissA 50 (1989s) 2526-A; RelStR 16,189.

King Philip J., Hosea 1988 ➤ 3838.

3792 **Limburg** James, Hosea [through] Micah: Interpretation comm. 1988 ➤ 4,3922; 0-8042-3128-1: ᴿSWJT 32,2 (1989s) 55 (R. L. *Smith*).

3793 *McCarthy* Dennis J.†, *Murphy* Roland E., Hosea: ➤ 384, NJBC (1989) 217-228.

3794 **Neef** H.-D., Heilstraditionen... Hosea: BZAW 169, 1987 ➤ 3,3683; 4,3925: ᴿOLZ 84 (1989) 684s (G. *Pfeifer*); Salesianum 51 (1989) 566s (M. *Cimosa*).

3795 **Stuart** D., Hosea-Jonah: Word-*Themes*. Dallas 1989, Word. x-121 p. $10. 0-8499-0789-6 [BL 90,93, G. I. *Emmerson*].

3796 *Thornton* Larry R., [Hosea and 4 other books] A biblical approach to establishing marital intimacy, II. God in the marriage motif in Scripture; III. Commands and commendations: CalvaryB 5,1 (1989) 43-62; 5,2 (1989) 30-74.

3797 **Yee** Gale A., Composition and tradition in the book of Hosea [diss. St. Michael's, ᴰ*Ceresko* A., Toronto 1985]: SBL diss 102, 1987 ➤ 3,3684; 4,3931: ᴿCBQ 51 (1989) 549-551 (J. D. *Newsome*).

3798 *Anderlini* Gianpaolo, *Gmr bt dblym* (Os 1,3): RivB 37 (1989) 305-311.

3799 *Schmitt* John J., The wife of God in Hosea 2: BiRes 34 (1989) 5-18.

3800 **Weems** Renita J., [Hos 2; Jer Ezek ...], Sexual violence as an image for divine retribution in the prophetic writings: diss. Princeton Theol. Sem. 1989. 298 p. 89-23112. – DissA 50 (1989s) 2100s-A; RelStR 16,189.

3801 *Weems* Renita, Gomer, victim of violence or victim of metaphor?: Semeia 47 (1989) 87-104.

3802 *Falke* Jane, Hosea speaks to Gomer, Israel, and women religious: RRel 48 (1989) 258-263.

3803 *Paolantonio* Marguerite, [Hos 2,8...] God as husband: BToday 27 (1989) 299-303.

3804 *Mosis* Rudolf, Die Wiederherstellung Israels; zur anthropologischen Dimension des verheissenen Heils nach Hos 2,16f: ➤ 45, ꟳDEISSLER A., Weg 1989, 110-133.

3804* *Raurell* Frederic, Os 4,7: De la 'doxa' a la 'atimia': ➤ 69*, ꟳGOMÀ I., RCatalT 14 (1989) 41-51; Eng. 51.

3805 *Mazor* Yair, Hosea 5:1-3; between compositional rhetoric and rhetorical composition: JStOT 45 (1989) 115-126.

3806 **Pryce** Bertrand C., The resurrection motif in Hosea 5:8-6:6: diss. Andrews, ᴰ*Davidson* R. Berrien Springs MI 1989. 412 p. 89-22842. – DissA 50 (1989s) 2116s-A; RTLv 21,541.

3807 *Morla Asensio* Víctor, El verbo *'āśāh* 'ofrecer' en la estructura literaria de Os 9,1-7: EstBíb 47 (1989) 119-129.

3808 *Steingrimsson* Sigurdur Ö., Zeit und Relationen in Ho 10,1-2; einige literaturwissenschaftliche Betrachtungen: SvEx 54 (1989) 188-198.

3809 *Arnold* Patrick M. [Hos 10,9; 9,8] Hosea and the sin of Gibeah: CBQ 51 (1989) 447-460; map.

3810 *Kreuzer* Siegfried, Gott als Mutter in Hosea 11?: TüTQ 169 (1989) 123-132.

3811 *Lust* Johan, FREUD, Hosea, and the murder of Moses; Hosea 12: ETL 65 (1989) 81-93.

3812 *Heintz* J.-G., Une tradition occultée? La déesse cananéenne 'Anat et son *'ašerâh* dans le livre du prophète Osée (chap. 14, v. 9b): Ktema 11 (1986) 3-13.
3813 *Loretz* O., 'Anat-Aschera (Hos 14,9) [*Wellhausen* J.] und die Inschriften von Kuntillet 'Ajrud: StEpL 6 (1989) 57-65.
3814 *Tångberg* K. Arvid, 'I am like an evergreen fir; from me comes your fruit'; notes on meaning and symbolism in Hosea 14,9b (MT): ScandJOT (1989,2) 81-93.

3815 **Bergler** Siegfried, Joel als Schriftinterpret: BeiATJ 16, 1988 → 4,3938: ᴿComViat 32 (1989) 103s (J. *Heller*); RHPR 69 (1989) 211-3 (J. G. *Heintz*; this and some few other reviews inconsistently give surname first in the title).
3816 *Dupont-Roc* Roselyne, Le livre de Joël et sa tradution grecque dans la Septante I: LOrA 2 (1989) 79-97.
3817 *Hiebert* Theodore, Joel: → 377, Books 1 (1989) 359-365.
3818 **Hubbard** David A., Joel and Amos: TyndaleOT. Leicester 1989, Inter-Varsity. 245 p. – ᴿExpTim 101 (1989s) 282 (C. S. *Rodd*).
3819 **Loretz** O., Regenritual und Jahwetag im Joelbuch; Kanaanäischer Hintergrund, Kolometrie, Aufbau und Symbolik eines Prophetenbuches: Ug-B Lit 4, 1986 → 4,3941; DM 60; 3-88733-068-4: ᴿZAW 101 (1989) 468s (H.-C. *Schmitt*).
3820 *Mallon* Elias D., Joel, Obadiah: → 384, NJBC (1989) 399-405.
3821 **Meer** Willem van der, Oude woorden worden nieuw; de opbouw van het boek Joël: diss. Kampen, ᴰ*Noort* E. Kampen 1989, Kok. x-346 p. 90-242-4821-3. – TsTNijm 29 (1989) 283; RTLv 21,342 sub Van: Old words become new; the structure of the Book of Joel. – ᴿStreven 57 (1989s) 756 (P. *Beentjes*).
3822 **Nash** Kathleen S., The Palestinian agricultural year and the Book of Joel: diss. Catholic Univ., ᴰ*Fitzgerald* A. Wsh 1989. 249 p. 89-12984. – DissA 50 (1989s) 980-A; RTLv 21,541.
3823 **Prinsloo** Willem S., The theology of the book of Joel: BZAW 163, 1985 → 1,3757... 4,3943: ᴿJTS 40 (1989) 158s (D. R. *Jones*); RBíbArg 51 (1989) 54-56 (J. S. *Croatto*); TLZ 114 (1989) 266s (G. *Wallis*).
3824 *a*) *Redditt* Paul L., The book of Joel, an overview; – *b*) *Nash* Kathleen S., The cycle of seasons in Joel; *c*) *Launderville* Dale, Joel, prophet and visionary; – *d*) *Nowell* Irene, The coming of the Spirit in the Book of Joel: BToday 27 (1989) 69-73 / 74-80 / 81-86 / 87-92.

3824* *Barker* Kenneth S., [Joel 1,4] Grasshoppers and grace; Joel: ExpTim 101 (1989s) 302s.
3825 *Shapiro* Ophra, Medieval Jewish commentary on Joel 2,1-11: → 116, ꟳLEEUWEN C. van 1989, 67-77.
3825* *VanGemeren* Willem A., [Joel 2,28-32] The spirit of restoration: WestTJ 50 (1988) 81-102.
3826 *Luria* B. Z., ⊕ The date of Joel 4: BethM 32 (1986s) 345-9 [OTAbs 11,176].

E9.4 **Amos.**

3827 **Andersen** F. J., *Freedman* D. N., Amos: AnchorB 24 A. GCNY 1989, Doubleday. xliii-979 p. $30. 0-385-00773-6 [BL 80, 49, A. G. *Auld*]. –

ᴿExpTim 101 (1989s) 276s (C. S. *Rodd*: at 125 p. per page of Amos, the Anchor Bible has lost its way).

3828 *Barré* Michael L., Amos: ↪ 384, NJBC (1989) 209-216.

3829 **Beyerlin** Walter, Reflexe der Amosvisionen im Jeremiabuch: OBO 93. FrB/Gö 1989, Univ./VR. 119 p. 3-7278-0658-3 / VR 3-525-53723-9 [BL 90,151].

3830 *a*) *Biguzzi* Giancarlo, L'elezione di Israele e dei popoli in Amos; – *b*) *Carnevale* Leonardo, La salvezza nel profetismo vetero-testamentario: ↪ 735, Salvezza 1988/9, 265-278 / 295-307.

3831 **Bjørndalen** Anders J., Untersuchungen zur allegorischen Rede der Propheten Amos und Jesaja: BZAW 185, 1986 ↪ 2,2886... 4,3947: ᴿBZ 33 (1989) 122-4 (R. *Mosis*); CBQ 51 (1989) 109-111 (M. A. *Sweeney*); OLZ 84 (1989) 554 (G. *Pfeifer*); ZkT 111 (1989) 88s (R. *Oberforcher*).

3832 **Doorly** William J., Prophet of justice; understanding the Book of Amos. NY 1989, Paulist. iv-92 p.; map. 0-8091-3089-0 [BL 90,152].

3833 *Ebo* D. J. I., Another look at Amos' visions: AfTJ 18 (1989) 17-27 [< TContext 7/1, 18].

3834 **Fleischer** Günther, Von Menschenverkäufern, Baschankühen und Rechtsverkehrern; die Sozialkritik des Amosbuches in historisch-kritischer, sozialgeschichtlicher und archäologischer Perspektive [kath. Diss. Bonn 1985, ᴰ*Hossfeld* F.]: BoBB 74. Fra 1989, Athenäum. xiv-486 p. DM 88. 3-610-09130-4.

3835 **Giles** Terry, Amos and the Law: diss. Michigan State. East Lansing 1989. 263 p. 89-23849. – DissA 50 (1989s) 2095-A.

Hubbard David A., Amos 1989 ↪ 3818.

3836 **Hunter** A. V., Seek the Lord... Amos... Hos... Zeph (ᴰ1981) 1982 ↪ 63,3824... 1,3763: ᴿBZ 33 (1989) 289s (N. *Lohfink*).

3837 *Jeremias* Jörg, Jakob im Amosbuch: ↪ 169, ᶠSCHARBERT J., Väter 1989, 139-154.

3838 **King** Philip J., Amos, Hosea, Micah — an archaeological commentary 1988 ↪ 4,3956: ᴿBA 52 (1989) 232 (J. C. *Moyer*); BL (1989) 56s (G. I. *Davies*; 'companion' rather than commentary, but splendid); OTAbs 12 (1989) 121 (B. F. *Batto*); VT 39 (1989) 255s (J. A. *Emerton*).

3839 *Parker* Simon B., Amos: ↪ 377, Books 1 (1989) 367-374.

3840 *Pfeifer* Gerhard, Das Ja des Amos: VT 39 (1989) 497-503.

3841 **Polley** Max E., Amos and the Davidic empire; a socio-historical approach. Ox 1989, UP. xii-243 p. £24. 0-19-505478-4 [BL 90,90, A.G. *Auld*].

3842 **Ruiz González** Gregorio, ᴱ*Ortega Monasterio* M. T., Comentarios hebreos medievales al libro de Amos 1987 ↪ 3,3711; 4,3960: ᴿBL (1989) 61 (F. *García Martínez*); JQR 80 (1989s) 369s (M. J. de *Azcárraga*).

3843 *Ruiz* Gregorio, Don Isaac ABRABANEL... Amos 1984 ↪ 65,3345... 2,2895: ᴿOLZ 84 (1989) 178s (G. *Pfeifer*).

3844 **Smith** Gary V., Amos, a commentary. GR 1986, Regency. 307 p. $18 [TR 86,162].

3845 **Soggin** J. Alberto, The prophet Amos [1982], ᵀ*Bowden* J. 1987 ↪ 3,3712; 4,3961: ᴿCBQ 51 (1989) 539-541 (H. *Gossai*); JBL 108 (1989) 334s (J. J. *Jackson*); ScripTPamp 21 (1989) 694s (S. *Ausín*).

3846 **Stoebe** Hans J., Der Prophet Amos und sein bürgerlicher Beruf [< WDienst 5 (1957) 160-181]: ↪ 162, Geschichte 1989, 145-166.

3847 **Nielsen** Eduard, Om formkritik som hjælpemiddel i historisk-genetisk forskning, belegt ved eksempler fra Amos 1-2 og Mika 1: ➤ 148, FOTZEN B., DanTTs 52 (1989) 243-350 [< ZIT 90,302].

3848 **Barstad** Hans M., The religious polemics of Amos 2,7s: VTSup 34, 1984 ➤ 65,3354 ... 3,3715: ᴿOLZ 84 (1989) 176-8 (G. *Pfeifer*); SMSR 55 (1989) 297-304 (T. *Podella*).

3849 *Jeremias* Jörg, Tod und Leben in Am 5,1-17: ➤ 45, FDEISSLER A., Weg 1989, 134-152.

3850 *Loretz* Oswald, Die babylonischen Gottesnamen Sukkut und Kajjamānu in Amos 5,26; ein Beitrag zur jüdischen Astrologie: ZAW 101 (1989) 286-9.

3851 *King* Philip J., [Am 6,7; Jer 16,5] The *marzeaḥ*; textual and archaeological evidence [? banquet]: ➤ 218, Mem. YADIN Y., ErIsr 29 (1989) 98*-106*; 5 fig.

3852 *Loretz* Oswald, Amos VI 12: VT 39 (1989) 240-2.

3853 **Beyerlin** Walter, [Amos 7,7-9] Bleilot, Brecheisen oder was sonst?: OBO 81, 1988 ➤ 4,3975: ᴿCBQ 51 (1989) 708s (P. L. *Redditt*); RB 96 (1989) 613s (R. J. *Tournay*); TLZ 114 (1989) 266 (D. R. *Daniels*); VT 39 (1989) 242s (H. G. M. *Williamson* warns of his own forthcoming alternative).

3854 *Stoebe* Hans-J., Noch einmal zu Amos VII 10-17: VT 39 (1989) 341-354.

3855 a) *Gese* Hartmut, Amos 8,4-8 — der kosmische Frevel händlerischer Habgier; – b) *Fritz* Volkmar, Amosbuch, Amosschule und historischer Amos; – c) *Jeremias* Jörg, Völkersprüche und Visionsberichte im Amosbuch: ➤ 105, FKAISER O., Prophet 1989, 59-72 / 29-43 / 82-97.

3856 *Kessler* Rainer, Die angeblichen Kornhändler von Amos VIII, 4-7: VT 39 [nicht 29 wie oben] (1989) 13-22.

3856* *Kooij* A. van der, De tent van David, Amos 9,11-12 in de Griekse bijbel: ➤ 116, FLEEUWEN C. van 1989, 49-56.

E9.5 **Jonas.**

3857 *Barkuizen* J. H., Jona; die rekonstruksie van 'n karakter: HervTS 44 (1988) 55-70 [< OTAbs 12,89].

3858 **Barnard** Will J., *Riet* Pieter van 't, Als een duif naar het land Assur; het boek Jona... rabbijnse traditie... Kampen 1988, Kok. 172 p. ƒ29.90. – ᴿStreven 56 (1988s) 759 (P. *Beentjes*).

3859 *Ceresko* Anthony R., Jonah: ➤ 384, NJBC (1989) 580-4.

3860 **Christensen** D. L., Narrative poetics and the interpretation of the book of Jonah: ➤ 2987, Directions 1987, 29-48.

3861 **Craig** Kenneth M.ᴶ, The poetics of the book of Jonah; toward an understanding of narrative strategy: diss. Southern Baptist Theol. Sem.; ᴰ*Watts* J., 1989. 215 p. 90-08961. – DissA 50 (1989s) 2931s-A.

3862 **Darr** Katheryn P., Jonah: ➤ 377, Books 1 (1989) 381-4.

3863 ᴱDuval Yves-Marie, JÉRÔME, Jonas: SChr 323, 1985 ➤ 1,3784 ... 4,3984: ᴿMnemosyne 64 (1989) 226-230 (A. M. *Bastiaensen*); RBén 99 (1989) 221-236 (H. de *Sainte-Marie* †); RivStoLR 25 (1989) 167-170 (G. *Visonà*).

3864 **Ebach** Jürgen, Kassandra und Jona 1987 ➤ 3,3729; 4,3086: ᴿLuthMon 29 (1989) 429 (D. *Aschenbrenner*); VT 39 (1989) 243 (R. P. *Gordon*).

3865 *Elata-Alster* Gerda, *Salmon* Rachel, The deconstruction of genre in the book of Jonah; towards a theological discourse: LitTOx 3,1 (1989) 40-60 [< ZIT 89,226].

3866 *Fass* D., Jonah's forgiveness of God: JRefJud 36,3 (San Antonio 1989) 23-34 [< Judaica 45,206].

3867 *Gese* Hartmut, Jona ben Amittai und das Jonabuch: TBei 16 (1985) 256-272 [< OTAbs 12,199].

Golka Friedemann W., Jonah, revelation of God: Int. Theol. Comm. with **Knight** G., Song of Songs 1988 → 3245.

3868 *Hastoupis* Athanasios P., ⑨ The book of Jonah: TAth 60 (1989) 77-93.

3869 *Hoop* R. de, The book of Jonah as poetry; an analysis of Jonah 1,1-16: → 410, Structural/poetry 1988, 156-171.

3870 **Lacocque** André & P.-E., Le Complexe de Jonas; une étude psychologique du prophète [The Jonah Complex 1981, reworked, with response to JUNG...]: Initiations. P 1989, Cerf. 320 p. F 180. 2-204-03075-9 [BL 90,83, R.P. *Carroll*: a fine book; 'pp. 2320']. – ᴿNRT 111 (1989) 934s (J.-L. *Ska*: 'étude psycho-religieuse' en titre).

3871 **Levi** Abramo, Il mostro e la sapienza; il libro di Giona. T 1989, Gribaudi. 205 p. Lit. 15.000.

3871* *Mendiboure* Bernard, Jonas retrouve le goût du présent: Christus 36 (P 1989) 59-66.

3872 *Paper* Herbert H., Jonah in Judeo-Persian [Hebrew characters]: → 30, Mem. BLANC H. 1989, 252-5.

3873 *Payne* Robin, The prophet Jonah; reluctant messenger and intercessor: ExpTim 100 (1988s) 131-4.

3874 **Potgieter** Johan H., A narratological approach to the book of Jonah: diss. Pretoria 1989, ᴰZyl H. van. – OTEssays 2,2 (1989) 77; DissA 50 (1989s) 1340-A ('Afrikaans').

Schüngel-Straumann Helen, Giona 1989 → 3905.

3875 *Schumann* Stefan, Jona und die Weisheit — das prophetische Wort in einer zweideutigen Wirklichkeit: TZBas 45 (1989) 73-80.

3876 *Thordarson* Thorir, Notes on the semiotic context of the verb *niḥam* in the book of Jonah: SvEx 54 (1989) 226-235.

3877 *Trudinger* Paul, Jonah; a post-exilic verbal cartoon?: DowR 107 (1989) 142s.

Wolff Hans W., Jonah, ᵀKohl M. 1986 → 3900.

3878 **Zandbelt** André. Jonas: BelichtingBB. Boxtel/Brugge 1987, KBS/Tabor. 53 p. Fb 300. – ᴿCollatVL 19 (1989) 231 (P. *Kevers*); Streven 55 (1987s) 753 (P. *Beentjes*).

3879 *Cohen* Jeffrey M., Jonah's race to Nineveh [3,4]. Dor 16 (1987s) 10-17 [< OTAbs 11,178].

3879* *Dozeman* Thomas B., [Jon 4,2; Joel 2,13 God repenting] Inner-biblical interpretation of Yahweh's gracious and compassionate character: JBL 108 (1989) 207-223.

E9.6 *Michaeas*, **Micah.**

3880 **Alfaro** Juan I. [O.S.B., San Antonio] Justice and loyalty; a commentary on the book of Micah: Int. Theol. Comm. GR/E 1989, Eerdmans/Handsel. x-85 p. $10 pa. 0-8028-0431-4 [TDig 37,147].

3880* *Barker* Kenneth S., A balanced faith; Micah [...'a man by the name of Mike... brought up in a small town, moved to the big city']: ExpTim 101 (1989s) 337-9.

King Philip J., Micah 1988 → 3838.

3881 *Laberge* Léo, Micah: → 384, NJBC (1989) 249-254.

3882 *Mays* James L., Micah: → 377, Books 1 (1989) 385-390.

3883 *Nielsen* Eduard, Mika–bogen – et trøsteskrift fra eksilet [JEPPESEN K.]?: DanTTs 51 (1988) 204-219 [< OTAbs 12,90].

3884 **Renaud** Bernard, Michée – Sophonie – Nahum 1987 ⇒ 3,3740; 4,4009: RAngelicum 66 (1989) 323s (P. *Zerafa*); Biblica 70 (1989) 126-130 (Ina *Willi-Plein*); CBQ 51 (1989) 726-8 (M. A. *Sweeney*).

3885 **Schibler** Daniel, Le livre de Michée. Vaux-sur-Seine 1989, Edifac. 152 p. F 97. 2-904407-10-3.

3886 **Schuman** N A., Micha: VBGed. Kampen 1989, Kok. 188 p. *f*28. – RStreven 57 (1989s) 1047 (P. *Beentjes*).

3887 **Stansell** Gary, Micah and Isaiah [Diss Heid 1981, D*Wolff* H. W.] 1988 ⇒ 4,4010: RJRel 69 (1989) 549s (B. *Halpern*).

3888 *Moor* J. C. de, Micah I; a structural approach: ⇒ 410, Structural/poetry 1988, 172-185.

3889 **Niccacci** Alviero, Un profeta tra oppressori e oppressi: analisi esegetica del capitolo 2 di Michea nel piano generale del libro: SBF Anal 27. J 1989, Franciscan. xi-211 p. $12.

3890 *Pixley* Jorge, Miqueas 2,6-11; ¿Qué quiso silenciar la casa de Jacob? Profecía y insurrección: RBíbArg 51 (1989) 143-162.

3891 *Brin* Gershon, Micah 2,12-13, a textual and ideological study: ZAW 101 (1989) 118-124.

3892 *Strydom* J. G., Micah 4:1-5 and Isaiah 2:2-5: who said it first? A critical discussion of A. S. van der WOUDE's view: OTEssays 2/2 (Pretoria 1989) 15-28.

3893 **Diggs** James B., Implications from ancient Near Eastern deportation practices for an understanding of the authorship of 'ad-Babel in Micah 4:10: diss. SW Baptist Theol. Sem. 1988. 342 p. 89-08441. – DissA 50 (1989s) 771-A.

3894 *Stoebe* Hans J., Und demütig sein vor deinem Gott; Micha 6,8 [< WDienst 6 (1959) 180-195]: ⇒ 362, Geschichte 1989, 209-223.

3895 *Luria* B. Z., For the statues of Omri are kept... (Micah 6:16): JBQ (= Dor) 18 (1989s) 69-73.

E9.7 *Abdias, Sophonias...* **Obadiah, Zephaniah, Nahum.**

3896 *a)* **Achtemeier** Elizabeth, Obadiah and Nahum; – *b)* **Bennett** Robert A., Zephaniah: ⇒ 377, Books 1 (1989) 375-380 / 397-404.
   Mallon Elias D., Obadiah 1989 ⇒ 3820.

3897 **Schelling** P., Obadja: VBGed. Kampen 1989, Kok. 72 p. *f*15. 90-242-4688-1 [TsTNijm 29,434].

3898 *Snyman* S. D., *a)* Cohesion in the book of Obadiah: ZAW 101 (1989) 59-71; – *b)* Obadja (on)preekbar?: NduitsGT 29 (1988) 216-223 [< OT-Abs 12,89].

3899 **Wehrle** Josef, Prophetie und Textanalyse; die Komposition Obadja 1-21 interpretiert auf der Basis textlinguistischer und semiotischer Konzeptionen: Mü Univ. AOtt 28, 1987 ⇒ 3,3750; 4,4023: RJBL 108 (1989) 507-9 (M. H. *Floyd*); OLZ 84 (1989) 551-3 (R. *Stahl*); TLZ 114 (1989) 724-6 (M. *Zlatohlávek*); TR 85 (1989) 12 (O. *Loretz*).

3900 **Wolff** Hans W., Obadiah and Jonah, comm. T*Kohl* Margaret 1986 ⇒ 3,3751: RCBQ 51 (1989) 139-141 (C. R. *Seitz*).

3901 **Ball** Ivan J., A rhetorical study of Zephaniah. Berkeley 1988 [= 1973 photcopied] ⇒ 4,4024 ['1983']: RExpTim 100 (1988s) 390 (R. *Carroll*, not bad for its age).

3902 **Ben Zvi** Ehud, The book of Zephaniah; an historical-critical analysis: diss. Emory, ^D*Tucker* G. Atlanta 1989. – RTLv 21, p. 539.

3903 **Deissler** A., Zwölfpropheten III. Zefanja, Haggai, Sacharja, Maleachi: NEchter 21, 1988 ➤ 4,4025: ^RZAW 101 (1989) 149 (H.-C. *Schmitt*).

3904 **House** Paul R., Zephaniah, a prophetic drama: JStOT supp. 60. 1988 ➤ 4,4026: ^RExpTim 100 (1988s) 349 (J. F. A. *Sawyer*); JTS 40 (1989) 529s (Meg *Davies*); ScriptB 20 (1989s) 21 (B. *Robinson*).

   Hunter A. V., Zephaniah 1982 ➤ 3836.

   Renaud B., Sophonie – Nahum 1987 ➤ 3844.

3905 **Schüngel-Straumann** Helen, Sofonia – Naum – Abacuc – Abdia – Giona; Israele – e gli altri?: Bibbia per tutti. Assisi 1989, Cittadella. 92 p.

3906 *Wahl* Thomas P., Zephaniah: ➤ 384, NJBC (1989) 255-8.

3907 *Spieckermann* Hermann, [Zeph 1,15] Dies irae; der alttestamentliche Befund und seine Vorgeschichte: VT 39 (1989) 194-208.

3908 *Grol* H. W. M. van, Classical Hebrew metrics and Zephaniah 2-3: ➤ 410, Structural/poetry 1988, 186-206.

3909 **Achtemeier** Elizabeth, Nahum [through] Malachi 1986 ➤ 3,3761; 4,4027: ^RWestTJ 50 (1988) 190-2 (D. A. *Brueggemann*).

3910 **Bonora** Antonio, Nahum – Sofonia – Abacuc – Lamentazioni; dolore, protesta e speranza: LoB 1/25. Brescia 1989, Queriniana. 134 p. Lit. 15.000. 88-399-1575-3. – ^RAntonianum 64 (1989) 607 (M. *Nobile*); HumBr 44 (1989) 901s (F. *Della Vecchia*);NRT 111 (1989) 935 (J. L. *Ska*).

3911 *Christensen* D., *a)* The Book of Nahum; the question of authorship within the canonical process: JEvTS 31 (1988) 51-58 [< ZAW 102, 130; Nah 1,1-10 a hymn of theophany]; – *b)* The Book of Nahum as a liturgical composition; a prosodic analysis: JEvTS 32 (1989) 159-170 [< ZIT 89,704].

3912 **Clark** David J., *Hatton* Howard A., A translator's handbook on the books of Nahum, Habakkuk, and Zephaniah: Helps for Translators. NY 1989, United Bible Societies. ix-221 p. $7.50. 0-8267-0130-2.

3913 *Nowell* Irene, Nahum: ➤ 384, NJBC (1989) 258-261.

3914 **Seybold** Klaus, Profane Profetie, Studien zum Buch Nahum: SBS 135. Stu 1989, KBW. 107 p. DM 26,80. 3-460-04351-2 [ZAW 102, 163, H.-C. *Schmitt*].

3915 *Valčanov* Slavčo, (Bulg.) Das Buch des Propheten Nahum; textkritische Forschung: AnOchr 29 (1988 für 1980) 67-162.

3916 *Seybold* Klaus, Vormasoretische Randnotizen in Nahum 1: ZAW 101 (1989) 71-85.

3916* *Charles* J. Daryl, Plundering the lion's den — a portrait of divine fury (Nahum 2:3-11): GraceTJ 10 (1989) 183-201.

E9.8   *Habacuc,* **Habakkuk.**

3917 *Ceresko* Anthony R., Habakkuk: ➤ 384, NJBC (1989) 261-4.

3918 *Roberts* J. J. M., Habakkuk: ➤ 377, Books 1 (1989) 391-6.

   Feltes H., Die Gattung der Habakuk-Kommentar 1986 ➤ a15.

3919 **Nitzan** Bilha, ❿ Pesher Habakkuk 1986 ➤ 2,2941 ... 4,4937: ^RCBQ 51 (1989) 532s (J. E. *Wright*); RÉJ 147 (1988) 227s (A. *Caquot*).

3920 *Prinsloo* G. T. M., Die identifikasie van die goddelose in Habakuk; 'n literêre benadering: JSem 1 (1989) 88-104; bibliog. 105-7; Eng. 88.

3921 **Széles** Mária E.,   Wrath and mercy ... HabZeph 1987 ➤ 4,4037:   ᴿCBQ
51 (1989) 542s (P. L. *Redditt*, also on OGDEN G. and DEUTSCH R.: in all
three, the exegesis ignores the author's international background).

3921* *Wever* T.,   Een inclusio van godsnamen in Habakuk 1,12-17?: ➤ 116,
ᶠLEEUWEN C. van 1989, 133-160.
3922 *Mursell* Gordon, [Hab 2,1-3; Is 21,11s] The Bible and ministry: TLond
92 (1989) 15-19.
3923 **Hiebert** Theodore,   God of my victory ... Hab 3: HarvSemMon 38, 1986
➤ 2,2945; 4,4080:   ᴿBO 46 (1989) 438-440 (A. G. *Auld*); ÉTRel 64 (1989)
618 (J. *Rennes*); OLZ 84 (1989) 679-683 (Eva *Osswald*); VT 39 (1989) 509s
(H. *Williamson*).
3924 *Hiebert* T.,   The use of inclusion in Habakkuk 3: ➤ 2987, Directions
1987, 118-149.
3925 *Tsumura* David T.,   Ugaritic poetry and Habakkuk 3 (1989) 24-48.
3926 *Giannarelli* Elena,   Abacuc [3,3], la montagna ombreggiata e Maria:
➤ 567, AnStoEseg 6 (1989) 77-88; Eng. 7.

E9.9   *Aggaeus,* **Haggai** – *Zacharias,* **Zechariah** – *Malachias,* **Malachi.**

3927 *Cody* Aelred,   Haggai Zechariah Malachi: ➤ 384, NJBC (1989) 349-361.
Deissler A.,   Haggai, Sacharja, Maleachi 1988 ➤ 3903.
3928 **Meyers** C. & E.,   Haggai, Zechariah 1-8: AnchorB 25B, 1987 ➤ 3,3781;
4,4044:   ᴿBA 52 (1989) 50-52 (H. G. M. *Williamson*); BibleBh 15 (1989)
199s (G. *Mangatt*); BL (1989) 58s (R. J. *Coggins*); CBQ 51 (1989) 722-4
(M. *Prokurat*); JRel 68 (1988) 582s (M. A. *Sweeney*).
3929 *Ollenburger* Ben C.,   Haggai, Zechariah and Malachi: ➤ 377, Books 1
(1989) 405-414.
3930 **Stendebach** Franz-Josef,   Aggeo-Zaccaria; Malachia-Gioele; profezia e
tempio [Prophetie und Tempel 1977], ᵀ*Filippi* Emilio: Bibbia per tutti.
Assisi 1989, Cittadella.   123 p. Lit. 12.000.
3931 **Stuhlmueller** Carroll,   Rebuilding with hope; a commentary on the books
of Haggai and Zechariah: IntTComm. 1988 ➤ 4,4048:   ᴿÉTRel 64 (1989)
111s (J. *Pons*: rather a good thing that the series does not live up to its
claim of actualization); ExpTim 100 (1988s) 189 (C. S. *Rodd*).
3932 *Vena* O. D.,   Visionarios vs. establishment en la comunidad judía
postexílica: Cuadernos de Teología 9 (BA 1988) 85-98 [< Stromata
45,499].
3933 **Verhoef** Pieter A.,   The books of Haggai and Malachi: NICOT 1987
➤ 3,3783; 4,4049:   ᴿAndrUnS 26 (1988) 310-2 (W. H. *Hessel*); GraceTJ
10 (1989) 86-88 (R. *Patterson*); ScriptB 20 (1989s) 20s (B. *Robinson*: the
author wrote in Dutch a more technical commentary on Mal 1972);
WestTJ 51 (1989) 160-2 (A. M. *Harman*).
3934 **Wyrick** Stephen V.,   Haggai's appeal to tradition; imagination used as
authority: ➤ 592, Systemic 1 (1989) 117-125.

3935 *Hildebrand* David R.,   Temple ritual; a paradigm for moral holiness in
Haggai II 10-19: VT 39 (1989) 154-168.

3936 *Amsler* Samuel,   Des visions de Zacharie à l'apocalypse d'Ésaïe 24-27:
➤ 614, Isaiah Lv 1987/9, 263-273.

3937 **Rokay** Zoltán, Die Nachtgesichte des Propheten Sacharja; eine einzelexegetische Untersuchung: Diss. ᴰ*Gamper* A. Innsbruck 1988s. – TR 85 (1989) 512; RTLv 21,541; ZkT 111 (1989) 521s.

3938 **Schöttler** Hans-G., [Zech 1-6] Gott inmitten seines Volkes: TrierTSt 43, ᴰ1987 → 3,3791: ᴿExpTim 100 (1988s) 430 (R. *Coggins*).

3939 *Redditt* Paul L., Israel's shepherds; hope and pessimism in Zechariah 9-14: CBQ 51 (1989) 631-642.

3940 **Willi-Plein** Ina, Prophetie am Ende; Untersuchungen zu Sacharja 9-14: HDiss. Basel 1988s. – TR 85 (1989) 511.

3941 *Hill* Andrew E., Dating Second Zechariah; a linguistic reexamination: HebAnR 6 (1982) 105-134 [< OTAbs 11,180].

3942 *Paul* Shalom M., A technical expression from archery in Zechariah IX 13a: VT 39 (1989) 495-7.

3943 *Gordon* R.P., Targumic '*dy* (Zechariah XIV 6) and the not so common 'cold': VT 39 (not 29 as bot.; 1989) 77-81.

3944 *Berquist* Jon L., The social setting of Malachi: BibTB 19 (1989) 121-6.

3945 *Bossman* David M., Kinship and religious system in the prophet Malachi: → 592, Systemic 1 (1989) 127-142.

3946 **Glazier-McDonald** Beth, Malachi: SBL diss. 98 [Chicago 1983], 1987 → 3,3793: ᴿCBQ 51 (1989) 517s (E. *Achtemeier*); JBL 108 (1989) 127s (B.V. *Malchow*).

3947 **Kaiser** Walter C., Malachi; God's unchanging love 1984 → 65,3423; 2,2964: ᴿCriswTJ 2 (1987s) 141-4 (G. *Galeotti*: best of 36 commentaries surveyed).

3948 *a*) *Klein* George L., An introduction to Malachi; – *b*) *Clendenen* E. Ray, The structure of Malachi; a textlinguistic study; – *c*) *Wells* C. Richard, The subtle crises of secularism; preaching the burden of Israel; – *d*) *Harrison* George W., Covenant unfaithfulness in Malachi 2: 1-16; – *e*) *Kaiser* Walter C., Divorce in Malachi 2:10-16; – *f*) *Davis* George D., [Mal 3,8s] Are Christians supposed to tithe?; – *g*) *Blomberg* Craig L., Elijah, election, and the use of Malachi in the NT: CriswTJ 2 (1987s) 19-37 / 3-17 / 39-61 / 63-72 / 73-84 / 85-97 / 99-117.

3949 *a*) *Smith* G.V., Alienation and restoration; a Jacob-Esau typology; – *b*) *Ricks* S.D., The prophetic literality of tribal reconstruction; – *c*) *Stuart* D.K., The prophetic ideal of government in the restoration era: → 77, ᶠHARRISON R., Israel's apostasy and restoration 1988, 165-174 / 273-281 / 283-292.

3949* *Utzschneider* Helmut, Kunder oder Schreiber? Eine These zum Problem der 'Schriftprophetie' auf Grund von Maleachi 1,6-2,9: BErfATJ 19. Fra 1989, Lang. 102 p. Fs 36 [TR 86,162]. 3-631-42294-6.

> IX. NT Exegesis generalis

F1. **New Testament Introduction.**

3950 *Aland* Barbara, Die Rezeption des neutestamentlichen Textes in den ersten Jahrhunderten → 606, Réception 1986/9, 1-38.

3950* *Andreatta* Bruno, Las dos edades en Virgilio; connotaciones cristianas: RBíbArg 51 (1989) 111-126.
3951 **Aune** David E., The NT in its literary environment 1987 ⇒ 3,3801; 4,4071; 0-664-21912-8; also C 1988, Clarke. £13; pa. 1989; 0-664-25018-1: RClasR 39 (1989) 388s (A. *Wedderburn*); CurrTM 16 (1989) 455 (E. *Krentz*, enthusiastic); Interpretation 43 (1989) 298-300 (Jouette M. *Bassler*: also enthusiastic despite mild reserves); JStNT 36 (1989) 124 (R. A. *Burridge*); ScotJT 42 (1989) 590s (D. C. *Parker*: not eulogistic); TLond 92 (1989) 325s (G. *Stanton*: excellent); TR 85 (1989) 290s (D. *Zeller*).
3952 **Bammel** Ernst, Jesu Nachfolger... des frühen Christentums, 1988 ⇒ 4,4072: RGregorianum 70 (1989) 797-9 (J. *Janssens*, ital.); JTS 40 (1989) 553s (M. E. *Glasswell*); TLZ 114 (1989) 436s (W. *Vogler*); TR 85 (1989) 374s (T. *Söding*); ZKG 100 (1989) 409-411 (J. C. *Salzmann*).
3953 **Baxter** M., The formation of the Christian Scriptures. Ph 1988, Westminster. 148 p. $9 [cf. ⇒ 4,4283; 4,4120; TS 50,212].
3954 **Berger** Klaus, Hermeneutik des NTs 1988 ⇒ 4,4076: RSWJT 32,2 (1989s) 62s (E. E. *Ellis*); TsTNijm 29 (1989) 288 (A. van *Diemen*).
3955 **Berger** Klaus, *Colpe* Carsten, Religionsgeschichtliches Textbuch zum NT 1987 ⇒ 3,3805; 4,4075: RCBQ 51 (1989) 145s (Pheme *Perkins*: 626 parallels, avoiding better-known ones like Thomas Gospel); Neotestamentica 23 (1989) 359 (W. S. *Vorster*).
3956 *Beyer* Klaus, Woran erkennt man, dass ein griechischer Text aus dem Hebräischen oder Aramäischen übersetzt ist?: ⇒ 126, FMACUCH R., Hokmôt 1989, 21-31 [Quellen der Synoptiker und der Apokalypse; Apg/Joh-Ev originalgriechisch aber unter semitischem Einfluss].
3957 **Boor** Werner de, *Pohl* Adolf, Neues Testament: Wuppertaler Studienbibel [begründet von *Rienecker* Fritz]. Wu/Giessen 1989, Brockhaus/ Brunnen. I. *Rienecker*, Ev.Mt. 1989. 555 p. 3-417-25141-9 / 3-7655-5431-6 [+ 6 vol. through Apc].
3958 *a) Brown* Schuyler, Jesus, history and the kerygma; a hermeneutical reflection; – *b) Kasper* Walter, Prolegomena zur Erneuerung der geistlichen Schriftauslegung; – *c) Schürmann* Heinz, Die neutestamentliche Bibelwissenschaft als theologische Disziplin; ein interdisziplinärer Gesprächsbeitrag: ⇒ 68, FGNILKA J., Vom Urchristentum 1989, 487-496 / 508-526 / 527-533.
3959 *Cady* S., *Taussig* H., Jesus and Sophia [or Sophia's child]: Daughters of Sarah 14,6 (Ch 1988) 7-11 [< NTAbs 33,197).
3960 **Carmody** John & Denise L., *Robbins* Gregory A., Exploring the NT 1986 ⇒ 3,3809: RHorizons 16 (1989) 376s (Mary R. *D'Angelo*).
3961 **Davies** Stevan L., The New Testament, a contemporary introduction 1988 ⇒ 4,4081: RSWJT 32,2 (1989s) 60 (E. E. *Ellis*).
EEpp Eldon J., *MacRae* George W., The New Testament and its modern interpreters 1989 ⇒ 394.
3962 **Ferguson** Everett, Backgrounds of early Christianity 1987 ⇒ 3,3817; 4,4086: RChH 50 (1989) 367 (J. K. *Brackett*: good for introductory NT courses); CriswT 3 (1988s) 214s (S. *Sheeley*); GraceTJ 10 (1989) 244-6 (D. B. *Sandy*).
3963 **Fernández Ramos** F., El Nuevo Testamento, I. presentación y contenido: Síntesis 1/1. M 1988, Atenas. 395 p. – RSalmanticensis 36 (1989) 379-381 (R. *Trevijano*); Studium 29 (1989) 346s (L. *López de las Heras*).
3964 **Ford** Josephine M., Bonded with the immortal; a pastoral introduction to the NT 1987 ⇒ 3,3818; 4,4087: RHorizons 16 (1989) 153s (J. A. *Grassi*).

3965 **Graaff** [➤ 4,4089 Graff] F. de,   Jezus de Verborgene; een voorbereiding tot inwijding in de mysteriën van het Evengelie.   Kampen 1987, Kok. 567 p. ƒ79,50. – ᴿBijdragen 50 (1989) 339s (W. G. *Tillmans*).

3966 **Grant** Patrick,   Reading the New Testament.   GR/Basingstoke 1989, Eerdmans/Macmillan.   ix-161 p.   £27.50 [JTS 41,354].   0-8028-0448-9 / 0-333-43618-0. – ᴿExpTim 101 (1989s) 84 (R. *Morgan*).

3967 **Grelot** Pierre, [*Dumais* Marcel, Actes], Homélies sur l'Écriture à l'époque apostolique: IntrNT² 8.   P 1989, Desclée.   320 p.   F 145.   2-7189-0413-5. – ᴿEsprVie 99 (1989) 547-550 (É. *Cothenet*).

3968 **Guijarro Oporto** Santiago,   La buena noticia de Jesús 1987 ➤ 3,3823; 4,4091:   ᴿSalmanticensis 36 (1989) 108s (F. F. *Ramos*).

3969 **Guillemette** Nil,   On the evening of the third day; how to study the New Testament [1980 ➤ 61,5067],ᵀ: Loyola Theology Textbook.   Makati, Philippines 1989, St. Paul.   xix-353 p.   971-504-092-6.

3970 **Guitton** J.,   Le Nouveau Testament, une nouvelle lecture.   P 1987, Desclée de Brouwer.   95 p.   F 60   pa.   2-220-02659-0 [NTAbs 33,236]. – ᴿLavalTP 45 (1989) 172 (R. *Sauvageau*).

3971 *Healey* Joseph G.,   Our stories as 'fifth gospels' [his 1981 'A fifth gospel; in search of black Christian values', etc.: brief history of the metaphor 'a fifth gospel']: AfER 30 (1988) 151-165.

3972 *Hodgson* Robertᴶ,   Valerius MAXIMUS [anthology of over 1000 chreia-type anecdotes published about 31 C.E., surviving in two 9th century manuscripts and two 5th century epitomes]: CBQ 51 (1989) 502-510.

ᴱ**Horsley** G. H. R.,   New documents illustrating early Christianity 4 (for 1979) 1987 ➤ b679 [5. Linguistic essays 1989 ➤ 401].

3973 **Hromadka** Josef L. ⓜ The Gospel in men's way, ᵀ*Huszti* Kálmán. – c. 1989, c. 300 p. – ᴿTSzem 32 (1989) 253s (J. *Szigeti*).

3974 **Johnson** Luke T.,   The writings of the NT 1986 ➤ 3,3828; 4,4094: ᴿCurrTM 16 (1989) 462 (W. C. *Linss*: a strange mixture); ScripTPamp 21 (1989) 350 (J. M. *Casciaro*).

3975 **Kegel** G.,   Und ich sah einen neuen Himmel und eine neue Erde; das Neue Testament und die Heilung der Welt [NT focus was not God's saving action in Jesus but the healing of the world].   Gü 1988, Mohn. 319 p. DM 78 pa.   3-579-00086-1 [NTAbs 33,121].

Kinneavy James L.,   Greek rhetorical origins of Christian faith 1987 ➤ g745.

3976 *Knox* John,   J. A. T. ROBINSON and the meaning of New Testament scholarship: TLond 92 (1989) 251-268.

3977 **Köster** Helmut,   Introducción al Nuevo Testamento; historia, cultura y religión de la época helenística e historia y literatura del cristianismo primitivo, ᵀ*Lacarra* Javier, *Piñero* Antonio [➤ 4,4095!]: BiblEstB 59, 1988:   ᴿActuBbg 26 (1989) 196s (J. *Boada*); CommSev 22 (1989) 264s (M. de *Burgos*); LumenVr 38 (1989) 337s (F. *Ortiz de Urtaran*); SalT 77 (1989) 595-7 (J. R. *Busto Saiz*).

3978 **Lips** Hermann von,   Weisheitliche Traditionen im Neuen Testament: ev. HDiss. ᴰ*Hahn* F.   München 1988s. – TR 85 (1989) 511; RTLv 21,546.

3979 **Lührmann** Dieter,   An itinerary for New Testament study [Auslegung 1984 ➤ 65,3717], ᵀ*Bowden* John.   L/Ph 1989, SCM/Trinity.   ix-131 p. $10.   0-334-02076-X [TDig 37,169].

3980 **MacArthur** John F.ᴶ,   The Gospel according to Jesus.   GR 1988, Zondervan. – ᴿBS 146 (1989) 21-40 (D. L. *Bock*: his opposition to combining 'being saved' with 'sinful life' is open to misunderstanding).

Mack B., *Robbins* V., Patterns of persuasion in the Gospels ➤ 4628.
MacRae George W., Studies in the New Testament and Gnosticism 1988
➤ a466.
3982 **Malherbe** A.J., Moral exhortation, a Greco-Roman sourcebook 1986
➤ 2,8902; 3,b146: ᴿCurrTM 16 (1989) 135 (F.W. *Danker*).
3983 *Malherbe* Abraham J., The world of the New Testament; Greco-Roman
religion and philosophy: ➤ 394, NT/Interpreters 1989, 3-26.
3984 *Malina* Bruce J., Christ and time; Swiss or Mediterranean? [CULL-
MANN O. 1946; BARR J. 1962...: CBA presidential address, Santa Clara
Aug. 15, 1988]: CBQ 51 (1989) 1-30; diagram 31.
3985 **Marinelli** Anthony J., Understanding the Gospels; a guide for
beginners. NY 1988, Paulist. iii-111 p. $5 pa. 0-8091-3037-8 [NTAbs
33,387].
3986 **Moloney** F.J., The living voice of the Gospel 1987 ➤ 3,3839; 4,4101:
ᴿIrTQ 55 (1989) 164 (S.P. *Kealy*); ScotJT 42 (1989) 575 (T.S.N.
Goubule: well worth reading).
3987 **Neill** Stephen [1964], ²*Wright* Tom, The interpretation of the NT
1861-1986: 1988 ➤ 4,4103; £22.50; pa. £7. – ᴿJTS 40 (1989) 729 (Morna
D. *Hooker*); NBlackf 70 (1989) 46s (C. *Rowland*).
3988 *Odelain* O. *Séguineau* R., Concordance thématique du NT. P 1989,
Cerf. 1100 p. F 249. – ᴿEsprVie 99 (1989) 294s (É. *Cothenet*).
3989 *Ogden* Schubert M., The problem of normative witness; a response:
PerkJ 41,3 (1988) 22-26 [< NTAbs 33,140].
3990 **Palmer** David G., Sliced bread [chiasmus and numerical schemes
dominating Gospels, Acts, Rev]. 1988, Ceridwen. 160 p. £6. 0-951-
3661-06. – ᴿExpTim 101 (1989s) 95 [C.S. *Rodd*: amuses, irritates].
3991 **Papineau** André, Lightly goes the Good News; making the Gospel your
own story. Mystic CT 1988, Twenty-Third. [xiii-]129 p. $8 [CBQ
51,785].
3992 **Penna** Romano, Letture evangeliche; saggi esegetici sui quattro vangeli
[Lezioni Univ. Lateranense]: StudRicB. R 1989, Borla. 238 p. 88-263-
0742-3.
3993 **Perkins** Pheme, Reading the NT² 1988 ➤ 4,4104: ᴿEstBíb 47 (1989)
569s (L.F. *García-Viana*); LvSt 14 (1989) 166s (R.F. *Collins*); NBlackf 70
(1989) 153s (E. *Franklin*: sometimes infuriating, always stimulating); RRel
48 (1989) 949s (Judette M. *Kolasny*).
3994 **Petzer** Kobus [= Jacobus], Die teks van die Nuwe Testament, 'n
inleiding in die basiese aspekte van die teorie en praktyk van die
tekskritiek van die Nuwe Testament: HervTSt supp 2. Pretoria 1990,
Fakulteit Teologie. xvii-353 p. [ETL 66,409, F. *Neirynck*].
3995 **Roetzel** Calvin J., The world that shaped the NT 1985 ➤ 2,3007...
4,4108: ᴿBibTB 19 (1989) 40 (Carolyn *Osiek*: uneven); ScripTPamp 21
(1989) 945 (J.M. *Casciaro*).
3996 **Schweitzer** Albert, Gespräche über das NT [< Ev.-p. Kirchenbote
1901-4], ᴱ*Dobertin* Winfried. Mü 1988, Bechtle. 215 p. DM 24. 3-
7628-0480-X [ÉTRel 64,629].
3997 **Schweizer** Eduard, Theologische Einleitung in das Neue Testament:
Grundrisse NT 7. Gö 1989, Vandenhoeck & R. 176 p. DM 26 pa.
3-525-51370-4 [NTAbs 33,381].
3998 **Segalla** Giuseppe, Panorama letterario/teologico del NT: LoB 3.6 1986/7
➤ 3,3852 / 3,9178; 4,a167: ᴿGregorianum 70 (1989) 151s (E. *Farahian*) &
152s (E. *Rasco*).

3999 **Segalla** Giuseppe, Panoramas del Nuevo Testamento [1986 → 3,3852], ᵀ*Ortiz García* A. Estella 1989, VDivino. 487 p. [NatGrac 36, 376, F. F. *Ramos*]. – ᴿBibFe 15 (1989) 486 (M. *Sáenz Galache*).

4000 *a) Sheeley* Steven, The narrator in the Gospels; developing a model; – *b) Sykes* John, Literary parables of divine redemption; a review article [of?: ᴢɪᴛ 90,164]: PerspRelSt 16 (1989) 213-224 / 157(-196?).

4002 **Strack** Jay, *Witty* Robert G., The New Testament way to revival. Nv 1989, Broadman. 144 p. – ᴿSWJT 32,2 (1989s) 80s (M. *McDow*).

4003 **Strecker** G., Neues Testament; *Maier* J., Antikes Judentum: Urban-TB 422, Grundkurs Theol. 2. Stu 1989, Kohlhammer. 192 p. DM 22 pa. 3-17-010266-4 [NTAbs 33,381].

4004 **Stuhlmacher** P., Vom Verstehen des NTs³ 1986 → 2,3012: ᴿProtestantesimo 44 (1989) 61s (F. *Ferrario*).

4005 *Stuhlmacher* P., *al.*, NT Hermeneutik: → 894, EvKL 2 (1988) 494-6 (-502).

4006 **Tuckett** Christopher, Reading the New Testament; methods of interpretation 1987 → 3,3858; 4,4113: ᴿCBQ 51 (1989) 167s (R. A. *Edwards*).

4007 [Oriol] **Tuñi i Vancells** Josep, *a*) Jesús en comunitat; el Nou Testament, un accés a Jesús: Horitzons 18. Barc 1988, Claret. 111 p. 84-7263-530-9. – *b*) Jesús en comunidad; el Nuevo Testamento medio de acceso a Jesús, ᵀ*Pericas* Rafael M.: Presencia Teológica. Santander 1988, Sal Terrae. 154 p. 84-3293-0822-9. – ᴿActuBbg 26 (1989) 200 (J. I. *González Faus*); BibFe 15 (1989) 323 (M. *Sáenz Galache*).

F1.2   *Origo Evangeliorum;* The Origin of the Gospels.

4007* *Black* Matthew, The use of rhetorical terminology in Pᴀᴘɪᴀs on Mark and Matthew: → 84, ᶠHɪʟʟ D., JStNT 37 (1989) 31-41.

4008 **Drane** J., Gesù e i quattro Vangeli 1986 [1979; franç. 1984 → 65,3538]: ᴿProtestantesimo 44 (1989) 58s (P. *Tognina*).

4009 **Gerhardsson** Birger, The Gospel tradition 1986 → 2,3027... 4,4127: ᴿScotJT 42 (1989) 118s (E. *Best*).

4010 **Grelot** Pierre, Évangiles et tradition apostolique [Tʀᴇsᴍᴏɴᴛᴀɴᴛ 1983] 1984 → 65,3488... 2,3028: ᴿDowR 107 (1989) 226s (A. G. *Murray:* perhaps pardonably strident, perhaps also less convincing on some points).

4011 **Grelot** P., L'origine des Évangiles... J. Cᴀʀᴍɪɢɴᴀᴄ 1986 → 2,3029... 4,4129: ᴿAnnTh 3 (1989) 379-382 (B. *Estrada*); IndTSt 25 (1988) 105-7 (L. *Legrand*).

4012 *Hahneman* Geoffrey, More on redating the Muratorian fragment [Sᴜɴᴅʙᴇʀɢ A. 1973: early 4th century; Cᴀᴍᴘᴏs J., 1960, 5th]: → 696, 10th Patristic, 19 (1989) 359-365.

4013 *Koester* Helmut, From the kerygma-gospel to written gospels [... origin of *euangelion* and of its use for 'gospel']: NTS 35 (1989) 361-381.

4014 *Marguerat* D., Raconter Dieu; l'évangile comme narration historique: → 385, Narration 1988, 83-106.

4015 **O'Grady** John F., The Four Gospels and the Jesus tradition. NY 1989, Paulist. vi-275 p. $12. 0-8091-3085-8.

4016 **Stanton** Graham N., The Gospels and Jesus: Oxford Bible Series. NY 1989, Oxford-UP. x-296 p. $50; pa. $13. 0-19-213240-7; 1-5 [TDig 37,188]. – ᴿExpTim 101,4 top choice (1989s) 97-100 (C. S. *Rodd*).

4017 *Williams* David S.,   Reconsidering MARCION's Gospel: JBL 108 (1989)
477-496.

F1.3   **Historicitas,** *chronologia* **Evangeliorum.**

4018 **Blomberg** Craig L.,   The historical reliability of the Gospels 1987
➤ 3,3886; 4,4139:   ᴿWestTJ 50 (1988) 357-9 (J. W. *Scott*).
4019 **Bruce** F. F.,   Gesù visto dai contemporanei; le testimonianze non
bibliche [Jesus and Christian origins 1974 ²1984], ᵀ*Corsani* Mirella; intr.
Tommasetto D.: Piccola bibl. teol. 19. T 1989, Claudiana. viii-209 p. Lit.
18.000. 88-7016-077-4. – ᴿStPatav 36 (1989) 623s (G. *Segalla*).
4020 *Cunningham* L. S.,   His story in history [DONAHUE J., KRIEG R.,
FREDRIKSEN P., SAWICKI M., SCHREITER R., all 1988]: Commonweal
115 (1988) 694-6.
4021 *Ellis* E. Earle,   Reading the Gospels as history: CriswT 3 (1988s) 3-15.
4022 *a) Grech* Prosper,   La storicità dei detti di Gesù; problemi e soluzioni; –
    b) Pesce Mauro,   Problemi aperti nello studio della tradizione
protocristiana; – *c) Montanari* Fausto,   La poesia del Vangelo: ➤ 572*,
Storia/ preistoria Vangeli 1986/8, 25-39 / 91-120 / 9-15.
4023 **Grelot** Pierre,   Los Evangelios y la historia, ᵀ*Arias* Isidro, 1988
➤ 4,4147:   ᴿLumenVr 38 (1989) 445s (U. *Gil Ortega*); RazFe 217 (1988)
556s (J. *García Pérez*); ScripTPamp 21 (1989) 943s (J. M. *Casciaro*).
4024 **Grelot** Pierre,   Los evangelios; origen, fechas, historicidad: CuadB 45,
1984 ➤ 65,3489:   ᴿRBíbArg 51 (1989) 45-47 (R. *Krüger*).
4025 **Grelot** P.,   Les paroles de Jésus: Intr. 3/7 1986 ➤ 2,3046... 4,4148:
ᴿÉglT 19 (1988) 256-8 (M. *Dumais*).
4026 **Grelot** Pierre,   Las palabras de Jesucristo 1988 ➤ 4,4140:   Carthaginensia 5 (1989) 286s (J. F. *Cuenca*); CiTom 116 (1989) 626 (J. L.
Espinel); EstAgust 24 (1989) 528 (C. *Mielgo*); RelCu 35 (1989) 140 (M. A.
Martín Juárez).
4027 **Grelot** Pierre,   Introduzione al NT, 6. Vangeli e storia; 7. Le parole di
Gesù Cristo. R 1988, Borla. 313 p.; 329 p. Lit. 25.000 ciascuno. –
ᴿBenedictina 36 (1989) 578-581 (L. *De Lorenzi*); CC 140 (1989,3) 94s (V.
Fusco).
4028 **Nanteuil** Hugues de,   Sur les dates de naissance et de mort de Jésus. P
1988, Téqui. 114 p. – ᴿScripTPamp 21 (1989) 702 (F. *Varo*).
4029 **Robinson** John A. T.,   Re-dater le NT 1987 ➤ 3,3898; 4,4151: ᴿBLitEc
90 (1989) 65 (S. *Légasse*); RHR 206 (1989) 310-2 (A. *Méhat*).

F1.4   *Jesus historicus* – **The human Jesus.**

4030 **Barclay** W.,   The mind of Jesus, crucified and crowned [< British
Weekly articles]. L 1988 = 1960, James. 190 p.; 192 p. £3 each. 0-
85305-291-3; 2-1 [NTAbs 33,242].
4031 **Barclay** William,   Los hombres del maestro [The master's men; the
apostles in general and in particular], ᵀC. P. M.: Biblioteca Catecumenal.
Bilbao 1988, Desclée de Brouwer. 258 p. – ᴿLumenVr 38 (1989) 189s (U.
Gil Ortega).
4032 *Barón* Enrique, Lo humano de la persona de Jesús: ➤ 7, ᶠALFARO J.,
EstE 64 (1989) 365-375.
4033 **Barton** Gerald,   The man who conquered the world. L 1988, Churchman. 87 p. £3. 1-85093-065-1 [ExpTim 100, 359].

4034 *Beaude* Pierre-Marie, Jesús de Nazaret, [T]*Darrical* Nicolas. Estella 1988, VDivino. 228 p. 84-7151-534-2. – [R]ActuBbg 26 (1989) 50 (J. *Boada*).

4035 **Bezançon** Jean Noël, Jésus le Christ. P 1989, Desclée de Brouwer. 154 p. – [R]EsprVie 99 (1989) 287 (P. *Jay*: admirable).

4036 **Biser** E., Der Freund; Annäherungen an Jesus. Mü 1989, Piper. 341 p. DM 20 [MüTZ 40,377].

4037 **Boers** Hendrikus, Who was Jesus? The historical Jesus and the synoptic gospels. SF 1989, Harper & R. xix-143 p. $25. 0-06-060809-9 [TDig 36,354].

4038 **Bordoni** Marcello, Gesù di Nazaret; presenza, memoria, attesa: Bibl-TeolContemporanea 57. Brescia 1988, Queriniana. 463 p. Lit. 39.000. 88-399-0357-7 [Greg 70,407]. – [R]StPatav 36 (1989) 584-7 (E. R. *Tura*).

4039 **Borg** M. J., Jesus, a new vision 1987 → 4,4155: [R]BibTB 19 (1989) 70 (M. *McVann*); CCurr 38 (1988s) 358-360 (D. F. *Gray*, also on M. de JONGE); Forum 5,4 (1989) 71-82 (D. M. *Smith*); Interpretation 43 (1989) 422.424 (C. C. *Black*); QRMin 9,1 (1989) 104-8 (P. F. *Aspan*); TTod 46 (1989s) 119s (B. *Chilton*).

4040 **Bowden** John, Jesus, the unanswered questions 1988 → 4,4157: [R]Exp-Tim 100 (1988s) 108s (J. A. *Ziesler*); Pacifica 2 (1989) 360-3 (A. *Hamilton*); TLond 92 (1988) 206s (C. C. *Rowland*).

4041 [TE]**Braaten** C. E., M. KÄHLER, The so-called historical Jesus and the historic biblical Christ [1896]: Fortress texts in modern theology. Ph 1988 = c. 1963, Fortress. viii-152 p. $9. 0-8006-1206-0 [NTAbs 33,248].

4042 **Bruce** F. F., The hard sayings of Jesus [69 from Synoptics, plus one] 1983 → 64,3915: [R]RExp 86 (1989) 626 (R. *Bailey*). /

4043 **Bruggen** Jakob van, Christus op aarde; zijn levensbeschrijving door leerlingen en tijdgenoten: CommNT NS 1, 1987 → 4,4160; *f* 49,50: [R]TLZ 114 (1989) 30 (M. *Rese*).

4044 **Carreira das Neves** Joaquim, Jesus Cristo, história e fé: Espírito e vida 2. Braga 1989, Franciscana. 322 p.

4045 **Coulot** Claude, Jésus et le disciple; étude sur l'autorité messianique de Jésus [diss. Strasbourg]: ÉtBN 8, 1987 → 3,3917; 4,4163; F 290: [R]ÉTRel 64 (1989) 633s (H. *Cousin*).

4046 **Cunningham** Philip A., Jesus and the Evangelists; the ministry of Jesus [and its portrayal] in the Synoptic Gospels 1988 → 4,4166: [R]ExpTim 100 (1988s) 432 (G. T. *Eddy*: radical); ScriptB 20 (1989s) 22s (H. *Wansbrough*).

4047 **Domeris** W., Matthew, 88 p. – **Guttler** M., Mark, 64 p. – **Germond** P., Luke, 96 p. – Domeris & *Wortley* R., John, 80 p.: Portraits of Jesus; a contextual [South Africa] approach to Bible study. L 1987s, Collins. £2 each. 0-00-599974-X; 3,1; 5-8; 6-6 [NTAbs 33,284].

4048 *Douglas* Hugh O. †, The humour of Jesus: ExpTim 101 (1989s) 204s.

4049 *Evans* Craig A., Authenticity criteria in Life of Jesus research: ChrSchR 19 (1989) 3-31 [< ZIT 89,763].

Fitzmyer J. A., Scripture and Christology 1986 → 7424*ab*; **Forte** B., Cristologia 1988 → 7495.

4050 **Floris** Ennio, Sous le Christ, Jésus; méthode d'analyse référentielle appliquée aux Évangiles 1987 → 4,4171: [R]RHPR 69 (1989) 220s (É. *Trocmé*).

4051 **Foley** Leonard, A story of Jesus, for those who have only heard rumors. Cincinnati 1988, St. Anthony Messenger. v-38 p. $3 pa. [Horizons 16,206].

4052 *Fowl* Stephen, Reconstructing and deconstructing the quest of the historical Jesus [*Sanders* E.P., Jesus and Judaism 1985, put into W. *Runciman* categories]: ScotJT 42 (1989) 319-333.

4053 **Fredriksen** Paula, From Jesus to Christ; the origins of the New Testament images of Jesus. NHv 1988, Yale Univ. xii-256 p. $22.50. – ᴿTS 50 (1989) 789 (A.C. *Mitchell*); TTod 46 (1989s) 218.220.222 (C.C. *Black*).

4054 **Goergen** Donald J., Mission and Ministry of Jesus 1986 → 4,4172: ᴿÉglT 19 (1988) 430s (R.P. *Hardy*, Eng.); RelStT 7,2s (1987) 88-90 (E. *Segal*).

4055 **Guelluy** R., Mais il y a Jésus-Christ. P 1989, Duculot. 197 p. Fb 540. – ᴿRTLv 20 (1989) 395s (G. *Thils* suggère sans éclaircir un rapport avec l'OCKHAM de sa spécialisation).

4056 *Hellwig* Monika, Re-emergence of the human, critical, public Jesus: TS 50 (1989) 466-480.

4057 **Herbst** K., Der wirkliche Jesus; das total andere Gottesbild. Olten 1988, Walter. 295 p. DM 33. 3-530-34551-2. – ᴿTsTNijm 29 (1989) 307 (R. *Cornelissen*: the author is a Catholic priest who moved from DDR to BR after 'a theological conflict with Church authorities').

4058 *Hollenbach* Paul, The historical Jesus question in America today: BibTB 19 (1989) 11-22.

4059 **Hollmann** Klaus, Gesucht: Jesus; eine Wegbeschreibung. Pd 1989, Bonifatius. 155 p. DM 16,80. 3-87088-561-0 [TPQ 137,183 adv.].

4060 *Holtz* Traugott, Jesus: → 894, EvKL 2 (1988) 824-831.

4061 *Howell* O.M., The humanity of Christ: Emmanuel 95,3 (NY 1989) 162-7 [< NTAbs 33,296].

4062 **Hurth** Elizabeth, In his name; comparative studies in the quest for the historical Jesus; Life of Jesus research in Germany and America [diss. Boston: Univ.; complement and corrective to SCHWEITZER A.: ᴰHall D. 650 p. 89-13765. – DissA 50 (1989s) 979s-A]: EurHS 23/367. Fra 1989, Lang. xv-336 p. Fs 75. – TR 86,251. 3-631-41955-4.

4063 **Knopp** Robert L., Finding Jesus in the Gospels; a companion to Mark, Matthew, Luke and John. ND 1989, Ave Maria. 326 p. $10. 0-87793-405-3 [TDig 37,166].

4064 **Kudasiewicz** Józef, ⊖ Jesus historii a Chrystus wiary 1987 → 3,3936; 4,4180: ᴿAtKap 112 (1989) 484-490 (Z. *Pawlak* ⊖).

4065 *Kudasiewicz* Józef, ⊖ Der Jesus der Geschichte und der Christus des Glaubens; aktueller Stand der Debatte: RoczTK 33,1 (1986) 47-68; deutsch 60.

4066 *Kümmel* Werner G., Jesusforschung seit 1981: TRu 54 (1989) 1-53.

4067 **Leivestad** Ragnar, Jesus in his own perspective; an examination of his sayings, actions, and eschatological titles, ᵀ*Aune* David E. 1987 → 3,3938; 4,4187: ᴿBibTB 19 (1989) 38s (R.L. *Mowery*); BS 146 (1989) 112s (R.P. *Lightner*: unreliable; conclusions inherent in liberal redaction criticism); Interpretation 43 (1989) 199s (Dorothy J. *Weaver*).

4067* **MacArthur** John F.ᴶ, The Gospel according to Jesus. GR 1988, Zondervan. 253 p. $15. – ᴿGraceTJ 10 (1989) 67-77 (H.A. *Kent*).

4068 **Magli** Ida, Gesù di Nazaret. Mi 1987, Rizzoli. 208 p. Lit. 8500. 88-17-13693-X. – ᴿCiVit 43 (1988) 299s (G. *Cesaro*).

4069 **Martín Descalzo** José Luis, Vida y misterio de Jesús de Nazaret: Nueva Alianza 114. Salamanca 1989, Sígueme. 1312 p. [= 1-3 → 4,4187]: ᴿLumenVr 38 (1989) 438 (F. *Ortiz de Urtaran*); SalT 77 (1989) 840s (T. *García*).

4070 **Mathaji** Vandana [➤ 4,4188 Mataji] Jesus the Christ; who is he? what is his message? 1987: ᴿBibleBh 15 (1989) 134s (J. *Maniketh*).

4071 *Meier* John P., Jesus: ➤ 384, NJBC (1989) 1316-1328.

4072 **Morin** Émile, Non-lieu pour Jésus [p. 178: toutes les reconstitutions tournent court]: Présence. P 1989, Flammarion. 236 p. F 85. – ᴿEsprVie 99 (1989) 290s (É. *Cothenet*).

4073 *Nabot* Jesús, ¿Revolucionario?: Verbo 299 (BA 1989) 11-20 [< Stromata 45,491].

4074 **O'Collins** Gerald, Para interpretar a Jesús 1986 ➤ 4,4192: ᴿScrip-TPamp 21 (1989) 353s (V. *Balaguer*).

4075 *Ostling* R. N., ¿Quién fue Jesús?: Documentos para el diálogo 14 (Medellín 1988) 32-43 [< Stromata 45,500].

4076 **Pelikan** Jaroslav, Jesus through the centuries; his place in the history of culture 1985 ➤ 1,3975... 4,4195: ᴿAsbTJ 44,1 (1989) 112-4 (R. D. *Rightmire*).

4077 **Pelikan** Jaroslav, Jésus au fil de l'histoire; sa place dans l'histoire de la culture, ᵀ*Malmoud* Catherine. P 1989, Hachette. 302 p. F 168. – ᴿÉtudes 371 (1989) 712s (R. *Marlé*).

4078 **Pelikan** Jaroslav, Jesús a través de los siglos; su lugar en la historia de la cultura, ᵀ*Iglesia* Juan A. Barc 1989, Herder. 303 p. – ᴿLumenVr 38 (1989) 447s (F. *Ortiz de Urtaran*).

4079 ᴱ**Pirola** Giuseppe, *Coppellotti* Francesco, Il Gesù storico 1985/8 ➤ 4,495*: ᴿCC 140 (1989,1) 616 (V. *Fusco*); FilT 3 (1989) 221s (F. *Bisio*).

4080 **Rey** B., Jésus le Christ. P/Québec 1988, Centurion/Paulines. 124 p. F 59. 2-227-30137-6 [ÉTRel 64,674].

4081 **Riesner** Rainer, Jesus als Lehrer²ʳᵉᵛ: WUNT 2/7, 1984 ➤ 62,4080... 4,4199: ᴿRB 96 (1989) 307s (B. T. *Viviano*).

4082 **Ross** C. Randolph, Common sense Christianity [no miracles, Incarnation, original sin]. 1989, Occam. 266 p. 0-929368-00-2.– ᴿExpTim 101 (1989s) 219 (G. T. *Eddy*).

4083 *Schille* Gottfried, Entstand die Jesus-Bewegung vor Ostern?: TVers 17 (1989) 45-49.

4084 **Schillebeeckx** Edward, Jesús en nuestra cultura [1986/7 ➤ 3,3059], ᵀ1987 ➤ 4,4206: ᴿEfMex 7 (1989) 132s (E. *Bonnín*).

4085 **Schweitzer** Albert, Storia della ricerca sulla vita di Gesù [1906, ³1984] ᵀ1986 ➤ 2,3103... 4,4208: ᴿAnStoEseg 6 (1989) 324 [M. *Pesce*]; Carthaginensia 5 (1989) 274 (R. *Sanz Valdivieso*); EstE 64 (1989) 576s (J. *Alonso Díaz*).

4086 **Schweizer** Eduard, Jesus Christ, the man from Nazareth and the exalted Lord ➤ 3,3962; 4,8544: (1984 Sizemore lecture, KC Midwestern Baptist Sem.), ᴱ*Gloer* H. Macon GA 1987, Mercer Univ./L 1989, SCM. vii-96 p. $19; pa. $10/£6. – ᴿExpTim 100,12 2d-top choice (1988s) 442s (C. S. *Rodd*); TLond 92 (1989) 323 (D. *Catchpole*: a course of lectures and an autobiography, each echoing the other); TLZ 114 (1989) 524s (T. *Holtz*).

4087 **Secondin** Bruno, Alla luce del suo volto, I. Lo splendore [1. prepotente ma disordinato 'ritorno a Gesù' nei diversi ambienti dentro e fuori il cristianesimo ufficiale...]. Bo 1989, Dehoniane. 298 p. Lit. 30.000. – ᴿCC 140 (1989,3) 439s (P. *Vanzan*).

Segundo Juan L., The historical Jesus of the Synoptics 1985 ➤ 7438; Jésus devant la conscience moderne 1988 ➤ 7442.

4088 **Sloyan** G. S., The Jesus tradition; images of Jesus in the West 1986 ➤ 2,3106... 4,4213: ᴿHorizons 16 (1989) 382s (Kathleen M. *Gaffney*).

4089 *Spencer* R. A., Jesus in the prophetic tradition: Faith and Mission 6,2 (Wake Forest NC 1989) 61-75 [< NTAbs 33,342].

4090 **Theissen** G., Der Schatten des Galiläers 1986 ➤ 2,3109... 4,4215: ᴿPrzPow 812 (1989) 142-5 (C. *Łukasz*).

4091 **Theissen** Gerd, The shadow of the Galilean; the quest of the historical Jesus in narrative form 1987 ➤ 4,3969: ᴿAsbTJ 44,1 (1989) 98s (J. B. *Green*); Interpretation 43 (1989) 90.92 (P. S. *Minear*).

4092 **Theissen** Gerd, L'ombre du Galiléen; récit historique. P 1988, Cerf. 270 p. F 120. 2-227-30141-4 [ÉTRel 64,674]. – ᴿEsprVie 99 (1989) 289s (É. *Cothenet*); EstFran 90 (1989) 515s (Madeleine *Taradach*).

4093 **Theissen** Gerd, La sombra del Galileo; las investigaciones históricas sobre Jesús traducidas a un relato, ᵀ*Ruiz Garrido* C.: Nueva Alianza 110, 1988 ➤ 4,4217: ᴿActuBbg 26 (1989) 200 (J. I. *González Faus*); BibFe 15 (1989) 328s (A. *Salas*); CiTom 116 (1989) 631s (J. *Huarte*); LumenVr 38 (1989) 81s (F. *Ortiz de Urtaran*).

4094 **Theissen** Gerd, A sombra do Galileu, ᵀ*Reis* Orlando dos. Petrópolis 1989, Vozes. 251 p. – ᴿREB 49 (1989) 484s (H. A. *Trein*).

4095 **Theissen** G., Ik moest van Pilatus achter Jezus aan; verslag van een speurtocht [Der Schatten des Galiläers],ᵀ. Baarn 1988, Ten Have. 260 p. ƒ25. 90-259-4355-1. – ᴿStreven 56 (1988s) 466s (P. *Beentjes*); TsTNijm 29 (1989) 89 (L. *Grollenberg*).

4096 **Thomas** R. L., *Gundry* S. N., The NIV harmony of the Gospels [revised *Broadus* J. 1893, *Robertson* A. T. 1903, 1922] with explanations and essays. SF 1988, Harper & R. 343 p.; 2 maps. 0-06-063523-1 [NTAbs 33,113].

4097 **Thompson** William M., The Jesus debate 1985 ➤ 1,3089*... 4,4128: ᴿBijdragen 50 (1989) 98s (J.-J. *Suurmond*, Eng.); RechSR 77 (1989) 547-9 (B. *Sesboüé*).

4098 **Toy** John, Jesus, man for God 1988 ➤ 4,4219: ᴿPrPeo 3 (1989) 353 (H. *Wansbrough*).

4099 **Tremmel** William C., The Jesus story in the twenty-seven books that changed the world: AmerUnivSt 7/50. NY 1989, Lang. [viii-]272 p. Fs 78 [TR 86,163]. 0-8204-0772-0.

4100 *Williams* D. T., The four-fold office of Christ [apart from prophet-priest-king: atoning servant]: ExpTim 100 (1988s) 134-7.

F1.5 *Jesus et Israel* – **Jesus the Jew.**

4101 **Ballarini** L., Gesù, nostro fratello ebreo; alla scoperta dell'umanità ebraica di Gesù; per un dialogo tra Cristiani ed Ebrei: Le Mie Vie. Mi 1987, Ist. Propaganda Libraria. 310 p. Lit. 15.000 pa [NTAbs 33,120].

4102 *Barié* H., Pharisäer — typisch für 'die Frommen'?: TBei 19,5 (1988) 257-267 [< NTAbs 33,201].

4103 *Baumbach* Günther, Randbemerkungen zu Jesu Judaizität: ➤ 197, ᶠTRILLING W., Christus bezeugen 1989, 74-83.

4104 **Berlin** George L., Defending the faith; nineteenth-century American Jewish writings on Christianity and Jesus. Albany 1989, SUNY. x-207 p. $54.50; pa. $18. 0-88706-920-7; -1-5 [TDig 37,149]. – ᴿJScStR 29 (1989) 127s (A. E. *Nudelman*).

4105 *Borowitz* E. B., How is the Church to confront Jesus' Jewishness?: Moment 14,2 (Wsh 1989) 40-47.53 [< NTAbs 33,296].

4106 **Bruners** Wilhelm, Wie Jesus glauben lernte. 1988 ²1989, Christophorus. 128 p. DM 17,80. 3-419-50829-8. – ᴿBiKi 44 (1989) 44s (T. *Staubli*).

4107 **Callan** T., Forgetting the root; the emergence of Christianity from Judaism 1986 ➤ 2,3124... 4,4224: ᴿRivB 37 (1989) 232s (P. *Stefani*); ScriptB 20 (1989s) 24 (Mary E. *Mills*).

4108 **Charlesworth** James H., Jesus within Judaism; new light from exciting archaeological discoveries 1988 ➤ 4,4225; also L 1989, SPCK. 0-281-04406-6 [BL 89,154]. – ᴿExpTim 100,12 first choice (1988s) 441s (C. S. *Rodd*); RExp 86 (1989) 624s (D. E. *Garland*: his 'new' has been around for a while).

4109 **Charlier** Jean-Pierre, Jésus au milieu de son peuple [I. 1987 ➤ 3,3979; 193 p.] II. La terre d'Abraham et de Jésus; III. Les jours et la vie: Lire la Bible (78) 84s. P 1989, Cerf. 130 p.; 180 p. F 90 + 98 (2-204-02700-6) 2-204-03100-3; -4026-6.

4110 **Chilton** Bruce, Profiles of a Rabbi; Synoptic opportunities in reading about Jesus: BrownJudSt 177. Atlanta 1989, Scholars. 225 p. 1-55540-362-X [ExpTim 101,344].

4111 **Chilton** Bruce, Targumic approaches to the Gospels 1986 ➤ 2,140*; 3,3981: ᴿJQR 80 (1989s) 421s (A. J. *Saldarini*); Sefarad 49 (1989) 407-411 (F. *Sen*).

4113 *Dubourg* Bernard, L'invention de Jésus, 1. L'hébreu du NT 1987 ➤ 3,3985; 4,4232; 2-07-071093-9: ᴿÉTRel 64 (1989) 633s (M. *Bouttier*: invention de Dubourg).

4114 *Dupuy* Bernard, Le *logion* de Jésus rapporté dans le Talmud (Gittin 57a); sens et portée d'une sentence de Rav Aha BEN ULLA: RÉJ 146 (1987) 255-264.

4115 **Freyne** Sean, Galilee, Jesus and the Gospels 1988 ➤ 4,4238: ᴿDocLife 39 (1989) 164s (J. *Taylor*); JStJud 20 (1989) 226-8 (Ruth M. *Vale*: more a literary study of the Gospels than anything on Galilee); NewTR 2,4 (1988) 97s (Carolyn *Osiek*); TLond 92 (1989) 320s (G. *Theissen*).

4116 *Fusco* Vittorio, Gesù di fronte alla Legge [< incontro Amicizia ebraico-cristiana, Napoli 12.I.1989]: RasT 30 (1989) 528-538.

4117 *Goodblatt* D., The place of the Pharisees in first century Judaism; the state of the debate: JStJud 20 (1989) 12-30.

4118 ᴱGrossi Vittorino, Cristianesimo e giudaismo; eredità e confronti: XVI incontro di Studiosi dell'Antichità Cristiana (7-9 maggio 1987) 1988 ➤ 4,570: ᴿRBíbArg 51 (1989) 181-8 (F. J. *Weismann*: análisis detallados).

4119 *Gryglewicz* Feliks, ℗ Faryzeusze: ➤ 891, EncKat 5 (1989) 55-57 (55, *Rosik* Seweryn, Faryzeizm).

4120 **Hagner** Donald A., The Jewish reclamation of Jesus 1984 ➤ 65,3605... 4,4241: ᴿBZ 33 (1989) 273s (Ingo *Broer*); CriswT 3 (1988s) 215-7 (C. C. *Newman*: recommended).

4121 *Hahn* Ferdinand, Warum die Christen nicht Juden geblieben sind: ➤ 177, ᶠSCHWARZ R., Von Wittenberg 1989, 47-61.

4122 *Harvey* A. E., Rabbis, evangelists — and Jesus: TLond 92 (1989) 244-251: DERRETT the real heavy-weight.

4123 *Hebblethwaite* B., The Jewishness of Jesus from the perspective of Christian doctrine: ScotJT 42 (1989) 27-44.

4124 **Heschel** Susannah, Abraham GEIGER on the origins of Christianity: diss. Pennsylvania, ᴰ*Kraft* R. Ph 1989. 402 p. 89-22516. – DissA 50 (1989s) 2105-A [RelStR 16,191 '*Heschel*, H. Susannah', ᴰDunning S.'].

4125 **Hilton** Michael, *Marshall* Gordian, The Gospels and rabbinic Judaism; a study guide 1988 ➤ 4,4243: ᴿHorizons 16 (1989) 375s (J. S. *Siker*); TLond 92 (1989) 313-5 (W. R. *Telford*: admirable).

4126 **Horsley** Richard A., Jesus and the spiral of violence 1987 ➤ 3,3995; 4,4244: ᴿHorizons 16 (1989) 380-2 (G. S. *Sloyan*); Interpretation 43 (1989) 320.322 (C. C. *Black*); JBL 108 (1989) 518-520 (H. W. *Attridge*); RExp 86 (1989) 272-4 (D. E. *Garland*).

4127 *a*) *Horsley* Richard A., Jesus and the spiral of violence; a summary; – *b*) *Smith* Dennis E., A review of...: Forum 5/4 (1989) 3-17 / 18-26.

4128 **Jossa** G., Gesù e i movimenti di liberazione della Palestina 1978 (1980 ➤ 61,9205): ᴿNicolaus 16 (1989) 319-331 (A. *Moda*).

4129 **Kippenberg** H., *Wewers* G., Testi giudaici per lo studio del NT 1987 ➤ 4,4248: ᴿAsprenas 36 (1989) 109s (C. *Marcheselli-Casale*).

4130 **Landmann** S., Jesus und die Juden oder Die Folgen einer Verstrickung [imbroglio]. Mü 1987, Herbig. 336 p.; 2 maps. DM 34. 3-7766-1444-7 [NTAbs 33,386: she treats lack of attention to Jesus in Jewish writings; conflicts...].

4131 **Le Déaut** Roger, The message of the New Testament and the Aramaic Bible: SubsBPont 5, 1982 ➤ 63,4109; 3,4000: ᴿRoczTK 33,1 (1986) 132s (J. *Szlaga*).

4132 **Lohfink** Norbert, Das Jüdische am Christentum 1987 ➤ 3,4003; 4,4252: ᴿBLtg 62 (1989) 61s (L. *Schwienhorst-Schönberger*); EstAgust 24 (1989) 259 (C. *Mielgo*); JEcuSt 26 (1989) 538s (W. J. *Urbrock*); Salesianum 51 (1989) 157 (M. *Cimosa*).

4133 **Maccoby** Hyam, Judaism in the first century. L 1989, Sheldon. vi-136 p. £5 pa. – ᴿTLond 92 (1989) 317-320 (J. *Muddiman*, also on ZEITLIN I., CHARLESWORTH J.).

4134 *MacRae* George, Messiah and Gospel: ➤ 7368, ᴱ*Neusner* J., Judaisms and their Messiahs 1987, 169-185 [< JStJud 20,252: MacRae 'is surprised to observe, not how central the messianic idea is to the gospels, but how it is in a sense peripheral'].

4134* *Mills* Mary E., *a*) Jesus of Nazareth in his Jewish background; – *b*) Galilee, Jesus and the Gospels: Month 250 (1989) 378-383 / 441-4.

4135 *Mowery* Robert L., Pharisees and scribes, Galilee and Jerusalem: ZNW 80 (1989) 266-8.

4136 *Müller* Mogens, Jødedommens Bibel på nytestamentlig tid og den kristne Bibel: DanTTs 51 (1988) 220-237 [< OTAbs 12,10].

4137 **Neusner** J., Christian faith and the Bible of Judaism 1987 ➤ 4,4255: ᴿBL (1989) 139 (R. *Hammer*).

4138 **Neusner** Jacob, Le judaïsme à l'aube du christianisme 1986 ➤ 2,3145... 4,4257: ᴿLatomus 48 (1989) 704s (C. *Aziza*).

4139 **Neusner** J., Judentum in frühchristlicher Zeit, ᵀ*Hudel* W., 1988 ➤ 4, 4258: ᴿBL (1989) 141 (C. J. A. *Hickling*).

4140 **Neusner** Jacob, Il giudaismo nei primi secoli del cristianesimo, ᵀ*Servi* Sandro & Silvia: Shalom. Brescia 1989, Morcelliana. 172 p. 88-372-1383-2. – ᴿHumBr 44 (1989) 902s (A. *Bonora*).

4141 **Neusner** Jacob, De Joodse wieg van het christendom 1987 ➤ 4,4259: ᴿStreven 55 (1987s) 182s (P. *Beentjes*).

4142 **Neusner** Jacob, Judaism and Christianity — their relationship then, their relationship to come: CCurr 39 (1989s) 10-20.

4143 *Novak* M., The quest for the Jewish Jesus: Modern Judaism 8,2 (Baltimore 1988) 119-138 [< NTAbs 33,152].

4144 **Paul** André, Il mondo ebraico al tempo di Gesù: Piccola Enciclopedia Biblica 6, 1983 ➤ 64,a288*b*... 3,b997: ᴿParVi 33 (1988) 473s (M. *Cimosa*, anche su PEB 8, 9, 10).

4145 **Pawlikowski** J., Jesus and the theology of Israel: Zacchaeus Studies. Wilmington 1989, Glazier. 99 p. $7. 0-89453-683-4 [NTAbs 33,408]. – ᴿPrzPow 820 (1989) 461-3 (W. *Chrostowski* ✪).

4146 **Perelmuter** Hayim G., Siblings; rabbinic Judaism and early Christianity at their beginnings. NY 1989, Paulist. v-217 p. $12. 0-8091-3104-8.

4147 **Poorthuis** M., De joodse groeperingen ten tijds van Jezus; oorsprong, inhoud en relatie tot Jezus: Oecumenereeks 892d. Bolsward 1989, Het Witte B. 48 p. *f* 6,50. – ᴿStreven 57 (1989s) 1046s (P. *Beentjes*).

4148 **Rowland** Christopher, Christian origins; from messianic movement to Christian religion 1985: → 2,3148 ... 4,4265*: ᴿHeythJ 29 (1988) 360s (M. J. *Walsh*); ScripTPamp 21 (1989) 698s (J. M. *Casciaro*).

4149 *Saldarini* Anthony J., Judaism and the NT: → 394, NT/Interpreters 1989, 27-54.

4150 **Sanders** E. P., Jesus and Judaism 1985 → 1,4028 ... 4,4267; ²1987: ᴿEstAgust 24 (1989) 258s (C. *Mielgo*).

4151 *Sievers* Joseph, Gesù di Nazareth visto da Ebrei di oggi [LAPIDE P., HAGNER D. ...]: NuovaUm 11,64s (1989) 125-136.

4152 *Stemberger* Günter, Jüdische Zugänge zum Neuen Testament: BLtg 62 (1989) 40-45.

4153 **Swidler** Leonard, Yeshua, a model for moderns 1988 → 4,4273: ᴿJEcuSt 26 (1989) 535s (Amy-Jill *Levine*).

4154 *Theissen* Gerd, Die Entstehung des Christentums aus dem Judentum [FLUSSER D.]: KIsr 4 (1988) 179-189.

4155 *Tresmontant* Claude, Le Christ hébreu; la langue et l'âge des évangiles [¹1983 → 64,4003 ... 1,4032]: ᴿDowR 107 (1989) 144-9 (A. G. *Murray*; a new edition, date not given, after the author had translated for himself all four Gospels into French).

4156 **Tresmontant** Claude, The Hebrew Christ; language in the age of the gospels, ᵀ*Whitehead* Kenneth H. Ch 1989, Franciscan. xv-323 p. $20. 0-8199-0876-2 [TDig 37,92].

4157 **Vogler** Werner, Jüdische Jesusinterpretation in christlicher Sicht: ArbKG 11. Weimar 1988, Böhlau. 151 p. M 18 [TLZ 115,103, W. *Wiefel*].

4158 **Werner** Eric, The sacred bridge II [HUC; ital. 1983 → 64,4009] 1984 → 3,d506: ᴿSecC 6 (1987) 249-251 (P. F. *Bradshaw*).

4159 *Wigoder* Geoffrey, ✪ The NT and Christianity in the light of Jewish-Israeli thought, ᵀ*Chrostowski* Waldemar: PrzPow 808 (1988) 344-358; 809 (1989) 36-49.

4160 **Wilson** Marvin R., Our father Abraham; Jewish roots of the Christian faith. GR 1989, Eerdmans. xxi-374 p. $16 pa. 0-8028-0423-3. – ᴿCalvinT 24 (1989) 388-390 (R. R. *DeRidder*); ExpTim 101 (1989s) 382 (M. *Braybrooke*).

4161 **Zatelli** Ida, La situazione linguistica in terra d'Israele nel I secolo [mostly Aramaic; also Hebrew and Greek, some little Latin]: → 572*, Storia e Preistoria dei Vangeli. Genova 1988, Univ. 'D.AR.FI.CL.ET', p. 17-24.

4162 **Zeitlin** Irving M., Jesus and the Judaism of his time 1988 → 4,4278: ᴿExpTim 100 (1988s) 309s (Judith M. *Lieu*).

4163 Aramaic-English interlinear New Testament [1. 1987] 2. Acts-Philemon; 3. Heb-Rev. New Knoxville OH 1988s, American Christian

Press. vii-687 p.; vii-281 p. $21; $19. 0-910068-74-7; 5-5. [NTAbs 33,395: 'each Aramaic word as it appears in the (Syriac) Peshitta'].

F1.6   *Jesus in Ecclesia* –   **The Church Jesus.**

4164 **Ellul** Jacques,   The subversion of Christianity 1986 ➤ 3,4032; 4,4286: ᴿEvQ 61 (1989) 178s (N. M. *Cameron*); WestTJ 50 (1988) 234-6 (J. W. *Scott*).

4165 *Evans* C. A.,   The historical Jesus and Christian faith; a critical assessment of a scholarly problem: ChrSchR 18,1 (GR 1988) 48-63 [< NTAbs 33,151].

4166 **Germain** Élisabeth,   Jésus-Christ dans les catéchismes; étude historique: JJC 27. P 1986, Desclée. 270 p. – ᴿRechSR 77 (1989) 542s (B. *Sesboüé*).

4167 **Gillabert** É., [➤ 4186] L'Évangile, voie de la connaissance: Mystiques et Religions. P 1987, Dervy. 207 p. F 92. 2-85076-066-8 [NTAbs 33,385: continues his claim that Jesus emphasized the interior kingdom accessible here and now, and was misunderstood and misused by the early Church].

4168 **Glebe-Möller** Jens,   Jesus and theology; critique of a tradition [a 'theological code' has explained away the central Gospel message], ᵀ*Hall* Thor. Minneapolis 1989, Fortress. xi-196 p. [TS 51,766].

4169 **Koestler** Martin,   Stirbt Jesus am Christentum? Ein Plädoyer für die ursprüngliche Verkündigung Jesu: Siebenstern 1417. Gü 1986, GVH. 192 p. [LuJb 56, p. 192].

4170 **Lohaus** G.,   Die Geheimnisse des Lebens Jesu in der Summa theologiae des heiligen Thomas von AQUIN [ᴰ1984] 1985 ➤ 1,4048*... 4,4289: ᴿKatKenk 26,2 (1987) 186-196 (S. *Takayanagi*, ❶).

Madec Goulven,   La Patrie et la Voie; le Christ dans la vie et la pensée de saint AUGUSTIN: JJC 36, 1989 ➤ g841.

4171 **Marzola** Oddone, Gesù Cristo centro vivo della fede — dall'esperienza religiosa all'annuncio cristiano 1986 ➤ 2,3169.6414: ᴿProtestantesimo 44 (1989) 153s (G. *Plescan*: parte dalla reazione al Catechismo dei Giovani CEI 1979).

4171* *Medisch* Richard,   Der historische Judas — und was aus ihm gemacht wurde: TGegw 31 (1988) 50-54. ➤ 4777s.

4172 **Trilling** Wolfgang,   L'annuncio di Gesù, orientamenti esegetici [1975-7 ➤ 58,6068],ᵀ: i. il messaggio di Gesù; ii. ecclesiologia implicita; iii. verità delle parole di Gesù: StBPaid 74. Brescia 1986, Paideia. 136 p. Lit. 17.000. – ᴿParVi 34 (1989) 311s (M. *Orsatti*); Protestantesimo 44 (1989) 297 (G. *Conte*).

F1.7   *Jesus 'anormalis':*   **to atheists, psychoanalysts, romance ...**

4173 **Arnaldez** Roger,   Jésus dans la pensée musulmane: JJC 32, 1988 ➤ 4, 4298: ᴿNRT 111 (1989) 601s (J. *Masson*); RThom 89 (1989) 505-7 (J. *Jomier*, aussi sur son Jésus prophète 1980).

4174 **Boyer** Régis,   Le Christ des barbares; le monde nordique, IXᵉ-XIIᵉ siècle: Jésus depuis Jésus 4. P 1987, Cerf. 159 p. F 107. 2-204-02766-9. – ᴿCrNSt 10 (1989) 623s (G. M. *Cantarella*); ExpTim 100 (1988s) 33 (J. *Kent*).

4175 **Breech** James,   Jesus and postmodernism. Minneapolis 1989, Fortress. 96 p. [CBQ 52,380].

4176 **Brown** Kelly D.,   'Who do they say that I am?' A critical examination of the black Christ: diss. Union. NY 1988. – RTLv 21,568.

4177 **Buddhadasa** V., Un bouddhiste dit le christianisme,...: JJC 31, 1987 ⇥ 4,4299; ᵀᴱ*Pezet* Edmond: ᴿÉtudes 370 (1989) 137 (P. *Magnin*); NRT 111 (1989) 290 (J. *Masson*).

4178 *Castelli* F., Il 'Gesù' di Khalil GIBRAN [Jesus the Son of Man c. 1925]: CC 140 (1989,4) 548-561.

4179 **Dart** John, The Jesus of heresy and history; the discovery and meaning of the Nag Hammadi gnostic library² [= ¹The laughing savior 1976 + Thomas-Gospel entire] 1988 ⇥ 4,4305: ᴿRelStR 15 (1989) 356 (J. L. *Price*).

4180 **Downing** F. Gerald, Christ and the cynics; Jesus and other radical preachers in first-century tradition: JStOT Manual 4, 1988 ⇥ 4,4306: ᴿBZ 33 (1989) 265s (H.-J. *Klauck*); ÉTRel 64 (1989) 292s (E. *Cuvillier*); ExpTim 100 (1988s) 350 (R. *Butterworth*: unconvincing); JTS 40 (1989) 550-3 (A. E. *Harvey*).

4181 **Downing** F. Gerald, Jesus and the threat of freedom 1987 [⇥ 3,8328; but it is on Cynic parallels); 0-334-00764-X: ᴿExpTim 100 1988s) 31 (B. G. *Powley*); TLond 92 (1989) 50-52 (S. C. *Barton*), reply p. 105s.

4182 *a*) *Draper* J. A., LACTANTIUS and the Jesus tradition in the Didache; – *b*) *Nicholson* Oliver, Flight from persecution as imitation of Christ; Lactantius' Divine Institutes IV. 18,1-2: JTS 40 (1989) 112-116 / 48-65 [66-94, *Davies* P. S., Origin and purpose of the persecution of AD 303 (Lactantius)].

4183 *Drijvers* H. J. W., Christ as warrior and merchant; aspects of MARCION's Christology: ⇥ 696, 10th Patristic 21 (1989) 73-85.

4184 **Epalza** Mikel de, Jésus ôtage... en Espagne: Jésus depuis Jésus 1, 1987 ⇥ 3,4055; 4.4308: ᴿCrNSt 10 (1989) 620-2 (K. *Reinhardt*).

4185 **Fox** Michael, The coming of the cosmic Christ, the healing of Mother Earth and the birth of a global renaissance 1988 ⇥ 4,8510: ᴿAmerica 161 (1989) 195.197 (G. *Peck*: does he mean Jesus or a 'cosmic idea'?); BibTB 19 (1989) 152 (J. F. *Craghan*); GraceTJ 10 (1989) 250-2 (R. A. *Young*).

4186 **Gillabert** Émile, [⇥ 4167] Jésus et la Gnose; préf. *Salvan* Paule: Mystiques et religions 1981 ⇥ 63,4176; 64,4049: ᴿÉTRel 64 (1989) 300s (J.-D. *Dubois*).

4187 **Grant** J., White women's Christ and black women's Jesus. Atlanta 1989, Scholars. 264 p. $33; pa. $22 [TS 51,383].

4188 **Grelot** Pierre, Un Jésus de comédie [MESSADIÉ (M.) G.] 'L'Homme qui devint Dieu' [⇥ 4199]. P 1989, Cerf. 64 p. F 25. – ᴿEsprVie 99 (1989) 411 (R. *Desvoyes*).

4189 *Hill* Nancy K., Jesus' death in childbirth; the Savior as woman: CCurr 39 (1989s) 1-9.

4190 **Ishan** —, *Vempeny* —, Krishna and Christ. ᴰ1988, Gujarat-SP. r 110. $20. – ᴿJDharma 14 (1989) 108.

4191 **Jaschke** Helmut, Psychotherapie aus dem NT; heilende Begegnungen mit Jesus: Herder-TB 1347, 1987 ⇥ 4,4314: ᴿBLtg 62 (1989) 120-2 (L. *Schwienhorst-Schönberger*); ErbAuf 65 (1989) 74s (C. *Maier*).

4192 *Jaschke* Helmut, Psychotherapie aus dem Neuen Testament: BLtg 62 (1989) 35-39.

4193 **Kryvelev** I., Christ, myth or reality?: Religious studies in the USSR 2. Moskva 1987, Acad. 224 p. [CBQ 51,590].

4194 **Lin Jui-Lung** Joseph, Christ as the Christian symbol of God's salvific action in the world; Christology in a religiously pluralistic era: diss. Drew, ᴰ*Courtney*. Madison NJ 1989. 252 p. 89-21809. – DissA 50 (1989s) 1705-A; RelStR 16,187.

4195 **Lochman** Jan Milič, Christ and Prometheus? A quest for theological identity [after 18 years of theology teaching in communist eastern Europe and equally long in the west]. Geneva 1988, WCC. 105 p. – ᴿRExp 86 (1989) 641s (T. *George*); ScripTPamp 21 (1989) 722s (P. *O'Callaghan*); TZBas 45 (1989) 376s (K. *Rennstich*).

4196 *Luttikhuizen* G.P., The evaluation of the teaching of Jesus in Christian Gnostic revelation dialogues: ➤ 606, Réception 1986/9, 363...

4197 **McCarthy** Vincent A., Quest for a philosophical Jesus... Rousseau... Hegel... 1986 ➤ 2,3192... 4,4320: ᴿJRel 68 (1988) 290s (J. *Yerkes*).

4198 **Menacherry** Cheryan, An Indian philosophical approach to the personality of Jesus 1986 ➤ 2,3194; 3,4067: ᴿScotJT 42 (1989) 411 (G. *Smith*).

4199 **Messadie** Gérald, L'homme qui devint Dieu. P 1988, Laffont. 610 p. F 125. – ᴿFoiVie 88 (1989) 81s (O. *Pigeaud*: roman). ➤ 4188.

4200 *Murphy* Francesca A., On finding the whole within the part; a reassessment of William F. Lynch, Christ and Apollo; the dimensions of the literary imagination: LitTOx 3 (1989) 242-... [< zit 89,583].

4201 *Piemontese* A.M., Storie di Maria, Gesù e Paolo nel commento coranico persiano di Sūrābādī: ➤ 4,144, Mem. Tucci G. (1988) 1101-1118.

4202 **Pomilio** Mário, O quinto evangelho: Romance Vozes. Petrópolis 1988, Vozes. 392 p. – ᴿREB 49 (1989) 235-7 (N. *Molinari*).

4203 *Ramsperger* Frank, The Rohrschach Jesus ['he *must* have... because *I* do']: RRel 48 (1989) 394-400.

4204 **Risse** Günter, 'Gott ist Christus, der Sohn der Maria' — eine Studie zum Christusbild im Koran [kath. Diss. ᴰ*Waldenfels*, Bonn 1988. – TR 85,514]. Bonn 1989, Borengässer. xi-274 p.; map. [RHE 85, p. 94*]. 3-923946-17-1.

4205 **Rizzardi** G., Il fascino del Cristo nell'Islam. Mi 1989, IPL. 262 p. Lit. 17.000. – ᴿStPatav 36 (1989) 618 (G. *Segalla*).

4206 *Rőzse* István, Ⓜ The image of Jesus in the Koran: TSzem 31 (1988) 202-4.

4207 **Sarale** Nicolino, Un uomo di fronte all'assoluto, Giuseppe di Nazareth. Cavallermaggiore CN 1987, Gribaudo. 326 p. Lit. 16.000. – ᴿCC 140 (1989,3) 440s (F. *Castelli*: libro di fede, di poesia...).

4208 **Schumann** Olaf H., Der Christus der Muslime; christologische Aspekte in der arabisch-islamischen Literatur² [¹Diss. Tü 1972]: Veröff. Rel. G. 13. Köln 1988, Böhlau. x-294 p. – ᴿDer Islam 66 (1989) 358 (B. *Spuler*).

4209 *Staehelein* Balthasar, Christus-Jesus-Therapie: ArztC 34 (1988) 57-66.

4210 **Stroker** William D., Extracanonical sayings of Jesus: SBL Resources 18. Atlanta 1989, Scholars. viii-341 p. 1-55540-055-8; pa. -442-1.

4211 *Vernette* Jean, 'Jésus' dans la nouvelle religiosité [... cf. ➤ 3,4087; 4,4322... retour du paganisme et de la gnose]: EsprVie 99 (1989) 97-109.

F2.1   *Exegesis creativa* – innovative methods.

4212 **Agua Pérez** A. del, El método midrásico y... NT 1985 ➤ 1,4112... 4,4334: ᴿScriptV 34 (1987) 218s (A. *Rodríguez Carmona*).

4213 **Berger** Klaus, Einführung in die Formgeschichte 1987 ➤ 3,4093: ᴿNT 31 (1989) 88-90 (R. *Schmitt*).

4214 **Berger** Klaus, Hermeneutik des NTs. Gü 1988, Mohn. 456 p. DM 68. 3-579-00088-8. – ᴿLuthMon 29 (1989) 429 (E. *Lohse*).

4215 ᴱ**Buehler** David, Lexegete, lectionary software for study of the Bible Year A gospels. Dartmouth MA 1986 ²1989, Tischrede. 22 p. + 3 disks. $59.50. – ᴿCurrTM 16 (1989) 461s (E. *Krentz*: offers also year B for same price).

4216 **Conzelmann** Hans, *Lindemann* Andreas, Interpreting the New Testament; an introduction to the principles and methods of NT exegesis [Arbeitsbuch zum NT⁸ 1985],ᵀ. Peabody MA 1988, Hendrickson. xix-389 p. 0-913573-80-9.

4217 **Chang** M. C., Space-time talk; New Testament hermeneutics, a philosophical and theological approach [diss. LA Pacific Western Univ.]. Virginia Beach VA 1988, Heritage Research. xiv-194 p. 14 fig. 0-912617-02-0 [NTAbs 33,375].

4218 **Egger** Wilhelm, Methodenlehre zum NT 1987 → 3,4096; 4,4338: ᴿCiTom 116 (1989) 189s (J. *Huarte*); TPhil 64 (1989) 581s (H. *Engel*); TPQ 137 (1989) 84s (A. *Stöger*).

4219 **Egger** Wilhelm, Metodologia del Nuovo Testamento; introduzione allo studio scientifico del NT [1987 → 3,4096], ᵀ*Forza* Gianfranco: StBDeh 16. Bo 1989, Dehoniane. 256 p. Lit. 30.000 [RivB 37,342 adv.]. 88-10-40716-4. – ᴿStPatav 36 (1989) 623s (G. *Segalla*).

4220 **Jasper** David, The New Testament and the literary imagination 1986 → 3,3827.4103; 4,4343: ᴿJRel 68 (1988) 482s (D. *Edgerton*); TLond 92 (1989) 131-3 (Meg *Davies*).

4221 *Kselman* John S., *Witherup* Ronald D., Modern New Testament criticism: → 384, NJBC (1989) 1130-1145.

4222 *Kudasiewicz* Jerzy, ❷ Formgeschichte, szkola historii form: → 891, EncKat 5 (1989) 397-400.

4223 *Lambrecht* Jan, Rhetorical criticism and the New Testament [mostly Paul]: Bijdragen 50 (1989) 239-253; Eng. 253.

4224 *a*) *McKnight* Edgar V., Form- and redaction-criticism; – *b*) *Beardslee* William A., Recent literary criticism; – *c*) *Brown* Schuyler, Philology: → 394, NT/Interpreters 1989, 149-174 / 175-198 / 127-147.

4225 **Mercer** Calvin R., Norman PERRIN's interpretation of the NT 1986 → 3,g837; 4,4340: ᴿHorizons 15 (1988) 385s (Mary Ann *Getty*); JRel 68 (1988) 587s (Adela Y. *Collins*).

4226 **Merkel** Helmut, Bibelkunde des Neuen Testaments, ein Arbeitsbuch³ʳᵉᵛ [¹1978 → 60,5304]. Gü 1988, Mohn. 297 p. 3-579-04031-6.

4227 **Meyer** Ben F., Critical realism and the NT: Princeton Theol. Mg. 17. Allison Park PA 1989, Pickwick. xv-225 p. $20 [CBQ 51,785].

Meynet Roland, L'analyse rhétorique; une nouvelle méthode pour comprendre la Bible 1989 → 1642 (Lc → 5069).

4229 **Moore** Stephen D., Literary criticism and the Gospels; the theoretical challenge. NHv 1989, Yale Univ. xxii-226 p.

4230 **Muñoz León** Domingo, Deras I. targúmico y neotestamentario 1987 → 3,4009.1610; 4,4349*: ᴿArTGran 52 (1989) 259s (A. *Torres*); BL (1989) 138s (F. *García Martínez*); BZ 33 (1989) 266-9 (M. *Rodríguez Ruiz*); Carthaginensia 5 (1989) 280s (R. *Sanz Valdivieso*); CBQ 51 (1989) 747s (E. J. *Fisher*); EstBíb 47 (1989) 139-142 (L. *Díez Merino*); EstE 64 (1989) 555s (J. *Iturriaga*); RivB 37 (1989) 367-370 (A. *Rolla*); Salmanticensis 36 (1989) 99-102 (J. M. *Sánchez Caro*); ScripTPamp 21 (1989) 923-6 (J. M. *Casciaro*).

4231 **Painter** John, Theology as hermeneutics; R. BULTMANN's interpretation of the history of Jesus 1987 → 3,4113; 4,4352: ᴿTPhil 64 (1989) 286s (J. *Beutler*).

4232 *Perkins* Pheme, Crisis in Jerusalem? Narrative criticism in New Testament studies: TS 50 (1989) 296-313.

4233 *Radcliffe* Timothy, Tradition and creativity; the paradigm of the NT: NBlackf 70,2 ('What counts as Catholic teaching?' 1989) 57-66.

4234 **Tuckett** Christopher, Reading the New Testament; methods of interpretation [Mk 3,1-6] 1987 ➔ 3,4117... 4,4358: ᴿCriswT 3 (1989) 387s (D. L. *Akin*: too liberal, and not the best even of that); CurrTM 16 (1989) 232 (E. M. *Krentz*); RelStR 15 (1989) 66 (T. L. *Donaldson*); ScotBEv 7 (1989) 49s (M. *Turner*); SvTKv 65 (1989) 35s (B. *Homberg*).

4235 **Wrege** Hans-Theo, Wirkungsgeschichte des Evangeliums; Erfahrungen, Perspektiven und Möglichkeiten. Gö 1981, Vandenhoeck & R. 290 p. DM 39,80. – ᴿTLZ 114 (1989) 197-9 (G. *Haufe*).

F2.2   *Unitas VT-NT:* **The Unity of the Two Testaments.**

4236 *Andia* Ysabel de, Modèles de l'unité des testaments selon IRÉNÉE de Lyon: ➔ 696, 10th Patristic 21 (1989) 49-59.

4237 **Buchanan** George W., Typology and the Gospels 1987 ➔ 3,4124: ᴿJQR 79 (1988s) 267s (L. T. *Johnson*).

4238 *a) Busto Saiz* José Ramón, La Biblia Hebrea y el Antiguo Testamento cristiano; – *b) Sánchez Caro* José M., La lectura cristiana del AT; reflexiones hermenéuticas sobre una cuestión clásica; – *c) Franco* Ricardo, El uso del AT en el trabajo teológico: EstBíb 47 (1989) 435-447 / 475-492 / 493-512; Eng. 435.475.493.

4239 *a) Cipriani* Settimio, La comunità a Maria; dall'Antico al Nuovo Testamento; – *b) La Potterie* Ignace de, La 'Figlia di Sion' nel mistero dell'Alleanza; – *c) Pacomio* Luciano, Dall'ascolto [VT] al discepolato: ➔ 611, Come leggere 1988/9, 152-173 / 102-122 / 123-137.

4240 **Cohen** N. M., Jewish Bible personages in the New Testament. Lanham MD 1989, UPA. xii-163 p. $19.75. 0-8191-7252-9 [NTAbs 33,413].

4241 *a) Collins* John J., Judaism as praeparatio evangelica in the work of Martin HENGEL; – *b) Long* William R., Martin Hengel and early Christianity: RelStR 15 (1989) 226-8 / 230-4.
    Derrett J, D. M., The sea-change of the Old Testament in the New: Studies in the NT 5, 1989 ➔ 253.

4242 *a) Di Sante* C., L'ancienne et la nouvelle alliance; – *b) Rossi de Gasperis* Francesco, La typologie est-elle encore acceptable?; – *c) Cocchini* F., La typologie des Pères de l'Église: Sidic 21 (R 1988) 12-18 / 4-8 / 9-11 [< Judaica 45,78].

4243 *Di Sante* C., The 'Old' and the 'New' Covenant; how to relate the two Testaments: Sidic 21,3 (R 1988) 12-17.

4244 ᴱFeinberg J., Continuity and discontinuity; perspectives on the relationship between the Old and New Testaments. Westchester IL 1988, Crossway. 410 p. $27.50; pa. $17.50 [TS 50,212].

4245 **Goppelt** Leonhard, Typos; die typologische Deutung des Alten Testaments im Neuen: Beiträge zur Förderung christlicher Theologie 2/43. AA 1989 = 1939, Univ. Michigan. ix-255 p.

4246 **Groves** Joseph W., Actualization and interpretation in the Old Testament, ᴰ1987 ➔ 3,1263: ᴿAsbTJ 44,2 (1989) 91-93 (L. G. *Stone*).

4247 *Hoffmann* Gottfried, Christus, der Herr der Schrift [LUTHER 1535]: LuthTKi 12 (1988) 122-8.

4248 *a) Holtz* Traugott, Das Alte Testament und das Bekenntnis der frühen Gemeinde zu Jesus Christus; – *b) Kühn* Ulrich, Kirche unter dem

rechtfertigenden Wort Gottes: → 197, FTRILLING W. 1989, 55-66 /
275-286.

4249 *Jantzen* G.M., The mystical meaning of Scripture; medieval and
modern presuppositions [... Christocentric interpretation]: KingsTR 11,2
(1988) 39-43 [NTAbs 33,142].

4250 **Juel** Donald, Messianic exegesis; Christological interpretations of the
Old Testament in early Christianity 1987 → 3,4136; 4,4375: RCBQ 51
(1989) 373-5 (J. *Marcus*); HorBT 11,1 (1989) 99s (Mary Rose *D'Angelo*);
JAAR 57 (1989) 198-200 (Rowan A. *Greer*); QRMin 9,1 (1989) 98-100
(J.A. *Darr*); TR 85 (1989) 296-8 (W. *Gross*).

4251 *Kaiser* Otto, Die Bedeutung des Alten Testaments für den christlichen
Glauben [Vortrag Marburg 1988]: ZTK 86 (1989) 1-17.

4252 **Kaiser** Walter C., Toward rediscovering the OT [significance for the
Christian Church]. GR 1987, Zondervan. 219 p. $18. – RAndrUnS 27
(1989) 235 p. (J. *Ray*: fourth of his 'toward' volumes [theology 1978,
exegesis 1981, ethics 1983).

4253 **Kaiser** W.J., The uses of the OT in the New 1985 → 1,4147; 2,3242:
RAsbTJ 44,1 (1989) 97s (V.P. *Hamilton*).

4254 **Koch** D.A., Die Schrift als Zeuge des Evangeliums: BeiHistT 69. Tü
1986, Mohr. xii-406 p. DM 198. – RSWJT 32,1 (1989s) 56 (E.E. *Ellis*).

4255 FLINDARS Barnabas, It is written; Scripture citing Scripture, ECarson
D.A., 1988→ 4,97: RExpTim 100,8 top choice (1988s) 281-3 (C.S.
Rodd); JStJud 20 (1989) 232-5 (F. *García Martínez*); NBlackf 70 (1989)
45 (Meg *Davies*).

4256 *Lubsczyk* Hans, Die Einheit der Schrift; zur hermeneutischen Relevanz
des Urbekenntnisses im Alten und Neuen Testament [< FKLEINEIDAM
Erich, Sapienter ordinare (Lp 1969) 73-104]: → 306, Einheit 1989, 71-102.

4257 *Moreno Martínez* José Luis, El molino de los dos Testamentos; un
símbolo de la exégesis patrística y medieval: EstBíb 47 (1989) 559-568;
Eng. 559 [... exégesis alegórica de Dt 24,6; Mt 24,41].

4258 **Motyer** Steve, Israel in the plan of God; light on today's debate.
Leicester 1989, Inter-Varsity. 172 p. 0-85110-671-4.

4259 *Oss* Douglas A., The influence of hermeneutical frameworks in the
theonomy debate [role of Mosaic law in Christianity]: WestTJ 51 (1989)
227-258.

4260 **Papandreou** Damaskinos, présent., L'Ancien Testament dans l'Église
[Ecumenical Patriarchate conference, Chambésy 1986]. Genève 1988,
Centre Orthodoxe. 234 p. Fs 45 [RelStR 16, 151, C. *Bernas*].

4261 **Pinto Cardoso** A., Da Antiga à Nova Aliança; relações entre o Antigo
y o Novo Testamento em Sebastião BARRADAS 1543-1615 [diss. FrB
1984]: Historia 9. Lisboa 1987, Inst. Nac. Inv. Cientifica. 538 p. – RSalmanticensis 36 (1989) 112-4 (J.M. *Sánchez Caro*).

4262 **Poythress** V.S., Christ the only savior of interpretation: WestTJ 50
(1988) 305-321 [< NTAbs 33,143].

4263 a) *Rendtorff* Rolf, Christologische Auslegung als 'Rettung' des Alten
Testaments? Wilhelm VISCHER und Gerhard von RAD; – b) *Vetter*
Dieter, Lernen und Lehren; Skizze eines lebenswichtigen Vorgangs für
das Volk Gottes: → 212, FWESTERMANN C., Schöpfung 1989, 191-203 /
220-232.

4264 *Rossi de Gasperis* Francesco, Christian typology, is it still valid? If so,
which typology?: Sidic 21,3 (R 1988) 4-8.

4265 *Runia* Klaas, Some crucial issues in biblical interpretation [salva-
tion-history; OT-NT; Law]: CalvinT 24 (1989) 300-315.

4266 *Seim* Jürgen, Das Christuszeugnis des ATs [IWAND H.-J. 1934-42]: KIsr (1989,2) 149-155.

4267 *Steyn* G. J., Die eksegetisering van Ou-Testamentiese stof in die Nuwe Testament — enkele probleme en 'n moontlike [possible] model: TEv 20,3 (Pretoria 1987) 29-37 [< OTAbs 12, 139].

4268 **Taylor** Edward (1642-1729), Upon the types of the Old Testament, E*Mignon* Charles W. Lincoln 1989, Univ. Nebraska. lxxx-1005 p. [2 vol.] $90. 0-8032-3075-3 [TDig 37,89].

4269 *Terino* Jonathan, Il popolo dell'Antico Testamento; presenza e testimonianza: STEv NS 1/1 (1989) 7-24.

4270 *Thüsing* Wilhelm, Zwischen Jahweglaube und christologischem Dogma; zu Position und Funktion der neutestamentlichen Exegese innerhalb der Theologie: TJb (1989) 45-64.

4271 **Villegas** Guillermo V., The OT as a Christian book [diss. Greg 1985] 1988 → 4,4383: RCBQ 51 (1989) 734s (D. J. *Harrington*).

4272 *Wong Yai-Chow* Teresa, ⊖ Relationship between OT and NT: Colc-FuJen 77 (1988) 411-9.

F2.5   *Commentarii* – **Commentaries on the whole NT.**

4273 Bibbia di Navarra, I quattro Vangeli (Neo Volgata ...),T. Mi 1988, Ares. xxv-1088 p. Lit. 60.000 [CC 140/1, copertina].

4274 E**Friedrich** G., Auslegungen der Reformatoren [41 NT] 1984 → 65,d699; 1,f813: RProtestantesimo 44 (1989) 145 (P. *Tognina*).

4275 *a)* **García Avilés** Rafael J., Llamados a ser libres; 'seréis dichosos', Ciclo A [B 1990]; – *b)* **Peláez** Jesús, La otra lectura de los Evangelios; Ciclo C: En torno al Nuevo Testamento 7; ... Córdoba 1989; 1987s. 244 p. / 2 vol. 84-86077-79-6 [83-4] /.

4276 **Giertz** Bo, Förklaringar till Nya testamentet: I. Mt-Lk; II. Jn-Kor; III. Gal-Upb. Lund 1984/5/5, Verbum. 377 p.; 445 p. 398 p. – RSvTKv 65 (1989) 170s (B. *Johnson*).

4277 *Gilicze* László, ⊛ 'Az ö zsinagógáikban prédikált [LAPIDE P., Ein Jude erklärt das Ev. 41983]: TSzem 32 (1989) 184s.

4278 **Lachs** Samuel T., A rabbinic commentary on ... MtMkLk 1987 → 3,4156; 4,4388: RBS 146 (1989) 111 (D. L. *Bock*); Judaica 45 (1989) 71s (S. *Schreiner*).

4279 *Lohfink* Gerhard, Kommentar als Gattung [< Bibel und Leben 15 (1974) 1-16]: → 300, Studien zum NT 1989, 363-381.

4280 **Mateos** J., **Alonso Schökel** L., Nuevo Testamento 1987 → 3,4157: RSalmanticensis 36 (1989) 102-8 (J. M. *Sánchez Caro*: nihil obstat de 1974 no corresponde al testo bastante cambiado).

4281 Nuevo Testamento (traducción y notas de la Casa de la Biblia. M 1989, Promoción Popular Cristiana etc. 810 p. – BibFe 15 (1989) 485 (M. *Sáenz Galache*).

4282 **Rummel** Erika, Erasmus' Annotations on the NT 1986 → 2,d650: RCurrTM 16 (1989) 133s (E. M. *Krentz*: magnificent, fascinating).

Solms E. de (*J.-Nesmy* C.) Les quatre Evangiles, commentaires: Bible chrétienne II* 1988 → 1802*.

4283 **Vesco** J.-L., Le Nouveau Testament, textes choisis [version TOB 1972, commentée]. P 1988, Livre de Poche. 224 p. – REsprVie 99 (1989) 239 (L. *Walter*).

4284 **Wellhausen** Julius, Evangelienkommentare [1909-14, ➤ 3,4162], [E]*Hengel*
Martin. B 1987, de Gruyter. xvi-746 p. DM 238. 3-11-010065-7. –
[R]ZRGg 41 (1989) 189s (L. *Flaig*).

| X. Evangelia |

F2.6 **Evangelia Synoptica;** *textus, synopses, commentarii.*

4285 **Boismard** M.-E., *Lamouille* A., Synopsis graeca IV evv. 1986
➤ 2,3253... 4,4393: [R]JTS 40 (1989) 176s (Morna D. *Hooker*: clarity
dubiously compensates no variants); RB 96 (1989) 391-4 (J. *Taylor*,
franç.).

4286 **Kloppenborg** John S., Q parallels, synopsis... 1988 ➤ 4,4395: [R]JBL 108
(1989) 720-2 (M. E. *Boring*); TLZ 114 (1989) 428s (J. K. *Elliott*).

4287 **Neirynck** F., Q-Synopsis 1988 ➤ 4,4397: [R]RHE 84 (1989) 528s (J.
Dupont).

4288 **Poppi** Angelico, Sinossi dei quattro Vangeli II, 1988 ➤ 4,4400:
[R]Asprenas 36 (1989) 110 (C. *Marcheselli-Casale*); DivThom 91 (1988)
474s (G. *Testa*); RivB 37 (1989) 222s (M. *Làconi*); Salesianum 51 (1989)
567s (B. *Carlo*); Teresianum 40 (1989) 272s (V. *Pasquetto*).

4289 **Sanders** E. P., *Davies* Margaret, Studying the Synoptic Gospels. L/Ph
1989, SCM/Trinity. ix-374 p. [JTS 41,354]. £15. 0-334-02342-4. –
[R]ExpTim 101,4,2d-top choice (1989s) 97-100 (C. S. *Rodd*).

F2.7 *Problema synopticum:* **The Synoptic Problem.**

4290 **Carmignac** Jean, La naissance des évangiles synoptiques 1984
➤ 65,3769... 4,4403: [R]IrTQ 55 (1989) 246s (A. *O'Leary*).

4291 *Collins* Adela Y., The Son of Man sayings in the Sayings source: ➤ 60,
[F]FITZMYER J., Touch 1989, 369-389.

4292 *Cunningham* S., The Synoptic Problem; a summary of the leading
theories: AfJB 1,1 (Ibadan 1986) 48-58 [< NTAbs 33,19].

4293 *Elliott* J. K., L'importance de la critique textuelle pour le problème
synoptique: RB 96 (1989) 56-70; Eng. 56.

4294 **Havener** Ivan, Q, the sayings of Jesus: Good News Studies 19, 1987
➤ 3,4182; 4,4406: [R]CBQ 51 (1989) 152 (J. G. *Lodge*: for college students
without Greek); RelStT 7,2s (1987) 96s (T. A. *Robinson*).

4295 **Henaut** Barry W., Is Q but the invention of Luke and Mark? Method
and argument in the GRIESBACH hypothesis: RelStT 8,3 (1988) 15-32.

4296 **Horsley** Richard A., Questions about redactional strata and the social
relations reflected in Q: ➤ 589, SBL Seminars 1989, 186-203; 204-215,
Kloppenborg John S., The formation of Q revisited.

4297 **Kloppenborg** John S., The formation of Q: Studies in Antiquity and
Christianity, 1987 ➤ 3,4184; 4,4407: [R]Biblica 70 (1989) 282-5 (R.
Hodgson: gratifying); Interpretation 43 (1989) 200s (H. *Boers*); JBL 108
(1989) 150-2 (A. D. *Jacobson*: raises level of Q-study).

4298 *Kosch* Daniel, Q; Rekonstruktion und Interpretation; eine metho-
denkritische Hinführung mit einem Exkurs zur Q-Vorlage des Lk: FreibZ
36 (1989) 409-425.

4299 *Lührmann* Dieter, The Gospel of Mark and the sayings collection Q
[reaction to D. F. *Strauss* challenge]: JBL 108 (1989) 51-71.

4300 *Neirynck* Frans, Synoptic problem: ➤ 384, NJBC (1989) 587-595.
4301 **Sato** Migaku, Q und Prophetie...: WUNT 2/29, 1988 ➤ 4,4412: ᴿTsTNijm 29 (1989) 64 (W.H. *Berflo*); TLZ 114 (1989) 669-672 (A. *Suhl*).
4302 *Scholer* David M., Q bibliography, 1981-1989: ➤ 589, SBL Seminars 1989, 23-37.
4303 **Stein** Robert H., The Synoptic Problem; an introduction 1987 ➤ 3,4189; 4,4415: ᴿAndrUnS 26 (1988) 308-310 (G.F. *Rice*); WestTJ 50 (1988) 213-5 (J.W. *Scott*).
4304 *Tuckett* C.M., A cynic Q?: Biblica 70 (1989) 349-376; franç. 376.

F2.8 *Synoptica:* **themata.**

4305 **Brindle** Wayne A., A definition of the title 'Son of God' in the Synoptic Gospels: diss. Dallas Theol. Sem. 1988. 356 p. 89-13828. – DissA 50 (1989s) 1337-A.
4306 **Dominique** Fr., Jésus disait, I. Présentation des paroles de Jésus conservées dans les Évangiles de Matthieu. Marc et Luc 1987 ➤ 3,4193: ᴿNRT 111 (1989) 943s (A. *Toubeau*).
4307 *Friedrichsen* Timothy A., The minor agreements of Matthew and Luke against Mark; critical observations on R.B. VINSON's statistical analysis [diss. Duke 1984, 'The significance of the minor...', ᴰ*Smith* D.M.]: ETL 65 (1989) 395-408.
4308 *Green* H. Benedict, Matthew, Clement and Luke; their sequence and relationship [dissatisfaction with Q...]: JTS 40 (1989) 1-25.
4309 **Jolliffe** Roland L., The woes on the Pharisees; a critical text and commentary on [...code-number (= ?Lk)] Q11: 46, 43, 52, 42, 39-40, 44, 47-48: diss. Claremont 1989, ᴰ*Robinson* J. – RelStR 16,189.
4310 *Kee* Howard C., Synoptic studies: ➤ 394, NT/Interpreters 1989, 245-269.
4311 **Martin** Raymond A., Syntax criticism of the Synoptic Gospels: StBEC 10, 1987 ➤ 3,4197; 4,4427: ᴿCBQ 51 (1989) 378-380 (E.C. *Maloney*).
4312 **Melbourne** Bertram L., Slow to understand; the disciples in Synoptic perspective [diss. Andrews]. Lanham MD 1988, UPA. xvii-206 p. $14.50 pa. [JBL 109,533s, R.H. *Gundry*].
4313 *Merk* O., Aus (unveröffentlichten) Aufzeichnungen Rudolf BULTMANNs zur Synoptikerforschung: ➤ 131, ᶠMARXSEN W., Jesu Rede 1989, 195-207.
4314 **Orchard** B., *Riley* H., The order of the Synoptics; why three synoptic gospels? 1987 ➤ 3,4198; 4,4429: ᴿBiblica 70 (1989) 555-8 (D.L. *Dungan*); CriswT 2 (1988) 441-3 (D.L. *Akin*); IrTQ 55 (1989) 77s (J. *McPolin*); JBL 108 (1989) 521s (W.O. *Walker*); JTS 40 (1989) 554-6 (J. *Muddiman*: an unrecognizable Mark, a papalist fundamentalism); ScotJT 42 (1989) 572 (C. *Tuckett*); TGL 79 (1989) 623 (J. *Ernst*); TLZ 114 (1989) 189-191 (H.-T. *Wrege*).
4315 **Reicke** Bo, The roots of the Synoptic Gospels 1986 ➤ 2,3290*... 4,4430: ᴿRHPR 69 (1989) 224s (J.-C. *Ingelaere*).
4316 *Rolland* Philippe, La question synoptique demande-t-elle une réponse compliquée?: Biblica 70 (1989) 217-223] [approche de M.-E. BOISMARD trop 'alambiquée'].
4317 **Theissen** Gerd, Lokalkolorit und Zeitgeschichte in den Evangelien; ein Beitrag zur Geschichte der synoptischen Tradition: NTOrb 8. FrS/Gö

1989, Univ./VR. x-335 p. [CBQ 51,593]. – ᴿTsTNijm 29 (1989) 406s (J. *Negenman*).

4318 **Tuckett** Christopher, Nag Hammadi and the Gospel tradition ... synoptic 1986 ⇒ 2,8609 ... 4,4434: ᴿJRel 68 (1988) 449s (J. A. *Trumbower*); Salmanticensis 36 (1989) 119-122 (R. *Trevijano*).

4319 *Tuckett* Christopher M., Synoptic tradition in the Didache: ⇒ 606, Réception 1986/9, 197-230.

4320 **Vouga** François, Jésus et la loi selon la tradition synoptique [diss. Genève, ᴰ*Bovon* F.]: MondeB. Genève 1988, Labor et Fides. 331 p. – ᴿRechSR 77 (1989) 400s (J. *Guillet*); STEv NS 1 (1989) 88 (G. *Emetti*); TLZ 114 (1989) 273s (D. *Kosch*).

Wisselink Willem F., Assimilation ... Mt Mk Lk 1989 ⇒ 1750.

F3.1 **Matthaei evangelium:** *Textus, commentarii.*

4321 **Aranda Pérez** Gonzalo, El Evangelio de San Mateo en copto sahídico [1984 ⇒ 2,3300]; texto de M 569 y aparato crítico. TEstCisn 45. M 1988, Cons. Sup. 150 p. – ᴿRSO 62 (1988) 154s (Caterina *Moro*).

4322 *Ballentyne* Adrian, A reassessment of the exposition on the Gospel according to St Matthew in Manuscript Alençon 26: RTAM 56 (1989) 19-57.

4323 **Bruner** Frederick D., The Christbook, Mt 1-12 1987 ⇒ 3,4209; 4,4438: ᴿCalvinT 24 (1989) 151-5 (D. E. *Holwerda*).

4324 *Crisci* Edoardo, Un frammento palinsesto del 'Commento al vangelo di S. Matteo' di ORIGENE nel codice Criptense *G.b.*VI: JbÖsByz 38 (1988) 95-112; 8 pl.

4325 **Davies** W., *Allison* D., ICC, The Gospel according to St. Matthew I (1-7) 1988 ⇒ 4,4439: ᴿAsbTJ 44,2 (1989) 96-98 (D. R. *Bauer*: sometimes helpful but not great); ÉTRel 64 (1989) 288s (E. *Cuvillier*); ExpTim 100 (1988s) 228-230 (C. S. *Rodd*); ScotJT 42 (1989) 574s (C. M. *Tuckett*).

4325* **France** R. T., The Gospel according to Matthew; an introduction and commentary. Leicester/GR 1989 = 1985, Inter-Varsity/Eerdmans. 416 p. 0-85111-870-4 / 0-8028-0063-7. ⇒ 4358.

4326 **Gnilka** J., Mt-Ev. II 1988 ⇒ 4,4440: ᴿBiblica 70 (1989) 526-538 (D. C. *Allison*: masterful, but with problems); NRT 111 (1989) 428s (X. *Jacques*); Salesianum 51 (1989) 357s (C. *Bissoli*); TGL 79 (1989) 620s (J. *Ernst*); TR 85 (1989) 200 (A. *Sand*).

4327 **Guijarro** Santiago, Evangelio según San Mateo, comentario: MensajeNT 1. S 1989, Sígueme. 229 p. 84-7151-635-7.

4328 **Howard** George, The Gospel of Matthew according to a primitive Hebrew text [Even Bohan 1380] 1988 ⇒ 3,4215; 4,4442: ᴿBS 146 (1989) 470 (D. K. *Lowery*); JBL 108 (1989) 722-6 (W. L. *Petersen*: interesting yes, primitive no); RTAM 56 (1989) 238s (R. *Winandy*).

4329 **Jeanne d'Arc** sr., Évangile selon Matthieu 1987 ⇒ 3,4216; 4,4444: ᴿÉTRel 64 (1989) 635s (M. *Bouttier*); Salesianum 51 (1989) 356 (B. *Amata*).

4330 **Limbeck** M., Matthäus-Evangelium 1986 ⇒ 2,3306 ... 4,4445: ᴿTLZ 114 (1989) 592s (U. *Luz*).

4331 ᴱ**Löfstedt** B., SEDULIUS Scottus, Kommentar zum Evangelium nach Matthäus i,l-xi,1: Vetus Latina Gesch. 14. FrB 1989, Herder. 306 p. [RHE 84, p. 359*]. 3-451-00498-4. – ᴿRÉLat 67 (1989) 277s (J. *Fontaine*).

4332 ᵀᴱ**Longobardo** Luigi, ILARIO, Commentario a Matteo 1988 ⇒ 4,4446: ᴿCC 140 (1989,3) 203s (A. *Ferrua*).

4333 **Luz** Ulrich, Matthew 1-7, a commentary [EkK 1985 ➤ 1,4213], ᵀ*Linss* Wilhelm C. Minneapolis 1989, Augsburg. 460 p. $37. 0-8066-2402-7 [TDig 37,169].

4334 **Maier** Gerhard, Matthäus-Evangelium II⁴ [16,21-28,20; ¹1980]: Bibel-Kommentar 2. Stu-Neuhausen 1989, Hänssler. 503 p. 3-7751-0524-7.

4334* **Montague** George T., Companion God; a cross-cultural commentary on the Gospel of Matthew. NY 1989, Paulist. x-188 p. $10 [TR 86,427].

4335 **Patte** Daniel, The Gospel according to Matthew; a structural commentary on Matthew's faith 1987 ➤ 3,4222: ᴿCriswT 3 (1988s) 218-220 (D.A. *Black*); Interpretation 43 (1989) 184-6 (G. *Stanton*); ScotJT 42 (1989) 451-3 (R.A. *Piper*).

4336 **Sand** Alexander, Das Evangelium nach Matthäus: RgNT 1986 ➤ 3, 4224; 4,4451: ᴿAntonianum 64 (1989) 610s (M. *Nobile*); BLitEc 89 (1988) 294s (S. *Légasse*); CrNSt 10 (1989) 150s (V. *Fusco*); Salesianum 51 (1989) 362 (C. *Bissoli*); ScripTPamp 21 (1989) 699 (K. *Limburg*).

4337 **Schnackenburg** R., Matthäusevangelium 16,21-28: NEchter 1987 ➤ 3, 4226; ᴿBLtg 62 (1989) 57s (T. *Söding*).

4338 **Smith** Robert H., Matthew: Augsburg Comm. Minneapolis 1989, Augsburg. 351 p. 0-8066-8854-8. – ᴿSWJT 32,3 (1989s) 51 (G. *Greenfield*).

4339 ᴱ**Vanetti** P., Matteo [< Bibbia CC / S. Fedele]: Il Vangelo dell'anno. CasM 1986, Piemme. 94 p.; ill. Lit. 6500. – ᴿNRT 111 (1989) 615 (A. H.).

4340 *Viviano* Benedict T., The Gospel according to Matthew: ➤ 384, NJBC (1989) 630-674.

F3.2 **Themata** *de Matthaeo*.

4341 *Barbaglio* Giuseppe, Paolo e Matteo; due termini di confronto: ➤ 597, RicStoB 1,2 (1987/9) 5-22.

4342 **Bauer** David R., The structure of Matthew's Gospel; a study in literary design [diss. Richmond Union 1985, ᴰ*Kingsbury* J.]: JStNT Sup 31, 1988 ➤ 4,4456: ᴿETL 65 (1989) 163s (P. *Neirynck*); ÉTRel 64 (1989) 289s (E. *Cuvillier*); ExpTim 100 (1988s) 471s (S. H. *Travis*); TLZ 114 (1989) 812s (W. *Schenk*).

4343 *Bauer* D. R., The interpretation of Matthew's Gospel in the twentieth century: ➤ 754, AmTLibProc 42 (St. Meinrad IN 1988) 119-145.

4344 *Beauchamp* Paul, L'évangile de Matthieu et l'héritage d'Isräel: RechSR 76 (1988) 5-37, Eng. 38.

4345 *Black* David A., Conjectural emendations in the Gospel of Matthew [5,3; 6,28; 7,6; 8,22; 21,41 ...]: NT 31 (1989) 1-15.

4346 *Bratcher* Robert G., 'Righteousness' in Matthew: BTrans 40 (1989) 228-235.

4347 **Brooks** Stephenson H., Matthew's community; the evidence of his special sayings material [diss. Columbia/Union]: JStNT Sup 16, 1987 ➤ 3,4233: ᴿCBQ 51 (1989) 363s (D.J. *Harrington*); EstBíb 47 (1989) 423s (J. *Guijarro*); ExpTim 100 (1988s) 310 (G. *Stanton*); Interpretation 43 (1989) 424.426 (D. R. *Bauer*); JBL 108 (1989) 523s (M.A. *Powell*); JTS 40 (1989) 556-560 (H. B. *Green*).

4348 *a) Brown* Schuyler, Universalism and particularism in Matthew's Gospel; a JUNGIAN approach; – *b) Mowery* Robert L., The activity of God in the Gospel of Matthew: ➤ 589, SBL Seminars 1989, 388-399 / 400-411.

4349 *Burnett* F. W., Characterization in Matthew; reader construction of the disciple Peter: McKendree Pastoral Review 4,1 (Lebanon IL 1987) 13-43 [< NTAbs 33,20].

4350 *a) Burnett* Fred W., Characterization and Christology in Matthew; Jesus in the Gospel of Matthew; – *b) Black* C. Clifton[III], Depth of characterization and degrees of faith in Matthew: ➤ 589, SBL Seminars 1989, 588-603 / 604-623.

4351 **Chung Hoon Taik** [Seoul Presbyterian], Aan de vruchten zult gij hen kennen [TR 86,251: een onderzoek naar het inwendig verband tussen ...] christelijk geloof en gelovige levenswandel bij Matteüs [diss. Kampen Geref. Theol. Hogeschool, [D]*Baarlink* H.] Kampen c. 1989, Kok. 431 p. *f* 59,50. 90-242-5269-5. – TsTNijm 29 (1989) 170; RTLv 21,544.

4352 **Crosby** Michael H., The Matthean house church and political economy; implications for ethics and spirituality then and now: diss. Graduate Theological Union, [D]*Short* W. Berkeley c. 1989. 679 p. 89-24367. – DissA 50 (1989s) 2111-A; RelStR 16,190.

4353 **Crosby** M., House of disciples; Church, economics, and justice in Matthew ➤ 4,4458; also GR/Exeter 1989, Eerdmans/Paternoster. 182 p. $15 [TS 51,381].

4354 **Edwards** Richard A., Matthew's story of Jesus 1985 ➤ 1,4236; 2,3318: [R]BibTB 19 (1989) 109s (Karen A. *Barta*); CurrTM 16 (1989) 386s (A. T. *Kenealy*, also on [2]KINGSBURY J.).

4355 **Ernst** Josef, Matthäus, ein theologisches Portrait. Dü 1989, Patmos. 152 p. 3-491-77780-1.

4356 *Estrada* Bernardo, L'importanza delle antitesi del primo Vangelo: AnnTh 3,1 (1989) 99-119.

4357 **Fischer** Bonifatius, Varianten zu Mt: Aus der Geschichte der lateinischen Bibel 13, 1988 ➤ 4,4460: [R]NRT 111 (1989) 751s (X. *Jacques*); RHE 84 (1989) 505s (P.-M. *Bogaert*).

4358 **France** Richard T., [➤ 4325*] Matthew, evangelist and teacher. Exeter 1989, Paternoster. 345 p. 0-8006-1891-2.

4359 *a) Gorman* Frank H.[J], When law becomes Gospel; Matthew's transformed Torah; – *b) Matera* Frank J., The ethics of the Kingdom in the Gospel of Matthew; – *c) Edwards* Richard A., Reading Matthew; the Gospel as Narrative; – *d) Pilch* John J., Reading Matthew anthropologically; healing in cultural perspective; Listening 24 (1989) 227-240 / 241-250 / 251-261 / 278-289 [< ZIT 90,14].

4360 *Grassi* Joseph A., *a)* Matthew's Gospel as a live performance: BToday 27 (1989) 225-232; – *b)* Matthew as a Second Testament Deuteronomy: BibTB 19 (1989) 23-29.

4361 *Harrington* D. J., A dangerous text; Matthew and Judaism: Canad-CathR 7,4 (Saskatoon 1989) 135-142 [< NTAbs 33,302].

4361* *Howard* George, The textual nature of SHEM-TOB's Hebrew Matthew [IBN-ŠAPRUT 1380, akin but not identical to J. de TILLET 1555]: JBL 108 (1989) 239-257.

4362 **Kingsbury** J. D., Matthew as story[2rev]. Ph 1988, Fortress. x-181 p. $11. 0-8006-2099-2 [NTAbs 33,107: 'Son of Man' revised; new chapters on the great speeches of Jesus and the story line of the religious leaders]. – [R]CurrTM 16 (1989) 130s (L. A. *Kauppl*).

4363 **Kingsbury** Jack D., Matthew; structure, theology, Kingdom. Minneapolis 1989, Fortress. xxx-178 p.

4364 *Kingsbury* Jack D., Matthew: ➤ 377, Books 2 (1989) 125-147.

4365 *Klein* Hans, Judenchristliche Frömmigkeit im Sondergut des Matthäus: NTS 35 (1989) 466-474.

4366 **Köhler** Wolf-Dietrich, Die Rezeption des Matthäusevangeliums in der Zeit vor IRENÄUS [ᴰ1986]: WUNT 2/24, 1987 ➤ 3,4241: ᴿCBQ 51 (1989) 562-4 (W. R. *Schoedel* compares with E. MASSAUX 1950 reprinted 1986); TGegw 32 (1989) 77s (H. *Giesen*).

4367 *Kuntz* Manfred, Eine Skizze zum Sabbatverständnis des Matthäusevangeliums: ➤ 65*, ᶠGEISSER H. 1988, 358-361.

4368 *Lillie* Betty Jane, Matthew's wisdom theology; old things and new: ProcGLM 9 (1989) 124-137.

Lowery David K., God as father (Mt) ᴰ1987 ➤ 7084*.

4369 **McIver** Robert K., The problem of Synoptic relationships in the development and testing of a methodology for the reconstruction of the Matthean community: diss. Andrews, ᴰ*Johnston* R. Berrien Springs MI 1989. 731 p. 90-07148. – DissA 50 (1989s) 3259s-A.; RTLv 21,546 '1988'.

4370 ᴱ**Mandruzzato** Enzo, Il buon messaggio seguendo Matteo: Il soggetto e la scienza 7. Pordenone 1989, Biblioteca dell'Immagine. xlv-186 p. Lit. 25.000.

4371 *Niedner* Frederick A.ᴶ, Rereading Matthew on Jerusalem and Judaism: BibTB 19 (1989) 43-47.

4372 **Njoroge** Peter D., An exegetical study of 'interiority; a dimension in the mission of Jesus' in selected texts of the Gospel of Matthew: diss. Pont. Univ. Gregoriana, ᴰ*Rasco* E. R 1989. 397 p. – RTLv 21,546.

4373 *Okeke* G. E., The after-life in St. Matthew and an aspect of Matthean ethics: Melanesian Journal of Theology 4,2 (1988) 35-45.

4374 **Orton** David E., The understanding scribe; Matthew and the apocalyptic ideal [diss. Sheffield]. Sheffield 1989, JStOT. 280 p. £25. 1-85075-181-1 [TDig 37,80]. – ᴿExpTim 101 (1989s) 121 (Margaret *Davies*).

4375 **Overman** John A., Matthew's Gospel and formative Judaism; a study of the social world of the Matthean community: diss. Boston 1989, ᴰ*Kee* H. 358 p. 89-11553. – DissA 50 (1989s) 711-A. [RelStR 16,189 title 'The Gospel of Matthew in formative Judaism ...'].

4376 *Pantle-Schieber* Klaus, Anmerkungen zur Auseinanderstzung von *ekklēsía* und Judentum im Matthäusevangelium: ZNW 80 (1989) 145-163.

4377 ᶠPESCH Wilhelm, ᴱ**Schenke** Ludger, Studien zum Mt-Ev 1988 ➤ 4,115: ᴿÉTRel 64 (1989) 634 (G. *Balestier-Stengel*, deçu).

4378 *Pesch* Wilhelm, Matthäus als Gemeindetheologe und Seelsorger: TGegw32 (1989) 277-289.

4379 *Phillips* Cary A., Training scribes for a world divided; discourse and division in the religious system of Matthew's Gospel: ➤ 592, Systemic 2 (1989) 51-74.

4380 *Popkes* Wiard, Die Gerechtigkeitstradition im Matthäus-Evangelium: ZNW 80 (1989) 1-23.

Pregeant Russell, Matthew's Christ in process hermeneutic 1978 ➤ 7057*.

4381 *Quesnel* Michel, Les citations de Jérémie dans l'Évangile selon saint Matthieu: EstBíb 47 (1989) 513-527; castellano/Eng. 513.

4382 *Rumianek* Ryszard, ⊘ Pastoral examples in the teaching of Jesus in Mt: STWsz 26,1 (1988) 245-9.

4383 *Savon* H., JÉRÔME et AMBROISE, interprètes du premier Évangile: ➤ 577*, Jérôme Occident/Orient 1986/8, 205-225.

4384 **Schenk** Wolfgang, Die Sprache des Matthäus [1691 words in alphabetical order] 1987 ➤ 3,4253; 4,4479: ᴿCBQ 51 (1989) 164s (F. W.

Burnett: gives sign-clusters but unclear on sentence-meanings); JBL 108 (1989) 341s (R. L. *Mowery*); TsTNijm 29 (1989) 64s (H. *Welzen*).

4385 **Sigal** P. (d. 1985), The Halakhah of Jesus according to Mt. 1986 ➤ 2,3338 ... 4,4481: ᴿJEcuSt 26 (1989) 530-5 (L. *Swidler*, M. *Chernick*, *Amy-Jill Levine*).

4386 **Thompson** William G., Matthew's story; good news for uncertain times. NY 1989, Paulist. ix-165 p. $9 pa [CBQ 52,199].

4387 **Stock** Klemens, [➤ 4474] Gesù annuncia la beatitudine; il messaggio di Matteo [Jesus – Kunder der Seligkeit 1986 ➤ 2,3340], ᵀ*Ronchitelli* Domenico: Bibbia e Preghiera 4. R 1989, Apostolato della Preghiera. 151 p. Lit. 15.000. 88-7375-077-1.

4388 **Wilkins** Michael J., The concept of disciple in Mt 1988 ➤ 4,4485: ᴿBibTB 19 (1989) 158 (L. E. *Frizzell*).

4389 **Zumstein** J., La condition du croyant ... Mt [ᴰ1974]: OBO 16, 1977 ➤ 58,4613; 60,5870: ᴿNicolaus 16 (1989) 263-5 (A. *Moda*).

F3.3 *Mt 1s* (*Lc 1s* ➤ F7.5) *Infantia Jesu* – **Infancy Gospels.**

4391 *Harrington* Daniel J., Birth narratives in Pseudo-PHILO's Biblical Antiquities and the Gospels: ➤ 60, FITZMYER J., Touch 1989, 316-324.

4392 **Hendrickx** Hermann, Los relatos de la infancia 1986 ➤ 3,4367: ᴿStudium 29 (M 1989) 552 (P. *Blázquez*).

4393 *Henninger* Joseph, *a*) 'Ein Kind ist uns geboren ...'; die Weihnachtsbotschaft im Lichte palästinischen Volksbrauches [< SchweizKZ 120 (1952) 641]; – *b*) Zum Erstgeborenenrecht bei den Semiten [< ᶠ*Caskel* W. (Leiden 1968) 162-183]; – *c*) ... im alten Südarabien [< EthnZts 2 (1972) 185-192]: ➤ 279, Arabica 1989, 454-7 / 139-167 / 168-179.

4394 **Horsley** Richard A., The liberation of Christmas 1989 ➤ 4,4500: ᴿTTod 46 (1989s) 222.224.226 (Sharon H. *Ringe*).

4395 *Horsley* R., Liberating Christmas [the original story was full of politics]: ChrisCris 48 (NY 1988) 436-8 [410-5, *Gubler* M.-L.; < NTAbs 33,155s].

4396 *Laurentin* René, I Vangeli del Natale 1987 ➤ 4,4503: ᴿAnnTh 3,1 (1989) 154-6 (B. *Estrada*).

4397 *a*) *Maier* Paul L., The date of the Nativity and the chronology of Jesus' life; – *b*) *Martin* Ernest L., The Nativity and Herod's death; – *c*) *Hoehner* Harold W., The date of the death of Herod the Great; – *d*) *Johnson* Douglas, 'And they went eight stades toward Herodeion' [JOSEPHUS Ant 17,199, Herod's funeral procession]; – *e*) *Vardaman* Jerry, Jesus' life; a new chronology [born 12 B.C.]: ➤ 58, ᶠFINEGAN J., Chronos 1989, 113-130 / 85-92 / 101-111 / 93-99 / 55-82; 8 fig.

4398 *Miyoshi* M., Die Theologie der Spaltung und Einigung Israels in der Geburts- und Leidensgeschichte nach Matthäus: AnJapB 15 (1989) 37-52.

4399 *a*) *Muñoz Iglesias* Salvador, Derás en Mt 1-2; – *b*) *Vernet* Joan M., Herodes el Gran; nova òptica històrica: ➤ 69*, ᶠGOMÀ I., RCatalT 14 (1989) 111-120 castellano; Eng. 121 / 99-109; Eng. 110.

4400 **Oberweis** Michael, Beobachtungen zum AT-Gebrauch in der matthäischen Kindheitsgeschichte: NTS 35 (1989) 131-149.

4400* **Paul** André, Il vangelo dell'infanzia secondo san Matteo [1986], ᵀ*Valentino* G. R 1986, Borla. 198 p. – ᴿBenedictina 35 (1988) 226s (L. *De Lorenzi*); Marianum 51 (1989) 655-7 (E. *Peretto*).

4401 **Segalla** G., Una storia annunciata 1987 ➤ 4,4509: ᴿAnnTh 3,1 (1989) 151-4 (M. A. *Tábet*); StPatav 36 (1989) 168-174 (A. *Moda*).

4402 *Thundy* Zacharias P., Intertextuality, Buddhism, and the Infancy Gospels: → 592, Systemic 1 (1989) 17-73.
4403 **Weren** W., *al.*, Geboorteverhalen van Jesus, feit en ficties. Boxtel/Brugge 1988, KBS/Tabor. 188 p. Fb 435. – RCollatVL 19 (1989) 239 (R. *Hoet*).

4404 *Van Elderen* Bastiaan, The significance of the structure of Matthew 1: → 58, FFINEGAN J., Chronos 1989, 3-14.
4405 *Fabris* Rinaldo, La vergogna redenta, Mt 1,1-17: ParSpV 20 (1989) 89-103.
4406 *Graves* Thomas H., Matthew 1:1-17 (exposition): RExp 86 (1989) 595-600.
4407 *Harrington* Daniel J., New and old in NT interpretation; the many faces of Matthew 1:18-25: NewTR 2,1 (1989) 39-49.
4408 *Stramare* Tarcisio, L'annunciazione a Giuseppe in Mt. 1,18-25; analisi letteraria e significato teologico: BbbOr 31 (1989) 3-14. 199-217.
4409 *López Rosas* Ricardo, San José en la Sagrada Escritura; la justicia de San José según Mateo 1,18ss: EfMex 7 (1989) 179-193.
4410 *Stefani* P., I sogni di Giuseppe, sposo di Maria: → 563c, Sogno 1988 ...
4411 **Brown** Raymond E., A concepção virginal e a ressureição corporal de Jesus, TToledo Steidel Yolanda de, São Paulo 1987, Loyola. 126 p. – RPerspT 20 (1988) 137s (F. *Taborda*).
4412 *Corpuz* Ruben, The validity of the virginal conception language in the ecumenical dialogue: Philippiniana Sacra 70 (1989) 91-111 [< TContext 7/1, 66].
4413 **Müller** Gerhard I., Was heisst: Geboren von der Jungfrau Maria? Eine theologische Deutung: QDisp 119. FrB 1989, Herder. 128 p. DM 29,80 [MüTZ 40,378]. 3-451-02119-6.
4414 *Jaki* Stanley L., The virgin birth and the birth of science: DowR 107 (1989) 255-273.
4415 **Schaberg** Jane, The illegitimacy of Jesus; a feminist interpretation of the infancy narratives 1987 → 3,4273; 4,4508: RAmerica 158 (1988) 435-7 (Pheme *Perkins*); CCurr 38 (1988s) 360s (Carolyn *Osiek*: case skilfully made); Horizons 16 (1989) 377s (Mary Ann *Getty*); Interpretation 43 (1989) 208 (R. S. *Dietrich*); JRel 69 (1989) 238s (Janice C. *Anderson*).
4416 *Buit* M. du, Quirinius: → 882, Catholicisme XII, 55 (1989) 402s.
4417 *Frankemölle* H., Die Geburt im Stall; die 'Weihnachtsgeschichte' im Widerstreit zwischen tiefenpsychologischer und historisch-kritischer Auslegung: Diakonia 19 (W 1988) 402-410 [< NTAbs 33,155].
4418 *Camprubí* Francese, El bou i l'ase en el pessebre [s. 4-15]: → 69*, FGOMÀ I., RCatalT 14 (1989) 441-451; 11 fig.; Eng. 451.
4419 *Couffignal* Robert, [Mt 2,1-12] Le conte merveilleux des mages et du cruel Hérode: RThom 89 (1989) 98-117.
4420 **Spartà** S., I Magi, tra storia e leggenda. Assisi 1987, Cittadella. 190 p.; 8 pl. Lit. 20.000 pa. [NTAbs 33,391].
4421 *Küchler* Max, 'Wir haben seinen Stern gesehen ..' (Mt 2,2) [archäologisch zu Sternen, zunächst der Dioskuren]: BiKi 44 (1989) 179-186; 10 fig.
4422 **Strobel** August, Der Stern von Bethlehem, ... ein Licht in unserer Zeit; Erwägungen zu Mt 2,1-12: 1985 → 2,3373: RTRu 54 (1989) 422-6 (H.-H. *Voigt*).

4423 *Voigt* H.-H.,   Astronomie, Astrologie, Theologie [*Strobel* A. 1985; Mt 2,1-12]: TRu 54 (1989) 422-6.

4424 ᴱStephenson F. R.,   *Walker* C. B. F.,   Halley's comet in history 1985 ➤ 1,446: ᴿOLZ 84 (1989) 292-4 (S. M. *Maul*).

4425 *a*) *Yamauchi* Edwin M.,   [Mt 2,1-12] The episode of the Magi; – *b*) *Ferrari-d'Occhieppo* Konradin,   The star of the Magi and Babylonian astronomy: ➤ 58, ᶠFINEGAN J., Chronos 1989, 15-39 / 55-82.

4426 **Aron** Robert,   Así rezaba Jesús de niño, ᵀ*Munera* Concha: Biblioteca Catecumenal.   Bilbao 1985, Desclée de Brouwer.   258 p. – ᴿLumenVr 38 (1989) 85s (F. *Ortiz de Urtaran*).

4427 *Carniti* Cecilia,   La sacra famiglia; 'i fratelli di Gesù': ➤ 587, Famiglia 1987/9, 189-197.

F3.4   *Mt 3 ... Baptismus Jesu*,   **Beginning of the Public Life.**

4428 *McVann* Mark,   The making of Jesus the prophet; Matthew 3:13-4:25: Listening 24 (1989) (223-6) 262-277 [< ZIT 90,14].

4429 *Ladaria* Luis F.,   [Mt 3,13-17] El bautismo y la unción de Jesús en HILARIO de Poitiers: Gregorianum 70 (1989) 277-290; franç. 290.

4430 *Smalbrugge* Matthias,   [Mt. 3,13-17 chez AUGUSTIN, Sermon 52, 'vestiges de la Trinité'; opposition de K. BARTH]: RHPR 69 (1989) 121-134; Eng. 241.

4431 *Corrigan* Kathleen,   The witness of John the Baptist on an early Byzantine icon in Kiev: DumbO 42 (1988) 1-11 + 11 fig.

4432 **Dobbeler** Stephanie von,   Das Gericht und das Erbarmen Gottes; die Botschaft Johannes des Täufers im Rahmen der Theologiegeschichte des Frühjudentums [kath. Diss. ᴰ*Merklein* H., Bonn 1987]: BoBB 70. Fra 1988, Athenäum.   258 p. DM 58.   3-610-09119-3. – ᴿTLZ 114 (1989) 737s (J. *Becker*).

4433 **Ernst** Josef,   Johannes der Täufer; Interpretation–Geschichte–Wirkungsgeschichte: BZNW 53. B 1989, de Gruyter. xv-427 p. 3-11-011707-X.

4434 *Ernst* Josef,   War Jesus ein Schüler Johannes' des Täufers?: ➤ 68, ᶠGNILKA J., Vom Urchristentum 1989, 13-33.

4435 **Infante** Renzo,   L'amico dello Sposo Giovanni Battista 1984 ➤ 65,3887: ᴿRivScR 3,1 (1989) 240s (A. *Pitta*).

4435* *Lucchesi* E.,   Un feuillet reconnu de l'Histoire de Gesius et Isidorus relative à l'invention du chef de saint Jean-Baptiste (BHO 485-486]: ➤ 820, Journée copte 1984/6, 15-19.

4436 **Lupieri** Edmondo,   Giovanni Battista nelle tradizioni sinottiche: StBPaid 82, 1988 ➤ 4,4536: ᴿÉTRel 64 (1989) 292 (E. *Cuvillier*); RivB 37 (1989) 370s (V. *Fusco*: stimolante, penetrante).

4437 *Lupieri* Edmondo F.,   John the Gnostic; the figure of the Baptist in ORIGEN and heterodox Gnosticism: ➤ 696, 10th Patristic, 19 (1989) 322-7.

4438 **Metzsch** Friedrich-August von,   Johannes der Täufer; seine Geschichte und seine Darstellung in der Kunst.   Mü 1989, Callwey.   230 p. [RHPR 70, 262, G. *Siegwalt*].

4439 *Thyen* Hartwig,   Johannes der Täufer: ➤ 894, EvKL 2 (1988) 834s.

4441 *Enout* J. E.,   As tentações de Jesus como tema teológico: Liturgia e Vida 209 (Rio 1988) 1-9 [< Stromata 45,491].

4442 *a*) *Esch* Arnold,   Versuchung; Predigt über Matthäus 4,1-11; – *b*) *Moltmann-Wendel* Elisabeth,   Alles haben oder ganz sein; Die Ver-

suchungen Jesu und unsere Versuchungen... Mt 4,1-13, Frauenforum:
EvT 49 (1989) 3-7 / 8-19.
4443 *Flusser* David, [Mt 4,1-11] Die Versuchung Jesu und ihr jüdischer
Hintergrund: Judaica 45 (1989) 110-128.
4444 *Hunter* A., Rite of passage; the implications of Matthew 4:1-11 for an
understanding of the Jewishness of Jesus: Christian-Jewish Relations 19,4
(L 1986) 7-22 [NTAbs 33,303].
4445 *Kruse* Heinz, ◑ The temptations of Jesus: KatKenk 28,55 (1989) 1-34;
Eng. 1s.
4446 *Lindemann* A., Die Versuchungsgeschichte Jesu nach der Logienquelle
und das Vaterunser: ⇥ 131, ᶠMARXSEN W., Jesu Rede 1989, 91-100.
4446* *Frankemölle* Hubert, [Mt 4,15...] Jesus als deuterojesajanischer
Freudenbote? zur Rezeption von Jes 52,7 und 61,1 im Neuen Testament,
durch Jesus und in den Targumim: ⇥ 68, ᶠGNILKA J. 1989, 34-67.
4447 *Busse* Ulrich, [Mt 4,17-22...] Nachfolge auf dem Weg Jesu; Ursprung
und Verhältnis von Nachfolge und Berufung im Neuen Testament: ⇥ 68*,
ᶠGNILKA J., Vom Urchristentum 1989, 68-81.

F3.5   Mt 5... Sermon on the Mount [... plain, Lk 6,17].

4447* **Betz** Hans D., Essays on the Sermon on the Mount 1985 ⇢ 1,4323...
4,4549: ᴿSvTKv 65 (1989) 169 (B. *Gerhardsson*).
4448 **Bretzke** James T., The notion of moral community in the 'Analects' of
Confucius and Matthew's Sermon on the Mount; a hermeneutical
approach for the inculturation of moral theology in Korea: diss. Pont.
Univ. Gregoriana, Nᵒ 3609, ᴰ*Dupuis* J. R 1989. 530 p.; extr. 160 p. –
RTLv 21,574.
4449 *Broer* I., Bergpredigt: ⇢ 902, NBL, Lfg. 2 (1989) 272-4.
4450 **Davenport** Gene L., Into the darkness; discipleship in the Sermon on the
Mount 1988 ⇢ 4,4554*: ᴿExpTim 101 (1989) 121 (E. *Franklin*).
4451 **Derrett** J. D. M., The ascetic discourse; an explanation of the Sermon
on the Mount. Eilsbrunn 1989, Ko'amar. 112 p. DM 24,80. 3-927136-
03-4 [ÉTRel 64,672]. – ᴿExpTim 101 (1989s) 120s (E. *Franklin*: heady
stuff).
4452 *Ellis* E. Earle, [Mt 5] How Jesus interpreted his Bible [... never opposed
Torah, only interpreted it better]: CriswT 3,2 (1989) 341-351.
Fusco Vittorio, Gesù e la legge 1989 ⇢ 4116.
4453 *a)* *Geyer* Hans-Georg, LUTHERs Auslegung der Bergpredigt; – *b)* *Blank*
Josef, Liebe und Glaube; die Bergpredigt nach dem Verständnis des
Matthäus; – *c)* *Mokrosch* Reinhold, Liebe und Glaube; wird Luthers
Auslegung der Bergpredigt dem Anspruch Jesu und des Matthäus-
Evangeliums gerecht?: ⇢ k114, ᴱ*Graf*, Werden und Wirkung der
Reformation 1983/6, 139-146 / 147-152 / 153-6.
4454 *Haufe* Günter, Umstrittene Bergpredigt — Positionen ihrer Auslegungs-
und Wirkungsgeschichte: TVers 17 (1989) 35-43.
4455 **Kodjak** A., A structural analysis of the Sermon on the Mount 1986
⇢ 2,3400: ᴿActuBbg 26 (1989) 43s (X. *Alegre* S.).
Kosch Daniel, Die eschatologische Torah des Menschensohnes; Untersuchungen zur Rezeption der Stellung Jesu zur Tora in Q 1989
⇢ 7626.
4456 **Lambrecht** J., 'Eh bien! Moi je vous dis': LDiv 125, 1986 ⇢ 2,3402...
4,4559: ᴿAnnTh 3 (1989) 156-9 (B. *Estrada*); ÉglT 19 (1988) 101s (M.

Dumais); EstBíb 47 (1989) 424s (D. *Muñoz León*); Gregorianum 70 (1989) 785s (E. *Farahian*); LavalTP 44 (1988) 123s (H.-M. *Guindon*); RAfrT 13 (1989) 110-4 (N. *Waswandi*).

4457 **Lohfink** Gerhard,   Wem gilt die Bergpredigt? Beiträge zu einer christlichen Ethik 1988 ➤ 4,4564:   ᴿLebZeug 43 (1988) 66 (R. *Jungnitsch*); Salesianum 51 (1989) 136s (G. *Abbà*); TXav 39 (1989) 171-3 (R. E. de *Roux*).

4458 **Schnackenburg** Rudolf,   Tutto è possibile a chi crede; Discorso della montagna e Padrenostro nell'intenzione di Gesù [Alles ... Bergpredigt 1984 ➤ 65,3923; ²1988], ᵀ*De Marchi* Valentino: StBPaid 89.   Brescia 1989, Paideia. 142 p. 88-394-0436-8.

4459 *a) Schüller* B.,   Zur Interpretation der Antithesen der Bergpredigt; – *b) Hoffmann* P.,   Jesu 'Verbot des Sorgens' und seine Nachgeschichte in der synoptischen Überlieferung: ➤ 131, ᶠMARXSEN W., Jesu Rede 1989, 101-115 / 116-141.

4460 *Sorani* Giuseppe,   'Avete udito ... ma io vi dico': StEcum 5 (1987) 221-235: Eng. 236.

4461 **Stoll** Brigitta, De virtute in virtutem; zur Auslegung ... der Bergpredigt 800-1200, ᴰ1988 ➤ 4,4570:   ᴿGGA 241 (1989) 258-264 (R. *Sprandel*).

4462 **Strecker** Georg,   The Sermon on the Mount [²1985], ᵀ*Dean* O. C. 1988 ➤ 4,4571:   ᴿTLond 92 (1989) 328s (M. *Goulder*: good, but many hypotheses).

4463 **Syreeni** Kari,   The making of the Sermon on the Mount [1987 ➤ 3,4360; 4,4572:   ᴿExpTim 100 (1988s) 66s (J. M. *Court*); JBL 108 (1989) 524-6 (L. R. *Donelson*).

4464 **Tilborg** Sjef van,   The sermon on the mount as an ideological intervention; a reconstruction of meaning.   Assen (Wolfeboro NH) 1986, Van Gorcum. vii-376 p. $20. – ᴿCBQ 51 (1989) 168s (N. J. *McEleney*: he uses L. ALTHUSER's Marxist philosophy to counter a too ethical/dogmatic interpretation; helpful but badly presented typescript).

4465 **Weder** Hans,   Die 'Rede der Reden' 1985 ➤ 3,4363:   ᴿProtestantesimo 44 (1989) 131s (U. *Eckert*).

4466 *Wright* Alexandra, rabbi,   The Sermon on the Mount, a Jewish view: NBlackf 70 (1989) 182-8.

F3.6   **Mt 5,3-11 (Lc 6,20-22) Beatitudines.**

4467 **Borao** Jesús,   El camino de las bienaventuranzas 1987 ➤ 4,4576: ᴿFranBog 30 (1988) 380 (E. V. D.).

4468 **Camacho** F.,   La proclama del Reino... Mt 5,3-10, 1987 ➤ 3,4367; 4,4580:   ᴿActuBbg 26 (1989) 35 (X. *Alegre* S.); Burgense 30 (1989) 283s (J. M. C.).

4469 *Coste* R.,   Le grand secret des Béatitudes 1985 ➤ 1,4352*... 4,4581: ᴿRTAfr 13 (1989) 119-122 (N. *Waswandi*).

4470 *DiLella* Alexander A.,   The structure and composition of the Matthean Beatitudes: ➤ 60, ᶠFITZMYER J., Touch 1989, 237-242.

4471 **López Melús** Francisco M.,   Las bienaventuranzas, ley fundamental de la vida cristiana: Nueva alianza 109, 1988 ➤ 4,4583:   ᴿActuBbg 26 (1989) 242s (R. de *Sivatte*); EstAgust 24 (1989) 259s (D. *Natal*); LumenVr 38 (1989) 83 (F. *Ortiz de Urtaran*); NRT 111 (1989) 940 (L.-J. *Renard*); QVidCr 145 (1989) 146 (Ll. *Juliá*); Teresianum 40 (1989) 624s (V. *Pasquetto*).

4472 *a*) *Mora* Gaspar, El regne de Déu, concepte clau de les benaurances; –
b) *Rovira Bellosa* Josep M., Benaurats els qui sofreixen persecució per la
justícia; – *c*) *Tena* Pere, Les benaurances en l'"Ordo lectionum Missae':
→ 69*, ᶠGOMÀ I., RCatalT 14 (1989) 279-290; Eng. 290 / 291-307; Eng.
307 / 467-476; Eng. 477.

4473 *Pantelis* Jorge, Los pobres en espíritu; bienaventurados en el Reino de
Dios; Mateo 5,3-12: RBibArg 51,33 (1989) 1-9.
Stock Klemens, Gesù annuncia la Beatitudine; il messaggio di Matteo 1989
→ 4387.

4474 *Stock* Klemens, Der Weg der Freude / Der Gott der Freude: Die acht
Seligpreisungen I-II: GeistL 62 (1989) 360-373. 433-446.

_____

4475 *Lana* Horacio, La bienaventuranza a los pobres (Lc 6,20b; Mt 5,3):
ProyCSE 1,1 (1989) 7-39.

4476 **Pobee** John S., Who are the poor? 1987 → 3,4369; 4,4585: ᴿAsiaJT 3
(1989) 358-361 (N. C. *Capulong*).

4477 *Li Young-Hún*, **◎** The exegetical interpretation of the Gospel of
Matthew 5:17-20: Sinhak Jonmang 85 (Kwangju 1989) 2-13 [< TContext
7/1, 60].

4478 *Boismard* Marie-Émile, [Mt 5,17.16.37] Une tradition para-synoptique
attestée par les Pères anciens: → 606, Réception 1986/9, 177-195.

4479 *a*) *Luz* Ulrich, [Mt 5,17] Das Matthäusevangelium und die Perspektive
einer biblischen Theologie; – *b*) *Limbeck* Meinrad, Vom rechten
Gebrauch des Gesetzes; – *c*) *Pesch* Otto H., Begriff und Bedeutung des
Gesetzes in der katholischen Theologie; – *d*) *Welker* Michael, Gesetz und
Geist: JbBT 4 ('Gesetz als Thema biblischer Theologie' 1989) 233-248 /
151-169 / 171-213 / 215-229.

4480 *Loader* William, [Mt 5,18s] Jesus left loose ends [... Torah obligations]:
Pacifica 2 (1989) 210-228.

4481 *Dewey* Arthur J., Quibbling over serifs; observations on Matt 5:18 /
Luke 16:17: → 160*, ᶠROBINSON J. = Forum 5,2 (1989) 109-120.

4482 *Casciaro* José M., Las antítesis de Mt 5,21-48; ¿Halakhot de la Torah o
algo más?; → 69*, ᶠGOMÀ I., RCatalT 14 (1989) 123-131, castellano;
Eng. 132.

4483 *Dupont* Jacques, [Mt 5,24] Laisse là ton offrande devant l'autel: → 141,
ᶠNOCENT A., Traditio 1988, 205-214.

4484 *Bockmuehl* Markus, Matthew 5.32; 19.9 in the light of pre-Rabbinic
Halakhah: NTS 35 (1989) 291-5.

4485 de la *Serna* Eduardo, [Mt 5,32; 19,9] ¿Divorcio en Mateo?: RBíbArg
51 (1989) 91-110.

4486 **Marucci** Corrado, [Mt 5,31...] Parole di Gesù sul divorzio 1982
→ 63,4453 ... 1,4368: ᴿRB 96 (1989) 304s (B. T. *Viviano*).

4487 *Funk* Robert W., [Mt 5,38-48; Lk 6,27-35: on love of enemies]
Unraveling the Jesus tradition; criteria and criticism: → 160*, ᶠROBINSON
J. = Forum 5,2 (1989) 31-62.

4488 *Vögtle* Anton, Ein 'unablässiger Stachel' (Mt 5,39b-42 par Lk 6,29-30):
→ 173, ᶠSCHNACKENBURG R., NT & Ethik 1989, 53-70.

4489 *Ellington* Paul, 'In secret' (Mt 6,4.6.18): BTrans 40 (1989) 446s: claims
extremely difficult; retains for Mt 6,4a, but in the others 'in the secret
place'.

4490 *Hemmerle* Klaus, Wandern mit deinem Gott — religionsphilosophische Kontexte zu Mt 6,8: ➤ 45, FDEISSLER A., Weg 1989, 234-250.

F3.7   *Mt 6,9-13 (Lc 11,2-4)* **Oratio Jesu,** Pater Noster, **Lord's Prayer** [H1.4].

4491 *Bell* David N., The commentary on the Lord's Prayer of Gilbert FOLIOT [c. 1180]: RTAM 56 (1989) 80-89; Latin text 89-101.
4492 *Buchan* William M., Research on the Lord's Prayer: ExpTim 100 (1988s) 336-9.
4493 *Delobel* Joël, The Lord's Prayer in the textual tradition; a critique of recent theories and their view on MARCION's role: ➤ 606, Réception 1986/9, 293-309.
4494 **Heinimann** Siegfried, Oratio dominica romanice; das Vaterunser in den romanischen Sprachen [111 Fassungen] von den Anfängen bis ins 16. Jhdt. ...: ZromanPgBeih 219. Tü 1988, Niemeyer. xii-224 p. DM 74. – RTüTQ 169 (1989) 140s (W. *Gross*).
4495 **Lochman** Jan M., Unser Vater, Auslegung. Gö 1988. 152 p. – RTZBas 45 (1989) 378-380 (A. *Jäger*).
   Lowery David K., God as father... Mt, D1987 ➤ 7084*.
4496 *Miller* Robert J., The Lord's Prayer and other items from the Sermon on the Mount: ➤ 160*, FROBINSON J. = Forum 5,2 (1989) 177-186.
4497 *Moor* J. C. de, The reconstruction of the Aramaic original of the Lord's Prayer: ➤ 410, Structural/poetry 1988, 397-422.
4498 *Perarnau* Josep, Sermó inèdit de Sant Vicent FERRER explicant el 'Pare Nostre' (Barcelona, Biblioteca de Catalunya, Ms. 477): ➤ 69*, FGOMÀ I., RCatalT 14 (1989) 527-532; Lat. 533-9; Eng. 540.
4499 *Plymale* Steven F., The Lucan Lord's Prayer: BToday 27 (1989) 176-182.
4500 **Sabugal** Santos, Il Padrenuestro nella catechesi antica e moderna [1982 ➤ 63,4470, con traduzioni italiane più recenti], ENicolosi Mauro, 1988 ➤ 4,4610: RCC 140 (1989,3) 306s (A. *Ferrua*); RasT 30 (1989) 490s (A. *Longobardi*).
4501 *Scognamiglio* Rosario, Il 'Padre nostro' nelle esegesi dei Padri: ParVi 34 (1989) 56-59. 136-140. 205-9. 286-8. 378-382. 451-5.
4502 *Standaert* Benoît, Crying 'Abba' and saying 'Our Father'; an intertextual approach to the dominical prayer: ➤ 95, FIERSEL B. van, 1989, 141-158.
4503 **Stritzky** Maria-Barbara von, Studien zur Überlieferung und Interpretation des Vaterunsers in der frühchristlichen Literatur [diss. 1988 ➤ 4,4613]: Münsterische BeiT 57, Münster 1989, Aschendorff. viii-208 p. DM 58 [RHE 84,96*]. 3-402-03962-1. – RRSPT 73 (1989) 465s (G.-M. de *Durand*); TGL 79 (1989) 628 (M. *Kunzler*); TLZ 114 (1989) 830s (E. *Mühlenberg*); TPhil 64 (1989) 589s (H. J. *Sieben*); VigChr 43 (1989) 305s (J. van *Winden*).
4504 **Strunk** Reiner, Das Gebet Jesu; Betrachtungen und Geschichten zum Vaterunser. Stu 1988, Quell. 239 p. DM 19,80. – RTGL 70 (1989) 95 (K. *Hollmann*).
4505 **Templeton** David, The Lord's Prayer as Eucharist in daily life: IrBSt 11,3 (1989) 133-140 [< ZIT 89,531].
4506 **Torresin** Pierluigi, Padre nostro capitale dei poveri. Lisiera, Vicenza c. 1988, Radio Orel. Lit. 10.000. – RSapCr 4 (1989) 363s (F. *Toniolo*).

4507 *Trudinger* Paul, The 'Our Father' in Matthew as apocalyptic eschatology: DowR 107 (1989) 49-54.

4507* *Brož* Luděk, [Mt 6,9] Theology of the first petition: ComViat 31 (1988) 243-251 [< IZBG 36, p. 151].

4508 **Luka** Ron, [Mt 6,10] 'Thy kingdom come...' What do we mean? A discussion-action guide for Catholic parishioners. Daytona Beach FL 1989, Pastoral Arts. $5 [TDig 37,169, no p.].

4509 *Serikoff* Nikolaus I., '...und deine Gewalt komme...'; die arabische Übersetzung des Vaterunsers in al-YA'QŪBĪ's Geschichte und die byzantinisch-arabische konfessionelle Polemik: JbÖsByz 38 (1988) 235-246.

4510 *Pasinya Monsengwo* [Mt 6,12] Incidence théologique d'une traduction: RAfT 12,23s (1988) 15-21 [NTAbs 33,305: current Bantu/Lingala version wrongly implies 'as we are *in the habit of forgiving*'].

4511 *Porter* Stanley E., Mt 6:13 and Lk 11:4, 'Lead us not into temptation': ExpTim 101 (1989s) 359-362.

4512 *Grelot* Pierre, [Mt 6,13] L'épreuve de la tentation [longue note sur 'a malo', préfère le masculin au neutre]: EsprVie 99 (1989) 280-4.

4513 *Làconi* M., 'Ma liberaci dal male' (Mt 6,13): ParSpV 19 (1989) 97-107.

4513* *a) Brooks* Stephenson H., Apocalyptic paraenesis in Mt 6,19-34; – *b) Scroggs* Robin, Eschatological existence in Matthew and Paul; coincidentia oppositorum; – *c) Cope* O. Lamar, 'To the close of the age'; the role of apocalyptic thought in the Gospel of Mt.: ➤ 130, ᶠMARTYN J., 1989, 95-112 / 125-146 / 112-124.

4514 *Healey* John F., Models of behavior: Matt 6:26 (∥ Luke 12:24) and Prov. 6:6-8: JBL 108 (1989) 497s.

4515 *a) Beasley-Murray* G.R., Matthew 6:33; the Kingdom of God and the ethics of Jesus; 'seek first his kingdom and righteousness, and all these things will be added to you'; – *b) Lohfink* Gerhard, Der präexistente Heilplan; Sinn und Hintergrund der dritten Vaterunserbitte: ➤ 173, ᶠSCHNACKENBURG R., NT & Ethik 1989, 84-98 / 110-133.

4516 *Llewelyn* Stephen, Mt 7:6A [pearls to swine]; mistranslation or interpretation?: NT 31 (1989) 98-103.

4517 *Goldsmith* Dale, [Mt 7,7-12...] 'Ask, and it will be given...'; toward writing the history of a logion: NTS 35 (1989) 254-265.

4518 **Piper** Ronald A., [Mt 7,7-11] Wisdom in the Q-tradition; the aphoristic teaching of Jesus: SNTS Mg 61. C 1989, Univ. ix-325 p. £30. 0-521-35293-2 [TDig 36,385]. – ᴿExpTim 100 (1988s) 431 (I.H. *Marshall*).

4519 *Parrot* Rod, Entering the narrow door; Matt 7:13-14 / Luke 13:22-24: Forum 5,1 (1989) 111-120.

4520 *Black* David A., Remarks on the translation of Matthew 7:14: FgNt 2 (1989) 193-5.

4521 **Carson** D.A., When Jesus confronts the world... Mt 8-10, 1987 ➤ 4,4652: ᴿCriswT 3 (1989) 388s (D.L. *Turner*); EvQ 61 (1989) 161-4 (R.P. *Menzies*).

4522 *Allison* Dale C.ᴶ, Who will come from East and West? Observations on Matt 8.11-12 — Luke 13.18-29: IrBSt 11 (Belfast 1989) 158-170 [171-185, *Knox* R.B., The Bible in Irish Presbyterianism].

4523 *Boring* M. Eugene, [Mt 8,11s] A proposed reconstruction of Q 13:28: ➤ 589, SBL Seminars 1989, 1-22.

4524 *a*) *Löning* Karl, Die Füchse, die Vögel und der Menschensohn (Mt 8,19f par 9,57f); – *b*) *Luz* Ulrich, Vom Taumellolch im Weizenfeld; ein Beispiel wirkungsgeschichtlicher Hermeneutik; – *c*) *Weder* Hans, Einblick ins Menschliche; anthropologische Entdeckungen in der Bergpredigt; – *d*) *Kuhn* Heinz-W., Das Liebesgebot Jesu als Tora und als Evangelium; zur Feindesliebe und zur christlichen und jüdischen Auslegung der Bergpredigt: ➤ 68, ᶠGNILKA J.: 1989, 82-102 / 154-171 / 172-193 / 194-230.

4525 *Charlet* Jean Louis, [Mt 8,23-27; 14,23-32] La tempête apaisée et la marche sur l'eau dans la poésie de PRUDENCE: ➤ 42, ᶠCOSTANZA S., Polyanthema 1989, 227-247.

4526 *Obeng*, [Mt 8,23] The miracle of the stilling of the storm and its implications for the Church in Africa: DeltioVM 18,1 (1989) 43-... [< ZIT 89,530].

4527 *Vattuone* G., [Mt 8,28-34] El endemoniado de Gérasa: Gladius 15 (BA 1989) 121-130 [< Stromata 45,500].

4527* **Dickason** C. Fred, [Mt 8,28] Demon possession and the Christian; a new perspective. Ch 1987, Moody. 355 p. $11 pa. – ᴿGraceTJ 10 (1989) 89-94 (T. *Davis*, unfavoring).

F4.1 *Mt 9-12; Miracula Jesu* – **The Gospel miracles.**

4528 *Abecassis* A., The Jewish miracle [bSab 21b ...]: Sidic 21,2 (R 1988) 4-8.

4529 *Amjad-Ali* Charles M., Freeing the paralysed [... healing miracles; Mk 2,1-12]: Al-Mushir 31,1 (Rawalpindi 1989) 28-31 [< TContext 7/1, 60].

4530 *Barbaglio* Giuseppe, Gesù e Paolo di fronte alla malattia e alla sofferenza: Servitium 3,64 (Bergamo 1989) 361-9.

4531 ᴱ**Berg** Sigrid & Horst K., Himmel auf Erden; Wunder und Gleichnisse: Biblische Texte verfremdet 11. Mü/Stu 1989, Kösel/Calwer. 95 p.; ill. 3-446-36376-4 / Stu 3-7668-3076-6.

4532 **Bouthillier** Denise, PETRI Cluniacensis, De miraculis libri duo: CCMed 83. Turnhout 1988, Brepols. 132 + 187 p. – ᴿRBén (1989) 193 (P.-I. *Fransen*); ScEspr 41 (1989) 252-4 (R. *Latourelle*).

4533 *a*) *Brady* J.R., Do miracles authenticate the Messiah?: EvRT 13,2 (Exeter 1989) 101-9 [< NTAbs 33,295]; – *b*) *Brady* James, The rôle of miracle working as authentication of Jesus as 'the Son of God': Churchman 103,1 (L 1989) 32-39 [< ZIT 89,365].

4534 **Brown** Colin, That you may believe 1987 ➤ 1,4414 ... 4,4630: ᴿRelStT 7,2s (1987) 101s (T. A. *Robinson*).

4535 *Brown* C., The other half of the Gospel? [healing miracles continue today]: ChrTod 33,7 (Carol Stream IL 1989) 26-29 [< NTAbs 33,344].

4536 *Buckley* Michael J., The true meaning of healing: PrPeo 3 (1989) 348-350.

4537 **Charlier** J.-P., Signes et prodiges; les miracles dans l'évangile 1987 ➤ 3,4418; 4,4632: ᴿNRT 111 (1989) 249-254 (P. *Haudebert*: 'symboles et paraboles?').

4538 **Dericquebourg** Régis, Religions de guérison; Antoinisme, Science chrétienne, Scientologie: Bref. P 1988, Cerf/Fides. 125 p. F 40. – ᴿEsprVie 99 (1989) 340-2 (L. *Debarge*).

4539 ᴱ**Doyle** Robert, Signs and wonders [movement] and evangelicals. Homebush West, NSW 1987, Lancer. 130 p. $6.50 pa. – ᴿBS 146 (1989) 457s (K. L. *Sarles*: fine).

4540 *a) Drewermann* Eugen, Missverständnisse und Irrwege der Wunder-auslegung; – *b) Füssel* Kuno, Der Schrei des Glaubens; erläuternde Hinweise zu einer materialistischen Lektüre der Bibel (Mk 10,46-52); – *c) Frankemölle* Hubert, Christlich glauben in ambivalenter Wirklichkeit; Handlungsanweisungen der Wundergeschichten am Beispiel von Mt 8-9): KatBlätt 114 (1989) 404-413 / 414-8 / 419-427.

4541 **Dzielska** Maria, APOLLONIUS of Tyana in legend and history 1986 ➤ 4,4634: ᴿJRS 79 (1989) 252-4 (E. L. *Bowie*).

ᴱ**Exum** J. Cheryl, Signs and wonders; biblical texts in literary focus 1989 ➤ 395.

4542 **Fiederlein** Friedrich M., Die Wunder Jesu und die Wundererzählungen der Urkirche 1988 ➤ 4,4636: ᴿTGL 79 (1989) 622s (J. *Ernst*).

4543 *García Norro* Juan José, La posibilidad de lo milagroso: Cartha-ginensia 5 (1989) 221-237.

4544 *Gero* S., The Ta'ämra 'Iyasūs [miracles of Jesus, related to earlier NT apocrypha]; a study of textual and source-critical problems: Proc 8th Ethiopian (Fra 1988) 1,165-170 [< NTAbs 33,227].

4545 *Gilman* James E., Reconceiving miracles: RelSt 25 (C 1989) 477-487.

4546 **Greer** Rowan A., The fear of freedom; a study of miracles in the Roman imperial church [... how the 4th-5th centuries understood Christ's miracles]. University Park PA 1989, Penn State Univ. xi-211 p. $25. 0-271-00648-X [NTAbs 33,416].

4547 **Groot** Adrianus de, Čudo u Bibliji: Riječ 17. Zagreb 1987, Kršćanska Sadašnost. 84 p. – ᴿBogSmot 59 (1989) 236s (A. *Rebić*).

4548 **Hark** Helmut, Jesus der Heiler; vom Sinn der Krankheit. Olten 1988, Walter. 275 p. DM 39,80. – ᴿTGL 79 (1989) 201s (W. *Beinert*).

4549 *Igenoza* Andrew Olu, Medicine and healing in African Christianity; a biblical critique: AfER 30 (1988) 12-25.

4550 **Jaki** Stanley I., Miracles and physics. Front Royal VA 1989, Chris-tendom. 111 p. $8. 0-931888-33-6 [TDig 37,64].

4551 *Kasher* R., Miracle, faith, and merit of the Fathers — conceptual development in the sages' writings [in first century B.C.E. and C.E., miracles were attributed to the faith of the people; in reaction to Christianity, changed to merits of the fathers]: Jerusalem studies in Jewish thought 5 (1986) 15-22 [< JStJud 20,278].

4552 **Knoch** Otto, Dem, der glaubt, ist alles möglich... Wundererzählungen... 1986 ➤ 4,4647: ᴿGregorianum 70 (1989) 156-8 (R. *Fisichella*).

4553 **Larmer** Robert A. H., Water into wine? An investigation of the concept of miracle 1987 ➤ 4,4648: ᴿSR 18 (1989) 372s (J. R. *Horne*).

4554 **Latourelle** René, Miracles de Jésus 1986 ➤ 2,3471... 4,4650: ᴿAn-gelicum 66 (1989) 646s (R. *Spiazzi*, anche ital.); Brotéria 126 (1988) 232s (I. *Ribeiro da Silva*); PrzPow 803s (1988) 227-9 (J. *Nawrocki*).

4555 **Latourelle** René, Miracoli di Gesù e teologia del miracolo 1987 ➤ 4,4651: ᴿParVi 34 (1989) 302 (G. *Coffele*).

4556 **Latourelle** R., Miracles of Jesus 1988 ➤ 4,4652: ᴿPrPeo 3 (1989) 334s (B. *Robinson*).

4557 **LiDonnici** Lynn R., Tale and dream; the text and compositional history of the corpus of Epidaurian miracle cures: diss. Pennsylvania, ᴰ*Kraft* R. Ph 1989. 321 p. 89-22557. – DissA 50 (1989s) 2105s-A [RelStR 16,189 title 'Studies in the corpus of Epidaurian miracle cures'].

4558 **McCready** William D., Signs of sanctity; miracles in the thought of GREGORY the Great: ST 91. Toronto 1989, Pont. Inst. Mediaeval Studies. xiii-316 p. $32 [JTS 41, 722, Benedicta *Ward*].

4559 **Mosetto** Francesco, I miracoli evangelici nel dibattito tra CELSO e ORIGENE: BiblScRel 76, 1986 ➤ 2,3474 ... 4,4660: ᴿGregorianum 70 (1989) 349s (R. *Fisichella*); RivStoLR 25 (1989) 184-7 (F. *Trisoglio*).

4560 *Mullin* Robert B., Horace BUSHNELL and the question of miracles: ChH 50 (1989) 460-473.

4561 **Nielsen** Helge K., Heilung und Verkündigung 1987 ➤ 3,4443; 4,4662: ᴿJBL 108 (1989) 718-720 (R. A. *Harrisville*).

4562 **Parsons** Stephen, The challenge of Christian healing. L 1986, SPCK. ix-166 p. £5. – ᴿScotJT 42 (1989) 136s (J. *Wilkinson*).

4563 *Reppert* V., Miracles and the case for theism: Int. J. Philosophy of Religion 25 (Haag 1989) 35-52 [< ZIT 89,423].

4564 *Richards* H. J., The miraculous: Sidic 21,2 (R 1988) 9-13 [NTAbs 33,15].

4565 **Robertson** Edwin, The biblical bases of healing. 1988, ... A. James. 125 p. £4. 0-85305-287-5. – ᴿExpTim 101 (1989s) 54 (J. *Wilkinson*); Furrow 40 (1989) 562 (D. *O'Neill*).

4566 a) *Rosenblatt* Marie-Eloise, Jesus as healer; – b) *Pilch* John J., Sickness and healing in Luke-Acts; – c) *Stuhlmueller* Carroll, Sickness and disease; an OT perspective: BToday 27 (1989) 10-20 / 21-27 / 5-9; ill. (modern scenes).

4567 **Rusecki** Marian, ❾ Believe my works; motivational function of miracles in 20th century theology. Katowice 1988, Ś. Jacka. vii-308 p. – ᴿAntonianum 64 (1989) 306s (C. *Teklak*).

4568 *Senior* Donald, Suffering as inaccessibility; lessons from the New Testament healing stories: NewTR 1,4 (1988) 5-14 [NTAbs 33,150].

4569 *Senior* Donald, The miracles of Jesus: ➤ 384, NJBC (1989s) 1369-73.

4570 **Shooman** A. P., An investigation of the concept of the miraculous: diss. Univ. Wales 1987. 214 p. BRDX-84951. – DissA 50 (1989s) 468-A.

4571 **Sibaldi** Igor, I miracoli di Gesù e la tecnica dei miracoli nei Vangeli canonici. Mi 1989, Mondadori. 256 p. Lit. 9000 [CC 140,3 dopo 448]. – ᴿStCattMi 33 (1989) 851 (U. *De Martino*).

4572 *Silva* S., Los milagros de Jesús, ¿sólo signos literarios?: Revista Católica 89 (Santiago/Chile 1989) 3-16. 185-9 [< Stromata 45,500].

4573 a) *Spiegel* Yorick, ...Wunder dauern etwas länger; biblische Heilungsgeschichten im heutigen Kontext; – b) *Theurich* Henning, 'Der Kranke will Heilung; Christus schenkt mehr, sein Heil': Theologia practica 24,1 ('Heilung – medizinische und theologische Aspekte' 1989) 34-39 / 40-44 [< ZIT 89,345].

4574 a) *Stock* Klemens, Le 'azioni potenti' di Gesù nella testimonianza dei Vangeli sinottici [Die Machttaten Jesu; ihr Zeugnis in den synoptischen Evangelien: IkaZ 18 (1989) 195-206], ᵀ*Burzacca* Paola; – b) *Verweyen* Hansjürgen, Senso e realtà dei miracoli di Gesù, ᵀ*De Luca* Lidia; – c) *Sudbrack* Josef, I miracoli e il miracolo; – d) *Marion* Jean-Luc, Nulla è impossibile a Dio, ᵀ*Ferraris* Anna: CommStrum 107 (1989) 10-23 / 24-32 / 33-56 / 57-73.

4575 *Suharyo* I., Sickness, sin and healing in Holy Scripture [Indonesian]: Rohani 35,11 (Yogyakarta 1988) 433-7 [< TContext 6/2, 40].

ᴱ**Swinburne** Richard, Miracles 1989 ➤ 523.

4576 **Williams** Benjamin E., Miracle – mission – competition? Miracle-working in the early Christian mission and its cultural environment: ev. Diss. ᴰ*Roloff*. Erlangen 1988s. – TR 85 (1989) 515; RTLv 21,547 'Raloeff J.'.

4577 *O'Callaghan* José, Tres casos de armonización en Mt 9: EstBíb 47 (1989) 131-4.

4578 **Weaver** Dorothy J., [Mt 9,35-11,1] The missionary discourse in the Gospel of Matthew; a literary critical analysis: Diss. Richmond Union 1987. x-310 p.

4580 *Luz* Ulrich, [Mt 10 ...] Die Jüngerrede des Matthäus als Anfrage an die Ekklesiologie oder, Exegetische Prolegomena zu einer dynamischen Ekklesiologie: → 197, FTRILLING W. 1989, 84-101.

4581 *Feldmann* Erich, [Mt 10,1 ...] Apostolus: → 879, AugL 1/3 (1988) 395-406.

4582 *Baarda* Tjitze, 'A staff only, not a stick', disharmony of the gospels and the harmony of Tatian (Mt 10,9f.; Mk 6,8f.; Lk 9,3 and 10,4): → 606, Réception 1986/9, 311-333.

4583 *Hampel* Volker, 'Ihr werdet mit den Städten Israels nicht zu Ende kommen'; eine exegetische Studie über Matthäus 10,23: TZBas 45 (1989) 1-28; Bibliog. 28-31.

4584 *Allison* Dale C., a) Matthew 10:26-31 and the problem of evil: SVlad 32 (1988) 293-308; – b) [Mt 10,30] 'The hairs of your head are all numbered': ExpTim 101 (1989s) 334-6.

4585 *Patterson* Stephen J., [Mt 10,34-36] Fire and dissension; ipsissima vox Jesu in Q [Luke] 12:49,51-53 ?: → 160*, FROBINSON J. = Forum 5,2 (1989) 121-139.

4586 *Derrett* J. D. M., [Mt 10,38] Taking up the cross and turning the cheek [< EHarvey A., Alternative approaches to NT Study 1985, 61-78]: → 253, Sea-Change 1989, 41-58.

4587 *Wink* Walter, Jesus' reply to John; Matt 11:2-6 / Luke 7:18-23: Forum 5,1 (1989) 121-8.

4588 *Frankemölle* H., Die 'Praxis Christi' (Mt 11,2) und die handlungsorientierte Exegese: → 131, FMARXSEN W., Jesu Rede 1989, 142-164.

4588* *Bredin* Eamonn, [Mt 11,5] The good news for the poor: Furrow 40 (1989) 25-31.

4589 *Moore* W. Ernest, [Mt 11,12 biázō, harpázō; details in NTS 21,519-543] Violence to the kingdom; Josephus and the Syrian churches: ExpTim 100 (1988s) 174-7.

4590 *Williams* James G., [Mt 11,12 ...] Neither here nor there; between wisdom and apocalypse in Jesus' Kingdom sayings: → 160*, FROBINSON J. = Forum 5,2 (1989) 7-30.

4591 a) *Smith* Dennis E., [Mt 11,16 ...] The historical Jesus at table; – b) *Corley* Kathleen E., Were the women around Jesus really prostitutes? Women in the context of Greco-Roman meals: → 589, SBL Seminars 1989, 466-486 / 487-521.

4592 *Cotter* Wendy J., Children sitting in the agora; Q (Luke) 7:31-35 [Mt 11,16-19]: → 160*, FROBINSON J. = Forum 5,2 (1989) 63-82.

4593 **Deutsch** Celia, Hidden wisdom and the easy yoke ... Mt 11,25-30: 1987 → 3,4488; 4,4688: RJBL 108 (1989) 526-8 (D. J. *Good*).

4594 **Mulloor** Augustine, Jesus' prayer of praise; a study of the meaning and function of Mt 11,25-30 in the First Gospel; diss. Pont. Ist. Biblico, DLentzen-Deis F. R 1989. 223 p. – Acta PIB 9,425; RTLv 21,546.

4595 *Bergant* Francisco, [Mt 12s] Discurso parabólico de Mateo; estudio de redacción e interpretación teológica: TArg 24 (1987) 5-27.

4596 *Chico* Gabriel, [Mt 12,22-32 | |] Jesús y Beelzebul; la presencia del Reino en un cuadro polémico: EfMex 7 (1989) 165-178.

4597 *Dunn* James D. G., Matthew 12:28 / Luke 11:20 — a word of Jesus?: → 21, FBEASLEY-MURRAY G., Eschatology 1988, 29-49.

4598 *Cattaneo* Enrico,   La bestemmia contro lo Spirito Santo (Mt 12,31-32) in S. ATANASIO: ➤ 696, 10th Patristic, 21 (1989) 420-5.

4599 *Chrostowski* Waldemar, ❷ Le blasphème contre le Saint-Esprit (Mt 12,31 et paral.): PrzPow 798 (1988) 208-221; franç. 221.

4600 *Murray* Gregory,   [Mt 12,38-41; 16,4] The sign of Jonah: DowR 107 (1989) 224s.

4601 *Hoffmann* Paul,   Die Auferweckung Jesu als Zeichen für Israel; Mt 12,39f und die matthäische Ostergeschichte: ➤ 197, FTRILLING W., Christus bezeugen 1989, 110-123.

4602 *McKerras* R., [Mt 12,39; 23,36] Who is 'this generation'? an alternative view: Notes on Translation 2,1 (Dallas 1988) 57-58 [< NTAbs 33,292].

F4.3   Mt 13 ...   *Parabolae Jesu* – the Parables.

4603 **Aerts** Lodewijk,   Gottesherrschaft als Gleichnis? Eine Untersuchung zur Auslegung der Gleichnisse Jesu nach Eberhard JÜNGEL: diss. Pont. Univ. Gregoriana, ᴰ*Lentzen-Deis* F.   Roma 1989. 379 p. – RTLv 21,543.

4604 **Avila** Charles,   Fische, Vögel und die Gerechtigkeit Gottes; Philippinische Bauern bedenken sich ihrer Lage im Licht von Gleichnissen Jesu, ᵀᴱ*Ruppell* G.   Erlangen 1981, Ev.-Luth. Mission. 48 p. DM 3,80. – ᴿBiKi 44 (1989) 132s (M. *Helsper*).

4605 **Baudler** Georg,   Jesus erzählt von sich; die Gleichnisse als Ausdruck seiner Lebenserfahrung: Tb 1616.   FrB 1989, Herder.   127 p. DM 10 pa. 3-451-08616-6 [NTAbs 33,381]. – ᴿCarthaginensia 5 (1989) 336s (R. *Sanz Valdivieso*).

4606 **Baudler** Georg,   Jesus im Spiegel seiner Gleichnisse 1986 ➤ 2,3504 ... 4,4696: ᴿSalesianum 51 (1989) 348 (C. *Bissoli*); ScripTPamp 21 (1989) 319-321 (K. *Limburg*); TPQ 137 (1989) 414s (F. *Kogler*).

4607 **Borsch** Frederick H.,   Many things in parables 1988 ➤ 4,4697: ᴿCBQ 51 (1989) 551s (M. L. *Soards*).

4608 ᴱ**Butts** J. R.,   The parables of Jesus; [black, gray, pink and] red-letter edition; a report of the Jesus Seminar [degree of probability of origin from Jesus himself, according to seminar directed by R. W. FUNK; other essays by B. B. *Scott*]. Sonoma CA 1988, Polebridge. xx-107 p.; 10 fig. $15 pa. 0-944344-07-0 [NTAbs 33,246].

4609 **Capon** Robert F.,   The parables of judgment. GR 1989, Eerdmans. vi-181 p. $16 [CBQ 52,380].   0-8028-3650-X.

4610 *Champion* James,   The parable as an ancient and a modern form: JLit&T 3,1 (Ox 1989) 16-39 [< NTAbs 33,300].

4611 *Cothenet* Éduard,   Du nouveau sur les paraboles [ACFÉB 1987]?: EsprVie 99 (1989) 606-8.

4612 **Cuervo** M., *Diéguez* J.   Al calor de las parábolas.   M 1989, PPC. 205 p. [Studium-M 29, 551].

ᴱ**Delorme** Jean,   Les paraboles évangéliques, perspectives nouvelles, ACFÉB 1987: LDiv 135, 1989 ➤ 576.

4613 **Donahue** John R.,   The Gospel in parable; metaphor, narrative, and theology in the Synoptic Gospels 1988 ➤ 4,4700: ᴿBibTB 19 (1989) 37 (C. C. *Black*); CCurr 39 (1989s) 238s (D. N. *Mosser*); CurrTM 16 (1989) 468s (R. H. *Smith*); RExp 86 (1989) 269s (D. E. *Garland*: not ground-breaking, but helpful); TS 50 (1989) 359s (J. D. *Kingsbury*: superb); TTod 46 (1989s) 248 (Pheme *Perkins*).

4614 *Donahue* John R.,   The parables of Jesus: ➤ 384, NJBC (1989s) 1364-9.

4615 **Dschulnigg** Peter, Rabbinische Gleichnisse und das NT ^{D}1988 → 4,4702: ^{R}TGL 79 (1989) 197s (J. *Ernst*).

4616 *Dschulnigg* Peter, Positionen des Gleichnisverständnisses im 20. Jahrhundert; kurze Darstellung von fünf wichtigen Positionen der Gleichnistheorie (JÜLICHER, JEREMIAS, WEDER, ARENS, HARNISCH): TZBas 45 (1989) 335-351.

4617 **Erlemann** Kurt, Das Bild Gottes in den synoptischen Gleichnissen: BW 126, 1988 → 4,4704: ^{R}TPQ 137 (1989) 196s (K. M. *Woschitz*).

4618 **Espinel** José Luis, La poesía de Jesús 1986 → 2,3512... 4,4705: ^{R}ÉTRel (J. *Alexandre*: la poésie biblique devient spécialité espagnole? ici le langage algébrosé comme parfois en français; mais on peut souhaiter une traduction d'ALONSO-SCHÖKEL); Salesianum 51 (1989) 355s (C. *Bissoli*).

4619 *a) Fusco* Vittorio, Tendances récentes dans l'interprétation des paraboles; – *b) Marguerat* Daniel, La parabole, de Jésus aux évangiles; une histoire de réception; – *c) Zumstein* Jean, Jésus et les paraboles; – *d) Gélas* Bruno, La parabole comme texte; – *e) Delorme* Jean, Récit, parole et parabole; – *f) Marty* François, Parabole, symbole, concept; – *g) Dubost* Michel, L'utilisation pastorale et pédagogique des paraboles: → 576, Paraboles 1987/9, 19-60 / 61-88 / 89-108 / 109-122 / 123-150 / 171-192 / 193-216.

4620 *Guevin* Benedict M., The moral imagination and the shaping power of the parables: JRelEth 17 (1989) 63-79.

4621 **Harnisch** Wolfgang, Las parábolas de Jesús, una introducción hermenéutica [1985 → 1,4485], ^{T}*Olasagasti* Manuel: BiblEstB 66. Salamanca 1989, Sígueme. 296 p. pt. 1200 [LumenVr 38,351]. – ^{R}Proyección 36 (1989) 326 (A. *Sánchez*).

Heininger B., Metaphorik... in den Sondergutgleichnissen bei Lukas, ^{D}1988s → 5092.

4622 **Hendricks** H., The parables of Jesus^2 1986 → 2,3514*; 4,4711: ^{R}ScripB 20 (1989s) 46s (T. *Welland*).

4623 *a) Hermans* C.A.M., Verstehen von Parabeln und Gleichnissen als Metaphern; – *b) Baudler* Georg, Jesus, das Gleichnis Gottes: RelPBei 23 (1989) 124-156 / 107-123 [< ZIT 89,272s].

4624 **Kjärgaard** Mogens S., Metaphor and parable... [diss. Aarhus 1984] 1986 → 2,3516: ^{R}JBL 108 (1989) 148-150 (J. D. *Crossan*: why is Prodigal Son a metaphor but Good Samaritan not?); TLZ 114 (1989) 672-4 (W. *Flach*).

4625 De kracht van parabels: Jota 3. Boxtel/Lv 1989, KBS / Vlaamse Bs. 64 p. – ^{R}Streven 57 (1989s) 854 (P. *Beentjes*).

4626 *La Verdiere* E., Teaching in parables [Mk 4 examples]: Emmanuel 94 (1988) 439-445.464 [< NTAbs 33,161].

4627 **Lowry** Eugene L., How to preach a parable; designs for narrative sermons. Nv 1989, Abingdon. 176 p. $13 [Interp 43,425 adv.].

4628 **Mack** Burton L., *Robbins* Vernon K., Patterns of persuasion in the Gospels [Hellenistic *chreia* parallels]: Foundations and Facets. Sonoma CA 1989, Polebridge. x-230 p. 0-944344-08-9.

4629 **Manigne** Jean-Pierre, Le maître des signes [... paraboles; vol. 1 de 3 sur la Christologie]: Théologies, 1987 → 3,4907: ^{R}RTLv 20 (1989) 91 (C. *Focant*); ScEspr 41 (1989) 389s (M. *Girard*); SR 18 (1989) 114 (Anne *Fortin-Melkevik*).

4630 **Mateos** Juan, *Camacho* Fernando, Evangelio, figuras y símbolos: En torno al NT 4. Córdoba 1989, Almendro. 253 p. pt. 848. 84-86077-75-3. – ^{R}FgNt 2 (1989) 214s (J. *Peláez*).

4631 **Pate** Ronald E., Preaching the parables of Jesus; an analysis of selected twentieth century sermons: diss. Baptist Theol. Sem. ᴰ*Bryson* H. New Orleans 1988. 180 p. 89-11181. – DissA 50 (1989s) 708s-A.

4632 **Scott** Brendan B., Hear then the parable; a commentary on the parables of Jesus. Minneapolis 1989, Fortress. xii-465 p. $30. 0-8006-0897-6 [TDig 37,185]. – ᴿBibTB 19 (1989) 156 (J. M. *Reese*); ExpTim 101 (1989s) 283s (Meg *Davies*: reader-response).

4633 *Tamás* Fabiny, ⓦ The sociological analysis of the parables of Jesus [... BAILEY K.]: TSzem 31 (1988) 198-202.

4634 **Taylor** Anthony B., The master-servant type scene in the parables of Jesus: diss. Fordham, ᴰ*Giblin* C. H. – Bronx 1989. 376 p. 89-17243. – DissA 50 (1989s) 1706-A; RelStR 16,189.

ᴱ**Thoma** Clemens, *Wyschogrod* Michael, Parable and story in Judaism and Christianity 1986-9 → 610.

4635 *a) Vouga* F., Jésus le conteur; – *b) Habermacher* J.-F., Jésus, conteur d'histoires; la narration dans les paraboles: → 385, Narration 1988, 107-130 / 131-144.

4636 **Wailes** S. L., Medieval allegories of [41 of] Jesus' parables: MedievRenSt 23. Berkeley 1987, Univ. California. x-270 p. $37,50. 0-520-05560-8 [NTAbs 33,394].

4637 *a) White* Roger, MACKINNON and the parables; – *b) Sherry* Patrick, Modes of representation and likeness to God; – *c) Surin* Kenneth, Some aspects of the 'grammar' of 'incarnation' and 'kenosis': → 701, ᶠMACKINNON D., 1986/9, 49-70 / 34-48 / 93-116.

4638 *Williams* Michael D., Jesus and the theological imagination in the work of Gordon D. KAUFMAN: JEvTS 32 (1989) 217-226 [< ZIT 89,704].

4639 **Young** Brad H., Jesus and his Jewish parables; rediscovering the roots of Jesus' teaching: Theological Inquiries. NY 1989, Paulist. v-365 p. $13. 0-8091-3031-9 [TDig 37,96].

4640 *Cazeaux* Jacques, La parabole attire la parabole ou le problème des séquences de paraboles (PHILON et Matthieu ch. 13): → 576, Paraboles 1987/9, 403-424.

4641 **Quacquarelli** A., Il triplice frutto della vita cristiana, 100, 60 e 30 (Matteo xiii,8 nelle diverse interpretazioni)². Bari 1989, Edipuglia. 127 p. [RHE 84, p. 347*].

4642 *Zeilinger* Franz, Redaktion in Mt 13,24-30: → 197, ᶠTRILLING W. 1989, 102-9.

4643 *Fleddermann* Harry, [Mt 13,31s] The mustard seed and the leaven in Q, the Synoptics, and Thomas: → 589, SBL Seminars 1989, 216-236.

4644 **Kogler** Franz, [Mt 13,31ss... Reich Gottes] Das Doppelgleichnis vom Senfkorn und vom Sauerteig...: ForBi 59, 1988 → 4,4733: ᴿETL 65 (1989) 440s (F. *Neirynck*: 'Deuteromarkan hypothesis'); TGL 79 (1989) 622 (J. *Ernst*).

4645 **Israel** Martin, [Mt 13,45] The pearl of great price; a journey to the Kingdom. L 1988, SPCK. xiv-126 p. £5 pa. – ᴿTLond 92 (1989) 148-150 (A. *Ecclestone*).

4646 *Schnackenburg* Rudolf, 'Jeder Schriftgelehrte, der ein Jünger des Himmelreiches geworden ist' (Mt 13,52): → 120, ᶠLOHSE E., Wissenschaft 1989, 57-69.

4647 *Kratz* R., [Mt 14,13-21...] Brotvermehrung: → 902, NBL Lfg. 2 (1989) 33s.

4648 *Dufton* Francis, [Mt 15,21-28] The Syrophoenician woman and her dogs [Greek-influenced pet-lover, unlike Semite Jesus]: ExpTim 100 (1988s) 417 only.

4649 *O'Day* Gail R., [Mt 15,28] Surprised by faith; Jesus and the Canaanite woman: Listening 24 (1989) 290-301 [< ZIT 90,14].

4650 *Schlichting* Wolfhart, Unwiderstehlicher Glaube (Mt 15,21-28): TBei 20 (Wu 1989) 57-61 [< ZIT 89,384].

F4.5 **Mt 16...** *Primatus promissus* – **The promise to Peter.**

4651 *Aguirre* Rafael, Pedro en el evangelio de Mateo: EstBíb 47 (1989) 343-361; Eng. 343.

4652 **Bessière** Gérard, Pierre, Pape malgré lui: Présence. P 1989, Flammarion. 204 p. F 89. – ᴿEsprVie 99 (1989) 669 (P. *Jay*).

4653 *Burgos Nuñez* Miguel de, Simón-Pedro; ideología e historicidad en las tradiciones neotestamentarias: CommSev 22 (1989) 355-380 [359, against THIEDE 'Life of Jesus' style combining of traditions].

4654 **Caragounis** Chrys C., Peter and the Rock: BZNW 58. B 1989, de Gruyter. viii-157 p. DM 64.

4655 *Chrostowski* Waldemar, ⊕ 'Tu es Pierre...' (Mt 16,17-19); les fondements bibliques de la primauté du pape dans l'Église: PrzPow 806 (1988) 7-23; franç. 23.

4656 *a)* *Dschulnigg* Peter, Gestalt und Funktion des Petrus im Matthäusevangelium; – *b)* *Korting* Georg, Binden oder lösen: SNTU 14 (Linz 1989) 161-184 / 39-92 [< ZIT 90,340].

4657 *Fábrega* Valentí, El papado como objeto de investigación en la teología católica actual de habla alemana (1974-1989): ActuBbg 26 (1989) 151-165 [HASLER A.: DENZLER J., POTTMEYER H., LEHMANN K. ...].

4658 *Hommel* Hildebrecht, Die Tore des Hades: ZNW 80 (1989) 124s.

4659 *a)* *Klein* Hans, Zur Traditionsgeschichte von Mt 16,16b.17; zugleich ein Beitrag zur Frühgeschichte der christlichen Taufe; – *b)* *Kähler* Christoph, Kirchenleitung und Kirchenzucht nach Matthäus 18: → 197, ᶠTRILLING W., Christus bezeugen 1989, 124-135 / 136-145.

4660 **Méhat** André, Simon dit Képhas; la vie clandestine de l'Apôtre Pierre, essai historique: BVieChr NS. P 1989, Lethielleux. 184 p. 2-283-61020-8.

4661 *Oss* Douglas A., The interpretation of the 'stone' passages by Peter and Paul; a comparative study: JEvTS 32 (1989) 181-200 [< ZIT 89,704].

4662 *Pousset* Édouard, Jésus-Christ, Simon-Pierre, histoire d'un trait d'union: Christus 35 (P 1988) 428-439.

4663 **Smith** Terence V., Petrine controversies 1985 → 1,4538... 4,4748: ᴿCommSev 22 (1989) 91s (M. de *Burgos*); CrNSt 9 (1988) 177-181 (E. *Norelli*); SecC 7 (1989s) 123-5 (M. W. *Meyer*).

4664 **Thiede** C. P., Simon Peter, from Galilee to Rome 1986 → 2,3557... 4,4749: ᴿSWJT 32,3 (1989s) 55s (E. E. *Ellis*: well-told with little speculation).

4665 **Tillard** J. M. R., O bispo de Roma [1982 → 63,903]. São Paulo 1985, Loyola. 218 p. – ᴿPerspT 20 (1988) 131-3 (G. I. *Rodríguez*).

4666 *González Faus* José I., Las tentaciones de Pedro [i. quedarse en el Tabor, Mc 9; ii. pensar de Dios como el hombre religioso y no como Jesús, Mc 8,33s; iii. sacar la espada, Jn. 18; iv. servir a Dios como le gusta, Jn 13; v. creerse el mejor, Mt 26; vi. controlar el carisma, Jn 21; vii. no hacer las reformas que crean problemas...]: SalT 77 (1989) 419-428.

4667 **McGuckin** John A., The transfiguration 1986 ➤ 2,1563: ᴿCBQ 51 (1989) 159s (Q. *Quesnell*: not as patristic as claimed).

4668 **Niemand** Christoph, Studien zu den Minor Agreements der synoptischen Verklärungsperikopen; eine Untersuchung der literarkritischen Relevanz der gemeinsamen Abweichungen des Matthäus und Lukas von Markus 9,2-10 für die synoptische Frage [Diss. *Linz* 1988, ᴰ*Fuchs* A. ➤ 4,4755; cf. SNTU 14,89]: EurHS 23/352. Fra 1989, Lang. 345 p. – ᴿETL 65 (1989) 441s (F. *Neirynck*: Deuteromarkan followup to KOGLER).

4669 **Sachot** Maurice, Les homélies grecques [LÉONCE...] sur la Transfiguration; tradition manuscrite. P 1987, CNRS. 132 p. F 40. – ᴿRHPR 69 (1989) 348 (D. A. *Bertrand*: inventaire); VigChr 43 (1989) 412 (C. *Datema*).

4670 **Wild** Robert, His face shone like the sun. NY 1986, Alba. 126 p. $6. 0-8189-0501-8. – ᴿHolyL 9 (1989) 217 (S. *Kirsch*).

4671 *Taylor-Wingender* P., Kids of the Kingdom (a study of Matthew 18:1-5 and its context): Direction 17,2 (Fresno 1988) 18-25 [< NTAbs 33,159].

4672 **Deloffre** Jean, L'enfant et le Royaume; recherche sur l'interprétation de Mt 18,3 à partir du Nouveau Testament et des œuvres de Saint AUGUSTIN: diss. Inst. Cath., ᴰ*Lévêque* J. P 1989. 286 p. – RICathP 32 (1989) 122-4; RTLv 21,544.

4673 *a*) *Fodor* György, Ⓜ 'Wenn ihr nicht wie Kinder werdet...' (Mt 18,3); – *b*) *Gubler* Marie-Louise, Ⓜ Werdet wie Kinder,... aber seid nicht Kinder im Denken, ᵀ*Bánhegyi* B. Mikra: TBud 22 (1988) 204-7 / 201-212.

4674 *Alves* H., Parábola da ovelha perdida (Mt 18,10-14; Lc 15,1-7; Ev. Tom. 107), estudo histórico-literário: HumT 9 (1988) 299-328 [< REB 49,506].

4675 *Burggraff* David L., Principles of discipline in Matthew 18: 15-17, II. An exegetical study; III. A practical study: CalvaryB 5,1 (1989) 1-11; 5,2 (1989) 1-29.

4676 *García Martínez* Florentino, La represión fraterna en Qumrán y Mat 18,15-17: FgNt 2,1 (1989) 23-39; Eng. 39s.

4677 *Carmody* Timothy R., Matt 18:15-17 in relation to three texts from Qumran literature (CD 9:2-8, 16-22; 1QS 5:25-6:13): ➤ 60, ᶠFITZMYER J., Touch 1989, 141-158.

4678 *a*) *Muñoz León* Domingo, 'Allí estoy yo en medio de ellos' (Mt 18,20); un ejemplo mateano de derás de traspaso; – *b*) *O'Callaghan* Josep, Consideracions crítiques sobre Mt 19,20-21; – *c*) *Taradach* Madeleine, Mt 21,5, une lecture midrashique de Za 9,9: ➤ 69*, ᶠGOMÀ I., RCatalT 14 (1989) 133-147 castellano, Eng. 148 / 149-154, Eng. 154 / 155-161 français, Eng. 162.

4678* ᴱ**Pizzolato** Luigi F., [Mt 19,16-22] Per foramen acus 1986 ➤ 2,3572...4,4769: ᴿBenedictina 35 (1988) 240-3 (G. *Picasso*). ➤ 4991.

4679 *Galot* Jean, [Mt 19,29] Lo stato di vita degli Apostoli [contro un parere prevalente che tutti salvo Giovanni fossero sposati: al momento della chiamata nessuno di loro poteva avere legami matrimoniali]: CC 140 (1989,4) 327-340.

F4.8 **Mt 20 ...** *Regnum eschatologicum* – **Kingdom eschatology.**

4680 *Culbertson* P. [Mt 20s] Reclaiming the Matthean vineyard parables: Encounter 49 (Indianapolis 1988) 257-283 [< NTAbs 33,159].

4681 *Evans* Craig A., [Mt 21,12s...] Jesus' action in the Temple and evidence of corruption in the first-century temple [SANDERS E. 1985...]: ➤ 589, SBL Seminars 1989, 522-539.

4682 *Broadhead* Edwin K., [Mt 21,28] An example of gender bias in UBS³ ['sons' for *tékna* in all mss.]: BTrans 40 (1989) 336-8 [338, R. *Bratcher* comment: would a girl be asked to go out and work in her father's vineyard? relevant *apokritheis* and *metamelētheis* in verse 29 are masc.].

4682* a) *Milavec* Aaron A., [Mt 21,33-46] A fresh analysis of the parable of the wicked husbandmen in the light of Jewish-Christian dialogue; – b) *Stern* David, Jesus' parables from the perspective of rabbinic literature; the example of the husbandmen; – c) *Thoma* Clemens, Literary and theological aspects of the rabbinic parables: ➤ 610, Parable and story 1986/9, 81-117 / 42-80 / 26-41.

4683 *Schweizer* Eduard, Auf W. Trillings Spuren zu Mt 22,1-14 [Gleichnis vom Hochzeitsmahl 1960]: ➤ 197, FTRILLING W., Christus bezeugen 1989, 146-9.

4684 a) *Beatrice* Pier Franco, [Mt 22,14] Une citation de l'Évangile de Matthieu dans l'épître de Barnabé; – b) *Verheyden* Joseph, L'ascension d'Isaïe [3,13-18] et l'Évangile de Matthieu: ➤ 606, Réception 1986/9, 231-245 / 247-274.

4685 *Noël* Timothy, [Mt 22,11] The parable of the wedding guest; a narrative-critical interpretation: PerspRelSt 16,1 (1989) 17-28 [< ZIT 89,446].

4686 **Newport** K. G. C., The sources and 'Sitz im Leben' of Matt 23: diss. Oxford 1988. – RTLv 21,546.

4687 a) *Viviano* Benedict T., The Pharisees in Matthew 23; – b) *Senior* Donald, The Gospel of Matthew and our Jewish heritage; – c) *Harrington* Daniel J., 'Not to abolish, but to fulfill'; – d) *Matera* Frank J., 'His blood be on us and on our children '; – e) *Pawlikowski* John T., Christian-Jewish dialogue and Matthew: BToday 27 (1989) 338-344/ 325-331 / 333-7 / 345-350 / 356-362.

4687* **Del Verme** Marcello, [Mt 23,23...] Giudaismo e Nuovo Testamento; il caso delle decime: Studi su Giudaismo e Cristianesimo Antico 1. N 1989, D'Auria. 281 p. 88-7092-045-3.

4688 *Miller* Robert J., [Mt 23,25s] The inside is (not) the outside; [Lk] Q 11:39-41 and GThom 89: Forum 5,1 (1989) 92-105.

4689 **MacArthur** John ᴶ, Mt 24-28. Ch 1989, Moody. viii-359 p. [JBL 109,378].

4690 **Dupont** Jacques, [Mt 24s] Les trois Apocalypses synoptiques: LDiv 121, 1985 ➤ 1,4572... 3,4582: ᴿBrotéria 126 (1988) 230 (I. *Ribeiro*); ScEspr 40 (1988) 239-241 (G. *Rochais*).

4690* *Turner* David L., The structure and sequence of Matthew 24:1-41; interaction with evangelical treatments: GraceTJ 10 (1989) 3-27.

4691 **Wenham** David, [Mt 24,1-36] The rediscovery of Jesus' eschatological discourse 1984 ➤ 65,4126... 4,4788: ᴿTLZ 114 (1989) 113-5 (N. *Walter*).

4692 *Taylor* Justin, 'The love of many will grow cold'; Matt. 24:9-13 and the Neronian persecution: RB 96 (1989) 352-7.

4693 *Stanton* Graham N., 'Pray that your flight may not be in winter or on a Sabbath' (Matthew 24,20]: ► 84, FHILL D., JStNT 37 (1989) 17-30.

4694 *Guenther* Heinz O., [Mt 24,27s ...] When 'eagles' draw together: ► 160*, FROBINSON J. = Forum 5,2 (1989) 140-150.

4695 *Jefford* Clayton N. [Mt 24,40s; GThom 61,1] The dangers of lying in bed; Luke 17,34-35 and parallels: Forum 5,1 (1989) 106-110.

4696 *Dewey* Arthur J., [Mt 24,45-51] A prophetic pronouncement, Q 12:42-46: ► 160*, FROBINSON J. = Forum 5,2 (1989) 99-108.

4697 *Légasse* Simon, La parabole des dix vierges (Mt 25,1-13); essai de synthèse historico-littéraire: ► 576, Paraboles 1987/9, 349-360.

4698 *Bauer* Johannes B., [Mt 25] Vidisti fratrem, vidisti dominum tuum (Agraphon 144 Resch und 126 Resch): ZKG 100 (1989) 71-76.

4699 *Dietzfelbinger* Christian, [Mt 25,14-30] Das Gleichnis von den anvertrauten Geldern: BTZ 6 (1989) 222-233.

4700 *Flusser* David, [Mt 25,14-30] Aesop's Miser and the parable of the talents: ► 610, Parable & story 1986/9, 9-25.

4701 *Lys* Daniel, [Mt 25,14-30] Contre le salut par les œuvres dans la prédication des talents [et contre la lecture anthropocentrique qui cherche dans la Bible des exemples, bons ou mauvais]: ÉTRel 64 (1989) 331-340.

4702 **Gray** Sherman W., The least of my brothers, Matthew 25:31-46; a history of interpretation: SBL diss. 114 [Catholic U. DFitzmyer J., Wsh 1987 ► 3,4590]. Atlanta 1989, Scholars. xxii-452 p. 1-55540-344-1; -5-X.

F5.1 Redemptio; Mt 26, *Ultima coena*; The Eucharist ► H7.4.

4703 **Alonso Schökel** Luis, Eucharistie feiern; biblische Meditationen zum Verständnis der heiligen Messe [Meditaciones 1986 ► 2,3601], TSedlmeier Franz: Hilfen zum christlichen Leben. Mü 1989, Neue Stadt. 150 p. DM 16,80 3-87996-231-6.

4704 *Alonso Schökel* Luis, Eucharystia, meditacje biblijne, 7. Epikleza; 8. Anamneza; 9. Konsekracja; 10. Ofiara: Współczesna Ambona 16,4 (1988) 165-172; 17,1 (1989) 121-7; 2,153-65.

4705 **Barth** Markus, Das Mahl des Herrn 1987 ► 3,4598; 4,4800: RJEcuSt 26 (1989) 364 (R. J. *Siebert*).

4706 **Barth** Markus, Rediscovering the Lord's Supper 1988 ► 4,4801 [< German, but 1986 Pittsburgh lectures]: RCurrTM 16 (1989) 47 (J. C. *Rochelle*).

4707 **Bermejo** Luis M., Body broken and blood shed 1986 ► 3,4600; 4,4802: RBibleBh 15 (1989) 274s (A. *Mannarkulam*); ScripB 20 (1989s) 39s (J. *McGuckin*: curious mixture of historical analysis and Catholic fundamentalism); Studies 78 (1989) 96-99 (D. *Deane*: clear; may his pen not be silenced).

4708 *Chadwick* H., Ego Berengarius [opening words of formula which Pope Nicholas II forced him to accept, which he then disavowed as self-contradictory, as even his critics admitted]: JTS 40 (1989) 414-445.

4709 *Colombo* Giuseppe, Per il trattato dell'Eucaristia II: TItSett 14 (1989) 105-136; Eng. 137.

4710 **Crockett** William R., Eucharist, symbol of transformation. NY 1989, Pueblo. x-286 p. $14.50. 0-916134-98-9 [TDig 37,48].

4711 *Dunnett* Dolores E., The Eucharist; representative views: JEvTS 32 (1989) 63-72 [< ZIT 89,509].

4712 **Franz** Egon, Das Opfersein Christi und das Opfersein der Kirche...
Lima 1983. Fra 1988, Lang. 144 p. Fs 34. – RTLZ 114 (1989) 627-9 (G.
Wenz).

4713 **Garijo-Guembe** Miguel, *al.*, Mahl des Herrn: Ökumenische Studien.
Fra/Pd 1988, Lembeck/Bonifatius. 338 p. DM 68. – RJEcuSt 26 (1989)
385s (B. A. *Asen*); TLZ 114 (1989) 916-9 (F. *Jacob*).

4714 **Giraudo** Cesare, Eucaristia per la Chiesa; prospettive teologiche
sull'eucaristia a partire dalla 'Lex orandi': Aloisiana 22. R/Brescia 1989,
Univ. Gregoriana/Morcelliana. xxi-679 p. Lit. 58.000 [CBQ 52,195].

4715 **Giraudo** Cesare, La struttura letteraria della preghiera eucaristica;
saggio sulla genesi letteraria di una forma: AnBib 92. R 1989 = 1981
[→ 62,4765], Pont. Ist. Biblico. xxiv-392 p. Lit. 38.000. 88-7653-092-4.

4716 *Giraudo* Cesare, La messa; ripresentazione o rappresentazione; 'anám-
nesis' o 'mímesis'? : RasT 30 (1989) 52-67.

4717 *Hanson* A., *a)* A conference on the Eucharist between Roman Catholics
and Anglicans [Yorkshire Apr. 1987]: – *b)* The Eucharist as sacrifice:
QLtg 69 (1988) 121-4 / 155-162.

4718 **Hardt** Tom G. A., Venerabilis et adorabilis Eucharistia; eine Studie
über die lutherische Abendmahlslehre im 16. Jahrhundert [diss. Uppsala
1971], TDiestelmann S.: ForKDg 42. Gö 1988, Vandenhoeck & R.
viii-355 p.; 5 fig. + 1 color. pl. DM 58. – RSixtC 20 (1989) 693s (K. D.
Lewis); TLZ 114 (1989) 685-8 (R. *Slenczka*).

4719 **Haunerland** Winfried, Die Eucharistie und ihre Wirkungen im Spiegel
der Euchologie des Missale Romanum [kath. Diss. München 1988,
DKaczynski R.]: LtgWQF 71. Münster 1989, Aschendorff. xxvi-479.
3-402-03857-9.

4720 *Hilberath* Bernd J., Abendmahlsgemeinschaft — Station auf dem Weg
zur Kirchengemeinschaft? Thesen aus katholischer Sicht: Catholica 43
(1989) 95-116.

4721 **Hönig** Elisabeth, Die Eucharistie als Opfer nach den neueren ökumenischen Erklärungen: KkKSt 54. Pd 1988, Bonifatius. 299 p. DM 38
[JTS 41, 803-5, E. J. *Yarnold*].

4722 *Jenks* G. C., Maundy Thursday and the Passover [the Last Supper was
not a passover meal, but was on the preceding day]: Australian Journal of
Liturgy 1,3 (Belair, S. Australia 1988) 110-120 [NTAbs 33,205].

4723 *Kobayashi* Reiko, sr., ◑ The doctrine of Saint IRENAEUS about the
Eucharist: KatKenk 28,56 (1989) 65-98; Eng. iv-vii.

4724 **Kodell** J., The Eucharist in the New Testament: Zacchaeus Studies NT.
Wilmington 1988, Glazier. 142 p. $8. 0-89453-663-X [NTAbs 33,264].

4725 **Kollmann** Bernd, Ursprung und Gestalt der frühchristlichen Mahlfeier:
Diss. DStegemann. Göttingen 1989. – RTLv 21,560.

4726 *Lee Hong-Gi*, ◎ The Lord's Supper according to the traditional report
of the Last Supper: Sinhak Jonmang 82 (Kwangju 1988) 96-113
[< TContext 6/2, 46].

4727 **Léon-Dufour** Xavier, Sharing the Eucharistic bread [1982] 1987
→ 3,4620; 4,4824: RBS 146 (1989) 355 (D. L. *Bock*); Consensus 14,2
(Waterloo ON 1988) 94-103 (J. *Reumann*) [< NTAbs 33,347]; NBlackf 70
(1989) 147s (K. *Grayston*); ScripB 20 (1989s) 39s (J. *McGuckin*: a joy and
delight); SVlad 32 (1988) 266-273 (P. *Weiche*: 'tends toward
Nestorianism').

4728 *Luke* K., *a)* The Eucharist words in some ancient oriental versions:
BibleBh 15 (1989) 58-69; – *b)* Sacred meals in Judaism: Living Word 94,4
(1988) 227-246 [< TContext 6/2, 33].

4729 **McAdoo** H. R., The Eucharistic theology of Jeremy TAYLOR [1654] today. 1988, Canterbury. 212 p. £10 pa. – ᴿTLond 92 (1989) 414s (R. *Askew*).

4730 **Margerie** Bertrand de, Vous ferez ceci en mémorial de moi; annonce et souvenir de la mort du Ressuscité: THist 80. Montréal/P 1989, Bellarmin/Beauchesne. 365 p. $28 [CBQ 52,380].

4731 **Matthew** David, The covenant meal. ... 1988, Harvestime. 155 p. £3.75. 0-947714-51-0. – ᴿExpTim 100 (1988s) 113 (J. G. *Davies*: partly rash).

4732 *Mello* Alberto, Questa è la nuova alleanza nel mio sangue: StEcum 5 (1987) 209-220; Eng. 220.

4733 *Moloney* Francis J., The Eucharist as Jesus' presence to the broken [i.e. sinners]: Pacifica 2 (1989) 151-174.

4734 *Nadler* Steven M., ARNAULD, DESCARTES, and Transubstantiation; reconciling Cartesian metaphysics and Real Presence: JHistId 49 (1988) 229-246.

4735 **O'Connor** James T., The hidden manna; a theology of the Eucharist. SF 1989, Ignatius. xiv-376 p. 0-89870-225-9 [TDig 37,79].

4736 *O'Rourke* Brian, The Eucharist in its social dimension: AfTJ 18 (Tanzania 1989) 28-35 [< TContext 7/1, 18].

4737 **Power** D. N., The sacrifice we offer 1987 → 3,4625; 4,4837: ᴿNRT 111 (1989) 446s (L. *Renwart*); ScotBEv 7 (1989) 52-54 (R. T. *Jones*); ScotJT 42 (1989) 268-270 (P. *Avis*); TLond 92 (1989) 43s (K. *Stevenson*: subtly undermines clichés).

4738 **Schmemann** Alexander, The Eucharist; sacrament of the Kingdom [℗ 1984], ᵀ*Kachur* Paul. Crestwood NY 1988, St. Vladimir. 245 p. – ᴿSVlad 32 (1988) 260-6 (P. *Lazor*).

4739 **Sheerin** Daniel, The Eucharist: Message of the Fathers 7, 1986 → 3,4632: ᴿScriptB 20 (1989s) 39 (J. *McGuckin*).

4740 **Smith** Barry, The words of institution; Jesus' death as eschatological Passover sacrifice: diss. McMaster, ᴰ*Meyer* B. Hamilton 1988. – RelStR 16,190.

4741 *Sottocornola* Franco, The prayer of Jesus over the bread and the cup at his Last Supper [... Japanese inculturation]: Japan Missionary Bulletin 41,1 (1989) 12-20 [< TContext 7/1, 50].

4742 **Stevenson** Kenneth, Accept this offering; the Eucharist as sacrifice today. L 1989, SPCK. 88 p. £4 pa. – ᴿStudies 78 (1989) 336-8 (Teresa *Clements*); TLond 92 (1989) 416 (R. *Askew*: rebarbative; not profane, but breezy).

4743 **Stevenson** Kenneth W., Eucharist and offering 1986 → 3,4637; 4,4842: ᴿScotJT 42 (1989) 280-3 (D. *Tripp*).

4744 *Stevenson* Kenneth W., Eucharistic sacrifice — an insoluble liturgical problem? [currently handled with 'creative ambiguity']: ScotJT 42 (1989) 469-492.

4745 *Takács* Béla, Ⓦ Scripture texts on the Lord's Table, on vessels and communion-cloths: TSzem 31 (1988) 344-8.

4746 *Temiño Sáiz* Ángel, La Eucaristía, sacrificio y sacramento, fuente y culmen de toda santificación: Burgense 30 (1989) 325-353.

4747 ᴱ**Tourn** G., G. Calvino, Il 'Piccolo trattato sulla S. Cena' nel dibattito sacramentale della Riforma: Testi della Riforma 15. T 1987, Claudiana. 159 p. Lit. 14.800. – ᴿProtestantesimo 44 (1989) 228s (F. *Ferrario*).

4748 *Wójtowicz* Henryk, ❷ De vocibus Eucharistiae apud sanctum AUGUSTINUM: VoxP 14 (1988) 225-265; lat. 266.

4749 **Zirkel** Patricia M., The Divine Child ['spiritually'; fostering a dynamic change within the participant] in Paschasius RADBERTUS' 'De corpore et sanguine Domini', ch. XIV: diss. Fordham, ᴰ*Cousins* E. Bronx 1989. 243 p. 89-17244. – DissA 50 (1989s) 1344-A; RelStR 16,188.

F5.3   **Mt 26,30 ...** || *Passio Christi;* **Passion-narrative.**

4750 **Allison** Dale C., The end of the ages has come 1987 ➤ 2,3648 ... 4,4847: ᴿActuBbg 26 (1989) 32s (X. *Alegre S.*); ScotJT 42 (1989) 429 (P. S. *Cameron*: doctorate subtitle was '... passion and resurrection of Jesus').

4751 **Bader** Günter, Symbolik des Todes Jesu: HermUntT 25, 1988 ➤ 4,4847: ᴿExpTim 100 (1988s) 380s (E. *Best*).

4752 **Beardslee** William A., *al.*, Biblical preaching on the death of Jesus. Nv 1989, Abington. 256 p. $16 [Interp 43,425 adv.].

4753 **Binz** S., The Passion and Resurrection narratives of Jesus; a commentary. Collegeville MN 1989, Liturgical. 127 p. 0-8146-1771-9 [NTAbs 33,282].

4754 *Biser* Eugen, Theologische Trauerarbeit; zu Hans BLUMENBERGs 'Matthäuspassion' [1988]: TR 85 (1989) 441-452.

4755 **Blumenberg** Hans, Matthäuspassion: Bibliothek 998, 1988 ➤ 4,4848; ᴿTR 85 (1989) 441-452 (E. *Biser*).

Crossan John D., The Cross that spoke [the apocryphal Gospel of Peter gives a more reliable earliest account of the Passion] 1988 ➤ 9983.

4756 **Dawe** Donald A., Jesus; the death and resurrection of God 1985 ➤ 3,4704: ᴿJRel 68 (1988) 126s (C. A. *Wilson*).

4757 *Derrett* J. D. M., *Archontes, archaí*; a wider background to the Passion narratives: FgNt 2 (1989) 173-184; castellano 184s.

4758 **Goergen** Donald, Death and resurrection of Christ 1988 (2d of 5 vol.) ➤ 4,4855: ᴿHorizons 16 (1989) 391s (Mary T. *Rattigan*).

4759 **Gourgues** Michel, Le crucifié; du scandale à l'exaltation: JJC 38. Montréal/P 1989, Bellarmin/Desclée. 178 p.

4760 **Green** J. B., The death of Jesus; tradition and interpretation in the Passion narrative [diss. Aberdeen 1985, ᴰ*Marshall* I.]: WUNT 2/33, 1988 ➤ 4,4856; 3-16-145349-2. – ᴿArTGran 52 (1989) 252s (A. *Segovia*); ExpTim 100 (1988s) 472 (J. A. *Ziesler*); TGegw 32 (1989) 314s (H. *Giesen*); TLZ 114 (1989) 891-3 (R. *Feldmeier*); TsTNijm 29 (1989) 408 (F. van *Helmond*).

4761 *Henrich* Reiner, Rationalistische Christentumskritik in essenischem Gewand; der Streit um die 'Enthüllungen über die wirkliche Todesart Jesu': ➤ 65*, ᶠGEISSER H. 1988, 308-322.

4762 *Hofrichter* Peter, Das dreifache Verfahren über Jesus als Gottessohn, König und Mensch: Kairos 30s (1988s) 69-81.

4763 *Hübner* Hans, Kreuz und Auferstehung im NT: TRu 54 (1989) 262-306 ...

4764 *a) Kokkinos* Nikos, Crucifixion in A.D. 36; the keystone for dating the birth of Jesus; – *b) Humphreys* Colin J., *Waddington* W. G., Astronomy and the date of the Crucifixion; – *c) Beckwith* Roger T., Cautionary notes on the use of calendars and astronomy to determine the chronology of the Passion: ➤ 58, ᶠFINEGAN J., Chronos 1989, 133-163 / 165-181 / 183-205.

4765 **Krotz** Fritz, ... für uns gestorben? Zugänge zur Geschichte von der Passion Jesu: Wege des Lernens 5, 1987 ➤ 3,4659: ᴿTsTNijm 29 (1989) 430 (F. *Peerlinck*).

4766 **Lapide** Pinchas, Wer war schuld an Jesu Tod? 1987 ➤ 4,4660: ᴿJEcuSt 26 (1989) 537s (J. *Mbiti*); LuthMon 29 (1989) 134 (A. *Peuster*).

4767 **Léon-Dufour** Xavier, Di fronte alla morte; Gesù e Paolo [1979 ➤ 60,6263] 1982 ➤ 63,4740: ᴿParVi 34 (1989) 220-3 (C. *Marcheselli Casale*, anche su *Schürmann* H. ital. 1983, *al.*).

4768 *Marcheselli-Casale* Cesare, Gesù di fronte alla sua morte e alla sua risurrezione; rassegna critica di alcuni studi recenti: Asprenas 36 (1989) 399-405.

4769 **Marshall** Michael, Just like him; the Passion of Christ in the Old Testament. ... 1989, Bible Reading Fellowship. 128 p. £3.50. 0-900164-79-4 [ExpTim 101,353].

4770 **Martin** Ernest L., Secrets of Golgotha; the forgotten history of Christ's crucifixion 1988 ➤ 4,4864: ᴿBibTB 19 (1989) 112 (L. J. *Hoppe*: absurd).

4771 **Matera** F. J., Passion narrative and Gospel theologies 1986 ➤ 2,3669 ... 4,4865: ᴿRivB 37 (1989) 109s (G. *Segalla*); ScripB 20 (1989s) 47s (D. *Way*).

4772 **Quenot** Yvette, Jean de LA CEPPÈDE, Les theorèmes sur le sacré mystère de nostre redemption [verse-meditations on the passion]. P 1988, Nizet. 273 p. – ᴿRHE 86 (1989) 832 (M. *Veissière*).

4773 **Stevenson** Kenneth, Jerusalem revisited; the liturgical meaning of Holy Week. ... 1988, Pastoral. 104 p. $7. 0-912405-53-8. – ᴿExpTim 101 (1989s) 92 (D. *Tripp* praises).

4774 *Turner* Geoffrey, Collective guilt and the Crucifixion: NBlackf 70 (1989) 124-136.

4775 *Feuillet* A., L'agonie de Gethsémani... PASCAL 1978 ➤ 58,6217; 60,6249: ᴿNicolaus 16 (1989) 338-340 (A. *Moda*).

4776 *Barkhuizen* J. H., Narrative apostrophe in the Kontakia of ROMANOS the Melodist, with special reference to his hymn 'On Judas': ActaClassica 29 (Pretoria 1986) 19-27.

4776* **Silvola** Kalevi, [Mk 14,3-9; Mt 26,13-16] Nardusvoide ja suudelma [Nardensalbe und Kuss, S. 257-265]: Traditio- ja redaktio-historiallinen tutkimus evankeliumien voitelukertomuksista: Suomen Eksegeettisen Seuran Julkaisuja 50. Helsinki 1989, Kirjapaino Raamattutalo. vii-265 p. 951-9217-05-3.

4777 **Klauck** Hans Josef, [Mt 26,14.47] Judas – ein Jünger des Herrn: QDisp 111, 1987 ➤ 3,4683; 4,4884: ᴿFranzSt 70 (1988) 119 (H. *Rusche*); TPQ 137 (1989) 81 (A. *Stöger*). ➤ 4171*.

4778 **Schwarz** Gunther, Jesus und Judas; aram. ...: BW 123, 1987 ➤ 4,4885: ᴿBL (1989) 153 (J. C. L. *Gibson*); CBQ 51 (1989) 574s (C. *Bernas*: boldest ever 'revisionist' view of Judas); ÉTRel 64 (1989) 633 (H. *Cousin*); TLZ 114 (1989) 29s (W. *Vogler*).

4779 *Saunderson* Barbara, Gethsemane; the missing witness [the fleeing youth of Mk 14,51s not excluded]: Biblica 70 (1989) 224-233.

4780 **Fricke** Weddig, Standrechtlich gekreuzigt... Prozess 1988 ➤ 2,3658; 4,4851: ᴿTR 85 (1989) 202-4 (A. *Kolping*).

4781 **Fricke** W., Il caso Gesù — il più controverso processo della storia. Mi 1988, Rusconi. 284 p. Lit. 30.000. – ᴿProtestantesimo 44 (1989) 226 (M. F. *Berutti*).

4782 **Imbert** Jean, Il processo di Gesù 1984 ➤ 1,4677: ᴿProtestantesimo 44 (1989) 60s (V. *Ribet*).

4783 **Pesch** Rudolf, Der Prozess Jesu geht weiter: Herderbücherei 1507, 1988
➤ 4,4890: ᴿJEcuSt 26 (1989) 363s (P. J. *Achtemeier*); TPQ 137 (1989) 197
(S. *Stahr*).

4784 *Luis Vizcaino* Pio de, Exégesis, apologética y teología; Poncio Pilato en
la obra agustiniana: EstAgust 24 (1989) 353-390.

4785 *Tilborg* Sjef van, Matthew 27.3-10; an intertextual reading: ➤ 95,
ᶠIERSEL B. van, 1989, 159-174.

4786 *Connolly-Weinert* Frank, [Lk 22,54s omits Mk 14,57s; Lk 23,26s omits
Mk 15,29s] Assessing omissions as redaction; Luke's handling of the
charge against Jesus as detractor of the Temple: ➤ 60, ᶠFITZMYER J.,
Touch 1989, 358-368.

4787 **Mora** V., Le refus d'Israël, Mt 27,25, 1986 ➤ 2,3692... 4,4895: ᴿRB
96 (1989) 147s (B. T. *Viviano*).

4788 *Schwank* Benedikt, 'Ecce homo' [Karfreitag]: ErbAuf 65 (1989) 199-209.

4789 *Hoppe* R., Barabbas: ➤ 902, NBL Lfg. 2 (1989) 239s.

4790 *Mertens* Herman-Emiel, Jesus as master of the Golgotha-situation; old
soteriological questions 'reposed': LvSt 14 (1989) 291-311.

4791 **Rossé** Gérard [Mt 27,46; Mk 15,34] The cry of Jesus on the Cross 1987
➤ 4,4899; ᵀ*Arndt* S. W.: ᴿBZ 33 (1989) 150s (R. *Schnackenburg*); CBQ
51 (1989) 381s (F. J. *Matera*); DocLife 39 (1989) 276s (F. *McCarthy*);
ExpTim 100 (1988s) 67 (J. *Muddiman*).

4792 *Grández* Rufino M., Las tinieblas en la muerte de Jesús; historia de la
exégesis de Lc 23,44-45a (Mt 27,45; Mc 15,33): EstBíb 47 (1989) 177-224;
Eng. 177.

4793 *Dubois* Jean-Daniel, Une variante copte de Matthieu 27,49 tirée du
Codex Scheide: ➤ 820, Journées coptes III, 1986/9, 32-45.

4794 *Brändle* Werner, Hinabgestiegen in das Reich des Todes: KerDo 35
(1989) 54-68; Eng. 68 '... into Hell'.

4795 *Spada* Domenico, [Mt 27,52...] La portata salvifica della discesa di
Cristo agli inferi: ➤ 735, Salvezza 1988/9, 517-530.

4796 *Yates* J., 'He descended into hell'; creed, article and Scripture:
Churchman 102 (L 1988) 240-250. 303-315 [NTAbs 33,352].

F5.6 **Mt 28 ‖ – Resurrectio.**

4797 *a) Aarde* A. G. van, *Ēgerthē apò tôn nekrôn* (Mt 28:7); a textual
evidence on the separation of Judaism and Christianity; – *b) Botha* P. J. J.,
Ouk éstin hōde ... Mark's stories of Jesus' tomb and history; – *c) Vorster*
W. S., The religio-historical context of the resurrection of Jesus and
resurrection faith in the New Testament: ➤ 617, Resurrection =
Neotestamentica 23,2 (1989) 219-233 / 195-218 / 159-175.

4798 *Alsup* J. E., Resurrection and historicity: Austin Seminary Bulletin 103,8
(1988) 5-18 [NTAbs 33,18].

4799 **Bagur Jover** Lorenzo, La resurrección de Cristo en los 'Tractatus in
Iohannis evangelium' de San AGUSTÍN: diss. ᴰ*Mateo-Seco* L. Pamplona
1989. 469 p. – RTLv 21,567.

4800 *Barón* Enrique, Cristo resucita en la Iglesia: Proyección 35 (1988)
105-113.

4801 **Bayer** Hans F., Jesus' predictions of vindication and resurrection...:
WUNT 2/20, 1986 ➤ 2,3277; 3,4697: ᴿJBL 108 (1989) 339-341 (M. E.
Boring).

4802 *Beaude* P. M., Les premiers chrétiens parlent du Ressuscité: DossB 27
(1989) 10-13 [-25, *al.*: 3-7, *Gruson* Philippe, Lueurs dans l'AT].

4803 **Bloem** Henk,   Die Ostererzählung des Mt... 27,57-28,20:   1987
➤ 3,4699: ᴿCBQ 51 (1989) 739s (F. J. *Moloney*: updated to 1979).
4804 ᴱ**Broer** Ingo... 'Der Herr ist wahrhaft auferstanden' (Lk 24,34 ...): SBS
134, 1988 ➤ 4,4903: ᴿGregorianum 70 (1989) 567s (G. *O'Collins*:
WERBICK and WENZ articles adequate); TLZ 114 (1989) 179s (R.
Marschner).
4805 *Bush* L. Russ,   Apostolic hermeneutics; 'proof texts' and the Resurrection: CriswT 2 (1987s) 291-307.
4806 **Carnley** Peter,   The structure of Resurrection belief 1987 ➤ 3,4702;
4,4908:   ᴿAustralasCR 66 (1989) 115-7 (P. *Gwynne*); CCurr 39 (1989s)
475-7 (P. *Giurlanda*); Colloquium 22,1 (1989) 45s (W. R. G. *Loader*);
EpworthR 15,3 (1988) 82-89 (J. H. *Jones*) [< NTAbs 33,18]; Gregorianum
70 (1989) 341-4 (G. *O'Collins*); JRel 69 (1989) 425s (P. E. *Devenish*);
JTS 40 (1989) 324-8 (C. F. *Evans*); ScotJT 42 (1989) 454s (D. *Fergusson*);
TS 50 (1989) 178s (G. *O'Collins*).
4807 *Clément* Olivier,   La joie de la Résurrection dont l'Église est la
fête: Christus 34 (1987) 269-273 [> SelT 28 (1989) 136-8, ᵀᴱ*Ribas*
Manuel].
4808 **Craig** William L.,   The historical argument for the resurrection of Jesus
during the Deist controversy 1985 ➤ 1,4715; 4,4912: ᴿJRel 68 (1988) 595
(S. C. *Pearson*); JTS 40 (1989) 309s (R. *Morgan*).
4809 **Craig** William L.,   Assessing the New Testament evidence for the
historicity of the Resurrection of Jesus: StBEC 16. Lewiston 1989,
Mellen. xix-442 p. 0-88946-616-5.
4810 **Craig** W. L.,   Knowing the truth about the Resurrection; our response
to the empty tomb [= ²The Son Rises 1981]. AA 1988, Servant.
xiv-153 p. $8. 0-89283-384-X [NTAbs 33,105]. – ᴿBS 146 (1989) 102 (R. P.
Lightner).
4810* *a*) *Cranfield* C. E. B.,   The Resurrection of Jesus Christ; – *b*) *Walker*
David A.,   Resurrection, empty tomb and Easter faith: ExpTim 101
(1989s) 167-172 / 172-5.
4811 *Doré* Joseph, *Mercier* Bernard,   Croire en la résurrection de Jésus-Christ:
Masses ouvrières 424 (1989) 65-77.
4812 *Eddy* G. T.,   The Resurrection of Jesus Christ; a consideration of
Professor CRANFIELD's argument: ExpTim 101 (1989s) [167] 327-9.
4813 **Espezel** Alberto,   El misterio pascual en H. U. v. BALTHASAR [diss.
Pont. Univ. Gregoriana, R 1987]. San Isidro ARG 1987, auct.   200 p. [TR
86, 35-38, M. *Tiator*].
4814 *Galvin* John P.,   On the third day he rose again; the centrality of Jesus'
Resurrection: PrPeo 3 (1989) 120-3.
4815 *Galvin* John P.,   Der Ursprung des Glaubens an die Auferstehung Jesu;
zwei neuere Perspektiven [< TS 1988, 25-44], ᵀ*Mirbach* S. *al.*: TGegw 32
(1989) 203-218.
4816 *Geisler* Norman L.,   The significance of Christ's physical resurrection:
BS 146 (1989) 148-170.
4817 **Greenacre** Roger, *Haselock* Jeremy,   The sacrament of Easter. Leominster 1989, Fowler Wright. vii-178 p.; 3 fig. £10 pa. [JTS 41,823].
4818 **Guilbert** Pierre,   Il ressuscita le troisième jour: Racines.   P 1988,
Nouvelle Cité. 256 p. F 116. – ᴿEsprVie 99 (1989) 45s (É. *Cothenet*).
4819 *Habermas* Gary R.,   Resurrection claims in non-Christian religions:
RelSt 25 (1989) 167-177.
4820 *Harvey* Nicholas P.,   Frames of reference for the Resurrection: ScotJT
42 (1989) 335-9.

4821 ᴱ*Hoffmann* Paul, Zur neutestamentlichen Überlieferung von der Auferstehung Jesu: WegFor 522, 1988 ➤ 4,311; 3-534-08006-8: ᴿActuBbg 26 (1989) 40s (V. *Fábrega*).

4822 *a*) *Hoffmann* P., Auferweckung Jesu; – *b*) *Görg* M., Auferstehung: ➤ 902, NBL Lfg. 2 (1989) 202-215 / 199-202.

4823 *Isidro Alves* M., A ressureição de Jesus; experiência e testemunho: HumT 9 (1988) 267-275 [< REB 49,507].

4824 **Kessler** Hans, La resurrección de Jesús; aspecto bíblico, teológico y sistemático [Sucht... 1985 ➤ 1,4727], ᵀ*Olasagasti* Manuel: Lux Mundi 65. S 1989, Sígueme. 373 p. 84-301-1069-0. – ᴿActuBbg 26 (1989) 214s (J. *Boada*); CommSev 32 (1989) 428 (M. de *Burgos*); LumenVr 38 (1989) 446 (A. M. *Navarro*); Proyección 36 (1989) 327s (E. *Barón*).

4825 *Kessler* Hans, Irdischer Jesus, Kreuzestod und Osterglaube [Sucht den Lebenden nicht bei den Toten 1985 = 1987; Reaktionen zu Rezensionen von *Schmied* A., *Verweyen* H.]: TGegw 32 (1989) 219-229.

4826 **Klasen** Franz-Josef, Über das Bild des Auferstandenen und seine Entleerung in der Geschichte der deutschen Kunst: Diss. ᴰ*Lehmann*. Freiburg/B 1988s. – TR 85 (1989) 515.

4827 *Kremer* Jacob, El testimonio de la Resurrección de Cristo en forma de narraciones históricas [< StiZt 61 (1988) 172-187], ᵀ*Torres* M. J. de: SelT 28 (1989) 323-9.

4828 *Kušar* Stjepan, The Paschal mystery and the Christian family (in Croatian); ObnŽiv 44,4 (XVIII. Obiteljska Ljetna Škola, Zagreb 23.-27. VIII. 1989) 510-524; Eng. 525.

4829 **Léon-Dufour** Xavier, Risurrezione di Gesù e messaggio pasquale. Mi 1987, Paoline. 381 p. Lit. 25.000. – ᴿSapCr 4 (1989) 276 (F. *Toniolo*).

4830 *Lona* Horacio, Ps. JUSTINS 'De resurrectione' und die altchristliche Auferstehungsapologetik: Salesianum 51 (1989) 691-768.

4831 **Lunny** William J., The sociology of the Resurrection. L/Victoria 1989, SCM/Heron. viii-146 p. £7 pa. 0-334-02335-1. – ᴱExpTim 101 (1989s) 83s (J. M. *Court*: little or no sociology); TLond 92 (1989) 332 (C. S. *Rodd*: re-formation of a 'gang'; young people understand how gangs operate).

4832 **McDonald** J. I. H., The Resurrection; narrative and belief. L 1989, SPCK. xii-161 p. £15. 0-281-04400-7. – ᴿExpTim 101 (1989s) 122 (J. L. *Houlden*).

4833 ᴱ**Miethe** T., (*Habermas-Flew*) Did Jesus rise? 1987 ➤ 3,4710; 4,4923: ᴿWestTJ 50 (1988) 360-2 (J. W. *Scott*).

4834 [ᶠVÖGTLE Anton], ᴱ**Oberlinner** Lorenz, Auferstehung Jesu/Christen...: QDisp 105, 1986 ➤ 2,120: ᴿSalesianum 51 (1989) 365s (A. *Amato*).

4835 **O'Collins** Gerald, Jesus risen; the Resurrection — what actually happened and what does it mean? 1987 ➤ 3,4718; 4,6930: ᴿJRel 69 (1989) 269 (R. *Zachman*: opposes the tendency to collapse the resurrection into the incarnation or vocation or kerygma); RelStT 7,2s (1987) 104s (T. A. *Robinson*); ScotJT 42 (1989) 105-7 (D. *Fergusson*); Studies 77 (1988) 245-7 (R. *Moloney*).

4836 **O'Collins** G., Jesús resucitado 1988 ➤ 4,4931; ᵀ*Martínez Riu* Antonio; 84-254-1620-5; ᴿActuBbg 26 (1989) 220s (J. *Boada*); BibFe 15 (1989) 170s (A. *Salas*); CiTom 116 (1989) 195s (E. *Rodríguez*); CommSev 22 (1989) 93s (M. de *Burgos*); FranBog 31 (1989) 213s (E. H.); LumenVr 38 (1989) 84 (F. *Ortiz de Urtaran*); NatGrac 36 (1989) 153 (A. *Villalmonte*).

4837 **O'Collins** Gerald, Gesù risorto; un'indagine biblica, storica e teologica sulla risurrezione di Gesù. Brescia 1989, Queriniana. 265 p. Lit. 32.000. – ᴿCC 140 (1989,4) 97s (F. *Lambiasi*); Lateranum 55 (1989) 262s (G. *Ancona*).

4838 *O'Collins* Gerald, Alcuni problemi attuali sulla risurrezione di Gesù [... apparizioni; sepolcro vuoto]: CC 140 (1989,2) 32-38.
O'Donovan Oliver, Resurrection and moral order 1986 ➤ 8348.

4839 *Osiek* Carolyn, *al.*, The Resurrection: BToday 27 (1989) 133-9 (167).

4840 *Pagola* José A., Resucitar lo muerto; la experiencia pascual como nueva posibilidad de vida: SalT 76 (1988) 175-185.

4841 **Palumbieri** Sabino, Cristo risorto, leva della storia. T 1988, SEI. 306 p. – ᴿLateranum 55 (1989) 486-8 (A. *Amato*); Salesianum 51 (1989) 416s (*ipse*).

4842 *Roberts* J., Galilean resurrection [means Jesus continued to work in his disciples as Herod Antipas thought John the Baptist to have done]: EpworthR 15,3 (1988) 44-46 [< NTAbs 33,18].

4843 *a) Scuka* Robert F., Resurrection; critical reflections on a doctrine in search of a meaning; – *b) Craig* William L., On doubts about the Resurrection: ModT 6 (1989s) 77-95 / 53-75.

4844 *Smith* Joseph J., *a)* The Resurrection and the empty tomb: Landas 1,2 (Manila 1987) 143-164 [< NTAbs 33,18]; – *b)* The resurrection appearances and the origin of the Easter faith: Landas 2,2 (1988) 204-237 [< NTAbs 33,152].

4844* *Vargas-Machuca* Antonio, Reflexiones en torno a la Resurrección de Jesús: RazF 217 (1988) 351-365.

4845 *Viney* D. W., Grave doubts about the resurrection [for the historian, though faith is not irrational]: Encounter 50,2 (Indianapolis 1989) 125-140 [< NTAbs 33,299].

4846 *Weder* H., [Die Auferstehung als] Gottes Einspruch gegen Leben aus eigener Macht: RefForum 3,11 (Z 1989) 11-13 [< NTAbs 33,299].

4847 *Weinrich* M., Christus als Zeitgenosse; von der Gegenwart der Parusie Jesu Christi: ZdialektT 4,2 (1988) 185-226 [< ZIT 89,805].

4848 *Wengst* K., 'Ein wirkliches Gleichnis...' [Ezech 37 nach Rabbinen]; Zur Rede von der Auferweckung Jesu Christi im NT: Zts für dialektische Theologie 4,2 (Kampen 1988) 149-183 [< NTAbs 33,300].

4849 **Trull** Joe E., The seven last words of the risen Christ. GR 1985, Baker. 110 p. $5 pa. – ᴿCriswT 2 (1988) 471s (A. B. *Luter*).

4850 *a) Bolognesi* Pietro, Matteo 28,16-20 e il suo contenuto; – *b) Packer* James I., Cos'è l'evangelizzazione? Evangelizzazione e teologia, ᵀ*Grottoli* C.; – *c) Schluchter* Antoine, Una controversia sull'evangelizzazione; WHITEFIELD-WESLEY [sintesi di tesi < RRéf 1986]: STEv NS 1/1 (1989) 25-39 / 41-60 / 61-68.

4851 **Lagrand** Jamesᴶ, The earliest Christian mission to 'all nations' in the light of Matthew's Gospel: diss. ᴰ*Stegemann* E. Basel 1989. – RTLv 21,545.

4852 *Masiá* Juan, [Mt 28,19] Id y aprended de todas las gentes: SalT 77 (1989) 665-672.

4853 *Perkins* Pheme, Christology and mission; Matthew 28:16-20: Listening 24 (1989) 302... [< ZIT 90,14].

4854 *Gonin* F., Recherches sur l'invocation du nom de Dieu au moment du baptême: RRéf 40,2 (1989) 43-47 [< NTAbs 33,346].

F6.1 **Evangelium Marci** – *Textus, commentarii.*

4855 **Aranda Pérez** G., El Evangelio de San Marcos en copto 1988 ➤ 4,4954: ᴿSalmanticensis 36 (1989) 391 (R. *Trevijano*).

4856 **Cole** R. Alan, The Gospel according to Mark; an introduction and commentary[2] [[1]1961]: Tyndale NT comm. Leicester/GR 1989, Inter-Varsity/Eerdmans. 340 p. 0-85111-871-2 / 0-8028-0481-0.

4857 **Drewermann** Eugen, Das Markus-Evangelium; Bilder von Erlösung [I. 1987 [2]1988 ➤ 4,4956]; II. Olten 1989, Walter. – [R]ExpTim 101 (1989s) 282s (E. *Best*).

4858 **Fischer** Bonifatius, Die lateinischen Evangelien bis zum 10. Jh., II. Varianten zu Markus: VLGesch 15. FrB 1989, Herder. 48*-555 p. [NRT 112,909, X. *Jacques*].

4859 **Georgeot** J.-M., Évangile selon saint Marc; contribution à la 'lectio divina': Spiritualité 2. Reiningue 1988, Documentation Cistercienne. I. c. 100 p. II. 66 p. III. 1989, Lexique A-K, 565 p. IV. (1990), I-Z; p. 571-1150: [R]Burgense 30 (1989) 589 (F. *Pérez Herrera*); EsprVie (1989) 653 (É. *Ricaud*).

4860 **Gnilka** Joachim, Marco 1987 ➤ 3,4744; 4,4957: [R]Antonianum 64 (1989) 473-5 (M. *Nobile*); Asprenas 36 (1989) 531s (S. *Cipriani*); CC 140 (1989,2) 88s (K. *Stock*).

4861 **Gnilka** J., El Evangelio según San Marcos II (8,27-16,20) 1986 ➤ 2,3731; 3,4743: [R]CiuD 202 (1989) 250s (J. *Gutiérrez*).

4862 **González Ruiz** J. M., Evangelio según Marcos; introducción, traducción, comentario. Pamplona 1988, VDivino. 238 p. pt. 1000. 84-7151-595-4 [NTAbs 33,385]. – [R]BibFe 15 (1989) 321 (A. *Salas*).

4863 **Guelich** Robert A., Mark 1-8,26: Word comm. 34a. Dallas 1989, Word. xliii-454 p. $25 [JBL 108,754]. 0-8499-0233-9.

4864 *Harrington* Daniel J., The Gospel according to Mark: ➤ 384, NJBC (1989) 594-629.

4865 **Iersel** Bastiaan M. F. van, Reading Mark [1986 ➤ 4,4957*], [T]*Bisscheroux* W. H. E 1989, Clark. 261 p. £10. 0-567-29159-6. – [R]Biblica 70 (1989) 558-560 (J. *Swetnam*); Neotestamentica 23 (1989) 360s (W. S. *Vorster*).

4866 **Iersel** Bastiaan M. F. Van, Leggere Marco: Parola di Dio. CinB 1989, Paoline. 388 p.

4867 **Jeanne d'Arc**, sr., Les Évangiles... Mc... 1986 ➤ 2,3735 (4,4387): [R]RÉG 101 (1988) 583 (P. *Nautin*).

4868 **Kilgallen** John J., A brief commentary on the Gospel of Mark. NY 1989, Paulist. iv-319 p. $15. 0-8091-3059-9 [EstBíb 47,578].

4869 **Lührmann** D., Das Markusevangelium: HbNT 1987 ➤ 3,4750; 4,4958: [R]JBL 108 (1989) 343-5 (M. E. *Boring*); JTS 40 (1989) 560-3 (E. *Best*); TsTNijm 29 (1989) 65 (W. *Weren*).

4870 **Mann** C. S., Mark: AnchorB 27, 1986 ➤ 2,3736... 4,4959: [R]CriswT 2 (1988) 443s (D. L. *Akin*: best and worst).

4871 **Mourlon Beernaert** P., S. Marc 1985 ➤ 1,4752*; 2,3738: [R]ScripTPamp 21 (1989) 945s (J. M. *Casciaro*).

4872 *Neirynck* F., Mark and his commentators, Mk 1,1-8,26 [LÜHRMANN D., 1987; GUELICH R. 1989]: ETL 65 (1989) 381-9.

4873 [T]**Pascual Torres** Joaquín, [E]*Guerrero Martínez* Fernando, San JERÓNIMO, Comentario al evangelio de san Marcos: BiblPatr 5. M 1989, Ciudad Nueva. 104 p. pt. 800. 84-86987-01-6. – [R]ActuBbg 26 (1989) 246s (J. *Vives*).

4874 **Pérez Herrero** Francisco, Evangelio según San Marcos: MensajeNT 2. S 1989, Sígueme. 173 p. 84-7151-636-5.

4875 **Pesch** R., Il Vangelo di Marco [1976s] 1980-2 ➤ 63,4851*b*... 3,4754: [R]Nicolaus 16 (1989) 245-258 (A. *Moda*).

4876 **Pickering** S. R., *Cook* R. R. E., Has a fragment of the Gospel of Mark been found at Qumran? [no]: Papyrology & Historical Perspectives 1. Sydney 1989, Macquarie Univ. Anc. Hist. Centre. viii-25 p.; 1 fig. 0-85837-635-0.

4877 ^E**Rummel** Erika; ERASMUS, ·Paraphrase on Mark; Works 49. Toronto 1988, Univ. xiv-235 p. $40 [RelStR 16, 158, M. *Hoffmann*].

4878 **Schenke** Ludger, Das Markusevangelium 1988 ➤ 4,4960*;   3-17-010182-X: ^RBiKi 44 (1989) 90s (M. *Helsper*); ÉTRel 64 (1989) 290s (E. *Cuvillier*); RHPR 69 (1989) 225s (É. *Trocmé*); TLZ 114 (1989) 349s (D. *Lührmann*); TPQ 137 (1989) 413s (F. *Kogler*); TsTNijm 29 (1989) 289 (P. J. *Farla*).

4879 **Wiersbe** Warren, [Mk] Be diligent. Wheaton 1987, Victor. 156 p. $6 pa. − ^RCriswT 2 (1988) 446s (D. J. *Akin*).

4880 **Zuurmond** Rochus, Novum Testamentum aethiopice; the synoptic Gospels, general introduction, edition of the Gospel of Mark: ÄthForsch 27. Stu 1989, Steiner. I. xv-406 p. 3-515-05269-0.

F6.2 *Evangelium Marci,* **Themata.**

4880* *Ambrozic* Aloysius M., Jesus as the ultimate reality in St. Mark's Gospel: Ultimate Reality and Meaning 12,3 (1989) 169-176 [< IZBG 36, p. 170].

4881 **Austin** Stephen W., [Mk on Pharisees] The coming of age of historical criticism; setting the parameters of objective research: diss. Duke, ^D*Via* D. Durham NC 1989. 323 p. 90-01051. − DissA 50 (1989s) 2523-A.

4882 *Balembo* Buetubela, Le péché dans l'Évangile de Marc: RAfT 12,23s (1988) 23-29 [< NTAbs 33,307].

4882* *Best* Ernest, Disciples and discipleship; studies in the Gospel according to Mark 1986 ➤ 2,132*; 3,4758: ^RBZ 33 (1989) 271-3 (Ingo *Broer*).

4883 *Best* Ernest, a) The Gospel of Mark; who was the reader?: IrBSt 11,3 (1989) 124-132 [< ZIT 89,531]; − b) Mark's narrative technique: ➤ 84, ^FHILL D., JStNT 37 (1989) 43-58.

4884 **Biguzzi** Giancarlo, 'Io distruggerò questo tempio'; il tempio e il giudaismo nel Vangelo di Marco 1987 ➤ 3,4759; 4,4965: ^RBurgense 30 (1989) 587-9 (F. *Pérez Herrero*); RivB 37 (1989) 374-381 (E. *Manicardi*); Salesianum 51 (1989) 349s (M. *Cimosa*).

4885 **Black** C. Clifton, The disciples according to Mark; Markan redaction in current debate [diss. Duke 1986, ^D*Smith* D. M.: JStNT Supp 27. Sheffield 1989, Academic. 392 p. £25. 1-85075-157-9 [JTS 41, 602-7, E. *Best*].

4886 **Blanch** Stuart, Encounters with Jesus [20 in Mk]. L 1988, Hodder & S. 237 p. £8. 0-340-42592-X [ExpTim 101,95].

Brock Rita N., Journeys by heart; a [Mark] Christology of erotic power 1988 ➤ 8860.

4888 **Cuvillier** C., La tragédie de Jésus; Marc raconte l'Évangile. Aubonne 1989, Moulin. 93 p. [RHPR 69,89].

4889 *Davis* Philip G., Mark's Christological paradox: JStNT 35 (1989) 3-18.

4890 a) *Delorme* Jean, Intertextualities about Mark; − b) *Jonge* Marinus de, Jesus, Son of David and Son of God: ➤ 95, ^FIERSEL B. van, 1989, 35-42 / 95-104.

4891 *Dewey* Joanna, Oral methods of structuring narrative in Mark: Interpretation 43 (1989) 32-44.

4892 **Doohan** Leonard, Mark, visionary of early Christianity 1986 ➤ 3,4771: ^RRelStT 8,3 (1988) 53s (E. L. *Segal*).

4893 **Dschulnigg** Peter, Sprache, Redaktion und Intention des Mk-Ev 1984
→ 1,4776... 3,4772: ᴿTZBas 45 (1989) 89-91 (G. D. *Kilpatrick*).

4894 *Eck* E. van, Galilea en Jerusalem as narratologiese ruimtes [toponyms]
in die Markusevangelium; 'n kontinuering van die LOHMEYER-LIGHT-
FOOT-MARXSEN ketting [chain]: HervTS 44 (Pretoria 1988) 139-163
[< NTAbs 33,26].

4895 *Edwards* James R., Markan sandwiches; the significance of interpolation
in Markan narratives: NT 31 (1989) 193-216.

4896 **Fander** Monika, Die Stellung der Frau im Markusevangelium, unter
besonderer Berücksichtigung kultur- und religionsgeschichtlicher Hintergründe [kath. Diss. ᴰ*Löning*. Münster 1988s. TR 85 (1989) 517].
Altenberge 1989, Telos. xi-395 p. DM 50 [TR 86,75]. 3-89375-017-7.

4897 *Fusco* Vittorio, Avversari di Paolo — avversari di Marco; un contatto
attraverso la 'cristologia del theios anēr'?; appunti sulla discussione:
→ 597, RicStoB 1,2 (1987/9) 23-42.

4898 *Gerhardsson* Birger, Mark and the female witnesses: → 183, ᶠSJÖBERG
Å., Dumu- 1989, 217-226.

4899 *González Ruiz* José M., Paralelos en las teologías marcana y paulina:
→ 69*, ᶠGOMÀ I., RCatalT 14 (1989) 323-332 castellano; Eng. 332.

4900 **Hengel** Martin, Studies in the Gospel of Mark 1985 → 1,4779; 2,3760:
ᴿHeythJ 30 (1989) 443s (Marion *Smith*).

4901 *Humphrey* Hugh M., Jesus as wisdom in Mark: BibTB 19 (1989)
48-53.

4902 *a) Iersel* B. M. F. van, The reader of Mark as operator of a system of
connotations; – *b) Fowler* Robert M., The rhetoric of direction and
indirection in the Gospel of Mark; – *c) Berg* Temma F., Reading in/to
Mark: Semeia 48 (1989) 83-114 / 115-133 / 187-206.

4903 **Kato** Zenji, Die Völkermission im Markusevangelium; eine redaktionsgeschichtliche Untersuchung: EurHS 23/252, 1986 → 2,3763; 3,4785:
ᴿActuBbg 26 (1989) 41s (X. *Alegre S.*).

4904 *Kee* Howard C., Mark: → 377, Books 2 (1989) 149-169.

4905 *a) Kee* Howard C., Christology in Mark's Gospel; – *b) Charlesworth*
J. H., From Jewish messianology to Christian Christology; some caveats
and perspectives: → 7368, ᴱNeusner J., Judaisms and their Messiahs 1987,
187-208 / 225-264 [< JStJud 20,252].

4906 *Kelber* Werner H., [Marc déconstruit, ne favorise pas le secret] Récit
et révélation; voiler, dévoiler et revoiler: RHPR 69 (1989) 389-410;
Eng. 509.

4907 **Kingsbury** Jack D., The Christology of Mark's Gospel. Ph 1989,
Fortress. xxi-207 p. [CBQ 52,197].

4908 **Kingsbury** Jack D., Conflict in Mark; Jesus, authorities, disciples.
Minneapolis 1989, Fortress. ix-150 p. [CBQ 52,197]. $9. 0-8006-2336-3.

4909 **Klerk** J. C. de, *Schnell* C. W., A new look at Jesus; literary and
sociological-historical interpretations of Mark and John. Pretoria 1987,
van Schaik. xi-272 p. $20. 0-627-01504-2 [NTAbs 33,244].

4910 *Klumbies* P.-G., Die Sabbatheilungen Jesu nach Markus und Lukas:
→ 131, ᶠMARXSEN W., Jesu Rede 1989, 165-178.

4911 **Longstaff** Thomas R. W., Evidence of conflation in Mark? [ᴰ1973]
1977 → 58,4831...: ᴿLA 39 (1989) 364 (V. *Mora*).

4912 *a) Lührmann* Dieter, Das Markusevangelium als Erzählung; – *b) Schröer*
Henning, Anders als die Schriftgelehrten? Eugen DREWERMANNS Aus-
legung des Markusevangeliums: EvErz 41 (Fra 1989) 212-221 / 222-230
[< ZIT 89,678].

4913 **Mack** Burton L., A myth of innocence; Mark and Christian origins 1988 ➤ 4,4988: ᴿAndrUnS 27 (1989) 236 (M. M. *Kent*: deprecates 'novelty' due to appearance of Jesus); JBL 108 (1989) 726-9 (Adela Y. *Collins*: very ambitious); Paradigms 5,1 (1989) 67s (Mitzi *Minor*); TLond 92 (1989) 329-334 (F. G. *Downing*: the book holds that Mark could have invented the eschatological figure of Jesus the Son of Man, thus producing the totally misleading and potentially destructive impression that there could be and was someone in charge of human history).

4914 *Mackowski* Richard M., Some colloquialisms in the Gospel according to Mark [in the 7 hapax legomena and 18 words not elsewhere in the Bible]: ➤ 175, Mem. SCHODER R., Daidalikon 1989, 229-238.

4915 **Mackrell** Gerald, The healing miracles in Mark's Gospel. Slough c. 1989, St. Paul's. 131 p. £5. – ᴿPrPeo 3 (1989) 409s (R. *Duckworth*).

4916 **Malbon** Elizabeth S., Narrative space and mythic meaning in Mark 1986 ➤ 2,3769; 4,4990: ᴿJRel 68 (1988) 584-6 (R. M. *Fowler*).

4917 *Malbon* Elizabeth S., The Jewish leaders in the Gospel of Mark; a literary study of Marcan characterization: JBL 108 (1989) 259-281.

4918 *Maloney* Elliott C., The historical present in the Gospel of Mark: ➤ 60, ᶠFITZMYER J., Touch 1989, 67-78.

4919 **Mansfield** Robert M., 'Spirit and Gospel' in Mark ᴰ1987 ➤ 3,4793: ᴿJBL 108 (1989) 152-4 (R. H. *Gundry*).

4920 **Marshall** Christopher D., Faith as a theme in Mark's narrative [diss. London 1985, ᴰ*Stanton* G.]: SNTS Mg 64. C 1989, Univ. xii-262 p. £27.50 [TR 86,340]. 0-521-36507-4.

4921 **Matera** Frank J., What are they saying about Mark? 1987 ➤ 3,4795; 4,4991: ᴿBibTB 19 (1989) 39 (M. *McVann*); RB 96 (1989) 148 (B. T. *Viviano*); TLZ 114 (1989) 883s (G. *Sellin*: vorbildlich).

4922 *Matera* F. J., Mystery and humanity; the Jesus of Mark: Church 5,1 (NY 1989) 20-23 [< NTAbs 33,308].

4922* *Minette de Tillesse* Caetano, Evangelho segundo Marcos: RBBras 5,3s (1988) 89-117 . 137-156.

4923 **Minor** Mitzi L., The spirituality of the Gospel of Mark: diss. Southern Baptist Theol. Sem. 1989, ᴰ*Borchert* G. 301 p. 90-04718. – DissA 50 (1989s) 2540-A.

4924 *Muddiman* John B., The end of Markan redaction criticism? A review article [BLACK C., KINGSBURY J., WAETJEN H., MARSHALL C., THOMPSON M., all 1989; SERGEANT J. 1988]: ExpTim 101 (1989s) 307-9.

4925 **Neirynck** Frans, Duality in Mark²ʳᵉᵛ. [¹1972, épuisée 1975] 1988 ➤ 4,4995: ᴿNRT 111 (1989) 748s (X. *Jacques*); RHE 84 (1989) 792s (J. *Dupont*: les Supplementary Notes p. 215-252 font le prix de cette édition).

4926 *Neirynck* Frans, The apocryphal gospels and the Gospel of Mark: ➤ 606, Réception 1986/9, 123-175.

4927 *Osborne* William L., The Markan theme of 'who is Jesus?': AsiaJT 3 (Singapore 1989) 302-314.

4928 **Peabody** David B., Mark as composer [1983 diss. Southern Methodist Univ.]: New Gospel Studies 1, 1987 ➤ 3,4801; 4,5001: ᴿCriswT 2 (1988) 444s (D. L. *Akin*); JAAR 57 (1989) 421-4 (C. C. *Black*).

4929 *Pérez Fernández* Miguel, Lectura del Antiguo Testamento desde el Nuevo Testamento; estudio sobre las citas bíblicas atribuidas a Jesús en el Evangelio de Marcos: EstBíb 47 (1989) 449-474; Eng. 449.

4930 **Riley** Harold, The making of Mark, an exploration. Macon GA 1989, Mercer Univ. xx-268 p. 0-86554-359-3.

4931 **Robinson** James M., Messiasgeheimnis und Geschichtsverständnis; zur Gattungsgeschichte des Markusevangeliums, ᵀ*Fröhlich* Karlfried: TBüch 81. Mü 1989, Kaiser. ix-158 p. DM 53 [TR 86,163].

4932 **Roth** Wolfgang, Hebrew Gospel [though in Greek]; cracking the code of Mark 1988 ➤ 4,5007; 0-940989-17-4; pa. -31-X: ᴿExpTim 100 (1988s) 232 (J. *Muddiman*); RHPR 69 (1989) 226s (É. *Trocmé*: artificial); ScotJT 42 (1989) 575s (E. *Best*: totally useless).

4933 ᴱ**Sabbe** M., L'Évangile selon Marc, tradition et rédaction²ʳᵉᵛ [Colloquium Biblicum Lovaniense 1971] 1988 ➤ 4,5008: ᴿNRT 111 (1989) 749 (X. *Jacques*).

4934 *Schreiber* Johannes, [Mk] WELLHAUSEN und WREDE; eine methodische Differenz: ZNW 80 (1989) 24-41.

4935 *Sellew* Philip, Composition of didactic scenes in Mark's Gospel: JBL 108 (1989) 613-634.

4936 **Sergeant** John, Lion let loose 1988 ➤ 4,5011: ᴿRHPR 69 (1989) 226 (É. *Trocmé*: brilliant title and cover; the cage is the idea that Mark is just a summarizer of Mt; but he is here too tamed).

4937 *a*) *Silva Airton* José da, O relato de uma prática — roteiro para uma leitura de Marcos; – *b*) *Oliveira de Azevedo* Walmor, Uma leitura do Evangelho de Marcos... articulação global; – *c*) *Soares* Paulo S., Uma experiência popular com Marcos — parábola do coco [*Mesters* C., a Biblia 'um coco de casca dura']; – *d*) *Messias de Oliveira* Emanuel, Apresentação de alguns estudos sobre Marcos: EstudosB 22 (1989) 11-23 [43-53] / 23-30 / 55-64 / 65-78.

4938 *Smith* Stephen H., The role of Jesus' opponents in the Markan drama [... modelled consciously or subconsciously on Greek tragic drama]: NTS 35 (1989) 161-182.

4939 **Stock** A., The method and message of Mark. Wilmington 1989, Glazier. iv-452 p. $30. 0-89453-642-7 [NTAbs 33,391].

4940 **Sweetland** Dennis M., Our journey with Jesus... Mark: Good News Studies 22, 1987 ➤ 3,4814; 4,5014: ᴿCurrTM 16 (1989) 294 (M. L. *Wegener*: medium good, like MATERA F.); NewTR 2,1 (1989) 105s (D. P. *Reid*).

4941 **Thimmes** Pamela, Fear as a reaction to Jesus in the Markan gospel: ProcGLM 9 (1989) 138-147.

4942 **Thompson** Mary R., The role of disbelief in Mark; a new approach to the 2nd Gospel. NY 1989, Paulist. x-188 p. $10 [TR 86,427]. 0-8091-3044-0.

4943 **Tolbert** Mary Ann, Sowing the Gospel; Mark's world in literary-historical perspective. Minneapolis 1989, Fortress. xvi-336 p. $28 [TR 86,427].

4944 **Trakatellis** Demetrios, Authority and Passion: Christological aspects of the Gospel according to Mark [1983], ᵀ*Duvall* G. K., *Vulopas* H. Brookline MA 1987, Holy Cross Orthodox. xii-245 p. $24; pa. $16. – ᴿCBQ 51 (1989) 384s (L. W. *Hurtado*).

4945 *Trotter* Irwin J., Preaching 'on the way'; homilies based on new interpretations of the Gospel of Mark QRMin 8,2 (1988) 90-108.

4946 **Via** Dan O., The ethics of Mark's Gospel — in the middle of time 1985 ➤ 1,4808 ... 4,5020: ᴿJRel 68 (1988) 476s (Troy *Martin*); TLZ 114 (1989) 525s (P. *Pokorný*).

4947 *a*) *Vouga* F., Die Entwicklungsgeschichte der jesuanischen Chrien und didaktischen Dialoge des Markusevangeliums; – *b*) *Sellin* G., Einige symbolische und esoterische Züge im Markus-Evangelium: → 131, FMARXSEN W., Jesu Rede 1989, 45-56 / 74-90.

4948 **Waetjen** Herman C., A reordering of power; a sociopolitical reading of Mark's Gospel. Minneapolis 1989, Fortress. xx-257 p. $20 [TDig 37,192]. 0-8006-2319-3.

4949 *Wallace* Mark I., Parsimony of presence in Mark; narratology, the reader and genre analysis in Paul RICŒUR: SR 18 (1989) 201-212.

4950 *Walsh* Richard G., Tragic dimensions in Mark: BibTB 19 (1989) 94-99.

4951 **Weiss** Wolfgang, 'Eine neue Lehre in Vollmacht'; die Streit- und Schulgespräche des Markus-Evangeliums [Diss. ᴰ*Brandenburger* E., Mainz 1986]: BZNW 52. B 1989, de Gruyter. xi-236 p. DM 136 [CBQ 51,593]. 3-11-011789-4.

4952 **Williams** James G., Gospel against parable; Mark's language of mystery 1985 → 2,3789... 4,5021: ᴿCBQ 51 (1989) 386s (Karen A. *Barta*); CurrTM 16 (1989) 137s (M. J. *Wegener*, unfavorable); JTS 40 (1989) 180s (J. *Drury*); RHPR 69 (1989) 227s (É. *Trocmé*).

4953 *Winkler* J., Jesus and Francis as gospel makers; an experience in kenosis [Mark shows Jesus as lowly]: RRel 47 (1988) 481-494.

4954 **Zwick** Reinhold, Montage im Markusevangelium; Studien zur narra-tiven Organisation der ältesten Jesuserzählung [kath. Diss. Rg., ᴰ*Schut-termayr* G.]: SBB 18. Stu 1989, KBW. xvi-652 p. DM 39 [TR 86,163]. 3-460-00181-X.

F6.3 **Evangelii Marci versiculi 1,1 ...**

4955 **Oyen** Geert van, De summaria in Marcus... 1,14-8,26 [diss. 1987, ᴰ*Neirynck* F.]: SNTAux 12, 1987 → 3,4824; 4,5029: ᴿCBQ 51 (1989) 760s (J. *Gillman*); JBL 108 (1989) 729s (H. *Boers*); RivB 37 (1989) 371-4 (V. *Fusco*); TsTNijm 29 (1989) 65 (P. J. *Farla*).

4955* a) *Marcus* Joel, 'The time has been fulfilled!' (Mark 1:15); – b) *Schaberg* Jane, Mark 14.52, early Christian Merkabah imagery? → 130, FMARTYN J., 49-68 / 69-94.

4956 *Bianchi* Enzo, Esci da costui! (Mc 1,21-28): ParSpV 19 (1989) 109-137.

4957 *Giesen* Heinz, Dämonenaustreibungen — Erweis der Nähe der Herr-schaft Gottes: Zu Mk 1,21-28: TGegw 32 (1989) 24-37.

4958 *Wojciechowski* Michał, The touching of the leper (Mark 1,40-45) as a historical and symbolic act of Jesus: BZ 33 (1989) 114-9.

4959 *Briscoe* Peter, Faith confirmed through conflict — the Matthean redaction of Mark 2:1-3:6 [= Mt 9,1-17 + 12:1-14]: → 165, Mem. RYAN D., Back to the sources 1989, 104-128.

4960 **Kiilunen** Jarmo, [Mk 2,1-3,6] Die Vollmacht im Widerstreit 1985 → 1,4822: ᴿStPatav 36 (1989) 625s (G. *Segalla*).

4961 a) *Luck* Ulrich, Was wiegt leichter? Zu Mk 2,9; – b) *Dormeyer* Detlev, Die Familie Jesu und der Sohn der Maria im Markusevangelium (3,20f.31-35; 6,3): → 68, FGNILKA J., Vom Urchristentum 1989, 103-8 / 109-135.

4962 *Koch* D.-A., Jesu Tischgemeinschaft mit Zöllnern und Sündern; Erwägungen zur Entstehung von Mk 2,13-17: → 131, FMARXSEN W., Jesu Rede 1989, 57-73.

4963 *Bianchi* Enzo, Gesù alla tavola dei peccatori, amico dei pubblicani e delle prostitute; Mc 2,13ss e par.: ParSpV 20 (1989) 127-149.

4964 *Mateos* Juan, [Mc 2,16s ...] Algunas notas sobre el evangelio de Marcos: FgNt 2 (1989) 197-204.

4965 *LaVerdiere* E., [Mk 2,23-6,6] Jesus and the New Israel: Emmanuel 94 (1988) 322-9 ... [< NTAbs 33,27].

4966 **Roure Muntada** Joan, Jesús y la figura de David en Mc 2,23-26; antecedentes y medios literarios: diss. Pont. Ist. Biblico, ᴰ*Lentzen-Deis* Fritzleo. R 1989s. – ActaPIB 9,6 (1989s) 518.

4967 *Wachinger* Lorenz, [Mk 3,1-6...] Kreativ werden; das Gefühl lockern: BLtg 62 (1989) 229-235.

4968 *Klauck* Hans-J., [Mk 3,14] Die Auswahl der Zwölf [< Dienender Glaube 60 (1984) 351-4] ➤ 292, Gemeinde 1989, 131-6.

4969 *Nkwoka* A.O., Mark 3:19b-21, a study on the charge of fanaticism against Jesus: BibleBh 15 (1989) 205-221.

4970 *a) Stock* Klemens, La famiglia di Gesù si vergogna di lui; Mc 3,20s; – *b) Mosetto* Francesco, 'Chi si vergognerà di me...' Mc 8,38: ParSpV 20 (1989) 105-126 / 151-163.

4971 *Fay* Greg, Introduction to incomprehension; the literary structure of Mark 4:1-34: CBQ 51 (1989) 65-81.

4972 *Wagner* Marc, Le langage imagé de la venue du Règne de Dieu; étude de Marc 4/1-34: ÉTRel 64 (1989) 1-11.

4973 *a) Beauchamp* Paul, Paraboles de Jésus, vie de Jésus; l'encadrement évangélique et scripturaire des paraboles (Mc 4,1-34); – *b) Fusco* Vittorio, Mc 4,1-34; la section des paraboles; – *c) Giroud* Jean-Claude, La parabole ou l'opacité incontournable; à propos de Mc 4,1-34: ➤ 576, Paraboles 1987/9, 151-170 / 219-234 / 235-246.

4974 *Lohfink* Gerhard, *a)* Die Metaphorik der Aussaat im Gleichnis vom Sämann (Mk 4,3-9) [< ᶠ*Dupont* J., À cause de l'Évangile 1985, 211-228]: – *b)* Das Gleichnis vom Sämann (Mk 4,3-9) [< BZ 30 (1986) 36-69]: ➤ 300, Studien zum NT 1989, 131-147 / 91-130.

4975 **Beavis** Mary Ann, Mark's audience; the literary and social setting of Mark 4,11-12 [diss. Cambridge, ᴰ*Hooker* Morna, 1987]: JStNT supp. 33. Sheffield 1989, Academic. 261 p. £25. 1-85075-215-X.

4976 *Collins* R.F., [Mk 4,26-29] The story of a seed growing by itself; a parable for our times: Emmanuel 94 (1988) 446-452 [< NTAbs 33,161].

4977 *Strelan* J.G., 'For thine are the statistic'? Sermon study on Mark 4,26-29 [not evolutionary growth]: LuthTJ 22,1 (Adelaide 1988) 32-36 [< NTAbs 33,28].

4979 *La Verdiere* E., [Mk 4,35-5,20] Journey to the Gentiles: Emmanuel 94 (NY 1988) 554-6 [95 (1989) 74-79. 138-144. 102-8 [< NTAbs 33,310].

4980 *Tromp* Nico, Zonder geloof vaart niemand wel: over Marcus 4,35-41: Geest en Leven 65 (1988) 215-7.

4980* *La Potterie* Ignace de, [Mk 6] Die wunderbare Brotvermehrung; ihr Sinn und ihre Bedeutung im Leben Jesu: IkaZ 18 (1989) 207-221.

4981 *Matera* Frank J., The incomprehension of the disciples and Peter's confession (Mark 6,14-8,30): Biblica 70 (1989) 153-172; franç. 172.

4982 *Neirynck* F., *a)* Marc 6,14-16 et par. [opposition soit de BOISMARD soit de ROLLAND à la suite de GRIESBACH, à une filiation directe entre les évangiles]; – *b)* Kaì élegon en Mc 6,14: ETL 65 (1989) 105-9 / 110-8.

4983 *Pereira da Silva* Querubim J., História – mediadora de Revelação; autenticidade histórica do milagre da Multiplicação dos Pães (Mc 6,30-44 e paralelos; Mc 8,1-10 e paralelos): HumT 9 (1988) 3-50.

4984 **Both** Roger P., [Mk 7] Jesus and the laws of purity: JStNT Sup 13, 1986 ➤ 2,3809 ... 4,5047: ᴿBZ 33 (1989) 145-8 (K. *Müller*).

4985 **Stock** Klemens, Il cammino di Gesù verso Gerusalemme, Marco 8,27-10,52. R 1989, Pont. Ist. Biblico. ii-162 p.

4986 a) *Maggioni* Bruno, [Mc 8,34] 'Chi vuole essere mio discepolo rinneghi se stesso'; – b) *Levi* Abramo, 'Sentitela alla maniera di Gesù Cristo' (Fil 2,5-11): Servitium 3,65 (Bergamo 1989) 491-8 / 499-509.

4987 *Rebell* Walter, 'Sein Leben verlieren' (Mark 8.35 parr.) als Strukturmoment vor- und nachösterlichen Glaubens: NTS 35 (1989) 202-218.

4988 *Marcus* Joel, Mark 9,11-13, 'as it has been written' [... problem of the violent fate of Elijah]: ZNW 80 (1989) 42-63.

4988* **Chu** Samuel W., [Mk 9,20] The healing of the epileptic boy in Mark; its structure and its theological implications: diss. Vanderbilt. Nv 1988. – RTLv 21,544.

4989 *Iersel* B. M. F. van, Mark 9,43-48 in a martyrological perspective: → 17, ᶠBARTELINK G., Fructus 1989, 333-342.

4990 *Làconi* Mauro, *Casali* Michele, [Mc 10,1-12; 7,8-13; Mt 10,11-14; 5,31s] Posizioni pastorali su matrimonio e famiglia nel Nuovo Testamento: → 627, SacDoc 34,3s (1989) 102-123.

4991 ᴱ**Pizzolato** Luigi F. [→ 4678*] Per foramen acus [Mc 10,25; Mt 19,24; Lc 18,25] 1986 → 2,3572. – ᴿMaia 41 (1989) 163-5 (F. *Giovannini*); MélSR 46 (1989) 48-50 (A.-G. *Hamman*).

4991* *Asmussen* J. P. [needle's eye, (not camel, through anchor-cable) in Arabic, Armenian etc.]: → 93, ᶠHUMBACH H. Studia iranica 1986...

4992 *Seeley* David, [Mk 10,45; 14,24] Was Jesus like a philosopher? The evidence of martyrological and wisdom motifs in Q, pre-Pauline traditions, and Mark: → 589, SBL Seminars 1989, 540-9.

4993 *Smith* Stephen H., The literary structure of Mark 11:1-12:40: NT 31 (1989) 104-124; p. 105, *Stock* K. sensitive to the situation.

4994 **Füssel** Kuno, [Mk 11,7-13,2] Drei Tage mit Jesus im Tempel; Einführung in die materialistische Lektüre der Bibel für Religionsunterricht, Theologiestudium und Pastoral. Münster 1987, Liberación. 172 p. DM 34,80 pa. – ᴿRelStR 15 (1989) 262 (J. H. *Elliott*).

4995 *Neusner* Jacob, [Mk 11,15-19 → 4,5058] a) Money-changers in the Temple; the Mishnah's explanation: NTS 35 (1989) 287-290; – b) Geldwechsler im Tempel — von der Mischna her erklärt, ᵀ*Betz* Isolde: TZBas 45 (1989) 81-84.

4996 *Evans* Craig A., [Mk 11,17] Jesus' action in the Temple; cleansing or portent of destruction?: CBQ 51 (1989) 237-270.

4997 **Dowd** Sharyn, Prayer, power, and the problem of suffering; Mark 11:22-25 in the context of Markan theology → 4,5059 [diss. Emory, Atlanta 1986, ᴰ*Holladay* C. R.: SBL diss. 105. Atlanta 1985, Scholars. x-186 p. $18; pa. $12. 1-555-40251-8; 2-6 [NTAbs 33,244]. – ᴿExpTim 100 (1988s) 389 (C. S. *Rodd*, also briefly on 10 other SBL new volumes).

4998 *Alegre* Xavier, La paràbola dels vinyaters homicides segons la versió de Marc (Mc 12,1-12): → 69*, ᶠGOMÀ I., RCatalT 14 (1989) 163-173; Eng. 174.

4999 a) *Trimaille* Michel, La parabole des vignerons meurtriers (Mc 12,1-12); – b) *Duplantier* Jean-Pierre, Les vignerons meurtriers; le travail d'une parabole: → 576, Paraboles 1987/9, 247-258 / 259-270.

5000 *Milavec* Aaron A., [Mk 12,1-11] Mark's parable of the wicked husbandmen as reaffirming God's predilection for Israel: JEcuSt 26 (1989) 289-312.

5001 **Kiilunen** Jarmo, Das Doppelgebot der Liebe in synoptischer Sicht; ein redaktionskritischer Versuch über Mk 12,28-34 und die Parallelen:

Annales B-250. Helsinki 1989, Acad. Sc. Fennica. 110 p. 951-41-0609-1.

5002 *Drączkowski* Franciszek, ❷ [Mc 12,30] 'Amare Dio con tutta la mente' secondo l'interpretazione di CLEMENTE Alessandrino: ➤ 51, [F]EBOROWICZ W. = VoxPa 15 (1988) 603-620; ital. 620.

5003 **Geddert** Timothy J., Watchwords; Mark 13 in Markan eschatology [diss. [D]*Marshall* I.]: JStNT supp 26. Sheffield 1989, JStOT. 352 p. £25. 1-85075-127-7.

5004 **Mateos** J., Marcos 13; el grupo cristiano en la historia 1987 ➤ 3,4871; 570 p.: [R]Proyección 35 (1988) 72s (F. *Contreras*).

5005 **Mussner** Franz, [Mk 13] Was lehrt Jesus über das Ende der Welt[3rev] [([1]1958) [2rev]1964 + 2 Adventspredigten 1985s]. FrB 1987, Herder. 92 p. DM 12. – [R]TR 85 (1989) 458 (T. *Söding*).

5006 *Ruiz de Gopegui* J. A., A vigilância escatológica em constante conflito com as especulações apocalípticas; ensaio de leitura teológica de Mc 13: PerspT 20,52 (1988) 339-358 [< NTAbs 33,312].

5007 *Dautzenberg* Gerhard, Das Wort von der weltweiten Verkündigung des Evangeliums (Mk 13,10) und seine Vorgeschichte: ➤ 197, [F]TRILLING W., Christus bezeugen 1989, 110-165.

5008 *Clements* Ronald E., [Mk 13,14] Apocalyptic, literacy, and the canonical tradition: ➤ 21, [F]BEASLEY-MURRAY G., Eschatology 1988, 15-27.

F6.8 **Passio secundum Marcum**, 14,1 ... [➤ F5.3].

5009 **Senior** Donald, The Passion of Jesus in the Gospel of Mark 1984 ➤ 1,4879; 2,3843: [R]TXav 39 (1989) 499-501 (R. *Schneck*).

5010 **Senior** Donald, La passione di Gesù nel vangelo di Marco 1988 ➤ 4,5067: [R]ParVi 34 (1989) 473s (M. *Orsatti*).

5011 **Smith** Richard, Hang Jesus [Mark's Passion as cartoon-strip]. L 1989, Bow Mission. 20 p. £0.95 pa. [TLond 92,350: significant].

5012 **Sommer** Urs, Die Passionsgeschichte des Markusevangeliums; Überlegungen zur Bedeutung der Geschichte für den Glauben: ev. Diss. [D]*Weder*. Zürich 1988s. – TR 85 (1989) 513.

5013 **Feldmeier** Reinhard, Die Krise des Gottessohnes; die Gethsemaneerzählung als Schlüssel der Markuspassion [D]1987 ➤ 3,4873; 4,5069: [R]ScripTPamp 21 (1989) 350s (K. *Limburg*); TLZ 114 (1989) 593-5 (A. *Suhl*: hervorragend).

5014 **Ruhland** Maria, Die Markuspassion aus der Sicht der Verleugnung [14,27-72] 1987 ➤ 3,4872; 4,5072: [R]CBQ 51 (1989) 571s (P. *Rogers*); JTS 40 (1989) 182-5 (W. R. *Telford*).

5016 *Viviano* Benedict T., The High Priest's servant's ear; Mark 14:47: RB 96 (1989) 71-80; franç. 71.

5017 **Herron** Robert W., Mark's account of Peter's denial of Jesus; a representative history of interpretation of Mark 14:54,66-72: diss. Rice, [D]*Nielson* N. Houston 1989. 313 p. 90-12808. – DissA 50 (1989s) 3984-A.

5018 *Marcus* Joel, Mark 14:61: 'Are you the Messiah-Son-of-God?': NT 31 (1989) 125-141.

5019 *Rodgers* P., Mark 15:28 [Is 53:12 citation authentic]: EvQ 61 (1989) 61-64.

5020 *Lincoln* Andrew T., The promise and the failure; Mark 16:7,8: JBL 108 (1989) 283-300.

5021 **Magness** J. Lee, Sense and absence ... ending of Mk 1986 → 2,3858 ...
4,5078: RTLZ 114 (1989) 884s (P. *Pokorny*).

XII. Opus Lucanum

F7.1 *Opus Lucanum* – **Luke-Acts**

5022 *Athyal* Abraham P., Towards a soteriology for the Indian society;
guidelines from Luke-Acts: Bible Bhashyam 14 (1988) 132-148.

5023 *Balch* David L., Comments on the genre and a political theme of
Luke-Acts; a preliminary comparison of two Hellenistic historians
[DIONYSIUS of Halicarnassus, model for JOSEPHUS Flavius]: → 589, SBL
Seminars 1989, 343-361.

5024 **Bock** Darrell L., Proclamation from prophecy and pattern; Lucan OT
Christology 1987 → 3,4898; 4,5081 [not 'theology']: RCBQ 51 (1989) 148s
(F. W. *Danker*); ÉTRel 64 (1989) 84s (B. *Corsani*); JBL 108 (1989) 346-8
(M. C. *Parsons*); TLZ 114 (1989) 115s (M. *Rese*).

5025 **Bovon** F., l'œuvre de Luc 1987 → 3,195; 4,5082: RProtestantesimo 44
(1989) 59s (P. *Tognina*); RBíbArg 51 (1989) 49-51 (R. *Krüger*); ScEspr 40
(1988) 382s (J.-Y. *Thériault*).

5026 **Bovon** F., Luc le théologien (1950-1975)²ʳᵉᵛ 1988 → 4,5082*: RCarthaginensia 5 (1989) 282 (J. F. *Cuenca*); CrNSt 10 (1989) 617s
(*Ngayihembako Mutahinga*); JBL 108 (1989) 345s (C. H. *Talbert*).

5027 **Brawley** Robert L., Luke-Acts and the Jews; conflict, apology, and
conciliation: SBL Mg 33, 1987 → 3,4902; 4,5084: RBiblica 70 (1989)
279-282 (R. C. *Tannehill*); CBQ 51 (1989) 552s (J. J. *Neyrey*); JBL 108
(1989) 348-350 (J. S. *Siker*); JQR 80 (1989s) 427-9 (D. R. *Schwartz*).

5028 **Carroll** John T., Response to the end of history; eschatology and
situation in Luke-Acts: SBL diss. 92 [Princeton 1986, DAdams D.] 1988
→ 4,5085: RBiblica 70 (1989) 276-8 (J. J. *Kilgallen*); CBQ 51 (1989) 553-5
(W. S. *Kurz*); JBL 108 (1989) 730-2 (A. J. *Mattill*); TLZ 114 (1989) 518s
(M. *Rese*).

5029 **Chance** J. Bradley, Jerusalem; the Temple and the New Age in
Luke-Acts 1988 → 4,5087; 0-86554-201-1: RRExp 86 (1989) 271 (J. E.
Jones).

5030 *Corsani* Bruno, Bulletin du Nouveau Testament; études lucaniennes:
ÉTRel 64 (1989) 83-93.

5031 **Crump** David M., Jesus the intercessor; prayer and Christology in
Luke-Acts: diss. Aberdeen. 560 p. BRDX-87294. – DissA 50 (1989s)
3266-A.

5032 **Dawsey** J., The literary unity of Luke-Acts; questions of style — a task
for literary critics: NTS 35 (1989) 48-66 [similarities yes, but also
differences to be taken into account].

5033 **Esler** Philip F., Community and Gospel in Luke-Acts; the social and
political motivations of Lucan theology: SNTS Mg 57, 1987 → 3,4908;
4,5090: RJBL 108 (1989) 161s (A. T. *Kraabel*); TLond 92 (1989) 52-54
(S. C. *Barton*); TS 50 (1989) 199s (R. J. *Cassidy*).

5034 **Fitzmyer** Joseph A., Luke the theologian; aspects of his teaching
[D'Arcy lectures, Oxford 1987]. NY 1989, Paulist. xiii-250 p. $8. 0-
8091-3058-0.

5035 *Fitzmyer* Joseph A., Preaching in the apostolic and subapostolic age:
→ 38, FBURGHARDT W., Preaching 1989, 19-35.

5036 **Frein** Brigid C.,   The literary significance of the Jesus-as-prophet motif in the Gospel of Luke and the Acts of the Apostles: diss. St. Louis Univ. 1989, ᴰ*O'Toole* R. 324 p. 90-00909. – DissA 50 (1989s) 2538-A.
Garrett Susan R.,   The demise of the devil; magic and the demonic in Luke's writings. Minneapolis 1989, Fortress.   ix-179 p. $17 → 5036*.

5037 **Gowler** David B.,   A socio-narratological character analysis of the Pharisees in Luke-Acts: diss. Southern Baptist Theol. Sem., ᴰ*Culpepper* R. A., 1989.   399 p. 90-08962. – DissA 50 (1989s) 2932-A.

5038 *Jackson* Don,   Luke and Paul; a theology of one spirit from two perspectives: JEvTS 32 (1989) 335-344.

5039 *Juel* Donald, Luke-Acts: → 377, Books 2 (1989) 171-202.

5040 **Kahl** Brigitte,   Armenevangelium und Heidenevangelium; 'Sola scriptura' und die ökumenische Traditionsproblematik im Lichte von Väterkonflikt und Väterkonsens bei Lukas 1987 → 3,4919: ᴿTLZ 114 (1989) 77 (R. *Stahl*).

5041 *Kilgallen* John J.,   'Peace' in the Gospel of Luke and Acts of the Apostles: StMiss 38 (1989) 55-79.

5042 **Klinghardt** Matthias,   Gesetz und Volk Gottes; das lukanische Verständnis des Gesetzes nach Herkunft, Funktion und seinem Ort in der Geschichte des Urchristentums [Diss. ᴰ*Berger* K., Heidelberg 1987: WUNT 2/32], 1988 → 4,5098;   DM 89 pa.: ᴿTR 85 (1989) 458-460 (F. *Mussner*); TsTNijm 29 (1989) 290 (G. *Bouwman*).

5043 **Koet** B. J.,   Five studies on interpretation of Scripture in Luke-Acts [< A light for revelation to the Gentiles and for glory to thy people Israel; five studies on interpretation of Scripture in Luke-Acts: diss. Heerlen Univ. voor Theol. en Past. 1989, ᴰ*Menken* M.: Lv, Univ./Peeters.   178 p. – TsTNijm 29 (1989) 283; RTLv 21,545]: StNTAux 14, Lv 1989, Univ./Peeters.   198 p. 90-6186-330-9 / 90-6831-189-1.

5044 **Korn** Manfred,   Die vergangene Geschichte Jesu als Grundlage und Norm der Zeugen- und Kirchengeschichte nach Lukas: ev. Diss. ᴰ*Luz* U. Bern 1988s. – TR 85 (1989) 513.

5045 **Làconi** Mauro, San Lucas y su Iglesia. Estella 1987, VDivino.   140 p. – ᴿHumT 9 (1988) 108s (J. *Monteiro*).

5045* *Larsson* Edvin,   Lukas och Pentateuch: TsTKi 60 (1989) 293-9 [< IZBG 36, p. 199].

5046 *Moore* Stephen D.,   Luke's economy of knowledge [*Dillon* R. 1978; ...'Luke-Acts: seeing is believing'; 'Look-Ax; Luke's cutting glance'...]: → 589, SBL Seminars 1989, 38-56.

5047 **Nola** Mike F.,   Towards a positive understanding of the structure of Luke-Acts: diss. Aberdeen 1987.   475 p. BRDX-87428. – DissA 50 (1989s) 3268-A.

5048 *a) Pervo* Richard I.,   Must Luke and Acts belong to the same genre?; – *b) Sterling* Gregory E.,   Luke-Acts and apologetic historiography; – *c) Jones* David L.,   Luke's unique interest in historical chronology: → 589, SBL Seminars 1989, 309-316 / 326-342 / 378-387.

5049 *Plooy* G. P. V. du,   The design of God in Luke-Acts: Scriptura 25 (Stellenbosch 1988) 1-6 [< NTAbs 33,163].

5050 **Sanders** Jack T.,   The Jews in Luke-Acts, 1987 → 3,4930; 4,5106: ᴿCurrTM 16 (1989) 464 (E. *Krentz*); JBL 108 (1989) 162s (A. T. *Kraabel*).

5051 Sanders [BRAWLEY R.] Response to R. HANN review of The Jews in Luke-Acts 1987: JEcuSt [25 (1988) 461s] 26 (1989) 341-4 (344-6, Hann rejoinder).

5052 **Taeger** Jens-W., Der Mensch und sein Heil... bei Lukas [D1978] 1982 ► 63,5006: RTLZ 114 (1989) 272s (W. *Wiefel*).
5053 *Talbert* Charles H., Luke-Acts: ► 394, NT/Interpreters 1989, 297-320.
5054 **Tannehill** Robert C., The narrative unity of Luke-Acts I, 1986 ► 2,3901 ... 4,5110: RInterpretation 43 (1989) 78.80.82 (F. W. *Danker*); WestTJ 50 (1988) 352-5 (F. S. *Spencer*).
5055 *Weatherly* Jon A., The Jews in Luke-Acts: TyndB 40 (1989) 107-117.
5056 **York** John O., The rhetorical function of bi-polar reversal in Luke: diss. Emory, DRobbins V. Atlanta 1989. 241 p. 89-24722. – DissA 50 (1989s) 2101s-A [RelStR 16,190 title 'The function of reversal in Luke', so also RTLv 21,547].

F7.3 **Evangelium Lucae** – *Textus, commentarii.*

5057 **Bovon** François, Das Evangelium nach Lukas I. 1.1-9.50: EkK NT 3/1. Z/Neuk 1989, Benziger/Neuk-V. viii-524 p. DM 128 [CBQ 52,379]. 3-545-23117-8 / Neuk 3-7887-1270-8.
5058 [TMaignan Ann, Soler P.] présent. **Butin** J. D. †, L'Évangile selon Luc commenté par les Pères: Les Pères dans la foi, 1987 ► 4,5120: RNRT 111 (1989) 616 (V. *Roisel*); SR 18 (1989) 110 (P.-H. *Poirier*).
5059 **Danker** Frederick W., Jesus and the New Age; a commentary on St. Luke's Gospel²rev [¹1972 ► 54,3234]. Ph 1988, Fortress. xx-410 p. $20. – RCurrTM 16 (1989) 132s (E. M. *Krentz*).
5060 EElliott J. K., The New Testament in Greek, Luke II 1987 ► 3,4941; 4,5121: RClasR 39 (1989) 198-200 (J. N. *Birdsall*).
5061 *Petzer* J. J., The Oxford Greek New Testament [Luke 1984/7] — a review article: Neotestamentica 23 (1989) 83-92.
5062 **Fitzmyer** Joseph A., The Gospel according to Luke I-II: AnchorB 28, 1981/5 ► 62,8051 ... 4,5122: RScotJT 42 (1989) 258-260 (C. J. A. *Hickling*: 'no pages so moving as those on Peter's denial').
5063 **Fitzmyer** Joseph A., El evangelio según Lucas, I. Introducción general, TMinguez Dionisio 1986 ► 4,5123; II. 1-8,21; 764 p. III. (8,22-18,14). M 1987, Cristiandad. 84-7057-408; -23-X. – RActuBbg 26 (1989) 36 (X. *Alegre S.*).
5064 **García-Viana** Luis F., Evangelio según San Lucas, comentario: MensajeNT 3. S 1989, Sígueme. 232 p. 84-301-1084-4 [VDiv 84-7151-637-3).
5065 **Gooding** David, According to Luke; a new exposition of the Third Gospel. GR/Leicester 1987, Eerdmans/Inter-Varsity. 362 p. $13. – RCBQ 51 (1989) 151s (C. H. *Talbert*: for college, not fully up-to-date); CriswT 3 (1988s) 221s (S. *Sheeley*); EvQ 61 (1989) 263s (D. *Crump*).
5066 **Goulder** Michael D., Luke, a new paradigm; I. The Argument; II. Commentary Luke 1,1-9.50 / 9.51-24.53: JStNT sup 20. Sheffield 1989, JStOT. xi-452 p.; 372 p. $60 [Cornell]. 1-85075-101-3 [TDig 35,55: holds Q is a total error]. – RCommSev 22 (1989) 426s (M. de *Burgos*); ExpTim 101 (1989s) 711s (I. H. *Marshall*).
5067 *Karris* Robert J., The Gospel according to Luke: ► 384, NJBC (1989) 675-721.
5068 **Masini** Mario, Luca, il vangelo del discepolo: LoB 2.3, 1988 ► 4,5125: RAsprenas 36 (1989) 408s (A. *Rolla*); ParVi 34 (1989) 399 (C. *Ghidelli*); RivB 37 (1989) 510s (M. *Làconi*).
5069 **Meynet** Roland, L'Évangile selon saint Luc, analyse rhétorique I-II, 1988 ► 4,5126: RBiblica 70 (1989) 561-4 (R. C. *Tannehill*).

5070 Navarre Bible [^ECasciaro José M., al.; ^{TE}McCarthy Brian], St. Luke's Gospel, RSV and Neo-Vulgata with commentary. Dublin 1988, Four Courts. 285 p.; map. 1-85182-041-8; pa. 0-X.

5071 **Nolland** John, Luke 1-9:20: Word comm. Dallas 1989, Word. lxvi-459 p. [TS 51,572]. 0-8499-0234-7. – ^RExpTim 101 (1989s) 374s (C. S. Rodd).

5072 **Powell** Mark A., What are they saying about Luke? NY 1989, Paulist. 151 p. $6.

5073 **Sabourin** Léopold, L'Évangile de Luc, introduction et commentaire 1985 → 1,4946... 4,5129: ^RÉTRel 64 (1989) 87s (B. Corsani).

5074 **Sabourin** Léopold, Il Vangelo di Luca, introduzione e commento [1985 → 1,4946], ^T· R/CasM 1989, Pont. Univ. Gregoriana / Piemme. 392 p. Lit. 48.000. 88-7652-594-7 / 88-384-1347-9. – ^RCC 140 (1989,4) 402s (V. Fusco); ParVi 34 (1989) 398 (C. Ghidelli).

5075 **Stock** Klemens, Jesus – die Güte Gottes; Betrachtungen zum Lukas-Evangelium² [¹1984 → 65,4492]. Innsbruck 1989, Tyrolia. 159 p. [ActaPIB 9,460].

5076 **Tiede** David L., Luke: Augsburg Comm. 1988 → 4,5130; ^RRExp 86 (1989) 622 (J. E. Jones).

5077 **Vesco** Jean-Luc, Jérusalem/Luc 1988 → 4,5131: 0-8066-8858-0: ^RAngelicum 66 (1989) 329s (S. Jurič); ÉTRel 64 (1989) 92s (B. Corsani: good bibliography with no German titles); VSp 143 (1989) 489 (H. Cousin).

5078 **Zahn** T., Das Evangelium des Lukas⁴ [1920 + praef. Hengel M.] 1988 → 4,5134: ^RSWJT 32,1 (1989s) 54 (E. E. Ellis).

F7.4   *Lucae themata*   –   **Luke's Gospel, topics.**

5079 *a) Abraham* M. V., Good news to the poor in Luke's Gospel; – *b) Hemraj* S., Having nothing as one's own: Bible Bhashyam 14,1s (1988, all on poverty in Scripture) 65-77 / 50-64.

5080 **Aletti** Jean-Noël, L'art de raconter Jésus-Christ; l'écriture narrative de l'Évangile de Luc. P 1989, Seuil. 265 p. 2-02-010929-8 [EstBíb 47,577]. F 120.

5081 *Bataillon* L.-J., Les sources patristiques du commentaire de Bo-NAVENTURE sur Luc et HUGUES de Saint-Cher: → 33, ^FBOUGEROL J., Bonaventuriana 1988, 17-32.

5082 **Beck** Brian E., Christian character in the Gospel of Luke. L 1989, Epworth. viii-232 p. £7. 0-7162-0463-0. – ^RExpTim 101 (1989s) 312 (I. H. Marshall).

5083 **Beydon** France, En danger de richesse; le chrétien et les biens de ce monde selon Luc. Aubonne 1989, Moulin. 98 p. – ^RRHPR 69 (1989) 229 (J. C. Ingelaere).

5084 *Bundy* David, The anti-Marcionite commentary on the Lucan parables (Pseudo-EPHREM A): images in tension: Muséon 103 (1989) 111-123.

5085 *Casalegno* Alberto, Pobreza e riqueza no evangelho de Lucas, ^TOtacílio Leite José: PerspT 20 (1988) 9-33.

5086 *Dawsey* James M., Mathetaí (autoû) and Luke's concern for the sound of his Gospel [hoi mathetaì autoû occurs 30 times in Mt and 32 in Mk; Luke omits autoû when another aut- is near, or to avoid similar jangle, or just for metre]: MeliT 40,1 (1989) 59-62.

5087 *Derrett* J. D. M., New resolutions... Luke 1986 → 2,3923; 4,5137: ^RJRel 68 (1988) 586 (F. W. Danker); Salesianum 51 (1989) 352s (C. Bissoli); TLZ 114 (1989) 731s (C. Burchard).

5088 **Donnelly** Noel S.,   The Gospel of Luke; the pieties of its sources and author: diss. Edinburgh 1988. 300 p. BRD-86401. – DissA 50 (1989s) 1702-A.

5089 *Gowler* David B.,   Characterization in Luke; a socio-narratological approach: BibTB 19 (1989) 54-62.

5090 **Grassi** Joseph A.,   God makes me laugh; a new approach to Luke 1986 ↪ 2,3924; 4,5138*: ᴿBibTB 19 (1989) 38 (E. L. *Bode*).

5091 **Gueuret** Agnès,   La mise en discours... Luc ᴰ1987 ↪ 3,4967; 4,5139: ᴿÉTRel 64 (1989) 91s (B. *Corsani*).

5092 **Heininger** Bernhard R.,   Metaphorik, Erzählstruktur und szenisch-dramatische Gestaltung in den Sondergutgleichnissen bei Lukas: kath. Diss. ᴰ*Klauck*. Würzburg 1988s. – TR 85 (1989) 520.

5093 **Hirunuma** Toshio,   The praxis of New Testament textual studies; how to use apparatus criticus Luke (I). Osaka 1989, Shin-Yaku-Kenkyu-Sya. x-294 p.

5094 *Klein* G. L.,   The challenge of Luke's Gospel: Emmanuel 95 (NY 1989) 250-5 [< NTAbs 33,313].

5095 **Lentini** Gerlando,   Il Vangelo di Luca oggi 1986 ↪ 3,4949: ᴿParVi 34 (1989) 303 (C. *Ghidelli*).

5096 *Lentzen-Deis* Fritzleo,   Arm und reich aus der Sicht des Evagelisten Lukas: ↪ 402, ᴱ*Kamphaus* F., ... und machen einander reich 1989, 17-68.

5097 **Moxnes** Halvor,   The economy of the Kingdom; social conflict and economic relations in Luke's Gospel: OvBT 1989 ↪ 4,5141*: ᴿExpTim 101 (1989s) 99s (C. S. *Rodd*: if only Luke knew as much about 'Palestinian society' as EISENSTADT-RONIGER and SAHLINS); TTod 46 (1989) 468 (L. T. *Johnson*).

5098 **Nebe** Gottfried,   Prophetische Züge im Bilde Jesu bei Lukas [Hab.-Diss. Bochum 1986 ᴰ*Burchard* C. J.: BW 127. Stu 1989, Kohlhammer. vii-127 p. DM 64 [TR 86,75]. 3-17-010576-0.

5099 ᴱ**Neirynck** F.,   L'Évangile de Luc²ʳᵉᵛ = ¹1973, 12 art., avec notes 1989, et supplément 7 art.: *Friedrichsen* T. A. on Mt-Lk agreements 335-391(-8); *Schreck* C. J., Lk 4,16-30, 399-471; *Judge* P. J., Lk 7,1-10, 473-489; *Verheyden* J., Lk 21, 491-516; *Matera* F. J., Lk 22s, 517-551; *Bouwman* G., Act 1,1, 553-565]: BiblETL 32. Lv 1989, Univ./Peeters. x-590 p. Fb 2200. 90-6186-280-9 / 90-6831-196-4.

5100 *Rodríguez Carmona* Antonio,   Leer a San Lucas en el ciclo litúrgico C: Proyección 36 (1989) 27-39.

5101 **Scheffler** Eben H.,   Suffering in Luke's Gospel: diss. Pretoria 1989, ᴰ*Toit* A. du. – DissA 50 (1989s) 1342-A.

5102 **Segbroeck** Frans van,   The Gospel of Luke; a cumulative bibliography 1973-1988: BiblETL 88. Lv 1989, Univ./Peeters. 241 p. Fb 1200. 90-6186-327-9.

5102* *a)* **Steyn** G. J.,   Die manifestering van Septuaginta-invloed in die Sondergut-Lukas; – *b)* **Zyl** D. M. van,   Die onkunde van die Jode en hulle verwerping van die evangelie [Lk]: HervTS 45 (Pretoria 1989) 864-873 / 44 (1988) 909-916 [< IZBG 36, p. 179s].

5103 *Wallis* E. E.,   Aristotelian echoes in Luke's discourse structure: OPTAT 2,2 (Dallas 1988) 81-88 [< NTAbs 33,314].

5104 **Welzen** H.,   [Beschrijving van de methode p. 1-21; Lc 12,13-21, p. 83-109: conclusion-synthesis p. 281-321 embodying also his doctorate on Lk 15,1-17,10; the rest of the articles (infra) are applications to separate parables of Luke]: Parabelverhalen in Lucas: van semiotiek naar pragmatiek: TFT 8. Tilburg 1987, Univ. xiii-321 p. ƒ47.50. – RCBQ 51 (1989) 772s (W. A. *Vogels*).

5105 **Wojcik** Jan, The road to Emmaus; reading Luke's Gospel. West Lafayette 1989, Purdue Univ. vi-168 p. $21.50 [JBL 109,381].

F7.5 *Infantia, cantica* – **Magnificat, Benedictus: Luc. 1-3.**

5106 **Muñoz Iglesias** S., Nacimiento e infancia de Juan y de Jesús en Lucas 1-2: EvInf 3, 1987 ➤ 3,4996; 4,5151 [I. 1983 ➤ 64,4929; II. 1986 ➤ 3,4981]: RCommSev 22 (1989) 92s (M. de *Burgos, 2s); EstE 64 (1989) 564 (F. Pastor Ramos*); RBíbArg 51 (1989) 47-49 (R. *Krüger*); ScripT-Pamp 21 (1989) 927-9 (J. M. *Casciaro*).

5107 **Berlingieri** Giovanni, Il lieto annuncio della nascita e il concepimento del precursore di Gesù (Lc 1,5-23.24-25) nel quadro dell'opera lucana; uno studio tradizionale e redazionale: diss. Pont. Univ. Gregoriana, DRasco E. R 1989. 403 p. – RTLv 21,544.

5108 *Levi* Abramo, [Lc 1,5...] Esempi di vocazione nel NT: Servitium 3,61 (Bergamo 1989) 24-34.

5109 *Browne* Gerald M., The Sunnarti Luke [1,27, Old Nubian]: ZPapEp 77 (1989) 293-6; facsim.; pl. IV-B.

5110 *a) Vicent Cernuda* Antonio, La intención de *en gastrí* en Lc 1,31; – *b) Simón Muñoz* Alfonso, El camino de la visitación; precisiones a Lc 1,39; – *c) Guerra Gómez* Manuel, [➤ 5126*ab*] '... *Eudokía* (bondad, benevolencia) en medio de los hombres', nombre o designación de Jesucristo en el himno de los Ángeles (Lc 2,14 y comienzo del 'Gloria...' de la Misa): ➤ 69*, FGOMÀ I., RCatalT 14 (1989) 175-184 / 185-200 / 202-221; castellano; Eng. 184.201.222.

5111 *Legrand* Lucien, [Lk 1,32s] The angel Gabriel and politics; Messianism and Christology: IndTSt 26 (1989) 1-21.

5112 *Marín Heredia* Francisco, Difícil equilibrio en Lc 1,35*b*: Carthaginensia 5 (1989) 19-30.

5113 *Serra* Aristide M., 'Benedetto il frutto del tuo seno!' (Lc 1,42); il grembo materno, luogo della benedizione di Dio: ➤ 611, Come leggere 1988/9, 78-101.

5114 *González Novalín* José Luis, Los comentarios al 'Magnificat' en el período renacentista: ➤ 69*, FGOMÀ I., RCatalT 14 (1989) 541-551 castellano; Eng. 552.

5115 *Herrera Aceves* J. Jesús, El Magníficat, canto de liberación: EfMex 6 (1988) 367-390.

5116 *Krüger* R., El Magníficat de Lucas 1,46-55... recuerdo agradecido convertido en anuncio de una auténtica alternativa para la humanidad: CuadT 9,1 (BA 1988) 77-83 [< NTAbs 33,164].

5117 TELöfström Inge, Marias Lovsång, M. LUTHERs tolkning av 'Magnificat'. SH 1987, Proprius. 113 p.; ill. [LuJb 56, p. 167].

5118 **López Melús** F. M., María de Nazaret, la Virgen del Magnificat 1988 ➤ 4,5147: RStLeg 29 (1988) 347 (F. F. *Ramos*).

5119 *Mezzacasa* F., El cántico de liberación de María; una reflexión catequética de Lc. 1,46-56: CuadT 9,2 (BA 1988) 133-150 [< NTAbs 33,314].

5120 *Spencer* A. B., [Lk 1,46-55] Mary's influence on Jesus' message: Daughters of Sarah 14,6 (Ch 1988) 28s [< NTAbs 33,165].

5121 **Valentini** Alberto, Il Magnificat 1987 ➤ 3,4993; 4,5162: RCBQ 51 (1989) 759s (S. B. *Marrow*); CC 140 (1989,2) 304s (K. *Stock*); ÉTRel 64 (1989) 291 (E. *Cuvillier*); Marianum 51 (1989) 643-6 (O. *da Spinetoli*).

5122 **Farris** Stephen, The hymns 1985 ➤ 1,4990 ... 4,5156: ᴿÉTRel 64 (1989) 88s (B. *Corsani*).

5123 **Zeilinger** Franz, Zum Lobpreis seiner Herrlichkeit; exegetische Erschliessung der neutestamentlichen Cantica im Stundenbuch. W 1988, Herder. 256 p. DM 36,80. – ᴿTPQ 137 (1989) 301s (H. *Giesen*); ZkT 111 (1989) 223s (M. *Hasitschka*).

5124 *Kilpatrick* G. D., Luke 2,4-5 and Leviticus 25,10: ZNW 80 (1989) 264s.

5125 *Heggen* F. J., 'Vrees niet, want zie, ik verkondig u een blijde boodschap die bestemd is voor heel het volk' (Lk 2,10): PrakT 16 (1989) 553 ... [< ZIT 90,131].

5126 *Guerra Gómez* Manuel, *a*) Análisis filológico-teológico y traducción del himno de los ángeles en Belén (Luc 2,14 y comienzo del 'Dóxa-Gloria' ... ➤ 5110*c*): Burgense 30 (1989) 31-86; – *b*) 'Hominibus bonae voluntatis', análisis filológico-teológico y traducción (Lc 2,14 y 'Gloria' de la Misa): ScripTPamp 21 (1989) 755-774; lat. 774; Eng. 775.

5126* *Dettloff* Werner, [Lk 2,16] Franziskus und die Weihnachtskrippe; der theologiegeschichtliche Hintergrund der Krippenfeier des hl. Franziskus von Assisi: FranzSt 70 (1988) 225-234.

5127 *Schlemmer* Cordula, Simeon und Hanna — der zwölfjährige Jesus im Tempel; Unterrichtshilfe zu Lukas 2,22-52: CLehre 42 (1989) ... 185-9 [< ZIT 90,196].

5128 *a) Longobardo* L., 'Una spada ti trafiggerà l'anima'; l'interpretazione di Lc 2,35 in ORIGENE: – *b*) *Mattai* G., Mater dolorosa; Maria e le sofferenze degli uomini; – *c*) *Ragozzino* G., La maternità verginale di Maria nel Corano; – *d*) *Rolla* A., Maria nell'ebraismo antico e recente: ➤ 721*b*, Maria nel cammino = Asprenas 36 (1989) 224-232 / 153-163 / 208-223 / 193-207.

5129 *Brown* R. E., Die dritte Weihnachtsgeschichte, Lukas 2,41-52 [< An adult Christ at Christmas 1985, 37-50]: TGegw 31 (1988) 209-217.

5130 *Crampsey* J. A., [Lk 2,41-51 ...] Jesus and discernment [how he came to a sense of himself]: Way Sup 64 (1989) 19-28 [< NTAbs 33,313].

5131 **Spensley** Barbara E., Luke 3 [exc. genealogy]; structure, interpretation and functions: diss. Leeds 1989. 350 p. BRD-88416. – DissA 50 (1989s) 3940-A.

5132 *Bartina* S., ¿El padre de la Virgen María se llamó Joaquín o Eliaquín? (Lc 3,23): EphMar 39 (1989) 95-99.

5133 *Steyn* Gert J., [Lk 3,36] The occurrence of 'Kainam' in Luke's genealogy; evidence of Septuagint [Gn 11,12] influence?: ETL 65 (1989) 409-411.

F7.6 **Evangelium Lucae 4,1 ...**

5134 *Gutiérrez* G., [Lc 4,16-30] La primera declaración mesiánica: Páginas 13,92 (Lima 1988) 6-9.

5135 **Shin Kyo-Seon** Gabriel, Die Ausrufung des endgültigen Jubeljahres durch Jesus in Nazaret (Lk 4,16-30): Diss. ᴰ*Kirchschläger* W. Luzern 1989. – RTLv 21,547 (> Fra, Lang).

5136 **Noorda** Sijbolt J., Historia vitae magistra; een beoordeling van de geschiedenis van de uitleg van Lucas 4,16-30 als bijdrage aan de hermeneutische discussie: diss. Utrecht 1989, ᴰ*Baarda* T. Amst 1989, Vrije Univ. 344 p. ƒ72.50 – TsTNijm 29 (1989) 285; RTLv 21, p. 538. 90-6256790-8.

5137 *Kilgallen* John J., Provocation in Luke 4,23-24: Biblica 70 (1989) 511-6.

5138 *Rius-Camps* Josep, [Lc 5,1; 9,51...] El *kai autós* en los encabezamientos lucanos, ¿una fórmula anafórica?: FgNt 2 (1989) 187-192.

5139 *Levi* Abramo, [Lc 6,13.9] 'non potete servire a Dio e a mammona'; del denaro 'so io quello che farò': Servitium 3,62 (Bergamo 1989) 165-176.

5140 *Vaage* Leif E., [Lk 6,20-49; KLOPPENBORG J. 1987] Composite texts and oral myths; the case of the 'Sermon' ([Q] 6:20b-49]: ➤ 589, SBL Seminars 1989, 424-439.

5141 *Kremer* Jacob, Mahnungen zum innerkirchlichen Befolgung des Liebesgebotes; textpragmatische Erwägungen zu Lk 6,37-45: ➤ 68, FGNILKA, Vom Urchristentum 1989, 231-245.

5142 *Sabugal* Santos, 'Joven, te lo digo, levántate' (Lc 7,11-17), análisis histórico: EstAg 23 (1988) 469-482.

5143 *Ferry* Bernard-Marie, La pécheresse pardonnée (Lc 7,36-50); pourquoi verse-t-elle des pleurs?: EsprVie 99 (1989) 174-6.

5144 *Hurst* Antony, [Lk 7,36-50] The woman with the ointment: ExpTim 101 (1989s) 304.

5145 *Weren* W., *a)* De parabel van het zaad (Lc 8,1-21) [only]; – *b)* ... van de wijnbouwers (Lc 19,1-27): ➤ 5104, *Welzen* H. 1987, 22-54 / 251-280.

5146 *Sim* David C., The women followers of Jesus; the implications of Luke 8:1-3: HeythJ 30 (1989) 51-62.

5147 *Westendorf* Craig, The parable of the sower (Luke 8:4-15) in the seventeenth century: Lutheran Quarterly 3,1s (Ridgefield NJ 1989) 49-64 [< ZIT 89,646].

5148 *Vaage* Leif E., [Lk 7,33...] Q¹ and the historical Jesus; some peculiar sayings (7:33-34; 9:57-58, 59-60; 14:26-27): ➤ 160*, FROBINSON J. = Forum 5,2 (1989) 159-176.

5149 *Neirynck* F., *Friedrichsen* T.A., Note on Luke 9,22 [not un-Lukan]; a response to M.D. GOULDER: ETL 65 (1989) 390-4.

5150 *Reid* Barbara O., What were they talking about at the Transfiguration? A redaction-critical study of Luke 9:28-36: BiRes 34 (Ch 1989) 19-31.

5151 *Kilgallen* John J., [Lk 9,46-48] This child 'in my name': ➤ 175, Mem. SCHODER R., Daidalikon 1989, 183-192.

F7.7 *Iter hierosolymitanum* – *Lc 9,51...* – **Jerusalem journey.**

5152 **Kozar** Joseph F., An investigation of the narrative frame of a journey to Jerusalem in the Lucan travel narrative: diss. St. Michael, DGuenther H. Toronto 1989 [microfiche Ottawa Nat. Library]. – RTLv 21,545.

5153 **Moessner** David P., Lord of the banquet; the literary and theological significance of the Lukan travel narrative [Diss. Basel 1983, DReicke B.: Jesus like Moses in Luke-Acts]. Minneapolis 1989, Fortress. xviii-358 p. 0-8006-0893-3. – RExpTim 101 (1989s) 346s (Margaret *Davies*); SWJT 32,3 (1989s) 56 (E. E. *Ellis*).

5154 *Brodie* Thomas L., The departure for Jerusalem (Luke 9,51-56) as a rhetorical imitation of Elijah's departure for the Jordan (2 Kgs 1,1-2,6): Biblica 70 (1989) 96-109.

5155 *Steinhauser* Michael G., Putting one's hand to the plow; the authenticity of [Luke] Q 9:61-62: ➤ 160*, FROBINSON J. = Forum 5,2 (1989) 141-8.

5156 *Brodie* Thomas L., Luke 9:57-62; a systematic adaptation of the divine challenge to Elijah (1 Kings 19): ➤ 589, SBL Seminars 1989, 237-245.

5156* **Uro** Risto, [Lk 10,2-16... Mt 9,37-10,40...] Sheep among the wolves; a study on the mission instructions of Q, 1987 ➤ 3,4207: RCBQ 51 (1989)

757-9 (H. *Fleddermann*); JBL 108 (1989) 337-9 (J. S. *Kloppenborg*); JTS 40 (1989) 185-7 (D. R. *Catchpole*); TLZ 114 (1989) 890 (G. *Haufe*).

5157 *Schaik* T. van, [Lc 10,25-37; 13,1-9] *a*) De barmhartige Samaritaan; – *b*) Die vijgeboom met kans op vruchten [The fig tree that might bear]: ⇥ 5104, *Welzen* H., Parabelverhalen 1987, 55-82 / 110-132.

5158 *Cooke* R. A., [Lk 10,29-37] What is a person worth? The Good Samaritan problem reconsidered [such generosity cannot be legislated]: Listening 23,3 (Glenview IL 1988) 198-213 [< NTAbs 33,166].

5159 *Matthieu* L., *al.*, Le bon Samaritain: Évangile Aujourd'hui 141 (1989) [< REB 49,764].

5160 **Légasse** Simon, 'Et qui est mon prochain?' Étude sur l'agapè dans le NT: LDiv 136. P 1989, Cerf. 183 p. [RHPR 69,91]. 2-204-03044-9.

5161 *Beydon* France, À temps nouveau, nouvelles questions; Luc 10,38-42 [unum necessarium]: FoiVie 88,5 (CahBib 28, 1989) 25-32.

5162 *Brutschek* Jutta, Lukanische Anliegen in der Maria-Marta-Erzählung; zu Lk 10,38-42: *a*) GeistL 62 (1989) 84-96; – *b*) TJb (1989) 65-75.

5163 *Wall* Robert W., Martha and Mary (Luke 10,38-42) in the context of a Christian Deuteronomy: JStNT 35 (1989) 19-35.

5164 *Fritsch-Oppermann* Sybille, [Lk 10,40] Maria und Marta; eine Aufforderung zum geschwisterlichen Streit: Diakonie 15 (Stu 1989) 215-9 [< ZIT 78,677].

5165 *Tuckett* C. M., [Lk 11,5-8] Q, prayer, and the Kingdom: JTS [34 (1983) 407-424, *Catchpole* D. R.] 40 (1989) 367-376; rejoinder 377-388.

5166 *Kloppenborg* John S., [Lk 12,2-7...] The Q sayings on anxiety (Q 12: 2-7): ⇥ 160*, ᶠROBINSON J., Forum 5,2 (1989) 83-98.

5167 **Ammanathukunnel** Kurian, Abandonment to the Kingdom and God's care; an interpretation of Lk 12,13-34: diss. Pont. Univ. Gregoriana, nᵒ 3594, ᴰ*Lentzen-Deis* F., Roma 1989. 117 p. – RTLv 21,543.

5168 *Làconi* Mauro, *a*) [Lc 12,13-21] Ricchi davanti a Dio [... Luca ha scritto proprio così?]; – *b*) [Lc 13,1-9] La pazienza di Dio: SacDoc 34 (1989) 5-41 / 437-472.

5169 *a*) *März* Claus-Peter, Zur Vorgeschichte von Lk 12,35-48; Beobachtungen zur Komposition der Logientradition in der Redequelle; – *b*) *Pokorný* Petr, Lukas 15,11-32 und die lukanische Soteriologie: ⇥ 197, ᶠTRILLING W., Christus bezeugen 1989, 166-178 / 179-192.

5170 *Smit* D. J., Those were the critics, what about the real readers? An analysis of 65 published sermons and sermon guidelines on Luke 12:35-48 [blessed the servant found watchful]: Neotestamentica 23 (1989) 61-82, continuation of 22 (1988)...

5171 *Derrett* J. D. M., Christ's second baptism (Lk 12:50; Mk 10:38-40): ExpTim 100 (1988s) 294s.

5172 *a*) *Welzen* Huub, Loosening and binding; Luke 13,10-21 as programme and anti-programme of the gospel of Luke; – *b*) *Weren* Wim, Psalm 2 in Luke-Acts; an intertextual study: – *c*) *Schenk* Wolfgang, Luke as reader of Paul; observations on his reception: ⇥ 95, ᶠIERSEL B. van, Intertextuality 1989, 175-187 [187 on HAMM D.] / 189-203 / 127-139.

5173 *Green* Joel B., Jesus and a daughter of Abraham (Luke 13:10-17); test case for a Lucan perspective on Jesus' miracles: CBQ 51 (1989) 643-654.

5174 *Schüssler Fiorenza* Elisabeth, Lk 13:10-17; interpretation for liberation and transformation [St. Louis Univ. 33d Bellarmine lecture 1989, unabridged]: TDig 36 (1989) 303-319.

5175 *Giesen* Heinz, Verantwortung des Christen in der Gegenwart und Heilsvollendung; Ethik und Eschatologie nach Lk 13,24 und 16,16: TGegw 31 (1988) 218-228.

5176 *Isola* Antonino, Note sull'esegesi di Lc 13,24 nei Padri dei primi secoli: ➤ 759, Sangue VI, 1987/9, 741-753.

5177 *Tilborg* S. van, [Lc 14,1-24; 19,1-27] *a*) De parabel van de grote feestmaaltijd; – *b*) De koning en de tien slaven: ➤ 5104, *Welzen* H., Parabelverhalen 1987, 133-167 / 217-250.

5178 *Noël* T., [Lk 14,7-11] The parable of the wedding-guest; a narrative-critical interpretation: PerspRelSt 16,1 (1989) 17-27 [< NTAbs 33,316].

5179 *Stein* Robert H., Luke 14:26 and the question of authenticity: ➤ 160*, ᶠROBINSON J. = Forum 5,2 (1989) 187-192.

5180 *Agnew* Francis H., [Lk 15] The parables of divine compassion: BToday 27 (1989) 35-40.

5181 *Sheerin* Daniel, The theotokion *ho tēn eulogēmenēn* [incipit of a hymn]; its background in patristic exegesis of Luke 15.8-10, and western parallels: VigChr 43 (1989) 166-187.

5182 ᴱ**Galli** Giuseppe, [Lc 15,11-32] Interpretazione e invenzione... Figlio prodigo 1986/7 ➤ 3,543; 4,5197: ᴿRTLv 20 (1989) 89s (C. *Focant*).

5183 *Casey* Patrick J., A parable of God's love for sinners; Luke 15:11-32: CalvaryB 5,1 (1989) 28-42.

5184 *Cloete* G. D., *Smit* D. J., Luke 15:11-32, 'rejoicing with God': JTSAf 66 (1989) 62-73 [< ZIT 89,443].

5185 *Corlett* Tom, 'This *brother* of yours' [Lk 15,32 without italics would wrongly sound contemptuous, as the exact same idiom is generally rendered in Lk 15,30]: ExpTim 100 (1988s) 216.

5186 **Ireland** Dennis J., Stewardship and the kingdom of God; an exegetical and contextual study of the parable of the unjust steward in Luke 16:1-13: diss. Westminster Theol. Sem. ᴰ*Silva* M., 1989. 423 p. 89-18228. – DissA 50 (1989s) 1330-A.

5187 *Ireland* Dennis J., A history of recent interpretation of the parable of the unjust steward (Luke 16:1-13): WestTJ 51 (1989) 293-318.

5188 **Wilson** Paul S. [Lk 16,1-13] The lost parable of the generous landowner and other texts for imaginative preaching: QRMin 9,3 (1989) 80-99.

5189 *Kloppenborg* John S., The dishonoured master (Luke 16:1-8a): Biblica 70 (1989) 474-494; franç. 495.

5190 *Loader* William, Jesus and the rogue in Luke 16,1-8A; the parable of the unjust steward: RB 96 (1989) 518-532; franç. 518.

5191 *Reinmuth* Eckart, Ps.-PHILO, Liber antiquitatum biblicarum 33,1-5 und die Auslegung der Parabel Lk 16,19-31: NT 31 (1989) 16-38.

5192 *Vogels* Walter, Having or longing; a semiotic analysis of Luke 16:19-31: ÉglT 20 (1989) 27-46.

5193 *Iersel* B. van, [➤ 3,4968; 4,5139*; Lc 18,1-14] *a*) De rechter en de weduwe; – *b*) De Farizeeër en de tollenaar: ➤ 5104, *Welzen* H., Parabelverhalen 1987, 168-193 / 194-216.

5194 *Haudebert* P., Publicain: ➤ 882, Catholicisme XII,55 (1989) 269-272.

5195 *a*) *Schlosser* Jacques, Le pharisien et le publicain (Lc 18,9-14); – *b*) *Gueuret* Agnès, Le pharisien et le publicain et son contexte: ➤ 576, Paraboles 1987/9, 271-288 / 289-307.

5196 *a*) *Aletti* Jean-Noël, Lc 19,11-28; parabole des mines et/ou parabole du roi; remarques sur l'écriture parabolique de Luc; – *b*) *Panier* Louis, La parabole des mines; lecture sémiotique (Lc 19,11-27) [mais en tête des pages 'approche de l'organisation discursive']: ➤ 576, Paraboles 1987/9, 309-332 / 333-347.

5197 **McDaniel** Martin C., [Lk 19,12-27] Parables in context; Luke's parables of the Minas and the Wicked Tenants and their literary contexts: diss. Vanderbilt, ᴰ*Patte* D. Nv 1989. 381 p. 89-19706. – DissA 50 (1989s) 1690-A; RelStR 16,190.

5199 *Koester* Craig, [Lk 21,20] The origin and significance of the flight to Pella tradition [EUSEBIUS Hist. 3.5.3, not invented cf. Recog. Clem. 1,37.39; Lk 21:20-22] CBQ 51 (1989) 90-106.

5200 **Giblin** Charles H., The destruction of Jerusalem... Lk: AnBib 107, 1985 ➤ 1,5952... 4,5214: ᴿTLZ 114 (1989) 885s (M. *Rese*).

F7.8 Passio – Lc 22...

5201 *Cousin* Hugues, *al.* [Passion], L'originalité de Luc: DossB 22 (1988) 12-14. 19 [3-27].

5202 **Senior** Donald,   The Passion of Jesus in the Gospel of Luke: Passion Series 3. Wilmington 1989, Glazier. 192 p. $11 pa. 0-89453-461-0 [NTAbs 33,390].

5202* **Soards** Marion L.,   The Passion according to Luke (22) [ᴰ1984]: JStNT Sup 14, 1987 ➤ 3,5063; 4,5261: ᴿJBL 108 (1989) 154-6 (J. B. *Green*).

5203 **Tyson** Joseph B.,   The death of Jesus in Luke-Acts 1986 ➤ 2,4007: ᴿCBQ 51 (1989) 575s (D. *Senior*).

5204 *Heil* John P.,   Reader-response and the irony of Jesus before the Sanhedrin in Luke 22:66-71: CBQ 51 (1989) 271-284.

5205 *Matera* Frank J.,   Luke 22,56-71, Jesus before the *presbyterion*: ETL 65 (1989) 43-59.

5206 *Manus* Chris U.,   The universalism of Luke (23:6-12) and the motif of reconciliation; reflections on their implications in the African cultural context: AsiaJT 3 (Singapore 1989) 192-205.

5207 *Stock* Klemens,   Jesus der Retter nach Lk 23,35-43: ➤ 735, Salvezza 1988/9, 531-541.

5208 *Powell* J. Enoch, [Lk 23,46] 'Father, into thy hands...': JTS 40 (1989) 95s.

5209 *Gubler* M.-L., [Lk 24,1-53] *a)* Eine biblisch orientierte Pastoral: Diakonia 20,1 (W 1989) 11-15 [< NTAbs 33,317]: – *b)* A biblically oriented pastoral theology, TDig 36 (1989) 8-10.

5210 *a)* *Engelbrecht* J.,   The empty tomb (Lk 24:1-12) in historical perspective; – *b)* *Scheffler* E.H.,   Emmaus – a historical perspective: ➤ 617, Resurrection = Neotestamentica 23,2 (1989) 235-249 / 251-267.

5211 *Rousseau* François,   Un phénomène particulier d'inclusions dans Luc 24,13-35: Studies in Religion 18,1 (Toronto 1989) 67-79.

5212 *Milne* D.,   Luke 24:46-49; Luke's great commission: VoxRef 51 (Melbourne 1988) 24-28 [< NTAbs 33,218].

XII. Actus Apostolorum

F8.1 **Acts** – *text, commentary, topics.*

5212* **Arrington** F. L.,   The Acts of the Apostles, an introduction and commentary. Peabody MA 1988, Hendrickson. xlvi-298 p. $17. 0-913573-73-6 [NTAbs 33,242].

5213 **Benéitez** Manuel, 'Esta salvación de Dios' (Hech 28,28); análisis narrativo estructuralista de 'Hechos' 1986 ➤ 2,4023.4127; 3,5084: ᴿCBQ 51 (1989) 362s (J. C. *Turro*).

5214 *Betori* Giuseppe, Alla ricerca di un'articolazione per il libro degli Atti: RivB 37 (1989) 185-205.

5215 **Bruce** F. F.,   The book of the Acts²ʳᵉᵛ [¹1954]: NICNT 1988 ➤ 4,5227: ᴿBTrans 40 (1989) 339-341 (I. H. *Marshall*); ÉTRel 64 (1989) 293s (E. *Cuvillier*); TLZ 114 (1989) 597s (G. *Schille*).

5216 *Bruce* F. F.,   Commentaries on Acts: BTrans 40 (1989) 315-321 [BARRETT C. K. in ICC awaited].

5217 *a) Bruce* F. F., Eschatology in Acts; – *b) Barrett* C. K., The Gentile mission as an eschatological phenomenon: ➤ 21, ᶠBEASLEY-MURRAY G., Eschatology 1988, 51-63 / 65-75.

5218 **Cassidy** Richard J.,   Society and politics in Acts 1987 ➤ 3,5088; 4,5228: ᴿAndrUnS 27 (1989) 80-82 (A. *Hernandez*); Biblica 70 (1989) 424-8 (R. F. *O'Toole*); CBQ 51 (1989) 555s (R. J. *Karris*); Horizons 16 (1989) 154s (Pheme *Perkins*); Interpretation 43 (1989) 324.326 (S. *Fabris*); RB 96 (1989) 419-422 (J. *Taylor*); ScotJT 42 (1989) 577-9 (J. M. G. *Barclay*); StPatav 36 (1989) 629s (G. *Segalla*).

5219 **Conzelmann** Hans,   Acts [1963, ²1972], ᵀLimburg J.: Hermeneia Comm. 1987 ➤ 3,5089; 4,5229: ᴿCBQ 51 (1989) 556-8 (D. *Hamm*); Interpretation 43 (1989) 187s (R. I. *Pervo*); RelStR 15 (1989) 263 (R. H. *Fuller*: outdated).

5220 **Delebecque** E.,   Les deux Actes: ÉtBN 6, 1986 ➤ 2,4028... 4,5230: ᴿRBgPg 67 (1989) 191s (H. *Savon*).

5221 *Devine* A. M.,   Manuscripts of St. John CHRYSOSTOM's Commentary on the Acts of the Apostles; a preliminary study for a critical edition: AncW 20 (Ch 1989) 111-125.

5222 *Dillon* Richard J.,   Acts of the Apostles: ➤ 384, NJBC (1989) 722-767.

5223 **Dupont** Jacques,   Nouvelles études sur les Actes 1984 ➤ 65,184... 3,5093: ᴿTLZ 114 (1989) 276-8 (M. *Rese*).

5224 **Ferguson** E.,   Acts of Apostles; the message of the NT: Way of Life 164s. Abilene TX 1986, Christian Univ. iii-83 p.; iii-85 p. 0-915547-93-7; -16-5 [NTAbs 33,106].

5225 **Gasque** W. Ward,   A history of the interpretation of the Acts of the Apostles [= 1975 + Interp 42 (1988)]. Peabody MA 1989, Hendrickson. viii-359 p. 0-943575-12-5.

5225* *Gasque* W. Ward, The historical value of Acts: TyndB 40 (1989) 136-157.

5226 *Geer* Thomas C.,   The two faces of Codex 33 in Acts [less 'ancient' than its Gospels]: NT 31 (1989) 39-47.

5227 **Gourgues** Michel, Misión y comunidad, Hch 1-12: QuadBib 60, 1988 ➤ 4,5235; pt. 280.   84-7151-551-2: ᴿActuBbg 26 (1989) 40 (R. de *Sivatte*); EfMex 6 (1988) 458s (E. *Serraima*).

5228 **Gourgues** M.,   L'Évangile aux païens (Ac 13-28): CahÉv 67. P 1989, Cerf. 66 p. F 24. – ᴿMondeB 60 (1989) 71 (F. *Brossier*).

5230 **Harrison** Everett F.,   Interpreting Acts; the expanding Church 1986 ➤ 3,5097: ᴿCalvinT 24 (1989) 316-322 (W. P. *DeBoer*, comparing KRODEL G. 'more stimulating').

5231 **Hemer** Colin J., [† 1987] The Book of Acts in the setting of Hellenistic history, ᴱGempf Conrad H. [only introd. and brief conclusion]: WUNT 49. Tü 1989, Mohr. xiv-482 p. DM 128. 3-16-145451-0 [TDig 37,60]. –

RArTGran 52 (1989) 253s (A. S. *Muñoz*); SWJT 32,3 (1989s) 52 (E. E. *Ellis*).

5232 **Krodel** Gerhard A., Acts: Augsburg Comm. 1986 ➤ 3,5100; 4,5239: RCBQ 51 (1989) 157s (W. J. *Harrington*).

5233 *Larsson* Edvin, Apostlagärningarnas historiska värde; synpunkter på den aktuella debatten: SvTKv 65 (1989) 145-155.

5234 **L'Éplattenier** Charles, Gli Atti degli Apostoli, quadro delle origini cristiane [1987 ➤ 3,5101], T: Lettura Pastorale della Bibbia. Bo c. 1989, Dehoniane. 218 p. Lit. 24.000 [RivB 37,498 adv.].

5235 **Levinsohn** Stephen H., Textual connections in Acts [diss. Reading UK]: SBL Mg 31. Atlanta 1987, Scholars. xviii-187 p. $19; sb/pa. $14. – RJBL 109 (1989) 350-2 (S. E. *Porter*).

5236 **Lüdemann** Gerd, Das frühe Christentum nach... Apg 1987 ➤ 3,5103; 4,5244: RJBL 108 (1989) 530-2 (C. R. *Matthews*); JTS 40 (1989) 567-9 (C. K. *Barrett*); ScotJT 42 (1989) 260-3 (A. J. M. *Wedderburn*); TR 85 (1989) 201s (A. *Weiser*).

5237 **Lüdemann** Gerd, Early Christianity according to the traditions in Acts, a commentary [1987 ➤ 3,5103], T*Bowden* John: Augsburg Comm. NT. Minneapolis 1989, Fortress. ix-277 p. $20 pa. 0-8006-2314-2 [TDig 37,71].

5238 **Luzzi** G., Fatti degli apostoli; commentario esegetico-pratico del NT [1899]. T 1988, Claudiana. 270 p. Lit. 20.000. 88-7016-074-2 [NTAbs 33,387: 1899, only on Acts].

5238* **McDonnell** John, Acts to Gospels; a New Testament path. Lanham MD 1989, UPA. xii-243 p. $32.50 [TR 86,523].

5239 **Marshall** I. Howard, The Acts of the Apostles, an introduction and commentary: Tyndale NT Comm. Leicester/GR 1989, Inter-Varsity/ Eerdmans. 427 p. 0-85111-634-5 / GR 0-8028-1423-9.

5240 **May** Flavius J., The book of Acts and church growth: diss. Fuller. Pasadena 1989. 120 p. 89-23002. – DissA 50 (1989s) 2097-A.

5241 [ECasciaro J. M., *al.*; TEGavigan James, *al.*] Navarre Bible, Acts of the Apostles, RSV, New Vulgate, Comm. Dublin 1989, Four Courts. 272 p.; maps. 1-85182-045-0; pa. 4-2.

5242 **O'Reilly** Leo, Word and sign in Acts: AnGreg 243, D1987 ➤ 3,5106; 4,5247: RInterpretation 43 (1989) 105 (J. D. *Kingsbury* along with 4 other volumes).

5243 **Pastor** Federico, Hechos de los Apóstoles, comentario: MensajeNT 5. S 1989, Sígueme. 203 p.; maps. 84-301-1097-6 (Verbo Divino 84-7151-653-5).

5244 **Pervo** Richard J., Profit with delight [D1979] 1987 ➤ 3,5108; 4,5248: RCBQ 51 (1989) 162-4 (S. *Davies*: witty, but with a wary eye to the sunset of NT fundamentalism); CurrTM 16 (1989) 294s (F. W. *Danker*: Luke sometimes inventive?); Interpretation 43 (1989) 407-410 (M. C. *Parsons*: 'the book of Acts as an ancient novel'; controversial confidence in genre conventions); JBL 108 (1989) 353-5 (D. R. *Edwards*); JRel 69 (1989) 399s (D. E. *Aune*); JTS 40 (1989) 569-571 (J. *Jervell*); ScotJT 42 (1989) 423s (Ruth B. *Edwards*).

5245 **Pesch** Rudolf, Die Apostelgeschichte (1-12) 1986 ➤ 2,4037... 4,5249: RCiTom 116 (1989) 630 (J. *Huarte*); NRT 111 (1989) 753s (R. *Pesch*).

5246 **Rius-Camps** Josep, De Jerusalén a Antioquía, génesis de la Iglesia cristiana; comentario lingüístico y exegético a Hch 1-12. Córdoba 1989, Almendro. 190 p. pt 2862. 84-86077-76-1. – RFgNt 2 (1989) 213s (J. *Peláez*).

5247 **Scaglioni** A., I racconti dei miracoli negli Atti degli Apostoli e loro significato teologico [diss. Angelicum, Roma], 1987 ➤ 4,5250: ᴿRivB 37 (1989) 110-2 (M. *Làconi*).

5248 **Schille** G., Die Apostelgeschichte des Lukas 1983 ➤ 64,5033: ᴿTLZ 114 (1989) 32s (A. *Weiser*).

5249 *Seifrid* Mark A., Messiah and mission in Acts; a brief response to J.B. TYSON [NTS 1987]: JStNT 36 (1989) 47-50.

5250 **Strange** E.A., The problem of the text of Acts: diss. Oxford 1989. – RTLv 21,547.

5251 *Sugirtharajah* R.S., Luke's second volume and the Gentiles: ExpTim 100 (1988s) 178s. 181.

5252 **Willimon** William H., Acts: Interpretation Comm. 1988 ➤ 4,5262: ᴿTTod 46 (1989s) 354.356 (Gail R. *O'Day*: homiletically fine, exegetically lean).

5253 **Wright** Neil, [Acts in verse] ARATOR's use of Caelius SEDULIUS; a re-examination: Eranos 87 (1989) 51-64,

5254 **Zawadzki** Marek, ⊘ Pojęcie zbawienia [the concept of salvation] w Dziejach Apostolskich; eksplikacja derywatów rdzenia sōs-: diss. ᴰ*Langkammer* H. Lublin 1989. 188 p. – RTLv 21,547.

F8.3   *Ecclesia primaeva Actuum:*   **Die Urgemeinde.**

5255 **Achtemeier** Paul J., The quest for unity in the NT church 1987 ➤ 3,5121; 5,5264: ᴿActuBbg 26 (1989) 31s (X. *Alegre* S.); Interpretation 43 (1989) 191-4 (C.J. *Roetzel*: vigorous, provocative, not too speculative).

5256 **Aguirre** Rafael, Del movimiento de Jesús a la Iglesia cristiana 1987 ➤ 3,5122: ᴿSalT 76 (1988) 73-75 (J.M. *González Ruiz*); ScripTPamp 21 (1989) 354s (J.M. *Casciaro*).

5257 **Becker** Jürgen, *al.*, Die Anfänge des Christentums; alte Welt und neue Hoffnungen 1987 ➤ 3,326: ᴿHZ 249 (1989) 399-402 (C. *Gizewski*); TPhil 64 (1989) 260s (A. *Brendle*).

5258 **Billheimer** Paul E., Für den Thron bestimmt; Gebet und Vollmacht der Gemeinde Jesu³ [1973] ᵀ1983: Telos 360. Stu-Neuhausen 1989, Hänssler. 123 p. 3-7751-0844-0.

5259 **Böcker** Tobias, Katholizismus und Konfessionalität; das Frühkatholizismusproblem in der protestantischen Theologie als Frage nach der Berechtigung der konfessionellen Partikularität: kath. Diss. ᴰ*Petri* H. Regensburg 1988s. – TR 85 (1989) 518; RTLv 21,566.

5260 *Bremmer* J., Why did early Christianity attract upper-class women?: ➤ 17, ᶠBARTELINK G., Fructus 1989, 37-48.

5261 **Brown** Raymond E., L'Église héritée des apôtres: Lire la Bible 1987 ➤ 3,5127; 4,5272: ᴿBLitEc 90 (1989) 59s (S. *Légasse*); EstAg 23 (1988) 202 (C. *Mielgo*; español T. *Marcos*); LavalTP 45 (1989) 308-310 (P.-H. *Poirier*); RHPR 69 (1989) 233s (C. *Grappe*).

5262 **Brown** Raymond E., Las Iglesias que los Apóstoles nos dejaron 1986 ➤ 3,5128; 4,5273: ᴿLumenVr 38 (1989) 539s (A.M. *Navarro*).

5263 **Brown** R.E., Meier J.P., Antioche et Rome, berceaux du christianisme [1983 ➤ 64,5048], ᵀ: LDiv 131, 1988 ➤ 4,5274: ᴿAngelicum 66 (1989) 324s (S. *Jurič*); LVitae 44 (1989) 236s (L. *Partos*); NRT 111 (1989) 766 (X. *Jacques*, 'Meier' correct dans le texte et p. 1103, non 'Meyer' comme titre p. 766); RechSR 77 (1989) 411s (J. *Guillet*); VSp 143 (1989) 831s (H. *Cousin*).

5264 **Brown** R. E., *Meier* J. P., Antiochia e Roma 1987 ➤ 3,5131; 4,5275: RSalesianum 51 (1989) 142s (B. *Amata*).

5265 *Brown* R. E., Early Church: ➤ 384, NJBC (1989s) 1338-46.

5266 **Cragg** Kenneth, What decided Christianity? Event and experience in the New Testament. L 1989, Churchman. 178 p. £6. 1-85093-113-5. – RExpTim 101 (1989s) 51 (B. G. *Powley*).

5267 **Cwiekowski** Frederick J., The beginnings of the Church 1988 ➤ 4,5279: RNewTR 2,2 (1989) 96 (Carolyn *Osiek*); PrPeo 3 (1989) 73 (J. B. *Scott*); RB 96 (1989) 618 (J. J. *Taylor*); RTLv 20 (1989) 219s (J. *Ponthot*).

5268 **Dudley** Carl S., *Hilgert* Earle, New Testament tensions and the contemporary Church 1987 ➤ 3,5134*; 0-8006-1955-2: RCBQ 51 (1989) 150s (Carolyn *Osiek*); ExpTim 100 (1988s) 352 (S. C. *Barton*).

5269 *Frohnhofen* Herbert, Die frühe Kirche als Leitbild der Erneuerung: MüTZ 40 (1989) 211-222.

5270 **Goppelt** L., L'età apostolica e subapostolica: CommNT Sup 5, 1986 ➤ 4,5282: RProtestantesimo 44 (1989) 226s (P. *Ribet*).

5271 **Grappe** Christian, D'un Temple à l'autre; Pierre et l'Église primitive de Jérusalem: diss. prot. Strasbourg 1989, DTrocmé E. 764 p. (2 vol.). – RTLv 21,545.

5272 **Grossi** V., *Siniscalco* P., La vita cristiana dei primi secoli: Spiritualità cristiana 2, 1988 ➤ 4,5283: RProtestantesimo 44 (1989) 299s (G. *Plescan*).

5273 *Gubler* Marie-Louise, Lebendige Vielfalt des Anfangs: Diakonia 20 (1989) 385-391 [> Eng. TDig 37,115s, TEAsen B.].

5274 **Guillet** J., Entre Jésus et l'Église 1985 ➤ 1,5109 ... 4,5284: RScripTPamp 21 (1989) 354 (V. *Balaguer*).

5275 **Hoornaert** Eduardo, Die Anfänge der Kirche in der Erinnerung des christlichen Volkes: Theologie der Befreiung 1987 ➤ 4,5289; DM 40; 3-491-77714-3: RTsTNijm 29 (1989) 68s (J. Van *Nieuwenhove*).

5276 **Hoornaert** Eduardo, The memory of the Christian people [Portuguese], TBarr Robert R.: Theology and liberation. xii-304 p. $27; pa. $14. 0-88344-574-3; 3-5 [TDig 36,373].

5277 *Jáuregui* José Antonio, La Iglesia de Jerusalén; origen, autoconciencia y estructuras eclesiales: EstDeusto 18,41 (1988) 21-49.

5278 *a)* *Kertelge* K., 'Frühkatholizismus' im Neuen Testament als Herausforderung für die Ökumene; – *b)* *Paulsen* H., Auslegungsgeschichte und Geschichte des Urchristentums — die Überprüfung eines Paradigmas: ➤ 131, FMARXSEN W., Jesu Rede 1989, 344-360 / 361-374.

5279 *Liampawe* Lucien, Meaning of priesthood in the primitive Church community: Pastoral Orientation Service (Tanzania 1989,1) 10-18 [< TContext 7/1, 20].

5280 **Lohse** Eduard, The first Christians 1983 ➤ 64,5068b; 1,5113: RAsbTJ 44,2 (1989) 98s (A. H. M. *Zahniser*).

5281 **MacDonald** Margaret Y., The Pauline churches D1988 ➤ 4,5296: RÉTRel 64 (1989) 297s (E. *Cuvillier*); EvQ 61 (1989) 271-3 (I. H. *Marshall*); NRT 111 (1989) 761s (X. *Jacques*); Salmanticensis 36 (1989) 383-6 (R. *Trevijano*); SvTKv 65 (1989) 132s (B. *Homberg*); TsTNijm 29 (1989) 289 (L. *Visschers*).

5282 *Marczewski* Marek, ⊙ Anteil der Ehe am Missionswerk im NT — die Hauskirche: ➤ 51, FEBOROWICZ W. = VoxPa 15 (1988) 575-583; deutsch 583.

5283 *a)* *Monsengwo* Pasinya, L'inculturation dans le Livre des Actes; – *b)* *Onaiyekan* John, Ministries in the Acts; – *c)* *Amewowo* Wynnand, The

Christian community in the Acts: RAfT 13,25 (1989) 31-40 / 41-57 / 59-66 [< TContext 7/1, 27].
5284 **Nouailhat** René, Les premiers christianismes. P 1988, Errance. – [Masses Ouvrières 432, 87, F. *Dumortier*].
Ries J., Les chrétiens parmi les religions, des Actes des Apôtres à Vatican II 1987 ➤ a683.
5286 *a) Sarah* Robert, Les Actes des Apôtres et les jeunes églises: RAfT 13, 25 (1989) 7-16; – *b) Akpunonu* Peter D., The church and churches in the Acts of the Apostles [Jerusalem to Antioch, Rome; < TContext 7/1, 26].
5287 *Sumney* J., The role of historical reconstructions of early Christianity in identifying Paul's opponents: PerspRelSt 16,1 (1989) 45-53 [< NTAbs 33,327].
5288 **Tigcheler** Jo, Gemeenschappen in het Nieuwe Testament 1987 ➤ 3,5158; 4,5311; ᴿStreven 55 (1987s) 469 (P. *Beentjes*).
5289 **Vögtle** Anton, Die Dynamik des Anfangs; Leben und Fragen der jungen Kirche 1988 ➤ 4,5315: ᴿTLZ 114 (1989) 120s (E. *Reinmuth*).
5290 *Wainwright* Geoffrey, Early Jewish Christianity — a lost chapter?: AsbTJ 44,2 (1989) 17-29.
5291 **Webber** Randall C., An analysis of power in the Jerusalem church in Acts: diss. Southern Baptist Theol. Sem. 1989, ᴰ*Polhill* J. 248 p. 89-25776. – DissA 50 (1989s) 2108-A.
5292 **Wright** Edgar L., A critical examination of the origin and development of house churches and their significance for contemporary evangelism: diss. New Orleans Baptist Theol. Sem. 1989, ᴰ*Thiele* W. E. 236 p. 89-21984. – DissA 50 (1989s) 2101-A.

F8.5   **Ascensio, Pentecostes; ministerium Petri** – *Act 1 …*

5293 *Mealand* David L., The phrase 'many proofs' in Acts 1,3 and in Hellenistic writers: ZNW 80 (1989) 133s.
5294 *Capmany Casamitjana* Josep, El perfil del obispo en la elección de Matías (Hch 1,15-26): ➤ 69*, ᶠ*Gomà* I., RCatalT 14 (1989) 309-321 castellano; Eng. 321.
5295 *Colpe* Carsten, Himmelfahrt [… auch Christi]: ➤ 905, RLA 7,3s (1989) 213-9.
5296 *Geerlings* Wilhelm, Ascensio Christi: ➤ 879, AugL 1/3 (1989) 475-9 (mentis, 465-475, *Madec* Goulven).
5297 *Green* E. A., Enoch, Lent and the Ascension of Christ: ➤ 430, De ore Domini 1989, 13-25.
5298 *O'Collins* G., Christ's resurrection and ascension: America 160 (NY 1989) 262s [< NTAbs 33,299: 'The ascension reminds us that Jesus' resurrection was more than a mere coming back to life under the normal conditions of human existence'].
5299 **Parsons** Mikeal C., The departure of Jesus in Luke-Acts; the Ascension … JStNT sup 21, 1987 ➤ 4,5321: ᴿCBQ 51 (1989) 753-5 (R. J. *Miller*: a ten-page summary would be all anyone needs to know about these two passages); ÉTRel 64 (1989) 91 (B. *Corsani*); ExpTim 100 (1988s) 67s (I. H. *Marshall*); JBL 108 (1989) 528-530 (S. G. *Wilson*); JTS 40 (1989) 187-9 (C. F. D. *Moule*); RExp 86 (1989) 115s (S. *Sheeley*); TLZ 114 (1989) 886-8 (C.-P. *März*).
5300 *Rius-Camps* Josep,. Els tres sumaris dels Fets dels Apòstols (Ac 2,41-47; 4,32-5,16 i 19,11-19): ➤ 69*, ᶠ*Gomà* I., RCatalT 14 (1989) 243-255; Eng. 256.

5301 **Brakemeier** Gottfried, [At 2-5] O 'socialismo' da primeira cristiandade [2,4092]; uma experiência e um desafio para hoje. São Leopoldo 1985, Sinodal. 59 p. 85-233-0058-9. – ᴿPerspT 20 (1988) 257s (G. I. *Rodríguez*).

5302 **Brakemeier** G., Der 'Sozialismus' der Urchristenheit; Experiment und neue Herausforderung: KV-Reihe 1535. Gö 1988, Vandenhoeck & R. 60 p. DM 9,80. 3-525-33545-8 [TsTNijm 29,90].

5303 *Abogunrin* S. O., [Act 2,44...] The community of goods in the Early Church and the distribution of national wealth: AfJB 1,2 (1986) 74-94 [< NTAbs 33,40].

5304 *Horst* Pieter W. van der, Hellenistic parallels to Acts (chapters 3 and 4): JStNT 35 (1989) 37-46.

5305 *Crouzel* Henri, [At 3,21] L'apocatastasi in Origene [= Origeniana Quarta 1985/7, 283-290], ᵀ*Tiana* Luigi E. ParSpV 19 (1989) 209-223.

5306 *Szűcs* Ferenc, [Acts 3,21] ⓌApokatásztazisz tón pantón; the problem of the salvation of all in the history of theology and today: TSzem 32 (1989) 259-263.

5307 *Ellul* Danielle, Actes 3/1-11: ÉTRel 64 (1989) 95-99.

5308 **Danter** Albert F., Acts 4:25-31, a model for enduring persecution: diss. St. Louis Univ. 1989, ᴰ*O'Toole* R. 243 p. 90-00903. – DissA 50 (1989s) 2536-A.

5309 *Salyer* Gary D., [Act. 4,32-5,11; DOUGLAS M., MALINA B., ground-grid model] Famine in the land and dishonesty among the faithful; the story of Ananias and Sapphira in sociological perspective: Paradigms 5,1 (Louisville 1989) 32-50.

5310 **Tosco** Lorenzo, Pietro e Paolo ministri del giudizio di Dio; studio del genere letterario e della funzione di At 5,1-11 e 13,4-12 [diss. 1986, ᴰ*Lentzen-Deis* F.]: RivB supp. 19. Bo 1989, Dehoniane. 240 p. Lit. 28.000 [RivB 37,328 adv.]. 88-10-30207-9.

5311 *Roosen* A., Service de la Parole et service des pauvres dans Actes 6,1-7 et 20,32-35: Studia Moralia 27,1 (R 1989) 43-76 [< ZIT 89,618].

5312 *Schüssler Fiorenza* Elisabeth, 'Waiting at table'; a critical feminist theological reflection on diakonia: Concilium 198 (E 1988) 84-94.

5313 *Arai* S., Stephanusrede – gelesen vom Standpunkt ihrer Leser: AnJapB 13 (1989) 53-85.

5314 *Kilgallen* John J., The function of Stephen's speech (Acts 7,2-53): Biblica 70 (1989) 173-193; franç. 193.

5315 *Bruce* F. F., Philip and the Ethiopian: → 200, ᶠULLENDORFF E., JSS 34 (1989) 377-386.

5316 *Rouiller* Grégoire, Sur les pas du Ressuscité; une lecture d'Ac 8,25-40: ÉchSM 19 (1989) 213-224.

5317 *Martin* Clarice J., [Acts 8,26-40] A chamberlain's journey and the challenge of interpretation for liberation: Semeia 47 (1989) 105-135.

5318 *Porter* R. J., [Acts 8,37] What did Philip say to the eunuch?: ExpTim 100 (1988s) 54s.

5319 **Spencer** Franklin S., Philip the evangelist in Lucan perspective: diss. Durham 1989. – RTLv 21,547.

5320 *Steuernagel* Gert, *Akoúontes mèn tês phōnês* (Apg 9.7); ein Genitiv in der Apostelgeschichte: NTS 35 (1989) 619-624.

5320* **Eck** J. van, [Act 9,15] Paulus en de koningen; politieke aspecten van het boek Handelingen. Franeker 1989, van Wijnen. 143 p. ƒ22.75. 90-5194-014-9 [TsTNijm 30,310, P. J. *Farla*].

5321 *Stuehrenberg* Paul F., [Acts 10s; 13,50] The 'God-fearers' in Martin
LUTHER's translation of Acts: SixtC 20 (1989) 407-415.

5322 *Ordon* Hubert, ℗ Peter's catechesis at Caesarea (Acts 10,34-43):
RoczTK 33,1 (1986) 101-114; deutsch 115.

5323 *Fonseca* R. H., Comentario exegético teológico a los Hechos de los
Apóstoles 11,19-26: FranBog 30 (1988) 155-202 [< Stromata 45,499].

F8.7 **Acts 13... *Itinera Pauli,* Paul's Journeys.**

5324 *Reumann* John, The 'itinerary' as a form in classical literature and the
Acts of the Apostles: → 60, ᶠFITZMYER J., Touch 1989, 335-357.

5325 *Sabugal* Santos, ¡Dios cumplió la promesa patriarcal, resucitando a
Jesús! (Act 13,16-41); análisis redaccional e histórico-tradicional: Est-
Agust 24 (1989) 549-583.

5326 *a) Böcher* Otto, [Apg 15,20] Das sogenannte Aposteldekret; – *b) Dauer*
Anton, 'Ergänzungen' und 'Variationen' in den Reden der Apostelgeschichte gegenüber vorausgegangenen Erzählungen; Beobachtungen zur
literarischen Arbeitsweise des Lukas: → 68, ᶠGNILKA J., Vom Urchristentum 1989, 325-336 / 307-324.

5327 *Cohen* Charles L., [Acts 16,14s, Lydia; David and Ps 51] Two biblical
models of conversion; an example of Puritan hermeneutics: ChH 58
(1989) 182-196.

5328 *Stock* A., [Acts 16,14...] Lydia and Prisca: Emmanuel 9 (NY 1988)
514-521.525 [< NTAbs 33,174].

5329 *Edwards* M.J., Three exorcisms [i. Solomon, Ant. 8.4.5; ii. Python Acts
16,16-20; iii. Indian boy, Life of Apollonius 3,38] and the New Testament
world: Eranos 87 (1989) 117-126.

5330 *Trebilco* Paul R., Paul and Silas — 'servants of the Most High God'
(Acts 16,16-18): JStNT 36 (1989) 51-73.

5331 *a) Schmidt* Daryl D., [Act 16,10...] Syntactical style in the 'we'-sections
of Acts; how Lukan is it?; – *b) Dawsey* James M., Characteristics of
folk-epic in Acts; – *c) Edwards* Douglas R., Acts of the Apostles and the
Graeco-Roman world; narrative communication in social context: → 589,
SBL Seminars 1989, 300-8 / 317-325 / 362-377.

5332 *Spencer* R.B., Is biblical scholarship really objective ['we' in Acts and
Jn 1,1-4 means eyewitness testimony]: HomP 89,7 (NY 1989) 52-58.

5333 **Wehnert** Jürgen, Die Wir-Passagen der Apg; ein lukanischer Stilmittel
aus jüdischer Tradition [Diss. 1988 → 4,5379]: GöTheolArb 40. Gö 1989,
Vandenhoeck & R. vii-300 p. [BZ 34, 281s, G. *Schneider*]. 3-525-87394-8.

5334 *Weiss* Hans-Friedrich, Verkündigter Verkündiger; das Paulusbild der
Wir-Stücke in der Apostelgeschichte; seine Aufnahme und Bearbeitung
durch Lukas: TLZ 114 (1989) 705-720.

5335 *Onwu* N., Ministry to the educated; reinterpreting Acts 17:16-34 in
Africa: Chiea 4,4 (Nairobi 1988) 61-71 [< TContext 7/1, 18].

6336 *a) Ukachukwu Manus* Chris, The Areopagus speech (Acts 17,16-34); a
study on Luke's approach to evangelism and its significance in the African
context; – *b) Ukpong* Justin, Mission in Acts of the Apostles; a study
from the perspective of the evangelized; – *c) Arowele* P.-J., Mission and
evangelisation in Acts and the African experience; – *d) Waliggo* John M.,
The Acts of the Apostles and a hundred years of Catholic evangelization
in Africa: RAfT 13 (1989) 155-170 / 171-192 / 193-207 / 209-222.

5337 *Zweck* Dean, The exordium of the Areopagus speech, Acts 17.22,23:
NTS 35 (1989) 94-103.

5338 *a*) *Horst* P. W. van der, The unknown God (Acts 17:23); – *b*) *Mussies* G., Identification and self-identification of gods in classical and Hellenistic times; – *c*) *Baarda* T., 'If you do not sabbatize the Sabbath ...' ; the Sabbath as God or Word in Gnostic understanding (Ev. Thom. Log. 27); – *d*) *Stone* M. E., The way of the Most High and the injustice of God in 4 Ezra; – *e*) *Dillon* J. M., The knowledge of God in ORIGEN; – *f*) *Stead* G. C., ... in EUSEBIUS and ATHANASIUS; – *g*) *Tardieu* M., La conception de Dieu dans le Manichéisme: ↠ 639, Knowledge of God 1986/8, 19-42 / 1-18 / 178-201 / 132-142 / 219-228 / 229-242 / 262-290.

5339 *Horst* P. W. van der, The altar of the 'Unknown God' in Athens (Acts 17:23) and the cult of 'Unknown Gods' in the Hellenistic and Roman periods: ↠ 878, ANRW 2/18/2 (1989) 1426-1456.

5339* *Plötz* Karl, Die Areopagrede des Apostels Paulus: IkaZ 17 (1988) 111-7.

5340 *Stoops* Robert F.[J], Riot and assembly; the social context of Acts 19:23-41: JBL 108 (1989) 73-91.

5341 **Tajra** H. W., The trial of St. Paul; a judicial exegesis of the second half of the Acts of the Apostles (Diss. Geneva 1988): WUNT 2/33. Tü 1989, Mohr. xvii-225 p. DM 79 [TRu 55,112 adv.]. 3-16-145443-X.

5341* *Hemer* Colin J. †, *a*) [Acts 20,17-38] The speeches of Acts, I. The Ephesian elders at Miletus; II. The Areopagus address [Acts 17]: TyndB 40 (1989) 77-85 . 239-260.

5342 **Aejmelaeus** Lars, Die Rezeption der Paulusbriefe in der Miletrede (Apg 20:18-35) 1987 ↠ 3,5217; 4,5381: [R]Biblica 70 (1989) 140-2 (J. *Dupont*); CBQ 51 (1989) 738s (V. P. *Branick*); ExpTim 100 (1988s) 433s (E. *Best*); JBL 108 (1989) 532-4 (R. L. *Brawley*); JTS 40 (1989) 572-4 (I. H. *Marshall*: strong case for Luke not knowing letters of Paul); RB 96 (1989) 416-9 (J. *Taylor*); TLZ 114 (1989) 429-431 (T. *Holtz*); TR 85 (1989) 460-2 (Maria-B. von *Stritzky*).

5343 **Lentz** John C.[J], Luke's portrayal of St. Paul as a man of high social status and moral virtue in the concluding chapters of Acts: diss. Edinburgh 1988. 428 p. BRD-85031. – DissA 50 (1989s) 469-A.

5344 *Agouridis* Savas, ☉ Paul the prisoner (Acts 21,27-28,31): DeltioVM 18,1 (1989) 5-29 [< ZIT 89,530].

5345 **Warnecke** Heinz, [Act 27s] Die tatsächliche Romfahrt des Apostels Paulus, [D]1987 ↠ 3,5226: [R]IndTSt 25 (1988) 107s (L. *Legrand*); JBL 108 (1989) 536s (C. R. *Matthews*: threat to render our maps obsolete is remote).

5346 *Uhlig* Siegbert, [Apg 28] Ein pseudepigraphischer Actaschluss in der äthiopischen Version: OrChr 73 (1989) 129-136.

XIV. Johannes

G1 *Corpus Johanneum* .1 **John and his community.**

5347 *Beutler* Johannes, Krise und Untergang der johanneischen Gemeinde; das Zeugnis der Johannesbriefe: ↠ 606, Réception 1986/9, 85-103.

5348 *Brown* Raymond E., The Johannine world for preachers: Interpretation 43 (1989) 58-65.

5349 **Burge** Gary M., The anointed community; the Holy Spirit in the Johannine tradition 1987 ↠ 3,5230; 4,5392: [R]Interpretation 43 (1989) 426.428 (J. W. *Aageson*); JBL 108 (1989) 158-160 (M. R. *Mansfield*);

RechSR 77 (1989) 272-4 (X. *Léon-Dufour*); RTLv 20 (1989) 90s (J.-P. *Kaefer*); ScripB 20 (1989s) 49s (H. *Wansbrough*); STEv NS 1 (1989) 91 (E. *Beriti*); WestTJ 50 (1988) 355-7 (M. *Silva*).

5350 *Domeris* W. R., Christology and community; a study of the social matrix of the Fourth Gospel: JTSAf 64 (1988) 49-56 [< NTAbs 33,168].

5351 **Marzotto** Damiano, L'unità degli uomini nel vangelo di Giovanni 1978 ➤ 58,5318 ... 65,4741: ᴿNicolaus 16 (1989) 288-291 (A. *Moda*).

5352 *Munitiz* Joseph A., BLEMMYDES' encomium on St. John the Evangelist (BHG 931): AnBoll 107 (1989) 285-346 [cf. 238, *Zanetti* U. on a related Munitiz book).

5353 **Panimolle** S. A., L'evangelista Giovanni 1985 ➤ 1,5184... 3,5232: ᴿScripTPamp 21 (1989) 314-7 (A. *Garcia-Moreno*).

5354 **Quast** Kevin, Peter and the beloved disciple; figures for a community in crisis: JStNT supp. 32. Sheffield 1989, JStOT. 236 p. £25. 1-85075-217-6. – ᴿExpTim 101 (1989s) 214 (Margaret *Davies*: complementary roles).

5355 **Rensberger** David, Johannine faith and liberating community 1988 ➤ 4,5400: ᴿTTod 46 (1989s) 241s (G. S. *Sloyan*).

5356 **Rensberger** David, Overcoming the world; politics and community in the Gospel of John. L 1989, SPCK. 168 p. £10. 0-281-04429-5. – ᴿExp-Tim 101 (1989s) 213s (S. S. *Smalley*, also on L. MORRIS).

5357 **Schnelle** Udo, Antidoketische Christologie ... in der johanneischen Schule: FRL 144, 1987 ➤ 3,5237; 4,5401: ᴿNRT 111 (1989) 948s (Y. *Simoens*).

5358 **Smith** D. Moody, Johannine Christianity 1984 ➤ 65,4745 ... 3,5238: ᴿJRel 68 (1988) 94s (R. *Scroggs*); ScotJT 42 (1989) 119-121 (S. W. *Need*).

5359 **Taeger** Jens-W., Johannesapokalypse und johanneischer Kreis; Versuch einer traditionsgeschichtlichen Ortsbestimmung am Paradigma des Lebenswasser-Thematik [ev. Hab. Diss. Münster 1986, ᴰ*Klein* G.]: BZNW 51. B 1989, de Gruyter. xi-236 p. 3-11-011359-7. – ᴿÉTRel 64 (1989) 443s (E. *Cuvillier*); TLZ 114 (1989) 813-5 (M. *Karrer*).

5360 **Tuñi Vancells** J.-O., Jesús y el evangelio en la comunidad juanica ...: Biblia y catequesis 13, 1987 ➤ 4,5403: ᴿNRT 111 (1989) 616s (L.-J. *Renard*).

5361 **Tuñi** J. O., Las comunidades juánicas 1988 ➤ 4,5404: ᴿScripTPamp 21 (1989) 949 (A. *García Moreno*).

G1.2 **Evangelium Johannis:** *textus, commentarii.*

5362 **Beasley-Murray** George R., John: WordComm 36, 1987 ➤ 3,5243; 4,5411: ᴿAndrUnS 27 (1989) 75s (J. *Paulien*); CBQ 51 (1989) 144s (P. J. *Cahill*); CriswT 3 (1989) 382-4 (E. *Rowell*); ETL 65 (1989) 166s (F. *Neirynck*); ExpTim 100 (1988s) 230s (C. S. *Rodd* still prefers LINDARS); Interpretation 43 (1989) 201s (P. S. *Berge*); JBL 108 (1989) 732s (R. *Kysar*); JTS 40 (1989) 189-192 (B. *Lindars*); RB 96 (1989) 463s (M.-É. *Boismard*); WestTJ 50 (1988) 355-7 (M. *Silva*).

5363 ᵀᴱ**Berrouard** M. F., AUGUSTIN, Homélies sur l'Évangile de Saint Jean, XXXIV à XLIII: Œuvres 73A, 1988 ➤ 4,5411*; 2-85121-103-X: ᴿEsprVie 99 (1989) 134-*jaune* (J. *Pintard*); RBén 99 (1989) 337s (L. *Wankenne*); RSPT 73 (1989) 480s (G.-M. de *Durand*).

5364 **Blank** Josef, O Evangelho segundo João: ᵀ*Gomes Mourão de Castro* Miguel: NT comentário e mensagem 4/2. Petrópolis 1988, Vozes. 320 p. – ᴿREB 49 (1989) 483s (E. F. *Alves*).

5365 **Delebecque** Édouard, Évangile de Jean, texte traduit et annoté; préf. *Guitton* Jean: CahRB 23, 1987 ➤ 3,5250; 4,5415: ᴿÉtClas 57 (1989) 367s (X. *Jacques*); RThom 89 (1989) 478s (L. *Devillers*).

5366 **Fatica** L., I commentari a Giovanni di TEODORO M. e CIRILLO A. 1988 ➤ 4,5418: ᴿAsprenas 36 (1989) 535-8 (L. *Longobardo*).

5366* **Gruenler** Royce C., The Trinity in the Gospel of John, a thematic commentary 1985 ➤ 2,4147... 4,5421: ᴿCriswT 2 (1987s) 168s (J. L. *Burns*).

5367 ᵀᴱ**Heine** Ronald E., ORIGEN, Commentary on the Gospel according to John, books 1-10: Fathers 80. Wsh 1989, Catholic University of America. xi-344 p. $35. 0-8132-0080-6 [TDig 37,79].

5368 **Jenkins** D. L., Windows on the Gospel of John. Nv 1988, Broadman. 211 p. $7. 0-8054-1540-8 [NTAbs 33,248].

5369 **Kieffer** René, Johannesevangeliet [1-10, 1987 ➤ 3,5257] 11-21. Uppsala 1988, EFS. p. 261-513: ᴿRB 96 (1989) 306 (I.-M. *Dewailly*).

5370 *Koester* H., Johannes-Evangelium: ➤ 694, EvKL 2 (1988) 840-3 (838s, Briefe, G. *Strecker*; 835-8, Apk, *Strecker*).

5371 **Làconi** Mauro, Il racconto di Giovanni. Assisi 1989, Cittadella. 426 p. Lit. 33.000. – ᴿTeresianum 40 (1989) 627 (V. *Pasquetto*).

5372 **Léon-Dufour** Xavier, Lectures de... Jean 1-4, 1987 ➤ 3,5259; 4,5425: ᴿBiblica 70 (1989) 137-9 (J. *Beutler*); EstE 64 (1989) 573s (J. *Luzárraga*); RechSR 76 (1988) 618-620 (É. *Cothenet*); RThom 89 (1989) 479-481 (L. *Devillers*); StPatav 36 (1989) 626-8 (G. *Segalla*); TsTNijm 29 (1989) 65s (L. *Grollenberg*).

5373 ᵀᴱ**Libera** A., *al.*, M. ECKHART, Le commentaire de l'Évangile selon Jean; Le Prologue (ch. 1,1-18): Œuvre latine 6. P 1989, Cerf. xxx-1844 + 109 p. 88-10-80225-X [Greg 70,615].

5374 **Mateos** Juan, *Barreto* Juan, O Evangelho de São João, análise lingüística e comentário exegético, ᵀ*Costa* Alberto, São Paulo 1989, Paulinas. 923 p. – ᴿREB 49 (1989) 482s (L. *Garmus*).

5375 **Michaels** J. Ramsey, John; NIntBComm 4. Peabody MA 1989, Hendrickson. xii-386 p. $10 [TR 86,427].

5375* Navarre Bible [ᴱ*Casciaro* José M., ᵀᴱ*Gavigan* James, *al.*] Saint John's Gospel with RSV & Neo-Vulgata. Dublin 1989, Four Courts. 247 p. 0-906127-97-1; pa. -8-X.

5376 *Perkins* Pheme, The Gospel according to John: ➤ 384, NJBC (1989) 942-985.

5377 **Phillips** J., Exploring the Gospels: John. Neptune NJ 1988, Loizeaux. 425 p. $20. 0-87213-658-2 [NTAbs 33,388].

5378 *Porsch* Felix, Johannes-Evangelium: KLK NT 4, 1988 ➤ 4,5443: ᴿTR 85 (1989) 287s (T. *Söding*).

5379 *Quecke* Hans, Das Johannesevangelium saïdisch 1984 ➤ 65,4769... 4,5434: ᴿRB 96 (1989) 460 (M.-É. *Boismard*).

5380 [*Fernández*] **Ramos** Felipe, Evangelio según San Juan: MensajeNT 4. S 1989, Sígueme. 213 p. 84-301-1085-2 (VDivino 84-7151-638-1, etc.).

5380* **Quéré** France, Une lecture de l'Évangile de Jean 1987 ➤ 3,5261: ᴿRHPR 69 (1989) 231s (R. *Mehl*: né de la rencontre entre cette théologienne protestante et un metteur en scène, Dominique Quétrec).

5381 ᵀ**Rettig** John W., St. AUGUSTINE, Tractates on the Gospel of John 1-10: Fathers 78, 1988 ➤ 4,5436: ᴿETL 65 (1989) 180 (A. de *Halleux*).

5382 **Salvail** G., En busca de la luz; evangelio según San Juan. M 1988, Paulinas. 107 p. – ᴿBibFe 15 (1989) 326s (A. *Salas*).

5383 **Schnackenburg** Rudolf, El Evangelio según San Juan [I-III, 1980 ➤ 61,6635*d*] IV, 1987 ➤ 3,5263: ᴿScripTPamp 21 (1989) 306-310 (A. *García-Moreno*).

5384 **Tilborg** S. van, Johannes: Belichting van het Bijbelboek. Boxtel/Brugge 1988, Kath. B-St./Tabor. 232 p. *f* 24,75. 90-6173-440-1. – ᴿStreven 57 (1989s) 180s (P. *Beentjes*); TsTNijm 29 (1989) 176 (A. van *Deuren*).

5385 **Wengert** T. L., P. MELANCHTHON's Annotationes in Johannem 1987 ➤ 3,5267; 4,5441: ᴿScotJT 42 (1989) 430 (D. C. *Parker*).

5386 **Zevini** Giorgio, Commenti spirituali del NT, Vangelo secondo Giovanni I-II 1984/7 ➤ 65,4782... 4,5442: ᴿBenedictina 35 (1988) 227s (L. *De Lorenzi*); NRT 111 (1989) 943s (Y. *Simoens*); ScEspr 41 (1989) 382s (L. *Sabourin*); RivB 37 (1989) 112s (G. *Danieli*); ScotJT 42 (1989) 422s (A. W. *Morrison*).

G1.3 **Introductio** in Evangelium Johannis.

5387 **Barberis** Giovanni, L'ora della vita; leggere Giovanni: Incontro alla Parola 4. Mi 1988, Paoline. 204 p. Lit. 12.000. – ᴿParVi 34 (1989) 314s (S. *Migliasso*).

5388 **Beasley-Murray** G. R., John: Word Biblical *Themes*. Dallas 1989, Word. xii-116 p. 0-8499-0624-5 [NTAbs 33,381].

5389 *a*) *Beaude* Pierre-Marie, Lire Jean dans le canon des écritures; – *b*) *Bourg* Dominique, L'entrée en littérature des textes chrétiennes; – *c*) *Morgen* Michèle, L'exégèse johannique à l'heure actuelle; quelques orientations: ➤ 381, Variations 1989, 193-210 / 211-239; 2 fig. / 243-263.

5390 **Belle** Gilbert Van, Johannine bibliography 1988 ➤ 4,876: ᴿETL 65 (1989) 164s (F. *Neirynck*: more adequate than G. WAGNER 1987, which however gives summaries); NRT 111 (1989) 750s (X. *Jacques*: ne précise pas les 'bibliographies en cours' employées, à part cet Elenchus déjà dépouillé par E. MALATESTA 1967); NT 31 (1989) 383s (J. K. *Elliott*).

5391 **Bittner** Wolfgang J., Jesu Zeichen im Joh.-Ev. [Diss. Basel 1986]: WUNT 2/26, 1987 ➤ 3,5274; 4,5444: ᴿCBQ 51 (1989) 147s (R. E. *Brown*: joins strong current movement rejecting pre-Johannine signs-source); JBL 108 (1989) 735-7 (Marianne M. *Thompson*); TGegw 32 (1989) 72s (H. *Giesen*); TLZ 114 (1989) 30s (R. *Riesner*).

5392 **Bjerkelund** Carl J., Tauta egeneto; die Präzisierungssätze im Joh.-Ev.: WUNT 40, 1987 ➤ 3,5275; 4,5445: ᴿScripTPamp 21 (1989) 352s (K. *Limburg*); StPatav 36 (1989) 203s (G. *Segalla*); JBL 108 (1989) 738s (C. H. *Giblin*).

5393 **Countryman** L. William, The mystical way in the Fourth Gospel 1987 ➤ 3,5276; 4,5451: ᴿCBQ 51 (1989) 149s (Rea *McDonnell*).

5394 **Eller** Vernard, The beloved disciple; his name, his story, his thought. GR/Exeter 1987, Eerdmans/Paternoster. 124 p. £7.35. 0-8028-0275-3. – ᴿExpTim 100 (1988s) 239 [C. S. *Rodd*: fascinating].

5395 **Fortna** Robert T., The fourth gospel and its predecessor 1988 ➤ 4,5454; also E 1989, Clark; 0-567-09496-0: ᴿETL 65 (1989) 167-170 (F. *Neirynck*); TTod 46 (1989s) 358s (M. C. *de Boer*).

5396 **Ghiberti** Giuseppe, L'origine del vangelo di Giovanni: ➤ 572*, Storia/preistoria Vangeli 1986/8, 41-61.

5397 **Grob** Francis, Faire l'œuvre de Dieu; Christologie et éthique dans l'Évangile de Jean ᴰ1986 ➤ 3,5280; 4,5455: ᴿRThom 89 (1989) 481s (L. *Devillers*).

5397* **Hengel** Martin,   The Johannine question [1987 Princeton conferences].
L/Ph 1989, SCM/Trinity. 240 p. [RHPR 70, 264-7, P. *Prigent*].

5398 **Hinrichs** Boy,   'Ich bin' 1988 → 4,5456:   ᴿBogSmot 59 (1989) 483-5 (M.
Zovkić).

5399 **Kügler** Joachim, [Joh 13,23] Der Jünger, den Jesus liebte [→ 4,5460]; literarische, theologische und historische Untersuchungen zu einer Schlüs-
selgestalt johanneischer Theologie und Geschichte, mit einem Exkurs über
die Brotrede in Joh 6 [Diss. Bamberg, ᴰ*Hoffmann* P.]: SBB 16. Stu 1988,
KBW.   520 p. – ᴿArTGran 52 (1989) 257s (A.S. *Muñoz*); RivB 37 (1989)
351-363 (G. *Segalla*: tipica ipertrofia tedesca difficilmente accettabile).

5400 *Kurz* William S., The Beloved Disciple and implied readers; a socio-narratological approach: BibTB 19 (1989) 100-7.

5401 **Landier** Jean, *al.*,   Avec Jean; pour accompagner une lecture de
l'évangile, ch. 1-12.   P 1988, Ouvrières.   292 p. F 98. – ᴿRB 96 (1989) 465
(M.-É. *Boismard*).

5401* *Léon-Dufour* Xavier,   Bulletin: L'Évangile de Jean [16 livres]:   RechSR
77 (1989) 261-280.

5402 **Mlakuzhyil** George,   The Christocentric literary structure of the Fourth
Gospel: AnBib 117, ᴰ1987 → 3,5286; 4,5462:   ᴿBiblica 70 (1989) 286-290
(G. *Segalla*); CBQ 51 (1989) 749s (F.F. *Segovia*: good but claims too
much); EstBíb 47 (1989) 285-7 (D. *Muñoz León*); JTS 40 (1989) 192-4
(S.S. *Smalley*); RechSR 77 (1989) 264-6 (X. *Léon-Dufour*).

5403 **Robinson** J.A.T.,   The priority of John 1985 → 1,5234... 4,5466:
ᴿHeythJ 30 (1989) 444s (J.O. *Tuñí*: disappointing); JBL 108 (1989)
156-8 (D.M. *Smith*); StPatav 36 (1989) 202s (G. *Segalla*).

5404 **Ruckstuhl** Eugen,   Die literarische Einheit 1987 [= ᴰ1951 avec
supplément bibliog.]: NTOrb 5 → 3,5292; 4,5467:   ᴿETL 65 (1989) 170s
(F. *Neirynck*); ZkT 111 (1989) 222 (M. *Hasitschka*).

5405 **Segalla** Giuseppe, *a*) 'Il discepolo che Gesù amava' [Gv 13,23] e la
tradizione giovannea: TItSett 14 (1989) 217-243; Eng. 244; – *b*) Il
'discepolo che Gesù amava' cancellato dalla storia [KÜGLER J. 1988
→ 5399]: RivB 37 (1989) 361-363.

5406 *a*) *Silva* Moisés,   Approaching the Fourth Gospel; – *b*) *Parker* James,
The incarnational Christology of John; – *c*) *Morris* Leon,   The atonement
in John's Gospel; – *d*) *Borchert* Gerald L.,   The Spirit and salvation; – *e*)
Cook W. Robert,   Eschatology in John's Gospel; – *f*) *Mathews* Kenneth
A.,   John, Jesus and the Essenes; trouble at the Temple; – *g*) *Lea* Thomas
D.,   Preaching from John; – *h*) *Burns* John A., Commentaries: CriswT
3,1 (1988) 17-29 / 31-48 / 49-64 / 65-78 / 79-99 / 101-126 / 161-184 /
185-197.

5406* *Silva Santos* Bento,   A autoria [authorship] do Quarto Evangelho:
RBBras 5,4 (1988) 157-181 [< IZBG 36, p. 186].

5407 *Smith* D. Moody,   Johannine studies: → 394, NT/Interpreters 1989,
271-298.

5408 **Stible** Mark,   The artistry of John; the Fourth Gospel as narrative
Christology: diss. Nottingham.   345 p. BRD-87408. – DissA 50 (1989s)
3269-A.

5409 **Trudinger** P.,   The cool gospel; [14] essays on St. John's Gospel for
reflection and resource.   Kingston ON 1988, R.P. Frye.   vii-137 p.
0-919741-03-7 [NTAbs 33,254: 'cool' in M. MᶜLᴜʜᴀɴ categories].

5410 **Wahlde** Urban C. von,   The earliest version of John's Gospel; recovering
the gospel of signs. Wilmington 1989, Glazier.   216 p. $19.   0-89453-
694-X [TDig 37,93].

5411 **Wengst** Hans, Interpretación del evangelio de Juan [contra BULTMANN, KÄSEMANN]: Biblia y catequesis 11. Salamanca 1988, Sígueme. 146 p. – ^RLumenVr 38 (1989) 82 (F. *Ortiz de Urtaran*).

5412 *Zumstein* J., Analyse narrative, critique rhétorique et exégèse johannique: → 385, Narration 1988, 37-56.

G1.4 *Johannis themata,* topics.

5413 **Bahr** Ann-Marie, 'Knowing God' in the Fourth Gospel; the household and the Word: diss. Temple, ^D*Sloyan* G. Ph 1989. 447 p. 90-07337. – DissA 50 (1989s) 3258-A; RelStR 16,189.

5413* *Barth* Markus, Ultimate reality and meaning in the light of John's Gospel: Ultimate Reality and Meaning 12,2 (1989) 84-103 [< IZBG 36, p. 190].

5414 *Beaude* P. M., Le Jésus de saint Jean: DossB 26 (1989) 20s [3-24, *al.*].

5415 **Belle** G. Van, Les parenthèses 1985 → 1,5243 ... 4,5473: ^RRB 96 (1989) 462s (M.-É. *Boismard*).

5416 **Boismard** M.-É., Moïse ou Jésus? [Essai de Christologie joh. + 3 reprints]: BiblETL 84. Lv 1988, Peeters. → 4,5474; xvi-241 p. Fb 1000. 90-6831-145-X: ^RExpTim 101 (1989s) 315 (E. *Best*); RB 96 (1989) 465s (B. T. *Viviano*).

5417 *a) Brumlik* Micha, Johannes; das judenfeindliche Evangelium; – *b) Stegemann* Ekkehard, Die Tragödie der Nähe; zu den judenfeindlichen Aussagen des Joh.-Evs.: KIsr (1989,2) 102-113 / 114-122.

5418 **Burkett** Delbert R., The Son of Man in the Gospel of John: diss. Duke, ^D*Smith* D. M. Durham NC 1989. 309 p. 90-06727. – DissA 50 (1989s) 3258-A; RelStR 16,190.

5419 *Carroll* John T., Present and future in Fourth Gospel 'eschatology': BibTB 19 (1989) 63-69.

5420 **Cirillo** Antonio, Cristo rivelatore del Padre nel Vangelo di S. Giovanni secondo il commento di S. Tommaso d'AQUINO, ^D1988 → 4,3479: ^RAnnTh 3 (1989) 163s (M. A. *Tábet*).

5421 **Crowe** James R.^J, Avatāra and incarnation; a paradigm analysis and comparison of their respective meanings in the Bhagavadgītā and in the Gospel of John: diss. Rice, ^D*Nielson* N. Houston 1989. 316 p. 90-12792. – DissA 50 (1989s) 3986-A. → 5433.

5422 **Diel** P., *Solotareff* J., Symbolism in the Gospel of John [c. 1984], ^T*Marans* N. SF 1988, Harper & R. viii-222 p. $20 pa. 0-86683-509-1 [NTAbs 33,106].

5423 **Dodd** Charles H., La tradition historique du quatrième évangile [1963 → 45,1163], ^T*Montabrut* Maurice & Simone: LDiv 128. P 1987, Cerf. 563 p. – ^RBLitEc 90 (1989) 62s (S. *Légasse*); ScripTPamp 21 (1989) 310-2 (A. *García-Moreno*).

5424 **Dorado** G. G., Moral y existencia cristiana en el IV Evangelio y en las Cartas de Juan. M 1989, 'PS'. 207 p. – ^RBibFe 15 (1989) 320 (A. *Salas*).

5425 **Duke** Paul D., Irony in the Fourth Gospel 1985 → 1,5250 ... 4,5483: ^RCriswT 2 (1988) 436s (D. S. *Dockery*).

5426 **Ferraro** Giuseppe, La gioia di Cristo nel quarto Vangelo 1988 → 4, 5488: ^RCC 140 (1989,2) 87s (N. *Spaccapelo*); Gregorianum 70 (1989) 607s (*ipse*); Irénikon 62 (1989) 121s (E. *Lanne*); RivB 37 (1989) 515s (A. *Bonora*).

5427 **Ferraro** Giuseppe, Lo Spirito e Cristo nel Vangelo di Giovanni: StBPaid 70, 1984 ➤ 65,4809 ... 3,5310: ᴿScripTPamp 21 (1989) 312s (A. *García-Moreno*).

5428 *Ferraro* Giuseppe, La pneumatologia di San Tommaso d'AQuino nel suo commento al quarto Vangelo: Angelicum 66 (1989) 193-263.

5429 *Gangemi* Attilio, L'utilizzazione del c. 55 del Libro di Isaia nel Vangelo di Giovanni: Synaxis 7 (Catania 1989) 7-90.

5430 *Garcia-Moreno* Antonio, La Palabra en la Liturgía; aspectos joánicos: ➤ 69*, ᶠGoMÀ I., RCatalT 14 (1989) 485-491 castellano; Eng. 492 [479-484, *Llopis* Joan].

5431 **Ghiberti** Giuseppe, Spirito e vita cristiana in Giovanni: StBPaid 84. Brescia 1989, Paideia. 189 p. Lit. 20.000. 88-394-0419-8. – ᴿTeresianum 40 (1989) 626 (V. *Pasquetto*).

5432 *Giblet* Jean, La puissance satanique selon l'Évangile de saint Jean: ➤ 728, Anges et démons 1987/9, 291-300.

5433 *Gorospe* V. R., Krishna avatars in the Bhagavad Gita and Christ incarnate in John's Gospel: Dialogue & Alliance 1,2 (NY 1987) 53-72 [< NTAbs 33,169]. ➤ 5421.

5434 *Grayston* Kenneth, Who misunderstands the Johannine misunderstandings?: ScriptB 20 (1989s) 9-15.

5434* *Gyllenhaal* C. Edward, Terminological connections between the Gospel of John and the Dead Sea Scrolls: The New Philosophy 90 (1987) 393-414 [< IZBG 36, p. 187].

5435 *a*) *Harrington* Daniel J., 'The Jews' in John's Gospel; – *b*) *Osiek* Carolyn, The 'liberation theology' of the Gospel of John: BToday 27 (1989) 203-9 / 210-8.

5436 ᴱ**Hartman** L., *Olsson* B., Aspects on the Johannine literature 1986/7 ➤ 3,546; 4,5491: ᴿExpTim 100 (1988s) 31 (Judith *Lieu*); NRT 111 (1989) 945s (Y. *Simoens*).

5437 **Hasitschka** Martin, Befreiung von Sünde nach dem Johannesevangelium [1,29 ...]; eine bibeltheologische Untersuchung [Diss. ᴰ*Stock* K. 1986]: InnsbTStud 27. Innsbruck 1989, Tyrolia. 439 p. DM 62 [TR 86,163].

5438 *Heine* Ronald E., The Gospel of John and the Montanist debate at Rome: ➤ 696, 10th Patristic, 21 (1989) 95-100 [cf. ➤ 4,5492].

5439 *Hengel* Martin, Die Schriftauslegung des 4. Evangeliums auf dem Hintergrund der urchristlichen Exegese: JbBT 4 (1989) 249-288.

5439* *Hoffman* T. A., A.M.D.G. according to John: RRel 48 (1989) 594-8.

5440 **Kieffer** René, Le monde symbolique de saint Jean: LDiv 137. P 1989, Cerf. 119 p. F 88 [CBQ 52,382]. 2-204-03148-0. – ᴿPrOrChr 39 (1989) 216 (P. *Ternant*).

5441 *Kieffer* René, Olika nivåer i johanneiskt bildspråk [varying levels of Johannine imagery]: SvTKv 65 (1989) 9-15.

5442 *Koester* Craig, Hearing, seeing, and believing in the Gospel of John: Biblica 70 (1989) 327-348; franç. 348.

5443 *Konings* Johan, A memória de Jesus e a manifestação do Pai no quarto evangelho: PerspT 20,51 (1988) 177-200 [< TContext 6/2, 58].

5444 *Langkammer* Hugolin, ❷ From among the problems of the ethic of the Gospel of St. John: RoczTK 33,1 (1986) 69-77.

5445 *La Potterie* Ignace de, *a*) Simbologia della famiglia in S. Giovanni: ➤ 587, Famiglia 1987/9, 225-240; – *b*) Teología del cuerpo y de la sexualidad en los escritos de Juan: ➤ 572, Masculinidad 1989, 825-897.

5445* *a*) *Larsen* J., The use of *hina* in the New Testament, with special reference to the Gospel of John: Notes on Translation 2,2 (Dallas 1988)

28-34 [< NTAbs 33,282]: – *b*) *Pope* T., The use of the present indicative to signal future time in NT Greek, with special reference to the Gospel of John: OPTAT 2,2 (Dallas 1988) 27-38 [< NTAbs 33,292].

5446 **Loader** William, The Christology of the Fourth Gospel; structure and issues: BeitBExT 23. Fra 1989, Lang. 303 p. Fs 65. 3-631-41912-9. – ᴿExpTim 101 (1989s) 312 (S. S. *Smalley*).

5447 **Maloney** George A., Entering into the Heart of Jesus; meditation on the indwelling Trinity in St. John's Gospel. NY 1988, Alba. xx-170 p. 0-8189-0527-1.

5447* **Martini** Carlo M., Il Vangelo secondo Giovanni nell'esperienza degli esercizi spirituali [1974, ²1979], ᴱ*Stancari* Pino⁵: Letture bibliche. R 1984, Borla. 217 p.

5448 *Moloney* Francis J., Johannine theology: ⇥ 384, NJBC (1989) 1417-1426.

5448* *Monshouwer* D., Het vierde evangelie en de joodse eredienst opnieuw bezien: AmstCah 8 (1987) 117-135 [< GerefTTs 89,61].

5449 *a*) *Moore* Stephen D., Rifts in (a reading of) the fourth gospel; or: does Johannine irony still collapse in a reading that draws attention to itself?; – *b*) *Tilborg* Sjef van, The Gospel of John; communicative processes in a narrative text: Neotestamentica 23 (Bloemfontein 1989) 5-17 / 19-31.

5450 **Morris** Leon, Jesus is the Christ; studies in the theology of John. GR/Leicester 1989, Eerdmans/Inter-Varsity. vii-224 p. [TR 86,251]. 0-8028-0452-7 / 0-85111-574-8.

5451 **O'Day** Gail R., Revelation in the Fourth Gospel [diss. Emory, ᴰ*Beardslee* W.] 1986 ⇥ 2,4203; 4,5511: ᴿJRel 68 (1988) 450s (R. A. *Culpepper* wishes all dissertations were so successful).

5452 **Odiam** Alan R., The rhetoric of the Fourth Gospel; a key to preaching: diss. Southern Baptist Theol. Sem. 1989, ᴰ*Cox* J. 90-08963. – DissA 50 (1989s) 2945-A.

5453 *Pereyra* R., El significado de Ioudaioi en el evangelio de Juan: Theologika 3,2 (Lima 1988) 116-136 [< NTAbs 33,319].

5454 **Rabiej** Andrzej, ❷ Christological meaning of the biblical formula 'ego eimi': diss. ᴰ*Bartnik* C. Lublin 1989. xxxiii-300 p. – RTLv 21,570.

5455 *Rao* O. M., Soteriology in the Fourth Gospel: Bible Bhashyam 14 (1988) 149-162.

5457 *a*) *Reinhartz* Adele [⇥ 5506], Jesus as prophet; predictive prolepses in the Fourth Gospel; – *b*) *Painter* John, Quest and rejection stories in John: JStNT 36 (1989) 3-16 / 17-46.

5458 *Robertson* P. E., Glory [*dóxa*] in the Fourth Gospel: TEdr 38 (New Orleans 1988) 121-131 [NTAbs 33,170].

5459 **Rodríguez Ruiz** M., Der Missionsgedanke des Joh.-evs...: ForBi 55, 1987 ⇥ 3,5329; 4,5515: ᴿSalmanticensis 36 (1989) 111s (F. F. *Ramos*); ScripTPamp 21 (1989) 701s (K. *Limburg*); ZkT 111 (1989) 223 (M. *Hasitschka*).

5460 *Segalla* Giuseppe, La Scrittura nel Quarto Vangelo: StPatav 36 (1989) 89-112; Eng. 113.

5461 *Silva Santos* B., A fórmula 'egō eimi' no Quarto Evangelho: Liturgia y Vida 210 (Rio 1989) 12-23 [< Stromata 45,499].

5462 *a*) *Simmons* B. E., A Christology of the 'I am' sayings in the Gospel of John; – *b*) *Winbery* C. L., Abiding in Christ; the concept of discipleship in John; – *c*) *Sullivan* R., Jesus' suffering, death, and resurrection in the Fourth Gospel: TEdr 38 (1988) 94-103 / 104-120 / 145-153 [< NTAbs 33,170].

5463 **Stanley** David M., 'I encountered God!'; The Spiritual Exercises with the Gospel of St. John, 1986 ➤ 2,4208; 3,5337: [R]HeythJ 30 (1989) 219 (A. *Parish*).

5464 **Tew** William M., Judgment as present and future in the Gospel of John: diss. Baptist Theol. Sem., [D]*Simmons* B. New Orleans 1988. 129 p. 89-11189. – DissA 50 (1989s) 716-A.

5465 **Thompson** Marianne Meye, The humanity of Jesus in the Fourth Gospel [diss. Duke, [D]*Smith* D. M.; against KÄSEMANN E.] 1988 ➤ 4,5523: [R]ExpTim 100 (1988s) 392 (S. S. *Smalley*); JBL 108 734s (F. F. *Segovia*: 'Professor Meye Thompson'); TS 50 (1989) 397s (J. W. *Holleran*).

5466 *Tialet* Noël, Les étapes de la foi dans l'Évangile de Jean: Christus 36 (P 1989) 306-319.

5467 **Trumbower** Jeffrey A., Born from above; the anthropology of the Gospel of John: diss. [D]*Betz* H. Chicago 1989. OIAc Ja90; RelStR 16,190.

5468 *Watt* J. G. van der, The use of *aiōnios* in the concept *zōē aiōnios* in John's Gospel: NT 31 (1989) 217-228.

5469 **Whitacre** Rodney A., Johannine polemic [diss. C, [D]*Hooker* M.] 1982 ➤ 63,5372... 4,5526: [R]TLZ 114 (1989) 432-3 (H.-M. *Schenke*).

5470 **Yee** Gale A., Jewish feasts and the Gospel of John: Zacchaeus Studies. Wilmington 1989, Glazier. 93 p. $7 [TDig 36,194].

5471 *Yousif* Pierre, La Vierge Marie et le disciple bien-aimé chez saint ÉPHREM de Nisibe: OrChrPer 55 (1989) 283-316.

5472 *Zevini* Giorgio, Il 'peccato' e il credente negli scritti giovannei: ParSpV 19 (1989) 163-177.

G1.5 Johannis Prologus 1,1 ...

5473 *Bandera* A., [Jn 1] Una eclesiología trinitaria y sapiencial, el Prólogo de San Juan II: Vida y Espiritualidad 10 (Lima 1988) 15-32 [< Stromata 45,499].

5474 **Barth** K., Witness to the Word... Jn 1 [1925-55] 1986 ➤ 2,4224... 4,5530: [R]StPatav 36 (1989) 631s (G. *Segalla*).

5475 **Beutel** Albrecht, In dem Anfang war das Wort; eine Untersuchung zu LUTHERs Sprachverständnis im Anschluss an seine Auslegung des Johannes-Prologs von 1522: Diss. [D]*Jüngel* E. Tübingen 1989. x-351 p.; 275 p. – TLZ 115,773-5.

5476 *Chico* Gabriel, [Jn 1] Mito y palabra; nota hermenéutica de desmitologización: EfMex 6 (1988) 391-400.

5477 **Cholin** Marc, Le Prologue de l'Évangile selon Jean; structure et formation: ScEspr 41 (1989) 189-205. 343-362.

5478 **Clark** Gordon H., The Johannine Logos; the mind of Christ[2] [[1]1972]. Jefferson MD 1989, Trinity Fd. ix-155 p. 0-940931-22-2.

5479 *Fatica* Luigi, Il commento di TEODORO di Mopsuestia a Giovanni 1,1-18: Koinonia 13 (N 1989) 61-78.

5480 *García-Moreno* Antonio, Aspectos teológicos del Prólogo de S. Juan: ScripTPamp 21 (1989) 411-430.

5481 **Hofrichter** Peter, Im Anfang war der 'Johannesprolog' 1986 ➤ 2,4217... 4,5534: [R]Salesianum 51 (1989) 358 (C. *Bissoli*).

5482 *Kalinich* Lila J., The logos in LACAN [Jacques, psychoanalyst, † 1981]: SVlad 32 (1988) 367-383.

5483 *Lyman* Rebecca, Arians and Manichees on Christ: JTS 40 (1989) 493-503.

5484 *Ménard* Jacques É., Le Logos de la Prôtennoia trimorphe et celui du
IVᵉ Évangile: ➤ 820, Journées Coptes III, 1986/9, 128s.

5485 *Meynet* Roland, Analyse rhétorique du Prologue de Jean: RB 96
(1989) 481-510; Eng. 481.

5486 *Ruh* K., Die Homilie über den Prolog des Johannes-Evangeliums des
Johannes ERIUGENA: Würzburger Diözesangeschichtsblätter 51 (1989)
491-500 [< RHE 84, p. 359*].

5487 **Theobald** Michael, Die Fleischwerdung des Logos: NTAbs 20, 1988
➤ 4,5536: ᴿBZ 33 (1989) 275-8 (R. *Schnackenburg*); RHR 206 (1989)
429-431 (A. *Méhat*).

5488 *Weder* Hans, ⓌThe myth of the logos; thoughts in connection with the
(objective) problem of de-mythologization, ᵀ*Fóris* Mrs. Eva: TSzem 32
(1989) 32-43.

5489 *Korting* Georg, Joh 1,3 [*oudén* = 'keineswegs', nicht ein Substantiv]: BZ
33 (1989) 97-104.

5490 **Miller** Ed L., Salvation-History in the Prologue of John; the significance
of John 1:3/4: NT supp 60. Leiden 1989, Brill. ix-119 p. *f* 60.
90-04-08692-7. – ᴿExpTim 101 (1989s) 248s (Ruth B. *Edwards*: model of
clarity, almost persuades).

5491 *Galot* Jean, Maternité virginale de Marie et paternité divine; que dit le
Prologue de S. Jean 1,13 [contre le témoignage unanime des manuscrits,
lire 'lui qui ne fut' au lieu de 'ceux qui ne furent' engendré(s) des sangs]:
EsprVie 99 (1989) 57-64.

5491* *a) Kotzé* P.P.A. [Jn 1,14-18] Die betekenis en konteks van genade en
waarheid in Johannes 1:14-18; – *b) Watt* J.W. van der, Die strukturele
komposisie van die proloog aan die Johannesevangelie heroorweeg: Skrif
en Kerk 8,1 (1987) 38-51 / 68-84 [< IZBG 36, p. 192].

5492 *Devillers* Luc, Exégèse et théologie de Jean 1,18: RThom 89 (1989)
181-217 [N.B. p. 475, correction des errata p. 184 et 206].

5493 *Hofius* Otfried, 'Der in des Vaters Schoss ist' Joh 1,18: ZNW 80 (1989)
163-171.

5494 *Robert* René, Le mot final du prologue johannique; à propos d'un
article récent [*La Potterie* I. de, Biblica 69 (1988) 340-370]: RThom 89
(1989) 279-280 [encore 90, 634-9].

5494* *Nortjé* S., [Jn 1,28, Bethania trans Jordanem] Johannes die Doper in
Betanië oorkant die Jordaan: HervTS 45 (1989) 573-585 [< IZBG 36,
p. 191].

5495 *Charles* J. Daryl, 'Will the court please call in the prime witness?';
John 1:29-34 and the 'witness-' motif: TrinJ 10,1 (1989) 71-83.

5496 *Dschulnigg* Peter, Die Berufung der Jünger Joh 1,35-51 im Rahmen des
vierten Evangeliums: FreibZ 36 (1989) 427-447.

5497 *Kuhn* H.-J., Christologie und Wunder; Untersuchungen zu Joh. 1,35-51
[Diss. Trier, ᴰ*Eckert* J.]: BibUnt 18, 1987 ➤ 4,5547: ᴿClaretianum 29
(1989) 424-6 (B. *Proietti*); EstAgust 24 (1989) 257 (C. *Mielgo*); NRT 111
(1989) 947s (Y. *Simoens*); Salmanticensis 36 (1989) 109s (F.F. *Ramos*); TLZ 114 (1989) 434 (J. *Becker*); TsTNijm 29 (1989) 66 (A. van
Diemen).

5498 *Breton* Stanislas, [Jn 1,35-40; 15,9; 14,8] Esquisse de commentaire de
quelques textes de saint Jean: ➤ 381, Variations 1989, 85-106.

5499 *Gomes* Peter J., John 1:45-51 (expository): Interpretation 43 (1989)
282-6.

5500 **Aus** Roger, Water into wine and the beheading of John the Baptist;
early Jewish-Christian interpretation of Esther 1 [and its rabbinic

adaptations] in John 2:1-11 and Mark 6:17-29: BrownJudSt 150. Atlanta 1988, Scholars. x-96 p. $30. 1-55540-245-3 [TDig 36,349].

5501 *Derrett* J.D.M., [Jn 2,1-11] Der Wasserwandel in christlicher und jüdischer Perspektive: ZRGg 41 (1989) 193-214.

5502 *Moloney* Francis J., Mary in the Fourth Gospel; woman and mother: Salesianum 51 (1989) 421-440.

5503 **Moreira Azevedo** Carlos A., O milagre de Caná na iconografia paleocristã I-II [diss. Pont. Univ. Gregoriana, R 1986]. Porto 1986, auct. (Largo P. Vitorino 2). 285 p.; Eng. Summary. – ᴿJbAC 32 (1989) 219-221 (Beatrix *Asamer*).

5504 *Seckel* Marianne, La mère de Jésus dans le 4ᵉ évangile; de la lignée des femmes-disciples?: FoiVie 88,5 (CahBib 28, 1989) 33-41.

5505 **Serra** Aristide, E c'era la Madre di Gesù... [Gv 2,1]; Saggi di esegesi biblico-mariana (1978-1988). Cernuso 1989, Cens-Marianum. v-671 p. Lit. 50.000.

5506 *Reinhartz* A., [Jn 2,1-11; 4,46-54; 11,1-44] Great expectations; a reader-oriented approach to Johannine Christology and eschatology: LitTOx 3,1 (1989) 61-76 [< NTAbs 33,320].

5507 *Zappella* M., Gv 2,1-12; la figura della madre di Gesù nel conflitto delle interpretazioni; rassegna bibliografica (1970-1988): Quaderni Monfortani 5 (R 1987) [< NTAbs 33,321].

5508 *a) Burmeister* J., Exegetical and translation issues in John 2:4 [3:29]; – *b) Steele* M., Where does the speech quotation end in John 3:1-21; – *c) Larsen* J., Did Peter enter the boat? (John 21:11); – *d) Jarvis* E., The key term 'believe' in the Gospel of John: NotesTr 2,2 (1988) 16-24 [25-28] / 51-58 / 34-41 / 46-51 [< NTAbs 33,319-323].

5509 *Brearley* Denis, The allegorical identification of the Architriclinus (Jn 2.9-10) in early mediaeval exegesis: → 696, 10th Patristic, 19 (1989) 337-344.

5510 *Bauer* Johannes B., [Joh 2,13-22; Mk 11,15-18] Christus sidereus; die Tempelaustreibung, HIERONYMUS und das Nazaräerevangelium: → 197, ᶠTRILLING W. 1989, 257-266.

5511 **Rebolledo** René, 'In tre giorni io lo sveglierò' (Gv 2,19); teologia, spiritualità e pastorale del 'Tempio Nuovo': < diss. Pont. Univ. Urbaniana, ᴰ*Federici* T. R 1989. xlvii-209 p.

5512 *Hartman* Lars, 'He spoke of the temple of his body' (Jn 2:13-22): → 147, ᶠOTTOSSON M., SvEx 54 (1989) 70-79.

G1.6 Jn 3ss... Nicodemus, Samaritana.

5513 *Bassler* Jouette M., Mixed signals; Nicodemus in the Fourth Gospel: JBL 108 (1989) 635-646.

5514 *Bauer* Dieter, 'Wenn jemand nicht von neuem geboren wird...'; ein Versuch, 'New Age' mit den Augen des Johannesevangeliums zu sehen: BiKi 44,1 ('New Age' und Bibel, 1989) 14-21.

5515 *Bonvin* Bernard, Nicodème ou l'invitation à renaître, Jn 3,1-21: NVFr 64 (1989) 68-71.

5516 *Born* J.B., Literary features in the Gospel of John (an analysis of John 3:1-21): Direction 17,2 (Fresno 1988) 3-17 [< NTAbs 33,171].

5517 **Smidt** Jacobus C. de, Die Johannesevangelie en die 'sakramente'; die eksegese van Johannes 3:3-7.22-25 en 6:22-59: diss. ᴰ*Lombard* H. Pretoria 1989 [microfilm from Unisa]. RTLv 21,544.

5518 *a*) *Osburn* Carroll D., Some exegetical observations on John 3:5-8; – *b*) *Pack* Frank, The Holy Spirit in the Fourth Gospel: RestQ 31 (Abilene 1989) 129-138 / 139-148 [-164, *Brooks* Pat].

5519 *Witherington* Ben[III], The waters of birth; John 3.5 and 1 John 5.6-8: NTS 35 (1989) 155-160.

5520 *Hollis* H., [Jn 3,14 + 3 times] The root of the Johannine pun — *hypsō-thēnai*: NTS 35 (1989) 475-8.

5521 *Dockery* David S., Reading John 4:1-45; some diverse hermeneutical perspectives: CriswT 3 (1988s) 127-140.

5522 *Hock* Gundikar [Jn 4,1-26] Das Gespräch mit Jesus wagen: GeistL 62 (1989) 38-40.

5523 *Hunger* Herbert, [Jn 4] Das lebenspendende Wasser; ROMANOS Melodos, Kontakion 9. Jesus und die Samariterin: JbÖsByz 38 (1988) 125-157.

5524 **Poffet** Jean-Michel, Méthode exégétique... ORIGÈNE/Jn 4, 1985 ➤ 1, 5308... 4,5563: [R]TR 85 (1989) 107s (N. *Brox*).

5525 **Okure** Teresa, The Johannine approach to mission... 4,1-42: WUNT 2/31, 1988 ➤ 4,5564: [R]ExpTim 100 (1988s) 431s (Judith *Lieu*); SWJT 32,2 (1989s) 60 (E. E. *Ellis*); TGL 79 (1989) 198s (J. *Ernst*); TPhil 64 (1989) 582s (J. *Beutler*).

5526 *a*) *Ritt* Hubert, Die Frau als Glaubensbotin; zum Verständnis der Samaritanerin von Joh 4,1-42; – *b*) *Ruckstuhl* Eugen, Jesus und der geschichtliche Mutterboden im vierten Evangelium; – *c*) *Mussner* Franz, Die 'semantische Achse' des Johannesevangeliums; ein Versuch: ➤ 68, [F]GNILKA J., Vom Urchristentum 1989, 287-306 / 256-286 / 246-255.

5527 *Ukachukwu Manus* Chris, The Samaritan woman (Jn 4:7); reflections on female leadership and nation building in modern Africa: Chiea 4,4 (Nairobi 1988) 73-84 [< TContext 7/1, 19].

5528 *Vitório* J., Jesus, a festa y a morte; leitura de Jo 5,1-18: PerspTeol 21 (1989) 199-220 [< Stromata 45,500].

G1.7 **Panis Vitae** – *Jn 6*...

5529 **Morris** Leon, The Bread of Life, John 6-10: Reflections/Jn, 2. GR 1987, Baker. 200 p. $9. – [R]CriswT 3 (1989) 391 (T. D. *Lea*).

5530 *a*) *Grosjean* Jean, Selon Jean, chapitre 6 [lecture / le style johannique]; – *b*) *Manigne* Jean-P., Question de signes; une lecture de Jean 6; – *c*) *Kristeva* Julia, Des signes au sujet; – *d*) *Sublon* Roland, Voix; variations sur l'évangile de Jean, chapitres 5 et 6: ➤ 381, Variations 1989, 17-60 / 127-136 / 137-146 / 147-155 / 61-83.

5531 *Sevrin* Jean-Marie, L'écriture du IVe évangile comme phénomène de réception; l'exemple de Jn 6: ➤ 606, Réception 1986/9, 69-83.

5531* *Snyman* G. F., Die wonders in Johannes 6 verklaar aan die hand van die vertellerperspektiefanalise: HervTS 44 (1988) 708-733.

5532 *Voelz* J. W., The discourse on the Bread of Life in John; is it eucharistic?: ConcordiaJ 15,1 (St. Louis 1989) 29-37 [< NTAbs 33,172].

5533 *Painter* John, Tradition and interpretation in John 6: NTS 35 (1989) 421-450.

5534 **Wehr** Lothar, Arznei der Unsterblichkeit... Ignatius/Joh.-ev. [Diss. Mü, [D]*Gnilka* J.]: NTAbh NS 18, 1987 ➤ 4,5574: [R]JBL 108 (1989) 739s (D. E. *Aune*); StPatav 36 (1989) 205s (G. *Segalla*).

5535 *Hurst* Antony, [Jn 6,1-14; Phlp 4,10-20] Feeding the five thousand [... 'the Church is in a bit of a quandary about miracles at the moment']: ExpTim 101 (1989s) 80s.

5536 *Grigsby* Bruce, [Jn 6,20] The reworking of the lake-walking account in the Johannine tradition: ExpTim 100 (1988s) 295-7.

5537 *Giblin* Charles H.,   St. John's Jesus, sign seekers, and Gnostics; a reading of John 6:22-71: → 175, ᶠSCHODER R., Daidalikon 1989, 125-130.

5538 *Roberge* Michael,   Jean 6,26 et le rassasiement eschatologique: LavalTP 45 (1989) 339-349.

5539 *Cosgrove* Charles H., [Jn 6,52...] The place where Jesus is; allusions to baptism and the eucharist in the Fourth Gospel: NTS 35 (1989) 522-539.

5540 *Kilmartin* Edward J.,   The Eucharistic gift; AUGUSTINE of Hippo's tractate 27 on John 6:60-72: → 38, ᶠBURGHARDT W.,   Preaching 1989, 162-182.

5541 *Schenke* Ludger,   John 7-10; eine dramatische Szene: ZNW 80 (1989) 172-192.

5542 *a) Culbertson* Diana,   'Are you also deceived?' Reforming the reader in John 7; – *b) Reinhartz* Adele,   The shepherd and the sheep; John 10:1-5 reconsidered: ProcGLM 9 (1989) 148-160 / 161-177.

5543 *Comfort* Philip, [Jn 7,53-8,11] The pericope of the adulteress: BTrans 40 (1989) 145-7.

5544 *Baylis* Charles P., [Jn 8] The woman caught in adultery; a test of Jesus as the greater prophet: BS 146 (1989) 171-184.

5545 *Trumbower* Jeffrey A.,   ORIGEN's exegesis of John 8:19-53; the struggle with Heracleon over the idea of fixed natures: VigChr 43 (1989) 138-154.

5546 *Robert* René,   Étude littéraire de Jean VIII, 21-59:   RThom 89 (1989) 71-84.

5547 *Porsch* Felix,   'Ihr habt den Teufel zum Vater' (Joh. 8,44); Antijudaismus im Johannesevangelium?:   BiKi 44 (1989) 50-57.

5548 *a) Dockery* D. S.,   John 9:1-41; a narrative discourse study; – *b) Myers* D. E.,   Irony and humor in the Gospel of John: OPTAT 2,2 (Dallas 1988) 14-26 / 1-13 [< NTAbs 33,323.319].

5549 *Atal sa Angang*, [Jn 9,1-4] Foi et conversion [TContext 6/2,22].

5550 *García Romero* Francisco A.,   Breve comentario a Jn 9,1-3; objeciones al supuesto cristianismo de TRIFIODORO [*Hálōsis Ilíou*]:   FgNt 2,1 (1989) 93-97.

5550* *Dimitrov* Ivan Z., (Bulg.) Der Herr Jesus Christus — einziger neutestamentlicher Erzhirt und Hoherpriester; exegetische Forschung in Joh 10,11-16... Heb]: AnOchr 29 (1988 für 1980) 165-197; deutsch 198.

5551 *Dschulnigg* Peter,   Der Hirt und die Schafe (Joh 10,1-18):   SNTU 14 (1989) 5-24 [< ZIT 90,406].

5552 *a) Genuyt* François,   La Porte et le Pasteur (Jn 10,1-21); étude sémiotique; – *b) Léon-Dufour* Xavier,   Jésus le bon pasteur: → 576, Paraboles 1987/9, 375-387 / 361-373.

5553 *Otranto* Giorgio, [Gv 10] Tra letteratura e iconografia; note sul Buon Pastore e sull'Orante nell'arte cristiana antica (II-III secolo):   *a)* → 567, AnStoEseg 6 (1989) 15-39; Eng. 5; – *b)* VetChr 26 (1989) 69-87 + 7 fig.

5554 *Regopoulos* G.,   Jesus Christ, 'the Good Shepherd' (interpretative approach): DeltioVM 18 (1989) 5-48.

5555 *Homcy* Stephen L., [Ps 82,6 → 3138; Jn 10,4] 'You are gods'? Spirituality and a difficult text: JEvTS 32 (1989) 485-492 [493-502, *Dahms* John V.,   The generation of the Son [< ZIT 90,228].

5556 *Barsi* Balázs, (Joh 10,10) Ⓜ 'Ich bin gekommen, damit sie das Leben haben':   TBud 22 (1988) 6-10.

5557 *Pratt* Douglas,   The Imago Dei in the thought of John MACQUARRIE; a reflection on John 10:10:   AsiaJT 3 (1989) 79-83.

5558 *Kysar* Robert, John 10:22-30 (expository): Interpretation 43 (1989) 66-69.
5559 *Morujão* Geraldo, A unidade de Jesus com o Pai em Jo 10,30: EstBíb 47 (1989) 47-64; castellano/Eng. 47.
5560 *Phillips* W. Gary, An apologetic study of John 10:34-36: BS 146 (1989) 405-419.
5561 *Manns* Frédéric, Lecture midrashique de Jean 11: LA 39 (1989) 49-76.
5562 *Cueto Carmelo* R. del, La Resurrección de Lázaro es signo de vida para el cristiano: StLeg 29 (1988) 75-92.
5563 **Marchadour** Alain, Lazare 1988 ⇒ 4,5592:   ᴿAngelicum 66 (1989) 328s (S. *Jurič*); BLitEc 90 (1989) 60-62 (L. *Légasse*); CBQ 51 (1989) 160 (J. J. *O'Rourke*: interesting, not major); LVitae 44 (1989) 238s (L. *Partos*); NRT 111 (1989) 951s (Y. *Simoens*); RechSR 77 (1989) 277-9 (X. *Léon-Dufour*); RThom 89 (1989) 482s (L. *Devillers*); StPatav 36 (1989) 628s (G. *Segalla*).
5564 *a) Marchadour* Alain, Lazare; du silence à la parole; – *b) Eslin* Jean-Claude, Proses évangéliques: ⇒ 381, Variations 1989, 175-189 / 119-124.
5565 *Sabugal* Santos, La resurrección de Lázaro (Jn 11,1-54): EstAgust 24 (1989) 55-70.
5566 *Uthemann* Karl-Heinz, Die Lazarus-Predigt des LEONTIOS von Arabissos (BHG 2219u): Byzantion 59 (Bru 1989) 291-331; Text + deutsch gegenüber, 332-353.
5567 **Partyka** Jan, La résurrection de Lazare dans les monuments funéraires des catacombes de Rome: diss. ᴰ*Myszor* W., Wsz 1988. 647 p. – RTLv 21,559.
5568 **Wagner** Josef, Auferstehung und Leben; Joh 11,1 - 12,19 als Spiegel johanneischer Redaktions- und Theologiegeschichte [Diss. Fra 1987s ⇒ 4,5588a]: BibUnt 19, 1988 ⇒ 4,5588b: ᴿActuBbg 26 (1989) 201s (X. *Alegre S.*); Claretianum 29 (1989) 437-9 (B. *Proietti*); ErbAuf 65 (1989) 75 (B. *Schwank*); TLZ 114 (1989) 275s (U. *Schnelle*).
5569 **Calleja** Joseph, Jesus, resurrection and life for all his believers (structure and meaning of John 11): Diss. Seraphicum 72, ᴰ*Mees* M. R 1989, Miscellanea Franciscana. 199 p.
5570 *Robert* René, [Jo 11,44 *soudarion*] Le 'suaire' johannique; réponse à quelques questions: RThom 89 (1989) 599-608.
5571 *a) Michaels* J. Ramsey, John 12:1-11; – *b) Jeske* Richard L., John 12:20-36 (expositions): Interpretation 43 (1989) 287-291 / 292-5.
5572 *Rundgren* Frithiof, [Jn 12,3] Odor suavitatis [Eng.; really on questions of Syriac in Acts 1s and Teaching of the Apostles]; on the phenomenon of intertextuality: OrSuec 36s (1987s) 85-97.
5574 *Menken* M. J. J., Die Redaktion des Zitates aus Sach 9,9 in Joh 12,15: ZNW 80 (1989) 193-209.

G1.8   Jn 13 ... Sermo sacerdotalis et Passio.

5575 *Story* Cullen I. K., The bearing of Old Testament terminology on the Johannine chronology of the final passover of Jesus: NT 31 (1989) 316-324.
5576 **Wiersbe** Warren, [Jn 13-21] Be transformed. Wheaton 1986, Victor. 151 p. $6 pa. – ᴿCriswT 2 (1988) 445s (T. D. *Lea*).
5576* *Fourie* Sam, *Rousseau* Jacques, 'Eenheid' in Johannes 13-17: Scriptura 29 (1989) 19-35 [< IZBG 36, p. 196].

5577 a) *Bartlett* David L.,   John 13:21-30; – b) *Hubbard* David A.,   John 19:17-30; – c) *Matera* Frank J.,   John 20:1-18 (expository articles): Interpretation 43 (1989) 393-7 / 397-401 / 402-6.

5578 *Schnelle* Udo,   Die Abschiedsreden im Johannesevangelium: ZNW 80 (1989) 64-79.

5579 **Brownson** James V.,   The first farewell; a redaction-critical reconstruction of the first farewell discourse in the Gospel of John: diss. Princeton Theol. Sem. 1989, ^D*de Boer* M. – RelStR 16,189.

5580 **Woll** D. Bruce,   Johannine Christianity in conflict; authority, rank, and succession in the First Farewell Discourse: SBL diss. 60, 1981 ➤ 62,6123 ... 65,4918: ^RStPatav 36 (1989) 204s (G. *Segalla*).

5581 **McCaffrey** James,   The house with many rooms; the Temple theme in Jn. 14.2-3 [diss. 1981]: AnBib 114, 1988 ➤ 4,5606: ^RIndTSt 26 (1989) 86s (L. *Legrand*).

5582 a) *Fee* Gordon D.,   John 14:8-17; – b) *Hesselink* I. John,   John 14:23-29; – c) *Gruenler* Royce G.,   John 17:20-26 (expository articles): Interpretation 43 (1989) 170-4 / 174-7 / 178-183.

5583 *Dietzfelbinger* C.,   Die grösseren Werke (Joh 14.12f.): NTS 35 (1989) 27-47.

5584 *Domeris* Bill, [Jn 15 ...] The paraclete as an ideological construct; a study in the farewell discourses: JTSAf 67 (Rondebosch 1989) 17-23 [< TContext 7/1, 22].

5585 *Ritt* Hubert,   Der christologische Imperativ; zur Weinstock-Metapher in der testamentarischen Mahnrede Joh 15,1-17: ➤ 173, ^FSCHNACKENBURG R., NT & Ethik 1989, 136-150.

5586 *Laney* J. Carl,   Abiding is believing; the analogy of the vine in John 15:1-6: BS 146 (1989) 55-66.

5587 *Tragan* Pius-Ramon,   Jn 15,1-2; testimoni d'una eclesiologia antiga; reflexions exegètiques i teològiques: ➤ 69*, ^FGOMÀ I., RCatalT 14 (1989) 223-240; Eng. 241.

5588 **Feuillet** André,   Les promesses johanniques de l'Esprit Paraclet: Pont. Accad. Teol. Romana, Coll. Teologica 1. Vaticano 1989, Editrice. 90 p. Lit. 8000. – ^REsprVie 99 (1989) 550-2 (É. *Ricaud*).

5589 **Franck** Eskil,   Revelation taught ... Paraclete/John 1985 ➤ 1,5363 ... 4,5609: ^RTLZ 114 (1989) 519-521 (H. *Hübner*).

5590 *Gordon* T.W.,   The Paraclete in the Fourth Gospel: Search 11,2 (Dublin 1988) 72-82 [< NTAbs 33,168].

5591 **Kim Sawkyoung** Stephen,   The judgment function of the Paraclete; an exegetical study of John 16:7-11: diss. Calvin Sem. ^D*Holwerda* D. GR 1989. v-93 p. + bibliog. – CalvinT 24 (1989) 398.

5592 *Aycock* D.M.,   John 17 and Jesus' prayer for unity: TEdr 38 (1988) 132-144 [< NTAbs 33,172].

5593 *Black* David A.,   On the style and significance of John 17: CriswT 3 (1988s) 141-159.

5594 *Rossé* G., [Gv 17] L'ultima preghiera di Gesù dal Vangelo di Giovanni: Collana Scritturistica. R 1988, Città Nuova. 195 p. Lit. 18.000 pa. 88-311-3611-9 [NTAbs 33,390].

5595 *Ukpong* Justin S.,   Jesus' prayer for his followers (Jn. 17) in mission perspective: AfTJ 18 (1989) 49-60 [< TContext 7/1, 18].

5596 **La Potterie** I. de,   La passion ... de Jean 1986 ➤ 2,4290 ... 4,5616: ^RCr-NSt 10 (1989) 153-5 (E. *Schweizer*: eine Reihe überraschender neuer Einsichten); EstBíb 47 (1989) 570-3 (A. *Garcia-Moreno*); IndTSt 25 (1988) 104s (L. *Legrand*); RHPR 69 (1989) 229s (J. C. *Ingelaere*).

5597 **La Potterie** Ignace de,   La Passione di Gesù secondo il vangelo di Giovanni; Testo e Spirito 1988 ⇨ 4,5617:   RLetture 44 (1989) 879s (G. *Ravasi*); SapCr 4 (1989) 371-4 (F. *Toniolo*); StPatav 36 (1989) 206s (G. *Segalla*).

5598 **La Potterie** Ignace de,   The hour of Jesus; the Passion and the Resurrection of Jesus according to St. John; Text and Spirit, T*Murray* G. NY/Slough 1989, Alba / St. Paul.   233 p. $13/£9 [AcPIB 9/5, 360]. 0-8189-0575-1. – RExpTim 101 (1989s) 127 [C. S. *Rodd*]; PrPeo 3 (1989) 234s (B. *Robinson*: keen on symbolism).

5599 **Nicholson** D.,   Death as departure – Joh. 1983 ⇨ 64,5358... 1,5350: RTLZ 114 (1989) 595s (H.-F. *Weiss*).

5600 *Neirynck* Frans,   Parentheses in the Fourth Gospel [adds Jn 18,24... BJERKELUND C. 1987 to G. VAN BELLE 1985]: ETL 65 (1989) 119-123.

5601 *Derrett* J. Duncan M.,   Christ, king and witness (John 18,37):   BbbOr 31 (1989) 189-198.

5602 **Urbán** Ángel,   El origen divino del poder; estudio filológico e historia de la interpretación de Jn 19,11a [diss. M Complutense D*Piñero* J. (*Mateos* J.)]: Est FgNt 2. Córdoba 1989, Almendro. 458 p. pt 2500; $35. 84-86077-73-7. – RFgNt 2,1 (1989) 113 (J. *Peláez*: *exousía* 'libertad' no 'poder'; tenía en cada siglo algunos defensores, no pocos tenidos por herejes).

5603 **Panackel** C.,   Idou ho anthropos (Jn 19,5b) D1988 ⇨ 4,5621:   RJTS 40 (1989) 565-7 (S. S. *Smalley*); NRT 111 (1989) 952s (Y. *Simoens*); StPatav 36 (1989) 570-3 (G. *Segalla*).

5604 *Beaude* Pierre-Marie,   [Jn 19,23-27...] De Marie de Magdala à la Madeleine; la formation d'une figure mystique: ⇨ 381, Variations 1989, 157-173.

5605 **Blank** Josef,   Als sie den Herrn sahen, freuten sie sich; Österliche Wirklichkeit nach Johannes.   FrB 1988, Herder.   80 p.   DM 10,80. – RBiKi 44 (1989) 131s (M. *Helsper*).

   Bagur Jover L.,   La Resurrección en AUG. In Joh. D1989 ⇨ 4799.

5606 *O'Day* Gail R.,   Claiming the world of the risen Jesus; Easter lections from the Gospel of John: QRMin 9,1 (1989) 78-95.

5607 **Gangemi** Attilio,   I racconti post-pasquali nel Vangelo di S. Giovanni I. Gesù si manifesta a Maria Maddalena (Gv 20,1-18): Synaxis Documenti e Studi 2. Acireale 1989, Galatea.   287 p.

5608 *Borse* Udo,   Joh 20,8: österlicher oder vorösterlicher Glaube?:   SNTU 14 (Linz 1989) 151-160 [< ZIT 90,407].

5609 *Delebecque* Édouard,   Retour sur Jean XX,9:   RB 96 (1989) 81-93; Eng. 81; p. 93s, corrigenda pour son Év. Jean 1987.

5610 *Iglesias* Ignacio,   [Jn 20,21] 'Como el Padre me envió, os envío Yo también'; el Resucitado pone en marcha la misión: SalT 76 (1988) 195-208.

5611 *Read* David H. C.,   [Jn 20,21] The Resurrection conspiracy [without sinister implications]: ExpTim 100 (1988s) 227s.

5612 *Samuel* S.,   [Jn 20,21] The Johannine perspective on mission in Christ's praxis: BangaloreTheolF 20,3 (1988) 8-16 [< NTAbs 33,173].

5613 *a) Pelser* G. M. M.,   Rudolf BULTMANN's programme of demythologising and the resurrection narratives in John; – *b) Schnell* C. W., Tendencies in the Synoptic resurrection tradition; R. Bultmann's legacy and an important Christian tradition: ⇨ 617, Resurrection = Neotestamentica 23,2 (1989) 269-286 / 177-194.

5614 *Codina* Victor, [Jn 21] ¡Es el Señor! La parábola del lago: SalT 76 (1988) 187-194.
5615 *Schneiders* Sandra M., John 21:1-14 (expository): Interpretation 43 (1989) 70-75.
5616 *Gee* D.H., Why did Peter spring into the sea? (John 21:7) [because he was ashamed and did not wish to face Jesus]: JTS 40 (1989) 480-9.
5617 *Owen* O.T., [Jn 21,11 ‖ Nm 11; 27] One hundred and fifty three fishes: ExpTim 100 (1988s) 52-54 [374, *Ross* J.M.].

G2.1   **Epistulae Johannis.**

5618 **Brown** Raymond E., Le lettere di Giovanni [1982] 1986 ⇥ 2,4311; 3,5449: ᴿAsprenas 36 (1989) 532s (S. *Cipriani*); Benedictina 35 (1988) 232-4 (S. *Spera*); CiuD 202 (1989) 780-2 (J. *Gutiérrez*).
5619 **Burdick** Donald W., The letters of John the Apostle; an in-depth commentary. Ch 1985, Moody. 488 p. $13. – ᴿCriswT 2 (1987s) 166-8 (E. R. *Clendenen*).
Kistemaker S., James and 1-3 John 1986 ⇥ 6449.
5620 **Morgen** Michèle, Las cartas de Juan [1987 ⇥ 4,5644], ᴰ*Darrical* Nicolás: CuadBíb 62. Estella 1988, VDivino. 71 p. 84-7151-594-6. – ᴿActuBbg 26 (1989) 197 (R. de *Sivatte*).
5621 *Perkins* Pheme, *a)* The Johannine epistles: ⇥ 384, NJBC (1989) 986-995; – *b)* I, II and III John: ⇥ 377, Books 2 (1989) 359-365.
5622 **Stott** John R.W., The letters of John, an introduction and commentary[2] [[1]1964]: Tyndale NT comm. Leicester/GR 1989 = 1988, Inter-Varsity/Eerdmans. 234 p. 0-85111-588-7 / GR 0-8028-0368-7.
5623 **Strecker** Georg, Die Johannesbriefe: KeK NT 14. Gö 1989, Vandenhoeck & R. 381 p.; DM 98; sb. 88,20. 3-525-51621-5. – ᴿNRT 111 (1989) 944s (Y. *Simoens*); SWJT 32,3 (1989s) 51s (E. E. *Ellis*).

─────────

5624 **Edanad** Antony, [1 Jn; Jer 31 ...] Christian existence and the New Covenant [diss. ᴰ*Mollat* D.] 1987 ⇥ 4,5650: ᴿCBQ 51 (1989) 366-8 (J. E. *Bruns*); StPatav 36 (1989) 630s (G. *Segalla*).
5625 *Edwards* M.J., Martyrdom and the First Epistle of John: NT 31 (1989) 164-171.
5626 *Giaconi* E., Il volgarizzamento toscano dei Sermoni sopra la Prima Lettera di S. Giovanni di Frate Girolamo Sᴀᴠᴏɴᴀʀᴏʟᴀ; impianto linguistico ed elementi stilistici: Memorie Domenicane 19 (1988) 111-189 [< RHE 85,50*].
Goldhahn-Müller Ingrid, Die Grenze der Gemeinde ... zweite Busse [1 Jn] ᴰ1989 ⇥ g728.
5627 **Staden** Petrus J. van, [Afrikaans] The structure of the first letter of St. John: diss. ᴰ*Pelser* G. Pretoria 1989. – DissA 50 (1989s) 1343s-A.
5628 *Vellanickal* Matthew, Life and fellowship with God; an introduction to the First Epistle of John: BibleBh 15 (1989) 170-181.
5629 *Klauck* Hans-Josef, Der 'Rückgriff' auf Jesus im Prolog des ersten Johannesbriefs (1 Joh 1,1-4): ⇥ 68, ᶠGɴɪʟᴋᴀ J., Vom Urchristentum 1989, 433-451.
5630 *Azzali Bernardelli* Giovanna, *Cacciari* Antonio, 1 Gv 1,7 e 1 Pt 1,18-19 nell'esegesi dei primi tre secoli: ⇥ 759, Sangue VI, 1987/9, 795-849.

5631 *Watson* Duane F., 1 John 2,12-14 as *distributio, conduplicatio,* and *expolitio*; a rhetorical understanding: JStNT 35 (1989) 97-110.
5632 *Klauck* Hans-Josef, *a)* Der Antichrist und das johanneische Schisma; zu 1 Joh 2,18-19: ➤ 197, ᶠTRILLING W., Christus bezeugen 1989, 237-248; – *b)* In der Welt, aus der Welt (1 Joh 2,15-17); Beobachtungen zur Ambivalenz des johanneischen Kosmosbegriffs: FranzSt 71 (1989) 58-68 > In the world, of the world ᵀᴱ*Asen* B., TDig 37,209-214.
5633 *Hiebert* D. Edmond, An exposition of 1 John 2:18-28 / 2:29-3:12 / 3:13-24 / 4:1-6 [parts 4-7 of 10-part series]: BS 146 (1989) 76-93 / 198-216 / 420-436.
5634 *Klauck* Hans-Josef, Brudermord und Bruderliebe; ethische Paradigmen in 1 Joh 3,11-17: ➤ 173, ᶠSCHNACKENBURG R., NT & Ethik 1989, 151-169.
5635 *Louis-Combet* Claude, Celui qui aime... connaît Dieu (1 Jn 4,7): ➤ 381, Variations 1989, 107-117.
5636 *Boer* M. C. de, [1 Jn 5,6] Het bloed en het water van Jezus Christus in de eerste Johannesbrief: GerefTTs 89 (1989) 131-9.
5637 *Hills* Julian, 'Little children, keep yourselves from idols'; 1 John 5:21 reconsidered: CBQ 51 (1989) 285-310.

5638 **Lieu** Judith, The Second and Third Epistles of John [diss. Birmingham 1980]: StNT&W 1986 ➤ 3,5468; 4,5662: ᴿHeythJ 30 (1989) 191-3 (R. E. *Brown*); JBL 108 (1989) 546-9 (M. C. *de Boer*); StPatav 36 (1989) 174-6 (G. *Segalla*).
5639 *Watson* Duane F., A rhetorical analysis of 2 John according to Greco-Roman convention: NTS 35 (1989) 104-130.
5640 *Price* Robert M., The Sitz-im-Leben of Third John; a new reconstruction: EvQ 61 (1989) 109-119.
5641 *Watson* Duane F., A rhetorical analysis of 3 John; a study in epistolary rhetoric: CBQ 51 (1989) 479-501.

G2.3   *Apocalypsis Johannis* – **Revelation: text, introduction.**

5642 **Becker** Siegbert W. † 1984, Revelation [➤ 3,5475]; the distant triumph song 1985: ᴿLuthTKi 12 (1988) 74 (V. *Stolle*).
5643 **Boring** M. Eugene, Revelation: Interpretation comm. Louisville 1989, Knox. viii-236 p. $19. 0-8042-3150-8 [TDig 37,150]. – ᴿSWJT 32,3 (1989s) 54 (T. D. *Lea*).
5644 **Burger** Edward K., JOACHIM of Fiore, Enchiridion super Apocalypsim: ST 78, 1986 ➤ 3,5476; 4,5664: ᴿRelStR 15 (1989) 77 (D. *Burr*).
5645 **Collins** Adela Y., The Apocalypse (Revelation): ➤ 384, NJBC (1989) 996-1016.
5646 **Courreau** J., L'Apocalypse expliquée par CÉSAIRE d'Arles [+] *Bouquet* S., Scholies attribuées à ORIGÈNE; intr. *La Potterie* I. de, *Hamman* A.-G.: Les Pères dans la foi. P 1989, D-Brouwer. 222 p. F 99. – ᴿEsprVie 99 (1989) 547 (É. *Cothenet*).
5647 **Foulkes** Ricardo, El Apocalipsis de San Juan; una lectura desde América Latina: Nueva Creación. GR/Buenos Aires 1989, Eerdmans/ Nueva Creación. xxii-253 p. 0-8028-0907-3.
5648 **González Ruiz** José M., Apocalipsis de Juan, el libro del testimonio cristiano: Biblia y Lenguaje 9, 1987 ➤ 4,5667: ᴿActuBbg 26 (1989) 38s (X. *Alegre S.*); SalT 76 (1988) 737-9 (M. *Benéitez*).
     Macé de la Charité, Apocalypse, ᴱ*Lops* Ritt, 1986 ➤ 1887.

5649 **Prigent** Pierre, L'Apocalypse de saint Jean[2] 1988 ➤ 4,5672: ᴿÉTRel 64 (1989) 299s (E. *Cuvillier*: [2]corrigée, 'non revisée ou augmentée!').

5650 ᴱ**Romero-Posé** E. S. BEATI a Liebana Comm. in Apc. 1985 ➤ 1,5427; 2,5488: ᴿNT 31 (1989) 92 (G. D. *Kilpatrick*).

5651 **Steinhauser** Kenneth B., The Apocalypse commentary of TYCONIUS; a history of its reception and influence: EurHS 23/301, 1987 ➤ 4,5675: ᴿTR 85 (1989) 298-300 (N. *Brox*).

5652 **Still** William, 'A vision of glory'; an exposition of the book of Revelation. Glasgow 1987, Gray. 160 p. – ᴿEvQ 61 (1989) 164s (D. J. *Graham*: devotion, light exposition; millennial).

5653 **Vanni** Ugo, L'Apocalisse; ermeneutica, esegesi, teologia: RivB supp 17, 1988 ➤ 4,5676: ᴿBenedictina 36 (1989) 583-6 (L. *De Lorenzi*); Biblica 70 (1989) 432-8 (P. *Prigent*: un des plus remarquable spécialistes... livre se dérobant à toute classification); CC 140 (1989,1) 509s (G. *Ferraro*); EsprVie 99 (1989) 545-7 (É. *Cothenet*); Marianum 51 (1989) 657s (S. *Sabugal*); Protestantesimo 44 (1989) 298s (D. *Bouchard*: competente); RivB 37 (1989) 511-3 (E. *Bosetti*); Stromata 45 (1989) 240; Teresianum 40 (1989) 521s (V. *Pasquetto*); ZkT 111 (1989) 450-3 (C. *Marucci*: hervorragende Qualität).

5654 **Vögtle** Anton, Das Buch mit den sieben Siegeln; die Offenbarung des Johannes in Auswahl gedeutet. FrB 1989 = 1981, Herder. 187 p. 3-451-19426-0.

G2.4 *Apocalypsis,* **Revelation, topics.**

5655 **Alonso Merlino** Pedro J., El cántico nuevo en el Apocalipsis; perspectiva bíblico-teológica: diss. Pont. Univ. Gregoriana Nº 3654, ᴰ*Vanni* U. Roma 1989. 429 p. – RTLv 21,543.

5656 *Amat* J., La valutazione dell'Apocalisse di Giovanni nella Chiesa antica: ➤ 748, Sogni 1988 = AugR 29 (1989) 171-191.

5657 *Augustinovich* A., ¿María madre en el Apocalipsis?: Testimonio 3 (Caracas 1988) 39-53 [< Stromata 45,499].

5658 *Barnett* Paul, Polemical parallelism; some further reflections on the Apocalypse: JStNT 35 (1989) 111-120.

5658* *a) Bauckham* R., The Book of Revelation as a Christian War Scroll; – *b) Botha* P.J.J., God, emperor worship and society; contemporary experiences and the Book of Revelation; – *c) Vorster* W.S., 'Genre' and the Revelation of John; a study in text, context and intertext: Neotestamentica 22,1 (1988) 17-40 / 87-102 / 103-123.

5659 **Beagley** Alan J., The 'Sitz im Leben' of the Apocalypse [diss. Fuller 1983, ᴰ*Martin* R.]...: BZNW 50, 1987 ➤ 3,5494; 4,5679: ᴿAndrUnS 27 (1989) 229s (J. *Paulien*); CBQ 51 (1989) 142-4 (L.J. *Thompson*); Interpretation 43 (1989) 94.96 (B. *Crawford*); JBL 108 (1989) 169-171 (C. *DuRousseau*).

5660 ᴱ**Bloom** Harold, The Revelation of St, John the divine; modern critical interpretation ➤ 4,5682 [ABRAMS M. 1984, MAY J. 1972, LAWRENCE D. 1931, FARRER A. 1963, FRYE N. 1982, COLLINS A.Y. 1984, SHAFFER E. 1975]. NHv 1988, Chelsea. viii-150 p. $24.50. 0-87754-916-8 [NTAbs 33,255].

5661 *Bodinger* Martin, Le mythe de Néron, de l'Apocalypse de saint Jean au Talmud de Babylone: RHR 206 (1989) 21-40; Eng. 21.

5662 **Boesak** Allan, 'Schreibe dem Engel Südafrikas'; Trost und Protest in der Apokalypse des Johannes [1987 ➤ 3,5497], ᵀ. 158 p. DM 19,80. – ᴿÖkRu 38 (1989) 117s (Ako *Haarbeck*).

5663 ᴱ*Contreras* Francisco, Luis del ALCÁZAR, Vestigatio arcani sensus in Apocalypsi (1614), presentación, estudio y comentarios: ArTGran 58 (1989) 51-168 [5-50 biobibliog. Alcázar (1554-1613), *Olivares* Estanislao].

5664 **Corsani** Bruno, L'Apocalisse, guida alla lettura 1987 ➤ 3,5505; Lit. 12.000: ᴿProtestantesimo 44 (1989) 299 (A. *Adamo*); RivStoLR 25 (1989) 372s (Giuliana *Iacopino*); StEcum 6 (1988) 143s (Tecle *Vetrali*).

5665 *Corsani* Bruno, Il discepolato cristiano secondo l'Apocalisse: Protestantesimo 44 (1989) 242-254.

5666 *Delebecque* Édouard, 'J'entendis' dans l'Apocalypse: RThom 89 (1989) 85-90.

5667 *Elliott* J.K., Manuscripts of the Book of Revelation collated by H.C. HOSKIER [and concordances to GREGORY and TISCHENDORF]: JTS 40 (1989) 100-111.

5668 **Fekkes** John, Isaiah and prophetic tradition in the Book of Revelation; visionary antecedents and their development: diss. Manchester 1989, ᴰ*Lindars* B. 319 p. – RTLv 21,544.

5669 **Gentry** Kenneth L., Before Jerusalem fell; dating the Book of Revelation. Tyler TX 1989, Inst. Christian Economics. xix-409 p. [TrinJ 10,241].

5670 **Gnatkowski** Mel W., The implied reader in the Book of Revelation: diss. Baptist Theol. Sem., ᴰ*Winbery* C. New Orleans 1988. 137 p. 89-11184. – DissA 50 (1989s) 706-A.

5671 **Guthrie** Donald, The relevance of John's Apocalypse [1985 Didsbury Lectures] 1987 ➤ 4,5694; also GR, Eerdmans: ᴿExpTim 100 (1988s) 279 [C.S. *Rodd* or whoever: 'not without some success'].

5672 **Harris** Michael A., The literary function of hymns in the Apocalypse of John: diss. Southern Baptist Theol Sem. 1989, ᴰ*Blevins* J. 355 p. 89-15269. – DissA 50 (1989s) 979-A.

5674 *a*) *Holtz* Traugott, Die 'Werke' in der Johannesapokalypse; – *b*) *Lona* Horacio E., 'Treu bis zum Tod'; zum Ethos des Martyriums in der Offenbarung des Johannes; – *c*) *Gnilka* Joachim, Apokalyptik und Ethik; die Kategorie der Zukunft als Anweisung für sittliches Handeln: ➤ 173, ꟳSCHNACKENBURG R., NT & Ethik 1989, 426-441 / 442-461 / 464-481.

5675 [*Hre*] *Kio* Stephen, The Exodus symbol of liberation in the Apocalypse and its relevance for some aspects of translation: BTrans 40 (1989) 120-135.

5676 **Huber** Paul, Apokalypse; Bilderzyklen zur Johannes-Offenbarung in Trier, auf dem Athos und von Caillaud d'Angers. Dü 1989, Patmos. 296 p., 307 (color.) fig. 3-491-77770-4.

5677 *Klein* Peter, ['étudie un fragment d'une Apocalypse ottonienne tardive conservée à Bâle ... en particulier pour certains thèmes comme "l'agneau sur la montagne", "le fils de l'homme sur le nuage" et "les anges portant l'Évangile"' RHE 84 (1989) 293]: ➤ 24, ꟳBEER Ellen J. 1986, 27-36.

5678 *a*) *Knoch* Otto B., Apokalyptische Zukunftsängste und die Botschaft der Offenbarung des Johannes: – *b*) *Marböck* Johannes, Gottes Plan und Herrschaft; zu den Anfängen apokalyptischen Schrifttums: TPQ 137 (1989) 327-334 / 335-345.

5679 *Kvanvig* Helge S., The relevance of the biblical visions of the end time; hermeneutical guidelines to the apocalyptical literature: HorBT 11,1 (Pittsburgh 1989) 35-58 [< ZIT 90,333].

5680 **La Rocca** T., Es ist Zeit; Apocalisse e storia, studio su Thomas MÜNTZER. Bo 1988, Cappelli. 212 p. – ᴿProtestantesimo 44 (1989) 281-3 (E. *Campi*).

5681 **LaRondelle** Hans K., Chariots of salvation 1987 ➤ 3,5519: ᴿAndrUnS 27 (1989) 89s (K. L. *Vine*).

5682 *LaRondelle* Hans K., The Middle Ages within the scope of apocalyptic prophecy: JEvTS 32 (1989) 345-354 [< zɪт 90,6].

5683 **Mazzaferri** Frederick D., The genre of the Book of Revelation from a source-critical perspective [< diss. Aberdeen]: BZNW 54. B/Hawthorne ɴʏ 1989, de Gruyter. xix-486 p. DM 168. 3-11-011518-2 / 0-89925-460-8 [TDig 37,74]. – ᴿExpTim 101 (1989s) 123s (J. M. *Court*); Salmanticensis 36 (1989) 388-391 (R. *Trevijano*).

5684 *Moore* Hamilton, New Testament Apocalyptic in twentieth century discussion: IrBSt 11 (1989) 197-206 [< zɪт 89,726].

5685 **Paley** Morton D., The apocalyptic sublime [18th-19th century British paintings mostly on Rev.] 1986 ➤ 2,4367*: ᴿJRel 68 (1988) 162 (J. W. *Dixon*).

5686 *Peterson* D. G., Worship in the Revelation to John: RefTR 47,3 (Melbourne 1988) 67-77 [< NTAbs 33,340].

5687 **Peterson** E. H., Reversed thunder... the praying imagination 1988 ➤ 4,5713: ᴿTTod 46 (1989s) 86s (M. E. *Boring*).

5688 *Ponthot* Joseph, L'angélologie dans l'Apocalypse johannique: ➤ 728, Anges 1987/9, 301-312.

5689 *Porter* Stanley E., The language of the Apocalypse in recent discussion: NTS 35 (1989) 582-603.

5690 *Poucouta* Paul, La misión de la Iglesia en el Apocalipsis [< NRT 110 (1988) 38-57], ᵀᴱ*Suñol* Miquel: SelT 28 (1989) 341-9.

5691 **Prevost** J. P., Para terminar con el miedo; el Apocalipsis. M 1987, Paulinas. 115 p. – ᴿBibFe 15 (1989) 324 (M. *Sáenz Galache*).

5692 *Sand* A., Jüdische und christliche Apokalyptik; exegetische Fragen und theologische Aspekte: Renovatio 45,1 (Bonn 1989) 12-24 [< NTAbs 33,340].

5693 **Schüssler Fiorenza** Elisabeth, The book of Revelation; justice and judgment 1985 ➤ 1,5466... 4,5719: ᴿActuBbg 26 (1989) 47s (X. *Alegre S.*).

5694 *Schüssler Fiorenza* Elisabeth, Revelation: *a)* ➤ 394, NT/Interpreters 1989, 407-427; – *b)* ➤ 377, Books 2 (1989) 367-381.

5695 *Surridge* Robert, Redemption in the structure of Revelation: ExpTim 101 (1989s) 231-4.

5696 **Thompson** Steven, The Apocalypse and Semitic syntax: SNTS Mg 52, 1985 ➤ 1,5469... 4,5723*: ᴿBZ 33 (1989) 282-4 (K. *Müller*: not exactly sensational); FgNt 2 (1989) 207-211 (G. *Mussies*).

5697 *Trevett* Christiane, Apocalypse, ɪɢɴᴀᴛɪᴜs, Montanism; seeking the seeds: VigChr 43 (1989) 313-338 [Ignatius' acquaintance with Apocalypse doubtful but suggestive].

5698 *Trummer* Peter, Offenbarung in Bildern; zur Bildersprache der Apokalypse; eine Skizze: ➤ 367, Aufsätze 1987, 207-220.

5699 *Vanni* Ugo, Paolinismo o antipaolinismo nell'Apocalisse? ➤ 597, RicStoB 1,2 (1987/9) 65-75.

5700 *Verde* A. F., Le lezioni o i sermoni sull'Apocalisse di Girolamo Sᴀᴠᴏɴᴀʀᴏʟᴀ (1490); nova dicere et novo modo: Memorie domenicane 19 (1988) 5-109; 2 pl. [< RHE 85,50*].

5700* *Vetrali* Tecle, [Apc] Non ci sarà più male: ParSpV 19 (1989) 179-195.

5701 *a)* *Villiers* P. de, The Lord was crucified in Sodom and Egypt; symbols in the Apocalypse of John [11,8]; – *b)* *Rand* J. A. du, The imagery of the heavenly Jerusalem (Rev 21,9-22,5); – *c)* *Draper* J. A., [Rev 21,14] The twelve Apostles as foundation stones of the heavenly Jerusalem and the foundation of the Qumran community: Neotestamentica 22,1 (1988) 125-138 / 65-86 / 41-63.

5702 **Weber** Hans-Ruedi, The way of the Lamb; Christ in the Apocalypse: Risk. Geneva 1988, WCC. 58 p. £3.25. 2-8254-0918-9 [ExpTim 100,199].

5703 a) *Wengst* Klaus, Erfahrungen und Bilder vom Krieg und Frieden in der Offenbarung des Johannes; – b) *Gutheil* Jörn-Erik, Gerechtigkeit, Frieden und Bewahrung der Schöpfung: ⇒ 47*, ᶠDEMBOWSKI H. 1989, 98-116 / 117-135.

5704 *Wojciechowski* Michał, ❷ Church as Israel according to the Revelation of St. John: STWsz 26,1 (1988) 221-233; Eng. 233s.

G2.5   *Apocalypsis,* **Revelation 1,1 ...**

5705 **Fredericks** Richard L., A sequential study of Revelation 1-14 emphasizing the judgment motif, with implications for Seventh-Day Adventist apocalyptic pedagogy: diss. Andrews, ᴰ*Naden* R. Berrien Springs MI 1988. 404 p. 89-11523. – DissA 50 (1989s) 714-A.

5706 **Woschitz** Karl M., Erneuerung aus dem Ewigen; Denkweisen – Glaubensweisen in Antike und Christentum nach Offb 1-3, 1987 ⇒ 3,5588; 4,5731: ᴿTPQ 137 (1989) 80s (O. S. *Knoch*).

5707 *Sieg* Franciszek, [Apc 1,12-16; 19,11-15] ❷ 'Like a Son of Man'; comparative analysis: STWsz 26,1 (1988) 250-5.

5707* *Enroth* Anne-Marit, [Apk 2,7 + 7-mal] Kuulemisformeli Ilmestys-kirjassa [Die Weckformel in der Offenbarung]: Teologinen Aikakauskirja 94,1 (Helsinki 1989) 8-14 [< IZBG 36, p. 247].

5708 *Trevett* Christine, The other letters to the Churches of Asia; Apoc-alypse and IGNATIUS of Antioch: ⇒ 84, ᶠHILL D., JStNT 37 (1989) 117-135.

5709 *Roloff* Jürgen, 'Siehe, ich stehe vor der Tür und klopfe an'; Be-obachtungen zur Überlieferungsgeschichte von Offb 3,20: ⇒ 68, ᶠGNILKA J., Vom Urchristentum 1989, 452-466.

5710 *Bachmann* Michael, Die apokalyptischen Reiter; DÜRERs Holzschnitt und die Auslegungsgeschichte von Apk 6,1-8: ZTK 86 (1989) 33-58; 8 phot.

5711 *Strand* Kenneth A., The 'spotlight-on-last-events' sections in the Book of Revelation [7]: AndrUnS 27 (1989) 201-221.

5712 *Winkle* Ross E., Another look at the list of tribes in Revelation 7: AndrUnS 27 (1989) 53-67.

5713 **Ulfgard** Håkan, Feast and future; Revelation 7:9-17 and the Feast of Tabernacles [diss. ᴰ*Gerhardsson* B. Lund 1989. – RTLv 21,547]: ConBib NT 22. Sto 1989, Almqvist & W. 196 p. 91-22-01263-X [EstBib 47,580]. – ᴿExpTim 101 (1989s) 123 (J. M. *Court*); SvTKv 65 (1989) 141s (*ipse*); SWJT 32,2 (1989s) 57s (E. E. *Ellis*).

5714 *Storniolo* L., A propaganda da idolatria (a besta de Ap 13,11-17): Vida Pastoral 144 (São Paulo 1989) 2-11 [< Stromata 45,499].

5715 *Loasby* Roland E.†, ᴱ*Running* Leona G., 'Har-Magedon' according to the Hebrew in the setting of the seven last plagues of Revelation 16: AndrUnS 27 (1989) 129-132.

5716 *LaRondelle* Hans K., The etymology of Har-Magedon (Rev 16:16): AndrUnS 27 (1989) 69-73.

5718 **Ruiz** Jean-Pierre M., Ezekiel in the Apocalypse; the transformation of prophetic language in Revelation 16,17-19,10 [diss. Roma, Pont. Univ. Gregoriana, ᴰ*Vanni* U., N° 3563; extr. 182 p. – RTLv 21,546]: EurHS 28, 375. Fra 1989, Lang. xx-607 p. Fs 93 [TR 86,75]. 3-631-42217-2. – ᴿExpTim 101 (1989s) 248 (J. M. *Court*); LA 39 (1989) 349-352 (G. *Bissoli*).

5719 *White* R. Fowler, Reexamining the evidence for recapitulation in Rev. 20:1-10: WestTJ 51 (1989) 319-344.

G2.7 Millenniarismus, Apc 21...

5720 *Caffiero* Marina, La fine del mondo; profezia, apocalisse e millennio nell'Italia rivoluzionaria: CrNSt 10 (1989) 389-441; Eng. 442.

5721 **Doan** Ruth A., The Miller heresy, millennialism, and American culture [< 1984 diss. Chapel Hill NC] 1987 ↠ 3,5559; ᴿChH 58 (1989) 249s (T. P. *Weber*).

5722 **House** H. Wayne, *Ice* Thomas, Dominion theology, blessing or curse? [activist version of premillennialism; Gary *North*...] Portland OR 1988, Multnomah. 460 p. $16. – ᴿSWJT 32,1 (1989s) 69s (L. R. *Bush*: important warning against a danger).

5723 *Katz* D., Milleniarism, the Jews, and biblical criticism in seventeenth-century England: Pietismus und Neuzeit 14 (Gö 1988) 166-184 [149-165, *Williamson* A.: < Judaica 45,205].

5724 *Sailer* W. S., Francis BACON among the theologians; aspects of dispensational hermeneutics: EvJ 6,2 (Myerstown 1988) 71-82 [< NTAbs 33,9].

5725 ᴱ**Numbers** R. L., *Butler* J. M., The disappointed... millenarianism 1987 ↠ 3,5562*: ᴿAndrUnS 27 (1989) 149-151 (G. R. *Knight*); ChH 58 (1989) 247-9 (B. J. *Leonard*).

5726 **Poythress** Vern S., Understanding dispensationalists 1987 ↠ 4,5761: ᴿAndrUnS 27 (1989) 151-3 (H. K. *LaRondelle*: Poythress is 'himself a covenant theologian').

5727 *Simonetti* Manlio, L'Apocalisse e l'origine del millennio: VetChr 26 (1989) 337-350 [> ᶠIACOBANGELI R.].

5728 *Wessel* H., Le livre de l'Apocalypse et la fin des temps: RRéf 39,156 (1988) 1-8 [< NTAbs 33,195].

5729 *Winkler* Gerhard R., Chiliastische Ideen und christliche Wirklichkeit: TPQ 137 (1989) 360-8 [> Eng. TDig 37,132-6, ᵀᴱ*Asen* B.].

5730 **Dumbrell** William J., The end of the beginning; Revelation 21-22 and the Old Testament 1985 ↠ 2,4403; 4,5763: ᴿCalvinT 24 (1989) 137-9 (A. J. *Bandstra*); WestTJ 50 (1988) 216s (M. *Kreft*).

5731 *Topham* Michael, a) [Rev 21,15-17] The dimensions of the New Jerusalem [change stades to cubits, 12,000 (= 30 stades) as length of all four sides together]; – b) [Rev 21,17] 'A human being's measurement, which is an angel's' [... Sargon; gematria]: ExpTim 100 (1988s) 417-9 / 217.

5732 **Bishop** John, [Rev 22,13] Jesus, the First and Last [inexhaustible, indispensable, invincible]: ExpTim 101 (1989s) 76-79.

5733 *Grossi* Vittorino, Apocalisse 22,14 nella tradizione latina antica: ↠ 759, Sangue VI, 1987/9, 851-8.

5734 *Aune* David E., The prophetic circle of the John of Patmos and the exegesis of Revelation 22.16: ↠ 84, ᶠHILL D., JStNT 37 (1989) 103-116.

5735 *Thomas* Robert L., The spiritual gift of prophecy in Rev 22:18: JEvTS 32 (1989) 201-216 [< ZIT 89,704].

XIII. Paulus

G3.1 **Pauli vita, stylus, chronologia.**

5736 **Barbaglio** Giuseppe, Paolo di Tarso e le origini cristiane 1985 ➤ 1,5511 ... 3,5570: ᴿCBQ 51 (1989) 141s (R. A. *Wild*); ÉTRel 64 (1989) 442s (A. *Moda*: admirable); HumBr 44 (1989) 602 (M. *Orsatti*); RHPR 69 (1989) 234s (J. C. *Ingelaere*).

5737 *Barrett* Charles K., Paulus als Missionar und Theologe: ZTK 86 (1989) 18-32.

5738 *Bartnicki* Roman, ℗ Apostolat a charyzmat Pawła: STWsz 26,1 (1988) 147-163; Eng. 163.

5739 **Becker** Jürgen, Paulus, der Apostel der Völker. Tü 1989, Mohr. vii-524 p. DM 48. 3-16-145500-2 [TsTNijm 30,201, L. *Grollenberg*].

5740 **Beker** J. Christiaan, Paul the Apostle; the triumph of God in life and thought 1980 ➤ 61,6997: reprint E 1989, Clark; £12.50.

5741 **Best** Ernest, Paul and his converts [lectures to pastors, Richmond 1985] 1988 ➤ 4,5770: ᴿExpTim 100 (1988s) 310 (L. *Alexander*); JTS 40 (1989) 577 (A. *Lincoln*); Salmanticensis 36 (1989) 381-3 (R. *Trevijano*).

5742 **Bornkamm** G., Paul apôtre de JC. Genève 1988, Labor et Fides. 340 p. 2-8309-0130-4 [ÉTRel 64,481].

5743 **Breton** Stanislas, Saint Paul 1988 ➤ 4,5773: ᴿLumièreV 38,192 (1989) 110 (A. *Lion*); RThom 89 (1989) 686 (J. G. *Ranquet*).

5745 *a) Busto Saiz* José Ramón, Pablo y su experiencia de la gracia; – *b) Tornos* Andrés, Vino nuevo – nuevo ser; la gracia como 'novedad': SalT 77 (1989) 347-357 / 359-368.

5746 **Dietzfelbinger** C., Berufung: WM 58, 1985 ➤ 2,4418 ... 4,5778: ᴿZkT 111 (1989) 221 (E. *Ruschitzka*).

5747 *Engberg-Pedersen* Troels, Et paulinsk annus mirabilis?: DanTTs 52 (1989) 21-40 [< ZIT 89,217].

5748 **Fabris** Rinaldo, Paolo catechista. Bo 1988, Dehoniane. 96 p. Lit. 8500. – ᴿHumBr 44 (1989) 602s (A. *Nassini*).

5749 *Fitzmyer* J., Paul: ➤ 384, NJBC (1989s) 1329-37.

5750 *Furnish* Victor P., Paul the *martys*: ➤ 143, ᶠOGDEN S., Witness 1989, 73-90.

5751 **Gerleman** G., Der Heidenapostel; ketzerische Erwägungen zur Predigt des Paulus, zugleich ein Streifzug in der griechischen Mythologie ['Paul' is Hermes instructing his fellow-gods; 1 Cor vices are those of Olympians, not of a Christian community]: Lund Acad. Scripta Minora 1987s/2. Sto 1989, Almqvist & W. 120 p. [ClasR 40,479, J. *Barclay*].

5752 **González Ruiz** J. M., El Evangelio de Pablo²: Presencia teológica 47. Santander 1988, Sal Terrae. 270 p. 84-293-0811-3. – ᴿActuBbg 26 (1989) 39s (J. *Giménez Meliá*); BibFe 15 (1989) 322 (A. *Salas*); Proyección 36 (1989) 163 (J. L. *Sicre*).

5753 *Gruson* Michel, Pourquoi j'aime Paul: DossB 24 (1988) 3s [-25, *al.*].

5754 **Gorman** Michael J., The self, the Lord, and the other; the significance of reflexive pronoun constructions in the letters of Paul, with a comparison to the 'Discourses' of EPICTETUS: diss. Princeton Theol. Sem. 1989. 843 p. 89-23115. – DissA 50 (1989s) 2095-A; RelStR 16,190.

5755 *Guillemette* Nil, Saint Paul and women: EAPast 26 (Quezon City 1989) 121-133 [< TContext 7/1, 64: 'Attempt to exonerate St. Paul of the accusation to be a misogynist by exegetical means'].

5756 **Harrington** Wilfrid, Jesus and Paul signs of contradiction 1987 ➤ 2,4423 ... 4,5784: ᴿBogSmot 59 (1989) 481-3 (M. *Zovkić*).

5757 **Hubaut** Michel A., Paul de Tarse: Bibliothèque de l'Histoire du Christianisme 18. P 1989, Desclée. 145 p. F 98. – ᴿEsprVie 99 (1989) 190-*jaune* (É. *Vauthier*).

5758 **Johnson** Sherman E., Paul ... and his cities 1987 ➤ 3,5589; 4,5786: ᴿCurrTM 16 (1989) 127 (R. P. *Carlson*: IDB better).

5759 *a*) *Keck* Leander E., Images of Paul in the New Testament; – *b*) *Beker* J. Christiaan, Paul the theologian; major motifs in Pauline theology; – *c*) *Kilner* John F., A Pauline approach to ethical decision-making; – *d*) *Brown* Charles E., [1 Cor 15,26] 'The last enemy is death'; Paul and the pastoral task: Interpretation 43 (1989) 341-351 / 352-365 / 366-379 / 380-392.

5760 *Klessmann* M., Zum Problem der Identität des Paulus: Wege zum Menschen 41 (Gö 1989) 156-... [< ZIT 89,346].

5760* **Knox** John, Chapters in a life of Paul² [¹1950], ᴱ*Hare* Douglas R. A. L 1989, SCM. xxii-137 p. £7. 0-334-01918-4.

5761 **Lapide** P., *Stuhlmacher* P., Paulus, rabbi en apostel. Kampen 1988, Kok. 67 p. ƒ 12,90. – ᴿStreven 57 (1989s) 567s (P. *Beentjes*).

5762 *Larsson* Edvin, Zur Diskussion über die neue Paulus-Chronologie: ➤ 183, ᶠSJÖBERG Å., Dumu- 1989, 337-347.

5763 *Legrand* Lucien, From apostle to pastor; St. Paul's pastoral itinerary: IndTSt 26 (1989) 152-170.

5764 *Lindemann* Andreas, Der Apostel Paulus im 2. Jahrhundert: ➤ 606, Réception 1986/9, 39-67.

5765 **Luedemann** Gerd, Opposition to Paul in Jewish Christianity [FRL 130, 1983 ➤ 64,5523], ᵀ*Boring* M. Eugene. Minneapolis 1989, Fortress. xxii-368 p. 0-8006-0908-5.

5766 **Maccoby** Hyam, The mythmaker; Paul and the invention of Christianity 1986 ➤ 2,4437; 3,5596: ᴿJQR 79 (1988s) 248-250 (J. G. *Gager*).

5767 **Maestri** William F., Paul's pastoral vision; pastoral letters for a pastoral Church today. Staten Island 1989, Alba. xx-220 p. $13. 0-8189-0556-6 [TDig 37,170].

5768 **Malherbe** Abraham J., Paul and the popular philosophers. Minneapolis 1989, Fortress. xvi-192 p. $20 [TrinJ 10,242].

5769 *Moda* Aldo, Paolo prigioniero e martire; per una cronologia degli ultimi anni: BbbOr 31 (1989) 50-181.

5770 *a*) *Moody* Dale, A new chronology for the life and letters of Paul [Spain (Cadiz) 60-64; executed 68 (2 Tim 4,17s)]; – *b*) *Dockx* S. [† 2.XI.1985] The first missionary voyage of Paul; historical reality or literary creation of Luke?, ᵀ*Yamauchi* E.: ➤ 58, ᶠFINEGAN J., Chronos 1989, 223-240 / 209-221.

5770* *Mosconi* Luís, Paulo Apóstolo, fidelidade a Jesus Cristo e ao Reino no meio dos conflitos: EstudosB 12 (1986) 24-30 [< IZBG 36, p. 208].

5771 *Müller* Paul-Gerhard, Judenbeschimpfung und Selbstverfluchung bei Paulus: BiKi 44 (1989) 58-65.

5772 *Nagy* László, ⓜ Der betende Paulus: Református Szemle 80 (1987) 370-9 [< TLZ 115,238].

5773 [Oriol] **Tuñí** Josep, Pablo y Jesús; la vida de Jesús y la vida de Pablo: RLatAmT 5 (Salvador 1988) 285-305.

5774 **Pak Yeong Sik** James, Paul a missionary; a comparative study of missionary discourse in Paul's epistles and selected contemporary Jewish texts: diss. PIB 1989s, ᴰ*Vanhoye* A. – ActaPIB 9 (1989s) 517.

5775 *Papathomas* Gregory D., ℗ Did St. Paul visit Spain? [yes]: TAth 60 (1989) 754-774; Eng. 585.

5776 *Peters* Georg, Der Seelsorgerdienst des Paulus: ➤ 28*, ᶠBEYERHAUS P., Martyria 1989, 83-87.

5777 **Plevnik** Joseph, What are they saying about Paul? 1986 ➤ 2,4445... 4,5797: ᴿBibTB 19 (1989) 40 (R. *Jewett*).

5778 **Rodgers** Lloyd W.ᴵᴵᴵ, An examination of [pre-conversion] Paul as persecutor [Gal 1, Phlp 3, 1 Cor 15, 1 Tim 1,12]: diss. Southern Baptist Theol. Sem. 1989, ᴰ*Garland* D. 298 p. 90-04721. – DissA 50 (1989s) 2541-A.

5779 **Schnelle** Udo, Wandlungen im paulinischen Denken: SBS 137. Stu 1989, KBW. 108 p. DM 29,80 [TR 86,75]. – ᴿBogSmot 59 (1989) 488s (M. *Zovkić*).

5781 **Templeton** D. A., Re-exploring Paul's imagination; a cynical lay-woman's guide to Paul of Tarsus 1988 ➤ 4,5807: ᴿJTS 40 (1989) 575-7 (J. *Ashton*: his style is as quirky as his subtitle, but enjoyable).

5782 ᴱ**Vanhoye** A., L'apôtre Paul 1984/6 ➤ 2,398... 4,5810: ᴿRechSR 77 (1989) 118 (J.-N. *Aletti*); TLZ 114 (1989) 601s (tit. pp.).

5783 *Vos* J. S., Nieuw licht op de Apostel Paulus; tendenties in het huidige onderzoek: GerefTTs 89 (1989) 23-40.

5784 *Wedderburn* Alexander J. M., Paul and Jesus... [< NTS 34 (1988) 61; ScotJT 38 (1985) 189-203]: ➤ 615, Paul and Jesus 99-115 / 117-143 (161-195), [17-50 *Furnish* V., 51-80, *Walter* N.; 81-98 + 145-160, *Wolff* C., reprinted essays].

5785 **Zmijewski** J., Paulus... Amt 1986 ➤ 3,5615: ᴿBZ 33 (1989) 278-280 (Ingo *Broer*).

G3.2   **Corpus paulinum;** *introductio, commentarii.*

5785* **Artola** Antonio M., Curso de exegesis sobre San Pablo (volumen I) [San Pablo en la estructura del Cristianismo; la conversión; Tes Gal Rom]: Teología Deusto, Manuales 5. Bilbao 1989, Univ. Deusto. 211 p.

5786 **Berardi** G., [1904-1973] Le lettere del Nuovo Testamento, 1. Lettere paoline; 2. lettere non paoline, ᴱ*Costantini* M., *Gasperoni* A.: Fano, Sem. Marchigiano. Vaticano 1987, Libreria. 447 p.; 403 p. 88-209-1669-X; 8-1 [NTAbs 33,115]. – ᴿRivB 37 (1989) 223-5 (G. *Crocetti*).

5787 *Bercovitz* J. Peter, Two letters chronologies: ProcGLM 9 (1989) 178-194.

5788 **Clabeaux** J. J., A lost edition of the letters of Paul; a reassessment of the text of the Pauline Corpus attested by MARCION: CBQ Mg 21. Wsh 1989, Catholic Biblical Association. xiv-183 p. $8.50. 0-915170-20-5 [NTAbs 33,397].

5789 **Fallon** Michael, The letters of Paul. Eastwood NSW, 1989, Parish Ministry. x-555 p. 0-949807-72-9.

5790 *Frankowski* Janusz, ℗ Le problème de l'origine et de la réception par l'Église du Corpus Paulinum [d'après H. M. SCHENKE 1974s]: STWsz 26,1 (1988) 180-203; franç. 203s [Le procès, 235-244].

5791 **Fuerst** Norbert, Der Schriftsteller Paulus. Da 1989, Wiss. 138 p. [CBQ 52,381]. 3-922981-49-6.

5792 *Furnish* Victor P., Pauline studies: ➤ 394, NT/Interpreters 1989, 321-350.

5793 **Garrido** J., Relectura ['modernizada'] de las cartas de san Pablo. M 1987, Paulinas. – ᴿBibFe 15 (1989) 170 (M. *Saenz de Santa Maria*).

5794 *Gillman* J., Recent perspectives in Pauline studies: Living Light 24 (Wsh 1988) 255-266 [NTAbs 33,43].

5795 **Hays** Richard B., Echoes of Scripture in the letters of Paul. NHv 1989, Yale Univ. xiv-240 p. $30. 0-300-04471-2 [TDig 37,59].

5796 **Johnson** David W., Purging the poison; the revision of Pelagius' Pauline commentaries by CASSIODORUS and his students: diss. Princeton Theol. Sem. 1989. 323 p. 89-23108. – DissA 50 (1989s) 2105-A [RTLv 21,548 as ➤ 4,5816 without 'purging the poison'].

5797 **Keck** L. E., Paolo e le sue lettere [1979 ➤ 65,5114] ᵀᴱ*Masini* M.: Strumenti 37. Brescia 1987, Queriniana. 146 p. Lit. 15.000. – ᴿAsprenas 36 (1989) 93s (S. *Cipriani*).

5798 *Kühschelm* R. [*Görg* M. AT], Brief, -formular: ➤ 902, NBL Lfg. 2 (1989) 325-7.

5799 **Locke** John, ᴱ*Wainwright* Arthur W., Paraphrase and notes 1705-7: 1987 ➤ 3,5634: ᴿRivB 37 (1989) 230-2 (P. C. *Bori*); TLZ 114 (1989) 342-4 (W. *Wiefel*); TR 85 (1989) 304-6 (H. *Hübner*).

5800 **Lovering** Eugene H.ᴶ, The collection, redaction, and early circulation of the Corpus Paulinum: diss. Southern Methodist, ᴰ*Furnish* V. 1988. 407 p. 89-09268. – DissA 50 (1989s) 466-A; RelStR 16,190.

5801 **Malherbe** Abraham J., Ancient epistolary theorists [< Ohio Journal of Religious Studies; translations from nine writers]: SBL Sources Bib. Study 19, 1988 ➤ 4,5820: ᴿExpTim 100 (1988s) 33 (C. S. *Rodd*).

5802 *Marin* Marcello, Sulla successione delle epistole paoline in Mario VITTORINO: VetChr 26 (1989) 377-385.

5803 **Marrow** Stanley B., Paul, his letters... 1986 ➤ 2,4473... 4,5821: ᴿAsbTJ 44,1 (1989) 116-8 (F. D. *Layman*); HeythJ 30 (1989) 189s (F. F. *Bruce*); WestTJ 51 (1989) 173s (D. J. W. *Milne*).

5804 *Mealand* David L., Positional stylometry reassessed; testing a seven epistle theory of Pauline authorship: NTS 35 (1989) 266-286 [Philippians is the seventh].

5805 **Popowski** Remigiusz, ⊕ Imperatiwus na tle indikatiwu... L'imperativo sullo sfondo dell'indicativo nelle Epistole di Paolo di Tarso [Diss. Hab. Lublin]. Lublin 1985, KUL. 412 p. – ᴿSalesianum 51 (1989) 161 (S. *Felici*).

5806 **Schmeller** Thomas, Paulus und die 'Diatribe' [kath. Diss. München 1985, ᴰ*Gnilka* J.] 1987 ➤ 3,5628; 4,5824: ᴿJBL 108 (1989) 538-542 (S. K. *Stowers*: uncritical); JTS 40 (1989) 197-200 (H. D. *Betz*); Salesianum 51 (1989) 162s (J. *Heriban*); TR 85 (1989) 370-2 (A. de *Oliveira*).

5807 **Schnider** F. *Stenger* W., Studien zum neutestamentlichen Briefformular 1987 ➤ 3,5629; 4,5825: ᴿNRT 111 (1989) 430s (X. *Jacques*); TLZ 114 (1989) 195-7 (W. *Schenk*).

5807* **Soards** M., The apostle Paul 1987 ➤ 3,5630; 4,5827: ᴿRelStT 8,1s (1988) 82 (T. A. *Robinson*).

5808 **Stein** R. H., Difficult passages in the Epistles. GR 1988, Baker. 162 p. $9. 0-8010-8293-5 [NTAbs 33,260: also author of Difficult sayings in the Gospels 1985 ➤ 1,3986].

5809 **Stowers** Stanley K., Letter writing in Greco-Roman antiquity 1986 ➤ 2,4482... 4,5829: ᴿCalvinT 24 (1989) 143s (A. J. *Bandstra*).

5810 **Trobisch** David, Die Entstehung der Paulusbriefsammlung; Studien zu den Anfängen christlicher Publizistik: NTOrb 10. FrS/Gö 1989. Univ/VR. ix-163 p. Fs 42 [RivB 37,531].

5811 *Zincone* Sergio, L'esegesi paolina di SEVERIANO di Gabala: ➤ 567, AnStoEseg 6 (1989) 51-75; Eng. 6.

G3.3 Pauli theologia.

5812 *Bassler* Jouette M., Paul's theology; whence and whither? A synthesis (of sorts) of the theology of Phlm, 1 Thess, Phlp, Gal, and 1 Cor: ➤ 589, SBL Seminars 1989, 412-423.

5813 **Beaudean** J. W., Paul's theology of preaching [diss. Drew, ᴰ*Doughty* D., Madison NJ]: Baptist prof. diss. 6. Macon GA 1988, Mercer Univ. xi-216 p. $19. 0-86554-341-0 [NTAbs 33,396].

5814 **Breytenbach** Cilliers, Versöhnung, eine Studie zur paulinischen Soteriologie [ev. Hab-Diss. Mü, ᴰ*Hahn* F.]: WM 60. Neuk 1989, Neuk.-V. xv-260 p. DM 75. 3-7887-1269-4. – ᴿComViat 32 (1989) 287s (P. *Pokorný*).

5815 *De Lorenzi* L., Il Dio di Paolo: ScuolCat 117 (1989) 231-286 [RHE 85,95*].

5816 **Dobbeler** Axel von, Glaube als Teilhabe...: WUNT 2/22, 1987 ➤ 3, 5641; 4,5840: ᴿGregorianum 70 (1989) 564s (R. *Penna*); TLZ 114 (1989) 119s (J. *Reumann*, Eng.).

5817 **Doohan** H., Paul's vision of the Church: Good News Studies 32. Wilmington 1989, Glazier. xi-262 p.; 4 maps. $13 pa. 0-89453-746-6 [NTAbs 33,256].

5818 *a*) *Eckert* Jost, Christus als 'Bild Gottes' und die Gottebenbildlichkeit des Menschen in der paulinischen Theologie; – *b*) *Kertelge* Karl, Autorität des Gesetzes und Autorität Jesu bei Paulus: ➤ 68, ᶠGNILKA J., Vom Urchristentum 1989, 337-357 / 358-376.

5819 **Ellis** E. Earle, Pauline theology; ministry and society. GR/Exeter 1989, Eerdmans/Paternoster. xv-182 p. 0-8028-0451-9 / 0-85364-503-5.

5820 *Fitzmyer* Joseph A., Pauline theology: ➤ 384, NJBC (1989) 1382-1416 [=] Paul and his theology, a brief sketch². ENJ 1989, Prentice Hall. xviii-119 p. 0-1365-4419-3.

5821 **Gundry** Robert H., Studies in biblical theology, with emphasis on Pauline anthropology [against BULTMANN Theology of NT]. GR 1987 = 1976, Zondervan. 279 p. $13 pa. – ᴿAndrUnS 27 (1989) 86s (A. *Dupertuis*: against holistic definition of *sōma*).

5822 **Harper** George D., Repentance in Pauline theology: diss. McGill. Montreal 1988. – DissA 50 (1989s) 175-A.

5823 *Hay* David M., *Pistis* as 'ground for faith' in Hellenized Judaism and Paul: JBL 108 (1989) 461-476.

5824 **Kreitzer** L. Joseph, Jesus and God in Paul's eschatology [diss. London King's College]: JStNT Sup 19, 1987 ➤ 3,5648; 4,5847: ᴿCBQ 51 (1989) 156s (L. T. *Johnson*); ExpTim 100 (1988s) 31s (J. D. G. *Dunn*); Interpretation 43 (1989) 202s (F. *Thielman*); JBL 108 (1989) 534-6 (R. *Morton*); JTS 40 (1989) 206-8 (J. M. G. *Barclay*).

5825 **McLean** Bradley H., Scapeman and scapebeast; soteriology in the letters of Paul: diss. St. Michael, ᴰ*Guenther* H. Toronto 1989 [microfiche Ottawa, Nat. Library]. – RTLv 21,546.

5826 **Mell** Ulrich, Neue Schöpfung; eine traditionsgeschichtliche und exegetische Studie zu einem soteriologischen Grundsatz paulinischer Theologie [Diss. ᴰ*Becker* J., Kiel 1987s ➤ 3,5650*]: BZNW 56. B 1989, de Gruyter. xv-436 p. 3-11-011831-9.

5827 *a*) *Merk* Otto, Nachahmung Christi; zu ethischen Perspektiven in der paulinischen Theologie; – *b*) *Lohse* Eduard, Die Berufung auf das

Gewissen in der paulinischen Ethik; – c) *Hahn* Ferdinand, Prophetie und Lebenswandel; Bemerkungen zu Paulus und zu zwei Texten der Apostolischen Väter: ➤ 173, FSCHNACKENBURG R., NT & Ethik 1989, 172-206 / 207-219 / 527-537.

5828 *Plevnik* Joseph, The center of Pauline theology: CBQ 51 (1989) 461-478: knowledge of God born of his Damascus experience.

5829 **Pobee** John S., Persecution and martyrdom in the theology of Paul: JStNT Sup 6, 1985 ➤ 1,5604... 4,5853: RHeythJ 30 (1989) 445s (F. F. *Bruce*: able and original).

5830 **Röhser** Günter, Metaphorik und Personifikation der Sünde; antike Sündenvorstellungen und paulinische Hamartia: WUNT 2/25, D1987 ➤ 3,5777: RCBQ 51 (1989) 755s (R. *Scroggs*: ignores gnosticism in favor of linguistic/rhetorical analysis of Macht); Gregorianum 70 (1989) 566 (R. *Penna*); JTS 40 (1989) 208-210 (A. J. M. *Wedderburn*).

5831 **Schade** Hans-H., Apokalyptische Christologie bei Paulus...: GöTheolArb 18, D1981 ➤ 62,6319... 65,5141: RJTS 40 (1989) 577s (E. *Bammel*).
 Segundo Juan L., The humanist Christology of Paul: Jesus Yesterday and Today 3, 1986 ➤ 7439.

5832 **Shogren** Gary S., The Pauline proclamation of the Kingdom of God and the Kingdom of Christ within its New Testament setting: diss. Aberdeen. 586 p. BRDX-86892. – DissA 50 (1989s) 3269-A.

5834 **Sinclair** Scott G., Jesus Christ according to Paul: BIBAL Mg. 1. Berkeley 1988, BIBAL. ii-150 p. $13 pa. [CBQ 52,198]. 0-941037-08-8. – RExpTim101 (1989s) 284 (J. A. *Ziesler*).

5835 *Söding* Thomas, a) Gottesliebe bei Paulus: TGL 79 (1989) 219-242; – b) Taufe, Geist und neues Leben; eine Orientierung an Paulus: BLtg 62 (1989) 179-186.

5836 **Styers** Norman, Truth and delusion in Eric VOEGELIN's analysis of the Pauline consciousness [... vision of the Resurrected]: diss. Boston Univ. 1989, DRouner L. 233 p. 8904166. – DissA 49 (1988s) 3401-A [RelStR 16,188 gives title as 'E. VOEGELIN's theory of symbolization and the nature of theological doctrine'].

5837 **Theissen** Gerd, Psychological aspects of Pauline theology 1987 ➤ 3,5658; 4,5856: RCBQ 51 (1989) 165-7 (B. A. *Malina*: excellent in its way, 'treating Paul as a 20th-century German'; requires pre-reading of D. E. STANNARD, Shrinking history; on FREUD and the failure of psychohistory, 1980); Pacifica 2 (1989) 112-5 (B. *Byrne*: rich, refreshing); ScotJT 42 (1989) 579-584 (A. *Wedderburn*: usually-reliable translation of an important and substantial work).

5838 **Wedderburn** A. J. M., Baptism and resurrection... Pauline theology [< diss. Cambridge]: WUNT 44, 1987 ➤ 3,5661; 4,5860: RActuBbg 26 (1989) 202s (X. *Alegre S.*); BZ 33 (1989) 151-3 (H.-J. *Klauck*); CBQ 51 (1989) 762-4 (W. *Willis*); ÉTRel 64 (1989) 121s (E. *Cuvillier*); EvQ 61 (1989) 265-8 (M. M. B. *Turner*); ExpTim 100 (1988s) 68 (J. J. *Houlden*); JBL 108 (1989) 742-5 (W. A. *Meeks*); NRT 111 (1989) 431s (X. *Jacques*); SvTKv 65 (1989) 133s (B. *Homberg*); TR 85 (1989) 364-6 (D. *Zeller*).

5839 *Wintle* Brian, 'Salvation' in the Pauline letters: Bible Bhashyam 14 (1988) 163-175.

G3.4 Themata paulina [Israel et Lex ➤ G4.6].

5840 **Bertau** Ingeborg, Unterscheidung der Geister; Studien zur theologischen Semantik der gotischen Paulusbriefe [Diss. Erlangen 1987]: Erlanger

Studien 72. Erlangen 1987, Palm & E. vii-251 p. DM 40 pa. 3-7896-0172-1 [NTAbs 33,115]. – ᴿTLZ 114 (1989) 19s (O. *Haendler*).

5840* *a*) *Boer* Martinus C. de, Paul and Jewish apocalyptic eschatology; – *b*) *Hays* Richard B., 'The righteous one' as eschatological deliverer; a case study in Paul's apocalyptic hermeneutics; – *c*) *Duff* Nancy J., The significance of Pauline apocalyptic for theological ethics: ⇥ 130, ᶠMARTYN J., 169-190 / 191-215 / 279-296.

5841 *Bosch* David, Paul on human hopes [... social justice]: JTSAf 67 (1989) 3-16 [< TContext 7/1, 22].

5842 *Brandenburger* Egon, Der Leib-Christi-Gedanke bei Paulus: ÖkRu 38 (1989) 389-397.

5843 **Branick** Vincent P., The house church in the writings of Paul: Zacchaeus NT. Wilmington 1989, Glazier. 143 p. $7 pa. [CBQ 51,782].

5844 *Breytenbach* Cilliers, Die Identität eines Christenmenschen — im Anschluss an Paulus: ZevEth 33 (1989) 263-277.

5845 *Cipriani* Settimio, Matrimonio e famiglia in San Paolo: ⇥ 587, Famiglia 1987/9, 199-223.

5846 *Clark* Andrew C., Apostleship; evidence from the New Testament [chiefly Paul, though 'apostle' occurs 34 times in Luke] and early Christian literature: VoxEvca 19 (1989) 49-82.

5847 *Davison* James E., The patterns of salvation in Paul and in Palestinian Judaism: JRelSt 15,1s (Cleveland 1987) 99-118 [< ᴢɪᴛ 89,633].

5848 *Derrett* J. D. M., 'Running' in Paul; the midrashic potential of Hab 2:2 [< Biblica 66 (1985) 560-7]: ⇥ 253, Sea-Change 1989, 188-195.

5849 *a*) *Dockery* David S., An outline of Paul's view of the spiritual life; foundation for an evangelical spirituality; – *b*) *Demarest* Bruce, *Raup* Charles, Recovering the heart of Christian spirituality: CriswT 3,2 (1989) 327-339 / 321-6.

5850 **Flood** Edmund, All is ours; Paul's message to all Christians. NY 1987, Paulist. 219 p. $5. – ᴿLVitae 44 (1989) 351s (G. Van *Hoomissen*).

5851 **Franco** Ettore, Comunione 1986 ⇥ 2,4516 ... 4,5873: ᴿEstBíb 47 (1989) 426 (F. *Pastor-Ramos*).

5852 *Fuller* Reginald H., Jesus, Paul and Apocalyptic: AngTR 71 (1989) 134-142 [< ᴢɪᴛ 89,639].

5853 *a*) *Furnish* V. P., Der 'Wille Gottes' in paulinischer Sicht; – *b*) *Schrage* W., Heiligung als Prozess bei Paulus; – *c*) *Schmithals* W., Paulus als Heidenmissionar und das Problem seiner theologischen Entwicklung: ⇥ 131, ᶠMARXSEN W., Jesu Rede 1989, 208-221 / 222-234 / 235-251.

5854 **Gebauer** Roland, Das Gebet bei Paulus; Forschungsgeschichtliche und exegetische Studien. Giessen 1989, Brunnen. xiv-393 p. 3-7655-9349-4. – ᴿExpTim 101 (1989s) 315 (E. *Best*).

5855 **Grams** Rollin G., Gospel and mission in Paul's ethics: diss. Duke, ᴰ*Price* J. Durham NC 1989. 499 p. 90-06733. – DissA 50 (1989s) 3267-A; RelStR 16,190.

5856 **Hanson** Anthony T., The paradox of the Cross in the thought of St. Paul: JStNT sup 17, 1987 ⇥ 3,5681; 4,5875: ᴿCBQ 51 (1989) 559s (E. *Hensell*); ExpTim 100 (1988s) 233 (J. K. *Riches*); JTS 40 (1989) 578-80 (C. J. A. *Hickling*); ScotJT 42 (1989) 427s (J. *Barclay*: too hastily written). **Hofius** O., Paulusstudien 1989 ⇥ 280.

5857 **Jones** F. Stanley, 'Freiheit' in den Briefen des Apostels Paulus ...: GöTArb 34, ᴰ1987 ⇥ 3,5688; 4,5878: ᴿBiblica 70 (1989) 428-432 (J. D. G. *Dunn*); CBQ 51 (1989) 372s (J. *Plevnik*); RelStR 15 (1989) 161 (C. *Bernas*); TLZ 114 (1989) 36s (M. *Rissi*).

5858 *a) Jovino* Paolo, Il 'ministero' di salvezza dell'apostolo Paolo; – *b) Fabris* Rinaldo, Lo spirito che ama in noi [... Paolo ecc.]: ➤ 751, Spiritualità oblativa 1989, 77-99 / 25-45.

5859 *Karrer* Martin, Petrus im paulinischen Gemeindekreis: ZNW 80 (1989) 210-231.

5860 *a)* **Kitzberger** Ingrid R., Bau der Gemeinde... paulin. *oikodomē* 1986 ➤ 4,a682: RJBL 108 (1989) 544-6 (H. *Boers*); – *b)* Paulinische Perspektiven zu Friede-Gerechtigkeit-Schöpfung: BiKi 44 (1989) 163-170.

5861 *Klauck* Hans-J., Kultische Symbolsprache bei Paulus [< F*Plöger* J., Freude 1983, 107-118]: ➤ 292, Gemeinde 1989, 348-358.

5862 **Koch** D.-A., Die Schrift als Zeuge des Ev... bei Paulus: BeiHistT 69, 1987 ➤ 2,4525... 4,5880: RRechSR 77 (1989) 119-121 (J. *Aletti*).

5863 *Légasse* Simon, La polémique antipaulinienne dans le judéo-christianisme hétérodoxe: BLitEc 90 (1989) 5-22. 85-100.

5863* *Leonarda* Salvatore, La gioia nelle lettere di Paolo: diss. Urbaniana 1987, D*Federici* T. – RBenedictina 35 (1988) 183-9 (L. *De Lorenzi*).

5864 **Liebenow** Mark, Is there fun after Paul? A theology of clowning [diss.]... Resource/Columba. 150 p. £8 pa. – RDocLife 38 (1988) 389s (F. *Kelly:* sense of humor yes, clown no).

5865 *López de las Heras* L., ¿Hay una mística paulina?: Studium 29 (M 1989) 61-106.

5866 **Low** Douglas A., Apocalyptic motivation in Pauline paraenesis: diss. Southern Baptist Theol. Sem. 1988, D*Polhill* J. 330 p. 89-09291. – DissA 50 (1989s) 470-A.

5867 *Meagher* Patrick, The absence of 'the Poor' in the Pauline letters: Bible Bhashyam 14 (1988) 78-97 [for his Vidyajyoti reviews see our next volume].

5868 **Meeks** W.A., Los primeros cristianos urbanos; el mundo social del apóstol Pablo 1988 ➤ 4,5884: RBibFe 15 (1989) 323 (A. *Salas*); CiTom 116 (1989) 191-3 (J. *Huarte*); CiuD 202 (1989) 251s (J. *Gutiérrez*); CommSev 22 (1989) 90s (M. de *Burgos*); Proyección 36 (1989) 240 (B.A.O.); ScripTPamp 21 (1989) 655-9 (C. *Basevi*); Studium-M 29 (1989) 378 (C. G. *Extremeño*).

5869 *Meeks* W.A., The polyphonic ethics of the Apostle Paul: Annual of the Society of Christian Ethics (Knoxville TN 1988) 17-29 [< NTAbs 33,178].

5870 **Ménard** Camil, L'Esprit de la Nouvelle Alliance chez saint Paul [diss. Laval 1983]: Recherches NS 10, 1987 ➤ 3,5697; 4,5885: RBijdragen 50 (1989) 444 (T.C. de *Kruijf*); EsprVie 99 (1989) 291-3 (É. *Cothenet*); EstBíb 47 (1989) 574s (F. *Pastor-Ramos*); ÉTRel 64 (1989) 294s (Danielle *Ellul*); Gregorianum 70 (1989) 155s (J. *Galot*); LavalTP 44 (1988) 262s (P.-E. *Langevin*); RTPhil 121 (1989) 341 (R. *Petraglio*).

5871 **Newman** Carey C., 'Glory of God in the face of Jesus'; a tradition-historical investigation into the origin of Paul's identification of Christ as *dóxa*: diss. Baylor 1989. 384 p. 89-19930. – DissA 50 (1989s) 1697-A.

5872 **Ngundu** Onesimus Annos, Toward a Pauline model of progressive sanctification: diss. Dallas Theol. Sem. 1988. 230 p. 89-13853. – DissA 50 (1989s) 1330-A.

5873 *Porter* Stanley E., WITTGENSTEIN's classes of utterance and Paul's ethical texts: JEvTS 32 (1989) 85-98 [< ZIT 89,509].

5874 **Robert** Micheline, Au principe de l'amélioration des conditions humaines chez Paul: diss. D*Côté* P. Montréal 1989. 404 p. – RTLv 21,546.

5875 *Roberts* J. H., Belydenisuitsprake as Pauliniese briefoorgange: HervTSt 44 (Pretoria 1988) 81-97 [< NTAbs 33,45: Credal statements as Pauline epistolary transitions].

5876 **Segundo** Juan Luis, [➤ 7443] Le christianisme de S. Paul; l'histoire retrouvée [= La historia perdida y remplazada 2; 1 = Jésus devant la conscience moderne 1988; 'constitue une version nouvelle et améliorée de El hombre de hoy ante Jesús de Nazareth, (vol. 2, avec un peu de vol. 1-3; ...lesquels) avaient suscité divers problèmes, en partie sans doute à cause d'un manque de clarté, de concision et d'ordre dans la rédaction', NRT 111,763, X. *Jacques*]. P 1988, Cerf. 335 p. F 210.

5877 **South** James T., Corrective discipline in the Pauline communities: diss. Virginia, ᴰ*Gamble* H. 1989. 359 p. 90-08183. – DissA 50 (1989s) 3263s-A; RelStR 16,190.

5878 **Stark** Judith C., The Pauline influence on AUGUSTINE's notion of the will: VigChr 43 (1989) 345-361.

5879 (Cohen) *Stuart* G. H., Tweestrijd; strijd tussen goed en kwaad bij Paulus en zijn tijdgenoten [The struggle in man, diss. Amst 1984]. Kampen 1988, Kok. 143 p. ƒ 22,50. – ᴿStreven 56 (1988s) 757 (P. *Beentjes*).

5880 **Vollenweider** Samuel, Freiheit als neue Schöpfung; eine Untersuchung zur Eleutheria bei Paulus und in seiner Umwelt [Hab.-Diss. Zürich]: FRL 147. Gö 1989, Vandenhoeck & R. 451 p. DM 120. 3-525-53828-6. – ᴿTsTNijm 29 (1989) 410 (J. *Smit*).

G4 **Ad Romanos** .1 *Textus, commentarii.*

5881 **Black** Matthew, Romans² (¹1973): NCent. GR/L 1989, Eerdmans/ Marshall-MS. xv-224 p. $14. 0-8028-0374-1/. [TDig 37,150].

5882 **Bruce** F. F., The letter of Paul to the Romans² [¹1963]. Tyndale NT comm. Leicester/GR 1989, Inter-Varsity/Eerdmans. 274 p. 0-85111-875-5 / GR 0-8028-0062-9.

5883 ᵀᴱ**Cocchini** Francesca, ORIGENE, Commento alla Lettera ai Romani II (lib. 7-10) 1986 ➤ 3,5724; 4,5903: ᴿProtestantesimo 44 (1989) 136-8 (A. *Landi*).

5884 **Cranfield** C., Romans shorter 1985 ➤ 1,5669; 2,4553: ᴿCriswT 2 (1987s) 172s (D. S. *Dockery*); RelStT 7,1 (1987) 67s (G. *Hamilton*); TLZ 114 (1989) 33-35 (N. *Walter*).

5885 **Dunn** James D. G., Romans 1-8 / 9-16: Word Comm. 38A-B, 1988 ➤ 4,5904: ᴿSWJT 32,1 (1989s) 46s (J. A. *Brooks*).

5886 *Fitzmyer* Joseph A., The letter to the Romans: ➤ 384, NJBC (1989) 830-868 [768-771, epistles introd.].

5887 ᴱ**Fraenkel** Pierre, *Perrotet* Luc, Théodore de BÈZE, Cours sur les épîtres aux Romains et aux Hébreux, 1564-66: TravHumRen 226, 1988 ➤ 4,5905: Genève 1988, Droz. 443 p. – ᴿJTS 40 (1989) 678-681 (Irena *Backus*); RivStoLR 25 (1989) 565s (M. *Richter*).

5888 **Heil** John P., Paul's letter to the Romans, a reader-response commentary 1987 ➤ 3,5729; 4,5906: ᴿCBQ 51 (1989) 743s (D. M. *Sweetland*: valuable); RelStR 15 (1989) 161s (L. E. *Keck*).

5889 **Heither** Theresia, [Röm; HAMMOND-BAMMEL C. 1983] ORIGENES — ein moderner Exeget: ErbAuf 65 (1989) 359-375.

5890 ᴱ**Junack** K., *al.*, Das NT auf Papyrus [I. kath. 1986 ➤ 2,4972], II. Die paulinischen Briefe, Teil 1, Röm. 1 Kor. 2 Kor; Einf. *Aland* B.: Arb-NTTextf 12. B 1989, de Gruyter. lvi-418 p. DM 148. 3-11-012248-0. –

ᴿETL 65 (1989) 439s (F. *Neirynck*: grande précision); NT 31 (1989) 381-3 (J. K. *Elliott*).

5891 **Klaiber** Walter, *al.*, Rechenschaft über den Glauben; Römerbrief: Bibelauslegung für die Praxis 21. Stu 1989, KBW. 159 p. 3-460-25211-1.

5892 ᴱ**Lagarrigue** Georges, Martin LUTHER, Commentaire de l'Épître aux Romains II (3,2 à 16): Œuvres 12. Genève 1985, Labor et Fides. 364 p. – ᴿScriptB 20 (1989s) 21s (L. *Swain*); TVida 29 (1988) 88s (Annelies *Meis*).

5893 **Legée** Jacqueline, Jean CHRYSOSTOME commente saint Paul; homélies choisies sur l'épître aux Romains / [*Winling* Raymond] sur la 1ᵉʳᵉ lettre aux Corinthiens: Les Pères dans la foi [ᴱ*Hamman* A.]. P 1988, Desclée de Brouwer. 369 p. F 128. – ᴿEsprVie 99 (1989) 44s (É. *Cothenet*]; VSp 143 (1989) 130s (G. *Berceville*).

5894 **Morris** Leon, The epistle to the Romans 1988 → 4,5911: ᴿCBQ 51 (1989) 750-2 (J. P. *Heil*); BTrans 40 (1989) 344-6 (R. L. *Omanson*); JBL 108 (1989) 740-2 (F. *Thielman*).

5895 *Pani* Giancarlo, John COLET e l'Expositio ad Romanos (1498): → 567, AnStoEseg 6 (1989) 235-259; Eng. 10.

5896 **Parker** T. [11] Commentaries on Romans 1532-1542: 1986 → 2,4564... 4,5912: ᴿScotJT 42 (1989) 604-6 (J. L. *North*); TLZ 114 (1989) 45-47 (S. *Strohm*).

5897 **Philip** James, The power of God; an exposition of Paul's letter to the Romans. Glasgow 1987, Gray. 222 p. – ᴿEvQ 61 (1989) 164 (D. J. *Graham*: no reference to recent work).

5898 **Ponsot** H., Une introduction à la lettre aux Romains: Initiations. P 1988, Cerf. 218 p. – ᴿEsprVie 99 (1989) 552-4 (L. *Walter*).

5899 **Schmithals** W., Römerbrief 1988 → 4,5913; DM 128: ᴿLuthMon 29 (1989) 377 (E. *Lohse*); TsTNijm 29 (1989) 290 (H. van de *Sandt*).

5900 ᴱ**Strohm** Stefan, Johannes BRENZ, Explicatio ep. Pauli ad Rom. 1, 1986 → 2,4567... 4,5914: ᴿTLZ 114 (1989) 373s (H. J. E. *Beintker*).

5901 **Stuhlmacher** Peter, Der Brief an die Römer: NTD 6. Gö 1989, Vandenhoeck & R. 237 p. 3-525-51372-0.

5902 ᴱ**Verdeyen** Paul, GUILLELMUS S. Theodorici, Expositio super epistolam ad Romanos: Opera I, CCMed 86. Turnhout 1989, Brepols. lxxxiii-210 p. 2-503-03861-1; pa. -2-2.

5903 **Ziesler** John, Paul's letter to the Romans: TPI NT Comm. L 1989, SCM. xv-382 p. [JTS 41, 615-7, C. E. B. *Cranfield*]. 0-334-02297-5; pa. -6-7.

G4.2 *Ad Romanos: themata*, **topics.**

5904 **Abbott** Thomas M., Paul's Christology in Romans: diss. Drew. ᴰ*Doughty*. Madison NJ 1989. 199 p. 89-21804. – DissA 50 (1989s) 1701-A; RelStR 16,187.

5905 *Beker* J. Christiaan, Romans: → 377, Books 2 (1989) 229-243.

5906 *Crawford* Barry, Reading Romans as a Christianity: → 592, Systemic 2 (1989) 1-15.

5997 **Davies** Glenn N., Faith and obedience in Romans: diss. Sheffield 1987. 369 p. BRDX-88449. – DissA 50 (1989s) 3989-A.

5908 **Elliott** R. Neil, The rhetoric of Romans [1-8]; argumentative constraint and strategy and Paul's 'dialogue with Judaism': diss. Princeton Theol. Sem. 1989, ᴰ*Beker* J. 340 p. 89-23105. – DissA 50 (1989s) 2104-A; RelStR 16,190 ('Rodger N.', 'strategy and constraint').

5909 **Elorriaga** C., La fuerza del evangelio; sentido de la existencia humana en la carta a los Romanos. M 1988, Paulinas. 172 p. – ᴿBibFe 15 (1989) 320 (M. *Sáenz Galache*).

5910 *Keck* Leander E., 'Jesus' in Romans: JBL 108 (1989) 443-460.

5911 *a) Lyonnet* Stanislas, L'universalisme de S. Paul d'après l'Épître aux Romains [conférence Milan avril 1961]; – *b*) La connaissance naturelle de Dieu, Rom. 1,18-23; – *c*) La justification par la foi selon Rom. 3,27-4,8 [< lat. Quaestiones in Rom. I, 57-88. 104-145, ᵀ*Morel* Charles]: ⇥ 307, Études sur Rom, 1989, 1-13 / 43-70 / 107-143.

5912 *Müller* M., Ånden of loven, pagtsteologi i Romerbrevet: ⇥ 181, ᶠOᴛᴢᴇɴ B., DanTTs 52,4 (1989) 251-267 [< ZNW 81,149].

5913 *Penna* Romano, Narrative aspects of the epistle of St. Paul to the Romans: ⇥ 610, Parable & story 1986/9, 191-204.

5914 **Ponsot** Hervé, Une introduction à la lettre aux Romains 1988 ⇥ 4,5924: ᴿRThom 89 (1989) 686 (J.-G. *Ranquet*).

5915 *Roukema* Riemer, The diversity of laws in Augustine's commentary on Romans. Amst 1988, Vrije Univ. 118 p. – ᴿZKG 100 (1989) 419s (H. *Chadwick*, Eng.).

5916 *Roukema* R., Oʀɪɢᴇɴᴇs' visie op de rechtvaardiging volgens zijn Commentaar op Romeinen: GerefTTs 89 (1989) 94-105.

5917 **Ruschke** Werner M., Entstehung und Ausführung der Diastasentheologie in Karl Bᴀʀᴛʜs zweitem 'Römerbrief' [ev. Diss. Münster 1978, ᴰ*Stoll* G.E.]: Neuk BeitSysT 5. Neuk 1987. x-229 p. DM 64 pa. 3-7887-1207-4 [NTAbs 33,119]. – ᴿTLZ 114 (1989) 137 (M. *Beintker*).

5918 **Schneider** Nelio, Die 'Schwachen' in der christlichen Gemeinde Roms: Diss. ᴰ*Barth* G. Wuppertal 1989. 266 p. – RTLv 21,547.

5918* *Stuhlmacher* Peter, The theme of Romans: AustralBR 36 (1988) 31-44 [< IZBG 36, p. 212].

5919 *Varo* Francisco, El léxico del pecado en la Epístola de san Pablo a los Romanos: ScripTPamp 21 (1989) 99-116.

5920 **Wedderburn** A.J.M., The reasons for Romans 1988 ⇥ 4,5926: ᴿTLond 92 (1989) 333s (J.M.G. *Barclay*); TLZ 114 (1989) 674-6 (W. *Schmithals*); TR 85 (1989) 366s (D. *Zeller*).

G4.3 *Naturalis cognitio Dei ... Rom 1-4.*

5921 *Toit* A.B. du, Persuasion in Romans 1:1-17: BZ 33 (1989) 192-209.

5922 *a) Pesch* Rudolf, Das Evangelium Gottes über seinen Sohn; zur Auslegung der Tradition in Rom 1,1-4; – *b) Walter* Nikolaus, Gottes Zorn und das 'Harren der Kreatur'; zur Korrespondenz zwischen Römer 1,18-32 und 8,19-22; – *c) Dunn* James D.G., Paul's knowledge of the Jesus tradition; the evidence of Romans: ⇥ 197, ᶠTʀɪʟʟɪɴɢ W., Christus bezeugen 1989, 208-217 / 218-226 / 193-207.

5923 *Baasland* Ernst, Cognitio Dei im Römerbrief: SNTU 14 (Linz 1989) 185-218 [< zɪᴛ 90,407].

5924 **Dubarle** A.-M., La manifestation naturelle de Dieu d'après l'Écriture: LDiv 91, 1977 ⇥ 58,7670 ...: ᴿNicolaus 16 (1989) 307-310 (A. *Moda*).

5925 *Theobald* Michael, Glaube und Vernunft; zur Argumentation des Paulus im Römerbrief: TüTQ 169 (1989) 287-301.

5926 *a) Dockery* David S., Romans 1:16-17 (exposition); – *b) Leonard* Bill J., A place to believe (Romans 1:16-18): RExp 86 (1989) 87-91 / 93-98.

5927 *Vouga* F., Romains 1,18-3,20 comme narratio: ⇥ 385, Narration 1988, 145-162.

5928 **Vives** Josep, *al.*, El segrest de la veritat; els homes segresten la veritat amb llur injustícia (Rom 1,18): Horitzons 14. Barc 1986, Claret. 151 p.: ᴿTR 85 (1989) 372-4 (A. de *Oliveira*).

5929 *Hooker* Morna D., [Rom 3,2 + 6 times outside Rom 3] *Pístis Christoû* [presidential address SNTS Cambridge August 1988]: NTS 35 (1989) 321-342.

5930 *Penna* Romano, I diffamatori di Paolo in Rm 3,8: → 597, RicStoB 1,2 (1987/9) 43-53.

5931 *De Lorenzi* Lorenzo, 'Tutti sotto il peccato' (Rm 3,9): ParSpV 19 (1989) 139-162.

5932 **Campbell** Douglas A., The rhetoric of righteousness [in /; an analysis of] Romans 3:21-26: diss. ᴰ*Longenecker* R. Toronto 1989. DissA 50 (1989s) 2943-A ['in']; RelStR 16,190.

5933 *Ramaroson* Léonard, [Rom 3,21-26...] Trois études récentes sur 'la foi de Jésus dans saint Paul' [lui-même et *Williams* S. 1987; *Johnson* L. 1982]: ScEspr 40 (1988) 365-377.

5934 **Lambrecht** J., *Thompson* R. W., Justification by faith; the implications of Romans 3:27-31 [< Thompson's diss. Lv 1985, ᴰ*Lambrecht*]: Zacchaeus Studies. Wilmington 1989, Glazier, 94 p. $7. 0-89453-665-6 [NTAbs 33,400].

5935 *Stowers* Stanley K., *Ek písteōs* and *dià tês písteōs* in Romans 3:30: JBL 108 (1989) 665-674.

5936 *Bravo* Ernesto, [Rom 4,5s...] La justificación por la fe sola; un enfoque nuevo para un viejo problema [< Las respuestas del católico, próximo a publicarse]: RBibArg 51 (1989) 11-36.

5937 *Toit* A. B. du, Gesetzesgerechtigkeit und Glaubensgerechtigkeit in Röm 4:13-25; in Gespräch mit E. P. SANDERS: HervTSt 44 (1988) 71-80 [NTAbs 33,46].

G4.4 *Peccatum originale; redemptio cosmica:* **Rom 5-8.**

5938 *Ricœur* Paul, Ⓜ Jesus' logic; Rom 5 [Revue de Montpellier (1980) 420-5], ᵀ*Fáy* Tünde: TSzem 32 (1989) 75-77.

5939 **McDonald** Patricia M., Romans 5:1-11; the structure and significance of a bridge: diss. Catholic Univ. of America, ᴰ*Meier* J. Wsh 1989. 282 p. 89-17031. – DissA 50 (1989s) 1340-A; RTLv 21,546.

5940 *a) Mela* Roberto, [Rm 5,6-11] Amare i 'nemici'; i peccatori e la compassione evangelica; – *b) Fabris* Rinaldo, Lo spirito che ama in noi: → 751, Sp. oblativa 1988/9, 47-55 / 25-45.

5941 **Seemuth** David P., Adam the sinner and Christ the righteous one; the theological and exegetical substructure of Romans 5:12-21: diss. Marquette, ᴰ*Stockhausen* Carol. Milwaukee 1989. 298 p. 90-14062. – DissA 50 (1989s) 3991-A.

5942 *Harbert* B., Romans 5,12; Old Latin and Vulgate in the Pelagian controversy: → 696, StudPatr 10/22 (1987/9) 261-4.

5943 *Giblin* Charles H., A qualifying parenthesis (Rom 5:13-14) and its context: → 60, ᶠFITZMYER J., Touch 1989, 305-315.

5944 *Kreitzer* Larry, [Rom 5,14...] Christ and Second Adam in Paul: ComViat 32 (1989) 55-101.

5945 *Grelot* Pierre, Une homélie de saint Paul sur le baptême (Rom. 6,1-23): EsprVie 99 (1989) 155-9.

5946 *Fischbach* Stephanie M., Der neue Mensch; zu Röm 6,1-14: GeistL 62 (1989) 1-3.

5947 *Schlarb* Robert, Röm 6:1-11 in der Auslegung der frühen Kirchenväter: BZ 33 (1989) 104-113.

5948 *Luck* Ulrich, Das Gute und das Böse in Römer 7: ➤ 173, FSCHNAC-KENBURG R., NT & Ethik 1989, 220-237.

5949 *Ring* Thomas G., Römer 7 in den *Enarrationes ad Psalmos*: ➤ 13, FMAYER C., Signum pietatis 1989, 383-407.

5950 *Weder* Hans, Der Mensch im Widerspruch; eine Paraphrase zu Röm 7,7-28: GLern 4 (1989) 130-142 [< ZIT 90,62].

5951 **Kim Jung-Joo**, The Spirit of God as witness to the redemption in Christ; a tradition-historical analysis of Paul's pneumatology in Romans 8: diss. SW Baptist Theol. Sem. 1989, DKoester H. 283 p. 89-25425. – DissA 50 (1989) 2114-A; RelStR 16,190.

5952 *Tamez* Elsa, Now no condemnation; a meditation on Romans 8[,1]: EcuR 41 (1989) 446-453.

5953 *Schütz* Christian, 'Nach dem Geist leben' (Röm 8,4): TPQ 137 (1989) 395-8.

5954 **Rossi** Benedetto, La redenzione cosmica in Romani 8,18-25; la ktisis in San Paolo tra protologia ed escatologia: diss. SBF, DBuscemi A. M. J 1989. 424 p. – LA 39 (1989) 381s.

5955 *a) Cross* Frank M., The redemption of nature; – *b) Willis-Watkins* E. David, Creation and human creativity: PrincSemB 10 (1989) 94-104 / 105-118 [< ZIT 89,649].

5956 *Lambrecht* Jan, De kreunende schepping; een lezing van Rom. 8,19-22: CollatVL 19 (1989) 292-310.

5957 *Hommel* Hildebrecht, Denen, die Gott lieben... Erwägungen zu Römer 8,28: ZNW 80 (1989) 126-9.

G4.6   *Israel et Lex;* **The Law and the Jews,** *Rom 9-11.*

5958 *Campbell* W. S., Did Paul advocate separation from the synagogue? a reaction to Francis WATSON [... sociological approach 1986]: ScotJT 42 (1989) 457-467.

5959 **Cassirer** Heinz, [➤ 4,5959] EWeitzman Ronald, Grace and Law [... Paul, KANT; 1959]. E/GR 1989, Handsel/Eerdmans. xvi-176 p. £6.50. 0-905312-78-3 / 0-8028-0317-2. – RExpTim 100 (1988s) 475 (D. A. *Pailin*).

5960 *Donaldson* Terence L., Zealot and convert; the origin of Paul's Christ-Torah antithesis [Phlp 3,6; Gal 1,13s...]: CBQ 51 (1989) 655-682.

Fusco Vittorio, Gesù e la legge 1989 ➤ 4116.

5961 **Gaston** Lloyd, Paul and the Torah [10 art., 7 reprinted] 1987 ➤ 4,196: RCBQ 51 (1989) 769-772 (K. P. *Donfried*); RelStR 15 (1989) 161 (R. B. *Hays*); RelStT 8,1s (1988) 80s (A. E. *Milton*); TLZ 114 (1989) 191s (H. *Räisänen*: eine Revolution... Akt der Verzweiflung); TS 50 (1989) 360s (R. J. *Dillon*: 'exegesis after Auschwitz' a program to which all textual evidence must cede).

5962 *Geer* Thomas C., Paul and the Law in recent discussion: RestQ 31 (1989) 93-... [< ZIT 89,651].

5963 *Hofius* O., *a)* Das Evangelium und Israel, Erwägungen zu Römer 9-11 [< ZTK 83 (1986) 297-324]; – *b)* 'Rechtfertigung des Gottlosen' als Thema biblischer Theologie [< JbBT 2 (1987) 79-105]; – *c)* Wort Gottes und Glaube bei Paulus [ineditum]; – *d)* Erwägungen zu Gestalt und Herkunft des paulinischen Versöhnungsgedankens [< ZTK 77 (1980) 186-199]: ➤ 280, Paulusstudien 1989, 175-202 / 121-147 / 148-174 / 1-14.

5964 *Holtz* Traugott, Das Gericht über die Juden und die Rettung ganz Israels: ➤ 120, ᶠLOHSE E., Wissenschaft 1989, 119-131.

5965 **Johnson** E. Elizabeth, The function of apocalyptic and wisdom traditions in Romans 9-11: SBL diss 109. Atlanta 1989, Scholars. 260 p. $17; sb./pa. $11. 1-55540-226-7; 7-5 [TDig 37,66].

5966 **Kaylor** R. David, Paul's covenant community; Jew and Gentile in Romans. Louisville 1988, Westminster/Knox. 260 p. $15. 0-8042-0220-6 [TDig 36,376].

5967 **Liebers** Reinhold, Das Gesetz als Evangelium; Untersuchungen zur Gesetzeskritik des Paulus [Diss. Kiel 1986, ᴰ*Luck* U.]: ATANT 75. Z 1989, Theol.-V. 257 p. 3-290-10041-3.

5968 *Longenecker* Bruce W., Different answers to different issues; Israel, the Gentiles and salvation history in Romans 9-11: JStNT 36 (1989) 95-128.

5969 **Martin** Brice L., Christ and the Law in Paul: NT supp. 62. Leiden 1989, Brill. xi-186 p. ƒ115 [JBL 109,378].

5970 **Motyer** Steve, Israel in the plan of God; light on today's debate. Leicester 1989, Inter-Varsity. 172 p. £5.

5971 **Mussner** Franz, Traité sur les Juifs: CogF 109, 1981 ➤ 62,6488*b*; 63,5845: ᴿRTPhil 121 (1989) 100s (Esther *Starobinski*).

5972 *Mussner* Franz, Warum muss es den Juden post Christum noch geben?; Reflexionen im Anschluss es an Röm 9-11: ➤ 197, ᶠTRILLING W., 1989, 67-73.

5973 **Osten-Sacken** Peter von der, Die Heiligkeit der Tora; Studien zum Gesetz bei Paulus. Mü 1989, Kaiser. 179 p. DM 48 [TLZ 115, 274-6, W. *Wiefel*]. 3-419-01787-2.

5974 **Panimolle** Salvatore A., La libertà dalla legge di Mosè negli scritti dei Padri dalla fine del II secolo: studi e ricerche bibliche. R 1989, Borla. 224 p. 88-263-0702-4.

5975 *Pastor-Ramos* Federico, Liberación y libertad de la ley: SalT 76 (1988) 29-37.

5976 **Räisänen** Heikki, Paul and the Law²ʳᵉᵛ, WUNT 29, 1987 [¹1983 ➤ 64,5532 ... 4,5971]: ᴿScripTpamp 21 (1989) 660-2 (C. *Basevi*).

5977 *Sanders* Ed P., Paolo, la legge e il popolo giudaico [1983 ➤ 64,5537], ᵀ*Borbone* Pier G.: StBPaid. Brescia 1989, Paideia. 363 p. Lit. 38.000. 88-394-0430-9.

5978 **Siegert** Folker, Argumentation bei Paulus... Röm 9-11: WUNT 34, 1985 ➤ 1,5766 ... 4,5977: TLZ 114 (1989) 350-2 (N. *Walter*).

5979 **Thielman** Frank, From plight to solution; a Jewish framework for understanding Paul's view of the Law in Galatians and Romans: NT supp. 61. Leiden 1989, Brill. ix-159 p. ƒ100 [TR 86,163].

5980 *Vouga* François, Paulus und die Juden; Interpretation aus der Zeitstimmung: WDienst 20 (1989) 105-120.

5981 *Wagner* Günter, The future of Israel; reflections on Romans 9-11: ➤ 21, ᶠBEASLEY-MURRAY G., Eschatology 1988, 77-112.

5982 **Watson** Francis, Paul, Judaism and the Gentiles, a sociological approach 1986 ➤ 2,4634* ... 4,5980: ᴿHeythJ 30 (1989) 193s (J. *Coventry*); JBL 108 (1989) 160s (A. T. *Kraabel*); JTS 40 (1989) 200-206 (N. T. *Wright*); RechSR 77 (1989) 115-7 (J.-N. *Aletti*); SvTKv 65 (1989) 131s (B. *Homberg*).

5983 **Westerholm** Stephen, Israel's Law and the Church's faith; Paul 1988 ➤ 4,3981: ᴿÉTRel 64 (1989) 442 (E. *Cuvillier*); ExpTim 101 (1989s) 284

(J. *Barclay*); LA 39 (1989) 368-371 (A.M. *Buscemi*); TLond 92 (1989) 334s (J.A. *Ziesler*); WestTJ 51 (1989) 174-7 (M. *Silva*).

5984 *Parmentier* Martin, Greek Church fathers on Romans 9: Bijdragen 50 (1989) 139-154.

5985 *Dewey* Arthur J., Acoustics of the Spirit; a hearing of Romans 10: ProcGLM 9 (1989) 212-230.

5986 *Rese* M., Israels Unwissen und Ungehorsam und die Verkündigung des Glaubens durch Paulus in Römer 10: → 131, FMARXSEN W., Jesu Rede 1989, 252-266.

5987 *Obijole* O.O., The Pauline concept of the Law (Gal 3,19-4,7; Rom 10,4): IndTSt 26 (1989) 22-34.

5988 *Schutter* William L., PHILO's psychology of prophetic inspiration and Romans 10:20: → 589, SBL Seminars 1989, 624-633.

5989 *Bloesch* Donald G., [Rom 11,25s] 'All Israel will be saved'; super-sessionism and the biblical witness: Interpretation 43 (1989) 130-142.

5990 **Carbone** Sandro, La misericordia universale di Dio in Romani 11,30-32: diss. SBF, DBuscemi A. J 1988. 366 p. – LA 39 (1989) 379s.

G4.8 Rom 12...

5990* **Schegget** G.H. ter, Het moreel van de gemeente; essays over de ethiek van Paulus volgens Romeinen 12 en 13. Baarn 1985, Ten Have. 104 p. f16,50 pa. 90-259-4289-X [NTAbs 33,119].

5991 *Voss* Gerhard, In Christus Gemeinschaft bilden; eine Auslegung des 12. Kapitels des Römerbriefes: UnSa 43 (1988) 277-283. 342 [< IZBG 36,216].

5991* *Betz* Hans Dieter, The foundations of Christian ethics according to Romans 12:1-2: → 143, FOGDEN S., Witness 1989, 55-73.

5992 *Baumert* Norbert, [Röm 12,2-8] Zur 'Unterscheidung der Geister': ZkT 111 (1989) 183-195.

5993 **North** James L., Romans 12.11; a textual, lexical and ethical study: diss. Durham 1989. – RTLv 21,546.

5993* **Munro** Winsome, [Rom 13,1-9] Authority in Paul and Peter 1983 → 65,5743... 2,4648: RTLZ 114 (1989) 278-280 (O. *Merk*).

5994 *McDonald* J.I.H., Romans 13.1-7, a test case for New Testament interpretation: NTS 35 (1989) 540-9.

5995 *Draper* J.A., 'Humble submission to Almighty God' and its biblical foundation; contextual exegesis of Romans 13:1-7: JTSAf 63 (1988) 30-38 [< NTAbs 33,182].

5996 *Merklein* Helmut, Sinn und Zweck von Röm 13,1-7; zur semanti-schen und pragmatischen Struktur eines umstrittenen Textes: → 173, FSCHNACKENBURG R., NT & Ethik 1989, 238-270.

5997 *Stein* Robert H., The argument of Romans 13:1-7: NT 31 (1989) 325-343.

5998 *Black* David A., The Pauline love command; structure, style, and ethics in Romans 13,9-21: FgNt 2,1 (1989) 3-21; español 21s.

5999 *Marcus* Joel, [Rom 14...] The circumcision and the uncircumcision in Rome: NTS 35 (1989) 67-81.

6000 *Barrett* C.K., [...Rom 14,23] The reign of evil [Asbury Ryan lecture 1988]: AsbTJ 44,2 (1989) 5-16.

6001 *Müller* Peter, Grundlinien paulinischer Theologie (Röm 15,14-33): KerDo 35 (1989) 212-234; Eng. 235.

6002 *Sotomayor* Manuel, [Rom 15,24] Leyenda y realidad en las orígenes del cristianismo hispano: Proyección 36 (1989) 179-198.

6003 *Zappella* Marco, A proposito di Febe *próstatis* (Rm 16,2): RivB 37 (1989) 167-171.

6004 *Gill* David W.J., [Rom 16,23] Erastus the aedile [on Corinth slab]: TyndB 40 (1989) 293-300; plan 301.

G5.1 **Epistulae ad Corinthios** (I vel I-II) – *textus, commentarii.*

6005 **Barbaglio** Giuseppe, 1-2 Corinzi: LoB 2.7. Brescia 1989, Queriniana. 145 p. Lit. 15.000. 88-399-1583-4. – [R]ParVi 34 (1989) 471 (F. *Mosetto*); StPatav 36 (1989) 207s (G. *Segalla*).

6006 **Bartolomé** Juan José, '¡Ay de mí si no evangelizara! (1 Cor 9,16); una lectura de la primera carta a los Corintios para apóstoles de Cristo: Espiritualidad 8, 1986 ➤ 2,4656: [R]Salesianum 51 (1989) 150s (R. *Vicent*).

6007 [E]**Fatica** Luigi, AMBROSIASTER, Commento alla Prima Lettera ai Corinzi: TPatr 78. R 1989, Città Nuova. 255 p. 88-311-3078-1.

6008 **Fee** Gordon D., The First Epistle to the Corinthians: NICNT 1987 ➤ 3,5842; 4,6010: [R]BibTB 19 (1989) 110 (C.J. *Roetzel*); BS 146 (1989) 101s (D.L. *Bock*); CriswT 3 (1988s) 209s (D.L. *Allen*: finest available); Interpretation 43 (1989) 203s (R. *Carlson*); JBL 108 (1987) 164-6 (W. *Baird*); JTS 40 (1989) 580-3 (F. *Watson*); NT 31 (1989) 185s (J.K. *Elliott*); SR 18 (1989) 366s (P. *Richardson*); WestTJ 51 (1989) 390-3 (M. *Silva*: the best in any language).

6009 **Harrisville** Roy A., I Corinthians: Augsburg Comm. 1987 ➤ 3,5843: [R]CBQ 51 (1989) 370-2 (Marie-Eloise *Rosenblatt*); CurrTM 16 (1989) 135s (E.M. *Krentz*: admirable); Interpretation 43 (1989) 92.94 (W.F. *Taylor*: the series 'has carved for itself a productive niche').

6011 **Morris** Leon, The First Epistle of Paul to the Corinthians[2] [[1]1958]: Tyndale NT comm. Leicester/GR 1985 = 1989, Inter-Varsity/Eerdmans. 244 p. 0-85111-876-3 / GR 0-8028-0064-5.

6012 **Murphy-O'Connor** Jerome, The first/second letter to the Corinthians: ➤ 384, NJBC (1989) 798-815 / 816-829.

6013 **Strobel** August, Der erste Brief an die Korinther: Z BK NT 6/1. Z 1989, Theol.-V. 284 p. [TLZ 115,30, C. *Wolff*]. 3-290-10027-8.

6014 **Talbert** Charles H., Reading Cor 1-2 1987 ➤ 3,5851; 4,6016: [R]Interpretation 43 (1989) 301-3 (C.J. *Roetzel*).

Winling Raymond, CHRYSOSTOME, homélies sur 1 Cor 1988 ➤ 5893.

G5.2 *1 & 1-2 ad Corinthios* – *themata*, **topics.**

6015 *Betz* Hans D., Korintherbriefe: ➤ 894, EvKL 2 (1989) 1448-53.

6015* *Boshoff* P.B., Die reels en tussen die reels [the lines and between the lines] van die Korintierbrieve: HervTS 45 (1989) 302-327 [< IZBG 36, p. 218].

6016 *Byars* Ronald P., Sectarian division and the wisdom of the Cross; preaching from First Corinthians: QRMin 9,4 (1989) 65-97.

6017 *Davis* James A., The interaction between individual ethical conscience and community ethical consciousness in 1 Corinthians: HorBT 10,2 (1988) 1-18 [< ZIT 89,725].

6018 *Dobbs* F. [1 Cor] The Church; the Body of Christ: Search 11,2 (Dublin 1988) 82-86 [< NTAbs 33,183].

6019 **Fitzgerald** John T., Cracks in an earthen vessel: SBL diss. 99, 1988 ➤ 4,6019: ᴿJBL 108 (1989) 745-8 (R. F. *Hock*); TLZ 114 (1989) 431s (A. *Lindemann*).

6020 *a*) *Furnish* Victor P., Theology in 1 Corinthians; initial soundings; – *b*) *Fee* Gordon D., Toward a theology of 1 Corinthians: ➤ 589, SBL Seminars 1989, 246-264 / 265-281.

6020* *Harding* Mark, Church and Gentile cults at Corinth: GraceTJ 10 (1989) 203-223.

6021 *Klauck* Hans-J., Der Gottesdienst in der Gemeinde von Korinth [< Pastoralblatt Aachen 36 (1984) 11-20]: ➤ 292, Gemeinde 1989, 46-58.

6022 *McGraw* Larry, The city of Corinth: SWJT 32,1 (1989s) 5-10.

6023 **Marshall** Peter, Enmity in Corinth ᴰ1987 ➤ 3,5860; 4,6025: ᴿEstE 64 (1989) 567-9 (A. M. *Artola*); JBL 108 (1989) 542-4 (D. B. *Martin*: excellent); TLZ 114 (1989) 117-9 (M. *Theobald*); TsTNijm 29 (1989) 67 (L. *Grollenberg*).

6024 **Mitchell** Margaret Mary, Paul and the rhetoric of reconciliation; an exegetical investigation of the language and composition of 1 Corinthians: diss. ᴰBetz H. Chicago 1989. – OIAc Ja90; RTLv 21,546.

6025 *Mitchell* Margaret M., Concerning *perì dé* in 1 Corinthians: NT 31 (1989) 229-256.

6026 *Moore* R., The letters to Corinth: Friends' Quarterly 25,3 (Ashford, Kent 1988) 125-133 [< NTAbs 33,48].

6027 **Murphy-O'Connor** Jérôme, Corinthe au temps de saint Paul [1983], ᵀ1986 ➤ 2,4663... 4,6027: ᴿLatomus 48 (1989) 931 (P. *Prigent*: was so much uncontroverted and uncomplementary documentation needed?).

6028 *Sampley* J. Paul, I and II Corinthians: ➤ 377, Books 2 (1989) 245-269.

6028* *Schenk* Wolfgang, Korintherbriefe: ➤ 911, TRE 19 (1989) 620-640 [< IZBG 36, p. 217].

6029 (de la) *Serna* Eduardo, La iniciativa divina en 1 Cor: RBíbArg 51 (1989) 39-44.

6030 *Ubieta* José Ángel, Significación neotestamentaria de la Iglesia de Corinto: ➤ 69*, ᶠGOMÀ I., RCatalT 14 (1989) 333-344 castellano; Eng. 344.

6031 **Voigt** Gottfried, Gemeinsam glauben, hoffen, lieben; Paulus an die Korinther I: Biblisch-theologische Schwerpunkte 4. Gö 1989, Vandenhoeck & R. 167 p. 3-525-61285-0.

6032 *Young* F., Mission in the Corinthian correspondence: EpworthR 16,1 (1989) 76-84 [< NTAbs 33,329].

G5.3 **1 Cor 1-7:** *sapientia crucis... abusus matrimonii.*

6032* *Gregersen* Vilhelm, [1 Cor 1,4-9] Det apostoliske ord og den apostoliske myndighed: DanTTs 52 (1989) 92-105 [< IZBG 36, p. 217].

6033 *Kovacs* Judith L., The archons, the Spirit, and the death of Christ; do we need the hypothesis of Gnostic opponents to explain 1 Cor 2.6-16?: ➤ 130, ᶠMARTYN J., 1989, 217-236.

6033* *Willis* Wendell, The 'mind of Christ' in 1 Corinthians 2,16: Biblica 70 (1989) 110-122.

6034 **Kuck** David W., Judgment and community conflict; Paul's use of apocalyptic judgment language in 1 Corinthians 3:5-4:5: diss. Yale, NHv 1989. 348 p. – 90-10665. – DissA 50 (1989s) 3626-A; RTLv 21,545.

6035 *Schwarz* Eberhard, Wo's Weisheit ist, ein Tor zu sein; zur Argumentation von 1 Kor 4-6: WDienst 20 (1989) 219-235.

6036 *Plunkett* Mark A., Eschatology at Corinth (1 Cor 4:8; 15:12-58): ProcGLM 9 (1989) 195-211.

6037 **Plank** Karl A., [1 Cor 4,9-13] Paul and the irony of affliction [ᴰ1983] 1987 ⇥ 3,5887; 4,6043: ᴿJRel 68 (1988) 352 (Margaret M. *Mitchell*).

6038 *Spencer* William D., The power in Paul's teaching (1 Cor 4:9-20): JEvTS 32 (1989) 51-62 [< ZIT 89,509].

6039 *Klein* George L., Hos 3:1-3 — background to 1 Cor 6:19b-20?: CriswT 3,2 (1989) 373-5.

6040 *a) Dautzenberg* Gerhard, *Pheúgete tēn porneían* (1 Kor 6,18); eine Fallstudie zur paulinischen Sexualethik in ihrem Verhältnis zur Sexualethik des Frühjudentums; – *b) Broer* Ingo, 'Darum: Wer da meint zu stehen, der sehe zu, dass er nicht falle'; 1 Kor 10.12f im Kontext von 1 Kor 10,1-13: ⇥ 173, ᶠSCHNACKENBURG R., NT & Ethik 1989, 271-298 / 299-325.

6041 *Ross* Susan A., 'Then honor God in your body' (1 Cor 6:20); feminist and sacramental theology on the body: Horizons 16 (1989) 7-27.

6042 *Basevi* Claudio, La santità nel matrimonio; una riflessione su 1 Cor 7: StCattMi 33 (1989) 498-504.

6043 **Wimbush** Vincent L., Paul, the worldly ascetic... 1 Cor 7, 1987 ⇥ 3,5894; 4,6049: ᴿJBL 108 (1989) 355-7 (D. R. *Cartlidge*).

6044 *Zaleski* Jan, ❷ Unauflöslichkeit nach dem 1 Kor 7,10-11: STWsz 26,1 (1988) 137-146; deutsch 146.

6045 *Payette-Bucci* D., [1 Cor 7,25-40] Voluntary childlessness: Direction 17,2 (Fresno 1988) 26-41 [< NTAbs 33,184].

6046 *Botman* H. R., *Smit* D. J., Exegesis and proclamation, 1 Corinthians 7:29-31, 'To live... as if it were not!': JTSAf 65 (Rondebosch 1988) 73-79 [< NTAbs 33,184; TContext 6/2, 19].

G5.4 *Idolothyta... Eucharistia:* 1 Cor 8-11.

6047 *Fisk* Bruce N., Eating meat offered to idols; Corinthian behavior and Pauline response in 1 Corinthians 8-10 (a response to Gordon FEE): TrinJ 10,1 (1989) 49-70.

6048 **Magee** Bruce R., A rhetorical analysis of First Corinthians 8:1-11:1 and Romans 14:1-15:13: diss. Baptist Theol. Sem., ᴰPerkins D. New Orleans 1988. 321 p. 89-11186. – DissA 50 (1989s) 710-A.

6049 *Kennedy* Charles A., 1 Corinthians 8 as a Mishnaic list: ⇥ 592, Systemic 2 (1989) 17-24.

6050 **Rainbow** Paul A., Monotheism and Christology in 1 Corinthians 8.4-6: diss. Oxford 1987. 382 p. BRD-87825. – DissA 50 (1989s) 3630-A.

6051 *Adamo* David T., The Lord's Supper in 1 Corinthians 10:14-22; 11:17-34: AfTJ 18 (1989) 36-48 [< TContext 7/1, 18].

6052 *Porter* C. L., An interpretation of Paul's Lord's Supper texts; 1 Corinthians 10:14-22 and 11:17-34: Encounter 50,1 (Indianapolis 1989) 29-45 [< NTAbs 33,184].

6053 *Sebothoma* W., Koinonia in 1 Cor. 10:16; its significance for liturgy and sacrament: QLtg 70 (Lv 1989) 243-250 [< ZIT 90,202].

6054 *Watson* Duane F., 1 Corinthians 10:23-11:1 in the light of Greco-Roman rhetoric; the role of rhetorical questions: JBL 108 (1989) 301-318.

6055 *Walker* William O.ᴶ, The vocabulary of 1 Corinthians 11:3-16; Pauline or non-Pauline?: JStNT 35 (1989) 75-88.

6056 *Ellul* Danielle, 'Sois belle et tais-toi!' Est-ce vraiment ce que Paul a dit? À propos de 1 Co 11,2-16: FoiVie 88,5 (CahBib 28, 1989) 49-58.

6057 *Fitzmyer* Joseph A., Another look at *kephalē* in 1 Corinthians 11,3: NTS 35 (1989) 503-511.

6057* **Schori** [nicht Schari wie 4,6068] Kurt, Das theologische Problem der Tradition; eine Untersuchung zum Traditionsproblem mit Hilfe linguistischer Kriterien anhand der Abendmahlsperikope 1 Kor. 11,17-34: Diss. ᴰ*Wegenast* K. Bern 1989. 404 p. – RTLv 21,567 (> Stu, Kohlhammer).

6058 *Cousin* Hugues [1 Co 11,17-21] 'A tous les saints qui sont à Corinthe': VSp 143 (1989) 39-44.

6059 *Frank* Karl S., Vom Nutzen der Häresie; 1 Kor 11,19 in der frühen patristischen Literatur: → 4,7, ꟳBäUMER R., Ecclesia 1988, I, 23-35.

6060 *Derrett* J.D.M., Intoxication, joy, and wrath; 1 Cor 11:21 and Jn 2:10: FgNt 2,1 (1989) 41-55; español 55s.

6061 *Farmer* William R., Peter and Paul, and the tradition concerning 'the Lord's Supper' in 1 Cor 11:23-26: CriswTJ 2 (1987s) 119-140.

6062 *Klauck* Hans-J., *a*) Präsenz im Herrenmahl, 1 Kor 11,23-26 im Kontext hellenistischer Religionsgeschichte [< 'Sammelband USA']; – *b*) Eucharistie und Kirchengemeinschaft bei Paulus (1 Kor 11 ...): → 292, Gemeinde 1989, 313-330 / 331-347.

6063 *Hofius* Otfried, Tò sôma tò hypèr hymôn 1 Kor 11,24: ZNW 80 (1989) 80-88.

6064 *Perrot* Charles, 'C'est pourquoi il y a parmi vous beaucoup de malades' (1 Co 11,30): SuppVSp 170 ('Religion et maladie; le Sida' 1989) 45-54.

G5.5   **1 Cor 12s... Glossolalia, charismata.**

6065 *Aizpurua* Fidel, El perfil profético de Jesús y su comunidad; contribución a la teología del profetismo en el NT: Lumen 38 (1989) 193-221.

6066 *Asi* Emmanuel, Concept, charism and practice of the prophetic: Focus 8,3 (Pakistan 1988) 155-166 [G. *Evers* (Eng.) summary in TContext 7/1, 107].

6067 *Bacq* Philippe, Le prophétisme dans l'Écriture et dans l'Église: LVitae 43 (1988) 173-183.419-429; Eng. 183.429.

6068 *Brueggemann* Walter, Prophetic ministry; a sustainable alternative community: HorBT 11,1 (1989) 1-33.

6069 ᴱ**Burgess** Stanley M., *McGee* Gary B., Dictionary of Pentecostal and Charismatic movements: Regency Reference Library. GR 1988, Zondervan. 914 p. $30. 0-310-44100-5. – ᴿAndrUnS 27 (1989) 78-80 (G.R. *Knight*); CalvaryB 5,2 (1989) 99 (C.J. *Banz*); ExpTim 101 (1989s) 221s (W.J. *Hollenweger*: fills a gap).

6070 **Carson** D.A., Showing the Spirit... 1 Cor 12-14, 1989 → 3,5921; 4,6076: ᴿBS 146 (1989) 112 (W.H. *Harris*); ÉTRel 64 (1989) 636s (E. *Cuvillier*: pastorale fondamentaliste); STEv 1,2 (1989) 212s (P. *Finch*).

6071 **Coiffet** Denis, Le renouveau charismatique est-il d'Église? P 1988, Nouv. éd. latines. 128 p. – ᴿEsprVie 99 (1989) 29-*jaune* (M. *Trémeau*).

6072 **Dayton** Donald W., Theological roots of Pentecostalism 1987 → 3,5923; 4,6077: ᴿExpTim 100 (1988s) 154 (J. *Kent*); JAAR 57 (1989) 185-7 (R.V. *Pierard*); RRel 48 (1989) 151s (J. *Gros*); TrinJ 10,1 (1989) 119-121 (D. *Smeeton*).

6073 *Ellacuría* Ignacio, Diez afirmaciones sobre 'utopía' y profetismo: SalT 77 (1989) 889-893 [851-935, Martirio en El Salvador, 16.XI.1989].

6074 *Gaede* Charles S., Glossolalia at [Los Angeles 1906] Azusa Street; a hidden presupposition?: WestTJ 51 (1989) 77-92.

6075 **Giesriegl** Richard, Die Sprengkraft des Geistes; Charismen und Apostolischer Dienst des Paulus im 1. Korintherbrief. Thaur 1989, Österr. Kulturv. 362 p. DM 42 [TR 86,251].

6076 **Grazier** Jack, The power beyond; in search of miraculous healing. NY 1989, Macmillan. xvi-302 p. $18. 0-02-545180-4 [TDig 37,159].

6077 *Grossi* Vittorino, Il profeta 'ecclesiastico' nelle antiche raccolte eresiologiche: ► 748, Sogni 1988 = AugR 29 (1989) 71-80.

6078 **Grudem** Wayne, The gift of prophecy in the NT and today [diss. 1978, D*Moule* C.] 1988 ► 4,6082 [0-89107-495-3]: RRExp 86 (1989) 623s (D. S. *Dockery*); EvQ 61 (1989) 276-9 (G. R. *Houston*).

6079 *Hellstern* Mark, The 'me gospel'; an examination of the historical roots of the prosperity emphasis within current charismatic theology: FidesH 21,3 (1989) 78 ... [< ZIT 90,46].

6080 **Hocken** Peter [cf. diss. 1986 ► 3,5930], One Lord, one Spirit, one body [charismatic movement/renewal]. Exeter 1987, Paternoster. 129 p. £4. 0-85364-436-5. – RExpTim 100 (1988s) 279 (C. S. *Rodd* in 7 lines: important).

6081 *Hollenweger* Walter J., Healing through prayer; superstition or forgotten Christian tradition?: TLond 92 (1989) 166-174.

6082 *a*) *Hübner* Hans, The Holy Spirit in Holy Scripture; – *b*) *Bobrinsky* Boris, The Holy Spirit — in the Bible and the Church; – *c*) *Rosato* Philip J., The mission of the Spirit within and beyond the Church; – *d*) *Osei-Bonsu*, The Spirit as agent of renewal; the NT testimony: EcuR 41 (1989) 324-338 / 357-362 / 388-397 / 454-460 [*al.* 339-356 / 363-387 / 398-445].

6083 *Karasszon* István, Ⓜ The Charismatics and the Bible: TSzem 32 (1989) 290-293.

6084 *Klauck* Hans-J., Die Autorität des Charismas; zehn neutestamentliche Thesen zum Thema [< E*Klinger* E. (► 4,391), Kirche der Laien 1987, 25-37]: ► 292, Gemeinde 1989, 223-231.

6085 *Kleinig* J.W., The nature and use of the charismata; some theses, questions, and a conclusion: LuthTJ 23,1 (Adelaide 1989) 32-36 [< NTAbs 33,347].

6086 *Körtner* Ulrich H.J., Der Geist der Prophetie: WDienst 20 (1989) 281-307.

6087 *a*) *Kovács* Gàbor, Ⓜ Im Heiligen Geist und in dem Feuer; die Hauptzüge der katholischen charismatischen Erneuerung; – *b*) *Horváth* Lóránt, Ⓜ Die Kirche des Geistes [... Egyházában]: TBud 22 (1988) 81-85 / 85-89.

6088 **Kydd** Ronald A.N., Charismatic gifts in the Early Church. Peabody MA 1984, Hendrickson. x-100 p. – RSecC 7 (1989) 117s (V. L. *Wimbush*).

6089 **Lederle** Henry I., Treasures old and new; interpretations of 'Spirit-baptism' [► 6234] in the charismatic renewal movement [diss. Unisa]. Peabody MA 1988, Hendrickson. xx-264 p. $15. 0-913573-75-2 [TDig 36,378].

6090 *Lohfink* Norbert, *a*) ¿Dónde están hoy los profetas? [< StiZt 206 (1988) 183-192], TE*Aleu* José: SelT 28 (1989) 305-311; – *b*) Gdzie są dziś prorocy? T*Humeński* Julian: PrzPow 815 (1989) 59-71 ► 4,6089.

6091 **McDonnell** Kilian, Open the windows; the popes and charismatic renewal. South Bend IN 1989, Greenlawn. xxvii-67 p. $6. 0-937779- 06-7 [TDig 37,177].

6092 **Malony** H. N., *Lovekin* A. A., Glossolalia 1985 ➤ 2,4720 ...4,6090: ᴿBijdragen 50 (1989) 103s (J.-J. *Suurmond*, Eng.).

6093 **Martin** Ralph P., The Spirit and the congregation ... 1 Cor 12-15: 1984 ➤ 65,5375 ... 3,5938: ᴿTLZ 114 (1989) 352-4 (E. *Reinmuth*).

6094 **Mather** Anne R., The theology of the charismatic movement in Britain from 1964 to the present day: diss. Univ. Wales, 1983. 540 p. BRDX-87928. – DissA 50 (1989s) 3629s-A.

6095 **Neitz** Mary Jo, Charisma and community; a study of religious commitment within the charismatic renewal [3-year 24-interview observation of 'Precious Blood prayer group'] 1987 ➤ 4,6093: ᴿJRelRes 31 (1989s) 217s (Nancy T. *Ammerman*).

6096 *Onunwa* U., Biblical basis for some healing methods in African traditional society: EAfJE 7,1 (1988) 56-63 [< NTAbs 33,68].

6097 **Park** Young-don Daniel, The fullness of the Holy Spirit: diss. Calvin Sem, ᴰ*Klooster* F. GR 1989. v-236 p. + bibliog. – CalvinT 24 (1989) 400s.

6098 **Ruthven** Jon M., On the cessation of the charismata; the Protestant polemic of Benjamin B. WARFIELD: diss. Marquette, ᴰ*Carey* P. Milwaukee 1989. 392 p. 90-14061. – DissA 50 (1989s) 3990s-A.

6099 ᴱ**Sandidge** Jerry L., Roman Catholic/Pentecostal dialogue (1977-82) 1987 ➤ 3,7888: ᴿEcuR 41 (1989) 638s (F. A. *Sullivan*).

6100 **Satre** Lowell J., All Christians are charismatic; sharing faith, fruit, charisms. Ph 1988, Fortress. 96 p. $6 pa. 0-8006-2023-2. – ᴿCurrTM 16 (1989) 57 (J. C. *Rochelle*).

6101 *Schwarzwäller* Klaus, Erkennen, welcher Geist uns bestimmt; auch die charismatische Bewegung gründet im Kirchentum: LuthMon 29 (1989) 79-85.

6102 **Secondin** Bruno, Segni di profezia nella Chiesa; comunità, gruppi, movimenti, 1987 ➤ 3,5953; 4,6098: ᴿGregorianum 70 (1989) 610s (*ipse*).

Sicre José Luis, *al.*, La Iglesia y los profetas 1989 ➤ 3447.

6103 ᴱ**Smedes** Lewis B., Ministry and the miraculous 1987 ➤ 4,415: ᴿAndrUnS 27 (1989) 168s (K. A. *Strand*).

6104 *Sullivan* Francis A., Charismes et renouveau charismatique [1982] ᵀ1988 ➤ 4,6099: ᴿRThom 89 (1989) 679s (H.-D. de *Spéville*); VSp 143 (1989) 499s (H. *Bourgeois*).

6105 *Sullivan* Francis A., La guarigione carismatica, ᵀ*Di Meo* Margherita: CommStrum 107 (1989) 74-80.

6106 ᴱ**Springer** Kevin, Power encounters ['with the Holy Spirit' p. xi, recounted by the experiencers] among Christians in the western world. SF 1988, Harper & R. 218 p. $11 pa. – ᴿCalvinT 24 (1989) 360-2 (R. R. *Recker*).

6107 *Szabó* Imre, ⓜ Charismatic renewal in the Hungarian Reformed Church: TSzem 31 (1988) 365-372.

6108 *Smit* Joop, De rangorde in de kerk; retorische analyse van 1 Kor. 12: TsTNijm 29 (1989) 325-342; Eng. 342s 'The hierarchy ..'

6109 *Morton* R., [1 Cor 12,31] Paul's use of the image of the 'Body of Christ' in 1 Corinthians 12: Kardia 3 (Portland OR 1988) 15-26 [< NTAbs 33,49].

6110 *Petzer* J. H., Contextual evidence in favour of *kauchēsomai* in 1 Corinthians 13.3: NTS 35 (1989) 229-253.

6111 *Grudem* Wayne A.,   Why Christians can still prophesy [... 1 Cor 13,9s; 14,3]: Christianity Today 32,13 (Carol Stream IL 1988) 29-31.34s [< NTAbs 33,66].

6112 **Gooch** Paul W. [1 Cor 13,12] Partial knowledge 1987 ➤ 3,5857: ScotJT 42 (1989) 584-6 (J. *Barclay*).

6113 *a) Bammel* C.P., [1 Kor 14,1] Die Prophetie in der patristischen Exegese zum ersten Korintherbrief; – *b) Bammel* Ernst, Prophetie und Deutung: ➤ 748, Sogni 1988 = AugR 29 (1989) 157-169 / 601-610.

6114 *Bammel* C.P., [1 Cor 14,6] ORIGEN's definitions of prophecy and gnosis: JTS 40 (1989) 489-493.

6115 *Albus* Michael, 'Ihr redet nur in den Wind' (1 Kor 14,9); Worte der Kirche — Sprache der Welt: BLtg 62 (1989) 194-201.

G5.6   **Resurrectio;** *1 Cor 15*... [➤ F5.6; H9].

6116 **De Boer** Martinus C.,   The defeat of death... 1 Cor 15; Rom 5, 1988 ➤ 4,6115:   ᴿÉTRel 64 (1989) 295s (E. *Cuvillier*).

6117 *Dumortier* Francis,   La résurrection en débat! 1 Co.15:   Masses ouvrières 424 (1989) 57-64.

6118 *Green* M., [1 Cor 15] Why the Resurrection matters: ChrTod 33,5 (1989) 28-32 [< NTAbs 33,330].

6119 ᴱ**Hoffmann** Paul,   Zur ntlichen Überlieferung von der Auferstehung Jesu: WegFor 522, 1988 ➤ 4,311:   ᴿTLZ 114 (1989) 600s (R. *Marschner*).

6120 *Kreitzer* L., [1 Cor 15; Rom 5] Adam as analogy; help or hindrance? King'sTR 11,2 (1988) 59-62 [< NTAbs 33,178].

6121 *a) Vorster* J.N.,   Resurrection faith in 1 Corinthians 15; – *b) Toit* A.B. du,   Primitive Christian belief in the resurrection of Jesus in the light of Pauline resurrection and appearance terminology: ➤ 617, Resurrection = Neotestamentica 23,2 (1989) 287-307 / 309-358.

6122 ᴱ**De Lorenzi** Lorenzo,   Résurrection du Christ et des chrétiens (1 Co 15) 1983/5 ➤ 1,466... 3,5973:   ᴿRelStT 8,1s (1988) 83s (B. F. *Meyer*).

6123 *Langkammer* Hugolinus, [1 Cor 15,3-5...] Jesus in der Sprache der neutestamentlichen Christuslieder: ➤ 68,   ꟳGNILKA J.,   Vom Urchristentum 1989, 467-486.

6124 *Voigt* Simão,   Cristo já entregou o Reino? O prefácio de Cristo Rei e a reinologia de 1 Cor 15,24:   REB 49 (1989) 640-660.

6125 *Perriman* A.C.,   Paul and the Parousia; 1 Corinthians 15.50-7 and 2 Corinthians 5:1-5:   NTS 35 (1989) 512-521.

6126 *Vicuña* M.,   1 Corintios 15:54b-57, un canto anticipado de victoria sobre la muerte — un midrash en el NT: Theologika 3,1 (Lima 1988) 2-19 [< NTAbs 33,331].

G5.9   **Secunda epistula ad Corinthios.**

6127 **Barnett** Paul,   The message of 2 Corinthians: The Bible Speaks Today. DG 1988, InterVarsity. 188 p. $10. – ᴿSWJT 32,3 (1989s) 52s (E. E. *Ellis*).

6128 *a) Borchert* Gerland L.,   Introduction to 2 Cor; – *b) Hafemann* Scott, [2 Cor 1-3] The comfort and power of the Gospel; – *c) Polhill* John B., [2 Cor 4-7] Reconciliation at Corinth; – *d) Bridges* Linda M.,   2 Cor 4:7-15; – *e) Gloer* W. Hulitt,   2 Cor 5,14-21; – *f) Talbert* Charles H. [2 Cor 8s] Money management in early Mediterranean Christianity; – *g) Garland* David E.,   Paul's apostolic authority; the power of Christ sustaining weakness (2 Cor 10-13); – h) Shoemaker H. Stephen, 2 Cor 11:1-21: RExp 86 (1989) 313-324 / 325-344 / 345-357 / 391-6 / 397-405 / 359-370 / 371-389 / 407-414.

6129 **Carrez** Maurice, La deuxième Épître de saint Paul aux Corinthiens: CommNT 8, 1986 ➤ 3,5988; 4,6124: RBenedictina 35 (1988) 229-231 (L. De Lorenzi); RHPR 69 (1989) 235s (J. C. Ingelaere); TLZ 114 (1989) 521s (C. Wolff); TR 85 (1989) 368s (A. de Oliveira).

6130 **Crafton** Jeffrey A., The agency of the apostle; a dramatic analysis of Paul's response to conflict in 2 Corinthians: diss. Northwestern, DJewett R. Evanston IL 1989. 263 p. 90-01791. – DissA 50 (1989s) 2524-A.

6131 **Danker** Frederick W., II Corinthians: Augsburg Comm. Minneapolis 1989, Augsburg. 223 p. 0-8066-8868-8. – RSWJT 32,2 (1989s) 56s (J. A. Brooks: distinctive: parallels from ancient writings).

6132 TEFatica Luigi, AMBROSIASTER, Commento alla Seconda Lettera ai Corinzi: TPatr 79. R 1989, Città Nuova. 168 p. 88-311-3079-X.

6133 **Furnish** Victor P., II Cor.: AnchorB 32A, 1984 ➤ 65,5416... 4,6125: RIrTQ 55 (1989) 78s (M. Hogan).

6134 **Georgi** Dieter, The opponents of Paul in Second Corinthians 1986 ➤ 2,4763... 4,6126: RCriswT 3 (1989) 392-4 (C. C. Newman: not frustrating, though stems from 'the likes of BULTMANN'); ScotJT 42 (1989) 426s (C. J. A. Hickling).

6135 — Welborn L. L., [2 Cor] GEORGI's Gegner; reflections on the occasion of its translation [1986; ten translators indicated]: JRel 68 (1988) 566-574.

6136 **Martin** R. P., 2 Corinthians. Word Comm. 40. Dallas 1986, Word. – RIrTQ 55 (1989) 165s (S. P. Kealy); JTS 40 (1989) 194-7 (C. J. A. Hickling); ScotJT 42 (1989) 424s (C. K. Barrett).

6137 **Pesch** R., Paulus kämpft... drei weitere Briefe [2 Kor] 1987 ➤ 3,5996; 4,6131: RJTS 40 (1989) 583s (C. J. A. Hickling); RivB 37 (1989) 114s (G. Barbaglio); Salesianum 51 (1989) 160s (J. Heriban); TLZ 114 (1989) 820 (T. Holtz); TR 85 (1989) 369s (A. de Oliveira).

6138 a) Price Craig, Critical issues in 2 Corinthians; – b) Rainey Frankie E., A pastor bares his heart; an outline of 2 Corinthians; – c) Evans James W., Interpretation of 2 Cor; – d) Young James A., Preaching values in 2 Cor; – e) Dutile Gordon, Bibliog.: SWJT 32,1 (1989s) 11-17 / 18-21 / 22-32 / 33-40 / 41-43.

6139 **Sakkos** Sergios N., ⊚ Hoi anónymoi adelphoí... On II Cor. Thessaloniki 1989. 91 p.

6140 **Young** Frances M., Ford David F., Meaning and truth in 2 Corinthians (SPCK 1987 ➤ 3,5999; 4,6133), also GR 1988, Eerdmans. 289 p. $16. 0-8028-0351-2 [TDig 37,195].

6141 Kruse Colin G., The relationship between the opposition to Paul reflected in 2 Corinthians 1-7 and 10-13: EvQ 61 (1989) 195-202.

6142 Belleville Linda L., A letter of apologetic? Self-commendation; 2 Cor 1:8-7:16; NT 31 (1989) 142-163.

6143 Jong M. de, [2 Cor 2,12-4,6], Paulus, struikelblok of toetsteen; een studie van 2 Korintiërs 2:12-4:6 als bijdrage in het gesprek met Israël [Prot. diss. Bru 1989, DNielsen J. T. – RTLv 21,544]. Kampen 1989, Mondiss. 215 p. ƒ37,50. 90-6651-104-4 [NTAbs 33,398]. – RTsTNijm 29 (1989) 409s (L. Visschers).

6144 *Colafemmina* Cesare, Il mancato incontro di Paolo con Tito a Troade (2 Cor 2,12-13) nell'esegesi patristica: ➔ 567, AnStoEseg 6 (1989) 89-98; Eng. 7.

6145 **Hafemann** Scott J., Suffering and the Spirit ... 2 Cor 2,14-3,3: WUNT 2/19, 1986 ➔ 2,4775 ... 4,6138: ᴿÉTRel 64 (1989) 637s (M. *Bouttier*); ScripTPamp 21 (1989) 946s (C. *Basevi*).

6146 *Hofius* Otfried, Gesetz und Evangelium nach 2. Korinther 3: JbBT 4 (1989) 105-149.

6147 **Conceição (da) Souza** Ivo, The New Covenant in the Second Letter to the Corinthians [3,1-4,6; 5,14-21]: diss. Pont. Univ. Gregoriana, R 1977, ᴰ*Lyonnet* S. R 1978. lxxiii-273 p.

6148 **Stockhausen** Carol K., *a)* Moses' veil and the glory of the New Covenant; the exegetical substructure of II Cor. 3,1 - 4,6 [diss. Marquette, Milwaukee 1984 ➔ 65,5424]: AnBib 116. R 1989, Pont. Ist. Biblico. ix-199 p. Lit. 40,500. 88-7653-116-5; – *b)* Early interpretation of II Corinthians 3; an exegetical perspective: ➔ 696, 10th Patristic, 19 (1989) 392-9.

6149 *Srampickal* T., The ministry of the New Covenant; an exegetical study of 2 Cor 3:6 and 7:1-18: diss. ᴰ*Lambrecht* J. Leuven 1989. 402 p. – TsTNijm 30,190; RTLv 21,547 ('and 7-18').

6150 *Jüngel* Eberhard, La colère de l'Apôtre et le Dieu incomparable; un sermon sur 2 Corinthiens 4,5-10, ᵀ*Lacoste* Jean-Yves: FoiVie 88 (1989) 13-22 [5-11; 23-31 aussi de Jüngel].

6151 *a) Bouttier* Michel, La souffrance de l'apôtre, 2 Co 4,7-18; – *b) Deutzenberg* Gerhard, 'Glaube' oder 'Hoffnung' in 2. Kor 4,13-5,10? – *c) Lambrecht* Jan, 'Reconcile yourselves ...'; a reading of 2 Cor 5,11-21; – *d) Wolff* Christian, Gedankengang und Kontextbezug in 2. Kor. 4,7-7,4; – *e) Patte* Daniel, Place et rôle de 6:11-7:4 dans 2 Cor 2:14-7:4; – *f) Legrand* Lucien, Alcuni aspetti missionari di 2 Corinti: ➔ 575, Diakonia 1987/9, 29-49 (-74, discussion) 75-9 (-104) / 161-191 (-209) / 211-220 / 221-264 (-290) / 305-325.

6152 *a) Kertelge* Karl, Jesus Christus verkündigen als den Herrn (2 Kor 4,5); – *b) Hübner* Siegfried, 'Heimgesucht über unsere Kraft' — Ernstfall im Glauben: ➔ 197, ᶠTRILLING W., Christus bezeugen 1989, 227-236 / 287-298.

6153 *Beale* G. K., The Old Testament background of reconciliation in 2 Corinthians 5-7 and its bearing on the literary problem of 2 Corinthians 5.14 - 7.1: NTS 35 (1989) 550-581.

6154 *Lambrecht* Jan, The favorable time; a study of 2 Cor 6,2a in its context: ➔ 68, ᶠGNILKA J., Vom Urchristentum 1989, 377-391.

6155 *Cranfield* C. E. B., The grace of our Lord Jesus Christ [and the need of money], 2 Cor 8,1-9: ComViat 32 (1989) 105-9.

6156 *Ginami* Corrado, Gli 'pseudo-apostoli' in 2 Cor 11,13: ➔ 597, RicStoB 1,2 (1987/9) 55-64.

6157 *Trocmé* Étienne, [2 Cor 11,32s) Le rempart de Damas; un faux pas de Paul?: RHPR 69 (1989) 475-9: his failure to say goodbye to his hosts isolated his personal disciples from the rest of the Damascus church.

6158 **Tabor** James D., [2 Cor 12,2-4] Things unutterable; Paul's ascent ... [ᴰ1981] 1986 ➔ 2,4791 ... 4,6158: ᴿAndrUnS 27 (1989) 159-162 (H. *Weiss*); JRel 68 (1988) 451-3 (A. J. *Droge*); Numen 36 (1989) 283-6 (P. *Schäfer*: ingeniös).

6159 *De Lorenzi* Lorenzo, L'ignominia di Paolo alla luce di 2 Cor 12,7b-10: ParSpV 20 (1989) 179-203.

6160 *Martin* Ralph P., The Spirit in 2 Corinthians in light of the 'fellowship of the Holy Spirit' in 2 Cor 13:14: ➤ 21, ᶠBEASLEY-MURRAY G., Eschatology 1988, 113-128.

G6.1 Ad Galatas.

6161 **Barclay** John M. G., Obeying the truth; a study of Paul's ethics in Galatians: StNW 1988 ➤ 4,6165: ᴿExpTim 100,7s 2d-top choice (1988s) 243s (C. S. *Rodd*).

6162 **Betz** H. D., Der Galaterbrief [1979] ᵀ1988 ➤ 4,6166: ᴿTLZ 114 (1989) 599s (H. *Hübner*).

6163 **Buscemi** A. M., L'uso delle preposizioni / Gal 1987 ➤ 3,6033; 4,6168: ᴿSalesianum 51 (1989) 180 (R. *Sabin*).

6164 **Cole** R. Alan, The letter of Paul to the Galatians² [¹1965]: Tyndale NT comm. Leicester/GR 1989, Inter-Varsity/Eerdmans. 240 p. 0-85111-878-X / GR 0-8028-0478-0.

6165 *Corsani* Bruno, Gli avversari di Paolo nella lettera ai Galati: ➤ 597, RicStoB 1,2 (1987/9) 97-119.

6166 *Fitzmyer* Joseph A., The letter to the Galatians: ➤ 384, NJBC (1989) 780-790.

6167 **Fung** Ronald Y., Epistle of Paul to the churches of Galatia: NICNT, 1988 ➤ 4,6173: ᴿWestTJ 51 (1989) 390-2 (M. *Silva*).

6168 **Giavini** Giovanni, Gálatas; liberdade e lei na Igreja, ᵀ*Almeida* J. M. de; Peq. Com. B. NT. São Paulo 1987, Paulinas. 130 p. 85-05-00707-0. – ᴿPerspT 20 (1988) 274s (A. *Casalegno*).

6169 *a) Gillet* Michel, Vivre sans loi?; – *b) Refoulé* François, Approches de l'Épître aux Galates; – *c) Méhat* André, 'Quand Képhas vint à Antioche...'; que s'est-il passé entre Pierre et Paul?; – *d) Vouga* François, Jean et Paul, controverse sur la liberté; – *e) Klumbies* Paul-G., La liberté de penser Dieu autrement; – *f) Secretan* Philibert, Réflexions sur la liberté; – *g) Radcliffe* Timothy, Libres en Église; – *h) Duquoc* Christian, Liberté chrétienne et institution ecclésiale: LumièreV 38/192 (1989) 5-14 / 15-28 / 29-44 / 45-64 / 65-72 / 73-84 / 85-96 / 97-108.

6170 **Hansen** G. Walter, Abraham in Galatians; epistolary and rhetorical contexts [diss. Toronto 1985, ᴰ*Longenecker* R.]: JStNT supp. 29. Sheffield 1989, Academic. 224 p. £23,50. 1-85075-171-4.

6171 *Hays* Richard B., Cristología y ética en Gálatas; la ley de Cristo [< CBQ 49 (1987) 268-290], ᵀᴱ*Forcades* Teresa: SelT 28 (1989) 125-136.

6172 **Herman** Zvonimir I., Liberi in Cristo... Gal 1986 ➤ 2,4803 ... 4,6174: ᴿEstBíb 47 (1989) 143s (J. L. *Larrabe*); JBL 108 (1989) 166-8 (G. *Smiga*: no theology, as he warned; but that does not guarantee objectivity); RechSR 77 (1989) 110s (J.-N. *Aletti*); RHPR 69 (1989) 237s (J. C. *Ingelaere*).

6173 *Hyldahl* Niels, Paulus. Galaterbrev i hans annus mirabilis: DanTTs 52 (1989) 106-109 [< ZIT 89,507].

6174 *Kertelge* Karl, Freiheitsbotschaft und Liebesgebot im Galaterbrief: ➤ 173, ᶠSCHNACKENBURG R., NT & Ethik 1989, 326-337.

6175 *Koester* C., Opportunity to do good; the letter to the Galatians; WWorld 9,2 (1989) 183-9 [< NTAbs 33,331].

6176 *Lategan* Bernard C., Levels of reader instructions in the text of Galatians [< (Journal of) Literary Studies Ox 3 (1987) 47-59]: Semeia 48 (1989) 171-184.

6177 **MacArthur** John F., Galatians: NTComm. Ch 1987, Moody. 221 p. $13. – ᴿBS 146 (1989) 470s (S. D. *Toussaint*).

6178 *Martyn* J. Louis, Galatians: ➤ 377, Books 2 (1989) 271-283.

6179 **Mussner** Franz, La lettera ai Galati: CommT [1974, ⁴1981], ᵀ*Favero* R., ᴱ*Soffritti* O., 1987 ➤ 3,6047; 4,6179: ᴿParVi 34 (1989) 474s (E. *Franco*); Salesianum 51 (1989) 159s (J. *Heriban*).

6180 **Rommel** K., Der zornige Apostel, Paulus und die Galater: Geschichten des Glaubens neu erzählt. Stu 1988, Quell. 48 p.; 4 fig. DM 4,80 pa. 3-7918-5902-X [NTAbs 33,118].

6181 ᴱ**Sheppard** Gerald T., A commentary on Galatians [1616] by William PERKINS [1558-1602]; intr. *Childs* Brevard, *al*.: Pilgrim Classic Commentaries. NY 1989, Pilgrim. lxxvii-584 + 21 p. 0-8298-0790-X; pa. -86-1.

6182 **Smiles** Vincent M., The Gospel and the Law in Galatia; Paul's response to Jewish Christian separatism and the threat of Galatian apostasy: diss. Fordham, ᴰ*Dillon* R. Bronx 1989. 361 p. 89-17242. – DissA 50 (1989s) 1342s-A; RelStR 16,189.

6183 **Smit** J., Brief aan de Galaten: Belichting. Boxtel/Lv 1989, KBS/ Vlaamse. 109 p. *f*21. 90-6173-450-9 / 90-6597-164-5. – ᴿTsTNijm 29 (1989) 410 (L. *Visschers*).

6184 *Smit* Joop, The letter of Paul to the Galatians; a deliberative speech: NTS [21 (1975) 353-379, *Betz* H.] 35 (1989) 1-26.

6185 *Suhl* A., Die Galater und der Geist — kritische Erwägungen zur Situation in Galatien: ➤ 131, ᶠMARXSEN W., Jesu Rede 1989, 267-296.

6186 *Szymanek* Edward, ⊘ Galaci (list): ➤ 891, EncKat 5 (1989) 808-10 (810, Galacja, *Langkammer* H.).

6187 *Tarazi* Paul N., The addresses and the purpose of Galatians: SVlad 33 (1989) 159-179.

6188 **Taube** Roselies, Gott und das Ich, erörtert in einer Auseinandersetzung mit LUTHERs Lehre über Glaube und Liebe in seinem Galaterkommentar (1531/35): EurHS 23/259. Fra 1986, Lang. 612 p. Fs 84. – ᴿTLZ 114 (1989) 208-210 (R. *Mau*).

6189 *Dubuis* E., Paul et la narration de soi en Galates 1 et 2: ➤ 385, Narration 1988, 163-176.

6189* *Craffert* Peter F., Paul's Damascus experience as reflected in Galatians 1; call or conversion?: Scriptura 29 (Stellenbosch 1989) 36-47 [< IZBG 36, p. 226].

6190 *Marxsen* Willi, [Gal 2,11] Sündige Tapfer; wer hat sich beim Streit in Antiochien richtig verhalten?: EvKomm 20 (1987) 81-84 [> SelT 28 (1989) 122-4, ᵀᴱ*Aleu* J.].

6191 **Bartolomé** Juan J., El evangelio y su verdad [ᴰ1985]... Gal 2,5-14, 1988 ➤ 4,6188: ᴿEstBib 47 (1989) 575s (F. *Pastor-Ramos*); LA 39 (1989) 371-3 (A. M. *Buscemi*); Salesianum 51 (1989) 415 (*ipse*).

6192 *Cameron* Peter S., An exercise in translation, Galatians 2,11-14: BTrans 40 (1989) 135-145.

6193 *May* Gerhard, [Gal 2,11-14] Der Streit zwischen Petrus und Paulus in Antiochien bei MARKION: ➤ 177, ᶠSCHWARZ R., Von Wittenberg 1989, 204-211.

6193* *Soards* Marion L., Seeking (*zēteîn*) and sinning (*hamartōlós* & *hamartía*) according to Galatians 2.17: ➤ 130, ᶠMARTYN J., 1989, 236-254.

6194 **Farahian** Edmond, Le 'je' paulinien ... Gal 2,19-21: AnGreg 253, 1988
➤ 4,6191: ᴿEsprVie 99 (1989) 251-3 (P. *Grelot*); Gregorianum 70 (1989)
401s (*ipse*); Lateranum 55 (1989) 471-3 (R. *Penna*); NRT 111 (1989) 755-7
(X. *Jacques*); RThom 89 (1989) 687 (H. *Ponsot*).

6195 *Zedda* Silverio, 'Morto alla legge mediante la legge' (Gal 2,19a); testo autobiografico sulla conversione di San Paolo?: RivB 37 (1989)
81-95.

6196 **Robertson** Glenn E., Paul and the Abrahamic tradition ... Gal 3-4;
Rom. 4: diss. SWBaptist. 266 p. 89-08436. – DissA 50 (1989s) 176-A.

6197 *Ukpong* J. S., *Asahu-Ejere*, [Gal 3-4] The letter to the Galatians and the
problem of cultural pluralism in Christianity: RAfT 12,23s (1988) 67-77
[< NTAbs 33,332].

6198 *Arroniz* José Manuel, Experiencia del espíritu y salvación (Gal 3,1-5);
ScriptV 34 (1987) 67-101.

6199 *Williams* Sam K., [Gal 3,2.5] The hearing of faith, *akoē písteōs* in
Galatians 3: NTS 35 (1989) 82-93.

6200 *Caneday* Ardel, 'Redeemed from the curse of the Law'; the use of Deut
21:22-23 in Gal 3:13: TrinJ 10 (1989) 185-209.

6201 *Schreiner* Thomas R., [Gal 3,15/5,14...] The abolition and fulfillment of
the law in Paul: JStNT 35 (1989) 47-74.

6202 *Bandstra* Andrew J., The law and angels; [Jos. F.] Antiquities 15.136
and Galatians 3:19: CalvinT 24 (1989) 223-240.

6203 *Gordon* T. David, A note on *paidagōgós* in Galatians 3.24-25: NTS 35
(1989) 150-4.

6204 **MacDonald** Dennis R., [Gal 3,26-28; 1 Cor 11,2-16] There is no male and
female; the fate of a dominical saying in Paul and Gnosticism:
HarvDissRel 20, 1987 ➤ 2,4818; 4,6199: ᴿCBQ 51 (1989) 376-8 (B.
Fiore); JBL 108 (1989) 168s (R. *Scroggs*).

6205 **Byrne** Brendan, [Gal 3,28] Paul and the Christian woman. Homebush
1988, St. Paul. xviii-109 p. $9. – ᴿAustralasCR 66 (1989) 373 (W.
Hoekstra).

6206 *Maahs* K. H., [Gal 3,28 ...] Male and female in Pauline perspective; a
study in biblical ambivalence: Dialogue and Alliance 2,3 (NY 1988)
17-34 [< NTAbs 33, 178: equality yes; but implanting of the Kingdom
had priority].

6207 *Motyer* Stephen, The relationship between Paul's Gospel of 'all one in
Christ Jesus' (Gal 3:28) and the 'Household Codes': VoxEvca 19 (1989)
33-48.

6208 *Moore-Crispin* Derek R., Galatians 4:1-9; the use and abuse of parallels:
EvQ 61 (1989) 203-223.

6209 *Thornton* T. C. G., Jewish new moons and festivals, Galatians 4:3-11
and Colossians 2:16: JTS 40 (1989) 97-100.

6210 *Pitta* Antonio, L'allegoria di Agar e Sara e la libertà dalla Legge (Gal
4,21-5,1): RivScR 3,1 (1989) 15-56.

6211 *Steinhauser* Michael G., Gal 4,25*a*; evidence of targumic tradition in
Gal 4,21-31?: Biblica 70 (1989) 234-240.

6212 *Ricart i Fàbregas* Ignasi, El 'discerniment cristià' en la carta als Galates,
estudi de Ga 6,4.5: RCatalT 13 (1988) 1-22; Eng. 22.

G6.2 Ad Ephesios.

6213 **Arnold** Clinton E., Ephesians; power and magic, the concept of power
in Ephesians in light of its historical setting: SNTS Mg 63. C 1989,

Univ. xliv-244 p. $34.50. 0-521-36236-9 [TDig 36,348]. – ᴿExpTim 100 (1988s) 472s (C. M. *Tuckett*).

6214 *Binder* Hermann, ⑩ Ephesus, das Zentrum der Mission des Paulus: Református Szemle 80 (1987) 208-221 [< TLZ 115,238].

6215 *Bruffey* L. Mark, A study of verb forms in the Book of Ephesians: CalvaryB 5,1 (1989) 86-100.

6216 **Foulkes** Francis, The letter of Paul to the Ephesians; an introduction and commentary[2] [[1]1963]: Tyndale NT Comm. 10. Leicester/GR 1989, Inter-Varsity/Eerdmans. 189 p. $8 pa. [CBQ 52,195]. 0-85111-879-8 / GR 0-8028-0312-1.

6217 *Frerichs* W. W., Reconciled in Christ; ministry in light of Ephesians: WWorld 8 (1988) 293-300 [< NTAbs 33,51].

6218 *Hendrix* Holland, On the form and ethos of Ephesians: UnSemQ 42,4 (1988) 3-16 [< ZIT 89,658].

6220 *Kobelski* Paul J., The letter to the Ephesians: ➤ 384, NJBC (1989) 883-890.

6221 **Lemmer** Hermanus R., Pneumatology and eschatology in Ephesians — the role of the eschatological Spirit in the Church: diss. Unisa, ᴰ*Roberts* J. Pretoria 1988. – DissA 50 (1989s) 2947-A.

6222 *Luz* Ulrich, Überlegungen zum Epheserbrief und seiner Paränese: ➤ 173, ᶠSCHNACKENBURG R., NT & Ethik 1989, 376-396.

6223 *Penna* Romano, La lettera agli Efesini: Scritti delle origini cristiane 10, 1988 ➤ 4,6206: ᴿAsprenas 36 (1989) 111 (C. *Marcheselli-Casale*).

6224 **Pfammatter** Josef, Epheserbrief, Kolosserbrief: NEchter 10.12, 1987 ➤ 3,6080; 4,6208: ᴿBLtg 62 (1989) 59s (T. *Söding*).

6225 *Roussel* B., L'Épître aux Éphésiens, de Laurent Valla à Sixte de Sienne; quelques aspects de l'histoire des écrits bibliques au xvie s.: ➤ 4,1253: ᴱTardieu M., Les règles d'interprétation 1982/7, 173-194: 'Le xvie s. des biblistes commence entre 1440 et 1460. Il se clot entre 1590 et 1615' [< RHE 85,217].

6226 *Saffrey* H. D., Paul à Éphèse, patrie d'Artémis: MondeB 57 (1989) 43 (58, 42-48; 59, 42-48; 60, 50-56; 61, 50-56 ... ailleurs).

6227 *Sloyan* Gerard S., Ephesians / Colossians: ➤ 377, Books 2 (1989) 285-292 / 301-310.

6228 **Stockhausen** Carol L., Letters in the Pauline tradition; Eph Col 1-2 Tim Tit: Message of Biblical Spirituality 13. Wilmington 1989, Glazier. 208 p. $13 pa. [CBQ 52,198]. 0-89453-579-X.

6229 **Stuart** R. D., Ephesians, a study manual. Phillipsburg NJ 1987, Presbyterian & R. 108 p. $5. – ᴿCriswT 3 (1989) 391s (T. D. *Lea*).

6230 **Usami** Kōshi, Somatic comprehension of unity ᴰ1983 ➤ 64,5948 ... 2,4829: ᴿTLZ 114 (1989) 732s (P. *Pokorný*).

_____

6231 *Gamber* K., [Eph 1,3-14] Älteste Eucharistiegebete 9. Die paulinischen Dankgebete im Epheser- und Kolosserbrief: HDienst 42 (Salzburg 1988) 171-6 [< NTAbs 33,333].

6232 *Grelot* Pierre, La structure d'Éphésiens 1,3-14: RB 96 (1989) 193-209; Eng. 193.

6233 **Thanner** Nathanael H., Das Mysterium der Vollendung der Gesamtschöpfung in ihrer Vereinigung in Christus (Eph. 1,9-10): Diss. Pont. Univ. S. Thomae, ᴰ*Duroux* P., 1988. R 1989. xxvi-517 p.

6234 **Eaton** Michael A., [Eph 1,13; Rom 8,16; Jn 1,33] Baptism with the Spirit; the teaching of Dr. Martin LLOYD-JONES: diss. Unisa, [D]*Lederle* H., Pretoria. Leicester 1989, Inter-Varsity. 253 p. £7. 0-86110-663-3.

6235 *Hübner* Hans, Glossen in Epheser 2: ↠ 68, [F]GNILKA J., Vom Urchristentum 1989, 392-406.

6236 *a) Radmacher* Earl D., [Eph 2] The Church; God's building; – *b) Davis* George B., Whatever happened to Church discipline?; – *c) Saucy* Robert, The locus of the Church: ↠ 44*, [F]CRISWELL W.A., CriswTJ 1 (1987) 335-344 / 345-361 / 387-399.

6237 *Schweitzer* Wolfgang, Überlegungen zum Verhältnis von Christen und Juden nach Epheser 2,11-22: WDienst 20 (1989) 237-264.

6238 *Smith* Derwood C., Cultic language in Ephesians 2,19-22, a test case: RestQ 31 (1989) 207-218 [< ZIT 90,168].

6239 *Tábet* Miguel Angel, Ef 3,4-6 e l'Epifania storica della salvezza, secondo San TOMMASO: ↠ 735, Salvezza 1988/9, 543-551.

6240 **Kobayashi** T., Ps 68 in Eph 4: diss. 1989. – CalvinT 24 (1989) 299.

6241 *a) Montagnini* Felice, Echi di parenesi cultuale in Ef 4,25-32; – *b) Conti* Valentina, Paolo ad Efeso: RivB 37 (1989) 257-281; Eng. 282 / 283-303; Eng. 303.

6242 *Wallace* Daniel B., *Orgizesthe* in Ephesians 4:26; command or condition?: CriswT 3,2 (1989) 353-372.

6243 *Engberg-Pedersen* Troels, Ephesians 5,12-13; *elénchein* and conversion in the New Testament: ZNW 80 (1989) 89-110.

6244 *Varmarasi* Jotama, [Eph 5,18] Wine or spirit? [South Pacific] Rotuman understanding of a controverted text: BTrans 40 (1989) 241-3.

6245 *Vanhoye* Albert, Il 'grande mistero'; la lettura di Ef. 5,21-33 nel nuovo documento pontificio [Mulieris dignitatem 15.VIII.1988]: ↠ 429, OssRom Quad 9 (1989) 146-153.

6246 *Wessels* François, Ephesians 5:21-33, 'Wives, be subject to your husbands; husbands, love your wives...': JTSAf 67 (1989) 67-76 [< ZIT 89,581].

6247 **Miletic** Stephen F., 'One flesh', Eph 5,22-24; 5,31, marriage and the new creation [diss. 1985]: AnBib 115, 1988 ↠ 4,6221: [R]ExpTim 100 (1988s) 32s (Margaret *Davies*); CurrTM 16 (1989) 307 (E. *Krentz*); JStNT 35 (1989) 125 (A.T. *Lincoln*, unconvinced); JTS 40 (1989) 732 (J.M.G. *Barclay*); NRT 111 (1989) 759s (X. *Jacques*); RivBib 37 (1989) 381s (R. *Penna*); SR 18 (1989) 368 (W. *Klaassen*).

G6.3   **Ad Philippenses.**

6248 *Byrne* Brendan, The letter to the Philippians: ↠ 384, NJBC (1989) 791-7.

6249 **Ernst** Josef, Le lettere ai Filippesi Flm Col Ef: NT commento, 1986 ↠ 2,4842... 4,6224: [R]Laurentianum 30 (1989) 227-9 (L. *Martignani*); ParVi 34 (1989) 399s (E. *Franco*).

6250 *Getty* Mary Ann, Philippians / Philemon: ↠ 377, Books 2 (1989) 293-9 / 325s.

6251 *Gryglewicz* Feliks, 𝕺 Filipian (list): ↠ 891, EncKat 5 (1989) 209s (221, Filippi, *Gawlikowski* M.).

6252 *a) Klein* G., Antipaulinismus in Philippi — eine Problemskizze; – *b) Ulonska* H., Gesetz und Beschneidung — Überlegungen zu einem paulinischen Ablösungskonflikt: ↠ 131, [F]MARXSEN W., Jesu Rede 1989, 267-296 / 297-313.

6253 *Loveday* Alexander,   Hellenistic   letter-forms   and   the   structure   of Philippians: ➤ 84, ᶠHILL D., JStNT 37 (1989) 87-101.

6254 **Martin** Ralph P.,   The epistle of Paul to the Philippians²ʳᵉᵛ [¹1959]; Tyndale NT Comm. 11.   Leicester/GR 1987, Inter-Varsity/Eerdmans. 187 p. $6.   0-85111-880-1 / GR 0-8028-0310-5 [NTAbs 33,259].

6255 **Masini** M.,   Filippesi-Col-Ef-Flm: LoB 2/9, 1987 ➤ 3,6102; 4,6227: ᴿRivB 37 (1989) 115s (A. *Minissale*).

6256 **Portefaix** Lilian,   Sisters rejoice... Phlp Lk: ConBibNT 20, 1988 ➤ 4,6228: ᴿÉTRel 64 (1988) 122s (E. *Cuvillier*); JTS 40 (1989) 584-6 (Judith *Lieu*); NRT 111 (1989) 757s (X. *Jacques*).

6257 *Pretorius* E.A.C.,   A key to the literature on Philippians: Neo-testamentica 23 (1989) 125-153.

6257* *Droge* A.J., [Phlp 1,22...] Did Paul commit suicide?: BR 5,6 (1989) 14-21.42.

6258 *Moreno García* Abdón,   Aproximación al sentido de Filipenses 2,1-5: EstBíb 47 (1989) 529-558; Eng. 529.

6259 *Black* David A.,   The authorship of Philippians 2:6-11; some lit-erary-critical observations: CriswTJ 2 (1987s) 269-289.

6260 *Briggs* Sheila,   Can an enslaved God liberate? Hermeneutical reflections on Philippians 2:6-11: Semeia 47 (1989) 137-153.

6261 *Gonzaga do Prado* José L.,   Filipenses 2,6-11; doutrina ou caminho?: EstudosB 22 (1989) 79-86.

6262 *Ogliari* Donato, [Flp 2,6-11] Esordio e sviluppi della 'teoria chenotica' in Gran Bretagna, Charles GORE [1889] e Hugh Ross MACKINTOSH [1912]: Asprenas 36 (1989) 331-350.

6263 *Harnisch* Wolfgang, [Phlp 2,7] Kenosis: ➤ 894, EvKL 2 (1989) 1027-30.

6264 *Giesen* Heinz,   'Furcht und Zittern' – vor Gott? Zu Philipper 2,12: TGegw 31 (1988) 86-94.

6265 *a) Dormeyer* Detlev,   The implicit and explicit readers and the genre of Philippians 3:2-4:3,8-9; – *b*) [*Combrink* H.J. Bernard] *Voelz* James W., Some things old, some things new; a response to Wolfgang SCHENK, Philipperbrief (1984): Semeia 48 (1989) 147-159 / [135-146] 161-9.

6266 *Schoenborn* Ulrich, [Flp 3,2s...] El yo y los demás en el discurso paulino: RBíbArg 51 (1989) 163-180.

6267 *Lührmann* Dieter, [Phlp 3,5s] Paul and the Pharisaic tradition: JStNT 36 (1989) 75-94.

6268 *Doignon* Jean,   Comment HILAIRE de Poitiers a-t-il lu et compris le verset de Paul Philippiens 3,21?: VigChr 43 (1989) 127-137.

G6.4 **Ad Colossenses.**

6269 **Bruce** F.F.,   The epistles to the Colossians Phlp Eph: NICNT 1984 ➤ 65,5515... 3,2123: ᴿRHPR 69 (1989) 238 (J.C. *Ingelaere*).

6270 **Clark** G.H. †1985,   Colossians; another commentary on an inex-haustible message². Jefferson MD 1989, Trinity Found. 157 p. $6 pa. 0-940931-25-7 [NTAbs 33,397].

6271 **Furter** D.,   Les épîtres de Paul aux Colossiens et à Philémon: CEB 8. Vaux/Seine 1988, Édifac. 271 p. F 107. – ᴿNRT 111 (1989) 758s (X. J-*acques*).

6271* *Hoppe* Rudolf,   Das Mysterium und die Ekklesia; Aspekte zum Mysterium-Verständnis im Kolosser- und Epheserbrief: in ᴱ**Schilson** A.,

Gottes Weisheit im Mysterium (Mainz 1989, Grünewald) 81-101 [< IZBG 36, p. 229].

6272 *Horgan* Maurya P., The letter to the Colossians: ⇥ 384, NJBC (1989) 876-882.

6272* **Hughes** R., Colossians and Philemon. Westchester IL 1989, Crossway. 185 p. $11 [TS 51,186].

6273 *Nash* Robert S., Heuristic Haustafeln; domestic codes as entrance to the social world of early Christianity; the case of Colossians: ⇥ 592; Systemic 2 (1989) 25-50.

6274 ᵀᴱ**Parker** D. C., Philip MELANCHTHON, Paul's Letter to the Colossians: HistTInt. Sheffield 1989, Almond. 126 p. $21.50 [CBQ 52,383].

6275 *Pongutá H.* Silvestre, Autenticidad de la Carta a los Colosenses; un examen: TXav 39 (1989) 433-441.

6276 **Schweizer** Eduard, La carta a los Colosenses: BiblEstB 58, 1987 ⇥ 4,6247: ᴿEstE 64 (1989) 563s (A. M. *Artola*).

6277 **Wright** N. T., The epistles of Paul to the Colossians and Philemon: Tyndale NT comm., 1986 ⇥ 3,6135; 4,6249: ᴿSTEv NS 1 (Padova 1989) 88s (M. *Clemente*).

_____

6278 *Marcheselli Casale* Cesare, Der christologische Hymnus Kol 1,15-20 im Dienste der Versöhnung und des Friedens [Vortrag Bonn 1985]: Teresianum 40 (1989) 3-21.

6279 *Zabala* Artemio M., Advent reflections on Colossians 1:15-20 in the Philippine setting: AsiaJT 3 (Singapore 1989) 315-329.

6280 *Fossum* Jarl, Colossians 1.15-18a in the light of Jewish mysticism and gnosticism: NTS 35 (1989) 193-201.

6281 *Obijole* Bayo, [Col 1,16...] St. Paul's concept of principalities and powers: *a)* BibleBh 15 (1989) 25-39; – *b)* ... in African context: AfJT 17,2 (1988) 118-129 [< NTAbs 33,325].

6282 **Eller** Vernard [Col 1,16] Christian anarchy; Jesus' primacy over the powers 1987 ⇥ 3,6126: ᴿJRel 69 (1989) 270 (D. K. *Friesen*).

6283 *Brungs* Robert A., [Col 1,19; Christogenesis, TEILHARD...] Biology and the future; a doctrinal agenda: TS 50 (1989) 698-717.

6284 *a)* **Schweizer** Eduard, Askese nach Kol 1,24 oder 2,20f?; – *b)* Strecker Georg, Die neutestamentlichen Haustafeln (Kol 3,18-4,1 und Eph 5,22-6,9): ⇥ 173, ᶠSCHNACKENBURG R., NT & Ethik 1989, 340-8 / 349-375.

6285 **Merk** Otto, Erwägungen zu Kol 2,6f: ⇥ 68, ᶠGNILKA J., Vom Urchristentum 1989, 407-416.

6286 **Yates** Roy, Christ triumphant; a study of Colossians 2:13-15: diss. ᴰ*Lindars* B. Manchester 1989. – RTLv 21,547.

6287 *Schweizer* Eduard, Altes und Neues zu den 'Elementen der Welt' in Kol 2,20; Gal 4,3.9: ⇥ 120, ᶠLOHSE E., Wissenschaft 1989, 111-8.

6288 *Levison* John R., 2 Apoc. Bar. 48:42-52:7 and the apocalyptic dimension of Colossians 3:1-6: JBL 108 (1989) 93-108.

6289 *Delebecque* Édouard, Sur un problème de temps, chez Saint Paul (Col 3,1-4): Biblica 70 (1989) 389-395.

6290 Une lecture féministe des 'codes domestiques' [Col 3,18s; Eph 5,21-33; 1 Pt 3,1-7; Tit 2,3-5; 1 Tim 2,9-15; 5,9-15] par un groupe [Orsay, de féministes protestantes]: FoiVie 88,5 (CahBib 28, 1989) 59-69.

6291 **Saxer** Victor, Domus ecclesiae, *oîkos tês ekklēsías* in den frühchristlichen literarischen Texten [Col 4,15; Phlm 2; 1 Tim 4,19; Phlp 4,22:

nicht Kulthäuser wie Apg 2,46; 12,12; 20,7-12]: ➤ 732, RömQ 83 (1988) 167-179.

G6.5   *Ad Philemonem*   –   **Slavery in NT background.**

6292 *Bielman* Anne,   *Lytra*, prisonniers et affranchis: MusHelv 46 (1989) 25-41.

6293 **Bradley** Keith R.,   Slavery and rebellion in the Roman world, 140 B.C.-70 B.C.   Bloomington/L 1989, Indiana Univ./Batsford.   xiii-186 p. 0-253-35259 / L 0-7134-6561-X.

6294 **Collange** Jean-François,   L'Épître de S. Paul à Philémon 1987 ➤ 3,6147; 4,6261:   ᴿRHPR 69 (1989) 81 (*ipse*).

6295 **Corcoran** Gervase,   St. AUGUSTINE on slavery [< diss. 1978; earlier parts (NT) in MilltSt 1980/4] 1985 ➤ 1,6044... 3,6148:   ᴿHeythJ 30 (1989) 197s (J. F. *Maxwell*: too little on OT and Roman penal law).

6296 **Dumont** Jean C.,   Servus; Rome et l'esclavage sous la République: Coll.Éc.Fr. 103.   R 1987, École française.   834 p.   2-7283-0155-7 [AntClas 59,512, J.A. *Straus*].   – ᴿAthenaeum 67 (1989) 638s (A. *Marcone*).

6297 *Fitzmyer* Joseph A.,   The letter to Philemon: ➤ 384, NJBC (1989) 869s.

6298 *Gardner* Jane F.,   The adoption of Roman freedmen: Phoenix 43 (Toronto 1989) 236-257.

6299 *Garlan* Yvon,   Slavery in ancient Greece 1988 ➤ 4,6266; ᵀ*Lloyd* Janet: ᴿRelStR 15 (1989) 259 (Marleen B. *Flory*).

6300 *Gryglewicz* Feliks, ❷ Filemon (list): ➤ 891, EncKat 5 (1989) 194.

6301 *Kim Hee-Zung*, ❸ The fundamental ideas of the early Church about reformation of society from the point of view of the teaching of John CHRYSOSTOM regarding the problem of slavery: Sinhak Jonmang 85 (1989) 36-54 [< TContext 7/1, 60].

6302 **Klein** Richard,   Die Sklaverei in der Sicht der Bischöfe AMBROSIUS und AUGUSTINUS 1988 ➤ 4,6269:   ᴿDLZ 110 (1989) 713-7 (Liselot *Huchthausen*); JbAC 32 (1989) 191-4 (E. *Dassmann*); MusHelv 46 (1989) 267 (J.-P. *Borle*); TR 85 (1989) 376-9 (C. *Jacob*).

6303 *Klein* Richard,   Zum Verhältnis von Herren und Sklaven in der Spätantike: ➤ 209, ᶠWERNER R., Xenia 22 (1989) 229-258.

6304 *Manning* C.E.,   Stoicism and slavery in the Roman Empire: ➤ 878, ANRW 2/26/3 (1989) 1518-1543.

6305 *Martini* Remo,   'Servus perpetuus mercennarius est':   Labeo 35 (1989) 189-194.

6306 *Migliazza* B.L.,   Text analysis observations from Philemon using FLEMING's stratificational model: NotesTr 2,4 (Dallas 1988) 36-48 [< NTAbs 33,335].

6307 **Mora Paz** César A.,   Dimensión socio-religiosa de la carta a Filemon; su función comunicativa y su contenido [diss. Pont. Ist. Biblico 1987s ➤ 3,6157]. R 1988 (extractum). – Biblica 70 (1989) 146.

6308 **Petersen** Norman R.,   Rediscovering Paul; Philemon and the sociology of Paul's narrative world 1985 ➤ 1,6057... 4,6274:   ᴿSvTKv 65 (1989) 77-79 (B. *Holmberg*).

6309 *Prachner* Gottfried,   Bemerkungen zu den ältesten römischen Sklaveninschriften: ➤ 150, ᶠPEKÁRY T., Migratio 1989, 201-217.

6310 *Samson* Ross,   Rural slavery, inscriptions, archaeology and MARX; a response to Ramsay MACMULLEN's 'Late Roman Slavery': Historia 38 (1989) 99-110.

6311 **Štaerman** E. M., Die Sklaverei in den westlichen Provinzen des römischen Reiches im 1.-3. Jahrhundert, ᵀ*Kriz* J., *al.* [fourth of five translations from the Russian on ancient slavery]. Stu 1987, Steiner. x-269 p. DM 64. – ᴿClasR 39 (1989) 315-7 (Barbara M. *Levick*).

G6.6 Ad Thessalonicenses.

6312 **Ahn Yong-Sk** Joseph, The Parousia in Paul's letters to the Thessalonians, the Corinthians, and the Romans, in relation to its Old Testament-Judaic background: diss. Fuller, ᴰ*Martin* R. Pasadena 1989. 376 p. 89-19388. – DissA 50 (1989s) 1336-A.

6313 *Bassler* Jouette M., I and II Thessalonians: → 377, Books 2 (1989) 311-8.

6314 *Bohlen* Reinhold, The unity of 1 Thessalonians [< TrierTZ 96 (1987) 313-7], ᵀᴱ*Asen* B. A.: TDig 36 (1989) 132-4.

6315 *Bonsack* Bernhard, Literarkritische Kaprizen zu den Thessalonicherbriefen: → 65*, ᶠGEISSER H. 1988, 180-190.

6316 *Collins* Raymond F., [*Giblin* Charles H.], The first [second] letter to the Thessalonians: → 384, NJBC (1989) 772-9 [871-5].

6317 **Jewett** Robert, The Thessalonian correspondence 1986 → 2,4895...4, 6288: ᴿTLZ 114 (1989) 888-890 (T. *Holtz*: anregend, kaum überzeugend).

6318 **Johanson** Bruce C., To all the brethren... 1 Thess: ConBib NT 16, 1987 → 3,6174; 4,6289: ᴿEstBib 47 (1989) 425s (F. *Pastor-Ramos*); TLZ 114 (1989) 192s (G. *Haufe*).

6319 **Malherbe** Abraham, Paul and the Thessalonians; the philosophic tradition of pastoral care 1987 → 3,6178; 4,6292: ᴿAndrUnS 26 (1988) 302-4 (J. *Paulien*); JBL 108 (1989) 359-9 (C. J. *Roetzel*); TR 85 (1989) 12s (T. *Söding*).

6320 **Marxsen** Willi, La prima lettera ai Tessalonicesi: Parole per l'uomo di oggi, 1988 → 4,6293: ᴿParVi 34 (1989) 470s (A. *Barbieri*: 'Marxen').

6321 *Míguez Néstor* O., La composición social de la Iglesia en Tesalonica: RBibArg 51 (1989) 65-89.

6322 **Morris** Leon, [comm. 1956 ²1984 → 4,6294] 1, 2 Thessalonians: Word Biblical *Themes*. Dallas 1989, Word. x-105 p. 0-8499-0797-7 [NTAbs 33,401].

6323 *Perkins* Pheme, 1 Thessalonians and Hellenistic religious practices: → 60, ᶠFITZMYER J., Touch 1989, 325-334.

6324 **Pesch** R., La scoperta della più antica lettera di Paolo: StBPaid 80, 1987 → 4,6295: ᴿRivB 37 (1989) 225-7 (A. *Bonora*).

6325 *Gilliard* Frank D., The problem of the antisemitic comma between 1 Thessalonians 2.14 and 15: NTS 35 (1989) 481-502.

6326 *McGehee* Michael, A rejoinder to two recent studies dealing with 1 Thess 4:4 [YARBROUGH O. 1985; COLLINS R. 1983]: CBQ 51 (1989) 82-89.

6327 **Yarbrough** O. Larry, [1 Thes 4,5...] Not like the Gentiles... marriage in... Paul ᴰ1985 → 3,6191; 4,6299*: ᴿRechSR 77 (1989) 124-6 (J.-N. *Aletti*); TLZ 114 (1989) 676s (E. *Reinmuth*).

6328 **Mason** John P., Paul's understanding of resurrection in 1 Thess 4:13-18: diss. Southern Baptist Theol. Sem. 1989, ᴰ*Borchert* G. 208 p. 90-04716. – DissA 50 (1989s) 2540-A.

6329 *Langevin* Paul-Émile, L'intervention de Dieu, selon 1 Thes 5,23-24; déjà le salut par grâce: ScEspr 41 (1989) 71-92.

6330 **Holland** Glenn S., The tradition that you received from us; 2 Thessalonians in the Pauline tradition [diss. Chicago, ᴰ*Betz* H.-D.]: Herm-UntT 24, 1988 ➤ 4,6302: ᴿExpTim 100 (1988s) 110 (M. *Goulder*: few conclusions convincing); JBL 108 (1989) 748 (D. F. *Watson*).

6331 **Hughes** Frank W., Early Christian rhetoric and 2 Thessalonians: JStNT Sup 30. Sheffield 1989, Academic. 156 p. £22.50. 1-85075-137-4 [NTAbs 33,400]. – ᴿÉTRel 64 (1989) 639 (E. *Cuvillier*: 'particulièrement stimulant'; ISBN faux); ExpTim 100 (1988s) 473 (J. *Proctor*).

6332 **Müller** Peter, Anfänge der Paulusschule, dargestellt am zweiter Thessalonicherbrief und am Kolosserbrief: ATANT 24. Z 1987, Theol.-V. 346 p. Fs 53. 3-290-10033-2. – ᴿTLZ 114 (1989) 354-7 (A. *Lindemann*).

6333 *Winter* Bruce W., 'If a man does not wish to work...'; a cultural and historical setting for 2 Thessalonians 3:6-16: TyndB 40 (1989) 303-315.

G7 **Epistulae pastorales.**

6334 **Brox** Norbert, Die Pastoralbriefe⁵ʳᵉᵛ [¹1950, *Freundorfer* J., ⁴1969 Brox]. Rg 1989, Pustet. 356 p. 3-7917-0140-1.

6335 **Donelson** Lewis R., Pseudepigraphy and ethical argument in the Pastoral Epistles 1986 ➤ 2,4909 ... 4,6307: ᴿHeythJ 30 (1989) 190s (F. F. *Bruce*); JRel 69 (1989) 235-7 (D. L. *Balch*).

6336 **Houlden** J. L., The Pastoral Epistles; I and II Timothy, Titus: TPI NT commentaries. L 1989, SCM. 168 p. $15 pa. 0-334-01327-5.

6337 **Johnson** Luke T., 1-2 Timothy, Titus: Preaching Guides 1987 ➤ 3,6206: ᴿCriswT 3 (1989) 389s (A. Boyd *Luter*).

6338 **Kidd** Reggie M., Wealth and beneficence in the Pastoral Epistles; an inquiry into a 'bourgeois' form of early Christianity: diss. Duke, ᴰ*Young* F. Durham ɴᴄ 1989. 327 p. 90-06737. – DissA 50 (1989s) 3262s-A.

6339 **Knoch** Otto, 1. und 2. Timotheusbrief; Titusbrief: NEchter, 1988 ➤ 4,6311: ᴿÉTRel 64 (1989) 297 (E. *Cuvillier*).

6340 **Lenkey** Mrs. Klara Semsey, Ⓜ *A Timóteushoz* ... Explanation of 1 Tim: ᴿTSzem 32 (1989) 125s (J. *Pásztor*).

6341 *Lohfink* Gerhard, Paulinische Theologie in der Rezeption der Pastoralbriefe [< ᴱ*Kertelge* K., Paulus...-rezeption: QDisp 89 (1981) 70-121]: ➤ 300, Studien zum NT 1989, 291-343.

6342 **Miller** James D., The pastoral letters as composite documents: diss. Edinburgh 1988, 241 p. BRD-87601. – DissA 50 (1989s) 3266-A.

6343 **Oden** Thomas C., First and Second Timothy and Titus. Louisville 1989, Westminster/Knox. 192 p. $17 [TS 51,381].

6344 *Sánchez Bosch* Jordi, Jesucrist, el Senyor, en les cartes pastorals: ➤ 69*, ᶠGOMÀ I., RCatalT 14 (1989) 345-359; Eng. 360.

6345 **Schlarb** Egbert, Die gesunde Häresie und Wahrheit im Spiegel der Pastoralbriefe: Diss. ᴰ*Lührmann* D. Marburg 1989. – RTLv 21, 546.

6346 **Towner** Philip H., The goal of our instruction; the structure of theology and ethics in the Pastoral Epistles: JStNT Supp 34. Sheffield 1989, Academic. 321 p. £26.50. 1-85075-216-8. – ᴿExpTim 101 (1989s) 312 (L. *Houlden*).

6347 *Wild* Robert A., The pastoral letters: ➤ 384, NJBC (1989) 891-902.

6348 *Wimbush* Vincent L., I and II Timothy, Titus: ➤ 377, Books 2 (1989) 319-326.
6349 *Wolfe* B. Paul, Scripture in the Pastoral Epistles; pre-Marcion Marcionism?: PerspRelSt 16,1 (1989) 5-16 [< ZIT 89,445].
6350 **Wolter** Michael, Die Pastoralbriefe als Paulustradition: FRL 146, ᴰ1988 ➤ 4,6316: ᴿNRT 111 (1989) 760s (X. *Jacques*); Salmanticensis 36 (1989) 386-8 (R. *Trevijano*); SWJT 32,1 (1989s) 54s (E. E. *Ellis*); TLZ 114 (1989) 45s (P. *Trummer*); TsTNijm 29 (1989) 67 (L. *Visschers*).

G7.2 **1-2 ad Timotheum.**

6351 *Wolter* Michael, Paulus, der bekehrte Gottesfeind; zum Verständnis von 1. Tim. 1:13: NT 31 (1989) 48-66.
6352 **Küchler** Max, [1 Tim 2,8-15] Schweigen, Schmuck und Schleier 1986 ➤ 2,4924; 4,6320: ᴿBZ 33 (1989) 302-7 (J. *Maier*); Henoch 11 (1989) 119-122 (R. *Penna*); RHR 206 (1989) 298-300 (M. *Carrez*); TLZ 114 (1989) 735-7 (C. *Wolff*).
6353 *Barnett* Paul W., Wives and women's ministry (1 Timothy 2:11-15): EvQ 61 (1989) 225-238.
6354 *Schöllgen* Georg, Die *diplê timē* von 1 Tim 5,17: ZNW 80 (1989) 232-9.
6355 *Quinn* Jerome D., †, TERTULLIAN and 1 Timothy 5:22 on imposing hands; Paul GALTIER revisited: ➤ 696, 10th Patristic, 21 (1989) 268-270.
6356 **Prior** M., Paul the letter-writer and the second letter to Timothy. Sheffield 1989, Academic. 303 p. £25. 1-85075-147-1 [ÉTRel 64,674]. – ᴿScriptB 20 (1989s) 23s (R. *Morgan*).
6357 *Trummer* Peter, 'Treue Menschen' (2 Tim 2,2); Amtskriterien damals und heute: ➤ 367, Aufsätze 1987, 95-135.
6358 *McCoy* B., Secure yet scrutinized; 2 Timothy 2:11-13: Journal of the Grace Evangelical Society 1,1 (San Antonio 1988) 21-33 [< NTAbs 33,192].
6359 *Donfried* Karl P., [2 Tim 4,13] Paul as Skenopoios and the use of the codex in early Christianity: ➤ 197, ᶠTRILLING W., Christus bezeugen 1989, 249-256.

6360 *Weiser* Alfons, Titus 2 als Gemeindeparänese: ➤ 173, ᶠSCHNACKEN-BURG R., NT & Ethik 1989, 397-414.
6361 *Santos Otero* Aurelio de, Der Pseudo-Titus-Brief: ➤ 417, ᴱ*Schnee-melcher* W., Neutestamentliche Apocryphen II. Tü 1989, 50-70.

G8 **Epistula ad Hebraeos.**

6361* *Anderson* Charles P., Who are the heirs of the new age in the epistle to the Hebrews?: ➤ 130, ᶠMARTYN J., 1989, 255-277.
6362 **Attridge** Harold W., The epistle to the Hebrews: Hermeneia commentary, ᴱ*Koester* Helmut. Minneapolis 1989, Fortress. xxviii-437 p. $40. 0-8006-6021-8 [NTAbs 33,396].
6363 *Attridge* Harold W., New Covenant Christology in Hebrews: QRMin 8,3 (1988) 89-108.
6364 *Bourke* Myles M., The epistle to the Hebrews: ➤ 384, NJBC (1989) 920-941.
6365 **Bruce** F. F., La epístola a los Hebreos [1964], ᵀ*Márquez de Campanelli* Maria, *Feser de Padilla* Catharine [texto Reina-Valera 1960]: GR/Buenos

Aires 1987, Eerdmans/Nueva Creación. 428 p. 0-8028-0900-6. – ᴿActu-Bbg 26 (1989) 191 (X. *Alegre* S.).

6366 *Caballera Cuesta* José M., Para mejor comprender la 'Carta a los Hebreos': Burgense 29 (1989) 367-415.

6367 *Collins* R.F., Letters that Paul did not write; Heb... 1988 ⇒ 4,6331: ᴿBogSmot 59 (1989) 485-8 (M. *Zovkić*); LvSt 14 (1989) 62s (J. *Lambrecht*).

6368 **Evans** C.F., The theology of rhetoric; the epistle to the Hebrews: Williams Lecture 42. L 1988, Dr. Williams Trust. 20 p. 0305-3962 [NTAbs 33,399].

6369 ᴱ**Feld** Helmut, Wendelini STEINBACH Comm. in Epistolam ad Hebraeos II: Opera 3, 1987 ⇒ 4,6335: ᴿGregorianum 70 (1989) 153-5 (J. *Wicks*); RTPhil 121 (1989) 116-8 (M. *Engammare*); TR 85 (1989) 31s (Irena *Backus*: Bd. 4, Register, erwartet).

6370 *Fischer* J., Covenant, fulfilment and Judaism in Hebrews: EvRT 13,2 (Exeter 1989) 175-187 [< NTAbs 33,336].

6371 ᴱ**Frede** Hermann J., Vetus Latina 25/2, Epistulae ad Thessalonicenses... Hebraeos [Lfg. 5, 1988 ⇒ 4,6337] Lfg. 6, Hbr 5,8-7,10. FrB 1989, Herder. p. 1237-1316. – ᴿNRT 111 (1989) 755 (X. *Jacques*, 5); RHE 84 (1989) 505 (P.-M. *Bogaert*, 3-5).

6372 *Freyne* Seán, Reading Hebrews and Revelation intertextually: ⇒ 95, ᶠIERSEL B. Van, 1989, 83-93.

6373 **Gooding** David, An unshakeable kingdom; the letter to the Hebrews for today. GR 1989, Eerdmans. 255 p. 0-8028-0471-3.

6374 *Horak* Tomasz, ❷ Les titres donnés à Jésus dans la Lettre aux Hébreux et leur signification christologique: AtKap 112 (1989) 54-65.

6375 *Hughes* Philip E., The epistle to the Hebrews: ⇒ 394, NT/Interpreters 1989, 351-370.

6376 *Jelonek* Tomasz, Regulae revelationis biblicae; continuitas et transpositio in epistola ad Hebraeos: AnCracov 20 (1988) 165-171 [< ZIT 89,431].

6377 *Johnson* Ricky L., Heavenly strength for an earthly journey; the system of Hebrews: ⇒ 592, Systemic 2 (1989) 75-87.

6378 *Lane* William L., Call to commitment; responding to the message of Hebrews 1985 ⇒ 1,6138... 3,6234: ᴿCriswT 2 (1988) 434-6 (C. L. *Blomberg*).

6379 *Laws* Sophie, Hebrews: ⇒ 377, Books 2 (1989) 327-338.

6380 **Lehne** Susanne, The concept of the New Covenant in the Epistle to the Hebrews: diss. Columbia, ᴰ*Somerville* R. NY 1989. 314 p. 90-05903. – DissA 50 (1989s) 3268-A; RelStR 16,190.

6381 *Lindars* Barnabas, The rhetorical structure of Hebrews: NTS 35 (1989) 382-406.

6382 *MacLeod* David J., *a*) The literary structure of the Book of Hebrews; – *b*) The doctrinal center of the Book of Hebrews: BS 146 (1989) 185-197 / 291-300.

6383 **März** Claus-Peter, Hebräerbrief: NEchter 16. Wü 1989, Echter. 88 p. 3-429-01213-9.

6384 **Malone** Fred A., A critical evaluation of the use of Jeremiah 31:31-34 in the letter to the Hebrews: diss. SW Baptist Theol. Sem. 1989. 326 p. 90-04364. – DissA 50 (1989s) 2947s-A.

6385 *Melbourne* Bertram L., An examination of the historical-Jesus motif in the Epistle to the Hebrews: AndrUnS 26 (1988) 281-297.

6386 **Rathel** Mark A., An examination of the soteriological terminology in the Epistle to the Hebrews: diss. Baptist Theol. Sem., ᴰ*Simmons* B. New Orleans 1988. 228 p. 89-11188. – DissA 50 (1989s) 707-A.

6387 **Rissi** Mathias. Die Theologie des Hebräerbriefs: WUNT 41, 1987 ➤ 3,6242; 4,6347: ᴿBiblica 70 (1989) 564-6 (A. *Vanhoye*: le lecteur restera sur sa faim); CBQ 51 (1989) 380s (R. D. *Witherup*); Gregorianum 70 (1989) 565 (R. *Penna*).

6388 *Rose* Christian, Verheissung und Erfüllung; zum Verständnis von *epangelia* im Hebräerbrief: BZ 33 (1989) 60-80.178-191.

6389 *Schick* Edwin A., Priestly pilgrims; mission outside the camp in Hebrews: CurrTM 16 (1989) 372-6.

6390 *Standaert* Benoit, Het verbond in het Nieuwe Testament: ➤ 412, Sleutelen 1989, 75-96.

6391 **Swetnam** James, Jesus and Isaac... Heb in the light of the Aqedah: AnBib 94, 1981 ➤ 63,6789... 1,6145: ᴿRThom 89 (1989) 486-8 (L. *Devillers*: prudent).

6392 *Swetnam* James, Christology and the Eucharist in the Epistle to the Hebrews: Biblica 70 (1989) 74-94; franç. 95.

6393 *Tetley* Joy, [cf. diss. 1987 ➤ 4,6352] The priesthood of Christ in Hebrews: Anvil 5,3 (Nottingham 1988) 195-206 [< NTAbs 33,192].

6394 *Thompson* J., The beginnings of Christian philosophy... Heb: CBQ Mg 13, 1982 ➤ 63,6163... 1,6146: ᴿTLZ 114 (1989) 357s (H.-F. *Weiss*).

6395 **Vanhoye** Albert, Structure and message of the Epistle to the Hebrews² [= Traduction structurée 1963 + Le Message 1971], ᵀ*Swetnam* James: SubsBPont 12. R 1989, Pont. Ist. Biblico. ix-120 p. Lit. 16.000. 88-7653-571-3 [BL 90, 143, D. G. *Deboys*: refreshingly bereft of footnotes or bibliography].

6396 *Vanhoye* Albert, Il superamento della vergogna nella Lettera agli Ebrei: ParSpV 20 (1989) 205-218.

6397 **Übelacker** Walter G., Der Hebräerbrief als Appell, I. Untersuchungen zu 'exordium', 'narratio' und 'postscriptum ' (Hebr 1-2 und 13,22-15) [Diss. ᴰ*Gerhardsson* B. Lund 1989. – RTLv 21,547 ('NTAbs 34,1-4'); SvTKv 65,140]: ConBib NT 21. Sto 1989, Almqvist & W. 256 p. 91-22-01251-1.

6398 *Garuti* Pablo, Il prologo della Lettera agli Ebrei (Eb 1,1-4): SacDoc 34 (1989) 533-556.

6399 *Łach* Jan, ❷ Jesus Christus als Mittler des Neuen Bundes (Hebr. 1,1-4): STWsz 26,1 (1988) 205-219; deutsch 219s.

6400 *Dormandy* Richard, Hebrews 1:1-2 and the parable of the wicked husbandmen: ExpTim 100 (1988s) 371-5.

6401 *Laub* Franz, 'Schaut auf Jesus' (Hebr 3,1); die Bedeutung des irdischen Jesus für den Glauben nach dem Hebräerbrief: ➤ 68, ᶠGNILKA J., Vom Urchristentum 1989, 417-432.

6402 *Peter* Navamani E., Bible study, practical exhortation: Hebrews 3;7-15: AsiaJT 3 (1989) 576-581.

6403 *Grässer* E., Hebräer 4,12-13 — Etüde für einen Kommentar: ➤ 131, ᶠMARXSEN W., Jesu Rede 1989, 332-343.

6404 **Casalini** Nello, Dal simbolo alla realtà; l'espiazione dall'Antica alla Nuova Alleanza secondo Ebr 9,1-14; una proposta esegetica [diss. ᴰ*Grelot* P., Inst. Cath., Paris 1986 ➤ 2,4962]: SBF Anal. 26. J 1989,

Franciscan. 276 p. [NTAbs 33,256]. – RScEspr 41 (1989) 381s (L. *Sabourin*: lucide, convaincant).

6405 *Vanhoye* Albert, [Eb 10,19] Sangue di Cristo e sacerdozio dei fedeli nel Nuovo Testamento: ↠ 759, Sangue VI, 1987/9, 771-785.

6406 **Colton** C. E., [Heb 11] The faithfulness of faith. Nv 1985, Broadman. 124 p. $6 pa. – RCriswT 1 (1987) 403 (T. D. *Lea*).

6407 *Cosby* Michael R., The rhetorical composition and function of Hebrews 11 in light of example-lists in antiquity 1988 ↠ 4,6363: RCurrTM 16 (1989) 472 (E. *Krentz*).

6408 *Oberholtzer* Thomas K., The failure to heed his speaking in Hebrews 12:25-29 [last of 5-part series]: BS 146 (1989) 67-75.

6409 *Klauck* Hans-J., *Thysiastērion* in Hebr 13,10 und bei IGNATIUS von Antiochien [< SBF Studia Hieros. 3 (1987) 147-158]: ↠ 292, Gemeinde 1989, 359-372.

G9.1   1-2 Petri.

6410 *Achtermeier* Paul J., Newborn babes and living stones; literal and figurative in 1 Peter: ↠ 60, FFITZMYER J., Touch 1989, 207-236.

6411 a) *Achtermeier* Paul J., 1 Peter; – b) *Matera* Frank J., II Peter, Jude: 377, Books 2 (1989) 345-351 / 353-7.

6412 **Adinolfi** Marco, La Prima Lettera di Pietro nel mondo greco-romano 1987 ↠ 4,6365: RAngelicum 66 (1989) 329s (M. *Làconi*); ArTGran 52 (1989) 242 (A. *Segovia*); CC 140 (1989,2) 205s (K. *Stock*); NRT 111 (1989) 763s (X. *Jacques*).

6413 EAland Kurt, *al.*, Text und Textwert der griechischen Handschriften des NTs, I. Die katholischen Briefe 1-3: ArbNTTextf 9-11, 1987 ↠ 3,6264; 4,6366: RBASP 25 (1988) 179s (T. H. *Tobin*); RB 96 (1989) 455s (M.-É. *Boismard*).

6414 EAland Barbara, [*Juckel* A.], Das NT in syrischer Überlieferung, 1. Die grossen Katholischen Briefe: ArbNTTextf 7, 1986 ↠ 2,1246... 4,6396: RRB 96 (1989) 457s (M.-É. *Boismard*).

6415 *Aranda Pérez* Gonzalo, El apóstol Pedro en la literatura gnóstica: EstBíb 47 (1989) 65-92; Eng. 65.

6416 *Dalton* William J., The first epistle of Peter: ↠ 384, NJBC (1989) 903-8.

6417 **Dixon** Michael C., Discipleship in 1 Peter as a model for contextual mission: diss. Southern Baptist Theol Sem. 1989, DHicks W. B. 179 p. 89-15267. – DissA 50 (1989s) 713s-A.

6418 **Frankemölle** Hubert, 1. Petrusbrief, 2. Petrusbrief, Judasbrief: NEchter 1987 ↠ 3,6269; 4.6368: RActu Bbg 26 (1989) 36s (X. *Alegre S.*).

6420 **Grudem** Wayne A., The First Epistle of Peter, an introduction and commentary. Tyndale NT 17, 1988 ↠ 4,6369: RWestTJ 51 (1989) 394-6 (D. G. *McCartney*: a gem).

6421 **Halas** Stanisław, Risurrezione e vita secondo la prima lettera di Pietro: diss. Pont. Ist. Biblico, DVanhoye A. R 1989. – AcPIB 9,5 (1988s) 384.423; Biblica 70,443.

6422 **Ho Sang** D. A., The New Age and the interpretation of First Peter: diss. Oxford 1989. – RTLv 21,545.

6423 **Lamau** Marie-Louise, Des chrétiens dans le monde; communautés pétriniennes: LDiv 134, 1988 ↠ 4,6374: RÉTRel 64 (1989) 298s (E. *Cuvillier*); MélSR 46 (1989) 173s (G.-H. *Baudry*); MondeB 59 (1989) 63 (F. *Brossier*); NRT 111 (1989) 764s (X. *Jacques*).

6424 **McCartney** Dan G., The use of the OT in the first epistle of Peter: diss. Westminster Theol Sem. ^D*Silva* M. 1989. 315 p. 89-18223. – DissA 50 (1989s) 1340-A.

6425 **Michaels** J. Ramsey, 1 Peter: Word Comm. 49, 1988 ⇒ 4,6375: ^RAndrUnS 27 (1989) 148s (M. *Kent*); SWJT 32,1 (1989s) 49 (E. E. *Ellis*).

6426 **Reichert** Angelika Eine urchristliche praeparatio ad martyrium; Studien zur Komposition, Traditionsgeschichte und Theologie des 1. Petrusbriefes [kath. Diss. Münster 1988 ⇒ 4,6377]: BeitBExT 22. Fra 1989, Lang. v-614 p. 3-631-41796-9.

6427 **Renoux** Charles, La chaîne arménienne sur les Épîtres catholiques [I. Jacques ⇒ 3,6306] II.... Pierre: Patrol.Or. 44,2/198. Turnhout 1987, Brepols. 231 p. – ^RMuséon 102 (1989) 205s (B. *Coulie*).

6428 **Schutter** William L., Hermeneutic and composition in 1 Peter [diss. Cambridge ^D*Lindars* B.]: WUNT 2/30. Tü 1989, Mohr. iv-218 p. DM 79. 3-16-145118-X [TDig 37,86]. – ^RExpTim 101 (1989s) 214s (C. J. A. *Hickling*); TsTNijm 29 (1989) 410s (H. *Welzen*).

6429 *Swetnam* James, Alcune osservazioni su 1 Pt 1,2 e il sangue di Cristo: ⇒ 759, Sangue VI, 1987/9, 787-793.

6430 *Warden* D., The prophets of 1 Peter 1:10-12 [contemporaries]: RestQ 31,1 (1989) 1-12 [< NTAbs 33,337].

6431 *Botha* J., [1 Pt 1,13-25] Christian and society in 1 Peter: Scriptura 24 (Stellenbosch 1988) 27-37 [< NTAbs 33,56].

6432 *Evang* Martin, Ek kardías allēlous agapēsate ektenôs; zum Verständnis der Aufforderung und ihrer Begründungen in 1 Petr 1,22f.: ZNW 80 (1989) 111-123.

6433 *Kayaparampil* Thomas, Christian people, a royal priesthood; a study on 1 Peter 2:9: BibleBh 15 (1989) 154-169.

6434 **Jones-Haldeman** Madelynn, [⇒ 4,6387] The function of Christ's suffering in 1 Peter 2:21: diss. Andrews. Berrien Springs MI 1988. 342 p. 89-19889. – AndrUnS 27 (1989) 226 (^D*Knight* G.); DissA 50 (1989s) 1704-4 (^D*Johnston* R.).

6435 *Gross* Carl D., Are the wives of 1 Peter 3.7 Christians? [probably not]: JStNT 35 (1989) 89-96.

6436 **Dalton** William J., Christ's proclamation to the spirits; a study of 1 Peter 3:18 - 6^{2rev} [¹1965, ^D*Zerwick* M. ⇒ 46,2174]: AnBib 23. R 1989, Pont. Ist. Biblico. 276 p. Lit. 42.000. 88-7653-023-1. – ^RExpTim 101 (1989s) 215 (J. *Proctor*: could not take GRUDEM into account).

6437 **Giesen** Heinz, Hoffnung und Heil für alle — Heilsgegenwart für die Glaubenden (1 Petr. 3,18-22): SNTU 14 (1989) 93-150 [< ZIT 90,407].

6438 *Dschulnigg* Peter, Der theologische Ort des Zweiten Petrusbriefes [Hab.-Vorlesung Luzern 1988]: BZ 33 (1989) 161-177.

6439 **Green** Michael, The second epistle general of Peter and the general epistle of Jude; an introduction and commentary^{2rev} [NIV text; ¹1968]: Tyndale NT Comm. Leicester/GR 1989 = 1987, Inter-Varsity/Eerdmans. 208 p. 0-85111-8879 / GR 0-8028-0078-5.

6440 *Kahmann* Johannes, The Second Letter of Peter and the Letter of Jude; their mutual relationship: ⇒ 606, Réception 1986/9, 105-121. ⇒ 6471s.

6441 *Neyrey* Jerome H., The second epistle of Peter: ➤ 384, NJBC (1989) 1017-1022.

G9.4 Epistula Jacobi ... data on both apostles James.

6442 **Adamson** James B., James, the man and his message [companion to, not replacement of, his 1976 commentary]. GR 1989, Eerdmans. xxii-553 p. $30. 0-8028-0167-6 [NTAbs 33,395]. – ᴿTrinJ 10,1 (1989) 121-4 (S. *McKnight*: a joy to read).

6443 **Becquet** Gilles, *al.*, La carta de Santiago, lectura sociolingüística 1988 ➤ 4,6397*: ᴿBibFe 15 ⊙ (1989) 172 (M. *Sáenz Galache*).

6444 **Boumis** Panagiotis I., ⊙ Who are the authors of the epistles of James and Jude (canonical evidence)?: TAth 60 (1989) 305-335; Eng. 883.

6445 **Deppe** D.B., The sayings of Jesus in the Epistle of James: diss. Amsterdam Vrije Univ., ᴰ*Van Elderen* B., 1989. (> AA, Bookcrafters). – TsTNijm 30,83; RTLv 21,544.

6445* *Fabris* Rinaldo, Figura e ruolo di Giacomo nell'antipaolinismo [non a causa di Gc 2,14-26]: RicStoB 1,2 (1989) 77-92 [< IZBG 36, p. 1682].

6446 *Hartin* Patrick J., James and the Q-sermon on the mount/plain: ➤ 589, SBL Seminars 1989, 440-457.

6447 **Hoppe** Rudolf, Jakobusbrief: KʟK NT 15. Stu 1989, KBW. 120 p. 3-460-15451-9.

6448 *Karrer* Martin, Christus der Herr und die Welt als Stätte der Prüfung; zur Theologie des Jacobusbriefs: KerDo 35 (1989) 166-187; Eng. 188.

6449 **Kristemaker** Simon J., James and 1-3 John: 1986 ➤ 3,6302; 4,6401: ᴿCriswT 2 (1987s) 165s (T.D. *Lea*).

6450 *Leahy* Thomas W., The epistle of James: ➤ 384, NJBC (1989) 909-916.

6451 **Maggioni** Bruno, La lettera di Giacomo; un itinerario di maturità cristiana: Bibbia per tutti. Assisi 1989, Cittadella. 163 p. Lit. 13.000. – ᴿTeresianum 40 (1989) 627s (V. *Pasquetto*).

6452 *Maier* Gerhard, Inwiefern ist der Jakobusbrief missionarisch?: ➤ 28*, ꟳBEYERHAUS P., Martyria 1989, 88-92.

6453 **Manns** F., Jacob, le Min, selon la Tosephta Hulin 2.22-24; contribution à l'étude du christianisme primitif: CrNSt 10 (1989) 449-465.

6454 *Marcus* Joel, James: ➤ 377, Books 2 (1989) 339-343.

6455 **Maynard-Reid** Pedrito U., Poverty and wealth in James 1987 ➤ 3,6303; 4,6405: ᴿCrNSt 10 (1989) 155s (R. *Fabris*).

6456 *Mussner* Franz, Die ethische Motivation im Jakobusbrief: ➤ 173, ꟳSCHNACKENBURG R., NT & Ethik 1989, 416-423.

6457 *Panackel* Charles, The option for the poor in the letter of St. James: BibleBh 15 (1989) 141-153.

6458 *Pearson* Birger A., James, 1-2 Peter, Jude: ➤ 394, NT/Interpreters 1989, 371-406.

6459 *Popkes* Wiard, Adressaten, Situation und Form des Jakobusbriefes 1986 ➤ 2,4999; 4,6406: ᴿIndTSt 26 (1989) 184s (L. *Legrand*).

6460 **Pratscher** Wilhelm, Der Herrenbruder Jakobus und die Jakobustra-dition: FRL 139, ᴰ1987 ➤ 3,6305: ᴿBiblica 70 (1989) 142-5 (R.M. *Wilson*); CBQ 51 (1989) 368-370 (M.E. *Boring*); ExpTim 100 (1988s) 380 (E. *Best*).

6461 *Schnider* Franz, Der Jakobusbrief 1987 ➤ 3,6309; 4,6407: ᴿBLitEc 90 (1989) 64s (S. *Légasse*); BLtg 62 (1989) 60s (R. *Hoppe*); BZ 33 (1989) 280-2 (auch R. *Hoppe*); CBQ 51 (1989) 756s (G.W. *Buchanan*: for cultivated non-scholars); EstBíb 47 (1989) 142s (J.P. *Tosaus*); MüTZ 40

(1989) 250s (J. *Gnilka*); RBíbArg 51 (1989) 51s (R. *Krüger*); TGegw 32 (1989) 316s (H. *Giesen*); TLZ 114 (1989) 280s (N. *Walter*); TPhil 64 (1989) 584s (H. *Engel*); TPQ 137 (1989) 195s (A. *Fuchs*); TR 85 (1989) 14s (W. *Pratscher*).

6462 *Spencer* A. B., The function of the miserific and beatific images in the letter of James: EvJ 7,1 (Myerstown PA 1989) 3-14 [< NTAbs 33,337].

6463 *Strecker* G., Jakobus-Brief: → 894, EvKL 2 (1988) 794s.

6464 **Vouga** François, L'Épître de Saint Jacques 1984 → 65,5700... 3,6311: ÉglT 19 (1988) 426-8 (L. *Laberge*); RThom 89 (1989) 484s (L. *Devillers*).

6465 *Marconi* Gilberto, Una nota sullo specchio di Gc 1,23: Biblica 70 (1989) 396-402.

6466 *Scannerini* Stefano, Giustificazione per la fede, giustificazione per le opere; linee di storia dell'esegesi di Giacomo 2,20-24 e 26: → 567, AnStoEseg 8 (1989) 165-187; 8.

6467 *Prockter* Lewis J., James 4.4-6, midrash on Noah: NTS 35 (1989) 625-7.

6468 *Marconi* Gilberto, La debolezza in forma di attesa; appunti per un'esegesi di Gc 5,7-12: RivB 37 (1989) 173-183. ['Peter DAVIDS ha prodotto certamente uno dei migliori commentari della Lettera di Giacomo dell'ultimo decennio'; si riferisce al 'commentario sul testo greco' Eerdmans/Paternoster 1982 → 63,6223; ma Davids ha anche il Good News comm., Harper 1983 → 64,6145].

6469 *Shogren* Gary S., Will God heal us? — a re-examination of James 5:14-16a: EvQ 61 (1989) 99-108.

G9.6 **Epistula Judae.**

6470 *Buono* A. M., [Jude] A golden letter: HomP 89,2 (1988) 59-62 [< NTAbs 33,195].

6471 *Cothenet* E., La tradition selon Jude et 2 Pierre: NTS 35 (1989) 407-420.

6472 *Dunnett* W. M., The hermeneutics of Jude and 2 Peter; the use of ancient Jewish traditions: JEvTS 31 (1988) 287-292 [< NTAbs 33,57].

Green M., Jude 1987 → 6439.

6472* *Joubert* S., Die Judas brief; 'n simboliese universum in gedrang [a symbolic universe endangered]: HervTS 44 (1988) 613-635 [< IZBG 36, p. 245].

Kahmann J., Jude 1988/9 → 6440.

6473 **Maton** T., Commentary on Jude [Puritan 1658]. GR 1988, Kregel. 384 p. $20; pa. $14. 0-8254-3240-5; 39-1 [NTAbs 33,258].

6474 **Merkel** H., Judasbrief: → 894, EvKL 2 (1988) 850s.

6475 *Neyrey* Jerome H., The epistle of Jude: → 384, NJBC (1989) 917-9.

6476 *Thekkekara* Mathew, Contend for the faith; the letter of Jude: BibleBh 15 (1989) 182-198.

6477 **Watson** Duane F., Invention, arrangement, and style; rhetorical criticism of Jude and 2 Peter [diss. Duke, ᴰ*Strong* F. 1986]: SBL Diss. 104. Atlanta 1988, Scholars. 220 p. $21; pa. $14. 1-55540-155-4; -6-2. – ᴿTLZ 114 (1989) 523 (T. *Fornberg*).

6478 *Wolthuis* Thomas R., Jude and the rhetorician; [imaginary dialogue with Cicero] on the rhetorical nature of the epistle of Jude: CalvinT 24 (1989) 126-134.
6479 *Ross* J. M., Church discipline in Jude 22-23: ExpTim 100 (1988s) 297s.

Desunt hoc anno – N⁰ 6480-6999 – **not used this year.**

XV. **Theologia Biblica**

H1   **Biblical Theology** .1 [OT] **God**

7000 *Ararat* Nisan, ❺ The name of God (*dîn*) and the name of existence (*raḥᵃmîm*): BethM 34,17 (1988s) 153-175.
7001 **Birnbaum** David, God and evil, a Jewish perspective. Hoboken 1989, KTAV. 287 p. $20 [JAAR 57,887].
7002 *Boshof* Willem, Die monoteïsme; vroeë rigtinggewer of laat aankomeling in die godsdiensgeschiedenis van Israel [Early tendency or late arrival in the religious history...] ?: TEv 21,3 (Pretoria 1988) 2-14 [< OTAbs 12,201].
7002* **Bouyer** Louis, Gnosis; la connaissance de Dieu dans l'Écriture: Théologies 1988 ⇒ 4,a662: ᴿTsTNijm 29 (1989) 404s (L. *Grollenberg*: p. 185 claims that in France there was a veritable conspiracy of exegetes to prevent publishing a translation of J. A T. ROBINSON's 'Redating').
7003 **Brettler** Marc Z., God is king; understanding an Israelite metaphor: JStOT supp. 76. Sheffield 1989, Academic. 239 p. 1-85075-224-9.
7004 *Brito* Émilio, La beauté de Dieu [...pas un attribut chez AQUIN ou HEGEL; BARTH si]: RTLv 20 (1989) 141-161; Eng. 280.
7005 *Brzegowy* Tadeusz, ❺ Teofanie w sanktuariach Izraela: AtKap 112 (1989) 39-53.
7006 **Buber** Martin, La regalità di Dio, Genova 1989, Marietti. 216 p. Lit. 32.000 [RivB 37,529].
7007 **Buckley** Michael, At the origins of modern atheism 1987 ⇒ 4,8010: ᴿThomist 53 (1989) 144-9 (D. J. M. *Bradley*).
7008 **Burrell** David B., Knowing the unknowable God 1986 ⇒ 2,5017 ... 4,8012: ᴿGrOrTR 33 (1988) 409s (G. C. *Papademetriou*); JRel 68 (1988) 302-5 (R. L. *Weiss*).
7009 *Cattin* Yves, Dieu d'amour, Dieu de colère ... justice et miséricorde dans le Proslogion (ch. VI-XI) d'ANSELME de Canterbury [sic]: RHPR 69 (1989) 265-284 . 423-450; Eng. 383.
7010 **Cazelles** Henri, La Bible et son Dieu: JJC 40. P 1989, Desclée. 194 p. 2-7189-0434-8.
7011 **Coratelli** Bruno, Il Dio terribile; una storia elementare di Javè da Adamo alla rovina di Gerusalemme. R 1989, Laripress. 294 p.
7012 **Díaz** Carlos, Preguntarse por Dios es razonable; ensayo de teodicea: Ensayos 52. M 1989, Encuentro. 522 p. – ᴿCiTom 116 (1989) 614-6 (L. *Lago Alba*).
7012* **Gross** Lora M., God, world, spirit; [TEILHARD, PANNENBERG] trajectories toward a new synthesis: diss. ᴰ*Hefner* P., Lutheran School of Theology. Ch 1989, 189 p. 90-00851. – DissA 50 (1989s) 2945s-A.
7013 *Gruson* Philippe, *al.,* La Bible raconte Dieu: DossB 28 (1989) 31 p.
7014 *Halpern* Baruch, 'Brisker pipes than poetry'; the development of Israelite monotheism: ⇒ 3,355, ᴱ**Neusner** J., Judaic perspectives 1987, 77-115.

7015 *Henrix* H.H., Auschwitz und Gottes Selbstbegrenzung; zum Gottesverständnis bei Hans JONAS: TGegw 32 (1989) 129-143.

7015* *Hurwitz* Siegmund, Das dunkle Antlitz Gottes im Judentum: Judaica 45 (1989) 83-94.

7016 *Kaiser* Otto, Der Gott des alten Testaments: Amtsblatt ev.-luth. K. Thüringen 41 (1988) 109-116 [< ZAW 101,125].

7017 **Köckert** M., Vätergott und Väterverheissungen; eine Auseinandersetzung mit Albrecht ALT und seinen Erben: FRL 142, 1988 → 4,8023: RBL (1989) 83 (A.D.H. *Mayes*); BO 46 (1989) 694-7 (P. *Höffken*); SvTKv 65 (1989) 128-130 (S. *Hidal*); TR 85 (1989) 453s (O. *Loretz*); TüTQ 169 (1989) 68-70 (W. *Gross*); ZAW 101 (1989) 159 (H.-C. *Schmitt*). → 2255.

7018 *Krötke* Wolf, Gott auf der Suche nach dem Menschen; Erwägungen zu einer biblischen Metapher: ZTK 86 (1989) 517-532.

7019 **Lash** Nicholas, Easter in ordinary: reflections on human experience and the knowledge of God. Charlottesville 1988, Univ. Virginia. 304 p. $30. – RTS 50 (1989) 378-80 (M.J. *Buckley*: a singularly important scrutiny of leading thinkers; title 'crafted' from HOPKINS 'Let him easter in us' plus HERBERT '[prayer is] heaven in ordinarie').

7020 **Leuze** Reinhard, Gotteslehre. Stu 1988, Kohlhammer. 183 p. DM 35. 3-17-010301-6. – RGregorianum 70 (1989) 790s (F.-A. *Pastor*).

7021 **Levenson** Jon D., Creation and the persistence of evil; the Jewish drama of divine omnipotence 1988 → 4,8026: RBS 146 (1989) 229-231 (R.C. *Cover*); JRel 69 (1989) 192s (J.S. *Kselman*); Paradigms 5,1 (1989) 70s (M. *McEntire*: Gn 1 and Ps 104 attempt to demythologize creation); TS 50 (1989) 397 (J.C. *Endres*).

7022 *Lippi* Adolfo, Conoscere il Dio vivente nel pensiero ebraico; ermeneutica e teologia del nostro secolo: SapCr 4 (1989) 51-70.

7023 **McFague** Sallie, Models of God 1987 → 3,6354; 4,8028: RAmerica 159 (1988) 234s (D.D. *Wiebe*); JAAR 57 (1989) 656-661 (Nancy C. *Ring*); JRel 69 (1989) 256s (Karen L. *Bloomquist*); Themelios 14 (1988s) 109s (Sally *Alford*); TLZ 114 (1989) 613-5 (J. *Langer*); TR 85 (1989) 308s (J. *Schmid*).

7024 **Meurers** Joseph, Gott – bist du? Erleben, Fragen, Antworten. Graz 1984, Styria. 244 p. DM 29,80. – RTR 85 (1989) 502-7 (D. *Brünn*).

7025 EMorris Thomas V., The concept of God 1987 → 4,8032: RAsbTJ 43,2 (1988) 138-140 (J.L. *Walls*).

7026 **Nam Daegeuk**, The 'throne of God' motif in the Hebrew Bible: diss. Andrews, DHasel G. Berrien Springs MI 1989. 606 p. 89-22840. – AndrUnS 27 (1989) 228; DissA 50 (1989s) 2115s-A.

7027 **Podella** Thomas, Ṣôm-Fasten; kollektive Trauer um den verborgenen Gott im AT [Diss. 1987, DWelten P. → 3,6365]: AOAT 224. Neuk/Kevelaer 1989, Neuk-V./Butzon & B. xi-327 p. 3-7887-1309-7 / 3-7666-9368-6.

7028 *Preuss* Horst D., Gotteslehre AT [*Roloff* Jürgen, NT]: → 894, EvKL 2 (1988) 296-300 [-304; -316, *al.*].

7029 *Schäfer* Rolf, Ein Lehrbuch zwischen LUTHER und BARTH [*Joest* W., Die Wirklichkeit Gottes 1984, Der Weg Gottes 1986]: TRu 54 (1989) 196-202.

7030 **Seebass** Horst, Il Dio di tutta la Bibbia [1982] 1985 → 2,5056; 3,6371: RProtestantesimo 44 (1989) 55s (Lucilla *Peyrot*).

7031 *Starobinski-Safran* Esther, Hermann COHEN [1842-1918] et les défis du monothéisme: NVFr 63 (1988) 289-308.

7031* **Staton** C.P., 'And Yahweh appeared...'; a study of the motifs of 'seeing God' and of 'God's appearing' in Old Testament narratives: diss. Oxford 1988. – RTLv 21,542.

7032 **Swinburne** Richard, Die Existenz Gottes [The existence of God, Oxford 1979, 296 p.], T*Ginters* Rudolf: Universal-Bibliothek 8434[6]. Stu 1987, Reclam. 414 p. Sch. 122. – RZkT 111 (1989) 66-76 (E. *Runggaldier*).

7033 *Szathmáry* Sándor, Ⓜ The problem of theodicy; on five models of solution: TSzem 32 (1989) 77-83.

7034 EThoma C., *Wyschogrod* M., Das Reden vom einen Gott bei Juden und Christen, 1982/4 ↠ 2,5061: RJudaica 44 (1988) 116-8 (H.L. *Reichrath*); TsTNijm 29 (1989) 185 (H. *Häring*).

7035 **Thompson** Alden, Who's afraid of the Old Testament God? Exeter 1988, Paternoster/GR 1989, Zondervan; 0-310-51921-7. 173 p. [RHPR 69,95].

7036 **Whitner** Barry L., What are they saying about God and evil? NY 1989, Paulist. 129 p. $6 [JAAR 57,893].

H1.3 *Immutabilitas* – God's suffering; process theology.

7037 **Basinger** David, Divine power in process theism; a philosophical critique 1988 ↠ 4,8044: REvQ 61 (1989) 376 (P. *Helm*); SWJT 32,1 (1989s) 64 (I.R. *Bush*).

7037* *Bayes* Jonathan, Divine *apátheia* in IGNATIUS of Antioch: ↠ 696, 10th Patristic 21 (1989) 27-31.

7038 **Bracken** Joseph A., The triune symbol; persons, process and community 1985 ↠ 1,6280 ... 3,6388: RHeythJ 30 (1989) 434 (J. *O'Donnell*: opening lines give title variously as 'The Triune symbol', 'The Triued God'); IrTQ 55 (1989) 344-6 (sr Aengus *O'Donovan*).

7039 *Brown* Delwin, Thinking about the God of the poor; questions for liberation theology from process thought: JAAR 57 (1989) 267-282.

7040 *Buit* M. du, Puissance de Dieu: ↠ 882, Catholicisme XII,55 (1989) 288-293.

7041 **Carroll** Denis, A pilgrim God for a pilgrim people: Theology & Life 24. Wilmington 1989, Glazier. 193 p. $13 pa. [Horizons 16,204] = Dublin 1988, Gill & M., £8: in projected 14-vol. series entitled Theology of a Pilgrim People. – RDocLife 39 (1989) 222s (B.F. *O'Connor*); PrPeo 3 (1989) 153s (M.E. *Williams*).

7041* **Case-Winters** Anna, The problem of omnipotence; a theological exploration of the meaning of power: diss. Vanderbilt. Nv 1988. – RTLv 21,568.

7042 **Creel** Richard E., Divine impassibility 1986 ↠ 2,5072...4,8048: RHeythJ 30 (1989) 239s (B. *Davies*).

7043 **Fiddes** Paul S., The creative suffering of God 1988 ↠ 4,8051: RExpTim 100 (1988s) 312 (D.W. *Hardy*); Interpretation 43 (1989) 216-8 (P. *Sponheim*); RExp 86 (1989) 637-9 (D.R. *Stiver*); ScripTPamp 21 (1989) 724 (L.F. *Mateo-Seco*); TLond 92 (1989) 448s (D. *Cohn-Sherbok*); TS 50 (1989) 380-2 (M.R. *Tripole*).

7044 TEFreddoso Alfred J., Luis de MOLINA, On divine foreknowledge (Concordia IV). Ithaca NY 1988, Cornell Univ. xii-286 p. $35 [RelStR 16, 160, Y. *Watson*]. 0-8014-2131-4. – RAsbTJ 44,2 (1989) 93-95 (J.L. *Walls*).

7045 **Frohnhofen** Herbert, Apatheia tou theou 1987 ↠ 3,6394; 4,8054: RJTS 40 (1989) 232-4 (M. *Slusser*); TLZ 114 (1989) 448-450 (K.-W. *Tröger*).

7046 God and change; process thought and the Christian doctrine of God [articles from 1978-87]. Lv 1987, Centrum/Metafysica. 35+108 p. 90-71061-05-1. – ᴿTsTNijm 29 (1989) 186 (Palmyre *Oomen*).

7046* **Gordon** Bobby Joe, The role of process theology in the Christologies of W. N. PITTENGER and W. PANNENBERG; an analysis of the doctrine of the person of Christ: diss. SW Baptist Theol. Sem. 1989. 283 p. 90-04361. – DissA 50 (1989s) 2946-A.

7047 *Grey* Mary, Naar nieuwe verbondenheid; feministisch proces-denken als belofte voor de theologie [kath. Univ. Nijmegen, 1.II.1989], ᵀ*Borgman* E.: TsTNijm 29 (1989) 114-130; Eng. 130, Weaving new connections.

7047* *Grijs* Ferdinand de, Over de vraag of God de wereld regeert: Bijdragen 50 (1989) 358-371; Eng. 371s.

7048 *Hallman* Joseph M., Divine suffering and change in ORIGEN and Ad Theopompum: SecC 7 (1989s) 85-98.

ꟳHARTSHORNE Charles, process philosophy and theology 1989 → 674.

7049 **Jaeckel** T., Anything but a quiet life; ideas of God in the Bible, ᵀ*Bowden* J. L 1989, SCM. x-100 p. £5 0-334-02767-3 [BL (1989) 155].

7049* **Jaggar** William L., The passibility of God as atonement motif in the theology of Martin LUTHER: diss. SW Baptist Theol. Sem. 1989, 221 p. 90-04363. – DissA 50 (1989s) 2945s-A.

7050 **Keane** Angela C. H., The pathos of God as the theological basis for a servant model of church: diss. Unisa, ᴰ*Konig* A. Pretoria 1987. – DissA 50 (1989s) 2113-A.

7050* **Knaebel** Simon, Abaissement et mort de Dieu; le défi hégélien dans la théologie contemporaine: diss. cath. ᴰ*Wackenheim* C. Strasbourg 1989. 358 p. – RTLv 21,569.

7051 **Kreuzer** Siegfried, Der lebendige Gott ... BW 116, 1983 → 64,6184 ... 3,6401: ᴿAfO 35 (1988) 232-4 (H. *Vorländer*).

7051* **Kvanvig** Jonathan L., Unknowable truths and the doctrine of omniscience: JAAR 57 (1989) 485-507.

7052 *Li Byúng-Ho,* ❻ The 'unchangeability' of God and Christology [*Gervais* M.]: Sinhak Jonmang 83 (Kwangju 1988) 2-24 [< TContext 6/2, 47].

7052* *Lochmann* Jan M., Ein Zeuge der Menschlichkeit Gottes [*Hromadka* J.]: Orientierung 53 (1989) 110-3.

7053 **Meessen** Frank N., Unveränderlichkeit und Menschwerdung Gottes; eine theologiegeschichtlich-systematische Untersuchung: Diss. ᴰ*Lehmann*. Freiburg/B 1988s. – TR 85 (1989) 515.

7053* *Moonan* Lawrence, On dispensing with omnipotence: ETL 65 (1989) 60-80.

7054 **Neusner** J., The incarnation of God [anthropomorphism]; the character of divinity in formative Judaism. Minneapolis 1988, Fortress. 256 p. $25. 0-8006-2086-0. – ᴿExpTim 100 (1988s) 356s (W. *Horbury*).

7054* *Núñez de Castro* Ignacio, Biología e imagen de Dios [... más cercana al 'Dios vivo' de la tradición judeo-cristiana a la que heredamos de la tradición occidental griega]: Proyección 36 (1989) 15-26.

7055 **Oden** Thomas C., The living God 1987 → 3,6362: ᴿCCurr 38 (1988s) 477-480 (T. *Peters*); Interpretation 43 (1989) 304-6 (G. P. *Guthrie*); JAAR 57 (1989) 869-871 (T. *Peters*); JRel 68 (1989) 429s (J. R. *Pool*).

7055* **Pailin** David A., God and the processes of reality; [process-] foundations of a credible theism. L 1989, Routledge. x-235 p. £30. – ᴿTLond 92 (1989) 449s (N. *Pittenger*).

7056 *Pikaza* Xabier, ¿Dónde está tu Dios? ¿Es El quien se ha marchado o nosotros los que tenemos que lavar su rostro?: [... el sufrimiento de Dios]: SalT 76 (1988) 437-449.

7057 **Pittenger** Norman,   Freed to love; a process interpretation of redemption. Wilton CT 1987, Morehouse-Barlow. ix-129 p. $9. – RAngl-TR 70 (1988) 277-9 (J. E. *Skinner*).

7057* **Pregeant** Russell,   Christology beyond dogma; Matthew's Christ in process hermeneutic 1978 ➤ 58,4587* ... 61,5595:   RLA 39 (1989) 363 (V. *Mora*).

7058 *Regan* Thomas J.,   La 'process theology' y la fe cristiana contemporanea [< Études 368 (1988) 81-92],   TE*Pascual* E.:   SelT 29 (1988) 225-230.

7059 E**Rudavsky** Tamar,   Divine omniscience and omnipotence in medieval philosophy; Islamic, Jewish and Christian perspectives 1984 ➤ 2,336: RJQR 79 (1988s) 269s (R. C. *Kiener*).

7059* *Russell* John M.,   Impassibility and pathos in BARTH's idea of God: AnglTR 70 (1988) 221-232.

7060 *Schoonenberg* P.,   De lijdende God in de Britse theologie: GerefTTs 89 (1989) 154-170.

7061 **Suchocki** Marjorie H.,   The end of evil; process eschatology in historical context [< diss. 1973]. Albany 1988, SUNY. $34.50; pa. $11. – RHorizons 16 (1989) 198s (J. A. *Bracken*); TS 50 (1989) 406s (J. *Farrelly*); TTod 46 (1989s) 92-94 (L. S. *Ford*).

7061* **Sugarman** Alvin M.,   God and finitude; toward a covenant of mutual affirmation [process; ... HESCHEL A.]: diss. Emory,   D*Blumenthal* D. Atlanta 1988.   286 p. – DissA 50 (1989s) 981-A.

7062 *Summers* H. C.,   Going back home; process theology goes political: JTSAf 64 (Rondebosch 1988) 57-63 [B. *Abeng* (Eng.) summary, TContext 6/2,100].

7063 *Taliaferro* Charles,   The passibility of God: RelSt 25 (1989) 217-224.

7064 *Thaidigsmann* Edgar,   Die Weltlichkeit Gottes; zum Spätwerk von Leonhard RAGAZ: EvT 49 (1989) 161-179.

7065 *Thelakat* Paul,   God suffers evil [< diss.]: LvSt 14 (1989) 16-25.

7066 **Trethowyn** Illtyd,   Process theology and the Christian tradition 1985 ➤ 1,6310 ... 4,8072:   RHeythJ 30 (1989) 235s (T. J. *Regan*: disappointing in comparison with N. CLARKE 1989 and fine essays of ESIA 1986).

7067 **Veken** Jan Van der,   God en wereld; basisteksten uit de procestheologie: Sleutelteksten in godsdienst 7. Haag 1989, Meinema. Fb. 500. – RStreven 57 (1989s) 179s (G. *Dekeyser*).

7068 **Weinandy** Thomas G.,   Does God change? [diss. London King's College 1975, D*Mascall* E.]: Studies in Historical Theology 4, 1985 ➤ 1,6993 ... 4,8074:   RHeythJ 30 (1989) 362-4 (J. P. *Galvin*: few will share his convictions).

7069 **Williams** Trevor,   Form and vitality in the world and God 1985 ➤ 2,5097 ... 4,8075:   RHeythJ 30 (1989) 75s (B. *McNeil*); JRel 68 (1988) 301s (J. T. *Pawlikowski*).

7069* **Wilson** Paul E.,   The bearing of process thought on the problem of theodicy: diss Tennessee, D*Edwards* R. 1989. 297 p. 89-19868. – DissA 50 (1989s) 1686-A.

7070 **Zoppoli** E.,   'Mistero della sofferenza di Dio'? Il pensiero di S. TOMMASO: Studi tomistici 34. Vaticano 1988, Editrice.   85 p. Lit. 10.000. – RAsprenas 36 (1989) 97s (P. *Orlando*).

H1.4   *Femininum in Deo* – **God as father and as mother** [➤ F3.7; H8,8s].

7071 *a*) *Abraham* Dulcie,   Feminine images of God [Malaysia]; – *b*) *Faria* Stella, ... in traditional religions; – *c*) *Wansbrough* Ann, ... in the West; – *d*) *Chui* Jane C. N., ... Chinese folk religion; – *e*) *Choi Man Ja*, ... in

Korea: In God's image (Hong Kong, June 1989) 3-7 / 7-17 / 18-22 / 24-26 / 30-36 [< TContext 7/1,33].

7072 *Benjamin* Don C., Israel's God; mother and midwife: BibTB 19 (1989) 115-120.

7073 *Berger* K., Die Männlichkeit Gottes: EvKomm 21 (Stu 1988) 712-4 [< NTAbs 33,201: 'the male metaphor suggests that God is the origin of life in a non-human way'].

7074 **Bloesch** Donald G., The battle for the Trinity; the debate over inclusive God-language 1985 ➤ 1,6316 ... 4,8077: ᴿThemelios 14 (1988s) 32s (G. R. *Palmer*).

7075 **Boff** Leonardo, The maternal face of God; the feminine and its religious expressions 1987 ➤ 3,6430; 4,8078: ᴿTS 50 (1989) 179-181 (P. *Bearsley*: Mariology on a broad canvas).

7076 *Brouwer* T., *Folkertsma* D., Een antwoord aan Jill ROBSON, God, een huisvrouw?: Mara 2,2 (1989) 25-28 [< GerefTTs 89,64].

7077 *Clarkson* Shannon, [Male] Language about God: SR 18 (1989) 37-49.

7078 *Corrington* Gail P., The 'divine woman': propaganda and the power of celibacy in the NT apocrypha; a reconsideration: AnglTR 70 (1988) 207-220.

7078* **Croce** Vittorio, Il Padre di Gesù, Dio di tutti. CasM 1989, Piemme. 184 p. – ᴿLateranum 55 (1989) 261s (N. *Ciola*).

7079 **Duck** Ruth C., The trinitarian baptismal formula; gender and the name of God [a new formula must be used with no sex-exclusive terms]: diss. Boston Univ. 1988, ᴰAllen H. 409 p. 89-04846. – DissA 49 (1988s) 3762-A.

7079* **Durrwell** F.-X., Le Père 1987 ➤ 3,6436; 4,8081: ᴿBLitEc 90 (1989) 154s (B. de *Guibert*); ScripTPamp 21 (1989) 373s (J. L. *Lorda*).

7080 *Frye* Roland M., Language for God and feminist language; a literary and rhetorical analysis: Interpretation 43 (1989) 45-57: the assumption that we can exchange certain biblical figures for others that, for whatever reason, may seem preferable is not only linguistically and literarily wrong, but leads to conclusions that are false both historically and theologically.

7081 **Gerstenberger** Erhard S., Jahwe – ein patriarchaler Gott? Traditionelles Gottesbild und feministische Theologie 1988 ➤ 4,8084: ᴿTLZ 114 (1989) 516s (W. *Herrmann*); TPQ 137 (1989) 311 (Irmtraud *Fischer*); TR 85 (1989) 100-3 (Marie-Theres *Wacker*); TsTNijm 29 (1989) 419 (C. *Halkes*); ZAW 101 (1989) 315s (H.-C. *Schmitt* bedauert, nichts mögliches über widersprechenden TIGAY).

7081* *a)* **Helminiak** Daniel A., Doing right by women and the Trinity too: America 160 (1989) 110.112.119; – *b)* *Griffith* Joan D., When God is woman, too: DocLife 39 (1989) 181-6.

7082 *a)* *Kaufmann* Ludwig, Kein Gott der männlichen Grimassen [Nederland 8.-Mai-Bewegung]; – *b)* *Keel* Othmar, Jahwe in der Rolle der Muttergottheit: Orientierung 53 (1989) [113-6] 138-142 / 89-92.

7082* *Kimbrough* S. T.ᴶ, Bible translation and the gender of God: TTod 46 (1989s) 195-202.

7083 *a)* *King* Ursula, The divine as mother; – *b)* *McFague* Sallie, Mother God: Concilium 206 (E 1989) 128-137 / 138-143 [= IZT 25 (1989) 539-545, Das Göttliche als Mutter / 545-9] ➤ 7096.

7083* **Kinkel** Gary S., Count ZINZENDORF's doctrine of the Holy Spirit as mother: diss. Iowa, ᴰForell G. Iowa City 1988. 354 p. 89-13193. – DissA 50 (1989s) 975s-A; RelStR 16,190.

7084 **Koop** Raymond C., God as Father in the Synoptic Gospels and Pauline literature; a comparison and differentiation: diss. Golden Gate Baptist Theol. Sem. 1989, ᴰ*Brooks* O. 259 p. 89-23158. – DissA 50 (1989s) 2539-A.

7084* **Lowery** David K., God as father with special reference to Matthew's Gospel: diss. Aberdeen 1987. 392 p. BRDX-88500. – DissA 50 (1989s) 3989s-A.

7085 *Macias* M., Dios es padre, pero sobre todo madre: Nuevo Mundo 138 (Caracas 1988) 367-372 [< TContext 6/2,83].

7086 *Mattison* R.D., God/Father; tradition and interpretation: RefR 42,3 (1989) 189-206 [< NTAbs 33,303].

7087 **Miller** John W., Biblical faith and fathering; why we call God 'Father'. NY 1989, Paulist. 165 p. $10.

7088 *Miller* Patrick D., The absence of the goddess in Israelite religion: HebAnR 10 (1986) 239-248.

7089 **Mulack** Christa, Die Weiblichkeit Gottes; matriarchale Voraussetzungen des Gottesbildes 1983 ➤ 64,6200 ... 1,6341: ᴿJudaica 44 (1988) 248-250 (S. *Hurwitz*).

Mulack Christa, Im Anfang war die Weisheit; feministische Kritik des männlichen Gottesbildes 1988 ➤ 326*.

7090 **Nilsson** Kristina, Den himmelska Föräldern; ett studium av kvinnans betydelse i och för Lars Levi LAESTADIUS' teologie och förkunnelse: Acta. U 1988, Univ. – ᴿSvTKv 65 (1989) 79s (Kirsti *Suolinna*).

7091 **Oddie** William, What will happen to God? 1984 ➤ 65,7541 ... 4,8092: ᴿThomist 53 (1989) 515-8 (W.J.A. *Soule*).

7091* **Page** Ruth, Ambiguity and the presence of God 1985 ➤ 2,5049; 3,6456: ᴿHeythJ 30 (1989) 69s (J. *Coventry*: ambivalent).

7092 **Raurell** Frederic, Der Mythos vom männlichen Gott, ᵀ*Moll* Ursula, *Ruh* Ulrich: Frauenforum. FrB 1989, Herder. 224 p. DM 28,80 [TüTQ 169,332].

7093 *a*) *Raurell* Frederic, Les bases bibliques per una verbalització femenina de Déu; – *b*) *Rovira Belloso* Josep M., Les dimensións paterna i materna de Déu: QVidCr 144 (1988) 63-77 / 59-62.

7094 *Rupprecht* Friederike, 'Den Felsen, der dich gebär, täuschtest du'; Gott als gebärende Frau in Dtn 32,18 und anderen Texten der hebräischen Bible: KIsr 3 (1988) 53-64.

7094* **Spanier** Ktziah, Aspects of fratriarchy in the OT [patriarchal system]: diss. ᴰ*Gordon* C.H. NYU 1989. 255 p. 90-04242. – DissA 50 (1989s) 2876s-A.

7095 **Trible** Phyllis, *a*) God en sekse-gebonden taalgebruik Hilversum 1988, Gooi & S. 191 p. ƒ 37,50. – ᴿStreven 56 (1988s) 560 (P. *Beentjes*). – *b*) ◐ God and the rhetoric of sexuality [1978], ᵀ*Kawano* N. Tokyo 1989, Yorudan-sha. 337 p. Y 3300 [BL 90,116].

7096 *a*) *Wacker* Marie-Theres, Dieu mère? Signification d'un symbole biblique pour la théologie féministe, ᵀ*Guétho* Marie-Thérèse; – *b*) *Schaberg* Jane, Les aïeules et la mère de Jésus; – *c*) *King* Ursula, La divinité mère; – *d*) *McFague* Sallie, Dieu mère; ᵀ*Divault* André: ➤ 454, Concilium 226 (1989) 125-133 / 135-143 / 153-163 / 165-171.

7097 *Walker* Megan, The challenge of feminism to the Christian concept of God [as male]: JTSAf 66 (Rondebosch 1989) 4-20 [< TContext 7/1,21].

7098 **Wren** Brian, What language shall I borrow? 1989 ➤ 4,a864: ᴿTTod 46 (1989s) 432. 434s (W. *Brueggemann*).

7099 *Zgobo* Lynell, Pronouns for God; he, she, or it? ['Not every pronoun system matches the ones found in Hebrew, Greek, and English']: BTrans 40 (1989) 401-5.

H1.7 **Revelatio.**

7101 *Bertuletti* Angelo, Pensiero dell'alterità e teologia della rivelazione [*Resweber* J., *Delzant* A., *Lafon* G.]: TItSett 14 (1989) 199-216. 285-316; Eng. 216.317 ('recent French destructive theology').

7102 **Buzaka** Nikola, Rivelazione e teologia in Gottlieb Söhngen. R 1985, Città Nuova. 328 p. – ᴿSalesianum 51 (1989) 366 (L. A. *Gallo*).

7103 *Caragounis* C., Divine revelation: EvRT 12 (Exeter 1988) 226-239 [< NTAbs 33,4].

7104 **Dartigues** A., La Révélation 1985 ➤ 4,8102: ᴿLavalTP 44 (1988) 124s (R.-M. *Roberge*).

7105 *Del Zotto* Cornelio, Per una teologia delle rivelazioni private: Antonianum 64 (1989) 308-329; Eng. 308.

7106 *Demarest* Bruce A., *Harpel* Richard J., Don RICHARDSON's 'Redemptive analogies' and the biblical idea of Revelation: BS 146 (1989) 330-340.

7106* **Feucht** Robert C., The center that holds; PANNENBERG's understanding of revelation as the unifying center of his theology of synthesis: diss. Lutheran School of Theology, ᴰ*Hefner* P. 90-00850. – DissA 50 (1989s) 2537-A.

7107 **Fisichella** Rino, La Revelación, evento y credibilidad; ensayo de teología fundamental [1985 ➤ 2,5162], ᵀ*Ortiz García* Alfonso: Lux Mundi 63. Salamanca 1989, Sígueme. 406 p. [LumenVr 38,351]. pt. 1600. – ᴿCiTom 116 (1989) 610s (L. *Lago Alba*); CommSev 22 (1989) 449 (A. *González de León*); Proyección 36 (1989) 325 (B.A.O.).

7108 **Fisichella** Rino, La révélation et sa crédibilité; essai de théologie fondamentale: Recherches NS 22. Montréal/P 1989, Bellarmin/Cerf. 384 p. 2-89007-676-8 / P 2-204-62564-X.

7109 *Gootjes* N. H., General revelation in its relation to special revelation: WestTJ 51 (1989) 359-368.

7109* **Harnett** Anne Marie, The role of the Holy Spirit in constitutive and ongoing revelation according to Yves CONGAR: diss. ᴰ*Dulles* A. Catholic Univ. of America. Wsh 1989. 365 p. 89-25988. – DissA 50 (1989s) 2095s-A; RTLv 21,567 without 'constitutive and ongoing'.

7110 **Heywood** David S., Revelation and Christian learning: diss. Durham 1989. – RTLv 21,567.

7110* **Jiménez Ortiz** Antonio, Teología fundamental; la revelación y la fe en Heinrich FRIES [diss. R, Univ Salesiana]: Bibl. Salm. Est. 106. Salamanca 1988, Univ. Pontificia. 517 p. pt. 3200. [TR 85,527]. – ᴿCiTom 116 (1989) 611-4 (L. *Lago Alba*).

7111 **Kessler** Michael, Kritik aller Offenbarung ... FICHTE 1986 ➤ 2,5184 ... 4,8108: ᴿRTLv 20 (1989) 228 (É. *Brito*); TLZ 114 (1989) 211-3 (U. *Kern*).

7112 **Kraus** Georg, Gotteserkenntnis ohne Offenbarung und Glaube? Natürliche Theologie als ökumenisches Problem: KkK 30, 1987 ➤ 3,6553. 7833: ᴿETRel 63 (1988) 322 (J.-L. *Klein*); TPhil 64 (1989) 130-2 (R. *Sebott*).

7113 **Kuhn** Peter, *a)* Offenbarungsstimmen im Antiken Judentum; Untersuchungen zur Bat Qol und verwandten Phänomenen: TStAJ 20. Tü

1989, Mohr. xii-425 p. DM 258. 3-16-145167-8 [BL 90, 137, N. de *Lange*]. – *b*) Bat Qol, die Offenbarungsstimme in der rabbinischen Literatur; Sammlung, Übersetzung und Kurzkommentierung der Texte: Eichstätter Materialien (0722-1010) 13/5. Rg 1989, Pustet. 110 p. 3-7917-1233-0.

7113* **McGrath** F. J., NEWMAN on revelation and its existence outside Christianity: diss. Oxford 1988. – RTLv 21,585.

7114 **Maesschalek** Marc, Philosophie et révélation dans l'itinéraire de SCHELLING, préf. *Tilliette* X.: BiblPhLv 33. P 1989, Vrin. 768 p. – ᴿZkT 111 (1989) 453s (E. *Coreth*).

7115 *Maesschalek* Marc, Philosophie et révélation chez SCHELLING: RTLv 20 (1989) 281-307; Eng. 419.

7116 *Matthiae* Gisela, La rivelazione nel dibattito postbarthiano: Protestantesimo 44 (1989) 101-113.

7117 **Mavrodes** George J., Revelation in religious belief. Ph 1988, Temple Univ. vii-161 p. $20 [JTS 40,362].

7117* **Muis** Jan, Openbaring en interpretatie; het verstaan van de heilige Schrift volgens K. BARTH en K. H. MISKOTTE [Offenbarung und Interpretation; das Verständnis ...]: diss. ᴰ*Knijft* [RTLv 21, p. 538].

7118 *Odero* José M., Experiencia y revelación; reflexiones sobre la teología de la revelación [*Torres Queiruga* A. 1987]: ScripTPamp 21 (1989) 185-195.

7119 **Schmitz** Josef, Offenbarung: Leitfaden Theol. 19, 1988 → 4,8116; 3-491-77914-6: ᴿTsTNijm 29 (1989) 73 (Ad *Brants*).

7120 **Segundo** Juan Luis, El dogma que libera; fe, revelación, magisterio dogmático: Pres. Teol. 53. Santander 1989, Sal Terrae. 407 p. pt. 1980. – ᴿBibFe 15 (1989) 327 (A. *Salas*); CommSev 22 (1989) 470s (J. *Duque*); Proyección 36 (1989) 328 (A. *Sánchez*).

7121 *Segundo* Juan Luis, Revelación, fe, signos de los tiempos: RLatAmT 5 (Salvador 1988) 123-144 [< Stromata 45,489].

7121* **Senn** Felix, Orthopraktische Ekklesiologie? Karl RAHNERS Offenbarungsverständnis und seine ekklesiologischen Konsequenzen im Kontext der neueren katholischen Theologiegeschichte: kath. Diss. ᴰ*Selvatico* P. Fribourg/S 1988s. 816 p. – TR 85 (1989) 513; RTLv 21,567.

7122 *Speyer* Wolfgang, Himmelsstimme: → 904, RAC 15,114 (1989) 286-303.

7123 *Studer* Basil, Apparitio: → 879, AugL 1/3 (1988) 407-416.

7124 **Thiemann** Ronald F., Revelation and theology; the Gospel as narrated promise 1985 → 1,6442 ... 4,8120: ᴿHeythJ 30 (1989) 73s (G. *O'Collins*).

7124* **Torres Queiruga** A., La revelación de Dios en la realización del hombre 1987 → 3,6498: ᴿRazF 217 (1988) 1257 [-? 109] (A. *Álvarez Bolado*).

H1.8   Theologia fundamentalis.

7125 **Allen** Diogenes, Philosophy for understanding theology 1985 → 2,5133; 3,6501: ᴿHeythJ 30 (1989) 96s (T. *Murphy*).

7126 **Avis** Paul, The methods of modern theology; the dream of reason 1986 → 3,6503; 4,8127: ᴿHeythJ 30 (1989) 221-3 (B. R. *Brinkman*).

7127 ᴱ**Avis** Paul, The threshold of theology 1988 → 4,338; 0-551-01567-5. – ᴿExpTim 100 (1988s) 112 (C. S. *Rodd*).

7127* *a*) **Bachl** Gottfried, Der Glaube sucht das Denken; – *b*) *Singer* Johannes, Verantwortung unserer Hoffnung [... Von der Apologetik zur Fundamentaltheologie]: TPQ 137 (1989) 122-6 / 127-137.

7128 **Bentué** Antonio, La opción creyente ... teol. fundamental 1986 ➤ 2,5140; 84-301-1010-0: ᴿActuBbg 25 (1988) 36-38 (F. *Manresa*).

7129 **Brown** David, Continental philosophy and modern theology; an engagement. Ox 1987, Blackwell. 250 p. £27.50. – ᴿScotJT 42 (1989) 255s (P. *Avis*); Themelios 14 (1988s) 108s (G. *Bray*); TR 85 (1989) 128-130 (E. *Arens*).

7130 *Callahan* Annice, The relation between spirituality [... experience] and theology: Horizons 16 (1989) 266-274.

7131 **Casale** U., L'avventura della fede; saggio di teologia fondamentale: Saggi di teologia. T-Leumann 1988, Elle Di Ci. 180 p. Lit. 13.000. – ᴿAsprenas 36 (1989) 300s (A. *Terracciano*).

7132 **Collins** Raymond F., Models of theological reflection [or, Is ministry truly theological? p. 215] Lanham MD 1984, UPA. 224 p. – ᴿRTLv 20 (1989) 391 (E. *Brito*).

7133 *Cunningham* David S., Clodovis BOFF on the discipline of theology: ModT 6 (1989s) 137-158.

7134 **Dalferth** Ingolf U., Theology and philosophy 1988 ➤ 4,8136: ᴿExpTim 100 (1988s) 276 (P. *Byrne*).

7135 **Dumont** Fernand, L'institution de la théologie; essai sur la situation du théologien: Héritage et projet 38. Montréal 1987, Fides. 292 p. – ᴿÉglT 19 (1988) 438-440 (B. *Garceau*); LavalTP 45 (1989) 131-5 (R.-M. *Roberge*) & 135-142 (J. *Richard*) & 143-151 (R. *Lemieux*).

7135* **Egan** Joseph, The nature of fundamental theology: diss. Pont. Univ. Gregoriana, ᴰ*Dupuis* J. R 1989. 714 p. – RTLv 21, p. 537.

7136 **Franck** Olof, The criteriologic [sic] problem; ... A. FLEW, J. HICK, *al.*: diss. Sto 1988, Almqvist & W. 287 p. – SvTKv 65 (Lund 1989) 90.

7136* *Gómez-Hinojosa* José F., La praxis (unidad teoría-práctica) como criterio de verdad; condiciones de posibilidad para una filosofía mexicana del conocimiento: EfMex 6 (1988) 5-26.

7137 **Hackmann** Daniel W., Validation and truth; Wolfhart PANNENBERG and the scientific status of theology: diss. ᴰ*Forell* G. Iowa City 1989. 293 p. 90-04911. – DissA 50 (1989s) 2946-A; RelStR 16,187.

7137* ᶠHANSON Richard P. C., Scripture, tradition and reason, ᴱ**Bauckham** R. 1988 ➤ 4,60: ᴿScripTPamp 21 (1989) 978s (C. *Izquierdo*).

7138 *Houziaux* Alain, L'ébranlement des fondements de la science et de la théologie: RSPT 73 (1989) 205-232; Eng. 232.

7138* *Jörns* Klaus-Peter, Theologie studieren; Vorschläge für eine Neuorientierung: BTZ 6 (1989) 22-40.

7139 *Kasper* Walter, Zustimmung zum Denken; von der Unerlässlichkeit der Metaphysik für die Sache der Theologie: TüTQ 169 (1989) 257-271.

7140 **Kenny** Anthony, Reason and religion; essays in philosophical theory [6 reprints, 5 new] 1987 ➤ 3,241; 4,8150: ᴿThomist 53 (1989) 709-713 (P. L. *Quinn*).

7141 *Kolvenbach* Peter-Hans, 'Pietas' et 'eruditio' nella ricerca teologica: CC 140 (1989,3) 252-264.

7142 **Kuitert** H. M., Filosofie van de theologie: Wetenschapsfilosofie. Leiden 1988, Nijhoff. 119 p. f 22,50. 90-6890-095-1. – ᴿTsTNijm 29 (1989) 182 (M. van den *Nieuwenhuizen*).

7143 *Lago Alba* Luis, Teología fundamental, hoy [i. IV Jornadas, Valencia 8-10, VI, 1989; ii. Libros]: CiTom 116 (1989) 601-620.

7143* ᴱ**Lauret** Bernard, *Refoulé* François, Iniciación a la práctica de la teología [I. 1984 ➤ 64,335; II-III. 1984s ➤ 1,6406] IV. Etica 1985;

V. Práctica 1986. 462 p.; 480 p. M, Cristiandad. 84-7057-379-9; 92-6 (obra completa -48-9).

7144 **Lonergan** B., Método en teología, [T]*Remolina* G. Salamanca 1988, Sígueme. 380 p. – [R]Carthaginensia 5 (1989) 302s (F. *Martínez Fresneda*).

7145 **Mackey** James P., Modern theology; a sense of direction 1987 ➤ 3,6560; 4,8157: [R]ScotJT 42 (1989) 241-3 (N. *Lash*).

7146 **Magne** Jean, Logique des dogmes: Origines chrétiennes 4. P 1989, auct. 249 p. F 148.

7147 *Marlé* René La théologie admet-elle le pluralisme?: Études 371 (1989) 675-688.

7148 **Marquardt** Friedrich-Wilhelm, Von Elend und Heimsuchung der Theologie; Prolegomena zur Dogmatik. Mü 1988, Kaiser. 468 p. DM 89, 3-459-01740-6 – [R]ActuBbg 26 (1989) 216s (J. *Boada*); KIsr 4,1 (1989) 66-72 (H. H. *Henrix*).

7149 **Moltmann** Jürgen, Theology today 1988 ➤ 4,8161: [R]TLond 92 (1989) 447s (J. *Mark*).

7150 **Mondin** Battista, Scienze umane e teologia. R 1988, Pont. Univ. Urbaniana. 510 p. Lit. 30.000. – [R]HumBr 44 (1989) 905 (G. *Penati*).

7151 **Moreland** J. P., Scaling the secular city; a defense of Christianity. GR 1987, Baker. 256 p. $13. – [R]BS 146 (1989) 223s (R. P. *Richard*: high praise).

7152 **Morris** Thomas V., Francis SCHAEFFER's apologetics; a critique[2rev] [[1]1976]. GR 1987, Baker. 133 p. $6. – [R]BS 146 (1989) 104 (F. R. *Howe*).

7153 **Mueller** J. J., What are they saying about theological method? 1984 ➤ 1,g307: [R]CurrTM 16 (1989) 302s (T. *Peters*: very good; but 'methodology', not 'method', reflects on method).

7154 **Müller** Bernhard, Vernunft und Theologie; eine historisch-systematische Untersuchung zum Verhältnis von Denken und Glauben bei Stephan WIEST (1748-1797): Eichstätter Studien NF 26. Rg 1988, Pustet. 536 p. DM 98. – [R]TR 85 (1989) 394s (P. *Schäfer*).

7155 **Müller** Hans-Peter [53-67 AT], Was ist Wahrheit? Stu 1989, Kohlhammer. 119 p. DM 40. 7 other art. [JBL 108,755].

7156 *Narcisse* Gilbert, Bulletin de théologie fondamentale: RThom 89 (1989) 655-665.

7157 [E]Neufeld K. H., Problemas y perspectivas de la teología dogmática [1983 ➤ 1,387],[T]: Verdad e imagen 92. Salamanca 1987, Sígueme. 527 p. – [R]Proyección 35 (1988) 152 (R. *Franco*).

7158 *Neufeld* Karl-Heinz, Über fundamentaltheologische Tendenzen der Gegenwart: ZkT 111 (1989) 26-44 [i. Aporien; ii. Hermeneutik; iii. Sprachphilosophie; iv. Praxisorientiert; v. Handlungstheorie].

7159 *Niemann* Franz-Josef, Paradigmenwechsel in der Fundamentaltheologie: TGegw 32 (1989) 64-71.

7160 *O'Collins* Gerald, Fundamental theology; an agenda for the 1990s: Pacifica 1,3 (1988) 290-7 [< ZIT 89,159].

7160* **Ohlig** K. H., Fundamentaltheologie im Spannungsfeld von Christentum und Kultur ➤ 2,5639 ... 4,8534: [R]KatKenk 28,55 (1989) 191-8 (S. *Takayanagi*).

7161 **Phillips** D. Z., Faith after foundationalism [philosphers' universal unjustified assumption that faith to be rational requires 'self-evident' propositions as foundation]. L 1988, Routledge. xviii-341 p. £40. 0-415-00333-4. – [R]ExpTim 100 (1988s) 236 (G. *Pattison*).

7162 **Pie i Ninot** Salvador, Tratado de teología fundamental; dar razón de la esperanza (1 Pe 3,15): Agape 7. Salamanca 1989, Segr. Trinitario. 426 p. – ᴿCiTom 116 (1989) 607-610 (L. *Lago Alba*).

7162* *Reckinger* François, Beglaubigt durch Wunder und Zeichen (Vgl. Apg. 2,22); ist die traditionelle Fundamentaltheologie 'ins Mark getroffen'?: ForumKT 4 (1988) 111-125.

7163 *Ricœur* Paul, Entre philosophie et théologie; la Règle d'Or en question: ⇒ 734, Sagesse, éloquence 1988 = RHPR 69 (1989) 3-9 [43-49, *Reboul* Olivier, L'université et le savoir]; Eng. p. 85.

7164 *Roberge* René-Michel, al., De la situation du théologien à la structure de la théologie [*Dumont* F. 1987]: LavalTP 45 (1989) 131-151.

7165 *Rose* Mary C., Christianity and revisionist theologies; a defence of traditional Christian theology: PrPeo 3 (1989) 387-393.

7166 **Runzo** Joseph, Reason, relativism, and God. NY 1986, St. Martin's. 308 p. $30. – ᴿJRel 68 (1988) 305s (W. L. *Proudfoot*).

7166* *Rusecki* Marian, ❷ Fundamentalna teologia: ⇒ 891, EncKat 5 (1989) 764-772.

7167 *a) Seifert* Josef, Philosophie und Glaube im gegenwärtigen kulturellen Kontext; – *b) Mondin* G. Battista, Relazioni tra filosofia e teologia: Seminarium 31 (R 1981) 5-25 / 26-36.

7168 **Thompson** W. M., Fire and light; on consulting the saints, mystics and martyrs in theology. NY 1987, Paulist. v-201 p. $9. 0-8091-2891-8. – ᴿTsTNijm 29 (1989) 183s (J. A. P. *Peters*).

7169 **Van Huysteen** Wentzel, Theology and the justification of faith. GR 1989, Eerdmans. $19. – ᴿTrinJ 10 (1989) 161-184 (J. S. *Feinberg*).

7170 **Vergote** Antoon, Cultuur, religie, geloof [... evolution; 1989 Dondeyne lectures]. Lv 1989, Univ. 124 p. – ᴿETL 65 (1989) 460s (T. *Merrigan*).

7171 **Zimmer** Christoph, Was ist unter einer theologischen Aussage zu verstehen?: FreibZ 36 (1989) 311-340.

H2.1   **Anthropologia theologica**   –   VT & NT.

7172 **Alfaro** Juan, De la cuestión del hombre a la cuestión de Díos 1988 ⇒ 4,8193: ᴿActuBbg 26 (1989) 67s (J. M. *Fondevila*); Burgense 30 (1989) 286-9 (J. A. *Sayés*); CommSev 22 (1989) 100s (M. *Sánchez*); RazF 218 (1988) 252s (J. *Gómez Caffarena*).

7173 **Álvarez Turienzo** Saturnino, Regio media salutis, imagen del hombre y su puesto en la creación; S. AGUSTÍN: Bibl. Salm. Est 108. Salamanca 1988, Univ. Pontificia. 369 p. [TR 85,524]. – ᴿScripTPamp 21 (1989) 705s (C. *Basevi*).

7174 *Békési* Andor, ⓜ The Protestant view of man: TSzem 81 (1988) 331-4.

7174* **Bokwa** Ignacy, Christologie als Anfang und Ende der Anthropologie; über das gegenseitige Verhältnis zwischen Christologie und Anthropologie bei Karl RAHNER: diss. Pont. Univ. Gregoriana, Nº 3613, ᴰ*Neufeld* K. R 1989. 390 p. – RTLv 21,567 (> Fra, 367 p.).

7175 *Borrego* Enrique M., Idea de sexualidad y crisis de la antropología: Proyección 36 (1989) 215-232.

7176 *Britt* William G. III, God's holiness and humanity's self esteem: JPsy&T 16 (1988) 213-221 [< OTAbs 12,130].

7177 *Budillon* Jean, Loi naturelle et anthropologie biblique: Istina 32 (1987) 258-273 [> SelT 28 (1989) 205-212, ᵀᴱ*Gari* José A.].

ᴱ**Bühler** Pierre, Humain à l'image de Dieu ... l'anthropologie 1989 ⇒ 447.

7178 *Coda* Piero, *a)* Antropologia teologica e agire umano nel mondo nella 'Gaudium et Spes': Lateranum 55 (1989) 176-207; – *b)* L'antropologia trinitaria; una chiave di lettura della 'Gaudium et spes'; – *c)* Teologia e antropologia nella 'Mulieris dignitatem' NuovUm 10,56 (R 1988) 17-47, 11,61 (1989) 9-32.

7179 **Colzani** Gianni, Antropologia teologica; l'uomo, paradosso e mistero: corso di teologia sistematica 9. Bo 1988, Dehoniane. 464 p. [TR 85,170].

7180 **Comblin** José, Antropologia cristiana [1985 ➤ 3,6614],[T]. Assisi 1987, Cittadella. 272 p. – [R]Laurentianum 30 (1989) 233-5 (E. *Covi*); Teresianum 40 (1989) 594-9 (F. *Di Giacomo*).

7181 *Congourdeau* Marie-Hélène, L'animation de l'embryon humain chez MAXIME le Confesseur: NRT 111 (1989) 693-709.

7182 *Constantelos* Demetrios J., IRENAEOS of Lyons and his central views on human nature: SVlad 33 (1989) 351-363.

7183 **Deissler** Alfons, L'uomo secondo la Bibbia [1985 ➤ 1,6472],[T]. R 1989, Città Nuova. 102 p. Lit. 9000 [CC 149,3 dopo 448].

7184 [E]**Felici** S., Crescita dell'uomo nella catechesi dei Padri (età postnicena); convegno di studio, Pont. Inst. Altioris Latinitatis, Roma 20-21 marzo 1987: BiblScRel 80, 1988 ➤ 4,562: [R]Claretianum 29 (1989) 396-8 (B. *Proietti*); Lateranum 55 (1989) 493s (O. *Pasquato*); NRT 111 (1989) 1065 (A. *Harvengt*); RBén 99 (1989) 210s (L.-J. *Wankenne*); StPatav 36 (1989) 643s (O. *Pasquato*).

7185 *González de Cordedal* Olegario, Evangelio de Dios y humanidad del hombre: ➤ 7, [F]ALFARO J., EstE 64 (1989) 495-523.

7186 **González Faus** José I., Proyecto de hermano; visión creyente del hombre 1987 ➤ 4,8215: [R]SalT 76 (1988) 239-241 (J. R. *Busto Saiz*).

7187 **Gozzelino** Giorgio, Vocazione e destino dell'uomo in Cristo; saggio di antropologia teologica fondamentale 1985 ➤ 1,6480…3,6626: [R]Protestantesimo 44 (1989) 65s (A *Moda*).

7188 **Hamman** A.-G., L'homme image de Dieu; essai d'une anthropologie chrétienne dans l'Église des cinq premiers siècles 1987 ➤ 4,8218: [R]BLitEc 90 (1989) 142s (H. *Crouzel*); NRT 111 (1989) 263s (V. *Roisel*); VigChr 43 (1989) 95s (J. van *Winden*).

7189 *Henriksen* Jan-Olav, Body, nature and norm; an essay exploring ways of understanding the integrity of creation […the body as the image of God Gn 1,26]: IrTQ 55 (1989) 307-323.

7190 **Hughes** Philip E., The true image; the origin and destiny of man in Christ. GR/Leicester 1989, Eerdmans/Inter-Varsity. ix-430 p. $20. 0-8028-0314-8 / IVP 0-85110-680-3 [NTAbs 33,406].

7190* **Kuhn** Wolfgang, Zwischen Tier und Engel; die Zerstörung des Menschenbildes durch die Biologie. Stein, Schweiz 1988, Christiana. 199 p. – [R]TGL 79 (1989) 325-7 (R. M. *Bucher*).

7191 **Lane** George L., Historicality and repentance; a philosophical reconstruction of Reinhold NIEBUHR's Christian anthropology: diss. [D]*Tracy* D. Chicago 1989. – RelStR 16,187.

7191* **Lobet** Benoît, La joie d'être sauvé, introduction à l'anthropologie chrétienne: Racines. P 1989, Nouvelle Cité. 115 p. F 60. – [R]EsprVie 99 (1989) 284s (P. *Jay*).

7192 *Lys* Daniel, Vingt-trois minutes pour un testament [AT … anthropologie]: ÉTRel 64 (1989) 161-173.

7193 **Macquarrie** John, In search of humanity; a theological and philosophical approach. NY 1985, Crossroad. 280 p. $12 pa. – [R]JRel 68 (1988) 466s (D. D. *Evans*: twenty dimensions; excellent].

7193* **Mahan** Susan M. Thrift,   The Christian anthropology of JULIAN of Norwich: diss. Marquette. Milwaukee 1988. 285 p. 89-04273. – DissA 50 (1989s) 406-A.

7194 **Meslin** M.,   L'expérience humaine du divin, fondements d'une anthropologie religieuse.   P 1988, Cerf. 421 p. [RHPR 69,92].

7195 **Nellas** Panayotis [† 1986 aet. 50],   Le vivant divinisé; anthropologie des Pères de l'Église 1989 → 4,8230:   REsprVie 99 (1989) 476s (P. *Jay*); RHPR 69 (1989) 487 (G. *Siegwalt*).

7196 *O'Daly* Gerald J. P.,   Anima-animus: → 879, AugL 1/3 (1988) ... 321-337. [340-350, *Zumkeller* A., 'De anima'].

7197 **Pannenberg** W.,   Anthropologie 1983 → 64,6259 ... 4,8234:   RTsTKi 59 (1988) 316-8 (I. *Asheim*); ZevEth 32 (1988) 75-78 (K. *Nürnberger*).

7198 **Pesch** Otto H.,   Frei sein aus Gnade; theologische Anthropologie 1983 → 65,5909. – RZkT 111 (1989) 382-5 (L. *Lies*, auch über andere Leistungen des kath. Theologen in prot. Fakultät).

7199 *Peters* Albrecht †,   Christliche Seelsorge im Horizont der drei Glaubensartikel; Aspekte einer theologischen Anthropologie: TLZ 114 (1989) 641-660.

7200 *Rizzerio* Laura,   Le problème des parties de l'âme et de l'animation chez CLÉMENT d'Alexandrie: NRT 111 (1989) 389-416.

7201 **Rogerson** J. M.,   Antropologia e Antico Testamento [1978 → 60,8503] 1984 → 1,f126:   RParVi 34 (1989) 154s (C. *Marcheselli Casale*, anche su MORK F. 1971; WOLFF H. W. 1975).

7202 **Ruiz de la Peña** Juan Luis,   Imagen de Dios; antropología teológica fundamental 1988 → 4,4243:   RActuBbg 26 (1989) 237 (J.I. *González Faus*); BibFe 15 (1989) 171 (M. *Sáenz Galache*); Burgense 30 (1989) 294-6 (J. de *Sahagún Lucas H.*); Gregorianum 70 (1989) 353s (L. F. *Ladaria*); Proyección 36 (1989) 165 (J. *Vílchez*); SalT 76 (1988) 817s (J. A. *García*).

   Rulla Luigi M., Anthropology of the Christian vocation I; II. (with *Ridick* J., *Imoda* F.) 1986-9 → 8246.

7203 **Spinsanti** Sandro,   Guarire tutto l'uomo; la medicina antropologica di Viktor von WEIZSÄCKER. CinB 1988, Paoline. 158 p. Lit. 10.000. – RCC 140 (1989,3) 198-200 (P. *Cattorini*).

7204 **Splett** Jörg,   Freiheitserfahrung ... Anthropo-theologie 1986 → 3,6658; 4,8248:   RMüTZ 40 (1989) 253s (G. L. *Müller*).

7205 *Stolle* Volker,   Die ungeborenen Kinder in Gottes bedachten Händen [i. die biblische Terminologie; ii. der biblische Sitz im Leben; iii. die Ganzheit der menschlichen Existenz; iv. ethisch; v. Beten fur sie]:   LuthTKi 12 (1988) 1-17.

7205* **Thielicke** Helmut,   Esencia del hombre; ensayo de antropología cristiana 1985 → 2,5291; 3,6666:   RTVida 29 (1988) 87s (Annelies *Meis*).

7206 *Watson* Gerard,   Souls and bodies in ORIGEN's *Peri Archon*:   IrTQ 55 (1989) 173-192.

7206* *Yates* John C.,   The origin of the soul; new light on an old question: EvQ 61 (1989) 121-140.

7207 **Zincone** Sergio,   Studi sulla visione dell'uomo in ambito antiocheno. L'Aquila 1988, Japadre. 116 p. Lit. 15.000. 88-7006-155-8. – RRHPR 69 (1989) 348s (P. *Maraval*: l'originalité de dégager leur conception de l'homme de leur exégèse).

7208 *Zung Tae-Hyoun*, ✪ Anthropology of the Bible with a view to salvation: Samok 121 (Seoul 1989) 19-32 [< TContext 7/1,56].

H2.8 Œcologia VT & NT – saecularitas.

7209 **Altner** G., Die Überlebenskrise in der Gegenwart; Ansätze zum Dialog mit der Natur in Wissenschaft und Theologie: WB-Forum 10, 1988 ➤ 4,8254: ᴿActuBbg 26 (1989) 49s (J. *Boada*); TsTNijm 29 (1989) 184 (T. *Brattinga*).

7209* **Altner** Günter, Die grosse Kollision; Mensch und Natur: Herkunft und Zukunft 9. Graz 1987, Styria. 144 p. 3-222-11616-4. – ᴿActuBbg 26 (1989) 48s (J. *Boada*).

7210 **Auer** Alfons, Etica dell'ambiente; un contributo teologico al dibattito ecologico [1984 ²1985 ➤ 3,6673]ᵀ, 1988 ➤ 4,8256: ᴿCC 140 (1989,3) 325s (F. *Cultrera*).

7211 **Austin** Richard C., Hope for the land; nature in the Bible: Environmental Theology 3. Atlanta 1988, Knox. ix-262 p. 0-8042-0861-1.

7211* **Auvenshine** Donnie G., The theological significance of beauty [in God; in nature...] in the OT: diss. SW Baptist Theol. Sem. 1987. 239 p. 88-06934. DissA 49 (1988s) 526s-A.

7212 **Barbaglio** G., La laicità del credente; interpretazione biblica: Orizzonti Biblici. Assisi 1987, Cittadella. 164 p. Lit. 15.000 [NTAbs 33,404: how a believer lives in a de-sacralized world].

7213 **Barbaglio** Giuseppe, Le sens biblique de la laïcité [... sécularité], ᵀ*Vulliez*: Lire la Bible 83. P 1989, Cerf. 176 p. F 80. – ᴿEsprVie 99 (1989) 654s (É. *Ricaud*).

7214 **Barros** M. de, *Caravias* J.L., Teología de la tierra: Cristianismo y Sociedad 14. M 1989, Paulinas. 444 p. pt. 1750. – ᴿBibFe 15 (1989) 482 (A. *Salas*); Proyección 36 (1989) 325 (I. *Camacho*).

7214* **Bartl** Klaus, Theologie und Säkularität; die theologischen Ansätze Friedrich GOGARTENS und Dietrich BONHOEFFERS zur Analyse und Reflexion der säkularisierten Welt: ev. Diss. ᴰ*Sauter*. Bonn 1988s. – TR 85 (1989) 514.

7215 *Biser* Eugen, Das Schicksal der religiösen Ideen im Säkularisierungsprozess: StiZt 207 (1989) 697-709.

7216 *Bizeul* Yves, Étude critique; justice, paix et sauvegarde de la création; un processus 'conciliaire' [Conférence des Églises Européennes, Bâle 15-21.V.1989]: RHPR 69 (1989) 325-330. ➤ 732.

7217 *Brinkman* Martien, De ambivalentie van het begrip 'behoud van de schepping': Geest en leven 65 (1988) 100-107; 108, fig. (Chartres).

7217* *Bucher* Rainer M., Die ökologische Krise – eine Schöpfungskrise; Ansätze und Perspektiven einer Theologie des Überlebens: TGL 79 (1989) 19-41.

7218 *Coda* Piero, Spirito Santo, cosmo e storia; a proposito della questione ecologica: NuovaUm 11,66 (R 1989) 27-46.

7219 *a) Dal Ferro* Giuseppe, Religioni ed ecologia; – *b) Bertalot* Renzo, Il problema ecologico; prospettive ecumeniche; – *c) Vetrali* Tecle, S. FRANCESCO ecologista; esteta o teologo: StEcum 5 (1987) 491-511; Eng. 511 / 483-490; Eng. 490 / 513-527; Eng. 527.

7220 *a) Deuser* Herrmann, Schöpfung und Schöpfungsethik; Argumente amerikanischer Religionsphilosophie (C. PEIRCE, W. JAMES, A. WHITEHEAD);

– b) *Frey* Christofer, Neue Perspektive; Literaturbericht: ZevEth 33 (1989) 176-185 / 217-232.

7221 a) *Gábriš* Karol, Die Theologie der Schöpfung im Zusammenhang mit dem ökologischen Problem; – b) *Möller* Werner, Wir Menschen; Teil der Schöpfung und Verwalter der Schöpfung; – c) *Müller-Fahrenholz* Geiko, Gefährdete Schöpfung — Lob des Schöpfers; – d) *Heubach* Joachim, LUTHER über Schöpfung, Gerechtigkeit, Frieden: Lutherische Kirche in der Welt 36 (Neuendettelsau 1989) 31-50 / 51-67 / 68-79 / 16-30 [< ZIT 89,347].

7222 *Gaillard* Jean, L'église catholique et la protection animale: SuppVSp 167 (1988) 173-192.

7223 **Ganoczy** Alexandre, Théologie de la nature. P 1988, Desclée. 116 p. F 69. – ᴿEsprVie 99 (1989) 286 (P. *Jay*); Études 370 (1989) 569s (R. *Marlé*); NRT 111 (1989) 792 (A. *Toubeau*).

7224 *Gibellini* R., Dalla modernità alla solidarietà; oltre la teología della secolarizzazione: RasT 30 (1989) 121-144.

7225 *Gironés* Gonzalo, Dios pertenece al mundo secular: AnVal 15 (1989) 301-310.

7225* **Granberg-Michaelson** Wesley, Ecology and life. Waco 1988, Word. 200 p. 0-8499-0579-6. – ᴿExpTim 100 (1988s) 478 [C. S. *Rodd*: a flip from biblical references to immediate policies bypassing theology].

7226 *Guerra* Santiago, Ecología y cristianismo: RazF 219 (1989) 605-625.

7227 **Hall** Douglas J., Imaging God; dominion as stewardship 1986 ⇥ 3,6684: ᴿRHPR 69 (1989) 490s (G. *Vahanian*: 'every 24 hours, US citizens consume 2250 animals in the form of McDonald hamburgers').

7228 ᴱ**Hargrove** Eugene C., Religion and environmental crisis 1987 ⇥ 3,412: ᴿJRel 68 (1988) 183 (W. *French*).

7229 **Hedstrom** Ingemar, ¿Volverán las golondrinas? La reintegración de la creación desde una perspectiva latinoamericana. San José CR 1988, Dep. Ecum. Inv. 248 p. – ᴿEfMex 7 (1989) 105-111 (M. A. *Sobrino*).

7229* a) *Helland* Jonathan, The earth is the Lord's; Judaism and environmental ethics; – b) *Brotton* Susan P., Christian ecotheology and the OT; – c) *LaBar* Martin, A biblical perspective on nonhuman organisms; values, moral considerability and moral agency; – d) *Jakowska* Sophie, Roman Catholic teaching and environmental ethics in Latin America; – e) *Ayers* Robert H., Christian realism and environmental ethics; – f) *Cobb* John B., Christian existence in a world of limits: ⇥ 3,412, ᴱ*Hargrove* E., Religion and environmental crisis 1986, 38-52 / 53-75 / 76-93 / 127-153 / 154-171 / 172-187.

7230 ⑩ II. JÁNOS PAL Pápa levele Carlo MARTINI biboroshoz (letter for Basel peace conference 15-21-V-1989), ᵀ*Fükő* Dezső: TSzem 32 (1989) 326 [*al.* 321-374 (361-6, *Etchegaray* card. Roger)].

7230* a) *Jans* H., Ecologische ethiek; een volstrekt nieuwe uitdaging voor het (wereld) geweten; – b) *Tavernier* J. De, De oecumenische ontmoeting 'vrede en gerechtigheid voor de gehele schepping' (Bazel, 15-21 mei 1989): CollatVL 19 (1989) 344-369 / 370-388.

7231 *Koch* Traugott, Das Risiko der Verantwortung in der Gentechnologie bei Pflanzen und Tieren: ZevEth 33 (1989) 278-282.

7232 Der konziliare Prozess über Gerechtigkeit, Frieden und Bewahrung der Schöpfung; a) StiZt 207 (1989) 353-6 (Georg *Schütz* deals not specifically with any one book of that title, but with a series of meetings); – b) *Hintzen* Georg, Die ekklesiologische Bedeutung des konziliaren Prozesses für Frieden, Gerechtigkeit und Bewahrung der Schöpfung: ÖkRu 38

(1989) 289-297; – c) *Slenczka* Reinhard, Das Forum 'Gerechtigkeit, Frieden und Bewahrung der Schöpfung'; dogmatische Beurteilung eines 'konziliaren Prozesses': KerDo 35 (1989) 316-335, not on ecology but on what 'dogma' and 'conciliar' mean; → 7216 and 8013 infra.

7233 **Krolzik** U., Säkularisierung der Natur; Providentia-Dei-Lehre und Naturverständnis der Frühaufklärung [Diss. 1984]. Neuk 1988. 220 p. DM 54. 3-7887-1227-9. – ᴿCrNSt 10 (1989) 644s (M. *Seckler*, deutsch); TsTNijm 29 (1989) 306 (N. *Schreurs*).

7233* **Kruithof** Jaap, Christendom en ecologie: → 412, Sleutelen 1989, 169-184.

7234 **Linzey** Andrew, Christianity and the rights of animals 1987 → 3,6692; 4,8276: ᴿÉTRel 64 (1989) 139 (A. *Gounelle*: better than his 'Compassion for animals' selections 1988); ScotBEv 7 (1989) 47s (C. P. *White*); Themelios 14 (1988s) 35 (E. C. *Lucas*).

7235 **Lötzsch** Frieder, Was ist 'Ökologie'? REIMARUS ... Köln 1987, Böhlau. 36 + 350 p. – ᴿSvTKv 65 (1989) 37s (B. *Hägglund*); LuthMon 28 (1989) 44 (U. *Asendorf*).

7236 *López Azpitarte* Eduardo, La moral ecológica; una defensa del hombre: Proyección 36 (1989) 91-103.

7236* **Losinger** Anton, Die rechte Autonomie der irdischen Wirklichkeiten: kath. Diss. ᴰ*Rauscher*. Augsburg 1988s. – TR 85 (1989) 513.

7237 *McPherson* Jim, The integrity of creation; science, history, and theology [*Moltmann* J., *Peacocke* A., on environment]: Pacifica 2 (1989) 333-355.

7238 **Manenschijn** G., Geplunderde aarde, getergde hemel; ontwerp voor een christelijke milieu-ethiek. Baarn 1988, Ten Have. 206 p. *f* 25. 90-259-4398-5. – ᴿTsTNijm 29 (1989) 313 (T. *Veerkamp*).

7239 *Marini-Bettolo* Giovanni B., Scienza e coscienza di fronte al problema ecologico: Asprenas 36 (1989) 508-521.

7240 **Moltmann** Jürgen, God in creation ... the ecological crisis [Gifford Lectures 1984s] 1985 → 2,5315 ... 4,8281: ᴿHeythJ 30 (1989) 232-4 (Anne *Primavesi*).

7241 **Moltmann** Jürgen, Gott in der Schöpfung² 1985 → 1,6536 ... 3,6701: ᴿKatKenk 26,52 (1987) 1-26; Eng. i-ii (S. *Takayanagi* ❶); TsTKi 59 (1988) 231s (J.-O. *Henriksen*).

7242 **Moltmann** Jürgen, Dieu dans la création, traité écologique, ᵀ*Kleiber* M.: CogF 146, 1988 → 4,8282: ᴿBLitEc 90 (1989) 418s (B. de *Guibert*); ETL 65 (1989) 208-210 (E. *Brito*); Istina 34 (1989) 242-4 (B. *Dupuy*); RTLv 20 (1989) 382s (R. *Guelluy*).

7243 **Moltmann** J., a) Dios en la creación 1987 → 4,8283: ᴿBurgense 30 (1989) 590-2 (G. del *Pozo Abejón*); – b) Dio nella creazione 1986 → 3,6703: ᴿFutUom 15,1 (1988) 91-95 (L. *Galleni*).

7244 — *French* William C., Returning to creation; MOLTMANN's eschatology naturalized [Eng. 1985]: JRel 68 (Ch 1988) 78-86.

7245 — *Marlé* René, A teologia da criação de J. MOLTMANN [franç. 1988]: Brotéria 127 (1988) 3-15.

7246 *Oderberg* David S., Animals – the need for a new Catholicism: NBlackf 70 (1989) 245-8.

7246* **Osborn** Lawrence H., The kingdom of nature; God's providential care for the non-human creation: diss. London 1989. 376 p. – RTLv 21,570.

7247 **Pannenberg** Wolfhart, Christianity in a secularized world, ᵀ*Bowden* John. NY 1989, Crossroad. ix-62 p. $12 pa. 0-8245-0936-6 [TDig 37,81].

7248 *Pavan* Mario, Ⓜ The role of Christians in a world-wide ecology, 'egy milliárd keresztyén mozgósítva' [subtitle given in English and German as 'at the time of creation'], ᵀ*Fóris* Mrs. Eva; TSzem 32 (1989) 354-361.

7248* **Pieratt** Alan B., Secularization or reoccupation? A debate over the influence of theology in western history: Diss. Iowa, ᴰ*Klemm* D. Iowa City 1989, 215 p. 90-04941. – DissA 50 (1989s) 2933s-A.

7249 *a*) *Pikaza* Xabier,   Carácter sacramental del mundo; reflexión filosófico-teológica; – *b*) *Gallego* Epifanio, Mundo y reino, ayer y hoy; – *c*) *Garrido Sanz* Alfonso,   Profanidad y trascendencia en el 'primer mundo'; – *d*) *Andrés* Laureano, El 'tercer' mundo, hoy; problemática humana y religiosa; – *e*) *Salas* Antonio, El mundo y su destino; – *f*) *Galende* Francisco,   'Dios-Hombre-Mundo';   ¿ relación estática o dinámica? aporte de San AGUSTÍN: BibFe 15,45 (1989) 332-369 / 381-404 / 405-420 / 421-436 / 437-466 / 467-481.

7250 *Rendtorff* Trutz,   Vertrauenskrise? Bemerkungen zum Gebrauch des Topos 'Bewahrung der Schöpfung': ZevEth 32 (1988) 245-9; *Lüpke* Johannes von, Fragen: 33 (1989) 233-5 (-7, Rendtorff).

7251 *Ringeling* H.,   Leben im Anspruch der Schöpfung: St. theol. Ethik 24. FrB/FrS 1988, Herder/Univ. 163 p. – ᴿTGegw 32 (1989) 153 (B. *Häring*).

7252 *Rizzi* Armido,   'Oikos'; la teologia di fronte al problema ecologico: RasT 30 (1989) 22-35 . 145-164.

7252* **Rock** Martin, Die Umwelt ist uns anvertraut: Sachbücher des Glaubens 1987 ↠ 3,6713: ᴿTPQ 137 (1989) 431 (K. *Rohregger*).

7253 *a*) *Ruh* Hans,   Tierrechte – neue Fragen der Tierethik; Literaturbericht; – *b*) *Wolf* Jean Claude, Kritische Bemerkungen dazu: ZevEth 33 (1989) 59-71 / 303-5.

7254 **Sachse** Hans,   Ökologische Philosophie; Natur, Technik, Gesellschaft. Da 1984, Wiss. IX-141 p. DM 34; sb. 21. – ᴿZevEth 33 (1989) 314-6 (K. *Nürnberger*).

7255 *Sahi* Jyoti, The ecological voice of the earth: Vidyajyoti 52 (1988) 341-5.

7256 *Schrenk* Martin, Die Sonne tönt; Umwelt-Ökologie – Mitwelt-Ökologie: Universitas 44 (Stu 1989) 255-261.

7257 **Teutsch** G. M., [Lexikon der Umweltethik 1985 „‚] Mensch und Tier; Lexikon der Tierschützethik. Gö 1987, Vandenhoeck & R. 301 p. DM 28. 3-525-50171-4. – ᴿTsTNijm 29 (1989) 196 (G. *Manenschijn*).

7258 *Weizsäcker* Carl F. von,   Friede – Gerechtigkeit – Bewahrung der Schöpfung: Universitas 44 (Stu 1989) 817-822.

7258* **Westermann** Claus, Schöpfung; wie Naturwissenschaft fragt – wie die Bibel antwortet. Tb (= Stu 1971, Kreuz). FrB 1989, Herder. 206 p. DM 12,90. – ᴿBiKi 44 (1989) 134 (M. *Helsper*).

H3.1 *Foedus* – **the Covenant;** the Chosen People.

7259 *Abe* G. O.,   The community of God and its mission in the OT: AfTJ 17 (Tanzania 1988) 150-161 [< TContext 7/1,77].

7260 *Ábrego* José M.,   El 'resto' de Israel; la gratuidad y la búsqueda, elementos fundantes de una nueva relación con Dios: SalT 77 (1989) 709-718.

7260* **Ahn Keumyoung,** The Sinaitic covenant and law in the theology of Dispensationalism [meaning and history of D.: 'most covenant theologians reject the dispensationalist idea of the covenant of works']: diss. Andrews, ᴰ*LaRondelle* H. Berrien Springs MI 1989. 454 p. 89-22836 – DissA 50 (1989s) 2109-A; RTLv 21,537.

7261 a) *Ashby* Godfrey, The chosen people [... and apartheid], Is 40-55; – b) *Hartin* Patrick J., Apartheid and the Scriptures [*Geyser* A.]: JTSAf 64 (Rondebosch 1988) 34-38 / 20-33 [< TContext 6/2,18].

7262 **Beaucamp** Évode, Les grands thèmes de l'Alliance: Lire la Bible 81, 1988 → 4,8302: ᴿÉTRel 64 (1989) 275s (D. *Lys*); VSp 143 (1989) 313s (J. *Asurmendi*).

7262* a) *Beentjes* Panc, Het verbond in de Bijbel; Boog, besnijdenis en sabbat, wat wij 'tekenen van het verbond' noemen; – b) *Hoogen* Toine van den, Over de strijd van het bestaan; aanzetten tot een verbondstheologie; – c) *Houtepen* Anton, Gods verbond van vrede; – d) *Halkes* Catharina, Verbond met heel de aarde en elkaar; – → 412, Sleutelen 1989, 33-51 / 99-124 / 125-148 / 149-168.

7263 *Breitbart* Sidney, The problem of the 'chosen people': JBQ (= Dor) 18 (1989s) 165-171.

7264 **Bühlmann** W., Les peuples élus; pour une nouvelle approche de l'élection [1981 → 63,6356] 1986 → 2,5330: ᴿNRT 111 (1989) 1054s (J. M.).

7264* *Campbell-Jack* W.C., Prolegomena for reprobation [... scholastic Calvinism]: EvQ 61 (1989) 39-50.

7265 *Cangh* Jean-Marie van, Le pluralisme théologique de l'Ancien Testament [*Vermeylen* J., Dieu de la promesse 1986]: CrNSt 10 (1989) 129-143; Eng. 144.

7265* *Collani* Claudia von, Das Problem des Heils der Heiden [*Mascarell* V. 1701]: NZMissW 45 (1989) 17-36. 93-109.

7266 **Damrosch** David, The narrative covenant 1987 → 3,6734; 4,8305: ᴿBibTB 19 (1989) 71s (Chris *Franke*); Horizons 16 (1989) 374s (Alice L. *Laffey*); Paradigms 5,1 (1989) 72s (M.W. *Gregory*); RelStR 15 (1989) 304s (R. *Polzin*); TTod 46 (1989s) 118 (D.T. *Olson*).

7266* *Davidson* Robert, Covenant ideology in ancient Israel: → 387, World 1989, 323-347.

7267 **Farley** Benjamin W., The providence of God. GR 1988, Baker. 257 p. $17. – ᴿWestTJ 51 (1989) 397-400 (J.M. *Frame*).

7268 *Fisher* Eugene J., Covenant theology and Jewish-Christian dialogue: AmJTP 9,1s [W. Lafayette IN 1988) 5-39 [< NTAbs 33,65].

7268* **Fruchtenbaum** Arnold G., Israelology; the missing link in systematic theology [three covenant approaches plus dispensationalism examined]: diss NYU 1989, ᴰ*Thompson* Norma H. 496 p. 89-16021. – DissA 50 (1989s) 1338-A.

7269 **Graafland** C., Van Calvijn tot Barth, oorsprong en ontwikkeling van de leer der verkiezing [Election] in het Gereformeerd Protestantisme. Haag 1987, Boeken-C. 609 p. *f*89,50. 90-239-04060. – ᴿBijdragen 50 (1989) 457s (J.B.M. *Wissink*).

7270 **Guillén Torralba** Juan, La fuerza oculta de Dios; la elección en el AT: SJer 15, 1983 → 64,6320 ... 4,8309: ᴿCiTom 116 (1989) 626s (J.A.M.).

7270* *Hopkins* D.D., God's continuing covenant with the Jews and the Christian reading of the Bible: Prism 3,2 (St. Paul 1988) 60-75 [< NTAbs 33,205].

7271 *Igenoza* A.O., Universalism and New Testament Christianity: EvRT 12 (Exeter 1988) 261-275 [< NTAbs 33,66: tropical Africa situation ... to promote universalism is alien to the spirit of the NT].

7272 **Joubert** Michael D., The election of Israel from Old Testament to rabbinical times (a terminological study): diss Unisa, ᴰ*Dreyer* H. Pretoria 1987. – DissA 50 (1988s) 2113-A.

7272* *Karlberg* M.W., The significance of Israel in biblical [... covenant] typology: JEvTS 31 (1988) 257-269 [< NTAbs 33,66].

7273 *Kitchen* Kenneth A., The fall and rise of covenant, law, and treaty [*Nicholson* E., God and his people 1986]: TyndB 40 (1989) 118-135.

7273* **Lettinga** Cornelius H., Covenant theology [*Hammond* H. 1644] and the transformation of Anglicanism: diss. Johns Hopkins. Baltimore 1987. 405 p. 88-07443. – DissA 49 (1988s) 525-A.

7274 **Lohfink** Norbert, Der niemals gekündigte Bund [The never-abrogated covenant, at Zion Sisters Studientagung, Rome 3-7.I.1989]; exegetische Gedanken zum christlich-jüdischen Gespräch. FrB 1989, Herder. 120 p. 3-451-21597-7 [Jer 31; Röm 9-11; 2 Kor 3,14...]. – ᴿÖkRu 38 (1989) 595s (F.-W. *Marquardt*).

7274* *Lubsczyk* Hans, Der Bund als Gemeinschaft mit Gott; Erwägungen zur Diskussion über den Begriff 'berit' im AT [< ᴱ*Ernst* W., Dienst der Vermittlung (EThSt 37) Lp 1977, 61-96]: ⇒ 306, Einheit 1989, 185-220.

7275 **Lustiger** Jean-Marie Aron, card. La elección de Dios [con *Missika* Jean-Luis, *Wolton* Dominique]. Barc 1989, Planeta. 408 p. – ᴿSalT 77 (1989) 337-340 (C. *Sarrias*).

7276 **Luz** U., al., La théologie de l'alliance dans la Bible et la tradition. Bern 1987, Féd.Éc.Prot. 90 p. – ᴿÉTRel 64 (1989) 137 (A. *Gounelle*).

7277 *Marchadour* Alain, al., La Bible, histoire d'alliance et de péché: DossB 25 (1988) 3-6 [-26].

7278 **Mathew** P. C., Berith; the Semitic concept of divine human relationship. Kottayam 1987, Ashram. 213 p. R 120 [ExpTim 100,279].

7279 **Nicholson** E. W., God and his people 1986 ⇒ 2,5342 ... 4,8318: ᴿJRel 69 (1989) 233s (E. F. *Campbell*); TsTNijm 29 (1989) 62s (L. *Grollenberg*).

7280 *Olthuis* James H., The covenanting metaphor of the Christian faith and the self psychology of Heinz KOHUT: SR 18 (1989) 313-324.

7280* *Pallatty* Paul, Discipleship and the Covenant: BibleBh ... 15 (1989) 40-57. 254-272.

7281 *Roehrs* Walter R., Divine covenants; their structure and function: ConcordiaJ 14 (1988) 7-27 [< OTAbs 12,138].

7282 **Sperling** S. David, Rethinking covenant in late biblical books [Ezra-Neh, Chr, Ps 106, Dan 9,4-19; Hag-Zech; Is 54,9s; 56,1-7]: Biblica 70 (1989) 50-72; franç. 73.

7283 **Storms** C. Samuel, Chosen for life; an introductory guide to the doctrine of election 1987 ⇒ 4,8324: ᴿBS 146 (1989) 225 (R. P. *Lightner*: reserves).

7284 **Strehle** Stephen, Calvinism, federalism, and scholasticism; a study of the Reformed doctrine of covenant: BaBS 58. Bern 1988, Lang. – ᴿCalvinT 24 (1989) 366-371 (A. *König*: 'price unknown', pp. also).

7285 **Vermeylen** Jacques, Le Dieu de la promesse 1986 ⇒ 2,5344 ... 4,8325: ᴿBrotéria 126 (1988) 113 (I. *Ribeiro da Silva*); Sefarad 49 (1989) 186s (J. R. *Busto Saiz*).

7285* **Ward** James D., The doctrine of election in the theologies of F. SCHLEIERMACHER and K. BARTH: diss. ᴰGerrish B. Chicago 1989. – RelStR 16,188.

Werner Wolfgang, Studien zur alttestamentlichen Vorstellung vom Plan Jahwes 1988 ⇒ 7403.

H3.3 *Fides in VT* - **Old Testament faith.**

7286 **Dumbrell** William J., The faith of Israel; its expression in the books of the Old Testament [.. theology of each] 1988 ⇒ 4,8328: ᴿBL (1989) 104 (A. G. *Auld*); CalvinT 24 (1989) 337-340 (G. N. *Knoppers*); GraceTJ 10 (1989) 243s (M. *Grisanti*).

7287 *Kim Hak-Moo,* ❸ Faith in the Bible [OT-NT]: Samok 126 (Seoul 1989) 4-25 [< TContext 7/1,59].

7288 *Ritschl* Dietrich, Glaube [AT, *Löwenclau* Ilse von; NT, *Lührmann* Dieter]: → 894, EvKL 2 (1988) 186-8 [-190-4; 206, *al.*].

7289 **Schmidt** W. H., Alttestamentlicher Glaube in seiner Geschichte[6rev] [1c. 1968; 2c. 1975; Eng. 1983 → 64,6338]: Studienbücher 6, 1987 → 3,6763; 3-7887-1263-5: RBL (1989) 115 (R. E. *Clements*: nova on ethics, law, postexilic universalism).

7290 *Zobel* Hans-Jürgen, Der frühe Jahwe-Glaube in der Spannung von Wüste und Kulturland: ZAW 101 (1989) 342-365.

H3.5 *Liturgia, spiritualitas VT* – OT prayer.

7290* **Aron** R., Así rezaba Jesús de niño, T*Munera* C. Bilbao 1988, D-Brouwer. 258 p. – RRelCu 35 (M 1989) 138s (M. A. *Martín Juárez*).

7291 *Balentine* Samuel E., Prayers for justice in the Old Testament; theodicy and theology: CBQ 51 (1989) 597-616.

7292 *Beentjes* Panc, Synagoge en kerk in gebed en liturgie [5 books]: Streven 57 (1989) 367-9.

7293 E**Bonora** Antonio, Spiritualità dell'AT. Bo 1987, Dehoniane. 559 p. – RRasT 30 (1989) 393s (L. *Borriello*).

7294 **Clements** R. E., The prayers of the Bible [17 OT, 8 NT here; there are over 100 in all outside Psalms] 1986 → 2,5355; 3,6769: RHeythJ 30 (1989) 442s (B. P. *Robinson*).

7295 **Di Sante** C., La prière d'Israël; aux sources de la liturgie chrétienne [1985 → 2,5358 ... 4,8335],T. P/Montréal 1986, Desclée/Bellarmin. 247 p. F 125. – RNRT 110 (1988) 764s (Y. *Simoens*).

7295* E**Fanuli** A., La spiritualità dell'AT: StSpG, Borla 1988 → 909: RBbbOr 31 (1989) 182s (E. *Jucci*).

7296 *Flusser* David, ❸ 'He has planted it [i.e. the Law (torah)] as eternal life in our midst' [the 'it as', still in MAIMONIDES, has got lost in the current blessing pronounced after a Torah reading]: Tarbiz 58 (1988s) 147-153; Eng. I.

7296* *Galot* Jean, Rivelazione di Cristo e liturgia giudaica: CC 140 (1989,1) 16-30.

7297 **Gammie** John G., Holiness in Israel: OvBT. Minneapolis 1989, Fortress. xv-215 p. $13. 0-8006-1549-2 [TDig 37,158]. – RJRel 69 (1989) 443s (M. A. *Signer*) & 445s (D. *Ellenson*: II. 1988).

7298 E**Green** Arthur, Jewish spirituality 1986 → 2,5361 ... 4,8338: RBA 52 (1989) 48s (E. L. *Greenstein*); Commonweal 115 (1988) 380s (Mary *Gerhart*, also on 3 other EWSp vols.).

7299 **Heinemann** J., La preghiera ebraica, T*Mello* Alberto. Magnano VC 1986, Comunità di Bose. 192 p. Lit. 8000. – RParVi 34 (1989) 155s (M. *Perani*).

7300 *Henrix* Hans H., Von der Nachahmung Gottes; Heiligkeit und Heiligsein im biblischen und jüdischen Denken: ErbAuf 65 (1989) 177-187.

7301 *Homerski* Józef, ❸ Die Berufung und ihre Rolle in der religiösen Formation des alttestamentlichen Gottesvolkes: RoczTK 33,1 (1986) 37-46; deutsch 46.

7302 **Jarach** Paola, Shemà Israel; l'ebreo orante. Mi 1988, Àncora. 134 p. Lit. 11.000. – RHumBr 44 (1989) 600s (M. *Orsatti*); StCattMi 33 (1989) 178 (R. *Fabris*).

7303 *Kavanagh* Aidan, Scripture and worship in synagogue and church: ➤ 3,356, ᴱO'Connor M., Backgrounds 1987, 73-87 [< JBL 108,174].

7304 *Kimelman* Reuven, The daily 'Amidah and the rhetoric of redemption: JQR 79 (1988s) 165-197.

7305 **Manns** Frédéric, La prière d'Israël à l'heure de Jésus 1987 ➤ 2,5370 ... 4,8342: ᴿRelStR 15 (1989) 81 (T. *Zahavy*: fine; replaces IDELSON 1932); Salesianum 51 (1989) 360 (C. *Bissoli*).

7306 *Monloubou* Louis, Signification du culte selon l'Ancien Testament; célébrer pour connaître: EsprVie 99 (1989) 27-30.

7307 **Nigosian** Solomon, Judaism, the way of holiness ➤ 3,6788: Wellingsborough, UK 1986, Aquarian. 224 p. – ᴿSR 18 (1989) 86s (J. D. *Cook*).

7308 **Petuchowski** J. J., Le feste del Signore [ebraiche con relazione al cristianesimo; 1984 ➤ 65,6015],ᵀ. N 1987, Dehoniane. 149 p. Lit. 9000. – ᴿParVi 33 (1988) 235-7 (L. *Villoresi*).

7309 *Ravasi* Gianfranco, 'Il tuo amore è più dolce della vita'; distacco e rinnegamento di sé nell'AT: Servitium 3,65 (1989) 481-490.

7309* *a) Rudd* Philip J., Holiness and cult: ➤ 387, World 1989, 275-289; – *b) Safrai* Shmuel, Gathering in the synagogues on festivals, sabbaths and weekdays: ➤ 845, Synagogues 1987/9, 7-15.

7310 **Sestieri** Lea, La spiritualità ebraica 1987 ➤ 3,6782; 4,8350: ᴿHenoch 11 (1989) 123-5 (M. *Perani*); RBgPg 67 (1989) 219-222 (J. *Klener*, Eng.); RivStoLR 25 (1989) 375s (Elena *Loewenthal*).

7311 **Shelemay** Kay K., Music, ritual and Falasha history: Ethiopian Series 17. East Lansing 1986, Univ. African Studies Center. xv-415 p. $23. – ᴿWorship 62 (1988) 87-90 (P. *Jeffery*).

7312 **Vigée** C., La manna e la rugiada; feste della Torah; Spighe. R 1988, Borla. 272 p. Lit. 20.000. – ᴿStPatav 36 (1989) 622 (G. *Segalla*).

H3.7 *Theologia moralis VT* – **OT moral theology.**

7313 **Baruk** Henri, La Bible hébraïque devant la crise morale d'aujourd'hui. P 1987, Colbo. 100 p. – ᴿRÉJ 147 (1988) 488 (Élisabeth *Couteau*).

7313* **Birch** Bruce C., What does the Lord require; the OT call to social witness 1985 ➤ 1,6630*; 2,5381*: ᴿSWJT 32,1 (1989s) 64s (R. E. *Higgins*).

7314 *Díez Macho* Alejandro, La sexualidad en el Targum [... antropología ... Apócrifos]: ➤ 572, Masculinidad 1989, [423–] 463-552.

7315 **Friedman** Mordechai A., ⊕ Jewish polygamy in the Middle Ages. J 1986, Bialik. 380 p. + 80 photostats. – ᴿRÉJ 147 (1988) 422-4 (J. *Shatzmiller*).

7316 **Goldstein** Andrew, Kings, prophets and exile. L 1988, Religious and moral education. 64 p. £4.45. 0-08-036016-5. – ᴿExpTim 100 (1988s) 478 [C. S. *Rodd*: applications to peace and justice today].

7317 *Jakobovits* I., Los experimentos médicos con seres humanos en la legislación judía: Etica y ciencia 2 (BA 1988) 19-22 [< Stromata 45,498].

7318 *Johnson* B., ṣedeq 'Gerechtigkeit', ṣādaq, ṣᵉdāqāh, ṣaddīq: ➤ 913, TWAT 6,8s (1989) 898-924.

7319 **Lapide** Pinchas, Können wir die Fremden lieben? Mainz 1988, Grünewald. 125 p. – ᴿTGegw 32 (1989) 152s (B. *Häring*).

7320 *Pons* J., L'oppression dans l'AT 1981 ➤ 62,7030 ...: ᴿProtestantesimo 44 (1989) 47 (J. A. *Soggin*).

7321 **Reeder** John P., Source, sanction, and salvation; religion and morality in Judaic and Christian traditions. ENJ 1988, Prentice-Hall. x-140 p. $16 pa. – ᴿHorizons 16 (1989) 401s (A. *Battaglia*).

7322 **Roth** Sol, Halakhah and politics; the Jewish idea of a state. Hoboken 1988, Ktav. 205 p. $17. 0-88125-129-1. – ᴿExpTim 100 (1988s) 437 (Julia *Neuberger*: muddled).

H3.8 *Bellum et pax VT-NT* – **War and peace in the whole Bible.**

7322* *Allen* Pauline, War and the early Greek church historians: → 696, 10th Patristic, 19 (1989) 3-7.

7323 **Aukerman** Dale, Darkening valley, a biblical perspective on nuclear war; foreword *Wallis* Jim. Scottdale PA 1989, Herald. xix-236 p. $15. 0-8361-3501-6.

7324 *Bregman* Lucy, Two imageries of peace; popular psychology and charismatic Christianity: Horizons 16 (1989) 79-96.

7325 **Budzik** Stanisław, Doctor pacis; Theologie des Friedens bei AUGUSTINUS: InnsTheolSt 24. Innsbruck 1988, Tyrolia. 412 p. DM 58 pa. – ᴿTüTQ 169 (1989) 317s (H. J. *Vogt*).

7326 *a) Carroll* Robert P., War; – *b) Lang* B., Segregation and intolerance: → 418, What the Bible really says 1989, 147-170 / 115-135.

7327 *a) Chester* Andrew, The concept of peace in the Old Testament; – *b) Williams* Rowan, Resurrection and peace; – *c) Young* Frances, The early Church; military service, war and peace: TLond 92 (1989) 466-481 / 481-490 / 491-503.

7328 *Cleve* Frederic, Gesetz und Evangelium als die theologische Grundlage für die Friedensarbeit der Kirchen: Lutherische Kirche in der Welt 36 (1989) 125-157 [< ZIT 89,348].

7329 *Coste* René, La doctrine de la paix de JEAN-PAUL II: EsprVie 99 (1989) 594-605.609-616.

7330 *a) Cox* Dermot, Peace and peacemakers in the 'writings' of the Old Testament; – *b) Farahian* Edmond, Aux sources de la véritable paix, Jésus-Christ: StMiss 38 ('Peace; Christianity and other religions' 1989) 1-20 / 21-53.

7330* *Duke* D. N., Asking the right questions about war; a lesson from C. H. SPURGEON: EvQ 61 (1989) 71-80.

7331 **Ebach** Jürgen, L'eredità della violenza 1986 → 3,6823: ᴿÉTRel 63 (1988) 101s (J. *Pons*).

7332 *Ebeling* Hans, Die Strategic Defense Initiative und die Kunst des Sterbens; über Bedingungen der Abschiedlichkeit der Philosophie und des Menschen: → 763, Ars moriendi 1988, 166-175.

7333 *Espinel* José Luis, Nuevo Testamento y pacifismo: RazF 219 (1989) 67-79.

7333* *Esser* Hans H., Die Verantwortung der Kirche für den Frieden der Menschheit und der Schöpfung unter dem Frieden mit Gott: → 120, ᶠLOHSE E., Wissenschaft 1989, 235-258.

7334 *Gensichen* Hans-W., Ⓜ Weltreligionen und Weltfriede: TSzem 31 (1988) 254-6 + cover (ᵀ*Fóris* Eva).

7335 **Häring** Bernhard, Die Heilkraft der Gewaltfreiheit. Dü 1986, Patmos. [Eng. 1986 → 2,5405; 4,8366]. – ᴿTR 85 (1989) 65-67 (E. *Spiegel*: 'Kernstück des Evangeliums' p. 12 & 55; mit *Girard* R. p. 25.34ss, 57,64).

7336 **Hampsch** George H., Preventing nuclear genocide; essays on peace and war: AmerUnivSt 5/50. NY 1988, Lang. 170 p. – ᴿStudies 78 (1989) 229-231 (F. *Brennan*).

7337 **Hauerwas** Stanley, Against the nations 1985 → 2,5406; 3,6832: ᴿJTS 40 (1989) 339s (D. M. *MacKinnon*).

7337* **Hendricks** H., A time for peace; reflections on the meaning of peace and violence in the Bible [= Peace, anyone? 1986 ➤ 3,6834]. L 1988, SPCK. xi-101 p. £3. 0-281-04397-3 [NTAbs 33,263].

7338 *Hilpert* Konrad, [*al.*], Die Verpflichtung zum Frieden und die friedlose Realität: LebZeug 43 (1988) 5-19 [-65].

7338* **Joblin** Joseph, L'Église et la guerre (conscience, violence, pouvoir). P 1988, D-Brouwer. 352 p. F 143. – ᴿComViat 32 (1989) 202s (m.); EsprVie 99 (1989) 48s (R. *Coste*).

7339 *Jones* Gwilym H., The concept of holy war: ➤ 387, World 1989, 299-321: 'Israel means El fights, and Yahweh was the fighting El after whom the people named itself' (WELLHAUSEN).

7339* **Kang Sa-Moon**, Divine war in the OT and in the Ancient Near East [diss. J, Hebrew Univ., ᴰ*Haran, Weinfeld*]: BZAW 177. B/Hawthorne NY 1989, de Gruyter. xv-251 p. DM 118. 3-11-011156-X / 0-89925-278-8 [BL 90, 80, G. *Jones*; TDig 37,67].

7340 **Langendörfer** Hans, Atomare Abschreckung und kirchliche Friedensethik; eine Untersuchung zu neuesten katholischen Friedensverlautbarungen und zur ethischen Problematik heutiger Sicherheitspolitik 1987 ➤ 4,8375; DM 28: ᴿTS 50 (1989) 194-6 (G. S. *Harak*).

7341 *a*) *Lienemann* Wolfgang, Krieg; Gewalt, Gewaltlosigkeit; – *b*) *Stolz* Fritz, Heiliger Krieg: ➤ 894, EvKL 2 (1989) 1474-82 (-85 *al.*). 163-9/446s.

7342 **Lohfink** Norbert, *a*) Il Dio della Bibbia e la violenza 1985 ➤ 2,5418; 3,6845: ᴿProtestantesimo 44 (1989) 225 (J. A. *Soggin*: dovrebbe essere accompagnato dal resto di QDisp 96, 1983 ➤ 64,407*); – *b*) La 'guerra santa' e il 'bando' nella Bibbia come educazione alla pace, ᵀ*Babini* Ellero: CommStrum 104 (1989) 15-25.

7343 *López Azpitarte* Eduardo, Moralidad de la guerra; reflexiones históricas: Proyección 36 (1989) 259-274.

7344 *Luria* B. Ş., ☉ Conquest in patriarchal times: BethM 34,117 (1988s) 97-120.

7345 **Mayhew** Peter, A theology [in defense] of force and violence. L 1989, SCM. xii-112 p. £6 pa. – ᴿTLond 92 (1989) 588 (J. E. *Powell*).

7346 **Mellon** C., I cristiani di fronte alla guerra e alla pace 1986 ➤ 3,6848; Lit. 15.000: ᴿProtestantesimo 44 (1989) 75s (G. *Plescan*: sbilanciato).

7347 ᴱ**Moltmann** Jürgen, Friedenstheologie – Befreiungstheologie; Analysen – Berichte – Meditationen: Kaiser Tb. 26, 1988 ➤ 4,613: ᴿTsTNijm 29 (1989) 421 (A. van *Iersel*).

7347* (Yoder) **Neufeld** Thomas R., God and saints at war; the transformation and democratization of the Divine Warrior in Isaiah 59, Wisdom of Solomon 5, 1 Thes 5, and Eph 6: diss. Harvard, ᴰ*Koester* H. CM 1989. 179 p. 89-25426. – DissA 50 (1989s) 2108-A (under Yoder); RelStA 16,189 (under Neufeld).

7348 ᴱ**Pucciarelli** Enrico, I cristiani e il servizio militare; testimonianze dei primi tre secoli: Bibliotheca Patristica 9, 1987 ➤ 3,6854; 4,8384: ᴿAevum 63 (1989) 137s (A. *Barzanò*); Gnomon 61 (1989) 629-631 (E. *Heck*); RHPR 69 (1989) 335 (P. *Maraval*: 18 textes).

7349 **Ramsey** Paul, Speak up for just war or pacifism; a critique of the [1986] United Methodist Bishops' pastoral letter 'In defense of creation'; epilogue *Hauerwas* Stanley. University Park 1988, Pennsylvania State Univ. vii-214 p. $25; pa. $13. – ᴿQRMin 9,1 (1989) 96-98 (J. *Goodhue*: HAUERWAS's epilogue the best part); TS 50 (1989) 393-5 (J. L. *Allen*)

7350 **Ricca** Paolo, Le chiese evangeliche e la pace. – 1989, Cultura della Pace. – ᴿTSzem 32 (1989) 183s (Karla *Tamás*).

7351 **Spiegel** Egon, Gewaltverzicht; Grundlagen einer biblischen Friedenstheologie 1987 → 3,6859; 4,8387: ᴿDivThom 91 (1988) 488 (G. *Testa*); LebZeug 43 (1988) 66s (J. *Kreiml*); NRT 111 (1989) 941s (L. *Volpe*); TLZ 114 (1989) 761 (C.P. *März*); TPQ 137 (1989) 103s (G. *Wildmann*).

ᴱ**Tambasco** Anthony J., Blessed are the peacemakers; biblical perspectives on peace and its social foundations 1989 → 609.

7352 **Thompson** Henry O., World religions in war and peace. Jefferson NC 1988, McFarland. 241 p. $22. – ᴿJEcuSt 26 (1989) 355s (H. *Gordon*).

7353 **Thorogood** Bernard, The flag and the Cross [is nationalism a war-spawning and freedom-restricting device which religion ought to oppose more courageously?]. L 1988, SCM. 88 p. £5. 0-334-00490-X. – ᴿExpT 100 (1988s) 3s (C.S. *Rodd* would incline to a more affirmative answer).

7354 *Verstraeten* Johan, From just war to proportionate defense; a critical reassessment of a significant tradition: → 102, ᶠJANSSENS L., Personalist 1988, 301-317.

7355 **Weigel** George, Tranquillitas ordinis 1987 → 3,6866; 4,8392: ᴿJRel 68 (1988) 609s (J. *Langan*).

7356 **Wengst** Klaus, Pax romana, Anspruch und Wirklichkeit 1986 → 2.5441 ... 4,8594: ᴿTR 85 (1989) 197-9 (R. *Kampling*: hochinteressant); ZevEth 32 (1988) 152s (W. *Rebell*).

7357 **Wengst** Claus, Pax romana and the peace of Jesus Christ 1987 → 3,6869; 4,8395: ᴿCurrTM 16 (1989) 459 (E. *Krentz*: good but one-sided and overoptimistic); Interpretation 43 (1989) 318.320 (W.E. *Pilgrim*, favorable); JTS 40 (1989) 212 (A.E. *Harvey*: on the whole enlightening).

7358 **Wilkinson** A., Dissent or conform? War, peace and the English churches 1900-1945: 1986 → 2,5442; 3,6870: ᴿCrNSt 10 (1989) 210-2 (Catherine *Guicherd*, franç.).

7359 **Will** James F., A Christology of peace. Louisville 1989, Knox. 154 p. [CBQ 52,385].

7359* **Wink** Walter, Violence and nonviolence in South Africa; Jesus' third way. Ph 1987, New Society. 95 p. – ᴿQRMin 9,2 (1989) 106-9 (D. *Mosser*).

7360 **Yoder** John H., 'To your tents, O Israel'; the legacy of Israel's experience with holy war: SR 18 (1989) 345-362.

H4.1 Messianismus.

7361 **Betz** Otto, Jesus, der Messias Israels; Aufsätze zur biblischen Theologie: WUNT 42, 1987 → 3,190: ᴿProtestantesimo 44 (1989) 130s (U. *Eckert*).

7362 *Clements* R.E., The messianic hope in the Old Testament: JStOT 43 (1989) 3-19.

7363 **Coppens** Joseph, Le Messianisme et sa relève prophétique; les anticipations vétérotestamentaires; leur accomplissement en Jésus²ʳᵉᵛ [¹1974]: BiblETL 38. Lv 1989, Univ. xiii-265 p. Fb 1000. 90-6186-312-0.

7364 *Dehandschutter* B., 'Le Messie est déjà venu'; à propos du thème de la double venue du Messie chez les Pères de l'Église: Bijdragen 50 (1989) 314-320.

7365 *Harrelson* W., Messianic expectations at the time of Jesus: StLuke 32,1 (Sewanee TN 1988) 28-42 [< NTAbs 33,220].

7366 *Katz* Jacob, Messianismus und Zionismus: KIsr 3 (1988) 19-31.

7367 *Moenikes* Ansgar, Messianismus im Alten Testament (vorapokalyp-
tische Zeit): ZRGg 40 (1988) 289-306.
7368 ᴱNeusner Jacob, [Mishnah and Messiah p.265-282], *al.* [*Green* W.,
present. 1-13] Judaisms and their Messiahs 1987 ➤ 4,494: ᴿBL (1989)
140 (J. C. *O'Neill*); JStJud 20 (1989) 248-252 (A. S. van der *Woude*: a
major contribution; tit. pp. lengthy analyses); Month 250 (1989) 103 (J.
Ashton).
7368* *a) Stefani* Piero, Note sul messianismo ebraico postbiblico [*al.*, ...
russo, polacco, americano, africano, secolare]; – *b) Prandi* Carlo, Popoli
'messianici' e popoli 'non-messianici'; un problema storico-religioso [*Rizzi*
A., Radici antropologiche]; – *c) Fabris* Rinaldo, Originalità del messianismo biblico-cristiano [... ed ecclesiologia: *Dianich* S.; *Bof* G.]: ➤ 603,
Popoli messianici 1984/7, 41-77 [–191] / 193-207 [227-233] / 215-226
[235-255 / 257-268].

H4.3   *Eschatologia VT*   –   OT hope of future life.

7369 **Boxel** Piet van, Sjabbatskind; vroegjoodse tradities over leven en dood.
Hilversum 1987, Gooi & S. 96 p. *f* 19,50. – ᴿStreven 55 (1987s) 179 (P.
Beentjes).
7370 *Burns* John B., Some personifications of death in the Old Testament:
IrBSt 11 (1989) 23-34: hunter Qoh 7,26; 9,12; robber Jer 9,20 ...
[< OTAbs 12,130].
7371 **Gowan** Donald E., Eschatology in the OT 1986 ➤ 2,5445 ... 4,8409:
ᴿÉTRel 63 (1988) 451s (D. *Lys*); Gregorianum 70 (1989) 150s (D. *Cox*);
ScotJT 42 (1989) 116-8 (S. H. *Travis*).
7372 *Knibb* Michael A., Life and death in the Old Testament: ➤ 387,
ᴱ*Clements* R. E., World of Ancient Israel 1989, 395-415.
7373 **Krieg** Matthias, Todesbilder im AT oder 'Wie die Alten den Tod
gebildet': ATANT 73, 1988 ➤ 4,8411: DM 72: ᴿBiblica 70 (1989) 274s
(L. *Alonso Schökel*); CBQ 51 (1989) 522s (W. *Brueggemann*: too dense);
RTPhil 121 (1989) 450s (M. *Rose*).
7374 **Martin-Achard** Robert, La mort en face selon la Bible hébraïque 1988
➤ 4,8414: ᴿIrénikon 62 (1989) 285 (J. C.); Protestantesimo 44 (1989) 292
(B. *Costabel*); TLZ 114 (1989) 515s (L. *Wächter*).
7374* *Podella* Thomas, Grundzüge alttestamentlicher Jenseitsvorstellungen,
Šᵉ'ôl: BibNot 43 (1988) 70-89.
7375 *a) Ribera Florit* Joseph, La resurreció dels morts segons la tradició
jueva targúmica: ➤ 69*, ᶠGᴏᴍÀ I., RCatalT 14 (1989) 87-92; Eng. 93; –
b) Schunck Klaus D., Die Korrelation von Sünde und Gericht im AT
[< Theologie im Kontext von Kirche und Gesellschaft (Rostock 1987)
70-88]: ➤ 349, AT 1989, 229-242.

H4.5   *Theologia totius VT*   –   General Old Testament theology.

7375* **Baumann** Rolf, Gottes Gerechtigkeit – Verheissung und Herausforderung für diese Welt: Tb. FrB 1989, Herder. 253 p. DM 16. – ᴿBiKi 44
(1989) 193s (M. *Helsper*).
ᴱ**Brekelmans** C., ²*Vervenne* M., Questions disputées d'Ancien Testament
1989 ➤ 383.
7376 **Childs** Brevard, OT theology in a canonical context 1985 (SCM)
➤ 1,6759 ... 4,8419: ᴿHeythJ 30 (1989) 184s (J. *Blenkinsopp*: mo-
notonous).

7377 **Childs** Brevard S., Teologia dell'Antico Testamento in un contesto canonico [1985 → 1,6759], ᵀScorsone Massimo A.: Parola di Dio. CinB 1989, Paoline. 306 p. Lit. 20.000 [RivB 37,529]. 88-215-1794-2.

7378 Collins John J., Biblical theology and the history of Israelite religion: → 165, Mem. RYAN D., Back to the sources 1989, 16-32.

7379 **De Vries** Simon J., The achievements of biblical religion, a prolegomenon to OT theology 1983 → 64,6490; 1,6762: ᴿExpTim 99 (1987s) 382 [C. S. Rodd: lots of defects].

7380 **Fohrer** Georg, Storia della religione israelitica [1969 → 50,4430] 1985 → 1,6764; 2,5473: ᴿProtestantesimo 44 (1989) 56s (D. Garrone).

7381 **Gese** H., Sulla teologia biblica [1977 ²1983 → 2,164]. ᵀᴱOdasso G.: BiblCuRel 54. Brescia 1989, Paideia. 288 p. Lit. 30.000. – ᴿStPatav 36 (1989) 214s (G. Segalla).

7382 **Gnuse** Robert, Heilsgeschichte as a model for biblical theology; the debate concerning the uniqueness and significance of Israel's worldview: College Theology Soc. Studies in Religion 4. Lanham MD 1989, UPA. viii-179 p. $24.75; pa. $12.75. 0-8191-7245-6; pa. 6-4.

Gottfriedsen C., ... Differenz der Theologie in den beiden Landesteilen [Israels] 1985 → g99.

7383 Günther Hartmut, Die Bibel der Christenheit; Erwägungen zur Diskussion über neue 'Biblische Theologie' seit Gerhard von RAD: LuthTKi 12 (1988) 35-49.

7384 **Hayes** J. H., Prussner F. C., OT theology 1985 → 1,6767 ... 4,8421: ᴿAsbTJ 43,1 (1988) 95s (A. J. Meenan); Protestantesimo 44 (1989) 127s (J. A. Soggin).

7385 **Høgenhaven** Jesper, Problems and prospects of Old Testament theology: Biblical Seminar 6. Sheffield 1988, Academic. 136 p. £8. 1-85075-180-7. – ᴿBL (1989) 107 (R. Davidson); CBQ 51 (1989) 518 (R. E. Murphy); ÉTRel 64 (1989) 113s (J. Pons); ExpT 100 (1988s) 2s (C. S. Rodd); JTS 40 (1989) 512s (G. Auld); VT 39 (1989) 384 (J. A. Emerton).

7386 **House** H. Wayne, Ice Thomas D., Dominion theology [Gn 1,28]: blessing or curse? Portland OR 1988, Multnomah. 460 p. $16. – ᴿBS 146 (1989) 226s (N. L. Geisler: favors Mosaic law for modern society; 'voluntary slavery', gold-based economy, death penalty also for incorrigible children ...).

7387 Jeppesen Knud, The study of the Israelite religion and Old Testament; where do we stand and where should we go?: ScandJOT (1989,2) 140-5.

ᴱ**Johnston** Robert K., The use of the Bible in theology; evangelical options 1985 → 1381.

7387* **Kittel** Gisela, Der Name über alle Namen; Biblische Theologie AT: Biblisch-theologische Schwerpunkte 2. Gö 1989, Vandenhoeck & R. 227 p. DM 29,80. 3-525-61283-4 [BL 90,103, R. E. Clements: 2d volume awaited].

7388 Kramer Werner, 'Eine ebenso freie als biblische Theologie': → 65*, ᶠGEISSER H. 1988, 354-7.

7388* **Legrand** Lucien, Le Dieu qui vient 1988 → 4,8427: ᴿBiblica 70 (1989) 295-8 (J. Swetnam); ÉTRel 64 (1989) 475 (M. Spindler: excellent; à ajouter sa propre bibliographie, Bible and Mission, Leiden 1981); MélSR 46 (1989) 97s (M. Huftier); VSp 143 (1989) 657 (H. Cousin).

7389 a) **Lemke** Werner E., Is Old Testament theology an essentially Christian theological discipline? [so Childs; and so it has in fact been since its inception around 1800]; – b) Walker-Jones Arthur W., The role of theological imagination in biblical theology: HorBT 11,1 (1989) 59-71 / 73-97.

7390 *Levenson* Jon D., Why Jews are not interested in biblical theology:
➤ 3,355, ᴱNeusner J., Judaic perspectives 1987, 281-307.

7391 *McKenzie* John L., Aspects of Old Testament thought: ➤ 384, NJBC
(1989s) 1284-1315 [1310s added by R. E. *Brown*].

7392 **Maillot** A., Gros plan sur l'Ancien Testament; ses thèmes et ses défis
1989 ➤ 4,1079: ᴿBL (1989) 110 (C. J. A. *Hickling*).

7392* **Murrell** Nathaniel S., A critical appraisal of the significance of James
BARR's critique of biblical theology: diss. Drew. Madison NJ 1988. –
RTLv 21, p. 538.

7393 **Pawlikowski** John, Jesus and the theology of Israel: Zacchaeus Theol.
Wilmington 1989, Glazier. 99 p. $7 [BibTB 19/4 cover].

7394 **Rad** Gerhard von, ❷ Teologia Starego Testamentu [⁶1975] ᵀ*Widła*
Bogusław, 1986 ➤ 3,6922: ᴿPrzPow 799 (1988) 444-7 (W. *Chrostowski*).

7395 **Reventlow** H., Problems of OT theology 1985 ➤ 1,6780*b*; 2,5481:
ᴿHeythJ 30 (1989) 72s (R. E. *Clements*).

7395* *Rendtorff* Rolf, The future of biblical theology; a Jewish and Christian
interpretation: TorJT 5 (1989) 280-292 [< ZAW 102,289].

7396 *Scharbert* Josef, Die biblische Theologie auf der Suche nach ihrem
Wesen und ihrer Methode: MüTZ 40 (1989) 7-26.

7396* *Schmid* Hans H., Vers une théologie du Pentateuque. ᵀ*Pury* Albert de:
➤ 601, Pentateuque 1987/9, 361-386.

7397 *Schmidt* Werner H., Pentateuch und Prophetie; eine Skizze zu
Verschiedenartigkeit und Einheit alttestamentlicher Theologie: ➤ 105,
ᶠKAISER O., Prophet 1989, 181-195.

7397* **Shear-Yashuv** Aharon, The theology of Salomon L. STEINHEIM:
Studies in Judaism in modern times 7. Leiden 1986, Brill. 116 p. *f*68.
90-04-07670-0. – ᴿBijdragen 50 (1989) 446 (F. De *Meyer*).

7398 ᴱ**Sitarz** E., Höre Israel ... Theologie des ATs 1987 ➤ 4,327: ᴿBL (1989)
116 (R. A. *Mason*).

7398* *Stoebe* Hans J., Überlegungen zur Theologie des Alten Testaments
[< ᶠ*Hertzberg* H. 1965, 200-220]: ➤ 362, Geschichte 1989, 268-288.

7399 *Strange* John, Heilsgeschichte *und* Geschichte; ein Aspekt der biblischen
Theologie, ᵀ*Olsen* Christa M.: ScandJOT (1989,2) 100-113 (114-135,
N. P. *Lemche*; 136-9, Replik).

7399* *Stuhlmacher* Peter, Die Mitte der Schrift — biblisch-theologisch
betrachtet: ➤ 120, ᶠLOHSE E., Wissenschaft 1989, 29-56.

7400 **Thoma** Clemens, Teologia cristiana dell'Ebraismo [1978 ➤ 60,8804;
Eng. 1980 ➤ 61,5470]: Radici 3. CasM 1983, Marietti. xxxiv-233 p. Lit.
23.000. – ᴿProtestantesimo 44 (1989) 233 (J. A. *Soggin*).

7400* **Ulrich** Peter, Die alttestamentliche Theologie Hermann SCHULTZ' im
Zusammenhang seines Lebens und Werkes: Diss. ᴰ*Smend* R. Göttingen
[RTLv 21,542 sans date]. 243 p.

7401 **Van Buren** Paul, Theology of the Jewish-Christian reality III. Christ in
context 1980-8 ➤ 61,k176 ... 4,8436.8555: ᴿCCurr 38 (1988s) 496-9
(Mary J. *Ryles*); Horizons 16 (1989) 379s (J. *Koenig*, 3); JEcuSt 26 (1989)
362 (D. J. *Lasker*, 3: 'there is a sense of unease in watching a Christian
attempting to rewrite his religion in such a manner'); TS 50 (1989) 174s
(D. J. *Harrington*: remarkably creative recovering, 3).

7402 **Vermeylen** J., Het geloof van Israël; theologie van het OT. Boxtel/
Brugge 1989, KBS/Tabor. 434 p. *f*49,50. – ᴿStreven 57 (1989s) 372s (P.
Beentjes).

7403 **Werner** Wolfgang, Studien zur alttestamentlichen Vorstellung vom Plan
Jahwes: BZAW 173. B 1988, de Gruyter. xii-334 p. DM 140. 3-11-

011255-8. – ᴿBL (1989) 129 (W. L. *Houston*); BLitEc 90 (1989) 128s (M. *Delcor*); RHPL 69 (1989) 197-9 (J. G. *Heintz*); TLZ 114 (1989) 585-7 (L. *Wächter*).

7403* **Westermann** Claus, Elements of OT theology [1978 ➤ 60,8807], ᵀ*Stott* Douglas W. 1982 ➤ 63,6488: ᴿRelStT 8,3 (1988) 45s (D. B. *MacKay*).

H5.1   Deus – NT – God [as Father ➤ H 1.4].

7404 **Gesché** Adolphe, Waarom ik in God geloof: CollatVʟ 19 (1989) 52-75.

7405 **Hurtado** Larry W., One God, one Lord; early Christian devotion and ancient Jewish monotheism 1988 ➤ 4,8842: ᴿExpTim 100,7 2d-top choice (1988s) 242s (C. S. *Rodd*); JBL 108 (1989) 712-4 (Beverly R. *Gaventa*); SR 18 (1989) 369s (Mary M. *Schaefer*); TLond 92 (1989) 321s (L. *Houlden*); TS 50 (1989) 198s (J. J. *Collins*).

7406 **Joest** Wilfried, Der Weg Gottes mit dem Menschen: Dogmatik [1, Die Wirklichkeit Gottes ²1987] 2. Gö 1986, VR. xii-697p. DM 28,80. 3-525-03264-1. – ᴿTsTKi 59 (1988) 64-66 (J.-O. *Henriksen*).

7407 **Kasper** Walter, Is God obsolete? [Irish Theol. Asn. 14-15 April 1989, ᵀ*Breslin* Eamonn]: IrTQ 55 (1989) 85-98 (99-113, 114-124, responses *O'Hanlon* G., *Daly* G.).

7407* **Koch** Kurt, Dunkle Facetten im Gottesbild des Christentums: Judaica 45 (1989) 95-109.

7408 **Li** *Young-Hún*, ❻ God in the Bible [NT compared with OT]: Samok 124 (Seoul 1989) 4-20 [< TContext 7/1,57].

7408* *a) Lohfink* Gerhard, Gott in der Verkündigung Jesu [< ᴱ*Hengel* M., Heute von Gott reden 1977, 50-65]: ➤ 300, Studien zum NT 1989, 27-44; – *b) Lähnemann* J., Jesu Rede von Gott — als christlicher Beitrag im Gespräch mit Menschen anderen Glaubens: ➤ 131, ᶠ*Marxsen* W., Jesu Rede 1989, 443-456.

7409 **Macky** Peter W., The metaphors of God's mercy and justice in the New Testament; how are they related: ProcGLM 9 (1989) 231-245.

7410 **Minear** P. S., The God of the Gospels; a theological workbook. Atlanta 1988, Knox. 144 p. $10. 0-8042-0545-0 [NTAbs 33,251].

7411 **Muñoz** Ronaldo, Dios de los Cristianos 1986 ➤ 3,6950; 4,8445: ᴿEfMex 6 (1988) 462-5 (J. F. *Gómez Hinojosa*); SalT 76 (1988) 242 (R. N. de Z.); TVida 29 (1988) 303-6 (M. *Arias Reyero*).

7412 **Muñoz** Ronaldo, Der Gott der Christen, ᵀ*Goldstein* Horst: Bibliothek Theologie der Befreiung 2. Dü 1987, Patmos. 232 p. DM 38,80. – ᴿTR 85 (1989) 132s (A. *Tafferner*).

7413 **Schlosser** Jacques, Le Dieu de Jésus, étude exégétique: LDiv 129, 1987 ➤ 3,6952; 4,8446: ᴿBLitEc 90 (1989) 66s (S. *Légasse*); Burgense 30 (1989) 585s (F. *Pérez Herrero*); CrNSt 10 (1989) 152s (V. *Fusco*); ÉTRel 63 (1988) 290 (A.-G. *Martin*); IndTSt 25 (1988) 94-101 (L. *Legrand*); RTLv 20 (1989) 89 (C. *Focant*); ScEspr 41 (1989) 116s (L. *Sabourin*); ScripTpamp 21 (1989) 351s (J. L. *Lorda*).

7414 **Simonis** Walter, Gott in Welt; Umrisse christlicher Gotteslehre. St. Ottilien 1988, EOS. 391 p. DM 38. – ᴿNRT 111 (1989) 911-3 (L. *Renwart*).

7415 **Smith** Francis R., The God question, a Catholic approach. NY 1988, Paulist. ix-240 p. $15. – ᴿNRT 111 (1989) 955 (R. *Escol*); TLZ 114 (1989) 914-6 (F. *Mildenberg*: eindrücklich).

7416 **Van Roo** William A., Telling about God I-3, 1986s ➤ 2,3248 ... 4,8448: ᴿArTGran 52 (1988) 290s (R. *Franco*, 3); Bijdragen 50 (1989) 220s (W. G.

Tillmans, 1-3); BLitEc 90 (1989) 157s (H. *Crouzel,* 2); JRel 69 (1989) 426s (J. *Carlson:* interesting project, limited realization); TLZ 114 (1989) 474-6 (J. *Roloff,* 3).

7417 **Vives** Josep, 'Si oyerais su Voz...'; exploración cristiana del misterio de Dios: PresT 48. Santander 1988, Sal Terrae. 366 p. 84-293-0814-8. – ᴿGregorianum 70 (1989) 576 (L. F. *Ladaria*); SalT 77 (1989) 429s (F. *Manresa*).

7417* **Vorgrimler** Herbert, Doctrina teológica de Dios 1987 ⮕ 3,6954*b*: ᴿTVida 29 (1988) 310s (C. *Casale*).

7418 *Zur Mühlen* Karl-Heinz, Zur Gotteslehre M. LUTHERS auf dem Hintergrund der mittelalterlichen Theologie: Luther 19 (1988) 53-68.

H5.2 **Christologia ipsius NT.**

7419 **Berten** Ignace, Christ pour les pauvres; Dieu à la marge de l'histoire: Théologies. P 1989, Cerf. 128 p. F 69. – ᴿRTLv 20 (1989) 383s (R. *Guelluy:* christologie inspirée presqu'uniquement des Synoptiques ... méthode des théologies de la libération).

7420 CAIRD George B. mem., The glory of Christ in the NT; studies in Christology, ᴱHurst L. ... 1987 ⮕ 3,35: ᴿBZ 33 (1989) 141-3 (R. *Schnackenburg*); ScotJT 42 (1989) 591-3 (Frances M. *Young:* 17 of the 21 are superb).

7421 **Dreyfus** François, Did Jesus know he was God? [1984 ⮕ 65,6193 ... 4,8450*], ᵀ*Wrenn* Michael J. Ch 1988, Franciscan Herald. xiii-154 p. $14 pa. 0-8199-0899-1 [NTAbs 33,406]. – ᴿHomP 89,9 (1988s) 77s (K. *Baker:* thoroughly Catholic exegesis).

7422 **Dunn** James D. G., Christology in the making; a New Testament inquiry into the origins of the doctrine of the Incarnation² [¹1980 ⮕ 61,8088 ... 2,5553]. L 1989, SCM. xlvi-443 p. £15. 0-334-00237-0.

7423 ᴱ**Dupont** Jacques, Jésus aux origines de la christologie²ʳᵉᵛ [= ¹1975 + J. *Lambrecht,* Jesus and the Law, Mk 7,1-23 < ETL 53 (1975) 24-82, ici 358-415]: BiblETL 40. Lv 1989, Univ. 458 p. Fb 1500.

7424 **Fitzmyer** Joseph A., *a)* Scripture and Christology 1986 ⮕ 2,5518; 4,8451: ᴿTrinJ 10 (1989) 226-233 (D. S. *Huffman*); – *b)* Geloven in vraag en antwoord; de historische Jezus en de Christus van het geloof,ᵀ. Kapellen 1987, Patmos. 170 p. Fb 595. – ᴿStreven 55 (1987s) 665s (P. *Beentjes*).

7425 *González* Carlos I., Herejías cristológicas en la comunidad del Nuevo Testamento: Medellín 14,55 (1988) 386-427 [< TContext 6/2,69].

7426 **Hengel** Martin, Il figlio di Dio; l'origine della cristologia 1984 ⮕ 2,5528; StBPaid 67: ᴿNicolaus 16 (1989) 349s (A. *Moda*).

7427 **Hultgren** Arland J., New Testament Christology; a critical assessment and annotated bibliography [1917 items]: Bibliographies and indexes in religious studies 12. Westport CT 1988, Greenwood. XIV-485 p. $65. 0-313-25188-6 [TDig 36,374].

7428 **Jonge** Marinus de, Christology in context; the earliest Christian response to Jesus 1988 ⮕ 4,8455*: ᴿCBQ 51 (1989) 365s (S. P. *Kealy*); Horizons 16 (1989) 158s (D. P. *Gray*); JBL 108 (1989) 707-710 (L. W. *Hurtado*); TS 50 (1989) 171s (P. J. *Achtemeier*).

7429 **Jossa** Giorgio, Dal Messia al Cristo; le origini della cristologia: StBPaid 88. Brescia 1989, Paideia. 192 p. Lit. 20.000. 88-394-0433-3.

7430 **Krieg** Robert A., Story-shaped Christology 1988 ⮕ 4,8456: ᴿGregorianum 70 (1989) 162s (J. *McDermott*); Horizons 16 (1989) 170s (J. A.

La Barge); PrPeo 3 (1989) 291 (M. *Evans)*; ScripTPamp 21 (1989) 725s (P. *O'Callaghan)*.

7431 **Luck** Ulrich, Der Anfang der Christologie, die Sache Jesu und die Gottesherrschaft: ➤ 131, FMARXSEN W., Jesu Rede 1989, 28-44.

7432 **McDonald** H.D., Jesus, human and divine; an introduction to New Testament Christology. Lanham MD 1989, UPA. 144 p. $10.25. 0-8191-7236-7 [NTAbs 33,265].

Manigne Jean-Pierre, Le maître des signes [... paraboles: vol. 1 de 3 sur la Christologie] 1987 ➤ 4629.

7433 **Padrón** D., *al.,* Cristología biblica: IUSI-Tesis 3. Caracas 1989, Trípode. 286 p. 980-208-123-X. – RTXav 39 (1989) 374 (A. *Echeverri)*.

7434 **Richard** Earl, Jesus, one and many; the Christological concept of New Testament authors 1988 ➤ 4,8459: RJBL 108 (1989) 710-2 (L.W. *Hurtado)*; TS 50 (1989) 575s (C. *Bernas)*.

7435 **Sabourin** Léopold, La christologie à partir de textes clés 1986 ➤ 2,5537 ... 4,8460: RRBibArg 51 (1989) 127s (A.J. *Levoratti)*; RechSR 77 (1989) 110s (B. *Sesboüé)*; Salesianum 51 (1989) 376 (A. *Amato)*; TLZ 114 (1989) 121-3 (W. *Wiefel)*.

7436 **Scroggs** Robin, The reality and revelation of God; Christology in Paul and John 1988 ➤ 4,8461: RCalvinT 24 (1989) 357-360 (W.P. *DeBoer)*; Interpretation 43 (1989) 327. 330 (D.R. *Edwards)*.

7437 **Segalla** Giuseppe, La cristologia del NT 1985 ➤ 1,6854 ... 4,8462: RNicolaus 16 (1989) 351s (A. *Moda)*.

7438 **Segundo** Juan L., The historical Jesus of the Synoptics: Jesus Yesterday and Today 2 [of 5], 1985 ➤ 1,6855* ... 4,8563: RHeythJ 30 (1989) 355s (J. *Coventry)*; TorJT 4 (1988) 143-5 (H. *Wells)*.

7439 **Segundo** Juan L., The humanist Christology of Paul: Jesus Yesterday and Today 3 [of 5], 1986 ➤ 2,5542 ... 4,8563: £10.50: RHeythJ 30 (1989) 356-8 (J.P. *Galvin)*; RelStR 15 (1989) 45-47-51 (A.T. *Hennelly*; Marsha A. *Hewitt*: 1-3).

7440 **Segundo** Juan L., The Christ of the Ignatian Exercises: Jesus Yesterday and Today 4 [of 5], TEDrury John. L 1988, Sheed & W. 147 p. £10.50. – RHeythJ 30 (1989) 358-360 (J.A. *Munitiz)*; Month 250 (1989) 148-150 (P. *Endean*: agreeably outrageous).

7441 **Segundo** Juan Luis, An evolutionary approach to Jesus of Nazareth [= El hombre de hoy 2/4, 1982], TDrury John: Jesus Yesterday and Today 5. Mkn 1988, Orbis. vii-148 p. 0-88344-588-3.

7442 **Segundo** Juan Luis, Jésus devant la conscience moderne; l'histoire perdue [El hombre de hoy ante Jesús de Nazareth 3]: CogF 148. P 1988, Cerf. 399 p. F 239. – RÉTRel 64 (1989) 650 (C. *Izard*, aussi sur vol. 2, Paul); LavalTP 45 (1989) 453s (M. *Rondeau)*; MélSR 46 (1989) 171-3 (B. *Rey)*; NRT 111 (1989) 913-5 (L. *Renwart*, aussi sur Le Christ des Exercices Engl.).

7443 **Segundo** Juan-Luis, Le christianisme de Paul; l'histoire retrouvée [El hombre de hoy, abregé et revisé], TGuibal Francis: CogF 151. P 1988, Cerf. – REsprVie 99 (1989) 293s (É. *Cothenet)*; Études 370 (1989) 831-6 (R. *Marlé)*; RTLv 20 (1989) 358-363 (C. *Focant)*. ➤ 5876.

7444 — **Marlé** René, Foi, idéologie, religion chez J.-L. SEGUNDO: RechSR 76 (1988) 267-282.

Tèze Jean-M., Théophanies du Christ 1988 ➤ d377.

7446 **Tuñí** J.O., Jesús en comunidad; el Nuevo Testamento, medio de acceso a Jesús: PresTeol 52. Santander 1988, Sal Terrae 154 p. pt. 690. – RProyección 36 (1989) 328 (E. *Barón)*.

7446* a) *Zeller* Dieter, Die Menschwerdung des Sohnes Gottes im Neuen Testament und die antike Religionsgeschichte; – b) *Schilson* Arno, 'Gott wird immer mehr Mensch' (D. SÖLLE); Aspekte eines postchristlichen Humanismus: ➤ 769, Menschwerdung 1986/9, 141-176 / 177-215.

H5.3   *Christologia praemoderna* – Patristic through Reformation.

7447 *Arnau* Ramón, Determinantes cristológicos en las eclesiologías del siglo XIV: ➤ 7, FALFARO J., EstE 64 (1989) 335-364.

7447* *Baxter* Anthony, Chalcedon, and the subject in Christ: DowR 107 (1989) 1-21.

7448 a) *Bienert* Wolfgang A., Zur Logos-Christologie des ATHANASIUS von Alexandrien in Contra Gentes und De Incarnatione; – b) *Wolinski* Joseph, L'emploi de *triás* dans les 'Traités contre les Ariens' d'Athanase d'Alexandrie: ➤ 696, 10th Patristic 21 (1989) 402-419 / 448-455.

7448* **Brandy** Hans C., Die späte Christologie des Johannes BRENZ: ev. Diss. D*Baur*. Göttingen 1988s. – TR 85 (1985) 516.

7449 **Brennecke** Hanns C., Studien zur Geschichte der Homöer; der Osten bis zum Ende der homöischen Reichskirche [Hab. Tü 1986]: BeitHistT 73. Tü 1988, Mohr. x-280 p. 3-16-145246-1. – RTLZ 114 (1989) 822-4 (H. G. *Thümmel*).

7450 **Contri** Antonio, Gesù Cristo figlio di Dio e salvatore ... patristico 1985 ➤ 1,6867 ... 3,6991: RProtestantesimo 44 (1989) 301s (G. *Scuderi*).

7451 *Cross* Richard, Nature and personality in the Incarnation [*Freddoso* Alfred, Faith and Philosophy 3 (1986) 27-53, on AQUINAS and SCOTUS-OCKHAM]: DowR 107 (1989) 237-254.

7452 **Drobner** Hubertus R., Person-Exegese und Christologie bei AUGUSTINUS [Diss. R 1984] 1986 ➤ 4,8470: REstAg 23 (1988) 707s (P. de *Luis*); Salesianum 51 (1989) 368s (A. *Amato*).

7453 *Drobner* Hubertus R., Outlines of the Christology of St. AUGUSTINE: MeliT 40,1 (1989) 45-58.

7454 *Galot* Jean, 'Une seule personne, une seule hypostase'; origine et sens de la formule de Chalcédoine: Gregorianum 70 (1989) 251-275; Eng. 276.

7455 *Geerlings* W., Die Christologie AUGUSTINS; zum Stand der Forschung: ➤ 707, Symposium 1987/9, 219-230.

7456 **Gilg** Arnold, Weg und Bedeutung der altkirchlichen Christologie: Tb 59. Mü 1989, Kaiser. 109 p. DM 10,80. – RÖkRu 38 (1989) 485s (H. *Vorster*).

7457 *Gould* Graham, CYRIL of Alexandria and the formula of reunion: DowR 106 (1988) 235-252.

7458 **Grillmeier** Alois, Jesus der Christus im Glauben der Kirche 2/1, 1986 ➤ 2,5557 ... 4,8473: RKatKenk 26,52 (1987) 178-185 (S. *Takayanagi* ❶).

7459 **Grillmeier** Alois, a) Jesus der Christus im Glauben der Kirche [I, 1979 ➤ 60,8909] 2/2 Die Kirche von Konstantinopel im 6. Jahrhundert. FrB 1989, Herder. 616 p. DM 95 [TR 86,253]; – b) Christ in Christian tradition 2/1, 1987 ➤ 3,7001; 4,8474: RAnglTR 70 (1988) 367-9 (L. *Urban*); Horizons 16 (1989) 159s (J. C. *Cavadini*); RechSR 77 (1989) 538-540 (B. *Sesboüé*).

7460 **Hanson** R. P. C., The search for the Christian doctrine of God; the Arian controversy 318-381: 1988 ➤ 4,8475; £35: RRSPT 73 (1989) 466-9 (G.-M. de *Durand*); TLond 92 (1989) 405-7 (A. *Louth*).

7461 *Hattrup* Dieter, Ekstatik der Geschichte; Identität im Licht der Christologie BONAVENTURAS: ➤ 92, FHünermann P., Christologie 1988, 59-87.

7462 *a) Havrilak* Gregory, Chalcedon and orthodox Christology today; – *b)*
Breck John, Reflections on the 'problem' of Chalcedonian Christology:
SVlad 33 (1989) 127-145 / 147-157.

7463 **Henne** Philippe, À propos de la Christologie du Pasteur d'Hermas; la
cohérence interne...: diss. LvN, ᴰ*Halleux* A. de: ➤ 986, Travaux de
doctorat en théologie 12 (1989) fasc 11 [< RSPT 72 (1988) 569-578].

7464 *Kannengiesser* Charles, Le Verbe de Dieu selon Aᴛʜᴀɴᴀsᴇ d'Alexandrie:
LavalTP 45 (1989) 229-242.

7465 **Ladaria** Luis F., La cristología de Hɪʟᴀʀɪᴏ de Poitiers: AnGreg 255.
R 1989, Pont. Univ. Gregoriana. xx-324 p. Lit. 45.000. 88-7652-605-6.

7466 *Lawrenz* M. E.ᴵᴵᴵ, The Christology of John CHRYSOSTOM: ➤ 696,
StudPatr 10/22 (1987.9) 148-153.

7467 ᵀᴱ**Leonardi** Claudio, Il Cristo 3. Testi teologici e spirituali in lingua
latina da Agostino ad Anselmo di Canterbury: Scrittori greci e latini.
1989, Mondadori. – ᴿRBén 99 (1989) 338 (P. *Verbraken*).

7468 *McGuckin* John A., Did Aᴜɢᴜsᴛɪɴᴇ's Christology depend on Tʜᴇᴏ-
ᴅᴏʀᴇ of Mopsuestia?: RivStoSR 25 (1989) 444-457.

7469 *Maraval* Pierre, La lettre 3 de Gʀᴇɢᴏɪʀᴇ de Nysse dans le débat
christologique: RevSR 61 (1987) 74-89.

7470 *Meyendorff* John, Chalcedonians and non-Chalcedonians; the last steps
to unity: SVlad 33 (1989) 319-329.

7471 **Nielsen** Lauge O., Theology ... G. PORRETA ... Incarnation 1982
➤ 65,6247; 1,6893: ᴿBTAM 14 (1989) 704s (G. *Mathon*).

7472 *Pieszczech* Szczepan, ❷ Una caratteristica della cristologia di
sant'Aɢᴏsᴛɪɴᴏ: VoxP 14 (1988) 185-195; ital. 195.

7473 **Pifarré** Cebrià, Aʀɴᴏʙɪᴏ el Joven [5º sec.] y la cristología del
'conflictus': Scripta et Documenta 35. Montserrat 1988, Abadia. 261 p.
– ᴿETL 65 (1989) 180-3 (A. de *Halleux*); NRT 111 (1989) 895s (L.
Renwart); RSPT 73 (1989) 341 (J.-P. *Jossua*).

7473* **Piret** Pierre, Le Christ et la Trinité selon Mᴀxɪᴍᴇ le Confesseur 1983
➤ 64,6651...1,6896: ᴿÉglT 19 (1988) 108-111 (J. K. *Coyle*).

7474 *Sanders* J., Le traité 'De l'incarnation' du ms. Paris B. N. syr. 371, F.
107ᵛ-125ʳ [syriaque avec français en face] (2ᵈᵉ partie): Muséon 102 (1989)
147-163.

7475 *Schmidt* Andrea B., Die Refutatio des Timotheus Aelurus gegen das
Konzil von Chalcedon; ihre Bedeutung für die Bekenntnisentwicklung der
armenischen Kirche Persiens im 6, Jh.: OrChr 73 (1989) 149-165.

7476 *Schönborn* Christoph, La conscience du Christ; approches histo-
rico-théologiques: EsprVie 99 (1989) 81-7.

7476* **Séguenny** André, The Christology of Caspar SCHWENKFELD; spirit and
flesh in the process of life transformation: TStRel 35, 1987 ➤ 4,8487:
ᴿChH 50 (1989) 387-9 (W. *Klaassen*).

7477 **Sesboüé** Bernard, Gesù Cristo nella tradizione della Chiesa; per una
attualizzazione della cristologia di Calcedonia [1982 ➤ 64,6654],ᵀ. CinB
1987, Paoline. 343 p. – ᴿSalesianum 51 (1989) 377s (A. *Amato*).

7477* *Torrance* Iain R., Christology afer Chalcedon; Sᴇᴠᴇʀᴜs of Antioch
and Sᴇʀɢɪᴜs the Monophysite 1988 ➤ 4,8490*; £24.50: ᴿDowR 107
(1989) 67-69 (A. *Louth*); JTS 40 (1989) 641s (L. R. *Wickham*); ScotJT 42
(1989) 598-600 (A. *Heron*).

7478 **Wéber** Édouard-Henri, Le Christ selon saint Thomas d'AQᴜɪɴ: JJC 35
P 1989, Desclée. 336 p. F 165. – ᴿFreibZ 36 (1989) 489-493 (J.-P. *Torrell*); NRT 111 (1989) 896-8 (L. *Renwart*).

7479 [ᴱ*Welte* B.] *Schlier* H., *al.* [Tagung Untermarchtal 1969] La storia della cristologia primitiva [1970] 1986 ➤ 2,5545*: ᴿProtestantesimo 44 (1989) 133s (F. *Ferrario*); ScripTPamp 21 (1989) 317-9 (J. M. *Casciaro*).

7480 *a) Wesche* Kenneth P., Christological doctrine and liturgical interpretation in Pseudo-Dɪᴏɴʏsɪᴜs: SVlad 23 (1989) 53-73; – *b) Williams* Rowan D., *al.,* Inkarnation: ➤ 894, EvKL 2 (1988) 665-682.

H5.4   (*Commentationes de*) *Christologia* **moderna.**

7481 **Amato** Angelo, Gesù il Signore; saggio di cristologia: Teol. Sist. 4. Bo 1988, Dehoniane. 504 p. Lit. 35.000. 88-10-50304-X. – ᴿAntonianum 64 (1989) 475 (V. *Battaglia*); Gregorianum 70 (1989) 791-4 (R. *Fisichella*); NRT 111 (1989) 901-3 (L. *Renwart,* avec deux réflexions qui 'etendent la discussion').

7482 **Auer** Johann, *a*) Jesus Christus, Gottes und Mariä 'Sohn' 1986 ➤ 2,5582: ᴿBijdragen 50 (1989) 339 (W. G. *Tillmans*); – *b*) Jesucristo, hijo de Dios y hijo de María [Jesu und Mariä 'Sohn' 1986 ➤ 2,5582],ᵀ. Barc 1989, Herder. 548 p. [SalT 77,841].

7483 *Beaudin* Michel, Une christologie d'Amérique Latine [Soʙʀɪɴᴏ J. 1986]: ScEspr 41 (1989) 361-9.

7484 **Bordoni** M., Gesù di Nazaret; presenza, memoria, attesa: BiblTeolContemp 57. Brescia 1988, Queriniana. 464 p. Lit. 39.000. – ᴿAsprenas 36 (1989) 538s (B. *Forte*).

7485 *a) Bordoni* Marcello, Problemi ed orientamenti dell'attuale cristologia sistematica; – *b) Tilliette* Xavier, Sulla cristologia idealistica; – *c) Sorrentino* Sergio, La cristologia di Sᴄʜʟᴇɪᴇʀᴍᴀᴄʜᴇʀ; saggio di lettura critica; – *d) Coda* Piero, L'attualità inattuale della cristologia hegeliana; – *e) Berlendis* Alfredo, Dal problema del 'Gesù storico' al significato cosmico di Cristo; itinerari della cristologia protestante contemporanea: FilT 3 (1989) 3-22 / 23-39 / 40-69 / 70-90 / 91-109.

7486 **Borghesi** Massimo, La figura di Cristo in Hᴇɢᴇʟ 1983 ➤ 64,6663; 1,6919: ᴿFilT 3 (1989) 219s (Isabella *Garavagno Barbero*).

7487 **Brambilla** Franco G., La cristologia di Sᴄʜɪʟʟᴇʙᴇᴇᴄᴋx; la singolarità di Gesù come problema di ermeneutica teologica [diss. Pont. Univ. Gregoriana 1985, ᴰ*Alfaro* J.]: Pont. Sem. Lombardo Roma pubbl. 30. Brescia 1989, Morcelliana. 620 p. Lit. 60.000. 88-372-1363-8. – ᴿNRT 111 (1989) 900s (L. *Renwart*).

Brock Rita N., Journeys by heart; a Christology of erotic power [... Mark] 1988 ➤ 8860.

7489 *Brown* R. E., Christology [Resurrection, etc.]: ➤ 384, NJBC (1989s) 1354-59 [1323-81].

7491 **Chesnut** Glenn F., Images of Christ; an introduction to Christology 1984 ➤ 65,6279 ... 2,5596: ᴿIrTQ 55 (1989) 247s (W. G. *Jeanrond*).

7492 **Coakley** Sarah, Christ without absolutes; a study of the Christology of Ernst Tʀᴏᴇʟᴛsᴄʜ [diss.1982]. Ox 1988, Clarendon. 214 p. £25. 0-19-826670-7. – ᴿÉTRel 64 (1989) 455s (A. *Gounelle*); ExpTim 100 (1988s) 312 (T. J. *Gorringe*); NRT 111 (1989) 898 (L. *Renwart*); RelSt 25 (1989) 399-401 (D. A. *Pailin*); TLond 92 (1989) 324s (R. *Morgan*); TLZ 114 (1989) 692-4 (F. W. *Graf*); TS 50 (1989) 803-5 (M. L. *Stackhouse*); TsTNijm 29 (1989) 294 (T. *Schoof,* also on ᴱ*Renz* H. ➤ 727*).

7492* *Coda* Piero, Un'introduzione storica e metodologica alla cristologia di S. Bᴜʟɢᴀᴋᴏᴠ: Lateranum 55 (1989) 435-469.

7493 **Danet** Henriette, Gloire et croix de Jésus-Christ; l'analogie chez H. Urs von BALTHASAR comme introduction à sa christologie [diss. Paris, Inst. Cath.]: JJC 30. P 1987, Desclée. 320 p. F 148. – RIrénikon 62 (1989) 300 (S. N.).

7494 *a) Doré* Joseph, Jésus-Christ, l'aujourd'hui de Dieu; – *b) Léon-Dufour* Xavier, Du présent à la présence, selon l'Évangile: Christus 36 (P 1989) 6-15 / 46-58.

7494* **Dorries** David W., Nineteenth century British Christological controversy, centring upon Edward IRVING's doctrine of Christ's human nature: diss. Aberdeen 1987. 515 p. – BRDX-81370. – DissA 49 (1988s) 527-A (no summary).

7495 *Forte* Bruno, *a)* Cristologia [risposta alla recensione *de Rosa* Giuseppe]: DivThom [89s (1986s) 3-133] 91 (1988) 361-6 (367-374, de Rosa); – *b) Forte*, risposta in Asprenas 36 (1989) 282-7.

7496 **Frangipane** D., Alla destra di Dio o l'apoteosi di Gesù I. Caltanisetta 1988, Krinon. 463 p. Lit. 40.000. – RHumBr 44 (1989) 301s (R. *Tononi*: cristologia ma di genere letterario non facile da definire).

7496* **Garascia** M. Martha, The search for an ascending Christology ... John B. COBB: diss. Iliff/Denver 1988, DBrown D. 233 p. 88-09291. – DissA 49 (1988s) 846-A.

7497 **Gertler** Thomas, Jesus Christus – die Antwort der Kirche auf die Frage nach dem Menschsein 1986 ➤ 2,5611; 4,8512: RGregorianum 70 (1989) 158-160 (R. *Fisichella*).

7498 **González** Carlos I., Cristologia; Tu sei la nostra salvezza: TeolFund-Dogm. CasM 1988, Piemme. 428 p. Lit. 45.000. 88-384-2047-1. – RAntonianum 64 (1989) 476s (V. *Battaglia*); NRT 111 (1989) 904s (L. *Renwart*); Teresianum 40 (1989) 248s (M. *Caprioli*).

7498* **Habra** Georges, La foi en Dieu incarné, I. Justification rationnelle. P 1989, Cariscript. 273 p. 2-902161-06-9.

7499 *Hamilton* Andrew, Recent issues in Christology: AustralasCR 66 (1989) 94-103.

7499* **Hatchett** Randy L., Towards a post-critical Christological hermeneutic; an analysis of the hermeneutics of Raymond E. BROWN: diss. SWBaptist Theol. Sem. 1989. 274 p. 89-22314. – DissA 50 (1989s) 2108-A.

7500 **Hattrup** Dieter, Die Bewegung der Zeit; naturwissenschaftliche Kategorien und die Christologie; Vermittlung von Sein und Geschichte: Münst Beit Theol 56. Münster 1988, Aschendorff. x-296 p. DM 58 [JTS 49,742].

7501 *Haubner* Reinhard, Christologie und metaphysischer Gottesbegriff bei Werner ELERT: KerDo 35 (1989) 128-162; Eng. 163.

7502 **Hebblethwaite** Brian, The Incarnation; collected essays in Christology 1987 ➤ 3,235: RPacifica 2 (1989) 236-8 (P. F. *Carnley*).

7503 **Helminiak** Daniel A., The same Jesus; a contemporary Christology 1986 ➤ 2,5619 ... 4,8519: RHeythJ 30 (1989) 361s (J. P. *Galvin*); RRel 48 (1989) 948s (T. J. *Tekippe*).

7503* **Horrell** John S., Analysis of the deity of Christ in BOFF and SEGUNDO: diss. Dallas Theol. Sem. 1988. 480 p. 89-13834. – DissA 50 (1989s) 1703-A.

7504 *a) Hospital* Clifford G., Toward a Christology for global consciousness; – *b) Duffy* Stephen J., The Galilean Christ; particularity and universality: JEcuSt 26 (1989) 45-57 / 154-174.

7505 **Herbst** Karl, Der wirkliche Jesus; das total andere Gottesbild². Olten 1988, Walter. 300 p.

7506 **Hünermann** Peter, Offenbarung Gottes in der Zeit; Prolegomena zur Christologie [20 years' studies but not a Sammelwerk]. Münster 1989, Aschendorff. vi-199 p. [TPhil 64,479]. 3-402-03293-2.

7506* **Junker** Maureen, Das Urbild des Gottesbewusstseins; zur Entwicklung der Christologie SCHLEIERMACHERS von der ersten zur zweiten Auflage der Glaubenslehre: kath. Diss. ᴰMetz. Münster 1988s. – TR 85 (1989) 517.

7507 **Kaiser** Alfred, Der christologische Neuansatz 'von unten' bei Piet SCHOONENBERG; Versuch einer Darlegung und kritischen Würdigung seines christologischen Entwurfs und dessen Weiterentwicklung mit Blick auf die Theologie des Nikolaus von KUES: Diss. ᴰHaubst. Trier 1988s. – TR 85 (1989) 518.

7507* **Küng** Hans, The incarnation of God ... HEGEL [1970] 1987 ➤ 3,7061; 4,8522: ᴿCCurr 39 (1989s) 371-3 (A. Dragstedt); Thomist 53 (1989) 693-700 (T. Weinandy).

7508 **Kulisz** Józef, ❷ En quête d'une christologie nouvelle [... TEILHARD]: PrzPow 806 (1988) 73-83; franç. 83.

7509 **Lambiasi** F., Credo ... Cristologia 1988 ➤ 4,8523: ᴿAsprenas 36 (1989) 96s (N. Ciola).

7510 **La Potterie** Ignace de, **Schindler** David, Il paradosso dell'Incarnazione: ➤ 715, ᴱNeri Emma, Meeting 89, 207-214-217.

7511 **Lefebure** Leo D., Towards a contemporary Wisdom Christology ... RAHNER ... PITTENGER [diss. 1987 ➤ 3,6968*]. Lanham MD 1988, UPA. 298 p. 0-8191-7151-4; pa. 2-2. – ᴿExpTim 100 (1988s) 434 (T.J. Gorringe).

7512 **McGrath** Alister E., The making of modern German Christology 1986 ➤ 2,5626 ... 4,8529: ᴿHeythJ 30 (1989) 360s (R. Morgan); JAAR 57 (1989) 415-7 (B.D. Marshall); TsTKi 59 (1988) 134s (T. Austad).

7512* **Madonia** Nicolò, Ermeneutica e cristologia in Walter KASPER: diss. Pont. Univ. Gregoriana, ᴰDupuis J. R 1989. 467 p. – RTLv 21, p. 538.

7513 **Marshall** Bruce, Christology in conflict [➤ 3,7069]; the identity of a savior in RAHNER and BARTH 1987: ᴿInterpretation 43 (1989) 436 (A.M. Olson); JAAR 57 (1989) 866-9 (E. TeSelle); JTS 40 (1989) 700-3 (P.S. Fiddes: elegance, simplicity); Thomist 53 (1989) 149-153 (J.J. Buckley).

7514 **Martorell** José, La palabra encadenada: Jesús Mesías I (de 3). Valencia 1988, auct. 210 p. – ᴿNRT 111 (1989) 906s (L. Renwart).

7514* **Marxsen** Willi, The limit to the possibility of Christological assertions: ➤ 143, ᶠOGDEN S., Witness 1989, 43-54.

7515 **Moltmann** Jürgen, Der Weg Jesu Christi; Christologie in messianischen Dimensionen. Mü 1989, Kaiser. 379 p. DM 48 pa. 3-459-01294-5 [Greg 70,831]. – ᴿTsTNijm 29 (1989) 422 (H.-E. Mertens).

7516 — **Fernández García** Bonifacio, Cristo de esperanza; la cristología escatológica de J. MOLTMANN: Bibl./Est. 105. Salamanca 1988, Univ. Pontificia. 323 p. – ᴿCiuD 202 (1989) 256s (J.M. Ozaeta); ETL 65 (1989) 466s (E. Brito); NRT 111 (1989) 898s (L. Renwart).

7517 **Morris** Thomas V., a) The logic of God Incarnate 1986 ➤ 2,5634; 3,7072: ᴿHeythJ 30 (1989) 449s (G. O'Collins: brilliant); ModT 6 (1989s) 112s (D. Brown); RelSt 25 (1989) 409-423 (J. Hick); ScotJT 42 (1989) 243-6 (Grace M. Jantzen). – b) Understanding God incarnate: AsbTJ 43,2 (1988) 63-77.

7517* **Noceda García** Carmen, El Yo de Jesucristo; la controversia teológica en España: diss. ᴰMateo-Seco L. Pamplona 1989. 325 p. – RTLv 21,570.

7518 **Odell-Scott** David W., Logic and metaphysics; the Christological de-structuring of metaphysical theism [... HEIDEGGER M.]: diss. Vanderbilt, ᴰScott C. Nashville 1989. 406 p. 90-06855. – DissA 50 (1989s) 3252-A.

7518* **Ohlig** Karl-H., Christologie I-II: Texte, Dogmatik 4/1s. Graz 1989, Styria. 227 p.; 239 p. 3-222-11832-9; 86-8 [Greg 70,828].

7519 *Pattison* George, Idol or icon? some principles of an aesthetic Christology: LitTOx 3,1 (1989) 1-15 [< ᴢɪᴛ 89,225].

7520 *Pérez Valera* J. Eduardo, ◑ The fruits from LONERGAN's Insight; an example from Christology: KatKenk 26 (1987) 75-122; 343-385. Eng. viii-ix; xi-xiii.

7520* **Posset** Franz, LUTHER's Catholic Christology according to his Johannine lectures of 1527, diss. 1988 ➤ 4,8485; 0-8100-0275-2. – ᴿBijdragen 50 (1989) 455-7 (T. *Bell*).

7521 *Puthur* Bosco, Christological developments after Vatican II: Living Word 94/6 (Alwaye 1988) 349-362 [< TContext 6/2,33].

7522 **Ramm** Bernard L., An evangelical Christology, ecumenic and historic 1985 ➤ 3,7078; 4,8536: ᴿWestTJ 50 (1988) 226-230 (R. G. *Gruenler*).

7524 *Renwart* Léon, 'Premier-né de toute créature'; chronique de christologie: NRT 111 (1989) 895-918.

7524* **Reumann** John, Jesus and Christology: ➤ 394, NT/Interpreters 1989, 501-564.

7525 **Rey** Bernard, Jésus le Christ [➤ 4,8538]: Dieu se donne un visage: Parcours. P/Québec 1988, Centurion / Paulines. 124 p. – ᴿScEspr 41 (1989) 387 (G. *Langevin*: aide-mémoire plutôt qu'initiation).

7526 *a*) *Sanna* Ignazio, Karl RAHNER, una cristologia antropologica; – *b*) *Bosco* Nynfa, Le cristologie processuali; – *c*) *Piovesana* Gino K., Cristo nel pensiero russo: FilT 3 (1989) 132-146 / 147-176 / 110-131.

7527 **Semplici** Stefano, Socrate e Gesù; HEGEL dall'ideale della grecità al problema dell'Uomo-Dio. Padova 1987, Cedam. – ᴿFilT 3 (1989) 217-9 (Chiara *Giacometti*).

7528 **Snyder** Mary H., The Christology of Rosemary R. RUETHER; a critical introduction. Mystic CT 1988, Twenty-Third. xv-152 p. $13 pa. 0-89622-358-2 [NTAbs 33,137]. – ᴿRelStR 15 (1989) 345s (T. W. *Tilley*).

7530 *Thompson* William M., Jesus' unsurpassable uniqueness; a theological note: Horizons 16 (1989) 101-115 [responses, *Swidler* Leonard, *Hick* John, 116-120 / 121-4; rejoinder 125-130].

7531 **Thurmer** John, The Son in the Bible and the Church 1987 ➤ 4,8553: ᴿThemelios 14 (1988s) 107s (H *Bigg*); TLond 92 (1989) 133s (T. *Williams*).

7532 **Tilliette** Xavier, La christologie idéaliste: JJC 28, 1986 ➤ 2,5666; 3,7090: ᴿFilT 3 (1989) 195-200 (M. *Pagano*); RelStR 15 (1989) 246s (T. F. *O'Meara*).

7533 *Tilliette* Xavier, Die Vielfalt der christologischen Ansätze im Frühwerk Maurice BLONDELS: TPhil 64 (1989) 199-209.

7534 *Tinker* Melvin, Truth, myth and incarnation: Themelios 14 (1988s) 11-17.

Van Buren Paul M., Christ in context 1988 ➤ 7401.

7536 **Verweyen** Hansjürgen, Christologische Brennpunkte²ʳᵉᵛ: Christliche Strukturen in der modernen Welt 20. ... 154 p. – ᴿTR 85 (1989) 46s (H. *Waldenfels*).

7537 *Vető* Miklós, De la hiérophanie jusqu'à la christophanie; le problème d'une religion chrétienne: RThom 89 (1989) 40-70.

7538 **Vidal Taléns** José, El mediador y la mediación; la cristología de Walter KASPER en su génesis y estructura: Ferrer Valentina 21. Valencia 1988, Soler. 498 p. pt 2800 [TR 85,527]. – ᴿCarthaginensia 5 (1989) 296s (F. *Martínez Fresneda*); ScripTPamp 21 (1989) 725 (L. F. *Mateo-Seco*).

7539 *Vogler* Werner, Der historische Jesus und die nachösterliche Christusverkündigung; zum Verhältnis von expliziter und impliziter Christologie: ➤ 197, ᶠTRILLING W., Christus bezeugen 1989, 43-54.

7540 **Willers** Ulrich, Friedrich NIETZSCHES antichristliche Christologie; eine theologische Rekonstruktion [Diss. Tübingen]: InnsbTSt 23. Innsbruck 1988, Tyrolia. 383 p. DM 86 [TR 85,432].

7541 **Wong** Joseph H. P., Logos-symbol in the Christology of K. RAHNER 1984 ➤ 1,6997 ... 3,7096: ᴿJRel 68 (1988) 465s (O. *Heintz*).

H5.5   *Spiritus Sanctus; pneumatologia*   –   The Holy Spirit.

7541* **Anderson** James, A Vatican II pneumatology of the paschal mystery [on the missionary activity of the Church]; the historical-doctrinal genesis of Ad gentes I,2-5 [diss. Gregorian] 1988 ➤ 4,8558. – ᴿTS 50 (1989) 403 (K. *McDonnell*).

7542 **Bauman** Harold E., Presence and power; releasing the Holy Spirit in your life and church. Scottdale PA 1989, Herald. 124 p. $8. 0-8361-3493-1.

7543 **Bermejo** Luis M., The spirit of life; the Holy Spirit in the life of the Christian 1987 ➤ 4,8561: ᴿAmerica 161 (1989) 192s (L. *Dupré*); TS 50 (1989) 207s (J. F. *Russell*).

7544 **Boespflug** F., Dio nell'arte [1984 ➤ 65,6357], ᵀ*Rizzi* A. Genova 1986, Marietti. 356 p. Lit. 40.000. 88-211-6774-7. – ᴿCrNSt 9 (1988) 205-8 (A. *Natali*).

7545 *Borchert* G. L., The Spirit and salvation: CriswellT 3,1 (Dallas 1988) 65-78 [< NTAbs 33,168].

7545* *Byatt* Anthony, The Holy Spirit — a further examination [of D. P. FRANCIS' statistics]: ExpTim [96 (1984s) 136s] 100 (1988s) 215s.

7546 **Comblin** José, Der Heilige Geist [1983s ➤ 2,5688], ᵀ*Goldstein* H. Dü 1988, Patmos. 235 p. DM 44. – ᴿTLZ 114 (1989) 381s (E. *Lessing*).

7547 **Comblin** José, The Holy Spirit and liberation, ᵀ*Burns* Paul. Maryknoll NY 1989, Orbis. xvi-213 p. $14. 0-88344-367-8 [TDig 36,362].

7548 *Cottier* Georges, Le Saint-Esprit, Maître de sagesse: NVFr 63 (1988) 161-178.

7548* **Dabney** Delmar L., Die Kenosis des Geistes; Kontinuität zwischen Schöpfung und Erlösung im Werk des Heiligen Geistes: ev. Diss. ᴰ*Moltmann* J. Tübingen 1988s. 307 p. – TR 85 (1989) 518; RTLv 21,568.

7549 **Durrwell** F. X., *a*) Der Geist des Herrn; Tiefe Gottes – schöpferische Weite 1986 ➤ 3,7108; ᵀ*Schmid* Alois: ᴿFreibZ 35 (1988) 268s (A. *Schenker*); – *b*) El Espíritu Santo en la Iglesia 1986 ➤ 2,5691; 3,7107: ᴿTVida 29 (1988) 307s (Annelies *Meis*).

7550 **Ferraro** G., Lo Spirito Santo ... AGOSTINO 1987 ➤ 4,8567: ᴿNRT 111 (1989) 306 (L. J. *Renard*).

7550* **Ferreira de Farias** José J., O Espírito e a história; o Pneuma Divino no recente debate sobre as pessoas da Trindade: diss. Pont. Univ. Gregoriana, ᴰ*Rosato* P. R 1989. 446 p. – RTLv 21,569.

7551 *Ford* J. M., The Holy Spirit and mission in the New Testament: Missiology 16 (Scottdale PA 1988) 439-453 [< NTAbs 33,203].

7552 **Granado** Carmelo, El Espíritu Santo en la teología patrística 1987 ⇥ 3,7112; 4,8571: ᴿRazF 218 (1988) 253s (J. *Corella*); TVida 29 (1988) 306s (Annelies *Meis*).

7553 **Gresham** John L.ᴶ, Charles G. FINNEY's doctrine of the baptism of the Holy Spirit 1987 ⇥ 4,8572; $7: ᴿBS 146 (1989) 114 (K. L. *Sarles*: Pentecostal precursor).

7553* **Jackson** Pamela E., The Holy Spirit in the catechesis and mystagogy of CYRIL of Jerusalem, AMBROSE, and John CHRYSOSTOM: diss. Yale. NHv 1988. – RTLv 21, p, 548.

7554 *Henriksen* Jan-Olav, [Norw.] Spirit and [human] nature; pneumatology and the understanding of nature in W. PANNENBERG: TsTKi 59 (1988) 175-188; Eng. 188.

Kinkel G., Holy spirit as mother, ᴰ1988 ⇥ 7083*.

7554* **Kallarangatt** Joseph, The Holy Spirit, bond of communion of the churches; a comparative study of the ecclesiology of Yves CONGAR and Nikos NISSIOTIS: diss. Pont. Univ. Gregoriana, Nº 3596, ᴰ*Dupuis* J. R 1989. 693 p.; extr. 182 p. – RTLv 21,566.

7555 **Lambiasi** F., Lo Spirito Santo; mistero e presenza 1987 ⇥ 4,8574: ᴿLateranum 55 (1989) 258-260 (N. *Ciola*); ParVi 33 (1988) 159s (C. *Ghidelli*); ScEspr 41 (1989) 122s (R. *Fisichella*).

7556 **Lavatori** R., Lo Spirito Santo ... BASILIO 1986 ⇥ 2,5705: ᴿAngelicum 66 (1989) 347-9 (G. M. *Salvati*); ScEspr 40 (1988) 385s (G. *Pelland*); TVida 29 (1988) 87 (Annelies *Meis*).

7557 **Lessmann** Thomas, Rolle und Bedeutung des Heiligen Geistes in der Theologie John WESLEYS: Beit. Gesch. ev.-meth. Kirche 30. Stu 1987, Christliches-VH. 174 p. DM 10. – ᴿTPQ 137 (1989) 290 (L. *Pöll*); TR 85 (1989) 395 (Teresa *Berger*).

7557* **Meis Wörmer** sr. Annelies, La formula de la fe 'Creo en el Espíritu Santo' en el Siglo II [diss. 1978]: AnChile 29/2, 1980 ⇥ 64,6771: ᴿForumKT 4 (1988) 77-79 (A. *Ziegenaus*).

7558 *Milet* Jean, 'Je crois au Saint-Esprit': EsprVie 99 (1989) 129-137. 145-154, 161-4.

7559 **Moysa** Stefan, ⊕ '*Teraz zaś*' Now there remain these three [theological virtues]. Wsz 1986, AkadTK. 341 p. – ᴿSTWsz 26,1 (1989) 274-7 (L. *Balter*).

7559* *Orazem* France, [in Slovene] The action of the Holy Spirit in the sacraments: BogVest 47 (1987) 89-103.

7560 *a)* *Outler* Albert, A focus on the Holy Spirit; Spirit and spirituality in John Wesley; – *b)* *Hellwig* Monika K., In Spirit and in truth; a Catholic perspective on the Holy Spirit: QRMin 8,2 (1988) 3-18 / 36-48.

7560* *Rebić* Adalbert, Experientia religiosa Spiritus Sancti in Sacra Scriptura: BogSmot 59,1s (congressus de Spiritu Sancto, 1989) 40-66 croat.; 66 deutsch.

7561 *Salachas* Dimitri, Il ruolo dello Spirito Santo nei sacramenti dell'iniziazione cristiana secondo il documento di Bari: ⇥ 703, Atti VII, Nicolaus 16 (1989) 19-31.

7562 **Santos Ferreira** José Manuel dos, Teologia do Espírito Santo em AGOSTINHO de Hipona [diss. Univ. Cat. Portuguesa]: Fac. Teol. Fundamenta 3. Lisboa 1987, Didaskalia. 115 p. – ᴿGregorianum 70 (1989) 178 (J. *Galot*); ScEspr 41 (1989) 120s (B. de *Margerie*).

7563 ᴱ**Saraiva Martins** José, Credo in Spiritum Sanctum 1982/3 ⇥ 64,531; 1,7032: ᴿCarmelus 35 (1988) 240s (L. P. *Rogge*).

7564 **Schütz** Christian, Einführung in die Pneumatologie 1985 ⇥ 1,7034 ... 3,7127: ᴿTPQ 137 (1989) 87 (O. B. *Knoch*).

7565 *Schütz* Christian, Wir glauben an den Heiligen Geist, den Herrn und Lebensspender: TPQ 137 (1989) 58-60.

7567 *Sesboüé* Bernard, Pneumatologie; bulletin de théologie dogmatique: RechSR 76 (1988) 115-128.

7568 *Siegwalt* Gérard, Le Saint Esprit créateur, puissance de relation: ÉTRel 64 (1989) 235-248.

7568* **Strong** Barry R., The economy of the Spirit in ecumenical perspective: diss. Pont. Univ. Gregoriana, ᴰ*Dupuis* J. R 1989. 492 p. – RTLv 21,566.

7569 *Takayanagi* Shunichi, ❶ The poetry of Gerard Manley HOPKINS and pneumatology: KatKenk 28,55 (1989) 59-96; Eng. v-vii.

7569* **Thompson** Michael D., The Holy Spirit and human instrumentality in the training of new converts; an evaluation of the missiological thought of Roland ALLEN: diss. Golden Gate Baptist Theol. Sem., ᴰ*DuBose* F., 1989, 170 p. 89-23304. – DissA 50 (1989s) 2118-A.

7570 *Valentini* Alberto, Presenza ed esperienza dello Spirito: ➤ 611, Come leggere 1988/9, 138-151.

7570* *Verheul* A., Les symboles de l'Esprit Saint dans la Bible et la liturgie: QLtg 69 (1988) 67-94; Eng. 94s.

7571 *Welker* Michael, a) Der Heilige Geist: EvT 49 (1989) 126-141; – b) The Holy Spirit: TTod 46 (1989s) 5-20.

7572 **Wells** David F., God the evangelist 1987 ➤ 4,8585: ᴿEvQ 61 (1989) 179s (F. *Cotterell*); Themelios 14 (1988s) 109 (C. *Hingley*).

7573 *Zimmermann* Gunter, Die pneumatologische Tradition in der reformierten Bekenntnisbildung: TZBas 45 (1989) 352-374.

H5.6 *Spiritus et Filius*; **'Spirit-Christology'.**

7573* *Berthold* George C., CYRIL of Alexandria and the Filioque: ➤ 696, 10th Patristic, 19 (1989) 143-7.

7574 **Dupuy** Michel, L'Esprit, Souffle du Seigneur: JJC Résonances, 1988 ➤ 4,8587: ᴿVSp 142 (1988) 598s (P.-T. *Camelot*).

7575 **Durrwell** F.-X., L'Esprit du Père et du Fils. Maranatha 18. P/Montréal 1989, Médiaspaul/Paulinas. 73 p. F 54. 2-7122-0344-5 [ÉTRel 64,672].

7576 *Halleux* André de, a) Manifesté par le Fils; aux origines d'une formule pneumatologique: RTLv 20 (1989) 3-31; Eng. 139; – b) La question de la procession du Saint-Esprit; aspect théologique: PrOrChr 38 (1988) 6-17.

7576* *Kupiec* Kazimierz, ❷ Filioque: ➤ 891, EncKat 5 (1989) 196-9.

7577 **Lavatori** Renzo, Lo Spirito Santo dono del Padre e del Figlio; ricerca sull'identità dello Spirito Santo. Bo 1987, Dehoniane. 300 p. Lit. 30.000. – ᴿCC 140 (1989,1) 303s (G. *Blandino*: perplessità forse non giustificata).

7578 *Martin* Vincent, Aspects théologiques du 'Filioque': Irénikon 62 (1989) 37-50; Eng. 50.

7579 *O'Donnell* John, In him and over him; the Holy Spirit in the life of Jesus: Gregorianum 70 (1989) 25-45; franç. 45.

7580 *Schneider* Alfred, Christus unctus Spiritu Sancto: BogSmot 59 (1989) 89-101 (croat.); 101-3 deutsch.

7581 *Suttner* Ernst C., Ist das 'filioque' noch kirchentrennend?: TPQ 137 (1989) 248-258.

H5.7 *Ssma Trinitas* – **The Holy Trinity.**

7581* **Black** Arthur B.S., The Trinity and the contemporary doctrine of God; towards a new model for understanding the nature of the Christian

God: diss. Westminster UK, 1988. 327 p. BRDX-84635. – DissA 49 (1988s) 3760-A.

7582 **Bobrinskoy** Boris, Le mystère de la Trinité 1986 ➤ 3,7150; 4,8598*: ᴿRET 49 (1989) 318-320 (M. *Gesteira*).

7583 **Boff** Leonardo, La Trinidad, la sociedad, la liberación[2] 1987 ➤ 3,7151; 4,8599: ᴿEfMex 7 (1989) 146-9 (J. *Trinidad González*).

7584 **Boff** Leonardo, Trinity and society [... e la libertação 1986 ➤ 2,5734], ᵀ*Burns* Paul. Mkn/L 1988, Orbis / Burns-Oates. 272 p. $14/£9. – ᴿCCurr 39 (1989s) 502.504 (L. *Doohan*); NewTR 2,3 (1989) 104s (S. *Bevans*); PrPeo 3 (1989) 110s (M. *Evans*); TTod 46 (1989s) 205s (Shirley C. *Guthrie*).

7585 **Boff** Leonardo, Der dreieinige Gott: Bibl. Theologie der Befreiung. Dü 1987, Patmos. 279 p. DM 44. 3-491-77711-9. – ᴿTsTNijm 28 (1989) 75s (E. *Borgman*, auch über Muñoz und Comblin).

7586 *Cain* James, The doctrine of the Trinity and the logic of relative identity: RelSt 25 (1989) 141-152.

7586* *Ciola* Nicola, Monoteismo cristiano come monoteismo trinitario: Lateranum 55 (1989) 208-257 (409-434).

7587 **Coda** Piero, *a*) Il negativo e la Trinità; ipotesi su Hegel 1987 ➤ 4,8604: ᴿFilT 3 (1989) 238-242 (V. *Mancuso*). – *b*) La via del negativo e la Trinità; per una risposta alla 'sfida' hegeliana: Asprenas 36 (1989) 315-330.

7588 **Courth** Franz, Trinität – in der Scholastik: HbDG 2/1b, 1985 ➤ 1,7058 ... 3,7157: ᴿForumKT 4 (1988) 156-8 (E. *Schadel*).

7588* **Daniélou** J., La Trinità e il mistero dell'esistenza [1968, ital. 1969]. Brescia 1989, Queriniana. 76 p. – ᴿLateranum 55 (1989) 473-6 (N. *Ciola*).

7589 **Forte** Bruno, Trinidad como historia 1988 ➤ 4,8609: ᴿRLatAmT 6,16 (1989) 132s (J. V.).

7590 **Forte** Bruno, La Trinité comme histoire; essai sur le Dieu chrétien. ... 1989, Nouvelle Cité/Méristème. 265 p. F 176. – ᴿEsprVie 99 (1989) 475 (P. *Jay*).

7591 **Forte** Bruno, The Trinity as history; the saga of the Christian God, ᵀ*Rotondi* Paul. Staten Island NY 1989, Alba. xi-250 p. $15. 0-9189-0552-2 [TDig 37,53].

7592 **Hilberath** Bernd J., Der Personbegriff der Trinitätstheologie ... Rahner/ Tertullian, ᴰ1986 ➤ 2,5753 ... 4,8615: ᴿGregorianum 70 (1989) 160s (F.-A. *Pastor*, también sobre Sheehan T., Rahner); TPQ 137 (1989) 85s (A. *Seigfried*).

7593 **Ladaria** Luis, S. Hilario, La Trinidad 1986 ➤ 2,5759 ... 4,8620: ᴿRBibArg 29 (1988) 61-64 (F. *García Bazán*); RTLv 20 (1989) 224s (A. de *Halleux*, aussi sur Rocher A.).

7593* **Mason** George A.ᴶ, God's freedom as faithfulness; a critique of Jürgen Moltmann's social trinitarianism: diss. SW Baptist Theol. Sem. 1987. 276 p. 88-06938. – DissA 49 (1988s) 527-A.

7594 *Miell* David K., Barth on persons in relationship [also within God]; a case for further reflection?: ScotJT 42 (1989) 541-555.

7595 **Miller** David L., Three faces of God; traces of the Trinity in literature and life 1986 ➤ 2,5763; 3,7174: ᴿJRel 68 (1988) 124s (Ruth E. *Saffar*).

7596 *Molnar* Paul D., The function of the immanent Trinity in the theology of Karl Barth; implications for today: ScotJT 42 (1989) 367-399.

7597 **Moltmann** Jürgen, Trinidad y reino de Dios 1986 (1980 ➤ 62,7453a) ➤ 1,7083: ᴿTXav 39 (1989) 123-9 (M. *Gutiérrez J.*).

7598 **O'Donnell** John J., The mystery of the triune God 1988 ➤ 4,8626: ᴿHeythJ 30 (1989) 64-67 (B. R. *Brinkman*); IrTQ 55 (1989) 243s (G.

O'Hanlon); NRT 111 (1989) 955s (L.-J. *Renard*); Pacifica 2 (1989) 120-2 (A.J. *Kelly*); TS 50 (1989) 207 (H.J. *Ryan*).

7599 **O'Donnell** John J., Il mistero della Trinità,ᵀ. R 1989, Pont. Univ. Gregoriana/Piemme. 176 p. Lit. 25.000. 88-7652-603-X / 88-384-1391-6.

7600 *O'Donnell* John, La Trinidad como comunidad divina [< Gregorianum 69 (1988) 5-34], ᵀ*Aute Puiggari* Germán, ᴱ*Sivatte* R. de; SelT 28 (1989) 185-196.

7601 **Salman** Elmar, Neuzeit und Offenbarung; Studien zur trinitarischen Analogik des Christentums: StudAnselm 94, 1986 ➤ 4,8633: ᴿTR 85 (1989) 219s (B J. *Hilberath*).

7602 *Salvati* Giuseppe M., Teologia trinitaria della croce [diss. R, Angelicum]. T-Leumann 1987, Elle Di Ci. 216 p. – ᴿSapienza 41 (1988) 312-6 (G. *Turco*).

7603 **Schadel** Erwin, Bibliotheca trinitariorum II, 1988 ➤ 4,979: ᴿFreibZ 35 (1988) 257-261 (S. M. *Wittschier,* 1); Lateranum 55 (1989) 264 (N. *Ciola*); TPhil 64 (1989) 295s (J. *Splett*).

7604 *Schoonenberg* Piet, Eine Diskussion über den trinitarischen Personbegriff, Karl RAHNER und Bernd Jochen HILBERATH: ZkT 111 (1989) 129-162.

7605 *Takahashi* Wataru, ◉ The Trinitarian theology of St. AUGUSTINE: KatKenk 28,55 (1989) 35-58; Eng. ii-v.

7606 **Torrance** Thomas F., The Trinitarian faith; the evangelical theology of the ancient Catholic Church [< 1981 Princeton Warfield lectures] 1988 ➤ 4,8640: £17.50: ᴿHeythJ 30 (1989) 64-66 (B. R. *Brinkman*); NRT 111 (1989) 917s (L. *Renwart*).

7607 **Willis** W. Waite, Theism ... trinity: BARTH, MOLTMANN 1987 ➤ 3,7191: ᴿWestTJ 50 (1988) 374-8 (R. E. *Otto*).

H5.8   *Regnum messianicum, Filius hominis* – **Messianic kingdom, Son of Man.**

7608 *Aguirre* Rafael, El mensaje de Jesús y los ideales del Reino de Dios: LumenVr 38 (1989) 449-473.

7609 **Beasley-Murray** G. R., Jesus and the Kingdom of God 1986 ➤ 2,5782 ... 4,8646: ᴿBibTB 19 (1989) 108 (Karen A. *Barta*); HeythJ 30 (1989) 448s (B. *Lindars*: conservative); TLZ 114 (1989) 599s (G. *Haufe*: die ganze Menschensohnthematik).

7610 **Böhm** Manfred, Gottes Reich und Gesellschaftsveränderung; Traditionen einer befreienden Theologie im Spätwerk von L. RAGAZ; Vorw. *Fuchs* O. Münster 1988, Liberación. 314 p. DM 36,50. – ᴿÖkRu 38 (1989) 494s (K. *Raiser*).

7611 *Bowman* John, David, Jesus son of David and son of man: AbrNahrain 27 (1989) 1-22.

7612 **Cantalamessa** Raniero, *a*) La vita nella signoría de Cristo. Mi 1988, Àncora. – *b*) La vida en el señorío de Cristo, ᵀ*Monter* José. Valencia 1988, Edicep. 315 p. – ᴿLumenVr 38 (1989) 344s (U. *Gil Ortega*).

7613 **Caragounis** Chrys C., The Son of Man 1988 = 1986 ➤ 2,5786 ... 4,8649: ᴿHeythJ 30 (1989) 188s (B. *Lindars,* unfavorable); RechSR 77 (1989) 399s (J. *Guillet*).

7614 *Caragounis* Chrys C., Kingdom of God, Son of Man and Jesus' self-understanding: TyndB 40 (1989) 3-23 . 223-238 [not vol. 49 as announced p. 23].

7615 **Chilton** Bruce D., God in strength; Jesus' announcement of the Kingdom: Bib. Seminar. Sheffield 1987, JStOT. 347 p. 1-85075-162-5.

7616 *Cook* Michael L.,   Iglesia y reinado de Díos: TVida 29 (1988) 73-86.

7617 **Ehler** Bernhard, Die Herrschaft des Gekreuzigten ... E. KÄSEMANN [kath. Diss. Augsburg] ...: BZNW 46, 1986 ➤ 2,5790 ... 4,8652: RJBL 108 (1989) 549-551 (R. B. *Hays*); JTS 40 (1989) 699s (R. *Morgan*).

7618 *Ellington* John, 'Son of Man' and contextual translation: BTrans 40 (1989) 201-8.

7619 **Ellul** Jacques, The presence of the kingdom[2] [[1]1948, Eng. 1967], with new comments by Ellul and by *Clendenin* Daniel B. Colorado Springs 1989, Helmers & H. xliii-145 p. $11 pa. 0-939443-14-7 [TDig 37,50].

7620 **Forck** Gottfried, Die Königsherrschaft Jesu Christi bei LUTHER[2rev] [[1]1959 < [D]1956]; Beitrag *Lohse* B. B 1988, Ev.-V. 167 p. M 18. – RTLZ 114 (1989) 362s (G. *Heintze*).

7621 **González-Carvajal** L., Los signos de los tiempos; El Reino de Dios está entre nosotros...: PresTeol 39, 1987 ➤ 3,7212: RProyección 35 (1989) 239s (A. *Sánchez*).

7622 *Horvath* Tibor, Jesus Christ, the eschatological union of time and eternity: ScEspr 40 (1988) 179-192; franç. 192.

7623 **Kearns** Rollin, Das Traditionsgefüge um den Menschensohn 1986 ➤ 2,5796 ... 4,8656: RJStJud 20 (1989) 238-240 (K. *Koch*); ScripTPamp 21 (1989) 700s (K. *Limburg*).

7624 **Kearns** Rollin, Die Entchristologisierung des Menschensohnes 1988 ➤ 4,8657: RArTGran 52 (1989) 255s (E. *Barón*); TLZ 114 (1989) 734s (M. *Karrer*).

7625 **Kerkhofs** J., De smalle weg; over 'het Rijk' dat komen zal als bron van alle zingeving. Kapellen 1988, Pelckmans. 182 p. Fb 595. 90-289-1358-0. – RTsTNijm 29 (1989) 197 (E. *Henau*).

7626 **Kosch** Daniel, Die eschatologische Torah des Menschensohnes; Untersuchungen zur Rezeption der Stellung Jesu zur Tora in Q: NTOrb 12. FrS/Gö 1989, Univ./VR. 512 p. Fs 98.

7627 *Liszka* Piotr, ❷ Christus als der Schöpfer des Reiches Gottes auf Erden nach Leonardo BOFF: RoczTK 33,2 (1986) 133-142; deutsch 142.

7628 *Lohfink* Gerhard, Die Not der Exegese mit der Reich-Gottes-Verkündigung Jesu: TüTQ 168 (1988) 1-15 [➤ 4,8660], [TE]*Giménez* Josep, ¿Que quería decir Jesús cuando predicaba el Reino de Dios?: SelT 28 (1989) 312-8.

7629 *Lord* Elizabeth, Human history and the Kingdom of God; past perspectives and those of J. L. SEGUNDO: HeythJ 30 (1989) 293-203 [355-360, *al.,* reviews of Segundo].

7630 **Margerie** Bertrand de, Liberté religieuse et Règne du Christ 1988 ➤ 4,8662: RMélSR 46 (1989) 175s (M. *Huftier*); MiscFranc 89 (1989) 624-6 (L. *Iammarrone*); RTLv 20 (1989) 97s (G. *Thils* s'oppose à son idée d'une 'certaine compétence' de l'État et matière religieuse).

7631 *Marshall* I. Howard, Jesus as Lord; the development of the concept: ➤ 21, [F]BEASLEY-MURRAY G., Eschatology 1988, 129-145.

7632 a) *Matthias* Anton, Biblical notion of the Kingdom of God; – b) *Nicholas* J., The Kingdom of God and culture: Iraiyiyal Kolangal 5,1 (Sri Lanka) both in Tamil; Eng. summ. p. 49 / p. 50 [< TContext 7/1, 69].

7632* a) *Nkoua Kek* Aloys, Hospitality and solidarity as mediations of the Kingdom of God: diss. Duquesne, [D]*Hanigan* J. Pittsburgh 1989. 435 p. 90-00828. – DissA 50 (1989s) 2540-A. – b) **Palmer** Timothy P., John CALVIN's view of the Kingdom of God: diss. Aberdeen, UK, 1988. 368 p. 89-14319. – DissA 50 (1989s) 976-A.

7633 *Pawlas* Andreas, Zwei-Reiche-Lehre und Lehre von der Königsherrschaft Christi in der neueren theologiegeschichtlichen Diskussion: Luther 19 (1988) 89-105.
7634 *Poythress* Vern S., God's Lordship in interpretation: WestTJ 50 (1988) 27-64.
7635 *Quirk* Michael J., Jesus and interpretation; SHEEHAN's hermeneutic radicalism: ModT 6 (1989s) 197-209.
7636 *Selman* Martin, The Kingdom of God in the Old Testament: TyndB 40 (called 40,2 though vol. 40 was not called 40,1; 1989) 161-183.
7637 **Sheehan** Thomas, The first coming; how the Kingdom of God became Christianity 1986 ⇥ 2,3172 ... 4, 8668: ᴿHeythJ 30 (1989) 448s (B. *Lindars*: gripping, totally unconvincing).
7638 *Subilia* Victor †, Le Royaume de Dieu dans la perspective du XVIIᵉ siècle piétiste et puritain: RHPR 68 (1988) 275-291.
7639 **Taylor** John V., Kingdom come. L/Ph 1989, SCM/Trinity ix-114 p. 0-334-00841-7.
7640 **Viviano** Benedict T., The Kingdom of God in history 1988 ⇥ 4,8671: ᴿLA 38 (1988) 496-8 (J. *Majercik*); TS 50 (1989) 405s (B. *Fiore*: informative and fair).
7640* *Vögtle* Anton, Eine überholte 'Menschensohn'-Hypothese?: ⇥ 120, ᶠLOHSE E., Wissenschaft 1989, 70-95.

H6.1   *Creatio, sabbatum NT* [⇥ E3.5]; **The Creation** [⇥ E1.6; H2.8].

7641 *Ansaldi* Jean, La doctrine de la création au futur antérieur: ÉTRel 64 (1989) 249-262.
7642 *a)* ᶠBAUMGARTNER Jakob, Der Sonntag, ᴱAltermatt A.M., al. 1986 ⇥ 2,10: ᴿTR 85 (1989) 312-4 (M. *Probst*). – *b)* **Dione** Hyacinthe, Jésus et le sabbat; contribution à la recherche historique sur Jésus de Nazareth: diss. cath. ᴰ*Schlosser* J. Strasbourg 1989. 481 p. (2 vol.) – RTLv 21,544.
7643 *Bayer* Oswald, Schöpfung als Anrede und Anspruch: Luther 19 (1988) 133-144.
7643* *a)* **Berkey** Merlin D., Creation evangelism [OT background; NT, Paul]: diss. Dallas Theol. Sem. 1988. 245 p. 89-13827. – DissA 50 (1989s) 1327-A. – *b)* *Coutagne* Paul, TEILHARD de Chardin et le 'tragique' de la création: SuppVSp 167 ('Conflits du monde et paix de Dieu' 1988) 149-164.
     Eberlein K., Gott der Schöpfer ᴰ1986 ⇥ 1960.
7644 **Greshake** Gisbert, Gott in allen Dingen finden; Schöpfung und Gotteserfahrung 1986 ⇥ 3,7248: ᴿSalesianum 51 (1989) 371 (L. A. *Gallo*).
7645 **Katz** David S., Sabbath and sectarianism in seventeenth-century England: St. Intell. Hist. 10. Leiden 1988, Brill. xiv-224 p. $60. – ᴿChH 50 (1989) 516s (K. L. *Parker*).
7646 *L'Éplattenier* C., *Bouttier* M., Le thème de la création dans le NT: ⇥ 450, ᴱ*Cardon* P., Dieu 1987/8, ...
7647 *Nethöfel* Wolfgang, Biotechnik zwischen Schöpferglauben und schöpferischem Handeln: EvT 49 (1989) 179-199.
7648 **Parker** Kenneth L., The English sabbath; a study of doctrine and discipline from the Reformation to the Civil War. C 1988, Univ. xii-250 p. £27.50. 0-521-30535-5. – ᴿCalvinT 24 (1989) 354-7 (A. P. F. *Sell*); ExpTim 100 (1988s) 274 (D. *Cornick*).
7649 **Porter** H. B., The day of light; the biblical and liturgical meaning of Sunday. Wsh 1987, Pastoral. xi-84 p. $7 [JTS 40,361].

7649* **Rodriguez Jarque** Fernando, El tratado teológico de la creación; desarrollo histórico y situación actual: diss. ᴰ*Morales Marín* J. Pamplona 1989. 361 p. – RTLv 21,570.

7650 **Ruiz de la Peña** José, Teología de la creación [... écologie; créativité sécularisée; Gn Ps Sap 2Mcb]: Presencia teológica 24, 1986 ➤ 2,5820; 3,7256: ᴿForumKT 5 (1989) 314-6 (A. *Ziegenaus*); RTLv 20 (1989) 94s (E. *Brito*).

7650* *a*) **Scheffczyk** L., Einführung in die Schöpfungslehre². Da 1987, Wiss. ix-185 p. – ᴿForumKT 4 (1988) 160 (A. *Ziegenaus*). – *b*) *Soom* Willy Van, Omdat God ons draagt; een systematisch-theologische bezinning op het scheppingsgeloof: CollatVL 19 (1989) 311-343.

7651 **Scott** Robbie H.ᴶ, Jesus and the Sabbath; an investigation on the Sabbath in Jewish literature from 200 B.C. to A.D. 100 and its impact upon the ministry of Jesus: diss. SW Baptist theol. sem. 1988. 260 p. 89-08443. – DissA 50 (1989s) 76-A.

7651* *Strohm* Theodor, Sonntagsarbeit aus technischen und wirtschaftlichen Gründen?: ZevEth 33 (1989) 47-53.

7652 **Tanner** Kathryn, God and creation in Christian theology; tyranny or empowerment? Ox 1988, Blackwell. vii-196 p. £25. 0-631-15994-0 [NTAbs 33,282]. – ᴿJTS 40 (1989) 322-4 (M. *Wiles*).

7653 **Trigo** P., Creación e historia en el proceso de liberación: Cristianismo y Sociedad 13. M 1988, Paulinas. 358 p. pt. 1450. – ᴿProyección 36 (1989) 165 (B. A. O).

H6.3 *Fides, veritas in NT* – Faith and truth.

7654 *a*) *Aletti* Jean-Noël, L'acte de croire pour l'apôtre Paul; – *b*) *Zumstein* Jean, L'évangile johannique, une stratégie du croire: RechSR 77 (1989) 233-250; Eng. 161s / 217-232; Eng. 161 [13-111, 165-216, *al.*, L'acte de croire ➤ 711].

7655 *Barr* James, La foi biblique et la théologie naturelle: ÉTRel 64 (1989) 355-368 [353s, doctorat honoris causa, Fac. Prot. (Montpellier)].

7656 Belg. Bischöfe, ᵀᴱ*Schütz* U., Unser Glaube; wie wir ihn bekennen, feiern und leben. FrB 1988, Herder. 200 p. DM 19,80 pa. – ᴿTGL 79 (1989) 202s (W. *Beinert*).

7656* *Bohren* Rudolf, Glaube und Ästhetik — ein vergessenes Kapitel der Theologie: BTZ 6 (1989) 2-7.

7657 **Brossier** François, Relatos bíblicos y comunicación de la fe. Estella 1987, VDivino. 181 p. – ᴿHumT 9 (1988) 106s (J. *Monteiro*).

7657* ᶠ**Buri** Fritz: Weltoffenheit des christlichen Glaubens, ᴱ*Abbt* Imelda, *Jäger* Alfred 1987 ➤ 3,33: ᴿTZBas 45 (1989) 381s (W. A. *Sommer*).

7658 *a*) *Busto Saiz* José R., Guardar la fe; actitudes frente a los impactos de una cultura nueva; – *b*) *Ibáñez* Fernando, La fe en un tiempo sin ideales: SalT 77 (1989) 695-707 / 719-729.

7658* *Cozzoli* Mauro, I presupposti antropologici della fede: Lateranum 55 (1989) 329-343.

7659 **Cunningham** Lawrence S., The Catholic faith. NY 1987, Paulist. v-184 p. $5 pa. – ᴿHorizons 16 (1989) 166-8 (D. M. *Doyle*, also on Cunningham's cognate 1987).

7660 **Dobbeler** Axel von, Glaube als Teilhabe ... WUNT 2/22, 1987 ➤ 3,7266: ᴿSalesianum 51 (1989) 153 (J. *Heriban*).

7661 **Fabris** Rinaldo, L'esperienza di fede nella Bibbia: Andate e annunciate 7, 1987 ➤ 3,7268: ᴿParVi 34 (1989) 146-150 (A. *Dalbesio*).

7662 **Fischer** Kathleen R., *Hart* Thomas N., Christian foundations; an introduction to faith in our time. NY 1986, Paulist. v-222 p. $10 pa. – ^RHorizons 16 (1989) 168s (Barbara *Finan*).

7663 *a*) *Galot* Jean, La profession de foi et le serment de fidélité [... formules prescrites par la Congrégation pour la Foi 25.II.1989]: EsprVie 99 (1989) 694-8. → 7670 infra; 1401, 1411* supra. – *b*) *Held* Heinz J., Glaube und Liebe in der Erlangung des Heils: → 120, ^FLOHSE E., Wissenschaft 1989, 288-304.

Henn William, The hierarchy of truths ... CONGAR ^D1987 → k526.

7664 **Johnson** Alan F., *Webber* Robert E., What Christians believe; a biblical and historical summary. GR 1989, Zondervan Academie. 480 p. $20. 0-310-36730-4 [TDig 37,65].

7665 **Kruhöffer** Gerald, Grundlinien des Glaubens; ein biblisch-theologischer Leitfaden. Gö 1989, Vandenhoeck & R. 326 p. 3-525-6128-6.

7666 **Lubac** Henri de, The Christian faith; an essay on the structure of the Apostles' Creed [¹1970] → 2,5843; also SF 1986, Ignatius. 353 p. – ^RVidyajyoti 52 (1988) 253 (G. *Gispert-Sauch*).

7667 **Nash** Ronald H., Faith and reason; searching for a rational faith. GR 1988, Zondervan. 295 p. $18. – ^RAndrUnS 27 (1989) 258-260 (F. L. *Canale*).

7668 **Poterie** René, L'aube d'une liberté humaine [... sa foi en Jésus]. P 1988, Nouvelle Cité. 304 p. F 100. – ^REsprVie 99 (1989) 208 (M. *Trémeau*: réserves).

7669 **Schillebeeckx** E., On Christian faith (Amst lectures) 1987 → 3,7296: ^RAnglTR 70 (1988) 189s (J. G. *Brewster*); Interpretation 43 (1989) 106s (W. D. *White*); JRel 69 (1989) 119s (D. G. *Murphy*).

7670 *Sullivan* Francis A., *a*) Note sulla nuova formula per la professione di fede: CC 140 (1989,3) 130-9; – *b*) Some observations on the new formula for the profession of faith: Gregorianum 70 (1989) 549-558.

7671 *Vandenbulcke* Jaak, Geloof op basis van ervaring; naar aanleiding van A. VERGOTE's 'Cultuur, Religie, Geloof' [Lv 1989, Univ.]: TsTNijm 29 (1989) 270-8; Eng. 278.

7672 **Viladesau** Richard, Answering for faith; Christ and the human search for salvation. NY 1987, Paulist. xiii-312 p. $13. 0-8091-2882-9. – ^RGregorianum 70 (1989) 360s (A. *Wolanin*: ragionevolezza dell'atto di fede); NRT 111 (1989) 101s (J. *Masson*).

7673 *Walls* Jerry L., The moral obligation of belief: AsbTJ 43,2 (1988) 79-94.

7674 **Werbick** Jürgen, Glaube im Kontext; Prolegomena und Skizzen zu einer elementaren Theologie. Z 1983, Benziger. 599 p. DM 59. – ^RTR 85 (1989) 474s (E. *Rolinck*).

7675 *Zimany* Roland D., Believing in God today [... truth comes down to what you are willing to commit yourself to]: CurrTM 16 (1989) 267-276.

H6.6   *Peccatum NT* – **Sin, Evil** [→ E1.9].

7676 *Bastianel* Sergio, Strutture di peccato; riflessione teologico-morale: CC 140 (1989,1) 325-338.

7677 **Delumeau** Jean, Il peccato e la paura; l'idea di colpa in Occidente dal XIII al XVIII secolo,^T: Le occasioni XI. Bo 1987, Mulino. 1008 p. – ^RFilT 3 (1989) 232-5 (A. *Vuolo*); Salesianum 51 (1989) 332s (M. *Müller*).

7678 *a*) *Eichinger* Werner, 'Strukturen der Sünde', zur theologischen Argumentation von Sollicitudo rei socialis; – *b*) *Nuscheler* Franz,

Weltwirtschaft als 'Struktur der Sünde': → 464, Sollicitudo 1988, 117-136 / 205-218.

7679 *Finance* Joseph de, Dieu punit-il en ce monde? [*La Fontaine,* Fables 7,1, peste]: ScEspr 40 (1988) 279-294.

7680 *Haacker* K., Schuld und Schuldverarbeitung in biblischer Sicht und im Kontext deutscher Zeitgeschichte [... sins of the fathers]: TBei 19,3 (1988) 230-250 [< NTAbs 33,204].

7681 *Häring* Bernhard, Sin in post-Vatican II theology: → 102, ᶠJANSSENS L., Personalist 1988, 87-107.

7682 *Henriksen* Jan O., [Norw.] Sin and death [relation in OSBERG, THIELICKE, JÜNGEL, PANNENBERG]; remarks on the problem of empirical experience in theology: TsTKi 59 (1988) 81-96; Eng. 96.

7683 *Hilpert* Konrad, Schuld in ihrer sozialen Erscheinungsform; Verschiebungen im Verantwortungsverständnis: TGegw 32 (1989) 38-52.

7683* *Jüngel* Eberhard, Zur Lehre vom Bösen und von der Sünde: → 120, ᶠLOHSE E., Wissenschaft 1989, 177-188.

7684 [*Lindström* F., AT] *Limbeck* M., Böse: → 902, NBL, Lfg 2 (1989) 314-6.

7685 *Makarushka* Irena, Teaching a course on evil; an interdisciplinary approach: CouStR 18 (1989) 1-3.

7687 **Millás** José M., Die Sünde in der Theologie R. BULTMANNS (ᴰ1983) 1987 → 3,7324: ᴿTLZ 114 (1989) 839-841 (H. *Hübner*).

7688 **Millás** José M., Pecado y existencia cristiana ... en BULTMANN 1989 [→ 4,8718]. – ᴿGregorianum 70 (1989) 609s (*ipse*).

7689 *Millás* José M., Pecado y perdón en la existencia cristiana; estudio de la relación entre el pecado y el perdón en la teología de Rudolf BULTMANN: Gregorianum 70 (1989) 321-340; franç. 340.

7689* *Mynatty* H., From 'fundamental option' to 'social sin'; a search for an integrated theology of sin: diss. ᴰ*Selling* J. Leuven 1989. xxxviii-458 p. – TsTNijm 30,190; RTLv 21,570.

7690 *a*) *Ritt* Hubert, Sünde – Umkehr – Vergebung; neutestamentliche Leitlinien; – *b*) *Neufeld* Karl-Heinz, Unkehr [index; Freudian slip?] und Busse im Denken Karl RAHNERS: WAntw 30,1 (Mainz 1989) 12-15 / 30-33 [< ZIT 89,241].

7691 *a*) *Rosik* Seweryn, ℗ Die Sünde im Licht der biblischen Prämissen; – *b*) *Greniuk* Franciszek, ℗ Contemporanea teologia del peccato: RoczTK 32,3 (1985) 57-79; deutsch 59 / 81-100; ital. 101s.

7692 **Sabugal** Santos, Pecado y reconciliación en el mensaje de Jesús 1985 → 1,7217 ... 3,7334: ᴿGregorianum 70 (1989) 163s (J. M. *Millás*).

7693 *Schulte* Christoph, Die Wiederkehr des Bösen; über radikale Vorstellungen vom Bösen in der Moderne: ZRGg 41 (1989) 33-51.

7694 **Sievernich** M., Schuld und Sünde in der Theologie der Gegenwart [cf. Diss. Münster 1987 → 4,8722]: FraTSt 29,1982 → 64,6898 ... 1,7220: ᴿStPatav 36 (1989) 669s (G. *Trentin*).

7695 *Trevijano* Pedro, Pecado y opción fundamental: Salmanticensis 36 (1989) 363-378; Eng. 378.

H7 Soteriologia NT.

7695* *Akin* Daniel L., BERNARD of Clairvaux, evangelical of the twelfth century (a critical analysis of his soteriology): diss. ᴰ*Lackner* K., Univ. Texas. Arlington 1989. 247 p. 90-00949. – DissA 50 (1989s) 2610s-A.

7696 *Allison* Christopher C., The pastoral and political implications of Trent on justification; response to ARCIC: Churchman 103,1 (L 1989) 15-31 [< ZIT 89,365] = ► 4,8728 (StLuke 31,204-222).

7696* **Breytenbach** Cilliers, Versöhnung; eine Studie zur paulinischen Soteriologie [Hab. München]: WM 60. Neuk 1989. xv-260 p. DM 75. – TR 86,251.

7697 *Champagne* Claude, Salut, religions mondiales et mission de l'Église selon Hans KÜNG: ► 735, Salvezza 1988/9, 309-318.

7697* **Criswell** W. A., [sermons, ᴱ*Patterson* Paige], Soteriology: Great doctrines of the Bible 5. GR 1985, Zondervan. 154 p. $10. – ᴿCriswT 2 (1987s) 177s (B. *Vinson*) [425s, T. S. *Rainer* on vol. 6, Stewardship].

7698 **Daly** Gabriel, Creation and redemption. Dublin 1988, Gill & M.; Wilmington 1989, Glazier. 230 p. $16. – ᴿStudies 78 (1989) 334-6 (G. *O'Hanlon*); TS 50 (1989) 827 (S. *Bevans*).

7699 *Decock* Paul A., A 'this-worldly' or an 'other-worldly' salvation: Grace and Truth 8,4 (Hilton SAf 1988) 168-180 [B. *Abeng* (Eng.) summary, TContext 6/2, 98].

7700 *Demmer* Klaus, Die Lebensgeschichte als Versöhnungsgeschichte: FreibZ 36 (1989) 375-393.

7701 **Driver** John, Understanding the Atonement for the mission of the Church 1986 ► 3,7347; 4,8738: ᴿThemelios 14 (1988s) 77 (G. *Woolard*).

7702 *Evans* G. R., *Vis verborum*; scholastic method and finding words in the debate on justification of the Council of Trent: DowR 106 (1988) 264-275.

7703 **Gillis** Chester, A question of final belief; John HICK's pluralistic theory of salvation. NY 1989, St. Martin's. xiv-186 p. $40. – ᴿJEcuSt 26 (1989) 217s (J. *Berthrong*); TS 50 (1989) 826 (T. W. *Tilley*). – ► a595s.

7703* **Göll** Hans-Peter, Versöhnung und Rechtfertigung; eine Untersuchung zur Funktion der Rechtfertigungslehre in der theologischen Argumentation Martin KÄHLERS: Diss. ᴰSAUTER G. Bonn 1989s. – RTLv 21,569.

7704 **González** Carlos I., Él es nuestra salvación; Cristología y soteriología: CELAM Textos Sem. 3. Bogotá/México 1987. 582 p. 958-625-045-8. – ᴿGregorianum 70 (1989) 194 (*ipse*).

7705 *González de Cardedal* Olegario, La soteriología contemporánea: Salmanticensis 36 (1989) 267-316; Eng. 316s.

7706 **Greshake** Gisbert, Erlöst in einer unerlösten Welt?: Topos-Tb. Mainz 1987, Grünewald. 170 p. DM 9,80. – ᴿTPQ 137 (1989) 86s (A. *Habichler*).

7707 **Gunton** Colin E., The actuality of atonement; a study of metaphor, rationality and the Christian tradition. GR 1989, Eerdmans. xlv-222 p. 0-8028-3664-X.

7708 **Hallonsten** Gösta, Meritum bei TERTULLIAN, ᵀ*Hofmann* Manfred 1985 ► 3,7357; 4,8745: ᴿSecC 7 (1989s) 108s (R. D. *Sider*).

7709 *Hart* Trevor, Humankind in Christ and Christ in humankind; salvation as participation in our substitute in the theology of John CALVIN: ScotJT 42 (1989) 67-84.

7709* *Hart* Trevor A., The two soteriological traditions of Alexandria: EvQ 61 (1989) 239-259.

7710 **Heinz** Johann, Justification and merit; Luther vs. Catholicism: Andrews diss. 8, 1984 ► 2,5901; 3,7359: ᴿTR 85 (1989) 211-3 (J. *Wicks*).

7711 **Hultgren** Arland J., Christ and his benefits 1987 ► 3,7364; 4,8748: ᴿCurrTM 16 (1989) 131s (F. W. *Danker*); JBL 108 (1989) 146-8 (L. W. *Hurtado*).

7712 **Jegen** Carol F., Restoring our friendship with God; the mystery of redemption from suffering and sin: Zacchaeus Studies, Theology. Wilmington 1989, Glazier. 99 p. $7. 0-89453-757-1 [NTAbs 33,422].
Janowski Bernd, Rettungsgewissheit... 'am Morgen'...: WM 59, 1989 ➤ 9245.

7713 *a)* *Kasper* Walter, Die soteriologische Rolle der Kirche und die Sakramente des Heils; – *b)* *Dhavamony* Mariasusai, Today's challenge; salvation offered by non-Christian religions; – *c)* *Testa* Emmanuele, 'Una salvezza per tutti, la volontà salvifica di Dio'; 'il piano salvifico e universale di Dio in Cristo Gesù': ➤ 735, Salvezza 1988/9, 33-60 / 81-100 / 151-5.

7714 *Kretschmar* Georg, Das Heil als Befreiung – eine Anfrage an die Lutherische Theologie: ➤ 177, ᶠSCHWARZ R., Von Wittenberg 1989, 162-189.

7715 *Kraus* Georg, Der Mittler zwischen Gott und Mensch; zur soteriologischen Bedeutung der Gottessohnschaft Jesu Christi: TPQ 137 (1989) 48-57.

7716 **McGrath** Alister E., Iustitia Dei, a history of the Christian doctrine of justification I, 1986 ➤ 3,7373; 4,8753: ᴿJAAR 57 (1989) 204-6 (G.H. *Tavard*); JEcuSt 26 (1989) 565-7 (R.E. *McLaughlin*: quirky insights); Salesianum 51 (1989) 578s (P.T. *Stella*).

7717 *a)* *Mathew* M.J., Soteriology; prophetic and apocalyptic perspectives; – *b)* *Joseph* M.J., 'Jesus Christ and him crucified'; – *c)* *Luke* K., The impact of Egyptian ideas on the formulation of NT soteriology; – *d)* *Mark* John, Rejection of salvation as depicted in the Gospels: Bible Bhashyam 14,3s (1988) 103-116 / 176-184 / 185-194 / 195-209.

7718 *Meyendorff* John, New life in Christ; salvation in Orthodox theology: TS 50 (1989) 481-499.

7719 *a)* *Ouwerkerk* C. van, Uniciteit van Christus; Tragiek der exclusiviteit?; – *b)* *Denaux* Adelbert, Eén God, één Heer; over de joodse wortels van de christelijke visie op Jesus' uniciteit; – *c)* *Logister* Wiel, Aan de overkant van exclusiviteit en inclusiviteit: TsTNijm 29 (1989) 365-8 / 369-378 / 379-387 (–389): Eng. [replies to L. *Bakker* 29 (1989) 211-231 reacting to 28 (1988) 211-289].

7720 *a)* *Poythress* V.S., Christ the only savior of interpretation; – *b)* *VanGemeren* W.A., The spirit of restoration: WestTJ 50 (1988) 305-321 / 81-102.

7721 *Preez* Jannie du, Indications of Sola Gratia in Judaism and Islam? [law/grace; a comparative study of the term 'salvation']: JStRel 2,1 (Natal 1989) 3-13 [< TContext 7/1,21].

7721* **Pröpper** Thomas, Erlösungsglaube und Freiheitsgeschichte 1985 ➤ 3, 7384: ᴿForumKT 5 (1989) 75-77 (P. *Schäfer*).

7722 **Rickauer** Hans-C., Rechtfertigung und Heil; die Vermittlung von Glaube und Heilshandeln in der Auseinandersetzung mit der reformatorischen Lehre bei Konrad KLINGE (1483/4-1556): ErfurterTSt 53. Lp 1986, St. Benno. xxii-273 p. M 25,50. – ᴿDivThom 91 (1988) 256s (L.J. *Elders*); TLZ 114 (1989) 684s (H. *Smolinsky*).

7723 *a)* *Roloff* Jürgen, Heil, biblisch; – *b)* *Dietrich* Walter [AT], *Luz* Ulrich, Gerechtigkeit NT: ➤ 894, EvKL 2 (1988) 413-6 (–432 *al.*) / [87–] 90-92 [–101, *al.*].

7724 **Schwager** Raymund, Der wunderbare Tausch; zur Geschichte und Deutung der Erlösungslehre 1986 ➤ 2,219; ... 4,8764: ᴿJTS 40 (1989) 703-5 (A. *Louth*); RechSR 77 (1989) 554s (B. *Sesboüé*); TsTNijm 29 (1989)

189 (H. *Häring*: buitengewoon interessant; maar de toepassing van
GIRARD blijft aan de buitenkant; eine theoretische confrontatie vindt niet
plaats. 'In feite formuleert S. vanuit Girard slechts kritiek die ook van
hedendaagse katholieke theologen bekend is, terwijl het problem van
sacralisering – bij Girard een van de hoofdproblemen – niet eens genoemd
wordt').

7725 *Schwarzwäller* Klaus,   Rechtfertigung und Ekklesiologie in den schmal-
kaldischen Artikeln :   KerDo 35 (1989) 84-104; Eng. 104s.

7725* **Seaford** Stephen V.,   Jesus as Savior in the New Testament: diss. New
Orleans Baptist Theol. Sem. 1987, D*Simmons* B.   193 p. – 88-10256. –
DissA 49 (1988s) 944-A.

7726 **Sésboüé** Bernard,   Jésus-Christ l'unique médiateur; essai sur la rédemption et le salut, 1. Problématique et relecture doctrinale: JJC 33,
1988 ⮕ 4,8765:   R ETL 65 (1989) 462-6 (E. *Brito*); ÉTRel 64 (1989) 462s
(A. *Gounelle*: lucide, un peu grisâtre); NRT 111 (1989) 908-910 (L.
Renwart); RET 49 (1989) 333-6 (M. *Gesteira*); RHPR 69 (1989) 487-9 (G.
Siegwalt: riche, lisible); RSPT 73 (1989) 524-7 (B. *Rey*); ScEspr 41 (1989)
243-5 (G. *Langevin*); Spiritus 30 (1989) 217s (H. *Frévin*); TPhil 64 (1989)
620s (W. *Löser*); ZkT 111 (1989) 110-2 (K. H. *Neufeld*).

7727 **Sloyan** Gerard S.,   Jesus; redeemer and divine Word: Theology & Life
28.   Wilmington 1989, Glazier.   160 p. $15; pa. $13 [CBQ 52,384].

7728 **Snook** Lee E.,   The anonymous Christ; Jesus as savior in modern
theology 1986 ⮕ 3,7394;   0-8066-2220-2:   R ÉTRel 64 (1989) 460s (A.
Gounelle).

7729 **Steindl** Helmut,   Genugtuung; biblische Versöhnungsdenken – eine
Quelle für ANSELMS Satisfaktionstheorie? [Diss FrS 1988 ⮕ 4,8767]:
StFrib NF 71.   FrS 1989, Univ.   xiv-338 p. Fs 46   3-7278-0631-1.

7729* **Steinert** Hermann,   Begegnung und Erlösung; der Mensch als sote-
riologisches Wesen – das Existenzproblem bei Martin BUBER: kath. Diss.
Würzburg 1988s, D*Klinger*. – TR 85 (1989) 520.

7730 *Stoeckle* Bernhard,   Gesundheit und Heil; Überlegungen zu einem von
der Theologie vernachlässigten Thema: ⮕ 45, F DEISSLER A., Weg 1989,
310-325.

7730* *Strehle* Stephen,   The extent of the atonement and the Synod of Dort:
WestTJ 51 (1989) 1-23 (345-357, on *Amyraut* M.).

7731 **Studer** Basil,   Dieu sauveur; la rédemption dans la foi de l'Église
ancienne [1985 ⮕ 1,7290], T*Hoffmann* J.   P 1989, Cerf.   350 p. –
R Irénikon 62 (1989) 125 (E. *lanne*); RHPR 69 (1989) 335 (S. *Siegwalt*);
RSPT 73 (1989) 453-5 (G.-M. de *Durand*).

7732 **VanGemeren** Willem,   The progress of redemption.   GR 1988, Zondervan.   544 p. $20. – R BS 146 (1989) 465 (E. H. *Merrill*).

7733 *Versnel* H. S.,   Jezus soter – neos Alkestis? Over de niet-joodse
achtergrond van een christelijke doctrine [vicarious death]: Lampas 22
(1989) 219-242 [< JStJud 20,285].

7734 *Viciano* Alberto, · Grundzüge der Soteriologie TERTULLIANS: TGL 79
(1989) 147-161.

7734* **Viladesau** Richard,   Answering for faith; Christ and the human search
for salvation 1987 ⮕ 3,7404*:   R Themelios 14 (1988s) 110 (R. *Sturch*: in
RAHNER-LONERGAN jargon, makes other religions say what he wants to
hear).

7735 **Vitoria Cormenzana** F. Javier, ¿Todavía la salvación cristiana? ... cuatro
cristologías actuales 1986 ⮕ 3,7406:   R TLZ 114 (1989) 376-9 (A. *Gon-
zález-Montes*).

7736 *Vitoria Cormenzana* F. Javier, Salvación de Jesucristo y soteriologías cristianas; aproximación a cuatro diseños [*Moltmann* J., *Kasper* W., *González Faus* J., *Sobrino* J.]; RLatAmT 4,12 (Salvador 1987) 199-216 [< TContext 6/2,67].

7737 *a*) *Vives* Josep, ¿Liberación o salvación? más allá de interpretaciones reduccionistas; – *b*) *Sobrino* Jon, Liberación del pecado: SalT 76 (1988) 3-14 / 15-28.

7738 *Volf* Miroslav, Materiality of salvation; an investigation in the soteriologies of liberation and Pentecostal theologies: JEcuSt 26 (1989) 447-467.

7739 **Von Rohr** John, The covenant of grace in Puritan thought 1986 → 3,7403.g668: RJAAR 57 (1989) 437-9 (C. F. *Hambrick-Stowe*); JRel 68 (1988) 111s (M. *McGiffert*); ScotJT 42 (1989) 610-2 (M. *Jenkins*).

7740 *Watson* G., A study in St. ANSELM's soteriology and Karl BARTH's theological method: ScotJT 42 (1989) 493-517.

7741 TE**Wilson** John F., Jonathan EDWARDS, A history of the work of redemption [1739; 30 sermons on Is 51,8]: Edwards Works 9. NHv 1989, Yale Univ. ix-594 p. $65. 0-300-04155-1 [TDig 37,50].

7742 *Zimmermann* Gunter, CALVINS Auseinandersetzung mit OSIANDERS Rechtfertigungslehre: KerDo 35 (1989) 236-256; Eng. 256.

H7.2 *Crux, sacrificium* – **The Cross.**

7742* *a*) *Amadasi Guzzo* Maria Giulia, Sacrifici e banchetti; Bibbia ebraica e iscrizioni puniche; – *b*) *Burkert* Walter, Sacrificio-sacrilegio; il 'trickster' fondatore: ⊁ 7758*, Sacrificio 1983/8, 97-122 / 163-175.

7743 **Ashby** Godfrey, bp., Sacrifice, its nature and purpose. L 1988, SCM. 151 p. £7.50. 0-334-01437-9. – RExpTim 100,5 first choice (1988s) 161s (C. S. *Rodd*: 'slight Protestant bias'; the review does not mention GIRARD); PrPeo 3 (1989) 292s (sr. M. Cecily *Boulding*).

7744 **Bader** Günter, Symbolik des Todes Jesu [ANSELM]: HermUnT 25. Tü 1988, Mohr. x-258 p. DM 89. 3-16-145363-8 [NTAbs 23,261]. – RTLZ 114 (1989) 540s (W. *Schüssler*).

7745 **Balmary** Marie, Le sacrifice inerdit; FREUD et la Bible 1986 ⊁ 3,7413; 4,8778: RÉTRel 64 (1989) 653-6 (P.-A. *Harlé*).

7746 **Battaglia** Vincenzo, Croce, Trinità, creazione: Antonianum 64 (1989) 246-307; Eng. 246.

7747 **Baudler** Georg, Erlösung vom Stiergott; christliche Gotteserfahrung im Dialog mit Mythen und Religionen [GIRARD R.; BURKERT W.]. Mü/Stu 1989, Kösel/Calwer. 432 p. DM 48. 3-466-36326-8 / 3-7668-3032-5. – RCarthaginensia 5 (1989) 288 (J. *García Hernández*); MiscFranc 89 (1989) 621s (J. *Imbach*, ital.).

7748 *Baudler* Georg, Am Anfang war das Wort [*Herbig* J. 1984] – oder der Mord? [*Girard* R., *Burkert* W., bei H. nicht beabsichtigt]; die Faszination des Lebens und die Faszination der Tötungsmacht am Ursprung der Religion: ZkT 111 (1989) 45-56.

7749 *Biessen* Leon, [Joost van den] VONDELS Lucifer en Renè GIRARD: Streven 57 (1989s) 423-432.

7749* **Burkert** W., Anthropologie des religösen Opfers; die Sakralisierung der Gewalt: Siemens-Vortrag 1983. Mü 1984, Siemens-Stiftung [zieht Verbindungslinien mit Girard; ZkT 111,45].

7750 *Burrell* David B., René GIRARD, Violence and sacrifice [Scapegoat Eng.; SCHWAGER; Festschrift; all 1986]: CCurr 38 (1988s) 443-7.

7750* *Daly* Robert J., Sacrifice in ORIGEN and AUGUSTINE; comparisons and contrasts: ➤ 696, 10th Patristic, 19 (1989) 148-153.

7751 a) *Desplanque* Christophe, Pourquoi Jésus a-t-il dû mourir? La réponse de René Girard; – b) *Locoge* Bernard, Psychanalyse et substitution sacrificielle; quels apports, quelles limites?; – c) *Pella* Gérard, 'Pourquoi m'as-tu abandonné?' Marc 15,33-39 – d) *Bénétreau* Samuel, La mort du Christ selon l'épître aux Hébreux: Hokhma 39 ('Mort en sacrifice?' 1ère partie, 1988) 48-62 / 63-92 / 3-24 / 25-47.

7751* *Dinkler-von Schubert* Erika, Kreuz: ➤ 894, EvKL 2 (1989) 1462-8.

7752 *Dumais* Marcel, Le sens de la croix de Jésus d'après Jon SOBRINO; questions d'exégèse et d'herméneutique: ÉglT 19 (1988) 323-347.

7753 *Exem* A. Van, The sacrifice and the meal in the light of Sarna ritual: Vidyajyoti 52 (1988) 122-136.

7754 *Falusi* G. K., Sacrifice in the NT [and in traditional African religion]: Orita 20,2 (Ibadan 1988) 79-90 [–126, *al*: < TContext 7/1,24].

7754* *Galot* Jean, Sangue e sofferenza di Dio; la chiesa che Dio si è acquistata con il suo sangue: ➤ 759, Sangue VI, 1987/9, 755-770.

7755 *Galvin* John P., The marvelous exchange; Raymund SCHWAGER's interpretation of the history of soteriology [1986; *Girard* R.]; Thomist 53 (1989) 675-691.

7756 **Gauthier** Jean-Marc, Le Dieu des victimes; une lecture théologique de René GIRARD: diss. ᴰ*Parent* R. Montréal 1989. 350 p. – RTLv 21,569.

7756* *Gesteira Garza* Manuel, La Eucaristía como sacrificio incruento en la tradición patrística: ➤ 7, ᶠALFARO J., EstE 64 (1989) 401-432.

7757 **Girard** René, *al.*, Things hidden since the foundation of the world 1987 ➤ 3,7420: ᴿJAAR 57 (1989) 640-2 (T. V. *Peterson* objects chiefly to his making Christian revelation central).

7758 **Gourgues** Michel, Le crucifié; du scandale è l'exaltation: JJC 38. Montréal/P 1989, Bellarmin/Desclée. 178 p. 2-89007-6811-4 / P 2-7189-0420-8.

7758* *Grottanelli* Cristiano, a) Aspetti del sacrificio nel mondo greco e nella Bibbia ebraica; – b) Uccidere, donare, mangiare; problematiche attuali del sacrificio antico: ➤ 790*, Sacrificio e società nel mondo antico [in parte, convegno Univ. Siena, Pontignano 23-25 sett. 1983 (Bari 1988, Laterza)]. 123-162 / 3-53; p.23 [citando 'tendenza gnosticheggiante' criticata da NORTH] 'la scientificità manca di tutto a questo inventore di generalizzazioni' ... 'brade' anziché 'interpretative'].

7759 **Hengel** Martin, Crocifissione ed espiazione [1976, Eng. rev. 1977, franç. 1981 (qui)]ᵀ, 1988 ➤ 4,8785*: ᴿRivB 37 (1989) 517s (A. *Bonora*); StPatav 36 (1989) 624s (G. *Segalla*).

7760 ᴱ**Juilland** Alphonse, To honor René GIRARD 1986 ➤ 3,61: ᴿJRel 68 (1988) 155-7 (155-7 (P. G. *Williams*: detailed also on Girard's work in general).

7761 **Lascaris** André, Advocaat van de zondebok; het werk van René GIRARD en het evangelie van Jezus 1987 ➤ 3,7430*; 4,8791: ᴿBijdragen 50 (1989) 221 (W. G. *Tillmans*: humans are for others at once model and obstacle; they get superficial relief from scapegoats; Girard follows this up in OT, Job; Lascaris seeks to supply NT).

7761* *Lorizio* Giuseppe, Ipotesi e testi per una theologia crucis ROSMINIANA: Lateranum 55 (1989) 134-175 (369-392).

7762 **McGrath** Alister E., The mystery of the Cross 1988 ➤ 4,8795 [➤ 3,7431]; 182 p. $12: ᴿAndrUnS 27 (1989) 90-92 (J. *Paulien*).

7762* **McGuckin** Terence A., The eschatological effect of the Cross of Christ in the NT commentaries of St. Thomas AQUINAS: diss. Pont.

Univ. Gregoriana, N⁰ 3564, ᴰ*Rosato* P. J. R 1989. 554 p.; extract 242 p. – RTLv 21,550.

7763 *a*) *Marinatos* Nanno, The imagery of sacrifice, Minoan and Greek; – *b*) *Bergquist* Birgitta, The archaeology of sacrifice: Minoan-Mycenaean versus Greek: ➤ 792, Greek cult 1986/8, 9-20 / 21-44.

7764 *a*) *Mariotti* Maria Giovanna, Il sacrificio a Palmira; – *b*) *Mauriello* Domenico, Il sangue nel culto della dea araba Allāt; – *c*) *Lacerenza* Giancarlo, Il sangue e la lana nel culto del betilo; un'ipotesi di sostituzione rituale: ➤ 759, Sangue VI, 1987/9, 25-40 / 41-74 / 75-87.

7765 *Martins Terra* J., Significado del sufrimiento en el Nuevo Testamento: Senderos 34 (Costa Rica 1989) 15-24 [< Stromata 45,499].

7766 *Mertens* Herman-Emile, Jezus de Golgotha-situatie meester geworden; oude vragen omtrent de soteriologie opnieuw gesteld: TsTNijm 29 (1989) 131-147; Eng. 147.

7767 **Morris** Leon, The Cross of Jesus [Australian's lectures to U.S. Southern Baptists] 1988 ➤ 4,8797: ᴿExpTim 100 (1988s) 67 (J. *Muddiman*: without abandoning his rigorous penal substitution base, he here ventures into more humane aspects).

7768 **Padovese** L., Lo scandalo della croce; la polemica anticristiana nei primi secoli. R 1988, Dehoniane. 216 p. Lit. 22.000. – ᴿNRT 111 (1989) 593 (A. *Harvengt*).

7768* **Priest** Douglas D., The problem of animal sacrifice among Massai Christians [Kenya-Tanzania; compared with OT sacrifices]: diss. Fuller, ᴰ*Kraft* C. Pasadena 1989. 306 p. 89-18248. – DissA 50 (1989s) 1330-A.

7769 **Rey** Bernard, Nous prêchons un Messie crucifié [il constate 'une désaffection à l'égard de la Croix' p. 11]. P 1989, Cerf. 156 p. F 75. – ᴿEsprVie 99 (1989) 149s-*jaune* (L. *Barbey*); NRT 111 (1989) 910s (L. *Renwart*); RBíbArg 51 (1989) 249-251 (A. J. *Levoratti*).

7770 **Schalkwijk** Hendrikus Jacobus van, Kruisen; een studie over het gebruik van kruistekens in de ontwikkeling van het godsdienstig en maatschappelijk leven [Crosses; a study of the use of cross-signs in the development of religious and social life: diss. ᴰ*Broek* R. van den. Utrecht 1989. – RTLv 21,559]. Hilversum c. 1989, Gooi & S. 362 p. 90-304-04868. – ᴿTsTNijm 29 (1989) 413 (L. *Goosen*).

7771 *Smith* Brian K., *Doniger* Wendy, Sacrifice and substitution; ritual mystification and mythical demystification: Numen 36 (1989) 189-223.

7771* **Stokes** David L., BARTH and the atoning narratives; the figure of the cross in the 'Church Dogmatics': diss. Princeton Theol. Sem. 1989. 404 p. 89-23112. – DissA 50 (1989s) 2942-A; RelStR 16,188.

7772 **Stott** John R. W., The Cross of Christ 1986 ➤ 2,5957; 4,8800: ᴿSWJT 32,1 (1989s) 56 (B. *Dominy*: defense of penal substitution).

7772* **Trausnitz** Johann, Die Kreuzestheologie; eine Theologie der Nachfolge: Diss., ᴰ*Darlap* A. Innsbruck 1988s. 248 p. – TR 85 (1989) 512; RTLv 21,583; ZkT 111,523.

7773 **Valeri** Valerio, Kingship and sacrifice; ritual and society in ancient Hawaii 1985 ➤ 4,8804: ᴿJRel 68 (1988) 488s (Katharine *Luomala*).

7774 *a*) *Vanhoye* Albert, L'oblazione di Gesù sacerdote; – *b*) *Bordoni* Marcello, La teologia della redenzione: ➤ 751, Sp. oblativa 1988/9, 57-75 / 115-127.

7775 **Varone** François, Ce Dieu censé aimer la souffrance 1984 ➤ 65,6615 .. 3,7445: ᴿTR 85 (1989) 474s (K. J. *Tossou*).

7776 **Varone** F., El dios 'sádico'? Ama Dios el sufrimiento? Santander 1988, Sal Terrae. 259 p. – ᴿActuBbg 26 (1989) 27-29 (J. I. *González* Faus);

Carthaginensia 5 (1989) 306s (F. *Martínez Fresneda*); Proyección 36 (1989) 241 (R. *Franco*); RazF 219 (1989) 441s (María *Paz P. Campanero*).

7777 **Wittschier** Sturmius-F., Kreuz–Trinität–Analogie; trinitarische Ontologie unter dem Leitbild des Kreuzes, dargestellt als ästhetische Theologie: Bonner Dogmatische Studien 1. Wü 1987, Echter. 347p. – ᴿTPhil 64 (1989) 294s (W. *Löser*).

7778 **Zeninotto** Gino, Giusto Lɪᴘsɪo, Il supplicio della croce (De cruce 1593). R 1988, Giovinezza. 226p. Lit. 30.000. – ᴿRHE 84 (1989) 264 (J. *Ruysschaert*).

H7.4 **Sacramenta,** *Gratia.*

7778* *Adam* Gottfried, Konfirmation, Konfirmandenunterricht: ➤ 894, EvKL 2 (1989) 1370-77.

7779 *Aleixandre* Dolores, Tres lugares para acoger la gracia [i. la casa ... Heb 2,12; ii. el desierto, Os 2,16; iii. el camino, Prov 20,24]: SalTerrae 77 (1989) 377-386.

7780 **Barrett** C. K., Kerk, ambt en sacramenten in het Nieuwe Testament [1983/5 ➤ 1,7343], ᵀDe *Ru.* Haag 1988, Boeken-C. 110p. ƒ19,50. 90-239-0099-5. – ᴿTsTNijm 29 (1989) 177 (L. *Visschers*).

7781 **Barth** G., *a)* Il battesimo in epoca protocristiana: StBPaid 79, 1987 ➤ 4,8808a; Lit. 18.000: ᴿProtestantesimo 44 (1989) 134s (F. *Ferrario*). – *b)* El bautismo en el tiempo del cristianismo primitivo. REB 60, 1986 ➤ 2,5967 ... 4,8808b: ᴿCiuD 202 (1989) 252 (J. *Gutiérrez*).

7782 **Baumann** Urs, Die Ehe – ein Sakrament? [Diss. 1987 ➤ 4,8810*]. Z 1988, Benziger. 512p. DM88. – ᴿTGL 79 (1989) 91s (W. *Beinert*).

7783 **Blanchette** Claude, Pénitence et eucharistie; dossier d'une question controversée: Recherches NS 21. Montréal/P 1989, Bellarmin/Cerf. 336p. [CBQ 52,379].

7784 *Brinkman* M. E., De verwevenheid van schepping en sacrament; nieuwe perspectieven vanuit de oecumenische discussie: TsTNijm 29 (1989) 38-54; Eng. 54.

7785 **Brooks** Oscar S., The drama of decision; baptism in the New Testament. Peabody MA 1987, Hendrickson. 177p. [GraceTJ 9,313]. $10 pa. – ᴿWestTJ 51 (1989) 171-3 (J. W. *Scott,* also on M. Gʀᴇᴇɴ).

7786 **Carpenter** James A., Nature and grace; toward an integral perspective. NY 1988, Crossroad. xi-229p. $22.50. – ᴿTS 50 (1989) 580s (S. *Duffy*).

7787 **Cecchinato** Angelo, Celebrare la confermazione; rassegna critica dell'attuale dibattito teologico sul sacramento: Caro Salutis Cardo 3. Padova 1987, Messaggero / S. Giustina. 323p Lit. 28.000. – ᴿNRT 111 (1989) 991s (A. *Toubeau*).

7788 *Cenzón* María Andrelita, Ecclesial dimension of baptism through the Augustinian category Ecclesia mater: AnnTh 3 (1989) 315-345.

7789 **Chauvet** Louis M, Symbole et sacrement; une relecture sacramentelle de l'existence chrétienne: CogF 144, 1987 ➤ 4,8813: ᴿActuBbg 26 (1989) 69 (J. M. *Fondevila*); REB 49 (1989) 230-2 (J. *Ariovaldo da Silva*); NRT 111 (1989) 255-7 (P. *Lebeau*: diss. summa cum laude, P 1986); RTLv 20 (1989) 194-203 (G. *Fourez*); RTPhil 121 (1989) 211-223 (H. *Mottu*).

7790 **Cipriani** Settimio, Evangelizzare i Sacramenti; riflessioni biblico-liturgiche per la celebrazione dei sacramenti: Parola e Liturgia 20, CinB 1988, Paoline. 321p. Lit. 14.000. – ᴿAsprenas 36 (1989) 98s (P. *Pifano*).

7790* **Cordileone** Salvatore, General absolution; a study of the present norms in their theological and historical context: diss. Pont. Univ. Gregoriana, N° 3582, ᴰ*Navarrete* U. R 1989. 290 p. – RTLv 21,587.

7791 *Cozzoli* Mauro, Partecipi della natura divina; vita e virtù teologali: RivScR 3,1 (1989) 57-80.

7792 **Dale** James W., Classic baptism; *baptizō*, an inquiry into the meaning of the word as determined by the usage of classsical Greek writers [1867], new pref. *Adams* J. E., *Countess* R. H. Wauconda IL / Phillipsburg NJ 1989, Bolchazy-Carducci / Presb. & R. 354 p. $25. 0-86516-224-7 / 0-87552-230-3 [TDig 37,48: one of his 4 volumes on baptism].

7793 *Denis* Henri, *al.*, Guérir de la mort; réflexions sur le Sacrement de l'Onction des Malades [... laboratoire de recherche]: Fac. Théol. Lyon, Essais. Lyon 1986, Profac. 143 p. – ᴿRHPR 69 (1989) 491s (B. *Kaempf*).

7794 *Dixon* Richard D., *al.*, Asking the 'born-again' question [Gallup poll: question is inadequate unless alternative is provided]: RRelRes 30 (1988) 33-39 [< BS 146 (1989) 96, S. S. *Cook*].

7795 **Downey** Michael, Clothed in Christ; the sacraments and Christian living 1987 → 3,7461: ᴿHorizons 16 (1989) 173s (B. *Cooke,* also on OSBORNE K.).

7796 **Espeja** Jesús, Sacramentos y seguimiento de Jesús: Glosas 12. Salamanca 1989, S. Esteban. 186 p. – ᴿCiTom 116 (1989) 621s (D. *Salado*).

7796* ᴱ**Fahey** Michael A., Catholic perspectives on BEM 1986 → 3,7465: ᴿStEcum 6 (1988) 297s (M. *Favretto*).

7797 **Ferraro** Giuseppe, I sacramenti e l'identità cristiana 1986 → 4,8815*; Lit. 25.000; ᴿParVi 33 (1988) 233s (P. *Dacquino*: spirituale, catechetico).

7797* **Fugel** Adolf, Tauflehre und Taufliturgie bei Huldrych ZWINGLI: Diss. ᴰ*Baumgartner* J. FrS 1989. – RTLv 21,566 (> EurHS 23/380).

7798 **Gaboriau** Florent, Chrétiens 'confirmés'; le sacrement de la croissance: Théologie Nouvelle 8, 1987 → 4,8816*: ᴿGregorianum 70 (1989) 356s (J. *Galot*); RThom 89 (1989) 125-8 (G.-M. *Marty*).

7799 **Ganoczy** Alexandre, Aus seiner Fülle haben wir alle empfangen; Grundriss der Gnadenlehre. Dü 1989, Patmos. 376 p. DM 50. – ᴿTGL 79 (1989) 328 (W. *Beinert*); TR 85 (1989) 475-7 (G. L. *Müller*).

7800 **Ganoczy** Alexandre, An introduction to Catholic sacramental theology 1989 → 1,7362; 4,8818: ᴿRExp 86 (1989) 648s (T. *George*).

7801 **Gelpi** Donald L., Grace as transmuted experience and social process, and other essays in North American theology 1988 → 4,197; 0-8191-6367-8. – ᴿGregorianum 70 (1989) 578s (J. *O'Donnell*: oversimplifications); LVitae 44 (1989) 355s (G. van *Hoomissen*).

7801* *Hahn* Ferdinand, Kindersegnung und Kindertaufe im ältesten Christentum: → 68, ᶠGNILKA J., Urchristentum 1989, 497-507.

7802 *Hawkings* David G., Infant baptism; a view from the font: ExpTim 100 (1988s) 461s.

7803 *Heller* Jan, Die altneue Frage nach Kindertaufe: ComViat 32 (1989) 1-4.

7803* *Hempelmann* Reinhard, Sakrament als Ort der Vermittlung des Heils: Diss. ᴰ*Ritschl*. Heidelberg 1988s. – TR 85 (1989) 516.

7804 **Hotz** Robert, Los sacramentos en nuevas perspectivas [1979] 1986 → 4,8822: ᴿFranBog 30 (1988) 241 (J. M. *Siciliani*); VerVida 116 (1988) 162 (D. *Cervera*).

7805 *Irwin* Kevin W., Recent sacramental theology III (Message of the Sacraments series, ᴱ*Hellwig* Monika): Thomist 53 (1989) 281-313.

7805* *Kasper* Walter, Il messaggio della remissione dei peccati, ᵀ*Simoncioni* Paolo: CommStrum 103 (1989) 13-23.

7806 **Kavanagh** Aidan, Confirmation 1988 ➤ 4,8825: ᴿAnglTR 70 (1988) 379-381 (P. V. *Marshall*); CalvinT 24 (1989) 181-3 (C. E. *Zylstra*); JTS 40 (1989) 720-2 (P. *Bradshaw*: grew out of Mass-dismissal); NewTR 2,2 (1989) 111s (M. R. *Francis*); TS 50 (1989) 184-6 (B. *Cooke*, also on TURNER P.).

7806* **Kavanagh** Aidan, Batismo, rito de iniciação cristã; tradição, reformas, perspectivas, ᵀ*Lamego* Maria: Líturgia e Teologia. São Paulo 1987, Paulinas. 195 p. 85-05-00624-0. – ᴿPerspT 20 (1988) 127-9 (F. *Taborda*).

7807 *Kavanagh* Aidan, The origins and reform of Confirmation [Schmemann lecture 1988]: SVlad 23 (1989) 5-20.

7808 *Kilmartin* Edward J., Sacraments as liturgy of the Church: TS 50 (1989) 527-547.

7810 **Kuhrt** Gordon, Believing in baptism. L 1987, Mowbray. v-186 p. £6 pa. – ᴿTLond 92 (1989) 41s (J. *Halliburton*).

7811 **Laporte** Jean-Marc, Patience and power; grace for the First World [also 2d/3d in ch.2]. NY 1988, Paulist. iv-297 p. $15. – ᴿTS 50 (1989) 811-3 (S. *Duffy*); ZkT 111 (1989) 375-7 (K. H. *Neufeld*: serious objections).

7812 *Larrabe* José Luis, La confesión de los pecados en las culturas y religiones extrabíblicas: StLeg 29 (1988) 93-104.

7813 **Lawler** Michael G., Symbol and sacrament; a contemporary sacramental theology 1987 ➤ 4,8827*: ᴿThomist 53 (1989) 732-4 (K. W. *Irwin*); TS 50 (1989) 590s (G. *McCauley*).

7814 **Magne** Jean, Logique des sacrements: Origines chrétiennes 3. P 1989, auct. 247 p. F 148.

7815 **Maldonado** Luis, Sacramentalidad evangélica; signos de la presencia para el camino 1987 ➤ 4,8830: ᴿRET 49 (1989) 453-6 (J. M. *Canals*); SalT 76 (1988) 413-5 (F. de *Carlos Otto*).

7816 *Mottu* Henry, Les sacrements selon Karl BARTH et Eberhard JÜNGEL: FoiVie 88 (1989) 33-55 [57-93, *Lienhard* F., *Bizeul* Y., encore sur Jüngel].

7817 *Mühlen* Heribert, Das Verhältnis von 'innerer Taufe' und Taufsakrament; gehört das persönliche Taufbekenntnis zum Wesen der Taufe?: TGL 79 (1989) 552-567.

7818 *Obijole* Bayo, Infant baptism, a critical review [... of the facts]: AfER 30 (1988) 299-312.

7819 **Osborne** Kenan B., Sacramental theology 1988 ➤ 4,8837: ᴿLvSt 14 (1989) 63 (L. *Leijssen*); TLZ 114 (1989) 53s (G. *Wenz*); Worship 62 (1988) 551s (E. J. *Cutrone*).

7820 **Osborne** Kenan B., The Christian sacraments of initiation 1987 ➤ 3,7496; 4,8836: ᴿDocLife 38 (1988) 105s (L. G. *Walsh*); PrPeo 3 (1989) 269-271 (O. F. *Cummings*).

7821 **Philips** G., L'union personnelle avec le Dieu vivant; essai sur l'origine et le sens de la grâce créée: BiblETL 36. Lv 1989 = œuvre postume 1974, Univ./Peeters. 299 p. [RHE 85, 161, R. *Aubert*].

7821* ᴱ**Pinnock** Clark H., The grace of God, the will of man; a case for Arminianism. GR 1989, Zondervan. xiv-318 p. $15 pa. – ᴿAndrUnS 27 (1989) 241s (S. P. *Vitrano*: 'symposium' – not clearly a meeting).

7822 **Reckinger** François, Baptiser des enfants, à quelles conditions? Réflexions théologiques et pastorales. Bru 1987, Nauwelaerts. 236 p. Fb 620. 2-8038-0011-X. – ᴿGregorianum 70 (1989) 355s (J. *Galot*); RTLv 20 (1989) 242 (A. *Haquin*); ScEspr 41 (1989) 117-120 (J.-M. *Dufort*).

7823 **Richter** Klemens, Was die sakramentalen Zeichen bedeuten; zu Fragen aus der Gemeinde von heute: Gemeinde im Gottesdienst. FrB 1988, Herder. 159 p. DM 18,80 [TR 86, 41, M. *Probst*].

7824 **Rocchetta** Carlo, I sacramenti della fede; saggio di teologia biblica sui sacramenti quali 'meraviglie di salvezza' nel tempo della Chiesa 1982 ➤ 64,7040 ... 2,5999: ᴿParVi 33 (1988) 232s (P. *Dacquino*: malgrado la fatica, non è veramente una teologia biblica).

7825 *Roloff* Jürgen, Gnade, biblisch: ➤ 894, EvKL 2 (1988) 222-5 [-239, *al.*].

7826 *Ruokanen* Miikka, Das Problem der Gnadenlehre in der Dogmatik G. EBELINGS: KerDo 35 (1989) 2-22; Eng. 22.

7826* **Saraiva Martins** José, I sacramenti della Nuova Alleanza: Subs. Urbaniana 22, 1987 ➤ 3,7498: ᴿTeresianum 40 (1989) 257s (J. *Castellano*).

7827 *Schmied* Augustin, Kindertaufe und Erbsünde: TGegw 31 (1988) 171-8.

7828 **Sedgwick** Timothy F., Sacramental ethics; paschal identity and the Christian life. Ph 1987, Fortress. 118 p. $11.15; pa. $8. – ᴿRelStR 15 (1989) 62 (L. H. *Steffen*).

7829 **Smith** Patricia, Teaching sacraments: Theology & Life 17. Wilmington 1987, Glazier. 196 p. $9 pa. – ᴿHorizons 16 (1989) 172 (J. *Martos*).

7829* **Snela** Bogdan, Kindertaufe; ja oder nein?; Plädoyer für die Erwachsenentaufe: Evangelium konkret, 1987 ➤ 3,7503: ᴿQLtg 69 (1988) 108s (J. *Lamberts*).

7830 **Steffen** U., Taufe; Ursprung und Sinn des christlichen Einweihungsritus: Symbole. Stu 1988, Kreuz. 188 p.; 4 color. fig. DM 29,80. 3-7831-0939-6. – ᴿActuBbg 26 (1989) 71s (J. *Boada*); Stromata 45 (1989) 236s.

7831 **Stuhlhofer** Franz, Symbol oder Realität? Taufe und Abendmahl 1988 ➤ 4,8847; Fs 7: ᴿForumKT 5 (1989) 317s (P. C. *Düren*); TPQ 137 (1989) 419s (F. *Reckinger*).

7831* *a) Tragan* Pius-Ramon, Le radici bibliche del sacramento della Confermazione; – *b) Peri* Vittorio, La cresima ieri e oggi; considerazioni storiche e pastorali: RivLtg 76 (1989) 214-231 / 151-213.

7832 **Vorgrimler** Hubert, Sakramententheologie: Leitfaden Theologie 17, 1987 ➤ 3,7509; 4,8852: ᴿTLZ 114 (1989) 306-9 (F. *Jacob*).

7833 **Walsh** Liam J., The sacraments of initiation; baptism, confirmation, Eucharist: Theology Library 7. L 1988, Chapman. xii-317 p. £12 pa. 0-225-66499-2 [Greg 70,202].

7834 **Wenz** Gunther, Einführung in die evangelische Sakramentenlehre. Da 1988, Wiss. viii-267 p. DM 42. – ᴿTLZ 114 (1989) 841-3 (M. *Plathow*); TR 85 (1989) 478-480 (A. *Moos*).

7835 **Werbick** Jürgen, Schulderfahrung und Busssakrament. Mainz 1985, Grünewald. 172 p. DM 26,80. 3-7867-1199-2. – ᴿGregorianum 70 (1989) 577s (J. M. *Millás*).

7835* **Ziegenaus** Anton, *a)* Christus begegnen im Sakrament der Krankensalbung. Leutesdorf 1989, Johannes. 29 p. – ᴿForumKT 5 (1989) 231s (G. *Staudigl*); – *b)* Das Busssakrament als Brennpunkt der Umkehr: ForumKT 4 (1988) 282-297.

H7.6   *Ecclesiologia, theologia missionis, laici* – The Church.

7836 **Alberigo** Giuseppe, La Chiesa nella storia: BiblCuRel 51. Brescia 1988, Paideia. 335 p. Lit. 35.000. 88-394-0411-2 [Greg 70,196]. – ᴿCrNSt 10 (1989) 625-8 (O. *Capitani*).

7837 **Antón** Ángel, El misterio de la Iglesia 1986s ➤ 3,7517; 4,8859: ᴿActuBbg 26 (1989) 62s (J. *Boada*, 2); Angelicum 66 (1989) 342s (G. *Phan Tan Thanh*, 2); DivThom 91 (1988) 478s (B. *Ardura*,1); NRT 111 (1989) 104s (R. *Escol*, 1s); RasT 30 (1989) 81-86 (A. *Marranzini*); RTLv 20 (1989)

234s (A. de *Halleux*, 1); Salesianum 51 (1989) 845s (D. *Valentini*: 1s; sub 'Angel A.' también Indice); TüTQ 169 (1989) 249s (P. *Walter*, 2).

7838 *Antón* Ángel, O mistério da Igreja na evolução histórica das ideias eclesiológicas: Brotéria 128 (1989) 181-195.

7839 **Arnau-García** Ramón, San Vicente FERRER y las eclesiologías del Cisma 1987 ▶ 3,7519; 4,8861: ᴿSalmanticensis 36 (1989) 393 (J. I. *Tellechea Idigoras*).

7839* **Baier** Walter, Die Kirche ... A. BERLAGE 1984 ▶ 1,7407; 2,6021: ᴿForumKT 4 (1988) 74-76 (L. *Scheffczyk*).

7840 **Barbaglio** G., La laicità del credente; interpretazione biblica. Assisi 1987, Cittadella. 162 p. Lit. 15.000. – ᴿParVi 34 (1989) 296s (M. *Semeraro*).

7840* *Barrett* C. K., School, conventicle, and Church in the New Testament: ▶ 120, ᶠLOHSE E., Wissenschaft 1989, 96-110.

7841 *a) Barth* Hans-Martin, 'Il sacerdozio universale' secondo M. LUTHER; – *b) Sartori* Luigi, Il 'sensus fidelium' del popolo di Dio e il concorso dei laici nelle determinazioni dottrinali: StEcum 6 (1988) 9-31; Eng. 31s / 33-57; Eng. 57s.

7841* *Berger* Klaus, Kirche NT: ▶ 911, TRE 18 (1989) 198-218 (–344 *al*.; 227-252 kath., *Finkenzeller* Josef).

7842 **Blázquez** R., La Iglesia del Concilio Vaticano II: Verdad e imagen 107. Salamanca 1988, Sígueme. 510 p. 84-301-1056-9. – ᴿActuBbg 26 (1989) 226 (I. *Riudor*); NatGrac 36 (1989) 144 (A. *Villalmonte*); NRT 111 (1989) 960 (L.-J. *Renard*).

7843 **Boff** Leonardo, Church, charism and power 1985 ▶ 1,7413 ... 3,7358: ᴿHeythJ 30 (1989) 77s (Elizabeth *Lord*).

7844 *Boff* Leonardo, CEBs: que significa 'novo modo de toda a Igreja ser?': REB 49 (1989) 546-562.

7845 *Bojorge* Horacio, El fiel laico en el horizonte de su pertenencia; aspectos bíblicos de la teología del laicado II: Stromata 45 (1989) 191-233.

7846 *Bühler* Pierre, L'Église réformée; une Église sans mystère?: Irénikon 61 (1988) 485-505; Eng. 506.

7847 *Bueno de la Fuente* Eloy, ¿Rediscubrimiento de los laicos o de la Iglesia? [bibliog.] II: RET 49 (1989) 69-99.

7848 *a) Campbell* R. A., Essential aspects of the Church in the Bible; – *b) Kuen* A., The free or gathered Church: EvRT 13,1 (Exeter 1989) 5-22 / 23-29 [< NTAbs 33,342s].

7849 ᴱ**Carson** D. A., *a)* Biblical interpretation and the Church 1982/5 ▶ 1,459; 2,243; – *b)* The Church in the Bible and the world 1984/7 ▶ 3,526: ᴿAndrUnS 27 (1989) 137s (B. *Norman*).

7849* **Cenzon Santos** Maria Andrelita, Baptismal ecclesiology of St. AUGUSTINE: diss. Ateneo S. Croce, ᴰ*Miralles* A. R [no date, RTLv 21,568]. 540 p.

7850 **Chantraine** G., Les laïcs, chrétiens dans le monde 1987 ▶ 3,7556; 4,8879: ᴿNRT 111 (1989) 457s (P. *Lebeau*).

7851 *Chevallier* Max Alain, La Iglesia, tensión entre unidad y pluralidad [< L'unité plurielle de l'Église d'après le NT: RHPR 66 (1986) 3-20], ᵀᴱ*Rocafiguera* Josep M.: SelT 28 (1989) 19-28.

7852 **Ciola** Nicola, Il dibattito ecclesiastico [o? ecclesiologico ▶ 2,6035 ... 4,8882] in Italia – uno studio bibliografico (1963-84). R 1986, Pont. Univ. Lateranense. 263 p. – ᴿProtestantesimo 44 (1989) 233s (C. *Tron*: 'ecclesiastico').

7853 *Congar* Yves, Vatican I questioned; review of conciliar ecclesiology [mostly on *Bermejo* L., 1984 < RSPT 68 (1984) 449-456], ᵀ*Gispert-Sauch* G.: Vidyajyoti 52 (1988) 45-53 [247-9, Bermejo's reaction].

7854 *Cosmao* Vincent, Problématique du développement; défi à l'Église: LavalTP 44 (1988) 3-18.

7855 ᵀᴱ**Dattrino** Lorenzo, OTTATO da Milevi, La vera Chiesa 1988 ➤ 4,8894; Lit. 20.000: ᴿLateranum 55 (1989) 494s (O. *Pasquato*). StPatav 36 (1989) 634s (anche O. *Pasquato*).

7856 **Descamps** A., Jésus et l'Église [1958-80] 1987 ➤ 3,213: ᴿRivB 37 (1989) 235-240 (M. *Pesce*).

7857 **Descy** Serge, Introduction à l'église melkite II/1,1986 ➤ 3,7573: ᴿBLitEc 90 (1989) 79 (S. *Légasse*); FreibZ 35 (1988) 549-551 (M. *Brun*).

7858 **Dianich** Severino, Iglesia en misión; hacia una eclesiología dinámica [1985]: Verdad e imagen 108, 1988 ➤ 4,8898; pt. 1200: ᴿActuBbg 26 (1989) 226 (J. I. *González Faus*); Proyección 36 (1989) 239 (A. *Sánchez*).

7859 **Diez** Karlheinz, Christus und seine Kirche; zum Kirchenverständnis des Petrus CANISIUS: KkKSt 51, 1987 ➤ 3,7575; 4,8899: ᴿNRT 111 (1989) 103s (A. *Toubeau*).

7860 **Drushal** M. E., Implementing theory Z in the Church; managing people as Jesus did: AshlandT 20 (1988) 47-62 [< NTAbs 33,342].

7861 *a) Duda* Bonaventura, Ecclesia utpote communio-koinonia; – *b) Aračiá* Pero, Sacerdos in populo Dei (en croate): ➤ 4,93, ᶠLADIKA J. = BogSmot 58,4 (1988) 143-8 / 132-142.

7862 **Dulles** Avery, The reshaping of Catholicism; current challenges in the theology of Church [12 art.] 1988 ➤ 4,183: ᴿAmerica 160 (1989) 65 (R. *Weakland*: uses 'secular' vaguely); CalvinT 24 (1989) 334-7 (P. G. *Schrotenboer*: encouraging); NewTR 2,2 (1989) 106 (Mary E. *Hines*); RExp 86 (1989) 453 (E. G. *Hinson*); TS 50 (1989) 385s (P. *Chirico*).

7863 *Dulles* Avery, A half-century of ecclesiology: Theological Studies 50,3 (Fiftieth Anniversary volume, Systematics issue, 1989) 419-442.

7863* *Eijk* A. H. C. van, The Church; mystery, sacrament, sign, instrument, symbolic reality: Bijdragen 50 (1989) 178-202.

7864 **Elberti** Arturo, Il sacerdozio regale dei fedeli nei prodromi del Concilio Ecumenico Vaticano II (1903-1962): AnGreg 254. R 1989, Pont. Univ. Gregoriana. xxiv-300 p. Lit. 45.000. 88-7652-601-3.

7865 **Espeja** J., L'Église, mémoire et prophétie [1983] 1987 ➤ 3,7585; 4,8902: ᴿNRT 111 (1989) 260s (A. *Toubeau*).

7866 **Estrada** Juan A., Del misterio de la Iglesia al pueblo de Dios; sobre las ambigüedades de una Iglesia mistérica: Verdad e Imagen 104, 1988 ➤ 4,8903: ᴿLumenVr 38 (1989) 87-89 (U. *Gil Ortega*: problemas reales y de suma importancia); NRT 111 (1989) 960s (A. *Toubeau*).

7867 **Estrada** Juan A., La Iglesia, identidad y cambio 1985 ➤ 1,7452 ... 3,7587: ᴿEfMex 6 (1988) 302-5 (M. *Olimón Nolasco*).

7867* *Fahlbusch* Erwin, *al*, [*Döring* Heinrich, R.-Kath.], Kirche: ➤ 894, EvKL 2 (1989) 1046-1094 [1069-73].

7868 'Fare chiesa': ParVi 34 (1989): fasc. 1, Il progetto di Gesù (*Boggio* G., *Vallauri* E., *Filippini* R., *Mosetto* F., *Maggioni* B.); 2. Le prime realizzazioni (*Fabris* R., *Lenoci* M., *Marconcini* B., *Cimosa* M.); 3. Camminando insieme (*Franco* E., *Sacchi* A., *Pasquetto* V., *Dalbesio* A.); 4. In continua conversione (*Nobile* M., *Infante* R., *Cipriani* S., *Bianchi* M.); 5. Nella novità evangelica (*Monari* L., *Biguzzi* G., *Barbi* A., *Valentini* A., *Làconi* M.); 6. Verso la Gerusalemme celeste (*Ghidelli* C., *Migliasso* S. *Masini* M., *Cantore* Stefania).

7869 *Feldkaemper* Ludger, The Bible and our missionary work: Word & Worship 21 (Bangalore 1988) 212-8. 243-250 [296-304, *Herrera* C.; < TContext 6/2, 36s].

7869* *Fung* Raymond, Mission in Christ's way; the Strachan lectures [Costa Rica 1988]: IntRMiss 78 (1989) 4-29.

7870 *Galeota* Gustavo, *Mancia* Anita, Dall'unità nucleare della Chiesa alla 'cristianità santa'; la chiesa locale in Lutero: StEcum 5 (1987) 325-370; Eng. 370s [455-482, la famiglia nucleo della Chiesa].

7870* *Galli* Carlos M., Tres de la eclesiología conciliar del Pueblo de Dios [GUARDINI R., ADAM K., PINSK J.]: TArg 25 (1988) 171-203.

7871 **Garijo-Guembe** Miguel M. Gemeinschaft der Heiligen; Grund, Wesen und Struktur der Kirche. Dü 1988, Patmos. 309 p. DM 39,80. – RGregorianum 70 (1989) 389 (J. E. *Vercruysse*); NRT 111 (1989) 961s (A. *Toubeau*: équilibré); TLZ 114 (1989) 632-4 (W. *Huber*); TS 50 (1989) 407 (L. *Örsy*).

7872 **Gherardini** Brunero, La Chiesa mistero e servizio 1988 → 4,8913: RAnnTh 3 (1989) 388-391 (E. *Juliá*); Lateranum 55 (1989) 519s (*ipse*).

7873 **Giglioni** Paolo, La missione sulle vie del Concilio; il pensiero missionario di GIOVANNI PAOLO II. R 1988, Pont. Univ. Urbaniana. 210 p. Lit. 24.000. – RCC 140 (1989,2) 203 (G. *Caprile*).

7874 **Gil** Josep, Sígnes de pertinença a l'Església: Els daus 85. Barc 1987, Claret. – RQVidCr 140 (1988) 120 (E. *Vilanova*).

7875 **Gil Sousa** José Antonio, La eclesiología de Bartolomé CARRANZA DE MIRANDA [diss.] Toledo 1986, Seminario. 252 p. – RScripTPamp 21 (1989) 369 (J. R. *Villar*).

7876 **Grenholm** Carl-Henric, Vad skall kyrkan bekänna? Frågor till et rådslag om kyrkans identitet. Älvskö 1986, Verbum. 175 p. – RTsTKi 59 (1988) 133s (H. *Hegstad*).

7877 **Grootaers** J., Le chantier reste ouvert; les laïcs dans l'Église et dans le monde. P 1988, Centurion. 180 p. F 89. – RNRT 111 (1989) 459s (L.-J. *Renard*).

7878 **Hanson** Paul D., The people called 1986 (1987) → 2,6072 ... 4,8920: RBibTB 19 (1989) 38 (Betty Jane *Lillie*); Paradigms 5 (1989) 158s (M. *McEntire*); Worship 62 (1989) 558-560 (D. *Launderville*).

7879 **Hinson** E. Glenn, Understandings of the Church: Sources of Early Christian Thought 1986 → 4,8922: RIntRMiss 78 (1989) 226-8 (H. *Rowold*); SecC 7 (1989s) 113-5 (D. *Tripp*).

7880 *Hirth* Volkmar, Gedanken über den Beitrag des ATs zu einer Lehre vom Gemeindeaufbau: TLZ 114 (1989) 93-98.

7881 **Hübner** Eberhard, Theologie und Empirie der Kirche; Prolegomena zur praktischen Theologie 1985 → 1,7485; 3,7616: RZevEth 32 (1988) 234s (C. *Frey*).

7882 **Hume** Basil, Towards a civilization of love; being Church in today's world [1988 Australia lectures]. L 1988, Hodder & S. xi-177 p. £7. – RTLond 92 (1989) 423s (A. *Webster*).

7883 **Hutchison** William R., Errand to the world; American Protestant thought and foreign missions 1987 → 4,8926.9690: RAndrUnS 27 (1989) 87-89 (G. R. *Knight*); Horizons 16 (1989) 161s (Amanda *Porterfield*); JAAR 57 (1989) 194-6 (G. T. *Miller*); JRel 69 (1989) 254s (T. *Swanson*).

7884 **Karrer** Leo, Aufbruch der Christen; das Ende der klerikalen Kirche ['die 0.05% männlichen Amtsträger für die 99.95% Frauen und Männer in der Kirche ... allein definieren, was in der Kirche offiziell von Belang ist']: Evangelium konkret. Mü 1989, Kösel. 189 p. DM 24,80. – ᴿTPQ 137 (1989) 421s (M. *Lehner*).

7885 *Kerkhofs* Jan, Omgaan met de leegte; pastoraltheologie als een bevrijdingstheologie: CollatVL 19 (1989) 156-174.

7886 *a) Killus* Dorothea R., Die missionstheologische Dynamis des ATs; – *b) Scheurer* Erich, Der Bogen auf der Erde und in den Wolken; – *c) Betz* Otto, Das Gnadenamt des Jüngers und Apostels; – *d) Hille* Rolf, Ist Missio intolerant?: ➤ 28*, ᶠBEYERHAUS P., Martyria 1989, 58-63 / 64-71 / 72-82 / 45-51.

7887 *Komonchak* Joseph A., The local church: ChSt 28 (1989) 320-335.

7888 **Krikonis** Christos T., ☉ The mystery of the Church; patristic views. Thessaloniki 1989. 118 p. [= Kleronomía 18,1 (1986) 5-93]. – ᴿTAth 60 (1989) 856-8 (M. A. *Siotis*).

7889 *a) Krusche* Werner, Die Kirche im Spannungsfeld von Charisma und Institution; – *b) Forte* Bruno, Kirche, Charismen und Dienste in der Erneuerung der katholischen Ekklesiologie; – *c) Volf* Miroslav, Kirche als Gemeinschaft; ekklesiologische Überlegungen aus freikirchlicher Perspektive; – *d) Luz* Ulrich, Charisma und Institution in neutestamentlicher [*Lohmann* Theodor, aus religionswissenschaftlicher] Sicht; EvT 49 (1989) 20-38 / 39-52 / 52-76 / 76-94 [95-110].

7890 *LaVerdiere* E., 'To the ends of the earth', a biblical perspective [use of Scripture in U.S. Bishops' pastoral on world mission]: Emmanuel 95,5 (1989) 262-9. 284 [< NTAbs 33,347].

7891 *Levoratti* Armando J., Un aporte fundamental a la eclesiología [*Lohfink* G., español 1986]: RBíbArg 30s (1988) 295-319.

7892 **Lienhard** M., L'évangile et l'Église selon LUTHER. P 1989, Cerf. 287 p. F 145. 2-204-03080-5 [ÉTRel 64,673].

7893 ᴱ**Limouris** Gennadios, Church, Kingdom, world; the Church as mystery and prophetic sign 1985/6 ➤ 3,665: ᴿIrénikon 61 (1988) 310-2 (E. *Lanne*); RTPhil 121 (1989) 124s (L. *Rumpf*).

7894 *Linn* Gerhard, Dein Wille geschehe; Mission in der Nachfolge Jesu Christi: ÖkRu 38 (1989) 128-146 [147-156, *Löffler* P. über NEWBIGIN L.].

7894* ᴱ**Löser** Werner, Die römisch-katholische Kirche: Kirchen der Welt 20, 1986 ➤ 2,323; 3,7638: ᴿTsTKi 59 (1988) 233-5 (Ola *Tjørhom*).

7895 **Lohfink** Gerhard, Jesus in community; the social dimension of Christian faith [Wie hat Jesus Gemeinde gewollt? 1982 ➤ 63,5118], ᵀ*Galvin* John P. 1985 ➤ 1,7507 ... 3,7644: ᴿHeythJ 30 (1989) 76 (J. *Coventry*).

7896 **Lohfink** Gerhard, Gesù come voleva la sua comunità; la Chiesa quale dovrebbe essere 1987 ➤ 3,7643: ᴿCC 140 (1989,1) 617 (K. *Stock*); RivAscM 13 (1988) 280 (G. *D'Urso*).

7897 *Luz* U., Kirche ist Alternativgesellschaft der Liebe: Reformiertes Forum 3,17 (Z 1989) 12s [< NTAbs 33,348, where perhaps in fidelity to the original it is not made clear what 'society (? of love)' is the alternative to the Church].

7897* **Malanowski** G., É. MERSCH.../ Church: diss. 1988. – DissA 49 (1988s) 353-A.

7898 **Martini** Carlo M., *a)* Der immer neue Antlitz der Kirche. Graz 1988, Styria. 176 p. DM 24,80. – *b)* Es ist der Herr – Christus begegnen. FrB c. 1989, Herder. 96 p. DM 11,50. – ᴿTPQ 137 (1989) 106 (J. *Hörmandinger*).

7898* **Martini** Carlo Maria, Uomini di pace e di riconciliazione: Meditazioni sulla coscienza missionaria: Letture bibliche. R 1985, Borla. 136 p.

7899 *Michiels* Robrecht, *a)* The self-understanding of the Church after Vatican II: LvSt 14 (1989) 83-105; – *b)* Kerk van Jesus Christus II [...Wie hat Jesus Gemeinde gewollt?...]: CollatVL 19 (1989) 24-51.

7899* **Miller** E.J., J.H. NEWMAN on the idea of the Church 1987 ⟶ 3,7653: ᴿChH 58 (1989) 118s (P. *Misner*).

7900 **Neglia** A., Laici senza complessi; intuizioni profetiche di Antonio ROSMINI. Messina 1988, 'E.S.U.R.' iii-167p. Lit. 15.000. – ᴿNRT 111 (1989) 962s (L.-J. *Renard*).

7901 **Neuner** Peter, Der Laie und das Gottesvolk 1988 ⟶ 4,8965; DM 32. 3-7820-0572-4: ᴿTPQ 137 (1989) 200 (M. *Lehner*); TsTNijm 29 (1989) 77 (P. *Valkenberg*).

7902 *Ochoa* José M., [JUAN PABLO II] La exhortación apostólica 'Christifideles laici'; riqueza y cuestión pendiente: LumenVr 38 (1989) 353-381.

7902* **Panizzolo** S., *a)* Coscienza di Chiesa nella teologia e nella prassi; indirizzi ecclesiologici nei documenti della Conferenza episcopale italiana dal 1965 al 1980. Bo 1989, Dehoniane. 282p. – *b)* (con *Castellucci* E.) Noi chiesa; introduzione all'ecclesiologia. R 1989, Paoline. 218p. – ᴿLateranum 55 (1989) 483-5 (M. *Semeraro*).

7903 ᴱ**Petit** Jean-Claude, *Breton* Jean-Claude, La laïcat; les limites d'un système; Actes du Congrès de la Société Canadienne de Théologie, Montréal 17-19 oct. 1986: Héritage et projet 36, 1987 ⟶ 3,692: ᴿScEspr 41 (1989) 131-3 (A. *Beauregard*).

7904 *Phan* Peter C., God as holy mystery and the quest for God-equivalents in interreligious dialogue: IrTQ 55 (1989) 277-290.

7905 *a) Pie y Ninot* Salvador, Eclesiología fundamental, 'status quaestionis': RET 49 (1989) 361-403; – *b) Quacquarelli* Antonio, L'ecclesiologia nella esegesi di CROMAZIO: VetChr 26 (1989) 5-22 (201-6).

7905* **Poisson** Raymond, Église et Eucharistie dans la pensée de Pierre TEILHARD de Chardin: diss. Pont. Univ. Gregoriana, Nᵒ 3575, ᴰ*Rosato* P.J. R 1989. 438p. – RTLv 21,553.

7906 **Pozzo** Guido, Lumen Gentium; costituzione dogmatica sulla Chiesa: Collana Conc. Vat. II, 3. CasM 1988, Piemme. 260p. – ᴿLateranum 55 (1989) 481-3 (P. *Scabini*).

7906* *Rau* Gerhard, Volkskirche heute – im Spiegel ihrer theologischen Problematisierung [444 Schriften]: VerkFor 32 (1987) 2-31 (–83).

7907 *Rebeiro* M., Origin of the Church; 'did Jesus found a church?'; a historical survey and a theological discussion, [*Küng* H., *Rahner* K....]: LivingWord 95 (1989) 139-169 [< TContext 7/1,39].

7908 **Rommen** Edward, Die Notwendigkeit der Umkehr; Missionsstrategie und Gemeindeaufbau in der Sicht evangelischer Missionswissenschaftler Nordamerikas [ev. Diss. München 1986]. Giessen 1987, Brunnen. x-284p. DM 32 pa. – ᴿTR 85 (1989) 490s (N.M. *Borengässer*).

7909 **Rosmini** Antonio, The five wounds of the Church [1832, publ. 1848], ᵀ*Cleary* Denis. L 1987, Fowler Wright. xii-257p. $9 pa. – ᴿTLond 92 (1989) 134-6 (R. *Kollar*: fine translation; proposed remedies partly naive or outdated).

7910 **Sabugal** S., La Iglesia, sierva de Dios; hacia una eclesiología servicial. Zamora 1987, Monte Casino. 171p. – ᴿProyección 35 (1988) 153 (A. *Sánchez*); TLZ 114 (1989) 609s (W. *Nagel*).

7911 *Sartori* Luigi, Storia dell'ecclesiologia; A. ANTÓN [1986s] riempie un vuoto: StPatav 36 (1989) 149-154.

7911* **Schächtele** Traugott, Das Verständnis des allgemeinen Priestertums bei AUGUSTIN: Diss. ᴰ*Ritter*. Heid 1989. – RTLv 21,549.

7912 *Schelbert* Georg, Eine biblische Missionstheologie [*Legrand* L. 1988 ➤ 7388*]: NZMissW 45 (1989) 131-7.

7912* **Scherer** James A., Gospel, Church, and Kingdom; comparative studies in world mission theology. 1987 ➤ 3,7691; 4,8983: ᴿCalvinT 24 (1989) 164-6 (J. A. *DeJong*).

7913 ᴱ**Schreiner** J., Unterwegs zur Kirche, AT...: QDisp 110, 1985/7 ➤ 3,563; 4,8987: ᴿBLtg 62 (1989) 254s (L. *Schwienhorst-Schönberger*); Salesianum 51 (1989) 163s (M. *Cimosa*).

7914 **Shenk** D. W., *Stutzman* E. R., Creating communities of the Kingdom; New Testament models of church planting. Scottdale PA 1988, Herald. 229 p. $10. 0-8361-3470-2 [NTAbs 33,267].

7914* **Solomone** K. A., The People of God in the Second Vatican Council; the biblical antecedents of the notion and its reception: diss. ᴰ*Schrijver* G. De. Leuven 1989. lv-553 p. (2 vol.) – TsTNijm 30,190; RTLv 21,565.

7915 **Soulages** Gérard, Divisions ou pacification dans l'Église. P 1989, C.L.D. 128 p. F 78. – ᴿEsprVie 99 (1989) 159 (C. *Jean-Nesmy*).

7916 *Stamoulis* James J., The imperative of mission in Orthodox theology: GrOrTR 33 (1988) 63-80.

7917 **Stötzel** Arnold, Kirche als 'neue Gesellschaft'; die humanisierende Wirkung des Christentums nach J. CHRYSOSTOMOS: Münsterische BeitT 51, 1984 ➤ 1,7566 ... 4,8994: ᴿTLZ 114 (1989) 206s (P. F. *Burton*).

7918 *Štrukelj* Anton, [in Slovene] Institution and authority in the Church: BogVest 47 (1987) 43-55.

7918* **Subilia** Vittorio, 'Solus Christus'; il messaggio cristiano nella prospettiva protestante 1985 ➤ 1,7567: ... 3,7707. – ᴿFilT 3 (1989) 222-4 (A. *Cislaghi*); StEcum 5 (1987) 175-7 (T. *Vetrali*).

7919 **Sudbrack** Josef, a) Neue Religiosität; Herausforderung für die Christen. Mainz 1987 ²1988, Grünewald. – b) La nuova religiosità, una sfida per i cristiani: GdT 186. Brescia 1988, Queriniana. 344 p. Lit. 28.000. 88-399-0686-X [Greg 70,412].

7920 **Sullivan** Francis A., The Church we believe in; one, holy, catholic and apostolic. NY/Dublin 1989, Paulist/Gill & M. vi-241 p. 0-8091-3039-4. – ᴿGregorianum 70 (1989) 824s (*ipse*); PrPeo 3 (1989) 368 (J. *Tolhurst*); TS 50 (1989) 829 (L. *Örsy*).

7921 *Tarocchi* Stefano, Laici e laicità fra Antico e Nuovo Testamento: RivAscM 13 (1988) 157-172.

7922 **Thaler** Anton, Gemeinde und Eucharistie; Grundlegung einer eucharistischen Ekklesiologie: Praktische Theologie im Dialog 2. FrS 1988, Univ. xvi-558 p. Fs 49. – ᴿTR 85 (1989) 477s (W. *Beinert*); ZkT 111 (1989) 360-4 (H. B. *Meyer*).

7923 *Thomas* Owen C., On stepping twice into the same church [are we in the same church as the apostles ...?]; essence, development, and pluralism: AnglTR 70 (1988) 293-306.

7924 **Thomas** Pascal, Ces chrétiens que l'on appelle laïcs: Théologie/Repères 1988 ➤ 4,8998; F 120: ᴿNRT 111 (1989) 460 (A. *Toubeau*).

7925 **Thornhill** John, Sign and promise; a theology of the Church for a changing world. L 1988, Collins. xiii-234 p. $18 pa. – ᴿAustralasCR 66 (1989) 114s (G. *Kelly*).

7926 a) *Tillard* J.-M. R., L'Universel et le local; réflexion sur Église universelle et Églises locales, II. Le statut ecclésiologique de la différence; – b) Autorité et mémoire dans l'Église: Irénikon 61 (1988) 28-40; Eng. 40 / 332-346 . 481-4; Eng. 484.

7926* **Timko** Philip S.,   The ecclesiology of MONETA [O.P.] of Cremona's 'Adversus Catharos et Valdenses': diss. Catholic Univ., ᴰDulles A. Wsh 1989. 357 p. 89-13823. – DissA 50 (1989s) 981-A.

7927 **Tolhurst** James,   The Church ... a communion – in the preaching and thought of J. H. NEWMAN [diss. Salamanca]. L 1988, Fowler Wright. xiv-232 p. £10. – ᴿJTS 40 (1989) 311s (G. *Rowell*); PrPeo 3 (1989) 291s (F. J. *Selman*).

7928 *Triacca* Achille M.,   Christi sanguis arrha Ecclesiae; significativa testimonianza di EUSEBIO Gallicano: → 759, Sanguis VI, 1987/9, 909-962.

7928* **Vanhoutte** Koenraad,   L'Église du Christ; étude systématique de l'ecclésiologie d'Émile MERSCH à la lumière de la théologie du Corps Mystique: diss. Pont. Univ. Gregoriana Nᵉ 3585, ᴰAntón A. R 1989. Extr. 109 p. – RTLv 21,565.

7929 ᴱ**Vanzan** Piersandro,   Il laicato nella Bibbia e nella storia 1987 → 3,572; 4,9003: ᴿSalesianum 51 (1989) 865-8 (G. *Abbà*).

7930 **Wolanin** Adam,   Teologia della Missione, temi scelti. CasM 1989, Piemme. 189 p.; Lit. 25.000. – ᴿCC 140 (1989,4) 619 (E. *Farahian*).

7931 **Zizioulas** John D.,   Being as communion 1985 → 1,7385 ... 4,9009: ᴿScotJT 42 (1989) 101-5 (R. *Williams*).

H7.7 *Œcumenismus* – The ecumenical movement.

7932 ᴱ**Amirtham** S., *Moon* C., The teaching of ecumenics 1987 → 3,7735: ᴿTLZ 114 (1989) 853s (H. *Krüger*).

7933 ᴱ(**Andresen** Carl), **Benrath** Gustav A.,   ... Ökumenizität: HbDTg 3, 1984 → 65,739* ... 2,589: ᴿTRu 54 (1989) 432-4 (J. *Wirsching*).

7934 *Arrieta* Jesús S.,   ❾ Ways of belonging to the Church and salvation in the Church according to the II. Vatican Council: KatKenk 28,55 (1989) 97-126; Eng. vii-x.

7935 **Arx** Urs von,   Koinonia auf altkirchlicher Basis; deutsche Gesamtausgabe der gemeinsamen Texte des orthodox-altkatholischen Dialogs 1975-1987 mit französischer und englischer Übersetzung: IkiZ 49,4 Beih (1989). 229 p.

7936 **Avis** Paul,   Ecumenical theology and the elusiveness of doctrine 1986 → 1,7404 ...4,9012: ᴿHeythJ 30 (1989) 67-69 (B. R. *Brinkman*).

7937 *Baillargeon* Gaëtan,   Jean ZIZIOULAS, porte-parole de l'Orthodoxie contemporaine: NRT 111 (1989) 176-193.

7938 *Barth* Hans-M.,   Wort und Bild; ein Beitrag zum Gespräch zwischen Orthodoxie und Luthertum: KerDo 35 (1989) 34-53; Eng. 54.

7939 **Baubérot** Jean,   Le protestantisme doit-il mourir? La différence protestante dans une France pluriculturelle. P 1988, Seuil. 283 p. F 110. 2-02-010365-6. – ᴿÉTRel 64 (1989) 472s (A. *Gounelle*); FoiVie 88 (1989) 148-154 (O. *Millet*).

7940 *Bavaud* Georges,   'Hors de l'Église, pas de salut'; comment la compréhension de cette doctrine a-t-elle évolué?: NVFr 63 (1988) 137-148.

7941 **Beck** Nestor,   The doctrine of faith ... Augsburg confession ... 1987 → 3,7744; 4,9013: ᴿTLZ 114 (1989) 534-7 (M. *Seils*).

7942 *Beinert* Wolfgang,   a) Das Finden und Verkunden der Wahrheit in der Gemeinschaft der Kirche; – b) Möglichkeiten und Umfang ökumenischer Konsense: Catholica 43 (1989) 1-30 / 268-294.

7943 **BEM**, réponse: La Documentation Catholique 70,2 (1988) 102-119 [> CollatVL 19 (1989) 76-113 vlaams].

7944 *Bent* Ans J. van der, Diversity, conflict and unity in ecumenical theology: EcuR 41 (1989) 201-212.

7945 **Bermejo** Luis M., Towards Christian reunion, Vatican I. Obstacles and opportunities. Lanham MD 1987, UPA [Pune 1984 unchanged → 65,6696]. iv-316p. – ᴿRTLv 20 (1989) 236s (A. de *Halleux*: his proposal to eliminate the 'petra scandali' by renouncing ecumenicity of Vatican I cannot help ecumenicity insofar as it is disloyal to his own tradition); Salesianum 51 (1989) 846-8 (D. *Valentini*).

7946 *Bertalot* Renzo, Risposte al BEM [6 vol. 1986-9 → 8035 infra]: Protestantesimo 44 (1989) 171-7.

7947 *Betti* Umberto, A proposito del pluralismo dell'appartenenza ecclesiale; aporie dell'ecumenismo: Antonianum 64 (1989) 489-500; Eng. 489.

7948 **Birmelé** André, 'Sola gratia'; Le salut... dans les dialogues œcuméniques ᴰ1986 → 2,6163... 4,9017: ᴿRechSR 77 (1989) 308-311 (B. *Sesboüé*); Salesianum 51 (1989) 849s (D. *Valentini*).

7949 **Birmelé** A., *Ruster* T., Allein seligmachend? Das Thema Kirche im Gespräch der Kirchen: Arbeitsbuch Ökumene 4. Wü/Gö 1988, Echter / VR. 103p. DM 15,80. 3-429-01130-2 / VR 3-525-56829-0. – ᴿTsTNijm 29 (1989) 309 (H.-E. *Mertens*).

7950 *Birmelé* André, À l'ordre du jour des futurs dialogues œcuméniques: RHPR 69 (1989) 136-151; Eng. 241.

7951 *Blei* K. [secr. Ned. Hervormde Kerk], *al.*, De nederlandse kerken en het Lima-rapport; vergelijking van visies op doop, eucharistie en ambt: TsTNijm 29 (1989) 148-163; Eng. 163 (including Catholic Bishops' conference).

7951* *Böckle* Franz, *al.*, Die konfessionsverschiedene Ehe; Problem für Millionen — Herausförderung für die Ökumene. Rg 1988, Pustet. 139p. – ᴿTPhil 64 (1989) 627s (R. *Sebott*).

7952 ᴱ**Brandt** Hermann, Kirchliches Lehren in ökumenischer Verpflichtung... Rezeption 1986 → 3,7758; 4,9022: ᴿTLZ 114 (1989) 854s (M. *Sens*).

7953 *Brown* Raymond E., The contribution of historical biblical criticism to ecumenical church discussion: → 591*a*, Ratzinger 1988/9, 24-49.

7954 **Brun** Maria, Orthodoxe Stimmen zum II. Vatikanum, ein Beitrag zur Überwindung der Trennung, praef. *Papandreou* D.: FreibZ ÖkBeih 16. FrS 1988, Univ. XLI-230p. Fs 56. – ᴿTR 85 (1989) 479s (S. O. *Horn*).

7955 *Butselaar* G. J. van, 'Evangelicals' en 'ecumenicals'; waar ligt nu het echte verschil?: GerefTTs 89 (1989) 171-183.

7956 *a)* *Carbonnier* Jean, 1938-1988: et après?; – *b)* *Longeiret* Maurice, Un projet en marche; – *c)* *Courthial* Pierre, Brève réflexion sur un cinquantenaire: RRéf 40,1 ('Regard sur le catholicisme contemporain' 1989) 42-45 / 46-48 / 49... [< ZIT 89,234].

7957 **Castro** Emilio, When we pray together: Risk Book 40. Geneva 1989, WCC. 86p. – ᴿTSzem 32 (1989) 384 and cover (I. *Karasszon*).

7958 *Chronique des Églises*: Irénikon 62 (1989) 76-120. 242-284. 382-430. 550-592 [Relations entre les Communions 58-75. 213-242. 355-381. 531-549].

7959 **Clément** Olivier, La Chiesa ortodossa [³1985 Que sais-je?], ᵀᴱ*Manna* Salvatore: Strumenti 43. Brescia 1989, Queriniana. 118p. Lit. 15.000. – ᴿETL 65 (1989) 461s (A. de *Halleux*).

7960 *Cross* Peter R., 'Although we cannot fully meet'; the Roman Catholic response to BEM: Pacifica 2 (1989) 249-268.

7961 **Cullmann** Oscar, Unity through diversity [1986] 1988 → 4,9036: ᴿRExp 86 (1989) 122s (E. G. *Hinson*); Worship 62 (1988) 465s (J. *Gros*).

7962 *Czajkowski* Michał, **℗** Die Heilige Schrift und der Ökumenismus: STWsz 26,1 (1988) 164-178; deutsch 178s.

7963 ᴱ**Dionne** J. Robert, The papacy and the Church; a study of praxis and reception in ecumenical perspective [seven papal teachings, of which he is here presented as 'editor', balanced passively and actively by *sensus fidelium*] 1987 ➤ 3,7776; 4,9042: ᴿAnglTR 70 (1988) 177-185 (E. *Sullivan*, also on ᶠHOWE); CCurr 38 (1988s) 366-8 (J. R. *Morris*); JTS 40 (1989) 708s (E. J. *Yarnold*); StPatav 36 (1989) 181-4 (L. *Sartori*); Studium 29 (M 1989) 161 (P. *Blázquez*); TLZ 114 (1989) 477s (H. *Kirchner*).

7964 Dombes, groupe de, Pour la communion des Églises. P 1988, Centurion. 234 p. F 75. – ᴿTS 50 (1989) 621s (J. *Gros*).

7965 *Dubois* Elfrieda, Pierre-François LE COURAYER (1681-1776), canon regular of Ste-Geneviève in Paris, and the defence of the validity of Anglican orders: DowR 107 (1989) 127-141.

7966 *Ducruet* Jean, La foi chrétienne dans une situation de pluralisme culturel [conférence Djakarta]: RTLv 20 (1989) 32-58; Eng. 139s.

7967 **Dulles** Avery, The catholicity of the Church 1987 ➤ 1,7443 ... 4,9044: ᴿScripTPamp 21 (1989) 383 (J. R. *Villar*).

7967* *Duprey* Pierre, Quelques réflexions sur l'infaillibilité: ➤ 136, ᶠMEYER H., Einheit der Kirche 1988, 113-9.

7968 **Duquoc** Christian, Chiese provvisorie [1985 ➤ 1,7446], ᵀ*Savoldi* F. Brescia 1985, Queriniana. 150 p. Lit. 100.000. – ᴿSalesianum 51 (1989) 853s (D. *Valentini*).

7969 *Erny* P., L'Orthodoxie [... l'Orient plutôt]: pourquoi?: FoiVie 88 (1989) 41-53.

7970 *Evans* Gillian, Having authority to act unilaterally; the Anglican situation [... unilateral 'decision-making' about matters of faith may be seen as a hiccough in the process of reception and something which the Holy Spirit will put right in time; but in matters which affect other communities (women's ordination ...) the situation is more delicate]: DowR 107 (1989) 119-126.

7970* *Fahlbusch* Erwin, Katholisch, Katholizität: ➤ 894, EvKL 2 (1989) 991-6 [(1003-) 1007-20, Katholizismus].

7971 *Ferraro* Giuseppe, La 'oratio dogmatica de unione' del BESSARIONE e il concilio di Firenze [1439]: CC 140 (1989,1) 220-231.

7972 *Forte* Bruno [*al.*], Il trattato di ecclesiologia; una impostazione ecumenica: StEcum 6 (1988) 153-165; Eng. 165 [167-205].

7973 *Frend* W. H. C., ARCIC; a new start necessary? [19.XI.1988 Rome decree a severe setback]: TLond 92 (1989) 383-8.

7974 **Frieling** Reinhard, *Schöpsdau* Walter, Lehrverurteilungen damals und heute: eine evangelische [ökum.] Arbeitshilfe; Bensheimer 67. Gö 1987, VR. 54 p. DM 8,80. – ᴿÖkRu 38 (1989) 243s (H. *Vorster*).

7975 **Fries** H., *Rahner* K., Unione della chiese ... con bilancio, approvazione e critica (Fries): QDisp 1986 ➤ 2,6197 ... 4,9055. – ᴿEstE 64 (1989) 581s (J. J. *Alemany*); Protestantesimo 44 (1989) 312s (A. *Moda*). – ᴿHumT 10 (1989) 267s (A. de *Pinho*, español 1987).

7976 *Galeota* Gustavo, *Mancia* Anita, *a*) La chiesa locale nel dialogo ecumenico; modelli e forme di unità; – *b*) La comunione anglicana in dialogo; sulla Lambeth Conference 1988: Asprenas 36 (1989) 443-468 / 50-68.

7977 **Gregson** Vernon, LONERGAN, spirituality, and the meeting of religions 1985 ➤ 2,6204: ᴿJEcuSt 26 (1989) 552s (Walter *Harrington*).

7978 *Guérin* Nicolas, La réception du BEM; une évaluation des réponses des Églises aux quatre questions de sa préface: FreibZ 36 (1989) 173-192.

7979 *Gunten* A.F. von, Les ordinations anglicanes — le problème affronté par LÉON XIII: NVFr 63 (1988) 1-21.

7980 *Halleux* André de, Foi, baptême et unité; à propos du texte de Bari: Irénikon 61 (1988) 155-187; Eng. 188.

7980* *Hauke* Manfred, Luthertum und Ökumene in Finnland: ForumKT 4 (1988) 126-135.

7981 *Hebblethwaite* Peter, An Anglican visit to [MONTINI in] Milan; September 1956: TLond 92 (1989) 374-383.

7982 **Heiser** Lothar, Die georgische Orthodoxe Kirche und ihr Glaubenszeugnis: Sophia 26. Trier 1989, Paulinus. 248 p.; 32 color. pl. DM 68. 3-7902-1413-2 [TPQ 137,29: adv.].

7983 *Henrich* Stefan, Der ökumenische Arbeitskreis evangelischer und katholischer Theologen, Dokumentation [places and participants of meetings since 1946]: KerDo 35 (1989) 258-295.

7984 **Hillman** Eugene, Many paths; a Catholic approach to religious pluralism: Faith meets faith. Mkn 1989, Orbis. xi-95 p. $30; pa. $15. 0-88344-542-6; 8-4 [TDig 37,163].

7985 *Hinson* E. Glenn, The influence of fundamentalism on ecumenical dialogue: JEcuSt 26 (1989) 468-482.

7985* **Irvin** Dale T., Rendering account of the ecumenical past; the theology of history and historical consciousness of the ecumenical movement: diss. Union Theol. Sem., ᴰ*Koyama* K. NY 1989. – RelStR 16,191.

Kallarangatt J., The Holy Spirit, bond of communion of the churches, ᴰ1989 → 7554.

7986 *a) Kasper* Walter, Lehrverurteilungen — kirchentrennend? Überlegungen zu der Studie der Ökumenischen Arbeitskreises; – *b) Scheele* Paul-Werner, Die Rezeption ökumenischer Dokumente als geistliches Geschehen; – *c) Papandreou* Damaskinos, Auf dem Weg zur Gemeinschaft; Überlegungen zum letzten ökumenischen Konzil von Nizäa (787): → 120, ᶠLOHSE E., Wissenschaft 1989, 189-203 / 259-277 / 278-287.

7986* **Kirmse** Anne-Marie R., The Church and the churches; a study of ecclesiastical and ecumenical developments in the writings of Avery DULLES: diss. Fordham, ᴰ*Kilian* S. Bronx 1989. 284 p. 89-18638. – DissA 50 (1989s) 980-A; RelStR 16,187.

7987 *a) Klän* Werner, Skizzen aus der ökumenischen Landschaft heute: LuthTKi 12 (1986) 66-73; – *b) Kindt-Siegwalt* Irmgard, Die Antwort der Kirchen auf Lima und ihre Auswertung: ÖkRu 38 (1989) 1-13 [14-29, *Witzel* Johann H.; 30-46, *Wenz* Günther].

7988 **Klappert** Bertold, Bekennende Kirche in ökumenischer Verantwortung: Ök. Existenz heute 4. Mü 1988, Kaiser. 126 p. DM 16,80. – ᴿÖkRu 38 (1989) 494 (H. *Röhr*).

Klauck Hans-Josef, Gemeinde-Amt-Sakrament; NT Perspektiven 1989 → 292.

7989 **Klausnitzer** Wolfgang, Das Papstamt im Disput zwischen Lutheranern und Katholiken; Schwerpunkt von der Reformation bis zur Gegenwart [Diss]: InnsbTSt 20, 1987 → 3,7831; 4,9077: ᴿNRT 111 (1989) 132-4 (R. *Escol*); ÖkRu 38 (1989) 244s (G. *Schütz*); TPQ 137 (1989) 89s (G.B. *Winkler*); TS 50 (1989) 187s (R. *Kress*: well written); ZkT 111 (1989) 78-82 (W. *Kern*: Standardwerk).

7990 *König* Franz Kard., Die Theologie angesichts des religiösen Pluralismus: TPQ 137 (1989) 115-121.

7991 **Küng** Hans,   Theologie im Aufbruch; eine ökumenische Grundlegung 1987 ➤ 4,213:   ᴿDLZ 110 (1989) 319-322 (H. *Mohr*).

7992 *a*) *Küng* Hans,   Dialogfähigkeit und Standfestigkeit; über zwei komplementäre Tugenden; – *b*) *Knitter* Paul F.,   Nochmals die Absolutheitsfrage; Gründe für eine pluralistische Theologie der Religionen; – *c*) *Bernhardt* Reinhold,   Ein neuer LESSING? Knitter ...; – *d*) *Moltmann* Jürgen,   Dient die 'pluralistische Theologie' dem Dialog der Weltreligionen?; – *e*) *Marx* Bernhard,   Dialogik als ethisches Prinzip: EvT 49 (1989) 492-504 / 505-516 / 516-528 / 528-536 / 537-550.

7992* *Lane* Tony,   Evangelicalism and Roman Catholicism: EvQ 61 (1989) 351-364.

7993 ᴱ**Lehmann** Karl,   *Pannenberg* Wolfhart,   The condemnations of the Reformation era; do they still divide? [1986 ➤ 3,661; 4,9083], ᵀ*Kohl* Margaret.   Minneapolis 1989, Fortress. $20 [TrinJ 10,242].

7994 *Lindbeck* George,   Two kinds of ecumenism, unitive and interdenominational [2d McCarthy lecture, April 1989]: Gregorianum 70 (1989) 647-660; franç. 660.

7995 **Link** C. *al.*,   Sie aber hielten fest an die Gemeinschaft... Einheit der Kirche als Prozess... 1988 ➤ 4,596:   ᴿÖkRu 38 (1989) 483-5 (K. *Raiser*).

7996 **Lochhead** David,   The dialogical imperative; a Christian reflection on the interfaith encounter.   L 1988, SCM.   104 p. £5.50.   0-334-01969-9. – ᴿExpTim 100 (1988s) 356 (Ursula *King*).

7997 *Lovsky* F.,   Le peuple d'Israël et l'ecclésiologie œcuménique: FoiVie 88 (1989) 55-70.

7997* **Lowery** Mark D.,   The hierarchy of truths [Vatican II decree on Ecumenism] and doctrinal particularity: diss. Marquette. Milwaukee 1988. 337 p. 89-25434. – DissA 50 (1989s) 2539-A.

7998 *Macquarrie* John,   The papacy in a unified Church: Pacifica 2 (1989) 123-134.

7998* **Mader** Josef,   Kirche innerhalb und ausserhalb der Kirchen: kath. Diss. ᴰ*Neuner*. Passau 1988s. – TR 85 (1989) 518.

7999 *Martini* Carlo M.,   L'ecumenismo e il futuro dell'Europa; cinque tappe ecumeniche: Asprenas 36 (1989) 370-380.

8000 *Meyer* Harding,   Eine Gemeinschaft in Gegensätzen? Streit um Rezeption und ökumenischen Minimalismus: EvKomm 21 (1988) 260-4.

8001 *Meyer* Harding,   Sündige Kirche? Bemerkungen zum ekklesiologischen Aspekt der Debatte um eine katholisch/evangelische 'Grunddifferenz': ÖkRu 38 (1989) 397-410. ➤ 136.

8002 *a*) *Mojzes* Paul,   Universality and uniqueness in the context of religious pluralism; – *b*) *Meynell* Hugo A.,   The conditions of Christian ecumenism; – *c*) *Ingram* Paul O.,   Two western models of interreligious dialogue; – *d*) *Panikkar* Raimundo,   The crux of Christian ecumenism; can universality and chosenness be held simultaneously?: JEcuSt 26 (1989) 1-7 / 58-71 / 8-28 / 82-99.

8003 **Montefiore** Hugh,   So near and yet so far [ARCIC] 1986 ➤ 2,6234... 4,9099:   ᴿEcuR 41 (1989) 137s (W. G. *Rusch*).

8004 *Neufeld* Karl H.,   Der Umgang mit der Geschichte als Weg zur Ökumene, gezeigt am Beispiel des Bollandisten P. de BUCK: TPQ 137 (1989) 155-166.

8005 *a*) *Nossol* Alfons,   Schwerpunkte der Ökumene heute und ihre Bedeutung für die Theologie; – *b*) *Knoch* Wendelin,   Das Verhältnis von 'fides qua' und 'fides quae' im ökumenischen Gespräch; – *c*) *Schütte* Heinz,   Auf dem Weg zu einem gemeinsamen Ausdruck des apostolischen Glaubens heute: Catholica 43 (1989) 153-175 / 176-194 / 209-230.

8006 *a) Oeyen* Christian, Ekklesiologische Fragen in den orthodox-altkatholischen Kommissionstexten; – *b) Papandreou* Damaskinos, Theologischer Konsens und kirchlicher Gemeinschaft: ➤ 629, Innsbruck 1988 = IkiZ 49 (1989) 237-265 / 44-52.

8006* **O'Neill** Maura, A world of difference; examining gender issues in interreligious dialogue: diss. Claremont 1989. 238 p. 90-00189. – DissA 50 (1989s) 2535-A.

8007 *Ottlyk* Ernő, ⓌThe ecumenical significance of St. AUGUSTINE: TSzem 32 (1989) 215-220.

8008 **Panikkar** Raimundo, Il dialogo interreligioso. Assisi 1988, Cittadella. 207 p. Lit. 14.000. – ᴿHumBr 44 (1989) 437 (T. *Goffi*).

8009 *a) Papandreou* Damaskinos, Die Frage nach den Grenzen der Kirche im heutigen ökumenischen Dialog; – *b) Nikolaou* Theodor, Stand und Perspektiven des Orthodox-Lutherischen Dialogs: – *c) Ioniţa* Viorel, Die Heilige Schrift in der Rumänischen Orthodoxen Kirche: ➤ 174, ᶠSCHNEEMELCHER W., Oecumenica et Patristica 1989, 21-32 / 33-60 / 61-69.

8010 **Persenius** Ragnar, Kyrkans identitet; en studie i kyrkotänkandets profilering inom Svenska kyrkan i ekumeniskt perspektiv, 1937-1952. Lund 1987, Verbum. 320 p. – ᴿSvTKv 65 (1989) 40-43 (C. A. *Aurelius*).

8011 *Persson* Per E., Konfessionerna, ekumeniken och den systematiska teologin: SvTKv 65 (1989) 117-124.

8012 *Ráskai* Ferenc, Ⓦ On the theology of the ecumenical movement of Taizé: TSzem 32 (1989) 249-253 [241-9 *Alföldy-Boruss* Dezső, (Taizé) A spiritual adventure].

8013 *a) Ritter* A. Martin, Patristische Anmerkungen zur Frage 'Lehrverurteilungen — kirchentrennend?' am Beispiel des Konzils von Chalkedon; – *b) Kallis* Anastasios, Konziliarer Prozess gegenseitiger Verpflichtung (Bund) für Gerechtigkeit, Frieden und die Integrität der Schöpfung; eine ekklesiologisch-oecumenische Würdigung aus orthodoxer Sicht: ➤ 174, ᶠSCHNEEMELCHER W., Oecumenica 1989, 269-279 / 339-350.

8014 **Rössler** Andreas, Positionen, Konfessionen, Denominationen; eine kleine Kirchenkunde. Stu 1988, Calwer. DM 16,80. – ᴿTGL 79 (1989) 201 (W. *Beinert*).

8015 **Rusch** William G., Reception, an ecumenical opportunity. Ph 1988, Fortress. 78 p. $3.25 pa. – ᴿAnglTR 70 (1988) 378s (A. A. *Vogel*); CurrTM 16 (1989) 298-300 (T. *Peters*, also on CULLMANN O.).

8016 *a) Saayman* W. A., Mission and disunity; the Reformed reality; – *b) Kritzinger* J. N. J., The Kairos document, a call to conversion: Missionalia 16,3 (Pretoria 1988) 119-125 / 126-145 [< TContext 6/2, 19].

8016* **Sabra** G., Thomas AQUINAS' vision of the Church; fundamentals of an ecumenical ecclesiology [diss. prot.]: TüTheolSt 27, 1987 ➤ 3,7885; 4,9115: ᴿNRT 111 (1989) 102s (R. *Escol*).

8017 **Sartori** Luigi, Teologia ecumenica, saggi 1987 ➤ 3,288; 4,9120: ᴿStEcum 5 (1987) 568s (T. *Goffi*).

8018 **Santa Ana** Julio de, Ecumenismo y liberación; reflexiones sobre la relación entre la unidad cristiana y el reino de Dios: Cristianismo y Sociedad 6, 1987 ➤ 3,7889; 4,9119: ᴿLumenVr 38 (1989) 335s (U. *Gil Ortega*); Protestantesimo 44 (1989) 235s (E. *Bernardini*).

8019 **Schäfer** Gerhard K.,   Eucharistie im ökumenischen Kontext... 1927-82: ForSysÖk 55. Gö 1988, Vandenhoeck & R. x-351 p. – ᴿTLZ 114 (1989) 150-2 (K.-H. *Kandler*).

8019* *Schäfer* Philipp,   Eine neue Initiative auf dem Weg zur Einheit [ᴱ*Lehmann* K., Lehrverurteilungen 1986]: ForKT 4 (1988) 218-232.

8020 *Schäfer* Rolf,   Die Einheit der Kirche im Studiendokument 'Den einen Glauben bekennen': ÖkRu 38 (1989) 47-61.

8021 ᶠSCHEELE Paul W.,   ᴱ**Schreiner** Josef, *Wittstadt* Klaus, Communio sanctorum; Einheit der Kirche 1988 → 4,129: ᴿTGL 79 (1989) 192-6 (W. *Breuning*).

8022 *Schlüter* Richard,   'Ökumenisches Lernen' — zur Übereinstimmung der Konzeptionen in den Kirchen: Catholica 43 (1989) 138-158.

8023 *Schmidt-Lauber* Hans C.,   Das Gottesverständnis M. LUTHERs im ökumenischen Kontext; TLZ 114 (1989) 321-338.

8024 ᴱSchrotenboer Paul G.,   Roman Catholicism, a contemporary evangelical perspective. GR 1987, Baker. 99 p. $6 pa, – ᴿBS 146 (1989) 227s (J. A. *Witmer*).

8025 **Seils** Michael,   Lutheran convergence?... [27] responses to BEM. Geneva 1988, Lutheran World Federation. 174 p. – ᴿJEcuSt 26 (1989) 384s (J. L. *Empereur*).

8026 **Sélis** Claude,   Les Syriens orthodoxes et catholiques: Fils d'Abraham. Turnhout 1988, Brepols. 304 p. – ᴿRTLv 20 (1989) 390s (L. *Leloir*).

8027 **Shriver** Peggy L.,   Having gifts that differ; profiles of ecumenical churches. NY 1989, Friendship. xi-178 p. $8. 0-377-00199-6 [TDig 37,187].

8028 *Sieben* Hermann J.,   Ferrara/Florenz (1438/9) und vier weitere konziliare Reunionsversuche: TPhil 64 (1989) 514-556.

8029 *a) Siegwalt* Gérard,   Dogmatique pour la catholicité évangélique; ses caractéristiques; – *b) Richard* Jean, La théologie évangélique et philosophique de G. Siegwalt; – *c) Grondin* Nicole, L'idée d'une théologie de la culture chez P. TILLICH et G. Siegwalt; – *d) Pelchat* M., Le principe scripturaire d'après H. de LUBAC et G. Siegwalt; – *e) Langevin* Gilles, La portée œcuménique...; – *f) Couture* André, La théologie des religions non-chrétiennes...: LavalTP 45 (1989) 3-9 / 11-30 / 31-38 / 39-53 / 55-62 / 63-72.

8030 *Silva* António da,   Quarenta anos do conselho mundial das Igrejas: Brotéria 127 (1988) 421-437

8031 *Spuler* Bertold,   Die Orthodoxen Kirchen 99-100 (Schluss); IkiZ 49 (1989) 1-28. 210-236.

8032 **Stavridis** Vassilios T.,   ⊚ History of the ecumenical movement²: AnVlat 47. Thessaloniki 1984 [¹1964], Patriarchal Inst. Patr. 419 p. – ᴿGregorianum 70 (1989) 820s (J. E. *Vercruysse*).

8032* *Steinacker* Peter,   Katholizität: → 911, TRE 18 (1989) 72-80.

8033 *Thils* Gustave,   Le fondement naturel et universel de la 'liberté religieuse': RTLv 20 (1989) 59-66; Eng. 140.

8034 **Thomas** M.M.,   Risking Christ for Christ's sake 1987 → 3,7906; 4,9131: ᴿWestTJ 51 (1989) 421-4 (T. *Hard*).

8035 ᴱThurian Max,   Churches respond to BEM, V-VI: Faith & Order 143s, 1988 → 4,9132: ᴿJEcuSt 26 (1989) 382s (J.P. *Gaffney*); RTLv 20 (1989) 75-80 (A. de *Halleux*); TLZ 114 (1989) 629-632 (C. *Hinz*, 4-6).

8036 *Tillard* J.-M. R.,   Église d'Églises 1987 → 3,7911; 4,9133: ᴿAsprenas 36 (1989) 412-4 (A. *Mancia*); BLitEc 90 (1989) 73-75 (J. *Rigal*); ETL 65 (1989) 201-3 (J. E. *Vercruysse*: important, bien documenté); IndTSt 26

(1989) 93s (L. *Lits*); JRel 69 (1989) 260s (J. *Gnos*); OrChrPer 55 (1989) 235s (E. R. *Hambye*).

8037 **Tillard** J.-M. R., Chiesa di chiese; l'ecclesiologia di comunione [1987]: BiblTeolContemporanea 59. Brescia 1989, Queriniana. 388 p. Lit. 38.000. 88-399-0359-3 [Greg 70,620].

8038 *Tillard* J.-M. R., Sacrements et communion ecclésiale; les cas de Lambeth et d'Écône: NRT 111 (1989) 641-663.

8039 **Torrance** Thomas F., Theological dialogue between Orthodox and Reformed churches 1985 ↠ 2,511; 4,9136: ᴿHeythJ 30 (1989) 78-80 (R. H. *Roberts*).

8040 *Tsuchiya* Yoshimasa, ◑ The ecumenical meaning of the 'Traditio apostolica' of HIPPOLYTUS: KatKenk 26,52 (1987) 77-102; Eng. vii-ix.

8041 *Vanzan* Piersandro, Vocazione e missione dei 'fedeli laici' nella Chiesa e nella società, oggi: RivScR 3,1 (1989) 81-97.

8042 *Vercruysse* Jos E., Rilevanza per l'ecumenismo della 'teologia della Croce' di LUTERO: CC 140 (1989,4) 16-29.

8043 ᴱ**Voicu** S., Cereti G., Enchiridion oecumenicum I, Dialoghi internazionali 1986 ↠ 3,7920. – II. locali. Bo 1988, Dehoniane. 1844 p. Lit. 80.000. 88-10-80221-7; -5-X. – ᴿProtestantesimo 44 (1989) 159s (F. *Ferrario*) & 238s (G. *Scuderi*).

8044 *Wainwright* Geoffrey, From pluralism towards catholicity? The United Methodist Church after the General Conference of 1988: AsbTJ 44,1 (1989) 17-27.

8044* *Waldenfels* Hans, Mission und interreligiöser Dialog; was steht auf dem Spiel?: ZMissRW 73 (1989) 182-194.

8045 *Weisse* Wolfram, Ökumenisches Lernen; Möglichkeiten und Grenzen einer neuen pädagogischen Dimension: ÖkRu 38 (1989) 181-199.

8045* **Wi Hyung Yoon**, Die Taufe als ökumenisches Sakrament; heutige Taufpraxis und Taufpredigt als Frage an die Kircheneinheit: ev. Diss. ᴰ*Müller*. Tübingen 1988s. – TR 85 (1989) 518.

8046 *Zachariah* Mathai, The changing face of ecumenism; – *b*) *Kamath* Ravi S., The WCC, the RC Church and the unity of the Church; – *c*) *Bermejo* L. M., The churches respond to BEM: Vidyajyoti 52 (1988) 4-11 / 13-25 / 27-43.

8047 *Zeddies* Helmut, 'Einheit vor uns' [Kath./ev.-luth. 1985] — im Spiegel der Leuenberger Konkordie betrachtet: TLZ 114 (1989) 161-174.

8048 ᴱ**Ziegler** Josef G., 'In Christus'; Beiträge zum ökumenischen Gespräch; MoraltStSyst 14, 1987 ↠ 4,430: ᴿÖkRu 38 (1989) 121-3 (W. *Müller*).

H7.8 Amt – *Ministerium ecclesiasticum*.

8049 *Amjad Ali* Christine, Ministry in the New Testament: Al-Mushir 31,2 (1989) 61-71 [< TContext 7/1, 61].

8049* **Andrewarths** John M., Elder, bishop, pastor; a descriptive study of the terms and their implications for a contemporary ecclesiology: diss. SW Baptist Theol. Sem. 1989. 279 p. 90-04359. – DissA 50 (1989s) 2930-A.

8050 **Antón** Ángel, Conferencias episcopales, ¿instancias intermedias? El estado teológico de la cuestión: Verdad e imagen 111. Salamanca 1989, Sígueme. 495 p. – ᴿCiTom 116 (1989) 193s (A. *Bandera*); Gregorianum 70 (1989) 606s (*ipse*); LumenVr 38 (1989) 183s (F. *Ortiz de Urtaran*); NatGrac 36 (1989) 143s (A. *Villalmonte*); NRT 111 (1989) 1038s (L. *Volpe*).

8051 *Antón* Ángel,   a) Fundamentación teológica de las Conferencias Episcopales; – b) ¿Ejercen las conferencias episcopales un munus magisterii?; – c) ...horizonte teológico y criterios de valorización: Gregorianum 70 (1989) 205-232; Eng. 232 / 439-492; Eng. 493s / 741-776; Eng. 777s.

8052 *Antón* Ángel,   A fundamentação teológica das conferências episcopais: Brotéria 129 (1989) 27-42.

8053 **Betti** Umberto,   La dottrina sull'episcopato del Concilio Vaticano II 1984 ➤ 1,7592; 3,7940:   ᴿSalesianum 51 (1989) 848 (D. *Valentini*).

8054 *Bürki* Bruno,   Entre Jean CALVIN et le texte de Lima; le fonctionnement des ministères dans les Églises réformées francophones: FreibZ 35 (1988) 469-484 [485-505, *Lemopoulos* G., Lima/Eucharistie].

8055 **Card** Terence,   Priesthood and ministry in crisis 1988 ➤ 4,9154: ᴿExpTim 100 (1988s) 73s (B. L. *Horne*).

8056 *Carroll* Thomas D.,   The human person in ministry; [Luigi] RULLA's contribution: ➤ 446, Challenges 1989, 219-241.

8057 **Chalendar** Xavier de,   Le prêtre, hier, aujourd'hui et pour demain: L'horizon du croyant 7.   P/Ottawa 1989, Desclée/Novalis. 187 p. – ᴿEsprVie 99 (1989) 665 (P. *Jay*).

8058 *Chauvet* Patrick,   Le presbytère à travers la correspondance de saint BASILE; sainteté et théologie du caractère: NRT 111 (1989) 682-692.

8059 *Cholij* Roman,   Clerical celibacy in the Western Church and defense of his 'Celibacy, a tradition of the Eastern churches': PrPeo 3 (1989) 301-312 and 69-71 [2 (1988) July].

8060 **Dianich** S.,   Teología del ministerio ordenado; una interpretación eclesiológica. M 1988, Paulinas.   342 p. – ᴿBibFe 15 (1989) 318s (A. *Salas*); EfMex 7 (1989) 314s (E. *Bonnín*).

8061 **Domínguez Sánchez** Benito,   El ministerio y su repercusión en la unidad 1984 ➤ 2,6289:   ᴿÉTRel 63 (1988) 322s (J. *Rennes*: serious though without imprimatur or publisher, and it could have all been said in 250 p.).

8062 **Dourley** John P.,   Love, celibacy, and the inner marriage. Toronto 1987, Inner City.   122 p. – ᴿSR 18 (1989) 253 (Sean M. *Kealy*: classical Jungian).

8063 *Estrada* Juan A.,   Los ministerios laicales; posibilidades actuales: Proyección 35 (1988) 185-200.

8064 *Eyt* Pierre,   Autour des conférences épiscopales: NRT 111 (1989) 345-359.

8064* *Favale* Agostino,   Il ministero presbiterale; analisi dottrinali, pastorali, spirituali: Studi di spiritualità 7.   R 1989, LASalesianum. 375 p. Lit. 25.000.   88-213-0182-6. – ᴿActuBbg 26 (1989) 230s (A. M. *Tortras*); Teresianum 40 (1989) 584s (M. *Caprioli*).

8065 **Freitag** Josef,   'Sacramentum ordinis'; die Entwicklung des Ordo-Verständnisses im Konzil von Trient und ihre Bedeutung: Diss. ᴰGreshake G. FrB 1989. 666 p. – RTLv 21,569.

8065* *Ganzer* Klaus,   Gallikanische und römische Primatsauffassung im Widerstreit; zu den ekklesiologischen Auseinandersetzungen auf dem Konzil von Trient: HistJb 109 (1989) 109-163 [< ZIT 89,398].

Garrido J.,   Grandeza y miseria del celibato cristiano 1987 ➤ 8234.

8067 **Genn** Felix,   Trinität und Amt nach AUGUSTINUS 1986 ➤ 2,6297; 3,7967:   ᴿBogVest 47 (1987) 69-72 (A. *Strle*, in Slovene).

8068 **Giles** Kevin,   Patterns of ministry among the first Christians. Melbourne 1989, Collins Dove. ix-247 p. 0-85924-729-5.

8069 **González Dorado** A., Sacerdotes dignos de crédito; perspectiva latinoamericana: Servidores y testigos 37. Santander 1988, Sal Terrae. 103 p. pt. 420. 84-293-0806-7. – ᴿActuBbg 26 (1989) 70 (R. de *Sivatte*); Proyección 36 (1989) 71 (P. *Castón*).

8070 **González Faus** José I., Hombres de la comunidad; apuntes sobre el ministerio eclesial. Santander 1989, Sal Terrae. 163 p. – ᴿAnVal 15 (1989) 214-7 (R. *Arnau*); RelCu 35 (1989) 486 (A. De *Mier*).

8071 *González Faus* J. I., Sobre el ministerio eclesial: RLatAmT 5 (1988) 307-320; 6 (1989) 44-88. 185-221 (la clericalización del ministerio).

8072 *Gosker* Margriet, Het kerkelijk ambt; centrum van eenheid of struikelblok in de oecumene?: GerefTTs 89 (1989) 65-93.

8073 **Granfield** Patrick, The limits of the Papacy 1987 → 3,4537; 4,9162: ᴿEcuR 41 (1989) 139s (J. R. *Dionne*); ExpTim 100 (1988s) 69 (J. *Kent*: despite plea for moderation in dissents, proves what it grants: the papacy, with its limits rightly understood, remains a major barrier to ecumenism); TR 85 (1989) 41s (W. *Beinert*).

8074 **Granfield** Patrick, Das Papsttum, Kontinuität und Wandel. Münster 1984, Aschendorff. 292 p. – ᴿTsTKi 59 (1988) 144s (Ola *Tjørhom*: '1984').

8075 **Grelot** Pierre, Les ministères dans le peuple de Dieu [encore Schillebeeckx]; lettre à un théologien: Apologique, 1988 → 4,9164: ᴿEstE 64 (1989) 573 (J. Antonio *Estrada*); ETL 65 (1989) 194-7 (A. de *Halleux*: embarrassé, mais pas défavorable à Schillebeeckx); LavalTP 45 (1989) 165-7 (C. *Renauld*); NRT 111 (1989) 767s (X. *Jacques*).

8076 **Grootaers** Jan, Primauté et collégialité... G. Philips: BiblETL 72, 1986 → 3,7969; 4,9165: ᴿRTLv 20 (1989) 96s (M. *Simon*).

8077 **de Gruchy** John W., Theology and ministry in context and crisis; a South African perspective. L 1987, Collins. 183 p. £8. 0-00-599969-3. – ᴿExpTim 99 (1987s) 349 (B. L. *Horne*).

8078 *a*) *Grumm* Meinert, Ministry; the OT background; – *b*) *Housholder* David, An evangelical doctrine...; – *c*) *Foster* Christine M., ... and motherhood: CurrTM 16 (1989) 104-7 / 108-113 / 95-103.

8079 *Guerra Gómez* Manuel, *a*) 'In solidum' o 'colegialmente' (De unit. Eccl. 4); la colegialidad episcopal y el Primado romano según S. Cipriano, obispo de Cartago (aa. 248-258), y los Papas de su tiempo: AnnTh 3 (1989) 219-285; – *b*) El obispo de Roma y la 'Regula fidei' en los tres primeros siglos de la Iglesia: Burgense 30 (1989) 355-432.

8080 **Hill** Edmund, Ministry and authority in the Church [... creeping infallibilism] 1988 → 4,9171: ᴿNewTR 2,3 (1989) 117s (J. E. *Linnan*).

8081 ᴱ**Hoffmann** Paul [im NT p. 12-61; Schluss], Priesterkirche: Theologie zur Zeit 3, 1987 → 4,370: ᴿTLZ 114 (1989) 152 (E. *Winkler*); TR 85 (1989) 277-281 (E. *Dassmann*); ZkT 111 (1989) 82-84 (R. *Schwager*: criticisms pessimistic, proposals uncritically optimistic).

8082 *Hünermann* Peter, Der römische Bischof und der Weltepiskopat; systematisch-theologische Überlegungen: TüTQ 169 (1989) 272-286.

8082* **Kasik** Simeon M., The changing role of the Catholic priest in a traditional church; an ethnographic study: diss. Gonzaga. Spokane 1989. 225 p. 89-26349. – DissA 50 (1989s) 2529-A.

8083 *Kealy* Seán P., Is Jesus a model for ministry?: IrTQ 55 (1989) 253-276.

8084 *Komonchak* Joseph A., Episcopal conferences: ChSt 27 (1988) 311-328.

8085 *a*) *Laberge* Léo, Ministères et sacerdoce; quelques leçons de l'AT; – *b*) *Drilling* Peter J., The priest, prophet and king trilogy; elements of its

meaning in the Lumen Gentium and for today; – *c*) *Zimmermann* Joyce
A., Priesthood through the eyes of a non-ordained priest: ÉglT 19
(1988) 159-178 / 179-206 / 223-240.

8086 **Laudage** Johannes, Priesterbild und Reformpapsttum im 11. Jhdt:
ArKulturG Beih 22. Köln 1984, Böhlau. 338 p. DM 94. – ᴿRHE 84
(1989) 174s (G. *Fransen*: nouvelle figure du prêtre introduite par
l'hagiographie et mise à la base de la réforme pontificale).

8087 **Laurance** J. D., Priest / CYPRIAN 1984 ➤ 65,6881... 2,6311:   ᴿSecC 6
(1987s) 255s (T. *Halton*).

8088 **Lienhard** Joseph T., Ministry: Message of the Fathers 1984 ➤ 65,6884:
ᴿÉTRel 64 (1989) 125 (J. *Dubois*).

8089 **McBrien** R., Ministry 1987 ➤ 3,7979; 4,9181:   ᴿWorship 62 (1988)
375-7 (R. L. *Kinast*).

8090 *McGarry* Cecil, Ministry in the Church; post-Vatican II theology of
ministry [... role of the local churches]: Chiea 5,2 (Nairobi 1989) 65-80
[< TContext 7/1,19].

8091 **McKee** Else A., Diakonia in the classical Reformed tradition and today.
GR 1989, Eerdmans. xii-139 p. $13 pa. [TrinJ 10,242].

8092 **Marcus** Émile, *a*) Les prêtres. Desclée. – *b*) I preti, ᵀ*Palazzi* Claudia.
Mi 1988, Àncora. 129 p. Lit. 10.000. 88-7610-241-8 [Greg 70,199]. –
ᴿClaretianum 29 (1989) 427s (J. *Rovira*); Salesianum 51 (1989) 856s (A.
Favale).

8093 **Marronche** J., L'homme interdit [le prêtre attirant l'affectivité fé-
minine...]. P 1987, Nouvelle Cité. 199 p. F 69. – ᴿNRT 111 (1989) 316
(A. *Toubeau*).

8094 **Martelet** Gustave, Teologia del sacerdozio; duemila anni di Chiesa in
questione [1984] 1986 ➤ 3,7985; ᵀ*Savoldi* Fausto: ᴿCC 140 (1989,3) 96s
(F. A. *Pastor*; contributo significativo).

8095 *Martínez Albiach* Alfredo, La colegialidad episcopal al inicio del
pontificado de Juan Pablo II: Burgense 30 (1989) 235-251.

8096 **Martini** Carlo M., Coenae tuae; itinerario sacerdotale. Mi 1988,
Àncora. 221 p. Lit. 14.000. – ᴿHumBr 44 (1989) 729s (G. *Colombi*).

8097 **Martini** Carlo M., Qualche anno dopo; riflessioni sul ministero
presbiterale: Centro ambrosiano 1987 ➤ 3,7986; (anche) Piemme; Lit.
9500:   ᴿHumBr 44 (1989) 155s (G. *Colombi*).

8098 **Marzotto** D., Celibato sacerdotale 1987 ➤ 4,230: ᴿSalesianum 51 (1989)
857 (A. *Favale*).

8098* **Mayer** Bernhard, *Seybold* Michael, Die Kirche als Mysterium in ihren
Ämtern und Diensten: Extemporalia 5. Eichstätt 1987, Sales. 88 p. –
ᴿForumKT 4 (1988) 158s (A. *Ziegenaus*).

8099 *Meulenberg* Leonardo, 'Quem deve presedir a todos, deve também ser
eleito por todos' (Leão Magno); anotações históricas sobre a eleição de
um bispo: REB 49 (1989) 400-4.

8100 *Miralles* Antonio, Prospettiva ministeriale della posizione attiva dei
fedeli laici nella vita della Chiesa: AnnTh 3.1 (1989) 53-70.

8101 *Moellering* H. A., Some New Testament aspects of the ministry
identified and applied: Concordia Journal 14 (St. Louis 1988) 229-247
[< NTAbs 33,62].

8102 *Müller* Gerhard L., Theologische Überlegungen zur Weiterentwicklung
des Diakonats [sic S. 129; sonst Diakonates]: MüTZ 40 (1989) 129-143.

8102* **Naab** Erich, Kirchen- und Amtsverständnis bei Valentin THALHOFER
[1825-1891]: ForumKT 5 (1989) 291-301.

8103 *Nagórny* Janusz, ❷ Der Priester als Diener des Neuen Bundes: RoczTK 33,3 (1986) 55-71; deutsch 71.

8104 *Naud* André, Dans le prolongement du Colloque de Salamanque [ᴱ*Legrand* H., al., 1988]; le magistère contesté des conférences épiscopales: ScEspr 41 (1989) 93-114.

8105 *O'Daly* Gerard, Hierarchie; ↦ 904, RAC 15,113 (1989) 41-73.

8106 **O'Meara** Thomas F., Theology of ministry 1983 ↦ 64,7216... 3,7994: ᴿTLZ 114 (1989) 315s (G. *Gassmann*).

8107 **Osborne** Kenan B., Priesthood; a history of ordained ministry in the Roman Catholic Church. NY 1989, Paulist. vii-388 p. $15 pa. 0-8091-3032-7 [TDig 36,384]. – ᴿAmerica 161 (1989) 433s (D. L. *Gelpi*).

8108 *Palacio* Carlos, Da autoridade na igreja; formas históricas e eclesiologias subjacentes: PerspTeol 19 (1987) 151-179 [> SelT 28 (1989) 111-121, ᵀᴱ*Suñol* Miquel].

8109 *Papademetriou* George C., [Eng.] The prophetic ministry of the priest: TAth 60 (1989) 403-415.

8110 ᴱ**Prinz** Friedrich, Herrschaft und Kirche; Beiträge zur Entstehung und Wirkungsweise episkopaler und monastischer Organisationsformen; Mg-GeschMA 33. Stu 1988, Hiersemann. viii-391 p. DM 290.

8111 *Rambaldi* Giuseppe, La sostanza del sacramento dell'Ordine e la validità delle ordinazioni anglicane secondo E. DE AUGUSTINIS S.J. [membro della commissione di Leone XIII 1896]: Gregorianum 70 (1989) 47-89; Eng. 90; abbrev. 91.

8111* *Rankin* D. I., TERTULLIAN'S consistency of thought on ministry: ↦ 696, 10th Patristic 21 (1989) 271-6.

8112 **Rausch** Thomas P., Authority and leadership in the Church; past directions and future possibilities. Wilmington 1989, Glazier. 158 p. $16. – ᴿTS 50 (1989) 829s (D. J. *Grimes*).

8113 *Rausch* Thomas P., Priesthood today; from sacral to ministerial model: IrTQ 55 (1989) 206-214.

8113* *Riedlinger* Helmut, Zur geistlichen Übertragung alttestamentlicher Priestertexte auf Amtsträger der christlichen Kirche: ↦ 45, ᶠDEISSLER A., Weg 1989, 275-293.

8114 *Santos Marto* Antonio das, Sacerdócio comun e sacerdócio ministerial em comunhâo: HumT 9 (1988) 51-67.

8114* **Schillebeeckx** E., Plaidoyer 1987 ↦ 3,8008; 4,9198: ᴿLavalTP 45 (1989) 464 (R.-M. *Roberge*); LVitae 44 (1989) 233-5 (P. *Tihon*, sur les critiques de P. GRELOT); RHR 206 (1989) 208 (I. H. *Dalmais*); TXav 39 (1989) 495-8 (I. *Madera*); VSp 142 (1988) 467s (H. *Bourgeois*).

8115 **Schillebeeckx** Edward, Christliche Identität und kirchliches Amt 1985 ↦ 1,7681... 3,8007: ᴿTsTKi 59 (1988) 235s (Ola *Tjørhom*).

8115* *Schnackenburg* R., Bischof: ↦ 902, NBL Lfg. 2 (1989) 301s.

8116 *Schoovaerts* Gustaaf, Le motif du célibat ecclésiastique selon les lettres d'YVES de Chartres: ScEspr 40 (1988) 193-208.

8117 *Schreiber* Paul L., Priests among priests; the office of the ministry in the light of the Old Testament priesthood: ConcordiaJ 14 (1988) 215-228 [< OTAbs 12,98].

8118 *Seweryniak* Henryk, ❷ Les conférences épiscopales, un nouveau sujet de débat dans l'Église: PrzPow 813 (1989) 194-205; franç. 205.

8119 *Sternberg* Thomas, Der vermeintliche Ursprung der westlichen Diakonien in Ägypten und die Conlationes des Johannes CASSIAN: JbAC 31 (1988) 173-209; 4 fig.

8119* *Stein* Albert, Klerus und Laien: ↦ 894, EvKL 2 (1989) 1306-10.

8120 *Tillard* J.-M. R.,   Conférences épiscopales et catholicité de l'Église: CrNSt 9 (1988) 523-538; Eng. 539.
8120* *Uprichard* R. E. H., The Eldership in Martin BUCER and John CALVIN: EvQ 61 (1989) 21-37.
8121 *Whitehead* Evelyn E. & James D., Women and men; partners in ministry: ChSt 27 (1988) 159-172.
8122 *Wilfred* Felix,   Episcopal conferences — their theological status; a contribution to the current debate: Vidyajyoti 52 (1988) 471-494.
8123 *Winogradsky* Alexandre A.,   Réflexions sur le rétablissement du diaconat latin: Istina 33 (1988) 126-145.

   H8   *Liturgia; oratio, vita spiritualis* – NT –   **Prayer.**

8124 *Andia* Ysabel de,   Simplicité, Écriture [*al.*]: ➤ 886, DictSpir 14,92s (1989) 892-903 [-921].
8125 **Applebee** Denis,   When I tread the verge of Jordan.   Marion IN 1988, World Gospel. 78 p.   0-9620406-2-2. – RAsbTJ 44,1 (1989) 102-5 (L. W. *Wood*: devotional lectures, good but not perfect).
8126 **Arzubialde** S. G.,   Theologia spiritualis; el camino espiritual del seguimiento a Jesús.   M 1989, Univ. Comillas.   265 p. – RCarthaginensia 5 (1989) 300 (F. *Martínez Fresneda*).
8127 *Axe* Tony,   Is discipleship an option? A Scriptural approach for today: PrPeo 3 (1989) 162-9.
8128 *Baigent* J.,   Worship; essence and form in Scripture and today: Christian Brethren Review 39 (Exeter 1988) 9-28 [< NTAbs 33,62].
8129 **Baldovin** John F.,   The urban character of Christian worship... stational liturgy: OrChrAn 228, 1987 ➤ 3,8037; 4,9217*: RJTS 40 (1989) 634-6 (K. *Stevenson*); RÉByz 47 (1989) 289s (J. *Wolinski*); SVlad 33 (1989) 407-9 (J. *Meyendorff*); TS 50 (1989) 365s (E. J. *Cutrone*).
8130 **Barry** W. A.,   'Seek my face'; prayer as personal relationship in Scripture.   NY 1989, Paulist.   v-100 p. $5 pa.   0-8091-3025-4 [NTAbs 33,404].
8131 *Barth* Hans-M.,   Gebet: ➤ 894, EvKL 2 (1988) 8-21.
8132 **Berger** Klaus,   Wie ein Vogel ist das Wort 1987 ➤ 3,8041: RTR 85 (1989) 15 (R. *Pesch*).
8133 **Berger** Teresa,   Theologie in Hymnen? Zum Verhältnis von Theologie und Doxologie am Beispiel der 'Collection of Hymns for the use of the people called Methodists' (1780) [kath. Diss] Münsteraner Theol. Abh. 6. Altenberge 1989, Telos. 234 p. DM 29,80 [TR 86, 42-45, P. *Harnoncourt*].
8133* **Bernabé Ibáñez** M.,   El evangelio olvidado: Col. Acanto de Espiritualidad.   M 1987, PPC.   229 p. – RStudium 29 (M 1989) 159 (P. *Juan*).
8134 **Boguniowski** Józef,   Domus ecclesiae; der Ort der Eucharistiefeier in den ersten Jahrhunderten; Tatsachen und theologische Sicht und Folgerungen daraus für heute [diss. S. Anselmo, DNeunheuser B.] 1986 ➤ 4,9222: RVoxPa15 (1988) 1102-5 (J. J. *Kopeć*).
8135 **Brock** Sebastian,   The Syriac Fathers on prayer and the spiritual life 1987 ➤ 3,8047; 4,9224: RChH 50 (1989) 502s (B. E. *Daley*); Worship 62 (1988) 455-7 (A. *Cody*).
8136 **Burini** Clara, *Cavalcanti* Elena,   La spiritualità della vita quotidiana negli scritti dei Padri: ➤ 908, StoSp 3c, 1988 ➤ 4,9226; Lit. 22.000. 88-10-30415-2: RAnnTh 3 (1989) 395-400 (E. *Juliá*); Gregorianum 70 (1989) 168s (M. *Ruiz Jurado*).

8136* **Burton-Christie** Douglas E., Scripture and the quest for holiness in the 'Apophthegmata Patrum': diss. Graduate Theological Union, ᴰ*Schneiders* S. Berkeley 1988. 451 p. 89-06364. – DissA 49 (1988s) 3761-A; RelStR 16,190.

8137 **Cabaniss** Allen, Pattern in early Christian worship. Macon GA 1989, Mercer. 122 p. $17.50 [JAAR 57,887].

8138 **Canopi** A. M., Incontri con Gesù; meditazioni sul Vangelo. T-Leumann 1989, Elle Di Ci. 108 p. Lit. 7000 [RivB 37,529].

8139 **Casas García** Victoriano, Cristo al encuentro del hombre; hacia una espiritualidad cristiano-evangélica 1988 → 4,9229: ᴿVerVid 46 (1988) 369 (J. *Pujol i Bardolet*).

8140 **Castillo** José M., El seguimiento de Jesús 1986 → 3,8050; 4,9230: ᴿEfMex 6 (1988) 121-5 (E. *Serraima*).

8141 **Coombs** Stephen, The Eucharistic prayer in the orthodox west; a reappraisal of its ancient and modern history, peculiarities, and possibilities [France, Spain ...], with an excursus, the Priscillian Tractatus XI an illatio. Dorchester 1987, auct. – ᴿRHE 84 (1989) 248s (A. van *Bunnen*).

8142 **Corbon** Jean, The wellspring of worship [Rev 22,1s 'river of life'], ᵀ*O'Connell* Matthew J. NY 1988, Paulist. vi-200 p. $13 pa. – ᴿHorizons 16 (1989) 390 (G. S. *Worgul*); TS 50 (1989) 208s (J. D. *Laurance*).

8143 *Costa* Maurizio, Gli 'esercizi spirituali' del Card. MARTINI [Carlo M.; 20 corsi già pubblicati]: CC 140 (1989,3) 140-153.

8144 *Coste* René, Solidarité [mot 'pas absent de la littérature des siècles passés, cependant ...']: → 886, DictSpir 14,92s (1989) 999-1006.

Cothenet E., Exégèse et liturgie: LDiv 133, 1988 → 247 (4,9233).

8145 *Cunningham* Agnes, Horizons of [feminist] spirituality: ChSt 28 (1989) 89-102.

8146 **Cusson** Gilles, Biblical theology and the Spiritual Exercises [1968] 1988 → 4,9235: ᴿRRel 48 (1989) 789s (R. F. *Harvanek*); TS 50 (1989) 596s (D. *Stanley*: superlative).

8147 **Cusson** Gilles, The Spiritual Exercises made in everyday life; a method and a biblical interpretation [Conduis-moi sur le chemin de l'éternité 1983], ᵀ*Roduit* Mary Angela, *Ganss* George E.: Modern scholarly studies about the Jesuits in English translations 2/8. St. Louis 1989, Institute of Jesuit Sources. ix-161 p. $16.

8148 **Dal Covolo** Enrico, Letture bibliche per la preghiera e per la vita ... ANT 1987 → 3,8055: ᴿCC 140 (1989,3) 446 (G. *Giachi*).

8148* *De Zan* Renato, Silenzio, ascolto e parola di Dio; appunti di spiritualità biblica: RivLtg 76 (1989) 340-351.

8149 **Dieter** Melvin E., *al.*, Five views on sanctification 1987 → 4,9238: ᴿGraceTJ 10 (1989) 94-98 (D. L. *Turner*); RExp 86 (1989) 116s (B. J. *Leonard*: good that the Keswick movement is included, by J. R. McQUILKIN; but not that Pietism and Catholic mysticism are omitted).

8150 **Drewermann** Eugen, Wort des Heils — Wort der Heilung; von der Befreienden Kraft des Glaubens I-II. Dü 1988, Patmos. 212 p.; 224 p. DM 29,80; 32,80. – ᴿLuthMon 29 (1989) 517 (J. *Jeziorowski*, 1); TGL 79 (1989) 99. 331 (K. *Hollmann*: spirituelle Theologie).

8151 ᴱ**Dupré** Louis, *Saliers* Don E., Christian spirituality, post-Reformation and modern: EWSp 18. NY 1989, Crossroad. xxvi-566 p. 0-8245-0766-5. P. 174ss, *Pacini* David S., Excursus on reading Holy Writ.

8152 **Earkle** R., Sanctification in the New Testament. KC 1988, Beacon Hill. 70 p. $3. 0-8341-1237-X [NTAbs 33,262].

8153 **Empereur** James, Worship; exploring the sacred. Wsh 1988, Pastoral. ix-238 p. $12. – ᴿTS 50 (1989) 407s (J. H. *McKenna*).

8154 *Esquierda Bifet* Juan, Dimensión soteriológica de la contemplación cristiana y no cristiana: Burgense 30 (1989) 87-104.

8155 ᴱ**Fabris** R., La spiritualità del NT: → 909, StSpG, 2, 1985 [→ 2,6738*]: ᴿParVi 33 (1988) 470s (C. *Ghidelli*).

8156 **Farrell** Edward, Free to be nothing. Collegeville MN 1989, Glazier. 152 p. $9. 0-89453-780-6 [TDig 37,156; biblical reflections on poor-parish apostolate].

8157 **Fiand** Barbara, Releasement; spirituality for ministry; pref. *Chittesten* sr. Joan. NY 1987, Crossroad. 108 p. $12. – ᴿNewTR 2,1 (1989) 101 (Mary *McCarthy*).

8158 **Forte** Bruno, Théologie priée. P/Montréal 1989, Médiaspaul. 63 p. F 30. – ᴿEsprVie 99 (1989) 173 (P. *Jay*).

8159 **Galilea** Segundo, The way of living faith; a spirituality of liberation. SF 1988, Harper & R. 160 p. $15. – ᴿTTod 46 (1989s) 111s (D. A. *Smith*).

8160 **Gjergji** Lush, Tutta la nostra vita a dire 'grazie' e 'perdono'. Bo 1989, SERMIS/EMI. 125 p. Lit. 9000. 88-307-0228-5.

8161 **Goettmann** A. & R., Prière de Jésus, prière du cœur: Béthanie. P 1988, Dervy. 224 p. F 98. 2-85076-296-2. – ᴿÉTRel 64 (1989) 640s (J. *Ansaldi*: aurait pu combler un vide; agréable mais simplifie trop les Pères).

8162 ᴱ**Gray** Donald, The Word in season; the use of the Bible in liturgy. ... 1988, Canterbury. 141 p. £6. 1-85311-011-9. – ᴿExpTim 100 (1988s) 194 (K. *Stevenson*).

8167 **Grossi** V., La vita cristiana nei primi secoli: → 907, ᴱ*Ancilli* V., La spiritualità cristiana, Storia e Testi 2. R 1988, Studium. 315 p. [200 estratti]. – ᴿRHE 84 (1989) 256s (R. *Aubert*: la série comporte 20 vol. dont 2 sur la spiritualité byzantine et russe, 1 protestante; mais La spiritualità non cristiana forme une collection parallèle de 5 vol.).

8168 **Guelluy** Robert, Mais il y a Jésus-Christ. LvN 1989, Duculot. 198 p. Fb 540. – ᴿEsprVie 99 (1989) 224 (P. *Delhaye*).

8169 *Guillet* Jacques, La volonté de Dieu dans l'Écriture Sainte: Christus 36 (P 1989) 414-425 [426-438, en Islam, *Pouzet* Louis].

8170 **Guiver** George, Company of voices; daily prayer and the people of God. NY 1988, Pueblo. 280 p. $19.50. – ᴿTS 50 (1989) 594-6 (J. F. *Baldovin*).

8170* **Hamman** Adalbert-G., Das Gebet in der alten Kirche, ᵀ*Spoerri* Annemarie: Traditio Christiana 7. Bern 1989, Lang. xlvii-234 p. [TR 86, 252].

8171 **Hebblethwaite** Margaret, Finding God in all things [LOYOLA I.]. L 1987, Collins Fount. 240 p. £3. 0-00-627077-8. – ᴿExpTim 100 (1988s) 38 (sr. Dorothy *Bell*: one of the better ones among the 20,000 books on spirituality in print).

8172 **Jacquemet** Maurice, La prière chrétienne en saint AUGUSTIN et saint Thomas d'AQUIN. P 1989, Téqui. 72 p. F 30. – ᴿEsprVie 99 (1989) 150-*jaune* (J. *Daoust*).

8173 **Johnson** Arthur L., Faith misguided; exposing the dangers of mysticism. Ch 1988, Moody. 156 p. $7. – ᴿWestTJ 51 (1989) 180-3 (S. *Oliphint*).

8174 *Johnston* William, Being in love [a book about prayer]. L 1988, Collins. 171 p. £11. 0-00-215086-7. – ᴿExpTim 100 (1988s) 318 (G. S. *Wakefield*).

8174* **Josuttis** Manfred, Der Traum des Theologen; Aspekte einer zeit-genössischen Pastoraltheologie [1, 1982] 2. Mü 1988, Kaiser. 237 p. DM 36. – ᴿBTZ 6 (1989) 272-281 (M. *Germer*, J. *Hermelink*).

8175 **Jungmann** Josef A., The place of Christ in liturgical prayer [1925, ²1962], ᵀ*Peeler* A.; pref. *Fischer* Balthasar. L/Collegeville 1989 = 1965, Chapman/Liturgical. xx-300 p. £12.50. 0-225-66528-X / US 0-8146-1916-9.

8176 *Kelsay* John, Prayer and ethics; reflections on CALVIN and BARTH [... Why pray?]: HarvTR 82 (1989) 169-184.

8177 **Kolvenbach** Peter-Hans, Der österliche Weg; Exerzitien zur Lebenserneuerung [italienisch, Vaticano 1987], ᵀ*Kohlhaus* Radbert (O.S.B.). FrB 1988, Herder. 240 p. – ᴿSalesianum 51 (1989) 388 (B. *Amata*).

8178 **La Potterie** Ignace de, Il mistero del Cuore trafitto; fondamenti biblici della spiritualità del Cuore di Gesù 1988 ➤ 4,9263: ᴿCC 140 (1989,1) 307 (G. *Giachi*); HumBr 44 (1989) 303s (T. *Goffi*); ParVi 34 (1989) 304s (C. *Ghidelli*: 7 art. già pubblicati).

8179 **La Potterie** Ignace de, La preghiera di Gesù, il Messia, il Servo di Dio, il Figlio del Padre [Het gebed, conferenze Bonheiden 14-15.IX.1985], ᵀ*Berényi* Gabriella: Bibbia e Preghiera 2. R 1989, Apostolato della Preghiera. 148 p. Lit. 18.000. – ᴿCC 140 (1989,4) 543 (G. *Giachi*); Letture 44 (1989) 879-891 (G. *Ravasi*).

8180 **Lauriola** G., Spiritualità laicale. Noci 1987, Scala. 120 p. – ᴿAnnTh 3 (1989) 400-3 (E. *Juliá*).

8180* **Llamas Martínez** Román, La Biblia del B. Francisco PALAU [I. c. 1987] II. Temas bíblicos: Cuadernos Palautianos 5. Tarragona 1988, Carmelitas. 342 p. – ᴿTeresianum 40 (1989) 604s (M. D. *Sánchez*).

8181 ᴱ**McGinn** B. *al.*, Christian spirituality 1985 ➤ 1,271*... 4,9265: ᴿEcuR 41 (1989) 304s (P. G. *Henry*); HeythJ 30 (1989) 367s (P. *Sheldrake*).

8182 *Martin* Ralph P., Patterns of worship in NT churches: ➤ 84, ᶠHILL D. 37 (1989) 59-85.

8182* **Masini** Mario, Iniziazione alla 'lectio divina'; teologia, metodo, spiritualità, prassi. Padova 1988, Messaggero. 123 p. – ᴿTeresianum 40 (1989) 277 (V. *Pasquetto*).

8183 ᴱ**Miquel** Pierre, Cinq mille ans de prière; textes choisis. P 1989, D-Brouwer. 528 p. 17-50 Égypte, Babylone; 90-130 AT; 179-271 chrét. anc. 2-220-03044-X.

8184 **Moore** Sebastian, Jesus the liberator of desire. NY 1989, Crossroad. xi-122 p. $12. 0-8245-0939-0 [TDig 37,75].

8185 **Moore** Sebastian, Let this mind be in you; the quest for identity through Oedipus to Christ 1985 ➤ 2,6416: ᴿHeythJ 30 (1989) 81s (W. *Reiser*).

8185* *Mooren* Thomas, Theology at the crossroads [with anthropology]; the case of mission spirituality: NZMissW 45 (1989) 1-16.

8186 *Navone* John, The Gospel norm of true love: PrPeo 3 (1989) 276-282.

8187 **Nelson** James B., The intimate connection; male sexuality, masculine spirituality. Ph 1988, Westminster. 140 p. $9 pa. – ᴿHorizons 16 (1989) 188 (J. *Carmody*: more psychology than theology); RelStR 15 (1989) 251 (J. R. *Bowlin*).

8187* **Nicks** Elizabeth J., Biblical and experiential images of the Divine as aids in the worship experience: diss. Claremont 1989. 119 p. 89-24382. – DissA 50 (1989s) 2116-A.

8188 **Nicol** Martin, Meditation bei LUTHER [Diss. Erlangen]: ForKDg 14, 1984 ➤ 2,6419: ᴿLuther 19 (1988) 105s (Ingetraut *Ludolphy*).

8189 **Pacomio** Luciano, Lectio divina; accostarsi della Bibbia; leggere, meditare, pregare, contemplare, amare: Azione Pastorale. CasM 1986, Piemme. 66 p. – ᴿSalesianum 51 (1989) 361 (C. *Bissoli*).

8190 *Painadath* Sebastian, Contemplative and liberative action: Vidyajyoti 52 (1988) 210-223.

8191 **Panimolle** Salvatore A., *al.*, Ascolto della Parola e preghiera; la lectio divina 1987 ⇒ 3,8097; Lit. 20.000: ᴿParVi 33 (1988) 156s (E. *Bianchi*).

8192 *Placer Ugarte* Félix, Espiritualidad sacramental: LumenVr 38 (1989) 382-408.

8193 **Purcell** William, Anglican spirituality, a continuing tradition. L 1988, Mowbray. vii-112 p. £5. – ᴿTLond 92 (1989) 413s (G. S. *Wakefield*).

8194 *Ross* E. M., The use of Scripture and the spiritual journey in Walter HILTON's *Scale of Perfection*: AugLv 39 (1989) 119-131 [< RHE 85,51*].

8195 *Satura* Vladimir, Gotteserfahrung in der Bibelmeditation: GeistL 62 (1989) 201-212.

8196 *Schneiders* Sandra M., Spirituality and the Academy: TS 50 (1989) 676-697.

8197 **Schreiter** Robert J., In water and in blood; a spirituality of solidarity and hope. NY 1988, Crossroad. xii-141 p. $11 pa. – ᴿCommonweal 115 (1988) 695s (L. S. *Cunningham*); Horizons 16 (1989) 186s (Annice *Callahan*).

8197* Kirchenjahr: *a*) *Schulz* Frieder, ⇒ 894, EvKL 2 (1989) 1115-26; – *b*) *Jörns* Klaus-Peter, *Bieritz* Karl-Heinrich, ⇒ 911, TRE 18 (1989) 575-599.

8198 **Secondin** Bruno, Alla luce del suo volto; 1. Lo splendore: Cammini dello Spirito. Bo 1989, EDB. 298 p. Lit. 30.000. – ᴿNRT 111 (1989) 907s (B. *Studer*).

Segundo Juan L., The Christ of the Ignatian exercises 1988 ⇒ 7440.

8199 ᴱ**Senn** Frank C., Protestant spiritual traditions 1986 ⇒ 2,339; 3,8111: ᴿIrTQ 55 (1989) 168s (A. D. *Falconer*).

8200 **Sheldrake** Philip, Images of holiness; exploration in contemporary spirituality. L 1987, Darton-LT. 118 p. £3.50. – ᴿThemelios 14 (1988s) 78s (C. *Marchant*).

8201 **Sobrino** Jon, Tracce per una nuova spiritualità [1985 ⇒ 2,6439],ᵀ: Spighe. R 1987, Borla. 264 p. Lit. 18.000. – ᴿStPatav 36 (1989) 678s (G. *Toffanello*).

8201* *Solignac* Aimé, Spiritualité: ⇒ 886, DictSpir 14 (1989s) 1142...

8202 *Spanneut* Michel, SÉNÈQUE [... influence]: ⇒ 886, DictSpir 14,92s (1989) 570-598.

8203 *Špidlík* Thomas, La spiritualité de l'Orient chrétien, 2. La prière: OrChrAn 230, 1988 ⇒ 4,9288: ᴿGeistL 62 (1989) 77s (J. *Sudbrack*); Irénikon 61 (1988) 437s [E. *Lanne*]; JTS 40 (1989) 722-4 (G. *Gould*); StMon 30 (1988) 442s (L.-O. d'*Aydi*); TS 50 (1989) 591-3 (J. *Meyendorff*: scholarly and ecumenical); ZkT 111 (1989) 493s (H. B. *Meyer*).

8204 *Stolle* Volker, Apostelbriefe und Evangelien als Zeugnisse für den urchristlichen Gottesdienst; zu den neutestamentlichen Grundlagen und Kriterien des christlichen Gottesdienstes: LuthTKi 12 (1988) 50-65.

8205 **Taft** Robert, The liturgy of the hours in East and West 1986 ⇒ 2,6444... 4,9290: ᴿHeythJ 30 (1989) 460s (B. D. *Spinks*); HumT 10,1 (1989) 128s (J. da *Silva Peixoto*); LtgJb 38 (1988) 165-172 (A. *Gerhards*).

8206 **Taft** R., La Liturgia delle ore in Oriente e in Occidente: Tesi di teologia 4. CinB 1988, Paoline. 544 p. Lit. 30.000. – ᴿAsprenas 36 (1989) 307s [A. *Petti*].

8207 **Thils** Gustave, Existencia y santidad en Jesucristo 1987 ⇒ 4,9291: ᴿEf-Mex 6 (1988) 149-151 (E. *Serraima Cirici*).

8208 ᴱTonelli Riccardo, Essere cristiani oggi; per una ridefinizione del progetto cristiano: BiblScRel 77, 1986 → 3,731: ᴿGregorianum 70 (1989) 350-2 (R. *Fisichella*).

8209 **Toon** Peter, [Biblical] Meditating upon God's Word. L 1988, Darton-LT. 103 p. £4. 0-232-51755-X. – ᴿExpTim 100 (1988s) 37s (R. *Howe*).

8210 **Topel** L. John, El camino hacia la paz; liberación a través de la Biblia: Nuevo Mundo 4. M 1989, Biblia y Fe. pt. 1110. – ᴿBibFe 15 (1989) 329 (A. *Salas*).

8211 ᴱTriacca A. M., *Pistoia* A., Les bénédictions et les sacramentaux dans la liturgie: S. Serge 34, 1987/8 → 4,643: ᴿCarthaginensia 5 (1989) 295 (J. M. *Lozano*).

8212 **Vandevelder** Frank R., The biblical journey of faith; the road of the sojourner. Ph 1988, Fortress. 126 p. [CBQ 51,593].

8213 *Vaz* Armindo, Jesus o orante e mestre de oração: Espiritualidade 4. Oeiras 1987, Carmelo. 115 p.

8214 *Walter* Louis, Les liens [couverture 'rapports'] entre la liturgie de la fin du Iᵉʳ siècle et les textes du Nouveau Testament [*Cothenet* E. 1988]: EsprVie 99 (1989) 235-8.

8215 *Wicks* Jared, Living and praying as *simul iustus et peccator*; a chapter in Luᴛʜᴇʀ's spiritual teaching: Gregorianum 70 (1989) 521-547; ital. 548.

H8.1 Vocatio, *vita religiosa communitatis* – *Sancti;* the Saints.

8216 **Augé** Matias, *Sastre Santos* Eutimio, *Borriello* Luigi, Storia della vita religiosa. Brescia 1988, Queriniana. 508 p. Lit. 60.000 [RHE 85,247s, P. H. *Daly*]. 88-3990079-9. – ᴿTeresianum 40 (1989) 590-4 (C. *Pérez Milla*).

8217 *a) Baumeister* Theofried, Der aktuelle Forschungsstand zu den Pachomiusregeln; – *b) Frank* Karl S., Abbas Poimen — Versuch über die Apophthegmata Patrum: MüTZ 40 (1989) 313-321 / 337-347.

8218 **Benne** Robert, Ordinary saints; an introduction to the Christian life. Ph 1988, Fortress. x-212 p. $14 pa. – ᴿHorizons 16 (1989) 397s (D. *Di Domizio*: classical Protestant).

8219 ᴱBianchi U., La tradizione dell'enkrateia 1982/5 → 1,542... 4,9302*: ᴿCrNSt 10 (1989) 160-3 (D. *Pazzini*); RÉG 101 (1988) 529s (P. *Nautin*).

8220 *Bonny* Johan, Het aktieve religieuse leven: CollatVL 19 (1989) 194-212. **Bretón** Santiago, Vocación y misión 1987 → 3415.

8221 **Brown** Peter, The body and society; men, women and sexual renunciation in early Christianity 1988 → 4,9306: ᴿNYReview of Books (2.II.1989) 39-41 (W. H. C. *Frend*); NY Times Book Review (25.XII.1988: 1) 20s (E. P. *Sanders*); Times Literary Sup (L 23.IX.1988) 1411s (H. *Chadwick*) [< NTAbs 33,226]; TLond 92 (1989) 338-340 (Rowan *Williams*); TS 50 (1989) 361-5 (D. G. *Hunter*).

8222 **Byrne** Lavinia, Sharing the vision; creative encounters between [Catholic] religious and lay life [...'we need women ministers, ordained and unordained']. L 1989, SPCK. viii-101 p. £5. – ᴿTLond 92 (1989) 424 (R. *McCurry*).

8223 *Cecire* Robert, Encratism, an ascetic extremist movement within early Christianity: ResPLit 10 (1987) 47-50.

8224 **Codina** Victor, *Zevallos* Noe, Vida religiosa, historia y teología: Cristianismo y sociedad 9. M 1987, Paulinas. 204 p. – ᴿLumenVr 38 (1989) 440s (U. *Gil Ortega*); RLatAmT 5 (1988) 219s (J. *Sobrino*).

8225 **Conti** M., La vocazione e le vocazioni nella Bibbia 1985 ➤ 1,7726...
3,8128: ᴿCiuD 202 (1989) 755s (J. *Gutiérrez*).

8226 *a*) *Conti* Martino, I santi e la Bibbia; San FRANCESCO d'Assisi; – *b*)
Cremaschi Lisa, La parola e la preghiera nei Padri del Deserto; – *c*)
Melotti Luigi, Santa CATERINA da Siena; – *d*) *Prete* Benedetto, San
DOMENICO di Guzman; – *e*) *Ghiberti* Giuseppe, La Sacra Scrittura in
Santa TERESA: ParVi 34 (1989) 50-55 / 128-135 / 200-204 / 280-5 /
442-450.

8227 ᴱ**di Meglio** Salvatore, ABELARDO, L'origine del monachesimo femminile. Padova 1988, Messaggero. 252 p. Lit. 14.000. – ᴿHumBr 44
(1989) 732s (B. *Belletti*: scritto per Eloisa; biblico, dialettico).

8228 **Dinet** Dominique, Vocation et fidélité (Le recrutement des réguliers
dans les diocèses d'Auxerre, Langres et Dijon aux XVIIᵉ et XVIIIᵉ
siècles); préf. *Jacquart* Jean. P 1988, Economica. 335 p.; ill. F 155. –
ᴿEsprVie 99 (1989) 248-250 (H. *Platelle*: un beau livre).

8229 *Egender* Nikolaus, Palästina im Übergang vom Asketentum zum
Mönchtum: ErbAuf 65 (1989) 95-106.

8230 *Escallada* Alberto, Lineas fundamentales sobre el sentido y valor de la
vida religiosa hoy: CiTom 116 (1989) 69-98.

8231 *Fros* Henryk, ❷ Les objectifs et les conséquences de la réforme post-
conciliaire du culte des saints: PrzPow 807 (1988) 233-245; franç. 245.

8232 **Galot** Jean, Vivre avec le Christ; la vie consacrée selon l'Evangile. Lv
1986, Sintal. 240 p. – ᴿRThom 89 (1989) 516s (Benoit-Dominique de *la
Soujeole*, aussi sur Vivre avec Marie 1988).

8233 **Galot** Jean, Vivere con Cristo; i fondamenti evangelici della vita
consacrata 1986 ➤ 3,8134*b*: ᴿDivThom 91 (1988) 479-482 (E. *Juliá*);
Salesianum 51 (1989) 357 (C. *Bissoli*).

8233* **García Trapiello** J., Servir a la mejor causa; llamada divina y respuesta
humana según el pensamiento bíblico. M 1987, Atenas. 285 p. – ᴿRelCu
35 (1989) 482s (M. A. *Martín Juárez*).

8234 **Garrido** Javier, Grandeza y miseria del celibato cristiano. Santander
1987, Sal Terrae. 288 p. – ᴿProyección 35 (1988) (E. *López Azpitarte*);
SalT 76 (1988) 567s (J. *Ciervide*).

8234* *Gerlitz* Peter; *Pratscher* Wilhelm, Keuschheit: ➤ 911, TRE 18 (1989)
113-9-120 (-130, *Beatrice* P. F., Alte Kirche; -134, *Dominian* J.).

8235 **Guy** Jean-Claude, La vie religieuse mémoire évangélique de l'Église,
préf. *Madelin* Henri. P 1987, Centurion. 195 p. DM 35. – ᴿGeistL 62
(1989) 79s (J. *Sudbrack*).

ᴱ**Hawley** John S., Saints and virtues 1987 ➤ 471; ᴱ**Hilhorst** A., Heiligenverering 1986/8 ➤ 675; ᴱ**Kieckhefer - Bond**, Sainthood 1988 ➤ 480;
ᴱ**Marx** J., Sainteté 1989 ➤ 491.

8236 **Holtz** Leonhard, Geschichte des christlichen Ordenslebens. Z 1986,
Benziger. 405 p. – ᴿZkT 111 (1989) 231 (H. *Rotter*).

8237 *Honecker* Martin, Askese — Renaissance eines theologischen und
antiken Begriffs?: ➤ 174, ᶠSCHNEEMELCHER W., Oecumenica 1989,
317-327.

8238 *Jászai* G. [*Restle* M.] Heilige A. Westkirche [B. Ostkirche]: ➤ 901,
LexMA 4 (1989) 2014-8 [-2020]; al. 1840-62, Hagiographie.

8239 **Luzárraga** Jesús, Espiritualidad bíblica de la vocación²: Por el Reino 5.
M 1989, Paulinas. 350 p. 84-285-0989-1.

8240 **Maloney** George A., *a*) Communion of Saints. Hauppauge NY 1988,
Living Flame. 192 p. $5. 0-914544-73-X. – *b*) God's incredible mercy.
Staten Island 1989, Alba. xvii-183 p. $10. 0-8189-0544-2 [TDig 36,380].

8241 *Meeks* W. A.,   When celibates were a brash new elite [*Brown* P., Body and society]: Commonweal 116 (1989) 246s [< NTAbs 33,370].

8242 **Nürnberg** Rosemarie,   Askese als sozialer Impuls; monastisch-asketische Spiritualität als Wurzel und Triebfeder sozialer Ideen und Aktivitäten der Kirche in Südgallien im !. Jahrhundert: Hereditas 2.   Bonn 1988, Borengässer. xxx-354 p. 3-923946-11-2 [Greg 79,618].

8242* **Penco** Gregorio, Spiritualità monastica; aspetti e momenti: Scritti Monastici 9. Praglia 1988, Abbazia. 536 p. – ᴿStMon 30 (1988) 444s (R. *Badia*).

8243 *Rodríguez-Melgarejo* Guillermo, Elementos para el discernimiento de la vocación al ministerio ordenado de la Iglesia: TArg 25 (1988) 119-131.

8243* *Rosso Ubigli* Liliane,   Israël et la communion des saints; esquisse d'une nouvelle approche du problème: QuatreF 25s (1988) 7-15 [< JStJud 20,286].

8244 *Rubiano G.* Luis E.,   La 'llamada' de Dios en la Biblia y en la Iglesia católica: FranBog 31 (1989) 9-43.

8245 **Rulla** L. M.,   Anthropology of the Christian vocation I, 1986 → 3,6655: ᴿIrTQ 55 (1989) 249-251 (M. *McGuire*).

8246 **Rulla** Luigi M., *Ridick* sr. Joyce, *Imoda* Franco, Anthropology of the Christian vocation, II. Existential confirmation. R 1989, Pont. Univ. Gregoriana. 500 p. Lit. 48.000. 88-7652-598-X.

8247 *Sánchez-Marco* Francisco, El celibato de Jesús: SalT 76 (1988) 381-396.

8247* *Scheuer* Manfred,   Die evangelischen Räte; Strukturprinzip systematischer Theologie bei H. U. von BALTHASAR, K. RAHNER, J. B. METZ, und in der Theologie der Befreiung: Diss. ᴰ*Greshake* G. FrB 1989. 468 p. – RTLv 21,581.

8248 *Trummer* Peter,   Was heisst 'Armut um des Evangeliens willen'?: → 367, Aufsätze 1987, 7-37.

8249 *Vinke Dovale* Ramón,   La veneración de los santos: Tiusi 4 (Caracas 1989) 66-97.

H8.2   Theologia moralis NT.

8250 **Adinolfi** Marco, *Geraci* Paola,   Bibbia e ginecologia a confronto. CasM 1989, Piemme. 176 p. Lit. 24.000 [CBQ 52,194]. – ᴿAsprenas 36 (1989) 533-5 (A. *Rolla*); NRT 111 (1989) 1089 (A. *Toubeau*).

8251 **Aubert** Jean Marie,   Diritti umani e liberazione evangelica. Brescia 1988, Queriniana. 238 p. Lit. 24.000. – ᴿHumBr 44 (1989) 924 (M. *Perrini*).

8252 *a) Aubert* Jean-Marie,   Morale chrétienne et morale laïque; – *b) Poulat* Émile,   La morale au test historique de la laïcité: SuppVSp 164 (1988) 73-82 / 117-122.

8253 **Beach** Waldo,   Christian ethics in the Protestant tradition. Atlanta 1988, Knox. [vi-] 149 p. $10 [CBQ 51,782].

8254 *a) Becker* Jürgen,   Das Ethos Jesu und die Geltung des Gesetzes; – *b) Pesch* Rudolf,   Jesus und das Hauptgebot; – *c) Schneider* Gerhard, Imitatio Dei als Moriv der 'Ethik Jesu'; – *d) Grässer* Erich, Zum Stichwort 'Interimsethik'; eine notwendige Korrektur: → 173, ᶠSCHNACKENBURG R., NT & Ethik 1989, 31-52 / 99-109 / 71-83 / 16-30.

8255 ᴱ**Beckley** Harlan R., *Swezey* Charles M.,   James M. GUSTAFSON's theocentric ethics; interpretations and assessments. Macon GA 1988, Mercer Univ. 254 p. $35. – ᴿTTod 46 (1989s) 326. 328. 330s (R. R. *Reng*).

8256 *Beougher* Tim, The Puritan view of marriage; the nature of the husband-wife relationship in Puritan England as taught and experienced by a representative Puritan pastor, Richard BAXTER: TrinJ 10 (1989) 131-160.

8257 *a*) *Bernard* Christiane, *al.*, Le statut de l'embryon humain dans l'Antiquité gréco-romaine; – *b*) *Croteau* Jacques, Le fœtus humain, une personne?: LavalTP 45 (1989) 179-195 / 197-208 (209-227, *Murray* Warren).

8258 *a*) *Bindemann* W., Gedanken zur biblischen Botschaft von der Gerechtigkeit; – *b*) *Gerstenberger* E., Der Realitätsbezug alttestamentlicher Exegese: ZeichZt 42 (1988) 190-6 / 144-8.

8259 **Birch** Bruce C., *Rasmussen* Larry L., Bible and ethics in the Christian life²ʳᵉᵛ [¹c. 1976]. Minneapolis 1989, Augsburg. 239 p. $13. 0-8066-2397-7 [NTAbs 33,261]. – ᴿTTod 46 (1989s) 438-440 (E. *Mount*).

8260 **Bloesch** Donald G., Freedom for obedience; evangelical ethics for contemporary times. SF 1987, Harper & R. 342 p. $25. – ᴿCalvinT 24 (1989) 144-150 (D. J. *Schuurman*); Interpretation 43 (1989) 208.210 (R. W. *Palmer*: save your $25); JRel 69 (1989) 438s (J. H. *Yoder*).

8261 *a*) *Breck* John, Bio-medical technology; of the Kingdom or of the cosmos?; – *b*) *Harakas* Stanley S., The integrity of creation and ethics: SVlad 32 (1988) 5-26 / 27-42.

8261* *Builes* U. Miguel Ángel, El matrimonio en CLEMENTE Alejandrino: FranBog 29 (1987) 159-221.

8262 *Carey* Jonathan S., D. S. BAILEY [1954 Homosexuality] and 'the name forbidden among Christians': AnglTR 70 (1988) 152-173.

8263 *Cartwright* M. G., The practice and performance of Scripture; grounding Christian ethics in a communal hermeneutic: Annual of the Society of Christian Ethics (Knoxville TN 1988) 31-53 [< NTAbs 33,202].

8264 *a*) *Casciaro* José M., La sexualidad en los evangelios sinópticos con especial referencia a la predicación de Cristo (apuntes exegéticos para una Teología del cuerpo humano y del sexo); – *b*) *Basevi* Claudio, ... corpus paulinum; – *c*) *Caffara* Carlo, La sexualidad en el Antiguo y Nuevo Testamento desde la perspectiva ética: → 572, Masculinidad 1989, 556-669 / 671-823 / 901-933.

8265 **Chilton** Bruce, *McDonald* J. I. H., Jesus and the ethics of the Kingdom 1987 → 3,8176; 4,9352: ᴿJBL 108 (1989) 714-6 (R. H. *Hiers*); ScotJT 42 (1989) 421s (P. *Harvey*); ScripB 20 (1989s) 48 (J. *McGuckin*); TLond 92 (1989) 48-50 (J. *Muddiman*).

8266 *Clancy* J. B., Liberating the chained; Jesus' attitude toward divorce [he was rather against making it easier for the husband than for the wife]: Daughters of Sarah 15,1 (Ch 1989) 10-13 [< NTAbs 33,202].

8266* **Comstock** Gary D., Violence against Lesbians and gay men in post-World War II North America; an empirical and biblical-ethical study: diss. Union Theol. Sem., ᴰ*Shinn* R. NY 1989. – RelStR 16,188.

8267 **Countryman** L. William, Dirt, greed and sex; sexual ethics in the NT and their implications for today 1988 → 4,9356; 0-334-00327-X: ᴱExpTim 100,9 first choice (1988s) 321-4 (C. S. *Rodd*: the title is vulgar, but the usual terms tend to remove the reality from our own experience); NewTR 2,4 (1989) 98s (Carolyn *Osiek*); TLond 92 (1989) 336-8 (S. C. *Barton*).

8268 **Cupitt** Don, The new Christian ethics. L 1988, SCM. 176 p. £7 pa. – ᴿTLond 92 (1989) 538s (A. *Dyson*: he has a point).

8269 **Curran** Charles E., Directions in fundamental moral theology. ND 1985, Univ. 304 p. $10 pa. 0-268-00854-X. – RHeythJ 30 (1989) 334 (B. R. *Brinkman*).

8270 **Dacquino** Pietro, Storia del matrimonio cristiano alla luce della Bibbia [I. 1984 → 65,6629], II. Inseparabilità e monogamia. T-Leumann 1988, LDC. 413 p. Lit. 24.000. – RCC 140 (1989,2) 93s (F. *Giunchedi*); Claretianum 29 (1989) 409-412 (J. *Rovira*).

8270* EDaly Robert J., Christian biblical ethics 1984 → 65,7049...3,8184: RCriswT 2 (1987s) 174-6 (R. V. *Rakestraw*: important).

8271 **Danesi** Giacomo [AT, cammino d'Israele], *Garofalo* Salvatore, Migrazioni e accoglienza nella Sacra Scrittura 1987 → 3,8185; 4,9359: RCC 139 (1988,1) 619 (U. *De Mielesi*).

8272 *Daubercies* Pierre, Théologie et droits de l'homme [i. Des sources scripturaires?...]: EsprVie 99 (1989) 305-313.

8273 *Dorschel* Andreas, Die darwinische Pointe aller moralischen Pointen; zur neodarwinistischen Ethologie: Bijdragen 50 (1989) 24-39.

8274 **Drinan** Robert F., Cry of the oppressed; the history and hope of the human rights revolution. SF 1987, Harper & R. $18. – RCCurr 39 (1989s) 232-4 (W. L. *Holleman*).

8275 **Dussel** Enrique, Ética comunitária². Petrópolis 1987, Vozes. 288 p. – RREB 49 (1989) 486-9 (J. *Hernández Pico*: ed. note, English-Spanish-Italian-German already circulating).

8276 **Dussel** Enrique, Etica comunitaria, TEPompei Giuseppina: Teologia della Liberazione 8. Assisi 1988, Cittadella. 288 p. Lit. 20.000. – RCC 140 (1989,3) 310s (P. *Cultrera*); Laurentianum 30 (1989) 443-7 (E. *Covi*).

8277 **Dussel** Enrique, Ethik der Gemeinschaft; die Befreiung in der Geschichte: Bibliothek Theol. Befr. Dü 1988, Patmos. 239 p. [TR 86, 47-49, F. *Furger*]. – RZMissRW 73 (1989) 249s (G. *Kruip*).

8278 **Dussel** Enrique, Ethics and community. Mkn/L 1988, Orbis/Burns & O. xii-260 p. £9. 0-86012-162-3. – RExpTim 100 (1988s) 395 (A. M. *Suggate*).

8279 *Ellis* W. G., A scriptural viewpoint on divorce: TEdr 38 (New Orleans 1988) 33-40 [< NTAbs 33,203: Jesus spoke against the divorcing and the divorcers rather than the divorced; the Bible recognizes the legitimacy of divorce].

8281 EFerraro Sergio, Morale e coscienza storica; in dialogo con Josef FUCHS: Saggi 26. R 1988, Veritas. 210 p. – RCarthaginensia 5 (1989) 307 (J. L. *Parada*).

8284 **Fuchs** Joseph [→ 263], Christian morality; the Word becomes flesh [essays 1981-7], TMcNeil P., *Keenan* J. Dublin/Wsh 1987, Gill&M / Georgetown Univ.: RExpTim 99 (1987s) 344s (J. *McDonald*, warmly recommended); JTS 40 (1989) 331-7 (O. *O'Donovan*); Studies 77 (1988) 375-7 (J. *Healy*).

8287 **Gallagher** John, The basis for Christian ethics. NY 1985, Paulist. 271 p. $9. – RHeythJ 30 (1989) 336 (R. *Preston*: 'He thinks there is a crisis of authority in the Roman Catholic Church and that pluralism is not a state to be rested in').

8288 **Gatti** G., Morale sessuale, educazione dell'amore: TeolMor 3. T-Leumann 1988, Elle Di Ci. 197 p. – RClaretianum 29 (1989) 417s (J. *Rovira*).

8290 **Gaudemet** Jean, Le mariage en Occident 1987 → 3,8206; 4,9372: RCrNSt 10 (1989) 157-9 (G. *Cereti*: 75% delle nullità vengono pronunziate negli Stati Uniti, che hanno solo il 7% dei cattolici del mondo); NRT 111 (1989) 109s (B. *Joassart*).

8291 **Geisler** Norman L., Christian ethics. GR 1989, Baker. 335 p. $17 pa. [TrinJ 10,241].

8292 *Gibert* Pierre, Y a-t-il un statut biblique de l'embryon humain?: SuppVSp 165 (1988) 149-161.

8293 **Gill** Robin, A textbook of Christian ethics ➤ 2,6498 ['certain biblically consonant values held in tension']. E 1985, Clark. xiii-571 p. £10. – ᴿHeythJ 30 (1989) 335 (R. *Preston*).

8294 *Glinka* Luis, Indisolubilidad y divorcio en las Iglesias Ortodoxas, una contribución al diálogo ecuménico: TArg 25 (1988) 59-69.

8295 **Goldsmith** D., New Testament ethics, an introduction. Elgin IL 1988, Brethren. vi-185 p. $10 pa. 0-87178-605-2 [NTAbs 33,263].

8296 *Grayston* K., Adultery and sodomy; the biblical sources of Christian moral judgment: EpworthR 15,3 (1988) 54-70 [< NTAbs 33,66].

8297 **Guroian** Vigen, Incarnate love; essays in Orthodox ethics. ND 1987, Univ. xii-212 p. $25. – ᴿWestTJ 51 (1989) 187-193 (P. J. *Letthart*).

8297* **Haas** John M., The holy and the good; the relationship between religion and morality in the thought of Rudolf OTTO and Joseph PIEPER: diss. Catholic University of America, ᴰ*May* W. Wsh 1988. 88-14945. – DissA 49 (1988s) 1850-A.

8298 *Häring* Bernhard, [Grito de alarme, contra o rigorismo de Mons. Carlo CAFFARA (Humanae Vitae)]: REB 49 (1989) 464s.

8299 **Hallett** Garth L., Christian neighbor-love; an assessment of six rival versions. Wsh 1989, Georgetown Univ. viii-177 p. $25; pa. $13. 0-87840-479-1; 80-5 [TDig 37,57].

8300 *Hamann* H.P., Problems in the use of Scripture as an authoritative guide for Christian living today: LuthTJ 23,1 (Adelaide 1989) 11-18 [< NTAbs 33,288].

8301 **Hanigan** James P., Homosexuality 1988 ➤ 4,9383: ᴿÉglT 20 (1989) 141-4 (A. *Guindon*); LvSt 14 (1989) 65 (E. J. *Cooper*).

8302 **Happel** Stephen, *Walter* James J., Conversion and discipleship; a Christian foundation for ethics and doctrine 1986 ➤ 3,8219: ᴿJRel 68 (1988) 477 (J. W. *Fowler*: emerging genre in Roman Catholic ecumenical scholarship).

8303 **Harrison** Brian W., Le développement de la doctrine catholique sur la liberté religieuse (un précédent pour un changement vis-à-vis de la contraception)? Bouère 1988, D. M. Morin. 206 p. F 120. – ᴿEsprVie 99 (1989) 47 (R. *Coste*: 'Harrisson').

8304 *Herrenbrück* Reinhard, 'Die Ehe währet siebzehn Jahre, und wenn's hoch kommt, so sind's achtzehn Jahre'... Welche kirchliche Begleitung in der Scheidung? [Marriage lasts 17 years, at most 18; what Church accompaniment is there for divorce?]: WDienst 20 (1989) 353-375.

8305 *Hoffmann* Daniel, Bemerkungen zum Begriff des Nächsten und des Feindes im Anschluss an COHEN [H. 1935] und LÉVINAS: ZTK 86 (1989) 236-260.

8305* *Hoffmann* Gerhard, Solidarity with strangers as part of the mission of the Church: IntRMiss 78 (1989) 53-61.

8306 *Horsley* Richard, *Myers* Max, Idols, demons, and the hermeneutics of suspicion; biblical traditions informing ethics: ➤ 589, SBL Seminars 1989, 634-655.

8307 **Hughes** Gerard J., Authority in morals; an essay in Christian ethics. Wsh 1986, Georgetown Univ. xix-136 p. $7 pa. – ᴿJRel 68 (1988) 321s (T. A. *Byrnes*).

8308 *Hyldahl* Niels, *Salomonsen* Børge, Hinrichtung [death-penalty]: ⇒ 904, RAC 15,115 (1989) 342-365.

8309 *a*) *Istas* Michel, Une morale chrétienne plurielle?; – *b*) *Macina* M. R., Un modèle pour délier les divorcés remariés; l''admission provisoire' des *lapsi* par CYPRIEN de Carthage († 258): SuppVSp 165 (1988) 94-134.

8310 *Johnson* R. O., What the Bible says about homosexuality [refutation of six statements claiming not against]: Dialog 28,2 (St. Paul 1989) 49s [< NTAbs 33,346].

8311 **Kaiser** Robert B., The encyclical that never was; the story of the [Vatican] Commission on Population, Family and Birth, 1964-66 [= ³US 1985, The politics of sex and religion]. L 1987, Sheed & W. xii-307 p. – RAustralasCR 66 (1989) 243s (P. D. *Smith*); DocLife 38 (1988) 167s (L. *McRedmond*); NRT 111 (1989) 109s (L.-J. *Renard*).

8312 **Kammer** Charles L., Ethics and liberation; an introduction. L 1988, SCM. xi-243 p. £10.50. 0-334-00397-0. – RExpTim 100 (1988s) 306s (R. G. *Jones* compares with V. MACNAMARA); TsTNijm 29 (1989) 425 (H. *Spee*).

8313 *Kern* Udo, Dimensionen der Ehe in Theologie und Philosophie; Mann und Frau in ihrer theologischen dialogisch-leiblichen Verwiesenheit: ZRGg 40 (1988) 1-23.

8314 **Kirchschläger** Walter, Ehe und Ehescheidung im NT 1987 ⇒ 3,8232: RAtKap 113 (1989) 151-4 (M. *Marczewski*); ZkT 111 (1989) 209-211 (C. *Marucci*).

8315 **Knijff** H. W. de, Venus aan de leiband; Europa's erotische cultur en christlijke sexuele ethiek. Kampen 1987, Kok. 318 p. *f*65. 90-242-4799-3. – RTsTNijm 29 (1989) 427 (B. de *Groot-Kopetzky*).

8316 **Kötting** Bernhard, Die Bewertung der Wiederverheiratung (der zweiten Ehe) in der Antike und in der frühen Kirche [< Diss. Bonn 1982]: Rh/Wf Akad Vorträge G 292. Opladen 1988, Westd.-V. 43 p. DM 14. – RTR 85 (1989) 108s (P. *Mikat*).

8317 *Krüger* R., Reconciliación: Cuadernos de Teología 8 (Buenos Aires 1987) 153-8 [< NTAbs 33,57].

8318 *Lamarche* Paul, Bible [*al.*], Sexualité: ⇒ 886, DictSpir 14,92s (1989) 768-772 [-787].

8319 *Larue* Gerald A., Marriage and divorce: ⇒ 418: What the Bible really says 1989, 75-98.

8320 **Legrain** Michel, Les divorcés remariés; dossier de réflexion: Amour humain. P 1987, Centurion. 191 p. – RLavalTP 44 (1988) 407-410 (J. *Flamand*).

8321 *L'Huillier* Peter, bp., The indissolubility of marriage in Orthodox law and practice: SVlad 32 (1988) 199-221.

8322 **Lohse** Eduard, Theologische Ethik des NTs 1988 ⇒ 4,9394: RStPatav 36 (1989) 311s (G. *Segalla*); TPQ 137 (1989) 407s (J. *Janda*).

8323 *a*) *McCormick* Richard A., Moral theology 1940-1989; an overview; – *b*) *Gustafson* James M., Roman Catholic and Protestant interaction in ethics; an interpretation: TS 50,1 (Fiftieth Anniversary volume, Moral/Ethics issue 1989) 3-24 / 44-69.

8324 *McCormick* Richard A., ¿Se puede disentir en teología moral? [< TS 48 (1987) 87-105], TPascual Eduard: SelT 28 (1989) 245-255.

8325 *MacIntyre* Alasdair, Der Verlust der Tugend; zur moralischen Krise der Gegenwart, TRiehl W.: Theorie und Gesellschaft 5. Fra 1987, Campus. 381 p. DM 58. – RTLZ 114 (1989) 382s (H. *Kress*).

8326 **MacNamara** Vincent, The truth in love 1988 ➤ 4,9398: ᴿStudies 78 (1989) 105-7 (B. *Cosgrave*).

8327 **McNeill** John J., Taking a chance on God. Boston c. 1988, Beacon. 213 p. $13. – ᴿAmerica 160 (1989) 227-9 (L. *Griffini*, also on ᴱGRA-MICK); Commonweal 116 (1989) 90-92 (J. A. *O'Donohue*: also on his cognate Church & Homosexual³ and its censure).

8328 *Magesa C.* Laurenti, Sexual orientation and preference; recent development in Christian thought on homosexuality: ChAfChr 5,4 (1989) 3-45.

8329 **Maguire** Daniel C., The moral revolution 1986 ➤ 3,254; 4,9399: ᴿHorizons 16 (1989) 402s (Bonnie J. *Miller-McLemore*); JRel 68 (1988) 322s (Elizabeth *Bettenhausen*: 'lucid, loving prose').

8330 **Mahoney** John, The making of moral theology 1987 ➤ 3,8247; 4,9400: ᴿAmerica 159 (1988) 70s (W. C. *Spohn*); ETL 65 (1989) 210s (J. *Jans*: superb, insightful; Magisterium is shown to have been the function of those who were teaching); HeythJ 30 (1989) 331-3 (M. *Reidy*); NRT 111 (1989) 107 (L. *Volpe*); ScotJT 42 (1989) 130s (D. *Brown*).

8331 **Malherbe** Abraham J., Moral exhortation; a Greco-Roman sourcebook 1986 ➤ 2,6525 ... 4,9401: ᴿJBL 108 (1989) 359s (S. K. *Stowers*).

8332 *Mann* P. S., Toward a biblical understanding of polygamy: Missiology 17 (1989) 11-26 [< REB 49,507; NTAbs 33,206].

8333 *Marrow* Stanley B., Marriage and divorce in the NT: AnglTR 70 (1988) 3-15 [➤ 4,9402]: BS 146 (1989) 219-221, long summary by B. M. *Fanning* concludes that Marrow simply cuts rather than unties the Gordian knot of diversity of opinion among Catholics.

8334 **Marxsen** Willi, 'Christliche' und christliche Ethik im Neuen Testament. Gü 1989, Mohn. 272 p. DM 98. 3-579-00089-6 [NTAbs 33,407]. – ᴿRivB 37 (1989) 461-7 (G. *Segalla*: 'cristliche' und cristliche Ethik ...).

8335 **Mattioli** Anselmo, Le realtà sessuali nella Bibbia: Storia e dottrina. CasM 1987, Piemme. 262 p. – ᴿSalesianum 51 (1989) 158 (G. *Gatti*); Teresianum 40 (1989) 278s (P. *Mantovani*).

8336 *Mauerhofer* E., Sexualität aus der Perspektive des Alten und Neuen Testaments: Fundamentum (1989,1, on AIDS/SIDA) 17-23.

8337 **May** William E., Moral absolutes; Catholic tradition, current trends, and the truth: Père Marquette Theology lecture. Milwaukee 1989, Marquette Univ. vi-93 p. $8. 0-87462-544-0 [TDig 37,171].

8338 *a) Merino* José Antonio, L'etica di KANT nel pluralismo del suo tempo; – *b) Todisco* Orlando, ... nel pluralismo etico attuale: Antonianum 64,1 (Kant, 1989) 131-152 / 153-195.

8339 **Meurers** Joseph, Matrimonium perenne; Ehe gestern, heute und morgen: EurHS 23/239. Fra 1988, Lang. DM 26. – ᴿTGL 79 (1989) 20 (W. *Beinert*).

8340 **Moral** Antonio, *Leers* Bernardino, Teología moral, conflictos y alternativas: Cristianismo y sociedad 8. M 1987, Paulinas. 323 p. – ᴿScripTPamp 21 (1989) 731s (J. M. *Yanguas*).

8341 **Müller** Wunibald, Homosexualität; eine Herausforderung für Theologie und Seelsorge [kath. Diss. Würzburg 1984; bibelexegetisch ...]; Vorwort *Pompey* Heinrich. Mainz 1986, Grünewald. 240 p. DM 32 pa. – ᴿForumKT 4 (1988) 307-9 (J. *Rief*); TPQ 137 (1989) 293s (A. *Laun*: wissenschaftlich aber gegen die Lehre der Kirche); TR 85 (1989) 235-8 (A. van de *Spijker*).

8342 **Munier** Charles, *a)* Mariage et virginité dans l'Église ancienne: Traditio christiana 6. Bern 1987, Lang. lxxi-333 p. – ᴿBLitEc 90 (1989)

143s (H. *Crouzel*); RBén 98 (1988) 239s (L.-J. *Wankenne*); – *b*) Ehe und Ehelosigkeit in der Alten Kirche, ^T*Spoerri* Annemarie: Traditio christiana 4, 1987 ➔ 4,9405: ^RTPhil 64 (1989) 264s (H. J. *Sieben*).

8343 *Munier* Charles, La sollicitude pastorale de l'Église ancienne en matière de divorce et de remariage: LavalTP 44 (1988) 19-30 [> SelT 28 (1989) 213-221, ^T*Pericas* R. M.; ^E*Messa* J.].

Navone John; L'amore... teologia narrativa 1986 ➔ 9880; *Nelson* P., Narrative and morality ➔ 9881.

8345 **Nethöfel** Wolfgang, Moraltheologie nach dem Konzil; Personen, Programme, Positionen. Gö 1987, Vandenhoeck & R. 251 p. – ^RFreibZ 36 (1989) 503-6 (H. *Hirschi*).

8346 *Nyiredy* Maurus, Ⓜ Das Dilemma der Kirche (Dürfen die wiederverheirateten Geschiedenen das Sakrament der Busse empfangen?): TBud 22 (1988) 10-15.

8347 *O'Callaghan* Paul, La fórmula 'resurrección de la carne' y su significado para la moral cristiana: ScripTPamp 21 (1989) 777-803; Eng. 803.

8348 **O'Donovan** Oliver, Resurrection and moral order; an outline for evangelical ethics 1986 ➔ 2,6540... 4,9410: ^RHeythJ 30 (1989) 338s (G. J. *Hughes*); JAAR 57 (1989) 419-421 (T. F. *Sedgwick*); ScotJT 42 (1989) 131-4 (M. *Reidy*) & 564-8 (Helen *Oppenheimer*, orally to his seminar: 'authoritative, learned, judicious').

8349 *Østnor* Lars, [Norw.] An ecumenical ethics? Criteria for a common Catholic-Protestant ethics considered on the background of [^E*Hertz* A., al., 1978/82] 'Handbuch der christlichen Ethik': TsTKi 59 (1988) 189-204; Eng. 204.

8350 ^E**Perrin** Michel, Le Pardon, Actes du colloque, Centre d'histoire des idées, Univ. Picardie 1985/7 ➔ 3,691: ^RScEspr 41 (1989) 390s (G. *Novotny*).

8351 *Post* Stephen G., *Andolsen* Barbara, Recent works on reproductive technology [nine, none with apparent biblical orientation]: RelStR 15 (1989) 210-8.

8352 **Pozo Abejón** Gerardo del, Lex evangelica; estudio histórico-sistemático del paso de la concepción tomista a la suareciana: BiblTGran 29. Granada 1988, Fac. Teol. 367 p.

8353 **Ranke-Heinemann** Uta, Eunuchen für das Himmelreich; katholische Kirche und Sexualität. Ha 1988, Hofmann & C. 386 p. – ^RTPQ 137 (1989) 431s (W. *Blasig*).

8354 **Rebell** Walter, Neutestamentliche Ethik — Anmerkungen zum gegenwärtigen Diskussionsstand: ZevEth 32 (1988) 143-151.

8355 **Rendtorff** Trutz, Ethics I., Basic elements and methodology in an ethical theology, ^T*Crim* Keith. Ph 1986, Fortress. 193 p. – ^RJAAR 57 (1989) 427-9 (J. B. *Nelson*).

8356 **Richard** Lucien, Is there a Christian ethics? NY 1988, Paulist. 139 p. $8. – ^RHorizons 16 (1989) 189s (R. M. *Gula*); ScotJT 42 (1989) 617s (S. *Fowl*); SWJT 32,2 (1989) 75 (R. E. *Higgins*); TTod 46 (1989s) 102.104s.108 (M. Cathleen *Kaveny*).

8357 *Rigali* Norbert J., The story of Christian morality: ChSt 27 (1988) 173-180 [198-220, *Pollock* James R., book-reviews].

8358 *Rigby* Paul, *O'Grady* Paul, Agape and altruism; debates in theology and social psychology: JAAR 57 (1989) 719-737.

8359 *Rooke* M., Beyond the Bible: Faith and freedom 41,2 (Oxford 1988) 73-82 [➔ NTAbs 33,208: the Bible does not really show restraint in sex].

8360 **Schnackenburg** Rudolf, Die sittliche Botschaft des NTs I., 1986
➤ 2,6553; 3,8287; II., 1988 ➤ 4,9422: ᴿBogSmot 59 (1989) 490s (M.
Valković, 2); NRT 111 (1989) 429s (X. *Jacques*, 2); StPatav 36 (1989)
209-211 (G. *Segalla*, 2); TGegw 31 (1988) 129 (F. *Rosenberg*, 1); TGʟ 79
(1989) 620 (J. *Ernst*, 2); TPQ 137 (1989) 197s (J. *Janda*, 2); TsTNijm 29
(1989) 291 (T. *Veerkamp*, 2); ZevEth 33 (1989) 305s (W. *Rebell*, 2); ZkT
111 (1989) 244s (H. *Rotter*, 1s).

8361 **Schnackenburg** R., Il messaggio morale del NT, I. Da Gesù alla chiesa
primitiva [1986 ➤ 2,6553], ᵀ*Panini* M. A.: CommTeolNT Sup 1. Brescia
1989, Paideia. 351 p. Lit. 40.000. – ᴿStPatav 36 (1989) 624s (G. *Segalla*).

8362 **Schockenhoff** Eberhard, Bonum hominis; die anthropologischen und
theologischen Grundlagen der Tugendethik des Thomas von Aᴏᴜɪɴ:
TüTSt 28. Mainz 1987, Grünewald. 614 p. – ᴿRThom 89 (1989)
118-125 (S. *Pinckaers*: excellent).

8363 **Schrage** Wolfgang, The ethics of the NT [1982 ➤ 63,7294] 1988
➤ 4,9423: ᴿRExp 86 (1989) 440s (P. D. *Simmons*); ScotJT 42 (1989) 594-7
(J. I. H. *McDonald*); TLond 92 (1989) 335s (L. *Houlden*); TrinJ 10 (1989)
233-8 (P. T. *Denton*); TS 50 (1989) 172-4 (R. J. *Daly*).

8364 *a) Schrage* Wolfgang, Komparative Ethik im NT: – *b) Roloff* Jürgen,
Themen und Traditionen urchristlicher Amtsträgerparänese; – *c) Jonge*
Marinus de, Die Paränese in den Schriften des NTs und in den
Testamenten der Zwölf Patriarchen; einige Überlegungen: ➤ 173,
ᶠSᴄʜɴᴀᴄᴋᴇɴʙᴜʀɢ R., NT & Ethik 1989, 482-506 / 507-526 / 538-550.

8365 *Schwab* Claude, Morale protestante et morale catholique d'après Paul
Tɪʟʟɪᴄʜ: ÉTRel 64 (1989) 225-234.

8366 **Spicq** Ceslas, Connaissance et morale dans la Bible: Ét. Éthique
Chrétienne 13, 1985 ➤ 1,7938... 4,9429: ᴿRoczTK 33,3 (1986) 105-9 (S.
Warzeszak).

8367 **Spong** John S. [Episcopal bishop of Newark], Living in sin? A bishop
rethinks human sexuality. SF 1988, Harper & R. 256 p. $16. 0-06-
067505-5. – ᴿCCurr 39 (1989s) 213-7 (Christine *Gudorf*, also on three
cognate books); Horizons 16 (1989) 190s (J. P. *Hanigan*); JRel 69 (1989)
582s (E. V. *Vacek*: not so much about sex as about prejudice; also
considers Yahweh's victory as women's defeat); RExp 86 (1989) 138s
(P. D. *Simmons*: daring; canceled by Abingdon).

8368 **Stout** Jeffrey, Ethics after Babel; the languages of morals and their
discontents. Boston 1988, Beacon. 338 p. $27.50. – ᴿTTod 46 (1989s)
55-58 (C. *Dykstra*) & 59-61 (G. *Lindbeck*) & 61-64 (J. *McClendon*, Nancey
Murphy) & 64-66 (Sheila *Briggs*) & 66-68 (C. *West*); 69-73, Stout replies.

8369 *Szathmáry* Sándor, Ⓦ The New Testament (nova lex) as an ethical
source: TSzem 32 (1989) 221-7.

8370 **Tettamanzi** D., I due saranno una carne sola; saggi teologici su
matrimonio e famiglia. T-Leumann 1986, Elle Di Ci. 326 p. Lit. 19.000.
– ᴿDivThom 91 (1988) 482-4 (L. *Ciccone*).

8371 *Tischner* Jósef, Called to freedom [< Wezwani do wolności, Znak
37,362s (1985) 204-212], ᵀᴱ*Czosnyka* Helena J.: TDig 36 (1989) 37-41.

8372 **Tödt** Heinz E., Perspektiven theologischer Ethik. Mü 1988, Kaiser.
288 p. DM 48. – ᴿGerefTTs 89 (1989) 123s (F. de *Lange*); TLZ 114 (1989)
618s (J. *Wiebering*).

8372* *Troianos* Spyros, Kirchliche und weltliche Rechtsquellen zur Homosexualität in Byzanz: JbÖsByz 39 (1989) 29-48.

8373 *Vacek* Edward C., Divorce; making a moral decision: AnglTR 70
(1988) 310-322.

8374 *Valadier* Paul,   Pequeña apología de la conciencia [Petite apologie de la conscience: Études 370 (1989) 371-382], ᵀᴱ*Ferrer* Pi Pedro: SelT 28 (1989) 269-273.

8375 **Verhey** Allen, The great reversal 1984 ⇥ 65,7122 ... 3,8304:   ᴿWestTJ 50 (1988) 206-213 (D. W. *Clowney*).

8376 *a) Wehrle* J.,   Barmherzigkeit; – *b)* [*Bons* E. AT] *Kampling* R., Begierde; – *c) Hoppe* R., Bruderliebe: ⇥ 902, NBL, Lfg 2 (1989) 241-4 / 259-262 / 335s.

8377 *Wiemeyer* Joachim,   Renaissance der Wirtschaftsethik [9 volumes, none with perceptible relation to Scripture]: TR 85 (1989) 89-100.

8378 *Wilcken* J.,   Reconciliation; a scriptural and theological approach: Australian Journal of Liturgy 1,4 (Belair SAu 1988) 164-9 [< NTAbs 33,209].

8379 **Wogaman** J. Philip,   Christian moral judgment [= ²A Christian method of ... 1976; omits final chapter on social strategy; adds others]. Louisville 1989, Westminster/Knox. 192 p. $15. 0-664-25004-1 [TDig 37,95]. – ᴿTTod 46 (1989s) 438-440 (E. *Mount*).

8380 ᵀᴱ**Womer** Jan L.,   Morality and ethics in early Christianity: Sources 1987 ⇥ 4,9434:   ᴿTLZ 114 (1989) 450s (H. *Opitz*).

8380* *Wright* David F.,   Homosexuality; the relevance of the Bible: EvQ 61 (1989) 291-300.

8381 *Ziegler* Josef G.,   Neuere Veröffentlichungen zur Geschlechtsmoral [*Haag-Elliger, Kertelge* biblisch]: TR 85 (1989) 177-190.

8381* *Ziegler* J. G.,   Vom 'Sein in Christus' zum 'Leben in Christus'; das Strukturgesetz einer Gnadenmoral: ForumKT 4 (1988) 1-18 [5 (1989) 69-71, ᴿ*Rief* J.].

H8.4   *NT ipsum de reformatione sociali* – **Political action in Scripture.**

8382 *a) Aguirre* Rafael, El Evangelio como 'juicio' a la cultura del consumo; – *b) González Faus* José I.,   La 'filosofia de la vida' de Jesús de Nazaret: SalT 76 (1988) 265-274 / 275-289.

8383 *Akpunou* P.D.,   Religion and politics in the Old Testament and in the intertestamentary era; NigJT 1,4 (1988) 78-90 [< TContext 7/1,24].

8384 *Amjad-Ali* Charles,   The option for the poor in the Old Testament: Al-Mushir 30,2 (Rawalpindi 1988) 51-59 [< TContext 6/2, 47].

8385 *a) Artom* Emanuele,   Gli oppressi nella Bibbia; – *b) Ortona* Silvia, Poveri nella società regia biblica; i contadini; – *c) Valacca Pagella* Vivetta, Dio e gli stranieri; – *d) Bianchi* Enzo, I derelitti nella Bibbia: ⇥ 921, Deboli 1987/8, 77-89 / 93-122 / 47-74 / (fasc. inserito) 1-21.

8386 ᴱ**Bammel** Ernst, *Moule* C.F.D.,   Jesus and the politics of his day 1984 ⇥ 65,267 ... 3,8316:   ᴿCrNSt 9 (1988) 170-2 (G. D. *Cova*).

8387 **Bandow** Doug,   Beyond good intentions; a biblical view of politics. Westchester IL 1988, Crossway. xiv-271 p. $10. – ᴿWestTJ 51 (1989) 419-421 (P. J. *Leithart*).

8388 **Bartnik** Czesław S., [⇥ 3,6505 théologie 'poiétique'] Formen der politischen Theologie in Polen: Eichstätter Materialien 4/8. Rg 1986, Pustet. 159 p. DM 39. – ᴿTR 85 (1989) 472s (J. *Piegsa*).

8388* **Battenhouse** Paul F.,   Theology in the social gospel, 1918-1946: diss. Yale. NHv 1950. 416 p. – DissA 50 (1989s) 978-A.

8389 **Bauckham** Richard,   The Bible in politics; how to read the Bible politically: Third Way Book. L 1989, SPCK. x-166 p. £7 pa. 0-281-

04402-3. – RExpTim 100,11 first choice (1988s) 401-3 (C.S. *Rodd*: instructive on Rev 18); TLond 92 (1989) 343 (D. *Cohn-Sherbok*).

8390 **Baum** Gregory, Theology and society [16 reprints] 1987 → 4,162: RHorizons 16 (1989) 179s (F. *Keck*); SR 18 (1989) 97-99 (R. *Haight*).

8391 **Berten** Ignace, Christ pour les pauvres. P 1989, Cerf. 128 p. F 69. 2-204-03018-X [ÉTRel 64,481].

8392 *Beyerhaus* Peter, *a)* A teologia do pobre na perspectiva biblica: Atualização 19 (Belo Horizonte 1988) 441-452 [< Stromata 45,500]; – *b)* La teología de los pobres en perspectiva bíblica: Tierra Nueva 17,66 (1988s) 41-49.

8393 *Bindemann* W., Gedanken zur biblischen Botschaft von der Gerechtigkeit: ZeichZt 42 (B 1988) 190-6 [< NTAbs 33,201].

8394 *Cartaxo Rolim* Francisco, Neoconservadorismo eclesiástico e uma estratégia política: REB 49 (1989) 259-281.

8395 **Cort** J.C., Christian socialism; an informal history 1987 → 4,9466; 0-88344-573-5: RTsTNijm 29 (1989) 292 (J. van *Laarhoven*: 'In every Christian lives a socialist, in every socialist a Christian').

8396 *Cristianesimo e potere* [Seminario 1985]: Ist. Trentino di Cultura 10. Bo 1986, Dehoniane. 191 p. [21-36 AT, *Bonora* A.; 37-42 NT, *Segalla* G.]. – RAevum 62 (1988) 152s (A. *Barzanò*).

8397 *De Benedetti* Paolo, Povero e povertà nella Bibbia: HumBr 44 (1989) 363-374.

8398 **Elliott** Charles, Praying the Kingdom; towards a political spirituality 1985 → 2,6591 ... 4,9453: RVidyajyoti 52 (1988) 224 (P.M. *Meagher*).

8399 *a) Fabris* R., Dio e Cesare; soggetti, forme e criteri della politica nel NT; – *b) Bonora* A., Storia e principi della politica nell'Antico Testamento: Credere Oggi (1989,2) 26s / 15-25 [< REB 49,764].

8400 **Farina** Marcella, Chiesa di poveri e Chiesa dei poveri [II.] La memoria della Chiesa: Prisma 7, 1985 → 4,9456; Lit. 30.000: RClaretianum 29 (1989) 414-6 (B. *Proietti*); CrNSt 9 (1988) 429s (J. *Dupont*); RivScR 3,1 (1989) 241s (L.M. de *Palma*); Salesianum 51 (1989) 168s (O. *Pasquato*); Teresianum 40 (1989) 597-9 (F. *Di Giacomo*).

8401 **Forrester** Duncan B., Theology and politics; Signposts in theology. Ox 1988, Blackwell. ix-182 p. £25; pa. £8. 0-631-15282-2; pa. 3-0 [NTAbs 33,262]. – RExpTim 100,3 first choice (1988s) 81s (C.S. *Rodd*); TLond 92 (1989) 536-8 (J. *Atherton*).

8402 EForrester Duncan B., Skene Danus, [Church of Scotland report], Just sharing; a Christian approach to the distribution of wealth, income and benefits. L 1988, Epworth. xi-131 p. £5.50 pa. – RTLond 92 (1989) 222s (Ruth *McCurry*).

8403 *Fraijo* Manuel, Jesús frente al sistema de su época: RazF 219 (1989) 626-638.

8404 *France* R.T., La libération dans le Nouveau Testament [< EvQ 1986, 3-23], Tanonyme: Hokhma 37 (1988) 1-24.

8404* **Gladwin** John, The good of the people; a Christian reflection on living with the modern state: London Lectures in Contemporary Christianity. Basingstoke 1988, Marshall Pickering. viii-102 p. £8 [JTS 40, 743].

8405 **Glebe-Möller** Jens, A political dogmatic [*Metz* J.-B.; *Habermas* J. ...], THall Thor, 1987 → 4,9461: 0-8006-2053-4. – RExpTim 100 (1988s) 394 (R. *Bauckham*); TR 85 (1989) 130-2 (E. *Arens*).

8406 **González** Carlos I., Pobreza y riqueza en obras selectas del cristianismo primitivo: 'Sepan cuantos' 564. Méx 1988, Porrúa. xxxviii-182 p. 968-452-289-4. – RGregorianum 70 (1989) 195 (*ipse*).

8406* **Gordon** Barry, The economic problem in biblical and patristic thought: VigChr supp 9. Leiden 1989, Brill. x-144 p. *f* 70 [TR 86, 252].

8407 *Graf* Friedrich W., Vom munus propheticum Christi zum prophetischen Wächteramt der Kirche? Erwägungen zum Verhältnis von Christologie und Ekklesiologie: ZevEth 32 (1988) 88-106.

8407* *a) Grant* Robert M., Kirche und Staat, Urchristentum; – *b) Honecker* Martin, Kirche und Welt; ➤ 911, TRE 18 (1989) 354-365 (-405, *al.*) / 405-421.

8408 *Guillemette* Nil, Jesus, politics, and violence: Landas 1,2 (Manila 1987) 183-205 [< NTAbs 33,17].

8409 *Guillén* Antonio, El planteamiento económico neo-conservador; análisis crítico-teológico: SalT 77 (1989) 551-564.

8410 **Haan** R., The economics of honour; biblical reflections on money and property: Oikoumene. Geneva 1988, WCC. x-71 p. Fs 10. – RNRT 111 (1989) 614s (C. M.).

8411 *Hartin* P. J., Apartheid and the Scriptures; the contribution of Albert GEYSER [more scholarly than DU PEREZ] in this polemic: JTSAf 64 (Rondebosch 1988) 20-23 [4s, Geyser 1918-1985].

8412 *Hausmanninger* Thomas, Politisch engagierter Glaube im Streit [*Ockenfels* W,; *Büchele* H.; E*Hofmann* R.: alle 1987]: MüTZ 40 (1989) 71-75.

8413 *Herczeg* Pál, Ⓜ Liberty, libertinism (*szabadosság*) and self-restraint in gospel and apostolic teaching: TSzem 31 (1988) 172-7.

8414 *Herms* Eilert, Die Bedeutung des Gesetzes für die lutherische Sozialethik: ➤ 177, FSCHWARZ R., Von Wittenberg 1989, 62-89.

8415 *Hobbs* T. R., Reflections on 'the poor' and the OT: ExpTim [99 (1987s) 1-14, *Coggins* R.] 100 (1988s) 291-4.

8416 **Hoppe** Leslie J., Being poor; a biblical study 1987 ➤ 3,8338 ... 4,9468: RPacifica 2 (1989) 107-112 (J. *Wright*: many errors in index and Scripture-references); RRel 48 (1989) 630s (C. *Bernas*).

8417 **Jäger** Alfred, Diakonie als christliches Unternehmen; theologische Wirtschaftsethik im Kontext diakonischer Unternehmenspolitik. Gü 1986, Mohn. 365 p. – RTZBas 45 (1989) 382-4 (W. *Neidhart*).

8418 *Kautil* Kasek, A political theology; Melanesian milieu: Melanesian Journal of Theology 5,1 (PapuaNG 1989) 20-26 [H. *Janssen* summary in TContext 7/1,111].

8419 **Kee** Alistair, Domination or liberation; the place of religion in social conflict. L 1986, SCM. xiii-126 p. – RNBlackf 68 (1987) 366 (R. *Ruston*).

8420 *a) Kresina* Ante, Conspectus biblico-theologicus problematum socialium; – *b) Krašovec* Jože, Analysis philologica conceptus justitiae [< diss. 1988]: BogSmot 59 (1989) 268-276, croat.; 276 deutsch / 277-284.

8421 **Lascaris** André, Uitsicht voor een oude wereld; West-Europa op een keerpunt. Kampen 1987, Kok Agora. 183 p. *f* 29,50. 90-242-7552-0. – RBijdragen 50 (1989) 221s (W. G. *Tillmans*: GIRARD-based analysis of explosion awaited from third-world mimesis of Europe's desire/needs).

8422 *Le Grys* Alan, The pastor's opportunities, XVIII. Social and political issues [... OT; NT]: ExpTim 99 (1987s) 355-9.

8423 **Lohfink** Norbert, Gott auf der Seite der Armen; Biblisches zur 'optio praeferentialis pro pauperibus'. Fra 1985, St. Georgen. 124 p.

8424 **Lohfink** Norbert F., Option for the poor ... in the light of the Bible 1987 ➤ 3,8348; 4,9480: RCBQ 51 (1989) 337-9 (J. *Limburg*: also on HOPPE L.; for both, poverty in the Bible is real, not 'spiritual'); ExpTim 99 (1987s)

340 (C. S. *Rodd*); RBibArg 51 (1989) 52-54 (J. S. *Croatto*); Vidyajyoti 52 (1988) 58 (R. J. *Raja*).

8425 *Lohfink* Norbert, Voorkeur voor de armen, het leidmotief van de bevrijdingstheologie: Streven 55 (1987) 483-496.

8426 **Manenschijn** G., Geldzucht — de wortel van alle kwaad? Economie tussen moralisme en amoraliteit 1987 ➤ 3,8355*: RCollatVL 19 (1989) 229s (E. *Lagae*).

8427 *Matura* Thaddée, Les pauvres et la pauvreté dans la Bible: Christus 35 (P 1988) 23-38.

8428 **Medhurst** Kenneth N., *Moyser* George H., Church and politics in a secular age. Ox 1988, Clarendon. xvii-392 p.; 6 fig. £35. – RJTS 40 (1989) 717-9 (P. *Hinchliff*).

8429 **Meeks** M. Douglas, God the economist; the doctrine of God and political economy. Minneapolis 1989, Fortress. xiii-257 p. $13 pa. 0-8006-2329-0 [TDig 37,172].

8430 **Minnerath** Roland, Jésus et le pouvoir: PoinT 46, 1987 ➤ 3,8362; 4,9486: RBrotéria 127 (1988) 475 (F. *Pires Lopes*); ScEspr 41 (1989) 115 (L. *Sabourin*).

8431 **Molnar** Thomas S., Twin powers; politics and the sacred. GR 1988, Eerdmans. ix-147 p. $10 pa. 0-8028-0303-2 [TDig 37,173: W. C. *Heiser*: Catholic philosopher, on desacralization of power].

8432 *Mott* S. C., Because Jesus was homeless for us... a biblical study on our responsibility to the homeless [Job 24,1-12; Mt 8,18-22; Lk 14,12-24; Ps 107,4-9.33-43]: Christian Social Action 2,2 (Wsh 1989) 4-15 [< NTAbs 33,349].

8433 *Munier* Charles, Les doctrines politiques de l'Église ancienne: RevSR 62 (1988) 42-53.

8434 **Neal** sr. Marie Augusta, The just demands of the poor [9 reprinted 1972-85] essays in socio-theology. NY 1987, Paulist. 142 p. $9. 0-8091-2845-4. – RRelStT 7,2s (1987) 97 (D. *Skoyles*); PrPeo 3 (1989) 36s (P. *Phillips*); RExp 86 (1989) 639 (Diana S. R. *Garland*).

8434* **Nelson-Pallmeyer** Jack, The politics of compassion 1986 ➤ 3,8367: RPhilipSa 27 (1987) 320-2 (P. T. *Tiong*).

8435 *a) Neutzling* Inácio, Jesus e os marginalizados do seu tempo — uma meditação bíblica; – *b) Zanini* Ovidio, Opção pelas categorias de marginalizados em Paulo; – *c) Wolff* Günter, A chave de leitura do Novo Testamento; – *d) Silva* Valmor da, Os marginalizados constroem a história; – *e) Tavares Zabatiero* Julio P., O Estado e o empobrecimento do povo — reflexões a partir dos profetas do VIII século aC: EstudosB 21 (1989) 47-55 / 56-69 / 33-46 / 9-22 / 23-32.

8436 **North** Gary, Dominion and common grace; the biblical basis of progress. Tyler TX 1987, Institute for Christian Economics. XV-295 p. $9. – RWestTJ 50 (1988) 323-337 (M. W. *Karlberg*: theonomy; 'covenant and common grace').

8437 **Oakman** Douglas K., Jesus and the economic questions of his day 1986 ➤ 2,6627; 4,9494: RCBQ 51 (1989) 564-6 (P. *Hollenbach*); CurrTM 16 (1989) 463 (E. *Krentz*).

8437* **Ockenfels** Wolfgang, Politisierte Glaube?: Politeia 33. Walderberg 1987, 'IfG'. 346 p. – RForumKT 5 (1989) 67-69 (J. *Giers*).

8438 **Pracher** Christian, Ökonomie der Nächstenliebe; Kirche als Dienstleistungsbetrieb: Sozialwissenschaftliche Materialien 13. Linz 1987, Trauner. 284 p.; 73 fig. DM 29. – RTPQ 137 (1989) 201 (P. *Gradauer*).

8439 **Prior** David, Jesus and power: Jesus Library 11, 1987 ⇥ 4,9497; also L 1987, Hodder & S. 192 p. £7. – ᴿThemelios 14 (1988s) 106 (B. *Houston*).

8440 **Ratzinger** J., Chiesa, ecumenismo e politica 1987 ⇥ 4,9501: ᴿAnnTh 3,1 (1989) 165-174 (E. *Juliá*).

8441 **Ratzinger** J., Iglesia, ecumenismo y política; nuevos ensayos de eclesiología 1987 ⇥ 4,9500: ᴿCiuD 202 (1989) 517 (J. M. *Ozaeta*).

8442 **Ratzinger** Joseph [⇥ 342]. Church, ecumenism and politics. NY 1988, Crossroad. 256 p. $20. 0-8245-0859-9. – ᴿCommonweal 115 (1988) 572s (J. A. *Komonchak*); Tablet 242 (1988) 274 (E. *Yarnold*); TS 50 (1989) 386s (J. *Gros*).

8443 **Rief** Josef, Christliche Verantwortung nur als Politik?: MüTZ [39 (1988) 259-280, *Zottl* A.] 40 (1989) 233-247.

8444 *Rodrigo* Michael, Bible and the liberation of the poor: Dialogue 15,1s (Sri Lanka 1988) 61-83 [< TContext 7/1, 69].

8445 **Rowland** Christopher, Radical Christianity, a reading of recovery. L 1988, Polity. vi-199 p. £27.50; pa. £8. – ᴿExpTim 100 (1988s) 394s (W. J. *Hollenweger*: begins with Paul's well-to-do Gentiles already embarrassed by Jesus' contacts with guerilla Judaism); TLond 92 (1989) 342s (F. G. *Downing*: other-worldliness demanding social practice, as found interestingly in the British bishop Fastidius, ed. *Haslehurst* R. 1927).

8446 *Rowland* C., Reading the Bible in the struggle for justice and peace: Way Sup 63 (1988) 25-37 [< NTAbs 33,144].

8447 *Salemink* Theo, Economische theologie; object en methode: TsTNijm 29 (1989) 344-364; Eng. 364: 'A. T. van LEEUWEN's Economic Theology' [deals with modern economics, not patristic *oikonomía*].

8448 **Schillebeeckx** Edward, Jesus in... politics 1987 ⇥ 4,9511: ᴿVidyajyoti 52 (1988) 143 (G. *Lobo*).

8449 **Schmidt** Thomas E., Hostility to wealth in the Synoptic gospels: JStNT sup 15, 1987 ⇥ 3,8383; 4,9512: ᴿCBQ 51 (1989) 572-4 (H. C. *Kee*: aims to discredit sociological methods); EvQ 61 (1989) 93-95 (J. *Peck*).

8450 *Schmidt* T., *al.*, Rich wisdom; NT teachings on wealth [consistently negative]: ChrTod 33,8 (1989) 28-30 [*Grudem* W., 31-34; *Van Leeuwen* R. C., 34-70; *Maynard-Reid* P. U., 37-39; *Kantzer* K. S., 39: < NTAbs 33,360].

8451 **Scholder** Klaus, The Churches and the Third Reich, 2. The year of disillusionment; 1934, Barmen and Rome. L 1988, SCM. x-392 p. £25. – ᴿTLond 92 (1989) 532-4 (E. *Robertson*: Scholder died at this point, but his student Gerhard BESIER will continue in three volumes to 1949).

8452 *Segalla* J., El Nuevo Testamento y el Estado: Didascalia 420 (Rosario ARG 1989) 4-9 [< Stromata 45, 499].

8453 ᴱ**Sheils** W. J., *Wood* Diana, The Church and wealth 1986/7 ⇥ 3,721: ᴿExpTim 100 (1988s) 273s (J. A. *Newton*); Tablet 242 (1988) 212s (M. *Richards*); Vidyajyoti 52 (1988) 415 (D. G.).

Sicre J. L., 'Con los pobres de la tierra' 1984 ⇥ 3445 (-8).

8454 *Sider* Ronald L., Toward a biblical perspective on equality; steps on the way toward Christian political engagement: Interpretation 43 (1989) 156-169.

8455 *Silva* V. da, *al.*, Categorias de marginalidade na Biblia: EstudosB 21 (1989) [< REB 49,764].

8456 *Sivatte* Rafael de, 'No soporto vuestras fiestas'; quando la fe se desentiende de la justicia; SalT 77 (1989) 683-693.

8457 *Staats* R., Die Ortskirche soll reich sein; ein Grundsatz frühchristlicher Wirtschaftsethik: Diakonia 19 (Wien 1988) [230-6, *Thomas* J.] 236-244

[< NTAbs 33,69: 'The early Christians were more concerned with the responsible use of property and wealth than with the dangers of possessions. They assumed that the local Church should have large sums of money at its disposal' (D. J. *Harrington*)].

8457* **Stackhouse** Max I., Public theology and political economy; Christian stewardship in modern society 1987 ➤ 3,8389; 4,9519:   ᴿJRel 69 (1989) 134s (J. P. *Gunnemann*).

8458 *Susin* L. C., Jesus, o 'Cristo' e seu projeto político: Teocomunicação 80 (1988) 135-147 [< Stromata 45,500].

8459 *Szabó* Csaba, ⓂCritical political questions according to the NT: TSzem 31 (1988) 340-4.

8460 ᴱTaubes Jacob, Religionstheorie und politische Theologie, 2. Gnosis und Politik 1982/4 ➤ 1,654; DM 78:   ᴿBijdragen 50 (1989) 211s (Hanneke *Reuling*).

8461 *Ukachukwu Manus* Chris, New Testament theological foundations for Christian contribution to politics in Nigeria: BEcuT 2,1 (Enugu 1989) 7-30 [< TContext 7/1,23].

8462 **Walsh** James P. M., The mighty from their thrones 1987 ➤ 3,2608; 4,9534: ᴿGregorianum 70 (1989) 783-5 (G. L. *Prato*); Interpretation 43 (1989) 218s [also 420.422] (R. D. *Witherup*: too puissant and feckless); ScotJT 42 (1989) 570s (Vicky *Raymer*).

8463 **Weber** Hans-Ruedi, Power; focus for a biblical theology [... six trajectories]. Geneva 1989, WCC. xi-204; ill.; 11 maps. $12.90. 2-8254-0925-1 [NTAbs 33,410].

8464 **Wogaman** J. Philip, Christian perspectives on politics. L/Ph 1988, SCM/Fortress. ix-309 p. £12.50 pa. 0-334-01920-6/. – ᴿExpTim 100 first choice (1988s) 82s (C. S. *Rodd*); TLond 92 (1989) 536-8 (J. *Atherton*).

8465 **Zsifkovits** Valentin, Politik ohne Moral?: Soziale Perspektiven. Linz 1989, Veritas. 136 p. – ᴿBogSmot 59 (1989) 498s (M. *Valković*).

H8.5   Theologia liberationis latino-americana.

8466 **Acosta** José de, De procuranda [Perú 1539-1600] Indorum salute, I. Pacificación y colonización; II. Educación y evangelización: Corpus Hispanorum de Pace 23s. M 1987, Cons. Sup. Inv. 734 p.; 321 p. – ᴿTPhil 64 (1989) 273s (M. *Sievernich*).

8467 *Agera* Cassian R., Liberation theology today [*Boff* L. & C., Introducing 1987]: Indian Missiological Review 11,1 (Shillong 1989) 96-100 [< TContext 7/1, 35].

8468 **Alegre** X. [exégesis de Rom 1,18-32], *al.*, El segrest de la veritat... (Rom 1,18) [original de El secuestro 1984s ➤ 2,6650a] 1986 ➤ 2,6650b: ᴿEstE 64 (1989) 565 (F. *Pastor Ramos*).

8469 **Altmann** Walter, Confrontación y liberación; una perspectiva latinoamericana sobre Martín LUTERO; conferencias Carnahan 1983: Vox Evangelii 2. BA 1987, Asoc. Interconfesional. 254 p. – ᴿTLZ 114 (1989) 233 (R. *Frieling*).

8470 *Andonegui* Javier, La ética a propósito de la conquista de América: ScripV 35 (1988) 320-385.

8471 **Araya Guillén** Victorio, God of the poor 1987 ➤ 3,8403:   ᴿPacifica 2 (1989) 229-231 (J. *Sweeney*).

8472 *Asi* Emmanuel, Liberation theology; a Pakistani perspective: Logos 28,1 (Colombo 1989) 1-53 [G. *Evers* (Eng.) summary in TContext 7/1, 107].

8473 *Bartha* Tibor, Ⓜ A felszabadítás teológiajáról... Liberation theology: TSzem 32 (1989) 110-114.

8474 **Bastian** Jean-Pierre, Breve historia del protestantismo en América latina; Historia Mínima 25s. México 1986, CUSPA. 190 p. – ᴿÉTRel 64 (1989) 133s (J. *Alexandre*).

8474* **Batstone** David B., From conquest to struggle; Jesus of Nazareth in the liberation Christology of Latin America: diss. Graduate Theological Union, ᴰ*Reist* B. Berkeley 1989. 316 p. 89-24365. – DissA 50 (1989s) 2110-A; RelStR 16,187.

8475 **Berryman** Phillip, Liberation theology 1987 → 3,8406; 4,9532: ᴿInterpretation 43 (1989) 434s (D. A. *Diekema*: no-violence claim not fully in accord with the facts); WestTJ 51 (1989) 424s (H. M. *Conn*).

8476 **Biancucci** Duilio, Einführung in die Theologie der Befreiung 1987 → 4,9534: ᴿTPhil 64 (1989) 311s (M. *Sievernich*).

8477 **Blue** John R., Origin of G. GUTIÉRREZ' 'A theology of liberation': diss. ᴰ*Studerus* L. H. Univ. Texas at Arlington 1989. 285 p. 90-10432. – DissA 50 (1989s) 3628-A.

8478 *Boero* Mario, Materiales sobre la transformación de la teología contemporánea; la teología de la liberación en América Latina: EstFranc 90 (1989) 1-71; fig. p. 72.

8479 **Boff** Clodovis, Theology and praxis; epistemological foundations 1987 → 3,8410; 4,9537: $20. 0-88344-416-X. – ᴿDoctLife 39 (1989) 166s (B. *Hearne*); ExpTim 100 (1988s) 36 (R. G. *Crawford*); IntRMiss 78 (1989) 97-101 (S. S. *Mackie*: 'advanced level' like SEGUNDO); Vidyajyoti 52 (1988) 112 (G. *Lobo*).

8480 **Boff** L., Passion of Christ, passion of the world; the facts, their interpretation, and their meaning, yesterday and today 1987 → 3,8414: ᴿIndTSt 26 (1989) 84-86 (L. *Legrand*); Vidyajyoti 52 (1988) 563s (R. J. *Raja*).

8481 *Boff* Leonardo, Libertad y liberación; puntos de contacto y de fricción en el primer y tercer mundo: RLatAmT 5 (1988) 187-205 [207-217, *Metz* J.-B.].

8482 **Boff** L. & C., Liberation theology, from confrontation to dialogue 1986 → 2,6669; 3,8425: ᴿRExp 86 (1989) 278s (Molly *Marshall-Green*: 'Blodovis' in both title and text).

8483 **Boff** L. & C., Wat is theologie van de bevrijding 1986 → 3,8428: ᴿBijdragen 50 (1989) 338s (W. G. *Tillmans*).

8484 ᴱ**Bourdarias** Jean [CELAM, conseil épiscopal latino-américain, colloque 1985], Église populaire et théologie de la libération, ᵀ*Dauge* Viviane. P 1988, Fayard. 300 p. F 120. – ᴿRTLv 20 (1989) 392 (P. *Wéber*: très informatif; mais traduction détestable, et préface de Bourdarias soulignant uniquement le caractère pervers de la TL).

8485 **Brown** Robert M., Spirituality and liberation; overcoming the great fallacy 1988 → 4,9548: ᴿCurrTM 16 (1989) 139s (Jane *Seagren*); Horizons 16 (1989) 185s (Margaret *Brennan*); NewTR 2,3 (1989) 119 (J. M. *Lozano*); TPhil 64 (1989) 315s (M. *Sievernich*).

8486 **Cadorette** Curt, From the heart of the people; the theology of G. GUTIERREZ. Oak Park IL 1988, Meyer-Stone. $35; pa. $15. 0-940989-27-1; 18-2. – ᴿExpTim 100 (1988s) 114 (W. J. *Hollenweger*).

8487 *Calvez* Y., Théologie de la libération après les deux Instructions [< NRT 108 (1986) 845-859] Slovene, ᵀ*Stres* A.: BogVest 47 (1989) 171.

8488 *Campbell* James L., Liberation theology and the thought of William TEMPLE; a discussion of possibilities: ScotJT 42 (1989) 513-539.

8489 *Casaldáliga* Pedro, A los quinientos años, 'descolonizar y desevangelizar'; entrevista con J. M. VIGIL: RLatAmT 6,16 (1989) 115-130.

8490 **Chopp** Rebecca, The praxis of suffering 1986 ➤ 2,6674 ... 4,9553: ᴿRelStR 15 (1989) 123-5 (D. R. *Blumenthal*).

8491 **Cohn-Sherbok** Dan, On earth as it is in heaven 1987 ➤ 3,8440; 4,9556: ᴿVidyajyoti 52 (1988) 358s (M. V. *Chinnappan*).

8492 *a*) *Colom Casta* Enrique, Entre la opción por los pobres y el marxismo; – *b*) *Spieker* Manfred, La tentación de la utopía; sobre la relación entre fe y política en la teología de la liberación: Tierra Nueva 16,64 (1987s) 5-23 / 24ss.

8493 *Cooper* John W., TEILHARD, MARX, and the worldview of prominent liberation theologians: CalvinT 24 (1989) 241-262.

8494 **Cox** Harvey, The silencing of Leonardo BOFF; the Vatican and the future of world Christianity. Oak Park IL 1988, Meyer-Stone. x-208 p. $10. – ᴿCCurr 38 (1988s) 491s (J. *Cunneen*); JEcuSt 26 (1989) 572s (M. J. *Kerlin*: not unsympathetic to RATZINGER); Month 250 (1989) 279s (B. B. *McClorry*); RAfrT 13 (1989) 271s (R. De *Haes*); TS 50 (1989) 404s (A. T. *Hennelly*).

8495 *a*) *Díaz Mateos* Manuel, Medellín, voz profética; – *b*) *Brown* Robert M., El futuro de la teología de la liberación, ᵀUrdanivia Eduard: Páginas 13,92 (1988) 11-27 / 13,93 (1988) 25-39.

8496 *Duarte* Raúl, Reflexión bíblica sobre la Teología de la Liberación: EfMex 6 (1988) 249-258.

8497 **Dupertuis** Attilio René, Liberation theology; a study in its soteriology: diss. Andrews 9. Berrien Springs MI 1987, Andrews Univ. xiii-361 p.

8498 **Duquoc** Christian, Libération et progressisme; un dialogue théologique entre l'Amérique Latine et l'Europe: Théologies. P 1987, Cerf. 142 p. F 85. – ᴿNRT 111 (1989) 461s (A. *Toubeau*); SR 18 (1989) 117 (F. *Dumont*).

8499 **Duquoc** Christian, Liberación y progresismo; un diálogo teológico entre América Latina y Europa: Presencia Teológica 57. Santander 1989, Sal Terrae. 132 p. pt. 795. – ᴿProyección 36 (1989) 325 (J. A. *Estrada*); Sal T 77 (1989) 765s (J. A. *García*); TXav 39 (1989) 371-3 (A. *Parra*).

8500 **Durán Flórez** Ricardo, La utopía de la liberación, ¿teología de los pobres? 1988 ➤ 4,9562: ᴿRLatAmT 5 (1988) 321-3 (J. I. *González Faus* against the attack on GUTIÉRREZ G.).

8501 **Dussel** Enrique, Die Geschichte der Kirche in Lateinamerika. Mainz 1988, Grünewald. 435 p.; 12 maps. DM 48. – ᴿMüTZ 40 (1989) 251s (P. *Neuner*); NZMissW 45 (1989) 227-9 (J. *Baumgartner*); ÖkRu 38 (1989) 115s (R. *Müller*); TPQ 137 (1989) 208s (F. *Schragl*).

8502 *Eichinger* Werner, Katholische Soziallehre und Theologie; zur Kritik einiger Vertreter der kath. Soziallehre an der Theologie der Befreiung: TGegw 31 (1988) 102-112.

8503 *Ellacuría* Ignacio, Utopía y profetismo desde América Latina; un ensayo concreto de soteriología histórica: RLatAmT 6 (1989) 141-184 [205-333, el pueblo crucificado].

8504 *Feller Vitor* Galdino, A pergunta por Deus na teologia da libertação: PerspT 20,51 (1988) 151-175 [< TContext 6/2, 58].

8505 **Ferm** Deane W., Profiles in liberation; 36 portraits of Third World theologians ➤ 4,9555: ᴿTS 50 (1989) 404 (P. T. *Giordano*).

8505* **Fornet-Betancourt** Raúl, Philosophie und Theologie der Befreiung; Vorw. *Dussel* Enrique. Fra 1988, Materialis. 112 p. – ᴿZMissRW 73 (1989) 250-2 (G. *Maihold*).

8506 *Fornet-Betancourt* Raúl, Hundert Jahre Marxismus in Lateinamerika; Anmerkungen zur philosophischen Rezeption: TPhil 64 (1989) 364-383.

8507 *Fuente* Alfonso de la, El problema de la pobreza en la Biblia: RET 49 (1989) 431-448.

8507* *Galeano A.* Adolfo, La crítica del pensamiento totalizador an Enrique DUSSEL (Para una liberación de la ideología totalizante en América Latina): FranBog 30 (1988) 123-153.

8508 **Garcia** Ismael, Justice in Latin American theology of liberation, ᴰ1987 ⇒ 3,8468; 4,9572: ᴿCurrTM 16 (1989) 467s (M. *Hoy*); Horizons 16 (1989) 395-7 (John R. *Connolly*: also on BERRYMAN P. 1987); JRel 69 (1989) 424s (J. A. *Colombo*).

8509 **Goizueta** Roberto S., Liberation method and dialogue; Enrique DUSSEL and North American theological discourse [diss.] 1988 ⇒ 4,9574: ᴿTS 50 (1989) 620 (J. P. *Hogan*).

8510 *González F.* Antonio, El problema de la historia en la teología de G. GUTIÉRREZ: RLatAmT 6 (1989) 335-364.

8511 **González Faus** José I., La interpelación de las Iglesias latinoamericanas a la Europa postmoderna y a las Iglesias europeas: Fe y Justicia 8. 1988. S. Maria. – ᴿScripTPamp 21 (1989) 729s (L. F. *Mateo-Seco*).

8512 *González Faus* J. I., Individuo y comunidad en la teología europea y en la teología de la liberación: RLatAmT 5 (1988) 163-186.

8513 *Grácio das Neves* Rui M., El Dios del Sistema frente al Dios de la Sociedad Alternativa: CiTom 116 (1989) 457-494.

8514 *Guibal* Francis, La force subversive de l'Évangile; sur la pensée théologique de Gustavo GUTIÉRREZ: RechSR 77 (1989) 483-508; Eng. 481s.

8515 **Gutierrez** Gustavo, Dios o el oro en las Indias (siglo XVI) [Bartolomé de LAS CASAS]: Pedal 204. S/Lima 1989, Sígueme/Centro de Estudios. 177 p. [TContext 7/1, 23, M. *Sievernich*]. – ᴿCommSev 22 (1989) 433-5 (F. *Sánchez-Hermosilla Peña*); RTLim 23 (1989) 357s (A. *Nieto Vélez*).

8516 **Gutiérrez** Gustavo, Drinken uit de eigen bron; de geestelijke reis van een volk. Kampen/Averbode 1988, Kok/Altiora. 170 p. *f* 30. 90-242-0867-9 / Belg. 90-317-0734-1 [Bijdragen 49,474]. – ᴿTsTNijm 29 (1989) 79 (R. G. van *Rossum*).

8517 *Gutiérrez* Gustavo, Comentario bíblico: Páginas 13 (Lima 1988): fasc. 89s, 6-9; 91, 7-11; 92, 6-10; 93, 7-13 [14-23, *Gómez de Sousa* Luis A., forza de Gutiérrez]; 94, 6-11.

8518 *a) Gutiérrez* Gustavo, La evangelización de América Latina ante el año 2000; – *b) Hernández* Ramón, Doctrina americanista de Domingo BAÑEZ; – *c) Sastre Varas* Lázaro, Teoría esclavista de Tomás de MERCADO: CiTom 116 (1989) 365-378 / 235-269 / 317-332.

8519 **Harvey** John, Bridging the gap; has the Church failed the poor? 1987, St. Andrew's. 128 p. £5. 0-7152-0607-9. – ᴿExpTim 99 (1987s) 350 (J. J. *Vincent*).

8520 **Herzog** Frederick, God-walk; liberation shaping dogmatics. Mkn 1988, Orbis. xxxii-272 p. $27; pa. $14. – ᴿTS 50 (1989) 830 (J. A. *Colombo*).

8521 *Idígoras* José L., Balance de la teología de la liberación: RTLim 23 (1989) 331-351.

8522 **Kaufmann** Ludwig, **Klein** Nikolaus, Die Bibel den Armen wieder wegnehmen? Konflikte im Vorfeld von Santo Domingo 1992 [< *Antoine* C., L'Actualité Religieuse (juillet 1989) 29s]: Orientierung 53 (1989) 252-6.

8523 *Koch* Kurt, Befreiungstheologische Lektüre der Bibel: StiZt 207 (1989) 771-784.

8524 *Kreck* Walter, Das Menschenrecht auf Freiheit und die Freiheit eines Christenmenschen: EvT 49 (1989) 417-428.

8524* **Lee Sang Rin,** The dialectics of liberation theology; a Marxist critique ['to many, Marxism and liberation theology seem to be identical']: diss. Temple, ᴰ*Raines* J. Ph 1989. 182 p. 89-20271. – DissA 50 (1989s) 1700-A; RelStR 16,188.

8525 *Leers* Bernardino, Homosexuais e ética da libertação; uma caminhada: PerspT 20,52 (1988) 293-316 [< TContext 6/2, 58].

8525* **Legido** Marcelino, *Arranz* Eloy, *Martín* Ramón, Evangelio a los pobres [... historia de la salvación]: Pedal 189s, 1987 ⮞ 3,8499 (II. 295 p.): ᴿCiTom 116 (1989) 190s (E. *Rodríguez*).

8526 **Levi** Werner, From alms to liberation; the Catholic Church, the theologians, poverty, and politics. NY 1989, Praeger. vi-175 p. $36. 0-275-93171-4 [TDig 37,71].

8527 *Lippert* Peter, Theologie der Befreiung — wie ihre Herausforderung aufnehmen?: TGegw 32 (1989) 178-192 (163-177, *Anjos* M. dos).

8528 *Löbig* Gustavo, ¿ Ebionismo hoy?: Nuevo Mundo 138 (Caracas 1988) 337-342 [< TContext 6/2, 82].

8529 *Lorscheider* Aloisio, La comunidad eclesial, sacramento de liberación [< Orientierung 51 (1987) 110-2], ᵀᴱ*Torres* M. J.: SelT 28 (1989) 36-40.

8530 **McGovern** Arthur F., Marxism, an American Christian perspective. Mkn 1984 (1980), Orbis. 339 p. $13 pa. – ᴿCalvinT 24 (1989) 135-7 (S. H. *Rooy*).

8531 *Maduro* Otto, La desacralización del Marxismo en la teología de la liberación: Cristianismo y Sociedad 26,4 (México 1988) 69-84 [37-60, *Dussel* E.; R. *Fornet-Betancourt*, Eng. summaries in TContext 6/2, 101s].

8532 *Mardones* José M., ¿ El capitalismo como liberación? La teología política neoconservadora: RazF 220 (1989) 357-369.

8533 **Marlé** René, Introduction à la théologie de la libération 1988 ⮞ 4,9603: ᴿETL 65 (1989) 469-471 (V. *Neckebrouck*: le meilleur entre sept; mais il ne traite que de l'Amérique latine); TPhil 64 (1989) 310s (M. *Sievernich*).

8534 *Martínez Heredia* Fernando, ¿ Revolución en el cristianismo? Un estudio cubano de la Teología de la Liberación latinoamericana, de sus condicionamientos y su situación actual: RLatAmT 4,11 (Salvador 1987) 129-164 [R. *Fornet-Betancourt* Eng. summary, TContext 6/2 (1989) 96].

8535 ᴱ**Meier** Johannes, Zur Geschichte des Christentums in Lateinamerika. Mü 1988, Schnell & S. 96 p. DM 18. – ᴿTPQ 137 (1989) 207s (F. *Gruber*).

8536 *Menard* Camil [*Laberge* Léo], L'ecclésiologie [l'éthique] des théologiens de la libération: ÉglT 19 (1988) 349-372 [373-400] (114-6).

8536* ᶠMᴇᴛᴢ Johann-B.: Mystik und Politik; Theologie im Ringen um Geschichte und Gesellschaft, ᴱ**Schillebeeckx** E. 1988 ⮞ 4,106: ᴿForumKT 5 (1989) 305 (A. *Rauscher*).

8537 ᴱ**Metz** J.-B., *Rottländer* Peter, Lateinamerika und Europa 1988 ⮞ 4,611: ᴿTGegw 32 (1989) 233s (B. *Häring*); TPQ 137 (1989) 207 (F. *Gruber*).

8538 *a)* *Min* Anselm K., How not to do a theology of liberation; a critique of Schubert Oɢᴅᴇɴ: – *b)* *Taylor* Mark L., The boundless love of God and the bounds of critical reflection; Schubert Ogden's contribution to a theology of liberation: JAAR 57 (1989) 83-102 / 103-147.

8539 **Mires** Fernando, La colonización de las almas; misión y conquista en Hispanoamérica. San José CR, 1987, Dep. Ecum. Inv. 228 p. – ᴿTPhil 64 (1989) 605-7 (K. *Schatz*).

8540 *a) Nessan* Craig J., Liberation theology's critique of LUTHER's two kingdoms doctrine; – *b) Persaud* Winston D., The article of justification and the theology of liberation: CurrTM 16 (1989) 257-266 / 361-371.

8540* **Nickoloff** James B., The Church and human liberation; the ecclesiology of G. GUTIERREZ: diss. Graduate Theological Union, ᴰ*Gelpi* D. Berkeley 1989. 417 p. 89-06587. – DissA 49 (1988s) 376s-A; RelStR 16,187.

8541 *Ortiz de Urtaran* Félix, 'Descubrir el potencial evangelizador de los pobres': LumenVr 38 (1989) 474-506.

8542 *Parra* Alberto, La hermenéutica palabra-vida, hermenéutica de los pobres: RLatAmT 6 (1989) 365-377.

8543 **Pasquetto** Virgilio, Mai più schiavi... concetto biblico di liberazione 1988 → 4,9613: ᴿAnnTh 3,1 (1989) 159-163 (M.A. *Tábet*); CC 140 (1989,3) 101s (C. *Di Sante*); Teresianum 40 (1989) 266-9 (B. *Moriconi*).

8544 *Pastor* F., Cristo solitario; aportación desde san Pablo a la teología de la liberación: RLatAmT 5 (1988) 145-161 [< NTAbs 33,44].

8545 *Pastor* Félix A., Ortopraxis y ortodoxia; el debate teológico sobre Iglesia y liberación en la perspectiva del Magisterio eclesial: Gregorianum 70 (1989) 689-738; franç. 739.

8546 *Pásztor* János, ⓦ The Christian-Marxist dialogue in Latin American view: TSzem 31 (1988) 205-213 [297-302, Debrecen meeting 5-8.IV.1988, *Szathmáry* Sándor].

8547 *Pieris* Aloysius, Human rights language and liberation theology: Vidyajyoti 52 (1988) 522-536 [604, reaction of *Roberts* H.R.T.].

8548 **Pixley** J., *Boff* C., Opción por los pobres²: Cristianismo y sociedad 1. M 1988, Paulinas. 286 p. – ᴿEfMex 6 (1988) 459-462 (J. *Crespo*).

8549 [Porfirio] **Miranda** José, Apelo a la razón; teoría de la ciencia y crítica del positivismo [...juicios morales, ética]: Hermeneia 27. Salamanca 1988, Sígueme. 508 p. – ᴿLumenVr 38 (1989) 443s (U. *Gil Ortega*: obra profunda, erudita y de gran actualidad; el autor se confiesa comunista).

8550 *Possenti* Vittorio, Il metodo della 'teologia della liberazione' e le scienze sociali: Sapienza 41 (1988) 405-427.

8551 *Ranly* Ernest W., Latin American spirituality [5 books]: CCurr 39 (1989s) 458-462.

8552 **Ratzinger** Joseph, Politik und Erlösung; zum Verhältnis von Glaube, Rationalität und Irrationalem in der sogenannten Theologie der Befreiung: Rh/Wf Akad Szb 295 / Vorträge G 279. Opladen 1986, Westd.-V. 36 p. – ᴿTPhil 64 (1989) 314s (M. *Sievernich*).

8552* **Regan** David, Church for liberation. Dublin 1987, Dominican. 238 p. £8 pa. – ᴿDocLife 39 (1989) 108 (B. *Hearne*).

8553 **Richard** Pablo, La fuerza espiritual de la Iglesia de los pobres 1987 → 4,9619: ᴿEfMex 6 (1988) 445-7 (E. *Bonnin*).

8554 ᴱ**Roos** Lothar, *Vélez Correa* Jaime, Befreiende Evangelisierung und katholische Soziallehre: Entwicklung und Frieden 45. Mainz/Mü 1987, Grünewald/Kaiser. 149 p. – ᴿTPhil 64 (1989) 313s (M. *Sievernich*).

8555 *Russell* Anthony J., Theology in context and 'the right to think' in three contemporary theologians; GUTIÉRREZ, DUSSEL, and [L.] BOFF: Pacifica 2 (1988) 282-322.

8556 *Saranyana* Josep-Ignasi, Teología académica y teología profética americanas (siglo XVI): ScripTPamp 21 (1989) 483-509 [-586, al.].

8557 *Scheffczyk* Leo, Acerca de la hermenéutica bíblica de 'La teología de lo político' [1984] según Clodovis BOFF: Tierra Nueva 17,67 (Bogotá 1988s) 37-45.

8558 *Schrijver* Georges De, Theologie van de bevrijding met MARX of LEVINAS ?: Streven 55 (1987) 3-14.

8559 **Scott Eunson** Kenneth D., Privileged Peru; the Israelites of the New Universal Covenant: diss. Aberdeen 1988 [pp. 348-373^T = RTLim 23 (1989) 265-276].

8560 ᴱ**Sievernich** Michael, Impulse der Befreiungstheologie für Europa; ein Lesebuch: Forum Politische Theologie 2. Mainz/Mü 1987, Grünewald/Kaiser. 196 p. DM 22,80 pa. – ᴿTPhil 64 (1989) 312s (K. *Mertes*); TPQ 137 (1989) 206s (F. *Gruber*).

8561 **Sobrino** Jon, Jésus en Amérique latine; sa signification pour la foi et la christologie: CogF 140, 1986 ↠ 3,8544; 4,9633: ᴿScEspr 41 (1989) 363-9 (M. *Beaudin*).

8562 **Sobrino** Jon, Spirituality of liberation; toward a political holiness, ᵀ*Barr* R. Mkn 1988, Orbis. 224 p. $25; pa. $13. 0-88344-617-0; 6-7. – ᴿCCurr 38 (1988s) 502-4 (H. *Lacey*, also on HERZOG F.); Horizons 16 (1988) 131-5 (P. F. *Knitter*) & 135-7 (K. J. *Egan*) & 137-140 (Elizabeth *Koenig*); 140-150, Sobrino response.

8563 **Sobrino** Jon, Bevrijding met Geest; notities voor een nieuwe spiritualiteit. Averbode/Kampen 1988, Altiora/Kok. 240 p. ƒ34,50. 90-317-0667-1. – ᴿTsTNijm 29 (1989) 314s (G. van *Rossum*).

8564 *a)* *Sobrino* Jon, Sanctuary [right of Latin Americans to seek refuge in the U. S.]; a theological analysis, ᵀ*Petry* Walter; – *b)* *Clasby* Nancy T., Malcolm X and liberation theology: CCurr 23 (1988s) 164-172 / 173-184.

8565 *Sobrino* Jon, Hacer teología en América Latina: TXav 39/91 (1989) 139-156.

8566 *Sobrino* Jon, Los 'signos de los tiempos' en la teología de la liberación: ↠ 7, ᶠALFARO J., EstE 64 (1989) 249-269 [193-221, *Hernández Pico* Juan; 223-249, *Manzanera* Miguel].

8567 *Spieker* Manfred, Libertad y liberación en la política; sobre las controversias entre la teología de la liberación y la doctrina social de la Iglesia: Tierra Nueva 17,68 (1989) 52-62 ...

8568 *Stone* Ronald H., Paulus [Paul TILLICH] and GUSTAVO; religious socialism and liberation theology: LavalTP 44 (1988) 155-167; franç. 155.

8569 **Tamayo-Acosta** J. J., Para comprender la·teología de la liberación. Estella 1989, VDivino. 295 p. – ᴿBibFe 15 (1989) 328 (A. *Salas*); Carthaginensia 5 (1989) 305 (F. *Martínez Fresneda*); CiuD 202 (1989) 766s (T. *Viñas*: calurosa apología); RazF 220 (1989) 123 (J. *Gómez Caffarena*).

8570 **Thomas** Gloria B., Ecclesial authority; a study of the conflicting perspectives of Leonardo BOFF, liberation theologian [... consonant with Vatican II] and the Congregation for the Doctrine of the Faith: diss. Drew. Durham NC 1988. 243 p. 89-06809. – DissA 50 (1989s) 176-A; RelStR 16,188.

8570* **Trigo** Pedro, Creación e historia en el proceso de la liberación: Cristianismo y sociedad 13. M 1988, Paulinas. 358 p. – ᴿRLatAmT 5 (1988) 325 (J. V.).

8571 **Vanderhoff Boersma** F., Organizar la esperanza; teología campesina. México 1986, Centro Estud. Ecum. 360 p. – ᴿTsTNijm 29 (1989) 74 (J. Van *Nieuwenhove*).

8571* **Venter** Rian, [Afrikaans] The paradigmatic function of the Resurrection to disclose structurally a soteriology of liberation: diss. ᴰ*Heyns* J. Pretoria 1989. – DissA 50 (1989s) 1344-A: concludes questioning Latin American methodology.

8572 **Warren** William H.[III], *Kairos* and *logos*; critical comparison of the theologies of history of Paul TILLICH and selected Latin American liberation theologians: diss. Emory, [D]*Saliers* D. Atlanta 1989. 410 p. 89-24716. – DissA 50 (1989s) 2120-A; RTLv 21,554.

H8.6 Theologiae emergentes – 'Theologies of' emergent groups.

8572* **Ackerman** Susan E., *Lee* Raymond L. M., Heaven in transition; non-Muslim religious innovation and ethnic identity in Malaysia. Honolulu 1988, Univ. Hawaii. – [R]Asia JT 3 (1989) 357 (R. *Ching*).

8573 *Ariarajah* S. Wesley, Christology in Asia; perspectives from Hindu-Christian dialogue; CTC Bulletin 7,3 (Hong Kong 1987) 32-36 [< TContext 6/2, 27].

8573* [E]**Arokiasamy** S., *Gispert-Sauch* G., Liberation in Asia; theological perspectives 1987 → 4,337: [R]BibleBh 15 (1989) 133s (J. *Kottackal*).

8574 *a) Aykara* Thomas, *Chethimattam* John B., Church of St. Thomas in India; its history, problems and hopes; – *b) Timm* Jeffrey R., Vallabha, Vaiṣṇavism and the western hegemony of Indian thought: JDharma 14 (1989) 62-73 [74-92, *Mundadan* A.] / 6-36; 1 fig.

8575 *Banawiratma* J. B., *Jacobs* Tom, Doing theology with local resources; an Indonesian experiment: EAPastR 26,1 (Quezon City 1989) 51-72 [G. *Evers* (Eng.) summary in TContext 7/1,114].

8576 *Bediako Kwame*, The roots of African theology: IntBMiss 13,2 (1989) 58-65 [< TContext 7/1,104; Eng. summary by B. *Abeng*; periodical not listed p. 10].

8577 **Beken** A. van der, L'Évangile en Afrique, vécu et commenté par les Bayaka [... région rurale du Zaïre]: Inst. Missiol. SVD. Nettetal 1986, Steyler. 328 p. DM 48. – [R]NRT 111 (1989) 147s (J. M.).

8578 **Beltran** Benigno, Philippinische Theologie in ihrem kulturellen und gesellschaftlichen Kontext: Theologie Interkulturell 3. Dü 1988, Patmos. 172 p. – [R]TContext 6,2 (1989) 112 (G. *Evers*).

8578* *Bergmann* Ulrich, Hat die Bibel eine Botschaft für den ganzen Menschen? Die Frage melanesischer Christen an Theologie und kirchliche Praxis in Europa, Amerika und Australien: → 212, [F]WESTERMANN C., Schöpfung 1989, 251-261.

8579 [E]**Binsbergen** W. van, *Schoffeleers* M., Theoretical explorations in African religion 1985 → 1,543: [R]HeythJ 30 (1989) 87s (M. F. C. *Bourdillon*: social anthropology).

8580 *Bosch* David, L'évangélisation; courants et contre-courants dans la théologie d'aujourd'hui: Perspectives missionnaires 17 (1989) 12-32 [B. *Abeng* Eng. summary in TContext 7/1,110].

8581 **Bujo** Bénézet, Teologia africana nel suo contesto sociale [Afrikanische Theologie 1986 → 3,8587], [T]: GdT 185. Brescia 1988, Queriniana. 216 p. Lit. 18.000. 88-399-0685-1. – [R]Asprenas 36 (1989) 303s (G. *Mattai*); Gregorianum 70 (1989) 599-601 (A. *Wolanin*); StPatav 36 (1989) 242s (G. *Segalla*).

8582 *Bujo* Bénézet, Gibt es eine spezifisch afrikanische Ethik? Eine Anfrage an westliches Denken: StiZt 207 (1989) 591-606.

8583 **Butselaar** J. van, Africains, missionnaires et colonialistes — les origines de l'Église Presbytérienne du Mozambique (Mission Suisse) 1880-1896. Leiden 1984, Brill. 237 p. – [R]ÉTRel 64 (1989) 665-8 (P. *Couprie*).

8584 *a) Cannon* Katie G., Slave ideology and biblical interpretation; – *b) Wimbush* Vincent L., Historical/cultural criticism as liberation; a

proposal for an African American biblical hermeneutic; – *c*) *Gilkes* Cheryl
T., 'Mother to the motherless, father to the fatherless'; power, gender,
and community in Afrocentric biblical tradition; – *d*) *Kwok Pui Lan*,
Discovering the Bible in the non-biblical world: Semeia 47 (1989) 9-23 /
43-55 / 57-85 / 25-42.

8585 **Carrier** Hervé, Évangile et cultures. Vaticano 1987, ed. 276 p. –
ᴿRThom 89 (1989) 129s (P. de *Laubier*).

8586 **Chan Kim-Kwong**, Towards a contextual theology; the Catholic Church
in the People's Republic of China (1979-1983); its life and theological
implications 1987 ↠ 4,9657: ᴿNewTR 2,2 (1989) 109s (P. *Fleming*).

8587 **Chenu** B., Teologie cristiane dei terzi mondi: GdT 181, 4,9659: ᴿNRT
111 (1989) 769 (J. *Masson*).

8589 **Chenu** Bruno, Teologías cristianas de los terceros mundos [1987
↠ 3,8594], ᵀ*Medrano* L. Barc 1989, Herder. 244 p. – ᴿCarthaginensia 5
(1989) 337s (F. *Martínez Fresneda*); NatGrac 36 (1989) 145 (A.
Villalmonte).

8590 **Cohen** Eric, The missionary as stranger; a phenomenological analysis of
Christian missionaries' encounter with folk religions: JRelRes 31 (1989s)
337-350.

8591 ᴱ**Collet** Giancarlo, Der Christus der Armen; das Christuszeugnis der
lateinamerikanischen Befreiungstheologie. FrB 1988, Herder. 231 p. –
ᴿNZMissW 45 (1989) 225s (J. G. *Piepke*); ZMissRW 73 (1989) 248s
(Christiane *Hetterich*).

8592 **Curran** C. E., Toward an American Catholic moral theology 1987
↠ 3,210: ᴿAnglTR 70 (1988) 193s (J. W. *Turnbull*); ScotJT 42 (1989)
447s (J. *McDonald*).

8593 *Czajkowski* M., Die Inkulturation des Evangeliums Jesu im NT [and
other essays largely focusing Poland]: Collectanea Theologica Wsz. 58
(1988) 217 p. [< RelStR 16, 143].

8594 *Das* Somen, A general survey of Asian Christian theology: Bangalore
Theol. Forum 20, 4 (1988) 1-23 [G. *Evers* summary in TContext 7/1,105].

8595 *Delotavo* Allen, Toward a Christ-centred way of doing theology in
Asia: AsiaJT 3,1 (1989) 330-4 [G. *Evers* (Eng.) summary in TContext
7/1,105].

8596 *Doran* John, Towards an Africanized Church: Shalom 6,2 (Nigeria
1988) 220-240 [< TContext 7/1,24].

8596* ᴱ**Doré** J., *al.*, *a*) Chemins de la christologie africaine [1982 papers]: JJC
25. P 1986, Desclée. 317 p. F 139. 2-7189-0295-7. – ᴿMilltSt 23 (1989)
108-112 (R. *Moloney*); RAfrT 13 (1989) 127-9 (M. *Lukombo*). – *b*)
Cristologia africana 1987 ↠ 3,396: ᴿFilT 3 (1989) 224s (Isabella *Garavagno Barbero*).

8597 *Douglas* Mary, The problem of evil among the Lele; sorcery, witch-hunt
and Christian teaching in Africa: Chiea 4,3 (1988) 21-38 [< TContext
6/2,16].

8598 **Eilers** Frans-Josef, Communicating between cultures; an introduction to
intercultural communication. R 1988, Gregoriana. 137 p. Lit. 6500. –
ᴿTR 85 (1989) 308 (E. *Arens*).

8599 **Ela** Jean-Marc, Mein Glaube als Afrikaner; Das Evangelium in
schwarzafrikanischer Lebenswirklichkeit: Theologie der Dritten Welt 10,
1987 ↠ 3,8619; 4,9676: ᴿTPQ 137 (1989) 108s (K. J. *Tossou*).

8600 **Éla** Jean-Marc, My faith as an African [1987 ↠ 3,8619; 4,9676], ᵀ*Brown*
John P., *Perry* Susan. Mkn/L 1989, Orbis/Chapman. xx-187 p. $10.
0-88344-631-6 / [TDig 36,368].

8601 **Elavathingal** Sebastian, Inculturation in India; the expression of Christian life in the traditional art and symbolism of India: diss. Pont. Univ. Gregoriana, Nᵒ 3583, ᴰ*Dupuis* J. R 1989. 412 p.; extr. 83 p. – RTLv 21,582.

8602 *England* John C., Towards the charting of Asian theologies: Interreligio 14 (Nagoya 1988) 55-62 [< TContext 6/2, 41].

8603 *Estepa* Pio, Theology as a social force; a sociological reading of two Third-World-Theologies: Diwa 13,1 (Tagaytay 1988) 19-29 [G. *Evers* summary (Eng.), TContext 6/2,94].

8604 **Felder** C. H., Troubling biblical waters; race, class, and family [... correctives on use of the Bible in relation to ancient Africa and black people today]: Turner Studies in N. Am. Black religion 3. Mkn 1989, Orbis. xviii-233 p. $15 pa. 0-88344-535-2 [NTAbs 33,406]. – ᴿTTod 46 (1989) 345s.348 (V. L. *Wimbush*: Howard Univ. NT prof.).

8605 *a)* For God and his glory alone, a contribution relating some biblical principles to the situation in Northern Ireland. Hollywood, Down 1988, ECONI. 18 p. £1. – *b)* *Murphy* H. P., The Bible and Northern Ireland: Furrow 40 (1989) 349 (E. de *Bhaldraithe*) / 243s.

8606 *Friedli* Richard, Die Ortskirche als Ort evangelisierenden Handelns; Sinn, Notwendigkeit and Grenzen von Inkulturation: FreibZ 36 (1989) 159-172.

8607 **Gelpi** Donald L., Inculturating North American theology; an experiment in foundational method 1988 → 4,9683: ᴿTS 50 (1989) 389s (W. E. *Conn*).

8607* *George* Francis E., Ecclesiological presuppositions in inculturating the faith: NZMissW 45 (1989) 256-264.

8608 **Govender** S. P., In search of tomorrow; the dialogue between black theology and Marxism in South Africa. Kampen 1987, Kok. 171 p. *f*27.50. 90-242-3334-8. – ᴿTsTNijm 29 (1989) 74s (T. *Witvliet*).

8609 **Guerrero** G. Andrés, A Chicano theology. Mkn 1987, Orbis. 186 p. – ᴿTGL 79 (1989) 209-211 (K. J. *Tossou*).

8609* *Gutheinz* Luis, Ost und West sprechen miteinander [*Küng* H., *Ching* Julia, 1988 → b258]: NZMissW 45 (1989) 57-60.

8610 *Hage* Wolfgang, Literatur zur Geschichte und gegenwärtigen Situation der Thomaschristenheit Indiens: TRu 54 (1989) 169-189.

8611 **Hall** Douglas J., Thinking the faith; Christian theology in a North American context. Minneapolis 1989, Augsburg. 465 p. $30. – ᴿTTod 46 (1989s) 312s (Susan B. *Thistlethwaite*).

8612 **Hesselgrave** David J., *Rommen* Edward. Contextualization [other Christians' term for what Catholics call inculturation]; meanings, methods, and models. Leicester 1989, Apollos. xii-281 p. 0-85111-413-X.

8613 **Hopkins** Dwight N., Black theology; U. S. A. and South Africa political and cultural liberations: diss. Union. NY 1988. – RTLv 21,569.

8614 *Ilogu* Edmund C., Christ and crisis in Africa: ChSt 27 (1988) 113-122.

8615 **Jesudasan** I., Gandhian theology of liberation: Jesuit Theological Forum, Studies 3. Anand 1987 [= Mkn 1984 → 65,7339], Fujarat-SP. xiv-318 p. – ᴿNRT 111 (1989) 463 (J. *Masson*).

8616 *Jørgensen* Torstein, [Norw.] Some perspectives on Christianity in Africa: TsTKi 59 (1988) 123-131.

8617 **Khawam** René, L'Univers culturel des Chrétiens d'Orient 1987 → 4,9699: ᴿIslamochristiana 15 (1989) 271s (H. G. *Moussalli*).

8618 *Kim* Jeong-Soo, ❻ The Korean history of the Catholic faith: Sinhak Jonmang 81 (Kwangju 1988) 81-99 [< TContext 6/2, 46].

8619 **Kirwen** Michael C., The missionary and the diviner 1987 ➤ 3,8652: ᴿTContext 6,2 (1989) 113 (B. *Abeng*).

8620 ᴱ*Langevin* Gilles, *a*) [Commission théologique internationale], La foi et l'inculturation 1988: EsprVie 99 (1989) 65-76 [p. 76, liste des 14 auteurs signés]; – *b*) Commissio theologica internationalis, Fides et inculturatio: Gregorianum 70 (1989) 625-646; – *c*) Le Christ et les cultures: ScEspr 40 (1988) 269-277.

ᴱ**Lee Jung Young**, An emerging theology in world perspective; commentary on Korean Minjung theology 1988 ➤ 485.

8622 *Lee* Robert, From ancient Jerusalem to modern Tokyo; contextualization in Japanese culture and society: Japanese Missionary Bulletin 42,3 (Tokyo 1988) 127-140 [G. *Evers* (Eng.) summary, TContext 6/2, 93 'Japanese' Miss. B.; p. 10 & 42 'Japan' MB].

8623 **Link-Wieczorek** Ulrike, Zur Phänomenologie des Redens von Gott in der afrikanischen Theologie; mit einem vergleichenden Teil über die südkoreanische Minjung-Theologie: Diss. Heidelberg 1989. – TContext 7/1, 121 (Eng. summ, B. *Abeng*).

8624 *Lovett* Brendan, On earth as in heaven; corresponding to God in Philippine context: Pacifica 2 (1989) 1-25.

8625 **Luneau** René, Laisse aller mon peuple; églises africaines au-delà des modèles? 1987 ➤ 4,9709: ᴿBrotéria 127 (1988) 235 (F. *Pires Lopes*).

8626 *Luneau* René, Une tradition africaine de la foi?: Études 370 (1989) 657-665 [B. *Abeng* Eng. summ. in TContext 7/1,104].

8627 **Luzbetak** Louis J., The Church and cultures; new prospectives in missiological anthropology. Mkn 1988, Orbis. xx-464 p. $20. 0-88344-625-1. – ᴿAmerica 161 (1989) 168 (B. *Cooke*); NewTR 2,4 (1989) 1165 (A. J. *Gillins*).

8628 *Mackie* Steven G., God's people in Asia; a key concept in Asian theology: ScotJT 42 (1989) 215-240.

8629 *Madigan* Dan, Pakistan's emerging theology: Focus 8,2 (Multan 1988) 21-36 [G. *Evers* summary (Eng.), TContext 6/2, 94].

8630 *a*) *Maimela* Simon S., Faith that does justice ['What would LUTHER say if he would find himself in S. Africa?']; – *b*) *Moila* Moeahabo P., The role of Christ in Jon SOBRINO's liberation theology; its significance for black theology in South Africa: JBlackT 3,1 (Attaridgeville 1989) 1-14 / 15-22.

8631 ᴱ**Malone** Peter, Discovering an Australian theology [essays < Compass...]. Homebush 1988, St. Paul. 239 p. $17. – ᴿAustralasCR 66 (1989) 229s (M. *Slattery*).

8632 *Mangatt* George, The Thomas Christians and the Persian church: Vidyajyoti 52 (1988) 437-446.

8633 *Mante* Gabriel, Christian and African traditional values and [i.e. incorporated into] priestly formation: West African journal of ecclesial studies 1,1 (Nigeria 1989) 54-70 [< TContext 7/1,25].

8634 **Masson** Joseph, Père de nos pères [Afrique] 1988 ➤ 4,9712: ᴿCC 140 (1989,1) 92s (A. *Seumois*); Gregorianum 70 (1989) 369s (J. *Galot*); NRT 111 (1989) 287s (L. de *Sousberghe*); Spiritus 30 (1989) 332s (H. *Mourier*).

8635 **Mbiti** John S., Bible and theology in African Christianity 1986 ➤ 3,8663; 4,9717: ᴿLvSt 14 (1989) 74 (R. F. *Collins*).

8636 **Mbiti** John S., Bibel und Theologie im afrikanischen Christentum [NY General Theol. Sem. lectures], ᴱ*Löwner* Gudrun: Theologie der Ökumene 22. Gö 1987, Vandenhoeck & R. – ᴿNZMissW 45 (1989) 71s (L. *Clerici*); TContext 6,2 (1989) 106 (B. *Abeng*); ZMissRW 73 (1989) 88 (J. *Kuhl*).

8637 *Mbon* Friday M., Christianity, a bone of contention in Nigeria [Olumbe Ola movement claiming the Church is a foreign intrusion]: JDharma 14 (1989) 247-258.

8638 *Morozumi* Katsuo, Japanese people and the Hebrew way of thinking — an ontological consideration: KatKenk 51,1 (1987) 123-154; Eng. x-xii.

8639 ᴱ*Mulago gwa Cikala* Musharhamina, Afrikanische Spiritualität und christlicher Glaube; Erfahrungen der Inkulturation 1986 ➤ 3,8677; 4,9722: ᴿTLZ 114 (1989) 553s (J. *Althausen*).

8640 *Mundadan* A. Mathias, Meeting of two theologies [(apostle) Thomas/ scholastic] in India in the 16th/17th century: JDharma 14,1 (1989) 74-92 [G. *Evers* (Eng.) summary in TContext 7/1,107].

8641 *Mveng* Engelbert, Spiritualité et libération en Afrique [< EATWOT 4th African meeting, Cairo Aug. 24-28, 1985]. P 1987, Harmattan. 123 p. – ᴿTContext 6,2 (1989) 106 (N. *Bitoto Abeng*).

8642 *Nazar* David E., Inculturation; meaning and method: diss. ᴰ*Peelman* A. Ottawa 1989. 267 p. – RTLv 21,583.

8643 *Neckebrouck* Valeer, La Tierce Église devant le problème de la culture: NZMissW Beih 36, 1987 ➤ 4,9723: ᴿNRT 111 (1989) 768s (J. *Masson*); TLZ 114 (1989) 554-6 (S. *Krügel*).

8644 *Newbigin* Lesslie, Foolishness to the Greeks 1986 ➤ 2,6890...4,9725: ᴿEvQ 61 (1989) 374s (T. *Hart*); ScotBEv 7 (1989) 54s (S. *Williams*); Vidyajyoti 52 (1988) 58s (M. V. *Chinnappan*).

8645 *Ngili-Bofeko* Batsu, Jésus-Christ dans la théologie africaine; la pertinence de l'expression 'christologie africaine' dans le discours théologique aujourd'hui: diss. ᴰ*Gabus* J. Bru 1988. 535 p. (2 vol.) – RTLv 21,570.

8646 *Ngindu Mushete* A., La teologia africana in cammino. Bo 1986, Dehoniane. 136 p. Lit. 16.000. – ᴿStPatav 36 (1989) 241s (G. *Segalla*).

8647 *Ngindu Mushete* A., L'évangélisation à l'épreuve de la modernité; questions venues de l'Afrique: ' AuCAf 28,4 (Burundi 1988) 248-268 [< TContext 6/2, 20; p. 97, Concilium 1988].

8648 *Nthamburi* Zablon, The Donatist controversy as a paradigm for Church and state [as an indigenous form of Christianism vis-à-vis Catholicism]: AfTJ 17 (Tanzania 1988) 196-206 [< TContext 7/1,17].

8648* *Nwabueze* P. Emeka, The image of the missionary priest in modern African fiction: NZMissW 44 (1988) 285-295.

8649 *Nyamiti* Charles A., A critical assessment on some issues in today's African theology: Chiea 5,1 (1989) 5-18 [< TContext 7/1,9].

8650 *Oduyoye* Mercy Amba, Hearing and knowing... Christianity in Africa 1986 ➤ 3,8692: ᴿAsiaJT 3 (1989) 363-5 (C. S. *Song*); RAfrT 13 (1989) 129s (R. De *Haes*).

8650* **Oduyoye** Mercy A., Wir selber haben ihn gehört; theologische Reflexionen zum Christentum in Afrika. FrS 1988, Exodus. 228 p. – ᴿNZMissW 45 (1989) 310 (F. *Kollbrunner*).

8651 *Onaiyekan* John, Tendencias cristológicas en la teología africana contemporánea; estudio y valoración provisional: ScripTPamp 21 (1989) 169-184.

8651* **Onwurah** E., The quest, means, and relevance of African Christian theology: ChieaÀfChr 4,3 (1988) 5-19; deutsch TKontext 10/2 (1989) 92.

8652 **Park Il-Young**, Minjung, Schamanismus und Inkulturation; schamanistische Religion und christliche Orthopraxis in Korea [Diss. 1987 ➤ 4,9734]. Seoul 1988. 441 p. – ᴿTContext 6,2 (1989) 111 (G. *Evers*).

8653 **Parratt** John, A reader in African Christian theology 1987 ⟶ 4,9735: ᴿThemelios 14 (1988s) 113s (G. *Molyneux*).

8654 ᴱ**Pathil** Kuncheria, Mission in India today; the task of the Thomas Christians [Aug. 1987 meeting] 1988 ⟶ 4,621: ᴿTContext 6,2 (1989) 116 (G. *Evers*).

8654* **Peelman** Achiel, L'inculturation; l'Église et les cultures: L'horizon du croyant 8. P 1989, Desclée/Novalis. 197 p. [TR 86, 257].

8655 **Pieris** Aloysius, [⟶ b272] *a*) An Asian theology of liberation: Faith Meets Faith. Mkn 1988, Orbis. 220 p. $27; pa. $14. 0-88344-627-8; -6-X. – ᴿExpTim 100 (1988s) 397s (D. B. *Forrester*: praise); Month 250 (1989) 223 (M. *Barnes*); TTod 46 (1989s) 236-8 (P. H. *Van Ness*, also on his Love meets wisdom). – *b*) Theologie der Befreiung in Asien 1986 ⟶ 2,6901... 4,9736: ᴿEvKomm 21 (1988) 53s (W. *Kröger*; Rubrik 'Buddhistische Christologie').

8656 *Plathow* Michael, Einheit des christlichen Glaubens und kulturelle Verschiedenheit; zur Frage einer 'Theologie der Kultur': TZBas 45 (1989) 53-68.

8657 *Pobee* John S., I am first African and second a Christian?: Indian Missiological Review 10,3 (Shillong 1988) 268-277 [< TContext 6/2, 29].

8658 **Poupard** Paul, Iglesia y culturas; orientación para una pastoral de inteligencia [1985], ᵀ*Ureña* Pastor Manuel. Valencia 1988, Edicep. 242 p. – ᴿLumenVr 38 (1989) 343s (U. *Gil Ortega*).

8659 *Renik* Krzysztof, ❶ Des chrétiens exotiques [pré-portugais de l'Inde]: PrzPow 814 (1989) 327-341; franç. 341.

8660 *Robinson* Gnana, *a*) Jesus Christ, the open way and the fellow-struggle; a look into the Christologies in India: AsiaJT 3 (1989) 403-415; – *b*) Solidarität als Missionsprinzip — eine asiatische Perspektive: ÖkRu 38 (1989) 157-168.

8660* ᴱ**Röser** Johannes, Gott kommt aus der Dritten Welt; Erfahrungen und Zeugnisse. FrB 1988, Herder. 238 p. NZMissW 45 (1989) 145s (J. *Bommer*); ZMissRW 73 (1989) 156s (M. *Hakenes*).

8661 *Rosny* Éric de, Renouveau charismatique et transe en Afrique: Études 370 (1989) 667-678.

8662 **Rücker** Heribert, 'Afrikanische Theologie,' Darstellung und Dialog: InnsbTSt 14, 1985 ⟶ 1,8342... 4,9744: ᴿTR 85 (1989) 401-3 (K. J. *Tossou*).

8663 *Ruiz* Samuel, bp., Popular religiosity and evangelization in Latin America: Sedos Bulletin 89 (1989) 155-166 [G. *Evers* (Eng.) summary in TContext 7/1,115].

8664 *Sahi* Jyoti, Popular spirituality in India: Sedos Bulletin 89 (1989) 146-154 [G. *Evers* summary in TContext 7/1 p. 106; periodical not listed p. 12].

8665 **Salas** A., Fe cristiana y cultura secular. M 1989, Biblia y Fe. 247 p. – ᴿBibFe 15 (1989) 326 (M. *Sáenz Galache*).

8666 **Salvoldi** V., *Kizito Sesana* R., Africa; the Gospel belongs to us; problems and prospects for an African council 1986 ⟶ 3,8714: ᴿNRT 111 (1989). 146 (J. M.).

8667 *Samir* Khalil, Pour une théologie arabe contemporaine; actualité du patrimoine arabe chrétien: PrOrChr 38 (1988) 64-98.

8668 ᴱ**Samuel** Vinay, *Sugden* Chris, Der ganze Christus für eine geteilte Welt; evangelische Christologie in der Zwei-Drittel-Welt [Bangkok 22.-25. III.1982] Erlangen 1987, Ev.-Luth. Mission. 283 p. DM 49. – ᴿÖkRu 38 (1989) 245s (G. *Fritz*).

8669 **Sanneh** Lamin, Translating the message; the missionary impact on culture. Mkn 1989, Orbis. 255 p. $18. – ᴿTTod 46 (1989s) 444s (A. *Ross*).

8670 *Savagnone* Giuseppe, Il problema dell'inculturazione: Ho Theológos 4 (1986) 219-228 [1-256 sulla programmazione della teologia in Sicilia].

8671 *Schnabel* E., Theologie und Bibelwissenschaft in Asien; Erfahrungen auf den Philippinen: TBei 20,2 (Wu 1989) 79-93 [< NTAbs 33,284].

8671* *Schreiner* Lothar, Kontextuelle Theologie: ➤ 894, EvKL 2 (1989) 1418-22.

8672 *Schreiter* Robert J., Faith and cultures; challenges to a world church: TS 50 (1989) 744-760.

8673 **Shorter** Aylward, Toward a theology of inculturation ➤ 4,9749; also Mkn 1988, Orbis. xii-291 p. $17. 0-88344-536-0. – ᴿCommonweal 116 (1989) 539s (L. S. *Cunningham*); Tablet 243 (1989) 1249s (J. *Wijngaards*); TS 50 (1989) 834 (J. C. *McKenna*).

8674 *a) Smith* Henry N., Christianity and ancestor practices in Hong Kong; – *b) Nelson* Reed E., Five principles of indigenous Church organization; – *c) Swanson* Allen J., Decisions or disciples? A study of evangelism effectiveness in Taiwan: Missiology 17 (Pasadena 1989) 27-38 / 39-52 / 53-68.

8674* *Smith* Thee, W/Riting black theology: Forum 5/4 (1989) 41-70.

8675 **Song** C. S., Theology from the womb of Asia 1986 ➤ 3,8724: ᴿNBlackf 70 (1989) 148s (A. *Kee*); Pacifica 2 (1989) 231-3 (I. S. *Williams*); PhilipSa 27 (1987) 322s (F. *Fernando*).

8676 **Stackhouse** Max, Apologia; contextualization, globalization, and mission in theological education 1988 ➤ 4,9753. ᴿHorizons 16 (1989) 178s (J. *Gros*); TLZ 114 (1989) 232s (O. *Pläner-Friedrich*).

8677 **Staffner** Hans, The significance of Jesus Christ in Asia 1985 ➤ 4,9754: ᴿBible Bhashyam 14 (1988) 210-3 (P. *Maroky*).

8678 *Starkloff* Carl, Indigenous peoples and the experience of Christianity: Pacifica 2 (1989) 323-332.

8679 *Suess* Paulo, Inculturação; desafios — caminhos — metas: REB 49 (1989) 81-120.

8680 *Święcicki* Andrzej, ❷ La culture et l'évangélisation: AtKap 112 (1989) 367-380.

8681 ᴱ**Terazono** Yoshiki, *Hames* Heyo E., Brennpunkte in Kirche und Theologie Japans; pref. *Sundemeier* T. Neuk 1988. 235 p. – ᴿTContext 6,2 (1989) 110 (G. *Evers*).

8682 **Tabata** Takeshi, The contemporary significance of *Iēsoûs Kýrios* confession of early Church in Japanese context: diss. Lutheran Theol. Sem, Kobe 1988. – AsiaJT 3 (1989) 354-6.

8683 *a) Tracy* David, Église universelle et catéchisme universel; le problème de l'eurocentrisme, ᵀ*Divault* André; – *b) Alberich* Emilio, Le catéchisme universel, obstacle ou catalysateur dans le processus d'inculturation, ᵀ*Dumont* sr. Jacqueline: ➤ 454, Concilium 224 (P 1989) 33-43 / 97-106.

8684 **Trompf** Garry W., The Gospel is not western 1987 ➤ 3,734; 4,9760: ᴿNRT 111 (1989) 770s (J. *Masson*); Pacifica 2 (1989) 356-360 (H. *Taylor*); Themelios 14 (1988s) 111 (J. *Chapman*).

8685 *Turner* William C.ᴶ, Black evangelicalism; theology, politics, and race: JRelTht 45 (1989) 40-56 [< BS 146 (1989) 452s, E. B. *Lane*].

8685* *Udeafor* Innocent, Inculturation path to African Christianity: Diss. ᴰ*Kern* W. Innsbruck 1988s. 278 p. – TR 85 (1989) 512; RTLv 21,585.

8686 ^E**Uzukwu** Elochukwu E., Religion and African cultures, 1. Inculturation, a Nigerian perspective. Enugu 1988, Spiritan. 208 p. [TContext 7/1, 120 B. *Abeng*].

8687 *Walt* Bennie J. van der, On being human and being a Christian in Africa; communalism, socialism and communism in a struggle for an African anthropology: Orientation 49 (Potchefstrom 1988) 34-98 [< TContext 6/2, 19].

8688 **Wilfred** Felix, *a)* Verlass den Tempel; Antyodaya — indischer Weg zur Befreiung: Theologie der Dritten Welt 11. FrB 1988, Herder. 208 p. [Mundus 25,143]. – *b)* The emergent Church in a new India. Trivandrum 1988, Jayamatha. 305 p. [TContext 7/1, 122, G. *Evers*].

8689 *Wilfred* Felix, *a)* Inculturation as a hermeneutical question: Vidyajyoti 52 (1988) 422-436; – *b)* Asia and western Christianity: Pacifica 2 (1989) 268-281.

8689* **Williams** Lewin L., The indigenization of theology in the Caribbean: diss. Union Theol. Sem., ^D*Morse* C. NY 1989. – RelStR 16, 188.

8690 **Witvliet** Theo, The way of the black Messiah 1987 → 3,8748; 4,9764: ^RDocLife 38 (1988) 222s (D. *Regan*); TLond 92 (1989) 128s (A. *Kee*).

8691 **Yoo Boo-Woong**, Korean Pentecostalism; its history and theology [diss. Birmingham, ^D*Hollenweger* W.]: Studien zur interkulturellen Geschichte des Christentums 52. Fra 1988, Lang. 283 p. [TContext 7/1,129, G. *Evers*].

H8.7   *Mariologia* — **The mother of Jesus in the NT.**

8692 **Anitua** S. de, Reflexiones sobre la Virgen Maria [... Lc 1,26s; 2,7s]. Costa Rica 1987, Libro libre. 334 p. 99-77901-63-5 [NTAbs 33,105].

8693 **Auer** Johann, [→ 7482] Jesus Christus, Heiland der Welt; Maria, Christi Mutter im Heilsplan Gottes: Kl.kath.Dogmatik 4/2. Rg 1988, Pustet. 509 p. DM 38. 3-7917-1147-4. – ^RGregorianum 70 (1989) 584s (J. *Galot*); NRT 111 (1989) 903s (L. *Renwart*).

8694 **Balthasar** Hans Urs von, Mary for today, ^T*Nowell* Robert, 1988 → 4,9772: ^RSpirLife 34 (1988) 237-240 (E. J. *Sullivan*, also on five cognate works).

8695 *a)* *Baril* Gilbert, Marie et la feminité; une perspective ecclésiologique englobante; – *b)* *Militello* Cettina, Maria e la diaconia della donna nella Chiesa: → 721*a*, Simposio 7, 1988/9, 387-408 / 117-183.

8696 *Barón* Enrique, María en la historia de la salvación: Proyección 35 (1988) 23-37.

8697 **Beinert** Wolfgang, Unsere Liebe Frau und die Frauen: Frauenforum. FrB 1989, Herder. 207 p. DM 24,80. – ^RTR 85 (1989) 404s (Teresa *Berger*).

8697* **Bengoechea** I., *Martínez Blat* V., Lo mejor sobre María; pequeña enciclopedía popular. San José 1987, Centro S. Juan de la Cruz. 125 p. – ^RTeresianum 40 (1989) 256s (J. *Castellano*).

8698 **Bertetto** D. † Maria la serva del Signore; trattato di Mariologia: Teologia a confronto 7, 1988 → 4,9775; Lit. 38.500: ^RAsprenas 36 (1989) 290s (P. *Pifano*).

8699 **Besutti** Giuseppe M., Bibliografia mariana 1978-1984: 1988 → 4,930: ^RCC 140 (1989,1) 95s (G. *Caprile*).

8699* [*Beyer* J., present.] Maria esule, itinerante, pia pellegrina; figura della Chiesa in cammino. Padova 1988, Messaggero. 317 p. – ^RTeresianum 40 (1989) 255s (J. *Castellano*).

8700 **Bojorge** Horacio, The image of Mary according to the Evangelists. Bombay 1987 = 1978, St. Paul. 61 p. rs 10. – RVidyajyoti 52 (1988) 153 (P. *Arokiadass*: could not have used the ecumenical 'Mary in the NT', but could have interpreted Mark from Mark instead of from John).

8700* *Borges de Pinho* J. E., O lugar de María numa perspectiva ecuménica: HumT 9 (1988) 139-168.

8701 *Ceresa-Gastaldo* Aldo, Maria di Nazaret nelle opere di MASSIMO Confessore: → 42, FCOSTANZO S., Polyanthema 1989, 379-385.

8702 *Chorão Lavajo* Joaquim, María e o islamismo: Brotéria 129 (1989) 309-329.

8703 *Cipriani* Settimio, Maria figura del credente; riflessioni bibliche alla luce della 'Redemptoris Mater': → 721*b*, Maria nel cammino = Asprenas 36 (1989) 123-138.

8703* *Courth* Franz [*al.*], Ökumenische Impulse der Enzyklika Redemptoris Mater: LebZeug 43 (1988) 5-15 [-66].

8704 *da Spinetoli* Ortensio, Lettura mariologica della Bibbia? Criteri e prospettive: → 611, Come leggere 1988/9, 7-26.

8705 **De Fiores** Stefano, Maria nella teologia contemporanea² 1987 → 4,9794: RCC 140 (1989,2) 508s (V. *Caporale*).

8706 **De Fiores** S., *Meo* S., Nuovo dizionario di Mariologia 1985 → 2,609*; RRivLtg 75 (1988) 136-142 (L. *Melotti*).

8707 **Dumas** André & Francine, Marie de Nazareth: Entrée Libre. Genève 1989, Labor et Fides. 105 p. – RFoiVie 88 (1989) 102s (O. *Millet*); RHPR 69 (1989) 489s (G. *Siegwalt*).

8708 *D'Urso* Giacinto, Occhi negli occhi; incontri di sguardi tra Gesù e Maria: SacDoc 34 (1989) 141-168 (557-584, Betlemme).

8708* **Dwyer** Peter, Mary, a history of devotion. Dublin 1988. – RMilltSt 23 (1989) 115-121 (D. *Ó Laoghaire*).

8709 **Esquerda Bifet** Juan, Mariologia per una Chiesa missionaria 1988 → 4,9799: RSalesianum 51 (1989) 168s (D. *Bertetto*); Teresianum 40 (1989) 255 (J. *Castellano*).

8710 *Fauth* Wolfgang, Himmelskönigin: → 904, RAC 15,114 (1989) 220-233.

8711 **Felici** Sergio, La Mariologia nella catechesi dei Padri: BiblScRel 88. R 1988, LAS. 260 p. – RMarianum 51 (1989) 663-6 (E. *dal Covolo*).

8712 **Forte** Bruno, Maria, la donna icona del mistero; saggio di teologia simbolico-narrativa: Prospettive teologiche 8. CinB 1989, Paoline. 272 p. Lit. 16.000. – RAsprenas 36 (1989) 291-4 (Diana *Pacelli*); StPatav 36 (1989) 661-3 (E. R. *Tura*).

8713 *a) Forte* Bruno, Maria, la donna icona del mistero; un progetto di mariologia; – *b) Pacelli* Diana, Maria in CALVINO; riflessioni teologiche intorno ai 'Sermoni sulla Natività': → 721*b*. Maria nel cammino = Asprenas 36 (1989) 178-192 / 245-260.

8714 *Frieling* Reinhard, Maria und die Ökumene: Im Lichte der Reformation 32 (Gö 1989) 85-101 [< ZIT 89,278].

8715 *Fries* Heinrich, Maria — Stein des Anstosses oder Chance für die Ökumene?: StiZt 207 (1989) 158-170.

8716 **Galot** Jean, Maria, la donna nell'opera di salvezza 1984 → 65,7409 ... 2,6958: RMarianum 51 (1989) 673s (M. *Semeraro*).

8717 *Galot* Jean, *a)* La relation de Marie avec l'Esprit Saint [i. le problème: titre d'épouse ...]: EsprVie 99 (1989) 440-7; – *b)* La vergine Maria e lo Spirito Santo: CC 140 (1989,3) 209-222.

8718 *García de Dios* Joaquim M., Maria de Nazareth, un desafío para os catequistas onestos: Encrucillada 12 (Pontevedra 1988) 170-7 [> SelT 28 (1989) 349-352, ᵀᴱ*Marcet* Carles].

8719 *García Pérez* Juan, La Virgen en el diálogo ecuménico actual: RazF 219 (1989) 547-552.

8720 **Gebara** I., [Lucchetti] *Bingemer* M. C., Maria, mujer profética; ensayo teológico a partir de la mujer y de América Latina. M 1988, Paulinas. 205 p. pt. 975. – ᴿBibFe 15 (1989) 483 (M. *Sáenz Galache*); Proyección 36 (1989) 326 (E. *Barón*).

8721 **Gebara** Ivone, *Lucchetti Bingemer* Maria C., Maria, die Mutter Gottes und Mutter der Armen, ᵀ*Lauble* M., *Petermann* S.: Bibl. Theol. Befr. Dü 1988, Patmos. 196 p. DM 38, sb. 34. – ᴿTGL 79 (1989) 205 (W. *Beinert*).

8722 ᴱ**Gharib** Georges, *al.*, Testi mariani del primo millennio; I. Padri e altri autori greci 1988 → 4,9806; Lit. 95.000: ᴿArTGran 52 (1989) 277s (A. *Segovia*); Marianum 51 (1989) 660-3 (P. *Langa*); NRT 111 (1989) 965s (L.-J. *Renard*).

8723 ᴱ**Gharib** Georges, Testi mariani del primo millennio, II. [I. 1988 → 4,9806] Padri e altri autori bizantini (VI-XI sec.). R 1989, Città Nuova. 1098 p. Lit. 110.000. – ᴿStPatav 36 (1989) 638s (C. *Corsato*).

8724 **Gironés-Guillem** Gonzalo [→ 4,9908], La humanidad salvada y salvadora; tratado dogmático de la Madre de Cristo² [¹1969]. Valencia 1987, Fac. S. V. Ferrer. 186 p. 84-600-5289-3. – ᴿEstE 64 (1989) 556-8 (J. *Iturriaga*).

8725 **Gonzalez** Carlos I., Mariología; Maria madre e discepola 1988 → 4,9809: ᴿAsprenas 36 (1989) 289s (P. *Pifano*); HumBr 44 (1989) 605s (A. *Biazzi*); NRT 111 (1989) 964s (R. *Escol*); ScripTPamp 21 (1989) 276s (J. L. *Bastero*).

8726 *González* Carlos I., El título 'theotokos' en torno al Concilio de Nicea: TXav 39 (1989) 335-352. 443-471.

8727 **González Dorado** Antonio, De María conquistadora a María liberadora 1988 → 4,9810: ᴿPáginas 13,93 (Lima 1988) 126-9 (Ana *Gispert-Sauch*); RazF 218 (1988) 480s (R. de *Andrés*); RLatAmT 6 (1989) 238-240 [R. *Cardenal*].

8727* **Gorski** Helmut, Die Niedrigkeit seiner Magd... LUTHER 1987 → 4, 9811: ᴿForumKT 5 (1989) 153s (L. J. *Elders*).

8728 **Graef** Hilda, Mary, a history of doctrine and devotion: Westminster 1987 = 1963-5, Christian Classics. xxii-371 + 160 p. 0-7220-5220-0.

8729 **Grassi** Joseph A., Mary, mother and disciple 1988 → 4,9812: ᴿHorizons 16 (1989) 383s (Anita M. *Hyslop*, also on BRENNAN W.).

8730 *Guarducci* Margherita, La più antica icone di Maria. R c. 1989, Ist. Poligrafico. – ᴿStCattMi 33 (1989) 733s (L. *Tirelli Barilla*).

8731 **Heister** Maria Sybilla, Maria aus Nazareth 1987 → 4,9819: ᴿTZBas 45 (1989) 91s (E. *Buess*).

8732 *Henle* Robert J., The Rosary as a religious art form: SpirLife 34 (1988) 202-6.

8733 *Henn* William, Interpreting Marian doctrine [Rome McCarthy lecture, 14.XII.1988]: Gregorianum 70 (1989) 413-436; franç. 437.

8734 *a)* *Hennaux* Jean-M., Les aspects œcuméniques de l'Encyclique 'Redemptoris Mater' [25.III.1987]; – *b)* *Gabus* Jean-Paul, Le chéminement de la foi de Marie et le nôtre; une lecture protestante du 'Redemptoris Mater': NRT 111 (1989) 24-45. 161-175 / 46-61 (corrections p. 175).

8735 *Huguet* Marie-Thérèse, Miryam et Israël; le mystère de l'Épouse 1987 [→ 3,8793]; ᴿNRT 111 (1989) 271s (L.-J. *Renard*).

8736 *Johnson* Elizabeth A., Mary and the female face of God: TS 50 (1989) 500-526.

8737 *Kudasiewicz* Józef, ❷ Racines bibliques de la théologie mariale: Ateneum Kapłańskie 110,3 ('Redemptoris mater I' 1988) 362-380 (-443, *al.*). [II: AtKap 111,1 (1988) 3-124, mostly about pilgrimages].

8738 **Läpple** Alfred, Maria in der Glaubensverkündigung. St. Ottilien 1988, EOS. 154 p. DM 9,80. 3-88096-702-4. – ᴿGregorianum 70 (1989) 797 (C. I. *González*).

8739 **La Potterie** I. de, Marie dans le Mystère de l'Alliance: JJC 34, 1988 → 4,9833; F 158: ᴿEsprVie 99 (1989) 555-7 (B. *Billet*); NRT 111 (1989) 963s (L.-J. *Renard*: équilibrer l'aspect masculin de l'Église); RTLv 20 (1989) 384 (R. *Guelluy*: érudit; souci de donner raison à ce que la piété souhaite).

8740 **La Potterie** Ignace de, Maria nel mistero dell'Alleanza: Dabar 6, 1988 → 4,9834: ᴿAsprenas 36 (1989) 288s (P. *Pifano*); BogSmot 59 (1989) 475s (A. *Rebić*); HumBr 44 (1989) 906s (A. *Biazzi*); Marianum 51 (1989) 647-651 (M. *Masini*); StPatav 36 (1989) 208s (G. *Segalla*); Teresianum 40 (1989) 247s (M. *Caprioli*).

8741 **Laurentin** René, *a)* Breve trattato su la Vergine Maria: Alma Mater 1. CinB 1987, Paoline. 380 p. Lit. 16.000. – *b)* Breve mariologia. Brescia 1988, Queriniana. 58 p. Lit. 7.500. – ᴿAsprenas 36 (1989) 294s (P. *Pifano*).

8742 *Lavin* Thomas P., Christianity's Mary complex: ChSt 27,1 ('Miryam, woman of Nazareth' 1988) 32-47.

8743 *Little* Joyce A., Mary and feminist theology: Thought 62 (1987) 343-357.

8744 ᴱ**Llamas** E., Maria, Madre de la reconciliación. 1985. ᴿForum KT 4 (1988) 76s (A. *Ziegenaus*).

8745 **López Melús** Francisco Mª., María de Nazareth en el Evangelio. M 1989, Promoción Popular. 267 p. pt. 960. 84-288-0934-8. – ᴿActuBbg 28 (1989) 85 (I. *Riudor*); Vida Nueva 1668 (1989) 55 (E. *Martín Nieto*).

8746 *Madey* Johannes, Maria und der Heilige Geist in ostkirchlicher Perspektive: Catholica 43 (1989) 117-137.

8746•**Maggi** Alberto, Nostra Signora degli eretici (Maria e Nazaret). Assisi 1988, Cittadella. 204 p. Lit. 19.000. – ᴿTeresianum 40 (1989) 623s (V. *Pasquetto*).

8747 [*Rostagno* Sergio, 6 al., Chiese evangeliche] Maria nostra sorella 1988 → 4,9862]. ᴿBbbOr 31 (1989) 43s [F. *Sardini*]; Protestantesimo 44 (1989) 150-2 (A. *Sonelli*).

8748 **Martini** Carlo M., The woman among her people [1984 → 4,9841],ᵀ. Slough 1989, St. Paul's. 136 p. £6. – ᴿPrPeo 3 (1989) 370s (sr. M. Cecily *Boulding*).

8749 **Mavrofidis** S. ❺ *Hē mētéra toû Iēsoû*, La madre di Gesù nel NT. Athenai 1989, Poreía Pneumatikí. 207 p.

8749* *Mazzoleni* Danilo, La mariologia nell'epigrafia cristiana antica: VetChr 26 (1989) 59-68 + 20 fig.

8750 *Mezzasalma* C., La Vergine Maria e la Chiesa secondo AGOSTINO: CiVit 43 (1988) 123-134.

8751 **Moloney** Francis J., Mary, woman and mother [NT texts]. Homebush 1988, St. Paul. 71 p. $7. – ᴿAustralasCR 66 (1989) 503 (T. *Johns*); Pacifica 2 (1989) 241-3 (Veronica *Lawson*).

8752 ᴱ**Moltmann-Wendel** Elisabeth *al.*, Was geht uns Maria an? 1983/8 → 4,388: ᴿTGL 79 (1989) 206 (W. *Beinert*).

8753 *Müller* Gerhard, Evangelische Marienverehrung: Luther 19 (1988) 2-13.
8754 *Nardi* Isabella, Alcune immagini di Maria nella letteratura contemporanea: NuovaUm 11,66 (1989) 97-110.
8755 *Norris* Thomas, Mariology a key to the faith: IrTQ 55 (1989) 192-305.
8756 **Obregón Barreda** Luis, María en los padres de la Iglesia, antologia 1988 ⇒ 4,9852: ᴿHumT 10,1 (1989) 123s (A. de *Pinho*); ScripTPamp 21 (1989) 708s (J. L. *Bastero*).
8757 **O'Dwyer** Peter, Mary, a history of devotion in Ireland. Dublin 1988, Four Courts. 331 p. $45. – ᴿTS 50 (1989) 593s (E. R. *Carroll*).
8758 **Ordóñez Márquez** J., Maternidad plena de María; teología de la espiritualidad mariana. Toledo 1987, CETE. 466 p. – ᴿBurgense 30 (1989) 290s [N. *López Martínez*].
8759 ᴱ**Peretto** E., Maria nell'ebraismo e nell'Islam oggi 1986/7 ⇒ 4,624: ᴿAsprenas 36 (1989) 298s (P. *Pifano*); DivThom 91 (1988) 476s (G. *Testa*); Salesianum 51 (1989) 174s (D. *Bertetto*).
8760 **Perry** Nicholas, *Echeverria* Loretto, Under the heel of Mary. L 1988, Routledge. 442 p. $40 [JAAR 57,889].
Petri H., Divergenzen in der Mariologie 1987; Mariolog. Studien 7 ⇒ 723.
8761 **Pinkus** L., El mito de María, aproximación simbólica: Cristianismo y Sociedad 16, 1987 ⇒ 4,9856: ᴿProyección 35 (1988) 322 (E. *Barón*: no mito sino símbolos); RazF 218 (1988) 481 (J. M. *Vallarino*).
8762 **Pinkus** Lucio, Il mito di Maria, un approccio simbolico: materiale per la comprensione della psicodinamica del femminile nell'esperienza cristiana: Ricerche teologiche. R 1986, Borla. 153 p. Lit. 15.000. 88-263-0633-8. – ᴿCarmelus 35 (1988) 234-7 (A. *Pacciolla*).
8763 *Pratscher* Wilhelm, Das neutestamentliche Bild Marias als Grundlage der Mariologie: KerDo 35 (1989) 189-210; Eng. 211.
8764 **Prévost** J. P., La mère de Jésus 1987 (⇒ 4,9857 '1988'); ᴿNRT 111 (1989) 143 (A. *Toubeau*: Vatican II entre l'hypertrophie et le féminisme).
8765 **Radkiewicz** Jan, Auf der Suche nach einem mariologischen Grundprinzip; eine historisch-systematische Untersuchung über die letzten hundert Jahre: Diss. ᴰ*Lehmann* K. Freiburg/B, 1988s. 546 p. – TR 85 (1989) 515; RTLv 21,570 (> Konstanz, Hartung-Gorre).
8766 **Räisänen** H., Die Mutter Jesu im Neuen Testament². Helsinki 1989 = 1969, Suomalainen Tiedeakatemia. 217 p. 951-41-0591-5 [NTAbs 33,408].
8767 **Ratzinger** Joseph, *Balthasar* Hans Urs von, Marie première église [Maria — Kirche im Ursprung],ᵀ. P/Montréal 1987, Médiaspaul/Paulines. 78 p. – ᴿRTAM 56 (1989) 239 (J. *Winandy*: titre allemand plus approprié).
8768 **Rubio** Miguel, Un rostro nuevo de mujer; la figura cristiana de María a la hora de los feminismos: 'EAS' 27. M 1989, 'PS'. 197 p. – ᴿBibFe 15 (1989) 485 (A. *Salas*); Lumen Vr 38 (1989) 338s (F. *Ortiz de Urtaran*).
8769 *Sartori* Luigi, [al.]., 'Storia della salvezza' e 'storia dell'umanità' nell'enciclica 'Redemptoris Mater': Marianum 51 (1989) 19-32 [-466, 19 altri commenti sull'Enciclica].
8769* *a) Schaberg* Jane, The foremothers and the mother of Jesus; – *b) Maeckelberghe* Els, 'Mary', maternal friend or virgin mother, ᵀ*Smith* D.: Concilium 206 (E 1989) 112-9 / 120-7 = Concilium 222 (P 1989) 135-143 / 145-152 = IZT 25 (1989) 529-533 / 534-8.
8770 **Schelkle** K. H., La madre del Salvatore; la figura di Maria nel NT [²1970], ᵀ*Strada* M. R 1985, Città Nuova. 88 p. Lit. 6000. 88-311-4511-8. – ᴿMarianum 51 (1989) 638-640 (Adriana *Bottino*).

8771 **Schipflinger** Thomas,   Sophia-Maria; eine ganzheitliche Vision der Schöpfung. Mü 1988, Neue Stadt. 348 p.; 20 fig. + 41 color. DM 38. – [R]TGL 79 (1989) 630s (M. *Kunzler*).

8772 **Schlichting** Wolfhart,   Maria, die Mutter Jesu in Bibel, Tradition und Feminismus: ABC-team. Wu 1989, Brockhaus. 176 p. 3-417-12431-X.

8773 [E]**Schmitt-Lieb** Willy,   Das Marienbild im Wandel von 1300-1800 [Kevelaer Weltkongress 1987, Ausstellung]. Wü 1987, Echter. 800 p. 353 + 103 fig. DM 98. – [R]TGL 79 (1989) 212s (W. *Beinert*: Wirrwarr).

8773* [E]**Schoepsdau** W. [p. 7-12], Mariologie und Feminismus: Benzheimer Hefte 64. Gö 1985, Vandenhoeck & R. 141 p. – [R]Protestantesimo 44 (1989) 152 (A. *Moda*).

8774 **Scott** Philip M.,   A virgin called woman 1986 ➤ 3,8829; 4,9868: [R]DowR 107 (1989) 63-65 (A. G. *Murray*: most important on 'Mary in Mark').

8775 *Sponsa mater uirgo* 1985 ➤ 3,527*: [R]Latomus 48 (1989) 496 (Simone *Deléani*).

8776 [E]**Stacpoole** Alberic,   Mary and the Churches [Ecumenical Society of Mary 7th meeting, Chichester c. 1986] 1987 ➤ 3,84: [R]IrTQ 55 (1989) 83s (A. M. *Allchin*).

8777 *Thompson* William M., *Chirico* Peter F.,   Mary, virgin and wife; a dialogue: ChSt 28 (1989) 137-159.

8778 **T'Joen** Michel T.,   Marie et l'Esprit dans la théologie de Hans Urs von BALTHASAR: diss. LvN, [D]*Perre* A. Vander: ➤ 986, Travaux de doctorat 9 (LvN 1989) Théologie 10 [< Marianum 49 (1987) 161-195 ➤ 4,9873d].

8779 *Tromp* Nico,   Zie uw Moeder; zes bijbelse portretten van Maria: Geest en Leven 65 (1988) 159-167.

8780 **Valentini** Alberto,   Esperienza cristiana con Maria; 30 riflessioni bibliche per il nostro tempo. R 1980, Monfortiane. – [R]ParVi 34 (1989) 471s (Maria *Ko*).

8780* *Waldenfels* Hans,   Maria zwischen Talmud und Koran: ZMissRW 73 (1989) 97-108.

8781 *Wilckens* Ulrich,   Maria, die Mutter des Herrn — in evangelischer Sicht: UnSa 43 (1988) 166-176.

8782 **Zavalloni** Roberto, *Mariani* Eliodoro,   La dottrina mariologico di G. Duns SCOTO 1987 ➤ 4,9880: [R]VerVid 47 (1989) 511 (G. *Calvo Moralejo*).

H8.8   *Feminae NT* – Women in the NT and early Church.

8783 *Ahl* Ruth,   *a*) Frauengeschichte im frühen Christentum [*Schüssler Fiorenza* E.]; – *b*) Antijudaismus in feministischer Theologie?: StiZt 207 (1989) 713-6/210-2.

8783* *Arjava* Antti,   Jerome and women: Arctos 23 (1989) 5-18.

8784 **Bacchiocchi** Samuele,   Women in the Church., a biblical study 1987 ➤ 3,8848: [R]BS 146 (1989) 105 (H. W. *House*); Worship 62 (1988) 90-92 (Mary Ann *Getty* does not recommend).

8785 *a*) *Bavel* T. J. Van,   Woman as the image of God in AUGUSTINE's *De Trinitate* XII; – *b*) *Soennecken* S.,   Die Rolle der Frau in Augustins *De Genesi ad litteram*: ➤ 132, [F]MAYER C., Signum pietatis 1989, 267-288 / 289-300 [< RHE 85,38*].

8786 *Bavel* T. J. van,   AUGUSTINE's view of women: AugLv 39 (1989) 5-53 [< RHE 85,99*].

8787 *Bingemer Lucchetti* Maria Clara, Jesus Christ and the salvation of the women: Voices from the Third World 11,2 (Colombo 1988) 125-142 [< TContext 7/1, 72].

8789 ᵀᴱBrock S. P., *Harvey* Susan A., Holy women of the Syrian Orient [14 Syriac inedita in English + one from John of Ephesus] 1987 ⮕ 3,g352; 4,h926: ᴿMuséon 102 (1989) 389s (B. *Coulie*).

8790 *Brunelli* Delir, La liberación de la mujer; enfoques bíblicos: Testimonio 113 (Santiago/Chile 1989) 13-25 [R. *Fornet-Bétancourt* Eng. summary in TContext 7,111].

8790* **Burrus** Virginia, Chastity as autonomy; women in the stories of apocryphal Acts: Studies in Women and Religion 23, 1987 ⮕ 3,8853: ᴿCBQ 51 (1989) 364s (R. L. *Pervo*).

8791 **Byrne** Brendan, Paul and the Christian woman [Gal 3,28; 1 Cor 7; 11; 14; 'Was Paul married?']. Collegeville MN 1989, Liturgical. xviii-109 p. $7. 0-8146-1846-4 [TDig 37,151].

8792 *Callaway* Mary [*Kovacs* Judith L.] Women OT [NT]: ⮕ 418, What the Bible really says 1989, 197-211 / 213-227.

8793 **Carmody** Denise L., Biblical woman; contemporary reflections on Scriptural texts 1988 ⮕ 4,9892: ᴿSWJT 32,1 (1989s) 66 (G. *Greenfield*).

8794 *Carnelley* Elizabeth, ᵀᴱᴿᵀᵁᴸᴸᴵᴬᴺ and feminism: TLond 92 (1989) 31-35.

8794* *Casadio* Giovanni, Gnostic womanhood; preliminary notes for a typology of the feminine in second century Gnosticism: ⮕ 696, 10th Patristic, 19 (1989) 307-312.

8795 **Clark** Elizabeth A., Ascetic piety and women's faith [13 1977-85] essays on late ancient Christianity 1987 ⮕ 3,204; 4,9893: ᴿVigChr 43 (1989) 411s (J. den *Boeft*).

8795* *Corrington* Gail P., The 'Divine Woman'? [⮕ 4,8079]; Propaganda and the power of celibacy in the NT apocrypha; a reconsideration: AnglTR 70 (1988) 207-220.

8796 **Costello** Melanie S., Women's mysticism and reform; the adaptation of biblical prophetic conventions in fourteenth century hagiographic and visionary literature: diss. Northwestern, ᴰ*Kleckhefer* R. 1989. 264 p. 90-09632. – DissA 50 (1989s) 3025s-A.

8797 *Cunningham* Agnes, Women and preaching in the patristic age: ⮕ 38, ᶠBURGHARDT W., Preaching 1989, 53-72.

8798 *Dumais* Marcel, présent. [groupe ASTER, ᴰ*Légaré* C.] De Jésus et des femmes 1987 ⮕ 4,292: ᴿÉglT 19 (1988) 262s (M. *Girard*); LavalTP 45 (1989) 319s (G. *Bouchard*); NRT 111 (1989) 939s (A. *Fossion*); ScEspr 40 (1988) 379s (J. *Duhaime*); SR 18 (1989) 95 (Sylvie *Prévost* indique Clément Légaré comme 'directeur': du livre? ou de la série Recherches NS?).

8799 *Dumais* Marcel, Langage sexiste et traductions de la Bible: ÉglT 19 (1988) 241-253.

8800 **Dumais** Monique, Las mujeres en la Biblia; experiencias e inter-pelaciones. M 1987, Paulinas. 125 p. – ᴿBibFe 14 (1988) 480 (M. *Sáenz Galache*).

8801 **Emmanuele** Marie sr., *Bonanate* Mariapia, Appuntamento con Maria Maddalena. T 1988, Abele. 162 p. Lit. 18.000. – ᴿStCattMi 33 (1989) 375s (C. *Toscani*).

8802 *Evenson* Ardy, Mary of Magdala: BToday 27 (1989) 219-224.

8803 **Fabris** Rinaldo, La femme dans l'Église primitive 1987 ⮕ 4,9897; F 67: ᴿNRT 111 (1989) 293s (A. *Toubeau*).

8804 *Fabris* Rinaldo, La donna nel NT: ➤ 4,699, [E]**Uglione** Renato, La donna nel mondo antico [convegno Torino 21-23. IV. 1986], 1987, p. 209-221.

Fander Monika, Die Stellung der Frau im Mk.-Ev., Diss. Münster 1989 ➤ 4896.

8805 **Faricy** Robert, The Lord's dealing; the primacy of the feminine in Christian spirituality. NY 1988, Paulist. vi-113 p. $7 pa. [Horizons 16,206]. – [R]PrPeo 3 (1989) 371s (Lavinia *Byrne*).

8806 **Ford** David C., Misogynist or advocate? St. John CHRYSOSTOM and his views on women: diss. Drew, [D]*Pain*. Madison NJ 1989. – RelStR 16,190.

8807 *Gerhardsson* Birger, Kvinnorna som vittnen vid korset och graven [women as witnesses at Cross and tomb]: SvTKv 65 (1989) 49-57.

8808 **Grassi** Joseph A., The hidden heroes of the Gospels; female counterparts of Jesus. Collegeville MN 1989, Liturgical. 143 p. $8. 0-8146-1591-0 [NTAbs 33,385].

8809 **Hayter** Mary, The new Eve in Christ; use and abuse of the Bible 1987 ➤ 3,8865; 4,9901: [R]CBQ 51 (1989) 153s (M. C. *Boys*: she oversimplifies radical feminists); Interpretation 43 (1989) 326s (Mary Ellen *Ross*: dismisses feminists); JEcuSt 26 (1989) 559s (R. A. *Boisclair*); OTAbs 12 (1989) 346 (W. J. *Urbrock*); Salesianum 51 (1989) 154 (R. *Vincent*); ScotBEv 7 (1989) 48 (Ann *Allen*).

8810 **Heeney** Brian † 1983, The women's movement in the Church of England 1850-1930. Ox 1988, Clarendon. xi-144 p. £19.50. 0-19-822671-3. – [R]ExpTim 100 (1988s) 118 (Mary *Hayter*).

8811 **Heine** Susanne, Wiederbelebung der Göttinnen? 1987➤ 2,2007... 4,9990: [R]ÉTRel 63 (1988) 309s (H. *Schoenhals*); TLZ 114 (1989) 219-222 (Christine *Janowski*).

8812 **Heine** Susanne, *a*) Frauen der frühen Christenheit[1] 1986 ➤ 2,7007; 4,9991; *b*) Wiederbelebung der Göttinnen? ([2]1987) ➤ 8811 supra: [R]TR 85 (1989) 47-51 (Maria *Kassel* describes them as vol. I and II).

8812* *Heine* S., Eine Person von Rang und Namen — historische Konturen der Magdalenerin: ➤ 131, [F]MARXSEN W., Jesu Rede 1989, 179-194.

8813 *House* H. Wayne, Distinctive roles for women in the second and third centuries [fifth part in a series on Women in the Ministry]: Bibliotheca Sacra 134 (1989) 41-54.

8814 *Housley* K., [Mary of Magdala] Solid citizen or prostitute? Two millennia of misinformation: Dialog 27 (St. Paul 1988) 295-7 [< NTAbs 33,150: 'a template'].

8814* *Klauck* Hans-J., Vom Reden und Schweigen der Frauen in der Ur-kirche [> Symposion Würzburg]: ➤ 292, Gemeinde 1989, 232-245.

8815 **Landercy** Mathilde, Figures de femmes au sein du peuple de Dieu 1987 ➤ 3,8872: [R]RThom 89 (1989) 518s (H.-F. *Rovarino*).

8816 **Lang** Judith, Ministers of grace; women in the early Church. Slough 1989, St. Paul's. 151 p. £6.25. – [R]PrPeo 3 (1989) 371 (sr. M. Cecily *Boulding*).

8817 **Leclercq** Jean, *a*) Women and Saint BERNARD of Clairvaux; – *b*) A second look at Bernard of Clairvaux: both [T]*Saïd* Marie-Bernard: Cistercian Studies 104s. Kalamazoo 1989s, Cistercian. 175 p./150 p. $17 + 20. 0-87907-404-3; 4-1 [TDig 37,47].

8818 *Loss* Nicolò M., Il tema della 'donna' nella Bibbia: ➤ 611, Come leggere 1988/9, 27-77.

8819 *Lubich* Chiara, La radicale novità e la profonda libertà di Gesù nel rapporto con le donne: ➤ 429, OssRom Quad 9 (1989) 125-9.

8820 **Martini**, Carlo M., Women and reconciliation [...six biblical themes], ᵀ*Griffin* L.: Cathedral Series 3. Dublin 1987, Veritas. 66 p. £ 3.25 pa. 0-86217-239-X [NTAbs 33,109].

8821 **Massey** Lesly F., Women and the New Testament; an analysis of Scripture in light of New Testament era culture. Jefferson NC 1989, McFarland. vii-152 p. $25. 0-89950-438-8 [TDig 37,74].

8822 *Milhaven* J. Giles, A medieval lesson on bodily knowing; women's experience and men's thought [*Bynum* C., *Ziegler* J.]: JAAR 57 (1989) 341-372.

8823 *a) Moxnes* Halvor, Feminist reconstruction of early Christian history / Social integration and the problem of gender in St. Paul's letters; – *b) Schüssler Fiorenza* Elisabeth, Biblical interpretation and critical commitment / Text and reality — reality as text; the problem of a feminist historical and social reconstruction based on texts: ST 43,1 (1989) 1-3.99-113 / 5-18.19-34 [-163 *al.* ➤ 8827 infra].

8824 **Newman** Barbara, Sister of wisdom; St. HILDEGARD's theology of the feminine 1987 ➤ 3,8886: ᴿChH 58 (1989) 223-5 (G. W. *Olsen*); Horizons 16 (1989) 386s (Mary Jo *Weaver*); JAAR 57 (1989) 217-9 (T. *Head*).

8825 *Osborne* Grant R., Women in Jesus' ministry: WestTJ 51 (1989) 259-291.

8826 **Pirot** Jean, Trois amies de Jésus [Marie de Lc 7,36 n'est pas celle de 10,39 ni la Magdeleine]: Lire la Bible 74,1986 ➤ 2,7021:3,6888: ᴿRTLv 19 (1989) 89 (Alice *Dermience*: fondamentalisme avec imagination).

8827 *a) Portefaix* Lilian, Women and mission in the New Testament; some remarks on the perspective of audience, a research report; – *b) Lindboe* Inger M., Recent literature; development and perspectives in New Testament research on women; – *c) Seim* Turid K., Ascetic autonomy? New perspectives on single women in the early Church; – *d) Montgomery* Hugo, Women and status in the Greco-Roman world: ST 43,1 (1989) 141-152 / 153-163 / 125-140 / 115-124.

8828 *Reynolds* Lyndon, BONAVENTURE on gender and godlikeness: DowR 106 (1988) 171-194.

8829 **Rieplhuber** R., Die Stellung der Frau in den neutestamentlichen Schriften und im Koran [Diss. 1984, Salesianer Hochschule]: Studien 5. 1986 ➤ 3,552; 3-88733-002-5 [NTAbs 33,122].

8830 *Rigazio* Emiliano †, Santità femminile nella Chiesa apostolica: Riv-AscM 13 (1988) 328-340.

8831 *Rossé* Gérard, La donna nel NT: NuovaUm 11,62 (1989) 17-29 / 11,63 (1989) 9-21.

8834 ᴱ**Russell** Letty M., Feminist interpretation of the Bible 1985 ➤ 3,1515: ᴿHeythJ 30 (1989) 71s (M. *Barker*).

8835 **Schüssler Fiorenza** Elisabeth, En memoria de ella; una reconstrucción teológico-feminista de los orígenes del cristianismo [1983 ➤ 64,7405 ... 3,8892], ᵀ*Tabuyo* María: Cristianismo y sociedad 18. Bilbao 1989, D-Brouwer. 416 p. [LumenVr 38,351]. – ᴿActuBbg 26 (1988) 118s (J. I. *González Faus*); CiuD 202 (1989) 760s (J. M. *Ozaeta*); NatGrac 36 (1989) 156 (A. *Villalmonte*); RazF 219 (1989) 663s (J. M. G.).

8836 **Schüssler Fiorenza** Elisabeth, Zu ihrem Gedächtnis — eine feministisch-theologische Rekonstruktion der christlichen Ursprünge, ᵀ*Schaumberger* Christine, Mü/Mainz 1988, Kaiser/Grünewald. 424 p. DM 50. – ᴿBiKi 44 (1989) 91-93 (S. *Schroer* < Reformatio 1989); TGL 79 (1989) 208s (W. *Beinert*).

8837 **Schüssler Fiorenza** E., Ter herinnering aan haar 1987 → 3,8895: RStreven 55 (1987s) 1033s (P. *Beentjes*).

8838 *Snell* P., The women from Galilee: Sisters Today 60,8 (Collegeville MN 1989) 483-5 [< NTAbs 33,314].

8839 *Strahm* Doris, De Bijbel en de bevrijding van de vrouw: Streven 56 (1988s) 195-203.

8840 *Stuard* R.M., From women to woman; new thinking about gender c. 1140: Thought 64 (1989) 208-219 [< RHE 85,101*].

8841 *Synek* Eva M., Heilige Frauen der Frühen Kirche; ein Beitrag über Frauenbilder hagiographischer Texte der Kirchen des Ostens: UnSa 43 (1988) 289-298.

8842 **Tung** S., Brève histoire des femmes chrétiennes [rôle dans l'Église, à partir des origines..]: Parole présente. P 1989, Cerf. 296 p. F 124. – RNRT 111 (1989) 1080 (A. *Harvengt*: réserves).

8843 EWalter Karin, Donne alla riscoperta della Bibbia [1986→ 2,270], TGaiotti Oxenius P., EBartolomei Maria Cristina, 1988 → 4,9936; Lit. 17.000; 88-399-1749-7: RNRT 111 (1989) 612s (A.*Harvengt*); Protestantesimo 44 (1989) 288s (F. *Ferrario*).

8844 **Walter** Karin, Zwischen Ohnmacht und Befreiung; biblische Frauengestalten: Frauenforum. FrB 1988, Herder. 200 p. DM 19,80. – RTPQ 137 (1989) 311s (Herline-Anna *Pissarek*).

8845 *Willaert* F., HADEWIJCH en Maria Magdalena [...homily attributed to Origen but really of 12th century]: → 4,33, FDESCHAMPS J., Miscellanea Neerlandica II (1987) 57-69 [< BTAM 14 (1989) p. 722 (G. *Hendrix*)].

H8.9 *Theologia feminae* – **Feminist theology.**

8846 **Andolsen** Barbara H., Daughters of Jefferson / ...bootblacks 1986 → 2,7035...4,9940: RJRel 68 (1988) 457s (Kristine A. *Culp*).

8847 **Aubert** Jean-Marie, L'exil féminin; antiféminisme et christianisme: [= 2La femme 1975]. Recherches Morales. P 1988, Cerf. 274 p. F 125 [NRT 111, 467]. – RETL 65 (1989) 199s (A. de *Halleux*); MélSR 46 (1989) 95 (L. *Debarge*).

8848 **Aubert** Marie-Josèphe, Des femmes diacres...: PoinT 47, 1987→ 4,9946: RScEspr 41 (1989) 124 (G. *Novotny*).

8849 *Azevedo* Marcello, Le versant féminin de l'Église: VieCons 60 (1988) 323-336.

8850 *Barton* Stephen C., Impatient for justice; five reasons why the Church of England should ordain women to the priesthood: TLond 92 (1989) 403-5.

8851 **Beers** William R., Women and sacrifice; male narcissism and the psychology of religion: diss. DHomans P. Chicago 1989. – RelStR 16,186.

8852 **Behr-Sigel** Elisabeth, Le ministère de la femme dans l'Église 1987 → 4,9947: RMélSR 46 (1989) 173 (G.-H. *Baudry*).

8853 EBeinert W., Frauenbefreiung und Kirche 1987 → 4,9948: RTGegw 31 (1988) 205s (F. *Rosenberg*).

8854 *Bellosillo* Pilar, Carta de JUAN PABLO II sobre la dignidad de la mujer y su vocación. ¿Cómo se llegó hasta aquí?: SalT 76 (1988) 765-776 [747-763.777-784.793-803, al.].

8855 **Bennett** Gillian, Traditions of belief; women, folklore and the supernatural today. L 1987, Penguin. x-222 p. $8. – RRelStR 15 (1989) 339s (Volney P. *Gay*).

8856 *Berger* Teresa, Liturgiewissenschaft und Frauenforschung; getrennte Schwestern?: TR 85 (1989) 353-362.

8857 *Biffi* Inos, Per una teologia dell'"uomo-donna'; metodologia e linguaggio: TItSett 14 (1989) 172-178.

8858 **Böhrig** Marga, *a)* Die unsichtbare Frau und der Gott der Väter; eine Einführung in die feministische Theologie. Stu 1987, Kreuz. 135 p. DM 19.80. – ᴿTLZ 114 (1989) 688-690 (K. *Lüthi*). – *b)* Donne invisibili e Dio patriarcale; introduzione alla teologia femminista [1987], ᵀ*Abate Liebbrand* Mirella: Nostro tempo 48. T 1989, Claudiana. 120 p. Lit. 13.000. – ᴿStPatav 36 (1989) 661 (G. *Segalla*).

8858* **Borrowdale** Catherine A., In search of a feminist theology of work: diss. Durham 1988. – RTLv 21,584.

8859 *Bouchard* Guy, L'hétéropolitique féministe: LavalTP 45 (1989) 95-120.

8860 **Brock** Rita N., Journeys by heart; a Christology of erotic power. NY 1988, Crossroad. xvii-130 p. $17. – ᴿHorizons 16 (1989) 394s (Susan A. *Ross*); NewTR 2,3 (1989) 107s (Marie-Eloise *Rosenblatt*); RExp 86 (1989) 645 (Molly *Marshall-Green*: Christ without Jesus); TTod 46 (1989s) 206.208 (Mary Ellen *Ross*).

8861 *Burggraf* Jutta, Una contemplazione essenziale dell'immagine cristiana della donna... Mulieris dignitatem: AnnTh 3,1 (1989) 3-33.

8862 **Byrne** Lavinia, Women before God. 1988 → 4,9955s also L 1988, SPCK; xiii-111 p.; £5: ᴿHeythJ 30 (1989) 329s (Monica *Furlong*); PrPeo 3 (1989) 35s (Mary *Mills*); TLond 92 (1989) 147s (Hannah *Ward*).

8863 **Cannon** Katie G., Black womanist ethics 1988 → 4,9956: ᴿHorizons 16 (1989) 193 (Christine *Gudorf*).

8864 *a) Carmody* Denise L., Integrating feminist perspectives with the religious studies curriculum; setting the question; – *b) Weaver* Mary Jo, Widening the sphere of discourse...: Horizons 16 (1989) 292-301 / 302-315.

8865 **Carr** Anne E., Transforming grace; Christian tradition and women's experience 1988 → 4,9957: ᴿAmerica 160 (1989) 178-180 (Marie Anne *Mayeski*); BibTB 19 (1989) 70s (Carolyn *Osiek*); CCurr 39 (1989s) 364-6 (Beth *Palmer*); JRel 69 (1989) 573s (Susan B. *Thistlethwaite*); NewTR 2,2 (1989) 102s (Susan A. *Ross*); TS 50 (1989) 387s (Bernadette *Topel*).

8866 **Chopp** Rebecca S., The power to speak; feminism, language, God. NY 1989, Crossroad. 167 p. $18. 0-8245-0940-4 [TDig 37,46].

8867 **Chung Kyun-Kyung**, Struggle to be the sun again; emerging Asian women's liberation theology: diss. Union Theol. Sem., ᴰ*Cone* J. NY 1989. – RelStR 16,187: 'to be the sun'.

8868 *Cisło* Mieczysław, ❷ W poszukiwaniu... Dans la recherche de la théologie de la femme: AtKap 110,2 ('La femme dans l'Église' 1988) 180-193 (— 285, al.; aucun sur l'Écriture).

8869 ᴱ**Cooey** Paula M., al., Embodied love; sensuality and relationship as feminist values [14 art.] 1988 → 4,352: ᴿHorizons 16 (1989) 410-2 (Demaris *Wehr*); NewTR 2,3 (1989) 115-7 (Susan A. *Ross*).

8869* *Cooey* Paula M., Experience, body, and authority: HarvTR 82 (1989) 325-342.

8870 *Corpas de Posada* Isabel, Compromiso social y eclesial de la mujer: TXav 99 (1989) 305-316.

8871 [5 auct.] Lust-gratie; over Mary DALY: Lesbisch cultureel tijdschrift 7 (1985) [< Geest en Leven 65 (1988) 172, B. de *Groot-Kopetzky*: een plezier voor het oog].

8872 **DeBerg** Betty A., American fundamentalism and the disruption of traditional gender roles, 1880-1930: diss. Vanderbilt. Nv 1988. – RTLv 21,555.

8873 *Derks* M., Wat bewoog zoveel vrouwen? Een indruk van vijf jaar theologie in het perspectief van feminisme en christendom: Mara 2,2 (1989) 19-24 [3-10, *Sölle* D.: < GerefTTs 89,64].

8874 *Dietrich* Gabriele, Women, ecology and culture: Bangalore Theol. Forum 21,1 (1989) 1-23 [G. *Evers* (Eng.) summary in TContext 7/1,115].

8875 Dignità e vocazione della donna; per una lettura della 'Mulieris dignitatem' [GIOVANNI PAOLO II], testo e commenti: → OssRom Quad 9, 1989; 110-6, *La Potterie* I. de < OssRom 15.X.1988 p. 1.8.

8875* *Dockery* David S., The role of women in worship and ministry: some hermeneutical questions: → 44*, FCRISWELL W. A., CriswTJ 1 (1987) 363-386.

8876 La donna nella Chiesa e nella società; *Monticone* A., present. R 1986, AVE. 184 p. – RSalesianum 51 (1989) 887 (D. *Valentini*).

8877 **Dowell** Susan, *Hurcombe* Linda, Dispossessed daughters of Eve; faith and feminism[2rev] [[1]1981 → 62,8377]. L 1987, SCM. – RScotJT 42 (1989) 274 (Helen *Cameron*).

8878 **Dunfee** Susan N., Beyond servanthood; Christianity and the liberation of women [diss. Claremont]. Lanham MD 1989, UPA. xvi-175 p. $24.75; pa. $14.25. 0-8191-7224-3 [TDig 37,50]. – RTTod 46 (1989s) 353s (F. J. *Matera*).

8879 **Duquoc** Christian, La femme, le clerc et le laïc; œcuménisme et ministère: Entrée libre 4. Genève 1989, Labor et Fides. 80 p. – RETL 65 (1989) 473s (A. *Haquin*).

8879* *Durlak* Ewa, *Szmydki* Ryszard, Feminizm: → 891, EncKat 5 (1989) 115s.

8880 **Eisler** Riane, The chalice and the blade; our [feminist] history, our future. SF 1987, Harper & R. xxiii-261 p. $17. – RAnglTR 70 (1988) 287-290 (Laurie L. *Patton*).

EFarnham Christie, The impact of feminist research on the Academy 1987 → 460.

8882 **Frykberg** Elizabeth A., Spiritual transformation and the creation of humankind in the image of God, male and female; a study of Karl BARTH's understanding of the 'analogia relationis' correlated with psychosexual and psychosocial developmental theory: diss. Princeton Theol. Sem. 1989, DLoder J. – RelStR 16,186.

8883 *a) García Álvarez* Emilio, Ser mujer ahora; glosa crítica a 'Mulieris dignitatem' de JUAN PABLO II; – *b) Gallegos* Presentación, La mujer es también una persona: CiTom 116 (1989) 535-552 / 553-572.

8884 **Gentili** Antonio, Se non diventerete come donne 1987 → 4,9974: RClaretianum 29 (1989) 418-420 (J. *Rovira*); Salesianum 51 (1989) 387s (M. *Midali*).

8885 **Gerber** Uwe, Die feministische Eroberung der Theologie 1987 → 3,8950; 4,9975: RTPQ 137 (1989) 313 (Marie-Louise *Gubler*).

8886 *Gerhart* Mary, Theologians and feminism [6 books]: Commonweal 115 (1988) 635-8.

8887 **Gerl** Hanna-Barbara, Die bekannte Unbekannte; Frauen-Bilder in der Kultur- und Geistesgeschichte. Mainz 1988, Grünewald. 160 p. DM 24,80. – RTPQ 137 (1989) 312 (Lina *Börsig-Hover*).

8888 *Giglioni* Paolo, Donna; ministero e missione: EuntDoc 42 (1989) 450-469.

8889 EGössmann Elisabeth, Archiv für Philosophie- und Theologiegeschichtliche Frauenforschung, I. Das wohlgelahrte Frauenzimmer; 2. Eva Gottes
Meisterwerk; 3. Johann Casper EBERTI, Eröffnetes Cabinet Dess
Gelehrten Frauen-Zimmers [1706]; 4. Ob die Weiber Menschen seyn, oder
nicht. Mü 1984/5/6/8. 213 p.; 290 p.; xiii-36 + 384 p.; 337 p. – RTPhil 64
(1989) 615-7 (J. *Splett*).

8889* EGössmann Elisabeth, JOHANNES PAUL II., Die Zeit der Frau,
Apostolisches Schreiben 'Mulieris dignitatem'; Einf. *Ratzinger* J. FrB
1988, Herder. 150 p. DM 16,80 [TLZ 115,549, H. *Kirchner*].

8890 Goritschewa Tatiana, Hiobs Töchter (Ⓑ), TButz Birgit: Frauenforum.
FrB 1988, Herder. 141 p. DM 16,80. – RTR 85 (1989) 51s (Corona
Bamberg).

8891 Goritcheva Tatiana, Filles de Job; les féministes de 'Maria'. P 1989,
Nouvelle Cité. 157 p. F 79. – RIrénikon 62 (1989) 441s (J. C.).

8892 Green Elizabeth, Ecologia, feminismo y teología; el pensamiento de
Rosemary R. RUETHER en el contexto del debate actual; diss. DRuiz de la
Peña J. Salamanca 1989. – RTLv 21,569.

8893 *Grelot* Pierre, Y aura-t-il des 'femmes-prêtres' dans l'Église?: NRT
111 (1989) 842-865.

8894 *Hannaford* Robert, Women and the human paradigm; an exploration of
gender discrimination: NBlackf 70 (1989) 226-233.

8895 Harris Maria, Dance of the spirit; the seven steps of women's
spirituality. NY 1989, Bantam. xiv-224 p. $19 [CBQ 52,196].

8896 Hauke Manfred, Women in the priesthood? A systematic analysis in
the light of the order of creation and redemption [against Haye van der
Meer approved by K. *Rahner* 1969],T. SF 1988, Ignatius. 497 p. –
RAngelicum 66 (1989) 352-5 (B. *Cole*: definitive).

8897 *Hauke* Manfred, Zielbild 'Androgyn'; Anliegen und Hintergründe
feministischer Theologie: ForumKT 5 (1989) 1-24.

8899 Heine Susanne, Matriarchs, goddesses, and images of God; a critique of
a feminist theology [1987 ➤ 3,8966], TBowden John. Minneapolis 1989,
Augsburg. vi-183 p. $13. 0-8066-2421-3 [TDig 37,60]. – = ? Christianity
and the goddesses; systematic criticism of feminist theology 1988: RHeythJ
30 (1989) 327-9 (Monica *Furlong*).

8900 *Heine* Susanne [➤ 8812] a) Rechte des Menschen oder Mächte des
Weiblichen? zum Problem einer feministischen Anthropologie: Zeitwende 60,1 (Karlsruhe 1989) 36-... [< ZIT 89,389]; – b) Das 'Mannsbild'
in der feministischen Theologie ➤4,a1b: Diakonia 19 (1988) 162-7
[> TDig 36,11-14, 'The "male" in feminist theology'].

8901 Henderson Susan K., Women in the pews and feminist theologians
speak about God, Jesus, and ethics: diss. Minnesota, DYates Gayle G.
Minneapolis 1989. 207 p. 89-18280. – DissA 50 (1989s) 1329s-A.

8902 EHiggins Michael W., Letson Douglas R., Women and the Church; a
sourcebook ➤ 3,415: Toronto 1986, Griffin. x-234. 26 selections. – RSR
18 (1989) 252s (Elizabeth *Bellefontaine*: no biblical article).

8903 a) *Holler* Linda, Is there a 'thou' within nature? A feminist dialogue with H. Richard NIEBUHR; – b) *Bruland* Esther B., Evangelical and
feminist ethics; complex solidarities: JRelEth 17 (1989) 81-102 /
139-160.

8904 Hourcade Janine, La femme dans l'Église; étude anthropologique et
théologique des ministères féminins: Croire et Savoir 7. P 1986, Téqui.
343 p. F 160. – RIrénikon 62 (1989) 298s (E. Lt.: 'féminisation du
féminisme').

8905 EJardin Alice, *Smith* Paul, Men in feminism [20 art., half by women] 1987 → 4,371: RJRel 68 (1988) 614s (Kathryn *Rabuzzi*).

8906 *a) Johnson* Elizabeth A., Feminist hermeneutics; – *b) Cook* Michael L., The image of Jesus as liberating for women; ChSt 27 (1988), 123-135 / 136-150.

8907 *Jones* Alan W., Men, women and sex; make way for the image of God: Worship 62 (1988) 25-44.

8908 EKassel M., Feministische Theologie; Perspektive zur Orientierung 1988 → 4,a2; 3-7831-0914-0: RTsTNijm 29 (1989) 303s (C. *Claassen*).

8908* King Ursula, Women and spirituality; voices of protest and promise: Women in Society. L 1989, Macmillan Education. xii-273 p. – RExpTim 100 (1988s) 474 (N. *Slee*); ZMissRW 73 (1989) 316s (Donate *Pahnke*).

8909 Klotz Verena, 'Mit dir, statt gegen dich'; ein feministisch-theologischer Beitrag zur relationalen Selbstvergewisserung der Frauen in einer androzentrischen Kultur: kath. Diss. DFuchs O. Bamberg 1988s. 515 p. – TR 85 (1989) 513; RTLv 21,586.

8910 EKolbenschlag Madonna, Women in the Church I [conference Wsh Oct. 10-12, 1986]. Wsh 1987, Pastoral. vi-250 p. $12. – RTS 50 (1989) 183s (Mary Ann *Donovan*).

8911 Krockow Christian von [nach Erzählungen seiner Schwester], Die Stunde der Frauen; Berichte aus Pommern 1944-7. Stu 1988, Deutsche-VA. 256 p.; ill. DM 32. – RStiZt 207 (1989) 205-7 (Elisabeth von der *Lieth*).

8912 *La Cugna* Catherine M., The baptismal formula, feminist objections, and Trinitarian theology: JEcuSt 26 (1989) 235-250.

8913 *Lindgren* Ura, Wege der historischen Frauenforschung: HistJb 109 (1989) 211-9 [< ZIT 89,399].

8914 Loades Ann, Searching for lost coins 1987 → 4,a13: RExpTim 100 (1988s) 474 (Sue *Birchmore*: a survey of the place of women within the Christian tradition); RelSt 25 (1989) 538s (R. H. *Bell*); Studies 77 (1988) 475s (Teresa *Clements*).

8915 Lunen-Chenu Marie-Thérèse van, *Gibellini* Rosino, Donna e teologia: GdT 182. Brescia 1988, Queriniana. 193 p. Lit. 15.000. 88-399-0682-7. – RÉTRel 64 (1989) 463s (Bettina *Cottin*); StPatav 36 (1989) 147s (L. *Sartori*: due art. già pubblicati ma ricchi di informazioni).

8916 *a) Lunen-Chenu* M. Thérèse van, Moviments de dones en l'Esglesia, estils de reciprocitat entre els sexes i llur dimensió ecumènica; – *b) Pintos* Margarita, Les grans tendències de la teologia feminista: QVidCr 144 (1988) 28-48 / 49-58.

8917 McGraw Barbara Lee, A theology for women in church leadership; problems and practical solutions: diss. Fuller Theol. Sem. Pasadena 1989. 212 p. 89-23018. – DissA 50 (1989s) 2526-A.

8918 *Maselli* Domenico, La donna: → 563a, Debole 1987/8, 27-44.

8919 *Mattai* Giuseppe, Nuovo discorso sulla donna nella lettera apostolica 'Mulieris dignitatem': Asprenas 36 (1989) 69-79.

8920 *May* Melanie A., The ordination of women; the churches' responses to Baptism, Eucharist, and Ministry: JEcuSt 26 (1989) 251-269.

8921 *Militello* Cettina, La donna nella Chiesa; problemi aperti: StEcum 6 (1988) 59-102; Eng. 102s.

8922 Miller Page P., A claim to new roles [200 Presbyterian women; diss. Univ. Maryland]: ATLA Mg 22. Metuchen NJ 1985, Scarecrow. 253 p. $17.50. 0-8108-1809-4. – RRExp 86 (1989) 280s (Molly *Marshall-Green*).

8923 ᴱMillhaven Annie L., The inside stories, 13 valiant women challenging the Church [Mary Hunt, Elisabeth Schüssler Fiorenza ...] 1907 ► 4,386: ᴿNewTR 2,1 (1989) 115-7 (Ann O. Graff).

8924 Milne Pamela J., Women and words; the use of non-sexist, inclusive language in the Academy: SR 18 (1989) 25-35.

8925 ᴱMollenkott Virginia R., Women of faith in dialogue 1987 ► 4,e387: ᴿHorizons 16 (1989) 412s (Dolores Greeley).

8926 Monaghan Patricia, Le donne nei miti e nelle leggende; dizionario delle dee e delle eroine. Como 1987, Red. 453 p. Lit. 14.000. – ᴿCC 140 (1989,3) 197s (P. Vanzan: scritto 1968-78; settimo volume di una collana junghiana).

8927 Moore Karen D., Rape and worship; toward a feminist theology [but answering the view that Christianity's patriarchalism fosters rape]: diss. Claremont 1989. 143 p. 89-24380. – DissA 50 (1989s) 2097s-A.

8928 Morley Janet, All desires known; women in theology. L 1988, Movement for the ordination of women. 60 p. £2.50 pa. 0-9513039-0-2. – ᴿTLond 92 (1989) 67 (C. C. Rowland).

8929 Oden Amy C., Secularization theory and the ordination of women: Paradigms 5,1 (1989) 51-62.

8930 a) Pandharipande Rajeshwari, Spiritual dimension of fertility cult and power in women; – b) Ananda Sri, Religio-cultural approach to the gender problem in India: JDharma 13 (1988) 267-281 / 351-381.

8931 Paterson Torquil, The ordination of women ... Church of the Province of Southern Africa: JTSAf 66 (Rondebosch 1989) 21-33 [34-47, Swart-Russell Phoebe, < TContext 7/1,21].

8932 Paul Camille, Christifideles laici — a feminist's response: AustralasCR 66,4 ('The synod on the laity' 1989) 412-9 [400-6, Esther Doyle; 387-431, other articles on the document].

8933 Paul Camille, A plethora of Phoebes [Rom 16,1: women in ministry]: ► 446, Challenges 1989, 75-86.

8934 ᴱPeberdy Alyson, Women priests. Basingstoke 1988, Marshall Pickering. 84 p. £4. – ᴿPrPeo 3 (1989) 35 (Sr M. Cecily Boulding: restrained essays).

8935 Piotet Françoise, al., La différence des sexes: LumièreV 38/194 (1989) 5-90.

8936 Porcile Santiso Maria Teresa, Misión de la mujer en la Iglesia; una perspectiva antropológica: dis. cat. ᴰSchenker A. Fribourg/S 1988s. – TR 85 (1989) 513.

8937 Prelinger Catherine M., Charity, challenge, and change; religious dimensions of the mid-nineteenth century women's movement in [Catholic Hamburg-area] Germany: Contributions in women's studies 75. Westport CT 1987, Greenwood. xx-205 p. $30 [RelStR 16, 58, Dawn De Vries].

8938 a) Ramos-Lissón Domingo, Le rôle de la femme dans la théologie de saint IRÉNÉE; – b) Trevett Christine, IGNATIUS and the monstrous regiment of women; – c) Torjesen Karen Jo, TERTULLIAN's 'political ecclesiology' and women's leadership; – d) Burrus Virginia, Hierarchalization and genderization of leadership in the writings of IRENAEUS: ► 696, 10th Patristic 21 (1989) 163-174 / 202-214 / 277-282 / 42-48.

8938* ᴱRauscher Anton, Die Frau in Gesellschaft und Kirche, Kath. Kommission 1986 ► 3,450: ᴿZevEth 33 (1989) 76s (Susanne Dimpker).

8939 Ruether Rosemary R., Women-Church 1985 ► 2,7105 ... 4,a28: ᴿJRel 68 (1988) 332s (Kristine A. Culp).

8940 *Ruether* Rosemary R., *a*) The development of my theology: RelStR 15 (1989) 1-4 [4-8-11, further on Ruether by *Rabuzzi* Kathryn A., *Chopp* Rebecca S.]; – *b*) Mary's pence; promoting women's ministries: CCurr 39 (1989s) 97-102.

8941 **Russell** Letty M., Household of freedom; authority in feminist theology 1987 → 3,9018; 4,131: ᴿCCurr 39 (1989s) 119-121 (Beth *Palmer*); JRel 69 (1989) 571-3 (Christine F. *Hinze*).

8942 *Schneiders* Sandra M., Feminist ideology criticism and biblical hermeneutics: BibTB 19 (1989) 3-10.

8943 *Schöpp-Schilling* Hanna B., Frauenforschung: → 952, Frauenlexikon² 1989, 334-338.

8944 **Schüssler Fiorenza** E., Bread not stone (1984) 1986 → 1,8622... 3,9023: ᴿCurrTM 16 (1989) 131 (Jessica *Crist*).

8945 **Schüssler Fiorenza** Elisabeth, Brot statt Steine; die Herausforderung einer feministischen Interpretation der Bibel, ᵀ*Hermans* Karel. FrS 1988, Exodus. 237 p. Fs 30,80. – ᴿTR 85 (1989) 375s (H. *Frankemolle*).

8946 *Schüssler Fiorenza* Elisabeth, Commitment and critical inquiry: HarvTR 82 (1989) 1-11.

8947 *Scopello* Madeleine, Femme et société dans les notices des Pères contre les Gnostiques: → 820*b*, Journées coptes III, 1986/9, 115-123.

8948 *Smith* Frank J., Petticoat Presbyterianism; a century of debate in American Presbyterianism on the issue of the ordination of women: WestTJ 51 (1989) 51-76.

8949 *Spelman* Elizabeth V., Inessential woman; problems of exclusion in feminist thought. Boston 1989, Beacon. xiii-221 p. $23 [RelStR 16, 138, Kathryn A. *Rabuzzi*].

8950 *Stolz* Fritz, Feministische Religiosität — feministische Theologie; religionswissenschaftliche Perspektiven: ZTK 86 (1989) 477-516.

8951 **Starkey** Elaine, What's right with feminism 1985 → 2,7119; 3,9027: ᴿScotJT 42 (1989) 274-6 (Helen *Alexander*).

8952 **Stowe** Margaret L., Conceiving justice; an examination of the concept of justice in the writings of four Christian feminist ethicists: diss. Boston Univ. 1988. – RelStR 16,188.

8953 ᴱ**Tamez** Elsa, Against machismo 1987 → 3,469: ᴿHorizons 16 (1989) 194 (P. *Berryman*).

8954 **Támez** Elsa, Teólogos de la liberación hablan sobre la mujer. San José 1986, DEI. 183 p. – ᴿRLatAmT 5 (1988) 117s (J. *Sobrino*).

8955 ᴱ**Tamez** Elsa, Through her eyes; women's theology from Latin America. Mkn 1989, Orbis. viii-168 p. $12. 0-88344-373-2 [TDig 37,191].

8956 **Tapia** Elizabeth, S., The contribution of Philippine Christian women to Asian women's theology: diss. Claremont 1988, ᴰ*Moore* M. 218 p. 90-00194. – DissA 50 (1989s) 3269-A; RelStR 16,189.

8957 *Traitler* Reinhild, Bleibt uns nur die andere Sicht der Dinge? Fragen und Wünsche an die ökumenische Dekade 'Solidarität der Kirchen mit den Frauen': ÖkRu 38 (1989) 373-388.

8958 *Trible* Phyllis, Five loaves and two fishes; feminist hermeneutics and biblical theology: TS 50 (1989) 279-295.

8959 **Valenze** Deborah M., Prophetic sons and daughters; female preaching and popular religion in industrial England 1985 → 2,d746: ᴿEngHR 104 (1989) 224s (W. R. *Ward*); JRel 68 (1988) 115s (Ann *Taves*).

8960 *Wainwright* Elaine, In search of the lost coin; toward a feminist biblical hermeneutic: Pacifica 2 (1989) 135-150.

8961 **Wartenberg-Potter** Bärbel von, We will not hang our harps on the willows (1987) 1988 ➤ 4,a48: ᴿAsiaJT 3 (1989) 367-9 (Diane *D'Souza*).

8962 **Wahr** Demaris S., JUNG and feminism; liberating archetypes. Boston 1987, Beacon. xii-148 p. $18. – ᴿCCurr 39 (1989s) 477-480 (Carolyn M. *Craft*); Horizons 16 (1989) 196s (Sally A. *Kenel*).

8963 **Weiden** Colleen A., A feminist critique of the theological anthropology of the papal encyclicals from 1740 to 1989 [they show women's nature as inferior and subordinate to man's]: diss. Duquesne, ᴰ*Hanigan* J. Pittsburgh 1989. – 420 p. 90-11327. – DissA 50 (1989s) 3991-A.

8963* **Wilson** H. T., Sex and gender; making cultural sense of civilization: Mg SociolAnthrop 24. Leiden 1989, Brill. xi-227 p. 90-04-08546-7.

8964 *Worgul* George S.ᴶ, Ritual, power, authority and riddles; the anthropology of Rome's declaration on the ordination of women: LvSt 14 (1989) 38-61.

8965 **Young** Pamela D., Feminist theology / Christian theology. Ph c. 1989, Fortress. $8. [TTod 46,455 adv.].

8966 *Young* Pamela D., Elisabeth SCHÜSSLER FIORENZA's feminist hermeneutic: Grail 4,2 (Waterloo ON 1988) 27-35 [< NTAbs 33,10].

8967 *a) Zumstein* Jean, Pourquoi s'intéresser à l'exégèse féministe?; – *b) Schüssler Fiorenza* Elisabeth, Les douze dans la communauté des disciples égaux; contradiction ou malentendu, ᵀ*Babut* Jacqueline, *Beydon* France; – *c) Salles* Catherine, La diversité de la situation des femmes dans l'Empire romain aux 1ᵉʳ et 2ᵉ siècles; – *d) Kaestli* J.-D., Les Actes apocryphes et la reconstitution de l'histoire des femmes dans le christianisme ancien: FoiVie 88,5 (Cahier Biblique 28, 1989) 1-11 / 13-24 / 43-48 / 71-79.

H9 Eschatologia NT, *spes*, hope.

8968 **Accattoli** Luigi, La speranza di non morire. Mi 1988, Paoline. 186 p. Lit. 14.000. – ᴿCC 140 (1989,2) 405 (G. *Salvini*).
Allison Dale C., The end of the ages has come 1985 ➤ 4750.

8969 **Balthasar** H. Urs von, L'enfer, une question. P 1988, D-Brouwer. 92 p. – ᴿEsprVie 99 (1989) 10-12 (P. *Jay*).

8970 *Balthasar* Hans Urs von, Sperare per tutti [Was dürfen wir hoffen? 1966] ᵀ*Frattini* Maria & Luigi: Già e non ancora 165. Mi 1989, Jaca. 137 p. 88-16-30165-1.

8971 *Bauckham* Richard, MOLTMANN's Theology of hope revisited: ScotJT 42 (1989) 199-214.

8972 **Beck** Heinrich, Reinkarnation oder Auferstehung, ein Widerspruch?: Grenzfragen 14, 1988 ➤ 4,a58: ᴿTPhil 64 (1989) 140 (R. *Sebott*).

8973 *Becker* Bertilo F., Ressureição 18,80 (1988) 189-196 [< TContext 6/2, 61].

8974 **Beker** J. Christiaan, Suffering and hope 1987 ➤ 3,9054; 4,a60; 0-8006-1999-4. – ᴿExpTim 99 (1987s) 344 (E. *Franklin*).

8975 *Bietenhard* Hans, Hoffnung in der Bibel: ➤ 894, EvKL 2 (1988) 543-5 [-7, *Stock* K.].

8976 **Bloch** Ernst, The principle of hope 1986 ➤ 4,a61: ᴿRelStR 15 (1989) 112-6 (F. *Dallmayr*).

8977 **Bordoni** Marcello, *Ciola* Nicola, Gesù nostra speranza; saggio di escatologia 1988➤ 4,a62: ᴿCC 140 (1989,1) 90s (P. *Vanzan*).

8978 *Bourgeois* Henri, Faites-vous attention à la réincarnation?: Masses ouvrières 424 (1989) 46-55.

8979 **Bridges** J.T., Human destiny and resurrection in PANNENBERG and RAHNER: AmerUnivStud 7/32. NY 1987, Lang. 249 p. $32.50. 0-8204-0485-3. – ᴿTsTNijm 29 (1989) 71 (W. *Logister*).

8980 **Bruce** Graham A., Apocalyptic eschatology and reality — an investigation of cosmic transformation: diss. Unisa, ᴰ*König* A. Pretoria 1987. – DissA 50 (1989s) 2110-A.

8981 *Busto Saiz* José R., Liberados de la muerte: SalT 76 (1988) 39-48.

8982 *a) Chareire* Isabelle, Croire à la résurrection des morts; – *b) Bourgeois* Henri, Réincarnation, résurrection; présupposés et fondements: LumièreV 38/195 (1989) 61-72 / 73-84 [1-60 *al.*].

8983 *Collins* Adela Y., Eschatology and apocalypticism: ⇥ 384, NJBC (1989s) 1359-64.

8984 **Cooper** J.W., Body, soul, and life everlasting: biblical anthropology and the monism-dualism debate. GR 1989, Eerdmans. xiii-262 p. $17. 0-8028-0435-7. – ᴿSWJT 32,3 (1989s) 59 (E. E. *Ellis*).

8985 **Croce** Vittorio, Quando Dio sarà tutto in tutti; escatologia: Capire e vivere la fede 1987 ⇥ 4,a71: ᴿScripTPamp 21 (1989) 726s (P. *O'Callaghan*).

8986 *dal Covolo* Enrico, Appunti di escatologia origeniana con particolare riferimento alla morte e al martirio: Salesianum 51 (1989) 769-784.

8987 **Damiano** Kathryn A., On earth as it is in heaven; eighteenth century Quakerism as realized eschatology: diss. Union for Experimenting Colleges 1988. 259 p. 89-13771. – DissA 50 (1989s) 979s-A.

8988 *Davis* Charles, Death and the sense of ending: SR 18 (1989) 51-60.

8989 *Davis* Stephen T., Universalism [belief that all will be saved], hell, and the fate of the ignorant: ModT 6 (1989s) 173-186.

8990 **Drewermann** Eugen, Ich steige hinab in die Barke der Sonne; Meditationen zu Tod und Auferstehung. Olten 1989, Walter. 322 p. DM 43. – ᴿTGL 79 (1989) 331s (K. *Hollmann*).

8991 *Dubied* Pierre-Luigi, L'avenir de la mort: ÉTRel 64 (1989) 321-330.

8992 **Durst** Michael, Die Eschatologie des HILARIUS 1987 ⇥ 3,9069; 4,a74: ᴿActuBbg 26 (1989) 14s (V. *Fábrega*); EstE 64 (1989) 590-2 (C. *Granado*); Salesianum 51 (1989) 167s (B. *Amata*); TR 85 (1989) 379-381 (P.T. *Camelot*, ᵀ*Gaukesbrink* M.).

8993 **Fabris** Rinaldo, Attualità della speranza: BMinCuR 32, 1984 ⇥ 65,7585 ... 2,7263: ᴿÉTRel 63 (1988) 118 (A. *Moda*).

8994 **Fechner** Gustav T., Le petit livre de la vie après la mort; anatomie comparée des anges [1836], ᵀ*Ouerd* Michèle, *Yaiche* Annick. – Les inédits et les introuvables de Patio-Psychanalyse. Montpellier 1987, Éclat. 127 p. – ᴿRHPR 69 (1989) 491-3 (B. *Kaempf*: worth making known; influenced FREUD).

8995 *Fernández del Riesgo* Manuel, La muerte y la teodicea; una reflexión socioantropológica: EstAg 23 (1988) 129-156.

8996 *Formet* E., El maniqueismo y la escatología de S. AGUSTIN: ⇥ 624, Jornadas 347-375.

8997 *Frohnhofen* Herbert, Reinkarnation und frühe Kirche: StiZt 207 (1989) 236-244.

8998 *a) Ghoos* Jozef, Death in contemporary Christian understanding; – *b) Tavernier* Johan De, Eschatology and social ethics: ⇥ 102, JANSSENS L., Personalist 1988, 213-222 / 279-300.

8999 *Giesen* Heinz, Eschatologie und Naherwartung im Neuen Testament: TPQ 137 (1989) 346-359.

9000 **Giovetti** P., Inchiesta sul Paradiso [televisiva]. Mi 1986, Rizzoli. 237 p. Lit. 16,500. – ᴿProtestantesimo 44 (1989) 78 (P. *De Petris*).

9001 *Góźdź* Krzysztof, ❷ Escatologia nell'avvenimento di Gesù Cristo [... PANNENBERG]: RoczTK 33,2 (1986) 121-132; ital. 132.

9002 **Greshake** Gisbert, Tod — und dann? Ende — Reinkarnation — Auferstehung; der Streit der Hoffnungen: H-Bücherei 1504. FrB 1988, Herder. 93 p. DM 8. – ᴿTPhil 64 (1989) 139s (R. *Sebott*); TR 85 (1989) 311s (W. *Beinert*).

9003 **Greshake** G., *Kremer* J., Resurrectio mortuorum 1986 ➤ 2,7167; 3,9084: ᴿRechSR 77 (1989) 559-561 (B. *Sesboüé*).

9004 **Hällstrom** G., Carnis resurrectio; the interpretation of a credal formula. Helsinki 1988, Finnish Acad. 106 p. [RHPR 69,90].

9005 **Hummel** Reinhart, Reinkarnation; Weltbilder des Reinkarnationsglaubens und das Christentum: Unterscheidung. Mainz/Stu 1988, Grünewald/Quell. 128 p. DM 18,80. 3-7918-2270-5. – ᴿActuBbg 26 (1989) 254s (J. *Boada*); GeistL 62 (1989) 63s (B. *Grom*); TPQ 137 (1989) 109 (J. *Janda*).

9006 *Jones* P., Sauver et détruire; un aspect de l'enseignement biblique sur l'enfer et la vie éternelle: RRéf 39,156 (SGLaye 1988) 41-63 [< NTAbs 33,206].

9007 **Kehl** Medard, Eschatologie 1986 ➤ 2,7179 ... 4,a93: ᴿForumKT 4 (1988) 318 (P. *Schäfer*).

9008 **König** Adrio, The eclipse of Christ in eschatology; toward a Christ-centered approach [Jesus die Laaste 1980]. GR/L 1989, Eerdmans/Marshall-MS. viii-248 p. $17 pa. [TrinJ 10,242]. 0-8028-0356-3 / L 0-551-01922-0.

9009 **Kramer** Kenneth P., The sacred art of dying; how world religions understand death. NY 1988, Paulist. vi-226 p. $12. 0-8091-2942-0. – ᴿETL 65 (1989) 204s (V. *Neckebrouck*: arbitraire; beaucoup sur l'ancienne Mésopotamie, rien sur l'Afrique bien vivante); TsTNijm 29 (1989) 310 (J. H. *Kamstra*).

9010 **Lana Solano** José L., Eschatology and utopia; the relationship between the eschaton and utopia in a historical perspective: diss. Graduate Theological Union. Berkeley 1988. 479 p. 89-06585. – DissA 49 (1988s) 3763-A.

9011 **Lannert** Berthold, Die Wiederentdeckung der neutestamentlichen Eschatologie durch Johannes WEIS: Diss. ᴰ*Berger*. Heidelberg 1988s. – TR 85 (1989) 516; RTLv 21,546.

9012 *Lapide* Pinchas, Apokalypse als Hoffnungstheologie; Anmerkungen zu Ernst BLOCHS 'Prinzip Hoffnung': UnSa 43 (1988) 93-100.

9013 *Le Goff* Jacques, Your money or your life; [Purgatory (p. 92)], economy and religion in the Middle Ages, ᵀ*Ranum* Patricia. CM 1988, MIT. 116 p. $19. – ᴿRelStR 15 (1989) 358 (T. F. X. *Noble*).

9014 *Leuze* Reinhard, Das Ziel der Geschichte — Reinkarnationslehre und christlicher Glaube: ➤ 177, ᶠSCHWARZ R., Von Wittenberg 1989, 190-203.

9015 **Libânio** João B., [Lucchetti] *Bingemer* M. C., Christliche Eschatologie: Bibl. Befreiung. Dü 1987, Patmos. 283 p. DM 44. 3-491-77716-X. – ᴿTierra Nueva 16,64 (1988) 92-96 (B. de *Margerie*); TPhil 64 (1989) 316s (M. *Sievernich*: 'Luchetti'); TsTNijm 29 (1989) 78 (E. *Borgman*).

9016 **Lohmann** Hans, Drohung und Verheissung; exegetische Untersuchungen zur Eschatologie bei den Apostolischen Vätern: BZNW 55. B 1989, de Gruyter. viii-266 p. 3-11-012018-6.

9017 *Lumpe* Adolf, *Bietenhard* Hans, Himmel: ⇒ 904, RAC XV,114 (1989) 173-202.

9018 **Luyten** Norbert A., † 1986, ᴱ*Christoffels* Hildegard, Ewigkeit des Menschen; eine kritische Auseinandersetzung mit den Theorien über das Leben nach dem Tod. FrS 1988, Univ. 189 p. Fs 24. – ᴿMüTZ 40 (1989) 163 (E. *Zwick*); TPQ 137 (1989) 417 (J. *Janda*).

9019 **McDannell** Colleen, *Lang* Bernhard, Heaven, a history 1988 ⇒ 4,a106: ᴿTLond 92 (1989) 438-440 (J. *McManners*); TS 50 (1989) 588s (Z. *Hayes*); TTod 46 (1989s) 209.212 (J. H. *Moorhead*).

9020 *McGuire* E. P., Purgatory, the communion of saints, and medieval change: Viator 20 (1989) 61-64 [RHE 85,101*].

9021 *MacIntosh* J. J., Reincarnation and relativized identity: RelSt 25 (1989) 153-165.

9022 *Mann* Walther, Der Beruf im Lichte letzter Dinge: Luther 19 (1988) 122-131.

9023 **Marcheselli-Casale** Cesare, Risorgeremo, ma come? Risurrezione dei corpi, degli spiriti o dell'uomo? per un contributo allo studio della speculazione apocalittica in epoca greco-romana, II sec. a. C. - II sec. d. C.: RivB supp. 18, 1988 ⇒ 4,a110; Lit. 72.000: ᴿBbbOr 31 (1989) 183-6 (E. *Jucci*).

9024 **Marguerat** Daniel, Vivre avec la mort; le défi du NT. Aubonne 1987, Moulin. 91 p. – ᴿRHPR 69 (1989) 491s (B. *Kaempf*, en relation avec *Müller* D., Réincarnation 1986).

9025 **Marmorstein** Arthur R., Marking well the end; eschatological solutions to dilemmas faced by the ante-Nicene Church: diss. Univ. California, Davis 1988, ᴰ*Spyridakis* S. 269 p. 89-03730. – DissA 49 (1988s) 3839-A.

9026 **Martin-Achard** Robert, La mort en face selon la Bible hébraïque. Genève 1988, Labor et Fides. 136 p. – ᴿÉTRel 64 (1989) 613 (D. *Lys*: auteur de dissertation 'De la mort à la résurrection AT' 1956, et SDB 'Résurrection AT').

9027 **Miller-McLemore** Bonnie J., Death, sin and the moral life; contemporary cultural interpretations of death: diss. Ch (AAR). Atlanta 1988, Scholars. 196 p.; $30; sb./pa. $20. – ᴿTS 50 (1989) 211 (R. M. *Gula*); TTod 46 (1989s) 76s (K. L. *Vaux*).

9028 **Murphy** Maria, New images of the last things; Karl RAHNER on death and life after death. NY 1988, Paulist. 96 p. $7 pa. [Horizons 17, 161, J. J. *Bacik*].

9029 **Nachtwei** Gerhard, Dialogische Unsterblichkeit; eine Untersuchung zu J. RATZINGERS Eschatologie und Theologie: Erfurter TheolSt 54. Lp 1986, St. Benno. xxiv-340 p. – ᴿTPQ 137 (1989) 416s (P. *Schoonenberg*: R., ein 'progressiver' Theologe, der 'konservativ' geworden ist).

9030 *Nayak* Anand, La réincarnation dans les religions I: ÉchSM 19 (1989) 259-270.

9030* *Noemi C.* Juan, Significado teológico de la muerte: TVida 29 (1988) 261-291.

9031 *O'Callaghan* Paul, Hope and freedom in Gabriel MARCEL and Ernst BLOCH: Ir TQ 55 (1989) 215-239.

9032 **Pae Kyung-Sik**, Eschatologie bei Johann T. BECK: ev. Diss. ᴰ*Moltmann* J. Tübingen 1988s. – TR 85 (1989) 518; RTLv 21, p. 538; TLZ 115,76s.

9033 *Pattin* A., Les lendemains de la mort [... philosophie thomiste]: DivThom 91 (1988) 355-360.

9034 *Perrot* C., *al.*, Le retour du Christ 1984 ⇒ 4,a127: ᴿRevSR 61 (1987) 246 (R. *Winling*).

9035 **Phan** Peter C., Eternity in time; a study of Karl RAHNER's eschatology. Cranbury NJ 1988, Susquehanna Univ. 269 p. $35. – ᴿTS 50 (1989) 581-3 (H. D. *Egan*).

9036 *Pignet* Dominique, Immortalité de l'âme ou résurrection de la chair: ÉchSM 19 (1989) 141-9.

9037 **Puente Santidrián** Pablo, La terminología de la Resurrección en TERTULIANO 1987 → 4,a131: ᴿGregorianum 70 (1989) 178s (J. *Galot*).

9038 ᴱ**Raffaelli** R., Rappresentazioni della morte: Letteratura e antropologia 1. Urbino 1987, Quattro Venti. 357 p.; 8 pl. – ᴿRFgIC 117 (1989) 490-5 (M. *Salvadore*).

9039 *Ratschow* Carl-Heinz, Von des Christen Hoffnung: → 105, ᶠKAISER O., Prophet 1989, 173-180.

9040 **Ratzinger** Joseph, Eschatology; death and eternal life [1977 with updating appendices], ᵀ*Waldstein* Michael, 1988→ 4,a132: ᴿNewTR 2,2 (1989) 99-101 (Z. *Hayes*); TS 50 (1989) 583-5 (B. E. *Hinze*).

9041 **Reboux-Caubel** Anne, Peut-on ressusciter? Les chrétiens l'affirment. Et si c'était vrai?: Coll. C'est-à-dire 4. P 1989, Centurion. 124 p. F 54. – ᴿEsprVie 99 (1989) 474 (P. *Jay*).

9042 *a)* *Riga* Peter J., Einige Bedenken gegen die Kremation; – *b*) *Bergsmann* Johann, Positive Erfahrungen mit der Feuerbestattung: TPQ 137 (1989) 176-9 / 179 s.

9043 *a)* *Rolfes* Helmuth, Ars moriendi — eine Sterbekunst aus der Sorge um das Ewige Heil; – *b*) *Barth* Hans-Martin, Leben und sterben können; Brechungen der spätmittelalterlichen 'ars moriendi' in der Theologia M. LUTHERS: → 763, Ars moriendi 1989, 15-44 / 45-66.

9044 **Ruiz de la Peña** J.L., La otra dimensión; escatología cristiana³ʳᵉᵛ: Presencia Teológica 29. Santander 1986, SalTerrae. – ᴿProyección 35 (1988) 74 (J. M. *Hernández*).

9045 *Schmithals* Walter, Eschatologie und Apokalyptik: VerkFor 33 (1988) 64-82.

9046 *a)* *Schneiders* Sandra M., Der Tod in der Gemeinde des ewigen Lebens [< Interpretation 41 (1987) 44-56, ᵀ*Gottfried* Herbert]; – *b*) *Schmied* A., Der Christ vor der Reinkarnationsidee: TGegw 31 (1988) 27-36 / 37-49.

9047 *Schweizer* Eduard, The significance of eschatology in the teaching of Jesus: → 21, ᶠBEASLEY-MURRAY G., Eschatology 1988, 1-13.

9048 *Seifert* Josef, Gibt es ein Leben nach dem Tod? Philosophische Gedanken zur Unsterblichkeit: ForumKT 5 (1989) 241-254.

9049 *Serraima Cirici* Enrique, Reacción del cristiano ante la muerte; dos textos de los Padres de la Iglesia [JERÓNIMO carta 39 a Paula; BERNARDO]: EfMex 7 (1989) 207-223.

9050 *Smith* Wolfgang, The near-death experience; what does it mean? how interpret the contemporary surge of interest?: HomP 88 (1987s) 52-59 [< ZIT 88,633].

9051 **Srohl** Jane E., LUTHER's eschatology; the last times and the last things: diss. ᴰ*Gerrish* B. Chicago 1989. – RelStR 16,191.

9051* **Stanczyk** Stanisław, Konzeptionen der Hölle in der katholischen Theologie im 20. Jh. im deutschen Sprachraum: Diss. Innsbruck ᴰ*Schwager* R 1988s. 251 p. – TR 85 (1989) 512; RTLv 21,571; ZkT 111,522.

9052 *Strle* Anton, [in Slovene] Immortality of soul and thesis on 'resurrection in death': BogVest 47 (1987) 19-41.

9053 *Strobel* A., Weltangst und Weltende [*Körtner* U.]; was Theologie weithin nicht kümmert, aber den Menschen zutiefst beschäftigt: TBei 20,1 (Wu 1989) 23-28.

9054 **Sullivan** Clayton,   Rethinking realized eschatology.   Macon GA 1988, Mercer Univ. $20.   0-86554-302-X. – ᴿBS 146 (1989) 469s (D. L. *Bock*) RExp 86 (1989) 270s (J. E. *Jones*: beating a dead horse? 'Marcan priority has not been disproved, but has suffered a plausibility depletion').

9055 *Szennay* András,   ⓂErwachsenenbildung   in   der   Dimension   der Hoffnung: TBud 22 (1988) 135-7.

9056 **Tatum** William C.,   MOLTMANN's eschatological perspective in relationship to selected doctrines: diss.   Southern Baptist Theol.   Sem., ᴰ*Mueller* D. 1989. 328 p. 89-25775. – DissA 50 (1989s) 2118-A.

9057 **Tornos** A.,   Escatología I: P.U.P.   M 1989, Comillas.   177 p. – ᴿCarthaginensia 5 (1989) 299 (F. *Martínez Fresneda*); RET 49 (1989) 323-8 (E. *Tourón*).

9058 ᴱ**Triacca** A.,   *Pistoia* A.,   Eschatologie et liturgie 1984/5 ↠ 4,640: ᴿWorship 62 (1988) 85s (Mary M. *Schaefer*).

9059 ᴱ**Verbeke** Werner, *al.*,   The use and abuse of eschatology in the Middle Ages ↠ 4,426:   ᴿRBén 99 (1989) 212s (P.-M. *Bogaert*: tit. pp.); TR 85 (1989) 525 (tit. pp.).

9060 **Vernette** Jean,   Réincarnation, résurrection; communiquer avec l'au-delà; les mystères de la vie après la vie. 1988, Salvator.   188 p. F 89. – ᴿÉtudes 370 (1989) 568s (R. *Marlé*); VSp 143 (1989) 500s (H. *Bourgeois*).

9060* *a)* *Vogt* Hermann J.,   Die Exegese des ORIGENES in Contra Celsum; das neue Interesse an der Eschatologie; – *b)* *O'Brien* Denis, L'immortalité chez saint ATHANASE (De incarnatione Verbi cap. 4. 5; PG 25, col. 104B-C): ↠ 696, 10th Patristic 21 (1989) 356-373 / 426-437.

9061 **Wilkens** Steven R.,   The afterlife considered in the light of biblical teaching concerning the resurrection of the body: diss. Fuller Theol. Sem., ᴰ*Brown* C. Pasadena 1988. 322 p. 88-16097. – DissA 49 (1988s) 1856-A.

9062 *Williams* Arthur H.,   Theology in an eschatological matrix: ScotJT 42 (1989) 289-302.

9063 *Williams* Stephen N.,   On giving hope in a suffering world; response to MOLTMANN: ↠ 544, Issues 1987/9, 3-19.

9064 ᴱ**Xella** P.,   Archeologia dell'inferno 1987↠ 3,844:   ᴿProtestantesimo 44 (1989) 49 (J. A. *Soggin*).

9065 *Zung Tae-Hyoun*,   ⓈThe eschatology of Jesus [*Lee Whan-Zin*, OT]: Samok 119 (Seoul 1988) 23-30 [16-22; < TContext 6/2, 45].

H9.5   *Theologia totius [V] NT* –   **General [O] NT Theology.**

9066 **Baumann** Rolf,   'Gottes Gerechtigkeit' — Verheissung und Herausforderung für diese Welt: Tb 1643.   FrB 1989, Herder.   253 p. DM 16. – ᴿBibel Heute 25 (Stu 1989) 94 (N. *Lohfink*: Bibelbuch zum Zentralthema des 'konziliaren Prozesses').

9067 **Beeck** Franz J. Van,   God encountered: a contemporary Catholic systematic theology 1 [of 3]. SF 1989, Harper & R.   xiii-338 p. $28. – ᴿHorizons 16 (1989) 388s (J. A. *Colombo*).

9068 **Bouyer** Louis,   Cosmos; the world and the glory of God [fourth and final volume on economy of salvation], ᵀ*Fontnouvelle* Pierre de.   Petersham MA 1988, St. Bede.   xii-274 p. $18.   0-932506-66-6 [TDig 36,355].

9069 *Casas García* Victorino,   Dios nos salva por Jesucristo; aspectos teológicos del Nuevo Testamento.   M 1989, S. Pio X.   199+43 p. – ᴿBibFe 15 (1989) 318 (A. *Salas*); VerVid 47 (1989) 363 (C. *Bermejo*).

9070 *Donahue* John R.,   The changing shape of New Testament theology: TS 50 (1989) 314-335.

9071 **Dunn** James D. G., *Mackey* James P., New Testament theology in dialogue; Christology and ministry 1987 ➤ 3,9161; 4,a156: – ᴿCBQ 51 (1989) 740s (Lauree H. *Meyer*); Pacifica 2 (1969) 238-240 (C. *Mostert*).

9072 **Dwyer** John C., The Word was made flesh; an introduction to the theology of the New Testament. KC 1989, Sheed & W. viii-152 p. $11 pa. 1-55612-251-9 [TDig 37,155].

9072* *Fuller* Reginald H., New Testament theology: ➤ 394, NT/Interpreters 1989, 565-584.

9073 **Gnilka** Joachim, Neutestamentliche Theologie; ein Überblick: NEchter Egb 1. Wü 1989, Echter. 158 p. DM 32 [CBQ 52,381].

9074 *Kampling* Rainer, Exegese und Theologie des Neuen Testaments — Randbemerkungen zu einem problematischen Verhältnis: TGL 79 (1989) 107-113.

9075 **Kegel** Günter, Und ich sah einen neuen Himmel und eine neue Erde; das NT und die Heilung der Welt [... Neuansatz der Theologie, S. 46]. Gü 1988, Mohn. 319 p. DM 78. – ᴿTLZ 114 (1989) 893s (W. *Vogler*).

9076 **Kudasiewicz** J., ⓞ Teologia Nowego Testamentu, 1. ewangelii synoptycznych. Lublin 1986, KUL. 120 p. zł 300. 83-222-0067-3 [NTAbs 33,108].

9077 **Ladd** George E., Theology of the NT 1974➤ 56,6300 (franc. 1984 ➤ 1,8733): ᴿTSzem 32 (1989) 60-62 (L. *Muzsnai*).

9078 **Langkammer** Hugolin, ⓞ Teologia Nowego Testamentu I 1985; II 1984➤ 3,8774s: ᴿRoczTK 33,1 (1986) 132-4 (R. *Rubinkiewicz*).

9079 **Lohse** Éduard, Théologie du NT [1974, ³1984], ᵀ*Jundt* Pierre: MondeB, 1987 ➤ 4,a158: ᴿBLitEc 90 (1989) 63s (S. *Légasse*); RHPR 69 (1989) 217-9 (J.-C. *Ingelaere*).

9080 **McCurley** Foster R., *Reumann* John, Witness of the Word; a biblical theology of the Gospel 1986 ➤ 2,7232; 3,9170: ᴿBibTB 19 (1989) 112 (C. C. *Black*); RExp 86 (1989) 623 (Molly *Marshall-Green*).

9081 **McKenzie** Peter, The Christians, their beliefs and practices [UK: 'practices and beliefs']. L/Nv 1988, SPCK/Abington. xiii-345 p. £15 pa. 0-687-07661-7. – ᴿExpTim 100 (1988s) 159 (R. *Gill*: an adaptation of F. HEILER's untranslated Phenomenology of Religion); TLond 92 (1989) 212-4 (G. *D'Costa*: a must).

9081* *McNamara* Martin, Celtic Christianity; creation and apocalypse, Christ and Antichrist ['title sufficiently broad to embrace the entire presentation of Christianity', p. 5]: MilltSt 23 (1989) 5-39.

9082 **Malmede** Hans, Die Lichtsymbolik im NT: Studies in Oriental Religions 15, 1986 ➤ 3,9171: ᴿCarthaginensia 5 (1989) 276s (R. *Sanz Valdivieso*).

9082* *Meier* J. P., The Bible as a source for theology: PrCTSAm 43 (1988) 1-14: J. SOBRINO never really engages the basic problems of Jesus-research, and his treatment of Jesus is socioeconomically naive; J. SEGUNDO's reconstruction of history is dictated by his desires ...]; p. 15-18, response by J. *Nilson*.

9083 *Merk* Otto, Gesamtbiblische Theologie; zum Fortgang der Diskussion in den 80er Jahren: VerkFor 33 (1988) 19-40.

9084 *Moore* M. K., A theology of light from the words of Jesus: Kardia 2 (Portland OR 1986) 43-55 [< NTAbs 33, 15].

9085 **Morris** Leon, NT theology 1986 ➤ 2,7234; 4,a162: ᴿCriswT 2 (1987s) 173s (D. L. *Turner*); ScotBEvT 7 (1989) 59s (J. *Proctor*); WestTJ 50 (1988) 200-6 (D. E. *Johnson*).

9086 **Panimolle** Salvatore A., La libertà cristiana; teologia sapienziale [NT]. Vaticano 1988, ed. 228 p. Lit. 20.000. 88-209-1653-2 [NTAbs 33,408].

H9.5 General New Testament theology 557

9087 **Pannenberg** Wolfhart, Systematische Theologie I. Gö 1988, Vandenhoeck & R. 515 p. DM 98. – ᴿScotJT 42 (1989) 401-3 (S. *Grenz*); TGʟ 79 (1989) 90s (W. *Beinert*).
9088 La proclamación del mensaje cristiano [IV Simp. 1986] 1986. – ᴿRET 49 (1989) 336-8 (F. de *Carlos Otto*).
9089 *Riches* J., Biblical theology and the pressing concerns of the Church: Modern Churchman 30,3 (Leominster 1988) 6-12 [< NTAbs 33,341].
9090 **Segalla** Giuseppe, Panorama teologico NT: LoB 3.7, 1987 ➤ 3,9178; 4,a167: ᴿStPatav 36 (1989) 213s (A. *Moda*).
9091 **Siegwalt** Gérard, Dogmatique pour la catholicité évangélique I-II, 1986s➤ 3,6581; 4,a168: ᴿIstina 34 (1989) 236-8 (B. *Dupuy*); TLZ 114 (1989) 303s (F. *Heyer*).
9092 *a*) *Tamayo-Acosta* Juan J., El hombre de hoy ante los valores religiosos; – *b*) *Folgado Flórez* Segundo, ... ante los valores trascendentes; – *c*) *Torres* Julio, ... ante la injusticia; – *d*) *González Ruiz* José M., ... ante la posmodernidad; – *e*) *Salas* Antonio, ... ante su destino; – *f*) bibliog.: BibFe 15,44 (1989) 176-205 / 206-232 / 233-258 / 259-278 / 279-314 / 315s.
9093 **VanDevelder** F. R., The biblical journey of faith; the road of the sojourner. Ph 1988, Fortress. 126 p. $9. 0-8006-2318-5 [NTAbs 33,268].

XVI. **Philologia biblica**

Jl **Hebraica** .1 *grammatica*.

9094 **Andersen** F., *Forbes* A., Spelling in the Hebrew Bible: BibOrPont 41, 1986 ➤ 2,2742 ... 4,a172: ᴿScripTPamp 21 (1989) 345 (S. *Ausín*: ignores copyists' role).
9095 **Barr** James, The variable spellings of the Hebrew Bible: Schweich Lectures. Ox 1989, Univ. for British Academy. 239 p. £27.50 [TR 85,250]. 0-19-726068-3.
9096 *Barr* James, 'Determination' and the definite article in biblical Hebrew: ➤ 200, ᶠULLENDORFF E., JSS 34 (1989) 307-335.
9097 **Benoit** L. de, Première découverte de l'hébreu biblique. St-Légier 1986, Emmaüs. 102 p. – ᴿSTEv 11,21 (1988) 155s (P. *Bolognesi*).
9098 **Döhmer** Klaus, Die Affixe des Hebräischen in alphabetischer Darstellung 1988 ➤ 4,a180: ᴿBeiNam 24 (1989) 461 (H.-P. *Müller*); TüTQ 169 (1989) 70s (W. *Gross*); VT 39 (1989) 121s (G. I. *Davies*); ZAW 101 (1989) 313s (H. W. *Hoffmann*).
9099 **Eckardt** Walter, Computergestützte Analyse althebräischer Texte; algorithmische Erkennung der Morphologie [program SALOMO = Searching algorithm on morphology]: AOtt 29, 1987 ➤ 3,9193: ᴿCBQ 51 (1989) 320s (S. *Segert*).
9100 **Garr** W. Randall, Dialect geography of Syria-Palestine 1000-586 B.C., 1985 ➤ 1,8791*b* ... 4,a185: ᴿTLZ 114 (1989) 179s (H.-J. *Zobel*).
9101 **Gross** Walter, Die Pendenskonstruktion 1987 ➤ 3,9197; 4,a186: ᴿCarthaginensia 5 (1989) 271s (R. *Sanz Valdivieso*); CBQ 51 (1989) 326-9 (D. *Pardee*: 5 proposals for improvement); OLZ 84 (1989) 561s (Jutta *Körner*); RÉJ 148 (1989) 160s (J. *Margain*); TLZ 114 (1989) 506-8 (H. *Schweizer*: easy to get used to, e.g. Gn 13,15 = (...) 'at + {**NGr** ... 3 e **PP**} // **PV + V + e PP [O*]** (...) –; WeltOr 20s (1989s) 312-5 (J. A. *Naudé*: some inconsistencies).

9101* **Grossmann** Hans-Christoph,   Grundriss der hebräischen Grammatik:
    Fra 1988, Haag & H.   81 p. [Mundus 25,55].
9102 **Hamilton** Jeffries M.,   *Rogers* Jeffrey S.,   A grammar for biblical
    Hebrew; Handbook, answer keys and study guide. Nv 1989, Abingdon.
    iv-104 p.   0-687-15685-8 [OIAc N89].
9103 **Kittel** Bonnie P., *al.*,   Biblical Hebrew, a text and workbook.   NHv
    1989, Yale Univ.   xxiii-429. $21 + cassette $10.   0-300-04394-5. – [BL 90,
    148, H. G. M. *Williamson*: sumptuous and user-friendly, but better to
    plagiarize than to use].
9104 **Köhn** Rosemarie,   Hebraisk grammatikk³ 1988 ➤ 4,a192:   ᴿSvTKv 65
    (1989) 34s (S. *Norin*).
9105 **La Maisonneuve** Sr. Dominique de,   L'hébreu biblique par les textes [Jg
    13; 1 Sam 3; Gn 22; Ex 3,22]; I. Analyse, commentaires, précis de
    grammaire, lexique. P. 1988, Desclée.   268 p.   2-7189-0387-2.   – ᴿÉTRel
    64 (1989) 429 (D. *Bourguet*: le cobaye l'a trouvé difficile); NRT 111 (1989)
    938 (J.-L. *Ska*); RB 96 (1988) 413-5 (J. *Margain*, sévère sur 30 lacunes
    ou erreurs).
9106 **Levi** Jaakov,   Die Inkongruenz im biblischen Hebräisch 1987 ➤ 3,9209;
    4,a193; Diss. Heidelberg: ᴿJBL 108 (1989) 499-501 (G. A. *Rendsburg*);
    JSS 34 (1989) 197s (P. *Wernberg-Møller*); ZAW 101 (1989) 161 (H. W.
    Hoffmann).
9107 **Martins Ramos** José Augusto,   O sufixo verbal não-acusativo em
    hebraico antigo no contexto semítico do noroeste: diss. ᴰ*Augusto Tavares*
    A. Lisboa 1988.   572 p.
9108 **Meyer** Rudolf,   Gramática de la lengua hebrea [c. 1969], ᵀ*Sáenz-Badillos*
    Ángel. Barc 1989, Riopedras.   490 p. – ᴿCiTom 116 (1989) 627s (M.
    García Cordero).
9109 **Niccacci** Alviero,   Sintassi del verbo ebraico 1986 ➤ 62,8716... 3,9213:
    ᴿAbrNahrain 27 (1989) 187-193 (T. *Muraoka*: stimulating).
9109* *Niccacci* Alviero,   An outline of the Hebrew verbal system in prose: LA
    39 (1989) 7-26.
9110 *Omanson* Roger L.,   What's in a name [list of people and place names
    with meaning for the narrative]: BTrans 40 (1989) 109-119 [416-9, further
    on Lazarus and Simon; further 447, J. *Sterk* on popular etymology].
9111 **Parker** C. Halder,   Biblical Hebrew, an exegetical approach 1987
    ➤ 4,a198:   C$22.   0-919741-66-5:   ᴿExpTim 100 (1988s) 29 (C. S. *Rodd*).
9112 **Qimron** Elisha,   The Hebrew of the Dead Sea Scrolls 1986 ➤ 2,7262...
    4,a199*: ᴿBO 46 (1989) 445-7 (A. *Vivian*); JNES 48 (1989) 143-5 (M. O.
    Wise: indispensable); JSS 34 (1989) 205s (P. *Wernberg-Møller*); OLZ 84
    (1989) 430-2 (J. *Körner*).
9113 *Revell* E. J.,   a) The system of the verb in standard biblical prose:
    HUCA 60 (1989) 1-37; – b) The conditioning of word order in verbless
    clauses in biblical Hebrew: JSS 34 (1989) 1-24.
9114 **Richter** Wolfgang,   Grundlagen einer althebräischen Grammatik I-III
    1978-80 ➤ 60,a173... 64,7832:   ᴿKirSef 61 (1986s) 919-924 (J. *Blau* ❸).
9115 **Seow** C. L.,   A grammar for biblical Hebrew 1987 ➤ 3,9224:   ᴿJBL 108
    (1989) 117s (J. B. *Burns*).
9116 *Stern* Naftali,   The infinitive as a complement of a predicate of
    incomplete predication: HebAnR 10 (1986) 337-349.
9117 **Waldman** Nahum M.,   The recent study of Hebrew; a survey of the
    literature with selected bibliography: Bibliographica Judaica [0067-6853]
    10. Cincinnati/Winona Lake IN 1989, HUC / Eisenbrauns.   xx-464 p.
    0-87820-908-5 [OIAc Ja90].

9118 **Wallace** Constance V., Broken and double plural formations in the Hebrew Bible: diss. NYU 1988, ᴰ*Gordon* C. H. 141 p. 89-10613. – DissA 50 (1989s) 125-A.

9118* *Westermann* Claus, Bedeutung und Funktion des Imperativs in den Geschichtsbüchern des Alten Testaments: ➤ 45, ᶠDEISSLER A., Weg 1989, 13-27.

9119 **Zuber** Beat, Das Tempussystem 1986 ➤ 1,8822... 4,a209: ᴿOLZ 84 (1989) 186-9 (J. *Körner*); RHPR 69 (1989) 196s (J. de *Waard*: à corriger et compléter).

J1.2 Lexica et inscriptiones hebraicae; later Hebrew.

9120 **Alonso Schökel** Luis [*Morla* V., *Collado* V., *Esquivias* J., *Bretón* S., *al.*], Diccionario bíblico hebreo-español, one of five new Hebrew dictionaries being prepared [Gesenius/*Meyer-Donner*; *Clines* in Sheffield and *Roberts* in Philadelphia; *Reymond* at Lausanne: ZAltH report on SBL 1989 meeting].

9120* **Andersen** F. I., Forbes A. D., The vocabulary of the OT. R 1989, Pontifical Biblical Institute. viii-721 p. Lit. 73.500. [ZAW 102, 295, H. W. *Hoffmann*].

9121 **Avishur** Yitzhak, Stylistic studies of word-pairs in biblical and ancient Semitic literatures: AOAT 210, 1984 ➤ 65,5711... 3,9239: ᴿCBQ 51 (1989) 512-4 (M. L. *Barré*); JAOS 109 (1989) 684s (D. *Marcus*).

9121* *a)* **Bar-Asher** Moshe, *b)* *Morag* Shelomo, *c)* *Sharvit* Shimon, ❽ The study of Mishnaic Hebrew: ➤ 564*, 9th Congress, 1985/8, B2, 3-37 / 39-53 / 61-73.

9122 **Bat-El** Outi, Phonology and word structure in modern Hebrew: diss. UCLA 1989, ᴰ*Anderson* S. 219 p. 89-12841. – DissA 50 (1989s) 935-A.

9122* *Bothma* T. J. D., Computerized syntactic data bases in the Semitic languages: JSem 1 (1989) 23-38.

9123 *Broshi* Magen, *Qimron* Elisha, ❽ An I. O. U. note from the time of the Bar Kokhba revolt: ➤ 218, Mem. YADIN Y., ErIsr 20 (1989) 246-261; 2 fig.; Eng. 204* and > IsrEJ.

9124 *Eilers* Wilhelm †, Zu Resch als Wurzeldeterminativ (*r-*): OrSuec [23s (1984) 215-230, *Kechrida* H.] 36s (1987s) 38-45.

9124* *Eldar* Ilan, Description aéro-cinétique des voyelles a, u, i en hébreu [d'après des grammaires médiévales]: Orientalia 58 (1989) 525-532.

9125 *a)* *Eldar* Ilan, ❽ Pronunciation traditions of Hebrew; – *b)* *Gamliel* Chanoch, ❽ The verb-system in an old Yemenite manuscript; – *c)* *Dodi* Amos, ❽ A morphological study of verba primae alef in Targum Onqelos; – *d)* *Mishor* Mordechay, ❽ Ashkenazi traditions; toward a method of research: Massorot 3s (1989) 3-36; Eng. ix-x / 37-71; Eng. x / 73-86; Eng. xi-xii / 87-127; Eng. xii.

9126 **Elwolde** John F., Aspects of the collocational analysis of meaning with special reference to some biblical Hebrew anatomical idioms: diss. Hull 1987. 508 p. BRDX-85382. – DissA 50 (1989s) 676-A.

9127 *a)* *Eph'al* Israel, *Naveh* Joseph, Hazael's booty inscriptions [from Samos and Eritrea]; *b)* *Barkay* Gabriel, Another palaeo-Hebrew ossuary inscription: IsrEJ 39 (1989) 192-200; 2 fig.; pl. 25-26 / 201-3; 2 fig.

9128 *Faber* Alice, On the nature of proto-Semitic *L [only phonological; relation to *š*...]: JAOS 109 (1989) 33-36.

9129 *a)* ᴱ**Fohrer** Georg, *Hoffmann* Hans W., *al.*, Hebräisches und aramäisches Wörterbuch zum Alten Testament²ʳᵉᵛ. B 1989, de Gruyter. xii-331 p. 3-

11-012112-3. – *b*) **Fohrer** Georg, ᵀᴱ*Krüger* René, Diccionario del hebreo y arameo bíblicos. Buenos Aires 1982, Aurora. 345 p. – ᴿRBíbArg 51 (1989) 251s (H.-H. *Mallau*).

9130 **Fowler** Jeaneane D., Theophoric personal names in ancient Hebrew ➤ 4,a221 [diss. Liverpool, ᴰ*Millard* A.]: JStOT Sup 49, 1988: ᴿExpTim 100 (1988s) 231 (M. E. J. *Richardson*); OTAbs 12 (1989) 328s (J. F. *Wimmer*); SvTKv 65 (1989) 32-34 (S. *Norin*); VT 39 (1989) 246-8 (J. A. *Emerton*: serious criticisms); ZAW 101 (1989) 458 (H. C. *Schmitt*).

9131 *Garr* W. Randall, The *seghol* and segholation in Hebrew: JNES 48 (1989) 109-116.

9132 **Glinert** Lewis, The grammar of modern Hebrew. C 1989, Univ. xxviii-580 p. 0-521-25611-9.

9133 *a*) *Glinert* Lewis, A unified framework for identity and similarity structures: Israeli Hebrew *kmo*; – *b*) *Berman* Ruth A., The role of blends in modern Hebrew word-formation; ➤ 30, Mem. BLANC H. 1989, 104-9 / 45-61.

9134 **Greenspahn** F. E., Hapax legomena in biblical Hebrew ᴰ1984 ➤ 65,7726 … 3,9255: ᴿAulaO 7,1 (1989) 134-6 (G. del *Olmo Lete*); TLZ 114 (1989) 347s (Jutta *Körner*).

9135 *Hoberman* Robert D., Initial consonant clusters in Hebrew and Aramaic [... *še*ᵗ*tayim* is the only word in Hebrew with dagesh after (initial) *še*wa]: JNES 48 (1989) 25-29 (*štayim* was original, also *šnayim*; also Syriac *štā*, '6').

9136 *Hookerman* Yaᶜaqov, ⊕ Biblical etymological notes 15: BethM 34,121 (1989s) 131-7.

9137 *Ilan* Tal, Notes on the distribution of Jewish women's names in Palestine in the Second Temple and Mishnaic periods: JJS 40 (1989) 186-200.

9138 *Israel* Felice, Studi di lessico ebraico epigrafico I; i materiali del nord: LOrA 2 (1989) 37-67.

9139 **Jobin** Gérard, Concordance des particules cooccurrentes de la Bible Hébraïque [noted in margins of Leningrad ms]: JudUmw 25. Fra 1988, Lang. xxv-14 p. Fs 43. 3-631-41818-3 [BL 90, 147, J. C. L. *Gibson*: odd but significant].

9140 **Khan** G., Studies in Semitic syntax [... casus pendens]: London Oriental Series 38. Ox 1988, UP. xxxix-252 p. £37.50. 0-19-713607-9 [BL 90, 147, J. C. L. *Gibson*].

9141 **Klein** E., A comprehensive etymological dictionary of the Hebrew language for readers of English. NY/L 1987, Macmillan/Collier. xix-721 p. $90. 0-032-917431-7 [NTAbs 33,130: he is author of 1966 Comprehensive Etymological Dictionary of the English Language].

9141* *Lemaire* A., Les inscriptions palestiniennes d'époque perse; un bilan provisoire: TEuph 1 (1989) 87-105 [< ZAW 102,434].

9142 *Merkin* Reuven, *al.*, The historical dictionary of the Hebrew language: LitLComp 4 (Ox 1989) 271-3.

9143 [*Gesenius* W., ¹⁷*Buhl* F.] ¹⁸**Meyer** R., *Donner* H., Hebräisches und aramäisches Handwörterbuch zum AT 1, 1987 ➤ 4,a232: ᴿBiblica 70 (1989) 413-6 (A. *Gianto*); BL (1989) 150 (D. J. A. *Clines*: ought to be now an outright dictionary of *all* attested ancient Hebrew); TLZ 114 (1989) 659-662 (R. *Stahl*); VT 39 (1989) 104-110 (J. A. *Emerton*); ZkT 111 (1989) 94s (J. M. *Oesch*).

9144 **Mozeson** Isaac E., The word; the dictionary that reveals the Hebrew source of English. NY 1989, Shapolsky. [viii-] 310 p. 0-933503-44-X.

9145 **Murtonen** A., [Non-masoretic] Hebrew in its West Semitic setting I-A: StSemLLing 13, 1986 ➤ 2,7306; 4,a235: ᴿBO 46 (1989) 686s (C. van der *Merwe*); JAOS 109 (1989) 295-7 (A.S. *Kaye*). JStJud 20 (1989) 246-8 (E. *Qimron*: not comprehensive, and other defects for a work of this importance).

9146 *a*) *Nathan* Hayya, ⊕ Did Mishnaic Hebrew lose the distinction between the pronominal suffixes of the third person feminine singular and plural?: – *b*) *Zurawel* Talma, The Qal conjugation in Samaritan Hebrew: Massorot 1 (1984) 121-134 / 135-151.

9147 *Ratshabi* Yehuda, ⊕ Biblical names for human private parts: BethM 34,121 (1989s) 192-6.

9148 *Revell* E.J., The Tiberian reflexes of short *i in closed syllables: JAOS 109 (1989) 183-203.

9149 **Sáenz-Badillos** A., Historia de la lengua hebrea: Estud. Or. 2. Sabadell 1988, AUSA. 362 p. – ᴿAulaO 7,1 (1989) 143-5 (J.R. *Magdalena Nom de Déu*).

9150 **Sagarin** James L., Hebrew noun patterns 1987 ➤ 3,9279: ᴿBijdragen 50 (1989) 337 (F. De *Meyer*); JAOS 109 (1989) 118s (A.S. *Kaye*).

9151 **Sidi** Smadar S., The complete book of Hebrew baby names. SF 1989, Harper & R. xii-176 p. 0-06-254850-6.

9152 *Simon* Marie, [Leopold] ZUNZ als Begründer der Onomastik im Rahmen der Wissenschaft des Judentums: Kairos 30s (1988s) 121-132.

9153 *Sirat* Colette, Les papyrus en caractères hébraïques trouvés en Égypte 1985 ➤ 1,8858 ... 3,9286*: ᴿJEA 75 (1989) 297 (J.B. *Segal*).

9154 *Sivan* Daniel, Biblical Hebrew roots and quiescents according to Judah HAYYUJ's grammatical works: HUCA 60 (1989) 115-127.

9155 **Sperber** Daniel, A dictionary of Greek and Latin legal terms in rabbinic literature 1984 ➤ 65,7744; 2,7320: ᴿJStJud 20 (1989) 195-206 (R. *Katzoff*).

9156 *Stamm* Johann J., Bericht über den Stand der Arbeit an der 3. Auflage des hebräischen und aramäischen Wörterbuches von Ludwig KOEHLER und Walter BAUMGARTNER, mit einem Rückblick auf die 1. und 2. Auflage: TZBas 45 (1989) 277-289.

9157 **Stioul** Roger, Yissud ha-'ibbur [basis of intercalation], le calendrier hébreux. P 1988, Colbo. 259 p. – ᴿRÉJ 148 (1989) 162s (G. *Nahon* gives title first in Hebrew, but no further indication whether this 'clear presentation' is in French).

9158 *Tsereteli* Konstantin, ⊕ A lexical opposition in Semitic languages: ➤ 126, ᶠMACUCH R., Ḥokmôt 1989, 343-351.

9158* *Vriezen* K., Wegen en wegaanleg; opmerkingen naar aanleiding van het vocabulaire in de Profeten en de Geschriften: ➤ 116, ᶠLEEUWEN C. van 1989, 129-132.

9159 **Wexler** Paul, Explorations in Judeo-Slavic linguistics: Contributions to the Sociology of Jewish Language 2. Leiden 1987, Brill. xix-286 p. – ᴿRÉJ 148 (1989) 169s (J. *Margain*).

9160 **Zadok** Ran, The pre-Hellenistic Israelite anthroponymy and prosopography: OrLovAn 28. Lv 1988, Peeters. xxv-465 p. 90-6831-120-4.

J1.3 Voces ordine alphabetico *consonantium* hebraicarum.

9161 ***abba*:** *VanGemeren* W., Abba in the OT: JEvTS 31 (1988) 385-398 [< ZAW 102, 130].

9162 *'ôb:* **Jeffers** Steven L., The cultural power of words; occult terminology [words for witch, magician] in the Hebrew, Greek, Latin and English Bibles: diss. Florida State, ᴰ*Darst* D. 1989. 282 p. 90-12918. – DissA 50 (1989s) 3984-A.

9163 *'ôr:* **Reece** William D., The concept of light in the OT, a semantic analysis: diss. UCLA 1989, ᴰ*Segert* S. 242 p. 89-06133. – DissA 49 (1988s) 3707s-A.

9164 *eḥad: Lund* Jerome A., Syntax of 'One' ... Amoraic Aramaic: JAOS [106 (1986) 413-423] 108 (1988) 211-7.

9165 *êk: Hyman* Ronald T., The multiple functions of 'how' in the Tanakh: JBQ (= Dor) 18 (1989s) 84-91.

'el scambiato con *'al* (*min* con *bᵉ* ecc.) in Cron.: *Lorenzin* T. ⇒ 2887.

9166 *amēn: Cohen* N. J., Analysis of an exegetic tradition in the Mekhilta de-Rabbi ISHMAEL; the meaning of *'amanah* in the second and third centuries: AJS 9,1 (CM 1984) 1-25 [< NTAbs 33,79].

9167 *'rk:* **Richter** Wolfgang, Untersuchungen zur Valenz I. 'rk; II. ... 1985s ⇒ 1,8957 ... 4,a247.a257: ᴿCBQ 51 (1989) 347-9 (S. D. *Sperling*); REJ 148 (1989) 158s (J. *Margain*).

9168 *ēš:* **Morla Asensio** V., El fuego en el AT 1988 ⇒ 4,a249: ᴿNRT 111 (1989) 935-7 (J.-L. *Ska:* une acribie qui force l'admiration).

9168* *Kienast* Burkhart, The Old Assyrian *be'alātum* ['pledge-loan' rather than 'available capital']: JCS 41 (1989) 87-95.

9169 *bārak:* **Mitchell** Christopher W., The meaning of brk ... [diss. Wisconsin 1983, ᴰ*Fox* M.]: SBL diss. 95, 1987 ⇒ 3,9307; 4,a254: ᴿCBQ 51 (1989) 528s (D. H. *Little*).

9170 *ga'al: Cimosa* Mario, '*Go'ēl ha-dām,* vendicatore del sangue' nella traduzione greca dei LXX e in alcune traduzioni moderne: ⇒ 759, Sangue VI, 1987/9, 719-739.

9171 *gmn: Watson* W. E., What does Ugaritic *gmn* mean? [mourning]: AulaO 7,1 (1989) 129-131.

9172 *dam: Raineri* Osvaldo, *a) Dam* (sangue) in alcuni testi etiopici di lingue semitiche; – *b)* (con *Tedla da Hebo* Agostino) La voce *dam* (sangue) nell'uso corrente della lingua tigrina: ⇒ 759, Sangue VI, 1987/9, 207-308 / 309-322.

9172* *dôr: Steiner* Gerd, Die Dauer einer 'Generation' nach den Vorstellungen des Alten Orients: ⇒ 831*, High/Low III (1989) 170-196: 35 (-40) years.

9173 *dāraš:* **Deshayes** Henry † 13.X.1988, Chercher Dieu dans la Bible. P 1989, Letouzey & A. xii-195 p. F 120. 2-7063-0174-0.

9174 *zākar: mazkir, sōpēr, śar* ...: **Rüterswörden** U., Beamter: ⇒ 902, NBL, Lfg. 2 (1989) 252-4.

9175 *z̄'q/ṣ'q:* **Boyce** Richard N., The cry to God in the OT: SBL diss 103, 1988 ⇒ 4,8009: ᴿRB 96 (1989) 603-5 (J. *Loza*).

9175* *ḥesed:* **Sakenfeld** Katharine D., Faithfulness in action 1985 ⇒ 1,8893; 2,7345: ᴿCriswT 1 (1987) 411s (G. L. *Klein*).

9176 *yāda':* **Westhuizen** J. P. van der, Three nuances of sexual intercourse: *yada'* – *ba' el* – *šakab im*: JBQ (= Dor) 18 (1989s) 92-100.

9177 *Yāwān:* **Brinkman** J. A., The Akkadian words for 'Ionia' [*yawan(u)*] and 'Ionian': ⇒ 175, Mem. SCHODER R., Daidalikon 1989, 53-71.

9178 *yārā':* **Costacurta** Bruna, La vita minacciata; il tema della paura nella Bibbia Ebraica: AnBib 119, 1988 ⇒ 4,a264: ᴿBL (1989) 102 (J. R. *Porter*); Gregorianum 70 (1989) 400s (*ipsa*); NRT 111 (1989) 937s (J.-L.

Ska: maîtrise); OTAbs 12 (1989) 212 (C. T. *Begg*); TXav 39 (1989) 256; ZAW 101 (1989) 312 (J. A. *Soggin*: Übersetzung erwünscht).

9178* **yāšēn: McAlpine** Thomas H., Sleep, divine and human, in the OT 1987 ➔ 3,9138*: ᴿEvQ 61 (1989) 88 (R. W. L. *Moberly*).

9179 **kābôd: Struppe** Ursula, Die Herrlichkeit Jahwes in der Priesterschrift; eine semantische Studie zu *kᵉbod* YHWH [Diss. W 1984] 1988 ➔ 4,a270: ᴿBL (1989) 93 (A. D. H. *Mayes*); CBQ 51 (1989) 731-3 (R. *Gnuse*); NRT 111 (1989) 577s (J. L. *Ska*); RB 96 (1989) 607s (J. *Loza*); TLZ 114 (1989) 104-6 (Jutta *Körner*).

9180 **kābîr:** *Gosse* Bernard, L'emploi de *kbyr* dans le livre d'Isaïe, un problème de méthodologie [Is 10,13H; 16,14; 17,12; 28,2 liés entre eux; ailleurs seul Job]: BZ 33 (1989) 259s.

9181 **kîdōn:** *Heltzer* M., Akkadian *katinnu* and Hebrew *kîdōn*, 'sword': JCS 41 (1989) 65-68.

9181* **kāpal:** *Kline* Meredith J., Double trouble [the Greek and Hebrew terms rendered 'double' should be 'equivalent']: JEvTS 32 (1989) 171-189 [< ZAW 102,279].

kisse ...: **Nam Daegeuk,** The 'throne of God' motif in the Hebrew Bible: ᴰ1989 ➔ 7026.

9182 **krṣ:** *Mayer* Walter, *Kirṣītum* 'abgeschlossenes Gebäude' – kein Phantomwort: UF 21 (1989) 269s.

9183 **lᵉ: Pinto León** Adolfo, Lamed y sus relaciones; indicaciones para su traducción [diss. Pont. Ist. Biblico 1989s, ᴰ*Alonso Schökel* L.]. R 1989. 126 p. (estratto) [ActaPIB 9,481.517].

9184 **lō': Whitney** G. E., **L'** ('not') as 'not yet' in the Hebrew Bible: Hebrew Studies 29 (Madison WI 1988) 43-48 [< OTAbs 12,263].

9185 **lô[']: Ognibeni** [➔ 4,2547!] Bruno, Tradizioni orali di lettura e testo ebraico della Bibbia; studio dei diciassette ketiv L'/qere LW: Studia Friburgensia NS 72. FrS 1989, Univ. xvii-274 p. Fs 38. 2-8271-0426-1 [BL 90,148, A. *Gelston*]. – ᴿLA 39 (1989) 340-6 (A. *Mello*).

9186 **Lwt:** *Margain* Jean, Note sur *lwt* et *lyd* dans le Targum samaritain: ➔ 126, ꟻMACUCH R., Ḥokmôt 1989, 161-5.

9187 **mah:** *Khan* Geoffrey, The pronunciation of *mah-* before *dageš* in the medieval Tiberian Hebrew reading tradition: ➔ 200, ꟻULLENDORFF E., JSS 34 (1989) 433-441.

9188 **melek:** *Renger* Johann, Zur Wurzel MLK in akkadischen Texten aus Syrien und Palästina: ➔ 831, Eblaite names 1985/8, 165-172.

9189 **Miṣrayim:** *Fontinoy* Charles, Les noms de l'Égypte en hébreu et leur étymologie: ➔ 204, Mém. WALLE B. van de, CdÉ 64 (1989) 90-97.

9190 **mrq,** *tmryq* (Prov. 20,30) 'Kränkung': ZaltH 2 (1989) 81-82 (W. von *Soden*).

9191 **mṯḥ:** *Sanmartín* J., Glossen zum ugaritischen Lexikon (VI) [*mṯḥ*, **ṯeḥû*; *mqdm d nyn*; *nʿr*, *nṯq*, *ṯrtn*]: UF 21 (1989) 335-348.

9192 **meṯ:** *Aartun* Kjell, Zur Deutung der Sprachbelege *mṯ* / *mṯṯ* im ugaritischen Material: ➔ 126, ꟻMACUCH R. 1989, 1-8.

9193 **nēder:** *Schenker* Adrian, Gelübde im AT [Jer 19,21 ...]: unbeachtete Aspekte: VT 39 (nicht 29 wie p. 87 unten; 1989) 87-91.

9194 **nāṭāh:** *maṭṭeh* – *šebeṭ*: *Mojola* A. Osotsi, Translating the term 'tribe' in the Bible with special reference to African languages: BTrans 40 (1989) 208-211.

9195 **na'ar:** *Wolfers* David, The verb *na'ar* in the Bible: JBQ (= Dor) 18 (1989s) 27-31.

9196 *nepeš:* Rankin J., The corporeal reality of *nepeš* and the status of the unborn: JEvTS 31 (1988) 153-160 [< ZAW 102,130].

9196* *nš':* Kessler Rainer, Das hebräische Schuldenwesen; Terminologie und Metaphorik: WDienst 20 (1989) 181-195. *Sōpēr* ➤ 9174.

9197 *'eber:* Loretz Oswald, Habiru-Hebräer ...: BZAW 160, 1984 ➤ 65,7843 ... 4,a284: ᴿAulaO 7,1 (1989) 138s (G. del *Olmo Lete*); Protestantesimo 44 (1989) 48 (J. A. *Soggin*); TR 85 (1989) 9-12 (K. *Koch*).

9198 *'ayin:* Watson Wilfred G. E., The unnoticed word pair 'eye(s)' ‖ 'heart': ZAW 101 (1989) 398-408.

9199 *'am:* Good Robert M., The sheep of his pasture ᴰ1983 ➤ 64,7981 ... 3,9378: ᴿÉglT 19 (1988) 99-101 (L. *Laberge*).

9200 *'āmad* (= *lᵉhitqayyem*): BethM 32,111 (1986s) 383-6 (Y. *Gottlieb* ❸).

9201 *'āmad* 'endure': BethM 32 (1986s) 383-6 (Y. *Gottlieb,* ❸).

9201* Lipiński E., 'Cellériers' [*phw'* sur sceaux] de la province de Juda: TEuph 1 (1989) 107-9 [< ZAW 102,434].

9202 *pālal:* Berlin Adele, On the meaning of *pll* in the Bible [Ex 21,22-25 'accountable, redevable', advancing *Westbrook* R.]: RB [93 (1986) 52-69] 96 (1989) 345-351.

9203 *şāe'ᵃᵉşā'īm* 'Sprössling': ➤ 913, TWAT 6,8s (1989) 868-871 (D. *Kellermann*).

9204 *şābā', şᵉbā'ôt* 'Heer': ➤ 913, TWAT 6,8s (1989) 871-6 (H. *Ringgren*), 876-892 (H.-J. *Zobel*).

9205 *şedeq:* Krašovec J., La justice (sdq) de Dieu 1988 ➤ 4,a307: ᴿArTGran 52 (1989) 256s (J. L. *Sicre*); ZAW 101 (1989) 159s (H.-C. *Schmitt*).

9206 *şŏhᵒrājīm* 'Mittag': ➤ 913, TWAT 6,8s (1989) 924-6 (H. *Niehr*); one line missing from the top of col. 926 is supplied in fasc. 11, p. [667].

9207 *şwh* [*mişwāh*] 'Befehl': ➤ 913, TWAT 6,6s (1989) 936-9 (F. *García-López*).

9208 *şûm, şôm* 'Fasten': ➤ 913, TWAT 6,8s (1989) 959-963 (H. D. *Preuss*), ➤ 7027.

9209 *şôq* usw. 'Bedrängnis': ➤ 913, TWAT 6,8s (1989) 963-8 (H. *Lamberty-Zieliński*).

9210 *şûr* 'Fels' [*şûr,* 4 verschiedene Wurzeln, 'einbinden']: ➤ 913, TWAT 6,8s (1989) 973-83 (H.-J. *Fabry*) [968-974 (W. *Thiel*)].

9211 *şawwār* 'Hals': ➤ 913, TWAT 6,8s (1989) 927-9 (J. *Hausmann*).

9212 *şah* [? 'glühen' Name eines Monats]: ➤ 913, TWAT 6,8s (1989) 983-6 (S. *Talmon*).

9213 *şijjāh* 'trocken': ➤ 913, TWAT 6,8s (1989) 991-4 (G. *Fleischer*).

9214 *şālah* 'gelingen': ➤ 913, TWAT 6,8s (1989) 1042-6 (J. *Hausmann*).

9215 *şel* 'Schatten' [auch *ţālal*]: ➤ 913, TWAT 6,8s (1989) 1034-1042 (E. *Schwab*); 1056-9 *şalmawet* (H. *Niehr*).

9216 *şāme'* 'dürsten': ➤ 913, TWAT 6,8s (1989) 1065-8 (D. *Kellermann*).

9217 *şāna '* 'bedachtsam, klug sein': ➤ 913, TWAT 6,8s (1989) 1078-1080 (H. *Ringgren*).

9218 *şā'ad* '(hinauf) schreiten': ➤ 913, TWAT 6,8s (1989) 1080-3 (D. *Kellermann*).

9219 *şā'ir* 'klein': ➤ 913, TWAT 6,8s (1989) 1083-7 (M. *Sæbø*).

9220 *şā'aq:* Meier Samuel A., A Ugaritic convention in biblical dialogue (*ş'q* 11 times out of 3100 recorded 'citations' in the Bible]: UF 21 (1989) 277-282.

9221 *şāpāh* 'verbergen' [*şapôn* ➤ a962]: ➤ 913, TWAT 6,8s (1989) 1087-1093 (G. *Steins*): *şpn, maşpôn* 1107-1112 (S. *Wagner*).

9222 ṣar 1. 'Enge' 2. 'Feind': ➤ 913, TWAT 6,8s (1989) 1113-1122-6 (H.-J. Fabry; H. Ringgren).

9223 ṣārap 'schmelzen, melt': ➤ 913, TWAT 6,8s (1989) 1133-8 (M. Sæbø).

9224 qābab 'verwünschen' [curse, but the root is a variant of NQB]: ➤ 913, TWAT 6,6s (1989) 1138s (H. Ringgren).

9225 qābal 'annehmen': ➤ 913, TWAT 6,8s (1989) 1139-1143 (F. Reiterer).

9225* Ribera J., Evolución semántica y funcional de la partícula aramea 'qbl': AulaO 7 (1989) 263-8.

9226 qābaṣ 'sammeln': ➤ 913, TWAT 6,8s (1989) 1144-9 (P. Mommer).

9227 qad: Kinberg Naphtali, Some modal, aspectual, and syntactic constraints on the use of qad in the verbal system of classical Arabic: ➤ 30, BLANC H., mem. 1989, 170-9.

9228 qādad 'sich beugen': ➤ 913, TWAT 6,8s (1989) 1157-9 (M.J. Mulder).

9229 qodqod 'Scheitel, top of head': ➤ 913, TWAT 6,8s (1989) 1174-6 (E. Schwab).

9230 qādīm 'Osten', qædæm 'Frühzeit', qādam 'vorn sein': ➤ 913, TWAT 6,8s (1989) 1159-63-69-74 (T. Kronholm).

9231 qādar 'schmutzig sein, trauern': ➤ 913, TWAT 6,8s (1989) 1176-8 (H. Schmoldt).

9231* qdš: Alexandre Monique, La constitution d'un lexique du sacré dans le Pentateuque des Septante: ➤ 786, Écrivains/sacré 1988/9, 270-2.

9232 qaw 'Messschnur': ➤ 913, TWAT 6,8s (1989) 1223-5 (K.-M. Beyse).

9233 qwh 'hoffen', miqwæh, tiqwāh: ➤ 913, TWAT 6,8s (1989) 1225-1234 (G. Waschke).

9234 qûṭ 'verabscheuen': ➤ 913, TWAT 6,8s (1989) 1234-8 (H. Schmoldt).

9235 qôl 'Stimme': ➤ 913, TWAT 6,8s.11 (1989) 1237-1252 (B. Kedar-Kopfstein).

9236 qûm 'stehen': ➤ 913, TWAT 6,11 (1989) 1252-1274 (J. Gamberoni).

9237 rōeh: Hoffmann E., Das Hirtenbild im AT: Fundamentum 4 (Riehen, Switzerland 1987) 33-50 [OTAbs 12,6].

9238 ruaḥ: Dreytza Manfred, Der theologische Gebrauch von RWH im AT: Diss. ᴰJenni E. Basel 1988s. – TR 85 (1989) 513; RTLv 21, p.540: 'Dreyza'.

9239 Sekki Arthur E., The meaning of ruaḥ at Qumran: SBL diss. 110 [Madison WI 1987, ᴰSchoville K.] Atlanta 1989, Scholars. x-261 p. 1-55540-351-4.

9240 rîb: Bovati Pietro, Ristabilire la giustizia [ᴰ1985]: AnBib 110, 1986 ➤ 2,7458 ... 4,a317: ᴿArTGran 52 (1989) 246s (J.L. Sicre); BL (1989) 101 (F.F. Bruce: illuminating, also widely on psalms-prophets juridical language); CiuD 202 (1989) 499s (J. Gutiérrez); JTS 40 (1989) 141 (A. Gelston: lucid exposition of 'controversy' as an alternative to legal process); RechSR 76 (1988) 577 (J. Briend); ScripTPamp 21 (1989) 690s (F. Varo).

9241 Rᵃpā'îm: Healey John F., The last of the Rephaim: ➤ 165, Mem. RYAN D., Back to the Sources 1989, 33-44.

9242 Rubinkiewicz Ryszard, ⊕ Giganci: ➤ 891, EncKat 5 (1989) 1072.

9243 Rüterswörden Udo [➤ 9174] Die Beamten ... śr 1985 ➤ 1,8983 ... 4,a321: ᴿTPhil 64 (1989) 257 (N. Lohfink).

9244 šadday: Delcor Mathias, Des inscriptions de Deir'Alla aux traditions bibliques, à propos des šdyn, des šedim et de šadday: ➤ 169, ᶠSCHARBERT J., Väter 1989, 33-40.

9245 šākam: Janowski Bernd, Rettungsgewissheit und Epiphanie des Heils; das Motiv der Hilfe Gottes 'am Morgen' im Alten Orient und im Alten

Testament: WM 59. Neuk 1989. I. Alter Orient, xiii-215 p. 3-7887-1230-9. – ᴿTüTQ 169 (1989) 138s (W. *Gross*).

9246 *maškim* (*rābiṣu*) 'Kommissar' ➤ 905, RLA 7,5s (1989) 449-455 (D. *Edzard,* A. *Wiggermann*).

9247 *šāmā:* **Arambarri Echaniz** Jesús. Der Stamm šmʿ und seine Sprechhandlungen im AT; semantische Differenzierungen durch präpositionale und nichtpräpositionale Formen: kath. Diss. ᴰ*Mosis.* Mainz 1988s. – TR 85 (1989) 516; RTLv 21, p. 539 > SBB.

9248 *špṭ:* **Niehr** H., Herrschen und Richten 1986 ➤ 2,7471 ... 4,a325: ᴿExpTim 99 (1987s) 329 (R.J. *Coggins*); TLZ 114 (1989) 587-9 (G. *Sauer*).

9249 *šqy: Tropper* Josef, Ugaritisch *šqy;* 'trinken' oder 'tränken'?: Orientalia 58 (1989) 233-242: drink, except in D– [Š] stem.

9250 *Tōpēt: Görg* Manfred, Topæt (Tofet) 'Die (Stätte) des Feuergottes'?: BibNot 43 (1988) 12s.

J1.5   *Phoenicia, ugaritica* –   **North-West Semitic [➤** T5.4].

9251 *Aitken* K.T., *a*) Oral formulaic composition and theme in the Aqhat narrative; – *b*) Word pairs and tradition in an Ugaritic tale: UF 21 (1989) 1-16 / 17-38.

9252 **Bordreuil** Pierre, *Pardee* Dennis, *al., La trouvaille épigraphique de l'Ougarit,* 1. Concordance: RS-Ougarit 5 / Mém 86. P 1989, RCiv 457 p. 2-86538-202-4. – ᴿUF 21 (1989) 476 (M. *Dietrich,* O. *Loretz*).

9253 ᵀᴱ**Caquot** André, *Tarragon* Jean-Michel de, [*Cunchillos* Jesús-Luis], Textes ougaritiques 2. Textes religieux et rituels [Correspondance]: LAPO 14. P 1989, Cerf. 480 p. [CBQ 52,380].

9254 **Cunchillos-Illari** J. Luis, Estudios de epistolografía ugarítica: Fuentes de la ciencia bíblica 3. Valencia 1989, Inst. S. Jerónimo. xiii-329 p. 84-86067-29-4 [EstBíb 47,577]. – ᴿArTGran 52 (1989) 355s (A. *Torres*); AulaO 7 (1989) 281-4 (W. G. E. *Watson*).

9255 *Cunchillos* Jesús L., 'Todos los reyes me hicieron padre'; nueva interpretación de un pasaje fenicio, Karatepe 1:12: Sefarad 49 (1989) 153-6.

9256 **Dahood** Mitchell, Ugaritic-Hebrew philology; marginal notes on recent publications [second reprint, corrected]: BibOrPont 17. R 1989, Biblical Institute. viii-90 p. 88-7653-345-1.

9256* *Dearman* A. (p. 155-210), *Drinkard* J. (p. 132-154), *Graham* M. (p. 41-92), *Jackson* K. (p. 96-130), *Mattingly* G. (religion, p. 211-238), *Miller* J. (p. 1-40), Studies in the Mesha inscription 1989 ➤ 392.

9257 *Dietrich* M., *Loretz* O., *a*) The cuneiform alphabets of Ugarit; – *b*) Die Wasserflut Addus von unten šrʿ thmtm (KTU 1.19 I 45) – šdj trwmt (II Sam. 1,21) im Licht mesopotamischer Quellen; – *c*) Rāpiʾu und Milku aus Ugarit — neuere historisch-geographische Thesen zu *rpu mlk 'lm* (KTU 1.108: 1) und *mt rpi* (KTU 1.17 I 1); – *d*) (mit *Mayer* Walter) Sikkanum 'Betyle': UF 21 (1989) 101-112 / 113-121 / 123-131 / 133-9.

9258 *a*) *Dijkstra* M., Marginalia to the Ugarit letters in KTU (II); – *b*) *Loretz* O., Hexakola im Ugaritischen und Hebräischen — zu KTU 1.3 IV 50-53 *et par:* UF 21 (1989) 237-240.

9259 *Fensham* Frank C. †, Ugaritic studies and South Africa: JSem 1 (1989) 156-167; bibliog. 167-173.

9260 **Garbini** Giovanni, Il semitico nordoccidentale; studi di storia linguistica [reprints: ... ii. varietà; iii. filologia ebraica; ... v. lingua di

Ya'udi (Sam'al) ; ... vii. lingua degli Ebrei]: StSemitici NS 5. R 1988, Univ. ix-172 p.

9261 **Garbini** G., Venti anni di epigrafia punica nel Magreb (1965-1985) 1986 ➤ 4,a336: ᴿUF 21 (1989) 467-9 (M. *Heltzer*).

9262 *Garbini* G., Alfabeto ugaritico e alfabeto cananaico [*Lundin* A. 1987; *Dietrich-Loretz* 1988]: RStFen 8 (1989) 127-131.

9262* *a) Greenfield* Jonas C., NW Semitic epigraphy and the Bible; accomplishments and tasks; – *b) Kaufman* Stephen A., Classification of NW Semitic dialects: ➤ 564*, 9th Congress 1985/8, B2, 1-8 / 41-57.

9263 **Huehnergard** John, Ugaritic vocabulary in syllabic transcription 1987 ➤ 3,9468: ᴿAndrUnS 27 (1989) 232s (J. E. *Miller*); CBQ 51 (1989) 718-720 (M. S. *Smith*); JBL 108 (1989) 320-2 (S. B. *Parker*: 168 Akkadian texts contain at least one Ugaritic form); UF 21 (1989) 357-364 (D. *Sivan*: numerous disputable reconstructions).

9264 *Israel* Felice, Die Sprache des Ostrakons aus Nimrud: UF 21 (1989) 233-5.

9265 **Jackson** K. P., The Ammonite language 1983 ➤ 64,8944 ... 3,9471: ᴿAulaO 7 (1989) 293s (G. del *Olmo Lete*).

9265* *Kruger* P. A., On non-verbal communication in the Baal epic: JSem 1 (1989) 54-69.

9266 *Lackenbacher* Sylvie, Trois lettres d'Ugarit: ➤ 183, ᶠSJÖBERG Å., Dumu– 1989, 317-320.

9266* *Lipiński* Edward, *a)* L'élément 'RŠ dans l'anthroponymie carthaginoise: ➤ 126, ᶠMACUCH R., Hokmôt 1989, 141-8; – *b)* Les racines ǵzr et '*dr* dans l'onomastique amorite: ➤ 59, ᶠFINET A., Reflets 1989, 113-6.

9267 *Long* G. A., *Pardee* D., Who exiled whom? Another interpretation of the Phoenician inscription from Cebel Ires Dağı: AulaO 7 (1989) 207-214.

9267* **Margalit** Baruch, The Ugaritic poem of AQHT, text, tr., comm.: BZAW 182. B 1989, de Gruyter. xvii-534 p. 34 pl., map. 3-11-011632-4 [OIAc N89]; US 0-89925-472-1. – ᴿUF 21 (1989) 476s (M. *Dietrich, O. Loretz*).

9268 **Padró i Parcerisa** Josep, Egyptian-type documents from the Mediterranean littoral of the Iberian Peninsula before the Roman conquest [I. 1980 ➤ 61, q287 ... 1,b72 = e95]; II. Languedoc to Murcia; III. Andalusia: ÉPR 65 [➤ 3,b703]. Leiden 1983/5, Brill. vi-146 p.; pl. XXIX-LXV / viii-160 p.; pl. LXVI-CXLVI. ƒ90 + 110. – ᴿBO 46 (1989) 625s (E. *Gubel*).

9268* **Pardee** Dennis, Les textes para-mythologiques 1988 ➤ 4,a349: ᴿOrientalia 58 (1989) 559-561 (W. G. E. *Watson*).

9269 *Pardee* Dennis, (Rather dim but nevertheless appreciable) Light from (a very obscure) Ugaritic (Text) on (the) Hebrew (Bible): ➤ 60, ᶠFITZMYER J., Touch 1989, 79-89 [...*prš* Ezek 17,21; *hšlym* (')*l* Jos 11,19; Job 5,23; *zr'* + hsl Dt 28,38; '*zz* '1 Jg 3,10].

9270 **Parker** Simon B., The pre-biblical [Ugaritic] narrative tradition; Essays on the Ugaritic poems 'Keret' and 'Aqhat': SBL Resources 24. Atlanta 1989, Scholars. 248 p. $30; sb./pa. $20. 1-55540-300-X; 1-8 [BL 90, 125, N. *Wyatt*].

9271 *Renfroe* Fred H., Arabic and Ugaritic lexicography: diss. Yale. NHv 1989. 276 p. 90-11384. – DissA 50 (1989s) 3567-A.

9272 **Segert** Stanislav, A basic grammar of the Ugaritic language 1985 ➤ 65,7912 ... 3,9487: ᴿHeythJ 30 (1989) 117 (J. F. *Healey*: too lavish).

9273 *Shea* William H., The inscribed tablets from Tell Deir'Alla: AndrUnS 27 (1989) 21-37 . 97-120.

9274 **Sivan** Daniel, Grammatical analysis and glossary of the Northwest Semitic vocables in Akkadian texts of the 15th-13th c. B.C. from Canaan and Syria [diss. TA, ᴰ*Rainey* A.]: AOAT 214, 1984 ➤ 65,7914 ... 2,7493: ᴿBO 46 (1989) 645-651 (W. H. van *Soldt*).

9275 *Smit* E. J., The Tell Siran [Ammonite] inscription; linguistic and historical implications: JSem 1 (1989) 108-117.

9276 *Spronk* K., The legend of Kirtu (KTU 1 14-16); a study of the structure and its consequences for interpretation: ➤ 410, Structural/poetry 1988 62-82.

9277 **Verreet** E., Modi ugaritici; eine morpho-syntaktische Abhandlung über das Modalsystem im Ugaritischen: OrLovAn 27, 1988 ➤ 4,a357: ᴿBiblica 70 (1989) 572-5 (A. *Gianto*).

9278 *Vittmann* G., Zu den in den phönikischen Inschriften enthaltenen ägyptischen Personennamen: GöMiszÄg 113 (1989) 91-96.

9279 *a) Watson* W. G. E., Notes on some Ugaritic words; – *b) Israel* F., Note ammonite, I. Gli arabismi nella documentazione onomastica ammonita: StEpL 6 (1989) 47-52 / 91-96 [< ZAW 102,285].

9280 *a) Watts* J. W., Ḥnt, an Ugaritic formula of intercession; – *b) Tropper* Josef, Ugaritisch *wm* (KTU 3,9:6) und der Schwund von anlautendem *h* im Semitischen: UF 21 (1989) 443-9 / 421-3.

9281 *Zwickel* Wolfgang, Das 'edomitische' Ostrakon aus Ḥirbet Gazza (Ḥorvat 'Uza): BibNot 41 (1988) 36-39; facsim. 40.

J1.6   **Aramaica.**

9282 **Abou-Assaf** Ali, *al.*, La statue de Tell Fekherye et son inscription bilingue assyro-araméenne 1982 ➤ 63,8067*a* ... 2,7501: ᴿLOrA 2 (1989) 273-5 (R. *Lebrun*); RBgPg 67 (1989) 229-231 (G. *Bunnens*); RSO 62 (1988) 171s (F. *Israel*).

9283 *Anderson* Francis I., *Freedman* David N., *a)* Aleph as a vowel letter in old Aramaic; – *b)* The spelling of Samaria Papyrus I: ➤ 60, ᶠFITZMYER J., Touch 1989, 3-14 / 15-32.

9284 **Arnold** W., *a)* Lehrbuch des Neuwestaramäischen: Semitica Viva didact. 1. Wsb 1989, Harrassowitz. xvii-137 p. DM 40. 3-447-02910-2; – *b)* Das Neuwestaramäische, I. Texte aus Bax'a: Semitica Viva 4/1. Wsb 1989, Harrassowitz. 3-447-02949-8 [BL 90,145 (J. F. *Healey*) & 151].

9285 *Aufrecht* Walter E., *Hamilton* Gordon J., The Tell Fakhariyah bilingual inscription; a bibliography: News Targ supp. 4 (1988) 1-7.

9286 *Ben-Ḥayyim* Ze'ev, Verdrängung der ersten Person durch die dritte im Aramäischen der Targumim?: ➤ 126, ᶠMACUCH R., Ḥokmôt 1989, 9-19.

9287 **Beyer** K., Die aramäischen Texte 1984 ➤ 65,7925 ... 3,9501: ᴿProtestantesimo 44 (1989) 294s (J. A. *Soggin*).

9288 *Brock* S. B., Three thousand years of Aramaic literature: Aram 1,1 (Ox 1989) 11-23 [< ZAW 102,264].

9289 *Dankwarth* G., *Müller* C., Zur altaramäischen 'Altar'-Inschrift vom Tell Ḥalaf: AfO 35 (1988) 73-78; 4 fig.

9290 **Fales** Mario, [61 brief] Aramaic epigraphs on clay tablets of the Neo-Assyrian period 1986 ➤ 2,7512; 4,a365*: ᴿJAOS 109 (1989) 97-102 (S. A. *Kaufman*: Assyro-Aramaica).

9291 **Greenfield** Jonas C., *Porten* Bezalel, The Bisitun inscription, Aramaic version: Corpus Inscr. Iranicarum 1/5/1, 1982 ➤ 65,7931 ... 2,7517:

RJAOS 109 (1989) 685s (M. *Sokoloff*); WZKM 77 (1987) 209-213 (R. *Schmitt*).

9292 *Greenfield* Jonas C., Idiomatic ancient Aramaic: ➤ 60, FFITZMYER J., Touch 1989, 47-51.

9293 *a*) *Greenfield* J. C., *Sokoloff* M., Astrological and related omen texts in Jewish Palestinian Aramaic; – *b*) *Porten* Bezalel, Fragmentary Aramaic deeds of obligation and conveyance; new collations and restorations: JNES 48 (1989) 201-214 / 161-177 + 5 facsim.

9294 *Hoberman* Robert D., The history of the modern [northeastern-neo-] Aramaic pronouns and pronominal suffixes: JAOS 108 (1988) 557-575.

9295 *a*) *Hoberman* Robert D., Agglutination and composition in Neo-Aramaic verb inflection; – *b*) *Sabar* Jona, Substratal and adstratal elements in Jewish Neo-Aramaic: ➤ 30, Mem. BLANC H. 1989, 145-155 / 264-276.

9296 *Hopkins* Simon, Neo-Aramaic dialects and the formation of the preterite: ➤ 200, FULLENDORFF E., JSS 34 (1989) 413-431 + map.

9297 *Jones* Richard N., A new reading of the [Nabataean] Petra temple inscription: BASOR 275 (1989) 41-46; facsim.

9298 *Kara* Yechiel, ❶ Tradition yéménite de l'araméen babylonien; unité et diversité: ➤ 564, Massorot 2 (1986) 79-102.

9299 *Krotkoff* Georg, A Neo-Aramaic dialect of Kurdistan 1982 ➤ 1,9045; 3,7518: RJSS 33 (1988) 340-6 (R. D. *Hoberman*).

9299* *Lemaire* André, *a*) Remarques à propos du monnayage cilicien d'époque perse et de ses légendes araméennes: ➤ 782*, L'or perse = RÉAnc 91 (1989) 141-154 + 3 pl.; – *b*) Aramaic literature and Hebrew literature — contacts and influences in the First Millenium B.C.: ➤ 564*, 9th Congress 1985/5, B2, 9-24.

9300 *Levias* Caspar (d. 1934), ❶ A grammar of Galilean Aramaic, ESokoloff Michael. NY 1986, Jewish Theol. Sem. xxxii-343 p. [RelStR 16, 273, D. M. *Golomb*: an oddity].

9300* *Lipiński* Edward, Prohibitive and related law formulations in biblical Hebrew and Aramaic: ➤ 564*, 9th Congress 1985/8, B2, 25-39.

9301 *Luz* M., Salam, Meleager? [Meleager Anth. Gr. 7,419 wrote of himself a valediction in Greek, Aramiac and Phoenician]: StItFgC 81 (1988) 222-231 [< JStJud 20,293].

9302 *Margain* Jean, Les particules dans le targum samaritain de Genèse-Exode; jalons pour une histoire de l'araméen samaritain: diss. Paris-III 1988. – RÉJ 148 (1989) 193-5.

9303 *MacAdam* Henry I., *Graf* David F., [Nabatean and Greek] Inscriptions from the southern Hawrān survey, 1985 (Dayfana, Umm al-Quṭṭayn, Dayr al-Qinn): ADAJ 33 (1989) 177-197; 13 fig.; pl. XXV-XXX.

9304 *Naccach* Albert F., A ninth century A.D. Judeo-Aramaic epitaph from [1987, near] B'albak: Orientalia 58 (1989) 243-5; facsimile; pl. 5.

9305 *Naveh* Joseph, ❶ The Aramaic and Hebrew inscriptions from ancient synagogues: ➤ 218, Mem. YADIN Y., ErIsr 20 (1989) 302-310; 9 fig.; Eng. 206*.

9306 *Naveh* Joseph, *Shaked* Shaul. [Aramaic] Amulets and magic bowls 1985 ➤ 1,9051 ... 4,a372: ROLZ 84 (1989) 38-41 (J. *Oelsner*).

9306* *Odisho* Edward Y., The sound system of modern Assyrian (Neo-Aramaic): Semitica Viva 2. Wsb 1988, Harrassowitz. xv-146 p. DM 64. – RMundus 25 (1989) 35s (R. M. *Voigt*).

9307 *Porten* Bezalel, *Yardeni* Ada, Textbook of Aramaic documents from ancient Egypt, newly copied, edited, and translated into Hebrew and

English [1. 1986 → 2,7529]; 2. Contracts: History Texts. J 1989, Hebrew Univ. 965-350-003-1 [OIAc S89].

9308 *Porten* Bezalel, Five fragmentary Aramaic marriage documents; new collations and restorations: Abr Nahrain 27 (1989) 80-105.

9309 *Puech* Émile, Une inscription araméenne sur un couvercle de sarcophage ['il a fermé; il a dit de ne pas changer, et personne ne doit être enseveli avec lui dans le sarcophage']: → 218, Mem. YADIN Y., ErIsr 20 (1989) 161*-165*; 3 fig.

9310 *Rooy* H. F. van, The structure of the Aramaic treaties of Sefiré: JSem 1 (1989) 133-9.

9311 **Rosenthal** Franz, Grammaire de l'araméen biblique, [T]*Hébert* P., [E]*Margain* J.: Religions 19. P 1988, Beauchesne. 133 p. F 96. 2-7010-1178-7. – [R]ÉTRel 64 (1989) 272 (C.-B. *Amphoux*); RThom 89 (1989) 475s (L. *Devillers*).

9312 *Somekh* Alberto, Targumismi nel testo della Ketubbah [aramaica]: → 567, AnStoEseg 6 (1989) 39-50; Eng. 6.

9313 *Tadmor* Hayim, ⊙ On the use of Aramaic in the Assyrian Empire; three observations on a relief of Sargon II [in Yadin's 'Art of warfare']: → 218, Mem. YADIN Y., ErIsr 20 (1989) 249-252; 2 fig.; Eng. 203*.

9314 **Tepstad** Gunn K., Contributions to the study of the Aramaic Legal Papyri from Elephantine: diss. [D]*Segert* S. UCLA 1989. xi-229 p.; bibliog. p. 185-202. 89-15860. – DissA 50 (1988s) 1291-A; OIAc Ja90.

9315 *Vittmann* Günther, Zu den ägyptischen Entsprechungen aramäisch überlieferter Personennamen: Orientalia 58 (1989) 213-229.

9316 **Yadin** Yigael, *a*) with *Naveh* Joseph, Masada I. The Aramaic and Hebrew ostraca and jar inscriptions; – *b*) with *Greenfield* Jonas C., Aramaic and Nabatean signatures and subscriptions (*Meshorer* Yaacov, The coins of Masada). J 1989.

9316* *Yardeni* Ada, ⊙ New Jewish Aramaic ostraca from Israel: Tarbiz 58 (1988s) 119-134; 5 facsim.; 2 pl.; Eng. vi [all reports on food-deliveries].

J1.7 Syriaca.

9317 **Çiçek** Julius Y., Tenhōtō d-Ṭūr 'Abdin [anthology]. Glane 1987, Bar-Hebraeus. 159 p. – [R]JSS 34 (1989) 216-8 (S. *Brock*).

9318 *Diem* Werner, Syrische Kleinigkeiten [*nebboz*; *ḥammeš*; *hdādē*; Kurzvokale]: → 126, [F]MACUCH R. 1989, 65-78.

9319 **Gignoux** Philippe, Incantations magiques syriaques: Coll. RÉJ, 1987 → 3,9543; 4,a387*: [R]JAOS 109 (1989) 292s (M. *Sokoloff*); JJS 40 (1989) 121-4 (S. *Brock*).

9320 *Joosten* Jan, *a*) The predicative adjective in the *Status emphaticus* in Syriac: BO 46 (1989) 19-24; – *b*) The function of the so-called Dativus ethicus in classical Syriac: Orientalia 58 (1989) 473-492.

9321 **Kiraz** George A., Syriac for beginners. LA 1985, St. Ephraim youth organization. 257 p. – [R]JNES 46 (1989) 319 (M. O. *Wise*: from church traditions alien to current approaches).

9322 **Kiraz** George A., The Syriac primer; reading, writing, vocabulary and grammar [? = Oxford 1988, → 4,a389], with exercises and cassette activities: JStOT Manuals 5. Sheffield 1989, Academic. xii-273 p.; one cassette. £9. 1-85075-199-4. – [R]JJS 40 (1989) 247s (A. *Salvesen*, D. *Taylor*: for children).

9323 **Muraoka** Takamitsu, Classical Syriac for Hebraists 1987 → 3,9550; 4,a391: [R]BO 46 (1989) 150-2 (M.J. *Mulder*); JSS 34 (1989) 215 (S. *Brock*).

9324 *Palmer* Andrew, The Syriac letter-forms of Tūr 'Abdīn and environs: OrChr 73 (1989) 68-89; 4 pl.

9325 *Preissler* Holger, Altsyrische heidnische Namen in der frühen syrischen Literatur: ➤ 73, ᶠGÜNTHER R. = Klio 71/2 (1989) 503-7.

9326 **Riad** Eva, Studies in the Syriac Preface: Ac U 11. U 1988, Almqvist & W. 270 p. – ᴿMuséon 102 (1989) 199-201 (A. de *Halleux*).

9327 *Segal* J. B., *Quššaya* and *rukkaka* [corrections to NÖLDEKE Syriac Grammar, Eng. 1904]; a historical introduction: ➤ 200, ᶠULLENDORFF E., JSS 34 (1989) 483-491.

9327* *Todt* Susanne R., Die syrische und die arabische Weltgeschichte des BAR HEBRAEUS – ein Vergleich: Der Islam 65 (1988) 60-80.

J2.1 **Akkadica** (sumerica).

9328 *Boisson* Claude P., Contraintes typologiques sur le système phonologique du sumérien: BSLP 84,1 (1989) 201-233.

9329 **CAD:** Chicago Assyrian Dictionary, ᴱ**Brinkman** J., 13, 'Q', 1982 ➤ 63,784: ᴿOrientalia 58 (1989) 255-267 (K. *Deller,* Neu- und Mittelassyrisch; Nuzi) & 267-275 (W. R. *Mayer*; Nuzi Babylonisch) & 275-282 (J. *Oelsner,* Neu- und Spätbabylonisch).

9330 **Cavigneaux** A., *al.,* The series Erim-huš...: MSL 17, 1985 ➤ 1,9087: ᴿAfO 35 (1988) 173-5 (W. von *Soden*).

9331 **Civil** M, *al.,* The Sag-Tablet: MSL SS 1, 1986 ➤ 2,7543*; 4,a395*: ᴿAfO 35 (1988) 173-5 (also W. von *Soden*).

9332 *Cochavi-Rainey* Zippora, Canaanite influence in the Akkadian texts written by Egyptian scribes in the 14th and 13th centuries B.C.E.: UF 21 (1989) 39-46.

9333 *a) Freydank* H., Zur Paläographie der mittelassyrischen Urkunden; – *b)* *Nissen* H. J., Schrift als geschriebene Sprache (Das Beispiel des frühen Babylonien); – *c) Nováková* N., Die akkadischen Verbalwurzeln und das akkadische Verbum vom statistischen Gesichtspunkt; – *d) Prosecký* J., À propos de l'interprétation du texte [Sultantepe] STT 2,177: ➤ 874, Šulmu 1986/8, 73-84 / 225-233 / 235-241 / 287-299.

9334 *Gerardi* Pamela, Thus, he spoke; direct speech in Esarhaddon's royal inscriptions: ZAss 79 (1989) 245-260.

9335 **Groneberg** Brigitte R. M., Syntax, Morphologie und Stil der jung-babylonischen 'hymnischen' Literatur I-II: FreibAltorSt 14, 1987 ➤ 4,a400: ᴿBO 46 (1989) 384-6 (M. E. *Vogelzang*); JAss 89 (1989) 118-121 (E. *Reiner*).

9336 *Harrak* Amir, Middle Assyrian *bit ḫašimi* [reading also for *pit ḫašimi,* granary]: ZAss 89 (1989) 61-72; 1 fig.

9337 *a) Heimpel* Wolfgang, The Babylonian background of the term 'milky way'; – *b) Pedersén* Olof, Some morphological aspects of Sumerian and Akkadian linguistic areas; – *c) Yoshikawa* Mamoru, The Sumerian verbal aspects: ➤ 183, ᶠSJÖBERG Å., Dumu- 1989, 249-252 / 429-438 / 585-590.

9338 *Horowitz* Wayne, *a)* An Assyrian source for [Sumerian-Akkadian lexical] Urra 21: KAV 80+90+137 (+) 89: AfO 35 (1988) 64-72; 5 facsim.; – *b)* The Akkadian name for Ursa minor, ᵐᵘˡmar. gíd. da. an. na = *eriqqi šamê/šamāmi:* ZAss 79 (1989) 242-4; 1 pl.

9340 **Huehnergard** John, The Akkadian of Ugarit: HarvSemSt 34. Atlanta 1989, Scholars. xxiii-473 p. $30. 1-55540-316-6.

9341 **Hunger** Hermann, *Pingree* David, MUL.APIN; an astronomical compendium in cuneiform: AfO Beih 24. Horn 1989, Berger. 164 p.; xxviii pl.

9342 *Kossmann* Maarten, The case-system of West-Semitized Amarna Akkadian: JbEOL 30 (1987s) 38-60.

9343 **Labat** René, [6]*Malbran-Labat* Florence: Manuel d'épigraphie akkadienne. P 1988, Geuthner. xiv-346 p.

9344 *Lambert* W. G., *a)* A new interpretation of Enlîl and Namzitarra [*Civil* M., AfO 25 (1977) 65-71]: Orientalia 58 (1989) 308s.; – *b)* An Old Akkadian list of Sumerian personal names: ➤ 166, Mem. SACHS A. 1988, 251-8 + 2 pl.

9345 [E]**Livingstone** Alasdair, Court poetry and literary miscellanea: SAA 3. Helsinki 1989, Univ. xxxvii-185 p.; 35 fig., xvi pl. 951-570-044-2; pa. 3-4.

9346 **Livingstone** Alasdair, Mystical and mythological explanatory works of Assyrian and Babylonian scholars 1986 ➤ 2,7557*: [R]BO 46 (1989) 107-114 (W. *Farber*).

9347 *Lundin* A. G. Ⓞ A tablet from Beth-Shemesh [against *Loretz* O.]: VDI 188 (1989) 146-149; 1 fig.; Eng. 149-150 [as p. 269, not on p. 136 before Theorikan as Eng. index p. 271].

9348 *Maeda* Tohru, Ⓞ Mu-tūm obligation in the Ur III dynasty: Orient-Japan 32,1 (1989) 67-81; Eng. 67.

9349 *Mayer* Werner R., Die Verwendung der Negation im Akkadischen zur Bildung von Indefinit- bzw. Totalitätsausdrücken: Orientalia 58 (1989) 145-170.

9350 *Michel* Cécile, *Foster* Benjamin R., Trois textes paléo-assyriens de New York et les affaires confuses d'Iddin-Ištar: JCS 41 (1989) 34-52; facsimiles 53-56.

Moran William L., Les lettres d'Amarna: LIPO 13, 1987 ➤ e381.

9351 *Muntingh* L. M., Problems in connection with the verbal forms in the Amarna letters from Jerusalem, with special reference to EZ 286: JSem 1 (1989) 244-256.

9352 *a)* *Pingree* David, *Walker* Christopher, A Babylonian star-catalogue, BM 78161; – *b)* *Nemet-Nejat* Karen R., Cuneiform mathematical texts as training for scribal professions; – *c)* *Rochberg-Halton* F., Benefic and malefic planets in Babylonian astrology; – *d)* *Toomer* C. J., Hipparchus and Babylonian astronomy: ➤ 166, Mem. SACHS A., A scientific humanist 1988, 313-322 / 285-300 / 323-8 / 353-362.

9353 *Rawi* F. N. H. al-, *Black* J. A., The second tablet of 'Išum and Erra' [*Cagni* L. 1969]: Iraq 51 (1989) 111-122; 2 fig.; pl. XX.

9354 **Rochberg-Halton** Francesca, Aspects of Babylonian celestial divination; the lunar eclipse tablets of Enuma Anu Enlil [< diss. Chicago 1980]: AfO Beih 22. Horn 1989, Berger. 296 p. – OIAc N89; but Ja90 gives title differently as 'The treatment of lunar eclipses in Babylonian omen astrology ...'.

9355 *Saporetti* Claudio, Analisi elettronica del cuneiforme; prospettive di una ricerca: Note di informatica IBM 19. R 1988, Direzione Scientifica e Tecnologia; p. 4-14.

9355* [E]**Sjöberg** Åke W., Pennsylvania Sumerian dictionary 1984 ➤ 65,7989 ... 3,9597: [R]WeltOr 20s (1989s) 264-8 (J. *Marzahn*).

9356 **Soden** W. von, Einführung in die Altorientalistik 1985 ➤ 1,9116 ... 4,a413: [R]ArOr 57 (1989) 284s (Jana *Pečírková*, Eng.).

9357 **Soden** Wolfram von, Introduzione all'orientalistica antica [1985], [T]*Marchini* Laura, [E]*Mora* Clelia. Brescia 1989, Paideia. 281 p.; map. Lit. 35.000. 88-394-0432-5.

9358 *Soldt* W. H. van, An orthographic peculiarity in the Akkadian letters of Tušratta: ➤ 122, [F]LOON M. van. 1989, 103-115.

9359 *Stein* Diana L., A reappraisal of the 'Saustatar letter' from Nuzi: ZAss 89 (1989) 36-60.

9360 **Thomsen** Marie-Louise, The Sumerian language 1984 ➤ 65,7992 ... 4,a417: ᴿOLZ 84 (1989) 538-541 (B. *Hruška*).

9361 **Volk** Konrad, Die Balag-Komposition Uru Am-ma-ir-ra-bi; Rekonstruktion und Bearbeitung der Tafeln 18 (19 ff) 19,20 und 21 der späten kanonischen Version: FreibAltOrSt 18. Stu 1989 Steiner-Wsb. xiv-283 p.; XI (foldout) pl. 3-515-05091-4.

9362 **Walker** C. B. F., Cuneiform: Reading the Past, 1987 ➤ 3,9602; 4,a419: ᴿAncHRes 19 (1989) 165s (M. R. *Adamthwaite*); OrAnt 28 (1989) 155-7 (Vesna *Davidović*).

9363 *Westhuizen* J. P. van der, A re-interpretation of a Nippur loan document (CBS 7256) and its formal components: JSem 1 (1989) 287-298.

J2.7 Arabica.

9364 **Ahmed** Mokhtar, Lehrbuch des ägyptisch-arabischen 1981 ➤ 2,7569: ᴿOLZ 84 (1989) 189-191 (H. *Elsässer*).

9365 *Ambros* Arne A., Eine Lexikostatistik des Verbs im Koran: WZKM 77 (1987) 9-36.
Arabic bibliography ➤ 1109, 1114s, 1120.

9366 **Asbaghi** Asya, Die semantische Entwicklung arabischer Wörter im Persischen ᴰ1987 ➤ 3,9603; 4,a423: ᴿOLZ 84 (1989) 707-9 (F. *Meier*).

9366* **Asbaghi** Asya, Persische Lehnwörter im Arabischen. Wsb 1988, Harrassowitz. xix-286 p. DM 88. 3-447-02757-6. – ᴿWeltOr 20s (1989s) 315-321 (J. *Niehoff*).

9367 *a*) **Behnstedt** Peter, Zum Gebrauch von '*am* und *ṣana* im Arabischen; – *b*) *Peled* Yishai, Modifying verbs in full-verb constructions in literary Arabic; – *c*) *Palva* Heikki, Linguistic sketch of the Arabic dialect of El-Karak; – *d*) *Corriente* Federico, South Arabian features in Andalusī Arabic; – *e*) *Jastrow* Otto, The Judeo-Arabic dialect of Nusaybin/ Qāmᵉšli; – *f*) *Versteegh* Kers, A sociological view of the Arabic grammatical tradition; grammarians and their profession: ➤ 30, Mem. *Blanc* H. 1989, 27-44 / 256-263 / 225-251 / 94-103 / 156-178 / 289-302.

9368 *Bellamy* James A., Two pre-Islamic Arabic inscriptions revised; Jabal Ramm and Umm al-Jimāl: JAOS 108 (1988) 369-378.

9369 **Bloch** Ariel A., Studies in Arabic syntax and semantics 1986 ➤ 3, 9611:. ᴿBSOAS 51 (1988) 548s (J. *Wansbrough*).

9370 **Breydy** Michael, Geschichte der syro-arabischen Literatur der Maroniten vom VII.-XVI. Jahrhundert 1985 ➤ 3,g351; DM 44: ᴿOLZ 84 (1989) 195s (P. *Kawerau* †).

9371 **Corriente** F., Gramática árabe⁴. Barc 1988, Herder. 392 p. 84-252-1649-9. – ᴿCarthaginensia 5 (1989) 338s (R. *Sanz Valdivieso*); ScripTPamp 21 (1989) 683s (P. *Monod*).

9372 *a*) **Fischer** Wolfdietrich, Sprachwissenschaft; *b*) **Gätje** Helmut, Literaturwissenschaft: Grundriss der arabischen Philologie I-II. [➤ 4,a431] Wsb 1982/7, Reichert. xiv-326 p.; xiv-560 p. DM 118 + 280. 3-88226-144-7; -5-5. – ᴿBO 46 (1989) 194-7 (G. H. A. *Juynboll*: monumental; some notable errors); JSS 33 (1988) 300-309 (A. F. L. *Beeston*, Fischer).

9373 *Garbini* G., Ḥbl e ḥmr in sudarabico: ➤ 164, ᶠRUBINACCI R. 1985, I, 309-316.

9374 **Gary** Judith O., *Gamal-Eldin* Saad, Cairene Egyptian colloquial Arabic: Lingua Descriptiva Studies. Amst/L 1983, North-Holland/Croom-Helm. 141 p. 0-7099-3815-2. [Highly theoretical; not for learners.]. – ᴿJAOS 109 (1989) 437s (A. S. *Kaye*).

9375 *Griffith* S. H., The monks of Palestine and the growth of Christian literature in Arabic: Muslim World 78 (1988) 1-28 [RHE 84,105*].

9377 **Hopkins** Simon, Studies in the grammar of early Arabic 1984 ➤ 1,9145 ... 3,9623: ᴿJAOS 108 (1988) 166s (J. A. *Bellamy*).

9378 *Kinberg* Naphtali, Some temporal, aspectual, and modal features of the Arabic structure *la-qad* + prefix-tense verb: JAOS 108 (1988) 291-5.

9379 *Noja* Sergio, Über die älteste arabische Inschrift, die vor kurzem entdeckt wurde [*Negev* A., IsrEJ 36 (1986) 59s; aus der Nähe von Avdat; zwei Zeilen ganz arabisch, in nabatäischer Schrift; Datum 7. v.Chr. bis 125 n.Chr., also 200-300 Jahre älter als die Inschrift von Nemara]: ➤ 126, ᶠMACUCH R., Ḥokmôt 1989, 187-194; facsim.

9380 **Pellat** Charles, Cinq calendriers égyptiens 1986 ➤ 4,a439: ᴿJAOS 109 (1989) 696 (D. M. *Varisco*); JSS 33 (1988) 321-4 (M. J. L. *Young*).

9381 *Petráček* K., Pour une stratigraphie linguistique de la péninsule arabique: ➤ 874, Šulmu 1986/8, 257-271.

9382 [ᴱ**Pirenne** J.; AIBL] Corpus des inscriptions et antiquités sud-arabes; I, 1. Inscriptions; 2. [➤ 3,9634*] Antiquités; II, 1-2, Musée d'Aden; Tables (aussi pour I; *Fauveaud-Brassard* Catherine). Lv 1986, Peeters. 5 vols.; 3 vols. Fb 4500 + 3000. – ᴿMuséon 102 (1989) 219s (J. *Ryckmans*).

9383 **Qahtani** Duleim M. al-, Semantic valence of Arabic verbs: diss. Georgetown. Wsh 1988. 725 p. 89-13255. – DissA 50 (1989s) 934-A.

9384 **Ricks** Stephen D., Lexicon of inscriptional Qatabanian [diss. 1982, Berkeley GTU ➤ 65,8032]: StPohl 14. xii-244 p. Lit. 25.000. 88-7653-570-5 [OIAc Ja90]. – ᴿRSO 63 (1989) 316-320 (Alessandra

9385 **Roman** André, Étude de la phonologie et de la morphologie de la koïné arabe 1983 ➤ 2,7584: ᴿRSO 62 (1988) 155s (O. *Durand*). *Avanzini*).

9385* *Rundgren* Frithiof, The form of the definite article in Arabic: ➤ 126, ᶠMACUCH R., Ḥokmôt 1989, 257-269.

9386 **Samir** Khalil, Actes ... arabes-chrétiennes II, 1984/6 ➤ 3,651; 4,a442: ᴿMuséon 102 (1989) 385s (J. *Grand'henry*).

9387 **Schregle** Götz (*Rizk* Sayed M.), Arabisch-deutsches Wörterbuch, Lfg. 9-13: DMG-Beirut, 1985 ➤ 4,a444; je Lfg DM 43: ᴿDLZ 110 (1989) 281s (Wiebke *Walther*).

9388 **Smart** J. R., Arabic: Teach Yourself 1986 ➤ 3,9642: ᴿDer Islam 65 (1988) 159s (M. *Woidich*); JSS 33 (1988) 338-340 (Najah *Shamaa*).

9389 *a*) *Stetkevych* Jaroslav, Arabic hermeneutical terminology; paradox and the production of meaning; – *b*) *Frantz-Murphy* Gladys, A comparison of Arabic and earlier Egyptian contract formularies 5, Formulaic evidence: JNES 48 (1989) 81-96 / 97-107.

9390 *Touratier* Christian, Structure de la phrase simple en arabe: BSLP 84,1 (1989) 345-350.

9391 **Ullmann** Manfred, Wörterbuch der klassischen arabischen Sprache, Band II, Lfg. 18. Wsb 1989, Harrassowitz. p. 1059-1122. 3-447-02958-7 [OIAc Ja90]. [= (62 p.)] Vorläufiges Literatur- und Abkürzungsverzeichnis zum zweiten Band.

9392 **Versteegh** Kees, Pidginization and creolization; the case of Arabic: StThHistLing 4 / Current Issues 33. Amst 1984, Benjamins. xiii-194 p. – ᴿBSO 51 (1988) 124s (J. *Wansbrough*).

9393 **Voigt** Rainer M., Die infirmen Verbaltypen des Arabischen und das Biradikalismus-Problem 1988 ⟶ 4,a448: RAulaO 7,1 (1989) 151s (F. *Corriente*); BO 46 (1989) 482-6 (L. O. *Schuman*: 'Voigt' in text, 'Vogt' in title and contents); RSO 63 (1989) 344-7 (O. *Durand*).

9394 **Wehr** Hans, ⁵*Kropfitsch* L., Arabisches Wörterbuch für die Schriftsprache der Gegenwart 1985 (¹1952) ⟶ 3,9173: ROLZ 84 (1989) 690-3 (G. *Werner*, also on 4th English ed. ᵀ*Cowan* J. M. 1979).

J3 Ægyptia.

9395 *Abdalla* A. M., Beginnings of insight into the possible meanings of certain Meroitic personal names [1. 1988 ⟶ 4,a450] (2), Verbal sentences and sentences that are partly verbal and partly non-verbal: BeiSudan 4 (1989) 9-62 (63-74, *Browne* G. M., Notes on Old-Nubian texts).

9396 *Aufrère* Sydney, *a)* Remarques sur la transmission des noms royaux par les traditions orales et écrites; – *b)* ḥmwt/ḥmjt, 'Steatine, serpentine?' (Lexicologie et histoire naturelle 27): BIFAO 89 (1989) 1-14 / 15-24.

9397 *Baines* John, Communication and display; the integration of early Egyptian art and writing: Antiquity 63 (1989) 471-482; 5 fig.

9398 *Barta* Winfried, *a)* Zur Apposition vom Typ AmB [mit *m* 'der Äquivalens' vor dem apponierten Nomen]: GöMiscÄg 109 (1989) 17-19; – *b)* Zur Konstruktion der ägyptischen Königsnamens V-VI: ZägSpr 116 (1989) 1-9. 111-137.

9399 *a) Barta* Winfried, Beispiele der Sargtexte für *jn* als Pleneschreibung der Präposition *n*; *b) Fischer* Henry G., Occurrences of *yn*, agential and dative: GöMiszÄg 107 (1989) 55-58 / 69-76; 3 fig.

9400 **Beinlich** Horst, **Saleh** Mohamed, Corpus der hieroglyphischen Inschriften aus dem Grab des Tutanchamun; mit Konkordanz der Nummernsysteme. Ox 1989, Ashmolean/Griffith. xvi-282 p. 0-900416- 53-X.

9401 *Betrò* Maria Carmela, L'inno crittografico del Libro del Giorno (= Medinet Habu VI 421A-420B = Taharqa 18A): EgVO 12 (1989) 37-54.

9402 **Bonhême** Marie-Ange, Les noms royaux 1987 ⟶ 3,9659: RJAmEg 26 (1989) 250-2 (K. A. *Kitchen*).

9403 *a) Borghouts* Joris F., Aspectual values of the second tenses in Middle Egyptian; – *b) Eyre* Christopher J., Tense or aspect in Middle Egyptian?: ⟶ 823, Akten IV 3 (1985/9) 29-42 / 51-65.

9404 **Brovarski** Edward, The inscribed material from Naga ed-Der: diss. Chicago 1989. – OIAc Ja90.

9405 **Brunner** Hellmut, Grundzüge einer Geschichte der altägyptischen Literatur⁴ʳᵉᵛ. Da 1986, Wiss. xi-116 p. DM 29. – ROLZ 84 (1989) 404-6 (Elke *Blumenthal*).

9405* **Buurman** J., *Grimal* N., al., Informatique et égyptologie²ʳᵉᵛ. P 1986-, CNRS. 2, 1986, 47 p.; 3, 1987, 29 p.; 4, 1988, 124 p.; 5 (Uppsala 1988) 92 p.; 6 (P 1988) 17 p.; 7 (1990, *Grimal* N., al.), 169 p.

9406 **Callender** J. B., Studies in the nominal sentence in Egyptian and Coptic 1984 ⟶ 2,7597; 3,9665: RJNES 48 (1989) 230-2 (M. *Gilula*).

9407 **Cauville** Sylvie, al., Catalogue de la fonte hieroglyphique de l'imprimerie de l'I.F.A.O.² [¹1907, *Chassinat* É.] (7104 single or complex signs). P 1983, IFAO. viii-503 p. – ROLZ 84 (1989) 162s (J. *Hallof*).

9408 **Černy** Jaroslav, [I c. 1935] II. ᴱ*Koenig* Yvan, Papyrus hiératiques de Deir El-Médineh, catalogue complété: DocFouilles 22. Le Caire 1986, IFAO. vi-7 p.; 24 pl. 2-7247-0028-7. – RBO 46 (1989) 31s (S. *Allam*).

9409 **Chappaz** Jean-Luc, Écriture égyptienne: Éd. d'histoire. Genève 1986, Musée d'art. 2-8306-0025-8 [OIAc S 89].

9410 **Davies** W. V., Egyptian hieroglyphs 1987 → 3,9672: ᴿOLZ 84 (1989) 657s (J. *Hallof*).

9411 *a) Depuydt* Leo, The contingent tenses of Egyptian; – *b) Shisha-Halevy* Ariel, Work-notes on demotic syntax I: Orientalia 58 (1989) 1-27 / 28-60.

9412 *Derchain* Philippe, [*Sḏm.n.f*] À propos de performativité; pensers anciens et articles récents: GöMiszÄg 110 (1989) 13-18.

9412* **Dondelinger** Edmund, Das Totenbuch des Schreibers Ani. Graz 1987, Akad. 135 p.; 32 color. ill. – ᴿMundus 25 (1989) 8s (Ingrid *Gamer-Wallert*).

9413 **Doret** Eric, The narrative verbal system of Old and Middle Egyptian 1986 → 2,7603; 4,2470: ᴿAfO 35 (1988) 237-244 (W. *Schenkel*); BO 46 (1989) 567-573 (F. *Junge*); RSO 62 (1988) 147-151 (F. *Tiradritti*).

9414 *Doret* Éric, Phrase nominale, identité et substitution dans les textes des sarcophages I: → 39, Mém. CLÈRE J., RÉgp 40 (1989) 49-62; Eng. 63.

9415 ᴱ**Englund** Gertie, *Frandsen* Paul-John, Crossroad; chaos or the beginning of a new paradigm; papers from the conference on Egyptian grammar, Helsingfør 28-30 May 1986: 1986 → 3,780: ᴿJNES 48 (1989) 232-5 (E. S. *Meltzer*).

9416 ᵀ**Faulkner** Raymond O. [1972 → 1,9194] ²ʳᵉᵛ*Andrews* Carol, The ancient Egyptian Book of the Dead 1985 → 2,7605: ᴿOLZ 84 (1989) 146-9 (Ursula *Rössler-Köhler*).

9417 *Fischer* Henry G., On some reinterpretations of royal names [Tuthmosis III; errors and pitfalls of *Iversen* E. 1988]: GöMiszÄg 108 (1989) 21-29.

9418 *a) Fischer* Henry G., The transcription of the royal name Pepy; – *b) Darnell* John C., The chief baker [(another) Pepy]: JEA 75 (1989) 214s / 216-9.

9419 *Fournet* Jean-Luc, Les emprunts du grec à l'égyptien: BSLP 84,1 (1989) 56-80.

9420 *Frandsen* Paul J., A word for 'causeway' and the location of 'the Five Walls' [south rather than north as *Ventura* R. 1986]: JEA 75 (1989) 113-123.

9421 *Gallo* Paolo, Ostraca demotici da Medinet Madi [Fayum]: EgVO 12 (1989) 99-120 + 5 fot.

9422 *Gessler-Löhr* Beatrix, Bemerkungen zu einigen *wbȝw njswt* [royal butler] der Nach-Amarnazeit: GöMiszÄg 112 (1989) 27-34.

9423 *Gnirs* Andrea M., *Seidlmayer* Stephan J., Report on a 'philologisch-prosopographisches [computer-encoding] Texterschliessungssystem' (PPTES): GöMiszÄg 111 (1989) 19-32.

9424 **Graefe** E. Mittelägyptische Grammatik für Anfänger²ʳᵉᵛ (¹1987). Wsb 1988, Harrassowitz. xxii-252 p. DM 48. – ᴿLA 38 (1988) 474-7 (A. *Niccacci*).

9425 **Grenier** Jean-Claude, Les titulatures des empereurs romains dans les documents en langue égyptienne: PapBrux 22. Bru 1989, Fd.Reine Élisabeth. 122 p. [OIAc Ja90]. – ᴿCdÉ 64 (1989) 354 (J. *Bingen*).

9426 *Helck* Wolfgang, Grundsätzliches zur sogenannten 'syllabischen Schreibung': StAltÄgK 16 (1989) 121-143.

9427 *Hintze* Fritz, Meroitisch und Nubisch; eine vergleichende Studie: BeiSudan 4 (1989) 95-106.

9428 *Inconnu-Bocquillon* Danielle, Les titres *ḥry idb* [maître de largesse] et *ḥry wḏb* [provider of ritual food] dans les inscriptions des temples gréco-romains: ➤ 39, Mém. CLÈRE J., RÉgp 40 (1989) 65-88; Eng. 89.

9430 *Jansen-Winkeln* Karl, a) Die Inschriften der Schreiberstatue des Nespapaschuti: MiDAI-K 45 (1989) 203-205; facsim.; pl. 23; – b) Zu einigen 'Trinksprüchen' auf ägyptischen Gefässen: ZägSpr 116 (1989) 143-153.

9431 **Johnson** Janet H., Thus wrote 'Onchsheshonqy; an introductory grammar of demotic: SAOC 45, 1986 ➤ 2,7615; 4,a478: ᴿBO 46 (1989) 576-9 (C. J. *Martin*).

9432 *Jones* P. M. E., The nature of the hieroglyph [for] 'pr ['scribal kit-bag' rather than just 'equip(-ment for offerings')]: JEA 75 (1989) 245s.

9433 **Junge** Friedrich, 'Emphasis' and sentential meaning in Middle Egyptian: GöOrF 4/20. Wsb 1989, Harrassowitz. 130 p. 3-447-02975-7.

9434 *Kurth* Dieter, Zum *'šdm.n.f'* in Tempeltexten der griechisch-römischen Zeit: GöMiszÄg 108 (1989) 31-44; 113 (1989) 55-64+phot.

9435 *Lalouette* Claire, Textes sacrés et textes profanes de l'ancienne Égypte I-II, 1984/7 ➤ 4,a483: ᴿBO 46 (1989) 84s.

9436 *Lapp* Günther, Die Papyrusvorlagen der Sargtexte: StAltÄgK 16 (1989) 171-202.

9437 *Leahy* Anthony, Taniy, a seventh century lady (Cairo CG 20564 and Vienne 192): GöMiszÄg 108 (1989) 45-54+2 fig.

9438 **Lesko** Leonard H. & Barbara S., A dictionary of Late Egyptian 4 (completes Egyptian-English). Providence 1989, B. C. Scribe. viii-170 p. 0-930548-10-8 [OIAc N89].

9439 *Lichtheim* Miriam, The stela of Taniy, CG 20564, its date and character: StAltÄgK 16 (1989) 203-215; pl. 1-2 [independently reached exactly the same date, 7th cent. under Montemhet, as A. *Leahy* supra ➤ 9437].

9440 **Loprieno** Antonio, Topos und mimesis; zum Ausländer in der ägyptischen Literatur [Hab.Gö 1984]: ÄgAbh 48, 1988 ➤ 4,a484: ᴿOrAnt 28 (1989) 159 (S. *Donadoni*); RHPR 69 (1989) 191s (J. G. *Heintz*: 'imbrication' de deux objets de recherche 'déjà ésotériques en eux-mêmes').

9441 *Loprieno* Antonio, Book-reviews once more [defense of his article in Crossroad against R. H. *Pierce* claim of 'unusable jargon']: GöMiszÄg 112 (1989) 35-61.

9442 **Malaise** Michel, Du mot *ḥw* exprimant le caractère 'exceptionnel' des divinités ou des êtres: ➤ 204, Mém. WALLE B. van de, CdÉ 64 (1989) 111-120.

9443 **Niwinski** A., Studies on the illustrated Theban funerary papyri of the 11th and 10th centuries B.C.: OBO 86. FrS/Gö 1989, Univ./VR. xxxii-402 p.; 49 pl. F 118. 3-7278-0613-3 / 3-525-53716-6 [BL 90, 125, K. A. *Kitchen*].

9444 **Posener** Georges, Le papyrus Vandier 1985 ➤ 1,9216: ᴿJAOS 109 (1989) 421-435 (A. *Shisha-Halevy*: an early demotic literary text?); Orientalia 58 (1989) 535-9 (R. A. *Caminos*: a new work of fiction on the back of part of the Book of the Dead).

9445 **Sadek** Abdel-Aziz F., Contribution à l'étude de l'Amdouat...: OBO 65, 1985 ➤ 1,a647*; 3,b337: ᴿAfO 35 (1988) 248-250 (Waltraud *Guglielmi*); BO 46 (1989) 39-41 (J. G. *Griffiths*: reassuringly presented by E. HORNUNG, the acknowledged authority); RB 96 (1989) 441s (R. *Beaud*).

9446 **Schlott** Adelheid, Schrift und Schreiber im Alten Ägypten: Archäol. Bibliothek. Mü 1989, Beck. 3-406-33602-7 [OIAc S89].

9447 *Shisha-Halevy* Ariel, [on *Doret* É. 1986:] The narrative verbal system of Old and Middle Egyptian: Orientalia 58 (1989) 247-254.

9448 **Smith** M., Mortuary texts of papyrus BM 10507; Catalogue of demotic papyri 3. L 1987, British Museum. 191 p.; 11 pl. £120. – ᴿCdÉ 64 (1989) 175-7 (H. de *Meulenaere*).

9449 **Smith** H. S., *Tait* W. J., Saqqâra demotic papyri I, 1983 ⇒ 65,8081; 4,a513: ᴿOLZ 84 (1989) 279-281 (B. *Menu*).

9450 *Sturtewagen* Christian, *Goelet* Ogden, The [IBM-compatible microcomputer] Egyptian vocabulary project: GöMiszÄg 109 (1989) 95.

9451 *Thelwell* R., Meroitic and African language prehistory; prelude to a synthesis: ⇒ 814, Meroitica 1984/9, 567-607 + 8 fig.

9452 *Vandersleyen* Claude, Les inscriptions 114 et 1 du Ouadi Hammamât (11ᵉ dynastie): ⇒ 204, Mém. WALLE B. van de, CdÉ 64 (1989) 148-158.

9453 *Vandersleyen* Claude, *W3ḏ-wr* ['great green', 180 examples] never means the sea [often Delta, also Fayûm; once Nile-flood]: ⇒ 859, Delta 1988/9, 244-250, ᵀ*Haneborg-Lühr* Maureen [p. 243, *Nibbi* A., finds support for her view].

9454 **Vernus** Pascal, Le surnom au Moyen Empire; répertoire, procédés d'expression et structures de la double identité au début de la XIIᵉ Dynastie à la fin de la XVIIᵉ Dynastie: StPohl 13, 1986 ⇒ 2,7632; 4,a516: ᴿBO 46 (1989) 307-9 (O. *Berlev*); JNES 48 (1989) 224s (W. A. *Ward*: 350 cases).

9455 ᴱ**Vleeming** S. P., Aspects of demotic lexicography 1984/7 ⇒ 4,715: ᴿBO 46 (1989) 573-6 (M. *Smith*: summary of each art. with tit. pp.).

9455* **Ward** William A., Essays on feminine titles of the Middle Kingdom and related subjects 1986 ⇒ 2,7633; 4,a520: ᴿJNES 48 (1989) 225s (W. J. *Murnane*: on the social status of women).

9456 *Ward* William A., *a*) Egyptian *ṯbs*, a Hurrian loan-word in the vernacular of Deir el-Medineh: GöMiszÄg 109 (1989) 73-82; 2 fig.; – *b*) Some foreign personal names and loan-words from the Deir el-Medineh ostraca: ⇒ 106, ᶠKANTOR H., Essays 1989, 287-303.

9457 *Westendorf* Wolfhart, Der dreigliedrige Nominalsatz Subjekt-*pw*-Prädikat; Konstatierung oder emphatisch?: GöMiszÄg 109 (1989) 83-94.

9458 **Winand** Jean, Le voyage d'Ounamon ... concordance 1987 ⇒ 3,9703: ᴿCdÉ 64 (1989) 174s (M. *Green*).

9459 *Winand* Jean, L'expression du sujet nominal au présent I en néo-égyptien: ⇒ 204, Mém. WALLE B. van de, CdÉ 64 (1989) 159-171.

9460 *Winter* Erich, Hieroglyphen: ⇒ 904, RAC 15,113 (1989) 83-103.

9461 *Yoyotte* Jean, Le nom égyptien du 'ministre de l'économie' – de Saïs à Meroé: CRAI (1989) 73-88 (-90, *Leclant* J.).

9462 **Browne** Gerald M., Introduction to Old Nubian: Meroitica 11. B 1989, Akademie. xii-59 p. 3-05-000829-6.

9463 **Browne** Gerald M., Old Nubian texts from Qasr Ibrīm [I. *Plumley* J. M. & Browne, Ninth Mem. 1986]; II: Texts from Excavations 10. L 1989 Egypt Expl. 87 p. 0-85698-10[0-1] 8-7.

9464 **Hintze** Fritz, *Reineke* Walter F., *al.*, Felsinschriften aus dem Sudanesischen Nubien: Nubien-Expedition 1961-3, 1. B 1989, Akademie. 3-05-000369-3 [OIAc S89].

J3.4 **Coptica.**

9465 *Cannuyer* Christian, Un mot copte absent des dictionnaires; *hōseb* (s. 'cordeau'): GöMiszÄg 104 (1988) 71-73.

9466 *Gabra* Gawdat, *tehen* 'grün' und *tehnē* 'Saat (junges Getreide?)':
GöMiszÄg 105 (1988) 11-13.

9467 **Gardner** Iain, Coptic theological papyri II. (appendix, The docetic
Jesus): Rainer NS 21. W 1988, Nationalbibliothek (Hollinek). 85 p.; vol.
of 38 pl. 3-85119-217-6 [OIAc Ja90].

9468 **Giversen** S., Kephalaia / Homilies / Psalmbook I-II: Manichaean Coptic
Beatty papyri 1-4 1986 (➤ 1,7643) 1988: [Cah. Orientalisme 14s: Genève
1986, Cramer]: ᴿLavalTP 45 (1989) 154-6 (P.-H. *Poirier*).

9469 ᴱ**Hasitzka** Monika R. M., Koptische [... ökonomische] Texte: Corpus
Papyrorum Raineri 12. W 1987, Hollinek. 100 p. + vol. 32 pl. – ᴿMuséon
102 (1989) 198s (P.-H. *Poirier*).

9470 *a) Kasser* Rodolphe, Sigles des dialectes coptes; propositions pour
une convention permettant d'unifier les divers usages systématiques ac-
tuellement en vigueur; – *b) Boud'hors* Anne, Manuscrits coptes 'chypriotes' à la B. N. Paris: ➤ 820, Journées coptes III 1986/9, 1-10 / 11-20.

9471 **Layton** B., Catalogue of Coptic literary mss 1987 ➤ 4,a533: ᴿRB 96
(1989) 458 (M.-É. *Boismard*).

9472 *Mikhail* Louis B., The second tenses in practice: ZägSpr 116 (1989)
60-71.

9473 *Pelsmaekers* J., Het gebed in de teksten op koptische grafplaten:
bemerkingen en vragen: BBelgRom 59 (1989) 31-42.

9474 *Pietersma* A., *Comstock* S. T., Coptic martyrdoms in the Chester Beatty
library: BASP 24 (1987) 143-155 + 8 pl.

9475 **Polotsky** H. J., *a)* Grundlagen des koptischen Satzbaus I: AmStPapyr
28, 1987 ('Nᵒ 27') ➤ 4,a536: ᴿRelStR 15 (1989) 264 (B. A. *Pearson*). – *b)*
Zur Determination im Koptischen: Orientalia 58 (1989) 464-472.

9475* POLOTSKY H. anniv. ❺ ʿIyyûnîm [bibliog. 51-66; *Goldenberg* N., 7-18;
Groll S., 19-37; *Rosén* D., 38-60]. J 1988.

ᴱ**Rosenstiehl** Jean-Marc, Journées d'Étude Coptes 1984/6, 1986/9 ➤ 820 *ab*.

9476 **Shisha-Halevy** Ariel, The proper name; structural prolegomena to its
syntax; a case study in Coptic: WZKM Beih 15. W 1989, WVGO. 143 p.
3-85369-734-8 [OIAc S89].

9477 *Störk* Lothar, Aurispizien III [Zur Bedeutung des Ohres in den
altägyptischen Sexualvorstellungen; spätere Belege]: GöMiszÄg 108 (1989)
65-74; 4 fig.

9478 **Vergote** Jozef, Grammaire copte; morphologie syntagmatique, syntaxe;
IIa. Partie synchronique; IIb. Partie diachronique 1983 ➤ 64,8249:
ᴿOLZ 84 (1989) 272-8 (H.-M. *Schenke*).

9479 *Vogüé* Adalbert de, Les fragments coptes de l'Histoire Lausiaque;
l'édition d'Amélineau et le manuscrit: Orientalia 58 (1989) 326-332.

9480 *Vycichl* Werner, Dictionnaire étymologique de la langue copte 1983
➤ 64,8250 ... 4,a540: ᴿOLZ 84 (1989) 155-9 (H. *Satzinger*).

9481 **Zanetti** Ugo, Les manuscrits de Dair Abû Maqâr; inventaire: Cah-
Orientalisme 11. Genève 1986, Cramer. 102 p. – ᴿBSOAS 51 (1988) 619
(M. *Smith*).

J3.8 Æthiopica.

9481* *Angoujard* J. P., *Denais* M., Le pluriel brisé en Tigrigna: LOrA 2
(1989) 99-148.

9482 *Appleyard* D. L., The relative verb in focus constructions; an Ethiopian
areal feature: ➤ 200, ᶠULLENDORFF E., JSS 34 (1989) 291-305.

ᴱ**Goldenberg** G., Ethiopian studies 1980/6 ➤ 817.

9483 **Hammerschmidt** E., *Six* V., Äthiopische Handschriften [1.1983 ➤ 64, 8252] 2. Die Handschriften der Bayerischen Staatsbibliothek: Verzeichnis der orientalischen Handschriften in Deutschland 20/5. Stu 1980, Steiner. 200 p. DM 150 [RHE 85, 82]. – ᴿRSO 63 (1989) 160-3 (P. *Marrassini*).

9483* **Kapeliuk** Olga, Nominalization in Amharic: ÄthFor 23. Stu 1988, Steiner. 173 p.

9484 **Leslau** Wolf, Comparative dictionary of Ge'ez 1987 ➤ 3,9734; 4,a546: ᴿOLZ 84 (1989) 389-394 (S. *Uhlig*); WeltOr 20s (1989s) 326-8 (R. *Voigt*).

9485 *Leslau* Wolf, Analysis of the Ge'ez vocabulary; Ge'ez and Cushitic: RasEtiop 32 (1988) 59-109.

9486 **Neugebauer** Otto, Chronography in Ethiopic sources: Szb ph/h 512. W 1989, Österr. Akad. 151 p. 3-7001-1469-9.

9487 **Raz** Shlomo, Tigre 1983 ➤ 64,8258 ... 1,9252: ᴿJSS 33 (1988) 151-3 (F. R. *Palmer*).

9488 **Richter** Renate, Lehrbuch der amharischen Sprache 1987 ➤ 3,9740; 4,a548; 3-324-00172-2: ᴿBO 46 (1989) 218-221 (Olga *Kapeliuk*); WeltOr 20s (1989s) 328-332 (R. *Voigt*).

9489 **Ullendorff** Edward, *a)* Studia aethiopica et semitica 1987 ➤ 3,313: ᴿJAOS 109 (1989) 716s (G. *Haile*); – *b)* The two Zions; reminiscences of Jerusalem and Ethiopia 1988 ➤ 4,a552: ᴿJJS 40 (1989) 110-2 (A. *Wasserstein*); Orientalia 58 (1989) 437s (P. J. L. *Frankl*).

J4 Anatolica.

9490 **Bernabé** Alberto, Textos literarios hetitas. M 1987, Alianza. xvi-316 p. [JAOS 108,675].

9491 **Boley** Jacqueline, The sentence particles and the place words in Old and Middle Hittite: IBeiSprW 60. Innsbruck 1989, Univ. Inst. SprW. 401 p. 3-85124-606-3.

9492 *Finkelberg* Margalit, From Ahhiyawa to Achaioí: Glotta 66 (1988) 127-134.

9493 **Girbal** Christian, Beiträge zur Grammatik des Hattischen: EurHS 21/50. Fra 1986, Lang, v-201 p. Fs 47. 3-8402-8540-6. – ᴿBO 46 (1989) 669-671 (G. *Beckman*); OLZ 84 (1989) 261-9 (P. *Taracha*).

9494 ᶠGÜTERBOCK Hans G.: Kaniššuwar, ᴱHoffner H., ... 1986 ➤ 3,42; 4,a558: ᴿBO 46 (1989) 653-9 (F. *Starke*: long commented summaries with tit. pp.); OLZ 84 (1989) 411-5 (R. *Lebrun*).

9495 **Güterbock** Hans G., Hoffner Harry A., Hittite dictionary 3/3, 1986 ➤ 4,a559: ᴿBO 46 (1989) 661-9 (F. *Starke*).

9496 *Güterbock* Hans G., Marginal notes on recent Hittitological publications [against *Badalì* E. BbbOr 1984 influence on three recent researches]: JNES 48 (1989) 307-311.

9497 *Haas* Volkert, Ein Preis auf das Wasser in hurritischer Sprache: ZAss 79 (1989) 261-271.

9498 **Hagenbuchner** Albertine, Die Korrespondenz der Hethiter, I. Die Briefe, unter ihren kulturellen, sprachlichen und thematischen Gesichtspunkten: Texte der Hethiter 15. Heid 1989, Winter. xxix-175 p. 3-533-04153-9 [OIAc S89].

9499 *a) Ivanov* V., Relations between the ancient languages of Asia Minor; – *b) Rikov* G., Zur Entstehung der hethitischen hi-Konjugation; – *c) Vavroušek* P., Einige Bemerkungen zu den hethitischen Pronominaladverbien; – *d) Mačavariani* I., Die Subjekt-Objekt-Beziehungen im Hurri-Urartäischen; – e) *Ardzinba* V. ◉ Observations on Hittite Laws § 168: ➤ 874, Šulmu 1986/8, 133-144 / 319-327 / 337-348 / 195-210 / 1-18.

9500 *Kalaç* Mustafa, *Hawkins* J. D., The hieroglyphic Luwian rock inscription from Malpınar [between Adıyaman and Akpınar]: AnSt 39 (1989) 107-112; 2 fig.; pl. XXIII-XXV.

9501 [*Friedrich* Johannes †] **Kammenhuber** Annelies, Hethitisches Wörterbuch²ʳᵉᵛ 1984 ➤ 58,a342b ... 65,8118: ᴿJAOS 109 (1989) 87-95 (H. A. *Hoffner*: hopefully in 2114, when vol. 14 is likely to be completed, there will still be Hittitologists interested in reading these 1974 observations).

9502 **Kammenhuber** Annelies, Materialien zu einem hethitischen Thesaurus [10, 1981 ➤ 62,8993] 11. Heid 1989, Winter. iv-159 p. [BO 46,228].

9503 [*Kronasser* Heinz] Etymologie der hethitischen Sprache [1], **Neu** Erich, (Band 2), Indices zu Band 1, 1987 ➤ 3,9775; DM 198: ᴿBSLP 84,2 (1989) 253s (Françoise *Bader*); Kratylos 34 (1989) 183s (R. *Schmitt*).

9504 *Laroche* Emmanuel, a) Luwier, Luwisch, Lu(w)iya: ➤ 905, RLA 7,3s (1988) 181-4; – b) La version hourrite de la liste AN de Meskéné-Émar: CRAI (1989) 8-12.

9504* *Mascheroni* Lorenza M., A proposito delle cosiddette Sammeltafeln etee: ➤ 154, ᶠPuGLIESE CARRATELLI G., 1988, 131-145.

9505 **Neu** Erich, a) Zum Alter der personifizierenden -*ant*-Bildung des Hethitischen; ein Beitrag zur Geschichte der indogermanischen Genuskategorie: HistSprF [ex-ZVglSp] 102 (1989) 1-15 [16-20 -*al*; 21s, *Hamp* E. P., *alpu, dampu*]; – b) Zur Grammatik des Hurritischen auf der Grundlage der hurritisch-hethitischen Bilingue aus der Boğazköy-Grabungskampagne 1983: ➤ 817*, Hurriter 1988, 95-115.

9505* **Neu** Erich, Das Hurritische; eine altorientalische Sprache in neuem Licht [Boğazköy bilingual]: Abh g/soz 1988/3. Stu 1988, Steiner. 48 p. DM 24. – ᴿMundus 25 (1989) 124 (N. *Boysan-Dietrich*).

9506 *Ono* Satoshi, ◉ Clauses of tribute in Hittite vassal-treaties: Orient-Japan 32,1 (1989) 82-92.

9507 **Peckeruhn** Kerstin, Die Handschrift A der hethitischen Gesetze: Diss. ᴰ*Schuler* E. von. Würzburg 1988. vi-236 p. – OIAc N89.

9508 a) *Plank* Frans, Das Hurritische und die Sprachwissenschaft; – b) *Wilhelm* Gernot, Gedanken zur Frühgeschichte der Hurriter und zum hurritisch-urartäischen Sprachvergleich: ➤ 817*, Hurriter 1988, 69-93 / 43-67.

9508* *Poetto* Massimo, *Dinçol* A. & B., A new seal in hieroglyphic Luwian: Akkadica 62 (1989) 21s; 5 fig.

9509 **Polvani** Anna Maria, La terminologia dei minerali nei testi ittiti, I: Civiltà Or.Ant. 3. F 1988, E(d.)L(ibr.)IT(al.)E(stere). 193 p. [OIAc N89].

9510 **Rüster** Christel, **Neu** Erich, Hethitisches Zeichenlexicon; Inventar und Interpretation der Keilschriftzeichen aus den Boğazköy-Texten: Studien zu den Boğazköy-Texten Beih 2. Wsb 1989, Harrassowitz. 284 p.; 7 fig. 3-447-02794-0 [OIAc Ja90].

9510* *Smit* D. W., Achilles, Aeneas and the Hittites; a Hittite [KBo III 4] model for Iliad XX 191-194?: Talanta 20s (1988s) 53-64.

9511 **Starke** Frank, Die keilschrift-luwischen Texte in Umschrift 1985 ➤ 1,9277 ... 4,a569: ᴿOLZ 84 (1989) 542-4 (M. *Popko*).

9512 *Ünal* Ahmet, The power of narrative in Hittite literature: BA 52 (1989) 130-143; ill.; glossary 143-5.

9513 *Villar* V., Los pronombres personales hetitas: AulaO 7,1 (1989) 117-122; Eng. 117.

9514 **Weltenberg** Joseph J. S., Die hethitischen U-Stämme 1984 ⊳ 65,8138 ... 2,7675: ᴿOLZ 84 (1989) 422-7 (O. *Carruba*).

9515 *Windekens* A. J. Van †, Études de phonétique et d'étymologie hittites: ArOr 57 (1989) 333-342.

9516 **Yoshida** Daisuke, Die Syntax des alt-hethitischen substantivischen Genitivs: Texte der Hethiter 13, 1987 ⊳ 3,9764: ᴿHistSprF 102 (1989) 307s (G. *Neumann*).

J4.4 Phrygia, Lydia, Lycia.

9517 **Brixhe** Claude, **Hodot** René, L'Asie Mineure du nord au sud; inscriptions inédites [koinè, mais p. 165-234 pamphylien]: Études d'Archéologie Classique 6. Nancy 1988, Univ. 256 p.; 36 pl. – ᴿGnomon 61 (1989) 431s (G. *Neumann*).

9518 **Brixhe** Claude, Essai sur le grec anatolien au début de notre ère²ʳᵉᵛ [¹1984 ⊳ 65,8162 ... addenda]. Nancy 1987, Univ. 171 p. – ᴿBSLP 84,2 (1989) 267s (Françoise *Bader*); RÉG 101 (1988) 547-9 (O. *Masson*). **Bryce** T. R., The Lycians in literary and epigraphic sources 1986 ⊳ g243.

9519 *Faucouneau* J., À propos de la lecture des inscriptions cariennes: Kadmos 28 (1989) 174s.

9520 *Fauth* Wolfgang, Mykenisch *du-ma*, phrygisch *dum-*: HistSprF 102 (1989) 187-206.

9520* *a)* **Gusmani** Roberto, An epichoric inscription from the Lydio-Phrygian borderland; – *b)* **Heubeck** Alfred, Lykisch *tuhēi* in N 74c; – *c)* **Masson** Olivier, Noms cariens à Iasos; – *d)* **Neuman** Günter, Beobachtungen an karischen Ortsnamen: ⊳ 154, ꟳPUGLIESE CARRATELLI G. 1988, 67-73 / 75-78 / 155-7 / 183-191.

9521 *Hamp* Eric P., The Lydian locative in -L: HistSprF 101 (1988) 89-91.

9521* *Lubotsky* Alexander, *a)* New Phrygian *eti* and *ti*; – *b)* The syntax of the new Phrygian inscription No. 88: Kadmos 28 (1989) 79-88 / 146-155.

9522 *Melchert* H. Craig, New Luvo-Lycian isoglosses: HistSprF 102 (1989) 23-45 [46-57, *Heubeck* Alfred, Zur lykischen Inschrift von Çagman].

9523 **Neumann** Günter, Phrygisch und Griechisch: Szb W 499, 1988 ⊳ 4,a575; DM 10: ᴿBSLP 84,2 (1989) 254-7 (C. *Brixhe*); Kratylos 34 (1989) 185s (R. *Werner*).

9524 *Neumann* G., Lydien/Lykien [... iv. Sprache]: ⊳ 905, RLA 7,3s (1988) 184-6 / 189-191.

9525 *Otkupščikov* Yuri B., ❻ Carian and Greek language; genetic and ethno-cultural relations: ⊳ 794, Zentrum 1986 = Klio 71,1 (1989) 66-69.

9526 *Sanz Mingote* L., La escritura licia; una propuesta de transcripción; AulaO 7,1 (1989) 95-101; Eng. 95.

9527 **Jansky** Herbert, ¹¹*Landmann* Angelika, Lehrbuch der türkischen Sprache. Wsb 1986, Harrassowitz. x-222 p. – ᴿDer Islam 65 (1988) 184-7 (L. *Johanson*).

J4.8 Armena, georgica.

9528 **Diakonoff** I. M., *Starostin* S. A., Hurro-Urartian as an Eastern Caucasian language: MüStSprW Beih 12, 1986 ⊳ 4,a576; 3-920645-39-1: ᴿBO 46 (1989) 259-279 (R. *Smeets*).

9529 ᵀᴱGarsoïan Nina G., The epic histories attributed to PᵉAWSTOS BUZAND. CM 1989, Harvard Univ. xvii-665 p.; maps.
9530 **Kévorkian** Raymond H., Catalogue des 'incunables' arméniens (1511.1695) ou chronique de l'imprimerie arménienne 1986 ➤ 3,9774; 4,a577: ᴿOLZ 84 (1989) 206-8 (E. *Schütz*); OrChrPer 55 (1989) 217s (V. *Poggi*).
9531 *Mačaariani* Irakli G., Zur Rekonstruktion des Konjugationssystems der urartäischen Sprache der vorschriftlichen Periode: ArOr 57 (1989) 57-65.
9532 *Olsen* Birgitte A., A trace of Indo-European accent in Armenian; on the development of *-nt-* with an excursus on Greek *-ad-*: HistSprF 102 (1989) 220-240.
9533 *Schmidt* Karl H., On Armenian phonology and Indo-European reconstruction: ➤ 153, ᶠPOLOMÉ E., Languages 1988, 601-610.

9534 **Aronson** Howard J., Georgian; a reading grammar. Columbus OH 1984, Slavica. 526 p. $26. – ᴿJAOS 108 (1988) 322s (S. P. *Cowe*).
9535 *Schmidt* Karl H., Zur relativen Chronologie in den Kartvelsprachen: HistSprF 102 (1989) 129-152 [... 245-259].

J5 Graeca .1 *grammatica, onomastica, inscriptiones.*

9536 [*Bauer* Walter] ⁶**Aland** K. & B., Griechisch-Deutsches Wörterbuch ... NT 1988 ➤ 4,a579: ᴿArTGran 52 (1989) 352s (A. *Segovia*); BZ 33 (1989) 261-3 (R. *Schnackenburg*); FgNt 2,1 (1989) 100-2 (J. K. *Elliott*); GGA 241 (1989) 103-146 (R. *Borger*); JbAC 32 (1989) 186-8 (G. *Schöllgen*); NRT 111 (1989) 427s (X. *Jacques*); RB 96 (1989) 303s (J. J. *Taylor*); TR 85 (1989) 289s (D. *Zeller*); TS 50 (1989) 576-8 (J. A. *Fitzmyer*); TüTQ 169 (1989) 141-3 (M. *Reiser*); VigChr 43 (1989) 201-3 (J. van *Winden*).
9537 **Allen** W. Sidney, Vox graeca, a guide to the pronunciation of classical Greek³ [¹1968]. C 1987, Univ. xx-179 p.; 8 fig.; 1 pl. £9. 0-521-33555-8. – ᴿAntClas 58 (1989) 376 (A. *Martin*); Salesianum 51 (1989) 392s (R. *Della Casa*).
9538 *Arena* Renato, Varianti grafiche e morfologiche in area greca: Acme 42 (1989) 5-8.
9539 *Arnaud* Pascal, Une deuxième lecture du 'bouclier' de Doura-Europos: CRAI (1989) 373-387; 3 fig.
9540 **Bartoletti Colombo** A. M. (**Archi** I. G.) Legum Iustiniani Imperatoris vocabularium, Novellae I-IV, 1984-8. (*-ho*) ➤ 4,a580: ᴿByzantion 59 (1989) 540-5 (Giuliana *Lanata*).
9541 **Berkowitz** Luci, *Squitier* Karl A., Thesaurus linguae graecae, canon of Greek authors and works 1986 ➤ 3,9785; $25: ᴿNT 31 (1989) 90s (G. D. *Kilpatrick*: alternative to an impractical new LIDDELL-SCOTT); RelStR 15 (1989) 164 (A. T. *Kraabel*: ³1989 awaited).
9542 **Bernand** Étienne, Recueil des inscriptions grecques du Fayoum II-III, 1981 ➤ 63,8273; 65,8157: ᴿBO 46 (1989) 77-82 (H. *Heinen*).
9543 *Bile* M., *al.,* Bulletin de dialectologie grecque: RÉG 101 (1988) 74-112.
9544 **Biville** Frédérique, Graphie et prononciation des mots grecs en latin: Bibliothèque de l'Information Grammaticale 1987 ➤ 4,a584; F 58: ᴿAntClas 58 (1989) 376s (G. *Purnelle*).
9544* **Boel** Gunnar De, Goal accusative and object accusative in HOMER; a contribution to the theory of transitivity: Verh. Belg. Acad. Lett. 150/125. Bru 1988, Acad. 196 p. – ᴿClasR 39 (1989) 403s (A. C. *Moorhouse*).

9545 *Borger* Rykle, Zum Stande der neutestamentlichen Lexikographie; die Neuarbeitung des Wörterbuchs von W. BAUER: GGA 241 (1989) 103-146.

9545* *a)* *Boyer* James L., Noun clauses in the Greek New Testament; – *b)* *Young* Richard A., A classification of conditional sentences based on speech act theory: GraceTJ 10 (1989) 225-239 / 29-49.

9546 **Buonocore** Marco, Le iscrizioni latine e greche (Vaticano) 1987 ⇒ 4,g823: ᴿAntClas 58 (1989) 421s (Marie-Thérèse *Raepsaet-Charlier*); Arctos 23 (1989) 268 (M. *Kajava*); Gnomon 61 (1989) 637-9 (H. *Freis*).

9547 **Buzzetti** Carlo, (*Corsani* Bruno), Dizionario base del Nuovo Testamento (con statistica-base) [testo greco 1971, *Newman* B.M.]. R 1989, Libreria S. Scritture. 190 p. 88-237-8030-6.

9548 **Carrière** Jean, Stylistique grecque; l'usage de la prose attique³: Tradition de l'humanisme 6. P 1983, Klincksieck. x-247 p. 2-252-02439-9.

9549 *a)* *Ceresa-Gastaldo* Aldo, Lingua greca e categorie semitiche del testo evangelico; – *b)* *Zatelli* Ida, La situazione linguistica in terra d'Israele nel I secolo: ⇒ 572*, Storia/preistoria Vangeli 1986/8, 121-141 / 17-24.

9549* *Cignelli* Lino, *Bottino* Giovanni C., Il complemento d'agente nel greco biblico (LXX e NT): LA 39 (1989) 37-48.

9550 ᴱ**Coles** R.A., *al.,* The Oxyrhynchus Papyri 54, Memoir 74, 1987 ⇒ 4,a591: ᴿClasR 39 (1989) 124-6 (Wolfgang *Luppe*, deutsch).

9550* **Conybeare** F.C., *Stock* S.G., Grammar of Septuagint Greek, with selected readings from the Septuagint according to the text of SWETE. Peabody MA 1988 = 1905, Hendrickson. vi-313 p. $15. 0-913573-93-0 [NTAbs 33,270].

9551 Corpus dei papiri filosofici greci e latini; testi e lessico dei papiri di cultura greca e latina, I. autori noti 1*: Ac Toscana / Unione Accad. Naz. F 1989, Olschki. iv-479 p. 88-222-3638-6.

9551* **Corsani** Bruno (*Buzzetti* C.), Guida allo studio del greco del NT 1987 ⇒ 3,9797; 4,a592: ᴿLA 39 (1989) 352-363 (L. *Cignelli*: correzioni per quasi ogni pagina).

9552 **Cotton** Hannah M., *Geiger* Joseph, Masada II: The Latin and Greek documents. J 1989, Israel Expl. x-246 p.; ill.

9553 **Cuvigny** Hélène, *Wagner* Guy, Les ostraca grecs de Douch II, 1988 ⇒ 4,a595: ᴿRÉG 102 (1989) 576s (P. *Cauderlier*).

9553* **Daniel** Robert W., *al.,* Griechische und demotische Papyri der Universitätsbibliothek Freiburg: Mitteilungen 4: PapyrTAbh 38, 1986 ⇒ 2,7707; DM124: ᴿClasR 39 (1989) 122s (R. *Coles*).

9554 *a)* *Davison* M.E., New Testament Greek word order; – *b)* *Huynh-Armanet* V., *Pineira-Tresmontant* C., La description contextuelle des mots et l'ordinateur: LitLComp 4 (Ox 1989) 19-28 / 12-18.

9555 **Dobson** J.H., Learn New Testament Greek. GR 1989, Baker. xiii-306 p. $12. 0-8010-2992-9 [NTAbs 33,234]. 0-564-07872-7. £5; cassette £4; both £8. – ᴿExpTim 100 (1988s) 270 (C.S. *Rodd*).

9556 **Dubois** Laurent, Recherches sur le dialecte arcadien [I-III, 1975 diss. P, ᴰ*Masson* O.]. Lv 1986, Cabay ⇒ 4,a599: ᴿHistSprF 102 (1989) 311-6 (J.L. *García-Ramón*).

9557 **Dubois** Laurent, Inscriptions grecques dialectales de Sicile; contribution à l'étude du vocabulaire grec colonial: Coll.Éc.Fr.R. 119. R 1989, École Française. xv-305 p. 2-7283-0185-9.

9558 **Dunn** Graham, Enclitic pronoun movement and the ancient Greek sentence accent: Glotta 67 (1989) 1-19.

9559 **Fantoni** Georgina, Greek papyri of the Byzantine period: Corpus Papyrorum Raineri 15, Griechische Texte 10. W 1989, Nationalbiblio-

thek (Hollinek). 121 p.; 50 pl. 3-85119-233-8 [OIAc N89]. – ᴿBASP 25 (1988) 169-171 (J. G. *Keenan*).
9560 **Fisher** William F., The participle in the Greek Pentateuch, a descriptive analysis and comparison to NT usage: diss. SW Baptist Theol. Sem. 1989. 352 p. 90-04360.
9561 ᴱ**Fraser** P. M., *Matthews* E., A lexicon of Greek personal names I, The Aegean islands, Cyprus, Cyrenaica 1987 ➤ 3,9805; 4,a602: ᴿClasR 39 (1989) 300-2 (C. *Tuplin*); RHE 84 (1989) 613s (N. *Zeegers-Vander Vorst*); RPg 62 (1988) 326-8 (J.-L. *Perpillou*).
9561* **Frösen** J., *al.*, Papyri helsingienses 1. Ptolemäische Urkunden: Comm. Hum.Lit. Fenn. 80, 1986 ➤ 3,9806. – ᴿClasR 39 (1989) 159 (Dorothy J. *Thompson*).
9562 **Gignac** Francis T., *a*) The development of Greek phonology; the fifteenth century B.C. to the twentieth century after Christ: ➤ 175, Mem. SCHODER R., Daidalikon 1989, 131-7; – *b*) Phonological phenomena in the Greek Papyri significant for the text and language of the New Testament: ➤ 60, ᶠFITZMYER J., Touch 1989, 33-46.
9562* ᴱ**Gronewald** M., *al.*, Kölner Papyri 6: Rh/Wf Akad, PapyrolCol 7, 1987 ➤ 4,a606; DM 64: ᴿClasR 39 (1989) 356-98 (G. O. *Hutchinson*).
9563 **Guerra** Manuel, Diccionario morfológico del Nuevo Testamento² [¹1978 + suplemento] 1988 ➤ 4,a607: ᴿEfMex 7 (1989) 133-5 (R. H. *Lugo Rodríguez*); EstE 64 (1989) 558s (J. *Iturriaga*: novedad, transcripción castellana de nombres propios).
9564 **Guillemette** P., The Greek New Testament analyzed. Kitchener ᴼⁿ 1986, Herald. xlii-435 p. – ᴿÉglT 19 (1989) 102-4 (G. *Bloomquist*, Eng.); NRT 111 (1989) 617 (A. *Harvengt*).
9565 **Hansen** Mogens H., *Dêmos, ekklēsia* and *dikastērion*; a reply to M. OSTWALD and J. OBER: ClasMedK 40 (1989) 101-6.
9565* ᴱ**Harlfinger** D., *al.*, Specimina sinaitica; die datierten griechischen Handschriften 1983 ➤ 64,8334...2,7721: ᴿRCatalT 13 (1988) 507-9 (S. *Janeras*).
9566 *a*) *Harstad* M. J., Greek-English word processing on MS-DOS computers; – *b*) *Kilpatrick* G. D., Text and language in the Greek New Testament: Classical Review 65,1s (Chicago 1989) 3-16 / 64,3s (1988) 71s [< NTAbs 33,290s].
9567 **Haslam** M. L., The Oxyrhynchus Papyri 53: Greco-Roman Memoirs 73, 1986 ➤ 3,9814: ᴿBASP 24 (1987) 165-177 (H. S. *Schibli*); JHS 109 (1989) 247s (M. *Davies*).
9568 **Hewett** S. A., NT Greek 1986 ➤ 4,a611: ᴿSVlad 32 (1988) 185 (J. E. *Rexine*).
9569 **Hoffmann** Ernst G., *Siebenthal* Heinrich von, Griechische Grammatik zum NT 1985 ➤ 3,9818: ᴿJBL 108,185 (187 again under *von* Hoffmann).
9569* ᴱ**Karageorghis** J., *Masson* O., The history of the Greek language in Cyprus; Proceedings of an International Symposium, Larnaca 8-13 Sept. 1986. Larnaca 1988, Pierides. xl-222 p. – ᴿBSLP 84,2 (1989) 260-6 (Françoise *Bader*); ClasR 39 (1989) 276s (J. T. *Hooker*: V. Karageorghis speculates idly about 'Sea-Peoples').
9570 *Krämer* H., Zur Bedeutung von Wünschsätzen im Neuen Testament: ➤ 131, ᶠMARXSEN W., Jesu Rede 1989, 375-8.
9570* **Kramer** Bärbel, *Hagedorn* Dieter, Griechische Texte der Heidelberger Papyrus-Sammlung 1986 ➤ 2,7734: ᴿBO 46 (1989) 332s (J. M. *Diethart*).
9571 **Lewis** Naphtali, Greek Papyri: Documents from the Bar Kokhba period in the Cave of Letters. J c. 1989, Israel Expl.

9572 ᴱLouw Johannes P., *Nida* Eugene A., Greek-English lexicon of the New Testament based on semantic domains, I. Introduction and domains; 2. Indices, 1988 → 4,a617: ᴿBiblica 70 (1989) 438-442 (J.J. *Welch*: beautifully produced and clearly expressed); JBL 108 (1989) 705-7 (H. *Boers*); NT 31 (1989) 379s (J.K. *Elliott*); Salesianum 51 (1989) 359s (C. *Buzzetti*); TLZ 114 (1989) 817-820 (N. *Walter*); WestTJ 51 (1989) 163-7 (M. *Silva*).

9573 **MacDonald** William G., Greek enchiridion; a concise handbook of grammar for translation and exegesis 1986 → 3,9826: ᴿRelStR 15 (1989) 262 (B.D. *Ehrman*); SVlad 32 (1989) 186s (J.E. *Rexine*).

9574 ᴱMcKechnie P.R., *Kern* S., Hellenica Oxyrhynchia. Wmr 1988, Aris & P. 187 p.

9575 **Mateos** Juan, Método de análisis semántico aplicado al griego del Nuevo Testamento: Est FgNt 1. Córdoba 1989, Almendro. 186 p. pt. 1590; $20. 84-86077-72-9. – ᴿFgNt 2,1 (1989) 111s (J. *Peláez*).

9576 *Meier-Brügger* Michael, Verbaute schwundstufige -s- Neutra in der griechischen Wortbildung: HistSprF 102 (1989) 58-61.

9577 *Mussies* Gerard, Eine Architravinschrift aus Umm Qēs (Gadara) in Jardanien: ZDPV 105 (1989) 124-8.

9577* *Nicolau* Francese, Nota sobre l'aspecte verbal de l'imperfet en el grec del Nou Testament: → 69*, ᶠGOMÀ I., RCatalT 14 (1989) 273-8; Eng. 278.

9578 *Noret* Jacques, Faut-il écrire oúk eisin ou ouk eisín? [after *kaì, ei, hōs* and several other tiny words, not only *estí* but also *eisí* and *eimí, esmén, esté* are 'orthotonic']: Byzantion 59 (Bru 1989) 277-280.

9579 *Packman* Zola M., Masculine and feminine; use of the adjectives in the documentary papyri: BASP 25 (1988) 137-148.

9580 **Perschbacher** Wesley J., The new [*Wigram* G. 1852 fully revised] Analytical Greek lexicon. Peabody MA 1989, Hendrickson. 542 p. $30 [Interp 43,431 adv.].

9580* **Petzl** G., Die Inschriften von Smyrna [1. 1982 → 63,8312] 2/1: Kleinasien 24. Bonn 1987, Habelt. – ᴿClasR 39 (1989) 350s (D.M. *Lewis*).

9581 **Porter** Stanley E., Verbal aspect in the Greek of the New Testament, with reference to tense and mood: Studies in Biblical Greek 1. NY 1989, P. Lang. xii-582 p.

9582 *Radney* J.R., Some factors that influence fronting [putting a noun before the verb] in koine clauses: OPTAT 2,3 (Dallas 1988) 1-79 [< NTAbs 33,293].

9583 **Rca** J.R., Oxyrhynchus papyri 55: Mem 75, L 1988, Egypt Expl. – ᴿBASP 25 (1988) 157-168 (R. *Katzoff*); VDI 190 (1989) 295-215 (V.N. *Yarkho*).

9584 **Rehkopf** F., Septuaginta-Vokabular. Gö 1989, Vandenhoeck & R. ix-318 p. DM 38. 3-525-50172-2 [BL 90,46]. – ᴿTüTQ 169 (1989) 321s (W. *Gross*).

9585 **Rijksbaron** Albert, The syntax and semantics of the verb in classical Greek. Amst 1984, Gieben. 186 p. – ᴿAnzAltW 42 (1989) 17-20 (T. *Krisch*).

9585* **Rosén** Haiim B., Early Greek grammar and thought in HERACLITUS; the emergence of the article: Proc 7/2. J 1988, Israel Acad. 42 p. – ᴿBSLP 84,2 (1989) 269s (Françoise *Bader*); ClasR 39 (1989) 404s (A.C. *Moorhouse*).

9586 *Rosén* Haiim B., Der griechische 'dativus absolutus' und indogermanische 'unpersönliche' Partizipialkonstruktionen: HistSprF 101 (1988) 92-103.

9586* *Sasse* Hans-Jürgen,   Wortumfang und Wortform; zur Weiterentwicklung einsilbiger Imperative im nachklassischen Griechisch: HistSprF 102 (1989) 212-5.

9587 **Scheelhas** L. B., Wie 't kleine niet eert ... Het gebruik van het lidwoord bji persoonsnamen in het Nieuwe Testament: Cah 60, 1987 ➤ 4,a638: ᴿStreven 55 (1987s) 180s (P. *Beentjes*).

9588 ᶠSOISALON-SOININEN I.,   Studien zur Septuaginta-Syntax, ᴱAejmelaeus A., *Sollamo* R. 1987 ➤ 3,305: ᴿSalesianum 51 (1989) 346s (M. *Cimosa*).

9589 **Spicq** Ceslas,   Note di lessicografia neotestamentaria [I. A-K] 1988 ➤ 4,a640: ᴿCC 140 (1989,2) 206 (S. *Votto*); Gregorianum 70 (1989) 788s (G. *Ferraro*); RivB 37 (1989) 504-510 (Anna *Passoni Dell'Acqua*: traduzione spesso 'calco' o 'targumica'); Salesianum 51 (1989) 570 (R. *Sabin*); StCattMi 33 (1989) 284 (U. *De Martino*).

9590 **Teeter** Timothy M.,   Ten Christian papyri in the Columbia collection [Mt 6,4-12; Ps 150...]: diss. Columbia. NY 1989. 169 p. 90-05944. – DissA 50 (1989s) 3329-A.

9591 *Thorley* John,   Aktionsart in New Testament Greek; infinitive and imperative: NT 31 (1989) 290-315.

9592 **Trench** Richard C.,   Synonyms of the New Testament (1876), ᴱHoerber Robert G.   GR 1989, Baker. 425 p. $25. 0-8010-8890-9 [TDig 37,191].

9593 **Turner** Eric G., ²*Parsons* P. J.,   Greek manuscripts of the ancient world 1987 ➤ 4,a642: ᴿCdÉ 64 (1989) 337s (J. *Lenaerts*); RÉG 101 (1988) 543s (P. *Cauderlier*).

9594 *Villa* Jesús de la,   Caractérisation fonctionnnelle du datif grec: Glotta 67 (1989) 20-40.

9594* **Windekens** A. J. van,   Dictionnaire étymologique complémentaire de la langue grecque 1986 ➤ 3,9861; 4,a647:   ᴿBSLP 84,2 (1989) 258-260 (C. *Brixhe*).

9595 **Wouters** Alfons,   The Chester Beatty codex AC 1499, a Graeco-Latin lexicon on the Pauline epistles and a Greek grammar 1988 ➤ 4,a647: ᴿAegyptus 69 (1989) 277-280 (Anna *Passoni Dell'Acqua*); BSLP 84,2 (1989) 273s (P. *Swiggers*); RelStR 15 (1989) 264 (B. D. *Ehrman*); ÉtClas 57 (1989) 178s (aussi P. *Swiggers*); RHE 84 (1989) 714-7 (W. *Clarysse*).

J5.2   **Voces graecae** (*ordine alphabetico* **graeco**).

9596 *agápē*: **Légasse** S.,   'Et qui est mon prochain?' Étude sur l'*agapè* dans le NT: LDiv 136. P 1989, Cerf. 184 p. F 125. 2-204-03044-9. – ᴿEsprVie 99 (1989) 651s (L. *Walter*); Gregorianum 70 (1989) 786s (J. *Galot*).

9597 *hágios*: **Nuchelmans** J.,   À propos de *hagios* avant l'époque hellénistique: ➤ 17, ᶠBARTELINK G., Fructus 1989, 239-258.

9598 *Brenk* Frederick,   Plus saint que chez Homère; *sanctus* chez Virgile: XII Congrès international de l'Association G. Budé, Bordeaux 1988 (Paris 1989) 305-7 [ActaPIB 9,455].

9599 *aiōn*: RoczTK 33,1 (1986) 79-99 (A. S. *Jasiński* ●; 99 deutsch).

9600 *állōs*: **Veyne** Paul,   Les emplois d'*állōs* dans le grec d'époque impériale: RPLH 62 (1988) 209-216.

9600* *hamartía*: **Ullmann** Reinholdo A.,   'Hamartia' [cultura grega]; erro, culpa ou pecado?: Teocomunicação 19 (1989) 151-8 [< TContext 7/1, 80].

9601 **Ostwald** Martin, *anánkē* in THUCYDIDES: AmerClasSt 18. Atlanta 1988, Scholars. vii-82 p. $18; pa. $12 [AmJPg 111, 277-9, P. A. *Stadter*].

9601* *Merkel* F., **Anámnēsis** — eine liturgiewissenschaftliche Studie: ⇥ 131, ᶠMARXSEN W., Jesu Rede 1989, 414-423.

9602 *áxios*: **Pöschl** Viktor, Der Begriff der Würde im antiken Rom und später: Szb ph/h Heid. 1989,3. Heid 1989, Winter. 67 p.

9602* *apotélesma*: *Biscardi* Arnaldo, 'Quod Graeci "apotelesma" vocant': Labeo 35 (1989) 163-171.

9603 *Calduch Benages* Núria, El término *áphesis* en los papiros griegos [84 veces] y en el Nuevo Testamento [17 veces]: ⇥ 69*, ᶠGOMÀ I., RCatalT 14 (1989) 267-271 castellano; Eng. 272.

9603* *Montevecchi* Orsolina, **achreîos - áchrēstos - akyrōsimos**: JJurPap 20 (1988) 113-8.

9604 *býrsa*: *Habermann* Wolfgang, Lexikalische und semantische Untersuchung am griechischen Begriff býrsa [Ledergewerbe, leatherwork]: Glotta 66 (1988) 93-99.

9605 *bouleutēs*: *Sijpesteijn* P. J., A female *bouleutēs*: BASP 24,3 (1987) 141s.

9606 *glaukós*: *Perotti* Pier Angelo, Sur les adjectifs *glaukós, glaukôpis*: Ét-Clas 57 (1989) 97-109.

9607 *diá*: *Luraghi* Silvia, Cause and instrument expressions in classical Greek; remarks on the use of *diá* in HERODOTUS and PLATO: Mnemosyne 42 (1989) 294-307.

9608 *douleúō*: *Hilhorst* A., 'Servir Dieu' dans la terminologie du judaïsme hellénistique et des premières générations chrétiennes de langue grecque: ⇥ 17*, ᶠBARTELINK G., Fructus 1989, 177-192.

9609 *doxázō*: *Brückner* K., A word study of *doxázō* in the Gospel of John: NotesTr 2,2 (Dallas 1988) 41-46 [< NTAbs 33,318].

9610 *ekklēsía*: *Peri* Israel, *Ecclesia* und *synagoga* in der lateinischen Übersetzung des Alten Testamentes: BZ 33 (1989) 245-251.

9611 *Héllēn*: *Vannicelli* Pietro, Il nome *Héllēnes* in Omero: RivFgIC 117 (1989) 34-48.

9612 *embrímion* / embrýmion (papyrus, textes monastiques): RÉG 101 (1988) XIII (Geneviève *Husson*; ⇥ 4,a671).

9613 *exomológēsis*: *Bardski* Krzysztof, 'Exomologesis' en san Paciano de Barcelona: ScripTPamp 21 (1989) 117-124.

9614 *epēreia*: *Blanc* Alain, La volonté de nuire; étude sur *epēreia* et *epēreázō*: RÉG 102 (1989) 175-182.

9615 *érchomai*: *Létoublon* Françoise, Il allait 1985 ⇥ 3,9887: ᴿMnemosyne 64 (1989) 146-153 (C. J. *Ruijgh*); RPg 62 (1988) 330s (J.-L. *Perpillou*).

9616 *erōtáō*: *Elliott* J. K., erotân and eperōtân in the NT: FgNt 2 (1989) 205s.

9617 *éschatos*: *Kastner* Wolfgang, éschatos – enkata: MusHelv 46 (1989) 9-14 [cf. ⇥ 4,a674].

9618 *héōs* (ion. *ēos*): *Powell* Marvin A., Aja ~ Eos: ⇥ 183, ᶠSJÖBERG Å., Dumu- 1989, 447-455.

9619 *theós*: *Ullmann* Reinholdo A., O significado de 'Theos' em Grego: Teocomunicação 16,79 (1988) 7-26 [< TContext 6/2,60].

9620 *Starowieyski* Marek, Le titre *theotókos* avant le concile d'Éphèse: ⇥ 696, 10th Patristic, 19 (1989) 236-242.

9620* *thýrion*: *Derda* Tomasz, Thýrion, a new occurrence of a rare word: JJurPap 20 (1988) 41-46.

9621 *Louth* Andrew, The use of the term *ídios* in Alexandrian theology from Alexander to Cyril: ⇥ 696, 10th Patristic, 19 (1989) 198-202.

9622 *Otterloo* R. Van, Towards an understanding of 'Lo' and 'behold'; functions of *idou* and *ide* in the Greek New Testament: OPTAT 2,1 (Dallas 1988) 34-64 [NTAbs 33,293, giving the accents *idoú* and *íde*).

9623 *hiláskomai:* *Vivoli* Rita, Hiláskomai nei testi epigrafici dell'Asia Minore: ➤ 759, Sangue VI, 1987/9, 137-161.

9624 *Ioudaîos:* *Kraemer* Ross S., On the meaning of the term 'Jew' in Greco-Roman inscriptions: HarvTR 82 (1989) 35-53.

9625 *kephalē:* *Cervin* Richard S., Does *kephalē* mean 'source' [hardly] or 'authority over' [no, pace *Grudem* W. and *Fitzmyer* J.]; a rebuttal: TrinityJ 10,1 (1989) 85-112.

9626 *kérygma:* *Virgulin* Stefano, 'Kerigma' e 'didaskalia' nel NT: Seminarium 31 (1989) 319-333; Eng. 287; franç. 293.

9627 *kýrios:* *Gagos* Trajanos, A brief note on the nomen sacrum *kýrios* in the Codex Manichaicus coloniensis: ZPapEp 77 (1989) 273s.

9628 *límiton:* *Mayerson* Philip, The meaning of the word *limes (límiton)* in the papyri: ZPapEp 77 (1989) 287-291.

9629 *maraínō:* *Meier-Brügger* Michael, Zu griechisch *maraínō-omai* und *móros:* HistSprF 102 (1989) 62-67.

9629* *metánoia:* **Gaventa** Beverly R., From darkness ... conversion NT 1986 ➤ 2,7786 ... 4,a679: [R]JRel 69 (1989) 237s (J. D. *Tabor*).

9630 *metaphorá:* *Fruyt* Michèle, Métaphore, métonymie et synecdoque dans le lexique latin: Glotta 67 (1989) 106-122.

9631 *oîkos:* *MacDowell* Douglas M., The *oîkos* in Athenian law: ClasQ 83 = 39 (1989) 10-21.

9631* *órgia:* HistSprF 101 (1988) 104-7 (M. *Meier-Brügger*).

9632 *órthros:* *Wallace* Robert W., *órthros* ['(pre-) dawn']: AmPgTr 119 (1989) 201-7.

9633 *ouranós:* *Worthen* Thomas, The idea of 'sky' in archaic Greek poetry, Iliad 18,485: Glotta 66 (1988) 1-19.

9634 *páthos:* *Garro* Paola, La concezione dei *páthē* da ZENONE e CRISIPPO a PANEZIO: SMSR 55 (1989) 183-195.

9635 *pastós:* *Lane* Eugene N., Pastós [bridal nook; not *pástos* salted meat]: Glotta 66 (1988) 100-123.

9636 *pístis:* *Dewey* Arthur J., The Synoptic use of *pistis*: an appeal for a context-sensitive translation: Forum 5/4 (1989) 83-86.

9637 *pólis:* *Aloni* Antonio, *Negri* Mario, Il caso di *ptólis* [like *ptólemos* etc.]: Minos 24 (1989) 139-144.

9638 *Sarakēnos:* *Mayerson* Philip, The word Saracen (*sarakēnos*) in the papyri: ZPapEp 79 (1989) 283-7.

9639 *skándalon:* *Mateos* Juan, Análisis semántico de los lexemas skandalízō y skándalon: FgNt 2,1 (1989) 57-91; Eng. 92.

9640 *smarís:* *Knobloch* Johann, Der Fischname smarís [its tough skin served as sandpaper]: HistSprF 102 (1989) 68s.
sôs-: [D]Zawadzki M. ➤ 5254.

9641 *tolmēría:* *Brunner* Theodore F., *tolmēría* [boldness]: Glotta 67 (1989) 191-3.

9642 *phálanx:* *Pattison* John H., Le sémantisme de *phálanx:* ➤ 190, [F]TAILLARDAT J. 1988, 205-212.

9643 *philóponos:* *Sijpesteijn* P. J., New light on the *philoponoi*: Aegyptus 69 (1989) 95-99.

9644 *psychē:* **Jahn** Thomas, Zum Wortfeld 'Seele-Geist' in der Sprache

Homers: Zetemata 83. Mü 1987, Beck. xvi-328 p. – ᴿGGA 241 (1989) 147-157 (R. *Führe*).

J5.5   **Cypro-Minoa** [➤ T9.1-4].

9645 *Adrados* Francisco R., ¿ Sincretismo de casos en micénico?: Minos 24 (1989) 169-185.

9645* *Baumbach* Lydia, Names of shepherds at Knossos: Acta Classica 30 (Pretoria 1987) 5-10.

9646 *Bennett* Emmett L., *al.*, 436 raccords et quasi-raccords de fragments inédits dans KT5: Minos 24 (1989) 199-242.

9647 ᴱ**Best** Ian, *Woudhuizen* Fred, Ancient scripts from Crete and Cyprus: Frankfort Foundation 9, 1988 ➤ 4,a694; £20 pa.: ᴿAntiquity 63 (1989) 181 (J. *Chadwick*: unsuccessful attempt to relate to Luwian).

9648 **Bile** Monique, Le dialecte crétois ancien; étude de la langue des inscriptions...: Ét. Crétoises 27. P 1988, Geuthner. 405 p.; 8 pl.

9649 *Bile* Monique, Le vocabulaire du village dans les inscriptions crétoises: Ktema 11 (1986) 137-144.

9650 ᴱ**Chadwick** John, *al.*, Corpus of Mycenaean inscriptions from Knossos I (1-1063): Incunabula Graeca 88, 1986 ➤ 2,7813; 4,a695: ᴿAJA 93 (1989) 294-6 (T. G. *Palaima*); RÉG 101 (1988) 195-7 (P. *Faure*).

9651 **Chadwick** John, Linear B and related scripts: Reading the Past series, 1, 1986 ➤ 4,a696; also Berkeley 1987, Univ. California. 64 p.; 39 fig. $7. 0-520-06019-9. – ᴿBAR-W 15,4 (1989) 11 (C. A. *Moore,* also on three other British Museum booklets); ÉchMClas 33 (1989) 263s (F. H. *Casler*).

9652 ᶠCHADWICK J., Studies in Mycenaean and classical Greek, ᴱ**Killen** J. T....: Minos 20ss, 1987 ➤ 3,37: ᴿKratylos 34 (1989) 79-85 (J.-L. *Perpillou*).

9653 *Deroy* Louis, Quelques réflexions sur le cadastre mycénien de Pylos: Minos 24 (1989) 125-130.

9654 *Gallagher* William R., A reconsideration of *o-no* [not 'payer, price' but h^e*mor* 'ass'] in Mycenaean Greek: Minos 23 (1988) 85-106; 1 fig. [107-115, *Janda* Michael, Zeichen 47; 147-162, *Milani* Celestina, *we/u*; 163-182, *Guidi* Michele, *i-qo* = *hippos*].

9655 *Godart* Louis, *Tzedakis* Iannis, La storia del Lineare B e le scoperte di Armenoi e La Canea: RFgIC 117 (1989) 385-409.

9656 *Guidi* Michele, Gli scribi della Serie O di Micene: Minos 24 (1989) 69-88.

9657 *a) Hallager* Erik, *Godart* Louis, *Olivier* Jean-Pierre, La rondelle en Linéaire A d'Haghia Triada We 3024 (HM 1110); – *b) Farnoux* Alexandre, *Olivier* J.-P. Trois nouveaux fragments de tablettes en écriture hiéroglyphique crétoise à Malia: BCH 113 (1989) 431-7 / 97-100; ill.

9658 **Herrmann** Peter, Tituli Asiae Minoris 5. Lydiae 2 NW. W 1989, Akad.

9659 **Killen** John T., *Olivier* Jean-Pierre, The Knossos tablets, a transliteration⁵ [¹1955, ²1956, ⁴1971: but with varying editors]: Minos supp. 11. Salamanca 1989, Univ. xxii-489 p.

9660 *a) Kopaka* Katerina, Une nouvelle inscription en linéaire A de Zakros; – *b) Neumann* Günter, Beiträge zum Kyprischen X/XI: Kadmos 28 (1989) 7-13 / 89-95. 168-173.

9661 **Masson** Olivier, *Mitford* Terence B., Les inscriptions syllabiques de Kouklia-Paphos 1986 ➤ 3,9950; 4,a702: ᴿHistSprF 102 (1989) 309s (A. *Heubeck* †); RArchéol (1988) 149-151 (A. *Hermary*).

9662 *Masson* Olivier, Les inscriptions syllabiques chypriotes de Golgoi, fouilles 1969-1972: Kadmos 28 (1989) 156-167.

9663 *Maurice* Nicole, Analogie et flexion nominale en grec mycénien, I. le datif-locatif pluriel des thèmes en -n-; – II, Les noms en -(t)er-; Minos 23 (1988) 117-146; 24 (1989) 145-168.

9664 *Militello* Pietro, Gli scribi di Haghia Triada; alcune osservazioni: ParPass 245 (1989) 126-147.

9665 **Morpurgo Davies** Anna, **Duhoux** Yves, Linear B 1984/5 ➤ 1,768; 3,9952: ᴿAntClas 58 (1989) 412-4 (P. *Wathelet*, sans pp., sur la religion mycénienne, CHADWICK J., HÄGG R., DIETRICH B.); RÉG 101 (1988) 545-7 (O. *Masson*).

9665* *a) Neuss* O., Addenda zu Struktur und Interpretation des Diskos von Phaistos; – *b) Woudhuizen* F.C., The recently discovered Greek-Sidetic bilingue from Seleucia: Talanta 20s (1988s) 75-80 + 8 fig / 87-96.

9666 *Nicolaou* Ino, Inscriptiones cypriae alphabeticae 28, 1988: RepCyp (1989) 141-7 + 3 fig.; pl. XXXIII-XXXVIII.

9666* **Palaima** Thomas G., The scribes of Pylos: Incunabula Graeca 87. R 1988, Ateneo. 287 p.; 26 fig.

9667 *Palaima* Thomas G., Ideograms and supplementals and regional interaction among Aegean and Cypriote scripts: Minos 24 (1989) 29-54.

9668 *Patria* Enrica, The misunderstanding of Linear A: Minos 23 (1988) 15-37.

9669 *Redondo* Jordi, Mycénien *da-pu-ri-to, de-re-u-ko*; une seule question de phonétique: Minos 24 (1989) 187-198.

9670 ᶠRISCH E., o-o-pe-ro-si, ᴱEtter A. 1986 ➤ 2,95: ᴿKratylos 34 (1989) 34-41 (H. *Hettrich*).

9671 *Sacconi* Anna, Filologia micenea: ➤ 775, Filologia 1984/9, 3-32.

9671* *a) Sacconi* A., Le marche di vasaio; questioni di metodo; – *b) Franceschetti* A., L'allume [aluminium-compound] nei documenti micenei: ➤ 811, Momenti 1985/8, 147-155 + 2 charts / 163-7.

9672 **Stavrianopoulou** Eftychia, Untersuchungen zur Struktur des Reiches von Pylos; die Stellung der Ortschaften im Lichte der Linear-B-Texte: Diss. Heidelberg 1987. – Chiron 19 (1989) 556.

9673 *Tegyey* Imre, Some problems of the status of the working groups on Linear B tablets: AnClasDeb 24 (1988) 3-8.

9674 **Trümpy** Catherine, Vergleich des Mykenischen mit der Sprache der Chorlyrik [Diss. ᴰRisch E.] 1986 ➤ 3,9954; 4,a707: ᴿKratylos 34 (1989) 85-91 (C.J. *Ruijgh*).

9675 **Ventris** Michael, Work notes on Minoan language research and other unedited papers, ᴱSacconi Anna: Incunabula Graeca 90. R 1988, Ateneo. viii-396 p.

9676 *Xhardez* Didier, Le scribe 2 de Pylos; sur deux questions controversées [Linéaire B]: AntClas 58 (1989) 5-16.

J6 **Indo-Iranica.**

9677 *Beekes* R.S.P., Old Persian *p-θ-i-m* ['path']: MüStSprW 50 (1989) 7-13.

9678 **Camps** A., *Muller* J.-C., Sanskrit grammar of H. ROTH 1988 ➤ 4,a709: ᴿKratylos 34 (1989) 177 (H.M. *Hoenigswald*).

9679 **Davari** G. Djelani, Baktrisch, ein Wörterbuch. Heid 1982, Gross. 306 p. – ᴿStIran 17 (1988) 111s (P. *Gignoux*).

9680 **Diakonoff** I.M., *Livshitz* V.A., Parthian economic documents from Nisa, ᴱMacKenzie D.M.: Corpus Inscriptionum Iranicarum 2/2. L 1976s, Lund Humphries. II. Parthian, 80 p. + vol. of 330 pl.

9680* **Filliozat** Pierre-Sylvain,   Grammaire sanskrite pāninéenne: Connaissance des Langues.   P 1988, Picard.   185 p.   F 180. – ᴿJRAS (1989) 166s (*J. L. Brockington*).

9681 **Gignoux** Philippe,   Noms propres sassanides [diss.]: Iranisches Personennamenbuch 2/2, 1986. – ᴿIndIraJ 32 (1989) 311-3 (P. *Huyse*); JAOS 109 (1989) 127-9 (P. O. *Skjærvø*); OLZ 84 (1989) 579-588 (S. *Zimmer*) auch 589-591 über 4/2, Münzen, *Alram* A.).

9681* *Giovinazzo* G.,   L'expression *haduš haduka* dans les textes [élamites] de Persepolis: Akkadica 63 (1989) 12-26.

9682 **Grillot-Susini** Françoise, (*Roche* Claude),   Éléments de grammaire élamite: Synthèse 29.   P 1989, RCiv.   80 p. – ᴿBSLP 84,1 (1989) 333-343 & 84,2 (1989) 412-425 (Florence *Malbran-Labat*); JAOS 109 (1989) 670s (H. H. *Paper*: a valiant effort, but misses the mark); JRAS (1989) 149-151 (*J. A. Black*).

9683 *Mayrhofer* Manfred,   Über die Verschriftung des Altpersischen: Hist-SprF 102 (1989) 174-186.

9684 **Shokoohy** Mehrdad,   Rajasthan I: Corpus Inscriptionum Iranicarum 4/49/1.   L 1986, Lund Humphries.   93 p.   87 pl. – ᴿAcOrK 49 (1988) 146-8 (B. *Utas*).

9685 ᴱSkalmowski W., *Tongerloo* A. Van,   Middle Iranian studies 1982/4 → 65,668 ... 4,a716: ᴿStIran 16 (1987) 281-292 (E. M. *Jeremias*; very detailed summaries).

J6.5   **Latina.**

9685* *a)* **Salomies** Olli,   Die römischen Vornamen; Studien zur römischen Namengebung: Comm.Hum.Lit. 82.   Helsinki 1987, Soc.Scientiarum Fennica.   466 p. – ᴿClasR 39 (1989) 93-95 (A. R. *Birley*); – *b)* **Solin** Heikki, *Salomies* Olli,   Repertorium nominum gentilium et cognominum Latinorum: Alpha-Omega 80.   Hildesheim 1988, Olms.   x-474 p.   DM 128. – ᴿClasR 39 (1989) 327-9 (T. J. *Cadoux*).

9686 Thesaurus linguae latinae X fasc. 2-5 / XI,1 fasc. 4.   Lp 1984-7, Teubner.   Col. 161-782 / 431-640. – ᴿBBudé (1988) 283s & (1989) 92 (G. *Serbat*).

J8.1   **Philologia generalis.**

9687 **Amsler** Mark,   Etymology and grammatical discourse in late antiquity and the early Middle Ages: Studies in the History of the Language Sciences 44.   Amst 1989, Benjamins.   xi-280 p.   90-272-4527-4.

9688 ᴱBest Ian, *Woudhuizen* Fred,   Lost languages of the Mediterranean: Frankfort Fd 101.   Leiden 1989, Brill.   179 p.; 5 pl.   90-04-08934-9 [OIAc N89].

9689 ᶠBRÄUER Herbert, 65. Gb., ᴱOlesch Reinhold, *Rothe* Hans: Slavistische Forschungen 53.   1986 → 3,28: ᴿKratylos 34 (1989) 204-6 (Annelies *Lagreid*).

9689* **Brucker** Charles,   L'étymologie: Que sais-je 1122, 1988 → 4,a732: ᴿBSLP 84,2 (1989) 114-6 (P. *Swiggers*: 'plagiat' de 6 auteurs).

9690 *Burkert* Walter,   Schweiz; die klassische Philologie: → 775, La filologia greca e latina nel secolo XX, 1984/9, 75-127.

9691 ᴱComrie Bernard,   The world's major languages.   L 1989, Routledge.   xiii-1025 p.; maps.   0-415-04516-9.   50 art.

Derchain Philippe, À propos de performativité; pensers anciens et articles récents 1989 → 9112.

9694 **Katzner** Kenneth, The languages of the world. L 1989 = 1977 Routledge. x-376 p. 0-415-04604-1.

9695 **Klein** Ernest, A comprehensive etymological dictionary of the English language , dealing with the origin of words and their sense development, thus illustrating the history of civilization and culture. Amst 1986 = 1971 (2 vol. 1966s), Scientific. xxv-844 p. 0-444-40930-0.

9696 **Klose** Albrecht, Sprachen der Welt. Mü 1987, Saur. xlviii-410 p. DM 360. – ᴿKratylos 34 (1989) 159-161 (Rüdiger *Schmitt*).

9697 ᶠLAUSBERG Heinrich: Text-Etymologie; Untersuchungen zu Textkörper und Textinhalt, 75. Gb., ᴱArens Arnold, 1987 → 4,94: ᴿSalesianum 51 (1989) 393s (R. *Gottlieb*, tit. senza pp.).

9698 *Merwe* C.H.J. van der, The vague term 'emphasis': JSem 1 (1989) 118-132.

9698* **Miller** J., Semantics and syntax; parallels and connections 1985 → 3,9988; £25: ᴿBSLP 84,2 (1989) 84-86 (H. B. *Rosén*: le titre serait mieux formulé 'lexique et grammaire').

9699 *Modini* Paul, Historical typology and language classification: ArOr 57 (1989) 343-6.

9700 ᶠNEUMANN Günter: Serta indogermanica, ᴱTischler Johann: Innsb. Beit. SprW 40, 1982 → 64,85: ᴿAnzAltW 42 (1989) 1-14 (G. R. *Solte*).

9700* *Rosén* Hannah, On the plausibility of ancient etymologies: HistSprF 101 (1988) 116-126.

9701 *Shields* Kennethᴶ, The origin of the thematic vowel: IndogF 94 (1989) 7-20.

9701* **Svenbro** Jasper, Phrasikleia; anthropologie de la lecture en Grèce ancienne: Textes à l'appui. P 1988, Découverte. 268 p. F 185. 2-7071-1768-4. – ᴿRÉLat 67 (1989) 312s (Florence *Dupont*).

9702 *Testa Bappenheim* Italo, Rilevazioni antropologico-linguistiche sugli influssi jonico-etruschi nella scrittura medio-adriatica in ambito demo-piceno: BbbOr 31 (1989) 15-40.223-244.

9702* **Thomas** Rosalind, Oral tradition and written record in classical Athens: Cambridge Studies in Oral and Literate Culture 18. C 1989, Univ. xiii-321 p. 0-521-35025-5.

J8.2 Grammatica comparata.

9704 *Adrados* Francisco R., Agglutination, suffixation or adaptation? For the history of Indoeuropean nominal inflexion: IndogF 94 (1989) 21-44.

9705 *Alonso Schökel* Luis, Hebreo + Español; notas de semántica comparada II: Sefarad 49 (1989) 11-19.

9706 **Barr** James, Comparative philology and the text of the OT 1987 [¹1968] → 3,9992: ᴿBS 146 (1989) 106s (E. H. *Merrill*: indispensable).

9707 *Blažek* Václav, Lexica nostratica, addenda et corrigenda I: ArOr 57 (1989) 201-210.

9708 *Bliese* Loren F., Does the verb come last in your language?: BTrans 40 (1989) 219-227 ['translators soon learn to work from opposite ends of the sentence'].

9708* *Bomhard* Allan R., Recent trends in the reconstruction of the Proto-Indo-European consonantal system: HistSprF 101 (1988) 2-25.

9709 **Diakonoff** I. M., Afrasian languages [to replace Semito-Hamitic languages 1965]. Moskva 1988, Nauka. 143 p. – ᴿAulaO 7 (1989) 287s (W. G. E. *Watson*).

9710 *a*) *Gamkrelidze* Thomas V., Ex oriente lux; on the problem of an Asiatic homeland of the Proto-Indo-Europeans; – *b*) *Hamp* Eric P., The Indo-European terms for 'marriage'; – *c*) *Adrados* Francisco R., On the origins of the Indo-European dative-locative singular endings: ➤ 153, ᶠPOLOMÉ E., 1988, 161-7 / 179-182 / 29-41.

9711 *Gamkrelidze* T.V., *Ivanov* V.V., ❽ First Indo-Europeans in history; ancestors of the Tokharians in the Ancient Near East: VDI 188 (1989) 14-38; Eng. 38s.

9712 *Hart* Gillian R., Anatolian evidence and the origins of the Indo-European mediopassive: BSOAS 51 (1988) 69-95.

9713 *Hintze* Fritz, Das Ägyptische und das SAE ['Standard Average European', *Whorf* B.L.]: ZägSpr 115 (1988) 39-41.

9714 ᴱJungraithmayr Herrmann, *Müller* Walter W., Proceedings of the fourth Hamito-Semitic Congress 1983: Amst. Theor. Ling. 4/44. Amst 1987, Benjamins. xiv-609 p. – ᴿOLZ 84 (1989) 688-690 (J. *Oelsner*).

9715 *Kienast* Burkhart, Zur Nominalbildung im Semitischen: ➤ 183, ᶠSJÖBERG Å., Dumu- 1989, 277-287.

9716 *Lavalade* Paul †, Noms de parties du corps en égyptien et en indo-européen: ➤ 823, Akten IV,3 (1985/9) 67-75.

9717 **Loprieno** A., Das Verbalsystem im Ägyptischen und im Semitischen 1986 ➤ 2,7842; 4,a758: ᴿJSS 34 (1989) 187-195 (Frithiof *Rundgren*).

9718 *Lühr* Rosemarie, Ist die Basiskategorie TEMPORAL als Ausgangspunkt für konjunktionale Bedeutungen ein Universale? Zur Polyfunktionalität von Konjunktionen in indogermanischen Sprachen: HistSprF 102 (1989) 153-173.

9719 **Mallory** J.P., In search of the Indo-Europeans; language, archaeology and myth. L 1989, Thames & H. 288 p.; 175 fig. £24. – ᴿAntiquity 63 (1989) 843-7 (C. *Renfrew*); EWest 39 (1989) 317s (G. *Stacul*); GreeceR 36 (1989) 250 (P. *Walcot*).

9720 **Mann** Stuart E., An Indo-European comparative dictionary. Ha 1984/7, Buske. XIV-1684 col. DM 720. – ᴿKratylos 34 (1989) 41-45 (M. *Mayrhofer*).

9721 **Martinet** André, L'indoeuropeo; lingue, popoli e culture: Universale 207. Bari 1987, Laterza. xii-291 p. – ᴿSalesianum 51 (1989) 906s (R. *Bracchi*).

9722 **Mayrhofer** M., Sanskrit und die Sprachen Alteuropas: NachGö 1983/5, Gö 1983 ➤ 1,9479: ᴿArGlotIt 71 (1986) 135-145 (D. *Maggi*).

9723 **Meid** Wolfgang, Archäologie und Sprachwissenschaft; Kritisches zu neucren Hypothesen der Ausbreitung der Indogermanen: BeiSprW 43. Innsbruck 1989, Univ. 40 p. – ᴿBeiNam 24 (1989) 434s (J. *Knobloch*).

9724 **Nussbaum** Alan J., Head and horn in Indo-European 1986 ➤ 3,a8: ᴿBSLP 84,2 (1989) 218-222 (Françoise *Bader*); JAOS 108 (1988) 186s (D.A. *Ringe*); Kratylos 34 (1989) 55-59 (R.S.P. *Beekes*); Latomus 48 (1989) 922s (Marie-José *Reichler-Béguelin*).

9725 *O'Connor* Michael, Semitic *mgn* ['give'] and its supposed Sanskrit origin: JAOS 109 (1989) 25-32.

9726 **Olsen** Birgit A., The Proto-Indo-European instrument noun suffix *tlom* and its variants: Hist./filos. Med. 55, 1988 ➤ 4,a760: ᴿRPg 62 (1988) 328 (M. *Menu*).

9727 *Pârvulescu* Adrian, Blood and Indoeuropean kinship terminology: IndogF 94 (1989) 67-88.

9728 *Pezzi* Elena, Aportaciones para un estudio de lingüística ario-semítica (II): La expresión del movimiento: BAsEspOr 24 (1988) 153-169.

9729 *Rendsburg* Gary A., Sabaic notes to Hebrew grammar: Abr Nahrain 27 (1989) 106-119.

9730 **Renfrew** Colin, Archaeology and language; the puzzle of Indo-European origins. L 1988 (2d reprint), Cape. xv-446 p. – ᴿAJA 93 (1989) 466s (Susan N. *Skomal*); Salesianum 51 (1989) 832 (R. *Della Casa*).

9731 **Retsö** Jan, Diathesis in the Semitic languages; a comparative morphological study: StSemitLangLing 14. Leiden 1989, Brill. xvii-254 p. 90-04-08818-0.

9732 *Rundgren* Frithiof, Aspectology in the light of text linguistics: OrSuec 36s (1987s) 57-76.

9733 **Szemerényi** Oswald, Einführung in die vergleichende Sprachwissenschaft[3rev]. [¹1970]. Da 1989, Wiss. xxv-370 p. – ᴿBeiNam 24 (1989) 483s (J. *Tischler*).

9734 ᴱ**Vennemann** Theo, The new sound of Indo-European; essays in phonological reconstruction: Trends in Linguistics 41. B/NY 1989, Mouton de G. xvi-300 p. 3-11010-536-5 / US 0-89925-521-3.

9735 *Voigt* Rainer, Zur semitohamitischen Wortvergleichung: GöMiszÄg 107 (1989) 87-95: 7 Beispiele.

9736 **Wexler** Paul, Explorations in Judeo-Slavic linguistics: Contributions to the Sociology of Jewish Languages 2. Leiden 1987, Brill. xix-286 p. ƒ160. – ᴿOLZ 84 (1989) 41-45 (H. *Simon*).

9737 *Wyatt* Nicholas, Near Eastern echoes of Āryan tradition: SMSR 55,1 (1989) 5-29.

J8.3 Linguistica generalis.

9738 **Anttila** Raimo, Historical and comparative linguistics[2rev]: Current Issues in Linguistic Theory 6. Amst 1989, Benjamins. xv-462 p.; ill. 90-272-3556-2; pa. 7-0.

9739 *Bailey* Charles J. N., Two true/false principles of language change: IndogF 94 (1989) 1-4.

9740 **Black** David A., Linguistics for students of NT Greek 1988 → 4,a766: ᴿExpTim 100 (1988s) 432 (Ruth B. *Edwards*; mercifully without roadblocks like 'morphemes' 'allophones' but at cost of ancient pronunciation etc.): RExp 86 (1989) 434s (D. S. *Dockery*).

9740* **Bloomfield** Leonard, Language [1933], pref. *Hockett* C. F., Ch 1988, Univ. xvi-564 p. – ᴿBSLP 84,2 (1989) 20-23 (P. *Swiggers*).

9741 ᴱ**Breivik** Leiv E., *Jahr* Ernst H., Language change; contributions to the study of its causes: Trends in Linguistics 43. B/NY 1989, Mouton de G. 281 p. 3-11010-536-5 / US 0-89925-521-3.

9742 *Bronk* Andrzej, ☻ Filozofia języka: → 891, EncKat 5 (1989) 257-261 (798s, GADAMER).

9743 **Cardona** Giorgio R., Introduzione alla sociolinguistica. T 1987, Loescher. 182 p. – ᴿSalesianum 51 (1989) 398s (R. *Della Casa*).

9744 **Comrie** Bernard, Language universals and linguistic typology; syntax and morphology[2]. Ch 1989, Univ. xiv-264 p.

9745 **Coseriu** Eugenio, Einführung in die allgemeine Sprachwissenschaft. Tü 1988, Francke. 329 p. – ᴿBeiNam 24 (1989) 367 (R. *Schützeichel*: ein Desiderat).

9746 **Cotterell** Peter, *Turner* Max, Linguistics and biblical interpretation. L 1989, SPCK. 348 p. £10. 0-281-04358-2. – ᴿExpTim 100 (1988s) 470 (C. S. *Rodd*); TLond 92 (1989) 302s (D. de *Lacey*: not easy to discover finally the Linguistics/Bible relation); WestTJ 51 (1989) 389s (M. *Silva*).

9747 **Crystal** David, The Cambridge encyclopaedia of linguistics. C 1987, Univ. vii-472 p. £25. 0-521-26438-3. – ᴿBTrans 40 (1989) 342s (D. *Kenrick*).

9747* **Demers** Richard A., *Farmer* Ann K., A linguistics workbook. CM 1986, MIT. xii-275 p. 0-262-54045-2. – ᴿBSLP 84,2 (1989) 118s (R. *Hodot*).

9748 **Dressler** Wolfgang, Morphonology; the dynamics of derivation: Linguistica extranea 12. AA 1985, Karoma. ix-439 p. – ᴿIndogF 94 (1989) 328-333 (J. *Lenerz*).

9749 **Dressler** Wolfgang U., Semiotische Parameter einer textlinguistischen Natürlichkeitstheorie: Szb W ph/h 529. W 1989, Österr. Akad. 63 p. 3-7001-1587-3.

9750 ᴱ**Fisiak** Jacek, Historical dialectology, regional and social [Błażejewsko, Poland, May 7-10, 1986]: Trends in Linguistics 37 B/NY 1988, Mouton de G. xiii-694 p. 3-11-011550-6 / US 0-89925-434-9.

9751 *Fontaine-De Visscher* L., La linguistique et les sciences humaines: Revue Philosophique de Louvain 86 (1988) 378-392 [< RSPT 73 (1989) 141].

ᴱ**Gessinger** Joachim, *Rahden* Wolfert von, Theorien vom Ursprung der Sprache 1989 ➤ 541.

9752 *Goldenberg* Gideon, The contribution of Semitic languages to linguistic thinking: JbEOL 30 (1987s) 107-115.

9752* **Guillaume** Gabriel, [*Chabot* Caroline, *Douet* Anne-Thérèse], Langages et langue; de la dialectologie à la systématique [diss. d'État, Paris-IV 1987]: Marche Armoricaine 6. xxxiv-284 p. – ᴿBSLP 84,2 (1989) 323-5 (P.-Y. *Lambert*).

9753 ᴱ**Haiman** John, *Thompson* Sandra A., Clause combining in grammar and discourse: Typological Studies in Language 18. Amst/Ph 1988, Benjamins. xiii-442 p. 90-272-2893-0; pa. 4-9 / US 1-55619-0220; 3-9.

9754 ᴱ**Harris** Martin, *Ramat* Paolo, Historical development of auxiliaries: Trends in Linguistics 35. B/NY 1987, Mouton de G. viii-368 p. 3-11-010990-5.

9755 ᴱ**Hattori** Shirō, *Inoue* Kazuko, Proceedings of the XIIIth International Congress of Linguists 1982/3 ➤ 2,532: ᴿHistSprF 102 (1989) 297-302 (N. *Oettinger*: many summaries).

9756 **Helbig** Gerhard, Entwicklung der Sprachwissenschaft seit 1970. Lp 1986, VEB Bibliographisches Institut. 323 p. – ᴿBeiNam 24 (1989) 235-240 (Rosemarie *Lühr*).

9757 ᴱ**Heydrich** Wolfgang, *al.*, Connexity and coherence; analysis of text and discourse: Research in Text Theory 12. B 1989, de Gruyter. xi-404 p. 3-11-011102-0.

9758 **Horn** George M., Essentials of functional grammar; a structure-neutral theory of movement, control, and anaphora: Trends in Linguistics 38. B/NY 1988, Mouton de G. 404 p. 3-11-011286-8 / US 0-899-25348-2.

9759 **Lazzeroni** Romano, Linguistica storica: Lettere 25. R 1987, Nuova Italia. 179 p. – ᴿSalesianum 51 (1989) 905s (R. *Gottlieb*).

9760 ᴱ**Lyons** John, New horizons in linguistics I-II: Pelican. Hmw 1987 = 1970, Penguin, I. 367 p. II. vi-465 p. 0-14-022786-5; II. 0-14-022612-5.

9761 **Mounin** Georges, Histoire de la linguistique des origines au XXᵉ siècle⁴ [¹1967]: Le Linguiste. P 1985, PUF. 230 p. 2-13-039216-4.

9762 **Mulder** Jan W. F., Foundations of axiomatic linguistics: Trends in Linguistics 40. B/NY 1989, Mouton de G. xii-475 p. 3-11011-234-5 / US 0-899-25323-7.

9763 *a) Partee* Barbara H., Possible worlds in model-theoretic semantics; a linguistic perspective; – *b) Enkvist* Nils E., Connexity, interpretability, universes of discourse, and text worlds: → 773, Possible worlds 1986/9, 93-123 [-161] / 162-186 [-218].

9764 ᴱ**Perron** Paul, *Collins* Frank, Paris school semiotics: Semiotic Crossroads 1s. Amst/Ph 1989, Benjamins. I. xxvi-257 p. 90-272-1942-7 / US 1-55619-040-9.

9765 *Porter* Stanley E., Studying ancient languages from a modern linguistic perspective; essential terms and terminology: FgNt 2 (1989) 147-177; castellano 177s.

9766 **Radford** Andrew, Transformational grammar, a first course: Textbooks in Linguistics. C 1988, Univ. xiv-625 p. 0-521-34506-5; pa. 750-5.

9767 **Runggaldier** Edmund, Zeichen und Bezeichnetes; sprachphilosophische Untersuchungen zum Problem der Referenz. B 1985, de Gruyter. xi-360 p. – ᴿTPhil 64 (1989) 460s (F. *Ricken*).

9768 *Sandor* Andras, Signification, meaning and the text level of language [... *Benveniste* É.]: IndogF 94 (1989) 45-66.

9769 **Saussure** Ferdinand de, *a)* Cours de linguistique générale 1, édition critique, *Engler* Rudolf. Wsb 1989 = 1968, Harrassowitz. xii-515 p. 3-447-00798-2; – *b)* Course in General Linguistics, ᴱ*Bally* Charles, *al.* [1972, ᵀ*Harris* Roy 1983]. La Salle IL 1989, Open Court. xx-236 p. 0-8126-9023-0.

9770 **Saville-Troike** Muriel, The ethnography of communicaton, an introduction²: Language in Society 3. Ox 1989, Blackwell. ix-315 p. 0-631-16678-5.

9771 ᴱ**Schubert** Klaus (*Maxwell* Dan), Interlinguistics; aspects of the science of planned languages: Trends in linguistics 42. B/NY 1989, Mouton de G. 348 p. 3-11011-910-2 / US 0-899-25548-5.

9772 **Searle** John R., Les actes de langage; essai de philosophie de langage [Speech acts 1969], ᵀ*Pauchard* Hélène: Savoir. P 1988, Hermann. 261 p. 2-7056-5727-4.

9773 **Sözer** Önay, Leere und Fülle; ein Essay in phänomenologischer Semiotik. Mü 1988, Fink. 162 p.; 2 fig. DM 48. – ᴿDLZ 110 (1989) 529-531 (G. *Lerchner*).

9774 ᴱ**Tobin** Yishai, From sign to text; a semiotic view of communication: Foundations of Semiotics 20. Amst 1989, Benjamins. xiii-545 p. 90-272-3292-X. 23 art. Eng. + 10 français.

J8.4 *Origines artis scribendi* – The Origin of Writing.

9775 *Briquel* Dominique, Les traditions sur l'origine de l'écriture en Italie: RPg 62 (1988) 251-271.

9776 **Cardona** Giorgio R., Storia universale della scrittura [= lo scrivere]²: Le Palme. Mi 1987, Mondadori. 332 p. – ᴿArGlotIt 72 (1987) 154-8 (G. *Costa*); Salesianum 51 (1989) 187s (R. *Bracchi*).

9777 *Daniels* Peter T., 'Proto-Euphratic' and the syllabic origin of writing: ProcGLM 9 (1989) 23-33.

9778 **Defrancis** John, Visible speech; the diverse oneness of writing systems. Honolulu 1989, Univ. xiv-306 p. 0-8248-1207-7 [OIAc N89].

9779 ᴱ**Detienne** Marcel, Les savoirs de l'écriture en Grèce ancienne [1984]: CahPg Lille 3/14. Lille 1988, Univ. 545 p. F 160. 2-85939-322-6. – ᴿClasR 39 (1989) 242s (C. G. *Thomas*); ÉTRel 64 (1989) 266s (Jacky *Argaud*: 'écriture' dans le texte, 'É' dans le titre).

9780 **Dietrich** M., *Loretz* O., Die Keilalphabete 1988 → 4,a801: ᴿVT 39 (1989) 119s (J. A. *Emerton*).

9781 **Fales** Frederick M., *al.* Prima dell'alfabeto; la storia della scrittura attraverso testi cuneiformi inediti: StDoc 4. Venezia 1989, Erizzo. 269 p.; (color.) ill. 88-7077-026-5.

9782 **Gamkrelidze** Thomas V., Alphabetic writing and the Old Georgian script; a typology and provenience of alphabetic writing systems. Tbilisi 1989, Univ. 351 p.

9783 *Haarmann* Harald, Hieroglyphen- und Linearschriften; Anmerkungen zu alteuropäischen Schriftkonvergenzen: Kadmos 28 (1989) 1-6.

9784 **Halvorsen** Barry D., Scribes and scribal schools in the Ancient Near East; a historical survey: diss. Grace Theol. Sem., ᴰ*Fowler* Donald L., Winona Lake IN 1981. – OIAc Ja90.

9784* *Heinz* Marlies, Die Steingefässe aus Süd- und Mittelmesopotamien als Inschriftenträger der frühdynastischen Zeit: BaghMit 20 (1989) 197-224; 17 fig.

9785 **Jean** Georges, L'écriture mémoire des hommes: Découvertes. P 1987, Gallimard. 290 p. F 66. 2-07-053040-X. – ᴿÉTRel 64 (1989) 101 (Jacky *Argaud*).

9786 **Mendenhall** George E., The syllabic inscriptions from Byblos 1985 → 1,d728 ... 4,a809: ᴿBASOR 276 (1989) 85s (S. A. *Kaufman*: fails on all counts); Orientalia 58 (1989) 134-8 (É. *Puech*: L'auteur se montre conscient des nombreuses incertitudes).

9787 **Naveh** J., Early history of the alphabet 1982 → 64,8514 ... 1,9518: ᴿRSO 62 (1988) 172s (F. *Israel*).

9788 *Powell* Barry, Why was the Greek alphabet invented? The epigraphical evidence: ClasAnt 8 (1989) 321-350.

9789 *Sass* [Za's] Benjamin, The Egyptian Middle Kingdom system for writing foreign names and the beginnings of the West-Semitic alphabet: → 218, Mem. YADIN Y., ErIsr 20 (1989) 44-50; Eng. 195*.

9790 ᴱ**Senner** Wayne M., The origins of writing. Lincoln 1989, Univ. Nebraska. vii-245 p. 0-8032-4202-6. 12 art.; p. 77-90, *Cross* F. M., alphabet; 59-76, *Fischer* H. G., hieroglyphs; 43-57, *Green* E. W., cuneiform; 27-41, *Schmandt-Besserat* D., tokens.

9791 *Speyer* Wolfgang, Geheimgehaltene Überlieferungen und Schriften der Antike: → 547, ᴱ*Neukam* P., Die Antike als Begleiterin. [c. 1989, Bayerischer Schulbuch-V.] 91-109.

9791* *Vajman* A. A., Beiträge zur Entzifferung der archaischen Schriften Vorderasiens I: BaghMit 20 (1989) 94-133 [-139, *Damerow* P., *Englund* R., Bemerkungen].

9792 *Vanstiphout* Hermann, Enmerkar's invention of writing revisited: → 183, ᶠSJÖBERG Å., Dumu- 1989, 515-524.

9793 *a) Wachter* Rudolf, Zur Vorgeschichte des griechischen Alphabets; – *b) Lejeune* Michel, Un abécédaire corinthien du Vᵉ s. en Dardanie: Kadmos 28 (1989) 19-78 / 14-19.

J9.1 *Analysis linguistica loquelae de Deo* – **God-talk.**

9794 *Adams* Daniel J., Reconciling theological opposites; a linguistic model: AsiaJT 3 (1989) 96-107.

9795 *Albano* Peter J., Freedom, truth and hope; the relationship of philosophy and religion in the thought of Paul RICŒUR. Lanham MD 1987, UPA. xvi-252 p. $27.50; pa. $13.70. – ᴿJRel 68 (1988) 471s (D. *Pellauer*).

9796 *Bayer* Oswald, Theologie im Konflikt der Interpretationen; ein Gespräch mit Paul RICŒUR: ComViat 32 (1989) 223-230.

9797 **Betti** E., L'ermeneutica come metodica generale delle scienze dello spirito, ᵀᴱ*Mora* Gaspare, 1987 ➤ 3,a65:   ᴿAnStoEseg 6 (1989) 319s (A. N.).

9798 *Bielfeldt* Dennis, LUTHER, metaphor, and theological language: ModT 6 (1989s) 121-135.

9798* **Bori** Pier Cesare, L'interpretazione infinita; l'ermeneutica cristiana antica e le sue trasformazioni 1987 ➤ 3,a67; 4,a868:   ᴿAnStoEseg 6 (1989) 311-3 (M. *Pesce*).

9799 **Bourg** Dominique   Transcendance et discours: CogF 132, 1985 ➤ 2,7893; 3,a68:   ᴿRevSR 61 (1987) 92s (J. *Joubert*).

ᴱ**Braaten** Carl E.,   Our naming of God; problems and prospects of God-talk today 1986/9 ➤ 637.

9800 *Carminati* Giancarlo,   Una teoria semiologica del linguaggio liturgico; una verifica sull'Ordo Missae: EphLtg 102 (1988) 184-233.

9801 **Cathey** Robert A.,   Foundations with faces; a prolegomenon to a postliberal doctrine of God: diss. Duke, ᴰ*Wainwright* G. Durham NC 1989. 779 p. 90-01053. – DissA 50 (1989s) 2536-A.

9802 **Cooke** Bernard J.,   The distancing of God; the ambiguity of symbol in history and theology. Ph c. 1989, Fortress. $25. [TTod 46,455 adv.].

9803 **Dillistone** F.M.,   The power of symbols in religion and culture 1986 ➤ 3,a77; 4,a823:   ᴿJRel 68 (1988) 343 (J.W. *Heisig*: an academic sermon).

9804 *Dumont* Heinrich, Theologische Bedeutung der Symbole: TGegw 32 (1989) 255-265.

9805 **Eliade** Mircea,   Spezzare il tetto della casa; la creatività e i suoi simboli [1986], ᵀᴱ *Scagno* Roberto: Di fronte e attraverso 211. Mi 1988, Jaca. xxi-260 p. 88-16-40211-3.

9806 **Ellul** Jacques,   What I believe, ᵀ*Bromiley* Geoffrey W. GR 1989, Eerdmans. 233 p. $20 [TrinJ 10,240].

9807 *Evans* Jeanne,   Paul RICŒUR's hermeneutics; the imagination as the creative element of religious literacy: diss. St. Michael, ᴱ*Farris* W. Toronto 1989. 186 p. – RTLv 21, p. 537.

9808 *Findeis* Hans-Jürgen, Languages of religions and intercultural communication; a contribution to the intercultural philosophy of religious language: ZMissRW 73 (1989) 257-283.

9809 **Geffré** Claude,   The risk of interpretation 1987 ➤ 3,a84; 4,a826: ᴿAmerica 158 (1989) 217 (Nancy C. *Ring*); LVitae 44 (1989) 231 (A.T. *Godin*); RelStT 7,2s (1987) 100 (H. *Meynell*); RRel 48 (1989) 631-3 (G.T. *Finnegan*); Thomist 53 (1989) 156-160 (M.J. *Dodds*); TLZ 114 (1989) 462s (M.J. *Suda*).

9810 *Giustiniani* Pasquale, Paul RICŒUR; ermeneutica e teologia: Asprenas 36 (1989) 494-507.

9811 *Harvey* Michael G., WITTGENSTEIN's notion of 'theology as grammar'; RelSt 25 (C 1989) 89-103.

9812 **Hogan** John P., COLLINGWOOD and theological hermeneutics: CTS StRel 3. Lanham MD 1989, UPA. vii-238 p. $27.50; pa. $14.75 [CBQ 152,196].

9813 *a)* *Holifield* E. Brooks,   On saying too much and saying too little; – *b)* *Terrien* Samuel, A theological look at [BECKETT S.] Waiting for Godot: TTod 46 (1989s) 130-8 / 139-151.

9814 **Jeanrond** Werner G.,   Text and interpretation as categories of theological thinking 1988 ➤ 2,7910 ... 4,a832: ᴿCCurr 39 (1989s) 219-221

(J. E. *Thiel*); Horizons 16 (1989) 174s (J. *McCarthy*); JRel 69 (1989) 562s (D. *Jasper*); RExp 86 (1989) 449 (J. D. W. *Watts*).

9815 *Jossua* Jean-Pierre, L'apport de la littérature pour un renouvellement du langage religieux: ÉchSM 19 (1989) 101-117.

9816 *Joy* Morna, DERRIDA and RICŒUR; a case of mistaken identity (and difference): JRel 68 (1988) 508-526.

Laurant J.-P., Symbolisme et écriture; le cardinal PITRA et [i.e rédacteur 1884 de] la 'Clef' de MÉLITON de Sardes 1988 ➤ 1274.

9818 **Long** Charles, Significations ... in religion 1986 ➤ 2,187 ... 4,a838: RJRel 68 (1988) 341-3 (Lisa B. *Raskind*); TR 85 (1989) 143-5 (S. *Wisse*).

9819 **Loose** Donald, God ter sprake brengen; een semantiek van de analogie en de metafoor: diss. DVergote A., Leuven 1989. xiii-746 p. – RTLv 21, p. 538, L'évocation de Dieu; une sémantique de l'analogie et de la métaphore; TsTNijm 29 (1989) 171s.

9820 FMcINTYRE John: Religious imagination, EMackey James P., 1986 ➤ 2,63: RJRel 68 (1988) 468-470 (L. D. *Bouchard*).

9821 *Mora* Gaspare, Interpretare e comprendere; attualità ermeneutica di S. TOMMASO: III. Ermeneutica e ontologia della parola: NuovaUm 11,61 (1989) 57-80.

9822 *Morgan* Drew P., Hermeneutical aspects of J. H. NEWMAN's Essay on the development of Christian doctrine: Horizons 16 (1989) 223-243.

9823 **Morgan** George A., Speech and society; the Christian linguistic and social philosophy of Eugen ROSENSTOCK-HUESSY. Gainesville 1987, Univ. Florida. – RRHPR 69 (1989) 55s (G. *Vahanian*).

9824 *Morrissey* Michael P., Reason and emotion; modern and classical views on religious knowing: Horizons 16 (1989) 275-291.

9825 **Müller** Wolfgang W., Das Symbol in der dogmatischen Theologie, unter besonderer Berücksichtigung der Symboltheorien bei Karl RAHNER, Paul TILLICH, Paul RICŒUR und Jacques LACAN: kath. Diss. DMüller G. München 1989. 455 p. – RTLv 21,370 (> Fra, Lang).

9825* *Muruzáhal* Saturnino, Acercamiento al lenguaje religioso, hoy: An-Calas 30 (1988) 9-83.

9826 ENoppen Jean-Pierre van, Erinnern, um Neues zu sagen; die Bedeutung der Metapher für die religiöse Sprache 1988 ➤ 4,a848; DM 58: RTLZ 114 (1989) 459-461 (W. *Krötke*); ZAW 101 (1989) 151 (tit. pp.); ZRGg 41 (1989) 283s (K. *Ebert*).

9827 **Ohly** Friedrich, Süsse Nägel der Passion; ein Beitrag zur theologischen Semantik [= FGRIPPER Helmut, Collectanea Philologica, EHeintz Günter, *Schmitter* Peter: Saecula spiritalia 15 (Baden-Baden) 403-613]: Saecula Spiritalia 21. Baden-Baden 1989, Koerner [RHE 85, 147, G. *Hendrix*].

9828 **Pastor** Félix A., La lógica de lo Inefable, una teoría teológica sobre el lenguaje del teismo cristiano 1986 ➤ 2,7929; 3,a108: RTR 85 (1989) 470 (I. *Escribano-Alberca*).

9829 *Santos* Emil M., Theology OF communication, theology AND communication; two comprehensive approaches linking theology and communication: Salesianum 51 (1989) 89-111.

9830 *Smith* Roy H. S., The denial of mystery; object relations theory and religion: Horizons 16 (1989) 243-265.

9831 **Soskice** Janet M., Metaphor and religious language 1987 ➤ 1,9626 ... 4,a856: RTTod 46 (1989s) 352s (A. M. *Olson*).

9832 **Steiner** George, Real presences; is there anything IN what we say? ['any coherent account of the capacity of human speech to communicate meaning and feeling is, in the final analysis, underwritten by the assumption of God's presence']. Faber & F. 236 p. £13. – ᴿDowR 107 (1989) 292-6 (L. *Bell*).

9833 **Tracy** David, Plurality and ambiguity; hermeneutics, religion, hope 1987 ➤ 3.a117 = a997; 4,a858: ᴿCCurr 38 (1988s) 352s (P. *Giurlanda*); DocLife 39 (1989) 277s (S. P. *Kealy*); Interpretation 43 (1989) 412-4 (D. G. *Dawe*: ethical sanity cum ambiguity towards revelation); JRel 69 (1989) 85-91 (R. J. *Bernstein*); RelStR 15 (1989) 218-221-223 (W. G. *Jeanrond, M. Wiles*); RExp 86 (1989) 444s (W. L. *Hendricks*); TLond 92 (1989) 446s (P. *Avis*); WestTJ 50 (1988) 217-222 (K. *Vanhoozer*).

9834 **Treitler** Wolfgang, Gotteswort im Menschenwort; das Problem theologisch-methodischen Redens nach Hans Urs von BALTHASAR: kath. Diss. ᴰ*Reikerstorfer*. Wien 1988s. – TR 85 (1989) 513.

9835 **Vahanian** Gabriel, Dieu anonyme, ou la peur des mots. P 1989, Desclée de Brouwer. 186 p. F 95. – ᴿRHPR 69 (1989) 506s (*ipse*).

9836 *Vitre* Marie-Madeleine, À la recherche d'une herméneutique du symbole [l'analyse du symbole chez LEIBNIZ et BLONDEL impliquerait un recours à la Médiation du Christ, Forme universelle, Lien unissant la multiplicité des éléments du monde]: NRT 111 (1989) 500-521.

9837 **Zimmermann** Joyce Ann, Liturgy as language of faith; a liturgical methodology in the mode of Paul RICŒUR's textual hermeneutics. Lanham MD 1988, UPA. xvii-263 p. $30 [TR 85,176].

J9.2 *Hermeneutica paratheologica* – **Wider linguistic analysis.**

9838 *Abrams* M. H., *a)* Behaviorism and deconstruction; – *b)* Construing and deconstructing: ➤ 223, Doing things 1989, 252-268 [< Critical inquiry 4 (1977) 181-193] / 297-333 [1983 < ᴱ*Eaves* M. Romanticism, 1986].

9839 *Anglet* Kurt, Die Erschöpfung der Wörter; Jacques DERRIDAS Abbruch der philosophischen Methodik: TPhil 64 (1989) 397-408.

9840 **Baratin** M., *Desbordes* F., L'analyse linguistique dans l'Antiquité classique, I. Les théories 1981 ➤ 65,8351; 2,7850: ᴿRTAM 56 (1989) 240s (P. *Swiggers*).

9841 *Bayer* Oswald, Wahrheit oder Methode?: ZTK 86 (1989) 179-203.

9842 **Biehl** Peter, *al.*, Symbole geben zu lernen; Einführung in die Symboldidaktik anhand der Symbole Hand, Haus und Weg: Wege des Lernens 6. Neuk 1989, Neuk.-V. 264 p.; 43 fig. 3-7887-1290-2.

9843 *Bouma-Prediger* Steve, [1979 Richard] RORTY's pragmatism and GADAMER's hermeneutics: JAAR 57 (1989) 313-324.

9844 **Brown** Gillian, *Yule* George, Discourse analysis: Textbooks in Linguistics. C 1989, Univ. xii-288 p. 0-521-24144-8; pa. 8475-9.

9845 ᴱ**Ciani** Maria Grazia, [*Schön* Alberto *al.*], The regions of silence; studies of the difficulty of commnicating: London Studies in Classical Philology 17. Amst 1987, Gieben. 160 p. *f*70. 90-70265-17-6. – ᴿAntClas 58 (1989) 401s (Marie-France *Bodson*).

9846 ᴱ**Eco** Umberto, *Marmo* Costantino, On the medieval theory of signs: Foundations of Semiotics 21. Amst/Ph 1989, Benjamins. ix-224 p. 90-272-3293-8; pa. 2108-1 / US pa. 1-55610-075-1.

9847 *Eco* Umberto, Wer ist schuld an der Konfusion von Denotation und Bedeutung? Versuch einer Spurensicherung: ZSemiot 10 (1988) 189-208.

9848 **Fong Heatherbell** Nancy, The stony idiom of the brain; a study in the semantics and syntax of metaphors; diss. Univ. California ᴰ*Longacker* R. San Diego 1989. 256 p. 89-14184. – DissA 50 (1989s) 937-A.

9849 **Forni** Guglielmo, Studi di ermeneutica; SCHLEIERMACHER, DILTHEY, CASSIRER: Ermeneutica e Fenomenologia 1. Bo 1985, Clueb. – ᴿFilT 3 (1989) 242-7 (P. *Boschini*).

Fürst G., Sprache als metaphorischer Process; J.G. HERDERS hermeneutische Theorie 1988 ➤ k253.

9850 **Genette** Gérard, Figures I-III: Tel Quel, poétique. P 1966-72, Seuil. I. 1976, F 115; 2-02-001933-7; II. 1969; III. 1972.

9851 *Greisch* Jean, Le cercle et l'ellipse; le statut de l'herméneutique de PLATON à SCHLEIERMACHER: RSPT 73 (1989) 161-184; Eng. 184.

9852 *Grunfeld* Joseph, GADAMER's hermeneutics [Eng. 1985]: ScEspr 41 (1989) 231-6.

9853 **Gusdorf** Georges, Les origines de l'herméneutique: Bibliothèque scientifique. P 1988, Payot. 428 p. F 280. 2-228-88008-6.

9854 **Heidegger** Martin, Ser e tempo [1927], ᵀ*Sá Cavalcanti* Márcia de. Petrópolis 1988s, Vozes. 326 + 262 p. – ᴿREB 49 (1989) 744-7 (G. *Fagel*).

9855 *Höhn* Hans-Joachim, Vernunft – Kommunikation – Diskurs; zu Anspruch und Grenze der Transzendentalpragmatik als Basistheorie der Philosophie: FreibZ 36 (1989) 93-128.

9856 *Innis* Robert E., Die Überwindung der Assoziationspsychologie durch zeichentheoretische Analyse; JAMES, PEIRCE, HUSSERL, BÜHLER: ZSemiot 10,4 ('Semiotische Kontroversen der Jahrhundertwende' 1988) 331-355.

9857 *Lagopoulos* Alexandros P., Über die Möglichkeit einer materialistischen Soziosemiotik: ZSemiot 10,1s ('Semiotik und Marxismus' 1988) 9-17.

9858 *Mark* James, GADAMER and the consensus of experience: TLond 92 (1989) 366-374.

9858* *Michel* Paul, Figurative speech; function, form, exegesis – a linguistic approach: ➤ 610, Parable & story 1986/9, 136-158.

9859 *Müller* Ulrich, Sprachspiele und Begriffskonstellationen; über ADORNO und WITTGENSTEIN als dialektische Hermeneutiker: TPhil 64 (1989) 53-85.

9860 *Oyarzabal* Auginagalde M., El lenguaje significante según L. *Wittgenstein*: LumenVr 38 (1989) 287-303.

9861 *Petöfi* János S., *Olivi* Terry, Understanding literary texts; a semiotic textological approach: ➤ 545, Comprehension 1989, 190-225.

9862 **Ricœur** Paul, Die lebendige Metapher [La métaphore vive, 1975 < séminaire Toronto 1971], ᵀ*Rochlitz* Rainer: Übergänge 17. Mü 1986, Fink. 324 p. – ᴿZkT 111 (1989) 485 (J. *Thorer*).

9863 *Ricœur* Paul, Éloge de la lecture et de l'écriture: ÉTRel 64 (1989) 395-405 [393s, doctorat honoris causa, Montpellier].

9864 **Rondal** J.-A., al., Le langage des signes: Psychologie et Sciences Humaines 155. Bru 1986, Mardaga. 224 p. – ᴿRThom 89 (1989) 130-2 (P.-D. *Guitteny*).

9865 **Schouwey** Jacques, Herméneutique; ontologie ou méthodologie? Quelques questions à propos du livre de Paul RICŒUR, 'Du texte à l'action' [Essais d'herméneutique 2 (P 1986, Seuil) 414 p.]: RTPhil 120 (1988) 75-87.

9866 **Voorsluis** B., Taal en relationaliteit; over de scheppende en verbindende kracht van taal volgens Eugen ROSENSTOCK-HUESSY: Vrije Univ. Bezinningscentrum 16. Kampen 1988, Kok. 256 p. ƒ45. 90-242-3264-3. – ᴿTsTNijm 29 (1989) 70 (P. *Leenhouwens*).

9867 *Wachterhauser* Brice R., Must we be what we say? GADAMER on truth in the human sciences [ineditum, amid 10 reprints (some 8 by or about

Gadamer)]: → 3,368, Hermeneutics and modern philosophy 1986 [0-88706-295-4], 219-240; *Ricœur, Habermas*; (5-61); other titles (none on Bultmann, even in bibliog. p. 487-502) with pp. in JBL 108 (1989) 561; ᴿRExp 86 (1989) 119s (C. J. *Scalise*).

9868 **Warnke** Georgia, GADAMER; hermeneutics, tradition and reason. SF 1987, Stanford Univ. 206 p. $35; pa. $12. – ᴿJAAR 57 (1989) 879-882 (J. *Weinsheimer*).

9868* *Wierciński* Andrzej, ❷ Die Funktion der Sprache in der Hermeneutik von H.-G. GADAMER: RoczTK 33,2 (1986) 21-36; deutsch 36.

J9.3 *Critica reactionis lectoris* – **Reader-response criticism.**

9869 *a*) *Schmidt* Siegfried J., Der beobachtete Beobachter; zu Text, Kommunikation und Verstehen; – *b*) *Wahl* Heribert, Empathie und Text; das selbstpsychologische Modell interaktiver Texthermeneutik: TüTQ 169 (1989) 187-200 / 201-222.

J9.4 **Structuralismus,** deconstructio.

9869* ᴱ**Buttigieg** Joseph A., Criticism without boundaries; directions and crosscurrents in postmodern critical theory (1984 Ward-Phillips lectures). ND 1987, Univ. 256 p. $29. – ᴿJRel 69 (1989) 456s (T. *Murray*: against deconstruction).

9870 **Caputo** John D., Radical hermeneutics ... deconstruction 1988 → 4, a903: ᴿRelStR 15 (1989) 138 (M. K. *Taylor*); Thomist 53 (1989) 722-5 (R. E. *Lauder*); TS 50 (1989) 181-3 (M. J. *Kerlin*).

9871 **Culler** Jonathan, On deconstruction; theory and criticism after structuralism. L 1989, Routledge. 307 p. 0-415-04555-X (*p*); 0-7100-9502-3 (*c*).

9872 **Harland** Richard, Superstructuralism; the philosophy of structuralism and post-structuralism: New Accents. NY 1987, Methuen. x-213 p. $37.50; pa. $11. [RelStR 16, 134, D. *Jobling*].

9873 **Lévi-Strauss** Claude, Tristes tropiques: Terre humaine poche 3009. P 1989, Plon. 504 p.

9874 **Scott** Charles E., [DERRIDA, deconstruction] The language of difference. 1987, Humanities. 180 p. $35. – ᴿJAAR 57 (1989) 430-3 (Lisa D. *Campolo*).

9874* **Taylor** Mark C., Altarity. Ch 1987, Univ. xxxiv-371 p. $42.50; pa. $16. – ᴿJRel 69 (1989) 455s (C. *Winquist*).

J9.6 *Analysis narrationis* – **Narrative-analysis.**

9875 **Calame** Claude, Le récit en Grèce ancienne; énonciations et représentations de poètes; préf. *Coquet* J.-C.: Sémiotique. P 1986, Klincksieck. 222 p. 2-86563-154-0.

9876 **Donaldson** Mara E., Holy places are dark places; C. S. LEWIS and Paul RICŒUR on narrative transformation. Lanham MD 1988, UPA. xxvi-146 p. $22.50 [RelStR 16, 146, T. M. *Ledbetter*].

9876* **Ricœur** Paul, Time and narrative I-II, [1983-5], ᵀ*McLaughlin* Kathleen, *Pellauer* David; III, ᵀ*Blamey* Kathleen, Pellauer, 1985-8 → 3,a180; 4,a917: ᴿJRel 69 (1989) 92-98 (Mary *Gerhart*).

9877 **Stanzel** Franz K.,   Theorie des Erzählens[4rev] [[1]1979]: Uni-Tb 904.   Gö
1989, Vandenhoeck & R.   339 p.   3-525-03208-0.

J9.8   *Theologia narrativa*   –   **Story-theology.** ➤ 3133.

9878 *Goldberg* Michael,   God, action, and narrative; *which* narrative? *which*
action? *which* God?:   JRel 68 (Ch 1988) 39-56.
9879 *Habermacher* J. F.,   Promesses et limites d'une 'théologie narrative':
➤ 385, Narration 1988, 57-82.
9879* **Kort** Wesley A.,   Story, text and Scripture; literary interests in biblical
narrative 1988 ➤ 4,a914:   [R]JRel 69 (1989) 298 (T. R. *Wright*).
Krieg Robert A.,   Story-shaped Christology 1988 ➤ 7430.
9880 **Navone** John,   L'amore evangelico, una teologia narrativa [1984], [T]*Del
Genio* M., *Borriello* L.,   1986 ➤ 2,8025; 3,a201;   88-263-0641-9:   – [R]Be-
nedictina 35 (1988) 221s (L. *De Lorenzi*); RivAscM 13 (1988) 141s (G.
Podio).
9881 **Nelson** Paul, Narrative and morality 1987 ➤ 3,a204; 4,a928:   [R]ExpTim
99 (1987s) 349 (T. *Baird*);   Interpretation 43 (1989) 96.98 (G. B.
Hammond); JAAR 57 (1989) 213-7 (G. *Comstock*); JRel 69 (1989) 298s
(J. D. *Barbour*); RelSt 25 (1989) 393-6 (J. *Milbank*); TLond 92 (1989)
62-64 (H. *Willmer*).
9882 **Stegner** William R.,   Narrative theology in early Jewish Christianity.
Louisville 1989, Westminster/Knox.   141 p. $12.   0-8042-0265-6 [TDig
37,188].

━━━━━━━━━━━━━━━━━━━━
(IV). Postbiblica
━━━━━━━━━━━━━━━━━━━━

κ1   **Pseudepigrapha** [= catholicis 'Apocrypha'] .1 *VT, generalia.*

9883 **Block** Per, *al.,*   'God och nyttig läsning' [good and useful reading
(LUTHER)];   om Gamla testamentets Apokrypher.   Sto 1988, Proprius.
234 p.; ill.   91-7118-624-7 [BL 90, 128, G. W. *Anderson*]. – [R]SvTKv 65
(1989) 130s (B. *Olsson*).
9884 **Charlesworth** J. H.,   The OT Pseudepigrapha and the NT 1985 ➤ 1,9649
... 4,a937:   [R]JRel 68 (1988) 93s (J. J. *Collins*); StPhilonAn 1 (1989) 127s
(D. M. *Hay*).
9885 **Denis** A. M. (*Janssens* Yvonne; CETEDOC) Concordance grecque des
pseudépigraphes d'AT 1987 ➤ 3,a212:   [R]EstBíb 47 (1989) 272-4 (J.
Trebolle); ETL 65 (1989) 124-130 (J. *Verheyden*); ETRel 64 (1989) 436s
(D. *Lys*); JStJud 20 (1989) 219-221 (A. *Hilhorst*: monumental; more than
a concordance, a statistical analysis); RHE 84 (1989) 97-100 (L. *Leloir*:
pertinence de LYONNET S., Biblica 1939, 131); RTLv 20 (1989) 204-7
(P. M. *Bogaert*).
9886 *Denis* Albert-Marie, Les genres littéraires des pseudépigraphes d'AT;
essai de classification: ➤ 585, FolOr 25 (1987/8) 99-112.
9887 [E]**Díez Macho** A., Apócrifos AT 5, Testamentos y discursos de adios 1987
➤ 3,335:   [R]BL (1989) 128 (R. *Murray*); JStJud 20 (1989) 253s (A.
Hilhorst).
9888 [E]**Dupont-Sommer** A., ... La Bible, Écrits intertestamentaires 1987
➤ 3,a214; 4,a940:   [R]AbrNahrain 27 (1989) 170-4 (T. *Muraoka*); BO 46
(1989) 697-701 (M. de *Jonge*); CiuD 202 (1989) 503s (J. *Gutiérrez*); JStJud
20 (1989) 214-6 (A. S. van der *Woude*: trotz einer Reihe von Bedenken,
eine grossartige Leistung); Protestantesimo 44 (1989) 50s (J. A. *Soggin*).

9889 ᴱ**Jonge** M de, Outside the OT: CamCW 4, 1985 ➤ 2,254 ... 4,a942: ᴿRelStT 7,1 (1987) 72-74 (T. *Robinson*); Sefarad 49 (1989) 183s (F. *Sen*).

9890 *Perkins* Pheme, Apocrypha: ➤ 384, NJBC (1989s) 1055-1068 [parts of 1066s by R. E. *Brown*].

9891 **Rubinkiewicz** Ryszard, ❷ Wprowadzenie [introd] do apokryfów ST 1987 ➤ 3,a220: ᴿCBQ 51 (1989) 728-730 (J. J. *Pilch*).

9892 **Russell** D. S., The Old Testament pseudepigrapha; patriarchs and prophets in early Judaism 1987 ➤ 3,a221; 4,a945: ᴿCBQ 51 (1989) 538s (W. W. *Frerichs*); Interpretation 43 (1989) 316.318 (Susan G. *De George*); Themelios 14 (1988s) 105s (K. *Hacking*).

9893 ᴱ**Sacchi** Paolo, Apocrifi dell'Antico Testamento [I. 1981 ➤ 62,350] II: Classici della religione T 1989, UTET. 660 p. Lit. 85.000. – ᴿRivB 37 (1989) 487-497 (Anna *Passoni Dell'Acqua*).

9894 *Santos Otero* Aurelio de, Alttestamentliche Pseudepigrapha und die sogenannte 'Toljovaja Paleja' [TP]: ➤ 174, ᶠSCHNEEMELCHER W., Oecumenica 1989, 107-122.

9895 *Starowieyski* Marek, ❷ Libri recentes de apocryphis: VoxPa 15 (1988) 1074-1084.

9895* ᴱ**Stone** M. E., Jewish writings ... Apocrypha, PHILO: CompNT 2/2, 1984 ➤ 65,311 ... 3,a224: ᴿProtestantesimo 44 (1989) 53 (J. A. *Soggin*); RelStT 7,2s (1987) 85-87 (W. O. *McCready*).

9896 **Weidinger** Erich, Die Apokryphen; verborgene Bücher der Bibel. Augsburg 1989, Pattloch. 590 p. 3-629-91319-9.

9897 *Wermelinger* Otto, Apocrypha: ➤ 879, AugL 1/3 (1988) 385-391.

κ1.2   Henoch.

9898 **Barker** Margaret, The lost prophet ... Enoch 1988 ➤ 4,a947: ᴿExpTim 100 (1988s) 270 (J. R. *Bartlett*: high praise); JStJud 20 (1989) 207s (Eibert *Tigchelaar*: popularizing of her Older Testament; here does not sufficiently distinguish writings from traditions); TLond 92 (1989) 310-2 (P. R. *Davies*).

9899 *García Martínez* F., Tigchelaar E. J. C., The Books of Enoch (1 Enoch) and the Aramaic fragments from Qumran: RQum 14 (1989) 131-146 [147-174, Enoch bibliog, 1970-88].

9900 **Jones** Arthur H., Enoch and the fall of the Watchers; I Enoch 1-36: diss. Vanderbilt, ᴰ*Harrelson* W. Nv 1989. 421 p. 89-19699. – DissA 50 (1989s) 1689-A; RelStR 16,189: '*Jones* A. Heathᴵᴵᴵ'.

9901 ᵀᴱ**Mopsik** Charles, Le livre hébreu d'Hénoch ou Livre des Palais + *Idel* Moché, 'Hénoch c'est Métatron': Les dix paroles. Lagrasse 1989, Verdier. 420 p. 2-86432-088-6.

9902 *Nickelsburg* G. W. E., Salvation without and with a Messiah; developing beliefs in writings ascribed to Henoch: ➤ 7368, ᴱ**Neusner** J. *al.*, Judaisms and their Messiahs 1987, 49-68 [< JStJud 20,249].

9903 *Ricciardi* Alberto, *a*) Algunos pasajes de las parábolas [no evangélicas, aparentemente] en recientes versiones del libro etiópico de Henoc: – *b*) 'Traducción' y 'interpretación' en el 'Libro de las Parábolas de Henoc': RBibArg 29 (1988) 33-60 / 219-231.

κ1.3   Testamenta.

Niebuhr Karl-W., Gesetz und Paränese; katechismusartige Weisungsreihen in der frühjüdischen Literatur [Ph.-Phocylides, Test. XII, Philo] 1987 ➤ a119.

9905 *Safrai* Z., **❹** Midraš Wayisaw; the war of the sons of Jacob in southern Samaria [Test. Judah 3-7; Jub 34,1-9]: Sinai 100 (1987) 612-627 [< JStJud 20,293].

9906 *Baarda* T., De namen van de kinderen van Levi; de duiding van de namen Gersjôn, Qehath, Merari en Jochebed in het Testament van Levi 11: AmstCah 8 (1987) 87-107 [< GerefTTs 89,61].

9907 **Schmidt** F., Le testament grec d'Abraham 1986 → 2,8055; 3,a242: ᴿHenoch 11 (1989) 375s (B. *Chiesa*).

9908 ᴱ**Knibb** Michael A., *Horst* Pieter W. van der, Studies on the Testament of Job [also by *Haas* C., *Schaller* B. *Römer* C. & *Thissen* H.]: SNTS Mg 66. C 1989, Univ. vii-172 p. 0-521-37216-X.

ᴋ1.4 Salomonis psalmi et odae.

9909 *Jonge* Marinus de, The expectation of the future in the Psalms of Solomon [1965], ᵀ*Villiers* P. G. R. de: Neotestamentica 23 (1989) 93-117; updating note p. 103-5.

9910 **Trafton** Joseph L., The Syriac version of the Psalms of Solomon: SBL SeptCog 11, 1985 → 1,8694 ... 4,a966: ᴿJQR 79 (1988s) 286-290 (O. *Wintermute*).

9911 **Pigué** Stanley C., **❻** The Syriac apocryphal psalms; text, texture, and commentary: diss. Southern Baptist Theol. Sem. ᴰ*Smothers* T. 1988, 253 p. 89-09292. – DissA 50 (1989s) 463-A.

9912 **Blaszczak** Gerald R., A formcritical study of selected Odes of Solomon: HarvSemMg 36, 1985 → 1,9695 ... 4,a967: ᴿBO 46 (1989) 701-3 (J. W. van *Henten*); SecC 7 (1989s) 101s (Kathleen E. *McVey*).

9913 *Franzmann* sr. M., The parable of the vine in Odes of Solomon 38,17-19?; a response to Richard *Bauckham*: NTS [33 (1987) 84-101] 35 (1989) 604-8.

9914 *Hess* Hamilton, Salvation motifs in the Odes of Solomon: → 696, StudPatr 10/20 (1987/9) 182-190.

9915 **Lattke** Michael, Die Oden Salomos 1986 → 2,8069; 4,a968: ᴿKairos 30 (1988s) 247s (K. W. *Tröger*); OLZ 84 (1989) 438-440 (W. *Wiefel*).

9916 *a)* *Lattke* Michael, Salomo-Ode 13 im Spiegelbild der Werke von EPHRAEM Syrus; – *b)* *Franzmann* Majella, Strangers from above; an investigation of the motif of strangeness in the Odes of Solomon and some Gnostic texts: Muséon 102 (1989) 255-266 / 27-41.

ᴋ1.6 Jubilaea, Adam, Aḥiqar, Asenet.

9917 *Doran* R., The non-dating of Jubilees; Jub 34-38; 23:14-32 in narrative context: JStJud 20 (1989) 1-11.

9918 **Endres** John C., Biblical interpretation in the book of Jubilees: CBQ Mg 18 [ᴰ1982] 1987 → 3,a254; 4,a969: ᴿJTS 40 (1989) 174-6 (M. A. *Knibb*).

9919 ᵀᴱ**VanderKam** James C., The Book of Jubilees, a critical text: CSCOr 510s, aethiop. 87s. I. xviii-301 p. (Ethiopic etc.); II. xxxvii-368 p. 0070-0398.

9920 *Zuurmond* R., De misdaad van Ruben volgens Jubileeën 33:1-9: AmstCah 8 (1987) 108-116 [< GerefTTs 89,61].

9921 **Doty** Susan E. H., From ivory tower to city of refuge; the role and function of the protagonist in 'Joseph and Aseneth' and related narratives:

diss. Iliff, ᴰ*MacDonald* D.   Denver 1989. 243 p. 89-24292. – DissA 50 (1989s) 2043-A.

9922 *Dschulnigg* Peter,   *a*) Gleichnis vom Kind, das zum Vater flieht (JosAs 12,8); – *b*) Überlegungen zum Hintergrund der Mahlformel in JosAs; ein Versuch [... 1 Cor 10; Jn 6]:   ZNW 80 (1989) 269-271 / 272-7.

9923 **Croisier** Faïka,   L'histoire de Joseph d'après un manuscrit oriental [arabe 16ᵉ s.]: Arabiyya 10.   Genève 1989, Labor et Fides.   x-253 p. – ᴿRHPR 69 (1989) 340s (D. A. *Bertrand*).

K1.7   Apocalypses, ascensiones.

9924 ᴱ**Loerzer** Sven,   Visionen und Prophezeiungen; die berühmtesten [apokryphen usw.] Weissagungen der Weltgeschichte.   Aschaffenburg 1988, Pattloch. 423 p. – ᴿTR 85 (1989) 385 (J. *Sudbrack*: RAHNER cited at outset does not guide his presentation).

9925 *Parrott* Douglas M.,   The 13 Kingdoms of the Apocalypse of Adam; origin, meaning and significance: NT 31 (1989) 67-87.

9926 *Beaux* Nathalie,   Pour une paléographie du papyrus Chester Beatty 2018 [Apocalypse d'Élie, ᴱ*Pietersma* A. 1981]: ➤ 820, Journées coptes III, 1986/9, 41-49.

9927 **Bertrand** Daniel A.,   La Vie grecque d'Adam et Ève 1987 ➤ 3,a265; 4,a976: ᴿBZ 33 (1989) 120-2 (W. *Schenk*); JBL 108 (1989) 135-7 (L. W. *Hurtado*); JStJud 20 (1989) 210-4 (Liliana *Rosso Ubigli*); JTS 40 (1989) 172-4 (R. *Bauckham*); RÉG 102 (1989) 614s (A. *Wartelle*);RÉj 148 (1989) 163s (J. *Schwartz*); RHR 206 (1989) 84s (P. *Nautin*); Salesianum 51 (1989) 395s (B. *Amata*).

9928 *Levison* John R.,   The exoneration of Eve in the Apocalypse of Moses 15-30: JStJud 20 (1989) 135-150.

9929 **Acerbi** Antonio,   L'ascensione d'Isaia; cristologia e profetismo in Siria nei primi decenni del II sec.: StPatrMediolan 17.   Mi 1989, ViPe. xii-327 p. [RHE 85,39*]. 88-343-0177-3; pa. -6-5.

9930 *Kazhdan* Alexander,   Where, when and by whom was the Greek Barlaam and Ioasaph not written: ➤ 215, ᶠWIRTH G., Zu Alexander 2 (1988) 1187-1207 [it *was* written in Palestine around 800].

K2.1   Philo judaeus alexandrinus.

9931 **Amir** Yehoshua,   Die hellenistische Gestalt des Judentums bei Philon 1983 ➤ 64,8681 ... 2,8085:   ᴿStPhilonAn 1 (1989) 144-8 (D. T. *Runia*).

9932 **Belkin** Samuel,   The Midrash of Philo; the oldest recorded midrash, written in Alexandria by Philo (c. 20 B.C. E. – 45 C.E.) before the formulation of tannaitic literature.   NY 1989, Yeshiva Univ. I. 32 + ⓞ 298 p. 0-88125-149-6.

9933 *Belletti* Bruno,   *a*) Il 'Commentario allegorico alla Bibbia' di Filone Alessandrino [5 vol. ᴱ*Reale* Giovanni, I. 1987 II. 1984, III. 1988. IV. 1981, *Radice* R.; V. 1986, *Kraus Reggiani* C.]:   HumBr 44 (1989) 591-4; – *b*) Sui rapporti fra Dio, Logos e idee in Filone di Alessandria: Asprenas 36 (1989) 39-49.

9934 **Burkhardt** Helmut,   Die Inspiration heiliger Schriften bei Philo von Alexandrien [Diss. Gö, ᴰ*Stegemann* H.]: TVG-Mg 340.   Giessen 1988, Brunnen.   xi-265 p. DM 39 [ZAW 101, 311, H. C. *Schmitt*].

9935 *Decharneux* Baudouin,   Anges, démons et Logos dans l'œuvre de Philon d'Alexandrie: ➤ 728, Anges 1987/9, 147-175.

9936 *Drączkowski* Franciszek, ❷ Filon z Aleksandrii: ➤ 891, EncKat 5 (1989) 236-9.

9937 *Fishwick* Duncan, [PHILO on] The temple of Caesar at Alexandria; AmJAncH 9,1 (for 1984) 131-4.

9938 **Grabbe** L. L., Etymology in early Jewish interpretation; the Hebrew names in Philo [166 with etymologies]: BrownJudSt 115. Atlanta 1988, Scholars. xvi-268 p. $50. 1-55540-080-9 [BL 90, 134, H. *Williamson*: from Claremont project].

9939 *Hecht* R. D., Philo and Messiah: ➤ 7368, E*Neusner* J., Judaisms and their Messiahs 1987, 139-168 [< JStJud 20,251].

9940 [E*Kraus Reggiani* Clara ...] Filone di Alessandria, L'uomo e Dio 1986 ➤ 4,a984: R Protestantesimo 44 (1989) 136 (G. *Vetrano*: nessun altro traduttore indicato).

9941 *Kraus Reggiani* C., L'In Flaccum et la Legatio ad Gaium di Filone alessandrino: ➤ 595, Storiografia 1983/7, 153-161.

9942 *McIver* Robert K., 'Cosmology' as a key to the thought-world of Philo of Alexandria: AndrUnS 26 (1988) 267-279.

9943 **Marín** J. Pablo, Filón de Alejandría y la génesis de la cultura occidental 1986 ➤ 3,a276; 4,a986: R JSS 34 (1989) 209s (G. J. *Brooke*); JStJud 20 (1989) 100 (A. *Hilhorst*: reasoning 'elegant', documentation good); RBibArg 51 (1989) 57-59 (J. M. B.).

9944 *Matín* José P., Filón y las ideas cristianas del siglo II; estado de la cuestión: RBibArg 30s (1988) 263-294.

9945 **Méasson** Anita, Du char ailé de Zeus à l'Arche d'alliance; images et mythes platoniciens chez Philon d'Alexandrie [diss. 1982] 1986 ➤ 2,8095; 4,a989: R Mnemosyne 64 (1989) 203s (R. *Ferwerda*); StPhilon 1 (1989) 153-5 (D. T. *Runia*).

9946 **Ménard** Jacques, La gnose de Philon 1987 ➤ 3,a277; 4,a990: R BZ 33 (1989) 155 (H.-J. *Klauck*: berührt nur ganz am Rande dieses Thema; Verlag behandelt Freimaurerei, Nostradamus usw.); JTS 40 (1989) 602-4 (R. *Williamson*).

9947 **Mendelson** A., Philo's Jewish identity: BrownJudSt 161. Atlanta 1988, Scholars. xiii-158 p. $29; sb. $18. 1-55540-307-7 [BL 90, L. L. *Grabbe*].

9948 *a) Nikiprowetzky* Valentin †, Thèmes et traditions de la lumière chez Philon d'Alexandrie; – *b) Laporte* J., Sacrifice and forgiveness in Philo of Alexandria; – *c) Weiss* Herold D., A schema of 'the Road' in Philo and LUCAN; – *d) McKnight* Scot, De vita Mosis 1.147; lion proselytes in Philo?; – *e) Schwartz* D. R., Philonic anonyms of the Roman and Nazi periods; two suggestions: StPhilonAn 1 (1989) 6-33 / 34-42 / 43-57 / 58-62 / 63-73.

9949 **Pépin** Jean, La tradition de l'allégorie de Philon d'Alexandrie à Dante. P 1987, Ét. Augustiniennes. 382 p. – R RSPT 73 (1989) 457-9 (G.-M. de *Durand*).

9950 **Radice** R. [1983 ➤ 64,852 updated], *Runia* D. T., Philo of Alexandria, an annotated bibliography 1937-1986: VigChr Sup 8, 1988 ➤ 4,a993: R JStJud 20 (1989) 254-6 (A. *Hilhorst*).

9951 *Radice* Roberto, Platonismo e creazionismo in Filone di Alessandria, intr. *Reale* Giovanni: Metafisica del Platonismo 7. Mi 1989, ViPe. 444 p. Lit. 40.000. 88-343-0262-1 [Greg 70,833].

9952 *Reinmuth* Eckart, Beobachtungen zum Verständnis des Gesetzes im Liber antiquitatum biblicarum (Pseudo-Philo): JStJud 20 (1989) 151-170.

9953 **Riedweg** Christoph, Mysterienterminologie ... 1987 ➤ 3,a284; 4,a994: R Athenaeum 67 (1989) 340s (B. *Chiesa*); JbAC 32 (1989) 188-190 (J.

Frickel); Judaica 45 (1989) 264s (C. *Thoma*); RBgPg 67 (1989) 190 (E. des *Places*); StPatav 36 (1989) 610s (F. *Mora*); WienerSt 102 (1989) 290s (H. *Schwabl*).

9954 *Rosso Ubigli* Liliana, L'immagine d'Israele in Filone d'Alessandria: → 597; RicStoB 1,1 (1987/9) 81-97.

9955 *Runia* David T., *a*) Philo, Alexandrijn en Jood: Lampas 22 (1989) 205-218 [< JStJud 20,285]; – *b*) Polis and Megalopolis; Philo and the founding of Alexandria: Mnemosyne 64 (1989) 398-412.

9956 SANDMEL Samuel mem., Nourished with peace; studies in Hellenistic Judaism, ᴱGreenspahn F. E., al. 1984 → 65,128: ᴿStPhilonAn 1 (1989) 149-153 (D. T. *Runia*).

9957 **Siegert** Folker, Philon ... Feuer (De Deo): WUNT 46, 1988 → 3,a987: ᴿVigChr 43 (1989) 398-405 (D. T. *Runia*: pure-gold nugget).

9958 *Siegert* Folker, Der armenische Philon; Textbestand, Editionen, Forschungsgeschichte: ZKG 100 (1989) 353-369.

9959 *Una Juárez* Agustín, Hermenéutica de las ideas; de Platón a Ockham pasando por Filón y San AGUSTÍN: CiuD 202 (1989) 173-230.

9960 **Williamson** Ronald, Jews in the Hellenistic world, 2. Philo [1.was Josephus etc.]: CamCW 1/2. C 1989, Univ. xii-314 p. $54.50; pa. $20. 0-521-20511-X; 48-X [TDig 37,95].

K2.4 *Evangelia apocrypha* – Apocryphal Gospels.

9961 ᴱSchneemelcher W., Neutestamentliche Apokryphen⁵ 1987 → 3,a298* (I; II → supra 417): ᴿAnBoll 107 (1989) 454-6 (M. van *Esbroeck*); JStJud 20 (1989) 109s (A. *Hilhorst*); JTS 40 (1989) 217-9 (R. M. *Wilson*); NT 31 (1989) 186-9 (J. K. *Elliott*); TPQ 137 (1989) 196 (F. *Kogler*).

9962 *Wilson* R. M., New Testament apocrypha: → 394, NT/Interpreters 1989, 429-455.

9963 **Yusseff** M. A., The Dead Sea scrolls, the Gospel of Barnabas [more reliable portrayal of Jesus] and the NT. Indianapolis 1985, American Trust. xv-137 p. $8 [RelStR 16, 272, S. *Goranson*].

9963* ᵀᴱCoune Michel, Het voorevangelie van Jakobus; een apokrief evangelie van de tweede eeuw. Brugge 1988, Zevenkerken. 33 p. Fb 150. – ᴿCollatVL 19 (1989) 496 (L. *Lemmens*).

9964 *Berthold* Michael, Zur Datierung des Pseudo-Matthäus-Evangeliums [ᴱSantos Otero A. de 1956, 221]: WienerSt 102 (1989) 247-9.

9965 **Moraldi** Luigi, Nascita e infanzia di Gesù nei più antichi codici cristiani: Uomini e religioni. Mi 1989, Mondadori. 318 p. 88-04-32044-3.

9966 *Izydorczyk* Zbigniew, The unfamiliar Evangelium Nicodemi: Manuscripta 8 (1989) 169ss.

9967 *Philippart* Guy, Les fragments palimpsestes de l'Évangile de Nicodème [... gesta Pilati] dans le Vindobonensis 563 (Vᵉ s.?): AnBoll 107 (1989) 171-188.

9968 *Dubois* Jean-Daniel, L'affaire des étendards de Pilate [JOSEPHUS F., A 18,3,1: B 2,9,2] dans le premier chapitre des Actes de Pilate: → 696, 10th Patristic, 19 (1989) 351-8.

9969 *Siker* Jeffrey S., Gnostic views on Jews and Christians in the Gospel of Philip: NT 31 (1989) 275-288.

9970 **Manns** Frédéric, Le récit de la dormition de Marie (Vatican grec 1982);

contribution à l'étude des origines de l'exégèse chrétienne: SBF pubbl. 33.
J 1989, Franciscan. 255 p.; photo du ms.; foldout texte/tr.

9971 *Mimouni* Simon C., 'Histoire de la Dormition et de l'Assomption de
Marie'; une nouvelle hypothèse de recherche: ➤ 696, 10th Patristic, 19
(1989) 372-380.

K2.7 **Alia pseudepigrapha NT.**

9972 *a*) *Beinert* Wolfgang A., Das Apostelbild in der altchristlichen
Überlieferung; – *b*) *Schneemelcher* W., [*al.*], Apostolische Pseudepi-
graphen, Kerygma Petri, Laodicenerbrief; – *c*) *Schäferdiek* Knut, *al.*,
Johannesakten; – *d*) *Drijvers* H., Thomasakten; – *e*) *Prieur* J., *al.*,
Andreasakten; – *f*) *Schneemelcher, al.*, Paulusakten, Petrusakten; – *g*)
Schenke Hans M., Die Taten des Petrus und der zwölf Apostel: ➤ 417,
Apokryphen II⁵ 1989, 6-28 / 29-44 /138-193 / 289-367 / 193-289 / 368-380.

9973 **Leloir** Louis, Écrits apocryphes sur les apôtres I: CCApocr 3, 1986
➤ 2,8117 ... 4,b11:   ᴿBLitEx 90 (1989) 69 (H. *Crouzel*); JTS 40 (1989)
226-8 (S. P. *Cowe*); LavalTP 44 (1988) 121-3 (P. H. *Poirier*); RBén 98
(1988) 221s (P.-M. *Bogaert*); RHE 84 (1989) 106s (P.-H. *Poirier*);
RivStoLR 25 (1989) 338-342 (W. *Schneemelcher*).

9974 *a*) *Vielhauer* Philipp †, *Strecker* Georg, Apokalyptik des Urchristentums;
– *b*) *Müller* G., Himmelfahrt des Jesaja, Offenbarung des Petrus; – *c*)
Treu Ursula, Christliche Sibyllinen; ➤ 417, Apokryphen II⁵ 1989,
491-547 / 547- 578 / 591-619.

9975 ᴱ**Prieur** Jean-Marc, Acta Andreae; praefatio – commentarius – textus:
CChrApocr 5s. Turnhout 1989, Brepols. I. praef. comm. xxvi-416 p.; II.
textus 848 p. 2-503-41051-0; pa. –2-9; II. –61-8; pa. –8-6.

9976 **Van Voorst** Robert E., The ascents of James; history and theology of a
Jewish Christian community; SBL diss. 112 (NY Union 1988, ᴰ*Martyn*
J). Atlanta 1989, Scholars. xi-202 p. $15; pa. $10 [JAAR 57,893].
1-55540-293-3; pa. –4-1.

9977 *Luttikhuizen* Gerard, Intertextual references in readers' responses to the
Apocryphon of John [not 'to John' as page-headings]: ➤ 95, ᶠIERSEL B.
van, 1989, 117-126.

9978 **Onuki** Tadashi, Gnosis und Stoa; eine Untersuchung zum Apokryphon des Johannes: NTOrb 9. FrS/Gö 1989, Univ./VR. x-197 p. [CBQ
51,392]. 3-7278-0606-0 / VR 3-525-53909-6.

9979 **Schneider** Paul, The mystery of the Acts of John; an interpretation
of the hymn of the dance in light of the Acts theology: diss. Columbia,
ᴰ*Scroggs* R. NY 1989. – RelStR 16,190.

9980 *Rosenstiehl* Jean-Marc, Tartarouchos-temelouchos; contribution à
l'étude de l'Apocalypse apocryphe de Paul [visio Pauli]: ➤ 820, Deuxième
Journée d'Études Coptes, Strasbourg 25 mai 1984 [Cah. Bibliothèque
Copte 3; Lv 1986, Peeters] 29-56.

9981 *Rordorf* Willy, Was wissen wir über Plan und Absicht der Paulusakten?: ➤ 174, ᶠSCHNEEMELCHER W., Oecumenica 1989, 71-82.

9982 **Buchholz** Dennis D., Your eyes will be opened; a study of the Greek
(Ethiopic) Apocalypse of Peter: SBL diss. 97 [Claremont 1984] 1988
➤ 4,b20: ᴿETL 65 (1989) 442-4 (B. *Dehandschutter*).

9983 **Crossan** John D., The Cross that spoke [apocr. Pt.]; the origins of the
Passion narrative. SF 1988, Harper & R. 224 p. $20. – 0-06-254843-3. –
ᴿCCurr 39 (1989s) 499s. 502 (G. *Aichele*); Horizons 16 (1989) 478s (J. P.

Meier: no, and badly edited); JRel 69 (1989) 398s (C. C. *Black*); NewTR 2,1 (1989) 106s (D. *Senior*).

9983* — *Dewey* Arthur J., 'And an answer was heard from the Cross...', a response to J. D. Crossan [...continuing in the spirit of such a constructive effort (at coping with H. Koester's challenge)]: Forum 5,3 (1989) 103-111.

9984 *Bouvier* Bertrand, *Bovon* François, Actes de Philippe, I, d'après un manuscrit inédit: ➤ 174, FSchneemelcher W., Oecumenica 1989, 367s.392-4; 370-391, texte grec, français en face.

9985 *Santos Otero* A. de, Die Thomas-Apokalypse; – *b*) [mit *Duensing* Hugo †] Die Apokalypse des Paulus: ➤ 417, ESchneemelcher W., NTliche Apokryphen II (1989) 675-7 / 644-676.

9986 **Lipinski** M., Konkordanz zu den Thomasakten [*Lipsius-Bonnet* Greek text 1959 = 1903, here reprinted in appendix]: BoBB 67. Fra 1988, Athenäum. xiii-605 p. DM 128. 3-610-09103-7 [NTAbs 33,275].

9987 *Römer* Cornelia, Der Briefwechsel zwischen Seneca und Paulus: ➤ 417, Apokryphen II⁵ 1989, 44-50.

9988 *Duensing* Hugo †, *Santos Otero* Aurelio de, Das 5. und 6. Buch Esra: ➤ 417, ESchneemelcher W., NTliche Apokryphen II., 1989. 581-590.

9989 *Santos Otero* Aurelio de, Jüngere Apostelakten: ➤ 417, ESchneemelcher W., NTliche Apokryphen II., 1989. 381-438.

9990 *Haile Getatchew*, The legend of Abgar in Ethiopic tradition: OrChrPer 55 (1989) 375-410.

9991 *Colonna* Aristide, Una profezia del Cristo attribuito a Sofocle: ➤ 42, FCostanza S., Polyanthema 1989, 113-5.

9992 **Herbert** Máire, *McNamara* Martin, Irish biblical apocrypha; selected texts in translation. E 1989, Clark. 196 p. £20. 0-567-09524-X [EstBíb 47,578].

K3 Qumran .1 generalia.

9993 *Brown* Raymond E., Dead Sea Scrolls: ➤ 384, NJBC (1989s) 1068-1079.

9994 *Fröhlich* Ida, Recherches sur Qumrân en Hongrie: ➤ 585, FolOr 25 (1988) 75-78; bibliog 79-83.

9995 **Fujita** Neil S., A crack in the jar ... NT 1986 ➤ 2,8128 ... 4,b25*: RBA 52 (1989) 54s (E. *Yamauchi*: despite K. Rudolph, there is no evidence that the Mandaeans 'flourished' earlier than the 2d century); CurrTM 16 (1989) 233 (W. C. *Linss*); RivB 37 (1989) 234s (Anna *Passoni Dell'Acqua*).

9996 *Garcia Martínez* F., Estudios Qumránicos 1975-1985; panorama crítico (V) / (VI): EstBíb 47 (1989) 93-118. 225-266; Eng. 93.225.

9997 *Garcia Martinez* Florentino, Lista de mss procedentes de Qumran [updating *Fitzmyer* DSS² 1987; < libro atteso]: Henoch 11 (1989) 149-232; 243-270, indice italiano-inglese, *Rosso Ubigli* Liliana.

9998 **Knibb** Michael A., The Qumran community: CamCW 2, 1987 ➤ 3,a314; 4,b27: RCBQ 51 (1989) 712s (C. *Bernas*); Salesianum 51 (1989) 155s (R. *Vicent*); Sefarad 49 (1989) 46s (F. *Sen*).

9999 *Lichtenberger* Hermann, Literatur zum Antiken Judentum [Qumran; ... Schürer-Vermes]: VerkFor 33 (1988) 2-19.

a1 *Schuller* Eileen, The 40th anniversary of the Dead Sea Scrolls: SR 18 (1989) 61-65.

a2 *Shanks* Hershel, At least publish the Dead Sea Scrolls timetable [... *Milik*; *Strugnell*, new Israel Antiquities director A. *Drori*]: BAR-W 15,3 (1989) 56-58.

a3 *Shanks* Hershel, *a*) Dead Sea Scrolls scandal – Israel's Department of Antiquities joins conspiracy to keep scrolls secret: – *b*) What should be done about the unpublished Dead Sea Scrolls?; – *c*) New hope: BAR-W 15,4 (1989) 18-21.55 / 15,5 (1989) 18-23 / 15,6 (1989) 55s.74; ill.

a4 *Stone* G. R., Enhancing the image [by interplanetary spacecraft methods] of a Dead Sea Scroll [GnApoc]: Buried History 24,2 (Melbourne 1988) 32.35 [< NTAbs 33,76].

a5 *Talmon* Shemaryahu, ❺ Fragments of scrolls from Masada [< Eng. final report]: ➤ 218, Mem. YADIN Y., ErIsr 20 (1989) 278-286; 6 fig.

a6 **Vermes** Geza, The Dead Sea Scrolls in English³ 1987 ➤ 3,a318; 4,b31: ᴿTZBas 45 (1989) 89 (K. *Seybold*).

a7 *Woude* Adam S. van der, Fünfzehn Jahre Qumranforschung (1974-1988): TRu 54 (1989) 221-261 ...

K3.4   *Qumran,* **Libri biblici** [➤ singuli] et pseudo-biblici; **Commentarii.**

a8 *Cook* J., Toepassings op die gerekenariseerde databasis van die Bybelse Dooie See-rolle: JSem 1 (1989) 193-203; Eng. 193.

a9 *Vermes* Geza, *a*) Bible interpretation at Qumran: ➤ 218, Mem. YADIN Y., ErIsr 20 (1989) 184*-191*; – *b*) Biblical proof-texts in Qumran literature: ➤ 200, ᶠULLENDORFF E., JSS 34 (1989) 493-508.

a10 *Giese* R. L., Further evidence for the bisection of 1QIsᵃ: Textus 14 (1988) 61-70 [< NTAbs 33,217].

a11 *Horgan* Maurya P., *Kobelski* Paul J., The Hodayot (1QH) and New Testament poetry: ➤ 60, ᶠFITZMYER J., Touch 1989, 179-193.

a12 *Qimron* E., A new reading in 1QH XV 15 and the root GYL in the Dead Sea Scrolls: RQum 14 (1989) 127s.

a13 **Schuller** Eileen M., Non-canonical psalms from Qumran ...: HarvSemSt 28, 1986 ➤ 2,8145 ... 4,b32: ᴿJJS 40 (1989) 115s (G. *Vermes*); JStJud 20 (1989) 110-5 (F. *García Martínez,* franç.).

a13* *Wacholder* B. Z., David's eschatological psalter; 11QPsalmsᵃ: HUCA 59 (1988) 23-72.

a14 **Brooke** G. J., Exegesis at Qumran; 4QFlorilegium ...: JStOT Sup 29, 1985 ➤ 1,9789 ... 4,b38: ᴿHeythJ 30 (1989) 446s (R. *Hayward*).

a15 **Feltes** Heinz, Die Gattung des Hab-K. [ᴰ1984] 1986 ➤ 2,8137; 4,b41: ᴿCBQ 51 (1989) 533-5 (J. E. *Wright*).

a15* *Talmon* S., Yom hakippurim in the Habakkuk scroll [< Biblica 32 (1951) 549-563]: ➤ 365, Qumran 1989, 186-199.

a16 *Nebe* G., Wilhelm, Ergänzende Bemerkung zu 4Q 176, Jubiläen 23,21: RQum [12 (1987) 529-536, *Kister* M.] 14 (1989) 129s.

K3.5   *Rotulus Templi –* **The Temple Scroll,** *al.*

a17 *Eisenman* Robert, The historical provenance of the 'three nets of Belial' allusion in the Zadokite Document and Balla'/Bela' in the Temple Scroll: ➤ 585, FolOr 25 (1987/8) 51-66.

a18 *Hamilton* Gordon J., A new interpretation of the end of 11QT III 3: VT 39 (1989) 485-8.

a19 *a*) *Laperrousaz* Ernest-M., Does the Temple Scroll date from the first or second century BCE? [c. 80 BCE]; – *b*) *Thiering* Barbara, The date of composition of the Temple Scroll [time of Herod the Great]; – *c*) *Delcor* Mathias, Is the Temple Scroll a source of the Herodian Temple? ᵀ*Brooke* G.: ➤ 568, Temple Scroll 1987/9, 91-97 / 99-120 / 67-89.

a20 **Maier** Johann, The Temple scroll, [T]*White* R. 1985 → 1,9801 ... 3,a339: [R]BA 52 (1989) 45 (D.P. *Wright*); ÉTRel 64 (1989) 623s (Françoise *Smyth*); JNES 48 (1989) 40s (M. *Wise*: unmentioned English translator erred only in taking 37,14 'Herde' as 'flocks' instead of 'stoves').

a21 *Schiffman* Lawrence H., *Shelamim* sacrifices in the Temple Scroll: → 218, Mem. YADIN Y., ErIsr 20 (1989) 176*-183*.

a22 *a) Schiffman* Lawrence H., The Temple Scroll and the systems of Jewish law of the Second Temple period; – *b) Burgmann* H. [< Die essenischen Gemeinden Kap. 7, awaited 1989] 11QT: the Sadducean *Torah*; – *c) Lehmann* Manfred R., The beautiful war bride (*ypt t'r*) and other Halakhoth in the Temple Scroll; – *d) Kapera* Zdzisław J., A review of East European studies on the Temple Scroll: → 568, Temple Scroll 1987/9, 239-255 / 257-263 / 265-271 / 275-286.

a23 *a) Stegemann* Hartmut, The literary composition of the Temple Scroll and its status at Qumran; – *b) Callaway* Phillip R., Extending divine revelation; micro-compositional strategies in the Temple Scroll; – *c) Davies* Philip R., The Temple Scroll and the Damascus Document; – *d) VanderKam* James C., The Temple Scroll and the Book of Jubilees: → 568, Temple Scroll 1987/9, 123-148 / 149-162 / 201-210 / 211-236.

a24 *a) Tyloch* Walter, La provenance et la date du Rouleau du Temple; – *b) Schiffman* Lawrence H., The Law of the Temple Scroll and its provenance: → 585, FolOr 25 (1987/8) 33-40 / 89-98.

a25 **Wacholder** Ben Zion, [Temple Scroll] The dawn of Qumran 1983 → 64,8791 ... 3,a346: [R]JNES 48 (1989) 72-74 (D. *Pardee*: overlooks Messianism and Essene origins).

a26 *Westling* Judith L., Unraveling the relationship between 11QT[emple], the eschatological Temple, and the Qumran community: RQum 14 (1989) 61-73.

a27 *Wise* Michael O., The covenant of Temple Scroll XXIX, 3-10: RQum 14 (1989) 49-60; franç. 60.

a28 **Yadin** Y., The Temple Scroll 1-III 1983/1977 → 65,8615 ... 2,8157: [R]Protestantesimo 44 (1989) 128s (J. A. *Soggin*).

a29 *Kustár* Peter †, Ⓜ Appraisal of the Qumran 'War of the sons of darkness against the sons of light': TSzem 31 (1988) 221-4.

a30 **Schiffman** Lawrence H., The eschatological community of the Dead Sea Scrolls; a study of the Rule of the Congregation: SBL Mg 38. Atlanta 1989, Scholars. xi-101 p. $23; sb./pa. $15. 1-55540-329-8; pa. –30-1.

K3.6 Qumran et NT.

a31 *Alonso Schökel* Luis M., ¿El manuscrito más antiguo del NT? Entrevista con José O'CALLAGHAN: RazF 219 (1989) 503-510.

a32 *Brooke* George J., The Temple Scroll and the New Testament: → 568, Temple Scroll 1987/9, 181-199.

a33 *Carmignac* Jean, Ⓟ Le Nouveau Testament à la lumière des documents des rives de la mer Morte, [T]*Rapak* W.: PrzPow 809 (1989) 50-66.

a33* *Cothenet* Édouard, La secte de Qumran et la communauté chrétienne: EsprVie 99 (1989) 488-494.

a34 **Eisenman** Robert H., James the Just in the Habakkuk pesher 1986 → 2,8136: [R]JAOS 109 (1989) 297s (J. *Kampen*); JSS 33 (1988) 276-8 (F. F. *Bruce*).

a34* *a) García Martínez* Florentino, Significado de los manuscritos de Qumrán para el conocimiento de Jesucristo y del Cristianismo; –

b) *Stegeman* Hartmut,   Jesucristo y el Maestro de Justicia de Qumrán [curso Escorial 1989]: ComSev 22 (1989) 331-342 / 343-354.

a35 *Golb* Norman, Who wrote the Dead Sea Scrolls? A new answer suggests a vital link behween Judaism and Christianity: The Sciences (Apr. 1987) 40-49; ❷ ᵀ*Fiala* E., PrzPow 217 (1989) 294-310; 310-2, bibliog.

a36 *Lichtenberger* Herman, Reflections on the history of John the Baptist's communities: ➤ 585, DSS Colloquium 1987, FolOr 25 (1988) 45-49.

a36* *Manns* F., Note sur l'origine des impropères du Vendredi Saint [1QS 1:16-2:18]: EphLtg 103 (1989) 275-7.

a37 *Murphy-O'Connor* Jerome, *a*) The New Covenant in the letters of Paul and the Essene documents: ➤ 60, ᶠFITZMYER J., Touch 1989, 194-204; – *b*) Qumran and the New Testament: ➤ 394, NT/Interpreters 1989, 55-71.

a38 **Pickering** S. R., **Cook** R. R. E., Has a fragment of the Gospel of Mark been found at Qumran? [O'CALLAGHAN J. 1972; especially Mk 6,52s = 7Q5 (no)]: Papyrology and Historical Perspectives 1. Sydney 1989, Macquarie Univ. viii-23 p.; 1 fig. A$ 4.50; elsewhere $6.50. 0-85837-635-0.

a39 **Thiede** Carsten P., ¿ El manuscrito más antiguo de los Evangelios?; el fragmento de Marcos en Qumrán y los comienzos de la tradición escrita del Nuevo Testamento [1986 ➤ 2,8168] ᵀ*Fornari Carbonell* Isabel. Valencia 1989, Inst. S. Jerónimo. 94 p. 84-86067-33-2.

     K3.8 **Historia et doctrinae Qumran.**

a40 **Burgmann** Hans, Die essenischen Gemeinden von Qumran und Damaskus in der Zeit der Hasmonäer und Herodier (130 ante – 68 post): ArbNTJ [7, 1987 ➤ 4,b63] 8. Fra 1988, Lang. 541 p.; ill. 3-8204-9905-9 [NTAbs 33,412].

a41 *Burgmann* Hans, Who was the 'Wicked Priest'? [Jonathan Maccabeus]: ➤ 585, FolOr 25 (1987/8) 41-44.

a42 **Callaway** Phillip R., The history of the Qumran community ...: JPseud Sup 3, 1988 ➤ 4,b64: ᴿJJS 40 (1989) 116s (G. *Vermes*); JStJud 20 (1989) 216-9 (F. *García Martínez*); TLZ 114 (1989) 667s (G. *Stemberger*).

a43 *Chmiel* Jerzy, La conscience de communauté et l'attitude sectaire à Qoumrân; remarques herméneutiques: ➤ 585, FolOr 25 (1987/8) 137-141.

a44 *Collins* John J., The origin of the Qumran community; a review of the evidence: ➤ 60, ᶠFITZMYER J., Touch 1989, 159-178.

a45 **Flusser** David, The spiritual history of the Dead Sea sect [❷], ᵀ*Glucker* Carol. TA 1989, MOD. 97 p. $8 [Jerusalem Perspective 3/4, 12, S. *Schmidt*].

a46 *a*) *García Martínez* Florentino, Il problema della purità; la soluzione qumranica; – *b*) *Jucci* Elio, Il genere 'pesher' e la profezia; – *c*) *Sacchi* Paolo, La conoscenza presso gli Ebrei da Amos all'essenismo: ➤ 567, RicStoB 1,1 (1987/9) 169-191 / 151-168 / 123-149.

a47 *a*) *García Martínez* Florentino, Qumran origins and early history; a Groningen hypothesis; – *b*) *Collaway* Phillip, The history of the Qumran community, an investigaton: ➤ 585, FolOr 25 (1987/8) 113-136 / 143-150.

a48 *Golb* N., Les manuscrits de la Mer Morte; une nouvelle approche du problème de leur origine [pas sectaire; judaïsme normatif]: Annales Économies Sociétés Civilisations 5 (1985) 1133-1149; 1305-12, objections de *Laperrousaz* E.-M., 1313-20, réponse [< JStJud 20,271].

a49 **Knibb** Michael A., Jubilees and the origins of the Qumran communty: inaugural 17.I.1989. L 1989, King's College. 20 p.

a50 **Kreiger** Barbara, Living waters; myth, history, and politics of the Dead Sea; pref. *Perrin* Noel. 1988, Continuum. 226 p. [TR 85,522].

a51 *Laperrousaz* Ernest-Marie, L'établissement de Qoumran près de la mer Morte; forteresse ou couvent? (avec évocation du 'Rouleau de cuivre', 3Q 15): → 218, Mem. YADIN Y., ErIsr 20 (1989) 118*-123*.

a52 *Lipiński* Édouard, Le repas sacré à Qumran et à Palmyre: → 218, Mem. YADIN Y., ErIsr 20 (1989) 130*-134*.

a53 *Mędala* Stanisław, ☉ Nouvelle hypothèse concernant l'origine des manuscrits de la région de la mer Morte [*Golb* N. 1980: bibliothèque du Temple, cachée 66 ap. J.-C.]: STWsz 26,1 (1988) 117-135; franç. 136.

a54 *Talmon* S., Waiting for the Messiah; the spiritual universe of the Qumran covenanters: → 7368, ᴱNeusner J., Judaisms and their Messiahs 1987, 111-137 [< JStJud 20,251]: reprinted → 365, Qumran 1989, 273-300.

a55 *Wacholder* Ben Zion, Rules of testimony in Qumranic jurisprudence; CD 9 and 11Q Torah 64: JJS 40 (1989) 163-174.

a56 *Weinfeld* Moshe, The organizational pattern and the penal code of the Qumran sect 1986 → 2,8188 ... 4,b71: ᴿBZ 33 (1989) 299s (J. *Maier*); CBQ 51 (1989) 361 (J. *Duhaime*); JNES 48 (1989) 142s (M. O. *Wise*); JSS 34 (1989) 206-8 (G. J. *Brooke*); RÉG 101 (1988) 583s (P. *Nautin*); RQum 14 (1989) 147s (É. *Puech*).

K4.1 Esseni, Zelotae.

a57 **Beall** Todd S., JOSEPHUS' description of the Essenes ... DSS [diss. Wsh Cath. U. 1984 ᴰ*Fitzmyer*]: SNTS Mg 58, 1988 → 4,b72: ᴿÉTRel 64 (1989) 284s (E. *Cuvillier*); ExpTim 100 (1988s) 309 (R. *Mason*); JStJud 20 (1989) 84-88 (F. *García Martínez*, franç.).

a58 *Braun* Willi, Were the New Testament Herodians Essenes? A critique of an hypothesis [*Daniel* C. 1967; *Yadin* Y.]: RQum 14 (1989) 75-88.

a59 **Hengel** Martin, The Zealots; investigations into the Jewish freedom movement in the period from Herod I until 70 A.D. [1961], ᵀ*Smith* David. E 1989, Clark. xxiv-487 p. £30. 0-567-09372-2 [TDig 37,60]. – ᴿTLond 92 (1989) 316s (Judith *Lieu*).

a60 **Laperrousaz** Ernest-M., Gli Esseni secondo le loro testimonianze dirette 1988 → 4,b76: ᴿAsprenas 36 (1989) 109 (A. *Rolla*); CC 140 (1989,3) 304s (G. L. *Prato*).

a61 *Mędala* Stanisław, Le camp des Esséniens à Jérusalem à la lumière des récentes recherches archéologiques: → 585, FolOr 25 (1988) 67-74.

a62 ᵀᴱ**Székely** Edmond B., Das Evangelium der Essener I-IV, die Originaltexte aus dem Aramäischen und Hebräischen ['Gospel of Peace' etc. not linked with (Qumran/Josephus) Essenes]. Südergellersen 1988= 1978, B. Martin. 350 p.

a63 **Vermes** Geza, *Goodman* Martin D., The Essenes according to the classical sources: Oxford Centre Textbooks 1. Sheffield 1989, JStOT. xi-103 p. 1-85075-139-0. – ᴿJStJud 20 (1989) 259s (F. *García Martínez*).

K4.3 Samaritani.

a64 **Ben-Hayyim** Z., *Tibât Mârqe*, a collection of Samaritan midrashim. J 1988, Israel Acad. 84-v-411 p. – ᴿKairos 30s (1988s) 240-2 (F. *Dexinger*).

a65 **Boid** Iain R. M., Principles of Samaritan Halachah: StJudLA 38. Leiden 1989, Brill. xiv-362 p. ƒ155. 90-04-07479-1 [BL 90, 129, R. J. *Coggins*].

a66 **Egger** Rita, JOSEPHUS F. und die Samaritaner 1986 → 2,8195 ... 4,b85: ᴿBZ 33 (1989) 300-2 (J. *Maier*); JJS 40 (1989) 117-9 (Tessa *Rajak*).

a67 *Girón* Luis F., Estudios samaritanos 1985-8: Sefarad 49 (1989) 167-178.

a68 **Hall** Bruce W., Samaritan religion from John Hyrcanus to Baba Rabba [diss. 1986]: Studies in Judaica 3. Sydney 1987, Univ. Mandelbaum Trust. viii-352 p. – ᴿRÉJ 148 (1989) 162 (J.-P. *Rothschild*: consciencieux).

a69 *a) Mor* M., [Samaritan history] 1. Persian, Hellenistic, Hasmonaean period; 2. Bar-Kokhbah revolt [*al.*, 3.-7., later periods]; – *b) Pummer* R., *Sixdenier* G. D., Archeology and inscriptions; numismatic; – *c) Stenhouse* P., the Samaritan Chronicle; – *d) Dexinger* F., Samaritan Eschatology; – *e) Anderson* B. T., Samaritan Pentateuch: → 389, ᴱ*Crown* A., The Samaritans 1989, 1[-134] / 135-194 / 218-265 / 266-292 / 390- ...

a70 *Naveh* Joseph, *a)* Some considerations on the ancient Samaritan inscriptions: → 126, ꜰMACUCH R., Ḥokmôt 1989, 179-185; – *b)* Did ancient Samaritan inscriptions belong to synagogues?: → 845, Synagogues 1987/9, 61-63.

a71 *Panimolle* Salvatore A., Il battesimo e la Pentecoste dei Samaritani: → 141, ꜰNOCENT A., Traditio 1988, 413-436.

a72 **Pummer** R., The Samaritans: IconRel 23/5, 1987 → 3,a399; 4,b88: ᴿJQR 79 (1988s) 231-4 (A. D. *Crown*); JSS 34 (1989) 212s (R. *Coggins*); RHR 206 (1989) 84 (J.-P. *Rothschild*).

a73 **Rabello** Alfredo M., GIUSTINIANO, ebrei e samaritani alla luce delle fonti storico-letterarie, ecclesiastiche e giuridiche [Vocabolario di Giustiniano] 1987 → 4,b89: ᴿHenoch 11 (1989) 377s (Sergio J. *Sierra*); Sefarad 49 (1989) 423 (J. J. *Alarcón Sainz*).

a74 *Rothschild* Jean-Pierre, Deux manuscrits liturgiques samaritains (copiés à Naplouse 1872 et c. 1750]: RÉJ 148 (1989) 93-102.

a75 **Schur** Nathan, History of the Samaritans: BErfAJ 18. Fra 1989, Lang. 305 p. Fs 65. 3-631-40340-2 [BL 90,41, R. J. *Coggins*].

a76 *Wedel* Gerhard, Aspekte der Etablierung des Arabischen als Literatursprache bei den Samaritanern: → 126, ꜰMACUCH R., Ḥokmôt 1989, 397-407.

a77 **Whaley** Ernest B., Samaria and the Samaritans in JOSEPHUS'S 'Antiquities' 1-11: diss. Emory, ᴰ*Hayes* J. Atlanta 1989. 539 p. 89-24720. – DissA 50 (1989s) 2076-A; RelStR 16,189; RTLv 21,543: 'in the Josephan corpus'.

a78 *Zertal* Adam, The wedge-shaped decorated bowl and the origin of the Samaritans: BASOR 276 (1989) 77-84; 5 fig.

K4.5 Ṣadoqitae, Qaraitae – Cairo Genizah; Zadokites, Karaites.

a79 *Attias* Jean-Christophe, Mordekhai KOMTINO, exégète enseignant judéo-byzantin, et le karaïsme (XVᵉ siècle): RHPR 69 (1989) 249-264: Eng. 383.

a80 **Friedman** Mordechai A., ⊕ *Ribbui nashim* ... Jewish polygyny in the Middle Ages; new documents from the Cairo Geniza. J/TA 1986, Bialik Inst. Univ. 380 p.; ill. – ᴿJAOS 109 (1989) 713s (M. R. *Cohen*).

a81 **Gil** Moshe, ⊕ Palestine during the first Muslim period (634-1099); I. Studies; II. Cairo Geniza documents; III. Cairo Geniza documents, indexes: Diaspora Research Institute Publ. 47.57.58. TA 1983, Univ./Ministry of Defense. 688 p.; 762 p.; 742 p. – ᴿJAOS 109 (1989) 138-140 (N. A. *Stillman*).

a82 *Kraemer* Joel L.,   Return to Messina; a letter from the Cairo Geniza: Medit HistR 4 (1989) 364-374.

a83 **Trevisan Semi** Emanuela,   Gli Ebrei Caraiti tra etnia e religione 1984 ➤ 1,9856:   ᴿRÉJ 146 (1987) 197s (C. *Tapia*).

K5   Judaismus prior vel totus.

a84 *Ayali* Meir,   Die Apostasie des [Tannaiten] Elischa BEN ABUYA: Kairos 30s (1988s) 31-40.

a84* **Ballarini** Luigi,   Israele fratello mio, chi sei? 1986 ➤ 3,a407:   ᴿStPatav 36 (1989) 620-2 (M. *Milani*).

a85 *Caquot* André, *al.,* [ᴱ*Puech* H.-C.]   L'ebraismoᵀ: Universale 221.   R 1988, Laterza. 289 p.; map. 88-420-3031-7.

a86 **Chouraqui** André,   Il pensiero ebraico [²1975],   ᵀ*Bigarelli* Alberto: LoB 3,10.   Brescia 1989, Queriniana.   113 p. 88-399-1690-3.

a87 *Cohen* Shaye J. D.,   Crossing the boundary and becoming a Jew: Harv-TR 82 (1989) 13-33: seven degrees or steps.

a87* *Cortès* Enric,   L'amor a l'estudi en la literatura rabínica antiga: ➤ 69*, ᶠGOMÀ I., RCatalT 14 (1989) 75-84; Eng. 85.

a88 *Ebach* Jürgen,   Der Treulosen Treue; Versuch über Jochanan BEN ZAKKAI: Einwürfe 5,28-39 [< TLZ 114, 271 ohne Datum].

a89 *Edgerton* Dow,   The exegesis of tears [... sacredness of Jewish texts]: TTod 46 (1989s) 21-38.

a90 **Ego** Beate,   Im Himmel wie auf Erden; Studien zum Verhältnis von himmlischer und irdischer Welt im rabbinischen Judentum [Diss.Tü]: WUNT 2/34. Tü 1989, Mohr.   220 p. DM 58 [TR 86,74]. 3-16-145403-0.

a91 **Faur** José,   Golden doves with silver dots; semiotics and textuality in Rabbinic tradition 1986 ➤ 2,7289; 3,9250:   ᴿJRel 68 (1988) 158s (Shira *Wolosky*).

a92 ᴱ**Frerichs** Ernst S., *Neusner* Jacob,   GOODENOUGH On the history of religion and on Judaism: BrownJudSt 121, 1986 ➤ 268*:   ᴿRB 95 (1988) 421 (tit. pp.).

a93 **Geiger** Abraham,   Judaism and its history [1911 < Judentum 1864]: Brown Classics in Judaica.   Lanham MD 1985, UPA. – viii-406 p. [KirSef 61,599].

a94 *Goodman* Martin,   Proselytising in rabbinic Judaism: JJS 40 (1989) 175-185.

a95 ᴱ**Green** W. S.,   Approaches to ancient Judaism 1983 ➤ [I.-III. 1978-81 ➤ 60,440 ... 64,269] IV. 1983 ➤ 65,288 [V. 1985 ➤ 1,286]:   ᴿSefarad 49 (1989) 179-182 (F. *Sen*: IV., análisis detallados.).

a96 **Green** William S.,   The traditions of Joshua BEN-HANANIAH I. 1981 ➤ 62,9552 ... 64,8856:   ᴿOLZ 84 (1989) 306-8 (G. *Mayer*).

a97 *Greenspahn* Frederick E.,   Why prophecy ceased [p. 49 'Rabbinic (self-protecting) statements about the removal of the holy spirit parallel the early church's repudiation of Montanism ...']:   JBL 108 (1989) 37-49.

a98 *Hayman* Peter,   Was God a magician? Sefer Yeṣira and Jewish magic: JJS 40 (1989) 224-237.

a99 ᴱ**Henten** J. W. Van, *al.*   Die Entstehung der jüdischen Martyrologie: StPostB 38.   vii-271 p. 90-04-08978-0.

a100 ᴱ**Kraft** R. A., *Nickelsburg* G. W. E.,   Early Judaism and its modern interpreters 1986 ➤ 2,255 ... 4,b117:   ᴿJRel 68 (1988) 139s (L. J. *Greenspoon*: 'Alexander to Hadrian'); RelStR 15 (1989) 327-333 (J. C. *VanderKam*).

a101 **Lange** Nicholas de, Judaism, 1986 ➤ 2,8228; 3,a427: ᴿJRel 68 (1988) 336s (R. L. *Cohn*: good for college; enough but not too much); JSS 34 (1989) 241s (A. *Unterman*).

a102 **Lange** Nicholas de, Judendomen, ᵀ*Schueler* Kaj. Södertälje 1988, Nordstendt. 200 p. – ᴿSvTKv 65 (1989) 30 (B. *Johnson*).

a103 **Lenhardt** Pierre, *Osten-Sacken* Peter von der, Rabbi Aᴋɪᴠᴀ 1987 ➤ 4,b119: ᴿTLZ 114 (1989) 187s (W. *Wiefel*).

a103* **Levine** Lee I., The rabbinic class of Roman Palestine in late antiquity. J/NY 1989, Yad Ben Zvi / Jewish Theol. Sem. 223 p.

a104 **Loth** Heinz-Jürgen, Judentum: Religionen 4. Gö 1989, Vandenhoeck & R. 112 p. 3-525-77807-4. – ᴿJudaica 45 (1989) 260s (E. *Bons*).

a105 ᴱ**Maccoby** Hyam, Early Rabbinic Writings: CamCW 3, 1988 ➤ 4,b122: ᴿEvQ 61 (1989) 275s (I. H. *Marshall*); JTS 40 (1989) 732s (L. L. *Grabbe*); Sefarad 49 (1989) 417-420 (F. *Sen*); SWJT 32,2 (1989s) 59s (E. E. *Ellis*: 'Baccoby').

a106 **Maccoby** H., Judaism in the first century: Issues in Religious Studies. L 1989, Sheldon. viii-136 p. £5. 0-85969-550-6 [BL 90, 139, T. *Rajak*].

a107 *Mendes de Castro* J., MÃO DE JUDEU, Versão medieval inédita do Pirqué Abot: HumT 10,1 (Porto 1989) 89-100.

a108 *Meyer* Rudolf, Tradition und Neuschöpfung im antiken Judentum, dargestellt an der Geschichte des Pharisäismus [< Szb Lp p/h 110/2, 1965]: ➤ 320, Zur Geschichte 1989, 130-187.

a109 **Navarro Peiró** María Ángeles, Abot de Rabbi Natán 1987 ➤ 3,a432; 4,b124: ᴿArTGran 52 (1989) 362 (A. *Torres*); EstBíb 47 (1989) 430-2 (L. *Girón*); ScripTPamp 21 (1989) 347s (S. *Ausín*: espléndido); Sefarad 49 (1989) 184 (M.-J. de *Azcárraga*).

a110 **Neusner** Jacob, The economics of Judaism; the initial stage [to follow his philosophical analysis of the 80s (historical 50s, religious 60s), announced in his Method and Meaning 4,ix). Ch 1989, Univ.

a111 **Neusner** Jacob, The formation of the Jewish intellect; making connections and drawing conclusions in the traditonal system of Judaism: BrownJudSt 151. Atlanta 1988, Scholars. xiii-178 p. $47. 1-55540-255-0 [NTAbs 33,277].

a112 **Neusner** J., Formative Judaism ... a nascent religion [1982/4 ➤ 64,8886 ... 2,8238] 5, 1985: ᴿRelStT 7,1 (1987) 77 (W. O. *McCready*).

a113 **Neusner** Jacob, From description to conviction; essays on the history and theology of Judaism: BrownJudSt 86, 1987 ➤ 4,b127: ᴿJRel 69 (1989) 441s (A. J. *Yuter*).

a114 **Neusner** Jacob, Judaism and its social metaphors; Israel in the history of Jewish thought [... how the name was thought of 70-300 and later]. C 1989, Univ. xiv-258 p. $34.50. 0-521-35471-4 [NTAbs 33,419]. – ᴿJScStR 29 (1989) 272s (B. *Beit-Hallahmi*).

a115 ᴱ**Neusner** Jacob, Judaic perspectives on ancient Israel 1987 ➤ 3,355: ᴿHorizons 16 (1989) 152s (R. *Gnuse*); KirSef 62 (1988s) 28-30 (B. J. *Schwartz* ❸).

a116 **Neusner** Jacob, A religion of pots and pans? Modes of philosophical and theological discourse in ancient Judaism; essays and a program: BrownJudSt 156. Atlanta 1988, Scholars. xix-200 p. 1-55540-283-0.

a117 **Neusner** Jacob, Understanding seeking faith; the case of Judaism: Soundings 71 (Vanderbilt 1988) 329-346 [< OTAbs 12,96].

a118 **Neusner** Jacob, *Green* William S., Writing with Scripture; the authority and uses of the Hebrew Bible in the Torah of formative Judaism. Minneapolis 1989, Fortress. xii-188 p. 0-8006-2330-4.

a119 **Niebuhr** Karl-Wilhelm, Gesetz und Paränese ... [Diss. Halle 1986] WUNT 2/28, 1987 ⇥ 3,3242; 4,b139: ᴿCBQ 51 (1989) 732s (J. J. *Collins*); JBL 108 (1989) 514-6 (J. C. *VanderKam*); JStJud 20 (1989) 100-4 (A. S. van der *Woude*: eine hervorragende Leistung); TGegw 31 (1988) 276s (H. *Giesen*).

a120 **Novoseller** Shalom, Rabban Simon BEN GAMALIEL nasi at Usha [140-180 C.E.], a study in tannaitic literature: diss. Annenberg Inst. 1988. 160 p. 89-21892. – DissA 50 (1989s) 2917-A.

a121 *Pawlikowski* John T., Judaism, the genius of self-renewal (5 NEUSNER books): Commonweal 115 (1988) 434-6.

a122 **Pérez Fernández** M., Los capítulos de r. Eliezer 1984 ⇥ 65,8679 ... 2,8248: ᴿKirSef 61 (1986s) 628 (Shifra *Sznol*).

a123 *Perrot* Charles, Images et paraboles dans la littérature juive ancienne: ⇥ 576, Paraboles 1987/9, 380-401.

a124 ᴱ**Reeg** G., Die Geschichte von den zehn Märtyrern: TStAntJ 10, 1985 ⇥ 1,9892 ... 4,b144: ᴿBijdragen 50 (1989) 212s (M. *Poorthuis*); Gregorianum 70 (1989) 347-9 (G. L. *Prato*).

a125 *Rosenfeld* B. Z., ⊕ Sages and 'House-Owners' in Jabne [rather in Lydda] during the Jabne-period: Sinai 103,1 (1988) 60-71 [< JStJud 20,293].

a126 **Roth** Joel, The halakhic process 1986 ⇥ 2,8252; 3,a448: ᴿRRel 48 (1989) 311s (A. J. *Saldarini*); JQR 80 (1989s) 391-5 (M. B. *Lerner*).

a127 ᴱ**Safrai** Shmuel, The literature of the sages I. Oral Tora ... Talmud: CompNT 2/3, 1987 ⇥ 3,a449; 4,8148: ᴿBijdragen 50 (1989) 445s (R. C. A. *Deen*); BL (1989) 143 (G. *Vermes*); Interpretation 43 (1989) 418.420 (A. J. *Saldarini*); Protestantesimo 44 (1989) 53s (J. A. *Soggin*); RBén 98 (1988) 220s (P.-M. *Bogaert*); RelStR 15 (1989) 82 (M. S. *Jaffee*: misleads beginners by ignoring NEUSNER); RExp 86 (1989) 274 (D. E. *Garland*: good but hard on *Neusner*).

a128 **Scholem** G., Concetti fondamentali dell'ebraismo [1970; conferenze], ᵀ1986 ⇥ 2,8255; 4,b149: ᴿParVi 33 (1988) 456-8 (M. *Perani*).

a129 *Schwarzschild* Steven S., Judentum, ᵀ*Voorgang* D.: ⇥ 894, EvKL 2 (1988) 857-867 [-887 *al.*; 913-5 Kabbala].

a130 **Sigal** Phillip, Judentum [summary of unfinished Emergence of contemporary Judaism 1977-1984],ᵀ: Urban-Tb 359, 1986 ⇥ 2,8256: ᴿTPhil 64 (1989) 585-7 (H. *Engel*).

a131 *Sigal* P. [d., 1985], Judaism, the evolution of a faith [⇥ 4,b153], ᴱ*Sigal* L. [his wife, with 25-p. appendix on women in Judaism]. GR 1988, Eerdmans. xxii-326 p. $22; pa. $15. 0-8028-3661-5; 0345-8 [NTAbs 33,421: 'distillation' of his proposed 5-volume Emergence of Contemporary Judaism, NTAbs 25, p. 322].

a132 *a) Silberman* Lou H., From apocalyptic proclamation to moral prescript; Abot 2,15-16; – *b) Schäfer* Peter, Once again the status quaestionis of research in rabbinic literature; an answer to Chaim MILIKOWSKY; – *c) Newman* Louis E., Virtue and supererogation in the Halakha; the problem of 'Lifnim Mishurat Hadin' reconsidered: JJS 40 (1989) 53-60 / 89-94 / 61-88.

a133 *Spiro* J., Formative process in Jewish tradition: RelEdn 82 (Ch 1987) 547-554 [Judaica 44,126].

a134 **Stefani** Piero, Il nome e la domanda; dodici volti dell'ebraismo: Shalom. Brescia 1988, Morcelliana. 340 p. – ᴿRivB 37 (1989) 228-230 (M. *Perani*).

a134* *Talmon* Shemaryahu, Between the Bible and the Mishna: ⇥ 365, Qumran 1989, 11-52 [ineditum? p. 324].

a135 **Tyloch** Witold, Judaism 1987 → 4,b157: ᴿPrzPow 799 (1988) 439-444 (W. *Chrostowski*).
a136 **Urbach** E. E., The Sages, Harvard 1987 reprint of Hebrew Univ. 2 vol. → 3,a452: ᴿRelStT 8,1s (1988) 66-74 (J. *Neusner*).
a137 *Willems* Gerard F., Le juif TRYFON et Rabbi TARFON: Bijdragen 50 (1989) 278-291; Eng. 292: not the same person.

 κ6 **Mišna,** *tosepta; Tannaim.*

a138 *Bar-Asher* Moshe, ⊕ On vocalization errors in Codex Kaufman of the Mishna: Massorot 1 (1984) 1-17.
a139 **Bunte** Wolfgang, Toharot: Ohalot, Zelte: Die Mischna 6/2; 1988 → 4,b161: ᴿNRT 111 (1989) 441s (X. *Jacques*); TLZ 114 (1989) 729s (S. *Schreiner*: unanswered questions remain).
a140 **Correns** D., Tanijot, Fastentage: Die Mischna 2/9. B 1989, de Gruyter. vii-154 p. DM 128. 3-11-002439-X [BL 90, 130, P. S. *Alexander*].
a141 **Eilberg-Schwartz** Howard, The human will in Judaism 1986 → 2,8266 ... 4,b162: ᴿJRel 68 (1988) 140s (R. *Brody*).
a142 ᴱ**Goldberg** Abraham, Mishna treatise Eruvin, 1986 → 4,b164; $35: ᴿJAOS 108 (1988) 471-4 (J. *Goldin*).
a143 *Kirschner* Robert, Three recensions of a baraitha [Tosefta Terumot 7,20, jTerumot 8, 10, 46; Gen. Rabbah 94]; an analysis and theory of development: JSS 33 (1988) 37-52.
a144 *Mandell* Sara, The Jewish Christians and the Temple tax; *ha-Kuti* and *ha-Ya'abod Kokabbim* in Mishnah Seqalim 1:5: SecC 7 (1989s) 76-84.
a145 **Manns** Frédéric, Pour lire la Mishna 1984 → 65,8690 ... 4,b167: ᴿEstBib 47 (1989) 137-9 (L. *Díez Merino*).
a146 **Manns** Frédéric, Leggere la Mishnah [1984], ᵀ1987 → 4,b168: ᴿParVi 33 (1988) 317s (I. *Zatelli*); Protestantesimo 44 (1989) 51s (J. A. *Soggin*).
a147 *Manns* Frédéric, Jacob, le Min, selon la Tosephta Hulin 2,22-24; contribution à l'étude du christianisme primiitif: CrNSt 10 (1989) 449-465; Eng. 465; ital. i.
a148 *Muchowski* P., ⊕ Traktat Miszny Nazir: Euhemer 31,2 (Wsz 1988) 17-32 [< NTAbs 33,364].
a149 **Neusner** Jacob, Making the classics in Judaism; the three stages of literary formation: BrownJudSt 180. Atlanta 1989, Scholars. xiv-282 p. 1-55540-377-8.
a150 **Neusner** Jacob, The philosophical Mishnah 1. The initial probe; 2. The tractates' agenda, from Abodah Zarah through Moed Qaton: Brown JudSt 163s. Atlanta 1988s, Scholars. xv-303 p. 1-55540-326-3 [NTAbs 33,419]. II. 1989: 1-55560-310-7.
a151 **Neusner** J., A history of the Mishnaic law of appointed times 1-5; StJudLA 34, 1981-3 → 62,9536 ... 65,8692s: ᴿOLZ 84 (1989) 180-3 (G. *Meyer*).
a152 *Neusner* Jacob, *a*) Accommodating Mishnah to Scripture in Judaism; the uneasy union and its offspring: → 3,356, ᴱO'Connor M., Backgrounds 1987, 39-53 [< JBL 108,174]; – *b*) The Mishnah's generative mode of thought: Listenwissenschaft and analogical-contrastive reasoning: → 592, Systemic 1 (1989) 167-195.
a153 *Neusner* J., *a*) The amazing Mishnah: Moment 14,1 (Wsh 1989) 18-23 [< NTAbs 33,222: its inaccessibility is its safeguard; its utopia reflected a basic structure of life for Jewish people anywhere]; – *b*) The constitution

of Judaism in ancient times; the Pentateuch and the Mishnah: JRefJud 36,2 (NY 1989) 55-63 [< NTAbs 33,364].

a154 *Neusner* Jacob, Sifra [document uniting the written Torah and the oral Mishnah] and the problem of the Mishnah: Henoch 11 (1989) 17-39; franç. 39s.

a155 **Porton** Gary G., Goyim; Gentiles and Israelites in Mishnah-Tosefta: BrownJudSt 155. Atlanta 1988, Scholars. xii-356 p. 1-55540-278-X.

a156 *Saldarini* Anthony J., Jewish literature [Mishna ... Targum; also PHILO, JOSEPHUS]: ➤ 384, NJBC (1989s) 1079-1082.

a157 **Segal** Peretz, The 'divine death penalty' in the Hatra inscriptions and the Mishnah: JJS 40 (1989) 46-52.

a158 **Tijn** M. van, Een historische inleiding op de Misjna; Vrede en er is geen vrede! (naar Jer. 6:14; 8:11). Haag 1988, Boeken-C. 246 p. ƒ29,90. 90-239-1591-2. – ᴿTsTNijm 29 (1989) 318 (K. *Waaijman*: leest als een roman).

a159 **Valle Rodríguez** Carlos del, La Misna 1981 ➤ 62,9546 ... 65,8701: ᴿOLZ 84 (1989) 555-7 (G. *Mayer*).

a160 **Zahavy** Tzvee, The Mishnaic law of blessings and prayers; tractate Berakhot: Brown JudSt 88, 1987 ➤ 3,a472: ᴿBL (1989) 147 (P.S. *Alexander*).

a161 **Zlotnick** Dov, The iron pillar – Mishnah; redaction, form, and intent. J 1988, DAF-Noy. 273 p. 965-324-516-1. [RelStR 16, 272, J. *Neusner*: ignorant, an oddity].

K6.5 **Talmud; midraš.**

a162 *Adler* R., The virgin in the brothel and other anomalies; character and context in the legend of Beruriah [woman talmudic scholar who married Rabbi Meir but came to a shameful end]: Tikkun 3,6 (Oakland 1988) 22-32 . 102-5 [< NTAbs 33,218].

a163 **Avery-Peck** Alan J., Tractate Beṣah: American Talmud 7, 1986 ➤ 2,8282*: ᴿJQR 79 (1988s) 271s (L. C. *Kravitz*).

a164 *Bahbout* Scialom, Il midrash; pensiero logico e analogico e la tradizione narrativa ebraica: ➤ 571, L'Ebraismo 1986/7, 61-78.

a165 **Banon** David, La lecture infinie ... midrachique ᴰ1987 ➤ 3,a477: ᴿScripTPamp 21 (1989) 346s (V. *Balaguer*).

a166 *Block* R.A., As people say, *'amri enashei* [119 cases], proverbs in the Babylonian Talmud: JRefJud 36,1 (NY 1989) 67-84 [< NTAbs 33,219].

a167 **Datner** Szymon, *Kamieńska* Anna, ❷ Z mądrości [from the wisdom of] Talmudu. Wsz 1988, PIW. 400 p. – ᴿPrzPow 808 (1988) 451-5 (W. *Chrostowski*).

a168 *Fishbane* Michael, *a)* Extra-biblical exegesis; the sense of not reading in rabbinic midrash; – b) From scribalism to rabbinism; perspectives on the emergence of classical Judaism; – c) The teacher and the hermeneutical task; a reinterpretation of medieval exegesis: ➤ 259, Garments of Torah (1980-)1989, 19-32 / 64-78 / 112-120.

a169 **Freeman** Gordon M., The heavenly kingdom; aspects of political thought in the Talmud and Midrash 1986 ➤ 2,8285; 4,b184: ᴿScripTPamp 21 (1989) 347 (F. *Varo*).

a170 *Friedman* T., Breaking new ground in Talmudic studies [*Steinsaltz* A., Peah]: ConsJud 40,3 (NY 1988) 59-63 [< NTAbs 33,220].

a171 **Hauptmann** Judith, Development of the Talmudic sugya [cf. ➤ 3,a489]; relationship between Tannaitic and Amoraic Sources. Lanham MD 1988, UPA. 243 p. $27.50. – ᴿJJS 40 (1989) 249-251 (L. *Jacobs*).

a172 **Hüttenmeister** Frowald G., Megilla, Schriftrolle;   Übersetzung des Talmud Yerushalmi 2/10, 1987 ⇥ 3,a490; DM 124 + 89. – ᴿNRT 111 (1989) 442s (X. *Jacques*).

a173 **Jaffee** Martin S.,   Tractate Horayot: American Talmud 26, BrownJSt 90, 1987 ⇥ 3,a491: ᴿJQR 79 (1988s) 235-242 (H. *Fox*).

a174 *Kraemer* David, On the reliability of attributions in the Babylonian Talmud: HUCA 60 (1989) 175-190.

a175 **Levine** L. I., ❶ The rabbinic class in Palestine during the Talmudic period. J 1985, Yad Ben Zvi. 154 p. – ᴿJStJud 20 (1989) 240-3 (M. *Mach*).

a176 **Loewe** Raphael, The Rylands haggadah 1988 ⇥ 4,b218: ᴿJJS 40 (1989) 252s (J. B. *Segal*).

a177 **Loopik** M van, De wegen der wijzen en de weg van de wereld [< Bab. Talmudᵀ]: Na de Schriften 5. Kampen 1989, Kok. 107 p. *f* 125. – ᴿStreven 57 (1989s) 754 (P. *Beentjes*).

a178 *Luz* M., A description of the Greek Cynic in the Jerusalem Talmud [... as he appeared to third-century Jewish sages]: JStJud 20 (1989) 49-60.

a179 **Middleton** Deborah F., A critical edition of the 'Midrash Aleph Beth' with an English translation, commentary and introduction: diss. Edinburgh 1988. 439 p. BRD-86420. – DissA 50 (1989s) 1675-A.

a179* **Morag** Shelomo, Vocalized Talmudic manuscripts in the Cambridge Genizah collections I, 1988 ⇥ 4,b189: ᴿJTS 40 (1989) 733 (S. P. *Brock*).

a180 **Neusner** J., From tradition to imitation; the plan and program of Pesiqta deRab Kahana 1987 ⇥ 3,a497: ᴿBL (1989) 139 (P. S. *Alexander*).

a181 **Neusner** Jacob, Invitation to midrash; the workings of rabbinic Bible interpretation; a teaching book. SF 1989, Harper & R. xv-336 p. $26. 0-06-066107-0 [NTAbs 33,418].

a182 **Neusner** J., The peripatetic saying 1985 ⇥ 1,9938; 3,a498: ᴿRechST 76 (1988) 69s (A. *Paul*: 'la révolution neusnérienne').

a183 **Neusner** J., Berakhot: American Talmud 1984 ⇥ 65,8721; 1,9940: ᴿAbr-Nahrain 27 (1989) 185-7 (T. *Muraoka*).

a184 **Neusner** J., What is Midrash? 1987 ⇥ 3,a500; 4,b193: ᴿGregorianum 70 (1989) 141-3 (G. L. *Prato*); Interpretation 43 (1989) 416 (J. *Scholer*); JRel 69 (1989) 439-441 (S. D. *Fraade*); RExp 86 (1989) 275s (D. R. *Garland*).

a185 **Neusner** Jacob, Why no Gospels in Talmudic Judaism?: BrownJudSt 135, 1988 ⇥ 4,b194: ᴿRivB 37 (1989) 233s (M. *Perani*).

a186 *Neusner* Jacob, The word and the world; midrash, literature, and theology: RelStT 7,2s (Edmonton 1987) 48-55 [< NTAbs 33,223].

a186* *Ostow* M., [bḤag 14] Four entered the garden; normative religion versus illusion [gnostic-mystic threat to faith, sanity, life]: ConsJud 40,4 (1988) 35-46 [< NTAbs 33,365].

a187 ᵀᴱ**Perani** Mauro, Il Midrash Temurah ['dello Scambio', dialettica degli opposti]. Bo 1986, Dehoniane. 105 p. Lit. 12.000. – ᴿParVi 34 (1989) 475s (Ida *Zatelli*).

a188 *Poorthuis* Marcel, 'Beide zijn woorden van de levende God'; over het belang van het meningsverschil in de Talmoedhermeneutiek van LEVINAS: Bijdragen 50 (1989) 394-412; Eng. 413.

a189 **Ratner** Dov B. [1852-1917], Midrash Seder Olam, photostatic ᴱ*Slonimsky* Sarah. Brooklyn 1988, Moznaim.

a190 **Steinsaltz** Adin, The Talmud, a reference guide and commentary. NY 1989, Random. I. 252 p. 0-394-57666-7.

a191 [*Strack* H. L.] **Stemberger** G., Introducción a la literatura talmúdica y midrásica [1982] ᵀ*Pérez Fernández* Miguel: Biblioteca Midrásica 3.

Valencia 1988, Inst. S. Jerónimo. 492 p. [JStJud 20,258]. 84-86067-28-6. – ᴿActuBbg 26 (1989) 199 (R. de *Sivatte*).

a192 **Stemberger** Günter, Il Talmud; introduzione, testi, commenti [1982], ᵀ*Moretti* Donata; pref. *Vivian* A. Bo 1989, Dehoniane. 456 p. Lit. 50.000. 88-10-40784-9. – ᴿBbbOr 31 (1989) 245s (E. *Jucci*).

a193 **Stemberger** Günter, Midrasch; von Umgang der Rabbinen mit der Bibel; Einführung, Texte, Erläuterungen. Mü 1989, Beck. 241 p. [TR 86,74]. 3-406-33910-7.

a194 *Stemberger* G., Münchhausen und die Apokalyptik; Baba Batra 73a-75b als literarische Einheit: JStJud 20 (1989) 61-83.

a195 **Taradach** Madeleine, El midrash; introducció a la literatura midràshica, als targumim i als midrashim: Col·lectània Sant Pacià 38. Barc 1989, Fac. Teol. de Catalunya / Herder / Scrinia. 236 p. 84-86065-16-X.

a196 ᵀᴱ**Wewers** Gerd A., Horayot / Entscheidungen: Übersetzung des Talmud Yerushalmi 4/8, 1984 ➤ 1,9949; 2,8309: ᴿTR 85 (1989) 364 (G. D. *Kilpatrick*, ᵀ*Tensundern* G.).

a197 ᵀᴱ**Wewers** Gerd A., Makkot-Geisselung, Shevuot-Schwüre: TYer 4/5s, 1983 ➤ 64,8937; 65,8729: ᴿRÉJ 147 (1988) 231s (J.-P. *Rothschild*).

K7.1 Judaismus mediaevalis, *generalia*.

a198 **Altmann** Alexander, Von der mittelalterlichen zur modernen Aufklärung; Studien zur jüdischen Geistesgeschichte. Tü 1987, Mohr. vii-336 p. DM 128. – ᴿTLZ 114 (1989) 27s (E. *Bammel*).

a199 *Bareket* Elinoar, ❻ Struggles over Jewish leadership in Fustat in the mid-eleventh century: Zion 59 (1989) 161-178: Eng.v.

a200 **Biale** David, Power and powerlessness in Jewish history 1986 ➤ 3,a516; 4,b212: ᴿAmHR 94 (1989) 708s (D. *Vital*).

a201 *Chiesa* Bruno, Testi e studi di letteratura ebraica medievale, 2: Henoch [7 (1985) 207-226] 11 (1989) 67-101.

a202 *Favreau* Robert, Les Juifs en Poitou et dans les pays de la Charente au Moyen-Âge: RÉJ 147 (1988) 5-29.

a203 *Greenspahn* Frederick E., Jewish scholars, medieval and modern: ➤ 3,355, ᴱ**Neusner** J., Judaic perspectives 1988, 245-258.

a204 **Haxen** Ulf, Facsimile-Ausgabe der 3. Darmstädter Pesach-Haggada, Cod Or 7, Hessische L-HS-Bibliothek. Graz 1989, Akademische DVA. Sch 11.500. – ᴿKairos 30 (1988s) 248-250 (K. *Schubert*).

a205 **Janowitz** Naomi, The poetics of ascent; theories of language in a rabbinic ascent text: SUNY Judaica. Albany 1989, SUNY. xv-154 p. $39.50; pa. $13 [CBQ 52,196].

a206 *Lerner* Myron B., ❻ Collected exempla; studies in aggadic texts published in the *Genuzot* series: KirSef 61 (1986s) 867-891.

a206* *Levy* Ze'ev, Between Yafeth and Shem; on the relation between Jewish and general philosophy. NY 1987, Lang. 253 p. $40. – ᴿJAAR 57 (1989) 864-6 (K. R. *Seeskin*).

a207 *Miletto* Gianfranco, Un manoscritto 'Hillelita' della biblioteca palatina di Parma: Henoch 11 (1989) 271-291; franç. 292; pl. p. 293.

a208 **Mutius** Hans-Georg von, Rechtsentscheide rheinischer Rabbinen vor dem ersten Kreuzzug: JudUmw 13. Fra 1984s, Lang. 2 vol. Fs 44 + 47. 3-8204-5578-7; 686-4. – ᴿNedTTs 42 (1988) 77s (K. A. D. *Smelik*).

a209 **Navarro Peiro** Ángeles, Literatura hispanohebrea (siglos X-XIII), panorámica: Estudios de Cultura Hebrea 5. Córdoba 1988, Almendro. 125 p.; ill. 84-86077-60-5.

a210 ᴱPeláez del Rosal Jesús, Los judíos y Lucena; historia, pensamiento y poesía: Estudios de Cultura Hebrea 9. Córdoba 1988, Almendro. 130 p. 84-86077-64-8.

a211 ᴱPeláez del Rosal Jesús, De Abrahán a Maimónides III; los judíos en Córdoba (ss. X-XII): Estudios de Cultura Hebrea 3. Córdoba 1988, Almendro. 195 p. 84-86077-38-9.

a212 Potok Chaim, Wanderings; history of the Jews. NY 1986, Knopf. xv-431 p. $40. – ᴿProtestantesimo 44 (1989) 295 (G. Vetrano: splendidamente illustrato).

a213 Saenz Badillos Ángel, Targarona Borras Judit, Poetas / Gramáticos hebreos de Al-Andalus (siglos X-XII): Estudios de Cultura Hebrea 4.6. Córdoba 1988, Almendro. 232 p.; 192 p. 84-86077-57-5.

a213* Saltman Avrom, HERMANN's Opusculum de conversione sua [1130; publ. 1687 and in Monumenta Germaniae Historica 1963]; truth or fiction?: RÉJ 147 (1988) 31-56.

a214 Saperstein Marc, Jewish preaching 1200-1800, an anthology: Yale Judaica 26. NHv 1989, Yale Univ. xiii-470 p. 0-300-04355-4.

a215 Schwarzfuchs Simon, Le Kahal, la communauté juive médiévale. P 1986. 157 p. – ᴿRÉJ 146 (1987) 173-5 (D. Tollet).

a216 Sephiha Haïm V., Le ladino (judéo-espagnol calque); structure et évolution d'une langue liturgique, I. Théorie du ladino; II. Textes et commentaires [diss. d'État 1979]. P 1982, Vidas Largas. 26-xlvi-190 p.; 740 + 10 p., 72 pl. – ᴿRÉJ 146 (1987) 405-8 (Monique Boaziz-Aboulker).

a217 Sibony Moïse [mathématicien; disciple du Rav Hakham Dahan], Le jour dans le judaïsme; son histoire et ses moments significatifs. P 1986, auct. (Tours Fac. Sciences). 354 p., dont 170 tableaux. – ᴿRÉJ 146 (1987) 381s (J. Margain).

a218 Sirat Colette, A history of Jewish philosophy in the Middle Ages [1983]ᵀ 1985 → 1,9960: ᴿRelStT 8,3 (1988) 41-43 (F. Landy).

a219 ᴱTwersky Isadore, Studies in medieval Jewish history and literature II. CM 1984, Harvard. 455 p. – ᴿRÉJ 146 (1987) 389-393 (M.-R. Hayoun).

a220 Yante J.-M., Les Juifs dans le Luxembourg au moyen âge: Bulletin de l'Institut Archéologique du Luxembourg 62 (1986) 3-33 [< BTAM 14 (1989) 715s (ipse)].

ᴋ7.2 Maimonides.

a220* Alexander Tamar, Romero Elena, Erase una vez ... Maimónides; cuentos tradicionales hebreos, antología: Estudios de Cultura Hebrea 8. Córdoba 1988, Almendro. 280 p.; ill. 84-86077-65-6.

a221 Freudenthal Gad, Pour le dossier de la traduction latine médiévale du Guide des Égarés: RÉJ 147 (1988) 167-172.

a222 Funkenstein Amos, Maïmonide; nature, histoire et messianisme, ᵀChalier Catherine; préf. Goetschel Roland. La nuit surveillée. P 1988, Cerf. 124 p. – ᴿRÉJ 148 (1989) 170s (J.-P. Rothschild).

a223 Goldfield Lea N., Maimonides' treatise on Resurrection 1986 → 2,8326 ... 4,b226: ᴿJRel 68 (1988) 104s (C. M. Raffel).

a224 Green Kenneth H., The return to Maimonides in the Jewish thought of Leo STRAUSS: diss. Brandeis. Boston 1989, 241 p. 89-22188. – DissA 50 (1989s) 1681-A.

a224* Kasher Hannah, 'Torah for its own sake', 'Torah not for its own sake' [... Maimonides] and a third way: JQR 79 (1988s) 153-163.

a225 **Katchen** Aaron L., Christian Hebraists and Dutch Rabbis... Maimonides: Harvard Judaic Texts 3. CM 1984, Harvard Univ. 391 p. $28. – ᴿJEcuSt 26 (1989) 364s (Susan *Frank*).

a226 *Levenson* Jon D., The [Maimonides] eighth principle of Judaism and the literary simultaneity of Scripture: JRel 68 (1988) 205-225.

a227 *Lévy* Tony, Le chapitre 1,73 du Guide des égarés et la tradition mathématique hébraïque au moyen âge; un commentaire inédit de Salomon B. ISAAC: RÉJ 148 (1989) 307-336.

a228 **Münz** J., Moses ben Maimon (Maimonides) – sein Leben und seine Werke. Z reprint 1986, Morascha. 335 p. – ᴿJudaica 44 (1988) 58s (S. *Schreiner*).

a229 **Niewöhner** Friedrich, Maimonides; Aufklärung und Toleranz im Mittelalter: Kl. Schriften zur Aufklärung 1. Wolfenbüttel / Heid 1988, Lessing-Akad. / Schneider. 60 p. DM 29. – ᴿTLZ 114 (1989) 517s (P. *Heidrich*).

a230 ᴱ**Rakover** Nahum, Maimonides as codifier of Jewish law [Proc. 2d international Law seminar, August 1985] J 1987, Library of Jewish Law. 325 p.; p. 61-73, *Saenz-Badillos* A., Biblical foundations.

a231 [**Romano** David], Maimonides y su época [catálogo de exposición] Palacio de la Merced, Córdoba 1986. 184 p. – ᴿRÉJ 147 (1988) 458-460 (G. *Nahon*).

a232 **Roth** Norman, Maimonides, essays and texts, 850th anniversary [Roth reprints]. Madison WI 1985, Hispanic Seminar. 169 p. – ᴿRÉJ 146 (1987) 175s (J. *Shatzmiller*).

a233 **Strauss** Leo, Maïmonide, essais, ᵀᴱ*Brague* Rémy. P 1988, PUF. 376 p. – ᴿRÉJ 148 (1989) 146-8 (M.-R. *Hayoun*).

a234 **Dana** Nissim, Rabbi Abraham BEN MOSHE ben Maimon [Maimuni, son of Maimonides, 1186-1237], Sefer ha-Maspik ... 2/2, ⊙⊕ Ramat-Gan 1989, Bar-Ilan Univ. 346 p.; 4 pl. 965-226-080-0. – ᴿJJS 40 (1989) 253-8 (D. *Frank*).

a235 **Fenton** Paul B., Deux traités de mystique juive [OVADIA, grandson of Maimonides, 1228-1265; and DAVID II 'last work of the Maimonidean dynasty']: Les Dix Paroles. Lagrasse 1987, Verdier. 334 p. – ᴿRÉJ 148 (1989) 418-420 (D. R. *Blumenthal*).

a236 *Fenton* Paul B., Carmoly [Getschel BAER 1802-75] et le dernier des Maïmonide: RÉJ 148 (1989) 367-375.

K7.3 Alii magistri Judaismi mediaevalis.

a237 RASHI: **Banitt** Menahem, Rashi interpreter of the biblical letter 1985 ➤ 1,9979; 3,a557: ᴿRÉJ 147 (1988) 415-7 (J.-P. *Rothschild*).

a238 **Pearl** Chaim, Rashi: Jewish Thinkers. L 1988, Halban. x-113 p.; maps. £11; pa. £5.25. – ᴿJBQ (= Dor) 18 (1989s) 48-50 (S. *Bakon*); JJS 39 (1988) 283s (D. *Frank*).

a239 SAADIA: *Avishur* Yitzhak, ⊕ 'Difficult words' in Saadia's translation to the Torah and modern translation in the Orient: Massorot 3s (1989) 131-146; Eng. xiii-xiv.

a240 ᵀ**Rosenblatt** Samuel ['from Saadia Gaon, the Arabic and the Hebrew'], The book of beliefs and opinions. NHv c. 1989 pa., Yale Univ. $18 [JBL 108, 72 adv.].

a241 NAHMANIDES: *Fox* Marvin, Nahmanides on the status of Aggadot; perspectives on the disputation at Barcelona, 1263: JJS 40 (1989) 95-109.

a242 *Perani* Mauro, *a*) Storia e prefigurazione tipologica nell'esegesi biblica di Naḥmanide: RivB 37 (1989) 329-341; – *b*) Esegesi biblica e storia del Sefer ha-ge'ulla di Nahmanide: ⟶ 595, Storiografia 1983/7, 89-104.

a243 ᵀᴱ**Feldman** Seymour, Levi Ben Gershom (GERSONIDES) [1288-1344], The wars of the Lord [1 ⟶ 65,8741 ... 4,b234]. Ph 1984/7, Jewish Publ. Soc. viii-256 p.; ix-278 p. $24 each. – ᴿJAOS 109 (1989) 712s (A. L. *Ivry*); RÉJ 146 (1987) 400-3 (G. *Freudenthal*, 1) & 148 (1989) 379-384 (G. *Freudenthal*, 2: unsatisfactory).

a244 ᵀᴱ**Cattani** Luigi, Jehudah HALEVI, Liriche religiose e Canti di Sion: Tradizione d'Israele 2 [⟶ 4,b236]: R 1987, Città Nuova. 192 p. Lit. 25.000. – ᴿParVi 34 (1989) 300-2 (M. *Perani*).

a245 *Fleischer* Ezra, ⊙ On r. Yehuda Hallevi's early years and his first contacts with r. Moshe IBN EZRA: KirSef 61 (1986s) 893-910; p. 894, photo of Arie *Vilsker* 1919-1978.

a246 **Sáenz-Badillos** Ángel, Menahem BEN SARUQ, Mahberet 1986 ⟶ 4,b238: ᴿRÉJ 147 (1988) 412-4 (J.-P. *Rothschild*).

a247 ᴱ**Yahalom** J., Engel E., Mahzor Eretz Israel, a Geniza codex [9th century Palestine liturgy]. J 1987, Hebrew Univ. 42 p. ⊙; 84 pl. + 16 p. – ᴿRÉJ 148 (1989) 165s (Colette *Sirat*: excellent).

a248 *Yudlov* Isaac, ⊙ 'Tefilla le-David', a collection of prayers from Jerusalem, Constantinople 5295 or 5298: KirSef 61 (1986s) 929-932.

a249 **Cohen** Martin S., The Shiʿur Qomah 1983 ⟶ 64,8941 ... 4,b239: ᴿRÉJ 147 (1988) 235s (Colette *Sirat*: the title means 'measure of the divine stature').

K7.4   *Qabbalâ, Zohar, Merkabâ* – **Jewish mysticism.**

a250 **Dan** Joseph, Gershom SCHOLEM and the mystical dimension of Jewish history 1987 ⟶ 3,a578: ᴿJRel 69 (1989) 442s (H. *Maccoby*); RÉJ 146 (1987) 449s (M.-R. *Hayoun*).

a251 *Dan* J., Kabbala, ᵀ*Müller* E.: ⟶ 894, EvKL 2 (1988) 913-5.

a252 **Ginsburg** Elliot K., The Sabbath in the classical Kabbalah. Albany 1989, SUNY. xx-341 p.; 7 fig. $44.50; pa. $15. 0-88706-778-6; pa. –9-4. [RelStR 16, 174, D. C. *Matt*, also on Meir ibn GABBAL, Sod ha-Shabbat, ᴱ*Ginsburg* 1989].

a253 **Gruenwald** Ithamar, From apocalypticism to gnosticism; studies in apocalypticism, Merkavah mysticism and gnosticism: BeiErfAJ 14. Fra 1988, Lang. vii-294 p. 3-8204-1087-2. – ᴿComViat 32 (1989) 102 (J. *Heller*).

a254 **Halperin** David J., The Merkabah in rabbinic literature: AmerOrSer 62, 1980 ⟶ 63,8841: ᴿBO 46 (1989) 704s (J.-C. *Lebram*).

a255 *Holdrege* Barbara A., The bride of Israel; the ontological status of Scripture in the rabbinic and kabbalistic traditions: ⟶ 695, Re-thinking 1989 ...

a256 **Idel** Moshe, Kabbalah, new perspectives 1988 ⟶ 4,h248: ᴿJJS 40 (1989) 251s (L. *Jacobs*).

a257 **Idel** Moshe, Language, torah and hermeneutics in Abraham ABULAFIA [⊙], ᵀ*Kallus* Menahem. Albany 1988, SUNY. xvii-212 p. – ᴿJJS 40 (1989) 251s (L. *Jacobs*).

a258 **Idel** Moshe, Studies in ecstatic Kabbalah 1988 ⟶ 4,b248:: ᴿJJS 40 (1989) 251s (L. *Jacobs*).

a259 **Lachower** Fischel, *Tishby* Isaiah, The wisdom of the Zohar, an anthology of texts systematically arranged and rendered into Hebrew: Littman Library of Jewish Civilization. Ox 1989, Univ.

a260 *McBride* James, Marooned in the realm of the profane; Walter BEN-JAMIN's synthesis of Kabbalah and communism: JAAR 57 (1989) 241-266.

a261 *Meghnagi* David, La kabbalah come metafora dell'esilio: ⟶ 571, L'Ebraismo 1986/7, 79-85.

a262 ᵀᴱ**Mopsik** Charles, Lettre sur la sainteté; le secret de la relation entre l'homme et la femme dans la cabale [+ *Idel* Moché]: Les dix paroles, 1986 ⟶ 4,b251: ᴿRÉJ 147 (1988) 197-200 (J.-P. *Rothschild*).

a263 **Nangeroni** Alessandro, I segreti della Cabbalà; storia di una tradizione mistica. Mi 1988, Xenia. 191 p. Lit. 20.000. – ᴿCC 140 (1989,3) 537s (S. M. *Katunarich*).

a264 **Ruderman** David, Kabbalah, magic, and science; the cultural universe of a sixteenth-century Jewish physician. CM 1988, Harvard. xii-232 p. $30. [RelStR 16, 274, E. K. *Ginsburg*].

a265 *Rudolph* Kurt, Mystik im Judentum: Judaica 44 (1988) 31-46.

a266 **Schäfer** P., Hekhalot-Studien 1988 ⟶ 4,b255: ᴿKairos 30s (1988s) 242-4 (G. *Stemberger*); NRT 111 (1989) 443s (X. *Jacques*); TLZ 114 (1989) 811s (S. *Schreiner*).

a267 **Schäfer** Peter, (*Reeg* G.) Konkordanz zur Hekhalot-Literatur I. 1986; II. 1988: TStAJ 12 ⟶ 2,8361; 4,b253: ᴿGregorianum 70 (1989) 345-7 (G. L. *Prato*); JJS 40 (1989) 125-8 (P. S. *Alexander*); TLZ 114 (1989) 270s (S. *Schreiner*).

a268 ᴱ**Schäfer** Peter, (*Herrmann* Klaus, *al.*), Übersetzung der Hekhalot-Literatur [II. 1987 ⟶ 3,a594; 4,b254] III. 335-597: TStAJ 22. Tü 1989, Mohr. xliii-339 p. 3-16-145565-7.

a269 *Schäfer* P. (p.1-22), *Grözinger* K.-E. (p.23-42), *al.* [Hekhalot, < Scholem Conference 1984ᵀ]: FraJudBei 13 (1985). 146 p. – ᴿRÉJ 146 (1987) 382-6 (N. *Séd*).

a270 **Scholem** Gershom, Origins of Kabbalah, ᵀ*Arkush* Allan, 1987 ⟶ 3,a596; 4,b258: ᴿJRel 69 (1989) 139s (E. R. *Wolfson*); Numen 36 (1989) 131-5 (P. *Schäfer*); RBgPg 67 (1989) 222s (J. *Klener*).

a271 ᵀᴱ**Séd** Nicolas, Le livre Bahir. Mi 1988, Arché. 210 p. – ᴿRÉJ 148 (1989) 172s (M.-R. *Hayoun*: in French, with some 'fâcheuses coquilles due to Italian publisher').

a272 **Swietlicki** Catherine, Spanish Christian Cabala 1986 ⟶ 4,b280: ᴿSefarad 49 (1989) 184-6 (N. *Fernández Marcos*).

a273 *Tishby* Isaiah, ⊕ Upheaval in the research of Kabalah [*Idel* M.]: Zion 59 (1989) 209-222. 469-491; reply 223-240. 493-508.

a274 **Wald** S.G., The doctrine of the divine name; an introduction to classical kabbalistic theology: BrownJudSt 149. Atlanta 1988, Scholars. xi-187 p. $36. 1-55540-242-9 [NTAbs 33,136].

a274* **Wineman** Aryeh, Beyond appearances; stories from the Kabbalistic ethical writings. Ph 1988, Jewish Publ. xi-174 p. $20. 0-8276-0307-X [TDig 36,394].

a275 **Zafrani** Haïm, Kabbale, vie mystique et magie; Judaïsme d'Occident musulman 1986 ⟶ 2,8369: ᴿJSS 34 (1989) 237-241 (D. J. *Schroeter*); RÉJ 146 (1987) 157s (R. *Goetschel*); RTPhil 121 (1989) 454-6 (J. *Borel*).

K7.5 Judaismus saec. 14-18.

a276 *Band* Arnold, The politics of Scripture; the Hasidic tale: ⟶ 3,356, ᴱ**O'Connor** M., Backgrounds 1987, 55-71 [< JBL 108,174].

a277 ᵀᴱBaumgarten Jean, Jacob ben Isaac ASHKENAZI, Le commentaire sur la Torah (Tseenah uReenah) [yiddish 17ᵉs., surtout pour les femmes]: Les Dix Paroles. Lagrasse 1987, Verdier. 944 p. – ᴿRÉJ 147 (1988) 468-470 (B. *Vaisbrot*).

a278 *a*) *Benayahu Meir,* Ⓝ The character of Rabbi Moshe Hayim LUZZATTO [b.1707] as reflected in new sources; – *b*) *Jacobson* Yoram, Ⓞ M.H. Luzzatto's doctrine of divine guidance and its relation to his Kabbalistic teachings: ➤ 745, Italia Judaica 3 (1986/9) 11-25 / 27-46; Eng. 223s.

a279 **Bowman** Steven B., The Jews of Byzantium (1204-1453) 1985 ➤ 2,8731; 3,a602: ᴿCrNSt 9 (1988) 440-4 (A. *Rigo*); RÉJ 147 (1988) 419-422 (J.-C. *Attias*).

a280 *a*) *Chiesa* Bruno, Il supercommentario di 'Ovadyah da Bertinoro a Raši; ➤ *b*) *Tamani* Giuliano, La diffusione del commento alla Mišnah di 'Ovadya Yare da Bertinoro: ➤ 570, Bertinoro 1988/9, 35-46 / 47-56.

a281 **Edwards** John, The Jews in Christian Europe 1400-1700. L 1988, Routledge. 190 p. £25. 0-415-00864-6. – ᴿExpTim 100 (1988s) 436s (N. *Solomon*).

a282 IBN FALAQUERA (13th cent. popularizer): *a*) **Jospe** Raphael, Torah and Sophia; the life and thought of Shem Tov ~ : HUC Mg 11. Cincinnati 1988. 505 p. $45. [RelStR 16, 167, D.J. *Lasker*]; – *b*) **Harvey** Steven, Falaquera's 'Epistle of the debate', an introduction to Jewish philosophy. CM 1987, Harvard. xvi-155 p. $22.50; pa. $14. – ᴿJRel 69 (1989) 611s (B.S. *Kogan*).

a283 **Hayoun** Maurice R., Moshe NARBONI [1300-1362]: Texts and Studies in Medieval and Early Modern Judaism 1. Tü 1986, Mohr. 184 p. DM 78. – ᴿJudaica 44 (1988) 109s (S. *Schreiner*: auch über 2. ALTMANN A. Aufsätze).

a284 *Iancou-Agou* Danièle, Une vente de livres hébreux à Arles en 1434; tableau de l'élite juive arlésienne au milieu du XVᵉ siècle: RÉJ 146 (1987) 5-62.

a285 **Israel** Jonathan I., European Jewry in the age of mercantilism 1550-1750: 1985 ➤ 4,b267: ᴿJudaica 44 (1988) 119s (S. *Schreiner*); RÉJ 147 (1988) 207-210 (G. *Nahon*).

a286 ᴱKrabbenhoft Kenneth, Abraham COHEN de Herrera [d.1635], Puerta del Cielo. M 1987, Fund. Univ. 272 p. – ᴿRÉJ 147 (1988) 210-2 (C. *Mopsik*).

a287 **Leibovici** Sarah, Christophe Colomb juif; défense et illustration. P 1986, Maisonneuve. – ᴿRÉJ 147 (1988) 243s (R.S. *Sirat*).

a288 *a*) ᴱMéchoulan Henry, *Nahon* Gérard, Menasseh BEN ISRAEL, The hope of Israel [Miqweh I. 1650], ᵀ*Wall* Moses [1652] 1987 ➤ 4,b263: ᴿJSS 33 (1988) 149-151 (N. de *Lange*); RÉJ 147 (1988) 246-8 (J.-P. *Osier*); – *b*) ᴱKaplan Yosef, *al.,* Menasseh ben Israel and his world: Studies in Intellectual History 15. Leiden 1989, Brill. x-278 p.; portr.

a289 **Méchoulan** Henry, Abraham PEREYRA, [Certeza del Camino 1666; diss. Salamanca 1983] Hispanidad y Judaismo en tiempos de Espinoza. Salamanca 1987, Univ. 343 p. – ᴿRÉJ 147 (1988) 248-250 (J.-P. *Osier*).

a289* **Mirsky** David, The life and work of Ephraim LUZZATTO [1727-1792]. NY 1987, KTAV. 98 p. + Ⓞ 93. 0-88125-139-9.

a290 [Basch] **Moreen** Vera, Iranian Jewry's hour of peril and heroism; a study of Bābāī IBN LUTF's Chronicle (1617-1662): Texts and Studies 6. NY 1987, American Academy for Jewish Research. xv-247 p. – ᴿStIran 17 (1988) 261-3 (P. *Gignoux*).

a291 *Rigo* Caterina, Un passo sconosciuto di ALBERTO Magno [citato presso AQUINAS] nel *Sefer 'eṣem ha-shamayim* di Yehudah b. MOSHEH (14 sec.): Henoch 11 (1989) 295-318; franç. 318.

a292 *a) Rosa* Mario, Tra tolleranza e repressione; Roma e gli ebrei nel '700; – *b) Badini* Gino, L'archivio dell'Università israelitica di Reggio Emilia: → 745, Italia Judaica 3 (1986/9) 81-98 / 179-182; Eng 209s/216.

a293 *Schubert* Kurt, [AT] Apostasie aus Identitätskrise – Nikolaus DONIN: Kairos 30s (1988s) 1-10 [*Simon* Heinrich 53-63; 64-68 *tohu wᵉbohu*].

a294 **Shenhav-Gollan** Shoshana, Le gestion de la communauté selon le 'Registre des décrets de l'honorable conseil de la sainte communauté de Rome' (de 1573-1577): RÉJ 147 (1988) 289-307.

a295 **Toaff** Ariel, The Ghetto of Rome in the XVIth century; ethnical and social conflicts. Ramot-Gan 1984, Bar-Ilan Univ. xvii-99 p. – ᴿJQR 79 (1988s) 281s (H. *Sukenic*).

a296 *Washofsky* Mark, The commentary of r. Nissim b. Reuven GERONDI ['Ran' d. 1376] to the Halakot of ALFASI; a study in halakhic history: HUCA 60 (1989) 191-257.

a297 **Zinguer** Ilana, Historiographes juifs de la renaissance italienne; lecteurs d'Antonio DE GUEVARA: RÉJ 146 (1987) 281-297.

κ7.7 Judaismus saeculi XIX.

a298 ᴱ**Abramson** Glenda, The Blackwell companion to Jewish culture, from the eighteenth century to the present [topics, mostly persons (with portraits) alphabetically]. Ox 1989, Blackwell. xxiii-853 p. 0-631-15111-7.

a299 *Barnai* Jacob, Some clarifications on the Land of Israel's stories of 'In praise of the Baal Shem Tov': RÉJ 146 (1987) 367-380.

a300 ᵀᴱ**Gourévitch** Édouard, Jeudah BEN CHEMOUEL, Guide des Hasidim (part), préf. *Eisenberg* Josy: Patrimoines Judaïsme. P 1988, Cerf. 510 p. – ᴿRÉJ 147 (1988) 456-8 (M.-R. *Hayoun*).

a301 *Hayoun* Maurice R., Von Moses MENDELSSOHN zu Moritz GOLDSTEIN, ᵀ*Locher* C., *Cunz* M., Judaica 44 (1988) 160-176.

a301* **Heschel** Abraham J., The circle of the Baal Shem Tov; studies in Hasidism, ᵀᴱ*Dresner* Samuel H. Ch 1985, Univ. xlv-213 p. $25. – ᴿJRel 68 (1988) 145s (N. *Polen*).

a302 **Katz** Jacob, The 'shabbes goy', a study in halakhic flexibility, ᵀ*Lerner* Yoel: Mendelson book. Ph 1989, Jewish Publ. viii-253 p. $23. 0-8276-0320-7 [TDig 37,165].

a304 **Safran** Bezalel, Hasidism, continuity or innovation? JudTSt 5. CM 1985, pa. 1989, Harvard. $10, pa. $6. 0-674-38120-3; 1-1. – ᴿJRel 69 (1989) 586s (L. A. *Segal*).

a305 *Schwarzfuchs* Simon, La situation du judaïsme français en 1883; le rapport ISIDOR: RÉJ 146 (1987) 299-355: 147 (1988) 57-144.

a306 *Seltzer* R. M., The secular appropriation of Hassidism by the East European Jewish intellectual; DUBNOW, RENAN and the Besht: Polin, a journal of Polish-Jewish studies 1 (Oxford 1986) 151-162 [résumé RÉJ 146 (1987) 414-6, aussi des 15 autres art.].

a306* *Simon* Heinrich, Wissenschaft vom Judentum in der Geschichte der Berliner Universität: Kairos 30s (1988s) 133-142.

a307 *Simon-Nahum* Perrine, Une famille d'intellectuels juifs en République, les REINACH: RÉJ 146 (1987) 245-254.

a308 *Tamani* Giuliano, Il chassidismo; un movimento mistico presso gli ebrei dell'Europa orientale (sec. XVIII-XIX): ➤ 571, L'Ebraismo 1986/7, 87-107.
a309 ᴱWiesemann Falk, Zur Geschichte und Kultur der Juden in Rheinland [*Kober* Adolf, *al.*, < Zts des Rheinischen Vereins für Denkmalpflege 1916 & 1931]. Dü 1985, Schwann. xvii-219 p.; 150 pl. – ᴿRÉJ 146 (1987) 411-4 (J.-P. *Rothschild*).

K7.8 **Judaismus contemporaneus.**

a310 **Belcove-Shalin** Janet S., A quest for wholeness; the Hasidim of Boro Park [Brooklyn]: diss. Cornell. Ithaca NY 1989. 216 p. – 90-01298. – DissA 50 (1989s) 2956-A.
a311 **Bleich** J. David, Contemporary halakhic problems I-III: Library of Jewish Law 4.10.16. NY 1983-9, KTAV. I. 1983.; 0-87068-450-7. – II. 1983, 423 p. 0-87068-451-5. – III. 1989, xv-415 p.
a312 *Bourel* Dominique, Bulletin du Judaïsme moderne [52 livres]: RechSR 77 (1989) 453-469.
a313 **Chill** Abraham, The *minhagim*; the customs and ceremonies of Judaism, their origins and rationale. NY 1989, Sepher-Hermon. xxvi-339 p.
a314 **Cohn-Sherbok** Dan, The Jewish heritage. Ox 1988, Blackwell. 204 p. £27.50; pa. £8.50. 0-631-15413-2; -4-0. – ᴿExpTim 100 (1988s) 158 (F. *Morgan*: mission unaccomplished); TLond 92 (1989) 315s (B. *Ettlinger*).
a315 **Einstein** Stephen J., *Kukoff* Lydia, Every person's guide to Judaism. NY 1989, 'UAHC'. xii-195 p. $9 pa. 0-8074-0434-9 [TDig 36,368].
a316 **Ellis** Marc H., *a*) Een joodse bevrijdingstheologie? [1987 ➤ 3,a620],ᵀ. – Baarn 1989, Ten Have. 200 p. *f* 25. – ᴿCollatVL 19 (1989) *f* 5. (J. De *Kesel*); Streven 57 (1989s) 371s (P. *Beentjes*). – *b*) Hacia una teología judía de la liberación. San José, Costa Rica 1988, Dep. Ecum. 168 p. – ᴿFranBog 30 (1988) 374 (A. *Morales D.*).
a317 ᴱEndelman Todd M., Jewish apostasy in the modern world 1987 ➤ 4,356; $39.50: ᴿJEcuSt 26 (1989) 367 (Alice L. *Eckardt*); JRel 69 (1989) 446 (Marsha *Rozenblit*).
a317* **Friedman** Maurice S., A dialogue [of the past 25 years] with Hasidic tales; hallowing the everyday. NY 1988, Human Sciences. 170 p. $25. 0-89885-407-5 [TDig 36,370].
a318 *Goitein-Galperin* Denise-Rachel, Albert COHEN revisité; la vision cohénienne de l'existence juive: RÉJ 148 (1989) 205-219.
a319 **Goldscheider** Calvin, *Zuckerman* Alan S., The transformation of the Jews [impact of modernization ...]. Ch 1985, Univ. xii-279 p. $25. – ᴿJRel 68 (1988) 141s (S. M. *Cohen*).
a320 **Graves** Robert, *Patai* Raphaël, Les mythes hébreux [c. 1971], ᵀ*Landais* Jean-Paul. P 1987, Fayard. 294 p. – ᴿRÉJ 148 (1989) 161 (M.-R. *Hayoun* partage les doutes de G. VAJDA).
a321 *Gutwirth* Jacques, Les Juifs américains; l'ère de la quatrième génération: Études 370 (1989) 107-116.
a322 **Helmreich** William B., The world of the Yeshiva; an intimate portrait of orthodox Jewry. NY 1982, Free Press [1986 Yale ➤ 2,8391]. 412 p. $15. – ᴿJRel 68 (1988) 142-4 (S. *Heilman*).
a323 *Homolka* Walter, Continuity in change – liberal Jewish theology in a Christian society: ➤ 177, ᶠSCHWARZ R., Von Wittenberg 1989, 90-119.
a324 *Ish-Shalom* Benjamin, Rav KUK; Pluralismus und Toleranz aus einer jüdisch-orthodoxen Perspektive: Judaica 45 (1989) 169-193 [*al.* 145-168].

a325 *Kühntopf-Gentz* Michael, Der im Judentum ignorierte Gott; Theodor LESSINGS religiöse Philosophie: ZRGg 41 (1989) 134-145.

a326 **Leshem** Moshe, Balaam's curse; how Israel lost its way, and how it can find it again. NY 1989, Simon & S. 304 p. $20 [JAAR 57,888].

a327 **Meyer** Michael A., Response to modernity; a history of the reform movement in Judaism 1988 ➤ 4,b286: ᴿJAAR 57 (1989) 661-3 (Paula E. *Hyman*).

a328 *Morgan* Michael L., Jewish thought today [*Cohen* A., *Mendes-Flohr* P. 1987]: JRel 68 (1988) 575-580.

a329 **Nadell** Pamela S., Conservative Judaism in America; a biographical dictionary and source book. NY 1988, Greenwood. xvi-409 p. $55. [RelStR 16, 86, J. D. *Sarna*].

a330 **Neusner** Jacob, Death and birth of Judaism 1987 ➤ 3,a634; 4,b287: ᴿJRel 68 (1988) 613s (A. *Eisen*).

a331 **Neusner** Jacob, The enchantments of Judaism 1987 ➤ 4,b288: ᴿAndr-UnS 27 (1989) 92-94 (R. *Brooks*).

a332 **Neusner** Jacob, Reading and believing; ancient Judaism and contemporary gullibility. Atlanta 1986, Scholars. 129 p. $20.50 pa. – ᴿJRel 68 (1988) 333 (E. P. *Sanders*: a flagrant example of what Neusner rightly attacks is Neusner's own 1984 treatment of Yoḥanan B. ZAKKAI).

a333 **Oren** Dan A., Joining the club; a history of Jews and Yale. NHv 1986, Yale Univ. xiv-440 p. $20. – ᴿJRel 68 (1988) 147s (F. *Jaher*).

a334 *Pawlikowski* J. T., Judaism; the genius of self-renewal [NEUSNER skilfully faces the faith-modernity problem]: Commonweal 115 (1988) 434-6 [< NTAbs 33,83].

a335 **Peláez del Rosal** Jésús, La sinagoga: Estudios de Cultura Hebrea 7. Córdoba 1988, Almendro. 180 p. 84-86077-63-X.

a336 **Pinkus** Benjamin, The Jews of the Soviet Union; the history of a national minority. C 1988, Univ. xviii-398 p. – ᴿIrénikon 62 (1989) 440 (E. *Lanne*).

a337 **Raphael** Marc L., Profiles in American Judaism 1985 ➤ 1,a38 ... 3,2637: ᴿJRel 68 (1988) 338 (J. *Harris*); RExp 86 (1989) 126 (B. J. *Leonard*: fine).

a338 *Rash* Yehoshua, Immobilisme et dynamisme dans la culture d'Israël: RechSR 77 (1989) 323-346; Eng. 321.

a339 **Reines** Alvin J., Polydoxy [branch-sect of reform Judaism, of his invention]; explorations in a philosophy of liberal religion. Buffalo 1987, Prometheus. 107 p. $23. – ᴿJAAR 57 (1989) 667-9 (S. D. *Breslauer*).

a340 ᴱ**Reinharz** Jehuda, *Schatzberg* Walter, The Jewish response to German culture [1983 Clark Univ. meeting]. Hanover NH 1985, Univ. Pr. New England. xii-362 p. £23.50. – ᴿEngHR 104 (1989) 227s (D. *Johnson*).

a340* **Sarna** Jonathan D., JPS, the Americanization of Jewish culture, 1888-1988. Ph 1989, Jewish Publication Society. xiii-430 p.; ill. [RelStR 16,167, I. *Robinson*].

a341 *Toscano* Mario, Il giudaismo emancipato; la svolta dell'illuminismo: ➤ 571, L'Ebraismo 1986/7, 109-125.

a342 **Tolédano** Joseph, Les Juifs maghrébins: Fils d'Abraham. Turnhout 1989, Brepols. 312 p. 27 (color.) fig. 2-503-50032-3.

a343 *Trevisan Semi* Emanuela, Le sriet, un rite d'investiture sacerdotale chez les Beta Esra'el (Falachas) [avant 1936, mission Viterbo C. A.]: RÉJ 146 (1987) 101-124.

a344 **Udovitch** Abraham L., *Valensi* Lucette, The last Arab Jews; the communities of Jerba, Tunisia: Social Orders 1. NY 1984, Harwood. 178 p. $36. – ᴿJAOS 109 (1989) 134s (W. M. *Brinner*: important).

a345 ᴱWertheimer Jack, The American synagogue, a sanctuary transformed 1987 ➤ 4,329; 0-521-33290-7: ᴿExpTim 100 (1988s) 238 (F. Morgan: essays also on other aspects of development; high praise); JRel 69 (1989) 587s (S. Schafler).

a345* Winer Mark L., al., Leaders of Reform Judaism; a study of Jewish identity, religious practices and beliefs, and marriage patterns. NY 1987, Union Hebr. Congr. xix-154 p. – ᴿJScStR 28 (1989) 380 (B. A. Phillips).

a346 Zohn Harry, Identitätsprobleme deutsch-jüdischer Einwanderer in den Vereinigten Staaten: Kairos 30s (1988s) 11-24.

κ8 Philosemitismus – Judeo-Christian rapprochement.

a347 ᴱAlmog Shmuel, Antisemitism through the ages [Jerusalem symposia and lectures], ᵀReisner Nathan M. NY 1987, Pergamon [for Hebrew Univ. Sassoon Center]. xi-419 p. $55; pa. $25. 0-08-034792-4; 5850-0 [TDig 36,348]. – ᴿÉTRel 64 (1989) 439 (J. Pons).

a348 Andel C. P. van, Rome en Jerusalem; over de veranderingen in de rooms-katholieke sociale leer na Auschwitz. Voorberg 1988, Prot.St.Bibl-wezen. 135 p. ƒ28,50. 90-6495-165-9 [TsTNijm 29,90].

a349 Bakker Leo, Heil door Jezus alleen? Jezus' uniciteit en de afweerhou-ding tegen de joden: TsTNijm 29 (1989) 211-230; Eng. 230s.

a349* Barromi Joel, L'antisemitismo moderno, pref. Roest Crollius Ary. Genova 1988, Marietti. 136 p. Lit 17.000. – ᴿLetture 44 (1989) 278s (S. Fugazza).

a350 Ben-Chorin Schalom, Zusammenstoss zweier Welten: EvT 49 (1989) 290-7 [286-9, Laudatio, 75. Gb., Hahn F.].

a351 Berg Dieter, Servitus Judaeorum; zum Verhältnis des Thomas von AQUIN und seines Ordens zu den Juden in Europa im 13. Jahrhundert: ➤ 771, Aquin/Werk 1986/8, 439-458 [< BTAM 14 (1989) p. 743s (R. Wielockx)].

a352 ᴱBergmann Werner, Error without trial, psychological research on antisemitism: Current Research on Antisemitism 2. B 1988, de Gruyter. xii-546 p.; 11 fig. DM 138 [RelStR 16, 86, J. D. Sarna].

a353 Berlin George L., Defending the faith; nineteenth-century American Jewish writings on Christianity and Jesus. Albany 1989, SUNY. 217 p. [JAAR 57,682].

a354 a) Bernardin Joseph, Emerging Catholic attitudes toward Judaism; – b) Arkoun Mohammed, New pespectives for a Jewish-Christian-Muslim dialogue: JEcuSt 26 (1989) 437-446 / 523-9.

a355 Bianchi Enzo, Israele e la Chiesa: CrNSt 10 (1989) 77-105; Eng. 106.

a356 Boureau Alain, L'inceste de Judas; essai sur la genèse de la haine antisémite au XIIᵉ siècle: Nouvelle Revue de Psychanalyse 33 (1986) 25-41 [< BTAM 14 (1989) 672s (G. Dahan)].

a357 Bowler Maurice G., Claude MONTEFIORE [1858-1938] and Christianity: Brown JudSt 157. Atlanta 1988, Scholars. ix-107 p. $38. 1-55540-286-0 [NTAbs 33,232].

a358 Braybrooke Marcus, The pastor's opportunities, XVII. Relations with Jews: ExpTim 99 (1987s) 324-7.

a359 Brockway Allan, al. (P. Van Buren, R. Rendtorff...) The theology of the churches and the Jewish people. Geneva 1988, WCC. 186 p. $12.90 pa. – ᴿCalvinT 24 (1989) 371s (M. Stover).

a360 ᴱBrooks Roger, Unanswered questions 1988 ➤ 4,b306: ᴿCCurr 39 (1989s) 241-4 (D. Biale); JRel 69 (1989) 448s (J. C. Rylaarsdam).

a361 **Bunte** W., Juden und Judentum in der mittelniederländischen Literatur, 1100-1600: JudUmw 24. Bern 1989, Lang. 592 p.; ill.; maps. Fs 83 [RHE 85,131*].

a362 *Certeau* Michel de, Le Judaïsme dans le monde chrétien: RechSR 76 (1988) 232-5 [163-266 et 321-404, deux fascicules dediés à M. de CERTEAU, co-rédacteur 1966-86, sa bibliographie, p. 405-457].

a363 **Chazan** Robert, Daggers of faith; thirteenth-century Christian missionizing and Jewish response. Berkeley 1989, Univ. California. $40. 0-520-06297-3 [TDig 37,46].

a364 **Chevallier** Yves L'antisémitisme; le Juif comme bouc émissaire: Sciences humaines et religions 125. P 1988, Cerf. 464 p. F 125. 2-204-02912-2. – ᴿEsprVie 99 (1989) 80 (L. *Debarge*); ÉTRel 64 (1989) 440 (J. *Pons*); NRT 111 (1989) 988s (L.-J. *Renard*).

a365 *Chrostowski* Waldemar, ❷ a) Nouvelle approche des juifs et du judaïsme par le christianisme – une théologie nouvelle: PrzPow 805 (1988) 263-278; franç. 278; – b) Dialog z Żydami i judaizmem a posłannictwo Kościoła: PrzPow 815 (1989) 44-58 [817 (1989) 395-9, *Gebert* K.: response].

a366 *Cottier* Georges, Der Antisemitismus von Karl MARX, ᵀ*Locher* Clemens: Judaica 45 (1989) 211-220.

a367 **Cutler** Allan H. & Helen E., The Jew as ally of the Muslim 1985 → 2,8429 ... 4,b318: ᴿRÉJ 147 (1988) 201s (J. *Shatzmiller*: speculations evaluated in place of proofs); RelStT 8,3 (1988) 33-35 (B. *Firestone*); Thought 62 (1987) 435-443 (L. J. *Simon*).

a368 *Dahan* Gilbert, BERNARD de Clairvaux et les Juifs: Archives juives 23 (1987) 59-64 [< BTAM 14 (1989) 702s (H. *Silvestre*)].

a369 *Dahan* Gilbert, Judaïsme et christianisme; le débat au moyen âge; cadre et méthodes de la 'disputatio': Juifs et chrétiens, un vis-à-vis permanent [Publ 42; Bru 1988, Fac. Univ. St.-Louis; 190 p.] 27-53 [< BTAM 14 (1989) 671s].

a369* **Davies** Alan, Infected Christianity, a study of modern racism. Montreal 1988, McGill-Queen Univ. 160 p. $25. – ᴿJEcuSt 26 (1989) 536s (R. *Modras*: cites without favor 'There's no business like *Shoah* business').

a370 *Dehandschutter* B., Anti-Judaism in the Apocrypha: → 696, 10th Patristic, 19 (1989) 345-350.

a371 *Di Sante* Carmine, Il dialogo cristiano-ebraico; cammino, problemi e speranze: StEcum 5 (1987) 239-259; Eng. 259s.

a372 *Donnelly* John P., Antonio POSSEVINO and Jesuits of Jewish ancestry: ArchHistSI 55 (1986) 3-31 [he may have been Jewish himself, and vigorously opposed 5th General Congregation decree 1593 excluding members of Jewish origin: RHE 84 (1989) 866s].

a373 *Duffy* Michael F., *Mittelmann* Willard, NIETZSCHE's attitudes toward the Jews: JHistId 49 (1988) 301-317.

a374 *Dujardin* Jean, Catholiques, qu'avons-nous compris? À propos du Carmel d'Auschwitz [... résistance à son transfert est un scandale ... l'histoire, en Pologne, depuis la guerre, n'a jamais présenté le camp d'Auschwitz comme le symbole de la Shoah; ... responsabilité que l'Église assume devant le peuple polonais]: NRT 111 (1989) 522-536.

a375 *Eckardt* A. Roy, Jews and Christians; the contemporary meeting 1986 → 2,8437 ... 4,b324: ᴿJRel 68 (1988) 339 (A. *LaCocque*: provocative).

a376 *Eckert* Willehad P., Antijüdische Motive in der christlichen Kunst und ihre Folgen: BiKi 44 (1989) 72-79; 5 fig. [65-70, *Klein* Charlotte, im Theologiestudium].

a377 **Edwards** John, The Jews in Christian Europe 1400-1700: Christianity and society in the modern world. NY 1988, Routledge. x-190 p. $35. 0-415-00864-6 [TDig 36,367]. – ᴿJJS 40 (1989) 258s (L. *Kochan*: what one can do without knowing Hebrew or Yiddish).

a378 *Eijk* A. H. C. van, The Jewish people and the Church's self-understanding: Bijdragen 50 (1989) 373-392.

a379 **Evearitt** Daniel J., Jewish-Christian missions to the Jews, 1820-1935: diss. Drew, ᴰ*Handy*. Durham NC 1988. 404 p. 89-06804. – DissA 50 (1989s) 171-A; RelStR 16,190.

a380 ᴱ**Fein** Helen, The persisting question; sociological perspectives and social contexts of modern antisemitism: Current Research on Antisemitism 1. B 1987, de Gruyter. XIV-430 p. DM 106 [RelStR 16, 86, J. D. *Sarna*].

a381 *Feldman* L. H., Is the New Testament anti-Semitic? [not the earliest parts; and the others were not used in that way before the Crusades]: Humanities 21 (Tokyo 1987) 1-14 [< NTAbs 33,345].

a382 Fifteen years of Catholic-Jewish dialogue 1970-1985 (Lateran/Vatican) 1988 → 4,h326: ᴿCC 140 (1989,3) 308s (S. M. *Katunarich*); PrzPow 809 (1989) 140-3 (W. *Chrostowski*).

a383 **Fornberg** Tord, Jewish-Christian dialogue and biblical exegesis: StMissionalia 47, 1988 → 4,b328: ᴿSvTKv 65 (1989) 30-32 (B. *Fjärstedt*).

a384 **Friedrich** Martin, Zwischen Abwehr und Bekehrung; die Stellung der deutschen evangelischen Theologie zum Judentum im 17. Jahrhundert: BeiHistT 72. Tü 1988, Mohr. viii-222 p. DM 118. – ᴿProtestantesimo 44 (1989) 129s (J. A. *Soggin*); TLZ 114 (1989) 526-8 (E. *Koch*).

a385 *Garrone* Daniele, Protestanti ed ebrei; alcuni nodi del confronto attuale: Protestantesimo 44 (1989) 82-95 [96-100, documenti].

a386 *Golomb* Jacob, NIETZSCHE's Judaism of power [not anti-Semitic as claimed by A. *Bäumler* 1934, C. *Brinton* 1965]: RÉJ 147 (1988) 353-385.

a387 *a) Gross* Rita M., Religious pluralism; some implications for Judaism; – *b) Pawlikowski* John T., Toward a theology for religious diversity; perspectives from the Christian-Jewish dialogue: JEcuSt 26 (1989) 29-44 / 138-153.

a388 *Hellig* J., The negative image of the Jew and its New Testament roots: JTSAf 64 (Rondebosch 1988) 39-48 [< NTAbs 33,205].

a388* **Henry** Marie Luise, Der jüdische Bruder und seine hebräische Bibel 1988 → 4,b343: ᴿBiKi 44 (1989) 43s (M. *Helsper*).

a389 **Hoffmann** Christhard, Juden und Judentum im Werk deutscher Althistoriker des 19. und 20. Jahrhunderts: Studies in Judaism in Modern Times 9. Leiden 1988, Brill. xii-302 p. *f* 106. – ᴿClasR 39 (1989) 378s (Margaret H. *Williams*).

a389* *Horst* Ulrich, *Faes de Mottoni* Barbara, Die Zwangstaufe jüdischer Kinder im Urteil scholastischer Theologen: MüTZ 40 (1989) 173-199.

a390 **Ioly Zorattini** P. C., Processi del S. Uffizio di Venezia contro Ebrei et giudaizzanti 3-4, 1984s → 62,331; 63,8946 (3,a608): ᴿRÉJ 147 (1988) 202-7 (A. *di Leone Leoni*).

a391 *Johnson* E. E., Jews and Christians in the New Testament; John, Matthew, and Paul: RefR 42,2 (Holland MI 1988s) 113-128 [< NTAbs 33,205].

a392 *Johnson* Luke T., The New Testament's anti-Jewish slander and the conventions of ancient polemic: JBL 108 (1989) 419-441.

Juden (Luther-Bibliographie): LuJb 56 (1989) 192.

a393 *a) Karski* K., LUTHER, das Luthertum und die Juden; – *b) Krüger* H., CALVIN und die Juden; – *c) Tranda* B., Die reformierte Theologie und das jüdische Volk; – *d) Karski* K., Die ökumenische Bewegung und die Juden; – *e) Czajkowski* M., Christlicher Antisemitismus schon im Neuen Testament?: Jednota (Monatsschrift für Religion und Gesellschaft) 9s (Wsz 1987) 4-7 / 8-11 / 11-14 / 15-18 / 19-22 [< Judaica 44,128; the titles (including the subtitle of the periodical) are all given in German, with no indication of whether the originals are in Polish].

a394 **Katunarich** S. M., Breve storia dell'ebraismo e dei suoi rapporti con la cristianità 1988 ➤ 3,a679; 4,b352: RBL (1989) 19 (N. R. M. de *Lange*: 'a breathless and inevitably superficial romp'; impressive sincerity and enthusiasm, somewhat low on Byzantinism/Reformation); ParVi 33 (1988) 394 (M. *Perani*).

a395 **Katz** Jacob, Exclusion et tolérance, chrétiens et juifs du Moyen Âge à l'ère des Lumières [**❿**; Eng. c. 1961], ᵀ*Rozenberg* Léna, *Perret* Xavier. P..., Lieu commun. 284 p. – RRÉJ 147 (1988) 471s (M.-R. *Hayoun* gives renvoi to RÉJ 1962 recension but no date for ❿, Eng., or French).

a396 **Katz** Jacob, Vom Vorurteil bis zur Vernichtung; der Antisemitismus 1700-1933. Mü 1989, Beck. 375 p. DM 48. – RJudaica 45 (1989) 262s (A. *Pfahl-Traughber*).

a397 *Kessler* E., Claude MONTEFIORE: Christian Jewish Relations 21,4 (L 1988) 6-17 [< NTAbs 33,282].

a398 **Krämer-Badoni** Rudolf, Judenmord, Frauenmord, heilige Kirche. Mü 1988, Knesebeck & S. DM 34. – RJudaica 45 (1989) 263 (A. *Pfahl-Traughber*).

a399 **Kraus** Hans-Joachim, Denken aus Umkehr [*Marquardt* F.-W., Von Elend und Heimsuchung der Theologie 1988 ... 'aus jüdisch-christlichem Dialog']: EvT 49 (1989) 564-571.

a400 *a) Kraus* Hans-Joachim, 'Israel' in der Theologie CALVINS; Anstösse zu neuer Begegnung mit dem AT und dem Judentum; – *b) Riegner* Gerhart M., Verpasste Chancen im christlich-jüdischen Dialog vor der Scho'a [= a428]; – *c) Hermle* Siegfried, 'Wo ist dein Bruder Israel?' [*Freudenberg* A.]: KIsr 4,1 (1989) 3-13 / 14-30 / 42-59.

a401 ᴱ**Kremers** Heinz, *al.*, Die Juden / LUTHER 1985 ➤ 1,602* ... 4,b355: RJudaica 44 (1988) 245s (P. *Maser*).

a402 ᴱ**Kremers** Heinz, *Schoeps* Julius H., Das jüdisch-christliche Religions-gespräch 1986/8 ➤ 4,b356: RKIsr 4 (1988) 105-8 (Julie *Kirchberg*).

a403 *a) Lambert* Ian M., Reflections on the Council of Christians and Jews; – *b) Murrell* N. Samuel, Linking Auschwitz to the demise-of-Jesus tradition in Jewish-Christian dialogue; – *c) Levitt* Laura, Political power; learning a new Jewish theological vocabulary: Paradigms 5 (1989) 77-87 / 101-116 / 143-154.

a404 *Leavy* Stanley K., Jews in the Church: CCurr 39 (1989s) 196-203.

a405 *Levine* Robert, Why praise Jews? [it was a safe way of attacking some Christians]; satire and history in the Middle Ages: Journal of Medieval History 12 (1986) 291-6 [< RHE 84 (1989) 645, H. *Silvestre*].

a406 **Lewis** Bernard, Semites and Antisemites; an inquiry into conflict and prejudice 1986 ➤ 3,a691: RBAsEspOr 23 (1987) 418-421 (V. *Morales Lezcano*).

a407 **Lindeskog** Gösta, Das jüdisch-christliche Problem; Randglossen zu einer Forschungsepoche 1986 ➤ 2,8481 ... 4,b362: RJAAR 57 (1989) 408 (L. *Gaston*); Judaica 44 (1988) 110s (S. *Schreiner*).

Lohfink Norbert, Der niemals gekündigte Bund; exegetische Gedanken zum christlich-jüdischen Gespräch 1989 ➤ 7274.

a408 Lubac Henri de, Résistance chrétienne à l'antisémitisme; souvenirs 1940-44: 1988 ➤ 4,b363: ᴿRivStoLR 25 (1989) 308-335 (G. Miccoli); ZkT 111 (1989) 232s (K. H. Neufeld).

a408* Lucas L., Zur Geschichte der Juden im vierten Jahrhundert; der Kampf zwischen Christentum und Judentum, Hildesheim 1985=1910, Olms. 14+134p. – ᴿArTGran 52 (1989) 342s (A. Torres).

a409 MacLennan Robert S., Four early Christian texts on Jews and Judaism in the second century C.E. [in the context of the city in which they were written, itself a 'text' which can be read]: diss. Minnesota. Minneapolis 1988. 368 p. 89-11010. – DissA 50 (1989s) 520s-A.

a410 Manns Frédéric, Israël dans la réflexion des Pères de l'Église: RivScR 3,1 (1989) 129-142.

a411 Martola N., The Rabbinate in a historical perspective: NordJud 10,1 (Åbo 1989) 11-26 svensk; Eng. summ. [< Judaica 45,268].

a412 Massing Paul W., Vorgeschichte des politischen Antisemitismus [1949], ᵀWeil Felix J.: Tb Syndikat/EVA 78. Fra 1986. Europ.-V. viii-285 p. DM 19,80. – ᴿJudaica 45 (1989) 252s (S. Schreiner).

a413 May John D., 'The only great ecumenical question'; Christian-Jewish relations: Studies 77 (Dublin 1988) 300-8.

a414 Miller Ronald H., Dialogue and disagreement; Franz ROSENZWEIG's relevance to contemporary Jewish-Christian understanding. Lanham MD 1989, UPA. xix-213 p. $37.50; pa. $21.75. 0-8191-7539-0; 49-8 [TDig 37,75].

a415 Misiurek Jerzy, ❷ Filosemityzm: ➤ 891, EncKat 5 (1989) 239s.

a416 Müller Karlheinz, Zur Datierung rabbinischer Aussagen: ➤ 173, ᶠSCHNACKENBURG R., NT & Ethik 1989, 551-587.

a417 Neudecker Reinhard, Die vielen Gesichter des einen Gottes; Christen und Juden im Gespräch: ÖkExH 6. Mü 1989, Kaiser. 133 p. [AcPIB 9/5,359]. DM 19,80. – ᴿÖkRu 38 (1989) 506s (F.-W. Marquardt).

a418 Neusner Jacob, The absoluteness of Christianity and the uniqueness of Judaism [to use the correct language of their respective theologies]; why salvation is not of the Jews: Interpretation 43 (1989) 18-31: there can be no dialogue between an entity sui generis and any other entity; genuine dialogue falls beyond the limits of logical discourse, blurring of the boundaries.

a419 Novak David, Jewish-Christian dialogue; a Jewish justification. NY 1989, Oxford-UP. xiii-194 p. $25. 0-19-505084-3 [TDig 37,176].

a420 Pawlikowski John T., The re-Judaization of Christianity – its impact on the Church and its implications for the Jewish people: ➤ 408, Immanuel 22s (1989) 60-74.

a421 Petuchowski J.J., Thoma C., Lexikon der jüdisch-christlichen Begegnung. FrB 1989, Herder. 256p. DM 38. – ᴿOrientierung 53 (1989) 223s (C. Locher).

a422 a) Petuchowski J.J., Verso una teologia ebraica del cristianesimo [< ᴱMcInnes A., Renewing 1987, 41-52, ᵀStefani Piero]; – b) Fabris Renzo, Il sentimento della fratellanza verso gli Ebrei nella coscienza della Chiesa: HumBr 44 (1989) 181-194 / 195-207.

a423 Pfisterer R., Von A bis Z; Quellen zu Fragen um Juden und Christen [1971], ²Mybes F. Neuk 1985, Schriftenmission. 491 p. DM 38. – ᴿTGegw 31 (1988) 206 (A. Schmied).

a424 **Poliakov** Léon, Geschichte des Antisemitismus [franç.],[T] [5. 1983 ➤ 1,a114]; 6. Emanzipation und Rassenwahn, Worms 1987, Heintz. 361 p. DM 48. – [R]ZkT [106 (1984) 463-7] 111 (1989) 232 (R. *Oberforcher*);– TGegw 32 (1989) 144-151 (J. *Pistorius* 1-8).

a425 **Rausch** David A., Building bridges; understanding Jews and Judaism. Ch 1988, Moody. $8. 0-8024-1076-6. – [R]JEcuSt 26 (1989) 545s (H. H. *Cohn*).

a425* *Raveaux* Thomas, Adversus Iudaeos — Antisemitismus bei AUGUSTINUS?: ➤ 132, [F]MAYER C., Signum 1989, 37-51.

a426 **Rendtorff** Rolf, Hat denn Gott sein Volk verstossen?: Die evangelische Kirche und das Judentum seit 1945; ein Kommentar: AbhChrJü-Dial 18. Mü 1989, Kaiser. 130 p. 3-459-01820-8.

a427 [E]**Rendtorff** Rolf, *Henrix* Hans H., Die Kirchen und das Judentum, Dokumente von 1945-1985 ➤ 4,b381: [R]TLZ 114 (1989) 426-8 (C. *Hinz*); TR 85 (1989) 407s (F. *Mussner*).

a428 *Riegner* Gerhart M., Verpasste Chancen zu einem christlich-jüdischen Dialog von der Shoah: TLZ 114 (1989) 81-94.

a429 *Riggans* W., Towards an evangelical doctrine of the Church; the Church and Israel: Churchman 103,2 (L 1989) 129-135 [< Judaica 45,268].

a430 **Robinson** Jack H., John CALVIN and the Jews: diss. St. Louis Univ. 1989. 246 p. 90-00933. – DissA 50 (1989s) 2541-A.

a431 *Rottenberg* I. C., Christian fulfilment and Jewish-Christian dialogue [E. J. *Fisher* ill-reconcilable with NT]: ChrCent 106,12 (Ch 1989) 387-391 [< NTAbs 33,349].

a432 *Rueff* A. L., Den Christen jüdische Theologie erklärt [biobibliographical assessment of S. *Ben Chorin*]: RefF 3,2 (Z 1989) 25 [< NTAbs 33,140].

a433 **Schalom** für Österreich; christlich-jüdische Begegnungen in Wien. [12./26. Okt. 1986]. W 1986, Herold. 96 p. – [R]TPQ 137 (1989) 101s (J. *Lettl*).

a434 *a*) *Scholl* Reiner, LUTHERS Stellung zu den Juden; – *b*) *Gritsch* Eric W., Luther and Israel; trial and error; a neuralgic theme; ➤ 177, [F]SCHWARZ R., Von Wittenberg 1989, 212-228 / 38-46.

a435 *a*) *Schottroff* Luise, Passion Jesu — Passion des jüdischen Volkes; – *b*) *Wigoder* Geoffrey, Der christlich-jüdische Dialog in Israel; – *c*) *Barkenings* Hans-J., Dem Antijudaismus widersprechen; Anmerkungen zu einer neuen Kirchenverfassung [Ev.-Ref. Bayern/NW Deutschland 9.VI.1988]: KIsr (1989,2) 91-101 / 156-165 / 172-4.

a436 *a*) *Schreiner* Stefan, Ⓜ The re-discovery of the fellow-believer; on the aim and problems of the Jewish-Christian dialogue; – *b*) *Papp* Vilmos, Ⓜ Protestantism and Judaism: TSzem 31 (1988) 272-5 / 157-168 ([T]*Karasszon* István).

a437 **Shermis** Michael, Jewish-Christian relations; an annotated bibliography and resource guide. Bloomington 1988, Indiana Univ. xv-291 p. $30. 0-253-33153-6 [NTAbs 33,267]. – [R]RExp 86 (1989) 281 (F. *Stagg*).

a438 *Siker* Jeffrey S., From Gentile inclusion to Jewish exclusion; Abraham in early Christian controversy with Jews: BibTB 19 (1989) 30-36.

a439 **Simonsohn** Shlomo, The Apostolic See and the Jews; documents [I. 492-1404 ➤ 4,b392; C$49], II. 1294-1464. Toronto 1989, Pontifical Institute of Mediaeval Studies. p. 551-1132. – [R]Aevum 63 (1989) 403s (G. M. *Cantarella*); RÉJ 148 (1989) 428-430 (G. *Nahon*, 1s; more volumes awaited); RHE 84 (1989) 563s (R. *Aubert*).

a440 *Simonsohn* Shlomo, Some well-known Jewish converts during the Renaissance: R EJ 148 (1989) 17-52.

a441 *Smith* J., The conversion of the Jews: RelEdn 82 (Ch 1987) 592-605 [< Judaica 44,126].

a442 **Sobel** B.Z., Hebrew Christianity, the thirteenth tribe [... attraction of Protestant sects for Young American Jews rejecting the industrial society]. NY 1974, Wiley. 413 p. – ᴿRÉJ 147 (1988) 489s (Colette *Sirat*).

a443 *Sonnet* Jean-Pierre, Figure di resistenza etica in Israele: CC 139 (1988,4) 348-361.

a444 **Springer** Anthony J., AUGUSTINE's use of Scripture in his anti-Jewish polemic: diss. Southern Baptist Theol. Sem., ᴰ*Hinson* E.G. 1989. 203 p. 90-08964. – DissA 50 (1989s) 2940-A.

a445 *a) Stow* Kenneth R., I Papi, gli Ebrei e la Legge; – *b) Dahan* Gilbert, L'Église et les Juifs au moyen âge (XIIᵉ-XIVᵉ siècles); – *c) Sermoneta* Giuseppe, L'incontro culturale tra Ebrei e Cristiani nel Medioevo e nel Renascimento; – *d) Boesch Gajano* Sofia, Identità ebraica e stereotipi cristiani: ➤ 700, Ebrei/Cristiani 1988, 141-153 / 19-43 / 183-207 / 45-61.

a446 ᴱ**Strauss** Herbert A., *Kampf* Norbert, Antisemitismus; von der Judenfeindschaft zum Holocaust [Tagung 1983, Technische Univ. wBerlin]: Bundeszentrale für politische Bildung 213. Bonn 1985. 288 p. – ᴿRÉJ 146 (1987) 462-4 (M.-R. *Hayoun*).

a447 *Swidler* L., Contemporary implications of the Jewish-Christian dialogue on Jesus Christ: Dialogue & Alliance 2,3 (NY 1988) 95-108 [< NTAbs 33,152].

a448 *Timmer* David E., Biblical exegesis and the Jewish-Christian controversy in the early twelfth century: ChH 58 (1989) 309-321.

a449 *Valadier* Paul, Juifs et chrétiens; indépassable rivalité?: Études 371 (1989) 509-520.

a450 **Vreekamp** H., Zonder Israël niet volgroied; visie op de verhouding tussen de kerk en joodse volk van Hervormde zijde. Kampen 1988, Kok. 113 p. *f* 16,90. – ᴿStreven 56 (1988s) 662s (P. *Beentjes*).

a451 *Wigoder Geoffrey*, Jewish-Christian relations since the Second World War. Manchester 1988, Univ. 184 p. £22.50. – ᴿTablet 242 (1988) 1068s (D. *Nicholl*); TS 50 (1989) 403s (J.T. *Pawlikowski*).

Williamson Clark M., *Allen* Ronald J., Interpreting difficult texts; anti-Judaism and Christian preaching 1989 ➤ 1446*.

a452 **Zuidema** Willem, God's partner, an encounter with Judaism, ᵀ*Bowden* J. 1987 ➤ 3,a745; 4,b405: ᴿSalesianum 51 (1989) 844 (R. *Vicent*).

a452* **Zuidema** Willem, Partenaire de Dieu; à la rencontre du Judaïsme, ᵀ*Passelecq* Georges: Bible et Vie Chrétienne NS. P 1987, Lethielleux. 256 p. – ᴿBLitEc 90 (1989) 57s (S. *Légasse*).

XVII,3 Religiones parabiblicae

M1.1 **Gnosticismus classicus.**

a453 *Beltz* Walter, Zur Geschichtsbild der Gnosis: ZRGg 40 (1989) 362-6.

a454 **Boehlig** A., Gnosis und Synkretismus I. Tü 1989, Mohr. 370 p. DM 128. [ÉTRel 64,671].

a455 **Buckley** Jorunn J., Female fault and fulfillment in Gnosticism 1986 ➤ 2,8545 ... 4,b408: ᴿJRel 68 (1988) 330s (Deirdre *Good*); JTS 40 (1989) 234-8 (Anne *McGuire*).

a456 **Culianu** Ioan P., Gnosticismo ... H. JONAS 1985 ➤ 2,8546 ... 4,b409: ᴿRÉG 102 (1989) 255s (P. *Nautin*).

a457 *Edwards* M. J.,   New discoveries and Gnosticism; some precautions: OrChrPer 55 (1989) 257-272 [< RHE 85,40*].

a458 *Filoramo* Giovanni,   Diventare Dio; visione e regenerazione nello Gnosticismo: → 748, Sogni 1988 = AugR 29 (1989) 81-121.

a459 **Guillaumont** Antoine & Claire,   ÉVAGRE le Pontique, Le gnostique ou à celui qui est devenu digne de la science; édition critique des fragments grecs,[T] au moyen des versions syriaques et arméniennes: SChr 356. P 1989, Cerf. 208 p. 2-204-03190-9.

a460 *Hanratty* Gerald T.,   JUNG and the Gnostics: MilltSt 23 (1989) 54-70.

a461 *Hinlicky* E. & P.,   Gnosticism old and new: Dialog 28,1 (St. Paul 1989) 12-17 [< NTAbs 33,229].

a462 *Hombert* Pierre-M.,   Simone PÉTREMENT et les origines du Gnosticisme: MélSR 46 (1989) 71-87.

a463 **Jonas** Hans,   Gnosis und spätantiker Geist, 1. Die mythologische Gnosis[4]: FRL 33.   Gö 1988 = 1934 [[1]1954, [3]1964], Vandenhoeck & R. xvi-456 p. DM 128.   3-525-53123-0 [NTAbs 33,273].

a464 *La Potterie* Ignace de,   La gnosi; il percorso dalle origini: Synesi 6 ('Immagini dell'uomo del XX secolo' 1989) 57-76 [< ActaPIB 9,459].

a465 [TE]**Layton** Bentley,   The Gnostic scriptures 1987 → 3,a759; 4,b414:   [R]BA 52 (1989) 49s (P. A. *Mirecki*); CBQ 51 (1989) 746s (D. *Johnson*: only 14 of the 42 NH, but others also, some non-Gnostic); JStJud 20 (1989) 95s (I. P. *Culianu*: Layton talks about Gnosticism as a Gnostic; claims a knowledge endowed by powers unknown to other human minds); RB 96 (1989) 113-6 (L. *Painchaud*); TLZ 114 (1989) 101-4 (H.-M. *Schenke*).

a465* *Luttikhuizen* Gerard P.,   The evaluation of the teaching of Jesus in Christian Gnostic revelation dialogues: → 606, Réception 1986/9, 363-372 = NT 30 (1988) 158-168.

a466 **MacRae** George W.,   Studies in the NT and Gnosticism.   Wilmington 1988, Glazier. $13.   0-89453-648-6. – [R]RelStR 15 (1989) 73 (B. A. *Pearson*).

a467 **Moraldi** Luigi,   La gnosi e il mondo; raccolta di testi gnostici[2]: I tascabili degli Editori Associati 16.   Mi 1988 [[1]1982], TEA. xx-127 p. 88-7819-016-0.

a468 *Nagel* Peter,   Gnosis, Gnostizismus: → 894, EvKL 2 (1988) 241-7.

a469 **Onuki** Takashi,   Gnosis und Stoa, eine Untersuchung zum Apokryphon des Johannes: NTOrbA 9.   FrS 1989, Univ. x-196 p. – [R]ETL 65 (1989) 444 (B. *Dehandschutter*).

a470 **Pagels** Elaine,   I vangeli gnostici [1979 → 61,k252], [TE]*Moraldi* Luigi. Mi 1987, Mondadori.   235 p. Lit. 8000. – [R]CC 140 (1989,1) 311 (B. *Groth*).

a471 [E]**Pearson** B., *Goehring* J.,   The roots of Egyptian Christianity 1983/6 → 2,484 ... 4,b18:   [R]HeythJ 30 (1989) 195-7 (P. *Rousseau*).

a472 *Perkins* Pheme,   Gnosticism: → 384, NJBC (1989s) 1350-3.

a473 *Pétrement* Simone,   Le Dieu séparé; les origines du gnosticisme 1984 → 65,8001 ... 4,b421:   [R]BO 46 (1989) 98-101 (G. G. *Stroumsa*); EWest 38 (1988) 331s (G. *Gnoli*).

a474 **Schmithals** Walter,   NT & Gnosis: ErtFor 208, 1984 → 65,8904 ... 2,8558:   [R]RB 96 (1989) 624s (J. J. *Taylor*: reviews possible relevance to every NT book, always with BULTMANN outlook).

a475 **Stroumsa** G. G.,   Another seed 1984 → 65,8995 ... 4,b425:   [R]Numen 36 (1989) 127-131 (K. *Rudolph*).

a476 *Stryjecki* Janusz, *Myszor* Wincenty, ❷ Gnostycyzm: → 891, EncKat 5 (1989) 1201-5-8 (–1218, Gnoza, *Myszor* al.).

a477 *Sumney* Jerry L., The letter of EUGNOSTOS and the origins of Gnosticism: NT 31 (1989) 172-181.

a478 *Szabó* Andor, ⑩ The Old Testament and gnosis: TSzem 32 (1989) 70-73.

a479 **Tardieu** M., *Dubois* J.-D., Introduction à la littérature gnostique I, 1986 ➤ 2,8562 ... 4,b426: ᴿSalmanticensis 36 (1989) 125-7 (R. *Trevijano*).

a480 *a*) *Thoma* Clemens, Rabbinische Reaktionen gegen die Gnosis; – *b*) *Stroumsa* Gedaliahu G., Mythos und Erinnerung; jüdische Dimensionen der gnostischen Revolte gegen die Zeit: Judaica 44 (1988) 2-14 / 15-30.

a481 *Vincent* Gilbert, Le corps de l'hérétique; la critique de la gnose par IRÉNÉE: RHPR 69 (1989) 411-421; Eng. 509.

a482 **Williams** Michael A., The immovable race [ᴰ1977] 1985 ➤ 1,a181 ... 4,b430: ᴿRB 96 (1989) 621 (G.J. *Norton*: mature).

M1.2   *Valentinus* – *Pistis sophia,* Elchasai.

a483 *Edwards* M.J., Gnostics and Valentinians in the Church Fathers: JTS 40 (1989) 26-47.

a484 **Frickel** Josef, Hellenistische Erlösung in christlicher Deutung; die gnostische Naassenerschrift 1984 ➤ 65,8914 ... 4,b443: ᴿCrNSt 10 (1989) 619s (C. *Gianotto*); TLZ 114 (1989) 418-420 (K.-W. *Tröger*).

a485 *Irmscher* Johannes, Das Buch des Elchasai: ➤ 417, Apokryphen II⁵ 1989, 619-623.

a486 *Jackson* Howard M., The origin in ancient incantatory *voces magicae* of some names in the Sethian gnostic system: VigChr 43 (1989) 69-79.

a487 *Ménard* J.É., Termes et thèmes valentiniens de l'Exposé Valentinien (ExpVal) et des Fragments du Baptême et de l'Eucharistie du Codex XI de Nag Hammadi: ➤ 820, Journée copte 1984/6, 161-8.

a488 *Strecker* Georg, Der Kölner Mani Kodex, Elkesai und das Neue Testament: ➤ 174, ᶠSCHNEEMELCHER W., Oecumenica 1989, 123-134.

a489 *Thomassen* Einar, The Valentinianism of the Valentinian Exposition (NHC XI,2): Muséon 102 (1989) 225-236.

M1.3   **Corpus hermeticum; Orphismus.**

a490 *Borgia* Alessandra, Unità, unicità, totalità di Dio nell'ermetismo antico: SMSR 55 (1989) 197-211.

a491 **Büchli** Jörg, Der Poimandres, ein paganisiertes Evangelium [Diss. Z]: CorpHerm 1/WUNT 2/27, 1987 ➤ 3,a793 ... 4,b438: ᴿÉTRel 64 (1989) 641 (M. *Bouttier*); NRT 111 (1989) 444-6 (X. *Jacques*); Salmanticensis 36 (1989) 132-5 (R. *Trevijano*).

a492 *Casadio* Giovanni, Antropologia gnostica e antropologia orfica nella notizia di IPPOLITO sui Sethiani: ➤ 759, Sangue VI 1987/9, 1295-1350.

a493 **Fowden** Garth, The Egyptian Hermes; a historical approach to the late pagan mind 1986 ➤ 3,a797; 4,b439: ᴿAntClas 58 (1989) 407-9 (Michèle *Mertens*); BO 46 (1989) 335-340 (P. *Derchain*); RHR 206 (1989) 295-8 (Nicole *Genaille*); Salesianum 51 (1989) 535 (P. *Canaccini*).

a494 *Levi della Vida* Giorgio, 'La dottrina e i dodici legati di stomathalassa', uno scritto di ermetismo popolare in siriaco e in arabo [< Lincei Mem 8/3 (1950s) 477-542 + Ricerche Religiose 18 (1947) 350-362]: ➤ 297, Pitagora (1989) 125-190 (112-124).

a495 *Mahé* J.-P., *Palingenesía* et structure du monde supérieur dans les Hermetica et le traité d'Eugnoste de Nag Hammadi: ➤ 820, Journées coptes 1984/6, 137-149.

a496 *Mahé* Jean-Pierre,   Paraphrase de Sem et corpus hermétique: ➤ 820, Journées coptes III, 1986/9, 124-7.

a497 **Moreschini** Claudio,   Dall'*Asclepius* al Crater Hermetis; studi sull'ermetismo latino tardo-antico e rinascimentale [studi articolati]. Pisa 1985, Giardini. – ᴿFilT 3 (1989) 230-2 (C. *Licata*).

a498 *Motte* Laurent,   Orphica aegyptiaca I: LOrA 2 (1989) 253-272.

a499 *Quispel* Gilles,   Hermes Trismegistus and TERTULLIAN: VigChr 43 (1989) 188-190.

a500 *Tröger* Karl-W.,   Hermetica ➤ 911, TRE 18 (1989) 749-752 (Nachtrag).

M1.5   **Mani**, *dualismus;* **Mandaei.**

a501 *Bianchi* Ugo,   Il male nel dualismo gnostico: ParSpV 19 (1989) 199-208.

a502 *Böhlig* Alexander,   Neue Initiative zur Erschliessung der koptisch-manichäischen Bibliothek von Medinet Madi: ZNW 80 (1989) 240-262.

a503 *Böhlig* Alexander, *a)* Das Neue Testament und die Idee des manichäischen Mythos [< ᶠ*Wilson* R. 1983, 90-104]; – *b)* Jakob als Engel in Gnostizismus und Manichäismus [< ᴱ*Wiessner* G., Erkenntnisse 1978, 1-14]; – *c)* Das Problem aramäischer Elemente in den Texten von Nag Hammadi: ➤ 236, Gnosis und Synkretismus 1989, 586-612 / 164-180 / 414-453.

a504 *Buckley* Jorunn J.,   Why once is not enough; Mandean baptism (*maṣbuta*) as an example of a repeated ritual: HistRel 29 (1989s) 23-34.

a505 **Culiano** Ioan P.,   I miti dei dualismi occidentali; dai sistemi gnostici al mondo moderno [Les gnoses dualistes 1987], ᵀ*Cosi* Dario, *Saibene* Luigi: Di fronte e attraverso 227. Mi 1989, Jaca. 326 p. 88-16-40227-X.

a506 *Decret* F.,   Aspects de l'Église manichéenne; remarque sur le Manuscrit de Tébessa: ➤ 132, ᶠMAYER D., Signum pietatis 1989, 123-151.

a507 **Doresse** J. *al.*,   Gnosticismo e manicheismo [1970-6; II. 364-645], ᵀ*Novella Pierini* Maria: Universale 223. R 1988, Laterza. vii-313 p. 88-420-3225-5.

a508 **Fontaine** P. F. M.,   The light and the dark [I, 1986 ➤ 4,b448] II, 1987; III. 1988. Amst, Gieben; *f*70+65: ᴿClasR 103 = 39 (1989) 268s (R. W. *Jordan*); Salesianum 51 (1989) 594s (E. *Fontana*).

a509 *Franzmann* Majella,   Living water, mediating element in Mandaean myth and ritual: Numen 36 (1989) 156-172.

a510 **Giversen** Søren,   [➤ 9468] The Manichaean Coptic papyri, I. Kephalaia; 2. Homilies...: 1986 ➤ 2,7643: ᴿBSOAS 51 (1988) 569s (W. *Sundermann*).

a511 *a) Greenfield* Jonas C.,   On Mandaic poetic technique; – *b) Segert* Stanislav, Parallelism in the *Qolasta*: ➤ 126, ᶠMACUCH C., Ḥokmôt 1989, 101-8 / 283-301.

a511* **Klimkeit** Hans-Joachim,   Hymnen und Gebete der Religion des Lichts; iranische und türkische liturgische Texte der Manichäer Zentralasiens; eingeleitet und aus dem Mittelpersischen, Parthischen, Sogdischen und Uigurischen (Alttürkischen) übersetzt: Abh Rh/Wf Akad 79.   Opladen 1989, Westdeutscher-V.   280 p.   3-531-05096-6.

a512 **Koenen** L., *Römer* C.,   Der Kölner Mani-Codex 1985 ➤ 1,a204... 4,b450: ᴿOrChrPer 55 (1989) 237s (J. D. *Baggarly*).

a513 ᵀᴱ**Koenen** Ludwig, *Römer* Cornelia,   Der Kölner Mani-Kodex, Über das Werden seines Leibes: PapyrolCol 14. Opladen 1988, Westdeutscher-V. (Rh/Wf Akad).   xxxii-119 p.; 2 pl.   3-531-09924-8. – ᴿTLZ 114 (1989) 820-2 (H. M. *Schenke*).

a514 **Macuch** Rudolf, (*Boekels* Klaus), Neumandäische Chrestomathie, mit grammatischer Skizze, kommentierter Übersetzung und Glossar: Porta Linguarum Orientalium NS 18. Wsb 1989, Harrassowitz. xxii-263 p. 3-447-02859-9.

a515 **Ménard** Jacques, De la Gnose au Manichéisme 1986 ➤ 2,8596; 3,a818: ᴿBO 46 (1989) 515s (K.-H. *Uthemann*); EWest 38 (1988) 332s (G. *Gnoli*); Salmanticensis 36 (1989) 127-9 (R. *Trevijano*).

a516 **Merkelbach** Reinhold, Mani und sein Religionssystem 1986 ➤ 3,a819: ᴿBO 46 (1989) 512-5 (K.-H. *Uthemann*).

a517 *a*) *Patschkovsky* Alexander, Katharer: ➤ 894, EvKL 2 (1989) 988-990; – *b*) *Müller* Daniela, Katharer: ➤ 911, TRE 18 (1989) 21-30; map.

a518 *Philonenko* Marc, La philosophie de PLOTIN et la gnose mandéenne: CRAI (1989) 18-27.

a519 *Ries* Julien, La formation de la pensée manichéenne — de l'elchaïsme à la gnose: ➤ 696, 10th Patristic, 19 (1989) 328-334.

a520 **Runciman** Steven, Häresie und Christentum; der mittelalterliche Manichäismus [1947], ᵀ*Jatho* H. Mü 1988, Fink. 255 p. DM 48. – ᴿTLZ 114 (1989) 125s (G. *Haendler*).

a521 *Scott* David, Manichaean responses to Zoroastrianism: RelSt 25 (C 1989) 435-457.

a522 *Sunaga* Umeo, ❿ The thought of Mani and genealogy of apocalyptic literature: Orient-Japan 31,2 (1988) 140-152.

a523 **Tardieu** Michel, *a*) Études manichéennes, bibliographie critique 1977-1986 [< Abstracta Iranica I-Xʳᵉᵛ]: Hors Série 4. Lv 1988, Peeters. 159 p. 0240-8910. – *b*) La diffusion du Bouddhisme dans l'empire Kouchan, l'Iran et la Chine, d'après un kephalaion manichéen inédit: StIran 17 (1988) 153-182; pl. I.

М2.1 Nag' Ḥammadi, *generalia*.

a524 **Dart** John, The Jesus of heresy and history... Nag Hammadi (= 1976 revised) 1988 ➤ 4,4305: ᴿBibTB 19 (1989) 154s (C. R. *Matthews*).

a525 ᴱ**Hedrick** C. W., *Hodgson* R., Nag Hammadi Gnosticism and early Christianity 1986 ➤ 2,374... 4,b462: ᴿAndrUnS 27 (1989) 144-6 (A. *Terian*).

a526 *Malachi* Zvi, Jewish parallels to visions and revelations in the Nag Hammadi texts: ➤ 748, Sogni = AugR 29 (1989) 147-155.

a527 *Myszor* Wincenty, ANTONIUS-Briefe und Nag-Hammadi-Texte: JbAC 32 (1989) 72-88.

a528 **Siegert** Folker, Nag-Hammadi-Register [koptisch, deutsch]: WUNT 26, 1982 ➤ 64,9184; 65,8954: ᴿTLZ 114 (1989) 193-5 (H.-M. *Schenke*).

a529 **Tuckett** Christopher, Nag Hammadi and the Gospel tradition 1986 ➤ 3,4205... 4,b465: ᴿScotJT 42 (1989) 573s (R. *Hart*).

М2.2 *Evangelium etc. Thomae* – **The Gospel** (etc.) **of Thomas.**

a530 **Alcalá** Manuel, El evangelio copto de Tomás; palabras ocultas de Jesús: BiblEstB 67. Salamanca 1989, Sígueme. 113 p. [LumenVr 38,351]. – ᴿCiTom 116 (1989) 624 (M. *García Cordero*).

a530* **Baarda** T., Early transmission of the words of Jesus; Thomas... 14 art. ᴱ*Helderman* J., *Noorda* S. 1983 ➤ 64,134*...: ᴿRSO 63 (1989) 339-344 (R. *Contini*).

a531 **Doresse** J., L'Évangile selon Thomas, 'les paroles secrètes de Jésus'[2rev] [[1]1957 + new 30 p. introd. ...] Monaco 1988, Rocher. xxix-221 p. F 125 pa. 2-268-00622-0 [NTAbs 33,129].

a531* **Fieger** Michael, Das Thomasevangelium; Einleitung, Kommentar und Systematik: kath. Diss. [D]*Gnilka* J. München 1989. – TR 85 (1989) 517; RTLv 21,545 (> Münster, Aschendorff).

a532 **Henderson** I. H., 'Sententiae Jesu'; gnomic sayings in the tradition of Jesus: diss. Oxford 1989. – RTLv 21,545.

a533 **Jackson** H. M., The lion becomes man [Thomas logion 7] 1985 ➤ 1,a162 ... b,470: [R]RB 96 (1989) 620s (G. J. *Norton*: undisciplined).

a534 **Kuntzman** Raymond, *Dubois* Jean-Daniel, Nag Hammadi, Evangelio según Tomás; textos gnósticos de los orígenes del cristianismo: Documentos en torno a la Biblia 16, 1988 ➤ 4,b471. 84-7151-585-7: [R]ActuBbg 26 (1989) 44 (R. de *Sivatte*); EfMex 7 (1989) 154-6 (E. *Serraima*).

a535 **Lelyveld** Margaretha, Les logia de la vie dans EvT: NHS 34, 1987 ➤ 3,a842; 4,b472: [R]RevSR 62 (1989) 10-13 (J. E. *Ménard*: Lelyveld p. 13, Lellyveld p. 10); Salmanticensis 36 (1989) 114-6 (R. *Trevijano*); RelStR 15 (1989) 162 (B. A. *Pearson*).

a536 **Lipinski** Matthias, Konkordanz zu den Thomasakten [chosen for computer-sample because BONNET index is inadequate and other small apocrypha already have concordances]: BoBB 67. Fra 1988, Athenäum. xiii-605 p. DM 128. – [R]VigChr 43 (1989) 196s (A. F. J. *Klijn*).

a537 [T][McGregor] **Ross** Hugh M. The Gospel of Thomas 1987 ➤ 4,b47: [R]Gerión 6 (1986) 300s (G. *Fernández*).

a538 **McNarie** Alan D., [Yeshua], the Gospel of St. Thomas [not about the Gospel of Thomas but a novel]; an exploration of role playing and the creative process: diss. Missouri, [D]*Morgan* S. Columbia 1988. 460 p. 88-26596. – DissA 49 (1988s) 2644-A.

a539 *Sevrin* Jean-Marie, Un groupement de trois paraboles contre les richesses dans l'Évangile selon Thomas 63; 64; 65: ➤ 576, Paraboles 1987/9, 425-439.

a539* *Trevijano* Ramón, La madre de Jesús en el Evangelio de Tomás (Logg. 55, 99, 101 y 105): ➤ 69*, [F]GOMÀ I., RCatalT 14 (1989) 257-266 castellano; Eng. 266.

a540 **Winterhalter** R., The fifth Gospel; a verse-by-verse New Age commentary on the Gospel of Thomas. SF 1988, Harper & R. 122 p. $9. 0-06-250972-1 [NTAbs 33,137].

---

a541 **Kuntzmann** R., Le livre de Thomas (NH II,7) 1986 ➤ 2,8614 ... 4,b480: [R]RechSR 77 (1989) 288s (Madeleine *Scopello*); RHR 206 (1989) 433s (P. *Nautin*).

a452 [TE]**Schenke** Hans-Martin, Das Thomas-Buch (Nag-Hammadi-Codex II,7): TU 138. B 1989, Akademie. xvi-221 p.

M2.3 *Singula scripta* – Nag' Hammadi, various titles.

a543 *Agouridis* Savas, [G] The Gospel of Philip, introduction and Greek translation: DeltioVM 17,2 (1988) 44-67.

a544 **Attridge** Harold W., Nag Hammadi Codex I ['Jung', including Ev. Ver.] 1985 ➤ 1,a238; 3,a849: [R]OLZ 84 (1989) 532-8 (H.-M. *Schenke*).

a544* *García Bazán* Francisco, El Evangelio de la Verdad; traducción, introducción y notas: RBíbArg 51,36 (1989) 193-248.

a545 **Bethge** Hans-Gebhard, 'Der Brief des Petrus an Philippus', ein neutestamentliches Apokryphon aus dem Funde von Nag Hammadi (NHC VIII,2): Diss. Berlin 1985, 205 p. – TLZ 114 (1989) 396-8.

a546 **Cameron** Ron, Sayings traditions in the Apocryphon of James: HarvTSt 34, 1984 ➤ 65,8970 ... 3,a854: ᴿSecC 7 (1989s) 115-7 (Anne *McGuire*).

a547 **Cherix** Pierre, Le concept/Puissance (CG VI,4): OBO 47, 1982 ➤ 63,9045 ... 4,b496: ᴿTLZ 114 (1989) 523s (H.-M. *Schenke*).

a548 *Davies* Stevan, Gnostic idealism and the Gospel of Truth: ➤ 592, Systemic 1 (1989) 83-94.

a549 *Dubois* J.-D., Contribution à l'interprétation de la Paraphrase de Sem: ➤ 820, Journée copte 1984/6, 150-160.

a550 *a) Funk* Wolf-Peter, Koptisch-gnostische Apokalypse des Paulus; – *b) Werner* Andreas, ... des Petrus: ➤ 417, NT Apokryphen II⁵ 1989, 628-633 / 633-643.

a551 *García Bazán* Francisco, El 'Nombre' según la enseñanza del Tractatus Tripartitus (Códice de Nag-Hammadi 1,5) y su contexto gnóstico y hebreocristiano: RBíbArg 30s (1988) 233-261.

a552 **Gilhus** Ingvild S., The nature of the archons... (CG II,4) 1985 ➤ 1,a242; 3,a862: ᴿSalmanticensis 36 (1989) 116-9 (R. *Trevijano*).

a553 ᵀᴱ**Kirchner** Dankwart, Epistula Jacobi apocrypha; die zweite Schrift aus Nag-Hammadi-Codex I: TU 136. B 1989, Akademie. xvi-163 p.

a554 **Moraldi** Luigi, Le apocalissi gnostiche [5 from 52 NH tractates] 1987 ➤ 3,a762; 4,b416: ᴿBL (1989) 138 (T. *Rajak*); Salesianum 51 (1989) 347 (C. *Semeraro*).

a555 **Morard** Françoise, L'apocalypse d'Adam (NH V,5): BCNH-T 15, 1985 ➤ 1,a249 ... 4,b495: ᴿBO 46 (1989) 96-98 (A. I. *Elanskaya*).

a556 *Motte* Laurent, *a)* L'hiéroglyphe, d'Esna à l'Évangile de Vérité; – *b)* [Hermès Trismégiste dans NH Codex VI] La vache multicolore et les trois pierres de la régénération: ➤ 820, Journées Coptes II, 1984/6, 111-6 / 130-149.

a557 **Rouleau** D., L'Épître apocryphe de Jacques (NH I,2) [avec *Roy* L., Acte de Pierre] 1987 ➤ 3,a855; 4,b486: ᴿJTS 40 (1989) 606-611 (M. *Smith*); RechSR 77 (1989) 292-6 (Madeleine *Scopello*); RHPR 69 (1989) 341 (D. A. *Bertrand*). ➤ a562.

a558 *Scopello* M., Jacques de SAROUG et l'Exégèse de l'Âme: ➤ 820, Journée copte 1984.6, 130-6.

a559 **Sevrin** Jean-Marie, Le dossier baptismal séthien 1985 ➤ 1,a256 ... 4,b501: ᴿQLtg 69 (1988) 108 (L. *Leijssen*); RechSR 77 (1989) 300s (Madeleine *Scopello*).

a560 ᴱ**Thomassen** Einar, ᵀ*Painchaud* Louis, Le traité tripartite (NH 1,5): BCNH-T 19. Québec 1989, Univ. Laval. xviii-535 p. 2-7637-7143-2: ᴿBZ 33 (1989) 263-5 (R. *Schnackenburg*); RSPT 73 (1989) 463s (G.-M. de *Durand*).

a561 *Trautmann* C., Le schème de la croix dans l'Évangile selon Philippe: ➤ 820, Journée copte 1984/6, 123-9.

a562 **Veilleux** Armand, 1-2 Apocalypse de Jacques (NH V.3s) 1986 ➤ 3,a856; 4,b487: ᴿBZ 33 (1989) 139-141 (R. *Schnackenburg*, auch über ROULEAU D.-ROY L.); JTS 40 (1989) 604-6 (M. *Smith*); OrChrPer 55 (1989) 499-500 (V. *Poggi*); RB 96 (1989) 622s (J. J. *Taylor*, also on cognate volumes); RechSR 77 (1989) 289-292 (Madeleine *Scopello*); RHPR 69 (1989) 339s (D. A. *Bertrand*); TLZ 114 (1989) 815-7 (H.-M. *Schenke*); TR 85 (1989) 105s (H.-J. *Klauck*, also on ROULEAU/ROY).

a563 **Williams** Jacqueline A.,   Biblical interpretation in the Gnostic Gospel of Truth from Nag Hammadi: SBL diss. 79 [Yale 1983, ᴰ*Layton* B.] 1988 ➤ 4,b494: ᴿBL (1989) 147 (P.W. *Coxon*); RB 96 (1989) 623s (J.J. *Taylor*).

M3   **Religiones comparatae** – *Historia religionum*.

a564 *a*) *Abe* Masao, 'There is no common denominator for world religions'; the positive meaning of this negative statement; – *b*) *Grenz* Stanley J., Commitment and dialogue; PANNENBERG on Christianity and the religions: JEcuSt 26 (1989) 72-81 / 196-210.

a565 **Aldanow** Boris,   The human predicament; I. The secular ideologies [... international politics]; II. Theory of religion.   New Delhi 1988, Ashish/Vikas. 618 p.; 550 p. [TPhil 64, 318, 632].

a566 *Allen* Douglas, ELIADE and history: JRel 68 (1988) 545-565.

a567 *Antes* Peter,   Religionswissenschaftliche Neuerscheinungen: TRu 54 (1989) 54-68.

a568 *Aquino* Marcelo F. de,   O conceito de religião em HEGEL.   São Paulo 1989, Loyola. 368 p. [RTLv 21,479].

a569 **Ariarajah** S. Wesley,   The Bible and people of other faiths 1985 ➤ 1,a264 ... 4,b506:   ᴿRelStR 15 (1989) 197-204 (F.X. *Clooney*, also on 13 cognate works).

a570 **Arkush** Allan M.,   The philosophical account of religion and Judaism in the thought of Moses MENDELSSOHN: diss. Brandeis. Boston 1988. 316 p. 88-19742. – DissA 49 (1988s) 3059-A.

a571 **Balthasar** H. U. v.,   Il cristianesimo e le religioni universali; uno sguardo d'insieme [1979], ᵀ*Coppellotti* F., *Graziotto* R. CasM 1988, Piemme. 31 p. – ᴿHumBr 44 (1989) 901 (A. *Moda*).

a572 **Bataille** Georges [1897-1962], Theory of religion [1976], ᵀ*Hurley* Robert. NY 1989, Zone [CM, MIT]. 126 p. $18 [TDig 36,351].

a573 **Becker** Gerhold,   Die Ursymbole in den Religionen 1987 ➤ 3,a874; 4,b508:   ᴿActuBbg 26 (1989) 104s (J. *Boada*); Mundus 25 (1987) 94 (H. *Biedermann*); ZMissRW 73 (1989) 151s (M. *Baumann*).

a574 **Berger** P. L.,   L'imperativo eretico; possibilità contemporanee di affermazione religiosa [1980 ➤ 62,9880],ᵀ; intr. *de Nicola* G.: La ricerca religiosa. T-Leumann 1987, ElleDiCi. 182 p. – ᴿAntonianum 64 (1989) 204s (T. *Larrañaga*); Claretianum 29 (1989) 404s (S. M. *González Silva*).

a575 **Bernand** Carmen, *Gruzinski* Serge, De l'idolâtrie; une archéologie des sciences religieuses.   P 1988, Seuil. 260 p. F 150. 2-02-010255-2. – ᴿÉTRel 64 (1989) 601 (Jacky *Argaud*).

a576 **Bernhardt** Reinhold,   Der Absolutheitsanspruch des Christentums; Modelle theologischer Verhältnisbestimmung zwischen dem Christentum und den nicht-christlichen Religionen: Diss. ᴰ*Ritschl* D. Heidelberg 1988s. – RTLv 21,585.

a577 *Beyerhaus* Peter,   Theologisches Verstehen nichtchristlicher Religionen: KerDo 35 (1989) 106-126; Eng. 127.

a578 *a*) *Bonsor* Jack A.,   Irreducible pluralism; the transcendental and hermeneutical as theological options; – *b*) *Fiorenza* Francis S., Theology; transcendental or hermeneutical; – *c*) *Lawrence* Fred L., On the relation ...; – *d*) Joy Morna, ... feminist/pluralistic: Horizons 16 (1989) 316-328 / 329-341 / 342-5 / 346-352.

a579 **Bowker** John,   Licensed insanities; religions ... 1987 ➤ 3,a879; 4,b511; ᴿScotJT 42 (1989) 559-561 (B. *Russell*).

a580 **Brelich** A., *Meslin* M., Religione e storia delle religioni: Universale 227. R 1988, Laterza. vii-117 p. 88-420-3294-8.

a581 **Brown** L. B., The psychology of religious belief 1987 → 4,b512; £30: ᴿRelSt 25 (1989) 543s (Kate *Loewenthal*).

a582 *Brück* M. von, Religious pluralism and our understanding of God, with special reference to LUTHER's theology: IndTSt 26 (1989) 35-47.

a583 **Byrnes** Joseph F., The psychology of religion 1985 → 1,a278 ('1984'): ᴿJRel 68 (1988) 164s (H. N. *Malony*).

a584 *Cantone* Carlo, Per una filosofia della vita spirituale; alle radici metafisiche dell'esperienza religiosa: Salesianum 51 (1989) 515-522.

a584* **Carrier** Hervé, Psico-sociologia dell'appartenenza religiosa,² ᵀ*Battaglia* G. T-Leumann 1988, ElleDiCi. 286 p. Lit. 19.000. – ᴿLetture 44 (1989) 377s (Daniela *Patrignani*).

a585 *Chagnon* Roland (1939-1989), Religion, sécularisation et déplacements du sacré [< ᴱ*Desrosiers* Yvon, Religion et culture au Québec (Montréal 1986, Fides) 21-51]: SR 18 (1989) 127-151.

a586 **Christian** William A., Doctrines of religious communities [i. e. religions]; a philosophical study. NHv 1987, Yale Univ. 234 p. £25. – ᴿInterpretation 43 (1989) 98.100 (D. G. *Dawe*); JAAR 57 (1989) 857-9 (D. A. *Crosby*).

a587 **Clark** Stephen R. L., The mysteries of religion: Philosophical Introductions, 1986 → 4,b515: ᴿModT 6 (1989s) 114s (P. *Sherry*); ScotJT 42 (1989) 561-3 (A. *Millar*).

a588 *Clooney* Francis X., Christianity and world religions; religion, reason, and pluralism: RelStR 15 (1989) 197-204 on 14 books.

a589 ᴱ**Colin** P., *Mongin* O., Un monde désenchanté? Débat avec M. GAUCHET: Thèses. P 1988, Cerf [RThom 89,461].

a590 **Coward** Harold, Sacred word and sacred text; Scripture in world religions 1988 → 4,b517: ᴿBibleBh 15 (1989) 277s (V. O. *Kathanar*); ExpTim 100 (1988s) 278 (Ursula *King*); SR 18 (1989) 89s (S. A. *Nigosian*); ZMissRW 73 (1989) 153s (H. *Waldenfels*).

a591 *a*) *Cowdell* Scott, Hans KÜNG and world religions; the emergence of a pluralist; – *b*) *Simpson* R. T., The new dialogue between Christianity and other religions: TLond 92 (1989) 85-92 / 92-102.

a592 **Cragg** Kenneth, The Christ and the faiths 1987 → 2,8665... 4,b519: ᴿHorizons 16 (1989) 413s (J. *Renard*); ScotJT 42 (1989) 445-7 (D. A. *Scott*).

a593 *Dakouras* Dionysios G., ᴳ The language of symbols in religion [esp. Buddhism]: TAth 60 (1989) 117-156.

a594 *Dawson* Lorne, OTTO and FREUD on the uncanny and beyond: JAAR 57 (1989) 283-311.

a595 **D'Costa** Gavin, John HICK's theology of religions, a critical evaluation. Lanham MD 1987, UPA. 252 p. £28; pa. $15. 0-8191-6617-0; 8-9. – ᴿIntRMiss 78 (1989) 463-5 (J. P. *Rajashekar*); JEcuSt 26 (1989) 218 (H. *Obayashi*). → 7703.

a596 **D'Costa** Gavin, Theology and religious pluralism; the challenge of other religions 1986 → 2,8667... 4,b521: ᴿGregorianum 70 (1989) 179-182 (J. *Dupuis*: based on J. P. SCHINELLER TS 1976); NZMissW 44 (1988) 62 (F. *Frei*).

a597 **Dean** William, [Chicago Univ. ...] American religious empiricism 1986 → 3,a895; 4,b522: ᴿZygon 24 (1989) 382-5 (M. C. *Shaw*).

a598 *Debarge* Louis, Le syncrétisme religieux; druidisme et christianisme: MélSR 46 (1989) 5-21; Eng. 21.

a599 *de Menezes* Rui, The Bible in relation to other religions: BibleBh 15 (1989) 222-253.

a600 **De Rosa** Giuseppe, Cristianesimo, religioni e sètte non cristiane a confronto. R 1988, Città Nuova. 298 p. Lit. 22.000. – ᴿCC 140 (1989,2) 301s (F. *Castelli*).

a601 **Díaz Murugarren** José, La religión y los 'Maestros de la Sospecha': Paradosis 5. Salamanca 1989, S. Esteban. 211 p. – ᴿCiTom 116 (1989) 413s (L. *Lago*).

a602 *Dörmann* Johannes, La verdad una y las muchas religiones III/IV/V/VI: Tierra Nueva 16/60 (1987s) 20-34 / 16/62, 68-78 / 16/63, 61-72 / 17/65 (1988s) 41-52.

a603 *Dourley* John P., The challenge of Jung's psychology for the study of religion: SR 18 (1989) 297-311.

a604 **Ejizu** Christopher, Nigeria's three religions; patterns and prospects of their interaction: AfTJ 17 (Tanzania 1988) 179-195 [< TContext 7/1, 17].

a605 **Eliade** Mircea, Erinnerungen 1907-1937. Fra 1987, Insel. 439 p. DM 86. – ᴿTPQ 137 (1989) 99 (J. *Janda*).

a606 **Ellwood** Robert, The history and future of faith; religion past, present, and to come 1988 → 4,b527: ᴿRelStR 15 (1989) 237 (F. X. *Clooney*).

a607 *Fédou* Michel, Théologie des religions et pluralisme: Études 370 (1989) 821-831.

a608 **Fenn** Richard, The dream of the perfect act; an inquiry into the fate of religion in a secular world 1987 → 4,b529: ᴿJRel 69 (1989) 125s (H. H. *Penner*).

a609 ᵀᴱ**Ferrara** Riccardo, G. W. F. Hegel, Lecciones sobre Filosofía de la religión 1-3. M 1984-7. viii-379 p.; x-642 p.; xl-360 p. – ᴿRTLv 20 (1989) 378s (E. *Brito*: magistral; la seule oeuvre de Hegel pas encore traduite en espagnol).

a610 **Finegan** Jack, Myth and mystery; an introduction to the pagan religions of the biblical world. GR 1989, Baker. 335 p. $25 [TrinJ 10,241].

a611 *Flasche* Rainer, Einige Bemerkungen zum Umgang mit den sogenannten 'Jugendreligionen': ZRGg 40 (1988) 44-83.

a612 *Fonner* Michael G., Christology, the central issue in Christian theologies of religions: AsiaJT 2,2 (Singapore 1988) 327-341 [G. *Evers* (Eng.) summary in TContext 6/2, 104].

a613 *Forward* Martin H. F., Through another's eyes; a Christian vision of God in a world of religions: ExpTim 100,6 (1988s) 208-212.

a614 *Gächter* Othmar, *Quack* Anton, Symbole, Magie und Religion: Anthropos 84 (1989) 521-9 [> Eng. TDig 37,109-114, ᵀᴱ*Asen* B.].

a615 **Gaskin** J. C. A., [David] Hume's philosophy of religion. L 1988, Macmillan. 250 p. 0-333-42329-1; pa. 39346-5. – ᴿExpTim 100 (1988s) 115 (W. D. *Hudson*).

a616 **Gauchet** Marcel, Le désenchantement du monde; une histoire politique de la religion: Bibliothèque des sciences humaines 1985 → 1,a298: ᴿNRT 111 (1989) 361-388 (Y. *Labbé*: 'la religion socialement finie?'); RThom 89 (1989) 461-7 [Y. *Floucat*, citant récensions Autrement 75 (1985) 12-17. 191-4; Esprit (1986,4s) 95-101. 201-212 (451-474, 'La philosophie et ses sources religieuses')].

a617 **Geisler** Norman L. [1974], ²*Corduan* Winfried, Philosophy of religion 1988 → 4,b537; 0-8010-3821-9: ᴿBS 146 (1989) 226 (J. A. *Witmer*); ExpTim 100 (1988s) 276 (P. *Vardy*).

a618 *Gensichen* Hans-Werner, Erwartungen der Religionen an das Christentum: ZMissRW 73 (1989) 195-209.

a618* *Gil i Ribas* Joseph, Teologia de la religió II-III: RCatalT [12 (1987) 337-411] 13 (1988) 59-114. 315-363; Eng. 114. 364.

a619 *Görg* Manfred, Religionsgeschichtliches Vergleichen: MüTZ 40 (1989) 63-69.

a620 **Goodman** Felicitas D., Ecstasy, ritual, and alternative reality; religion in a pluralistic world. Bloomington 1988, Indiana Univ. xii-193 p. $35. 0-253-31899-8 [TDig 37,55]. – ᴿRelStR 15 (1989) 339 (R. *Ellwood*).

a621 *Goudoever* Jan van, La religion d'Isaac NEWTON [l' 'unitarisme' peut signifier aussi l'unité profonde des religions]: ÉTRel 64 (1989) 13-22.

a622 **Goulet** Jacques, Construire une science de la religion. Montréal 1984, Fides. 329 p. – ᴿSR 18 (1989) 377s (J. *Pierre*).

a623 **Graham** William A., Beyond the written word; oral aspects of Scripture in the history of religion 1987 → 3,a912; 4,b539; £25: ᴿAmerica 160 (1989) 203-5 (W. J. *Ong*); BL (1989) 16s (R. P. *Carroll*); ExpTim 100 (1988s) 107 (G. H. *Bebawi*).

a624 *a)* *Grant* Colin, The threat and prospect in religious pluralism; – *b)* *Hoedemaker* Bert, [Hendrik] KRAEMER reassessed: EcuR 41 (1989) 50-63 / 41-49.

a625 **Grant** R.-M., Gods and the one God 1986 → 2,8683... 4,b340: ᴿJRel 68 (1988) 286s (R. I. *Pervo*); Latomus 48 (1989) 705-7 (R. *Braun*).

a626 **Greschat** Hans-Jürgen, Was ist Religionswissenschaft?: Urban-Tb 390, 1988 → 4,b542: ᴿTPQ 137 (1989) 305 (J. *Janda*); ZRGg 41 (1989) 282 (M. *Baumann*).

a627 **Guareschi** P., Perspectivas psicosociais para a análise do fenómeno religioso: Teocomunicação 18 (1988) 439-454 [< Stromata 45, 489].

a628 **Guerra** Manuel, Storia delle religioni. Brescia 1989, Scuola. 576 p. Lit. 38.000. – ᴿHumBr 44 (1989) 728s (A. *Nassini*).

a629 **Guilhou** Nadine, La vieillesse des dieux [traduction d'ornementation de tombes]. Montpellier 1989, Univ. 2-905-4397-403.

a630 *Hallencreutz* Carl F., Den mångdimensionella religionsteologien: Sv-TKv 65 (1989) 109-116.

a631 **Hick** John, An interpretation of religion; human responses to the transcendent (Gifford Lectures 1986s). NHv 1989, Yale Univ. 412 p. $35. – ᴿExpTim 101,2 top choice (1989s) 33-35 (C. S. *Rodd*: magnificent; too optimistic); SWJT 32,3 (1989s) 48s (Y. *Woodfin*); TTod 46 (1989s) 461s (G. *Green*).

a632 **Hick** John, **Knitter** Paul F., The myth of Christian uniqueness 1988 → 4,b546: ᴿEcuR 41 (1989) 468s (L. *Newbigin*) & 470s (A. van der *Bent*); HeythJ 30 (1989) 325-7 (M. *Barnes*); Horizons 16 (1989) 176 (J. *Carmody*); ModT 6 (1989s) 217-9 (G. *Loughlin*); TLond 92 (1989) 444-6 (also G. *Loughlin*).

a633 *Hick* John, Straightening the record; some response to critics [*D'Costa* G. 1987, *Gillis* C. 1989; not *Mathis* T. 1985 'muddled']: ModT 6 (1989s) 187-195.

a634 *Hierzenberger* Gottfried, 'Neues Bewusstsein' [...'New Age'; 5 Bücher] und christliche Tradition: TPQ 137 (1989) 271-6.

a635 *Hodgson* Peter C., Logic, history, and alternative paradigms in HEGEL's interpretation of the religions: JRel 68 (Ch 1988) 1-20.

a636 **Horváth** Árpád, Sozialismus und Religion; die Religion und ihre Funktion im Spiegel sozialistischer Ideologien I. 1835-1909. Bern 1987, Lang. 505 p. – ᴿTPhil 64 (1989) 477s (J. *Oswald*); TR 85 (1989) 320s (F. *Furger*).

a637 **Hubbeling** H.G., Principles of the philosophy of religion: PhRel 25. Assum 1987, van Gorcum. x-285 p. f57.50. – RBijdragen 50 (1989) 347 (B. *Vedder*).

a638 **Jaeschke** Walter, Die Vernunft in der Religion ... HEGELS 1986 ➤ 3,a925; 4,b547: RTR 85 (1989) 145-8 (H. *Verweyen*).

a639 *a) Jellici* Silvana, L'opera di Wilhelm SCHMIDT negli scritti di Mircea ELIADE: – *b) Renzetti* Emanuela, W. Schmidt e Franz BOAS; opinioni a confronto sul metodo della scienza della cultura: ➤ 804, Schmidt 1986/9, 213-7 / 191-202.

a640 **Jenkins** Vicki L., Paradox and the ways of religion: diss. ND 1989. 315 p. 90-11418. – DissA 50 (1989s) 3980-A.

a641 *Johannesson* Rudolf, Individualistisk och holistisk religionsuppfattning: SvTKv 65 (1989) 58-63.

a642 **Kehrer** Günther, Einführung in die Religionssoziologie. Da 1988, Wiss. 192 p. – RZMissRW 73 (1989) 315s (F. *Usarski*).

a643 **Kelly** James J., Baron F. von HÜGEL's philosophy of religion: Bibl-ETL 62, 1983 ➤ 64, e460; ... 1,f966: RRTLv 20 (1989) 108s (Brigitte *Waché*).

a644 **Kilcullen** John, Sincerity and truth; essays on ARNAULD [Antoine, against Jesuit 'philosophic sin'], BAYLE and Toleration. Ox 1988, Clarendon. 228 p. £25. 0-19-826691-X. – RÉTRel 64 (1989) 307s (H. *Bost*: complexité aplatie).

a645 **Kitagawa** Joseph M., The history of religions 1987 ➤ 1,369; 3,a29: RJRel 69 (1989) 451s (R. J. Z. *Werblowsky*).

a646 **Klinkhammer** K. E., Was mich auf Jesus von Nazareth verweist; 'Religion' Buddha/Mohammed/Zarathustra/Jesus [/die Synagoge]. Aachen 1987, Einhard. 281 p. DM 32 pa. [TR 86, 63s, L. *Hagemann*].

a647 **Knitter** Paul F., No other name 1985 ➤ 1,a319 ... 3,a931: RRelStT 7,1 (1987) 80s (R. *Neufeldt*).

a648 **Knitter** Paul F., Ein Gott – viele Religionen [< (first Cath.) DMarburg 1974] 1988 ➤ 4,b411: RKIsr (1989,2) 183-5 (Julie *Kirchberg*); TüTQ 169 (1989) 76s (P. *Hünermann*).

a649 *Knitter* Paul F., Making sense of the many (review of 8 books): RelStR 15 (1989) 204-7; 202s [review of Knitter (-Hick) by F. *Clooney*].

a650 *Koch* Günter, Neue Religiosität ausserhalb der Kirche; Bedrohung oder Chance für den Glauben?: TGegw 31 (1988) 67-75.

a651 EKüng H., *Moltmann* J., Christianity among world religions 1986 ➤ 3,a936 ('Christianity and the ... 1987'): RJEcuSt 26 (1989) 220 (N. *Smart*).

a652 **Küng** Hans, *Jens* Walter, Poesia e religione [Dichtung und Religion 1985 ➤ 3,1550] TGaraventa Roberto. Genova 1989, Marietti. 296 p. Lit. 35.000. – RLetture 44 (1989) 783s (A. *Carrara*).

a653 **Lähnemann** Johannes, Weltreligionen im Unterricht I. Fernöstl. II. Islam: 1986 ➤ 2,8713: RZRGg 40 (1988) 263-7 (H. *Grothaus*).

a654 *Lähnemann* Johannes, Begegnungen mit den Weltreligionen im Unterricht: VerkFor 32 (1987) 21-43.

a655 *Lau* Stephen, Paul TILLICH and the Frankfurt School's critical theory of religion; a dialogue: LvSt 14 (1989) 3-15.

a656 *Laurenzi* Maria Cristina, Il Dio altro è Dio di altri: HumBr 44 (1989) 636-646.

a657 **Lewis** R. M., Ecstatic religion; a study of shamanism and spirit possession[2] [[1]1971]. L 1989, Routledge. 200 p. £11. 0-415-00799-2 [BL 90, 105, R. P. *Carroll*: thoroughly revised but photos omitted].

a658 ᴱLinders Tullia ..., Gifts to the gods 1985/7 ➤ 3,666: ᴿArchaeologia 39 (Wrocław 1988) 243s (K. *Milewska*, Eng.); BO 46 (1989) 467-9 (P. *Xella*); RArchéol (1989) 364s (Louise *Bruit*).

a659 **Lott** Eric J., Vision, tradition, interpretation; theology, religion, and the study of religion: Religion and Reason 35, 1988 ➤ b560; 3-11-009761-3: ᴱExpTim 100 (1988s) 195 (P. *Byrne*); NRT 111 (1989) 599s (J. *Masson*).

a660 **Lübbe** Hermann, Religion nach der Aufklärung 1986 ➤ 4,b562: ᴿTPhil 64 (1989) 127-130 (H.-L. *Ollig*); ZevEth 32 (1988) 153 (Annette & H. *Hamann*).

a661 **Madelin** Henri, La menace idéologique: Parole présente. P 1988, Cerf. 190 p. F 69. – ᴿEsprVie 99 (1989) 79s (L. *Debarge*, aussi p. 76-8, Idéologie et religion).

a662 **Mahaffey** Patrick J., Religious pluralism and the question of truth; an inquiry in the philosophy of religious worldviews: diss. 1988, Univ. California, ᴰ*Smart* N. – RelStR 16,187.

a663 **Mancini** I., Filosofia della religione.³ Genova 1986 ¹1966, Marietti. xvi-396 p. Lit. 35.000. – ᴿProtestantesimo 44 (1989) 64 (G. *Vetrano*).

a664 **Martin** Stoddard, Orthodox heresy; the rise of 'magic' as religion and its relation to literature. NY 1989, St. Martin's. $30. 0-312-02389-8 [TDig 37,171, no p.].

a665 **Ménard** Jacques, Introduction à l'histoire des religions 1987 ➤ 3,a952: ᴿETL 65 (1989) 205 (V. *Neckebrouck*: not only too brief, but full of blanks; for whom?); TR 85 (1989) 494s (L. *Hagemann*).

a665* **Meštrović** Stjepan G., Reappraising DURKHEIM's Elementary forms of the religious life, in the context of SCHOPENHAUER's philosophy: JScStR 28 (1989) 255-272.

a666 **Meyer** Heinz, Religionskritik, Religionssoziologie und Säkularisation. Fra 1988, Lang. 478 p. DM 76. 3-8204-1370-7. – ᴿActuBbg 26 (1989) 217s (J. *Boada*).

a666* **Nabe** Clyde, Mystery and religion; NEWMAN's epistemology of religion. Lanham MD 1988, UPA. 64 p. – ᴿRelStR 15 (1989) 343 (R. *Penaskovic*).

a667 **Newport** John P., Life's ultimate questions; a contemporary philosophy of religion. Dallas 1989, Word. 644 p. – ᴿSWJT 32,3 (1989s) 46s (T. *George*).

a668 **Oberhammer** Gerhard, Versuch einer transzendentalen Hermeneutik religiöser Traditionen: de Nobili 3. W 1987, Univ. Inst. Indology. 47 p. [RelStR 16,135, J. W. *Laine*].

a669 *Ogden* Schubert M., Problems in the case for a pluralistic theology of religions: JRel 68 (1988) 493-507.

a670 *Olson* Carl, Theology of nostalgia; reflections on the theological aspects of ELIADE's work: Numen 36 (1989) 98-112.

a671 **Oppenheim** Frank M., Josiah ROYCE'e mature philosophy of religion 1987 ➤ 3,a960; 4,b377: ᴿRelStR 15 (1989) 57 (P. C. *Hodgson*).

a671* **Pacini** David S., The cunning of modern religious thought 1987 ➤ 3,a965: ᴿJAAR 57 (1989) 222-5 (D. E. *Linge*).

a672 **Paden** William E., Religious worlds; the comparative study of religion. Boston 1988, Beacon. viii-192 p. $20; pa. $10. 0-8070-1210-6; 21-4 [TDig 37,80].

a673 *Pannenberg* Wolfhart, Die Religionen als Thema der Theologie; die Relevanz der Religionen für das Selbstverständnis der Theologie: TüTQ 169 (1989) 99-110.

a674 **Paranilam** Zacharias, Christian openness to the world religions. Alwaye 1988, Pontifical Institute. xvi-183 p. rs 20. – ᴿBibleBh 15 (1989) 273 (G. *Mangatt*); IndTSt 26 (1989) 187s (R. *De Smet*); JDharma 13 (1988) 414s (A. *James*).

a674* *Pepper* George, Peter BERGER; modernization and religion: CCurr 38 (1988s) 448-456.

a675 *Plantinga* Richard J., W. B. KRISTENSEN and the study of religion: Numen 36 (1989) 173-188.

a676 *a) Plantinga* Richard J., In the beginning; P. D. CHANTEPIE de la Saussaye on Religionswissenschaft and theology; – *b) Webb* Eugene, Recent French psychoanalytic thought and the psychology of religion; – *c) Sheard* Robert B., Let God be God; the historical dimension of religious truth: RelStT 8,1s (1988) 24-30 / 31-44 / 45-54.

a677 **Platt** David, Intimations of divinity [...grounding religious belief in experience]. NY 1989, Lang. 248 p. $36. – ᴿTTod 46 (1989s) 449s (Kathryn E. *Tanner*).

a678 **Poupard** Paul, Las religiones [compendio de Diccionario de las r. 1987 ➤ 4,865 < 1984 ➤ 65,788]. Barc 1989, Herder. 140 p. – ᴿCarthaginensia 5 (1989) 337 (F. *Martínez Fresneda*); ScripTPamp 21 (1989) 876s (C. J. *Alejos*).

a679 **Prades** José A., Persistance et métamorphose du sacré; actualiser DURKHEIM et repenser la modernité: Sociologie d'aujourd'hui, 1987 ➤ 4,b582: ᴿSR 18 (1989) 234s (J.-P. *Rouleau*: enthousiaste mais convaincant).

a680 **Preus** J. Samuel, Explaining religion; criticism and theory from Bodin to Freud 1987 ➤ 3,a971; 4,b583: ᴿInterpretation 43 (1989) 102 (R. *Hjelm*); HistRel 29 (1989s) 7-73 (G. D. *Alles*); JAAR 57 (1989) 173-180 (Hans H. *Penner*); RelStR 15 (1989) 334-7 (R. A. *Segal*).

a681 *Proudfoot* Wayne, From theology to a science of religions; Jonathan EDWARDS and William JAMES on religious affections: HarvTR 82 (1989) 149-168.

a682 *Richard* Jean, La révélation finale d'après Paul TILLICH; une voie théologique pour la rencontre du christianisme avec les religions du monde: ÉTRel 64 (1989) 211-224.

a683 **Ries** Julien, Les chrétiens parmi les religions, des Actes des Apôtres à Vatican II 1987 ➤ 3,a977; 4,8979: ᴿNRT 111 (1989) 285s (J. *Masson*); RTPhil 121 (1989) 104s (J.-C. *Basset*); TR 85 (1989) 494s (A. T. *Khoury*).

a684 *Ries* Julien, Chronique d'histoire des religions; la recherche comparée [I. 1987] II: EsprVie 99 (1989) 625-635.

a685 **Riess** Klaus, Gott zwischen Begriff und Geheimnis; zu einem Ende natürlicher Theologie als Aufgang neuzeitlicher Religionsphilosophie: kath. Diss. ᴰ*Heinzmann*. München 1988s. – TR 85 (1989) 517.

a686 **Rizzardi** G., Le religioni [... Islam] come tema della cultura e della teologia. Pavia 1987, Casa del Giovane. 334 p. Lit. 22.000. – ᴿStPatav 36 (1989) 613-5 (G. *Basetti-Sani*).

a687 **Rossano** Pietro, I perché dell'uomo e le risposte delle grandi religioni: Le Religioni 5. CinB 1988, Paoline. 136 p. Lit. 10.000. – ᴿHumBr 44 (1989) 606s (G. *Colombi*); Lateranum 55 (1989) 270 (*ipse*).

a688 **Rudolph** Kurt, Historical fundamentals and the study of religions (Haskell lectures, Univ. Chicago). NY 1986, Macmillan. xiii-123 p. $17. – ᴿHeythJ 30 (1989) 351s (E. *Hulmes*).

a689 **Saldanha** Chrys, Divine pedagogy; a patristic view of non-Christian religions: BiblScR 57, 1984 ➤ 65,9073 ... 3,a986:   ᴿJRel 68 (1988) 288s (R. M. *Grant*: from 1979 Maynooth dissertation).

a690 *Scannone* Juan Carlos, Fenomenología y religión: ➤ 7, ᶠALFARO J., EstE 64 (1989) 133-9.

a691 *Schadel* Erwin, Anthropologischer Zugang zum Glauben [*Beck* H., Religionsphilosophie 1979]: FreibZ 36 (1989) 129-158.

a692 **Schlamm** Leon P., Rudolph OTTO's theory of religious experience in 'The idea of the holy'; a study in the phenomenology and philosophy of religion: diss. Kent. Canterbury 1988. 442 p. BRDX-87183. – DissA 50 (1989s) 2941s-A.

a693 **Schlesinger** George N., New perspectives on old-time religion. Ox 1988, Clarendon. vii-196 p. £17.50. – ᴿJTS 40 (1989) 709s (B. *Hebblethwaite*: ponderous, Pelagian, but partly good).

a694 **Schmitz** Joseph, Filosofia della religione [1964; español 1987 ➤ 3,a989], ᵀᴱ*Bartolomei* Maria C.: GdT 183. Brescia 1988, Queriniana. 220 p. Lit. 18.000. – ᴿAsprenas 36 (1989) 103s (G. *Ragozzino*); ETL 65 (1989) 460 (E. *Brito*); StPatav 36 (1989) 607s (V. *Bortolin*).

a695 *Schoen* Ulrich, Denkwege auf dem Gebiet der Theologie der Religionen: VerkF 34,1 (1989) 61-87.

a696 *Schröder* Richard, Gottesdienst, Afterdienst, Fetischdienst; zum kritischen Gebrauch einer religionsgeschichtlichen Kategorie bei KANT und MARX: BTZ 6 (1989) 146-160.

a697 *Schweiker* William, Beyond imitation; mimetic praxis in GADAMER, RICOEUR, and DERRIDA: JRel 68 (Ch 1968) 21-38 [no mention of GIRARD].

a698 *a)* *Seckler* Max, Synodos der Religionen; das 'Ereignis von Assisi' und seine Perspektiven für eine Theologie der Religionen; – *b)* *Limbeck* Meinrad, Die Religionen im NT: TüTQ 169 (1989) 5-24 (-34, *Waldenfels* H.) / 44-56 (-67, *Hünermann* P.).

a699 *Segal* Robert A., *Wiebe* Donald, Axioms and dogmas in the study of religion: JAAR 57 (1989) 591-605.

a700 **Sell** Alan P. F., The philosophy of religion 1975-1980 ➤ 4,b596; L 1988, Croom Helm, 252 p. £35. 0-7099-5458-1. – ᴿExpTim 100 (1988s) 116 (P. *Vardy*); RelSt 25 (1989) 402s (H. P. *Owen*).

a701 *a)* *Sheridan* Daniel P., Distinct by God's Word; diversity and the theology of religions; – *b)* *De Sousa* Pio, Mysticism in different religious traditions: JDharma 13 (1988) 105-115.

a702 *Siegwalt* Gérard, Pourquoi et comment la foi chrétienne est-elle concernée par les autres religions?: FoiVie 88 (1989) 21-39.

a702* *Simpson* R. T., The new dialogue between Christianity and other religions: TLond 92 (1989) 92-102 [297 J. *Hick* reactions to citations from him].

a703 **Smart** Ninian, The world's religions — old traditions and modern transformations. C 1989, Univ. 580 p. £25. 0-521-34005-5. – ᴿÉTRel 64 (1989) 601 (Jacky *Argaud*).

a704 *a)* *Smart* Ninian, Humanismo transcendental, ᵀ*González Velasco* M.; – *b)* *Murty* K. S., El Dios del Hinduismo, ᵀ*O'Connor* Aurora; – *c)* *Dhirasekera* Jotiya, El Dios del Budismo, ᵀ*Serrano* Raúl; – *d)* *Idrid* Gaafar S., El Dios del Islam, ᵀ*Serrano*; – *e)* *Muñoz León* Domingo, El Dios del Judaismo; – *f)* *Casas* Victoriano, El Dios de Jesús; – *g)* *Salas* Antonio, El Dios del Cristianismo; – *h)* bibliog.: BibFe 15,43 ('¿Qué es

Dios? Responden las grandes religiones' 1989) 9-20 / 21-38 / 39-51 / 52-63 / 64-89 / 90-116 / 117-164 / 165-8.

a705 **Stark** Rodney, *Bainbridge* William S., A theory of religion 1987 ⮕ 4,b603: ᴿHistRel 29 (1989s) 418-420 (J. A. *Coleman*: sees religion only as a market); TS 50 (1989) 578-580 (D. J. *Casey*).

a706 **Stolz** Fritz, Grundzüge der Religionswissenschaft: VR Kleine Reihe 1527, 1988 ⮕ 4,b605: ᴿTLZ 114 (1989) 101 (P. *Heidrich*); ZRGg 41 (1989) 283 (M. *Baumann*).

a707 **Strolz** Walter, Heilswege der Weltreligionen 3. Quellentexte... 1987 ⮕ 3,a993; 4,b606: ᴿTPQ 137 (1989) 100s (J. *Janda*); TüTQ 169 (1989) 73-75 (M. *Seckler*).

a708 *Surin* Kenneth, Toward a 'materialist' critique of 'religious pluralism'; a polemical examination of the discourse of John HICK and Wilfred C. SMITH: Thomist 53 (1989) 655-673.

a709 ᴱ**Sutherland** Stewart, *al.*, The world's religions 1988 ⮕ 4,418; also L, Routledge/Croom Helm; 0-415-00324-5: ᴿExpTim 100 (1988s) 347s (P. D. *Bishop*).

a710 ᴱ**Swidler** Leonard, Toward a universal theology of religion 1987 ⮕ 3,a994; 4,b607: ᴿCalvinT 24 (1989) 167-171 (J. W. *Cooper*); ÉTRel 64 (1989) 461s (A. *Gounelle*); Horizons 16 (1989) 177s (C. *Chapple*).

a711 *Terrin* Aldo N., Scienza delle religioni; un fascio di problemi ancora irrisolti: TItSett 14 (1989) 154-170; Eng. 171.

a712 *Tilley* Terrence W., The prudence of religious commitment [i. e. to the practice of a religion; not to the religious vows]: Horizons 16 (1989) 45-64.

a713 *Vandenbulcke* Jaak, Een niet-kognitieve omschrijving van de godsdienst [... definition of religion]? Vragen aan Arnold BURMS en Herman De DIJN: Bijdragen 50 (1989) 322-335; Eng. 335s.

a714 **Vergote** Antoine, Guilt and desire; religious attitudes and their pathological foundations, ᵀ*Wood* M. H. NHv 1988, Yale. x-254 p. $32.50. – ᴿJRel 69 (1989) 588s (J. *Byrnes*).

a715 *Verweyen* Hansjürgen, Methodik der Religionsphilosophie; [M. BLONDEL], 'L'Action' (1893) im Spiegel der 'Lettre' (1896): TPhil 64 (1989) 210-221.

a716 *a) Victorin-Vangerod* Nancy M., Reflections on religious pluralism; the new face no one has seen before; – *b) Brown* Carol, The nature of evil; a comparative study of Buddhist and Christian temptation narratives: Paradigms 5 (1989) 88-100 / 117-142.

a717 **Vidal** Jacques, Symboles et religions; cours de l'année académique 1986-7, ᴱ*Ries* Julien, *al.*: Homo Religiosus cahiers 1. LvN 1989, Centre Hist. Rel. xvii-417 p.

a718 **Vroom** H. M., Religies en de waarheid. Kampen 1988, Kok. 334 p. ƒ59,50. 90-242-3314-3. – ᴿTsTNijm 29 (1989) 433 (R. *Bakker*).

a719 **Wallace** Raymond P., Reference, method, and religious pluralism; 'The Encyclopedia of Religion and Ethics' and 'Die Religion in Geschichte und Gegenwart' [how they tried to integrate comparative religion into theological reflection]: diss. Graduate Theological Union, ᴰ*Welch* C. Berkeley 1989. 311 p. 89-24373. – DissA 50 (1989s) 2119-A.

a720 *Warburg* Margit, William ROBERTSON SMITH and the study of religion: Religion 19,1 (L 1989) 41-62 [< ᶻⁱᵀ 89,352].

a721 **Watts** Fraser, *Williams* Mark, The psychology of religious knowing. C 1988, Univ. 169 p. £19.50. 0-521-32610-9. – ᴿExpTim 100 (1988s) 195s (D. Z. *Phillips*); TTod 46 (1989s) 358 (C. V. *Gerkin*: not as reductionistic as other clinical psychologists).

a721* *Welti* Manfred,   Das Zwischenspiel zwischen Humanismus und Konfessionalismus: HZ 249 (1989) 19-52.

a722 **Whaling** Frank,   Christian theology and world religions 1986 ➤ 3,b8: ᴿThemelios 14 (1988s) 114s (M. *Goldsmith*).

a723 **Whitehead** Alfred N.,   Wie entsteht Religion? [Religion in the making 1926], ᵀ. Fra 1985, Suhrkamp. 127 p. – ᴿTPhil 64 (1989) 464s (H.-J. *Höhn*).

a724 **Whitehead** Alfred N.,   De dynamiek van de religie [Religion in the making 1926], ᵀ*Veken* J. van der. Kapellen/Kampen 1988, Pelckmans/ Kok. 185 p. Fb 495. 90-289-1364-5 / 90-242-7610-1. – ᴿTsTNijm 29 (1989) 205 (H. *Berger*).

a724* *Wilfred* Felix,   World religions and Christian inculturation: IndTSt 25 (1988) 5-25.

a725 *Wilken* Robert L.,   Who will speak *for* the religious traditions? [AAR 1989 presidential address]: JAAR 57 (1989) 699-717.

a726 *Zdybicka* Zofia, ➋ *a*) Fenomenologia religii; – *b*) Filozofia religii: ➤ 891, EncKat 5 (1989) 126-8 / 264-8.

a727 **Zdybicka** sr. Zofia S.,   ➋ Religia i religioznawstwo. Lublin 1988, KUL. 447 p. – ᴿAtKap 113 (1989) 158-160 (M. *Rusecki*).

a728 **Zirker** H.,   Critica della religione: GdT 187. Brescia 1989, Queriniana. 286 p. Lit. 24.000. – ᴿStPatav 36 (1989) 608-610 (V. *Bortolin*).

M3.5 Mythologia.

a729 **Assmann** Jan, *al.*,   Funktionen und Leistungen des Mythos...: OBO 48, 1982 ➤ 63,2079... 2,8781*: ᴿWZKM 77 (1987) 179-182 (H.-P. *Müller*).

a730 *Bartmiński* Jerzy, ➋ Folklor: ➤ 891, EncKat 5 (1989) 368-374.

a731 **Behre** Maria,   'Des dunkeln Lichtes voll'; HÖLDERLINs Mythokonzept Dionysos. Mü 1987, Fink. 282 p. – ᴿTR 85 (1989) 331-4 (G. *Schmiz*).

a732 **Biallas** L. J.   Myths, gods and saviors 1986 ➤ 3,b16: ᴿAnglTR 70 (1988) 383-6 (T. J. *Kodera*).

a733 **Elworthy** Frederick T.,   The evil eye; an account of this ancient and widespread superstition. NY 1989, Bell. xlv-471 p.; 187 fig. 0-517-67944-2.

a734 **Fisch** H.,   Un futuro ricordato; saggio sulla mitologia letteraria. Bo 1988, Mulino. 240 p. – ᴿRivB 37 (1989) 97-102 (G. *Ravasi*; l'autore si dedica al rapporto tra letteratura inglese e tradizione ebraico-biblica nell'Università Bar-Ilan; non viene spiegato come l'abbiamo in italiano).

a735 **Gibson** James E.,   Mimetic action; hermeneutic and therapeutic applications of mythical re-enactment [LAEUCHLI S.]: diss. ᴰ*Laeuchli*, Temple Univ. Ph 1989. 306 p. 89-12431. – DissA 50 (1989s) 971s-A.

a736 **Hübner** Kurt,   Die Wahrheit des Mythus 1985 ➤ 1,a412... 4,b637: ᴿZRGg 40 (1988) 80-87 (G. *Lüling*).

a737 *Hübner* Kurt,   Die moderne Mythos-Forschung; eine noch nicht erkannte Revolution: BTZ 6 (1989) 8-21.

a737* *Imhoof* Stefan,   Le chemin du mythe à la philosophie: RTPhil 121 (1989) 91-96.

a738 **Kajanto** Iiro,   Humanism in a Christian society, I. The attitude to classical mythology and religion in Finland 1640-1713: Toimituksia B 248. Helsinki 1989, Soc. Scientiarum Fennica. 204 p. 951-41-0592-3.

a738* **Kaufmann** Rolf,   Das ewig Christliche; Glaubensbekenntnis und Mythos; Vorw. *Pflüger* Peter M.: Theol.-tiefenpsychologische Deutungen. FrB 1989, Walter. 235 p. 3-530-42321-1. – ᴿActuBbg 26 (1989) 212s (J. *Boada*).

a739 **Kolakowski** Leszek, The presence of myth [1966, 1972], ᵀ*Czerniawski* Adam. Ch 1989, Univ. xii-138 p. 0-226-45041-4.

a740 **Krolick** Sanford, Recollective resolve: a phenomenological under-standing of time and myth. Macon GA 1987, Mercer Univ. 125 p. [RelStR 16, 236, R. R. *Williams*].

a741 *Kulisz* Józef, ❷ L'homme, cet animal mythique: PrzPow 818 (1989) 74-87.

a742 *Le Glay* Marcel, Mythes, légendes et réalités cultuelles [*Bonnet* C., Melqart 1988]: Latomus 48 (1989) 581-9.

a743 **Lévêque** Pierre, Colère, sexe, rire; le Japon des mythes anciens 1988 ⇒ 4,b640*: ᴿAntClas 58 (1989) 409s (L. *Lacroix*).

a744 ᴱ**Lindfors** Bernth, Forms of folklore in Africa; narrative, poetic, gnomic, dramatic. AA 1989, Univ. Michigan. viii-281 p.

a745 *Mactoux* Marie-Madeleine, Panthéon et discours mythologique; le cas d'APOLLODORE: RHR 206 (1989) 245-270.

a746 *Masuzawa* Tomoko, Original lost; an image of myth and ritual in the age of mechanical reproduction: JRel 69 (1989) 307-325.

a747 ᴱ**Metzger** Michael M., *Mommsen* Katharina, Fairy tales as ways of knowing; essays on Märchen in psychology, society and literature: Germanic Studies in America 41. Bern 1981, Lang. 198 p.

a748 ꟳMUTH Robert: Mythos, Deutung und Bedeutung; Dies philologicus Aenipontanus (1986) 5, 1987 ⇒ 4,110: ᴿSalesianum 51 (1989) 339s (B. *Amata*).

a749 *Plácido* Domingo, Realidades arcaicas de los viajes míticos a Occidente: Gerión 7 (1989) 41-51.

a750 **Puhvel** Jaan, Comparative mythology 1987 ⇒ 4,b649: ᴿÉtClas 57 (1989) 265s (Corinne *Bonnet*); HistRel 29 (1989s) 184-9 (E. C. *Polomé*: textbook; Dumézilian perspective; excellent); IndoIraJ 32 (1989) 206-8 (J. W. de *Jong*).

a751 *Pulak* David, An image of myth / The mythic vision of Joseph CAMPBELL: JDharma 13,2 ('Mythical and Mystic in Religions' 1988) 178-183.

a752 *Richter* Hans-Friedemann, Zum Problem des Mythos: ZRGg 40 (1988) 24-43.

a752* **Roux** Jean-Paul, Le sang; mythes, symboles et réalités. P 1988, Fayard. 410 p. F 130. 2-213-02090-6. – ᴿÉtRel 64 (1989) 103 (Jacky *Argaud*).

a753 **Schindler** Wolfgang, Mythos und Wirklichkeit in der Antike. Lp 1987, Ed. Lp. 202 p.; 146 (color.) fig. – ᴿDLZ 110 (1989) 250-3 (M. *Op-permann*).

ᴱ**Schmidt** H. H., Mythos und Rationalität 1987/8 ⇒ 741*.

a753* *Williams* James G., Mythos, aphorism and the Christ as sign: Forum 5,1 (1989) 73-91 [45-72, *Shea* Chris, The myth of Arthur (not Athur as p. 1) updated and undone].

M4 Religio romana.

a754 ᵀᴱ**Bara** Joëlle-Frédérique, VETTIUS Valens d'Antioche, Anthologies I; ÉPR 111. Leiden 1989, Brill. xv-245 p. 90-04-08643-9.

a755 *Bömer* Franz, Isis und Serapis in der Welt der Sklaven: Gymnasium 96 (1989) 97-109.

a756 ᴱBonfante L., Etruscan life and afterlife 1986 ➤ 3,485; 4,b658: ᴿLatomus 48 (1989) 722s (J.-R. *Jannot*).

a757 Bremmer J. N., *Horsfall* N. M., Roman myth and mythography: Bulletin Supp. 52, 1987 ➤ 3,b48*; 4,b659: ᴿGreeceR 36 (1989) 253 (P. *Walcot* praises).

a758 Brouwer H. H. J., Bona dea; the sources and a description of the cult: ÉPR 110. Leiden 1989, Brill. xxvii-507 p.; 2 fig.; 52 pl.; 2 maps. 90-04-08606-4.

a758* Carozzi Claude, Le voyage de l'âme dans l'au-delà d'après la littérature latine (Vᵉ-XIIIᵉ siècles): diss. Paris-IV 1989. – RÉLat 67 (1989) 36.

a759 Castner Catherine J., Prosopography of Roman Epicureans; from the second century B.C. to the second century A.D.: StKlasPg 34. Fra 1988, Lang. xix-116 p. 3-8204-9933-4.

a760 Champeaux Jacqueline, Fortuna; recherches sur le culte de la Fortune à Rome... II. Les transformations de Fortuna sous la république: Coll.ÉcFrR 64, 1987 ➤ 4,b661: ᴿGnomon 61 (1989) 27-31 (G. *Radke*).

a761 Cleveland Ingrid T., The Egyptian cults in ancient Rome; a study of the diffusion and popularity of the cults in Roman society: diss. Central Missouri State Univ. Warrensburg 1987. 90 p.

a762 Coarelli Filippo, I santuari del Lazio in età repubblicana. R 1987, Nuova It. Scientifica. 195 p.; 49 fig. Lit. 24.000. – ᴿAJA 93 (1989) 301s (P. *Harvey*); Gnomon 61 (1989) 278s (T. P. *Wiseman*); JRS 79 (1989) 180-2 (J. *Scheid*).

a763 Colish Marcia L., The Stoic tradition I-II 1985 ➤ 3,b52; 4,b663: ᴿCrNSt 9 (1988) 618-622 (M. *Spanneut*); Latomus 48 (1989) 701-3 (G. *Scarpat*).

a764 *Dorcey* Peter F., The role of women in the cult of Silvanus: Numen 36 (1989) 143-155.

a765 Dubourdieu Annie, Les origines et le développement du culte des Pénates à Rome: Coll. 118. R 1989, Éc. Française. x-566 p.; 2 pl. 2-7283-0162-X.

a766 Eden P. T., SENECA, Apocolocynthosis. C 1984, Univ. xii-169 p. – ᴿAntClas 58 (1989) 342s (D. *Pikhaus*).

a767 *Elsas* Christoph, Hellenistisch-römische Religion: ➤ 894, EvKL 2 (1988) 481-8 [335-7 griechische, *Fauth* Wolfgang].

a768 Fishwick Duncan, The imperial cult in the Latin West [revised reprints]: ÉPR 108, 1987 ➤ 3,b57; *f* 220: ᴿClasR 39 (1989) 321s (J. *Liebeschuetz*); Gnomon 61 (1989) 466-8 (P. *Gros*); JRS 79 (1989) 239s (Élisabeth *Smadja*, français).

a768* Giancotti Francesco, Religio, natura, voluptas; studi su LUCREZIO con un'antologia di testi annotati e tradotti: Ed. Saggi FgClas 37. Bo 1989, Pàtron. xxiii-661 p. [RFgIC 118,89-94, C, *Di Giovine*].

a769 Goulet-Cazé Marie-Odile, L'ascèse cynique; un commentaire de Diogène LAËRCE VI 70-71: Histoire des doctrines de l'antiquité classique 10, 1986 ➤ 4,b669: ᴿRivFgIC 117 (1989) 74-79 (Caterina *Licciardi*).

a770 Grimal Pierre, Jupiter, Anchise et Vulcain; trois révélations sur le destin de Rome: ➤ 35, ᶠBRINK C. 1989, 1-13.

a771 Haudry Jean, La religion cosmique des Indo-Européens: Ét.Ind.-Eur. 2. P 1987, Archè/BLettres. 329 p. F 180. – ᴿClasR 39 (1989) 144s (M. L. *West*); RÉLat 67 (1989) 369-371 (P. *Flobert*); RHR 206 (1989) 183-8 (Émilia *Masson*).

a772 *Herz* Peter, Der römische Kaiser und der Kaiserkult; Gott oder primus inter pares?: ➤ 769, Menschwerdung 1986/9, 115-140.

a773 ᴱHinard François, La mort, les morts et l'au-delà dans le monde romain; Actes du colloque de Caen, 20-22 nov. 1985. Caen 1987, Univ. 376 p.; 35 fig. F 210. – ᴿClasR 39 (1989) 325-7 (G. *Davies*); Phoenix 43 (Toronto 1989) 384-6 (Y. *Grisé*).

a774 **Hörig** Monika, *Schwertheim* Elmar, Corpus cultus Iovis Dolicheni: ÉPR 106, 1987 ➤ 3,b64: ᴿClasR 39 (1989) 146 (S. R. F. *Price*); RArchéol (1989) 417s (R. *Turcan*).

a775 **Irwin** Terence, Classical [... religious] thought: History of Western Philosophy 1. Ox 1989, Univ. xii-266 p. 0-19-219196-9; pa. 77-4.

a775* *Jocelyn* H. D., LUCRETIUS, his copyists, and the horrors of the underworld [as depicted: really suffered in this life] (De Rerum Natura 3, 978-1023): Acta Classica 29 (Pretoria 1986) 43-56.

a776 **Krause** Bernd H., Iuppiter O. M. Saturnus; ein Beitrag zur ikonographischen Darstellung Saturns: Trierer Winck-P. 5, 1983 ➤ 1,a441: ᴿAnzAltW 42 (1989) 120-2 (K. *Schauenburg*).

a777 **Krauskopff** Ingrid, Todesdämonen und Totengötter im vorhellenistischen Etrurien; Kontinuität und Wandel: Biblioteca di Studi Etruschi 16. F 1987, Olschki. 148 p.; 20 pl. – ᴿAntClas 58 (1989) 211-220 (F. de *Ruyt*: vaste érudition).

a778 **Lane** E. N., Corpus Cultus Iovis Sabazii 3. Conclusions: ÉPR 100. Leiden 1989, Brill. ix-68 p.; II pl. 90-04-08974-8.

a779 *Leach* Eleanor W., The implied reader and the political argument in SENECA's Apocolocyntosis and De clementia: Arethusa 22 (1989) 197-230.

a780 *Long* Charlotte R., The gods of the [Roman] months in ancient [Egyptian, Greek] art: AJA 93 (1989) 589-595; 3 fig.

a781 **Meer** L. B. van der, The bronze liver of Piacenza; analysis of a polytheistic structure 1987 ➤ 4,b682: ᴿAntClas 58 (1989) 551-5 (F. De *Ruyt*); Gnomon 60 (1988) 561-3 (M. *Cristofani*, ital.; non leído).

a782 **Merkelbach** Reinhold, Die Hirten des Dionysos; die Dionysos-Mysterien der römischen Kaiserzeit und der bukolische Roman des Longus. Stu 1988, Teubner. 290 p.; 88 fig. – ᴿGGA 241 (1989) 169-192 (R. *Turcan*: mystères de Lesbos).

a783 **Montanari** Enrico, Identità culturale e conflitti religiosi nella Roma repubblicana: Filologia e critica 54, 1988 ➤ 4,b683: ᴿAevum 63 (1984) 107s (A. *Barzanò*); RÉLat 67 (1989) 372-4 (J.-C. *Richard*).

a784 **Pailler** Jean-Marie, Bacchanalia; la répression de 186 av. J.-C. à Rome et en Italie; vestiges, images, tradition: BÉF 270. R 1988, École Française. 868 p.; 15 fig. 2-7283-0161-1. – ᴿRÉLat 67 (1989) 332-5 (R. *Turcan*).

a785 **Paladino** Ida, Fratres arvales; storia di un collegio sacerdotale romano. R 1988, Bretschneider. 317 p. – ᴿSMSR 55,1 (1989) 165-8 (Claudia *Santi*).

a786 *Paladino* Ida, Modello 'fatale' e modello funzionale nel comportamento delle gentes: SMSR 55,1 (1989) 31-43.

a787 **Porte** Danielle, Les donneurs du sacré; le prêtre à Rome: Realia. P 1989, BLettres. 266 p. F 135. 2-251-23806-3. – ᴿRÉLat 67 (1989) 367s (H. *Le Bonniec*).

a788 *Prosdocimi* Aldo, Sacerdos 'qui sacrum dat', *sacrum dare* and *sacra facere* in ancient Italy: ➤ 153, ᶠPOLOMÉ E., 1988, 509-523.

a789 **Radke** Gerhard, Zur Entwicklung der Gottesvorstellung und der Gottesverehrung in Rom; ImpulsForsch 50. Da 1987, Wiss. xiv-340 p. – RAnzAltW 42 (1989) 48-51 (R. *Schilling*); HZ 248 (1989) 672-4 (C. J. *Classen*).

a790 **Sabbatucci** Dario, La religione di Roma antica; dal calendario festivo all'ordine cosmico: Cultura 67, 1988 ➤ 4,b688: RRHR 206 (1989) 69-73 (R. *Turcan*).

a791 **Schowalter** Daniel N., The relationship between the emperor and the gods; images from PLINY's 'Panegyricus' and other sources from the time of Trajan: diss. Harvard, DKoester H. CM 1989. 268 p. 89-25427. – DissA 50 (1989s) 2533-A.

a792 *Seweryniak* Lucyna, ❷ Fortuna, bogini szczęścia: ➤ 891, EncKat 5 (1989) 410-2.

a793 ESordi Marta, Politica e religione nel primo scontro tra Roma e l'Oriente [15 art.]: Ist. Storia Antica 8. Mi 1982, ViPe. ix-203 p. Lit. 24.000. – RAntClas 58 (1989) 465s (J.-M. *Hannick*).

a794 *Syme* Ronald, A dozen early priesthoods: ZPapEp 77 (1989) 241-259.

a795 *Ternes* Charles-Marie, Y a-t-il une démonologie romaine?: ➤ 728, Anges 1987/9, 253-268.

a796 **Turcan** R., Religion romaine; I. Les dieux; II. Le culte: IconRel 17,1s, 1988 ➤ 4,b694: RStPatav 36 (1989) 611s (F. *Mora*).

a797 **Turcan** Robert, Les cultes orientaux dans le monde romain: Histoire. P 1989, BLettres. 397 p.; 24 pl. 2-251-38001-9.

a797* **Vanggaard** Jens H., The Flamen, a study in the history and sociology of Roman religion. K 1988, Mus. Tusc. 175 p. Dk 171 [AmJPg 111, 118-121, Agnes *Michels*].

a798 **Vermaseren** M. J., Corpus cultus Cybelae Attidisque 5 [Aeg. ...]: ÉPR 50, 1986 ➤ 2,8953: RBonnJbb 189 (1989) 647-651 (W. *Eck*).

a800 *Webster* Graham, Deities and religious scenes on Romano-British pottery: JRPot 2 (Ox 1989) 1-28; 9 fig.

a801 *Wiseman* T. P., Roman legend and oral tradition [Bremmer J., Horsfall N. 1987]: JRS 79 (1989) 129-137.

a802 **Zannini** *Quirini* Bruno, Rassegna, religione romana: StRom 36 (1988) 97-107 (91-96, storia, *Malavolta* Mariano) / 37 (1989) 128-130.

a803 **Zuntz** Günther, Aion, Gott des Römerreiches: Abh Heid ph/h 1989/2. Heid 1989, Winter. 67 p.

M4.5 **Mithraismus.**

a804 **Beck** Roger, Planetary gods and planetary orders in the mysteries of Mithras: ÉPR 109, 1988 ➤ 4,b698; ƒ115: RGreeceR 36 (1989) 253 (P. *Walcot*).

a805 *Décréaux* Joseph, Le culte de Mithra en orient: Archéologia 243 (1989) 48-57; ill.

a806 **Dumézil** Georges, Mitra-Varuna, TColtman Derek. ... 1988, Zone. 250 p. $22 [JAAR 57,446].

a807 *Martin* Luther M., Roman Mithraism and Christianity: Numen 36 (1989) 2-15.

a808 **Ulansey** David, The origin of the Mithraic mysteries; cosmology and salvation in the ancient world. NY 1989, Oxford-UP. xii-154 p.; ill. 0-19-505402-4.

a809 *Zwirn* S. R.,   The intention of biographical narration on Mithraic cult
images: Word & Image 5,1 (L 1989) 2-18 [< NTAbs 33,369].

M5 **Religio graeca.**

a810 *Alderink* Larry J.,   The Eleusinian mysteries in Roman imperial times:
→ 878, ANRW 2/18/2, 1457-1498 [-1598 *al.*, plus several articles on
Mithraism *etc.* in Dacia and Pannonia].
a811 **Aleshire** Sara B.,   The Athenian Asklepieion; the people, their
dedications, and the inventories. Amst 1989, Gieben. xii-385 p.; 3 fig.;
12 pl. 90-5063-025-1.
a812 **Alroth** Brita,   Greek gods and figurines; aspects of the anthropomorphic dedications: Boreas 18. U 1989, Almqvist & W. 120 p.
91-554-2367-1.
a813 *Athanassakis* Apostolos,   From the phallic cairn to shepherd god and
divine herald [Hermes]: Eranos 87 (1989) 33-49.
a814 ᴱ**Baldassari** Mariano,   Le testimonianze minori del secolo II d. C.;
EPITTETO PLUTARCO GELLIO APULEIO: La logica stoica, testimonianza e
frammenti 7B. Como 1987. 112 p.
a815 **Barrett** Harold,   The sophists; rhetoric, democracy and PLATO's idea of
sophistry. Novato CA 1987, Chandler & S. ix-85 p. $7. – ᴿClasR 39
(1989) 143 (G. B. *Kerferd*).
a816 *Bassi* Karen,   The poetics of exclusion in CALLIMACHUS' Hymn to
Apollo: AmPgTr 119 (1989) 219-231.
a817 **Berges** Dietrich,   Hellenistische Rundaltäre Kleinasiens 1986 → 3,b94:
ᴿGnomon 61 (1989) 376s (Heide *Lauter-Bufe*).
a818 **Blundell** Mary W.,   Helping friends and harming enemies; a study in
SOPHOCLES and Greek ethics. C 1989, Univ. xii-298 p. 0-521-35116-2.
a819 **Böhme** Gernot,   Der Typ Sokrates. Fra 1988, Suhrkamp. 222 p. –
ᴿTPhil 64 (1989) 409-411 (H.-L. *Ollig*).
a820 *Bompaire* Jacques,   Le sacré dans les discours d'Aelius ARISTIDE
(XLVII-LII Keil): RÉG 102 (1989) 28-39.
a821 ᴱ**Bremmer** J.,   Interpretations of Greek mythology [10-40, *Burkert*
Walter, Oriental parallels] 1987 → 3,b99: ᴿHistRel 29 (1989s) 58-64 (C.
Grottanelli); StPatav 36 (1989) 165-8 (F. *Mora*).
a822 **Broek** R. Van den, *al.*,   Knowledge of God in the Graeco-Roman world:
ÉPR 112, 1988 → 4,b712: ᴿClasR 39 (1989) 401 (A. H. *Armstrong*).
a823 *Bruit* Louise,   Les dieux aux festins des mortels; théoxénies et *xeniai*:
→ 796, Polythéismes 1989, 13-24; Eng. 25.
a824 *Brulé* Pierre,   La fille d'Athènes... religion 1987 → 4,b713: ᴿAntClas 58
(1989) 405-7 (Vinciane *Pirenne-Delforge*); ÉTRel 64 (1989) 603s (Jacky
Argaud); RÉG 102 (1989) 208 (Yvonne *Vernière*).
a825 **Buchheim** Thomas,   Die Sophistik als Avantgarde normalen Lebens. Ha
1986, Meiner. ix-164 p. – ᴿGnomon 61 (1989) 147s (C. J. *Claassen*).
a826 *Buck* Robert J.,   Mycenaean human sacrifice: Minos 24 (1989) 131-7.
a827 **Burkert** Walter,   Ancient mystery cults 1987 → 3,b103; 4,b715: ᴿAJA
93 (1989) 297s (S. *Johnston*); AmJPg 110 (1989) 658-660 (B. M. *Metzger*);
ChH 58 (1989) 983s (R. M. *Grant*); ClasJ 84 (1988s) 167 (H. A.
Pohlsander); ClasR 39 (1989) 58-61 (B. C. *Dietrich*); Gnomon 61 (1989)
289-292 (F. E. *Brenk*); HZ 248 (1989) 401s (R. *Merkelbach*); RHR 206
(1989) 291-5 (R. *Turcan*); TS 50 (1959) 200s (D. G. *Hunter*).

a828 **Burkert** Walter, Greek religion, archaic and classical 1985 → 1,a464...
4,b716: ᴿHeythJ 30 (1989) 99 (J. *Ferguson*: will now become the standard
handbook).

a829 **Burkert** Walter, Die orientalisierende Epoche in der griechischen
Religion und Literatur: Szb Heid 1984/1 → 2,8864... 4,b718: ᴿAnzAltW
42 (1989) 42-44 (K. H. *Kinzl*); Gymnasium 96 (1989) 158-160 (P.
Habermehl).

a830 *a*) *Burkert* Walter, *Katagōgia-anagōgia* and the goddess of Knossos; – *b*)
Parker Robert, Demeter, Dionysus and the Spartan pantheon; – *c*)
Mazarakis Ainian A. J., Early Greek temples; their origin and function; –
d) *Romano* Irene B., Early Greek cult images and cult practices: → 792,
Greek cult 1986/8, 81-88 / 99-103 / 105-119 / 127-134.

a831 ᴱ**Calame** Claude, Métamorphoses du mythe en Grèce antique: Religions
et perspectives 4, 1988 → 4,b719: ᴿEsprVie 99 (1989) 351s (L. *Debarge*);
RTPhil 121 (1989) 442s (S. *Imhoof*).

a831* *Camps i Gaset* Montserrat, La felicitat humana segons EPICTET:
→ 69*, ᶠGOMÀ I., RCatalT 14 (1989) 493-8; Eng. 498.

a832 *a*) *Connelly* Joan B., Votive offering from Hellenistic Failaka; evidence
for Heracles cult; – *b*) *Callot* Olivier, Failaka à l'époque hellénistique; –
c) *Teixidor* Javier, À propos d'une inscription araméenne de Failaka
[Ekarra, temple de Dilmun]; – *d*) *Petersmann* Hubert, Le culte du soleil
chez les Arabes selon les témoignages gréco-romains: → 816, L'Arabie
1987/9, 145-158; 28 fig. / 127-143; 6 fig. / 169-171; 1 pl. / 401-412.

a833 *Davison* Jean W., Egyptian influence on the Greek legend of Io: → 859,
Delta 1988/9, 61-74; discussion 75-79.

a834 **Descat** Raymond, L'acte et l'effort; une idéologie du travail en Grèce
ancienne (VIIIᵉ-Vᵉ s. av. J.-C.): Univ. Besançon, Annales litt. 339 (hist.
73). P 1986, BLettres. 342 p. 2-251-60339-5. – ᴿAntClas 58 (1989) 449
(G. *Raepsaet*).

a835 **Dietrich** Bernard C., Tradition in Greek religion 1986 → 2,8872...
4,b728: ᴿClasR 39 (1989) 51-58 (C. *Sourvinou-Inwood*); WienerSt 102
(1989) 279s (Christine *Harrauer*).

a837 **Dörrie** H., Platonismus I, 1987 → 3,b117; 4,b734: ᴿJTS 40 (1989) 239-2
(C. *Stead*).

a838 **Durand** Jean-Louis, Sacrifice et labour en Grèce ancienne; essai
d'anthropologie religieuse 1986 → 3,b118: ᴿClasPg 84 (1989) 149-151
(Anne *Burnett*); JRel 68 (1988) 620s (V. *Valeri*).

a839 **Edlund** Ingrid E. M., The gods and the place; location and function of
sanctuaries in the countryside of Etruria and Magna Graecia (700-400
B.C.): Svenska Inst. Rom 43. Sto 1987, Åström. 156 p.; 16 fig.; 16 plans.
– ᴿAJA 93 (1989) 299s (R. R. *Holloway*).

a840 **Erbse** Hartmut, Untersuchungen zur Funktion der Götter im
homerischen Epos 1986 → 2,8875... 4,b735: ᴿJHS 109 (1989) 208s (B. C.
Dietrich).

a841 **Erskine** Andrew, The Hellenistic Stoa; political thought and action: diss.
Oxford 1988, 361 p. BRD-84930. – DissA 50 (1989s) 229s-A.

a842 **Evans** Arthur, The god of ecstasy; sex-roles and the madness of
Dionysos. NY 1988, St. Martin's. 286 p.; 11 fig. $20. – ᴿClasR 39
(1989) 145 (R. *Seaford*).

a843 **Freyburger-Galland** M. L., *al.*, Sectes religieuses en Grèce et à Rome
dans l'antiquité 1986 → 2,8877... 4,b741: ᴿJRS 78 (1988) 207s (J.
Linderski).

a844 **Furley** David, [➤ 1999] Cosmic problems; essays on Greek and Roman philosophy of nature [essays during 20 years]. C 1989, Univ. xiv-258 p. 0-521-33330-X.

a845 **Gadamer** Hans-Georg,   The idea of the good in Platonic-Aristotelian philosophy [1974/6 'zwischen P und A' ➤ 58,d906], ᵀ*Smith* T. Christopher. NHv 1986, Yale Univ. xxxi-182 p. 0-300-03463-6; pa. 4114-4. – ᴿÉchMClas 33 (1989) 368-370 (Martha *Husayn*: too casual).

a846 *Gaiser* Konrad †,   Das Gold der Weisheit; zum Gebet des Philosophen am Schluss des Phaidros: RheinMus 132 (1989) 105-140.

a847 **Garland** Robert,   The Greek way of death 1985 ➤ 2,8880... 4,b743: ᴿSMSR 55 (1989) 171-4 (G. A. *Samonà*).

a848 **Graf** Fritz,   Nordionische Kulte; religionsgeschichtliche und epigraphische Untersuchungen zu den Kulten von Chios, Erythrai, Klazomenai und Phokaia: Bibl. Helv. Rom. 21, 1985 ➤ 2,8885: ᴿAnzAltW 42 (1989) 44-48 (G. *Radke*).

a849 ᴱ**Griswold** Charles L.,   Platonic writings, Platonic readings. L 1988, Routledge. xi-321 p. £25; pa. £12. – ᴿClasR 39 (1989) 252s (C. *Gill*).

a850 *Guerra* Manuel,   Antropología sexual en la antigüedad griega; la sexualidad y el amor como 'koinonía': ➤ 572, Masculinidad 1989, 287-421.

a851 **Guthrie** William,   I Greci e i loro dei [1954], ᵀ. Bo 1987, Mulino. – ᴿFilT 3 (1989) 225-7 (Giuliana *Scalera McClintock*).

a852 **Hager** Fritz-Peter,   Gott und das Böse im antiken Platonismus: Elementa 43 [➤ 3,b132]: Wü/Amst 1987, Königshausen/Rodopi. 165 p. – ᴿTPhil 64 (1989) 98 (F. *Ricken*).

a853 *Harrauer* Christine,   Meliouchos; Studien zur Entwicklung religiöser Vorstellungen in griechischen synkretistischen Zaubertexten: WienerSt Beih 11, 1987 3,b133: ᴿAntClas 58 (1989) 404s (Maryse *Waegeman*); ClasR 39 (1989) 62s (J. G. *Griffiths*).

a854 *Herrmann* Peter,   Rom und die Asylie griechischer Heiligtümer; eine Urkunde des Diktators Caesar aus Sardeis: Chiron 19 (1989) 127-158; 6 pl.

a855 ᴱ**Isnardi Parente** Margherita,   Stoici antichi: Classici della Filosofia. T 1989, UTET. I. 686 p. II. p. 683 (*sic*)-1311. 88-02-04318-3.

a856 **Jürss** Fritz,   Vom Mythos der alten Griechen; Deutungen und Erzählungen: Universalbibliothek 1230. Lp 1988, Reclam. 213 p.; 22 fig. M 2,50. – ᴿDLZ 110 (1989) 668-670 (Zs. *Ritoók*); TLZ 114 (1989) 260s (G. *Haufe*).

ᴱ**Kraemer** R. S.,   Maenads, martyrs, matrons, monastics; a sourcebook on women's religions in the Greco-Roman world [135 texts 300 B.C.-500 A.D. translated] 1988 ➤ 482.

a858 **Lamberton** Robert,   Homer the theologian; Neoplatonist allegorical reading and the growth of the epic tradition 1986 ➤ 3,b140; 4,b757: ᴿAntClas 58 (1989) 239s (Monique *Mund-Dopchie*).

a859 **Lefkowitz** Mary R.,   Women in Greek myth 1986 ➤ 3,b141; 4,b758: ᴿPhoenix 43 (Toronto 1989) 165-9 (Jane *Cahill*, also on LORAUX N.).

a860 *Lindner* Ruth, *al.*,   Hades: ➤ 951, LIMC 4 (1989) 167-406; phot. p. 209-235.

a861 **Long** A. A., *Sedley* D. N.,   The Hellenistic philosophers I-II, 1987 ➤ 3,b142; 4,b759:   ᴿAncHRes 19 (1989) 113s (H. *Tarrant*); ClasR 39 (1989) 49-51 (G. B. *Kerferd*).

a862 **Luck** Georg,   Arcana Mundi... texts 1985 ➤ 2,8901; 3,b144: ᴿClasJ 84 (1988s) 168-170 (D. *Martinez*).

a863 **Lyons** Deborah J., Heroic configurations of the feminine in Greek myth and cult: diss. Princeton 1989. 282 p. 89-17762. – DissA 50 (1989s) 1296-A.

a864 *Maaskant-Kleibrink* Marianne, The stuff of which Greek heroines are made: Babesch 64 (1989) 1-49.

a865 ᴱMacDowell Douglas, Andokides, On the Mysteries. Ox 1989 = 1962, Clarendon. xii-223 p. 0-19-814692-2.

a866 **Malkin** Irad, Religion and colonization in ancient Greece: Studies in Greek and Roman Religion 3, 1987 ⇒ 4,b762: ᴿAntClas 58 (1989) 402-4 (Vinciane *Pirenne-Delforge*); ClasR 39 (1989) 271s (R. *Parker*); RÉG 102 (1989) 561-3 (C. *Rolley*).

a867 *Mansfeld* Jaap, Stoic definition of the good (Diog. LAERT. VII 94): Mnemosyne 42 (1989) 487-491 (88s: VII 92).

a868 **Manuwald** Bernd, Studien zum Unbewegten Beweger in der Naturphilosophie des Aristoteles: Abh. Mainz, geist/soz 1989/9. Mainz 1989, Akad. 130 p.

a869 **Maranhão** Tullio, Therapeutic discourse and Socratic dialogue; a cultural critique. Madison 1986, Univ. Wisconsin. xv-276 p. $22.50. – ᴿAmJPg 110 (1989) 161-4 (B. E. *Goldfarb*, also on STOKES M. 1986).

a870 **Martin** Luther H., Hellenistic religions, an introduction, 1987 ⇒ 3,b151; 4,b765: ᴿGreeceR 36 (1989) 252 (P. *Walcot*); HZ 248 (1989) 412-4 (F. *Graf*).

a871 *Mašlanka Soro* Maria, La legge del *pathei mathos* nel Prometeo incatenato di Eschilo: Sandalion 12s (1989s) 5-25.

a872 *a) Mauduit* Christine, Le sauvage et le sacré dans la tragédie grecque; – *b) Fromentin* Valérie, L'attitude critique de DENYS d'Halicarnasse face aux mythes; – *c) Boudon* Véronique, GALIEN et le sacré: BBudé (1988) 303-317 / 318-326 / 327-337.

a873 *Mertens* Michèle, Pourquoi Isis est-elle appelée *prophêtis*? : CdÉ 64 (1989) 260-6.

a874 **Molnar** Thomas, The pagan temptation [modern compared with pre-Christian Hellenism]. GR 1987, Eerdmans. 201 p. £9.50 (Paternoster). – ᴿThemelios 14 (1988s) 110 (L. H. *Osborn*).

a875 *Morris* Ian, Attitudes toward death in archaic Greece: ClasAnt 8 (1989) 296-320.

a876 *a) Motte* André, La catégorie platonicienne du démonique; – *b) Pirenne-Delforge* Vinciane, Eros en Grèce; dieu ou démon?; – *c) Vernière* Yvonne, Nature et fonction des démons chez PLUTARQUE: ⇒ 728, Anges 1987/9, 205-221 / 223-239 / 241-251.

a877 *a) Motte* André, L'expression du sacré chez PLATON; – *b) Gaudin* Claude, Rhétorique et dialectique à propos de l'opposition *phýsis-nómos* dans le Gorgias de Platon: RÉG 102 (1989) 10-27 / 308-330.

a878 **Muth** Robert, Einführung in die griechische und römische Religion. Da 1988, Wiss. XI-347 p. 3-534-03839-8. – ᴿArTGran 52 (1989) 345s (A. *Segovia*).

a879 **Naumann** Friederike, Die Ikonographie der Kybele in der phrygischen und der griechischen Kunst: IstMit 28, ᴰ1983 ⇒ 3,b160: ᴿBO 46 (1989) 724-8 (J. M. *Hemelrijk*).

a880 *a) Niemeier* Wolf-Dietrich, Zur Ikonographie von Gottheiten und Adoranten in den Kultszenen auf minoischen und mykenischen Siegeln; – *b) Marinatos* Nanno, The tree as a focus of ritual action in Minoan glyptic art; – *c) Sourvinou-Inwood* Christiane, Space in Late Minoan religious scenes in glyptic; some remarks: ➤ 858, Fragen 1985/9, 163-186; 6 fig. / 127-143; 22 fig. / 241-257; 4 fig.

a881 **Onians** Richard B., The origins of European thought about the body, the mind, the soul, the world, time and fate; new interpretations of Greek, Roman and kindred evidence, also of some basic Jewish and Christian beliefs [1951, ²1953]. C 1988, Univ. xviii-583 p. £35; first pa. £12.50. 0-521-35122-7; 4794-7. – ᴿAntClas 58 (1989) 383s (R. *Joly*: classique d'érudition et de cohérence d'interprétation).

a882 *Papadis* Dimitris,   Der Begriff der Seele bei PLATON zwischen Dialektik und Mythos: Eranos 87 (1989) 21-32.

a883 *a) Parise* Nicola F.,   Sacrificio e misura del valore nella Grecia antica; – *b) Lissarague* François, (Schmitt) *Pantel* Pauline,   Spartizione e comunità nei banchetti greci,   ᵀ*Scheid* J.; – *c) Durand* Jean-Louis,   Sacrificare, dividere, ripartire: – *d) Detienne* Marcel,   I limiti della spartizione, ᵀ*Molinari* M.:   ➤ 790*, Sacrificio 1983/8, 253-265 / 211-229 / 193-202 / 177-191.

a884 **Parke** H. W.,   Athenische Feste 1987 ➤ 4,b784:   ᴿAulaO 7,1 (1989) 141-3 (M. *Camps-Gaset*); HZ 249 (1989) 133s (W. *Burkert*).

a884* **Parke** H. W.,†,   Sibyls and Sibylline prophecy in classical antiquity, ᴱ*McGing* B. C.: Croom Helm Clas. St. L 1988, Routledge. ix-236 p. £25. – ᴿJHS 109 (1989) 241 (R. A. *Tomlinson*).

a885 **Patzer** Andreas,   Der Sophist Hippias als Philosophiehistoriker.   FrB 1986, Alber. 128 p.

a886 *Petrioli* Emiliana,   Il mito del Minotauro; un'interpretazione storico-religiosa: StClasOr 29 (1989) 203-256.

a886* *Places* Édouard des,   Chronique de la philosophie religieuse des Grecs (1987-1989): BBudé (1989) 406-426.

a887 *Pochmarski* Erwin,   Motiv- und Typengeschichte dionysischer Gruppen: MGraz 2 (1988) 198-219; pl. 14-18.

a887* *Poe* Joe P.,   The altar in the fifth-century theater: ClasAnt 8 (1989) 116-139.

a888 ᴱ**Puech** Henry-Charles,   Le religioni nel mondo classico [1970-6]ᵀ: Storia e Società.   R 1987, Laterza. 349 p. 88-420-2818-5.

a889 *Pugliese Carratelli* Giovanni,   La *theá* di Parmenide: ParPass 43 (1988) 337-346 (L'intero volume, fasc. 238-243, contiene articoli su Parmenide in vista di un convegno 'Marina di Ascea' 5-7.VI.1989).

a890 ᴱ**Raffaelli** Renato,   Rappresentazioni della morte: Letteratura e Antropologia 1.   Urbino 1987, Quattro Venti. 257 p.; 10 fig. Lit. 25.000 pa. – ᴿClasR 39 (245-7 (R. *Garland*).

a891 **Reesor** Margaret E.,   The nature of man in early Stoic philosophy. L 1989, Duckworth. ix-179 p. 0-7156-2256-0.

a891* **Regen** Frank,   Formlose Formen — PLOTINS Philosophie als Versuch, die Regressprobleme des platonischen PARMENIDES zu lösen: NachGö ph/h 1988. Gö 1988, Vandenhoeck & R. 51 p.

a892 **Romilly** Jacqueline de,   Les grands sophistes dans l'Athènes de Périclès. P 1988, de Fallois. 335 p. 2-87706-003-9.

a893 *Rose* Joseph J.,   The concept of *aretē* in PLUTARCH's Parallel Lives: diss. State Univ. NJ, ᴰ*Tripolitis* Antonia. New Brunswick 1988. 188 p. 88-27388. – DissA 49 (1988s) 3018-A.

a894 *Sackett* Hugh, *MacGillivray* Sandy,   Boyhood of a god; statuette found in Crete suggests Minoan link to classical mythology: Archaeology 42,5 (1989) 26-31; ill.

a895 ᴱSaffrey H. D., *Westerink* L. G., PROCLUS, Théologie platonicienne 5: Coll Budé. P 1987, BLettres. ciii-226 (d.) p. – ᴿClasR 39 (1989) 206s (L. *Siorvanes*).

a896 **Salmona** B., Le spiritualità dell'antica Grecia: ➤ 907, Spiritualità non cristiana 3, 1986 ➤ 3,b180: ᴿRHE 84 (1989) 257 (R. *Aubert*).

a897 **Santas** Gerasimos, PLATO and FREUD, two theories of love. Ox 1988, Blackwell. xi-195 p. £25. – ᴿClasR 39 (1989) 255s (C. *Gill*).

a898 ᴱ**Savino** Ezio, Platone, Apologia di Socrate, Critone, Fedone, il Convito¹², ᵀ*Marziano* Nino [¹1975/81]: I grandi libri 135. Mi 1988, Garzanti. xxv-262 p. 88-11-58135-7.

a898* *a) Scheid* John, La spartizione sacrificale a Roma; – *b) Santini* Carlo, Il lessico della spartizione nel sacrificio romano: ➤ 790*, Sacrificio 1983/8, 267-292 / 293-302.

a899 **Sergent** Bernard, Homosexuality in Greek myth [1984 ➤ 65,9209], ᵀ*Goldhammer* Arthur 1987 ➤ 3,b188: ᴿJRel 68 (1988) 485-7 (J. *Boswell*: dubious).

a900 **Sfameni Gasparro** Giulia, Misteri e culti mistici di Demetra: Storia delle religioni 3, 1986 ➤ 4,b796: ᴿClasR 39 (1989) 61-s (Emily *Kearns*).

a901 **Sfameni Gasparro** Giulia, Soteriology and mystic aspects in the cult of Cybele and Attis [1979]: ÉPR 103, 1985 ➤ 1,a522; $20 pa.: ᴿSecC 7 (1989s) 118-120 (L. M. *White*).

a902 ᴱ**Sørensen** Jørgen P., Rethinking religion; studies in the Hellenistic process [symposium for U. *Bianchi*, K Apr. 1984]: Opuscula Graecolatina 30. K 1989, Museum Tusculanum. 101 p. 87-7289-079-7.

a903 *Sogomonov* A. Yu., ⓖ Oriental sources of early Greek culture after the studies of Walter BURKERT; VDI 191 (1989) 146-155.

a904 *Stol* M., Greek *deiktērion*: the lying-in-state of Adonis [< *kulkumu*; *taklimtu* 'display' of the body of Tammuz]: ➤ 78, ᶠHEERMA VAN VOSS M., Funerary 1988, 127s.

a905 *a) Straten* Folkert van, The god's portion in Greek sacrificial representations; is the tail doing nicely? – *b) Clinton* Kevin, Sacrifice at the Eleusinian Mysteries; – *c) Cole* Susan G., The uses of water in Greek sanctuaries: ➤ 792, Greek cult 1986/8, 51-68 / 69-80 / 161-5 (167-71, *Tomlinson* R.).

a906 **Sutton** D. F., Papyrological studies in Dionysiac literature; P. Lit. Lond. 77, a post-classical satyr play; and P. Ross. Georg. 1.11, a hymn to Dionysus. Oak Park IL 1987, Bolchazy-Carducci. 106 p. $30; pa. $15. 0-86516-197-6; 8-4 [NTAbs 33,135].

a907 ᴱ**Tobin** Thomas H., TIMAIOS of Locri, On the nature of the world and the soul: SBL TTr 8, 1985: ᴿSecC 7 (1989s) 120s (R. F. *Hock*).

a908 *Trombley* Frank, Prolegomena to the systemic analysis of Late Hellenic religion; the case of the aretalogy of Isis at Kyme: ➤ 592, Systemic 1 (1989) 95-113.

a909 *Vernant* Jean-Pierre, Artémis et le sacrifice préliminaire au combat: RÉG 101 (1988) 221-239.

a910 *a) Vernière* Yvonne, Les deux pôles du sacré chez PLUTARQUE; – *b) Bompaire* Jacques, Le sacré dans les discours d'Aelius ARISTIDE: ➤ 786, Écrivains/Sacré 1988/9, 273s / 275s.

a910* **Vernon-Hunt** Sarah, Minoan religion; a comparative analysis of the cult material from a sample of shrine sites in Bronze Age Crete: diss. Bristol 1988. 730 p. BRDX-85241. – DissA 50 (1989s) 474-A.

a911 **Véron** Robert, PLATON; une introduction à la vie de l'esprit. P 1987, BLettres. 209 p. ᴿRÉG 102 (1989) 249s (Véronique *Boudon*).

a912 ᴱVersnel H.S., Faith, hope and worship; aspects of religious mentality in the ancient world: Studies in Greek and Roman Religion 2, 1981 ➤ 63,9234: ᴿRelStR 15 (1989) 163 (J.M. *Sasson*).

a913 *Vogel* Joseph, EPICTÈTE et son dieu: ÉchSM 19 (1989) 96-100.

a914 **Waegeman** Maryse, Amulet and alphabet; magical amulets in the first book of CYRANIDES. Amst 1987, Gieben. 231 p. – ᴿSalesianum 51 (1989) 149 (B. *Amata*).

a915 **Warren** Peter, Minoan religion as ritual action [Neubergh Lecture 1986]: SIMA pocket 72. Göteborg 1988, Univ. 39 p.

a916 **Wasson** R.Gordon *al.*, The road to Eleusis; unveiling the secret of the mysteries. NY 1978, Harcourt-BJ. 126 p.: ᴿRÉG 102 (1989) 563s (Hélène *Cassimatis*).

a917 ᵀᴱ**Waterfield** Robin, The theology of arithmetic; on the mystical, mathematical and cosmological symbolism of the first ten numbers, attributed to IAMBLICHUS; pref. *Chrichtlow* Keith. GR 1988, Phanes. 130 p. $25; pa. $14. – ᴿClasR 39 (1989) 266s (I. *Bulmer-Thomas*: well done).

a917* **Weber** Frans Josef, Fragmente der Vorsokratiker: Uni-Tb 1485. Pd 1988, Schöningh. 304 p. DM 14,80. – ᴿClasR 39 (1989) 250-2 (D.W. *Graham*: called first edition, but clearly a reworking of 1964 and 1976).

a918 **Wendell** Laura K., Aspects of *nómos* in the Histories of HERODOTUS; patterns of aggression and restraint: diss. ᴰ*Wallace* M. Toronto 1989. – DissA 50 (1989s) 1770-A.

a919 **Yunis** Harvey, A new creed; fundamental religious beliefs in the Athenian polis and Euripidean drama: Hypomnemata 91. Gö 1988, Vandenhoeck & R. 188 p. 3-525-25190-4.

M5.5   Religiones anatolicae.

a920 *Beckman* Gary, The religion of the Hittites: BA 52 (1989) 98-108; ill.

a921 *Bernabé* A., Generaciones de dioses y sucesión interrumpida; el mito hitita de Kumarbi, la 'Teogonía' de Hesíodo y la del 'Papiro de Derveni': AulaO 7 (1989) 159-181.

a922 *a*) de *Martino* Stefano, L'atto di 'baciare' nel culto e nella vita quotidiana degli Ittiti: – *b*) *Laroche* Emmanuel, Observations sur le rituel anatolien provenant de Meskéné-Émar; – *c*) *Masson* Emilia, La formule 'aimé des dieux' dans les hiéroglyphes louvites; – *d*) *Polvani* Anna Maria, Un oggetto del culto ittita, (*giš*) *zahurti*: ➤ 154, ᶠPUGLIESE CARRATELLI G., 57-65 / 111-7 / 147-153 / 209-219.

a923 *Haas* V., Magie und Zauberei B. bei den Hethitern: ➤ 905, RLA 7,3s (1988) 234-255.

a924 *a*) *Haas* Volkert, Die hurritisch-hethitischen Rituale der Beschwörerin Allaituraḫ(ḫ)i und ihr literarhistorischer Hintergrund; – *b*) *Wegner* Ilse, Grammatikalische und lexikalische Untersuchungen hurritischer Beschwörungsformeln aus Boğazköy: ➤ 817*, Hurriter 1988, 117-143 / 145-155.

a925 **Hutter** M., Behexung, Entsühnung und Heilung; das Ritual der Tunnawiya für ein Königspaar aus mittelhethitischer Zeit (KBo XXI 1 – KUB IX 34 – KBo XXI 6): OBO 82, 1988 ➤ 4,b815: ᴿBL (1989) 29 (J.F. *Healey*); ZAss 89 (1989) 293-7 (P. *Taracha*).

a926 **Jacob-Rost** Liane, Hethitische Rituale und Festbeschreibungen: KUB 59. B 1989, Akademie. x + 50 pl. 3-05-000710-9.

a927 **Loon** Maurits van, Anatolia in the second millennium B.C.: IconRel 15/12, 1985 ➤ 3,b222: ᴿBO 46 (1989) 158-165 (Jeanny V. *Canby*); OLZ 84 (1989) 33-35 (K. *Bittel*).

a928 **Masson** Emilia, Les douze dieux de l'immortalité; croyances indo-européennes à Yazilikaya: Vérité des mythes. P 1989, BLettres. x-231 p.; 32 pl.; map. F 150. 2-251-32417-8. – ᴿRÉLat 67 (1989) 368s (J. *Haudry*).

a929 **Popko** Maciej, Keilschrifturkunden aus Boghazköy 58, Hethitische Rituale 1988 ➤ 4,b824: ᴿOrAnt 28 (1989) 163-7 (G. F. *Del Monte*); Orientalia 58 (1989) 557-9 (Inge *Hoffmann*) ➤ e549*.

a930 **Popko** Maciej, ❷ Mitologia hetyckiej Anatolii. Wsz 1987, Artystyczne. 206 p. 83-221-0103-1 [OIAc Ja90].

a931 **Popko** Maciej, ❷ *Wierzenia* ... Beliefs of the peoples of ancient Asia Minor. Wsz 1989, Młodzieżowa. 171 p.; 15 color. pl. 83-203-2972-8 [OIAc Ja90].

a932 *a) Popko* M., Die Götter von Zippalanda; – *b) Arešjan* G., Éléments indoeuropéens dans la mythologie du Plateau Arménien et du Caucase du Sud au IIᵉ mil. av. J.-C.; – *c) Voos* J., Bemerkungen zum syrohethitischen Totenkult der frühen Eisenzeit: ➤ 874, Šulmu 1986/8, 273-285 / 19-37; 10 fig. / 349-360.

a933 **Vermaseren** M. J., Corpus cultus Cybelae Attidisque I. Asia Minor: ÉPR 50, 1987 ➤ 3,b230: ᴿRArchéol (1989) 186s (R. *Turcan*).

a934 **Woodley** Mary Sue, The sacred precincts of Cybele [first around Karkamiš, spreading to Phrygia ...]: diss. UCLA 1989, ᴰ*Downey* Susan B. 247 p. 89-08587. – DissA 50 (1989s) 720-A.

a935 **Zinko** Christian, Betrachtungen zum AN TAH SUN –Fest (Aspekte eines hethitischen Festrituals: Scientia 8. Innsbruck 1987, Scientia 1010-612X [OIAc S89].

M6   Religio canaanaea, syra.

a935* *Acquaro* Enrico, Il tempio nella colonizzazione fenicia: ➤ 811, Momenti 1985/8, 187-9.

a936 **Amir** David, ❺ Gods and heroes; Canaanite epics from Ugarit 1986 ➤ 2,8953; 4,b829: ᴿCBQ 51 (1989) 703s (F. E. *Greenspahn*).

a937 **Barker** Margaret, The older testament ... royal cult 1987 ➤ 3,b237; 4,b836: ᴿInterpretation 43 (1989) 196s (K. C. *Hanson*); ScotJT 42 (1989) 256s (C. *Rowland*).

a938 *a) Bechmann* U., Aschera; – *b) Rauschenbach* B., Astarte; – *c) Röllig* W., Baal: ➤ 902, NBL, Lfg. 2 (1989) 184-6 / 193-5 / 223.

a939 **Block** Daniel I., The gods of the nations; studies in Ancient Near Eastern national theology: [J]EvTS Mg 2. Jackson MI 1988, EvTS. xlv-214 p. $14. 0-932055-02-8.

a940 **Bonnet** Corinne, Melqart; cultes et mythes de l'Héraclès tyrien en Méditerranée: Bibl. Ph/lett Namur 69/StPhoen 8, 1988 ➤ 4,b839; Fb 2950: ᴿGnomon 61 (1989) 142-7 (W. *Huss*); Orientalia 58 (1989) 567-9 (Anna Maria *Bisi* †).

a941 *Bonnet* C., Le dieu solaire Shamash dans le monde phénico-punique: StEpL 6 (1989) 97-115 [< ZAW 102,285].

a942 *Bonnet* C., L'onomastique de Melqart; en appendice, l'inscription punique CIS, 1,4612: RStFen 8 (1989) 31-40; pl. V.

a943 *Brzegowy* Tadeusz, ❷ Théophanies dans les sanctuaires d'Israël: AtKap 112 (1989) 39-53.

a944 **Caquot** A., *Tarragon* J.-M. [*Cunchillos* J.-L.], Textes religieux, Rituels [Correspondance]: Textes Ougaritiques [1. c. 1974] 2 / LAPO 14. P 1989, Cerf. 478 p. 2-204-02916-5 [BL 90,118, A. *Curtis*].

a945 *Carlson* R. A., (svensk) Templum et somnium: SvEx 54 (1989) 50-56.

a946 FCROSS Frank M., Ancient Israelite religion, EMiller P. D., *al.*, 1987 ➤ 3,42; 4,b842: RBO 46 (1989) 121-3 (M. J. *Mulder*); JRel 68 (1988) 581s (B. *Halpern*); OTAbs 12 (1989) 106-9 (T. P. *McCreesh*).

a947 **Daum** W., Ursemitische Religion 1985 ➤ 1,a566; 2,8957: RRSO 62 (1988) 152-4 (G. *Garbini*).

a948 **Day** John, Molech, a god of human sacrifice in the Old Testament: Oriental Publ. 41. C 1989, Univ. ix-115 p. 0-521-36474-4.

a949 *Dietrich* Manfried, Das Einsetzungsritual der Entu von Emar (Emar VI/3, 369): UF 21 (1989) 47-100.

a950 *Dijk* Jacobus van, The Canaanite god Ḥauron and his cult in Egypt: GöMiszÄg 107 (1989) 59-68.

a951 **Drijvers** H. J. W., Cults and beliefs at Edessa: ÉPR 82, 1980 ➤ 61,m155... 3,b243: ROLZ 84 (1989) 183-6 (J. *Oelsner*).

a952 *Fauth* Wolfgang, Hierodulie: ➤ 904, RAC 15,113 (1989) 73-78 [79-82, *Stritzky* Maria-Barbara von, Christlich (auch AT)].

a953 **Grosby** Steven E., Religion and nationality; the worship of Yahweh and ancient Israel: diss. Chicago 1989. – OIAc Ja90.

a954 *Gross* Walter, YHWH und die Religionen der Nicht-Israeliten: TüTQ 169 (1989) 34-44.

a955 **Heider** George C., The cult of Molek 1985 ➤ 1,a572... 4,b857: RHeythJ 30 (1989) 185s (J. *Blenkinsopp*).

a956 **Hubmann** Axel F., Betyl. W 1978.

a957 *Hübner* Ulrich, Das Fragment einer Tonfigurine vom Tell el-Milḥ; Überlegungen zur Funktion der sog. Pfeilerfigurinen in der israelitischen Volksreligion: ZDPV 105 (1989) 47-55; pl. 7.

a958 KOCH Klaus (60. Gb.), [seine] Studien zur alttestamentlichen und altorientalischen Religionsgeschichte, EOtto E. 1988 ➤ 4,212: RBL (1989) 109 (P. R. *Ackroyd*).

a959 *Lang* Bernhard, Der vergöttlichte König im polytheistischen Israel: ➤ 769, Menschwerdung 1986/9, 37-59.

a960 *LaRocca* Elizabeth C., Archaeology and 'Asherah: BToday 27 (1989) 288-292.

a961 **Lewis** Theodore J., Cults of the dead in ancient Israel and Ugarit: HarvSemMg 39. Atlanta 1989, Scholars. xv-230 p. $21; sb. $14. 1-55540-325-5 [BL 90,105, N. *Wyatt*].

a962 *Lipiński* E., ṣāpôn '(Baal) Saphon': ➤ 913, TWAT 6,6s (1989) 1094-1102.

a963 **Maier** Walter A.III, Ašerah [diss. 1984] 1986 ➤ 2,8974; 4,b865: RÉTRel 64 (1989) 106s (D. *Lys*: savant et facile); JNES 48 (1989) 140s (Diana *Edelman*); JTS 40 (1989) 168-171 (J. F. *Healey*).

a964 *Margalit* Baruch, *a*) Some observations on the inscription and drawing from Khirbet el-Qôm: VT [37 (1987) 39-49, *Hadley* Judith] 39 (1989) 370-8; – *b*) KTU 1.92 (Obv.); a Ugaritic theophagy: AulaO 7,1 (1989) 67-80; 1 fig.

a965 **Moor** Johannes C., An anthology of religious texts from Ugarit / [with *Spronk* K.] A cuneiform anthology... 1987 ➤ 3,b265a; 4,a347: RBO 46 (1989) 681-3 (F. C. *Fensham* refers only 'Anthology' to Religious Texts Translation Series Nisaba 16; 'Cuneiform Anthology' to Semitic Studies 6); ÉTRel 64 (1989) 270s (D. *Lys*).

a966 *North* Robert, Yahweh's Asherah: → 60, ᶠFITZMYER J., Touch 1989, 118-137; 4 fig.

a967 **Nunes Carreira** José, Estudos de cultura pré-clássica; religião e cultura na antiguidade oriental: Biblioteca de textos universitários 76, 1985 → 1,222: ᴿRB 95 (1988) 439s (F. J. *Gonçalves*).

a968 *Olmo Lete* G. del, *a*) Anatomía cultual en Ugarit; ofrenda de visceras en el culto ugarítico; – *b*) Liturgía sacrificial y salmodía en Ugarit (KTU 1,119); – *c*) Rituales sacrificiales de plenilunio y novilunio (KTU 1.109/1.46): AulaO 7,1 (1989) 123-5 / 27-35; Eng. 27 / 181-8.

a969 **Olyan** Saul, Ashera and the cult of Yahweh in Israel 1988 → 4,b871: ᴿRB 96 (1989) 584-8 (E. *Puech*).

a970 *Otzen* Benedikt, Inskrifterne fra Kuntillet Ajrud; tekst – form – funktion: SvEx 54 (1989) 151-164.

a971 *Pardee* Dennis, An evaluation of the proper names from Ebla from a West Semitic perspective; pantheon distribution according to genre: → 831, Eblaite names 1985/8, 119-151.

a972 **Ribichini** Sergio, Il Tofet e il sacrificio dei fanciulli: Atlante Sardegna Fen. Pun. 2. Sassari 1987, Chiarella. 63 p. [OIAc N89].

a973 **Ringgren** Helmer, Die Religionen des Alten Orients [1979] ᵀ*Klaus-Credé* H. B 1987, Ev.-V. 255 p. M 10,80. – ᴿTLZ 114 (1989) 180s (K.W. *Tröger*).

a974 *Ringgren* Helmer, (*Kornfeld* W.), *qôdœš*, 'heilig' usw.: → 913, TWAT 6,8s (1989) 1179-1204.

a975 *Sarianidi* V.I., ⊕ Syro-Hittite deities in Bactria and Margiana: SovArch (1989,4) 17-24; Eng. 24.

a976 **Schroer Ammann** Silvia, Die Zweiggöttin in Palästina/Israel und ihr Nachleben im Alten Testament: kath.-Diss. FrS 1988s, ᴰ*Keel* O. – TR 85 (1989) 511.

a977 **Segarra Crespo** Diana, La ofrenda en Ebla; el caso de MUL: diss. M 1989, Univ. Complutense. 493 p.

a978 *Stern* Ephraim, What happened to the cult figurines? Israelite religion purified after the Exile [two *favissae*, pits containing cult-statues, were found at Tel Dor]: BAR-W 15,4 (1989) 22-29.53s; color. ill.; map.

a979 **Talmon** S., King, cult, and calendar in ancient Israel 1986 → 2,227; 3,2695: ᴿJNES 48 (1989) 44s (Diana *Edelman*: in English, 2 new from Hebrew and 2 from German).

a980 **Taylor** James G., Solar worship in the Bible and its world: diss. Yale, NHv 1989. 488 p. 90-11396. – DissA 50 (1989s) 3627-A.

a981 **Tigay** Jeffrey H., You shall have no other gods; Israelite religion in the light of Hebrew inscriptions: HarvSemSt 31, ᴰ1986 → 3,b276; 4,b879 [> Israelite Religion, ᶠCROSS 1987, 157-194]: ᴿBZ 33 (1989) 298s (H. *Niehr*); JTS 40 (1989) 143-6 (G. I. *Davies*).

a982 *Tsafrir* Yoram, Further evidence of the cult of Zeus Akraios at Beth Shean (Scythopolis): IsrEJ 39 (1989) 76-78; pl. 10c.

a983 **Tubach** Jürgen, Im Schatten des Sonnengottes... Edessa... Hatra 1986 → 2,3989... 4,b880: ᴿDLZ 109 (1988) 284s (B. *Brentjes*).

a984 *a*) *Waterston* Alastair, 'Death and resurrection in the A.B. cycle'; – *b*) *Loretz* O., Stelen und Sohnespflicht im Totenkult Kanaans und Israels; *skn* (KTU 1.17 I 26) und *jd* (Jes 56,5); – *c*) *Ribichini* Sergio, L'aruspicina fenicio-punica e la divinazione a Pafo [... Atti 13,6-11]; – *d*) *Soldt* W. H. van, *'Atn prln*, ''Attā/ēnu the diviner'; – *e*) *Wyatt* N., Quaternities in the mythology of Ba'al; – *f*) *Yon* Marguerite, Šḥr mt, la chaleur de Mot: UF 21 (1989) 425-434 / 241-6 / 307-317 / 365-8 / 451-9 / 461-6.

M6.5   Religio aegyptia.

a985 **Altenmüller** Brigitte, Synkretismus in den Sargtexten: GöOrF 4/7. Wsb 1975, Harrassowitz. viii-361 p. ⇒ 58,d057; 3-447-01662-0: ᴿWZKM 77 (1987) 139-146 (W. *Schenkel*: severe).

a986 **Armour** Robert A., Gods and myths of ancient Egypt 1986 ⇒ 2,8992: ᴿJNES 48 (1989) 235 (Rivkah *Harris*: enthusiastic, uncritical).

a987 *Armstrong* A. H., JAMBLIQUE et l'Égypte [... théurgie ancienne]: Études Philosophiques 42 (1987) 521-532 [< RSPT 73,126].

a987* **Assaad** Fawzia, Préfigurations égyptiennes de la pensée de NIETZSCHE; essai philosophique 1986 ⇒ 3,b285 ('-on -enne'): ᴿBO 46 (1989) 309-314 (Johanna *Schmitz*: her first chapter starts out 'Absurd project? Irrelevant?' but she provides analyses useful for Egyptologists).

a988 **Assmann** Jan, Re und Amun; die Krise des polytheistischen Weltbilds ...: OBO 51, 1983 ⇒ 64,9524 ... 3,b286: ᴿBO 46 (1989) 33-38 (D. van der *Plas*); RB 96 (1989) 439s (R. *Beaud*).

a989 *Banna* Essam el-, À propos des aspects héliopolitains d'Osiris: BIFAO 89 (1989) 101-126.

a990 **Barta** Winfried, Die Bedeutung der Jenseitsbücher für den verstorbenen König 1985 ⇒ 1,a594 (nicht 'Jenseitstexte'!): ᴿCdÉ 64 (1989) 189-192 (J. G. *Griffiths*).

a991 **Beinlich** Horst, Die 'Osirisreliquien' 1984 ⇒ 65,9295 ... 2,9001: ᴿOLZ 83 (1988) 405-7 (W. *Barta*); WeltOr 19 (1988) 156-9 (C. D. G. *Müller*).

a992 **Budge** E. A. Wallis, Egyptian religion; Egyptian ideas of the future life. L 1989 = 1889, Arkana. x-198 p. 1-85063-084-4.

a993 **Cauville** Sylvie, La théologie d'Osiris à Edfou 1983 ⇒ 64,9539 ... 3,b295: ᴿOLZ 83 (1988) 658-660 (L. *Kákosy*).

a994 *Clarysse* Willy, *al.*, The eponymous priests of Ptolemaic Egypt 1983 ⇒ 64,9540; 3,b300: ᴿWZKM 77 (1987) 147-155 (W. *Brunsch*).

a995 *Dembska* Albertyna, Papyrus Berlin P 3051 A and C [prayers]: ZägSpr 116 (1989) 9-36 [29-35 facsimile].

a996 **Derchain-Urtel** Maria-Theresia, Priester im Tempel; die Rezeption der Theologie der Tempel von Edfu und Dendera in den Privatdokumenten aus ptolemäischer Zeit: GöOrF 4/19. Wsb 1989, Harrassowitz. 276 p.; 2 inserts. 3-447-02867-X [OIAc N89].

a997 **Derchain-Urtel** Maria-Theresia, Thot à travers ses épithètes 1981 ⇒ 63,9325; 64,9544: ᴿJNES 48 (1989) 318s (M. *Smith*).

a998 *De Salvia* Fulvio, The Cypriots in the Saïte Nile Delta; the Cypro-Egyptian religious syncretism: ⇒ 859, Delta 1988/9, 81-113 + 15 fig.

a999 *a) Dolzani* Claudia, Aspetti e problemi del culto degli animali nella religione egiziana; – *b) Wessetzky* Vilmos, Tier, Bild, Gott; über die Affen des Thot; – *c) Shirun-Grumach* Irene, On 'revelation' in ancient Egypt: ⇒ 823, Akten IV 3 (1985/9) 231-240 / 425-430; pl. 6 / 379-384.

b1 *Donadoni Roveri* Anna Maria, Civiltà degli Egizi; le credenze religiose: Torino, Museo Egizio. Mi 1988, Electa. 261 p.; 343 color. fig.

b2 *Dunand* Françoise, Du séjour osirien des morts à l'au-delà chrétien; pratiques funéraires en Égypte tardive: Ktema 11 (1986) 29-37.

b3 *Fazzini* R. A., Egypt, Dynasty XXII-XXV: IconRel 16/10, 1988 ⇒ 4,b901: ᴿBL (1989) 124 (K. A. *Kitchen*); ÉTRel 64 (1989) 270 (D. *Lys*).

b4 **Fenoglio** Alberto, I misteri dell'antico Egitto; viaggio nella scienza e nei culti iniziatici degli Egizi: Manuali del Mistero e dell'Occulto 47. Padova 1989, MEB. 317 p.; ill. 88-7669-243-6 [OIAc S89].

b5 *Flis* Jan, ℗ Antidämonische Praktiken im alten Ägypten: RoczTK 33,1 (1986) 117-128; deutsch 129.

b6 *Förster* Dagmar, A late period statue of an overseer of priests of Horus of Hierakonpolis: GöMiszÄg 111 (1989) 47-51 + 3 fig.; 3 pl.

b7 **Gasse** Annie, Données nouvelles administratives et sacerdotales sur l'organisation du domaine d'Amon, XXᵉ-XXIᵉ dynasties, à la lumière des papyrus Prachov, Reinhardt et Grundbuch (avec édition princeps des papyrus Louvre AF 6345 et 6346-7]: BibÉt 104. Le Caire 1989, IFAO. x-274 p.; 105 pl. 2-7247-0070-8 [OIAc N89].

b8 **Gillar** Johannes, Symbol oder Fetisch? Ausgewählte Beispiele der kultischen Verehrung heiliger Gegenstände in der ägyptischen Religion [Magisterarbeit Heid 1989]. – OIAc S89.

b9 **Goyon** Jean-Claude, Les dieux-gardiens et la genèse des temples égyptiens (d'après les textes égyptiens d'époque gréco-romaine); les soixante d'Edfou et les soixante-dix-sept dieux de Pharbaethos: BÉt 93, 1985 ➤ 1,a612; 4,b905: ᴿJEA 75 (1989) 281-3 (J. G. *Griffiths*); Orientalia 58 (1989) 128s (L. *Kákosy*).

b10 *a) Goyon* Jean-Claude, Momification et recomposition du corps divin; Anubis et les Canopes; – *b) Zandee* J., Sargtexte, Sprüche 363-366 (Coffin Texts V 23-28); – *c) Janssen* J.J., Two Egyptian commandments [Book of the Dead...]; – *d) Borghouts* J.F., An early book of Gates, Coffin Texts, spell 336: ➤ 78, ꟳHEERMA VAN VOSS M., Funerary 1988, 34-44 / 165-182 / 52-59 / 12-22.

b11 *Grimm* Alfred, Der Tod im Wasser; rituelle Feindvernichtung und Hinrichtung durch Ertränken: StAltÄgK 16 (1989) 111-9; 3 fig.

b12 **Hart** George, A dictionary of Egyptian gods and goddesses 1986 ➤ 2,9024... 4,b907: ᴿAncHRes 19 (1989) 26s (B. *Ockinga*: excellent).

b13 ᴱ**Helck** Wolfgang, Tempel und Kult: ÄgAbh 46, 1986/7 ➤ 3,818.b313; 4,b908: ᴿBO 46 (1989) 300-2 (J.-C. *Goyon*).

b14 *a) Hölbl* Gunther, Wer ist König in der Endphase der ägyptischen Religion?; – *b) Velde* Herman te, Mut, the eye of Re; – *c) Sadek* Ashraf I., Les fêtes personnelles au Nouvel Empire: ➤ 823, Akten IV 3 (1985/9) 261-8 / 395-403 / 353-368.

b15 **Hoffmeier** James K., Sacred in the vocabulary of ancient Egypt... *dsr*: OBO 59, 1985 ➤ 1,a623... 3,b314: ᴿOLZ 84 (1989) 281s (L. *Kákosy*).

b16 **Hornung** Erik, Das Buch von den Pforten des Jenseits 1980 [II. 1984 ➤ 4,b912]: ᴿOLZ 84 (1989) 13-18 (Karin *Götte*).

b17 **Horst** Pieter W. van der, Chaeremon, Egyptian priest and Stoic philosopher: ÉPR 101, 1984 ➤ 65,9333... 4,b915: ᴿOLZ 84 (1989) 22-24 (L. *Kákosy*).

b18 **Junker** Hermann, Die Onurislegende [1917]; die Stundenwachen in den Osirismysterien [1910]; das Götterdekret über das Abaton [1913]: Denkschrift Wien 59,1s; 54,1; 56,4. Hildesheim 1988, Olms. x-169 + vi-127 + viii-188 p. 3-487-07995-X.

b19 *Kanawati* Naguib, The chronology of the overseers of priests at el-Qusiya in the Sixth Dynasty: GöMiszÄg 111 (1989) 75-80.

b20 **Kaplony-Heckel** Ursula [ᴱ*Lüddeckens* E.], Ägyptische Handschriften 3. [papyrus religieux de Berlin]: Verzeichnis Or. H. Deutschland 19/3, 1986 ➤ 2,7617*; DM 84. 3-515-02442-5: ᴿBO 46 (1989) 32s (M. *Patané*).

b21 **Koch** Klaus, Das Wesen altägyptischer Religion im Spiegel ägyptologischer Forschung: Jungius-Ges. 7/1. Ha 1989, J. Jungius Ges. Wiss. 106 p. 3-525-86239-3.

b22 **Kolansky** Roy D., Graeco-Egyptian magic lamellae; an introduction, corpus, and commentary on the phylacteries and amulets principally engraved on gold and silver: diss. ᴰ*Betz* H. Chicago 1988. xiv-718 p. (3 vol.). – OIAc N89.

b23 **Kruchten** Jean-Marie, Les annales des prêtres de Karnak (XXI-XXIIIᵐᵉˢ dynasties) et autres textes contemporains relatifs à l'initiation des prêtres d'Amon [archéol. *Zimmer* Thierry]: OrLovAn 32. Lv 1989, Univ. Dep. Oriëntalistiek.   viii-306 p.; 32 pl. Fb 1980. 90-6831-170-0 [BO 46,759].

b24 ᴱ**Lalouette** Claire, Textes sacrés et textes profanes de l'ancienne Égypte [I. 1984] II. Mythes, contes et poésies; introd. *Grimal* Pierre: Connaissance de l'Orient [54] 63. P 1987, Gallimard. 276 p. F 128. – ᴿEsprVie 99 (1989) 14 (C. *Jean-Nesmy*).

b25 **Lapp** Günther, Die Opferformel des Alten Reiches 1986 → 2,9034: ᴿOLZ 84 (1989) 399-401 (W. *Barta*).

b26 **Leclant** J., *Clerc* G., Inventaire bibliographique des Isiaca, L-Q: ÉPR 18, 1985 → 1,1087: ᴿBO 46 (1989) 72-74 (J. G. *Griffiths*); JEA 75 (1989) 285s (also J. G. *Griffiths*); OLZ 84 (1989) 658s (Ilse *Becher* †).

b27 **Lüscher** Barbara, Totenbuch Spruch I 1986 → 4,b922; KlÄgT, Wsb, Harrassowitz; x-74 p.; 3-447-02646-4: ᴿBO 46 (1989) 583 (H. *Milde*).

b28 **Mahdy** Christine el-, Mummies, myth and magic in ancient Egypt. L 1989, Thames & H. 192 p. 0-500-05055-4 [OIAc Ja90].

b29 *a) Meeks* Dimitri, Un manuel de géographie religieuse du Delta; – *b)* *Borghouts* Joris P., A new Middle Kingdom netherworld guide: → 823, Akten IV 3 (1985/9) 297-303 / 131-7 + 2 facsims.

b30 **Meyer** Gudrun, Untersuchungen zum Hirtenlied in den Gräbern des Alten Reiches: Mag.-Diss. Ha 1989, Univ. Archäol. Inst. 120 p. [OIAc Ja90].

b30* **Migahid** Abd-el-Gawad, Demotische Briefe an Götter, von der Spät- bis Römerzeit; ein Beitrag zur Kenntnis des religiösen Brauchtums im alten Ägypten: Diss. Würzburg 1987. – ᴿMundus 25 (1989) 30s (Renate *Müller-Wollermann*).

b31 **Müller** Hans W., Eine ungewöhnliche Metallfigur eines blinden ägyptischen Priesters: Szb Bayr. Akad. ph/h 1989/5. Mü 1989, Bayr. Akad. 33 p.

b32 **Myśliwiec** Karol, Eighteenth Dynasty before the Amarna period: IconRel 16/5. Leiden 1985, Brill. xi-31 p.: ᴿBO 46 (1989) 579-582 (Betsy M. *Bryan*).

b33 *Niwiński* Andrzej, *a)* Mummy in the coffin as the central element of iconographic reflection of the theology of the 21st Dynasty in Thebes: GöMiszÄg 109 (1989) 53-66; 10 fig.; 2 pl.; – *b)* The solar-Osirian unity as principle of the theology of the 'State of Amun' in Thebes in the 21st dynasty: JbEOL 30 (1987s) 89-106; 20 fig.

b33* *Nolli* Gianfranco, Sexualidad y corporeidad en el antiguo Egipto [*Cunchillos* J. L., ... en Ugarit]: → 572, Masculinidad 1989, 171-268 [269-286].

b34 *Plas* Dirk van der, 'Voir' Dieu — quelques observations au sujet de la fonction des sens dans le culte et la dévotion de l'Égypte ancienne: BSocFrÉg 115 (1989) 4-35; 11 fig.

b35 *Ramadan* Wagdy, Was there a chapel of Nehebkaw in Heliopolis?: GöMiszÄg 110 (1989) 55-61; 3 fig.; 4 phot.

b36 a) *Roccati* Alessandro, Concezioni rituali e terminologia sociale nell'antico Egitto; – b) *Pestman* P. W., Il patrimonio di una società di choachiti ['sacerdoti dei morti'] (Tebe, II secolo a. C.): ⮕ 877, Lavoro 1988, 73-78 / 111-127.

b37 *Rowell* Sheila, The Alexander cult and Ptolemaic ruler-worship: AncHRes 19 (1989) 82-86.

b38 **Ryhiner** Marie-Louise, L'offrande du Lotus dans les temples égyptiens d'époque tardive 1986 ⮕ 4,b930: ᴿBO 46 (1989) 302-7 (P. *Germond*).

b40 **Sauneron** Serge †, Les prêtres de l'ancienne Égypt²ʳᵉᵛ [¹1957] 1988 ⮕ 4,b932: ᴿÉTRel 64 (1989) 269 (Jacky *Argaud*).

b41 **Schumacher** Inke W., Der Gott Šopdu — der Herr der Fremdländer [< Diss.]: OBO 79, 1988 ⮕ 4,b933: ᴿBL (1989) 127 (K. A. *Kitchen*: 'authoress').

b42 **Schwarz** Fernand, Initiation aux Livres des Morts égyptiens: Spiritualités vivantes. P 1988, Michel. 248 p. F 45. – ᴿÉtudes 370 (1989) 373s (B. *Matray*).

b43 **Sternberg** Heike, Mythische Motive und Mythenbildung in den ägyptischen Tempeln und Papyri der griechisch-römischen Zeit [Diss. Tübingen]: GöOrFor 4/14, 1985 ⮕ 1,a656; 3,b340: ᴿJEA 75 (1989) 283-5 (J. G. *Griffiths*).

b44 *Störk* Lothar, Aurispizien III [Ohr und Seele]: GöMiszÄg 108 (1989) 65-74; 4 fig.; Kopt. Faksimile.

b45 **Stricker** B. H., De geboorte van Horus V: MedEOL 26. Leiden 1989, Ex Oriente Lux. p. 595-773. 90-72690-02-8.

b46 ᵀᴱ**Thissen** Heinz J., Die demotischen Graffiti von Medinet Habu; Zeugnisse zu Tempel und Kult im ptolemäischen Ägypten: Demotische Studien 10. Sommerhausen 1989, Zauzich. viii-264 p. 3-924151-03-2.

b47 **Tobin** Vincent A., Theological principles of Egyptian religion, pref. *Bonnel* Roland G.: AmerUnivSt 7/59. NY 1989, Lang. xix-223 p. Fs 59,60. 0-8204-1082-9 [OIAc Ja90].

b48 **Troy** Lana, Patterns of queenship in ancient Egyptian myth and history 1986 ⮕ 3,b344: ᴿBO 46 (1989) 43-49 (A. *Dodson*: erudite but a bit premature).

b49 *Valloggia* Michel, Le Papyrus Bodmer 107 ou les reliefs tardifs d'une conception de l'éternité: ⮕ 39, Mém. CLÈRE J., RÉgp 40 (1989) 131-144; 5 fig.; pl. 5; Eng. p. 144.

b50 **Van Siclen** Charles C.ᴵᴵᴵ, The alabaster shrine of King Amenhotep II, 1986 ⮕ 2,9052: ᴿBO 46 (1989) 53-55 (R. *Tefnin*).

b51 *Vernus* Pascal, L'eau sainte de Xois [Khois, ḫ3sww = t. Sakha; but the article is about a Saqqara amphora]: ⮕ 859, Delta 1988/9, 323-333 (-335, discussion).

b52 **Versluis** Arthur, The Egyptian mysteries: Arkana pa. L 1988, Routledge. vi-169 p. £ 4. – ᴿClasR 39 (1989) 402 (J. G. *Griffiths*).

b53 *Viola* Lucien, Deities and dignitaries in ancient Egyptian art. NY 1989, L'Ibis. 20 p. [OIAc N89].

b54 **Watterson** Barbara, The gods of ancient Egypt. L 1984, Batsford. 208 p.; 54 fig. $34. 0-7134-4523-8. – ᴿAncHRes 19 (1989) 27-29 (B. *Ockinga*: severe).

b55 a) *Westendorf* Wolfhart, Der Priestertitel wʿh ḫr(j)-s3; – b) *Scheel* Bernd, Ptaḥ und die Zwerge; – c) *Feucht* Erika, Der Weg des Verstorbenen bis zur Rechtfertigung nach Darstellungen in ramessidischen Gräbern: ⮕ 80, ᶠHELCK W. 1989, 189-193 / 159-164 / 23-34 + 5 fig.

b56 *Wimmer* S., Ägyptische Tempel in Kanaan und im Sinai: JbEvHL 1 (1989) 30-55 [< ZAW 102,278].

b57 *Wulleman* R., *al.*, Passage to eternity [a ramble in the Theban necropolis]. Knokke, Belgium 1989, Mappamundi. 191 p.

b58 *Yoyotte* Jean, Le roi Mer-Djefa-Ré et le dieu Sopdou; un monument de la XIVᵉ dynastie [...complexe question de théologie]: BSocFrÉg 114 (1989) 17-63; 14 fig.

M7 Religio mesopotamica.

b59 *Abusch* T., Maqlû ['burning' incantations; Eng.]: ➤ 905, RLA 7,5s (1989) 346-351.

b60 **Barucq** A., *al.*, Prières de l'Ancien Orient: Documents autour de la Bible. P 1989, Cerf. 99 p. F 53. 2-204-03085-6 [BL 90,118, N. *Wyatt*: rather '*hymns* and prayers', 18 Akkadian, 5 Ugaritic ...].

b61 **Behrens** Hermann, Enlil und Ninlil; ein sumerischer Mythos aus Nippur: StPohl 8, 1978 ➤ 58,d743; 61,m412: ᴿOLZ 84 (1989) 669s (H. *Neumann*).

b62 **Bottéro** Jean, Mésopotamie; l'écriture, la raison et les dieux [15 adapted reprints] 1987 ➤ 3,194: ᴿBO 46 (1989) 349-352 (H. *Freydank*); RB 95 (1988) 125s (R. *Tournay*).

b63 **Bottéro** Jean, Mythes et rites de Babylone 1985 ➤ 2,137; 3,b356: ᴿOLZ 84 (1989) 295s (B. *Alster*).

b64 **Bottéro** Jean, *Kramer* Samuel N., Lorsque les dieux faisaient l'homme; mythologie mésopotamienne: Bibliothèque des histoires. P 1989, Gallimard. 755 p. F 330. – ᴿRB 96 (1989) 596s (M. *Sigrist*).

b65 *Bottéro* Jean, Magie A: ➤ 905, RLA 7,3s (1988) 200-234.

b66 **Bruschweiler** Françoise, Inanna; la déesse triomphante et vaincue dans la cosmologie sumérienne; recherche lexicographique [diss. Genève 1986, ᴰ*Kramer* S.]: CEPOA Cah. 4. Lv 1987, Peeters. 233 p.

b67 **Charpin** Dominique, Le clergé d'Ur au siècle d'Hammurabi 1986 ➤ 2,9061 ... 4,b947: ᴿAfO 35 (1988) 191-7 (I. M. *Diakonoff*); JCS 41 (1989) 237-252 (M. Van De *Mieroop*).

b68 *a) Cooper* Jerrold S., Warrior, devastating deluge, destroyer of hostile lands; a Sumerian Šuila to Marduk; – *b) Kramer* Samuel N., BM 96679, a new Inanna Iršemma; – *c) Moren* Sally, *Foster* Benjamin R., Eagle omens from Šumma alu; – *d) Owen* David J., A unique late Sargonic river ordeal: ➤ 166, Mem. SACHS A., A scientific humanist 1988, 83-90 + 3 pl. / 243-8 + 2 facsim. / 277-281 + 2 facsim. / 305-310 + 1 pl.

b69 **Farber** Walter, Schlaf, Kindlein, schlaf; mesopotamische Baby-Beschwörungen und Rituale: Mesopotamian Civilizations 2. WL 1989, Eisenbrauns. xii-196 p.; 16 pl. 0-831464-44-7 [RelStR 16,248, J. M. *Sasson*].

b70 *Farber* W., (W)ardatlilî(m) [i. eine altbabylonische Beschwörung]: ZAss 89 (1989) 14-35.

b71 *a) Farber* Walter, Vorzeichen aus der Waschschüssel; zu den akkadischen Bade-Omina (*Šumma ālu*, 43, *nishu*); – *b) Rochberg-Halton* Francesca, Babylonian horoscopes and their sources: Orientalia 58 (1989) 86-101 / 102-123; pl. 1-2.

b72 *a) Foxvog* Daniel A., A manual of sacrificial procedure; – *b) Frayne* Douglas, A duplicate of a Rīm-Sîn hymnal excerpt; – *c) Geller* Markham, A new piece of witchcraft; – *d) Jacobsen* Thorkild, The *lil₂* of ᵈ*En-lil₂*; – *e) Lambert* W. G., A Babylonian prayer to Anūna; – *f) Mieroop* Marc van de, Gifts and tithes to the temple in Ur; – *g) Römer*

W. H. P., Eine Beschwörung gegen den 'Bann'; – *h*) *Selz* Gebhard, Nissaba(k), 'die Herrin der Getreidezuteilungen': ➤ 183, ᶠSJÖBERG Å., Dumu- 1989, 167-173 + 3 facsim. / 181-3 / 193-203 + 2 facsim. / 267-276 / 321-336 / 397-401 / 465-479 / 491-7.

b73 *Funck* Bernd, Aus den Erinnerungen einer babylonischen Priesterin; zur Geschichte der Autobiographie [Harran, < ILN]: Altertum 34 (1988) 53-60; 3 fig.

b74 **Geller** Markham J., Forerunners to Udug-Hul; Sumerian exorcistic incantations: FreibOrSt 12. Stu 1985, Steiner. vii-172 p.; 20 pl. – ᴿOLZ 84 (1989) 666-9 (A. *Cavigneaux*).

b75 **Golzio** K. H., Der Tempel im alten Mesopotamien und seine Parallelen in Indien: BZRG 25, 1983 ➤ 64,b87... 2,9067: ᴿAulaO 7,1 (1989) 133s (G. del *Olmo Lete*).

b75* *a*) *Invernizzi* Antonio, The investiture of Nemesis-Allat in Hatra; – *b*) *Salihi* Wathiq al-, Stele of Brmryn from Hatra: Mesopotamia-T 24 (F 1989) 129-176; phot. 61-114 / 177-180; phot. 115.

b76 *Jacobsen* Thorkild, God or worshipper [male and female statues from Tell Asmar]: ➤ 106, ᶠKANTOR H., Essays 1989, 125-130 + pl. 20-22.

b77 **Jeyes** Ulla, Old Babylonian extispicy omen texts in the British Museum: Uitgaven 64. L 1989, Nederlands Historisch-Archaeologisch Instituut. xiii-219 p. 90-6258-064-5 [OIAc S89].

b78 **Kinnier Wilson** J. V., The legend of Etana; a new edition 1985 ➤ 1,9105... 4,b953: ᴿJAOS 109 (1989) 81-86 (B. *Alster*: the textual history); JNES 48 (1989) 155s (W. *Farber*: falls short of its goals).

b79 *Kobayashi* Toshiko, Was Mesandu the personal deity of Enentarzi?: Orient-Japan 25 (1989) 22-42.

b80 *Lambert* W. G., A Late Babylonian copy of an expository text [with his 1987 copy, supplying signs and rulings missing in C. GORDON's 1952 used by A. LIVINGSTONE's Mystical... works 1986, p. 64-66]: JNES 48 (1989) 215-221; facsim.

b81 *Lambert* W. G., Manzi'at, the goddess 'Rainbow' [Eng.]: ➤ 905, RLA 7,5s (1989) 344-6.

b82 *a*) *Limet* Henri, Les fantaisies du dieu Enki; essai sur les techniques de la narration dans les mythes; – *b*) *Westenholz* Joan G., Enheduanna, En-priestess, Hen of Nanna, spouse of Nanna; – *c*) *Guinan* Ann, The peril of high living; divinatory rhetoric in Šu-Sin and an Adab of Nergal: ➤ 183, ᶠSJÖBERG Å., Dumu- 1989, 357-365 / 539-556 / 303-316.

b83 **Majercik** Ruth, The Chaldean oracles; text, translation, and commentary: Studies in Greek and Roman Religion 5. Leiden 1989, Brill. xiv-247 p. 90-04-09043-6.

b83* *a*) *Matthiae* Paolo, Le temple ailé et le taureau; origine et continuité de l'iconographie de la grande déesse à Ebla; – *b*) *Gubel* Éric, À propos du *marzeaḥ* d'Assurbanipal: ➤ 59, ᶠFINET A., Reflets 1989, 127-135; 20 fig. / 47-53; 8 fig.

b84 *Moortgat-Correns* Ursula, Ein Kultbild Ninurtas aus neuassyrischer Zeit: AfO 35 (1988) 117-133; 8 fig.

b85 **Naccach** Albert F. H., *Zeineh* Husni, ⊕ *'Uḥda Kiš*, The spell of Kish = MAD 5,81: Diwan an-Nuṣuṣ 1. Beirut 1989, Tawzi. 123 p.

b86 *Römer* W. H. P., Miscellanea sumerologica I. Zur sumerischen Dichtung 'Heirat des Gottes Mardu': UF 21 (1989) 319-334.

b87 *Roth* Martha T., *ina amat* DN, *u* DN, *lišlim* [by the command of the god DN may this be successful]: JSS 33 (1988) 1-9.

b88 *Saporetti* Claudio,   Una comunità di aruspici paleo-babilonesi nella valle della Dijala: ➤ 877, Lavoro 1988, 31-35.

b89 **Seidl** U.,   Die babylonischen Kudurru-Reliefs; Symbole mesopotamischer Gottheiten: OBO 87.   FrS/Gö 1989, Univ./VR.   235 p.; 33 pl. Fs 64. 3-7278-0603-6 / VR 3-525-53717-4 [BL 90, 127, W. G. *Lambert*].

b90 **Shao** Joseph Too,   A study of Akkadian royal hymns and prayers; diss. HUC, ᴰ*Weisberg* D.   Cincinnati 1989, HUC-JIR.   xviii-396 p.; bibliog. p. 371-396.   89-18297. – DissA 50 (1989s) 1291-A; OIAc Ja90.

b91 **Shreibman** Henry M.,   Studies in comparative religion and literature of the ancient Near East; an interpretation of *Šurpu* and Spell 125: diss. Columbia, ᴰ*Marcus* D. – NY 1988.   383 p. 89-06084. – DissA 49 (1988s) 3699-A.

b92 *Soden* Wolfram von,   *a)* 'Als die Götter (auch noch) Mensch waren'; einige Grundgedanken des altbabylonischen Atramḫasis-Mythos [< Orientalia 38 (1969) 415-432]; – *b)* Die Terminologie des Tempelbaus [< Kolloquium 1972; CRAI 20 (1975) 133-143]; – *c)* Tempelstadt und Metropolis im Alten Orient [< ᴱ*Stoob* H., Die Stadt² (Köln 1985) 37-82]: ➤ 360, Aus Sprache 1989, 147-164 / 203-213 / 293-335.

b93 *Soden* Wolfram von,   *a)* Religion und Sittlichkeit nach den Anschauungen der Babylonier [< ZDMG 89 (1935) 143-169]; – *b)* Religiöse Unsicherheit, Säkularisierungstendenzen und Aberglaube zur Zeit der Sargoniden [< AnBib 12 (1959) 356-367]: ➤ 360, Aus Sprache 1989, 1-27 / 97-108.

b94 *Sommerfeld* W.,   Marduk: ➤ 905, RLA 7,5s (1989) 360-370 [-372 in Kleinasien, *Kammenhuber* A.; 372-4 archäologisch, *Rittig* D.]; 433-440 Martu (Mardu), *Edzard* D. O.

b95 *Stolz* Fritz,   Tradition orale et tradition écrite dans les religions de la Mésopotamie antique: ➤ 442, Mémoire 1988, 21-35.

b96 *Szarzyńska* Krystyna,   Some of the oldest cult symbols in archaic Uruk: JbEOL 30 (1987s) 3-21.

b97 **Thomsen** Marie-Louise,   Zauberdiagnose und Schwarze Magie in Mesopotamien 1987 ➤ 4,b966: ᴿOLZ 84 (1989) 170-3 (V. *Haas*, D. *Prechel*).

b98 *Toorn* Karel van der,   La pureté rituelle au Proche-Orient ancien: RHR 206 (1989) 339-356.

M7.4   Religio persiana, *Iran*.

b99 **Boyce** M.,   A history of Zoroastrianism, II. Under the Achaemenians: HbOr 1/8/1/2A, 1982 ➤ 64,9662 ... 3,b397: ᴿRHR 206 (1989) 188-193 (Rika *Gyselen*).

b99* *Capezzone* L.,   Lo Zoroastrismo islamizzato: RSO 63 (1989) 81-92.

b100 **Choksy** Jamsheed K.,   Purity and pollution in Zoroastrianism; triumph over evil.   Austin 1989, Univ. Texas. $22.50. – ᴿJScStR 29 (1989) 288s (A. L. *Greil*).

b101 *Colpe* Carsten,   Iranische Religionen: ➤ 894, EvKL 2 (1988) 717-722 (831-3, Yeziden).

b101* **Firby** Nora K.,   European travellers and their perceptions of Zoroastrians in the 17th and 18th centuries [diss. Manchester]: ArchMIran Egb 14.   B 1988, Reimer. 246 p. DM 88. – ᴿMundus 25 (1989) 10s (Rüdiger *Schmitt*).

b102 *Gropp* Gerd, Ein Elamischer Baderitus [not a text, but comments on portrayals and excavated plans]: → 28, ᶠBERGHE L. Vanden 1989, 239-262; 11 fig.

b103 **Guest** John S., The Yezidis 1987 → 3,b520; 4,b972:   ᴿBO 46 (1989) 212s (G.*Kreyenbroek*); JAOS 109 (1989) 447s (Matti *Moosa*).

b104 *Humbach* Helmut, Herrscher, Gott und Gottessohn in Iran und in angrenzenden Ländern: → 769, Menschwerdung 1986/9, 89-114.

b104* *Russell* J. R., Parsi Zoroastrian *garbās* and *monājāts*: JRAS (1989) 51-63.

b105 *Sarianidi* V. I., ❸ A proto-Zoroastrian temple in Margiana [in the Karakum desert] and the problem of origin of Zoroastrianism: VDI 188 (1989) 152-169; Eng. 169; 170-181. various comments ❸, also in 189 (1989) 170-181.

M8   **Religio islamica** *et proto-arabica.*

b107 **Abu-Husayn** Abdul-Rahim, Provincial leaderships in Syria, 1575-1650. Beirut 1985, American Univ. x-220 p. – ᴿJNES 48 (1989) 131-5 (A. *Rafeq*).

b108 **Amin** Husayn A. *al.*, Le défi du fondamentalisme islamique; regards sur l'occidentalisation: Arabya 2. Genève 1988, Labor et Fides. 117 p. 2-8309-0108-8. – ᴿÉTRel 64 (1989) 104s (J.-P. *Gabus*: seul article valable, KELLER C. A. 11-33, vraiment magistral).

b109 **Antoun** Richard T., *Hegland* Mary Elaine, Religious resurgence; contemporary cases in Islam, Christianity, and Judaism 1987 → 4,515 (= 335): ᴿJRel 69 (1989) 416s (J. *Peacock*).

b110 *Anyanwu* Herbert O., Human dimensions of religion in Islam and Christianity: JDharma 14,2 ('Humanism and religion' 1989) 165-172.

b111 **Argyriou** Astérios, Macaire MAKRÈS et la polémique contre l'Islam; édition princeps de l'Éloge et de ses deux oeuvres anti-Islamiques précédée d'une étude critique: ST 314, 1986 → 2,9087*: ᴿJTS 40 (1989) 669s (B. F. *Breiner*).

b112 **Arkoun** Mohammed, L'Islam, morale et politique 1982/6 → 4,b980: ᴿDer Islam 66 (1989) 371-4 (Rotraud *Wielandt*).

b113 **Arkoun** Mohammed, Ouvertures sur l'Islam. P 1989, Grancher. 189 p. – ᴿIslamochristiana 15 (1989) 257-9 (M. *Borrmans*).

b114 **Arkoun** Mohammed, Pour une critique de la raison islamique: Essais d'hier et d'aujourd'hui 24. P 1984, Maisonneuve & L. 378 p. F 120. – ᴿÉTRel 64 (1989) 605s (Françoise *Smyth*); NRT 111 (1989) 602s (J. *Scheuer*).

b115 **Arnaldez** R., L'Islam: L'horizon du croyant 4. P/Ottawa 1988, Desclée/Novalis. 206 p. F 65. – ᴿNRT 111 (1989) 601 (J. *Masson*).

b116 *Arnaldez* Roger, Bulletin d'Islamologie [19 livres]: RechSR 77 (1989) 431-452.

b117 **Assiouty** Sarwat A. al-, Origines égyptiennes du Christianisme et de l'Islam; résultat d'un siècle et demi d'archéologie; Jésus, réalités historiques; Muḥammad, évolution dialectique: Recherches Comparées sur le Christianisme Primitif et l'Islam Premier, 3. P 1989, Letouzey & Â. 296 p. F 118. 2-7063-0175-9 [BL 90,8, F. *Bruce*].

b118 *Basetti-Sani* Giulio, *a)* Autenticità della missione profetica di Muhammad, un'ipotesi di lavoro; – *b)* Un trattato di teologia musulmana [*Caspar* R. 1987]: StPatav 36 (1989) 545-551 / 155-161.

b119 *Batumalai* S., Responses to Islamic resurgence in Malaysia; from a Christian perspective: AsiaJT 3 (Singapore 1989) 1-14.

b120 **Bennassar** B. & L., Les Chrétiens d'Allah — l'histoire extraordinaire des renégats, XVIᵉ-XVIIᵉ siècle. P 1989, Perrin. 493 p. – ᴿIslamochristiana 15 (1989) 260s (J.-M. *Gaudeul*).

b121 **Bianquis** Thierry, Damas et la Syrie sous la domination Fatimide (359-468 / 969-1076); essais d'interprétation de chroniques arabes médiévales [diss. Paris-I, 1984]: IFD 120 [➤ 3,b411]+121. Damas 1986, Institut Français. I. xxii-387 p.; II. p. 389-804; 5. foldout maps.

b121* ᴱ**Biggar** Nigel, *al.*, Cities of Gods; faith, politics and pluralism in Judaism, Christianity and Islam 1986 ➤ 2,409; ᴿSR 18 (1989) 387s (D. *Stover*: parochial rather than pluralist).

b122 **Blichfeldt** Jan-Olaf, Early Mahdism 1985 ➤ 4,b985: ᴿOLZ 84 (1989) 446s (D. *Sturm*).

b123 **Bonnet-Eymard** F. Bruno, Le Coran, traduction et commentaire systématique, I. Sourate 1, Bénédiction; Sourate 2, Dieu des délivrances. S. Parres-lès-Vaudes 1988, Contre-Réforme Catholique. 344 p. – ᴿIslamochristiana 15 (1989) 262s (M. *Lagarde*: influencé par Georges de NANTES et Hanna Zakarias THÉRY: œuvre d'un Juif; la Tradition musulmane est toute apocryphe).

b124 **Borrmans** M., Orientamenti per un dialogo tra Cristiani e Musulmani [non 2ᵃ ed. del ¹1970]. R 1988, Pont. Univ. Urbaniana. 202 p. – ᴿStPatav 36 (1989) 616-8 (G. *Basetti-Sani*).

b125 *a)* ᵀᴱ**Bosworth** Clifford E., The reunification of the Abbasid Caliphate. – *b)* ᵀ**Fields** Philip M., ᴱ*Lassner* Jacob, The 'Abbasid recovery: TABARI, History 32.37. NY 1987, SUNY. xvi-281 p., 2 maps; xv-195 p. – ᴿDer Islam 65 (1988) 337-9 (B. *Spuler*, also on *Perlmann* M., 4; *Watt* W. M., 7).

b126 **Bouman** Johan, Das Wort vom Kreuz und das Bekenntnis zu Allah; die Grundlehren des Korans als nachbiblische Religion 1980 ➤ 62,a279 ... 3,b412: ᴿÉTRel 64 (1989) 604s (F. *Smyth*).

b127 ᴱ**Brinner** William M., *Ricks* Stephen D., Studies in Islamic and Judaic traditions [Denver Univ. meetings] 1986 ➤ 3,523: ᴿJRel 69 (1989) 447 (M. S. *Stern*).

b128 **Caspar** Robert, Traité de théologie musulmane, I. Histoire de la pensée religieuse musulmane: Studi arabo-islamici 1, 1987 ➤ 3,b414: ᴿRThom 89 (1989) 151s (J. *Jomier*).

b129 *Claverie* Pierre-Lucien, Conoscere meglio l'Islam: NuovaUm 10,60 (1988) 19-39; 11,61 (1989) 31-56.

b130 **Cragg** Kenneth, Muhammad and the Christian, a question of response [ital. 'un problema che attende risposta' 1986 ➤ 3,b418] 1984 ➤ 65,9446; 1,a758: ᴿNRT 111 (1989) 631 (J. *Scheuer*).

b131 **Cragg** Kenneth, Readings in the Qur'ān (2/3). L 1988, Collins Liturgical. 389 p. £9. 0-00-599087-4. – ᴿExpTim 100 (1988s) 158s (Susan *Wilding*).

b132 **Crespi** G., Maometto il profeta. CinB 1988, Paoline. 240 p. Lit. 18.000. – ᴿAsprenas 36 (1989) 423-5 (G. *Ragozzino*).

b133 **Crone** Patricia, *Hinds* Martin, God's caliph 1986 ➤ 3,b418*; 4,b991: ᴿDer Islam 66 (1989) 361-3 (H. *Motzki*); JNES 48 (1989) 135s (M. G. *Morony*); OLZ 84 (1989) 442s (T. *Nagel*).

b134 **Crone** Patricia, Roman, provincial and Islamic law; the origins of the Islamic patronate. C 1987 [JNES 48,185].

b134* **Eaton** Charles Le Gai, Der Islam und die Bestimmung des Menschen; Annäherung an eine Lebensform, ᵀ*Schmid* Eva-Liselotte. Köln 1987,

Diederichs. 447 p. DM 58. 3-424-00918-0. – ᴿActuBbg 26 (1989) 105s (J. *Boada*).

b135 **Endress** Gerhard, An introduction to Islam, ᵀ*Hillenbrand* Carole, 1988 ➤ 4,b994: ᴿJSS 34 (1989) 222s (C. *Melville*).

b136 ᵀ*Esperonnier* Maryse, QALQAŠANDI, Les fêtes civiles et les cérémonies d'origine antique sous les Fatimides d'Égypte: Der Islam 65 (1988) 46-59.

b137 **Farrugia** Joseph, The Church and the Muslims (...documents of Vatican II). Malta 1988, Media Centre. 88 p. – ᴿAsprenas 36 (1989) 549s (G. *Ragozzino*); Islamochristiana 15 (1989) 268s (M. *Borrmans*).

b138 *Farrugia* Joseph, The genesis of the conciliar statements regarding the Muslims: MeliT 40,1 (1989) 1-26.

b139 *Frank* Richard M., Knowledge and *taqlīd*; the foundations of religious belief in classical Ash'arism: JAOS 109 (1989) 37-62.

b140 **Gabrieli** F., *Walter* G., Maometto; testimonianze storiche; ritratto di Maometto. Novara 1989, De Agostini. 372 p. Lit. 26.000. – ᴿStPatav 36 (1989) 612s (G. *Basetti-Sani*).

b141 **Garaudy** Roger, Promessas do Islã; o Islã e suas contribuições presentes, passadas e futuras à nossa civilização. RJ 1988, Nova Fronteira. 192 p. – ᴿREB 49 (1989) 742s (A. H. *Campolina Martins*).

b142 *Garaudy* Roger, Islam y teología de la liberación: RLatAmT 4,11 (Salvador 1987) 165-175 [< TContext 6/2, 67].

b143 **Gardet** L., L'Islam e i cristiani; convergenze e differenze: Dialogo. R 1988, Città Nuova. 206 p. Lit. 23.000. – ᴿAsprenas 36 (1989) 547-9 (G. *Ragozzino*).

b144 *Gaudeul* Jean-Marie, Encounters and clashes; Islam and Christianity in history I-II: Pont. Ist. Studi Arabici e Islamici 1984 ➤ 3,b426: ᴿGrOrTR 33 (1988) 343-5 (D. J. *Sahas*).

b145 **Gimaret** Daniel, Les noms divins en Islam; exégèse lexicographique et théologique, 1988 ➤ 3,b997: ᴿNRT 111 (1989) 602 (J. *Scheuer*); RThom 89 (1989) 507s (J. *Jomier*).

b146 **Glassé** Cyril, The concise encyclopedia of Islam. SF 1989, Harper & R. 472 p. $60. 0-06-063123-6. – ᴿParadigms 5 (1989) 155s (R. *Fuller*).

b147 **Gramlich** Richard, Die Wunder der Freunde Gottes; Theologien und Erscheinungsformen des islamischen Heiligenwunders: FreibIslamSt 11. Wsb 1987, Steiner. 505 p. – ᴿDer Islam 65 (1988) 282-300 (F. *Meier*, 'Bemerkungen zu einem grossen buch': the entire long review is written in German without capitalizing substantives).

b147* ᵀᴱ**Gramlich** Richard, Das Sendschreiben al-QUŠAYRIS über das Sufitum: FreibIslamSt 12. Stu 1989, Steiner. 659 p. DM 240. – ᴿOrientalia 58 (1989) 569-572 (G. *Böwering*).

b148 *Gramlich* Richard, *a)* Indifferenz, eine Haltung der islamischen Frömmigkeit; – *b)* Nur Gott allein, ein Wesenszug islamischer Mystik [> ᶠSUDBRACK J. 1990]: GeistL 62 (1989) 241-5 / 459-469.

b149 **Greer** Gary M., A phenomenological study of Muḥammad for contemporary missiology: diss. Southern Baptist Theol. Sem. ᴰ*Jonsson* J. 1989. 348 p. 89-25770. – DissA 50 (1989s) 2104s-A.

b150 *Grohs* Gerhard, Christentum, Islam und die Menschenrechte: ÖkRu 38 (1989) 298-304.

b151 [Groupe de recherches islamo-chrétien 1978-82], ᵀ*Brown* Stuart E.: Faith meets faith. Mkn 1989, Orbis. vii-104 p. $27; pa. $14. 0-88344-651-0; 0-2 [TDig 37,77].

b152 *Hagemann* Ludwig, Zur Auseinandersetzung des Christentums mit dem Islam im Mittelalter und in der Reformationszeit: VerkFor 32 (1987) 43-62.

b153 **Hartmann** Richard, Die Religion des Islam, eine Einführung. Da 1987 = 1944, Wiss. vii-168 p. DM 40. 3-534-01664-5. – RAfO 35 (1988) 222 (H. *Eisenstein*).

b154 **Havenith** Alfred, Les Arabes chrétiens nomades au temps de Mohammed: Coll. Cerfaux-Lefort 7. LvN 1988, Centre Hist. Rel. 154 p. – RIslamochristiana 15 (1989) 269s (A. *Ferré*).

b155 **Hawting** G. R., The first dynasty of Islam; the Umayyad Caliphate A.D. 661-750. Carbondale/L 1987, Southern Illinois Univ. / Croom Helm. xx-141 p.; maps. $24. – RDer Islam 65 (1988) 122s (B. *Spuler*); JAOS 109 (1989) 448s (M. *Bonner*: intended to make easier but not replace WELLHAUSEN's great narrative history); JSS 33 (1988) 294-6 (Carole *Hillenbrand*).

b156 **Hedin** Christer, Alla är födda muslimer [everyone is born Muslim]; Islam som den naturliga religionen enligt fundamentalistisk apologetik: diss. Sto 1988, Verbum. – SvTKv 65 (Lund 1989) 89s.

b157 **Hijab** Nadia, Womanpower; the Arab debate on woman at work: Middle East Library. C 1988, Univ. xiv-176 p. 0-521-26443-8; pa. 992-X. – RBO 46 (1989) 495-9 (Wiebke *Walther*).

b158 *Hillenbrand* R., *al.*, Masdjid [mosque]: → 889, EncIslam 6,109s (1989) 644-708.

b159 **Hock** Klaus, Der Islam im Spiegel westlicher Theologie 1986 → 2,9112 ... 4,d3: RIslam 66 (1989) 148s (P. *Antes*); NZMissW 45 (1989) 124-130 (J. *Henninger*).

b160 *Hulmes* Edward, Walter MILLER and the Isawa; an experiment in Christian-Muslim relationships: ScotJT 41 (1988) 233-246.

b161 **Jansen** J. J. G., Inleiding tot de Islam. Muiderberg 1987, Coutinho. 190 p.; 4 pl. 90-6283-695-X. – RBO 46 (1989) 197s (A. *Wessels*).

b162 **Jomier** Jacques, Pour connaître l'Islam. P 1988, Cerf. 194 p. – RIslamochristiana 15 (1989) 270 (M. *Borrmans*).

b163 **Jomier** Jacques, How to understand Islam. L 1989, SCM. 168 p. £7. – RPrPeo 3 (1989) 445s (E. *Hulmes*).

b164 *Jomier* Jacques, Mystique, théologie et problèmes actuels de l'Islam [*Caspar* R., *Ascha* G. 1987]: RThom 89 (1989) 148-153.

b165 **Juynboll** Gauthier H. A., Muslim Tradition; studies in chronology, provenance and authorship of early hadith: Studies in Islamic Civilization, 1983 → 65,9461 ... 2,9116: RDer Islam 65 (1988) 326-9 (A. *Noth*).

b166 **Kaptein** N. J. G., Het geboortefeest van de profeet Mohammed; oorsprong en verspreiding in het Nabije Oosten tot het begin van de 7e/13e eeuw, invoering en geschiedenis in de Maghrib en el-Andalus tot an de dood van AL-WANŠARĪSĪ (914/1508): diss. Leiden, DLeertouwer L. Leiden 1989, auct. [Box 9515]. 302 p. – TsTNijm 29 (1989) 283.

b167 **Kennedy** Hugh, The Prophet and the age of the caliphates; the Islamic Near East from the sixth to the eleventh century: A history of the Near East 1 [of 7, up to the present]. L 1986, Longman. xii-424 p. £22; pa. £12. 0-582-49312-9; 3-7. – RBO 46 (1989) 198s (I. R. *Netton*).

b168 [*Kerr* D., Christianity and Islam, *al.*] Living among Muslims; experience and concerns, 5-12 July 1987 [World Reformed Alliance]: John Knox Series. Genève c. 1988, Centre Réf. 210 p. – RÉTRel 64 (1989) 104 (J.-P. *Gabus*: peu utilisable).

b169 **Khalidi** Tarif,   Classical Arab Islam; the culture and heritage of the golden age 1985 ➤ 1,a785... 4,d7: ᴿOLZ 84 (1989) 320-3 (D. *Bellmann*).

b170 *Khodr* Georges,   La communication du message en terre d'Islam: ÉTRel 64 (1989) 373-391 [367-371, doctorat honoris causa, Fac. Prot. (Montpellier)].

b171 **Khoury** Adel T.,   Der Islam; sein Glaube, seine Lebensordnung, sein Anspruch: Tb 1602. FrB 1988, Herder. 238 p. DM 12,90. – ᴿLuthMon 29 (1989) 137 (A. *Vieth*).

b172 **Khoury** Adel T.,   So sprach der Prophet; Worte aus der islamischen Überlieferung: Siebenstern 785. Gü 1988, Mohn. 368 p. DM 34 pa. – ᴿTLZ 114 (1989) 799s (K.-H. *Bernhardt*); TR 85 (1989) 330s (P. *Heine*).

b173 **Khoury** Adel T.,   Mohammed für Christen, eine Herausforderung. FrB 1984, Herder. 190 p. DM 9. – ᴿOLZ 84 (1989) 315-7 (K.-W. *Tröger*).

b174 **Khoury** Paul,   Matériaux pour servir à l'étude de la controverse théologique islamo-chrétienne de langue arabe du VIIIᵉ au XIIᵉ siècle: WüForMRWiss 2/11. Wü/Altenberge 1989; Echter/Telos. 407 p. [TR 86,154, P. *Heine*].

b175 *Kinberg* Leah,   Compromise of commerce; a study of early [Muslim] traditions concerning poverty and wealth: Der Islam 66 (1989) 193-212.

b176 **Lessner** Jacob,   Islamic revolution and historical memory; an inquiry into the art of 'Abbāsid apologetics: AmerOrSeries 66. NHv 1986, American Oriental Soc. xv-156 p. – ᴿDer Islam 65 (1988) 123s (B. *Spuler*); JAOS 109 (1989) 123s (C. E. *Bosworth*).

b177 **Levrat** Jacques,   Une expérience de dialogue; les Centres d'études chrétiens en monde musulman: Studien 9. Altenberge 1987, C(hristlich)-I(slamisches) Schriftum. 392 p. DM 70. – ᴿJEcuSt 26 (1989) 356s (T. J. *O'Shaughnessy*).

b178 **Longton** Joseph,   Fils d'Abraham; panorama des communautés juives, chrétiennes et musulmanes. Turnhout 1988, Brepols. 264 p. – ᴿRThom 89 (1989) 161s (D. *Cerbelaud*); SR 18 (1989) 87s (R. *Chagnon*); VSp 142 (1988) 764s (J. *Hoffmann*).

b179 *McDonough* Sheila,   Modern Muslim Qur'an commentaries in relation to gender roles and distinctions: RelStT 7,2s (1987) 56-69.

b180 *Makdisi* George,   Scholasticism and humanism in classical Islam and the Christian West [presidential address, American Oriental Society, Chicago 22.III. 1988]: JAOS 109 (1989) 175-182.

b181 **Marcuzzo** Giacinto B.,   Le dialogue d'ABRAHAM de Tibériade [moine chrétien] avec Abd al-Raḥman AL-HAŠIMI à Jérusalem vers 820... éd. critique [diss. Pont. Univ. Lateranensis, ᴰ*Samir Khalil*]. TÉtOrChr 3. R 1986, Univ. Lateran. 642 p. – ᴿRB 96 (1989) 116-9 (M. M. *Bar Asher*).

b182 *Michel* Thomas,   Jesuit writings on Islam in the seventeenth century: Islamochristiana 15 (1989) 57-85.

b183 **Molla** Claude F.,   L'Islam, c'est quoi? Cent cinquante questions et réponses: Entrée Libre 1. Genève 1989, Labor et Fides. 94 p. – ᴿRThom 89 (1989) 665s (-675, J. *Jomier*).

b184 *Mooren* Thomas,   Hermeneutische Strategien im gegenwärtigen Islam: ZMissRW 73 (1989) 210-234; Eng. 236.

b185 *Morris* James W.,   The spiritual ascension; IBN 'ARABĪ and the mi'rāj [of Muḥammad]: JAOS 108 (1988) 63-77.

b186 **Muṭahharî** Shahid A. M.,   I diritti della donna nell'Islam [◉ 1974; Eng. 1981], ᵀ*Palazzi* Abdu i-Hadi: Studi Islamici 30. R 1988, Centro Islamico. 299 p.

b187 **Nagel** Tilman, Die Festung des Glaubens; Triumph und Scheitern des islamischen Rationalismus im 11. Jahrhundert. Mü 1988, Beck. 422 p. DM 94. – ᴿDLZ 110 (1989) 1028-30 (G. *Strohmaier*).

b188 *Nagel* Tilman, Der Inhalt des Korans als Problem der historischen Forschung [*O'Shaughnessy* T. J. Creation 1985; Eschatological 1986]: OLZ 84 (1989) 133-142.

b189 ᴱ**Nasr** Seyyed H., Islamic spirituality: EWSp 19, 1987 ➤ 3,b460; 4,d18: ᴿJRel 69 (1989) 589s (M. *Sells*).

b190 **Nazir-Ali** Michael, Frontiers in Muslim-Christian encounter. Ox 1987, Regnum. 191 p. £6.50. – ᴿThemelios 14 (1988s) 112s (Vivienne *Stacey*).

b191 **Nettler** Ronald L., Past trials and present tribulations; a Muslim Fundamentalist's view of the Jews: Sassoon Center for the Study of Antisemitism. Ox 1988, Pergamon. – ᴿDer Islam 66 (1989) 164s (Gudrun *Krämer*).

b192 **Newby** Gordon D., The making of the last prophet; a reconstruction of the earliest biography of Muhammad. Orangeburg 1989, Univ. South Carolina. 263 p. $35 [JAAR 57,889].

b192* **Niewöhner-Eberhard** Elke, Saʿda [N-Yemen]; Bauten und Bewohner in einer traditionellen islamischen Stadt: TAVO Beih B64, 1985 ➤ 1,a796; 2,9129: ᴿOLZ 84 (1989) 200-2 (B. *Brentjes*).

b193 **Nigosian** Solomon, Islam, the way of submission. Wellingsborough, England 1987, Antiquarian. 216 p. – ᴿSR 18 (1989) 86 (J. D. *Cook*).

b194 **Ormsby** Eric L., Theodicy in ... GHAZĀLI 1984 ➤ 2,9130: ᴿOLZ 84 (1989) 447s (Renate *Jacobi*).

b195 **O'Shaughnessy** T. J., Eschatological themes in the Qur'an 1986 ➤ 3,b461: ᴿAbr-Nahrain 27 (1989) 193s (A. H. *Johns*); JSS 34 (1989) 220s (Penelope *Johnstone*).

b196 *Pastner* Carroll M., The emergence of Umma Muslima; religious ecology in Sura 22 of the Qur'an: ➤ 592, Systemic 1 (1989) 3-15.

b197 *Peirone* F. J., *Rizzardi* G., La spiritualità islamica: ➤ 907, Spiritualità non cristiana 5. R 1986, Studium. 212 p. – ᴿRHE 84 (1989) 257 (R. *Aubert*).

b198 ᴱ**Pines** S., *al.*, From Jāhiliyya to Islam 4s, 1984 ➤ 65,662: ᴿJNES 48 (1989) 65-68 (M. G. *Morony*).

b199 **Powers** David S., Studies in Qur'an and Hadith — the formation of the Islamic law of inheritance. Berkeley 1986, Univ. California. 263 p. $30. – ᴿDer Islam 65 (1988) 117-120 (H. *Motzki*).

b200 *Powers* David S., On bequests in early Islam [*Crone* P. 1987]: JNES 48 (1989) 185-200.

b201 **Rahmena** Zeinolabedin, Payambar, the messenger [= ? Le Prophète 1984 ➤ 65,9488], ᵀ*Elwell-Sutton* L. P. R 1984, Centro Islamico. xv-591 p.

b202 *Reeber* Michael, Les 'Versets sataniques' [*Rushdie* S.]; une affaire désolante qui amène au grand jour un réel conflit de valeurs: Masses Ouvrières 426 (1989) 47-55 [< Documents du Service des Relations avec l'Islam 7 (mars 1989)].

b202* ᵀᴱ**Rippin** Andrew [➤ 821], *Knappert* Jan, Textual sources for the study of Islam. Manchester 1986, Univ. xi-309 p. £6.75. – ᴿDerIslam 65 (1988) 121 (H. *Motzki*).

b203 **Rizzardi** G., Islam; processare o capire. Pavia 1988, Casa del Giovane. 332 p. Lit. 22.500. – ᴿStPatav 36 (1989) 615s (G. *Basetti-Sani*).

b204 **Rotter** Ekkehart, Abendland und Sarazenen; das okzidentale Araberbild und seine Entstehung im Frühmittelalter: Islam Beih. 11, 1986 ➤ 3,b471: ᴿIslam 66 (1989) 146-8 (P. *Kunitsch*).

b205 *Rudolph* Kurt, Juden – Christen – Muslime; zum Verhältnis der drei monotheistischen Religionen in religionswissenschaftlicher Sicht: Judaica 44 (1988) 214-232.

b206 *Ryckmans* Jacques, Le pantheón de l'Arabie du Sud préislamique; état des problèmes et brève synthèse: RHR 206 (1989) 151-170; Eng. 151: Athtar, a male Venus-god of irrigation and thunderstorm, had superseded Il as supreme god.

b207 **Saba** Michael P., Muslim-Christian relation, a program of interactive dialogue: diss. Union/Experimenting 1989. 443 p. 89-14873. – DissA 50 (1989s) 2612-A.

b208 **Sabbagh** Abdulkarim [cf. *Sabah* F. ↣ 2,9137], Frauen im Islam. Wü 1986, auct. 3-9801348-06. – ᴿBO 46 (1989) 499-502 (Wiebke *Walther*).

b209 **Schimmel** Annemarie, And Muhammad is his messenger; the veneration of the Prophet in Islamic piety 1985 ↣ 3,b477; 4,d29: ᴿJAOS 108 (1988) 492s (M. *Swartz*).

b210 **Schimmel** Annemarie, Mystische Dimensionen des Islam [USA 1975, erweitert], her ownᵀ. Köln 1985, Diederichs. 734 p.; ill. – ᴿDer Islam 66 (1989) 363-5 (F. *Sobieroj*).

b211 *Schoeter* Gregor, *a)* Mündliche Thora und Ḥadīt; Überlieferung, Schreibverbot, Redaktion; – *b)* Weiteres zur Frage der schriftlichen oder mündlichen Überlieferung der Wissenschaften im Islam: Der Islam 66 (1989) 213-251 / 38-67.

b212 **Schuon** Frithjof, Den Islam verstehen; eine Einführung in die innere Lehre und die mystische Erfahrung einer Weltreligion. Mü 1988, Barth. 222 p. DM 32. – ᴿLuthMon 29 (1989) 333 (A. *Vieth*).

b213 **Sharon** Moshe, Black banners from the East... Abbasid state 1983 ↣ 65,d374: ᴿJNES 48 (1989) 70-72 (W. *Madelung*).

b214 **Smith** Peter, The Babi and Baha'i religions 1987 ↣ 4,d33: ᴿBSO 51 (1988) 557s (D. *MacEoin*); JAOS 109 (1989) 452s (also D. *MacEoin*).

b215 *Soubeyrand* Pierre-Marie, L'Islam en question: Ces questions qu'on nous pose. Nouan-le-Fuzelier 1989, Lion de Juda. 120 p. – ᴿRThom 89 (1989) 666 (J. *Jomier*; bulletin d'Islam).

b216 **Speight** R. Marston, God is one; the way of Islam. NY 1989, Friendship. 139 p. $6. 0-377-00196-1 [TDig 37,188].

b217 **Sultana** Fehmida, Romantic orientalism and Islam; SOUTHEY, SHELLEY, MOORE, and BYRON: diss. Tufts 1989. 222 p. 89-20027. – DissA 50 (1989s) 1670-A.

b218 **Talbi** Mohamed, *Bucaille* Maurice, Réflexions sur le Coran. P 1989, Seghers. 245 p. – ᴿIslamochristiana 15 (1989) 283-5 (M. *Borrmans*: Bucaille voudrait que ses efforts soient ouverts au dialogue avec l'Église).

b219 **Thyen** Johann-D., Bibel und Koran; eine Synopse gemeinsamer Überlieferungen. Kölner Veröff. Rel.-G. 19. Köln 1989, Böhlau. XXIX-349 p. DM 58 [TR 86,169].

b219* **Turbiani** E., Il Sikhismo; la religione dei divini maestri: Lincei Mem. mor/st/fg. 8/29/3. R 1987. p. 331-391. – ᴿRSO 62 (1988) 177s (G. *Milanetti*).

b220 **Venzlaff** Helga, Der islamische Rosenkranz 1985 ↣ 3,b487: ᴿJAOS 108 (1988) 491s (K. *Reinhart*).

b221 **Verkuyl** J., Met Moslims in gesprek over het evangelie 1985 ↣ 1,a824*a*: ᴿJEcuSt 26 (1989) 546 (W. A. *Bijlefeld*).

b222 **Waardenburg** Jacques, L'Islam, une religion; suivi d'un débat, Quels types d'approches requiert le phénomène religieux? Genève 1989, Labor et Fides. 154 p. [RHPR 69,95]. – ᴿIslamochristiana 15 (1989) 289-291 (M. *Borrmans*).

b223 **Watt** William M., Islamic fundamentalism and modernity. NY 1989, Routledge. 158 p. £25. 0-415-00623-6. – ᴿExpTim 100 (1988s) 437s (S. *Wilding*); Islamochristiana 15 (1989) 291-3 (M. *Borrmans*: brilliant and open-minded).

b224 **Watt** W. Montgomery, Muhammad's Mecca; history in the Qur'ān: Islamic Surveys. E 1988, Univ. [NY 1989, Columbia]. vii-113 p. $35. 0-85334-565-3 [TDig 37,93].

b225 **Watt** W. Montgomery, *McDonald* M. V., El-ṬABARI History 6, Muhammad at Mecca: Bibl. Persica. Albany 1988, SUNY. xlvi-178 p. 0-88706-707-7 [OIAc Ja90].

Woodberry J. Dudley, [544] Muslims and Christians on the Emmaus road 1989 → 766.

b227 **Zirker** Hans, Christentum und Islam; theologische Verwandtschaft und Konkurrenz. Dü 1989, Patmos. 203 p. – ᴿMiscFranc 89 (1989) 626-9 (J. *Imbach*, ital.).

M8.5 **Religiones Indiae** et variae.

b228 **Abe** Masao, Zen and western thought 1985 → 2,9150; 3,b492: ᴿNumen 36 (1989) 286s (Y. *Hoffmann*).

b229 **Acharuparambil** Daniel [cf. 1982 → 1,a832], La spiritualità dell'Induismo: → 907, Sp. non cristiana 1. R 1986, Studium. 258 p. – ᴿProtestantesimo 44 (1989) 156 (A. *Moda*).

b230 *Akizuki* Ryomin [Zen-Buddhist monk], Christian-Buddhist dialogue; Interreligio 14 (Nagoya 1988) 38-54 [< TContext 6/2, 41].

b231 *Anyika* Francis, The supreme God in Igbo traditional religious thought and worship: ComViat 32 (1989) 5-20.

b233 **Basham** Arthur L., 1914-1986, The origins and development of classical Hinduism [lectures at ten universities 1984s], ᴱZysk Kenneth, with general and Basham bibliog. Boston 1989, Beacon. xix-159 p. $19. 0-8070-7300-8 [TDig 36,351].

b234 **Bassuk** Daniel E., Incarnation in Hinduism and Christianity; the myth of the God-Man 1987 → 3,b500; 4,d40: ᴿJRel 68 (1988) 177s (F. X. *Clooney*: hidden agenda).

b235 *Bell* Catherine, Religion and Chinese culture; toward an assessment of 'popular religion' [... five recent books]: HistRel 29 (1989s) 35-57.

b235* *Ben Yosef* A., Confucianism and Taoism in [a systematic Jewish theology] 'The star of redemption'; JStRel 1,2 (Pietermaritzburg SAf 1988) 25-36 [< TContext 6/2, 17].

b236 **Chakravarti** Uma, The social dimensions of early Buddhism. Ox 1987, Univ. 238 p. $27.50. – ᴿJRel 69 (1989) 592 (J. S. *Walters*).

b237 ᵀᴱ**Cleary** Thomas, LIU I-MING, Awakening to the Tao [1816]. Boston 1988, Shambhala. xvi-105 p. $10. 0-87773-447-X [TDig 36,378].

b238 **Cobb** John B., Bouddhisme – Christianisme; au-delà du dialogue? [c. 1983], ᵀ*Deshays* Marc; préf. *Gisel* Pierre: Lieux théologiques 13. Genève 1988, Labor et Fides. 178 p. 2-8309-0117-7. – ᴿETL 65 (1989) 203s (V. *Neckebrouck*: beau, honnête, riche); ÉTRel 64 (1989) 135 (A. *Gounelle*).

b239 *Collins* Steven, Louis DUMONT and the study of religions [of India]: RelStR 15 (1989) 14-20 (22-29, *Strenski* Ivan).

b240 ᴱCoward Harold, *al.*, Readings in Eastern religions. Waterloo ON 1988, W. Laurier Univ. vii-368 p. $30. – ᴿRelStR 15 (1989) 237 (C. *Chapple*).

b241 *De Smet* Richard V., [Bhagavad-]Gita/Gospel convergencies: Sevartham 14 (1989) 13-19 [< TContext 7/1, 40].

b242 **Dharmasiri** Gunapala, *a*) A Buddhist critique of the Christian concept of God; – *b*) Fundamentals of Buddhist ethics. Antioch CA 1988s, Golden Leaves. xx-313 p.; $42.85 pa. / xv-157 p.; $12 pa. 0-942353-00-5; 2-1 [TDig 36,366].
ᴱ**Eber** I., Confucianism 1983/6 → 815.

b243 *Eilert* Håkan, Konfucius som 'klockkläpp': SvTKv 65 (1989) 21-28.

b244 *a) Griffiths* Paul J., Buddha and God; a contrastive study in ideas about maximal greatness: – *b*) *Clooney* Francis X., Evil, divine omnipotence, and human freedom; Vedānta's theology of Karma: JRel 69 (1989) 502-529 / 530-548.

b245 *Hasumi* Kazuo, Eine kritische Betrachtung japanischer Theologien: Ev T49 (1989) 550-560.

b246 **Healey** Patricia, Belief and culture in Australia [aborigines' mythology]: Nelen Yubu 39 (Melville NT 1989) 3-19 [H. *Janssen* (Eng.) summary in TContext 7,114].

b247 ᴱ**Heissig** Walther, *Klimkeit* Hans-J., Synkretismus in den Religionen Zentralasiens; Ergebnisse eines Kolloquiums 24.-26.V.1983 Bonn-St. Augustin: StOrRel 13, 1987 → 3,642: ᴿTLZ 114 (1989) 582s (K.-W. *Tröger*).

b248 **Henry** Patrick G., *Swearer* Donald K., For the sake of the world; the spirit of Buddhist and Christian monasticism. Minneapolis/ Collegeville 1989, Fortress/Liturgical. 256 p. – ᴿTS 50 (1989) 833s (J. D. *Redington*).

b249 ᴱ*Hoyu* Ishida, OTTO's theory of religious experience as encounter with the numinous and its application to Buddhism: Japanese Religions 15,3 (Kyoto 1988s) 19-33.

b250 **Ingram** Paul O., The modern Buddhist-Christian dialogue; two universalistic religions in transformation: Studies in Comparative Religion 2. Lewiston NY 1988, Mellen. xvii-441 p. $80; sb. $40. 0-88946-490-1 [TDig 36,375].

b251 **Jackson** Robert, *Killingley* Dermot, Approaches to Hinduism [for teachers]. L 1988, Murray. 245 p. 0-7195-4362-2. – ᴿExpTim 100 (1988s) 197 (P. D. *Bishop*).

b252 *Kadowaki* Kakichi, From Chuang-Tzu's way to Jesus Christ as the way [... contextual Japanese theology]: Inter Religio 15 (Nagoya 1989) 2-20 [< TContext 7/1, 49].

b253 *Keidel* Anne G., Some reflections on Christianity's encounter with Zen; a need for ongoing discernment: IMA Monastic Bulletin 42 (1987) 117-137 (aussi français/español); deutsch Erbe und Auftrag 65 (Beuron 1989) 122-140.

b254 *King* Ursula, Some reflections on sociological approaches to the study of modern Hinduism: Numen 36 (1989) 72-97.

b255 *Kischkel* Heinz, Max WEBER und das Tao; zu einem neuen taoistischen Paradigma der Religionswissenschaft: ZRGg 40 (1988) 335-357.

b256 **Kitagawa** Joseph M., Understanding Japanese religions 1987 → 4,211*: ᴿAnglTR 70 (1988) 199s (W. *Davis*: lucid English).

b257 **Klostermaier** Klaus K., A survey of Hinduism. Albany 1989, SUNY. xv-649 p. $19. 0-88706-807-3 [Greg 70,831].

b258 **Küng** Hans, *Ching* Julia, *a*) Christentum und chinesische Religion. Mü 1988, Piper. 319 p. DM 39,80. – ᴿDLZ 110 (1989) 1026-8 (J. *Irmscher*); – *b*) Christianity and Chinese religion. GCNY 1989, Doubleday. 309 p. $24. 0-385-26022-9. – ᴿJEcuSt 26 (1989) 347 (C. W. *Swain*); TContext 6,2 (1989) 109 (G. *Evers*).

b259 **Langer-Kaneko** C., Das reine Land; zur Begegnung von Amida-Buddhismus und Christentum: ZRGg Beih 29. Leiden 1986, Brill. xii-193 p. *f* 70. – ᴿNRT 111 (1989) 291 (J. *Masson*).

b259* *a*) *Lee Jung Young*, Yin-Yang as a theological paradigm; – *b*) *Park A. Sung*, The theology of Han ('the abyss of pain'): QRMin 9,1 (1989) 36-47 / 48-62.

b260 **Lefebure** Leo, Life transformed; meditations on the Christian scriptures in light of Buddhist perspective. Ch 1989, ACTA. xii-186 p. $10 pa. [TrinJ 10,242].

b261 **McLeod** W. H., The Sikhs; history, religion, and society: Lectures on the History of Religion 14. NY 1989, Columbia Univ. ix-161 p. $25. 0-231-06814-X [TDig 37,73].

b262 **Mitra** Kana, Catholicism-Hinduism; Vedantic investigation of R. PANIKKAR's attempt at bridge building 1987 → 3,b538; 4,d67: ᴿJDharma 13 (1988) 192s (T. *Kadankavil*); LvSt 14 (1989) 76 (Catherine *Cornille*).

b263 **Moti Lal** Pandit, Saivism, a religio-philosophical history: New Delhi 1987, Th. Res. 218 p. rs 70. – ᴿIndTSt 26 (1989) 90s (A. *Kolencherry*).

b264 *Moti Lal* Pandit, Some common mystical themes in Trika Shaivism and Christianity: IndTSt 26 (1989) 48-70.

b265 **Nguyen Van Toy** Pierre, Le Bouddha et le Christ; parallèles et ressemblances dans la littérature canonique et apocryphe chrétienne [diss. Pont. Univ. Urbaniana, R 1987, ᴰ*Erbetta* M.]: Collectio Urbaniana 3284. R 1987, Urbaniana Univ. 139 p., 3 maps [NTAbs 33,252]. – ᴿTeresianum 40 (1989) 234s (E. *Pacho*).

b266 *Odin* Steve, ABE MASAO and the Kyoto school on Christian kenosis and Buddhist sunyata: Japanese Religions 15,3 (Kyoto 1988s) 1-18 [G. *Evers* (Eng.) summary in TContext 7,116].

b267 ᴱ**Padoux** André, Mantras et diagrammes rituels dans l'Hindouisme: L'Hindouisme 249. P 1986, CNRS. 230 p.; ill. F 240. – ᴿJAOS 109 (1989) 659s (K. W. *Bolle*).

b268 *Pallis* Marco, Espectro luminoso del budismo: Rota mundi 6, 1986 → 3,b542: ᴿLumenVr 38 (1989) 90s (U. *Gil Ortega*).

b269 **Panikkar** Raimundo, The silence of God; the answer of the Buddha, ᵀ*Barr* Robert R. Mkn 1989, Orbis. xxvi-268 p. $30; pa. $17. – ᴿCCurr 39 (1989s) 469-471 (T. *Anderson*).

b270 **Panikkar** R., Il silenzio di Dio, la risposta del Buddha. R 1985, Borla. 558 p. Lit. 25.000. – ᴿStPatav 36 (1989) 180s (L. *Sartori*).

b271 *Phan Tan Thanh* G., [? *Castanedo* Jacinto, *Liom* Vincente, c. 1780 Viet-Nam meeting-report] The Council of four religions; mission and dialogue in the Far East: Angelicum 66 (1989) 563-576.

b272 **Pieris** Aloysius, Love meets wisdom; a Christian experience of Buddhism. Mkn 1988, Orbis. xii-161 p. – ᴿCalvinT 24 (1989) 185-8 (R. R. *DeRidder*); CCurr 39 (1989s) 217-9 (D. P. *Sheridan*); Horizons 16 (1989) 414s (G. T. *Carney*); TS 50 (1988) 409s (F. X. *Clooney*).

b273 **Pieris** Aloysius, Liebe und Weisheit; Begegnung von Christentum und Buddhismus, ᵀᴱ*Siepen* Wolfgang. Mainz 1989, Grünewald. 263 p. 3-7867-1412-6 [Greg 70,832].

b273* **Pitzer-Reyl** Renate, Die Frau im frühen Buddhismus: Marburger Afr/As.-Kunde B7. B 1984, Reimer. 104p. DM22 [TLZ 115,95s K.-W. *Tröger*].

b274 **Rai** Priya M., Sikhism and the Sikhs; an annotated bibliography: Bibliog. Rel. St. 13. Westport CT 1989, Greenwood. xv-257p. $45. 0-313-26130-X [TDig 37,83].

b275 **Richman** Paula, Women, branch stories, and religious rhetoric in a Tamil Buddhist text [by Cittalai CĀTTAŊĀR]: Facs South Asian 12. Syracuse 1989, Univ. 288p. $20.50 [0-915894-3: RelStR 15,223 adv.].

b276 *Sheridan* Daniel P., Maternal affection for a divine son; a spirituality of the *Bhāgavata Purāṇa*: Horizons 16 (1989) 65-78.

b277 ᴱ**Sivaraman** Krishna, Hindu spirituality; Vedas through Vedanta: EWSp 6. NY 1989, Crossroad. xliv-447p. $50. 0-8245-0755-X [TDig 37,61].

b278 *Smith* Henry N., Ancestor practices in contemporary Hong Kong; religious ritual or social custom: AsiaJT 3,1 (1989) 31-45 [G. *Evers* (Eng.) summary in TContext 7/1,109].

b279 **Spink** Kathryn, A sense of the sacred; a biography of Bede GRIFFITHS. L 1988, SPCK. 214p. £9 pa. 0-281-04333-7. – ᴿExpTim 100 (1988s) 40 (*Paidagogos*: autobiographical too, about ashrams); TLond 92 (1989) 214s (*I. Clark*).

b280 **Staffner** Hans, Jesus Christ and the Hindu community; is a synthesis of Hinduism and Christianity possible?: Pastoral 7/25. Anand 1988, GJ-Prakash. xii-253p. $9; pa. $8 [TDig 37,188].

b281 **Standaert** Nicolas, YANG TINGYUN, Confucian and Christian in late Ming China; his life and thought [< diss. Leiden]. Leiden 1988, Brill. 263p. $38.25. – ᴿTS 50 (1989) 369-371 (J. W. *Witek*).

b282 ᴱ**Thomas** R. Murray, Oriental theories of human development; scriptural and popular beliefs from Hinduism, Buddhism, Confucianism, Shinto, and Islam: AmerUnivSt 11/19. NY 1988, Lang. xix-345p. Fs64,20 [TR 85,527].

b283 *a*) *Vakathanam* Mathew, Mystery, myth, history; the dimensions of spirituality in the context of Avatara; – *b*) *Sekher* Vincent, The way of the Spirit — a Jain journey; – *c*) *Waldenfels* H., Way of Wisdom; a way of spirituality; – *d*) *Sharma* Arvind, A third way of spirituality beyond faith and reason in Buddhism: JDharma 13 (1988) 204-216 / 217-237 / 248-287 / 282-290.

b284 **Vempeny** Ishanand, Krsna and Christ in the light of some of the fundamental concepts and themes of the Bhagavad Gita and the NT. Anand 1988, Gujarat-SP. 498p. – ᴿTContext 6,2 (1989) 118 (G. *Evers*).

b285 ᴱ**Waghorne** Joanne P. *al.*, Gods of flesh / gods of stone... in India 1985 ➤ 2,9197: ᴿAsiaJT 3 (1989) 699-705 (Gnana *Robinson*: non-contextual).

b286 **Zago** M., La spiritualità buddhista: La Spiritualità non cristiana, Storia e testi 2, 1986 ➤ 4,d84: ᴿRHE 84 (1989) 257 (R. *Aubert*).

XVII,1. Historia Medii Orientis Biblici

Q1 *Syria, Canaan,* **Israel Veteris Testamenti.**

b287 **Ahlström** Gösta W., Who were the Israelites? 1986 ➤ 2,9202.b811... 4,d86: ᴿAfO 35 (1988) 234s (G. *Sauer*); BO 46 (1989) 408-410 (C. H. J.

de *Geus*: superficial); OLZ 84 (1989) 432-4 (H. *Seidel*: Ursprung und Geschichte des Namens 'Israel').

Alt A., Essays on OT history and religion, ^T*Wilson* R.A. 1989 = 1966 → 225.

b288 *Balla* Lajos, Contribution aux problèmes de l'histoire des Syriens et de leurs cultes dans la région danubienne: AcClasDeb 25 (1989) 85-90.

b289 **Basnizki** Ludwig, Der jüdische Kalender — Entstehung und Aufbau. Königstein 1986, Athenäum. 69 p. – ^RJudaica 44 (1988) 59s (S. *Schreiner*).

b290 **Blázquez** J. M., Los Hebreos: Alcal Historia del Mundo Antiguo 101. M 1989, Alcal. 84-7600-383-8 [OIAc S89).

b291 **Bock** S., Geschichte des Volkes Israel, von den Anfängen bis in die Zeit des NTes; Einl. *Lohfink* N.: Tb 1642. FrB 1989, Herder. 192 p. DM 12,90 [ZAW 102, 296, H.-C. *Schmitt*].

b292 **Castel** François, The history of Israel and Judah in OT times 1986 → 1,a904 ... 4,d90: ^RHeythJ 30 (1989) 352s (B. P. *Robinson*: unenthusiastic).

b293 **Cazelles** Henri, História política de Israel, desde as origens até Alexandro Magno [1982 → 63,9564], ^T*Gomes* Cácio: BiblCienciasBibl. São Paulo 1986, Paulinas. [→ 3,b563]; 254 p. 86-05-00482-5. – ^RPerspT 20 (1988) 133s (L. *Stadelmann*).

b293* *Cazelles* H., Israel among the nations [1981 revised^T]: Pacifica 2 (1989) 47-60.

b294 **Clauss** Manfred, Geschichte Israels, von der Frühzeit bis zur Zerstörung Jerusalems 1986 → 2,9210 ... 4,d93: ^RGGA 241 (1989) 1-5 (V. *Fritz*).

b295 **Donner** Herbert, Geschichte des Volkes Israel I-II, 1984-6 → 65,9546 ... 4,d94: ^RScripTpamp 21 (1989) 921-3 (K. *Limburg*); WeltOr 20s (1989s) 311s (W. *Röllig*).

b296 *Garrone* D., Antico Testamento e storia: Protestantesimo 42 (1987) 202-214 [→ 3,b594 (p. 203-214) as review of *Soggin* J. A., Storia d'Israele].

Görg Manfred, Beiträge zur Zeitgeschichte der Anfänge Israels; Dokumente – Materialien – Notizen: ÄgAT 21 [< Biblische Notizen]. 1989 → 265*.

b298 *Harding* A. F., *Tait* W. J., 'The beginning of the end'; progress and prospects in Old World chronology [^E*Åström* P. 1987; ^E*Aurenche* O. 1986/8 ...]: Antiquity 63 (1989) 147-152.

b299 *Gunneweg* Antonius H. J., Israel: → 894, EvKL 2 (1988) 759-771 (-782, modern) [460-468 Heilsgeschichte, *Wiederkehr* Dietrich].

b300 *Healey* J. F., Ancient Aramaic culture and the Bible: Aram 1,1 (Ox 1989) 31-37 [< ZAW 102,264].

b301 *Jong* T. De, *Soldt* W. H. Van, Redating an early solar eclipse record (KTU 1.78); implications for the Ugaritic calendar and for the secular accelerations of the earth and moon: JbEOL 30 (1987s) 65-77.

b302 *Knapp* A. Bernard, The history and culture of Ancient Western Asia [... Syria, Palestine] and Egypt. Ch 1988, Dorsey. xvi-284 p.; 43 fig.; 20 pl.; 11 maps. $30; pa. $15. 0-256-05698-6; 6217-X. – ^RAcPraeh 21 (1989) 131-3 (P. A. *Miglus*, F. M. *Stepniowski*); BO 46 (1989) 560-2 (Gerlinde *Maijer*).

b303 **Knauf** Ernst A. [→ 2338], Ismael 1985 → 1,a924 ... 4,d97: ^ROLZ 84 (1989) 434-6 (E. *Otto*).

b304 **Kreuzer** Siegfried, Die Frühgeschichte Israels in Bekenntnis und Verkündigung des Alten Testaments [ev. Diss. Wien, ᴰ*Sauer* G.]: BZAW 178. B 1989, de Gruyter. ix-301 p. DM 120. 3-11-011736-3. – ᴿZAW 101 (1989) 465s (H.-C. *Schmitt*).

b305 **Lemaire** André, Storia del popolo ebraico [1981 ➤ 62,a418... 65,9561; ²1985], ᵀ*Bigarelli* A.: LoB 3.9. Brescia 1989, Morcelliana. 124 p. Lit. 15.000. 88-399-1600-8 [Greg 70,617]. – ᴿAsprenas 36 (1989) 406-8 (A. *Rolla*); StPatav 36 (1989) 198s (G. *Segalla*).

b306 **Lemche** Niels P., Ancient Israel, a new history of Israelite society: Biblical Seminar 1988 ➤ 4,d98: ᴿETL 65 (1989) 151s (J. *Lust*: balanced); ÉTRel 64 (1989) 272-4 (D. *Lys*); ExpTim 100,7 first choice (1988s) 241s (C. S. *Rodd*); TLond 92 (1989) 306s (R. *Coggins*: supplies social background lacking in R. de VAUX's work of the same title).

b307 **Malamat** Abraham, Mari and the early Israelite experience [1984 Schweich Lectures]. Ox 1989, UP (British Academy). xiii-161 p. £22.50. 0-19-726072-1.

b308 **Matthiae** Karl, *Thiel* Winfried, Biblische Zeittafeln 1985 ➤ 1,a929; 3,b580: ᴿTLZ 114 (1989) 341s (H.-J. *Zobel*).

b309 **Mazar** B., The early biblical period; historical studies, ᴱ*Ahituv* S., *Levine* B., 1986 ➤ 2,191... 4,d100: ᴿHenoch 11 (1989) 367s (B. *Chiesa*); JNES 48 (1989) 38s (Diana *Edelman*: six articles not previously in English).

b309* **Metzger** M., Grundriss der Geschichte Israels [unchanged reprint of ⁶1983 ➤ 64,9823 (= ¹1963); ital. 1985 ➤ 2,9231]. Neukirchen 1988 [ZAW 101,161].

b310 **Michaud** Robert, De la entrada en Canaán al destierro en Babilonia, historia y teología [1982 ➤ 1,a932], ᵀ: Buena noticia 13. Estella 1983, VDivino. 190 p.; maps. 84-7151-345-5.

b311 **Miller** J. M., *Hayes* J. H., A history of ancient Israel and Judah 1986 ➤ 2,9232... 4,d103: ᴿBA 52 (1989) 47s (P. E. *Dion*); EstAg 23 (1988) 700 (C. *Mielgo*).

b312 [*Wright* A. G.], *Murphy* R. E., A history of Israel, OT: ➤ 384, NJBC (1989s) [1219-] 1224-1243.

b313 **Nagle** D. Brendan, The ancient world, a social and cultural history². ENJ 1989, Prentice Hall. viii-436 p. 0-13-036419-3 [OIAc N89].

b314 **Nibbi** Alessandra, Canaan and Canaanite in ancient Egypt. Ox 1989, DiscEgPubl. 128 p.; 29 fig.; XVI pl. 0-9510704-4-4.

b315 *a*) *Oller* Gary H., The inscription of Idrimi; a pseudo-autobiography?; – *b*) *Sigrist* Marcel, Le deuil pour Šu-Sin [Ur-III, roi]; – *c*) *Wilcke* Claus, Genealogical and geographical thought in the Sumerian King List; – *d*) *Winter* Irene J., The body of the able ruler; toward an understanding of the statues of Gudea; – *e*) *Klein* Jacob, From Gudea to Šulgi; continuity and change in Sumerian literary tradition: ➤ 183, ᶠSJÖBERG Å., Dumu- 1989, 411-7 / 499-505 / 557-571 / 573-583 / 289-301.

b316 **Pikaza** Xabier, Para leer la historia del Pueblo de Dios 1988 ➤ 4,d105; pt. 1400: ᴿActuBbg 26 (1989) 462 (R. de *Sivatte*); Proyección 36 (1989) 72s (J. L. *Sicre*).

b317 *Prato* Gian Luigi, A proposito di una 'nuova' storia di Israele [*Lemche* N. 1988]: RivB 37 (1989) 65-71.

b318 **Quarantini** Marco, Israele tra la profezia e la storia: Documenti. Cuneo 1989, Arciere. 125 p. Lit. 15.000.

b319 **Robbins** Ellen, Studies in the prehistory of the Jewish calendar: diss. ᴰ*Levine* B. NYU 1989. 230 p. 90-04237. – DissA 50 (1989s) 2939-A.

b320 **Schaefer** P., Histoire des juifs dans l'antiquité. P 1989, Cerf. 280 p. F 139. 2-204-02968-8 [ÉTRel 64,674].

b321 *Schwartz* Glenn M., The origins of the Aramaeans in Syria and northern Mesopotamia; research problems and potential strategies: ➤ 122, ꟳLooN M. van, To the Euphrates 1989, 275-291.

b322 ᴱ**Shanks** Hershel, Ancient Israel, a short history from Abraham to the Roman destruction of the Temple. L 1989, SPCK. £13. – ᴿTLond 92 (1989) 307s (R. P. *Carroll*: very well written, while claiming 'We would pretty much know what happened from the biblical text even without the archaeological discoveries. The reverse is not at all true').

b323 ᴱ**Sigrist** Christian, *Neu* Rainer, Vor- und Frühgeschichte Israels: Ethnologische Texte zum AT 1. Neuk 1989, Neuk.-V. 230 p. 3-7887-1289-9. 17 art.; biblical relevance remote.

b324 **Smelik** Klaas A. D., Historische Dokumente aus dem alten Israel 1987 ➤ 3,b592 ... 4,d108: ᴿScripTPamp 21 (1989) 693 (K. *Limburg*); TPQ 137 (1989) 77s (Borghild *Baldauf*).

b325 *Smelik* K. A. D., De Hebreeuwse Bijbel als historische bron [Societas Hebraica Amstelodemensis anniv. 25]: AmstCah 8 (1987) 9-22 [23-27 tegenreferaat, *Mulder* M. J.; < GerefTTs 89,61].

b326 *Smend* Rudolf, Zur ältesten Geschichte Israels, Gesammelte Studien 2 (1957-83), 1987 ➤ 4,265: ᴿÉTRel 64 (1989) 613s (T. *Römer*).

b327 *Smick* E., Old Testament cross-culturalism [relation to other cultures]; paradigmatic or enigmatic?: JEvTS 32 (1989) 3-16 [< ZAW 102,279].

b328 **Smith** Morton, Palestinian parties 1987² [¹1971] ➤ 3,b593a: ᴿEstAg 23 (1988) 699s (C. *Mielgo*); ExpTim 99 (1987s) 340s (I. W. *Provan*: should have taken account of the severe criticisms); Protestantesimo 44 (1989) 47s (J. A. *Soggin*, ital. ➤ 65,9572; 3,b593); TLond 91 (1988) 526s (R. *Coggins*).

b329 **Soggin** J. Alberto, A history of ancient Israel 1984 ➤ 65,9573 ... 4,d109: ᴿCriswT 2 (1988) 428s (G. L. *Klein*); RelStT 7,1 (1987) 78s (L. *Eslinger*); TPhil 64 (1989) 253-6 (N. *Lohfink*).

b330 *Soggin* J. A., *al.*, Le origini di Israele 1986/7 ➤ 3,564; 4,d112: ᴿRivB 37 (1989) 207-211 (A. *Bonora*).

b331 *Thomson* Robert W., The [... biblical; Armenian] historical compilation of Vardan AREWELC'I: DumbO 43 (1989) 125-226.

b332 **Weiler** Gershon, Jewish theocracy. Leiden 1988, Brill. xiv-332 p. [TR 85,522].

b334 *Woude* A. S. van der, Zur Geschichte der Grenze zwischen Juda und Israel: ➤ 129, ꟳMULDER M., New avenues 1989, 38-48.

Q2 Historiographia – *theologia historiae.*

b335 **Bartnik** Czesław S., Chrystus jako sens historii / Historia ludzka i Chrystus 1987 ➤ 3,b602: ᴿTR 85 (1989) 470-2 (S. *Rabiej*).

b336 *Bartnik* Czesław S., ⊕ Zur Historiologie des heiligen AUGUSTINUS: ➤ 51, ꟳEBOROWICZ W. = VoxPa 15 (1988) 787-800; deutsch 801.

b337 **Boschi** Bernardo G., Le origini di Israele nella Bibbia fra storia e teologia; la questione del metodo e la sfida storiografica: RivB supp. Bo 1989, Dehoniane. 128 p. Lit. 15.000 [RivB 37,312 adv.].

b338 *Brandfon* Frederic R., Small pasts in Syro-Palestine; E. LeRoy LADURIE and the writing of local history [more applicable to Palestine coast than similar Mediterranean-Europe theorizing of Fernand BRAUDEL (summary)]: ➤ 830, AIA 90th, AJA 93 (1989) 263.

b339 **Breebaart** A. B., Clio and antiquity; history and historiography of the Greek and Roman world: Amst Hist. Reeks 2. Hilversum 1987, Verloren. 128 p. f 35. 90-6550-310-2 [JRS 78,273].

b340 **Carena** Ómar, History of the Near Eastern historiography and its problems I. 1852-1945: AOAT 218. Neuk/Kevelaer 1989, Neuk-V./Butzon & B. 143 p. 3-7887-1293-7 / 3-7666-9637-8.

b341 **Carr** Edward H. (1892-1982), Qu'est-ce que l'histoire? [successful Cambridge lectures 1961, only now translated, partly because paralleled by H. MARROU's 1954 De la connaissance historique; but with Carr's new notes prepared for a revised edition which never appeared]: Armillaire. P 1988, Découverte. 233 p. F 120. – ᴿRHE 84 (1989) 827 (J.-P. Hendrickx).

b342 **Cesana** Andreas, Geschichte als Entwicklung? Zur Kritik des geschichtsphilosophischen Entwicklungsdenkens: Quellen und Studien zur Philosophie 22. B 1988, de Gruyter. 405 p. – ᴿGGA 241 (1989) 275-281 (O. G. Oexle).

b343 **Conyers** A. J., God, hope, and history; Jürgen MOLTMANN and the Christian concept of history. Macon GA 1988, Mercer Univ. xiii-227 p. $40; pa. $30. 0-87554-297-X; 324-0 [TDig 36,362].

b344 ᴱ**Crawford** M., al., Fuentes para el estudio de la Historia Antigua [1983 ➤ 65,380.9583],ᵀ. M 1986, Taurus. 255 p.; 22 fig. – ᴿGerión 6 (1988) 292-5 (J. Gómez-Pantoia).

b345 ᴱ**Croke** Brian, **Emmett** Alanna M., History and historians in late antiquity 1981/3 ➤ 3,755; 4,d127: ᴿCrNSt 10 (1989) 168s (J. M. Alonso-Núñez).

b346 a) **Davidse** J., Geschiedenis is ook niet meer wat het geweest is; uit de lotgevallen van een begrip; – b) **Talstra** E., Clio en de 'agenda van de toekomst'; het Oude Testament van verhaalkunstenaars, gelovigen en historici: GerefTTs 89 (1989) 196-211 / 212-225 (-258, al.).

b347 **Dihle** Albrecht, Die Entstehung der historischen Biographie: Szb Heid ph/h 1986/3. Heid 1987, Winter. 90 p. DM 50. – ᴿAntClas 58 (1989) 348-350 (J. Wankenne).

b348 **Finley** M. I., Problemi e metodi di storia antica [1985], ᵀLo Cascio E. R 1987, Laterza. 210 p. Lit. 22.000. 88-420-2903-3. – ᴿOpus 5 (1986) 127-132 (C. R. Whittaker) & 133-7 (P. Garnsey) & 139-142 (C. Ampolo), dal convegno R 1988.

b349 **Garbini** Giovanni, Storia e ideologia nell'Israele antico 1986 ➤ 2,9256... 4,d130: ᴿAntClas 58 (1989) 443s (C. Orrieux: ord. de philologie sémitique, n'est pas bibliste et s'en fait gloire... pugnacité fort peu universitaire); Carthaginensia 5 (1989) 275 (J. F. Cuenca); CiuD 202 (1989) 746 (J. Gutiérrez); ExpTim 99 (1987s) 327s (R. Coggins); Eng. p. 340 (R. N. Whybray: polemical scepticism); ScripTPamp 21 (1989) 344s (S. Ausín: precipitación).

b350 **Garbini** Giovanni, History and ideology in ancient Israel 1988 ➤ 4,d131: ᴿBibTB 19 (1989) 110s (L. A. Sinclair: G. dismisses all Christian scholars as prejudiced); BS 146 (1989) 349 (E. H. Merrill: nihilistic); Horizons 16 (1988) 162 (Alice L. Laffey); OTAbs 11 (1988) 310 (R. E. Murphy: more provoking than provocative); RelStR 15 (1989) 256 (W. L. Humphreys: pricks others' balloons while overinflating his own); Themelios 14 (1988s) 105 (A. R. Millard: flawed reasoning page after page); TLond 92 (1989) 304-6 (J. Barton: cruel sport against sacred cows;

the pot calling the kettle black; pursuit of the untenable by the un-provable); TS 50 (1989) 168s (F. L. *Moriarty*).

b351 **Garcia Archilla** Aurelio A., Truth in history; theology of history and apologetic historiography in Henrich BULLINGER: diss. Princeton Theol. Sem. 1989, DDowey E. 494 p. 89-23107. – DissA 50 (1989s) 2112-A; RelStR 16,190.

b352 *Geerlings* Wilhelm, Vom Prinzip Bewährung zum Prinzip Offenbarung; die Umbildung der antiken Geschichtsphilosophie: TPhil 64 (1989) 87-95.

b353 EGibson M., *Biggs* R. D., The organization of power; aspects of bureaucracy in the Ancient Near East 1987 → 3,781: RAJA 93 (1989) 292s (B. R. *Foster*).

b354 *Gossman* L., Towards a rational historiography: AmPhTr 79,3 (Ph 1989) 1-68.

b355 **Góźdź** Krzysztof, Jesus Christus als Sinn der Geschichte bei W. PANNENBERG: Eichstätter St. 25. Rg 1988, Pustet. 284 p. DM 68 [TR 86,13s, G.-L. *Müller*]. – RActuBbg 28 (1989) 210 (J. *Boada*); TLZ 114 (1989) 539s (G. *Wenz*).

b356 **Hafstad** Kjetil, Wort und Geschichte; das Geschichtsverständnis Karl BARTHs: BeitEvT 98, 1985 → 3,b622; 4,d138: RGerefTTs 89 (1989) 124-7 (C. van der *Kooi*).

Halpern Baruch, The first historians; the Hebrew Bible and history 1988 → 1910.

b357 **Heil** W., Das Problem der Erklärung in der Geschichtswissenschaft; ein Beitrag zum Selbstverständnis und zur Objektivität der Geschichtswis-senschaft [Diss.]. Fra 1988, Fischer. 203 p. DM 28 [RHE 84,187*].

b358 **Hengel** Martin, La storiografia protocristiana: StBPaid 73, 1985 → 1,a978; 2,9263: RProtestantesimo 44 (1989) 132s (G. *Conte*).

b359 **Hodgson** Peter C., God in history [not 'the mythos of salvation-history']; shapes of freedom. Nv 1989, Abingdon. 287 p. $22. – RTTod 46 (1989s) 442-4 (G. D. *Kaufman*: brilliant).

b360 **Koch** Kurt, Der Gott der Geschichte; Theologie der Geschichte bei W. PANNENBERG als Paradigma einer philosophischen Theologie in öku-menischer Perspektive [kath. Diss. Luzern]. Mainz 1989, Grünewald. 459 p. DM 64. 3-7867-1370-7 [ÉTRel 64,673]. – RJEcuSt 26 (1989) 218s (R. P. *Scharlemann*); MüTZ 40 (1989) 164 (E. *Zwick*).

b361 *Kracik* Jan, ⊖ Secularization of the concept of church history in the Enlightenment: STWsz 26,2 (1988) 253-262.

b362 **La Capra** Dominick, History and criticism. Ithaca NY 1987, Cornell Univ. 145 p. $22; pa. $7 [RelStR 16,135, D. *Jobling*].

b363 *Latta* Bernd, Die Ausgestaltung der Geschichtskonzeption SALLUSTS, vom *Bellum iugurthinum* zu den *Historien*: Maia [40 (1988) 271-288] 41 (1989) 41-57.

b364 *Lettieri* Gaetano, Il senso della storia in AGOSTINO d'Ippona; il 'sae-culum' e la gloria nel 'De Civitate Dei': Cultura cristiana antica. R 1988, Borla. 346 p. Lit. 30.000. – RRSPT 73 (1989) 483-5 (G.-M. de *Durand*).

b365 *Martin* F., Literary theory, philosophy of history and exegesis: Thomist 52 (1988) 575-604.

b366 a) *McConville* J. Gordon, History, criticism and biblical theology; – b) *Blocher* Henri, Biblical narrative and historical reference; – c) *Kearsley* Roy, Christ and history; an early version: → 544, Issues 1987/9, 68-86 / 102-122 / 87-101.

b367 EMoxon I. S., *al.*, Past perspectives 1983/6 → 3,768; 4,d151: RAnzAltW 42 (1989) 75-78 (H. *Grassl*).

b368 *a*) *Nagl-Dockal* Herta, Geschichtsphilosophie; – *b*) *Smend* Rudolf, AT...; – *c*) *Holtz* Traugott, NT, Geschichtsschreibung: ➤ 894, EvKL 2 (1988) 115-7 / 117-9 / 119-121 [-7; 127-131, Geschichtstheologie, *Ringleben* Joachim; 461-7, Heilsgeschichte, *Wiederkehr* Dietrich].

b369 *Neusner* Jacob, The birth of history in Christianity and Judaism: ➤ 329, Method and Meaning 4 (1989) 229-242.

b370 **Nicolai** W., Versuch über HERODOTs Geschichtsphilosophie: Bibl. Klas. Alt-Wiss. 2/77, 1986 ➤ 2,9279; DM 19,80: ᴿGymnasium 96 (1989) 76s (K. H. *Kinzl*, Eng.).

b371 *Pannenberg* Wolfhart, Hermeneutics and universal history [< JTC 4 (1967) 122-152]: ➤ 3,368, ᴱ*Wachterhauser* Brice R., Hermeneutics and modern philosophy 1986, 111-146.

b372 *Peddle* Francis, Historical and transhistorical tension in VICO's philosophy of history: ScEspr 40 (1988) 127-149.

b373 **Plass** Paul, Wit and the writing of history; the rhetoric of historiography in imperial Rome. Madison 1988, Univ. Wisconsin. 182 p. $37.70; pa. $17.50. 0-299-11800-2; 4-5 [Antiquity 63,79].

b374 **Ratzinger** Joseph, La théologie de l'histoire de saint BONAVENTURE [1959], ᵀ*Givord* R.: Théologiques 1. P 1988, PUF. 206 p. F 168. 2-13-041828-7. – ᴿÉTRel 64 (1989) 446 (H. *Bost*); RHPR 69 (1989) 356s (G. *Siegwalt*: ouvrage excellent, traduction remarquable).

b375 **Rike** R. I., Apex omnium — religion in the Res Gestae of AMMIANUS 1987 ➤ 3,b640: ᴿAthenaeum 67 (1989) 340 (A. *Marcone*).

b376 *Russell* Peter A., The challenge of writing Christian history: Fides et Historia 21,1 (1989) 8-19 [< ZIT 89,326].

b377 *Sicré* José L., ¿Hay verdaderos historiadores en el antiguo Israel? [... no mitificar la historiografía griega]: Proyección 36 (1989) 55-67.

b378 **Shtayerman** E. M., *al.*, ❸ The current tasks facing the Journal of Ancient History: VDI 188 (1989) 3-13.

b379 **Stannard** David E., Shrinking history; on FREUD and the failure of psychohistory. NY 1980, Oxford-UP [CBQ 51,167].

b380 **Starr** Chester G., Past and future in ancient history: Asn Ancient Historians 1. Lanham MD 1987, UPA. x-70 p. $7.25. – ᴿRelStR 15 (1989) 162 (C. F. *Aling*).

b381 *Starr* Chester G., The birth of history: ParPass 249 (1989) 446-462.

b382 **Toynbee** A. J., A study of history, new abridgment with *Caplan* J. L 1988, Thames & H. 576 p.; 417 fig. + 90 color.; 23 maps. £15. 0-500-27539-4 [JRS 79,279].

b383 *Verbrugghe* Gerald P., On the meaning of *annales*, on the meaning of annalist: Philologus 133 (1989) 192-230.

b383* **Whitrow** G. J., Time in history; views of time from prehistory to the present day. Ox 1988, Univ. 217 p.; 8 fig.; £15. 0-19-215361-7 [Antiquity 63,100].

b384 *Wiles* Maurice, In what contexts does it make sense to say 'God acts in history?': ➤ 143, ᶠOGDEN S., Witness 1989, 190-9.

b384* **Wood** Richard A., Event and record; Old Testament historiography in the light of analytical philosophy of history: diss. Southern Baptist Theol. Sem. 1989, ᴰ*Watts* J. 285 p. 90-08965. – DissA 50 (1989s) 2936-A.

Q3 *Historia Ægypti* – Egypt.

b385 **Aldred** Cyril, The Egyptians²ʳᵉᵛ [= 1984 ¹1961]: Ancient Peoples and Places. L 1988, Thames & H. 216 p.; 139 fig. + viii colour. 0-500-27345-6.

b386 *Amelotti* Mario, L'Egitto augusteo tra novità e continuità: JJurPap 20 (1988) 19-24.

b387 *Aston* D. A., Takeloth II — a king of the 'Theban Twenty-Third Dynasty'? [after 825, not before]: JEA 75 (1989) 139-153.

b388 **Bastianini** Guido, *Whitehorne* John, Strategi and royal scribes of Roman Egypt; chronological list and index: Papyrol. Flor. 15, 1987 → 3,b656; Lit. 160.000: ᴿCdÉ 64 (1989) 350s (J. *Bingen*).

b389 **Bonhême** Marie-Ange, Le livre des rois de la troisième période intermédiaire I, XXIᵉ Dynastie: IFAO BÉt 99, 1987 → 3,b660: ᴿBO 46 (1989) 52s (W. J. *Murnane*: surpasses outdated H. GAUTHIER but with cumbersome arrangement).

b390 **Bourguet** Pierre du, Les Coptes² (corrigée) [¹1988]. Que sais-je? 2398. P 1989, PUF. 125 p. 2-13-042503-8. – ᴿOrChrPer 55 (1989) 227s (R.-G. *Coquin*); RHPR 69 (1989) 333s (D. A. *Bertrand*).

b391 **Bowman** Alan K., Egypt after the Pharaohs 332 B.C.-A.D. 642: 1986 → 2,9302... 4,d179: ᴿAncHRes 19 (1989) 94-96 (J. *Whitehorne*); BA 52 (1989) 52-54 (R. V. *McCleary*); BonnJbb 189 (1989) 651-5 (Heinz *Heinen*); Gerión 6 (1988) 296 (G. *Fernández*).

b392 **Cesaretti** Maria Pia, Nerone e l'Egitto; messaggio politico e continuità culturale: Studi di Storia Antica 12. Bo 1989, CLUEB. 120 p.; 12 pl.

b393 *Cesaretti* Maria Pia, In nota a Sinuhe, B 274: StEgPun 4 (1989) 31-42.

b394 *De Salvia* Fulvio, Cultura egizia e cultura greca in età pre-ellenistica; attrazione e repulsione: EgVO 12 (1989) 125-138.

b395 *DeVries* LaMoine, The Hyksos: BibIll 14,2 (1988) 62-65 [< OTAbs 12,37].

b396 *Fishwick* Duncan, Statues taxes in Roman Egypt [a special tax for upkeep of imperial statues]: Historia 38 (1989) 335-347.

b397 **Foertmeyer** Victoria A., Tourism in Graeco-Roman Egypt: diss. Princeton 1989. 366 p. 89-20342. – DissA 50 (1989) 1650-A.

b398 **Gestermann** Louise, Kontinuität und Wandel in Politik und Verwaltung des frühen Mittleren Reiches in Ägypten: GöOrF 4/18, 1987 → 3,b675; 4,d193: ᴿBO 46 (1989) 584-590 (S. *Quirke*).

b399 *Gnirs* Andrea, Haremhab — ein Staatsreformator?: StAltÄgK 16 (1989) 83-110.

b400 *Görg* Manfred, 'Bundesterminologie' im Seevölkertext Ramses' III: BibNot 42 (1988) 19-26.

b401 *Gordon* Andrew, Who was the southern vizier during the last part of the reign of Amenhotep III? [(another, Thebes-tomb) Amenhotep, and Ramose northern, inverting the current consensus]: JNES 48 (1989) 15-23.

b402 **Gutgesell** Manfred, Arbeiter und Pharaonen; Wirtschafts- und Sozialgeschichte im Alten Ägypten. Hildesheim 1989, Gerstenberg. 261 p. (color.) ill. 3-8067-2026-0.

b403 **Helck** Wolfgang, Politische Gegensätze im alten Ägypten: Hildesheimer ÄgBeit 23, 1986 → 2,9382; 4,d197: ᴿCdÉ 64 (1989) 177-181 (M. *Malaise*).

b404 *Helck* Wolfgang, Nochmals zur angeblichen Mitregentenschaft Sesostris' I. mit seinem Vater Amenemhet I.: Orientalia 58 (1989) 315-7.

b405 **Hornung** Erik, Geist der Pharaonenzeit. Z 1989, Artemis. 224 p.; ill. 3-7608-1005-5.

b406 **James** T. G. H., Ancient Egypt, the land and its legacy 1988 → 4,d201: ᴿBO 46 (1989) 562 (B. *Vachala*).

b407 **Jansen-Winkeln** Karl, Ägyptische Biographien der 22. und 23. Dynastie 1985 → 1,b49: ᴿJNES 48 (1989) 227s (E. S. *Meltzer*).

b408 **Kambitsis** Sophie, Le Papyrus Thmouis I, colonnes 68-160: Sorbonne-Papyrologie 3, 1985 ➤ 2,9331; 3,1855; x-196 p.; 16 pl. 2-8594-4101-8. – ᴿJEA 75 (1989) 288a (J. D. *Thomas*: not a dull receipt, but full of information).

b409 **Kemp** Barry J., Ancient Egypt; anatomy of a civilization. L 1989, Routledge. vii-356 p.; ill. 0-415-01281-3 [OIAc S89].

b410 **Kitchen** K. A., Ramesside inscriptions 7,1-8, 1986s ➤ 3,b688*; 4,d206: ᴿOLZ 84 (1989) 151-3 (J. von *Beckerath*).

b411 **Kitchen** Kenneth A., Ramesside inscriptions 7, 13-16. Ox 1989, Blackwell. 0-946344-30-2; 1-0; 2-9; 3-7 [OIAc S89].

b412 **Kitchen** Kenneth A., Ramesside inscriptions, historical and biographical, 8 (indexes)/2. Ox 1989, Blackwell. p. 33-64. 0-946344-35-3 [OIAc N89].

b413 **Klose** Dietrich O. A., *Overbeck* Bernhard, Ägypten zur Römerzeit; antikes Leben aufgrund der numismatischen Quellen; Mü 1989, Staatliche Münzsammlung. viii-108 p.; 273 + 28 fig.; p. 93-103, *Schoske* Sylvia, Vergleichsstücke. 3-9800744-8-X.

b414 **Krauss** Rolf, Sothis- und Monddaten 1985 ➤ 1,b56; 3,b690: ᴿOLZ 84 (1989) 401-4 (J. v. *Beckerath*).

b415 *Krauss* Rolf, Alte und neue Korrekturen zu Ronald A. WELLS 'Amarna Calendar Equivalent': GöMiszÄg 109 (1989) 33-36.

b416 **Kutzner** Edgar, Untersuchungen zur Stellung der Frau im römischen Oxyrhynchos: Diss. Münster 1987. – Chiron 19 (1989) 555.

Leahy Anthony, Taniy, a seventh century lady 1989 ➤ 9347; *Lichtheim* M. ➤ 9349.

b418 **Lewis** Naphtali, Greeks in Ptolemaic Egypt 1986 ➤ 3,b692; 4,d209: ᴿAntClas 58 (1989) 430s (A. *Martin*); Athenaeum 67 (1989) 328-331 (Alessandra *Gara*); ÉtClas 57 (1989) 85 (J. A. *Straus*); Gymnasium 96 (1989) 247s (K. H. *Kinzl*).

b419 **Lewis** Naphtali, Life in Egypt under Roman rule 1983 ➤ 64,a39... 3,b693: ᴿGnomon 61 (1989) 176-8 (H. *Heinen*).

b420 **Lewis** Naphtali, La mémoire des sables (La vie en Égypte sous la domination romaine) [1983], ᵀ*Chuvi* Pierre. P 1988, Colin. 222 p. – ᴿRÉG 102 (1989) 579s (P. *Cauderlier*).

b421 *Luft* Ulrich, Illahunstudien IV; zur chronologischen Verwertbarkeit des Sothisdatums: StAltÄgK 16 (1989) 217-233.

b422 **Lloyd** Alan B., HERODOTUS, Book II, commentary 99-182: ÉPR 43, 1988 ➤ 4,d363: ᴿClasR 39 (1989) 191-3 (Stephanie *West*).

b423 ᴱ**Lloyd** Alan B., ERODOTO, le storie volume II, libro II, l'Egitto: Scrittori greci e latini. Fond. Valla. Mi 1989, Mondadori. lxxviii-409 p. 88-04-30666-1.

b424 **Malek** Jaromir, In the shadow of the Pyramids; Egypt during the Old Kingdom [Norman 1986 ➤ 2,9340], also: Echoes of the Ancient World. L 1986, Orbis. 128 p. £8. 0-85613-965-3. – ᴿBO 46 (1989) 290-8 (M. *Eaton-Krauss* adds list of museum objects cited); JNES 48 (1989) 56s (Ann M. *Roth*: spectacularly attractive but very scholarly).

b425 *Malek* Jaromir, An early eighteenth dynasty monument of Sipair from Saqqara [...Memphis under the Hyksos]: JEA 75 (1989) 61-76; 2 fig.; pl. VII-VIII.

b426 **Manniche** Lise, Sexual life in ancient Egypt 1987 ➤ 3,b697; 4,d211*: ᴿJAmEg 26 (1989) 240s (R. S. *Bianchi*).

b427 *Martin-Pardey* Eva, Die Verwaltung im Alten Reich; Grenzen und Möglichkeiten von Untersuchungen zu diesem Thema [*Strudwick* N. 1985]: BO 46 (1989) 533-552.

b428 *a) Meyer* Christine, Zur Verfolgung Hatschepsuts durch Thutmosis III; – *b) Altenmüller* Hartwig, Die 'Geschichte des Schiffbrüchigen' — ein Aufruf zum Loyalismus?: ➤ 80, ᶠHELCK W., Miscellanea 1989, 119-126 / 7-21.

b429 **Moftah** Ramses, Studien zum ägyptischen Königsdogma im Neuen Reich 1985 ➤ 2,9346; 4,d215: ᴿOLZ 84 (1989) 282s (W. *Barta*).

b430 **Murnane** William J., The road to Kadesh... Sety I at Karnak 1985 ➤ 1,b71: ᴿCdÉ 64 (1989) 184-8 (M. *Green*); JEA 75 (1989) 276s (K. A. *Kitchen*); JNES 48 (1989) 48-50 (A. R. *Schulman*).

b431 *Murnane* William J., Rhetorical history? The beginning of Thutmose III's first campaign in Western Asia: JAmEg 26 (1989) 183-9.

Nibbi Alessandra, Canaan and Canaanites in Ancient Egypt 1989 ➤ b314.

b432 **Obsomer** Claude, Les campagnes de Sésostris dans Hérodote; essai d'interprétation du texte grec à la lumière des réalités égyptiennes. Bru 1989, Connaissance de l'Égypte ancienne. 215 p.; maps. 2-87268-000-4 [OIAc S89].

b433 **Parant** Robert, L'affaire Sinouhé... justice répressive égyptienne 1982 ➤ 63,9692... 65,9662: ᴿOLZ 84 (1989) 149-151 (Elke *Blumenthal*).

Pellat Charles, Cinq calendriers égyptiens 1986 ➤ 9380.

b435 **Piacentini** Patrizia, Gli 'amministratori di proprietà' nell'Egitto del III millennio a. C.: StEgPun 6 (intero fasc.). Pisa 1989, Giardini. 244 p.

b436 **Redford** Donald B., Pharaonic king-lists, annals and day-books; a contribution to the study of the Egyptian sense of history: JSStEg [ssea] 4, 1986 ➤ 4,d219*: ᴿBASOR 276 (1989) 93s (J. *Baines*); RB 96 (1989) 435s (R. *Beaud*).

b436* **Rice** E. E., The grand procession of Ptolemy Philadelphus 1983 ➤ 65,9666... 2,9351: ᴿCdÉ 64 (1989) 360s (J. *Lenaerts*).

b437 *Rössler-Köhler* Ursula, Gab es 'Todesanzeigen' in der 26. Dynastie? Zur Bedeutung der saitischen jm3ḫw-ḫr-njswt-Formel: StAltÄgK 16 (1989) 255-274.

b438 **Ruprechtsberger** Erwin M., Die Garamanten, Geschichte und Kultur eines libyschen Volkes in der Sahara: AntWelt Sondernummer 20a (1989). 72 p. 108 (color.) fig.

b439 **Samson** Julia, Nefertiti and Cleopatra 1985 ➤ 3,b712: ᴿCdE 64 (1989) 181-3 (R. S. *Bianchi*).

b440 **Sonnabend** Holger, Fremdenbild und Politik; Vorstellungen der Römer von Ägypten und dem Partherreich in der späten Republik und frühen Kaiserzeit [Diss. Hannover 1985]: EurHS 3/286, 1986 ➤ 2,9619; 3,b717: ᴿAthenaeum 67 (1989) 624s (D. *Asheri*); ClasR 39 (1989) 86s (Dorothy J. *Thompson*); JRS 79 (1989) 196 (S. *Mitchell*).

b441 **Trigger** B. G., *al.*, Ancient Egypt, a social history [< Cambridge History of Africa, except A. B. Lloyd on Late Period] 1983 ➤ 64,a66... 2,9358*: ᴿJNES 48 (1989) 226s (W. J. *Murnane*: escapes weaknesses of GARDINER and others, but lacks pedagogical framework).

b442 **Trigger** B. G., *Kemp* B. J., *al.*, Historia del Egipto Antiguo 1985 ➤ 2,9359: ᴿBAsEspOr 23 (1987) 426-8 (G. *Carrasco Serrano*).

b443 *a) Trigger* Bruce G., Egypt; a fledgling nation; – *b) Berg* David A., Early 18th dynasty expansion into Nubia; – *c) Redford* Donald B., The Tod inscription of Senwosret I and early 12th dynasty involvement in Nubia and the south: ➤ 181, ᶠSHINNIE P., JSSEg 17,1s (1987) 58-66 / 1-14 / 36-55; 5 fig.; pl. IV-IX.

b444 **Troy** Lana, Patterns of queenship in ancient Egyptian myth and history: Boreas 14, 1986 ➤ 2,9360; 3,b724: ᴿJAmEg 26 (1989) 242-4 (P. *Dils*).

b445 *Vernus* Pascal, La stèle du Pharaon *Mntw-htpi* à Karnak, un nouveau témoignage sur la situation politique et militaire au début de la d. p. i.: ➤ 39, Mém. CLÈRE J., RÉgp 40 (1989) 145-161; pl. 6-7; Eng. 161.

b446 *Wells* R. A., On chronology in Egyptology: GöMiszÄg 108 (1989) 87-95.

b447 *Whale* Sheila, *a)* 'Women's lib' in ancient Egypt; – *b)* Royal consorts and female Pharaohs [< 'The woman in the ancient Mediterranean world', Macquarrie Univ., May 1988]: AncHRes 19 (1989) 138-144; 58-64; 4 fig.

b447* **Zibelius-Chen** Karola, Die ägyptische Expansion nach Nubien; eine Darlegung der Grundfaktoren: TAVO Beih-B78. Wsb 1988, Reichert. – ᴿMundus 25 (1989) 138 (W. *Manshard*).

b448 *Zibelius-Chen* Karola, Überlegungen zur ägyptischen Nubienpolitik in der Dritten Zwischenzeit: StAltÄgK 16 (1989) 329-345.

Q4   Historia Mesopotamiae.

b449 *Afanasieva* V. K., ❸ Akkadian rulers in the Sumerian epic; Sargon the great: VDI 189 (1989) 3-12; Eng. 12s.

b450 **Archer** Carla, The Assyrian Empire. 1986, ᴿAncHRes 19 (1989) 166-8 (F. D. *Fiegert*).

b451 **Asher-Greve** Julia M., Frauen in altsumerischer Zeit 1985 ➤ 1,h87: ᴿArOr 57 (1989) 184s (B. *Hruška*).

b452 **Beaulieu** Paul-Alain, The reign of Nabonidus king of Babylon 556-539 B.C. [diss. Yale, ᴰ*Hallo* W.]: NERes 10. NHv 1989, Yale Univ. xiv-270 p. 0-300-04314-7.

b453 **Boncquet** Jan, DIODORUS Siculus (II.1-34) over Mesopotamië; een historische Kommentaar [diss. Lv 1983]: Verh. lett 122. Bru 1987, Acad. Wetenschappen. 243 p. (Eng. 213-5). Fb 1050. 90-6569-384-X. – ᴿAnt-Clas 58 (1989) 441-3 (R. *Tefnin*); RÉG 102 (1989) 253s (B. *Eck*).

b454 **Breuer** Stefan, Imperien der Alten Welt: Urban-Tb 385, 1987 ➤ 3,b731; DM 28. 3-17-009661-3: ᴿBO 46 (1989) 279-282 (H. *Freydank*); HZ 248 (1989) 380-2 (A. *Heuss*).

b455 *a)* **Burian** J., Das Gebiet Mesopotamiens in der Machtstruktur der Spätantike; – *b)* *Dandamajev* M., The Neo-Babylonian popular assembly; – *c)* *Charvát* P., The origins of Sumerian state; a modest proposal; – *d)* *Pečirková* J., The character of political power in Assyria; – *e)* *Zawadzki* S., Umman-manda; Bedeutung des Terminus und Gründe seiner An-wendung in der Chronik von Nabupolassar: ➤ 874, Šulmu 1986/8, 39-47 / 63-71 / 101-132 / 243-255 / 379-387.

b456 **Capomacchia** Anna Maria G., Semiramis, una femminilità ribaltata 1986 ➤ 2,9366; 4,d234: ᴿAntClas 58 (1989) 439-441 (R. *Tefnin*); BO 476 (1989) 651-3 (J. *Bremmer*); ÉtClas 57 (1989) 82s (Corinne *Bonnet*); Latomus 48 (1989) 469s (H. *Limet*); RÉG 101 (1988) 531 (Yvonne *Vernière*).

b457 **Carena** O., History of Near Eastern [Mesopotamian-Hittite] histo-riography and its problems 1852-1985; part I, 1852-1945: AOAT 218. Neuk/Kevelaer 1989, Neuk/Butzon & B. xviii-143 p. DM 67. 3-7887-1293-7 / 3-7666-9637-8 [BL 90,37, G. I. *Davies*].

b458 *Castellino* Giorgio, Il concetto della regalità in Mesopotamia dai testi autobiografici: ➤ 877, Lavoro 1988, 9-16.

b459 *Cogan* Mordechai, Ashurbanipal prisms K and C; further restorations: JCS 41 (1989) 96-99.

b460 *Conradie* A. F.,   The so-called standard titulary of the Ashurnasirpal II (883-859 B.C.) inscriptions: JSem 1 (1989) 174-192.

b461 **Cooper** Jerrold S.,   Sumerian and Akkadian royal inscriptions[T], I. Presargonic 1986 ➔ 2,9369:   [R]BO 46 (1989) 637-641 (J. *Bauer*); CBQ 51 (1989) 313s (D. W. *Baker*).

b462 **Glassner** J.-J.,   La chute d'Akkadé; l'événement et sa mémoire 1986 ➔ 2,9373:   [R]ArOr 57 (1989) 288 (Jana *Pečírková*, Eng.).

b463 **Grayson** A. K.,   Assyrian rulers of the third and second millennium B.C. (to 1115 B.C.):   RIMA 1, 1987 ➔ 3,b736:   [R]JCS 41 (1989) 117-126 (Pamela *Gerardi*); RAss 82 (1988) 88s (D. *Charpin*).

b464 *a) Hallo* William W.,   The Nabonassar era and other epochs in Mesopotamian chronology and chronography; – *b) Michalowski* Piotr, Sin-iddinam and Iškur; – *c) Neugebauer* Otto, A Babylonian lunar ephemeris from Roman Egypt: ➔ 166, Mem. SACHS A. 1988, 175-190 / 265-273 + 2 pl. / 301-304; 2 pl.

b465 *Harrak* Amir,   Historical statements in Middle Assyrian archival sources: JAOS 109 (1989) 205-9.

b466 **Heinsohn** Gunnar,   Die Sumerer gab es nicht 1988 ➔ 4,d244:   [R]ArOr 57 (1989) 289-291 (B. *Hruška*, deutsch: to pass over in silence).

b467 *a) Hienhold-Krahmer* Susanne,   Zu Salmanassars I. Eroberungen im Hurritergebiet; – *b) Moortgat-Correns* Ursula,   Zur ältesten historischen Darstellung der Assyrer; Tukulti-Ninurtas I. Sieg über das Land der Uqumeni (?):   AfO 35 (1988) 79-104 / 111-6; 2 fig.

Hruška B.,   Pod babylónskou věží (Under the tower of Babylon) 1987 ➔ b927.

b469 *Kennedy* D. L.,   The garrisoning of Mesopotamia in the Late Antonine and Early Severan period: Antichthon 21 (1987) 57-66.

b470 *Klinger* Jörg,   Überlegungen zu den Anfängen des Mitanni-Staates: ➔ 817*, Hurriter 1988, 27-41.

b471 **Knapp** A. Bernard,   The history and culture of ancient Western Asia and Egypt 1988 ➔ 4,d248 ('of' culture):   [R]AJA 93 (1989) 470s (B. R. *Foster*).

b472 **Kraus** F. R.,   Königliche Verfügungen in altbabylonischer Zeit 1984 ➔ 65,9700 ... 3,b738*:   [R]BSO 51 (1988) 118-120 (W. G. *Lambert*); JAOS 108 (1988) 153-7 (S. *Greengus*); WZKM 77 (1987) 195-8 (O. R. *Gurney*: reedition of his 'unique and extraordinary' Ammi-Ṣaduqa 1958 with its supplements).

b473 *Kümmel* Hans M.,   Ein Kaufvertrag aus Ḫana mit mittelassyrischer līmu-Datierung: ZAss 79 (1989) 191-200; 2 fig.; 2 pl.

b474 [E]**Lévêque** Pierre,   Les premières civilisations, I. Des despotismes orientaux à la cité grecque [état complètement inédit du volume homonyme de 1926]: Peuples et civilisations.   P 1987, PUF.   627 p.; 11 maps. [R]AntClas 58 (1989) 434-6 (C. *Delvoye*).

[E]**Lévy** Edmond,   Le système palatial en Orient, en Grèce et à Rome 1985/7 ➔ d46.

b476 *Lieberman* Stephen J.,   Royal 'reforms' of the Amurrite dynasty [*Kraus* F. R., Königliche Verfügungen 1984]: BO 46 (1989) 241-259.

b476* **Magen** U.,   Assyrische Königsdarstellungen [Diss. Fra [D]*Beran* T.] 1986 ➔ 3,b742; 4,d252:   [R]ArOr 57 (1989) 286s (Jana *Pečírková*, Eng.: art and documents compared); BL (1989) 126 (W. G. *Lambert*: lavish format and price, DM 180).

b477 *Medvedskaya* I. N.,   ⊕ The route of Sargon's campaign of 714 B.C.:   VDI 189 (1989) 100-116; Eng. 116s; map (Lake Urmia).

b478 **Moortgat** Anton, Die Entstehung der sumerischen Hochkultur [1945], ᴱ*Solyman* Toufic. Bonn/Tartus 1987, Habelt/Amani. xxxvi-164 p.; (neue) Aufnahmen.

b479 ᴱ**Nissen** H.-J., *Renger* J., Mesopotamien und seine Nachbarn 1978/82 ⇥ 63,701; 1,b111: ᴿJNES 47 (1988) 71s (P. *Michalowski*).

b480 **Nissen** Hans J., The early history of the Ancient Near East, 9000-2000 B.C. [1983 ⇥ 64,a95]ᵀ. Ch 1988, Univ. xiv-215 p.; 75 fig. $35 [JNES 48,78].

b481 **Perlmann** Moshe, al-Tᴀʙᴀʀɪ, History 4., The ancient kingdoms: Bibl. Persica. Albany 1987, SUNY. xiii-205 p. 0-88706-182-6 [OIAc Ja90].

b482 **Pettinato** Giovanni, Babilonia, centro dell'universo. T 1988, Rusconi. 315 p. 88-18-88007-X [OIAc Ja90]. – ᴿBbbOr 31 (1989) 43 [F. *Sardini*]; Lettura 44 (Mi 1989) 83-86 (G. *Ravasi*).

b483 **Pettinato** G., Semiramide 1985 ⇥ 1,b114 ... 4,d257: ᴿProtestantesimo 44 (1989) 155s (J. A. *Soggin*); RivB 37 (1989) 105-7 (R. *Gelio*); RStorAnt 17s (1987s) 303-6 (C. *Zaccagnini*, anche su Cᴀᴘᴏᴍᴀᴄᴄʜɪᴀ A.).

b484 *Pomponio* Francesco, a) The Reichskalender of Ur III in the Umma texts: ZAss 89 (1989) 10-13; – b) La rivale di Lagaš: RSO 63 (1989) 25-37.

b485 *Postgate* N., Ancient Assyria a multi-racial state: Aram 1,1 (Ox 1989) 1-10 [< ZAW 102,264].

b486 ꜰRᴇɪɴᴇʀ E., Language, literature, and history, ᴱ**Rochberg-Halton** F. 1987 ⇥ 3,136: ᴿBO 46 (1989) 629-637 (W. H. P. *Römer*: tit. pp., some summaries with comment).

b487 *Röllig* W., [*Görg* M.] Assyrien / Babylonien: ⇥ 902, NBL, Lfg. 2 (1989) 191s, map [Assur 190s] / 227; map [228-233, Kultur; 226s Babel].

b488 **Saggs** H. W. F., Civilization before Greece and Rome. L/NHv 1989, Batsford/Yale Univ. 322 p.; 15 fig.; 25 pl., 4 maps. £20. 0-7134-5277-3 [Antiquity 63,294]. – ᴿClasR 39 (1989) 406s (A. R. *Burn*); Orientalia 58 (1989) 533s (H. *Freydank*).

b489 **Sigrist** Marcel, Isin year names: Assyriological series 2. Berrien Springs ᴍɪ 1988, Andrews Univ. iii-63 p.

b490 *Steinkeller* P. [*Strommenger* E.], Man-ištūšu philologisch [archäologisch]: ⇥ 905, RLA 7,5s (1989) 334s [-339].

b491 *Stolper* Matthew W., The governor of Babylon and Across-the-River in 486 B.C.: JNES 48 (1989) 283-305 [p. 302 casually mentions Ezra 4,8, Rehum].

b492 a) *Storck* Herbert A., The Lydian campaign of Cyrus the Great in classical and cuneiform sources; – b) *Devine* A. M., The Macedonian army at Gaugamela; its strength and the length of its battle-line: AncW 19 (1989) 69-76 / 77-80.

b492* *Tuman* V. S., Astrological omens from lunar eclipses as a source for Babylonian chronology, confirms the long chronology: ⇥ 832*, High/Low III (1988) 197-206.

b493 *Veenhof* Klaas R., The sequence of the 'overseers of the merchants' at Sippar and the date of the year-eponymy of Habil-Kēnum: JbEOL 30 (1987s) 32-37.

b494 **Waschkies** Hans-Joachim, Anfänge der Arithmetik im Alten Orient und bei den Griechen. Amst 1989, Grüner. 386 p.; 42 fig. 90-6032-036-0.

b495 **Watanabe** K., Die adê-Vereidigung anlässlich der Thronfolgeregelung Asarhaddons: BagMitBeih 3, 1987 ⇥ 3,b760: ᴿAulaO 7,1 (1989) 153 (W. G. E. *Watson*: very successful revision of Wɪsᴇᴍᴀɴ 1955); BL (1989) 128 (W. G. *Lambert*).

b496 a) *Weisberg* David B., Zabaya, an early king of the Larsa dynasty; – b) *Donbaz* Veysel, *Harrak* Amir, The Middle Assyrian eponymy of Kidin-Aššur: JCS 41 (1989) 194-7; 3 fig. / 217-225; 2 facsim.

b497 **Wilhelm** Gernot, The Hurrians [1982 ➤ 61,9978* updated], T*Barnes* J.: + *Stein* Diana L. on art, religion, literature. Wmr 1989, Aris & P. ix-132 p. £8.75. 0-85668-442-2 [BL 90, 127, J. F. *Healey*].

b498 **Zawadzki** Stefan, The fall of Assyria and Median-Babylonian relations in light of the Nabupolassar Chronicle: Historia 149. Poznań/Delft 1988, Univ./Eburon. 176 p. 82-232-0122-6 / 90-5166-034-0.

b499 *Zawadzki* Stefan, The first year of Nabupolassar's rule according to the Babylonian Chronicle BM 25127 [*Wiseman* D. 1956; *Grayson* A. 1975]; a reinterpretation of the text and its consequences: JCS 41 (1989) 57-64.

Q4.5 *Historia Persiae,* Iran.

b500 *Bader* A. N., ❾ The problem of the emergence and political structure of the Parthian kingdom in modern historiography: VDI 188 (1989) 216-231.

b501 **Balcer** Jack M., HERODOTUS and Bisitun; problems in ancient Persian historiography: Hist. Einz. 49, 1987 ➤ 3,b765; 4,d268: R*RPg* 62 (1988) 338-340 (M. *Menu*).

b501* *Balcer* Jack M., The Persian wars against Greece; a reassessment: Historia 38 (1989) 127-143.

b502 **Carter** Elizabeth, *Stolper* Matthew W., Elam; surveys of political history and archaeology 1984 ➤ 1,419... 4,d270: R*JAOS* 108 (1988) 514-6 (D. *Fleming*).

b503 **Dandamaev** Muhammad A., A political history of the Achaemenid empire, [❾ 1985] T*Vogelsang* W. J. Leiden 1989, Brill. xv-373 p.; 14 pl., 2 maps.

b504 **Dandamaev** Muhammad A., *Lukonin* Vladimir G., The culture and social institutions of ancient Iran, TE*Kohl* Philip L. C 1989, Univ. xv-463 p.; 45 fig. 0-521-32107-7.

b505 *Fischer* Hagen, Fragen der Beziehungen zwischen Rom und Parthien und ihre Widerspiegelung in der damaligen Literatur (Mitte des I. Jh. v. u. Z. bis Mitte des I. Jh. u. Z.): ➤ 73, F*GÜNTHER* R. = Klio 71/2 (1989) 367-373.

b506 **Frye** Richard N., The history of ancient Iran: HbAltW 3/7, 1984 ➤ 65,9731... 3,b773: R*AcPraeh* 20 (1988) 203-6 (W. *Messerschmidt*); JAOS 108 (1988) 324s (J. R. *Russell*).

b507 *Heltzer* M., The Tell el-Mazar inscription N° 7 and some historical and literary problems of the Vth Satrapy: TEuph 1 (1989) 111-8 [< ZAW 102, 434].

b508 **Kevers-Pascalis** Claude, L'œil du roi; Vie de Cyrus. Nancy/P 1989, Univ./Cerf. 369 p. 2-86480-391-7 / P 2-204-03188-7.

b509 *Mattila* R., The political status of Elam after 653 B.C. according to ABL 839: SAAB 1/1 (1987) 27-30.

b510 *Peat* Jerome, Cyrus 'King of Lands', Cambyses 'King of Babylon'; the disputed co-regency; JCS 41 (1989) 199-216.

b511 *Pomeroy* Sarah B., The Persian King and the Queen Bee: AmJAncH 9/2 (for 1984, in 1990) 98-108.

b512 **Rigginson** Timothy, Greek attitudes to Persian kingship down to the time of XENOPHON: diss. Oxford 1987. 301 p. BRD-85461. – DissA 50 (1989s) 772-A.

b513 ᴱSancisi-Weerdenburg Heleen, al., Achaemenid history I-III, Proceedings 1983-5: 1987s ➤ 3,787; 4,713: ᴿBO 46 (1989) 671-8 (M. A. Dandamayev: tit. pp. summaries).

b514 a) Sancisi-Weerdenburg Heleen, The personality of Xerxes, King of Kings; – b) Wolski Josef, Sur l'impérialisme des Parthes arsacides: ➤ 28, ᶠBERGHE L. Vanden, Archaeologia 1989, 549-561 / (II) 637-650.

b515 Schwarz Franz F., Flammen über Baktrien [gegen Holt F. 1988]: GrazBei 16 (1989) 125-142.

b516 ᶠSTÈVE M.-J., Fragmenta historiae Aelamicae 1986 ➤ 3,a153: ᴿBO 46 (1989) 403-6 (U. Seidl).

b517 Tatum James, XENOPHON's imperial fiction; on the education of Cyrus. Princeton 1989, Univ. xiv-301. $32.50. – ᴿAmJPg 110 (1989) 665-8 (P. A. Stadter).

b518 Trümpelmann Leo, Zur Herkunft von Medern und Persern: ArchMIran 21 (1988) 79-90; 11 fig.

b519 Weiskopf Michael, The so-called 'Great Satraps' Revolt' 366-360 B.C.; concerning local instability in the Achaemenid Far West: Hist. Einz. 63. Stu 1989, Steiner. 112 p. 3-515-05387-5 [OIAc Ja90].

b520 Winter Engelbert, Die sāsānidisch-römischen Friedensverträge 1988 ➤ 4,d287: ᴿHZ 248 (1989) 146s (E. Kettenhofen).

b521 Wolski Jósef, Les commencements de l'Empire parthe: Gerión 6 (1988) 9-19.

b522 ᴱYarshater E., TABARI, History in 38 vol. ➤ 3,b782; 18, 26, 35, 38: 1985: ᴿBSO 51 (1988) 126-8 (G. R. Hawting).

Q5   Historia Anatoliae: Asia Minor, Hittites [➤ T8.2], Armenia [➤ T8.9].

b523 Astour Michael C., Hittite history and absolute chronology of the Bronze Age: SIMA pocket 73. Partille 1989, Åström. iv-152 p. 91- 86098-86-1.

b524 Bryce Trevor R., a) Ahhiyawans and Mycenaeans — an Anatolian viewpoint: OxJArch 8 (1989) 297-310; – b) The nature of Mycenaean involvement in Western Anatolia: Historia 38 (1989) 1-20; map p. 21; – c) Some observations on the chronology of Šuppiluliuma's reign: AnSt 39 (1989) 18-30.

b525 De Martino Stefano, Hattušili I e Haštayar; un problema aperto: OrAnt28 (1989) 1-24.

b526 Hout Theo P. J. van den, A chronology of the Tarhuntassa treaties: JCS 41 (1989) 100-114.

b527 a) Klengel Horst, Aspetti dello sviluppo dello stato ittita; – b) Carruba Onofrio, Stato e società nel Medio Regno eteo; – c) Mora Clelia, I proprietari di sigillo nella società ittita: ➤ 877, Lavoro 1988, 183-194 / 195-224 / 249-269.

b528 McGing B. C., The foreign policy of Mithridates VI 1986 ➤ 3,b794; 4,d297: ᴿGnomon 61 (1989) 67-69 (E. Olshausen); Latomus 48 (1989) 466-8 (A. Valvo).

b529 McMahon Gregory, The history of the Hittites: BA 52 (1989) 62-77.

b530 Macqueen J. G., The Hittites and their contemporaries in Asia Minor²ʳᵉᵛ 1986 ➤ 3,f688; 4,d298: ᴿBA 52 (1989) 46s (G. Beckan); JAOS 109 (1989) 283-7 (A. Ünal: archeological sources over-interpreted; non-English scholarship overlooked).

b531 Panitschek Peter, Zu den genealogischen Konstruktionen der Dynastien von Pontos und Kappadokien [c. 300-100 v. Chr.]: RStorAnt 17s (1987s) 73-95.

b532 **Rémy** Bernard, L'évolution administrative de l'Anatolie aux trois premiers siècles de notre ère: Centre d'Ét. Romaines 1986 ➤ 3,b798; 4,d303: ᴿLatomus 48 (1989) 929 (P. *Salmon*).

b533 *Rigsby* Kent, Provincia Asia: AmPgTr 118 (1988) 123-153.

b534 *Strubbe* J. H. M., Joden en Grieken; onverzoenlijke vijanden? De integratie van Joden in Kleinaziatische steden in de keizertijd: Lampas 22 (1989) 188-204.

b535 *a*) *Zaccagnini* Carlo, A note on Hittite international relations at the time of Tudẖaliya IV; – *b*) *Imparati* Fiorella, Armaziti; attività di un personaggio nel tardo impero ittita; – *c*) *Rosi* Susanna, Gli addetti alla sorveglianza nella società ittita; – *d*) *Del Monte* Giuseppe F., Il mese hittita: ➤ 154, ᶠPUGLIESE CARRATELLI G., 1988, 295-9 / 79-94 / 227-236 / 51-56.

Q6   Historia graeca et hellenistica incluso Alexandro.

b536 **Ager** Sheila L., International arbitration in the Greek world, 337-146 B.C.: diss. British Columbia, ᴰ*Harding* P. – DissA 50 (1989s) 4061-A.

b537 *Alfieri Tonini* Teresa, Atene e Mitilene nel 367 a. C. (IG II² 107): Acme 42 (1989) 47-61.

b538 *Alonso-Núñez* J. A., Historiographie hellénistique pré-polybienne: RÉG 102 (1989) 160-174.

b539 ᴱ**Asheri** David, ERODOTO, Le storie I. La Lidia e la Persia, ᵀ*Antelami* Virginio: Fond. Valla, ScrGrLat. Mi 1988, Mondadori. cxlviii-400 p.; 20 maps. – ᴿClasR 39 (1989) 189s (Stephanie *West*).

b540 *Ball* A.-J., Capturing a bride; marriage practices in classical Sparta [the common view that Spartan women were relatively 'liberated' is based on sources written by neither Spartans nor women]: AncHRes 19 (1989) 75-81.

b541 **Bengtson** H., Die Diadochen 1987 ➤ 4,d311: ᴿAntClas 58 (1989) 464s (Jean A. *Straus*); Athenaeum 67 (1989) 331s (D. *Ambaglio*).

b542 **Bengtson** Hermann, Die hellenistische Weltkultur. Stu 1988, Steiner. 202 p.; 6 pl. DM 38. – ᴿClasR 39 (1989) 286-8 (Amélie *Kuhrt*).

b543 **Bengtson** Hermann, History of Greece from the beginnings to the Byzantine era [⁵1976], ᵀᴱ*Bloedow* Edmund F. Ottawa 1988, Univ. xx-817 p.; ill.; maps. – ᴿRPg 62 (1988) 315s (É. *Will*).

b544 **Bichler** Reinhold, 'Hellenismus' 1983 ➤ 64,9762; 3,b810: ᴿZRGg 41 (1989) 285s (J. M. *Alonso-Núñez*).

b545 **Bosworth** A. B., From Arrian to Alexander; studies in historical interpretation. Ox 1988, Clarendon. x-225 p. £25. – ᴿAmJPg 110 (1989) 376-8 (P. A. *Stadter*); ClasR 39 (1989) 21-23 (N. G. L. *Hammond*); Gnomon 61 (1989) 554-6 (W. *Will*).

b546 **Bosworth** A. B., [➤ 239] Conquest and empire; the reign of Alexander the Great. C 1988. xiii-330 p. £10. 0-521-34320-8; pa. 823-4. – ᴿArctos 23 (1989) 279s (K. *Karttunen*); ClasR 39 (1989) 290s (A. R. *Burn*).

b547 ᴱ**Brenk** F. E., *Gallo* A., Miscellanea Plutarchea 1985/6 ➤ 2,521; 4,d319: ᴿArctos 23 (1989) 257s (R. *Westman*).

b548 *Bruyn* Odile de, L'Aréopage et la Macédoine à l'époque de Démosthène: ÉtClas 57 (1989) 3-12.

b549 *Burstein* Stanley M., The Greek tradition from Alexander to the end of antiquity: ➤ 558, ᴱ*Thomas* Carol G., Paths from ancient Greece 1988, 27-50.

b550 **Cartledge** Paul, Agesilaos and the crisis of Sparta. L 1987, Duckworth. xii-508 p.; 24 fig. £39.50. – RClasR 39 (1989) 283s (J. F. *Lazenby*).

b551 ᴱ**Crawford** Michael, Sources for ancient history 1983 ➤ 1,421: RGnomon 61 (1989) 550s (F. G. *Maier*).

b552 **Cunliffe** R. W., Greeks, Romans and barbarians; spheres of interaction. L 1988, Batsford. xii-243 p.; 76 fig. 0-7134-5273-0. – RGreeceR 36 (1989) 113 (T. *Wiedemann* wants 'Margreb' corrected to 'Mahgreb' inter alia); JRS 79 (1989) 236-9 (G. *Woolf*, also on RANKIN H. and ᴱROWLANDS M. 1987); RÉLat 67 (1989) 358-360 (R. *Adam*).

b553 *Devine* A. M., The generalships of Ptolemy and Demetrius Poliorcetes at the battle of Gaza (312 B.C.): AncW 20 (1989) 29-38.

b553* **Drews** Robert, The coming of the Greeks; Indo-European conquests in the Aegean and the Near East 1988 ➤ 4,d330; $30: RJAOS 109 (1989) 671s (J. A. C. *Greppin*: not competent to analyse linguistic data).

b554 **Droysen** Johann D., Ⓖ Geschichte des Hellenismus, I. Geschichte Alexanders des Grossen, ᵀ(Neugriechisch). Athen 1988, Trapeza Pistos. 837 p. – RBonnJbb 189 (1989) 573-5 (P. *Zachariadou*).

b555 **du Bois** Page, Sowing the body; psychoanalysis and ancient [... Greek] representations of women 1988 ➤ 4,d331: RHistRel 29 (1989s) 191 (Jorunn J. *Buckley*).

b555* **Effenterre** H. Van. Les structures politiques des premiers établissements grecs: ➤ 811, Momenti 1975/8, 169-176.

b556 **Errington** Malcolm, Geschichte Makedoniens 1986 ➤ 3,d333: RClasPg 84 (1989) 160-5 (A. B. *Bosworth*); DLZ 109 (1988) 282s (M. *Oppermann*); RÉG 102 (1989) 213-5 (P. *Cabanes*).

b557 **Farrar** Cynthia, The origins of democratic thinking; the invention of politics in classical Athens. C 1989, Univ. x-301 p. 0-521-34054-3; pa. -7584-3.

b558 **Flory** Stewart, The archaic smile of HERODOTUS 1987 ➤ 4,d335: RAmHR 94 (1989) 107s (Mabel L. *Lang*); JHS 109 (1989) 217s (C. W. *Fornara*); Phoenix 43 (Toronto 1989) 172-4 (J. M. *Bigwood*); RPg 62 (1988) 336s (M. *Menu*).

b559 **Gagarin** Michael, Early Greek law. Berkeley 1986, Univ. California. ix-167 p. $27.50. – RAmJPg 110 (1989) 362-7 (R. W. *Wallace*, R. *Westbrook*).

b560 *Gasparov* M. L., Ⓑ Incompleteness and symmetry in HERODOTUS' 'History': VDI 189 (1988) 117-122; Eng. 122.

b561 *Gerolymatos* André, The *proxenia* and the development of diplomacy in classical Greece: ➤ 70, ᶠGORDON C. 1987, 65-67.

b562 *Goralski* Walter J., ARRIAN's Events after Alexander; summary of PHOTIUS and selected fragments: AncW 19 (1989) 81-108.

b563 **Grant** Michael, The rise of the Greeks 1987 ➤ 4,d340; also NY 1988, Scribner's. xv-391 p. $27.50. – RClasR (1989) 64s (N. G. L. *Hammond*); Gnomon 61 (1989) 631-3 (J. *Weiler*); RelStR 15 (1989) 163 (A. *Avramides*).

b564 **Gray** Vivienne, The character of XENOPHON's Hellenica: Baltimore 1989, Johns Hopkins Univ. x-219 p. $32.50 [AmJPg 111, 408-410, W. C. *West*].

b565 *a)* **Green** Peter, The dog that barked in the night; revisionist thoughts on the diffusion of Hellenism; – *b*) *Eliot* C. W. J., Kleisthenes of Athens and the disputed case of the paternity of democracy; – *c*) *Barnes* T. D., The Constantinian reformation: ➤ 787, ᴱ*Fancy* M., Crake lectures 1984/6, 1-26 / 27-37 / 39-57.

b566 *Habicht* Christian,   Athen und die Seleukiden: Chiron 19 (1989) 7-26.

b567 *a) Hackl* Ursula,   Alexander der Grosse und der Beginn des Hellenistischen Zeitalters; – *b) Klein* Richard,   Zur Beurteilung Alexanders des Grossen in der patristischen Literatur: ➤ 215, ᶠWIRTH G., Zu Alexander 2 (1988) 693-716 / 925-989.

b568 *a) Halfmann* Helmut,   Die politischen Beziehungen zwischen Griechenland und den Diadochen; – *b) Kneppe* Alfred,   Timarchos von Milet — ein Usurpator im Seleukidenreich: ➤ 151, ᶠPEKÁRY T., Migratio 1989, 19-36 / 37-49.

b569 **Hammond** N. G. L.,   *Walbank* F. W.,   A history of Macedonia [I. 1973; II. 1978 ➤ 61,q729] III. (last) 336-167 B.C. Ox 1988, Clarendon. xxx-654 p.; 70 fig.; 4 pl. £65. – ᴿClasR 39 (1989) 288-290 (R. M. *Errington*); RÉLat 67 (1989) 331s (J.-L. *Ferrary*).

b570 **Hammond** Nicholas G. L.,   The Macedonian state; origins, institutions, and history. Ox 1989, Clarendon. xx-413 p.; end-maps. 0-19-814883-6.

b571 **Hammond** N. G. L.,   Arms and the king; the insignia of Alexander the Great: Phoenix 43 (Toronto 1989) 217-224.

b572 **Hansen** Mogens H.,   The Athenian assembly in the age of Demosthenes 1987 ➤ 4,d346;   0-631-15485-X. – ᴿAntClas 58 (1989) 456s (D. *Viviers*).

b573 **Hansen** Mogens H.,   Was Athens a democracy? Popular rule, liberty and equality in ancient and modern political thought: Dansk. Videnskab. Meddel. 59.   K 1989, Munksgaard.   47 p.

b574 **Heckel** Waldemar,   The last days and testament of Alexander the Great; a prosopographic study: Historia Einz. 56.   Stu 1988, Steiner.   xiv-114 p. – ᴿRÉG 102 (1989) 215 (A. *Billault*).

b575 **Hoff** Michael C.,   Civil disobedience and unrest in Augustan Athens: Hesperia 58 (1989) 267-276.

b576 **Holt** Frank L.,   Alexander the Great and Bactria [➤ 3,b832]; the formation of a Greek frontier in central Asia: Mnemosyne supp. 104. Leiden 1988, Brill. x-114 p. *f* 50. – ᴿClasR 39 (1989) 292s (P. M. *Fraser*); Gymnasium 96 (1989) 245-7 (Henriette *Harich*).

b577 *Hooker* James T.,   The coming of the Greeks [first Greek-speakers in Greece], III. Minos 24 (1989) 55-68.

b578 ᴱ**Hopkinson** N.,   A Hellenistic anthology 1988 ➤ 4,d351*:   ᴿJHS 109 (1989) 236s (G. O. *Hutchinson*: an outstanding service).

b579 **Hornblower** S.,   THUCYDIDES 1987 ➤ 4,d352:   ᴿAthenaeum 67 (1989) 617-9 (Laura *Boffo*); ÉchMClas 33 (1989) 408-413 (Catherine R. *Rubincam*); JHS 109 (1989) 219 (P. J. *Rhodes*).

b580 *Horsley* G. H. R.,   Teaching inscriptions in the classroom [and making squeezes] as an aid to the study of ancient history: AncHRes 19 (1989) [57;] 65-74.

b581 *Hunter* Virginia,   Women's authority in classical Athens; the example of Kleoboule and her son [DEMOSTHENES 27-29. in his Against Aphobus 1-3]: ÉchMClas 33 (1989) 39-48.

b582 *a) Irmscher* Johannes,   Die punischen Kriege in griechischer Sicht; – *b) Schepens* Guido,   Polybius on the Punic Wars; the problem of objectivity in history: ➤ 784, Punic Wars 1988/9, 307-316 / 317-327.

b583 *Jäkel* Siegfried,   THUKYDIDES als Historiker und Literat: Arctos 23 (1989) 67-90.

b584 **Jones** Nicholas F.,   Public organization in ancient Greece; a documentary study: AmPh Memoir 176,   Ph 1987, American Philosophical. xxiv-403 p. $35. – ᴿAmJPg 110 (1989) 660-3 (D. *Whitehead*).

b585 **Keuls** Eva C., Il regno della fallocrazia; la politica sessuale ad Atene [²1985], ᵀ*Carpi* Marino. Mi 1988, Saggiatore. 466 p. Lit. 50.000. – ᴿGitFg 40 (1988) 269s (Patrizia L. *Furiani*); Sileno 14 (1988) 288 (Anna *Quartarone Salanitro*).

b586 *Klein* Richard, Zur Beurteilung Alexanders des Grossen in der patristischen Literatur: ➤ 215, ᶠWIRTH G. 1988, 925-989 [< BTAM 14 (1989) 573, E. *Smits*].

b587 *Knoepfler* Denis, Le calendrier des Chalcidiens de Thrace; essai de mise au point sur la liste et l'ordre des mois eubéens: JSav (1989) 23-59.

b588 ᴱ**Kuhrt** Amélie, *Sherwin-White* Susan, Hellenism in the East; the interaction of Greek and non-Greek civilizations from Syria to Central Asia after Alexander [London Univ. seminar 1984] 1987 ➤ 4,d358: ᴿClasR 39 (1989) 80-82 (E. E. *Rice*); JHS 109 (1989) (M. M. *Austin*).

b589 *Levine* Molly M., *al.*, The challenge of Black Athena [*Bernal* M. 1987 ➤ 3,b809]: Arethusa (whole special issue 1989) 7-16 (-114); 17-37, Black Athena and the APA (reply to all the papers).

b590 **Long** Timothy, Repetition and variation in the short stories of HERODOTUS: BeihKlasPg 179. Fra 1987, Athenäum. 200 p. – ᴿPhoenix 43 (Toronto 1989) 172s (J. M. *Bigwood*).

b590* **Loraux** Nicole, Les expériences de Tirésias, le féminin et l'homme grec: Essais. P 1989, Gallimard. 397 p. [RÉG 103, 275, Yvonne *Vernière*].

b591 *Loreto* Luigi, Per la storia del protoellenismo [*Bengtson* H., Die Diadochen 1987]: AtenRom 34 (1989) 194-202.

b592 **McGregor** Malcolm F., The Athenians and their empire 1987 ➤ 4,d366: ᴿHZ 248 (1989) 411s (W. *Schuller*).

b593 **Macurdy** G. H., Hellenistic queens; a study of woman-power in Macedonia, Seleucid Syria, and Ptolemaic Egypt 1984 = 1932 ➤ 1,h196: ᴿNTAbs 33 (1989) 131.

b594 ᴱ**Maltese** Enrico V., Georgios G. PLĒTHŌON, c. 1355-1452, Opuscula de historia graeca. Lp 1989, Teubner. xii-46 p. 3-322-00674-3.

b595 **Mehl** Andreas, Seleukos Nikator und sein Reich, I. Seleukos und die Entwicklung seiner Machtposition: St. Hellenistica 28, 1986 ➤ 4,d367*: ᴿBO 46 (1989) 507-512 (Amélie *Kuhrt*); Gymnasium 96 (1989) 174-6 (H. *Halfmann*).

b596 *Meister* Klaus, Das Bild Alexanders des Grossen in der Historiographie seiner Zeit: ➤ 209, ᶠWERNER R. Xenia 22 (1989) 63-79.

b597 **Mossé** Claude, La vita quotidiana della donna nella Grecia antica [1983], ᵀ*Pelà* Rosanna. Mi 1988, Rizzoli. 200 p. – ᴿGitFg 41 (1989) 267-9 (Patrizia L. *Furiani*).

b598 **Musti** Domenico, Storia greca, linee di sviluppo dall'età micenea all'età romana. Bari 1989, Laterza. 989 p.; 100 fig. – ᴿRStorAnt 17s (1987s) 334-8 (G. A. *Mansuelli*).

b599 *Oikonomides* A. N., *a)* The portrait of King Philip II of Macedonia; – *b)* The elusive portrait of Antigonos I, the 'one-eyed' king of Macedonia: AncW 20 (1989) 5-16 / 17-20.

b600 **Oliva** Pavel, Solon — Legende und Wirklichkeit 1988 ➤ 4,d369*; 3-87940-331-7: ᴿAntClas 58 (1989) 449s (D. *Viviers*); HZ 248 (1989) 667s (M. *Stahl*).

b601 **Ostwald** Martin, From popular sovereignty to the sovereignty of law... Athens 1986 ➤ 4,d371 [not 'rule' of law]: ᴿAmHR 94 (1989) 725s (R. *Garner*); AmJPg 110 (1989) 367-371 (M. *Gagarin*); ClasR 39 (1989) 279-281 (D. M. *Lewis*); Phoenix 43 (Toronto 1989) 365-375 (N. *Robertson*).

b602 **Pearson** Lionel,   The Greek historians of the west, TIMAEUS... 1987
➤ 4,d372:   ᴿRÉG 101 (1988) 568 (F. *Chamoux*).

b603 **Portanova** Joseph J.,   The associates of Mithridates VI of Pontus: diss.
Columbia, ᴰ*Smith* Morton. NY 1988. 715 p. 88-27630. – DissA 49 (1988s)
3126-A.

b604 **Powell** Anton,   Athens and Sparta; constructing Greek political and
social history from 478 B.C.:   Croom Helm Classical Studies 1988
➤ 4,d375:   ᴿClasR 39 (1989) 77s (P. *Cartledge*); JHS 109 (1989) 251 (S.
Hodkinson).

b605 **Raaflaub** Kurt, Die Entdeckung der Freiheit 1985 ➤ 3,b851*; 4,d377*:
ᴿAnzAltW 42 (1989) 192-5 (K.H. *Kinzl*); JHS 109 (1989) 250 (R.
Seager); RÉG 102 (1989) 211s (G. *Lachenaud*).

b606 *Raaflaub* Kurt, Die Anfänge des politischen Denkens bei den Griechen:
HZ 248 (1989) 1-32.

b607 *Raubitschek* Anthony,   What the Greeks thought of their early history:
AncW 20 (1989) 39-45.

b608 ᴱ**Rhodes** P.J., THUCYDIDES Gr./Eng. II. Wmr 1988, Aris & P.   200 p.
$50; pa $20.   0-85668-396-5; -7-3.

b609 ᴱ**Rosén** Haiim B.,   HERODOTI historiae libr. I-IV, 1987 ➤ 3,b854:
ᴿClasR 39 (1989) 187s (D. *Fehling*).

b610 — *McNeal* Richard A., ROSÉN's Herodotus: Klio 71 (1989) 555-570.

b611 **Samuel** Alan E.,   The promise of the west... and Judaism 1988
➤ 4,d384:   ᴿRPg 62 (1988) 351s (E. des *Places*: somptueux).

b612 *Scaife* Ross,   Alexander I in the Histories of HERODOTUS: Hermes 117
(1989) 129-137.

b613 **Sinclair** R.K.,   Democracy and participation in Athens. C 1988, Univ.
288 p. $42.50.   0-521-33357-1. – ᴿClasR 39 (1989) 69-76 (M.H. *Hansen*).

b614 **Snodgrass** Anthony,   La Grèce antique; le temps des apprentissages,
ᵀ*Schnapp-Gourbeillon* A.   P 1986, Hachette.   197 p.; 15 fig.; 42 pl. –
ᴿRÉG 101 (1988) 531s (F. *Chamoux*).

b615 *Speyer* Wolfgang,   Die Griechen und die Fremdvölker; Kulturbegegnun-
gen und Wege zur gegenseitigen Verständigung: Eos 77 (1989) 17-29.

b616 **Stahl** Michael,   Aristokraten und Tyrannen im archaischen Athen; Untersuchungen zur Überlieferung, zur Sozialstruktur und zur Entstehung
des Staates.   Stu 1987, Steiner.   xiv-287 p.; 3 maps. DM 78.   3-515-
04501-5. – ᴿAntClas 58 (1989) 451s (D. *Viviers*).

b617 **Strauss** Barry S.,   Athens after the Peloponnesian War; class, faction
and policy 403-386 BC 1986 ➤ 4,d397; also   Ithaca NY 1987, Cornell
Univ.   xiii-191 p. $32.45.   0-8014-1942-5. – ᴿAntClas 58 (1989) 454s (D.
Viviers).

ᴱ**Thomas** Carol G.,   Paths from ancient Greece 1988 ➤ 558.

b618 **Thomas** Rosalind,   Oral tradition and written record in classical Athens:
C Studies in Oral and Literate Culture.   C 1989, Univ.   xiii-321 p. £27.50.
– ᴿGreeceR 36 (1989) 251 (P. *Walcot*).

b619 **Traill** John S., Demos and Trittys ... Attica 1986 ➤ 4,d401:   ᴿClasR 39
(1989) 67-69 (K.H. *Kinzl*); Gymnasium 96 (1989) 560s (auch K.H. *Kinzl*);
JHS 109 (1989) 253s (R.S. *Stroud*).

b620 ᴱ**Virgilio** Biagio,   Studi ellenistici II, 1987, Giardini.   216 p. Lit. 70.000.
– ᴿAntClas 58 (1989) 461-3 (G. *Schepens,* Eng.).

b621 *Werner* Jürgen,   Kenntnis und Bewertung fremder Sprachen bei den
antiken Griechen I. Griechen und 'Barbaren'; zum Sprachbewusstsein und
zum ethnischen Bewusstsein im frühgriechischen Epos: Philologus 133
(1989) 169-176.

b622 **Whitehead** David, The demes of Attica, 508/7 – ca. 250 B.C.; a political and social study. Princeton 1986, Univ. xxviii-485 p. – ᴿParPass 247 (1989) 311-320 (Maria Carla *Giammarco Razzano*).

b623 **Will** W., Alexander der Grosse: Gesch. Mak. 2, 1986 ⇒ 4,d408: ᴿDLZ 109 (1988) 276-284 (M. *Oppermann*).

b623* **Wirth** Gerhard, Philipp II: Geschichte Makedoniens 1, Urban-Tb 369, 1985 ⇒ 3,b871; DM 22: ᴿDLZ 109 (1988) 276-282 (M. *Oppermann*). ꜰWIRTH G., Zu Alexander, ᴱ**Will** W. 1988 ⇒ 215.

b624 **Wood** Ellen M., Peasant-citizen and slave; the foundations of Athenian democracy. L 1988, Verso. x-210 p. £23.

Q7 **Josephus Flavius.**

b624* *Abrudan* D., Iosif Flaviu (in Rumanian) ... Hiistoriker der Epoche zwischen den Testamenten: Mitropolia Ardealului 32,3 (1987) 8-10 [< TLZ 115,477].

b625 *a)* *Amir* Yehoshua, *Theokratía* as a concept of political philosophy; Josephus' presentation of Moses' Politeía; – *b)* *Fuks* Gideon, Some remarks on Simon bar-Giora: ScrClasIsr 8s (1988) 83-105 / 106s.

b625* *Anderson* Robert T., Josephus' accounts of Temple building; history, literature or politics?: ProcGLM 9 (1989) 246-257.

b626 **Bartlett** John R., Jews in the Hellenistic world; Josephus...: CamCW 1, 1985 ⇒ 1,b222 ... 3,b874: ᴿHeythJ 30 (1989) 495 (J. F.).

b627 **Bilde** Per, Flavius Josephus between Jerusalem and Rome; his life, his works, and their importance: JPseud Sup 2, 1988 ⇒ 4,d412: ᴿBL (1989) 34 (M. A. *Knibb*); JTS 40 (1989) 535s (F. G. *Downing*).

b627* *Cohen* Shaye J. D., Parallel historical tradition in Josephus and rabbinic literature: ⇒ 564*, 9th Congress 1985/6, B-1.

b628 **Bohrmann** M., Flavius Josèphe, les Zélotes et Yavné; pour une relecture de la Guerre des Juifs. Bern 1989, P. Lang. 256 p.; maps. [RHE 85,34*].

b629 ᴱ**Feldman** Louis H., *Hata* Gohei, Josephus, Judaism and Christianity [first half of the English edition of a work intended to introduce Josephus to the Japanese] 1987 ⇒ 3,338: ᴿJAOS 109 (1989) 677s (D. *Goodblatt*); Phoenix 40,1 (Toronto 1990) 95-97 (G. M. *Paul*).

b630 **Feldman** Louis H., Josephus, supplementary bibliog. 1986 ⇒ 2,9504; 4,d418: ᴿBO 46 (1989) 448s (P. W. van der *Horst*).

b631 *Feldman* L. H., Josephus and modern scholarship: Haifa Univ. Jewish History ☻ 1,2 (1986) 67-74; additions p. 75-74 (M. *Mor,* U. *Rappaport*) [< JStJud 20,279].

b631* *Garnet* Paul, If the Testimonium Flavianum contains alterations, who originated them?: ⇒ 696, 10th Patristic, 19 (1989) 57-61.

b632 *Gnuse* Robert, [32] Dream reports in the writings of Flavius Josephus: RB 96 (1989) 358-390.

b633 **Gross** Carl D., A grammar of Josephus' 'Vita': diss. Duke, ᴰ*Peters* M. Durham NC 1988. 307 p. 89-15461. – DissA 50 (1989s) 972-A.

b635 **Hadas-Lebel** Mireille, Flavius Josèphe, le Juif de Rome. P 1989, Fayard. 300 p. F 110. 2-213-02307-6. – ᴿÉtudes 371 (1989) 415 (P. *Vallin*).

b636 ᴱ**Maier** Paul L., Josephus, the essential writings; a condensation of Jewish Antiquities and The Jewish War [pivotal passages word-for-word; omits speeches, Egypt-Mesopotamia activities, etc.]. GR 1988, Kregel. 413 p.; 7 maps. $16. 0-8254-2963-3 [NTAbs 33,275].

b637 *Mason* S. N., Was Josephus a Pharisee? A re-examination of Life 10-12: JJS 40 (1989) 31-45.

b638 *Meyer* Rudolf, Bemerkungen zum literargeschichtlichen Hintergrund der Kanontheorie des Josefus [< ^F*Michel* O., Josefus-Studien (1974) 285-299]: ↠ 320, Zur Geschichte 1989, 196-207.

Moore W. Ernest [Mt 11,12] Josephus and the Syrian churches 1989 ↠ 4589.

b639 *a) Nodet* Étienne, [Ant 3,108] Table delphique au Temple; – *b) Saulnier* Christiane, Flavius Josèphe et la propagande flavienne: RB 96 (1989) 534-544, Eng. 534 / 545-562; Eng. 545.

b640 **Paul** André, Le judaïsme ancien et la Bible 1987 ↠ 3,b893; 4,d430: ^RCBQ 51 (1989) 567s (L. J. *Hoppe*); ÉTRel 64 (1989) 283s (Danielle *Ellul*); JStJud 20 (1989) 104s (E. J. C. *Tigchelaar*); JTS 40 (1989) 539-543 (N.R.M. de *Lange*: frustrating ambivalent use of the term 'Judaism'); NRT 111 (1989) 437s (X. *Jacques*); RechSR 76 (1988) 614-6 (P. *Vallin*); RÉJ 148 (1989) 401-3 (Madeleine *Petit*); RThom 89 (1989) 488s (L. *Devillers*); ScEspr 41 (1989) 241s (L. *Boisvert*).

b641 ^{TE}**Scardigli** Barbara (*Delbianco* Paola), NICOLAO di Damasco, Vita di Augusto: Univ. Siena. F 1983, Nardini. 276 p. Lit. 30.000. – ^RGnomon 61 (1989) 45-48 (G. *Dobesch*).

b642 *Toher* Mark, On the use of Nicolaus' historical fragments: ClasAnt 8 (1989) 159-172.

b643 *a) Troiani* Lucio, L'identità di Israele in Flavio Giuseppe e nella letteratura giudaico-ellenistica; – *b) Passoni Dell'Acqua* Anna, Differenze nell'uso del nome 'Israele' nel confronto tra il testo ebraico e la versione dei LXX: ↠ 597, RicStoB 1,1 (1987/9) 67-79 / 229-256.

b644 *a) Troiani* L., Per una esegesi unitaria delle Antichità giudaiche di Giuseppe Flavio; – *b) Schmidt* F., Chronologies et périodisations dans Flavius Josèphe et dans l'Apocalyptique juive; – *c) Hadas-Lebel* M., Anoia et aponoia des ennemis de Rome selon Flavius Josèphe: ↠ 595, Storiografia 1983/7, 9-12 / 125-138 / 197-212.

b645 **Villalba i Varneda** Père, The historical method of Flavius Josephus [diss. (Catalán) Barc. 1981]^T: ArbGHJ 19, 1986 ↠ 3,b904; 4,d436: ^RAulaO 7 (1989) 300s (G. del *Olmo Lete*); Emerita 57 (1988) 197s (M. Victoria *Spottorno*); Henoch 11 (1989) 374s (B. *Chiesa*); RÉJ 147 (1988) 229-231 (M. *Petit*).

Q8   *Historia epochae NT* – Seleucids to Bar-Kochba.

b646 *Applebaum* Shimon, The Hasmonaeans – logistics, taxation and the constitution [*Bar-Kokhva* B. 1977]: ↠ 227, Judaea 1989, 9-29.

b647 *Barnes* T. D., Trajan and the Jews [Toronto/Princeton lecture]: JJS 40 (1989) 145-162.

b648 **Bartelink** G. J. M., Het vroege christendom en de antieke cultuur. Cuitinho/Epo 1986, Muiderberg / Berchem. 188 p. Fb 625. – ^RStreven 56 (1988s) 179s (P. *Beentjes*).

b649 **Baumann** Uwe, Rom und die Juden; die römisch-jüdischen Beziehungen von Pompeius bis zum Tode des Herodes (63 v. Chr. – 4 v. Chr.)² [=¹1983]. Fra 1986, Lang. 294 p. [RelStR 16, 171, D. *Rhoads*].

b650 **Bickerman** Elias J., The Jews in the Greek age 1988 ↠ 4,d444: ^RRÉG 102 (1989) 569-571 (A. Le *Boulluec*).

b652 **Bombelli** Luciano, I frammenti degli storici [7] giudaico-ellenistici. Arch/Fg 103. Genova 1986, Univ. 193 p. – ^RManuscripta 8 (1989) 64.

b653 *Botha* P.J.J., The historical Domitian; illustrating some problems of historiography: Neotestamentica 23 (1989) 45-59.

b654 *Carleton* Samuel, The Nero kerygma [his popularity despite SUETONIUS and TACITUS, and the hope of Nero redivivus]: ➤ 592, Systemic 1 (1989) 75-82.

b655 **Cate** B.L., A history of the Bible lands in the interbiblical period. Nv 1989, Broadman. 176 p. $11. 0-8064-1154-2 [BL 90,38].

b655* **Chamoux** François, Marcus Antonius, der letzte Herrscher des griechischen Orients [1986]ᵀ. Gernsbach 1989, Katz. 396 p. [HZ 251, 673, W. *Rapp*].

b656 *Champlin* Edward, The testament of Augustus: RheinMus 132 (1989) 154-165.

b657 *Cotton* Hannah M., The date of the fall of Masada; the evidence of the Masada papyri [YADIN Y. 1965; spring 74 as ECK 1969, rather than 15 Xanthikos 73 as Josephus War 7,401]; ZPapEp 78 (1989) 157-162.

b658 *Culham* Phyllis, Archives and alternatives in republican Rome: ClasPg 84 (1989) 100-116.

b659 **Dal Covolo** Enrico, I Severi e il cristianesimo; ricerche sull'ambiente storico-istituzionale delle origini cristiane tra il secondo e il terzo secolo: BiblScR 87. R 1989, LAS(alesianum). 118 p. Lit. 15.000. 88-213-0188-5 [Greg 70,828]. – ᴿSalesianum 51 (1989) 933s (*ipse*); StPatav 36 (1989) 634 (O. *Pasquato*); VetChr 26 (1989) 387-9 (A. *Isola*).

b660 *De Filippis Cappai* Chiara, I rapporti tra Agricola e Domiziano nella biografia tacitiana: CivClasCr 10 (1989) 273-282.

b661 **Delling** Gerhard, Die Bewältigung der Diasporasituation 1987 ➤ 3, b928; 4,d458*: ᴿScripTPamp 21 (1989) 697 (K. *Limburg*).

b662 *De Nardis* Mauro, SENECA, PLINIO e la spedizione neroniana in Etiopia: Aegyptus 69 (1989) 123-152.

b663 **Dihle** Albrecht, Die griechische und lateinische Literatur der Kaiserzeit, von Augustus bis Justinian. Mü 1989, Beck. 651 p. 3-406-33794-5.

b663* *a) Drews* Robert, The lacuna in TACITUS book 5 [29-31] in the light of Christian traditions; – *b) Fishwick* Duncan, PLINY and the Christians: AmJAncH 9,1 (1990 for 1984) 112-122 / 123-130.

b664 **Epstein** David F., Personal enmity in Roman politics 218-43 B.C. L 1987, Croom Helm. vi-183 p. 0-7099-5394-6. – ᴿJRS 79 (1989) 189s (K.-J. *Hölkeskamp*).

b665 **Ferguson** Everett, Backgrounds of early Christianity ➤ 4,d463 [i. the great empires, Persia, Greece, Rome; ii. Roman social organization; iii. religions; iv. philosophy; v. Judaism; vi. pagan authors and archeology on Christianity]. GR 1987, Eerdmans. xvii-515 p. – ᴿCBQ 51 (1989) 369s (T. M. *Finn*); RHE 84 (1989) 217 (M. *Tylor*); RHPR 69 (1989) 219 (P. *Maraval*).

b666 **Freis** Helmut, Historische Inschriften 1984 ➤ 3,b934: ᴿAnzAltW 42 (1989) 84-86 (H. *Galsterer*).

b667 **Fitzmyer** Joseph A., A history of Israel ... from Pompey to Bar Cochba: ➤ 384, NJBC (1989s) 1243-52.

b668 *Giovannini* A., Review-discussion; Roman eastern policy in the Late Republic [*Gruen* E., *Sherwin-White* A.]: AmJAncH 9,1 (CM 1984) 33-42 [< NTAbs 33 (1989) 86].

b669 *Goodblatt* D., ❻ Agrippa I and Palestinian Judaism in the first century: Jewish History 2,1 (Haifa Univ. 1987) 4-32 [< JStJud 20,279].

b670 **Goodman** Martin, The ruling class of Judaea 1987 ➤ 4,d472 [not 'Judaism']: ᴿAmHR 94 (1989) 1352s (L. H. *Feldman*); CiuD 202 (1989)

748 (J. *Gutiérrez*); ClasR 39 (1989) 88s (Margaret H. *Williams*); JBL 108 (1989) 702-5 (D. R. *Edwards*: substantive and provocative); JSS 34 (1989) 211s (F. F. *Bruce*); JRS 79 (1989) 246s (B. D. *Shaw*); JTS 40 (1989) 213-7 (E. *Bammel*: challenging; distrusts JOSEPHUS); RHR 206 (1989) 200-2 (R. *Turcan*); Zion 59 (1989) 125-129 (M. *Stern, zal*).

b671 **Grimal** Pierre, Cicero; Philosoph, Politiker, Rhetor, ᵀ*Stamm* R. Mü 1988, List. 590 p. – ᴿGrazBei 16 (1988) 310-8 (F. F. *Schwarz*).

b672 **Gunneweg** A. H. J., Geschichte Israels von den Anfängen bis Bar Kochva⁶ [= ⁵ + 'und von Theodor Herzl bis zur Gegenwart', 40 p.]: Theologische Wissenschaft 2. Stu 1989, Kohlhammer. 253 p.; 2 maps. DM 26. 3-17-010511-6 [BL 90,39].

b673 **Hengel** Martin, (*Markschies* Christoph), The 'Hellenization' of Judaea in the first century after Christ [Zum Problem ... 1989], ᵀ*Bowden* John. L 1989, SCM. 114 p. 0-334-00602-3.

b674 *Henten* J. W. van, Jodendom versus hellenisme; een valse tegenstelling [supports HENGEL]: Lampas 22 (1989) 149-167 [< JStJud 20,284].

b675 *Hermon* E., L'impérialisme romain républicain; approches historiographiques et approche d'analyse [ᴱ*Harris* W., Imperialism in mid-Republican Rome 1984; ... (? deux colloques ➤ 2,531)]: Athenaeum 67 (1989) 407-416.

b676 **Hillman** Thomas P., The reputation of Cn. Pompeius Magnus among his contemporaries from 83 to 59 B.C.: diss. Fordham, ᴰ*Penella* R. Bronx 1989, 203 p. 89-17235. – DissA 50 (1989s) 1407-A.

b678 **Holladay** Carl R., Fragments from Hellenistic Jewish authors, II. Poets; the epic poets THEODOTUS and PHILO and EZEKIEL the tragedian: SBL TTr 30, Pseud 12. Atlanta 1989, Scholars. x-529 p. $26; sb./pa. $17. 1-55540-317-4; pa. -8-2.

b679 ᴱ**Horsley** G. H. R., New documents illustrating early Christianity (5. Linguistic essays 1989 ➤ 401 supra) 4, for 1979: 1987 ➤ 4,4987.a611*: ᴿCBQ 51 (1989) 154-6 (D. E. *Smith*); Pacifica 2 (1989) 244-6 (M. *Fitz-Patrick*).

b680 **Jacobs** Manfred, Das Christentum in der antiken Welt; von der frühkatholischen Kirche bis zu Kaiser Konstantin: Zugänge zu Kirchengeschichte 2, 1987 ➤ 3,b955: Gö 1987, Vandenhoeok & R. – ᴿRHPR 69 (1989) 331 (P. *Maraval*).

b681 **Jagersma** Hendrik, Israels Geschichte II. Von der hellenistischen bis zur römischen Zeit [1985], ᵀ*Thiele* F.: Bibel-Kirche-Gemeinde 27. Konstanz 1987, Christliche-VA. 279 p. DM 42,50. – ᴿTLZ 114 (1989) 514s (D. *Conrad*).

b682 **Jagersma** H., A history of Israel from Alexander to Bar Kochba 1986 ➤ 2,9576 ... 4,d486: ᴿBA 52 (1989) 146s (J. R. *Mueller*); CriswT 1 (1987) 412s (G. L. *Klein*); HeythJ 30 (1989) 186s (N. *King*).

b683 **Jehne** Martin, Der Staat des Dictators Caesar: Passauer Hist. For. 3, 1987 ➤ 4,d487; DM 98: ᴿClasR 39 (1989) 84-86 (R. *Seager*); HZ 248 (1989) 414s (Marieluise *Deissmann*).

b684 **Johnson** W. R., Momentary monsters; LUCAN and his heroes [Cato, Pompey, Caesar; 1984 Martin Lectures]. Ithaca NY 1987, Cornell Univ. xiii-145 p. $18. – ᴿAmJPg 110 (1989) 371-5 (M. *Morford*).

b685 *Jones* Brian W., *a*) Titus, his reign and significance: AncHRes 19 (1989) 21-25; – *b*) Titus in Judaea, A.D. 67: Latomus 48 (1989) 127-134.

b686 The Judean-Syrian-Egyptian conflict of 103-101 B.C.; a multilingual dossier concerning a 'war of sceptres': Collectanea Hellenistica 1. Bru 1989, Acad. 172 p.; 16 pl. Fb 950. 90-6569-403-X [BO 46,259, no ᴱ].

b687 **Kahn** Arthur D., The education of Julius Caesar 1986 ➤ 2,9579: RAmJAncH 9 (1990 for 1984) 135-152 (A. M. *Eckstein* compares with C. MEIER 1982).

b688 **Kasher** A., ⊕ *K⁽ᵉ⁾na'an, Pelešet* ... Canaan, Philistia, Greece and Israel; Jews and the Hellenistic cities in the Second Temple period, 332 B.C.E. – 70 C.E. J 1988, Ben-Zvi. – ᴿZion 59 (1989) 509-514 (G. *Fuks* ⊕).

b689 **Kasher** Aryeh, The Jews in ... Egypt 1985 ➤ 1,b298 ... 4,d490. – ᴿHZ 248 (1989) 669-671 (K. *Bringmann*).

b690 **Kasher** A., Jews, Hasmonaeans and ancient Arabs; relations of the Jews in Eretz-Israel with the nations of the frontier and the desert during the Hellenistic and Roman era (332 B.C.E. – 70 C.E.): TStudAJ 18. Tü 1988, Mohr. xix-264 p. DM 118. 3-16-145240-2 [BL 90, 136, T. *Rajak*].

b691 **Kolb** Frank, Untersuchungen zur Historia Augusta: Antiquitas 4/20. Bonn 1987, Habelt. vii-165 p. DM 98. 3-7749-2316-7. – ᴿAthenaeum 67 (1989) 639s (A. *Marcone*); Gnomon 61 (1989) 639-641 (B. *Baldwin*); RÉLat 67 (1989) 351s (J.-P. *Callu*).

b692 **Künzl** Ernst., Der römische Triumph; Siegesfeiern im antiken Rom. Mü 1988, Beck. 171 p. 100 fig. – ᴿArchAustriaca 73 (1989) 234s (O. *Harl*).

b693 **Linder** Amnon, The Jews in Roman imperial legislation: intr. tr. comm. 1987 ➤ 4,d504: ᴿJStJud 20 (1989) 97-99 (G. *Stemberger*); Salesianum 51 (1989) 839 (R. *Vicent*).

b694 **Lounsbury** Richard C., The arts of SUETONIUS; an introduction. NY 1987, Lang. xi-187 p. $31.50. – ᴿClasJ 84 (1988s) 367s (B. *Baldwin*: elegant, also typographically).

b695 **Martin** Alain, La titulature épigraphique de Domitien: BeitKlPG 181, 1987 ➤ 3,b986; 3-610-09006-5: ᴿAntClas 58 (1989) 423s (Marie-Thérèse *Raepsaet-Charlier*).

b695* *Martin* Régis F., Les paradoxes de l'empereur Claude: RÉLat 67 (1989) 149-162.

b696 *Meyers* Eric M., *White* I. Michael, Jews and Christians in a Roman world: Archaeology 42,2 (1989) 26-33 [< Bibliotheca Sacra 146 (1989) 342s (D. K. *Lowery*)].

b697 *Millar* Fergus, *a*) Political power in mid-Republican Rome; curia or comitium? [ᴱ*Raaflaub* K. 1986; *Hölkeskamp* K. 1987]: JRS 79 (1989) 138-150; – *b*) 'Senatorial' provinces; an institutionalized ghost: AncW 20 (1989) 93-97.

b698 **Momigliano** Arnaldo, Die Juden in der Alten Welt [ital. Eng.], ᵀ*Kempter* Martina: Kleine Kulturw. Bibliothek 5. B 1988, Wagenbach. 92 p.

b699 **Nash** Ronald H., Christianity and the Hellenistic world 1984 ➤ 1,b137 ... 3,b991 ('1985'): ᴿTLZ 114 (1989) 434-6 (N. *Walter*).

b700 NIKIPROWETZKY Valentin 1919-1983, mem. Hellenica et judaica, ᴱCaquot A., *al.*, 1986 ➤ 2,81; 4,d511: ᴿHenoch 11 (1989) 369-373 (B. *Chiesa*); RÉJ 147 (1988) 179-184 (E.-M. *Laperrousaz*); StPhilonAn 1 (1989) 155-9 (D. *Winston*).

b701 **Nippel** W., Aufruhr und 'Polizei' in der römischen Republik. Stu 1988, Klett-Cotta. 334 p. 3-608-91434-X [JRS 79,275].

b702 **Niswonger** R. L., New Testament history. GR 1988, Zondervan. 332 p.; 9 maps. $20. 0-310-31200-0 [NTAbs 33,278].

b703 *North* J. A., The Roman counter-revolution [*Brunt* P. A. 1988 ➤ 241]: JRS 79 (1989) 151-6.

b704 *Oppenheimer* A., Talmudic literature as a historical source for the Bar Kokhba revolt: ➤ 595, Storiografia 1983/7, 139-151.

b705 a) *Orth* Wolfgang, Demos-freundliche Tendenzen in der Zeit des Kaisers Claudius; – b) *Sünskes* Julia, Astrologie und Aufstand; die Angst der römischen Kaiser vor Machtverlust: → 151, [F]PEKÁRY T., Migratio 1989, 50-59 / 60-67.

b706 **Paul** André, Le monde des Juifs à l'heure de Jésus; histoire politique 1981 → 62,a76; 63,9930...: [R]RTLv 20 (1989) 218s (J. *Ponthot* attendait le promis Écrits des Juifs).

b707 [E]**Pelling** C. B. R., PLUTARCH, Life of Antony: Greek and Latin classics. C 1988, Univ. xiv-338 p.; 4 maps. £25; pa. £10. 0-521-24066-2; 8418-X. – [R]ClasR 39 (1989) 201s (H. *Seager*); JRS 79 (1989) 211s (J. M. *Carter*).

b708 **Pisi** Giordana, Il medico amico in Seneca; *Torti* Giovanni, Il suo regno non avrà mai fine [... pax romana e cristianesimo]. R 1983 Balzoni. 83 p. Lit. 8000. – [R]Latomus 48 (1989) 256 (B. *Stenuit*).

b709 **Poliakoff** Denali M. S., The acculturation of Jews in the Roman Empire; evidence from burial places: diss. Boston Univ. 1989, [D]*Reinhold* M. 172 p. 89-11555. – DissA 50 (1989s) 772-A.

b710 *Pucci Ben Ze'ev* Maria, Greek attacks against Alexandrian Jews during Emperor Trajan's reign: JStJud 20 (1989) 31-48.

b711 **Ramage** Edwin S., The nature and purpose of Augustus' 'Res gestae' 1987 → 4,d519: [R]AmJPg 110 (1980) 177-180 (D. *Kienast*); Athenaeum 67 (1989) 633-5 (E. *Noè*); Gnomon 61 (1989) 635-7 (D. *Flach*); JRS 79 (1989) 204 (B. M. *Levick*).

b712 *Reinhartz* Adele, Rabbinic perceptions of Simeon bar Kosiba: JStJud 20 (1989) 171-194.

b713 **Reinhold** Meyer, From republic to principate; an historical commentary on CASSIUS DIO's Roman History, Books 49-52 (36-29 B.C.): AmPgMg 34 (Dio comm. 6). Atlanta 1988, Scholars. xxii-261 p. $33; sb./pa. $25. 1-55540-112-0; pa. 246-1. – [R]ClasR 39 (1989) 204s (J. *Carter*); JRS 79 (1989) 251s (J. W. *Rich*).

b714 **Roberts** A., Mark Antony, his life and times. Upton 1988, Malvern. lxxviii-361 p.; 3 pl.; 7 maps. £15. 0-7134-5860-7 [JRS 79,277].

b715 [E]**Safrai** S., *al.*, ❶ The Jewish people in the first century [1974, first 6 ch.], [T]*Nagakubo* S., al. Tokyo 1989, Shinchi-shobō. [L]-492 p.; 7 maps. Y 8755. 4-88018-1390-C301-6 [BL 90,143].

b716 *Sartre* M., Organisation du territoire et pouvoirs locaux dans la Syrie hellénistique et romaine: TEuph 1 (1989) 119-128 [< ZAW 102,435].

b717 **Saulnier** Christiane, Histoire d'Israël 3, 1985 → 1,a940 ... 4,d530: [R]Latomus 48 (1989) 236s (E. *Lipiński*); ParVi 34 (1989) 299s (A. *Rolla*).

b718 **Schäfer** Peter, Histoire des Juifs dans l'antiquité [Geschichte ... von Alexander 1983], [T]*Schulte* Pascal: Patrimoines, Judaïsme. P 1989, Cerf. 280 p. F 139. [JStJud 20,257].

b719 *Schürer* Emil, [E]**Vermes** Geza, *al.*, History of ... the age of Jesus Christ → 4,d534: [R]Christian Jewish Relations 21,4 (L 1988) 49-59 (S. *Stern*) [< NTAbs 33,367]; JJS 40 (1989) 112-5 (A. *Cameron*, 3/2); RExp 86 (1989) 275 (D. E. *Garland*, 3/2); ScotJT 42 (1989) 121-3 (J. D. G. *Dunn*, 3/1s).

b720 [*Schürer* Emil] [E]**Vermes** Geza al., Storia del popolo giudaico al tempo di Gesù Cristo I, 1985; II. 1987: → 4,d315: [R]CC 140 (1989,2) 305s (G. L. *Prato*); Latomus 48 (1989) 237s (E. *Lipiński*, 1).

b720* [*Schürer* E.,] [E]**Vermes** G., *al.*, Historia del pueblo judío en tiempos de Jesús 1-11, 1985 → 3,d15: [R]PerspT 20 (1988) 273 (J. *Vitória*: no 'em' tiempos!).

b721 **Schuller** Wolfgang, Frauen in der römischen Geschichte 1987 ➤ 3,d16; 4,d533: ᴿAntClas 58 (1989) 489s (M.-Thérèse *Raepsaet-Charlier*); Phoenix 43 (Toronto 1989) 84-88 (Suzanne *Dixon,* also on CANTARELLA E. and GARDNER J.); VDI 189 (1989) 203-7 (O. B. *Lopuchova,* gr.) & 207s (A. V. *Padossinov*).

b722 *Schwartz* Jacques, Une fantaisie impie dans l'histoire Auguste [395 A.D. [the name (Bar-) Panther of the alleged father of Jesus is from confusion with *carpentarius,* trade of the soldier-father]: RHPR 69 (1989) 481-3.

b723 **Schwier** Helmut, Tempel und Tempelzerstörung; Untersuchungen zu den theologischen und ideologischen Faktoren im ersten jüdisch-römischen Krieg (66-74 n. Chr.) [< Diss. Heid 1988 ➤ 4,d538]: NTOrb 11. Fr/Gö 1989, Univ./VR. xii-421 p.; 9 maps. Fs 98 [CBQ 52,198]. 3-7278-0641-9 / VR 3-525-53912-6.

b724 **Segal** Alan, Rebecca's children; Judaism and Christianity in the Roman world 1986 ➤ 2,9613 ... 4,d539: ᴿBA 52 (1989) 43-45 (S. *Schwartz*); HeythJ 30 (1989) 194s (J. K. *Riches*); Istina 34 (1989) 235 (B. *Dupuy*); JQR 80 (1989s) 405-8 (Barbara H. G. *Nathanson*).

b725 ᴱ**Sherk** Robert K., The Roman Empire, Augustus to Hadrian: Translated Documents of Greece and Rome 6, 1988 ➤ 4,d542; £30; pa. £11. 0-521-33025-4; 887-5: ᴿAntClas 58 (1989) 475s (Marie-Thérèse *Raepsaet-Charlier*); ClasR 39 (1989) 314s (T. J. *Wiedemann*); Gnomon 61 (1989) 748-750 (H. *Freis*).

b726 **Simon** Erika, Augustus; Kunst und Leben in Rom um die Zeitwende 1986 ➤ 3,d24; 4,d546: ᴿAJA 93 (1989) 156s (R. *Winkes*); JRS 78 (1988) 226s (J. *Carter*).

b727 *Smelik* K.A. D., Tussen tolerantie en vervolging; reacties op het Jodendom in de Hellenistisch-Romeinse periode: Lampas 22 (1989) 168-187 [< JStJud 20,284].

b728 **Sordi** Marta, The Christians and the Roman Empire [1983] ᵀ1986 ➤ 2,9621; 3,d26: ᴿJRel 68 (1988) 96s (S. *Benko*); Latomus 48 (1989) 694-6 (J. F. *Drinkwater,* praise despite audacity).

b729 **Syme** Ronald, The Augustan aristocracy. Ox 1986, Clarendon. vi-504 p. £40. 0-19-814859-3. – ᴿAmHR 94 (1989) 416 (R. *Saller*); Ant-Clas 58 (1989) 476s (Marie-Thérèse *Raepsaet-Charlier:* includes 27 family trees); JRS 79 (1989) 201-3 (H. *Galsterer*).

b730 TACITUS: *a)* Annalium, ᴱ**Fisher** C. D. Ox 1986 = 1906, Clarendon. viii-422 p. 0-19-814633-7. – *b)* Histoires, ᵀᴱ**Le Bonniec** Henri, notes *Helle-gouarc'h* Joseph: Coll. Budé. P 1989, BLettres (livre I, 1987) lxix-249 (d.) p.; foldout map. – (livres II-III, 1989) xvi-326 p.; map. 2-251-01340-7; -1-4. – *c)* Historiae, ᴱ**Wellesley** Kenneth. Lp 1989, Teubner. II/1: xxii-222 p. 3-322-06671-9. ➤ b740.

b730* TACITUS: *a)* **Shotter** D. C. A., Annals IV. Wmr 1989, Aris & P. xvii-206 p. – *b)* **Lund** Allan A., Germania: Wiss. KommGL. Heid 1988, Winter. 283 p.; 24 pl. – ᴿRÉLat 67 (1989) 283-5 (J. *Hellegouarc'h*).

b731 **Tassin** Claude, El judaismo, desde el destierro hasta el tiempo de Jesús: CuadBib 85, 1986 ➤ 2,9630; 3,d33: ᴿScripTPamp 21 (1989) 346 (F. *Varo*).

b732 **Vanderbroeck** Paul J. J., Popular leadership and collective behavior in the Late Roman Republic (ca. 80-50 B.C.): DutchMgHist 3, 1987 ➤ 4,d555; 90-5063-001-4: ᴿClasH 39 (1989) 83s (J. W. *Rich*); JRS 79 (1989) 191s (K.-J. *Hölkeskamp*); Salesianum 51 (1989) 148s (B. *Amata*).

b733 **Vardiman** E. E., La grande svolta; la Giudea tra ellenismo e primo cristianesimo. Mi 1987, Garzanti. 179 p.; ill. Lit. 16.000. 88-11-54897-7. – ᴿCC 140 (1989,1) 91s (G. L. *Prato*).

b734 **Vielberg** Meinolf, Pflichten, Werte, Ideale; eine Untersuchung zu den Wertvorstellungen des TACITUS: Hermes Einz 52. Stu 1987, Steiner. 199 p. DM 46. – [R]ClasR 39 (1989) 37s (R. H. *Martin*); HZ 248 (1989) 144s (A. *Mehl*).

b735 *Wallace-Hadrill* Andrew, Rome's cultural revolution [*Zanker* P. 1988]: JRS 79 (1989) 157-164.

b736 *Weber* M., Augustus: ➤ 902, NBL, Lfg. 2 (1989) 216-8.

b737 **Wendland** Paul, La cultura ellenistico-romana [1907, 1972], [T]1986 ➤ 2,9635; 4,d560: [R]Protestantesimo 44 (1989) 63s (U. *Eckert*).

b738 **Will** É., *Orrieux* C., Ioudaismos-Hellenismos 1986 ➤ 2,9639 ... 4,d563: [R]EsprVie 99 (1989) 633s (J. *Ries*); RechSR 76 (1988) 62s (A. *Paul*).

b739 *Williams* Margaret H., The expulsion of the Jews from Rome in A.D. 19: Latomus 48 (1989) 765-784.

b740 [E]**Wuilleumier** Pierre, Le *Bonniec* Henri, Tacite, Histoires I, 1987 ➤ 4,d566: [R]Gymnasium 96 (1989) 241s (S. *Borzsák*). ➤ b730, b730*.

b741 *Yuval* Shahar, ⊕ Clashes between Jewish and non-Jewish settlements during the War of Destruction [66-70 C.E.]: CHistEI 51 (1989) 3-20; Eng. 195.

Q9 *Historia imperii romani* – Roman-Byzantine Empire.

b742 **Alföldy** Geza, [cf. 1975; also 1986 ➤ 3,177] The social history of Rome [T]*Braund* D., *Pollock* F., 1985 = 1988 ➤ 4,d569: [R]AncHRes 19 (1989) 115-8 (R. *Pitcher*).

b743 **Andreae** B., Laokoon und die Gründung Roms: KgAW 39. Mainz 1988, von Zabern. 220 p.; 14 fig.; 13 pl. + 27 color.; map. DM 50. 3-8053-0989-9 [JRS 79,267].

b744 *Babcock* W. S., Image and culture; an approach to the Christianization of the Roman Empire: Perkins Journal 41,3 (Dallas 1988) 1-10 [< NTAbs 33,209].

b745 *Bagnall* Roger S., *al.*, Consuls of the later Roman empire: AmPgMg 36, 1987 ➤ 3,d49; 4,d571: [R]JRS 79 (1989) 254s (J. R. *Martindale*).

b746 *Bauman* R. A., Oh no, not Roman law!: AncHRes 19 (1989) 131-7.

b747 **Birley** A. R., The African emperor Septimius Severus[2]. L 1988, Batsford. xi-291 p.; 16 pl.; 3 maps. £20. 0-7134-5694-9 [JRS 79,268].

b748 **Birley** Anthony, Marcus Aurelius, a biography[2rev] [[1]1966). L/NHv 1987, Batsford/Yale Univ., 320 p.; 16 pl., 3 maps. £20. 0-71-345428-8 / 0-300-03844-5. – [R]AntClas 58 (1989) 481s (Monique *Dondin-Payre*); ÉchMClas 33 (1989) 76-81 (B. *Baldwin*).

b749 *Bisbee* G. A., Pre-Decian Acts of Martyrs and Commentarii: Harvard Diss. Rel. 22. Ph 1988, Fortress. xv-187 p. $15. 0-8006-7074-4 [NTAbs 33,126: light on Christianity's confrontation with the Empire].

b750 [TE]**Bloch** Raymond, *Guittard* Charles, Tite-Live, Historie romaine VIII, 1987 ➤ 4,d596: [R]RPg 62 (1988) 369-371 (P. M. *Martin*).

Boatwright Mary T., HADRIAN and Rome / Italian cities 1979 ➤ e750/ e796.

b751 *Boeft* J. den, *al.*, Philological and historical commentary on AMMIANUS Marcellinus XX. Groningen 1987, E. Forster. 338 p.; 4 maps. – [R]Gnomon 61 (1989) 677-680 (J. *Szidat*); RÉLat 67 (1989) 308s (G. *Sabbah*).

b752 **Bonamente** G., GIULIANO l'Apostata e il 'Breviario' di EUTROPIO: Univ. Macerata. R 1986, Bretschneider. 223 p. – [R]GitFg 41 (1989) 133s (C. *Santini*).

b753 *Borkowski* Zbigniew, Local cults and resistance to Christianity: JJur-Pap 20 (1988) 25-30.

b754 *Bouffartigue* Jean, L'état mental de l'empereur JULIEN: RÉG 102 (1989) 529-539 [entre fou et sain comme plusieurs ...].

b755 **Bretone** M., Storia del diritto romano: Storia e Società. B 1987, Laterza. viii-507 p. 88-420-2934-3. – ᴿJRS 79 (1989) 192s (O. F. *Robinson*: his enjoyable teaching material; he must have unusually good students).

b756 **Cosi** Dario M., Casta Mater Idaea, GIULIANO e ... sessualità 1986 → 3,d63; 4,d578*: ᴿRPg 62 (1988) 376 (J. *Bouffartigue*).

Cunliffe Barry, Greeks, Romans and barbarians; spheres of interaction 1988 → b552.

b757 **Demandt** A., Die Spätantike; römische Geschichte von Diocletian bis Justinian, 284-565 n.Chr.: HbAltW 3/6. Mü 1989, Beck. xviii-612 p.; maps. DM 178 [RHE 85,64*]. 3-406-07992-X.

b758 *Demarolle* Jean-Marie, Le Contre les Galiléens; continuité et rupture dans la démarche polémique de l'empereur JULIEN: Ktema 11 (1986) 39-46; 47 'La Bible de Julien', passages qu'il cite.

b759 *Diesner* Hans-Joachim, Der Untergang Roms im Zwielicht; das Westreich zwischen zentrifugalen und zentripetalen Kräften: JbAC 32 (1989) 7-22.

b760 *DiMaio* Michael, The emperor JULIAN's edicts of religious tolerance: AncW 20 (1989) 99-110.

b762 **Ermatinger** James W., The economic reforms of Diocletian: diss. Indiana Univ., ᴰ*Fears* R. 1988. 488 p. 89-14810. – DissA 50 (1989s) 1054-A.

b763 **Ferrill** Arther, The fall of the Roman Empire; the military explanation 1986 → 3,d67*: ᴿGnomon 61 (1989) 596-9 (H. *Castritius*).

b764 *Finamore* John F., Theoi theôn; an Iamblichean doctrine in JULIAN's Against the Galileans: AmPgTr 118 (1988) 393-401.

b765 *a) Gabba* Emilio, Allora i Romani conobbero per la prima volta la ricchezza [Sabine takeover 290 a.C., STRABO 5,3,1]; – *b) Burnett* A. M., The beginnings of Roman coinage: AnIstNum 36 (1989) 9-17 / 33-64.

b766 **Garnsey** Peter, *Saller* Richard, The Roman empire; economy, society and culture 1987 → 3,d72: £24; pa. £10; 0-7156-2145-9; –7-5 / US 0-520-06066-0; –7-9: ᴿAmHR 94 (1989) 109s (D. *Engels*: excellent); JRS 78 (1988) 223s (G. *Burton*); ClasW 82 (1988s) 136s (S. E. *Sidebotham*).

b767 **Goffart** W., Rome's fall and after. L 1989, Hambledon. ix-371 p. [RHE 85,66*].

b768 **Goldmann** Bernhard, Einheitlichkeit und Eigenständigkeit der Historia Romana des APPIAN: BeiAltW 6. Hildesheim 1988, Olms-Weidmann. vi-147 p. DM 36. 3-487-09007-4. – ᴿClasR 39 (1989) 202s (C. B. R. *Pelling*); JRS 79 (1989) 250 (K. *Brodersen*).

b768* *a) Graf* David F., Rome and the Saracens; reassessing the nomadic menace; – *b) Dangel* Jacqueline, Du Nil à l'Euphrate dans l'imagerie des poètes latins d'époque républicaine: → 816, L'Arabie 1987/9, 341-400 / 321-339.

b769 **Hartke** Werner: Ideologie und Geschichte im alten Rom: Szb. Akad DDR. B 1988. 35 p. [AnPg 59, p. 972].

b770 **Herrin** Judith, The formation of Christendom 1987 → 3,d81: ᴿChH 58 (1989) 86-88 (H. *Rosenberg*); DowR 107 (1989) 65-67; Horizons 15 (1988) 390 (G. S. *Sloyan*); JRel 69 (1989) 239s (D. *Olster*); JTS 40 (1989) 270-3

(Rosamund *McKitterick*); Phoenix 43 (Toronto 1989) 88-94 (T. G. *Elliott*); RBén 98 (1988) 229s [L. *Wankenne*].

b771 **Hillgarth** Jocelyn N., Christianity and paganism, 350-750 [²The conversion of western Europe 1969]. Ph 1986, Univ. Pennsylvania. xvii-215 p. – ᴿBTAM 14 (1989) p. 582 (H. *Silvestre*).

b772 **Hussey** J. M., The Orthodox Church in the Byzantine Empire 1986 → 2,9668 ... 4,d598: ᴿHeythJ 30 (1989) 465s (G. *Every*).

b773 **Jeffreys** E. & M., The chronicle of John MALALAS 1986 → 4,d598*: ᴿBijdragen 50 (1989) 455 (M. *Parmentier*); ByZ 81 (1988) 295s (H. *Thurn*).

b774 **Keaveney** A., Rome and the unification of Italy. L 1987, Croom Helm. viii-231 p.; map. 0-7099-3121-2. – ᴿJRS 78 (1988) 202-5 (T. J. *Cornell*, also on POTTER T., 1987).

b775 **Keay** S., Roman Spain: Exploring the Roman World 2. L 1988, British Museum. 240 p.; 80 pl. + 8 colour. £17.50. – ᴿClasW 39 (1989) 318s (J. S. *Richardson*).

b776 **Lane Fox** Robin, Pagans and Christians → 3,d87; 4,d602; also SF 1986, Harper & R. 799 p. $17. 0-06-062852-0. – ᴿClasJ 83 (1987s) 347s (H. A. *Pohlsander*); ExpTim 100 (1988s) 68s (G. *Huelin*: brilliant wealth of learning); JRS 78 (1988) 173-182 (G. *Fowden*); RelStR 15 (1989) 356 (J. H. *Sieber*); RExp 86 (1989) 633s (E. G. *Hinson*).

b777 **MacMullen** R., Corruption and the decline of Rome 1988 → 4,d609: ᴿNYReview of Books (16.IV.1989) 6-13 (J. *Griffin* compares to B. CUNLIFFE and to 'full mastery' of E. J. BICKERMAN) [< NTAbs 33,353].

b778 *Mitchell* Stephen, Maximinus and the Christians in A.D. 312; a new Latin inscription [from Kuşbaba on Burdur-Antalya road]: JRS 78 (1988) 105-124; map; pl. XVI.

b779 *Noè* Eralda, Considerazioni sull'impero romano in STRABONE e in CASSIO DIONE: Rendiconti Ist. Lombardo let/mor/stor 122 (1988) 101-124.

b780 **Pabst** Angela, Divisio regni; der Zerfall des Imperium Romanum in der Sicht der Zeitgenossen: Diss. Alte Gesch. 23. Bonn 1986, Habelt. xi-491 p. DM 58. – ᴿClasR 39 (1989) 151s (D. *Braund*).

b781 *Papademetriou* Nona D., ☉ The wise chronographers of Malala [i. e. used by John MALALAS]: TAth 60 (1989) 672-700.

b782 *Paschoud* François, 'Se non è vero, è ben trovato'; tradition littéraire et vérité historique chez AMMIEN Marcellin: Chiron 19 (1989) 37-54.

b783 *Petolescu* Constantin C., (roum) Quelques remarques concernant les légions des provinces de Moesia Secunda et Scythia: StIstVArh 40 (1989) 165-9; franç. 169s.

b784 *Poucet* J., Les origines de Rome 1985 → 4,d612: ᴿAnzAltW 42 (1989) 218-222 (J. M. *Rainer*); Gymnasium 96 (1989) 180-2 (H.-D. *Richter*); Latomus 48 (1989) 231-3 (P. *Desy*).

b785 ᵀᴱPrato C., *Micalella* D., GIULIANO imperatore, Contro i cinici ignoranti: StTLatG 4. Lecce 1988, Univ. xl-127 p.

b786 **Quacquarelli** Antonio, Reazione pagana ...: VetChr Quad 19, 1986 → 2,9689; 3,d102: ᴿVigChr 43 (1989) 198s (J. den *Boeft*: original, controversial, difficult).

b787 *Rabello* A. M., GIUSTINIANO, Ebrei e Samaritani alla luce delle fonti storico-letterarie, ecclesiastiche e giuridiche: Mg Vocabolario di Giustiniano 1s. Mi 1987s, Giuffrè. ix-491 p.; viii-484 p. Lit. 40.000 + 42.000. – ᴿRevHDroit FrançÉt 67 (1989) 487-9 (N de *Lange*) [< RHE 85,66*].

b788 *Rémy* Bernard, Les carrières sénatoriales dans les provinces romaines d'Anatolie au haut-empire (31 av. J.-C. – 284 ap. J.-C.); Pont-Bithynie,

Galatie, Cappadoce, Lycie-Pamphylie et Cilicie; préf. *Chastagnol* André:
Varia Anatolica 2. Istanbul/P 1989, Inst. Franç. Ét. Anatoliennes / Divit.
2-906059-04-X [OIAc S89; Ap89 'Les fastes sénatoriaux des...'].

b789 **Ritter** Hans Werner, Rom und Numidien; Untersuchungen zur
rechtlichen Stellung abhängiger Könige [seit 3. Jh. v. Chr.]. Lüneburg
1987, AL.BE.CH. 152 p.; 11 pl. DM 85 0-926623-01-2. − ᴿJRS 79 (1989)
195s (C. R. *Whittaker*: 'Röm; abhängige' in title); Mundus 25 (1989) 39s
(J. *Thiel*).

b790 **Runciman** Steven, La teocrazia bizantina [1971 Weil Institute lectures,
Cincinnati; 1977],ᵀ. F 1988, Sansoni. xiv-143 p. Lit. 18.000. − ᴿCC 140
(1989,3) 533s (C. *Capizzi*).

b791 *Salzman* Michele R., The role of aristocratic women in the
Christianization of the Roman aristocracy in the Latin West in the years
after Constantine; the epigraphical evidence [summary]: ➤ 830, AIA 90th,
AJA 93 (1989) 256s.

b792 *Sazanov* A. V., ⊕ The Bosporan chronology in the early Byzantine time:
SovArch (1989,4) 41-60; Eng. 60.

b793 *Seeliger* Hans R., Die Verwendung des Christogramms durch Konstantin im Jahre 312: ZKG 100 (1989) 149-168.

b794 **Shahîd** Irfan, Byzantium and the Arabs in the fifth century 1984
➤ 65,9974 ... 4,d617: ᴿBASOR 275 (1989) 71-73 (D. F. *Graf*); Der Islam
65 (1989) 146 (B. *Spuler*); JRS 79 (1989) 248s (R. *Browning*); JSS 33
(1988) 290-3 (A. R. *Birley*); LA 39 (1989) 286-8 (M. *Piccirillo*); Muséon
102 (1989) 387s (J. *Mossay*).

b795 *Shtayerman* E. M., ⊕ On the problem of the rise of the State in Rome:
VDI 189 (1989) 76-93; Eng. 94.

b796 **Stemberger** Günter, Juden und Christen im Heiligen Land; Palästina
unter Konstantin und Theodosius 1987 ➤ 3,d110; 4,d620: ᴿZKG 100
(1989) 406-9 (E. *Dassmann*).

b797 **Syme** Ronald, Roman Papers IV-V, ᴱ*Birley* Anthony R. 1988 ➤ 4,269;
0-19-814873-9; 85-2. − ᴿAntClas 58 (1989) 482s (M.-Thérèse *Raepsaet-
Charlier*); Gnomon 61 (1989) 246-8 (J.-C. *Richard*).

b798 *Testard* Maurice, Observations sur le passage du paganisme au christianisme dans le monde antique: BBudé (1988) 140-161.

b799 *Turcan* Robert, Héliogabale précurseur de Constantin?: BBudé (1988)
38-52.

b800 ᵀ**Veh** Otto, ᴱ*Brodersen* Kai, APPIAN von Alexandria, Römische Geschichte I: BiblGrLit 23. Stu 1987, Hiersemann. viii-506 p. DM 298. −
ᴿClasR 39 (1989) 202s (C. B. R. *Pelling*).

b801 ᴱ**Veyne** Paul, A history of private life I. From pagan Rome to
Byzantium 1987 ➤ 3,d113; 4,d622: ᴿAmHR 94 (1989) 705-7 (R. *Saller*);
Antiquity 62 (1988) 822.824 (N. *Hammond*); RelStR 15 (1989) 169 (A. T.
Kraabel).

b802 **Virlouvet** Catherine, Famines et émeutes à Rome 1985 ➤ 2,9632 ...
4,d622*: ᴿJRS 78 (1988) 221s (P. *Garnsey*).

b803 **Walsh** Michael, Christen und Caesaren; die Geschichte des frühen
Christentums, ᵀ*Wollmann* Gabriele. Fr 1988, Ploetz. 256 p. − ᴿTPQ 137
(1989) 88 (G. *Feige*).

b804 **Weiss** Günter, Byzanz; kritischer Forschungs− und Literaturbericht
1968-1985: HZ Sonderheft 14. Mü 1986, Oldenbourg. ix-351 p. DM 98.
− ᴿDLZ 110 (1989) 50-53 (K.-P. *Matschke*).

b805 **Winkelmann** Friedhelm [Geschichte], *Gomolka-Fuchs* Gudrun [Kunstge-
schichte], Frühbyzantinische Kultur. Lp 1987, Ed.Ep. 219 p.; 166

(color.) fig. – ᴿDLZ 110 (1989) 717s (K. *Onasch*); ZkT 111 (1989) 230s (L. *Lies*).

b806 **Wohl** L. de, '¡Venciste, Galileo!' Historia del emperador JULIANO el Apóstata. M 1988, Palabra. 398 p. – ᴿCiuD 202 (1989) 537s (L. *González*).

XVIII. Archaeologia terrae biblicae

T1.1   **General biblical-area archeologies.**

b807 **Adam** Jean-Pierre, Le passé recomposé; chroniques d'archéologie fantastique. P 1988, Seuil. 251 p. F 110. – ᴿMondeB 59 (1989) 64 (J.-L. *Huot*: utile, mais de seconde main hors de sa sphère romaine).

b808 *a) Anikovich* M. V., ❷ The archaeological culture; how a definition of the concept affects the research procedure; – *b) Gening* V. V., ❷ Towards a universal archaeological definition of the feature and the type: SovArch (1989,4) 115-126 / 128-142; Eng. 127/142.

b809 ᴱ**Biran** A., Biblical archeology today 1984/5 → 3,902; 4,d630: ᴿBASOR 273 (1989) 87-96 (A. F. *Rainey*); OLZ 84 (1989) 557-560 (E. A. *Knauf*); TLZ 114 (1989) 297-300 (K.-D. *Schunck*).

b810 **Binford** L. R., En busca del pasado. Barc 1988, Crítica. 283 p. – ᴿArch-EspArq 62 (1989) 325s (V. *Lull*).

b811 ᴱ**Christenson** Andrew L., Tracing archaeology's past; the historiography of archaeology. Carbondale 1989, Southern Illinois Univ. xi-252 p. 0-8093-1523-8. 17 art., some America, none mid-east.

b812 *a) Deetz* James, Archaeography, archaeology, or archeology?: – *b) Wiseman* James R., Archaeology today; from the classroom to the field and elsewhere; – *c) Fagan* Brian M., The backward-looking curiosity; a glance at archaeology in the Year of Our Lord 1989; – *d) Davis* Hester A., The future of archaeology; dreamtime, crystal balls, and reality: plenary session papers of First Archaeological Congress, Baltimore 5-9.I. 1989: AJA 93 (1989) 429-435 / 437-444 / 445-9 / 451-7.

b813 ᶠDESHAYES Jean: De l'Indus aux Balcans, ᴱ**Huot** J.-L., *al.* 1985 → 3,45*: ᴿBO 46 (1989) 177-183 (Elisabeth C. L. *During-Caspers*: analyse de plusieurs articles importants).

b814 *Dever* William G., Archaeology in Israel today; a summation and critique: → 543, AASOR 49 (1989) 143-152.

b815 *a) Dever* William G., [vocal adversary of ALBRIGHT-style 'biblical archeology'], 'Yigael YADIN, prototypical biblical archaeologist' [to Israel what Albright was to USA]; – *b) Meyers* Carol & Eric, Expanding the frontiers of biblical archaeology: → 218, Mem. YADIN Y., ErIsr 20 (1989) 44*-51* / 140*-147*.

b816 ᴱ**Dowley** Tim, Discovering the Bible 1986 → 2,9711 ... 4,d633: ᴿRelStT 7,2s (1987) 99 (G. *Hamilton*).

b817 *Drinkard* Joel F.ᴶ, The position of biblical archaeology within biblical studies: RExp 86 (1989) 603-615.

b818 Excavation opportunities [each year; e.g.] 1989: BAR-W 15,1 (1989) 16-28, all in Israel [32-34, a poet at Ashkelon, *Sargent* Lois].

b819 *a) Flanagan* James W., Archaeology and the Bible; – *b) King* Philip J., OT examples; – *c) Hoppe* Leslie J., Synagogue and church in Palestine: BToday 27 (1989) 263-9 / 270-7 / 278-287 (+261s).

b820 *a) Foley* Robert A., The search for early man; – *b) Jochim* Michael A., From hunters to farmers; – *c) Wright* Henry T., The rise of civilizations; Mesopotamia to Mesoamerica; – *d) Bass* George F., Classical archaeology; the great tradition looks ahead: Archaeology 42,1 (special issue: technical progress foreseen for 2050: 1989) 26-32 / 42-45. 84-86 / 46-48. 96-100 / 50-55. 102s.

b821 **Frank** Harry T., Discovering the biblical world, ²ʳᵉᵛ*Strange* James F. [¹1975]. Maplewood NJ 1987, Hammond. → 3,d133; 288 p.; 110 fig. + 170 color.; 40 terrain-model maps; 27 plans. $30; pa. $17. – ᴿBA 52 (1989) 148s (L. *DeVries*); BAR-W 15,1 (1989) 12s (P. J. *King*: not just archeology).

b823 *Gallay* Alain, Logicism; a French view of archaeological theory founded in computational perspective: Antiquity 63 (1989) 27-39.

b824 *Garner* G. G., Archaeology as a tool [... cannot prove the word of God]: VoxRef 50 (1988) 39-47 [< NTAbs 33,71].

b825 **Gibbon** Guy, Explanation in archaeology: Social Archaeology. Ox 1989, Blackwell. ix-206 p. 0-631-16802-8; pa. 931-8

b826 *a) Greeves* Tom, Archaeology and the Green movement; a case for perestroika [... chief of human artefacts to be preserved is the landscape]; – *b) Carver* M. O. H., Digging for ideas: Antiquity 63 (1989) 659-665 / 666-674.

b827 ᴱ**Hodder** I., The meaning of things; material culture and symbolic expression: One World Archaeology. L 1989, Unwin Hyman. 265 p.; 68 fig. £30 [PrPrehSoc 56, 337, J. *Thomas*].

b828 **Hodder** Ian, Reading the past; current approaches to interpretation in archaeology 1986 → 2,9722; 3,d139: ᴿFornvännen 34 (1989) 107s (S. *Welinder*).

b829 **Hodder** I., Interpretación en arqueología; corrientes actuales. Barc 1988, Crítica. 236 p. – ᴿArchEspArq 62 (1989) 325s (V. *Lull*).

b830 *a) Hodder* Ian, Writing archaeology; site reports in context; – *b) Tilley* Christopher, Excavation as theatre [... why is it so exciting, and its reports so dull?]: Antiquity 63 (1989) 268-274 / 275-280.

b831 *Jamieson-Drake* David W., Text vs. [excavated] tell; which sets the agenda?: → 589, SBL Seminars 1989, 458-465.

b832 *Kempinski* Aharon, Die Archäologie als bestimmender Faktor in der israelischen Gesellschaft und Kultur: Judaica 45 (1989) 2-20; 4 fig.

b833 ᴱ**Laperrousaz** Ernest-M., Archéologie, art et histoire de la Palestine 1986/8 → 4,753: ᴿCC 140 (1989,3) 305s (A. *Gianto*); RÉJ 148 (1989) 157s (A. *Lemaire*).

b834 *Leventen* Alan C., A workable proposal to regulate antiquities trade: BAR-W 15,4 (1989) 44-58.

b835 **Miley** Barbara, *Schultz* Lorraine O., Biblical archaeology for teens. San Diego 1988, Rainbow. 4 colorfully covered booklets, each 64 p. $7. – ᴿBAR-W 15,1 (1989) 12 (K. N. *Schoville*: adult reading too).

b836 **Millard** A., Trésors des temps bibliques, ᵀ1986 → 3,d15: ᴿScEspr 40 (1988) 383s (P.-É. *Langevin*).

b837 **Millard** Alan, Archeologia e Bibbia 1988 → 4,d654: ᴿSTEv 1,2 (1989) 209-211 (D. *Valente*).

b838 **Mitchell** T. C., Biblical Archaeology; documents from the British Museum 1988 → 4,d655: ᴿBAR-W 15,5 (1989) 6 (J. A. *Armstrong*).

b839 *Mithen* Steven, Evolutionary theory and post-processual archaeology [... whatever be the judgment on social darwinism, evolutionary theory still has an important place in archaeological thought]: Antiquity 63 (1989) 483-494.

b840 *Nel* W. A. G.,   Die belang van argeologie vir die Bybelwetenskap: TEv 20,3 (1987) 18-28 [< OTAbs 12,143].

b841 *North* Robert, *King* Philip J.,   Biblical archaeology: → 384, NJBC (1989s) 1196-1218.

b842 **Patten** Donald W.,   Catastrophism and the Old Testament [six events caused by nearness of Mars, equated with biblical Ba'al]. Seattle 1988, Pacific Meridian. 289 p. $15 pa. – ᴿBS 146 (1989) 345s (F. R. *Howe*).

b843 **Rogerson** John, *Davies* Philip,   The Old Testament World. C 1989, Univ. 384 p.; (colour) ill. £19.50 [JTS 40,747]. 0-521-34006-3.

b843* ᴱ**Rowlands** Michael *al.*, Centre and periphery 1987 → 3,836; 4,d658: ᴿClasR 39 (1989) 97s (Susan E. *Alcock*).

b844 **Shanks** M., *Tilley* Christopher Y., Re-constructing archaeology; theory and practice: New Studies in Archaeology 1987 → 4,d660: ᴿFornvännen 34 (1989) 86-89 (S. *Welinder*).

b845 *Shay* Talia,   Israeli archaeology – ideology and practice [... isolated by nationalism]: Antiquity 63 (1989) 768-772.

b846 ᴱ**Shennan** S.,   Archaeological approaches to cultural identity: One World Archaeology. L 1989, Unwin Hyman.   317 p.; 46 fig. £33 [PrPrehSoc 56, 337, J. *Thomas*].

b847 *Shennan* Stephen,   Archaeology as archaeology or as anthropology? CLARKE's Analytical archaeology [1968; ²*Chapman* R.] and the BINDORFS' New perspectives in archaeology [1968] 21 years on: Antiquity 63 (1989) 831-5.

b848 *Small* David B.,   Toward a competent structuralist archaeology; a contribution from historical sources; Journal of Anthropological Archaeology 6 (1987) 105-121 [< BASOR 274,89].

b849 *Spencer* John R.,   Whither the Bible and archaeology? [presidential address, Eastern Great Lakes soc., Columbus 7.IV.1989]: ProcGLM 9 (1989) 1-20.

b850 ᴱ**Spriggs** Matthew,   Marxist perspectives in archaeology 1984 → 65,398 ... 4,d663: ᴿSovArch (1989,1) 235-246 (V. *Gulyaev*, E. N. *Chernykh*) & 247-252 (Y. N. *Zakharuk*).

b851 **Thompson** Henry O.,   Biblical archaeology; the world, the Mediterranean, the Bible 1987 → 3,d167: ᴿBA 52 (1989) 149s (D. C. *Benjamin*).

b852 **Trigger** Bruce G.,   A history of archaeological thought. C 1989, Univ. xv-500 p.   0-521-33878-9; pa. –18-2.

b853 *Van Beek* Gus,   Total retrieval and maximum reconstruction of artifacts; an experiment in archaeological methodology: → 218, Mem. YADIN Y., Eretz Israel 29 (1989) 12*-29*; 12 fig.

b854 *Zakharuk* Y. N., ⊕ Whether archaeology is a historical or a source study science: SovArch (1989,3) 207-214 [215-228, *Gening* V. F., on *Klein* L.].

τ1.2   **Musea, organismi, expositiones.**

b855 **Bianchi** Robert S., *al.*, [→ 4,d671] Kleopatra: Ägypten um die Zeitenwende [Hypo-Kulturstiftung, München Jun.-Sept. 1988]. Mainz 1989, von Zabern. 324 p. 3-8053-1014-5; 65-X [OIAc Ja90].

b856 **Boorn** G. P. F. van den, Oud Iran ... Rijksmuseum te Leiden, exhibition 1983 → 65,a37 ... 3,d177: ᴿBO 46 (1989) 454 (H. H. *Curvers*).

b857 *Bourriau* Janine,   [Egyptian antiquities, United Kingdom] Museum acquisitions, 1987: JEA 75 (1989) 209-211; pl. XXX.

b857* *Bulk* Martijn, Tentoonstelling, Een verhaal voor het oprapen [a story for the plucking]. Opgravingen te Deir'Alla in de Jordaanvallei 1989s, Rijksmuseum Leiden: Akkadica 63 (1989) 36.

b858 ᴱCarlsson Anders, Swedish archeology 1981-1987. Sto 1987, Svenska Arkeologiska Samfundet. 224 p.; 3 maps. DM 42. – ᴿPraehZts 64 (1989) 272 (T. *Capelle*).

b859 **Dewachter** Michel, Collections égyptiennes de l'Institut de France; antiquités, documents d'archives, manuscrits, lettres, dessins, estampes, livres, photographies et objets divers. Condé 1987, Sand/Conti. 40 p.; 36 fig.

b860 ᴱDonadoni Roveri Anna Maria, Passato e futuro del Museo Egizio di Torino; dal Museo al Museo: Archivi di archeologia. T 1989, Allemandi. 239 p. (→ 4,d683).

b861 *a*) **Drenkhahn** Rosemarie, Ägyptische Reliefs im Kestner-Museum; – *b*) **Berger** Frank, Die Münzen der Römischen Republik im Kestner-Museum Hannover; 100 Jahre Kestner-Museum 1889-1989: Sammlungskatalog 5.7. Hannover 1989, Museum. 154 p.; 49 (color.) pl. / 539 p.; 3952 fig. 3-924029-113; 2-1.

b862 *a*) *Evans* John D., The first half-century — and after; – *b*) *Parr* Peter J., Bloomsbury, Baghdad and beyond; – *c*) *Talbot* Geraldine, Memories; the Institute 1946-7; – *d*) *Potter* T. W., The Institute and Roman archaeology, past, present and future — an outsider's view; – *e*) *Drewett* P. L., The Institute of Archaeology and field archaeology [... computer, *Alvey* R. A. F.]; – *f*) *Redknap* Mark, *Croome* Angela, A Bloomsbury pharos; the Institute and nautical archaeology; – *g*) *Millet* Martin, A question of time? Aspects of the future of pottery studies: BInstArch Golden Jubilee Bulletin 24 (London 1987) 1-26; 19 fig. + 2 colour. / 29-42 / 27s / 71-84 / 127-139; 4 fig. [205-212] / 141-160; 9 fig. / 99-108; 2 fig.

b862* **Fazzini** Richard A., *al.*, Ancient Egyptian art in the Brooklyn museum. NY 1989, Brooklyn Museum. xv-99 p.; 100 color. phot.

b863 *Galter* Hannes D., *Scholz* Bernhard, Altvorderasiatisches in österreichischen Sammlungen: AfO 35 (1988) 30-47; 31 fig.

b864 **Gamwell** Lynn, *Wells* Richard, Sigmund Freud and art; his personal collection of antiquities; intr. *Gay* Peter. Binghamton/L 1989, suny/ Freud Museum. 192 p. [OIAc Ja90].

b865 **Gordon** Cyrus H., The Pennsylvania tradition of Semitics: SBL BSNAm 13, 1986 → 2,9768; 3,d190: ᴿCBQ 51 (1989) 325s (A. *Gianto*); JBL 108 (1989) 132 (S. D. *Sperling*: some Albright foibles).

b865* ᴱGoyon Jean-Claude, [*Gabolde* Marc (OIAc S89)] Les réserves du Pharaon; l'Égypte dans les collections du Musée des Beaux-Arts de Lyon, 15.XII.1988. Lyon 1988, Musée. 103 p.; ill.; map. 2-901306-20-9.

b866 **Greenfield** Jeanette, The return of cultural treasures. C 1989, Univ. xviii-361 p. 3 microfiches. 0-521-33319-9.

b867 **Guglielmi** Waltraud, Das Diakonie-Museum [mostly collection of T. Fliedner 1857]. Kaiserswerth 1988, Diakoniewerk. ix-102 p.; (color.) ill. [BO 46,628].

b868 Jarhresbericht 1988 des DAI [Berlin, Rom, Athen, Kairo, Istanbul, Madrid, Sanaa, Damaskus...]: ArchAnz (1989) 635-707; Personelle Gliederung, 708-717.

b869 *Limme* Luc, La collection égyptienne des M(usées) R(oyaux d') A(rt et d') Histoire (à Bruxelles); notes additionnelles sur les étapes marquantes de son développement: → 204, Mém. Walle B. van de, CdÉ 64 (1989) 98-110.

b870 *Loon* M. N. van, *al.,* Gids voor de afdeling West-Azië, Allard Pierson Museum Amsterdam = PhoenixEOL 34,1 (1988). 96 p.; (color. ill.; 68-71, Palestina.

b871 *Metzger* Henri, [*Delumeau* Jean], Rapport sur l'activité de l'École française d'Athènes [de Rome] 1988: CRAI (1989) 608-616 [617-631, map].

b872 *Napoli,* La collezione egiziana del Museo Archeologico Nazionale [ᴱ*Cantilena* Renata, *Rubino* Paola]. N 1989. Soprintendenza. vi-316 p.; 26 color. fig.; XVIII pl. Lit. 40.000.

b873 **Needler** Winifred, Predynastic and archaic Egypt in the Brooklyn Museum 1984 ➤ 65,a61; 4,d698: ᴿCdÉ 64 (1989) 197s (S. *Hendrickx*).

b874 **Reeder** Ellen D., Hellenistic art in the Walters Art Gallery. Baltimore/Princeton 1988. 259 p.; 366 fig. $75. 0-691-04069-9 [AJA 93,627].

b875 **Roland** Berthold, Max SLEVOGT, Ägyptenreise 1914; Ausstellung Dresden. Mainz 1989, von Zabern. 64 p. 3-8053-1094-3 [OIAc N89].

b876 **Rosovsky** Nitza, *Ungerleider-Mayerson* Joy, The museums of Israel. NY 1989, Abrams. 256 p.; 170 phot. (Harris D.); 9 maps. $15 pa. – ᴿBAR-W 15,6 (1989) 10 (S. S. *Weinberg*).

b877 *Sancisi-Weerdenburg* Heleen, Persepolis en Pasargadae in wisselend perspectief; Iraanse oudheden bechreven en getekende door Europese reizers [Catalogus Tentoonstelling Univ. Groningen apr.mei 1989] = Phoenix 35,1. Groningen 1989, Ex Oriente Lux. 106 p.; 44 fig. (map). 90-367-0136-8 [OIAc S89].

b878 **Satzinger** Helmut, Ägyptisch-orientalische Sammlung, Kunsthistorisches Museum Wien. Mü 1987, Magazin. 130 p. 0341-8634.

b879 **Schultz** Frederick, Egyptian art; the essential objects [exposition 1987]. Acanthus NY 1987, Schultz/Ancient Art. 48 p. [OIAc Ja90].

b880 **Seefried** Monique, *Woodward* Mary Cozine, The fascination with the East; early photographs of Egypt: Musum exhibition 1986-7. Atlanta 1989, Emory Univ. [OIAc S89].

b880* **Sturtewagen** Christian, Concordance of numbering systems in the [Vatican] Museo gregoriano egizio: Orientalia 58 (1989) 497-507.

b881 **Tefnin** Roland, Statues et statuettes de l'ancienne Égypte: Guides ég. 7. Bru 1989, Musée Royaux [OIAc S89].

b882 **Ucko** Peter, Academic freedom and apartheid; the story of the World Archaeological Congress [banning South Africans, Southampton 1986] 1987 ➤ 4,d706: ᴿBerytus 36 (1988) 189-192 (J. *Wilson*: Israel next).

b883 *Vesco* J. (présenté par *Will* Ernest), Rapport sur l'état et les activités de l'École Biblique et Archéologique de Jérusalem pendant l'année 1988-9: CRAI (1989) 584-8.

b884 **Waterhouse** Helen T., The British School at Athens; the first hundred years 1988 ➤ 3,d213; 4,d709 ('1986'): ᴿArchaeology 42,2 (1989) 69s (H. A. *Thompson*).

b885 **Whitley** Sarah, Ruin upon ruin; a colorful exhibit of rare and illustrated archaeology books. Ph 1982, Library Co. [OIAc S89].

T1.3 *Methodi,* **Science in archeology.**

b885* **David** A. Rosalie, Science in Egyptology: symposia Manchester 1979/84: 1986 ➤ 4,730: ᴿJAmEg 26 (1989) 244s (W. B. *Harer*).

b886 **Dorell** Peter, Photography in archeology and conservation. C 1989, Univ. 262 p. 99 fig. £27.50. 0-521-32797-0. – ᴿAntiquity 63 (1989) 869s (Gwil *Owen*).

b887 *Eisner* Michael,   Zukunftsperspektiven archäologischer Wissensdarstellung auf dem Computer: ➤ 49, ᶠDRERUP H., Bathron 1988, 115-120.

b888 *Farquhar* Ronald M., *Vitali* Vanda,   Lead isotope measurements and their application to Roman lead and bronze artifacts from Carthage: Masca 6 (Ph 1989) 39-45; 3 fig.

b888* *Fischer* Peter M.,   SIMS studies of teeth; a new dating technique?:
➤ 831*, High/Low III (1989) 142-9.

b889 **Gardin** J.-C., *al.*,   Systèmes experts [computer-programs] et sciences humaines.   P 1987, Eyrolles.   xiii-269 p. – ᴿAJA 93 (1989) 461s (M. *Fotiadis*).

b890 *Geyh* Mebus A., *al.*,   Zur absoluten Chronologie des Alten Reiches und der I. Zwischenzeit nach konventionellen und kalibrierten ¹⁴C-Daten: StAltÄgK 16 (1989) 65-81; 3 fig.

b891 *Gilead* Isaac, *Goren* Yuval,   Petrographic analyses of fourth millennium B.C. pottery and stone vessels from the northern Negev, Israel: BASOR 275 (1989) 5-14.

b892 ᴱ**Hackens** Tony *al.*,   Wood and archaeology, Acts of the European Symposium LvN Oct. 1987: Pact 22. Strasbourg 1988. 400 p.; ill Fb 3000. 0257-8725. 10 art. dendrochronology; 21 art. anthracology etc.

b893 *Helskog* Knut, *Schweder* Tore,   Estimating the number of contemporaneous houses from ¹⁴C dates [given a collection of absolute dates from individual structures on a settlement site, how many might have been occupied at any one time?]: Antiquity 63 (1989) 166-172; 1 fig.

b894 *Housley* Rupert A., *al.*,   AMS and radiometric dating of an Etruscan linen book and associated [Egyptian] mummy: ➤ 868, Radiocarbon 31 (1988/9) 970-5.

b895 *Jones* G.A., *al.*,   Radiocarbon dating of deep-sea sediments; a comparison of accelerator mass spectrometer and beta-decay methods: Radiocarbon 31 (1989) 105-116.

b896 **Leute** Ulrich,   Archaeometry; an introduction to physical methods in archaeology and the history of art 1987 ➤ 4,d724:   ᴿAcPraeh 21 (1989) 150s (G. *Schneider*); Qadmoniot 22 (1989) 53 (M. *Broshi*).

ᴱ**Liberati Silverio** Anna Maria, Archeologia e informatica, convegno 1988 ➤ 830.

b897 *Mellars* Paul, *Tixier* Jacques,   Radiocarbon-accelerator dating of Ksar 'Aqil (Lebanon) and the chronology of the Upper Palaeolithic sequence in the Middle East: Antiquity 63 (1989) 761-8; 3 fig.

b897* *a) Mills* C.,   Dendrochronology; the long and the short of it; – *b) Tite* M.S.,   The study of ancient ceramic technologies; past achievements and future prospects; – *c) Scott* E.M., *al.*,   The comparability of results across a sub-section of radiocarbon laboratories: ➤ 866, Glasgow 1987/8, 549-566 / 9-26 / 581-590.

b898 *Niejtsch* Reinhold, *a)* Die archäologische Datenbank 'Mufdarch'; – *b)* Datenerfassung und Datenmanipulation in der Luftbildarchäologie: ArchAustriaca 73 (1989) 1-12; 8 fig. / 14-34; 15 fig.

b899 *Oddone* Massimo, *Savio* Adriano,   Indagine, mediante analisi per attivazione neutronica strumentale, del contenuto di alcuni tetradrammi alessandrini di Nerone: RitNum 91 (1989) 131-150; 1 fig.

b899* *Olsson* Ingrid U.,   Carbon-14 dating and interpretation of the validity of some dates from the Bronze Age in the Aegean: ➤ 831*, High/Low II (1987) 4-38.

b900 ᴱ**Parrini** Paolo L.,   Science and conservation, ᵀ*Scipioni* Mary.   Mi 1986, Arcadia. 171 p.; ill. – ᴿAJA 93 (1989) 285s (Barbara *Moore*).

b901 *Perizonius* W. R. K., *Goudsmit* J., Ancient DNA and archaeo-virology; a question of samples: GöMiszÄg 110 (1988) 47-53.

b902 ᴱ**Phillips** Patricia, The archaeologist and the laboratory: Research Report 58. L 1985, Council for British Archaeology. 70 p.; 25 fig.; 55 color. phot. microfiches. – ᴿBonnJbb 189 (1989) 539s (G. *Eggert*).

ᴱ**Rahtz** S. P. Q., Computer and quantitative methods in archaeology: BAR-Int 446, 1988 ⇥ 865.

b903 **Riley** Derrick N., Air photography and archaeology 1987 ⇥ 4,d736; also Ph 1987, Univ. Pennsylvania. 151 p.; 102 fig. – ᴿAJA 93 (1989) 599s (J. W. *Myers*).

b904 **Sease** Catherine, A conservation manual for the field archaeologist 1987 ⇥ 3,d246; $16: Antiquity 63 (1989) 869 (Esther *Cameron*).

b905 **Wilkinson** Edward M., *al.,* Technische und naturwissenschaftliche Beiträge zur Feldarchäologie: Archaeo-Physika 5. Köln/Bonn 1974, Rheinland/Habelt. 437 p.; ill.

b906 *Yellin* Joseph, *Gunneweg* Jan, Instrumental neutron activation analysis and the origin of Iron Age I collared-rim jars and pithoi from Tel Dan: ⇥ 543, AASOR 49 (1989) 133-141.

T1.4   *Exploratores* – **Excavators, pioneers.**

b907 **Ackerman** Robert, J. G. Fʀᴀᴢᴇʀ, his life and work 1987 ⇥ 3,d251: ᴿJAAR 57 (1989) 625-7 (R. A. *Segal*); JTS 40 (1989) 692-4 (J. *Barr*); RelStR 15 (1989) 340 (I. *Strenski*).

b908 *Agache* Roger, Les grands archéologues: Jacques Bᴏᴜᴄʜᴇʀ de Crèvecœur de Perthes (1788-1868): Archéologia 243 (1989) 71-73; ill.

b909 *Allison* P., *al.,* Australians in the field of classical archaeology [Cyclades Zagora & Siphnos; N. Greece Torone; Pompeii, Salento]: AncHRes 19 (1989) 145-154.

b910 **Andrae** Walter, Lebenserinnerungen eines Ausgräbers[2] [[1]1961]. Stu 1988, Freies Geistesleben. xi-320 p.; 49 (color.) fig.; end-maps. 3-7725-0457-4.

b911 *Andrae* Ernst W., *Boehmer* Rainer M., Die Orientbilder [Malerei] von Walter Aɴᴅʀᴀᴇ: BaghMit 20 (1989) 1-89; 21 fig.; pl. 1-128.

b912 *Armerding* Carl E., Confessions of a failed archaeologist: Crux 25,1 (Vancouver 1989) 5-7 [< OTAbs 12,141].

b913 *Barnett* R. D., Lᴏғᴛᴜs, William K., 13.XI.1820 – 27.XI.1858: ⇥ 905, RLA 7,1s (1987) 102s.

b914 **Berchem** Denis van, L'égyptologue genevois Édouard Nᴀᴠɪʟʟᴇ; années d'études et premiers voyages en Égypte 1862-1870: Journal de Genève. Genève 1989, Georg. xiv-147 p. 2-8257-0182-3.

b915 **Blinderman** Charles, The Piltdown inquest. Buffalo 1986, Prometheus. 261 p. $23. 0-87975-359-5. – ᴿAmHR 94 (1989) 412s (Philippa *Levine*).

b916 *Bloedow* Edmund F., *al.,* Sᴄʜʟɪᴇᴍᴀɴɴ at Mycenae [Tʀᴀɪʟʟ attacks unconvincing or peripheral]: ÉchMClas 33 (1989) 147-165; 2 fig.

b917 **Bohrer** Frederick N., A new antiquity; the English reception of Assyria: diss. ᴰHeller R. Chicago 1989, Univ. xviii-548 p.; bibliog. 452-463. – OIAc Ja90.

b918 *Borger* R., Lᴜᴄᴋᴇɴʙɪʟʟ David D., 21.VI.1881 – 5.VI.1927: ⇥ 905, RLA 7,1s (1987) 107.

b919 *Chapman* William, The organizational context in the history of archaeology; [Augustus] Pɪᴛᴛ Rɪᴠᴇʀs and other British archaeologists in the 1860s: AntiqJ 69 (1989) 23-42.

b920 *Curto* Silvio, Giovanni KMINEK-SZEDLO e l'egittologia italiana del secondo ottocento: StudEgPun 2 (1987) 1-18 (–71, anche su lui: *Pernigotti* S., *Cesaretti* M. P., *Morigi Govi* C.).

b921 *Dewachter* Michel, *a*) Les manuscrits de l'ingénieur [Jean-B. P.] JOLLOIS et la correspondance relative à sa première année en Égypte (1798-1799); – *b*) Le prétendu portrait de CHAMPOLLION à Naples, peint par François Bouchot en 1828: ➤ 39, Mém. CLÈRE J., REgp 40 (1989) 201-215; 4 fig. / 215-8; 1 fig.

b922 **Dörner** Friedrich K. & Eleonore, Von Pergamon zum Nemrud Dağ; die archäologischen Entdeckungen Carl HUMANNS: KuGAW 40. Mainz 1989, von Zabern. xv-342 p.; 8 pl.

b923 **Drower** Margaret S., Flinders PETRIE, a life in archaeology 1985 ➤ 1,b564 ... 3,d263: ᴿBA 52 (1989) 146 (W. G. *Dever*).

b924 **Eccles** Robert S., E. R. GOODENOUGH 1985 ➤ 1,b565 ... 4,d754: ᴿRB 96 (1989) 617s (B. T. *Viviano*).

b925 **Ghali** Ibrahim A., VIVANT DENON [Dominique, 1747-1825; Voyage (avec Napoléon) 1802] ou la conquête du bonheur; préf. *Vatin* Jean-Claude: RechArch 31. Le Caire 1986, IFAO. 304 p. 2-7247-0040-6. – ᴿBO 46 (1989) 282-4 (P. A. *Clayton*).

b926 ᴱ**Henze** Dietmar, Enzyklopädie der Entdecker und Erforscher der Erde III, 12, la Ro – Law/Low, 1988 ➤ 4,d757: ᴿDLZ 110 (1989) 237s (K.-R. *Biermann*).

b927 **Hruška** Blahoslav, Pod babylónskou věži [mit Bildteil, 19 der bedeutendsten Orientalisten p. 349-354]. Prag 1987, Práce. 375 p. Kčs 40. – ᴿArOr 57 (1989) 186s (Jana *Pečirková*); OLZ 84 (1989) 679s (J. *Klíma*).

b928 **Käfer** Markus, WINCKELMANNS hermeneutische Prinzipien 1986 ➤ 4, d762: ᴿGymnasium 96 (1989) 91-93 (H. *Sichtermann*).

b929 ᴱ**Laurens** Henry, KLÉBER en Égypte 1798-1800: Voyageurs occidentaux en Égypte 25. Le Caire 1988, IFAO. 576 p.; 4 maps [JAOS 109,724].

b930 **Lecouture** Jean, Champollion, une vie de lumières. P 1988, Grasset & F. 529 p.; 16 pl. 2-246-41211-0 [OIAc Ja90].

b931 *Lehrer* Mark, Die aufschlussreichen Mängel von Heinrich SCHLIEMANNS Selbstbiographie: Klio 71 (1989) 650-6.

b932 *Lehrer* Mark, *Turner* David, The making of an Homeric archaeologist; SCHLIEMANN's diary of 1868: AnBritAth 84 (1989) 221-268.

b933 ᴱ**Lullies** R., *Schiering* W., Archäologenbildnisse; Porträts und Kurzbiographien von klassischen Archäologen deutscher Sprache. Mainz 1988, von Zabern. xxx-341 p.; 165 fig. DM 78. 3-8053-0971-6 [JRS 79,274].

b934 *a*) **Männchen** Julia, Gustaf DALMANS Leben und Wirken in der Brüdergemeine, für die Judenmission und in der Universität Leipzig 1855-1902: AbhDPV. Wsb 1987, Harrassowitz. vii-158 p. DM 68. 3-447-02750-9. – ᴿTLZ 114 (1989) 366-8 (M. *Trensky*). – *b*) **Rieckman** Wernfried, Der Beitrag Gustaf DALMANS zur Topographie des Ostjordanlandes: Diss. Greifswald 1987. v-200 p. – TLZ 114 (1989) 634s.

b935 *Most* Glenn W., Zur Archäologie der Archaik [... *Winckelmann*; *Brunn*]: AntAb 35 (1989) 1-23.

b936 **Olmo Lete** G. del, Semitistas catalanes del siglo XVIII: OrBarc 5, 1988 ➤ 4,d774: ᴿAulaO 7 (1989) 284-7 (M. *Delcor*).

b937 **Palmer** Ulrich, Ernst SELLIN – Alttestamentler – Religionsgeschichtler – Archäologe: Diss. ᴰ*Schunck*. Rostock 1988s. – TR 85 (1989) 520.

b938 **Rahn** Paul, Bluff your way in archaeology [... ghost-writers]. Horsham 1989, Ravette. 62 p. £2. 1-85304-102-5. – ᴿAntiquity 63 (1989) 851.853 (P. *Halstead*: enjoyable).

b939 *a) Reade* Julian, Reflections on LAYARD's archaeological career; – *b) Fales* Frederick M., Layard's observations of Iraq: ➤ 849, Layard symposium 1983/7, 47-53 / 55-77.

b940 **Rocher** Rosane, Orientalism, poetry, and the millennium; the checkered life of Nathaniel Brassey HALHED, 1751-1830. Delhi 1983, Motilal Banarsidas. xi-354 p.; 10 fig. rs 350 – ᴿJAOS 109 (1989) 142s (F. *Wilhelm*: Persian texts from Sanskrit).

b941 **St. Clair** William, Lord ELGIN, l'homme qui s'empara des marbres du Parthénon [²1983], ᵀ*Carlier* Jeannie & Marielle. P 1988, Macula. 317 p.; 10 fig. F 130. 2-86589-022-8. – ᴿAntClas 58 (1989) 512s (C. *Delvoye*).

b943 **Schimmel** Annemarie, Friedrich RÜCKERT [... Orientalist]: Lebensbild und Einführung in sein Werk. FrB 1987, Herder. 155 p. DM 10. – ᴿJAOS 109 (1989) 706s (Ingeborg H. *Solbrig*).

b944 **Shepherd** Naomi, The zealous intruders 1987 ➤ 3,d280: ᴿBA 52 (1989) 231s (M. P. *Graham*); ChH 50 (1989) 523s (J. H. *Glassman*); JEcuSt 25 (1988) 459s (E. J. *Fischer*); Tablet 242 (1988) 91s (E. C. *Hodgkin*).

b945 **Simon** Róbert, Ignác GOLDZIHER; his life and scholarship as reflected in his works and correspondence : Library of the Hungarian Academy of Sciences, 1986 ➤ 4,d782 ᴿJAOS 109 (1989) 439s (M. *Perlmann*).

b946 **Stark** Freya, Over the rim of the world; selected letters, ᴱ*Moorehead* Caroline. L 1988, Murray. 0-7195-4619-2 [OIAc S89].

b946* *Swallow* D. A., Oriental art and the popular fancy; Otto SAMSON, ethnographer, collector and museum director: JRAS (1989) 5-31.

b947 **Szemerényi** Oswald, Hounded out of Academe ...; the sad fate of a genius [Emil O. FORRER]: ➤ 154, ᶠPUGLIESE CARRATELLI G., 1989, 257-294.

b948 **Thausing** Gertrude, TARUDET, ein Leben für die Ägyptologie. Graz 1989, Akad. 149 p. 3-201-01456-7 [OIAc S89].

b949 **Tushingham** A. D., K. M. KENYON 1906-1978 [< ProcBritAcad 71] 1985 ➤ 2,e398; 3,d281: ᴿBO 46 (1989) 464-6 (Hanna *Blok*).

b950 *Vercoutter* Jean, Notice sur la vie et les travaux de Claude SCHAEFFER-FORRER [6. III. 1898 - 25. VIII. 1982]: CRAI (1989) 179-188; phot. 178.

b951 **Wilfong** Terry G., The Egyptological papers of Klaus BAER, an annotated inventory [OI archive; typescript]. Ch 1989, Univ. Or. Inst. [OIAc S89].

b952 **Wilkinson** Richard H., Directory of North American Egyptologists. Tucson 1989, American Research Center in Egypt [OIAc S89].

T1.5 *Materiae primae* – **metals, glass.**

b953 *Knapp* A. B., *Muhly* J. D. & P. M., To hoard is human; Late Bronze Age metal deposits in Cyprus and the Aegean: RepCyp (1988,1) 233-262 (–265, lead ingots).

b954 **Limet** Henri, Textes administratifs relatifs aux métaux: ARM 25, 1986 ➤ 3,d287: ᴿBL (1989) 29 (J. F. *Healey*); BO 46 (1989) 362-378 (Karin *Reiter*: long lists of corrections); Orientalia 58 (1989) 428-432 (W. von *Soden*).

b955 *Molina* M., Las piedras preciosas en los textos económicos de Ur de la tercera dinastía: AulaO 7,1 (1989) 81-93; Eng. 81.

b956 *Aes*, BRONZE, COPPER: *Emanuele* D., Aes corinthium; fact, fiction, and fake [carrying forward cogent observations of J. *Murphy-O'Connor* 1983]:

Phoenix 43 (Toronto 1989) 347-357; p. 358, list of ancient references, only some fifty.

b957 **Knapp** A. Bernhard, Copper production and divine protection; archaeology, ideology and social complexity on Bronze Age Cyprus: SIMA pocket 42, 1986 ➤ 2,9859: ᴿRÉG 102 (1989) 217 (A. *Hermary*).

b958 Malachit: ➤ 905, RLA 7,3s (1988) 273-5 (G. *Weisgerber*).

b959 *Argentum*, SILVER: ᴱ**Baratte** Françoise, Argenterie romaine et byzantine; actes de la Table Ronde, Paris 11-13 octobre 1983 [➤ 4,720]; CNRS Centre Merlin, Archéologie de l'Antiquité Tardive. P 1988, de Boccard. 231 p.; ill. 2-7018-0038-2 [JRS 79,270].

b960 *Marchetti* Patrick, Quelques réflexions sur l'équivalence entre l'or et l'argent: ➤ 791, Histoire économique 1985/7, 135-149.

b961 *Aurum*, GOLD: **Éluère** Christiane, Les ors préhistoriques: L'âge de bronze en France 2, 1982 ➤ 63,a196; 65,a153: ᴿAJA 93 (1989) 603-5 (J. D. *Muhly*: far more than a catalogue of the 400 objects).

b962 **Wolters** Jochem, Die Granulation; Geschichte und Technik einer alten Goldschmiedekunst. Mü 1983, Callway. 331 p.; 45 fig.; 399 pl. DM 248. – ᴿAJA 93 (1989) 601s (J. D. *Muhly*).

b963 *Ferrum*, IRON: *Maluquer de Motes i Nicolau* Juan [1915-1988], Problemática general del hierro en Occidente: Zephyrus 49 (S 1986s) (7–) 9-15.

b964 *Vitrum*, GLASS: **Hayes** John W., Greek and Italian black-glass and related wares .. Toronto, catalogue, 1984 ➤ 2,9870: ᴿBO 46 (1989) 728s (S. L. *Wynia*).

b965 **Kaczmarczyk** A., *Hedges* R. E., Ancient Egyptian faience 1983 ➤ 64, a586 ... 4,d811: ᴿBASOR 275 (1989) 79-81 (S. *Heil*).

b965* *Lunsingh Scheurleer* Robert A., Faience from Memphis, Egypt; the bowls: ➤ 838, Pottery, Copenhagen 1987/8, 558-567; 8 fig.

b966 *Meyer* Carol, *a*) Byzantine and Umayyad glass from Jerash; battleship curves: ADAJ 33 (1989) 235-243; – *b*) Crown window panes; Constantinian or Justinian [sic]?: ➤ 106, ᶠKANTOR H., Essays 1989, 213-9.

T1.6   *Silex, os*: **'Prehistory' — flint and bone industries.**

b967 *Andel* Tjeerd H. van, *Sutton* S., *al.*, Landscape and people of the Franchthi [21,000-3000 B.C., Argolid] region: Excavations at Franchthi Cave 2. Bloomington 1987, Indiana Univ. 92 p.; 28 fig.; 13 pl. $25. – ᴿAJA 93 (1989) 287s (J. *Chapman*, R. *Shiel*).

b968 **Campana** D. V., Natufian and protoneolithic bone tools; the manufacture and use of bone implements in the Zagros and the Levant: BAR-Int 494. Ox 1989. 156 p.; 157 pl. £10. – ᴿBAngIsr 9 (1989s) 58s (Y. *Garfinkle*).

b969 **Cazzella** Alberto, Manuale di archeologia; le società della preistoria: Manuali 2. R 1989, Laterza. xi-329 p.; ill.

b970 ᴱ**Garrard** A. H., *Gebel* H. G., The prehistory of Jordan; the state of research in 1986: BAR 396, 1988 ➤ 4,d821: ᴿBAngIsr 9 (1989s) 54-56 (Y. *Garfinkle*).

b971 *Gopher* Avi, *Orrelle* Estelle, The flint industry of Naḥal Zehori I, a Wadi Raba site in the Menashe hills: BASOR 276 (1989) 67-76; 8 fig.

b972 ᴱ**Hoffecker** J. F., *Wolf* C. A., The early Upper Paleolithic; evidence from Europe and the Near East: BAR-Int 137. Ox 1988. viii-277 p.

b973 **Holmes** Diane L., The predynastic lithic industries of Upper Egypt; a comparative study of the lithic traditions of Badari, Nagada and

Hierakonpolis: BAR-Int 469. Ox 1989. I. xi-321 p.; ill. (list p. xi-xiii); II. p. 322-466. 0-86054-601-2.

b974 *Isaac* Glynn, *a*) Squeezing blood from stones [< ᴱ*Wright* R., Stone tools as cultural markers (Canberra 1977) 5-12]; – *b*) Foundation stones; early artefacts as indicators of activities and abilities [< ᴱ*Bailey* G., Stone Age prehistory (C 1986) 221-241] ➤ 283, Archaeology of human origins 1989, 339-351 / 352-379.

b975 *Kondo* Jiro, ❶ Stone arrowheads of prehistoric Egypt; present state of the question: Orient-Japan 32,1 (1989) 108-118.

b976 **Leroi-Gourhan** André, ᴱ*Garanger* José, Dictionnaire de la préhistoire 1988 ➤ 4,d826: ᴿAntiquity 63 (1989) 647s (A. *Sherratt*); Études 370 (1989) 373 (A. *Jeannière*).

b977 *Minissi* Nullo, Una teoria interdisciplinare unificata della preistoria: ParPass 249 (1989) 401-445.

b978 **Roodenberg** J. J., Le mobilier en pierre de Bouqras ... néolithique 1986 ➤ 2,9888: ᴿAfO 35 (1988) 225 (W. *Antl-Weiser*); AJA 93 (1989) 605s (D. V. *Campana*).

b979 *Rosen* Steven A., Pottery neolithic flint artifacts from Tel Lachish: TAJ 15s (1988s) 193-6; 2 fig.

b980 *Sass* Benjamin, Inscribed Babylonian arrowheads of the turn of the second millennium and their Phoenician counterparts: UF 21 (1989) 349-356.

b981 *Shea* John J., Spear points from the Middle Paleolithic of the Levant: JField 15 (1988) 441-450.

b982 ᴱ**Sieveking** G. D., *Newcomer* Mark H., The human uses of flint and chert [4th (Brighton) symposium 10-15 April 1983, second volume (first was Sieveking's Scientific Study 1986)] 1987 ➤ 4,771: ᴿAJA 93 (1989) 601s (Pamela R. *Willoughby*); Antiquity 62 (1988) 609 (T. F. *Lynch*).

b983 *Vachala* Břetislav, *Svoboda* Jiří, Die Steinmesser aus Abusir: ZägSpr 116 (1989) 174-181.

b984 *Vlasov* V. G., ❻ On the calendar of the Upper Palaeolithic; SovArch (1989,2) 3-22; Eng. 23.

b985 **Whittle** Alasdair, Problems in neolithic archaeology: New Studies in Archaeology. C 1988, Univ. 232 p.; ill. £27 [PrPrehSoc 56, 343-5, L. P. *Louwe Kooijmans*].

T1.7 Technologia antiqua.

b986 *Andreau* Jean, Recherches récentes sur les mines à l'epoque romaine: RNum 31 (1989) 86-112.

b987 *Bongrani Fanfoni* Luisa, On the [number of bricks carried for the] *'snbt* [smelting-furnace, not just sloping wall (nor *Reisner*'s 'chapel')] inside the walls of Amenemhet-*m3'-ḫrw'* [Kerma, found 1914]: GöMiszÄg 110 (1989) 7-11.

b987* *Born* Hermann, Antike Bohrung in Metall: AcPraeh 21 (1989) 117-130; 11 fig.

b988 **Burford** Alison, Künstler und Handwerker in Griechenland und Rom, ᵀ*Felten* Wassiliki: KuGAW 24, 1985 ➤ 1,b639*; 32 pl. + 50 color. DM 68: ᴿDLZ 110 (1989) 895-8 (Gudrun *Gomolka-Fuchs*).

b989 *Collini* P., Studi sul lessico della metallurgia nell'ebraico biblico e nelle lingue siro-palestinesi del II e I millennio a.C.: StEpL [4 (1987) 9-43] 6 (1989) 23-45.

b990 *De Fidio* Pia, L'artigianato del bronzo nei testi micenei di Pilo: ➤ 794, Zentrum 1986 = Klio 71/1 (1989) 7-27.

b991 *Deroy* Louis, Sur deux poèmes grecs d'époque romaine décrivant un verrier au travail: AntClas 58 (1989) 178-184.

b992 *Fischer* Henry G., An Old Kingdom expedient for anchoring inlaid eyes: JEA 75 (1989) 213s; 2 fig.

b993 *Hauptmann* Andreas, *al.*, Ancient copper production in the area of Feinan, Khirbet en-Nahas, and Wadi el-Jariye, Wadi Arabah, Jordan: Masca 6 (1989) 6-16; 7 fig.

b994 *Kantzia* Charis, *Zimmer* Gerhard, Rhodische Kolosse; eine hellenistische Bronzegusswerkstatt: ArchAnz (1989) 497-523; 23 fig.

b995 **Klein** Michael J., Untersuchungen zu den kaiserlichen Steinbrüchen an Mons Porphyrites und Mons Claudianus in der östlichen Wüste Ägyptens: Diss, AlteGesch. 26. Bonn 1988, Habelt, x-208 p. 3-7749-2369-8 [BO 46,227].

b996 *Kramer* Diether, Kupfer-Bergbau, Verhüttung, Verarbeitung (ein Überblick); MGraz 2 (1988) 161-176 + 5 fig.

b997 *Levy* Thomas E., *Shalev* Sariel, Prehistoric metalworking in the southern Levant; archaeometallurgical and social perspectives: WorldArch 20,3 (1989) 352-367; 5 fig.; bibliog. p. 367-372.

b998 **McNutt** Paula M., The symbolism of ironworking in ancient Israel: diss. Vanderbilt, ᴰ*Knight* D. Nv 1989. 404 p. 90-06852. – DissA 50 (1989s) 3263-A; RelStR 16,189.

b999 *Mazzoni* Stefania, Strategie adattive e sviluppi artigianali; qualche esempio di diversità tra Siria e Mesopotamia: ➤ 877, Lavoro 1988, 302-312.

d1 *Meyer* Laure, La métallurgie dans le Proche-Orient antique: Archéologia 246 (1989) 20-27; ill.

d2 **Mieroop** M van de, Crafts in the early Isin period...: OrLovAn 24, 1987 ➤ 3,d328: ᴿAulaO 7,1 (1987) 147-9 (M. *Civil*).

d3 *Moorey* P. R. S., The Hurrians, the Mittani and technological innovation [spells Mittani throughout, and with 'the' though calling it a state]: ➤ 28, ᶠBERGHE L. Vanden 1989, 273-286.

d4 **Neumann** Hans, Handwerk in Mesopotamien 1987 ➤ 3,d330; 4,d850: ᴿZAss 89 (1989) 299s (M. *Sigrist*).

d5 **Oleson** John P., Bronze Age, Greek and Roman technology, a select annotated bibliography. NY 1986, Garland. xvi-515 p. $71. – ᴿLatomus 48 (1989) 729 (J. *Debergh*).

d6 ᴱ**Powell** Anton, Classical Sparta; techniques behind her success: Oklahoma Classical Culture 3. Norman/L 1989, Univ./Routledge. 196 p. £25. 0-8061-2177-7 / L 0-415-00339-3 [Antiquity 63,294].

d7 **Preti** Alberto, L'estrazione degli obelischi egizi. T 1988, Soc. Ed. Internaz. 91 p. 88-05-05051-2 [OIAc Ja90].

Rolley C., *al.*, Techniques antiques de bronze; faire un vase – faire un casque – faire une fibule: Centre Techniques gréco-romaines 12, 1988 ➤ 548.

d8 *Rutschowscaya* M.-H., Introduction à l'étude de l'artisanat du bois en Égypte chrétienne à travers la collection du Musée du Louvre: ➤ 820, Journée Copte 1984/6, 81-92.

d9 **Saladino** Vincenzo, Arte e artigianato in Grecia, dall'età del Bronzo alla fine dell'età classica: Studi e Testi 9. F 1988, Univ. xiii-352 p.

d10 **Scheel** Bernd, Egyptian metalworking and tools: Shire Egyptology 13. Aylesbury 1989, Shire. 68 p. 0-7478-0001-4 [OIAc Ja90].

d11 *Stocks* Denys A., Ancient factory mass-production techniques; indications of large-scale stone bead manufacture during the Egyptian New Kingdom period: Antiquity 63 (1989) 526-531; 4 fig.

d12 *Stos-Gale* Zofia, Oxhide ingots and Egyptian metallurgy: ➤ 859, Delta 1988/9, 285-290; 2 fig.

d13 **White** K. D., Greek and Roman technology 1984 ➤ 65,a198 ... 4,d857: ᴿClasJ 85 (1989s) 63-80 (G. W. *Houston,* also on recent cognate works).

d14 *Zaccagnini* Carlo, Asiatic mode of production and Ancient Near East: ➤ 876, Production 1981/9, 1-126.

T1.8   **Architectura.**

d15 (Usman) *Anabolu* Mukerrem, ❶ Architectural relations between Anatolia and Sicily: TürkArk 23 (1989) 41-47 + 52 fig.

d16 *Bajoni* Maria Grazia, VITRUVIO fra letteratura e scienza: AcClasDeb 24 (1988) 47-49.

d17 *Bassi* Carlo, Tre capitoli per una meditazione sull'architettura della chiesa [... Sergio QUINZIO]: HumBr 44 (1989) 477-485.

d18 **Boysan-Dietrich** Nilüfer, Der hethitische Lehmhaus aus der Sicht der Keilschriftquellen [Diss. Wü 1984]: Texte der Hethiter 12, 1987 ➤ 3,d339; DM 95; pa. 65: ᴿJAOS 109 (1989) 689 (G. *Beckman*).

d19 *Braun* Eliot, The problem of the apsidal house; new aspects of Early Bronze I domestic architecture in Israel, Jordan, and Lebanon: PEQ 121 (1989) 1-25 + 24 fig. (map) + 4 pl.

d20 **Brodribb** Gerald, Roman brick and tile. Gloucester 1987, Sutton, xi-164 p.; 62 fig.

d21 *Bruce* Larry D., An eighth century B.C. house: BibIll 15,1 (Nv 1988) 52-57 [< OTAbs 12,247].

d22 ᴱCallebat L., *Fleury* P., VITRUVE, Architecture X 1986 ➤ 2,9913 ... 4,d861: ᴿLatomus 48 (1989) 908 (R. *Verdière*).

d23 *Coleman* Robert O., City gates: BibIll 14,3 (1988) 62-66 [< OTAbs 12,36].

d24 *Compernolle* Thierry van, Architecture et tyrannie [datation de temples de Sicile ...]: AntClas 58 (1989) 44-70; 8 fig.

d25 *De Laine* Janet, Some observations on the transition from Greek to Roman baths in Hellenistic Italy: ➤ 196, ᶠTRENDALL D., MeditArch 2 (Sydney 1989) 111-125; 8 fig.

d26 **Downey** Susan B., Mesopotamian religious architecture; Alexander through the Parthians, 1988 ➤ 4,d866: ᴿAJA 93 (1989) 612 (J. M. *Bloom*); Mesopotamia-T 24 (F 1989) 181-6 (A. *Invernizzi*).

d27 a) *Farber* Gertrud, al-tar im Edubba; notwendige Arbeitsgänge beim Bau eines Schulhauses; – b) *Gerardi* Pamela, Assurbanipal and the building of the Egigunû: ➤ 183, ᶠSJÖBERG Å., Dumu– 1989, 137-147 / 207-215.

d28 *Forest* Jean-Daniel, La grande architecture obéidienne; sa forme et sa fonction: ➤ 3,822, Préhistoire/Hamrin 1984/7, 385-423; 9 fig. [379-383, *Oates* D., temple architecture].

d29 **Franz** Heinrich G., Palast, Moschee 1984 ➤ 65,a217; 1,b680 ... 4,d870: ᴿArOr 57 (1989) 82-84 (Adéla *Křikavová,* deutsch).

d30 **Golvin** Jean-Claude, L'amphithéâtre romain; essai sur la théorisation de sa forme et de ses fonctions: Centre Pierre Paris 18. P 1988, Boccard. 458 p.; vol. of 71 pl.

d31 ᴱHägg R, *Konsola* D., Early Helladic architecture and urbanization 1985/6 ➤ 3,817; 4,d873: ᴿMusHelv 46 (1989) 177s (F. van der *Wielen*).

d32 *Hellmann* Marie-Christine, Le vocabulaire architectural grec; bilan de plus de cent ans de recherches: RÉG 102 (1989) 549-560.

d33 **Herrmann** J. J., The Ionic capital in late antique Rome: Archaeologica 56. R 1988, Bretschneider. x-215 p.; 28 fig.; 147 pl. 88-7689-021-1 [JRS 79,273].

d34 **Herzog** Z., Das Stadttor 1986 → 2,9923 ... 4,d879: ᴿAulaO 7,1 (1989) 136s (E. *Olávarri Goicoechea*).

d35 *Hinkel* Friedrich W., Säule und Interkolumnium in der meroitischen Architektur; metrologische Vorstudien zu einer Klassifikation der Bauwerke: → 814, Meroitica 1984/9, 231-252 + 14 fig.

d36 **Hirschfeld** Yizhar, ❹ Dwelling houses in Roman and Byzantine Palestine [→ 3,d350]; pref. *Tsafrir* Y.; Arabic glossary *Frankel* T. J 1987, Ben Zvi. 222 p. – ᴿJStJud 20 (1989) 230 (M. *Mach*).

Höpfner W., *Schwandner* E., Haus und Stadt im klassischen Griechenland 1985 → g491.

d37 *Jones* Mark W., Principles of design in Roman architecture; the setting out of centralised buildings: PBritSR 57 (1989) 106-151.

d38 **Jouffrou** Hélène, La construction publique en Italie et dans l'Afrique romaine: ÉtTrav 2. Strasbourg 1986, AECR. 537 p.; 6 fig.; 56 maps. 2-904337-12-1. – ᴿArchaeologia 38 (1987) 214s (J. *Kolendo* ❺); ClasR 39 (1989) 346-8 (R. J. A. *Wilson*); JRS 79 (1989) 233 (R. P. *Duncan-Jones*).

d39 **Kirchoff** Werner, Die Entwicklung des ionischen Volutenkapitells im 6. und 5. Jhd. und seine Entstehung: Diss. Klas. Arch. 22. Bonn 1988, Habelt. xii-334 p. – ᴿRArchéol (1989) 376-8 (Marie-C. *Hellmann*).

d40 **Kleiss** Wolfram, Die Entwicklung von Palästen und palästartigen Wohnbauten in Iran: Abh 524. Wien 1989, Österr. Akad. 23 p.; 82 fig. DM 40. – ᴿZAss 89 (1989) 300s (L. *Bier*: overambitious).

d41 *a) Kobielus* Stanisław, ❺ Fondements bibliques et symboliques d'une construction sacrale; – *b) Brzegowy* Tadeusz, ❺ La demeure de Dieu sur la terre à la lumière des Psaumes: AtKap 113 (1989) 3-13 / 14-24.

d42 **Kuban** Doğan, Muslim religious architecture [I. 1974] II. Development of religious architecture in later periods. Leiden 1986, Brill. x-49 p.; 48 pl. *f*72. – ᴿBSO 51 (1988) 561-3 (G. R. D. *King*).

d43 **Lackenbacher** Sylvie, Le roi bâtisseur 1982 → 63,a270...2,9928: ᴿWZKM 77 (1987) 175-8 (Hannes D. *Galter*).

d44 **Leick** Gwendolyn, A dictionary of Ancient Near Eastern architecture. L 1988, Routledge. xix-261 p. $52.50 [JAOS 109,722].

ᴱ**Leriche** Pierre, *Tréziny* Henri, La fortification dans l'histoire du monde grec: Colloque CNRS Valbonne déc. 1982. P 1986 → d97.

d46 ᴱ**Lévy** Edmond, Le système palatial en Orient, en Grèce et à Rome 1985/7 → 3,825; 4,d888: ᴿAJA 93 (1989) 468-470 (John *Bennet*); BO 46 (1989) 173-5 (M. *Stol*); RArchéol (1989) 361-3 (Y. *Grandjean*).

d47 **Liebhart** Richard F., Timber roofing spans in Greek and Near Eastern monumental architecture during the Early Iron Age: diss. Univ. North Carolina, ᴰ*Sams* G. Chapel Hill 1988. 324 p. 89-14444. – DissA 50 (1989s) 2123-A.

d48 *Lohuizen-Mulder* Mab van, The two-zone capitals: Babesch 64 (1989) 193-202; 20 fig.

d49 **Lukaszewicz** Adam, Les édifices publics dans les villes de l'Égypte romaine; problèmes administratifs et financiers: Studia Antiqua. Wsz 1986, Uniw. 184 p. zł 120. 0133-0583. – ᴿBO 46 (1989) 340-2 (G. *Husson*).

d50 **MacDonald** William L. The architecture of the Roman Empire 2, 1986
➤ 2,9929 ... 4,d890: ᴿLatomus 48 (1987) 710s (R. *Chevallier*).

d51 ᴱ**Macready** Sarah, *Thompson* F. H., Roman architecture in the Greek
world ➤ 4,454; [Soc. Antiquaries one-day seminar, L 1985] 1987: ᴿAJA
93 (1989) 622s (Barbara *Tsakirgis*); ClasR 39 (1989) 415 (G. B.
Waywell).

d52 **Maggi** S., Anfiteatri della Cisalpina romana (Regio IX; Regio XI): Univ.
Pavia Let/f 43. F°1987, Nuova Italia. 91 p.; XLII pl. – ᴿAthenaeum 67
(1989) 610-3 (Daniela *Scagliarini Corlaita*).

d53 **Marta** Roberto, *a*) Architettura romana. R 1985, Kappa. 193 p.; 444
fig.; map. Lit. 25.000. – *b*) Tecnica costruttiva romana, Roman building
techniques. R 1986, Kappa. 81 p.; ill. Lit. 16.500. – ᴿLatomus 48 (1989)
498 (J. *Debergh*).

d54 **Martin** Roland, Architecture et urbanisme. 1987 Coll. ÉFR 99. R 1987,
École Française. xii-624 p.; ill. – ᴿGnomon 61 (1989) 179s (V. *Kockel*);
RArchéol (1989) 159-161 (M. *Sève*).

d55 **Martin** Susan P., Building contracts in classical Roman law: diss.
Michigan. AA 1986. vi-163. – ᴿIvra 37 (1986) 134-7 (G. *MacCormack*).

d56 *Mazarakis-Ainian* A., Late Bronze Age apsidal and oval buildings in
Greece and adjacent areas: AnBritAth 84 (1989) 269-288.

d57 *Meijer* D. J. W., Ground plans and archaeologists; on similarities and
comparisons: ➤ 122, ᶠLOON M. van, To the Euphrates 1989, 221-236;
19 fig.

d58 **Mielsch** Harald, Die römische Villa, Architektur und Lebensform:
ArchäolBibliothek. Mü 1987, Beck. 181 p.; 106 fig. DM 38. – ᴿClasR
39 (1989) 158s (J. *Percival*); JRS 78 (1988) 244s (R. J. A. *Wilson*).

d59 **Müller** Werner, Architekten in der Welt der Antike. Z 1989, Artemis.
242 p.; map. 3-7608-8071-1 [OIAc Ja90].

d60 **Müller-Wiener** Wolfgang, Griechisches Bauwesen in der Antike: Archäol.
Bibliothek. Mü 1988, Beck. 221 p.; 113 fig. DM 38. – ᴿDLZ 110
(1989) 1065s (W. *Schindler*).

d61 *a*) *Müller-Wiener* Wolfgang, Das 'Sigma', eine spätantike Bauform; – *b*)
Lloyd Seton, Palaces of the second millenium B.C.: ➤ 5, ᶠAKURGAL E.
= Anadolu 20 (1987 for 1978ss) 121-129; 3 pl. / 197-201; 2 pl.

d62 **Pedersen** Poul, The Parthenon and the origin of the Corinthian capital:
ClasSt 13. Odense 1989, Univ. 48 p. 87-7492-706-0.

d63 *Pedersen* Poul, Some general trends in architectural layout of 4th C.
Caria: ➤ 852, Caria 1987/9, 9-14 [63-68, Roos Paavo, Rock-tombs].

d64 **Pesando** Fabrizio, Oikos e ktesis; la casa in Grecia 1987 ➤ 4,d894:
ᴿAJA 93 (1989) 478s (M. H. *Jameson*); JHS 109 (1989) 264s (R. A.
Tomlinson); RArchéol (1989) 370-2 (Y. *Grandjean*); RÉG 102 (1989) 209
(G. *Husson*); Salesianum 51 (1989) 831s (R. *Della Casa*).

d65 *Reber* Karl, Zur architektonischen Gestaltung der Andro^nes in den
Häusern von Eretria: AntKu 32 (1989) 1-7; 4 fig.; franç. p. 7.

d65* *Rickert* Franz, Zu den Stadt- und Architekturdarstellungen des
Ashburnham Pentateuch (Paris, Bibl. nat. NAL 2334): ➤ 827, 11ᵉ Arch.
Chrét. 1986/9, (II) 1341-1354.

d66 **Roik** Elke, Das altägyptische Wohnhaus und seine Darstellung im
Flachbild 1988 ➤ 4,d899: ᴿBO 46 (1989) 322-4 (C. *Tietze*).

d67 **Romano** Elisa, La capanna e il tempio; VITRUVIO o dell'architettura 1987
➤ 4,d900: ᴿAevum 63 (1989) 130 (M. G. *Bajoni*).

d68 **Seiler** Florian, Die griechische Tholos 1986 ➤ 4,d902: ᴿAntClas 58
(1989) 521 (G. *Raepsaet*).

d69 *Silberman* Neil A., Stones in many shapes and sizes – ashlars, bosses, margins, headers and stretchers: BAR-W 15,4 (1989) 59s.

d70 **Tunça** Önhan, L'architecture religieuse protodynastique en Mésopotamie 1984 ➤ 1,b705; 2,9937: ᴿJNES 48 (1989) 158-160 (Sally *Dunham*: useful and stimulating); OLZ 84 (1989) 29-31 (U. *Seidl*).

d71 **Vemi** Vassiliki, Les chapiteaux ioniques à imposte de Grèce à l'époque paléochrétienne: Éc. Franç. Athènes BCH Sup. 17. P 1989, de Boccard. 238 p. + ⊚ 5 p.; 96 pl. 2-86958-022-3.

d72 *Wallace-Hadrill* Andrew, The social structure of the Roman house: PBritSR 56 (1988) 43-97; 20 fig.

d73 **Wright** G. R. H., Ancient building in South Syria and Palestine: HbOr 7/I/2B/3, 1985 ➤ 1,b709 ... 3,d374: ᴿBO 46 (1989) 463s (D. J. W. *Meijer*).

T1.9 *Supellex*; **Furniture; objects of daily life.**

d74 **Bimson** John, The compact handbook of Old Testament life. Minneapolis 1988, Bethany. 172 p. $6. – ᴿBS 146 (1989) 351 (F. D. *Lindsay*).

d74* a) *Burkhardt* Adelheid, 'Gründe dir einen Hausstand...'; Streiflichter aus dem altägyptischen Familienleben; – b) *Kluwe* Ernst, Haus und Herd in der griechischen Antike: Altertum 34 (1988) 69-76; 7 fig. / 77-86; 9 fig.

d75 **Chalkia** Eugenia, Le mense paleocristiane; tipologia e funzione delle mense secondarie nelle chiese paleocristiane: diss. Pont. Ist. Arch. Cr. R [sans date RTLv 21,558]. 403 p.; 146 pl.

d76 **Étienne** Robert, La vita quotidiana a Pompei [³1986] ᵀ*Andreose* Mario, *Proietti* Simona. Mi 1988, Mondadori. 363 p. Lit. 23.000 [HZ 251, 672, E. *Pack*].

d77 **Gubel** E., Phoenician furniture: StPhoen 7, 1987 ➤ 4,d915: ᴿRHPR 69 (1989) 193s (J. G. *Heintz*).

d78 **Hamman** A. G., La vita quotidiana nell'Africa di S. AGOSTINO; complementi alla storia della Chiesa [1979 ➤ 60,y677]: Già e non ancora 170. Mi 1989, Jaca. 336 p. Lit. 54.000. – ᴿStPatav 36 (1989) 636s (C. *Corsato*).

d79 *Hübner* U., Bett: ➤ 902, NBL, Lfg 2 (1989) 288s.

d80 **Jenkins** Ian, Greek and Roman life [inside the home] 1986 ➤ 4,d917: ᴿAncHRes 19 (1989) 41 (Pamela *Erwin*).

d81 **Maffre** Jean-Jacques, La vie dans la Grèce classique: Que sais-je? 231. P 1988, PUF. 126 p.; 7 fig.; map. – ᴿAntClas 58 (1989) 444s (C. *Delvoye*); RArchéol (1989) 366 (F. *Queyrel*).

d82 *Malek* J., *Miles* A., Early squeezes made in the tomb of Khaemhet (TT 57) [babies carried in a sling, according to drawings of M. E. *Cox*]: JEA 75 (1989) 227-9; 3 fig.; pl. XXXI-XXXII.

d83 **Matthews** Victor H., Manners and customs in the Bible; an illustrated guide to daily life in Bible times. Peabody MA 1988, Hendrickson. xxvi-283 p. $15. – ᴿBA 52 (1989) 150s (J. A. *Dearman*).

d84 **Rogers** Mary Eliza, Domestic life in Palestine. L 1989 = 1862, Kegan Paul. xii-416 p. 0-7103-0290-8 [OIAc N89].

T2.1 *Res militaris*; **weapons.**

Birley Eric, The Roman army 1988 ➤ 234.

d85 **Blois** Lukas de, The Roman army and politics in the first century before Christ. Amst 1987, Gieben. vi-112 p. f30. 90-70265-43-5 [JRS

78,273]. – ᴿClasR 39 (1989) 150s (J. F. *Lazenby*); Salesianum 51 (1989) 144s (B. *Amata*).

d86 *Born* Hermann, Antike Herstellungstechniken; gegossene Brustpanzer und Helme aus Italien: AcPraeh 21 (1989) 99-115; 26 fig.

d87 *Chevereau* Pierre-Marie, Contribution à la prosopographie des cadres militaires de l'Ancien Empire... B. Titres nautiques: → 39, Mém. *Clère J.* = RÉgp 40 (1989) 3-36.

Davies Roy W., Service in the Roman army 1989 → 252.

d88 **Davison** D. P., The barracks of the Roman army from the 1st to 3rd centuries A.D.; a comparative study of the barracks from fortresses, forts and fortlets with an analysis of building types and construction, stabling and garrisons [diss. Oxford 1987 → 4,d930]: BAR-Int 472. Ox 1989. xxii-914 p.; 129 fig.; 31 maps. £5. 0-86054-606-3 [JRS 79,271].

d89 *Devine* A. M., AELIAN's Manual of Hellenistic military tactics; a new translation: AncW 19 (1989) 31-64.

d90 *Eph'al* Israel, ❿ Lexical notes on some ancient military terms: → 218, Mem. YADIN Y., ErIsr 20 (1989) 115-9; Eng. 198*.

d91 **Foss** Clive, *Winfield* David, Byzantine fortifications; an introduction. Pretoria 1986, Unisa. xxvii-298 p.; 235 fig. – ᴿAJA 93 (1989) 309-311 (Sheila *Bonde*).

d92 **Franzoni** C., Habitus atque habitudo militis; monumenti funerari di militari nella Cisalpina romana. R 1987, Bretschneider. 151 p.; XXXVI pl. – ᴿAthenaeum 67 (1989) 609s (S. *Maggi*).

d93 *Fritz* V., Befestigung: → 902, NBL Lfg. 2 (1989) 257-9.

d94 *Hallo* William W., More on bows: → 218, Mem. YADIN Y., ErIsr 20 (1989) 68*-71*.

d95 *Hammond* N. G. L., Casualties and reinforcements of citizen soldiers in Greece and Macedonia: JHS 109 (1989) 56-68.

d95* **Kolias** Taxiarchis G., Byzantinische Waffen; ein Beitrag zur byzantinischen Waffenkunde von den Anfängen bis zur lateinischen Eroberung: ByzVindob 17. W 1988, Österr. Akad. 285 p. DM 90 [HZ 251, 679, P. *Schreiner*].

d96 *Lassen* Hanne, *al.*, A bronze sword from Luristan with a proto-Arabic inscription: AfO 35 (1988s) 136-152; 16 fig.

d97 ᴱLeriche Pierre, *Tréziny* Henri, La fortification dans l'histoire du monde grec: Valbonne déc. 1982. P 1986, CNRS. 651 p.; 331 fig.; 16 pl. F 490. – ᴿHZ 248 (1989) 404-6 (B. *Näf*); RArchéol (1989) 369s (Michèle *Brunet*).

d98 *Liberati* Anna Maria, *Silverio* Francesco; Con la forza dell'artiglieria;strumenti bellici dell'esercito romano: ArchViva 8,8 (1989) 28-33; color. ill.

d99 *Meshel* Zeev, ❿ A siege system and an ancient road at Alexandrium: → 218, Mem. YADIN Y., ErIsr 20 (1989) 292-301; 14 fig.; Eng. 205*.

d100 **Miller** D., *al.*, Domination and resistance: One World Archaeology 3. L 1989, Unwin Hyman. 332 p.; 43 fig. £35. 0-04-445022-2 [Antiquity 63,246].

d101 **Müller** Hans W., Der 'Armreif' des Königs Ahmose und der Handgelenkschutz des Bogenschutzen im Alten Ägypten und Vorderasien: DAI-K Sonderschrift 25. Mainz 1989, von Zabern. 3-8053-1055-2 [OIAc S89].

d102 *a)* *Muscarella* Oscar W., Multi-piece iron swords from Luristan; – *b)* *Overlaet* Bruno J., Swords of the Sasanians; notes on scabbard tips: → 28, ᶠBERGHE L. Vanden 1989, 349-365 + 3 fig. / (II) 741-750 + 4 fig.; II pl.

d103 **Nicolle** D.C., Arms and armour of the crusading era, 1050-1350. White Plains NY 1988, Kraus. xxi-574+575-1038, illustrations. – ᴿSpeculum 64 (1989) 1016-8 (D. *De Vries*) [< RHE 85,69*].

d104 *Pecorella* Paolo E., Ethnos e società; tracce di una unità a cavallo dello Zagros settentrionale durante l'Età del Ferro: → 877, Lavoro 1988, 288-301.

d105 *Rebuffat* René, À propos des libritores [slingers of stones, by hand or sling; not wielders of *libra*]: RPg 62 (1988) 283-9.

d106 *Sekunda* Nicholas, Achaemenid military terminology: ArchMIran 21 (1988) 69-77.

d107 **Spalinger** Anthony J., Aspects of the military documents of the ancient Egyptians 1982 → 63,a102... 3,d409: ᴿJEA 75 (1989) 259-261 (W.J. *Murnane*).

d108 **Wheeler** Everett L., Stratagem and the vocabulary of military trickery: Mnemosyne supp. 108. Leiden 1988, Brill. xviii-124 p. – ᴿOpus 5 (1986) 179-183 (M. *Bettalli*).

τ2.2 **Vehicula**.

d109 *a*) *Bienkowski* Piotr, The division of Middle Bronze IIB-C in Palestine; – *b*) *Hoffmeier* James K., Reconsidering Egypt's part in the termination of the Middle Bronze Age in Palestine: Levant 21 (1989) 169-176 (-8, Jericho, *Chapman* R.L.); bibliog. p. 178s / 181-191; -193 bibliog.

d110 **Bugh** Glenn R., The horsemen of Athens. Princeton 1988, Univ. ix-271 p.; 8 pl. $32.50 [AmJPg 111, 274-7, Cynthia S. *Clemons*].

d111 *Camps* Gabriel, Les chars sahariens; images d'une société aristocratique: AntAfr 265 (1989) 11-40; 20 fig. (map).

d112 *Crouwel* J.H., *Tatton-Brown* Veronica, Ridden horses in iron age Cyprus: RepCyp (1988,2) 77-87; 2 fig.; pl.XXIV-XXVI [(1989) 109s, pl.XXI].

d113 *Giesecke* H.-E., Der mykenische Wagen: Talanta 20s (1988s) 17-39; 7 fig.

d114 **Liebowitz** Harold, Terra-cotta figurines and model vehicles; the Oriental Institute excavations at Selenkahiye, Syria: BiblMesop 22. Malibu CA 1988, Undena. xiv-59 p.; 34 pl. 0-89003-105-3; pa. -4-5.

d115 **Littauer** M.A., *Crouwel* J.H., Chariots and related equipment from the tomb of Tut'ankhamun 1985 → 1,b764...4,d959; ᴿAntiquity 63 (1989) 638s (A.R. *Schulman*).

d116 *a*) *Littauer* M.A., *Crouwel* J.H., Metal wheel tyres from the ancient Near East; – *b*) *Özgüç* Tahsin, Horsebits from Altıntepe; – *c*) *Herrmann* Georgina, Parthian and Sasanian saddlery; new light from the Roman West: → 28, ᶠBERGHE L. Vanden, Archaeologia 1989, 111-121+4 fig.; II pl. / 409-413+VI pl. / (II) 757-782+7 fig.; XX pl.

d117 *Margueron* J.-C., Problèmes de transport au début de l'âge du Bronze: → 59, ᶠFINET A., Reflets 1989, 119-126.

d118 *Meischner* Jutta, Zwei Gewichtbronzen [für Hebelschnellwagen] in Form von Kaiserporträts: MiDAI-R 96 (1989) 407-418; pl.109-111.

d119 *Messerschmidt* Wolfgang, Der ägäische Streitwagen und seine Beziehungen zum Nordeurasisch-vorderasiatischen Raum: AcPraeh 20 (1988) 31-44; 8 fig.; Eng. 31; franç. 31s.

d120 *Pare* Christopher, From Dupljaja [Yugoslavia; *Bošković* D. 1959] to Delphi; the ceremonial use of the wagon in later prehistory: Antiquity 63 (1989) 80-100; 17 fig. (2 maps).

d121 *Raepsaet* G., Archéologie et iconographie des attelages dans le monde gréco-romain; la problématique économique: ⇥ 791, Histoire économique 1985/7, 29-48; 18 fig.

d122 *Stary* Peter F., Eisenzeitliche [...?phönizische] Wagengräber auf der Iberischen Halbinsel: MadMit 30 (1989) 151-183; 9 fig.

T2.3 Nautica.

d123 *Archontidou-Argyri* Aglaia, *al.*, The underwater excavation at the ancient port of Thasos, Greece: IntJNaut 18 (1989) 51-59; 14 fig. (1 foldout).

d124 *Arnold* Béat, Architecture navale en Helvétie à l'époque romaine; les barques de Bevaix et d'Yverdon: HelvArch 20,77 (1989) 2-27; ill. [29-37, *Renaud* J.-D.].

d125 *Avilia* Filippo, *Godart* Louis, La padrona dei mari, la trireme greca...: ArchViva 8,5 (1989) 10-17; color. ill.

d126 *Basile* Beatrice, A Roman wreck with a cargo of marble in the bay of Giardini Naxos (Sicily): IntJNaut 17 (1988) 133-142; 10 fig.

d127 *Bass* George F., *al.*, The Bronze Age shipwreck at Ulu Burun [Kaş, Turkey]: 1986 campaign: AJA 93 (1989) 1-29; 33 fig. [12-16, *Collon* D., cylinder seals; 17-29, gold scarab of Nefertiti].

d128 *Bauer* G., Berichte vom Roten Meer: ⇥ 814, Meroitica 1984/9, 389-398.

d129 **Blot** Jean-Yves, Archéologie sous-marine. P 1988, Arthaud. 253 p. (59 fig.) – ᴿIntJNaut 18 (1989) 187s (Honor *Frost*).

d130 *Bound* Mensun, A wreck at Dattilo, Panarea (Aeolian Islands) [Sicily-Lipari, c. 300 B.C.]; a preliminary note: IntJNaut 18 (1989) 27-32; 8 fig.

d131 *Broodbank* Cyprian, The longboat and society in the Cyclades in the Keros-Syros culture: AJA 93 (1989) 319-337; 6 fig.

d132 *Deman* A., Réflexions sur la navigation fluviale dans l'antiquité romaine: ⇥ 791, Histoire économique 1985/7, 79-106; 1 fig.

d133 **Eiseman** Cynthia J., *Ridgway* Brunilde S., The Porticello shipwreck 1987 ⇥ 3,d430*; 4,d971: ᴿIntJNaut 18 (1989) 346s (Honor *Frost*); JHS 109 (1989) 257 (J. F. *Lazenby*).

d134 **Ericsson** C. H., Navis oneraria 1984 ⇥ 65,a297... 4,d972: ᴿAnzAltW 42 (1989) 87-89 (H. *Aigner*); Mnemosyne 64 (1989) 238s (H. T. *Wallinga*).

d135 *Eschebach* Liselotte, Hafenstadt Pompeji: AntWelt 20,1 (1989) 40-54; ill.

d136 **Garland** Robert, The Piraeus, from the fifth to the first century B.C. 1987 ⇥ 4,d973: ᴿAmHR 94 (1989) 1350s (L. *Casson*); ClasR 39 (1989) 281-3 (G. *Shipley*); JHS 109 (1989) 251s (R. *Osborne*); RelStR 15 (1989) 71 (C. R. *Phillips*).

d137 *Gibbins* D. J. L., The Roman wreck of c. AD 200 at Plemmirio, near Siracusa (Sicily): second interim report: IntJNaut 18 (1989) 1-25; 16 fig.

d138 *a) Guerrero Ayuso* Victor M., *al.*, L'épave di Binisafuller (Minorque), un bateau de commerce punique du IIIᵉ siècle av. J.-C.; – *b) Frost* Honor, The prefabricated Punic warship: ⇥ 784, Punic Wars 1988/9, 115-125; 16 fig. / 127-135; 3 fig.

d139 *Hegyi* Dolores, ⓂⒺ Anatolische Elemente im griechischen Wortschatz der Piraterie: ⇥ 129, ᶠMARÓTI E., 1987, 47-49; deutsch 49.

d140 *Hillard* T. W., A Hellenistic quay in Caesarea's north bay?: ⇥ 196, ᶠTRENDALL D., MeditArch 2 (1989) 143-6; 3 fig.

d141 *Howard-Carter* Theresa, Voyages of votive vessels in the Gulf: ⇥ 183, ᶠSJÖBERG Å., Dumu- 1989, 253-266; 11 fig.

d142 *Jansen-Winkeln* Karl, Zur Schiffsliste aus Elephantine: GöMiszÄg 109 (1989) 31 nur.

d142* **Jones** Dilwyn, A glossary of ancient Egyptian nautical titles and terms: Studies in Egyptology. L 1988, Kegan Paul. 294 p. £45. – ᴿOrientalia 58 (1989) 539-541 (A. R. *Schulman*: Nile, the life of Egypt — and beyond).

d143 *Liritzis* Veronica M., Seafaring craft and cultural contact in the Aegean during the 3d millennium B.C.: IntJNaut 17 (1988) 237-256; 19 fig.

d144 **Lockery** Andy, Marine archaeology and the diver. Toronto 1985, Atlantis. 141 p.; 24 fig.; 15 phot. $13. – ᴿIntJNaut 17 (1988) 196-8 (S. A. *Easton*).

d144* **McCaslin** Dan E., Stone anchors in antiquity: SIMA 61, 1980 ➤ 61,s325 ... 64,a720 ...: ᴿOriginiR 12 (1983) 677s (M. *Liverani*).

d145 **McGrail** Sean, Ancient boats in N. W. Europe 1987 ➤ 3,d443; 4,d987: ᴿAntClas 58 (1989) 569s (G. *Raepsaet*).

d146 *Matei* Christian, Notes on the activity in the port of ancient Tomis [Constanţa in Rumania]: MünstHand 8,1 (1989) 39-54; 5 fig.; deutsch 54s, franç. 55.

d147 *Matthäus* Hartmut, *Schumacher-Matthäus* Gisela, Zyprische Hortfunde; Kult und Metallhandwerk in der späten Bronzezeit: ➤ 134, Mem. MERHART G. v. 1986, 129-211; 10 fig.

d148 **Meijer** Fik, A history of seafaring in the classical world 1986 ➤ 4,d990: ᴿMeditHistR 4 (1989) 375s (P. F. *Johnston*).

d149 **Misch-Brandl** Osnat, 'From the depth of the sea'; cargoes of ancient wrecks from the Carmel coast. J 1985, Israel Museum. 22 + 23 p.; 43 fig.

d150 **Morrison** J. S., *Coates* J. F., The Athenian trireme pa. 1987 ➤ 2,a18 ... 4,d992: ᴿAmHR 94 (1989) 726s (B. *Jordan*).

d151 *Morrison* John, The sea trials of the trireme; Paros 1987: IntJNaut 17 (1988) 173-5(-8).

d152 *Müller* H.-P., şî 'Schiff; Wüstenwesen, Wildkatz': ➤ 913, TWAT 6,6s (1989) 987-991.

d153 *Murray* William M., Lord of the prows — Augustus and the rostra of the Roman Forum [summary]: ➤ 830, AIA 90th, AJA 93 (1989) 259.

d154 *Murray* William M., *Petsas* Photios M., The spoils of Aetium [Roman memorial at Nikopolis with technical data on shipbuilding]: Archaeology 41,5 (1988) 28-35 [< OTAbs 12,25].

d155 *Oleson* John P., The technology of Roman harbours: IntJNaut 17 (1989) 147-157; 6 fig.

d156 **Palmer** Bob, Underwater expeditions. L 1986, Royal Geographical Soc. 125 p., spiral-bound. – ᴿIntJNaut 17 (1988) 276s (J. *Green*).

d157 *Raban* Avner, *a)* The boat from Migdal Nunia [Magdala] and the anchorages of the Sea of Galilee from the time of Jesus: IntJNaut 17 (1988) 311-329; 18 fig.; – *b)* The Medinet Habu ships; another interpretation: IntJNaut 18 (1989) 163-171.

d158 *a) Raban* Avner, Coastal processes and ancient harbour engineering; – *b) Collombier* Anne-Marie, Harbour or harbours of Kition on southeastern coastal Cyprus: ➤ 864, Coastal changes 1986/8, 185-208; 17 fig. / 35-46; 4 fig.

d159 **Reddé** Michel, Mare nostrum. R 1986, École Française. 737 p.; 73 fig. – ᴿGymnasium 96 (1989) 182s (K.-W. *Welwei*); IntJNaut 18 (1989) 76s (P. *Llewellyn*); Latomus 48 (1989) 927-9 (L. *Foucher*).

d160 *Rickman* G. E., The archaeology and history of Roman ports [... Rome itself]: IntJNaut 17 (1988) 257-267; 7 fig.

d160* **Riesner** Rainer, Das Boot vom See Gennesaret: HLand 119,1 (1987) 2-6.

d161 *a) Salles* Jean-François, La circumnavigation de l'Arabie dans l'Antiquité classique; – *b) Rougé* Jean, La navigation en mer Érythrée dans l'Antiquité: ➤ 822, Arabie/mers 1985/8, 75-102; map / 59-74; map.

d162 **Sperber** Daniel, Nautica talmudica 1986 ➤ 4,e1*: ᴿIntJNaut 18 (1989) 80s (B.S.J. *Isserlin*); JQR 80 (1989s) 433-5 (A. *Wasserstein*); RÉJ 147 (1988) 232s (J.-P. *Rothschild*).

d163 **Starr** Chester G., The influence of sea power on ancient history. Ox 1989, Univ. Pr. xi-105 p. $17 [RelStR 16,341, J.S. *Ruebel*].

d164 *Steiner* Gerd, 'Schiffe von Aḫḫijawa' oder 'Kriegsschiffe' von Amurru im Šauškamuwa-Vertrag?: UF 21 (1989) 393-411.

d165 *Stronk* J.P., A Thracian thalassocracy? [stone anchors in Sozopol museum, Bulgaria]: Talanta 20s (1988s) 65-69 + 5 fig.

T2.4 *Athletica*, sport, games, dancing.

d166 ᴱ**Angeli Bernardini** Paolo, Lo sport in Grecia: Storia e società. R 1988, Laterza. xxxvii-262 p.; 27 fig.

d167 ᴱ**Battini** Maria C., *al.*, L'archeologia racconta lo sport nell'antichità [Palazzo Strozzi febb.-apr. 1988]. F 1988, Cantini. 127 p.; 68 fig.; XXXII color. pl. 88-7737-028-9.

d168 **Bohus** Julius, Sportgeschichte; Gesellschaft und Sport von Mykene bis heute: BLV-sportwiss. 413. Mü 1986, BLV. 167 p.; ill. [AnPg 59, p. 960].

d169 *a) Briquel* Dominique, Ludi/Lydi; jeux romains et origines étrusques; – *b) Thuillier* Jean Paul, Les danseurs qui tuent... et autres athlètes étrusques: Ktema 11 (1986) 161-7 / 211-9; 2 fig.; IV pl.

d170 **Brödner** Erika, Die römischen Thermen und das antike Badewesen 1983 ➤ 65,a211: ᴿLatomus 48 (1989) 732s (F. *Bertrandy*).

d171 *Carter* John M., The study of medieval sports 1927-1987: Stadion 14 (St. Augustin 1988) 149-161.

d172 *Csepregi* Gabor, Le sport a-t-il un sens?: ScEspr 40 (1988) 209-225.

d173 *Crowther* N.B., *a)* Boy victors at Olympia [...16 new names in *Moretti* L., Sup. 2, 1987; Elis boys more successful (on home turf)]: AntClas 58 (1989) 206-210; – *b)* The Sebastan games in Naples (IvOL 56): ZPapEp 79 (1989) 100-102.

d174 **de Martino** Stefano, La danza nella cultura ittita: Eothen 2. Firenze 1989, ELITE. 103 p.

d175 **Di Donato** Michele, *Teja* Angela, Agonistica e ginnastica nella Grecia antica. R 1989, Studium. 377 p. Lit. 27.000. 88-382-3609-7.

d176 *Dunbabin* Katharine M.D., Baiarum grata voluptas; pleasures and dangers of the baths: PBritSR 57 (1988) 6-46; pl. III-XV.

d177 *Fittà* Marco, Dedicato a Olimpia; lo stadio di Domiziano [color foldout reconstruction]: ArchViva 7,2 (1988) 40s.

d178 *Floriani Squarciapino* Maria, Un altro mosaico ostiense con atleti: Rendiconti Pont. Accad. Arch. 59 (1986s) 161-179; 7 fig.

d179 *a) Freyne* Sean, Early Christianity and the Greek athletic ideal: Concilium 205 (E 1989) 93-100; = L'antiquité chrétienne et l'idéal athlétique grec, ᴶ*Divault* A. Concilium 225 (P 1989) 111-9; = IZT 25 (1989) 427-432, ᵀ*Berz* A.; – *b) Ryan* Thomas, Vers une spiritualité du sport; ᵀ*Divault* André: ➤ 454, Concilium 225 (1989) 131-140.

d180 **Frisch** Peter, Zehn agonistische Papyri 1986 ➤ 3,d466; 4,e22: ᴿAnz-AltW 42 (1989) 230-2 (I. *Weiler*); GGA 241 (1989) 12-21 (J. *Ebert*).

Golvin J.-C., L'amphithéâtre romain 1988 ➤ d30.

d181 *Hausmann* Ulrich, Schauspieler und Masken auf hellenistischen Reliefbechern Kleinasiens: ➤ 5, [F]AKURGAL E. = Anadolu 21 (1987 for 1978ss) 143-156; 4 pl.

d182 *Horn* Heinz G., Si per me misit, nil nisi vota feret; ein römischer Spielturm aus Froitzheim: BonnJbb 189 (1989) 139-160; 22 fig.

d183 *Hunter* Richard, Bulls and boxers in APOLLONIUS and VIRGIL: ClasQ 83 = 39 (1989) 557-561.

d184 *Isidori Frasca* Rosella, Educazione e libera espressione nel rito menadico: Stadion 14 (1988) 103-123.

d185 **Kyle** Donald G., Athletics in ancient Athens: Mnemosyne Sup 95, 1987 ➤ 3,d471; 4,e30: [R]AmHR 94 (1989) 106s (D. C. *Young*); ÉtClas 57 (1989) 186s (H. *Leclercq*); HZ 248 (1989) 140-2 (P. *Weiss*); RelStR 15 (1989) 165 (W. C. *Kurth*).

d186 *La Lomía* María R., Il giovane di Mozia è un danzatore?: ParPass 248 (1989) 377-396; 8 fig.

d187 *Langdon* Merle K., Scoring the ancient pentathlon; final solution? [*Sweet* Waldo, Sport and recreation in ancient Greece (NY 1987) 56-59]: ZPapEp 78 (1989) 117s.

d188 **Laser** Siegfried, Sport und Spiel: Archaeologia Homerica 'T'. Gö 1987, Vandenhoeck &R. 204 p.; 60 fig.; 8 pl. – [R]AnzAltW 42 (1989) 232-7 (E. *Maróti*); Salesianum 51 (1989) 146 (B. *Amata*).

d189 *Matoušová-Rajmová* Marie, Der Tanz auf kappadokischen Siegelbildern: ArOr 57 (1989) 247-256.

d190 *Meinberg* Eckhard, Plädoyer für eine neue Ethik des Sports: Universitas 44 (1989) 690-7.

d191 **Petersen** Arne F., Why children and young animals play; a new theory of play and its role in problem-solving: Hist.-filos. Meddelelser 54. K 1988, Danish Acad. 57 p. – [R]RPg 62 (1988) 344s (M. *Menu*).

d192 **Poliakoff** Michael B., Combat sports in the ancient world; competition, violence, and culture 1987 ➤ 3,d477; 4,e38: [R]AmHR 94 (1989) 186 (D. G. *Kyle*); ClasR 39 (1989) 107-9 (H. W. *Pleket*); JHS 109 (1989) 256s (S. *Instone*); JRel 68 (1988) 621s (K. *Sacks*).

d193 *Poliakoff* Michael B., Pēlōma and kērōma; refinement of the Greco-Roman gymnasium [a mud-salve, synonym for gymnasium as forbidden on sabbath mShab 22,6]: ZPapEp 79 (1989) 289-291.

d194 *Powels* Sylvia, Zur Geschichte des Schachspiels bei Indern und Arabern: ➤ 126, [F]MACUCH R., Ḥokmôt 1989, 201-212.

d195 [E]**Raschke** Wendy J., The archaeology of the Olympics 1984/8 ➤ 4,767: [R]ClasR 39 (1989) 297-300 (V. J. *Matthews*); RFgIC 117 (1989) 466-473 (F. *Guizzi*).

d196 *Rittig* D., Maske: ➤ 905, RLA 7,5s (1989) 448s; 2 fig.

d197 **Sansone** David, Greek athletics and the genesis of sport 1988 ➤ 4,e40: [R]Stadion 14 (1988) 275-8 (C. *Ulf*).

d198 **Simonnot** P., Homo sportivus; sport, capitalisme et religion: Au vif du sujet. P 1988, Gallimard. 197 p. F 82. – [R]NRT 111 (1989) 467 (C. M.).

d199 **Slowikowski** Synthia S., Sport and culture in the ancient Macedonian society: diss. Penn State, [D]Borza E. 1988. 186 p. 88-26821. – DissA 49 (1988s) 2776-A.

d200 **Swaddling** Judith, The ancient Olympic games 1988 = 1980 (➤ 1,b841) ➤ 3,d483: [R]AncHRes 19 (1989) 37-39 (G. *Duncan*: Greeks did not 'play' [< 'child'] games, but took them with adult seriousness).

d201 **Thomas** Renate, Athletenstatuetten 1981 ➤ 64,a927... 1,b842: [R]DLZ 110 (1989) 607-9 (E. *Paul*).

d202 *Thuillier* Jean-Paul,   Les jeux dans les premiers livres des Antiquités romaines: MÉF 101,1 (Autour de DENYs d'Halicarnasse, 1989) 229-242.

d203 *Van Beek* Gus W.,   The buzz; a simple toy from antiquity: BASOR 275 (1989) 53-58.

d204 **Wörrle** Michael,   Stadt und Fest im kaiserzeitlichen Kleinasien; Studien zu einer agonistischen Stiftung aus Oinoanda: Vestigia 39, 1988 ➤ 4,e48; DM 108. – RClasR 39 (1989) 355 (N. P. *Milner*).

d205 **Young** David C.,   The Olympic myth of Greek amateur athletics 1985 ➤ 2,a61; 3,d488:   RAmJPg 110 (1989) 166-171 (M. B. *Poliakoff*).

T2.5   **Musica**.

d206 **Albrecht** Michael von, *Schubert* Werner,   Musik in Antike und Neuzeit [18 études]: Quellen und Studien zur Musikgeschichte 1.   Fra 1987, Lang. 348 p. – RÉtClas 57 (1989) 259 (Y. *Lenoir*).

d206* **Barker** Andrew,   Greek musical writings [I. 1984 ➤ 65,a333] II. Harmonic and acoustic theory. C 1989, Univ.   viii-581 p. [RÉG 103, 290, J. *Irigoin*].

d207 **Bélis** Annie,   ARISTOXÈNE de Tarente et ARISTOTE; le Traité d'harmonique: Ét. et Comm. 100.   P 1986, Klincksieck.   274 p.   RRArchéol (1989) 171-3 (F. *Lasserre*).

d208 *Bélis* Annie,   *a*) Néron musicien: CRAI (1989) 747-763 (-768, *Irigoin* J., *al.*); – *b*) Les termes grecs et latins désignant las spécialités musicales: RPg 62 (1988) 227-250; – *c*) L'organologie [étude des instruments] des instruments de musique de l'antiquité; chronique bibliographique: RArchéol (1989) 127-142; 9 fig.

d209 E**Berti** Fede, *Restani* Donatella,   Lo specchio della musica; iconografia musicale nella ceramica attica di Spina.   Bo 1988, Nuova Alfa.   xxvi-93 p.; ill.

d210 *Bonefas* Suzanne,   The musical inscription from Epidauros: Hesperia 58 (1989) 51-62; pl. 14.

d211 *Burnim* Mellonee,   La séance de gospel music noire comme transformation, T*Divault* André: ➤ 454, Concilium 222 (P 1989) 63-73.

d212 *Černý* M. K.,   Probleme der Musikaufzeichnung aus Ugarit — Versuch einer neuen Interpretation des 'Hymnus h 6': ➤ 874, Šulmu 1986/8, 49-62.

d212* **Collins** Mary,   Music and the experience of God: Concilium 202 (E 1989) 3-8 [-151, *al.*] = Musik und Gotteserfahrung: IZT 25 (1989) 97-101 (-194) = Concilium 222 (P 1989) 7-13(-174).

d213 **Comotti** Giovanni,   Music in Greek and Roman culture, T*Munson* R. V.: Ancient Society and History. Baltimore 1989, Johns Hopkins Univ. xii-186 p.; 13 fig. $23 [JRS 79,270].

d214 **Corbin** Solange,   La musica cristiana dalle origini a Gregorio [1960, L'Église à la conquête de sa musique],T, 1987 ➤ 4,e56;   246 p. Lit. 26.000: RParVi 33 (1988) 319s (A. *Demonte*).

d215 *Duchesne-Guillemin* Marcelle,   Sur la lyre-kithara géante: ➤ 28, FBERGHE L. Vanden 1989, 127-131 + II pl.

d216 **During** Jean,   La musique iranienne, tradition et évolution: RCiv Mémoire 38.   P 1984, Inst. Français d'Iranologie.   243 p. – RDer Islam 65 (1988) 379 (G. *Braune*).

d217 **Flender** Reinhard,   Der biblische Sprechgesang und seine mündliche Überlieferung in Synagoge und griechischer Kirche: Quellenkataloge zur Musikgeschichte 20.   Wilhelmshaven 1988, Noetzel.   216 p.; 8 pl. DM 130. – RVT 39 (1989) 244s (L. R. *Wickham*).

d218 **Gentili** Bruno, *Pretagostini* Roberto,   La musica in Grecia.   R 1988, Laterza. 317 p. – ᴿRÉG 102 (1989) 586s (G. *Liberman*).

d219 **Hickmann** Hans,   Miscellanea musicologica [13 art. ASAE 1949-54], ᴱ*Abou-Ghazi* Diaᵉ M.: Vies et Travaux 1. Cairo 1980, Org. Antiquités. 291 p.; ill. – ᴿOLZ 84 (1989) 19s (R. *Krauspe*).

d220 *Katz* Ruth,   Samaritan Music: ➤ 389, ᴱ**Crown** A., The Samaritans 1989, 743-770.

d221 *Koitabashi* Matahisa, ❶ A Hurrian song with musical notation from Ugarit: Orient-Japan 32,1 (1989) 93-107.

d222 *a*) *Lasserre* François,   Musica babilonese e musica greca; – *b*) *Comotti* Giovanni,   I problemi dei valori ritmici nell'interpretazione dei testi musicali della Grecia antica: ➤ 790, Musica in Grecia 1985/8, 72-95 / 17-25.

d222* **Maas** Martha, *Snyder* Jane M.,   Stringed instruments of ancient Greece. NHv 1989, Yale Univ. xx-261 p.; 148 fig. $54 [Gnomon 62, 739, A. *Bélis*; RelStR 16,342, B. R. *Butler*].

d223 *a*) *Moberg* Carl-Axel,   On music archaeology; – *b*) *Schneider* Albrecht, *Archaiologeō*; some comments on methods and sources in music archaeology; – *c*) *Stockmann* Doris,   On the early history of drums and drumming in Europe and the Mediterranean: ➤ 853, Music archaeology 1984/6, I, 237-9 / 195-224 / 11-28; 11 fig. (-48, *al.*).

d224 *Montero Honorato* María Pilar,   La música en San AGUSTÍN: StOvet 16 (1988) 156-176.

d225 *Music* [sic, his surname] David W.,   The trumpet [*šôpār, qeren, yôbēl, hᵃṣōṣᵉrâ*]: BibIll 14,4 (Nv 1988) 30-33 [< OTAbs 12,266].

d226 ᵀᴱ**Neubecker** Annemarie J.,   PHILODEMUS, Über die Musik IV, 1986 ➤ 4,e69; Lit. 40.000: ᴿGymnasium 96 (1989) 77s (F. X. *Herrmann*).

d227 **Rashid** Subhi A.,   Mesopotamien: Musikgeschichte in Bildern 2/2, 1984 ➤ 2,a77; 4,e71: ᴿAfO 35 (1988) 205 (F. *Födermayr*).

d228 ᴱ**Riethmüller** Albrecht, *Zaminar* Frieder,   Die Musik des Altertums: NHbMusikWiss 1.   Laaber 1989, Laaber-V. x-358 p.   3-89007-031-0 [OIAc Ja90].

d229 *Rop* Yves De,   Sur le problème du tempérament musical; description des principaux systèmes utilisés depuis l'Antiquité jusqu'à nos jours: RArtLv 20 (1987) 75-99.

d230 **Seidel** Hans,   Musik in Altisrael; Untersuchungen zur Musikgeschichte und Musikpraxis Altisraels anhand biblischer und ausserbiblischer Texte: BeiErfAJ 12.   Fra 1989, Lang. 352 p. 3-8204-9887-2.

d231 *Thissen* Heinz J.,   Der verkommene Harfenspieler: ZPapEp 77 (1989) 227-240.

d232 *Waele* Eric De,   Musicians and musical instruments on the rock reliefs in the Elamite sanctuary of Kul-e Farah (Izeh) [125 km NE Ahwaz]: Iran 27 (1989) 29-38; VI pl.

d233 **Werner** Eric,   Il sacro ponte I, 1983 ➤ 1,6628 ... 3d506: ᴿRivLtg 76 (1989) 315-7 (S. *Rosso*).

d234 *a*) *Witkowska-Zaremba* Elżbieta, ❷ The Pythagorean system as formulated by Jean de MURIS; – *b*) *Piotrowska* Maria, ❷ Music and epiphany (hermeneutical fragments): ➤ 137, ꟳMROWIEC K., RoczTK 34,7 (1987) 285-292; Eng. 292 / 19-31; Eng. 32.

T2.6 **Textilia**, *vestis*, clothing.

d235 **Bezantakos** N. P., ❺ *Hē archaîa Hellenikē mítra* [during 1330 years, piece of cloth of various shapes on different parts of men's or women's body]. Athenai 1987, Kardamista. – ᴿClasR 39 (1989) 101-3 (A. G. *Geddes*).

d236 *Boëls-Janssen* Nicole, La prêtresse au trois voiles [*flammeum, uenenatum, rica*, à part le ruban/chignon *tutulus*]: RÉLat 67 (1989) 117-133.

d237 **Bolzot** Alain, Histoire, costumes, bijoux de l'Égypte ancienne. P 1987, Grancher. 84 p. [OIAc Ja90].

d238 *Calmeyer* Peter, Die elamisch-persische Tracht: Zur Genese altiranischer Motive X: ArchMIran 21 (1988) 27-51; 12 fig.; pl. 11-29.

d239 *David* Ephraim, Dress in Spartan society: AncW 19 (1989) 3-13.

d240 *Kokovkin* A., Ⓑ Early Coptic embroideries in the Hermitage: SGErm 52 (1987) 40-42; 4 fig.; Eng. 59.

d241 *Maes* A., L'habillement masculin à Carthage à l'époque des guerres puniques: → 784, Punic Wars 1988/9, 15-24; 4 fig.

d242 **Morrow** Katherine D., Greek footwear and the dating of sculpture 1985 → 3,d517: ᴿPhoenix 43 (Toronto 1989) 265-8 (Evelyn B. *Harrison*).

d243 **Ribichini** Sergio, *Xella* Paolo, La terminologia dei tessili nei testi di Ugarit: Coll. StFen 20, 1985 → 3,d521; 4,e94: ᴿBO 46 (1989) 118-120 (M. *Baldacci*: some 20 emendations, including *mḥs* 'smite' not 'weaver').

d244 *Ribichini* Sergio, *Xella* Paolo, Osservazioni sull'industria tessile nel regno di Ugarit: → 877, Lavoro 1988, 313-322.

d245 **Salvi** Pierre, *al.*, Tissu et vêtement; 5000 ans de savoir-faire [exposition 1986]: Monde Antique et Médiéval. Guiry-en-Vexin 1987, Musée. 198 p. [OIAc Ja90].

d246 **Symons** D. J., Costume of ancient Rome. L 1987, Batsford. 64 p.; 100 fig.; 8 colour. pl.; 2 maps. £9. 0-7134-5327-3 [JRS 78,283].

Terminologie und Typologie mittelalterlicher ... Kleidung 1986/8 → 872.

d247 **Tölle-Kastenbein** Renate, Frühklassische Peplosfiguren 1986 → 2,a106; 4,e102: ᴿDLZ 110 (1989) 609-611 (E. *Paul*).

d248 *Vogelsang-Eastwood* Gillian M., A note on the so-called 'spinning bowls' [bowl with a handle of four openings on its inner bottom]: JbEOL 30 (1987s) 78-88; 7 fig.

T2.7 *Ornamenta corporis*, jewelry, mirrors.

d249 a) *Calmeyer* Peter, Gute Geister [sechs goldene Ohrringe mit Eroten; aus Hamadan 1854]; – b) *Metdepenninghen* Catheline, The Urartian belts; a reconstruction and the evidence about some Urartian belt-workshops; – c) *Goldman* Bernard, The imperial jewel at Taq-i Bustan: → 28, ᶠBERGHE L. Vanden, Archaeologia 1989, (II) 605-615 + VI pl. (map) / (I) 421-434 + 3 fig.; II pl. / (II) 831-843 + 3 fig.; I pl.

d249* **de Puma** Richard D., Corpus speculorum etruscorum USA. Ames 1987, Iowa State Univ. 241 p.; 120 fig. $37 [Gnomon 62, 632-7, Ines *Jucker*].

d250 **Furlong** Iris, Divine headdresses of Mesopotamia 1987 → 3,d534: ᴿZAss 79 (1989) 278-283,6 fig. (R. M. *Boehmer*).

d251 *Garbini* Giovanni, Un'iscrizione fenicia su un anello d'oro: RStFen 8 (1989) 41-53; pl. VI.

d252 *Glaze* Joseph E., Ancient Egyptian jewelry: BibIll 15,1 (Nv 1988) 18-21 [< OTAbs 12,264].

d254 *Hofmann* Inge, Zur Herkunft der meroitischen Spiegeltypen: → 80, ᶠHELCK W. 1989, 97-118; 14 fig.; pl. V-VII.

d255 a) *Khlopin* I. N., *Khlopina* L. I., Double-spiral headpins in the Middle East [not pins for head or hair, but straight pins with the head in form of a spiral on each side]; – *b*) *Coessens* Bart, Bent pins in the Near East in the third millennium B.C.: → 28, ᶠBERGHE L. Vanden 1989, 99-107 + 2 fig. / 85-87 + 1 fig.

d256 **Limper** Klaudia, Uruk; Perlen, Ketten, Anhänger; Grabungen 1912-1985: Uruk-Warka Endberichte 2. Mainz 1989, von Zabern. 3-8053-1047-1 [OIAc S89].

d257 **Maaskant-Kleibrink** Marianne, The engraved gems, Roman and non Roman... in Rijksmuseum. Nijmegen 1986, Ministry of Welfare. xv-124 p. – ᴿBonnJbb 189 (1989) 631-4 (Antje *Krug*).

d258 **McGovern** Patrick E., Late Bronze Palestinian pendants [diss. Penn]: ASOR Mg 1, 1985 → 2,a116...7,e116: ᴿBASOR 275 (1989) 83-88 (Ora *Negbi*); JAOS 109 (1989) 115s (H. A. *Liebowitz*).

d259 **Megow** W.-R., Kameen von Augustus bis Alexander Severus: DAI-Antike Münzen 11. B 1987, de Gruyter. xvi-326 p.; 51 pl. – ᴿAc-ClasDeb 24 (1988) 61-66 (T. *Gesztelyi*); Archaeologia 39 (Wrocław 1988) 247s (Z. *Kiss*).

d260 *Mumcuoglu* Kostas Y., *Zias* Joseph, [combs...] How the ancients de-loused themselves: BAR-W 15,6 (1989) 66-69; color. ill.

d261 **Musche** Brigitte, Vorderasiatischer Schmuck zur Zeit der Arsakiden und der Sasaniden: HbOr 7/I/2B/5. Leiden 1988, Brill. 90-04-07874-6 [OIAc S89]. – ᴿMesopotamia-T 24 (F 1989) 212-6 (A. *Invernizzi*).

d261* **Platz-Horster** Gertrud, Die antiken Gemmen aus Xanten...: Kunst und Altertum am Rhein 126. Köln / Bonn 1987, Rheinland / Habelt. xxxii-162 p.; 253 fig.; 51 pl. [Gnomon 62, 641-4, Erika *Zwierlein-Diehl*].

d262 **Schumacher-Matthäus** Gisela, Studien zu bronzezeitlichen Schmuck-trachten im Karpatenbecken; ein Beitrag zur Deutung der Hortfunde im Karpatenbecken: Marburger St.VFrG 6. Mainz 1985, von Zabern. 266 p.; 77 pl.; 51 maps. – ᴿArchAustriaca 73 (1989) 228-30 (Zoja *Benkovsky-Pivovarova*).

d263 **Török** László, The royal crowns of Kush: BAR-Int 338, 1987 → 3, d542: ᴿBO 46 (1989) 67-70 (H. *Tomandl*).

T2.8   Utensilia.

d264 *Abka'i-Khavari* Manijeh, Die achämenidischen Metallschalen: ArchM-Iran 21 (1988) 91-113; 114-137, 13 fig. with facing description.

d265 *Amiran* Ruth, An Early Bronze I basalt cult-bowl with ibex reliefs: IsrMusJ 8 (1989) 17-23; 8 fig.

d266 *Aston* David, Ancient Egyptian 'fire dogs' – a new interpretation [like hearth-andirons, but to support a rounded-base jar]: MiDAI-K 45 (1989) 27-32; 2 fig.; pl. 1.

d267 *Avigad* Nahman, The inscribed pomegranate from the 'House of the Lord': *a*) IsrMusJ 8 (1989) 7-16; 18 fig. – *b*) ❶ Qadmoniot 22 (1989) 95-102; ill.

d268 *Biran* Avraham, Tel Dan scepter head; prize find: BAR-W 15,1 (1989) 29-31; (color.) ill.

d269 *Braun-Holzinger* E. A., REC 447. LÁ = Libationsbecher [des Gudea aus Tello]: ZAss 89 (1989) 1-6 + 3 fig.

d270 **Ciałowicz** Krzysztof, Les têtes de massues des périodes prédynastique et archaïque dans la Vallée du Nil: Acta 829. Kraków 1987, Univ. Jagiełłonski. 68 p.; 4 pl. zł 120. 83-01-07544-9. – ᴿBO 46 (1989) 55-61 (B. *Midant-Reynes*).

d271 *D'Angelo* M. C., Una scodellina eburnea da Acebuchal: RStFen 8 (1989) 117-125; fig. 1; pl. IX-XI.

d272 *Dar* Shimon, [Metal] Axes from the Early Bronze Age at a site near Nahal Alexander: BAngIsr 9 (1989s) 46-52; 5 fig. (map).

d273 *Dothan* Trude, ❽ Iron knives from Tel Miqne-Ekron: ➤ 218, Mem. YADIN Y., ErIsr 20 (1989) 154-163; 20 fig.; Eng. 199*.

d274 *Dunham* Sally, Metal animal-headed cups at Mari: ➤ 122, ᶠLOON M. van, To the Euphrates 1989, 213-220.

d274* *Fitton* J. Lesley, *Esse quam videri*; a reconsideration of the Kythnos hoard of early Cycladic tools [only 8 of the 10 claimed part of British Museum 1884 acquisition, along with four now in Copenhagen, all from Naxos, not Kythnos]: AJA 93 (1989) 31-39; 2 fig.

d275 *Gal* Zvi, Loom weights or jar stoppers?: IsrEJ 39 (1989) 281-3; 3 fig.

d276 *Gaon* Nora, Three Early Bronze zoomorphic clay vessels from Anatolia: IsrMusJ 8 (1989) 59-62; 5 fig.

d277 *Gill* David W. J., *Vickers* Michael, Pots and kettles [of metal influencing pottery, queried by *Boardman* J.]: RArchéol (1989) 297-303; 1 fig. ➤ d559.

d278 *Goz-Zilberstein* B., ❽ [Theriomorph] Drinking vessels from Tel Dor: Qadmoniot 22 (1989) 39-41.

d279 **Greene** Barbara A., Ancient Egyptian stone vessels; materials and forms: diss California 1989. 479 p. 90-06337. – DissA 50 (1989s) 3272-A.

d280 **Markoe** Glenn, Phoenician bronze and silver bowls from Cyprus and the Mediterranean 1985 ➤ 4,e146: ᴿBO 46 (1989) 167-172 (Gloria M. *Bellelli*: ajoute correspondances avec *Matthäus* J. 1985).

d281 *Mousli* Majed, Ein Räucherständer [spät-3.Jrtausend] aus Terrakotta im Museum zu Homs: AcPraeh 20 (1988) 27-30; 4 fig.; Eng. franç. 27.

d281* **Muscarella** O. W., Bronze and iron; ancient Near Eastern artifacts in the Metropolitan Museum. NY 1989, Met. 504 p.; 791 fig.; 7 maps. $75. 0-87099-525-1. – ᴿAkkadica 62 (1989) 32s (Marilyn *Able*).

d282 *Negahban* Ezat O., Mosaic, glass, and frit vessels from Marlik [Mt. Elburz in Gilan, Iran]: ➤ 106, ᶠKANTOR H., Essays 1989, 221-7; fig. 39-40; pl. 34-37.

d283 *Patrich* Joseph, *Arubas* Benny, A juglet containing balsam oil(?) from a cave near Qumran: IsrEJ 39 (1989) 43-55 (55-59, chemical analyses); 4 fig.; pl. 6.

d284 *Pinnock* Frances, A proto-Syrian [lion-head stone] bowl in the Brooklyn museum: JNES 48 (1989) 31-34; 3 fig.

d286 *Potts* T. E., Foreign stone vessels of the late third millennium B.C. from southern Mesopotamia; their origins and mechanisms of exchange [< diss. Oxford 1987]: Iraq 51 (1989) 123-156; 13 fig.; bibliog. p. 159-164.

d287 **Sinn** Friederike, Stadtrömischen Marmorurnen 1987 ➤ 4,e152: ᴿArchaeologia 39 (Wrocław 1988) 248-251, 2 fig. (T. *Mikocki* ❽); ArchAust 73 (1989) 235 (G. *Harl*); BonnJbb 189 (1989) 623-8 (Guntram *Koch*).

d288 *a) Tanabe* Katsumi, An Achaemenid silver Pegasus-rhyton; – *b) Harper* Prudence O., A Kushano-Sasanian silver bowl: ➤ 28, ᶠBERGHE L. Vanden 1989, 525-533; 2 fig.; II pl. / (II) 847-860 + VI pl.

d289 *Thuillier* Jean-Paul, Les strigiles de l'Italie antique [Table Ronde 1989]: RArchéol (1989) 339-342.

d290 *Trokay* Madeleine, Les deux documents complémentaires en basalte du tell Kannās; base de tournette ou meule?: ➤ 59, ᶠFINET A., Reflets 1989, 170-5; 10 fig.

d291 *Yazici* M., *Lightfoot* C. S., Two Roman samovars (*authepsae*) from Caesarea in Cappadocia: Antiquity 63 (1989) 343-7.349; 5 fig.; colour pl.

d292 *Yellin* Joseph, *Gunneweg* Jan,   The flowerpots from Herod's winter garden at Jericho: IsrEJ 39 (1989) 85-90; pl. 11.

T2.9   *Pondera et mensurae*   –   **Weights and measures.**

d293 *Del Monte* Giuseppe F.,   Una nuova suddivisione del 'sūtu' a Boğazköy: EgVO 12 (1989) 139-144.

d294 *Heltzer* Michael,   Some questions of the Ugaritic metrology and its parallels in Judah, Phoenicia, Mesopotamia and Greece: UF 21 (1989) 195-208.

d295 *Hoftijzer* J.,   Six shekel and a half (notes on the Hermopolis papyri 2 and 6): StEpL 6 (1989) 117-122 [< ZAW 102,285].

d296 *Joannès* Francis,   La culture matérielle à Mari (IV), les méthodes de pesée, à propos d'un ouvrage récent [*Limet* H. ARMT 25]: RAss 83 (1989) 113-151; Eng. 152.

d297 *Kloner* Amos, ◐ Lead weights of Ben-Kosba's administration: ➤ 218, Mem. YADIN Y., ErIsr 20 (1989) 345-351; 7 fig.; Eng. 207*.

d298 *Leonhardt* Jürgen,   Die beiden metrischen Systeme des Altertums: Hermes [1899, F. LEO] 117 (1989) 43-62.

d299 Masse und Gewichte: ➤ 905, RLA 7,5s (1989) 457-480...; 5 fig.

d300 *Molina* M.,   Una mina de Narām-Sīn: AulaO 7,1 (1989) 125-7; 3 fig.

d301 *Parise* Nicola,   *a)* The mina of Ugarit, the mina of Karkemish, the mina of Khatti: ➤ 876, Production 1981/9, 333-341, map. – *b)* Una serie ponderale 'minoica' e 'micenea' per tessuti: AIONClass (ArchStAnt) 9 (1987) 1-8.

d302 *Rao* Maria,   *a)* *Kordantēs*; semantica ed ideologia di un calco [*Hultsch* F., Scriptores metrologici 1971]: Koinonia 13 (N 1989) 79-84. – *b)* Sulla polisemia di *tálanton* (Pollux 9, 52, 4 - 9, 54,20): AnPisa 19 (1989) 1283-9.

d303 *Siegelmann* Asriel,   Two lead weights from *Tel Šōš* (*Tell Abū Šūše*): ZDPV 105 (1989) 123 nur; pl. 16.

T3.1   **Ars, *motiva, pictura.***

d304 ᴱ**Adams** Doug, *Apostolos-Cappadona* Diana,   Art as religious studies 1987 ➤ 3,371:   ᴿHorizons 16 (1989) 200s (Maria *Harris*).

d305 **Aldred** Cyril,   Egyptian art in the days of the Pharaohs 3100 – 320 B.C.: World of Art. L 1988 = 1980, Thames & H.   252 p.; 179 fig. + 20 colour. 0-500-20180-3.

d306 '*Amr* Abdel-Jalil,   Four Byzantine symbolic elements from Jerash: ADAJ 33 (1989) 353-6; 3 fig.

d307 **Anati** Emmanuel,   Origini dell'arte e della concettualità. Mi 1988, Jaca. 200 p.; 68 fig. [88-16-40128–..., Antiquity 63,224].

d308 *Azarpay* Guitty,   The Neo-Sumerian canon of proportions in art: ➤ 328, ᶠBERGHE L. Vanden 1989, 163-170 + 11 fig.

d309 ᶠBAAREN T. P. van,   Commemorative figures, ᴱ**Kippenberg** H. G. = Visible Religion 1, 1982 ➤ 65,9:   ᴿTLZ 114 (1989) 261-3 (K.-W. *Tröger*).

d310 *Babolin* Sante,   La teologia orientale dell'icona: Credere oggi 6,36 (1986) 65-78 [> SelT 28 (1989) 63-68, ᵀᴱ*Angles* Jaime].

d311 **Beigbeder** Olivier,   Lessico dei simboli medievali [1979], ᵀ*Robberto* Elio: Già e non ancora, arte 90. Mi 1989, Jaca. 305 p.; 111 fig.; 155 pl. + 1 color.   88-16-60090-X.

d312 *Beltrán* Antonio, L'art préhistorique español; nouveaux horizons et problèmes; état de la question: BCentPrei 24 (1988) 13-44; fig. 4-29.

d313 **Bérard** Claude, *Vernant* Jean-P., *al.*, Die Bilderwelt der Griechen; Schlüssel zu einer 'fremden' Kultur [La cité des images, catalogue d'exposition], ᵀ*Sturzenegger* Ursula: KuGAntW 31. Mainz 1985, von Zabern. 259 p.; 185 fig. 46 color. DM 50. – ᴿDLZ 109 (1988) 310-2 (Verena *Paul-Zinserling*).

d314 **Bernus-Taylor** Marthe, L'art en terres d'Islam, 1. Les premiers siècles: Louvre, Grandes Étapes. P 1988, Desclée de Brouwer. 195 p. F 195. 2-220-02728-7. – ᴿÉTRel 64 (1989) 606s (Jacky *Argaud*).

d315 **Blocher** Felix, Untersuchungen zum Motiv der nackten Frau in der altbabylonischen Zeit: Vorderas. St. 4, 1987 → 3,d586: ᴿMundus 25 (1989) 6s (Eva *Braun-Holzinger*); OLZ 84 (1989) 547-9 (E. *Klengel-Brandt*).

d316 *Boardman* John, *al.* Herakles: → 951, LIMC 4 (1989) 728-838; phot. p. 444-559.

d317 ᴱ**Boespflug** F., *Lossky* N., Nicée II, 787-1987, douze siècles d'images religieuses 1986/7 → 3,592; 4,e175: ᴿRechSR 77 (1989) 470s (P. *Vallin*); RET 49 (1989) 104-7 (M. *Gesteira*); RHPR 69 (1989) 353-5 (J.-G. *Heintz*).

d318 *Bogyay* Thomas von, Bemerkungen zur Deesis-Forschung: → 210, Mem. WESSEL K., 1988, 49-55; 2 phot. p. 303.

d319 *Bonfante* Larissa, Nudity as a costume in classical art ['The Greeks saw their custom of athletic male nudity as something that set them apart from the barbarians, as well as from their own past']: AJA 93 (1989) 543-570.

d320 **Breuil** Paul du, Des dieux de l'ancien Iran aux saints du bouddhisme, du christianisme et de l'Islam; histoire du cheminement allégorique et iconographique de l'image divine : Mystiques et Religions. P 1989, Dervy. 139 p.; 6 fig.; 4 color. phot. 2-85076-297-0.

d321 **Crowley** Janice L., The Aegean and the East; an investigation into the transference of artistic motifs between the Aegean, Egypt, and the Near East in the Bronze Age: SIMA pocket 51. Jonsered 1989, Åström. xii-507 p.; ill. 91-86098-55-1.

d321* *Crowley* Janice L., Minoan influence on Mycenaean art; chronological problems with the prototypes: → 831*, High/Low III (1989) 124-139 + 2 pl.

d322 **Davis** Whitney, The canonical tradition in ancient Egyptian art: New Art History & Criticism. C 1989, Univ. xx-272 p.; ill. 0-521-36590-2.

d323 **Davis-Kimball** Jeannine, Proportions in Achaemenid art: diss. California. Berkeley 1989. 943 p. 90-06299. – DissA 50 (1989s) 3271s-A.

d324 **Der Nersessian** Sirarpie, L'art arménien 1977 → 60,u129: ᴿByzantion 59 (1989) 524-7 (C. *Delvoye*).

d325 ᴱ**Distante** Giovanni, La legittimità del culto delle icone ... III Convegno storico interecclesiale, 11-13. V. 1987, Bari: 1988 → 4,552; Lit. 35.000. – ᴿRivScR 3,1 (1989) 245-7 (M. *Semeraro*).

ᴱ**Dohmen** Christoph [Ex 32, p.11-23], *Sternberg* Thomas, ... kein Bildnis machen; Kunst und Theologie im Gespräch [Dialog ...] 1987 → 2442.

d327 **Ehrhardt** Wolfgang, Stilgeschichtliche Untersuchungen an römischen Wandmalereien von der späten Republik bis zur Zeit Neros: DAI. Mainz 1987, von Zabern. xviii-170 p.; 14 fig.; 118 pl.– ᴿBonnJbb 189 (1989) 628-631 (R. *Ling*); RArchéol (1989) 419s (A. *Barbet*).

d328 *Ferraro* Giuseppe, Scrittura e Padri negli atti del Niceno II: Ho Theológos 4 (1986) 335-351 [271-315-333, *Santi Cucinotta* Filippo, *Lanne* Emmanuele, Niceno II (... iconi)].

d328* **Franz** Heinrich G., Von Baghdad bis Córdoba; Ausbreitung der islamischen Kunst 850-1050: Univ. Inst. Kunstgeschichte 6. Graz c.1988, Akademische-DV. 211 p. Sch 340. – ᴿMundus 25 (1989) 107s (K. *Fischer*).

d329 *García del Toro* Javier R., La pintura rupestre en Murcia: Revista de arqueología 10,98 (1989) 10-15; ill.

d330 *Gesztelyi* Tamás, ⑩ Politische Symbole zur Zeit der Entstehung des Prinzipats: ➤ 129, ᶠMARÓTI E. 1987, 23-29; deutsch 39.

d331 **Goodenough** E. R., Jewish symbols in the Greco-Roman period [13 vol. 1953-69] abridged ᴱ*Neusner* J. Princeton 1988, Bollingen. 384 p. $35. 0-691-09967-7. – ᴿStPhilonAn 1 (1989) 128-134 (D. M. *Hay,* also on ECCLES R. S., Goodenough biography).

d331* *Goodenough* Erwin R., Jewish symbolism [1970]: ➤ 268*, ᴱ*Frerichs* E., Goodenough 1986, 95-105.

d332 *Grimm* Alfred, Sonnenlauf und Vogelflug; das Motiv der Schwalbe mit der Sonnenscheibe: ZägSpr 116 (1989) 138-142; 8 fig.

d333 *Hachlili* Rachel, Unidentical symmetrical composition in synagogal art: ➤ 845, Synagogues 1987/9, 65-67 + pl. XXXI-XXXIX (p. 1-6; pl. I-X).

d334 **Hall** Emma S., The Pharaoh smites his enemies: MüÄgSt 34, 1986 ➤ 2,a179; 3,d606: ᴿBO 46 (1989) 615s (Jadwiga *Lipińska*); RHPR 67 (1987) 204 (J. G. *Heintz*).

d335 **Hannestad** Niels, Roman art and imperial policy 1986 ➤ 2,a180; 4,e195: ᴿAnzAltW 42 (1989) 112s (B. *Hebert*); ClasR 39 (1989) 344-6 (M. A. R. *Colledge*); JRS 79 (1989) 217s (D. C. *Bellingham,* A. *Watson*); RArchéol (1989) 189s (R. *Turcan*).

d336 **Holberton** Paul, The Bible in twentieth-century art, intr. *Usherwood* Nicholas. L 1987, Pagoda. 111 p.; 17 double-page pictures OT, 23 NT. £16. – ᴿTLond 92 (1989) 72s (T. D. *Jones*).

d337 **Humbert** Jean-Marcel, L'Égyptomanie dans l'art occidental; préf. *Tulard* J., *Leclant* J. P-Courbevoie 1989, ACR. 336 p. 2-86770-037-X [OIAc Ja90].

d337* **Jastrzebowska** Elżbieta, ❷ *Sztuka* ... Early Christian art. Wsz 1988, Wydownictwa Artystyczne. 298 p., 130 fig. + 8 color. – ᴿVoxPa 15 (1988) 1087-1102 (P. *Warsiński* ❷).

d338 **Koch-Harnack** Gundel, Erotische Symbole; Lotosblüte und gemeinsamer Mantel auf antiken Vasen. B 1989, Mann. 199 p., ill. 3-7861-1531-1.

d339 **Lafontaine-Dosogne** Jacqueline, Histoire de l'art byzantin et chrétien d'Orient 1987 ➤ 4,e204: ᴿRÉByz 47 (1989) 317 (C. *Walter*); RHPR 69 (1989) 332s (P. *Maraval*).

d340 *Langdon* Susan, The return of the horse-leader [Argive vase painting stylization echoed at Akrotiri, Ugarit ...]: AJA 93 (1989) 185-201; 14 fig.

d341 **Lange** Günter, Kunst zur Bibel; 32 Bildinterpretationen. Mü 1988, Kösel. 271 p. DM 39,80. – ᴿTGL 79 (1989) 97 (K. *Hollmann*).

d342 **Leach** Eleanor W., The rhetoric of space; literary and artistic representations of landscape in republican and Augustan Rome. Princeton 1988, Univ. 400 p.; 45 fig. $65. 0-691-04237-3 [AJA 93,626].

d343 *Lebeau* P., Aux origines de l'art chrétien: Le temps de lire. P 1988, Lumen Vitae. 103 p. – ᴿNRT 111 (1989) 1031 (J. *Hennaux*).

d344 *Limouris* Gennadios, The apocalyptic character and dimension of the icon in the life of the Orthodox Church: GrOrTR 33 (1988) 245-273.

d345 **Mansuelli** G. A., La fine del mondo antico: Storia universale dell'arte. T 1988, UTET. vii-274 p.; ill.; 6 maps. – ᴿAthenaeum 67 (1989) 318s (C. *Saletti*).

d346 *Markoe* Glenn E.,   The 'lion attack' in archaic Greek art; heroic triumph: ClasAnt 8 (1989) 86-115; XXVII pl.

d347 *Martens* Didier,   L'illusionnisme spatial dans la peinture grecque [de vases] des VIIe et VIe siècles: AntClas 58 (1989) 17-31; IX pl.

d348 **Martin** Roland,   La Grecia e il mondo greco; dalle origini all'età classica; dall'età classica all'ellenismo: Storia universale dell'arte. T 1984, UTET.

d349 *Meinardus* Otto F. A.,   Die koptische Kunst im Wandel der letzten drei Jahrhunderte: OrSuec 36s (1987s) 11-27; ill.

d350 ^EMentré Mireille,   L'art juif au Moyen Âge, textes et documents; préf. *Bompaire* J., introd. *Meslin* J. P 1988, Berg. 235p. – ^RAulaO 7,1 (1989) 139s (J. *Casanovas*); RÉJ 148 (1989) 410-3 (D. *Tollet*: en marge du colloque P 1987 'politique et religion dans le judaïsme antique et médiéval' dont les Actes par Tollet sont sous presse).

d351 *Mikuda* B.,   Josephskult und Josephsikonographie im österreichisch-schlesischen Gebiet: Archiv für schlesische Kirchengeschichte (Jahr 50) 44 (1986) 93-106 [< RHE 85,153].

d352 **Milburn** Robert,   Early Christian art and architecture 1988 ➤ 4,e213: ^RBAR-W 15,4 (1989) 8 (D. E. *Smith*: useful overview but unsatisfactory on pre-Constantinian); CurrTM 16 (1989) 471 (E. *Krentz*); TS 50 (1989) 821 (B. *Ramsey*).

d353 **Morgan** Lyvia,   The miniature wall paintings of Thera; a study in Aegean culture and iconography. C 1988, Univ. xix-234p.; 200 fig.

d354 **Moscati** Sabatino (*Bisi* Anna Maria),   Le civiltà periferiche del Vicino Oriente Antico; mondo anatolico e mondo siriano: Storia universale dell'arte, I. Civiltà antiche. T 1989, UTET. vii-270p.; ill.; 4 maps. 88-02-04238-1.

d355 *a) Niwiński* Andrzej,   Relativity in iconography; changes in the shape and value of some Egyptian funerary symbols dependent upon their date and authorship; – *b) Milde* H.,   It is all in the game; the development of an ancient Egyptian illusion: ➤ 78, ^FHEERMA VAN VOSS M., Funerary 1988, 96-104; 6 fig. / 89-95; 1 fig.

d356 **Nunn** Astrid,   Die Wandmalerei und der glasierte Wandschmuck im Alten Orient: HbOr 7/I/2B/6. Leiden 1988, Brill. 90-04-08428-2 [OIAc S89].

d357 *Openshaw* K. M.,   The battle between Christ and Satan in the Tiberius psalter: JWarburg 52 (1989) 14-33; pl. 5-11.

d358 *Perraymond* M.,   Alcune visioni nell'arte cristiana antica; Abramo, Giacobbe, Ezechiele, Pastore d'Erma, Felicità e Perpetua: ➤ 746, Sogni = AugR 29 (1989) 549-563; 6 pl.

d359 **Pipili** Maria,   Laconian iconography of the sixth century B.C. [diss.]: Committee for Archaeology Mg 12. Ox 1987, Univ. xiii-127p.; 114 fig. – ^RAJA 93 (1989) 473-6 (Jane B. *Carter*).

d360 *a) Pirenne* Jacqueline,   Des Grecs à l'aurore de la culture monumentale sabéenne; – *b) Will* Ernest,   De la Syrie au Yemen; problèmes de relations dans le domaine de l'art; – *c) Parlasca* Klaus,   Bemerkungen zu den archäologischen Beziehungen zwischen Südarabien und dem griechisch-römischen Kulturkreis: ➤ 916, L'Arabie 1987/9, 257-269 / 271-9; 3 fig. / 281-7; 12 fig.

d361 **Pollitt** J. J.,   Art in the Hellenistic age 1986 ➤ 2,a204 ... 4,e223: ^RGnomon 61 (1989) 539-544 (H. von *Hesberg*).

d362 *Posèq* Avigdor W. G.,   The mythic perspective in early Jewish art: JJS 40 (1989) 213-224.

d363 *Reilly* Joan, Many brides; 'mistress and maid' on Athenian lekythoi: Hesperia 58 (1989) 411-444; pl. 73-81.

d364 **Rombold** Günter, Der Streit um das Bild; zum Verhältnis von moderner Kunst und Religion. Stu 1988, KBW. 282 p.; 70 fig. + 32 color. – ᴿTPhil 64 (1989) 291-3 (J. *Splett*); TPQ 137 (1989) 193s (F. *Mennekes*).

d365 **Rousseau** D., L'icône, splendeur de ton visage: Théophanie, 1982 ➤ 1,d36: ᴿNRT 111 (1989) 1032s (Y. *Torly*).

d366 *Sahi* Jyoti, 'The glory of God is man fully alive'; Christian art and the image of God in the human person: Religion and Society 34,4 (Bangalore 1987) 3-13 [G. *Evers* (Eng.) summary in TContext 7/1, 112].

d367 *Schmaltz* Bernhard, Der 2. pompejanische Stil – zur Eigenart einer Dekorationsweise und zum Verständnis einer Entwicklungsstufe: Gymnasium 96 (1989) 217-238; pl. IX-XII.

d368 **Schönborn** Christoph, L'icône du Christ² 1986 ➤ 3,d646; 4,e231: ᴿScripTPamp 21 (1989) 363s (D. *Ramos-Lissón*).

d369 *a*) *Schubert* Kurt, Die Ikonographie der Vevezianischen Pesach-Haggada 1609/1629; – *b*) *Schubert* Ursula, Assimilations-Tendenzen in der jüdischen Bildkunst vom 3. bis 18. Jahrhundert: Kairos 30s (1988s) 143-151; 10 fig. / 162-178; 10 fig.

d370 **Sendler** Egon, The icon, image of the invisible [L'icône, also in German and Spanish], ᵀ*Bigham* Steve. Redondo Beach CA 1988, Oakwood. 282 p. – ᴿGrOrTR 33 (1988) 345-7 (J. *Thornton*).

d371 **Sourvinou-Inwood** Christiane, Studies in girls' transitions; aspects of the arkeia and age representations in Attic iconography. Athens 1988, Kardamitsa. 160 p.; 8 pl. $20 pa. 0-89005-496-7. – ᴿClasR 39 (1989) 272-4 (R. *Osborne*).

d372 **Spanel** Donald, Through ancient eyes; Egyptian portraiture 1988 ➤ 4,d704: ᴿAJA 93 (1989) 610 (R. S. *Bianchi*).

d373 *Spycket* Agnès, Malerei [peinture, en français]: ➤ 905, RLA 7,3s (1988) 287-300; 5 fig.

d374 *Stansbury-O'Donnell* Mark D., Polygnotos's Iliupersis [Delphi paintings described by *Pausanias*]; a new reconstruction: AJA 93 (1989) 203-215; 5 fig.

d375 **Strong** D., Roman art, ᴱ*Toynbee* J. M. C.: Pelican history of art. Hmw 1980, Penguin [JRS 79,278].

d376 *Taylor* Richard W., Jesus in Indian painting revisited: Religion and Society 34,4 (Bangalore 1987) 44-70 [< TContext 7/1, 40].

d377 **Tézé** J.-M., Théophanies du Christ [art chrétien des débuts – fin Moyen Âge]: JJC Résonances 4, 1988 ➤ 4,8550; 2-7189-0378-3: ᴿEsprVie 99 (1989) 22-*jaune* [E. *Vauthier*]; NRT 111 (1989) 1032 (A. *Wankenne*); RechSR 77 (1989) 535s (B. *Sesboüé*).

d378 **Thierry** Jean-Michel, *al.*, Les arts arméniens: L'Art et les Grandes Civilisations 17. P 1987, Mazenod. 623 p.; 705 fig. + 186 color.; 4 maps. 2-85088-107-5. – ᴿByzantion 59 (1989) 528-537 (C. *Delvoye*).

d379 **Thierry** Jean-Michel, *Donabédian* Patrick, Armenische Kunst, ᵀ*Rudeck* Claudia: Grosse Epochen der Weltkunst, Ars Antiqua 4/1. FrB 1988, Herder. 626 p.; 705 fig. + 186 color.; 5 maps. DM 350. – ᴿZkT 111 (1989) 503s (H. B. *Meyer*).

d380 *Thijs* L., Kunst als 'spoor van God'? (over de aktualiteit van G. van der Leeuw's theologische aesthetik): GerefTTs 89 (1989) 41-60.

d381 *Uscatescu* Jorge, El Oriente cristiano y la teología del Icono: VerVid 47 (1989) 317-329.

d382 **Vignaux** Anne-Laure,   Études d'iconographie séleucide: mémoire de license, Lv 1986, ᴰ*Hackens* T. – RArtLv 19 (1986) 347s.

d383 *Walters* C.C.,   Christian paintings from Tebtunis: JEA 75 (1989) 191-208; pl. XVI-XXIX.

d384 **Weber** Hans-Ruedi,   Voici Jésus l'Emmanuel; la venue de Jésus dans l'art et la Bible [1984 → 1,d59],ᵀ. Genève 1988, Labor et Fides / WCC. 123 p. – ᴿÉTRel 64 (1989) 479 (J. *Cottin*); RHPR 69 (1989) 219s (P. *Prigent*).

d385 **Woodrow** Martin, *Sanders* E.P.,   People from the Bible [100 new paintings based on archaeological and anthropological evidence].   Wilton CT 1988, Morehouse-Barlow. 180 p. $26. – ᴿBAR-W 15,6 (1989) 72 (R.D. *Hank*).

d385* **Zanker** Paul, *a)*   Augustus und die Macht der Bilder 1987 → 4,e251: ᴿArctos 23 (1989) 293-5 (P. *Castrén*); GGA 241 (1989) 192-8 (Angelika *Geyer*:... Statuen, Münzen); Gymnasium 96 (1989) 259s (F.K. *Herrmann*); HZ 248 (1989) 415-8 (D. *Kienast*). – *b)* The power of images in the age of Augustus, ᵀ*Shapiro* Alan.   Ann Arbor 1988,   385 p.; 351 fig. 0-472-10101-3. – ᴿJRS 79 (1989) 157-164 (A. *Wallace-Hadrill*).

d386 **Zenetti** Lothar,   Das Jesuskind; Verehrung und Darstellung.   Mü 1987, Wewel. 182 p.; 70 fig. + 16 color. DM 29,80. – ᴿColcFranc 59 (1989) 482s (S. *Gieben*).

d387 **Ziegler** Johanna E.,   The Word becomes flesh; radical physicality in religious sculpture of the Later Middle Ages: *a)* Holy Cross College Symposium 1985; – *b)* Exhibition catalogue.   Worcester 1985, Holy Cross College Cantor Art Gallery [JAAR 57 (1989) 372].

T3.2 **Sculptura.**

d388 *Auerbach* Elise,   Emphasis and eloquence in the reliefs of Tiglath-Pileser III: Iraq 51 (1989) 79-84; pl. IV-VII.

d389 **Baines** John,   Fecundity figures 1985 → 3,d661:   ᴿJEA 75 (1989) 255s (J.K. *Hoffmeier*).

d390 **Besques** Simone,   Musée du Louvre, Catalogue raisonné de figurines et reliefs en terre-cuite grecs [→ 4,e259], étrusques et romains, 4/1, époques hellénistique et romaine, Italie méridionale, Sicile, Sardaigne. P 1986, Réunion Musées Nat. xvi-161 p.; 165 pl. F 450. – ᴿGnomon 61 (1989) 752-4 (D. *Graepler*).

d391 **Boardman** John,   Greek sculpture; the classical period 1985 → 1,d76; 4,e260:   ᴿAncHRes 19 (1989) 110-2 (B. *Gollan*).

d392 *Boriskovskaya* S.,   A note on Cyprian archaic sculpture: SGErm 53 (1988) 28-30; 3 fig.; Eng. 54.

d393 **Börker-Klähn** Jutta,   Altvorderasiatische Bildstelen 1982 → 63,a512... 3,d666:   ᴿZAss 89 (1989) 149-151 (E. *Bleibtreu*).

d394 **Boschung** Dietrich,   Nobilia opera; zur Wirkungsgeschichte griechischer Meisterwerke im kaiserzeitlichen Rom: AntKu 32 (1989) 8-16; 4 pl.

d395 *Carter* Jane B.,   The chests of Periander [of Corinth after 600 B.C., claimed to have (possibly) commissioned Spartan artists to make the gold, silver, and bronze mythological statuettes found at Delphi in 1939]: AJA 93 (1989) 355-378; 28 fig.

d396 *a)* *Claridge* Amanda,   Roman statuary and the supply of statuary marble; – *b)* *Kozelj* Tony,   Les carrières des époques grecque, romaine et byzantine: → 843, Ancient marble 1986/8, 139-152; 16 fig. / 3-10 + 34 pl. with facing explanation.

d397 **Colbow** Gudrun, Zur Rundplastik des Gudea 1987 ⟶ 3,d670: ᴿMundus 25 (1989) 7s (Eva *Braun-Holzinger*); ZAss 89 (1989) 302-5 (auch E. A. *Braun-Holzinger*).

d398 **Connelly** Joan B., Votive sculpture of Hellenistic Cyprus. Nicosia 1988, Dept. Antiq./Getty Trust. xix-128 p.; 54 pl. – ᴿRÉG 102 (1989) 222s (O. *Masson*).

d399 **Dörig** José, Les trésors d'orfévrerie thrace. [⟶ e706] 1987 ⟶ 4,d796: ᴿArctos 23 (1989) 290-3 (Greti *Dinkova-Bruun*).

d400 — *Byvanck-Quarles van Ufford* L., À propos de l'orfèvrerie thrace [*Dörig* J. 1987]: Babesch 64 (1989) 205-219; 14 fig.

d400* **Dörig** José, The Olympia [sculpture] master and his collaborators: Monumenta GrRom 6, 1987 ⟶ 3,f124: ᴿAJA 93 (1989) 613s (R. R. *Holloway*).

d401 **Donohue** Alice A., Xoana and the origins of Greek sculpture: AmerClasSt 15. Atlanta 1988, Scholars. xxii-509 p. [RÉG 103, 283, F. *Chamoux*].

d401* ᴱ**Frel** Jiri, *al.,* [Essays on some] Ancient portraits in the J. Paul Getty museum: Occ. Papers on Antiquities 4. Malibu CA 1987, Museum. 142 p.; ill. – ᴿAJA 93 (1989) 154s (M. D. *Fullerton*: uneven).

d402 **Froning** Heide, Marmor-Schmuckreliefs mit griechischen Mythen im I. Jh. v.Chr 1981 ⟶ 64,a900: ᴿAnzAltW 42 (1989) 113-6 (G. *Schwarz*).

d403 **Getz-Preziosi** Pat, Sculptors of the Cyclades; individual and tradition in the third millennium 1987 ⟶ 4,e379: ᴿClasR 39 (1987) 331-4 (R. L. N. *Barber*).

d404 **Giuliani** Luca, Bildnis und Botschaft; hermeneutische Untersuchungen zur Bildniskunst der römischen Republik 1986 ⟶ 4,e280; 3-518-37818-9: ᴿHZ 249 (1989) 137s (H. P. *Laubscher*); JRS 79 (1989) 182s (P. *Zanker*).

d405 *Goedicke* Hans, The stela Brooklyn 71.37.2 [aesthetic and superbly-preserved 'heralding piece' of (R. *Bianchi* 1988) Cleopatra's Egypt exposition]: GöMiszÄg 111 (1989) 57-73.

d406 **Goodlett** Virginia C., Collaboration in Greek sculpture; the literary and epigraphical evidence: diss. NYU 1989, ᴰ*Harrison* Evelyn B. 287 p. 89-16070. – DissA 50 (1989s) 1054-A.

d407 *Grimm* Günter, Die Porträts der Triumvirn C. Octavius, M. Antonius und M. Aemilius Lepidus; Überlegungen zur Entstehung und Abfolge der Bildnistypen des Kaisers Augustus: MiDAI-R 96 (1989) 347-364; pl. 81-93.

d408 **Hein** Irmgard, *Satzinger* Helmut, Stelen des Mittleren Reichs [+ I.-II. Zw.Zt]: Wien, Corp. Ant. Aeg. 4. Mainz 1989, von Zabern. xxxi + 150 loose plates. 3-8053-1002-1 [OIAc Ja90].

d409 *Heintze* Helga von, Das Grabrelief [ind.: Grabmal] des Phaedrus [Zürich, Privatbesitz]: Gymnasium 96 (1989) 1-12; pl. I-VIII.

d410 **Higgins** R., Tanagra and the figurines 1987 ⟶ 4,e382: ᴿJHS 109 (1989) 263s (Lucilla *Burn*).

d411 *Howard* Seymour, Laocoon rerestored [elder son turned and fitted into space flanking altar blocks, in Vatican storeroom, shown in one of the photos]: AJA 93 (1989) 417-422; 7 fig.

d412 *Hübner* Ulrich, Die erste grossformatige Rundplastik aus dem eisen-zeitlichen Moab: UF 21 (1989) 227-231; 1 fig.

d413 *Hurwit* Jeffrey M., The Kritios boy; discovery, reconstruction, and date: AJA 93 (1989) 41-80; 32 fig.

d414 **Jaroš-Deckert** Brigitte, Statuen des Mittleren Reichs und der 18. Dynastie: Corpus Antiquitatum Aegyptiacarum, Wien 1. Mainz 1987, von Zabern. 166 p.; 15 pl. DM 78. 3-8053-09074. – ᴿBO 46 (1989) 622-4 (Elisabeth *Delange*).

d415 *Karageorghis* Vassos, A new 'Geryon' terracotta statuette from Cyprus [Paphos-Peyia]: ⇥ 218, Mem. YADIN Y., ErIsr 20 (1989) 92*-97*; 5 fig.

d416 *Kelly-Buccellati* Marilyn, A new third millennium sculpture from Mozan [Khabur triangle]: ⇥ 106, ᶠKANTOR H., Essays 1989, 149-154 + pl. 26.

d417 *Kleeman* Ilse, Frühe Bewegung I. Mainz 1984, van Zabern. xv-213 p.; 48 fig.; 68 pl. 3-8053-0511-7. – ᴿAnzAltW 42 (1989) 93-95 (T. *Lorenz*).

d418 ᴱ**Kyrieleis** Helmut, Archaische [Bd.I] und klassische [Bd.II] griechische Plastik [Athen 22.-25. April 1985] 1986 ⇥ 3,794; 4,e288: ᴿAntClas 58 (1989) 522-6 (D. *Viviers*); DLZ 110 (1989) 752-4 (W. *Schindler*).

d419 **Leander-Touati** A.-M., The great Trajanic frieze 1987 ⇥ 4,e290: ᴿJRS 79 (1989) 213-7 (R. R. R. *Smith*: also on three other types of early-Empire art).

d420 *Mackenzie* Judith S., The development of Nabataean sculpture at Petra and Khirbet Tannur: PEQ 120 (1988) 81-96 + 15 fig.

d421 **Maderna** Caterina, Iuppiter, Diomedes und Merkur als Vorbilder für römische Bildnisstatuen; Untersuchungen zum römischen statuarischen Idealporträt: Archäologie und Geschichte 1. Heid 1988, 264 p.; 108 fig.; 32 pl. – ᴿAJA 93 (1989) 618s (C. C. *Vermeule*).

Maeir Aren M., A note on a little-known Egyptian statue from Jerusalem 1989 ⇥ d757.

d423 *a*) *Matthiae* Paolo, Old Syrian ancestors of some Neo-Assyrian figurative symbols of kingship; – *b*) *Waele* Éric de, L'investiture et le triomphe dans la thématique de la sculpture rupestre sassanide: ⇥ 28, ᶠBERGHE L. Vanden 1989, 367-387 + IV pl. / (II) 811-827 + IV pl.

d424 **Mattusch** Carol C., Greek bronze statuary from the beginnings through the fifth century B.C. Ithaca NY 1989, Cornell Univ. 246 p.; 123 fig. £41.25. 0-8014-2148-9 [Antiquity 63,319].

d425 *Moormann* E. M., La pittura parietale romana come fonte di conoscenza per la scultura antica: Dutch Mg Hist 2. Assen 1988, van Gorcum. x-288 p. – ᴿClasR 39 (1989) 419s (R. *Ling*).

d426 **Myśliwiec** Karol, Royal portraiture of the Dynasties XXI-XXX. Mainz 1988, von Zabern xx-138 p.; 104 pl. DM 198. 3-8053-0939-2 [BO 46,227].

d427 *Orphanides* A. G., A classification of the Bronze Age terracotta anthropomorphic figurines from Cyprus: RepCyp (1988,1) 187-199 [1989, 89-91, chemical].

d428 **Pekáry** Thomas, Das römische Kaiserbildnis in Staat, Kult und Gesellschaft, dargestellt anhand der Schriftquellen: Das Römische Herrscherbild 3/5. B 1985, Mann. x-165 p.; 3 fig. DM 133. – ᴿDLZ 110 (1989) 776s (W. *Schindler*).

d429 **Pfrommer** Michael, Studien zu alexandrinischer und grossgriechischer Toreutik frühhellenistischer Zeit [... silver plate]: DAI Arch. For. 16. B 1987, Mann. xvi-312 p.; 2 fig.; 62 pl. DM 120. – ᴿClasR 39 (1989) 114-6 (D. W. J. *Gill*).

d430 **Pollini** John, The portraiture of Gaius and Lucius Caesar 1987 ⇥ 3,d698*: ᴿClasR 39 (1989) 119s (R. *Hannah*); RelStR 15 (1989) 261 (N. H. *Ramage*).

d431 **Porada** Edith, Problems of Late Assyrian reliefs: ⇥ 106, ᶠKANTOR H., Essays 1989, 233-248; pl. 38-44.

d432 **Posener** Georges, Cinq figurines d'envoûtement 1987 → 3,d699: ᴿBO 46 (1989) 29-31 (A. *Roccati*); JAmEg 26 (1989) 246-8 (H. G. *Fischer*); JAOS 109 (1989) 293s (W. A. *Ward*).

d432* **Prittwitz und Gaffron** Hans-Hoyer von, Der Wandel der Aphrodite; archäologische Studien zu weiblichen halbbekleideten Statuetten des späten Hellenismus: Diss. Klass. Arch. 25. Bonn 1988, Habelt. 136 p. 20 pl. [Gnomon 62, 619-25, W. *Neumer-Pfau*].

d433 *Rantz* Berthe, À propos de l'Égyptien au gestes perses [standing statue with joined hands in front]; RBgPg 67 (1989) 102-121; iv pl.

d434 [Jones] *Roccos* Linda, Apollo Palatinus [wearing peplos]; the Augustan Apollo on the Sorrento base: AJA 93 (1989) 571-588.

d435 *Rössler-Köhler* Ursula, Die rundplastische Gruppe der Frau Pepi und des Mannes Ra-Schepses (Bemerkungen zur Ikonographie von Familiendarstellungen des Alten Reiche): MiDAI-K 45 (1989) 261-274; 4 fig.; pl. 32-35.

d436 *Rolley* Claude, Les bronzes grecs et romains, recherches récentes 8-9: RArchéol (1989) 343-356; 4 fig.

d437 **Russmann** Edna R., Egyptian sculpture, Cairo and Luxor. Austin 1989, Univ. Texas. xi-230 p. (phot. *Finn* David). 0-292-70402-X [OIAc N89].

d438 *Sambin* Chantal, Génie [statuette] minoen et génie égyptien, un emprunt raisonné: BCH 113 (1989) 77-96; 30 fig.

d439 *Schneider* Gerwulf, Bronze casting at Olympia in classical times: Masca 6 (Ph 1989) 17-24; 7 fig.

d440 **Schuchhardt** W.-H. [griechisch], *Heintze* Hilge von [römisch], *Hutter* I. [frühchristlich], Griechische und römische Antike; Architektur, Skulptur, Malerei. Z 1987, Belser. 448 p.; 443 (color.) pl. DM 98; sb. 79. – ᴿGymnasium 96 (1989) 73s (L. *Voit*).

d441 **Schulman** Alan R., Ceremonial execution and public rewards ... on stelae: OBO 75, 1988 → 4,e312: ᴿOrientalia 58 (1989) 290s (A. *Roccati*); RB 96 (1989) 440s (R. *Beaud*); ZAW 101 (1989) 167s (Brigitte *Michallik*).

d442 **Seidl** Ursula, Die babylonischen Kudurru-Reliefs; Symbole mesopotamischer Gottheiten: OBO 87. FrS/Gö 1989, Univ./VR. 235 p.; 33 pl.; foldout. 3-7278-0603-6 / VR 3-525-53717-4.

d443 **Singer** Itamar, A new stele of Hamiyatas, king of Masuwari [Neo-Hittite, doubtless from T. Aḥmar; in TA Museum display 1987]: TAJ 15s (1988s) 184-192; 2 fig.; pl. 17s.

d444 **Smith** R. R. R., Hellenistic royal portraits: Ox Mg ClasArch 1988 → 4,e315; £60: ᴿBonnJbb 189 (1989) 581-5 (N. *Himmelmann*).

d445 *Stucchi* Sandro, La statua marmorea di Mozia e il viaggio aereo di Dedalo: Rendiconti Pont. Accad. Arch. 59 (1987s) 3-61; 42 fig.

d446 *Tefnin* Roland, Un chef d'œuvre de la fin de la 18ᵉ dynastie au Musée de Beyrouth: → 204, Mém. WALLE B. van de, CdÉ 64 (1989) 134-147; 3 fig.

d447 **Tran tam Tinh** V., Sérapis debout: ÉPR 94, 1983 → 64,a929: ᴿOLZ 84 (1989) 405-7 (K. *Parlasca*).

d448 *Verlinden* Colette, Les statuettes anthropomorphes en bronze et en plomb 1984 → 65,a496; 3,d716: ᴿRArchéol (1989) 152-6 (O. *Pelon*).

d449 *Whitehouse* David, The seasons vase [unjustly denied Augustus-age antiquity]: JGlass 31 (1989) 16-24; 9 fig.

d450 *Zagdoun* Mary-Anne, Bulletin archéologique: la sculpture, reliefs hellénistiques: RÉG 101 (1988) 113-169.

d451 *Zettler* Richard L., The statue of Šulgi-ki-ur₅-sag₉-kalam-ma: ➤ 183, ᶠSJÖBERG Å. Dumu- 1989, 65-77; 10 fig. [49-64, *Civil* Miguel, the inscription].

T3.3 *Glyptica:* stamp and cylinder seals, scarabs, amulets.

d452 *Amiet* Pierre, Les modes d'utilisation des sceaux à Suse au IVᵉ millénaire: ArchMIran 21 (1988) 7-16; 3 fig.; pl. 1-10.

d453 **Avigad** N., Hebrew bullae 1986 ➤ 2,a264 ... 4,e129: ᴿBO 46 (1989) 457-460 (C. H. J. de *Geus*: fascinating).

d454 *Avigad* Nahman, ❶ Two seals of women and [14] other Hebrew seals [of unknown provenance]: ➤ 218, Mem. YADIN Y., ErIsr 20 (1989) 90-96; 18 fig.; Eng. 197*.

d455 **Ben-Tor** Daphna, The scarab, a reflection of ancient Egypt: Catalogue 303. J 1989, Israel Museum. 84 p. 965-278-083-9 [OIAc Ja90].

d456 *Bollweg* Jutta, Protoachämenidische Siegelbilder: ArchMIran 21 (1988) 53-61; pl. 30-34.

d457 **Bordreuil** P., Catalogue des sceaux... 1986 ➤ 3,d730; 4,e337: ᴿAbr-Nahrain 27 (1989) 174-6 (G. *Bunnens*); BASOR 275 (1989) 74-79 (B. *Halpern*); RB 96 (1989) 588-592 (E. *Puech*: some 50 proposals); RStFen 8 (1989) 147s (Maria Giulia *Amadasi Guzzo*).

d458 *Brentjes* Burchard, Stempel– und Rollsiegel aus Baktrien und Chorasan: BaghMit 20 (1989) 315; pl. 132-142.

d459 **Buchanan** Briggs, *Moorey* P. R. S., Catalogue of Ancient Near Eastern Seals in the Ashmolean Museum, I. The Iron Age stamp seals (c. 1200-350 B. C.) Ox 1988, Clarendon. xviii-99 p.; 19 pl. $124 [JNES 48,75 '3350'].

d460 **Collon** Dominique, First impressions 1987 ➤ 3,d739; 4,e344: ᴱAfO 35 (1988) 214-7 (Marie *Matoušová*); Orientalia 58 (1989) 130-4 (Stefania *Mazzoni*: unmatchable precision); PEQ 121 (1989) 79 (Vronwy *Hankey*); ZAss 89 (1989) 151-6 (F. *Blocher*).

d461 *a) Effenterre* Micheline & Henri van, Pour une statistique thématique des sceaux créto-mycéniens; – *b) Krzyszkowska* Olga, Early Cretan seals; new evidence for the use of bone, ivory and boar's tusk; – *c) Tamvaki* Angela, The human figure in the Aegean glyptic of the Late Bronze Age; some remarks: ➤ 858, Fragen 1985/9, 27-37 / 111-126; 2 fig. / 259-273; 15 fig.

d462 *Eshel* Hanan, A *lmlk* stamp from Beth-El: IsrEJ 39 (1989) 60-62; 1 fig.; pl. 6*d-f*.

d463 *Farber* Walter, Dämonen ohne Stammbaum; zu einigen mesopotamischen Amuletten aus dem Kunsthandel: ➤ 106, ᶠKANTOR H., Essays 1989, 93-108; fig. 17-18; pl. 12-15.

d464 **Garrison** Mark B., Seal workshops and artists in Persepolis; a study of seal impressions preserving the theme of heroic encounter on the Persepolis Fortification and Treasury tablets: diss. Michigan, ᴰ*Root* Margaret C. AA 1988. 3 vol. 89-07034. – DissA 50 (1989s) 180-A.

d465 *Garrison* Mark B., An Early Dynastic III seal in the Kelsey Museum of Archaeology; the relationship of style and iconography in Early Dynastic glyptic: JNES 48 (1989) 1-13.

d466 **Gasse** Annie, Catalogue des ostraca figurés de Deir el-Médineh, nos. 3100-3372, 5ᵉ fasc. 1986 ➤ 3,d744; 4,e352: ᴿBO 46 (1989) 616s (Emma *Brunner-Traut*).

d467 **Gignoux** Philippe, Catalogue des sceaux, camées et bulles sassanides II, 1978 ➤ 61,a92 ... 63,a563: ᴿArOr 57 (1989) 167-9 (M. *Shaki*).

d468 **Gignoux** Philippe, *Gyselen* Rika, Bulles et sceaux sassanides de diverses collections 1987 ➤ 3,d745: ᴿStIran 17 (1988) 266-271 (Rüdiger *Schmitt*).

d469 *Gignoux* Philippe, *Gyselen* Rika, *a*) Sceaux de femmes à l'époque sassanide: ➤ 28, ᶠBERGHE L. Vanden 1989, (II) 877-893 + III pl. – *b*) Sceaux sassanides de la Walters Art Gallery à Baltimore: StIran 17 (1988) 183-9; pl. II.

d470 **Giveon** Raphael, Egyptian scarabs from Western Asia 1985 ➤ 1,d140 ... 4,e354: ᴿJNES 48 (1989) 50s (C. C. *Van Siclen*).

d471 **Giveon** R., ᴱ*Warburton* D., *Uehlinger* C., Scarabs from recent excavations in Israel: OBO 83, 1988 ➤ 4,e356: ᴿRivB 37 (1989) 500 (Anna *Passoni Dell'Acqua*).

d472 *Gubel* E., A group of Egyptian scarabs from Tell Rechidiyeh: Stud-EgPun 3 (1987) 67-88 + 12 fig. (map).

d473 *Hübner* Ulrich, Fälschungen ammonitischer Siegel [< Heidelberger Alttestamentler(innen)-Sozietät 2. Dez. 1988]: UF 21 (1989) 217-226; 3 fig.

d474 **Keel** O., *Schroer* S., Studien zu den Stempelsiegeln aus Palästina 1: OBO 67, 1985 ➤ 1,d152 ... 4,e362: ᴿJAOS 109 (1989) 298-300 (E. *Porada*).

d475 **Keel** Othmar, *al.*, Studien zu den Stempelsiegeln aus Palästina/Israel II: OBO 88. FrS/Gö 1989, Univ./VR. x-349 p.; 136 fig. 3-7278-0629-X / VR 3-525-53718-2. – ᴿUF 21 (1989) 481 (M. *Dietrich*, O. *Loretz*); WeltOr 20s (1989s) 300s (Ingrid *Gamer-Wallert*).

d476 *Kitchen* K. A., An early West-Semitic epigraph on a scarab from Tell Abu Zureiq?: IsrEJ 39 (1989) 278-280; 1 fig.

d477 *Lapp* Nancy L., Cylinder seals and impressions of the third millennium B.C. from the Dead Sea plain: BASOR 273 (1989) 1-15; 8 fig.

d478 *Lise* Giorgio, Amuleti egizi / Egyptian amulets: Itinerari d'immagini 8. Mi 1988, BE-MA. 135 p. 88-7143-055-7 [OIAc Ja90].

d479 *a*) *Martin* Harriet P., A monster mirrored; – *b*) *Biggs* Robert D., A recut Old Babylonian seal with a Sumerian prayer of the Kassite period: ➤ 106, ᶠKANTOR H., Essays 1989, 175-180; fig. 24-25 / 55s + pl. 9.

d480 **Müller-Winkler** Claudia, Die [6000+] ägyptischen Objekt-Amulette ...: OBO arch 5, 1987 ➤ 3,d767: ᴿBO 46 (1989) 617-620 (G. *Hölbl*); RB 96 (1989) 433s (R. *Beaud*); RStFen 8 (1989) 145s (Gabriella *Scandone Matthiae*); ZAW 101 (1989) 163 (Brigitte *Michallik*); ZDPV 105 (1989) 173s (Ingrid *Gamer-Wallert*).

d481 ᴱ**Oikonomidès** Nicolas, Studies in Byzantine sigillography. Wsh 1987, Dumbarton Oaks. 119 p. $18. – ᴿRÉByz 47 (1989) 309s (J.-C. *Cheynet*).

d482 **Pini** Ingo, *al.*, Kleinere europäische Sammlungen: Corpus der minoischen und mykenischen Siegel 11. B 1988, Mann. xl-363 p.; 354 fig. – ᴿGnomon 61 (1989) 373s (J. *Boardman*).

d483 ᶠPORADA Edith, Insight through images, ᴱ**Kelly-Buccellati** Marilyn 1986 ➤ 2,87: ᴿZAss 79 (1989) 286-291 (S. *Dunham*).

d484 *Quack* Joachim F., Die Datierung der Siegelabdrücke von Tel 'En Beṣōr: ZDPV 105 (1989) 18-26; 3 fig.

d485 *Sax* M., *Middleton* A.P., The use of volcanic tuff as a raw material for Proto-Elamite cylinder seals: Iran 27 (1989) 121-3; map; 4 phot.

d486 **Schaeffer-Fohrer** C. F.-A., Corpus I des cylindres-sceaux de Ras Shamra-Ugarit et d'Enkomi-Alasia 1983 ➤ 64,a992 ... 1,d166: ᴿAfO 35 (1988) 211s (R. M. *Boehmer*).

d487 *Soldt* W. H. van, Labels from Ugarit [seal-stamp impressions on clay]: UF 21 (1989) 375-388.

d488 a) *Sourvinou-Inwood* Christiane, Boat, tree and shrine; the Mochlos ring and the Makrygialos seal; – b) *Olivier* Jean-Pierre, Le 'disque de Mokhlos'; une nouvelle inscription en linéaire A sur un poids de plomb, HM 83/MOZf 1: Kadmos 28 (1989) 97-100 / 137-145.

d489 a) *Stein* Diana L., Mythologische Inhalte der Nuzi-Glyptik; – b) *Börker-Klähn* Jutta, Die archäologische Problematik der Hurriter-Frage und eine mögliche Lösung: ➤ 817*, Hurriter 1988, 173-190. 201-9 + 42 fig. / 211-247 + 53 fig.

d490 **Tufnell** Olga, Studies on scarab seals II [I. was by W. **Ward** 1978 ➤ 60,s266] 1984 ➤ 65,a534 ... 4,e378: ᴿBO 46 (1989) 620-2 (A. R. *Schulman*).

d491 *Wiggermann* F. A. M., Tišpak, his seal, and the dragon mušḫuššu [= 'Slaying of the Labbu' in *Heidel* A., Babylonian Genesis² 1951]: ➤ 122, ᶠLOON M. van, To the Euphrates 1989, 117-133.

d492 *Younger* John G., Aegean seals of the Late Bronze Age; stylistic groups VII, Concordance: Kadmos 28 (1989) 101-136.

d493 a) *Zeitler* Richard I., Sealings and administration in the Early Dynastic I Inanna temple at Nippur; – b) *Leinwand* Nancy W., Assyrian colony seal impressions; iconography and style in context; c) *Weingarten* Judith, Some connections between iconography, glyptic 'families' and the Minoan administrative elite in neopalatial Crete; – d) *Stein* Diana L., Archaeological and sociological study of the 14th century B.C. seal impressions from Nuzi [all summaries]: ➤ 830, AIA 90th, AJA 93 (1989) 281s.

d494 *Ziomecki* Juliusz, ✪ Gliptyka: ➤ 891, EncKat 5 (1989) 1109.

T3.4 **Mosaica.**

d495 [*Alexander* M. A.] **Ben Khader** A. *al.* Corpus des mosaïques de Tunisie [1,1980 ➤ 3,d784] 2, Thuburbo majus 2, 1985 ➤ 2,a324: ᴿLatomus 48 (1989) 500s (L. *Foucher*).

d496 ᴱ**Bertoli** Bruno, I mosaici di San Marco, iconografia dell'Antico e del Nuovo Testamento. Mi 1986, Electa. 210 p.; 172 (color.) fig. – ᴿCC 140 (1989,3) 99s (C. *Capizzi*).

d497 **Campbell** Sheila, The mosaics of Antioch 1988: Corpus of Mosaic Pavements in Turkey, Subsidia Mediaevalia 15. Toronto 1988, Pontifical Institute of Mediaeval Studies. 126 p.; 28 fig.; 234 pl. $41 pa. 0-88844-364-1 [AJA 93,491].

d498 [ᴱ*Christophe* Jeannine], Bibliographie 1985-1987 et complément des années antérieures: BMosAnt (AIEMA) 12 (1988s) 1-245.

d498* *Darder* Marta, *Ripoli* Gisela, Mosaicos bizantinos de Jordania [*Piccirillo* M., esposizione R B P etc.]: Revista de arqueología 10,98 (1989) 7-9; ill.

d499 **Daszewski** Wiktor A., Corpus of mosaics from Egypt, I. Hellenistic and early Roman period: Aegyptiaca Treverensia 3, 1985 ➤ 3,d788; 4,a191: DM 198. 3-8053-0482-X: ᴿBMosAnt 12 (1988s) 269-272 (J.-P. *Darmon*); JEA 75 (1989) 286-8 (D. M. *Bailey*).

d500 *Fehr* Burkhard, Zwei Lesungen des Alexandermosaiks [< Casa del Fauno; Neapel, Museum, Nachahmung pharaonischer Kunst]: ➤ 49, ᶠDRERUP H., Bathron 1988, 121-134; 4 fig.

d501 *Koranda* Christian, Menora-Darstellungen auf spätantiken Mosaikpavimenten; Untersuchungen zur neugefundenen Synagoge in Plovdiv: Kairos 30s (1988s) 218-228; 13 fig. p. 230-9.

d502 **Lavagne** Henri, *a*) Le mosaïque: Que sais-je? 2361: 1987 ➤ 4,e393: ᴿBMosAnt 12 (1988) 12 (1988s) 279 (D. E. *Johnston*). – *b*) Il mosaico attraverso i secoli [ᵀrevue par l'auteur]. Ravenna 1988, Longo. 154 p.; 16 fig. + 10 color.

d503 *Leyge* François, Mosaïques byzantines de Jordanie: Archéologia 246 (1989) 28-37; ill.; map.

d504 **Michaelides** Demetrias, Cypriot mosaics: Picture Book 7, 1987 ➤ 3,d794; 4,e393: ᴿBMosAnt 12 (1988s) 276s (Suzanne *Gozlan*).

d505 **Mouriki** Doula, The mosaics of Nea Moni on Chios. Athenai 1985, Commercial Bank. 343 pl. vol. of 224 pl. + 119 color. – ᴿJbÖsByz 39 (1989) 376s (H. *Buschhausen*).

d507 **Ovadiah** Ruth & Asher, Hellenistic ... mosaic pavements in Israel 1987 ➤ 4,e396: ᴿAJA 93 (1989) 157s (D. *Parrish*); Byzantion 59 (1989) 545-8 (Janine *Balty*); Gnomon 61 (1989) 177-9 (W. *Raeck*); Gymnasium 96 (1989) 258s (M. *Donderer*).

d508 **Russell** James, The mosaic inscriptions of Anemurium 1987 ➤ 4,e399: ᴿBMosAnt 12 (1988s) 268 (P. *Bruneau*); JbÖsByz 39 (1939) 369s (H. *Taeuber*).

d509 *a*) *Trilling* James, The soul of the empire; style and meaning in the mosaic pavement of the Byzantine imperial palace in Constantinople; – *b*) *Harding* Catherine, The production of medieval mosaics; the Orvieto evidence: DumbO 43 (1989) 27-72; 78 fig. / 73-102; 13 fig.

d510 *Tsakirgis* Barbara, The decorated pavements of Morgantina I, the mosaics: AJA 93 (1989) 395-416; 29 fig.

d511 *Valenziano* Crispino, Iconologia dei mosaici 'bizantini' di Sicilia: Ho Theológos 4 (1986) 261-9.

ᴛ3.5 *Ceramica,* **pottery** [➤ *singuli situs*].

d512 **Adams** Barbara, Sculptured pottery from Koptos in the Petrie collection 1986 ➤ 3,d807: ᴿBO 46 (1989) 62s (M. *Stoof*).

d513 **Adams** William Y., Ceramic industries of medieval Nubia [A.D. 200-1600]: UNESCO survey 1. Lexington 1986, Univ. Kentucky. xi-401 p.; 242 fig.; vii-p. 405-662; 92 fig. $75. – ᴿJNES 48 (1989) 57-59 (Helen *Jacquet-Gordon*).

d514 *Adams* William, From pottery to history; the dating of archaeological deposits by ceramic statistics: ➤ 814, Meroitica 1984/9, 423-446 + 5 fig.

d515 *Alp* Sedat, Eine Sphinxvase aus Karahöyük bei Konya: ➤ 5, ᶠAKUR-GAL E. = Anadolu 21 (1987 for 1978ss) 9-16; 2 pl.

d516 **Amyx** D. A., Corinthian vase-painting of the archaic period. Berkeley 1988, Univ. California. I. Catalogue, xxv-354 p.; II. Commentary, xviii + p. 355-700; III. indexes 701-809, pl. 143.

d517 *Arafat* Karim, *Morgan* Catherine, Pots and potters in Athens and Corinth; a review: OxJArch 8 (1989) 311-346; 7 fig.
Athenian agora pottery: **Moore** M. 1986 ➤ e679; **Rotroff** S. 1982 ➤ e680.

d518 **Betancourt** Philip P., The history of Minoan pottery 1985 ➤ 1,d202 ... 4,e408: ᴿClasJ 83 (1987s) 326s (J. B. *Rutter*); Gnomon 61 (1989) 720-4 (W.-D. *Niemeier*).

d519 *Bisi* Anna Maria, Un aspetto dell'economia punica; manifattura e commercio delle anfore 'a siluro' [torpedo jar] e 'greco-italiche' fra Nordafrica e Sicilia: ➤ 877, Lavoro 1988, 363-402 + 5 pl. (+ p. 408s).

d520 **Böhr** Elke, Der Schaukelmaler: Kerameus 2/4, 1982 ➤ 64,b25 ... 4,e410: ᴿDLZ 110 (1989) 898-901 (E. *Paul*).

d521 **Bothmer** Dietrich von, Greek vase painting[2rev] ([1]1972). NY 1987, Metropolitan Museum of Art. 71 p.; 123 fig. + 7 color. – [R]AJA 93 (1989) 613s (J. H. *Oakley*).

d522 *Brownlee* Ann B., Attic black-figure from Corinth II: Hesperia 58 (1989) 361-395; pl. 57-70.

d523 **Burn** Lucilla, The Meidias painter 1987 → 4,e417 (rather 1987): [R]ClasR 39 (1989) 338-340 (Elizabeth *Moignard*); Gnomon 61 (1989) 609-613 (Kalinka *Huber*); RArchéol (1989) 183-5 (H. *Metzger*).

d524 **Coulson** William D. E., The Dark Age pottery of Messenia: SIMA pocket 43, 1986 → 2,a343: [R]BO 46 (1989) 479-481 (O. *Dickinson*).

d525 **Cuomo di Caprio** Ninina, La ceramica in archeologia 1985 → 3,d823*; 4,e422 ([2]1988; DM 100): [R]AcPraeh 21 (1989) 152s (W. *Köpke*); RArchéol (1989) 359s (M. *Picon*).

[E]**Déroche** V., *Spieser* J. M., Recherches sur la céramique byzantine 1987/9 → 840.

d526 [E]**Empereur** J. Y., *Garlan* Y., Recherches sur les amphores grecques [Univ. Rennes/Athènes, 10-12 sept. 1984]. P 1986, ÉcFrA/de Boccard. – [R]Gnomon 61 (1989) 71-73 (V. *Stürmer*).

d527 *Eriksson* Kathryn, Pilgrim flasks; how were they made?: RepCyp (1988,1) 177-180.

d528 *Ese* Douglas, Village potters in Early Bronze Palestine; a case study [Beth Yeraḥ 'crackled' ware]: → 106, [F]KANTOR H., Essays 1989, 77-92; fig. 12-16 (map).

d529 *Fleming* David, Eggshell ware pottery in Achaemenid Mesopotamia: Iraq 51 (1989) 165-185; 4 fig. (map).

d530 *Frendo* Anthony J., H. J. FRANKEN'a method of ceramic typology; an appreciation: PEQ 120 (1988) 108-129.

d531 **Haerinck** E., La céramique en Iran pendant la période parthe 1983 → 64,b37 ... 4,e428: [R]RArtLv 18 (1985) 178-180 (R. *Donceel*).

d532 *Hannestad* Lise, Athenian pottery in Etruria c. 550-470 B.C,: AcArchK 59 (1988) 113-130.

d533 *Heiner* Robert, Eine Merkmalanalyse von Siedlungskeramik mit Hilfe faktoren- und clusteranalytischer Verfahren: AcPraeh 21 (1989) 41-51; 7 fig.

d534 *Helms* Svend, An EB pottery repertoire at Amman, Jordan: BASOR 273 (1989) 17-36; 8 fig.

d535 **Hoffmann** Herbert, Sexual and asexual pursuit; a structuralist approach to Greek vase painting: Occ. Paper 34. L 1977, Anthrop. Inst. 17 p.; 12 pl. – [R]AntClas 58 (1989) 532s (D. *Martens*).

d536 *Immerwahr* Sara A., The pomegranate vase, its origins and continuity: Hesperia 58 (1989) 397-410; 4 fig.; pl. 71-72.

d537 **Jones** R. E., *al.,* Greek and Cypriot pottery; a review of scientific studies: Fitch Paper 1, 1987 → 3,d840; 4,e431*: [R]ClasR 39 (1989) 109s (A. *Johnston*); JHS 109 (1989) 263 (P. P. *Betancourt*).

d538 **Kadous** Ezzat Z. H., Die Terra Sigillata in Alexandria; Untersuchungen zur westlichen und östlichen TS des Hellenismus und der frühen Kaiserzeit: Diss. Trier 1988. vii-392 p.; 183 fig.; 164 pl.

d539 *Kafafi* Zeidan, Late neolithic I pottery from 'Ain er-Rāhūk [13 k NE Irbid], Jordan: ZDPV 105 (1989) 1-13 + 5 fig.; pl. 1.

d540 **Karstens** Karsten, Typologische Untersuchungen an Gefässen aus altakkadischen Gräbern des Königsfriedhofes in Ur; ein Beitrag zur modernen archäologischen Methodik: Mü-Univ., Vorderas. St. 3, 1987 → 3,d842; DM 79: [R]ZAss 89 (1989) 141s (Marsa *Laird*).

d541 **Klenk** Gabriele B., Geologisch-mineralogische Untersuchungen zu Technologie frühbronzezeitlicher Keramik von Lidar Hüyük (Südost-Anatolien): Mü Geowissenschaftliche Abh. B-3. Mü 1987, Pfeil. 3-923871-23-6 [OIAc S89].

d541* *London* Gloria, Past present; the village potters of Cyprus: BA 52 (1989) 219-228.

d542 *Magrill* Pamela, An Assyrian glazed pottery vase from Lachish: BAngIsr 9 (1989s) 41-45; 2 fig.

d543 *Manacorda* Daniele, Schiavo 'manager' [*Di Porto* A.] e anfore romane; a proposito dei rapporti tra archeologia e storia del diritto: Opus 4 (1985) 141-151.

d544 *Metzger* Henri, Bulletin archéologique; céramique [258 écrits]: RÉG 102 (1989) 58-123.

d545 **Molitor** Martha A., Pots and potters of prehistoric Malta: diss. UCLA 1988. x-286 p.; 24 fig.; 6 pl.

d546 *Myśliwiec* Karol, Dreihenklige Gefässe in Ägypten: MiDAI-K 45 (1989) 239-247; 2 fig. pl. 26-28.

d546* *Phillipson* David W., Traditional pottery manufacture in the southern Sudan: OriginiR 13 (1984-7) 425-450.

d547 *Quesada Sana* Fernando, *López Grande* M. José, Talleres y producciones cerámicas actuales en Egipto; un estudio etno-arqueológico en Heracleopolis Magna: BAsEspOr 24 (1988) 325-355; 11 fig.

d548 Readers' solutions to mysterious [perforated] pot from Tell Batash: BAR-W 15,3 (1989) 10.12.

d549 **Rice** Prudence M., Pottery analysis, a source book. Ch 1987, Univ. 560 p. $45. 0-226-7118-8. – ᴿAJA 93 (1989) 143s (D. P. S. *Peacock*); Antiquity 63 (1989) 393s (D. E. *Arnold*: maybe replaces SHEPARD).

d550 ᴱRice Prudence M., Pots and potters 1984 ➤ 65,a582; 4,e451: ᴿBO 46 (1989) 720-2 (A. van *As*).

d551 *Rova* Elena, Die sogenannte 'Smeared-Wash Ware', ein Beitrag zur syrischen Keramik des III. Jahrtausends v. Chr.: BaghMit 20 (1989) 139-196; 10 fig.; map.

d552 *Savage* Joanna, Corinthian and Corinthianizing pottery in the University of Queensland: ➤ 196, ꟳTRENDALL D., MeditArch 2 (1989) 147-201; 90 phot.

d553 ᴱ*Schneider* Gerwulf, Naturwissenschaftliche Kriterien und Verfahren zur Beschreibung der Keramik: AcPraeh 21 (1989) 7-32; Bibliog. 32-39.

d554 *Serbeti* Eleftheria D., The Oinokles painter [Attic red-figure 460 B.C.]: Boreas 12 (Münster 1989) 17-46; 5 fig.; pl. 18-23.

d555 **Spivey** Nigel J., The Micali painter and his followers 1987 ➤ 4,e453: ᴿJHS 109 (1989) 265s (Elizabeth *Moignard*).

d556 **Thompson** Homer A. & Dorothy B., Hellenistic pottery and terracottas. Princeton 1987, Amer. Sch. Clas. Athens. 459 p. $40. – ᴿAJA 93 (1989) 300s (Rebecca M. *Ammerman*).

d557 **Trendall** Arthur D., The red-figured vases of Paestum² 1987 ➤ 4,e455: ᴿJHS 109 (1989) 270s (B. A. *Sparkes*: adds much to his 1935 Paestum Pottery); MusHelv 46 (1989) 179 (Margot *Schmidt*).

d558 *Vanschoonwinkel* Jacques, Les vases mycéniens du musée de Louvain-la-Neuve: ➤ 197*, ꟳTRIZNA J., RArtLv 20 (1987) 1-12; 8 fig.

d559 ᴱVickers Michael, Pots and pans, colloquium on precious metals and ceramics [... imitating metal vessels ➤ d277] 1985/7 ➤ 4,780: ᴿDer Islam 65 (1988) 382s (M. *Barrucand*).

d560 *Villanueva-Puig* Marie-Christine, Le vase des Perses, Naples 3253 (inv. 81947): ➤ 782*, L'or perse = RÉAnc 91 (1989) 277-298; 8 fig.

d561 **Vossen** Rüdiger, *Ebert* Wilhelm, Marokkanische Töpferei; Topferorte und -zentren; eine Landesaufnahme (1980). Bonn 1986, Habelt. 546 p.; ill.; map. DM 88. – ᴿAcPraeh 21 (1989) 147-9 (Annegret *Nippa*).

d561* *Walberg* Gisela, Kamares imitations in Egypt and their social and economic implications: ➤ 838, Pottery K 1987/8, 633-9.

d562 *Weisshaar* Hans-Joachim, Frühhelladische Tierkopfgefässe: ➤ 134, Mem. MERHART G.v. 1986, 327-335; pl. 14-16.

d563 *Williams* Bruce B., An early pottery jar with incised decoration from Egypt: ➤ 106, ꟳKANTOR H., Essays 1989, 305-320; fig. 41; pl. 61 [we may be pardoned for noting here a possible contemporary parallel: R. *North*, Ghassul's new-found jar-incision: ADAJ 8s (1964) 68-78].

d564 **Williams** Dyfri, Greek vases, British Museum 1985 ➤ 3,d869: ᴿAnc-HRes 19 (1989) 40 (Tina *Ashburner*).

d565 *Zettler* Richard L., Pottery profiles reconstructed from jar sealings in the lower seal impression strata (SIS 8-4) at Ur; new evidence for dating: ➤ 106, ꟳKANTOR H., Essays 1989, 369-387; fig. 49-52; pl. 67-72.

T3.6 **Lampas.**

d566 *Barbera* Mariarosaria, Lucerne africane nel Museo Nazionale Romano; riflessioni su iconografia e ideologia: Opus 4 (1985) 153-167 + 10 fig.

d567 *Bernard* Bruno, À propos d'un sub-archétype de lampe romaine: ÉchMClas 33 (1989) 241-9; 5 fig.; 2 pl.

d568 *Bussière* Jean, Les lampes phénicopuniques d'Algérie: AntAfr 25 (1989) 41-68; 24 fig. (map).

d569 *Fossey* John M., *Zoïtopoúlou* Eléni P., Vers une typologie de lampes égyptiennes de l'époque hellénistique: ➤ 70, ꟳGORDON C. 1987, 117-124; 3 fig.

d570 **Hellmann** Marie-Christine, Lampes antiques de la Bibliothèque Nationale 2. Fonds général; lampes pre-romaines et romaines 1987 ➤ 3,d876; 4,e465: ᴿClasR 39 (1989) 116s (D. M. *Bailey*).

d571 **Loffreda** Stanislao, Lucerne bizantine in Terra Santa con iscrizioni in greco: SBF 35. J 1989, Franciscan. xii-245 p.; 30 pl.

d572 **Modrzewska** I., Studio iconologico delle lucerne siro-palestinesi del IV-VII sec. d.C.: RivArchSup 4. R 1988, Bretschneider. 65 p.; 43 pl. 88-7689-043-2 [JRS 79,275].

d573 *Silvano* Flora, Lucerne fittili figurate da Saqqara: EgVO 12 (1989) 79-87; 88-91 = 4 fig., 3 pl.

T3.7 **Cultica.**

d574 **Aguirre** Rafael, La Iglesia de Antioquia de Siria / **Ubieta** José A., ... de Tesalonica / **Goitia** J de, ... de Roma: Iglesias del NT. Bilbao 1988, Desclée de Brouwer. 66 p.; 61 p. 49 p. – ᴿScripTPamp 21 (1989) 947s (C. *Basevi*).

d575 *a)* *Beck* Pirhiya, ❻ On the identification of the figure on the cult-stand from the 'city of David'; – *b)* *Amiran* Ruth, ❻ A cult-object in the Kh.Kerak ware culture: ➤ 218, Mem. YADIN Y., ErIsr 20 (1989) 147s; 3 fig.; Eng. 199* / 72-74; 5 fig.; Eng. 196*.

d576 *Ben-Pechat* Malka, The paleochristian baptismal fonts in the Holy Land; formal and functional study: LA 39 (1989) 165-188; 3 foldouts; pl. 27-34.

d577 *Brandenburg* Hugo, Kirchenbau, frühchristlich: → 911, TRE 18 (1989) 421-442 (–528, *al.*).

d578 **Broek** R. van den, *al.*, Kerk en kerken in Romeins-Byzantijns Palestina; archeologie en geschiedenis: Palestina Antiqua 6. Kampen 1988, Kok. 232 p. *f* 36. 90-242-4889-2. – ᴿStreven 57 (1989s) 274 (P. *Beentjes*); TsTNijm 29 (1989) 292 (L. *Goesen*).

d579 *Chen* Doron, Antike Synagogen in Palästina; Anlage und Datierung der Synagoge von Horvat Rimmon, ᵀ*Locher* Clemens: Judaica 45 (1989) 57-67; 8 fig.

d580 **Cipriano** Palmira, Templum: BiblRicLingFg 13. R 1983, Univ. 155 p. – ᴿÉtClas 57 (1989) 368s (J. *Grot*).

d581 **Davies** J. G., Temples, churches and mosques [→ 65,a605]; a guide to the appreciation of religious architecture. Ox 1982, Blackwell. x-262 p. $17.50. – ᴿRelStT 7,2s (1987) 70s (P. J. *Cahill*).

d582 *Epstein* Claire, ⊕ Temple models and their symbolism: → 218, Mem. YADIN Y., ErIsr 20 (1989) 23-30; 18 fig.; Eng. 193*.

d583 **Ferguson** John, Among the gods; an archaeological exploration of ancient Greek religion. L 1989, Routledge. xviii-249 p.

d584 *Fiey* J. M., Sanctuaires et villages syriaques orientaux de la vallée de la Sapna (Kurdistan iraquien): Muséon 102 (1989) 43-67.

d585 *Fracchia* Helena M., *Gualtieri* Maurizio, The social context of cult practices in pre-Roman Lucania [Magna Graecia 420-280 B.C.]: AJA 93 (1989) 217-232; 14 fig.

d586 *Gitin* Seymour, Incense altars from Ekron, Israel and Judah; context and typology: → 218, YADIN Y. Mem., ErIsr 20 (1989) 52*-67*; 2 fig.

d586* *Hirschfeld* Yizhar, ⊕ Monasteries of the Judean Desert in the Byzantine Period: Qadmoniot 22 (1989) 58-87; ill. + color covers.

d587 **Hubmann** Axel F., Betyl, Versuch eines Überblickes der Geschichte, Bedeutung und Verbreitung an Hand von ausgewählten Beispielen; Diss. Wien 1978, ᴰ*Kenner* Hedwig. 245 p.; vol. of 21 p. + 200 fig.

d588 **Jakobs** Peter H. F., Die frühchristlichen Ambone Griechenlands: Diss. Klas. Arch. 24. Bonn 1987, Habelt. XI-350 p.; 134 fig.; 40 pl. DM 78. – ᴿJbAC 32 (1989) 227-230 (S. de *Blaauw*).

d589 ᴱ**Kasher** A., *al.*, ⊕ Synagogues in antiquity [meeting 1984: 11-29, *Levine* L. I., Form and content of Second-Temple synagogue; 31-51, *Safrai* S., Temple and Synagogue; 53-75, *Urman* D., Synagogue same as Beth ha-Midrash?; 77-95, *Safrai* S., Financing synagogue construction; 97-115, *Ben-Shalom* I., Torah study for all or for the élite alone?; 119-132, *Kasher* A., Synagogues in Ptolemaic and Roman Egypt as community centres; 133-146, *Roth-Gerson* L., differences of Palestine and Diaspora Greek synagogue inscriptions; 147-154, *Oppenheimer* A., Babylonia synagogues; also 155-162, *Gafni* I.; 165-172, *Netzer* E., Massada, Herodium ... architecture; 173-9, *Foerster* G., Basilica-apsis plan; 181-4, *Applebaum* S., Beth-Yeraḥ; 185-202, *Ovadiah* A., Mosaics; 205-212, *Reich* R., Ritual bath; 213-230, *Dar* S., Carmel-Sumaqa; 231-266, *Ilan* Z., Meroth; 267-285 bibliog. (*Mor* M., *Rappaport* U.)]. J 1987, Yad Ben Zvi. 285 p. – ᴿJStJud 20 (1989) 235-8 (M. *Mach*).

d590 **Martin** Hans G., Römische Tempelkultbilder 1987 → 3,d889; 4,e476; Lit. 250.000: ᴿAJA 93 (1989) 302s (C. *Vermeule*); BonnJbb 189 (1989) 613-5 (H. *Gabelmann*); RArchéol (1989) 422-4 (P. *Gros*).

d591 *Perrot* C., *al.,* Les premières synagogues: MondeB 57 (1989) 5-8. 32-40 (20-31 Dura, *Levine* L.; 15-17, *Corbo* V.; 9-14, *Foerster* G.).

d592 *Piguet-Panayotova* Dora, Recherches sur les tetraconques à déambulatoire et leur décor en Transcaucasie au VIIe siècle: OrChr 73 (1989) 166-194 + 30 fig.

d593 *Podossinov* Alexander, Himmelsrichtung (kultische) [... Gräber, Tempel]: ➤ 904, RAC 15,114 (1989) 233-286.

d594 *a) Seager* Andrew R., The recent historiography of ancient synagogue architecture; – *b) Safrai* Zeev, Dukhan, Aron and Teva; how was the ancient synagogue furnished?; – *c) Yeivin* Ze'ev, Khirbet Susiya – the *bema* and synagogue ornamentation: ➤ 845, Synagogues 1987/9, 85-92; pl. XLIV-XLVIII / 69-84, ^T*Glatzer* M. / 93-98; pl. IL-LVIII.

d595 **Stähli** H.-P., Antike Synagogenkunst. Stu 1988, Calwer. 112 p. DM 29,80. 3-7668-0823-0. – ^RBL (1989) 145 (N. de *Lange*); KIsr 4,1 (1989) 85 (Julie *Kirchberg*).

d596 *Teteriatnikov* Natalia, Upper-story chapels near the sanctuary in churches of the Christian East: DumbO 42 (1988) 65-72 + 20 fig.

d597 *a) Will* Ernest, Temples, tombes et palais de la Jordanie antique; – *b) Zayadine* Fawzi, Les sanctuaires nabatéens: ➤ 869, Jordanie 1987, 75-92; 12 fig. / 93-108; 12 fig.

T3.8 **Funeraria;** *Sindon, the Shroud.*

d598 *Akkermans* Peter M. M. G., Halaf mortuary practices; a survey: ➤ 122, ^FLOON M. van, To the Euphrates 1989, 75-88.

d599 *Altenmüller* Hartwig, Kälberhirte und Schafhirte; Bemerkungen zur Rückkehr des Grabherrn: StAltÄgK 16 (1989) 1-19; 3 fig.

d600 **Arce** J., Funus imperatorum; los funerales de los emperadores romanos: Forma 68. M 1988, Alianza. 199 p.; 69 fig. 84-206-7068-5 [JRS 78,272]. – ^RArchEspArq 62 (1989) 329s (D. *Plácido*).

d601 *Batlogg* Andreas, (K)eine Spur von Jesus? Der Disput um das Turiner Grabtuch geht weiter: GeistL 62 (1989) 381-5.

d602 *Bietak* Manfred, Servant burials in the Middle Bronze Age culture of the Eastern Nile Delta: ➤ 218, mem. YADIN Y., ErIsr 20 (1989) 30*-43*; 21 fig. [all female, all from Dabʻa].

d603 **Boschung** Dietrich, Antike Grabaltäre aus den Nekropolen Roms 1987 ➤ 4,e496: ^RArchaeologia 39 (1988) 251s (T. *Mikocki* **Φ**); JRS 79 (1989) 220-2 (Glenys *Davies,* also on 1987 KLEINER D., SINN F., SCHEFFER C.); RArchéol (1989) 416s (R. *Turcan*).

d604 **Bruns-Özgan** Christine, Lykische Grabreliefs des 5. und 4. Jahrhunderts v. Chr.: IstMitt Beih 33, 1987 ➤ 3,d903; 4,e497: ^RBonnJbb 189 (1989) 570-3 (B. *Jacobs*); RÉG 102 (1989) 221s (A. *Hermary*).

d605 **Chappaz** Jean-Luc, Les figurines funéraires égyptiennes...: Aeg-Helv 10, 1982 ➤ 65,a632 ... 4,e499: ^ROLZ 84 (1989) 21s (Magdalena *Stoof*).

d606 **Currer Briggs** Noel, The shroud and the grail; a modern quest for the true grail. L 1987, Weidenfeld & N. 241 p. £11. – ^RHolyL 9 (1989) 129 (D. *Prail*).

a608 **D'Auria** Sue, *al.,* Mummies and magic; the funerary arts of ancient Egypt. Boston 1988, Museum of Fine Arts. 272 p.; ill. [JNES 48,76].

d609 *Gove* H. E., Progress in radiocarbon dating the shroud of Turin: ➤ 868, Radiocarbon 31 (1988/9) 965-9.

d610 *Geus* Francis, Enquêtes sur les pratiques et coutumes funéraires mé-
roïtiques; la contribution des cimetières non royaux; approche préliminaire: → 39, Mém. CLÈRE J., RÉgp 40 (1989) 163-184; map. 185.

d611 *Görg* M., Begräbnis: → 902, NBL Lfg. 2 (1989) 262-4.

d612 *Guarducci* Margherita, La sindone e i Vangeli: Rendiconti Pont.
Accad. Arch. 60 (1987s) 91-101.

d613 *Imoto* Eiichi, ❶ Man in the animal skin [in modern Iran as in neolithic
Egypt a dying man is wrapped in a goatskin or sheepskin to get vitality by
killing the deity itself]: Orient-Japan 31,2 (1988) 1-17; Eng. 1.

d614 **Joussaume** Roger, Des dolmens pour les morts; les mégalithismes à
travers le monde [Eng. 1988 → 4,e513],ᵀ. P 1985, Hachette.   398 p.; ill.
F 159. 2-01-008877-8. – ᴿFornvännen 34 (1989) 66s (Lili *Kadas*).

d615 **Kamel** Ibrahim, Coptic funerary stelae: Musée copte catalogue 5,
Nᵒ 1-253. Cairo 1987, Organisation des Antiquités. 271 p. 977-01-1571-1
[OIAc Ja90].

d616 **Kleiner** Diana E. E., Roman imperial funerary altars with portraits 1987
→ 3,d921; 4,e514: ᴿAJA 93 (1989) 483s (Natalie B. *Kampen*); Athenaeum
67 (1989) 606-9 (C. *Saletti*); Gnomon 61 (1989) 160-4 (H. R. *Goette*);
RArchéol (1989) 188s (R. *Turcan*).

d617 *Koch* Guntram, Der Import kaiserzeitlicher Sarkophage in den römischen Provinzen Syria, Palaestina und Arabia: BonnJbb 189 (1989)
161-211; 59 fig. (3 maps).

d618 *Koch* K., *qæbær* 'Grab': → 913, TWAT 6,8s (1989) 1149-1156.

d619 ᴱ**Laffineur** Robert, Thanatos; les coutumes funéraires en Égée à l'Âge
du Bronze 1986/7 → 4,752: ᴿGnomon 61 (1989) 271-3 (J. *Bouzek*).

d620 *Leitz* Christian, Die obere und die untere Dat: ZägSpr 116 (1989) 41-57.

d621 *Lüscher* Barbara, Eine Gruppe von Kanopenkästen: MiDAI-K 45
(1989) 207-228; 30 fig. Pl. 24-25.

d622 *Lukaszewicz* Adam, An Osiris 'cool water' inscription from Alexandria
[both *psychrón* and *hýdōr* are bracketed, but supported by parallels in R.
Wild]: ZPapEp 77 (1989) 195s.

d623 *Lull* Vicente, *Picazo* Marina, Arqueología de la muerte y estructura
social: ArchEspArq 62 (1989) 5-20; Eng. 5.

d624 *Marchesi* Giovanni, Un dibattito scientifico sulla sindone dopo l'esame
al carbonio 14: CC 140 (1989,3) 51-60.

d624* **May** Fabienne, Les sépultures préhistoriques; étude critique. P 1986,
CNRS. 264 p.; 51 pl. – ᴿOriginiR 13 (1984-7) 452 (Margherita *Mussi*:
Europe et Proche-Orient).

d625 *Mostafa* Doha M., The role of the Djed-pillar in New Kingdom private
tombs: GöMiszÄg 109 (1989) 41-50 + 6 fig.

d626 *Mostafa* Maha F., Eine aussergewöhnliche Totengerichtsszene im Grabe
des Mehu (TT 257) in Theben: StAltÄgK 16 (1989) 235-243; pl. 3s.

d627 **Neeft** C. W., Protocorinthian subgeometric aryballoi [focusing 193 of
the 3000 globular-to-conical objects found mostly in tombs]: Allard
Pierson series 7. Amst 1987, Allard Pierson Museum.   441 p.; 193 fig.;
3 pl. *f* 298. – ᴿClasR 39 (1989) 112-4 (A. *Johnston*).

d628 **Nickell** J., Inquest on the Shroud of Turin²ʳᵉᵛ [ᴵc. 1983]. Buffalo 1987,
Prometheus. 186 p.; ill. $14 pa. 9-87975-396-X [NTAbs 33,252].

d629 **Niwiński** Andrzej, Studies on the illustrated Theban funerary papyri of
the 11th and 10th centuries B.C.: OBO 86. FrS/Gö 1989, Univ./VR.
xxxiv-402 p.; 90 fig.; 49 pl. 3-7278-0613-3 / VR 3-525-53716-6.

d630 *a) Piccirillo* Michele, Un'iscrizione imperiale e alcune stele funerarie
di Madaba e di Kerak; – *b) Testa* Emanuele, Legislazione funeraria

greco-romana e le memorie degli eroi e dei martiri: LA 39 (1989) 105-118; 16 fig.; pl. 1-8 / 77-104.

d631 *Quaegebeur* Jan, Une stèle [funéraire] ptolémaïque d'Akhmim [collection privée]: GöMiszÄg 112 (1989) 43-52; 2 fig.

d632 *a)* *Quaegebeur* Jan, Lettres de Thot et décrets pour Osiris; – *b)* *Hornung* Erik, Zum Schutzbild im Grabe Ramses' VI; – *c)* *Kákosy* L., Magical bricks from [Thebes] TT 32: ⇥ 78, ᶠHEERMA VAN VOSS M., Funerary 1988, 104-126; 3 fig. / 45-51; 2 fig. / 60-72; 6 fig.

d633 **Reiser-Haslauer** Elfriede, Die Kanopen I-II: Corpus Ant. Aeg. 2s. Mainz 1989, von Zabern. xix + 177 loose leaves; xix + 201. 3-8053-1000-5; 1-3 [OIAc Ja90].

d634 *Rousseau* Jean, The problem of the consecrated numbers [in funerary architecture]: ⇥ 823, Akten IV 2 (1985/9) 113-123; 4 fig.

d635 *Saxer* V., La Sindone di Torino e la storia: Riv. Storia della Chiesa in Italia 43 (1989) 50-79 [< RHE 85,253].

d636 *Scavone* Daniel C., The Shroud of Turin in Constantinople; the documentary evidence: ⇥ 175, ᶠSCHODER R., Daidalikon 1989, 311-329; pl. 26-28; p. 311 'the Vatican's inexplicable acquiescence should not close ... the issue'.

d637 **Schmaltz** Bernhard, Griechische Grabreliefs: ErtFor 192, 1983 ⇥ 1, d312: ᴿRelStR 15 (1989) 165 (A. W. *Bulloch*).

d638 **Stewart** H. M., Mummy-cases and inscribed funerary cones in the Petrie collection 1986 ⇥ 2,a442; 3,d934: ᴿOLZ 84 (1989) 531s (Renate *Krauspe*).

d639 **Taylor** John H., Egyptian coffins: Shire Egyptology 11. Aylesbury 1989, Shire. 0-85263-977-5 [OIAc S89].

d640 *a)* *Van Lepp* Jonathan, The role of dance in funerary ritual in the Old Kingdom; – *b)* *Vliet* Jacques van der, Raising the Djed; a rite de marge; – *c)* *Fabián* Zoltan I., Heart-chapters in the context of the Book of the Dead: ⇥ 823, Akten IV 3 (1985/9) 385-394; 6 fig. / 405-411 / 249-259.

d641 *Vattioni* Francesco, Il sangue in una maledizione funeraria [greca] dell'Asia Minore: ⇥ 759, Sangue VI, 1987/9, 105-136.

d642 *Walter* Peter, Shaft-chambered tombs of the fourth millennium B.C. in the Mediterranean: Berytus 36 (1988) 143-167; 5 fig.

d643 **Walters** Elizabeth J., Attic grave reliefs that represent women in the dress of Isis: Hesperia sup. 22. Princeton 1988, Am. Sch. Athens. xvi-135 p.; 2 fig.; 52 pl. $40. – ᴿCdÉ 64 (1989) 361-3 (G. *Nachtergael*).

d644 **Weber** T., (*Chahad* J. *al.*) Syrisch-römische Sarkophagbeschläge; orientalische Bronzewerkstätten in römischer Zeit. Mainz 1989, von Zabern. viii-88 p.; 62 pl. – ᴿLA 39 (1989) 280 (P. *Kaswalder*).

d645 **Willems** Harco, Chests of life; a study of the typology and conceptual development of Middle Kingdom standard class coffins: MedEOL 25, Leiden 1988, EOL. 250 p.; foldout. *f*70. 90-72690-01-X [BO 46,228].

d646 *a)* *Youngblood* Clark R., The embalming process in ancient Egypt. BibIll 14,2 (1988) 80-83 [< OTAbs 12,43]; – *b)* *Grunert* Stefan, *Volke* Klaus, Zur altägyptischen Mumifizierung. Altertum 34 (1988) 197-209; 11 fig.

T3.9 *Numismatica,* coins.

d647 *a)* *Acquaro* Enrico, Rassegna di numismatica punica, 1986-1988; – *b)* *Viola* Mauro R., Monete puniche; mercato antiquario 1986-8: StEgPun 5 (1989) 7-65 / 67-147.

d648 **Akat** Yücel, Treasure of Incilpinar Definesi. İstanbul 1986, Arkeol.-Sanat. unnumbered pages and pl.

d649 **Alram** Michael, Nomina propria in nummis; Materialgrundlagen zu den iranischen Personennamen auf antiken Münzen: Iranisches Personennamenbuch 4. W 1986, Österr. Akad. 372 p.; vol. of 47 pl. DM 300. 3-7001-0790-0. – ᴿBO 46 (1989) 679s (P. G. *Kreyenbroek*); Orientalia 58 (1989) 138-140 (Heidemarie *Koch*).

d650 **Amandry** Michel, Le monnayage des duovirs corinthiens: BCH Supp. 15, 1988 ⇒ 4,e537: ᴿAJA 93 (1989) 487s (W. E. *Metcalf*); NumC 149 (1989) 199-208 (C. J. *Howgego*); RÉG 102 (1989) 585s (Dominique *Gerin*); RNum 31 (1989) 265s (D. *Nony*).

d651 *Amandry* M., La genèse de la réforme monétaire augustéenne en Occident: Bull. Cercle Ét. Numism. 23,2 (1986) 21-34 [< AcNum 17s, 340].

d652 *Ashton* Richard, Pseudo-Rhodian drachmas from Eretria (Euboia): RNum 31 (1989) 41-48; pl. IV.

d653 *Aulock* Hans von, Münzen und Städte Phrygiens 1980/7 ⇒ 4,e542: ᴿBonnJbb 189 (1989) 657-661 (J. *Nollé*); Gnomon 61 (1989) 37-40 (H. D. *Schultz*).

d654 *Baldus* Hans R., Zur Münzprägung von Dora/Phönizien zu Ehren Kleopatras VII. und Mark Antons: Chiron 19 (1989) 477-480; 2 fig.

d655 *Bianchi* Francesco, Bolli e monete ellenistici in Giudea: OrAnt 28 (1989) 25-40.

d656 *Burnett* A., Coinage in the Roman world 1987 ⇒ 4,e548: ᴿNumC 149 (1989) 244s (M. *Crawford*).

d657 *Buttrey* T. V., Greek ... coins from Sardis 1981 ⇒ 62,b496 ... 2,a461: ᴿRArchéol (1989) 373s (M. *Debidour*).

d658 **Cahn** Herbert A., *al.*, Griechische Münzen aus Grossgriechenland und Sizilien; Antikenmuseum und Sammlung Ludwig. Basel 1988. 276 p.; 605 fig.; 48 pl.; 2 maps. – ᴿRNum 31 (1989) 259-261 (D. *Bérend*).

d659 **Carradice** Ian, **Price** Martin, Coinage in the Greek world 1988 ⇒ 4,e551: ᴿNumC 149 (1989) 228-232 (H. B. *Mattingly*).

d660 **Christiansen** Erik, The Roman coins of Alexandria 1988 ⇒ 4,e554: ᴿAJA 93 (1989) 466s (W. E. *Metcalf*); ClasR 39 (1989) 349s (A. M. *Burnett*); RNum 31 (1989) 269-271 (S. *Bakhoum*).

d661 **Cooper** Denis, The art and craft of coin making; a history of minting technology. L 1988, Spink. 264 p. – ᴿAcNum 17s (Barc 1987s) 335s (Anna M. *Balaguer*).

d662 **Doyen** Jean-Marc, Les monnaies antiques de Tell Abou Danné et d'Oumm el-Marra ... Séleucides 1987 ⇒ 4,e561: ᴿRNum 31 (1989) 262s (G. *Le Rider*).

d663 *a)* **Duncan Jones** Richard P., Mobility and immobility of coin in the Roman Empire; – *b)* **Lo Cascio** Elio, Ancora sullo *stipendium* legionario dall'età politiana a Domiziano: AnIstNum 36 (1989) 121-137 / 101-120.

d664 *Elayi* J., Le monnayage de Byblos avant Alexandre; problèmes et perspectives: TEuph 1 (1989) 9-20 [< ZAW 102,433].

d665 *Elayi* J., **Lemaire** A., Numismatique: TEuph 1 (1989) 155-184.

d666 **Giard** J. B., Catalogue des monnaies de l'Empire romain [I. Auguste 1976] II. De Tibère à Néron. P 1988, Bibliotèque Nat. 183 p.; 56 pl. – ᴿRÉLat 67 (1989) 391s (H. *Zehnacker*)

d667 *Glushchenko* V. P., ⊕ A new hoard of Roman denarii: VDI 189 (1989) 68-74; Eng. 74: Belgorod, 100 coins, oldest Vespasian 69-70 A.D., latest Geta 203-8.

d668 *Hackens* Tony, L'apport de la numismatique à l'histoire économique: ➤ 791, Histoire économique 1985/7, 151-169.

d669 **Harl** Kenneth W., Civic coins and civic politics in the Roman East AD 180-275: Transformation of Clas. Heritage 12. Berkeley 1987, Univ. California. viii-253 p.; 36 pl. 0-520-05552-7. – ᴿAJA 93 (1989) 303s (W. E. *Metcalf,* also on SUTHERLAND C.); AmHR 94 (1989) 1353s (H. C. *Broen*); JRS 79 (1989) 243s (C. J. *Howgego*); NumC 149 (1989) 238-241 (K. *Butcher*); Phoenix 43 (Toronto 1989) 276-9 (N. M. *Kennell*).

d670 **Hendin** David, Guide to biblical coins 1987 ➤ 3,d965: ᴿBA 52 (1989) 45s (J. W. *Betlyon*).

d671 **Houghton** Arthur, Coins of the Seleucid Empire 1983 ➤ 65,a698 ... 4,e566: ᴿBASOR 276 (1989) 92s (P. A. *Mirecki*).

d672 *a*) *Houghton* Arthur, The royal Seleucid mint of Soli; – *b*) *Ashton* Richard, A series of Rhodian didrachms from the mid-third century BC: – *c*) *Levy* Brooks, Nero's 'Apollonia' series; the Achaean context; NumC 149 (1989) 15-32; pl. 6-10 / 1-13; pl. 1-5 / 59-68; pl. 18s.

d673 **Howgego** C. J., Greek Imperial countermarks 1985 ➤ 2,a471 ... 4,e568: ᴿRNum 31 (1989) 267-9 (F. *Rebuffat*).

d674 *Jenkins* Gilbert K., Hellenistic gold coins of Ephesos: ➤ 5, ᶠAKURGAL E. = Anadolu 21 (1987 for 1978ss) 185-188; 2 pl.

d675 **Kaenel** Hans-M. v., Münzprägung und Münzbildnis von Claudius 1986 ➤ 3,d970 ... 4,e572 ('des C.'): ᴿLatomus 48 (1989) 907 (J.-M. *Doyen*).

d676 *Knoepfler* Denis, Tétradrachmes attiques et argent 'alexandrin' chez Diogène Laërce, II: MusHelv [I: 44 (1987) 233-253] 46 (1989) 191-230.

d677 *Koch* Bernhard, Pflege der Numismatik in Österreich: NumZ 100 (1989) 209-218.

d678 *Kreitzer* Larry, The personification of Judaea; illustrations of the Hadrian travel *sestertii*: ZNW 80 (1989) 278s; 4 fig.

d679 *Le Rider* Georges, *Olcay* Nekriman, Le trésor de Tell Halaf (IGCH 1763): RNum 31 (1989) 25-40; pl. II-III.

d680 **Manfredi** Lorenza-Illa, Le monete della Sardegna punica: Atlante Sardegna Fen-Pun. 1. Sassari 1987, Chiarella. 39 p. [OIAc N89].

d681 **Martin** Thomas R., Sovereignty and coinage in classical Greece 1985 ➤ 2,a479 ... 4,e588: ᴿRivFgIC 117 (1989) 192-201 (Serafina *Pennestrì*).

d682 **Mildenberg** Leo, The coinage of the Bar Kokhba war 1984 ➤ 1,d36 ... 4,e593: ᴿBonnJbb 189 (1989) 655s (V. *Zedelius*); NumC 149 (1989) 241s (K. *Butcher*); RÉJ 147 (1988) 228s (A. *Lemaire*); RNum 31 (1989) 271-3 (M. *Amandry*).

d683 *Mildenberg* Leo, ◉ Rebel coinage in Roman times: CHistEI 52 (1989) 90-99; Eng. 189.

d684 *a*) *Mildenberg* L., Punic coinage on the eve of the first war against Rome; a reconsideration; – *b*) *Acquaro* Enrico, Les émissions du 'soulèvement libyen'; types, ethnies et rôles politiques: ➤ 784, Punic wars 1988/9, 5-14; 3 pl. / 137-144; 2 fig.

d685 *a*) *Mersch-Michaux* Francoise Van der, Le monnayage archaïque d'Égine; technique de frappe et critères de classement; – *b*) *Callatay* François de, Statistique et numismatique; les limites d'un apport: ➤ 366*, ᶠTRIZNA J., RArtLv 20 (1987) 13-21; 4 fig. / 76-96.

d686 *Meshorer* Yaakov, ◉ The mints of Ashdod and Ascalon during the Late Persian period: ➤ 218, Mem. YADIN Y., ErIsr 20 (1989) 287-291; 16 fig.; Eng. 205*.

d687 *a*) *Mogelonsky* Macia K., The dates of the earliest coinage; a response to Donald *Kagan*; – *b*) *Attas* Michael, The fineness of Tarentine didrachms; – c) Garmaise Michael, The mint sites of Caracalla's Syrian tetradrachmas; some problems in attribution: → 70, ᶠGORDON C. 1987, 51-63 / 99-115; 11 fig. / 139-154; 6 fig.

d688 ᴱOddy W. A., Metallurgy in numismatics [I. 1980] II. L 1988, Royal Numismatic Soc. 132 p. 11 pl. – ᴿRNum 31 (1989) 276-9 (M. Bompaire).

d689 Oeconomides Mando, Drossoyianni Phane, A hoard of gold Byzantine coins from Samos: RNum 31 (1989) 145-182; pl. XI-XVI.

d690 Picard Olivier, Innovations monétaires dans la Grèce du IVᵉ siècle: CRAI (1989) 673-685; 11 fig. (685-7, Pouilloux J., Le Rider Georges).

d691 a) Price Martin J., Darius I and the daric; – b) Descat Raymond, Notes sur l'histoire du monnayage achéménide sous le règne de Darius Iᵉʳ; – c) Tuplin Christopher J., The coinage of Aryandes; – d) Caccamo Caltabiano M., Radici Colace P., Darico persiano e nomisma greco; differenze strutturali, ideologiche e funzionali; – e) Baslez Marie-Françoise, La circulation et le rôle des dariques en Grèce ... apport des inscriptions phéniciennes et grecques; – f) Manganaro Giacomo, Darici in Sicilia e le emisioni auree delle poleis siceliote e di Cartagine nel V-III sec. a.C: → L'or perse = RÉAnc 91 (1989) 9-13 / 15-31 / 61-82 / 213-235 / 237-245 / 299-315.

d692 Raynor Joyce, Meshorer Yaakov, The coins of ancient Meiron: Excavation 4. WL 1988, Eisenbruns. VI-140 p.

d693 Sari S., 'Amr A. J., ❶ Ayyubid and Saljuk silver darahem and fulus from the Rujm el-Kursi excavations: ADAJ 33 (1989) ❶ 13-24; 2 pl.

d694 Savio Adriano, La coerenza di Caligola nella gestione della moneta: Univ. Milano, Publ. Lett./fil. 126. F 1988, Nuova Italia. 89 p; 5 pl. – ᴿRitNum 91 (1989) 314-6 (A. Saccocci).

d695 Schmitt-Korte Karl, Cowell Michael, Nabataean coinage, I. The silver content measured by X-ray fluorescence analysis; NumC 149 (1989) 33-58.

d696 a) Sellwood David, New Parthian coin types; – b) Butcher Kevin, Two notes on Syrian [Petra!] silver of the third century AD: NumC 149 (1989) 162-8; pl. 42 / 169-172; pl. 43.

d697 a) Seyrig Henri, In Syrien kontermarkierte Münzen [< Syria 35 (1958) 187-197], ᴿSchnur-Wellpott Margrit; – b) Sutherland C. H. V., Zur Verständlichkeit römischer kaiserzeitlicher Münztypen [< JRS 49 (1959) 46-55], ᵀWigg David G.; – c) Aulock Hans von, Kleinasiatische Münzstätten; die vermeintliche Stadt 'Sebaste in Paphlagonien' [< JbNumG 18 (1968) 43-46]; – d) Hall E. T., Mattingly H. B., Methoden chemischer und metallurgischer Untersuchung antiker Münzen [< Methods 1970/2, 315-326], ᵀNicolas K.: → 530, Methoden, WegFo 529 (1989) 144-156 / 157-179 / 228-232 / 359-379.

d698 a) Spaer Arnold, More on the 'Ptolemaic' coins of Aradus; – b) Troxell Hyla A., Kagan Jonathan H., Cilicians and neighbors in miniature: → 112, Mem. KRAAY-MORKHOLM 1989, 267-273; pl. LVIII-LXII 275-281; pl. LXIII-LXIV.

d699 Sutherland C. H. V., Roman history and coinage, 44 BC-AD 69, 1987 → 3,d995; 4,e613: ᴿClasR 39 (1989) 312s (C. E. King).

d700 a) Wallace Robert W., On the production and exchange of early Anatolian electrum coinages; – b) Cahn Herbert A., Le monnayage des satrapes; iconographie et signification [Moysey R. A., ... satrapic revolt]; – c) Davesne Alain, La circulation monétaire en Cilicie à l'époque achéménide; – d) Kinns Philip, Ionia, the pattern of coinage during the last century of the Persian empire; – e) Callatay F. De, Les trésors achéménides et les monnayages d'Alexandre; espèces immobilisées et espèces circulantes?: → 782*, L'or perse = RÉAnc 91 (1989) 87-95 / 97-106 [107-139] / 157-168 / 183-193 / 259-276.

d701 *Weiser* Wolfram, Die Eulen von Kyros dem Jüngeren; zu den ersten Münzporträts lebender Menschen: ZPapEp 77 (1989) 267-286; pl. XVI-XIX.

d702 *Zodda* Daniela, Contributo alla storia della monetazione di Erice nel V sec. a.C.: RitNum 91 (1989) 3-26; 3 pl.

T4   *Situs,* **excavation-sites**   .1   *Chronica,* **bulletins.**

d703 *Briend* J., *Sapin* J., Archéologie [... Cisjordanie, sites fouillés en ordre alphabétique]: TEuph 1 (1989) 147-154.

d704 Chronique archéologique: RB [95 (1988) 215-279] 96 (1989) 210-265; map.

d705 Excavations: IsrEJ 39 (1989) 91-120 (each signed, infra); map.

d706 *Ilan* David, *al.,* Plundered! the rampant rape of Israel's archaeological sites: BAR-W 15,2 (1989) 38-42; (color.) ill.

d707 ᴱ*Piccirillo* Michele, Ricerca storico-archeologica in Giordania, IX-1989: LA 39 (1989) 243-272; pl. 73-90; p. 272-301, book reviews. We are now using the more usual (and brief) acronym LA for SBFLA.

d708 ᵀᴱ*Pommerantz* Inna, *Hurowitz* Ann, Excavations and surveys in Israel 7s (1988s) [< ᴱ*Sussman* Ayala, *Greenberg* R., Hadashot Arkheologiyot]. x-209 p.; 169 fig.; 2 maps. 0334-1607.

T4.2   *Situs effossi,*   **syntheses.**

d709 **Arav** Rami, Hellenistic Palestine; settlement patterns and city planning, 337-31 B.C.E.: BAR-Int 485. Ox 1989. 262 p.; 99 fig. 0-86054-622-5 [OIAc S 89].

d710 *Bienkowski* Piotr, Prosperity and decline in LBA Canaan; a reply to *Liebowitz* and *Knapp*: BASOR [265 (1987) 3-24; 266 (1987) 1-30] 275 (1989) 59-63 [63s, 64-7, rejoinders]. → d109.

d710* *Bietak* Manfred, The Middle Bronze Age of the Levant; a new approach to relative and absolute chronologies: → 831*, High/Low III (1989) 78-108 + 17 fig.

d711 *Bimson* John J., defense of his date 1420 for end of MB against *Halpern* B.: BAR-W [13,6 (1987)] 14,4 (1988) 52-55 [on p. 54 there M. *Bietak* says that his own proposed date near 1500 at Dabʿa does not support Bimson: both in OTAbs 12,247].

d712 **Bloom** Joanne B., Material remains of the Neo-Assyrian presence in Palestine and Transjordan: diss. Bryn Mawr, ᴰ*Ellis* R. Ph 1988. 417 p. 89-08574. − DissA 50 (1989s) 718-A.

d713 **Chatonnet-Briquel** Françoise, Les relations entre Israël et les cités de la côte phénicienne du début du Iᵉʳ millénaire jusqu'à 587 av. J.-C.: diss. Paris I, 1988. − RÉJ 148 (1989) 459-462.

d713* *Dothan* Trude, Observations on the chronology of Canaan in the 13th-12th centuries B.C.E.: → 831*, High/Low II (1987) 87s.

d714 *a) Dothan* Trude, The arrival of the sea-peoples; cultural diversity in early Iron Age Canaan; − *b) Dothan* Moshe, Archaeological evidence for movements of the early 'Sea-Peoples' in Canaan: → 543, AASOR 49 (1989) 1-14; 9 fig. / 59-70; 2 fig.

d715 **Finkelstein** Israel, The archaeology of the Israelite settlement 1988
→ 4,e629: ᴿAJA 93 (1989) 289-292 (C. *Edens*); JJS 40 (1989) 238-240
(P. R. S. *Moorey*); RB 96 (1989) 600s (J.-M. de *Tarragon*); VT 39 (1989)
127 (G. I. *Davies*: one of the most important books of the decade); ZDPV
105 (1989) 178-186 (H. N. *Rösel*).

d716 *Görg* M., Bronzezeit: → 902, NBL, Lfg 2 (1989) 328-331.

d717 **James** P. J., *al.*, Bronze to Iron Age chronology 1987 → 4,d839: ᴿPEQ
121 (1989) 79-81 (T. *Watkins*).

d718 *Knapp* A. Bernard, Complexity and collapse in the North Jordan valley;
archaeometry and society in the Middle-Late Bronze ages: IsrEJ 39
(1989) 129-148; 8 fig.

d719 *Leonard* Albertᴶ, Archaeological sources for the history of Palestine; the
Late Bronze Age: BA 52 (1989) 4-40; ill.

d720 *London* Gloria, A comparison of two contemporaneous lifestyles of the
late second millenium B.C. [Canaanite/Israelite]: BASOR 273 (1989) 37-55;
8 fig.

d721 **Petrie** W. M. Flinders, Hyksos and Israelite cities: BritSchEg 12. L
1989 = 1906, Histories and Mysteries of Man. 1-854-17044-9 [OIAc
S89].

d722 *Shay* T., Intermediate Bronze period; a reply to G. PALUMBO: BASOR
[267 (1987) 43-59] 273 (1989) 84-86.

d723 [*Thompson* J. A.] New light on the Midianites: BurHist 24 (1988) 5-14
(35s) [< OTAbs 12,145].

d723* a) *Tsafrir* Yoram, Christian archaeology in Israel in recent years; – b)
Figueras Pau, Découvertes récentes d'épigraphie chrétienne en Israël; – c)
Foerster Gideon, Decorated marble chancel-screens in sixth-century
synagogues of Palestine and their relation to Christian art and architecture: → 827*, 11ᵉ Arch. Chrét. 1986/9, 1737-1770 / 1771-1785 /
1809-1820.

d724 **Weippert** Helga, Palästina in vorhellenistischer Zeit; Beitrag *Mildenberg*
L.: HbArch, Vorderasien 2/1, 1988 → 4,e639: ᴿDLZ 110 (1988) 892-5 (B.
Brentjes); Protestantesimo 44 (1989) 288s (J. A. *Soggin*: infinità di
illustrazioni); TR 85 (1989) 195s (E. *Zenger*); ZAW 101 (1989) 329s (O.
Kaiser).

т4.3 **Jerusalem,** *archaeologia et historia.*

d725 a) *Abecassis* Armand, Jérusalem dans la tradition mystique; – b)
Bogaert M., J. dans les apocalypses contemporaines de Baruch, d'Esdras
et de Jean; – c) *Chopineau* J., J., ville forte ou symbole? – d) *Dequeker*
L., L'iconographie du Temple de J. dans les synagogues de l'antiquité en
Palestine et en Syrie; – e) *Falk* Ze'ev, J. in Jewish law and religion; – f)
Goetschel R., J. ... Moyen-Âge; – g) *Guigui* Albert, J. dans le Talmud et le
Midrash; – h) *Safrai* S., Pèlerinages à J.; – j) *Schoors* A., Sion-J. en Is
40-55: → 4,e641, Jérusalem 1982/-, 7-13 / 15-23 / 25-32 / 33-55 / 57-61 /
63-80 / 81-96 / 97-108 / 109-127.

d726 **Atil** Esin, Süleymanname; the illustrated history of Süleyman the
Magnificent [... responsible for Old Jerusalem's present wall]: Wsh
National Gallery. NY 1986, Abrams. – ᴿDer Islam 66 (1989) 188-191
(K. *Schwarz*).

d727 **Bagatti** B., *Testa* E., Gerusalemme, la redenzione ...: Corpus Scriptorum
de Ecclesia Matre 4, 1982 → 63,a854; 65,a755: ᴿHenoch 11 (1989) 373s
(B. *Chiesa*: difficile giudicare senza gli altri volumi promessi).

d728 a) *Bagatti* B., Literary evidence for Mary's tomb in Jerusalem, not Ephesus [< New Discoveries at the tomb ... in Gethsemane]; – b) *Bagatti*, The tomb of the Virgin and the silence of the early centuries, ᵀ*Sullivan* J.; – c) *Cignelli* Lino, Our Lady's tomb in the Apocrypha, ᵀ*Sullivan* J.: HolyL 8 (1988) 73-79 / 80-87 / 87-91.

d729 *Bahat* Dan, ❸ The fuller's field and the 'conduit of the upper pool' [Is 7,3]: ➤ 218, Mem. YADIN Y., ErIsr 20 (1989) 253-5; 1 fig.; Eng. 203*.

d730 **Ben-Dov** Meir, In the shadow of the Temple; the discovery of ancient Jerusalem, ᵀ*Friedman* Ina, 1985 ➤ 2,a537 ... 4,e644: ᴿCBQ 51 (1989) 108s (H. D. *Lance*: fascinating information; too many typos).

d731 *Bieberstein* Klaus, Die Porta Neapolitana, die Nea Maria und die Nea Sophia in der Neapolis von Jerusalem: ZDPV 105 (1989) 110-122; 2 fig.

d732 *Bonanno* Raphael fr., al. The Holy Grail: HolyL 9 (1989) 117s (–128). 144-151.

d733 *Busse* Heribert, *Kretschmar* Georg, Jerusalemer Heiligtumstraditionen 1987 ➤ 3,a26; 4,e650: ᴿJbAC 32 (1989) 214-9 (U. & M. *Wagner*).

d734 *Camelot* P.-T., Hélène (mère de Constantin): ➤ 885, DHGE 23,135 (1989) 867-9.

d735 *Daoust* J., Au sommet du Mont des Oliviers [< MondeB 55 (1988)]: EsprVie 99 (1989) 55-57 [381s < *Puech* E.].

d736 *Decoster* Koen, Flavius JOSEPHUS and the Seleucid Acra in Jerusalem: ZDPV 105 (1989) 70-84.

d736* *Deichmann* F. W., Waren Eustathios und Zenobios die Architekten der Grabeskirche?: ByZ 82 (1989) 221-4.

d737 *Eibschitz* E., ❸ Pillar-halls and other buildings on the Temple mount in Herod's Temple [reflections on JOSEPHUS and Talmud]: Sinai 103,1 (1988) 1-20 [< JStJud 20,293].

d738 *Eisenberg* E., Naḥal Refa'im 3d, 1987: ExcSIsr 7 (1988s) 84-89, fig. 71-75 [p. 90-92, al., Mt. Scopus, Ramot].

d739 **Fleckenstein** Karl-Heinz, *Müller* Wolfgang, a) Jerusalem, die heilige Stadt der Juden, Christen und Muslime. FrB 1988, Herder. 224 p.; 31 fig. + 125 color.; maps. DM 50. – ᴿZkT 111 (1989) 117 (H. B. *Meyer*). – b) Jérusalem, ville sainte des trois monothéismesᵀ. P 1989, D-Brouwer. 234 p.; ill. [NRT 112, 474, A. *Wankenne*].

d740 *Follis* Elaine R., The Holy City as daughter ➤ 2987, Directions 1987, 173-184.

d741 **Gilbert** Martin, Jerusalem, rebirth of a city [since 1838] 1985 ➤ 1,d441 ... 3,e44: ᴿJJS 40 (1989) 275 (Sarah *Kochav*).

d742 *Griffith* Sidney H., Anthony David of Baghdad, scribe and monk of Mar Sabas; Arabic in the monasteries of Palestine; ChH 58 (1989) 7-19.

d743 *Harper* Richard P., *Pringle* Denys, Belmont Castle 1987, second preliminary report of excavations: Levant 21 (1989) 47-61; 14 fig.

d744 *Heid* Stefan, Der Ursprung der Helenalegende im Pilgerbetrieb Jerusalems: JbAC 32 (1989) 41-71.

d745 *Jacoby* Ruth, The ornamented stone near the [Jerusalem temple-area] fountain of Qaytbay; a sarcophagus or a frieze?: IsrEJ 39 (1989) 284-6; 2 fig.; pl. 35.

d746 **Jeremias** J., Gerusalemme al tempo di Gesù; ricerche di storia economica e sociale per il periodo neotestamentario [1923-7; 1967 franç.]. R 1989, Dehoniane. 648 p. Lit. 45.000. – ᴿStPatav 36 (1989) 622s (G. *Segalla*).

d747 **Jeremias** Joachim, Jerusalén en tiempos de Jesús; estudio económico y social del mundo del Nuevo Testamento [1969²], ᵀ*Luis Ballines* J. BiblBíblica. M 1985 = 1977, Cristiandad. 409 p. 84-7057-211-3.

d748 *Kalogeropoulou-Metallenou* Barbara, ❹ A report on the patriarchate of Jerusalem (1853): TAth 60 (1989) 801-825; Eng. 885.

d749 *Karavidopoulos* John, Jerusalem in the Orthodox theological tradition, ᵀ*Papademetriou* George C.: GrOrTR 33 (1988) 189-200.

d750 *Köhler* O., Deutscher Verband vom Heiligen Land: → 885, DHGE 23,135 (1989) 797-9.

d751 ᴱ**Küchler** Max..., Jerusalem; Texte-Bilder-Steine: NTOrb 6, 1987 → 3, a48; 4,e667: ᴿRÉJ 148 (1989) 406s (E.-M. *Laperrousaz*); RTPhil 121 (1989) 338 (T. *Römer*); ScripTPamp 21 (1989) 691s (K. *Limburg*); TLZ 114 (1989) 26s (C. *Dohmen*); ZDPV 105 (1989) 195-7 (U. *Hübner*).

d752 *Laperrousaz* E.-M., Jérusalem à l'époque perse; étendue et statut: TEuph 1 (1989) 55-65 [< ZAW 102,434].

d753 *Lea* Thomas, Jerusalem; BibIll 14,2 (1988) 42-49 [*al.*, Bethel, Shechem, etc.: < OTAbs 12,39].

d754 *Limor* Ora, The origins of a tradition; King David's tomb on Mount Zion: Traditio 44 (1988) 453-462.

d755 *Livne-Kafri* Ofer, ❺ On Jerusalem in early Islam: CHistEI 51 (1989) 35-66; Eng. 195.

d756 **Luṭfi** Huda, *Al-Quds* ... A history of Mamlûk Jerusalem based on the Ḥaram documents [found 1974-6]: Islamk. Unt. 113, 1985 → 3,e56; ᴿBSO 51 (1988) 122s (D. S. *Richards*); Der Islam 66 (1989) 365-7 (Monika *Gronke*); OLZ 84 (1989) 51s (W. *Madelung*).

d757 *Maeir* Aren M., A note on a little-Known Egyptian statue from Jerusalem [found and stored at Gallicante; whereabouts now unknown]: GöMiszÄg 110 (1989) 35-40.

d758 **Mare** W. Harold, The archaeology of the Jerusalem area 1987 → 3,e59; 4,e671: ᴿBA 52 (1989) 147s (Jane M. *Cahill*).

d759 *Margalit* Shlomo, Aelia Capitolina, ᵀ*Klostermann* G., *Luz* U.: Judaica 45 (1989) 45-56; 1 fig.

d760 **Mazar** Eilat & Benjamin, *al.* Excavations in the south of the Temple mount; the Ophel of biblical Jerusalem: Qedem 29. J 1989, Univ. xviii-187 p.; foldout plan. 0333-5844 [OIAc Ja90].

d761 a) *Mazar* Eilat, Royal gateway to [southeast] ancient Jerusalem uncovered, ᵀ*Schwarzman* Steven; – b) *Gonen* Rivka, Visualizing First Temple Jerusalem: BAR-W 15,3 (1989) 38-51 / 52-55; ill.

d762 *Norwich* John J., Three faces of Jerusalem: ILN 277 (Christmas 1989) 26-34; color. phot.

d763 *Ockinga* Boyo G., The inviolability of Zion – a pre-Israelite tradition?: BibNot 44 (1988) 54-60.

d764 **Onne** Eyal, *Wahrman* Dror, Jerusalem, profile of a changing city. J 1985, Mishkenot ša'Ananim. 72 p. 965-222-068-X. – ᴿHolyL 8 (1988) 155s (R. D. *Bonanno*).

d765 *Otto* Eckart, a) Jerusalem: → 894, EvKL 2 (1988) 809-813; – b) Ṣijjôn, 'Zion': → 913, TWAT 6,6s (1989) 994-1028.

d766 **Pellistrandi** Christine, Jérusalem, épouse et mère; préf. *Briend* Jacques: Lire la Bible 87. P 1989, Cerf. 223 p. 2-204-03163-1.

d767 *Pixner* Bargil, *Chen* Doron, *Margalit* Shlomo, Mount Zion; The 'Gate of the Essenes' re-excavated: ZDPV 105 (1989) 85-89 + 6 fig.; pl. 10-15; p. 96-104, *Pixner*, history of the area; 105-9, *Riesner* R., in JOSEPHUS.

d768 **Prag** Kay, Jerusalem: Blue Guide. L/NY 1989, Black / Norton. 331 p. (12 of maps by J. Flower). £12 / $20. 0-7136-2944-4 / 0-393-30480-9. – ᴿBL (1989) 39s (A. G. *Auld*).

d769 ᴱ**Prawer** Joshua, ❻ *Sefer Yerušalayim*... The history of Jerusalem, the early Islamic period (638-1099). J 1987, Ben-Zvi. 965-217-038-0 [OIAc S89].

d770 *Provera* Mario, La città di Davide: ParVi 33 (1988) 311-6; 2 fig.

d771 **Purvis** James D., Jerusalem, the Holy City; a bibliography [5827 items]: ATLA 20, 1988 ➜ 4,e680: ᴿJStJud 20 (1989) 107s (U. *Rappaport*: additions, especially writings in Hebrew or on numismatics); RelStR 15 (1989) 154 (W. T. *Pitard*).

d772 *Raedts* Peter, Jerusalem als Bild des Heiligen: Bijdragen 50 (1989) 122-138; Eng. 138.

d773 *Reich* Ronny *al.,* Jérusalem au temps de Jésus: MondeB 60 (1989) 20-33 (3-44).

d774 *Reich* Ronny, Two possible *miqwā'ot* [out of 37 subterranean cavities, others being cisterns, staircase-passages, or tombs] on the Temple mount: IsrEJ 39 (1989) 63-65; 1 fig.

d775 *Riesner* Rainer, Eine vorexilische Mauer auf dem Zionsberg: BiKi 44 (1989) 34-36.

d776 **Ritmeyer** Kathleen & Leen, Stone by stone, reconstructing Herod's Temple mount in Jerusalem: BAR-W 15,6 (1989) 23-53; color. ill.; plans.

d777 *Rosen-Ayalon* Miriam, The early Islamic monuments of al-Haram al-Sharif; an iconographic study: Qedem 28. J 1989, Hebrew Univ. 73 p.; 50 fig.; 15 colour. pl. $25. 0333-5844. – ᴿBAngIsr 9 (1989s) 56-58 (Géza *Fehérvári*).

d778 *Rosen-Ayalon* Myriam, ❻ An Ayyubid inscription in the Dome of the Rock: ➜ 218, Mem. YADIN Y., ErIsr 20 (1989) 360-370; 19 fig.; Eng. 208*.

d779 *Schleicher* W., Auf den Spuren König Davids; in memoriam Prof. Yigal SHILO: JbEvHL 1 (1989) 23-29 [< ZAW 102,278].

d779* *Schunck* Klaus-D., *a)* Juda und Jerusalem in vor- und früh-israelitischer Zeit [< ᶠ*Jepsen* A., Schalom 1971, 50-57]; – *b)* Zentralheiligtum, Grenzheiligtum und 'Höhenheiligtum' in Israel [< Numen 18 (1971) 132-140]: ➜ 349, AT 1989, 97-104 / 105-113.

d780 *Segal* Peretz, The penalty of the warning inscription from the Temple of Jerusalem: IsrEJ 39 (1989) 79-84.

d781 *Shiloh* Yigael, Judah and Jerusalem in the eighth-sixth centuries B.C.E.: ➜ 543, AASOR 49 (1989) 97-105; 5 fig.

d782 *a)* *Stachowiak* Lech, ❻ Gehenna; – *b)* *Rubinkiewicz* Ryszard, ❻ Gichon; Góra Oliwna; – *c)* *Tronina* Antoni, ❻ Golgota: ➜ 891, EncKat 5 (1989) 928s / 1054. 1372 / 1260s.

d783 *Steck* Odil H., Zion als Gelände und Gestalt; Überlegungen zur Wahrnehmung Jerusalems als Stadt und Frau im AT: ZTK 86 (1989) 261-281.

d784 *Stoebe* Hans J., Die Einnahme Jerusalems und der Ṣinnôr / Überlegungen zur Siloahinschrift [< ZDPV 73 (1957) 73-99; 71 (1955) 124-140]: ➜ 362, Geschichte 1989, 241-267 / 224-240.

d785 *Stone* G. R., The search for the authentic tomb of Jesus: BurHist 24,4 (Melbourne 1988) 84-97 [< NTAbs 33,297].

d786 *Strobel* A., Zur Geschichte des Lutherischen Hospizes in Jerusalem: JbEvHL 1 (1989) 79-99 [< ZAW 102,278].

d786* *Stuhlmacher* Peter, Die Stellung Jesu und des Paulus zu Jerusalem; Versuch einer Erinnerung: ZTK 86 (1989) 140-156.

d787 ᴱ**Tushingham** A. D., Excavations in Jerusalem 1961-1967, I, 1985 ➤ 1,d470 ... 4,e388: ᴿAJA 93 (1989) 610-2 (W. G. *Dever* defends KENYON); BO 46 (1989) 706-9 (H. J. *Franken*).

d788 *Tushingham* A. D., The 1961-67 excavations in the Armenian Garden, Jerusalem; a response [disagrees with M. *Gibson*'s re-interpretation in nearly every respect]: PEQ [119 (1987) 81-96] 120 (1988) 142-5.

d789 *Vilar Hueso* Vicente, El primer muro de Jerusalén antes del destierro: ➤ 61, ᶠFLETCHER D. (III), Archivo de Prehistoria Levantina 19 (1989) 429-435.

d790 **Wightman** G. J., The Damascus Gate, Jerusalem [BENNETT-HENNESSY excavations 1964-6]: BAR-Int 519. Ox 1989. 116 p.; 24 fig.; 239 pl. £28. – ᴿBAngIsr 9 (1989s) 61s (D. *Bahat*).

---

d791 *a) 'En Ya'el* (W Jerusalem) 3d, 1987, Roman villa: IsrEJ 39 (1989) 113-6; 2 fig. (mosaic floor: Y. *Rapuano*). – *b*) Yalu/Yael ('en, 1169.1278): RB 96 (1989) 248-251; fig. 16s; pl. XIII (mosaïque; G. *Edelstein*, Y. *Rapuano*).

d792 *Gibeon*: ➤ 891, EncKat 5 (1989) 1052s (A. *Tronina* ❷).

d793 *Manaḥat* 1670.1288, 5 k SW Jerusalem, 1st-2d, 1987-8, MB: ExcSIsr 7s (1988s) 117-123, fig. 98-104 (G. *Edelstein, al.*).

d794 Māliḥa (Manaḥat) 1987s: RB 96 (1989) 217-220; fig. 3s; pl. VII (G. *Edelstein*).

T4.4   *Situs alphabetice:* **Judaea, Negeb.**

d794* *Applebaum* Shimon, *a*) The Roman villa in Judaea, a problem; – *b*) Romanization and indigenism in Judaea; – *c*) The beginning of the Limes Palaestinae: ➤ 227, Judaea 1989, 124-131 / 155-165 / 132-142.

d795 *Aschdod / Aschkelon*: ➤ 902, NBL Lfg. 2 (1989) 182s / 186s (M. *Görg*).

d796 *Bataš* (Timna) 1987s: IsrEJ 39 (1989) 108-110; 1 fig. (G. *Kelm*, A. *Mazar*).

d797 *Kelm* George L., *Mazar* Amihai, Excavating in Samson country; Philistines and Israelites at Tel Batash: BAR-W 15,1 (1989) 36-49; (color.) ill.

d798 *Mazar* Amihai, ❶ Features of settlement in the northern Shephelah during MB and LB in the light of the excavations at Tel Batash and Gezer: ➤ 218, Mem. YADIN Y., ErIsr 20 (1989) 58-67; 13 fig.; Eng. 195*.

d799 *Beerscheba*: ➤ 902, NBL, Lfg. 2 (1989) 256s (M. *Görg*).

d800 **Herzog** Ze'ev, *al.*, Beer-Sheba II, Early Iron 1984 ➤ 65,a812 ... 4,e703: ᴿAfO 35 (1988) 235s (K. *Jaroš*).

d801 *Beit-Leyy*: *Mittmann* S., A confessional inscription from the year 701 praising the reign of Yahweh [Beit Leyy catacomb]: Acta Academica 21 (1989) 15-37 [< ZAW 102,422].

d802 *Betlehem / Bet-Schemesch*: ➤ 902, NBL Lfg 2 (1989) 283s/287s (M. *Görg*).

d803 *Milson* David, Byzantine architects at work at Herodium, Palaestina Prima: LA 39 (1989) 207-211; pl. 43-44.

d804 **Corbo** Virgilio C., Herodion I; gli edifici della Reggia-Fortezza: SBF 20. J 1989, Franciscan. 86 p.; 134 fig.; X color. pl.

d805 *Provera* Mario, La fortezza dell'Herodium: ParVi 33 (1988) 62-65; 2 fig.

d806 *Deir/Balaḥ:* *Schmitt* Götz, Gabbutunu [= Deir el-Balaḥ; Khorsabad reliefs]: ZDPV 105 (1989) 56-69; 10 pl.

d807 *Elusa:* a) *Negev* Avraham, The cathedral of Elusa and the new typology and chronology of the Byzantine churches in the Negev; – b) *Margalit* Shlomo, On the transformation of the mono-apsidal churches with two lateral pastophoria into tri-apsidal churches: LA 39 (1989) 143-164; pl. 21-26.

d808 *'En Beṣor:* a) *Gophna* Ran, ❻ The settlements in the 'En Besor oasis during Early Bronze I; – b) *Ben-Tor* Amnon, ❻ New light on the relations between Egypt and southern Palestine during the Early Bronze Age: ⇒ 218, Mem. YADIN Y., ErIsr 20 (1989) 37-43; 8 fig, Eng. 194* / 31-36.

d809 *Gaza:* ⇒ 891, EncKat 5 (1989) 903 (L. *Pawlak* ❿).

d810 *Katzenstein* H.J., Gaza in the Persian period: TEuph 1 (1989) 67-86 [< ZAW 102,434].

d811 *Gezer:* ᴱDever William G., Gezer IV 1986 ⇒ 2,a598; 4,e712: ᴿBL (1989) 25 (H.G.M. *Williamson:* ten years after Gezer II, best on Philistines; volume 5 'was scheduled for 1986', volume 6 for 1988; 3 in press, two others projected; but 'major interpretation is being held over for a final volume in the series'); Orientalia 58 (1989) 435-7 (A.J. *Frendo*).

d812 **Seger** Joe D., al., Gezer V, the Field I caves: HUC/Glueck Annual 5. J 1988. 0-87820-305-2 [OIAc S89].

d813 **Gilat:** *Alon* David, *Levy* Thomas E., The archaeology of cult and the chalcolithic sanctuary at Gilat [25 k NW Beersheba]: JMeditArch 2 (1989) 163-221; 13 fig. (maps).

d814 *Gilgal:* ⇒ 891, EncKat 5 (1989) 1078 (J. *Homerski* ❿).

d815 *Halif/*Lahav 1986: RB 96 (1989) 230-2; fig. 5; pl. VIII; X, b (J.D. *Seger,* O. *Borowski*).

d816 *Harṭuv* 1988: IsrEJ 39 (1989) 110-2 (A. *Mazar,* P. de *Miroschedji*).

d817 *Mazar* Amihai, *Miroschedji* Pierre de, ❻ Hartuv – an early Bronze Age I settlement in the Shephelah: Qadmoniot 22 (1989) 27-32; ill.

d818 *Hébron:* ⇒ 885, DHGE 23,133s (1989) 712-726 (D. *Stiernon*).

d819 *Ofer* Avi, ❻ Excavations at biblical Hebron: Qadmoniot 22 (1989) 88-93; 94, a 17-16 cent. cuneiform tablet, *Anbar* M.

d820 *Provera* Mario, La biblica Mamre presso Hebron: ParVi 33 (1988) 225-230; map; plan.

d821 *Ḥeṣi:* *Toombs* Lawrence E., The changing functions of a Palestine site, Tell el-Hesi: ÉchMClas 33 (1989) 125-146; 9 fig. (foldout plan); 6 pl.

d822 *Ḥever:* *Bar-Adon* Pesach, Excavations in the Judean Desert, ᴱ*Greenhut* Zvi: Atiqot ❻ 91 p.; ill.; Eng. 8* p.

d823 *Humayma,* aqueduc 1986s: RB 96 (1989) 244-8; fig. 14s; pl. XIV (J.P. *Oleson*).

d824 *Jalamé:* ᴱWeinberg Gladys D., Excavations at Jalame, site of a glass factory in Late Roman Palestine. Columbia 1988, Univ. Missouri. 0-8262-0409-0 [OIAc S89].

d825 *Jericho:* *Netzer* Ehud, Jericho und Herodium; verschwenderisches Leben in den Tagen der Hasmonäer und Herodes' des Grossen, ᵀ*Luz* U.: Judaica 45 (1989) 21-44; 17 fig.

d826 *Ussishkin* David, Notes on the fortifications of the Middle Bronze II period at Jericho and Shechem: BASOR 276 (1989) 29-53; 17 fig.

d827 *Eshel* Hanan, How I found a fourth-century B.C. papyrus scroll on my first time out [Ketef Jericho/Qurunṭal]: BAR-W 15,5 (1989) 44-53; ill.

d828 *Patrich* Joseph, Hideouts in the Judean wilderness – Jewish revolutionaries and Christian ascetics sought shelter and protection in cliffside caves: BAR-W 15,5 (1989) 32-42 [34, EB arrow-reed].

d829 Urkan er-Rub (N. Jericho 191.164), Kebaran: IsrEJ 39 (1989) 106-8 (E. *Hovers*, O. *Marder*).

d830 *Kadesh Barnea*: *Haiman* Mordechai, Preliminary report of the western Negev highlands [Qadeš Barnea area] emergency survey: IsrEJ 39 (1989) 173-191; 7 fig.; pl. 21-23.

d831 *Karkom*: *Anati* Emmanuel, New discoveries at Har Karkom 1986: BCentPrei 24 (1988) 113-8; fig. 76 [p.10-12 readers' letters, largely favoring Karkom as Sinai].

d832 *Khiam* (E Bethlehem): *González Echegaray* J., *Freeman* L.G., A reevaluation of El Khiam (Desert of Judea): AulaO 7,1 (1989) 37-66.

d833 *Kilia*: *Magen* Yishaq, ⊕ A Roman fort and a Byzantine monastery at Khirbet el-Kilia [Kfar Ramon 1487/1826]: Qadmoniot 22 (1989) 45-50; ill.

d834 *Lachish*: *Ussishkin* David, ⊕ The Assyrian attack on Lachish; the evidence from the southwest corner of the site: ➤ 218, Mem. YADIN Y., ErIsr 20 (1989) 97-114; 23 fig.; Eng. 197*.

d835 *a*) *Shalev* Sariel, *Northover* Peter, A cast bronze door hinge from Tel Lachish; an archaeometallurgical study; – *b*) *Drori* Israel, *Horowitz* Aharon, Tel Lachish; environment and subsistence during the Middle Bronze, Late Bronze and Iron Ages: TAJ 15s (1988s) 197-205; 4 fig.; pl. 19 / 206-211.

d836 *Kloner* Amos, ⊕ The hiding complexes in the Judean Shephelah. J 1987, Hameuhad. $20. ᴿBASOR 274 (1989) 81 (S. *Gitin*).

d837 *Loya*/Leḥi [5 k SE B. Guvrin), église: RB 96 (1989) 258-265; fig. 23-27; pl. XVI-XIX (J. *Patrich, Y. Tsafrir*).

d838 *Mampsis*: **Negev** A., The architecture of Mampsis, final report: 1, the middle and late Nabatean periods; 2, The Late Roman and Byzantine periods: Qedem 26s. J 1988, Univ. Inst. Archaeology. xvii-197 p.; xviii-116 p.; ill. $25 (vol. 2). 0333-5844 [NTAbs 33,418].

d839 *Masada*: *Cohen* S., What really happened at Masada?: Moment 13,5 (Wsh 1988) 28-35 [< NTAbs 33,80: archeology has confirmed much of JOSEPHUS' account, but his War 7,252-406 is implausible].

d840 *Hirschfeld* Yizhar, ⊕ Masada in the Byzantine period – the Marda monastery: ➤ 218, Mem. YADIN Y., ErIsr 20 (1989) 262-274; 17 fig.; Eng. 204*.

d841 *a*) *Netzer* Ehud, ⊕ The process of Masada's destruction [Zealot wood-earth barrier]; – *b*) *Foerster* Gideon, ⊕ Two bronze ornaments in the shape of rams' heads, from Masada: ➤ 218, Mem. YADIN Y., ErIsr 20 (1989) 311-320; 13 fig. / 333-6; 8 fig.; Eng. 206*.

YADIN Y. excavations final report, Masada ➤ 9552, **Cotton** H., documents 1989.

d842 *Meṣad ha-Šavyahu* [1207.1462] 3d, 1988: ErIsr 20 (1989) 228-232 ⊕; 5 fig.; Eng. 203* (R. *Reich*).

d843 *Wenning* Robert, Mesad Hašavyahu [1207.1462, J. *Naveh*, IEJ 1960-2], ein Stützpunkt des Jojakim [2 Kön 24]?: ➤ 220, ᶠZENGER E., Vom Sinai zum Horeb 1989, 169-196; 9 fig.; map.

d844 *Miqne*: *Gitin* Seymour, Tel Miqne-Ekron; a type-site for the inner coastal plain in the Iron Age II period: ➤ 543, AASOR 49 (1989) (15–) 23-58; 15 fig.

d845 *Mišmar*: a) *Tadmor* Miriam,   The Judean Desert Treasure from Naḥal Mishmar; a chalcolithic traders' hoard?; – b) *Beck* Pirhiya,   Notes on the style and iconography of the chalcolithic hoard from Naḥal Mishmar: → 106, [F]KANTOR H., Essays 1989, 249-261; pl. 45-49 / 39-47 + 249-261; pl. 45-49; fig. 4-10.

d846 *Muḥmas* wadi E. Jerusalem: RB 96 (1989) 235-9; fig. 11-13 (J. *Patrich*).

d847 *Negeb*:   *Lewin* Ariel,   La difesa del Negev in epoca tardoantica: Sileno 15 (R 1989) 161-174; map 175.

d848 *Schaefer* Jerry,   Archaeological remains from the medieval Islamic occupation of the northwest Negev desert: BASOR 274 (1989) 33-60 [61-69 *Betts* Alison, The Solubba, nonpastoral nomads in Arabia].

d849 *Oded* 1988 [S Makteš Ramon, 122.991], Late Byz.: IsrEJ 39 (1989) 117-120; 2 fig. (S. *Rosen, G. Avni*).

d850 *Qitmit*, E. Negev: *Beit-Arieh* Yitshak, ⊕ An Edomite shrine at Ḥorvat Qitmit: → 218, Mem. YADIN Y., ErIsr 20 (1989) 135-146; 15 fig.; Eng. 198*.

d851 *Beit-Arieh* Itzhaq,   New data on the relationship between Judah and Edom toward the end of the Iron Age: → 543, AASOR 49 (1989) 125-131; 4 fig.

d852 *Rimmon*: *Kloner* Amos,   The synagogues of Horvat Rimmon (Umm/ Ramamin 137.086):   → 845, Synagogues 1987/9,   43-48 + pl. XXV-XXVIII.

d853 *Garbrecht* Günther,   Die Wasserversorgung geschichtlicher Wüstenfestungen am Jordantal [Sartaba; Mird/Hyrcania ...]: AntWelt 20,2 (1989) 3-30; ill.

d854 *Šiqmîm* (N. Beersheba) chalcolithic, 2d 1988: IsrEJ 39 (1989) 115-7 (T. *Levy*, D. *Alon*).

d855 *Timna*: *Rothenberg* Beno,   The Egyptian mining temple at Timna 1988 → 4,e742. – [R]Antiquity 63 (1989) 658 (J. D. *Muhly*).

d856 *Yarmut* 5th-6th 1986s, EB: ExcSIsr 7s (1988s) 184-7; Fig. 154s (P. de *Miroschedji*).

d857 **Miroschedji** P. de,   Yarmouth I 1982/8 → 4,e744*:   [R]Qadmoniot 22 (1989) 118 (Ran *Gophna*).

T4.5   **Samaria, Sharon.**

d858 *Athlit*: *Blakeley* Jeffrey A., defense of his Straton's Tower against A. RABAN: BASOR [268 (1987) 71-88] 273 (1989) 79-82; response 83.

d859 *Azor*: *Dothan* Moshe, ⊕ A cremation burial at Azor – a Danite city: → 218, Mem. YADIN Y., ErIsr 20 (1989) 164-174; 21 fig.; Eng. 200*.

d860 *Bet-El*: → 902, NBL Lfg. 2 (1989) 281s (M. *Görg*).

d861 *Caesarea* Harbor 1987-8: ExcSIsr 7s (1988s) 33-42; fig. 32-41 (A. *Raban, al.*).

d862 **Raban** Avner,   The harbours of Caesarea Maritima, results ... 1980-5, I. The site and the excavations: BAR-Int 491 / Haifa Univ. Maritime Studies 3.   2 vol.   0-86054-628-4 [OIAc S89].

d863 *Levine* Lee I., *Netzer* Ehud, Excavations at Caesarea M. 1975, 1976, 1979: Qedem 21, 1986 → 2,a629; 4,e751:   [R]OLZ 84 (1989) 685-8 (P. *Welten*).

d864 **Blakeley** Jeffrey A.,   Caesarea Maritima; the pottery and dating of Vault 1;   horreum, Mithraeum, and later uses: Joint Expedition 4, 1987 → 3,e159; $150; sb. $100:   [R]Levant 21 (1989) 204 (P. *Bienkowski*); RelStR 15 (1989) 73 ('Blakey', 'Bault').

d865 **Bull** Robert J., *al.,* King Herod's dream, Caesarea on the sea. L 1988, Norton. 244 p.; ill. £22; pa £15. – ᴿIntJNaut 18 (1989) 86s (A. *Flinder*).

d866 *Schwartz* Daniel R., ⊕ 'Caesarea' and its 'sanctum': CHistEI 51 (1989) 21-34; Eng. 195.

d867 *Daoust* J. [< *Briend* J. MondeB 56, 1988] Césarée-sur-Mer: EsprVie 99 (1989) 319s.

d868 *Carmelus*: **Kuhnen** Hans-Peter, Studien zur Chronologie und Sied-lungsarchäologie des Karmel (Israel) zwischen Hellenismus und Spät-antike: TAVO B-22. Wsb 1989, Reichert. x-398 p.; vii-169 p., 84 pl.; 27 foldout plans. 3-88226-419-5.

d869 **Kuhnen** Hans-Peter, Nordwest-Palästina in hellenistisch-römischer Zeit ... Karmel 1987 ⇥ 3,e160; 4,e756: ᴿAcPraeh 20 (1988) 208s (Geraldine *Saherwala*); JRS 79 (1989) 245 (M. *Goodman* doubts that Carmel is typical of all Palestine as claimed).

d870 *Mittmann* Siegfried, Zur spätantiken Topographie der Karmelküste: ZDPV 105 (1989) 136-150.

d871 *Friedman* Elias, The monastery of the Carmelite Fathers, Mount Carmel, 1919-1931: Teresianum 40 (1989) 213-223.

d872 *Dor* 8th 1987, Iron to Roman: ExcSIsr 7s (1988s) 43-49, fig. 42-45 (E. *Stern, al.*); IsrEJ 39 (1989) 32-42; 2 fig.; pl. 5 (E. *Stern, al.*).

d874 *Gilboa* Ayelet, New finds at Tel Dor and the beginning of Cypro-Geometric pottery import to Palestine: IsrEJ 39 (1989) 204-218; 6 fig.; pl. 26 (219-227, origin, *Yellin* Joseph).

d875 *Stern* Ephraim, The beginning of the Greek settlement in Palestine in the light of the excavations at Tel Dor: ⇥ 543, AASOR 49 (1989) 107-124; 11 fig.

d876 *Stern* Ephraim, ⊕ Hazor, Dor and Megiddo in the time of Ahab and the Assyrian period: ⇥ 218, Mem. YADIN Y., ErIsr 20 (1989) 233-248; 10 fig.; Eng. 203*.

d877 *Far'a-N*: **Chambon** Alain, Tell el-Far'ah I. Fer 1984 ⇥ 65,a867; 4,e762: ᴿAfO 35 (1988) 236s (K. *Jaroš*).

d878 *Garizim*: ⇥ 891, EncKat 5 (1989) 870s (S. *Haręzga* ❷).

d879 *Jaffa*: **Kark** Ruth ⊕ Jaffa, a city in evolution 1799-1914. J 1984, Ben-Zvi. 297 p. – ᴿRÉJ 147 (1988) 438-440 (Esther *Benbassa*).

d880 *Kaplan* Jacob & Haya, ⊕ Remains of a Serapis cult in Tel Aviv: ⇥ 218, Mem. YADIN Y., ErIsr 20 (1989) 352-9; 17 fig.; Eng. 307*s.

d881 *Negbi* Ora, ⊕ The temples of Tel Qasila; additional comments on their architectural and cultic affinities: ⇥ 218, Mem. YADIN Y., ErIsr 20 (1989) 220-7; 9 fig.; Eng. 302*.

d882 *Lydda*: Schwartz J., ⊕ The town plan of Roman Lydda [in Talmudic sources and archeological remains]: Jewish History 2,1 (Univ. Haifa 1987) 33-36 [< JStJud 20,279].

d883 *Makmiš*: **Herzog** Ze'ev, Geschichte und Archäologie aus dem Tel Mikal [Makmiš 5 k N Qasile]: AntWelt 20,3 (1989) 35-31; ill.

d884 *Samaria*: **Zertal** Adam, ⊕ The wedge-decorated [N. Samaria] bowl and the origin of the Cuthaeans: ⇥ 218, Mem. YADIN Y., ErIsr 20 (1989) 181-7; 6 fig. (maps); Eng. 200*.

d885 *Applebaum* Shimon, *a)* Royal and imperial estates in the Sharon and Samaria; – *b)* Syria-Palaestina as a province of the Severan empire; – *c)* Jewish urban communities and Greek influences: ⇥ 227, Judaea 1989, 97-110 / 143-154 / 30-46.

d886 **Shiloh:** **Schley** Donald G., Shiloh, a biblical city in tradition and history [diss. Emory]: JStOT supp. 63. Sheffield 1989, Academic. 256 p. £25. 1-85075-161-7.

d887 *Holm-Nielsen* Svend, Silo – endnu en gang: SvEx 54 (1989) 80-89.

d887* *Finkelstein* Israel, The land of Ephraim survey 1980-1987; preliminary report: TAJ 15s (1988s) 117-179; 26 fig.; bibliog. 180-3.

d888 **Sichem:** **Cole** Dan P., Shechem I 1984 → 3,e177; 4,e775: ᴿBASOR 276 (1989) 86-88 (W. G. *Dever*).

d889 *Currid* John D., A note on the function of Building 5900 at Shechem – again: ZDPV 105 (1989) 42-46.

T4.6 **Galilaea;** pro tempore *Golan.*

d889* ʿ*Akko*: *Applebaum* Shimon, The Roman colony of Ptolemais-ʿAke and its territory: → 227, Judaea 1989, 70-96.

d890 **Arbel:** *Ilan* Zvi, *Izdarechet* Abraham, Arbel, an ancient town in the eastern Lower Galilee: Qadmoniot 22 (1989) 111-7.

d890* *Chen* Doron, Dating synagogues in Galilee; the case of Arbel: LA 39 (1989) 39-42.

d891 Et-Tell (**Bethsaida**) 1988: IsrEJ 39 (1989) 99s (R. *Arav*).

d891* **Bet-Schean:** → 902, NBL Lfg 2 (1989) 286s (M. *Görg*).

d892 *Applebaum* Shimon, When did Scythopolis become a Greek city?: → 227, Judaea 1989, 1-8.

d893 *Arav* Rami, The round church at Beth-Shan: LA 39 (1989) 189-197; pl. 35-38.

d894 Bet Shean project 1988: ExcSIsr 7s (1988s) 15-32; fig. 12-31 (G. *Foerster, Y. Tsafrir*; G. *Mazor*).

d895 **Bet Yeraḥ:** *Amiran* Ruth, Re-examination of a cult-and-art object from Beth Yerah: → 106, ᶠKANTOR H., Essays 1989, 31-33; pl. 5-8.

d896 **Cabul:** **Gal** Zvi, Hurbat Rosh Zayit, biblical Cabul: Catalogue 5. Haifa 1989, Hecht Museum. (❸–Eng.) [OIAc S89].

d897 **Capernaum:** **Tzaferis** Vassilios, Excavations at Capernaum I, 1978-82. WL 1989, Eisenbrauns (Pepperdine Univ.). xxi-234 p.; 14 loose plans. 0-931464-48-X [OIAc N89].

d898 *Foerster* Gideon, [Capernaum] Synagogue studies; metrology and excavations: ZDPV [102 (1986) 134-143, *Chen* D.] 105 (1989) 129-135.

d899 *Bloedhorn* Hanswulf, The capitals of the synagogue of Capernaum – their chronological and stylistic classification with regard to the development of capitals in the Decapolis and in Palestine: → 845, Synagogues 1987/9, 49-54; pl. XXVIII-XXIX.

d900 *Rough* Robert H., A new look at the Corinthian capitals at Capernaum: LA 39 (1989) 119-128; pl. 9-14.

d901 *Loffreda* Stanislao, Discovering Capharnaum: HolyL 8 (1988) 115-133.

d902 *Taylor* Joan E., Capernaum and its 'Jewish-Christians'; a re-examination of the Franciscan evidence: BAngIsr 9 (1989s) 7-28; 6 fig. [p. 26: if Jewish-Christians did live in Capernaum after the 1st century, they have left no trace, notably of veneration for Peter's home].

d903 *Dan* 1987s: IsrEJ 39 (1989) 93-96, 2 fig.; pl. 17-18 (A. *Biran*).

d904 *Biran* Avraham, ❸ The evidence for metal industry at Dan: → 218, Mem. YADIN Y., ErIsr 20 (1989) 120-134; 29 fig.; Eng. 198*.

d905 **Genezaret,** jezioro: ❾ → 891, EncKat 5 (1989) 960 (F. *Gryglewicz*).

d906 *Pixner* Bargil, Wege Jesu um den See Gennesaret: HLand 119,2s (1987) 1-14; 12 fig.; map.

d907 *Gischala*: *Groh* Dennis E., Judaism in Upper Galilee at the end of antiquity; excavations at Gush Halav and en-Nabratein: → 696, 10th Patristic, 19 (1989) 62-71.

d908 *Golan*: *a*) chalcolithic, 1987: IsrEJ 39 (1989) 91-93 (Claire *Epstein*); *b*) BInstArch 25 (1988) 179s (S. *Gibson*).

d909 *Ellenblum* Ronnie, Who built Qal'at al-Ṣubayba [today Q. Nimrud, S. Hermon]?: DumbO 43 (1989) 103-112 [113-9, inscriptions, *Amitai* R.].

d910 **Hartal** Moshe, ❻ Ha-Seqer... Northern Golan Heights; the archaeological survey as a source of regional history [diss. TA, ᴰ*Kochavi* M.]. Qazrin 1989, Israel Dept. Antiquities. vi-257 p.; xi-14 Eng. [OIAc N89].

d911 *Kochavi* Moshe, *a*) The land of Geshur project; regional archaeology of the southern Golan (1987-1988 seasons): IsrEJ 39 (1989) 1-17; 7 fig.; pl. 1-2; – *b*) ❻ The land of Geshur; the regional archaeology of the southern Golan Heights in the biblical period: Qadmoniot 22 (1989) 21-26; ill.

d912 *Zohar* Mattanyah, Rogem Hiri, a megalithic monument in the Golan: IsrEJ 39 (1989) 18-31; 3 fig.; pl. 3-4.

d913 *Hammeh*: Cahill J. al., ❻ Tell el-Hammeh in the tenth century BCE: Qadmoniot 22 (1989) 33-38; ill.

d914 *Hawam* / Haifa: réexamen de 1929-33 hellénistique-perse: RB 96 (1989) 224-235; fig. 6-10; pl. XI-XII (G. *Finkielsztejn*).

d915 *Hazor*: ᴱBen-Tor A., Hazor III-IV, an account of the third and fourth seasons of [Y. YADIN] excavation, 1957-58. J 1989, Israel Exploration Soc. 965-221-008-0.

d916 *a*) *Malamat* Avraham, ❻ Hazor and Mari; – *b*) *Kempinski* Aharon ❻ Reconstructing the [Hazor] Canaanite tower-temple; – *c*) *Tadmor* Miriam ❻, The 'cult-standard' from Hazor in a new light: → 218, Mem. YADIN Y., ErIsr 20 (1989) 68-71 / 82-85; 5 fig. / 86-89; 3 fig.; Eng. 196*s.

d917 *Malamat* A., Hazor once again in new Mari documents [ARM 23-25]: → 59, ᶠFINET A., Reflets 1989, 117s.

d918 *Iotapata*: Meshel Ze'ev, A fort at Yotvata from the time of Diocletian: IsrEJ 39 (1989) 228-238; 4 fig.; pl. 27-34 (239-260, Latin inscription, *Roll* Israel; 261-6, numismatic finds, *Kindler* Arie).

d919 *Jezreel*: Yizreel 1821.2180: 1987 / 1987s: ExcSIsr 7s (1988s) 189-191 (P. *Porat, al.*) / 191-5; fig. 159-162 (O. *Yogev*).

d920 *Goren* H., Erste Siedlungsversuche der deutschen Templer in der Jesreel-Ebene im 19. Jh.: JbEvHL 1 (1989) 100-130 [< ZAW 102,278].

d921 *Oeming* M., Der Tell Jesreel (Hirbet Zer'in); Studien zur Topographie, Archäologie und Geschichte: JbEvHL 1 (1989) 56-78 [< ZAW 102,278].

d922 *Portugali* Yubal, ❻ A field methodology for the West Jezreel valley survey 1981, ᵀ*Makino* Kumi: Orient-Japan 32,1 (1989) 119-139; plans.

d923 *Kinneret*/Ureimeh 1985: RB 96 (1989) 223s; pl. IX (F. *Fritz*).

d924 *Thompson* J. A., Kinnereth [*Fritz* V. since 1982]: BurHist 24 (1988) 14-24 [< OTAbs 12,145].

d925 *Hübner* Ulrich, Wohntürmen im eisenzeitlichen Israel? [*Fritz* V., 'Oreme]: BibNot 41 (1988) 23-30; 2 fig.

d926 *Kursi*: *Tzaferis* Vassilios, A pilgrimage to the site of the swine miracle: BAR-W 15,2 (1989) 44-51; (color.) ill.

d927 *Megiddo*: Kempinski A., Megiddo, a city-state and royal centre in North Israel: DAI-AVA Materialien. Mü 1989, Beck 224 p.; 59 fig.; 25 pl.; 14 plans. 3-406-31934-3. – ᴿBAngIsr 9 (1989s) 53s (G. J. *Wightman*).

d928 **Davies** Graham J., Megiddo 1986 → 2,a680 ... 4,e802: ᴿBA 52 (1989) 55 (H. O. *Thompson*); VT 39 (1989) 116s (J. L. *Peterson*).

d929 *Davies* G. I.,   Solomonic stables at Megiddo after all?: PEQ 120 (1988) 130-141; 5 fig.

d930 *Rast* Walter E.,   The problem of stratigraphy relating to David: → 219, Mem. YADIN Y., ErIsr 20 (1989) 166*-173*.

d931 *Ussishkin* David,   SCHUMACHER's shrine in building 338 at Megiddo [in 1903: he was right, and it is the finest shrine from the First Temple period known today]: IsrEJ 39 (1989) 149-172; 9 fig.; pl. 16-20.

d932 *Williams* Bruce, *Logan* Thomas J.,   Oriental Institute Museum notes, No. 14; a basalt royal or divine figure from Megiddo: JNES 48 (1989) 125-7 + 2 fig.

d933 *Milson* David,   Megiddo, Alalakh, and Troy; a design analogy between the Bronze Age temples: PEQ 121 (1989) 64-68; 3 fig.

d934 *a) Singer* Itamar, ❺ The political status of Megiddo VII A; – *b) Geva* Shulamit, ❺ The transition from Canaanite to Israelite hegemony in Palestine [... Megiddo VII A to V A...] – a suggestion: → 218, Mem. YADIN Y., ErIsr 20 (1989) 51-57; Eng. 195* / 149-153; Eng. 199*.

d935 *Daoust* J. [< *Thalman* J., MondeB], Megiddo, une grande cité royale: EsprVie 99 (1989) 647-9.

d936 *Briend* Jacques, *al.*, Megiddo, cité royale: MondeB 59 (1989) 14s. 33-38 (*al.* 6-40).

d937 *Me'ona* (Kh. Aliya E Akko, 174.264) 1988, EB II fort: IsrEJ 39 (1989) 96-98; 1 fig. (E. *Braun*); RB 96 (1989) 212-4; fig. 1; pl. V (E. *Braun*).

d938 *Meroth: Ilan* Zvi, *Damati* Emmanuel, The synagogue at Meroth; does it fix Israel's northern border in Second Temple times?:   BAR-W 15,2 (1989) 20-36; (color.) ill.

d939 *Tsafrir* Yoram, ❺ The synagogue at Meroth, the synagogue at Capernaum, and the dating of the Galilean synagogue; a reconsideration [3d century or early 4th, rather than under Julian 361]: → 218, Mem. YADIN Y., ErIsr 20 (1989) 337-344; 4 fig.; Eng. 207*.

d940 *a) Ilan* Zvi, The synagogue and Beth Midrash of Meroth; – *b) Dar* Shimon, *Mintzker* Johanan, The synagogue of Hurvat Sumaqa (Carmel): → 845, Synagogues 1987/9, 21-41 + pl. XVII-XXIV / 17-20 + pl. XI-XVI.

d941 *Nahariya:* **Dauphin** Claudine, *Edelstein* Gershon, L'Église byzantine de Nahariya (Israël), étude archéologique: Byzantina Mnemeîa 5, 1984 → 3,e218; 4,e805: ᴿBMosAnt (AIEMA) 12 (1988s) 284s (J.-P. *Sodini*); RHE 84 (1989) 253s (Jacqueline *Lafontaine-Dosogne*).

d942 *Nazareth:* **Santarelli** Giuseppe, La Santa Casa di Loreto, tradizioni e ipotesi [= ²Translazione 1984]. Loreto 1988, Congr. S. Casa. 194 p. – ᴿCC 140 (1989,4) 311 (M. *Paris:* merita considerazione l'ipotesi che il materiale della casa sia nazaretano).

d942* **Folda** Jaroslav, The Nazareth capitals 1986 → 2,a689; 4,e806: ᴿByZ 81 (1988) 316s (E. *Alliata*).

d943 *Qiri:* **Ben-Tor** Amnon, *al.*, Tell Qiri: Qedem 24, 1987 → 4,e809. – ᴿLevant 21 (1989) 203s (P. *Bienkowski*).

d944 *Safed:* Kfar Ḥananya (Ṣefat) 1987: IsrEJ 39 (1989) 98s (D. *Adan-Bayewitz*).

d945 *Sepphoris* 1987: RB 96 (1989) 240-3 (J. F. *Strange, al.*); IsrEJ 39 (1989) 104-6 (J. F. *Strange, al.*); 3d-4th 1987-8, Roman mansion mosaic...: ExcSIsr 7s (1988s) 169-173 (E. *Meyers, al.*).

d946 *Wawiyat* (N. Sepphoris) 1987: IsrEJ 39 (1989) 102-4 (J. P. *Dressel, al.*).

d947 **Miller** Stuart S., Studies in ... Sepphoris 1984 → 65,a920 ... 4,e814: ᴿRHR 206 (1989) 202-4 (S. *Schwarzfuchs*).

d948 **Taanach:** Görg Manfred, Zum Namen des Fürsten von Taanach: Bib-
Not 41 (1988) 15-18.

d948* **Tabor:** *Elitzur* Yoel, [Jos 19,12; 1 Chr 6,62: not the mount but a town],
The meaning of *epì lóphou* in POLYBIUS' writing and its effect on the
location of the town Tabor: ScrClasIsr 8s (1988) 79-82.

d949 *Tiberias:* **Dudman** Helga, *Ballhorn* Elisheva, Tiberias. J 1988, Carta.
240 p.; (color.) ill.; maps. $24.25. 965-220-141-3 [OIAc Ja90]. – ᴿBAR-W
15,4 (1989) 11.56 (N. A. *Silberman*).

d950 Horvat Arvel (Tiberias) 1988; synagogue: IsrEJ 39 (1989) 100-2- 2 fig.
(Z. *Ilan*).

d951 *Yiftaḥel* (Kh. Khaladiyeh) 1986: RB 96 (1989) 210. 212; pl. IV (E.
Braun).

d952 *Yoqne'am* et ses villages satellites: MondeB 61 (1989) 58-61, ill. (J.
Poulin).

d953 *Rubiato* María Teresa, Excavaciones arqueológicas en Tell Yoqne'am:
Sefarad 49 (1989) 217-9.

T4.8 *Transjordania:* **East-Jordan.**

d954 *Bartlett* J. R., The kingdom of Edom [... archeology surveys]: IrBSt 10
(1988) 207-223 [< OTAbs 12,155]. ⇥ g242.

d955 **Boling** Robert G., The early biblical community in Transjordan 1988
⇥ 4,e823*: ᴿBL (1989) 35 (J. R. *Bartlett*); ÉTRel 64 (1989) 107
(Françoise *Smyth*).

d956 *Desreumaux* Alain, La Jordanie byzantine : ⇥ 869, Jordanie 1987, 109-
119; 6 fig.

d957 *a) Dollfus* Geneviève, La Préhistoire récente en Jordanie; – *b) Thalmann*
Jean-Paul, Le IIIᵉ millénaire; les premières villes de Jordanie: ⇥ 869,
Jordanie 1987, 11-26; 6 fig. / 27-40; 6 fig.

d958 **Garrard** Andrew N., *Gebel* Hans G., The prehistory of Jordan; the state
of research in 1986: BAR 396. Ox 1988. ix-285 p.; p. 286-601.

d959 ᴱHadidi A., Studies in the history and archaeology of Jordan II, 1985
⇥ 1,849; 3,e240: ᴿLevant 21 (1989) 201-3 (P. *Dorrell*).

d960 **Homès-Fredericq** Denyse, *Hennessy* J. Basil, Archaeology of Jordan II.
Field reports 1s: Akkadica Sup. 7s. Lv 1989, Peeters. 650 p. Fb 3400.
90-6831-180-8 [BL 90, 32, J. R. *Bartlett*].

d961 ᶠHORN Siegfried H.: The archaeology of Jordan, ᴱGeraty L. ... 1986
⇥ 3,83: ᴿAndrUnS 27 (1989) 231s (J. B. *Storfjell*).

d961* *Piccirillo* M., *a)* Gruppi episcopali nelle tre Palestine e in Arabia; – *b)*
Recenti scoperte di archeologia cristiana in Giordania: ⇥ 822, 11ᵉ
Arch. Chrét. 1986/9, (I) 459-501 / (II) 1697-1735.

d962 **Schuldenrein** Joseph, Late quaternary paleo-environments and pre-
historic site distributions in the lower Jordan valley: diss. ᴰ*Butzer* Karl
W., dept. anthropology. Chicago 1983. xvii-568 p. (2 vol.) – OIAc
N89.

d963 **Timm** Stefan, Moab zwischen den Mächten; Studien zu historischen
Denkmälern und Texten [Hab-Diss. Kiel 1987]: ÄgAT 17. Wsb 1989,
Harrassowitz. vii-516 p. 3-447-02940-4.

─────────

d964 *'Abata* 2k SE Dead Sea 1988: ADAJ 33 (1989) 227-233; pl. XL-XLII
(K. D. *Politis*).

d965 *Abila* 1988, 7th century basilica: AJA 93 (1989) 260 (W. H. *Mare*); – RB 96 (1989) 251-7; fig. 18-22; pl. X (W. H. *Mare*).

d966 *Winter* Willard W., A centennial restudy of [Gottlieb] SCHUMACHER's temple at Tel Abil: ProcGLM 9 (1989) 258-272; 4 fig.

d967 *Amman* Citadel, lower terrace area A, 1988 (Jordan Antiquities Department and École Biblique]: ADAJ 33 (1989) 357-363; pl. LI (F. *Zayadine, al.*].

d968 Cittadella, Jebel Qal'ah 1988s: LA 39 (1989) 248-253 (J.-B. *Humbert, al.*).

d969 **Moawiyah** M. **Ibrahim**, *Gordon* Robert L., *al.*, A cemetery at Alia international airport: Yarmouk Univ. Arch/Anthrop 1. Wsb 1987, Harrassowitz. 98 p.; LIV pl; ❹ 5 p. DM 88. – ᴿJAOS 109 (1989) 689s (Carol *Meyers*).

d970 *Prag* Kay, A comment on the Amman citadel female heads: PEQ [120 (1988) 55-63, *Amr* measurements differ from *Dornemann's*] 121 (1989) 75s.

d971 *'Aqaba*-Ma'in survey 1988: LA 39 (1989) 253-5 (R. *Jobling*).

d972 *MacAdam* Henry I., Fragments of a Latin building inscription from Aqaba, Jordan: ZPapEp 79 (1989) 163-171; facsim; pl. IX.

d973 *Whitcomb* Donald, Coptic glazed ceramics from the excavations at Aqaba, Jordan: JAmEg 26 (1989) 167-182; 6 fig.

d974 *Bab ed-Dra*: **Schaub** R. Thomas, *Rast* Walter E., Bab edh-Dhra'; excavations in the cemetery directed by Paul W. LAPP (1965-7): Reports of the (ASOR) Expedition to the Dead Sea Plains, Jordan, 1. WL 1989, Eisenbrauns. xxv-598 p. 0-931464-51-X [OIAc N89].

d975 *Balu'* [NW Karak], 2d 1987: ADAJ 33 (1989) 111-121; pl. VII-VIII (U. *Worschech*).

d976 *Dananir* (umm, Baq'ah) 1987: ADAJ 33 (1989) 123-136; pl. IX-XIV (P. E. *McGovern*).

d977 *Faris* (18 k N Karak) post-Umayyad coins and glass, 1986/8: ADAJ 33 (1989) 245-258; pl. XLIII (J. *Johns*, A. *McQuitty*) [269-285, D. *Whitcomb*, Abbasid Mahesh ware; 305-322, ❹ 5-12, M. *Najjar*, from Muwaqqar].

d978 *Finan* [60k S Dead Sea, and to Qasr Tilah 20k N] Byzantine-Islamic survey 1982: ADAJ 33 (1989) 199-215; pl. XXXI-XXXV (G. R. D. *King* and 5 others).

d979 *Gadara*: MondeB 58 (1989) 49-51, ill. (T. *Weber*); – LA 39 (1989) 255-8 (T. *Weber*). – ➤ 891, EncKat 5 (1989) 799 (Maria *Wójcik* ❾).

d981 *Gazal*, 'ayn, 1988: ADAJ 33 (1989) 9-25, pl. I-V (G. O. *Rollefson, al.*).

d982 *Gerasa*: **Hackstein** Katharina, Ethnizität und Situation; Ǧaraš – eine vorderorientalische Kleinstadt: TAVO B 94. Wsb 1989, Reichert. xiii-164 p. 3-88226-469-1.

d983 Mutawwaq, 12 k SE Jerash, 1986: ADAJ 33 (1989) 137-144; pl. XV-XVI (J. W. *Hanbury-Tenison*).

d984 Mutawwah (Jerash): **Hanbury-Tenison** J. M., The Late Chalcolithic to Early Bronze I transition in Palestine and Transjordan: BAR-Int 311. Ox 1988. 309 p.; 38 fig. – ᴿLA 39 (1989) 274-86 (P. *Kaswalder*).

d985 *Ghassul*: *Tutundžić* Sava P., Relations between Late Predynastic Egypt and Palestine; some elements and phenomena: ➤ 857, Urbanisation 1986/9, 423-432.

d986 *Handaquq* 8k N Sa'idiyeh, 1987s: ADAJ 33 (1989) 59-95; 14 fig. (J. *Mabry*).

d987 *Harrana:* **Urice** Stephen K., Qasr Kharana in the Transjordan 1987 ➤ 3,e285: ᴿJAmEg 26 (1989) 254s (J. M. *Bloom*).

d988 *Hešbon*: ᴱGeraty Lawrence T., *Running* Leona G., (*Vyhmeister* Werner K.) Historical foundations; studies of literary references to Hesban and vicinity: Hesban 3. Berrien Springs MI 1989, Andrews Univ. ix-97 p. 0-943872-17-0. – ᴿLA 39 (1989) 278s (P. *Kaswalder*).

d989 **Ibach** Robert D.ᴶ, Archaeological survey of the Hesban region; catalogue of sites and characterization of periods: Hesban 5, 1987 → 4,e863: ᴿLA 39 (1989) 277s (P. *Kaswalder*).

d990 *Iktanu*: *Prag* Kay, Preliminary report on the excavations at Tell Iktanu, Jordan, 1987: Levant 21 (1989) 33-45; 11 fig.

d991 *Irbid*: *Lenzen* C.J., Tell Irbid and its context; a problem in archaeological interpretation: BibNot 42 (1988) 27-35.

d992 Yabis, wadi (Irbid) 1989 survey: LA 39 (1989) 246-8 (J. *Mabry*, al.).

d993 *Jawa*: *Helms* Svend, Jawa at the beginning of the Middle Bronze Age: Levant 21 (1989) 141-164; 13 fig.; bibliog. p. 164-8.

d994 *Kerak*: *Brown* Robin M., Excavations in the 14th century A.D. Mamluk palace at Kerak: ADAJ 33 (1989) 287-304.

d995 *Lehun*: *Homès-Fredericq* Denyse, Un temple nabatéen à Lehun (Jordanie) → 28, ᶠBERGHE L. Vanden 1989 (II) 575-580; 2 fig.

d996 *Limes Arabicus* project 1989: LA 39 (1989) 261-3 (S.R. *Parker*).

d997 *Madaba*: **Piccirillo** Michele, Chiese e mosaici di Madaba: SBF 34. J/CinB 1989, Franciscan/Paoline. 374 p.; ill. – ᴿLA 39 (1989) 290-301 (N. *Duval*, 'avril 1990').

d998 **Médébielle** Pierre, Madaba et son histoire chrétienne 1987 → 4,e875: ᴿRB 96 (1989) 150 (R.J. *Tournay*).

d999 'Umeiri ('Madaba plains project') 1987: ADAJ 33 (1989) 145-176; pl. XVII-XXIII (L.T. *Geraty* and 11 others).

e1 *Mahanaim*: *Coughenour* Robert A., A search for Mahanaim: BASOR 273 (1989) 57-66; 4 fig.

e2 *Maʿin*: *Vaccarini* Gioacchino, I capitelli di Maʿin: LA 39 (1989) 213-242; pl. 45-78.

e3 *Nebo* (Siyâgha, 'Uyun Musa) 1989: LA 39 (1989) 265s (M. *Piccirillo*).

e4 *Pella*: **Smith** H. Robert, *Day* P. Leslie, Pella of the Decapolis final report on Area IX, 2. The civic complex, 1978-1985. Wooster 1989, College. xxiv-168 p.; 47 fig.; 63 pl. 0-9604658-5-5. – ᴿLA 39 (1989) 283-6 (E. *Alliata*).

e5 Jisr Sheikh Hussein [Jordan river (bridge) 10 k NW Pella-Fahil], Tell Fendi 1986: ADAJ 33 (1989) 97-110 (J. *Kareem*).

e6 *Petra*: *Matthiae* Karl, Die Fassade von Ed-Der in Petra; ein Beitrag zur nabatäischen Felsarchitektur: Klio 71 (1989) 257-279; 6 fig.

e7 *Roche* Marie-Jeanne, Les niches cultuelles [c. 70 av. J.-C.] du Sadd al-Maʿjan à Pétra [bétyle]: ADAJ 33 (1989) 327-334; pl. XLV-L.

e8 ᴱLindner Manfred, Petra und das Königreich der Nabatäer; Lebensraum, Geschichte und Kultur eines arabischen Volkes der Antike⁵. Mü 1989, Delp. 336 p.; (color.) ill.; foldout map. [TLZ 115, 217, K. *Matthiae*].

e9 ᴱLindner Manfred, Petra; neue Ausgrabungen und Entdeckungen 1986 → 2,a746 ... 4,e887: ᴿAcPraeh 20 (1988) 207 (J. *Eiwanger*); AJA 93 (1989) 158s (S.T. *Parker*); OLZ 84 (1989) 397-9 (K. *Matthiae*); RArchéol (1989) 410s (J.-M. *Dentzer*).

e9* **Negev** Avraham, Nabataean archaeology today 1986 → 3,e316; 4,e892: ᴿByZ 82 (1989) 303s (P. *Grossmann*).

e10 **Stierlin** Henri, Städte in der Wüste; Petra, Palmyra und Hatra, Handelszentren am Karawanenweg: Antike Kunst im Vorderen Orient 1987 → 3,e310; DM 168: – ᴿMundus 25 (1989) 130-2 (K. *Schippmann*).

e11 *Funke* Peter,   Rom und das Nabatäerreich bis zur Aufrichtung der Provinz Arabia: → 151, ᶠPEKÁRY T., Migratio 1989, 1-18.

e12 *Daoust* J.,   Pétra, main de velours dans un gant de pierre [*Zeghidour* Slimane, Unesco spécial 13, 1588 (? pour 1988)]: EsprVie 99 (1989) 52s.

e13 **Wenning** Robert,   Die Nabatäer, Denkmäler und Geschichte: NTOrbA 3, 1987 → 3,e317; 4,e894:   ᴿIsrEJ 39 (1989) 122-7 (A. *Negev*); LA 39 (1989) 281s (P. *Kaswalder*); Mundus 25 (1989) 49s (K. *Schippmann*); RArchéol (1989) 170s (M. *Sartre*).

e14 *Gatier* Pierre-Louis, *Salles* J.-F.,   Aux frontières méridionales du domaine nabatéen: → 822, Arabie/mers 1985/8, 173-190; map.

e15 *Quweisma* church 1989:   LA 39 (1989) 264s (R. *Schick*, E. *Suleiman*).

e16 *Sa'idiyya*: **Pritchard** James B.,   Tell es–Saidiyeh 1985 → 1,d713 ... 4,e899*: ᴿTEuph 1 (1989) 191-3 (J. *Briend*); ZDPV 105 (1989) 189-195 (Helga *Weippert*).

e17 *Samra*: *Leonard* Albert,   A chalcolithic 'fine ware' from Kataret es Samara in the Jordan valley: BASOR 276 (1989) 3-14; 7 fig.

e18 *Ṣarbūṭ* (tell abu) 2 k NW Deir'Alla; 1988 Ayyubid-Mamluk: ADAJ 33 (1989) 323-6; pl. XLIV (H. de *Haas, al.*).

e19 *Šu'ayb*: *Simmons* A. H., *al.*,   Test excavations at Wadi Shu'eib, a major neolithic settlement in central Jordan: ADAJ 33 (1989) 27-43 [345-9, Katherine *Wright, al.*].

e20 *Umm Rasas* (Kastron Mefaa) 4th, 1989:   LA 39 (1989) 266-9 (M. *Piccirillo*); 268-270, inscription (E. *Puech*).

e21 *Elitzur* Yoel,   The identification of Mefa'at in view of the discoveries from Kh. Umm er-Raṣāṣ [PICCIRILLO M. 1986]: IsrEJ 39 (1989) 267-277.

e22 *Provera* Mario,   Gli scavi di Um er-Rasas in Giordania: ParVi 33 (1988) 459-462 + 4 fig.

e23 *Yasileh* 1st-2d, 1988-9:   LA 39 (1989) 271s (Z. Al-*Muheisen*).

e24 *Zara* (Callirhoe?) Dead Sea shore, 1986:   ADAJ 33 (1989) 217-225; pl. XXXVI-XXXIX (Christa *Clamer*).

e25 *Strobel* A.,   Die Grabungskampagne in ez-Zara (Kallirhoë) am Toten Meer (Jordanien):   JbEvHL 1 (1989) 173-6 [< ZAW 102,278].

e26 *Ziqlab*, wadi, 15 k N Zerqa, 1987: ADAJ 33 (1989) 43-58; pl. VI (E. H. *Banning* and 7 others).

T5.1   **Phoenicia** – *Libanus*, **Lebanon.**

e27 **Chamseddine** Ali,   Les sarcophages de l'époque romaine trouvés au Liban; importations et fabrications locales: diss. Paris-IV, 1989. – RÉLat 67 (1989) 36.

e28 **Elayi** Josette, Pénétration grecque en Phénicie [< diss. Nancy 1984, ᴰ*Will* É.] 1988 → 4,e911:   ᴿOLZ 84 (1989) 394-6 (E. *Lipiński*); RStFen 8 (1989) 149s (S. *Ribichini*); TEuph 1 (1989) 194-8 (J. *Sapin*).

e29 *Gawlikowski* Michał, ❷ Fenicja: → 891, EncKat 5 (1989) 118-122.

e30 **Salibi** Kamal,   A house of many mansions; the history of the Lebanon reconsidered.   L 1988, Tauris. vii-247 p. £17.50. – ᴿJRAS (1989) 319-321 (E. *Abushakra*: brilliant).

e31 *Ba'albek*: *Jakobs* Peter H. F., (*Imhof* Peter);   Bauplastik aus Baalbek [in Freiburg/Br]: ArchAnz (1989) 413-441; 31 fig.

e32 *Stiernon* D.,   Héliopolis de Célésyrie [/ d'Égypte]: → 885, DHGE 23,135 (1989) 911s [912-4, *Aubert* R.].

e33 *Kleiner* Gerhard, †, Baalbek und Palmyra: DamaszMit 4 (1989) 191-203.

e34 *Byblos: Scandone Matthiae* Gabriella, Due teste regali egiziane della XII dinastia a Biblo: RStFen 8 (1989) 7-14; pl. I-II.

e35 **Nibbi** Alessandra, Ancient Byblos reconsidered 1985 ➤ 1,d729 ... 4,e983: ᴿAntClas 58 (1989) 437-9 (R. *Tefnin,* also on her Wenamun).

e36 **Zegers** Catherine, Le sarcophage d'Ahiram: mémoire de licence, Lv 1986, ᴰ*Donceel* R. – RArtLv 19 (1986) 344-6.

e37 *Kāmid/Lōz:* **Poppa** R., Kāmid el-Lōz 2. Der eisenzeitliche Friedhof; Befunde und Funde 1978 ➤ 60,t306: ᴿTEuph 1 (1989) 181-4 (J. *Sapin*).

e38 *Sarafand:* **Anderson** William P., Sarepta I; – **Khalifeh** Issam A., Sarepta II; – **Koehl** Robert B., Sarepta III; – **Pritchard** James B., Sarepta IV. Beyrouth 1988, Univ. Libanaise. 707 p.; xx-436 p.; 209 p.; viii-125 p. [JAOS 109,721s].

e39 *Puech* Émile, Nouvelle inscription en alphabet cunéiforme court à Sarepta: RB 96 (1989) 338-344; pl. XX.

e40 *Sidon:* **Elayi** J., Sidon, cité autonome de l'Empire perse. P 1989, Idéaphane. [Akkadica 64,58].

e41 **Schmidt-Dounas** B., Der lykische Sarkophag aus Sidon 1985 ➤ 1,d742b ... 3,e352: ᴿRÉG 101 (1988) 191-3 (A. *Hermary*).

e42 **Stucky** R. A., Tribune d'Echmoun 1984 ➤ 65,b13 ... 3,e353: ᴿAfO 35 (1988) 252-4 (J. *Borchhardt*).

e43 *Tyrus:* **Aubet** M. E., Tiro y las colonias fenicias de Occidente. Barc 1987, Bellaterra. viii-323 p.; 70 fig.

e44 ᴱ**Schmeling** Gareth, Historia Apollonii regis Tyri 1988 ➤ 4,e942: ᴿMusHelv 46 (1989) 260 (K. *Müller*).

e44* *Spadaro* Giuseppe, Graeca mediaevalia VI. Ancora sul primo 'Apollonio di Tiro': SicGymn 42 (1989) 265-274.

e45 *Vattioni* Francesco, Note ... a proposito di un antroponimo di Tiro / di Iside nel mondo nabateo: AION 49 (1989) 75s.

T5.2   *Situs mediterranei* **phoenicei et punici.**

e46 *Bondì* Sandro F., Sull'organizzazione dell'attività commerciale nella società fenicia: ➤ 877, Lavoro 1988, 348-362.

e47 a) *Bresciani* E., Presenze fenicie in Egitto; – b) *Pernigotti* S., Aspetti dei rapporti tra la civiltà fenicia e la cultura egiziana; – c) *Tusa* V., La colonizzazione fenicia e le culture anelleniche di Sicilia: ➤ 811, Momenti 1985/8, 257-265 / 267-276 / 277-289.

e48 **Culican** William † 1984, Opera selecta, from Tyre to Tartessus 1986 ➤ 2,146: ᴿBO 46 (1989) 175-7 (E. *Gubel:* some 30 emendations).

e49 ᴱ**Delz** Josef, SILIUS Italicus, Punica. Stu 1987, Teubner. lxxviii-528 p. DM 168. – ᴿClasR 39 (1989) 215-8 (M. D. *Reeve*).

e50 *Gill* David W. J., Silver anchors and cargoes of oil; some observations on Phoenician trade in the Eastern Mediterranean: PBritSR 56 (1988) 1-12.

e51 **Gras** M., *al.,* L'univers phénicien, P 1989, Arthaud, 284 p.; 54 fig.; 16 color. pl.; 20 maps. – ᴿOrientalia 58 (1989) 561-6 (Maria Giulia *Amadasi Guzzo*); RÉLat 67 (1989) 315s (F. *Briquel-Chatonnet*).

e52 *Herrmann* Christian, Fünf phönizische Formen für ägyptische Fayencen: ZDPV 105 (1989) 27-41; 5 fig.; pl. 2-6.

e53 *Hölbl* Günther, Ägyptische Kunstelemente im phönikischen Kulturkreis des I. Jahrtausends v. Chr.: zur Methodik ihrer Verwendung: Orientalia 58 (1989) 318-325; 8 fig.; pl. XIV-XV.

e54 [E]**Lipiński** E. *al.*, Studia Phoenicia 3-5 (colloquia) 1985/7 ⇒ 3,826; 4,e944: [R]AulaO 7 (1989) 289-293 (E. del *Olmo Lete*).

e55 **Mazza** Federico, *Ribichini* S., *Xella* P., Fonti classiche per la civiltà fenicia e punica, I. Fonti letterarie greche dalle origini alla fine dell'età classica: Coll.StFen 27 / Testimonia Phoenicia 1. R 1988, Cons. Naz. Ricerche. 158 p.; 4 pl. [BL 90, 124, A. R. *Millard*].

e56 *a) Mazza* F., La 'precolonizzazione' fenicia; problemi storici e questioni metodologiche; – *b) Bisi* Anna M., Modalità e aspetti degli scambi fra Oriente e Occidente fenicio in età precoloniale; – *c) Bondì* S. F., Problemi della precolonizzazione fenicia nel Mediterraneo centro-occidentale: ⇒ 811, Momenti 1985/8, 191-203 / 205-226 / 243-255.

e57 **Moscati** Sabatino, Tra Tiro e Cadice; temi e problemi degli studi fenici: St.Punica 5. R 1989. Univ. 155 p.

e58 [E]**Moscati** Sabatino, [TE]*Niemeyer* Hans-G. & Doris, Die Phönizier [Ausstellung Venedig 1988]. Ha 1988, Hoffmann & C. 592 p.; 122 fig. + 683 color. DM 148. – [R]OLZ 84 (1989) 527-9 (H. *Klengel*).

e59 [E]**Moscati** Sabatino, The Phoenicians. NY 1988, Abbeville. 768 p.; ill. 0-89659-892-6. – [R]Archaeology 42,5 (1989) 74s. 80 (Patricia M. *Bikai*).

e60 *Moscati* Sabatino, Presenza fenicia nel Mediterraneo occidentale: RStFen 8 (1989) 133-8.

e61 **Schiffmann** Ilya, Phönizisch-punische Mythologie und geschichtliche Überlieferung in der Widerspiegelung der antiken Geschichtsschreibung: StFen coll. 17. R 1986, Cons. Naz. Ric. 103 p.

e62 *Creta*: **Shaw** Joseph W., Phoenicians in southern Crete: AJA 93 (1989) 165-183; 23 fig.

e63 *Cyprus*: **Bikai** Patricia M., *a)* The Phoenician pottery of Cyprus 1987 ⇒ 3,e370; 4,e950: [R]Gnomon 61 (1989) 727-731 (Gerta *Maass-Lindemann*); – *b)* Cyprus and the Phoenicians: BA 52 (1989) 203-9.

e64 **Markoe** Glenn, Phoenician bronze and silver bowls from Cyprus and the Mediterranean 1985 ⇒ 1,f755 ... 4,e950*: [R]JNES 48 (1989) 149s (Eleanor *Guralnick*).

e65 *Dor*: **Stern** E., ⊕ Phoenician discoveries at Tel Dor: Qadmoniot 22 (1989) 103-110; ill.

e66 *Hispania*: **Harrison** Richard J., Spain at the dawn of history; Iberians, Phoenicians and Greeks: Ancient Peoples and Places 105. L 1988, Thames & H. 176 p.; 112 fig. £18.50. 0-500-02111-2. – [R]Antiquity 63 (1989) 389-391 (G. *Ruiz Zapatero*).

e67 [E]**Olmo Lete** G. del, *Aubet Semmler* M. E., Los Fenicios en la península ibérica I-II, 1986 ⇒ 2,353: [R]BL (1989) 30 (N. *Wyatt*); BO 46 (1989) 470-2 (María Luisa *Ramos Sainz*).

e68 *Bisi* Anna Maria, I fenici nella penisola iberica [*Olmo Lete* E. del, *Aubet Semmler* Maria E., I-II 1986]: Orientalia 58 (1989) 283-8.

e68* [E]**González Blanco** Antonino, Arte y poblamiento en el Sureste peninsular durante los últimos siglos de la civilización romana: Antigüedad y Cristianismo 5. Murcia 1988, Univ. 679 p.

e69 *Rufete Tomico* Pilar, Die phönizische Rote Ware aus Huelva: MadMit 30 (1989) 118-134; 7 fig.

e70 *Suárez* Ángela, *al.*, Abdera, una colonia fenicia en el Sureste de la Península Ibérica: MadMit 30 (1989) 135-148; 10 fig.; pl. 11-12; deutsch 149s.

e71 *Wagner* Carlos G., The Carthaginians in ancient Spain; from administrative trade to territorial annexation: ➤ 784, Punic Wars 1988/9, 145-156.

e72 **Arteaga** O., *al.*, Forschungen zur [phönizischen] Archäologie und Geolo-
gie im Raum von Torre del Mar 1983/84. Mainz 1988, von Zabern.
viii-198 p. – ᴿOrAnt 28 (1989) 160-3 (F. *Fedele*).

e73 *Lusitania*: **Mello Beirão** C. M. de, Une civilisation prothohistorique du
sud du Portugal (Iᵉʳ âge du Fer) [36 new Phoenician-related cemetery
inscriptions, added to those publicized a century ago by *Estacio da Veiga*
S., *Carthailhac* É.]. P 1986, De Boccard. 168 p.; 15 pl. – ᴿAJA 93 (1989)
471 (R. J. *Harrison*: discoveries momentous; synthesis deficient).

e74 *Melita*: **Hölbl** Günther, Ägyptisches Kulturgut auf den Inseln Malta
und Gozo in phönikischer und punischer Zeit; die Objekte im Archäologischen Museum von Valletta: Szb W ph/h 538. Wien 1989,
Österr. Akad. 213 p.; 27 pl. 3-7001-1637-3 [OIAc N89].

e75 *Mozia* 1985 area 'K est': Sicilia Archeologica 60s (1989) 39-47, 20 fig.
(Antonella *Spanò Giammellaro*) & 48 (L. *Valente*).

e76 *Bondì* Sandro F., Mozia, tra i Greci e Cartagine: EgVO 12 (1989) 165-173.

e77 **Amadasi Guzzo** M. G., Scavi a Mozia – le iscrizioni 1986 ➤ 4,e956:
ᴿAulaO 7 (1989) 280s (G. del *Olmo Lete*); UF 21 (1989) 470 (M. *Heltzer*).

e78 *Falsone* Gioacchino, Da Nimrud a Mozia – un tipo statuario di stile
fenicio egittizzante: UF 21 (1989) 153-178 + 179-193, 32 fig. +
p. 161 + n. 60-63 supplied in UF 22,103s.

e79 *La Lomia* M. Rosaria, Il giovane di Mozia è un danzatore?: ParPass
248 (1989) 376-396; 8 fig.

e80 *a) Tusa* Vincenzo, Da Mozia a Marsala, un crocevia del Mediterraneo; –
b) Bondì S. F., Tra Cartagine e la Sicilia greca; momenti di storia
moziese; – *c) Acquaro* Enrico, Mozia 1985, ricerche e scavi; – *d) Ciasca*
Antonia, Considerazioni su Mozia fenicia; – *e) Amadasi Guzzo* Maria
Giulia, La scrittura fenicia a Mozia: ➤ 863, Da Mozia a Marsala 1987,
37-43 / 97-102 / 103-5; 2 pl. / 117-121 / 123-6.

e81 *Sardinia*: **Barrecca** Ferruccio, *al.*, Ricerca sugli antichi insediamenti
Fenici: Sardinian Coastal Project 1. Cagliari 1986, Soprintendenza
Archeol. 61 p.; 13 pl. [OIAc N89].

e82 **Gallin** Lenore J., Architectural attributes and inter-site variations; a case
study, the Sardinian nuraghi: diss. ᴰ*Earle* T. UCLA 1989. 621 p.
89-22211. – DissA 50 (1989) 1710-A.

e82* **Lilliu** G., La civiltà nuragica: Sardegna arch.st.mon. 1. Sassari 1982,
Delfino. 239 p. – ᴿOriginiR 12 (1983) 674-7 (A. *Cazzella*).

e83 *Manfredi* Lorenza-Ilia, Terracotte puniche di Sardegna: AION 49 (1989)
1-7; 2 pl.

e84 **Acquaro** Enrico, Gli insediamenti fenici e punici in Italia: Itinerari 1. R
1988, Libreria/Zecca dello Stato. 126 p.; 52 color. pl.

e85 *Bernardini* Paolo, Le origini di Sulcis e Monte Sirai: StEgPun 4 (1989)
45-59 + 7 fig.

e86 **Hölbl** Günther, Ägyptisches Kulturgut im phönikischen und punischen
Sardinien I-II: ÉPR 102, 1986 ➤ 2,a793; 4,e965: ᴿAfO 35 (1988) 250-2
(Ingrid *Gamer-Wallert*).

e87 *Tharros*: **Acquaro** E., Scavi al Tofet di Tharros; le urne dello scavo
Pesce-I [1962]: Coll.StFen 29. R 1980, CNR. 138 p.; 1 plan. – ᴿAION 49
(1989) 77 (S. *Lancel*).

e88 **Acquaro** Elena, *Finzi* Claudio, Tharros: Sardegna archeologica, Guida e
itinerari 5. Sassari 1986, Delfino [OIAc S89].

e89 ^E**Barnett** R.D., *Mendleson* C., Tharros ... tombs ... in British Museum 1987 ➤ 3,e391; 4,e972: ^RPEQ 121 (1989) 81s (B. *Isserlin*).

e90 *Manfredi* Lorenza-Ilia, Su un monumento punico da Tharros: Stud-EgPun 3 (1988) 93-195 + pl. 1-IV.

T5.3 Carthago.

e91 **Barceló** P.A., Karthago und die iberische Halbinsel vor den Barkiden; Studien zur karthagischen Präsenz im westlichen Mittelmeerraum von der Gründung von Ebusus (VII. Jh.v.Chr.) bis zum Übergang Hamilkars nach Hispanien (237 v.Chr.): Antiquitas 1.37. Bonn 1988, Habelt. ix-202 p.; map. DM 78. 3-7749-2354-X [JRS 79,267].

e92 *Barceló* Pedro, Zur karthagischen Überseepolitik im VI. und V. Jahrhundert v. Chr.: Gymnasium 96 (1989) 13-37.

e93 *Barnett* R.D., From Arad to Carthage; harvest rites and corn-dollies: ➤ 218, Mem. YADIN Y., ErIsr 20 (1989) 1*-11*; 10 fig.

e94 *Bomgardner* David L., The Carthage amphitheater; a reappraisal: AJA 93 (1989) 85-103; 11 fig.

e95 **Cirkin** Ju. B., ⑬ Karfagen i ego kul'tura. Moskva 1986. – ^RRStorAnt 17s (1987s) 322-4 (F. *Bosi*).

e96 *Clover* Frank M., Felix Karthago: ➤ 781, Tradition 1984/9, 129-169; 30 fig.

e97 *Cristofori* Alessandro, Colonia Carthago magnae in vestigiis Carthaginis (Plin., Nat. hist. V, 24): AntAfr 25 (1989) 83-93 [95-109, *Euzennat* Maurice, Maurétanie NH v, 2-18].

e98 *Hoyos* R.D., Hannibal's war; illusions and ironies: AncHRes 19 (1989) 87-92.

e99 **Huss** Werner, Geschichte der Karthager: HbAltW 3/8, 1985 ➤ 1,d789 ... 4,e983: ^RAmHR 94 (1989) 415s (J.R. *Fears*); Latomus 48 (1989) 258 (M. *Dubuisson*).

e100 *Jongeling* K., De verloren wetenschap van Phœniciërs en Carthagers: PhoenixEOL 35,2 (1989) 57-65.

e101 *a)* *Krings* Véronique, La destruction de Carthage; problèmes d'historiographie ancienne et moderne; – *b)* *Bonnet* Corinne, Les connotations sacrées de la destruction de Carthage; – *c)* *Dubuisson* Michel, 'Delenda est Carthago'; remise en question d'un stéréotype; – *d)* *Lancel* Serge, L'enceinte périurbaine de Carthage lors de la troisième guerre punique; réalités et hypothèses: ➤ 784, Punic Wars 1988/9, 329-344 / 289-305 / 279-287 / 251-278; 24 fig.

e102 ^E**Lipiński** E., Carthago; Acta colloquii Bru 2-3.V.1986: StPhoen 6, 1988 ➤ 4,754: ^RBO 46 (1989) 684-6 (E. *Gubel*); ClasR 39 (1989) 305-8 (H. *Hurst*); RStFen 8 (1989) 151-5 (P. *Xella*).

e103 *Niemeyer* Hans, Los comienzos de Cartago y la expansión fenicia en el área mediterránea: Gerión 7 (1989) 11-40.

e104 *a)* *Rakob* Friedrich, Karthago, die frühe Siedlung; neue Forschungen; – *b)* *Vegas* Mercedes, Archaische und mittelpunische Keramik aus Karthago, Grabungen 1987/88: MiDAI-R 96 (1989) 155-208; 20 fig.; pl. 34-49 / 209-265; 11 fig.

T5.4 Ugarit – Ras Šamra.

e104* **Callot** Olivier, Une maison à Ougarit 1983 ➤ 64,b601 ...4,e992: ^ROriginiR 12 (1983) 679-681 (M. *Liverani*).

e105 *Cunchillos* Jesús, Les tablettes trouvées à Ras Shamra (Ugarit) en 1929, 1930 et 1931; enquête critique des sources: Sefarad 49 (1989) 37-95; ill; Eng. español 96.

e106 **Dietrich** M., *al.*, Ugarit-Bibliographie, I-IV (1967-1971) 1973; V, AOAT 20/5, 1986 ➤ 55,6027 ... 4,e994: ᴿBO 46 (1989) 680s (W. *Herrmann*).

e107 **Grindstaff** Gwynn C., An analysis of five Late Bronze Age cities [Ugarit, Enkomi, Troy, Pylos, Zakros] in the ancient Mediterranean world: diss. Oklahoma State, ᴰ*Ospovat* A. 1988. 469 p. 89-15005. – DissA 50 (1989s) 1406s-A.

e108 *Soldt* W. H. van, Tbṣr, queen of Ugarit?: UF 21 (1989) 389-392.

e109 **Stucky** R. A., Ras Shamra, Leukos limen 1983 ➤ 64,b620 ... 4,g1: ᴿTEuph 1 (1989) 184-7 (J. *Sapin*).

e110 **Xella** Paolo, I testi rituali di Ugarit I, 1981 ➤ 62,b835: ᴿJNES 48 (1989) 42-44 (D. *Pardee*).

T5.5   **Ebla.**

e111 **Archi** A., Testi ... metalli e tessuti, L. 1769: ARET 7, 1988 ➤ 4,e77: ᴿOrientalia 58 (1989) 546s (B. R. *Foster*).

e111* *Archi* Alfonso, Integrazioni a testi eblaiti: Orientalia 58 (1989) 124-7: 7 facsimiles; pl. 3.

e112 *Baffi Guardata* Francesca, Bibliografia eblaita II [continuando ᴱ**Cagni** L. Ebla 1975-85 (N 1987) 429-456]: StEpL 6 (1989) 145-158.

e113 *a*) *Edzard* Dietz O., Semitische und nichtsemitische Personennamen in Texten aus Ebla; – *b*) *Krebernik* Manfred, Prefixed verbal forms in personal names from Ebla; – *c*) *Müller* Hans-Peter, Eblaitische Konjugation in Kontexten und Personennamen: ➤ 831, Eblaite names 1985/8, 25-34 / 45-69 / 71-87.

e114 *a*) *Fronzaroli* Pelio, Il culto degli Angubbu a Ebla; – *b*) *Durand* Jean-Marie, L'assemblée en Syrie à l'époque pré-amorite; – *c*) *Conti* Giovanni, Le fonti del vocabolario bilingue eblaita; – *d*) *Tonietti* Maria Vittoria, Le liste delle d a m   e n; cronologia interna; criteri ed elementi per una datazione relativa dei testi economici di Ebla; – *e*) *Tonietti*, Aggiornamenti alla cronologia dei n a r; – *f*) *Bonechi* Marco, Un atto di culto a Ebla; – *g*) *Catagnoti* Amalia, I NE.DI nei testi amministrativi: ᴱ**Fronzaroli** P., Miscellanea eblaitica 2: QuadSemit 16. F 1989, Univ. Dip. Linguistica; p. 1-26 / 27-44 / 45-78 / 79-115 / 117-129 / 131-147 / 149-201.

e115 *Gordon* Cyrus H., Ebla, Ugarit and the Old Testament: Orient-Japan 25 (1989) 134-168.

e116 *Klengel* Horst, Bemerkungen zur Rolle von Ebla in der frühen Bronzezeit Vorderasiens: ➤ 874, Šulmu 1986/8, 145-160.

e117 **Krebernik** Manfred, Die Beschwörungen aus Fara und Ebla 1984 ➤ 65,b82 ... 4,g12: ᴿOLZ 84 (1989) 287-9 (B. *Hruška*).

e118 **Krebernik** Manfred, Die Personennamen der Ebla-Texte: BBVO 7, 1988 ➤ 4,g13: ᴿAfO 35 (1988) 164-9 (F. *Pomponio*); BL (1989) 125 (A. R. *Millard*).

e119 *Lambert* W. C., Notes on a work of the most ancient Semitic literature [Ebla ARET 5, no. 6]: JCS 41 (1989) 1-32; translation 33.

e119* *Matthiae* Paolo, The destruction of Ebla Royal Palace; interconnections between Syria, Mesopotamia and Egypt in the Late EB IVA: ➤ 831*, High/Low III (1989) 163-9.

e120 *a) Millard* Alan R., Ebla personal names and personal names of the first millennium B.C. in Syria and Palestine; – *b) Gordon* Cyrus H., Notes on proper names in the Ebla tablets; – *c) Biggs* Robert D., The Semitic personal names from Abu Salabikh and the personal names from Ebla; – *d) Westenholz* Aage, Personal names in Ebla and in pre-Sargonic Babylonia: → 831, Eblaite names 1985/8, 159-164 / 153-8 / 89-98 / 99-117.

e121 **Pettinato** Giovanni, Ebla, nuovi orizzonti 1985 → 2,a841; 4,g19: ᴿJAOS 109 (1989) 120-3 (W. *Heimpel*: Ebla-fans will like it; Assyriologists will find it unfounded and exaggerated); RivB 37 (1989) 103-5 (R. *Gelio*).

e122 *Sollberger* E., Un cas possible de corégence à Ébla: → 59, ꜰFinet A., Reflets 1989, 161.

T5.8 **Situs effossi Syriae in ordine alphabetico.**

e123 *Amrît:* **Dunand** M., *Saliby* N., Le temple d'Amrith dans la pérée d'Arados 1985 → 3,d854: ᴿTEuph 1 (1989) 189-191 (J. *Elayi*).

e124 *Apameia:* **Balty** Jean-C., Apamea in Syria in the second and third centuries A.D.: JRS 78 (1988) 91-104; 2 maps; pl. X-XV.

e125 *Barri:* **Pecorella** Paolo E., Tell Barri, uno scavo italiano in Siria: ArchViva 8,3 (1989) [not 7,3 (1988) as in → 4,g29] 32-43; color. ill.

e126 *Boṣra:* **Freyberger** Klaus S., Einige Beobachtungen zur städtebaulichen Entwicklung des römischen Bostra: DamaszMit 4 (1989) 45-60; 1 fig.; pl. 7-16.

e127 *Damascus:* **Pitard** Wayne T., Ancient Damascus 1987 → 3,e466; 4,g36: ᴿBO 46 (1989) 146-150 (B. *Becking*); CBQ 51 (1989) 536-8 (R. S. *Boraas*); JAOS 109 (1989) 503s (M. *Liverani*: first-rate on literary sources, but there exist no new archeological data since UNGER 1957).

e128 *Freyberger* Klaus S., Untersuchungen zur Baugeschichte des Jupiter-Heiligtums in Damaskus: DamaszMit 4 (1989) 61-86; 7 (foldout) fig.; pl. 17-28.

e128* **Sack** Dorothée, Damaskus; Entwicklung und Struktur einer orientalisch-islamischen Stadt [< Diss.]: DamaszF 1. Mainz 1989, von Zabern. 142 p.; 32 pl.; 12 foldout plans [ByZ 88,445].

e129 **Sader** Hélène S., Les états araméens [diss. ᴰ*Röllig* W.] 1987 → 3,e467; 4,g38: ᴿArTGran 52 (1989) 346-8 (A. *Torres*); OLZ 84 (1989) 676-8 (W. *Herrmann*); WeltOr 20s (1989s) 301-3 (E. *Lipiński*).

e130 *Deir Seta:* **Khoury** Wedad, Deir Seta; prospection et analyse d'une ville morte inédite en Syrie: diss. Genève 1987. 160 p. 245 fig.

e131 *Dmeir:* **Klinkott** Manfred, Ergebnisse der Bauaufnahme am 'Tempel' von Dmeir: DamaszMit 4 (1989) 109-161; 12 fig.

e132 *Emar:* **Arnaud** Daniel, Recherches au pays d'Aštata: Emar VI 1986 → 2,a870; 4,g40: ᴿRAss 83 (1989) 163-191, à suivre (J.-M. *Durand*).

e133 **Civil** M., The texts from Meskene-Emar [*Arnaud* D. 1985-7 → 4,g40]: AulaO 7,1 (1989) 5-25.

e134 *Bunnens* Guy, Emar on the Euphrates in the 13th century B.C.: some thoughts about newly published cuneiform texts [*Arnaud* D. 1985s]: Abr-Nahrain 27 (1989) 23-36.

e135 *Hadidi:* **Dornemann** Rudolph H., Comments on small finds and items of artistic significance from Tell Hadidi and nearby sites in the Euphrates valley, Syria: → 106, ꜰKantor H., Essays 1989, 59-75; fig. 11; pl. 10-11.

e136 *Ḫalaf:* **Bartl** Karin, Die Datierung der altmonochromen Ware von Tell Halaf: → 122, ꜰLoon M. van, To the Euphrates 1989, 257-274; 4 fig.

790 Elenchus of Biblica 5, 1989 [XVIII. Archaeologia: situs

e136* *Winter* Irene J., North Syrian ivories and Tell Halaf reliefs; the impact of luxury goods upon 'major' arts: → 106, FKANTOR H., Essays 1989, 321-332; pl. 62-66.

e137 *Ḥama:* **Kristensen** Aristeia P., Hama 3/3, 1986 → 4,g44*: RGnomon 61 (1989) 652-4 (K. S. *Freyberger*).

e138 **Ploug** Gunhild, The Graeco-Roman Town: Hama 3/2, 1985 → 1,d881; 4,g45: RJNES 48 (1989) 45-47 (D. *Kennedy*).

e139 *Curvers* Hans H., The beginning of the third millennium in Syria: → 122, FLOON M. van, To the Euphrates 1989, 173-193; 4 fig.

e140 *Ḥamidiya:* **Eichler** Seyyare, *al.* Tall al-Hamīdīya I 1984: OBO arch. 4, 1985 → 1,d883... 4,g47: RArOr 57 (1989) 306s (P. *Charvát*, deutsch); OLZ 84 (1989) 549-551 (D. *Sürenhagen*).

e141 *Hammam/Turkman* (Balikh) 5th 1988: Akkadica 64 (1989) 1-6+8 fig. (D. W. J. *Meijer*).

e142 *Ḥazna:* **Munchayev** R. M., Ⓑ A Soviet archaeological expedition to Syria; the first results of research [t. Chazne, t. Nurek]: VDI 188 (1989) 181-5; 3 fig.

e143 *Ḥomṣ:* **Nitta** Ermenegilda, Antroponimi semitici nelle iscrizioni greche e latine della Emesene [Ḥomṣ]: CivClasCr 10 (1989) 283-302.

e144 *Sapin* J., Un domaine de la couronne dans la Trouée de Homs (Syrie); origines et transformations de Tiglat-Phalazar III à Auguste: TEuph I (1989) 21-54 [< ZAW 102, 434].

e145 *Ḥuwayra:* Chuera 1982-5: AfO 35 (1988) 155-163; 14 fig. (Ursula *Moortgat-Correns*).

e145* *Jabala:* **Tsugitaka** Sato, The Syrian coastal town of Jabala; its history and present situation: Studia culturae islamicae 35. Tokyo 1988, Inst. Asia-Africa. 102 p. [JNES 48,79]. – RJRAS (1989) 321s (L. I. *Conrad*).

e146 *Jazīra:* **Seeden** Helga, **Wilson** Jim, *a*) Processes of site formation in villages of the Syrian Ǧazīra: → a2.9, ICAES = Berytus 36 (1988) 169-188; – *b*) Rural settlement in the Syrian Ǧazīra from prehistoric to modern times: DamaszMit 4 (1989) 1-31; 9 fig.; pl. 1-4.

e147 *Kôm:* **Dornemann** Rudolf H., A neolithic village at Tell el Kowm 1986 → 2,a875... 4,g51: RAfO 35 (1988) 224s (Walpurga *Antl-Weiser*).

e148 [Kôm; N. Euphrates entre Mari et Malatya]: *Lebeau* Marc, Notes sur l'expansion urukéenne: → 28, BERGHE L. Vanden 1989, 33-48.

e149 *Mabbug:* **Drijvers** Han J. W., Hierapolis-Mabbog: → 904, RAC 15,113 (1989) 27-41.

e150 *Mari:* EDurand J.-M., [ECharpin D., *al.*, vol. 2], Archives épistolaires de Mari I,1s: ARM 26. P 1988, RCiv. xi-693 p., 3 fiches; 589 p., 3 fiches. F 236+229. 2-86538-189-7; 90-0 [BL 90, 120, W. G. *Lambert*].

e151 **Kupper** J.-R. [*Aynard* J.-M., *Spycket* A.] Mari, philologisch [archäologisch] tout en français: → 905, RLA 7,5s (1989) 382-390 [-418].

Malamat Abraham, Mari and the early Israelite experience, 1984 Schweich Lectures 1989 → b307.

e152 *Mayer* Walter, Ergänzungen zur Geschichte der Stadt Tuttul I [Mari]: UF 21 (1989) 271-6.

e153 *Sasson* Jack M., Shunukhra-Khalu [an official of Zimri-Lim's court]: → 166, Mem. SACHS A. 1988, 329-351.

e154 *a*) *Scouflaire* Marie-France, Premières réflexions sur l'organisation des 'prisons' dans le royaume de Mari; – *b*) *Malamat* A., Hazor once again in new Mari documents; – *c*) *Kraus* F.-R., Koppelungen in einer Gruppe von Briefen nach Mari: → 59, FFINET A., Reflets 1989, 157-160 / 117s / 83-88.

e155 *Feissel* Denis, *Gascou* Jean, Documents d'archives romains inédits [acquis dans le commerce des antiquités] du Moyen Euphrate (III siècle après J.-C.]: CRAI (1989) 535-561.

e156 MARI 5, RCiv 1987: ᴿBO 46 (1989) 101-7 (M. *Anbar*: 'riche' but some 150 improvements).

e157 *Melebiya* (Khabour) 4th 1987: Akkadica 61 (1989) 1-10+21 pl. (M. *Lebeau*, al.).

e158 *Munbaqa: Feyter* T. de,   The 'Aussenstadt' settlement of Munbaqa, Syria: ➤ 122, ᶠLOON M. van 1989, 237-256; 8 fig.

e159 *Nebi Mend* (Qadeš/Orontes): *Mathias* Virginia T., *Parr* Peter J.,   The early phases at Tell Nebi Mend; a preliminary account: Levant 21 (1989) 13-29; 12 fig.; 29-32, plants, *Moffett* Lisa.

e160 *Bruyn* M.J. de,   The battle of Qadesh; some reconsiderations: ➤ 122, ᶠLOON M. van, To the Euphrates 1989, 135-165; 5 maps.

e161 *Palmyra: Gawlikowski* Michel,   Le commerce de Palmyre sur terre et sur eau: ➤ 822, Arabie/mers 1985/8, 163-172; map.

e162 *Parlasca* Klaus,   *a)* Beobachtungen zur palmyrenischen Grabarchitektur: DamaszMit 4 (1989) 181-190; 1 fig.; pl. 49-52; – *b)* Palmyrenische Bildnisse aus dem Umkreis Zenobias: ➤ 209, ᶠWERNER R., Xenia 22 (1989) 205-9+4 fig.

e163 *Sadurska* Anna,   Die palmyrenische Grabskulptur: Altertum 34 (1988) 14-23; 8 fig.

e164 *Schmidt-Colinet* Andreas,   Flachdach und Giebel; zur Bekrönung des Tempelgrabes Nr. 86 von Palmyra: ➤ 62, ᶠFRANZ H. 1986, 329-331; 5 fig. p. 621-4.

e165 *Starcky* J. (1952), ²*Gawlikowski* M., Palmyre 1985 ➤ 3,e512; 4,g65: ᴿAJA 93 (1989) 159s (S.T. *Parker*).

e166 *Qamišli:* Meijer Diederik J.W.,   A survey in northeastern Syria 1986 ➤ 2,a848: ᴿJAOS 109 (1989) 506-8 (M.C. *Astour*).

e167 *Qara Qûzâq* 1988 [Euphrates 60k S frontier]: AulaO 7 (1989) 269-277; 2 maps; 4 phot. (G. del *Olmo Lete*).

e168 *Qaṣr/Ḥayr:* Schlumberger Daniel, *al.*,   Qasr el-Heir el Gharbi: BAH 120. P 1986, Geuthner. 36 p.; 84 pl. 2-7053-0258-1 [OIAc N89].

e169 *Qasrij:* Curtis John (*Collon* D., *al.*),   Excavations at Qasrij Cliff and Khirbet Qasrij: Western Asiatic Excavations 1. L 1989, British Museum. 79 p.; 4 p. ◐; 49 fig.; 13 pl. £25. 0-7141-1123-6.

e170 *Resāfa:* Mackensen Michael,   Eine befestigte... Resafa 1984 ➤ 65,b159 ... 4,g68: ᴿGnomon 61 (1989) 614-7 (F.W. *Deichmann*).

e171 Ulbert Thilo,   Resafa II. Basilika 1986 ➤ 2,a898 ... 4,g69: ᴿArchaeologia 38 (1987) 221s (S. *Parnicki-Pudelko* ◕); ByZ 82 (1989) 293-6 (U. *Peschlow*); JbAC 32 (1989) 230-3 (P. *Grossmann*); JbÖsByz 38 (1988) 499-501 (H. *Buschhausen*).

e172 *Sūkās:* Lund J.,   Sūkās VIII, The habitation quarters 1986 ➤ 3,e527; 4,g70: ᴿTEuph 1 (1989) 193s (J. *Sapin*).

e173 *Terqa: Rouault* Olivier, Terqa e il deserto: ArchViva 8,6 (1989) 58-64; color. ill.

T6.1   Mesopotamia: *generalia*.

e174 ᶠBRAIDWOOD Robert J., The hilly flanks and beyond, ᴱYoung T.C., *al.* 1983 ➤ 65,24; 4,g78: ᴿAcPraeh 20 (1988) 190-202 (P.P. *Vértesalji*).

e175 **Gasche** H., La Babylonie au 17ᵉ siècle avant notre ère; approche archéologique, problèmes et perspectives: Mesopotamian History and Environment 2/1. Ghent 1989, Univ. xii-161 p.; 46 pl.; 7 foldout plans. ᴱ**Huot** Jean-Louis (p. 293-303 Oueili), Préhistoire... Hamrin 1984/7 ➤ 3,822.

e176 *Matthews* Roger, Excavations in Iraq, 1987-88: Iraq 51 (1989) 249-262; map p. 251.

e177 *Millard* A. R., Mesopotamia and the Bible: Aram 1,1 (Ox 1989) 24-30 [< ZAW 102, 264].

e178 **Moortgat-Correns** Ursula, La Mesopotamia: Storia Universale dell'Arte. T 1989, Unione Tipografica. vii-295 p. 88-02-04237-3 [OIAc Ja90].

e179 *Whittaker* C. M., The absolute chronology of Mesopotamian archaeology, ca. 2000-1600 B.C. and Iron Age Iran: Mesopotamia-T 24 (F 1989) 73-116.

T6.3 *Mesopotamia, scripta effossa* – **Excavated Tablets.**

e180 **Archi** Alfonso, *Pomponio* F., Tavolette economiche neo-sumeriche [102,10 già pubblicata] dell'Università Pontificia Salesiana = VO 8/1 (1989), 112 p. 18 pl. – ᴿSalesianum 51 (1989) 319-323 (F. *Pomponio*).

Arnaud Daniel, Recherches au pays d'Aštata, Emar VI, Textes sumériens et accadiens [4 tombes; 1-3 1986] ➤ e132.

e181 **Cagni** L., Briefe aus dem Iraq Museum (TIM II): AltB Briefe 8, 1980 ➤ 61,t178...: ᴿJNES 48 (1989) 150-5 (Joan G. *Westenholz*, rather an original tabulation taking off also from AltBB 9, M. *Stol*, Letters from Yale 1981).

e182 **Dalley** Stephanie, *Postgate* J. N., The tablets from [Nimrud] Fort Shalmaneser 1984 ➤ 65,b181; 2,a915: ᴿAfO 35 (1989) 169-173 (O. *Pedersén*); ZAss 79 (1989) 272-8 (K. *Watanabe*: viele Verbesserungen).

e183 **Dijk** Jan van (*Falkenstein* A.†, ᴱ*Mayer* W. R.), Literarische Texte aus Babylon: B Museen Vorderas. Schriftdenkmäler 8, 1987 ➤ 3,e553: ᴿBO 46 (1989) 378-384; 3 facsim. (A. R. *George*); Mundus 25 (1989) 102s (W. *Farber*).

e183* *Dijk* J. van, [*Falkenstein* A., Nachlass] Ein spätbabylonischer Katalog einer Sammlung sumerischer Briefe: Orientalia 58 (1989) 441-452; 3 facsim.

e184 **Donbaz** Veysel, Keilschrifttexte in den Antiken-Museen zu Stambul II: FreibAltorSt 2. Stu 1989, Steiner. 128 p.; 45 pl. 3-515-05351-4.

e185 *Eidem* Jesper, Some remarks on the Iltani archive from Tell al Rimah [151 letters; 50 administrative texts]: Iraq 51 (1989) 67-78.

e186 **Forde** Nels W. (*Flaugher* W. Robert), Neo-Sumerian texts from South Dakota University, Luther and Union Colleges. Lawrence ᴋᴀ 1987, Coronado. 55 p. + 25 p. facsimiles. 0-87291-200-0.

e187 **Greengus** Samuel, Studies in Ishchali documents 1986 ➤ 4,g95: ᴿBO 46 (1989) 641-5 (Stephanie *Dalley*); Mesopotamia-T 24 (F 1989) 196-202 (L. *Cagni*).

e188 **Gurney** O. R., *a*) Literary and miscellaneous texts in the Ashmolean Museum: Cuneiform Texts 11. Ox 1989, Univ. 84 p.; 143 facsimiles. 0-19-815468-2 [OIAc N89]. – *b*) Middle Babylonian legal and economic texts from Ur 1983 ➤ 1,d959; 2,a929: ᴿOLZ 84 (1989) 167-9 (J. *Oelsner*).

e189 *Jacobsen* Thorkild, Lugalbanda and Ninsuna [Salabiḫ, *Biggs* R. 1974, Nº 327]: JCS 41 (1989) 69-86.

e190 **Joannès** Francis, Archives de Borsippa; la famille Ea-Ilûta-Bâni, étude d'un lot d'archives familiales en Babylonie du VIIIᵉ au Vᵉ siècles av. J.-C.: ÉPHÉH 2/25. Genève 1989, Droz. v-444 p.; 13 pl., 1 foldout [OIAc Ja90].

e191 **Kutscher** Raphael, The Brockmon tablets of the University of Haifa; Royal inscriptions: Zinman Inst. Shay series. Haifa 1989, Univ. 135 p. 956-311-004-7 / 3-447-02914-5 [OIAc N89].

e192 **Lacheman** Ernest R., *Maidman* Maynard P., Joint Expedition with the Iraq Museum at Nuzi 7, miscellaneous texts: Studies Nuzi/Hurrians [➤ 3,505] 3. WL 1989, Eisenbrauns. xii-307 p. catalogue 19-43; facsimiles 45-307. 0-931464-45-5 [OIAc N89].

e193 **Lafont** B., Documents administratifs sumériens... Tello/Louvre 1985 ➤ 1,d985... 4,g102: ᴿAfO 35 (1988) 179-181 (W. H. P. *Römer*).

e194 **Lafont** Bertrand, Tablettes cunéiformes de Tello au Musée d'Istanbul datant de l'époque de la IIIᵉ Dynastie d'Ur I (ITT II/1, 617-308) / Tabletleri...: Uitgaven 65. İstanbul 1989, Nederlands Hist./Arch. Instituut. 296 p.; p. 273-282 facsimiles; p. 283-296 photos. 90-6258-065-3.

e195 **Leichty** A., *Grayson* A. K., Tablets from Sippar 2, 1987 ➤ 3,e568: ᴿJAOS 109 (1989) 289 (M. A. *Dandamayev*).

e196 **Leichty** Erle, *al.*, Tablets from Sippar 3: Babylonian Tablets 8, 1988 ➤ 4,g103; £50; ᴿZAss 89 (1989) 102-117 (G. van *Driel*, 1-3).

e197 **Livingstone** Alasdair, Court poetry and literary miscellanies: State Archives of Assyria 3. Helsinki 1989, Univ. 951-570-044-2 [OIAc S89].

e198 **Mustafa** Abdul-Kader A., The Old Babylonian tablets from Me-Turan (Tell al-Sib and Tell Haddad) [Diyala; 145 tablets]: diss. Glasgow 1983. 397 p. BRDX-85620. – DissA 50 (1989s) 985s-A.

e199 **Roth** Martha T., Babylonian marriage agreements, 7th-3d centuries B.C. [18 inedita + 36]: AOAT 222. Neuk/Kevelaer 1989, Neuk./Butzon & B. xviii-154 p. DM 93. 3-7887-1311-9 / 3-7666-9636-X [BL 90,40].

e200 **Sachs** Abraham J.†, *Hunger* Hermann, Astronomical diaries and related texts from Babylonia I: Denkschr. 195, 1988 ➤ 4,g110: ᴿOLZ 84 (1989) 672-6 (J. *Oelsner*); Orientalia 58 (1989) 551-5 (Francesca *Rochberg-Halton*).

e201 *Sanati-Müller* Shirin, Texte aus dem [Warka] Sinkāšid-Palast, II. Fischtexte und Bürgschaftsurkunden: BaghMit 20 (1989) 225-313.

e202 **Selz** Gebhard J., Altsumerische Verwaltungstexte aus Lagaš I. Die altsumerischen Wirtschaftsurkunden der Eremitage zu Leningrad: Freib-AltorSt 15,1. Stu 1989, Steiner. 572 p. 3-515-05204-6.

e203 **Sigrist** Marcel, Textes économiques de... Syracuse: RCiv Mém 29, 1983 ➤ 64,b733; 4,g111: ᴿAulaO 7,1 (1989) 146s (M. *Civil*, también sobre Lafont B.).

e204 **Sigrist** Marcel, Neo-Sumerian account texts in the Horn Archaeological Museum; *Gavin* Carney E. S., seal impressions. Assyriol. [4,1984 ➤ 65,b207b] 6. Berrien Springs MI 1988, Andrews Univ. Inst. Archaeology. vi-101 p.; XCVI pl. 0-943872-31-6.

e205 **Sigrist** Marcel, *Vuk* Tomislav, Inscriptions cunéiformes, SBF Museum 4, J 1987, Franciscan. 62 p.; 15 pl. – ᴿOLZ 84 (1989) 416s (H. *Neumann*).

e206 **Spar** Ira, Cuneiform Texts in the Met I, 1987 ➤ 4,g112 ('1988'): ᴿZAss 89 (1989) 121-4 (D. O. *Edzard*).

e207 **Steinkeller** Piotr, Sale documents of the Ur-III period [diss. ᴰGelb I. Chicago 1977]: FreibAltorSt 17. Stu 1989, Steiner. xvi-395 p.; ill. 3-515-05327-1 [OIAc Ja90].

e208 **Stol** M., Letters from collections in Philadelphia, Chicago and Berkeley 1986 ➤ 2,a952 ... 4,g112*: ᴿOLZ 84 (1989) 289s (H. *Klengel*).

e209 *Stolper* M.W., Malamir [texts, Eng.]: ➤ 905, RLA 7,3s (1988) 276-281 (281-7 archäologisch, *Calmeyer* P.).

e210 *Stone* Garry R., New tablets at 'Ancient Times House': BurH 23 (1987) 53-55 [< OTAbs 11,242].

e211 **Watson** Philip J., Neo-Sumerian texts from Drehem ... Birmingham city museum 1 [Wmr not PBI!] 1986 ➤ 3,e584; 4,g116: ᴿJSS 34 (1989) 183-7 (Tohru *Gomi*).

e212 **Westenholz** Aage, Old Sumerian and Old Akkadian texts in Philadelphia, II, The 'Akkadian' texts, 1987 ➤ 3,e585: ᴿAfO 35 (1988) 176s (M.A. *Powell*); BO 46 (1989) 357-362; 2 facsim. (B.R. *Foster*); WeltOr 20s (1989s) 269s (F. *Pomponio*).

e213 **Whiting** Robert M., Old Babylonian letters [59 out of the 1400 documents] from Tell Asmar [< diss. ᴰ*Gelb* I.]: Assyriological Studies 22, 1987 ➤ 4,g118: ᴿAfO 35 (1988) 177-9 (M. *Stol*); Orientalia 58 (1989) 547-550 (D. *Charpin*).

e214 **Yang Zhi**, Sargonic inscriptions from Adab [diss. Chicago 1987]. Changchun 1989, Inst. History of Ancient Civilizations. xiii-449 p. [OIAc Ja90].

e215 ᴱ**Yıldız** Fatma, *al.*, Die Umma-Texte aus den archäologischen Museen zu Istanbul Nr. 1-600: Materiali per il vocabolario neosumerico 14. R 1988, Multigrafica. 167 p.

T6.5 **Situs effossi 'Iraq** *in ordine alphabetico.*

e216 *Aḫmar* (til Barsip) Melbourne Univ. project: Akkadica 63 (1989) 1-7+5 fig. (G. *Bunnens*).

e217 *Aššur:* **Pedersén** O., Archives and libraries in the city of Assur 1985 ➤ 1,d981 ... 4,g122: ᴿArOr 57 (1989) 285s (Jana *Pečírková*, Eng.).

e218 *Babylon:* **Finkel** Irving L., The hanging gardens of Babylon: ➤ 585, 7 Wonders 1988, 38-58; fig. 18-28.

e219 *Bauer* G.M., ☻ The site of Babylon in epigraphic sources: VDI 189 (1989) 153-7.

e220 *Bit Abu-Ilā'a:* *Fales* Frederick M., The Assyrian village of Bīt Abu-Ilā'a: ➤ 876, Production 1981/9, 169-200.

e221 *Brak:* **Oates** David & Joan, Akkadian buildings at Tell Brak: Iraq 51 (1989) 193-211; 8 fig.; pl. XXII-XXVIII [p. 213-215, *Bowman* S., *Ambers* J., radiocarbon dates; 217-224, *Clutton-Brock* J., dog and donkey skeletons ➤ e961*].

e222 *Hawa:* **Ball** Warwick, *al.*, The Tell al-Hawa project; archaeological excavations in the North Jazira 1986-87: Iraq 51 (1989) 1-66; 29 fig.; pl. I-III [p. 262-5 with map, other sites, *Wilkinson* T.].

e223 *Ḫuwayra:* **Moortgat-Correns** U., Tell Chuēra 1982s. 1985. B 1988, Mann. 99 p.; 42 fig.; 5 plans. DM 50. – ᴿZAss 89 (1989) 297s (U. *Seidl*).

e224 *Imlihīya:* **Boehmer** R.M., *Dämmer* H.-W., Tell Imlihīye... 1985 ➤ 1,g1 ... 4,g135: ᴿOLZ 84 (1989) 296-8 (R.-B. *Wartke*).

e225 *Iščali: Jacobsen* Thorkild, The Mesopotamian temple plan and the Kitîtum temple: ➤ 218, Mem. YADIN Y., ErIsr 20 (1989) 79*-91*; 4 fig.

e226 *Jamdat Naṣr:* **Matthews** R.J., Excavations at Jemdet Nasr, 1988: Iraq 51 (1989) 225-248; 12 fig.; pl. XXXIIIs.

e227 *Khorsabad:* **Albenda** Pauline, The palace of Sargon... wall-reliefs 1986 ➤ 2,a969; 4,g137: ᴿAfO 35 (1988) 212-4 (Erika *Bleibtreu*); AJA 93 (1989) 144s (G. *Beckman*); BASOR 276 (1989) 88-92 (J.M. *Russell*).

e228 *Algaze* Guillermo, Tepe Chenchi, an important settlement near Khorsabad: ⇥ 106, ᶠKANTOR H., Essays 1989, 1-25+4 pl.

e229 *Larsa:* **Kozyreva** Nelli V., ❸ *Drevnyaya*... Ancient Larsa; sketches of economic life: Kultura narodov Vostoka. Moskva 1988, Nauka. 206 p.

e230 *Nimrud:* **Paley** Samuel M., *Sobolewski* Richard P., The reconstruction of the relief representations and their positions in the northwest palace at Kalḫu (Nimrud) II. Rooms I,S,T,Z west wing: DAI BaghFor 10, 1987 ⇥ 3,e602; DM 135: ᴿBL (1989) 126 (D. J. *Wiseman*); Mundus 25 (1989) 37s (K. *Schippmann*: supplement to MEUSZYNSKI J., BaghFor 2, 1981).

e231 **Herrmann** Georgina, a) Ivories/Nimrud IV, 1986 ⇥ 2,a973...4,g144: ᴿWeltOr 20s (1989s) 281-5 (D. *Ciafaloni*); – b) The Nimrud ivories, 1. The flame and frond school: Iraq 51 (1989) 85-109; pl. VIII-XVIII.

e232 *Ninive: Invernizzi* Antonio, L'Héraclès Epitrapezios de Ninive [British Museum]: ⇥ 28, ᶠBERGHE L. Vanden 1989, (II) 623-633 + III pl.

e233 *Nippur: Charpin* Dominique, Un quartier de Nippur et le problème des écoles à l'époque paléo-babylonienne: RAss 83 (1989) 97-112...

e234 *Neumann* Hans, Umma und Nippur in altakkadischer Zeit [*Foster* B. 1982; *Westenholz* A. 1987]: OLZ 84 (1989) 517-527.

e235 **Armstrong** James A., The archaeology of Nippur from the decline of the Kassite Kingdom until the rise of the Neo-Babylonian empire: diss. ᴰ*Gibson* M. Chicago 1989. xi-337 p.; bibliog. p. 327-338. – OIAc Ja90.

e236 *Nuzi:* **Owen** D. I., *Morrison* M. A., ... Excavations at Nuzi 9/1. General studies and excavations. WL 1987, Eisenbrauns. ix-723 p. $65. 0-931464-08-0. – ᴿBO 46 (1989) 386-390 (W. von *Soden*).

e237 *Eichler* Barry L., Nuzi and the Bible; a retrospective: ⇥ 183, ᶠSJÖBERG Å., Dumu- 1989, 107-119.

e238 *Rubeideh:* ᴱ**Killick** R. G., Tell Rubeideh, an Uruk village in the Jebel Hamrin: Salvage Report 7/Iraq Arch. Rep. 2. Wmr 1989, Aris & P. 0-85668-431-7 [OIAc S89].

e239 *Sabra* (Hamrin), anthropologische Ergebnisse: Akkadica 62 (1989) 1-13 + VIII pl. (E. *Burger-Heinrich*).

e240 **Tunca** Ö., Tell Sabra (Hamrin): Akkadica supp. 5. Lv 1987, Peeters. 109 p.; 110 pl. – ᴿMesopotamia-T 24 (F 1989) 194-6 (P. *Mollo*).

e241 *Ṣalabiḫ:* **Martin** Harriet P. (ᴱ*Postgate* J. N.), Abu Salabikh 2, 1985 ⇥ 1,e18; 4,g155: ᴿJAOS 108 (1989) 116s (Elisabeth *Carter*); JNES 48 (1989) 62s (Margaret C. *Brandt*); OLZ 84 (1989) 31s (E. *Lindemeyer*).

e242 **Moon** Jane, Abu Salabīkh excavations, 3. Catalogue of Early Dynastic pottery. L 1987, British School in Iraq. 184 p.; 4 pl. £21 [JAOS 109,340].

e243 **Mander** Pietro, Il pantheon di Abu-Sālabīkh; contributo allo studio del pantheon sumerico arcaico: Studi Asiatici min. 26, 1986 ⇥ 4,g157: ᴿZAW 101 (1989) 161 (J. A. *Soggin*).

e244 *Sippar: Bruschweiler* Françoise, Un échange de terrains entre Nabuchodonozor II et un inconnu dans la région de Sippar: RAss 83 (1989) 153-162; 3 phot.

e245 *Ur:* **Karstens** Karsten, Typologische Untersuchungen an Gefässen aus altakkadischen Gräbern des Königsfriedhofs in Ur; ein Beitrag zur modernen archäologischen Methodik: Mü Univ. ph. 12/Vorderas. 3. Mü 1987, Profil. 246 p.; 104 fig.; 2 foldout maps. – ᴿAfO 35 (1989) 206s (P. R. S. *Moorey*).

e246 *Warka:* Archaische Keramik aus Uruk-Warka [cf. ⇥ 3,e621b]: BaghMit 18, 1987; 268 pl. DM 20. – ᴿMundus 25 (1989) 91 (Eva A. *Braun-Holzinger*).

e247 *Dandamayeva* M. M., *Chekhovich* N. O., ⑬ Results of the exploration in Uruk (1982-1985): VDI 191 (1989) 117-120.

e248 **Eichmann** Ricardo, Uruk; die Stratigraphie, Grabungen 1912-1977 in den Bereichen Eanna und Anu-Ziqqurrat: Uruk-Endberichte 3. Mainz 1989, von Zabern. I. 223 p.; 48 pl.; 106 Beilagen. 3-8053-1032-3.

e249 *Farber* Walter, Lamaštu, Enlil, Anu-iksur; Streiflichter aus Uruks Gelehrtenstuben: ZAss 79 (1989) 223-241.

e250 *Vértesalji* Peter Paul, Das Ende der Uruk-Zeit im Lichte der Grabungsergebnisse der sogenannten 'archaischen' Siedlung bei Uruk-Warka: ActaPraeh 20 (1988) 9-26; 7 fig.; Eng. franç. 9.

T6.7 **Arabia.**

e251 *a*) *Amirkhanov* K. A., ⑬ Ancient Arabia; complete settling and the protohistorical cultural substrate; – *b*) *Breton* J.-F., The work of the French archaeological mission in South Yemen; – *c*) *Maigret* A. de, The work of the Italian archaeological mission in North Yemen: VDI 190 (1989) 164-6 / 148-154; 5 fig.; Eng. 155 / 155-163; 6 fig. Eng. 163. Arabia/Arabic conferences ➜ 812.816.818.819.822.

e252 *Kettenhofen* Erich, Die Sarazenen in der Historia Augusta: ➜ 205, ᶠWALSER G., Labor 1989, 219-231.

e253 *Le Rider* Georges, Le golfe persique à l'époque séleucide; exploration archéologique et trouvailles monétaires: RNum 31 (1989) 248-252; map.

e254 **Parker** S. Thomas, Romans and Saracens (ᴰ1978) 1986 ➜ 2,a987; 3,e633: ᴿByZ 81 (1988) 308-310 (I. *Shahid*); RPg 62 (1988) 377s (A. *Chastagnol*).

e255 **Salibi** Kamal, La Bible est née en Arabie [1985 ➜ 1,e574], ᵀ*Mannoni* Gérard. P 1986, Grasset. 285 p.; 11 maps. – ᴿRÉJ 147 (1988) 173-6 (E.-M. *Laperrousaz*: the author, 'head of the department of history and archeology at Beirut American University' puts imagined excavations in Arabia on same plane as real excavations in Palestine which do not support him anyway).
Shahid Irfan, Rome/Byzantium and the Arabs 1984 ➜ b794.

e256 *Mayerson* Philip, Saracens and Romans; micro-macro relationships [*Banning* E. 1986 vs. *Parker* S. 1987]: BASOR 274 (1989) 71-79.

---

e257 *Dur* (Umm al-Quaiwayn) (U.A.E.) 1987-8: Mesopotamia-T 24 (F 1989) 1-69: Danish 13-26; français 29-56; Belgian 57-69.

e258 *Hadramaut: Griaznevitch* P. A., *al.*, ⑬ Ancient Hadramawt in the light of archaeological studies of the Soviet-Yemeni expedition: VDI 189 (1989) 129-135 [-153].

e259 *Hasa* (S. Arabia): **Potts** D. T., Miscellanea Hasaitica: Niebuhr Inst. 9. K 1989, Univ. 95 p. 87-7289-068-1.

e260 *Hayma:* **Vogt** Burkhard & Ute *Franke*-, Shimal [Ras al-Khaimah] 1985/1986: 1987 ➜ 3,e645: ᴿBO 46 (1989) 710-2 (D. T. *Potts*).

e261 *Himyar: Müller* Walter W., Himyar [SW-Südarabien]: ➜ 904, RAC 15,114s (1989) 303-331; map.

e262 *Failaka/Dilmun:* *a*) *Calvet* Yves, Le pays de Dilmoun au IIᵉ millénaire; découvertes récentes; – *b*) *Lombard* Pierre, Ages du Fer sans fer; le cas de la péninsule d'Oman au Iᵉʳ millénaire av. J.-C.; – *c*) *Parr* Peter J., Aspects of the archaeology of North-West Arabia in the first millennium B.C.; – *d*) *Livingstone* Alasdair, Arabians in Babylonia /

Babylonians in Arabia; some reflections à propos new and old evidence: ➤ 816, L'Arabie 1987/9, 15-24; 2 fig. / 25-37; map / 39-65 / 97-105; 2 fig.

e263 **Salles** Jean-François, *al.*, Failaka 1983, 1984s: 1984/6 ➤ 3,a639; 4,g189: ᴿAfO 35 (1988) 219-222 (D. T. *Potts*).

e264 *a*) *Sanlaville* Paul, Des mers au milieu du désert; mer Rouge et Golfe arabo-persique; – *b*) *Cleuziou* Serge, Dilmoun-Arabie [*Piesinger* C.]: ➤ 822, Arabie/mers 1985/8, 9-26 / 27-58.

e265 *San'a:* ᴱ**Schmidt** J., San'ā': DAI Yemen 3. Mainz 1987, von Zabern. vi-206 p.; 75 fig.; 75 pl.; 11 foldouts. DM 180. – ᴿAfO 35 (1988) 217-9 (Maria *Höfner*).

e266 *Yemen,* Madīnat al-Ahǧur 1981/4: OrAnt 28 (1989) 41-127; 28 fig.; pl. I-XIX (Sabina *Antonini*).

e267 **Maigret** A. de, Sabaean... Yemen. 1988 [OIAc S89].

T6.9   **Iran,** *Persia;*   Asia centralis.

e268 ᴱ**Hole** Frank, The archaeology of western Iran; settlement and society from prehistory to the Islamic conquest [1977 Seminar]. Wsh 1987, Smithsonian ➤ 4,744; g197: 0.87474-526-8, 3 art. by Hole, 8 others.

e269 **Kawami** Trudy S., Monumental art of the Parthian period in Iran: ActIran 26. Leiden 1987, Brill. xviii-272 p.; 32 fig.; 72 pl., 4 maps. – ᴿMesopotamia-T 24 (1989) 205-212 (A. *Invernizzi*).

e270 *a*) *Kuzmina* E. E., The motif of the lion-bull combat in the art of Iran, Scythia, and Central Asia and its semantics; – *b*) *Moscati* Sabatino, Arte storica nell'Eurasia: ➤ 4,144, Mem. Tucci G., Orientalia 2 (1987) 729-745 / 995-1004.

e271 *Masson* V. M., *Korobkova* G. F., Eneolithic stone sculpture in south Turkmenia [E of S Caspian Sea], ᵀ*Wright* Sarah: Antiquity 63 (1989) 62-70; 9 fig.

e272 *a*) *Schacht* Robert, Early historic cultures; – *b*) *Levine* Louis D., The iron age: ➤ 4,744, Archaeology of Western Iran 1977/87, 171-191 + fig. 44-56 / 229-244; fig. 66-73.

e273 *Hasanlu:* **Dyson** Robert H.ᴶ, *Muscarella* Oscar W., Constructing the chronology and historical implications of Hasanlu IV: Iran 27 (1989) 1-27; 17 fig.

e274 *Mārlīk,* tepe: ➤ 905, RLA 7,5s (1989) 426-9; 2 fig. (P. *Calmeyer*).

e275 *Naqš-i Rustam:* **Gall** Hubertus von, Das achämenidische Königsgrab; neue Überlegungen und Beobachtungen: ➤ 28, ᴱBERGHE L. Vanden 1989, 503-518 + 2 fig.; III pl.

e276 **Herrmann** Georgina, *al.*, The Sasanian rock reliefs at Naqsh-i Rustam 6, The Triumph of Shapur I (together with an account of the representations of Kerdir): Iranische Denkmäler 13 / Felsreliefs 1. B 1989, Reimer. Text volume with loose plates. 3-496-00931-4 [OIAc S89].

e277 **Seidl** Ursula, Die elamischen Felsreliefs von Kūrāngūn und Naqš-e Rustam 1986 ➤ 4,g206*: ᴿBO 46 (1989) 454-7 (É. de *Waele*); ZAss 89 (1989) 145-8 (Elisabeth *Carter*).

e278 *Persepolis:* **Sancisi-Weerdenburg** Heleen, Persepolis en Pasargadae in wisselend perspectief; Iraanse Oudheden beschreven en getekende door Europese reizigers [Tentoonstelling 1989]: Phoenix 35/1. Groningen 1989, Ex Oriente Lux. 90-367-0136-8 [OIAc S89].

e279 **Trümpelmann** Leo, Persepolis, ein Weltwunder der Antike [Ausstellung München Sept.-Dez. 1988]. Mainz 1988, von Zabern. 103 p.; 37 fig.

e280 *a*) *Root* Margaret C., The Persian archer at Persepolis; aspects of chronology, style and symbolism; – *b*) *Calmeyer* Peter, Das Datum der ältesten 'Bogenschützen': ➤ 782*, L'or perse 1989 = RÉAnc 91 (1989) 15-29 (-31, interventions) / 51-59; 6 fig.

e281 *Pušt-i Kuh*, Luristan: ➤ 3,822, Préhistoire/Hamrin 1984/7, 55-72 (E. *Haerinck*), 91-126 (L. Vanden *Berghe*), al.

e282 **Schmidt** Erich F., al., The Holmes expedition to Luristan: OIP 108. Ch 1989, Univ. Or. Inst. xv-594 p.; vol. of 265 pl. 0-918986-53-2 [OIAc N89].

e283 *Shiraz:* **Whitcomb** D.S., Before the roses... excavations at Shiraz 1985 ➤ 3,e672; 4,g212: ᴿOLZ 84 (1989) 327-9 (W. *Kleiss*).

e284 *Susa:* **Stève** M.-J., Ville royale de Suse 7, Nouveaux mélanges épigraphiques; inscriptions royales de Suse et de la Susiane: Dél. Arch. Iran Mémoir 53. Nice 1987, Serre. 111 p.; xviii pl. 2-86410-098-3 [OIAc Ja90].

e285 *Tureng:* **Boucharlat** Rémy, *Lecomte* Olivier, Fouilles de Tureng Tepe 1987 ➤ 4,g221: ᴿZAss 89 (1989) 149 (L. *Trümpelmann*).

e286 *Zagros:* **McDonald** Mary M.A., An examination of mid-Holocene settlement patterns in the Central Zagros region. T 1979, Univ. [OIAc S89].

---

e287 **Maillard** M., Grottes et monuments de l'Asie centrale. P 1983, J. Maisonneuve. 282 p.; 83 fig.; 185 pl.; 5 maps. F 680. – ᴿBO 46 (1989) 183-7 (Elisabeth C.L. *During-Caspers*).

e288 **Guillaume** Olivier, *Rougelle* Axelle, Fouilles d'Aï Khanoum 6. Le gymnase; 7. Les petits objets. P 1987, de Boccard. – ᴿRArchéol (1989) 177-9 (Marie-Christine *Hellmann*).

e289 *Brentjes* Burchard, Die 'baktrischen Bronzen', ihre Datierung und die Mitanni-Kunst: ➤ 62, ᶠFRANZ H. 1986, 15-20; 8 fig. p. 501-4.

e290 **Le Berre** Marc, Monuments pré-Islamiques de l'Hindukush central: Mém. 24. P 1987, RCiv. 2-86538-171-4. – ᴿAfO 35 (1988) 223s (K. *Jettmar*).

e291 ᴱ**Ligabue** Giancarlo, *Salvatori* Sandro, Bactria; an ancient oasis civilisation from the sands of Afghanistan. Venezia 1989, Erizzo. 187 p.; 9 fig.; 40 pl.; 4 maps. 88-7077-025-7. – ᴿAntiquity 63 (1989) 849s (K.R. *Maxwell-Hyslop*).

e292 *Ligabue* Giancarlo, *Salvatori* Sandro, Treasures of the Bactrian sands [Afghanistan 2000 B.C.]; ILN 277, 7092 (1989) 40-52; color. phot.

e293 ᵀᴱ**Begley** W.E., *Desai* Z.A., Taj Mahal, the illumined tomb; an anthology of seventeenth century Mughal and European documentary sources. CM/Seattle 1989, Aga Khan Program for Islamic Architecture/Univ. Washington. lvi-320 p.; 167 fig. 0-295-96944-X; pa. -5-8.

e293* **Schimmel** Annemarie, al., Vergessene Stadt am Indus; frühe Kulturen in Pakistan vom 8-2 Jahrtausend v. Chr. [Ausstellung Aachen Jun.-Sept. 1987]. Mainz 1987, von Zabern. 3-8053-0957-0 [? pa.] 82-X.

T7.1 **Aegyptus**, *generalia*.

e294 **Berger** Jean-Denis, Imago caeli; l'image de l'Égypte en Occident latin durant l'Antiquité tardive (IIIᵉ-VIIᵉ siècles: Diss. Paris-IV 1989. – RÉLat 67 (1989) 36.

e295 *Bietak* Manfred, *a*) Probleme, Aufgaben und Zukunft der Feldforschung in Ägypten; – *b*) Archäologischer Befund und historische Interpretation am Beispiel der Tell el-Yehudia-Ware: ↠ 823, Akten IV 2 (1985/9) 1-6 / 7-18 + 17 fig.

e296 **Bohm** Dorothy, Egypt ['text by Ian *Jeffrey*'], foreword *Durrell* Lawrence. L 1989, Thames & H. 112 p. $30. 0-500-54150-7 [OIAc S89].

e297 **Bourriau** Janine, Pharaohs and mortals; Egyptian art in the Middle Ages. C 1988, Univ. 167 p.; 191 fig. $49.50; pa. $18. 0-521-35319-X; 846-9 [AJA 93,491].

e298 **Brunner-Traut** Emma, Die alten Ägypter⁴. Stu 1987, Kohlhammer. 272 p.; 171 fig. + 20 color. DM 89. – ᴿBiKi 44 (1989) 133s (P.-G. *Müller*).

e299 ᶠDAUMAS François, Hommages 1986 ↠ 2,18: ᴿBO 46 (1989) 284-290 (L. *Pantalacci*).

e300 **David** A. Rosalie, Ancient Egypt. Ox 1988, Phaidon. viii-152 p.; (colour.) ill. 0-7148-2472-0.

e301 **Dorman** Peter F., The monuments of Senenmut; problems in historical methodology. L 1988, Kegan Paul. xvi-247 p.; 22 pl.

e302 *a*) *Egberts* A., Wetenschap in Egypte en Babylonië; – *b*) *Willems* H. O., Geleerde doden [Egypte]; Phoenix EOL 35,2 (1989) 5-20 / 21-38; 4 fig.

e303 *Eschweiler* Peter, Bildzauber im alten Ägypten; die Verwendung von Bildern und Gegenständen in magischen Handlungen nach den Textzeugnissen des Mittleren- und Neuen Reiches: Diss. Heid. 1989 [OIAc S 89: from 'working copy of a revision for the Ph.D. Degree'].

e304 **Fischer** H. G., L'histoire et l'art de l'Égypte ancienne... paléographie 1986 ↠ 2,7606: ᴿRHist 280,567 (1988) 238-340 (Y. *Kœnig*).

e305 *Glassner* Gottfried, Im Land der Mönchsväter; Eindrücke einer Reise zu den koptischen Klöstern (27. I. bis 10.II.1989): ErbAuf 65 (1989) 210-222.

e306 **Holzner** Anna, Die Bautätigkeit der 18. Dynastie bis zur Amarnazeit nach archäologischen und urkundlichen Belegen in Ägypten und Nubien: Diss. ᴰ*Arnold* D. Wien 1989. 219 p. – OIAc N89.

e307 **Kemp** Barry J., Ancient Egypt, anatomy of a civilization. L 1989, Routledge. 0-415-01281-3 [OIAc S89].

e307* *Kitchen* K. A., Supplementary notes on 'The basics of Egyptian chronology': ↠ 831*, High/Low [I (1987) 37-55] III (1989) 151-9.

e308 ᴱ**Kurth** Dieter, *Rössler-Köhler* Ursula, Zur Archäologie des 12. oberägyptischen Gaues... Surveys 1980-1: GöOrF 4/16, 1987 ↠ 3,e707: ᴿMundus 25 (1989) 29s (W. *Schenkel*).

e309 *Leclant* Jean, *Clerc* Gisèle, Fouilles et travaux en Égypte et au Soudan, 1987-1988: Orientalia 58 (1989) 335-427; pl. XVI-LXIX.

e310 *Loprieno* Antonio, Book reviews once more [defense of 'jargon' (in his 1986 'Crossroad' article) against R. H. *Pierce*, AcOr 49 (1988) 133-8]: GöMiszÄg 112 (1989) 35-41.

e311 ᶠPARKER Richard A., Egyptological studies, ᴱ**Lesko** L. H. 1986 ↠ 3,126: ᴿBO 46 (1989) 24-29 (S. *Pernigotti*: analisi dettagliate).

e312 *Pernigotti* Sergio, Dove scorre il Nilo; i grandi centri dell'Egitto antico: Archeo 55 (sett. 1989) 50-99; ill. Lit. 7500.

Petrie W. M. Flinders, Hyksos and Israelite Cities 1906 = 1989 ↠ d721.

e313 *Posener-Kriéger* Paule, Travaux de l'IFAO au cours de l'année 1988-1989: BIFAO 89 (1989) 291-341.

e314 *Redford* Susan & Donald B., Graffiti and petroglyphs old and new from the Eastern Desert: JAmEg 26 (1989) 3-49; 91 fig.

e315 **Romano** James F., The Bes-Image in pharaonic Egypt: diss. NYU, ᴰ*Bothmer* B. NY 1989. xii-879 p.; bibliog. p. 222-252. 89-16086. – OIAc Ja90.

e316 *Rutherford* John B., Construction stresses on obelisks: ➤ 823, Akten IV 2 (1985/9) 125-131 + 5 fig.

e317 **Schüssler** Karlheinz, Kleine Geschichte der ägyptischen Kunst: Tb 214. Köln 1988, DuMont. 382 p.; ill. DM 24. 3-7201-1602-X [BO 46,627].

e318 **Sourouzian** Hourig, Les monuments du roi Merneptah [diss. Éc. Louvre 1982]: DAI-K Sond. 22. Mainz 1989, von Zabern. ix-237 p.; 43 pl. 3-8053-1053-6 [OIAc Ja90].

e319 **Tzara** Tristan, L'Égypte face à face²; préf. *Leclant* J. Pierrevert 1988, Sved. 116 p.; photos d'Étienne Sved.

e320 **Valbelle** Dominique, La vie dans l'Égypte ancienne: Que sais-je? 1302. P 1988, PUF. 125 p.; 11 fig. 2-13-041730-2.

e321 ᶠVERCOUTTER J., Mélanges, ᴱ**Geus** F. ... 1985 ➤ 1,141: ᴿBO 46 (1989) 562-6 (B. *Vachala*, summary of each of the 34 articles in German, with pp. but without titles); CdÉ 64 (1989) 172s (Helen *Jacquet-Gordon*).

e322 **Wildung** Dietrich, Die Kunst des alten Ägypten (L'Art de l'Égypte),ᵀ. FrB 1988, Herder. 252 p.; 81 fig.; 95 pl.

e323 **Wreszinski** Walter, Atlas zur altägyptischen Kulturgeschichte: Classiques de l'Égyptologie. Genève 1988 (I = 1923), 1989 (II-III = 1925), Slatkine. 13 p.; 1000 pl. – ᴿRTPhil 121 (1989) 449 (M. *Patané*).

e324 *Yurco* Frank J., Were the ancient Egyptians black or white?: BAR-W 15,5 (1989) 24-29.58 [all shades]: 8.10.12, letters regarding Nefertiti.

T7.2 **Luxor,** *Karnak* [East Bank] – **Thebae** [West Bank].

e325 **Abdel-Raziq** Mahmud. Das Sanktuar Amenophis' III. im Luxor-Tempel: Studies in Egyptian Culture 3. Tokyo 1986, Waseda Univ. 113 p.; ill.; maps.

e326 **Abd el-Raziq** Mahmud, Die Darstellungen ... Alexanders, Luxor 1984 ➤ 4,g264: ᴿArOr 57 (1989) 194s (B. *Vachala*, deutsch).

e327 *Gamer-Wallert* Ingrid, Neue Funde im Tempel Amenophis' III. von Luxor: AntWelt 20,3 (1989) 3-8; color. ill.

e328 *Siliotti* Alberto, Nel segno di Amon [la scoperta di Luxor]: ArchViva 8,6 (1989) 8-21; (color.) ill.

e329 *Azim* Michel, Karnak et sa topographie: GöMiszÄg 113 (1989) 33-46.

e330 **Golvin** J.-C., *Goyon* J.-C., Les bâtisseurs de Karnak 1987 ➤ 3,e718: ᴿBO 46 (1989) 609-611 (J.-L. *Chappaz*).

e331 *Graindorge* Catherine, *Martinez* Philippe, Karnak avant Karnak; les constructions d'Aménophis Iᵉʳ et les premières liturgies amoniennes: BSocFrÉg 115 (1989) 36-55; 13 fig.; 9 pl.

e332 *Leclant* J., *Clerc* Gisèle, Karnak-Nord; rive gauche thébaine: ➤ e309, Orientalia 58 (1989) 379-395.

e333 *a) Le Fur* Daniel, *Delcroix* Gilbert, Caractérisation de matériaux et techniques de la peinture murale à Karnak à des fins de conservation et restauration; la palette d'un artisan peintre du Moyen Empire; – *b)* *Kákosy* László, Ungarische Grabungen in Theben - TT 32: ➤ 823, Akten IV 2 (1985/9) 101-112; 2 fig. / 211-4 + 1 fig.; pl. 18-20.

e334 *Peden* A. J., The usurped Karnak stela of Ramesses V [then X; Pylon IV south wing]: GöMiszÄg 110 (1989) 41-45 + phot.

e335 *Rondot* Vincent, *Golvin* Jean-Claude,   Restaurations antiques à l'entrée de la salle hypostyle ramesside du temple d'Amon-Rê à Karnak: MiDAI-K 45 (1989) 249-259; 5 fig.; pl. 29-31.

e336 **Therasse** Isabelle,   Ankhnesneferibré, dernière Divine Adoratrice et Divine Épouse de l'époque pharaonique (566-525 av. J.-C.) [fille de Psammétique II; chapelles de Karnak]: mémoire de license, Lv 1985, ᴰ*Vandersleyen* C. – RArtLv 18 (1985) 196s.

e337 **Traunecker** Claude, *al.*,   La chapelle d'Achôris à Karnak 1981 ➤ 64,b909 ... 2,b54: ᴿJNES 48 (1989) 315-8 (M. *Smith*).

e338 **Abitz** Friedrich,   Baugeschichte und Dekoration des Grabes Ramses' VI.: OBO 89. FrS/Gö 1989, Univ. / VR. 196 p. 3-7278-0637-0 / 3-525-53719-0 [OIAc S89].

e339 **Abitz** F.,   Ramses III in den Gräbern seiner Söhne ... OBO 72, 1986 ➤ 2,b59; 4,g271: ᴿRB 96 (1989) 437s (R. *Beaud*).

e340 *Abitz* Friedrich,   Die Entwicklung der Grabachsen in den Königsgräbern im Tal der Könige: MiDAI-K 45 (1989) 1-25; 14 fig.

e341 *Altenmüller* Hertwig,   Untersuchungen zum Grab des Bai (KV 13) im Tal der Könige von Theben [Arbeiten 1988 Univ. Hamburg]: GöMiszÄg 107 (1989) 43-54; 5 fig.

e342 **Beinlich** Horst, *Saleḥ* Mohamed,   Corpus der hieroglyphischen Inschriften aus dem Grab des Tutanchamun mit Konkordanz der Nummersysteme des Journal d'Entrée des Ägyptischen Museums Kairo, der Handlist to Howard CARTER's Catalogue of Objects in Tut'anchhamun's Tomb und der Ausstellungs-Nummer des Ägyptischen Museums Kairo. Ox 1989, Ashmolean. 0-900416-53-X [OIAc S89].

e343 *Blumenthal* Elke,   Der Tempel des Mentuhotep Nebhepetre in Deir el-Bahari [*Arnold* D. 1976-79-81]: OLZ 84 (1989) 5-12.

e344 **Brack** Annelies † & Arthur,   Das Grab des Tjanuni / Haremheb, Theben Nr. 74/78, 1977/80 ➤ 61,t356 / ➤ 62,k13: ᴿWZKM 77 (1987) 155-163; 8 fig. (Lise *Manniche*, 'to fill a few essential gaps in the otherwise excellent books').

e345 *Dodson* Aidan,   Hatshepsut and 'her father' Mentuhotpe II: JEA 75 (1989) 224-6; pl. XXIX.

e346 *Dodson* Aidan, *Janssen* J.J.,   A Theban tomb and its tenants: JEA 75 (1989) 125-138; 3 fig.; pl. X-XI.

e347 *Dziobek* Eberhard,   Eine Grabpyramide des frühen NR in Theben: MiDAI-K 45 (1989) 109-132; 7 fig.; pl. 4-8.

e348 **Eaton-Krauss** M., *Graefe* E.,   The small golden shrine from the tomb of Tutankhamun [Thebes] 1985 ➤ 1,e138; 3,e774: ᴿJEA 75 (1989) 271-3 (Kate *Bosse-Griffiths*); OLZ 84 (1989) 659-662 (W. *Westendorf*).

e349 *Eaton-Krauss* M.,   Walter SEGAL's [German] documentation of CG 51113, the throne of Princess Sat-Amun [from Tuyu-Yuya tomb; background of awaited 'Thrones, chairs, and stools from the tomb of Tutankhamun']: JEA 75 (1989) 77-88; 4 fig.; pl. IX.

e350 *Gabolde* Luc (& Marc), Les temples 'mémoriaux' de Thoutmosis II et Toutânkhamon (un rituel destiné à des statues sur barques): BIFAO 89 (1989) 127-178; 3 fig.; pl. XIII-XXIV.

e351 *Guidotti* M. Cristina,   Il tempio funerario di Tutmosi IV a Gurna; la ceramica della 'cappella superiore': EgVO 12 (1989) 55-68; 69-77, drawings partly in color.

e352 **Hari** Robert, La tombe thébaine du père divin Neferhotep (TT 30) 1985
➤ 1,e119; 4,g280: ᴿJEA 75 (1989) 273-5 (Lise *Manniche*); JNES 48
(1989) 228-230 (C.C. *Van Siclen*: Neferhotep was 'the god's father of
Amun').

e353 *Hassanein* Fathy, al., La nécropole de la Troisième Période Intermédiaire
du Ramesseum I/II implantée sur les aménagements périphériques du
temple et de ses annexes; étude architecturale: ➤ 823, Akten IV 2 (1985/9)
181-189-197; 3+3 fig.; pl. 14-16.

e354 *Leblanc* Christian, Architecture et évolution chronologique des tombes
de la Vallée des Reines: BIFAO 89 (1989) 227-247; pl. XXX-XXXI.

e355 **Manniche** Lise, City of the dead; Thebes in Egypt, British Museum 1987
➤ 3,e728; also Ch 1987, Univ. 146 p.; 100 fig. – ᴿJAmEg 26 (1989) 239s
(Arielle P. *Kozloff*).

e356 *Meulenaere* Herman De, Notes de prosopographie thébaine IV: ➤ 204,
Mém. WALLE B. van de, CdÉ 64 (1989) 55-73.

e357 **Polz** Daniel, Das Grab Nr. 54 in Theben: diss. Heid 1988. xii-414 p.; 54
pl. – OIAc Ja90.

e358 **Saleḥ** Mohamed, Das Totenbuch 1984 ➤ 3,e744: ᴿArOr 57 (1989) 194s
(B. *Vachala*, deutsch).

e359 **Shaheen** Alaa el-Din M., Historical significance of selected scenes
involving Western Asiatics and Nubians in the private Theban tombs
of the XVIIIth dynasty; diss. Pennsylvania, ᴰ*O'Connor* D. Ph 1988s.
xxviii-490 p. 89-08387. – OIAc N89.

e360 *Théodoridès* Aristide, Pèlerinage au Colosse de Memnon: CdÉ 64
(1989) 207-282.

e361 *Van Siclen* Charles C., New data on the date of the defacement of
Hatshepsut's name and image on the Chapelle Rouge [Karnak]:
GöMiszÄg 107 (1989) 85s; 1 fig.

e362 **Ventura** Raphael, 'Living in a city of the dead'...: OBO 69, 1986
➤ 3,e752; 4,g284: ᴿAfO 35 (1988) 246-8 (H. *Brunner*); JNES 48 (223s)
(J. G. *Manning*).

e363 **Wachsman** Shelley, Aegeans in the Theban tombs 1987 ➤ 3,e746;
4,g285: ᴿIntJNaut 18 (1989) 188 (Vronwy *Hankey*).

e364 *Wehausen* J.V., al., The Colossi of Memnon and Egyptian barges:
IntJNaut 17 (1988) 295-310.

e365 **Whale** Sheila, The family in the eighteenth dynasty of Egypt; a study of
the representation of the family in private tombs: Studies 1., Sydney
1989, Australian Centre for Egyptology. x-308 p.; 13 pl. 0-85837-670-9
[OIAc N89].

e366 *Witkowski* Maciej G., Le rôle et les fonctions des chapelles d'Anubis
dans le complexe funéraire de la reine Hatshepsout à Deir el Bahari:
➤ 823, Akten IV 3 (1985/9) 431-440 (2, 53-63, *Karkowski* Janusz,
restoration).

e367 *Worp* K.A., Studies on Greek ostraca from the Theban region [some
topographical ...]: ZPapEp 76 (1989) 45-62.

---

e368 **Fornari** Annamaria, *Tosi* Mario, Nella sede della verità; Deir el Medina
e l'ipogeo di Thutmosi III; pref. *Khadry* A.; *Donadoni* S. Mi 1987, F.M.
Ricci. 229 p.; 27 color. pl. insert. 88-216-0116-1.

e369 *Valbelle* Dominique, 'Les ouvriers de la tombe'; Deir el-Médineh à
l'époque ramesside: IFAO BibÉt 96, 1985 ➤ 1,e131; 4,g288: ᴿJAOS 109
(1989) 690-4 (C.A. *Keller*); JEA 75 (1989) 279s (M.L. *Bierbrier*).

Della Monica Madeleine, La classe ouvrière... Deir el Medineh² 1988 ➤ g292.

e370 **Jaroš-Deckert** Brigitte, *al.*, Grabung im Asasif 5. Jnj-jtj.f Wand-malereien ... 1984 → 65,b331; 3,e734: ᴿArOr 57 (1989) 296s (B. *Va-chala*, deutsch); BO 46 (1989) 592-601 (Marco *Willems*: clear, reliable).

T7.3 Amarna.

e371 **Aldred** Cyril, Akhenaten king of Egypt ['more than a revision' of 1968] 1988 → 4,g290: ᴿBA 52 (1989) 151s (G. *Alford*); BAR-W 15,3 (1989) 6.8 (S.T. *Hollis*: no documentation).
Eaton-Krauss M., *Graefe* E., The small golden shrine from the tomb of Tutankhamun 1985 → e348.

e372 *Edel* Elmar, Ägyptische Glossen in den Geschenklisten des Amar-nabriefes Nr. 14: StAltÄgK 16 (1989) 27-33.

e373 **Endruweit** Albrecht, Die Wohnhäuser in Amarna; zur architektonischen Resonanz auf die Erfordernisse eines Wüstenklimas: GöMiszÄg 112 (1989) 11-22.

e374 **Green** Lynda, Queens and princesses of the Amarna period; the social, political, and cultic role of the women of the royal family at the end of the Eighteenth Dynasty: diss. ᴰ*Redford* D. Toronto 1988. 604 p.; bibliog. 567-600; 50 pl. (or 7 microfiches). 0-315-46331-7 [OIAc Ja90].

e375 **Hari** Robert, New Kingdom Amarna period; the great Hymn to Aton: IconRel 16/6, 1985 → 1,e141; 3,e760: ᴿRB 96 (1989) 438s (R. *Beaud*).

e376 *Hess* Richard S., Cultural aspects of onomastic distribution in the Amarna texts [*Albright* W.; *Helck* W.]: UF 21 (1989) 209-216.

e377 *Ikram* Salima, Domestic shrines and the cult of the royal family at el-'Amarna: JEA 75 (1989) 89-101; 3 fig.

e378 **Kemp** Barry, Amarna reports [→ 65,b349 ... 4,g303ss] 5, 1989. L 1989, Egypt Expl. Soc. viii-290 p. 0-85698-109-5 [OIAc Ja90]. – ᴿBO 46 (1989) 601-7 (M. *Eaton-Krauss*, 3s); CdÉ 64 (1989) 194-6 (R. *Hari* †, 2).

e379 **Khouli** A. El-, *Kanawati* N., Quseir el-Amarna; the tombs of Pepy-ankh and Khewen-wekh: Reports 1. Sydney 1989, Australian Centre for Egyptology. 57 p.; 46 pl. 0-85837-663-6 [OIAc N89].

e380 *Leclant* J., *Clerc* Gisèle, Amarna 1988: → e309, Orientalia 58 (1989) 274s.

e381 **Moran** William L., Les lettres d'El-Amarna ...: LIPO 13, 1987 → 3,e766; 4,g308: ᴿBiblica 70 (1989) 566-572 (A.F. *Rainey*); OLZ 84 (1989) 670-2 (H. *Klengel*); RB 96 (1989) 599 (M. *Sigrist*); RSO 63 (1989) 168-171 (M. *Liverani*); ZAss 89 (1989) 128s (D.O. *Edzard*: Dank und Bewunderung).

e382 *Perepelkin* G.Ya., ❹ The kings' priest at the head of the state [from incomplete vol. 3 of Perevorot Amen-hotpa IV]: VDI 190 (1989) 4-28; Eng. 28.

e383 **Redford** Donald B., Akhenaten 1984 → 65,b351 ... 4,g310: ᴿArOr 57 (1989) 299-301 (L. *Young*).

e384 *Wells* R.A., The Amarna M,X,K boundary stelae date; ḥwt-itn ceremonial altar; initial results of a new survey [1988]: StAltÄgK 16 (1989) 289-327; 16 fig.; pl. 9-12.

e385 *Zonhoven* L.M.J., Toetanchamon en de dieven?: PhoenEOL 34,2 (1988) 59s.

T7.4 Memphis, *Saqqara* – Pyramides, *Giza* (Cairo).

e386 *a) Brinks* Jürgen, Die Entwicklung der Mastaba bis zum Ende des Alten Reiches; – *b) Walsem* René van, The mastaba project at Leiden University: → 823, Akten IV 2 (1985/9) 35-44; 3 fig. / 143-154.

e387 **Cherpion** Nadine, Mastabas et hypogées d'Ancien Empire; le problème de la datation. Bru 1989, Connaissance de l'Égypte Ancienne. 241 p.; 72 fig.; 48 pl. 2-87268-001-1.

e388 **Davies** W. V., *al.*, The mastabas of Mereri and Wernu 1984 → 65,b359 ... 4,g317: ᴿOLZ 84 (1989) 407-410 (E. *Martin-Pardey*).

e389 **Jeffreys** D. G., The survey of Memphis, I. The archaeological report 1985 → 1,e159: ᴿBO 46 (1989) 590s (A. R. *Schulman*); JEA 75 (1989) 256-9 (M. *Jones*).

e390 *Jeffreys* D. G., *Giddy* Lisa L., Memphis, 1988: JEA 75 (1989) 1-12; 6 fig.; pl. 1.

e391 **Khouli** A. El-, *Kanawati* N., Excavations at Saqqara II: Northwest of Teti's Pyramid. Sydney 1988, Macquarie Univ. Documentary Research Centre. 48 p.; 49 pl. 0-85837-626-1.

e392 *Leclant* J., *Clerc* Gisèle, (Giza) Saqqara, Memphis: → e309, Orientalia 58 (1989) 356-366.

e393 **Martin** Geoffrey T., Corpus of reliefs of the New Kingdom from the Memphite necropolis and Lower Egypt I, 1987 → 4,g329: ᴿOrientalia 58 (1989) 289s (H. G. *Fischer*).

e394 **Martin** Geoffrey T., The Memphite tomb of Ḥoremheb commander-in-chief of Tut'ankhamūn; I. The reliefs, inscriptions, and commentary: Memoir 55. L 1989, Egypt Expl. Soc. xxvii-182 p.; 175 pl. 0-85698-089-9.

e395 **Martin** Geoffrey T., *al.*, The tomb-chapels of Paser and Ra'ia at Saqqara 1985 → 1,e163; 4,g330: ᴿJEA 75 (1989) 278s (A.-P. *Zivie*, français).

e396 **Thompson** Dorothy J., Memphis under the Ptolemies 1988 → 4,g340; $37.50: ᴿAmJPg 110 (1989) 509-512 (J. F. *Oates*).

e397 *Zivie* Alain-Pierre, *a)* Recherches et découvertes récentes dans la tombe d'Aperia à Saqqarah: CRAI (1989) 490-505; 9 fig.; – *b)* Le trésor funéraire du vizir 'Aper-El [Saqqara]: BSocFrÉg 116 (1989) 31-44; 7 fig.

---

e398 *Clayton* Peter A., The great pyramid of Giza: → 535, 7 Wonders 1988, 13-37; fig. 1-17.

e399 **David** A. Rosalie, I costruttori delle piramidi; un'indagine sugli operai del Faraone [1986 → 2,b115],ᵀ. T 1989, Einaudi. xiii-251 p.; ill. 88-06-11589-8.

e400 **Davidovits** Joseph, *Morris* Margie, The pyramids; an enigma solved [the blocks are synthetic geopolymers, a type of concrete]. NY 1989, Hippocrene. 255 p. – ᴿArchaeology 42,4 (1989) 66s (R. S. *Bianchi*).

e401 — *Vandersleyen* Claude, *Putter* Thierry De, Pyramides de Giza; de la géopolymérisation à la géopoésie [...'opiniâtreté' de J. *Davidovits*, 1986 Revue des Questions Scientifiques de Bru-Namur]: GöMiszÄg 110 (1989) 65-74.

e402 *a)* *Hansen* Bent H., The construction of the Cheops Pyramid by means of a rope; – *b)* *Ryan* Donald P., Belzoni's rope from the tomb of Sethos I: → 823, Akten IV 2 (1985/9) 45-52; 2 fig. / 137-142; pl. 34.2.

e403 *Hatamori* Yasuko, ❶ The administration of Pyramid City and 'overseer of the Pyramid City' in the Old Kingdom: Oriento-Japan 32,1 (1989) 50-66; Eng. 50s.

e404 **Jacq** Christian, Le voyage aux pyramides. P 1989, Perrin. 141 p.; ill. 2-262-06639-3.

e405 **Jéquier** Gustave, Les pyramides des reines Neit et Apouit [Ṣaqqâra]. Le Caire 1933, reprint 1984, Org. Ég. du Livre. IV-63 p.; 37 fig.; 40 pl. – ᴿOLZ 84 (1989) 159-162 (E. *Martin-Pardey*).

e406 *Kákosy* László, The plundering of the pyramid of Cheops: StAltÄgK 16 (1989) 145-169; 1 fig.

e407 *Lally* Michael T., Engineering a pyramid: JAmEg 26 (1989) 207-218; 11 fig.

e408 **Lauer** Jean-Philippe, Le problème de la construction de la grande pyramide: ➤ 39, Mém. CLÈRE J., RÉgp 40 (1989) 91-111; 18 fig.; pl. 1-3; Eng. p. 111.

e409 *Legon* John A. R., *a*) The design of the [Giza Second] Pyramid of Khaefre: GöMiszÄg 110 (1989) 27-34; 2 fig.; – *b*) The geometry of the Great Pyramid [*Trench* J.]: GöMiszÄg [102 (1988) 85-94] 108 (1989) 57-64.

e410 **Lehner** Mark, The pyramid tomb of Hetep-heres and the satellite pyramid of Khufu: DAI-K Sonderschr. 19, 1985 ➤ 2,b120: ᴿCdÉ 64 (1989) 192-4 (R. *Tefnin*); JEA 75 (1989) 261-5 (I. E. S. *Edwards*).

e411 **Stadelmann** Rainer, Die ägyptischen Pyramiden 1985 ➤ 1,e169: ᴿJEA 75 (1989) 265s (E. *Graefe*, deutsch).

e412 *Trench* Jorge A., *Fuscaldo* Perla, Observations on the pyramidions [capstones that terminate a pyramid (no mention of obelisks)]: GöMiszÄg 113 (1989) 81-90.

e413 **Yoshimura** Sakuji, *al.*, Non-destructive pyramid investigation (2); Studies in Egyptian Culture 8. Tokyo 1988, Waseda Univ. [xvi-] 90 p.; 57 fig.; 11 color. pl.

e414 *Dahšur:* **Arnold** Dieter, Der Pyramidenbezirk des Königs Amenemhet III. in Dahschur, I. Die Pyramide 1987 ➤ 4,g352: ᴿBO 46 (1989) 316-9 (R. J. *Leprohon*).

e414* *Faltings* Dina, Die Keramik aus den Grabungen an der nördlichen Pyramide des Snofru in Dahschur ... 1983-6: MiDAI-K 45 (1989) 133-154; 11 fig.; pl. 9.

e415 *Lišt:* **Arnold** Dieter, *al.*, The pyramid of Senwosret I: South Cemeteries of Lisht 1. NY 1988, Met. 157 p.; 104 (foldout) pl. 0-87099-506-5.

---

e416 ᴱ**Beyer** Ursula, Kairo Mutter aller Stadt: Tb 696. Fra 1983, Insel. 3-458-32396-1 [OIAc S89].

e416* **Saad el-Din** Morsi, *al.*, Cairo, the site and the history. Baton Rouge 1988, Louisiana State Univ. 99 p.; ill. $25 [JNES 48,78].

e417 *Stricker* B. H., The empire of Heliopolis [*Sethe* K. 1930]: ➤ 859, Delta 1988/9, 293-300.

e417* *Awadalla* Atef, *Okasha* Sadek, Une paroi de la tombe du chancelier royal P3-Nḥsy à Héliopolis: Orientalia 58 (1989) 493-6; pl. LXXI-LXXII.

e418 *Ramadan* Wagdy, Was there a chapel of Nehebkaw in Helio-polis[-Matariyya; red quartzite statue of Ramesses II]? GöMiszÄg 110 (1989) 55-61 + 4 phot.

e419 *a*) **Kubiak** Władysław B., Al-Fustat; its foundation and early urban development. NY 1987, Columbia Univ. (for Cairo American Univ.). $20. 977-424-100-2. – ᴿJAmEg 26 (1989) 252-4 (Caroline *Williams*); – *b*) **Scanlon** George T., Fusṭāṭ Expedition Final Report, I. Catalogue of Filters; II. with *Kubiak* Władysław, Fusṭāṭ-C: AmResEg Reports

8.11.   WL 1989, Eisenbrauns.   ix-153 p.; 204 fig.; 24 pl. / x-101 p.; 113 fig.; plan apart.   0-936770-13-9.

T7.5   Delta Nili.

e420 *Favard-Meeks* Christine,   Le delta égyptien et la mer jusqu'à la fondation d'Alexandrie: StAltÄgK 16 (1989) 39-63.

e421 *Mokhtar* Gamal,   Classical archaeology of the Delta; a general survey: ➤ 859, Delta 1988/9, 217-226.

e422 *Panić* Miroslava,   Some evidence concerning the Delta of Egypt during the reign of Amenhotep III: ➤ 859, Delta 1988/9, 251-7.

e423 *Quirke* Stephen,   Frontier or border? The north-west Delta in Middle Kingdom texts: ➤ 859, Delta 1988/9, 261-273; discussion 274s.

---

e424 *Alexandria:* **Canfora** Luciano,   La véritable histoire de la bibliothèque d'Alexandrie.   P 1988, Desjonquères.   212 p.   2-904227-24-5 [OIAc N89].

e425 *Delia* Diana,   The population of Roman Alexandria: AmPgTr 118 (1988) 275-292; 1 fig.

e426 **Townsend** G.,   Caesar's war in Alexandria; Bellum civile iii. 102-112; Bellum alexandrinum 1-33.   Bristol / Wauconda 1988, Classical / Bolchazy-C.   vi-66 p.; map. £5.   1-85399-044-2 / US 0-86516-219-0 [JRS 79,269].

e427 *Marsa Matruk:* **Bates's** Island, 2d 1987: JAmEg 26 (1989) 87-114; 21 fig. (D. *White*; 115-126, Linda *Hulin*, ceramic).

e428 *Natrûn:* **Yamagata** Takao,   Coptic monasteries at Wadi al Natrun in Egypt; from the field notes on the Coptic monks' life: Studia Culturae Islamicae 20.   Tokyo 1983 [OIAc S89].

e429 *Pelusium:* **Carrez-Maratray** Jean-Yves,   Les relations entre l'épigraphie pélusienne et le Nord-Sinai: ➤ 859, Delta 1988/9, 53-60.

e430 *Qantîr:* **Pusch** Edgar B.,   Bericht über die sechste Hauptkampagne in Qantir/Piramesse-Nord, Herbst 1988: GöMiszÄg 112 (1989) 67-90 + 5 fig.; 1 foldout [no finds indicated as confirming the name Piramesse for the site]; 113 (1989) 7-24 + 9 fig., *Aston* David A., Pottery report 1988.

e431 *Ṣaḫa:* **Khachab** Abd el-Muhsin el-,   *Ta Sarapeia* à Ṣakha [Delta] et au Fayum, ou les Bains Thérapeutiques: ASAE Sup. 25.   Cairo 1978, Egyptian Museum.   210 p.; ill. – ᴿOLZ 84 (1989) 154s (K. *Parlasca*).

e432 *Tanis:* **Brissaud** Philippe, Tanis capitale du Delta: Archéologia 243 (1989) 22-38; ill.

e433 *Tumilat:* **Redmount** Carol Ann,   On an Egyptian/Asiatic frontier; an archaeological history of the Wadi Tumilat: diss. ᴰ*Stager* L.   Chicago 1989.   3 vol.; xv-978 p.; bibliog. p. 962-978. – OIAc Ja90.

e434 *Zagazig:* **Snape** Steven R.,   Six archaeological sites in Sharqiyeh province 1986 ➤ 3,e811; 4,g386: ᴿBO 46 (1989) 608s (K. *Martin*).

e435 *Bakr* Mohammed I.,   The Old Kingdom at Bubastis; excavations since 1978; outline: ➤ 859, Delta 1988/9, 29-49 + 3 pl.

T7.6   *Alii situs Aegypti* **alphabetice.**

e436 *Abu Mina:* **Grossmann** Peter,   Abu Mina I. Die Gruftkirche und die Gruft: DAI-K ArchV 44.   Mainz 1989, von Zabern.   3-8053-0508-7 [OIAc S89].

e437 *Abu Simbel:* **Navet** Dominique,   Les aspects de la reine Néfertari Mérenmouth [épouse de Ramsès II] d'après les reliefs du petit temple d'Abou Simbel; mémoire de license, Lv 1986, ᴰ*Vandersleyen* C. – RArtLv 19 (1989) 344.

e438 *Abydos:* a) *Baines* John, al., Techniques of decoration in the hall of barques [not 'baroques' as page-head] in the temple of Sethos I at Abydos; – b) *Leahy* Anthony,   A protective measure at Abydos in the thirteenth dynasty [Cairo stela found c. 1900]:   JEA 75 (1989) 13-30; pl. III-IV / 41-60; 2 fig.; pl. VI-VII.

e438* **Murray** Margaret A.,   The Osireion at Abydos. L 1989 = 1904, Quaritch [OIAc S89].

e439 *O'Connor* David,   New funerary enclosures (Talbezirke) of the Early Dynastic Period at Abydos: JAmEg 26 (1989) 51-86; 19 fig.

e440 a) *Silverman* David P.,   The so-called Portal Temple of Ramses II at Abydos: → 823, Akten IV 2 (1985/9) 269-277; 2 fig.; pl. 34.1; – b) *Lavier* Marie-Christine,   Les mystères d'Osiris à Abydos d'après les stèles du Moyen-Empire et du Nouvel-Empire: Akten IV 3 (1985/9) 289-295.

e441 **Caulfield** A. S.,   The temple of the kings at Abydos; chapter by *Petrie* W. M. F., drawings by Christie L. (1902): Brit. School Eg 8. Histories and Mysteries of Man. L 1989, Quaritch. 1-854-17040-6 [OIAc S89].

e442 *Aḥmîm:* *Quaegebeur* Jan,   Une stèle [funéraire] ptolémaïque d'Akhmim: GöMiszÄg 112 (1989) 43-52; 2 fig.

e443 *Akoris:* ᴱ**Kawanishi** Hinoyuki, *Tsujimura* Sumiyo,   Preliminary report, seventh/eighth season of the excavations at the site of Akoris [Minya], Egypt, 1987/8.   Kyoto 1988/9, Paleological Asn.   (1989) 56 p.; 21 fig. + Coptic mss.; 21 pl.

e444 *'Arabâ:* **Garstang** John,   El Arabah, a cemetery of the Middle Kingdom; survey of the Old Kingdom temenos; graffiti from the Temple of Sety: BritSchEg 6. L 1989 = 1900, Histories and Mysteries of Man. 1-854-17038-4 [OIAc S89].

e445 *Ašmunayn:* **Spencer** A. J., al.,   Excavations at El-Ashmunein II. The temple area. L 1989, British Museum. 90 p.; 112 pl. 0-7141-0950-9.

e446 *Szafrański* Zbigniew E., *Makramallah* Atta,   A new inscription of Nektanebū II from Ashmunein: GöMiszÄg 112 (1989) 65s.

e447 *Aswan;* Elephantine 17th, 1987: → e309, Orientalia 58 (1989) 397-9 (J. *Leclant,* G. *Clerc*).

e448 *Heilporn* Paul,   Les nilomètres d'Éléphantine et la date de la crue: CdÉ 64 (1989) 283-5.

e449 **Habachi** Labib,   Elephantine II. The sanctuary of Heqaib 1985 → 1,e208; 4,g194: ᴿJEA 75 (1989) 266-270 (Rita E. *Freed*).

e450 a) *Jaritz* Horst,   Nilkultstätten auf Elephantine: → 823, Akten IV 2 (1985/9) 199-209; 2 fig. – b) *Laskowska-Kusztal* Ewa,   Imhotep d'Éléphantine: Akten IV 3 (1985/9) 281-8.

e451 *Asyût:* **Ryan** Donald P.,   The archaeological excavations of David G. HOGARTH at Asyut, Egypt: diss. ᴰ*Lorton* D.   Cincinnati 1988, Union of Experimenting Colleges. 89-03766. – OIAc Ja90.

e452 *Spanel* Donald B.,   The Herakleopolitan tombs of Kheti I, *jt(-j)jb(-j),* and Kheti II at Asyut: Orientalia 58 (1989) 301-314; pl. VI-XIII.

e453 *Beni Hasan:* **Spanel** Donald,   Beni Hasan in the Herakleopolitan period: diss. Toronto 1985. Ottawa 1985, National Library, 5 microfiches. 0-315-18826-X [OIAc S89].

e454 *Dakhleh:* *Goedicke* Hans,   The Pepi II decree from Dakhleh: BIFAO 89 (1989) 203-212; pl. XXVIII.

e455 *Pantalacci* Laure, Les chapelles des gouverneurs de l'oasis et leurs dépendances (fouilles de l'IFAO à Balāṭ — 'Ayn Aṣīl, 1985-9) [Dakhla]: BSocFrÉg 114 (1989) 64-79; 9 fig.; 3 pl.

e456 **Valloggia** Michel, *al.*, Balat I 1986 ➤ 2,b151: ᴿBO 46 (1989) 314-6 (P. *Charvát*).

e457 *Valloggia* Michel, Nouvelles fouilles de l'IFAO dans la nécropole de Qila' el-Dabba (Balat); le dégagement du mastaba de Pepi-Ima: BSoc-FrÉg 116 (1989) 17-30; 9 fig.

e458 **Deir/Berša:** *Willems* Marco, Deir el-Bersheh [east of Mallawi]; preliminary report [Leiden Univ. 1988]: GöMiszÄg 110 (1989) 75-83; 12 fig.

e459 **Dendera:** **Castel** G., *al.*, Les fontaines de la Porte Nord: Dendara – Monuments de l'Enceinte Sacrée. Le Caire 1984, IFAO. viii-36 p.; 15 fig.; 18 pl.; 7 plans. – ᴿJAmEg 26 (1989) 241s (S. E. *Sidebotham*).

e460 *Cauville* Sylvie, La chapelle de Thot-Ibis à Dendera édifiée sous Ptolémée Iᵉʳ par Hor, scribe d'Amon-Rê: BIFAO 89 (1989) 43-66; pl. III-VII.

e461 *Winter* Erich, A reconsideration of the newly discovered building inscription on the Temple of Denderah [*Daumas* F. 1975]: GöMiszÄg 108 (1989) 75-85.

e462 *Dûš: Reddé* Michel, Le trésor de Douch: CRAI (1989) 427-445; 6 fig.

e463 **Elkab:** *Quaegebeur* Jan, Le petit obélisque l'Elkab et la Dame du terroir d'en haut: ➤ 204, Mém. WALLE B. van de, CdÉ 64 (1989) 121-133; 5 fig.

e463* *Farafra:* Barich Barbara E., *Hassan* Fekri A., The Farafra Oasis archaeological project (Western Desert, Egypt), 1987 field campaign: OriginiR 13 (1984-7) 117-191.

e464 *Fara'in: Way* Thomas von der, *al.*, Tell el-Fara'in-Buto, 4. Bericht: MiDAI-K 45 (1989) 275-318; 20 fig.; pl. 36.

e465 **Fayûm,** Kom Madi 1989: EgVO 12 (1989) 1 (E. *Bresciani*); 3-19 rilievo topografico di Medinet Madi (W. *Ferri*); 21-32, cappella di Alessandro a Kom Madi (G. *Nicola*, R. G. *Arosio*).

e466 **Garf Hussein:** **Tanbouli** M. A. L. el-, *Kuentz* C., *Sadek* A. A., Garf Hussein III. La grande salle (E), mur est, piliers et colosses. Le Caire 1975, Centre d'Études. 87 p.; 47 pl. à part. [OIAc N89].

e467 **Jabl Zeit:** **Castel** Georges, *Soukiassian* Georges, Gebel El-Zeit I. Les mines de galène (Égypte, IIᵉ millénaire av. J.-C.): Fouilles 35. Le Caire 1989, IFAO. 140 p.; ill. 2-7247-0090-2.

e468 **Heracleopolis:** *Pérez Die* M. C., Excavaciones en Heracleópolis Magna (Egipto), campaña de 1988: AulaO 7,1 (1989) 128s [132, correction to her 6 (1988) 62].

e469 **Hermopolis:** **Snape** Steven, *Bailey* Donald, The great portico at Hermopolis Magna; present state and past prospects: Occas. Paper 63. L 1988, British Museum. IX-122 p.; 54 pl.

e470 **Hudi:** **Sadek** Ashraf I., The amethyst mining inscriptions of Wadi el-Hudi II, 1985 ➤ 3,9693: ᴿJEA 75 (1989) 270s (E. S. *Meltzer*).

e471 **Idfu:** **Finnestad** Ragnhild B., Image of the world and symbol of the Creator ... Temple of Edfu: StOrRel 10 [diss. Bergen] ➤ 1,e224; 3,e837; x-174 p.; 9 pl. DM 44. 3-447-02504-2: ᴿBO 46 (1989) 41-43 (Sylvie *Cauville*).

e472 **Kellia:** **Makowiecka** Elżbieta, Excavations in Kellia, 1981-1986; ᵀ*Szonert* Agnieszka. Archaeologia 38 (Wrocław 1987) 185-200; 16 fig.

e473 **Kharga:** **Devauchelle** Didier, *Wagner* Guy, Les graffites du Gebel Teir; textes démotiques et grecques: Rech.Arch.Pg.Hist. 22. Le Caire 1984, IFAO. viii-61 p.; 34 pl.; map. – ᴿOLZ 84 (1989) 18s (S. P. *Vleeming*).

e474 *Cruz-Uribe* Eugene, [Kharga/Hibis] Oasis of the spirit: Archaeology 42,5 (1989) 48-53.

e475 *Kôm/Aḥmar:* *Gestermann* L., *al.*, al-Kōm al-aḥmar / Šārūna 1989: GöMiszÄg 111 (1989) 7-15 + 3 fig.

e476 *Kôm Abû Billu:* *Pelsmaekers* J., Studies on the funerary stelae from Kom Abou Billou: BBelgRom 59 (1989) 5-29.

e477 *Kôm/Ḥiṣn:* **Silverman** David P., The tomb chamber of Ḥsw the Elder; the inscribed material at Kom El-Ḥisn: AmResEg 10. WL 1988, Eisenbrauns. I. ix-146 p.; 131 fig. 0-936770-17-1.

e478 *Kôm Ombo:* **Wettengel** Wolfgang, Der Papyrussumpf als mythischer Ort; zu einem Relief im Tempel von Kom Ombo: Magisterarbeit, ᴰ*Wildung* D., München 1989. iii-85 p. [OIAc N89].

e479 *Ma'adi:* **Rizkana** Ibrahim, *Seeher* Jürgen, *al.*, Maadi III [Cairo Univ. 1930-53]; the non-lithic small finds and the structural remains of the predynastic settlement: DAI-Veröff 80. Mainz 1989, von Zabern. 141 p.; 32 pl. 3-8053-1050-1.

e480 *Malkata:* **Watanabe** Yasutada, *Seki* Kazuaki, The architecture of 'Kom el Samak' at Malkata-South; a study of architectural restoration: Studies in Egyptian Culture 5. Tokyo 1986, Weseda Univ. 40 p.; 36 fig.; 20 (color.) pl.

e481 *Mašayiḫ:* **Ockinga** Boyo C., *Masri* Yahya al-, Two Ramesside tombs at El Mashayikh, I. The tomb of Anhurmose; the outer room. Sydney 1988, Macquarie Univ. Ancient History Documentary Research Centre. xi-79 p.; 66 pl. 0-85837-632-6.

e482 *Naqada:* *Bard* Kathryn A., The evolution of social complexity in predynastic Egypt; an analysis of the Naqada cemeteries [27 k NW Luxor]: JMeditArch 2 (1989) 223-248.

e483 *Philae:* **Vassilika** Eleni, Ptolemaic Philae: OrLovAn 34. Lv 1989, Univ./Peeters. xxiv-403 p.; 44 pl. /90-6831-200-6 [OIAc Ja90].

e484 *Tebtunis: Gallazzi* Claudio, *Minaglou* G. Hadji, Fouilles anciennes et nouvelles sur le site de Tebtynis: BIFAO 89 (1989) 179-191-202; 6 fig.; pl. XXV-XXVII.

T7.7   **Antiquitates Nubiae et alibi.**

e485 **Curto** Silvio, Le sculture egizie... Ville Torlonia: ÉPR 105, 1985 ➤ 1,e258... 4,g436: ᴿAntClas 58 (1989) 558s (R. *Tefnin*).

e486 ᴱ**Hägg** Tomas, Nubian culture 1986/7 ➤ 4,740: ᴿBO 46 (1989) 324-7 (B. *Gratien*).

e487 **Hintze** Fritz, *al.*, Felsinschriften aus dem sudanesischen Nubien: 1963 Nubien-Expedition 1. B 1989, Akademie. 3-05-000369-3 [OIAc S89].

e488 **Manton** E. Lennox, Roman North Africa. L 1988, Seaby. 144 p.; 72 fig.

e489 ᶠMÜLLER C. Detlef G.: Nubia et Oriens Christianus, 60. Gb., ᴱScholz Piotr O., *Stempel* Reinhard: Bibliotheca Nubica I, 1988 (➤ 3,118 '1987'); DM 175: ᴿOrChr 73 (1989) 240-2 (H. *Kaufhold*).

e491 *Piacentini* Patrizia, Le stele di 'Horo sui coccodrilli' del Museo Civico Archeologico di Bologna: StEgPun 4 (1989) 1-15 + VII pl.

e492 *Ricci* Lanfranco, Appunti archeologici: RasEtiop 32 (1988) 129-165.

e493 **Scandone Matthiae** Gabriella, Egitto e Sardegna; contatti fra culture: Atlante Sardegna Fen.-Pun. 3. Sassari 1988, Chiarella. 49 p. [OIAc N89].

e493* **Török** László, Late antique Nubia; history and archeology of the southern neighbour of Egypt in the 4th-6th C. A.D.; pref. *Kirwan* L.: Antaeus 16, 1988 ➤ 4,g467: ᴿOrientalia 58 (1989) 542-6 (B. G. *Trigger*).

e494 a) *Török* László, Kush and the external world; – b) *Scholz* P. O., Kann die kuschitische Umwelt nur auf Ägypten und die Mittelmeerländer beschränkt werden? [zu Török]: ➤ 814, Meroitica 1984/9, 49-162 + 370 fig. / 317-346 + 6 fig.

e495 **Williams** Bruce B., Excavations between Abu Simbel and the Sudan frontier 2-4: Neolithic, A-group, and Post-A-group remains from cemeteries W, V, S, Q, T, and a cave east of cemetery K: Nubian Expedition 4. Ch 1989, Univ. Oriental Institute. xxvii-141 p. 0-918986-54-0.

e496 **Barkal** jabl: **Robisek** Christian, Das Bildprogramm des Muttempels am Gebel Barkal: Univ. Inst. Afrik. 52. Wien 1989, Afro. 123 p. 3-85043-052-9 [OIAc Ja90].

e497 **Vincintelli** Irene, Barkal, gebel (Sudan), palazzo di Natakamani 1987s: OrAnt 28 (1989) 129-150; + fig. 1-3; pl. XX-XXVII.

e498 **Būhēn:** **Gayar** El-Sayed El-, *Jones* M. P., A possible source of copper ore fragments found at the Old Kingdom town of Buhen [N. Sudan]: JEA 75 (1989) 31-40; 5 fig.

e499 **Dodekaschoinos:** **Burkhardt** Adelheid, Ägypter und Meroiten im Dodekaschoinos 1985 ➤ 1,9188; 4,g453:   ᴿArOr 57 (1989) 84-86 (E. *Strouhal,* Eng.); JAmEg 26 (1989) 245s (K. *Grzymski*).

e500 **Faras:** **Dzierzykray-Rogalski** Tadeusz, The bishops of Faras, an anthropological-medical study 1985 ➤ 3,e829:   ᴿBO 46 (1989) 329-332 (E. *Strouhal*).

e501 **Hasa:** a) *Tayeb* Mahmoud el-, Sculptured relief from al-Hasa (Sudan); – b) *Grzymski* Krzysztof, The Nubian collection in the Royal Ontario Museum, a survey; – c) *Haynes* Joyce L., *Leprohon* Ronald J., Napatan shawabtis in the Royal Ontario Museum; – d) *Millet* N. B., Nubian heraldry: ➤ 181, ᶠSHINNIE P., JSSEg 17,1 (1987) 56s; pl. X / 15-17 / 18-32 / 33-35; pl. I-III.

e502 **Kalabša:** **Wright** George R. H., The Ptolemaic sanctuary of Kalabsha; its reconstruction on Elephantine Island: ArchVeröff 3/1. Mainz 1987, von Zabern. 92 p. DM 120. – ᴿBO 46 (1989) 612-5 (J. *Karkowski*); Mundus 25 (1989) 137s (Ingrid *Gamer-Wallert*).

e503 **Strouhal** Eugen, W. Qitna and Kalabsha-S, I, 1984 ➤ 65,b440 ... 4,g456: ᴿAfO 35 (1988) 245s (M. *Bietak*).

e504 **Kerma:** a) *Ahmed* Saleh M., A Napatan residential building at Kerma; – b) *Bonnet* Charles, Un bâtiment résidentiel d'époque napatéenne à Kerma; premières interprétations: ➤ 614, Meroitica 1984/9, 843-848 + 6 fig. / 853-861.

e505 **Meroe:** **Hofmann** Inge, *Tomandl* Herbert, Unbekanntes Meroe: BeiSud Beih 1. W 1986, Univ. Inst. Afrikanistik. 132 p.; 173 (color.) fig. – ᴿBO 46 (1989) 65-67 (K, *Grzymski:* haphazard).

e506 ᴱ**Hintze** Fritz, Meroitistische Forschungen 1980/4 ➤ 65,708; 3,e889: ᴿOLZ 84 (1989) 284-7 (H. *Jacquet-Gordon*).

e507 a) *Leclant* Jean, Meroe et Rome; – b) *Kormysheva* E. Y., Political relations between the Roman Empire and Meroe; – c) *Török* László, Meroitic art; informations and illusions; ➤ 814, Meroitica 1984/9, 29-45 / 305-315 / 535-548.

e508 **Nag'/Šayma:** **Bietak** Manfred, *Schwarz* Mario, Nag' el-Scheima; eine befestigte christliche Siedlung und andere christliche Denkmäler in

Sayala-Nubien, I. Die österreichischen Grabungen 1963-1965: Berichte Unesco 8 / Österr. Akad. Denkschrift 191, 1987 → 3,e893; 216 p.; 65 fig.; 60 pl.; 10 foldout plans. DM 80. – ᴿOrientalia 58 (1989) 295-7 (P. *Grossmann*).

e508* *Saggai: Caneva* Isabella, *al.*, Pottery-using gatherers and hunters at Saggai (Sudan); preconditions for food production: OriginiR 12,1 (1983) 7-29 (-271); Eng. 275-8.

e509 *Tabo* (also called Argo): **Maystre** Charles, Tabo I, statue en bronze d'un roi méroïtique 1986 → 4,g478: ᴿAfO 35 (1989) 252 (Inge *Hofmann*); BO 46 (1989) 70-72 (P. L. *Shinnie*).

e510 *Qasr Ibrim: Driskell* Boyce N., Quantitative approach to Nile Valley basketry; basketry analysis at Qasr Ibrim: → 814, Meroitica 1984/9, 451-467.

e511 *Ukma:* **Vila** André, Le cimetière kermaïque d'Ukma Ouest 1987 → 3,e895: ᴿAulaO 7,1 (1989) 149-151 (V. M. *Fernández Martínez*); BO 46 (1989) 327-9 (Inge *Hofmann*); JAmEg 26 (1989) 248s (C. *Bonnet*).

---

e512 **Cyrene: Laronde** André, Cyrène et la Libye hellénistique; Libykai historiai. P 1987, CNRS. 524 p.; 185 fig.; map. – ᴿArchEspArq 62 (1989) 355s (M. A. *Elvira*); RNum 31 (1989) 263-5 (G. *Le Rider*).

e513 ᴱ**White** Donald, The extramural sanctuary of Demeter and Persephone at Cyrene, Libya [excavations 1969 & 1978]: Final Reports 2s. Ph 1985-7, Univ. Museum. xxii-140 p.; 18 fig.; 33 pl.; map / lii-131 p.; 36 fig.; 84 pl.; map, plan. ⊘ summaries. – ᴿAJA 93 (1989) 476s (Susan B. *Matheson*).

e514 *Ghirza:* **Brogan** Olwen, *Smith* D. J., *al.*, Ghirza, a Libyan settlement in the Roman period [fieldwork 1953-7]: Libya Antiqua 1. Tripoli 1984, Antiquities Dept. 327 p.; 115 fig.; 172 pl. – ᴿAJA 93 (1989) 486s (D. *White*); JRS 79 (1989) 233-5 (D. J. *Mattingly*); RArchéol (1989) 406s (R. *Rebuffat*).

e515 *Sabratha:* **Kenrick** Philip M., Excavations at Sabratha [KENYON K., WARD-PERKINS J. 1948-51] 1986 → 3,e882: ᴿJRS 78 (1988) 254s (Teresa *Clay*).

e516 **Sommerlatte** Herbert W. A., Gold und Ruinen in Zimbabwe [*Mauch* Karl 1871]. Gü 1987, Bertelsmann. xiv-304 p. DM 35. – ᴿMundus 25 (1989) 41s (E. *Beuchelt*).

T7.9 Sinai.

e516* *Figueras* Pau, The North Sinai road in the Graeco-Roman period: ScrClasIsr 8s (1988) 53-64; 65, map.

e517 *Gatier* Pierre-Louis, Les traditions et l'histoire du Sinaï du IVᵉ au VIIᵉ s.: → 816, L'Arabie 1987/9, 499-523.

e518 *Oren* E. D., *Shereshevski* J., ➌ Military architecture along the 'ways of Horus' — Egyptian reliefs and archaeological evidence [Karnak reliefs represent factually Egypt's military organization in northern Sinai]: → 218, Mem. YADIN Y., ErIsr 20 (1989) 8-22; 12 fig.; Eng. 193*.

e519 ᴱ**Rainey** Anson F., Egypt, Israel, Sinai 1982/7 → 3,834: ᴿAJA 93 (1989) 609s (J. M. *Weinstein*); BL (1989) 40 (K. A. *Kitchen*).

e520 **Solzbacher** Rudolf, Mönche, Pilger und Sarazenen; Studien zum Frühchristentum auf der südlichen Sinai-halbinsel, von den Anfängen bis zum Beginn islamischer Herrschaft [Diss. Münster 1987]: Münsteraner

Theol. Abh. 3. Altenberge 1989. 444 p.; 24 fig.; 13 maps. DM 80 [RHE 85, 88-91, C. *Cannuyer*].
e521 **Stewart** Frank H., Bedouin boundaries in central Sinai and the Southern Negev; a document from the Aḥaywāt tribe: Mediterranean Language and Culture Mg 2, 1986 ➤ 4,g485; DM 36: ᴿJAOS 109 (1989) 714s (C. *Bailey*: some inconsistencies).
e522 *Valbelle* Mlle Dominique, Recherches archéologiques récentes dans le Nord-Sinaï: CRAI (1989) 594-607; 9 fig.

T8.1 **Anatolia**, *generalia*.

e523 **Akşit** Ilhan, The civilisation of Western Anatolia. Schaumberg 1987, Merhaba. – ᴿAJA 93 (1989) 480 (R. L. *Pounder*; inaccurate and unmethodical; adds to AKURGAL only the many color photos).
e524 *Algaze* Guillermo, A new frontier; first results of the [Turkish] Tigris-Euphrates archaeological reconnaissance project, 1988: JNES 48 (1989) 241-255 + 14 plans; phot. fig. 15-36.
e524* **Belke** Klaus, *al.*, Galatien und Lykaonien: Tabula Imperii Byzantini 4 / Denkschr. 172, 1984 ➤ 1,e580: ᴿJRAS (1989) 312s (W. C. *Brice*: pattern of roads).
e525 **Durugönül** Serra, Die Felsreliefs im Rauen Kilikien: BAR-Int 511. Ox 1989. vi-260 p. 0-86054-652-7 [OIAc N89].
e526 **Edwards** Robert W., The fortifications of Armenian Cilicia: DumbO Studies 33, 1987 ➤ 4,g491: ᴿMuséon 102 (1989) 214-7 (J.-M. *Thierry*).
e527 **Elsner** Jacques, Sites antiques du sud-ouest de l'Anatolie: Bodrum Yachting Loisirs bleus. P 1987, de Boccard. 144 p. (ill. *Binhas* Yuda). – ᴿAntClas 58 (1989) 515s (C. *Delvoye*).
e528 *Işık* Fahri, ❶ Batı uyğarlığının kökeni... East-West cultural and artistic links of the early iron age: TürkArk 23 (1989) 1-24 + 28 phot.
e529 *Jasink* Anna Margherita, I Greci in Cilicia nel periodo neo-assiro: Mesopotamia-T 24 (F 1989) 117-128.
e530 *Kull* Brigitte, Untersuchungen zur Mittelbronzezeit in der Türkei und ihrer Bedeutung für die absolute Datierung der europäischen Bronzezeit: PraehZts 64 (1989) 48-73; 16 fig.
e531 **Laminger-Pascher** Gertrud, Lykaonien und die Phryger: Szb ph/h 532. W 1989, Österr. Akad. 56 p.; map. 3-7001-1627-6.
e532 ᶠLAROCHE E., Acta Anatolica, colloque 1985, ᴱLebrun R. = Hethitica 8, 1987 ➤ 3,824: ᴿOLZ 84 (1989) 174-6 (H. *Klengel*: tit. pp.).
e533 **Lloyd** Seton, Ancient Turkey; a traveller's history of Anatolia. L 1989, British Museum. 240 p.; 92 pl.; 8 maps. £17. 0-7141-1127-9 [Antiquity 63,827]. – ᴿScripB 20 (1989s) 40 (W. G. E. *Watson*).
e534 *Mellink* Machteld J., Archaeology in Anatolia: AJA 93 (1989) 105-133; 24 fig.; map.
e535 ᶠNASTER Paul: Archéologie et religions de l'Anatolie ancienne, ᴱDonceel R. .... 1983 ➤ 64,82: ᴿBO 46 (1989) 713-730 (J. V. *Canby*: some long summaries, no tit. pp.).
Padovese L., *al.*, Turchia, i luoghi delle origini cristiane 1987 ➤ g554.
e536 **Petzl** G., Die Inschriften von Smyrna: Inschriften griechischer Städte aus Kleinasien 24,1. Bonn 1987, Habelt. xi-337 p. DM 98. – ᴿJHS 109 (1989) 243-6 (A. G. *Woodhead*: also on Keramos 30; Klaudiu Polis 31; Hadrianoi 33; Mylesa 34/1).
e537 Recent archaeological research in Turkey [from reports duly attributed]: AnSt 39 (1989) 175-185.

e538 **Roos** Paavo,   Survey of rock-cut chamber-tombs in Caria, I.
South-eastern Caria and the Lyco-Carian borderland: SIMA 72.1.
Göteborg 1985, Åström. 129 p.; 73 pl. – [R]AnzAltW 42 (1989) 238s (J.
Borchhardt).

e539 **Sinclair** T. A.,   Eastern Turkey, an architectural and archaeological
survey [I. 1987 → 3,e920] II. L 1989, Pindar. xiii-453 p.; 62 pl.; 3 maps.
0-907132-33-2 [OIAc S89]. – [R]Byzantion 59 (1989) 537-9 (C. *Delvoye*, 1);
ByZ 89 (1989) 304-6 (N. *Thierry*, 1, franç.).

e540 **Smith** David N.,   HERODOTOS and the archaeology of Asia Minor; a
historiographic study: diss. Univ. Calif. Berkeley 1987. xx-291 p.

e541 **Waelkens** Marc,   Die kleinasiatischen Türsteine 1986 → 2,b207...
4,g505:   [R]Latomus 48 (1989) 722 (A. *Martin*); RBgPg 67 (1989) 227s (P.
Gros).

e542 **Wagner** Jörg,   Lykien; seine Kunstdenkmäler und archäologischen
Stätten: AntWelt Sondernummer 20b (1989).

e543 **Wagner** Jörg,   Türkei, die Südküste von Kaunos bis Issos: Cicerone. Z
1986, Artemis. 257 p. – [R]Der Islam 65 (1988) 183s (B. *Spuler*: nicht
Führer; Handbuch der Archäologie).

e543* *Wickert* U.,   Kleinasien: → 911, TRE 19 (1989) 244-265; foldout map.

T8.2   **Boğazköy**, *Hethaei* – **The Hittites.**

e544 *Alexander* Robert L.,   A great queen on the sphinx piers at Alaca
Hüyük: AnSt 39 (1989) 151-8; 3 fig.; pl. XXVIII-XXX.

e545 *a) Bittel* Kurt,   Der Schwertgott in Yazılıkaya; – *b) Neve* Peter,   Zur
sogenannten hethitischen Brücke in Hattuscha-Boğazköy: → 5, [F]AKUR-
GAL E. = Anadolu 21 (1987 for 1978ss) 21-28; 3 pl. / 67-70; foldout plan;
9 fig.

e546 *a) Gorny* Ronald L.,   Environment, archaeology, and history in Hittite
Anatolia; – *b) Canby* Jeanny V.,   Hittite Art: BA 52 (1989) 78-96; ill. /
109-129; ill.

e547 *a) Güterbock* Hans G.,   Bilingual moon omens from Boğazköy; – *b)*
Hoffner Harry A.[J],   A scene in the [Hittite] realm of the dead: → 166,
Mem. SACHS A. 1988, 161-173 / 191-199.

e548 **Klengel** Horst,   Die Keilschriftarchive von Boğazköy; Probleme der
Textüberlieferung und der historischen Interpretation: Szb DDR ges. w.
11-G (1987). B 1988, Akademie. 22 p. 3-05-000527-0.

e549 **Müller-Karpe** Andreas,   Hethitische Töpferei der Oberstadt von Hattuša
[... Boğazköy 1978-82]: StVFrG 10. Marburg 1988, Hitzerath. 197 p.; 5
fig.; 64 pl.; 72 plans.

e549* **Neu** Erich,   Althethitische Ritualtexte in Umschrift: StBoḡT 25, 1980
→ 64,9484... 3,h226: [R]Orientalia 58 (1989) 555-7 (H. A. *Hoffner* excuses
his own delay) → a929, Popko.

e550 *Neve* Peter J.,   *a)* Boğazköy-Hattusha; new results of the excavations in
the upper city: Anatolica 16 (1989s) 7-14 + 6 fig.; – *b)* Ausgrabungen
1988: ArchAnz (1989) 271-332; 333-7, Die hieroglyphen-luwische
Inschrift (*Otten* H.); – *c)* 1987: AJA 93 (1989) 108-111; 3 fig. (→ e534
supra).

e551 **Otten** Heinrich,   Die 1986 in Boğazköy gefundenen Bronzetafel, 1. Ein
hethitischer Staatsvertrag; 2. Zu den rechtlichen und religiösen Grundlagen des hethitischen Königtums: BeiSprW 42. Innsbruck 1989, Univ.
35 p. – [R]BeiNam 24 (1989) 430s (Liane *Jakob-Rost*).

e551* **Otten** Heinrich, Die Bronzetafel aus Boğazköy, ein Staatsvertrag Tuthalijas IV 1988 ➤ 4,g514: ᴿWeltOr 20s (1989s) 289-294 (G. *Beckman*).

T8.3 **Ephesus.**

e552 *a)* *Alzinger* Wilhelm, Die Lokalisierung des hellenistischen Rathauses von Ephesos; – *b)* *Naumann* Rudolf, Ein Greifenprotom vom Taxiarchis-Hügel in Didyma: ➤ 49, ᶠDRERUP H., Bathron 1988, 21-29; 10 fig. / 319-323; 6 fig.

e553 **Bammer** Anton, Das Heiligtum der Artemis von Ephesos 1984 ➤ 65,b466 ... 4,g518: ᴿRArtLv 19 (1986) 300 (Anne-Laure *Vignaux*).

e554 **Engelmann** Helmut, *Knibbe* Dieter, Das Zollgesetz der Provinz Asia; eine neue Inschrift aus Ephesos: EpAnat 14 (whole fascicle, 1989). x-195 p.; ❶ Özet 198-206; XIV pl. 0174-6545.

e555 *Habicht* Christian, Ein neues Bürgerrechtsdekret aus Ephesos: ZPapEp 77 (1989) 88-91.

e556 ᴱ**Oster** Richard E., A bibliography of ancient Ephesus: ATLA 19, 1987 ➤ 3,e943: ᴿCBQ 51 (1989) 566s (A. T. *Kraabel*).

e557 *Parman* Ebru, The pottery from St. John's Basilica at Ephesus: ➤ 840, Céramique byz. 1987/9, 277-289; 16 fig.

e557* **Rügler** Axel, Die Columnae Caelatae des jüngeren Artemisions von Ephesos [Diss. 1983]: IstMitt Beih 34. Tü 1988, Wasmuth. xi-194 p.; 9 fig.; 36 pl. [Gnomon 62, 61-65, Ulrike *Muss*].

e558 *Trell* Bluma L., The temple of Artemis at Ephesus: ➤ 535, 7 Wonders 1988, 78-99; fig. 39-49.

e559 *Vetters* Hermann, Neues zu den Hanghäusern in Ephesos: ➤ 5, ᶠAKUR-GAL E. 1987, 231-6; foldout plan.

T8.4 **Pergamum.**

e560 **Filgis** Meinrad N., *Radt* Wolfgang, *al.*, Das Heroon: Altertümer von Pergamon 16/1, 1986 ➤ 3,e951; 4,g528: ᴿArchaeologia 38 (1987) 212s (S. *Parnicki-Pudelko* ❷); BonnJbb 189 (1989) 588-591 (D. *Pinkwart*).

e561 **Garbrecht** Günther, *al.*, Die Wasserversorgung antiker Städte; Pergamon 1987 ➤ 3,e952: ᴿAJA 93 (1989) 307s (J. P. *Oleson*); Gnomon 61 (1989) 55-59 (P. *Leveau*).

e562 *Hafner* German, Der Alexanderkopf aus Pergamon und der 'Aichmophoros' des Lysippos: ➤ 5, ᶠAKURGAL E. = Anadolu 20 (1987 for 1978ss) 131-142; 6 fig.

e563 *Hoepfner* Wolfram, Zu den grossen Altären von Magnesia und Pergamon: ArchAnz (1989) 601-634; 34 fig.

e564 *Le Rider* Georges, La politique monétaire du Royaume de Pergame après 188: JSav (1989) 163-190.

e565 **Mandel** Ursula, Kleinasiatische Reliefkeramik der mittleren Kaiserzeit; die 'Oinophorengruppe' und Verwandtes: PergFor 5. B 1988, de Gruyter. xiv-270 p.; 44 pl. DM 220. 3-11-010648-5 [AJA 93,626]. – ᴿMusHelv 46 (1989) 181 (Katrin *Roth-Rubi*).

e566 **Meyer-Schliemann** Carsten, Die pergamenische Sigillata aus der Stadtgrabung von Pergamon, Mitte 2. Jh. v. Chr. - Mitte 2. Jh, n. Chr.: PergFor 6. B 1988, de Gruyter. xviii-274 p.; 27 fig.; 48 pl. – ᴿMusHelv 46 (1989) 180s (Katrin *Roth-Rubi*).

e567 *Müller* Helmut, Ein neues hellenistisches Weihepigramm aus Pergamon: Chiron 19 (1989) 499-553; 4 fig.

e568 *Nicolet-Pierre* Hélène, Monnaies de Pergame: → 113, Mem. KRAAY-MORKHOLM 1989, 303-317; pl. XLVII-XLIX.

e569 **Pinkwart** Doris, *Stamnitz* Wolf, Peristylhäuser westlich der Unteren Agora: Altertümer von Pergamon 14, 1984 → 3,e957: ᴿAnzAltW 42 (1989) 98-100 (Elisabeth *Unterkircher*); BonnJbb 189 (1989) 586-8 (M. *Kreeb*); ClasR 39 (1989) 412s (J.J. *Coulton*); RArchéol (1989) 393s (Y. *Grandjean*).

e570 **Radt** Wolfgang, Pergamon; Geschichte und Bauten; Funde und Erforschung einer antiken Metropole: Dokumente. Köln 1988, DuMont. 401 p.; 171 fig. + 34 color. (Elisabeth *Steiner*). DM 44. - ᴿDLZ 110 (1989) 208-210 (Elisabeth *Rohde*).

e571 *Radt* Wolfgang, *a)* Pergamon, Vorbericht über die Kampagne 1988: TürkArk 28 (1989) 225-242; + 261 fig.; ❶ 243s; - *b)* Vorbericht 1988: ArchAnz (1987) 387-412; 33 fig.; - *c)* Pergamon 1988: AnSt 39 (1989) 180-2; - *d)* AJA 93 (1989) 128-132; fig. 14-24.

e572 **Schalles** Hans-J., Untersuchungen zur Kulturpolitik der pergamenischen Herrscher im 3. Jdt. v.C.: IstFor 36, 1985 → 3,e960; 4,g534: ᴿBonnJbb 189 (1989) 576-581 (A.H. *Borbein*).

e573 *Spieser* Jean-Michel, Informatique et céramique; l'exemple de Pergame: → 840, Céramique byz. 1987/9, 291-302; 9 fig.

e574 *Wenster* Alexander F., Zur Datierung des Temenos für den Herrscherkult in Pergamon: ArchAnz (1989) 33-42; 2 fig.

т8.6 *Situs Anatoliae,* **Turkey sites** in alphabetical order.

e575 **Alalaḫ:** *McClellan* Thomas L., The chronology and ceramic assemblages of Alalakh: → 106, ᶠKANTOR H., Essays 1989, 181-212; fig. 26-38.

e575* *Gates* Marie-Henriette, Alalakh and chronology again: → 831*, High/Low II (1988) 60-86.

e576 *Amorium:* 1st 1988: AnSt 39 (1989) 167-174; 5 fig.; pl. XLIII-XLVIII (R.M. *Harrison*).

e577 *Amphipolis,* eine übersehene Paulus-Station: BiKi 44 (1989) 79-81 (R. *Riesner*).

e577* *Anemurium:* *Russel* James [*Campbell* Sheila, mosaics], Christianity at Anemurium (Cilicia): → 827, 11ᵉ Arch.Chrét. 1986/9, 1621-1637 [1639-45].

e578 *Apameia Phrygia: Christol* Michel, *Drew-Bear* Thomas, Un castellum romain près d'Apamée de Phrygie. W 1987, Österr. Akad. 59 p.; 3 fig.; 10 pl.; map. [Latomus 49,744, A. *Martin*].

e579 *Aphrodisias* 27th-28th, 1987s: AnSt 39 (1989) 175-7 (K. *Erim*); AJA 93 (1989) 121s (K. *Erim* → e534 supra).

e580 **Budde** Ludwig, St. Pantaleon von Aphrodisias in Kilikien: Beit. Kunst des christlichen Ostens 9. Recklinghausen 1987, Aurel Bongers. 127 p.; 115 fig.; 20 color. pl.; 3 plans. - ᴿAntClas 58 (1989) 585s (J. *Balty*).

e581 ᴱLa **Genière** Juliette de, *Erim* Kenan, Aphrodisias de Carie, Colloque Univ. Lille III, 1985/7 → 3,e971; F 80: ᴿAJA 93 (1989) 623 (Nancy H. *Ramage*); AntClas 58 (1989) 516-8 (C. *Delvoye*).

e582 *Erim* Kenan, The treasures of Aphrodisias: ILN 277, 7087 (Spring 1989) 100-103; ill.

e583 *Feldman* Louis H., Proselytes and 'sympathizers' in the light of the new inscriptions from Aphrodisias: RÉJ 148 (1989) 265-305.

e584 **Reynolds** Joyce, *Tannenbaum* Robert, Jews and Godfearers at Aphrodisias 1987 → 2,b236 ... 4,g547: ᴿAntClas 58 (1989) 419-421 (C. *Orrieux*);

Gymnasium 96 (1989) 177-9 (Kai *Brodersen*); JHS 109 (1989) 243 (A. G. *Woodhead*); JRS 78 (1988) 261s (M. *Goodman*).

e585 *Smith* R. R. R., Simulacra gentium; the *ethne* from the Sebasteion at Aphrodisias: JRS 78 (1988) 50-77.

e585* *Ariassos: Cormack* Sarah, A mausoleum at Ariassos, Pisidia: AnSt 39 (1989) 31-40; 3 fig.; pl. I-IV [63-77 *al.*, Ariassos and Sagalassos 1988].

e586 *Beşik: Korfmann* Manfred, Beşik-Tepe, Vorbericht 1987-8: ArchAnz (1989) 473-483; 6 fig.

e587 *Claros: La Genière* Juliette de, Les nouvelles fouilles de Claros sept. 1988, brève relation préliminaire: TürkArk 23 (1989) 287-292 + 12 fig.; ❶ 293-300.

e588 *Demirci:* ᴱKorfmann Manfred, Demircihüyük, die Ergebnisse der Ausgrabungen 1975-8; [I. 1983 ➤ 65,b490] II. Naturwissenschaftliche Untersuchungen [12 art.] III. 2, **Turan** Efe, The pottery 2C, EB from phase H. Mainz 1987, von Zabern. xix-77 p.; ill. DM 198. / xi-172 p.; 98 fig.; 74 pl. + 2 color. – ᴿMundus 25 (1989) 155-7 (K. *Schippmann*).

e589 *Deve:* **Moorey** P. R. S., Cemeteries of the first millennium B.C. at Deve Hüyük, near Carchemish (1913) 1980 ➤ 61,t510: ᴿAfO 35 (1988) 207-211 (R. *Hachmann*).

e590 *Didyma:* 1985s, Heilige Strasse von Milet: ArchAnz (1987) 143-217; 92 (foldout) fig. (J. *Knauss*).

e591 **Fontenrose** Joseph, Didyma, Apollo's oracle; cult and companions. Berkeley 1988, Univ. California. xxi-282 p.; 41 fig.; 3 maps. $40. 0-520-05845-3. – ᴿClasR 39 (1989) 270s (R. *Parker*).

e592 *Göreme:* **Kaspar** Elke & Hans-Dieter, Kappadokien und das Tal von Göreme; ein Reisehandbuch. Hausen 1988, Korient. 114 p.; ill.

e592* **Epstein** Ann W., Tokalı kilise 1986 ➤ 3,e986: ᴿByZ 82 (1989) 306-9 (N. *Thierry*, franç.).

e593 **Schön** Michael, *Kral* Herbert, Kappadokien. Graz 1987, Akademische DV. 97 p.; ill. Sch 49. – ᴿDLZ 110 (1989) 1066 (B. *Brentjes*).

e594 *Gordion:* **Prag** A. J. N. W., Reconstructing King Midas; a first report [body found 1957 in largest Gordion mound]: AnSt 39 (1989) 159-165; pl. XLI-XLII.

e595 *Goroş:* **Hackstein** Katharina, Ethnizität und Situation; Goroś — eine vorderasiatische Kleinstadt: TAVO B-94. Wsb 1989, Reichert. 3-88226-469-1 [OIAc S89].

e596 *Halicarnassus: Jeppesen* Kristiaan, What did the Maussoleion look like?: ➤ 852, Caria 1987/9, 15-22 [-62, *al.*].

e596* *Harran:* ➤ 885, DHGE 23,133s (1989) 405s (R. *Aubert*, J. M. *Fiey*, complément de 11,1123s, 'Carrae') ➤ e620 infra.

e597 *Ilıpınar* ('tepid spring', 2 k W Lake İznik) 1987-9; chalco. Roman-Byz.: Anatolica 16 (1989s) 61-122 + 29 fig., II pl. (J. *Roodenberg*, *al.*).

e598 *Inandik:* Özgüç Tahsin, ❶ Inandiktepe, an important cult center in the Old Hittite period: Yayınları 5/43. Ankara 1988, Türk Tarih Kurumu. xxxii-174 p.; 97 pl. + 16 color. 975-16-0071-5 [OIAc N89].

e599 *İstanbul: Larsson* Mats G., Nyfunna runor i Hagia Sofia: Fornvännen 34 (1989) 12-14; 3 fig.

e600 **Mainstone** Rowland J., Hagia Sophia 1988 ➤ 4,g579*: ᴿAJA 93 (1989) 489s (R. *Mark*).

e601 **Celik** Zeynep, The remaking of İstanbul; portrait of an Ottoman city in the nineteenth century. Wsh 1986, Wsh Univ. Press. 163 p. – ᴿDer Islam 66 (1989) 183-6 (W. *Müller-Wiener*).

e602 **Labraunda:** a) *Thieme* Thomas, Methodology and planning in Hekatomnid Labraunda; – b) *Gunter* Ann C., Sculptural dedications at Labraunda; – c) *Hellström* Pontus, Formal banqueting at Labraunda: ➤ 852, Caria 1987/9, 77-90 / 91-98 / 99-104; ill.

e603 **Miletus:** ᴱMüller-Wiener W., Milet 1899-1980: 1980/86 ➤ 2,568*; 3,f8: ᴿGymnasium 96 (1989) 87-89 (E. *Pochmarski*).

e604 **Errington** R. Malcolm, The peace treaty between Miletus and Magnesia (1. Milet 148): Chiron 19 (1989) 279-288.

e605 **Nicaea:** **Merkelbach** R., Nikaia in der römischen Kaiserzeit: Rh/Wf Akad Vorträge G289. Dü 1987, Westdeutscher-V. 41 p.; 5 fig.; 4 pl. + 4 color. DM 16. – ᴿClasR 39 (1989) 153 (S. *Mitchell*).

e606 **Oylum** höyük (S. Gaziantep), 1987, 1989, EB: Anatolica 16 (1989s) 20-25 + 7 fig.

e607 **Pamukkale:** **Ritti** Tullia, Hierapolis, scavi e ricerche I. Fonti letterarie ed epigrafiche [1985 ➤ 2,b252; 3,e992]; – II con **D'Andria** Francesco, Le sculture del teatro. R 1985, Bretschneider. xxviii-205 p.; 12 fig.; 53 pl. [Latomus 49, 237-9, A. *Martin*].

e608 **Perga:** İnan Jale, Thronende Isis von Perge: ➤ 5, ᶠAKURGAL E. = Anadolu 21 (1987 for 1978ss) 1-8; 3 pl.

e609 **Pessinus:** **Devreker** John, Pessinonte; histoire et fouilles: TürkArk 23 (1989) 165-170 + 8 fig.; map.

e610 **Priene:** *Tietze* Christian, Priene, Rekonstruktion einer antiken Stadt-planung: Altertum 34 (1988) 217-223; 6 fig.

e611 **Sardis** 1988: AnSt 39 (1989) 182-4 (C. H. *Greenewalt*).

e612 **Greenewalt** Crawford H.ᴶ, Excavations at Sardis, 1978-1988: TürkArk 28 (1989) 263-7 + 20 fig.

e613 ᴱ**Guralnick** Eleanor, Sardis, 27 years... 1987 ➤ 3,f27: ᴿAJA 93 (1989) 479s (R. L. *Pounder*); JNES 48 (1989) 61s (R. *Scranton*).

e614 **Ratté** Christopher J., Lydian masonry and monumental architecture at Sardis: diss. California, ᴰGreenewalt C. Berkeley 1989. 401 p. 90-06483. – DissA 50 (1989s) 3273-A.

e615 **Hanfmann** George, al., Sardis from prehistoric to Roman times 1983 ➤ 64,d74... 3,f23: ᴿÉchMClas 33 (1989) 264-7 (H. *Williams*).

e616 **Sinop:** **Conovici** Nicolae, (rum.) Probleme der Chronologie der gestem-pelten Sinope-Amphoren aus der IV. Gruppe (B. N. *Grakov*): IstVArh 40 (1989) 29-42; deutsch 42-44.

e617 **Tanais:** **Shelov** D. B. ⊕ The Hellenistic city of Tanais [Bosporan]: VDI 190 (1989) 47-53; Eng. 53s.

e617* **Tarsus:** ➤ 887, DMA 12 (1988) 599s (A. P. *Atamian*).

e618 **Troja:** ᴱ**Mellink** Machteld J., Troy and the Trojan War 1984/6 ➤ 3,837; 4,g615: ᴿJNES 48 (1989) 147-9 (I. *Morris*).

e619 **Urfa:** **Teixidor** Javier, Les derniers rois d'Édesse [après Abgar VIII 212] d'après deux nouveaux documents syriaques: ZPapEp 77 (1989) 219-222.

e620 **Laureano** Pietro, Nel tempio dei sette pianeti [Harran ➤ e596* supra]; alla ricerca del sapere perduto: ArchViva 7,2 (1988) 52-57; color. ill.

e621 **Yalvaç:** **Karamut** İsmail, ⊕ Sacrificing area of Men near Pisidian Antioch: TürkArk 23 (1989) 177-181 + 3 fig.; 4 phot.

T8.9   Armenia, Urartu.

e622 **Chahin** M., The kingdom of Armenia I. 1987 ➤ 4,g624: ᴿClasR 39 (1989) 308-311 (T. *Braun*).

e624 *Medvedskaya* Inna, The end of Urartian presence in the region of Lake Urmia: → 28, ᶠBERGHE L. Vanden 1989, 439-452 + 2 fig.

e625 *Roos* Paavo, Water-mills in Urartu?: EWest 38 (R 1988) 11-32; 12 fig.

e626 *Salvini* Mirjo, Sulla formazione dello stato urarteo: → 877, Lavoro 1988, 270-287.

e627 **Schottky** Martin, Media Atropatene und Gross-Armenien in hellenistischer Zeit: Diss. AltG 27. Bonn 1989, Habelt. 256 p.; 7 pl. 3-7749-2394-9 [OIAc N89].

e628 **Zimansky** Paul E., Ecology and empire; the structure of the Urartian state 1985 → 1,e371 ... 4,g633: ᴿAfO 35 (1988) 197-205 (I. M. *Diakonoff*, I. N. *Medvedskaya*); BO 46 (1989) 397-402 (M. *Salvini*).

ᴛ9.1 **Cyprus.**

e629 *Baurain* Claude, Passé légendaire, archéologie et réalité historique; l'hellénisation de Chypre: AnnalesESC 44 (1989) 463-477.

e630 *Béraud* Sylvain, Holy Land [Franciscan Custody] of Cyprus, ᵀ*Sullivan* James: HolyL 9 (1989) 27-42; 95s notes [5-24, biblical Cyprus varia].

e631 **Goring** Elizabeth, A mischievous pastime; digging in Cyprus in the nineteenth century. E 1988, Nat. Museum. viii-98 p.; 120 fig. £7. – ᴿClasR 39 (1989) 111s (D. *Hunt*).

e633 *a) Harris* Charles U., The role of CAARI (Cyprus American Archaeological research institute) on Cyprus; – *b) Davis* Thomas W., A history of American archaeology in Cyprus; – *c) Gaber* Pamela, The museums of Cyprus; – *d) Swiny* Stuart, Prehistoric Cyprus; a current perspective; – *e) Michaelides* Demetrios, The early Christian mosaics of Cyprus; – *f) Connelly* Joan B., Standing before one's God; votive sculpture and the Cypriot religious tradition: BA 52 (1989) 157-162 / 163-9 / 170-7 / 178-189 / 192-201 / 210-8.

e633* *Helck* W., Ein Ausgreifen des Mittleren Reiches in den zypriotischen Raum?: GöMiszÄg 109 (1989) 27-30.

e634 **Karageorghis** V., The archaeology of Cyprus... after Myres 1987 → 4,g639: ᴿAthenaeum 67 (1989) 323s (O. *Carruba*).

e634* **Karageorghis** Vassos, Blacks in ancient Cypriote art. Austin/Houston 1988, Univ. Texas/Menil. 62 p.; ill. – ᴿREG 102 (1989) 581s (Hélène *Cassimatis*).

e635 *Karageorghis* V., ⊕ New archaeological finds in Cyprus: VDI 191 (1989) 106-112; 9 fig.

e636 **Keswani** Priscilla F. S., Mortuary ritual and social hierarchy in Bronze Age Cyprus: anthropology diss. ᴰ*Wright* Henry T. AA 1989, Univ. Michigan. xvi-831 p.; bibliog. p. 792-831. 89-20561. – OIAc Ja90.

e637 *Pouilloux* Jean, L'époque classique à Chypre: JSav (1989) 147-162.

e638 **Schneider** Andreas, Zypern, 8000 Jahre Geschichte (archäologische Schätze, byzantinische Kirchen, gotische Kathedralen). Köln 1988. 373 p. – ᴿSileno 15 (1989) 321s (J. *Irmscher*).

e639 **Tatton-Brown** Veronica, Ancient Cyprus 1988 → 4,g645: ᴿAncHRes 19 (1989) 98s (R. S. *Merrillees*).

─────────

e641 *Amathous: a) Karageorghis* V., La nécropole d'Amathonte 3/1; *Hermary* A., Statuettes; École Française d'Athènes. Nicosia 1987, Leventis. 75 p.; 40 fig.; 52 pl. – ᴿGnomon 61 (1989) 644s (F. *Canciani*); – *b)* Céramiques non chypriotes. Leventis 1987. 65 p.; 38 pl. – *c*) **Bikai** Patricia M. *al.*, La nécropole d'Amathonte, tombes 113-367, – ᴿRArchéol (1989) 151s (A. *Hermary*).

e642 **Laffineur** R., Amathonte 3/3, L'orfèvrerie: ÉtChypr 7/Mém 67. P 1986, RCiv (Éc.Fr.Ath.). 196 p.; 133 fig. 2-86538-156-0. – ᴿAntClas 58 (1989) 518s (G. *Raepsaet*).

e643 **Queyrel** Anne, Amathonte IV. Les figurines hellénistiques 1988 → 4, g648: ᴿRÉG 102 (1989) 584s (Hélène *Cassimatis*).

e644 *Karageorghis* V., *Lo Schiavo* F., A West Mediterranean obelos from Amathus: RStFen 8 (1989) 15-24 + 5 fig. (map); pl. III-IV.

e645 **Ayia Paraskevi: Hennessy** J.B., *al.* [STEWART J.R.B.,† *al.*, excavations], Ayia Paraskevi e Vasilia: SIMA 82. Göteborg 1988, Åström. 111 p., incl. 63 fig. 91-8609879-9.

e646 **Enkomi: Courtois** J.-C., *al.*, Enkomi et le Bronze Récent à Chypre. Nicosia 1986, Leventis. xvi-204 p.; 8 fig.; 32 pl. C£10. – ᴿAJA 93 (1989) 608s (Elizabeth *Goring*); Gnomon 61 (1989) 273-5 (H. *Matthäus*); RÉG 101 (1988) 193s (A. *Hermary*).

e647 **Courtois** J.-C., Alasia 3, objets... d'Enkomi 1984 → 2,b308: ᴿAfO 35 (1988) 222s (V. *Stürmer*).

e648 *Keswani* Priscilla S., Dimensions of social hierarchy in Late Bronze Age Cyprus; an analysis of the mortuary data from Enkomi: JMeditArch 2 (1989) 49-86.

e649 **Episkopi: Swiny** Stuart, Kent State Expedition 2; SIMA 74/2, 1986 → 2,b310: ᴿBO 46 (1989) 472-7 (R.S. *Merrillees*).

e650 **Katydhata: Åström** Paul, Katydhata, a Bronze Age site in Cyprus: SIMA 86. Göteborg 1989, Åström. 131 p.; 207 fig.

e651 **Kition: Karageorghis** V., *al.*, Excavations at Kition V. The pre-Phoenician levels, area I and II. Nicosia 1985, Dept. Antiq. xix-448 p.; 493 p. + vol. of 239 pl. + vol. of 61 + 35 plans. – ᴿPEQ 121 (1989) 82-84 (E.J. *Peltenburg*); RÉG 102 (1989) 219-221 (A. *Hermary*).

e652 *Heltzer* Michael, *a*) Epigraphic evidence concerning a Jewish settlement in Kition (Larnaca, Cyprus) in the Achaemenid period (IV cent B.C.): AulaO 7 (1989) 189-206; 10 fig.; map glued in; – *b*) Kition according to the biblical prophets and Hebrew ostraca from Arad: RepCyp (1988,1) 167-172.

e653 *Pouilloux* Jean, Étrangers à Kition et Kitiens à l'étranger: RepCyp (1988,2) 95-99; 2 fig.

e654 **Yon** M., *Caubet* A., Kition-Bamboula III 1986 → 2,b316: ᴿArOr 57 (1987) 397s (P. *Charvát*).

e655 **Kourion:** ᴱ**Soren** David, The sanctuary of Apollo Hylates at Kourion, Cyprus 1987 → 4,g652: ᴿAJA 93 (1989) 623s (Mary B. *Hollinshead*).

e656 **Lemba: Peltenburg** E.J., *al.*, Excavations at Lemba Lakkous, 1976-1983: SIMA 70/1, 1985 → 1,e398... 4,g654: ᴿClasR 39 (1989) 334s (S. *Hood*: a landmark).

e657 **Paphos: Maier** Franz G., *Wartburg* Marie-Louise von, Ausgrabungen in Alt-Paphos; 15. Bericht 1987-8: ArchAnz (1989) 569-598; 37 fig.

e658 *Kouklia-Palaipaphos*; 15th, 1987s: RepCyp (1989) 177-193; 17 fig. pl. LVIII-LXIII [figurine phallique (1988,2) 53-58, pl. XVI, Gisèle *Clerc*].

e659 **Maier** F.G., *Karageorghis* V., *al.*, Paphos, history and archaeology 1984 → 1,e400; 2,b319: ᴿRArtLv 18 (1985) 176-8 (J. *Vanschoonwinkel*).

e660 *Salamis:* **Pouilloux** Jean, *al.*, Corpus épigraphique: Salamine de Chypre 13. P 1987, de Boccard. 151 p., dont 23 pl. – ᴿAntClas 58 (1989) 418s (J. *Bingen*).

т9.3 *Graecia*, **Greece** – mainland sites in alphabetical order.

e661 Chronikon (by periods) 1982: ☉ Archaiologikon Deltion 37, B1-2 (1989). 220 p., 132 pl.; maps + p. 221-417; pl. 133-284; maps.

e662 *Delvoye* Charles, Chronique archéologique: Byzantion 59 (Bru 1983) 508-539.

e663 *Fossey* John M., Settlement development in Greek prehistory: ⇒ 70, ᶠGORDON C. 1987, 17-33; 2 fig.

e664 ᴱ**French** E. B., *Wardle* K. A., Problems in Greek prehistory 1986/8 ⇒ 4,735: ᴿAntiquity 63 (1989) 642-644 (J. L. *Davis*).

e665 *Guralnick* Eleanor, Greece and the Near East; art and archaeology: ⇒ 175, Mem. SCHODER R., Daidalikon 1989, 151-176; 20 fig.

e666 *Pallas* Demetrios I., Die Baptisterien und das Kirchengebäude im altchristlichen Griechenland: ⇒ 210, Mem. WESSEL K. 1988, 215-230.

e667 **Snodgrass** Anthony M., An archaeology of Greece 1987 ⇒ 3,f86; 4,g662: ᴿAJA 93 (1989) 145s (C. *Runnels*: 'An' apt; unlikely to please); AmHR 94 (1989) 1349s (T. H. *Van Andel*); JHS 109 (1989) 248s (K. *Branigan*).

e668 *Touchais* Gilles, Chronique des fouilles et découvertes archéologiques en Grèce en 1988: BCH 113 (1989) 581-700 [701-788, *al.*, travaux de l'École française, Argos-Philippes-Délos-Malia; 789-853, *Karageorgis* V., Chypre; 854-910 *al.*, Éc. Fr. Amathonte].

———————————

e669 *Aegina:* **Margreiter** Ingrid, Die Kleinfunde aus dem Apollo-Heiligtum: Alt-Ägina 2/3. Mainz 1988, von Zabern. 86 p.; 18 fig.; 48 pl.

e670 *Aetolia:* **Bommelié** Sebastiaan, *al.*, Aetolia and the Aetolians; towards the interdisciplinary study of a Greek region: Studia Aetolica 1. Utrecht 1987, Parnassus. 176 p.; 17 fig. 90-720-1901-6. – ᴿAntClas 58 (1989) 432s (D. *Marcotte*).

e671 *Argos:* **Strøm** Ingrid, The early sanctuary of the Argive Heraion and its external relations (8th - early 6th cent. B.C.); the monumental architecture: AcArchK 59 (1988) 173-203; 20 fig.

e672 *Asine:* **Nordquist** G. C., A Middle Helladic village; Asine in the Argolid 1987 ⇒ 3,f91; 4,g666: ᴿAthenaeum 67 (1989) 605s (G. *Graziadio*).

e673 (Santillo) *Frizell* Barbro, Asine II, 1986 ⇒ 3,f90: ᴿArchaeologia 39 (1988) 239s (K. *Lewartowski* ☉).

e674 *Athenae:* **Kiilerich** Bente, The Athenian acropolis; the position of lions and leopards: AcArchK 59 (1988) 229-234; 4 fig.

e675 **Muss** Ulrike, *Schubert* Charlotte, Die Akropolis von Athen 1988 ⇒ 4,g675: ᴿAntClas 58 (1989) 511s (C. *Delvoye*); HZ 248 (1989) 410s (M. *Stahl*).

e676 **Hitchens** Christopher, *al.*, The Elgin Marbles 1987 ⇒ 4,g673: ᴿJHS 109 (1989) 279s (D. *Hunt*: if restored to the Parthenon they would quickly perish from atmosphere-contamination).

e677 ᴱ**Berger** Ernst, Parthenon-Kongress Basel 1982/4 ⇒ 65,b587; 4,g670: ᴿDLZ 110 (1989) 1034-7 (W. *Schindler*).

e678 **Camp** J. M.,   The Athenian agora, excavations... 1986 ➤ 2,b324...
4,g676: ᴿAncHRes 19 (1989) 34-37 (R. A. *Kearsley*); HZ 248 (1989) 409s
(J. *Bleicken*).

e679 **Moore** Mary B., *Philippides* Mary Z. P., The Athenian agora, 23. Attic
black-figured pottery, 1986 ➤ 3,f100; $60. 0-87661-223-0: ᴿAJA 93
(1989) 298s (Ann B. *Brownlee*).

e680 **Rotroff** Susan I.,   Hellenistic pottery; Athenian and imported mold-
made bowls: Athenian Agora 22, 1982 ➤ 65,b591; 1,e427; 0-87661-
222-2: ᴿAntClas 58 (1989) 547s (G. *Raepsaet*).

e681 *Levi* Doro,   I primi abitanti di Atene: ParPass 244 (1989) 5-14; 8 fig.

e682 *Athos:*   *Smyrnakes* Gerasimos, ⊜ *Tò hágion óros* [Athos].   Athos 1988
= 1903, Panselenas. xii-708-iii-108 p.; 62 fig. – ᴿJbÖsByz 39 (1989) 380
(J. *Koder*).

e683 *Beroea:*   *Tataki* Argyro B.,   Ancient Beroea, prosopography and society:
Meletemata 8. P 1988, de Boccard. 572 p.; 10 pl.

e684 *Chalcidice:*   *Cambitoglou* Alexander, *Papadopoulos* John K.,   Excavations at Torone [Chalkidike], 1986; a preliminary report: MeditArch 1
(1988) 180-217; 45 fig. [2 (1989) 9-44; 42 fig., iron age potters' kiln].

e685 *Corinthus:*   *Williams* Charles K.ᴵᴵ, [*Zervos* Orestes H., coins].   Corinth
1988; east of the theater: Hesperia 58 (1989) 1-36; 9 fig.; pl. 1-13
[p. 37-50].

e686 *Walbank* Mary E. H.,   PAUSANIAS, Octavia and Temple E at Corinth:
AnBritAth 84 (1989) 361-394.

e687 **Sturgeon** Mary C.,   Sculpture I [O. BRONEER excavations, Isthmus of
Corinth] 1952-1967: Isthmia 4.   Princeton 1987, American School of
Athens. xxiii-200 p.; 12 fig.; 87 pl.; 3 plans. $60. 0-87661-934-0. –
ᴿAntClas 58 (1989) 526-8 (D. *Viviers*).

e688 *Vermeule* Emily,   Carved bones from Corinth [270 fragments in Boston
Museum of Fine Arts since 1928]: ➤ 106, ꜰKANTOR H., Essays 1989,
271-286; pl. 54-60.

e689 ꜰAMYX Darrell A.,   Corinthiaca, ᴱ**Del Chiaro** Mario A., *Biers* William
R. 1986 ➤ 3,9: ᴿPhoenix 43 (Toronto 1989) 260-2 (G. P. *Schaus*: 23 art., 1
on vase-painting).

e690 *Hemans* Frederick P.,   The archaic roof-tiles at Isthmia; a re-examination: Hesperia 58 (1989) 251-266; 4 fig.

e691 *Avraméa* Anna, *Kyrkou* Maro,   Inventaire topographique de Corinthe et
sa région à l'époque chrétienne et byzantine: ➤ e807, ᴱ**Ahrweiler** H.,
Géographie du monde méditerranéen 1988, 31-45.

e692 *Delphi:*   **Daux** Georges, *Hansen* Erik,   Fouilles de Delphes 2. Topographie et architecture; le Trésor de Siphnos: Éc. Franç. Athènes, 1987
➤ 4,g693: ᴿAJA 93 (1989) 477s (W. R. *Biers*).

e692* *Deroche* V.,   Delphes, la christianisation d'un sanctuaire païen: ➤ 827,
11ᵉ Arch. Chrét. 1986/9, 2713-2723.

e693 *Roux* Georges,   Problèmes delphiques d'architecture et d'épigraphie:
RArchéol (1989) 23-64; 12 fig.

e694 *Kamaraki:*   *Cosmopoulos* Michael,   Kamaraki, an underwater site in [NE]
Attica, Greece: IntJNaut 18 (1989) 273-6; 4 fig.

e695 *Lerna:*   *Wiencke* Martha H.,   Change in Early Helladic II [Lerna III;
Caskey J. 1960]: AJA 93 (1989) 495-509.

e696 *Marathon:*   *Miles* Margaret M.,   A reconstruction of the temple of
Nemesis at Rhamnous [near Marathon]: Hesperia 58,2 (1989) 135-249
(whole fasc.); 32 fig.; pl. 29-48.

e697 *Mycenae:* **Mylonas Shear** Ione, The Panagia houses at Mycenae: Mg 68. Ph 1987 Univ. Museum. xx-172 p.; 52 pl.; 21 fig.; 2 foldouts. – RRArchéol (1989) 365s (P. *Darcque*).

e698 **Xénaki-Sakellariou** Agnès, Ⓖ Les tombes à chambre de Mycènes 1985 ➤ 2,b341; 3,f115: RRArchéol (1989) 157-9 (O. *Pelon*).

e699 **Taylour** W., I micenei [1964, ²1983 ➤ 64,d163],ᵀ; pref. *Benzi* M. F 1987, Giunti Barbèra. 215 p.; 150 fig.; 8 color. pl. – RSalesianum 51 (1989) 57s (R. *Della Casa*).

e700 *Philippi:* **Abrahamsen** Valerie, Bishop Porphyrios and the city of Philippi in the early fourth century: VigChr 43 (1989) 80-85.

e701 *Phocis:* **Fossey** John M., The ancient topography of eastern Phokis 1986 ➤ 2,b355 ... 4,g620*: RPhoenix 43 (Toronto 1989) 381s (T. E. *Gregory*).

e702 *Pylos:* **Coleman** John E., Excavations at Pylos 1986 ➤ 3,f126: RGnomon 61 (1989) 275-8 (Veronika *Mitsopoulos-Leon*).

e703 *Sparta:* **Stibbe** Conrad M., Beobachtungen zur Topographie des antiken Sparta: Babesch 64 (1989) 61-99; 33 fig.

e704 *Thebae:* **Braun** Karin, *Haevernick* Thea E., Bemalte Keramik und Glas aus dem Kabirenheiligtum bei Theben: DAI-Kab. 4, 1981 ➤ 1,e454; 2,b359: RDLZ 110 (1989) 154-6 (E. *Paul*).

e705 *Vergina:* **Rhomiopoulou** Katerina, *Kilian-Dirlmeier* Imma, Neue Funde aus der eisenzeitlichen Hügelnekropole von Vergina, Griechische Makedonien: PraehZts 64 (1989) 87-151; 51 fig.

e706 **Foi** Alexander, Dalla parte dei Traci; note e cultura nelle terre di Bulgaria: ArchViva 8,6 (1989) 22-31; color. ill.

T9.4 **Creta.**

e707 **Braune** Arnulf, Menes–Moses–Minos; die Altpalastzeit auf Kreta und ihre geschichtlichen Ursprünge. Essen 1988, Blaue Eule. 192 p.

e708 ᴱ**Cadogan** Gerald, The end of the Early Bronze Age in the Aegean [symposium for J. CASKEY 1979]: Cincinnati Classical Studies NS 6, 1986 ➤ 4,726: RBO 46 (1989) 188-194 (J. B. *Rutter*).

e709 ᴱ**Hägg** Robin, *Marinatos* Nanno, The function of the Minoan palaces 1984/7 ➤ 4,739: RClasR 39 (1989) 335-8 (Christiane *Sourvinou-Inwood*).

e710 **Gondicas** Daphne, Recherches sur la Crète occidentale ... Amst 1988, Hakkert. iii-365+60 p.; 28 pl.; 2 maps.

e711 **Kehnscherper** Günther, Kreta–Mykene–Santorin⁶. Lp 1986, Urania. 168 p., (color.) ill. M 15,80. – RSileno 15 (1989) 301s (R. *Witte*).

e712 *a)* **Vandenabeele** F., Les peuplements de la Crète; rupture et continuité; – *b) Antonelli* C., Alcune interferenze cultuali tra Creta e l'Egitto; – *c) Treuil* R., L'expansion minoenne en Méditerranée; problèmes d'interprétation historique; – *d) Godart* L., Minoici e Micenei; precolonizzatori e precolonizzati: ➤ 811, Momenti 1985/8, 57-64 / 157-162 / 37-41 / 43-55.

e713 *Knossos:* **Ashton** R. H. J., Knossos royal road south 1971 and 1972 excavations; the coins: AnBritAth 84 (1989) 49-60.

e714 **Popham** M. R., *al.*, The Minoan unexplored mansion at Knossos 1984 ➤ 65,b636 ... 3,f145: RGnomon 61 (1989) 605-8 (S. *Hiller*).

e715 **Raison** Jacques, Le palais du second millénaire à Knossos, 1, Le quartier nord: Ét. Crétoises 28. P 1988, Geuthnes.

e716 *Andreev* Yu. V., ❹ Minoan Daedalus: VDI 190 (1989) 29-46; Eng. 46.

e717 **Niemeier** W. D., Die Palaststilkeramik von Knossos 1985 ➤ 3,f144: ᴿJHS 109 (1989) 262s (P. A. *Mountjoy*).

e718 *Kommos:* a) *Watrous* L. Vance, Late Bronze Age Kommos; imported pottery as evidence for foreign contact; – b) *Shaw* Maria C., Late Minoan Buildings J/T and Late Minoan III buildings N and P at Kommos; – c) *Betancourt* Philip, A great Minoan triangle; the changing characters of Phaistos, Hagia Triadha, and Kommos: ➤ 847, Proc. Kommos Symposium 1984 = ScrMedit 6 (1985) 7-18 / 19-30 / 31-44 / 45-54.

e720 *Zakros:* **Platon** E. M., The workshops and working areas of Minoan Crete; the evidence of the palace and town of Zakros for a comparative study: diss. Bristol. 983 p. (3 vol.) BRDX-85980. – DissA 50 (1989s) 1347-A.

T9.5 Insulae graecae.

e720* *Hankey* Vronwy, The Aegean Late Bronze Age; relative and absolute chronology: ➤ 831*, High/Low II (1987) 39-59; III (1989) 150 + map.

e721 a) *Hiller* S., Die materielle Kultur der ägäischen Niederlassungen im Mittelmeerraum; – b) *Bernabò Brea* L., Le isole eolie e l'espansione egea in Occidente; ➤ 811, Momenti 1985/8, 73-90 / 103-7.

e722 **Press** Ludwika, ❷ *Budownictwo egejskie* ... Aegean architecture². Wsz 1986. 332 p.; 164 fig.; 3 maps. – ᴿArchaeologia 39 (1988) 240-3 (R. *Massalski* ❷).

e723 **Warren** Peter, *Hankey* Vronwy, Aegean Bronze Age Chronology. Bristol 1989, Classical. x-246 p. 0-906515-67-X [OIAc Ja90].

e724 *Chios:* ᴱ**Boardman** J., ... Chios conference 1984/6 ➤ 4,722: ᴿAJA 93 (1984) 148-150 (J. G. *Pedley*).

e725 *Delos:* *Büsing-Kolbe* Andrea, Ein neureiches Haus auf Delos: ➤ 49, ᶠDRERUP H., Bathron 1988, 99-106; 4 fig.

e726 **Will** E., Le sanctuaire de la déesse syrienne: Délos 35, 1985 ➤ 2,b392; 3,f156: ᴿGnomon 61 (1989) 645-8 (H. *Lauter*).

e727 **Barber** R. I. N., The Cyclades in the Bronze Age 1987 ➤ 4,g768: ᴿJHS 109 (1989) 258s (Elizabeth *Schofield*).

e728 **Ekschmitt** Werner, Kunst und Kultur der Kykladen I. Neolithikum und Bronzezeit; 2. Geometrische und archaische Zeit: KgAW 28, 1986 ➤ 2,b387: ᴿAJA 93 (1989) 293s (J. L. *Davis*: encyclopedic, rambling, inaccurate).

e729 *Karpathos:* **Melas** E. M., The islands of Karpathos, Saros and Kasos in the Neolithic and Bronze Age: SIMA 68, 1985 ➤ 2,b394; 3,f160: ᴿBO 46 (1989) 722-4 (Vronwy *Hankey*).

e730 *Keos:* **Brun** Patrice, L'île de Kéos et ses cités au IVᵉ siècle av. J.-C.: ZPapEp 76 (1989) 121-138.

e731 **Caskey** Miriam E., *al.*, The temple at Ayia Irini: Keos 2/1, 1986 ➤ 3,f146; 4,g762: ᴿGnomon 61 (1989) 339-343 (W. *Schiering*).

e732 **Cummer** W. Willson, *Schofield* Elizabeth, *al.*, Ayia Irini house A: Keos 3. Mainz 1984, von Zabern. xx-172 p. 66 + 572 fig.; 88 pl. – ᴿGnomon 61 (1989) 724-7 (S. *Hiller*).

e733 **Davis** Jack L.,   Ayia Irini: Keos 5, 1986 ⇥ 2,b396; 3,f162:   ᴿArchaeologia 38 (1987) 201s (Ludwika *Press* ❷).

e734 **Overbeck** John C., Ayia Irini, period IV, part 1. The stratigraphy and the find deposits; cemeteries, *Overbeck* Gatewood F.: Keos 7. Mainz 1989, von Zabern. xviii-233 p.; 104 pl. 3-8053-1024-2.

e735 *Lesbos: Williams* Caroline & Hector,   Excavations at Mytilene, 1988: ÉchMClas 33 (1989) 167. 181; 2 fig.; 6 pl.

e736 *Melos:* **Renfrew** Colin, The archaeology of cult ... Phylakopi (Melos) 1985 ⇥ 3,f165:   ᴿArchaeologia 39 (1988) 239 (B. *Rutkowski* ❷).

e737 *Patmos: Durand* Matthieu G. de, Le monastère de Patmos: ⇥ 32, Mém. BOUCHET J.-R., VSp 142 (1988) 665-677.

e738 **Kollias** Elias,   Patmos, ᵀ*Zigada* Hélène: Byzantine Art in Greece. Athens 1986, Melissa. 40 p.; ill. − ᴿByzantion 59 (1989) 521s (C. *Delvoye*).

e739 *Rhodus:* **Dietz** Søren, Escavations and surveys in southern Rhodes, the Mycenaean period 1984 ⇥ 65,b658 ... 4,g770:   ᴿBO 46 (1989) 477-9 (Vronwy *Hankey*).

e740 **Dietz** Søren, *Papachristodoulou* Ioannis,   Archaeology in the Dodecanese. K 1988, National Museum. 260 p.; ill.

e741 *Samos:* **Shipley** Graham,   A history of Samos, 800-188 B.C. 1987 ⇥ 4,g773: ᴿÉtClas 57 (1989) 188s (L. *Migeotte*); JHS 109 (1989) 252s (T. J. *Figueira*).

e742 *Tenos:* **Étienne** R., *Braun* J.-P.,   Tenos I ... Poséidon/Amphitrite 1986 ⇥ 3,f171; 4,g775: ᴿMusHelv 46 (1989) 181s (D. *Knoepfler*).

e743 *Thasos: Archontidou-Argyri* Aglaia, *al.*,   The underwater excavation at the ancient port of Thasos, Greece: IntJNaut 18 (1989) 51-59; 14 fig.

e744 **Wagner** G. A., *Weisgerber* Gerd,   Antike Edel- und Buntmetallgewinnung auf Thasos. Bochum 1988, Bergbaumuseum. 279 p.; 290 fig.; 8 foldouts.

e745 **Weill** Nicole, La plastique archaïque de Thasos 1985 ⇥ 3,f172; 4,g777: ᴿArchaeologia 39 (1988) 244-6 (Hanna *Szymańska* ❷).

e746 *Thera: Manning* Sturt W., The Santorina [Thera] eruption; an up-date: JMeditArch [1 (1988) 17-82] 2 (1989) 303-313.

e747 *Montero Ruiz* Ignacio, Santorini, consecuencias de una erupción: Revista de arqueología 10, 98 (1989) 16-24; ill.

e748 *Morris* Sarah P.,   A tale of two cities; the miniature frescoes from Thera and the origins of Greek poetry: AJA 93 (1989) 511-535.

T9.6 **Urbs Roma.**

e749 *a) Alföldy* Géza, Zu den Monumenta der römischen Provinzen auf dem Augustusforum; − *b) Stupperich* Reinhard, Gedanken zu Obelisk und Pulvinar in Darstellungen des Circus Maximus in Rom: ⇥ 151, ᶠPEKÁRY T., Migratio 1989, 226-234 / 265-279.

e749* **Benedettucci** Nicola, [Via] Appia Felix [drawings with all-hand-lettered comments]. R 1988, Sogno Neolatino. 207 p.

e750 **Boatwright** Mary T.,   Hadrian and the city of Rome 1987 ⇥ 3,f178; 4,g783: ᴿJRS 79 (1989) 218-220 (Janet *DeLaine*).

e751 ᴱ(Herausgeber) **Bol** Peter C., ᴱ(Bearbeiter) *Allroggen-Bedel* A., *al.*, Forschungen zur Villa Albani; Katalog der antiken Bildwerke I., Bildwerke im Treppenaufgang und im Piano nobile des Casino: Schriften des Liebieghauses. B 1989, Mann. 486 p.; 277 pl. 3-7861-1515-X.

e752 **Chevallier** Raymond, Ostie antique, ville et port. P 1986, BLettres. 289 p.; 39 fig.; XLI pl.; plan. F 170. – RLatomus 48 (1989) 492 (J. *Debergh*).

e753 **Coarelli** Filippo, Il Foro Boario dalle origini alla fine della Repubblica. R 1988, Quasar. 503 p.; 112 fig. – RAJA 93 (1989) 617s (F. S. *Kleiner*).

e754 *Cozza* Lucos, Roma; le Mura Aureliane dalla Porta Flaminia al Tevere: PBritSR 57 (1989) 1-5; 2 fig.; pl. I-II.

e755 **De Maria** S., Gli archi onorari di Roma e dell'Italia romana: Bibliotheca Archaeologica 7. R 1988, Bretschneider. 174 p.; 6 fig.; 120 pl. – RAthenaeum 67 (1989) 319-321 (C. *Saletti*).

e756 **Hibbert** C., Rome, the biography of a city. Hmw 1987 = 1985, Penguin. xi-387 p.; ill.; maps. £9. 0-14-007078-8 [JRS 78,278].

e757 *Kleiner* Fred S., An arch of Domitian in Rome on the coins of Alexandria: NumC 149 (1989) 69-81; pl. 20s.

e758 **Kleiner** Fred S., Arch of Nero 1985 → 1,e521* ... 4,g796: RAnzAltW 42 (1989) 116-120 (M. *Pfanner*); Gnomon 61 (1989) 186-8 (D. *Boschung*); Latomus 48 (1989) 939 (J. *Debergh*).

e759 *Kreitzer* Larry, Nero's Rome; images of the city on imperial coinage: EvQ 61 (1989) 301-9; 5 fig.

e760 **Leander Touati** Anne-Marie, The great Trajanic frieze; the study of a monument and the mechanisms of message transmission in Roman art: Act. Inst. Rom. Sueciae 45, 1987 → 3,f197: RAJA 93 (1989) 482s (R. A. *Gergel*); ClasR 39 (1989) 418s (F. A. *Lepper*).

e761 *Lepper* Frank, *Frere* Sheppard, Trajan's column 1988 → 4,g799*: RAntiqJ 69 (1989) 164s (J. J. *Wilkes*).

e762 *a)* *Nardi* Roberto, Il Tempio di Vespasiano; un palinsesto nella storia del Foro Romano; – *b)* *Rockwell* Peter, Carving instructions on the Temple of Vespasian: Rendiconti Pont. Accad. Arch 60 (1987s) 71-90; 3 fig.; 3 (foldout) pl. / 53-69; 3 fig.

e763 *Nielsen* Inge, The temple of Castor and Pollux on the Forum Romanum; a preliminary report on the Scandinavian excavations 1983-87 (II): AcArchK 59 (1988) 1-14; 14 fig.

e764 *Packer* James, Politics, urbanism, and archaeology in 'Roma capitale'; a troubled past and a controversial future; review article [5 books]: AJA 93 (1989) 137-141.

e765 ESettis Salvator, *al.*, La colonna traiana 1988 → 4,g802*; RAthenaeum 67 (1989) 313-6 (C. *Saletti*); RStorAnt 17s (1987s) 306-310 (S. *Tramonti*).

e766 *Wandschneider* Andrea, Das Pantheon; Raumerfahrung und Sakral-bestimmung: AntWelt 20,3 (1989) 9-24; ill.

T9.7 *Roma, Catacumbae.*

e767 **Baruffa** Antonio, Le catacombe di San Callisto; storia-archeologia-fede. T-Leumann 1988, Elle Di Ci. 190 p. → 4,g807; Lit. 16.000. 88-01-11090-1. – RCC 140 (1989,3) 103 (A. *Ferrua*); Gregorianum 70 (1989) 598s (J. *Janssens*).

e769 **Boschung** Dietrich, Antike Grabaltäre aus den Nekropolen Roms: Acta Bernensia 10. Bern 1987, Stämpfli. 136 p.; 61 pl. (997 fig.). DM 142. – RAJA 93 (1989) 306s (Diana E. E. *Kleiner*); BonnJbb 189 (1989) 620-3 (H. *Gabelmann*); Gnomon 61 (1989) 240-5 (Friederike *Sinn-Henninger*).

e770 *Chilton* Bruce, The epitaph of Himerus [monument of his wife Julia Alexandra from the Jewish catacomb of the Via Appia, re-discovered via antiquities dealer]: JQR 79 (1988s) 93-100.

e771 *Dal Bianco* Maria Grazia, Ad decimum [catacumba Via Latina]: ArchViva 8,8 (1989) 12-19; color. ill.

e772 **Deckers** Johannes G., *al.*, Die Katakombe 'Santi Marcellino e Pietro', Repertorium der Malereien 1987 → 3,f211; 4,g808: ᴿGGA 241 (1989) 198-243 (K.-D. *Dorsch*); TRu 54 (1989) 215s (E. *Mühlenberg*); TüTQ 169 (1989) 143-6 (H.-J. *Vogt*).

e773 — **Pillinger** Renate, Die Tituli Historiarum oder das sogenannte Dittochaeon des Prudentius: Denkschrift 142. W 1980, Österr. Akad. 142 p. – ᴿTuTQ 169 (1989) 146 (H.-J. *Vogt*: jetzt, wegen zwei Malereien 49 und 58 von S. Pietro e Marcellino nicht in Deckers).

e774 **Duval** Yvette, Auprès des saints corps et âme; l'inhumation 'ad sanctos' dans la chrétienté d'Orient et d'Occident du III au VIII siècle. P 1988, Ét. Aug. – ᴿArchEspArq 62 (1989) 356s (R. *Teja*).

e775 *Eck* Walter, Inschriften und Grabbauten in der Nekropole unter St. Peter: → 79, Heidelberger Jubiläum 1989, 55-90; XII pl.

e776 **Eisner** Michael, Zur Typologie der Grabbauten im Suburbium Roms 1986 → 3,f212; 4,g809: ᴿBonnJbb 189 (1989) 616-620 (W. K. *Kovacsovics*).

e777 **Fink** Josef [† 1984], ᴱ*Schmidinger* Heinrich M., Das Petrusgrab in Rom 1988 → 4,g813; 3-7022-1650-2: ᴿArchAustriaca 73 (1989) 235s (O. *Harl*); Gregorianum 70 (1989) 382s (J. *Janssens* non approva); ZkT 111 (1989) 221s (R. *Oberforcher*: Peter's 'grave' may mean 'the place where his resurrection is awaited').

e778 **Guarducci** Margherita, La tomba di San Pietro; una straordinaria vicenda. Mi 1988, Rusconi. 171 p.; 32 fig. – ᴿRHE 84 (1989) 863 (J. *Ruysschaert*: plaidoyer trop personnel, n'épargne pas PAUL VI, JEAN-PAUL II).

e779 **Guyon** Jean, Le cimetière Aux deux lauriers 1987 → 4,g814: ᴿJbAC 32 (1989) 221-5 (F. *Tolotti*).

e780 *Jastrzebowska* Elisabeth, Les sarcophages chrétiens d'enfants à Rome au IVᵉ siècle: MÉF 101 (1989) 783-804.

e781 *Konikoff* Adia, Sarcophagi from the Jewish catacombs of ancient Rome 1986 → 2,b437; 3,f219: ᴿRÉJ 147 (1988) 233s (François *Monfrin*).

e782 — *Vismara* C., Ancora sugli Ebrei di Roma [severe criticism of A. *Konikoff*, Sarcophagi from the Jewish catacombs of ancient Rome, Stu 1986]: Archaeologia Classica 38ss (1986ss) 150-161 [< JStJud 20,272].

e782* **Reekmans** Louis, Het Gaiuscomplex in de Callixtuscatacombe, een typisch voorbeeld van Romeinse crypten met vereerde paus- en martelarengraven: Analecta 49/2. Bru 1987, Acad. p. 53-73. – ᴿRHE 84 (1989) 529 (B. *Dehandschutter*).

e783 *Schumacher* Walter N., Die Grabungen unter S. Sebastiano 95 Jahre nach den Entdeckungen Anton de WAALS: → 732, RömQ 83 (1988) 134-166.

e784 **Tronzo** William, The Via Latina catacomb — imitation and discontinuity in fourth century Roman painting. Univ. Park 1986, Penn. State Univ. 78 p.; ill. – ᴿKairos 30s (1988s) 251-3 (K. *Schubert*).

T9.8 *Roma, Ars palaeochristiana.*

e785 **Arbeiter** Achim, Alt-St. Peter in Geschichte und Wissenschaft 1988 → 4,g822: ᴿByZ 82 (1989) 296-302 (F. W. *Deichmann*); JbAC 32 (1989) 225-7 (S. de *Blaauw*).

e786 *a) Carletti* Carlo, Origine, committenza e fruizione delle scene bibliche nella produzione figurativa romana del III sec.; – *b) Otranto* Giorgio, Alle origini dell'arte cristiana precostantiniana; interpretazione simbolica o storica? : VetChr 26 (1989) 207-219 / 287-306 + 9 fig.

e787 *Dassmann* Ernst, Archäologische Spuren frühchristlicher Paulusverehrung: ➤ 732, RömQ 84 (1989) 271-298.

e788 **Fiocchi Nicolai** Vincenzo, I cimiteri paleocristiani del Lazio I. Etruria meridionale: Monumenti di Antichità Cristiana 10. Vaticano 1988. 419-xviii p.; 388 fig.; 5 pl. – ᴿSMSR 55 (1989) 162-5 (Myla *Perraymond*).

e788* *a) Guidobaldi* Federico, Ricerche di archeologia cristiana a Roma (dentro le mura); – *b) Fasola* Umberto M., ...fuori le mura; – *c) Carletti* Carlo, ...epigrafia: ➤ 827, 11ᵉ Arch.Chrét. 1986-9, 2127-48 / 2149-76 / 2177-2200.

e789 **Korol** Dieter, Die frühchristlichen Wandmalereien.... Nola 1987 ➤ 3,f227; 4,g826: ᴿJTS 40 (1989) 262s (sr. C. *Murray*).

e790 *Menna* Maria Raffaella, Niccolò IV, i mosaici absidali di S. Maria Maggiore e l'Oriente: ʀɪɴᴀsᴀ 10 (1987) 201-224; 30 fig.

e790* **Sabbatini Tumolesi** Patrizia, Epigrafia anfiteatrale dell'Occidente romano, I. Roma. R 1988, Quasar. 188 p.; 19 pl. – ᴿCC 140 (1989,3) 442s (A. *Ferrua*).

e791 *Schlatter* Fredric W., The text in the mosaic of Santa Pudenziana: VigChr 43 (1989) 155-165.

e792 *Simonetti* Manlio, Roma cristiana tra II e III secolo: VetChr 26 (1989) 115-136.

e793 *Valerio Cosentino* Benedetto, L'atrio della Basilica di S. Clemente (< diss. Univ. Roma 1987): StRom 37 (1989) 309-323; 4 fig.

T9.9   *(Roma) Imperium occidentale,* **Europa.**

e794 **Baccrabère** Georges, Le Sanctuaire [romain] rural antique d'Ancely, commune de Toulouse: BLitEc Chr 1 Sup. Toulouse 1988, Inst. Cath. 576 p.; 87 fig.; 16 pl. – ᴿTR 85 (1989) 462s (H. *Brandenburg*: not much on how it came to be used for Christian worship).

e795 *Baldoni* Daniela, Dionysos si è fermato a Spina: ArchViva 8,8 (1989) 48-53; color. ill.

e796 *Boatwright* Mary T., Hadrian and Italian cities [he built at 29 outside Rome]: Chiron 19 (1989) 235-271.

e797 **Bonghi Jovino** Maria, L'insula VI/5: Pompei 5, 1984 ➤ 3,f232; 4,g833: ᴿJRS 78 (1988) 222s (R. *Ling*: an opportunity missed).

e798 *De Miro* Ernesto, *al.,* Agrigento: AntRArch 15,5 (1989) 4-8(-32).

e799 **Greco** E., *Theodorescu* D., Poseidonia-Paestum III. Forum nord 1987 ➤ 1,e550 ... 4,g837: ᴿGnomon 61 (1989) 233-240 (D. *Mertens*); JRS 79 (1989) 179s (R. M. *Harrison*).

e800 *Laidlaw* Anne, The first style in Pompeii; painting and architecture 1987 ➤ 3,f238: ᴿGnomon 61 (1989) 464-6 (H. von *Hesberg*).

e801 *Lange* Judith, Rovine a sud; Roma in Africa: ArchViva 7,1 (1988) 42-51; color. ill.

e802 *Marčenko* Konstantin, *Vinogradov* Yuri, The Scythian period in the northern Black Sea region (750-250 B.C.), ᵀ*Wright* Sarah, *Taylor* Timothy: Antiquity 63 (1989) 803-813; 5 fig.

e803 *Prosperi* Mario, Quella raffinata gente dell'antica Oplonti [villa di Poppea, Torre Annunziata]: AntRArch 15 (1989) 33-39; color. ill.

e804 **Richardson** L., Pompeii, an architectural history. Baltimore 1988, Johns Hopkins Univ. xxviii-445 p.; 53 fig.; 23 plans; map. $49.50. 0-8018-3533-X [JRS 79,276]. – ᴿAmJPg 110 (1989) 672-5 (R. *Brilliant*).

e805 *Whitehouse* Ruth D., *Wilkins* John B., Greeks and natives in south-east Italy; approaches to the archaeological evidence: ➤ 837, Centre 1986/9, 102-126.

e806 **Wojcik** Maria Rita, La villa dei padri ad Ercolano 1986 ➤ 2,b469; 4,g850: ᴿAntClas 58 (1989) 559-561 (J.C. *Balty*); Gnomon 61 (1989) 59-64 (R. *Neudecker*).

XIX. Geographia biblica

U1 **Geographies.**

e807 ᴱ**Ahrweiler** Hélène, Géographie historique du monde méditerranéen: Byzantina Sorbonensia 7 [p.17-29, *Avraméa* Anna, La géographie historique byzantine; 149-178, *Papazotos* A., Athos, topographie; 215-8, *Tsafrir* Y., Byzantine settlements in Israel]. P 1988, Sorbonne. 312 p. F 180. – ᴿByzantina 15 (1989) 490-6 (Alkmini *Stauridou-Zaphraka*); RÉByz 47 (1989) 293s (J.-C. *Cheynet*).

e808 **Bösen** Willibald, Galiläa als Lebensraum und Wirkungsfeld Jesu; eine zeitgeschichtliche und theologische Untersuchung 1985 ➤ 1,3855.e564; 3,f249: ᴿRelStR 15 (1989) 356 (J.H. *Elliott*).

e809 *Brown* Raymond E., [*North* Robert], Biblical Geography: ➤ 384, NJBC (1989s) [1175-] 1181-1195.

e810 **Deurloo** Karel, *Hemelsoet* Ben, Op bergen en in dalen; bijbelse geografie; de plaats waar geschreven staat. Baarn 1988, Ten Have. 180 p. ƒ25. – ᴿStreven 56 (1988s) 664s (P. *Beentjes*).

e811 ᴱ**Grothusen** Klaus-Detlev, Türkei [seit 1944; 37 Autoren]: Südosteuropa-Handbuch 4., 1985 ➤ 2,b475: ᴿDer Islam 65 (1988) 171-3 (A. *Schaendlinger*).

e812 **Haag** Herbert, Das Land der Bibel; Gestalt — Geschichte — Erforschung² [¹1976]. Stu 1989 = 1976, KBW. 188 p.; ill.; maps. 3-460-32791-X [NTAbs 34,131].

e813 *Jackson* Thomas A., The land and people of Canaan: BibIll 14,2 (1988) 66-69.

e814 **Johnson** Sherman E., Jesus and his towns: Good News Studies 29. Wilmington 1989, Glazier. 183 p. $13 pa. 0-89453-653-2 [TDig 37,66].

e815 *Muszyński* Jerzy, ⊕ Geografia biblijna: ➤ 891, EncKat 5 (1989) 979-981 [-82, historyczna chrześcijaństwa, *Kloczowski* Jerzy; 984 religii, *Bronk* Andrzej).

e816 **Quaresmi** Francesco [1583-1656], Elucidatio Terrae Sanctae, brani scelti e tradotti da Sabino De Sandoli: SBF 32. J 1989, Franciscan. xix-494 p.

e817 *Zadok* Ran, Notes on the historical geography of Mesopotamia and northern Syria: Abr-Nahrain 27 (1989) 154-169.

U1.2 **Historia geographiae.**

e818 *Babics* J., *Nobis* H.M., Die mathematisch-geographischen und kartographischen Ideen von ALBERTUS Magnus und ihre Stelle in der Geschichte der Geographie: ➤ 561, Kölner Univ. 1989, 97-110; 4 fig.

e818* ᴱBaladié Raoul, STRABON, Géographie, tome IV, livre VII: Budé. P 1989, BLettres. vii-335 (doubles) p. [ClasR 40, 14-16, P. *Levi*].

e819 *a) Baldacci* Osvaldo, Dalla topografia alla geocartografia in età romana; – *b) Janni* Pietro, Gli antichi e i punti cardinali; rileggendo PAUSANIA; – *c) Prontera* Francesco, La geografia dei greci fra natura e storia; note e ipotesi di lavoro: → 795, ᴱ*Janni* P., Geōgraphia 1985/8, 39-53 / 77-91 / 199-222.

e819* ᵀᴱCasson Lionel, The Periplus Maris Erythraei. Princeton 1989, Univ. xvii-320 p.; 18 maps. $50. [ClasR 40,16, S. E. *Sidebotham*].

e820 *Cranford* Jeff, Ancient knowledge of other worlds [... Babylonian astronomy]: BibIll 14,3 (1988) 30-32 [< OTAbs 12,36].

e821 [Gautier] **Dalché** Patrick, La 'Descriptio mappe mundi' de HUGUES de Saint-Victor, texte inédit intr. comm. P 1988, Ét. Augustiniennes. 228 p.; ill. – ᴿRBén 99 (1989) 195 (P.-I. *Fransen*: a description not of the world but of a map).

e822 *Danielyan* Edward, Cosmological ideas in antiquity and early medieval philosophical views: AcClasDeb 25 (Eirene 18 de philosophia antiqua, Budapest; 1989) 43-49.

e823 ᴱ**Desreumaux** Alain, *Schmidt* Francis, Moïse géographe; recherches sur les représentations juives et chrétiennes de l'espace: Études de Psychologie et de Philosophie 24. P 1988, Vrin. 262 p.; 14 fig. – ᴿRÉJ 148 (1989) 407-9 (Madeleine *Petit*: vaste problématique); RHPR 69 (1989) 336s (M. *Matter*).

e824 **Dilke** O. A. W., *a)* Greek and Roman maps 1985 → 1,e587 ... 4,g873: ᴿJNES 48 (1989) 59-61 (H. I. *MacAdam*); Klio 71 (1989) 307s (A. *Silbermann*); – *b)* Rome's contribution to cartography: Contr.Ist.Stor.Ant. 14 (1988) 194-201 [< ByZ 82,442].

e825 *Drory* Joseph, ❹ The chapters on Palestine in YAʿQUBI's Book of the Lands: CHistEI 51 (1989) 67-77; Eng. 194.

e826 **Frösén** Jaakko, *al.*, Ptolemäische Urkunden Papyri Helsingienses [aus Mumienkartonage] 1. Comm. Hum. Lit. 80, 1986 → 3,9806: ᴿDLZ 110 (1989) 670s (G. *Poethke*).

e827 *Gabba* Emilio, Sui sistemi catastali romani in Italia: Athenaeum 67 (1989) 567-570.

e828 **Habicht** Christian, PAUSANIAS und seine 'Beschreibung Griechenlands' [Eng. 1987 → 4,g878] 1985 → 3,f270: ᴿGymnasium 96 (1989) 176s (H.-P. *Drögemüller*); RArchéol (1989) 173-5 (J. *Pouilloux*).

e829 ᴱ**Harley** J.B., *Woodward* David, The history of cartography I 1987 → 3, 496; 4,g879: ᴿAmHR 94 (1989) 407s (R. J. A. *Talbert*: work begun 1975).

e830 *Isler* Martin, An ancient method of finding and extending direction: JAmEg 26 (1989) 191-206; 18 fig.

e831 **Karttunen** Klaus, India in early Greek literature: Studia Orientalia 65. Helsinki 1989, PunaMusta. 293 p.; maps. 951-9380-10-8.

e832 *Klein-Franke* Felix, Hat die Erde die Gestalt einer Kugel? Betrachtungen zum Verhältnis des Islam im Mittelalter gegenüber den physikalischen Wissenschaften [arabischer Text von Rašid FAḌLULLAH 1247-1318, deutsch gegenüber]: Muséon 102 (1989) 165-193.

e833 *Klemm* Dietrich & Rosemarie, Pharaonischer Goldbergbau im Wadi Sid und der Turiner Minenpapyrus: → 823, Akten IV 2 (1985/9) 73-87; 4 fig.; pl. 5-7.

e834 **Koch** Johannes, Neue Untersuchungen zur Topographie des babylonischen Fixsternhimmels. Wsb 1989, Harrassowitz. xl-157 p.; 22 fig. 3-447-02943-9.

e835 **Kunitzsch** Paul, [PTOLEMAEUS] Der Sternkatalog des Almagest; die arabisch-mittelalterliche Tradition, I. Die arabischen Übersetzungen 1986 → 4,g884: ᴿJAOS 109 (1989) 694-6 (G. *Saliba*).

e836 **Laut** Jena P., Materialien zu Evliya Çelebi I: Erläuterungen und Indices zur Karte B IX 6, 'Kleinasien im 17. Jahrhundert nach Evliya Çelebi': TAVO B-90. Wsb 1989, Reichert. 248 p. 3-88226-460-8.

e837 **Leitz** Christian, Studien zur ägyptischen Astronomie: ÄgAbh 49. Wsb 1989, Harrassowitz. ix-108 p. 3-447-02945-5.

e838 *a) Macadam* Henry I., STRABO, PLINY the Elder and PTOLEMY of Alexandria; three views of ancient Arabia and its peoples; – *b) Frézouls* Edmond, COSMAS Indicopleustès et l'Arabie; – *c) Desanges* Jehan, Arabes et Arabie en terre d'Afrique dans la géographie antique: → 816, L'Arabie 1987/9, 289-318; 2 maps / 441-460 / 413-429.

e839 **Maguire** Henry, Earth and ocean; the terrestrial world in early Byzantine art 1987 → 3,f276: ᴿBMosAnt 12 (1988s) 285-7 (J.-P. *Sodini*); BO 46 (1989) 166s (J. *Wilkinson*); JbÖsByz 39 (1989) 366-8 (H. *Hunger*); JHS 109 (1989) 274 (Lyn *Rodley*).

e840 *McGuirk* D.L.ᴶ, RUYSCH world map; census and commentary: Imago Mundi 41 (1989) 133-141; 1 fig.; 3 maps [< RHE 84, p. 339*].

e841 *Mason* Roger, The Medici-Lazara map of Alanya [Pisa? c.1609]: AnSt 39 (1989) 85-105; 3 fig.; pl. XIX-XXII.

e842 **Miller** Konrad, Mappae arabicae [1926-31] ᴱ*Gaube* Heinz: TAVO B-65, 1986 → 2,b499: ᴿZDPV 105 (1989) 200 (E. A. *Knauf*).

e843 **Nicolet** Claude, L'inventaire du monde 1988 → 4,g892: ᴿAmHR 94 (1989) 1351 (R. J. A. *Talbert*); AntClas 58 (1989) 474s (J. *Wankenne*); ÉtClas 57 (1989) 53-55 (J. M. *Alonso-Núñez*); Klio 31 (1989) 306s (A. *Silberman*); RPg 62 (1988) 309-314 (J. *Desanges*).

e844 ᵀ**Parroni** Piergiorgio, POMPONII Melae de chorographia libri tres: Storia e Letteratura 160, 1984 → 1,e608 ... 4,g894: ᴿAnzAltW 42 (1989) 36-38 (F. *Lasserre*).

e845 *Potts* D.T., Seleucid Karmania [southeast of Persepolis]: → 28, ᶠBERGHE L. Vanden 1989, (II) 581-600 + map; II pl.

e846 **Pryor** J.H., Geography, technology and war; studies in the maritime history of the Mediterranean, 649-1571. C 1988, Univ. xviii-236 p. £22.50. – ᴿTijdschrift voor Geschiedenis 102 (1989) 264s (R. Van *Uytven*) [< RHE 84, p. 339*].

e847 *Roller* Duane W., Columns in stone; ANAXIMANDROS' conception of the world: AntClas 58 (1989) 185-9.

e848 *Romm* James, HERODOTUS and mythic geography; the case of the Hyperboreans: AmPgTr 119 (1989) 97-113.

e849 *Rubin* Rehav, ⊙ The DE ANGELIS map of Jerusalem (1578) and its copies: CHistEI 52 (1989) 100-111 (-119).

e849* *Scarre* Chris, Hammond Past Worlds; the Times atlas of archaeology. Maplewood NJ 1988, Hammond. 319 p. $85. [BAR-W 16/4,4, B. J. *Beitzel*].

e850 *Silberman* Alain, Le premier ouvrage latin de géographie; la Chorographie de POMPONIUS Méla et ses sources grecques: Klio 71 (1989) 571-581.

e851 *Smith* Catherine D., Archaeology and maps in prehistoric art; the way forward: BCentPrei 24 (1988) 99-112.

e852 *a) Soldt* W.H. van, De Babylonische astronomie, het begin van een wetenschap; – *b) Jongeling* K., De verloren wetenschap van Phoeniciërs en Carthagers: PhoenixEOL 35,2 (1989) 39-56 / 57-65.

e853 **Thollard** Patrick,   Barbarie et civilisation chez STRABON; étude critique des livres III et IV de la Géographie: Ann. Litt. Besançon 365, Hist. Anc. 77.   P 1987, BLettres.   92 p.   2-251-60365-4. – ᴿAntClas 58 (1989) 292s (D. *Marcotte*).

e854 *Weber* Ekkehard,   Zur Datierung der Tabula Peutingeriana: ⇨ 205, ᶠWALSER G.   Labor 1989, 113-7.

U1.4   Atlas – maps.

e855 **Aharoni** Y., *Avi-Yonah* M.,   Atlante della Bibbia [1968 ²1977], ᵀ1987 ⇨ 3,f287; 4,g906:   ᴿParVi 34 (1989) 151 (G. *Biguzzi*).

e856 ᴱ**Baladier** Charles, Le grand atlas des religions. P 1988, Encyclopaedia universalis.   413 p.   F 580.   2-85229-920-8. – ᴿÉTRel 64 (1989) 263s (D. *Lys*: hardly an atlas in the dictionary sense of 'maps', only twelve); Études 370 (1989) 136s (P. *Valadier*); MondeB 59 (1989) 62 (J. *Potin*).

e857 **Beltrán Lloris** F., *Marco* Simón F.,   Atlas de historia antigua. Zaragoza 1987, Diputación Aragón / Pórtico.   127 p.; 72 color. maps.   84-85264-78-9 [JRS 79,268]. – ᴿGerión 7 (1989) 335 (J. *Alvar*).

e858 **Benvenisti** Meron, *Khayat* Shlomo, The [Palestine] West Bank and Gaza Atlas.   Jerusalem 1988, West Bank Data-Base Project.   965-356-602-6 [OIAc S89].

e859 **Blake** Gerald, *al.*,   The Cambridge Atlas of the Middle East and North Africa.   C 1987, Univ.   124 p.   [JAOS 109,341].

e860 **Brossier** François,   Atlante della storia biblica.   Brescia 1989, Queriniana.   62 p.   Lit. 15.000 [RivB 37,529].

e861 **Campbell** Joseph,   Historical atlas of world mythology [I. The way of the animal powers 1983 ⇨ 65,759] II.   SF 1989, Harper & R.   [I. 1983, 302 p. 440 fig.; 58 maps; 0-912383-00-3] II *a*) 1988, 127 p., 224 fig., 14 maps; *b*) p. 128-251; fig. 225-338; *c*) 1989, p. 252-387; fig. 339-551, maps 26-43. 0-90-55150-X; 8-5; 9-3.

e862 ᴱ**Chadwick** Henry, (*Evans* Gillian), Atlas van het Christendom [1987], ᵀ*Booij* P. J., 1987 ⇨ 4,g909:   ᴿBijdragen 50 (1989) 447s (J. G. *Hahn*).

e863 **Cornu** Georgette,   Atlas du monde arabo-islamique à l'époque classique, 9ᵉ-10ᵉ siècles; répertoires des toponymes: CNRS/Institut du Monde Arabe.   Leiden 1985, Brill.   228 p.; folder of 20 maps.   DM 105. – ᴿDer Islam 65 (1988) 385-7 (G. Dj. *Davary*).

e864 ᴱ**Jedin** Hubert, *al.*,   Atlas zur Kirchengeschichte²ʳᵉᵛ [¹1970] 1987 ⇨ 3,f296; 4,g915:   ᴿZkT 111 (1989) 231s (H. B. *Meyer*).

e865 **Littel** Franklin H., ᵀᴱ*Geldbach* Erich,   Atlas zur Geschichte des Christentums [1976],ᵀ, Wu 1989, Brockhaus.   160 p.   DM 19,80. – ᴿTPQ 137 (1989) 295 (R. *Zinnhobler*).

e866 ᴱ**May** H. G.,   Atlas Bíblico, Oxford.   Estella 1988, VDivino.   157 p. – ᴿBibFe 15 (1989) 486 (A. *Salas*).

e867 **Nebenzahl** Kenneth,   Maps of the Holy Land [60 maps since PTOLEMAEUS] 1986 ⇨ 3,f280; 4,g920:   ᴿBAR-W 15,2 (1989) 8s.11 (H. *Brodsky*); CurrTM 16 (1989) 233s (R. H. *Smith*: high praise, with a kind word also for R. NORTH 1979 ⇨ 60,u390).

e868 **Pacomio** L., *Vanetti* P.,   Kleiner Bibelatlas; Geschichte, Geographie, Archäologie der Bibel [1985 ⇨ 1,e620], ᵀ*Sommavilla* Guido. Pd 1987, Bonifatius.   DM 28,50. – ᴿTPQ 137 (1989) 75s (Borghild *Baldauf*).

e869 **Pritchard** J. B., Harper [= Times] Atlas of the Bible 1987 ⇨ 3,f305; 4,g921:   ᴿBS 146 (1989) 344s (F. Duane *Lindsey*); Interpretation 43 (1989)

307 (R. W. *Doermann*: far more than an atlas; 134 maps related to major historical events).

e870 [ᴱ**Pritchard** J. B. – Times 1987 ⇥ 3,f305], ᵀᴱ*Keel* O., *Küchler* M., Herders Grosser Bibelatlas. FrB 1989, Herder. 255 p.; 600 color. fig. DM 98. – ᴿBiKi 44 (1989) 93s (D. *Bauer*); TPQ 137 (1989) 415 (A. *Fuchs*); TüTQ 169 (1989) 242s (H. *Schweizer*).

e870* ᴱ**Pritchard** James B., Atlas du monde biblique [1987], ᵀ*Canal* Denis-Armand, *Féménias* Anne. P 1989, Larousse [RHPR 70,241, B. *Keller*].

e871 **Rasmussen** Carl G., Zondervan NIV atlas of the Bible; maps by Carta, Jerusalem. GR 1989, Zondervan Regency. 256 p. $40. 0-310-25160-5 [TDig 36,386].

e872 [Readers Digest, ᴱ*Frank* H.], ᵀᴱ*Rossi* F., Il grande atlante della Bibbia; la storia, i luoghi, i costumi della Terra Santa 1986 ⇥ 2,b521: ᴿParVi 34 (1989) 152s (G. *Biguzzi*, anche su RHYMER J., ital. 1986).

e873 **Rogerson** John, Atlante della Bibbia [1985 ⇥ 1,e622], ᵀᴱ*Cavedo* Romeo. Novara 1988, De Agostini. 240 p.; 67 fig. + 285 color.; 43 maps; 13 plans. ⇥ 4,g926: ᴿSalesianum 51 (1989) 568 (R. *Sabin*).

e874 **Rogerson** J., ❹ Shin Seisho-chizu [New atlas of the Bible 1985]. ᵀ*Onodera* K. Tokyo 1988, Asakura-shoten. 237 p.; ill.; maps. Y22.000. 4-254-16598 6 C 3325 [BL 90,40].

e875 **Sahab** A., Atlas of Iraq in ancient maps (in Persian): Documents and Maps on the Persian Gulf 2. Tehran 1985, Al-Iraq. 140 p. [OIAc Ja90].

e876 *Scippa* Vincenzo, Geografia e costumi della Terra Santa; a proposito di Atlanti biblici: Asprenas 36 (1989) 522-8.

e877 **Stohr** Volker, *Denk* Wolfgang, Die Kreuzfahrerstaaten im 13. Jahrhundert / Syrien und Palästina: map TAVO B-VIII-10. 1:2.000.000. Wsb 1989, Reichert [OIAc S89, with note of several outside-Palestine maps in this series]. Note now B.I.13, Ägypten, Neolith. 1988; B.II.7, Mesopotamien, frühdynast.; B.V.8, Römer und Parther 1988; B.V.17, Palästina unter römischer Vorherrschaft 1988.

e878 Stuttgarter Bibelatlas; historische Karten der Biblischen Welt. Stu 1988, Deutsche Bibelgesellschaft. 64 p. DM 25. – ᴿBiKi 44 (1989) 194 (D. *Bauer*).

u1.5 Photographiae.

e879 Allard Pierson Museum Archive, Early photographs from Egypt, 1880-1910. Leiden 1988 [OIAc S89].

e880 *Bates* James B., The [pastor's] use of visual aids: ExpTim 100 (1988s) 249-252: p. 251, 'Bible teaching can be helped, but also very much hindered ... Bible illustrations are to be avoided, not just because so many are bad ... but because their aim is wrong. You cannot re-create the scene as it happened'.

e881 **Brier** Bob, The glory of ancient Egypt; a collection of rare engravings from the Napoleonic edition. Millwood 1988, Kraus. xvi-182 p. 0-8115-4469-9 [OIAc Ja90].

e882 **Cole** Dan P., Biblical archaeology slide set / Jerusalem / NT [⇥ 2,b530]. Wsh 1985/3/6, BA Society. 134/140/180 slides; 32/36/48 p. booklet. $100/$119.50/159.50. – ᴿCurrTM 16 (1989) 230-2 (E. M. *Krentz*: there is a fourth set on Egypt-Sinai).

e883 ᴱ**Dewitz** Bodo von, An den süssen Ufern Asiens; Ägypten, Palästina, Osmanisches Reich; Reiseziele des 19. Jahrhunderts in frühen Photographien: Agfa-Foto-Historama, Ausstellung Köln Nov. 1988. Köln 1988, Agfa. 171 p. [OIAc Ja90].

e884 Les grands événements de la Bible [Marshall 1987],ᵀ. P 1988, Brepols. 200 p.; ill.; maps. F 265. 2-503-82345-9. – ᴿÉTRel 64 (1989) 115s (J. *Pons*: très bel album).

e885 **Gsellman** Hans, Türkei, Fotoerlebnisse zwischen Goldenem Horn und Ararat. Graz 1987, Styria. 168 p.; color. ill. – ᴿDer Islam 65 (1988) 183 (B. *Spuler*).

e886 **Masom** Caroline, *al.*, Bijbels beeldarchief 1987 → 4,g935: ᴿStreven 56 (1988s) 81 (P. *Beentjes*).

e887 **North** Robert, ᵀᴱ*Torta* Giorgio, Diapositive bibliche; didascalie per le Diapositive su Vicino Oriente antico e Terra Santa edite dal Pontificio Istituto Biblico. Bevera di Castello Br. (Como) 1988, Istituto Missioni Consolata. 265 p.

e887* The search for Herod's harbor — solving a 2000-year-old mystery [28 minute video tape]. NY c. 1989, Drew-Fairchild. $85 [BAR-W 16/2,10].

Seefried Monique, *Woodward* Mary C., The fascination with the East; early photographs of Egypt [Museum exhibition 1986s] 1989 → b880.

e888 **Stephens** William H., The New Testament world in pictures 1987 → 3,f315; 4,g939; also L 1988, Lutterworth; 0-7188-2701-5. – ᴿRelStR 15 (1989) 353 (A. T. *Kraabel*).

e889 *Szegedy-Maszak* Andrew, Picturing the past; photography's 150th anniversary: Archaeology 42,4 (1989) 38-47.

e889* **Tassel** Daniel, *Rosovsky* Nitza, The Holy Land then and now [with Bonfils etc.] 19th century photographs. CM 1984, Harvard Semitic Museum. 32 p. [OIAc N89].

e890 **Taylor** Jane, High above Jordan; aerial photographs [RAF for Glueck N., Saller S.; more recently Cleave]. L 1989, 64 p. – ᴿLA 39 (1989) 290 (M. *Piccirillo*).

e891 **Travlos** John, Bildlexikon zur Topographie des antiken Attika: DAI. Tü 1988, Wasmuth. xvi-486 p.; 602 fig. 3-8030-1036-5.

U1.6 Guide books, *Führer*.

e892 **Bock** Ulrich, Georgien und Armenien; zwei christliche Kulturlandschaften im Süden der Sowjetunion: Reiseführer-Dokumente. Köln 1988, DuMont. 357 p.

e893 **Bonnet** Marie-France, *Husson* Évelyne, Égypte: Guide Arthaud. P 1989, Arthaud. 2-7003-0689-9 [OIAc S89].

e894 **Brunner-Traut** Emma, Ägypten; Kunst- und Reiseführer⁶. Stu 1988, Kohlhammer. xxiii-834 p. DM 89. – ᴿBiKi 44 (1989) 45s (P.-G. *Müller*).

e895 ᴱ**Dexinger** F., *al.*, Jordanien 1985 → 1,280; 3,f321: ᴿOLZ 84 (1989) 397s (K. *Matthiae*).

e895* Egitto: Guide del Mondo. Mi 1987, Touring Club Italiano. 314 p.; ill., maps. 88-365-0056-0.

e896 **Gonen** R., Biblical holy places, an illustrated guide 1987 → 3,f322; 4,g944: ᴿPEQ 121 (1989) 84 (Kay *Prag*).

e897 **Gorys** Erhard, Das Heilige Land; historische und religiöse Stätten von Judentum, Christentum und Islam in dem 10.000 Jahre alten Kulturland zwischen Mittelmeer, Rotem Meer und Jordan: Kunst-Reiseführer. Köln

1984, DuMont. 494 p.; 130 fig.; 110 phot. + 64 color. DM 38. – ᴿZkT 111 (1969) 116s (F. *Mohr*).

e898 **Keel** O., *al.*, Orte und Landschaften der Bibel I, 1984 ➤ 65,b775 ... 2,b545: ᴿOLZ 84 (1989) 47-49 (G. *Pfeifer*) [II. 1982 ➤ 63,d816 ... 4,g944*].

e899 **Meyer** Marianne D., Ägypten: Richtig reisen 1987 ➤ 4,g946: ᴿDer Islam 65 (1988) 152 (B. *Spuler*).

e900 **Murphy-O'Connor** Jerome, The Holy Land; an archaeological guide from earliest times to 1700²ʳᵉᵛ 1986 ➤ 2,b546; 3,f329: ᴿBA 52 (1989) 42 (H. N. *Richardson*, also on S. DOYLE).
    Prag K., Jerusalem: Blue Guide 1989 ➤ d768.

e901 **Ravasi** G., La terra promessa; guida 1987 ➤ 3,f332: ᴿProtestantesimo 44 (1989) 54 (J. A. *Soggin*).

e902 **Schneider** Dux, Türkei; Reise-Handbuch: Richtig Reisen. Köln 1987, DuMont. 489 p. – ᴿDer Islam 65 (1988) 370s (B. *Spuler*).

e903 **Schüssler** Karlheinz [➤ e317], Ägypten; Altertümer, Koptische Kunst, Islamische Denkmäler². Cicerone. Mü 1987, Artemis. 247 p. – ᴿDer Islam 65 (1988) 150s (B. *Spuler*).

e904 **Tzaferis** Vassilios, The Holy Land². Athena 1988, auct. 237 p.; ill.

U1.7 **Onomastica.**

e905 **Aḥituv** Shmuel, Canaanite toponyms in ancient Egyptian documents [1979 J diss.] 1984 ➤ 65,b786 ... 4,g949: ᴿJNES 48 (1989) 35-38 (M. C. *Astour*: deficiencies); ZDPV 105 (1989) 174-7 (E. A. *Knauf*, C. J. *Lenzen*).

e906 *Beinlich* Horst, Spätzeitquellen zu den Gauen Oberägyptens: Gö-MiszÄg 107 (1989) 7-41.

e907 **Bell** Robert E., Place-names in classical mythology: Greece. Santa Barbara 1988, ABC-Clio. xiii-350 p. 0-87436-507-4.

e908 *Eilers* Wilhelm, Iranische Ortsnamenstudien: Szb W ph/h 465, 1987 ➤ 3,f345: ᴿJRAS (1989) 153s (C. E. *Bosworth*).

e909 *Krecher* Joachim, Observations on the Ebla toponyms: ➤ 831, Eblaite names 1985/8, 173-190.

e910 ᴱ**Lauffer** Siegfried, Lexikon der historischen Stätten, von den Anfängen bis zur Gegenwart. Mü 1989, Beck. 775 p.; 12 maps.

e911 *Miller* J. Maxwell, Six Khirbet el-Medeinehs in the region east of the Dead Sea: BASOR 276 (1989) 25-28; map.

e912 **Müller** Dietram, Topographischer Bildkommentar zu den Historien HERODOTS; Griechenland im Umfang des heutigen griechischen Staats-gebiets 1987 ➤ 3,f357; 1066 p.; 1052 fig.; 159 maps, foldout. DM 480. – ᴿAcPraeh 21 (1989) 145s (G. *Zimmer*); AnzAltW 42 (1989) 72-75 (R. *Bichler*).
    Na'aman Nadav, Studies in biblical geographical lists: Borders 7, 1986 ➤ g236.

e913 *Ohme* H., Der terminus *chōra* als 'Provinzbeziechnung' in synodalen Bischofslisten des 6.-8. Jahrhunderts: ByZ 82 (1989) 191-201.

e914 *Pruneti* Paola, Toparchie e *pagi*; precisazioni topografiche relative al nòmo Ossirinchite: Aegyptus 69 (1989) 113-8.

e915 *Reeg* Gottfried, Die Ortsnamen Israels nach der rabbinischen Literatur: TAVO B-51. Wsb 1989, Reichert. vii-696 p. 3-88226-456-X.

e916 **Thompson** T. L., *al.*, Toponymie palestinienne... Acre, Corridor de Jérusalem 1988 ➤ 4,g963: ᴿAION 49 (1989) 155 (F. *Vattioni*).

e916* *Zadok* Ran, On the onomastic material from Emar [mostly personal names, but with demographic conclusions]: WeltOr 20s (1989s) 45-61.

U2.1 **Geologia:** soils, mountains, volcanoes, earthquakes.

e917 **Andel** T. van, *Runnels* C., Beyond the Acropolis; a rural Greek past 1987 → 4,g967: ᴿÉchMClas 33 (1989) 267-272 (J. *Ober*).

e918 **Bartov** V., *Arad* V., Carmel and Carmel coast; bibliography of geological research: Geological survey of Israel report [0333-6069] 651/8/88. J 1988, Ministry of Energy [OIAc S89].

e919 *Edis* Jonathan, *al.*, An archaeologist's guide to classification of cropmarks and soilmarks: Antiquity 63 (1989) 112-126.

e920 *Gamil* Mahmoud M. El-, *Hassan* El-Khedr H., Geophysical investigations for holocene palaeohydrography in the northwestern Nile Delta: → 859, Delta 1988/9, 125-143 + 25 fig. (2 maps).

e921 **Mann** Ulrich, † 13.III.1989, Überall ist Sinai 1988 → 4,g976: ᴿTLZ 114 (1989) 719-722 (P. *Heidrich*).

e922 **Neev** D., *al.*, Mediterranean coasts of Israel and North Sinai; holocene tectonism from geology, geophysics and archaeology. NY 1988, Taylor & F. 130 p. – ᴿIntJNaut 18 (1989) 265-7 (A. *Ronen*).

e923 *a) Stachowiak* Lech, ❷ Góra [*har*, ST]; – *b) Szwarc* Urszula, [*óros*, NT]; – *c) Sakowicz* Eugeniusz, w religiach pozachrześcijańskich: → 891, EncKat 5 (1989) 1368s / 1369 / 1367s.

e924 **Vogel** Horst, Bodenerosion im Terrassenfeldbau; Kulturlandzerstörung durch Landzuntzungswandel im Haraz-Gebirge: Jemen-Studien 8. Wsb 1988, Reichert. 3-88226-427-6 [OIAc S89].

U2.2 *Hydrographia:* **rivers, seas, salt.**

e925 *Alpert* P., *Neumann* J., An ancient 'correlation' between streamflow and distant rainfall in the Near East: JNES 48 (1989) 313s.

e926 *Andel* Tjeerd H. van, Late Quaternary sea-level changes and archaeology: Antiquity 63 (1989) 233-245; 7 fig.

e927 *Baly* Denis, The river Nile [4132 miles, from Lake Victoria]: BibIll 14,3 (1988) 42-50 [< OTAbs 12,34].

e928 *Betts* A. V. G., *Helms* S. W., A water harvesting and storage system at Ibn el-Ghazzi in eastern Jordan; a preliminary report: Levant 21 (1989) 3-11; 9 fig.

e929 *Calvet* Yves, La maîtrise de l'eau à Ougarit: CRAI (1989) 308-326; 9 fig.

e930 **Garbrecht** Günther, Historische Talsperren. Stu 1987, Wittwer. vii-464 p. – ᴿGnomon 61 (1989) 641s (U. *Buske*).

e931 **Giddy** Lisa I., Egyptian oases (ᴰ1984) 1987 → 3,f389; 4,g981: ᴿOLZ 84 (1989) 529-531 (W. *Barta*).

e932 *Jundziłł* Julius, ❷ *Rola morza...* La mer dans la culture romaine; l'état actuel et les perspectives des recherches: Eos 77 (1989) 53-64.

e933 *Kleiss* Wolfram, Achaemenidische Staudämme in Fars: ArchMIran 21 (1988) 63-68; 6 (foldout) fig.; pl. 35-38.

e934 *McHugh* William P., *al.*, Neolithic adaptation and the Holocene functioning of Tertiary palaeodrainages in southern Egypt and northern Sudan: Antiquity 63 (1989) 320-336; 7 fig.; 1 colour. pl.

e935 *a) Mocchegiani Carpano* Claudio, La città e il fiume; le ricerche nel Tevere; – *b) d'Amato* Clotilde, I Romani alle terme; – *c) Marzatico*

Franco, *Perini* Renato, Gli uomini delle acque nell'età di bronzo [Fiave]: ArchViva 8,4 (1989) 20-27 / 28-33 / 34-55.

e936 *Nibbi* Alessandra, Some further remarks on the Haunebut: ZägSpr [114 (1987) *Iversen* E., taking *w3d-wr* as 'ocean'] 116 (1989) 153-160; 6 fig.; map.

e937 **Nomachi** Kazuyoshi, Le Nil; intr. *Moorhouse* Geoffrey. P 1989, Arthaud. 194 p., all color phot. 2-7003-0791-7.

e938 *Rodríguez Neila* Juan F., Aqua publica y política municipal romana: Gerión 6 (1988) 223-252.

e939 *Venit* Marjorie S., The pointed tomb from Wardian and the antiquity of the *sāqiya* [water-wheel] in Egypt: JAmEg 26 (1989) 219-222; 2 fig.

e940 **Wagner** Guy, Les oasis d'Égypte à l'époque grecque, romaine et byzantine d'après les documents grecs (recherches de papyrologie et d'épigraphie grecques): BiblÉt 100, 1987 → 3,f398: ᴿBO 46 (1989) 342-6 (R. S. *Bagnall*: useful despite quirks); JAmEg 26 (1989) 249s (Diana *Delia*); RÉG 102 (1989) 226s (P. *Cauderlier*).

Die Wasserversorgung antiker Städte (**Garbrecht** G., Pergamon 1987) → e561.

e941 **Werner** Dietrich, Wasser für das antike Rom 1986 → 3,f399: ᴿMGraz 2 (1988) 247-251 (M. *Hainzmann*).

U2.3 **Clima, pluvia.**

e942 *Rubin* Rehav, The debate over climatic changes in the Negev, fourth-seventh centuries C.E.: PEQ 121 (1989) 71-78; map.

U2.5 *Fauna;* **Animals.**

e944 *a) Allam* Schafik, Taxe (?) sur le bétail dans l'Égypte ancienne; – *b*) *Pecchioli Daddi* Franca, La condizione sociale del pastore (ˡᵘSIPAD) e dell'amministratore (ˡᵘAGRIG); esempi di 'diversità' presso gli Ittiti: → 877, Lavoro 1988, 52-70 + 2 fig. / 240-8.

e945 *Alster* Bendt, An Akkadian animal proverb (fox and dog) and the Assyrian letter ABL 555: JSC 41 (1989) 187-193.

e946 ᵀᴱ**Amann** Ludwig, Ausgewählte Kapitel über Chirurgie und Pferdezucht im Corpus Hippiatricorum Graecorum: Diss. Medic. Mü 1983. 161 p. [ähnliche 1981-4, **Beiter** Georg, **Schäffer** Johann, **Appal** Josef; **Göbel** Dieter, **Kämpf** Peter, **Rupp** Ulrich, **Zellwecker** Leopold].

e947 *Des animaux et des hommes*; témoignage de la préhistoire et de l'antiquité. Bru 1988, Soc. Protectrice des Animaux. 216 p.; 294 fig. – ᴿSalesianum 51 (1989) 523 (R. *Bratky*).

e948 *Archi* Alfonso, Société des hommes et société des animaux: → 154, ᶠPUGLIESE CARRATELLI G. 1988, 25-37.

e949 ᵀᴱ**Balme** D. M., ARISTOTLE, De partibus animalium I and De generatione animalium I (with passages from II,1-3). Ox 1985=1972, Clarendon. vii-173 p. 0-19-872059-9.

e950 *[Baltes* M.], *Lau* Dieter, Animal, tierkundlich / Aquila: → 879, AugL 1/3 (1988) [356-] 361-374 / 429-434.

e951 **Beavis** Ian C., Insects and other invertebrates in classical antiquity: Exeter Univ. Publ. Ox 1988, Alden. xv-269 p. £40. – ᴿClasR 39 (1989) 363-5 (E. K. *Borthwick*); Gnomon 61 (1989) 620s (L. *Gil*).

e952 **Behrmann** Almuth, Das Nilpferd in der Vorstellungswelt der Alten Ägypter: EurHS 38/22. Fra 1989, Lang. 3-8204-0212-8 [OIAc S89]. I. Katalog, 252 numbered items with drawings.

e953 *Bevan* Elinor, Water-birds and the Olympian gods: AnBritAth 84 (1989) 163-9.

e954 ᴱ**Bodson** Liliane, Anthropozoologica; l'animal dans l'alimentation humaine 1986/8 ➤ 4,723: ᴿRÉG 102 (1989) 207 (P. *Cauderlier*: POPLIN F. p. 163-170, L'anthropocentrisme des tabous alimentaires de l'AT).

e955 **Boessneck** Joachim, Die Tierwelt des alten Ägypten 1988 ➤ 4,h8: ᴿAntiquity 63 (1989) 386 (Juliet *Clutton-Brock*).

e956 **Brewer** Douglas J., Fishermen, hunters and herders; Zooarchaeology in the Fayum, Egypt (ca 8200-5000 B.C.) [diss. Tennessee 1986]: BAR-Int 478. 0-86054-615-2 [OIAc S89].

e957 **Brewer** Douglas J., *Friedman* Renée F., Fish and fishing in ancient Egypt: Natural History of Egypt 2. Wmr 1989, Aris & P. x-109 p.; 109 fig.; XIII pl. + 5 colour. 0-85668-399-X; pa. 485-6.

e957* *a*) *Burn* Lucilla, A heron on the left, by the Kodros painter; – *b*) *Lissarrague* François, Les satyres et le monde animal: ➤ 838, Pottery K 1987/8, 99-106; 4 fig. / 335-351; 13 fig.

e958 *a*) *Cannuyer* Christian, Du nom de la giraffe en ancien Égypte [p. 3; égyptien p. 7] et de la valeur phonétique du signe [*mm*, determinative of *śr*]; – *b*) *Schneider* Thomas, Mag.pHarris XII,1-5; eine kanaanäische Beschwörung für die Löwenjagd?: GöMiszÄg 112 (1989) 7-10 / 53-63.

e959 *Clark* Gillian, Animals and animal products in medieval Italy; a discussion of archaeological and historical methodology: PBritSR 57 (1989) 152-171.

e960 *Clason* A.T., The Bouqras bird frieze (SE Syria): Anatolica 16 (1989s) 209-211; 4 fig. [215-249, *Boerma* J.A.X., palaeo-environment].

e961 **Clutton-Brock** Juliet, The British Museum book of cats, ancient and modern. L 1988, Museum. 96 p.; 102 fig. £10. 0-7141-1664-5.

e961* *Clutton-Brock* Juliet, A dog and a donkey excavated at Tell Brak: Iraq 51 (1989) 217-224; fig. XXIX-XXXII.

e962 **Cohen** C., *Silvan* D., The Ugaritic hippiatric texts 1983 ➤ 64,d448 ... 2,b623: ᴿBASOR 275 (1989) 73s (S. B. *Parker*).

e963 **Collins** Billie Jean, The representations of wild animals in Hittite texts: diss. Yale. NHv 1989. 341 p. 90-10649. – DissA 50 (1989s) 3567-A.

e964 **Davies** Roy W., The supply of animals in the Roman army and the remount system [< Latomus 28 (1969) 429-459]: ➤ 252, Army 1989, 153-173, 274-280; 6 fig.

e965 **Davis** Simon J.M., The archaeology of animals 1987 ➤ 3,f431; 4,h21: ᴿAJA 93 (1989) 286s (Diana C. *Crader*); Archaeology 42,3 (1989) 67 (M. *Rose*).

e966 **Delorme** Jean, *Roux* Charles, Guide illustré de la faune aquatique dans l'art grec 1987 ➤ 3,f433: ᴿAntClas 58 (1989) 543s (Katrien *Maes*).

e967 **Derchain** Philippe, Harkhébis, le Psylle-Astrologue [charmeur de serpents]: ➤ 204, Mém. WALLE B. van de, CdÉ 64 (1989) 74-89.

e967* **Domagalski** Bernhard, Der Hirsch in spätantiker Literatur und Kunst, unter besonderer Berücksichtigung der frühchristlichen Zeugnisse: kath. Diss. ᴰ*Dassmann*. Bonn 1988s. – TR 85 (1989) 514.

e968 **Donkin** R.A., The Muscovy duck, *Cairina moschata domestica*; origins, dispersal and associated aspects of the geography of domestication. Rotterdam 1989, Balkema. viii-186 p.; 8 fig.; 18 maps. £21.50. 90-6191-544-9. – ᴿAntiquity 63 (1989) 630.632 (C. *Fisher*).

e969 **Dumas** Olivier, Les animaux domestiques dans la Bible; élevage et religion [diss.]. Alfort 1986, École Nationale Vétérinaire. 100 p. – ᴿÉTRel

64 (1989) 108 (D. *Lys*) [48 (1973) 528, *Maillot* A., thèse semblable non restreinte aux animaux domestiques].

e970 *Egberts* A., Python or worm? Some aspects of the rite of driving the calves: GöMiszÄg 111 (1989) 33-45.

e971 *Eisenstein* Herbert, Oryx, 'Elch' und Elefant; zu an-NUWAIRĪ's Bericht über die *lamṭ*-Antilope: Der Islam 66 (1989) 303-310.

e972 *Ellis* Maria D., An Old Babylonian *kusarikku* [mythic (?apotropaic) bison]: ➤ 183, ᶠSJÖBERG Å., Dumu- 1989, 121-135.

e973 **Engel** Burkhard J., Darstellungen von Dämonen und Tieren in assyrischen Palästen und Tempeln nach den schriftlichen Quellen. Mönchengladbach 1987, Hackbarth. xi-317 p. 3-9801509-9-2.

e974 *Greppin* John A. C., A bouquet of Armenian birds for Edgar Polomé: ➤ 153, ᶠPOLOMÉ E. 1988, 169-178.

e975 *Güterbock* Hans G., Hittite *kursa* 'hunting bag': ➤ 106, ᶠKANTOR H., Essays 1989, 113-9 + pl. 16-19.

e976 *Hanson* A. E., Declarations of sheep and goats from the Oxyrhynchite nome; Aegyptus 69 (1989) 61-70.

e977 *Hellwing* Salo (Shlomo), Faunal remains from the Early Bronze and Late Bronze ages at Tel Kinrot: TAJ 15s (1988s) 212-220.

e978 *Hintze* Fritz, Ein altes afrikanisches Wort für 'Elefant': ➤ 814, Meroitica 1984/9, 617-621.

e979 *Hoffmann* Friedhelm, Zu den 'Pirolen' [oriolus oriolus] auf dem Relief Kairo, Temporary Number 6/9/32/1: GöMiszÄg 107 (1989) 77-80; 3 fig.

e980 **Hofmann** Inge, *Tomandl* Herbert, Die Bedeutung des Tieres in der meroitischen Kultur vor dem Hintergrund der Fauna und ihrer Darstellung bis zum Ende der Napata-Zeit: BeiSudan Beih 2, 1987 ➤ 3,f445: ᴿOLZ 84 (1989) 662-4 (C. *Onasch*); Orientalia 58 (1989) 292-4 (P. *Červiček*).

e981 *Hollinshead* Mary B., The swallows and artists of room Delta 2 at Akrotiri, Thera: AJA 93 (1989) 339-354; 17 fig.

e982 *Horwitz* Liora K., Diachronic changes in rural husbandry practices in Bronze Age settlements from the Refaim Valley, Israel: PEQ 121 (1989) 44-54; 6 fig.

e983 **Houlihan** Patrick F., The birds of ancient Egypt 1986 ➤ 2,b640 ... 4,h41: ᴿAntiquity 63 (1989) 386s (Juliet *Clutton-Brock*).

e984 ᴱIngold Tim, What is an animal?: One World Archaeology 1. L 1988, Unwin Hyman. 189 p.; 21 fig. $40. 0-04-445012-5 [AJA 93,626].

e985 *a*) *Jameson* M. H., Sacrifice and animal husbandry in classical Greece; – *b*) *Cherry* J. F., Pastoralism and the role of animals in the pre- and protohistoric economies of the Aegean: ➤ 809, ᴱ*Whittaker* C., Pastoral economics 1986/8, 87-119 / 6-34.

e986 **Janssen** Rosalind & Jack, Egyptian household animals: Shire Egyptology 12. Aylesbury 1989, Shire. 68 p. 0-7478-0000-6 [OIAc N89].

e987 *Kádár* Zoltán, Some problems concerning the scientific authenticity of classical authors on Libyan fauna; Libyan animals in the work of STRABO of Amasea: AcClasDeb 24 (1988) 51-56.

e988 **Kanowski** Maxwell, Old bones; unlocking archaeological secrets 1987 ➤ 4,h45: ᴿArchaeology 42,3 (1989) 67s (M. *Rose*: for the younger set).

e989 **Kessler** D., Die heiligen Tiere und der König, I. Beiträge zur Organisation, Kult und Theologie der spätzeitlichen Tierfriedhöfe: ÄgAT 16. Wsb 1989, Harrassowitz. xi-303 p.; 10 pl. DM 78. 3-447-02863-7 [BL 90,122, K. A. *Kitchen*].

e990 ᴱLauvergne J. J., Populations traditionnelles et premières races standardisées d'Ovicaprinae dans le bassin méditerranéen [Colloque INRA 47, 1986]. P 1988, Institut National de la Recherche Agronomique. 298 p. 2-7380-0043-6 [OIAc N89].

e991 **Leone** Aurora, Gli animali da trasporto nell'Egitto greco, romano e bizantino: PapyrolCastroct 12, 1988 → 4,h54: ᴿAegyptus 69 (1989) 301s (O. *Montevecchi*); BASP 24 (1987!) 178s (J. F. *Ates*: inadequate); CdÉ 64 (1989) 355s (Hélène *Cuvigny*: prématuré).

e992 *McDermott* James P., Animals and humans in early Buddhism: IndIraJ 32 (1989) 269-280.

e993 *MacGinnis* J. D. A., Some inscribed horse troughs of Sennacherib: Iraq 51 (1989) 187-192.

e994 *MacGregor* Alexander P.ᴶ, The tigress and her cubs; tracking down a Roman anecdote: → 175, Mem. SCHODER R., Daidalikon 1989, 213-227; pl. 22-25.

e995 **McPhee** Ian, *Trendall* Arthur D., Greek red-figured fish-plates: AntKunst Beih. 14. Basel 1987, AntKunst Beih. 14. 176 p.; 5 fig.; 64 pl. + 4 colour. – ᴿAntClas 58 (1989) 539-543 (L. *Lacroix*); MusHelv 46 (1989) 180 (Margot *Schmidt*).

e996 *Madl* H., ṣᵉbî 'Zierde; Gazelle': → 913, TWAT 6,6ss (1989) 893-8.

e997 *Maiberger* P., Bär / Biene: → 902, NBL, Lfg 2 (1989) 235 / 293s.

e998 *Manzanedo* Marcos F., ¿Poseen inteligencia los animales?: CiTom 116 (1989) 99-128.

e999 *Matthews* Marie, Some zoological observations on ancient mosaics: BMosAnt 12 (1988s) 334-6 + 149 phot.

g1 *Mayer Modena* Maria Luisa, Zoonimia ebraica e sostrato mediterraneo; il nome della tarma [*šaš*, moth]: Acme 42 (1989) 11s.

g2 *Miller* R. L., *Dqr*, spinning and treatment of guinea worm in P. Ebers 875: JEA 75 (1989) 249-254; 2 fig.; pl. XXXVI.

g3 *Molin* G., Der Leviathan von Sumer bis zur Offenbarung des Johannes: Amt und Gemeinde 40 (1989) 142-6 [< ZAW 102, 263].

g4 *Nachtergael* Georges, Le chameau, l'âne et le mulet en Égypte gréco-romaine; les témoignages des terres-cuites: CdÉ 64 (1989) 287-336; 12 fig.; IV pl.

g5 *Nielsen* Eduard, [Lv 11,9s; Dtn 14,9s; Neh 3,3; Jon] Hvad syntes man om fisken?: SvEx 54 (1989) 146-150.

g6 *Oates* John F., Sale of a donkey: BASP 25 (1988) 129-135; 2 facsims.

g7 *Oeming* M., ṢWD, ṣajid 'jagen, fischen': → 913, TWAT 6,6s (1989) 930-6.

g8 **Pardee** Dennis, Les textes hippiatriques: Ugarit 2 / RCiv Mém 33, 1985 → 2,b661; 3,f464: ᴿAfO 35 (1988) 226-9 (J. *Sanmartín*); OLZ 84 (1989) 291s (W. *Herrmann*).

g9 **Pilali-Papasteriou** A., Die bronzenen Tierfiguren aus Kreta: Präh. Bronzefunde 1/3, 1985 → 2,b663; 4,h65: ᴿArchaeologia 38 (1987) 203s (B. *Rutkowski* ❷).

g10 *Pintus* Giovanna Maria, Il bestiario del diavolo; l'esegesi biblica nelle 'Formulae spiritualis intelligentiae' di EUCHERIO di Lione: Sandalion 12s (1989s) 99-114.

g11 **Prieur** Jean, Les animaux sacrés dans l'Antiquité: De mémoire d'homme. Rennes 1988, Ouest-France Univ. 201 p. – ᴿRÉG 102 (1989) 565s (P. *Cauderlier*).

g12 *Ratté* Christopher, Five Lydian felines [lions, 550-400 BC., found out of context]: AJA 93 (1989) 379-393; 9 fig.

g13 *Reese* David S.,   *a)* On Cassid lips and helmet shells: BASOR 275 (1989) 33-39; 9 fig.; – *b)* Faunal remains from the altar of Aphrodite Ourania, Athens: Hesperia 58 (1989) 63-70; 2 fig.; pl. 15-16.

g14 *Ritner* Robert K., So-called 'pre-dynastic hamster-headed' figurines in London and Hanover: GöMiszÄg 111 (1989) 85-95; 1 fig.

g15 *Romm* James S., ARISTOTLE's elephant and the myth of Alexander's scientific patronage [PLINY 8,17,44 held that Aristotle's biological treatises arose out of Alexander's conquests in the East]: AmJPg 110 (1989) 566-575.

g16 *Sandoz* Claude, Les noms latins de l'éléphant et le nom gotique du chameau: Latomus 48 (1989) 753-764.

g17 **Scharf** Joachim-Hermann, Anfänge von systematischer Anatomie und Teratologie im Alten Babylonien: Szb Lp, math. 120,3. 3-05-500481-7 [OIAc S89].

g18 *Schwab* E., *ṣippôr* 'Vogel': ➔ 913, TWAT 6,6s (1989) 1102-7.

g19 *Shapiro* H.A., Poseidon and the tuna: AntClas 58 (1989) 32-43; III pl.

g20 *Soldt* W.H. van, The Ugaritic word for 'fly' [*dabūbu*]: UF 21 (1989) 369-373.

g21 ᴱ**Spanier** Ehud, The royal purple and the biblical blue, *argaman* and *tekhelet* [*Herzog* Isaac, London diss. 1913 plus recent articles]. J 1987, Keter. $22. – ᴿBASOR 274 (1989) 85s (S. *Gitin*).

g22 *a) Stevens* K. Guy, Eine ikonographische Untersuchung der Schlange im vorgeschichtlichen Mesopotamien; – *b) Negahban* E.O., Horse and mule figurines from Marlik; – *c) Porada* Edith, A ram's head from Iran: ➔ 28*, ᶠBERGHE L. Vanden, Archaeologia 1989, 1-30 + 4 pl. / 287-304 + map; 3 pl. / 537-9 + 3 pl.

g23 **Stewart** Kathlyn M., Fishing sites of North and East Africa in the Late Pleistocene and Holocene; environmental change and human adaptation: Cambridge Mg Afr. Archaeology 34 / BAR-Int 521. Ox 1989. xiii-273 p. 0-86054-662-4.

g24 *Swiny* S., The pleistocene fauna of Cyprus and recent discoveries on the Akrotiri peninsula: RepCyp (1988,1) 1-14; 4 fig.; pl. 1.

g25 *Tammisto* Antero, The representations of the Capercaillie (Tetrao urogallus) and the Pheasant (Phasianus colchicus) in Romano-Campanian wall paintings and mosaics: Arctos 23 (1989) 223-247; 3 fig.

g26 ᵀᴱ**Terian** A., PHILON d'Alexandrie, Alexander... bruta animalia 1988 ➔ 4,h64: ᴿNRT 111 (1989) 438s (X. *Jacques*).

g27 *Tosi* M., ➋ The problem of domestication on the Arabian coast: VDI 188 (1989) 124s.

g28 **Toynbee** J.C.M., Tierwelt der Antike [Bestiarium romanum], ᵀR.-*Alföldi* Maria, *Misslbeck* Detlef: KuGAntW 17. Mainz 1983, von Zabern. xv-489 p. 3-8053-0481-1 [OIAc N89].

g29 *Tsuneki* Akira, The manufacture of *Spondylus* shell objects at neolithic Dimini, Greece: Orient-Japan 25 (1989) 1-21; 9 fig.; 1 pl.

g30 **Uerpmann** Hans-Peter, *al.*, Stammformen der Haustiere und frühe Domestikation: TAVO map A-VI-16. Wsh 1989, Reichert. 2 sheets. [OIAc S89, with data also on 10 other recent maps].

g31 *Vandersleyen* Claude, The *rekhyt* [long-legged crested bird, lapwing/vanneau/Kiebitz; *Nibbi* A. 1986] and the Delta: ➔ 859, Delta 1988/9, 301-310.

g32 *Vanek* Susannah, [Animals of] Marshland scenes in the private tombs of the eighteenth dynasty: ➔ 859, Delta 1988/9, 311-321.

g32* **Wheeler** Alwyne, *Jones* A. K. G., Fishes: Manuals in archaeology. C 1989, Univ. xiv-210 p. £32.50. 0-521-30407-5. – ᴿBInstArch 26 (1989) 303s (B. G. *Irving*).

g33 ᴱ**Wijngaarden-Bakker** Louise H. Van, Database management and zooarchaeology [Amsterdam workshop 1984]: PACT 14. Strasbourg 1986, Conseil de l'Europe. 206 p.; 2 foldouts. Fb 2000. – ᴿÉtClas 57 (1989) 94s (A. *Wankenne*).

g34 *Zimmermann* Jean-Louis, A geometric Greek horse in the [Sydney] Nicholson museum: Antichthon 21 (1987) 1-4; 5-8 = 6 fig.

U2.7 **Flora;** *plantae biblicae et antiquae.*

g35 ᵀᴱ**Amigues** Suzanne, *Théophraste*, Recherches sur les plantes I, 1988 → 4,h91: ᴿAntClas 58 (1989) 288-291 (A. *Touwaide*); RÉG 102 (1989) 247s (P. *Cauderlier*: admiration, améliorations).

g36 *Barrucand* Marianne, Gärten und gestaltete Landschaft als irdisches Paradies; Gärten im westlichen Islam: Der Islam 65 (1988) 244-263; Bibliog. 263-7; 12 fig.; 10 pl.

g37 *Brack* Artur, *Zoller* Heinrich, Die Pflanze auf der dekorierten Naqada-II-Keramik: Aloe oder Wildbanane (Ensete)?: MiDAI-K 45 (1989) 33-53; 7 fig.; pl. 2-3.

g38 *Cornelius* Izak, The garden in the iconography of the Ancient Near East; a study of selected material from Egypt: JSem 1 (1989) 204-228.

g39 **Dittmar** Johanna, Blumen und Blumensträusse als Opfergabe im alten Ägypten: MüÄgSt 43, 1986 → 2,b690; 3,f502: ᴿBO 46 (1989) 51s (Lise *Manniche*).

g40 **Donato** Giuseppe, *Seefried* Monique, The fragrant past; perfumes of Cleopatra and Julius Caesar: Atlanta Emory Univ. exhibition catalogue Apr.-Jun. 1989. R 1989, Ist. Poligrafico [OIAc S89].

g41 **Faure** Paul, Parfums et aromates de l'Antiquité: Nouvelles Études Historiques. P 1987, A. Fayard. 357 p.; 8 fig.; 2 plans. F 120. 2-213-01973-8 [OIAc S89]. – ᴿAntClas 58 (1989) 390s (S. *Byl*); ÉtClas 57 (1989) 83s (H. *Leclercq*); RÉG 101 (1988) 528s (D. *Arnould*).

g42 **Flattery** David S., *Schwartz* Martin, Haoma and Harmaline; the botanical identity of the Indo-Iranian sacred hallucinogen 'soma' and its legacy in religion, language and Middle Eastern folklore: Near Eastern Studies 21. Berkeley 1989, Univ. California. viii-211 p.; 5 fig. 0-520-09627-4. – ᴿEWest 39 (1989) 320-4 (G. *Gnoli*).

g43 **Gemünden** Petra von, Vegetationsmetaphorik im Neuen Testament und seiner Umwelt; eine Bildfeldanalyse: Diss. ᴰ*Theissen*. Heidelberg 1989. – TR 85 (1989) 516; RTLv 21,545.

g44 *Germer* Renate, Die Blutenhalskragen aus RT 54 [Reste der Balsamierung des Tutanchamun]: → 80, ᶠHELCK W. 1989, 89-95; pl. IV.

g45 **Germer** Renate, Die Pflanzenmaterialien aus dem Grab des Tutanchamun: HildÄgBeit 28. Hildesheim 1989, Gerstenberg. ix-94 p.; XIII pl. 3-8067-8113-3.

g46 **Hugonot** Jean-Claude, Le jardin dans l'Égypte ancien: EurHS 38/27. Fra 1989, Lang. x-321 p.; 256 fig.; map. 3-631-42009-9.

g47 *a)* **Jacob** Irene, Biblical plants; a guide to the Rodef Shalom biblical botanical garden. – *b)* Papyrus 1-3. Pittsburgh 1989, Rodef Shalom. 0-929699-01-7 [OIAc S89].

g48 **Keimer** Ludwig, ᴱ*Germer* Renate, Die Gartenpflanzen im alten Ägypten

[I 1924 ²1967] II: DAI-K Sonderschrift 13, 1984 ➤ 1,e851... 4,h117: ᴿBO 46 (1989) 49s (Marie-Francine *Moens*).

g49 *a) Klengel* Horst, Papaja, Kataḫzipuri und der *eja*-Baum; Erwägungen zum Verständnis von KUB LVI 17; – *b) Schuler* Einar von, Das 'gute Rohr': ➤ 154, ᶠPUGLIESE CARRATELLI G. 1988, 101-110 / 243-9.

g50 *Liphschitz* N., *Lev-Yadun* S., The botanical remains from Masada; identification of the plant species and the possible origin of the remnants: BASOR 274 (1989) 27-32; map.

g51 ᴱ**Macdougall** Elisabeth B., Ancient Roman villa gardens: History of Landscape Architecture, Dumbarton Oaks colloquium 10. Wsh 1987. 260 p. – ᴿAJA 93 (1989) 304-6 (Eleanor W. *Leach*).

g52 *Maggiulli* Gigliola, Amore e morte nella simbologia floreale: Maia 41 (1989) 185-197.

g53 **Manniche** Lise, An ancient Egyptian herbal. L/Austin 1989, British Museum/Univ. Texas. 176 p. 0-292-70415-1 [OIAc N89].

g54 **Miller** Anthony G., *Morris* Miranda, Plants of Dhofar, the southern region of Oman; traditional, economic, and medicinal uses. Oman 1988, Office of Environment. xxvii-361 p.; 148 color. fig.; 11 color. pl. – ᴿJRAS (1989) 338-340 (R. B. *Serjeant*).

g55 *Pasquazi* Anna, Sopra alcuni nomi di pianta nel 'De agri cultura' di CATONE: GitFg 41,1 (1989) 29-37.

g56 *Pomponio* Francesco, A Neo-Sumerian account about reeds: Orientalia 58 (1989) 230-2; pl. IV.

g57 *a) Ringgren* Helmer, ṣemaḥ 'Spross'; – *b) Rüterswörden* U., ṣemær 'Wolle': ➤ 913, TWAT 6,6s (1989) 1068-1072 / 1072-5.

g58 **Shelmerdine** Cynthia W., The perfume industry of Mycenaean Pylos: SIMA 34, 1985 ➤ 1,b656; 3,f126*: ᴿGnomon 61 (1989) 456s (K. *Kilian*).

g59 *Soysal* Oğuz, 'Der Apfel [hethitisch, luwisch, palaisch] möge die Zähne nehmen!': Orientalia 58 (1989) 171-192.

g60 *Steins* G., ṣiṣ 'Blume' [auch *neṣ*!]: ➤ 913, TWAT 6,8s (1989) 1029-1034.

g61 *Stronach* David, *a)* From Nineveh to Pasargadae; notes on the evolution and legacy of the Ancient Near Eastern garden [summary]: ➤ 830, AIA 90th, AJA 93 (1989) 277; – *b)* The royal garden at Pasargadae; evolution and legacy: ➤ 28, ᶠBERGHE L. Vanden 1989, 475-495 + 5 fig.; II pl.

g62 *Vitestam* Gösta, *Stýrax* and *ṣºrî*, an etymological study: OrSuec 36s (1987s) 29-37.

g63 *Wallert* A., *al.*, Mikroskopische Untersuchung von Papyrus und PLINIUS, Historia naturalis XIII, 74-83; eine anatomisch-morphologische Studie: ZPapEp 76 (1989) 39-45; pl. VI-VII.

g64 *Wilcke* Claus, Die Emar-Version von 'Dattelpalme und Tamariske' — ein Rekonstruktionsversuch: ZAss 79 (1989) 161-190.

U2.8   Agricultura, alimentatio.

g65 *Aaronson* Sheldon, Fungal parasites of grasses and cereals; their rôle as food or medicine, now and in the past: Antiquity 63 (1989) 247-257.

g66 **Abdel-Magid** Anwar, Plant domestication in the Middle Nile Basin; an archaeoethnobotanical case study: C Mg Afr 35 / BAR-Int 523. Ox 1989. xvi-356 p. 0-86054-664-0 [OIAc N89].

g67 *Alvar* Jaime, *Wagner* Carlos G., La actividad agrícola en la economía fenicia de la Península Ibérica: Gerión 6 (1988) 169-185.

g67* *Amir* Yehoshua, An anti-Semitic utterance of PLINY the Elder? [NH 13,46: M. STERN thinks so because he omits that it includes a reference to chydaeus, a kind of dates raised by Jews but sold for use in pagan worship]: ScrClasIsr 8s (1988) 130s.

g68 **Amouretti** Marie-Claire, Le pain et l'huile 1986 ➤ 3,f530:   ᴿAntClas 58 (1989) 548s (G. *Raepsaet*).

g69 *a) Ampolo* Carmine, Il pane quotidiano delle città antiche fra economia e antropologia; – *b) Bettini* Maurizio, *Pucci* Giuseppe, Del fritto e d'altro: Opus 5 (1986) 143-151 / 153-165.

g70 **Bacchiocchi** Samuele, Wine in the Bible; a biblical study on the use of alcoholic beverages: Biblical Perspectives 8. Berrien Springs MI 1989. 307 p. $13 [TDig 37,43].

g71 **Battaglia** Emanuela, 'Artos'; il lessico della panificazione nei papiri greci: AevAnt Bibl. 2. Mi 1989, ViPe. 252 p.; 10 pl. Lit. 30.000. – ᴿBASP 25 (1988!) 181s (J. J. *Farber*); CdÉ 64 (1989) 356s (Hélène *Cuvigny*).

g72 *a) Beloch* Karl J., [† ᴱ*Ampolo* C.] Die Landwirtschaft Athens I; – *b) Neeve* P. W. de, The price of agricultural land in Roman Italy and the problem of economic rationalism; – *c) Kolendo* Jerzy, Le attività agricole degli abitanti di Pompei e gli attrezzi agricoli ritrovati all'interno della città: Opus 4 (1985) 9-28 / 77-109 / 111-124.

g73 *Biagi* Paolo, *Nisbet* Renato, Ursprung der Landwirtschaft in Norditalien: ZfArch 21 (1987) 11-24; 4 fig.

g74 **Bietak** Manfred, Ein altägyptischer Weingarten in einem Tempelbezirk (Tell el-Dab'a 1. März bis 10. Juni 1985): AnzÖsterrAkad. 122/12. W 1986, Akad. 265-278; 12 (foldout.) fig.; pl. I-VIII.

g75 *a) Bockisch* Gabriele, Essen und Trinken im alten Rom; – *b) Grünert* Heinz, Was die Germanen assen und tranken: Altertum 34 (1988) 87-95; 7 fig. / 96-105; 7 fig.

g76 **Böcher** Otto, Der Wein und die Bibel: Kleine Weinbibliothek 1. Grünstadt 1989, Sommer. 48 p. 3-921395-20-8.

g77 **Borowski** Oded, Agriculture in Iron Age Israel [ᴰ1983] 1987 ➤ 3,f535; 4,h149: ᴿJAOS 109 (1989) 672s (M. A. *Powell*).

g78 *Bossu* C., L'objectif de l'institution alimentaire; essai d'évolution: Latomus 48 (1989) 372-382.

g79 **Bringmann** K., Die Agrarreform des Tiberius Gracchus: FraHistVorträge 10. Stu 1985, Steiner. 28 p. DM 14,80. – ᴿMnemosyne 64 (1989) 247s (A. van *Hooff*).

g80 *Christmann* Eckhard, Vᴀʀʀᴏs Definition von *seges, arvum,* und *novalis*: Hermes 117 (1989) 326-342.

g81 *a) Cooper* Jerrold S., Enki's member; Eros and irrigation in Sumerian literature; – *b) Robertson* John, Agriculture and the temple-estate economies of Old Babylonian Nippur; – *c) Donbaz* Veysel, Old Assyrian terms for bread (*akalu, kirrum*): ➤ 183, ᶠSᴊÖʙᴇʀɢ Å., Dumu- 1989, 87-89 / 457-464 / 91-97.

g82 *Cubberley* A. L., *al.*, Testa and clibani; the baking covers [sic: not 'ovens'] of classical Italy: PBritSR 56 (1988) 98-119; 3 fig.

g83 *Currid* John D., *Navon* Avi., Iron age pits and the Lahav (Tell Halif) grain storage project: BASOR 273 (1989) 67-78; 10 fig.

g84 *Dardaine* Sylvie, *Pavis d'Escurac* Henriette, Ravitaillement des cités et évergétisme annonaire dans les provinces occidentales sous le Haut-Empire: Ktema 11 (1989) 291-302.

g85 *Davies* Roy W., The Roman military diet [Britannia 2 (1971) 122-142]: ➤ 252, Service in the Roman army 1989, 187-206. 283-290. 6 fig.

g86 *a) Del Monte* Giuseppe, Razioni [alimentari] e classi d'età in Nippur medio-babilonese; – *b) Foraboschi* Daniele, Organizzazione delle semine e politica agraria in Egitto ellenistico; – *c*) *Bartoloni* Piero, Tracce di cultura della vite nella Sardegna fenicia: ➤ 877, Lavoro 1988, 17-30 / 138-144 / 410-412 + 1 pl.

g87 *De Martino* Francesco, Latifondo e agricoltura a schiavi [*Kolendo* J. ital. 1980; *Kuziščin* -, ital. 1982]: ParPass 246 (1989) 216-231.

g88 **Desportes** F., Le pain au Moyen Âge. P 1987, Orban. 231 p.; 14 fig.; 2 maps. F 96 [RHE 85,153*].

g89 **Detienne** Marcel, *Vernant* Jean-Pierre, *al.*, The cuisine of sacrifice among the Greeks, ᵀ*Wissing* Paula. Ch 1989, Univ. vii-276 p. $40; pa. $15. 0-226-14351-1; 3-8 [TDig 37,154].

g90 *a*) *Dickson* D. Bruce, Out of Utopia; RUNNEL's and ANDEL's non-equilibrium growth model of the origins of agriculture; – *b*) *Tangri* Daniel, On trade and assimilation in European agricultural origins: JMeditArch [1 (1988) 83-109] 2 (1989) 297-302 / 139-148.

g91 ᴱ**Dolce** Rita (p. 17-48), *Zaccagnini* Carlo (p. 101-116), Il pane del re; accumulo e distribuzione dei cereali nell'Oriente Antico: Studi di Storia Antica 13, 1989 ➤ 841: p. 49-63, *Frangipane* Marcello; p. 65-100, *Milano* Lucio; p. 117-132, *Grottanelli* Cristiano.

g92 *Driel* G. van, The edict of Belshazzar [*Dougherty* R., 1920; on agriculture]: JbEOL 30 (1987s) 61-64.
ᶠ**Dubuisson** Pierrette: Agronymes 1987 ➤ 50.

g93 *Edwards* Phillip C., Revising the Broad Spectrum Revolution [a proposed food-getting adaptation of the terminal Pleistocene], and its role in the origins of Southwest Asian food production [but mostly about Levant plant and animal food sites]: Antiquity 63 (1989) 225-246.

g94 *Fischer-Elfert* Hans-Werner, Zwei Akten aus der Getreideverwaltung der XXI. Dynastie (P. Berlin 14.384 und P. Berlin 23098): ➤ 80, ᶠHELCK W. 1989, 39-65; pl. I-III.

g95 *Franka* George F., Sitometria in the Zenon Archive; identifying Zenon's personal documents: BASP 25 (1988) 13-98.

g96 **Garnsey** P. D. A., Famine and food supply in the Graeco-Roman world; responses to risk and crisis 1988 ➤ 4,h164: ᴿGnomon 61 (1989) 135-142 (P. *Herz*); JRS 79 (1989) 174s (D. J. *Mattingly*); RÉG 101 (1988) 534 (M. D. *Grmek*).

g97 *Gibbs* Philip, Lepe, an exercise in horticultural theology [lepe-plant of young men's initiation may prefigure the life-giving power of Christ's death?]: Catalyst 18,3 (Papua-NG 1988) 215-234 [H. *Janssen* (Eng.) summary, TContext 6/2, 99].

g98 *Glassner* J. J., Mahlzeit [La nourriture, français]: ➤ 905, RLA 7,3s (1988) 259-267 [-270, hethitisch, *Ünal* A.; -271, archäologisch, *Calmeyer* P.].

g99 **Gottfriedsen** C., Die Fruchtbarkeit von Israels Land; die Differenz der Theologie in den beiden Landesteilen 1985 ➤ 3,f667: ᴿVT 39 (1989) 255 (H. *Williamson*).

g100 *Hadjisavvas* S., Olive oil production in ancient Cyprus: RepCyp (1988,2) 111-120; 6 fig.; pl. XXXIV-XXXVII.

g101 *Hanel* Norbert, Römische Öl- und Weinproduktion auf der Iberischen Halbinsel am Beispiel von Munigua und Milreu: MadMit 30 (1989) 204-238; 13 fig.; pl. 13-17.

g102 **Harris** D. R., *Hillman* G. C., Foraging and farming; the evolution of plant exploitation: One World Archaeology 13. L 1989, Unwin Hyman. 733 p.; 120 fig. £50; pa. £20. 0-04-445025-7; 235-7 [Antiquity 63,214].

g103 *a*) *Hassan* Fekri, Desertification and the beginnings of Egyptian agriculture; – *b*) *Krzyzaniak* Lech, Some remarks on the predynastic ecology and subsistence economy in the Eastern Nile Delta: → 823, Akten IV 2 (1985/9) 325-331 / 333-8.

g104 *Heine* Peter, Kulinarische Studien; Untersuchungen zur Kochkunst im arabisch-islamischen Mittelalter. Wsb 1988, Harrassowitz. 144 p. DM 64. – ᴿMundus 25 (1989) 111s (H. *Müller*).

g105 *Henry* Donald O., From foraging to agriculture; the Levant at the end of the Ice Age. Ph 1989, Univ. Pennsylvania. xix-277 p.; 72 fig. £31. 0-8122-8137-3. – ᴿAntiquity 63 (1989) 860s (A. *Ronen*).

g106 *Herring* Donald G., P. Trophitis; new Ptolemaic papyri relating to Egyptian alimentary and sale contracts; Greek abstracts from a 'kibōtos' archive edited and analyzed: diss. Texas, Austin 1989, ᴰ*Shelmerdine* Cynthia. 218 p. 90-05594. – DissA 50 (1989s) 3023-A.

g107 **Herz** P., Studien zur römischen Wirtschaftsgesetzgebung; die Lebensmittelversorgung: Historia Einz. 55. Stu 1988, Steiner. 403 p. DM 114. 3-515-04805-7 [JRS 79,273]. – ᴿMünstHand 8,2 (1989) 94s (T. *Pekáry*).

g107* *Hodder* Ian, Contextual archaeology; an interpretation of Çatal Hüyük and a discussion of the origins of agriculture: BInstArch 24 (jubilee 1987) 43-56.

g108 *Homès-Fredericq* Denyse, Cylindre néo-assyrien inédit avec représentation de banquet: → 59, ᶠFINET A., Reflets 1989, 55-59.

g109 *Hopf* Maria, Plant cultivation in the Old World — its beginning and diffusion: → a.2.9, ICAES = Berytus 36 (1988) 27-35; 5 fig.

g110 **Hopkins** David C., The highlands of Canaan; agricultural life... 1985 → 2,b773; 4,h173: ᴿBZ 33 (1989) 294-6 (W. *Thiel*); ExpTim 100 (1988s) 30 (J. *Healey*).

g111 a) *Hruška* B., Naturbedingungen und die traditionelle Landwirtschaft des alten Vorderen Orients; – b) *Wunsch* C., Zur Entwicklung und Nutzung privaten Grossgrundbesitzes in Babylonien während des 6. Jh. u. Z. nach dem Archiv des Ṭābija: → 874, Šulmu 1986/8, 85-100 / 361-378.

g112 **Katary** Sally L. D., Land tenure in the Ramesside period. L 1989, Kegan Paul. xxiv-322 p. 0-7103-0298-3 [OIAc N89].

g112* a) *Kedar* B. Z., The Arab conquests and agriculture; a seventh-century apocalypse, satellite imagery, and palynology: Asian and African Studies 9 (1985) 3s; – b) *Mayerson* Philip, P. Ness[ana] 58 and two *vaticinia ex eventu* [of the Arab conquest] in Hebrew: ZPapEp 77 (1989) 283-6.

g113 **Kehoe** Dennis P., The economics of agriculture on Roman imperial estates in North Africa: Hypomnemata 89, 1988 → 4,h176: 3-525-25188-2. – ᴿJRS 79 (1989) 235 (S. *Spurr*).

g114 *Kehoe* Dennis P., Approaches to economic problems in the 'Letters' of PLINY the Younger; the question of risk in agriculture: → 878, ANRW 2/33/1 (1989) 555-590.

g115 *Kellermann* M. Bier / Brot, → 902, NBL, Lfg. 2 (1989) 294/331s (-brechen 332s, *Klauck* H. J.).

g116 *Kramer* Samuel N., The churns' sweet sound; a Sumerian bucolic poem: → 218, ᶠYADIN Y., ErIsr 20 (1989) 113*-117*; 2 fig.

g117 *Kron* Uta, Kultmahle im Heraion von Samos archaischer Zeit; Versuch einer Rekonstruktion: → 792, Greek cult 1986/8, 135-148.

g118 ᴱLaBianca O., *Hopkins* D. [mem. BALY D.] Early Israelite agriculture 1988 → 832*.

g119 *LaBianca* Øystein S., Intensification of the food system in central Transjordan during the Ammonite period: AndrUnS 27 (1989) 169-178.

g120 *Laurenti* Renato, Diete vegetariane nei primi due secoli dell'era volgare nell'impero romano: ➤ 759, Sangue VI, 1987/9, 507-531.

g121 *a) Liverani* Mario, Economy of Ugarit royal farms; – *b) Milano* Lucio, Food and diet in pre-classical Syria; – *c) Grottanelli* Cristiano, The role of the guest in the epic banquet: ➤ 876, Production 1981/9, 127-168 / 201-271 / 272-332.

g122 *Marasco* Gabriele, L'ambasceria romana a Tolemeo [sic, but Eng. p. 225 'Ptolomy'] IV nel 210 a. C. per una richiesta di grano [respinta]: Opus 4 (1985) 43-48.

g123 *a) Merrillees* Robert S., Highs and lows in the Holy Land; opium in biblical times; – *b) Patrich* Joseph, *Arubas* Beni, ❸ A juglet containing balsam oil (?) from a cave near Qumran: ➤ 218, Mem. YADIN Y., ErIsr 20 (1989) 148*-153*; 3 fig.; 153*, chemical report, *Evans* John / 321-329; 11 fig.; 329-332, chemical report, *Eisenstadt* Zeev, *Eschengrau* Dorith.

g123* *a) Milano* Lucio, Codici alimentari, carne e commensalità nella Siria-Palestina in età pre-cristiana; – *b) Zaccagnini* Carlo, Divisione della carne a Nuzi: ➤ 790*, Sacrificio 1983/8, 55-85 / 87-96.

g124 *Molleson* Theya, Seed preparation in the Mesolithic; the osteological evidence [Tell Abu Hureyra]: Antiquity 63 (1989) 356-362; 6 fig.

g125 *Morgenstern* Frank, Die Auswertung des opus agriculturae des Palladius zu einigen Fragen der spätantiken Wirtschaftsgeschichte: ➤ 794, Zentrum 1986 = Klio 71,1 (1989) 179-192.

g126 **Narimanov** J. G., ❸ Culture of ancient land-tilling and cattle-breeding population of Azerbaijan (the eneolithic, the sixth-fourth millennia B.C.). Baku 1987. 259 p. – ᴿSovArch (1989,4) 290-293 (N. Ya. *Merpert*).

g127 *Nenci* Giuseppe, L'etnico Élymoi e il ruolo del panico nell'alimentazione antica: AnPisa 19 (1989) 1255-1265.

g128 *Palmer* Ruth, Subsistence rations at Pylos and Knossos: Minos 24 (1989) 89-124.

g129 *Peacock* D. P. S., The mills of Pompeii [... flour-production]: Antiquity 63 (1989) 205-214; 4 fig.

g130 *Pearson* T. A., Biblical foods and eating customs: BToday 27 (1989) 372-8.

g131 **Piperno** Dolores R., Phytolith analysis; an archaeological and geological perspective. San Diego 1988, Academic. 280 p.; 27 fig.; 96 pl. 0-12-557175-5 [AJA 93,627]. – ᴿAntiquity 63 (1989) 392 (Susan *Mulholland*, G. *Rapp*).

g132 **Purnelle** G., CATO, De agricultura; fragmenta omnia servata ...: Informatique Langues Anc. 15. Liège 1988, Centre Inf. Ph. Lett. xxiii-292 p. [JRS 79,269].

g133 **Recchia** Vincenzo, GREGORIO Magno e la società agricola: Verba Seniorum NS 8. R 1978, Studium. 190 p. Lit. 6400.

g134 *Rees* Sian, Agriculture and horticulture: ➤ 3,d36, ᴱ*Wacher* J., The Roman world 1987, 481-503 [< AnPg 59, p. 943].

g135 *Rossiter* J. J., *Hallenby* A. E., A wine-making plant in Pompeii insula II.5: ÉchMClas 33 (1989) 229-239; 2 fig.; 2 pl.

g136 **Sandy** D. Brent, The production and use of vegetable oils in Ptolemaic Egypt: BASP supp. 6. Atlanta 1989, Scholars. xi-136 p.; ill. 3-55540-0752-2.

g137 *Schmidt* Sabine, Zur Krise in der Getreideversorgung Roms im Jahre 68 n. Chr., Topos und Realität; einige Bemerkungen zu SUETON. Nero 45,1: MünstHand 8,1 (1989) 84-106; franç. Eng. 106.

g138 a) *Shnirelman* V. A., ❽ Main foci of early food-production in the light
of modern advances; – b) *Alexeyev* V. P., ❽ Micro-foci, foci, and areas of
influence in plant cultivation and behavioural prerequisites for animal
domestication; – c) *Kubbel* L. Y., ❽ Food production and political
organisation; – d) *Francfort* A. P., ❽ On proto-historical agriculture in
central Asia and its historical interpretation; – e) *Peyros* I. I. [*Militaryov*
Yu. A. additional], Concerning the correlation of archaeology and
linguistics in the study of food-production: VDI 188 (1989) 99-110, Eng.
111 / 111-114 / 117s / 121-124 / 126-8[-131].

g139 **Spurr** M. S.,   Arable cultivation in Roman Italy c. 200 B.C. - c. A.D. 100:
JRS Mg. 3, 1986 ➤ 4,h197:   ᴿParPass 246 (1989) 231-240 (F. *De
Martino*).

g140 *Stol* M., Malz: ➤ 905, RLA 7,5s (1989) 322-9.

g141 *Strubbe* J. H. M.,   The sitonia [state purchases of grain] in the cities of
Asia Minor under the principate II: EpAnat [10 (1987)] 13 (1989) 99-120;
map 121.

g142 **Tchernia** André,   Le vin de l'Italie romaine: BÉF 261, 1986 ➤ 2,b754;
4,h198:   ᴿAJA 93 (1984) 153s (B. W. *Frier*); Latomus 48 (1989) 896-8 (P.
Desy).

g143 a) *Trümpelmann* Leo,   Zum frühgeschichtlichen Silobau im alten Mesopotamien; – b) *Muyldermans* Robert,   Two banquet scenes in the
Levant; a comparison between the Ahiram sarcophagus from Byblos and
a North Syrian pyxis found at Nimrud: ➤ 28, BERGHE L. Vanden, 1989,
67-77 + 6 fig. / 393-406; 2 fig.

g144 *Uberti* Maria Luisa,   Qualche nota sull'alimentazione fenicia e punica; i
principali costituenti energetici: RStorAnt 17s (1987s) 189-197.

g145 *Virlouvet* Catherine,   Famines et émeutes à Rome 1985 ➤ 2,9632...
4,d622*: ᴿLatomus 48 (1989) 259 (P. *Salmon*); RStorAnt 17s (1987s)
301-3 (Gabriella *Poma*).

g146 *Währen* Max,   Brot und Gebäck von der Jungsteinzeit bis zur
Römerzeit: Helvetia Archaeologica 20,79 (1987) 82-110; 32 fig. [111-4,
Schärer M. R., Vevey Ernährungsmuseum].

g147 *Wagner* C. G., *Alvar* J.,   Fenicios en Occidente; la colonización agrícola:
RStFen 8 (1989) 61-102.

g148 *Weber* Thomas,   Damaskēna; landwirtschaftliche Produkte aus der Oase
von Damaskus im Spiegel griechischer und lateinischer Schriftquellen:
ZDPV 105 (1989) 151-165 [... Wein, Pflaume, Olive].

g149 *Winter* Bruce W.,   Secular and Christian responses to Corinthian
famines [... 1 Cor 7,31]: TyndB 40 (1989) 86-106.

g150 *Wojtilla* Guyla,   The Sanskrit terminology of the plough: AcOrH 42
(1988) 325-338.

g151 **Zohary** Daniel, *Hopf* Maria,   Domestication of plants in the Old World
[➤ 4,h204]; the origin and spread of cultivated plants in west Asia,
Europe and the Nile valley. Ox 1988, Univ. x-249 p.; 39 fig.; 25 maps.
£35. 0-19-854198-8. – ᴿAntiquity 63 (1989) 640-2 (G. *Hillman*); BAnglsr
8 (1988s) 70 (F. N. *Hepper*); ClasR 39 (1989) 160s (A. G. *Morton*);
RArchéol (1989) 360s (Susanne *Amigues*).

U2.9   **Medicina** *biblica et antiqua.*

g152 **Adinolfi** Marco, *Geraci* Paola,   Bibbia e ginecologia a confronto. CasM
1989, Piemme. 176 p. Lit. 24.000. 88-384-1380-0.

g153 [*Ahmed* Salah M., *al.*, **Honda** Gisho, *Miki* Wataru], Herb drugs and herbalists [in the Middle East 1980]; *Baser* K. H. C. ..., [in Turkey]; *Ushmanghani* Khan ..., [in Pakistan]: Studia Culturae Islamicae [8.] 27s. Tokyo 1986, Institute for ... Asia/Africa. 296 p., 361 fig.; 281 p., 291 fig. – ᴿJAOS 109 (1989) 697 (D. M. *Varisco*).

g154 **André** Jacques, Être médecin à Rome 1987 → 3,f587; 4,h206: ᴿClasAnt 58 (1989) 399s (A. *Touwaide*).

g155 Archéologie et médecine: VIIᵉᵐᵉˢ rencontres internationales d'archéologie et d'histoire d'Antibes, 23-25 Oct. 1986. Juan les Pins 1987, APDCA [AnPg 59, p. 947.950.952.953]: p. 17-26, *Guillermand* Jean, Les sanctuaires guérisseurs et les origines de la médecine scientifique; p. 95-107, *Hirt* Marguerite, Le statut social du médecin; p. 403-412, *Marganne-Mellard* Marie-Hélène, Les instruments chirurgicaux de l'Égypte gréco-romaine; p. 57-67, *Roesch* Paul, Médecins publics dans les cités grecques à l'époque hellénistique.

g156 *Behrens-Abouseif* Doris, The image of the physician in Arab biographies of the post-classical age: Der Islam 66 (1989) 331-343.

g157 *Borza* Eugene N., Malaria in Alexander's army: Ancient History Bulletin 1 (Calgary 1987) 36-38.

g158 **Brain** Peter, GALEN on bloodletting 1986 → 4,h213: ᴿAmHR 94 (1989) 110 (M. R. *McVaugh*).

g159 ᵀᴱ**Burguière** Paul, *al.*, SORANOS, Maladies des femmes 1988 → 4,h215: ᴿSalesianum 51 (1989) 834s (B. *Amata*).

g160 *Byl* Simon, L'odeur végétale dans la thérapeutique gynécologique du Corpus hippocratique: ᴿBgPg 67 (1989) 53-64.

g161 *Constantelos* Demetrios J., The interface of medicine and religion in the Greek and the Christian Greek Orthodox tradition: GrOrTR 33 (1988) 1-17 [19-43, *Harakas* Stanley S.].

g163 *Dasen* Veronique, Dwarfism in ancient Egypt and classical antiquity; iconography and medical history: Medical History 32 (L 1988) 253-276 [< AnPg 59, p. 948].

g164 *Davies* Roy W., The Roman military medical service [< Saalburg Jb 27 (1970) 84-104] → 252, Army 1989, 209-236, 290-8; 4 fig.

g165 *Dean-Jones* Lesley, Menstrual bleeding according to the Hippocratics and ARISTOTLE: AmPgTr 119 (1989) 177-191.

g166 *Debarge* Louis, Le religieux et le médical [... Le problème; l'antiquité ...]: EsprVie 99 (1989) 509-511.

g167 *De Felice* Maria Rosaria, Proprietà magiche e medicinali del sangue degli animali nel *Ḥayat al-Ḥayawan* di al-DAMĪRĪ: → 759, Sangue VI, 1987/9, 323-338.

g168 **Di Benedetto** Vincenzo, Il medico e la malattia; la scienza di IPPOCRATE 1986 → 3,f596; 4,h222: ᴿAnzAltW 42 (1989) 24s (V. *Langholf*).

g168* *Durling* Richard J., A guide to the medical manuscripts mentioned in KRISTELLER's Iter italicum I-II: Traditio 44 (1988) 485-536 [41 (1985) 341-365 was to volume III, which unlike I-II has no index].

g169 **Estes** J. Worth, The medical skulls of ancient Egypt. Canton MA 1989, Science History. xii-196 p.; 20 fig. 0-88135-093-1.

g170 **Fischer** Peter M., Prehistoric Cypriot skills: SIMA 75, 1986 → 2,b770; 4,h228: ᴿAJA 93 (1989) 142s (M. J. *Becker*).

g171 *Foster* G. V., *al.*, A Roman surgeon's tomb from Nea Paphos, 2. Ancient medicines; by-products of copper mining in Cyprus: RepCyp (1988,2) 229-234; 1 fig.; pl. LXX-LXXI.

g172 *Garofalo* Ivan, Addendum all'edizione delle 'Anatomicae administrationes' di GALENO; il codice arabo 4914 della Danishgāh di Teheran: AION 49 (1989) 149-153.

g173 **Gelpke** Almuth, Das Konzept des erkrankten Ortes in GALENs 'De locis affectis': Z Medizingesch. Abh 190. Z 1987, Juris. viii-129 p. Fs 35. 3-260-05179-1. – ᴿAntClas 58 (1989) 295s (A. *Touwaide*).

g174 *Gibbins* D. J. L., The Roman wreck of c. AD 200 at Plemmirio, near Siracusa (Sicily), second interim report; the domestic assemblage, 1. medical equipment and pottery lamps: IntJNaut 18 (1989) 1-25; 16 fig.

g175 *Giordano* Lisania, Morbus acediae; da Giovanni CASSIANO e GREGORIO Magno alla elaborazione medievale: VetChr 26 (1989) 221-245.

g176 **Goerke** Heinz, Arzt und Heilkunde; 3000 Jahre Medizin, vom Asklepiospriester zum Klinikarzt. Mü 1984, Callwey. 288 p. [AnPg 59, p. 949].

g177 **Grensemann** Hermann, Knidische Medizin II, 1987 → 3,f610; 4,h235: ᴿAmJPg 110 (1989) 164-6 (Lesley Ann *Jones*); Gymnasium 96 (1989) 161-3 (Jutta *Kollesch*).

g178 **Grmek** Mirko D., Diseases in the ancient Greek world, ᵀ*Muellner* M. & L., 1988 → 4,h286; xii-458. £29: ᴿGreeceR 36 (1989) 254 (J. *Walcot*: unfavoring).

g179 **Habrich** Christa, *al.*, Ein Leib für Leben und Ewigkeit; Medizin im alten Ägypten, Ausstellung Ingolstadt Medizinhist. Museum. Jul.-Sept. 1985. 54 p.

g180 **Hellweg** Rainer, Stilistische Untersuchungen zu den Krankengeschichten der Epidemienbücher I und III des Corpus Hippocraticum: Diss. KlasPg 35, 1985 → 3,f615: ᴿAnzAltW 42 (1989) 22-24 (F. *Loehner v. Hüttenbach*); Athenaeum 67 (1989) 644-9 (Daniela *Manetti*).

g181 *Herbero* Pablo, La thérapeutique mésopotamienne; Mém. 48. P 1984, RCiv. 139 p. F 200 pa. [JAOS 109,240].

g181* ᵀᴱHersant Yves, HIPPOCRATÈS, Sur le rire et la folie: Petite Bibl. 8. P 1989, Rivages. 129 p. – ᴿHumT 10 (1989) 403-6 (J. A. *Castro*).

g182 *Hershkovitz* Malka, ❶ A Roman cupping vessel [medical cucurbitula] from Masada: → 218, Mem. YADIN Y., ErIsr 20 (1989) 275-7; 8 fig.; Eng. 204*s.

g183 *Hohlweg* Armin, La formazione culturale e professionale del medico a Bisanzio: Koinonia 13 (N 1989) 165-188.

g184 **Iskander** Albert Z., On examinations by which the best physicians are recognized, ❹ + ᵀ: Corpus Medicorum Graecorum, Supp. Orientale 4. B 1988, Akademie. 313 p. M 72 [DLZ 111, 288, I. *Ormos*].

g185 **Jackson** Ralph, Doctors and diseases in the Roman Empire 1988 → 4,h242: ᴿGreeceR 36 (1989) 254 (P. *Walcot*); JRS 79 (1989) 224 (Helen *King*: fine, but not 'snapshots').

g186 *Jouanna* Jacques, Hippocrate, Des vents, de l'art: Coll. Budé. P 1988, BLettres. 282 (d.)p. – ᴿClasR 39 (1989) 185-7 (Vivian *Nutton*).

g187 *Jouanna* Jacques, a) Hippocrate de Cos et le sacré: JSav (1989) 3-22; – b) Note sur l'histoire de la subdivision du traité hippocratique Du régime en livres et sur le problème de l'existence de l'Hygieïon dans la collection hippocratique: StClasOr 29 (1989) 13-19.

g189 *Kornfeld* W., Beschneidung: → 902, NBL, Lfg 2 (1989) 276-9; fig. 6.

g190 **Korpela** Jukka, Das Medizinalpersonal im antiken Rom; eine sozialgeschichtliche Untersuchung: Ann. Acad. Fenn. hum. 45. Helsinki 1987, Suomalainen Tiedeakatemia. 235 p.

g191 *Kruse* Torsten, Ars moriendi; Aufgabe und Möglichkeiten der Medizin [i. Geschichtlich; Heilkunst/Religion]: → 763, Ars moriendi 1989, 99-116.

g192 **Kudlien** Fridolf, Die Stellung des Arztes in der römischen Gesellschaft 1986 ➤ 2,b781; 4,h248:   ᴿLatomus 48 (1989) 898-900 (J.-M. *André*).

g192* **Kühn** Josef-Hans, *al.* [sodales Thesauri Linguae Graecae Hamburgensis], ᴱ*Alpers* K., *al.*, Index Hippocraticus. Gö 1986-9, Vandenhoeck & R. 946 p. 3-525-25806-2.

g193 *Kurth* Dieter, Zu *t3-msh* ['Krokodilskot'?] in medizinischen Texten [vielmehr *thnt* 'Fayence']: GöMiszÄg 111 (1989) 81-83.

g194 *Lançon* B., Maladie et médecine dans la correspondance de JÉRÔME: ➤ 577*, Jérôme Occident/Orient 1986/8, 355-366.

g195 *a*) *Leichty* Erle, Guaranteed to cure; – *b*) *Jacobsen* Thorkild, The *asakku* [disease-causing demon] in Lugal-e; – *c*) *Behrens* Hermann, Eine Axt für Nergal: ➤ 166, Mem. SACHS A. 1988, 261-4 / 225-252 / 27-32.

g196 **Lloyd** Geoffrey E. R., The revolutions of wisdom; studies in the claims and practice of ancient Greek science [...Hippocratic corpus; Sather Lectures 52]. Berkeley 1987, Univ. California. xii-468 p. $45. – ᴿAmJPg 110 (1989) 499-502 (J. *Dillon*); ClasR 39 (1989) 361s (J. G. *Landels*).

g197 *McCoy* Glen, Lepers: BibIll 14,2 (1988) 30s [< OTAbs 12,40].

g198 **Maloney** Gilles, Concordantia in corpus hippocraticum (1986) VI. Index inverses.   Hildesheim 1989, Olms/Weidmann. 488 p. [Gnomon 62, 104-6, D. *Irmer*].

g198* **Maloney** Gilles, Cinq cent ans de bibliographie hippocratique. Québec 1982, Sphinx. v-291 p.

g199 *Mariani Canova* Giordana, Di sana pianta ... l'uso delle piante ritenute utili alla salute: ArchViva 8,3 (1989) 44-49; color. ill.

g200 *Mazzini* Innocenzo, La medicina nella letteratura latina: Aufidus (1988,4) 45-73 [< AnPg 59, p. 952].

g201 ᴱ**Meulenbeld** G. Jan, *Wujastyk* Dominik, Studies on Indian medical history: Wellcome Inst. international workshop 2-4.IX.1985. Groningen 1987, Forsten. vii-247 p. – ᴿIndIraJ 32 (1989) 322-7 (K. G. *Zysk*).

g202 *Müller* Erich, Die medizinisch-ärztliche Betreuung der christlichen Heiliglandpilger vor den Kreuzzügen: HLand 120,1 (1988) 15-18.

g203 **Nutton** Vivian, From Democedes to Harvey; studies in the history of medicine [1971-86, mostly Greco-Roman]. L 1988, Variorum. xi-323 p.; ill. [AnPg 59, p. 978].

g204 **Nutton** Vivian, John CAIUS and the manuscripts of GALEN: ProcPg Sup 13. C 1987, Univ. ix-117 p. 0-90601-409-3. – ᴿAntClas 58 (1989) 294s (S. *Byl*).

g205 *Ory* Thérèse, Deux études sur la médecine antique; 1. 'Poissons' et diététique dans le traité hippocratique Du Régime et sa transposition en latin [*Joly* R., *Mazzini* I.]; I testi di medicina [Congrès Macerata 1984/5]: ÉtClas 57 (1989) 147-153.

g206 **Palmer** Bernard, Medicine and the Bible 1986 ➤ 3,f640; 4,h260: ᴿBO 46 (1989) 128-130 (M. *Stol* focuses skin-diseases).

g207 *Pangas* J. C., La 'mano de un espectro', una enfermedad de la Antigua Mesopotamia: AulaO 7 (1989) 215-233 [neuropsychiatric].

g208 *Papagiannopoulos* John G., ⊕ Eye afflictions in the Old Testament and their sociological implications: TAth 60 (1989) 751-3.

g209 *Parmentier* M. F. G., Non-medical ways of healing in Eastern Christendom; the case of St. Dometios: ➤ 17, ᶠBARTELINK G., Fructus 1989, 279-296.

g210 *Perizonius* W. R. K., *Goudsmit* J., Ancient DNA and archaeo-virology; a question of samples: GöMiszÄg 110 (1989) 47-53.

g211 **Pigeaud** Jackie, Folie et cures 1987 → 4,h262: ᴿAntClas 58 (1989) 392-4 (S. *Byl*).

g212 *Pomponio* F., Épidémie et *revenants* à Ebla?: UF 21 (1989) 297-305.

g213 **Potter** Paul, A handbook of Hippocratic medicine. Sillery QU 1988, Sphinx. 59 p. $6 [ÉchMClas 33,442 adv.].

g214 *Rowling* J. Thompson, The rise and decline of surgery in dynastic Egypt: Antiquity 63 (1989) 312-9; 4 fig.

g215 ᴱ**Sabbah** Guy, *al.*, Bibliographie des textes médicaux latins; antiquité et haut Moyen Âge: Palerne Mémoires 6. S. Étienne 1987, Univ. 174 p. – ᴿAntClas 58 (1989) 398s (A. *Touwaide*).

g216 **Sabbah** G., Mémoires 8, Études de médecine romaine. St-Étienne 1988, Centre Palerne. 178 p. – ᴿLatomus 48 (1989) 479 (S.*Byl*).

g217 **Scharf** Joachim-Hermann, Anfänge von systematische Anatomie und Teratologie im Alten Babylonien: Szb sächs. Akad Lp, math/nat-w. 120/3. B 1988, Akademie. 63 p. 3-05-500481-7 [OIAc S89].

g218 **Schrijvers** P. H., Eine medizinische Erklärung der männlichen Homosexualität aus der Antike (Caelius AURELIANUS De morbis chronicis IV 9) 1985 → 3,f651: ᴿAnzAltW 42 (1989) 25-27 (V. *Langholf*); WienerSt 102 (1989) 305s (Edith *Specht*).

g219 **Seidl** T., *a*) Aussatz: → 902, NBL Lfg. 2 (1989) 218s; – *b*) ṣāra'at 'Aussatz, leprosy': → 913, TWAT 6,6s (1989) 1127-1133.

g220 **Skoda** Françoise, Médecine ancienne et métaphore; le vocabulaire de l'anatomie et de la pathologie en grec ancien: Ethnosciences 4. Lv/P 1988, Peeters/Selaf. xxiv-341 p. Fb 1200. 2-87723-001-5. – ᴿAntClas 58 (1989) 395s (A. *Touwaide*).

g221 **Skoda** Françoise, Les métaphores zoomorphes dans le vocabulaire médical, en grec ancien: → 190, ᶠTAILLARDAT J. Hediston 1988, 221-234.

g222 ᵀᴱ**Staden** Heinrich von, HÉROPHILUS, The art of medicine in early Alexandria. C/NHv 1989, Univ./Yale. xxvii-666 p. [RÉG 103,336, J. *Jouanna*].

g223 *Stol* M., *a*) Old Babylonian ophthalmology: → 59, ᶠFINET A., Reflets 1989, 163-6; – *b*) Leprosy; new light from Greek and Babylonian sources: JbEOL 30 (1987s) 22-31.

g224 *Tavares* A. Augusto, Medicina e médicos no antico Egipto e na Mesopotámia: Brotéria 126 (1988) 169-181.

g225 *Temkin* Owsei, Hippokrates: → 904, RAC 15, 115s (1989) 466-481.

g226 *Wolter* M., Arznei, Arzt: → 902, NBL Lfg. 2 (1989) 177-9.

g227 *Zias* Joseph, [Lv 13 ṣāra'at] Lust or leprosy; confusion or correlation: BASOR 275 (1989) 27-31.

U3 *Duodecim Tribus:* **Israel Tribes;** Land-Ideology.

g228 **Ainsworth** Gordon R., The tribe of Dan in biblical history and biblical prophecy: diss. Dallas Theol. Sem. 1988. 307 p. 89-13826. – DissA 50 (1989s) 1333-A.

g229 *Birkenfeld* Darryl L., Land; a place where justice, peace and creation meet: IntRMiss 78 (1989) 155-161.

g230 *Davies* Eryl W., Land; its rights and privileges: → 378, World 1989, 349-369.

g231 *a*) *Greenberg* Moshe, Theological reflections — land, people and the state: – *b*) *Pedersen* Kirsten H., 'The Holy Land' — history and reality of the term; – *c*) *Stöhr* Martin, People and land; — *d*) *Ronning* Halvor, The land of Israel — a Christian Zionist view; — *e*) *Dubois* Marcel, Jews,

Judaism and Israel in the theology of Saint AUGUSTINE — how he links the Jewish people and the land of Zion: ➤ 408, Immanuel 22s (1989) 25-34 / 35-40 / 50-59 / 120-132 / 162-214.

g232 ᴱHoffman Lawrence A., The land of Israel; Jewish perspectives 1986 ➤ 2,b818: ᴿBibTB 19 (1989) 152s (L. R. Frizzell); JRel 68 (1988) 337s (M. A. Sweeney).

g233 Kallai Zecharia, Historical geography of the Bible; the tribal territories of Israel 1986 ➤ 4,h284: ᴿBO 46 (1989) 127s (J. Negenman); CBQ 51 (1989) 333-5 (P. M. Arnold); CiuD 202 (1989) 249s (J. Gutiérrez); JTS 40 (1989) 136-140 (P. R. Davies; geography useful, history uncritical); TLZ 114 (1989) 24-26 (E.-J. Waschke); TRu 54 (1989) 331-3 (K.-D. Schunck).

g234 Mendels Doron, The Land of Israel as a political concept in Hasmonean literature 1987 ➤ 3,f669; 4,h285: ᴿJBL 108 (1989) 137-9 (J. J. Collins); JQR 79 (1988s) 259-263 (Betsy Halpern-Amaru); JStJud 20 (1989) 243-6 (A. S. van der Woude); Judaica 45 (1989) 253s (S. Schreiner); Salesianum 51 (1989) 839s (R. Vicent); ScrClasIsr 8s (1988) 188-191 (I. M. Gafni).

g235 Mulzer M., Benjamin: ➤ 902, NBL, Lfg. 2 (1989) 269-271.

g236 Na'aman N., Borders and districts in biblical historiography 1986 ➤ 2,b824; 4,g959: ᴿAbr-Nahrain 27 (1989) 176-184 (A. F. Rainey: rhetoric sans linguistics); BO 46 (1989) 406-8 (F. S. Frick); CBQ 51 (1989) 130s (F. E. Greenspahn); Henoch 11 (1989) 368s (B. Chiesa, anche su MENDELS D.).

g237 Niemann Hermann M., Die Daniten: FRL 135, 1985 ➤ 1,f11 ... 3,f670: ᴿCBQ 51 (1989) 724s (W. H. Irwin).

g238 a) Reali Louis, The land for the Moslems; – b) Heschel Abraham J., Engagement to the land: HolyL 9 (1989) 174-8. 187-193 / 183-6.

g239 Tournay Raymond J., La Terre promise, hier et aujourd'hui: PrOrChr 39 (1989) 35-59.

g240 Wolff Katherine E., 'Geh in das Land, das ich dir zeigen werde ...' Das Land Israel in den frühen rabbinischen Traditionen und im NT [diss. Fra St. Georgen]: EurHS 23/340. Fra 1989, Lang. 393 p. Fs 79 [TR 86, 250].

U4   Limitrophi, adjacent lands.

g241 André J., Filliozat J., L'Inde vue de Rome 1986 ➤ 4,h289: ᴿLatomus 48 (1989) 923s (P. Salmon); Maia 41 (1989) 171s (Marina Sechi 'Indie'); Sandalion 12s (1989s) 270s (anche Marina Sechi).

g242 Bartlett John R., Edom and the Edomites: JStOT supp 77. Sheffield 1989, Academic. 281 p. £14.50. 1-85075-205-2. ➤ d954.

g243 Bryce Trevor R., The Lycians 1986 ➤ 2,b839 ... 4,h292: ᴿClasR 39 (1989) 98-100 (Christian Le Roy, franç.).

g244 Garbini Giovanni, 'Popoli del mare', Tarsis e Filistei: ➤ 811, Momenti 1985/8, 235-242.

g245 Hidal S., Israel och Hellas; Studier kring Gamla testamentet och dess verkningshistoria: Religio 27 [0280-5723]. Lund 1988, Teologiska Institutionen [BL 90,153].

g246 Isaac Benjamin, The meaning of the terms limes and limitanei: JRS 78 (1988) 125-147.

g247 Kasher Arieh, ❶ Canaan, Philistia, Greece and Israel; relations of the Jews in Eretz-Israel with the Hellenistic cities (332 BCE- 70 CE). J 1988, Yad Ben-Zvi. 357 p. 965-217-056-9 [OIAc Ja90]. Eng. ➤ b690.

g248 **Lederman** Richard C., The designation of foreign territory in Assyrian royal inscriptions of the Sargonid period: diss. Annenberg Research Inst. 1989. 342 p. 89-21893. — DissA 50 (1989s) 2469s-A.

g249 **Lehmann** Gustav A., Die mykenisch-frühgriechischer Welt ... 'Seevölker' 1985 → 2,b850; 3,f686: ᴿCdÉ 64 (1989) 199s (K. A. *Kitchen*).

g250 *Lemaire* André, Ammon, Moab, Édom; l'époque de fer en Jordanie: → 869, Jordanie 1987, 47-74; 6 fig.

g251 **Margalith** O., ❺ The Sea Peoples in the Bible → 4,h296; 965-01-0233-7; ᴿBL (1989) 38 (H. G. M. *Williamson*).

g252 *Mund-Dopchie* Monique, *Vanbaelen* Sylvie, L'Inde dans l'imaginaire grec: ÉtClas 57 (1989) 209-226.

g253 **Nibbi** Alessandra, Lapwings and Libyans in ancient Egypt 1986 → 3,f691: ᴿAntClas 58 (1989) 436s (J.-M. *Kruchten*).

g254 *Piotrovsky* B.B., ❺ Scythians and Urartu: VDI 191 (1989) 3-10; Eng. 10.

g255 *Pogrebova* M.N., *Rayevsky* D.S., ❺ Concerning the 'breakaway Scythians': VDI 188 (1989) 40-65; Eng. 65.

g256 *Postgate* J.N., Mannäer [Eng.]: → 905, RLA 7,5s (1989) 340-2.

g257 *Puskás* Ildikó, Indo-mediterranica I: AnClasDeb 24 (1988) 15-22.

g258 **Rolle** Renate, The world of the Scythians [Die Welt der Scythen 1980 → 61,r225], ᵀ*Walls* Gayna. L 1989, Batsford. 141 p.; 97 fig.; 8 color. pl. – ᴿRÉLat 67 (1989) 329-331 (R. *Adam*).

g259 *Stucchi* Sandro, Problems concerning the coming of the Greeks to Cyrenaica and the relations with their neighbours: → 196, ᶠTRENDALL D., MeditArch 2 (1989) 73-84; map; 16 fig.

g260 *Wilhelm* G., Marijannu: → 905, RLA 7,5s (1989) 419-421.

U4.5 *Viae* – Routes, roads.

g261 *Aurig* R., Altstrassenreste als archäologische Denkmäler: AusgF 34 (1989) 1-4; 1 fig.; 1 pl.

g262 *Bauzou* T., Préparation du corpus des milliaires de Jordanie: LA 39 (1989) 259-261.

g263 **Chevallier** Raymond, Roman roads²ʳᵉᵛ (¹1976). L 1989, Batsford. 272 p.; 40 fig. – ᴿRÉLat 67 (1989) 367 (C.-M. *Ternes*).

g264 **Chevallier** Raymond, Voyages et déplacements dans l'empire romain. P 1988, Colin. 446 p. – ᴿGnomon 61 (1989) 560s (G. *Radke*: spinoff of his air-view studies of Roman roads).

g265 *Ehrensperger* Carl P., Römische Strassen; Characterisierung anhand der Linienführung: Helvetia Archaeologica 20,78 (1989) 42-77; 38 fig.

g266 **French** David, Roman roads and milestones of Asia Minor, 2/1s, An interim catalogue of milestones: BAR-Int 392. Ox 1988. viii-588 p.; ill.

g267 *Fuchs* Gerald, Antike Verkehrswege in der arabischen Wüste: MGraz 2 (1988) 1-12 + 2 fig.; map: pl. 1-3.

g268 *Gounaropolos* L., *Hatzopoulos* M.B., Les milliaires de la vie Egnatienne 1985 → 3,f703; 4,h306: ᴿLatomus 48 (1989) 487s (R. *Chevallier*).

g269 *Graf* David F., Les routes romaines d'Arabie Pétrée: MondeB 59 (1989) 54-56; ill.; map.

g270 **Halfmann** Helmut, Itinera principum; Geschichte und Typologie der Kaiserreisen im Römischen Reich 1986 → 4,h307: ᴿAntClas 58 (1989) 479s (Marie-Thérèse *Raepsaet-Charlier*); BonnJbb 189 (1989) 604-6 (L. *Wierschowski*).

g271 *Horsley* G. H. R., Two new milestones from Pisidia; AnSt 39 (1989) 79-84.

g272 **Klimkeit** Hans-Joachim, Die Seidenstrasse; Handelsweg und Kultur-brücke zwischen Morgen- und Abendland. Köln 1988, Du Mont. 270 p.; 70 fig. + 20 color. DM 40. – ᴿMundus 25 (1989) 119s (H. *Wilhelmy*).

g273 *Maele* Symphorien van de, La route antique du port mégarien de Pagai à la forteresse d'Aigosthenès: ÉchMClas 33 (1989) 183-8; 2 pl.

g274 *a)* *Mottas* François, Les voies de communication antiques de la Thrace égéenne; – *b)* *König* Ingemar, Wirtschaftsräume und Handelswege im römischen Westen: ➤ 205, ᶠWALSER G., Labor 1989, 82-104 / 70-81.

g275 **Nashef** Khaled, Rekonstruktion der Reiserouten zur Zeit der altassy-rischen Handelsniederlassungen: TAVO-B 83. 1987 ➤ 3,f706; DM 28: ᴿJAOS 109 (1989) 686-8 (M. C. *Astour*: his further fascicles awaited).

g276 *Potts* Daniel, Trans-Arabian routes of the pre-Islamic period: ➤ 822, Arabie/mers 1985/8, 127-162.

g277 *a)* *Rey-Coquais* Jean-Paul, L'Arabie dans les routes de commerce entre le monde méditerranéen et les côtes indiennes; – *b)* *Isaac* Benjamin, Trade-routes to Arabia and the Roman presence in the desert; – *c)* *Red-dé* Michel, *Bauzou* Thomas, Pistes caravanières de Syrie, d'Arabie et d'Égypte; quelques éléments de comparaison: ➤ 816, L'Arabie 1987/9, 225-239 / 241-256 / 485-497.

g278 *Tourovetz* Alexandre, De l'espace libre à la rue; origine, processus de formation et conception de la voie de circulation en Mésopotamie: ➤ 28, ᶠBERGHE L. Vanden 1989, 49-59 + 7 fig.

g279 *Tzedakis* Yannis, *al.*, Les routes minoennes; rapport préliminaire; défense de la circulation ou circulation de la défense?: BCH 113 (1989) 43-75; 44 fig.; foldout.

g280 [*Grassi* Paolo, *Biagi* Maria Cristina, present.] Le vie mercantili tra Mediterraneo e Oriente nel mondo antico [mostra Roma 1985s]. R 1986, Paleani. 182 p.; ill.

g281 *Zitterkopf* Ronald E., *Sidebothom* Steven E., Stations and towers on the Quseir-Nile road: JEA 75 (1989) 155-189; 4 fig.; pl. XII-XV.

U5 *Ethnographia,* **Sociologia** [servitus ➤ G6.5].

g282 *Baum* Gregory, Sociology and salvation; do we need a Catholic sociology?: TS 50 (1989) 718-743.

g283 **Berger** Peter L., Zur Dialektik von Religion und Gesellschaft; Elemente einer soziologischen Theorie, ᵀ*Plessner* M.: Fischer Tb. Fra 1988. xiii-193 p. DM 14,80. – ᴿTLZ 114 (1989) 800-2 (H. *Moritz*).

g284 **Berger** Peter L., *Luckmann* Thomas, La construcció social de la realitat; un tractat de sociologia del coneixement [The social construction of reality], ᵀ*Estruch* Joan. Barc 1988, Herder. 266 p. 84-254-1628-0. – ᴿActuBbg 26 (1989) 7-10 (Maria Carmen *López Saenz*).

g285 **Bily** Lothar, Die Religion im Denken Max WEBERS: kath. Diss. ᴰ*Kienzler*. Augsburg 1988s. – TR 85 (1989) 513.

g286 *a)* *Biscardi* Arnaldo, Contratto di lavoro e 'misthosis' nella civiltà greca del diritto; – *b)* *Aicher-Hadler* Gabriele, Das 'Urteil' des amtlichen Diaiteten; – *c)* *Phylaetou* Chrystalla, L'interprétation du concept de liberté politique athénienne: RIDA 36 (1989) 75-97 / 57-73 / 99-117.

g287 ᴱ**Blok** Josine, *Mason* Peter, Sexual asymmetry; studies in ancient society. Amst 1987, Gieben. 298 p. $40. – ᴿClasR 39 (1989) 103-5 (Gillian *Clark*); Gymnasium 96 (1989) 166s (Ines *Stahlmann*).

g287* *Buchberger* Hannes, Zum Ausländer in der altägyptischen Literatur — eine Kritik [*Loprieno* A. 1988]: WeltOr 20s (1989s) 5-34.

g288 *Cataudella* Michele R., Ricchi e ricchezze nell'antico cristianesimo (...Per foramen acus ➤ 2,3572): Sileno 14 (1988) 195-204.

g289 *a*) *Cohen* David, Seclusion, separation, and the status of women in classical Athens; – *b*) *Gardner* Jane F., Aristophanes and male anxiety; the defence of the *oikos*: GreeceR 36 (1989) 3-15 /51-62.

g290 **Comucci Biscardi** B. M., Donne di rango e donne di popolo nell''età dei Severi: Acc. Toscana Colombaria 88. F 1987, Olschki. 107 p. Lit. 23.000. 88-222-3508-8 [JRS 79,270].

g291 *Cracco Ruggini* Lellia, Juridical status and historical role of women in Roman patriarchal society: Klio 71 (1989) 604-619.

g292 **Della Monica** Madeleine, La classe ouvrière sous les Pharaons; étude du village de Deir el Medineh²*rev*. P 1988, A. Maisonneuve. 199 p.; ill.; map.

g293 *Diakonoff* Igor M., Three ways of development of ancient oriental society: ➤ 877, Lavoro 1988, 1-8.

g294 **Dixon** Suzanne, The Roman mother 1988 ➤ 4,h340; £25: ᴿClasR 39 (1989) 105-7 (Jane F. *Gardner*).

g295 **Douglas** Mary, How institutions think 1986 ➤ 4,h340*: ᴿJRel 68 (1988) 350s (R. *Segal*).

g296 **Drehsen** Volker, Neuzeitliche Konstitutionsbedingungen der praktischen Theologie; Aspekte der theologischen Wende zur sozialkulturellen Lebenswelt christlicher Religion. Gü 1988, Mohn. 622 p.; 602 p. DM 178. – ᴿZevEth 33 (1989) 306-9 (E. *Hübner*).

g297 **Ebertz** Michael N., Das Charisma des Gekreuzigten; zur Soziologie der Jesusbewegung [diss. Konstanz 1985]: WUNT 45, 1987 ➤ 3,f733; 4,h342: ᴿActuBbg 26 (1989) 52s (J. *Boada*); ArTGran 52 (1989) 273 (E. *Barón*); CBQ 51 (1989) 741-3 (B. J. *Malina* still doubts that WEBER-type charismatic leadership contributed anything to the Christian movement); EstE 64 (1989) 565-7 (A. *Vargas-Machuca*); JBL 108 (1989) 716-8 (W. A. *Meeks*); TLZ 114 (1989) 556-8 (G. *Baumbach*); ZkT 111 (1989) 219s (R. *Oberforcher*).

g298 **Eichenauer** Monika, Untersuchungen zur Arbeitswelt der Frau in der römischen Antike [Diss. Graz 1987]: EurHS 3/360. Fra 1988, Lang. 344 p. DM 70 [HZ 251,670, Beate *Wagner-Hasel*].

g299 **Faulkner** Thomas, Old age in Greek and Latin literature. Albany 1989, SUNY. xv-290 p. [RÉG 103, 309s, Yvonne *Vernière*].

g300 **Felder** Cain H., Troubling biblical waters; race, class, and family: Turner Studies in North American Black Religion 3. Mkn 1989, Orbis. xviii-233 p. $15 pa. 0-88344-535-2 [TDig 37,156].

g301 *Foxhall* Lin, Household, gender and property [page-headings only 'Ownership...'] in classical Athens: ClasQ 83 = 39 (1989) 22-44.

g302 **Gardner** Jane F., Women in Roman law and society 1986 ➤ 3,f740; 4,h354: ᴿÉchMClas 33 (1989) 89-93 (Beryl *Rawson*).

g303 ᴱ**Gibson** M., *Biggs* R., The organization of power; aspects of bureaucracy in the Ancient Near East 1983/7 ➤ 3,781: ᴿAfO 35 (1988) 181-7 (J. N. *Postgate*).

g304 *Gill* Robin, Theology, a social system; models for a systematic theology: ScotJT 42 (1989) 1-25.

g305 *Gottwald* Norman K., Religious conversion and the societal origins of ancient Israel [response to *Milgrom* J. JBL 1988]: PerspRelSt 15 (1988) 49-65 [< OTAbs 12,37].

g306 *Gous* I. G. P., Trajectories of tradition in the literature of Israel; OT [commentators'] attempts to understand reality in socio-economic and political context: OTEssays 2/2 (Pretoria 1989) 47-71.

g307 **Grant** Robert M., Cristianesimo primitivo e società (1977), [TE]*Firpo* G. 1987 ► 3,f745: [R]ParVi 34 (1989) 315s (H. *Wróbel*); RivStoLR 25 (1989) 373s (G. *Boccaccini*); ScripTPamp 21 (1989) 949s (D. *Ramos-Lissón);* StPatav 36 (1989) 633s (G. *Segalla*).

g308 **Günther** Rosemarie, Frauenarbeit — Frauenbindung; Untersuchungen zu unfreien und freigelassenen Frauen in den stadtrömischen Inschriften [Diss. Mannheim 1985]. Mannheim 1987, Univ. 380 p. DM 68. 3-7705-2496-9. – [R]Gnomon 61 (1989) 702-8 (L. *Schumacher*); JRS 79 (1989) 228s (Jane F. *Gardner*: sometimes breathtakingly cavalier).

g309 **Guidi** Alessandro, Storia della paletnologia: Universale 244. R 1988, Laterza. x-324 p.; 27 fig. Lit. 25.000 pa. 88-420-3224-7. – [R]Antiquity 63 (1981) 178 (D. *Ridgway*).

g310 **Hallett** Judith P., Fathers and daughters in Roman society 1984 ► 1,f82... 4,h361: [R]Arctos 23 (1989) 284s (Mika *Kajava).*

g311 *Hanson* K. C., The Herodians and Mediterranean kinship [*Todd* E.], I. Genealogy and descent; II. Marriage and divorce; III. ...: BibTB 19 (1989) 75-84 / 142-151 / ....

g312 **Hargrove** Barbara, The sociology of religion; classical and contemporary approaches[2] [[1]c. 1979]. Arlington Heights IL 1989, Harlan Davidson. 385 p. $19 pa. – [R]JRelRes 31 (1989s) 221s (A. *Lummis*).

g313 **Hennis** Wilhelm, Max WEBERs Fragestellung. Tü 1987, Mohr. 242 p. DM 58; pa. 34. – [R]Universitas 44 (1989) 1014s (D. *Senghaas*).

g314 *Hodgson* Robert[J], Valerius MAXIMUS and the social world of the New Testament: CBQ 51 (1989) 683-693.

g315 **Hölkeskamp** K.-J., Die Entstehung der Nobilität; Studien zur sozialen und politischen Geschichte der römischen Republik im 4. Jhdt. v. Chr. Stu 1987, Steiner. 303 p.; maps. 3-515-04621-6. – [R]JRS 79 (1989) 138-150 (F. *Millar*).

g316 *Hoffmann* Zsuzsanna, Der Wertbegriff *honos* in den Komödien von Plautus: AcClasDeb 24 (1988) 29-35.

g317 [F]HOIJER Harry, On the evolution of complex societies [UCLA lecture series 1982 [E]*Earle* T.]: Other Realities 6. Malibu CA 1984, Undena. 9-89033-138-X; pa. 9-8. – [R]BO 46 (1989) 449-453 (D. J. W. *Meijer*: H. T. WRIGHT largely on Iran and R. M. ADAMS on Mesopotamia).

g318 *Eising* Hermann, Bürger und Fremde in Israel: [F]HÖFFNER Joseph, Wissenschaft-Ethos-Politik (Rg 1966) 333-343.

g319 *Jones* Wayne, Parents' roles in the ancient world: BibIll 14,2 (1988) 39-41 [< OTAbs 12,38].

g320 **Kampenhausen** Georg, Hüter des Gewissens? Einfluss sozialwissenschaftlichen Denkens in Theologie und Kirche: Schriften zur Kultursoziologie 6. B 1988, Reimer. 337 p. – [R]TPhil 64 (1989) 290s (H. J. *Höhn*).

g321 **Kaster** Robert A., Guardians of language; the grammarian and society in late antiquity [... II. prosopography]: TransformationsClasHer 11. Berkeley 1988, Univ. California. xxi-524 p. 0-520-05535-7 [AncHB 4, 95-100, J. *Vanderspoel*].

g322 **Kee** Howard C., Knowing the truth; a sociological approach to New Testament interpretation. Minneapolis 1989, Fortress. vii-120 p. 0-8006-2335-5.

g323 *Kent* Dan O., Death of the firstborn [rather his privileged life]: BibIll 14,3 (1988) 76-78 [< OTAbs 12,7].

g324 *a) Klengel* Horst, 'Älteste' in den Texten aus Ebla und Mari; – *b) Naster* Paul, L'esclavage dans la série *ana ittišu*: ⇥ 59, [F]FINET A., Reflets 1989, 61-65 / 137-140.

g325 **Kyrtatas** Dimitris J., The social structure of the early Christian communities [diss. 1980] 1987 ⇥ 4,h376: [R]JSS 34 (1989) 213s (T. D. *Barnes*); RelStR 15 (1989) 265 (E. A. *Clark*: Marxist, good).

g326 *Lambert-Karlovsky* C.C., Ethnoarchaeology; legend, observations and critical theory: ⇥ 28, [F]BERGHE L. Vanden 1989 (II) 953-971 + 3 fig.

g327 *Lang* Graeme, Oppression and revolt in ancient Palestine; the evidence in Jewish literature from the Prophets to JOSEPHUS: Sociological Analysis (Rel.) 49,4 (Wsh 1989) 325-342 [< NTAbs 33,362].

g328 **Lapointe** Roger, Socio-anthropologie du religieux, I. La religion populaire au péril de la modernité: Travail de droit... d'anthropologie 156. Genève 1988, Droz. 258 p. – [R]ScEspr 41 (1989) 371-7 (B. *Lacroix*).

g329 *Laub* Fritz, Sozialgeschichtliche Exegese; Anmerkungen zu einer neuen Fragestellung in der historisch-kritischen Arbeit am Neuen Testament: MüTZ 40 (1989) 39-50.

g330 *Le Gall* Robert, Anthropologie et liturgie: QLtg 69 (1988) 96-104; Eng. 104.

g331 **Liverani** Mario, Antico Oriente; storia società economia 1988 ⇥ 4,h385: [R]Antonianum 64 (1989) 604-6 (M. *Nobile*); Gregorianum 70 (1989) 559-564 (G. L. *Prato*).

Loprieno Antonio, Topos und Mimesis; zum Ausländer in der ägyptischen Literatur: ÄgAbh 48, 1988 ⇥ 9440.

g333 *Malina* Bruce J., Dealing with biblical (Mediterranean) characters; a guide for U.S. consumers: BibTB 19 (1989) 127-141.

g334 *Martin* Alain, L'ostracisme athénien; un démi-siècle de découvertes et de recherches: RÉG 102 (1989) 124-143; 265 items; index p. 144s.

g335 **Massey** Michael, Women in ancient Greece and Rome. C 1988, Univ. iv-36 p.; 20 fig. £2.50. – [R]ClasR 39 (1989) 368 (S. *Freebairn-Smith*).

g336 *Mayak* I. L., ⊕ 'Populus', 'cives', and 'plebs' in the social structure of the early [Roman] republic: VDI 188 (1989) 66-80; Eng. 80-81.

g337 **Mayes** A. D. H., The Old Testament in sociological perspective. L 1989, Marshall Pickering. 0-551-01937-9.

g338 *a) Mayes* A. D. H., Sociology and the Old Testament; – *b) Rogerson* J. W., Anthropology and the Old Testament; – *c) Clements* Ronald E., Israel in its historical and cultural setting; – *d) Martin* James D., Israel as a tribal society: ⇥ 387, World 1989, 39-63 / 17-38 / 3-36 / 95-117.

g340 **Meeks** Wayne A., The moral world of the first Christians 1986 ⇥ 2,b908 ... 4,h393: [R]CurrTM 16 (1989) 292s (E. *Krentz*).

g341 *a) Menu* Bernadette, Une approche de la notion de travail dans l'Ancien Empire égyptien; – *b) Bresciani* Edda, Terminologia amministrativa nell'Egitto faraonico: ⇥ 877, Lavoro 1988, 94-110 / 36-43.

g341* *Meyer* Rudolf, Das Arbeitsethos in Palästina zur Zeit der werdenden Kirche [< Neues Sächsisches Kirchenblatt 42 (1935) 465-476]: ⇥ 320, Zur Geschichte 1989, 11-20 [21-39, Am ha-Areṣ 1947].

g342 *Mojola* A. O., Peasant studies [*Horsley* R., *Gottwald* N., *al.*] and biblical exegesis; a review with some implications for biblical translation [of 'tribe']: AfTJ 17,2 (Tanzania 1988) 162-173 [< NTAbs 33,287].

g343 *Morizot* Pierre, L'âge au mariage des jeunes Romaines à Rome et en Afrique: CRAI (1989) 656-668 (669, *Grimal* P.).

g344 **Morris** Brian, Anthropological studies in religion, an introductory text 1987 ➤ 4,h397: ᴿCBQ 51 (1989) 330-2 (M. S. *Moore*); RelSt 25 (1989) 255-7 (T. *Fitzgerald*); RelStR 15 (1989) 135 (V. P. *Gay*); TLond 92 (1989) 69s (C. S. *Rodd*: frankly atheist hostility to Catholic EVANS-PRITCHARD).

g345 *Nielsen* Thomas H., *al.*, Athenian grave monuments and social class: GrRByz 30 (1989) 411-420.

g346 *Osiek* Carolyn, The new handmaid; the Bible and the social sciences: TS 50 (1989) 260-278.

g347 **Oviedo** Lluis, La teoría de la secularización en Max WEBER; sus repercusiones teológicas: diss. Pont. Univ. Gregoriana, ᴰ*Groth* B.   R 1989. – TRLv 21,553.

g349 **Peppe** Leo, Posizione giuridica e ruolo sociale della donna romana in età repubblicana 1984 ➤ 3,f782: ᴿAntClas 58 (1989) 490 (M.-Thérèse *Raepsaet-Charlier*); JRS 78 (1988) 205s (F. *Gardiner*).

g350 **Perkins** Richard, Looking both ways... Christianity and sociology 1987 ➤ 3,f783; 4,h402: ᴿTTod 46 (1989s) 120.122 (J. A. *Varacalli*).

g351 *Powell* Jefferson, Social theory as exegetical tool: Forum 5/4 (1989) 27-40.

g352 ᴱ**Powell** Marvin A., Labor in the Ancient Near East 1978/87 ➤ 3,786: ᴿOLZ 84 (1989) 418s (H. *Limet*).

g352* **Prades** José A., Persistance et métamorphose du sacré; actualiser DURKHEIM et repenser la modernité: Sociologie d'aujourd'hui.   P 1987, PUF. 336 p. – ᴿLavalTP 45 (1989) 437-444 (J. P. *Rouleau*).

g353 ᴱ**Raaflaub** Kurt A., Social struggles in archaic Rome 1986 ➤ 4,458: ᴿGnomon 61 (1989) 304-318 (K.-J. *Hölkeskamp*: lengthy critical summaries).

g354 **Raebel** Bernd, Die Krise der jüdischen Führungselite in Palästina und der Ausbruch des Jüdischen Krieges; eine Untersuchung zur sozialen und religiösen Unruhe in der Umwelt des frühen Christentums: Diss. ᴰ*Theissen* G. Heid 1989s. – RTLv 21,543.

g355 ᴱ**Rawson** Beryl, The family in ancient Rome 1981/6 ➤ 3,507.f787; 4,h406: ᴿLatomus 48 (1989) 923 (J.-C. *Richard*).

g355* *Rebstock* Ulrich, Mathematische Quellen zur Rechtsgeschichte; das Problem des Hermaphroditen: WeltOr 20s (1989s) 99-114.

g356 **Reviv** Hanoch, The elders in ancient Israel; a study of a biblical institution. J 1989, Magnes. 222 p. $22.

g357 *a) Saller* Richard, Patronage and friendship in early imperial Rome; drawing the distinction; – *b) Rich* John, Patronage and international relations in the Roman Republic; – *c) Drummond* Andrew, Early Roman clientes; – *d) Hopwood* Keith, Bandits, elites and rural order: ➤ 808, Patronage 1984/9, 49-62 / 117-135 / 89-115 / 171-187 [+ 7 *al.*].

g358 **Schluchter** Wolfgang, Religion und Lebensführung, 2. Studien zu Max WEBERs Religions- und Herrschaftssoziologie. Fra 1988, Suhrkamp. 675 p. [127-196, Judaism; 197-260, Christianity: IZBG 35 (1987s) p. 334, N. 2219: not listed in the 'Rezensionenregister, Autoren der rezensierten Bücher' p. 358, which relates only to recensions from other periodicals cited there, not to the books of which IZBG itself gives a recension].

g359 **Schmeller** T., Brechungen; urchristliche Wandercharismatiker im Prisma soziologisch orientierter Exegese: SBS 136. Stu 1989, KBW.   128 p. DM 29,80. 3-460-04361-X [NTAbs 33,390].

g360 *Schneider* Diethelm, Theorien des Übergangs; materialistische und sozialgeschichtliche Erklärungen des Wandels im frühen Christentum und ihre Bedeutung für die Theologie [diss. Saarbrücken]: EurHS 23/355. Fra 1989, Lang. 359 p. Fs 71. – TR 86,252.

g361 **Schöllgen** G., Ecclesia sordida? 1984 → 65,d154... 4,h412: ᴿKlio 71,1 (1989) 301s (F. *Winkelmann*).

g362 *Schöllgen* Georg, Probleme der frühchristlichen Sozialgeschichte; Einwände gegen Peter LAMPEs Buch 'Die stadtrömischen Christen': JbAC 32 (1989) 23-40.

g363 **Sharot** Stephen, Messianism, mysticism, and magic; a sociological analysis of Jewish religious movements. Chapel Hill 1987, Univ. NC. x-306 p. $13 pa. – ᴿJRel 68 (1988) 287s (S. *Schimmel*: all from secondary sources, but excellent).

g364 **Shelton** Jo-Ann R., As the Romans did; a sourcebook in Roman social history. NY 1988, Oxford-UP. 512 p. $40; pa. $20. 0-19-504176-3; -7-1 [NTAbs 33,135].

g365 ᴱ**Sigrist** C., *Neu* R., Ethnologische Texte zum Alten Testament, I. Vor- und Frühgeschichte Israels. Neuk 1989. 230 p. DM 48. 3-7887-1289-9 [BL 90,41 A. *Mayes*].

g366 **Smith** Daniel L., The religion of the landless; the social context of the Babylonian Exile. NY 1989, Crossroad/Meyer Stone. xvii-250 p. $40; pa. $20.

g367 **Smith** Jonathan Z., To take place 1987 → 3,f799: ᴿHorizons 16 (1989) 199s (Mary Barbara *Agnew*).

g368 *a) Souček* V., Zur Struktur der hethitischen Gesellschaft; – *b) Klíma* J., Die Unfreien in der mittelassyrischen und neubabylonischen Gesetzen; – *c) Lipiński* E., La donation matrimoniale dans l'ancien droit hébraïque; – *d) Neumann* H., Einige Erwägungen zu Recht und Gesellschaft in Mesopotamien in frühstaatlicher Zeit: → 874, Šulmu 1986/8, 329-335 / 161-171 / 173-193 / 211-224.

g369 **Stambaugh** John E., *Balch* David L., The NT in its social environment 1986 → 3,f801; 4,h417: ᴿAsbTJ 44,1 (1989) 101s (D. R. *Bauer*); ClasJ 83 (1987s) 349s (Joan *O'Brien*); JRel 69 (1989) 234s (J. *Pastor*: 'Stambach' in title).

g370 **Steenken** John G., The holy and socio-political character of early Coptic monasticism: diss. Chicago 1987. iv-343 p. (2 vol.) [OIAc N89].

g371 **Tainter** Joseph A., The collapse of complex societies: New Studies in Archaeology, 1988 → 4,h419: ᴿAJA 93 (1989) 599-601 (P. N. *Kardulias*).

g372 **Theissen** Gerd, Studien zur Soziologie des Urchristentums³ʳᵉᵛ [¹1979 → 60,y73; ²1983 → 64,234]: WUNT 19. Tü 1989, Mohr. x-395 p. DM 49 [TLZ (107, 603-6; 109, 350f) 115, 111]. – ᴿGregorianum 70 (1989) 377s (B. *Kriegbaum*²).

g373 **Theissen** Gerd, Sociologia del cristianesimo primitivo. Genova 1987, Marietti. xvi-302 p. – ᴿBrotéria 130 (1989) 234 (F. *Pires Lopes*); Teresianum 40 (1989) 270s (V. *Pasquetto*).

g374 *Theissen* Gerd, Jesusbewegung als charismatische Wertrevolution: NTS 35 (1989) 343-360.

g375 **Thompson** Lloyd A., Romans and blacks. L/Norman 1989, Routledge/Oklahoma Univ. 265 p. £25. 0-415-03185-0 [Antiquity 63,470].

g376 *a) Vivian* Angelo, La valutazione del lavoro manuale nei testi giudaici antichi; – *b) Soggin* J. Alberto, L'Antico Israele — tentativo di analisi socio-economica dei testi e dei dati; – *c) Moraldi* Luigi, Esilio e post-esilio; motivi sociali-economici-religiosi: → 877, Lavoro 1988, 341-7 / 332-341 / 323-331.

g376* **Weiler** Gerda, Das Matriarchat im Alten Israel [= ^{2rev} 'Ich verwerfe im Lande die Kriege' 1984 ➤ 2,1097]. Stu 1989, Kohlhammer. 368 p. DM 29 [ZAW 102,464, H.-C. *Schmitt*].

g377 a) *Weiler* Ingomar, Fremde als stigmatisierte Randgruppe in Gesellschaftssystemen der Alten Welt; – b) *Lichocka* Barbara, Le barbare dans les représentations de Némésis en l'Égypte romaine; – c) *Kiss* Zsolt, Représentations de barbares dans l'iconographie romaine impériale en Égypte: ➤ 794, Zentrum 1986 = Klio 71/1 (1989) 51-59 / 115-126 / 127-137.

g378 ᴱ**Welskopf** Elisabeth C.†, Soziale Typenbegriffe im alten Griechenland und ihr Fortleben in der Sprachen der Welt, 1.-2. Belegstellen... 1985 ➤ 2,b944: ᴿIndogF 94 (1989) 354-8 (F. *Gschnitzer*).

g379 *Welten* Peter, Ansätze sozialgeschichtlicher Betrachtungsweise des Alten Testaments im 20. Jahrhundert: BTZ 6 (1989) 207-221.

g380 **Welwei** Karl-Wilhelm, Unfreie im antiken Kriegsdienst 3. Rom: Forsch. Ant. Sklaverei 21. Stu 1988, Steiner. 223 p. DM 54. – ᴿArctos 23 (1989) 286-8 (C. *Bruun*).

g381 **Wengst** Klaus, Demut — Solidarität der Gedemutigten 1987 ➤ 3,f811: ᴿÉTRel 64 (1989) 435s (J. *Pons*).

g382 **Wengst** Klaus, Humility, solidarity of the humiliated 1988 ➤ 4,h428: ᴿRExp 86 (1989) 441s (H. *Barnett*); TLond 92 (1989) 341 (J. *Muddiman*: a little gem).

g383 **Wiedemann** Thomas, Adults and children in the Roman Empire. NHv/ L 1989, Yale Univ./Routledge. xii-221 p. [AncHB 4, 90-94, M. *Golden*].

g384 *Yoffee* N., ⊕ 'Outsiders' in Mesopotamia: VDI 189 (1989) 95-100; Eng. 100.

g385 **Zeitlin** Irving M., Ancient Judaism; biblical criticism from Max Weber to the present 1984 ➤ 65,d173... 4,h434: ᴿRelStT 7,2s (1987) 80-82 (M. *De Roche*).

g386 a) *Zilinszky* János, Arbeit im archaischen Rom; – b) *Klingenberg* Georg, Die rechtsgeschäftliche Übertragung von Zwangsarbeit im römischen Ägypten: RIDA 36 (1989) 421-446 / 281-349.

U5.3 Commercium, oeconomica.

g387 **Andreau** Jean, La vie financière dans le monde romain; les métiers des manieurs d'argent (IVe siècle av.J.-C. - IIIe s.ap.J.-C.): BÉF 265, 1987 ➤ 4,h437: ᴿAthenaeum 67 (1989) 630-3 (Alessandra *Gara*); ClasR 39 (1989) 323s (A. M. *Burnett*); Gnomon 61 (1989) 318-323 (A. *Bürge*); JRS 79 (1989) 176s (D. *Nightingale*).

g388 ᴱ**Archi** Alfonso, Circulation of goods 1981/4 ➤ 65,694... 4,h438: ᴿOLZ 84 (1989) 419-422 (G. *Bunnens*).

g389 *Bagnall* Roger S., Fourth century [A.D. Egypt] prices; new evidences and further thoughts: ZPapEp 76 (1989) 69-76.

g390 a) *Betrò* M. Carmela. Ruolo economico della donna nella società faraonica tra Antico e Nuovo Regno; – b) *Pernigotti* Sergio, Per un capitolo di storia economica dell'Egitto antico; l'età saitica: ➤ 877, Lavoro 1988, 44-51 / 79-93.

g391 *Bogaert* R., Recherches sur la banque en Égypte gréco-romaine: ➤ 791, Histoire économique 1985/7, 49-77.

g392 *Bohn* Ilse, Arbeiten, um zu leben, oder leben, um zu arbeiten? Theologie im Kontext von Wirtschaft – Positionen und Perspektiven, dargestellt am Beispiel der Arbeitswelt: WDienst 20 (1989) 309-331.

g393 **Boochs** Wolfgang, Die Finanzverwaltung im Altertum 1985 ➤ 1,f181 ... 4,h446: ᴿHZ 248 (1989) 402-4 (H.-J. *Drexhage*).

g394 **Bousquet** Jean, Études sur les comptes de Delphes: BÉF 267. P 1988, de Boccard. 232 p.; ill.

g395 *Brandt* Hartwin, *Gês anadasmós* und ältere Tyrannis: Chiron 19 (1989) 207-220.

g396 *Cohen* Edward E., Athenian finance; maritime and landed yields: ClasAnt 8 (1989) 207-223.

g397 **Cozzo** Andrea, Kerdos 1988 ➤ 4,h453: ᴿClasR 39 (1989) 408s (M. J. *Edwards*).

g398 ᴱ**Crawford** Michael H., [Rome British School] L'impero romano e le strutture economiche e sociali delle province [Convegno Roma 1983]: Biblioteca di Athenaeum 4. Como 1986, New Press. 141 p. Lit. 30.000.

g399 *a) Dandamayev* M. A., Royal economy in the Achaemenid empire; – *b) Cagni* Luigi, Aspetti dell'economia regia nella Mesopotamia achemenide; – *c) Briant* Pierre, Guerre, tribut et forces productives dans l'Empire achéménide: ➤ 877, Lavoro 1988, 145-155 / 156-166 / 167-182.

g400 **De Martino** Francesco, Wirtschaftsgeschichte des alten Rom 1985 ➤ 1,f190 ... 4,h457: ᴿAnzAltW 42 (1989) 89-94 (I. *Weiler*).

g401 *Donbaz* Veyzel, The business of Ašēd, an Anatolian merchant: AfO 35 (1988) 48-63; 6 facsim.

g402 *Donlan* Walter, Homeric *témenos* and the land economy of the Dark Age: MusHelv 46 (1989) 126-145.

g403 **Drexhage** Raphaela, Untersuchungen zur römischen Osthandel. Bonn 1988, Habelt. vii-162 p.

g403* **Gabba** E., Del buon uso della ricchezza; saggi [16] 1988 ➤ 4,h464: ᴿRÉLat 67 (1989) 426 (J.-C. *Richard*).

g404 *a) Gara* Alessandra, Il significato economico della politica monetaria nell'Egitto ellenistico; – *b) Imparati* Fiorella, Interventi di politica economica dei sovrani ittiti e stabilità del potere: ➤ 877, Lavoro 1988, 128-137 / 225-239.

g405 *Garlan* Yvon, Guerre et économie en Grèce ancienne (4 inédits + 4). P 1989, Découverte. 226 p. – ᴿRÉG 102 (1988) 571s (P. *Cauderlier*).

Garnsey Peter, *Saller* Richard, The Roman Empire; economy, society and culture 1987 ➤ b766.

g406 *Ghiroldi* Angelo, Ruolo degli stranieri nei documenti economici medio-assiri (Assur-bel-Nisesu a Tukulti-Ninurta): EgVO 12 (1989) 145-152 + 11 pl. (map).

g407 **Goldsmith** R. W., Premodern financial systems; a historical comparative study [... Mesopotamia, Periclean Athens, Augustan Rome, Abbasids]. C 1987, Univ. xii-348 p. 0-521-32947-7. – ᴿJRS 79 (1989) 224 (D. *Nightingale*).

g408 **Gordon** Barry, The economic problem in biblical and patristic thought: VigChr supp. 9. Leiden 1989, Brill. x-144 p. 90-04-09048-7.

g409 **Gras** Michel, Trafics Tyrrhéniens archaïques 1985 ➤ 2,b970 ... 4,h468: ᴿMünstHand 8,2 (1989) 89-93 (P. *Kracht*); Opus 5 (1986) 171-4 (C. *Ampolo*); RÉG 101 (1988) 186 (L. *Dubois*).

g410 **Green** Henry A., The economic and social origins of Gnosticism: SBL diss. 77, 1985 ➤ 1,f212 ... 4,h469: ᴿRB 96 (1989) 619s (G. J. *Norton*); RelStT 7,2s (1987) 76s (T. A. *Robinson*); SecC 7 (1989s) 104-6 (M. A. *Williams*).

g411 **Greene** Kevin, The archaeology of the Roman economy 1986 → 4,h470: ᴿAJA 93 (1989) 184 (B. W. *Frier*); AntClas 58 (1989) 567-9 (G. *Raepsaet*); ClasR 39 (1989) 311s (K. D. *White*).

Gutgesell Manfred, Arbeiter und Pharaonen; Wirtschafts- und Sozialgeschichte 1989 → b402.

g412 *Haider* Peter W., Zu den ägyptisch-ägäischen Handelsbeziehungen zwischen ca. 1370 und 1200 v. Chr. II. Handelsgüter und Handelswege: Münst Hand 8,1 (1989) 1-26; franç. 27, Eng. 28.

g413 *Heltzer* Michael, *a*) The trade of Crete and Cyprus with Syria and Mesopotamia and their eastern tin-sources in the XVIII-XVII century B.C.: Minos 24 (1989) 7-28; – *b*) ❻ The royal economy of King David compared with the royal economy in Ugarit: → 218, Mem. YADIN Y., ErIsr 20 (1989) 175-180, Eng. 200.

g414 **Hendy** Michael F., Studies in the Byzantine monetary economy, c. 300-1450. C 1985, Univ. XXI-773 p.; 36 pl.; maps. 0-521-24715-2. – ᴿJRS 78 (1988) 198-202 (F. *Millar*).

g415 *a*) *Huxley* G. L., Kythera and the Minoan maritime economy; – *b*) *Hallager* E., Aspects of Aegean long-distance trade in the second millennium B.C.; – *c*) *Bunnens* G., Quelques aspects du commerce à longue distance des Syriens et des Phéniciens; – *d*) *Musti* Domenico, Sui problemi della frequentazione micenea nell'Italia meridionale e nel Lazio; – *e*) *Braccesi* L., Indizi per una frequentazione micenea dell'Adriatico: → 811, Momenti 1985/8, 65-71 / 91-101 / 227-234 / 113-122 (21-36) / 133-145.

g416 **Jongman** W., The economy and society of Pompeii: Dutch Mg. Hist. 4. Amst 1988, Gieben. 415 p.; 32 pl.; foldout map. 90-70265-24-9. – ᴿJRS 79 (1989) 229-231 (J. *Banaji*).

g417 *Kindler* Arie, Donations and taxes in the society of the Jewish villages in Eretz Israel during the 3rd to 6th centuries C.E.: → 845, Synagogues 1987/9, 55-59.

g419 *Lipiński* E., Societé et économie d'Ugarit aux XIVe-XIIIe [non XVe comme p. 5] siècles av.n.è.: → 791, Histoire économique 1985/7, 9-27.

g420 *Lowry* S. Todd, The archaeology of economic ideas; the classical Greek tradition 1987 → 4,h483: ᴿGnomon 61 (1989) 551-3 (T. *Pekáry*).

g421 *Maniscalco* Laura, Ocher containers and trade in the central Mediterranean Copper Age: AJA 93 (1989) 537-541.

g422 *Manning* J. G., *al.*, Chicago Oriental Institute Ostracon 12073 once again [debtor/creditor relationships]: JNES 48 (1989) 117-124.

g423 **Maselli** Giorgio, Argentaria; banche e banchieri nella Roma repubblicana 1986 → 3,f867: ᴿLatomus 48 (1989) 696s (R. *Delmaire*).

g424 **Meeks** M. Douglas, God the economist; the doctrine of God and political economy. Ph 1989, Fortress. $13 [CurrTM 16, 385 adv].

g425 **Migeotte** Léopold, L'emprunt public dans les cités grecques [diss. 1978] 1984 → 2,b994 ... 4,h487: ᴿAJA 93 (1989) 148s (Sara B. *Aleshire*).

g426 *Miró* Jordá, Ánforas arcaicas en el litoral catalán ... importaciones de vino (625-500 a.C.): ArchEspArq 62 (1989) 21-67; 30 fig.; 67-70, comentario de *Cabrera* Paloma.

g427 **Müller** Hansgünter, Untersuchungen zu místhōsis von Gebäuden im Recht der gräko-ägyptischen Papyri: Erlanger Juristische Abh. 33. Köln 1985, Heymanns. xliv-391 p.; map. DM 110. 3-452-20531-2. – ᴿBO 46 (1989) 87-89 (G. *Poethke*).

g428 ᴱNelson C. A., Financial and administrative documents from Roman Egypt 1983 → 64,d794 ... 3,f872: ᴿBO 46 (1989) 82s (K. A. *Worp*).

g429 **Nicolet** Claude, Rendre à César; èconomie et société dans la Rome antique: Bibliothèque des histoires. P 1988, Gallimard. 317 p. F 132. 2-07-071471-3 [JRS 79,275]. – ᴿRÉLat 67 (1989) 349-351 (J. *Hellegouarc'h*).

g430 **Orrieux** Claude, Zénon de Caunos 1985 ↠ 3,f873: ᴿBO 46 (1989) 83-87 (T. *Reekmans*).

g431 *Pankiewicz* Ryszard, ❷ Les prix, les salaires et l'argent dans le NT: ↠ 51, ᶠEBOROWICZ W. = VoxPa 15 (1988) 585-600; franç. 600s.

g432 **Piacentini** Patrizia, Gli 'amministratori di proprietà' nell'Egitto del III millennio a.c.: StEgPun 6 (Pisa 1989) 1-244.

g433 *a) Postgate* J. N., The ownership and exploitation of land in Assyria in the 1st Millennium B.C.; – *b) Limet* Henri, *Amurru-Šemi*, propriétaire foncier à Larsa; – *c) Kupper* J.-R., Les marchands à Mari: ↠ 59, ᶠFINET A., Reflets 1989, 141-152/99-111/89-93.

g434 *Rauh* Nicholas K., Finance and estate sales in republican Rome: Aevum 63 (1989) 45-76.

g435 *Renger* J., Zu aktuellen Fragen der mesopotamischen Wirtschaftsgeschichte: ↠ 874, Šulmu 1986/8, 301-317.

g436 *Ringstedt* Nils, A houschold-economic approach to archaeology with special reference to exchange and trade: Fornvännen 34 (1989) 135-141, svensk 141s.

g437 *Römer* Malte, Einige Anmerkungen zur Diskussion über die Ökonomie im Alten Ägypten: GöMiszÄg 108 (1989) 7-20.

g438 **Rostovtzeff** Michel I., Histoire économique et sociale de l'empire romain [Eng.], ᵀ*Demange* Odile; ᴱ*Andreau* Jean. P 1988, Laffont. lxxxiv-780 p.; maps.

g439 *a) Salles* Jean-François, Les échanges commerciaux et culturels dans le Golfe arabo-persique au Iᵉʳ millénaire av.-J.-C.; réflexions sur Makkan et Meluhha; – *b) Casson* Lionel, South Arabia's maritime trade in the first century A.D.; – *c) Sidebotham* Steven E., Ports of the Red Sea and the Arabia-India trade: ↠ 816, L'Arabie 1987/9, 67-96/187-194; map/ 195-223.

g440 **Schmitz** Winfried, Wirtschaftliche Prosperität, soziale Integration und die Seebundpolitik Athens...: Quellen und Forschungen zur antiken Welt 1, 1988 ↠ 4,h499: ᴿMünstHand 8,2 (1989) 73-81 (J. *Engels*).

g441 *a) Schneider* Hans-Christian, Italische *negotiatores* in Numidien; – *b) Metzler* Dieter, Kaiserkult ausserhalb der Reichsgrenzen und römischer Fernhandel: ↠ 150, ᶠPEKÁRY T., Migratio 1989, 218-225/196-200.

g442 **Sidebotham** Steven E., Roman economic policy in the Erythra Thalassa 30 B.C. – A.D. 217: Mnemosyne Sup 91, 1986 ↠ 4,h502: ᴿJRS 79 (1989) 249s (Paula *Turner*).

g443 **Siegelová** Jana, Hethitische Verwaltungspraxis im Lichte der Wirtschafts- und Inventardokumente I-III 1986 ↠ 3,f886: ᴿOLZ 84 (1989) 24-29 (M. *Popko*).

g444 **Silver** Morris, Economic structures of the Ancient Near East 1985 ↠ 1,f247 ... 4,h506: ᴿArOr 57 (1989) 185s (Jana *Pečírková*, Eng.).

g445 **Spek** Robartus J. van der, Grondbezit in het Seleucidische Rijk: diss. VU. Amst 1988, VUniv. x-392 p.*f*55. 90-6256-349-X. – ᴿBO 46 (1989) 390-7 (B. *Scholz*).

g446 **Stenger** Werner, 'Gebt dem Kaiser...'... Besteuerung Palästinas 1988 ↠ 4,h510: ᴿBZ 33 (1989) 270s (F. *Mussner*: einige Fragen ohne Antwort).

g447 **Stöver** Hans D.,   Macht und Geld im alten Rom.   Z 1989, Artemis.
    240 p. DM 40. – ᴿUniversitas 44 (1989) 805s (A. *Jaudzims*).
g448 **Stolper** Matthew W.,   Entrepreneurs and empire... Murašu [diss. 1974]
    1985 ↠ 4,h511:   ᴿArOr 57 (1989) 80s (Jana *Pečírková*, Eng.); Orientalia
    58 (1989) 297-9 (M. A. *Dandamayev*: painstaking and very stimulating);
    WeltOr 20s (1989s) 273-6 (R. *Zadok*).
g449 *Stolper* Matthew W.,   Registration and texation of slave sales in
    Achaemenid Babylonia: ZAss 89 (1989) 80-101; 4 fig.
g450 *a*) *Tausend* Klaus,   Die Reformen Solons und der attische Handel; – *b*)
    Strobel Karl,   Inflation und monetäre Wirtschaftsstrukturen im 3. Jh. n.
    Chr.; zu Daniel SPERBERS Bild der wirtschafts- und währungsge-
    schichtlichen Krise: MünstHand 8,2 (1989) 1-8; Eng. 8; franç. 9 / 10-30;
    Eng. 30; franç. 31.
g451 ꟳTRÉHEUX J.,   Comptes et inventaires dans la Cité grecque, ᴱ**Knoepfler**
    D. 1986/8 ↠ 4,698:   ᴿClasR 39 (1989) 352s (M. J. *Edwards*); RÉG 102
    (1989) 575s (P. *Cauderlier*).
g452 **Vannier** François,   Finances publiques et richesses privées dans le
    discours athénien aux Vᵉ et IVᵉ siècles: Univ. Besançon Annales Litt. 362.
    P 1988, BLettres.   245 p. – ᴿRPg 62 (1988) 349s (M. *Nouhaud*).
g453 *Wassink* A., The Roman monetary policy from 49 B.C. to the middle of
    the third century A.D.:   Babesch 64 (1989) 160-171.
g454 *Wegner* U.,   O que fazem os denários de César na Palestina? EstudosT
    29 (São Leopoldo 1989) 87-105 [< Stromata 45,500].
g455 **Weimert** H.,   Wirtschaft als landschaftgebundenes Phänomen; die antike
    Landschaft Pontos, eine Fallstudie.   Fra 1984. 259 p. – ᴿVDI 188 (1989)
    233-237 (C. Yu. *Saprikin*).
g456 *Wesch-Klein* Gabriele,   Private Handelsförderung im römischen Nord-
    afrika: MünstHand 8,1 (1989) 29-37; franç. 37s, Eng. 38.
g457 **Wickham** Chris,   Marx, Sherlock Holmes, and late Roman commerce
    [ᴱ*Giardina* A., Le merci 1986]: JRS 78 (1988) 183-193.
g458 *Wiseman* Donald J.,   A note on some prices in Late Babylonian
    astronomical diaries: ↠ 166, Mem. SACHS A. 1988, 363-7; 367-373
    facsimiles.
g459 *Zaccagnini* C.,   Markt (Market places, Eng.): ↠ 904, RAC 7,5s (1989)
    421-6.
g460 *a*) *Zahle* Jan,   Politics and economy in Lycia during the Persian period;
    – *b*) *Lewis* David M.,   Persian gold in Greek international relations; – *c*)
    Vickers Michael,   Persian gold in Parthenon inventories; – *d*) *Lombardo*
    Mario,   Oro lidio e oro persiano nelle Storie di ERODOTO: ↠ 782*, L'or
    perse = RÉAnc 91 (1989) 169-182 / 227-235 / 249-257 / 197-212.
g461 *Zarins* Juris,   Ancient Egypt and the Red Sea trade; the case for
    obsidian in the predynastic and archaic periods: ↠ 106, ꟳKANTOR H.,
    Essays 1989, 339-368; fig. 42-48 (map).

u5.7   **Nomadismus**; ecology.

g462 **Briant** Pierre,   État et pasteurs au Moyen-Orient ancien 1982 ↠ 63,d918
    ... 2,d22:   ᴿGnomon 61 (1989) 32-37 (E. *Kettenhofen*).
g463 *Donner* Fred M.,   The role of nomads in the Near East in late antiquity
    (400-800 C.E.): ↠ 781, Tradition/Late Ant. 1989, 73-85.
g464 **Downing** Gregory M.,   Pastoral in early Christianity, from the Gospels
    to Theodosius; a sample of an analytic history of pastoralism in culture:
    diss. ᴰ*Javitch* D. NYU 1989. 327 p. 90-04196. – DissA 50 (1989) 2888-A.

g465 *Edwards* Phillip C., Problems of recognizing earliest sedentism; the Natufian example: JMeditArch 2 (1989) 5-48.

g466 *Finkelstein* Israel, *Prevolotsky* Avi, ❹ Processes of sedentarization and nomadization in the history of the Negev and Sinai: CHistEI 52 (1989) 3-36; Eng. 190.

g467 *Frick* Frank S., Ecology, agriculture and patterns of settlement: ⇥ 378, Word 1989, 67-93; map.

g468 *Horwitz* Liora K., Sedentism in the Early Bronze IV; a faunal perspective: BASOR 275 (1989) 15-25.

g469 *Margueron* Jean-Claude, Les villages du Proche-Orient: Ktema 11 (1986) 97-116; 13 fig.

g470 *Matsuda* Toshimichi, ❹ The nomads as seen from the documents of Mt. Sinai: Orient-Japan 31,2 (1988) 153-164.

g471 *Soffer* Olga, Storage, sedentism and the Eurasian Palaeolithic record: Antiquity 63 (1989) 719-732; 6 fig.

g472 **Staubli** Thomas, Das Image der Nomaden im Alten Israel und in der Ikonographie seiner sesshaften Umwelt: kath. Diss. ᴰKeel O. Fribourg/S 1988s. – TR 85 (1989) 513; RTLv 21,542.

g473 *a)* *Sumner* William M., Anshan in the Kaftari phase; patterns of settlement and land use; – *b)* *Mortensen*, Inge *Demant-* & Peder, On the origin of nomadism in northern Luristan: ⇥ 28, ᶠBERGHE L. Vanden, Archaeologia 1989, 135-161 / (II) 929-941 + 5 fig. (maps); III pl.

g474 ᴱWhittaker C.R., Pastoral economies in classical antiquity [1986]: Proc Sup 14. C 1988, Pg.Soc. iii-218 p. 0-906014-13-1. – ᴿClasR 39 (1989) 95-97 (R. *Osborne*); JRS 79 (1989) 175s (S. *Spurr*); RÉLat 67 (1989) 324s (J.C. *Richard*).

U5.8 **Urbanismus.**

g475 *Alcock* Susan E., Archaeology and imperialism; Roman expansion and the Greek city: JMeditArch 2 (1989) 87-135.

g476 *Andreev* Y.V., Urbanization as a phenomenon of social history: OxJArch 8 (1989) 167-177.

g477 **Arav** Rami, Hellenistic Palestine, settlement patterns and city planning, 337-31 B.C.E.: BAR-Int 485. Ox 1989. 262 p.; 99 fig. £16. 0-86054-622-5 [OIAc S89]. – ᴿBAngIsr 8 (1988s) 69s (M. *Goodman*).

g478 **Arends** J.F.M., Die Einheit der Polis; eine Studie über PLATONS Stadt: Mnemosyne supp. 106. Leiden 1988, Brill. xxiv-466 p. ƒ170. 90-04-08785-0. – ᴿClasR 39 (1989) 254s (R.F. *Stalley*).

g479 **Bernhardt** Rainer, Polis und römische Herrschaft in der späten Republik 1985 ⇥ 2,d29 ... 4,h525: ᴿJRS 78 (1988) 219-221 (D. *Braund*: impressive).

g480 *Boos* Andreas, 'Oppidum' im caesarischen und im archäologischen Sprachgebrauch – Widersprüche und Probleme: AcPraeh 21 (1989) 53-73.

g481 *Braunstein-Silvestre* Florence, Des communautés rurales aux premiers villages: ⇥ 823, Akten IV 2 (1985/9) 305-311.

g482 *Cannuyer* Christian, Variations sur le thème de la ville dans les maximes sapientiales de l'ancienne Égypte: ⇥ 204, Mem. WALLE B. van de, CdÉ 64 (1989) 44-54.

g483 *Deininger* Jürgen, Die antike Stadt als Typus bei Max WEBER: ⇥ 209, ᶠWERNER R., Xenia 22 (1989) 269-289.

g483* *Frangipane* Marcella, *Palmieri* Alba, *al.*, Perspectives on protourbanization in Eastern Anatolia; Arslantepe (Malatya), an interim report on the 1975-1983 campaigns: OriginiR 12,2 (1983) 287-454 (–662), Eng. 666-8.

g484 *Froriep* Siegfried, Der antike Mensch und seine Stadt; bildliche und literarische Aussagen: AntWelt 20,1 (1989) 22-30; ill.

g485 EFukuyama Yoshio, The church in the city; Samuel C. KINCHELPE and the sociology of the city. Ch 1989, Exploration. – RJScStR 29 (1989) 265 (C. S. *Dudley*).

g486 Gawantka Wilfried, Die sogenannte Polis 1985 ➤ 1,f278 ... 4,h532: RAnzAltW 42 (1989) 197-204 (K.-J. *Hölkeskamp*).

g487 *Goldingay* John, The Bible in the city: TLond 92 (1989) 5-15.

g488 *Häussermann* Hartmut, *Siebel* Walter, Ökologie statt Urbanität?: Universitas 44 (1989) 514-525.

g489 *Hanbury-Tenison* J.W., Desert urbanism in the fourth millennium? [Jawa...]: PEQ 121 (1989) 55-63.

g489* **Harrison** R.K., Major cities of the biblical world 1985 ➤ 1,f279 ... 3,f916: RCriswT 2 (1987s) 171s (J. L. *Burns*).

g490 *Höhn* Hans-J., City religion [deutsch, zu *Baadte* G. *al.*]: Orientierung 53 (1989) 102-5.

g491 **Höpfner** Wolfram, *Schwandner* Ernst-Ludwig, Haus und Stadt im klassischen Griechenland: Wohnen in der klassischen Polis 1, 1985 ➤ 3,f918; 4,h537; DM 198: RAJA 93 (1989) 146-8 (W. *Rudolph*); Archaeologia 39 (1988) 246s (Aleksandra *Wąsowicz* ➋).

g492 *Jacoby* Ruth, ➌, The representation and identification of cities on Assyrian reliefs: ➤ 218, Mem. YADIN Y., 20 (1989) 188-197; 16 fig.; Eng. 201*.

g493 **Kolb** Frank, Die Stadt im Altertum 1984 ➤ 65,d248 ... 4,h540: RGnomon 61 (1989) 736s (R. *Martin*).

g494 **Lampe** Peter, Die stadtrömischen Christen ... Sozialgeschichte: WUNT 2/18, D1987 ➤ 3,f759; 4,h378; 2rev1989: RGnomon 61 (1989) 369-371 (W. A. *Meeks*); IBijdragen 50 (1989) 217s (M. *Schneiders*); BZ 33 (1989) 148-150 (M. *Theobald*); CBQ 51 (1989) 560-2 (J. H. *Elliott*); Gregorianum 70 (1989) 383-8 (J. *Janssens*); Interpretation 43 (1989) 296-8 (R. *Jewett*: 'a social profile of the early Christians at Rome'); TGegw 32 (1989) 74-6 (H. *Giesen*); ZkT 111 (1989) 220s (R. *Oberforcher*).

g495 **Leschhorn** Wolfgang, 'Gründer der Stadt' ... 1984 ➤ 2,d54; 3,f923: RRivFgIC 117 (1989) 332-4 (M. *Maggi*).

g496 **Letoublon** F., Fonder une cité, ce que disent les langues anciennes et les textes grecs et latins sur la fondation des cités. Grenoble 1987, Univ. 366 p. – RRÉG 102 (1989) 209s (L. *Pernot*).

g497 EMalkin Irad, *Hohlfelder* Robert L., Mediterranean cities; historical perspectives. Totowa NJ 1988, Cass. 200 p.; ill. 0-7146-3353-4. P. 37-53, Akko, *Kashtan* Nadav; 54-62, Caesarea-M, *Hohlfelder*, also 63-73, *Ringel* Joseph; 74-86, Jaffa, *Radan* George T.; 87-102, Tel Michal, *Herzog* Ze'ev; 186-197, CICERO on the disadvantages of a maritime city, *Vishnia* Rachel.

g498 **Müller** Reimar, Polis und res publica; Studien zum antiken Gesellschafts- und Geschichtsdenken. Weimar 1987, Böhlau. 384 p. M 48. – RDLZ 110 (1989) 359-363 (K.-D. *Eichler*).

g499 *a)* Oliva Pavel, Kolonisation und Entstehung der Polis; – *b)* Oudaltsova Z., Le rôle de la culture urbaine dans le développement de l'empire byzantin: ➤ 215, FWIRTH G., Zu Alexander, 2 (1988) 1099-1122/ 1179-1186.

g500 **Osborne** Robin, Classical landscape with figures; the ancient Greek city and its countryside 1987 ➤ 3,f927; 4,h549: ᴿClasJ 85 (1989s) 148-150 (Virginia *Hunter*); JHS 109 (1989) 249s (J. E. *Jones*).

g501 *Otto* E., Stadt und Land im spätbronzezeitlichen und früheisenzeitlichen Palästina; zur Methodik der Korrelierung von Geographie und antiker Religionsgeschichte: Geographia Religionum 6 (1988) 225-241 [< ZAW 102, 275].

g502 *a)* *Petersmann* Hubert, Die Urbanisierung des römischen Reiches im Lichte der lateinischen Sprache; – *b)* *Mielsch* Harald, Die römische Villa als Bildungslandschaft: ➤ 783, AltPgVerband 1988, Gymnasium 96,5 (1989) 406-428 / 444-456; pl. XIII-XVIII.

Piétri C., présent., L'urbs, espace urbain et histoire 1985/7 ➤ 873.

g504 **Rykwert** Joseph, The idea of a town; the anthropology of urban form in Rome, Italy and the ancient world. CM 1988, MIT. 242 p.; 169 fig. $15 pa. 0-262-68056-4 [JRS 79,277].

g505 **Sakellariou** M. B., The *polis*-state; definition and origins: Meletemata 4. Athens 1989 (P, de Boccard). 509 p.

g506 **Segal** A., Town planning and architecture in Provincia Arabia; the cities along the Via Traiana Nova in the 1st-3rd centuries C.E. [diss. ⊕ 1975]: BAR-Int 419. Ox 1988. xxi-126 p.; 176 fig. – ᴿMesopotamia-T 24 (F 1989) 216-8 (A. *Invernizzi*).

g507 ᴱ**Smith** Bordwell, *Reynolds* Holly B., The city as a sacred center; essays on six [Far] Asian contexts. Leiden 1987, Brill. vii-139 p. *f*50. – ᴿHistRel 29 (1989s) 412-5 (P. *Wheatley*).

g508 *Spieser* Jean-Michel, La christianisation de la ville dans l'Antiquité tardive: Ktema 11 (1986) 49-55.

g509 **Stambaugh** J. E., The ancient Roman city: Ancient Society and History 1988 ➤ 4,h557: ᴿClasJ 85 (1989s) 151s (G. M. *Woloch*); Gnomon 61 (1989) 649s (P. *Gros*). GreeceR 36 (1989) 252 (P. *Walcot*: painless).

g510 **Starr** Chester G., Individual and community; the rise of the polis 1986 ➤ 2,d67 ... 4,h558: ᴿHZ 248 (1989) 406-8 (M. *Stahl*).

g511 ᴱ**Uglione** Renate, La città ideale nella tradizione classica e biblica-cristiana [Toronto 2-4.V] 1985/7 ➤ 3,774; 4,h562: ᴿMaia 40 (1988) 296-8 (L. *Robertini*); RÉG 101 (1988) 532s (P. *Nautin*).

g512 **Watkin** Henry J., The development of cities in Cyprus from the Archaic to the Roman period: diss. Columbia. NY 1988. 598 p. 89-06094. – DissA 50 (1989s) 521-A.

g513 ᴱ**Weiss** Harvey, Origins of cities in dry farming Syria 1984/6 ➤ 2,d69; 4,h563: ᴿZAss 89 (1989) 136-9 (B. *Hrouda*).

U5.9 *Demographia,* population-statistics.

g514 *Dahlheim* Werner, Bevölkerungsgeschichte – die Herausforderung einer sozialwissenschaftlichen Disziplin an die Althistorie: ➤ 209, ᶠWᴇʀɴᴇʀ R., Xenia 22 (1989) 291-321.

g515 *Finkelstein* Israel, *a)* ⊕ The socio-demographic structure of the Intermediate Bronze Age: ➤ 218, Mem. Yᴀᴅɪɴ Y., ErIsr 20 (1989) 75-81; Eng. 196*; – *b)* Further observations on the socio-demographic structure of the Intermediate Bronze Age: Levant 21 (1989) 129-137; bibliog. 137-140.

g516 **Hansen** Mogens H., Demography and democracy ... Athens 4th c. B.C. 1986 ➤ 3,f947; 4,h572: ᴿAnzAltW 42 (1989) 204-7 (A. *Chaniotis*); RBgPg 67 (1989) 211s (J. A. *Straus*).

g517 **Morris** Ian, Burial and ancient society; the rise of the Greek city-state 1987 ➤ 4,h577: ᴿAJA 93 (1989) 296s (Carla M. *Antonaccio*); AntClas 58 (1989) 445-8 (D. *Viviers*); ClasR 39 (1989) 66s (R. *Garland*); Greece R 36 (1989) 110 (P.J. *Rhodes*); HZ 248 (1989) 138-140 (M. *Stahl*); RÉG 101 (1988) 533s (Yvonne *Vernière*).

g518 *Sellier* Pascal, Hypotheses and estiamators for the demographic interpretation of the chalcolithic population from Mehrgarh, Pakistan: EWest 39 (1989) 11-42.

U6 **Narrationes peregrinorum et exploratorum;** *Loca sancta.*

g519 *Alonso* Carlos, El primer viaje desde Persia a Roma del P. VICENTE de s. Francisco OCD (1609-1611): Teresianum 40 (1989) 517-550.

g520 **Artola** Antonio M., La Tierra, el libro, el espíritu; experiencia bíblica en TS 1986 ➤ 2,d83 ... 4,h579*; 84-330-0671-3: ᴿActuBbg 26 (1989) 33s (R. de *Sivatte*); RB 96 (1989) 295 (J. *Loza*).

g521 **Bellenger** Y., Jacques LESAGE, voyage en Terre Sainte d'un marchand de Douai en 1519. P 1989, Balland. 421 p.; ill. F 139 [RHE 85,57*].

g522 *Bosworth* C.E., The intrepid Victorian lady in Persia; Mrs. Isabella BISHOP's travels in Luristan and Kurdistan, 1890: Iran 27 (1989) 87-101.

g523 CHAMPOLLION: ᴱZiegler Christiane, L'Égypte de Jean-François ~; lettres et journaux de voyage (1828-1829); photographies de Hervé *Champollion* (1988-1989). Suresnes 1989, Image-magie. 403 p.

g524 *Dams* Thérèse, Le voyage en Orient de Diego de MÉRIDA (1507-1512), présenté, traduit et annoté I: MélSR 46 (1989) 131-157 [< RHE 85,57*].

g525 **Davies** J.G., Pilgrimage yesterday and today; why? where? how? L 1988, SCM: xiii-274 p. £15. 0-334-02254-1. – ᴿExpTim 100 (1988s) 156 (A. *Dunstan*); PrPeo 3 (1989) 297s (J.B. *Scott*); TLond 92 (1989) 416s (C. *Moody*: current limiting to Jerusalem and Rome overlooks Medjugorje).

g526 *Deluz* Christiane, Le livre de Jean de MANDEVILLE (1356), plagiat ou réécriture?: CRAI (1989) 394-402 (–403, *Mollat du Jourin* Michel).

g527 **Dunn** Ross E., The adventures of IBN BATTUTA, a Muslim traveler of the fourteenth century. Berkeley 1989, Univ. California. $13. 0-520-06743-6. – ᴿJSS 34 (1989) 233 (G.M. *Wickens*).

g528 **Dupront** Alphonse, Du sacré; croisades et pèlerinages, images et langages [1958-1986]: Bibliothèque des Histoires, 1987 ➤ 4,h583: 541 p. F 160: ᴿNRT 111 (1989) 129s (J. *Masson*); RHPR 68 (1988) 350 (P. *Maraval*).

g529 EGERIA: ᵀᴱJaneras Sebastiá, Egeria, Pelerinatge 1986 ➤ 2,98*; 3,f960: ᴿEstFranc 89 (1988) 680-2 (M.D.).

g530 **Väänänen** Veikko, Le journal-épître d'Égérie, étude linguistique 1987 ➤ 3,f964; 4,h601: ᴿBSLP 84,2 (1989) 343-5 (C. *Moussy*); Salesianum 51 (1989) 649s (R. *Bracchi*).

g531 **Blackman** D.R., **Betts** G.G., Concordantia in Itinerarium Egeriae: Alpha-Omega A-96. Hildesheim 1989, Olms-Weidmann. 204 p. 3-487-09075-9.

g531* *Natalucci* Nicoletta, Egeria e il monachesimo femminile: Benedictina 35 (1988) 37-46; 46-52, Un convegno ad Arezzo [25-23 ott.] sull'Itinerarium Egeriae.

g532 *Pérès* Jacques-Noël, Les Patriarches dans l'Itinéraire de la pèlerine Égérie: PosLuth 37,1 (1989) 41-50 [< ZIT 89,378].

g533 *Theodorou* Evangelos D., ⊕ Aetheria's 'Itinerary' and its significance for liturgies: TAth 60 (1989) 593-9 ...

g534 *Elm* Susanna, Perceptions of Jerusalem pilgrimage as reflected in two early sources on female pilgrimage (3d and 4th centuries A.D.): ➤ 696, StudPatr 10/20 (1987/9) 219-223.

g535 **Eriksen** E. O., Holy Land explorers. J 1989, Franciscan. [BL 90,152].

g536 **Erker-Sonnabend** Ulrich, Das Lüften des Schleiers; die Orienterfahrung britischer Reisender in Ägypten und Arabien; ein Beitrag zum Reisebericht des 19. Jahrhunderts. Hildesheim 1987, Olms. 310 p. – ᴿDer Islam 66 (1989) 154s (Karin *Hörner*).

g536* *Fischer* Moshe, An early Byzantine settlement at Kh. Zikhrin (Israel); a contribution to the archeology of pilgrimage in the Holy Land: ➤ 827, 11ᵉ Arch.Chrét. 1986-9, (II) 1787-1807.

g537 **Golding** William, An Egyptian journal. L 1985 = 1988, Faber & F. 208 p. + xxxii p. (color.) phot.

g538 *Graboïs* A., Louis VII pèlerin [Terre sainte 1145-8]: Revue d'histoire de l'Église de France 74 (1988) 5-22 [< RSPT 73,137].

g539 *Guth* Klaus, Heiliglandfahrt in frühislamischer Zeit; RTAM 56 (1989) 5-18. WILLIBALD von Eichstätt zum Gedenken († 787).

g540 ᴱ**Hämeen-Anttila** Jaakko, 'Alī N. AL-BARRĀNI, *Asnā*... nineteenth century grammatical commentary on ŠUBRĀWĪ (d. 1758), *Risāla*: StOr 66. Helsinki 1989, Puna Musta. 72 p. + ❹ 73-142 and facsimiles. 951-9380-11-6.

g540* **Hagen** Doris, Die Pilgerreise des Heiligen WILLIBALD [Ausstellung 1200. Todestag]. Eichstätt 1987, Bischöfl. Ordinariat; p. 63-74 [< ByZ 82,445].

g541 **Hakami** Nasrine, Pèlerinage de l'Emâm Rezâ, étude socio-économique: Studia culturae islamicae 38. Tokyo 1989; Inst. Asia-Africa. 286 p.

g542 **Halbwachs** Maurice, Memorie di Terrasanta [La topographie légendaire 1941 ²1971]: Via Lattea 2. Venezia 1988, Arsenale. 192 p. – ᴿRivStoLR 25 (1989) 546-8 (P. G. *Longo*).

g543 **Haynes** Jonathan, The humanist as traveler; George SANDYS's Relation of a journey begun An. Dom. 1610 [Holy Land, Egypt, Turkey...]. L 1986, Assoc. Univ.Pr. 159 p. £ 20. – ᴿEngHR 104 (1989) 488s (B. *Worden*).

g544 **Irby** Charles L., *Mangles* James, Travels in Egypt and Nubia, Syria and Asia Minor, during the years 1817 and 1818. L 1985 = 1823, Darf. XXXIII-560 p.; ill.

g545 **Kleitz** Dorsey R., Orientalism and the American Romantic imagination; the Middle East in the works of IRVING, POE, EMERSON, and MELVILLE: diss. Univ. New Hampshire 1988. 210 p. 89-07443. – DissA 50 (1989s) 685-A.

g546 *Kropp* Manfred, Reisediplomatie am Roten Meer im 17. Jahrhundert: OrChr 73 (1989) 137-148.

g547 *Kuntz* M. L., Voyages to the East and their meaning in the thought of Guillaume POSTEL: ➤ 780, Voyager 1983/7, 51-63.

g548 *Lewis* Christopher, On going to sacred places: TLond 92 (1989) 388-394.

g549 **Lumbreras** Juan M., En el país de Jesús; viaje a Tierra Santa. Bilbao 1989, Mensajero. 291 p. – ᴿRazF 220 (1989) 125 (R. de *Andrés*).

g550 **Magdalena Nom de Deu** José P., Relatos de viajes y epístolas de peregrinos judíos a Jerusalén (1481-1523): OrBarc 3, 1987 ➤ 4,h590: ᴿJSS 34 (1989) 236s (N. de *Lange*).

g551 *Matthews* John F., Hostages, philosophers, pilgrims and the diffusion of ideas in the Late Roman Mediterranean and Near East: ➤ 781, Tradition 1984/9, 29-49.

g552 *a) Mérigoux* J.-M., L'ouvrage d'un Frère Prêcheur florentin en Orient à la fin du XIIIᵉ siècle; RICCOLDO da Monte di Croce [†1320; Liber peregrinationis; Libellus ad nationes orientales] Libellus contra legem Sarracenorum: Memorie domenicane 17 (1986) 1-144; – *b) Panella* E., Ricerche su Riccoldo MC: ArchFrPraed 58 (1983) 5-85 [< RHE 84,865].

g552* *Koder* J., Early modern times travellers as a source for the historical geography of Byzantium; the diary of Reinhold LUBENAU: ➤ e807, Géog.Médit. 1988, 141-8 [< ByZ 82,443].

g553 **Nassir** Ghazi Q., A history and criticism of Samuel JOHNSON's oriental tales: diss. Florida State 1989, ᴰ*Davis* B. 315 p. 89-15757. – DissA 50 (1989s) 692-A.

g554 **Padovese** L., *al.*, Turchia, i luoghi delle origini cristiane 1987 ➤ 3,f983; 4,h595: ᴿEstFran 90 (1989) 307s (E. *Cortès*); NRT 111 (1989) 294s (N. *Plumat*).

g555 *Parijs* Michel Van, Abba SILVAIN et ses disciples; une famille monastique entre Scété et la Palestine à la fin du IVᵉ et dans la première moitié du Vᵉ siècle: Irénikon 61 (1988) 315-331. 451-480 [résumé RHE 85,163].

g556 **Pohanka** Reinhard, **Thurner** Ingrid, Der Khan aus Tirol, Albert J. GASTEIGER ... Diplomat, Ingenieur und Forschungsreisender am persischen Hof (1823-1890). W 1989, Bundesverlag. 3-215-06593-2 [OIAc S89].

g557 **Roberts** David, ᴱ*Culliford* Barbara, Carnets de voyage; Égypte, Terre Sainte. Arcueil 1989, Anthèse (also Eng. 'BLA'). 159 p.; 100 color. phot. 2-904-42044-4.

g558 **Serrano** V., Las huellas de sus pasos. M 1988, Paulinas. 94 p. – ᴿBibFe 15 (1989) 171s (M. *Sáenz de Santa María*).

g559 **Simoën** Jean-Claude, Le voyage en Égypte; les grands voyageurs au XIXᵉ siècle. P 1989, Lattès. 315 p.; p. 300-311, biog./phot. de 19 pionniers.

g560 **Stark** Freya, Over the rim of the world; selected letters, ᴱ*Moorehead* Caroline. L 1988, Murray. 0-7195-4619-2 [OIAc S89].

g561 **Strzelecka** Kinga sr., ⊕ Szalom. Wsz 1987, Verbinum. 214 p. – ᴿPrzPow 801 (1988) 293-7 (W. *Chrostowski*).

g562 *Teixidor* J., Géographies du voyageur au proche-orient ancien: AulaO 7,1 (1989) 106-115; Eng. 105.

g563 ᴱ**Wilkinson** John (*Hill* Joyce, *Ryan* W.F.), [Some twenty accounts from 1099 to 1185] Jerusalem pilgrimage: Hakluyt Series 2/167. L 1988, Hakluyt Soc. xi-372 p. £16. – ᴿRÉByz 47 (1989) 283-5 (B. *Flusin*: indicates inadequately the sources, also of the translations, some apparently just recopied from earlier Hakluyt); JRAS (1989) 136s (R. *Irwin*: thin gleanings).

g564 **Zink** Jörg, Tief ist der Brunnen der Vergangenheit; eine Reise durch die Ursprungsländer der Bibel 1988 ➤ 4,h603; 800 phot.: ᴿBL (1989) 33 (A. G. *Auld*: text as valuable as the photos); ScripTPamp 21 (1989) 692 (K. *Limburg*).

g565 **Zink** J., Voyage aux pays de la Bible; aux sources de notre histoire. P 1989, D-Brouwer. 400 p.; ill. – [NRT 112,473; A. *Wankenne*: un responsable de la télévision évangélique de Württemberg compare l'histoire biblique avec celle des régions].

U7 *Crucigeri* – **The Crusades.**

g566 *Ayalon* David, The auxiliary forces of the Mamluk Sultanate: Der Islam 65 (1988) 13-37.

g567 **Balard** Michel, Les croisades; les noms, les thèmes, les lieux. P 1988, 'MA'. 213 p.; 8 pl. F 150. – ᴿRÉByz 47 (1989) 288s (A. *Failler*).

g568 **Becker** Alfons, Papst URBAN II (1088-1099); der Papst, die griechische Christenheit und der Kreuzzug: MonGermHist Schr 19/11. Stu 1988, Hiersemann. xlii-457 p. DM 196. – ᴿRÉByz 47 (1989) 290s (A. *Failler*).

g569 *Bleck* R., Ein oberrheinischer Palästina-Kreuzzug 1267: Basler Zts für Gesch. und Altertumskunde 87 (1987) 5-27 [< RHE 84,234*].

g570 **Bordonove** Georges, Los Templarios, historia y tragedia. Breviarios 440. México 1988, Fondo de Cultura Económica. 332 p. – ᴿEfMex 7 (1989) 304s (E. *Serraima Cirici*).

g571 **Chazan** Robert, European Jewry and the first crusade 1987 ➤ 3,g1; 4,h605: ᴿChH 58 (1989) 90s (D. *Krug*); JJS 40 (1989) 128-130 (S. *Bowman*); JQR 79 (1988s) 254-8 (A. *Grabois*); RÉJ 147 (1988) 417-9 (J. *Shatzmiller*).

g572 *Despy* G., Godefroid de Bouillon, mythes et réalités [inverting the popular view, he was better as duke in Europe]: Bulletin de l'Acad. Belg. lett/mor 71 (1985) 249-275 [< RHE 84,795, R. *Aubert*].

g573 **Edbury** P.W., *Rowe* J.G., WILLIAM of Tyre, historian of the Latin East: Cambridge Studies in Medieval Life and Thought 4/8, 1988 ➤ 4,h606: ᴿJRAS (1989) 325s (P. *Jackson*).

g574 *Forey* A.J., The military orders and the Holy War against Christians in the thirteenth century: EngHR 104 (1989) 1-24.

g575 *Grabiner* Esther, Jérusalem aux mains des croisés; une église croisée, Abou-Gosh: MondeB 61 (1989) 27-36 [*al.*, 3-42, sur les Croisades].

g576 **Housley** Norman, The Avignon papacy and the Crusades, 1305-1378: 1986 ➤ 2,d128; 3,g8: ᴿMeditHistR 4 (1989) 376s (B. *Golding*).

g577 **Irwin** Robert, The Middle East in the middle ages; the early Mamluk Sultanate 1250-1382. L 1986, Croom Helm. 180 p. £ 20.

g578 *Kluncker* Karlans, Die Templer, Geschichte und Geheimnis: ZRGg 41 (1989) 215-247.

g579 **Kühnel** Gustav, Wall painting in the Latin Kingdom of Jerusalem: Fra Forschungen zur Kunst 14. B 1988, Mann. 224 p.; ill. [Mundus 25,56].

g580 **Lawrence** T.E., (1936) ²*Pringle* Denys, Crusade castles. Ox 1988, Clarendon. XL-154 p.; 108 fig.; 2 maps. £ 30 [HZ 251, 690, H. *Möhring*].

g581 *Legras* Anne-Marie, L'enquête dans le prieuré de France: [ᴱ*Glenisson* J.] L'enquête pontificale de 1373 sur l'ordre des hospitaliers de St.-Jean de Jérusalem. P 1987, CNRS. xii-524 p.; 32 pl. F 550. – ᴿRHE 84 (1989) 729-732 (J. *Pycke*).

g582 *McGinn* Bernard, Violence and spirituality; the enigma of the First Crusade [*Riley-Smith* J. 1986]: JRel 69 (1989) 375-9.

g583 **Macquarrie** Alan, Scotland and the Crusades, 1095-1560. E 1985, John Donald, xiii-154 p. £ 16. – ᴿHeythJ 30 (1989) 102 (I. B. *Cowan*).

g584 **Mayer** Hans E., The Crusades² 1988 ➤ 4,h612: ᴿCathHR 75 (1989) 144-6 (J. A. *Brundage*).

g585 *Prawer* Joshua, The history of the Jews in the Latin Kingdom of Jerusalem. Ox 1988, Clarendon. XV-310 p.; 5 maps. £ 32.50 [HZ 251, 691, H. *Möhring*].

g586 *Pringle* Denys, A Templar inscription from the Haram al-Sharif in Jerusalem: Levant 21 (1989) 197-201; fig. 4-7.

g587 *Richard* Jean, La Croisade de 1270, premier 'passage général'?: CRAI (1989) 510-523.

g588 **Riley-Smith** Jonathan, The First Crusade and the idea of crusading 1986 ➤ 2,d141 ... 4,h617: ᴿChH 50 (1989) 377s (T. E. *Morrissey*); HeythJ 30 (1989) 468s (B. *Hamilton*).

g589 *Roscher* Helmut, Kreuzzüge: ➤ 894, EvKL 2 (1989) 1470-4.

g590 **Rovik** Shefali S., The Templars in the Holy Land during the XIIth Century: diss. Oxford 1986. 441 p. BRD-88372. – DissA 50 (1989s) 3987-A.

g591 **Thorau** P., Sultan Baibars I. von Ägypten; ein Beitrag zur Geschichte des Vorderen Orients im XIII. Jht.: TAVO B-63. Wsb 1987, Reichert. 336 p. DM 128 [RHE 85,71*].

g592 *Thorau* Peter, Sultan Baibars im Urteil abendländischer Quellen: Saeculum 40 (1989) 56-69.

g593 **Tyerman** Christopher, England and the Crusades. Ch 1988, Univ. XVI-492 p. $40 [RelStR 16, 266, Victoria *Chandler*].

g594 ᴱ**Wienand** Adam, *al.*, Der Johanniterorden – Der Malteserorden ... vom Spital zu Jerusalem; seine Geschichte, seine Aufgaben³. Köln 1988, Wienand. 699 p.; ill. DM 88 [TR 86, 117-9, N. M. *Borengässer*].

U8   *Communitates Terrae Sanctae* – **The Status Quo.**

g595 **Ateek** Naim S., Justice and only justice; a Palestinian theology of liberation. Mkn 1989, Orbis. xvi-299 p. $19; pa. $10 [CBQ 52,194].

g596 **Boer** P.A.H. de, Religieuze aspecten van het Palestijnse vraagstuk. Leiden 1982, Brill. x-39 p. ƒ12. 90-04-06727-2. – ᴿExpTim 100 (1988s) 311s (J. W. *Rogerson*).

Bourguet Pierre, Les Coptes 1988 ➤ b390.

g597 **Cannuyer** Christian, Fils d'Abraham; les Baha'is, peuple de la Triple Unité. Turnhout 1988, Brepols. 220 p. – ᴿEsprVie 99 (1989) 570s (R. *Epp*).

g598 **Carter** Barbara L., The Copts in Egyptian politics 1986 ➤ 2,d156; ƒ25: ᴿDer Islam 65 (1988) 149s (B. *Spuler*).

g599 *Chrostowski* Waldemar, ❷ L'État d'Israël – les défis et les espoirs: PrzPow 810 (1989) 219-239.

g600 **Cohen** Amnon, Jewish life under Islam; Jerusalem in the sixteenth century [❷ 1982] 1984 ➤ 65,d341 ... 4,h628: ᴿRelStT 8,3 (1988) 43-45 (F. *Landy*).

g601 **Efthimiou** Miltiades B., Greeks and Latins on Cyprus in the thirteenth century. Brookline MA 1888, Hellenic College. 200 p.; 15 phot. $23; pa. $15 [RelStR 16, 78, D. *Jacoby*: unsatisfactory].

g602 **Friedman** Isaiah, Germany, Turkey, and Zionism 1897-1918. Ox 1977, Clarendon. 464 p. – ᴿRÉJ 147 (1988) 216-9 (A. *Boyer*: merited earlier review).

g603 **Friedman** Thomas L., From Beirut to Jerusalem. NY c.1989, Farrar-SG. 525 p. $23. – ᴿCommonweal 116 (1989) 508s (M. *Polner*).

g604 **Gorny** Yosef, Zionism and the Arabs 1882-1948, a study of ideology. Ox 1987, Clarendon. 342 p. £32.50. – ᴿDer Islam 65 (1988) 350s (P. *Freimark*); RÉJ 148 (1989) 151-3 (A. *Boyer*).

g605 **Hussar** Bruno, Ein Weg der Versöhnung; Juden, Christen und Moslems in Israel, ᵀ*Schiffler* M., *Engelhardt* P. Mainz 1988, Grünewald. 132 p. DM 8,80. – ᴿKIsr 4,1 (1989) 82s (Julie *Kirchberg*).

g606 *Karagila* Zvi, De l'origine des relations de la famille Rothschild de Paris avec les Juifs de Palestine au XIXᵉ siècle: RÉJ 146 (1987) 135-143.

g607 *Kuiper* A., *al.*, Veertig jaar Israël...: Ter Herkenning 16,3 (1988) 161-7 (–189; 190-202, *Adang* Camilla, Schriftvervalsing als thema in de islamitische polemiek tegen het Jodendom) [< Geref TTs 89,64].

g608 *Laskier* Michael M., Egyptian Jewry in the Post-World War II period: 1945-1948: RÉJ 148 (1989) 337-360.

g609 **Lewis** Bernard, Die Juden in der islamischen Welt; vom frühen Mittelalter bis ins 20. Jahrhundert [➔ 4,h644; 1984 ➔ 65,8735], ᵀ*Liselotte* Julius. Mü 1987, Beck. 216 p. – ᴿDer Islam 65 (1988) 346-8 (B. *Spuler*).

g610 **Minerbi** Sergio I., Il Vaticano, la Terra Santa e il Sionismo. Mi 1988. viii-341. Lit. 28.000. – ᴿProtestantesimo 44 (1989) 295s (J. A. *Soggin*).

g611 *Moscati Steindler* Gabriella, L'immagine dell'arabo nella letteratura israeliana [A. *ben Yehošua'*, *Ha-Me'ahev*]: Henoch 11 (1989) 327-336; franç. 337.

g611* **Patai** Raphael, The seed of Abraham; Jews and Arabs in contact and conflict. Salt Lake City 1986, Univ. Utah. xv-394 p. – ᴿJQR 80 (1989s) 430-2 (S. *Ward*).

g612 **Ruether** Rosemary R. & Herman J., The wrath of Jonah; the crisis of religious nationalism in the Israeli-Palestinian conflict. NY 1989, Harper & R. $17. – ᴿAmerica 161 (1989) 146-8 (M. H. *Bernstein*, also on SIMONS C.): CCurr 39 (1989s) 248-250 (G. E. *Irani*); Commonweal 116 (1989) 342s (G. *Baum*).

g612* *Ruether* Rosemary R., Christian Zionism is a heresy: JTSAf 69 (1989) 60 [< ZIT 90,159].

g613 *Rulli* Giovanni, La nascita dello Stato di Palestina [14.XI.1988 senza terra, governo, organi indispensabili p. 195]: CC 140 (1989,1) 187-195 [291-301, intensa attività diplomatica di Arafat].

g614 **Sa'd** Abujaber R., Pioneers over Jordan; the frontier of settlement in Transjordan 1850-1914. L 1989, Tauris. xviii-328 p. – ᴿLA 39 (1989) 289s (P. *Kaswalder*).

g615 **Schölch** Alexander †, Palästina im Umbruch 1856-1882; Untersuchungen zur wirtschaftlichen und soziopolitischen Entwicklung: Berliner Islamstudien 4, 1986 ➔ 2,d186: ᴿDer Islam 65 (1988) 351s (P. *Freimark*); OLZ 85 (1989) 202-4 (G. *Höpp*).

g616 **Sélis** Claude, Les Syriens orthodoxes et catholiques: Fils d'Abraham. Turnhout 1988, Brepols. 289 p.; 15 pl. [CBQ 51,592]. – ᴿAnBoll 107 (1989) 443s (R. de *Fenoyl*); EsprVie 99 (1989) 570 (R. *Epp*); RHPR 69 (1989) 334 (P. *Maraval*).

g617 *a) Sicking* Thom, Minorités religieuses et dialogue œcuménique; – *b) Dick* Ignace, Les relations interchrétiennes à Alep: PrOrChr 39 (1989) 60-90 / 113-126.

g618 *Simonsohn* Shlomo, Divieto di esportare Ebrei in Palestina [c. 1428]: ➔ 745, Italia Judaica 2 (1984/6) 39-53.

g619 *Stroumsa* Gedaliahu G., Religious contacts in Byzantine Palestine: Numen 36 (1989) 16-42.

g620 **Teveth** Shabtai, Ben-Gurion and the Palestine Arabs; from peace to war. NY 1985, Oxford-UP. x-134 p. £17.50 – ᴿEngHR 104 (1989) 168s (D. *Cesarani*).

g621 *Uhlig* Siegbert, DAMIANS Schrift über Glaube, Religion und Sitte der Äthiopier aus dem Jahre 1540 [Prester-John-Zeit; Damian a Goes, Lv]: BO 46 (1989) 552-560.

g622 **Yapp** M. E., The making of the modern Near East 1792-1923: History of the Near East. L 1987, Longman. xii-404 p.; 9 maps. £22.50; pa. £12. – ᴿJRAS (1989) 315s (W. J. *Olson*).

XX. Historia Scientiae Biblicae

Y1 **History of Exegesis** .1 **General.**

g623 **Beatrick** Pierre, Introduction aux Pères de l'Église 1987 ► 3,g79; aussi Vicence 1987, Inst.St-Gaétan. 351 p. F 70. 2-7122-0276-7: ᴿÉTRel 64 (1989) 303 (J.-D. *Dubois*).

g624 **Bellini** Enzo †, Los Santos Padres en la tradición cristiana, ᴱ*Saibene* Luigi: Libros de bolsillo 50. M 1988, Encuentro. 140 p. 84-7490-207-X. – ᴿActuBbg 26 (1989) 245 (J. *Vives*).

g625 **Bernardi** Jean, Les premiers siècles de l'Église 1987 ► 4,h659: ᴿNVFr 64 (1989) 115-133 (P.-L. *Carle*).

g626 **Brown** Harold O. J., Heresies; the image of Christ in the mirror of heresy and orthodoxy 1988 = 1944 ► 65,d381 ... 4,h660; 0-8010-0953-7: ᴿExpTim 100 (1988s) 271s (R. *Butterworth* thinks that heresy, as distinct from 'struggling orthodoxy', is boring); GraceTJ 10 (1989) 110s (J. E. *McGoldrick*); RExp 86 (1989) 631s (R. G. *Hinson*: missed his chance to make the reprint into a useful book).

g627 **Brox** Norbert, Storia della Chiesa, I. Epoca antica, ᵀᴱ*Mezzadri* Luigi, 1988 ► 4,h661: ᴿCC 140 (1989,3) 342 (C. *Capizzi*).

g628 **Camelot** P. T., *Maraval* P., Les conciles œcuméniques, I. Le premier millénaire; – II. **Christophe** P., *Frost* F., Le second millénaire: Bibliothèque d'Histoire du Christianisme 15s. P 1988, Desclée. 90 p., 1 map; 275 p., 7 maps. F 69 + 128. – ᴿNRT 111 (1989) 1005s (N. *Plumat*).

g628* *Curti al.*, La terminologia esegetica nell'antichità 1984/7 ► 3,534: ᴿGregorianum 70 (1989) 368s (G. *Pelland*).

g629 **Droge** Arthur J., Homer or Moses? Early Christian interpretations of the history of culture: HermUnT 26. Tü 1989, Mohr. xiv-220 p. DM 98. 3-16-145354-9 [TDig 36,367]. – ᴿNRT 111 (1989) 1018s (A. *Harvengt*).

g630 *Grant* Robert M., Kirchenväter, ᵀ*Mühlenberg* M.: ► 894, EvKL 2 (1989) 1186-92.

g631 Judendom och kristendom under de första århundradena: Nordiskt patristikerprojekt 1982-5, I-II. Oslo 1986, Bergen. 308 p.; 304 p. – ᴿSvT-Kv 65 (1989) 29 (B. *Johnson*).

g632 *Kannengiesser* Charles, Fifty years of patristics: TS 50 (1989) 633-656.

g633 **Kelly** John N. D., Początki doktryny chrześcijańskiej. Wsz 1988, PAX. ᴿAtKap 113 (1989) 377s (T. *Lenczewski* ❻).

g634 *Kertsch* Manfred, Patristische Zitate bei späteren griechisch-christlichen Autoren: JbÖsByz 38 (1988) 113-124.

g635 **Kozarzhevsky** A. ❻ *Istochnikovedcheskie* ... – Source-investigation problems of early Christian literature. Moskva 1985, MGU. – ᴿVDI 188 (1989) 215s (M. K. *Trophimova*).

g636 ᴱ**Lenzenweger** Josef, *al.*, Geschichte der katholischen Kirche, ein Grundkurs 1986 ► 3,430; 4,h677; 3-222-11647-4: ᴿGregorianum 70 (1989) 373-7 (M. *Chappin*, Eng.).

g637 ᴱ**Löser** Werner, *al.*, Dogmengeschichte und katholische Theologie 1985 ► 2,323*; 3,g100: ᴿTLZ 114 (1989) 47-50 (W.-D. *Hauschild*).

g638 **McGonigle** Thomas D., *Quigley* James F.,   A history of the Christian tradition from its Jewish origins to the Reformation. NY 1988, Paulist. vi-218 p. $11.   0-8091-2964-7 [TDig 36,379].

g639 ᴱ**Maraval** P., Lectures anciennes de la Bible 1987 ➤ 3,350: ᴿStPatav 36 (1989) 176-180 (C. *Corsato*).

g640 *Marin* Marcello,   Orientamenti di esegesi biblica dei Padri [< Complementi 1989 ➤ 503, p. 273-317]: VetChr 26 (1989) 247-274.

g641 **Moda** Aldo,   Il cristianesimo nel primo secolo, un itinerario e un dossier 1986 ➤ 4,h678:   ᴿParVi 34 (1989) 303s (E. *Dal Covolo*).

g642 **Mondésert** C.,   Pour lire les Pères...: SChr: Foi Vivante 230, 1988 ➤ 4,h679:   ᴿScripTPamp 21 (1989) 702s (C. *García Moyano*).

g643 *Padovese* Luigi,   La polemica anticristiana nei secoli II/IV; alcuni cenni illustrativi: ➤ 97, ᶠIRIARTE L. = EstFranc 89 (1988) 279-299.

g644 **Pierini** Franco,   Mille anni di pensiero cristiano, le letterature e i monumenti dei Padri, I. Alla ricerca dei Padri; introduzione e metodologia generale 1988 ➤ 4,h682:   ᴿCC 140 (1989,3) 534s (A. *Ferrua*); ETL 65 (1989) 172-4 (A. de *Halleux*: théorique mais pas fatiguant); Gregorianum 70 (1989) 590-2 (J. *Janssens*); RHE 84 (1989) 625 (R. *Gryson*: he would have done better to stick to catechism and leave patrology to its specialists).

ᴱ**Quacquarelli** Antonio,   Complementi interdisciplinari di patrologia, 1989 ➤ 503.

g645 **Ramsey** Boniface,   Beginning to read the Fathers 1985 ➤ 1,f467... 4,h684:   ᴿHeythJ 30 (1989) 460s (J. A. *McGuckin*: fine and usable, with some reserves on the Christology section).

Rinaldi Giancarlo,   Biblia gentium; primo contributo per un indice delle citazioni, dei riferimenti e delle allusioni alla Bibbia negli autori pagani, greci e latini, d'età imperiale 1989 ➤ supra 1872.

g647 *Rinaldi* Giancarlo,   *a*) Sognatori e visionari 'biblici' nei polemisti anticristiani [in margine a Biblia gentium 1989]: ➤ 748, Sogni 1988 = AugR 29 (1989) 7-30; – *b*) Tracce di controversie tra pagani e cristiani nella letteratura patristica delle 'quaestiones et responsiones': ➤ 567, AnStoEseg 6 (1989) 99-124; Eng. 7.

g648 **Rogerson** John [OT], *Rowland* C., *Lindars* B. [NT], The study and use of the Bible: History of Christian Theology 2, 1988 ➤ 4,h687:   ᴿRelStR 15 (1989) 154 (W. L. *Humphreys*).

g649 **Sawicki** Marianne,   The Gospel in history... Christian education 1988 ➤ 4,h691:   ᴿBibTB 19 (1989) 155s (M. *Warren*); ExpTim 100 (1988s) 274 (G. *White*).

g650 **Saxer** Victor,   Bible et hagiographie 1986 ➤ 3,g115; 4,h692:   ᴿLatomus 48 (1989) 457s (J. *Doignon*).

ᴱ**Sevrin** Jean-Marie,   The NT in early Christianity / La réception des écrits néotestamentaires 1987/9 ➤ 606.

g650* **Sider** Robert D.,   The Gospel and its proclamation: Message of the Fathers 10, 1983 ➤ 64,d968... 1,f470:   ᴿÉTRel 64 (1989) 301s (J.-D. *Dubois*).

g651 **Simonetti** Manlio,   Lettera e/o allegoria 1985 ➤ 1,f473... 4,h696:   ᴿRTPhil 121 (1989) 229 (F. *Rilliet*).

g651* **Trigg** Joseph W.,   Biblical interpretation: Message of the Fathers 9, 1988 ➤ 4,h701:   ᴿRExp 86 (1989) 643s (E. G. *Hinson*, also on vol. 15; 18; 21); TS 50 (1989) 612 (Pamela *Bright*).

g652 **Vilanova** Evangelista,   Historia de la teología cristiana I, 1987 ➤ 3,g125; 4,h704:   ᴿHumT 10,1 (1989) 125s (A. de *Pinho*); StMon 30 (1988) 172-8 (J. *Leclercq*). – II. ➤ k142.

g653 **Wojtowytsch** Myron, Papsttum und Konzile... bis 461, 1981 ➤ 63, e549...: ᴿRivStoLR 25 (1989) 144-153 (L. *Perrone*).

Y1.4   *Patres apostolici et saeculi II* – **First two centuries.**

g654 *Derrett* J.D.M., *Ho kýrios ebasíleusen apò toû xýlou* [asks *what* wood, and hints Is 8,24-9,6; Ps 95,11; but answers 'a Christian midrash preexisting Barnabas and Justin']: VigChr 43 (1989) 378-392.
g655 **Ferguson** E., Early Christians speak; faith and life in the first three centuries²ʳᵉᵛ [¹1981]. Abilene TX 1987, Christian Univ. 258 p.; 8 pl. 0-89112-044-0 [NTAbs 33,128: selections, then discussion of topics e.g. (immersion/infant) baptism].
g656 **Grant** Robert M., Greek apologists of the second century 1988 ➤ 4,h708: ᴿAndrUnS 27 (1989) 142-4 (R. M. *Johnston*); ExpTim 100 (1988s) 473s (R. *Butterworth*); JTS 40 (1989) 612s (L. W. *Barnard*); RExp 86 (1989) 448 (E. G. *Hinson*); TTod 46 (1989s) 250s (A. J. *Guerra*).
g657 **Grelot** P. (*Dumais* M.), Homélies sur l'Écriture à l'époque apostolique: Intr/NT 8. P 1989, Desclée. 320 p. F 145 [NRT 112, 900-2, X. *Jacques*].
g658 *Junod* Éric, Des apologètes à Origène; aux origines d'une forme de 'théologie critique': RTPhil 121 (1989) 149-164.
g659 *Kinzig* Wolfram, Der 'Sitz im Leben' der Apologie in der Alten Kirche: ZKG 100 (1989) 291-317.
g660 **Morcom** Donald L., The retention of the Jewish Scriptures in the self-definition of the second century Church: diss. Southern Baptist Theol. Sem. 1989, ᴰHinson D. G. 284 p. 89-25773. – DissA 50 (1989s) 2106-A.
g661 **Orbe** Antonio, Introducción a la teología de los siglos II y III, 1987 ➤ 3,g128; 4,h710: ᴿActuBbg 26 (1989) 91 (J. *Vives*); RivStoLR 25 (1989) 88-97 (M. *Simonetti*); ScripTPamp 21 (1989) 364s (D. *Ramos-Lissón*).
g662 *Osiek* Carolyn, Early Church [2d century writers]: ➤ 384, NJBC (1989s) 1346-50.
g663 **Schnabel** W., Die alte Kirche: Grundwissen zur Theologie und KG, eine Quellenkunde 1. Tü 1988, Mohn. 128 p. DM 24,80. 3-579-00143-4. – ᴿTsTNijm 29 (1989) 178 (A. *Davids*).
g664 *Schoedel* William R., The apostolic fathers: ➤ 394, NT/Interpreters 1989, 457-498.
g665 **Thomas** Mary Catherine, The influence of asceticism on the rise of Christian text, doctrine and practice in the first two centuries [... ascetic Christians altered the scriptural text to recruit]: diss. Brigham Young Univ. ᴰPixton P., 1989. 181 p. 90-00848. – DissA 50 (1989s) 2534-A.
g666 *Wartelle* André, Sur le vocabulaire du sacré chez les Pères Apologistes grecs: RÉG 102 (1989) 40-57.

---

g667 ATHÉNAGORAS: *a*) **Pouderon** B., Athénagoras d'Athènes, philosophe chrétien: THist 82. P 1989, Beauchesne. 354 p. F 195 [NRT 112, 923, G. *Navez*]. – *b*) *Schoedel* William R., Apologetic literature and ambassadorial activities: HarvTR 82 (1989) 55-78.
g668 CLEMENS A.: *a*) *Beers* J. Michael, Clement of Alexandria's world-view; the perspective of the knowing believer, *gnosis* builds on *pistis*; – *b*) *Milavec* Aaron, The pastoral genius of the Didache; an analytical translation and commentary: ➤ 592, Systemic 2 (1989) 127-137 / 89-125.

g669 *Torrance* Thomas F., The hermeneutics of Clement of Alexandria: Texts and Studies [for] Hellenism and Diaspora 7 (Athens 1988) 61-105 [< RTLv 20,388].

g670 CLEMENS R.: *Dehandschutter* B., Some notes on 1 Clement v,4-7: ➤ 17, FBARTELINK G., Fructus 1989, 83-89.

g671 a) *Herron* Thomas J., The most probable date of the first epistle of Clement to the Corinthians: – b) *Maier* H. O., I Clement 40-44; apostolic succession or legitimation? Insights from the social sciences: ➤ 696, 10th Patristic, 21 (1989) 106-121 / 137-141.

g672 *Peretto* Elio, Clemente Romano ai Corinti; sfida alla violenza: VetChr 26 (1989) 89-114.

g673 a) *Cirillo* Luigi, L'antipaolismo nelle Pseudoclementine; – b) *Grech* Prosper, Note sull'antipaolinismo nei Padri: ➤ 600, RicStoB 1,2 (1987/9) 121-137 / 93-95.

g674 *Irmscher* Johannes, *Strecker* Georg, Die Pseudoklementinen: ➤ 417, Apokryphen II⁵ 1989, 439-488.

g675 **Jones** Frederick S., Pseudo-Clementine Recognitions 1,27-71; early Jewish Christian perspectives on the nature and history of Christianity: diss. Vanderbilt, DLuedemann G. Nv 1989. 229 p. 90-06845. – DissA 50 (1989s) 3262-A; RelStR 16,190.

g676 *Marafioti* Domenico, La verginità in tempo di crisi; le due lettere pseudoclementine 'Ad virgines': CC 140 (1989,4) 434-448.

g677 CONST. AP.: TEMetzger Marcel, Les Constitutions Apostoliques II-III, SChr 329.336, 1986s ➤ 2,d264; 3,g141; 4,b722: RRB 96 (1989) 625s (M.-J. *Pierre*); RBgPg 67 (1989) 195s (J. *Schamp*); RCatalT 13 (1988) 251s (M. S. *Gros i Pujol*); TPhil 64 (1989) 587-9 (H. J. *Sieben*).

g678 *Fiensy* David A., Prayers alleged to be Jewish... BrownJudSt 65, 1985 ➤ 1,f493... 3,g142: RSecC 7 (1989) 122s (J. V. *Hills*).

g679 DIDACHE: ENiederwimmer Kurt, Die Didache: KommApV 1. Gö 1989, Vandenhoeck & R. 229 p. DM 94 [CBQ 52,197]. 3-525-51670-1.

g680 *Jefford* Clayton N., *Patterson* Stephen J., A note on Didache 12.2a (Coptic): SecC 7 (1989s) 65-75.

g681 AD DIOGNETUM: **Rizzi** Marco, La questione dell'unità dell''Ad Diognetum'. Mi 1989, ViPe. 203 p. Lit. 24.000. 88-343-0175-7; pa.–4-9. – RSileno 15 (1989) 347s (C. *Nicolosi*).

g682 HEGESIPPUS: *Dürst* Michael, Hegesipps 'Hypomnemata' [*Euseb* HE 4.8.2] – Titel oder Gattungsbezeichnung?: ➤ 732b, RömQ 84 (1989) 299-330.

g683 HERMAS: *Brox* Norbert, a) Die kleinen Gleichnisse im Pastor Hermae; MüTZ 40 (1989) 263-278; – b) Weggeworfene Steine im Pastor Hermae Vis III, 7,5: ZNW 80 (1989) 130-3.

g684 *Carlini* Antonio, La tradizione testuale del Pastore di Erma e i nuovi papiri: ➤ 533a, Strade del testo 1987, 21-43.

g685 *Henne* Philippe, La polysémie allégorique dans le Pasteur d'Hermas: ETL 65 (1989) 131-5.

g686 **Leutzsch** M., Die Wahrnehmung sozialer Wirklichkeit im 'Hirten des Hermas': FRL 150. Gö 1989, Vandenhoeck & R. 286 p. DM 76. 3-525-53832-4 [NRT 112, 924, A. *Harvengt*].

g687 *Lucchesi* Enzo, Le Pasteur d'Hermas en copte; perspective nouvelle: VigChr 43 (1989) 393-6.

g688 IGNATIUS A.: **Brent** Allen, History and eschatological mysticism in Ignatius of Antioch: ETL 65 (1989) 309-329.

g689 *Maier* Harry O., The charismatic authority of Ignatius of Antioch; a sociological analysis: SR 18 (1989) 185-199.

g690 **Paulsen** Henning, Die Briefe des Ignatius von Antiochia und der Polykarpbrief: 1985 ➤ 1,f500; 2,d269: ᴿRelStR 15 (1989) 130s (F. W. *Norris*).

g691 *Rius-Camps* Josep, a) Ignacio de Antioquía, ¿testigo ocular de la muerte y resurrección de Jesús?: Biblica 70 (1989) 449-472; Eng. 473. – b) ᵀᴱL'epistolari d'Ignasi d'Antioquia: RCatalT 13 (1988) 23-58.275-313; Eng. 58.314.

g692 **Schoedel** W. R., Ignatius... commentary 1985 ➤ 1,f502... 4,h730: ᴿIr-TQ 55 (1989) 79s (D. *Brown*); RelStR 15 (1989) 128-130 (F. W. *Norris*); Salesianum 51 (1989) 376s (Z. *Brzek*).

g693 *Stander* H. F., The Starhymn in the epistle of Ignatius to the Ephesians (19:2-3): VigChr 43 (1989) 209-214.

g694 *Trevett* Christine, Ignatius 'to the Romans' and 1 Clement LIV-LVI: VigChr 43 (1989) 35-52.

g695 IRENAEUS L.: **Greer** Rowan A., Broken lights... 1986 ➤ 2,d276... 4,h731: ᴿRechSR 77 (1989) 596s (Y.-M. *Duval*); SecC 7 (1989s) 106-8 (L. B. *Hennessey*).

g696 *Grego* Igino, Le 'due mani di Dio' nella storia della salvezza negli scritti di Ireneo di Lione: Asprenas 36 (1989) 469-483.

g697 **Orbe** Antonio, Teología de S. Ireneo V [1, 1985 ➤ 2,d278; 2. 1985 ➤ 4,h732], 3: BAC [25.29.]33. M 1988, Católica. xii-820 p. – ᴿETL 65 (1989) 174s (A. de *Halleux*); RBíbArg 51 (1989) 60s (F. *García Bazán*, 1); RThom 89 (1989) 646-8 (J. *Fantino*); Salesianum 51 (1989) 374s (B. *Amata*).

g698 **Orbe** Antonio, Espiritualidad de San Ireneo: AnGreg 256, Theol. A-33. R 1989, Pont. Univ. Gregoriana. xlii-340 p. Lit. 48.000. 88-7652-606-4.

g699 JUSTINUS: a) *Burini* Clara, L'ignominia della croce nel Dialogo con Trifone di Giustino; – b) *Maggioni* Bruno, La croce stoltezza e sapienza: ParSpV 20 (1989) 221-233 / 165-178.

g700 **Robillard** Edm, Justin, l'itinéraire philosophique: Recherches NS 23. Montréal/P 1989, Bellarmin/Cerf. 172 p. [NRT 112, 180, A. *Harvengt*].

g701 **Skarsaune** Oskar, The proof from prophecy... Justin 1987 ➤ 3,g166; 4,h737: ᴱEvQ 61 (1989) 165-7 (J. N. *Birdsall*); VigChr 43 (1989) 300-2 (J. van *Winden*).

g702 ᵀᴱ**Visonà** Giuseppe, S. Giustino, Dialogo con Trifone 1988 ➤ 4,h742: ᴿCC 140 (1989,4) 510s (A. *Ferrua*); RivStoLR 25 (1989) 556s (A. M. *Berruto*).

g703 ᵀᴱ**Wartelle** A., S. Justin, Apologies 1987 ➤ 3,g167; 4,h741: ᴿRÉG 102 (1989) 618s (J. *Irigoin*).

g704 POLYCARPUS: *Dehandschutter* Boudewijn, Polycarp's epistle to the Philippians; an early example of 'reception': ➤ 606, Réception 1986/9, 275-291.

g705 *Serraima Cirici* Enrique, Policarpo de Esmirna y su Carta a los Filipenses: EfMex 6 (1988) 401-415.

Y1.6 **Origenes.**

g706 *Brox* Norbert, Pascha und Passion; Eine neugefundene [Toura 1941, ᴱ*Guéraud* O. 1979 ...] Exegese des Origenes: ➤ 197, ᶠTRILLING W., Christus bezeugen 1989, 267-274.

g707 **Crouzel** Henri, *a)* Origen; the life and thought of the first great theologian [1985 → 1,f516], T*Worrall* A.S. SF 1989, Harper & R. 278 p. $40 [JAAR 57,683 'Courzel']. 0-06-061632-6. – RExpTim 101 (1989s) 216 (G. Bostock). – *b)* Chronique origénienne: BLitEc 90 (1989) 135-140.

g708 **Fédou** M., Christianisme et religions païennes dans le Contre Celse d'Origène: THist 81. P 1989, Beauchesne. 665 p. F 255. 2-7010-1200-7 [NRT 112, 925, A. *Toubeau*].

g708* **Hallström** Gunnar af, Charismatic succession; a study on Origen's concept of prophecy: Publ. 42. Helsinki 1986, Finnish Exeg.Soc. vi-76 p. [TLZ 115,34-36, W. *Ullmann*].

g709 *Hauck* R., The more divine proof; prophecy and inspiration in CELSUS and Origen. Atlanta 1989, Scholars. 158 p. $17; pa. $11 [TS 51,383].

g709* **Heimann** Peter, Erwähltes Schicksal; Präexistenz der Seele und christlicher Glaube im Denkmodell des Origenes [Diss Bern 1987]: TBeitF 5. Tü 1988, Katzmann. 292 p. DM 48 [TLZ 115, 896, K. *Treu*].

g710 **Lanata** Giuliana, CELSO, Il discorso vero [testo *Bader* R. Tü 1940, tradotto]: Adelphi Biblioteca 206. Mi 1987. 253 p. Lit. 14.000. – RProtestantesimo 44 (1989) 138s (G. *Conte*); RasT 30 (1989) 582-8 (L. *Paganelli*).

g710* — *Paganelli* Leonardo, Celso, un intellettuale contro il Cristianesimo [ELanata Giuliana, 1987]: RasT 30 (1989) 582-8.

g711 *Lienhard* Joseph T., Origen as homilist: → 38, FBURGHARDT W., Preaching 1989, 36-52.

g712 ELies Lothar, Origeniana quarta 1985/7 → 3,664b; 4,h758: RETL 65 (1989) 447s (B. *Dehandschutter*); RTLv 20 (1989) 210-5 (A. de *Halleux*); TLZ 114 (1989) 895-900 (W. *Ullmann*); TüTQ 169 (1989) 244-6 (H. J. *Vogt*).

g713 **Meis Wörmer** Anneliese, El problema del mal en Orígenes; importancia y significado teológico del tiempo en la argumentación sobre el mal del Peri Archon III, L,1-24: AnChile 37 (1986) cuad. 2. Santiago 1988, Pont. Univ. 136 p. [Greg 70,618]. $10.

g714 **Monaci Castagno** Adele, Origene predicatore e il suo pubblico 1987 → 4,h759; Lit. 30.000: RBLitEc 90 (1989) 136s (H. *Crouzel*); RÉByz 47 (1989) 298s (J. *Wolinski*).

g715 **Neuschäfer** Bernard, Origenes als Philologe: Schweize.Beit.AltW 18, 1987 → 3,g177; 4,h760: RClasR 39 (1989) 136 (N. G. *Wilson*).

g716 **Pietras** Henryk, L'amore in Origene 1988 → 4,h761: RSandalion 12s (1989s) 272-5 (Anna Maria *Piredda*).

g717 **Rabinowitz** Celia E., *Apokatastasis* and *sunteleia*; eschatological and soteriological speculation in Origen: diss. Fordham, DEttlinger G. Bronx 1989. 258 p. 89-17241. – DissA 50 (1989s) 1341-A; RelStR 16,187.

g718 *Sardella* Teresa, *Prognōsis* e *mantikē* in Origene: → 748, Sogni 1988 = AugR 29 (1989) 281-306.

g719 **Schockenhoff** Eberhard, Zum Fest der Freiheit – Theologie des christlichen Handelns bei Origenes: kath. H.-Diss. Tü 1988s, DKasper W. – TR 85 (1989) 511.

g720 **Schütz** Werner, Der christliche Gottesdienst bei Origenes 1984 → 1,7810 ... 3,g179: RJTS 40 (1989) 245-7 (C. P. *Bammel*).

g721 **Torjesen** Karen J., Hermeneutical procedure and theological method in Origen's exegesis 1986 → 2,d316 ... 4,h763: RRechSR 76 (1988) 591s (B. *Sesboüé*); TR 85 (1989) 106s (Maria-Barbara von *Stritzky*).

g722 **Tripolitis** Antonia, Origen, a critical reading 1985 → 2,d318; 3,g186: RSecC 7 (1989s) 110s (P.M. *Blowers*: not up to the level of existing works).

Y1.8 **Tertullianus.**

g723 *a) Braun* René, Sacralité et sainteté chez Tertullien [= BBudé (1989) 339-344]; – *b) Wartelle* A., Sur le vocabulaire du sacré chez les Pères apologistes grecs: → 786, Écrivains/Sacré 1988/9, 313s/277s.

g724 *Contreras* P. Enrique, Tertuliano 'Adversus Praxean', un tratado antimonarquiano: StOvet 16 (1988) 209-224.

g725 *Czesz* Bogdan, La 'tradizione' profetica nella controversia montanista: → 748, Sogni 1988 = AugR 29 (1989) 55-70.

g726 *Devoti* Domenico, All'origine dell'onirologia cristiana [... Tert. de anima 45-49]: → 748, Sogni 1988 = AugR 29 (1989) 31-53.

g727 **Franklin** Lloyd D., The spiritual gifts in Tertullian: diss. St. Louis Univ. 1989, DGreeley D. 165 p. 90-00908. – DissA 50 (1989s) 2538-A.

g728 **Goldhahn-Müller** Ingrid, Die Grenze der Gemeinde; Studien zum Problem der Zweiten Busse im Neuen Testament [1 Jn] unter Berücksichtigung der Entwicklung im 2. Jh. bis Tertullian [Diss.Gö 1988 DStrecker G.]: GöTheolAbh 39. Gö 1989, Vandenhoeck & R. ix-406 p. DM 84 pa. [CBQ 52,195]. 3-525-87392-1.

g729 **Gonzalez** Justo L., Christian thought revisited; three types of theology [Tertullian, ORIGEN, IRENAEUS]. Nv 1989, Abingdon. 185 p. $16. – RTTod 46 (1989) 465 (P. H. *Van Ness*).

g730 *Haendler* Gert, Tertullian und die Einheit der Kirche: → Einheit 1985/9, 80-92.

g731 **Heck** Eberhard, *Mē theomacheîn*... Bekämpfung römischer Religion bei Tertullian... 1987 → 4,b672.h767: RTR 85 (1989) 204-6 (N. *Brox*).

g732 **Heine** Ronald E., The Montanist oracles and testimonia: PatrMg 14. Macon GA 1989, Mercer Univ. xiv-190 p. $25. 0-86554-333-X.

g733 *Hill* C. E., Hades of HIPPOLYTUS [no] or Tartarus of Tertullian [yes]; the authorship of the fragment De universo [ps. Damascene]: VigChr 43 (1989) 105-126.

g734 **McGinn-Moorer** Sheila E., [Montanism]. The New Prophecy of Asia Minor and the rise of ecclesiastical patriarchy in second century Pauline traditions: diss. Northwestern. Evanston IL 1989. 396 p. 90-01839. – DissA 50 (1989s) 2532-A.

g735 **Mattei** Paul, Tertullien, Le mariage unique: SChr 343, 1988 → 4,h769: RJTS 40 (1989) 614s (M. *Winterbottom*).

g740 *Micaelli* Claudio, *a)* Note critiche ed esegetiche al testo del De resurrectione di Tertuliano: VetChr 26 (1989) 275-286; – *b)* Nuove ricerche sulla fortuna di Tertuliano: Koinonia 13 (1989) 113-126.

g741 ETWaszink J. H., Winden J.C.M. van, Tertullianus, de idololatria: VigChr Sup. 1. Leiden 1987, Brill. xii-317 p. *f* 148. – RJTS 40 (1989) 239s (M. *Winterbottom*).

Y2 *Patres graeci* – **The Greek Fathers.**

g742 **Armstrong** H., PLOTINUS VIs (Enneads 6; Loeb final Plotinus volume replacing *McKenna* 1917-30). CM/L 1988, Harvard/Heinemann. x-359 p.; x-345 p. £ 9.50 each. – RJTS 40 (1989) 616-8 (A. *Meredith*).

g743 **Christou** Panaghiotis K., ⊚ Greek patrology 3, 4-5 cent. Thessaloniki 1987, Meretakis. 599 p. – ᴿSalesianum 51 (1989) 367 (A. *Amato*).

g744 **Davis** Leo D., The first seven ecumenical councils 1987 ↦ 4,h776: ᴿChH 58 (1989) 218s (J. F. *Kelly*); SVlad 33 (1989) 413-5 (P. *Wesche*); TS 50 (1989) 202s (M. *Slusser*).

g744* *Gray* P., Forgery as an instrument of progress; reconstructing the theological tradition in the sixth century: ByZ 81 (1988) 284-9.

g745 **Kinneavy** James L., [*pístis, pisteúein*] Greek rhetorical origins of Christian faith 1987 ↦ 3,3830.g205; 4,h781: ᴿCBQ 51 (1989) 375s (C. C. *Black*, 'Kinneavey'); JTS 40 (1989) 211s (Margaret E. *Thrall*); TLond 92 (1989) 328 (F. G. *Downing*: 'pisteis' meaning 'proofs', a massive confusion, anyway not in NT).

g746 *Kolb* Anne, Das Symbolum Nicaeno-Constantinopolitanum; zwei neue Zeugnisse [Ostrakon, Heidelberg; Pergament, British Museum]: ZPapEp 79 (1989) 253-260; pl. VI.

g747 *Rist* J. M., Platonism and its Christian heritage [16 papers 1962-83]: Collected Studies 321, 1985 ↦ 1,234*; 2,d342: ᴿPhoenix 43 (Toronto 1989) 382-4 (I. G. *Westerink*).

g748 *Runia* David T., Festugière revisited; Aristotle in the Greek Patres: VigChr 43 (1989) 1-34.

g749 *Saranyana* Josep-Ignasi, Sobre el diálogo de los pensadores cristianos con las culturas no cristianas (siglos II al XIII): ScripTPamp 21 (1989) 125-139.

g750 *Simonetti* Manlio, Il problema dell'unità di Dio in Oriente dopo Origene: RivStoLR 25 (1989) 193-233.

g751 *Speigl* Jakob, Die Geschichte der vier ersten Ökumenischen Konzilien; wie Kaiser Justinian sie sah: MüTZ 40 (1989) 349-363.

g752 **Studer** Basil, La riflessione teologica nella Chiesa imperiale (sec. IV et V): Sussidi patristici 4. R 1989, Ist. Patr. Augustinianum. 244 p.

g753 **Thümmel** Hans Georg, Die Kirche des Ostens im 3. und 4. Jahrhundert: Kirchengeschichte in Einzeldarstellungen 1/4. B 1988, Ev.-V. 135 p. – ᴿTPhil 64 (1989) 262-4 (H. J. *Sieben*).

g754 **Weltin** E. G., Athens and Jerusalem 1987 ↦ 3,g212*; 4,h791: ᴿJAAR 57 (1989) 677-680 (T. A. *Kopecek*).

---

g755 ᴬᶜᴬᶜᴵᵁˢ: *Lienhard* J.T., Acacius of Caesarea, Contra Marcellum [340 A.D.]; historical and theological considerations: CrNSt 10 (1989) 1-21; ital. i; più dettagliato 22.

g756 ᴬᴾᴼᴸᴸᴵᴺᴬᴿᴵᵁˢ: **Hübner** Reinhard M., Die Schrift des Apolinarius von Laodicea gegen Photin (Pseudo-Athanasius, Contra Sabellianos) und Basilius von Caesarea [kath. Diss. Bonn]: PatrTSt 30. B 1989, de Gruyter. xii-322 p. [RHE 85, 140, A. de *Halleux*: one l in title but Apollinaire in Fr.text].

g757 ᴬᴿᴵᵁˢ: *Mara* Maria Grazia, Arriani, Arius: ↦ 879, AugL 1/3 (1988) 450-9.

g758 *Martin* Annick, Le fil d'Arius: 325-335: RHE 84 (1989) 297-333.

g759 **Williams** Rowan, Arius, heresy and tradition 1987 ↦ 3,g216; 4,h794: ᴿJRS 79 (1989) 256s (B. H. *Warmington*); JTS 40 (1989) 247-254 (R. C. *Gregg*); RHE 84 (1989) 616 (P. *Brady*); RHPR 69 (1989) 343s (W. *Fick*); RivStoLR 25 (1989) 153-7 (M. *Simonetti*); ScotJT 42 (1989) 263-7 (Frances M. *Young*); ScripTPamp 21 (1989) 703s (L. F. *Mateo Seco*).

g760 ATHANASIUS: **Kannengiesser** Charles, Athanase... Contre les Ariens: THist 70, 1983 → 64,e45... 1,f572: ᴿNRT 111 (1989) 593s (G. *Peters*).

g761 *Kannengiesser* Charles, *a*) The homiletic festal letters of Athanasius: → 38, ᶠBURGHARDT W., Preaching 1989, 73-100. – *b*) Questions ouvertes sur Athanase d'Alexandrie: → 51, ᶠEBOROWICZ W., VoxPa 15 (1988) 689-705 en français.

g762 *Martin* Annik, [Athanasius, Epiphanius]. Les relations entre Arius et Mélitios dans la tradition alexandrine; une histoire polémique: JTS 40 (1989) 401-413.

g763 BASILIUS C.: **Gain** B., L'Église de Cappadoce... Basile 1985 → 2,d353... 4,h804: ᴿREByz 45 (1987) 251s (J. *Darrouzès*); RivStoLR 25 (1989) 164-7 (Marcella *Forlin Patrucco*); VoxP 14 (1988) 481-4 (M. *Starowieyski*).

g764 *Lienhard* Joseph T., Basil of Caesarea, MARCELLUS of Ancyra, and 'SABELLIUS': ChH 58 (1989) 157-167.

g765 *Brennecke* Hanns Christof, Erwägungen zu den Anfängen des Neunizänismus [Bas.; Greg.Naz./Nyss.]: → 174, ᶠSCHNEEMELCHER W., Oecumenica 1989, 241-257.

g766 ᵀᴱ**Vaggione** Richard, Eunomius [Basil adversus...]; the extant texts ['Neo-Arianism']: Early Christian Texts, 1987 → 3,g224*; 0-19-825814-9: ᴿJRS 79 (1989) 257s (R. *Williams*).

g767 CHRYSOSTOMUS: **Aubineau** Michel, Chrysostome, SÉVÉRIEN, PROCLUS, HÉSYCHIUS et alii, patristique et hagiographie grecques; inventaires de manuscrits, textes inédits, traductions, études [30 art. en marge de ses éditions 1972-83]. L 1988, Variorum Reprints. xvi-366p. – ᴿRHPR 69 (1989) 350s (P. *Maraval*: de valeur).

g768 *Cameron* A., A misidentified homily of Chrysostom: Nottingham Medieval Studies 32 (1988) 34-48 [< RHE 85,35*].

g769 ᴱ**Malingrey** Anne-Marie, *al.*, PALLADIOS,... vie de Chrysostome I-II: SChr 341s, 1988 → 4,h812 (II. 3-487-06636-X): ᴿRHPR 69 (1989) 347s (D. A. *Bertrand*); RPg 62 (1988) 352s (É. des *Places*: quelques corrections); SMSR 55 (1989) 305s (S. *Zincone*); VigChr 43 (1989) 199-201 (G. *Bartelink*).

g770 **Malingrey** Anne-Marie, Indices chrysostomici II, De sacerdotio (avec *Guillaumin* M.-L.): Alpha-Omega A-31,2. Hildesheim 1989, Olms. x-329 p.

g771 *Andriopoulos* Panagiotis C., Ⓖ The New Testament text as hermeneutic principle of St. John Chrysostom's exegetical work: TAth 60 (1989) 476-492. 600-653.

g772 **Gärtner** Michael, Familienerziehung... Chrysostomus 1985 → 1,f577... 2,h810: ᴿBijdragen 50 (1989) 215s (G. J. *Bruins*).

g773 *Kecskeméti* Judit, Exégèse chrysostomienne et exégèse engagée: → 696, StudPatr 10/22 (1987/9) 136-147.

g774 *Meulenberg* Leonardo, 'Deus seja louvado por tudo'; as tribulações de João Crisóstomo, bispo da Igreja: REB 49 (1989) 371-399.

g775 **Schatkin** Margaret A., [cf. → 3,g227] John Chrysostom as apologist...: Analekta Vlatadon 50. Thessaloniki 1987, Fond. Patriarcale. 299 p. – ᴿRÉByz 47 (1989) 307 (J. *Wolinski*); RSPT 73 (1989) 475-7 (G.-M. de *Durand*).

g776 *Hunter* David G., Preaching and propaganda in fourth century Antioch; John Chrysostom's Homilies on the Statues: → 38, ᶠBURGHARDT W., preaching 1989, 119-138.

g777 *MacMullen* Ramsay, [Chrysostom, AUGUSTINE...]. The preacher's audience (AD 350-400): JTS 40 (1989) 503-511.

g778 CYRILLUS A.: *Pazzini* D., La critica di Cirillo Alessandrino alla dottrina origenista della preesistenza delle anime: CrNSt 9 (1988) 237-278; Eng. 278s.

g779 CYRILLUS H.: *Morales Villegas* Francisco José, Dios y Jesucristo en las catequesis bautismales de san Cirilo de Jerusalén; valor catequético actual: Tiusi 4 (Caracas 1989) 47-65.

g780 DAMASCENUS: **Kotter** Bonifatius, Die Schriften des Johannes von Damaskos, 5. Opera homiletica et hagiographica: PatrTStud [0553-4003] 29. B 1988, de Gruyter. xx-607 p. DM 340. 3-11-010173-4. – ᴿRHE 84 (1989) 172s (A. de *Halleux*).

g780* *Speck* Paul, Eine Interpolation in den Bilderreden des Johannes von Damaskus: ByZ 82 (1989) 114-7.

g781 DIONYSIUS Ps.-A. [➤ g916, k14-k17 infra]: ᴱ**Suchla** B. E., Pseudo-Dionysius Areopagita, Die Namen Gottes: Bibliothek der griechischen Literatur 26. Stu 1988, Hiersemann. ix-145 p. DM 120 [NRT 112, 619, R. *Escol*].

g782 EPIPHANIUS: **Dechow** Jon F., Dogma and mysticism in early Christianity; Epiphanius of Cyprus and the legacy of Origen: Patristic Mg 13, 1988 ➤ 4,h821; 0-86554-311-9. – ᴿRExp 86 (1989) 455s (E. G. *Hinson*).

g783 **Williams** Frank, The Panarion of Epiphanius of Salamis I (sect 1-46) 1987 ➤ 4,h824: ᴿBO 46 (1989) 224s (J. *Helderman*: premature; it is the English for the awaited revision of the K. *Holl* 1915 text by J. *Dummer*; but meanwhile a fully new text edition by P. *Nautin* is under way).

g784 **Holl** Karl, ²ʳᵉᵛ *Dummer* Jürgen, Epiphanius III, Panarion haer. 65-80, De fide. B 1985, Akademie. xiii-543 p. M 140. – ᴿAntClas 58 (1989) 361-5 (J. *Schamp*).

g785 EUSEBIUS: **Forrat** M. (*Places* É. des), Eusèbe, Contre Hiéroclès 1986 ➤ 2,d364... 4,h825: ᴿBijdragen 50 (1989) 451 (M. *Parmentier*: given the modern interest in the occult, ought to become a best-seller); JTS 40 (1989) 254-6 (E. D. *Hunt*); RÉG 101 (1988) 579s (P. *Nautin*); RTLv 20 (1989) 92s (A. de *Halleux*).

g786 *Places* Édouard des, Le Contre Hiéroclès d'Eusèbe de Césarèe á la lumière d'une édition récente (*Forrat* M. 1986): ➤ 696, 10th Patristic, 19 (1989) 37-42.

g787 **Places** Édouard des, Eusèbe, Préparation évangélique XIV-XV: SChr 338, 1987 ➤ 3,g240; 4,h827: ᴿAntClas 58 (1989) 360s (R. *Joly*: œuvre gigantesque); EsprVie 99 (1989) 227s (Yves-M. *Duval*); JEH 39 (1988) 628s (G. *Bonner*, 12s. 14s: immense erudition); LavalTP 45 (1989) 314-6 (P.-H. *Poirier*); RechSR 76 (1988) 594 (B. *Sesboüé*, aussi sur FORRAT M. SChr 333); RHR 206 (1989) 313s (A. *Le Boulluec*); RTAM 56 (1989) 241 (J. *Winandy*).

g789 **Gödecke** Monika, Geschichte als Mythos... Eusebius KG 1987 ➤ 3,g237; 4,h830: ᴿBLitEc 90 (1989) 146s (H. *Crouzel*); TR 85 (1989) 109-111 (H. R. *Seeliger*).

g790 *Allen* Pauline, Some aspects of Hellenism in the early Greek church historians: Traditio 43 (Fordham 1987) 368-381.

g791 *Timpe* Dieter, Was ist Kirchengeschichte? Zum Gattungscharakter der Historia Ecclesiastica des Eusebius: ➤ 209, ᶠWERNER R., Xenia 22 (1989) 171-204.

g792 *Bammel* E., Eine übersehene Angabe zu den Toledoth Jeschu [Euseb HE 1,11]: NTS 35 (1989) 479s.

g793 **Christensen** Torben, RUFINUS of Aquileia and the Historia Ecclesiastica Lib. VIII-IX of Eusebius: Vidensk. Selskab h/f Medd 58. K 1989, Munksgaard. 339 p. 87-7304-178-5.

g794 *Gallagher* Eugene V., Piety and polity; Eusebius' defense of the Gospel: ➤ 592, Systemic 2 (1989) 139-155.

g795 *Smith* Christine, Christian rhetoric in Eusebius' panegyric at Tyre: VigChr 43 (1989) 226-247.

g796 **Verheyden** Jozef, De vlucht van de christenen naar Pella; onderzoek van het getuigenis van Eusebius en EPIPHANIUS: Verh lett. 50/127, 1988 ➤ 4,h833: ᴿETL 65 (1989) 445s (A. de *Halleux*: acribie exemplaire, mais ne convaincra pas tous); Muséon 102 (1989) 208s (J. *Mossay*); RHPR 69 (1989) 240 (P. *Maraval*; from the English summary he holds it has no historical foundation whatever); RSPT 73 (1989) 459 (G.-M. de *Durand*: 'het christenen').

g797 FIRMUS: ᵀᴱ**Calvet-Sebasti** Marie-Ange, *Gatier* Pierre-Louis, Firmus de Césarée [Cappadoce vᵉ s.] Lettres: SChr 350. P 1989, Cerf. 206 p. 2-204-03069-4. – ᴿRHPR 69 (1989) 351 (P. *Maraval*); RPg 62 (1988!) 354s (É. des *Places*).

g798 GREGORIUS NAZ. [➤ 3,8325]: *Ettlinger* Gerard H., The orations of Gregory of Nazianzus; a study in rhetoric and personality: ➤ 38, ꟻBURGHARDT W., Preaching 1989, 101-118.

g799 *Palla* Roberto, Ordinamento e polimetria delle poesie bibliche di Gregorio Nazianzeno: WienerSt 102 (1989) 169-185.

g800 GREGORIUS NYSS.: **Apostolopoulos** Charalambos, Phaedo christianus [und] Gregor von Nyssa 'Über die Seele' 1986 ➤ 2,d372; 4,h836: ᴿRSPT 73 (1989) 471-3 (G.-M. de *Durand*).

g801 ᴱ**Downing** J. Kenneth, *McDonough* J. A., *Hörner* Hadwiga, Gregorii Nysseni Opera dogmatica minora 2. Leiden 1987, Brill. clxxviii-122 p. *f* 120 [JTS 41, 252-5, A. *Meredith*].

g802 **Altenburger** Margarete, *Mann* Friedhelm, Bibliographie zu Gregor von Nyssa 1988 ➤ 4,h838; DM 128: ᴿRSPT 73 (1989) 474s (G.-M. de *Durand*); TGL 79 (1989) 199-201 (H. *Drobner*).

g803 **Drobner** Hubertus R., Bibelindex zu den Werken Gregors von Nyssa. Pd 1988, auct. (Kamp 6, D-4790). 126 p. DM 44. – ᴿRÉG 102 (1989) 615 (P. *Nautin*); RHPR 69 (1989) 345s (A. *Hanriot-Coustet*, A. *Pautler*: full of the errors taken over from MG, GNO, SChr).

g804 *Maraval* Pierre, La lettre 3 de Grégoire de Nysse dans le débat christologique: RevSR 61 (1987) 74-89.

g805 ᴱ**Mateo-Seco** Lucas F., *Bastero* Juan L., El 'Contra Eunomium I', G. de Nisa [➤ 4,606], coloquio Pamplona 1986: Col. Teol. 59. Pamplona 1988, Univ. Navarra. 480 p. – ᴿETL 65 (1989) 175s (A. de *Halleux*).

g806 LUCIANUS S.: **Lauvergnat-Gagnière** Christiane, Lucien de Samosate et le lucianisme en France au XVIᵉ siècle; athéisme et polémique: TravHumRen 227. Genève 1988, Droz. 434 p. – ᴿRHPR 69 (1989) 357s (J. *Schwartz*: une bibliographie de Lucien va paraître en 1989, Univ. Strasbourg, à propos du De calumnia, par J.-M. *Massing*).

g807 MAXIMUS: ᵀᴱ**Berthold** George C., Maximus Confessor, selected writings [SPCK ➤ 3,g254]; introd. *Pelikan* J., pref. *Dalmais* I.-H.: Classics of Western Spirituality. NY 1985, Paulist. 240 p. $ 13; pa. $ 10. – ᴿSVlad 23 (1989) 205-8 (M. *Butler*).

g808 **Gatti** Maria Luisa, Massimo il Confessore, saggio di bibliografia 1987 ➤ 3,g256: ᴿAevum 63 (1989) 361-8 (P. *Conte*); OrChr 73 (1989) 233s (M.

van Esbroeck); RHPR 69 (1989) 352s (J.-C. *Larchet*); RPg 62 (1988) 353s (É. des *Places*: excellente initiation).

g809 NOETUS: *Hübner* Reinhard M., Die antignostische Glaubensregel des Noët von Smyrna (HIPPOLYT, Refutatio IX,10,9-12 und X,27,1-2) bei IGNATIUS, IRENAEUS und TERTULLIAN: MüTZ 40 (1989) 279-311.

g810 PAULUS SAMOSAT.: *Burrus* Virginia, Rhetorical stereotypes in the portrait of Paul of Samosata: VigChr 43 (1989) 215-225.

g811 PORPHYRIUS T.: *Sellew* Philip, Achilles or Christ? Porphyry of Tyre [Against the Christians, under Diocletian] and DIDYMUS [on Ecclesiastes] in debate over allegorical interpretation: HarvTR 82 (1989) 79-100.

g812 SOPHRONIUS H.; *Schönbron* Christoph, Sophrone de Jérusalem: ➤ 886, DictSpir 14,92s (1989) 1066-1073.

g813 STEPHANOS: *Wolska-Conus* Wanda, Stéphanos d'Athènes et Stéphanos d'Alexandrie [c. 600 ap. J.-C.]; essai d'identification et de biographie: RÉByz 47 (1989) 5-91.

g814 SYNESIUS: ᴱ**Garzya** A., Sinesio di Cirene, Opere; epistole operette inni: Classici greci 12. T 1989, UTET. 872 p. Lit. 95.000. – ᴿStPatav 36 (1989) 575-7 (C. *Corsato*).

g815 **Roques** Denis, Synésios de Cyrène... la Cyrénaïque 1987 ➤ 4,h846*: ᴿByZ 82 (1989) 258s (K. *Treu*); JbAC 32 (1989) 203-6 (W.H.C. *Frend*); RÉByz 47 (1989) 303-5 (B. *Flusin*); RÉG 101 (1988) 580s (F. *Chamoux*); RHE 84 (1989) 107-9 (Y.-M. *Duval*: 'centre d'un triptyque dont, malheureusement, les deux volets latéraux, indispensables, ne sont pas encore publiés'); RHPR 69 (1989) 349s (P. *Maraval*: important).

g816 THEODORETUS C.: *Viciano* Alberto, *Hómēron ex Homérou saphanízein*; Principios hermenéuticos de Teodoreto de Ciro en su Comentario a las Epístulas Paulinas: ScripTPamp 21 (1989) 13-60; Eng. 61.

g817 THEODORUS M.: *a*) *Reinink* G. J., Die Exegese des Theodor von Mopsuestia in einem anonymen nestorianischen Kommentar zum Neuen Testament. – *b*) *Rompay* L. Van, GENNADIUS of Constantinople as a representative of Antiochene exegesis: ➤ 696, 10th Patristic, 19 (1989) 381-391 / 400-5.

g818 **Zaharopoulos** Dimitri Z., Theodore of Mopsuestia on the Bible; a study of his Old Testament exegesis: Theological Inquiries. NY 1989, Paulist. vi-223 p. 0-8091-3091-2.

Y2.4   Augustinus

g819 *a*) ᵀᴱ**Babcock** William S., TYCONIUS, The book of rules: SBL TTr 31 / Early Christian Lit. 7. Atlanta 1989, Scholars. xiii-153 p. $15; sb./pa. $10. 1-55540-366-2; 7-0 [TDig 37,192]. – *b*) **Bright** Pamela, The book of rules of Tyconius; its purpose and inner logic: Christianity and Judaism in antiquity 2. ND 1988, Univ. 200 p. $19 [Manuscripta 8 (1989) 65]. – *c*) **Kannengiesser** Charles, A conflict of Christian hermeneutics in Roman Africa; TYCONIUS and Augustine, ᴱ*Bright* Pamela; *Wuellner* Wm. CHH 58. Berkeley 1989, Univ. California. 87 p. 0-89242-059-6.

g819* *a*) *Baptista* J. C., Santo Agostinho, evocação histórica; – *b*) *Pereira* D., Génese de 'A Cidade de Deus': Eborensia 2,3 (1989) 3-7 / 9-25 [< ZNW 81,149].

g820 *Beatrice* Pier Franco, Quosdam Platonicorum libros; the Platonic readings of Augustine in Milan: VigChr 43 (1989) 248-281.

g821 *Biedermann* Hermenegild M., Augustinus in der neueren griechischen
Theologie: ➤ 132, FMAYER C., Signum Pietatis 1989, 609-643 [< TAth
60 (1989) 511s (E. A. *Theodorou*)].

g822 **Bouman** J., Augustinus, Lebensweg und Theologie. Giessen 1987,
Brunnen. 349 p. DM 42. – RTLZ 114 (1989) 284s (H.-J. *Diesner*).

g823 ECaprioli Adriano, *Vaccaro* Luciano, Agostino e la conversione cristiana 1986/7 ➤ 4,518a: RRHR 206 (1989) 434 (J. *Doignon*).

g824 **Chadwick** H., Augustine 1986 ➤ 2,d387...4,h853: RHeythJ 30 (1989)
364 (D. F. *Wright*); VoxP 14 (1988) 473-8 (Agnieszka *Kijewska* ❷).

g825 **Chadwick** Henry, Augustin [deutsch] TMühlenberg Marianne 1987
➤ 3,g273: RTR 85 (1989) 16s (C. *Mayer*).

g826 [*Dagens* C.] Congrès augustinien (XVIe centenaire de la conversion)
30.I.-1.II.1987, Univ. cath. Toulouse: BLitEc 88,3s (1987) 161-352:
➤ 4,517b: RRHE 84 (1989) 606s (P.-A. *Deproost*). – b) Congresso I-III
AugR 1986/7 ➤ 4,517a: RStPatav 36 (1989) 581-4 (O. *Pasquato*).

g827 *Dassmann* Ernst, 'Tam AMBROSIUS quam CYPRIANUS' (c. Iul. imp.
4,112); Augustins Helfer im pelagianischen Streit: ➤ 174, FSCHNEE-
MELCHER W., Oecumenica 1989, 259-268.

g828 EDivjak J., Lettres 1*-29*; Œuvres de s. Augustin 6/46 B, 1987
➤ 3,g277: RRÉLat 67 (1989) 286s (J. P. *Bouhot*).

g829 *a) Dulaey* Martine, Songe et prophétie dans les Confessions d'Augustin;
du rêve de Monique à la conversion au jardin de Milan; – b) Zocca Elena,
Le visioni nei Sermones de sanctis agostiniani: ➤ 748, Sogni = AugR 29
(1989) 379-391 / 393-410.

g830 *Duval* Noel, Hippo regius, TKarol Dieter: ➤ 904, RAC 15,115 (1989)
442-466; 5 fig.

g831 TEEno Robert B., Augustine, Letters VI [*Divjak* J. 1980, 1*-29*]:
Fathers 81. Wsh 1989, Catholic University of America. xii-208 p. $30.
0-8132-0081-4 [TDig 37,43].

g832 *Eno* Robert B., Christian reaction to the barbarian invasion and the
sermons of Quodvultdeus [bishop of Carthage near Augustine's time]:
➤ 38, FBURGHARDT W., Preaching 1989, 139-161.

g833 *Etheridge* Barry, Augustine of Hippo addresses the Lambeth Conference: TLond 92 (1989) 287-294.

g834 **González** Sergio, La preocupación arriana en la predicación de San
Agustin: diss. DTrapè A. R 1987, Inst. Patristicum Augustinianum.
445 p. 84-85985-30-3.

g835 TEHill Edmund, Augustine, Sermons (1-19), on the OT: Works 3/1
[ERotelle John E.: 'A translation for the 21st century', first of about 40
foreseen volumes, first complete translation of all Augustine's known
works into English]. 399 p. $39. 0-911782-75-3 [TDig 37,43].

g836 **Kirwan** Christopher, Augustine. NY 1989, Routledge. viii-247 p. $75.
0-415-00812-3 [TDig 37,69].

g837 **Kriegbaum** Bernard, Kirche der Traditoren oder Kirche der Mär-
tyrer?... Donatismus 1986 ➤ 3,g286; 4,h858: RAevum 63 (1989) 119s (C.
Scaglioni); MilltSt 23 (1989) 113s (F. *O'Donoghue*).

g838 **La Bonnardière** Anne-Marie, Saint Augustin et la Bible: BTT 3, 1986
➤ 2,391...4,h859: RCrNSt 10 (1989) 165-8 (G. *Bonner*); RÉJ 148 (1989)
377-9 (P. *Jay*; excellent; coquilles gênantes).

g839 **Lawless** George P., Augustine of Hippo and his monastic rule. Ox
1987, Clarendon. xix-185 p. $49. – RJRel 69 (1989) 551s (J. P. *Burns*).

g840 **Lorin** Claude, Pour Saint Augustin. P 1988, Grasset. 263 p. – RRHPR
69 (1989) 62 (A. *Benoît*).

g841 **Madec** Goulven, La Patrie et la Voie; le Christ dans la vie et la pensée de saint Augustin: JJC 36. P 1989, Desclée. 346 p. F 165. – [R]EsprVie 99 (1989) 350s (J. *Pintard*); NRT 111 (1989) 595s (V. *Roisel*); RechSR 77 (1989) 556-8 (B. *Sesboüé*); RSPT 73 (1989) 478-480 (G.-M. *de Durand*).

g842 **Maier** J.-L., Dossier du Donatisme I, 1987 → 4,h864: [R]TS 50 (1989) 201 (R. B. *Eno*); ZKG 100 (1989) 417-9 (R. *Henke*).

g843 **Maier** Jean-Louis, Le dossier du donatisme II. De Julien l'Apostat à Saint Jean Damascène (361-750): TU 135. B 1989, Akademie. 462 p.; map. 3-05-000316-2.

g844 **Marafioti** D., L'uomo tra legge e grazia: Aloisiana 18, [D]1983 → 65,d536...4,h865: [R]NRT 111 (1989) 596 (D. *Dideberg*).

g845 **Marini** Angelo, La celebrazione eucaristica presieduta da Sant'Agostino; la partecipazione dei fedeli alla Liturgia della Parola e al Sacrificio Eucaristico. Brescia 1989, Pavoniana. xiv-182 p.; ill. Lit. 26.000.

g846 **Marshall** Michael (Anglican bp.), The restless heart; the life and influence of St. Augustine. GR 1987, Eerdmans. 151 p. $20. – [R]CalvinT 24 (1989) 159-162 (R. W. *Vunderink*).

g847 **O'Meara** John J., La jeunesse de Saint Augustin; introduction à la lecture des Confessions[2] [[1]1954, [2]1980], [T]*Marrou* Jeanne H. (= 1958). FrS/P 1988, Univ./Cerf. 279 p. – [R]RHPR 69 (1989) 62 (A. *Benoît*).

g848 [E]**Oroz Reta** J., S. Agustin, Meditación de su Centenario (Actas Salamanca 1987): Estudios 99. S 1987, Univ. 213 p. – [R]ScripTPamp 21 (1989) 704s (C. *Basevi*).

g849 **Paronetto** Vera, Augustinus, Botschaft eines Lebens, [T]*Hartmann* Arnulf: Aug.Heute 4, 1986 → 3,g298: [R]TüTQ 169 (1989) 310 (H. J. *Vogt*); VigChr 43 (1989) 197 (J. den *Boeft*).

g850 **Pelikan** Jaroslav, The mystery of continuity; time and history, memory and eternity in the thought of Saint Augustine, 1986 → 2,d404: [R]JAAR 57 (1989) 225-9 (P. J. *Gorday*).

g851 **Pollastri** Alessandra, *Cocchini* Francesca, Bibbia e storia nel cristianesimo latino [1. Agostino; 2. V secolo]. R 1988, Borla. [Lateranum 55,522].

g852 *Quacquarelli* Antonio, Il nesso 'sapientia-eloquentia' nel trattato esegetico di S. Agostino, De doctrina christiana IV: → 567, AnStoEseg 6 (1989) 189-202; Eng. 9.

[E]**Ranson** P., S. Augustin 1988 → 506.

g853 *Rava* Eva C., La ricerca di Dio; Albert CAMUS e Agostino a confronto: Lateranum 55 (1989) 69-133.

g854 **Raveaux** T., Augustinus, Contra adversarium legis et prophetarum; Analyse des Inhalts und Untersuchung des geistesgeschichtlichen Hintergrunds [Diss. Wü 1984]: Cassiciacum 37. Wü 1987, Augustinus. xix-224 p. – [R]RHE 84 (1989) 779 (P.-A. *Deproost*).

g855 **Rees** B. R., PELAGIUS, a reluctant heretic 1988 → 4,h873: [R]JTS 40 (1989) 623s (R. A. *Markus*); TLond 92 (1989) 407s (W. H. C. *Frend*).

g856 **Tack** Theodore, If Augustine were alive; Augustine's religious ideal for today. Staten Island 1988, Alba. x-163 p. $8. 0-8189-0539-5 [TDig 36,391].

g857 **Trapé** Agostino, Aurelius Augustinus, ein Lebensbild [[2]1979], [T]*Brehme* Ute 1988 → 4,h879: [R]TR 85 (1989) 18 (C. *Mayer*).

g858 **Vannini** Marco, Invito al pensiero di Sant'Agostino: Invito al pensiero 7. Mi 1989, Mursia. 200 p. [TR 86,341].

g859 *Wermelinger* O.,   Neue Forschungskontroversen um Augustinus und
PELAGIUS: ➤ 707, Symposium 1987/9, 189-217.

Y2.5   **Hieronymus.**

g859* *Balasch* Manuel,   Sant Jeroni, lector de Juvenal: ➤ 69*, FGOMÀ I.,
RCatalT 14 (1989) 511-5; Eng. 515.

g860 *Barnes* T. D.,   Jerome and the Origo Constantini Imperatoris [? before
381 or after]: Phoenix 43 (Toronto 1989) 158-161.

g861 *Bauer* E.,   Struktur und liturgische Aspekte des Ps.-Eusebius-[von
Cremona] Briefes über den Tod des Hieronymus: ➤ 684, Kartäuserliturgie
1987/8, 40-61 [< RHE 84 (1989) 189].

g862 *Hagendahl* Harald, *Waszink* Jan H.,   Hieronymus: ➤ 904, RAC 15, 113
(1989) 117-139.

g863 *Hellenga* Virginia K.,   The exchange of letters between Saint AUGUSTINE
and Saint Jerome: ➤ 175, Mem. SCHODER R., Daidalikon 1989, 177-182.

g864 *Jay* Pierre,   Combien Jérôme a-t-il traduit d'homélies d'ORIGÈNE?:
➤ 696, StudPatr 10/23 (1987/9) 133-7.

g865 *a) Romano* Domenico,   L'elemento classico nella Praefatio alla Vita
Hilarionis di Girolamo; – *b) Duval* Yves-Marie,   Les premiers rapports de
PAULIN de Nole avec Jérôme; moine et philosophe? poète ou exégète?:
➤ 42, FCOSTANZA S., Polyanthema 1989, 75-80 / 177-216.

Y2.6   **Patres Latini** alphabetice

g866 **Fontaine** J., *Piétri* C.,   Le monde latin antique et la Bible: BTT 2, 1985
➤ 1,f638 ... 3,g323:   RLatomus 48 (1989) 479-481 (P. *Salmon*); RÉJ 147
(1988) 184-8 (Mireille *Mentré*).

g866* *a) Ingremeau* Christiane,   LACTANCE et le sacré; l'Histoire Sainte ra-
contée aux païens... par les païens; – *b) Siniscalco* Paolo,   Le sacré et
l'expérience de l'histoire; AMMIEN Marcellin et Paul OROSE; – *c) Deproost*
Paul-Augustin,   Les fonctions apostoliques du sacré dans le poème
d'ARATOR; – *d) Fontaine* Jacques,   Le 'sacré' antique vu par un homme
du VIIe siècle; le livre des Étymologies par ISIDORE de Seville: BBudé
(1989) 345-354 / 355-366 / 376-393 / 394-405.

g867 TEGaudemet Jean, *Basdevant* Brigitte, (texte *Clercq* C. de),   Les canons
des conciles mérovingiens (VIe-VIIe siècles): SChr 353s. P 1989, Cerf.
348 p.; p. 345(sic)-636 + index. F 223. 2-204-03030-9; -185-2.

g868 *Gryson* Roger,   Éditions récentes des Pères latins, II: RHE 84 (1989)
691-9.

g869 **Hagendahl** Harald,   Cristianesimo latino e cultura classica [von Tertullian zu Cassiodor 1983, per ANRW],T; intr. *Siniscalco* P.   R 1988,
Borla.   228 p. – RRFgIC 117 (1989) 482s (A. *Traina*).

g870 **Lizzi** Rita,   Il potere episcopale nell'Oriente romano; rappresentazione
ideologica e realtà politica (IV-V sec. d.C.): Filologia e critica 53, 1987
➤ 3,g207:   RRivStoLR 25 (1989) 503-5 (Paola *Rivolta Tiberga*).

g871 **Pollastri** A., *Cocchini* F.,   Bibbia e storia nel cristianesimo latino:
Cultura cristiana antica.   R 1988, Borla.   252 p.

g872 ARATOR: *Sotinel* Claire,   Arator, un poète au service de la politique du
pape Vigile?:   MÉF 101 (1989) 805-820.

g873 ARNOBIUS: *Amata* Biagio, L'apologia cristiana di Arnobio di Sicca come ricerca della verità assoluta: Salesianum 51 (1989) 47-70.

g874 BOETHIUS: *Magee* J., Note on Boethius, Consolatio 1,1,5; 3,7; a new biblical parallel: VigChr 42 (1988) 79-82.

g875 CHROMATIUS: EBanterle Gabriele, Cromazio di Aquileia, I sermoni: Scriptores circa Ambrosium 3/1. R 1989, Città Nuova. 246 p.

g876 Truzzi Carlo, ZENO, GAUDENZIO e Cromazio 1985 ➤ 2,d434... 4,h897: RRivStoLR 25 (1989) 160-4 (G. *Cuscito*).

g877 CYPRIANUS: *Cavallotto* Stefano, Il magistero episcopale di Cipriano di Cartagine; aspetti metodologici: DivThom 91 (1988) 375-407; lat. 375.

g878 TEClarke G. W., Letters of Cyprian 3s: Ancient Christian Writers 46s. NY 1986-9, Newman. 345 p.; 345 p. [TS 51, 175, M. A. *Fahey*].

g879 *Folgado Flórez* S., La catolicidad, fórmula de identificación de la Iglesia en San Cipriano: CiuD 202 (1989) 593-611.

g880 Meulenberg Leo F. J., Cyprianus; de ene bron en de vele stromen. Kampen 1987, Kok. 101 p. ƒ17,50. 90-242-0868-8. – RBijdragen 50 (1989) 450s (M. *Parmentier*).

g881 GREGORIUS M.: Clark Francis, The Pseudo-Gregorian dialogues 1987 ➤ 3,g342; 4,h901: RChH 58 (1989) 88s (H. *Rosenberg*: hesitant acceptance).

g882 *Clark* Francis, The authorship of the Gregorian dialogues; an old controversy renewed [since COCCIUS 1551; survey of criticisms of his 1987 work]: HeythJ 30 (1989) 257-272 [365-7, H. *Wansbrough* review].

g883 EDonnini Mauro, Anonimo di Jumièges, I 'Dialogi' di Gregorio Magno, parafrasi in versi latini (sec. xiii): Mg Monastica 5. R 1988, Benedictina. 289 p. – RRBén 99 (1989) 195 (P.-I. *Fransen*).

g884 *Engelbert* Pius, Neue Forschungen zu den 'Dialogen' Gregors des Grossen; Antworten auf Clarks These: ErbAuf 65 (1989) 376-393.

g885 Evans Gillian R., The thought of Gregory the Great 1986 ➤ 2,d439; 4,h907: RHeythJ 30 (1989) 463s (J. *McGuckin*).

g886 EFontaine Jacques, al., Grégoire 1982/6 ➤ 2,433*; 4,h908: RBTAM 14 (1989) p. 613-5 (G. *Mathon*, tit. pp.).

g887 *Havener* Ivan †, The Greek prologue to the 'Dialogues' of Gregory the Great: RBén 99 (1989) 103-115; Greek text 115-7.

g888 Paronetto Vera, Gregorio Magno, un maestro alle origini cristiane d'Europa. R 1985, Studium. vi-182 p. Lit. 10.000. – RProtestantesimo 44 (1989) 139s (R. *Marchetti*).

g889 Straw Carole, Gregory the Great; perfection in imperfection 1988 ➤ 4,h910: RJTS 40 (1989) 261 (G. R. *Evans*); TS 50 (1989) 366s (D. J. *Grimes*); VigChr 43 (1989) 298-300 (G. *Bartelink*).

g890 HILARIUS: *Doignon* J., ➤ 904, RAC 15/113 (1989) 139 ...

g891 HIPPOLYTUS: Frickel Josef, Das Dunkel um Hippolyt von Rom; ein Lösungsversuch, die Schriften *Elenchos* und *Contra Noëtum*: GrazTheolSt 13. Graz 1988, Univ. Inst. Ök. 325 p. 3-900797-13-7 [Greg 70,198]. – RTPQ 137 (1989) 295s (F. *Schragl*).

g892 EMarcovich Miroslav, Hippolytus, Refutatio omnium haeresium: PatrTSt 25, 1986 ➤ 2,d447... 4,h916: RBO 46 (1989) 221-4 (J. *Helderman*); Gregorianum 70 (1989) 175 [?A. *Orbe*]; JbAC 32 (1989) 210-4 (D. *Hagedorn*); JTS 40 (1989) 243-5 (H. *Chadwick*).

g893 ENorelli Enrico, Ippolito, L'Anticristo 1987 ➤ 3,g345: RRHPR 69 (1989) 342s (P. *Maraval*).

g894 **Osborne** Catherine, Rethinking early Greek philosophy; Hippolytus of Rome and the Presocratics 1987 → 4,h918: ᴿJAAR 57 (1989) 666s (W. D. *Lindsey*); JTS 40 (1989) 240-243 (R. *Butterworth*).

g895 *Phillips* L. Edward, Daily prayer in the Apostolic Tradition of Hippolytus: JTS 40 (1989) 389-400.

g896 **Visonà** Giuseppe, Pseudo-Ippolito, In sanctum Pascha 1988 → 4,h918*: ᴿNRT 111 (1989) 967 (V. *Roisel*).

g897 LEO M.: *Murphy* Francis X., The sermons of Pope Leo the Great; content and style: → 38, ꜰBURGHARDT W., Preaching 1989, 183-197.

g898 PERPETUA: *Bodrato* Aldo, Lingua biblica e lingua letteraria nella 'Passio Perpetuae': HumBr 44 (1989) 374-390.

g899 SEDULIUS: **Springer** Carl P. E., Gospel as epic... Sedulius 1988 → 4,h924: ᴿJbAC 32 (1989) 197-203 (Christine *Ratkowitsch*).

g900 ᴱ**Simpson** Dean, Sedulius Scottus, Collectaneum miscellaneum; CCMed 67. Turnhout 1988, Brepols. XXXIX-410 p. – ᴿRÉLat 67 (1989) 279-281 (F. *Dolbeau*).

y2.8 Documenta orientalia

g901 **Carroll** Scott T., The Melitian schism; Coptic Christianity and the Egyptian church: diss. Miami (Ohio) Univ. 1989. 232 p. 89-20380. — DissA 50 (1989s) 1775-A.

g902 *a) Cowe* S. Peter, The Armeno-Georgian Acts of Ephesus — a reconsideration; – *b) Barnes* T. D., The date of the council of Gangra [in Paphlagonia]: JTS 40 (1989) 125-9 / 121-4.

g903 **Feydit** F., Amulettes de l'Arménie chrétienne [154 textes traduits et commentés]: Bibl. Gulbenkian. Venezia 1986, S.-Lazare. 385 p.; 24 pl. – ᴿMuséon 102 (1989) 206s (B. *Coulie*, aussi sur GIGNOUX P. et KEVORKIAN R.).

g904 **Isaac** Jacques, *Taḵsā D-Ḥūssāyā*; le rite du Pardon dans l'Église syriaque orientale [diss. 1970, ᴰ*Raes* A.]: OrChrAn 233. R 1989, Pont. Inst. Oriental. Stud. xl-244 p.

g905 *MacCoull* L. S. B., [C. *Wessely* 1914] Stud. Pal[äographie] XV 250 ab; a monophysite trishagion for the Nile flood: JTS 40 (1989) 129-135.

g906 **Mat'evosyani** A. S., *Hayeren...* 5.-12. Erevan 1988, Akad. Arm. SSR. 368 p.

g907 **Nasrallah** Joseph, Histoire du mouvement littéraire dans l'Église melchite, du Vᵉ au XXᵉs.; contributions à l'étude de la littérature arabe-chrétienne, II/2 [avec *Haddad* Rachid; quatrième volume paru]. Lv 1988, Peeters. xxxii-218 p. [RHE 85, 211-3, A. de *Halleux*].

g908 **Sauget** Joseph-Marie, Un Ghazza chaldéen disparu et retrouvé: ST 326, 1987 → 3,g374 (Gazza): ᴿBO 46 (1989) 155-7 (J. *Sanders*); RÉByz 47 (1989) 306s (B. *Flusin*).

g909 **Varghese** Baby, Les onctions baptismales dans la tradition syrienne: CSCOr 512, subs. 82. Lv 1989, Peeters. 0070-0044.

---

g910 AMMON: **Goehring** James E., The letter of Ammon and Pachomian monasticism: PatrTSt 27, 1986 → 2,7644: ᴿBO 46 (1989) 5-18 (Ewa *Wipszycka*, B. *Bravo*); JbAC 32 (1989) 190s (K. S. *Frank*); RTAM 56 (1989) 239s (J. *Winandy*).

g911 APHRAATES: *Aalst* A. J. van der, À l'origine du monachisme syrien; les 'ihidaye' chez Aphraat: ➤ 17, ^FBARTELINK G., Fructus 1989, 315-324.

g912 ^{TE}**Pierre** Marie-Joseph, Aphraate, Exposés I/II: SChr 349.359, 1988s ➤ 4,h935: ^RAnBoll 107 (1989) 438s (U. *Zanetti*); ETL 65 (1989) 448-451 (A. de *Halleux*); Irénikon 62 (1989) 123.594 (E. *Lanne*); NRT 111 (1989) 586s (V. *Roisel*); PrOrChr 39 (1989) 217-9 (P. *Ternant*).

g913 ATHANASIUS: **Camplani** Alberto, Le lettere festali di Atanasio di Alessandria; studio storico-critico: Corpus dei Manoscritti Copti Letterari. R 1989, CIM. v-340 p.

g914 BARHEBRAEUS: ^E**Çiçek** Julius Y., Barhebraeus *Huddāyē* (nono canon) / *Maktbanut Zabne* (secular chronography). Glane 1986s, Ephrem-Kloster. ii-335 p., DM 85; vii-548 p., DM 125. – ^RJSS 33 (1988) 286-8 (S. *Brock* describes manuscripts but does not say what 'nonocanon' means).

g915 BARSAUMA: **Gero** Stephen, Barsauma of Nisibis and Persian Christianity in the fifth century: CSCOr 426, Subs. 63, 1981 ➤ 62,m134 ... 64,e163: ^ROrChr 73 (1989) 235-7 (W. *Hage*).

g916 DIONYSIUS Ps.-A.: ^{TE}**Thomson** R. W., The Armenian version of the works attributed to Dionysius the Areopagite: CSCOr 488s / Arm 17s, 1987 ➤ 3,g368: ^RMuséon 102 (1989) 203-5 (B. *Coulie*).

g917 DIONYSIUS TM: **Witakowski** Witold, The Syriac chronicle of Pseudo-Dionysius of Tel-Mahre 1987 ➤ 3,g367; 4,h938: ^ROrSuec 36s (1987s) 135-9 (E. *Riad*).

g918 EPHRAEM: **Amar** Joseph P., The Syriac 'Vita' tradition of Ephrem the Syrian: diss. Catholic Univ., ^D*Griffith* S. H. Wsh 1988. 344 p. 89-19389. – DissA 50 (1989s) 1647-A.

g919 **Bou Mansour** Tanios, La pensée symbolique de saint Éphrem le Syrien [diss. Lv 1987]: Bibl. 16. Kaslik, Liban 1988, Univ. S. Esprit. xix-566 p. – ^RETL 65 (1989) 177-9 (A. de *Halleux*: bien, mais les auteurs cités ne sont pas toujours bien compris, comme lui-même une fois).

g920 **Brock** S., The luminous eye; the spiritual vision of St. Ephrem (Placid Lectures 6). R 1985, Center for Indian and Inter-Religious Studies. viii-166 p. $7. – ^RMuséon 102 (1989) 201-3 (A. de *Halleux*).

g921 *Leloir* L., Le commentaire d'Éphrem sur le Diatessaron; quarante et un feuillets retrouvés [chez deux antiquaires; achetés pour la collection Chester Beatty]: Muséon 102 (1989) 299-305.

g922 *Beck* Edmund, Der syrische Diatessaronkommentar zu der unvergebbaren Sünde wider den Heiligen Geist: OrChr 73 (1989) 1-37.

g923 ^{TE}**McVey** Kathleen E., Ephrem the Syrian, Hymns. NY 1989, Paulist. xiii-474 p. $18 [TS 51, 558, F. G. *McLeod*].

g924 **Perniola** Erasmo, Sant'Efrem Siro, dottore della Chiesa e cantore di Maria; pref. *Tagliaferri* Fiorino. Montefiascone VT 1989, Figli Imm. Conc. xv-386 p.; front.; bibliog. p. xi-xv. Lit. 32.000.

g925 **Petersen** William L., Diatessaron/Ephrem as sources of ROMANOS 1985 ➤ 65,d585 ... 3,g372: ^RJTS 40 (1989) 258-260 (R.P.R. *Murray*).

g926 *Yousif* Pietro, Il sangue eucaristico di Cristo; simbolismo e realismo secondo Sant'Efrem di Nisibi: ➤ 759, Sangue VI, 1987/9, 175-205.

g927 EVAGRIUS: *Bunge* Gabriel, Hénade ou monade? Au sujet de deux notions centrales de la terminologie [syriaque] évagrienne: Muséon 102 (1989) 69-91.

g928 *Quecke* Hans, Auszüge aus Evagrius' 'Mönschsspiegel' in koptischer Übersetzung: Orientalia 58 (1989) 453-463; pl. LXX.

g929 *Schenke* Hans-Martin,   Das Berliner Evagrius-Ostrakon (P. Berol.
14 700): ZägSpr 116 (1989) 90-107.

g930 *Vogüé* Adalbert, de   La version copte du chapitre XVII de l'Histoire
Lausiaque [vie de Pambo, Évagre; obsèques de Macaire inédit]; les deux
éditeurs et les trois manuscrits: Orientalia 58 (1989) 510-524.

g931 EZANA: *Munro-Hay* S.C.H.,   The dating of Ezana and FRUMENTIUS:
RasEtiop 32 (1988) 111-127.

g932 GREGORIUS ARM.:   *a*) *Chaumont* Marie-Louise, Sur l'origine de saint
Grégoire d'Arménie; – *b*) *Esbroeck* Michel van, Saint Grégoire d'Arménie et sa didascalie: Muséon 102 (1989) 115-130 / 131-145.

g933 HIPPOLYTUS: *Halleux* A. de,   Hippolyte en version syriaque: Muséon
102 (1989) 19-42.

g934 ISAACUS P.:   **Alcock** Anthony, The [Sahidic] life of Samuel of Kalamun
by Isaac the Presbyter. Warminster 1983, Aris & P. xii-140 p. £15.
0-85668-219-5. – ᴿBO 46 (1989) 89-96 (E. *Lucchesi*: some hundred
corrections, including one of the corrigenda).

g935 ĪŠŌ'DĀD: *Schall* Anton, Der nestorianische Bibelexeget Īšo'dād von
Merw (9. Jh. n. Chr) in seiner Bedeutung für die orientalische Philologie:
→ 126, ꜰMACUCH R., Ḥokmôt 1989, 271-282.

g936 JACOBUS S.:   *Alwān* Khalil, L'homme, était-il mortel ou immortel avant
le péché, pour Jacques de Saroug?: OrChrPer 55 (1989) 5-31.

g937 MAHWUB: **Heijer** Johannes Den, Mahwūb ibn Manṣūr ibn Mufarriğ
et l'historiographie copto-arabe; étude sur la composition de l'Histoire
des Patriarches d'Alexandrie: CSCOr 513, subs. 83. Lv 1989, Peeters.
xx-238 p. 0070-0044.

g938 NARSAI: **Sunquist** Scott W., Narsai and the Persians; a study in
cultural contact and conflict: diss. Princeton Theol. Sem. 1989, ᴰ*McVey*
K. – RelStR 16, 191.

g939 PACHOMIUS: *Lorenz* Rudolf, Zur Chronologie des Pachomius: ZNW
80 (1989) 280-3.

g940 PAULUS (Tamma):   ᴱ**Orlandi** Tito, Paolo di Tamma, Opere; introduzione, testo, traduzione e concordanze. R 1988, CIM. 197 p.

g941 SEVERIANUS: *Voicu* Sever J., Sévérien de Gabala c. 400: → 886, Dict-
Spir 14,92s (1989) 752-763.

g942 ZENOBIUS: *Johnson* David, The dossier of Aba Zenobius [in text
always Apa]: Orientalia 58 (1989) 193-312; Coptic text 199-205.

Y3   **Medium aevum,** *generalia.*

g943 **Ariès** Philippe, *Duby* Georges, A history of private life [11th-15th cent.].
CM 1988, Harvard-Belknap. xiii-650 p. $39.50 [RelStR 16, 266, G.H.
Shriver].

g944 *Berschin* W., [*Trapp* E.] Griechische Sprache: 901, LexMA 4 (1989)
[1708-]1710s.

g945 *Børresen* Kari E., Théologiennes au Moyen Âge: RTLv 20 (1989)
62-71; Eng. 140.

g946 **Brooke** Christopher V.L., The medieval idea of marriage. Ox 1989,
Clarendon. xviii-325 p.; 9 pl. £17 [JTS 41, 734-8, B.E. *Ferme*].

g947 **Brundage** James A., Law, sex and Christian society in medieval Europe
1988 → 4,h959: ᴿChH 58 (1989) 95-97 (P.I. *Kaufman*); JRel 69 (1989)
402s (Caroline *Bynum*); JTS 40 (1989) 275-9 (B. *Ferme*).

g948 **Calati** B., *al.*, La spiritualità del Medio Evo: → 909, StSpG 4. R 1988,
Borla. 516 p. Lit. 40.000. – ᴿStPatav 36 (1989) 645s (C. *Corsato*).

g949 **Cobban** Alan H., The medieval English universities, Oxford and Cambridge to ca. 1500. Berkeley 1988, Univ. California. xvii-465 p.; 16 pl. $55 [RHE 85, 100-3, J. *Paquet*].

g950 **Colette** Theresa, Naming the rose; Eco [→ 9846], medieval signs, and modern theory. Ithaca NY 1988, Cornell Univ. xi-212 p. $20. – ᴿJRel 69 (1989) 460s (C. *Wegener*).

g951 **Courtenay** William J., Schools and scholars in fourteenth century England [... Augustinian revival]. Princeton 1987, Univ. 435 p. – ᴿJAAR 57 (1989) 182-5 (J.J. *Ryan*).

g952 *Dyer* Joseph, Monastic psalmody of the Middle Ages: RBén 99 (1989) 41-74.

g953 **Eco** Umberto, Art and beauty in the Middle Ages [1959], ᵀ*Bredin* Hugh. NHv 1986, Yale Univ. x-131 p. $13. – ᴿJRel 68 (1988) 100s (J.C. *Jacobs*).

g954 **Eco** Umberto, Il pendolo di Foucault. Mi 1988, Bompiani. 516 p. Lit. 26.000. – ᴿCC 140 (1989,1) 116-129 (F. *Castelli*); Letture 44 (1989) 23-26 (A. *Scurani*); REB 49 (1989) 469-471 ('*Crônica*').

g955 **Erdoes** Richard, A.D. 1000; living on the brink of A-p-o-c-a-l-y-p-s-e. SF 1989, Harper & R. xvi-228 p. $20 [Horizons 16,205].

g956 **Ferruolo** Stephen C., The origins of the university; the schools of Paris and their critics, 1100-1215: 1985 → 3,g396; 4,h964: ᴿCrNSt 10 (1989) 178-181 (N. *Bériou*).

g957 *Flood* Bruce P.ᴶ, The Carmelite Friars in medieval English universities and society, 1299-1430: RTAM 55 (1988) 154-183 [résumé français, RHE 85,171s].

g958 **Funkenstein** Amos, Theology and the scientific imagination from the Middle Ages to the 17th century. Princeton 1986, Univ. xii-421 p. $47.50. – ᴿHZ 249 (1989) 115s (U. *Knefelkamp*); JRel 69 (1989) 107s (S. *Feldman*).

g959 *Gibson* Margaret T., The twelfth-century glossed Bible: → 696, StudPatr 10/23 (1987/9) 232-244.

g960 **Gold** Penny S., The lady and the virgin 1985 → 2,d487 ... 4,h969: ᴿJRel 68 (1988) 102 (Sharon *Farmer*).

g961 *Gonnet* Giovanni, Religione popolare e movimenti spirituali nel Medio Evo [*Manselli* R. 1985]: Protestantesimo 44 (1989) 42-46.

g962 **Haines** Roy M., Ecclesia anglicana; studies in the English Church of the later Middle Ages. Toronto 1989, Univ. xv-411 p. C$60 [TS 51, 532, T.E. *Morrissey*].

Kaster Robert A., Guardians of language; the grammarian and society in late antiquity 1988 → g321.

g964 *Kelly* Henry A., Inquisition and the prosecution of heresy; misconceptions and abuses: ChH 50 (1989) 439-451 [= → 4,b974].

g965 *Kelly* Joseph F., The Bible in early medieval Ireland: → 38, ᶠBURGHARDT W., Preaching 1989, 198-214.

g966 **Kleineidam** Erich, Univ. Erffordensis I, 1985 → 2,d490; 3,g403: ᴿZKG 100 (1989) 115-7 (A. *Zumkeller*).

g967 **Lorenz** Sönke, Studium generale erfordense; zum Erfurter Schulleben im 13. und 14. Jahrhundert: Mg GeschMA 34. Stu 1989, Hiersemann. xvi-403 p. DM 298 [TLZ 115, 514, G. *Haendler*].

g968 *Le Goff* Jacques, Le travail au Moyen Âge: CahSPR 6 (1989) 9-28.

g969 *Lomax* D.W., Heresy and orthodoxy in the fall of Almohad Spain: → 83, ᶠHIGHFIELD, God and man in medieval Spain 1989, 37-48.

g970 *López Silonis* Raphael, ❶ The relation between reason and faith in medieval thought: KatKenk 28,56 (1989) 35-64; Eng. ii-iv.

g971 **McKitterick** Rosamond, The Carolingians and the written word. C 1989, Univ. xvi-290 p. £30; pa. £10 [JTS 41, 732-5, Margaret *Gibson*].

g972 *Martin* John H., The four senses of Scripture; lessons from the thirteenth century: Pacifica 2 (1989) 87-106.

g973 **Meyer** Heinz, *Suntrup* Rudolf, Lexikon der mittelalterlichen Zahlenbedeutungen: Münsterische Mittelalter-Schriften 56. München 1987, Fink. xliv-1015 p. DM 298. 3-7705-2293-1. – ᴿGymnasium 96 (1989) 169 (W. *Harms*); RHE 84 (1989) 719-721 (D. *Iogna-Prat*).

g974 **Mollat** Michel, The poor in the Middle Ages [1978], ᵀ*Goldhammer* Arthur 1986 → 4,h984; 0-300-02789-3: ᴿJRel 68 (1988) 590s (J. *Kirshner*); RExp 86 (1989) 640s (T. *George*).

g975 **Moore** R. I., The formation of a persecuting society; power and deviance in Western Europe, 950-1250. Ox 1987, Blackwell. viii-168 p. £19.50 [HeythJ 31, 337-9, B. *Hamilton*].

g976 **Moore** R. I., Ketters, heksen en andere zondebokken; vervolging als middel tot macht 950-1120. Baarn 1988, Ambo. 158 p. Fb 595. – ᴿCollatVL 19 (1989) 490s (W. Van *Soom*).

g977 *Mühlenberg* Ekkehard, Katenen: → 911, TRE 18 (1989) 14-21.

g978 **Orabona** L., La Chiesa dell'anno mille; spiritualità tra politica ed economia nell'Europa medievale: La Spiritualità Cristiana, storia e testi, 1988 → 4,h987 [155 p. introd.; testi di BERNARDO 209-224; P. DAMIANO 163-198 ...]: ᴿRHE 84 (1989) 257 (R. *Aubert*; → 8167, série entière).

g979 **Pacaut** M., La théocratie; l'Église et le pouvoir au Moyen Âge: BiblHistChr 20. P 1989, Desclée. 197 p. F 128 [NRT 112, 632, N. *Plumat*: magistral].

g980 *Patschovsky* A., Häresie: → 901, LexMA 4 (1989) 1933-7.

g981 **Pelikan** Jaroslav, The excellent empire; the fall of Rome and the triumph of the Church 1987 → 4,h989; 0-06-254636-8: ᴿChH 50 (1989) 503s (R. M. *Grant*); Interpretation 43 (1989) 432 (T. R. *Skarsten*); RExp 86 (1989) 123 (E. G. *Hinson*); TS 50 (1989) 204s (R. L. *Wilken*).

g982 **Peters** Edward, Inquisition. NY 1988, Free Press. 362 p. $25. – ᴿJAAR 57 (1989) 424-7 (M. *McGaha*).

g983 ᴱ**Petroff** Elizabeth A., Medieval women's visionary literature 1986 → 4,h990a: ᴿJRel 68 (1988) 103s (K. *Emery*: 'woman's').

g984 ᴱ**Riché** Pierre, Lobrichon G., Lo studio della Bibbia nel medioevo latino [Le moyen âge et la Bible, BTT 1984 → 1,306], ᵀ*Rigo* Caterina: StBPaid 87. Brescia 1989, Paideia. 152 p. Lit. 18.000. 88-394-0428-7.

g985 **Roberts** Michael, Biblical epic and rhetorical paraphrase in late antiquity: ARCA 16, 1985 → 1,b719 ... 4,h992: ᴿAnzAltW 42 (1989) 254-7 (F. *Quadlbauer*).

g986 **Rubin** Miri, Charity and community in medieval Cambridge [... and beyond]: Studies in Medieval Life 4. C 1987, Univ. xiv-365 p. £30 [HeythJ 31, 339, N. P. *Tanner*].

g986* **Scase** Wendy, Piers Plowman and the new anti-clericalism. C 1989, Univ. xv-249 p. $44.50 [TS 51, 370, O. B. *Hardison*].

g987 (*Schneyer* J. B. †) ᴱ**Lohr** C., *al.*, Repertorium der lateinischen Sermones des Mittelalters für die Zeit von 1150-1350; Index der Textanfänge I-II: BeitGesch PTMA, TU 43/10s. Münster 1989s, Aschendorff. x-523 p.; 614 p. DM 178 + 198 [NRT 112, 779s, S. *Hilaire*].

g988 ᶠSMALLEY Beryl, The Bible in the medieval world, ᴱ**Walsh** K., ... 1985 → 1,131 ... 4,h995: ᴿJRel 69 (1989) 101s (B. *McGinn*).

g989 **Smalley** Beryl, The Gospels in the schools (5 studies 1978-80) 1985 → 3,299; 4,h996: ᴿEngHR 104 (1989) 178s (A. B. *Cobban*).

g990 **Stroll** Mary,   The Jewish Pope; ideology and politics in the papal schism of 1130: Studies in Intellectual History 1987 → 4,h998: ᴿChH 50 (1989) 504-6 (J. E. *Lynch*); RHE 84 (1989) 129-131 (M. *Pacaut*).

g991 **Swanson** R. N.,   Church and society in later medieval England.   NY 1989, Blackwell.   xii-427 p. $75 [TS 51, 533, T. E. *Morrissey*].

g992 **Tierney** Brian,   Origins of Papal infallibility 1150-1350; study on the concepts of infallibility, sovereignty and tradition in the Middle Ages [= 1972 + reaction to comments, p. 299-327]: Studies in the history of Christian thought 6.   Leiden 1988, Brill.   x-327 p. *f* 125 [TLZ 115, 515, H. *Zimmermann*].

g993 **Uytfanghe** Marc van,   Stylisation biblique et condition humaine dans l'hagiographie mérovingienne (600-750) [< diss. Gand 1979]: Verh. wet/lett 49/120.   Bru 1987, Academie.   286 p.   Fb 1400. – ᴿBTAM 14 (1989) 627-630 (H. *Silvestre*, long résumé); RHE 84 (1989) 110-2 (M. *Lauwers*).

g994 *Van Engen* John,   The Christian Middle Ages as an historiographical problem: AmHR 91 (1986) 519-552 ['the great majority were cut off from direct access to the written norms of a Christian culture...' but the dynamic inherent in acting on religious belief was based on Scripture... OT even more than Gospels, according to the admiring summary of H. *Silvestre*, RHE 84 (1989) 220-3; BTAM 14 (1989) 632-5].

g995 **Vauchez** André,   Les laïcs au Moyen Âge, pratiques et expériences religieuses 1987 → 4,h999: ᴿScEspr 41 (1989) 128-131 (P. *Boglioni*).

g996 **Vernet** André, (*Genevois* Anne-Marie),   La Bible au Moyen Âge, bibliographie.   P 1989, CNRS.   131 p.   F 96.   2-222-04343-3.

Y3.4   **Exegetae medievales** (hebraei → K7).

g998 ᴀɴsᴇʟᴍᴜs: ᴱ**Corbin** M., *Galonnier* A.   Anselme de Cantorbéry: Lettre sur l'Incarnation du Verbe; pourquoi un Dieu-Homme?: L'Œuvre 3.   P 1988, Cerf.   496 p.   F 185. – ᴿNRT 111 (1989) 968s (P. *Gilbert*); ScEspr 41 (1989) 385-7 (G. H. *Allard*).

g999 **Evans** Gillian R.,   Anselm: Outstanding Christian Thinkers [ᴱ*Davies* Brian].   Wilton ᴄᴛ / L 1989, Morehouse-Barlow / Chapman.   xiii-108 p. $16; pa. $9.   0-8192-1484-1; 3-3 [TDig 37,80].

k1 ᴀǫᴜɪɴᴀs: **Lacordaire** H. D., ᴱ*Piolanti* A.,   S. Tommaso il Dottore dei Dottori: Perennità di Tomismo 2.   Vaticano 1989, Libreria.   75 p.   Lit. 5000 [RHE 84, p. 406*].

k2 **Pesch** Otto-Hermann,   Thomas von Aquin; Grenze und Grösse mittelalterlicher Theologie 1988 → 4,k6: ᴿForumKT 5 (1989) 235-7 (R. *Elders*); FreibZ 36 (1989) 493-8 (J.-P. *Torrell*); Gregorianum 70 (1989) 580s (J. de *Finance*); Studium 29 (M 1989) 556s (M. F. de *Villacorta*); TR 85 (1989) 25s (G. L. *Müller*); TüTQ 169 (1989) 326-9 (M. *Seckler*).

k3 **Steenberghen** Fernand Van,   Le Thomisme: Que sais-je? 587.   P 1983, PUF.   127 p. – ᴿETL 65 (1989) 192 (R. *Wielockx* parle plutôt de 'Thomas' mais rien sur son exégèse).

k4 *Hünemörder* C.,   Thomas von Aquin und die Tiere: → 561, ᴱ*Zimmermann* A., Thomas 1988, 192-210.

k5 **Weisheipl** James A.,   Tommaso d'Aquino (Vita, pensiero, opere).   Mi 1988, Jaca.   426 p.   Lit. 45.000. – ᴿStCattMi 33 (1989) 956 (F. *Russo*).

k6 **Wohlman** Avital,   Thomas d'Aquin et Maïmonide 1988 → 4,k10: ᴿNRT 111 (1989) 981 (M. *Horowitz*); RÉJ 148 (1989) 423-5 (J.-P. *Rothschild*); RThom 89 (1989) 331s (S.-T. *Bonino*; 327-343 'Mediaevalia').

k8 BACON: *Lertora Mendoza* Celina A., Roger Bacon; sus ideas exegéticas: NatGrac 36 (1989) 195-372.

k9 BERNARDUS C.: **Heller** Dagmar, Schriftauslegung und geistliche Erfahrung bei Bernhard von Clairvaux: Diss. ᴰ*Ritter.* Heidelberg 1988s. – TR 85 (1989) 516; RTLv 21,549.

k10 BONAVENTURA: **Hoefs** Karl-Heinz, Erfahrung Gottes bei Bonaventura; Untersuchungen zum Begriff 'Erfahrung' in seinem Bezug zum Göttlichen: ErfurtTSt 57. Lp 1989, St. Benno. xvi-145 p.

k11 **Jehl** R., Melancholie und Acedia; ein Beitrag zu Anthropologie und Ethik Bonaventuras [Diss. München]: Grabmann-Institut NF 32. Pd 1984, Schöningh. xxxix-323 p. – ᴿCrNSt 10 (1989) 181-3 (Z. *Hayes:* competent).

k12 **Reist** Thomas, Saint Bonaventure as a biblical commentator... Luke XVIII, 34 - XIX, 42, 1988 [ᴰ1985] 1988 → 3,g434; 4,k12:   ᴿEstFranc 90 (1989) 295s (F. *Raurell*).

k13 CUMMIAN: Welsh Maura, *Ó Cróinín* Dáibhí, Cummian's letter De controversia paschali and the De ratione computandi: ST 86. Toronto 1988, Pont. Inst. Mediaeval St. X-264 p. $31 [JTS 41, 271-4, R. *Sharpe*].

k13* CUSANUS: **Meier-Oeser** Stephan, Die Präsenz des Vergessenen; zur Rezeption der Philosophie des Nicolaus Cusanus vom 15. bis zum 18. Jahrhundert: Cusanus-Ges. Buchreihe 10. Münster 1989, Aschendorff. viii-440 p.; 30 fig. DM 112 [TLZ 115, 844, K. H. *Kandler*].

k14 DIONYSIUS Ps.-A: ᴱ**Heil** Günter, Ps-Dionysius, Über die himmlische Hierarchie. Stu 1986, Hiersemann. xi-200 p. DM 160. – ᴿTLZ 114 (1989) 285s (G. *Haendler*); VigChr 43 (1989) 97 (J. van *Winden*).

k15 ᴱ**Hespel** Robert, Chronicon anonymum Pseudo-Dionysianum II gallice: CSCOr 507, syri 213. Lv 1989, Peeters. xvi-351 p. 0070-0452.

k16 **Louth** Andrew, Denys the Areopagite: Outstanding Christian Thinkers [ᴱ*Davies* Brian]. Wilton CT / L 1989, Morehouse-Barlow / Chapman. x-134 p. $17; pa. $10. 0-8192-1486-8; 5-X [TDig 37,80].

k17 *Tomasic* Thomas M., The logical function of metaphor and oppositional coincidence in the Pseudo-Dionysius and Johannes Scottus Eriugena: JRel 68 (1988) 361-376.

k18 ECKHART: *Goffi* Tullo, Meister Eckhart interprete mistico della S. Scrittura: StEcum 5 (1987) 395-405; Eng. 406.

k19 *Saranyana* Josep-Ignasi, Meister Eckhart y la controversia coloniense (1326); a propósito de la libertad de investigación teológica: ScripTPamp 21 (1989) 887-902 [903-918, *Lorda* J. L., La fe del teólogo].

k20 ERIUGENA: **O'Meara** John J., Eriugena 1988 → 4,k23: ᴿBTAM 14 (1989) 643s (J. *McEvoy*, Eng.); DowR 107 (1989) 153s (A. *Louth*); JTS 40 (1989) 651-4 (J. *Marenbon*); RHE 84 (1989) 618 (P. *Brady*); Studies 78 (1988) 226-9 (T. *O'Loughlin*).

k21 ᴱ**Jeauneau** Édouard, Études érigéniennes (reprints + 2 inedita). P 1987, Ét. Aug. 749 p. [JTS 41, 276-8, J. *Marenbon*].

k22 EUCHERIUS L.: *Mandolfo* Carmela, Osservazioni sull'esegesi di Eucherio di Lione [*Lubac* H. de, Exégèse médiévale 1 (1959) 193s]: → 567, AnStoEseg 6 (1989) 217-223; Eng. 9.

k23 FISHACRE: *Biffi* Inos, Figure della teologia medioevale; tra Scrittura e teologia o gli inizi della scuola domenicana a Oxford: I. Riccardo Fishacre † 1248: TItSett 14 (1989) 59-93; Eng. 93.

k24 GILBERTUS P.: *Colish* Marcia L., Early Porretan theology: RTAM 56 (1989) 58-79.

k25 GREGORIUS S.: *Rigo* Antonio, La vita e le opere di Gregorio Sinaita [esicasmo bizantino sec. XIII-XIV; *Balfour* D. 1982]: CrNSt 10 (1989) 579-607; Eng. 608.

k26 GUIBERTUS: E**Derolez** Albert, Guibertus Gemblacensis epistolae I-LVI: CCMed 66, 66A. Turnhout 1989, Brepols. 195 p.; 15 microfiches CETEDOC. 2-503-63662-4.

k27 HILDEGARD: **Épiney-Burgard** G., *Zum Brunn* E., Femmes troubadours de Dieu [Hildegarde de Bingen]: Témoins de notre histoire. Turnhout... Brepols. 235 p. F 100. – REsprVie 99 (1989) 367s (J. *Crépin*)).
Newman Barbara, Sister of wisdom, Hildegard's theology of the feminine 1987 → 8824.

k28 HRABANUS M.: *Clausi* Benedetto, 'Rerum naturae', 'verborum proprietates' e 'mystica significatio'; esegesi biblica e geografia nel De rerum naturis di Rabano Mauro: → 567, AnStoEseg 6 (1989) 203-216; Eng. 9.

k29 HUBERTUS A.: **Fanning** Steven, A bishop and his world before the Gregorian reform; Hubert of Angers, 1006-1047: AmPhTr 78/1. Ph 1988. 193 p. – RRHE 84 (1989) 122s (A. *Chédeville*).

k29* ISIDORUS H.: *Bat-Sheva* Albert, Isidore of Seville; his attitude towards Judaism and his impact on early medieval canon law: JQR 80 (1989s) 207-220.
Fontaine Jacques, Tradition et histoire chez Isidore de Seville 1988 → 260.

k30 JOACHIM F.: **Reeves** Marjorie, *Gould* Warwick, Joachim of Fiore and the myth of the eternal evangel in the nineteenth century 1987 → 3,g448; 4,k29: RRelStR 15 (1989) 80 (H. *Schwartz*).

k31 **Lee** Harold, *Reeves* Marjorie, *Silano* Giulio, Western Mediterranean prophecy; the school of Joachim of Fiore and the fourteenth-century 'Breviloquium': ST 88. Toronto 1989, Pont. Inst. Med. xii-346 p. – RScripTPamp 21 (1989) 960s (J. *Goñi Gaztambide*).

k32 **McGinn** Bernard, The Calabrian abbot, Joachim... 1985 → 1,f740 ...3,g445: RHeythJ 30 (1989) 471s (Jennifer *Britnell*).

k33 JULIANA N.: **Jantzen** Grace M., Julian of Norwich, mystic and theologian 1987 → 4,k31; also NY 1988, Paulist. x-230 p. $10. – RDowR 107 (1989) 73-75 (J. *Clark*); Horizons 16 (1939) 384-6 (Marie Anne *Mayeski*); ScotJT 42 (1989) 272-4 (sr. *Carol*); Studies 77 (1988) 479-481 (J. *Grennan*).

k34 **Pelphrey** B., Christ our mother; Julian of Norwich. Wilmington 1989, Glazier. 271 p. $15 [TS 51,189].

k35 KEMPE M.: *Despres* Denise L., The meditative art of Scripture interpolation in The book of Margery Kempe: DowR 106 (1988) 253-264 [107 (1989) 209-223 *Eberly* Susan].

k36 LYRANUS N.: *Reinhardt* Klaus, Das Werk des Nicolaus von Lyra im mittelalterlichen Spanien: Traditio 43 (Fordham 1987) 321-358.

k37 MATHIAS: E**Piltz** A., Magister Mathias, Vägen till Jerusalem; valda texter ur Homo conditus 1986 → 3,g451: RKyrkohistorisk Årsskrift 87 (1987) 192-6 (S. *Borgehammar*) [RHE 84,218*].

k38 MIRANDOLA: *Valcke* Louis, Humanisme et scolastique; le 'conflit des deux cultures' chez Jean Pic de la Mirandole: RTAM 56 (1989) 164-199.

k39 PÉREZ DE V.J.: **Peinado Muñoz** Miguel, La hermenéutica de Jaime Pérez de Valencia (1408-1490) en su perspectiva histórica: diss. DVilchez Lindez J. Granada 1989. 391 p. > ArTGran. – RTLv 21, p. 538.

k40 RUFUS R.: **Raedts** Peter, Richard Rufus of Cornwall and the tradition of Oxford theology: HistMg. NY 1987, Oxford-UP. 272 p. – RETL 65 (1989) 136-144 (R. *Wielockx*).

k41 RUPERTUS T.: **Arduini** Maria Lodovica, Rupert von Deutz (1076-1129) und der 'Status Christianitatis' seiner Zeit; symbolisch-prophetische Deutung der Geschichte: ArKulturG Beih 25. Köln 1987, Böhlau. xi-504 p. Kap. 5, Die Zeit der biblischen Armut. – ᴿRHE 84 (1989) 175s (H. *Silvestre* y trouve illustré: 'Le combat que le pauvre, ami de Jahvé, soutient contre le puissant et le détenteur intéressé du pouvoir est un des thèmes favoris de la Bible hébraïque. Dans la même perspective, Jésus de Nazareth annonça le triomphe eschatologique des pauvres en esprit'.

k42 *Curschmann* Michael, Imagined exegesis; text and picture in the exegetical works of Rupert of Deutz, HONORIUS Augustodunensis, and GERHOCH of Reichersberg: Traditio 44 (1989) 145-169.

Y4.1 Luther

k43 ᴱ**Aland** Kurt, Lutherlexikon⁴ ʳᵉᵛ [¹1967] reprint: Uni-Tb Theol. 1530. Gö 1989, Vandenhoeck & R. 438 p. DM 32,80 [TLZ 115,41, G. *Haendler*].

k44 **Asendorf** Ulrich, Die Theologie Martin Luthers nach seinen Predigten. Gö 1988, Vandenhoeck & R. 434 p. DM 64. 3-525-55411-7. – ᴿActuBbg 26 (1989) 227 (J. *Boada*); TLZ 114 (1989) 602-4 (E. W. *Gritsch*); TR 85 (1989) 118s (G. *Wenz*); TsTNijm 29 (1989) 414 (T. *Bell*).

k45 ᴱ**Behnken** Heinz, FREUD oder Luther? Versuch der Aufarbeitung einer (falschen?) Alternative [Tagung Loccum 1985]. Rehburg-Loccum 1986, Ev. Akad. 118 p.; p. 25-53, *Hermes* Eilert [= WegeMensch 39 (1987) 280-297] Luther und Freud; ein Theorievergleich; – p. 54-112, *Soeffner* Hans Georg, Luther, die Formierung eines protestantischen Individualtypus durch die Reformierung des biblischen Welt- und Menschenbildes.

k46 **Bell** T. M.; BERNHARDUS dixit; Bernardus van Clairvaux in Martin Luthers werken [diss. Kath. Univ. Amst. 1989, ᴰ*Boendermaker*]. Delft c. 1989, Eburon. 382 p. 90-55166-075-8. – TsTNijm 29 (1989) 169.

k47 *a*) *Beyer* Michael, Vulgatakonkordanzen als Hilfsmittel beim Übersetzen lateinischer Luthertexte; – *b*) *Brecht* Martin, Zum Problem der Identifizierung namentlich nicht gekennzeichneter Lutherschriften; – *c*) *Müller* Gotthold, Der junge GOETHE über Martin Luther und die Reformation: LuJb 56 (1989) 59-67 / 51-8 / 130-145.

k48 *a*) *Bienert* Wolfgang A., 'Im Zweifel näher bei AUGUSTIN?' — zum patristischen Hintergrund der Theologie Luthers; – *b*) *Geisser* Hans F., M. Luther; zwischen Sündenelend und Glaubensfestigkeit; die geistlichen Erfahrungen eines abendländischen Christen am Ende des Mittelalters und ihre theologische Bedeutung in einem ökumenischen Zeitalter: ➤ 174, ᶠSCHNEEMELCHER W., Oecumenica 1989, 281-294 / 295-316.

k49 **Brecht** Martin, M. Luther 2-3, 1986s ➤ 4,k43: ᴿLuJb 56 (1989) 148-155 (K.-V. *Selge*).

k50 ᴱ**Cavallotto** Stefano, Martin Lutero, Scritti pastorali minori, pref. *Ulianich* Boris 1987 ➤ 4,k45: ᴿGregorianum 70 (1989) 121-6 (J. *Wicks*: 'Lutero e la religiosità vissuta'); Protestantesimo 44 (1989) 141-3 (F. *Ferrario*); RHE 84 (1989) 633 (P. *Denis*: worth-while).

k51 **Currà** Gaetano, Il falso profeta; Lutero negli scritti di Tommaso CAMPANELLA. Cosenza 1989, Progetto 2000. 181 p. Lit. 20.000. – ᴿCC 140 (1989,4) 309s (G. *Mucci*).

k52 *Dickens* A. G., Luther and the humanists: ➤ 109, ᶠKOENIGSBERGER H. 1987 ...

k53 **Ebeling** Gerhard, Lutherstudien 3 [c. 1983] 1985 → 2,155*; 3,g469: ᴿRHPR 69 (1989) 64-66 (M. *Lienhard*); TPhil 64 (1989) 599-604 (P. *Knauer*).

k54 **Ebert** Helmut, Alltagssprache und religiöse Sprache in Luthers Briefen und in seiner Bibelübersetzung; eine satzsemantische Untersuchung am Beispiel von Aufforderungssätzen und Fragesätzen: EurHS 1/929. Fra 1986, Lang. iv-284 p. – ᴿRHPR 69 (1989) 365s (M. *Arnold*).

k55 **Edwards** Mark U., Luther's last battles; politics and polemics. Ithaca NY 1983, Cornell Univ. xiv-254 p. $20. – ᴿSWJT 32, 3 (1989s) 65 (W. R. *Estep*: asks how one can explain cited vilest vulgarities, and answers rather convincingly).

k56 ᴱ**Fabisch** Peter, **Iserloh** Erwin, Dokumente zur Causa Luthers (1517-1521) I, 1988 → 4,k50: ᴿTPhil 64 (1989) 270s (H. J. *Sieben*).

k57 **Febvre** Lucien, Martin Luther, un destin⁶ [¹1928; ² ʳᵉᵛ 1944, (³1945) 1951, ⁵1968]. P 1988, PUF-Quadrige. 210 p. – ᴿRHPR 69 (1989) 63 (M. *Chevallier*).

k58 **Führer** Werner, Das Wort Gottes in Luthers Theologie 1984 → 1,6381: ᴿTR 85 (1989) 207s (J. *Wicks*, ᵀ*Wiemeyer* E.)

k59 **Gerrish** B. A., Discerning the body; sign and reality in Luther's controversy with the Swiss: JRel 68 (1988) 377-395.

k60 ᴱ**Ghiselli** Anja, **Peura** Simo, *Tutkimuksia...* Beiträge zur Denkform Luthers: Teol. 154. Helsinki 1987, Teol. Kirjal. 136 p. [LuJb 56, p. 164].

k61 **Hahn** Gerhard, Evangelium als literarische Anweisung; zu Luthers Stellung in der Geschichte des deutschen kirchlichen Liedes: MTU 73. Mü 1981, Artemis. viii-318 p. – ᴿTRu 54 (1984) 218-220 (Inge *Mager*).

k62 ᴱ**Hammer** Gerhard, zur Mühlen Karl-Heinz, Lutherania, zum 500. Gb.: Archiv zur Weimarer-Ausgabe 5. Köln 1984, Böhlau. vii-483 p. DM 198 [TLZ 115, 281-3, S. *Bräuer*].

k63 ᴱ**Heine** Susanne, Europa in der Krise der Neuzeit; Martin Luther, Wandel und Wirkung seines Bildes 1986 → 4,366; DM 38: ᴿTR 85 (1989) 33s (R. *Decot*).

k64 **Heinz** Johann, Martin Luther and his theology in German Catholic interpretation before and after Vatican II: AndrUnS 26 (1988) 253-265.

k65 ᴱ**Herrmann** H., Luther in unserer Zeit: URANIA. Eggersdorf 1982, TASTOMAT. 31 p. [LuJb 56, p. 165].

k65* **Janz** Denis R., Luther on Thomas AQUINAS; the Angelic Doctor in the thought of the Reformer: Mainz Eur. Rel.-Gesch. 140. Stu 1989, Steiner. xi-124 p. DM 38 [TLZ 115, 903-5, L. *Grane*].

k66 **Jüngel** Eberhard, The freedom of a Christian; Luther's significance for contemporary theology, ᵀ*Harrisville* Roy A. Minneapolis 1988, Augsburg. 109 p. $10. 0-8066-2395-4 [TDig 37,67]. – ᴿCurrTM 16 (1989) 303 (J. C. *Rochelle*); TTod 46 (1989s) 352 (T. J. *Wengert*).

k67 **Kettunen** Ossi, Hade Martin Luther en teologisk metod?: SvTKv 65 (1989) 125-7.

k68 **Kisimba** Nyembo, La parole comme manifestation personnelle de Dieu dans les sacrements selon Martin Luther (1483-1546): Rech.Afr.Théol. 10. Kinshasa 1988, Fac.Théol.Cath. xiv-238 p. [NRT 112, 436s, L. *Renwart*].

k69 **Kittelson** James M., Luther the reformer; the story of the man and his career 1986 → 3,g484; 4,k54: ᴿAndrUnS 26 (1988) 300-2 (K. A. *Strand*); Interpretation 43 (1989) 188-191 (P. R. *Keifert*, also on MILDENBERGER F., Eng. 1986).

k70 ᴱ**Kraft** Heinrich, Luther als Prediger: Ratzeburg Luther-Akademie 9. Erlangen 1986, Luther. 135 p.; p. 53-76, *Kandler* K., Rechtfertigung;

102-135, *Beintker* H., Evangelium; 9-41, *Heckel* G., Oster; 89-101, *Asendorf* U., Die Bedeutung der Predigt für Luthers Theologie; 42-52, *Nembach* U., ML als Begleiter auf dem Weg von der Exegese zur Predigt [LuJb 56, p. 161 ... 181].

k71 ᴱKraft Heinrich, Schrift und Auslegung: Ratzeburg Luther-Akademie 10. Erlangen 1987, Luther. 127 p.; p. 60-87, *Bayer* Oswald, Schriftautorität und Vernunft, ein ekklesiologisches Problem; 15-29, *Beisser* Friedrich, Wort Gottes und Heilige Schrift bei Luther; 55-68, *Brecht* Martin, Zur Typologie in Luthers Schriftauslegung [LuJb 56, p. 161].

k72 ᴱLau Franz, Der Glaube der Reformatoren: Luther — ZWINGLI — CALVIN: Sammlung Dieterich 267. Wu 1988, Brockhaus. xvi-481 p. [LuJb 56, p. 167].

k73 *Lazareth* William H., Luther's 'Sola scriptura' traditions of the Gospel for norming Christian righteousness: ➤ 591*a*, Ratzinger 1988/9, 50-73.

k74 *Leske* Elmore, The mystery of Luther's 95 theses on indulgences; how 'Lutheran' are they?: Lutheran Theological Journal 20 (Adelaide 1985) 83-96 [LuJb 56, p. 170].

k75 Lienhard Marc, L'Évangile et l'Église chez Luther [complément de son Luther de 1983]. P 1989, Cerf. 287 p. – ᴿRHPR 69 (1989) 380 (*ipse*).

k76 Loewenich W. v., M. Luther, the man and his work 1986 ➤ 3,g487; 4,k57: ᴿScotJT 42 (1989) 603 (I. *Hazlett*: ranks with M. BRECHT, H. BORNKAMM, M. LIENHARD as the best recent Luther biographies).

k77 ᴱLohse Bernhard, Der Durchbruch der reformatorischen Erkenntnis bei Luther — neuere Untersuchungen [Fortsetzung vom Band 1968]: Mainz Inst.Europ. Gesch. Veröff. 25. Stu 1988, Steiner. xii-388 p. DM 54 [TLZ 115, 206-8, E W. *Gritsch*].

k78 Lohse B., M. Luther (1980), ᵀ*Schultz* R., 1986 ➤ 3,g487; 4,k58; also E 1987, Clark; £15: ᴿScotJT 42 (1989) 449-451 (W. P. *Stephens*).

k79 Lortz Joseph [†; 100. Gb.] Erneuerung und Einheit; [seine eigenen] Aufsätze zur Theologie und Kirchengeschichte, ᴱ*Manns* Peter: Mainz Eur.Geschichte 126 ➤ 305: p. 418-428, Zum Menschenbild Luthers (1934); 540-596, Römerbriefvorlesung, Grundanliegen; 678-717, Zum Kirchengedanken des jungen Luther (1967); 646-677, Sakramentales Denken beim j.L.; 429-484, ERASMUS — kirchengeschichtlich; 862-891, Ökumenismus ohne Wahrheit?

k80 ᴱLull Timothy F., Martin Luther's basic theological writings [25 complete treatises and 6 other items from vol. 31-54 of the 55-vol. American edition. Minneapolis 1989, Fortress. xix-755 p. $20 pa. 0-8006-2327-4 [TDig 37,72].

k81 Mannermaa Tuomo, *al.*, Thesaurus Lutheri; auf der Suche nach neuen Paradigmen der Luther-Forschung [HAIKOLA Lauri, Andenken, Luther-Symposium 11.-12.XI.1986]. Helsinki 1987, Luther-Agricola. 327 p. [LuJb 56, p. 162; *Ruokanan* M. 259-278 ➤ 4,1425; HeythJ 31, 246, J. *Wicks*].

k82 Manteufel Thomas E., Martin Luther and the concept of opus operatum: diss. Iowa, ᴰ*Forell* G. Iowa City 1988. – RelStR 16, 190.

k83 Maron Gottfried, Martin Luther und EPIKUR; ein Beitrag zum Verständnis des alten Luther: Szb Jungius-Ges. Ha 6. Gö 1988, Vandenhoeck & R. 66 p.; map. DM 16 [TLZ 115, 439, S. *Bräuer*].

k83* Mora Aldo, Martin Lutero, un decennio di studi (1975/6–1986-87) attorno a un centenario (1483-1983): O Odegos Quad. 8. Bari 1989, Centro Ecumenico S. Nicola. 223 p. [ETL 66,434, A. de *Halleux*].

k84 ᵀᴱNitti S., M. Lutero, Come si devono istituire i ministri nella Chiesa [1523]: Opere scelte 2. T 1987, Claudiana. 96 p. Lit. 9000. – ᴿProtestantesimo 44 (1989) 143s (F. Ferrari; 'ministri', ma tratta i ministeri, sacerdozio, episcopato).

k85 **Oberman** Heiko A., Martin Lutero, un uomo tra Dio e il diavolo [1982],ᵀ: Storia e società. Bari 1987, Laterza. viii-367 p. – ᴿSalesianum 51 (1989) 341s (M. Müller).

k86 **Preul** Reiner, Luther und die praktische Theologie; Beiträge zum kirchlichen Handeln in der Gegenwart: MarbTheolSt 25. Marburg 1989, Elwert. ix-131 p. DM 39 [TLZ 115, 299, E. Winkler].

k86* **Saarinen** Risto, Gottes Wirken auf uns; die transzendentale Deutung des Gegenwart-Christi-Motivs in der Lutherforschung: Mainz Eur.Rel. Gesch. 137. Stu 1989, Steiner. x-241 p. DM 42 [TLZ 115, 840-2, R. Slenczka].

k87 ᴱ**Schäferdiek** Knut, Martin Luther im Spiegel heutiger Wissenschaft: Studium Universale 4. Bonn 1985, Bouvier. vii-266 p. DM 58. – ᴿTR 85 (1989) 31s (R. Decot).

k88 ᴱ**Schulz** Hansjürgen, Mit Luther in Gespräch; heutige Konfrontationen. Mü 1983, Kaiser [B, Ev.-V.]. 156 p. DM 16. – ᴿLuthTKi 12 (1988) 28s (G. Rost: Studienbuch-Anthologie).

k89 **Schwarz** Reinhard, Luther: Die Kirche in ihrer Geschichte 3/1, 1986 → 3,g500; 4,k70: ᴿZKG 100 (1989) 121-6 (W. Härle).

k90 **Steinmetz** David C., Luther in context 1986 → 2,d571 ... 4,k74: ᴿChH 58 (1989) 100-2 (L. W. Spitz); TR 85 (1989) 210s (J. Wicks).

k91 **Stolt** Birgit, Lieblichkeit und Zier, Ungestüm und Donner; M. Luther im Spiegel seiner Sprache: ZTK 86 (1989) 282-305.

k92 **Turrado** Argimiro, Gracia y libre albedrio en S. AGUSTIN y en Lutero; la tragedia de la incomprensión en el s. XVI y la hermenéutica de las culturas: EstAg 23 (1988) 483-514.

k93 **[García] Villoslada** Ricardo, Martin Lutero: I. Il frate assetato di Dio; II. In lotta contro Roma. Mi 1985-8, IPL. 790 p. 843 p. Lit. 30.000 + 40.000. – ᴿLetture 44 (1989) 275-7 (N. Venturini).

k94 **Wingren** Gustaf, Konfrontationer [IRENAEUS ... Luther]. Hadsten, Denmark 1989, Mimer. 101 p. – ᴿSvTKv 65 (1989) 136s (L.-O. Armgard).

k95 **Wood** A. Skevington, Spirit and spirituality in Luther: EvQ 61 (1989) 311-333.

k96 **zur Mühlen** Karl-Heinz, Das Lutherjahr 1983 und die Lutherforschung: VerkF 34,2 (1989) (1-)3-23 [38-83, Mehlhausen Joachim, Barmen 1934].

Y4.3 Exegesis et controversia saeculi XVI.

k97 **Abrey** Lorna Jane, The people's reformation; magistrates, clergy and commons in Strasbourg, 1500-1958. Ithaca NY 1985, Cornell Univ. 272 p. – ᴿRHPR 69 (1989) 70-72 (M. Lienhard: original and well documented).

k98 **Allison** A. F., Rogers D. M., The contemporary printed literature of the English Counter-Reformation between 1558 and 1640, I. (with Lottes W.) Works in languages other than English. Aldershot, Hant. 1989, Scholar [Brookfield VT, Gower]. xxviii-291 p. $120. 0-85967-640-4 [TDig 36,347].

k99 **Anderson** Marvin W., Evangelical foundations; religion in England, 1378-1683 [... Bible studies and printing]: AmerUnivSt 7/33. NY 1987, Lang. xiv-488 p. $66. 0-8204-0486-1 [TDig 36,349].

k100 **Barnes** Robin B., Prophecy and gnosis; apocalypticism in the wake of the Lutheran Reformation 1988 → 4,k80: ᴿChH 50 (1989) 384s (E.W. *Gritsch*); RelStR 15 (1989) 78 (H. *Schwartz*); TS 50 (1989) 367-9 (M. *Murrin*).

k101 ᴱ**Bedouelle** Guy, *Roussel* Bernard, Le temps des Réformes et la Bible: BTT 5. P 1989, Beauchesne. 811 p.; 17 fig.; 15 facsim. F 480 [RHE 84,205*]. 2-7020-1092-6. – ᴿFoiVie 88 (1989) 92-94 (O. *Millet*).

k102 ᴱ**Bianco** Cesare, Il Sommario della Santa Scrittura e l'ordinario dei cristiani: Testi della Riforma 1988 → 4,k84. ᴿSTEv 1,2 (1989) 218 (P. *Cuccini*).

k103 **Brufau Prats** Jaime, La Escuela de Salamanca ante el descubrimiento del Nuevo Mundo: Biblioteca de Teólogos Españoles 33. Salamanca 1989, S. Esteban. 181 p. 84-85045-83-1. – ᴿGregorianum 70 (1989) 809s (F.P. *Sullivan*).

k104 **Bujanda** J.-M. de, *al.*, Index des livres interdits [→ 2,d581 ... 4,k86], II. de l'Université de Louvain, 1546, 1550, 1558. Sherbrooke/Genève 1986, Univ./Droz. 587 p. – ᴿRBgPg 67 (1989) 855s (R. *Crahay*); RHR 206 (1989) 193-5 (G. *Audisio*).

k105 **Bundschuh** Benno von, Das Wormser Religionsgespräch von 1557 unter besonderer Berücksichtigung der kaiserlichen Religionspolitik: RefGStT 124. Münster 1988, Aschendorff. xxviii-603 p. DM 158 pa. – ᴿTüTQ 169 (1989) 149s (R. *Reinhardt*).

Denis Philippe, Le Christ étendard... au temps des Réformes 1987 → 4,8469.

k106 **Dickens** A.G., *Tonkin* John M., The Reformation in historical thought 1985 → 3,g514 (not as 4,k92): ᴿJRel 68 (1988) 105s (M.L. *Edwards*).

k107 **Eire** Carlos M.N., War against the idols; the reformation of worship from Erasmus to Calvin 1986 → 2,d586: ᴿEngHR 104 (1989) 731s (H.M. *Höpfl*); RTLv 20 (1989) 245s (J.-F. *Gilmont*); ZKG 100 (1989) 240s (C. *Augustijn*: enttäuschend).

k108 **Estep** William R., The Reformation and Protestantism; a guided learning book. El Paso 1983, Carib Baptist. 183 p. [LuJb 56, p. 171].

k109 **Farge** James K., Orthodoxy and reform in early Reformation France; the faculty of theology of France, 1500-1543: Studies in Medieval and Reformation Thought 12, 1985 → 3,g520: ᴿRHE 84 (1989) 280s (P. *Denis*).

k110 **Farthing** John L., Thomas AQUINAS and Gabriel BIEL; interpretations of St. T.A. on the eve of the Reformation: MgMedRen 9. Durham NC 1988, Duke Univ. x-265 p. [RHE 85,207, P.H. *Daly*].

k110* **Friedman** Jerome, The most ancient testimony; sixteenth-century Christian-Hebraica in the age of Renaissance nostalgia 1983 → 64,9019; 1,f812: ᴿJQR 80 (1989s) 366-8 (Anna S. *Abulafia*).

k111 ᴱ**Füssel** Stephan, Bild und Wort; Mittelalter — Humanismus — Reformation: Pirckheimer Jb 1. Mü 1986, M. Fink. 121 p.; 12 fig.

k112 **George** Timothy, Theology of the Reformers 1988 → 4,k102: ᴿRelStR 15 (1989) 359 (R. *Kolb*); Paradigms 5/1 (1989) 63-65 (S.H. *Moore*).

k113 **Goertz** Hans-Jürgen, Pfaffenhass und gross Geschrei; die reformatorischen Bewegungen in Deutschland 1517-1529. Mü 1987, Beck. 300 p. 3-406-32195-X. – ᴿActuBbg 26 (1989) 18s (A. *Borràs y Feliu*).

k114 ᴱ**Graf zu Dohna** Lothar, *Mokrosch* Reinhold, Werden und Wirkung der Reformation, Ringvorlesung Da 1983s: THD-Wissenschaft & Technik 19. Da 1986, Technische Hochschule. 288 p.; ill.; p. 203-220, *Aretin* Karl O. von, Das Papsttum der Renaissance und M. Luther; 221-6, *Hoberg*

Rudolf, Luther und die deutsche Sprache; 157-181, *Decot* Rolf, Der Wandel des katholischen Lutherbildes; 95-116, *Graf zu Dohna*, STAUPITZ und Luther; → 4453.

k115 ᴱHaigh Christopher, The English Reformation revised [9 papers; it was only reluctantly accepted before 1580]. C 1987, Univ. x-229 p. £9 [HeythJ 31, 345-7, A. *Hamilton*].

k116 ᴱIserloh Erwin, Katholische Theologen der Reformationszeit 1-5, 1987 → 1,362...4,k104: ᴿColcFran 59 (1989) 173s (V. *Criscuolo*, 5); RHE 84 (1989) 171 (J.-F. *Gilmont*, 4s); RHPR 69 (1989) 67s (M. *Lienhard*, 3: besides CANISIUS, who 'lacked critico-historical sense' also on K. WIMPINA, T. MURNER, J. DRIEDO, J. MENSING, B. von CHEMSEE, M. CANO).

k117 **Jockenhovel** Klaus, Rom-Brüssel-Gottorf; ein Beitrag zur Geschichte der gegenreformatorischen Versuche in Nordeuropa 1622-1637: Quellen und Forschungen für Geschichte Schleswig-Holsteins 93. Neumünster 1989, Wachholtz. 245 p. – ᴿRHE 84 (1989) 782s (L.-M. *Dewailly*: posthumous).

k118 Katholische Reform und Gegenreformation: *a*) → 911, TRE 18 (1989) 45-72 (Gottfried *Maron*); – *b*) → 894, EvKL 2 (1989) 1003-7 (Heribert *Smolinski*).

k119 **Kirchner** Hubert, Reformationsgeschichte von 1532 bis 1555/1556: Festigung der Reformation, CALVIN, Katholische Reform und Konzil von Trient: Kirchengeschichte in Einzeldarstellungen 2/6. B 1988, Ev.-VA. 178 p. M 12. – ᴿDLZ 110 (1989) 204-7 (G. *Wendelborn*).

k120 **Kirk** J., Patterns of reform; continuity and change in the Reformation Kirk. E 1989, Clark. xxii-516 p. £25 [NRT 112,633, P. *Evrard*].

Klausnitzer Wolfgang, Das Papstamt im Disput zwischen Lutheranern und Katholiken ᴰ1987 → 7989.

k121 **Lecler** Joseph *al.*, Trient [I 1978] II [franç. 1981], ᵀ*Kolbe* F.: Gesch. Ök. Konzilien 11. Mainz 1987, Grünewald. 770 p. – ᴿTLZ 114 (1989) 604-6 (H. *Kirchner*).

k122 **Léonard** Émile G., Histoire générale du protestantisme; I. La réformation; II. L'établissement; III. Déclin et renouveau. P 1988, PUF-Quadrige. 401 p.; 449 p.; 782 p. F 181. – ᴿRHPR 69 (1989) 362s (M. *Arnold*).

k123 **Lods** Marc, Protestantisme et tradition de l'Église, ᴱ*Pérès* J.-N., *Dubois* J.-D.: Patrimoines. F 220. 2-204-03039-2 [JTS 40,743].

k124 **McGrath** Alister E., The intellectual origins of the European reformation 1987 → 3,g536; 4,k107: ᴿJRel 69 (1989) 248s (R. *Zachman*).

k125 **McGrath** Alister E., Reformation thought, an introduction 1988 → 4,k107*; 0-631-15802-2; 3-0: ᴿTLond 52 (1989) 218s (B. M. G. *Reardon*: style breezy but graceless; uses 'legitimate' as a verb).

k126 *Molnár* Amadeo, Ⓦ Contributions to a history of theology of Hussitism, ᵀ*Fóris* Mrs. Eva: TSzem 32 (1989) 18-22.

k127 *Morisi Guerra* Anna, Cultura ebraica ed esegesi biblica cristiana tra Umanesimo e Riforma: → 700, Ebrei/Cristiani 1988, 209-223 (G. *Dahan*).

k128 **Oberman** Heiko A., The dawn of the Reformation [essays 1962-78] 1986 → 3,g542; 4,k110: ᴿJRel 69 (1989) 403-5 (Susan E. *Schreiner*).

k129 **O'Day** Rosemary, The debate on the English reformation. 1986, Routledge-CH. 217 p. $13 pa. 0-416-72680-1 (9802). – ᴿJRel 68 (1988) 106s (W. J. *Tighe*).

k130 *Pani* Giancarlo, Alle origini della Riforma; un dialogo impossibile?: SMSR 55,1 (1989) 99-125.

k131 *Peronnet* Michel, Protestantisme et révolution; quelques réflexions: ÉTRel 64 (1989) 175-189.

k132 **Pettegree** Andrew, Foreign Protestant communities in sixteenth-century London: Oxford Hist. Mg. Ox 1986, Clarendon. 329 p. £27.50. – ᴿRTLv 20 (1989) 247-9 (J.-F. *Gilmont*).

k133 ᴱ**Raitt** Jill, *al.*, Christian spirituality; High Middle Ages and Reformation: EWSp 17, 1987 ➤ 3,862.g545; 4,k114: ᴿHorizons 16 (1989) 160s (G. *Macy*); JTS 40 (1989) 660-2 (A. *Louth*); SpirLife 34 (1988) 110-2 (Elizabeth *Dryer*).

k134 **Russell** Paul A., Lay theology in the Reformation; popular pamphleteers in southwest Germany 1521-5 [analysis of 40 pamphlets of the Tübingen Flugschriften project]. xiv-287 p. $39.50. – ᴿJRel 68 (1988) 107 (R. *Po-chia Hsia*; no publisher or date).

k135 *a*) *Scalise* Pamela J., The Reformers as biblical scholars: – *b*) *Leith* John H., CALVIN's doctrine of the proclamation of the Word and its significance for today in the light of recent research; – *c*) *George* Timothy, Reformation roots of the Baptist tradition; – *d*) *Mueller* David, Karl BARTH and the heritage of the Reformation: RExp 86 (1989) 23-25 / 29-44 / 9-22 / 45-63.

k136 *Selwyn* D. G., The 'Book of Doctrine'; the Lords' debate and the first prayer book of Edward VI; an abortive attempt at doctrinal consensus?: JTS 40 (1989) 446-480.

k137 **Simpler** Steven H., Roland H. BAINTON, an examination of his Reformation historiography: Texts and Studies in Religion 25, 1985 ➤ 2,d578: ᴿRHE 84 (1989) 823s (P. *Denis*: a worthy goal, but nothing new; in a lineup of book reviews).

k138 *a*) *Stauffer* Richard, Riforma e protestantesimo; – *b*) *Taveneaux* René, Il cattolicesimo post-tridentino: ➤ 502, ᴱ*Puech* H.-C., Cristianesimo 1988, 409-511 / 513-610.

k139 *Stein-Schneider* Herbert, La Renaissance dissidente: ÉTRel 64 (1989) 521-533.

k140 **Stinger** C. I., The Renaissance in Rome [1443-1527, distinct from those of Florence and northern Italy]. Bloomington 1985, Indiana Univ. xv-444 p. $37.50. – ᴿCrNSt 10 (1989) 191-3 (R. M. *Bell*).

k141 *Szablewski* Marian, The opposition of the 16th century Reformers to Mass without the participation of the people: AustralasCR 66 (1989) 206-222.

k142 **Vilanova** E., Historia de la teología cristiana [I ➤ g652]; II. [Pre-] Reforma 1986 ➤ 3,g553; 4,k128: ᴿEstFranc 89 (1988) 675-8 (A. *Bosch i Veciana*).

k143 **Wendebourg** Dorothee, Reformation und Orthodoxie; der ökumenische Briefwechsel zwischen der Leitung der Württembergischen Kirche und Patriarch Jeremias II. von Konstantinopel in den Jahren 1573-1581 [ev.Hab.Mü]: ForKDg 37. Gö 1986, VR. 425 p. DM 92. – ᴿTR 85 (1989) 385-394 (M. M. *Garijo-Guembe*: ausgezeichnet).

k144 **Willis** John D., 'Love your enemies'; sixteenth century interpretations: diss. ᴰ*Gerrish* B. Chicago 1989. – RelStR 16, 188.

ᴱ**Zambelli** Paola, 'Astrologi' ... in Luther's time 1984/6 ➤ 768.

Y4.4 Periti aetatis reformatoriae.

k145 ARMINIUS: *Muller* Richard A., Arminius [Jacob, 1559-1609] and the scholastic tradition: CalvinT 24 (1989) 263-277.

k146 ARNDT: **Sommer** Wolfgang, Gottesfurcht und Fürstenherrschaft; Studien zum Obrigkeitsverständnis Johann Arndts und lutherischer Hofprediger zur Zeit der altprotestantischen Orthodoxie. Gö 1988, Vandenhoeck & R. 351 p. – ᴿSvTKv 65 (1989) 177-9 (C. *Braw*).

k147 BELLARMINO: *a) Kuntz* Paul G. [➤ k591], The hierarchical vision [of being] of St. Roberto Bellarmino; – *b) Blumenthal* David R., LOVEJOY's Great chain of being and the medieval Jewish tradition: ➤ 4,375, Jacob's Ladder 1975/87, 111-128 / 179-190.

k148 ᵀᴱ**Donnelly** John P., *Teske* Roland J., Robert Bellarmine, spiritual writings. NY 1989, Paulist. 401 p. [TS 51,563, M. W. *Maher*].

k149 BEZA: ᴱ**Dufour** A., *Nicollier* B. (recueillie par H. *Aubert*) Correspondance de Théodore de Bèze [10s, 1980-3 ➤ 4,k132] 12, 1572: TravHumRen 229. Genève 1988, Droz. 312 p. Fs 120. – ᴿRHE 84 (1989) 292 (J.-F. *Gilmont*: c. 80 lettres).

k150 BUCER: **Pollet** J.V., M. Bucer, études... Pays-Bas 1985 ➤ 1,f838; 3,g563: ᴿRHPR 69 (1989) 370s (M. *Lienhard*).

k151 BUGENHAGEN: *Leder* Hans-Günter, Die Berufung Johannes Bugenhagens in das Wittenberger Stadtpfarramt: TLZ 114 (1989) 481-504.

k152 *Anderson* Niels K., Bugenhagen i Danmark: ➤ ᶠGRANE L., Teologi 1988, 111-130.

k153 **Cochlaeus** Johannes, Responsio ad Johannem Bogenhagium Pomeranum, ᴱ*Keen* R.: BibHumRef 44. Nieuwkoop 1988, de Graaf. 178 p. *f* 80 [TLZ 115,516, H.-G. *Leder*].

k154 CALVIN: *Anderson* Marvin, John Calvin, biblical preacher (1539-1564): ScotJT 42 (1989) 167-181.

k155 **Bell** Charles, Calvin and Scottish theology; the doctrine of assurance [ᴰ1982] 1985 ➤ 3,g568; 4,k140: ᴿScotJT 42 (1989) 127s (J. G. *Levack*).

k156 **Bouwsma** William J., John Calvin; a sixteenth-century portrait 1988 ➤ 4,k141: ᴿChH 58 (1989) 105s (B. G. *Armstrong*); GraceTJ 10 (1989) 108-110 (J. D. *Morrison*); JAAR 57 (1989) 845-8 (E. A. *Dowey*); JRel 69 (1989) 106s (P. I. *Kaufman*); JTS 40 (1989) 677s (B. R. *White*); TS 50 (1989) 188-190 (Jeannine *Olson*).

k157 *Brink* I., THOMAS en Calvijn tezamen ter communie: TsTNijm 29 (1989) 232-248; Eng. 248s.

k158 **Engel** Mary P., John Calvin's perspectival anthropology. Atlanta 1988, Scholars. xv-226 p. $27; pa. $18. – ᴿJRel 69 (1989) 553s (C. *Partee* doubts that he had one).

k159 **Ganoczy** Alexandre, The young Calvin [1966], ᵀ*Foxgrover* David, *Provo* Wade, 1987 ➤ 3,g571; 4,k145; 0-567-09486-3: ᴿExpTim 100 (1988s) 147 (W. I. P. *Hazlett*: in these 20 years he wrote 3 further high-quality monographs on Calvin); RHPR [48 (1968) 54-59, B. *Roussel*] 69 (1989) 69 (M. *Chevallier*).

k160 **Greef** W. de, Johannes Calvijn, zijn werk en geschriften. Kampen 1989, de Groot-G. 236 p. *f* 51 [TR 86,343].

k161 **Leith** John H., John Calvin's doctrine of the Christian life. Louisville 1989, Westminster/Knox. 230 p. $17 [TS 51,177, A. J. *Griffisen*].

k162 **McKee** Elsie Anne, Elders and the plural ministry; the role of exegetical history in illuminating John Calvin's theology. Geneva 1988, Droz. 237 p. – ᴿTTod 46 (1989s) 116 (T. *George*: sequel to her doctorate).

k163 **Perrot** Alain, Le visage humain de Jean Calvin 1986 ➤ 4,k147: ᴿRHPR 69 (1989) 361s (M. *Lienhard*).

k164 ᴱ**Prestwich** Menna, International Calvinism, 1541-1715: 1985 ➤ 3,448: ᴿJRel 68 (1988) 109s (W. F. *Graham*: useful).

k165 **Rutgers** F. L., Calvijns invloed op de Reformatie in de Nederlanden voor zoveel die door hemzelven is uitgeoefend, ᴱ*Spijker* W. van 't. Leeuwarden 1980 = 1901, De Tille. x-250 p. – ᴿRHE 84 (1989) 457s (M. *Gielis*).

k166 **Scheld** Stefan, Media Salutis; zur Heilsvermittlung bei Calvin [Hab.-Diss. Wü 1985, ᴰ*Ganoczy* A.]: Stu 1989, Steiner. ix-274 p. DM 88 [TS 51, 537, F. *Posset*].

k167 *Schützeichel* Heribert, Das altkirchliche Papsttum im Sicht Calvins: Catholica 43 (1989) 31-53.

k168 **Torrance** T. F., The hermeneutics of John Calvin 1988 → 4,k151: ᴿExpTim 100 (1988s) 352s (W. P. *Stephens*); ScotJT 42 (1989) 606s (D. C. *Parker*: title misleading; largely on SCOTUS, OCCAM, and MAJOR); WestTJ 51 (1989) 400-2 (R. C. *Gamble*).

k169 **Wallace** Ronald S., Calvin, Geneva and the Reformation; a study of Calvin as a social reformer, churchman, pastor and theologian 1988 → 4,k153: 0-7073-0512-8: ᴿCalvinT 24 (1989) 378-381 (R. C. *Gamble*); ExpTim 100 (1988s) 475s (P. N. *Brooks*); PrPeo 3 (1989) 235-7 (sr. Cecily *Boulding*).

k170 **Walt** Jansie van der, Calvin and his times. Potchefstrom 1985, Univ. 154 p. → 739. – ᴿEvQ 61 (1989) 283 (A. N. S. *Lane*).

k171 **Won Jong-Chun** Jonathan, Communion with Christ ... in Calvin and the English Puritans: diss. ᴰ*Ferguson* S., Westminster Theol. Sem. 387 p. 89-18224. – DissA 50 (1989s) 1344-A.

k172 CANO: *Horst* Ulrich, Die *Loci theologici* Melchior Canos und sein Gutachten zum *Catechismo Christiano* Bartolomé CARRANZAS: FreibZ 36 (1989) 47-92.

k173 COLET 1467-1519: **Pressley** Johnny G., John Colet and the Bible; guidelines for the interpretation of Scripture: diss. Westminster Theol. Sem., ᴰ*Barker* W. 1989. 451 p. 89-18225. – DissA 50 (1988s) 1340s-A.

k174 CRUCIUS: *Desmet-Goethals* M.-J., Levinus Crucius en de Reformatie [résumé diss. 1985]: De Franse Nederlanden 14 (1989) 11-23 [< RHE 85,183].

k175 DRUSIUS: *Fletcher* J. M., *Upton* C. A., John Drusius of Flanders [at Oxford 1572-6], Thomas BODLEY and the development of Hebrew studies at Merton College, Oxford: → 802, Academic relations 1987/9, 111-129.

k176 DUNGERSHEIM: ᴱ**Freudenberger** Theobald, Hieronymus Dungersheim, Schriften gegen Luther 1987 → 3,g587; 4,k154: ᴿRHE 84 (1989) 179 (P. *Denis*); RHPR 69 (1989) 366s (M. *Arnold*); TPhil 64 (1989) 271s (K. *Schatz*); TR 85 (1989) 117s (B. *Lohse*).

k176* **Freudenberger** T., H. Dungersheim von Ochsenfurt am Main 1465-1540; Theologieprof. in Leipzig, Leben und Schriften: RefGStT 126. Münster 1988, Aschendorff. xix-423 p. – ᴿTR 85 (1989) 465s (P. *Schäfer*).

k177 ECK: **Iserloh** E., Johannes Eck (1486-1543) im Streit der Jahrhunderte: RST 127. Münster 1988, Aschendorff. iv-274 p. [RHPR 69,91].

k178 ERASMUS: *Bierlaire* F., Érasme et RABELAIS; d'un anticléricalisme à l'autre?: ProbHistChr 18 ('Aspects de l'anticléricalisme du moyen âge à nos jours, ᴱ*Marx* J. 1988) 35-45 [+ 7 art., 197 p.: RHE 84,95*].

k179 **DeMolen** Richard L., The spirituality of Erasmus [8 reprints] 1988 → 4,k156: ᴿAndrUnS 27 (1989) 139s (K. A. *Strand*); ChH 50 (1989) 380-2 (J. M. *Weiss*: some weaknesses); TLZ 114 (1989) 127s (C. *Augustijn*).

k180 *Häring* Hermann, Naar een nieuwe omschrijving van vrijheid; Erasmus' diskussie met Luther: TsTNijm 29 (1989) 19-36; Eng. 36s.

k181 **Halkin** Léon-E., Érasme parmi nous: Grandes Études Historiques. P 1987, Fayard. 499 p. – RHZ 248 (1989) 699s (A. *Buck*); RHE 84 (1989) 743-6 (R. *Aubert*).

k182 **Krüger** Friedhelm, Humanistische Evangelienauslegung... Erasmus 1986 ➤ 3,g591; 4,k157: RSalesianum 51 (1989) 565s (P. T. *Stella*).

k183 **Schoeck** R. J., Erasmus grandescens; the growth of a humanist's mind and spirituality: BibHumRef 43. Nieuwkoop 1988, De Graaf. 260 p. – RRHE 84 (1989) 646 (L.-E. *Halkin*: agreeable).

k184 **Screech** M. A., Erasmus; ecstasy and the praise of folly. Hmw 1988, Penguin. xxiv-267 p. £6. 0-14-055235-9. – RExpTim 100 (1988s) 355s (W. P. *Stephens*).

k185 **Seidel Menchi** Silvana, Erasmo in Italia, 1520-1580: Nuova cultura 1, 1987 ➤ 4,k163: RFilT 3 (1989) 235-8 (Anna Maria *Negri*); RHE 84 (1989) 452-6 (J.-F. *Gilmont*); RivStoLR 25 (1989) 356-9 (L. *D'Ascia*).

k187 **Walter** Peter, Theologie aus dem Geist der Rhetorik; zur Hermeneutik des Erasmus von Rotterdam: kath. HDiss. DKasper W. Tübingen 1988s. – TR 85 (1989) 511.

k188 EWeiland Jan S., Erasmus von Rotterdam, die Aktualität seines Denkens [1986], THübner A. Ha 1988, Wittig. 183 p.; ill. [TLZ 115, 356-8, S. *Bräuer*].

k189 **Zweig** Stefan, Érasme, grandeur et décadence d'une idée: Les Cahiers Rouges 91. P 1988, Grasset. 252 p. F 43. – REsprVie 99 (1989) 95 (C. *Jean-Nesmy*).

k190 FLACIUS: **Keller** Rudolf, Der Schlüssel zur Schrift... bei M. Flacius 1984 ➤ 2,d653; 4,k166: RLuthTKi 12 (1988) 27s (M. *Roensch*).

k191 HOFFMAN: **Deppermann** Klaus, Melchior Hoffman 1987 ➤ 3,g600; 4,k168: RScotJT 42 (1989) 267s (D. *Butler*: good but needs G. WILLIAMS Radical Reformation as briefing).

k192 HUBMAIER: TEPipkin H. Wayne, *Yoder* John H. Balthasar Hubmaier, theologian of Anabaptism: Classics of the Radical Reformation 5. Scottsdale PA 1989, Herald. 608 p. $40. – RSWJT 32,2 (1989s) 52s (W. R. *Estep*).

Rickauer Hans-Christian, Rechtfertigung und Heil... K. KLINGE: ErfTSt 53, 1986 ➤ H7.

k193 LAMBERT: EFraenkel Pierre, [surtout *Bodenmann* Reinhard], Pour retrouver François Lambert [1486-1530, Frère Mineur devenu réformateur en Hesse], bio-bibliographie et études: Bibliotheca bibliographica aureliana 108. Baden-Baden 1987, Koerner. 303 p.; ill. – RRHE 84 (1989) 515s (J.-F. *Gilmont*).

k194 MALDONADO: **Schmitt** Paul, La réforme catholique; le combat de Maldonat (1534-1583): THist 74, 1985 ➤ 1,f589...4,k176: RSR 18 (1989) 384s (P. *Boglioni*).

k195 MOLLER: **Axmacher** Elke, Praxis Evangeliorum; Theologie und Frömmigkeit bei Martin Moller (1547-1606): ForKDG 43. Gö 1989, Vandenhoeck & R. 370 p.; 1 fig.; 1 pl. DM 78 pa. [TLZ 115,605, E. *Koch*].

k196 MÜNTZER: *a*) *Schwarz* Reinhard, Thomas Müntzers hermeneutisches Prinzip der Schriftvergleichung; – *b*) *Wolgast* Eike, Beobachtungen und Fragen zu T. Müntzers Gefangenschaftsaussagen 1525: LuJb 56 (1989) 11-25 / 26-50 [< TLZ 115,93, E. *Koch*: 'ergiebig'].

k196* *Bräuer* Siegfried, Die Kirche der Auserwählten; Thomas Müntzers Beitrag zur Reformation: EvKomm 22,7 (1989) 34-36.

k197 **Gritsch** Eric W., Thomas Müntzer [b. 1498]: a tragedy of errors. Minneapolis 1989, Fortress. xii-157 p. [TS 51, 371, F. *Posset*].

k197* *Waite* G. K., From apocalyptic crusaders to Anabaptist terrorists; Anabaptist radicalism after Müntzer 1535-1544: ArRelG 80 (1989) 173-193; map [< RHE 85,106*].

k198 *Wartenberg* Günther, Auslegung der Heiligen Schrift bei Thomas Müntzer und Martin Luther: Standpunkt 17 (1989) 79-... [< ZIT 89,382].

k199 MURNER: **Miskuly** John M. The defense of Catholic Eucharistic theology in the anti-Reformation writings of Thomas Murner, 'Unser hürt. hieter und Vorfechter der christlichen Schefflin' 1520-1529: Diss. D*Bäumer*. Freiburg/B 1988s. – TR 85 (1989) 515.

k200 PETRI L. *Dewailly* L.-M., a) [Index des thèmes et des citations bibliques] Kyrkohistorisk årsskrift (1986) 111-6; – b) Laurentius Petri et la Kyrkoordning de 1571: Istina 30 (1985) 228-320 [RHE 84 (1989) 831s (R. *Aubert*)]. – [livre 1984] RRHPR 68 (1988) 367-9 (R. *Kick*).

k200* PETRI O.: **Gardemeister** Christer, Den soveräne Guden; en studie i Olavus Petris teologi: STLund 43. Lund 1989, Univ. 304 p. SK 249 [TLZ 115, 751-3, B. *Hägglund*].

k201 SCHATZGEYER: **Schäfer** Philipp, Kaspar Schatzgeyer, Von der waren Christlichen und Evangelischen freyheit...: CCath 40, 1987 ⟶ 4,k180: RTR 85 (1989) 34s (B. *Lohse*).

k202 SCHWENCKFELD: *Derville* André, Schwenckfeld (Gaspard) 1489-1561: ⟶ 886, DictSpir 14,92s (1989) 451-3.

k203 **McLaughlin** R. E., C. Schwenckfeld, reluctant radical 1986 ⟶ 2,d664 ...4,k181: REngHR 104 (1989) 474s (H. M. *Höpfl*).

k204 SPALATIN: **Höss** Irmgard, Georg Spalatin, 1484-1545; ein Leben in der Zeit des Humanismus und der Reformation. Weimar 1989, Böhlau. xxxviii-478 p.; 9 pl. [JTS 41, 751-3, A. *McGrath*].

k205 TURRETTINI: *Bolognesi* Pietro, Un théologien oublié, François Turrettini: RRéf 40,2 (1989) 36-42 [< ZIT 89,381].

k206 TYNDALE: **Smeeton** Donald D., Lollard themes in... Tyndale 1986 ⟶ 3,g613; 4,k183: REvQ 61 (1989) 167s (D. F. *Wright*); ScotBEv 7 (1989) 125s (R. T. *Jones*).

k207 VELIUS: **Honée** Eugène, Der Libell des Hieronymus Velius zum Augsburger Reichstag 1530; Untersuchung und Text zur katholischen Concordia-Politik: rst 125. Münster 1987, Aschendorff. xvii-362 p. DM 98. – RTPQ 137 (1989) 89 (R. *Bäumer*); TüTQ 169 (1989) 149s (R. *Reinhardt*).

k208 VIRET: **Bavaud** G., Le Réformateur Pierre Viret; sa théologie 1986 ⟶ 2,d667; 3,g615: RNRT 111 (1989) 266s (P. *Evrard*); Protestantesimo 44 (1989) 229s (F. *Ferrario*).

k209 WYCLIF: **Hudson** Anne, The premature Reformation; Wycliffite texts and Lollard history 1988 ⟶ 4,k188*: RRHE 84 (1989) 250 (D. *Bradley*).

k210 EKenny Anthony, Wyclif in his time. Ox 1986, UP. 174 p. $42. 0-19-820088-9 [Not = 1985 ⟶ 1,f870]. – RHeythJ 30 (1989) 200-2 (N. P. *Tanner*); RechSR 76 (1988) 623s (P. *Vallin*).

k211 *Kenny* Anthony, Wyclif: Master-Mind lecture: ProcBritAcad 72 (1986) 91-113 [< RHE 84 (1989) 249 (R. *Aubert*)].

k212 *Holeton* David, Wyclif's Bohemian fate [i.e. success]: ComViat 32 (1989) 209-222.

k213 ZWINGLI: *Dellsperger* Rudolf, Das Zwinglijahr 1984 und die Zwingli-forschung: VerkF 34,2 (1989) 24-38.
k214 **Gäbler** Ulrich, Huldrych Zwingli, his life and work 1986 → 2,d671 ...4,k194: ᴿJTS 40 (1989) 672-6 (B. *Hall*, also on STEPHENS); ScotJT 42 (1989) 123-5 (W.P. *Stephens*).
k215 **Hamm** Berndt, Zwinglis Reformation der Freiheit. Neuk 1988, Neuk-V. xiii-154p. DM 28 [TLZ 115,116-8, J. *Rogge*].
k216 **Pollet** J.V., H. Zwingli: *a*) et le zwinglianisme. 1988. x-444p.; − *b*) biographie et théologie. 1988. 115p. − ᴿRHPR 69 (1989) 368s (J. *Rott*).
k217 **Stephens** W.P., The theology of H. Zwingli 1986 → 2,d674...4,k198: ᴿEvQ 61 (1989) 285s (D.F. *Wright*); HeythJ 30 (1989) 368-371 (J.K. *Cameron*); JRel 68 (1988) 108s (E.J. *Furcha*); TLZ 114 (1989) 900s (W.H. *Neuser*).

Y4.5 *Exegesis post-reformatoria* − **Historical criticism to 1800.**

k218 *Adriányi* Gabriel, Ⓜ Counter-Reformation or Catholic revival? The way of Catholic reform in 17th century Hungary, ᵀ*Fóris* Mrs. Éva: TSzem 32 (1989) 12ss.
k219 **Balmer** Randall, A perfect Babel of confusion; Dutch religion and English culture in the Middle Colonies: Religion in America. NY 1989, Oxford-UP. xi-258p. $25 [TrinJ 10,239].
k220 ᴱ**Belaval** Yvon, *Bourel* Dominique, Le siècle des Lumières et la Bible: BTT 7, 1986 → 2,237...4,k202: ᴿRÉJ 147 (1988) 250-2 (D. *Tollet*); ZAW 101 (1989) 169 (T. *Klein*).
k221 **Betts** C.J., Early Deism in France [...1564-1734], ᴰ1984 → 65,d741; 2,d679: ᴿRHPR 68 (1988) 370s (M. *Chevallier*).
k222 *Cabibbo* S., 'Ignoratio Scripturarum, ignoratio Christi est'; tradizione e pratica delle Scritture nei testi monastici femminili del XVII sec.: RSL 101 (1989) 85-124 [< RHE 85,116*].
k223 *Dickson* D.R., The complexities of biblical typology in the XVIIth cent.: Renaissance and Reformation 23 (1987) 253-272 [RHE 84,33*].
k224 ᴱ**Drury** John, Critics of the Bible 1724-1873: English Prose Texts. C 1989, Univ. ix-204p. 0-521-32992-2; pa.-3870-0. P. 21-45, *Collins* Anthony; 46-68, *Sherlock* Thomas; 69-102, *Lowth* Robert; 103s, *Blake* W.; 105-121, *Coleridge* S.T.; 122-136, *Arnold* Thomas; 137-151, *Jowett* Benjamin; 152-192, *Arnold* Matthew; 102-204 footnotes, bibliog.
k225 **Everdell** William R., Christian apologetics in France, 1730-1790; the roots of romantic religion. Lewiston NY 1987, Mellen. 353p. − ᴿRHR 206 (1989) 196s (Sylviane *Albertan-Coppola*).
k226 *Fernández Marcos* N., La Biblia y la revolución francesa [ᴱ*Belaval* Y., BTT 7, 1986]: Sefarad 49 (1989) 159-166.
k227 **Funkenstein** Amos, Theology and the scientific imagination... to 17th cent. 1986 → 4,k205: ᴿHeythJ 30 (1989) 242s (Sascha *Talmor*).
k228 *Hengst* Karl, Die Academia Theodoriana zu Paderborn; Westfalens älteste Universität [1614, 165 Jahre vor Münster; Jesuiten(-kolleg) seit 1580]: TGL 79 (1989) 350-378 [379-88-459, *Schmitz* Karl-J., kunsthistorisch; *al.*].
k229 *Karlberg* Mark W., Moses and Christ — the place of the Law in seventeenth-century Puritanism: TrinJ 10,1 (1989) 11-32.
k230 **Laplanche** François, L'Écriture, le sacré et l'histoire; érudits et politiques protestants devant la Bible en France au XVIIᵉ siècle 1986 → 2,d684; 4,k208: ᴿRechSR 76 (1988) 616-8 (P. *Vallin*); RÉJ 148 (1989)

442-5 (B. E. *Schwarzbach*); RTPhil 121 (1989) 120s (Maria-Cristina *Pitassi*).

k231 *Laplanche* François, Entre mythe et raison; l'exégèse biblique des Protestants français au XVIIe siècle: FoiVie 88 (1989) 3-20.

k232 **Martin** Jean-Pierre, Le puritanisme américain en Nouvelle-Angleterre (1620-1693). Bordeaux 1989, Presses Univ. 260 p.; map. – ^RFoiVie 88 (1989) 155-7 (J. *Blondel*).

k233 **Muller** Richard A., Post-Reformation Reformed dogmatics I, 1987 → 4,k210: ^RWestTJ 50 (1988) 364-370 (M. W. *Karlberg*).

k234 **Northeast** Catherine M., The Parisian Jesuits and the Enlightenment (1700-1762): diss. Oxford 1988. 350 p. BRD-86678. – DissA 50 (1989s) 2533-A.

k235 **Pelikan** Jaroslav J., Christian doctrine and modern culture (since 1700): The Christian tradition; a history of the development of doctrine [1-4, 1972-74-78-84] 5th and last volume. Ch 1989, Univ. xlix-361 p. $30. 0-226-6537[0-6; 2-2; 4-9; 6-5]-8-1 [TDig 37,81]. – ^RSWJT 32,3 (1989s) 59 (E. E. *Ellis*).

k236 **Podskalsky** Gerhard, Griechische Theologie... 1452-1821: 1988 → 3, g633; 4,k211: ^RFreibZ 36 (1989) 519-524 (M. *Brun*); OrChrPer 55 (1989) 230-3 (G. *Fedalto*); RÉByz 47 (1989) 302s (A. *Failler*); RechSR 77 (1989) 314-6 (P. *Vallin*).

k237 **Rupp** Ernest G., Religion in England 1688-1791: 1986 → 3,g635: ^RScotJT 42 (1989) 270-2 (G. S. *Wakefield*).

k238 **Simonutti** L., Arminianesimo e tolleranza nel Seicento olandese. F 1984, Olschki. 176 p. Lit. 34.000. – ^RProtestantesimo 44 (1989) 144s (G. *Long*).

k239 **Stam** F. P. van, The controversy over the theology of Saumur, 1635-1650; disrupting debates among the Huguenots in complicated circumstances, ^T*Vriend* John: Nijmegen Bayle Inst. St. 19. Amst 1988, APA-Holland. xiv-497 p. – ^RCalvinT 24 (1989) 376-8 (B. G. *Armstrong* mentions several recent researches on this squabble).

k240 **Trevor-Roper** Hugh, Catholics, Anglicans and Puritans; seventeenth century essays [5 inedita] 1988 → 4,274: ^RTS 50 (1989) 371s (J. E. *Booty*).

---

k241 BUNYAN (1628-1688): **Hill** Christopher, *a)* A turbulent, seditious, and factious people; John Bunyan and his church. Ox 1988, Clarendon. xxi-394 p. £19.50 [JTS 41, 759, B. *White*]. – *b)* A tinker and a poor man; John Bunyan and his church, 1628-1688. NY 1988, Knopf. xx-394 p. $23. – ^RRelStR 16 (1990) 354 (Loretta T. *Johnson*).

k242 CALMET: *Marsauche* P., La musique guérit les mélancolies; étude sur le Commentaire de dom Calmet [sur tous les livres de l'ANT 1707-1716]: → 1295, ^E*Tardieu* M., Les règles de l'interprétation 1987, 195-207 [< RHE 85,219].

k243 CAMUS J.-P. 1584-1642: *Bavaud* Georges, Un essai de dialogue œcuménique au XVIIe siècle: ÉchSM 19 (1989) 119-130.

k244 EDWARDS: **Holbrook** Clyde A., Jonathan Edwards, the valley and nature; an interpretive essay. Cranbury NJ 1987, Bucknell Univ. 151 p. $24.50. – ^RJRel 69 (1989) 250 (W. C. *Gilpin*).

k245 **Jenson** Robert W., America's theologian... J. Edwards 1988 → 4,k216: ^RChH 50 (1989) 520-2 (M. *Vetö*).

k246 **Murray** Iain H., J. Edwards. E 1987, Banner of Truth. xxxi-503 p. £11.
– ᴿEvQ 61 (1989) 168-170 (T. *Baxter*).

k247 **Vető** Miklós, La pensée de Jonathan Edwards 1987 ⇥ 3,g643:
ᴿFreibZ 36 (1989) 220-3 (R. *Kühn*); LavalTP 44 (1988) 416s (E. *Brito*);
RHPR 69 (1989) 75s (Marie-Jeanne *Kœnig*); TPhil 64 (1989) 103s (auch
R. *Kühn*).

k248 **Whittemore** Robert C., The transformation of the New England
theology [... Jonathan Edwards ... Samuel WILLARD, Samuel HARRIS]:
American Univ. Studies 7/232. NY 1987, Lang. viii-437 p. $55. –
ᴿCalvinT 24 (1989) 171-5 (P. Y. *DeJong*); EvQ 61 (1989) 366-8 (A. P. F.
Sell).

k249 ENGEL: *Lienhard* Marc, La foi chrétienne à l'heure de la Révolution;
l'itinéraire spirituel et politique du pasteur alsacien Mathias Engel
(1755-1811): RHPR 69 (1989) 461-473; Eng. 509.

k250 FÉNELON: *Leuenberger* Robert, Die Verurteilung Fénelons durch Rom
[1699], Darstellung eines Gewissenskonflikts: ZTK 86 (1989) 157-178.

k251 FRANCKE: *Peschke* Erhard, Die frühen Katechismuspredigten August
H. Franckes 1693-1695: TLZ 114 (1989) 561-578.

k252 HAMANN: **Lindner** Helgo, J. G. Hamann, Aufbruch zu biblischen Denken: Theologie und Dienst 54. Giessen 1988, Brunnen. 55 p. DM 7,80.
– ᴿTLZ 114 (1989) 210s (M. *Seils*).

k253 HERDER: **Fürst** G., Sprache als metaphorischer Process; J. G. Herders
hermeneutische Theorie der Sprache: TüTheolSt 31. Mainz 1988,
Grünewald. 436 p. [NRT 112, 438, B. *Pottier*].

k254 **Pältz** Eberhard, Zur Edition von J. G. Herders Briefen der Jahre
1788-1803 [*Dobbek* W., *Arnold* G. 1981-8]: TLZ 114 (1989) 401-414.

k255 ANNE HUTCHINSON: **Lang** Amy S., Prophetic woman; Anne Hut-
chinson and the problem of dissent in the literature of New England.
Berkeley 1987, Univ. California. xii-237 p. $28. – ᴿJRel 68 (1988) 456s
(J. F. *Maclear*).

k256 JANSENIUS: **Ceyssens** L., *Tans* J., Autour de l'Unigenitus 1987 ⇥ 3,
g648; 4,k225: ᴿCrNSt 10 (1989) 640s (J. *Le Brun*, franç.)

k257 *Ceyssens* Lucien, Autour de la bulle 'Unigenitus'; le cardinal André
Hercule de FLEURY (1653-1747): Bulletin de l'Institut historique belge de
Rome 58 (1988) 149-185 [< RHE 85,175].

k258 *Ceyssens* Lucien, Autour de la Bulle Unigenitus; la déclaration, dernière
illusion et ultime désillusion de Louis XIV: RHE 84 (1989) 1-29.

k259 *Ceyssens* Lucien, sur 'le Cardinal d'Alsace' [⇥ 4,k226b comme RBgPg
66,792] = Thomas-Philippe Liétard, archévêque de Malines; et plusieurs
autres études présentées en détail: RHE 84 (1989) 539-542 (R. *Aubert*).

k260 *Ceyssens* Lucien, La bulle *Vineam domini* (1705) et le jansénisme français:
Antonianum 64 (1989) 398-430; Eng. 398.

k261 ᴱ**Eijl** Edmond J. M. van, L'image de C. Jansenius 1985/7 ⇥ 4,557:
ᴿCarthaginensia 5 (1989) 324s (V. *Sánchez*); NRT 111 (1989) 267 (N.
Plumat); RHE 84 (1989) 466-9 (J. *Orcibal*); RTLv 20 (1989) 249s (J.-F.
Gilmont); ZkT 111 (1989) 109s (K. H. *Neufeld*).

k263 **Tans** Joseph A. G., Lexicon pseudonymorum jansenisticorum; répertoire des noms d'emprunt employés au cours de l'histoire du jansénisme et
de l'antijansénisme: InstrTheol 4. Lv 1989, Bibliotheek Fac. Godge-
leerdheid. 224 p. Fb 800 [TR 86,251].

k264 LA PEYRÈRE: **Popkin** R., I. La Peyrère 1987 ⇥ 4,k229: ᴿJTS 40
(1989) 685s (J. *Barr*).

k265 LE CLERC: **Pitassi** Maria Cristina, Entre croire et savoir; le problème de la méthode critique chez Jean Le Clerc: Kerkhistorische Bijdragen 14, 1987 ➤ 3,g658: ᴿChH 50 (1989) 396s (W. A. *Poe*); RÉJ 147 (1988) 470s (B. E. *Schwarzbach*).

k266 — ᴱ**Sina** Mario, J. Le Clerc, epistolario I, 1679-1689. F 1987, Olschki. 566 p. Lit. 87.000. – ᴿCrNSt 10 (1989) 642-4 (M. *Micheletti*: hostile to R. SIMON; finds Henry HAMMOND's NT Annotations incomparable).

k267 L'EMPEREUR: **Rooden** Peter T. van, Theology, biblical scholarship and rabbinical studies in the seventeenth century; Constantijn L'Empereur (1591-1648): Studies in the History of Leiden University 6. Leiden 1989, Brill. xi-268 p. 90-04-09035-5.

k268 LESSING: **Lüpke** Johannes, Wege der Weisheit; Studien zu Lessings Theologiekritik: GöTheolArb 41. Gö 1989, Vandenhoeck & R. 261 p. DM 54 [TLZ 115, 527-9, H. *Schultze*].

k269 **Michalson** G. E., Lessing's 'ugly ditch' 1985 ➤ 1,f906...4,k230: ᴿScot-JT 42 (1989) 253-5 (A. C. *Thiselton*).

k270 **Niewöhner** Friedrich, Veritas sive Varietas; Lessings Toleranzparabel und das Buch Von den drei Betrügern: Bibliothek der Aufklärung 5. Heid 1988, Schneider. 428 p. [TPhil 64,480].

MOLINA Luis de, on divine foreknowledge: **Freddoso** A. 1988 ➤ 7044.

k271 OWEN: *Smith* Christopher R., 'Up and be doing'; the pragmatic Puritan eschatology of John Owen: EvQ 61 (1989) 335-349.

k272 REIMARUS: *Gericke* Wolfgang. Zur theologischen Entwicklung von H. S. Reimarus: TLZ 114 (1989) 859-862.

k273 **Lötzsch** Frieder, Was ist 'Ökologie' [≅ göttliche Vorsehung bei] H. S. Reimarus; ein Beitrag zur Geistesgeschichte des 18. Jhts. Köln 1987, Böhlau. xxxvi-350 p. DM 78. – ᴿTLZ 114 (1989) 375s (G. *Hornig*: Titel nicht glücklich).

k274 SEMLER: **Schulz** H. H. R., Johann S. Semlers Wesensbestimmung des Christentums; ein Beitrag zur Erforschung der Theologie Semlers [Diss. Bochum, ᴰ*Hornig* G.]. Wü 1988, Königshausen & N. viii-255 p. DM 48. 3-88479-355-1 [NTAbs 33,266]. – ᴿTR 85 (1989) 306s (P. *Schäfer*).

k275 *Sommer* Wolfgang, Die Stellung Semlers und SCHLEIERMACHERS zu den reformatorischen Bekenntnisschriften, ein theologiegeschichtlicher Vergleich: KerDo 35 (1989) 296-315; Eng. 315.

k276 SIMON: **McKane** William, Selected Christian hebraists [ORIGEN, JEROME; ANDREW of St. Victor, G. MARTIN; R. Simon, A. GEDDES; Catholics except W. FULKE]. C 1989, Univ. 268 p. $49.50. 0-521-35507-8 [TDig 37,170].

k277 SPINOZA: *Dethloff* Klaus, Spinoza und das Problem der jüdischen Identität: Kairos 30s (1988s) 25-29.

k278 *Gire* Pierre, Spinoza devant le Christ: EsprVie 99 (1989) 577-582.

k279 ᵀ**Vallée** Gérard, al., The Spinoza conversations between LESSING and JACOBI; texts with excerpts from the ensuing controversy. Lanham 1988, UPA. 174 p. $26.50; pa. $13,75 [TLZ 115, 620-2, U. *Kern*].

k280 **Meyer** Louis [1630-1681, ami de Spinoza], La philosophie interprète de l'Écriture Sainte, ᵀ*Lagrée* Jacqueline, *Moreau* Pierre-F., P 1989, Intertextes. 267 p. F 149. 2-904593-02-0. – ᴿÉTRel 64 (1989) 448s (H. *Bost*); RSPT 73 (1989) 151-4 (L. *Bove* donne la date '1966 [?pour 1666], 4 ans avant le Tractatus' de Spinoza).

k281 STENSEN † 1686: *Wieh* H., *Jaschke* H.-J., *Scheele* P.-W., Niels-Stensen-Gedenken: TJb (1988) 277-295-307-326.

k282 TÖLLNER: **Pfizenmaier** M., Mit Vernunft glauben, fides ratione formata; die Umformung der Rechtfertigungslehre in der Theologie der deutschen Aufklärung dargestellt am Werk J. G. Töllners (1724-1744): Theol. Mg B-10. Stu 1986, Callwer. xxxiii-618 p. – ᴿCrNSt 10 (1989) 201 (Elisabeth *Kovács*).

k283 VICO (1668-1744): *Olivier* Paul, À propos de Vico [4 éditions, 4 études]: RechSR 76 (1988) 283-300.

k284 VOLTAIRE: ᵀᴱ**Capriglione** F., Voltaire, storia dell'affermazione del Cristianesimo [1726-9, inedito fino a 1785, ²1796: solo adesso in italiano]: Altair 36. Foggia 1987, Bastogi. 117 p. Lit. 12.000. – ᴿProtestantesimo 44 (1989) 232s (Elena *Bein Ricco*).

k285 **Whelan** Ruth, The anatomy of superstition; a study of the historical theory and practice of Pierre BAYLE: Studies on Voltaire 259. Ox 1989, Voltaire Found. xi-269 p. £44. 0-7294-0372-6. – ᴿÉTRel 64 (1989) 587-591 (H. *Bost*).

k286 WESLEY C. & J.: **Dallimore** Arnold A., A heart set free; the life of Charles Wesley (1707-1788). Westchester IL 1988, Crossway. 272 p. – ᴿCalvinT 24 (1989) 331s (Helen *Westra*).

k287 **Gunter** W. Stephen, The limits of 'love divine'; John Wesley's response to antinomianism and enthusiasm. Nv 1989, Abingdon. 368 p. $16 [TS 51, 341-3, J. D. *Nelson*].

k288 ᴱ**Outler** Albert C., [†1.IX.1989] The works of John Wesley, 1-4 (sermons). Nv, Abingdon. I. 1984, xxi-772 p.; II. 1985, xv-624 p.; III. 1986, xv-654 p.; IV. 1987, xix-638 p. $50 each. [RelStR 16, 120-3, J. D. *Nelson*].

k289 — *Tyson* John R., Sin, self and society; John Wesley's hamartiology reconsidered [108 sermons, ᴱ*Outler* A. 1984]: AsbTJ 44,2 (1989) 77-89.

k290 WIEST: **Müller** Bernhard, Vernunft und Theologie; eine historisch-systematische Untersuchung zum Verhältnis von Denken und Glauben bei Stephan Wiest (1748-1797) [Diss.]: Eichstätter Studien NF 26. Rg 1988, Pustet. 536 p. 3-7917-1177-6. – ᴿActuBbg 26 (1989) 218s (J. *Boada*).

Y5 *Saeculum XIX* – Exegesis – 19th Century.

k291 ᴱ**Armogathe** Jean-Robert, Le Grand Siècle et la Bible: BTT 6. P 1989, Beauchesne. 834 p. F 480 [CBQ 52,378].

k292 **Bebbington** David W., Evangelicalism in modern Britain; a history from the 1730s to the 1980s. L 1988, Unwin Hyman. xi-364 p. £35; pa. £12 [JTS 41, 765s, H. C. G. *Matthew*].

k292* **Berkhof** Hendrikus, Two hundred years of theology; report of a personal journey, ᵀ*Vriend* John. GR 1989, Eerdmans. xx-316 p. $25 [JTS 41,826].

k293 **Brown** Colin, Jesus in European Protestant thought, 1778-1860 [< diss. Bristol]. GR 1988, Baker. xxiv-359 p. 0-8010-0954-5. – ᴿExpTim 100 (1988s) 351 (N. T. *Wright*).

k294 **Cameron** N., Biblical higher criticism and the defense of infallibilism in 19th century Britain ᴰ1987 → 3,g684: ᴿScotJT 42 (1989) 613-5 (P. *Helm*).

k295 **Cashdollar** Charles D., The transformation of theology 1830-1890; Positivism and Protestant thought in Britain and America. Princeton 1989, Univ. xii-489 p. $35. – ᴿCommonweal 116 (1989) 540 (L. S. *Cunningham*); TTod 46 (1989s) 436-8 (J. H. *Moorhead*).

k296 **Corrington** Robert S., The community of interpreters; on the hermeneutics of nature and the Bible in the American philosophical

tradition [EMERSON, PEIRCE, ROYCE]. Macon GA 1987, Mercer Univ. xiii-
111 p. $25. – ᴿCCurr 39 (1989s) 230-2 (J. *Campbell*).
k297 **Faherty** William B.,   Rebels or reformers? Dissenting priests in
American life. Ch 1987, Loyola Univ. 123 p. $10. – ᴿChH 50 (1989) 411s
(J. M. *McShane*: breezy, serious).
k298 **Fogarty** Gerald P.,   American Catholic biblical scholarship; a history
from the early Republic to Vatican II, 1989 → 4,k245; 0-06-062666-0:
ᴿAmerica 161 (1989) 17s (J. *Blenkinsopp*); Commonweal 116 (1989) 511
(J. L. *McKenzie*); NewTR 2,4 (1989) 100s (C. *Stuhlmueller*); TTod 46
(1989s) 318s (R. E. *Murphy*: a gripping story, in which the reviewer
played a modest role).
k299 *Fogarty* Gerald P.,   American Catholic biblical scholarship; a review: TS
50 (1989) 219-243.
k300 ᴱ**Frerichs** Ernest S.,   The Bible and Bibles in America 1988 → 4,300:
ᴿAnStoEseg 6 (1989) 309s (*ipse*).
k301 *Goguel* Anne-Marie,   Les Protestants face au premier centenaire [1889!]
de la révolution française: ÉTRel 64 (1989) 489-519.
k302 *Hennesey* James,   Catholicism in an American environment; the early
years: TS 50 (1989) 657-675.
k303 **Hilton** Boyd,   The age of atonement; the influence of evangelicalism on
social and economic thought, 1795-1865.   Ox 1988, Clarendon.   xiii-
407 p. £35. – ᴿEngHR 104 (1989) 136-142 (G. E. *Rothenberg*).
k304 **Hughes** Richard T., *Allen* C. Leonard,   Illusions of innocence; Protestant
primitivism in America, 1630-1875: 1988 → 4,k248: ᴿTTod 46 (1989s)
234.236 (H. W. *Bowden*).
k305 **Marty** Martin E.,   Modern American religion I, 1986 → 2,d739
...4,k254: ᴿHeythJ 30 (1989) 214s (B. *Aspinwall*: refreshing).
k306 **Mead** Sidney E.,   Das Christentum in Nordamerika; Glaube und
Religionsfreiheit in vier Jahrhunderten [1963],ᵀ 1987 → 4,k254*; Einl.
Penzel K.; DM 48: ᴿTR 85 (1989) 488-490 (J. *Maier*).
k307 **Moore** R. Laurence,   Religious outsiders and the making of Americans
1986 → 3,g694: ᴿAndrUnS 26 (1988) 307s (G. R. *Knight*).
k308 ᴱ**Noll** M. A.,   The Princeton defense of plenary verbal inspiration [9
essays 1857-1926; one of a 45-volume facsimile series]: Fundamentalism
in American religion 1880-1950. NY 1988, Garland. xvii-278 p. $47.
0-8240-5020-7 [NTAbs 33,238].
k309 ᴱ**Smart** N. *al.*,   Nineteenth century religious thought 1985 → 1,399.f934
...4,k258: ᴿQRMin 9,3 (1989) 100-110 (F. J. *Streng*).
Smend Rudolf,   Deutsche Alttestamentler in drei Jahrhunderten 1989
→ 358.
k310 *Wartenberg* G.,   Zur Erforschung des Neuen Testaments an der
Leipziger theologischer Fakultät im 19, Jahrhundert: Abh Sächs. Akad.
ph/h 71 (B 1987,3) 227-235 [< NTAbs 33,2].
k311 **Welch** Claude,   Protestant thought in the nineteenth century [I. 1972] II.
1985 → 2,d794 ...4,k262: ᴿScotJT 42 (1989) 251-3 (K. *Surin*).

---

k312 BAUR: **Meijering** E. P.,   F. C. Baur als Patristiker 1986 → 2,d752:
ᴿVigChr 43 (1989) 204s (J. van *Winden*).
k313 CHAUNCY: **Corrigan** John,   The hidden balance; religion and the social
theories of Charles Chauncy and Jonathan MAYHEW. C 1987, Univ.
161 p. $30. – ᴿJAAR 57 (1989) 393s (L. E. *Schmidt*).

k314 DREY: **Kustermann** A.P., Die Apologetik J.S. Dreys [diss. 1987s
➤ 4,k268]...: Contubernium 36. Tü 1988, Mohr. 402 p. DM 78. 3-16-
445397-2. – ᴿActuBbg 26 (1989) 55s (J. *Boada*); TsTNijm 29 (1989) 293
(N. *Schreurs*); ZkT 111 (1989) 465-7 (W. *Kern*).

k315 *Kustermann* Abraham P., Der Name des Autors ist Drey; eine un-
vermeidliche Vorbemerkung zum Apologetik-Manuskript J.A. MÖHLERS:
Catholica 43 (1989) 54-76.

k316 **Tiefensee** E., Die religiöse Anlage und ihre Entwicklung; der religionsphilosophische Ansatz J.S. Dreys, 1777-1853: Erfurter TheolSt. 56.
Lp 1988, St. Benno. xxv-255 p. M 26 [RHE 84, p.401*].

k317 EKLUND J.: **Sundberg** Karl J., BACON, DILTHEY och svensk teologi;en studie i J.A. Eklunds teologiska metod [c. 1900]: SvTKv 65
(1989) 70-75 [156-161, Eklund H a r a l d 1901-1960, religionsfilosofi:
Hornig G.].

k318 FINNEY: **Hardman** Keith J., Charles Grandison Finney, 1792-1875,
revivalist and reformer. Syracuse NY 1987, Univ. 521 p. $45. – ᴿJAAR
57 (1989) 190-3 (D.N. *Williams*).

k319 FRANZELIN: *Śliwiński* Andrzej, ❷ Franzelin, Johannes Baptist SJ
(15.IV.1816-11.XII.1886): ➤ 891, EncKat 5 (1989) 693.

k321 HORT: **Patrick** G.A., F.J.A. Hort, eminent Victorian 1988 ➤ 4,k276:
ᴿBL (1989) 22 (D.G. *Deboys*: repetitious style; ignores GRIESBACH,
LACHMANN, TISCHENDORFF, COLWELL); JTS 40 (1989) 690-2 (I. *Ellis*);
RelStR 15 (1989) 363 (J.C. *Livingston*); ScotJT 42 (1989) 612s (P. *Avis*);
TLond 92 (1989) 411s (P. *Hinchliff*).

k322 JOWETT: **Hinchliff** Peter, Benjamin Jowett and the Christian religion
1987 ➤ 4,k278: ᴿChH 50 (1989) 405s (D.L. *Pals*); JRel 69 (1989) 555s
(J.C. *Livingston*).

k323 KIERKEGAARD: **Rosas** Louis J., The function of Scripture in the
thought of Søren Kierkegaard: diss. Southern Baptist Theol. Sem. 1988,
ᴰ*Rust* E. 334 p. 89-01501. – DissA 50 (1989s) 166-A.

k324 *Schröer* Henning, Kierkegaard, Søren Aabye (1813-1855): ➤ 911, TRE
18 (1989) 138-155.

k325 **Westphal** Merold, Kierkegaard's critique of reason and society. Macon
GA 1987, Mercer Univ. xii-129 p. $20. – ᴿJRel 69 (1989) 111 (T.
Jackson).

k327 MENDELSSOHN: *Weinberg* Werner, Moses Mendelssohns Übersetzungen und Kommentare der Bibel [< ᴱ*Bourel* D. BTT 7,1986]: ZRGg 41
(1989) 97-118 [.119-133, *Niewöhner* Friedrich].

k328 MÖHLER [➤ k315 supra]: *Wagner* Harald, J.A. Möhler — Fakten
und Überlegungen zu seiner Wirkungsgeschichte: Catholica 43 (1989)
195-208.

k329 NIETZSCHE: **Bucher** Rainer M., Nietzsches Mensch und Nietzsches
Gott; das Spätwerk als philosophisch-theologisches Programm: Wü-
StudFundT 1. Fra 1986, Lang. 407 p. – ᴿTPhil 64 (1989) 108-110 (U.
Willers).

k330 **Abel** Günter, Nietzsche; die Dynamik der [!] Willen zur Macht und die
ewige Wiederkehr: N-Forschung 15. B 1984, de Grüyter. 471 p. –
ᴿTPhil 64 (1989) 421-3 (U. *Willers*).

k331 **Kerger** Henry, Autorität und Recht im Denken Nietzsches: Schriften
zur Rechtstheorie 127. B 1988, Duncker & H. 212 p. – ᴿTPhil 64 (1989)
424s (N. *Brieskorn*).

k332 NIKODIMO: ᵀᴱ**Artioli** M. Benedetta, *Lovato* M. Francesca, Nicodimo
Aghiorita, MACARIO di Corinto [compilatori al monte Athos della vasta

antologia di testi patristici, classica greco-orientale e slavo-ortodossa] La
Filocalia I-IV. T 1982-7, Gribaudi. – ᴿParVi 34 (1989) 70-72 (R. *Scognamiglio*).

k333 PFLEIDERER: **Graf** F. W., Theonomie; Fallstudien zum Integrationsan-
spruch neuzeitlicher Theologie [... Pfleiderer O. † 1908]. Gü 1987, Mohn.
246 p. DM 64. 3-579-00265-1. – ᴿTsTNijm 29 (1989) 293 (T. *Schoof*).

k334 RÜCKERT: *Bobzin* Hartmut, Friedrich Rückert (1788-1866), ein ver-
gessener Alttestamentler und Hebraist: ZAW 101 (1989) 173-184.

k335 SCHEEBEN: M. J. Scheeben, teologo cattolico d'ispirazione tomista 1988
→ 4,k298b: ᴿGregorianum 70 (1989) 357-9 (J. de *Finance*); Laurentianum 30 (1989) 449s (B. de *Armellada*).

k336 *Horst* P. Ulrich. La doctrina de la infalibilidad papal en M. J. Scheeben
y su prehistoria: ScripTPamp 21 (1989) 151-167.

k337 SCHLEIERMACHER: [ᴱ**Rostagno** S.], *Birkner* H. J., al., Schleiermacher e
la modernità [Roma Fac. Valdese Goethe-Institut 26-27.X.1984] 1986
→ 4,637: ᴿLaurentianum 30 (1989) 237s (D. de *Torralba*).

k338 **Brandt** James M., RITSCHL's critique of Schleiermacher's theological
ethics: JRelEth 17,2 ('New Perspectives on Schleiermacher's Ethics' 1989)
[1-]51-72.

k339 **Clements** Keith W., F. Schleiermacher 1987 → 3,g731; 4,k290:   ᴿChH
50 (1989) 524-6 (D. *Jodock*).

k340 ᵀ**Crouter** Richard, F. Schleiermacher, On religion; speeches to its
cultured despisers: Texts in German philosophy. C 1988, Univ.   xii-
231 p. £25; pa. £9 [JTS 41, 761, J. *Clayton*].

k341 **Eckert** M., Gott — glauben und wissen; F. Schleiermachers philosophische Theologie: Schleiermacher-Archiv 1, 1987 → 3,g732: ᴿNRT
111 (1989) 447 (B. *Pottier*).

k342 **Hinze** Bradford E., Doctrinal criticism, reform, and development in the
work of Friedrich Schleiermacher and Johann S. DREY: diss. ᴰ*Kilian* S.
Ch 1989. – RelStR 16,187.

k343 **Riemer** Matthias, Bildung und Christentum; der Bildungsgedanke
Schleiermachers: ForSystÖ 58. Gö 1989, Vandenhoeck & R.   361 p.
DM 78 [TLZ 115, 753-5, H. *Peiter*].

k344 **Schleiermacher** Friedrich, Theologische Enzyklopädie [1831s], ᴱ*Sachs*
W.: S.-Archiv 4. B 1987, de Gruyter. xlii-256 p. DM 108. – ᴿDLZ 110
(1989) 645-7 (J. *Rachold*); ZkT 111 (1989) 100-2 (W. *Kern*, also on
Dialektik 1812 and 1814/33).

k345 ᴱ**Selge** Kurt-Victor, Internationaler Schleiermacher-Kongress Berlin
1984: 1985 → 2,500: ᴿJRel 68 (1988) 291-4 (J. *Brandt*, Dawn *DeVries*).

k347 STRAUSS: *Graf* Friedrich W., D. F. Strauss' radikaldemokratische
Christologie [*Massey* M. 1985]: ᴿTRu 54 (1989) 190-5 (F. W. *Graf*).

k348 **Lawler** Edwina G., D. F. Strauss and his critics 1986 → 2,d795
... 4,k297: ᴿJRel 68 (1988) 294s (W. *Madges*).

k349 *Madges* William, D. F. Strauss in retrospect; his reception among
Roman Catholics [p. 281, 'Hans KÜNG, Edward SCHILLEBEECKX, and
David TRACY all maintain fundamental continuity with their nineteenth-
century predecessors by rejecting Strauss's proposal for a Christianity
without Jesus']: HeythJ 30 (1989) 273-292.

k350 STUART: **Giltner** John H., Moses Stuart 1988 → 4,k300: ᴿJRel 69
(1989) 550s (Barbara B. *Kaiser*).

k351 UPHAM 1799-1872: **Salter** Darius L., Spirit and intellect; Thomas
Upham's holiness theology: Studies in Evangelicalism 7. Metuchen NJ

1986, Scarecrow. 278 p. $27.50. 0-8108-1899-X. – ᴿAsbTJ 44,1 (1989)
109s (N. *Murdoch*).

k352 WELLHAUSEN: *Smend* Rudolf, Wellhausen und die Kirche: ⇥ 120,
ᶠLOHSE E., Wissenschaft 1989, 225-234.

k353 ZIGLIARA: *Wilder* Alfred, Cardinal Zigliara and traditionalism: Angelicum 66 (1989) 517-562.

Y5.5 Crisis modernistica – The Modernist era.

k354 **Kurtz** Lester R., The politics of heresy 1986 ⇥ 2,d806 ... 4,k309: ᴿChH
58 (1989) 127-9 (R. S. *Appleby*).

k355 *Lease* Gary, Modernism and 'modernism'; Christianity as product of
its culture: JStRel 1,2 (Pietermaritzburg SAf 1988) 3-23 [< TContext
6/2, 17].

k356 **O'Gara** Margaret, Triumph in defeat; Infallibility, Vatican II, and the
French minority bishops 1988 ⇥ 4,k310: ᴿGregorianum 70 (1989)
568-570 (F. A. *Sullivan*); Horizons 16 (1989) 353-360 (J. T. *Ford*) & 360s
(R. F. *Costigan*) & 362-4 (F. S. *Fiorenza*) & 364-6 (Mary Jo *Weaver*);
366-372, O'Gara response.

k357 — *Thils* G., L'apport de la 'minorité' à Vatican I; à propos de
'Triumph in defeat' de Margaret O'GARA [1988]: ETL 65 (1989) 412-9.

k358 **Poulat** Émile, Liberté, laïcité 1987 ⇥ 4,k311: ᴿLVitae 43 (1988) 466s
(A. *Godin*, aussi sur L'Église, c'est un monde); NRT 111 (1989) 610 (B.
Joassart: 'heureusement n'est pas que pessimiste'); RechSR 76 (1988)
620-3 (H. *Madelin*); RHR 206 (1989) 441-3 (F. *Laplanche*); RTLv 20
(1988) 400s (B. *Waché*); RTPhil 121 (1989) 458s (L. *Rumpf*).

k359 **Stuart** Elizabeth B., Roman Catholic reactions to the Oxford
Movement and Anglican schemes for reunion, from 1833 to the
condemnation of Anglican Orders in 1896. Diss Oxford 1987, 378 p.
BRD-87237. – DissA 50 (1989s) 3264-A.

---

k360 ACTON: *Whisenant* James, Lord Acton's responses to the hierarchy in
the controversies of 1858-64: DowR 107 (1989) 34-48.

k361 BLONDEL: **Favraux** Paul, Une philosophie de médiateur; Maurice
Blondel, 1987; 2-283-61152-0: ᴿDowR 106 (1988) 149-156 (A. *Louth*).

k362 *Gilbert* Paul, Le phénomène, la médiation et la métaphysique; le dernier
chapitre de L'Action (1893) de Maurice Blondel: Gregorianum 70 (1989)
93-118 . 291-319; Eng. 119.319.

k363 *Hooff* Anton E. van, Die Innenseite des Modernismusstreits; die
persönliche Erfahrung Maurice Blondels — mehr als blosse Geschichte?:
StiZt 207 (1989) 667-676.

k364 *Izquierdo* Cesar, La tradición según Maurice Blondel: ScripTPamp 21
(1989) 63-96; Eng. 96.

k365 *a) Reiter* Josef, Geist und Buchstabe; Blondels Verständnis konkret-lebendigen Erkennens; – *b) Raffelt* Albert, Blondel, deutsch ... eine
Übersicht; – *c) Henrici* Peter, Blondels 'Action' im Lichte der klassischen
deutschen Philosophie: TPhil 64 (1989) 222-236 / 237-251 / 161-178.

k366 *Saint-Jean* Raymond, L'intelligence d'après Blondel et MARITAIN:
ScEspr 40 (1988) 5-34.

k367 *Sullivan* John, Living tradition [Blondel apud *Dulles* Models]: DowR
106 (1988) 59-66.

k368 **Theobald** Christoph, Maurice Blondel und das Problem der Modernität; Beitrag zu einer epistemologischen Standortbestimmung zeitgenössischer Fundamentaltheologie [Diss. Bonn]: FraTheolSt 35. Fra 1988, Knecht. 595 p. DM 90 [TR 85,434]. 3-7820-0576-7.

k368* CORNOLDI: **Malusa** L., [Cornoldi Giovanni Maria S.J. (1822-1892), scritti inediti], Neotomismo e intransigentismo cattolico, II. Testi e documenti per un bilancio del neotomismo: Ric. Filosofia 6. Mi 1989, IPL. xiii-479 p. Lit. 30.000 [NRT 112,153, N. *Plumat*].

k369 CURCI: *Mucci* Giandomenico, Una notizia sul Padre Curci [alla domanda del nipote ancora vivo, 'Perché si allontanò (o fu allontanato) dalla Civiltà Cattolica da lui fondata, intorno al 1864?': i motivi non sono stati fino ad oggi esaurientemente chiariti]: CC 140 (1989,1) 369-371.

k370 **Mucci** G., C. M. Curci 1988 ➤ 2,d821 ... 4,k320: ᴿHumBr 44 (1989) 451s (F. *Molinari*); StPatav 36 (1989) 224-7 (S. *Tramontin*).

k371 DÖLLINGER: **Plümmer** Alfred, Conversations with Dr. Döllinger 1985 ➤ 1,f995 ... 3,g769: ᴿLvSt 14 (1989) 66-68 (V. J. *Sansone*).

k372 von HÜGEL: *McGrath* John A., Fact and reality; von Hügel's response [... 'The eternal Christ and our successive Christologies', criticizing *Blondel*; given to *Bremond* to publish in French 1904]: HeythJ 30 (1989) 13-31.

k373 *Neuner* Peter, Laienspiritualität im Reformkatholizismus [... Modernismus]; F. von Hügel, Frömmigkeit und Weltverantwortung: MüTZ 40 (1989) 115-127.

k374 LEROY: **Mansini** Guy, 'What is a dogma?'... LeRoy 1985 ➤ 1,g2 ... 4,k323: ᴿJRel 68 (1988) 462s (J. T. *Ford*); TR 85 (1989) 397-9 (E. *Poulat*, who had optimistically promised a book on this subject 20 years ago).

k375 MANNING: **Gray** Robert, Cardinal Manning, a biography. L 1985, Weidenfeld & N. 366 p. £17. – ᴿAustralasCR 66 (1989) 236-242 (A. *Cooper*).

k376 de MANRESA: **Gasol** Joseph M. *Raurell* Frederic, *Serra* Valenti, Rupert M. de Manresa, pensador en temps de crísi [EstFran 90 (1989) 155-293; 169-252 Raurell, Com.Ct. ➤ 3251]. Barc 1989, Est.Franc. 200 p.; ill. – ᴿColcFran 59 (1959) 449s (V. *Criscuolo*); EstFranc 90 (1989) 525-8 (J. *Tusquets i Terrats*); QVidCr 147 (1989) 130-2 (J. *Llimona*); RCatalT 13 (1988) 509-511 (J. *Ferrer i Costa*).

k377 MUGNIER: ᴱDiesbach Ghislain de, Journal de l'abbé [Arthur] Mugnier (1879-1939) [... *Renan*]: Le temps retrouvé. P 1985, Mercure. 639 p. – ᴿRHE 84 (1989) 834s (H. *Silvestre*).

---

k378 NEWMAN, OXFORD MOVEMENT: **Biemer** G., John Henry Newman 1801-1890, Leben und Werk. Mainz 1989, Grünewald. 202 p.; 16 fig. DM 36. – ᴿNRT 111 (1989) 1027s (A. *Toubeau*).

k379 **Britt** John, J. H. Newman's rhetoric; becoming a discriminating reader: Amer.Univ.St. 14/2. NY 1989, Lang. x-218 p. [TR 85,432].

k380 **Chadwick** Owen, John-Henry Newman [1983 ➤ 65,d874], ᵀDayras Solange, *d'Haussy* Christiane; préf. *Guitton* J. P 1989, Cerf. 160 p. F 70. – ᴿEsprVie 99 (1989) 351 (J. *Pintard*).

k381 **Crumb** Lawrence N., The Oxford Movement and its leaders; a bibliography of secondary and lesser primary sources: ATLA bibliog. 24. Metuchen 1988, Scarecrow. xxviii-706 p. $62.50. 0-8108-2141-9. – 5688

items without KEBLE, PUSEY, and (except for 197 items on Apologia)
Newman [TDig 36,364].

k382 **Gauthier** Pierre, Newman et BLONDEL; tradition et développement du
dogme 1988 → 4,k335: ᴿActuBbg 26 (1989) 208s (J. *Boada*); BLitEc 90
(1989) 75s (A. *Dartigues*); CC 140 (1989,2) 92s (J. *Servais*); EsprVie 99
(1989) 623s (P. *Jay*); ÉTRel 64 (1989) 456 (A. *Gaillard*); RHPR 69 (1989)
56s (G. *Siegwalt*).

k383 *Hammond* David, Imagination and hermeneutical theology; Newman's
contribution to theological method: DowR 106 (1988) 17-34.

k384 **Honoré** Jean, Newman, sa vie et sa pensée: Bibl.Hist.Christianisme 17.
P 1988, Desclée. 132 p. F 90. – ᴿEsprVie 99 (1989) 240 (É. *Vauthier*:
'Newmann' 8 fois — et le tout repété p. 255); RBén 99 (1989) 372s (L.
Wankenne).

k385 **Ker** Ian, John H. Newman, a biography. Ox 1988, Clarendon. xiii-
762 p. £48. – ᴿIstina 34 (1989) 239s (B. *Dupuy*); Month 250 (1989) 186s
(O. *Rafferty*); Tablet 242 (1989) 126 (J. *Coulson*); TLond 92 (1989) 410s
(B. L. *Horne*).

k385* ᴱ**Ker** Ian, The genius of J. H. Newman; selections from his writings.
Ox 1989, Clarendon. xviii-341 p. £35 [JTS 41,825].

k386 *McRedmond* Louis, Freedom or faith? Newman's dilemma: DocLife
39 (1989) 137-142.

k387 **Merrigan** T., 'A theology of the religious imagination'; faith and reason
in the life and work of J. H. Newman: diss. kath. Univ. Leuven 1989,
ᴰ*Willaert* B. cvii-318 p. – TsTNijm 29 (1989) 284.

k388 **Nabe** Clyde, Mystery and religion; Newman's epistemology of religion.
Lanham MD 1988, UPA. xi-64 p. $13.25; pa. $7.75 [JTS 41,307, B.
Mitchell].

k389 *Nagakura* Reiko, ❹ John Henry Newman; his life and his meaning for
us to-day: KatKenk 28,55 (1989) 127-152; Eng. x-xii.

k390 *Smith* Jean, ᴱ*Smith* Rosemary (her sister-in-law) Newman and Sicily:
DowR 107 (1988) 155-181.

k391 **Thomas** Stephen C., Newman and heresy; the Anglican writings: diss.
Durham 1988. – RTLv 21,554.

k392 ᴱ**Weaver** Mary Jo, Newman and the modernists 1986 → 2,d844; 3,g790:
ᴿHeythJ 30 (1989) 372s (J. *Coulson*).

k393 **Zeno** Capuchin, J. H. Newman, his inner life. SF 1987, Ignatius.
335 p. $13 [RelStR 16, 81, M. S. *Burrows*].

k394 **Griffin** John R., John KEBLE, Saint of Anglicanism. Macon GA 1987,
Marcer Univ. viii-122 p. $25 [RelStR 16, 80, Julia *Gatta*].

k395 *Bedouelle* G., PUSEY (Edward Bouverie, 1800-1882): → 882, Catholicisme XII,55 (1989) 319-321.

k396 PIUS IX: **Martina** Giacomo, Pio IX (1851-1866): Misc.Hist.Pontificiae
51. R 1986, Pont. Univ. Gregoriana. 760 p. – ᴿCrNSt 10 (1989) 207-9
(G. *Battelli*: vol. 2; 1 nel 1974 trattava gli anni 1846-50).

k397 PORTAL: **Ladoux** Régis, Monsieur [Fernand] Portal et les siens
(1855-1926), préf. *Poulat* Émile. P 1985, Cerf. 521 p. F 145. – ᴿHeythJ
30 (1989) 107 (S. *Gilley*: not very original or bright, but friendly to LOISY
and Anglicanism).

k398 ROSMINI: *Dalledonne* Andrea, La critica fondamentale dell' 'Enigma
Rosmini': DivThom 91 (1988) 465-473.

k399 **Lorizio** Giuseppe, Eschaton e storia nel pensiero di A. Rosmini:
Aloisiana 21, 1988 → 4,k345: ᴿRivStoLR 25 (1989) 543-6 (G. *Tognon*).

k400 TYRRELL: **Butterworth** Robert, A Jesuit friendship [Tyrrell's letters to Herbert THURSTON]. Roehampton Inst. 1988, Digby Stuart College. – ᴿExpTim 100 (1988s) 440 (Paidagogos).

Y6 *Saeculum XX* – 20th Century Exegesis.

k401 ᴱ**Collins** John J., *Crossan* John D. [ᶠVAWTER B.]. The biblical heritage in modern Catholic scholarship 1986 ➤ 3,162: ᴿIrTQ 55 (1989) 329 (P. *Rogers*).

k402 *Doyle* B. R., Biblical studies in Australia, a Catholic contribution: Compass 22 (Melbourne 1988) 39-46 [< NTAbs 33,2].

k403 **Grunfeld** F. V., Profeti senza onore; l'intelligenza ebraica nella cultura tedesca nel '900 [= secolo 20]. Bo 1986, Mulino. xxiii-409 p. Lit. 38.000. – ᴿProtestantesimo 44 (1989) 73s (G. *Vetrano*).

k404 *La Potterie* Ignace de, Vatican II et la Bible: ➤ 652, Le deuxième concile du Vatican 1986/9, 477-496.

k405 *Pesce* Mauro, Esegesi storica ed esegesi spirituale nell'ermeneutica biblica cattolica dal pontificato di Leone XIII a quello di Pio XII: ➤ 567, AnStoEseg 6 (1989) 261-291; Eng. 10.

---

k406 BEA: *Rolla* Armando, *Pizzuti* Giuseppe M., Agostino Bea, il cardinale dell'Unità [*Schmidt* S. 1987]: Asprenas 36 (1989) 80-87.

k407 **Schmidt** Stjepan, Agostino Bea 1987 ➤ 3,g812; 4,k355: ᴿAnStoEseg 6 (1989) 323s [M. *Pesce*]; QVidCr 147 (1989) 136 (B. *Ubach*); Salesianum 51 (1989) 833s (D. *Valentini*).

k408 **Schmidt** Stjepan, Augustin Bea, der Kardinal der Einheit, ᵀ*Spath* Sigrid. Graz 1989, Styria. 1050 p. 3-222-11905-8.

k409 BRUCE: *Basque* W. W. & L., F. F. Bruce, a mind for what matters; a conversation with a pioneer of evangelical biblical scholarship: ChrTod 33,6 (Carol Stream IL 1989) 22-25 [< NTAbs 33,283].

k410 BUBER: **Becker** Dieter, K. BARTH und M. Buber [diss. Heid 1982] 1986 ➤ 2,d919: ᴿTR 85 (1989) 124-6 (E. *Sturm*).

k411 **Biser** Eugen, Buber für Christen; eine Herausforderung: Tb 1527. FrB 1988, Herder. 142 p. DM 10 [TLZ 114, 141]. – ᴿETL 65 (1989) 462 (A. de *Halleux*); TPQ 137 (1989) 428 (K. M. *Woschitz*); Tr 85 (1989) 126 (C. *Schütz*).

k412 *Brož* Luděk, Martin Buber: ComViat 32 (1989) 133-151.

k413 ᴱ**Gordon** Haim, The other Martin Buber; recollections of his contemporaries. 1988, Ohio Univ. xiii-186 p. $19. – ᴿJJS 40 (1989) 270-2 (P. *Vermes*).

k414 *Fishbane* Michael, *a)* Martin Buber's Moses (1988, 4-12); – *b)* The biblical dialogue of Martin Buber [< Judaism 27 (1978) 184-195]: ➤ 259, Garments of Torah 1989, 91-98.143 / 81-90.142s.

k415 **Friedman** Maurice, Martin Buber and the eternal 1986 ➤ 3,g816: ᴿJAAR 57 (1989) 861s (E. T. *Long*); JRel 68 (1988) 151s (M. *Wyschogrod*).

k416 *Mendes-Flohr* Paul, Nationalism as a spiritual sensibility; the philosophical suppositions of Buber's Hebrew humanism: JRel 69 (1989) 155-168.

k417 *Moore* Donald J., Buber's challenge to Christian theology: Thought 62 (1987) 388-399.

k418 **Oesterreicher** John M., The unfinished dialogue; Martin Buber and the Christian way 1986 → 2,d862; 4,k360: ᴿJRel 69 (1989) 115-7 (P. *Mendes-Flohr*).

k419 **Weinrich** Michael, Grenzgänger; Martin Bubers Anstösse zum Weitergehen: Abh. jüd.-chr. Dialog 17. Mü 1987, Kaiser. 240 p. DM 48. – ᴿBTZ 6 (1989) 282-5 (M. *Brumlik*).

k420 BULTMANN: **Bockmuehl** Klaus, The unreal God of modern theology; Bultmann, Barth and the theology of atheism, ᵀ*Bromiley* G. W. Colorado Springs 1988, Helmers & H. 192 p. $12 [TTod 46,99 adv.]. 0-939443-11-2.

k421 *Boutin* Maurice, Dieu et la projection non-objectivée; conséquences de la compréhension de Dieu dans la théologie de R. Bultmann: LavalTP 44 (1988) 221-246.

k422 **Evang** Martin, M. Bultmann in seiner Frühzeit: BeiHistT 74, 1988 → 4,k365: ᴿActuBbg 26 (1989) 15-17 (J. *Boada*); TLZ 114 (1989) 215-9 (H. *Hübner*).

k423 **Jaspert** Bernd, Sackgassen im Streit mit Rudolf Bultmann; hermeneutische Probleme der Bultmannrezeption in Theologie und Kirche 1985 → 3,g823; ᴿTRu 54 (1989) 333s (W. *Schmithals*).

k424 ᴱ**Johnson** Roger, R. Bultmann [anthology]; interpreting faith for the modern era: Making of Modern Theology, 1987 → 4,k367: ᴿCBQ 51 (1989) 744-6 (R. *Morton*); TTod 46 (1989s) 230s.234 (Dawn *De Vries*, also on the other three first volumes 'Making of Modern Theology').

k425 *Konings* Johan, Bultmann chega ao Brasil [Crer e comprender, ᵀ*Schlupp* W., *Altmann* W.; São Leopoldo 1987, Sinodal]: PerspT 20 (1988) 379-383.

k426 *a)* *Marlé* René, Bultmann e dopo Bultmann; *b)* *Costa* Filippo, Ent-Mytho-logisier-ung; – *c)* *Sorrentino* Sergio, Storia e storicità nel pensiero di Bultmann; – *d)* *Volpe* Giorgio, Al di là del Dio storico in Bultmann ed EBELING; – *e)* *Boschini* Paolo, Kerygma e storia; la critica di W. PANNENBERG a R. Bultmann: FilT 3 (1989) 257-262 / 263-283 / 285-309 / 310-341 / 342-361.

k427 *a)* *Lindemann* Andreas, Neutestamentler in der Zeit des Nationalsozialismus; Hans von SODEN und Rudolf Bultmann in Marburg; – *b)* *Crüsemann* Frank, Tendenzen der alttestamentlichen Wissenschaft zwischen 1933 und 1945: WDienst 20 (1989) 25-52 / 79-103 [13-23, *Ruhbach* Gerhard].

k428 *Schmithals* Walter, Der junge Bultmann [*Evang* M. 1988]: TRu 54 (1989) 203-211; 212-4, unveröffentlichter Brief.

k429 **Trocholepczy** Bernd, Rechtfertigung und Seinsfrage; Anknüpfung und Widerspruch in der HEIDEGGER-Rezeption Bultmanns: Diss. ᴰ*Lehmann* K. FrB 1989. 267 p. – TRLv 21, p. 539.

k430 CULLMANN: *Ferrario* Fulvio, La storia della salvezza nel pensiero di O. Cullmann [*Hersemann* H. 1979; *Schlaudraff* K. 1988]: Protestantesimo 44 (1989) 279-281.

k431 DEARMER: *Pilkington* John, Percy Dearmer's Lessons [On the Way 1920] for today: ExpTim 100 (1988s) 96-99.

k432 FRIEDRICH DELITZSCH: **Johanning** K., Der Bibel-Babel-Streit [De-litzsch 1902-4]: eine forschungsgeschichtliche Studie [ev. Diss. Marburg, ᴰ*Kaiser* O.]: EurHS 23/143. Fra 1988, Lang. xxiii-343 + 471 p. Fs 76 [ZAW 102,151, H.-C. *Schmitt*]. 0721-3409.

k433 **Lehmann** Reinhard G., Friedrich Delitzsch und der Babel-Bibel-Streit: ev. Diss. ᴰ*Diethelm* M. Mainz 1988s. – TR 85 (1989) 516; RTLv 21,541.

k434 FONCK: *Kudasiewicz* Józef, ❷ Fonck Leopold SJ (14.I.1865-19.X.1930):
➤ 891, EncKat 5 (1989) 375s.

k435 GUNKEL: **Lüdemann** G., *Schröder* M., Die religionsgeschichtliche Schule
in Göttingen [RITSCHL, DUHM, BOUSSET, Gunkel...]. Gö 1987, Vandenhoeck & R. 148 p. DM 19,80. 3-525-53582-1. – [R]ExpTim 100 (1988s)
69 (R. *Coggins*: fascinating new appreciation of these giants).

k436 HARPER: **Wind** James P., The Bible and the university... Harper 1987
➤ 3,g832; 4,k373: [R]CBQ 51 (1989) 376s (L. J. *Topel*); JRel 68 (1988)
295s (J. M. *Kitagawa*); RelStT 7,2s (1987) 87s (P. J. *Cahill*).

k437 HASTINGS: *Dempster* J. A. H., 'Incomparable encyclopaedist'; the life
and work of Dr. James Hastings [26.II.1852-15.X.1922; founder of ExpT]:
ExpT 100 (1988s) 4-9.

k438 HEINISCH: *Aubert* R., Heinisch (Paul) 25.III.1878-18.III.1956: ➤ 885,
DHGE 23,135 (1989) 832s.

k439 HESCHEL: **Moore** Donald, The human and the holy; the spirituality of
A. J. Heschel. NY 1989, Fordham. viii-215 p. $30. 0-8232-1235-1 [TDig
37,174].

k440 **Heschel** Abraham J., Israel — Echo der Ewigkeit, [T]*Olmesdahl* Ruth:
Information Judentum 9. Neuk 1988. 155 p. DM 26,80. – [R]KIsr 4,1
(1989) 81s (Julie *Kirchberg*).

k441 JANSSEN: **Holwerda** David E., Hermeneutical issues then and now; the
[Ralph] Janssen case revisited [removed from teaching at GR Calvin
seminary 1922, though H. HOEKEMA warned that his use of A. KUYPER's
teaching on common grace would ultimately prevail]: CalvinT 24 (1989)
7-34 [35-65, *Bavinck* Herman, Common Grace 1894, [T]*Leeuwen* Raymond
C. van].

k442 JONAS: *Müller* Wolfgang E., Zur Problematik des Verantwortungs-
begriffs bei Hans Jonas: ZevEth 33 (1989) 204-216.

k443 **Müller** W. E., Der Begriff der Verantwortung bei H. Jonas. Fra 1988,
Athenäum. 150 p. DM 48. 3-610-09114-2. – [R]Universitas 44 (Stu 1989)
90s (G. *Kleinschmidt*).

k444 *Oelmüller* Willi, Hans Jonas, een joodse stem: Streven 55 (1987s)
963-976.

k444* LAGRANGE: [E]**Montagnes** Bernard, Exégèse et obéissance; correspondance [maître-gén. Hyacinthe-M.] CORMIER – Lagrange (1904-1916):
ÉtBN 11. P 1989, Gabalda. 443 p.; portr. F 306. 2-85021-037-4.

k445 MARGOLIS: **Greenspoon** Leonard, Max L. Margolis 1987 ➤ 3,g836:
[R]JBL 108 (1989) 132s (S. D. *Sperling*).

k446 MOWINCKEL: [E]**Barstad** Hans M., *Ottosson* Magnus, The life and work
of Sigmund Mowinckel: ScandJOT (1988,2) 1-91; 95-168 bibliog., *Kvale*
Dagfinn [< TR 85,521].

k447 PERRIN: *Wilder* Amos N., Norman Perrin and the relation of
historical knowledge to faith [*Grässer* E., JRel 64 (1984) 484-500]:
HarvTR 82 (1989) 201-211.

k448 PETERS: *a) Gamberoni* Johann, Norbert Peters (1863-1938); sein
Eintreten für die Freiheit der katholischen Exegese [... Bibliog.]; – *b) Ernst*
Josef, Geschichte der Exegese und Theologie des Neuen Testamentes in
Paderborn 1614-1989: TGL 79 (1989) 498-516 / 517-539.

k449 PUECH: *Ries* J., Puech (Henri-Charles) 1902-1986: ➤ 882, Catholicisme
XII,55 (1989) 284s.

k449* VON RAD: *Derousseaux* L., Rad, Gerhard von (1901-1971): ➤ 882,
Catholicisme XII,55 (1989) 431-3.

k450 ROBINSON: ᴱJames Eric, God's truth [Robinson J. A. T.] 1988 = Life of R. 1987 → 3,g839: ᴿExpTim 100,4 first choice (1988s) 121s (C. S. *Rodd*); SWJT 32,1 (1989s) 72s (L. R. *Bush*).

k450* Kee Alistair, The roots of Christian freedom [Robinson J. A. T.]. L 1988, SPCK. 190 p. £9. 0-281-04338-8. – ᴿExpTim 100,4 also first choice (1988s) 122s (C. S. *Rodd*: exceptionally fine); TLZ 114 (1989) 211 (J. *Langer*).

k451 ROSENZWEIG: *Brocke* Michael, Die Schrift und Rosenzweig: KIsr 4,1 (1989) 31-41.

k452 *Fishbane* Michael, Speech and Scripture; the grammatical thinking and theology of Franz Rosenzweig: → 259, Garments of Torah 1989, 99-111.143-7.

k453 *Hoppe* Joachim, Neues Denken, neue Sprache; eine Einführung in das Lebenswerk von Franz Rosenzweig: BTZ 6 (1989) 41-52.

k454 Zak Adam, Vom reinen Denken zur Sprachvernunft; über die Grundmotive der Offenbarungsphilosophie Franz Rosenzweigs: Mü PhStud NF 1, 1987 → 4,k382: ᴿTPhil 64 (1989) 433-5 (J. *Splett*). → 604.

k455 SCHLIER: *Löser* Werner, Schlier (Heinrich) 1900-1978: → 886, DictSpir 14,92s (1989) 418-420.

Y6.4 Theologi influentes *in exegesim saeculi XX.*

k456 ᴱCarey Patrick, American Catholic religious thought [anthology of 11 items for college course] 1987 → 4,345; 0-8091-2884-5: ᴿGregorianum 70 (1989) 380s (C. *O'Neill*); Horizons 16 (1989) 163s (Arlene A. *Swidler*).

k457 Cholvy Gérard, *Hilaire* Yves-M., Histoire religieuse de la France contemporaine [I, 1800-1880: 1985; 351 p. II. 1986: -1930 → 3,g848]; III. 1930-1988: Bibliothèque historique. Toulouse 1988, Privat. 569 p. – ᴿNRT 111 (1989) 609s (B. *Joassart*).

k458 Clements Keith W., Lovers of discord 1988 → 4,k390: ᴿExpTim 100 (1988s) 111 (G. *Patrick*: good); HeythJ 30 (1989) 439s (S. *Gilley*: depressing).

k459 ᴱCoreth Emerich, al. ['Herausgeber'; *Schmidinger* Heinrich M., al. 'Redaktion'] Christliche Philosophie im katholischen Denken des 19. und 20. Jahrhunderts, I. Neue Ansätze im 19. Jht. Graz 1987, Styria. 299 p. – ᴿTPhil 64 (1989) 425-8 (H. *Schöndorf*).

k460 *Dumont* Camille, L'enseignement théologique au Collège Jésuite de Louvain; Louvain 1838 – Bruxelles 1988: NRT 111 (1989) 556-576.

k461 ᴱFord David F., The modern theologians [LONERGAN, TORRANCE, and 14 continental Europeans]; an introduction to Christian theology in the twentieth century. Ox 1989, Blackwell. xvi-342 p. + xii-300 p. £35; pa. $11 each. 0-631-15371-3, pa. -2-1; II. -6807-9; -8-7.

k462 Guillet Jacques, La théologie catholique en France de 1914 à 1960. P 1988, Médiasèvres. 60 p. – ᴿETL 65 (1989) 471s (A. *Haquin*: commence avec 'la fin du modernisme' mais en 1946 les jésuites les plus en vue sont soupçonnés de modernisme).

k463 Hummel Gert, Die Begegnung zwischen Philosophie und evangelischer Theologie im 20. Jahrhundert. Da 1989, Wiss. x-499 p. DM 98 [TLZ 115,759, M. *Trowitzsch*].

k464 Kent J., The unacceptable face 1987 → 3,g852; 4,k392: ᴿJTS 40 (1989) 312s (H. *Willmer*: too earnest).

k465 **Neusch** M., *Chenu* B., Au pays de la théologie; à la découverte des hommes et des courants[2] [¹1979]. P 1986, Centurion. 262 p. – ᴿRHE 84 (1989) 836s (R. *Aubert*).

k466 **O'Brien** David, Public Catholicism: Bicentennial History of the Catholic Church in America. NY 1989, Macmillan. xx-291 p. $25 [TS 51, 153-5, R. J. *Wister*].

k467 **Peden** Creighton, The Chicago school; voices in liberal religious thought. Bristol IN 1987, Wyndham Hall. 171 p. $25; pa. $16. – ᴿTTod 46 (1989s) 249 (W. *Dean*).

k468 **Reher** Margaret M., Catholic intellectual life in America: The Bicentennial History of the Catholic Church in America. NY 1989, Macmillan. xxiii-183 p. – ᴿTS 50 (1989) 597-9 (W. L. *Porter*).

k469 **Richardson** E. Allen, Strangers in this land; pluralism and the response to diversity in the U.S. NY 1988, Pilgrim. 270 p. $11 pa. 0-8298-0449-8. – ᴿTTod 46 (1989s) 341s (R. L. *Rogers*).

k470 **Simons** E., *Winkeler* L., Het verraad der clercken; intellektuellen en hun rol in de ontwikkelingen van het Nederlandse katholicisme na 1945: KDC 19. Baarn 1987, Arbor. 504 p. *f* 45. 90-5158-005-3. – ᴿTsTNijm 29 (1989) 72 (A. van *Harskamp*).

k471 ᴱ**Sykes** Stephen, *Booty* John, The study of Anglicanism [31 authors/essays] 1988 → 4,420; 0-281-04330-2 / Ph 0-8006-2087-9: ᴿExpTim 100 (1988s) 193 (B. *Horne*).

k472 *Winling* Raymond, [→ k721s] La théologie catholique en France au XXᵉ siècle, évolution et renouvellement: NRT 111 (1989) 537-555.

---

k473 ADAM: **Edwards** Thomas J. S., Karl Adam and Friedrich HELLER on the essence of Catholicism: diss. Catholic Univ. of America, ᴰ*Fiorenza* F. S. Wsh 1989. 389 p. 89-17019. – DissA 50 (1989s) 1227s-A.

k474 ASMUSSEN: **Lehmann** Wolfgang, Hans Asmussen; ein Leben für die Kirche. Gö 1988, Vandenhoeck & R. 387 p.; 21 fig. DM 68. – ᴿTR 85 (1989) 214-7 (L. *Klein*); ZkT 111 (1989) 229s (L. *Lies*).

k475 BALTHASAR: *Chantraine* Georges, Esegesi e contemplazione nell'opera di H. U. von Balthasar, ᵀ*Ferraris* Anna: CommStrum 105 (1989) 57-73.

k476 *a*) *Conzemius* Victor, Hans Urs von Balthasar o la memoria corta dei cattolici svizzeri; – *b*) *Ruggieri* Giuseppe Il principio estetico della teologia di B.; – *c*) *Guerriero* Elio, Teatro e teologia; la Teodrammatica ...: HumBr 44 (1989) 325-337 / 338-354 / 355-362.

k477 **Godenir** Joseph, Jésus, l'unique; introduction à la théologie de H. U. v. Balthasar 1984 → 2,d911; 4,k398: ᴿBogVest 47 (1987) 72-75 (A. *Strle*, in Slovene; further p. 145-160).

k478 *Marchesi* Giovanni, Il mistero di Cristo, centro della costellazione teologica di H. U. v. Balthasar: CC 140 (1989,2) 117-130.

k479 *Mengus* Raymond, L' 'épilogue' de H. Urs v. Balthasar (1905-1988): RevSR 62 (1988) 252-264.

k480 *Moda* Aldo, La ricezione dell'opera di Hans Urs von Balthasar in Italia: TItSett 14 (1989) 6-58; Eng. 58.

k481 **Naduvilekut** James, Christus der Heilsweg; Soteria als Theodrama im Werk Hans Urs von Balthasars 1987 → 4,8756*: ᴿTS 50 (1989) 383s (E. T. *Oakes*).

k482 — *Hoffmann* Fritz, Soteria als Theodrama [*Naduvilekut* J. 1987], in memoriam H. U. v. Balthasar: TLZ 114 (1989) 241-250.

k483 **Roberts** Louis, The theological aesthetics of H. U. v. Balthasar 1987 ➤ 3,g861; 4,k402: ᴿJRel 69 (1989) 263s (E. T. *Oakes*); ScotJT 42 (1989) 250s (Francesca *Murphy*); Studies 77 (1988) 478s (G. *O'Hanlon*).

k484 **Balthasar** Hans Urs von, Theodrama, theological dramatic theory, I. Prolegomena, ᵀ*Harrison* Graham. SF 1989, Ignatius. 663 p. $35. – ᴿAmerica 161 (1989) 432s (E. T. *Oakes*).

k485 **Balthasar** H. U. v., Glory... lay styles 1986 ➤ 3,g864; 4,k408: ᴿHeythJ 30 (1989) 450s (J. *O'Donnell*); Horizons 16 (1989) 392s (D. P. *Sheridan*); JRel 68 (1988) 601-3 (Susan A. *Ross*); ScotJT 42 (1989) 246-9 (G. S. *Wakefield*, 1-3; said to have been most cultured man in Europe).

k486 *Balthasar* Hans Urs von †, Die Heilige Schrift: TJb (1989) 34-44.

k487 BARTH: **Ahlers** R., The community of freedom; Barth and presup-positionless theology. NY 1989, Lang. 655 p. $85 [TS 51,187].

k488 **Bacik** James, [20] Contemporary theologians [... Barth, GUTIÉRREZ, M. L. KING, RUETHER, TEILHARD]. Ch 1989, More. 292 p. 0-88347-233-3 [TDig 36,350].

k489 **Bächli** Otto, Das AT in Barth KD 1987 ➤ 3,g868; 4,k412: ᴿTZBas 45 (1989) 377s (K. *Seybold*).

k490 **Blaser** K., K. Barth... combats... 1987 ➤ 4,k417: ᴿRTPhil 121 (1989) 121s (H. *Mottu*).

k491 **Frey** Christofer, Die Theologie K. Barths — eine Einführung 1988 ➤ 4,k424*: ᴿTPhil 64 (1989) 285s (W. *Löser*).

k492 ᴱ**Green** Clifford, Karl Barth, theologian of freedom [selections]: Making of Modern Theology 5. L 1989, Collins [SF, Harper]. 348 p. $20. 0-00-599129-3 [TDig 36,380].

k493 **Jüngel** E., Barth [1982], ᵀ*Paul* Garrett E. 1986 ➤ 2,d934... 4,k429: ᴿJAAR 57 (1989) 200-2 (R. D. *Zimany*); JRel 68 (1988) 464s (R. G. *Goetz*); JTS 40 (1989) 696-9 (P. S. *Fiddes*).

k494 **Kooi** Cornelis van der, Anfängliche Theologie; der Denkweg des jungen Karl Barth (1909 bis 1927) [Diss. Amst. 1985 ➤ 1,g154; 2,d935], ᵀ: BeiEvT 103. Mü 1987, Kaiser. 263 p. DM 68. – ᴿTLZ 114 (1989) 56-58 (M. *Beintker*).

k495 *Kraus* Hans-Joachim, Neue Begegnungen mit dem Alten Testament in Karl Barths Theologie: EvT 49 (1989) 429-443 [460-478, Versöh-nungslehre, *Klappert* B.].

k496 *Laurenzi* M. Cristina, Teologia naturale o responsabilità critica? Dal 'Nein:' di Barth a quesiti contemporanei: Protestantesimo 44 (1989) 162-170.

k497 **McCormack** Bruce L., A scholastic of a higher order; the development of Karl Barth's theology, 1921-31: diss. Princeton Theol. Sem. 1989. 710 p. 89-23109. – DissA 50 (1989s) 2540-A.

k498 *Merk* Otto, Karl Barths Beitrag zur Erforschung des Neuen Testa-ments: ➤ 120, ᶠLOHSE E., Wissenschaft 1989, 149-175.

k499 *Muller* Richard A., Karl Barth and the path of theology into the twentieth century; historical observations [his 'theology has never been examined by a neutral observer']: WestTJ 51 (1989) 25-50.

k500 **Reeling** Brouwer R. H., Over kerkelijke dogmatiek en marxistische filosofie; Karl Barth vergelijkenderwijs gelezen [diss.]. Haag 1988, Boeken-C. 338 p. ƒ47,50. 90-239-1259-4. – ᴿTsTNijm 29 (1989) 297 (A. van *Harskamp*: 'goed leesbaar, soms zelfs spannend').

k501 ᵀᴱ**Reymond** Bernard, Karl Barth — Pierre MAURY, Nous qui pouvons encore parler... correspondance 1928-1956: Symbolon, 1985 ➤ 2,d947b: ᴿRHPR 69 (1989) 78s (R. *Mehl*: Maury was not servile).

k502 *Rosato* Philip J., Karl Barth as spokesman and practitioner of the Christian concept of peace: StMiss 38 (1989) 113-132.

k503 *a) Rosato* Philip J., Ad limina apostolorum in retrospect; the reaction of Karl Barth to Vatican II; – *b) Roberts* Richard H., The reception of the theology of Karl Barth in the Anglo-Saxon world; history, typology and prospects; – *c) Dalferth* Ingolf Y., Karl Barth's eschatological realism; – *d) Gunton* Colin E., The triune God and the freedom of the creature: → 18, Barth centenary 1989, ...

k504 *Ruddies* Hartmut, Karl Barth und Ernst TROELTSCH, ein Literaturbericht: VerkF 34,1 (1989) 2-20 [-21, Troeltsch Bibliog., *Sauter* G.].

k505 *Wallace* Mark I., Karl Barth's hermeneutic; a way beyond the impasse: JRel 68 (1988) 396-410.

k506 **Barth** K., Volontà di Dio e desideri umani [scritti 1933-5],[T]. Torino 1986, Claudiana. 185 p. – [R]Laurentianum 30 (1989) 447-9 (E. *Covi*).

k507 **Köbler** R., In the shadow of Karl Barth; Charlotte von KIRSCHBAUM. Louisville 1989, Westminster/Knox. 156 p. $11 [TS 51,383].

k508 *Groó* Gyula, THURNEYSEN Eduard, 1888-1988: TSzem 31 (1988) 213-5.

k509 BERGSON: *Gire* Pierre, Bergson et le fait religieux chrétien: EsprVie 99 (1989) 684-8.

k510 BOEGNER: **Mehl** Roger, Le pasteur Marc Boegner, une humble grandeur. P 1987, Plon. 346 p. – [R]ZKG 100 (1989) 431s (K. *Blaser*).

k511 BONHOEFFER: **de Gruchy** John. D. Bonhoeffer, witness to Jesus Christ 1987 → 4,k444: 0-00599-58-0: [R]RExp 86 (1989) 443s (D. L. *Mueller*); TLond 92 (1989) 126s (K. W. *Clements*).

k512 *Feil* Ernst, Dietrich Bonhoeffers ökumenische Ethik, ein Gesprächsbeitrag angesichts restaurativer und revolutionärer Tendenzen: StiZt 207 (1989) 760-770.

k513 **Huntemann** Georg, Der andere Bonhoeffer; die Herausforderung des Modernismus: ABC-team. Wu 1989, Brockhaus. 318 p. DM 29,80 pa. [TLZ 115,607, M. *Kuske*].

k514 *Müller* Hans M., Bonhoeffer-Interpretationen: TRu 54 (1989) 307-314.

k515 [E]**Peck** William J., New studies in Bonhoeffer's ethics: TorontoSTh 30, 1987 → 3,g922: [R]Interpretation 43 (1989) 430 (C. M. *Swezey*).

k516 **Reynolds** Terrence, The coherence of life without God before God; the problem of earthly desires in the later theology of Dietrich Bonhoeffer [diss. Brown, [D]*Milhaven* G.]. Lanham MD 1989, UPA. xx-170 p. $23.50. – [R]TS 50 (1989) 825s (J. D. *Godsey*).

k517 **Robertson** Edwin, The shame and the sacrifice 1987 → 4,k446: [R]America 161 (1989) 220s (W. A. *Johnson*).

k518 **Robertson** Edwin H., Dietrich Bonhoeffer, Leben und Verkündigung, [T]*Mühlenberg* M.; Einf. *Bethge* R.(?) Gö 1989, Vandenheock & R. 335 p. DM 44 [TLZ 115,521, M. *Kuske*].

k519 *Tödt* Heinz E., Eberhard Bethge als Theologe und Zeitgeschichtsforscher [80. Gb.]: EvT 49 (1989) 397-416.

k520 BOUYER: **Walling** Richard, Metamorphosis of the sacred; Christian liturgy and the mystery of the Incarnation in the work of Louis Bouyer: diss. [D]*Power* D. Wsh 1989. – RTLv 21,560.

k521 BOYER: *Steenberghen* Fernand Van, Un incident révélateur au Congrès thomiste de 1950 [Boyer C.; quinque viae à la lumière de Humani generis 1950]: RHE 84 (1989) 379-390.

k522 BREMOND: *Duclos* Paul, L'abbé Louis BEAUDOU, un correspondant privilégié d'Henri Bremond: BLitEc 90 (1989) 113-124.

k523 CADOUX: **Kaye** Elaine, C. J. Cadoux, theologian, scholar and pacifist. E 1988, Univ. xiv-228 p. £15. 0-85224-603-X [NTAbs 33,378]. – RExpTim 100 (1988s) 240 [(C. S. *Rodd*) Presbyteros].

k524 CONE: **Stewart** C., God, Being and liberation; James Cone and Howard THURMAN. Lanham MD 1989, UPA. 324 p. $37.50 [TS 51,383].

k526 CONGAR: **Henn** William, The hierarchy of truths according to Yves Congar: AnGreg 246, 1987 ➤ 3,7276; 4,k457: RJRel 69 (1989) 567s (W. J. *Kelly*); NRT 111 (1989) 448s (J. *Famerée*); ÖkRu 38 (1989) 241 (T. *Bremer*); RTLv 20 (1989) 232s (aussi J. *Famerée*); StEcum 6 (1988) 447s (T. *Vetrali*).

k527 **Congar** Yves-Marie, Entretiens/Herbstgespräche [²1987],T 1988 ➤ 4, k458: RZkT 111 (1989) 225s (K. H. *Neufeld*).

k528 ELauret Bernard, Fifty years of Catholic theology; conversations with Yves Congar. L 1988, SCM. v-87 p. £5. – RTLond 92 (1989) 208s (R. *Greenacre*).

k529 **Nichols** Aidan, Yves Congar: Outstanding Christian Thinkers [EDavies Brian]. Wilton CT / L 1989, Morehouse-Barlow / Chapman. $20; pa. $13. 0-8192-1488-4; 7-6 [TDig 37,80].

Bunnenberg Johannes, Lebendige Treue zum Ursprung... Congar, D1988s ➤ 1474.

k530 COSTANTINI: **Butturini** Giuseppe, Alle origini del Concilio Vaticano secondo; una proposta di Celso Costantini [(non come ➤ 4,k450) segr. di Propaganda, 1939; riproposta 1949; poi è divenuto Papa il suo amico Roncalli ...]. Pordenone 1988, Concordia Sette. 349 p. Lit. 35.000. – RCC 140 (1989,3) 539s (G. *Caprile*: inesattezze); RHE 84 (1989) 764-6 (J. *Gadille*).

k531 CUPITT: **Cowdell** Scott, Atheist priest? Don Cupitt and Christianity. L 1988, SCM. xix-103 p. £6.50 pa. – RExpTim 100 (1988s) 312s (W. D. *Hudson*: by a young Australian, with Cupitt foreword); TLond 92 (1989) 443s (D. *Nineham*).

k532 **Hebblethwaite** Brian, The ocean of truth [against Cupitt ...] 1988 ➤ 4,8020: EExpTim 100 (1988s) 155s (W. D. *Hudson*: a bit triumphalistic).

k533 *Schrijver* Georges de, Don Cupitt; de christen als deconstructionist; kan theologie ook postmodern zijn?: Streven 55 (1987s) 698-710.

k534 DANIÉLOU: **Jacquin** Françoise, Histoire du Cercle St-Jean-Baptiste; l'enseignement du P. Daniélou; préf. *Rondeau* M.-J. P 1987, Beauchesne. 372 p. – RRHE 84 (1989) 165-8 (Y. *Tranvouez*).

k535 EBELING: *Schlögel* Heribert, 'Der Mensch ist Gewissen ...' Überlegungen zum Gewissensverständnis von G. Ebeling: Catholica 43 (1989) 79-94.

k536 EVDOKIMOV: **Phan** Peter C., Culture and eschatology; the iconographical vision of Paul Evdokimov [diss.] 1985 ➤ 1,8727: RHeythJ 30 (1989) 455s (Mary *Grey*).

k537 GARDEIL: *Petit* Jean-Claude, La compréhension de la théologie dans la théologie française au XXe siècle; la hantise de savoir et de l'objectivité; l'exemple d'Ambroise Gardeil: LavalTP 45 (1989) 379-391.

k538 GIFFORD: **Jaki** S., Lord Gifford and his lectures 1987 ➤ 3,g687; 4,k273: RScotJT 42 (1989) 111-3 (D. *Cairns*).

k539 GILKEY: *Walsh* Brian J., The dimension of ultimacy and theology of culture; a critical discussion of Langdon Gilkey: CalvinT 24 (1989) 66-92.

k540 GOGARTEN: *Graf* Friedrich W., Friedrich Gogartens Deutung der Moderne; ein theologiegeschichtlicher Rückblick: ZKG 100 (1989) 168-230.

k541 GOLLWITZER: *Stieber* Rolf, Helmut Gollwitzer — eine biographische Skizze: WDienst 20 (1989) 333-351.

k541* GORE [Charles, 1853-1932]: **Avis** Paul, Gore, construction and conflict. Worthing 1988, Churchman. v-123 p. £11 [JTS 40,361].

k542 GUARDINI: **Schmucker-von Koch** Joseph F., Autonomie und Transzendenz; Untersuchungen zur Religionsphilosophie Romano Guardinis 1985 → 1,g194: ᴿRTLv 20 (1989) 379s (E. *Brito*). **Theobald** M., Schriftauslegung Guardinis 1989 → 1414.

k543 ᴱ**Zucal** Silvano, La Weltanschauung cristiana di Romano Guardini: Trento IstScRel 13. Bo 1989, Dehoniano. 495 p. Lit. 35.000.

k544 HABERMAS: *Lakeland* Paul, Habermas and the theologians again [five books, one by Habermas and two by MCCANN D.]: RelStR 15 (1989) 104-9.

k545 *Simpson* Gary M., Theologia crucis and the forensically fraught world; engaging Helmut PEUKERT [Science, action 1984] and Jürgen Habermas: JAAR 57 (1989) 509-541.

k546 **Häring** Bernhard, Meine Erfahrung mit der Kirche 1989 → 3375; also in Italian [America 161,739] = ? Quelle morale? [RSPT 74,340, Y. *Congar*].

k547 HARNACK: ᴱ**Rumscheidt** Martin, Adolf von Harnack, liberal theology at its height [selections]: Making of Modern Theology 6. L 1989, Collins [SF, Harper]. 329 p. $20. 0-00-599131-5 [TDig 36,380].

k548 HAROUTUNIAN: *Crocco* Stephen, Joseph Haroutunian, neglected theocentrist [d. 1968; like AUGUSTINE, CALVIN, and Jonathan EDWARDS 'intoxicated by the majesty and mystery of God's sovereignty']: JRel 68 (1988) 411-425.

k549 HEIDEGGER: *Haeffner* Gerd, Heidegger [geb. 1889] über Zeit und Ewigkeit: TPhil 64 (1989) 481-517.

k550 *Jäger* Alfred, Das Erscheinen Gottes in der Spätphilosophie Martin Heideggers: TGL 79 (1989) 42-55.

k551 **Lotz** Johannes B., Martin Heidegger et Thomas d'AQUIN, ᵀ*Secretan* Philibert: Théologiques. P 1988, PUF. 232 p. [RTLv 21, 501s, E. *Brito*].

k552 ᴱ**Neske** Günther, *Kettering* Emil, Antwort; Martin Heidegger im Gespräch. Pfullingen 1988, Neske. 289 p. – ᴿTPhil 64 (1989) 448s (G. *Haeffner*).

k553 **Ott** Hugo, Martin Heidegger; Unterwegs zu seiner Biographie. Fra 1988, Campus. 355 p. – ᴿTPhil 64 (1989) 445-8 (G. *Haeffner*).

k554 HIRSCH: *Herms* Eilert, Emanuel Hirsch — zu Unrecht vergessen? II: Luther 60 (1989) 28-48.

k555 **Ericksen** Robert P., Theologen unter Hitler; das Bündnis zwischen evangelischer Dogmatik und Nationalsozialismus [Hirsch, G. KITTEL, ALTHAUS]. Mü 1986, Hanser. 343 p.

k555* **Ericksen** R. P., Theologians under Hitler 1985 → 1,g111 ... 4,k468: ᴿCurrTM 16 (1989) 50s (G. C. *Carter*: unmet expectations); RelSt 25 (1989) 247-250 (D. M. *MacKinnon*); ZKG 100 (1989) 288-290 (K. *Nowak*).

k556 HROMÁDKA: *Tóth* Károly (bp., on receiving honorary doctorate, inaugural, Praha 9.VI.1989), ⓦ J. L. Hromádka's theological heritage for the Christian peace conference: TSzem 32 (1989) 229-232.

k557 a) *Bent* Ans J. van der, The vital contribution of J. L. Hromádka to the ecumenical movement; – b) *Rumscheidt* Martin, Die Theologie Hromádkas auf dem Weg zur Kirche der kleinen Leute: ComViat 32 (1989) 153-165 / 167-179 [231-254, *al.*].

k558 IWAND: *Geyer* Klaus, Hans J. Iwands Erbe für heute: ComViat 32 (1989) 39-54.

k559 *Göll* Hans-Peter, [Hans J.] Iwand-Nachlass und Iwand-Studien: VerkF 34,1 (1989) 52-61.

k560 **Iwand** H.J., Frieden mit dem Osten; Texte 1933-1959, ᴱ*Hertog* G.C. den, Mü 1988, Kaiser. 236 p. – ᴿEvT 49 (1989) 389-394 (B. *Klappert*).

k561 *a*) *Thaidigsmann* Edgar, Geschehene und aufgegebene Versöhnung; die Stellung Hans J. Iwands zur Philosophie Hegels; – *b*) *Klappert* Bertold, Versöhnung, Reich Gottes und Gesellschaft; H.J. Iwands theologische Existenz im Dienst der einen Menschheit: EvT 49 (1989) 307-320 [-340, *Sänger* P.] / 341-369.

k562 JENKINS David, God, Jesus and life in the Spirit. L 1988, SCM. 147 p. £5. 0-334-02018-2. – ᴿExpTim 100 (1988s) 439 (R. *Lunt*: shocks with a fresh vision of God).

k563 JOHANNES XXIII: **Alberigo** G., ᵀᴱ*Pouilloux* É., Jean XXIII devant l'histoire [adaptation des plusieurs volumes italiens traitant le colloque L'età di Roncalli 1986]. P 1989, Seuil. 321 p. [RHE 85,227, C. *Soetens*].

k564 **Allegri** Renzo, [Giovanni XXIII] Il papa che ha cambiato il mondo; testimonianze sulla vita privata. Trento 1988, Reverdito. 352 p. Lit. 20.000. – ᴿStCattMi 33 (1989) 573 (M. *D'Avenia*).

k565 *Conzemius* Victor, Mythes et contre-mythes autour de Jean XXIII: CrNSt 10 (1989) 553-576; Eng. 577; ital. iii.

k566 JOHANNES PAULUS I: **Cornwell** J., A thief in the night; the mysterious death of Pope John Paul I. NY 1989, Simon & S. 366 p. $20 [TS 51,187].

k567 JOHANNES PAULUS II: **Del Rio** Domenico, *Accattoli* Luigi, Wojtyła, il nuovo Mosè 1988 → 4,k478: ᴿCC 140 (1989,2) 199-201 (G. *Caprile*); StCattMi 33 (1989) 377 (M. *Respinti*).

k568 **Giovanni Paolo** II, Io credo in Gesù Cristo Figlio dell'uomo, Figlio di Dio, ᴱ*Maggiolini* Sandro: Catechesi del mercoledì 5. CasM 1988, Piemme. 85 p. Lit. 8500. – ᴿParVi 34 (1989) 305s (L. *Melotti*).

k569 *Mattheuws* Alain, De la Bible à 'Humanae vitae'; les catéchèses de Jean-Paul II: NRT 111 (1989) 228-248.

k570 **Heaney** Stephen J., The concept of the unity of the person in the thought of Karol Wojtyła [Pope John Paul II]: diss. Marquette, ᴰ*Tallon* A. – Milwaukee 1988, 239 p. 89-04256. – DissA 50 (1989s) 163s-A.

k571 *Semeraro* Marcello, La 'communio' nel pensiero di Giovanni Paolo II: Lateranum 55 (1989) 393-407.

k572 JÜNGEL: **Kappes** Michael, ... keine Menschenlosigkeit Gottes; eine Auseinandersetzung mit Eberhard Jüngels Ansatz einer trinitarischen Kreuzestheologie jenseits von Theismus und Atheismus: kath. Diss. ᴰ*Vorgrimler*. Münster 1988s. – TR 85 (1989) 517.

k573 **Paulus** Engelbert, Liebe — das Geheimnis der Welt; formale und materiale Aspekte der Theologie Eberhard Jüngels: kath. Diss. ᴰ*Glässer* A. Eichstätt 1988s. xliii-408 p. – TR 85 (1989) 515; RTLv 21,570.

k574 **Webster** J.B., Eberhard Jüngel, an introduction to his theology 1986 → 2,e9 ... 4,k485: ᴿHeythJ 30 (1989) 228s (R.R. *Brinkman*); JAAR 57 (1989) 672-7 (R.D. *Zimany*); JRel 68 (1988) 123s (also R.D. *Zimany*: brilliant but insensitive to BARTH/HEIDEGGER influence); NRT 111 (1989) 270 (B. *Pottier*).

k575 JUNGMANN: *Meyer* Hans B., Der Liturgiewissenschaftler Josef A. Jungmann S.J. [100 Gb. 16.XI.1989]: ZkT 111 (1989) 258-273 [-359 al., seine Fachkompetenzen].

k576 KING: *Grosse* Heinrich W., King, Martin Luther (1929-1968): ➤ 911, TRE 18 (1989) 195-8.

k577 KÜNG Hans, Teologia in cammino, un'autobiografia spirituale 1987 ➤ 4,k493: ᴿTeresianum 40 (1989) 587-590 (C. *Laudazi*).

k578 **Küng** Hans, Pourquoi suis-je toujours [➤ 4,k494 'encore'] chrétien? P 1988, Centurion. 100 p. F 49. – ᴿSpiritus 30 (1989) 219s (F. *Nicolas*).

k578* **Kiewit** John, Hans Küng: Makers of modern theology 1985 ➤ 1,g201; 2,e17: ᴿCriswT 1 (1987) 431-4 (D. S. *Dockery*, also on HENRY and TILLICH earlier in the series).

k579 KUYPER: ᴱ**Augustijn** C., *al.*, Abraham Kuyper, zijn volksdeel, zijn invloed. Delft 1987, Meinema. 263 p. ƒ25. 90-211-3523-X. – ᴿBijdragen 50 (1989) 459s (J. *Jacobs*).

k580 **Stellingwerff** J., Dr. Abraham Kuyper en de Vrije Universiteit 1987 ➤ 4,k495: ᴿWestTJ 51 (1989) 403-6 (M. R. *Langley*: a bad book; how the Amsterdam Vrije Universiteit repudiated its founder).

k582 LEFEBVRE M.: **Penanster** Alain de, Un papiste contre les papes. P / Pontoise 1988, Table Ronde / Edifac. 233 p. F 110. – ᴿRSPT 73 (1989) 343 (Y. *Congar*).

k583 LEWIS: **Sayer** George, Jack [family nickname of] C. S. Lewis and his times. SF 1988, Harper & R. 278 p. $20. – ᴿWestTJ 51 (1989) 177-180 (T. N. *Brown*: excellent).

k584 LONERGAN: ᴱ**Gregson** Vernon, The desires of the human heart; an introduction to the theology of Bernard Lonergan. NY 1988, Paulist. $13. 0-8091-3002-5 [TDig 36,366 sans pp.].

k585 **Gregson** Vernon, Lonergan, spirituality, and the meeting of religions; pref. *Moore* Sebastian, 1985 ➤ 4,k501: ᴿHeythJ 30 (1989) 456-8 (G. *Walmsley*: reserves).

k586 ᴱ**Lawrence** Fred, Lonergan workshop 7. Atlanta 1988, Scholars. viii-360 p. – ᴿTPhil 64 (1989) 452-4 (G. B. *Sala*).

k587 **Lonergan** Bernard, Método en teología [²1973], ᵀ*Remolina* Gerardo: Verdad e Imagen 106. S 1988, Sígueme. 390 p. – ᴿEstAgust 24 (1989) 529-531 (A. *Turrado*); LumenVr 38 (1989) 347-9 (U. *Gil Ortega*).

k588 **Melchin** Kenneth F., History, ethics, and emergent probability; ethics, society and history in the work of Bernard Lonergan. Lanham MD 1987, UPA. xiv-281 p. $29.50; pa. $15.75. – ᴿJRel 69 (1989) 611 (D. J. *Fasching*).

k589 *Webb* Eugene, Metaphysics or Existenzerhellung; a comparison of Lonergan and VOEGELIN: RelStT 7,2s (1987) 36-47.

k590 LOVEJOY: *Duclow* Donald F., Rethinking The great chain of being with Huston SMITH: Listening 24,1 (1989) 3-7 (-70) [< ZIT 89,298].

k591 ᴱ**Kuntz** Marion L. & Paul G., Jacob's ladder and ... the great chain of being [LOVEJOY A. 1936, Kalamazoo meeting 1975] 1987 ➤ 4,375; 0-8204-0233-8. – ᴿChH 58 (1989) 97s (F. *Oakley*).

k592 de LUBAC: **Maier** Eugen, Einigung der Welt in Gott; das Katholische bei H. de Lubac 1983 ➤ 64,e602; 2,e12: ᴿBogVest 47 (1987) 75-78 (A. *Strle*, in Slovene).

k593 *Pelchat* Marc, P. TEILHARD de Chardin et H. de Lubac; pour une nouvelle synthèse théologique à l'âge scientifique: LavalTP 45 (1989) 255-273.

k594 **Lubac** Henri de, Mémoire sur l'occasion de mes écrits. Namur 1989, Culture et Vérité. 399 p. Fb 1450 [TR 86,256].

k595 **Lubac** H. de, ❿ Catholicisme, ᵀ*Odaka* T. – ᴿKatKenk 28,56 (1989) 163-6 (P. *Nemeshegyi*).

k596 **Russo** Antonio, Henri de Lubac; teologia e dogma nella storia; l'influsso di BLONDEL: kath. Diss. ᴰ*Kasper* W. Tübingen 1988s. – TR 85 (1989) 519.

k597 MISKOTTE: *Neven* Gerrit W., Miskotte und die Thora; ein systematischer Beitrag zur Interpretation seiner Theologie: BTZ 6 (1989) 53-76.

k598 MOLTMANN: **Bauckham** R.J., Moltmann, messianic theology in the making 1987 → 4,k512: ᴿNRT 111 (1989) 473 (Fr.J.); TLond 92 (1989) 47s (U. *Simon*).

k599 ᴱ**Burnham** Frederic R., *al.*, Love, the foundation of hope (the theology of Jürgen Moltmann and Elisabeth MOLTMANN-WENDEL). SF 1988, Harper & R. 160 p. $17. – ᴿParadigms 5 (1989) 166-9 (T. E. *Madison*).

k600 **Cornelison** Robert T., Realism and hope; the theologies of Jürgen Moltmann and Reinhold NIEBUHR in creative conflict: diss. Emory, ᴰ*Moltmann*. Atlanta 1989. – RelStR 16,187.

k601 *Marlé* René, Jürgen Moltmann: Études 370 (1989) 507-520.

k602 *Silva Gonçalves* Nuno da, Moltmann, esperança escatológica e empenho no mundo: Brotéria 126 (1988) 21-27.

k603 NEILL: *Yates* T., Stephen Neill; some aspects of a theological legacy: Anvil 5 (1988) 151-161 [< NTAbs 33,2].

k604 NEWBIGIN Lesslie, Unfinished agenda 1985 → 2,e35; 4,k515: ᴿAsiaJT 3 (1989) 369-371 (P. *Quek*).

k605 NIEBUHR: **Cooper** J.A., The theology of freedom; the legacy of Jacques MARITAIN and Reinhold Niebuhr. Macon GA 1985, Mercer Univ. ix-185 p. – ᴿProtestantesimo 44 (1989) 64s (M. *Rubboli*, anche su ZORZI G. 1984). → k600.

k606 **Fox** Richard W., Reinhold Niebuhr, a biography 1985 → 2,a39... 4,k517: ᴿCriswT 3 (1989) 401-4 (T.N. *Brown*); ExpTim 100 (1988s) 200 (*Paidagogos*: 'a superb intellectual biography'); JRel 68 (1988) 263-276 (L. *Gilkey*); SWJT 32,2 (1989s) 78s (J. L. *Garrett*).

k607 ᴱ**Harries** Richard, Reinhold Niebuhr and the issues of our time 1986 → 2,e40: ᴿJRel 68 (1988) 119s (R. *Sizemore*).

k608 ᴱ**Rasmussen** Larry, Reinhold Niebuhr, theologian of public life [selections]: Making of Modern Theology 7. L 1989, Collins [SF, Harper]. 297 p. $20. 0-00-599123-1 [TDig 36,380].

k609 OGDEN: *a) Ogden* Schubert M., Fundamentum fidei; critical reflections on Willi MARXSEN's contribution to systematic theology; – *b) Carlson* Jeffrey, Ogden's 'appropriateness' and religious plurality: ModT 6 (1989s) 1-14 / 15-28.

k610 **Ogden** Schubert M., On theology 1986 → 2,198; 3,270: ᴿJRel 68 (1988) 120-3 (G. L. *Goodwin*: 8 revised articles, not just 'about' theology).

k611 PANNENBERG: **Greiner** Sebastian, Die Theologie Wolfhart Pannenbergs: Bonner Dogmatische Studien 2. Wü 1988, Echter. 396 p. DM 48 pa. [TR 86,9-11, G. L. *Müller*].

Góźdź Krzysztof, Jesus Christus als Sinn der Geschichte bei W. Pannenberg 1986 → b355 supra.

k612 **Polk** David P., On the way to God; an exploration into the theology of Wolfhart Pannenberg [< diss. ᴰ*Cobb* J.B.]. Lanham MD 1989, UPA. xiv-333 p. $38.25. 0-8191-7229-4 [TDig 37,82].

k613 *Logister* W., Het systematisch karakter van Pannenberg's theologie .. recente publicaties: TsTNijm 29 (1989) 396-402.

ᴱBraaten Carl E., *Clayton* P., The theology of W. Pannenberg; twelve American critiques, with an autobiographical essay and response 1988 ⇥ 443.

k614 *Jüngel* Eberhard, Nihil divinitatis, ubi non fides [*Pannenberg* W., Systematische Theologie I, 1988]: ZTK 86 (1989) 204-235 [355-370, Antwort].

k615 *Rightmire* R. David, Pannenberg's quest for the proleptic Jesus: AsburyTJ 44,1 (1989) 51-75.

k616 PAULUS VI: *Ugenti* Antonio, Paolo VI, papa del dialogo: StCattMi 33 (1989) 211-8.

k617 PELIKAN: **Buschart** William D., Perspectives on Christian doctrine in the work of Jaroslav Pelikan; his vindication of the Christian tradition; diss. Drew, ᴰ*Pain*. Madison NJ 1988. – RelStR 16,190.

k618 **Pelikan** Jaroslav [⇥ k235], The melody of theology; a philosophical dictionary. CM 1988, Harvard Univ. x-274 p. $20. – ᴿHorizons 16 (1989) 387s (W. P. *Loewe*: autobiographical).

k619 RAGAZ: **Böhm** Manfred, Gottes Reich und Gesellschaftsveränderung; Traditionen einer befreienden Theologie im Spätwerk von Leonhard Ragaz [1868-1945; kath. Diss. Bamberg 1987]; Vorw. *Fuchs* O. Münster 1988, Liberación. 314 p. [TLZ 115,535, D. *Rostig*].

k620 RAHNER: **Bonsor** J.A., Rahner, HEIDEGGER, and truth; Karl Rahner's notion [of] Christian truth; the influence of Heidegger, Lanham MD 1987, UPA. xx-205 p. $25; pa. $12.75. – ᴿNRT 111 (1989) 121s (P. *Gilbert*).

k621 *Cavalcoli* Giovanni, Karl Rahner e il cristianesimo [Una risposta a 'La Civiltà Cattolica' (6 gen. 1989, *Neufeld* K.)]: SacDoc 34 (1989) 93-135.

k622 **Hines** Mary, The transformation of dogma; an introduction to Karl Rahner on doctrine. NY 1989, Paulist. 159 p. $8 pa. – ᴿHorizons 17 (1989) 60s (J. J. *Buckley*).

k623 **Imhof** P., *Biallowons* H., La fe en tiempos de invierno; diálogos con Karl Rahner, ᵀ*Albizu* José Luis: Cristianismo y Sociedad 17. Bilbao 1989, Desclée de B. 240 p. [LumenVr 38,351].

k624 *Ladaria* Luis F., Naturaleza y gracia; Karl Rahner y Juan ALFARO: ⇥ 7, ᶠAlfaro, EstE 64 (1989) 53-70.

k625 **Maher** Mary V., Historicity and Christian theology; J.-B. METZ's critique of K. Rahner's theology: diss. Catholic Univ., ᴰ*Hill* W. Wsh 1989. 436 p. 89-13815. – DissA 50 (1989s) 980-A.

k626 *Neufeld* Karl H., *a*) Lehramtliche Missverständnisse; zu Schwierigkeiten Karl Rahners in Rom: ZkT 111 (1989) 420-430; – *b*) Religiosità e teologia; lo sfondo spirituale del pensiero di Karl Rahner: CC 140 (1989,1) 46-54.

k627 *Phan* Peter C., Cultural pluralism and the unity of the sciences; Karl Rahner's transcendental theology as a test case: Salesianum 51 (1989) 785-809.

k628 *Russo* Gerry, Rahner and PALAMAS; a unity of grace: SVlad 32 (1988) 157-180.

k629 **Vorgrimler** Herbert, Understanding Karl Rahner 1986 ⇥ 2,e70... 4,k534: ᴿHeythJ 30 (1989) 458s (B. R. *Brinkman*: p. 94, 'he had only cold contempt for... a system of informers and talebearers'); JAAR 57 (1989) 439s (W. *Reiser*).

k630 **Vorgrimler** H., Entender a K. Rahner 1988 ⇥ 4,k536: ᴿRazF 218 (1988) 124 (M. *Alcalá*).

k631 RAMSEY: *Bonnel* M., Ramsey Arthur M. (1904-88): ⇥ 882, Catholicisme XII,55 (1989) 475s.

k632 RATZINGER: **Nichols** Aidan, The theology of J. Ratzinger, an introductory study 1988 ⇒ 4,k538: ᴿExpTim 100 (1988s) 113s (J. *Quinn*); Pacifica 2 (1989) 118 (A.J. *Kelly*); ScripTPamp 21 (1989) 323-9 (E. *Colom*); TLZ 114 (1989) 296s (H. *Kirchner*).

k633 **Rollet** Jacques, Le cardinal Ratzinger et la théologie contemporaine 1987 ⇒ 4,k540: ᴿAngelicum 66 (1989) 478-480 (A. *Nichols*: 'curiously conceived' as defending non-metaphysical post-conciliar line); LavalTP 45 (1989) 323-4 (M. *Pelchat*); ScripTPamp 21 (1989) 374s (L.-F. *Mateo-Seco*).

k634 *Ratzinger* Joseph, Les difficultés en matière de foi dans l'Europe d'aujourd'hui [< OssRom franç. 11.VII.1989]: EsprVie 99 (1989) 465-9.

k635 RAUSCHENBUSCH (1861-1918): **Minus** Paul W., Walter Rauschenbusch, American reformer 1988 ⇒ 4,k540*: ᴿJScStR 29 (1989) 137-140 (H. *Cox*); QRMin 9,4 (1989) 98-104 (C. *Cole*); TTod 46 (1989s) 96s (R.C. *White*).

k636 REU: *Weiblen* W.H., J. Michael Reu [1869-1943] — a self-made theologian [Dubuque Wartburg Lutheran sem.]: CurrTM 16 (1989) 341-5; phot.

k637 RÉVÉSZ: *Barcsza* József, Ⓜ Life-work of Imre Révész: TSzem 32 (1989) 193-7.

k638 RITSCHL: **Weyer-Menkhoff** Stephán, Aufklärung und Offenbarung... A. Ritschl: GöTheolArb 37. Gö 1988, Vandenhoeck & R. 258 p. DM 64. – ᴿTLZ 114 (1989) 833s (R. *Schäfer*).

k639 ROBERTS: **Harrell** David E.ᴶ, Oral Roberts, an American life. Bloomington 1985, Indiana Univ.; SF 1987, Harper & R. 622 p. $13. – ᴿJAAR 57 (1989) 193s (R.B. *Flowers*).

k640 RUNCIE Robert, One light for the world [37 discourses for various occasions, one on Biblical Study] 1988 ⇒ 4,254: 0-281-04334-5. – ᴿExpTim 100 (1988s) 198s [C.S. *Rodd* (presumably) says that he is a most attractive and sensitive speaker, but leaves unclear why TUTU's becoming bishop was such a difficult occasion].

k641 RUSSELL: *Rusling* G.W., David Syme Russell; a life of service [50 years ministry since 1939; apocrypha research]: BaptQ Sup (L 1989) 4-20 [< NTAbs 33,283].

k642 SCHILLEBEECKX: *Metz* Johann-B., Für eine neue hermeneutische Kultur: Orientierung 53 (1989) 256-9 [E. *Schillebeeckx*, 75. Gb.; cf. p. 225s].

k643 **Schillebeeckx** Edward, For the sake of the Gospel [homilies; sequel to God among us 1982s]. L 1989, SCM. ix-181 p. 0-334-01915-X.
ᴱ**Schreiter** Robert J., *Hilkert* Mary Catherine, The praxis of Christian experience; an introduction to the theology of Edward Schillebeeckx [8 other authors] 1989 ⇒ 514.

k644 SCHLATTER: **Bock** E., Adolf-Schlatter-Archiv, Inventar. Stu 1988, Landeskirchliches Archiv D40. xxi-248 p. – ᴿTLZ 114 (1989) 579-581 (W. *Neuer*).
ᴱ**Bockmühl** Klaus, Die Aktualität... Schlatters 1988 ⇒ 440.

k645 SCHWEITZER: *Grässer* Erich, Das theologische und ethische Erbe Albert Schweitzers: ⇒ 120, ᶠLOHSE E., Wissenschaft 1989, 212-224.

k646 R.G. SMITH: **Clements** Keith W., The theology of Ronald G. Smith 1986 ⇒ 2,e87; 4,k549: ᴿJTS 40 (1989) 316-9 (H. *Wardlaw*).

k647 *Williams* John A., Ronald Gregor Smith ['most important English-speaking theologian of (Lonergan's!) generation']; critical faith and the practice of religion: ScotJT 42 (1989) 85-100.

k648 SOMMERLATH: *Amberg* Ernst-Heinz, Ernst Sommerlath [1889-1983] und die Theologie des 20. Jahrhunderts: TLZ 114 (1989) 865-874.

k649 VON SPEYR: *Albrecht* Barbara, Speyr (Adrienne von) 1902-1967: ➤ 886, DictSpir 14,92s (1989) 1126-32.

k650 TEILHARD: **Becker** Thomas, Geist und Materie in den ersten Schriften P. Teilhard de Chardins: FreibTSt 134. FrB 1987, Herder. 239 p. – ᴿTPhil 64 (1989) 116s (R. *Koltermann*).

k651 TILLICH: ᴱAdams James L., *al.*, The thought of Paul Tillich 1985 ➤ 2,e92; 3,h21: ᴿJRel 68 (1988) 118s (C. A. *Kucheman*).

k652 **Ernst** Norbert, Die Tiefe des Seins; eine Untersuchung zum Ort der Analogia entis im Denken Paul Tillichs. St. Ottilien 1988, EOS. xiii-222 p. DM 58 [TS 51, 162-4, J. C. *Dwyer*].

k653 **Jasper** Bernd, *Ratschow* Carl Heinz, Paul Tillich, ein Leben für die Religion: Didaskalia 22. Kassel 1987, Ev. 85 p. [TLZ 114 (1989) 138].

k654 *Schüssler* Werner, Paul Tillich et Karl BARTH; leurs premiers échanges dans les années 20: LavalTP 44 (1988) 145-154.

k655 *Stone* Ronald H., Paul Tillich; on the boundary between Protestantism and Marxism: LavalTP 45 (1989) 393-404; franç. 393.

k656 ᴱ**Taylor** Mark K., P. Tillich, theologian of the boundaries 1987 ➤ 3,h30: ᴿRExp 86 (1989) 445 (D. L. *Mueller*).

k657 TROELTSCH: **Yasukata** Toshimasa, Ernst Troeltsch, systematic theologian of radical historicality [diss. Vanderbilt] 1986 ➤ 3,h34; 4,k563: ᴿJAAR 57 (1989) 883-6 (G. E. *Paul*); JRel 68 (1988) 463 (W. E. *Wyman*: part of Japanese Troeltsch scholarship documented in Mitteilungen der Troeltsch-Gesellschaft 3, Augburg 1984).

k658 **Dietrich** Wendell S., COHEN and Troeltsch; ethical monotheistic religion and theory of culture: BrownJudSt 120, 1986 ➤ 4,k561: ᴿJQR 80 (1989s) 384-7 (D. *Ellenson*).

Coakley Sarah, Christ without absolutes.. Troeltsch 1988 ➤ 7492; ᴱRenz H., Troeltsch-Kongress 1987 ➤ 727*.

k659 VALADIER: *Barthe* Claude, La stratégie du Père Valadier ['Donum vitae', 'écrit par une petite mafia de théologiens obscurs, anonymes', quintessence du refus du dialogue ... dépasse les bornes du supportable ...]: Catholica (P, nov. 1989) 2-7.

k660 VILLAIN Maurice, Vers l'Unité; itinéraire d'un pionnier [de l'oecuménisme], 1935-1975. Dinard 1986, G.S.O.E., xxii-342 p.; 8 color. pl. F 95 [RHE 85, 225, R. *Aubert*: BEA told him after JOHN XXIII's election 'Père, l'Encyclique (Humani Generis sur les frères séparés) se trompe'].

k661 WELTE Bernhard 1906-1983: *a*) **Feige** Ingeborg, Geschichtlichkeit; zu BWs Phänomenologie des Geschichtlichen auf der Grundlage unveröffentlichter Vorlesungen; – *b*) **Lenz** Hubert, Mut zum Nichts als Weg zu Gott; BWs religionsphilosophische Anstösse zur Erneuerung des Glaubens: FreibTSt 138s. FrB 1989, Herder. x-473 p.; DM 58 / xii-339 p. DM 46 [TLZ 115,219-221, H. *Vetter*].

k662 WERNER: *Balsiger* Max U., Un théologien méconnu, Martin Werner [né 1887]: ÉTRel 64 (1989) 23-44.

k663 WITTGENSTEIN: **Kerr** Fergus, Theology after Wittgenstein 1986 ➤ 2, e102 ... 4,k567: ᴿSvTKv 65 (1989) 179s (P. *Thalén*).

Y6.8	*Tendentiae exeuntis saeculi XX* – **Late 20th Century Movements.**

k664 ᴱ**Alberigo** G., *Jossua* J. P., Il Vaticano II e la Chiesa 1985 ➤ 1,g279a ... 4,k568: ᴿProtestantesimo 44 (1989) 76s (F. *Ferrario*).

k665 EAlberigo G., *Jossua* J. P., TE*Komonchak* J., The reception of Vatican II
[➤ 4,k568*], T*O'Connell* M. J.; Wsh; also Tunbridge Wells 1987, Burns &
O.: 0-8132-0654-5: RDocLife 39 (1989) 412-420 (G. *Daly*); ExpTim 100
(1988s) 315 (A. *Lovegrove*); SpirLife 35 (1989) 54-56 (F. R. *McManus*).

k666 [TEPottmeyer Hermann J.] *Alberigo* G., *Jossua* J.-P., Die Rezeption des
Zweiten Vatikanischen Konzils 1986 ➤ 3,e446: RTR 85 (1989) 36-41
(Dorothea *Sattler*).

k667 **Allen** Diogenes, Christian belief in a post-modern world; the full wealth
of conviction. Louisville 1989, Westminster/Knox. xii-238 p. $16 [TS
51, 520-2, J. H. *Wright*].

k668 **Bauberot** Jean, Le protestantisme doit-il mourir? P 1988, Seuil. 284 p.
– RRHPR 69 (1989) 79s (R. *Mehl*: sometimes hard on the Protestant
authorities).

k669 **Beeck** Frans J. van, Catholic identity after Vatican II 1985 ➤ 2,e107;
4,k573: RAngelicum 66 (1989) 497-9 (A. *Wilder*: ch. 1 a counterpoise to
RATZINGER, who wins); JRel 68 (1988) 610s (Ann O. *Graff*); RelStR 15
(1989) 170 (P. *Schineller*).

k670 *Biser* Eugen, ¿Qué futuro hay para la Iglesia? [< StiZt 205 (1987)
3-14], TE*Puig Massana* Ramón: SelT 28 (1989) 11-18 [231-8 (< 541-552)
para la teología].

k671 *a) Boadt* Lawrence, A biblically oriented Roman Catholic Church in the
twenty-first century; – *b) Fogarty* Gerald P., Catholicism, American
culture and the Bible; – *c) Marty* Martin E., The Bible and American
cultural values: NewTR 2,1 (1989) 84-91 / 16-38 / 6-15.

k671* *Bush* L. Russ, Defending the faith in the 21st century: ➤ 44*,
FCRISWELL W., CriswTJ 1 (1987) 269-280.

k672 **Davis** Charles, What is living, what is dead in Christianity today? 1986
➤ 2,e117... 4,k581: RSR 18 (1989) 102s (P. W. *Newman*).

k673 **Drummond** Richard H., Towards a new age in Christian theology:
American Soc. Missiology 8, 1985 ➤ 1,g291... 4,k584: RRelStT 7,1
(1987) 75s (M. *Bollenbaugh*).

k674 **Edwards** David L., The futures of Christianity 1987 ➤ 3,h53; 4,k585:
RScotJT 42 (1989) 431s (G. S. *Wakefield*).

k675 **Everett** W. J., God's Federal Republic; reconstructing our [USA]
governing symbol [God: 'Publisher and President'; Jesus 'Ecclesial
President' (p. 171; 174)]: Isaac Hecker Studies in Religion and American
Culture. NY 1988, Paulist. vi-204 p. $10. 0-8091-2938-8. – RTsTNijm
29 (1989) 308 (P. *Valkenberg*).

k676 *Fichter* Joseph H., The Church; looking to the future [... statistics show
that not all Catholic trends are downhill]: America 160 (1989) 189-192.

k676* *a) García* Ezequiel, A propósito de la modernidad y de la posmodernidad; – *b) Guerra* Augusto, Gaudium et spes; diálogo con el
mundo moderno: REspir 48,192 (1989) 353-388 / 389-414.

k677 *Goldie* Rosemary, *a)* Lay participation in the work of Vatican II,
Lateranum 40s (1974s) 503-525; = *b)* La participation des laïcs aux
travaux du Concile Vatican II: RevSR 62 (1988) 54-73.

k678 *Greinacher* N., ¿Invierno en la Iglesia? [< TüTQ 167 (1987) 182-195],
TE*Giménez* Josep: SelT 28 (1989) 3-10.

k679 **Griffin** David R., God and religion in the postmodern world; Essays in
Postmodern Theology 3. Albany 1989, SUNY. xv-175 p. $39.50; pa. $13.
– RNewTR 2,4 (1989) 107s (S. *Bevans*, also on 1 and 2, essays EGriffin);
TTod 46 (1989s) 337s (J. *DiCenso*).

k680 **Griffin** David R., *Smith* Huston, Primordial truth and postmodern theology. Albany 1989, SUNY. xiv-216 p. $13 pa. [TLZ 115,907, M. J. *Suda*].

k681 **Griffin** David R., *Beardslee* William A., *Holland* Joe, Varieties of postmodern theology. Albany 1989, SUNY. xiv-164 p. $15 [TLZ 115,294, M. *Suda*].

k682 **Groos** Helmut, Christlicher Glaube und intellektuelles Gewissen; Christentumskritik am Ende des zweiten Jahrtausends 1987 → 3,h55; 4,k593; 3-16-145245-3: ᴿActuBbg 26 (1989) 19-21 (J. *Boada*); TsTNijm 29 (1989) 89 (E. *Borgman*).

k683 **Hopper** Jeffery, Understanding modern theology [I. Cultural revolutions 1987 → 3,h61; 4,k598]; II. Reinterpreting Christian faith for changing worlds. Ph 1987, Fortress. vii-158 p. 0-8006-2050-X. – ᴿExpTim 100 (1988s) 237 (I. R. *Torrance*); JRel 69 (1989) 265s (Sheila G. *Davaney*).

k684 *Hünermann* Peter, ¿Amenaza una crisis modernista? [HerdKorr 43 (1989) 130-5], ᵀᴱ*Aleu* José: SelT 28 (1989) 279-286.

k685 **Hunter** James D., Evangelicalism; the coming generation 1987 → 3,h62; 4,k600: ᴿAndrUnS 27 (1989) 146-8 (R. L. *Staples*); EvQ 61 (1989) 180s (R. K. *Johnston*); Interpretation 43 (1989) 220 (R. *Hutchinson*); JRel 69 (1989) 257-9 (S. *Tipton*); TS 50 (1989) 817s (J. A. *Coleman*).

k686 *Jiménez* Antonio, A vueltas con la posmodernidad (I), Los rasgos de la sensibilidad posmoderna: Proyección 36 (1989) 295-311.

k687 **Kaufmann** Franz-Xaver, *Metz* Johann Baptist, Zukunftsfähigkeit; Suchbewegungen im Christentum. FrB 1987, Herder. 185 p. DM 19,80. – ᴿTR 85 (1989) 451-4 (J. *Werbick*).

k688 **Kennedy** Eugene, Tomorrow's Catholics / yesterday's Church 1988 → 4,k603: ᴿCCurr 39 (1989s) 236-8 (J. F. *Kane*).

k689 *Kobler* John F., Were theologians the engineers of Vatican II? [*Swidler* L., 'In essence the theologians wrote the Vatican II documents that the bishops voted on and signed', in The Church in Anguish 1987, p. 190]: Gregorianum 70 (1989) 233-250; franç. 250: doit être nuancé.

k690 ᴱ**Küng** Hans, *Swidler* Leonard, The Church in anguish; has the Vatican betrayed Vatican II? [12 German essays translated, plus 14 American; unanimously against John Paul II policies] 1987 → 4,k606: ᴿAmerica 160 (1989) 274s (T. H. *Sanks*); NewTR 2,1 (1988) 107s (R. J. *Schreiter*: shrill); RelStR 15 (1989) 146 (W. R. *Garrett*).

k691 **Küng** Hans, *Greinacher* N., Contro il tradimento del concilio; dove va la chiesa cattolica?: Nostro Tempo 44. T 1987, Claudiana. 412 p. Lit. 27.000. – ᴿDivThom 91 (1988) 230s (L. J. *Elders*: sad and lowclass; 29 papers sharply critical of RATZINGER); ÉTRel 64 (1989) 471s (A. *Moda*: irritant mais avec saveur de la vérité); Protestantesimo 44 (1989) 234s (anche A. *Moda*: fondato); Servitium 3,62 (1989) 238s (G. *Bacci*); StPatav 36 (1989) 238s (L. *Sartori*).

k692 **Küng** Hans, FREUD und die Zukunft der Religion: Piper 709, 1987 → 3,h69: ᴿLuthMon 29 (1989) 93 (H. *Alisch*).

k693 **Küng** H., Theology for the third millennium 1988 → 4,k607: ᴿAmerica 160 (1989) 379s (W. V. *Dych*).

k694 ᴱ**Ladrière** Paul, *Luneau* René, Le retour des certitudes; événements et orthodoxie depuis Vatican II. P 1987, Centurion. 312 p. F 135. – ᴿÉTRel 64 (1989) 147s (J.-M. *Prieur*: d'un grand intérêt); NRT 111 (1989) 464s (A. *Toubeau*).

k695 ᴱ**Latourelle** René, Vaticano II, bilancio e prospettive venticinque anni dopo, 1962-1987. Assisi 1987, ²1988, Cittadella. 2 vol. c. 1600 p.

Lit. 80.000 → 4,k608*: ᴿAntonianum 64 (1989) 611s (T. *Larrañaga*); Lateranum 55 (1989) 479-481 (S. *Lanza*); RHE 84 (1989) 638s (R. *Aubert*); Salesianum 51 (1989) 169-171 (D. *Bertetto*).

k696 ᴱ**Latourelle** René, Vatican II, bilan et perspectives I-II, 1988 → 4,379: ᴿNRT 111 (1989) 958-960 (R. *Escol*).

k697 ᴱ**Latourelle** René, Vatican II, assessment and perspectives [I. 1988 → 4,380] II-III. NY 1989, Paulist. II. xiii-528 p.; III. xiii-624 p. 0-8091-041[2-1] 3-X; 4-8. – ᴿAmerica 161 (1989) 41s (R. E. *Sullivan*); CalvinT 24 (1989) 392s (J. H. *Kromminga*, 2); TTod 46 (1989s) 246s (G. *Baum*: intramural Catholic); TS (1989) 602-4 (L. *Richard*, 1).

k698 ᴱ**Latourelle** René, Vaticano II; balance y perspectivas, veinticinco años después (1962-1987). S 1989, Sígueme. 1219 p. 84-301-1090-9.

k699 **Lindbeck** George A., The nature of doctrine... in a postliberal age 1984 → 1,g303 ... 4,k610: ᴿJRel 68 (1988) 87-92 (B. A. *Gerrish*).

k700 — **Kasper** Walter, Postmoderne Dogmatik? Zu einer neueren nord-amerikanischen Grundlagendiskussion [*Lindbeck* G. ...]: → 45, ᶠDᴇɪꜱꜱʟᴇʀ A., Weg 1989, 265-274.

k701 **Lochet** Louis, Vers une Église différente. P 1989, D-Brouwer. 152 p. F 73. – ᴿEsprVie 99 (1989) 133-*jaune* (L. *Barbey*).

k702 ᴱ**Logister** W. M. E., *al.*, Twintig jaar ontwikkelingen in de theologie; tendensen en perspectieven [... *Berger* H. H., Le postmodernisme en théologie]. Kampen 1987, Kok. 286 p. – ᴿRHE 84 (1989) 282s (G. *Thils*: Jᴇᴅɪɴ H. HbKG 1962 'ne porte pas la marque des événements en cours' mais ᴱ*Rogier* L., Geschiedenis van de Kerk 1963 élargisse les perspectives, 'Peuple de Dieu').

k703 *Lorizio* Giuseppe, Prospettive teologiche del postmoderno: RasT 30 (1989) 539-559.

k704 **Mardones** José M., Postmodernidad y cristianismo; el desafío del fragmento: Presencia Teológica 50. Santander 1988, Sal Terrae. 155 p. – ᴿBurgense 30 (1989) 593-5 (G. del *Pozo Abejón*); Carthaginensia 5 (1989) 305s (F. *Oliver Alcón*); Proyección 36 (1989) 164 (R. *Franco*); SalT 77 (1989) 169s (J. A. *García*).

k705 *Moore* Stephen D., The 'Post-' age stamp; does it stick? Biblical studies and the postmodernism debate: JAAR 57 (1989) 543-559.

k706 **Nemeshegyi** Peter, ⦿ The achievement of Vatican II and its reception: KatKenk 51,1 (1987) 155-196.

k707 **Neuhaus** Richard J., The Catholic moment; the paradox of the Church in the postmodern world 1987 → 3,h74; 4,k615*: ᴿCCurr 38 (1988s) 489-502 (L. *Doohan*); Horizons 16 (1989) 181s (M. J. *Hollerich*); JRel 69 (1989) 434s (J. A. *Coleman*).

k708 **O'Malley** John W., Tradition and transition; historical perspectives on Vatican II: Theology and Life 26. Wilmington 1989, Glazier. 191 p. $13. 0-89453-769-5 [TDig 36,384].

k709 *Otero* Herminio, Lo posmoderno y los posmodernos: LumenVr 38 (1989) 69-80.

k710 *Rabut* Olivier, Peut-on moderniser le christianisme?: Apologique 1986 → 3,b79: ᴿScEspr 40 (1988) 255 (R. *Potvin*).

k711 ᴱ**Richard** Lucien, Vatican II, the unfinished agenda 1987 → 3,h81; 4,k618: ᴿHorizons 16 (1989) 171s (R. *Modras*); TS 50 (1989) 193s (D. J. *Grimes*).

k712 ᴱ**Savart** C., *Aletti* J.-N., Le monde contemporain et la Bible 1985 → 1,311 ... 3,h84: ᴿScripTPamp 21 (1989) 690 (J. M. *Casciaro*: demasiado francés exc. Cᴀᴢᴇʟʟᴇꜱ).

k713 *Schorsch* Christof, Utopie und Mythos der Neuen Zeit; zur Problematik des 'New Age': TRu 54 (1989) 315-330.

k714 ᴱSeeber David, Brauchen wir ein neues Konzil? Erfahrungen mit dem II. Vatikanum: Tb 1400. FrB 1987, Herder. 191 p. DM 11. – ᴿTR 85 (1989) 218 (M. *Sievernich*).

k715 *Thiel* John E., Theological authorship; postmodern alternatives?: HeythJ 30 (1989) 32-50.

k716 *a*) *Tracy* David, The uneasy alliance reconceived; Catholic theological method, modernity, and postmodernity; – *b*) *Buckley* Michael J., Experience and culture; a point of departure for American atheism: TS 50 (1989) 548-570 / 443-465.

k717 **Walker** Peter bp., Rediscovering the middle way. L 1988, Mowbray. 164 p. £7. 0-264-6701-5. – ᴿExpTim 100 (1988s) 118 (G. *Patrick*: resists the current vogue of extreme views).

k718 **Weigel** George, Catholicism and the renewal of American democracy. NY 1989, Paulist. vi-218 p. $12 pa. [TLZ 115,550, D. L. *Huber*].

k719 **Welch** Wolfgang, Unsere postmoderne Moderne. Weinheim 1987. – ᴿTGL 79 (1989) 178-191 (R. M. *Bucher*: bemerkenswert).

k720 *Werbick* Jürgen, Kirche und Zukunftsfähigkeit [*Kaufmann* F.-*Metz* J.-B. 1987]: TR 85 (1989) 451-4.

k721 **Wiltgen** P. R. M., Der Rhein fliesst in den Tiber; eine Geschichte des Zweiten Vatikanischen Konzils [1987], ᵀ*Köck* I. Feldkirch 1988, Lins. 316 p. Sch. 178. – ᴿTLZ 114 (1989) 834-6 (S. *Hübner*).

k722 **Winling** Raymond, La théologie contemporaine, 1945-1980: 1983 ➤ 64,e649: ... 3,h99: ᴿRHE 84 (1989) 836 (R. *Aubert*).

k723 **Winling** Raymond, La teología del siglo XX; la teología contemporánea (1945-1980) [La théologie contemporaine 1983 ➤ 64,e649] 1987 ➤ 3,h100; 4,k628: ᴿCiTom 116 (1989) 197 (J. *Díaz Murugarren*); RazF 217 (1988) 553s (M. *Alcalá*); StLeg 28 (1987) 255s (C. R. del *Cueto*).

k724 **Wuthnow** Robert, The restructuring of American religion; society and faith since World War II. Princeton 1988, Univ. xiv-374 p. $25. – ᴿHorizons 16 (1989) 164s (D. J. *O'Brien*); JRel 69 (1989) 559s (M. *Silk*).

Y7 (*Acta*) *Congressuum* .2 *biblica*: **nuntii,** *rapports, Berichte.*

k725 *Agua* Agustín del, 44.ᵃ Asamblea General de la 'Studiorum Novi Testamenti Societas' (SNTS), Trinity College Dublin 24-28 Julio 1989 EstBíb 47 (1989) 417-421.

k726 *Basevi* Claudio, Il XXXVIII Colloquium Biblicum Lovaniense (Leuven 16-18 agosto 1988); le lettere ai Tessalonicesi: RivB 37 (1989) 249-253.

k727 *Buetubela* Balembo, IVᵉ Congrès de l'Association Panafricaine des exégètes catholiques [Nairobi, 24-29.VII.1989, 'Les communautés johanniques']: RTAfr 13 (1989) 227-9.

k728 *Catchpole* David R., Studiorum Novi Testamenti Societas, the forty-third general meeting, 8-12 August 1988: NTS 35 (1989) 296-8; 299-320, members' (residence-) addresses.

k728* Chronicles; XII Colloquium [O-]Ecumenicum Paulinum (25-30 September 1989): Deltio VM 18 (1989) 99-108.

k729 *Dal Covolo* Enrico, Una ricerca sulla storia dell'esegesi giudaica e cristiana antica [preistoria di AnStoEseg e sommario delle 6 convegni/ annate 1983/4 fino a 8/9; poi resoconto del settimo seminario, Sacrofano 18-20 sett. 1989]: ParVi 34 (1989) 463-9.

k730 *Evers* Georg,   Second Asian workshop for Bible apostolate,   Singapore 11-16.XII.1988: TContext 6,2 (1989) 125.

k731 *Fernández Marcos* N.,   III coloquio internacional de historia de la exégesis bíblica en el siglo XVII [31.VIII-3.IX.1988, Ginebra]: Sefarad 49 (1989) 211-3 [... *Hagen* K., ¿Que significa el termino *commentarius*?; *Steinmetz* D., CALVINO y Abrahán... Rom 4; *Barthélemy* D., Biblia de Vatablo].

k732 *Fernández Tejero* Emilia,   VIII congreso de la 'International Organization for Masoretic Studies' [Chicago 20-22.XI.1988]: Sefarad 49 (1989) 213-6.

k733 *Galian-Weiss* Sabine, *Oliel-Grausz* Évelyne,   'Sociétés juives en mutation aux XVIe et XVIIe siècles', colloque tenu à l'Institut van Leer (Jérusalem) 6-8 janvier 1986: RÉJ 147 (1988) 397-401.

k734 *Ghiberti* Giuseppe,   I convegni interdisciplinari, Associazione Biblica Italiana 1989, Prato 11-16 settembre: ParVi 34 (1989) 458-462.

k735 *Janssen* Hermann,   Kultur, Bibel und Kommunikation [Seminar der Evangelischen Allianz] Lae, Papua Neuguinea, 13.-18.III.1988: TKontext 10 (1989) 155s.

k736 *Kapera* Zdzisław J.,   The Manchester symposium of the Temple Scroll [Dec. 14-17, 1987]: → 585, FolOr 25 (1988) 241-6.

k737 *Leonardi* Giovanni,   Il Giovannismo alle origini cristiane, 3º Convegno Nazionale di Neotestamentaristi e Anticocristianisti, Prato (F) 14-16 sett. 1989: StPatav 36 (1989) 701-710.

k738 *Lust* Johan,   The XIIIth IOSOT Congress [Leuven 27 Aug.–1 Sept. 1989]: ETL 65 (1989) 489s.

k739 *Milani* Marcello, Pentateuco come Torah; storiografia e normatività religiosa nell'Israele antico, Prato 11-13 sett. 1989: StPatav 36 (1989) 697-700.

k740 ᴱ*Mosetto* Francesco,   *a)* La Bibbia e la sua interpretazione; simposio di Milano, giugno 1988 [2-4.VI: Associazione Biblica Italiana per il suo quarantesimo, insieme con la Fac. Teologica Ital. Sett. e il Dip. Scienze Religiose dell'Univ. Cattolica]: – *b)* La Missione nel mondo antico e nella Bibbia, XXX Settimana Biblica Nazionale, Roma 12-16 sett. 1988: ParVi 34 (1989) 73s.

k741 *Neirynck* F., SNTS 44th meeting, Dublin July 24-28, 1989: ETL 65 (1989) 494-5; usefully gives in full his presidential response to a State reception, detailing Ireland's relations to SNTS and to Leuven.

k742 ᴱ**Neirynck** F., Colloquium biblicum lovaniense... 1949-1989. Lv 1989, Univ. 100 p.; ill. 90-6186-311-2. Indexed contents of all the Acta.

k743 *ÓFearghail* Fearghus,   Society of New Testament Studies meets in Ireland [24-27 July]: DocLife 39 (1989) 379s.

k744 *a)* *Pani* Giancarlo,   III convegno internazionale di esegesi biblica nel XVI secolo [Ginevra 31.VIII-2.IX.1988]; – *b)* *Pesce* Mauro, Un convegno su Antropologia biblica e pensiero moderno (Modena 15-17.IX.1988): AnStoEseg 6 (1989) 301s / 302-7.

k745 *a)* *Pesce* Mauro, Un convegno su antropologia biblica e pensiero moderno (Modena 15-17 settembre 1988); – *b)* *Sacchi* Alessandro, XXX settimana biblica nazionale (Roma 12-16 settembre 1988): RivB 37 (1989) 117-124 / 124s.

k746 *Raurell* Frederic,   El XIII Congreso de la 'International Organization for the Study of the Old Testament' (Leuven 27 agosto–1 septiembre 1989): EstFran 90 (1989) 409-449.

k747 *Rothschild* Jean-Pierre, Le 'premier congrès général d'études samaritaines' (TA-J 11-13 avril 1988): RÉJ 148 (1989) 493-6.

k748 *Schwienhorst-Schönberger* Ludger, Bericht von der Tagung der AGAT [kath. Alttestamentler], 16.-20.VIII.1988 in Erfurt: *a*) BiKi 44 (1989) 42; – *b*) BZ 33 (1989) 313s.

k749 *Segalla* Giuseppe, Il 44º Congresso della SNTS a Dublino (24-28 luglio 1989): StPatav 36 (1989) 691-6.

k750 *Shanks* Hershel, DEVER stars at lackluster annual meeting [ASOR-SBL-AAR Chicago 19-22.IX.1988]: BAR-W 15,2 (1989) 52-54.

k751 *Söding* Thomas, 43. Meeting der Studiorum Novi Testamenti Societas vom 8.-12. August 1988 in Cambridge: BZ 33 (1989) 156-8.

k752 *Sullivan* John L., Report of the Fifty-Second general meeting of the Catholic Biblical Association of America [Aug 14-17, 1989, Syracuse NY]: CBQ 51 (1989) 694-8; 698-701, list of participants.

k753 *Troia* Pasquale, L'arte e la Bibbia; immagine come esegesi biblica; convegno internazionale di studi [laico: BIBLIA] (Venezia 14-16 ottobre 1988): RivB 37 (1989) 525-8.

Y7.4 (*Acta*) *theologica:* **nuntii.**

k753* AAR [American Academy of Religion] – SBL [Society of Biblical Literature], Annual Meeting 1989 [Nov. 18-21, Anaheim CA. Program only (p. 1-140; p. 241-259, index of sessions and participants; p. 140-239. 264 advertisements).

k754 *Abeng* Nazaire B., *a*) Dreissig Jahre Afrikanische Theologie; Ökumenisches Seminar, Bibelzentrum für Afrika und Madagaskar (BICAM), Nairobi 10.-19.IV.1988: TKontext 10,1 (1989) 139; – *b*) Third plenary assembly of the Ecumenical Association of African Theologians (AOTA): Inculturation and ecumenical dialogue in Africa today; Kinshasa, Zaire, 10.-16.XII.1988: TContext 6,2 (1989) 121-3.

k755 *a*) *Carroll* Eamon R., The 40th annual convention of the Mariological Society of America (Burlingame CA, May 31 and June 1, 1989); – *b*) *Bossard* Alphonse, 46ème session de la Société Française d'Études Mariales, Gap 4-6 sept. 1989; – *c*) *Courth* Franz, Maria und der Heilige Geist; Tagung Augsburg 5.-7.II.1989: Marianum 51 (1989) 628-630 / 630-2 [623-6 Paris] / 627 [624-639 España; 640s, Italia].

k756 *Castiau* Claude, Compte rendu de la session théologique 1986s, Le religieux en Occident / 1988, Réincarnation / 1989, Création et salut: CahSPR 1 (1987) 179 ... / 3 (1988) 107 ... / 5 (1989) 109-128.

k758 *Cavalcanti* Teresa, Produzindo teologia no feminino plural [III Encontro Nacional de Teologia, Rio 1-15.I.1988]: PerspT 20 (1988) 359-377.

k758* *Costa* Eugenio, Un convegno sul diavolo [Torino 17-21.X.1988]: RasT 30 (1989) 269-271.

k759 *a*) *Evers* Georg, Consultatie over interreligieuze dialoog in Azië [Hua Hin, Thailand, 23-29.IX.1988]: – *b*) *Schoors* A., Colloquium in Wégimont [België Inst. Iudaicum 10-11.XI.1988] over vormen van monotheïsme; – *c*) *Evers*, Inculturatie en oecumenische dialoog in Afrika [Kinshasa 10-16.XII.1988]; – *d*) *Evers*, Conferentie van pastorale instituten in Azië en Oceanië [Multan, Pakistan, 9-13.I.1989]; – *e*) *Hoogen* T. van den, Katholieke theologen over christelijk exclusivisme [14.I.1989, Werkgenootschap kath. Theologen]; – *f*) *Vandepitte* Marc, Kolloquium te Leuven over de heilige oorlog (1.III.1989): TsTNijm 29 (1989) 164 / 164s / 165s / 166 / 166s / 167s.

k760 *a) Evers* Georg, Oecumenische studiedagen over dertig jaar afrikaanse theologie [Nairobi april 1988]; – *b) Borgman* Erik, Studiedag over economische theologie [Intermat = materialistische Theologie, 29 okt. ...]; – *c) Hoogen* T. van den, Katholieke theologen over het recht van de leek [4 nov. 1988, ...]: TsTNijm 29 (1989) 55 / 55s / 56s.

k761 *Evers* Georg, Erste Schritte zu einer indischen Christologie, Seminar von indischen Theologen, Madras 16.-21.IV.1988: TKontext 10 (1989) 152s.

k762 *Evers* Georg, Seminar of Indian theologians; toward an Indian ecclesiology; Bangalore 17-21.V.1989: TContext 6,2 (1989) 126-8.

k763 *Gesteira Garza* Manuel, Crónica de la 2ª Semana de Teologia [RET / S. Dámaso, M 25-27.IX] 1989: RET 49 (1989) 449-452.

k764 *Giustiniani* Pasquale, Roberto BELLARMINO, teologo e pastore della riforma cattolica [convegno Capua 28 sett.–1 ott. 1988]: Asprenas 36 (1989) 88-92.

k765 *Grootaers* Jan, Bâle, mai 1989 [15-21 mai, Paix et justice], une conférence oecuménique pas comme les autres: Irénikon 62 (1989) 147-171; Eng. 171.

k766 *a) Hägglund* Bengt, Lutherforskarkongressen i Oslo [14-19 aug.] 1988; – *b) Bexell* Göran, Nordisk systematikerkonferens i Finland [Lärkulla-Karis 9-11.I. 1989]: SvTKv 65 (1989) 44s / 45s.

k767 *Haquin* André, Colloque Mgr. L. DUCHESNE, Origines du culte chrétien, Paris, Institut Catholique, 8.XII.1989: RHE 84 (1989) 839-841.

k768 *Hidal* Sten, Tredje nordiska patristikermötet [Lund 23-25 aug.]: SvTKv 65 (1989) 143.

k769 *Hoogen* T. van den, Katholieke theologen over islamitisch fundamentalisme [Werkgenootschap 21 april]; – *b) Vriesse* Jan De, Collegium te Leuven over volwassenencatechese [22 april]; – *c) Pattyn* Bart, Studiedag te Gent over ethiek en psychiatrie: TsTNijm 29 (1989) 279 / 279s / 280s.

k770 *a) Jaramillo* Pedro, El Congreso de espiritualidad sacerdotal; visión armónica de su contenido doctrinal [Madrid 11-15.IX]; – *b) Alcover* Norberto, 'Psicología y Ejercicios Ignacianos'; simposio en Salamanca [12-16.IX]; – *c) Tamayo* Alfredo, 'Iglesia y derechos humanos', IX Congreso de teología de Madrid [13-17.IX]: SalT 77 (1989) 741-752 / 753-8 / 759-764.

k771 *Kippenberg* Hans G., *a)* The history of religions and critique of culture in the days of Gerardus van der LEEUW (1890-1950) [Groningen conference 1-4.V.1989]; – *b)* with *Wiebe* D., Studies of religions in context of social sciences, Wsz 5-9. IX.1989: Numen 36 (1989) 257-9 / 280-2.

k772 Konferenzenberichte / Reports of conferences, by continent: [TKontext 10 =] TContext 6,1 (1989) 137-157 / 6,2 (1989) 129-134.

k772* *Kuschel* Karl-Josef, Weltreligionen und Menschenrechte; Bericht über ein Symposion in Paris [Unesco/Goethe Inst.]: EvKomm 234 (1989) 17-19.

k773 *Langford* Thomas A., [Methodist conference May 1988] Conciliar theology, a report: QRMin 9,2 (1989) 3-15 (-34, *Jones* L. G.).

k774 *Libânio* João Batista, VII encontro intereclesial das CEBs; povo de Deus na América Latina a caminho da libertação: REB 49 (1989) 515-534 [-585, *al.*].

k775 *Lüders* Ulrich, Auf der Suche nach geheimer Nähe; [20. Basel-] Leuenberger Jubiläumstagung zu 'BARTH und SCHLEIERMACHER': LuthMon 29 (1989) 477s.

k776 *a*) *Lukken* Gerard, Studieweek over semiotiek en christelijke uitings-vormen [Tilburg 26-29 mei 1989); – *b*) *Dröes* Freda, *Maeckelberghe* Els, Theologes uit Europa over godsbeelden [European Society of Women for Theological Research, 3d Arnoldsheim BR 22-26 sept. 1989]: TsTNijm 29 (1989) 291s / 293s.

k777 *Morren* Lucien, Science, technologie et valeurs spirituelles; un symposium à Tokyo [mai 1987]: NRT 111 (1989) 83-96.

k778 Newman Centenary Conference, St. Louis Univ. 'Tradition, values, and progress; the intellectual ethos of J. H. NEWMAN', Nov. 29–Dec. 2, 1990: TDig 36 (1989) 319, program.

k779 *Ntedika* Konde, 'Théologie africaine, bilan et perspectives'; XVII semaine théologique de Kinshasa [2-8.IV.1989]: RAfrT 13 (1989) 223-6.

k780 *Pahnke* Donate, Symposium 'The history of religions and critique of culture in the days of Gerardus van der LEEUW (1890-1950)', Groningen 1.-3. Mai 1989: ZMissRW 73 (1989) 309-311 (deutsch).

k781 *Poupard* Paul card., Conclusions, Colloque BLONDEL, Aix-en-Provence 4 mars 1989: EsprVie 99 (1989) 269-271.

k781* *Qualizza* Marino, Teologia e istanze di sapere oggi in Italia; XIII congresso ATI: RasT 30 (1989) 466-470 (473-8 *Molari* C.).

k782 Reports about theological conferences: TContext 6/2 (1989) 120-131; 7/1, 136-151, none perceptibly biblical.

k783 *Ricca* Paolo, Budapest 1989; il punto del cammino ecumenico alla luce dell'Assemblea plenaria di Fede e Costituzione [9-21 agosto]: Protestantesimo 44 (1989) 262-274.

k784 *Rostagno* Sergio, Kerygma paradosis ekklesia; convegno in ricordo di Vittorio SUBILIA, 14 aprile 1989: Protestantesimo 44 (1989) 114-6.

k785 *a*) *Ruiz Verdú* Pedro, XXIV simposio de teología trinitaria (Salamanca, 23-25.X.1989) / II Semana Española de Teología (Madrid 25-27.IX.1989); – *b*) *Romero García* Pedro, XX Congreso Franciscano Hispano-Portugués (Valencia, 10-15.IX.1989); – *c*) *Sánchez Gil* Victor, III Congreso Internacional sobre los Franciscanos en el Nuevo Mundo (La Rábida, Huelva, 18-23.IX.1989): Carthaginensia 5 (1989) 251-3.247-250 / 239-250 / 255-260.

k786 *Rusecki* Marian, ℗ 'Christ has freed us for freedom' [liberation theology]; 22d KUL ecclesiological week: ZeKUL 30,1 (1987) 67-71.

k787 *Salzano* Teresa, Israele e le genti, le genti e Israele; IX colloquio ebraico-cristiano, Camaldoli (Arezzo) 7-11 dic. 1988: StPatav 36 (1989) 255-260.

k788 *Sartori* Luigi, Teologia politica, convegno Trento 17s.V.1989: StPatav 36 (1989) 683-9.

k789 *Seidel-Menchi* S. ['initiative'], *Moeller* B. ['initiatrice'], *Guggisberg* H. R., Ketzerverfolgung im 16. und im frühen 17. Jhdt: Wolfenbüttel 2-4.X.1989 [on attend les Actes...]: RHE 84 (1989) 786s, plutôt détaillé (J.-F. *Gilmont*).

k790 *Tamayo Ayesterán* Alfredo, Utopía y profetismo en la sociedad y en la Iglesia; VIII Congreso de Teología [M 7-11.IX]: SalT 76 (1988) 647-655.

k791 *Tang* Edmond, Plural und kontextuell; alternative Modelle theologischer Ausbildung [... Asien, Afrika]: Pro Mundi Vita Studien 4 (1988) 1-12... [G. *Evers* (Eng.) summary, TContext 6/2, 103].

k792 *Trobajo* Antonio, XXI jornadas de teología [Salamanca 22-24.IX]: StLeg 29 (1988) 327-337.

k793 *Vettore* Carla, Dalla fenomenologia religiosa al pensiero religioso del mondo classico; Mircea ELIADE e Georges DUMÉZIL: Bressanone 11-12 oct. 1988: StPatav 36 (1989) 261-3.

k794 *Zander* Helmut, Katholische Aufklärung – Aufklärung im katholischen Deutschland; eine Tagung der 'Deutschen Gesellschaft für die Erforschung des 18. Jahrhunderts' vom 16.-18. November 1988 in Trier: ZKG 100 (1989) 231-9.

Y7.6   *Acta congressuum philologica:* **nuntii.**

k795 *Ankum* Hans, *Michel* Jacques-Henri, La XXXXIIème (42d) Session de la Société Internationale 'Fernand De Visscher' pour l'Histoire des Droits de l'Antiquité, Salzbourg, 20-23 septembre 1988: RIDA 36 (1989) 449-484.

k796 *Amande* Carlotta, *Graffigna* Paola [ᴰ*Cavallo* Guglielmo, *Tjäder* Jan-Olof], Convegno 'Scripts, books, and texts, in the provinces of the Byzantine Empire', 18-28.IX.1988, Erice: Maia 41 (1989) 149s.

k797 *Calder* William M., The Otto JAHN (1813-69) symposium [Bad Homburg 13-16 June 1988]: Gnomon 61 (1989) 380s.

k798 *Pesaresi* Raimondo, Secondo convegno nazionale di studi su La donna nel mondo antico [Torino 18-20.IV.1988]: AtenRom 34 (1989) 140-2.

k799 Société des Études Latines, liste des membres: RÉLat 67 (1989) IX-XXX; comptes-rendus 1-30.

k800 Veranstaltungen [-svorschau]: ZSemiot 11 (1989) 115-118 . 273-291. 421-435.

Y7.8   *Acta congressuum orientalistica et archaeologica:* **nuntii.**

k801 *a) Arat* M. Kristin, Armenien; Kultur-Liturgie-Spiritualität; interdisziplinäres ökumenisches Symposion in Mainz vom 17.-19. März 1988; – *b) Kropf* Manfred, 10ᵉ conférence internationale d'études éthiopiennes, Paris, 23.-26. August 1988; – *c) Müller* C., IVᵉ Congrès international d'études coptes; – *d) Kaufhold* Hubert, Symposium Syriacum 28.-31.VIII. / III. Kongress für christlich-arabische Studien 1-3.IX.1988 Leuven: OrChr 73 (1989) 213-6 / 217s / 221-3 / 218-220.

k802 *Avilova* L.I., *Terekhova* N.N., ❸ The Soviet-American symposium on 'The earliest metallurgy of the Old World' (Tbilisi-Signakhi, 1988): SovArch (1989,3) 290-6.

k803 *Avilova* L.I., ❸ 'Archaeology and linguistics; the Indoeuropean problem', Conference 18-19.XII.1986: SovArch (1989,2) 280-6.

k804 *a) Brice* William C., The eighteenth international Eirene congress at Budapest (29.VIII-2.IX.1988); – *b) Weingarten* Judith, First joint archaeological congress, Baltimore, Jan. 5-9, 1989: Kadmos 28 (1989) 96 / 175s.

k805 *Darmon* Jean-Pierre, Vᵉ colloque international sur la mosaïque antique, Bath 5-12 sept. 1987: BMosAnt 12 (1988s) 248-251.

k806 *Heintze* Helga von, Zweihundertfünfzig Jahre Herculaneum; convegno internazionale: Gymnasium 96 (1989) 153-7.

k807 *Ivanov* V., ❸ XXXIV Rencontre Assyriologique Internationale (Istanbul, July 1987): VDI 191 (1989) 187-190.

k808 *Kakovkin* A.Yu., ❸ Meeting on problems of Coptic Art, Leningrad Hermitage 14 Dec. 1988: VDI 191 (1989) 197s.

k809 *Konopatsky* A. K., ⊕ The 14th international congress on the history of Roman frontier defence construction (Bad-Deutsch-Altenburg, 1986): SovArch (1989,4) 294s.

k810 *Sapin* Y., Colloque [CNRS/Inst.Cath./Prot.] sur la Syrie-Palestine à l'époque perse, Paris, 29-31.III.1989: Akkadica 64s (1989) 39-43.

k811 *a) Shilov* V. P., *Masson* V. M. ⊕ The world archaeological congress [Southampton 1-7.IX.1986]; – *b) Ščapova* Y. L., ⊕ The second international symposium of archaeologists and historians of glass in Toruń [Oct. 1989]: SovArch (1989,1) 296-300 / 293-6.

Y8   *Periti,* **Scholars, Personalia, organizations.**

k812 **Brückmann** Hans, Bibelverbreitung im Rheinland; 175 Jahre Evangelisches Bibelwerk im Rheinland; gegründet als Bergische Bibelgesellschaft im Jahre 1814: Schr.Ver.Rh.Kirchengeschichte 95. Köln 1989, Rheinland-V. x-404 p. 3-7927-1095-1.

k813 *Buscemi* A. M., Studium Biblicum Franciscanum, cronaca 1988-1989: LA 39 (1989) 377-395.

k814 [ᴱ*Crocker* John, segr., *Valentino* Carlo, assist.] Acta Pontificii Instituti Biblici 9/6 (1989s) 431-520; 441-453, prolusione, R. P. Rettore *Vanhoye* Albert.

k815 *De Vries* Simon J., Bible and theology in the Netherlands[2]: Amer UnivStudies 7/22 [¹1968, Wageningen]. NY 1989, Lang. xi-171 p. $32. 0-8204-1052-7.

k816 *Fogarty* G. P., Biblical scholarship at the Catholic University of America: CathHR 75 (1989) 628-657 [< RHE 85,125*].

k816* Fünfzig Jahre Katholisches Bibelwerk in Deutschland. Stu c. 1988, KBW, 168 p.

k817 *Fuller* Reginald C., Golden jubilee of the [British] C. B. A.: ScriptB 20 (1989s) 34-37; phot.

k818 *Gatz* Erwin, Das Römische Institut der Görres-Gesellschaft 1888-1988: RömQ 83 (1988) 3-18.

k819 *Gutiérrez* Mario, Crónica de la Facultad de Teología [Bogotá] 1989: TXav 39 (1989) 473-493.

k820 **Handy** Robert T., A history of Union Theological Seminary in New York 1987 → 3,h265; 4,k738: ᴿJRel 69 (1989) 414s (D. A. *Hubbard,* of Fuller; p.415s, review of MARSDEN's Fuller → 3389); RHE 84 (1989) 759-761 (R. F. *McNamara,* franç.).

k820* Die Kirchliche Hochschule [Bethel/Bielefeld], Sommer 1987 bis Frühjahr 1989: WDienst 20 (1989) 379-416; 417-424, Veröffentlichungen der Professoren.

k821 *La Potterie* Ignace de, L'Istituto Biblico [Pontificio, di Roma] negli ottant'anni della sua storia: CC 140 (1989,4) 166-172.

k822 *Lewek* Antoni, ⊕ Kronika wydziału teologicznego: STWsz 26,1s (1988) 282-313 / 279-313.

k823 *Mailleux* Romain, *Conti* Martino, Chronica [Pontificio Ateneo Antonianum]: Antonianum 64 (1989) 621-635 / 636-657.

k824 *a) Muszyński* Henryk, Ks. Prof. Dr. Hab. Czesław JAKUBIEC jako biblista; – *b) Łach* Jan, Ks. Prof. Dr. Hab. Jan STEPIEŃ – Kilka uwag o jego działalności naukowe: STWsz 26,1 (1988) 5-11 / 12-14.

k824* *Pastor-Ramos* Federico, Ciencias bíblicas y increencia en España, hoy: RazF 217 (1988) 430-4.

k825 *Strobel* A., Der Lehrkurs 1987 in Jordanien und Syrien: JbEvHL 1 (1989) 131-172 [< ZAW 102, 278].

k826 STRUVE, Vassili Vassilevich 100th birthday: VDI 188 (1989) 244-7 (O.D. *Berlev, al.*).

Y8.5   *Periti,* in memoriam.

k827 In memoriam: ETL 65,2s (1989) 99*-101*; Necrologia: REB 49 (1989) 214-229.472-481.730-5.982-6; – Nécrologies: RHE 84 (1989) 130*s.283*s; 433s; NumLit 121 (1989) 144.

k829 Alfonsi, Luigi [→ 4,k753], 12.XI.1917-20.I.1987, collab.: SicGymn 42 (1989) 311s (S. *Pricoco*).

k830 Alonso Alonso, Pedro, abad, 20.II.1918-6.VII.1988; RHE 84 (1989) 579s (T. *Morál*).

k831 Amussin, Joseph [→ 65,e104; 1,g353], 29.XI.1910-12.VI.1984: RQum 14 (1989) 109-120 (N.L. *Gluskina*; bibliog. concerning Dead Sea Scrolls 121-6, Z.J. *Kapera*).

k832 Anastasiou, Ioannis, 1918-1987; Thessaloniki church historian: GrOrTR 33 (1988) 358s (G.C. *Papademetriou*).

k833 Apollonj Ghetti, Bruno Maria, 1905-27.V.1989: StRom 37 (1989) 347-9 (G. *Zander*).

k834 Ashmole, Bernard, 1894-25.II.1988; collateral descendant of Oxford Museum founder, director of British School in Rome: AnBritAth 84 (1989) ii-v; phot. – AJA 93 (1989) 135s (J. *Boardman*).

k835 Atiya, Aziz Suryal, 5.VII.1898-24.IX.1988: JAmEg 26 (1989) 1s (S.K. *Brown*).

k836 Balil Illana, Alberto, 1928-23.VIII.1989: ArchEspArq 62 (1989) 3s (J. *Arce*); Boletín del Seminario de Estudios de Arte y Arqueologia 55 (Valladolid 1989) 531-3, phot. (J.J. *Martín González*).

k837 Balthasar, Hans Urs von, HerdKom 42 (1988) 396s; IKZ 13 (1988) 249-256 (J. *Ambaum*); – ᴱ*Lehmann* Karl, *Kasper* Walter, Hans Urs von Balthasar – Gestalt und Werk. Köln 1989, Communio. 359 p. DM 48 [TLZ 115, 761-3, F. *Hoffmann*].

k838 Barbera, Francesco, 28.VI.1905-16.II.1988: StRom 36 (1988) 89s; phot. (N. *Vian*).

k839 Barnett, Richard D. [→ 2,e318; 3,h297], 23.I.1909-29.VII.1986; British Museum: RStFen 6 (1989) 3-6 (G. *Falsone*).

k840 Barrois, Georges A., [→ 4,k763] 17.II.1898-27.VIII.1987: GrOrTR 33 (1988) 243s (G. C. *Papademetriou*).

k841 Behrens, Peter, 19.VII.1931-11.II.1989; LexÄg Nacktheit, Phallus, Pfeil; Skorpion, Strauss, Widder...: GöMiszÄg 109 (1989) 8-11; phot. 7 (P. *Derchain*, U. *Verhoeven-van Elsbergen*): 12-15 Bibliog.

k842 Benoit, Pierre M., o.p. [→ 3,h305; 4,k776], 3.VIII.1906-23.IV.1987, Religious Life Review 28,135 (Dublin 1989) 4-6 (C. *Breen*).

k843 Ben-Sasson, Hayyim Hillel, ... Zion 59 (1989) 145-8 (M. *Stern,* ❸).

k844 Béranger, Jean, [→ 4,k771] 25.X.1903-13.IX.1988; Principat romain: CRAI (1989) 463s (B. *Guenée*); Gnomon 61 (1989) 285-7 (F. *Paschoud*).

k845 Beumer, Johannes, S.J., 1901-23.VI.1989: TPhil 84 (1989) 567-577 (R. *Berndt*, nur Bibliog.).

k846 Bialostocki, Jan, aet. 67, 25.XII.1988; historien d'art: RHE 84 (1989) 291 (R. *Aubert*).

k847 Bignami-Odier Jeanne, 30.X.1902-19.I.1988, collaboratrice de la Bibliothèque Vaticane: RHE 84 (1989) 277s (J. *Ruysschaert*).

k848 Blair, Dorothy Lilian, 10.IX.1890-16.III.1989; Corning Museum: JGlass 31 (1989) 124s, phot. (J. H. *Martin*).

k849 Bouärd, M. de, aet. 80, 28.IV.1989: RHE 84 (1989) 612 (L. *Genicot*).

k850 Bourguet, Pierre du, S.J., [➤ 4,k774], 1910-30.XII.1988: BSACopte 28 (1989) 1-4, portr. (R.-G. *Coquin*, bibliog.); RICathP 31 (1989) 121-5 (F. *Graffin*).

k851 Brásio, António, C.S.Sp., 8.VIII.1906-13.VIII.1985: RAfrT 13 (1989) 75-79 (F. *Bontinck*).

k852 Brown, Thomas Julian, 24.II.1923-19.I.1987; paleographer: ScrCiv 12 (1988) 305-316 (Michelle P. *Brown*).

k852* Bruin, C. C. de, 1905-1988: Nederlands Archief voor Kerkgeschiedenis 69,1 (1989) 1s; 3ss Bibliografie (*Woerden* A. van) [< ZIT 89,731].

k853 Brunn, Wilhelm Albert von, 17.IX.1911-8.V.1988: PraehZts 64 (1989) 1-4; bibliog. (Gisela *Schumacher-Matthäus*, Otto M. *Wilbertz*).

k854 Bucsay, Mihály, 8.VII.1912-1988: TSzem 31 (1988) 301s (M. *Márkus*).

k854* Bussagli, Mario [➤ 4,k777*], 23.IX.1917-14.VIII.1988: central Asian art: EWest 38 (R 1988) 317-321; bibliog.

k855 Callaway, Joseph A. [➤ 4,20.k778], 1920-23.VIII.1988; excavator of Ay: BASOR 275 (1989) 1-3, phot. (J. D. *Seger*).

k856 Carmignac, Jean [➤ 2,e336; 3,h315], 1914-2.X.1986; dir. RQum: FolOr 25 (1988) 233-240 (J. *Delcor*).

k857 Casas García, Victoriano, 27.X.1944-19.VIII.1989; exegeta; dir.: VerVid 47 (1989) 141-9, phot.; bibliog. (Segr. Prov.).

k858 Castagnoli, Ferdinando, 1917-28.VIII.1988: Mileto; Campi flegrei, Roma: RArchéol (1989) 357s (J. *Heurgon*); PBritSR 57 (1989) xi-xiv (L. *Cozza*).

k859 Celada, Benito, 4.III.1904-12.XII.1988; dir. Cultura Bíblica: Sefarad 49 (1989) 219s (F. *Sen*).

k860 Chagnon, Roland, 1939-1989, editor 1984-7: SR 18 (1989) 123-6 (T. *Sinclair-Faulkner*, Elisabeth J. *Lacelle*; bibliog.).

k861 Châtillon, Jean, 1912-29.IX.1988; médiévaliste: RHE 84 (1989) 245s (J. *Longère*); RICathP 30 (1989) 137-9 (S. *Breton*).

k862 Collins, John, O.M.I., 1933-20.II.1988: MilltSt 23 (1989) 40 (-53, his art. on suffering).

k863 Costas, Orlando E., 1942-1987: Missiology 17 (S. Pasadena 1989) 85 (S. *Escobar*; bibliog. 87-..., R. *Fernández Calienes*) [< ZIT 89,422].

k864 Cowley, Roger, aet. 48, 5.IV.1988: Times (9.IV.1988; E. *Ullendorff*); OrChr 73 (1989) 228 (M. *Kropp*).

k865 Cremaschi, Luigi, 11.VII.1896-27.VII.1989: RitNum 91 (1989) 301s, fot. (L. *Colombetti*).

k866 Daux, Georges, 21.IX.1899-23.XII.1988, dir. École Française d'Athènes 1950-69: BCH 113 (1989) iii-ix, bibliog. [P. *Aupert*]; CRAI (1989) 16s (B. *Guenée*).

k867 Der Nersessian, Sirarpie, 5.IX.1896-5.VII.1989; Armenian art: DumbO 43 (1989) IX-XI, portr. (J. *Allen, al.*); CRAI (1989) 531 (B. *Guenée*).

k868 Dinsmoor, William Bell,ᴶ, 2.VII.1923-7.VII.1988: AJA 93 (1989) 213s, phot. (J. M. *Camp*; bibliog.).

k869 Doumouras, Alexander, aet. 51, 15.XI.1987: SVlad 32 (1988) 195-7, phot. (P. *Lazor*).

k870 Drioton, Étienne, 1889-1961: BSocFrÉg 116 (1989) 5s (J. *Vercoutter*).

k871 Eilers, Wilhelm, 27.IX.1906-3.VII.1989; Keilschrift-Recht: AfO 35 (1988, sic) 255s, portr. (M. *Mayrhofer*). Mitarbeiter seit c. 1930: OLZ 84 (1989) 645 (H. *Klengel*).

k871* Fensham, Frank Charles, 13.X.1925-26.VII.1989: Old Testament Essays 2,3 (Pretoria 1989) 1-12, portr. (F. E. *Deist*: 'a theological evaluation', bibliog.); JSem 1 (1989) 145-155; portr. (H. J. *Dreyer*, Afrikaans; bibliog.).

k872 Fernández y Fernández, Doroteo, ep. Badajoz, aet. 86, 10.VII.1989: S.S.L.: AcPIB 9,5 (1988s) 420.

k872* Fernández-Galiano Manuel 1918-1988; filólogo, papirólogo: Emerita 57 (1988) 1-4 (J. *Lens Tuero*).

k873 Ferreira Gomes, Antonio, 1906-13.IV.1989: HumT 10,1 (Porto 1989) 3s (C. A. *Moreira Azevedo*).

k874 Fischer, Joseph Anton, prof. mgr., 5.V.1911-30.III.1989; patrologie, Augsburg: RHE 84 (1989) 522s (K. *Hausberger*).

k875 Franceschi, Filippo, vescovo † 30.XII.1988: StPatav 36 (1989) 5.

k876 Frei, Hans W., † 12.IX.1989; biblical narrative: ETL 65 (1989) 230 (R. F. *Collins*).

k877 Gaiser, Konrad, 26.XI.1929-3.V.1988: Gräzistik: Gnomon 61 (1989) 659-661, portr. (H. *Flashar*).

k877* Gammie, John G., † 26.XII.1989 [TS 51,366; ETL 66,248].

k878 Geyser, Albert S., 10.II.1918-13.VI.1985: JTSAf 64 (Rondebosch) 64 (1988) 4s [< TContext 6/2, 18].

k879 Gideon Virtus E., 29.XII.1926-14.XII.1988; NT: SWJT 32,1 (1989s) 1, phot.

k880 Gill, Joseph, S.J., 1901-15.X.1989; former rector of Pontifical Oriental Institute: RHE 84 (1989) 849 (C. *Fitzsimons*).

k881 Gochee, William J., prof. † 6.VIII.1989 [JBL 109,533].

k882 Gray, Basil, 1904-10.VI.1989; Islamic art: Iran 27 (1989) v-vi; phot. iv (R. *Pinder-Wilson*).

k882* Greifenhagen, Adolf, 31.XII.1905-27.I.1989; Greek pottery: Gnomon 61 (1989) 571-5 (W.-D. *Heilmeyer*).

k883 Griffith, Guy Thompson, 7.I.1908-12.IX.1985: AncW 20 (1989) 57-64 (A. M. *Devine*; bibliog.).

k884 Gutiérrez Inclan, José Manuel: StOvet 14 (1986) 7s, phot. (A. *Fernández García-Argüelles*); 'un historiador liberal' 9-18 (J. *Fernández Conde*).

k885 Halkin, François, S.J. [➤ 4,k814] 1.VII.1901-25.VII. 1988; Bollandiste: TAth 60 (1989) 826-8 (P. B. *Paschos* ☉; bibliog.).

k886 Hanson, Richard P. C., † 23.XII.1988: ExpTim 100 (1988s) 419-421 (W. H. C. *Frend*, also on his 1988 book).

k886* Hartdegen Stephen J., O.F.M., aet. 82, 19.XII.1989; editor-in-chief of NAB 1944-70: ETL 66,248.

k887 Havelock, Eric Alfred, 1903-4.IV.1988: ÉchMClas 33 (1989) 278 (R. S. *Kilpatrick*).

k887* Havener, Ivan, O.S.B. [➤ 4,k816], 1943-24.IV.1989; Q-theology: ETL 65 (1989) 229 (R. F. *Collins*).

k888 Heiming, Odilo Kurt, O.S.B., 7.IV.1898-21.IX.1988, Maria-Laach: OrChr 73 (1989) 230s (J. *Assfalg*: 'einer der bedeutendsten Liturgiewissenschaftler des Jahrhunderts').

k889 Henderson, Alastair A. R., 1937-1988: classical botany (unfinished): ÉchMClas 33 (1989) 427 (P. R. J.-P.).

k890 Herr, Moshe D., ... Zion 59 (1989) 264s ☉.

k891 Heubeck, Alfred [➤ 4,k819], 20.VII.1914-24.VII.1987: klas. Philologe: Minos 24 (1989) 243-7 (J. L. *García-Ramón*).

k891* Hintze, Ursula, 10.XI.1918-29.IV.1989: BeiSudan 4 (1989) 5-8; bibliog.

k892 Ijjas, Jószef, archiep. Kaloca (Ungheria), aet. 88, 29.IV.1989: AcPIB 9,5 (1988s) 420.

k893 Joachim, Paul B., O.S.B.Silv., aet. 48, 24.III.1989; S.S.L.: AcPIB 9,5 (1988s) 421.
k894 Kálmán, Csomasz Tóth, 30.IX.1902 - 1988: TSzem 32 (1989) 119 (J. *Máté*).
k895 Kaplan, Jacob, 1910-14.IV.1989: TA area archaeologist: BAngIsr 9 (1989s) 63s (R. *Gophna*); Qadmoniot 22 (1989) 55 (also R. *Gophna*, ❺).
k896 Kawerau, Peter, aet. 74, 8.IX.1988: OrChr 73 (1989) 229 (J. *Assfalg*).
k896* Khlobystin, Leonid Pavlovič, 2.III.1931-11.III.1988: SovArch (1989,2) 298s, phot. (V. M. *Masson, al.*).
k897 Kilpatrick, George Dunbar, 1910-1989: ClasB 65,3s (1989) 111-4 (A. M. *Devine*).
k897* Kipper, João Balduino, S.J., 28.I.1915-20.XI.1988; prof. exeg.: REB 49 (1989) 477s.
k898 Kirkman, James Spedding, 1906-26.IV.1989; editor 1982-9: IntJNaut 18 (1989) 189-190; portr. (Angela *Croome*).
k899 Kissling, Hans Joachim, 8.IX.1912-10.X.1985; Osmanisches Reich: Der Islam 65 (1988) 191-5; portr. (H. G. *Majer*); Bibliog. 196-9.
k900 Kobylina, Maria Michailovič, 17.X.1897-24.VIII.1988: VDI 190 (1989) 232s (N. A. *Sudorova*).
k900* Koerner, Reinhard, 27.VI.1926-23.IV.1987; Mitarbeiter; ArPapF 35 (1989) 5s, phot.; 117-9, Bibliog. (K. *Hallof*).
k901 Kornfeld, Walter, Prälat Prof. [➤ 4,k831], 18.IX.1917-11.XI.1988: lev. Gesetz; BiKi 44 (1989) 40s (G. *Braulik*).
k901* Kremers, Heinz, aet. 61, 26.V.1988: ZRGg 40 (1988) 259-262 (H.-J. *Barkenings*).
k902 Kutscher, Raphael, 1938-1989: Akkadian, Hebrew: TAJ 15s (1988s) 115s, portr. (A. *Kempinski*).
k903 Kuznetsov, Yuri Ivanovič, 1920-30.III.1984: SGErm 32 (1987) 95s (I. N. *Novosyelskaya*).
k904 Labib, Subhi Yanni, 27.III.1924-22.III.1987; prof. Kiel: Der Islam 65 (1988) 1-4; portr.; bibliog. (B. *Spuler*).
k905 Lah (Lach), Maksimilian, 27.IX.1897-1989: BogSmot 59 (1989) 471s. 472-4 (J. *Ćurić*, B. *Duda*).
k906 Lange-Seidl, Annemarie, 4.VII.1918-14.I.1989; Dir.: ZSemiot 11 (1989) 99-104, phot. (G. F. *Meier*, Bibliog.).
k907 Lefebvre, Charles, mgr. 29.VIII.1904-XI.1989; doyen émérite de la Ste-Rote Romaine: RHE 84 (1989) 841s (G. *Fransen*).
k908 Lehmann, Detlef, 20.VI.1934-15.VII.1988, Dir.: LuthTKi 12 (1988) 33s (H. *Günther, al.*).
k909 Lemerle, Paul Émile, 23.IV.1903-17.VII.1989; Byzantine hagiography, agrarian history: DumbO 43 (1989) xiii-xv; portr. (A. E. *Laiou*); CRAI (1989) 531-3 (B. *Guenée*); TAth 60 (1989) 828-832 (P. B. *Paschos*, ❻; bibliog.).
k910 Lentini, Anselmo, O.S.B., aet. 88, 16.X.1989: RHE 84 (1989) 882s (A. de *Vogüé*).
k911 Lentz, Otto Helmut Wolfgang [➤ 4,k834], 23.II.1900-8.XII.1986; Iranist: Der Islam 65 (1988) 7; bibliog. (W. *Eilers*).
k912 Lods, Marc, 1908-1988: PosLuth 37,1 (1989) 4-6 (J.-N. *Pérès*).
k913 Lonie, Iain Malcolm, 1932-18.VI.1988; Greek medicine: Gnomon 61 (1989) 190s (V. *Nutton*).
k914 Losev, Alexei Fedorovič, 23.IX.1893-24.V.1988: VDI 188 (1989) 250-2; phot. (S. S. *Averincev*).
k915 Lucot, Robert, 1903-1989: RÉLat 67 (1989) 31 (J. *Soubiran*).

k916 Lützeler, Heinrich, aet. 86, 13.VI.1988: ZRGg 41 (1989) 362-5 (F.-L. Kroll).

k917 Lukonin, Vladimir Grigorevič, 1932-10.IX.1984: SGErm 32 (1987) 97s (O. Vostoka).

k918 McKearin, Helen, 1898-20.X.1988: JGlass 31 (1989) 125s, phot. (Jane S. Spillman).

k919 Malula, J. A., card., 17.XII.1917-14.VI.1989: RAfrT 13,26 (1989) 151-3; portr.

k920 Mehlmann, João Evangelista, 7.II.1914-30.XII.1988: História de Palestina NT: REB 49 (1989) 218s.

k921 Mitrofanov, Alexei Grigorovič, 1912-c.1988: SovArch (1989,2) 296s, portr. (V. I. Šadryo).

k921* Mörsdorf, Klaus, aet. 80, 17.VIII.1989, peritus Vat. II: MüTZ 41 (1990) 99-102 (W. Aymans).

k922 Momigliano, Arnaldo Dante [→ 3,h396; 4,k850], 1908-1.IX.1987: ProcBritAcad 74 (1988) 405-442; portr.; StRom 36 (1988) 88; phot. (M. Pavan).

k923 Morey, Adrian, 1904-3.II.1989: RHE 84 (1989) 253 (A. Sillem).

k924 Morton, William Hardy, 29.I.1915-22.IX.1988, director ASOR-J.: BASOR 276 (1989) 1s, phot. (M. P. Matheney).

k925 Mylonas, George Emmanuel [→ 4,k855], 9.XII.1898-15.IV.1988: AJA 93 (1989) 215-7; 2 phot. (S. Iakovidis); correction p. 628.

k925* Nakahara, Yomokuro, aet. 88, 27.III.1988, founder of Sumerology in Japan: AcSum 11 (1989) v; phot. (M. Yoshikawa).

k926 Nikiprowetzky, Valentin [→ 1,g459], 15.IV.1919-19.XII.1983: StPhilonAn 1 (1989) 3-5 (J. Riaud).

k927 Nolli, Gianfranco, mons., aet. 70, 30.V.1989; S.S.L.: AcPIB 9,5 (1988s) 421.

k928 O'Connor, James J., S.J., aet. 77, 9.VII.1988: ETL 65 (1989) 229 (R. F. Collins).

k929 Onclin, Willy, msgr., 22.II.1905-15.VII.1989: effective in Vatican II because of his facility in Latin: ETL 65 (1989) 481-3; phot. p. 480 (L. De Fleurquin; bibliog.).

k930 Otto, Karl-Heinz, 9.XI.1915-29.V.1989: AusgF 34 (1989) 253s, phot. (J. Herrmann).

k931 Ottonello, Pellegrino, † 22.IX.1889 [auto; studente 1970-4, ActaPIB 9,516].

k932 Outler, Albert C., 17.XI.1908-1.IX.1989: JEcuSt 26 (1989) iii (Nancy E. Krody); America 161 (1989) 204 (D. S. Toolan).

k933 Perego, Angelo, S.J. [firmava anche con lo pseudonimo Zürich] (1913-1988), collaboratore: DivThom 91 (1988) 493-6 (G. Perini).

k934 Peters, Albrecht, 31.III.1924-26.X.1987; Eschatologie: LuJb 56 (1989) 7-10 (M. Plathow).

k935 Phillips, Kyle M.ᴶ, 20.V.1934-7.VIII.1988; Etruscologist: AJA 93 (1989) 239s (R. D. De Puma, al.).

k936 Pighi, Giovanni Battista, 1.V.1898-7.V.1978: Aevum 63 (1989) 139-144 (V. Cremona).

k937 Pleijel, Hilding, aet. 95, 15.XI.1988; Church life and systematic, Lund: SvTKv 65 (1989) 47s (C.-E. Normann).

k938 Pomerance, Leon, 2.VIII.1907-11.XI.1988; AJA 93 (1989) 459s (J. W. Shaw).

k939 Posener, Georges [→ 4,k869], 12.IX.1906-15.V.1988: ZägSpr 116 (1989) 109s, phot. (F. Hintze).

k940 Quinn, Jerome, msgr., 24.II.1927- .IX.1989: ETL 65 (1989) 230 (R. F. Collins).

k941 Ramsey, Arthur Michael, 14.XI.1904 [➤ 4,k875 'Michael... 1905... 1986']-23.IV.1988: Istina 34 (1989) 139-143 (B. Dupuy).

k942 Ramsey, Paul, aet. 74, 29.II.1989; moralista: ETL 65 (1989) 229 (R. F. Collins); ObnŽiv 44 (1989) 67s (V. Pozaić).

k943 Rappoport, Pavel Aleksandrovič, 29.VI.1913-11.IX.1988: SovArch (1989, 3) 297s (A. N. Kirpichnikov; bibliog. 299-303).

k944 Raubitschek, Isabelle Kelly, 2.IX.1914-1988; Isthmian objects, in press: AJA 93 (1989) 241 (Gladys D. Weinberg).

k945 Rawson, Elizabeth Donata, 1934-10.XII.1988; Roman Republic; honorary secretary: JRS 79 (1989) xi; portr. iv [Jorge Reynolds].

k946 Redig de Campos, Dioclecio, 6.III.1905-6.IV.1989, già direttore dei Musei Vaticani: RHE 84 (1989) 643s (J. Ruysschaert; OssR 16.IV.1989, C. Pietrangelo).

k947 Reese, James M., 27.V.1926-3.XII.1989; president-elect CBA: ETL 66, 248; CBQ 52,310.

k948 Revault, Jacques, 1902-8.IX.1986: AntAfr 25 (1989) 7-10, phot. (L. Golvin).

k949 Risch, Ernst, 9.X.1911-1.IX.1988, griechische Dialekten: Kratylos 34 (1989) 214-221 (B. Forssman; Bibliog.).

k950 Rossi, Amedeo, C.M., 1894-1986: DivThom 91 (1988) 490s.

k951 Rossi, Giovanni Felice, C.M., 1905-1987: DivThom 91 (1988) 492s.

k952 Rothuizen, Gerard, aet. 62, 29.VII.1988: GerefTTs 89 (1989) 1 (J. Firet; artikel volgt).

k953 Safrai, Shmuel: Zion 59 (1989) 267-9 ❺.

k954 Schachermeyr, Fritz [➤ 4,886], 10.I.1895-26.XII.1987; Ägäis, Mykene: AfO 35 (1988) 256-8, phot. (Sigrid Deger-Jalkotzy).

k955 Schallenberger, E. Horst, 14.VIII.1925-31.III.1987: ZRGg 40 (1988) 70s (J. H. Schoeps).

k956 Schelkle, Karl Hermann, 3.IV.1908-9.III.1988; NT-Theologie: BZ 33 (1989) 158-160 (H. Leroy).

k957 Schippers, Reinier, 1907-1989: GerefTTs 89 (1989) 129s (J. Veenhof).

k958 Schoder, Raymond V., S.J., † 1987 ➤ supra 175.

k959 Schölch, Alexander, 18.X.1943-29.VIII.1986; Ägypten; Palästina im Umbruch: Der Islam 65 (1988) 8-10 (F. Steppat).

k960 Scholl, fr. Paulo João, 14.IV.1946-22.XII.1989; minister-treasurer of the Pontifical Biblical Institute, Rome 1983-9: ActaPIB 9,515s.

k961 Schwartz, Daniel R.: Zion 59 (1989) 272 ❺.

k962 Seider, Richard, 9.III.1913-25.X.1988; Gründer des Heidelberger Instituts für Papyrologie: Aegyptus 69 (1989) 195s (D. Hagedorn).

k963 Seidl, Erwin, 1905-1987; collaboratore dal 1935: StDocHistJ 53 (1987) 505-7.

k964 Sersanti, Mario, F.D.P., aet. 74, † 1989 [studente 1940-2, ActaPIB 9,516].

k965 Shahovsky, John, abp., 23.VIII.1902-30.V.1989: SVlad 33 (1989) 315-7 (J. Meyendorff).

k966 Shiloh, Yigal [➤ 3,h428; 4,k890 '13.XI'], 6.VII.1937-14.XI.1987: RÉJ 148 (1989) 249-251, phot. (E.-M. Laperrousaz); BASOR 274 (1989) 1s, phot. (W. G. Dever).

k967 Sitter, Joseph, † 1987: CurrTM 16 (1989) 14-28 (P. Hefner, al.).

k968 Smuts, François, 1.IV.1916-27.III.1987: Acta Classica 30 (Pretoria 1987) 1-3; portr.

k969 Sollberger, Edmond, 12.X.1920-21.VI.1989; Assyriologist: AfO 35 (1988) 258-260, phot. (C. *Walker*).

k970 Solmsen, Friedrich, 4.II.1904-30.I.1989; foundations of Western thought: Gnomon 61 (1989) 757-9; portr. (Helen F. *North*).

k971 Speier, Hermine, 28.V.1898-11.I.1989: MiDAI-R 96 (1989) 1-6; phot. (B. *Andreae*, Bibliog.; C. *Pietrangeli*).

k972 Starcky, Jean [➤ 4,k897], 3.II.1909-9.II.1988; Petra, Palmyra: Orientalia 58 (1989) 333s, phot. (F. *Israel*); MondeB 58 (1989) 54 (É. *Puech*), aussi RQum 14 (1989) 3-6.

k973 Stern, Henri, † 4.IX.1988; fondateur: BMosAnt (AIEMA) 12 (1988s) v, phot.

k974 Stern, Menahem, 5.III.1925-22.VI.1989: Zion 59 (1989) 261-274 ❶; phot. p. 143; CHistEI 52 (1989) 185, phot. (A. *Oppenheimer* ❶).

k975 Stockmeier, Peter, prof. mgr., 29.XII.1925-19.XI.1988; Patrologie, München: RHE 84 (1989) 522 (K. *Hausberger*); K.-Gesch.: MüTZ 40 (1989) 3-5 (G. *Schweiger*); phot. 261; Bibliog. 365-371.

k976 Stroheker, Karl Friedrich, 1914-12.XII.1988, Mitbegründer: Historia 38 (1989) i-ii; phot.

k977 Struve, Karl Wilhelm, 12.II.1917-26.VI.1988: ActaPraeh 20 (1988) 7s, phot. (A. von *Müller*).

k978 Subilia, Vittorio [➤ 4,k899], 5.VIII.1911-12.IV.1988:   TSzem 32 (1989) 118 (L. *Szabó*).

k979 Superti Furga, Giulio, 12.VI.1904-18.XI.1989; monete gonzaghesche: RitNum 91 (1989) 303s (G. *Fenti*).

k980 Syme, Ronald, sir., 1903-4.IX.1989: AncW 20 (1989) 67-75 (A. M. *Devine*; 77-92, Syme and The Roman Revolution); AnSt 39 (1989) 17 (S. *Mitchell*); CRAI (1989) 533s (B. *Guenée*).

k981 Tadla, Agostinos, OFMCap, 26.VII.1921-28.IX.1989: RasEtiop 32 (1988) 195-7 (L. *Ricci*).

k982 Tosatto, Giuseppe, 15.VIII.1929-22.VIII.1988; laurea Atti Ap. 15; prof. S. Scr.: RivB 37 (1989) 126 (R. *Provera*).

k983 Tóth, Kalmán Csomasz, † 20.XI.1988: JbLtgHymn 32 (1989) vi (K. *Bardos*).

k984 Trümpelmann Leo, 1.IX.1931-15.VIII.1989; Jagddarstellungen: AfO 35 (1988) 280, phot. (B. *Hrouda*).

k985 Urbach, Ephraim E.: Zion 59 (1989) 264 ❶.

k986 Veiga, Jesús, S.J., 30.IV.1989: AcPIB 9,5 (1988s) 421.

k987 Vierck Hayo, 5.VIII.1939-16.III.1989: PraehZts 64 (1989) 159-163 (H. *Roth*; al. bibliog.).

k988 Villers, Robert, 8.V.1912-26.X.1989: RÉLat 67 (1989) 33 (P. *Grimal*).

k989 Vööbus, Arthur, 28.IV.1909-[26.IX➤ 4,k910?] 25.IX.1988: OrChr 73 (1989) 231 (J. *Assfalg*).

k990 Volterra, Edoardo [➤ 65,e284], 7.I.1904-19.VII.1984: JJurPap 20 (1988) 7-13 (L. *Capogrossi Colognesi*, ital.).

k991 Waggoner, Nancy Mann, 1924-10.IV.1989; American Numismatic soc. curator of Greek coins: AJA 93 (1989) 597s (W. E. *Metcalf*).

k992 Whiteley, Sim, 4.XII.1896-14.VI.1986: Acta Classica 29 (Pretoria 1986) 1s.

k993 Winder, Richard Bayly, 1920-6.VIII.1988: AmResEg 26 (1989) 1 (T. *Walz*).

k994 Wolff, Hans Julius, 1902-1983: JJurPap 20 (1988) 15-18 (H. *Kupiszewski*, ital.).

k995 Ziegler, Adolf Wilhelm, 9.III.1903-30.VIII.1989: MüTZ 41 (1990) 102-5 (M. *Weitlauff*).
k996 Ziegler, Charlotte, 8.III.1902-31.VIII.1988: Warka-Mitglied: BaghMit 20 (1989) 349s; phot. (M. A. *Brandes*).
k997 Ziegler, Joseph [➤ 4,k914], 15.III.1902-1.X.1988: Septuaginta: BZ 33 (1989) 160.311s (J. *Schreiner*).

Index Alphabeticus: Auctores – *Situs (omisso al-., tell, abu etc.)*
Ddiss./dir. Eeditor FFestschrift Mmentio, de eo Rrecensio Ttranslator † in mem.

Aageson J R5349
Aalst A van der g911
AAR-SBL 89 k753*
Aarde A van 4797a
Aarnink L 3036
Aaronson S g65
Abadie P 975*
Abata d964
Abate Liebbrand M 8858b
Abbà G R4457 7929 R 2908
Abbink J 976
Abbott T D5904
Abbt I E7657*
Abdalla A 9395 E810
Abdel-Magid A g66
–Raziq M e325 e326
Abdera e70
Abe G 1512 3536 7259 M a564a b228
Abecassis A 4528 d725a
Abel F R1617 G k330 M Rd281*
Abela A 1939 2267 D2243
Abelardus 8227
Abeng B. N 7062 7699 k754ab R201 516 682 8576 8580 8619 8623 8626 8636 8641 8686
Aberbach M R1723
Abila d965 d966
Abitz F e338-e340
Abka'i-Khavari M d264
Abma H 2645
Abogunrin S 5303
Abou-Assaf Ali 9282
–Ghazi D Ed219

Abrabanel I 3843
Abraham D 7071a M 5079a T Mb181
Abrahamsen V e700
Abram A R9681
Abramowitz C 1692ab
Abrams M 223 914 9838ab M5660
Abramsky C F3 R1691
Abramson G Ea298
Abrego J 2118 7260 R3410
Abrey L k97
Abrudan D b624*
Abu Goš g575
Abu-Husayn A b107
Abulafia A Ma257 Rk110*
Abu Mina e436
Abu Qorah O D2609
Abusch T b59
Abushakra E Re30
Abu Simbel e437
Abusir b983
Abydos e438-e440
Acacius Mg755
Accattoli L 8968
Acebuchal d271
Acerbi A 9929
Acharuparambil D b229
Achtemeier E 3896 3909 M1426R R3946 P 3434 5255 6410 6411a E915 M990 R4783 7428
Ackerman J R2332 R b907 S 3642 3703 8572*
Ackroyd P 3689 Ra958
Acosta J de 8466

Acquaro E a935* d647a d684b e80 e84 e87 e88 E811
Acre e916 ➤ *Akko*
Actes Arch Chrét 827
Actes RÉG 772
Acton Mk360
Actualité de la Réforme 618
Adab e214
Adam A E828 J b807 K Mk473 R g258 Rb552
Adamiak R M2184R
Adamo A R5664 D 1495* 6051
Adams 1417a B d512 D 1243 9794 Ed304 R5028 J E7792 k651 M1127 R Mg317R W d513 d514 R1418
Adamson J 6442
Adamthwaite M R9362
Adan-Bayewitz D d944
Adang C g607
Adey L 1558
Adinolfi M 2290c 6412 8250 g152
Adler R a162
Adorno M9859
Adrados F 9645 9704 9710c
Adriaen M M3361
Adriani A F4
Adriányi G k218
Adriaticum g415e
Aegaeum e721-e748
Aegina d685a e669
Aegyptus 1119 2333 3168 3433c a985-b58 b385-

ELENCHUS OF BIBLICA

5 (1989) - 1992

Index

ADDENDUM p. 954 post Aloni

Alonso C g519

— Alonso P †k830

— Díaz J R4085

— Merlino P D5655

— Núñez J b538 Rb345 b544 e843

— Schökel L 376 1179 1245 1246 1409R 2228*ab* 237?
2981 2982 3015 3076 4280 4703 4704 9705 9120 a3
D3415 9183 M3327 R7373

Barich B e463*
Barié H 4102
Baril G 8695a
Bar-Ilan M 2550
Barkal e496 e497
Barkay G 2543 9127b
Barkenings H a435c
k901*
Barker A d206* **D** R2881
K 3784* 3824* 3880*
M 2808b 9898 a937
R3677 8834 **W** Dk173
R1389
Bar-Kochva B 2960
Mb646
Barkuizen J 3857 4776
Barlé H 1419
Barlow P 1348 1818
Barnabas 4684a
Barnai J a299
Barnard L Rg656 **W**
3858
Barnes J Tb497 **M**
R8655a a632 **R** k100 **T**
b565c b647 g860 g902b
Rg325
Barnett H Rg382 **P** 5658
6353 b913 e93 Ee89
† k839
Barón E 4032 4800 8696
R960 4824 7446 7624
8720 8761 g297
Barouch G 1123
Barr J 1248 1249 7655
9095 9096 9706 M1301
3016 3984 7392* R1351
2093 b907 k264 **R** T359
5276 b269
Barradas S M4261
Barrāni A al- g540
Barré L 2850 **M** 3027
3828 R9121
Barres-Marlys M D1593
Barreto J 5374
Barrett CK 5217b 5737
6000 7780 7840* M5216
R5236 6136 **D** 1515 **H**
a815
Barri e125
Barrios D 2467
Barrois G † k840
Barromi J a349*
Barros M de 7214
Barrow J M2046
Barrucand M g36
Rd559

Barry P 1548 **R** 2020 **W**
8130
Barsauma Mg915
Barsi B 5556
Barsip e216
Barsotti D 2245
Barstad H 2635 3848
Ek446
Barta K R1322 4354
4952 7609 **W** 9398ab
9399a a990 Ra991 b25
b29 e931
Bartel A 2328
Bartelink G b648 F17
R3462 g769 g889
Barth G 7781ab D5918
H 7841a 7938 8131
9043b **K** 5474 7513
k135d k506 F18ac M458
1004g 1967 4430 5917
7004 7029 7059* 7117*
7285* 7596 7607 7740
7771* 7816 8176 8882
b356 k410 k420 k487-
k507 k574R k654 k775
L R2537 **M** 4705 4706
5413* R244
Bartha T 8473
Barthe C k659
Barthélemy D 2759 3705
k731 D1696 3588 E1656
Bartholomew D 2019
R2058b
Bartina S 5132
Bartl K e136 D7214
Bartlett D 5577a **J** 389
b626 d954 d960 g242
R2613 2960 9898 d955
Bartmiński J a730
Bartnicki R 5738
Bartnik C 8388 b335
b336 D5454
Bartoletti Colombo A
9540
Bartolomé J 6006 D6191
Bartolomei M E8843
Ta694
Bartolomeu Barros J
3643
Bartoloni P g26c
Barton G 4033 **J** 1280
1349 1636d 3408 D3694
R1194 1494 2712 b350
S 8850 R4181 5033
5268 8267
Bartov V e918

Barucq A 1131 1132 b60
Baruffa A e767
Baruk H 7313
Barzanò A R7348 8396
a783
Basdevant B Eg867
Baser K g153
Basetti-Sani G 2124
b118ab Ra686 b124
b140 b203
Basevi C 6042 8264b
k726 R334 5868 5976
6145 7173 d574 g848
Basham A b233
Basile B d126
Basilius C g763-g766
M7556 8058 g756
Basinger D 7037
Baskin J 1516
Baslez M d691e
Basnizki L b289
Bass D R1078 **G** b820d
d127
Basser H 2600
Basset J 1493c
Bassi C d17 **K** a816
Bassler J 5513 5812 6313
R3951
Bassuk D b234
Bastero J Eg805 R8725
Bastiaensen A E17
R3863
Bastian J 8474
Bastianel S 7676
Bastianini G b388
Bataille G a572
Bataillon L 1023a 5081
E776 R33 345 3180
Bataš d548 d796-d798
Bat-El O D9122
Bates J e880 R1225*
Batlogg A d601
Bat-Sheva A k29*
Batson B 1578
Batstone D D8474*
Battaglia A R7321 **E** g71
G Ta584* **V** 7746
R7198 7481
Battelli G k396
Battenfield J 2831*a
Battenhouse P D8388*
Batto B R3838
Batumalai S b119
Baubérot J 7939 k668

Ddiss./dir. Eeditor FFestschrift Mmentio, de eo Rrecensio Ttranslator † in mem.
Sub de, van etc.: cognomina *americana* (post 1979) et *italiana* (post 1984); non reliqua.

ᴰdiss./dir. ᴱeditor ᶠFestschrift ᴹmentio, de eo ᴿrecensio ᵀtranslator † in mem.
Sub de, van etc.: cognomina *americana* (post 1979) et *italiana* (post 1984); **non** reliqua.

Cognomina **italiana** et **americana** *sola* sub praefixo separato *da* etc.

Cognomina **italiana** et **americana** sola sub praefixo separato da etc.

Cognomina **italiana** et **americana** *sola* sub praefixo separato *da* etc.

Cognomina **italiana** et **americana** *sola* sub praefixo separato *da* etc.

Cognomina **italiana** et **americana** *sola* sub praefixo separato *da* etc.

Cognomina **italiana** et **americana** *sola* sub praefixo separato *da* etc.

Cognomina **italiana** et **americana** *sola* sub praefixo separato *da* etc.

Ddiss./dir. Eeditor FFestschrift Mmentio, de eo Rrecensio Ttranslator † in mem.
Sub **de, van** etc.: cognomina *americana* (post 1979) et *italiana* (post 1984); **non** reliqua.

Ddiss./dir. Eeditor FFestschrift Mmentio, de eo Rrecensio Ttranslator † in mem.
Sub de, van etc.: cognomina americana (post 1979) et italiana (post 1984); non reliqua.

ᴰdiss./dir. ᴱeditor ᶠFestschrift ᴹmentio, de eo ᴿrecensio ᵀtranslator † in mem.
Sub de, van etc.: cognomina americana (post 1979) et italiana (post 1984); non reliqua.

Ddiss./dir. Eeditor FFestschrift Mmentio, de eo Rrecensio Ttranslator † in mem.
Sub de, van etc.: cognomina *americana* (post 1979) et *italiana* (post 1984); **non** reliqua.

Ddiss./dir. Eeditor FFestschrift Mmentio, de eo Rrecensio Ttranslator † in mem.
Sub de, van etc.: cognomina americana (post 1979) et italiana (post 1984); non reliqua.

ᴰdiss./dir. ᴱeditor ꟳFestschrift ᴹmentio, de eo ᴿrecensio ᵀtranslator † in mem.
Sub **de, van** etc.: cognomina *americana* (post 1979) et *italiana* (post 1984); **non** reliqua.

Reddé M d159 e462 g277c
Redditt P 3824a 3939 ᴿ3853 3921
Redford D b436 b443c e314 e383 ᴰe374 ᴿ3413 S e314
Redig de Campos D † k946
Redington J ᴿb248
Redknap M b862f
Redmount C ᴰe433
Redondi P 2091 ᴹ2072b
Redondo J 9669
Red Sea g461 → *mare*
Reeber M 1202b
Reece W ᴰ9163
Reeder E b874 J 7321
Reeg G a267 e915 ᴱ3124
Reekmans L e782* ᴿg430
Reeling B ᴰk500
Reents C 1229 1236
Rees B g855 S g134
Reese D g13ab J ᴿ3379 4632 † k947
Reesor M a891
Reeve M ᴿ806 e49
Reeves M k30 k31
Refoulé F 6169b ᴱ7143*
Regan D ᴿ8690 T 7058 8552* ᴿ7066
Regen F a891*
Regopoulos G 5554
Regt L de 2582
Reher M k468 ᴱ477b
Rehkopf F 1758 9584
Rehov 2464
Reich R d589 d773 d774 d842
Reichert A 6426 J 3009
Reichler-Béguelin M ᴿ9724
Reichrath H ᴿ7034
Reicke B 4315 ᴰ5153
Reid B 5150 ᴿ394 1883 D ᴿ4940 P ᴿ3436 S 3752
Reidy M ᴿ8330 8348
Reif S ᴱ1009 ᴿ2514
Reikerstorfer ᴰ9834
Reiling J 1286
Reilly J d363
Reimarus H ᴹk272 k273

Reimer D 3620 ᴰ3657
Reinach S ᴹa307
Reineke W 9464 ᴱ850
Reinelt H 52 3024
Reiner E ꟳb486 ᴿ9335
Reinert W ᴿ8339 8721
Reines A a339
Reinhardt K 4184 k36 R ᴿ179 k105 k207
Reinhart K ᴿb220
Reinhartz A 5457a 5506 5542b b712
Reinharz J ᴱa340
Reinhold G ᴰ2843 ᴹ921 b713 ᴰb709
Reinholdo A 9601
Reinink G g817a
Reinlich H 9400
Reinmuth E 5191 ᴿ5289 6093 6327 R 9952
Reis O dos ᵀ4094
Reiser M ᴿ1825 9536 W ᴿ8185 k629
–Haslauer E d633
Reisinger F ᴿ314*
Reisner G ᴹb987 N ᵀa347
Reist B ᴰ8474* T k12
Reiter J k365a K ᴿb954
Reiterer F 9225
Religion sans retour 507
RelStR index 1075
Remelts G 2092
Remolina G ᵀ7144 k587
Remond R 1408
Rémy B b543 b788 G 2143b P 159
Renan E ᴹa306 k377
Renard J ᴿa592 L ᴿ506 622 882 886 4471 5360 7550 7598 7842 7877 7900 8311 8722 8735 8739 a364
Renaud B 3130 3884 ᴿ3092 J d124
Renauld C ᴿ8075
Rench G 1867a
Renckens H 1215
Rendelli M ᴿ830
Rendsburg G 1947 1948 2787 9729 ᴹ1939 ᴿ2740 9106
Rendtorff R 445 607 1161 1162 1973 3509a

4263a 7395* a359 a426 ᴱa427 ᴹ1146ᴿ 1451 1896 T 7250 8355
Renfrew C 9730 e736 ᴿ9719
Renfroe F 3323 ᴰ9271
Reng P ᴿ8255
Renger J b479 g435
Renik K 8659
Renkema J 3670
Rennes J ᴿ1138 1930 2130 3923 8061
Rennstich K ᴿ4195
Renoux C 6427
Rensberger D 5355 5356
Renwart L 1076 7524 ᴿ598 896 4737 7414 7442 7473 7478 7481 7487 7492 7498 7514 7516 7606 7726 7769 8693 k143
Renz H ᴱ727* ᴹ7492ᴿ
Renzetti E a639b
Répertoire Médiévistes 962
Rephaim d738 e982
Reports about theological conferences k782
Reppert V 4563
Resafa e170 e171
Rese M 5986 ᴿ4043 5024 5028 5200 5223
Respinti M ᴿk567
Restani D ᴱd209
Restle M 8238 ᴱ210
Resweber J 1287 ᴹ7101
Retsö J 9731
Rettig J ᵀ5381
Reu J k636
Reuling H ᴿ8460
Reumann J 5324 7524* 9080 ᴿ4727 5816
Revault J † k948
Revell E 9113ab 9148 ᴿ3585 3779
Reventlow H 7395 ᴱ602 1650 ᴿ2495 3647 3776
Révész I ᴹk637
Revista de Revistas 1077
RBíbArg indices 1010
Reviv H g356

ᴰdiss./dir. ᴱeditor ꟳFestschrift ᴹmentio, de eo ᴿrecensio ᵀtranslator † in mem.
Sub **de, van** etc.: cognomina *americana* (post 1979) et *italiana* (post 1984); **non** reliqua.

Riva F 1328
Rivero M R737
Rivolta Tiberga P Rg870
Rizk S 9387
Rizkana I e479
Rizzardi G 4205 a686
b197 b203
Rizzerio L 7200
Rizzi A 7252 7368*b
T7544 M g681
Robbins E Db319 G
1682 3960 E2171 V
4628 D5056 E963
Roberge M 5538 R 7164
R7104 7135 8114*
Robert L 344 M D5874
P M1801 P de R2651
3616 R 5494 5546 5570
R1847 R de R2867
Robertini L Rg511
Roberts M9120 A b714 C
1683 1988 D g557 H
8547 J 2093 3918 4842
5875 D6221 R1209 L
k483 M g985 O k639 R
k503b R8039
Robertson A M4096 E
4565 k517 k518 R8451
e53 G D6196 J g81b N
R202 b601 P 5458 R
1592
Robillard E g700
Robinson B 2547 R939
1206 1228 1409 1906
3904 3933 4556 5598
7294 b292 G 8660ab
Rb285 H 1441 I Ra340*
J 4029 4931 5403
D4309 a430 F160*
M3976 7002R k450
k450* L 1569 O Rb755
R D1409 T R4294 4534
4835 5807* 9889 g410
– Hammerstein H E730
Robisek C e496
Robles R R1181
Robson J 7076 E731
Rocafiguera J T7851
Roca-Puig R M1659
3071a
Rocca G E964
Roccati A b36a Rd432
d440
Rocchetta C 7824
Roccos L d434
Rochais G R4690

Rochberg-Halton F
9352c b71b D9354
Eb486
Roche C 9682 J R2079
2084 M e7
Rochelle J R4706 6100
k66
Rocher A M7593R L 636
R b940
Rochlitz R T9862
Rock M 7252*
Rockefeller S E698
Rockwell P e762b
Rodd C 1010* 4997
R418 640 521 562 926
1133 1150 1157 1280
1322 1349 1467 1920
2057 2065 2085 2086
2091 2614 2695 2704
2850 3173 3179 3251*
3280 3337 3364 3591
3602 3818 3827 3931
3990 4016 4086 4108
4255 4289 4325 4831
5071 5097 5362 5394
5598 5671 5801 6080
6161 7127 7225* 7316
7353 7379 7385 7405
7743 8267 8389 8401
8424 8464 9111 9555
9746 a631 b306 g344
k450 k450* k524 k640
Roddington A E834
Rodenberg O E489
Rodgers L D5778 P 5019
Rodilla Zanón A F161
2959
Rodley L Re839
Rodrigo M 8444
Rodríguez A E965
R3681 E R4836 8525*
G R4665 5301 J R3197
– Carmona A 5100 R4212
– Jarque F D7649*
– Melgarejo G 8243*
– Neila J e938
– Ruiz M 5459 R4230
– Somolinos J R1668
Roduit M T8147
Roebuck D R474
Röhr H R7988
Roehrs W 7281
Röhser G D5830
Röllig W b487 Rk295
Römer C 9908 9987
E512 513 M g437 T

1961b R1293 1960 1998
2013 2263 2270 2347
2915 3066 3092 b326
d751 W b72g b86 E912
Rb486 e193
Römheld KD D3298
3328
Roensch M Rk190
Roesch P g155
– Cajano S a445d
Rösel H Rd715 N R2615
Röser J E8660*
Rössler A 1384*b 8014
– Köhler U b437 d435
Ee308 R9416
Roest Crollius A
➤ a349*
Röthlin E R723
Roetzel C 3995 R5255
6008 6014 6319
Rőzse I 4206
Rofé A 2594 2762 3440
3578b 3621
Rogem Hiri d912
Rogers D k98 J 3502
9102 M d84 P R5014
k401 R Rk469
Rogerson J 607 1163
7201 b843 e873 e874
g338b g648 R301 355
602 1898 2356 2521
2533 2577 3699 g596
Rogge J R325* k215 L
R7563
Rogier L Mk702R
Rohde E Re570
Rohregger K R2104*
7252*
Roik E d66
Roisel V R45 457 1279
1888 5058 7188 g841
g896 g912
Roitman A 2950a
Rokay Z D3937
Rokesh M3432*
Roland B b875
Rolfes H 9043a
Rolinck E R7674
Roll I d918
Rolla A 5128d k406
R3390 4230 5068 8250
a60 b305 b717
Rolland M7982a P 4316
Rolle R 3203 g258

ᴰdiss./dir. ᴱeditor ᶠFestschrift ᴹmentio, de eo ᴿrecensio ᵀtranslator † in mem.
Sub **de, van** etc.: cognomina *americana* (post 1979) et *italiana* (post 1984); **non** reliqua.

ᴰdiss./dir. ᴱeditor ᶠFestschrift ᴹmentio, de eo ᴿrecensio ᵀtranslator † in mem.
Sub de, van etc.: cognomina americana (post 1979) et italiana (post 1984); non reliqua.

Ddiss./dir. Eeditor FFestschrift Mmentio, de eo Rrecensio Ttranslator † in mem.
Sub **de, van** etc.: cognomina *americana* (post 1979) et *italiana* (post 1984); **non** reliqua.

Cognomina **americana** *sola* ponuntur sub praefixo separato *van, von*

Vandenbulcke J 7641 a713
Vandepitte M k759*f*
Vanderbroeck P b732
Vanderhoff Boersma F 8571
VanderKam J 963 1709 a23*d* E9919 Ra100 a119
Vandersleyen C 9452 9453 e401 g31 De336 e437
Vanderspoel J Rg381
Van Develder F 1221 8212 9093
Van Dyk W R1423
Vanek S g32
Van Elderen B 58 4404 D6445
Van Engen J g994
Vanetti P e868 E4339
Van Gelder C R749
Van Gemeren W 3825* 7720*b* 7732 9161 R2355 3681
Vanggaard J a797*
Vanhetloo W 1468 R1453
Vanhoozer K R9833
Van Houten C D2477
Vanhoutte K D7928*
Vanhoye A 6245 6395 6396 6405 7774*a* k814 D6421 E5782 R5774 6387
Van Huysteen W 7169
Van Leeuwen R 3330 Tk441
Van Lepp J d640*a*
Van Ness P R8655*a* g729
Vanneste A F201
Vanni U 5653 5699 D5655 5718
Vannicelli P 9611
Vannier F g452*b* M 1949
Vannini M g858 E1175
Van Roo W 7416
Vanschoonwinkel J d558 Re659
Van Seters J 2185 M1950R 2259 R2332
Van Siclen C b50 e361 Rd470 e352
Vanstiphout H 9792
Van Till H 2108

Van Voorst R 9976
Van Winkle D 2822
Vanzan P 8041 E7929 R4087 8926 8977
Varacalli J Rg350
Vardaman J E58 R4397*e*
Vardiman E b733
Vardy P Ra617 a700
Vargas-Machuca A 4844* Rg297
Varghese B g909
Varisco D R9380 g153
Varmarasi J 6244
Varo F 5919 R1279 4028 9240 a169 b731
Varone F 7775 7776
Varro Mg80 R 1202*g* 3382*b*
Vasilia e645
Vassilika Eleni e483
Vatin J b925
Vattioni F 2929*b* 3217*ab* 3239 d641 e45 E759 R844 856 e916
Vattuone G 4527
Vauchez A g995
Vauthier É 2138*b* k384 R1189 1800 2181 2183 5757 d377
Vaux G de M2540 K R9027 R de 2656 M2495R Rb306
Vavroušek P 9499*c* E874
Vawter B 3456 Fk401
Vaz A 8213
Vazhuthanapally O 2588*a*
Vecchio S 2437
Vedder B Ra637
Veenhof J k957 K b493
Veerkamp T R366 7238 8360
Vegas M e104*b*
Veh O Tb800
Veiga J † k986
Veijola T 2296 2438 2450
Veilleux A a562
Veissière M R4772
Veken J van der 7067 Ta724
Vekene E van der E69
Velde H b14*b*
Velema 3074

Vélez Correa J E8554
Velius H Mk207
Vellanickal M 5628
Veltri G 1495
Vemi V d71
Vempeny I 4190 b284
Vena O 3932
Venit M e939
Vennemann T E9734
Venter J 3535* R D8571*
Ventris M 9675
Ventura R e362 M9420
Venturini N Rk93
Venzlaff H b220
Vera Chamaza G 2861
Veranstaltungen Semiotik k800
Verbeke W E760 9059
Verbrake F R13
Verbrugghe G b383
Vercellone C M2716R
Vercoutter J b950 k870 Fe321
Vercruysse J 8042 R310 7871 8032 8036
Verde A 5700
Verdeyen P E5902
Verdière R Rd22
Verey 1788*a*
Vergina e705
Vergote A 7170 a714 D9819 M7671 J 9478
Verheul A 7570*
Verhey A 8375
Verheyden J 4684*b* 5099 g796 R9885
Verhoef P 3933
Verhoeven-van Elsbergen U k841
Verkuyl J b221
Verlinden C d448
Vermaseren J a933 M a798
Vermes G a6 a9*ab* a63 Eb719 b720 M9999 R568 a13 Ra42 a127 J M2948 P Rk413
Vermeule C Rd421 d590 E e688
Vermeylen J 1913*c* 2186 3497*a* 7265 7285 7402 E614

Cognomina **americana** *sola* ponuntur sub praefixo separato *van, von*

VOCES

ordine **graeco**

Agapáō 6432
agápē 9596
hágios 9598
aiōn 9597
aiōnios 5468
akoúō 5320
akoē písteōs 6199
akyrōsimos 9603*
állōs 9600
hamartía 5830 9600*
anagōgía a830a
anadasmós g395
anankē 9601*
anámnēsis 1493c 4716
  9601
áxios 9602
apátheia 7037* 7045
apokatástasis 5305 5306
  g717
apokritheís 4682
apotélesma 9602*
aretē a893

ártos g71
arýballos d627
archē 4757
árchōn 4757
atimía 3804*
authepsa d291
autós 5138
áphesis 9603
Achaiós 9492
achreîos 9603*
áchrēstos 9603*

Baitylion a956
baptízō 7792
biázō 4589
bouleutēs 9605
býrsa 9604

Gastēr 5110a
glaukós glaukôpis 9606
gnôsis 7002* g662a

Deiktērion a904
deûro/deûte 2705
dêlos 2502
dêmos 9565
diá 9607
diakonía 575
didaskalía 9626
dikaiosýnē 4346
dikastērion 9565
diplē timē 6354
dóxa 3804* 5858 5871
doxázō 9609
douleúō 9608

Egérthē 4797a
ethnos e585
eimí 5454 5461
eirēnē 5041
ekklēsía 4376 9565 9610
elénchō 6243
eleuthería 5880
Héllēn 9611
embrimion 9612
exomológēsis 9613
exousía 5602R
epangelía 6388
epēreia 9614
epístamai 369
érchomai 9615
erōtáō 9616
éschatos 9617
euangélion 4013
eucharistía 4748
eudokía 5110c

eulogēménos 5181
héōs 9618

Theîos anēr 4897
theokrateía b625a
theomacheîn g731
theós 9619
thólos d68
theotókos 9620
thýrion 9620*
thysiastērion 6409

Idios 9621
idoú 9622
hiláskomai 9623
hína 5445*a
Ioudaîos 5453 9624
híppos 9654

Kairós 8572
kardía 6432
karpázō 4589
katagōgía a830a
kaucháō 6110
kénōsis 4637c 4953
kérdos g397
kérygma 489 9626
kērōma d193
kephalē 6057 9625
kibōtos g106
klíbanos g82
koinōnía a850
kordantēs d302*
ktêsis d64
ktísis 5954
kýrios 9627

Légō élegon 4982b
limiton 9628
lógos 5473-5488 7541 8572
lýtra 6292

Mathetai 5086
mantikē g718
marainō, móros 9629
mártys 5750
metamelētheis 4682
metánoia 9629*
metaphorá 9630
metonymía 9630
mímesis 4716 9440 g332
místhōsis g286a g427

Nómos a877b a918

Xýlon g654

Oikología k273
oikonomia 8447
oîkos   7252   9631   d64
 g289b
 -ekklēsías 6291
 -oikodome 5860a
horáō, eîdon 9622
orgízesthe 6242
oros e923b
órthros 9632
oudén 5489
ouranós 9633

Páthos 9634
páthei máthos a871
paidagōgós 6203
palingenesía a495
parousía 6125 6312
pastós 9635
perì 6025
pēlōma d193
pístis   5823   6199   9636
 g668a g745
 -Christoû 5929
 -ek/dià písteos 5935
polis g475-g511 (ptólis)
 9637
porneía 6040a
presbytérion 5205
prógnōsis g718
proxenía b561
próstatis 6003
prophḗtis a873

Sarakēnós 9638
sitonía g141
skándalon, -izō 9639
skēnopoiós 6359
smarís 9640
soudárion 5570
spóndylos g29
synagōgē 9610
synekdochē 9630
syntéleia g717
sōzo 5254
sōma 5821ᴿ 6063 (gra-
 phôn) 1303; (planta)
 g42
sotēría k481 k482

Tálanton d301
tartaroûchos 9980
témenos g402
tolméria 9641
tópos 9440 g332
triás 7448b

Hýdōr d622
hypér 6063
hypsōthēnai 5520

Phálanx 9642
pheúgō 6040a
philóponos 9643
phýsis a877b
phōnē 5320

Chreía 3972 4628 4947a
chōra e913

Psychē 9644
psychrós d622

ordine hebraico
†aram. ‡ug./ph. *akk. °arab.

aleph
abba † 4502 9161
ôb 9162
ôr 9163
eḥad 9164
êk 9165
akalu * g81c
'el 2887
amānah amēn 9166
asakku * 195b
asûr weazûb 2828
ephod 2727
argamān g21
mi'rāj ° b185
'rk 9167
-'rš- 9265
ēš 9168
Ašērâ 3812 3813 a938a
 a960 a963 a966 a969

beth
be 2887
be'alātum * 9168*
bgwtym 3398
bad 2727
bô' 9176
Ba'al a938c ṣāpôn a962
bārak 3425 9169
berît 7278
Bat Qôl 7113b

ghimel
gā'al: gō'ēl ha-dam 9170
gezerâ šāwā 1625
goyim a155
gyl a12

gōlēm 3168
gmn ‡ 9171

daleth
dabūbu ‡ g20
madhēbâ 3103
dabar zeh 3626
dôr 9172*
dîn 7000
dam 9172ab
dqr e2
darom 3649
dāraš 9173*
 daršan 1443

hē
hebel 3353ᴿ
hdādē † 9318
hāyâ, YHWH 416 2418
hkr 3398
halak 2251a 2705
hār e923a

waw
wawei 'amûdîm 1692b
wm ‡ 9280b

zayin
ze'ênâ/re'enâ 1922
zākar mazkīr 9174
zā'aq 9175
zemîrôt 3232
zârâ 3321
zera' 9269
zwi e996

ḥeth
ḥbl ° 9373
maḥzor 1672
ḥaṭṭa't 2522
ḥlb'ym 3103
ḥammeš † 9318
ḥemor 9654 ° 9373
ḥnt ‡ 9280a
ḥesed 9175*
ḥaṣoṣerâ d225
huqqîm 2591
ḥerem 425 2747 3535
ḥašimi (bit/pit) 9336

ṭeth
ṭbn ‡ 3139
ṭwb 3139
wayyaṭel 2764a

qôl 9235
qwm, hitqayyem 9200
  9236
maqlû * b59
taqlîd ° b139
qeren d225

rêš

rabiṣu * 9246
rādap, tirdop 3398
ruaḥ 3490 3690 9238
  9239
urwōt 2800
marzeaḥ 3703 3851
  b83*b
rāḥāb 2635
reḥob meqōmô 3229
raḥamîm 7000
roṭem 3230*

rîb 3126 3533 9240
rô'eh 9237
Repā'im 9241 ‡ 9257c

śin

śimḥa 3167
śar 9174 9243

šin

še'ol 7375
šebeṭ 9194
šadday 9244
šēdîm, šdyn 9244
šwb, lô yašub 3702
šakab 9176
šākam 9245 maškīm
  * 9246
ŠLM lišlim * b87 šelāmîm
  a21 hšlym ‡ 9269

šame (eriqqi) * 9339b
šama' 9247
šemiṭṭâ 2464
šnayim, štayim 9135
ši'ur qōmâ a249R
šāpaṭ 9248 mišpāṭîm
  2591
šōpār d225
šqy ‡ 9249
šurpu * b91
šaš g1

tau

tohu webohu a293
tekhelet g21
topet 9250 a972
ṭrtn ‡ 9191

Genesis

–: 1917-2343
1-11: 1952-2204
  2211
1-3: 2171 3222
1s: 1978 1993-
  2117
1: 1952-1980
  7021R
1,1: 2114
1,2: 1841a 1979
1,4: 1508 1980
1,26-28: 1991
1,26: 1841 1981-
  1990 7189
1,28: 7386
2-5: 2151
2s: 2118-2190
2,18-24: 2144b
2,19s: 2194
2,21: 2191
2,24: 2195
3,1-5: 2197
3,21: 2199
4s: 2210
4,1-26: 2200-2208
4,2-16: 2144a
4,9: 2205
5: 2209
5,24: 2213-2214
6s: 2216-2232
6,1-4: 2215
6,18: 2229
9,5: 2399

9,6: 2230
9,18-27: 2170b
9,20-27: 2144a
9,22-27: 2231
10: 2233
10,1-32: 2233-
  2234
11-13: 2244-2263
11,1-9: 2234-2240
11,4: 2241a
11,12: 5133
11,27-25-18: 2243
11,27-32: 2242a
12-35: 2276a
12-25: 2251a
12: 2264
12,10-20: 2251c
  2279c
13: 2267
14: 2268-2270
15: 1724 2271-
  2276
15,1-6: 2277
15,6: 2273c
15,13-16: 2274
15,18: 2591b
16: 2276b
16,11: 2279a
17,7: 2280
18s: 2282 2284
  2287
18,1-16: 2281
18,16-33: 2279b
18,23-32: 2288
19,1-11: 2680a

19,30-38: 2144a
  2170c
20: 2264-2266
  2271 2279c
20,1-18: 2276b
21,1-9: 2288a
21,8-21: 2276b
21,17: 2279a
22: 382 2289
  2292a-2298 9105
22,1-19: 2291
  2296*
24: 2300
24,12-14: 2299
25-31: 2302
25: 2301-2304
26: 2264 2266
26,1-33: 2276b
26,1-11: 2279c
26,8: 2303
26,26-31: 2304
27: 2305
27,1-45: 2306
28-30: 2309
28,5: 2310
28,10-22: 2311
28,12: 2312
29,1-32,2: 2313
31: 2314-2321
32: 2323 2324
32,10-13: 2322a
32,23-33: 2322b
  2325
34,12: 2327
35,1-15: 607

36: 2328
37-50: 1594
37:39-50: 2331-
  2336
37: 1724
37,13-19: 2337
37,28: 2338
38: 2329 2330
38,1-26: 1529b
39: 2340a
39,7: 2338*
40,1: 2339
43: 2211
46,1-5: 2340
49: 2341
49,8-12: 2342
49,18: 2343
49,22-26: 2342

Exodus

–: 607 2344-2509
1-12: 2359
1s: 2372-2387
2,11-15: 2388
3-14: 2391
3s: 2389-2394
3: 2274
3,1-23: 2395
3,14: 2397
3,22: 9105
4,24-26: 2400
4,25: 2399
6,28-11,10: 2401
7,1-11,10: 2402
11s: 2403-2405

1090 – Johannes

1,35-40: 5498
1,45-51: 5499
2,1-11: 5500-5507
2,1: 5505
2,4: 5508a
2,9s: 5509
2,10: 6060
2,13-22: 5510 5512
2,19: 5511
3,1-21: 5508b
  5513-5516
3,3-7: 5517
3,5-8: 5518a
3,5: 5519
3,14: 5520
3,22-25: 5517
3,29: 5508a
4,1-45: 5521-5526
4,1-26: 5522
4,7: 5527
4,46-54: 5506
5s: 5530d
5,1-18: 5528
6-10: 5529
6: 5531-5534
  9922b
6,1-14: 5535
6,20: 5536
6,22-71: 5537
6,22-59: 5517
6,26: 5538
6,52: 5539
6,60-72: 5540
7-10: 5541
7,53-8,11: 5543
7: 5542a
8: 5544
8,19-53: 5545
8,21-59: 5546
8,44: 5547
9,1-41: 5548a
9,1-4: 5549
9,1-3: 5550
10,1-18: 5551-5554
10,1-5: 5542
10,4: 5555
10,10: 5556 5557
10,11-16: 5550*
10,22-30: 5558
10,30: 5559
10,34-36: 3138
  5560
11,1-54: 5561-5567
11,1-44: 5506

11,44: 5570
12,1-11: 5571a
12,3: 5572
12,15: 5574
12,20-36: 5571b
13-21: 5576
13-17: 5576*
13: 4666
13: 5575
13,21-30: 5577a
13,23: 5399
  5405ab
14: 5578-5580
14,25: 5581
14,8-17: 5582a
14,8: 5498
14,12s: 5583
14,23-29: 5582b
15: 5584
15,1-17: 5585
15,1-8: 3507
15,1-6: 5586
15,1s: 5587
15,9: 5498
16,7-11: 5591
17: 5592-5595
17,20-26: 5582c
18s: 5596-5599
18: 4666
18,24: 5600
18,37: 5601
19,5: 5603
19,11: 5602
19,17-30: 5577b
19,23-27: 5604
20s: 5605-5613
20,1-18: 5577c
  5607
20,8: 5608
20,9: 5609
20,21: 5610-5612
21: 4666 5614
21,1-14: 5615
21,7: 5616
21,11: 5508c 5617

Actus Apostolorum

–: 3967 5022-5056
  5213-5292 a683
1-12: 5246
1s: 5572
1,1: 5099
1,3: 5293
1,15-26: 5294
1,23-26: 2299
2-5: 5301 5302

2,22: 7162*
2,41-47: 5300
2,44: 5303
2,46: 6291
3s: 5304
3,1-11: 5307
3,21: 5305 5306
4,25-31: 5308
4,32-5,16: 5300
4,32-5,11: 5309
5,1-11: 5310
6,1-7: 5311
6,2: 5312
7,2-53: 5314
8,25-40: 5316
8,26-40: 5317
8,37: 5318
10s: 5321
10,34-43: 5322
11,19-26: 5323
12,12: 6291
13s: 5324
13,4-12: 5310
13,6-11: a984c
13,16-41: 5325
13,50: 5321
15,20: 5326a
16,10s: 5331-5334
16,14s: 5327
16,14: 5328
16.16-20: 5329
16,16-18: 5330
17: 5341*
17,16-34: 5335
  5336a
17,22s: 5337
17,23: 5338a 5339
19,11-19: 5300
19,23-41: 5340
20,7-12: 6291
20,17-38: 5341*
20,18-35: 5342
20,32-35: 5311
21,27-28,31: 5344
27s: 5345
28: 5346
28,28: 5213

Ad Romanos

–: 5785* 5881-
  5920 6312 k79
1-8: 5908
1,1-17: 5921
1,1-4: 5922a
1,16s: 5926ab
1,18-3,20: 5927

1,18-32: 5922b
  8468
1,18-23: 5911b
1,18-22: 1969e
1,18: 5928
3,2: 5929
3,8: 5930
3,9: 5931
3,21-26: 5933
3,27-48: 5911c
3,27-31: 5934
3,30: 5935
4: 6196 k731
4,5s: 5936
4,13-25: 5937
5: 5938 6116 6120
5,1-11: 5939
5,6-11: 5940
5,12-21: 5941
5,12: 2176a 5942
5,13s: 5943
5,14: 5944
6: 1685*
6,1-23: 5945
6,1-14: 5946
6,1-11: 5947
7: 5948 5949
7,7-28: 5950
8: 5951
8,1: 5952
8,4: 5953
8,16: 6234
8,18-25: 5954
8,19-22: 5956
8,28: 5957
9-11: 5958-5983
  7274
9: 5984
10: 5985 5986
10,4: 5987
10,20: 5988
11,25s: 5989
11,30-32: 5990
12s: 5990*
12: 5991
12,1s: 5991*
12,2-8: 5992
12,11: 5993
13,1-7: 5994-5996
13,1-9: 5993*
13,1-7: 5997
13,9-21: 5998
14: 5999
14,1-15,13: 6048
14,23: 6000
15,14-33: 6001

FINIS – Elenchus of Biblica 5, 1989 – END OF INDEX

Finito di stampare il 3 aprile 1992
Tipografia Poliglotta della Pontificia Università Gregoriana
Piazza della Pilotta, 4 – 00187 Roma

AUGUSTINUS MERK S.J.

NOVUM TESTAMENTUM
GRAECE ET LATINE

APPARATU CRITICO INSTRUCTUM

editio undecima

(1992) pp. 48* + 1732. ISBN 88-7653-597-7.   Lit. 50.000

EDITRICE PONTIFICIO ISTITUTO BIBLICO – ROMA

FRANZ ZORELL

LEXICON GRAECUM
NOVI TESTAMENTI

editio quarta

(1990) pp. XXIV-(44)-752. ISBN 88-7653-590-X.   Lit. 75.000

EDITRICE PONTIFICIO ISTITUTO BIBLICO – ROMA

MAX ZERWICK – JOSEPH SMITH

BIBLICAL GREEK
ILLUSTRATED BY EXAMPLES

fifth reprint

(1990) xv-185 p. ISBN 88-7653-554-3.   Lit. 16.000

EDITRICE PONTIFICIO ISTITUTO BIBLICO – ROMA

FRANZ ZORELL – LUDOVICO SEMKOWSKI

LEXICON HEBRAICUM
VETERIS TESTAMENTI

fourth reprinting, completed

(1989) pp. 16*-1008. ISBN 88-7653-557-8.   Lit. 115.000

EDITRICE PONTIFICIO ISTITUTO BIBLICO – ROMA

PONTIFICAL BIBLICAL INSTITUTE PRESS 1991

ANALECTA BIBLICA

122. BOZAK Barbara: *Life 'Anew'. A Literary-Theological Study of Jer. 30-31.*
pp. XVIII-198. ISBN 88-7653-122-X   Lit. 33.500

126. O'FEARGHAIL Fearghus: *The Introduction to Luke-Acts. A Study of the Role of Lk. 1,1-4,44 in the Composition of Luke's Two Volume Work.*
pp. XII-256. ISBN 88-7653-126-2   Lit. 38.500

127. KOLARCIK Michael: *The Ambiguity of Death in the Book of Wisdom 1-6. A Study of Literary Structure and Interpretation.*
pp. XII-212. ISBN 88-7653-127-0   Lit. 34.500.

128. BARBIERO Gianni: *L'asino del nemico. Rinuncia alla vendetta e amore del nemico nella legislazione dell'Antico Testamento (Es. 23,4-5; Dt. 22,1-4; Lv. 19,17-18).*
pp. XII-420. ISBN 88-7653-128-9   Lit. 40.000

ANALECTA ORIENTALIA

42. von SODEN Wolfram – RÖLLIG Wolfgang: *Das Akkadische Syllabar.* 4ª ed. aggiornata.
pp. XLII-76-24*. ISBN 88-7653-257-9   Lit. 40.000

STUDIA POHL SERIES MAIOR

12. BLACK Jeremy A.: *Sumerian Grammar in Babylonian Theory.* 2ª ed. riveduta e corretta.
pp. XII-168. ISBN 88-7653-442-3   Lit. 29.000

SUBSIDIA BIBLICA

14. JOÜON Paul – MURAOKA T.: *A Grammar of Biblical Hebrew.*
Part One: Orthography of Biblical Hebrew.
Part Two: Morphology.
Part Three: Syntax. Paradigms and Indices.
2 volumi. pp. XLVI-780. ISBN 88-7653-595-0
Lit. 53.000

15. HILL Robert C.: *Breaking the Bread of the Word: Principles of Teaching Scripture.*
pp. XIV-186. ISBN 88-7653-596-9   Lit. 22.500

FUORI COLLANA

NORTH Robert (a cura di): *Elenchus of Biblica.* Vol. 4/1988.
pp. 1.056. ISBN 88-7653-594-2   Lit. 150.000

* * *

It is possible to subscribe standing orders

Orders and payments to:

AMMINISTRAZIONE PUBBLICAZIONI PUG/PIB
Piazza della Pilotta, 35 – 00187 Roma – Italia
Tel. 06/678.15.67 – Telefax 06/678.05.88

Conto Corrente Postale n. 34903005 – Compte Postal n. 34903005
Monte dei Paschi di Siena – Sede di Roma – c/c n. 54795.37

ISBN 88-7653-598-5